A DICTIONARY OF MODERN ITALIAN

A DICTIONARY
OF MODERN ITALIAN

Italian-English & English-Italian

by

JOHN PURVES

Reader Emeritus in Italian
University of Edinburgh

ROUTLEDGE & KEGAN PAUL
London, Boston and Henley

First published in 1953
by Routledge & Kegan Paul plc
14 Leicester Square,
London WC2H 7PH,
9 Park Street,
Boston, Mass. 02108, USA and
Broadway House, Newton Road,
Henley-on-Thames, Oxon RG9 1EN

Second impression 1956
Third impression 1959
Fourth impression (with some corrections) 1961
Fifth impression 1963
Sixth impression 1966
Seventh impression 1970
Eighth impression 1975

Reprinted and first published
as a paperback in 1980
Paperback reprinted in 1986

Printed in Great Britain by
The Guernsey Press Co. Ltd,
Guernsey, Channel Islands

ISBN 0 7100 1977 7 (c)
ISBN 0 7100 0602 0 (p)

CONTENTS

PREFACE

ALL languages are subject to a continuous process of growth and decay, but the modernization of Italian in the last fifty years has been unusually rapid. This is seen both in style and vocabulary.

Italian poetic style matured early, and its pattern was practically fixed by the 14th century in the work of Dante, Petrarch, and Boccaccio. But the development of prose as an easy and flexible instrument for the tasks of common life was scarcely accomplished before our own day. For long it remained under the influence of Latin, with its rhetorical and inflected structure, which Boccaccio adapted to the vernacular. Boccaccio's influence was immense, but his prose style, while suited to the leisurely and poetic needs of romance, was ill fitted to serve as a practical working medium for the needs of every day. During the Renaissance, too, respect for the Classics tended to harden into pedantry. There were of course some writers—of whom Machiavelli was the chief—who stamped their own personality on their work, and whose style thus acquired qualities of trenchancy and precision. But it was not until the rise of science in the 17th century that Galileo pointed the way to a prose of all work, simple in syntax and vocabulary, and suited both to scientific exposition and to the other tasks proper to that medium. Yet although Galileo is now considered the greatest prose-writer of his century, it is doubtful if his influence on the development of Italian prose was as great as that of the Royal Society on English. For many traces of the legacy of Latin and of Boccaccio still hung about narrative and imaginative writing in Italy for another two centuries at least, and a modern prose comparable to that of France or England had not yet been evolved. It is true that imitation of *The Spectator* and the influence of foreign travel had an appreciable effect on Italian literature in the 18th century, and that in the dialogue of comedy there was a decided advance towards a natural and conversational style ; yet only one writer, Giuseppe Baretti, shook himself sufficiently free of pedantry and affectation to merit, with some justice, the title of 'the father of modern prose'. Alfieri, too, whose education was wholly French, and who, as he tells us, had to learn Italian as a foreign language, wrote his Autobiography in a style of great efficacy, which owed much to his proud and independent character, but something also to his long residence in Tuscany. And when Alessandro Manzoni in 1827 decided to 'rinse his rags in the Arno', in other words to revise the text of *I Promessi Sposi* when in contact with the living language of Florence, he produced a masterpiece which remains a landmark of Italian literature. Yet the style of this novel is no more a modern style than that of Sir Walter Scott. And in the hands of his much inferior successors even the ground which Manzoni had won was lost. Few of the later novelists of the 19th century are remarkable either for matter or style until we come to Giovanni Verga, (1840–1922), whose best work resulted from his having come across a sailor's narrative which showed him the virtues of simplicity and truth to fact, and led him to reject the artificiality and pretension of his earlier fiction. Since then increased familiarity with contemporary literature, English, French, and American, has helped Italian prose to free itself of its inherited defects, and there has developed a style of native writing of a simplicity, naturalness, and syntactic ease unknown in earlier periods, and of an economy of means like that of the best Italian films.

And if pedantry and an undue respect for the past retarded the natural development of Italian prose, these same influences also hindered the free expansion of the Italian vocabulary. The 'questione della lingua', the question *i.e.* whether the origin and standard of literary Italian were to be sought in Tuscan (especially Florentine) or in another dialect or combination of dialects, or again whether, if Florentine, this standard should be the ancient or the living form of the language, continued to haunt Italian writers from Dante to Manzoni. But after 1870 these historical questions took on a certain unreality. The nation was united or on the way to being united, and linguistic unity seemed the desirable accompaniment of political unity. It was admitted that

Tuscan, and especially the Florentine dialect, had been the
nucleus of literary Italian, although it could not be allowed to
determine for all time the form and pattern of the language.
Florence, unlike Paris, as the great philologist Ascoli pointed
out, had never been the centre of all the activities of the national
life ; writers from every part of Italy had contributed to her
linguistic patrimony, which had been enriched from many
sources ; and the process must continue. Thus slowly at first
but with ever growing freedom new words were added to the
Italian vocabulary, until by the end of the century the number
of these neologisms was considerable. Since then the process of
change has been much more rapid. Old forms of expression have
fallen out of use, and a vast new terminology has sprung into
existence. The progress of science and technology, the influence
of the press, radio and the cinema, and the growing complexity
of social and professional life have all contributed to this.
Many of these new words were naturally offensive to purists
and those who had been brought up in an older tradition ; and
Alfredo Panzini, who had been a pupil of Carducci, no doubt
began his delightful *Dizionario Moderno* (1st ed. 1905) with the
intention of submitting these new elements in the vocabulary—
mostri and *mostricini* as he called them—to a playful and ironical
examination. But such was the success of the work that edition
after edition was called for, each larger than the former, until in
his preface to the 7th edition he was able, not without reason, to
speak of it as a ' panorama ' of the life and manners of the time.
With each fresh revision expressions that had failed to establish
themselves were rejected, but the crowd of new applicants
continued to increase, until in the latest (posthumous)
edition of 1950 Migliorini's appendix contains upwards of
8,000 words. It has thus become impossible, even if it were
desirable, to stem the flood of new additions to the language,
and the efforts of linguistic students such as Migliorini and
Devoto and the writers in *Lingua Nostra* are now directed
chiefly to bringing law and order into this vast new population.

In a small dictionary such as the present it is obviously impossible to include more than a limited proportion of these recent additions to the language, but an attempt has been made to provide a representative choice, and it is believed that this is much fuller than in any similar work of the kind. For the rest it should be understood that this is mainly a dictionary of modern *prose*. Poets such as Carducci, D'Annunzio, and Pascoli used such an individual and specialized vocabulary that each has his own lexicon. But it should not be difficult for a reader with the help of this dictionary to understand Leopardi or any of the simpler poets of the 19th century. None the less it has been chiefly to interpret the common language of the day that this work has been designed.

If personal dedications were in place in a dictionary, this one should have been dedicated to the memory of Professor Walter Bullock, who planned the work and carried it only a short way before his untimely death in 1944. All that is good in its execution is due to his initiative and example ; for its defects I am alone responsible.

J. P.

ABBREVIATIONS
USED IN THIS DICTIONARY

The swing dash (∼) signifies repetition in the singular of a leading vocabulary word (i.e. word printed in **bold type**). Followed by s (∼s) it indicates repetition in the plural.

The paragraph symbol (¶) also signifies repetition of a leading vocabulary word, when that is used as a different part of speech or with an altered gender.

Square brackets [ ] are used to indicate words, or parts of words, which may be used or omitted at will.

SUBJECT INDICATIONS

Aero.	Aeronautics	*Meas.*	Measurement; Measure
Agric.	Agriculture	*Mech.*	Mechanics
Anat.	Anatomy	*Med.*	Medicine; Medical
Arch.	Architecture	*Metall.*	Metallurgy
Arith.	Arithmetic	*Meteor.*	Meteorology
Artil.	Artillery	*Mil.*	Military
Astr.	Astronomy	*Min.*	Mining
Aviat.	Aviation	*Miner.*	Mineralogy
Bil.	Billiards	*Motor.*	Motoring; Motor car
Biol.	Biology	*Mus.*	Music
Bkkpg.	Bookkeeping	*Myth.*	Mythology
Bookb.	Bookbinding	*Naut.*	Nautical
Bot.	Botany	*Nav.*	Navy; Naval
Box.	Boxing	*Opt.*	Optics
Build.	Building	*Path.*	Pathology
Carp.	Carpentry	*Phar.*	Pharmacy
	& Joinery	*Phil.*	Philosophy
Chem.	Chemistry	*Phot.*	Photography
Com.	Commerce	*Phys.*	Physics
Cook.	Cookery	*Phys. Geog.*	Physical Geography
Cust.	Customs	*Poet.*	Poetry; Poetic
Danc.	Dancing	*Pol.*	Politics
Eccl.	Ecclesiastical	*Pros.*	Prosody
Elec.	Electricity, Electric	*Psych.*	Psychology
Emb.	Embroidery	*Radio*	Wireless
Engin.	Engineering	*Relig.*	Religion
Expl.	Explosives	*Rhet.*	Rhetoric
Fin.	Finance	*Rly.*	Railway(s)
Foot.	Football	*Sch.*	School
Geog.	Geography	*Ship.*	Shipping
Geol.	Geology	*Stk. Ex.*	Stock Exchange
Geom.	Geometry	*Surg.*	Surgery
Gram.	Grammar	*Teleg.*	Telegraphy
Her.	Heraldry	*Teleph.*	Telephony
Hist.	History; Historical	*Ten.*	Tennis
Hyd.	Hydraulics	*Theat.*	Theatre; Theatrical
Inc. Tax	Income Tax	*Theol.*	Theology
Insce.	Insurance	*Typ.*	Typography; Printing
Log.	Logic	*Univ.*	University
Mach.	Machinery; Machine	*Zool.*	Zoology
Math.	Mathematics		

TEXTUAL ABBREVIATIONS

a.	adjective
abb.	abbreviation
abs.	absolutely, i.e. (verb) used without its object
ad.	adverb
a.f.	adjective feminine only
a.m.	adjective masculine only
art.	article
att.	attributively, i.e. (noun) used as adjective
aux.	auxiliary (verb)
c.	conjunction
Cf.	Compare
col.	collectively, collective noun
comp.	compound ; comparative
def.	definite
defect.	defective
demons.	demonstrative
e.g.	for example
Eng.	England ; English
esp.	especially
expr.	expression
&	and
&c.	et cetera
f.	feminine (singular). In the Italian-English section *f.* = noun feminine singular
fam.	familiar
fig.	figuratively
f.pl.	feminine plural. In the Italian-English section *f.pl.* = noun feminine plural
Fr.	France ; French
i.	interjection
i.e.	that is to say
imp.	impersonal
indef.	indefinite
inv.	invariable (same in singular & plural)
ir.	irregular (verb)
iron.	ironical
It.	Italy ; Italian
lit.	literally. *Lit.* literary
m.	masculine (singular). In the Italian-English section *m.* = noun masculine singular
m.f.	masculine & feminine (noun)
m.pl.	masculine plural. In the Italian-English section *m.pl.* = noun masculine plural
n.	noun
neg.	negative ; used negatively
N.T.	New Testament
oft.	often
opp.	opposed to
O.T.	Old Testament
p.a.	participial adjective
pers.	person(s)
pl.	plural
pn.	pronoun
pop.	popular
p.p.	past participle
pr.	(of verbs) present indicative; preposition
pr.p.	present participle
s.	singular
sc.	(word) understood
Scot.	Scottish
sup.	superlative
v.i.	verb intransitive
v.refl.	verb reflexive
v.t.	verb transitive

THE ITALIAN ALPHABET
(Sounds & Letters)

THE VOWELS
(LE VOCALI)

The first column gives the ordinary symbol for each vowel with examples of words in which these occur, the second the same vowels in their accented form, and the third their phonetic equivalents.

a (*ara, aquila, avaro, calice, coda, fanteria, marmellata, traviata*).
    à (*bontà, capacità, età, pietà, società*).   [a]

e
open e (*e aperta, e larga*): *bello, erba, ero, evo, guerra, sapienza, tempo, sei, sette, piede, chiesa.*
    è (*è* (is), *tè* (tea), *caffè, gilè, lacchè, Mosè*).   [ɛ]

close e (*e chiusa, e stretta*): *e* (and), *cena, detto, pena, pineta, casetta, nebbia, te* (thee, you), *tre, tredici, trenta.*
    é (*perché, poiché, purché, credé*).   [e]

i (*il, mi, ti, si, di, fine, infinito, libri, medici, analisi, paralisi*).
    i (*così, finì, giurì, lì, morì*).   [i]

The letter *i* may be also (1) a diacritic sign to show that *c* or *g* is soft before the vowels *a, o,* & *u,* as in *abbraccio, ciancia, ciò, giù,* &c., or (2) semiconsonantal, as in *aia, più, miele, Pistoia,* &c.

o
open o (*o aperta, o larga*): *oca, poco, buono, giovinotto, nove* (nine).
    ò (*parlò, però, ciò, perciò*).   [ɔ]

close o (*o chiusa, o stretta*): *ora, signore, feroce, noi, voi, coloro.*
      [o]

u (*cura, furbo, luna, pure, comune*).
    ù (*caucciù, Corfú, giù, orsù, virtù*).   [u]

u is also semiconsonantal as in *cuòre, figliuòlo, oriuòlo, sangue,* &c.   [w]
Cf. below under digraph **qu**.

N.B.—Unaccented *e* & *o* are always close.

THE CONSONANTS
(LE CONSONANTI)

b (*bi*) can never be preceded by the consonant *n*; hence the prefix *in-* becomes in all such cases *im-*, *imboscare, imbucare,* &c.   [b]

c (*ci*)
palatal c, before *e* & *i*, e.g. *ce, ci, cera, fece, foce, cicerone, cioccolata. incidere.*   [tʃ]
guttural c, before *a, o, u, l, r,* & with the diacritic *h* before *e* & *i*; e.g. *capo, come, culla, clima, croce; che, chi, chiesa.*   [k]

d (*di*) *dare, dinamo, dinastia, doccia, duomo, addurre, erede, spedire, suddito,* &c.   [d]

f (*effe*) *fa, fece, fuoco, affare, effondere, fiero, francese, infusione, mafia,* &c.   [f]

g (*gi*)
palatal g, before *e* & *i*, e.g. *genio, gentile, già, giacca, giallo, giardino, gilè, maggio.*   [dʒ]
guttural g, before *a, o, u, l, r,* and with the diacritic *h* before *e* & *i*, e.g. *gabbia, galante, goccia, godere, gufo, guglia, globo, gloria, grado; ghetto, ghiaccia, ghianda.*   [g]

h (*acca*) survives as a vestigial form in parts of the verb *avere* (*ho, hai, ha, hanno*, from Lat. *habeo, habes, habet, habent*), & serves as a diacritic with *c* & *g* before *e* & *i*; otherwise it is found in some exclamations (*ah, eh, ahimè, ohimè,* &c.) and in a few foreign words. But it is invariably mute & forms no real part of the Italian alphabet.

j (*i lunga*) is similarly a dead letter in the modern alphabet, being replaced either by *i* or *g*.

l (*elle*) *labiale, leggiero, leone, liberale, lodare, logica, lunario, luogo, eleggere, infilare, palla, pallido,* &c.   [l]

m (*emme*) *mare, meccanica, mezzo, milizia, montaggio, motociclo, mughetto, mummia, commutatore, emisfero, immagine, infiamma-zione, parossismo, omeopatia,* &c.   [m]

n (*enne*)

    nave, ne, né, noi, nome, nucleo, nipote, &c.   [n]
    before *f* & *v* pronounced as *m*, although written as *n*, e.g. *anfora, enfatico, invadere, invece.*   [m]
    before [k] & [g] has a velar sound due to the proximity of these consonants, e.g. *anche, angolo,* &c.   [ŋ]

p (*pi*) *pace, palio, partire, impero, presentare,* &c.   [p]

r (*erre*) *radio, raffreddore, recente, ricorrere, rocchetto, rumore,* &c.   [r]

s (*esse*)

    voiceless s (*s aspra o sorda*), as in *sabbia. sedile, si, Sicilia, soggetto, suono, speranza, spesso, stato, casa, cosa, naso, riso, lapis,* &c.   [s]
    voiced s (*s dolce o sonora*), as in *roṣa, teṣoro, uṣo, uṣura, ṣnello, ṣregolato,* and in the termination -*iṣmo,* &c. This sound is indicated in the Dictionary by a dot over the letter *s*.   [z]

t (*ti*) *tale, tempo, titolo, tondo, tutto, otto, pietra,* &c.   [t]

v (*vu*) *vampa, vero, vita, voce, volto, vuoto, avere, avvenire, scevro; ṣvenevole, ṣvista* (always preceded by voiced *s*).   [v]

z (*zeta*)

    voiceless z (*z aspra, z sorda*), as in *zampa, zeppo, zia, zolfo, zucca, zucchero, marzo, spazio,* &c.   [ts]
    voiced z (*z dolce, z sonora*), as in *żaffiro, żeta, żibaldone, żigżag, żodiaco, żona, żoologo, żuavo, meżżo,* & verbs with the termination -*iżżare.* This sound is indicated in the Dictionary by a dot over the letter *z*.   [dz]

k (*cappa*), **w** (*doppia vu*), **x** (*ics or icchese*), & **y** (*ipsilon*) have no real place in the Italian alphabet, & are found only in foreign words. **k** is generally replaced by **c** or **ch** (*Corano, chilo*), **x** by **ss** or **s** (*ossigeno, silografia*), and **y** by **i** (*iarda, ciclo, ciclista*).

DIGRAPHS
(I DIGRAMMI)

ch has a single guttural (velar) sound, & is found only before *e* & *i*, e.g. *che, chi, chiamare, chiedere, cheto, duchi, ciechi, palchi, pochi,* &c.   [k]

gh similarly only found before *e* & *i*, has a guttural sound, like hard g, e.g. *ghetto, ghibellino, ghirlanda, luoghi, laghi, colleghi, dialoghi,* &c.   [g]

gl before *i* has a single palatal sound, as in *gli, figlio, famiglia, moglie, giglio,* &c. Exceptions are *glicine, glicerina, negligenza, angli-cano, ganglio,* where the sound is guttural, as it is before the vowels *a, e, o,* & *u,* as in *glabro, gleba, gloria, glutine,* &c.   [ʎ] / [gl]

gn has also a single palatal sound, as in *ogni, vergogna, vignetta, ingegno, gnocco, gnomo, gnomico,* &c. In German names, however, the sounds of *g* & *n* remain separate, as in *Wag/ner,* &c.   [ɲ] / [gn]

qu has the sound of *kw,* as in *acqua, equo, quasi, quinto, quota,* &c.   [kw]

sc before *e* & *i* has a single palatal sound (approximating to Eng. sh), [ʃ]
as in *scena, sciagura, scirocco, uscire*, &c. Before *a, o,* & *u* it
has a guttural sound, as in *scatola, scolaro, scuola*, &c. [sk]

DIPHTHONGS
(I DITTONGHI)

Diphthongs are formed (1) when the vowels *a, e,* or *o* are combined in a single emission of the breath with unaccented *i* or *u*, or (2) when *i* & *u* are combined in the same way with each other. In the former case the stress falls on *a, e,* or *o*, in the latter it falls sometimes on *i*, sometimes on *u*. E.g. *àura, biàda, èuro, fiàto, lièto, pièno, piòvere, pòi, suòno; fúi, colúi, guìda, guìsa*, &c.

Movable diphthongs (*Dittonghi mobili*). This name is given to the diphthongs *uo* & *ie*, since when the accent falls on another syllable they are reduced to the simple vowels *o* & *e*. E.g. *giuòco, giocàva; buòno, bonìssimo; sièdo, sedéva; mièle, melàto.*

Exceptions are the verbs *nuotare* & *vuotare*, which keep the diphthong even in the parts where it is not accented, to distinguish them from the verbs *notare* & *votare*; also the verbs *mietere* & *presiedere*.

ACCENTS AND ACCENTUATION

Italian words are classified according to the incidence of the tonic accent. When this falls on the last syllable they are styled **parole tronche**, e.g. *età, finché, però, servitú, andò, mori, temé, scimpanzè, trentatré*, &c.; when on the last syllable but one (the commonest type) **parole piane**, e.g. *amàre, bellézza, cioccolàta, docènte, figúra, illústre, onóre, riflèsso, siccòme*, &c.; when on the third last syllable **parole sdrucciole**, e.g. *agrìcolo, círcolo, diàlogo, fàbbrica, làmpada, màcchina, parèntesi, útile, verìssimo, versàtile, vòlgere*, &c.; when on the fourth last syllable **parole bisdrucciole**, e.g. *fàbbricano, rècitano, andàndosene, partèndosene*, &c.

ACCENTUAL SIGNS

There is considerable variation in current practice regarding the use of the written (or printed) accent. The only forms which invariably employ such an accent are:—

(1) Words of more than one syllable of which the last is accented (*parole tronche*)—see above.
(2) Monosyllables which have two senses & represent different parts of speech, e.g. *ché* (since or because) to distinguish it from *che* (conjunction & pronoun, that; who), *dà* (3rd sg. pr. indic. of *dare*), *da* (prep. from, by), *di* (poet. day), *di* (of), *là, li* (there), *la, li* (def. articles), *sí* (yes), *si* (refl. oneself, itself, himself, themselves), &c.
(3) Some monosyllables containing a diphthong, which might be considered disyllabic, e.g. *ciò, può, già, giú.*
(4) The parts *dànno* & *détti* of the verb *dare*, to distinguish them from the nouns *danno* & *detti*.
(5) Some words which change their meaning with a shift of the tonic accent, e.g. *àncora* (anchor), *ancóra* (yet, still); *bàlia* (nurse), *balìa* (power, mercy).

In many texts the only written accent is the 'grave' ('). As this gives no indication of the quality of the vowel on which the accent falls, & therefore of the pronunciation, it has been found better to reserve this for the open sounds, *a*, open *e* [ɛ], & open *o* [ɔ], & to mark the close sounds, *i*, close *e* & *o* [e, o] & *u*, with the 'acute' accent ('). This is the system adopted in this Dictionary.

Further, in Part I (Italian-English) the accent is inserted in *all* words, including the *parole piane*, where it is generally omitted in other dictionaries (since these words follow the normal type of accentuation). This has the advantage, among other things, of enabling the reader to distinguish easily between the numerous pairs of homonyms in Italian. But it should be understood that it is introduced merely as a convenience, & is not the general practice.

PARADIGMS
OF THE ITALIAN REGULAR VERB

FIRST CONJUGATION

Infinitive (*infinito*) -àre (am-àre, pari-àre, &c.).
Present Indicative (*indicativo presente*) -o, -i, -a, -iàmo, -àte, -ano.
Imperfect Indicative (*indicativo imperfetto*) -àvo, -àvi, -àva, -avàmo, -avàte, -àvano.
Preterite (*passato remoto*) -ài, -àsti, -ò, -àmmo, -àste, -àrono.
Future (*futuro*) -erò, -erài, -erà, -erémo, -eréte, -erànno.
Conditional (*condizionale*) -erèi, -erésti, -erèbbe, -erèmmo, -eréste, -erèbbero.
Present Subjunctive (*congiuntivo presente*) -i, -i, -i, -iàmo, -iàte, -ino.
Past Subjunctive (*congiuntivo imperfetto*) -àssi, -àssi, -àsse, -àssimo, -àste, -àssero.
Imperative (*imperativo*) -a, -i, -iàmo, -àte, -ino.
Present Participle (*participio presente*) -ànte.
Past Participle (*participio passato* (-àto.
Gerund (*gerundio*) -àndo.

SECOND CONJUGATION

Infinitive, -ére & -ere (tem-ére, créd-ere, ricév-ere, &c.).
Present Indicative, -o, -i, -e, -iàmo, -éte, -ono.
Imperfect Indicative, -évo, -évi, -éva, -evàmo, -evàte, -évano.
Preterite, -éi or -ètti, -ésti, -é or -ètte, -émmo, -éste, -érono or -èttero.
Future, -erò, -erài, -erà, -erémo, -eréte, -erànno.
Conditional, -erèi, -erésti, -erèbbe, -erèmmo, -eréste, -erèbbero.
Present Subjunctive, -a, -a, -a, -iàmo, -iàte, -ano.
Past Subjunctive, -éssi, -éssi, -ésse, -éssimo, -éste, -éssero.
Imperative, -i, -a, -iàmo, -éte, -ano.
Present Participle, -ènte.
Past Participle, -úto.
Gerund, -èndo.

THIRD CONJUGATION

Infinitive, -íre (dorm-íre, vest-íre; colp-íre, fin-íre, &c.).
Present Indicative, (dorm)-o, -i, -e, -iàmo, -íte, -ono; & (colp)-ísco, -ísci, -ísce, -iàmo, -íte, -íscono.
Imperfect Indicative, -ívo, -ívi, -íva, -ivàmo, -ivàte, -ívano.
Preterite, -íi, -ísti, -í, -ímmo, -íste, -írono.
Future, -irò, -irài, -irà, -irémo, -iréte, -irànno.
Conditional, -irèi, -irésti, -irèbbe, -irèmmo, -iréste, -irèbbero.
Present Subjunctive, -a, -a, -a, -iàmo, -iàte, -ano; & -ísca, -ísca, -ísca, -iàmo, -iàte, -íscano.
Past Subjunctive, -íssi, -íssi, -ísse, -íssimo, -íste, -íssero.
Imperative, -i, -a, -iàmo, -íte, -ano; & -ísci, -ísca, -iàmo, -íte, -íscano.
Present Participle, -ènte.
Past Participle, -íto.
Gerund, -èndo.

The great majority of verbs with infinitive in -ire are conjugated like *colpire* & *finire*, with present indicative in -isco, -isci, &c., & pres. subjunctive in -isca, &c., but those conjugated like *dormire* & *vestire* include such common verbs as *bollire, divertire, fuggire, partire, pentirsi, sentire, servire, sortire, tossire*.

A number can follow either pattern & these are duly recorded in their place in the Dictionary.

ITALIAN IRREGULAR VERBS

Order of tenses & parts:—

(1) = Present Indicative.
(2) = Imperfect Indicative.
(3) = Preterite.
(4) = Future
(5) = Conditional.
(6) = Present Subjunctive.
(7) = Imperfect Subjunctive.
(8) = Imperative.
(9) = Present Participle.
(10) = Past Participle.
(11) = Gerund.

Tenses & parts of the verb not included in the following list follow the pattern of the regular conjugations & prefixed verbs such as **accadére, accògliere, accórrere, amméttere, comprèndere, riprèndere, soddisfàre, intèndere, sottintèndere,** &c., are conjugated like the simple verbs forming their second or last element (**cadére, còglicre, córrere, méttere, prèndere, fàre, tèndere,** &c.).

accèndere. — (3) accési, accése, accésero. (10) accéso.

acclúdere. — (3) acclúsi, acclúse, acclúsero. (10) acclúso.

accoràrsi. — (1) mi accuòro, ti accuòri, *and so generally in all the parts where* o *is accented.*

accòrgersi. — (3) mi accorsi, si accorse, si accorsero. (10) accortosi.

accréscere. — *like* **créscere.**

addúrre. — (1) addúco, addúci, addúce, adduciàmo, adducéte, addúcono. (2) adducévo, adducévi, adducéva, adducevàmo, adducevàte, adducévano. (3) addussi, adducesti, adduse, adducemmo, adduceste, addussero. (4) addurrò, addurrai, addurrà, addurremo, addurrete, addurranno. (5) addurrei, addurresti, addurrebbe, addurremmo, addurreste, addurrebbero. (6) adduca, adduca, adduca, adduciamo, adduciate, adducano. (7) adducessi, adducessi, adducesse, adducessimo, adduceste, adducessero. (8) adduci, adduca, adduciamo, adducete, adducano. (9) adducente. (10) addotto. (11) adducendo.

affliggere. — (3) afflissi, afflisse, afflissero. (10) afflitto.

aggiúngere. — *like* **giungere.**

allúdere. — (3) allusi, alluse, allusero. (10) allušo.

andàre. — (1) vado *or* vo, vai, va, andiamo, andate, vanno. (4) andrò *or* anderò, andrai, andrà, andremo, andrete *or* anderete, andranno *or* anderanno. (5) andrei, andresti, andrebbe, andremmo, andreste, andrebbero. (6) vada, vada, vada, andiamo, andiate, vadano. (8) va', vada, andiamo, andate, vadano. (9) andante. (10) andato. (11) andando.

andàrsene. — *like* **andare.** *The auxiliary* essere *is used · in the compound tenses and is placed between* ne *and the* p.p. andato; *thus,* se n'è andato, ce ne siamo andati. (8) vattene, ce ne andiamo, andatevene.

annèttere. — (3) annettei *or* annessi, annetté *or* annesse, annetterono *or* annessero. (10) annesso.

apparíre. — (1) appaio *or* apparisco, appari *or* apparisci, appare *or* apparisce, appariamo, apparite, appaiono *or* appariscono. (3) apparii, apparvi *or* apparsi, appari, apparve *or* apparse, apparirono *or* apparvero *or* apparsero. (6) appaia *or* apparisca, appaiano *or* appariscano. (8) appari *or* apparisci, appaia *or* apparisca, appaiano *or* appariscano. (9) apparente *or* appariscente. (10) apparito *or* apparso.

appartenére. — *like* **tenere.**

appèndere. — (3) appesi, appese, appesero. (10) appeso.

applaudíre. — (1) applaudo, applaudi, applaude, applaudono. (6) applauda, applaudano.

aprire. — (1) apro, apri. (3) apersi *or* aprii, aperse *or* aprí, apersero *or* aprirono. (10) aperto.

àrdere. — (3) arsi, arse, arsero. (10) arso.

aspèrgere. — (3) aspersi, asperse, aspersero. (10) asperso.

assalíre. — (1) assalgo *or* assalisco, assali *or* assalisci, assale *or* assalisce, assalgono *or* assaliscono. (3) assalsi *or* assalii, assalse *or* assalí, assalsero *or* assalirono. (6) assalga *or* assalisca, &c. (10) assalito.

assídersi. — (3) mi assisi, si assise, si assisero. (10) assiso.

assístere. — (3) assistei or assistetti. (10) assistito.

assòlvere. — (3) assolvei or assolvetti or assolsi, assolvé or assolvette or assolse, assolverono or assolvettero or assolsero. (10) assoluto or assolto.

assorbíre. — (1) assorbo or assorbisco, assorbi or assorbisci, &c. (6) assorba or assorbisca, &c. (10) assorbito or assorto.

assúmere. — (3) assunsi, assunse, assunsero. (10) assunto.

avvertíre. — (1) avverto, avverti, avverte, avvertono. (6) avverta. &c.

avvíncere. — like **vincere**.

avvòlgere. — like **volgere**.

benedíre. — like **dire**.

bére. — (1) bevo, bevi, beve, beviamo, bevete, bevono. (2) bevevo, bevevi, &c. (3) bevvi or bevetti, bevve or bevette, bevvero or bevettero. (4) berrò, berrai, &c. (5) berrei, berresti, &c. (6) beva, beva, beva, beviamo, beviate, bevano. (7) bevessi, bevessi, bevesse, bevessimo, beveste, bevessero. (8) bevi, beva, beviamo, bevete, bevano. (10) bevuto. (11) bevendo.

bollíre. — (1) bóllo, bólli, bólle, or bollísco, bollísci, bollísce. (6) bólla, bólla, &c.

cadére. — (3) caddi, cadde, caddero. (4) cadrò, cadrai, cadrà, &c. (5) cadrei, cadresti, &c.

cèdere. — (3) cedetti or cessi, cedette or cesse, cedettero or cessero.

chiédere. — (1) chiedo or chieggo, chiedono or chieggono. (3) chiesi, chiese, chiesero. (6) chieda or chiegga, chiedano or chieggano. (10) chiesto.

chiúdere. — (3) chiusi, chiuse, chiusero. (10) chiuso.

cíngere. — (3) cinsi, cinse, cinsero. (10) cinto.

còigliere. — (1) colgo, cogli, coglie, cogliamo, cogliete, colgono. (3) colsi, colse, colsero. (4) coglierò or corrò, coglierai or corrai. (10) colto.

coincídere. — (3) coincisi, coincise or coincidette, coincisero or coincidettero. (10) coinciso.

comparíre. — like **apparire**.

cómpiere. — (1) compio, compi, &c. (2) compievo & compivo, &c.

(6) compia & compisca, &c. (10) compiuto. (11) compiendo. The alternate forms are from the infinitive compire, p.p. compito.

compórre. — like **porre**.

comprímere. — (3) compressi, compresse, compressero. (10) compresso.

concèdere. — (3) concedei or concedetti or concessi, concedette or concesse, concedettero or concessero. (10) conceduto or concesso.

concórrere. — like **correre**.

condúrre. — like **addurre**.

congiúngere. — like **giungere**.

connèttere. — like **annettere**.

conóscere. — (3) conobbi, conobbe, conobbero.

consumàre. — (3) consumai or consunsi, consumò or consunse, consumarono or consunsero. (10) consumato or consunto. The alternate forms are from a supposed infinitive consumere, conjugated like assumere.

contenére. — like **tenere**.

contúndere. — (3) contusi, contuse, contusero. (10) contuso.

convèrgere. — (3) convergei or conversi, convergé & converse, convergerono & conversero. No past participle.

convertíre. — like **avvertire**.

convíncere. — like **vincere**.

copríre. — like **aprire**.

corrèggere. — like **reggere**.

córrere. — (3) corsi, corse, corsero. (10) corso.

costruíre. — (3) costruii or costrussi, costruisti, costruí or costrusse, costruirono or costrussero. (10) costruito or costrutto.

créscere. — (3) crebbi, crebbe, crebbero. (10) cresciuto.

cucíre. — (1) cucio, cuciono. (6) cucia, cucia, &c. (8) cuci, cucia, cuciamo, cucite, cuciano.

cuòcere. — (1) cuocio, cuoci, cuoce, cociamo, cocete, cuociono. (2) cocevo, cocevi, &c. (3) cossi, cocesti, cosse, cocemmo, coceste, cossero. (4) cocerò, cocerai, &c. (5) cocerei, coceresti, &c. (6) cuocia, cuocia, cuocia, cociamo, cociate, cuociano. (7) cocessi, cocessi, &c. (8) cuoci, cuocia, cociamo, cocete, cuociano. (9) cocente. (10) cotto & (metaphorically) cociuto. (11) cocendo.

dàre. — (1) do, dài, dà, diamo, date, dànno. (2) davo, davi, &c. (3) diedi

& **detti,** desti, diede *&* **dette,** demmo, deste, diedero *&* dettero. (4) darò, darai, &c. (5) darei, daresti, &c. (6) dia, dia, dia, diamo, diate, diano. (7) dessi, dessi, desse, dessimo, deste, dessero. (8) da', dia, diamo, date, diano. (10) dato. (11) dando. *N.B.*—*The compound verb* **ridare** *is conjugated like* **dare.** **Circondare,** *however, is a regular verb of the First Conjugation.*

decídere. — (3) decisi, decise, decisero. (10) deciso.

decréscere. — *like* **crescere.**

difèndere. — (3) difesi, difese, difesero. (10) diféso.

dipèndere. — (3) dipesi, dipese, dipesero. (10) dipéso.

dipíngere. — (3) dipinsi, dipinse, dipinsero. (10) dipinto.

díre. — (1) dico, dici, dice, diciamo, dite, dicono. (2) dicevo, dicevi, &c. (3) dissi, dicesti, disse, dicemmo, diceste, dissero. (4) dirò, dirai, &c. (5) direi, diresti, &c. (6) dica, dica, &c. (7) dicessi, dicessi, &c. (8) di', dite. (10) detto. (11) dicendo.

dirígere. — (3) diressi, diresse, diressero. (10) diretto.

discórrere. — *like* **correre.**

discútere. — (3) discussi & discutei, discusse *&* discuté, discussero *&* discuterono. (10) discusso.

dispórre. — *like* **porre.**

dissòlvere. — (10) dissolto *&* dissoluto.

dissuadére. — *like* **persuadere.**

distínguere. — (3) distinsi, distinse, distinsero. (10) distinto.

distrúggere. — *like* **struggere.**

divídere. — (3) divisi, divise, divisero. (10) diviso.

dolérsi. — (1) mi dolgo, ti duoli, si duole, ci dogliamo, vi dolete, si dolgono. (3) mi dolsi, ti dolesti, si dolse, ci dolemmo, vi doleste, si dolsero. (4) mi dorrò, ti dorrai, &c. (5) mi dorrei, ti dorresti, &c. (6) mi dolga, ti dolga, si dolga, ci dogliamo, vi dogliate, si dolgano. (7) mi dolessi, ti dolessi, &c. (8) duoliti *or* dolgati, doletevi, *or* dolgavi. (9) dolentesi. (10) dolutosi. (11) dolendosi.

dormíre. — (9) dormente *&* dormiente.

dovére. — (1) devo *&* debbo, devi *or* dei, deve *or* dée, dobbiamo, dovete, devono *&* debbono. (3) dovei *&* dovetti, dovesti, dové *&* dovette, doverono *&* dovettero. (4) dovrò, dovrai, &c. (5) dovrei, dovi esti, &c. (6) deva *or* debba, dobbiamo, dobbiate, debbano. (10) dovuto. *No imperative.*

elèggere. — *like* **leggere.**

elídere. — (3) elisi, elidesti, elise *or* elidé, elisero *or* eliderono. (10) eliso.

emèrgere. — (3) emersi, emerse, emersero. (10) emerso.

empíre, émpiere. — (1) empio, empí, empié, &c. (3) empii, empiei *or* empietti, empisti *or* empiesti, empí, empié *or* empiette. (4) empirò, empirai, &c. (5) empirei, empiresti, &c. (6) empia, empia, &c. (7) empissi, empissi, &c. (8) empi, empite. (9) empiente, (10) empito *&* empiuto. (11) empiendo.

èrgere. — (3) ersi, erse, ersero. (10) erto.

eseguíre. — (1) eseguo *&* eseguisco, esegui *&* eseguisci, &c. *Regular in the other parts.*

esígere. — (10) esatto.

esplòdere. — (3) esplosi, esplose, esplosero. (10) esploso.

espórre. — *like* **porre.**

esprímere. — *like* **comprimere.**

fàre. — (1) fo *or* faccio, fai, fa, facciamo, fate, fanno. (2) facevo, facevi, &c. (3) feci, facesti, fece, facemmo, faceste, fecero. (4) farò, farai, &c. (5) farei, faresti, &c. (6) faccia, faccia, &c. (7) facessi, facessi, &c. (8) fa', faccia, facciamo, fate, facciano. (9) facente. (10) fatto. (11) facendo.

fèndere. — (3) fendei *or* fendetti. (10) fenduto *&* fesso.

fíggere. — (3) fissi, fisse, fissero. (10) fisso *or* fitto.

fíngere. — (3) finsi, finse, finsero. (10) finto.

fóndere. — (3) fusi, fuse, fusero. (10) fuso.

fràngere. — (3) fransi, franse, fransero. (10) franto.

fríggere. — (3) frissi, frisse, frissero. (10) fritto.

fuggíre. — (1) fuggo, fuggi, fugge. (6) fugga, fugga, &c. (8) fuggi.

giacére. — (1) giaccio, giaci, giace, giacciamo *&* giaciamo, giacete, giacciono. (3) giacqui, giacque, giacquero. (6) giaccia, giacciano.

giocàre. — (1) giuòco, giuòchi, *and so generally where o is accented.*

giùngere. — (3) giunsi, giunse, giunsero. (10) giunto.

godére. — (4) goderò *or* godrò.

incìdere. — (3) incisi, incise, incisero. (10) inciso.

incùtere. — (3) incutei & incussi, incuté *or* incusse, incuterono *or* incussero. (10) incusso.

insìstere. — *like* **assistere.**

intèndere. — *like* **tendere.**

interròmpere. — *like* **rompere.**

intrìdere. — (3) intrisi, intrise, intrisero. (10) intriso.

intrùdere. — (3) intrusi, intruse, intrusero. (10) intruso.

invàdere. — (3) invasi, invase, invasero. (10) invaso.

istruíre. — *like* **costruire.**

lèggere. — (3) lessi, lesse, lessero. (10) letto.

maledíre. — *like* **dire.**

mantenére. — *like* **tenere.**

mentíre. — (1) mento *or* mentisco, menti *or* mentisci, &c. (6) menta *or* mentisca, &c.

méscere. — (10) mesciuto & misto.

méttere. — (3) misi, mise, misero. (9) mettente & mittente. (10) messo.

mòrdere. — (3) morsi, morse, morsero. (10) morso.

moríre. — (1) muoio *or* muoro, muore, moriamo, morite, muoiono. (4) morrò, morrai, &c., *more rarely* morirò, morirai, &c. (5) morrei, morresti, &c. (6) muoia, moriamo, moriate, muoiano. (10) morto.

muòvere. — (1) muovo, muovi, muove, moviamo, movete, muovono. (2) movevo, movevi, &c. (3) mossi, movesti, mosse, movemmo, moveste, mossero. (4) moverò, moverai, &c. (5) moverei, moveresti, &c. (8) muovi, movete. (9) movente. (10) mosso. (11) movendo.

nàscere. — (3) nacqui, nascesti, nacque, nascemmo, nasceste, nacquero. (10) nato.

nascóndere. — (3) nascosi, nascondesti, nascose, nascondemmo, nascondeste, nascosero. (10) nascosto.

nuòcere. — (1) nuoccio *or* noccio, nuoci, nuoce, nociamo, nocete, nocciono, *or* nuocciono. (2) nocevo, nocevi, &c. (3) nocqui, nocesti,

nocque, nocemmo, noceste, nocquero. (4) nocerò, nocerai, &c. (5) nocerei, noceresti, &c. (6) noccia, noccia, noccia, nociamo, nociate, nocciano. (7) nocessi, nocessi, &c. (8) nuoci, noccia, nociamo, nocete, nocciano. (9) nocente. (10) nociuto. (11) nocendo.

nutríre. — (1) nutrisco *or* nutro, nutrisci *or* nutri, nutrisce *or* nutre, nutriamo, nutrite, nutriscono *or* nutrono. (6) nutrisca *or* nutra, nutriscano *or* nutrano.

occórrere. — *like* **correre.**

offèndere. — *like* **difendere.**

offríre. — (1) offro, offri, &c. (3) offrii *or* offersi, offristi, offrí *or* offerse, offrimmo, offriste, offrirono *or* offersero. (4) offrirò, &c. (5) offrirei, &c. (6) offra, offrano. (8) offri, offrite. (9) offrente & offerente. (10) offerto.

ottenére. — *like* **tenere.**

parére. — (1) paio, pari, pare, paiamo, parete, paiono. (3) parvi & parsi, paresti, parve & parse, paremmo, pareste, parvero & parsero. (4) parrò, parrai, &c. (5) parrei, parresti, &c. (6) paia, paia, paia, paiamo, paiate, paiano. (7) paressi, &c. (10) parso. *No imperative.*

percuòtere. — (1) percuoto, percuoti, percuote, percotiamo, percotete, percuotono. (3) percossi, percotesti, percosse, percotemmo, percoteste, percossero. (10) percosso.

pèrdere. — (3) persi *or* perdei *or* perdetti, perdesti, perse, perdé *or* perdette, perdemmo, perdeste, persero, perderono & perdettero. (10) perso *or* perduto.

perméttere. — *like* **mettere.**

persuadére. — (3) persuasi, persuadesti, persuase, persuademmo, persuadeste, persuasero. (10) persuaso.

piacére. — (1) piaccio, piaci, piace, piacciamo, piacete, piacciono. (3) piacqui, piacesti, piacque, piacemmo, piaceste, piacquero. (6) piaccia, piaccia, piaccia, piacciamo, piacciate, piacciano. (7) piaci, piaccia, piacciamo, piacete, piacciano. (10) piaciuto.

piàngere. — (3) piansi, pianse, piansero. (10) pianto.

piòvere. — (3) piovve, piovvero. (10) piovuto. *See list of Impersonal Verbs.*

pòrgere. — (3) porsi, porse, porsero. (10) porto.

pórre. — (1) pongo, poni, pone, poniamo, ponete, pongono. (2) pone, ponevi, &c. (3) posi, ponesti, pose, ponemmo, poneste, posero. (4) porrò, porrai, porrà, porremo, porrete, porranno. (5) porrei, porresti, &c. (6) ponga, ponga, ponga, poniamo, poniate, pongano. (7) ponessi, ponessi, &c. (8) poni, ponga, poniamo, ponete, pongano. (10) posto. (11) ponendo.

possedére. — like **sedere.**

potére. — (1) posso, puoi, può, possiamo, potete, possono. (3) potei, potesti, &c. (4) potrò, potrai, &c. (5) potrei, potresti, &c. (6) possa, possa, possa, possiamo, possiate, possano. (7) potessi, potessi, &c. (10) potuto. No imperative.

prediligere. — (3) predilessi, predilesse, predilessero. (10) prediletto.

prefiggere. — like **figgere.** (10) prefisso.

prelúdere. — like **alludere.**

prèmere. — (3) premei or pressi.

prèndere. — (3) presi, prese, presero. (10) preso.

presúmere. — (3) presumei or presunsi, presunse, presunsero. (10) presunto.

pretèndere. — like **tendere.**

prevalére. — like **valere.**

prevedére. — like **vedere.**

prevenire. — like **venire.**

prométtere. — like **mettere.**

protèggere. — (3) protessi, protesse, protessero. (10) protetto.

provvedére. — like **vedere.**

púngere. — (3) punsi, punse, punsero. (10) punto.

ràdere. — (3) rasi, rase, rasero. (10) raso.

recidere. — (3) recisi, recise, recisero. (10) reciso.

redigere. — (3) redassi, redasse, redassero. (10) redatto.

redimere. — (3) redensi, redense, redensero. (10) redento.

règgere. — (3) ressi, resse, ressero. (10) retto.

rèndere. — (3) resi, rendei or rendetti, rese, rendé or rendette, resero, renderono or rendettero. (10) reso or renduto.

resistere. — like **assistere.**

rídere. — (3) risi, rise, risero. (10) riso.

ridúrre. — like **addurre.**

riflèttere. — (10) riflesso & riflettuto.

rifúlgere. — (3) rifulsi, rifulse, rifulsero. No past participle.

rilúcere. — (3) rilussi or rilucei, rilusse, rilussero. No past participle.

rimanére. — (1) rimango, rimani, rimane, rimaniamo, rimanete, rimangono. (3) rimasi, rimase, rimasero. (4) rimarrò, rimarrai, &c. (5) rimarrei, rimarresti, &c. (6) rimanga, rimanga, rimanga, rimaniamo, rimaniate, rimangano. (8) rimani, rimanga, rimaniamo, rimanete, rimangano. (10) rimasto.

rincréscere. — like **crescere.**

riscuòtere. — like **scuotere.**

risòlvere. — like **assolvere.**

rispóndere. — (3) risposi, rispose, risposero. (10) risposto.

ródere. — (3) rosi, rose, rosero. (10) roso.

rómpere. — (3) ruppi, ruppe, ruppero. (10) rotto.

salíre. — (1) salgo, sali, sale, saliamo, salite, salgono. (3) salii, salisti, &c. (6) salga, salga, salga, saliamo, saliate, salgano. (8) sali, salga, saliamo, salite, salgano. (10) salito.

sapére. — (1) so, sai, sa, sappiamo, sapete, sanno. (3) seppi, sapesti, seppe, sapemmo, sapeste, seppero. (4) saprò, saprai, &c. (5) saprei, sapresti, &c. (6) sappia, sappia, sappia, sappiamo, sappiate, sappiano. (8) sappi, sappia, sappiate, &c. (9) sapiente. (10) saputo.

scégliere. — (1) scelgo, scegli, sceglie, scegliamo, scegliete, scelgono. (3) scelsi, scegliesti, scelse, scegliemmo, sceglieste, scelsero. (4) sceglierò, sceglierai, &c. (5) sceglierei, sceglieresti, &c. (6) scelga, scelga, scelga, scegliamo, scegliate, scelgano. (8) scegli, scelga, scegliamo, scegliete, scelgano. (10) scelto.

scéndere. — (3) scesi, scendesti, scese, scendemmo, scendeste, scesero. (10) sceso.

scèrnere. — (3) scernei, scernetti, & scersi, scerné, scernette, & scerse, scernerono, scernettero, & scersero. No past participle.

scíndere. — (3) scissi, scisse, scissero. (10) scisso.

sciògliere. — (1) sciolgo, sciogli, scioglie, sciogliamo, sciogliete, sciolgono. (3) sciolsi, sciogliesti, sciolse, sciogliemmo, scioglieste, sciolsero.

(4) scioglierò & sciorrò, scioglierai & sciorrai, &c. (5) scioglierei & sciorrei, scioglieresti & sciorresti, &c. (6) sciolga, sciolga, sciolga, sciogliamo, sciogliate, sciolgano. (8) sciogli, sciolga, scogliamo, sciogliete, sciolgano. (10) sciolto.

scolpíre. — (3) scolpii & sculsi. (10) scolpito & sculto.

scomméttere. — *like* **méttere.**

sconfíggere. — *like* **fíggere.**

sconvòlgere. — *like* **vòlgere.**

scrívere. — (3) scrissi, scrivesti, scrisse, scrivemmo, scriveste, scrissero. (10) scritto.

scuòtere. — (3) scossi, scotesti, scosse, scotemmo, scoteste, scosscro. (10) scosso.

śdrucíre. — (1) sdrucio & sdrucisco, &c. (6) sdrucia & sdrucisca, &c.

sedére. — (1) siedo & seggo, siedi, siede, sediamo, sedete, siedono & seggono. (6) sieda & segga, sediamo, sediate, siedano & seggano. (8) siedi, sieda & segga, sediamo, sedete, siedano & seggano. (10) seduto.

seppellíre. — (10) seppellito & sepolto.

soddisfàre. — (1) soddisfaccio *or* soddisfò, soddisfi (*or* soddisfai), soddisfa, soddisfacciamo, soddisfate, soddisfano *or* soddisfanno. (6) soddisfaccia *or* soddisfi, soddisfacciamo, soddisfacciate, soddisfacciano *or* soddisfino. *Otherwise like* fare.

soggiùngere. — *like* **giùngere.**

sórgere. — (3) sorsi, sorse, sorsero. (10) sorto.

spàndere. — (10) spanduto *or* spanto.

spàrgere. — (3) sparsi, sparse, sparsero. (10) sparso & sparto.

spégnere. — (1) spengo, spegni, spegne, spegniamo, spegnete, spengono. (3) spensi, spegnesti, spense, spegnemmo, spegneste, spensero. (6) spenga, spenga, spenza, spegniamo, spegniate, spengano. (8) spegni, spenga, spegniamo, spegnete, spengano. (10) spento.

spèndere. — (3) spési, spése, spésero. (10) spéso.

spíngere. — (3) spinsi, spinse, spinsero. (10) spinto.

stàre. — (1) sto, stai, sta, stiamo, state, stanno. (2) stavo, stavi, &c. (3) stetti, stesti, stette, stemmo, steste, stettero. (4) starò, starai, &c. (5) starei, staresti, &c. (6) stia, stia, stia, stiamo, stiate, stiano. (7) stessi, stessi, &c. (8) sta, stia, stiamo, state, stiano. (9) stante. (10) stato. *So,*

too, the compound **soprastare**, *while* **restare** & **contrastare** *are regular.*

stríngere. — (3) strinsi, strinse, strinsero. (10) stretto.

strúggere. — (3) strussi, strusse, strussero. (10) strutto.

succèdere. — *like* **concedere.**

śvèllere. — (1) śvello & śvelgo, śvelli & śvelgi, śvelle & śvelge, śvelliamo, śvellete, śvellono & śvelgono. (3) śvelsi, śvellesti, śvelse, śvellemmo, śvelleste, śvelsero. (6) śvelga, śvelga, śvelga, śvelliamo, śvelliate, śvellano. (8) śvelli, śvelga, śvelliamo, śvellete, śvelgano. (10) śvelto.

śveníre. — *like* **veníre.**

tacére. — (1) taccio, taci, tace, taciamo, tacete, tacciono. (3) tacqui, tacesti, tacque, tacemmo, taceste, tacquero. (6) taccia, taccia, taccia, taciamo, taciate, tacciano. (8) taci, taccia, taciamo, tacete, tacciano. (10) taciuto.

tèndere. — (3) tesi, tese, tesero. (10) téso.

tenére. — (1) tengo, tieni, tiene, teniamo, tenete, tengono. (3) tenni, tenesti, tenne, tencmmo, teneste, tennero. (4) terrò, terrai, &c. (5) terrei, terresti, &c. (6) tenga, tenga, teniamo, teniate, tengano. (8) tieni, tenga, teniamo, tenete, tengano. (10) tenuto.

tèrgere. — (3) tersi, terse, tersero. (10) terso.

tíngere. — (3) tinsi, tinse, tinsero. (10) tinto.

tògliere. — (1) tolgo, togli, toglie, togliamo, togliete, tolgono. (3) tolsi, togliesti, tolse, togliemmo, toglieste, tolsero. (4) toglierò & torrò, toglierai & torrai, &c. (5) toglierei & torrei, toglieresti & torresti, &c. (6) tolga, tolga, tolga, togliamo, togliate, tolgano. (8) togli, tolga, togliamo, togliete, tolgano. (10) tolto.

tòrcere. — (3) torsi, torcesti, torse, torcemmo, torceste, torsero. (10) torto.

tràrre. — (1) traggo, trai, trae, traiamo & tragghiamo, traete, traggono. (2) traevo, traevi, &c. (3) trassi, traesti, trasse, trassero. (4) trarrò, trarrai, &c. (5) trarrei, trarresti, &c. (6) tragga, tragga, tragga, traiamo & tragghiamo, traiate, traggano. (7) traessi, traessi, &c. (8) trai, tragga, traiamo, traete, traggano. (10) tratto.

uccídere. — (3) uccisi, uccise, uccisero. (10) ucciso.

udíre. — (1) odo, odi, ode, udiamo, udite, odono. (4) udirò or udrò, udirai or udrai, &c. (5) udirei or udrei, udiresti or udresti, &c. (6) oda, oda, oda, udiamo, udiate, odano. (8) odi, oda, udiamo, udite, odano.

úngere. — (3) unsi, unse, unsero. (10) unto.

uscíre. — (1) esco, esci, esce, usciamo, uscite, escono. (6) esca, esca, esca, usciamo, usciate, escano. (8) esci, esca, usciamo, uscite, escano.

valére. — (1) valgo, vali, vale, valiamo & vagliamo, valete, valgono. (3) valsi, valesti, valse, valemmo, valeste, valsero. (4) varrò, varrai, &c. (5) varrei, varresti, &c. (6) valga, valga, valga, valiamo, valiate, valgano. (10) valso. *No imperative.*

vedére. — (1) vedo & veggo, vedi, vede, vediamo, vedete, vedono & veggono. (3) vidi, vedesti, vide, vedemmo, vedeste, videro. (4) vedrò, vedrai, &c. (5) vedrei, vedresti, &c. (6) veda & vegga, veda & vegga, veda & vegga, vediamo, vediate, vedano & veggano. (8) vedi, veda, vediamo, vedete, vedano. (9) vedente & veggente. (10) veduto & visto.

veníre. — (1) vengo, vieni, viene, veniamo, venite, vengono. (3) venni, venisti, venne, venimmo, veniste, vennero. (4) verrò, verrai, &c. (5) verrei, verresti, &c. (6) venga, venga, venga, veniamo, veniate, vengano. (8) vieni, venga, veniamo, veniate, vengano. (9) veniente. (10) venuto.

víncere. — (3) vinsi, vincesti, vinse, vincemmo, vinceste, vinsero. (10) vinto.

vívere. — (3) vissi, vivesti, visse, vivemmo, viveste, vissero. (4) vivrò, vivrai, &c. (5) vivrei, vivresti, &c. (10) vissuto.

volére. — (1) voglio, vuoi, vuole, vogliamo, volete, vogliono. (3) volli, volesti, volle, volemmo, voleste, vollero. (4) vorrò, vorrai, &c. (5) vorrei, vorresti, &c. (6) voglia, voglia, voglia, vogliamo, vogliate, vogliano. (8) vogli, voglia, vogliamo, vogliate, vogliano. (10) voluto.

vòlgere. — (3) volsi, volgesti, volse, volgemmo, volgeste, volsero. (10) volto.

AUXILIARY VERBS

avére. — (1) ho, hai, ha, abbiamo, avete, hanno. (2) avevo, avevi, &c. (3) ebbi, avesti, ebbe, avemmo, aveste, ebbero. (4) avrò, avrai, avrà, avremo, avrete, avranno. (5) avrei, avresti, avrebbe, avremmo, avreste, avrebbero. (6) abbia, abbia, abbia, abbiamo, abbiate, abbiano. (7) avessi, avessi, avesse, avessimo, aveste, avessero. (8) abbi, abbia, abbiamo, abbiate, abbiano. (9) avente. (10) avuto. (11) avendo.

èssere. — (1) sono, sei, è, siamo, siete, sono. (2) ero, eri, era, eravamo, eravate, erano. (3) fui, fosti, fu, fummo, foste, furono. (4) sarò, sarai, sarà, saremo, sarete, saranno. (5) sarei, saresti, sarebbe, saremmo, sareste, sarebbero. (6) sia, sia, sia, siamo, siate, siano. (7) fossi, fossi, fosse, fossimo, foste, fossero. (8) sii, sia, siamo, siate, siano. (9) *No present participle.* (10) stato. (11) essendo.

veníre *may be used in the simple tenses as an auxiliary in place of* **essere** *(with a past participle) to form the passive, or with a gerund to indicate progressive action.*

andàre *may be similarly used with a past participle to indicate what should or ought to be done, & with the gerund to indicate repeated or continued action.*

DEFECTIVE VERBS

addírsi. — (1) si addice, si addicono. (2) si addiceva, si addicevano. (6) si addica, si addicano. (7) si addicesse, si addicessero.

ardíre. — *To avoid confusion with similar parts of the verb* ardere *the forms* ardiamo, ardiate, ardente, ardendo *have fallen out of use, & are replaced by the equivalent parts of the verb* osare.

arrògere. — (1) arroge. (8) arrogi.

calére. — (1) cale. (2) caleva. (3) calse. (6) caglia.

fèrvere. — (1) ferve, fervono. (2) fervea, ferveano. (7) fervesse, fervessero. (9) fervente. (11) fervendo.

gíre. — (2) gia *or* giva, givano. (4) girò, girai, giremo, girete, giranno. (7) gissi. (10) gito.

íre. — (1) ite. (2) ivo, iva. (3) isti, irono. (10) ito.

lèdere. — (1) lede. (2) ledeva. (3) lési *or* ledei, lése. (7) ledesse. (10) léso.

lícere. — (1) lice *or* lece. (2) liceva. (7) licesse. (10) licito.

lúcere. — (1) luce, lucono. (2) luceva, lucevano. (6) luca, lucano. (7) lucesse, lucessero. (9) lucente. (11) lucendo.

mólcere. — (1) molci, molce. (2) molcevo, molcevi, molceva, molcevamo, molcevate, molcevano. (6) molca, molcano. (7) molcessi, molcesse, molcessimo, molceste, molcessero. (11) molcendo.

solére. — (1) sòglio, suòli, suòle, sogliàmo, soléte, sògliono. (2) solevo, solevi, soleva, solevamo, solevate, solevano. (6) soglia, sogliamo, sogliate, sogliano. (7) solessi, solesse, solessimo, soleste, solessero. (10) sòlito. (11) solendo.

úrgere. — (1) urge, urgono. (2) urgeva, urgevano. (4) urgerà, urgeranno. (7) urgesse, urgessero. (9) urgente. (10) urgendo.

vèrtere. — (1) verte, vertono. (2) verteva, vertevano. (6) verta, vertano. (5) verterebbe, verterebbero. (7) vertesse, vertessero. (9) vertente. (11) vertendo.

vígere. — (1) vige, vigono. (2) vigeva, vigevano. (4) vigerà, vigeranno. (7) vigesse, vigessero. (9) vigente. (11) vigendo.

IMPERSONAL VERBS

These may be either descriptive of natural phenomena, as e.g. **albeggiare, annottare, balenare, grandinare, lampeggiare, nevicare, piovere, tuonare,** or verbs expressing occurrence, necessity, chance, possibility, concern, appearance, satisfaction, pleasure, regret, &c., when these are used impersonally, i.e. in the 3rd singular, e.g. *accade, succede, fa (freddo, caldo, &c), bisogna, conviene, importa, preme, tocca, pare, sembra, piace, giova, rincresce, dispiace, &c.*

ENGLISH IRREGULAR VERBS

Except as otherwise stated, order of parts is
(1) Infinitive (*i.*) & Present (*pr.*);
(2) Past (*p.*);
(3) Past Participle (*p.p.*).
Prefixed verbs not included in the list, such as **arise, regild**, follow the second or last element (**rise, gild**).

abide ; *p. & p.p.* abode *sometimes* abided.
awake; awoke; awoke, awaked.
i. **be**; *pr. indicative* am, art, is, *pl.* are; *p. ind.* was, wast *or* wert, was, *pl.* were; *pr. subjunctive* be; *p. subj.* were except 2 *sing.* wert; *imperative* be; *p.pr.* being; *p.p.* been. *Contractions:* 'm = am, 's = is, 're = are.

bear; bore; borne. *When referring to birth* born *&* borne, *e.g.,* born 19—; has borne a child; born of, borne by, woman.
beat; beat; beaten *sometimes* beat.
beget; begot; begotten.
begin; began; begun.
bend; bent; bent.
bereave; *p. & p.p.* bereaved *or* bereft.
beseech; besought; besought.
bespeak; bespoke; bespoke, -spoken.
bestride; bestrode; bestridden, bestrid, bestrode.
bid; bad, bade, bid; bidden, bid.
bind; bound; bound.
bite; bit; bitten *sometimes* bit.
bleed; bled; bled.
blend; *p. & p.p.* blended *or* blent.
blow; blew; blown.
break; broke; broken *sometimes* broke.
breed; bred; bred.
bring; brought; brought.
build; built; built.
burn; *p. & p.p.* burnt *sometimes* burned.
burst; burst; burst.
buy; bought; bought.

can.—*pr.* I, he, &c., can, thou canst. *neg.* cannot, can't. *p. & conditional,* I, he, &c., could, thou could[e]st. *i., p.pr. & p.p. wanting; defective parts supplied from* be able to.
cast; cast; cast.
catch; caught; caught.
chide; chid; chidden *or* chid.
choose; chose; chosen.

cleave; clove *or* cleft; cloven *or* cleft.
cling; clung; clung.
clothe; *p. & p.p.* clothed *or* clad.
come; came; come.
cost; cost; cost.
could. See *can*.
creep; crept; crept.
crow; crew *or* crowed; crowed.
cut; cut; cut.

dare; dared *&* durst; dared.
deal; dealt; dealt.
die; died; *p.pr.* dying; *p.p.* died.
dig; dug; dug.
i. **do**; *pr. indicative* do, doest (*as auxiliary* dost), does, *pl.* do; *p.* did, didst, did, *pl.* did; *p.p.* done. *Contractions:* don't = do not. doesn't = does not. didn't = did not.
draw; drew; drawn.
dream; *p. & p.p.* dreamt *or* dreamed.
drink; drank; drunk.
drive; drove; driven.
dwell; dwelt; dwelt.

eat; ate *or* eat; eaten.

fall; fell; fallen.
feed; fed; fed.
feel; felt; felt.
fight; fought; fought.
find; found; found.
flee; fled; fled.
fling; flung; flung.
fly; flew; flown.
forbear; forbore; forborne.
forbid; forbad *or* -bade; forbidden.
forget; forgot; forgotten.
forsake; forsook; forsaken.
freeze; froze; frozen.

get; got; got, *also* -gotten *in combination as* ill-gotten.
gild; *p. & p.p.* gilded *&* gilt.
gird; *p. & p.p.* girt *& poet.* girded.
give; gave; given.
go; *pr.* I go, thou goest, he goes, we, &c., go; *p.* went; *p.p.* gone.
grave; graved; graven *&* graved.
grind; ground; ground.
grow; grew; grown.

hang; *p. & p.p.* hung *&* hanged.
i. **have**; *pr.* I have, *archaic* thou hast, he has, we, you, they, have; *p.* had,

archaic thou hadst; *p.p.* had; *abb.*
I've, we've, &c.; I'd, we'd, &c.;
's = has; *colloquially neg.* haven't,
hasn't; hadn't.
hear; heard; heard.
heave; *p. & p.p.* heaved *or* hove.
hew; hewed; hewn *or* hewed.
hide; hid; hidden & hid.
hit; hit; hit.
hold; held; held.
hurt; hurt; hurt.

inset; *p. & p.p.* inset *or* insetted.

keep; kept; kept.
kneel; knelt; knelt.
knit; *p. & p.p.* knitted *or* knit.
know; knew; known.

lade; laded; laden.
lay; laid; laid.
lead; led; led.
lean; *p. & p.p.* leaned *or* leant.
leap; *p. & p.p.* leapt *or* leaped.
learn; *p. & p.p.* learnt, learned.
leave; left; left.
lend; lent; lent.
let; let; let.
lie; lay; *p.pr.* lying; *p.p.* lain.
light; *p. & p.p.* lit *or* lighted.
lose; lost; lost.

make; made; made.
pr. I may, he may; *p.* might.
mean; meant; meant.
meet; met; met.
melt; melted; melted, molten.
mow; mowed; mown.
pr. I must, he must; *p.* must.
pr. **ought;** *p.* ought.

outbid; outbid *or* -bade; outbid *or*
-bidden.
overhang; overhung; overhung.

pay; paid; paid.
put; put; put.

read; read; read.
reeve; *p. & p.p.* rove *or* reeved.
rend; rent; rent.
rid; ridded, rid; rid.
ride; rode; ridden.
ring; rang; rung.
rise; rose; risen.
rive; rived; riven.
run; ran; run.

saw; sawed; sawn.

say; said; said.
see; saw; seen.
seek; sought; sought.
sell; sold; sold.
send; sent; sent.
set; set; set.
sew; sewed; sewed *or* sewn.
shake; shook; shaken.
pr. **I shall,** thou shalt, he, &c., **shall;**
p. & conditional I should thou
should[e]st, he, &c., should; *neg.*
shall not *or* shan't; should not *or*
shouldn't.
shear; sheared; shorn.
shed; shed; shed.
shew; shewed; shewn.
shine; shone; shone.
shoe; shod; shod.
shoot; shot; shot.
should. See *shall.*
show; showed; shown.
shrink; shrank; shrunk.
shut; shut; shut.
sing; sang; sung.
sink; sank; sunk.
sit; sat; sat.
slay; slew; slain.
sleep; slept; slept.
slide; slid; slid.
sling; slung; slung.
slink; slunk; slunk.
slit; slit; slit.
smell; smelt; smelt.
smite; smote; smitten.
sow; sowed; sown *or* sowed.
speak; spoke; spoken.
speed; sped; sped.
spell; *p. & p.p.* spelt *or* spelled.
spend; spent; spent.
spill; *p. & p.p.* spilt *or* spilled.
spin; spun *or* span; spun.
spit; spat; spat.
split; split; split.
spread; spread; spread.
spring; sprang; sprung.
stand; stood; stood.
stave; *p. & p.p.* staved *or* stove.
steal; stole; stolen.
stick; stuck; stuck.
sting; stung; stung.
stink; stank *or* stunk; stunk.
strew; strewed; strewn, strewed.
stride; strode; (*rare*) stridden *or* strid.
strike; struck; struck *&* stricken.
string; strung; strung.
strive; strove; striven.
swear; swore; sworn.
sweep; swept; swept.
swell; swelled; swollen.
swim; swam; swum.
swing; swung; swung.

take; took; taken.
teach; taught; taught.
tear; tore; torn.
tell; told; told.
think; thought; thought.
thrive; throve; thriven.
throw; threw; thrown.
thrust; thrust; thrust.
tie; tied; *p.pr.* tying; *p.p.* tied.
tread; trod; trodden.

wake; woke, waked; waked, woken, woke.

wear; wore; worn.
weave; wove; woven *&* wove.
weep; wept; wept.
pr. I, he, &c., will *or* 'll, thou wilt *or* 'lt, *p.* *& conditional* I, he, &c., would *or* 'd, thou would[e]st *or* 'dst; *neg.* will not *or* won't; would not *or* wouldn't *or* 'd not.
win; won; won.
wind; wound; wound.
would. See *will.*
wring; wrung; wrung.
write; wrote; written.

A

A, a, *f.* letter A. **a.** *un'A maiuscola,* a capital A: *un'a minuscola,* a small (lower case) A.

a (sometimes **ad** for euphony before vowels), *pr.* to, at, in, within, into, on, by, with, for, from, of; according to, under; and. Combined with def. art. **al, all', allo, alla, ai, a', agli, alle.** *a uno a uno,* one by one. *a passo a passo,* step by step. *vendere a[lla] dozzina,* to sell by the dozen. When coupled with a noun, often rendered in English by noun used attributively, *e.g. pittura ad olio,* oil-painting. *treno a corridoio,* corridor-train. After a verb may indicate means or material, *andare a vela,* to sail. *costruire a mattoni,* to build in brick. *dipingere ad olio,* to paint in oil(s). *a braccia aperte,* with open arms. *a poco a poco,* little by little. *a bordo,* on board. *alla catena,* on the chain. *a piedi,* on foot. *a credito,* on credit. *a pronti,* for cash. When used as a prefix, requires the doubling of the consonant which follows it, *a-canto, accanto, a-lato, allato.*

àbaco (*pl.* **àbachi**), *n.* (*Arch.*) abacus. Cf. **àbbaco.**

abasía, *f.* (*Med.*) loss of the power of locomotion.

abàte, *m.* abbot; abbé (*Fr.*); priest.

abbacàre, *v.i.* (*aux.* avere) to dote, dream.

abbacchiàre, *v.t.* to knock down (*fruit, &c.*) with a pole (*bacchio*)); (*fig.*) bring down (prices); undersell; humiliate; depress.

abbàcchio, *m.* (*Cook.*) baby lamb.

abbacinàre (*pr.* -íno), *v.t.* to dazzle; blind; darken; (*fig.*) to deceive.

àbbaco (*pl.* **àbbachi**), *m.* calculating frame;(*Artil.*)artillery board,director.

abbagliaménto, *m.* glare, dazzle; dazzlement; error; confusion. **abbagliànte,** *p.a.* dazzling; blinding; fascinating. *faro anti-abbagliante,* anti-dazzle lamp. **abbagliàre,** *v.t. & abs.* to dazzle, blind; (*fig.*) fascinate; deceive; astonish. **abbàglio,** *m.* glare, dazzle; (*fig.*) error, slip.

abbaiàre, *v.i.* (*aux.* avere) to bark, bay, howl, yelp, snarl. **abbaiàta,** *f.* barking, baying, scolding. **abbaióne,** *m.* noisy fellow; great talker.

abbaíno, *m.* dormer window; skylight; garret window; garret.

abballàre, *v.t.* to pack, embale; stow away.

abballottàre, *v.t.* to toss about; handle roughly; mix, jumble.

abbandonàre, *v.t.* to abandon, leave, quit, desert, forsake; forgo; let go; drop, let fall; disuse; give up, relinquish, surrender; concede; throw away. **abbandonàrsi (a),** *v.refl.* to give way to, be addicted to; yield to, surrender to; indulge in. **abbandonàto,** *p.a.* abandoned, deserted, forsaken, neglected, given up. ¶ *m.* foundling. **abbandóno,** *m.* abandonment; desertion; dereliction; renouncement; relaxation, unconstraint; isolation, neglect. *nell' ~,* in confusion, in disorder; anyhow; derelict; in decay.

abbarbagliàre, *v.t.* to dazzle; daze; hallucinate.

abbarbicàre, *v.i.* (*aux.* avere) & **abbarbicàrsi,** *v.refl.* to take root, strike root; be implanted; cling; clutch; entwine. **abbarbicàto,** *p.a.* rooted; clinging; inveterate.

abbaruffàre, *v.t.* to mix up; embroil; jumble, upset. **abbaruffàrsi,** *v. refl.* to quarrel, wrangle; scuffle, come to blows.

abbassaménto, *m.* lowering; sinking; subsidence; sagging (*roof, &c.*); lessening, diminution; reduction; fall; decline; humiliation; (*Astr.*) depression; (*Naut.*) dip (*of horizon*). **abbassàre,** *v.t.* to lower, let down; drop (*voice*); dip (*flag*); turn down (*eyes, light, &c.*); pull down; reduce (*prices, Alg. equations*); draw down; lay down (*arms*); humble, abase; debase. *~ i fari,* to dim the headlights. *v.i.* (*aux.* essere) to fall, come down; lessen, diminish. **abbassàrsi,** *v.refl.* to fall, sink; sag; ebb; bow, stoop; humble oneself; condescend. **abbàsso,** *ad.* down, below; downwards; downstair… ¶ *i.* down! down with!

abbastànza, *ad.* enough, sufficiently; somewhat; rather, fairly, pretty.

abbàttere, *v.t.* to beat down, knock d., strike d.; throw d.; pull d.; bring d., shoot d. (*Aviat.*); cut d.; blow d.; break d.; hew d.; fell (*trees*); lay, clear; slaughter (*animals*), kill; destroy, demolish; (*fig.*) to depress, discourage, dishearten, dispirit; dismay; allay, abate; confute. **abbàttersi,** *v.refl.* to fall down, come d.; swoop d., pounce (*su* = [up]on); burst (*of storms*); (*fig*). be cast down, despondent, or depressed ; happen, succeed, fall out. ~ *in,* to fall in with, come across, meet. **abbattiménto,** *m* knocking down, pulling down, &c.; felling (*trees*); overthrow; destruction, demolition; prostration, dejection, depression; despondency; (*tax*) relief. **abbattúto,** *p.a.* dejected, depressed, low-spirited, downcast; despondent; crest-fallen; prostrate, fatigued; knocked down, felled, overthrown; destroyed.

abbazía, *f.* abbey ; abbacy.

abbecedàrio, *m.* first spelling-book; primer.

abbelliménto, *m.* embellishment, embellishing; decoration; improvement. **abbellíre** (*pr.* -ísco, ísci), *v.t.* to beautify, embellish, adorn. **abbellírsi,** *v.refl.* to adorn oneself; grow or seem (more) beautiful; improve in appearance.

abbeveràre, *v.t.* to water or give drink to (*horse, &c.*). **abbeveràrsi,** *v.refl.* to water; slake one's thirst (*fig.*). **abbeveratoio,** *m.* wateringplace, horse-pond, drinking trough.

abbicci, *m. inv.* ABC; spelling-book, primer; rudiments.

abbiènte *a.* well-to-do, prosperous. *gli* ~ *i e i non* ~ *i,* the haves & the have-nots.

abbigliaménto, *m.* dress, clothes, attire. ~ *da sera,* evening dress (*man's*). **abbigliàre,** *v.t. &* **abbigliàrsi,** *v.refl.* to dress, dress smartly. **abbigliatúra,** *f.* dressing; style of dress[ing].

abbinàre, *v.t.* to pair; unite (gen. two things of the same class).

abbindolàre, *v.t.* to cheat, dupe, deceive; (*fig.*) lead by the nose.

abbisognàre, *v.i.* (*aux.* avere) *& impers.* to want, be in want (of); require. *Mi abbisogna del denaro,* I want money.

abboccaménto, *m.* interview; conversation; talk. **abboccàre** (*pr.* **abbócco, abbócchi**), *v.t. & i.* to seize with the mouth; (*fish*) bite, bite at, swallow (*bait, hook*); (*fig.*) to be deceived, allured. *far* ~, to bring (people) to talk to each other. **abboccàrsi,** *v.refl.* to have an interview; talk, confer.

abbonacciàre, *v.t.* to appease, calm; quiet; soothe. **abbonacciàrsi,** *v.refl.* to become calm, grow calm; (*wind*) blow out (*Naut.*).

abbonaménto, *m.* subscription (*to concerts, theatre, journal, &c.*); reduction, allowance. *biglietto di* ~, season ticket. **abbonàre** (*pr.* **abbuòno**) to take out a subscription for (*someone else*); induce (someone) to subscribe; approve; allow (*discount*). **abbonàrsi,** *v.refl.* to subscribe, take out a subscription (*for oneself*). **abbonàto,** *m.* subscriber; seasonticket holder; consumer (*gas, elec.*).

abbondànte, *p.a.* abundant, plentiful, copious; rich, full, plenteous (*Lit.*), profuse. **abbondànza,** *f.* abundance, plenty, fullness. **abbondàre,** *v.i.* (*aux.* avere *&* essere) to abound. ~ *di,* ~ *in,* to abound in. **abbondévole,** *a.* (*Lit.*) abundant.

abbonire (*pr.* -ísco, -ísci), *v.t.* to calm, soften, appease; ripen; (*of land*) to cultivate, improve.

abbordàbile, *a.* approachable, accessible. **abbordàggio,** *m.* (*Naut.*) laying alongside; fouling; boarding. **abbordàre,** *v.t.* (*Naut.*) to board, lay alongside, close with, foul, collide with; (*fig.*) accost, approach, go up to; broach (*subject*). **abbórdo,** *m.* access, approach; (*Naut.*) boarding; collision. *di facile* ~, affable, approachable, accessible. *di* (or *sul*) *primo* ~, at first, first of all, to begin with.

abborracciàre, *v.t.* to botch, bungle, scamp (a piece of work). **abborraccióne,** *m.* bungler.

abbottonàre, *v.t.* to button, button up. **abbottonàrsi,** *v.refl.* (*fig.*) to become reserved, secretive, keep something to oneself. **abbottonatúra,** *f.* buttoning; row of buttons.

abbozzàre, *v.t.* to sketch, outline, make a rough draft of; (*sculpture*) rough-hew ; (*Naut.*) stopper (*a cable*). ~ *un sorriso,* to break into a smile. **abbozzàta,** *f.* rough sketch. **abbozzatíccio,** *a.* sketchy, slight, rough-cast. **abbozzo,** *m.* sketch, outline, rough model, rough draft; dwarf, manikin.

abbracciabòschi, *m. inv.* honey-suckle. **abbracciaménto,** *m.* embrace. **abbracciàre,** *v.t.* to embrace, clasp ; (*fig.*) to encircle, encompass; enclose; contain; include; adopt; choose; espouse (*cause, &c.*). **abbracciàta,** *f.* & **abbràccio,** *m.* embrace.

abbrancàre, *v.t.* to grasp, seize, grip; (*fig.*) steal. **abbrancàrsi,** *v.refl.* to catch hold (of); come to grips.

abbreviaménto, *m.* abbreviation, shortening; abridgement. **abbreviàre,** *v.t.* to abbreviate, shorten, contract; abridge. **abbreviatúra,** & **abbreviazióne,** *f.* abbreviation, abridgement, contraction.

abbrivàre, *v.i.* (*Naut.*) (*aux.* avere) to get under way; leave the shore (or moorings); make headway.

abbrividíre (*pr.* -ísco, -ísci), *v.i.* to shudder, shiver, quake.

abbrívo, *m.* (*Naut.*) course, headway, way (*of a ship*) *acquistare, pigliare* [*l'*] ~, to gather way, get under way. *perdere* [*l'*] ~, to lose way.

abbronzàre, *v.t.* to bronze, tan, scorch, sunburn. **abbronzàrsi,** *v.refl.* to grow brown, become sunburnt. **abbronzàta,** *f.* touch of brown. **abbronzatúra,** *f.* bronzing; sunburn. **abbronzíre** (*pr.* -ísco, -ísci), *v.i.* (*aux.* essere) to be or become sunburnt. **abbronzíto** or **abbronzàto,** *p.a.* sunburnt, sunburned; tanned (*fig.*).

abbruciacchiàre, *v.t.* to singe, scorch; discolour; parch.

abbruciàre, *v.t.* to burn, burn up; scorch; shrivel (*with heat or cold*). Cf. *bruciare.*

abbrunàre, *v.t.* to drape with black. **abbrunàrsi,** *v.refl.* to put on mourning. *bandiera abbrunata,* draped flag, flag at half-mast.

abbruníre, (*pr.* -ísco, -ísci) *v.t.* to darken, tan; *v.i.* (*aux.* essere) to become dark (*skin*).

abbrustolíre (*pr.* -ísco, -ísci), *v.t.* to toast; singe; scorch; roast (*coffee*).

abbrutiménto, *m.* degradation; brutishness, brutalization; sottishness, habitual drunkenness. **abbrutíre** (*pr.* -ísco, -ísci), *v.t.* to brutalize, degrade; coarsen.

abbuiàre, *v.t.* to obscure; darken; tarnish; hide; hush up.

abbuòno, *m.* allowance, special discount, deduction.

abburattàre, *v.t.* to bolt or sift

(*meal*); to choose, select; discuss at length; talk incoherently of.

abdicàre, *v.i.* (*aux.* avere) to abdicate. ~ *a,* to renounce, surrender, waive. **abdicazióne,** *f.* abdication.

aberrazióne, *f.* aberration.

abetàia, *f.* fir-plantation. **abéte,** *m.* fir[tree]. ~ *bianco,* silver fir. — ~ *rosso,* spruce [fir].

abiètto, *a.* abject, mean, low, despicable. **abiezióne,** *f.* abjectness, &c.

àbile, *a.* clever, capable, dexterous, skilful, able, talented; (legally) qualified, competent. **abilità,** *f.* ability, capacity, cleverness, skill, address. **abilitàre,** *v.t.* (*leg.*) qualify, enable, empower. **abilitazióne,** *f.* qualification; competence; proficiency. **abilménte,** *ad.* skilfully, cleverly.

Abissínia (l'), *f.* Abyssinia. **abissíno,** *a.* & *m.* Abyssinian.

abísso, *m.* abyss; gulf, chasm; bottomless pit; (*fig.*) mine, treasure.

abitàbile, *a.* habitable. **abitàcolo,** *m.* binnacle. **abitànte,** *m.f.* inhabitant, dweller; resident. **abitàre,** *v.t.* to inhabit, occupy, live in, l. at; *v.i.* (*aux.* avere) to live, dwell. **abitazióne,** *f.* house; dwelling. *crisi delle ~ i,* housing problem, *f.*

àbito, *m.* coat, dress, gown, frock; clothes; suit; garb, attire; uniform; (*fig.*) habit, custom; (*Med.*) constitution, habit of body. ~ *da sera,* dress-coat, evening dress. ~ *da società,* dress clothes (men). ~ *a coda di rondine,* swallow-tail coat, dress-coat. — ~ *da ballo,* dance frock. — ~ *da passeggio,* walking-out dress. ~ *da pomeriggio,* afternoon frock. (See also *veste, toletta.*)

abituàle, *a.* habitual, customary, usual. **abituàre,** *v.t.* to accustom. **abituàrsi** (a) *v.refl.* to get used (to), accustom oneself (to). **abitúdine,** *f.* habit; custom; rule, practice.

abitúro, *m.* mean dwelling; cottage; garret.

abiúra, *f.* abjuration. **abiuràre,** *v.t.* to abjure, forswear, renounce.

ablatívo, *m.* ablative [case].

ablazióne, *f.* removal, extraction; (*Geog.*) erosion.

abluzióne, *f.* ablution; purification.

abnegazióne, *f.* abnegation, self-denial.

abolíre (*pr.* -ísco, -ísci), *v.t.* to abolish, do away with; nullify; repeal. **abolizióne,** *f.* abolition; repeal.

abominàbile, or **abominévole**, also **abominàndo**, *a.* abominable, hateful; odious; nefarious. **abominàre**, *v.t.* to abominate, detest, abhor, loathe. **abominazióne**, *f.* abomination. **abomínio**, *m.* shame, abomination.

aborígeno, *a. & m.* aboriginal; (*m.pl.*) aborigines.

aborríre (*pr.* **abòrro** or **aborrísco**), *v.t.* to abhor, hold in abhorrence; loathe, detest; denounce. ~ *da*, to feel repugnance for, shrink from; hate, abhor.

abortíre (*pr.* **-ísco**, **-ísci**) (*aux.* avere), *v.i.* to miscarry, have a miscarriage; (*fig.*) fail, come to nothing. **abortívo**, *a.* abortive; premature. **abòrto**, *m.* abortion, miscarriage.

Abràmo, *m.* Abraham.

abraśióne, *f.* abrasion. **abraśívo**, *a. & m.* abrasive.

abrogàre, *v.t.* to abrogate, revoke, repeal. **abrogazióne**, *f.* abrogation, repeal, reversal.

abruzzése, *a.* of the Abruzzi. ¶ *m.* native of the A.; dialect of the A. **Abrúzzi (gli)**, *m.pl. &* **Abrúzzo (l')**, *m.* the Abruzzi (*Geog.*).

àbside, *f.* (*Arch.*) apse.

abulía, *f.* (*Psych.*) indecision, weakness of will.

abuśàre, *v.t. & i.* (*aux.* avere) *&* **abuśàrsi**, *v.refl.* to mis-use, indulge in excesses, make bad or excessive use of. (Not in the sense of 'revile', which is *ingiuriare* . . .) **abúśo**, *m.* misuse, excessive use, abuse.

acàcia, *f.* acacia.

acagiú, *m.* mahogany.

acànto, *m.* (*Bot. & Arch.*) acanthus.

àcaro, *m.* acarus, mite, tick.

àcca, *f.* letter H; a mere nothing. *non saperne un'* ~, to know nothing whatever of it.

accadèmia, *f.* academy; college, high school; university; school (*of fine arts, &*c.); academic taste; academy figure. **accadèmico** (*pl.* **-èmici**), *a.* academic(al). ¶ *m.* academician.

accadére, *v.i.* (*aux.* essere) to happen, take place, occur. **accadúto**, *p.p.* happened, taken place. ¶ *m.* what has happened, incident, event; case; matter.

accagliàre, *v.t. &* **accagliàrsi** *v.refl.* to curdle.

accalappiacàni, *m.inv.* dog-catcher. **accalappiàre**, *v.t.* to snare, ensnare, trap, catch; (*fig.*) to dupe, deceive.

accalcàre, *v.t.* to heap, crowd up. **accalcàrsi**, *v.refl.* to crowd, hustle, throng.

accaldàrsi, *v.refl.* to grow warm, become heated; become excited.

accaloràre, *v.t.* to excite (*feeling*); warm, heat; incite. **accaloràrsi**, *v.refl.* to become animated, excited, exasperated.

accampaménto, *m.* encampment, camping place, camp; camping.

accampanàto, *a.* bell-shaped.

accampàre, *v.i. & t.* to camp, pitch one's camp, encamp; (*fig.*) put forth; allege, assent. **accampàrsi**, *v.refl.* to encamp, pitch one's tent, go camping.

accampionàre, *v.t.* to sample; gauge; register.

accanalàre, *v.t.* to channel, flute, groove; chamber.

accaniménto, *m.* fury, persistence, pertinacity; animosity, bitterness. **accaníre** (*pr.* **-ísco**, **-ísci**), *v.t.* to infuriate, enrage, embitter. **accanírsi**, *v.refl.* to show furious determination, become enraged, be implacable; be desperately bent on. **accanitaménte**, *ad.* furiously. **accaníto**, *p.a.* dogged, inexorable, implacable; fierce; ruthless.

accànto, *ad. & pr.* near, nearby. ~ *a.* beside.

accantonaménto, *m.* billeting; billet; (*pl.*) cantonments. **accantonàre**, *v.t.* to billet, quarter; set aside (*sum of money*).

accaparràre, *v.t.* to corner, buy up, monopolize; forestall; book, secure; give earnest for. **accaparratóre**, *m.* hoarder, monopolist.

accapigliàrsi, *v.refl.* to seize or pull each other's hair; scuffle, come to blows; dispute.

accappatóio, *m.* loose bathing gown; wrap, wrapper.

accappiàre, *v.t.* to lasso, ensnare, catch or hold with a running knot. **accappiatúra**, *f.* slip-knot, running knot.

accapponàre, *v.i.* in the expr. *far* ~ *la pelle*, to make the flesh creep.

accarezzàre, *v.t.* to caress, fondle; cherish; (*fig.*) entertain (*an idea*).

accartocciàre, *v.t.* to twist (paper) into a cone or cornet; to shrivel; (*Arch.*) to form scrolls or spirals.

accaśàre, *v.t.* to settle a daughter in marriage, marry. **accaśàrsi**, *v.refl.* to get married; set up house; settle in life.

accasciaménto, *m.* despondency; dejection; weakness, prostration.

accasciàre, *v.t.* to crush; weaken; discourage, deject.

accatastàre, *v.t.* to pile, heap up, stack.

accattabríghe, *m.inv.* quarrelsome fellow; mischief-maker. **accattapàne,** *m.inv.* beggar. **accattàre,** *v.t.* to beg; collect alms; borrow. **accattonàggio,** *m.* begging, mendicancy. **accattóne,** *m.* beggar, mendicant.

accavalcàre (*pr.* -àlco, -àlchi), *v.t.* to place astride; climb over.

accavalciàre (*pr.* -àlcio, -àlci), *v.t.* to bestride; straddle; cross (*legs*); span (*river, &c.*). **accavalcióne &** **accavalcióni,** *ad.* astride, astraddle.

accavallàre, *v.t.* to superimpose; slip (*stitches*); stalk; inset (*Typ.*); stagger (*dates*).

accavigliàre, *v.t.* to wind on a bobbin.

accecaménto, *m.* blinding; blindness; darkness; (*fig.*) confusion; stoppage; obstruction. **accecàre** (*pr.* -ièco, -ièchi), *v.t.* to blind; dazzle; block, obstruct, stop (up), wall up; (*Mech.*) countersink. *v.i.* (*aux.* essere) & **accecàrsi,** *v.refl.* to become blind; blind oneself.

accecànte, *p.a.* blinding, dazzling.

accèdere (a), *v.i.* (*aux.* essere) to approach; enter; give access (to); accede (to), consent (to).

acceleràre, *v.t.* & *abs.* to accelerate, quicken; hasten. **acceleràto,** *p.a.* accelerated. *marcia accelerata,* quick march. ¶ *m.* for *treno a.,* ordinary train (*3 classes, stopping at all stations, but travelling at fair speed*). **acceleratóre,** *m.* accelerator. **accelerazióne,** *f.* acceleration.

accèndere, *v.t. ir.* to kindle, ignite, light, set fire to; (*fig.*) to fire, inflame, excite; open (*an account*). *l'ora d'accendere le luci,* lighting-up time. **accèndersi,** *v.refl.* to kindle, catch fire, light up, ignite; be excited; be enraged; blush; *accendersi d'amore per,* to fall in love with. **accendif[u]òco,** *m.inv.* fire-lighter. **accendisígaro,** *m.inv.* cigar lighter. ~ *a benzina,* petrol lighter. **accenditóio,** *m.* lighting-stick; pilot-burner.

accennàre (*pr.* -énno), *v.t.* & *v.i.* (*aux.* avere) to point out, indicate, allude to; beckon, nod, hint.

accénno, *m.* sign, indication, hint, nod.

accensióne, *f.* lighting, ignition; inflammation; flush, high colour; glow, animation. *candela d'* ~, sparking plug.

accentàre, *v.t.* to accent; accentuate, emphasize, stress. **accènto,** *m.* accent; stress; pronunciation; tone; (*Poet.*) voice; (*pl.*) strains.

accentràre, *v.t.* to centralize; gather, assemble.

accentuàre, *v.t.* to accentuate, stress, emphasize, lay emphasis on; (*Mus.*) play with expression.

accerchiaménto, *m.* encirclement. **accerchiàre,** *v.t.* to encircle, hem in; circumvent.

accertaménto, *m.* ascertainment; verification; assurance.

accertàre, *v.t.* to ascertain, to verify, assure. **accertàrsi,** *v.refl.* to make sure, assure oneself.

accéso, *p.p. of accendere.* ¶ *a.* alight; bright, vivid, lively, high-coloured (*complexion*). *rosso* ~, fiery red.

accessíbile, *a.* accessible; approachable. **accessióne,** *f.* accession; approach (*pers.*); increase, growth, addition. **accèsso,** *m.* access, accessibility; entry, approach; (*Min.*) adit; judicial visit; attack (of fever, &c.); transfer of vote in Papal election. **accessòrio,** *a.* & *m.* accessory.

accétta, *f.* hatchet; adze. *tagliato con l'* ~, coarsely made.

accettànte, *m.* acceptor. ~ *per intervento,* (*Com.*) acceptor for honour.

accettàre, *v.t.* to accept, approve, agree to; admit; undertake. **accettazióne,** *f.* acceptation, approval; acceptance. *mancata* ~, non-acceptance. **accettévole,** *a.* acceptable. **accètto,** *a.* welcome, agreeable. **accezióne,** *f.* acceptation, accepted meaning.

acchetàre, *v.t.* to quiet, pacify, appease; allay, hush; slake, put down, quell, suppress, calm.

acchiappàre, *v.t.* to catch, grasp, seize; take; overtake, entrap. **acchiapparèllo,** *m.* catch, tricky question. **acchiappatóio,** *m.* booby-trap.

acchitàre, *v.t.* & **acchitàrsi,** *v.refl.* (*Bil.*) to lead. **acchíto,** *m.* lead (*Bil.*) ~, at once, from the first. *di primo* ~, at the outset; at the first stroke.

acchiúdere, *v.t. ir.* (like *chiudere*) to enclose.

acciabattàre, *v.t.* to cobble, botch. **acciabattóne,** *m.* bungler.

acciaccàre, *v.t.* to crush, bruise. **acciaccàto,** *p.a.* crushed, bruised; broken down, ill, infirm. **acciàcco** (*pl.* **-acchi**), *m.* infirmity, misfortune, affliction, indisposition.

acciaiàre, *v.t.* to turn iron into steel; tip with steel; steel (*fig.*). **acciaieria,** *f.* steel-works. **acciàio,** *m.* steel. ~ *fuso,* cast steel. ~ *ad alta tensione,* high-tension s. ~ *inossidabile,* stainless s., rustless s. **acciaríno,** *m.* (*Mech.*) linch-pin. **acciàro,** *m.* (*Poet.*) steel, sword.

acciarpàre, *v.t.* to botch, bungle, cobble.

accidentàto, *a.* impotent; paralysed; uneven; hilly. *terreno* ~, broken ground. **accidènte,** *m.* accident, casualty; apoplectic fit. **accidènti !,** *i.* dash it all ! the deuce [take it] !

accídia, *f.* sloth, ennui.

accigliàrsi, *v.refl.* to frown, knit the brows. **accigliàto,** *a.* frowning, sullen, angry.

accíngersi (*pr.* **-ingo, -ingi** like *cingere*), *v.refl. ir.* to prepare (oneself), get ready, set about. **accínto,** *p.a.* prepared, disposed.

acciò, a ciò che, acciocché, *c.* in order that.

acciottolàre, *v.t.* to pave with cobbles; clatter (*plates, &c.*). **acciottolàto,** *m.* cobbled pavement, crazy p. **acciottolío,** *m.* clatter (*of dishes, &c.*).

acciuffàre, *v.t.* to seize by the hair; catch; grasp. **acciuffàrsi,** *v.refl.* to seize each other by the hair; come to blows.

acciúga (*pl.* **acciúghe**), *f.* anchovy. *pasta di acciughe,* anchovy paste. **acciugàta,** *f.* anchovy sauce.

acclamàre, *v.t.* to acclaim, applaud, cheer. **acclamazióne,** *f.* acclamation; applause.

acclimàre, *v.t.* to acclimatize. **acclimazióne,** *f.* acclimatization.

acclíve, *a.* sloping upward. **acclività,** *f.* acclivity; ascent.

acclúdere, *v.t. ir.* to enclose. **acclúsa,** *f.* enclosure (letter).

accoccàre, *v.t.* to fit the arrow to the bowstring; notch; strike. ~ *un colpo,* ~ *un pugno,* to deliver a blow. *accoccarla ad uno,* to trick someone. **accoccàrsi,** *v.refl.* to attach itself, be attached.

accoccolàrsi, *v.refl.* to crouch; to squat. **accoccolàto,** *p.a.* crouching, squatting.

accodàrsi, *v.refl.* to follow closely, follow in single file, fall in behind.

accogliènza, *f.* reception, welcome; (*Com.*) honouring a draft. **accògliere** (*pr.* **-còlgo, -cògli,** &c., like *cogliere*), *v.t. ir.* to receive, welcome, make welcome; accept; agree to; (*Com.*) honour (*draft or bill of exchange*).

accòlito, *m.* acolyte.

accollàre, *v.t.* to load; charge; yoke (oxen). (*v.i.*) (*aux. avere*) to fit close to the neck. **accollàrsi,** *v.refl.* to take upon oneself, undertake. **accollatàrio,** *m.* contractor.

accòlta, *f.* assembly, gathering.

accoltellàre, *v.t.* to knife, stab.

accomàndita, *f.* limited partnership. **accomandatàrio,** *m.* general partner (*Com.*).

accomiatàre, *v.t.* to dismiss. **accomiatàrsi,** *v.refl.* to take leave (of).

accomodaménto, *m.* accommodation (*Com.*); agreement, arrangement; settlement; composition (with creditors); reconciliation; adjustment; compromise. **accomodàre,** *v.t.* to mend, repair; arrange, adjust, put in order; settle; adapt; oblige. *Non mi accomoda,* it does not suit me, it is not convenient. **accomodàrsi,** *v.refl.* to come to terms; make oneself comfortable; sit down; take a seat.

accompagnaménto, *m.* accompaniment. **accompagnàre,** *v.t.* to accompany; attend, wait upon; escort; match, couple; harmonize; place side by side; (*Mus.*) accompany (*singer*). **accompagnàrsi,** *v.refl.* to keep company; match; join; take as a companion; (*Mus.*) accompany oneself.

accomunàre, *v.t.* to put together; put into the common stock; share in common, throw open to all. **accomunàrsi,** *v.refl.* to mix, associate familiarly, fraternize.

acconciaménte, *ad.* becomingly, fittingly; tidily, precisely; neatly. **acconciàre,** *v.t.* to arrange, set in order, prepare for use; deck, adorn; dress (*skins, &c.*); pickle. ~ (or *conciare*) *qualcuno pel di delle feste,* to give someone a (good) dressing down. **acconciàrsi,** *v.refl.* to dress (for some occasion), tidy oneself, adorn oneself. ~ *a,* to accom-

modate oneself to, adapt oneself to. ~ *per*, compose oneself for.
acconciatúra, *f.* arrangement; toilette; style of hair-dressing.
accóncio, *a.* suitable; serviceable; seasonable; seasoned; opportune; fit. ¶ *m.* advantage, opportunity; agreement.
acconsentíre (*pr.* -**ènto**), *v.i.* (*aux.* avere) to consent, assent; accede; (*Mech.*) spring, stretch; (*v.t.*) concede, grant.
accontentàre, *v.t.* to satisfy, content. **accontentàrsi**, *v.refl.* to be content (with).
accónto, *m.* instalment, part-payment, *in* ~, on account.
accoppiaménto, *m.* coupling; (*Mech.*) connection; pairing, matching. **accoppiàre**, *v.t.* to couple, join, match, pair, unite. **accoppiàrsi**, *v.refl.* to pair; marry; go in couples.
accoraménto, *m.* grief, sorrow, heart-ache; heartfelt sentiment. **accoràre**, *v.t.* to grieve, afflict, pierce to the heart. **accoràrsi**, *v.refl.* to be grieved, distressed, heartbroken.
accorciaménto, *m.* shortening; abbreviation; contraction. **accorciàre**, *v.t.* to shorten, curtail, abridge. **accorciàrsi**, *v.refl.* to contract, shrink. **accorciatívo**, *a. & m.* diminutive. **accorciatòia**, *f.* short cut.
accordàre, *v.t.* to grant; accord; tune, harmonize; reconcile. (*Gram.*) to make agree (with). **accordàrsi**, *v.refl.* to concur, be in accord, be in harmony; act in concert; (*Gram.*) to agree. **accordatóre**, *m.* (-**atríce** *f.*) tuner, piano-tuner. **accordatúra**, *f.* tuning. **accòrdo**, *m.* agreement; compromise, accord; (*Gram.*) concord. *d'*~, agreed, granted. *di comune* ~, by mutual consent, with one accord. *andare d'*~, to agree. ~ *fra gentiluomini*, gentlemen's agreement. *l'* ~ *di Monaco*, the Munich agreement. *in* ~ *con*, according to.
accòrgersi, *v.refl. ir.* to perceive, notice, become aware (of = *di*).
accorgiménto, *m.* shrewdness, perceptiveness; acuteness, circumspection, sagacity; subtlety, cunning.
accórrere, *v.i. ir.* (*aux.* essere) to run up, hasten, come running, come together. **accorr'uomo!** *i.* help! help!
accortaménte, *ad.* shrewdly, adroitly, cleverly, cunningly, astutely. **ac-**

cortézza, *f.* alertness, wariness, shrewdness, dexterity. **accòrto**, *a.* wary, alert; shrewd, keen, crafty; adroit, clever; prudent; cautious, suspicious (*of animals*). *mal* ~, awkward; unskilful; incautious.
accosciàrsi, *v.refl.* to squat, squat down, crouch.
accostàre, *v.t.* to bring near or nearer, put near; approach; be in close attendance on; leave ajar. ~ *al vento*, (*Naut.*) to come up to the wind. **accostàrsi**, *v.refl.* to approach, draw near; be intimate (with); resemble (in each case fol. by a). **accòsto**, *ad. & pr.* near, beside, close at hand. also *d'accosto*. ¶ *a.* neighbouring, nearby, adjoining.
accostumàre, *v.t.* to accustom; inure. **accostumàrsi**, *v.refl.* to accustom oneself, get used (to), get into the habit (of).
accozzàre, *v.t.* to jumble up; shuffle (*cards*); amass; collect, put together. ~ *i pentolini*, to picnic (*fam.*). **accozzàrsi**, *v.refl.* to get together; combine for mischief; clash. **accòzzo**, *m.* jumble, medley.
accreditàre, *v.t.* to accredit, confirm the truth of; (*Com.*) give letters of credit to; open a credit for. **accreditàrsi**, *v.refl.* to gain credit.
accréscere (*pr.* -**ésco**, &c., like *crescere*), *v.t. ir.* to increase, augment. **accréscersi**, *v.refl.* to increase. **accresciménto**, *m.* growth, increase. **accrescitívo**, *a. & m.* (*Gram.*) augmentative.
accrespàre, *v.t.* to curl, wrinkle.
accucciàrsi *or* **acciucciolàrsi**, *v.refl.* to crouch; lie curled up (*dog, &c.*).
accudíre (*pr.* -**ísco**, -**ísci**), *v.i.* (*aux.* avere) to attend (to household duties, &c.); assist.
accumulàre, *v.t.* to accumulate, heap up; gather, amass. **accumulatóre**, *m.* accumulator, [storage] battery (*Elec.*).
accuratézza, *f.* accuracy, exactitude, care, precision. **accuràto**, *a.* accurate; careful; correct.
accúsa, *f.* charge, accusation. *atto d'* ~, charge-sheet, indictment. **accusàre**, *v.t.* to accuse, charge; indict; impeach; blame; show, betray; bring out; complain of (*illness*); declare; acknowledge. ~ *ricevuta di*, to acknowledge receipt of. **accusàta**, *f.* (*at cards*) call, declaration. **accusatívo**, *m.* (*Gram.*)

accusative [case]. **accusàto, -a,** *n.*
accused, prisoner at the bar.
accusatóre, -tríce, *n.* accuser.
¶ *a.* accusing. *pubblico* ~, public
prosecutor.

acèfalo, *a.* headless; without a title.
libro ~, *manoscritto* ~, book,
manuscript lacking first page or
pages.

acèrbo, *a.* bitter, sour, unripe, green
(*fruit*); harsh, tart, pungent.

àcero, *m.* maple. ~ *di montagna,*
sycamore.

acèrrimo, *a.* very bitter, very harsh;
vehement, fierce. (sup. of *acre*).

acetàto, *a.* seasoned with vinegar.
¶ *m.* (*Chem.*) acetate.

acètico (*pl.* **-ètici**), *a.* acetic.

acetilène, *m.* acetylene.

acetíni, *m.pl.* pickles. **acéto,** *m.*
vinegar. *pigliar d'aceto,* (*fig.*) to be
piqued. *pigliar l'*~, to go sour.
acetósa, *f.* sorrel. **acetosèlla,** *f.*
wood-sorrel, wild-s. **acetosità,** *f.*
acidity, sourness. **acetóso,** *a.* acid,
vinegary. **Achílle,** *m.* Achilles.
tallone d'~, Achilles' heel. **aci-
détto, acídulo,** *a.* sourish; slightly
acid; acidulous. **acidézza** &
acidità, *f.* acidity; sourness. **àcido,**
a. acid; sour; sharp, tart. ¶ *m.* acid.
acidúme, *m.* sour stuff.

àcino, *m.* grape-stone; pip; grape.

àcqua, *f.* water. ~ *forte* (*pl.* **acque-
fòrti**), *f.* nitric acid; etching (also
incisione all' ~ *forte*). ~ *morta,*
stagnant water. ~ *pesante,* heavy
water. ~ *piovana,* rain water.
~ *potabile,* drinking water. ~ *dolce,*
fresh water; soft water. ~ *cruda,*
hard water. ~ *a monte,* head water
(*of stream*). ~ *di sentina,* bilge
water. *conduttura d'*~, *f.* water
main. ~ *in bocca!,* silence! *cassa
d'*~, water-tank. *camicia d'*~,
f. water-jacket. *filo dell'*~, part of
stream where current is strongest.
pelo dell'~, *m.* water surface.
far ~, to leak. *a fior d'*~, on the
surface, between wind and water.
andare contr'~, to stem the tide.
sott'~, (*fig.*) underhand. *far un
buco nell'*~, to beat the air. *stare
a pane ed* ~, to live on bread and
water. *lasciare andar l'* ~ *per la sua
china,* to let things take their course.
portare acqua al mare, to carry coals
to Newcastle (*fig.*). *mettere* ~ *nel
proprio vino* (*fig.*) to come to more
reasonable terms. *pestare l'*~ *nel*

mortaio, to act to no purpose. *tirar
l'*~ *al proprio mulino,* to bring grist
to one's mill.

acquafòrte, *f.* etching; (*Chem.*) aqua
fortis, nitric acid.

acquafortísta (*pl.* **-ísti**), *m.f.* etcher.

acquafrescàio, *m.* water-seller.

acquàio, *m.* sink.

acquai[u]òlo, *a.* aquatic; water (*att.*).
topo ~, water-rat. ¶ *m.* water-
carrier. **acquaplàno,** *m.* surf-
board. **acquàrio,** *m.* aquarium.

acquazzóne, *m.* heavy shower,
downpour.

acquartieràre, *v.t.* to quarter (*troops*).

acquasantièra, *f.* holy-water basin,
stoup. **acquàta,** *f.* shower; (*Mar.*)
store of fresh water.

acquattàrsi, *v.refl.* to crouch, squat
down; hide.

acquavíte, *f.* brandy.

acquedótto, *m.* aqueduct.

acquerellàre, *v.t.* to paint in water-
colour. **acquerellísta,** *m.f.* water-
colour painter. **acquerèllo,** *m.*
water-colour; water-colour painting;
thin, sour wine.

acquerúgiola, *f.* fine rain, drizzle.

acqu[i]etàre, *v.t.* to appease, pacify
calm, still. **acqu[i]etàrsi,** *v.refl.* to
become quiet, be appeased, resign
oneself, give in.

acquirènte, *m.f.* purchaser, buyer.

acquistàre, *v.t.* & *abs.* to acquire,
purchase, procure; advance, improve, gain ground. **acquísto,** *m.*
acquisition, purchase; buying; annexation.

acquitríno, *m.* marshy ground, swamp,
morass. **acquitrinóso,** *a.* marshy.

acquolína, *f. dim.* of *acqua,* a little
water; fine rain. *far venire l'* ~ *in
bocca,* to make one's mouth water.
acquóso, *a.* watery.

àcre, *a.* sharp, pungent; acrid, bitter,
sour; harsh, acrimonious, severe.
acrèdine, *f.* bitterness; acidity.
acrimònia, *f.* acrimony.

àcro, *m.* acre (4,840 sq. yds. or
4,046 sq. metres).

acròbata (*pl.* **-òbati**), *m.* acrobat.
acrobatísmo, *m.* acrobatics. **acro-
bazía,** *f.* acrobatics; (*Aviat.*) aero-
batics.

acromàtico (*pl.* **-àtici**), *a.* achromatic.

acròpoli, *f.* acropolis.

acuíre (*pr.* **-ísco**), *v.t.* sharpen, whet,
stimulate. **acuità,** *f.* sharpness;
acuteness (*pain,* &*c.*). **acúleo,** *m.*

sharp point; sting; goad; thorn; prickle; quill (*porcupine*). **acúme,** *m.* acumen, discernment; keenness, intensity; subtlety, penetration. **acuminàre,** *v.t.* to sharpen to a point.

acústica, *f.* acoustics. **acústico,** (*pl.* -ústici), *a.* acoustic. *cornetto* ~, ear-trumpet, *m.*

acutézza, *f.* acuteness; perspicuity, shrewdness. **acúto,** *a.* acute; keen; sharp; shrewd; pointed; piercing. *voce* ~*a,* shrill voice, *f.* *gli acuti,* (*Mus.*) the sharps; the high notes.

adacquàre, *v.t.* to water; irrigate. **adacquatóio,** *m.* watering-pot w.-can.

adagiàre, *v.t.* to lay down gently; set down; make comfortable. **adagiàrsi,** *v.refl.* to lie down, stretch oneself out, make oneself comfortable. **adàgio,** *a.* (*Mus.*) slow. ¶ *ad.* softly, slowly. ¶ *m.* adage; proverb.

Adàmo, *m.* Adam.

adattàbile, *a.* adaptable. **adattaménto,** *m.* adaptation; fitness; suitability; arrangement. **adattàre,** *v.t.* to adapt; adjust; apply; fit; suit. **adattàrsi,** *v.refl.* to adapt oneself; accommodate oneself; resign oneself; be applicable; suit, fit. **adàtto,** *sync. p.p.* fit, right, proper, suitable, adapted. ~ *al mare,* sea-going, sea-worthy.

addebitàre, *v.t.* to debit; charge (with = *di*), impute (to = *a*).

addentàre, *v.t.* to seize (*with the teeth, &c.*); bite; censure; carp at; (*Mech.*) to indent. **addentàto,** *p.a.* (*Mech.*) cogged, notched. **addentellàre,** *v.t.* to leave projecting stones in a wall for future extensions; to tooth. **addentellàto,** *m.* quoin or 'toothing', consisting of projecting bricks or stones left at the end of a wall to provide for its extension; uncompleted work; link.

addentràre, *v.t.* to drive in; put in. **addentràrsi,** *v.refl.* to penetrate; plunge into; study deeply. **addéntro,** *ad.* inside, well within.

addestraménto, *m.* training, instruction; drilling. **addestràre,** *v.t.* to train; drill; exercise; instruct; form by exercise; discipline; break in (*horse, &c.*).

addétto, *a.* belonging (to), attached (to). ¶ *m.* attaché. ~ *aeronautico,* air attaché.

addì, *or* a **dì,** the day of. *e.g.* ~ *dieci,* on the 10th.

addiacciaménto, *m.* freezing; icing. **addiacciàre,** *v.t.* to freeze; ice; keep the flock in the fold; bring the flock to the fold. **addiàccio,** *m.* sheep-fold. *dormire all'addiaccio,* to sleep in the open.

addiètro, *ad.* back, backward; behind; previously; ago. *anni* ~, years ago. *dar* ~, to draw back. ¶ *i.* ~! stand back! keep back! ¶ *m.* rear, hind part; stern (*ship*). *per l'* ~, in the past, formerly.

addío, *m. & i.* farewell, good-bye, adieu.

addirittúra, *ad.* absolutely, positively; actually, directly; plainly, frankly; immediately, at once.

addìrsi (*pr.* -díco, *&c.,* like *dire*), *v.refl.ir,* to be suitable, becoming; to be to one's taste.

addirizzàre, *v.t.* to straighten; set up; set right, direct; hold up; redress, rectify, correct.

additàre, *v.t.* to point out, point to, point at; indicate; designate, denote.

addizionàle, *a.* additional. **addizionàre,** *v.t.* to add, add up. **addizionatríce,** *f.* adding machine. **addizióne,** *f.* addition.

addobbaménto, *m.* decoration; ornament; furnishing. **addobbàre,** *v.t.* to decorate, furnish handsomely, adorn, deck; steep (*hids*). **addobbàrsi,** *v.refl.* to deck oneself in fine clothes, dress handsomely. **addobbatóre,** *m.* (-**trice** *f.*) decorator; upholsterer. **addòbbo,** *m.* decoration; fine furniture; handsome dress; bath of alum for steeping hides.

addolcíre (*pr.* -ísco, -ísci), *v.t.* to sweeten, soften, make milder; soothe, temper, alleviate; to mitigate, appease, calm, moderate.

addoloràre, *v.t.* to pain, hurt, distress, grieve. **addoloràrsi,** *v.refl.* to grieve, to be distressed, sorrow, mourn. **Addoloràta (l'),** *f.* the Virgin, the Mother of Sorrows.

addòme, *m.* abdomen. **addomINàle,** *a.* abdominal.

addomesticàre, *v.t.* to tame, domesticate; (*land*) to improve, prepare for cultivation.

addoppiàre (see also *raddoppiare*), *v.t.* to double, redouble, increase; fold.

addormentàre, *v.t.* to put to sleep, send to sleep; (*fig.*) to soothe, beguile, calm, compose. **addormentàrsi,** *v.refl.* to fall asleep, go to sleep.

addossàre, *v.t.* to lay upon (*a*), put upon; place on the back of, put on; to entrust; charge; load, burden; impute, pile up; to back. **addossàrsi**, *v.refl.* to take upon one, saddle oneself with, lean against (*a*); crowd upon. **addòsso**, *ad. & pr.* on, upon, on one's back; close by; above, over. *dare* ∼, to fall upon, attack. *stare* ∼, to stand over. *mettere* ∼, to impute. *portare* ∼, to wear (mettersi addosso). *tirarsi* ∼, to bring upon oneself. *levarsi d'* ∼, to take off; get rid of. *non ho denari* ∼, I have no money on me.

addòtto, *a. & pp.* of addurre, adduced; alleged.

addottoràre, *v.t.* to confer the degree of doctor. **addottoràrsi**, *v.refl.* to take a doctor's degree.

addottrinàre, *v.t.* to instruct; indoctrinate.

addúrre (*pr.* -úco, -úci, -úce), *v.t. ir.* to adduce; allege, assign, advance, cite; bring; bring forward; urge.

adeguaménto, *m.* equalization. **adeguàre** (*pr.* -éguo, -égui), *v.t.* to equalize; level; make proportionate. **adeguàrsi**, *v.refl.* to become equal, be considered equal, be proportionate. **adeguataménte**, *ad.* adequately; equally; proportionately. **adeguàto**, *a.* adequate; fair, reasonable, proportionate.

adémpiere (*pr.* -émpio, &c., like *empiere*) or **adempíre** (*pr.* -ísco, &c., like *empire*), *v.t.* to execute, accomplish, perform, fulfil, carry out, keep (*promise*). **adempiménto**, *m.* accomplishment, fulfilment, execution.

adenòidi, *f.pl.* adenoids.

aderènte, *a.m.* adherent. **aderènza**, *f.* adherence; adhesion; (*pl.fig.*) high connections, powerful protection. **aderíre** (*pr.* -ísco, -ísci, &c.), *v.i* (*aux.* avere) to adhere; cling; consent; ∼ *a*, (*fig.*) rally round, acquiesce in; grant (a request).

adescàre (*pr.* -ésco, -éschi), *v.t.* to lure, allure, entice, decoy, inveigle, beguile; tempt, bribe. ∼ *con amo*, to bait the hook for.

adesióne, *f.* adhesion; adherence; agreement; consent. *dare la propria* ∼ *a*, to give one's adhesion. **adesívo**, *a.* adhesive, sticky.

adèspoto, *a.* anonymous (*of MSS.*).

adèsso, *ad.* now, at present, at this moment; a moment ago; nowadays. ∼ ∼, in a moment, immediately,

at once, just now. *da* ∼ *in pai*, from this moment. *fino* ∼, hitherto.

adiacènte, *a.* adjacent.

adiànto, *m.* (*Bot.*) maiden-hair (fern).

adibíre (*pr.* -ísco, -ísci), *v.t.* to employ, destine for use, &c.; produce (*proofs, witnesses, &c.*).

adiràre, *v.t.* to enrage, anger, make angry, irritate. **adiràrsi**, *v.refl.* to get angry; fly into a passion; take offence. **adirataménte**, *ad.* angrily. **adiràto**, *a.* angry.

adire (*pr.* -ísco, -ísci), *v.t.* (*Law*) to present oneself before, address oneself to, apply to. ∼ *un'eredità*, to take possession of an inheritance. **àdito**, *m.* access; entry; right of access. **adizióne**, *f.* (*Law*) acceptance; taking possession of an inheritance.

adocchiàre, *v.t.* to eye attentively; espy; ogle; covet.

adolescènte, *a. & m.f.* adolescent. **adolescènza**, *f.* adolescence.

adombraménto, *m.* darkness, obscurity; shade, shading; (*fig.*) umbrage; suspicion, distrust. **adombràre**, *v.t.* to shade, darken; shade in; conceal; shadow forth; adumbrate; suggest; sketch; imagine. **adombràrsi**, *v.refl.* to become suspicious; take umbrage (at = *di*); get frightened; (*of horses*) to shy.

Adóne, *m.* Adonis. *un* ∼, a handsome youth.

adontàre, *v.t.* to affront; reproach; offend. **adontàrsi**, *v.refl.* to be offended, feel hurt.

adoperàre, *v.t.* to employ, use; exert, spend. **adoperàrsi**, *v.refl.* to apply oneself, busy oneself, exert oneself; take trouble; do one's best.

adoràre, *v.t.* to adore, venerate; pray to.

adornàre, *v.t.* to adorn, embellish, deck. **adórno**, *a.* adorned, trimmed, embellished; (*Poe.*) handsome; beautiful.

adottàre, *v.t.* to adopt. **adottívo**, *a.* adoptive, adopted. **adozióne**, *f.* adoption.

adrenalína, *f.* (*Med.*) adrenaline.

Adriàno, *m.* Hadrian.

Adriàtico, *a. & m.* Adriatic.

aduggiàre, *v.t.* to darken, obscure, overshade; blight, dull, embitter.

adulàre, *v.t.* to flatter, fawn upon, adulate. **adulatóre**, **-tríce**, *a.* flattering, &c. ¶ *m.f.* flatterer.

adúlteràre, *v.t.* to adulterate, taint,

debase, falsify, forge, corrupt, distort. **adultèrio,** *m.* adultery. **adúltero,** *a.* adulterous. ¶ *m.* adulterer, **-a,** *f.* adulteress.

adúlto, *a. & m.* adult, grown-up.

adunànza, *f.* assembly, meeting. **adunàre,** *v.t.* to assemble, convoke, muster, summon; gather, collect, unite. **adunàrsi,** *v.refl.* to assemble, meet. **adunàta,** *f.* meeting, assembly, rally; fall-in. ~ *all'aperto,* open-air meeting. ~ *in massa,* mass-meeting.

adúnco (*pl.* **-únchi**), *a.* hooked; curved, crooked.

adúnque, *c. & ad.* then, therefore; so.

adústo, *a.* scorched; dry, dried up; thin.

aeràre, *v.t.* to ventilate, air, aerate. **aerazióne,** *f.* airing, ventilation, draught, aeration. **àere,** *m.* (*Poet.*) air. **aeremòto,** *m.* whirlwind, tornado, hurricane. **aèreo,** *a.* aerial; airy; air (*att.*); overhead; vain, insubstantial. *posta* ~*a, f.* air mail. *per via* ~*a,* by air. *rilevamento* ~, *m.* air reconnaissance. *incursione* ~*a, f.* air-raid. *generale di squadra* ~*a,* air-marshal. *g. di divisione* ~*a,* air vice-marshal. ¶ *m.* aircraft. *nave porta-aerei, f.* aircraft carrier.

aerodinàmica, *f.* aerodynamics. **aerodinàmico** (*pl.* **-àmici**), *a.* aerodynamic; stream-lined. *vettura* ~*a, f.* stream-lined car.

aeròdromo, *m.* aerodrome, aviation ground, air-field.

aeròfaro, *m.* air beacon, air light-house.

aerolínea, *f.* air line.

aerolito, aereolíto, *m.* aerolite, meteorite.

aeronàuta, *m.* aeronaut. **aeronàutica,** *f.* aeronautics; aviation; air-force; air-fleet; aircraft (*pl.*). *Ministero dell'* ~, Air Ministry. *Regia* ~, Royal Air Force. **aeronàutico,** *a.* aeronautic(al), air (*att.*).

aeroplàno, *m.* aeroplane, (air)-plane, plane. ~ *di linea,* air liner. ~ *da caccia, caccia, m.* or *apparecchio da caccia,* fighter-plane. ~ *da carico,* ~ *da trasporto,* air freighter. ~ *da bombardamento* or *apparecchio da bombardamento,* bomber, bombing-plane. ~ *a reazione,* jet plane. **aeropòrto,** *m.* air-port, air-station. **aeroscàlo,** *m.* air-base, sea-plane base. **aerosilurànte,** *m.* torpedo-carrying plane. **aerotrasportàto,** *a.* air-borne. *truppe* ~*e,* air-borne

troops. **aerostàtica,** *f.* aerostatics; ballooning. **aeròstato,** *m.* lighter than air machine; balloon.

àfa, *f* closeness, sultriness, heavy heat; (*fig.*) breathlessness; tediousness, disgust.

afagía, *f.* (*Med.*) inability to swallow.

afasía, *f.* (*Med.*) aphasia, loss of speech.

affàbile, *a.* affable, agreeable, polite. **affabilità,** *f.* affability.

affaccendaménto, *m.* business, bustle, stir, stirring. **affaccendàrsi,** *v.refl.* to bustle, busy oneself, take (much) trouble. **affaccendàto,** *p.a.* very busy, much occupied, bustling; fussy.

affacchinàrsi, *v.refl.* to toil, drudge.

affacciàre, *v.t.* to bring forward, present, show. **affacciàrsi,** *v.refl.* to show oneself, come forward, appear, come out; address oneself (to).

affagottàre, *v.t.* to make into a bundle, bundle up, roll up, tuck up.

affaldàre, *v.t.* to pleat, fold into pleats.

affamàre, *v.t. & v.i.* (*aux.* essere) to starve. **affamàto,** *p.a.* hungry, starving, famished; (*fig.*) eager for, greedy for (= *di*).

affannànte, *p.a.* distressing; anxious; (*Med.*) asthmatic. **affannàre,** *v.t.* to distress, afflict, grieve, vex, weary. **affannàrsi,** *v.refl.* to toil, drudge, strive; to fret, grieve, be anxious. **affannàto,** *p.a.* out of breath, panting, asthmatic; uneasy, distressed. **affanno,** *m.* difficulty in breathing; severe exertion; distress, anxiety; trouble, exhaustion. **affannóso,** *a.* wearisome, troubled, oppressive.

affaràccio, *m.* bad business, ugly affair.

affardellàre, *v.t.* to pack up, make a bundle of.

affàre, *m.* matter; affair; job; bargain; business (*oft pl.*) (*gli affari*); speculation; predicament; importance; condition; quality. *un* ~ *da nulla,* a trifle, trifling affair. ~ *giudiziario,* law-suit. *uomo d'* ~*i,* business man; agent. *mettersi negli* ~*i,* to go into business, set up in business. *incaricato d'* ~*i,* chargé d'affaires (*dipl.*). **affarísta** (*pl.* **-ísti**), *m.* busybody; unscrupulous business man. **affaróne,** *m.* fine bargain, good stroke of business. **affaruccio,** *m.* petty affair.

affascinaménto, *m.* fascination, seduction, spell. **affascinànte,** *p.a.* fascinating, bewitching, charming, delightful. **affascinàre,** *v.t.* to fascinate, charm, delight; make up into faggots.

affastellàre, *v.t.* to tie up in bundles or sheaves, pile up, jumble up. **affastellío,** *m.* disorder, confusion.

affaticàre, *v.t.* to fatigue, tire, weary; overwork; strain; (*of land*) exhaust, impoverish. **affaticàrsi,** *v.refl.* to tire oneself out; take trouble, strive, toil.

affàtto, *ad.* quite, entirely, altogether. *niente* ~ (*or elip.* ~), not at all, nothing at all. *nulla* ~, nothing at all.

affatturàre, *v.t.* to bewitch; delude; adulterate, doctor (*wine*).

affazzonàre, *v.t.* to embellish, beautify, adorn.

affè, *i.* upon my word! in faith!

affermàre, *v.t.* to affirm, allege; confirm. **affermatíva,** *f.* affirmative. **affermatívo,** *a.* affirmative.

afferràre, *v.t.* to seize, grasp.

affettàre, *v.t.* to affect, feign, pretend; aspire to; covet. *v.t.* to slice, cut thin, cut down; fold in plaits. **affettàto,** *p.a.* affected; artificial; sliced. ¶ *m.* sliced ham or sausage. **affettazióne,** *f.* affectation. **affètto,** *m.* affection, love, feeling, emotion; malady, indisposition. ¶ *p.a.* affected, burdened, afflicted, (*Med.*) seized (with). **affettuóso,** *a.* affectionate.

affezionàre, *v.t.* to inspire affection in, dispose to affection; attach; gain the liking of. **affezionàrsi,** *v.refl.* ~ *a,* to become fond of, become attached to, feel affection for, take a liking to. **affezionàto,** *p.a.* affectionate; attached. **affezióne,** *f.* affection, attachment, love; (*Med.*) complaint, malady.

affiancàre, *v.t.* (*Mil.*) to flank, protect the flank[s].

affiatàre, *v.t.* to harmonize, bring together, train to work together (*actors, singers*). **affiatàrsi,** *v.refl.* to agree, get on well together; become familiar, feel at home [with].

affibbiàre, *v.t.* to buckle, clasp; play one a trick; deliver (*blow*); lay, bestow. **affibbiatúra,** *f.* set (row) of buckles, hooks and eyes; bookclasp.

affidàre, *v.t.* to entrust, commit,

confide; assure. **affidàrsi** (a), *v.refl.* to trust, have confidence in; be sure of, rely upon.

affievoliménto, *m.* weakening. **affievolíre** (*pr.* -ísco, -ísci), *v.t.* to weaken, *v.i.* (*aux.* essere) & **affievolírsi,** *v.refl.* to grow weak.

affiggere (*pr.* -íggo, &*c.*), like *figgere*), *v.t.* *ir.* to stick (up), post up, placard; affix, attach; expose, publish, announce; fix. **affíggersi,** *v.refl.* to gaze at (= a), give close attention to.

affilàre, *v.t.* to sharpen; strop; grind; set (*tools*), (*Agr.*) set in rows; taper. **affilàto,** *p.a.* sharpened, sharp; long; tapering, pointed.

affiliàre, *v.t.* to affiliate. **affiliàto,** *a.* & *m.* affiliated; associate.

affinàre, *v.t.* to refine; sharpen; improve; ripen (*fig.*); mature; purify. **affinatóio,** *m.* refining furnace. **affinatóre,** *m.* refiner. **affinatúra,** *f.* refining.

affinché, *c.* in order that, so that.

affíne, *a.* akin, allied, related; analogous; similar. ¶ *m.* kinsman; relative, relation. (*f.*) kinswoman, &c.

affíne di (*a fine di*), *c.* in order to, so as to.

affinità, *f.inv.* affinity; relationship; resemblance; connection.

affiochiménto, *m.* hoarseness; weakness. **affiochíre** (*pr.* -ísco, -ísci), *v.t.* to render hoarse; weaken; dim. *v.i.* (*aux.* essere) & **affiochìrsi,** *v.refl.* to become hoarse; grow weak; grow dim.

affioraménto, *m.* (*Min.*) outcrop.

affioràre, *v.i.* (*aux.* essere) to come to the surface, appear (on the surface); (*submarine*) surface.

affissàre, *v.t.* to fix; gaze at. **affissióne,** *f.* bill-posting; sticking up; application. *è proibita l'*~, stick no bills.

affísso, *p.p.* of *affiggere, p.a.* affixed, fixed, posted up. ¶ *m.* bill, play-bill, placard; poster; (*Gram.*) affix. ~ (*di finestra*), (window) sash.

affittacàmere, *m.* & *f. inv.* agent for furnished apartments; landlord, landlady. **affittaiuòlo,** *m.* tenant; tenant-farmer; leaseholder. **affittàre,** *v.t.* to let, lease; hire, rent; farm. **affíttasi,** house (or apartments) to let. **affitterèllo,** *m.* low rent. **affìtto,** *m.* rent; hire; lease. *prendere in* ~, *avere in* ~, to rent. *prezzo di* ~, rent[al]. *affitti e* *prestiti*, lend-lease. **affittuàrio**, *m.* tenant; leaseholder, lessee.

affliggere (*pr.* **-iggo, -iggi**), *v.t. ir.* to afflict, vex, distress; mortify; torment. **affliggersi**, *v.refl.* to grieve, fret; to be vexed, worried, tormented, distressed. **afflitto**, *p.a.* afflicted, vexed, tormented, pained, hurt. **afflizióne**, *f.* affliction, suffering, distress.

affloscire (*pr.* **-isco, -isci**), *v.i.* (*aux.* essere) and **affloscirsi**, *v.refl.* to become weak or flabby; lose strength.

affluènte, *a.* affluent; abounding. ¶ *m.* affluent; tributary. **affluènza**, *f.* affluence, abundance; concourse. **affluire** (*pr.* **-isco, -isci**), *v.i.* (*aux.* essere) to flow in; flock in.

afflussionàto, *a.* suffering from catarrh, with a cold in the head. **afflússo**, *m.* afflux, flow (*of blood*, *humours*, &c.).

affocàre (*pr.* **affuòco, affuòchi**), *v.t.* to inflame, set on fire; make red-hot, redden. **affocàrsi**, *v.refl.* to become inflamed, red-hot, enraged. **affocàto**, *a.* red-hot; flushed, fiery-red.

affogàre, *v.t.* to smother, stifle, choke, drown; (*Cook.*) poach; steam; plunge, submerge; quell, swamp, crush: (*fig.*) ruin. (*v.i.*) (*aux.* essere) be drowned; sink. *uovo affogato*, poached egg.

affollàre, *v.t.* to crowd, crowd round, throng, press, squeeze. **affollàrsi**, *v.refl.* to crowd; hasten. **affollataménte**, *ad.* tumultuously; precipitately, in haste.

affondàre, *v.t.* to sink, send to the bottom; thrust, drive in; plunge; submerge; deepen. ~ *l'àncora*, to drop the anchor. ~ *mine*, to lay mines. *v.i.* (*aux.* essere) & **affondàrsi**, *v.refl.* to sink; founder.

afforzaménto, *m.* reinforcement. **afforzàre**, *v.t.* to fortify; reinforce; encourage. **afforzàrsi**, *v.refl.* to exert oneself, persist.

affossàre, *v.t.* to ditch, trench; excavate, hollow out. **affossàrsi**, *v.refl.* to sink down, become hollow.

affrancàre (*pr.* **-ànco, -ànchi**), *v.t.* to free, set free, discharge; enfranchise; relieve, exempt; redeem; prepay, stamp (*letter*). **affrancatríce (macchina)**, *f.* stamping-machine (*post office*). **affrancatúra**, *f.* prepayment, postage. **affrancazióne**, *f.* enfranchisement; libera-

tion, release; (*fig.*) payment of postage.

affrànto, *a.* broken (in spirit), crushed, shattered, overcome.

affratellaménto, *m.* fraternization; intimacy; brotherly feeling. **affratellàrsi**, *v.refl.* to fraternize.

affrescàre, *v.t.* to paint in fresco. **affrésco** (*pl.* **-éschi**), *m.* fresco, fresco-painting.

affrettàre, *v.t.* to hasten, hurry; quicken. **affrettàrsi**, *v.refl.* to hasten, hurry, make haste. **affrettàto**, *a.* hasty, hurried; careless.

affrittellàre, *v.t.* to fry; poach (*eggs*); (*fig.*) crush, kill.

affrontàre, *v.t.* to front, confront, face; defy; meet (*expenses*). **affrontàrsi**, *v.refl.* to meet, encounter, attack one another; take offence (at = *di*). **affrónto**, *m.* affront, insult.

affumicàre, *v.t.* to smoke, blacken, fumigate; cure (*fish, flesh, meat*). *aringa affumicata, f.* kipper. *salmone affumicato*, smoked salmon. *prosciutto affumicato*, *m.* smoked ham. *occhiali* ~*i, m.pl.*, smoked glasses.

affusàre, affusolàre, *v.t.* to taper off. **affusolàto**, *p.a.* tapering; streamlined. *mano affusolata, dita affusolate*, tapering hand, tapering fingers.

affústo, *m.* gun-carriage.

Afg[h]ànistan (l'), *m.* Afghanistan. **afghàno**, *a.* & *m.* Afghan.

afonìa, *f.* (*Med.*) loss of speech. **àfono**, *a.* speechless, voiceless.

aforísma & **aforísmo**, *m.* aphorism.

afóso, *a.* sultry, heavy (*atmosphere*).

Àfrica (l'), *f.* Africa. ~ *meridionale*, ~ *del Sud*, South Africa. ~ *settentrionale*, North A. ~ *occidentale*, West A. ~ *orientale*, East A. **africàno**, *a.* & *m.* African.

àfro, *a.* bitter, sharp-tasting.

àfta, *f.* (*Med.*) aphtha. ~ *epizootica*, foot & mouth disease (*cattle*).

Agamènnone, *m.* Agamemnon.

agata, *f.* agate.

àgave, *f.* (*Bot.*) agave, American aloe.

agènda, *f.* pocket diary.

agènte, *a.* acting. ¶ *m.* agent; broker; representative; manager; medium; officer. ~ *di beni immobili*, estate agent. ~ *di cambio*, stockbroker. ~ *di commissione*, commission agent. ~ *di polizia*, policeman, police constable. ~ *di spedizione*, forwarding agent. ~ *delle tasse*, assessor of taxes. ~ *consolare*, consular agent. ~ *chimico* (*Chem.*), chemical agent.

~ *delle imposte,* tax collector. ~ *di trasporti marittimi,* shipping agent. ~ *unico,* ~ *esclusivo,* sole agent.

agenzía, *f.* agency, office, bureau. ~ *di trasporti,* forwarding agency. ~ *di trasporti marittimi,* shipping office. ~ *di viaggi,* travel agency. ~ *d'informazioni,* enquiry office, information bureau. ~ *delle tasse,* tax-office. ~ *di collocamento,* employment agency, registry.

agevolàre (*pr.* **-évolo**), *v.t.* to ease; facilitate; alleviate; assist. **agévole,** *a.* easy; manageable, handy; comfortable; mild, moderate; easy-tempered, conciliatory, compliant; unconstrained, ready-witted. **agevolazióne,** *f.* facilitation; facility (*oft. pl.*). **agevolézza,** *f.* ease, convenience, facilities; consideration, courtesy; fluency; readiness (*of speech*); (*Com.*) accommodation; (*pl.*) easy terms, consideration. **agevolménte,** *ad.* easily.

agganciàre (*pr.* **-àncio, -ànci**), *v.t.* to hook, seize, clasp; couple (*Rly. trucks*); hang up; (*Mil.*) engage, hold down.

aggéggio, *m.* trifle, thing (*of no account*).

aggentilíre (*pr.* **-ísco, -ísci**), *v.t.* to beautify, adorn.

aggettàre, *v.i.* (*aux.* essere), to project, jut out.

aggettívo, *m.* adjective.

aggètto, *m.* projection; (*Arch.*) overhang; (*Mech.*) boss, lug.

agghiacciàre, *v.t.* to freeze; congeal; ice.

agghiaiàre, *v.t.* to sprinkle with gravel, lay with gravel.

agghindàre, *v.t.* to dress up; (*Naut.*) to hoist sail.

àggio, *m.* exchange [premium], agio; discount charges. ~ *sui fondi pubblici,* stock-jobbing.

aggiogàre, *v.t.* to yoke; couple (*horses, oxen*).

aggiornaménto, *m.* adjournment; bringing up to date; (*Law*) summons, citation. **aggiornàre,** *v.i.* (*aux.* essere), to dawn, become daylight; *v.t.* to adjourn, postpone; bring up to date.

aggiotàggio, *m.* stock-jobbing, dealing on the exchange. **aggiotatóre,** *m.* exchange broker, stockbroker, speculator.

aggiraménto, *m.* turning, twisting, whirling; (*fig.*) evasion, shifting, fraud, embezzlement. (*pl.*) ~*i di parole,* beating about the bush. **aggiràre,** *v.t.* to turn, t. about, t. round; (*fig.*) deceive; (*Mil.*) outflank, turn (*position*), surround. **aggiràrsi,** *v.refl.* revolve, move in a circle; roam, wander. ~ *su,* to turn upon; be about. **aggiratóre,** *m.* dodger, trickster.

aggiudicàre, *v.t.* to adjudge, assign, award, decree, allot, grant. **aggiudicazióne,** *f.* adjudication, award; contract.

aggiúngere (*pr.* **-úngo,** &*c.*, like *giungere*), *v.t.* ir. to add; adjoin; appoint; join, connect, unite; ~ *a,* to attain, reach. **aggiúnta,** *f.* addition; adjunct; increase; (*Law*) rider; (*Com.*) make-weight. **aggiuntàre,** *v.t.* to attach, join, sew together. **aggiúnto,** *m.* assistant, deputy.

aggiustàbile, *a.* adjustable. **aggiustàggio,** *m.* (*Mech.*) adjustment; fitting. **aggiustaménto,** *m.* adjustment, arrangement, settlement. **aggiustàre,** *v.t.* to adjust, settle, put in order; tune; reconcile; aim; proportion; put right; lay out; dress, tidy, adorn. **aggiustatézza,** *f.* precision, accuracy, accurate adjustment; correction, good manners. **aggiustatóre,** *m.* (*Mech.*) fitter.

agglomeràre, *v.t.* & **agglomerarsi,** *v.refl.* to agglomerate. **agglomeràto,** *m.* agglomerate (*Geol.*); agglomeration; inhabited centre.

aggomitolàre, *v.t.* to wind into a ball, roll up, coil. **aggomitolàrsi,** *v.refl.* to curl up, crouch; gather in clusters.

aggottàre, *v.t.* to pump out; bale out.

aggraffàre, *v.t.* to scratch, seize with claws, snatch.

aggranchírsi (*pr.* **-ísco, -ísci**), *v.refl.* to get benumbed, become stiff with cold.

aggrandíre (*pr.* **-ísco, -ísci**), *v.t.* to aggrandize; enlarge, extend; magnify, augment, exaggerate, raise. **aggrandírsi,** *v.refl.* to increase; become greater, more powerful; increase one's importance.

aggrappàre, *v.t.* to grasp, grapple. **aggrappàrsi,** *v.refl.* to cling (to), lay hold of, grasp tightly.

aggraticciàre, *v.t.* to trellis, intertwine.

aggravaménto, *m.* aggravation; surcharge; increase of weight or penalty. **aggravàre,** *v.t.* aggravate;

overload; overburden; overcharge.
aggravàrsi, *v.refl.* to get worse; grow worse; overburden oneself; be weighed down (with = *di*). **aggràvio,** *m.* heavy burden (*as of taxes*), weight, charge, expense; (*fig.*) wrong, injury, imposition; imputation. ~ *fiscale,* tax.

aggraziàre, *v.t.* to render graceful or pleasing. **aggraziàrsi,** *v.refl.* to win, gain. ~ *l'animo di qualcuno,* to win someone's favour.

aggredíre (*pr.* **-ísco, -ísci**), *v.t.* to assail, attack.

aggregàre (*pr.* **-ègo, -èghi**), *v.t.* to admit (to a society); receive; unite, incorporate; to aggregate. **aggregàrsi,** *v.refl.* to join a society; to be united **aggregàto,** *p.a.* adjunct; united; incorporated. ¶ *m.* aggregate. ~ *di case,* block of houses. **aggregazióne,** *f.* aggregation.

aggressióne, *f.* aggression; assault. **aggressívo,** *a.* aggressive. **aggressóre,** *m.* **aggreditríce,** *f.* aggressor; assailant.

aggrinzàre, & **-íre** (*pr.* **-ísco, -ísci**), *v.t.* to wrinkle, rumple; ripple.

aggrottàre, *v.t.* ~ *le ciglia,* to frown, knit the brows.

aggrovigliàrsi, *v.refl.* to get entangled; curl up; shrink; get confused.

aggrumàre, *v.t.* to collect; curdle; heap up. **aggrumàrsi,** *v.refl.* to coagulate; clot; form a crust.

aggruppàre, *v.t.* to collect into a cluster; loop up; form a group.

aggruzzolàre, *v.t.* to hoard; save up; amass.

agguagliàre, *v.t.* to equalize, match; compare; make smooth or level; be equal to.

agguantàre, *v.t.* to seize; catch; lay hold of.

agguàto, *m.* ambush, snare, watch. *essere in* ~, to lie in wait. *stare in* ~, to be on the look-out.

agguerríre (*pr.* **-ísco, -ísci**), *v.t.* to inure to war; train to arms.

agguindolàre, *v.t.* to wind (reel or bobbin); reel off.

aghétto, *m.* (*metal*) tag, tagged lace (*boot, &c.*).

agiataménte, *ad.* comfortably, in easy circumstances; at ease, in easy fashion. **agiatézza,** *f.* comfort, moderate wealth, easy circumstances. **agiàto,** *a.* comfortable; well-to-do; easy, independent.

àgile, *a.* agile; alert; active, nimble.
agilità, *f.* agility.
àgio (*pl.* **àgi**), *m.* leisure, ease, comfort; time; opportunity; (*pl.*) conveniences, commodities, good fortune. *a bell'* ~, at one's convenience; in an easy going fashion. *gli* ~ *i della vita,* the comforts of life. *a mio* ~, at my convenience, as soon as I have leisure. *se avrò agio,* if I can spare time. *non trovarsi ad* ~, to be ill at ease, embarrassed or indisposed. *vivere nell'* ~, to live comfortably.

agiografía, *f.* hagiography.

agíre (*pr.* **-ísco, -ísci**), *v.i.* (*aux.* avere) to act; proceed; function.

agitàre, *v.t.* to agitate, perturb, shake, stir; excite; wave, wag. ~ *una lite,* to carry on a law-suit. ~ *una questione,* to raise a question. **agitàrsi,** *v.refl.* to be troubled; shake; stir; move about; bustle; turn round; turn upon. **agitàto,** *p.a.* agitated, troubled, excited; restless. *mare* ~, *m.* rough sea. **agitatóre,** *m.* agitator. **agitazióne,** *f.* agitation, &c.; unrest.

àgli, *pr.* & *def. art. pl. m.* = a gli, to the.

agliàio, *m.* garlic seller; garlic bed. **agliàta,** *f.* garlic sauce. **àglio,** *m.* garlic.

agnàto, *m.* relation in the male line.

agnèlla, *f.* ewe lamb. **agnellatúra,** *f.* lambing; lambing season. **agnèllo,** *m.* lamb.

agnosticísmo, *m.* agnosticism. **agnòstico** (*pl.* **-òstici**), *a.* & *m.* agnostic.

àgo (*pl.* **àghi**), *m.* needle; bodkin; hand (*of watch or clock*); tongue (*of balance or steelyard*); compass. *cruna dell'* ~, eye of the needle. ~ *magnetico,* ~ *calamitato,* magnetic needle. ~ *della bussola,* compass needle. *astuccio per aghi,* needle-case.

agognàre, *v.t.* to covet eagerly, long for, sue for, strive for. ~ *a,* to aspire to, strive after.

agonía, *f.* agony, dying breath, last gasp; death-struggle; anguish, anxiety, suspense. **agonizzànte,** *p.a.* agonizing, dying. **agonizzàre,** *v.i.* (*aux.* avere) to be in one's death-agony.

agorafobia, *f.* (*Med.*) agoraphobia, morbid dread of public places.

agoràio, *m.* needle-case.

agostàno, *a.* August (*hay, &c.*).
agostiniàno, *a.* & *m.* Augustinian.

agostíno, *a.* born in August; ripening in August. **Agostíno,** *m.* Augustine. **agósto,** *m.* August.

agraménte, *ad.* harshly, bitterly.

agrària, *f.* agriculture, agricultural science. **agràrio,** *a.* agrarian.

agrèste, *a.* rural, rustic; rude.

agrestíno, *a.* sourish, sharp. **agrèsto,** *a.* sour, bitter. ¶ *m.* sour grape; juice of unripe (sour) grapes.

agrétto, *a.* sourish, somewhat acid.

agrézza, *f.* sourness, acidity.

agricoltóre, *m.* farmer. **agricoltúra,** *f.* agriculture; tillage.

agrifòglio, *m.* holly.

agrimensóre, *m.* land surveyor. **agrimensúra,** *f.* land surveying, land measurement.

àgro, *a.* sour, bitter, acid, tart, sharp; pungent; (*fig.*) hard, unpleasant, distasteful. ¶ *m.* sourness, tartness; juice (of lemon); land, territory, plain round a city (*esp. Rome*), *l' ~ romano.* **agrodólce,** *a. & m.* bitter-sweet, sub-acid.

agronomía, *f.* agricultural science. **agrònomo,** *m.* agricultural specialist, scientific agriculturist.

agrúmi, *m.pl.* citrus fruits.

agúglia, *f.* spire; bar of a magnet; sail needle; gar-fish.

aguzzàre, *v.t.* to sharpen; whet; stimulate. **agúzzo,** *a.* sharp, s.-pointed; fine-edged.

ah! ahi! *ex.* oh! ah! O dear! (of pain).

ahimè! *ex.* alas!

àia, *f.* threshing-floor; governess. **Aia (l'),** *f.* The Hague.

Aiàce, *m.* Ajax.

àio, *m.* tutor.

airóne, *m.* heron.

aitànte, *a.* robust, vigorous; helpful.

aiuòla, *or* **aiòla,** *f.* flower-bed; parterre.

aiutànte, *m.* assistant; adjutant. *~ di bandiera,* flag lieutenant (*Nav.*). *~ di campo,* aide-de-camp. *~ maggiore,* (*Mil.*) adjutant. *~ medico,* assistant doctor. *~ di sanità,* medical orderly. **aiutàre,** *v.t.* to help, aid, assist; succour, tend. **aiutàrsi,** *v.refl.* to give mutual aid, help each other; help oneself; avail oneself (of = *di*); strive. **aiúto,** *m.* aid, help; assistant.

aizzàre, *v.t.* to incite, instigate, stir up, set on; provoke, stimulate.

àla (*pl.* **ali),** *f.* wing, blade (of an oar); (*Mil.*) flank; wing of a building; aisle. *far ~,* to make room; extend

the line. *stare sull'ali,* to be just going, just starting. *apertura d' ~ i,* (*Aero.*) wing-span.

alabàstro, *m.* alabaster.

àlacre, *a.* brisk, cheerful, active; ready, willing. **alacrità,** *f.* alacrity.

alamàro, *m.* braid on a uniform, ornamental lacing, loop; (*pl.*) frogs, braided fastenings.

alàno, *m.* bulldog.

alàre, *m.* gen. pl. *alari,* andirons, fire-dogs. **alàre,** *v.t.* (*Naut.*) to pull, heave, haul.

Alàsca (l'), *f.* Alaska.

alàto, *a.* winged.

àlba, *f.* dawn, day-break.

albagía, *f.* pride, vanity, self-conceit.

albanése, *a. & m.f.* Albanian. **Albanía (l'),** *f.* Albania.

albaspína, *f.* (*Poet.*) hawthorn, white-thorn.

àlbatra, *f.* arbutus berry. **àlbatro,** *m.* arbutus; albatross.

albèdine, *f.* whiteness, brightness.

albeggiàre, *v.i.* (*aux.* essere) to dawn, become bright or whitish.

alberàre, *v.t.* to raise (*mast or flag*), hoist, set up; plant (*trees*). **alberatúra,** *f.* masts of a ship; trees on a plantation or estate.

alberèlla, *f.* aspen-[tree].

alberèllo, *m.* salt-box; phial; paint-pot; small tree.

alberéto, *m.* plantation; avenue of poplars.

alberétto, *m.* dwarf-tree; royal or top-gallant mast.

albergàre (*pr.* -**èrgo,** -**èrghi),** *v.t. & i.* to lodge, harbour; put up at an inn. **albergatóre,** *m.* inn-keeper, hotel-keeper. **alberghièro,** *a.* hotel-keeping, hotel (*att.*). *l'industria ~ a,* the hotel industry. **albèrgo** (*pl.* **albèrghi),** *m.* hotel, inn; hostel, shelter; lodging. *~ diurno,* day hostel, d. hotel. *~ per la gioventù,* youth hostel.

alberíno, *m.* shrub, small tree; young poplar.

àlbero, *m.* tree; mast; shaft, axle (*Mech.*). *~ da frutti,* fruit tree; *~ genealogico,* pedigree, genealogical tree; *~ maestro,* main mast. *~ di mezzana,* mizzen mast; *~ di trinchetto,* fore-mast. *~ motore,* main shaft, driving s. *~ disinnesto,* disengaging shaft. *~ portaelica,* propeller shaft. *~ di trasmissione,* transmission shaft. [*~ di*]*rinvio,* *~ secondario,* countershaft. *~ a manovella,* crank shaft.

albicòcca, *f.* apricot. **albicòcco**, *m.* apricot tree.

albinismo, *m.* albinism. **albino**, *a.* & *m.* albino.

àlbo, *a.* white; tipsy. ¶ *m.* roll, register; list; album; notice-board.

albóre, *m.* brightness, white light, dawn. *ai primi ~i*, at dawn, at the first streak(s) of dawn.

àlbum (*pl.* **àlbi**), *m.* album, scrapbook. *~ da incollare*, paste-on album. *~ a passe-partout*, slip-in album.

albúme, *m.* albumen; white of egg. **albumína**, *f.* (*Med.*) albumin.

albúrno, *m.* alburnum.

àlcali, *m.* alkali. **alcalíno**, *a.* alkaline. **alcalòide**, *m.* alkaloid.

alcànna, *f.* henna.

àlce, *m.* elk. *~ americano*, moose.

alcèa, *f.* (*Bot.*) hollyhock.

alchímia, *f.* alchemy. **alchimísta** (*pl.* **-ísti**), *m.* alchemist.

alcióne, *m.* halcyon; king-fisher; gull.

àlcool, *m.inv.* a'*.*ohol, spirit[s]. *~ denaturato*, met'*.*ylated spirit. **alcoòlico** (*pl.* **-òlici**), *a.* alcoholic. **alcoolicità**, *f.* alcoholic content. **alcoolísmo**, *m.* alcoholism.

alcoràno, *m.* Koran.

alcòva, *f.* alcove; recess.

alcunché, *pn.* anything, something; a little bit.

alcúno, *a.* & *pn.* some, any; someone, anyone.

aldíno, *a.* Aldine.

àlea, *f.* (contingent) risk; game of chance. *correr l'~*, run the risk.

aleàtico (*pl.* **-àtici**), *m.* type of black grape; well-known red Tuscan wine.

aleggiàre (*pr.* **-éggio**, **-éggi**), *v.i.* (*aux.* avere) to flutter, flap (*wings*); flit; wave; quiver.

aleróne (*Aero.*), *m.* aileron.

alesàggio, *m.* boring, drilling, reaming; bore (*cylinder*). **alesàre**, *v.t.* to bore, drill; broach, ream. **alesatríce**, *f.* borer, boring machine; reamer.

Alessàndria, *f.* Alessandria (*Piedmont*). **Alessàndria d'Egitto**, *f.* Alexandria. **alessandríno**, *m.* alexandrine (*verse*). ¶ *a.* Alexandrian. **Alessàndro**, *m.* Alexander.

alétta, *f.* small wing; fin. *~ di rollio* (*Naut.*), bilge keel.

àlfa, *f.* alpha, Gk. letter A; alfa [grass], esparto [grass].

alfabètico (*pl.* **-ètici**), *a.* alphabetical. **alfabèto**, *m.* alphabe*.*

alfière, *m.* standard-bearer; ensign bishop (*chess*).

alfíne, *ad.* at last, finally; after all.

àlga (*pl.* **àlghe**), *f.* seaweed.

àlgebra, *f.* algebra. **algèbrico** (*pl.* **-èbrici**), *a.* algebraic(al).

Algéri, *f.* Algiers. **Algería (l')**, *f.* Algeria. **algeríno**, *a.* & *m.* Algerian.

àlgido, *a.* (*Poet.*) cold. **algóre**, *m.* (*Poet.*) icy cold.

algóso, *a.* abounding in seaweed; covered with seaweed.

aliànte, *m.* (*Aviat.*) glider.

alíce, *f.* anchovy.

alienàbile, *a.* alienable; transferable. **alienàre**, *v.t.* to alienate; transfer; deliver up; estrange, sever. **alienàto**, *p.a.* alienated, estranged; parted with; sold; mad, insane. ¶ *m.* madman, lunatic, -a, *f.* madwoman. **alienísta** (*pl.* **-ísti**), *m.* alienist; psychiatrist. **alièno**, *a.* alien, averse, disinclined. *~ da*, averse to.

alimentàre, **alimentàrio**, *a.* alimentary; nutritive. *pensione alimentaria*, alimony. *generi ~i*, *prodotti ~i*, foodstuffs. *condotto alimentario*, alimentary canal.

alimentàre, *v.t.* to feed, nourish; (*Mech.*) stoke, feed. **alimentazióne**, *f.* feeding; stoking. **aliménto**, *m.* nourishment, food, (*pl.*) alimony, support, subsistence. **alimònia**, *f.* (*Law*) alimony.

alínea, *f.* first line of a poem; new paragraph.

alipede, *a.* with winged feet.

alisèo, *a.* in *venti alisei*, tradewinds.

alitàre, *v.i.* (*aux.* avere) to breathe gently, blow softly. **àlito**, *m.* gentle breeze, breath, puff. *raccoglier l' ~*, *riaver l' ~*, to recover breath.

allacciabottóni, *m.inv.* button-hook. **allacciaménto**, *m.* lacing, linking, twining; (*Med.*) bandage, (*Rly.*) branch line. **allacciàre**, *v.t.* to lace, bind, tie; confine; entwine; leash, lasso; make fast, belay; [en]snare; [en]trap; deceive.

allagaménto, *m.* inundation. **allagàre**, *v.t.* to overflow, flood, submerge, form into a lake.

allampanàre, *v.i.* (*aux.* essere) to grow lean. **allampanàto**, *p.a.* emaciated, lean; starved. *essere ~ dalla fame*, to be ravenously hungry.

allappàre, *v.t.* to irritate, embitter, set one's teeth on edge.

allargaménto, *m.* enlargement, extension, spreading, widening. *~ della* *città*, growth of the town. **allargàre** (*pr.* **-àrgo, -àrghi**), *v.t.* to enlarge, widen, extend, stretch out, spread; increase; relax, loose, let go. ~ *la mano*, to be open-handed, liberal. **allargàrsi**, *v.refl.* to extend, spread out, grow; take a larger house; sheer off, put out to sea.

allarmànte, *p.a.* alarming. **allarmàre**, *v.t.* to alarm, startle. **allàrme**, *m.* alarm, warning, alert; fright. ~ *di incursione aerea*, air-raid warning. *dare un* ~, *suonare un* ~, raise an alarm, sound an alarm. *le sirene han dato il segnale del cessato* ~, the sirens have sounded the 'all clear'. **allarmìsta** (*pl.* **-ìsti**), *m.f.* alarmist.

allàto, a lato, *ad. & pr.* near, beside. ~ ~, *close beside.*

allattaménto, *m.* suckling, giving suck; nursing. **allattàre**, *v.t.* to suckle, nurse, give suck.

alleànza, *f.* alliance; league. **alleàrsi**, *v.refl.* to enter into an alliance; be allied. **alleàto**, *a.* allied; leagued. ¶ *m.* ally.

allegaménto, *m.* setting (*teeth*) on edge; mixture. **allegàre**, *v.t.* to cite, adduce; allege; assign; alloy; enclose, join; set on edge; (*v.i. aux. essere*) to take root, fructify. **allegàto**, *p.a.* alleged; cited, quoted. ¶ *m.* enclosure; schedule; codicil; insert; supplement. **allegazióne**, *f.* allegation; citation of proofs; alloy; setting on edge.

alleggeriménto, *m.* lightening; easing; alleviation, relief. **alleggerìre** (*pr.* **-ìsco, -ìsci**), *v.t.* to lighten; ease; mitigate; alleviate; soften; steal from; diminish; **alleggerìrsi**, *v.refl.* to put on lighter clothes; relieve oneself of a burden.

alleghíre (*pr.* **-ìsco, -ìsci**), *v.i.* (*aux. avere*) to take root. *fare* ~, to set on edge (*teeth*).

allegorìa, *f.* allegory. **allegòrico** (*pl.* **-òrici**), *a.* allegoric(al).

allegraménte, *ad.* gaily, cheerfully, merrily. **allegràre**, *v.t.* to gladden, delight, cheer. **allegràrsi**, *v.refl.* to rejoice, to be merry. **allegrézza**, *f.* cheerfulness, gaiety. **allegrìa**, *f.* mirth, gaiety, merriment. **allégro**, *a.* cheerful; merry; gay, lively.

allelúia, *m.inv.* hallelujah.

allenaménto, *m.* training; practice (*sport*). **allenàre**, *v.t.* to train; strengthen; invigorate. **allenatóre**, *m.* (*sport*) trainer; coach.

allentaménto, *m.* slackening. **allentàre**, *v.t.* to slacken, relax; loose, loosen; let siip, let go; diminish. **allentatúra**, *f.* hernia, rupture.

allergìa, *f.* (*Med.*) allergy. **allèrgico** (*pl.* **-èrgici**), *a.* allergic.

allessàre, *v.t.* to boil. **allésso**, *p.a. & m.* boiled; boiled meat, boiled beef.

allestiménto, *m.* preparation; (*ship*) fitting out; (*Typ.*) finishing. **allestìre** (*pr.* **-ìsco, -ìsci**), *v.t.* to prepare, get ready, make ready; fit out, rig, equip.

alletamàre, *v.t.* to manure.

allettaménto, *m.* allurement; attraction; charm, enticement. **allettàre**, *v.t.* to allure, entice, attract; decoy, ensnare; delight, charm, flatter; beat down; lay down. **allettàrsi**, *v.refl.* to take to one's bed, keep one's bed. **allettàto**, *p.a.* allured, enticed, charmed; bed-ridden.

allevaménto, *m.* bringing up; upbringing; rearing, breeding. **allevàre**, *v.t.* to rear, bring up; raise, breed; instruct, train. **allevatóre**, *m.* **-trìce**, *f.* breeder.

alleviaménto, *m.* alleviation; lightening; relief. **alleviàre** (*pr.* **-èvio, -èvi**), *v.t.* to alleviate; lighten; allay; soothe; relieve.

allib[b]íre (*pr.* **-ìsco, -ìsci**), *v.i.* (*aux. essere*) to turn pale; be dismayed.

allibratóre, *m.* bookmaker (*betting*).

allietàre (*pr.* **-èto**), *v.t.* to gladden, cheer, divert; enliven. **allietàrsi**, *v.refl.* to rejoice; cheer up; make merry.

allièvo, **-a**, *m.f.* pupil, scholar; school-boy, school-girl; cadet. ~ *ufficiale* (*Mil.*), cadet officer. ~ *della scuola navale*, naval cadet.

allignàre (*pr.* *aux. essere & avere*) to shoot; take root; grow; do well.

allineaménto, *m.* alignment; (*Mil.*) falling in. **allineàre**, *v.t.* to set in line; bring into line; range; (*Mil.*) rank, dress, draw up.

allit[t]erazióne, *f.* alliteration.

allividíre (*pr.* **-ìsco, -ìsci**), *v.i.* (*aux. essere*) to turn pale; become livid.

allòcco (*pl.* **-òcchi**), *m.* owl; (*fig.*) dolt, simpleton.

allocuzióne, *f.* speech, address.

allodiàle, *a.* allodial, free-hold. **allòdio**, *m.* free-hold estate.

allòdola, *f.* lark, sky-lark.

allogàre (*pr.* **-ògo, -òghi**), *v.t.* to place; deposit; invest; to let, lease;

commission; arrange; employ. ~ *una figliuola*, to marry (or give in marriage) a daughter. **alloggiàre** (*pr.* -**òggio**, -**òggi**), *v.t. & i.* to lodge; accommodate; put up; stay; encamp; billet, be billeted. **allòggio**, *m.* lodging(s), accommodation; quarters.

allontanaménto, *m.* removal; distance; absence; estrangement. **allontanàre**, *v.t.* to remove, send away, keep away; dismiss; estrange; avert; drive off. **allontanàrsi**, *v.refl.* to withdraw, move off, move away; wander; deviate; differ; become estranged. ~ *da terra*, (*Naut.*) to clear the land.

allopatía, *f.* allopathy (*Med.*).

allóra, *ad.* then. *d'* ~ *in poi*, thenceforward, from that time onwards. *fin* ~, until then. *fino da* ~, since then. *per* ~, for the time being; ~ (*in tal caso*), in that case.

allorché, *ad.* when, at the time when.

allòro, *m.* bay-tree, laurel; (*fig.*) laurel(s). *foglie di* ~, bay leaves.

allorquàndo, *ad.* when, at the time when.

allotropía, *f.* (*Chem.*) allotropy.

allottàre (*pr.* -**òtto**), *v.t.* to allot; apportion; put up to lottery.

allucinàre, *v.t.* to dazzle, deceive, bewitch, hallucinate. **allucinàrsi**, *v.refl.* to suffer from hallucinations, be mistaken, deceived. **allucinàto**, *p.a.* hallucinated, deluded. **allucinazióne**, *f.* hallucination, delusion.

allúdere, *v.i. ir.* (*aux.* avere), to allude; refer (to), hint (at).

allúme, *m.* alum. **allumièra**, *f.* alum pit, alum works. **allumína**, *f.* alumina; china clay.

alluminàre, *v.t.* (*Poet.*) to illuminate.

allumínio, *m.* aluminium.

allungàbile, *a.* extensible. **allungaménto**, *m.* lengthening. extension; prolongation; enlargement. **allungàre** (*pr.* -**úngo**, -**únghi**), *v.t.* to lengthen, elongate; prolong, extend; eke out; stretch [out]; dilute. ~ *il muso*, to pout; pull a long face. ~ *il collo*, to stretch out the neck; to hang. ~ *il passo*, to quicken one's step. ~ *il vino con acqua*, to dilute wine with water. **allungàrsi**, *v.refl.* to grow longer; lengthen; extend; stretch; grow tall; draw out (*days, &c.*). **allungàto**, *p.a.* elongated, lengthened, pro-

longed; diluted. **allúngo**, *m.* (forward) pass (*sport*).

allusióne, *f.* allusion, reference; hint. **allusívo**, *a.* allusive.

alluvióne, *f.* flood, inundation.

àlma, *f.* (*Poet.*) soul.

almanaccàre (*pr.* -**àcco**, -**àcchi**), *v.i.* to dream, build castles in the air; muse, ponder; puzzle one's head. **almanàcco** (*pl.* -**àcchi**), *m.* almanac; calendar. **almanaccóne**, *m.* idle dreamer.

almànco, **alméno**, *c.* at least.

àlmo, *a.* (*Poet.*) kindly, dear; beneficent; rich, fertile; glorious; divine.

àlno, *m.* alder [tree].

àloe, *m.* aloe.

alóne, *m.* halo.

àlpe, *f.* high mountain, alp. **alpèstre**, *a.* Alpine, mountainous; wild, rough. *giardino* —, *m.* rock-garden. **Àlpi (le)**, *f.pl.* the Alps. **alpigiàno**, *a.* Alpine. ¶ *m.* mountaineer; inhabitant of the Alps. **alpinísmo**, *m.* mountaineering, mountain-climbing. **alpinísta** (*pl.* -**ísti**), *m.* mountain-climber. **alpíno**, *a.* alpine; (*m.pl.*) Alpine troops (force created 15th October, 1872, to guard northern frontiers of the Kingdom of Italy).

alquànti, *a. & pn. pl.* some; a good many; several. **alquànto**, *a. & pn.* some, a good deal. ¶ *ad.* in some degree, somewhat, rather.

Alsàzia (l'), *f.* Alsace. **alsaziàno**, *a. & m.* Alsatian.

àlt! *i.* halt!

altaléna, *f.* see-saw; swing; swing-board; fluctuation, indecision. **altalenàre**, *v.i.* (*aux.* avere) & **altalenàrsi**, *v.refl.* to swing, see-saw.

altaménte, *ad.* highly; deeply; greatly.

altàna, *f.* open gallery or loggia on the roof of a house, belvedere.

altàre, *m.* altar. ~ *maggiore*, high altar.

altèa, *f.* marsh-mallow.

alteraménte, *ad.* proudly.

alteràre (*pr.* **àltero**), *v.t.* to alter; change; corrupt, distort; weaken, impair; falsify; forge. **alteràrsi**, *v.refl.* to alter; be upset or perturbed; become abnormal; get angry.

altercàre (*pr.* -**èrco**, -**èrchi**), *v.i.* (*aux.* avere) to dispute, wrangle, quarrel, have an altercation. **altèrco** (*pl.* -**èrchi**), *m.* altercation, quarrel, dispute.

alterézza, *f.* dignity, (legitimate) pride. **altèro**, *a.* proud, haughty.

alterígia, *f.* haughtiness, arrogance.

alternàre, *v.t.* to alternate. **alternaménte, alternataménte,** *ad.* alternately, in turn, in rotation. **alternatíva,** *f.* alternative; alternation. **alternatívo,** *a.* alternative; (*Mech.*) reciprocating. **alternàto,** *p.a.* alternate; (*Elec.*) alternating. *corrente* ~*a*, alternating current (*abb.* A.C.). **alternatóre,** *m.* alternator. ~ *ad alta frequenza* (*Elec.*) high-frequency a.

altézza, *f.* height; depth; dignity, impressiveness, loftiness; width (*of cloth*); loudness; (*Astr. & Geom.*) altitude; (*Naut.*) bearing, degree of latitude; (*in titles*) Highness. *essere all'* ~ *di*, to lie off (*shore or island*), be abreast of, be equal to (*task or responsibility*). *salto in* ~, *m.* high jump (*athletics*).

altíccio, *a.* tipsy, half seas over, merry (*in liquor*).

altímetro, *m.* altimeter.

altipiàno, *m.* table-land, plateau.

altisonàute, *a.* high-sounding; re-sounding.

altíssimo, *a. sup.* very high. ¶ *m.* *l'A* ~, the Most High.

altitonànte (l'), *m.* Jupiter, Jove, The Thunderer.

altitúdine, *f.* altitude; height.

altivolànte, *a.* high-flying.

àlto, *a.* high; tall; erect; (*Geog.*) upper; deep; loud; strong, sharp, clear; arduous, difficult, important; eminent; great; ancient. *l'A* ~ *Adige*, the Upper Adige. ~*a marea*, high water, high tide. ~*e maree*, spring tides. *in* ~ *mare*, on the high seas, on the open sea. *ad* ~*a voce*, aloud. *a testa* ~*a*, with head erect. *quest'anno la quaresima è* ~*a*, Lent is late this year. *a notte* ~*a*, late in the night. *l'* ~*a Italia*, North Italy. ¶ *ad.* loud, loudly; high, highly; up, above. *fare* ~ *e basso*, to do as one likes; assume authority. ¶ *m.* height, top, summit; heaven; (*Mil.*) halt (also *alt*). *farsi da* ~, begin at (or from) the beginning. *rifarsi da* ~, begin again from the beginning. *guardare dall'* ~ *in basso*, to look up and down, regard with condescension or contempt. *alti e bassi*, ups and downs.

altofórno (*pl.* **altiforni**), *m.* (*Metall.*) blast furnace.

altolocàto (*pl.* *altolocàti*), *a.* high placed; high ranking; of high social standing.

altoparlànte (*pl.* **-parlànti**), *m.* loud-speaker (*Radio*).

altresí, *ad.* likewise, also, too.

altrettàle, *a.* wholly similar, another such, (*pl.*) other such.

altrettànto, *a. & ad.* just as much, as much again; so much; equally, the same. **altrettànti,** *a. & pn. pl.* as many, so many.

àltri, *pn. indef. inv.* another, someone, anyone; others; some people. *noi* ~ *Inglesi*, we English. *noi* ~ *Scozzesi*, we Scots.

altrièri (l'), *ad.* the day before yesterday.

altriménti, *ad.* otherwise.

àltro, *a.* other; different; new; second; next; further. *da un'altra parte*, elsewhere. *senz'altre cerimonie*, without further ceremonies. *quest'altr'anno*, next year. ¶ *m.* another thing, something else; (*interr.*) anything else. *parliamo d'* ~, let us speak of something else. *non c'è altro*, there is nothing else. *per* ~, however; moreover. *senz'* ~, at once, without more ado; *tutt'* ~, on the contrary, far from it, not at all. *tutt'* ~ *che*, anything but. ¶ *pn.* other, (*pl.*) others; other one, other person. *un* ~, another. *nessun* ~, nobody else. *qualcun* ~, somebody else. *l'uno e l'* ~, both. *altro! i.* yes indeed! yes rather!

altrónde, *ad.* elsewhere. *d'* ~, on the other hand; besides.

altróve, *ad.* elsewhere, somewhere else.

altrúi, *pn.* another person, others. (*gen. in the oblique cases.*) *la roba* ~, other people's property. *senza giovare* ~, without benefiting one's neighbours.

altruísmo, *m.* altruism. **altruísta,** *m.* altruist. **altruístico** (*pl.* **-ístici**), *a.* altruistic.

altúra, *f.* high ground; eminence.

alúnno, *m.* **-a** *f.* pupil.

alveàre, *m.* bee-hive.

àlveo, *m.* river bed. **alvèolo,** *m.* socket, sheath; cell (*honeycomb*).

Alvèrnia (l'), *f.* Auvergne.

alvíno, *a.* abdominal. **àlvo,** *m.* abdomen; womb.

alzàia, *f.* tow-line; cable; hawser.

alzaménto, *m.* lifting, raising. **alzàre,** *v.t.* to raise, hoist, lift up; shrug (*shoulders*); elevate, exalt. **alzàrsi,** *v.refl.* to rise, get up, stand up. **alzàta,** *f.* rise; rising; raising; elevation; mound; raised bank. ~ *di spalle*, shrug of the shoulders.

alzàvola, *f.* teal.
àlzo, *m.* (*gun*) back sight. *dare l'~,* (*Artil.*) to range.
amàbile, *a.* amiable.
amàca, *f.* hammock.
amàlgama, *m.* amalgam, mixture. **amalgamàre,** *v.t.* to amalgamate.
amànte, *p.a.* loving, fond. ¶ *m.f.* lover; devotee, votary; (*f.*) mistress.
amanuènse, *m.f.* amanuensis; copyist.
amaraménte, *ad.* bitterly; painfully.
amàre, *v.t.* to love; be fond of, like.
amareggiàre, *v.t.* to embitter; sadden; vex; distress. **amareggiàrsi,** *v.refl.* to become bitter, feel bitter; grieve, fret, take to heart. **amarézza,** *f.* bitterness; grief; vexation; (*pl.*) sorrows. **amaritúdine,** *f.* bitterness, grief, distress. **amàro,** *a.* bitter; sharp; painful; hard. ¶ *m.* bitter, bitters; bitterness, grief, rancour, hatred. **amarógnolo,** *a.* bitterish, rather bitter. **amarúme,** *m.* bitter stuff; bitterness.
amàto, *p.a.* loved, beloved. ¶ *m.* & -a *f.* beloved. **amatóre,** *m.* connoisseur; amateur; lover (*gen.*).
amàżżone, *f.* horsewoman, amazon; riding-habit. *Rio delle Amàżżoni, m.* Amazon (*river*).
ambàgi, *f.pl.* circumlocution; evasions.
ambàscia (*pl.* **-àsce**), *f.* breathlessness; anxiety; distress.
ambasciàta, *f.* embassy; commission. **ambasciatóre,** *m.* ambassador. **ambasciatríce,** *f.* ambassadress; ambassador's wife.
ambedúe, *pn.* & *a. inv.* both.
ambiàre, *v.i.* to amble.
ambidèstro, *a.* ambidextrous.
ambientàrsi, *v.refl.* to find one's place (*in society*), settle down, get accustomed to one's surroundings.
ambiènte, *m.* surroundings, environment; surrounding atmosphere; circumference; enclosed space, room; setting.
ambiguità, *f.* ambiguity, ambiguousness. **ambíguo,** *a.* ambiguous; equivocal; doubtful.
ambíre (*pr.* **-ísco, -ísci**), *v.t.* & *i.* to covet, be ambitious (for), long for, seek after. **ambíto,** *p.a.* sought for, coveted, valued.
àmbito, *m.* circuit, compass, ambit; limits; competence; striving; intrigue.
ambivalènza, *f.* ambivalence.

ambizióne, *f.* ambition; eagerness; pretension. **ambizióso,** *a.* ambitious.
àmbo, *a. inv.* both. ¶ *m.* pair, double (*lottery*).
ambóne, *m.* (*Arch.*) ambo (*pl.* ambones), pulpit.
àmbra, *f.* amber, ambergris. **ambràto,** *a.* amber (-coloured).
Ambrògio, *m.* Ambrose.
ambrosiàno, *a.* Ambrosian, of St. Ambrose; Milanese. *Biblioteca ~a,* Ambrosian Library (founded at Milan by Cardinal Federigo Borromeo, early 17th cent.). *inno ~,* Te Deum.
ambulànte, *p.a.* walking; itinerant; wandering; strolling; travelling. *cattedra ~,* itinerant lectureship. *commediante ~i,* strolling players. *merciaio ~,* pedlar, itinerant dealer. *ufficio postale ~,* travelling post-office. **ambulànza,** *f.* ambulance. **ambulatòrio,** *m.* ambulatory; covered walk; cloister; (*Med.*) consulting room, surgery.
Ambúrgo, *f.* Hamburg.
amenaménte, *ad.* pleasantly, agreeably. **amenità,** *f.* amenity; charm; agreeableness; urbanity. **amèno,** *a.* pleasant, agreeable; delightful; amusing.
Amèrica (l'), *f.* America. *~ del Nord,* North A. *~ del Sud,* South A. **americàno,** *a.* & *m.* American.
ametísta, *f.* amethyst.
amichévole, *a.* friendly, amiable. **amicízia,** *f.* friendship. **amíco** (*pl.* **-íci**), *a.* friendly; harmonious; propitious. ¶ *m.* friend; lover; well-wisher. **amíca** (*pl.* **amiche**), *f.* female friend; sweetheart; mistress. **amichétto,** *m.* boy-friend.
àmido, *m.* starch. **amidóso,** *a.* starchy.
amistà, *f.* (*Poet.*) friendship.
Amlèto, *m.* Hamlet.
ammaccàre (*pr.* **-àcco, -àcchi**), *v.t.* to bruise; crush; pound; dent; flatten. **ammaccatúra,** *f.* bruise; contusion.
ammaestraménto, *m.* instruction; training; teaching; precept. **ammaestràre,** *v.t.* to train, teach, instruct; discipline; break in.
ammainàre (*pr.* **-aino**), *v.t.* to furl, lower, take in, strike (*sails*); haul down (*flag*).
ammalàre, *v.i.* (*aux.* essere) & **ammalàrsi,** *v.refl.* to fall ill. **ammalàto,** *a.* ill, sick, unwell.

ammaliaménto, *m.* witchery; enchantment; charm. **ammaliàre,** *v.t.* to bewitch; fascinate; enchant. **ammaliatóre,** *m.* enchanter. **ammaliatríce,** *f.* enchantress.

ammanettàre (*pr.* **-étto**), *v.t.* to handcuff; shackle.

ammanníre (*pr.* **-ísco, -ísci**), *v.t.* to prepare, get ready; (*paint*) prime. **ammanitúra,** *f.* priming.

ammansàre & **ammansíre** (*pr.* **-ísco, -ísci**), *v.t.* to tame; subdue; appease; calm; soften; allay. **ammansàrsi, -írsi,** *v.refl.* to grow tame; recover one's temper.

ammantàre, *v.t.* to mantle, clothe; cloak, hide, disguise.

ammaràggio, *m.* (*Aviat.*) alighting (*sea-plane*), landing (on water). *un* ~ *forzato,* a forced landing. **ammaràre,** *v.i.* (*Aviat.*) to alight, land, touch down (on water).

ammarràggio, *m.* (*Naut.* & *Aviat.*) mooring. *albero di* ~, mooring mast. *fune di* ~, mooring cable.

ammassàre, *v.t.* to amass; heap up; accumulate; pile up; stockpile; hoard; (*Mil.*) to mass. **ammassàrsi,** *v.refl.* to mass; muster; assemble. **ammàsso,** *m.* accumulation; pile; heap; mass; hoard.

ammatassàre, *v.t.* to wind into a skein; (*fig.*) to confuse. **ammatassàrsi,** *v.refl.* to become confused.

ammattiménto, *m.* (great) worry; embarrassment; care; difficulty. **ammattíre** (*pr.* **-ísco, -ísci**), *v.i.* (*aux.* essere) to go mad; become crazy or infuriated. *fare* ~, to drive mad.

ammattonàre, *v.t.* to pave with bricks. **ammattonàto,** *m.* brick floor or pavement; paved square.

ammazzàre, *v.t.* to kill, murder, slaughter; (*fig.*) to stun; crush; overwhelm; exhaust; (*cards*) play a better card than. **ammazzasètte,** *m.inv.* bully, braggart. **ammazzatóio,** *m.* slaughter-house; bludgeon; knock-out blow.

ammelmàre, *v.i.* (*aux.* essere) to sink in the mire.

ammenàre, *v.t.* to deliver (*a blow*), strike.

ammènda, *f.* fine; amends; ransom; correction. **ammendàre,** *v.t.* to make amends for; amend; correct.

ammésso, *p.a.* admitted; received; acknowledged.

nméttere (*pr.* **-étto,** &*c.*, like

mettere), *v.t. i.r.* to admit; receive; allow; grant; suppose.

ammezzaménto, *m.* halving; division in two. **ammezzàre,** *v.t.* to halve, cut in two; leave half-finished; clip (*words*).

ammiccàre (*pr.* **-ícco, -ícchi**), *v.i.* (*aux.* avere) to wink; beckon. **ammícco** (*pl.* **-ícchi**), *m.* wink; winking.

amministràre, *v.t.* to administrate; manage; direct; administer (*justice, sacraments, medicine,* &*c.*). **amministratóre,** *m.* (*f.* **trice** administrator, -trix, director. ~ *delegato,* managing director. **amministrazióne,** *f.* administration, management; direction; board, directorate; authorities. *consiglio d'* ~, board of directors. ~ *fiduciaria,* trusteeship.

ammiràglio, *m.* admiral. *Grande A* ~, Admiral of the Fleet. ~ *di Armata,* Admiral. ~ *di Squadra,* Vice-A. ~ *di Divisione,* Rear A. ¶ *a.* belonging to an admiral. *nave* ~*a,* flag-ship. *ufficiale* ~, flag officer (*Nav.*).

ammiràre, *v.t.* to admire, wonder at. **ammiratóre,** *m.* **-trice,** *f.* admirer. **ammirazióne,** *f.* admiration; wonder.

ammissíbile, *a.* admissible. **ammissióne,** *f.* admission, admittance; entrance; (*Mech.*) intake. *esame d'* ~, *m.* entrance examination.

ammobiliàre, *v.t.* to furnish.

ammodernàre, *v.t.* to modernize.

ammòdo, *a.* discreet, prudent, tactful. ¶ *ad.* gently, carefully; properly.

ammogliàre, *v.t.* to find a wife for; to marry, give in marriage; (*fig.*) to unite, couple, match. **ammogliàrsi,** *v.refl.* to take a wife, marry, get married; (*fig.*) to pair, match, tally. **ammogliàto,** *p.a.* married.

ammollàre, *v.t.* to steep, soak; soften; slacken, relax, let go.

ammolliménto, *m.* softening; slackening. **ammollíre** (*pr.* **-ísco, -ísci**), *v.t.* to soften; mollify; weaken. **ammollírsi,** *v.refl.* to mellow; become enfeebled.

ammoníaca, *f.* ammonia.

ammoníre (*pr.* **-ísco, -ísci**), *v.t.* to admonish; warn; reprimand. **ammonizióne,** *f.* admonition; reproof.

ammontàre, *v.t.* to amass, hoard up, heap up. *v.i.* (*aux.* essere) to amount. ~ *a,* to amount to.

ammontàrsi, *v.refl.* to accumulate, gather.

ammonticchiàre, *v.t.* to pile up, collect in small heaps.

ammorbàre (*pr.* -òrbo), *v.t.* to taint, infect; corrupt.

ammorbidíre (*pr.* -ísco, -ísci), *v.t.* to soften.

ammorsàre, *v.t.* to bite, nibble at; bit (*horse*).

ammorsatúra, *f.* (*Carp.*) scarf joint.

ammorsellàto, *m.* dish of minced meat and eggs.

ammortaménto, *m.* amortization; extinction; redemption (*Fin.*). *fondo di* ∼, sinking-fund.

ammortíre (*pr.* -ísco), *v.t.* to deaden; weaken; soften; parry (*blow*); allay.

ammortizzàre, *v.t.* to redeem, extinguish (*debt*), pay off by instalments (*interest & part of capital*). **ammortizzazióne,** *f.* amortization, redemption. *cassa di* ∼, sinking fund.

ammorzàre, *v.t.* to extinguish.

ammostàre, *v.t.* to press (*grapes*). **ammostatóio,** *m.* wine-press.

ammucchiàre, *v.t.* to heap up, pile up; cram; huddle together.

ammuffíre (*pr.* -ísco), *v.i. &* **ammuffirsi,** *v.refl.* to become mouldy.

ammutinaménto, *m.* mutiny; sedition. **ammutinàre,** *v.t.* to stir up mutiny. **ammutinàrsi,** *v.refl.* to mutiny, revolt.

ammutíre, ammutolíre (*pr.* -ísco), *v.i.* (*aux.* essere), to become dumb. *v.t.* to put to silence.

amnesía, *f.* loss of memory; amnesia (*Med.*).

amnistía, *f.* amnesty.

àmo, *m.* fish-hook.

amóre, *m.* love; affection; fondness; passion; (*pl.*) love affairs, amours. ∼ *mio!* my dear! my darling! ∼ *proprio,* self-respect, pride; self-esteem. *per* ∼ *vostro,* for your sake.

amoreggiàre (*pr.* -éggio, -éggi) *v.i.* (*aux.* avere) to make love; flirt. ∼ *con,* to flirt with, court. **amorétto,** *m.* love affair. **amorévole,** *a.* amiable; friendly; kindly; affectionate. **amorevolézza,** *f.* amiability; affection; kindness; mark of affection.

amòrfo, *a.* amorphous; shapeless.

amoríno, *m.* dear little thing, darling; (*Art*) child's figure; (*Bot.*) mignon-ette.

amoróso, *a.* loving; amorous; affectionate (*animal*). ¶ *m. & f.* (-a) lover; sweetheart.

amovíbile, *a.* removable.

ampère (*Elec.*), *m.* amp[ere]. **amperòmetro,** *m.* amp[ere]-meter.

ampiézza, *f.* ampleness; amplitude; largeness; width; range. **àmpio** (*pl.* -àmpi), *a.* (irreg. sup. *amplissimo*) ample, full, wide; large; roomy; spacious.

amplèsso, *m.* embrace.

ampliàre, *v.t.* to enlarge; amplify; extend, increase. **amplificàre** (*pr.* -ífico, -íchi), *v.t.* to amplify; exaggerate. **amplificatóre,** *m.* enlarger, magnifier; (*Radio*) amplifier. ¶ *a.* (*f.* -tríce) enlarging, amplifying. **amplitúdine,** *f.* amplitude.

ampólla, *f.* phial; cruet (*vessel*); (*Eccl.*) ampulla. **ampollièra,** *f.* cruet-stand. **ampollosità,** *f.* bombast; turgidity. **ampollóso,** *a.* inflated, bombastic, turgid; high-flown.

amputàre, *v.t.* to amputate, cut off.

amuléto, *m.* amulet, charm.

ànace, ànice, *m.* anise; aniseed.

anacorèta (*pl.* -èti), *m.* hermit, anchorite.

Anacreònte, *m.* Anacreon. **anacreòntico** (*pl.* -òntici), *a.* anacreontic.

anacronísmo, *m.* anachronism.

anàgrafe, *f.* register of births, deaths and marriages.

anagràmma (*pl.* -àmmi), *m.* anagram.

analfabèta (*pl.* -èti), *a. & m.f.* illiterate. **analfabetísmo,** *m.* illiteracy.

analgesía, *f.* (*Med.*) analgesia.

anàlisi, *f.* analysis; test; examination. ∼ *grammaticale,* parsing. ∼ *del sangue,* blood test. ∼ *spettroscopica,* spectrum analysis. **analísta** (*pl.* -ísti), *m.* analyst. **analítico** (*pl.* -ítici), *a.* analytic(al). **analizzàre,** *v.t.* to analyse; parse.

analogía, *f.* analogy. **anàlogo** (*pl.* -àloghi), *a.* analogous, like.

ananàsso, *m.* pineapple.

anarchía, *f.* anarchy; anarchism. **anàrchico** (*pl.* -àrchici), *a.* anarchic(al). ¶ *m.* anarchist.

anatèma (*pl.* -tèmi), *m.* anathema.

anatomía, *f.* anatomy. **anatòmico** (*pl.* -òmici), *a.* anatomic(al). **anatomísta** (*pl.* -ísti), *m.* anatomist.

ànatra, *f.* duck; *m.* drake. *dim.*

anatríno, anatròccolo, anatròtto, duckling; young duck.

ànca (*pl.* **ànche**), *f.* hip, haunch, leg (*chicken*); (*Naut.*) quarter. *misura delle anche,* hip measurement.

ancèlla, *f.* (*Poet.*) maid-servant; maid.

ànche, *ad. & c.* also; too; further, besides; still; even; yet. ~ *se, quand'* ~, even if, even though.

anchilòsi, *f.* anchylosis (*Med.*).

ancóna, *f.* altar-piece; niche for a statue.

àncora, *f.* anchor. ~ *di speranza* (*Naut.*), ~ *di salvezza* (*fig.*) sheet-anchor. *fondo all'* ~! let go the anchor! *affondare, gettare l'* ~, to cast anchor. *salpare l'* ~, to weigh anchor.

ancóra, *ad.* still, yet; again; more; longer; (*before comparative*) even.

ancoràggio, *m.* anchorage. **ancoràre** (*pr.* **àncoro**), *v.t. &* **ancoràrsi,** *v.refl.* to anchor.

ancorché, *c.* even if; although.

ancoròtto, *m.* kedge-anchor (*Naut.*).

ancúdine, *f.* anvil.

Andalúsia (l'), *f.* Andalusia.

andaménto, *m.* progress; rate of progress; proceeding; state. **andànte,** *a.* current; instant; smooth-going; uniform, steady; continuous; unbroken; plain; everyday; cheap. ¶ *m.* (*Mus.*) andante. ¶ *ad.* fluently. **andàre** (*pr.* vo or vàdo, vai, va, andiàmo, andàte, vànno), *v.i. ir.* (*aux.* essere) to go; move, run; be in demand; be current (*money*); proceed; do; get on; fare; please; fit; suit. *Before p.p.,* to be; require to be, ought to be. *Before gerund,* to indicate repeated or continuous action. ~ *a piedi,* to walk; go on foot. ~ *di seguito,* to run on (*fig.*). ~ *in bicicletta,* to cycle. ~ *a cavallo,* to ride. ~ *in automobile,* to motor. ~ *pian',* drive slowly (*traffic sign*). ~ *in carrozza,* to drive. ~ *in macchina,* to go to press (*Typ.*). ~ *in quota,* (*Aviat.*) to climb, gain height. ¶ *m.* going; gait. *a lungo* ~, in the long run. **andàrsene,** *v.refl.* to go (away), be off. **andàrne,** to be at stake. **andàta,** *f.* going, motion, movement; departure; journey; entrance. *biglietto di* ~, *m.* single ticket (*Rly.*), *b. di* ~ *e ritorno,* return ticket. **andàto,** *p.a.* gone; past; done for; ruined, gone bad. **andatúra,** *f.* gait; pace. **andàzzo,** *m.* bad habit; passing fashion; prevalence (*of epidemic*). **andirivièni,** *m.*

inv. coming & going; bustle (*of traffic*), intricate maze; (*fig.*) wandering talk.

àndito, *m.* passage; corridor.

andróne, *m.* lobby, entrance-hall.

anèddoto, *m.* anecdote.

anelànte, *p.a.* panting, gasping, breathless; eager (for). **anelàre** (*pr.* -èlo), *v.i.* (*aux.* avere) to pant; long (for). **anèlito,** *m.* panting, tremor; longing.

anèllo, *m.* (*pl. m.* -èlli, *f.* -èlla) ring; link (*chain*); ringlet (*hair*). *gioco degli* ~i, *m.* ring-quoits. **anèlla,** *f.pl.* curls.

anèlo, *a.* (*Poet.*) panting; yearning; exhausted.

anemía, *f.* anaemia, bloodlessness. **anèmico** (*pl.* -èmici), *a.* anaemic, bloodless.

anèmone, *m.* anemone; wind flower. **anemòmetro,** *m.* wind gauge.

aneròide, *a.* aneroid.

anesteśía, *f.* anaesthesia. **anestesísta** (*pl.* -ísti), *m.* anaesthetist. **anestètico** (*pl.* -ètici), *a. & m.* anaesthetic.

anéto, *m.* dill (*Bot., Cook.*).

aneurísma (*pl.* -ísmi), *m.* (*Med.*) aneurism.

anfíbio, *a.* amphibious. ¶ *a. & m.* amphibian (*Aviat., &c.*).

anfiteàtro, *m.* amphitheatre.

anfitrióne, *m.* generous host.

ànfora, *f.* jar; water-jar.

anfràtto, *m.* winding path; ravine; rocky defile. **anfrattuóso,** *a.* winding; craggy.

angariàre, *v.t.* to vex; harass; overtax; oppress.

angèlica, *f.* (*Bot.*) angelica. **angèlico** (*pl.* -èlici), *a.* angelic. **àngelo,** *m.* angel. ~ *custode,* guardian angel. *dim.* angiolíno, angiolétto.

angheria, *f.* imposition; outrage; abuse of power.

angína, *f.* angina; quinsy. ~ *pectoris,* angina pectoris.

angipòrto, *m.* blind alley, dead end.

anglicàno, *a. & m.* Anglican. **anglicísmo,** *m.* anglicism. **anglofobía,** *f.* anglophobia, anti-English feeling. **anglòfobo,** *m.* Anglophobe. **anglòmane,** *m.* passionate admirer of things English. **anglomanía,** *f.* Anglomania, craze for things English. **anglo-sàssone,** *m. & a.* Anglo-Saxon.

angolàre, *a.* angular; corner (*att.*). **àngolo,** *m.* angle, corner.

angòscia (*pl.* -òsce), *f.* anguish, pang; pain, grief. **angosciàre** (*pr.* -òscio,

-òsci), *v.t.* to distress, pain; grieve, vex. **angoscióso,** *a.* grievous, painful.

àngue, *m.* (*Poet.*) snake.

anguilla, *f.* eel. ~ *marina,* conger (eel).

angústia, *f.* poverty, misery; want, deficiency; pain, trouble, distress. **angustiàre,** *v.t.* to impoverish; distress; afflict, beset. **angústo,** *a.* narrow; stingy.

ànice, *m.* anise; aniseed.

anilína, *f.* aniline.

ànima, *f.* soul; spirit; heart, conscience; life, animation, liveliness; person; inhabitant; kernel, core. *stato d'* ~*e,* register of population. **animàle,** *a.* animal. ¶ *m.* animal, dumb animal, beast, brute; creature.

animàre, *v.t.* to animate, quicken, enliven, brighten, inspirit; give life to; provide with a core. *bastone animato,* sword-stick. **animàrsi,** *v.refl.* to become excited or lively; brighten; take courage. **animatóre,** *m.* (*f,* **-trice**) animator, moving spirit. ¶ *a.* animating; enlivening.

animèlla, *f.* sweet-bread.

ànimo, *m.* mind; courage; spirit, temper, disposition. *mal* ~, ill-will. **animosità,** *f.* prejudice, preconception; animosity, animus. **animóso,** *a.* courageous, brave; fiery-spirited; (*horse*) bold, spirited.

ànitra, *f.* duck. Cf. *anatra.* **anitrína,** *f.* duckweed. **anitròtto,** *m.* duckling; fat duck.

annacquàre, *v.t.* to water, dilute with water.

annaffiàre, *v.t.* to water (*plants*). **annaffiatóio,** *m.* watering-can.

annàli, *m.pl.* annals.

annaspàre, *v.t.* to reel, wind on a reel; (*fig.*) bungle, make a mess of. *v.i.* (*aux.* avere) to gesticulate wildly; act or think in a confused fashion.

annèta, *f.* year (*duration*), twelve-month; year's crop, salary, rent, numbers of a periodical, &c.

annebbiàre, *v.t.* to obscure, dim, cloud; blight. **annebbiàrsi,** *v.refl.* (*of sight*) to grow dim; (*sky*) be obscured, become foggy.

annegaménto, *m.* drowning. **annegàre,** *v.t.* to drown. *v.i.* (*aux.* essere) to drown, be drowned.

anneriménto, *m.* blackening. **anneríre** (*pr.* -ísco, -ísci), *v.t.* to blacken. *v.i.* (*aux.* essere) & **annerírsi,** *v.refl.* to become black or dark.

annessióne, *f.* annexation. **annèsso,** *a.* attached; annexed. ¶ *m.* annex[e;] appendage. **annèttere,** *v.t. ir.* to annex; attach; attribute.

annestàre, *v.t.* to graft; (*Mech.*) engage, insert. Cf. *innestare.*

Annìbale, *m.* Hannibal.

annichilaménto, *m.* annihilation. **annichilàre** (*pr.* -íchilo), *v.t.* to annihilate; crush; (*fig.*) dismay, humiliate. **annichilíre** (*pr.* -ísco, ísci). See *annichilare.*

annidàrsi, *v.refl.* to nestle; hide.

annientàre, *v.t.* to annihilate; bring to nought; destroy.

anniversàrio, *a. & m.* anniversary.

ànno, *m.* year. ~ *bisestile,* leap-year. *l'* ~ *prossimo, l'* ~ *venturo,* next year. *di* ~ *in* ~, from year to year. *ha dieci* ~*i,* he (she) is ten years old. *parer mill'* ~*i,* to desire greatly. ~ *luce* (*Astr.*). light-year.

annodàre, *v.t.* to knot; bind; tie; connect; clinch, settle conclusively. **annodàrsi,** *v.refl.* to form a knot; get entangled.

annoiàre, *v.t.* to trouble, annoy; bore; weary. **annoiàrsi,** *v.refl.* to be bored; grow tired. **annoiàto,** *a.* bored, wearied, sated; annoyed.

annòna, *f.* provisions, victuals (for a city).

annóso, *a.* old (*often but not excl. of trees*).

annotàre, *v.t.* to annotate. *v.i.* (*aux.* avere) to take (or make) notes.

annottàre, *v.i.* (*aux.* essere) to grow dark.

Annover (l'), *m.* Hanover (*prov.*). *A* ~, *f.* Hanover (*town*).

annoveràre, *v.t.* to number, count.

annuàle, *a.* annual, yearly. ¶ *m.* anniversary; annual festival. **annualità,** *f.* yearly payment, yearly instalment; annuity. **annuàrio,** *m.* year-book; annual; directory; list (*Army, Navy, &c.*).

annuíre (*pr.* -ísco, -ísci), *v.i.* (*aux.* avere) to assent, consent.

annullàre, *v.t.* to annul, nullify quash, cancel.

annunciàre, see *annunziare.*

annunziàre, *v.t.* to announce, advertise, proclaim, herald; signal; give out; betoken, foreshadow; inform, state; communicate; show in, usher in; preach; foretell. **Annunziàta,** *f.* Madonna; picture or festival of the Annunciation; chief Italian order of chivalry, founded 1362 by

Amedeo VI of Savoy. *collare dell'A~*, Collar of the A~.

annunziatóre, *m.* (*f.* **-tríce**) announcer (*Radio*, *&c.*); advertiser. **annunziazióne**, *f.* annunciation. *il giorno dell'A~*, the Annunciation, Lady-day (25 March). **annúnzio**, *m.* announcement; advertisement.

ànnuo, *a.* annual, yearly.

annusàre (*pr.* **-úso**), *v.t. & abs.* to smell, sniff (out); discover. *~ tabacco*, to take snuff.

annuvolàre, *v.t.* to cloud. **annuvolàrsi**, *v.refl.* to become clouded; (*fig.*) to become gloomy. **annuvolàto**, *a.* cloudy.

anodíno, *a.* anodyne. ¶ *m.* anodyne. **ànodo**, *m.* (*Elec.*, *Radio*) anode.

anomalía, *f.* anomaly. **anòmalo**, *a.* anomalous.

anònimo, *a.* anonymous. *societa ~a*, joint-stock company.

anormàle, *a.* abnormal. **anormalità**, *f.inv.* abnormality.

ànsa, *f.* handle (*vase*); (*fig.*) pretext, occasion; (*Geog.*) cove, creek.

ansàre, *v.i.* (*aux.* avere) to pant, breathe heavily.

ànsia, *f.* eager desire. **ansietà**, *f.* anxiety.

ànsima, *f.* shortness of breath, difficulty in breathing. **ansimàre**, *v.i.* (*aux.* avere) to pant, breathe heavily.

ansióso, *a.* anxious.

antagonísmo, *m.* antagonism. **antagonísta** (*pl.* **-ísti**), *m.* antagonist, opponent.

antàrtico (*pl.* **-àrtici**), *a.* antarctic.

antecedènte, *a. & m.* antecedent. **antecessóre**, *m.* predecessor.

anteguèrra, *f.* pre-war period.

antenàto, *m.* ancestor.

antènna, *f.* (*Zool.*) antenna, feeler, horn; (*Naut.*) yard; beam, pole; (*Radio*) aerial. *~ interna*, indoor aerial.

antepórre (*pr.* **-óngo**, **-óni**, &c.), *v.t. ir.* to place before; give precedence to; prefer.

antepríma, *f.* dress rehearsal; private view (*Art*).

anterióre, *a.* anterior, prior, previous; fore, former; front (*att.*).

antesignàno, *m.* leader, guide, forerunner.

antiaèreo, *a.* anti-aircraft. *cannone ~*, anti-aircraft gun. *difesa ~a*, air-raid defence.

antialcoòlico (*pl.* **-ólici**), *a.* teetotal, anti-alcoholic.

antibiòtico (*pl.* **-òtici**), *a. & m.* (*Med.*) antibiotic.

anticàglia, *f.* antique, old curiosity; (*pl.*) lumber, old rubbish. *negozio di ~e*, old curiosity shop.

anticàmera, *f.* antechamber, anteroom.

anticàrro, *a.inv.* anti-tank. *cannone ~*, *m.* anti-tank gun.

antichità, *f.* antiquity, ancient times; antique.

anticiclóne, *m.* anticyclone.

anticipàre (*pr.* **-ícipo**), *v.t.* to anticipate, forestall; advance, pay in advance. *v.i.* (*aux.* avere) to arrive earlier than usual. *contatore a pagamento anticipato*, *m.* slot-meter. **anticipatamente**, *ad.* beforehand; in advance. *pagare ~*, to pay in advance. **anticipazióne**, *f.* anticipation; advance.

antíco (*pl.* **antíchi**), *a.* ancient, old; old-fashioned; obsolete; antique. ¶ *m. l'~*, antiquity; antique (*style*). *gli antichi*, the ancients.

anticongelànte, *a.* anti-freezing. ¶ *m.* (*Motor*) antifreeze.

anticórte, *f.* forecourt.

anticrísto, *m.* antichrist.

antidatàre, *v.t.* to antedate.

antídoto, *m.* antidote.

antífona, *f.* antiphon; antiphony. **antifonàrio**, *m.* antiphonal.

antigas, *a.inv.* antigas, against (poison) gas. *maschera ~*, *f.* gas-mask.

Antílle (**le**), *f.pl.* the West Indies, the Antilles.

antílope, *f.* antelope.

antimeridiàno, *a.* morning, before noon (*abb.* a.m.).

antimònio, *m.* antimony.

antipàsto, *m.* hors-d'oeuvre.

antipatía, *f.* antipathy, dislike. **antipàtico** (*pl.* **-àtici**) *a.* antipathetic, disagreeable.

antipirína, *f.* (*Med.*) antipyrin.

antípodi, *m.pl.* Antipodes. *essere agli ~*, (*fig.*) to be poles apart.

antiquariàto, *m.* antiquarian trade; antiquarian bookseller's business.

antiquàrio, *m.* antiquary. ¶ *a. & m.* antiquarian.

antiquàto, *a.* antiquated, old-fashioned.

antirúggine, *a.inv.* rust-resisting.

antisdrucciolévole, *a.* (*Motor*) non-skid, anti-skid. *catena ~*, non-skid chain.

antisèttico (*pl.* **-èttici**), *a. & m.* antiseptic, disinfectant.

antítesi, *f.* antithesis.

antitossína, f. antitoxin.

antiúmido, a. damp-resisting.

antivedére (pr. **-éggo** or **-édo,** &c., like vedere), v.t. ir. to foresee. **antiveggènza,** f. foresight, prevision.

antivigília, f. day before the eve. l' ~ di, two days before (Christmas, Easter, &c.).

antología, f. anthology.

antràce, m. anthrax. **antracíte,** f. anthracite.

àntro, m. cave, den, lair; hovel; (Anat.) cavity.

antropòfago (pl. **-òfagi** & **-òfaghi**), a. & m. cannibal, man-eating, man-eater.

antropòide, m. & a. anthropoid.

antropòlogo (pl. **-òlogi** & **-òloghi**), m. anthropologist.

antropomòrfico (pl. **-òrfici**), a. anthropomorphic.

anulàre, a. annular. dito ~, m. ring finger, third f.

Anvérsa, f. Antwerp.

ànzi, c. (like Eng. nay (now archaic) may either reinforce, modify, or oppose a previous statement) indeed; even; (or) rather; on the contrary. ~ che, rather than. ¶ pr. before.

anzianità, f. seniority. avanzamento ad ~, promotion by seniority. **anziàno,** a. senior; old, aged. ¶ m. magistrate; alderman.

anziché, c. rather than. **anzidétto,** a. aforesaid, above-mentioned. **anzitútto,** ad. first of all; above all.

aòrta, f. (Physiol.) aorta.

apatía, f. apathy, indifference. **apàtico** (pl. **-àtici**), a. apathetic, indifferent, lackadaisical.

àpe, f. bee. ~ operaia, worker bee.

aperitívo, m. aperitif, appetizer; ¶ a. aperient.

apèrto, p.p. of aprire & a. open; (fig.) free; frank; candid; all' ~, in the open. **apertúra,** f. opening; aperture; orifice; hole; gap; spread; overture (diplom.).

apiàrio, m. apiary.

àpice, m. apex; summit; height; culminating point.

apicultóre, m. bee-keeper. **apicultúra,** f. bee-keeping.

Apocalísse & **Apocalíssi,** f. Apocalypse, Revelation (N.T.).

apòcrifo, a. apocryphal. gli scritti ~i, the Apocrypha.

apogèo, m. apogee; height; zenith; acme; high water-mark (fig.).

apòlide, a. stateless. ¶ m.f. stateless person.

apologètica, f. apologetics. **apologètico** (pl. **-ètici**), a. apologetic(al). **apología,** f. apology, justification; written or spoken defence. **apologísta,** m. apologist.

apòlogo (pl. **-òloghi**), m. apologue; fable.

apoplessía, f. apoplexy. **apolèttico** (pl. **-èttici**), a. & m. apoplectic. colpo ~, apoplectic fit.

apostasía, f. apostasy. **apòstata** (pl. **-òstati**), m. & att. apostate.

apostòlico (pl. **-òlici**), a. apostolic(al). **apòstolo,** m. apostle.

apostrofàre (pr. **-òstrofo**), v.i. (aux. avere) to apostrophize; address; (v.f.) mark with an apostrophe. **apòstrofe,** f. apostrophe (rhetorical figure). **apòstrofo,** m. apostrophe (orthographical sign).

apoteòsi, f. apotheosis.

appacificàre (pr. **-ífico, -ífichi**), v.t. to pacify; reconcile.

appagàre (pr. **-àgo, -àghi**), v.t. to satisfy; please; gratify.

appaiàre (pr. **-àio, -ài**), v.t. to pair, couple; yoke; match (colours, &c.).

appallottàre, appallottolàre, v.t. to make into a ball or balls. **appallottàrsi, appallottolàrsi,** v.refl. to roll itself up (hedgehog, armadillo, &c.).

appaltàre, v.t. to contract; let (out) on contract. **appaltàrsi,** v.refl. to take out a contract; subscribe. **appaltatóre,** m. contractor. **appàlto,** m. contract; lease; office of state monopolies; shop where such monopolies (e.g. salt and tobacco) are sold; subscription, season ticket.

appannàggio, m. appanage; prerogative.

appannàre, v.t. to dim, obscure; darken; tarnish.

apparàto, m. decoration; fittings; furnishings; requisites; apparatus; display. un conferenziere d' ~, a showy lecturer. discorso d' ~, parade of eloquence.

apparecchiàre, v.t. to prepare; lay (the table). **apparécchio,** m. preparation; lay-out; arrangement (of dinner-table); apparatus; set; machine; aeroplane. ~ da caccia, fighter plane. ~ da bombardamento, bomber. ~ radio, wireless set.

apparentàrsi, v.refl. to become related (by marriage); become intimate.

apparènte, a. seeming; apparent,

ostensible; visible; clear, evident, **apparènza,** *f.* appearance; show; outward appearance; look; guise; likelihood. *sotto l'* ~ *di,* (*fig.*) under cover of. **apparíre** (*pr.* **apparísco** *or* **appàio**), *v.i. ir.* (*aux* essere) to appear; seem; be visible; result, turn out. **appariscènte,** *a.* showy; gaudy; conspicuous; handsome. **apparíta,** *f.* (first) appearance. **apparizióne,** *f.* apparition; vision.
appartaménto, *m.* flat; apartments; suite of rooms. ~ *da scapolo,* bachelor flat.
appartàre, *v.t.* to set apart; put on one side; separate. **appartàrsi,** *v.refl.* to withdraw, stand aloof; retire. **appartàto,** *p.a.* secluded; set apart; separated.
appartenènte, *p.a.* belonging, pertaining. **appartenènza,** *f.* (*gen. pl.*) belongings, appurtenances, accessories. **appartenére** (*pr.* **èngo,** *&c.,* like *tenere*), *v.i. ir.* (*aux.* avere) to belong; befit; appertain; be related.
appassionàrsi, *v.refl.* to be deeply moved or excited; have a passion for (= *di*), be enamoured of (= *di*). **appassionàto,** *p.a.* passionate; ardent; strongly biassed.
appassíre (*pr.* **-ísco, -ísci**), *v.i.* (*aux.* essere) & **appassírsi,** *v.refl.* to fade, wither, decay; droop.
appellànte, *a. & m.f.* appellant. **appellàre,** *v.t.* to call, name, designate. *v.i.* (*aux.* avere) & **appellàrsi,** *v.refl.* to appeal. **appellativo,** *m.* term, designation, common name. **appèllo,** *m.* appeal; roll-call. *fare l'* ~, to call the roll. *fare* ~ *a,* to appeal to, invoke. *corte d'* ~, Court of Appeal. *senz'* ~, indisputable, without question.
appéna, *ad.* hardly, scarcely; as soon as, barely, almost immediately. (To indic. completed action in fut. requires a fut. perf. not simple fut. e.g. *appena sarò arrivato,* as soon as I arrive or shall arrive.) ~ *che,* as soon as.
appèndere, *v.t. ir.* to hang, hang up.
appendíce, *f.* appendix; literary page or column[s] in a newspaper. footnote. **appendicísta** (*pl.* **-ísti**) *m.* writer in the literary columns of a newspaper.
appendicíte, *f.* appendicitis.
appendízie, *f.pl.* dues, such as eggs, poultry, &c., furnished by a tenant farmer to the landlord.
Appenníno (l'), *m.* the Apennines.

appercezióne, *f.* apperception, mental perception.
appestàre, *v.t.* to infect, contaminate; cause to stink. **appestàto,** *p.a.* infected, tainted; plague-stricken.
appetíre (*pr.* **-ísco, -ísci**), *v.t.* to desire eagerly, long for. *v.i.* (*aux.* essere *or* avere) (of food) to stimulate the appetite. **appetíto,** *m.* appetite. **appetitóso,** *a.* appetizing; tempting.
appètto, a pètto, *ad. & ~ a, pr.* opposite; in comparison with.
appezzaménto, *m.* piece of ground (*usually separate fr. farm or other property*); plot, lot. **appezzàre,** *v.t.* to piece together.
Àppia (Via), *f.* Appian Way.
appianàre, *v.t.* to smooth, level; remove (difficulties or obstacles). **appianatóia,** *f.* plasterer's smoothing-board. **appianatóio,** *m.* ground roller.
appiastràre, *& appiastricciàre,** *v.t.* to plaster.
appiattaménto, *m.* flattening; levelling (*also fig. of salaries, &c.*).
appiattàre, *v.t.* to flatten; hide. **appiattàrsi,** *v.refl.* to hide oneself, crouch down, cower; squat.
appiccàgnolo, *m.* hook; (*fig.*) pretext.
appiccàre, *v.t.* to fasten; hang; hang up; begin; attach. ~ *il fuoco,* to set fire (to). ~ *la ad uno,* to play a trick on someone. ~ *lite,* to bring a law-suit (against). **appiccàrsi,** *v.refl.* to attach oneself; hang oneself; (*of contagious disease, &c.*) to attack, spread.
appiccatíccio (*pl.* **-ícci**), *a.* sticky; (*fig.*) importunate; contagious.
appicciàre, *v.t.* to kindle, light; string together (*figs, &c.*). ~ *le candele,* to burn the ends of wicks so that candles may light more easily.
appiccicàre, *v.t.* to paste, stick on; (*fig.*) to palm off; write things that do not agree; deliver. ~ *uno schiaffo,* to slap, box one's ears. *v.i.* (*aux.* avere) *& **appiccicàrsi,** *v.refl.* to stick; adhere. **appiccicatíccio,** *a.* sticky; adhesive; contagious. ¶ *m.* patchwork, hotchpotch.
appicciníre (*pr.* **-ísco, -ísci**), *v.t.* to lessen; belittle.
appicciolíre, *v.t.* to reduce in size, diminish.
appícco (*pl.* **-ícchi**), *m.* pretext; attachment.

appiè, a piè, *ad.* below, at the foot. *a piè di,* at the foot of.

appièno, *ad.* fully, completely, quite.

appigionaménto, *m.* letting. **appigionàre,** *v.t.* to let.

appigliàrsi, *v.refl.* to seize hold of; cling; take root; adhere (to) (*party, advice, course of action*). **appíglio,** *m.* (*pl.* -ígli), attachment, grip; (*fig.*) pretext, occasion, excuse.

appinzàre, *v.t.* to sting. **appínzo,** *m.* sting or bite of an insect; sour taste (*of wine or beer gone stale*).

appiómbo, *m.* perpendicular. ¶ *ad.* perpendicularly.

appioppàre, *v.t.* to buckle; stick on; give, inflict; palm off; plant poplars; tie (vines) to poplars. ~ *una bastonata,* give a drubbing, a thrashing.

appisolàrsi, *v.refl.* to doze, to be drowsy, take a nap.

applaudíre (*pr.* -àudo, *or* -audísco), *v.t. & i.* to applaud, cheer; praise; approve. **applàuso,** *m.* applause.

applicàre (*pr.* àpplico, àpplichi), *v.t.* to apply; lay on; enforce, impose; inflict; attribute; give; charge; devote. **applicàrsi,** *v.refl.* to apply oneself; set about; strive; study. **applicazióne,** *f.* application; attention; diligence. *scuola d'* ~, professional school (higher training school).

appoderàre, *v.t.* to prepare land for farming. **appoderàrsi,** *v.refl.* to settle on a farm.

appoggiacàpo, *m.inv.* head-rest; antimacassar.

appoggiamàno, *m.* (*painter's*) hand-rest.

appoggiàre, *v.t.* to lean; rest; prop; support (*also fig.*); stress, reinforce; deliver (*a blow, &c.*). **appoggiàrsi,** *v.refl.* to lean (*on, against* = a); to depend (on); confide (in).

appoggiatóio, *m.* support; prop; hand-rail; banister; arm-rest.

appoggiatúra, *f.* (*Mus.*) appoggiatura, grace-note; leaning. **appòggio** (*pl.* -òggi), *m.* support; prop; balustrade; buttress; protection; (*Gram.*) emphasis, stress. *nave* ~, (*Nav.*) *f.* tender. *nave* ~ *d'idrovolanti,* sea-plane tender.

appollaiàrsi, *v.refl.* to roost, go to roost; (*fig.*) settle. **appollaiàto,** *p.a.* perched; settled.

appoppàto, *a.* (*of a ship*) down by the stern.

appórre (*pr.* -óngo, *&c.*, like *porre*)

v.t. lr. to affix, append, add; set; (*fig.*) attribute, impute.

apportàre, *v.t.* to bring; carry; furnish; contribute; produce. **appòrto,** *m.* contribution.

appositaménte, *ad.* expressly, suitably, on purpose. **appòsito,** *a.* special, suitable, apposite, appropriate, prepared expressly.

apposizióne, *f.* affixing; appending (*of signature, &c.*), (*Gram.*) apposition.

appòsta, *or* **a pòsta,** *ad.* on purpose, purposely; expressly, just (for).

appostaménto, *m.* lying in wait; ambush. **appostàre,** *v.t.* to lie in wait for, to waylay, spy upon. **appostàrsi,** *v.refl.* to lie in wait, to lurk.

apprèndere (*pr.* -èndo, *&c.*, like *prendere*), *v.t. ir.* to learn; understand; hear; be informed of. **apprèndersi** (a), *v.refl.* to take hold (of), cling (to); adhere (to); apprehend, seize. **apprendiménto,** *m.* learning.

apprendísta (*pl.* -ísti), *m.* apprentice.

apprensióne, *f.* apprehension; fear. **apprensívo,** *a.* quick to perceive; apprehensive.

appressaménto, *m.* approach. **appressàre** (*pr.* -èsso), *v.t.* to approach; bring near. **appressàrsi,** *v.refl.* to approach; to be near; to come near[er].

apprèsso (also ~ a, ~ di), *pr.* near; before; close to; in the presence of. ¶ *ad.* near; near-by; shortly afterwards. *il giorno* ~, the following day, the day after.

apprestaménto, *m.* preparation; supply. **apprestàre,** *v.t.* to prepare; get ready; supply.

apprezzàbile, *a.* appreciable; valuable. **apprezzaménto,** *m.* appreciation; valuation; appraisement. **apprezzàre,** *v.t.* to appreciate; value; appraise.

approdàre, *v.i.* (*aux.* essere *or* avere) to land, disembark; come ashore; be useful; serve. **appròdo,** *m.* landing, landing-place; land-fall.

approfittàre (di), *v.i.* (*aux.* avere) to profit (by); benefit (from); take advantage (of). **approfittàrsi (di),** *v.refl.* to profit by; avail oneself of.

approfondíre (*pr.* -ísco, -ísci), *v.t.* to deepen; dive into; fathom. **approfondírsi (in),** *v.refl.* to go deeply into, become learned in.

approfondiménto, *m.* deepening; deep investigation, scrutiny.

approntàre, *v.t.* to make ready.

appropriàre, *v.t.* to adapt; render suitable or appropriate, suit. **appropriàrsi,** *v.refl.* to appropriate; convert to one's own use; embezzle.

appropriazióne, *f.* appropriation.

approssimàre, *v.t.* to approach; bring near. **approssimàrsi,** *v.refl.* to approach; come near[er]; approximate. **approssimatívo,** *a.* approximate. **approssimazióne,** *f.* approximation.

approvàre, *v.t.* to approve, countenance, confirm; recognize as fit or capable. **approvazióne,** *f.* approval.

approvvigionàre, *v.t.* to supply, store, stock, provision.

appruàto, *a.* (*of ship*) down by the head or prow.

appuntaménto, *m.* appointment; rendezvous.

appuntàre, *v.t.* to point; sharpen; tack; sew, stitch, pin; stick (*pin*) (*fig.*) to blame. **appuntàrsi,** *v.refl.* to be pointed; to be turned. **appuntàto,** *p.a.* pointed; stitched; formal, precise. ¶ *m.* (*Mil.*) lance-corporal. **appuntatóre,** *m.* marker, pointer. **appuntatúra,** *f.* pointing; censure.

appuntellàre, *v.t.* to prop, stay.

appúnto, *ad.* precisely, exactly. ¶ *m.* mark; note.

appuràre, *v.t.* to clear up, verify; ascertain; reconcile; wipe off (*debt*).

apribaràttolo, *m.* tin-opener.

aprìco (*pl.* -**ìchi**), *a.* sunny; exposed to the sun.

aprìle, *m.* April.

aprìre (*pr.* **àpro**), *v.t. & abs. ir.* to open; unlock; disburden; disclose, reveal; open up; cut; begin; head (*list, procession*); unfold; draw back (*curtains*); turn on, switch on (*tap, light*). **aprìrsi,** *v.refl.* to open.

aquàrio, *m.* aquarium. *A* ~, (*astr.*) Aquarius.

àquila, *f.* eagle.

aquilìno, *a.* aquiline; hooked, Roman (*nose*).

aquilóne, *m.* North wind; kite (*toy*).

aquilòtto, *m.* eaglet, young eagle.

Aquisgràna, *f.* Aachen; Aix-la-Chapelle.

àra, *f.* (*Poet.*) altar; are = 100 square metres or 119·60 sq. yds.

arabescàre, *v.t.* to decorate with arabesques. **arabescàto,** *a.* (*Typ.*)

fancy, ornamented. **arabésco** (*pl.* -**éschi**), *a.* arabic; arabesque. ¶ *m.* arabesque. **Aràbia** (l'), *f.* Arabia. ~ *Saudiana,* Saudi-Arabia. **aràbico** (*pl.* -**àbici**), *a.* arabic, Arabian.

aràbile, *a.* arable, tillable.

àrabo, *a.* Arab; Arabian; Arabic. *cifre* ~*e, f.pl.* Arabic numerals. ¶ *m.* Arabian, Arab; Arabic language.

aràchide, *f.* groundnut, peanut, monkey nut.

aragósta, *f.* lobster.

aràldica, *f.* heraldry. **aràldico** (*pl.* -**àldici**), *a.* heraldic. **aràldo,** *m.* herald.

araménto, *m.* ploughing; tillage.

arancéto, *m.* orange grove. **arància** (*pl.* -**ance**), *f.* orange. **aranciàio,** *m. & -a f.* orange-seller. **aranciàta,** *f.* orangeade. **aràncio** (*pl.* -**ànci**), *m.* orange-tree. **aràncio,** *a. & arancióne,* *a.inv.* orange coloured.

aràre, *v.t.* to plough. ~ *l'ancora,* (*Naut.*) to drag the anchor. **aratóre,** *m.* ploughman. **aratríce,** *f.* steam plough. **aràtro,** *m.* plough. **aratúra,** *f.* ploughing.

arazzería, *f.* tapestry-works; tapestry. **arazziére,** *m.* tapestry-maker. **aràzzo,** *m.* arras; piece of tapestry.

arbitràggio, *m.* arbitration; arbitrament. **arbitràre** (*pr.* **àrbitro**), *v.i.* (*aux.* avere) *& f.,* to arbitrate; arrange; referee, umpire. **arbitrariaménte,** *ad.* arbitrarily. **arbitràrio,** *a.* arbitrary; high-handed. ¶ *m.* arbitrariness; high-handedness. **arbitràto,** *m.* arbitration. *sottoporre all'* ~, to submit to arbitration. **arbitrio,** *m.* judgment; will; absolute power. **àrbitro,** *m.* arbitrator, arbiter; referee, umpire.

arbòreo, *a.* arboreal.

arboscèllo, *m.* shrub; bush.

arbústo, *m.* shrub.

àrca (*pl.* -**àrche**), *f.* tomb; ark; coffin, sarcophagus; bin.

arcàde, *m.* Arcadian; member of the Arcadia (*Lit.* academy founded at Rome in 1690). **arcàdico** (*pl.* -**àdici**), *a.* Arcadian.

arcàico (*pl.* -**àici**), *a.* archaic. **arcaísmo,** *m.* archaism.

arcàngelo, *m.* archangel.

arcàno, *a.* (*Lit.*) mysterious; secret.

arcàta, *f.* arcade; arch; archway.

archeggiàre, *v.i.* (*aux.* avere) to draw the bow across the strings (*violin*). *v.t.* to arch.

archeología, *f.* archaeology. **archeo-lògico** (*pl.* **-ògici**), *a.* archaeo-logical. **archeòlogo** (*pl.* **-òlogi** *or* **-òloghi**), *m.* archaeologist.

archètipo, *m.* archetype.

archétto, *m.* bow, fiddlestick; snare.

Archimède, *m.* Archimedes.

archipèndolo, -pènżolo, *m.* plum-met; plumb-line.

architettàre (*pr.* **étto**), *v.t.* to build, contrive; plot; design; form. **archi-tettònico** (*pl.* **-ònici**), *a.* architec-tonic; architectural.

architétto, *m.* architect.

architettúra, *f.* architecture.

architràve, *m.* or *f.* architrave; lintel.

archiviàre (*pr.* **-ívio, -ívi**), *v.t.* to register in the archives. **archívio,** *m.* also *pl.* **archívi,** archives; records. **archivísta,** *m.* archivist.

archivòlto, *m.* (*Arch.*) archivolt.

arci-, *prefix* = very; most; arch-; supremely. *e.g.* **arcibeàto,** very happy. **arcibèllo,** exceedingly beautiful. **arcifànfano,** *m.* arch-braggart.

arcidiàcono, *m.* archdeacon.

arcidúca (*pl.* **-úchi**), *m.* archduke. **arciduchéssa,** *f.* archduchess.

arcière, *m.* archer, bowman.

arcígno, *a.* gruff; surly.

arcióne, *m.* saddle-bow.

arcipèlago (*pl.* **-èlaghi**), *m.* archi-pelago.

arcivescovàdo, *m.* archbishopric; (archbishop's) palace. **arcivesco-víle,** *a.* archiepiscopal. **arci-véscovo,** *m.* archbishop.

àrco (*pl.* **àrchi**), *m.* bow; arc; arch. ~ *a sprone,* ~ *d'appoggio,* flying buttress. ~ *acuto,* pointed arch. ~ *gotico rialzato,* lancet a. *lampada ad* ~ *f.,* arc lamp.

arcobaléno, *m.* rainbow.

arcolàio, *m.* reel; winder; frame for winding wool.

arcuàto, *a.* curved, bent. *con le gambe* ~*e,* bow-legged.

ardènte, *a.* burning, hot, fiery, raging, blazing, live; ardent, keen, fervent, fervid, eager, earnest, spirited; passionate. **ardente-ménte,** *ad.* ardently, &*c.*

àrdere, *v.t.* & *i.,ir.* (*aux.* essere) to burn.

ardèsia, *f.* slate.

ardiglióne, *m.* tongue (*of a buckle*).

ardiménto, *m.* boldness; hardihood; daring. **ardire** (*pr.* **-ísco, -ísci**), *v.i.* (*aux.* avere) to dare. ¶ *m.* bold-ness; courage; daring. **ardita-ménte,** *ad.* boldly. **arditézza,** *f.*

boldness; temerity. **ardíto,** *a.* bold, daring.

ardóre, *m.* ardour, warmth, heat; zest.

arduaménte, *ad.* with difficulty, arduously. **àrduo,** *a.* arduous; difficult; steep, up-hill.

àrea, *f.* area; surface; zone; extent; ground. ~ *di rigore,* (*Foot.*) penalty area.

àrem, *m.inv.* harem.

aréna, *f.* arena, lists, ring; cock-pit; sand (*Poet.*). **arenàceo,** *a.* sandy. **ar[r]enàre,** *v.i.* (*aux.* essere) & **ar[r]enàrsi,** *v.refl.* to strand, ground, run ashore; be stranded (*lit.* & *fig.*). **arenària,** *f.* sandstone. **arenòso,** *a.* sandy.

areòmetro & **aeròmetro,** *m.* areo-meter. **areostàtica** & **aero-stàtica,** *f.* aerostatics.

àrgano, *m.* winch, windlass; capstan.

argentàre, *v.t.* to silver; silver-plate (*cf.* inargentare). **argentatúra,** *f.* silvering; silver-plating. **argènteo,** *a.* silvery, silver (*att.*). **argènteriá,** *f.* silver, s. plate. **argentièra,** *f.* silver-mine. **argentière,** *m.* silver-smith. **argentífero,** *a.* argenti-ferous. **Argentína** (l'), *f.* the Argentine, Argentina. **argentíno,** *a.* argentine, silvery, silvern (*Poet.*); silver (*att.*).

argénto, *m.* silver; money, cash. ~ *vivo,* quicksilver, mercury. ~ *battuto,* wrought silver. ~ *dorato,* silver-gilt. **argentóne,** *m.* nickel silver, German s.

argílla, *f.* clav. **argillóso,** *a.* clayey, argillaceous.

arginàre (*pr.* **àrgino**), *v.t.* to dyke, dam up, embank. **arginatúra,** *f.* dyking. **àrgine,** *m.* embankment; dyke; causeway.

argomentàre, *v.i.* (*aux.* avere) to argue, reason. **argomentazióne,** *f.* argumentation. **argoménto,** *m.* argument; synopsis; plot; theme, subject; sign; reason; business.

arguíre (*pr.* **-ísco, -ísci**), *v.t.* to infer, deduce, gather, conclude.

argutaménte, *ad.* wittily; keenly, sharply; subtly. **argutézza,** *f.* acuteness, keenness, sharpness, subtlety, wit. **argúto,** *a.* acute; keen, subtle; witty.

argúzia, *f.* witticism, witty remark; jest; sharpness, subtlety, wit.

ària, *f.* air; look, likeness; manner, way; mien; expression, atmosphere (*Art*); aria; tune, song, (*fig.*) climate;

country. *in* ~, in the air, airy (*schemes*); idle (*tales*); groundless (*fears*); empty (*threats*). *a mezz'aria*, in mid air (*fig.*). *sacca d'*~, *f.* air pocket, a. lock (*pipe*). *vuoto d'*~, *m.* air pocket (*Aviat.*).

aridità, *f.* aridity; dryness. **àrido**, *a.* arid, dry, barren.

arieggiàre, *v.t.* to air, *v.t. & i.* (*aux.* avere) to resemble.

ariète, *m.* ram; battering ram.

aringa (*pl.* -**inghe**), *f.* herring. ~ *affumicata*, kipper, bloater.

arióso, *a.* airy.

àrista, *f.* (*Cook.*) roast loin of pork.

aristocràtico (*pl.* -**àtici**), *a.* aristocratic(al). ¶ *m.* aristocrat. **aristocrazía**, *f.* aristocracy.

Aristòfane, *m.* Aristophanes. **Aristòtile**, *m.* Aristotle.

aritmètica, *f.* arithmetic. **aritmètico** (*pl.* -**ètici**), *a.* arithmetical. ¶ *m.* arithmetician.

arlecchinàta, *f.* harlequinade. **arlecchíno**, *m.* harlequin, clown; (*pop.*) cocktail.

àrma (*pl.* **àrmi**), *f.* arm, branch of the army. *l'*~ *di fanteria*, the infantry. ~ *del genio*, corps of engineers. ~ *aerea*, ~ *azzurra*, air force.

armacòllo (**ad**), *ad. expr.* in a sling; slung across the shoulders.

armàdio (*pl.* -**àdi**), *m.* wardrobe; cupboard.

armaiuòlo, *m.* armourer; gunsmith.

armaménto, *m.* armament; arming; equipment; fitting out; manning; shipping.

armàre, *v.t.* to arm; equip; fit out; man; commission (*ship*); reinforce; armour, sheathe.

armàta, *f.* army; navy, fleet. *corpo di* ~, army corps. *generale d'* ~ (*Mil.*) general. *g. di corpo d'*~, lieutenant general.

armatóre, *m.* (*ship*) owner; (registered) manager (*ship's*).

armatúra, *f.* armour, sheathing, plating; ribbing, trussing, bracing; fastening, strap;

àrme (*pl.* **àrmi**), *f.* arm, weapon; (*pl.*) arms (*Mil.*); (coat of) arms, (armorial) bearings. ~ *-i corte*, ~ *-i portatili*, small arms. *piazza d'*~*i*, drill ground. *all'armi! i.* to arms!

armeggiàre, *v.i.* (*aux.* avere) to handle arms; intrigue, manoeuvre. **armeggióne**, *m.* wire-puller, intriguer.

Armènia (**l'**), *f.* Armenia. **armèno**, *m. & a.* Armenian.

arménto, *m.* herd (*of cattle*).

armería, *f.* armoury, arsenal.

armière, *m.* (*Mil.*, *Aviat.*) gunner.

armistízio, *m.* armistice.

armonía, *f.* harmony. **armònica**, *f.* harmonica. **armònico** (*pl.* -**ònici**), *a. & m.* harmonic. **armònio**, *m.* harmonium. **armonióso**, *a.* harmonious, tuneful. **armonizzàre**, *v.t. & i.* (*aux.* avere) to harmonize; attune; tone.

arnése, *m.* tool; utensil; gear, tackle. *borsa degli* ~ *i*, *f.* tool-kit.

àrnia, *f.* beehive.

aròma (*pl.* -**òmi**), *m.* aroma. **aromàtico** (*pl.* -**àtici**), *a.* aromatic.

àrpa, *f.* harp.

arpagóne, *m.* grapnel; harpoon.

arpeggiàre, *v.i.* to harp; to play in arpeggio. **arpéggio**, *m.* arpeggio.

arpía, *f.* harpy.

arpicòrdo, *m.* harpsichord.

arpíno, *m.* boat-hook.

arpióne, *m.* hinge; spike; pivot-hook, grapnel.

arpísta, *m.f.* harpist.

àrra, *f.* pledge; deposit; token; earnest (money).

arrabattàrsi, *v.refl.* to endeavour; bestir oneself; strive (*without much success*).

arrabbiaménto, *m.* rage. **arrabbiàre**, *v.i.* (*aux.* essere) & **arrabbiàrsi**, *v.refl.* to be irritated, get angry, fly into a passion. **arrabbiàto**, *a.* furious, enraged; rabid.

arraffàre, *v.t.* to snatch, grasp, seize; get hold of.

arrampicàrsi, *v.refl.* to clamber, climb up.

arrancàre, *v.i.* (*aux.* avere) to hobble along, trudge, limp; (*Naut.*) pull away.

arrecàre (*pr.* -**èco**, -**èchi**), *v.t.* to occasion, bring about, produce.

arredàre (*pr.* -**èdo**), *v.t.* to furnish, equip; rig out. **arrèdo**, *m.* (*oft. pl.*) furnishings; fittings, outfit.

arrembàggio, *m.* boarding (*enemy's ship*). **arrembàre**, *v.t. & i.* to board.

arrenàre (*pr.* -**éno**), *v.i.* (*aux.* essere) & **arrenàrsi**, *v.refl.* to strand; run aground; (*fig.*) halt.

arrèndersi, *v.refl. ir.* to yield; surrender. **arrendévole**, *a.* yielding; compliant; supple. **arrendevolézza**, *f.* pliancy, suppleness.

arrestàre, *v.t.* to stop, arrest; seize; detain; fix. **arrestàrsi**, *v.refl.* to stop, stay; draw up (*carriage*). **arrèsto**, *m.* arrest; stoppage; seizure, detention.

arretràre, *v.i.* (*aux.* essere & avere) & **arretràrsi**, *v.refl.* to retire; draw back; recoil; withdraw; fall behind. **arretràto**, *a.* overdue, in arrear(s); outstanding, owing; behindhand; backward (*child*); old-fashioned. *area ~ a, f.* backward area, depressed a. **arretràti**, *m.pl.* arrears.

àrri! *i.* gee-up!

arricchiménto, *m.* enrichment. **arricchíre** (*pr.* -ísco, -ísci), *v.t.* to enrich. *v.i.* (*aux.* essere) & **arricchírsi**, *v.refl.* to grow rich. *nuovo arricchito*, upstart, parvenu.

arricciaménto, *m.* curling (of the hair); frowning. **arricciàre**, *v.t.* to curl; wrinkle; (*il naso*) frown, pout; (*wall*) rough-cast. **arricciatúra**, *f.* (hair) curling; rough-casting.

arrídere, *v.i. ir.* (*aux.* avere) to smile; smile upon. Used in such phrases as *la fortuna gli arrise*, fortune smiled upon him.

arrínga (*pl.* -rínghe), *f.* harangue; address; speech; (*law*) pleading. **arringàre**, *v.t.* & *i.* to harangue; address.

arríngo (*pl.* -inghi), *m.* lists; field; arena.

arrischiàre (*pr.* -íschio, -ischi), *v.t.* to risk; venture; (*v.i.*) to dare. **arrischiàrsi**, *v.refl.* to venture, to dare. **arrischiàto**, *a.* venturesome, daring, rash.

arrivàre, *v.i.* (*aux.* essere) to arrive; to be due (*train*); happen, befall. *~ a*, to reach; amount to; go so far as; succeed in. **arrivàto**, *a.* & *m.* (*fig.*) successful, s. man. **arrivísta**, *m.* arriviste. **arrivo**, *m.* arrival.

arroccàre, *v.t.* (*chess*) to castle; to fill the distaff (*for spinning*).

arrochíre, *v.i.* (*pr.* -ísco, -ísci), (*aux.* essere) & **arrochírsi**, *v.refl.* to become hoarse.

arrogànte, *a.* arrogant, insolent, over-bearing. **arrogànza**, *f.* arrogance; insolence; assumption.

arrogàre, *v.t.* (*Law*) to adopt. **arrogàrsi**, *v.refl.* to arrogate (to oneself), assume.

arrolaménto, *m.* enrolment. **arrolàre** (*pr.* -uòlo), *v.t.* to enrol, enlist.

arrosàrsi, *v.refl.* (*Poet.*) to become rosy.

arrossíre (*pr.* -ísco, -ísci), *v.i.* (*aux* essere) to blush, turn red; be ashamed.

arrostíre (*pr.* -ísco, -ísci), *v.t.* to roast; broil. *patate arrostite*, baked potatoes, roast p. **arròsto**, *m.* roast (meat). *~ di bue*, roast beef. *~ di castrato*, roast mutton. *~ d'agnello*, roast lamb.

arrotaménto, *m.* whetting; sharpening. **arrotàre** (*pr.* -uòto), *v.t.* to whet, sharpen, grind. **arrotatúra**, *f.* sharpening. **arrotíno**, *m.* knife-grinder.

arrotolàre (*pr.* -òtolo), *v.t.* to roll up.

arrotondàre (*pr.* -óndo), *v.t.* to round, make round; round off (*period*); supplement (*salary*).

arrovellàrsi, *v.refl.* to worry; strive; become angry, lose one's temper.

arroventàre, & **-íre** (*pr.* -ísco, -ísci), *v.t.* to make red-hot.

arrovesciàre, *v.t.* to turn upside down; overturn, upset; turn inside out; overthrow.

arrovèscio, **a rovèscio**, *ad.* the wrong side up, on the wrong side, upside down.

arrozzíre (*pr.* -ísco, -ísci), *v.i.* (*aux.* essere) to become coarse.

arruffapòpoli, *m.inv.* agitator; demagogue. **arruffàre**, *v.t.* to ru··e, r. up; make untidy. **arruffàrsi**, *v.refl.* to ruffle, dishevel (*one's hair*); become entangled. **arruffío**, *m.* confusion; disorder; mischief-making. **arruffóne**, *m.* mischief-maker; meddler.

arrugginíre (*pr.* -ísco, -ísci), *v.t.* to rust, make rusty. *v.i.* (*aux.* essere) & **arrugginírsi**, *v.refl.* to get rusty, rust.

arruvidíre (*pr.* -ísco, -ísci), *v.t.* to roughen; stiffen.

arsèlla, *f.* mussel.

arsenàle, *m.* arsenal; dockyard.

arsènico, *m.* arsenic.

arsicciàre, *v.t.* to singe; scorch. **arsíccio**, *a.* singed; scorched; dry; burnt.

àrso (*p.p.* of *ardere*), *a.* burnt.

arsúra, *f.* burning; burning heat; parching thirst.

àrte, *f.* art, skill; profession; artifice. *~ manuale*, handicraft.

artefàtto, *a.* artificial; adulterated.

artéfice, *m.* artificer.

artèria, *f.* artery; thoroughfare; arterial road. **arteriàle**, *a.* arterial. **arterioscleròsi**, *f.* hardening of the arteries (*Med.*).

arterióso, *a.* (*Med.*) arterial. *sangue* ~, arterial blood. *sistema* ~, arterial system.

artesiàno, *a.* artesian.

àrtico (*pl.* **àrtici**), *a.* arctic.

articolàre, *a.* articular. ¶ *v.t. & i.* to articulate; pronounce clearly; joint, link; utter. **articilàto,** *a.* distinct, articulate. *preposizione* ~*a*, (*Gram.*) preposition combined with the article. **articolazióne,** *f.* articulation; joint; knuckle; utterance.

artícolo, *m.* article; subject; matter; section, clause, point, item; entry; material, requisite; (*pl.*) wares.

artière, *m.* craftsman; artisan; (*Mil.*) pioneer, sapper.

artificiàle, *a.* artificial. **artificio,** contrivance, artifice; trick. **artificiosità,** *f.* artificiality. **artificióso,** *a.* artificial; artful, cunning, crafty.

artigiàno, *m.* artisan; craftsman; workman, operative; (*fig.*) originator, architect.

artiglière, *m.* artilleryman; gunner. **artiglieria,** *f.* artillery, ordnance; gunnery. ~ *da assedio,* siege artillery. ~ *da campagna,* field a.

artiglio, *m.* talon; claw.

artista (*pl.* **-isti**), *m.* artist; artiste; performer. **artístico** (*pl.* **-istici**), *a.* artistic.

àrto, *m.* joint; member (*Anat.*).

artrite, *f.* arthritis. **artrítico** (*pl.* **-itici**), *a.* arthritic. **Artù,** *m.* (King) Arthur.

arżigogolàre (*pr.* **-ògolo**), *v.i.* (*aux.* avere) to indulge one's fancy; quibble; follow a fantastic argument. **arżigògolo,** *m.* whim; caprice; quibble; sophistry

arżillo, *a.* lively; sprightly; vigorous; (*wine*) full-bodied; sparkling. ¶ *m.* pungency.

aśbèsto *m.* asbestos.

àscaro, *m. or* **àscari,** *m.inv.* native (African) soldier.

aścèlla, *f.* arm-pit.

ascendènte, *p.a.* ascending, upward. ¶ *m.* ascendant, -ent; ascendancy, -ency; (*pl.*) ancestry. **ascendènza,** *f.* ascendency.

ascéndere, *v.i. ir.* (*aux.* essere *or* avere) to climb, mount, ascend. **ascensióne,** *f.* ascent, climb; rising; a cension. *l'A*~, Ascension day. ~ *retta,* (*astr.*) right ascension. **ascensionísta,** *m.* climber, mountain c. **ascensóre,** *m.* (*passenger*)

lift. **ascensorísta** (*pl.* **-ísti**), *m.f.* liftman, -boy; lift-girl.

ascésa, *f.* (*Lit.*) ascent.

ascésso, *m.* abscess, gathering. ~ *alla gengiva,* *f.* gumboil.

ascèta (*pl.* **-èti**), *m. &* **ascètico** (*pl.* **-ètici**), *a.* ascetic.

àscia (*pl.* **àsce**), *f.* axe, hatchet. ~ *da ghiaccio,* ice-axe.

asciàre, *v.t.* to chip; rough hew.

asciàta, *f.* stroke of an axe.

asciugamàno, *m.* towel. **asciugaménto,** *&* **asciugatúra,** *f., m.* drying. **asciugàre,** *v.t. & i.* to dry; d. up; wipe; drain; **asciugatína,** *f.* wipe; air (linen). **asciugatóio** (*pl.* **-ói**), *m.* (bath) towel.

asciuttézza, *f.* dryness, drought. **asciútto,** *a.* dry, arid. ¶ *m.* drought; dry ground.

ascoltànte, *p.a.* listening. ¶ *m.f.* listener. **ascoltàre,** *v.t. & t.* to listen; hear; overhear; (*Med.*) sound. **ascoltatóre,** *m.* **-tríce,** *f.* listener; hearer. **ascoltazióne,** *f.* (*Med.*) auscultation. **ascólto,** *m.* hearing, listening. *dare* ~, *porgere* ~, to listen; pay attention.

ascóndere, *v.t ir.* (*Poet.*) to hide.

ascrívere, *v.t. ir.* to inscribe; register; enrol, ascribe, attribute.

asèttico (*pl.* **-èttici**), *a.* aseptic.

asfàlto, *m.* asphalt.

asfissía, *f.* asphyxia, suffocation; gassing. **asfissiànte,** *p.a.* asphyxiating. **asfissiàre,** *v.t.* to asphyxiate; choke, suffocate.

Àsia (l'), *f.* Asia. *l'A*~ *minore,* Asia minor. **aśiàtico** (*pl.* **-àtici**), *a. & m.* Asiatic. *morbo* ~, cholera.

aśilo, *m.* asylum; refuge; shelter; almshouse; sanctuary. ~ *infantile,* infant school, kindergarten.

àsina, *f.* she-ass. **asinàggine,** *f.* stupidity; silliness. **asinèllo,** *m.* young ass, foal of an ass. **asinésco** (*pl.* **éschi**), *a.* silly; dull, stupid. **asiníno,** *a.* asinine. *tosse* ~*a*, *f.* whooping-cough. **àsino,** *m.* ass, donkey.

asíntote, *f.* (*Geom.*) asymptote. **asintòtico** (*pl.* **-òtici**), *a.* asymptotic.

àśma, *f.* asthma. **aśmàtico** (*pl.* **-àtici**), *a.* asthmatic(al).

àśola, *f.* button-hole.

àśolo, *m.* gentle breath of air; light breeze.

aspàrago (*pl.* **-àragi**), *m.* asparagus.

aspèrgere, *v.t. ir.* to (be)sprinkle; strew.

asperità, *f.* asperity; roughness, harshness.

aspersióne, *f.* aspersion; sprinkling. **aspèrso,** *p.p.* of *aspergere,* sprinkled, strewn. **aspersòrio,** *m.* holy-water sprinkler.

aspettàre (*pr.* **-ètto**), *v.t. & i.* to await, wait, wait for. **aspettàrsi,** *v.refl.* to expect. **aspettatíva,** *f.* expectation; hope; temporary discharge. **aspettazióne,** *f.* expectation. **aspètto,** *m.* aspect, point of view; sight, appearance, look[s], bearing; complexion; waiting. *sala d'* ∼, waiting-room.

àspide, *m.* asp; aspic; (*fig.*) slanderer, back-biter.

aspirànte, *p.a.* aspiring, aiming; (*Mech.*) drawing up. *pompa* ∼, *tromba* ∼, suction pump. ¶ *m.* aspirant, suitor; applicant, candidate; (*Nav.*) midshipman. **aspira-pòlvere,** *m.inv.* vacuum-cleaner. **aspiràre,** *v.t.* to inspire, inhale; exhaust, suck, draw [in]; aspirate. *v.i.* (*aux.* avere) to aspire. **aspirazióne,** *f.* aspiration; yearning; inspiration; inhaling; suction (*Mech.*) *tubo d'* ∼, suction pipe. *valvola* ∼, inlet valve.

aspirína, *f.* aspirine.

àspo, *m.* reel.

asportàbile, *a.* exportable; removable. **asportàre,** *v.t.* to export; transport; remove.

aspraménte, *ad.* harshly, roughly. **aspreggiàre,** *v.t.* to treat roughly. **asprézza,** *f.* harshness; roughness.

asprígno, *a.* tart, sourish, rather acid. **àspro,** *a.* harsh, sour; rough; sharp.

assaggiaménto, *m. &* **assaggia-túra,** *f.* tasting; trial; proof. **assaggiàre,** *v.t.* to taste, try, sample. **assaggiatóre,** *m.* taster. **assàggio,** *m.* trial; tasting; sampling; sample.

assài, *ad. & a.* much; a great deal; plenty; very; very much; quite.

assàle, *m.* axle. ∼ *anteriore,* front axle. ∼ *posteriore,* back a. *tappo di* ∼, *m.* axle cap.

assalíre (*pr.* **-àlgo, -àli, -àle** *or* **-ísco, -isci, -ísce**), *v.t. ir.* to assail; assault; attack; seize. **assalitóre,** *m.* (*f.* **-tríce**), assailant.

assaltàre, *v.t.* to assail; assault. **assaltatóre,** *m.* (*f.* **-tríce**), assailant, agressor. **assàlto,** *m.* assault; storming; attack, onset; onslaught.

assaporaménto, *m.* relishing, tasting; relish, flavour. **assaporàre,** *v.t.* to relish; enjoy.

assaporíre (*pr.* **-ísco, -ísci**), *v.t.* to give a relish (to), season, flavour.

assassinaménto, *m.* assassination (*esp. fig.*). **assassinàre** (*pr.* **-íno**), *v.t.* to assassinate, murder, kill; (*fig.*) tire to death, bore, plague. **assassínio** (*pl.* **-íni**), *m.* murder, assassination. **assassíno,** *m.* murderer, assassin.

àsse, *f.* board; plank; shaft; axle (tree); axis; spindle (*cycl., wheel*). ∼ *a manovella,* ∼ *a gomito,* crank-shaft.

assecondàre, *v.t.* support; favour; uphold.

assediànte, *p.a.* besieging. ¶ *m.* besieger. **assediàre,** *v.t.* to lay siege to; besiege. **assediatóre** *m.* besieger. **assèdio,** *m.* siege.

assegnàbile, *a.* assignable. **assegnaménto,** *m.* allowance; allotment; assignation. *fare* ∼ *su,* to rely [up]on. **assegnàre,** *v.t.* to assign, settle, fix; allow, allot, award. **assegnàto,** *a.* moderate; thrifty; (*Com.*) unpaid; to be paid on delivery. **assegnazióne,** *f.* assignation; allowance; grant. **assègno,** *m.* allowance; payment; cheque (*a. bancario*). ∼ *a vuoto,* worthless cheque. *contro* ∼, cash on delivery. ∼ *in bianco,* blank cheque. ∼*sbarrato,* crossed cheque. ∼ *familiare,* family allowance.

assemblèa, *f.* assembly, meeting; conclave, congregation; meet (*Hunt*).

assembraménto, *m.* throng; concourse; assembling. **assembràre,** *v.t.* to assemble; collect, gather; summon; muster. **assembràrsi,** *v.refl.* to meet, assemble, congregate, flock.

assennataménte, *ad.* wisely; judiciously. **assennatézza,** *f.* good sense; judgment; discretion. **assennàto,** *a.* sensible; wary, prudent.

assènso, *m.* assent; consent. **assentàrsi,** *v.refl.* to absent oneself; keep away. **assènte,** *a.* absent, away (from home). ¶ *m.* absentee. **assenteísmo,** *m.* absenteeism; indifference.

assentiménto, *m.* assent, consent. **assentire** (*pr.* **-ènto**), *v.i.* (*aux.* avere) to consent; acquiesce.

assènza, *f.* absence. ∼ *con licenza,* leave of absence. ∼ *senza licenza,* absence without leave.

assènzio, *m.* absinth; (*plant*) wormwood; (*fig.*) bitterness.

asseríre (*pr.* -ísco, -ísci), *v.t. ir.* to affirm; assert.

asserragliàre, *v.t.* to barricade.

assèrto, *p.p.* affirmed; asserted. ¶ *m.* assertion. **asserzióne,** *f.* assertion.

assessóre, *m.* assessor.

assestaménto, *m.* arrangement; settlement. **assestàre,** *v.t.* to settle; set in order; to strike, deal (*blow*). **assestàto,** *p.a.* arranged, settled.

assetàto, *a.* dry; thirsty.

assettaménto, *m.* & **assettatúra,** *f.* arrangement, adjustment. **assettàre,** *v.t.* to arrange, adjust; put in order. **assètto,** *m.* order; arrangement.

asseveràre, *v.t.* to assert, affirm, declare (*solemnly, with conviction*).

assiàle, *a.* axial.

assicuraménto, *m.* assurance. **assicuràre,** *v.t.* to assure; insure; secure; fasten; declare. **assicuràrsi,** *v.refl.* to make sure (of); assure oneself; insure oneself; secure (for oneself); fasten oneself.

assicurazióne, *f.* assurance; confidence; security; pledge; insurance. ~ *contro gli incendi,* fire insurance. ~ *contro la disoccupazione,* unemployment i. ~ *contro i furti,* burglary i. ~ *contro gli infortuni,* accident i. ~ *contro gli infortuni sul lavoro,* workmen's compensation. ~ *contro i rischi dei trasporti,* travellers' i. ~ *marittima,* marine i., sea i. ~ *per la vecchiaia,* old age insurance. ~ *sulla vita,* life i. *polizza d'*~, insurance policy.

assideràre, *v.t.* to chill; freeze. **assideràto,** *p.a.* frozen; frozen to death; frost-bitten.

assídersi, *v.refl.* to sit down, take one's seat.

assiduaménte, *ad.* assiduously. **assiduità,** *f.* assiduousness, assiduity. **assíduo,** *a.* assiduous, sedulous, industrious; regular; (*Poet.*) thronging, quick-coming (*fears, &c.*).

assième, *ad.* together.

assiepàre, *v.t.* to fence, hedge [round]. **assiepàrsi,** *v.refl.* to crowd.

assillàre, *a.* axillary. ¶ *v.t.* to goad, incite; *v.i.* (*aux.* avere) to suffer tortures. **assillo,** *m.* gad-fly; (*fig.*) goad, painful thought.

assimilàre, *v.t.* to assimilate; absorb; compare. **assimilazióne,** *f.* assimilation.

assiòma (*pl.* -òmi), *m.* axiom.

Assíria (l'), *f.* Assyria. **assíro,** *a.* & **A**~, *n.* Assyrian.

assísa, *f.* sitting of a court (*Law*); uniform, livery; (*pl.*) assizes, courts of assize.

assíso, *p.a.* seated.

assistènte, *m.f.* assistant; bystander; onlooker. ¶ *a.* & *att.* assisting; assistant. **assistènza,** *f.* assistance, aid, help; presence, attendance; audience, public. *fondo di* ~, relief fund. **assístere,** *v.t.* to assist, aid, help; attend (*Med.*). *v.i.* (*aux.* avere) to be present; attend, witness.

assíto, *m.* flooring; partition; hoarding.

assiuòlo, *m.* horned owl. Also **chiú** (*in Tuscany*).

àsso, *m.* ace. ~ *dell'aviazione,* flying ace. ~ *di picche,* ace of spades (*cards*). ~ *di briscola,* ace of trumps; trump card (*fig.*). *essere l'*~, to be unique, to be tip-top. *lasciar in* ~, to leave in the lurch.

associàre, *v.t.* to associate; take into partnership. **associàrsi,** *v.refl.* to enter into partnership; subscribe; join (*society, &c.*). **associàto,** *p.a.* associated; associate. ¶ *m.* partner, subscriber; member, associate. **associazióne,** *f.* association; society; g[u]ild; partnership.

assodaménto, *m.* strengthening; consolidation. **assodàre,** *v.t.* to strengthen; consolidate; establish; boil (*eggs*) hard. **assodàrsi,** *v.refl.* to become solid.

assoggettaménto, *m.* subjection. **assoggettàre,** *v.t.* to subject; subdue; bind, tie down. **assoggettàrsi,** *v.refl.* to subject oneself; submit.

assolatío, -àto, *a.* sunny.

assolcàre, *v.t.* to furrow; plough.

assoldaménto, *m.* enlisting; engaging; recruitment. **assoldàre,** *v.t.* to enlist; recruit; engage. **assoldàrsi,** *v.refl.* to engage oneself; enter service, enlist.

assòlto, *p.p.* of *assolvere,* absolved; cleared, acquitted. **assolutaménte,** *ad.* absolutely. **assolúto,** *a.* absolute; hard & fast; positive; peremptory. **assoluzióne,** *f.* absolution; acquittal. **assòlvere,** *v.t. ir.* to absolve; acquit; forgive; relieve; free; pay (*debt*); perform (*task*).

assomigliànza. See *somiglianza, rassomiglianza, &c.*

assonànza, *f.* assonance.
assonnacchiàto, *a.* drowsy; dozing.
assonnàto, -íto, *a.* (very) sleepy, asleep.
assopiménto, *m.* drowsiness; doze, dozing. **assopíre** (*pr.* -ísco, -ísci), *v.t.* to make sleepy, lull to sleep.
assorbènte, *a. & m.* absorbent. **assorbiménto,** *m.* absorption. **assorbíre** (*pr.* -òrbo, -òrbi *or* -ísco, -ísci), *v.t.* to absorb.
assordaménto, -iménto, *m.* deafening. **assordànte,** *p.a.* deafening; stunning. **assordàre,** *v.t.* to deafen; stun. **assordíre** (*pr.* -ísco, -ísci), *v.t.* to deafen; *v.i.* (*aux.* essere) to grow deaf.
assortiménto, *m.* assortment; set; blend; match. **assortíre** (*pr.* -ísco, -ísci), *v.t. & i.* to assort, supply; sort, suit; draw lots.
assòrto, *p.a.* immersed; absorbed.
assottigliaménto, *m.* diminution. **assottigliàre** (*pr.* -íglio, -ígli), *v.t.* to diminish; thin; sharpen. **assottigliàrsi,** *v.refl.* to grow thin(ner).
assuefàre (*pr.* -fo *or* fàccio, -fai, -fa, *&c.*, like fare), *v.t. ir.* to accustom.
assùmere, *v.t. ir.* to assume; take; undertake; appoint, engage. **assúmersi,** *v.refl.* to assume; take; take upon oneself, undertake. **assúnto,** *p.p.* assumed; undertaken; appointed. ¶ *m.* charge, task; undertaking, enterprise; assumption. **Assunzióne,** *f.* Assumption (*Eccl.*).
assurdità, *f.* absurdity. **assúrdo,** *a.* absurd. ¶ *m.* absurdity.
àsta, *f.* staff; lance; stroke (*writing*); leg (*compasses*); boom (*Naut.*); auction. ~ *della bandiera,* flag-staff. ~ *di fiocco* (*Naut.*), jib-boom. *vendere all'* ~, to sell by auction.
astànte, *a. & m.f.* bystander; assistant. (*pl.*) spectators, onlookers. *medico* ~, doctor on duty (*hospital*). **astantería,** *f.* first aid post; staff on duty (*hospital*).
astèmio, *a.* abstemious.
astenènte, *p.a.* abstaining. **astenérsi,** *v.refl.* to abstain. **astensióne,** *f.* abstention.
astèrgere, *v.t. ir.* to wipe; clean.
astèria, *f.* star-fish.
asterísco (*pl.* -íschi), *m.* asterisk, star.
asteròide, *m.* asteroid.
astèrso, *p.p.* of **astergere,** cleansed, wiped.
astigiàno, *a.* of Asti, in Piedmont. *l'* ~, Vittorio Alfieri (1749-1803).

astigmatísmo, *m.* astigmatism.
astinènte, *a.* abstinent. **astinènza,** *f.* abstinence.
àstio, *m.* spite, rancour; grudge, resentment. **astióso,** *a.* spiteful, resentful, rancorous.
Asti spumante, *m.* sparkling wine of Asti, Italian champagne.
astràrre (*pr.* -àggo, *&c.*, like trarre), *v.t. ir.* to abstract. **astrattaménte,** *ad.* abstractly. **astrattézza,** *f.* abstractness. **astràtto,** *a.* abstract; inattentive; absent-minded. **astrazióne,** *f.* abstraction.
astrétto, *p.p.* of *astringere,* constrained; compelled. **astringènte,** *p.a. & m.* astringent. **astringènza,** *f.* astringency. **astríngere** (*pr.* -íngo, *&c.*, like stríngere), *v.t. ir.* to bind; tie down; compel, constrain.
àstro, *m.* star, luminary. ~ *del cinema,* film star (*male*). **astrofísica,** *f.* astrophysics. **astrología,** *f.* astrology; astronomy. **astrològico** (*pl.* -ògici), *a.* astrological. **astròlogo** (*pl.* -òlogi *or* -òloghi), *m.* astrologer.
astronomía, *f.* astronomy. **astronòmico** (*pl.* -òmici), *a.* astronomic(al). **astrònomo,** *m.* astronomer.
astrusaménte, *ad.* abstrusely. **astrúso,** *a.* abstruse, recondite.
astúccio (*pl.* -úcci), *m.* sheath; case. ~ *per gioielli,* jewel case.
Astúrie (le), *f.pl.* the Asturias.
astutaménte, *ad.* cunningly. **astutézza,** *f.* astuteness. **astúto,** *a.* astute, cunning, sly. **astúzia,** *f.* astuteness, artfulness, craftiness, cunning; guile; trick, wile.
atassía, *f.* (*Med.*) ataxy. ~ *locomotrice,* locomotor ataxy.
atavísmo, *m.* atavism.
ateísmo, *m.* atheism. **ateísta** (*pl.* -ísti) *& a*teo, *m.* atheist. **ateístico** (*pl.* -ístici), *a.* atheistic.
Atène, *f.* Athens. **atenèo,** *m.* athenaeum; academy; university; institute of higher studies. **ateniése,** *a. & m.* Athenian.
atlànte, *m.* atlas; (book of) plates. *A* ~, Atlas (*Myth.*).
atlàntico (*pl.* -àntici), *a.* Atlantic. *l'*[*Oceano*] *A* ~, the A. [Ocean].
atlèta (*pl.* -èti), *m.* athlete. **atlètico** (*pl.* -ètici), *a.* athletic.
atmosfèra, *f.* atmosphere. **atmosfèrico** (*pl.* -èrici), *a.* atmospheric.
àtomo, *m.* atom; mote. **atòmico** (*pl.*

-òmici), *a.* atomic. *bomba ~a,* atom[ic] bomb. *pila ~a,* atomic pile.

àtono, *a.* (*Gram.*) unstressed, unaccented; (*Med.*) toneless; weak, faint.

atrabiliàre, *a.* splenetic; moody; atrabilious.

àtrio, *m.* entrance hall; porch.

àtro, *a.* (*Poet.*) black, dark; gloomy, fearful.

atróce, *a.* atrocious, terrible, cruel; heinous, outrageous; excruciating. **atroceménte,** *ad.* atrociously. **atrocità,** *f.* atrocity.

atrofìa, *f.* atrophy, wasting away. **atrofizżàre,** *v.t.* & **atrofizżàrsi,** *v.refl.* to atrophy.

atropìna, *f.* (*Med.*) atropine.

attaccabrìghe, -lìte, *m.inv.* wrangler; quarrelsome person.

attaccaménto, *m.* attachment.

attaccànte, *m.* attacker; (*Foot.*) forward.

attaccapànni, *m.inv.* clothes-hook; hanger, coat-hanger; hat-stand.

attaccàre (*pr.* **-àcco, -àcchi**), *v.t.* to attack, set upon, assail; begin (*speech subject*); strike up (*band*); attach; tie, fasten, bind, yoke; insert; stick, paste, paste up; hang up; apply; convey (*infection*). *v.i.* (*aux.* essere) to stick, be sticky; be in contact; (*of ideas*) be popular, find favour. **attaccàrsi,** *v.refl.* to stick, cling, adhere; become attached; devote oneself; be contagious. ~ (*con.*), to scuffle, come to blows (with).

attagliàre, *v.t.* to adapt; cut (down). **attagliàrsi,** *v.refl.* to fit, suit.

attastàre, *v.t.* to touch; feel.

attecchiménto, *m.* sprouting; growth. **attecchìre** (*pr.* **-ìsco, -ìsci**), *v.i.* (*aux.* avere) to grow; sprout; take hold; root.

atteggiaménto, *m.* attitude. **atteggiàre,** *v.t.* to give appropriate action to; pose; express in gesture. **atteggiàrsi,** *v.refl.* to assume an attitude or expression; pose.

attempàto, *a.* elderly; up in years; aged.

attemperàre, *v.t.* to allay; temper; ease.

attendàrsi, *v.refl.* to camp; pitch tents.

attendènte, *p.a.* attending; attendant. ¶ *m.* (*Mil.*) orderly; batman. **attèndere** (*pr.* **-èndo,** &c.), like *tendere*), *v.t.* & *i. ir.* to attend, pay attention (to); wait for, await; apply oneself (to); expect; look after; look forward to; wait; stay. **attèndersi,** *v.refl.* to expect.

attenènte, *p.a.* adjoining; belonging. **attenènza,** *f.* appurtenance; appendage. **attenére** (*pr.* **-èngo,** &c., like *tenere*), *v.i. ir.* (*aux.* essere) to belong; concern, be reputed (to). *v.t.* to keep (*promise,* &c.). **attenérsi** (a), *v.refl.* to conform to, follow; keep; lean on.

attentaménte, *ad.* attentively. **attentàre,** *v.i.* (*aux.* avere) to make a (criminal) attempt. **attentàrsi,** *v.refl.* to dare. **attentàto,** *m.* attempt; outrage; assault; attempted murder. **attènti!** *i.* attention! *stare sull'~,* (*Mil.*) to stand at attention. **attènto,** *a.* attentive; alert, careful; mindful.

attenuàre, *v.t.* to attenuate; weaken, minimize; extenuate.

attenzióne, *f.* attention; notice; care-[fulness]; heed; caution. *fare ~,* to pay attention, mind.

attergàre, *v.t.* to docket.

atterràggio, *m.* landing (*Aviat.*). *campo d'~,* landing-ground. *pista d'~, f.* (*Aviat.*) runway ~ *forzato,* forced landing. ~ *di fortuna,* emergency landing. **atterraménto,** *m.* overthrow, demolition. **atterràre,** *v.t.* to bring down, throw down, demolish, (*fig.*) humiliate. *v.i.* (*aux.* avere) to land (*Aviat.*), make land (*Naut.*); alight. **atterràrsi,** *v.refl.* (*Poet.*) to prostrate oneself.

atterrìre (*pr.* **-ìsco, -ìsci**), *v.t.* to terrify. **atterrìrsi,** *v.refl.* to be terrified.

attésa, *f.* waiting; expectation; hope. *in ~ di,* awaiting. *sala d'~, f.* waiting-room.

attéso, *p.p.* of *attendere.* *a.* expected, awaited; considering, in consideration of (*used abs. in agreement with a noun*). ¶ considering. ~ *che,* seeing that.

attestàre, *v.t.* to attest; certify; vouch; witness, testify. **attestàrsi,** *v.refl.* (*Mil.*) to establish a bridgehead. **attestàto,** *m.* attestation; certificate; testimonial. ~ *di nascita,* birth-certificate. **attestazióne,** *f.* attestation; testimony.

atticciàto, *a.* squat; thick-set.

àttico (*pl.* **àttici**), *a.* Attic.

attìguo, *a.* near-by, adjoining, contiguous.

attillàre, *v.t.* to dress up, adorn.
attillàrsi, *v.refl.* to dress oneself up.
attillàto, *a.* elegant, foppish, dressed up; (*clothes*) well-fitting.
àttimo, *m.* instant, moment.
attinènte, *a.* pertaining, belonging; relating.
attinènza, *f.* relation; affinity.
attingere (*pr.* -íngo, *&c.*, like *tingere*), *v.t.* ir. to draw, derive; procure, get; reach, attain.
attiràre, *v.t.* to attract, draw; lure, win. **attiràrsi,** *v.refl.* to incur; win.
attitúdine, *f.* aptitude; disposition; inclination, turn.
attiváre, *v.t.* to set in action; speed up; quicken; exercise; work. **attività,** *f.inv.* activity; (*pl.*) assets. **attivo,** *a.* active, working, effective; energetic, diligent; busy. ¶ *m.* assets; credit account.
attizzàre, *v.t.* to stir up, poke; fan; (*fig.*) incite. **attizzatóio,** *m.* poker.
àtto, *a.* apt, fit. ~ *alla navigazione,* sea-worthy. ¶ *m.* act, action; attitude; sign, gesture; deed, indenture, instrument, document, agreement, contract; bond, certificate; licence; (*pl.*) legal proceedings; minutes *or* transactions (*of a society*). ~ *d'accusa,* bill of indictment. ~ *di nascita,* ~ *di morte,* entry in register of births, of deaths. ~ *di vendita,* bill of sale. ~ *operatorio,* (surgical) operation.
attònito, *a.* astonished, dumbfounded.
attòrcere (*pr.* -òrco, -òrci, *&c.*, like *torcere*), *v.t.* ir. to twist; wring.
attorcigliaménto, **attortigliaménto,** *m.* winding, twisting. **attorcigliàre,** **-tigliàre,** *v.t.* to twist; wind.
attóre, *m.* actor; plaintiff.
attorniàre, *v.t.* to surround. **attórno,** *ad.* around, roundabout.
attorràre, *v.t.* to stack; pile.
attòrta, *f.* strand (*of a rope*); sweet made of twisted pastry filled with almonds, chocolate & fruit.
attòrto, *p.p.* of *attorcere,* twisted.
attossicàre, *v.t.* to poison; infect; (*fig.*) embitter.
attraènte, *p.a.* attractive. **attràrre** (*pr.* -àggo, *&c.*, like *trarre*), *v.t.* ir. to attract; draw; allure. **attrattíva,** *f.* attraction, draw, appeal; (*pl.*) charms. **attrattività,** *f.* attractiveness. **attrattívo,** *a.* attractive. **attràtto,** *p.p.* of *attrarre,* attracted; drawn, allured.

attraversàre, *v.t.* to cross; traverse, pierce; pass through; thwart; oppose. **attravèrso,** *pr.* across; athwart; through. ¶ *ad.* cross-wise; badly, ill, amiss.
attrazióne, *f.* attraction.
attrezzàre, *v.t.* to rig; rig out; fit up. **attrezzatúra,** *f.* plant; rigging. **attrezzista** (*pl.* -ísti), *m.* (*Theat.*) scene-shifter. **attrézzo,** *m.* implement, tool, tackle; utensil; (*pl.*) hand-tools. *attrezzi da zappatore* (*Mil.*), entrenching tools.
attribuíre (*pr.* -ísco, *&c.*), *v.t.* to attribute, ascribe; delegate; predicate; father (*fig.*); allot. **attribuírsi,** *v.refl.* to claim. **attribúto,** *m.* attribute. **attribuzióne,** *f.* attribution; (delegated) power.
attríce, *f.* actress.
attristàre, *v.t.* to sadden.
attristíre (*pr.* -ísco, -ísci), *v.t.* to afflict, grieve. **attristírsi,** *v.refl.* to pine away.
attríto, *a.* (*Lit.*) worn out. ¶ *m.* attrition; abrasion; friction; (*fig.*) disagreement. **attrizióne,** *f.* attrition.
attruppaménto, *m.* trooping; assembly, crowd, mob. **attruppàre,** *v.t.* to assemble. **attruppàrsi,** *v.refl.* to troop; gather.
attuàbile, *a.* feasible, practicable.
attuàle, *a.* actual; present; for the time being. **attualità,** *f.inv.* actuality, present; (*pl.*) current news, questions of the hour; news. *cinema di* ~, news theatre. *film di* ~, news film or reel.
attualménte, *ad.* actually; now, at present.
attuàre, *v.t.* to effect; carry out; bring about, realize.
attuàrio, *m.* actuary; registrar.
attuazióne, *f.* bringing into effect, realization.
attuffàre, *v.t.* to plunge, dip. **attuffàrsi,** *v.refl.* to plunge, dip, dive.
attutíre (*pr.* -ísco, -ísci), *v.t.* to appease; calm; mitigate; deaden (*blow*).
audàce, *a.* audacious, bold, daring. **audàcia,** *f.* audacity, boldness, daring, hardihood.
auditóre, *m.* -**tríce,** *f.* hearer, listener, auditor, -tress. **audizióne,** *f.* audition; hearing; (*pl.*) broadcasting programme.
àuge, *m.* apogee; height; zenith; acme; (*fig.*) high water mark. *essere in* ~, to be in high favour, in high esteem.

augèllo, *m.* (*Poet.*) bird.

auguràle, *a.* augural; auspicious.

auguràre, *v.t.* to wish, wish for (someone). **auguràrsi,** *v.refl.* to hope. **àugure,** *m.* augur, prophet. **augùrio** (*pl.* -ùri), *m.* wish, omen, augury, presage.

augùsto, *a.* august; grand; venerable.

àula, *f.* hall; room (*Sch.*).

aulènte, *a.* (*Poet.*) scented, sweet-smelling.

àulico (*pl.* àulici), *a.* courtly; noble, illustrious.

aumentàre, *v.t.* to increase, augment, enlarge, enhance; supplement. *v.i.* (*aux.* essere) & **aumentàrsi,** *v.refl.* to increase; rise, grow. **aumentazióne,** *f.* augmentation; increase. **auménto,** *m.* growth; increase, rise.

àura, *f.* (*Poet.*) breeze, air.

auràto, *a.* (*Poet.*) gilt.

àurco, *a.* golden, gold (*att.*); (*fig.*) noble.

auréola, *f.* aureole, halo.

aurétta, *f.* gentle breeze; soft wind.

aurícola, *f.* auricle. **auricolàre,** *a.* auricular, ear (*att.*).

aurífero, *a.* auriferous, gold-bearing, gold (*att.*).

auròra, *f.* aurora, dawn, day break.

auśiliàre, *a.* & *m.* auxiliary. **auśiliàrio,** *a.* auxiliary. **auśílio,** *m.* help, assistance.

àuspice, *m.* patron; protector. **auspício,** *m.* auspice, omen; auspices.

austerità, *f.* austerity. **austèro,** *a.* austere; strict; unadorned.

austràle, *a.* south, southern.

Australàsia (l'), *f.* Australasia.

Austràlia (l'), *f.* Australia. **australiàno,** *a.* & *m.* Australian.

Àustria (l'), *f.* Austria. **austríaco** (*pl.* -íaci), *a.* & *m.* Austrian.

àustro, *m.* south wind; south.

autarchía, *f.* autarchy, self-sufficiency, independence.

autàrchico (*pl.* -àrchici), *a.* autarchic(al).

autèntica, *f.* authentic evidence, testimony. **autenticàre,** *v.t.* to authenticate. **autenticità,** *f.* authenticity. **autèntico** (*pl.* -èntici), *a.* authentic, genuine.

autísta, *m.* motor driver, chauffeur.

àuto-, *prefix,* auto-, self-, *e.g.* carta ~-*virante,* *f.* self-toning paper (*Phot.*).

àuto, *m.* (*abb.* of *automobile*) motor, motor car. **autoambulànza,** *f.* motor-ambulance. **auto-avviatóre,**

m. self-starter (*Motor*). **autobiografía,** *f.* autobiography. **autoblindàta,** *f.* (*Mil.*) armoured car; tank. **autobrúco,** *m.* (*Mil.*) tank (*pop.*). **àutobus,** *m.inv.* motor bus, motor coach. **autocàrro,** *m.* motor-lorry.

autòcrata, *m.* autocrat. **autocràtico** (*pl.* -àtici), *a.* autocratic. **autocrazía,** *f.* autocracy.

autodecisióne, *f.* self-determination.

autodidàtta (*pl.* -àtti), *m.* self-taught person.

autogíro, *m.* autogyro.

autogovèrno, *m.* self-government; self-control.

autògrafo, *a.* & *m.* autograph.

autoleśióne, *f.* self-inflicted wound.

autòma (*pl.* -òmi), *m.* automaton; robot. **automàtico** (*pl.* -àtici), *a.* automatic. *bottone* ~, press button. **automèẓẓo,** *m.* motor vehicle.

automòbile, *f.* motor[-car], car; automobile. *guidare un'* ~, to drive a (motor) car. *andare, viaggiare in* ~, to motor. ~ *scoperta,* open car. ~ *da corsa,* racing car.

autonomía, *f.* autonomy; self-government. **autònomo,** *a.* autonomous; self-governing; independent.

autoportàto, autotrasportàbile, *a.* lorry-borne (*troops,* &c,), motorized.

autopsía, *f.* autopsy; post-mortem [examination].

autóre, *m.* author; writer; composer; originator; progenitor; founder; perpetrator (*crime*); party at fault (*accident*).

autorévole, *a.* authoritative; reliable.

autoriméssa, *f.* (motor) garage.

autorità, *f.inv.* authority. **autorìtràtto,** *m.* self-portrait.

autoriẓẓàre, *v.t.* to authorize. **autoriẓẓazióne,** *f.* authorization.

autostràda, *f.* motor road, m. highway.

autosufficiènza, self-sufficiency, independence (*Econ.*).

autosuggestióne, *f.* autosuggestion.

autrice, *f.* authoress, woman writer.

autunnàle, *a.* autumnal. **autúnno,** *m.* autumn.

àva, *f.* grand-mother.

avallàre, *v.t.* to indorse; guarantee. **avàllo,** *m.* endorsement.

avambràccio (*pl.* -àcci), *m.* fore-arm.

avampósto, *m.* outpost.

avàna, *a.* & *m.* havana, h. cigar. l'A~, *f.* Havana.

avanguàrdia, *f.* van, vanguard.

avanía, *f.* affront; insult; ill-treatment; imposition.

avànti, *ad. & pr.* before. ¶ *i.* forward! come in! go on!

avantièri, *ad.* the day before yesterday.

avanzaménto, *m.* advancement; promotion. ~ *ad anzianità*, promotion by seniority. ~ *a scelta*, p. by selection. **avanzàre**, *v.t.* to advance; put forward; increase; surpass; lend; lay by. *v.i.* (*aux.* essere & avere) to go forward, advance. *v.i.* (*aux.* essere) to remain, be left over, be in excess. **avanzàrsi**, *v.refl.* to advance, go forward; project; stand out. **avanzata**, *f.* (*Mil.*) advance. **avanzatíccio**, *m.* remnant; leftover. **avanzàto**, *a. & p.p.* advanced; aged. **avànzo**, *m.* rest, remainder, relic; waste; (*pl.*) remains. (*ad.*) *d'* ~ to spare; left over.

avaràccio, *m.* sordid wretch, miser.

avaría, *f.* damage; average (*Marine Law*). ~ *grossa*, ~ *comune*, general average. *regolare l'* ~, to adjust average. **avariàre**, *v.t.* to damage. *merci avariate*, *f.pl.* damaged goods.

avarízia, *f.* avarice. **avàro**, *a.* avaricious; covetous; miserly. ¶ *m.* miser.

àve! *i.* hail! ave!

avellàna, *f.* filbert, hazel nut. **avellàno**, *m.* filbert tree.

avèllo, *m.* (*Poet.*) tomb.

avemaría, **avemmaría**, *f.* Ave Maria (prayer to the Virgin); sound of the morning or evening bell summoning to this prayer; hour at which it is rung; bead of the rosary.

avéna, *f.* oats; reed-pipe.

avére (*pr.* **ho, hai, ha, abbiàmo, avéte, hànno**), *v.t. & aux. ir.* to have; own, possess; (*in past def.*) get, obtain. ~ *da* (*with inf.*), to have to, ~ *in dosso*, to have on, wear, ~ *fame*, ~ *sete*, to be hungry, to be thirsty. *averla con uno*, to be angry with one, to bear one ill-will. *averla a fare con uno*, to have to deal with one. ¶ *m.* substance; property; credit; (*pl.*) possessions.

aviatóre, *m.* aviator; airman. *tenente* ~, Flight Lieutenant. *pilota* ~, pilot officer, air pilot. **aviatòrio**. *a.* flying, aviation (*att.*). **aviatríce**, *f.* air-woman. **aviazióne**, *f.* aviation, flying; air-force. *ufficiale d'* ~,

Flying Officer. *meccanico d'* ~ (or *motorista*), air-mechanic.

avidaménte, *ad.* greedily. **avidità**, *f.* avidity. **àvido**, *a.* greedy; eager.

avière, *m.* airman (*Mil.*). ~ *scelto*, leading airman.

aviolínea, *f.* air-line; airway. **avioriméssa**, *f.* hangar. **aviotraspòrto**, *m.* air transport.

avíto, *a.* hereditary, ancestral.

àvo, àvolo, *m.* ancestor; grandfather.

avocàre (*pr.* **àvoco, àvochi**), *v.t.* (*Law*) to evoke.

avòrio, *m.* ivory.

avúlso, *p.a.* uprooted, torn away (fr. *avellere*, found only in past def. *avulsi & p.p.*).

avvallaménto, *m.* landslip; sinking; trough (*of the waves*).

avvallàre, *v.t.* to lower; turn to the ground (*eyes*). *v.i.* (*aux.* essere) & **avvallarsi**, *v.refl.* to subside; sink.

avvaloraménto, *m. &* **avvalorazióne**, *f.* strengthening; improvement; increase of value. **avvaloràre** (*pr.* **-óro**), *v.t.* to strengthen; make valuable, give value to. **avvaloràrsi**, *v.refl.* to become stronger; increase in value.

avvampaménto, *m.* flame; blaze. **avvampàre**, *v.t.* to set ablaze; inflame. **avvampàrsi**, *v.refl.* to blaze up; burn.

avvantaggiàre, *v.t.* to benefit, favour, endow. **avvantaggiàrsi**, *v.refl.* to profit. **avvantàggio**, *m.* advantage. *d'* ~, more.

avvedérsi (*pr.* **-édo**, &c., like *vedere*), *v.refl.* *ir.* to perceive.

avvedutaménte, *ad.* shrewdly; sagaciously; adroitly; artfully. **avvedutézza**, *f.* shrewdness; discernment. **avvedúto**, *a.* wary; shrewd; sagacious; foreseeing; circumspect; provident.

avvelenaménto, *m.* poisoning. **avvelenàre**, *v.t.* to poison. **avvelenatóre**, *m.* **-tríce**, *f.* poisoner.

avvenènte, *a.* handsome, charming, comely, prepossessing, agreeable. **avvenènza**, *f.* charm; attraction.

avveniménto, *m.* event; accession (*to throne*). **avvenire** (*pr.* **-vèngo, -vièni**, &c., like *venire*), *v.i.* to occur, happen. ¶ *m.* (*Poet.*) future. **avvenírsi**, *v.refl.* to agree, suit; meet.

avventàre, *v.t.* to throw; hurl; venture. **avventàrsi**, *v.refl.* to rush. **avventàta**, *ad.* in *all'* ~ in-

considerately. **avventatàggine,** *f.*
-atézza, *f.* rashness, inconsiderateness. **avventataménte,** *ad.* inconsiderately. **avventàto,** *a.*
inconsiderate; imprudent, rash.
avventízio, *a.* adventitious, casual.
avvènto, *m.* advent; arrival; accession.
A ~, Advent (*Eccl.*).
avventóre, *m.* (*f.* **-tóra**) customer;
client.
avventúra, *f.* adventure. **avventu-
ràre,** *v.t.* to [ad]venture, risk.
avventuràrsi, *v.refl.* to venture.
avventuràto, *a.* fortunate; happy.
avventurière, *m.,* **-ièra,** *f.* adventurer, -ess. **avventuróso,** *a.*
adventurous.
avveraménto, *m.* verification. **av-
veràre,** *v.t.* to verify; establish,
prove. **avveràrsi,** *v.refl.* to happen,
come to pass, come true.
avverbiàle, *ad.* adverbial. **avvèrbio,**
m. adverb.
avverdíre (*pr.* **-ísco, -ísci**), *v.t.* to
make green, paint green. *v.i.* (*aux.*
essere) to become green, grow
green.
avversàre, *v.t.* to thwart; oppose.
avversàrio, *a.* contrary. ¶ *m.*
adversary, opponent, foe. **avversa-
tóre,** *m.* **-tríce,** *f.* opponent. ¶ *a.*
opposing.
avversióne, *f.* aversion, dislike.
avversità, *f.* adversity, misfortune.
avvèrso, *a.* adverse; averse; contrary, opposite; unfavourable.
avvertenteménte, *ad.* warily. **av-
vertènza,** *f.* notice, warning;
attention, care. **avvertiménto,** *m.*
warning, admonition; advertisement; notice; prefatory note. **avvertíre** (*pr.* **-èrto**), *v.t.* to notify,
(fore)warn, caution; admonish; call
attention to. *v.i.* (*aux.* avere) to
observe, notice, take care. **av-
vertíto,** *a.* aware.
avvezzàre, *v.t.* to accustom; bring up,
train. **avvézzo,** *a.* accustomed.
avviaménto, *m.* setting out, starting;
introduction (*to a subject*); patronage,
custom (*Com.*). *manovella d'* ~,
starting handle (*Mot.*). **avviàre,**
v.t. to start; set going; send off;
make ready; begin; get (*customers*).
avviàrsi, *v.refl.* to set out; move
(towards); get customers; thrive,
succeed (*in business*).
avviàto, *a.* begun; started; ready;
frequented.
avvicendaménto, *m.* alternation.
avvicendàre, *v.t.* to alternate.

avvicendàrsi, *v.refl.* to go by
turns; take turns; succeed each
other.
avvicinàre, *v.t.* to approach, bring
near. **avvicinàrsi,** *v.refl.* to draw
near, come near, approach.
avvignàre, *v.t.* to plant with vines;
prepare ground for vine-growing.
avviliménto, *m.* degradation; dejection. **avvilíre** (*pr.* **-ísco, -ísci**), *v.t.*
to debase; lower; degrade; depress.
avvilírsi, *v.refl.* to lose courage,
become depressed. **avvilíto,** *p.a.*
debased; discouraged.
avviluppaménto, *m.* envelopment.
avviluppàre, *v.t.* to envelope, wrap
up; entangle. **avviluppàrsi,** *v.refl.*
to envelop oneself; get entangled.
avviluppàto, *p.a.* enveloped; (*fig.*)
involved; deceived.
avvinàre, *v.t.* to season or flavour
with wine. **avvinàto,** *a.* tipsy.
avvíncere (*pr.* **-ínco,** *&c.,* like
vincere), *v.t.* *ir.* to bind; tie.
avvinghiàre, *v.t.* to clasp, grasp.
avvinghiàrsi, *v.refl.* to cling; clasp
each other.
avvínto, *p.a.* tied; clasped.
avvisàglia, *f.* skirmish.
avvisàre, *v.t.* to inform; give notice
of; advise; warn, admonish. *v.i.*
(*aux.* avere) to judge, think. **avvi-
sàrsi,** *v.refl.* to consider, believe.
avvisàto, *p.a.* informed; warned.
¶ *a.* shrewd. **avvisatóre,** *m.*
informant; announcer; call-boy
(*Theat.*). ~ *d'incendio,* fire-alarm
avvíso, *m.* opinion; notice; notification; placard; advice; warning.
come d' ~, *secondo* ~, as per advice
(*Com.*). *foglio d'* ~, *lettera d'* ~,
advice note. *star sull'* ~, to be on
the look-out.
avvistàre, *v.t.* to sight; catch sight of;
judge by first impressions. **av-
vistàto,** *p.p.* sighted, *&c.* ¶ *a.*
well-advised.
avvitaménto, *m.* screwing; (*Aero.*)
spin.
avvitàre, *v.t.* to screw; s. up.
avviticchiaménto, *m.* twining; twisting. **avviticchiàre,** *v.t.* to twine,
clasp. **avviticchiàrsi,** *v.refl.* to
twine (round); cling (to).
avvitíre (*pr.* **-ísco, -ísci**), *v.t.* to
plant with vines.
avvizziménto, *m.* fading, withering.
avvizzíre (*pr.* **-ísco, -ísci**), *v.i.* to
fade, wither.
avvocatéssa, *f.* woman barrister.
avvocàto, *m.* lawyer; barrister;

counsel; solicitor. **avvocatúra,** *f.*
lawyer's practice or profession.
avvòlgere (*pr.* **-òlgo,** *&c.*), like
volgere), *v.t.* to wind, roll up;
wrap (up); involve, implicate. **av-
vòlgersi,** *v.refl.* to wrap oneself up;
wind round one; embroil oneself,
become implicated. **avvolgíbile,** *f.*
roller blind; roll shutter (also
persiana ∼, *serranda* ∼). **avvolgi-
ménto,** *m.* envelopment; winding
(up), wrapping (up). **avvòlto,** *p.p.*
of *avvolgere*, enveloped; twisted.
avvoltóio, *m.* vulture.
avvoltolàre, *v.t.* to roll up; turn.
avvoltolàrsi, *v.refl.* to roll oneself
up; wallow.
aziènda, *f.* business, firm; management, administration.
azionàre, *v.t.* (*Mech.*) to operate.
azióne, *f.* action; act; deed; effect;
agency; (*Fin.*) share, (*pl.*) stock. ∼*i
al portatore,* bearer shares, b. stock.
∼*i privilegiate,* preference shares,
preferred stock. ∼*i nominative,*
registered shares, r. stock. ∼*i di
godimento,* bonus shares. ∼*i* [*interamente*] *versate,* fully paid shares.
∼*i postergate,* deferred shares.
azionísta (*pl.* **-ísti**), *m.* share-
holder.
azòtico, *a.* nitric. *acido* ∼, nitric
acid. **azòto,** *m.* nitrogen.
àzza, *f.* battle-axe.
azzannàre, *v.t.* to seize with the
fangs or teeth, snap, catch.
ażżardàre, *v.t.* to hazard, risk.
ażżardàrsi, *v.refl.* to ‧venture.
ażżàrdo, *m.* hazard; risk; chance;
presumption. **ażżardóso,** *a.* hazar-
dous, risky.
azzeccagarbúgli, *m.inv.* pettifogger.
azzeccàre, *v.t.* to hit, strike; bite.
ażżimàre, *v.t.* to dress up. **ażżi-
màrsi,** *v.refl.* to adorn oneself,
bedizen oneself. **ażżimàto,** *p.a.*
foppish, gaudily dressed, dressed up.
ażżimèlla, *f.* unleavened bread.
àzzimo, *a.* unleavened.
azzoppàre, -íre, *v.t.* to lame. *v.i.*
(*aux.* essere) to limp; go lame.
Ażżorre (**le**), *f.pl.* the Azores.
azzuffaménto, *m.* scuffle, scuffling;
fray. **azzuffàrsi,** *v.refl.* to scuffle,
come to blows.
ażżurreggiàre, *v.i.* (*aux.* avere) to be
bluish; tend towards blue. **ażżur-
rino,** *a.* sky-blue, light blue.
ażżúrro, *a.* azure, blue; deep blue.
arma ∼ *a,* *f.* air-force. ¶ *m.* azure;
clear sky. **ażżurrògnolo,** *a.* bluish.

B

B, b, (*bi*), *f.* the letter B.
babàu, *m.inv.* bugbear.
babbèo, *a.* silly, foolish. ¶ *m.* blockhead, fool.
babbióne, *m.* fool, simpleton, dolt.
bàbbo, *m.* daddy; papa, father.
babbuàsso, *m.* ninny, fool; clumsy
fellow.
babbúccia (*pl.* **-úcce**), *f.* bedroom
slipper.
babbuíno, *m.* baboon.
babèle, *f.* babel; (place of) confusion
& disorder. *torre di B* ∼, *f.* tower
of Babel. **babèlico** (*pl.* **-èlici**), *a.*
uproarious.
Babilònia (**la**), *f.* Babylon; (*fig.*) *b* ∼.
confusion, babel.
babórdo, *m.* port (side); larboard
(*Naut.*).
bacàre (*pr.* **-àco, -àchi**), *v.i.* (*aux.*
essere) *&* **bacàrsi,** *v.refl.* to go
rotten; become worm-eaten, decayed. **bacatíccio,** *a.* sickly,
maggoty. **bacàto,** *a.* worm-eaten;
decayed, rotten; (*fig.*) unsound.
bàcca (*pl.* **bàcche**), *f.* berry.
baccalà, *m.inv.* cod; codfish (*dried &
salted*).
baccanàle, *m.* orgy; noisy revel; row,
racket; (*pl.*) *B* ∼*i,* Bacchanalia.
baccàno, *m.* uproar; hubbub; row;
racket.
Baccànte, *f.* Bacchante.
baccarà, *m.* baccarat.
baccellieràto, *m.* bachelor's degree;
bachelorship. **baccellière,** *m.*
bachelor (*of Arts, Science, &c.*).
baccèllo, *m.* pod. **baccellóne,** *m.*
large pod; (*fig.*) blockhead.
bacchétta, *f.* rod; wand; staff; baton;
drumstick; ramrod; (*painter's*) mahl-
stick. **bacchettàre,** *v.t.* to beat;
flog. **bacchettàta,** *f.* stroke (or
blow) with a rod.
bacchettóne, *m.* **-óna,** *f.* bigot;
devotee; hypocrite. **bacchettone-
ría,** *f.* cant; hypocrisy; bigotry.
bacchiàre (*pr.* **bàcchio, -àcchi**), *v.t.*
to knock down (*fruit*) with a pole;
beat, strike. **bacchiata,** *f.* stroke
with a pole.
bàcchico (*pl.* **bàcchici**), *a.* Bacchic;
drinking (*song*).
bacchillóne, *m.* drone, good for nothing.
bàcchio, *m.* pole, long stick.

Bàcco, m. Bacchus.
bachèca (pl. -èche), f. show-case; glass-case.
bachelíte, f. bakelite.
bacheròzzo & bacheròzzolo, m. maggot, grub.
bachicultúra, f. silk-worm breeding.
baciamàno, m. kissing (of) hands; compliment. baciaménto, m. kissing. baciapíle, m. f. inv. hypocrite; bigot. baciàre, v.t. to kiss. baciàrsi, v.refl. to kiss one another, exchange kisses.
bacíle, m. wash-basin.
bacíllo, m. bacillus.
bacinèlla & bacinétta, f. small basin; (Phot.) tray.
bacíno, m. basin, bowl, pan; scale (pan); ornamental lake; dock; (Anat.) pelvis. ~ carbonifero, coal bed, c. basin. ~ di carenaggio, dry dock. ~ di raddobbo, graving dock. entrare in ~, to dock. diritti di ~, dock dues. ~ di marea, tidal basin.
bàcio (pl. bàci), m. kiss. bacióne, m. big kiss. baciòzzo, m. hearty kiss. baciucchiàre, v.t. to smother with kisses.
bàco (pl. bàchi), m. worm; grub; maggot; mite; silk-worm (also ~ da seta). bacología, f. science of silk-worm breeding. bacològico (pl. -ògici), a. dealing with the culture of silk-worms. bacòlogo (pl. -òlogi), m. expert in silk-worm culture.
Bacóne, m. Bacon.
bàda, f. waiting; delay; in the expr. tenere a ~, to check; baffle; keep in suspense; hold at bay. badàre, v.i. (aux. avere) to take care (of); pay attention (to); mind; look (after); listen (to) (followed in each case by pr. a.)
badéssa, f. abbess.
badía, f. abbey.
badíle, m. shovel; hoe.
bàffi, m.pl. moustache; (cat, &c.) whiskers. ridere sotto i ~, to laugh in one's sleeve. baffúto, a. moustached.
bagagliàio (pl. -ài), m. luggage-van (Rly).
bagàglio, m. luggage; baggage; kit, traps. ~ a mano, hand luggage. ~ pesante, heavy luggage. ufficio bagagli, m. luggage-office. consegna dei bagagli, f. left luggage office. visita dei ~ i, f. customs examination.
bagattèlla, f. bagatelle; trifle; bauble.

baggèo, m. booby; blockhead; fool; simpleton. baggianàta, f. foolish action; piece of nonsense. baggiàno, m. booby; fool.
bàglio, m. (Naut.) beam.
bagliére, m. gleam; glare; flash; beam; dazzling light.
bagnai[u]òlo, m. bath-attendant, bath-keeper. bagnànte, m.f. bather. bagnàre, v.t. to wet; moisten; soak, steep; bathe; dip; bath; sprinkle; suffuse. bagnàrsi, v.refl. to bathe; take a bath; get wet; welter. bagnaròla, f. bath-tub. bagnasciúga, f. (Naut.) [wind &] water-line. bagnàta, f. wetting, soaking. bagnàto, a. wet. bagnatúra, f. bathing; bathing season. bagnino, m. -a, f. bath attendant, bathing attendant. bàgno, m. bath; (pl. & s.) bathing; (pl.) watering-place, spa. fare un ~, to bathe; take a bath. stabilimento di bagni, m. bathing establishment, baths. stanza da ~, f. bath room. costume da ~, m. bathing costume. mutandine da ~, f.pl. bathing drawers. cabina da ~, f. bathing box, bathing-machine. ~ di fissaggio (Phot.), fixing-bath. bagnomaria, m. bain-marie; steam-cooker.
bagn[u]òlo, m. hot fomentation.
bagordàre (pr. -órdo), v.i. (aux. avere) to revel. bagórdo, m. orgy, revelry.
bàia, f. jest; joke; trick, prank; ridicule; bay, gulf. (pl.) nonsense! humbug! dar la ~ a, to banter; hoot. B~ di Biscaglia, Bay of Biscay. baiàta, f. hooting; uproar; joking.
baiétta, f. small bay; bolting cloth.
baílo, m. bailiff.
bàio, a. & m. bay (colour & horse).
baiòcco (pl. -òcchi), m. (fig.) farthing.
Baióna, f. Bayonne.
baionétta, f. bayonet. baionettàta, f. bayonet thrust.
bàita, f. (Alpine) hut.
balaústra & balaustràta, f. balustrade; hand-rail, rails.
balaústro, m. (Arch.) baluster.
balbettàre, v.i. (aux. avere) to stammer, stutter; (child) lisp, prattle; babble. v.t. to stammer out; speak (language) imperfectly. balbettío, m. stammering; (children) prattling, babbling.
bàlbo, a. stammering. balbutíre (pr. -ísco, -ísci), v.t. & i. (aux.

avere) to stammer. **balbúzie,** *f.inv.* stammer, stutter; stammering. **balbuziènte,** *a.* stammering. ¶ *m.f.* stammerer; stutterer.

Balcàni, (**I**) *m.pl.* the Balkans. **Balcànica (penisola)** *f.* Balkan Peninsula.

balconàta, *f.* (railed) balcony.

balcóne, *m.* balcony; window opening on to a balcony.

baldacchino, *m.* baldachin; canopy; tester.

baldaménte, *ad.* boldly.

baldànza, baldézza, *f.* boldness; assurance; self-confidence; daring; bold demeanour; impudence. **baldanzosaménte,** *ad.* boldly; haughtily. **baldanzóso,** *a.* bold; confident, fearless; haughty. **bàldo,** *a.* bold, daring, fearless.

baldoría, *f.* bonfire; revel; carousal; mirth. *far* ∼, to junket, make merry.

baldràcca, *f.* slut, strumpet.

Baleàri (Isole), *f.pl.* Balearic Islands.

balèna, *f.* whale. *osso di* ∼, *m.* whalebone. *olio di* ∼, *m.* whale-oil.

balenaménto, *m.* lightning (flash). **balenàre,** *v.i.* (*aux.* essere) to lighten, flash. **balenièra,** *f.* whaler (*ship*), whale-boat. **balenière,** *m.* whaler (*pers.*). **balenío,** *m.* (continual) lightning, flashing, flash. **baléno,** *m.* lightning; flash. *in un* ∼ in a flash, in a trice.

balèstra, *f.* cross-bow; (*Mech.*) spring. **balestràre,** *v.t. & i.* (*aux.* avere) to shoot with the cross-bow; (*fig.*) to throw about, send far away. **balestràta,** *f.* bow-shot. **balestrièra,** *f.* loophole.

balestrúccio, *m.* house martin.

bàlia, *f.* (wet) nurse, nurse; foster-mother.

balía, *f.* power; mercy; authority. *lasciare in* ∼ *di,* to leave at the mercy of.

baliàtico (*pl.* -**àtici**), *m.* suckling (*act*); nurse's wages.

bàlio, *m.* foster-father.

balística, *f.* ballistics.

bàlla, *f.* bale; package.

ballàbile, *a.* suitable for dancing. ¶ *m.* (*Mus.*) dance (*piece suitable for dancing*); brief ballet. **ballàre,** *v.t. & i.* (*aux.* avere) to dance. **ballàta,** *f.* dance; ballad.

ballatóio, *m.* gallery; platform.

ballerína, *f.* dancer; ballet dancer, ballet girl. **balleríno,** *m.* professional dancer; dancer.

ballétta, *f.* small parcel; packet.

ballétto, *m.* ballet. **bàllo,** *m.* ball; dance; dancing. ∼ *in costume,* fancy dress ball. ∼ *mascherato,* masked ball. ∼ *per sottoscrizione,* subscription dance. *maestro di* ∼, dancing-master. *tirare in* ∼, to call in question.

ballonzolàre, *v.i.* (*aux.* avere) to romp, trip; skip.

ballòtta, *f.* boiled chestnut.

ballottàggio, *m.* (second) ballot, ballotage. **ballottàre,** *v.t.* to ballot, put to the ballot. **ballottazióne,** *f.* voting by ballot, balloting.

balneàre & balneàrio, *a.* bathing (*att.*). *stazione balnearia,* watering place. *stagione balneare,* bathing season.

baloccàre, *v.t.* to amuse. **baloccàrsi,** *v.refl.* to amuse oneself (with trifles). **balòcco** (*pl.* -**òcchi**), *m.* plaything; toy; trifle. **baloccóne,** *m.* idle fellow.

balordàggine, *f.* stupidity; silliness. **balórdo,** *a.* silly; foolish; giddy. ¶ *m.* numskull; fool.

bàlsa, *f.* balsa. *zattera di* ∼, raft of balsa wood.

balsàmico (*pl.* -**àmici**), *a.* balmy. **bàlsamo,** *m.* balm.

bàlta (dàre di), *vb.expr.* to upset, be upset. ∼ *a,* to waste.

Bàltico (*Mare*) *m.* Baltic (Sea).

baluàrdo, *m.* bulwark; rampart.

bàlza, *f.* crag, cliff, rock; precipice; (*of dress*) flounce.

balzàna, *f.* flounce; fringe.

balzàno, *a.* crack-brained, strange.

balzàre, *v.i.* (*aux.* essere & avere) to spring; jump; leap; bound. **balzèllo,** *m.* little jump; hop, skip; tax, heavy duty. **balzellóne,** *m.* jump; sudden start. **balzellóni,** *v.i.* to hop, skip. *and*:*re a* ∼*i,* to skip about. **bàlzo,** *m.* bound, leap; hop; start; rebound. *prender* (*cogliere*) *la palla al* ∼, (*fig.*) to seize the opportunity.

bambàgia, *f.* cotton; cotton-wool. **bambagíno,** *a.* cotton. ¶ *m.* dimity.

bambagióne, *a.* clumsy. ¶ *m.* clumsy fellow; dunce.

bambína, *f.* baby; child; little girl. **bambinàggine, -àta, -ería,** *f.* childishness, childish action. **bambinàia,** *f.* nurse-maid; nursery-governess. **bambinèllo,** *m.* chubby child; baby. **bambinésco** (*pl.* -**éschi**), *a.* childish. **bambíno,** *m.*

baby; child; little boy. **bamboccià-ta**, *f.* childish action. **bambòccio** (*pl.* **-òcci**), *m.* great big baby; puppet; doll. **bàmbola**, *f.* doll. **bamboleggiaménto**, *m.* childish behaviour; play, romping. **bamboleggiàre**, *v.i.* (*aux.* avere) to behave like a child; amuse oneself with trifles.

bambú, *m.inv.* bamboo.

banàle, *a.* common; commonplace; banal. **banalità**, *f.inv.* banality; commonplaceness; triteness; platitude.

banàna, *f.* banana (*fruit*). **banàno**, *m.* banana tree.

bànca (*pl.* **bànche**), *f.* bank, banking-house, banking-establishment. ~ *di emissione*, bank of issu:. **banca-rèlla**, *f.* street stall; barrow; pavement display. **bancàrio**, *a.* bank, banking (*att.*). *commercio* ~, *operazione* ~*a*, banking, banking transaction. **bancarótta**, *f.* bankruptcy. *far(e)* ~, to go bankrupt.

banchettàre, *v.i.* (*aux.* avere) to banquet; feast. **banchétto**, *m.* banquet.

banchière, *m.* banker.

banchína, *f.* bench; wharf; quay; platform (*Rly.*).

bànco (*pl.* **bànchi**), *m.* bench, form, seat, settle; thwart; box (*jury, witness*); desk; counter; bank; bed, reef; shoal (*sand, fish*); floe (*ice*). ~ *di poppa*, stern seat (*boat*). ~ (*di chiesa*) pew. ~ *degli accusati*, dock. ~ *corallo*, coral reef. ~ *da lavoro*, work-bench. ~ *di nebbia*, fog bank.

bancogíro, *m.* clearing transaction (*Fin.*).

banconòta, *f.* banknote.

bànda, *f.* band, strip, belt, strap; bandage; streak; side; direction; place; time; leaf (*folding door or shutter*); troop, company (*Mus., &c.*); party; path; gang. *mettere da* ~, to put aside. *da* ~ *a* ~, through [& through]. *dare alla* ~, (*Naut.*) to heel over. *capo di* ~, (*Naut.*) freeboard.

bandèlla, *f.* sheet (*of metal*); iron brace.

banderuòla, *f.* banderol(e), streamer; vane; weathercock (*lit. & fig.*).

bandièra, *f.* flag; banner; colours (*pl.*). ~ *di partenza*, Blue Peter (*Naut.*). ~ *da segnali*, signal flag. ~ *di contumacia*, quarantine flag (*Naut.*). ~ *a mezz'asta*, flag at half-mast. *issare la* ~, to hoist the flag.

bandinèlla, *f.* roller towel; coach blind.

bandíre (*pr.* **-ísco**, **-ísci**), *v.t.* to proclaim; publish; put up; declare; announce; banish; exile; dismiss.

bandísta (*pl.* **-ísti**), *m.* musician; bandsman.

bandíta, *f.* preserve (*shooting or fishing*).

bandito, *p.a.* exiled, banished. ¶ *m.* bandit; outlaw; exile.

banditóre, *m.* public crier.

bàndo, *m.* ban; banishment, exile; proclamation, announcement.

bandolièra, *f.* bandolier; shoulder-belt. *a* ~, in a sling.

bàndolo, *m.* thread; knot of a skein.

bandóne, *m.* sheet iron, corrugated iron.

bar, *m.inv.* bar (*drinking*).

bàra, *f.* bier; coffin.

baràcca (*pl.* **-àcche**), *f.* booth; stall; hut; shed; shack.

baracchière, *m.* **-a**, *f.* stall (or shop) keeper.

baracchíno, *m.* mess-tin.

baraccóne, *m.* shed; big barrack.

baraónda, *f.* confusion; disorder; mess; hubbub.

baràre, *v.i.* (*aux.* avere) to cheat (*at play*).

bàratro, *m.* gulf; abyss; chasm.

barattaménto & **baràtto**, *m.* bartering; barter; exchange. **baràttare**, *v.t.* to barter; exchange; mistake, take by error. **barattatóre**, *m.* barterer.

barattería, *f.* (*Naut.*) barratry; swindling; embezzlement; fraud.

barattière, *m.* swindler; embezzler; rogue, cheat.

bàrba, *f.* beard; shaving; shave; barb (*feather*); awn; hair; root; (*pl.*) roots, rootlets. *farsi la* ~, to shave (oneself). *farsi radere la* ~, to get shaved. *Barba blu*, *m.* Bluebeard.

barbabiétola, *f.* beet; beetroot. ~ *da zucchero*, sugar beet.

barbacàne, *m.* barbican; buttress.

barbagiànni, *m.inv.* owl; blockhead.

barbàglio, *m.* dazzle.

barbaraménte, **-escaménte**, ad. barbarously.

barbàre, *v.i.* (*aux.* avere) to take root; put forth roots.

barbàrico (*pl.* **-àrici**), *a.* barbarous barbaric.

barbàrie, *f.inv.* barbarousness; barbarity.

barbaríŝmo, *m.* barbarism (*Gram.*).
bàrbaro, *a.* barbarous. ¶ *m.* barbarian.
barbàta, *f.* roots (of a plant).
barbàto, *a.* bearded; barbed.
barbazzàle, *m.* curb; curb-chain.
barbèra, *f.* black Piedmontese grape & the wine made from it.
bàrbero, *m.* barb (*horse*); Barbary horse.
barbétta, *f.* small beard; (*Naut.*) painter. ~ *a punta*, goatee.
barbicaménto, *m.* rooting. **barbicàre,** *v.i.* (*aux.* avere) to take root.
barbicèlla, *f.* small root.
barbière, *m.* barber; hair-dresser. **barbiería,** *f.* barber's shop.
barbóne, *m.* long beard; long-bearded man; poodle.
barbottàre, *v.i.* to grumble.
barbugliàre, *v.i.* (*aux.* avere) to stammer, stutter; falter. **barbuglióne,** *m.* stammerer.
barbúto, *a.* bearded.
bàrca (*pl.* **bàrche**), *f.* boat; barge; launch. ~ *peschereccia*, ~ *da pesca*, fishing boat. ~ *di salvataggio*, lifeboat. ~ *a motore*, motor-launch. ~ *da ponte*, pontoon. ~ *a remi*, row[ing] boat. *andare in* ~, to go boating. **barcàccia,** *f.* old boat, tub; (*Theat.*) stage box. **barcaiòlo,** *m.* boatman.
barcaròla, *f.* barcarolle (*Mus.*).
barcàta, *f.* boat-load.
Barcellóna, *f.* Barcelona.
barchétta, *f.* small boat; skiff; dinghy.
barchíno, *m.* midget (2 man) submarine.
barcollaménto, *m.* staggering; rocking; reeling; tottering. **barcollàre** (*pr.* **-òllo**), *v.i.* (*aux.* avere) to stagger; reel; rock; totter. **barcollío,** *m.* continual rocking, reeling, &c. **barcollóne,** *m.* stumble, stagger. *andar a* ~*i*, to stagger about.
barcóne, *m.* barge; lighter.
bardaménto, *m.* harnessing. **bardàre,** *v.t.* to harness, saddle. **bardatúra,** *f.* harness; horse-trappings. **bardèlla,** *f.* pack-saddle.
bàrdo, *m.* bard (*Poet.*).
barèlla, *f.* stretcher; litter; hand-cart. **barellàre,** *v.t.* to carry in a litter. *v.i.* (*aux.* avere) to stagger.
bargèllo, *m.* chief of police (*Med. Florence*); police headquarters.
bàrgia, *f.* dewlap (*oxen*).

bargíglio (*gen. pl.* **bargígli**), *m.* wattle (*of cocks*).
baricéntro, *m.* (*Phys.*) centre of gravity.
bariglióne, *m.* keg; barrel.
barilàio, *m.* cooper.
baríle, *m.* barrel; cask. **barilétto,** *m.* small cask. **barilòtto** & **barilòzzo,** *m.* keg.
bàrio, *m.* barium.
baríte, *f.* barytes (*Chem.*).
baritonàle, *a.* barytone (*att.*).
barítono, *a.* & *m.* barytone.
barlúme, *m.* glimmer; gleam.
bàro, *m.* swindler; cheat; trickster.
barocciàio (*pl.* **-ài**), *m.* carter. **baroccíno,** *m.* small cart; handcart; barrow. **baròccio,** *m.* cart.
baròcco (*pl.* **-òcchi**), *a.* baroque; (*fig.*) odd, queer, quaint. ¶ *m.* baroque (*style*).
barògrafo, *m.* barograph, recording barometer.
Baròlo, *m.* famous red wine of Piedmont.
baromètrico (*pl.* **-mètrici**), *a.* barometric(al). *pressione* ~*a*, baròmetric pressure. **baròmetro,** *m.* barometer, glass.
baronàle, *a.* baronial.
baróne, *m.* baron; rascal. **baronéssa,** *f.* baroness. **baronétto,** *m.* baronet. **baronía,** *f.* barony.
bàrra, *f.* bar, rod, rail; line, stroke; rudder, tiller (*b. del timone*). ~ *di direzione*, steering-rod (*Motor*).
barràre, *v.t.* to bar; obstruct.
barricàre, *v.t.* to barricade. **barricàta,** *f.* barricade.
barrièra, *f.* barrier; fence; bar; gate. ~ *scalabile*, stile.
barríre (*pr.* **-ísco, -ísci**), *v.i.* (*aux.* avere) to trumpet, roar (*elephant*).
barròccio, *m.* cart, large two-wheeled cart. Cf. *baroccio*.
barúffa, *f.* altercation; scuffle; fray.
barzellétta, *f.* jest, joke, witticism.
baŝàltico (*pl.* **-àltici**), *a.* basaltic, basalt (*att.*). **baŝàlto,** *m.* basalt.
baŝaménto, *m.* base; basement; pedestal; (*Mech.*) bed-plate. **basàre,** *v.t.* to ground; base; found.
bàsco (*pl.* **bàschi**), *a.* & *m.* Basque.
bascúlla, *f.* weighing-machine.
bàŝe, *f.* base; foundation; bed; basis, ground. ~ *aerea*, air base. *in* ~ *a*, on the ground of. *senza* ~, groundless.
baŝétta, *f.* moustache, whisker.
bàŝico (*pl.* **bàsici**), *a.* basic.
Baŝilèa, *f.* Basle (Basel).

basílica (*pl.* -íliche), *f.* basilica.
basílico, *m.* basil (*Bot.*, Cook).
basílisco, *m.* basilisk.
basiménto, *m.* swoon. **basíre** (*pr.*
-ísco, -ísci), *v.i.* (*aux.* essere) to
swoon; faint.
bàssa, *f.* plain; low ground.
bassaménte, *ad.* meanly; basely.
bassézza, *f.* meanness, baseness; vileness; humbleness (*birth*).
bàsso, *a.* low; lower, nether, down;
shallow; short; mean, vile, base,
degrading, vulgar; cheap. ¶ *ad.* low,
low down, down. *da ~*, downstairs.
in ~, down; downward(s); below; at
the bottom. *basso fondo*, shoal
water (*Naut.*). ¶ *m.* lower part;
bottom; foot; base; bass (*Mus.*).
alti e ~i, ups and downs.
bassofóndo, *m.* shallow; shallow
water; shoal water; (*pl.*) **bassifóndi**,
underworld (*city, society*).
bassóne, *m.* bassoon; deep voice.
bassopiàno (*pl.* **bassipiàni**), *m.* lowland.
bassorilièvo (*pl.* **bassorilièvi**), *m.*
bas-relief.
bassòtto, *a.* rather short; stout and
short. ¶ *m.* basset (*dog*).
bassúra, *f.* low land; low situation.
bàsta, *f.* tuck; hem. ¶ *ad. & i.*
enough! that's enough! (See
bastare.)
bastànte, *p.a.* enough, sufficient.
bastaneménte, *ad.* sufficiently,
enough.
bastardàggine, *f.* bastardy, illegitimacy; (*fig.*) spuriousness.
bastàrdo, *a. & m.* bastard; mongrel.
bastàre, *v.i.* (*aux.* essere) to suffice;
be enough, be sufficient. *basta!*
that will do! that's enough. **bastévole**, *a.* sufficient. **bastevolézza**, *f.*
sufficiency. **bastevolménte**, *ad.*
sufficiently.
bastíglia, *f.* bastille.
bastiménto, *m.* ship, vessel; shipload.
bastióne, *m.* bastion, rampart.
bàsto, *m.* pack-saddle. *cinghie di ~*,
f.pl. girths.
bastonaménto, *m.* -atúra, *f.* flogging,
beating, thrashing, caning. **bastonàre**, *v.t.* to flog, beat, cane, thrash.
bastonàta, *f.* flogging, cudgelling;
caning, beating; (*pl.*) blows (*with a
stick*). **bastóne**, *m.* stick; cudgel;
club; singlestick; baton; support
(*fig.*); (*pl.*) clubs (*cards*). *~ alpino*,
~ ferrato, alpenstock. *dim.*
bastoncello, bastoncino.

batacchiàre, *v.t.* to beat; knock
down. **batàcchio**, *m.* clapper
(*bell*).
batísta, *f.* cambric; batiste.
batòsta, *f.* blow; struggle; reverse.
battàglia, *f.* battle, fight, fray.
battagliàre, *v.i.* (*aux.* avere) to
fight; battle; struggle; wrangle.
battaglièro, *a.* warlike; bellicose.
battàglio, *m.* clapper (*of a bell*).
battagiióne, *m.* battalion.
battellière, *m.* boatman.
battèllo, *m.* boat. *~ a vapore*, steamboat. *~ faro*, lightship. *~ di
gomma*, rubber boat. *~ pilota*, pilot
boat. *~ di salvataggio*, lifeboat. *~ da traghetto*, ferry-boat,
ferry.
battènte, *m.* leaf, fold (*of door,
window, &c.*); shutter; knocker.
~ d'acqua, head of water.
bàttere, *v.t. & i.* (*aux.* avere & essere)
to beat, strike; knock; hit; batter;
scour (*country*); tread; thrash; thresh;
hammer; ram; coin, mint; stamp
(*foot*); clap (*hands*); fly (*national
flag*); tap (*keys of a typewriter*);
bang; clatter; flap; jar; throb, pulsate,
pant; tick (*clock*). **bàttersi**, *v.refl.*
to fight.
batteria, *f.* battery (*Artil., Elec.*);
outfit, set (*utensils*); striking
mechanism (*clock*). *~ di accumulatori*, (*Elec.*) storage battery. *~ di
costa*, coastal battery. *scoprire le ~e*,
(*fig.*) to give the show away.
battèrio, *m.* bacterium (*pl.* bacteria).
batteriología, *f.* bacteriology. **batteriòlogo** (*pl.* -òlogi), *m.* bacteriologist.
battesimàle, *a.* baptismal.
battésimo, *m.* baptism, christening.
nome di ~, *m.* Christian name.
battezzàre, *v.t.* to baptize, christen.
battibécco (*pl.* -écchi), *m.* altercation, dispute, squabble.
batticuòre, *m.* palpitation.
battifuòco, *m.* steel (*for striking
light*).
battilàna, *m.* woolcomber.
battilòro, *m.* gold-beater.
battimàno, -màni, *m.* hand-clap,
clapping (of hands), applause.
battiménto, *m.* beating, beat, &c.
(*cf. battere*).
battipàlo, *m.* ram; rammer; piledriver.
battiràme, *m.* coppersmith.
battistèro, *m.* baptistery.
battistràda, *m.inv.* leader; outrider;
scout; guide; tread (*tyre*). *ricostruire*

il ~, to retread (*a tyre*). *locomotiva*
~, *f.* pilot engine.

bàttito, *m.* throb, throbbing; beat,
beating; tick, ticking; (*Mech.*) rattle;
knocking (*piston, &c.*).

battitóre, *m.* beater; thresher; server
(*ball-game*). **battitríce,** *f.* threshing-
machine.

battitúra, *f.* beating; thrashing;
threshing.

bàttola, *f.* clapper (*of a mill*).

battúta, *f.* beat, beating; clapping;
stamping (*feet*); bar (*Mus.*); service
(*Ten.*); observation, remark.

battúto, *p.a.* beaten; threshed.

batúffolo *or* **batúfolo,** *m.* wad, flock;
bundle.

baúle, *m.* trunk; box. *dim. bauletto,*
small trunk; portmanteau.

baussíte *&* **bauxíte,** *f.* bauxite
(*Min.*).

bàva, *m.* slaver; foam.

bavaglíno, *m.* bib.

bavàglio, *m.* gag.

bavaróse, *a. & m.* Bavarian.

bavèlla, *f.* floss (*silk*).

bàvero, *m.* collar (*coat*). ~ *di pelo,*
fur collar.

Bavièra (la), *f.* Bavaria.

bavóso, *a.* slavering, slobbering;
foaming.

bazàr, *m.inv.* bazaar.

bàzza, *f.* projecting chin; good luck;
bargain.

bazzàna, *f.* sheepskin.

bazzècola, *f.* trifle, bagatelle.

bàzzica, *f.* pool (*game*); conversation,
company; bezique.

bazzicàre, *v.t. & i.* (*aux.* avere) to
frequent, haunt.

bazzòtto, *a.* soft; soft-boiled; half-
done.

beàre, *v.t.* to make happy. **beàrsi,**
v.refl. to rejoice, delight (in).

beatificàre (*pr.* -ífico, -ífichi), *v.t.*
to beatify. **beatificazióne,** *f.*
beatification. **beatífico** (*pl.* -ífici),
a. beatific.

beatitúdine, *f.* beatitude; blessedness;
(*pl.*) (the) Beatitudes (*N.T.*). *Sua
B~,* His Holiness (*Pope*).

beàto, *a.* happy; blessed.

beccàccia, *f.* wood-cock.

beccaccíno, *m.* snipe.

beccafíco (*pl.* -íchi), *m.* beccafico
(*bird*), warbler.

beccàio, *m.* butcher.

beccalíte, *m.* pettifogger; wrangler.

beccaménto, *m.* pecking.

beccamòrto, *m.inv.* grave-digger.

beccàre (*pr.* bécco, bécchi), *v.t.*

to peck; pick; pick up; gain;
catch.

beccastríno, *m.* mattock.

beccàta, *f.* peck; blow with the beak;
beakful.

beccatóio, *m.* trough.

beccheggiàre, *v.i.* (*aux.* avere) to
pitch (*Naut.*). **becchéggio,** *m.*
pitching.

beccheria, *f.* butcher's shop.

becchétto, *m.* small beak; point.

becchíme, *m.* birds' food.

becchíno, *m.* grave-digger.

bécco (*pl.* bécchi), *m.* beak, bill;
burner (*gas*); he-goat; cuckold.

beccúccio, *m.* spout. **beccúto,** *a.*
beaked.

beceràta, *f.* churlish action or
language. **bécero,** *m.* ill-bred
fellow; churl; cad.

beduíno, *m.* bedouin.

Befàna, *f.* Epiphany.

bèffa, *f.* trick; jest; mockery. *farsi
beffe di,* to deride; rally; make a
fool of. **beffàrdo,** *a.* mocking;
bantering; scoffing. ¶ *m.* mocker;
scoffer. **beffàre,** *v.t.* to mock; scoff
at; rally; banter; ridicule. **beffàrsi**
(**di**), *v.refl.* to laugh at; make a fool
of. **beffatóre,** *m.* jester; mocker;
banterer. **beffeggiaménto,** *m.*
mockery; scoffing; banter[ing].
beffeggiàre, *v.t.* to deride; ridicule,
mock (at); scoff at.

bèga (*pl.* bèghe), *f.* dispute, quarrel;
troublesome business.

begli, bel, bei. See *bello.*

belaménto, -àto, *m.* bleating.

belàre (*pr.* bèlo), *v.i.* (*aux.* avere)
to bleat. **belío,** *m.* (constant)
bleating.

bèlga (*pl.m.* belgi, *f.* belghe), *a. &*
m. Belgian. *il Congo Belga,* the
Belgian Congo.

Bèlgio (il), *m.* Belgium.

Belgràdo, *f.* Belgrade.

bèlla, *f.* mistress; lover; beautiful
woman.

belladònna, *f.* belladonna; deadly
nightshade.

bellaménte, *ad.* beautifully; politely;
quietly; skilfully.

bellétta, *f.* mire, mud.

bellétto, *m.* rouge, paint.

bellézza, *f.* beauty. *che* ~! how
lovely! how splendid! *la* ~ *di,*
as much as.

bèllico (*pl.* bèllici), *a.* warlike.

bellicóso, *a.* bellicose, aggressive;
combative.

belligerànte, *a. & m.* belligerent.

belligero, *a.* belligerent.

bellimbústo, *m.* dandy; fop.

bellíno, *a.* pretty; nice.

bèllo, *a.* (*m.pl.* **bei, begli**) beautiful, fine, handsome, fair, good-looking, pretty, comely; fashionable, smart; bright; palmy (*days*); queer. *le belle* ~*i*, the fine arts. ~ *spirito* (man of) wit. *bell'e fatto*, all ready. *Oh, bella!* You don't say so! *bel* ~, quietly, peacefully; slowly. ¶ *m.* (the) beautiful; lover, beau; beauty. *nel più* ~, just then. *nel più* ~ *che*, just when.

bellòccio, *a.* rather handsome; rather pretty.

bellumóre (*pl.* **begli umóri**), *m.* jolly fellow; wag.

bel paése, *m.* a well-known sweet cheese made in Brianza.

beltà, *f.* beauty.

bélva, *f.* wild beast.

belvedére, *m.* belvedere; look-out tower.

Belzebú, *m.* Beelzebub.

bemòlle, *m.* (*Mus.*) flat.

benalzàto! *i.* good morning, the top of the morning to you!

benamàto, *a.* (well) beloved.

benànche, *ad.* yet; still; also.

benarrivàto, *a.* welcome.

benché, *c.* though; although.

bencreàto, *a.* well-bred.

bènda, *f.* band; fillet; head-band; bandeau; bandage. **bendàggio,** *m.* (*Med.*) bandaging; (*sport*) wrapping round boxer's fist. **bendàre,** *v.t.* to bandage; bind; blindfold. **bendàto,** *p.a.* bandaged; blindfold[ed]. **bendatúra,** *f.* bandages; bandaging.

bène, *ad.* well; right, proper; nicely; all right; clearly; fully, thoroughly; much; very, far; fast; firm; indeed; duly; really; quite. ¶ *m.* good; welfare; peace; mercy; love; gift; happiness; blessing; affection; property; benefit. (*pl.*) goods, possessions, chattels, estate, substance. *voler* ~ *a*, to love; like. *il* ~ *e il male*, good & evil. *ogni ben di Dio*, all sorts of good things.

benedettíno, *a. & m.* Benedictine.

benedétto, *a.* blessed; holy. **B**~, *m.* Benedict.

benedíre (*pr.* **-íco, -íci**), *v.t., i.r.* to bless.

benedizióne, *f.* benediction, blessing; consecration.

beneducàto, *a.* well-bred, well-mannered.

benefattóre, *m.* **-fattríce,** *f.* benefactor, -tress.

beneficàre, *v.t. & abs.* to benefit.

beneficènza, *f.* beneficence; bounteousness; charity, donation(s). *serata di* ~, (*Theat.*) benefit night.

beneficiàle, *a.* beneficial.

beneficiàrio, *a. & m.* beneficiary.

beneficiàto, *a. & m.* beneficiary; (*Eccl.*) beneficed (*clergyman*). ¶ *m.* incumbent.

benefício, -fízio, *m.* favour; profit; advantage; gain; (*Eccl.*) benefice, living.

benèfico (*pl.* **-èfici**), *a.* beneficent; beneficial; charitable; useful.

benemerènza, *f.* worth; desert; merit; service.

benemèrito, *a.* praiseworthy; meritorious; well-deserving.

beneplàcito, *m.* consent; approval; permission.

benèssere, *m.* well-being; welfare; prosperity; comfort.

benestànte, *a.* well-to-do; prosperous. ¶ *m.f.* well-to-do person. **benestàre,** *m.inv.* comfort, prosperity; (*Com.*) approval, consent.

benevolènza, *f.* benevolence; kindness.

benevolménte, *ad.* benevolently.

benèvolo, *a.* benevolent; kind.

benfàtto, *a.* well-made; well-shaped; fine; handsome.

Bengàla (il), *m.* Bengal. **bengalése,** *a. & m.* Bengali.

beniamíno, *m.* benjamin; darling.

benignaménte, *ad.* benignly; graciously; kindly.

benignità, *f.* benignity; kindliness; kindness.

benígno, *a.* benignant; benign; kind; mild.

beníno, *ad.* fairly well; pretty well. *per* ~, accurately; properly.

benintéso che, *ad.* on the understanding that; provided [that].

beníssimo, *ad.* very well; perfectly well; all right.

bennàto, *a.* well-born; noble; well-bred.

benóne, *ad.* very well; all right.

benpensànte, *a.* judicious, sensible.

benpensànti (i), *m.pl.* the orthodox.

benportànte, *m.f.* healthy or hale person.

benservíto, *m.* testimonial, character.

bensì, *ad.* certainly, assuredly; really. ¶ *c.* but.

bentornàto, *a. & m.* welcome.

benvedúto, -vísto, *a.* liked, esteemed

benvenùto, *a. & m.*, welcome.
benvolére, *m.* benevolence. ¶ *v.t.* to like; love. *farsi* ~, to make oneself liked or loved. *prendere a* ~, to take a liking for, become attached to.
benvolùto, *a.* loved; liked.
benžína, *f.* petrol, motor-spirit; benzine. *serbatoio della* ~, petroltank. *latta per* ~, petrol can.
benzoíno, *m.* benzoin. benžòlo, *m.* benzol.
beóne, *m.* drunkard.
bequàdro, *m.* natural (*Mus.*).
bèrbero, *a. & m.* Berber.
berciàre, *v.i.* to scream, yell.
bére (*pr.* bévo, bévi, béve), *v.t. ir.* to drink; absorb; imbibe; swallow. ~ *a centellini*, to sip. ~ *un uovo*, to swallow an egg. ¶ *m.* drinking; drink.
bergamòtta, *f.* bergamot (*orange, pear*). bergamòtto, *m.* bergamot (tree) (orange).
beríllo, *m.* beryl.
berlína, *f.* coach; saloon-(car) (*Motor.*); pillory. *metter alla* ~, to pillory.
Berlíno, *f.* Berlin.
Bermúde (le), *f.pl.* Bermuda[s].
Bèrna, *f.* Berne.
Bernàrdo, *m.* Bernard.
bernésco (*pl.* -éschi), *a.* burlesque; of the school of Berni (1497–1535).
bernòccolo, *m.* bump; swelling; knot. bernoccolúto, *a.* bumpy; knotty.
berrétta, *f.* cap. ~ *da notte*, nightcap. berrettíno, *m.* child's cap. berrétto, *m.* cap. ~ *basco*, beret. ~ *a busta*, forage cap.
bersagliàre, *v.t.* to shoot at; harass.
bersaglière, *m.* sharpshooter; bersagliere.
bersàglio, *m.* target; mark; (*fig.*) laughing-stock. ~ *rimorchiato*, (*Nav.*) towed target.
bèrta, *f.* raillery; jest; joke; (*Mech.*) pile-driver. *dar la* ~, to banter; joke. *B*~, *f.* Bertha. *il tempo che Berta filava* (*prov.*), the good old times.
berteggiàre, *v.t.* to mock, rally; rail at; banter.
bertelle, see *bretelle*.
bertolòtto, *ad. mangiare a* ~, to live scot-free.
bertúccia (*pl.* -úcce), *f.* ape; monkey. bertuccióne, *m.* baboon.
bestémmia, *f.* blasphemy; oath; curse. bestemmiàre (*pr.* -émmio, -émmi), *v.i.* (*aux.* avere) to curse; swear; *v.t.* to blaspheme; (*fig.*) grumble at, murder (*a language*).

bestemmiatóre, *m.* blasphemer; swearer.
béstia, *f.* beast, animal; (*pl.*) cattle, &c.; (*fig.*) fool, idiot. ~ *da soma*, beast of burden. *andar in* ~, to go (get) into a rage. bestiàccia, *f.* nasty beast. bestiàle, *a.* bestial; brutish; beastly. bestialità, *f.* bestiality; stupidity. *dire delle* ~, to talk nonsense. *fare delle* ~, to do foolish things. bestiàme, *m.* cattle, live-stock.
Betlèmme, *f.* Bethlehem.
betonièrà, *f.* cement-mixer.
béttola, *j.* public-house; tavern; wine-shop. bettolière, *m.* tavernkeeper, publican.
bettònica, *f.* betony.
betúlla, *f.* birch (tree).
bevànda, *f.* drink; beverage.
beveràggio, *m.* beverage; drinkmoney, tip.
beveratóio, *m.* horse-pond.
beveríno, *m.* trough (*bird-cage*).
beveróne, *m.* drench; drink; potion.
bevíbile, *a.* drinkable.
bevitóre, *m.* drinker.
bevúta, *f.* draught; drinking.
bezzicàre, *v.t.* to peck; tease.
bézzo, *m.* (*Venetian*) farthing.
biàcca, *f.* ceruse, white lead.
biàda, *f.* oats; corn; feed (*animal*); fodder. le biade, *f.pl.* the crops; corn.
biadàre, *v.t.* to give oats to, feed with oats.
Biancanéve, *f.* Snow White. ~ *e i sette nani*, S. & the Seven Dwarfs.
biancàstro, *a.* whitish. biancheggiaménto, *m.* whitening; whiteness. biancheggiànte, *p.a.* whitening, growing white. biancheggiàre, *v.i.* (*aux.* avere) to appear white; grow white; (*sea*) foam. bianchería, *f.* linen. ~ *da tavola*, table linen. ~ *da letto*, bed linen. ~ *di sotto*, underwear, underclothing (*women's*). bianchétto, *m.* whitewash; bleaching powder. bianchézza, *f.* whiteness. bianchíccio, *a.* whitish. bianchiménto, *m.* whitening; bleaching. biànco (*pl.* -ànchi), *a.* white; hoary; blank; clean; fair (*skin*). *la Casa B*~*a*, the White House. *il Mar B*~, the White Sea. *il Monte B*~, Mont Blanc. *armi bianche*, *f.pl.* side arms. *sciopero* ~, *m.* stay-in strike. ¶ *m.* white (*colour, man, &c.*); blank, blank space. ~ *di calce*, whitewash. *assegno in* ~, blank cheque. ~ *alla base*, (*Typ.*)

beard. **biancospíno** (*pl.* **bianco-spíni**), *m.* hawthorn; whitethorn.

biasciàre, biascicàre, *v.t.* to chew; munch; mumble.

biaṣimàbile, -èvole, *a.* blamable.

biaṣimàre, *v.t.* to blame; censure; reprove, upbraid. **biàṣimo,** *m.* blame.

bíbbia, *f.* Bible.

bíbita, *f.* drink; beverage; (*pl.*) refreshments. ~ *non alcoolica,* soft drink.

bíblico (*pl.* **bíblici**), *a.* biblical; Bible (*att.*); solemn, prophetic.

bibliòfilo, *m.* bibliophil(e), book-lover. **bibliografía,** *f.* bibliography. **bibliogràfico** (*pl.* **-àfici**), *a.* biblio-graphical. **bibliògrafo,** *m.* biblio-grapher. **bibliòmane,** *m.* biblio-maniac. **bibliomanía,** *f.* biblio-mania. **bibliotèca** (*pl.* **-èche**), *f.* library; series (of books). ~ *circolante,* circulating library. ~ *di prestito,* lending library. ~ *pubblica di prestito,* public lending library. **bibliotecàrio,** *m.* librarian.

bica (*pl.* **biche**), *f.* stack; rick; heap, pile.

bicchieràta, *f.* round (*of glasses*); drink; party.

bicchière, *m.* glass; drinking-glass; tumbler; (*Chem.*) beaker. **bic-chieríno,** *m.* small glass. ~ *da liquori,* liqueur glass. **bicchieróne,** *m.* large glass; long drink.

bicèfalo, *a.* bicephalous; two-headed.

bicíclétta, *f.* bicycle, cycle. ~ *da corsa,* racer. ~ *da strada,* roadster. ~ *a due posti,* tandem. **bici-clettína,** *f.* fairy-cycle, child's bicycle.

bicípite, *m.* biceps. ¶ *a.* two-headed.

biclorúro, *m.* (*Chem.*) bichloride.

bicòcca, *f.* small hill fort; hut, hovel; shanty.

bicolóre, *a.* in two colours.

bidèllo, *m.* beadle; usher.

bidènte, *m.* pitchfork; two-pronged fork.

bidóne, *m.* can, drum. ~ *per olio,* oil can (*storage*).

biecaménte, *ad.* obliquely, askew; sullenly, fiercely.

bièco, (*pl.* **-èchi**) *a.* squinting; cross; sullen; fierce. ¶ *ad.* obliquely; crossly.

bièlla, *f.* connecting-rod; strut, brace.

biennàle, *a.* biennial; lasting two years; recurring every two years (exhibitions, &c., e.g. *la Biennale* of

Venice, for modern art). **biènnio,** *m.* space (or period) of two years.

biètola, *f.* beet. ~ *zuccherina,* sugar beet.

bietolóne, *m.* -a, *f.* blockhead, simpleton.

biétta, *f.* wedge; cotter.

bifólco (*pl.* **-ólchi**), *m.* peasant; ploughman; labourer.

biforcaménto, *m.* -atúra, *f.* -aziòne, *f.* bifurcation; branching off, forking; (*-azione*) fork (*road*). **biforcàrsi,** *v.refl.* to bifurcate; branch off. **biforcàto, -úto,** *p.a.* bifurcated.

bifórme, *a.* biform.

bifrónte, *a.* double-faced.

bíga (*pl.* **-bíghe**), *f.* chariot, ancient two-horsed c.

bigamía, *f.* bigamy. **bígamo,** *m.* -a, *f.* bigamist. ¶ *a.* bigamous.

bigattièra, *f.* silkworm nursery.

bigattière, *m.* silkworm breeder.

bighellonàre, *v.i.* (*aux.* avere) to lounge; saunter, stroll.

bighellóne, *m.* idler; lounger.

bigheríno, *m.* thread lace.

bigio (*pl. m.* **bigi,** *f.* **bígie**), *a.* grey; dull. *pane* ~, brown bread. **bigiògnolo,** *a.* greyish.

bíglia, *or* **bilia,** *f.* billiard-pocket; b. ball; marble.

bigliàrdo, see *biliardo.*

bigliettàrio & **bigliettinàio,** *m.* booking clerk. **biglietteria,** *f.* ticket office, booking o.; box o.

bigliétto, *m.* note; card; ticket; bill. ~ *di visita,* visiting card. ~ *di ingresso alla piattaforma,* platform ticket. ~ *per posto riservato,* reserved seat t. ~ *semplice,* ~ *di andata,* single ticket (*Rly., &c.*). ~ *di andata e ritorno,* return ticket. ~ *a prezzo ridotto,* ~ *a tariffa ridotta,* cheap ticket. ~ *turistico,* ~ *circolare,* tourist ticket. ~ *d'abbonamento,* season ticket. ~ *di coincidenza,* transfer [ticket] (*tram, &c.*). ~ *di banca,* bank note. ~ *d'alloggio,* billet (*Mil.*). ~ *di libero transito (sulle ferrovie),* free-pass (*Rly.*). *ufficio* ~*i,* ticket-office, booking office.

bigóncia (*pl.* **-ónce**), *f.* tub; vat; bucket.

bigòtta, *f.* bigot; devotee. **bigotteria,** *f.* **bigottísmo,** *m.* bigotry. **bigòtto,** *a.* bigoted. ¶ *m.* bigot.

bilància (*pl.* **-ànce**), *f.* balance; scales; steelyard; trawl (*net*).

bilanciaménto, *m.* balancing; swing-ing. **bilanciàre,** *v.t.* to balance;

ponder. **bilancière,** *m.* pendulum; balance; beam (*engine*).

bilancíno, *m.* small scales, gold-scales; assay-balance.

bilàncio (*pl.* **-ànci**), *m.* budget; balance; balance sheet.

bilateràle, *a.* bilateral.

bíle, *f.* bile; anger.

bilènco, *a.* bandy-legged.

bília, *f.* billiard pocket; crooked stick.

biliàrdo, *m.* billiards; billiard-table; billiard room.

biliàre, *a.* biliary; bilious.

bilicàre, *v.t.* to poise; hold balanced. **bilicàrsi,** *v.refl.* to swing; see-saw.

bílico (*pl.* **bílichi**), *m.* equipoise; balance. *in* ~, in equilibrium; (*fig.*) irresolute.

bilíngue, *a.* bilingual. **bilinguísmo,** *m.* bilingualism.

bilióne, *m.* billion (*million millions*).

bilióso, *a.* bilious; (*fig.*) peevish.

bilústre, *a.* lasting ten years; ten years long.

bímbo, *m.* **-a,** *f.* child; little child; baby.

bimensíle, *a.* fortnightly; appearing twice a month.

bimestràle, *a.* appearing every two months.

bimotóre, *m.* (*Aviat.*) two-engined plane.

binàrio, *m.* track; rails; line (*of rails*). ~ *a doppio scartamento,* double gauge line. ~ *a scartamento ridotto,* narrow gauge line. ~ *di corsa,* mainline. ~ *cieco,* dead-end, siding. ~ *morto,* siding. ¶ *a.* binary (*Arith.*).

binascènza, *f.* birth of twins.

binàto, *a.* coupled. ¶ *a. & m.* twin.

bínda, *f.* jack, screw-jack (*Mech.*).

bíndolo, *m.* reel; (skein) winder; water-wheel; cheat; swindler.

binòccolo, *m.* opera-glass[es], field-glass[es]; binocular[s].

biòccolo, *m.* flock (*of wool*); tuft; flake (*snow*); wreath (*smoke*).

biochímica, *f.* biochemistry.

biografía, *f.* biography. **biogràfico** (*pl.* **-àici**), *a.* biographical. **biò-grafo,** *m.* biographer.

biología, *f.* biology. **biològico** (*pl.* **-ògici**), *a.* biological. **biòlogo** (*pl.* **-òlogi**), *m.* biologist.

biondeggiànte, *p.a.* golden; yellowish; ripening. **biondeggiàre,** *v.i.* (*aux.* avere) to grow yellow; turn golden; appear light.

biondézza, *f.* fairness, lightness (*colour*).

biondíccio, *a.* fairish.

biondíno, *a. & m.* **-a,** *f.* fair-haired, fair-haired person.

bióndo, *a.* fair; light; flaxen; blond. ¶ *m. & * **-a,** *f.* fair skinned person; blonde.

biòscia, *f.* melting snow; swill.

biòssido, *m.* dioxide.

bipartíre (*pr.* **-ísco, -ísci**), *v.t.* to divide in two; halve. **bipartírsi,** *v.refl.* to branch off in two directions; diverge. **bipartíto,** *a.* bipartite; halved. **bipartizióne,** *f.* bipartition.

bípede, *a.* biped(al). ¶ *m.* biped.

bipènne, *f.* two-edged axe.

biplàno, *m.* biplane (*Aviat.*).

bipósto, *m.* two-seater (*car, &c.*).

birbànte, *m.* rogue, rascal, knave, scamp; (*pop.*) son of a gun. **birbanteggiàre,** *v.i.* (*aux.* avere) to act like a rogue; play mischievous tricks. **birbantería,** *f.* knavery; rascally trick. **birbantésco** (*pl.* **-éschi**), *a.* rascally; knavish. **birbésco** (*pl.* **-éschi**), *a.* roguish; sly. **bírbo,** *m.* rogue; urchin. **birbonàta,** *f.* knavery; malicious trick. **birbóne,** *m.* rogue; rascal; scoundrel. ¶ *f.* rascally, wicked. **birbonería,** *f.* rascality; roguery. **birbonésco** (*pl.* **-éschi**), *a.* scoundrelly; knavish.

bírcio, *a.* squint-eyed; short-sighted.

birichinàta, *f.* child's prank; trick. **birichíno,** *a.* sly, cunning; artful. ¶ *m.* little rogue; urchin; scamp.

bíríllo, *m.* skittle, ninepin.

Birmània (la), *f.* Burma. **birmàno,** *a. & m.* Burmese; Burman.

biròccino, *m.* chaise; tilbury; light two-wheeled carriage. **biròccio,** *m.* cart.

bírra, *f.* beer, lager [beer]; ale. ~ *di barile,* draught beer. ~ *in bottiglia,* bottled b. ~ *nera,* ~ *scura,* dark lager. ~ *chiara,* light lager. **birràio,** *m.* brewer; publican. **birrería,** *f.* beer-shop; ale-house; public-house. **birróne,** *m.* strong beer.

bís *ad.* (*Lat.*) twice, once more. ¶ *i.* encore !

bisàccia (*pl.* **-àcce**), *f.* bag, wallet; knapsack.

bisàva & bisàvola, *f.* great-grand-mother.

bisàvo, bisàvolo, *m.* great-grand-father.

bisbètico (*pl.* **-ètici**), *a.* crabbed; ill-tempered; shrewish. **bisbètica,** *f.*

shrew. *La B~ Domạta*, The Taming of the Shrew.

bisbigliaménto, *m.* whispering. **bisbigliàre**, *v.i.* (*aux.* avere) to whisper. **bisbigliatóre**, *m.* **-tríce**, *f.* whisperer. **bisbíglio**, *m.* whisper. **bisbiglióne**, *m.* **-a**, *f.* (constant) whisperer; tell-tale.

bísca (*pl.* **bísche**), *f.* gambling house; g.-den. **biscai[u]òlo**, *m.* gambler.

Biscàglia, *f.* Biscay. *golfo di ~*, Bay of Biscay.

biscànto, *m.* bisected angle; double corner.

biscazzàre, *v.i.* (*aux.* avere) to gamble. **biscazzière**, *m.* marker (*billiards*); keeper of a gambling house; gambler.

bíschero, *m.* peg (*of a stringed instrument*); belaying pin; (*fig.*) fool (*impolite*).

bischétto, *m.* cobbler's bench.

bíscia (*pl.* **bísce**), *f.* snake; adder.

biscióne, *m.* large snake.

biscottàre, *v.t.* to bake over again; anneal; (*fig.*) perfect. **biscottería**, *f.* biscuit shop; b.-factory; biscuits. **biscottifício**, *m.* biscuit factory. **biscottíno**, *m.* small biscuit. **biscòtto**, *a.* annealed; recooked. ¶ *m.* biscuit; rusk.

biscròma, *f.* (*Mus.*) semi-quaver.

bisdòsso, *ad. montare a ~*, to ride barebacked.

bisdrúcciolo, *a. & m.* word (or line) with the last three syllables unaccented.

bisecàre (*pr.* **-éco**, **-échi**), *v.t.* to bisect.

bisestíle, *a.* leap (year).

bisettríce, *f.* bisector, bisecting line.

bisezióne, *f.* bisection.

bisíllabo, *a.* dissyllabic. ¶ *m.* dissyllable.

bislàcco (*pl.* **-àcchi**), *a.* extravagant; queer; odd; fantastic.

bislúngo (*pl.* **-lúnghi**), *a.* oblong.

bismàlva, *f.* marsh-mallow.

bismúto, *m.* bismuth.

bisnipóte, *m.f.* grand-nephew (or -niece); great-grandson (or -daughter); (*pl.*) posterity. **bisnònno**, *m.* great-grandfather. **-a**, *f.* great-grandmother; (*pl.*) *bisnonni*, ancestors.

bisógna, *f.* (*Lit.*) business; affair; plight. **bisognàre**, *v.i. impers.* (*aux.* essere) to be necessary; be obliged; want; lack. **bisognévole**, *a.* needy; necessary. ¶ *m. il ~*, the needful; the necessaries. **bisógno**,

m. want, need; necessity; distress; poverty. **bisognóso**, *a.* poor; needy; indigent.

bisónte, *m.* bison.

bisquàdro, *m.* bevel.

bissàre, *v.t.* to encore; repeat.

bistècca (*pl.* **-ècche**), *f.* beef-steak; *~ alla fiorentina*, grilled veal cutlets.

bisticciàre, *v.i.* (*aux.* avere) & **bisticciàrsi**, *v.refl.* to quarrel.

bistíccio, *m.* pun; play upon words; teasing; dispute, altercation, quarrel.

bistòrto, *a.* crooked; tortuous; deceitful.

bistrattàre, *v.t.* to ill-treat; maltreat.

bístori *or* **bisturí**, *m.inv.* (*Surg.*) bistoury; scalpel.

bisúnto, *a.* very greasy.

bitòrzolo, *m.* pimple; (*Bot. & Zool.*) knot.

bitta, *f.* bollard (*Naut.*).

bitúme, *m.* bitumen. **bituminóso**, *a.* bituminous. *carbone ~*, soft coal.

bivaccàre, *v.i.* (*aux.* avere) to bivouac. **bivàcco** (*pl.* **-àcchi**), *m.* bivouac.

bivàlve, *a.* bivalve.

bívio (*pl.* **bívi**), *m.* cross-road[s]; (*fig.*) parting of the ways.

bizantíno, *a.* Byzantine.

bízza, *f.* caprice, freak; wayward action.

bizzarraménte, *ad.* oddly. **bizzarría**, *f.* extravagance; oddity; queerness; caprice; whim. **bizzàrro**, *a.* bizarre; odd; queer; whimsical; freakish. *cavallo ~*, high-mettled horse.

bizzeffe (**a**), *ad. expr.* in large quantity; abundantly.

bizzóso, *a.* irritable; freakish; wayward, capricious.

blandaménte, *ad.* gently; softly; slowly. **blandíre** (*pr.* **-ísco**, **-ísci**), *v.t.* to cajole; entice; soothe. **blandízie**, *f.pl.* caresses; flatteries, blandishments. **blàndo**, *a.* soft; mild; subdued (*light*); bland; mellow.

blasonàre, *v.t.* to blazon. **blasóne**, *m.* blazon; coat of arms.

blateràre, *v.i.* (*aux.* avere) to chatter, babble.

blàtta, *f.* cockroach.

blènda, *f.* blende, sulphide of zinc. *~ picea*, pitchblende.

blèso, *a.* lisping. ¶ *m.* lisper.

blindaménto, *m.* armour-plating. **blindàre**, *v.t.* to armour; sheet (with metal). *carro blindato*,

armoured car. **blindatúra,** *f.*
(*Aero.*) fuselage.
bloccàre, *v.t.* to blockade (*Mil.*);
block (up) (*Mech.*); jam; lock.
blòcco (*pl.* **blòcchi**), *m.* block;
lump; bulk (*Com.*); blockade;
coalition, bloc (*Pol.*). *in* ~, in bulk,
in the lump. *posto di* ~, road block.
blu, *a. & m.inv.* blue; dark blue.
bluàstro, *a.* dark bluish. *cenere* ~,
ashy blue.
blúsa, *f.* blouse; smock (frock).
bòa, *m.inv.* boa (*wrap. serpent*). ¶ *f.*
buoy. ~ *d'ormeggio,* mooring buoy.
~ *di salvataggio,* life-buoy.
boàro, *m.* cow-herd; cattle-driver.
boàrio, *a.* of cattle; cattle (*att.*).
boàto, *m.* lowing, bellowing; rumbling,
roaring.
bobìna, *f.* bobbin, reel, spool; coil
(*Elec.*). **bobinàggio,** *m.* (*Elec.*)
winding.
bócca (*pl.* **bócche**), *f.* mouth;
opening; muzzle (*gun*); hydrant,
plug; person to be fed. *a* ~ *aperta,*
open mouthed. ~ *da fuoco,* gun,
cannon; piece of ordnance. ~
d'incendio, fire hydrant, f. plug.
boccaccésco (*pl.* **-éschi**), *a.* in the
style of Boccaccio.
boccàccia, *f.* wry mouth; large ugly
mouth.
boccàglio, *m.* nozzle.
boccàle, *m.* tankard, jug.
boccapòrto (*pl.* **-òrti**), *m.* hatch,
hatchway (*Naut.*).
boccatíno. *m.* speaking-tube, voice
pipe.
boccàta, *f.* mouthful; slap (on the
mouth). ~ *di fumo,* puff of smoke.
boccétta, *f.* phial. **boccettína,** *f.*
small phial; scent bottle.
boccheggiaménto, *m.* breathlessness.
boccheggiànte, *a.* gasping; at one's
last gasp, dying. **boccheggiàre,** *v.i.*
(*aux.* avere) to pant; gasp; breathe
one's last.
bocchétta, *f.* small mouth; small
aperture.
bocchétto, *m.* reel; bobbin.
bocchíno, *m.* mouth-piece. ~ *per
sigarette,* cigarette holder.
bòccia (*pl.* **bòcce**), *f.* decanter; water
bottle; bowl (*ball*); bud; (*fig.*) head;
(*pl.*) bowls (*game*). **bocciàre,** *v.t.*
to bowl (*at skittles*); black-ball;
plough (*exams*). **boccíno,** *m.* jack
(*bowls*). **bocciòdromo,** *m.* bowling-
green, b. alley. **bocciòfilo,** *a.*
addicted to bowls. ¶ *m.* lover of
bowls.

bocci[u]òlo, *m.* bud.
bóccola, *f.* boss; nut (*of a screw*);
ear-ring; buckle; socket; bush
(*Mech.*).
bocconàta, *f.* mouthful.   **boc-
concèllo,** *m.* bit, morsel.   **boc-
concíno,** *m.* bit; dainty bit.
boccóne, *m.* mouthful; bite; piece;
morsel. *fare una cosa a pezzi e a*
~*i,* to do a thing by fits and starts.
boccóni, *ad.* face downwards.
bodoniàno, *a.* in the style of Bodoni
(famous Italian printer 1740–1813).
Boèmia (la), *f.* Bohemia.   **boèmo,**
a. & m. Bohemian.
boèro, *a. & m.* Boer (*S.A.*).
Boèzio, *m.* Boethius.
bofonchiàre, *v.i.* (*aux.* avere) to
grumble; mutter.   **bofónchio,** *m.*
bumble bee; hornet. (Cf. *calabróne.*)
bògia, *f.* skin-spot; speck.
bòia, *m.* hangman; executioner.
boicottàggio, *m.* boycott; boycotting.
boicottàre, *v.t.* to boycott.
bòlgia, *f.* bag; wallet; pit (*of hell, in
Dante*).
bòlide, *m.* meteor, fire-ball; (*pop.*) car
driven at excessive speed.
bolína, *f.* (*Naut.*) bowline.
bólla, *f.* bubble; blister; pimple;
[papal] bull; note; ticket.
bollàre, *v.t.* to stamp; seal; (*fig.*)
brand. **bollatúra,** *f.* stamping (*of
documents*); branding.
bollènte, *a.* boiling; ardent; hot; fiery.
bollétta, *f.* bill; receipt.
bollettàrio, *m.* receipt-book; counter-
foil-book.
bollettíno, *m.* bulletin; gazette; list;
note.
bollíre (*pr.* **bóllo, bólli**), *v.i.* (*aux.*
avere) to boil; (*fig.*) be excited.
bollíto, *a. & pp.* boiled, *manzo* ~,
boiled beef. ¶ *m.* boiled meat.
bollitúra, *f.* boiling; ebullition.
bóllo, *m.* stamp; seal. ~ *a secco,*
embossed stamp.   *marca da* ~,
f. revenue stamp. *tassa di* ~, *f.*
stamp-duty. ~ [*dell'ufficio*] *postale,*
postmark.
bollóre, *m.* boil, boiling; boiling-
point; (*fig.*) great heat, ardour.
excitement.
bòlo, *m.* pill; bolus.
bolsàggine, *f.* shortness of breath;
broken wind; (*Vet.*) heaves.
bolscevíco (*pl.* **-víchi**), *a.* Bolshevist.
¶ *m.* Bolshevik, Bolshevist. **bolsce-
vísmo,** *m.* bolshevism.
bólso, *a.* asthmatic; broken-winded.
bómba, *f.* bomb; b. shell; type of

sweet; (*children's game*) prisoners' base. *a prova di* ~, bomb-proof. *rastrelliera da* ~*e*, bomb-rack (*Aviat.*). ~ *antisommergibile*, depth-charge. ~ *atomica*, atom[ic] bomb. *raccontar* (*delle*) ~*e*, to draw a long bow, tell tall stories. *tornar a* ~, to return to the point.

Bombài, *f.* Bombay.

bombàrda, *f.* mortar, bombard.

bombardaménto, *m.* bombardment; bombing. *apparecchio da* ~, (*Aviat.*) bomber, bombing plane. ~ *in picchiata*, ~ *a tuffo*, dive bombing. **bombardàre**, *v.t.* to bomb; bombard; shell. **bombardière**, *m.* bomber (*Aviat.*); bombardier; bomb-aimer (*Aviat.*).

bombettàre, *v.i.* (*aux.* avere) to tipple.

bómbola, *f.* pitcher, jug; bottle; cylinder (*gas*).

bomprèsso, *m.* bowsprit.

bonàccia (*pl.* -àcce), *f.* calm; c. sea; c. weather; dead calm; prosperity. ~ *piena*, flat calm. **bonacciàrsi**, *v.refl.* to calm down; become calm. **bonaccióne**, *m.* good-natured fellow.

bonalàna (*pl.* **bonelàne**), *f.* scoundrel.

bonànima, *f.* spirit. *la* ~ *di mio padre*, my poor (late) father.

bonariaménte, *ad.* plainly, simply; good-naturedly; in a friendly fashion. **bonarietà**, *f.* good nature; simplicity; kindliness. **bonàrio**, *a.* simple; good natured; kind; friendly.

bongustàio, *m.* connoisseur; gourmet.

bonífica, *f.* -aménto, *m.* reclamation; land reclamation; improvement. **bonificàre** (*pr.* -ífico, -ífichi), *v.t.* to improve; drain; reclaim; (*Com.*) grant a reduction or discount. **bonifício**, *m.* (*Com.*) discount allowance.

bòno (*for* **buòno**), *a.* good. ¶ *m.* good; cheque; bill.

bonomía, *f.* good-nature; affability; geniality.

bonsènso, *m.* sense, good sense.

bontà, *f.inv.* goodness; kindness; (*pl.*) virtues, gifts, qualities.

bontempóne, *m.* jolly fellow; cheerful soul; kindly carefree person.

bòra, *f.* bora; north-east wind.

boràce, *m.* borax.

borboglío, *m.* murmuring, rumbling; gurgle, gurgling.

borbottaménto, *m.* grumbling; mur-muring; muttering. **borbottàre**, *v.i.* (*aux.* avere) to mumble, mutter; grumble; murmur. **borbottío**, *m.* (continual) murmuring; grumbling.

bòrchia, *f.* ornamental metal disk, sequin; boss.

bordàglia, *f.* mob; rabble.

bordàre, *v.t. & i.* (*aux.* avere) to strike; knock, hit; hem; plank (*vessel*); work hard. **bordàta**, *f.* border; broadside; volley; (*Naut.*) tack.

bordatúra, *f.* bordering; hemming; planking; lining.

bordeggiàre, *v.i.* (*aux.* avere) to tack, beat to windward (*Naut.*).

bordèllo, *m.* brothel; noise, uproar.

bórdo, *m.* edge, border, brink, verge, fringe, rim, margin; brim; bank, side, shore, coast, strand; board, side (*ship*); tack (*Naut.*). ~ *libero*, (*Naut.*) free board load line. *andar a* ~, to go on board. *fuori* ~, overboard. *giornale di* ~, log-book; ~ *di marciapiede*, kerb, k. stone.

bordolése, *m.* claret; dressing for vines.

bordóne, *m.* pilgrim's staff; (*Mus.*) bass accompaniment. *tener* ~ *a*, to chime in with, support.

bòrea, *m.* north wind; Boreas. **boreàle**, *a.* boreal, north[ern].

borgàta, *f.* village, hamlet.

borghése, *a.* middle class (*att.*); bourgeois; homely, plain (*cooking*, &c.); common, ordinary, private; civil[ian]. ¶ *m.* middle-class person. **borghesía**, *f.* middle class[es]; bourgeoisie.

borghétto, *m.* hamlet; small village. **borghigiàno**, *m.* villager.

bórgo (*pl.* **bórghi**), *m.* large village; small (country) town; suburb.

Borgógna (la), *f.* Burgundy. *vino di B*~, *or il B*~, *m.* Burgundy (wine).

borgomàstro, *m.* burgomaster; mayor.

bòria, *f.* arrogance, haughtiness; conceit. **borióso**, *a.* haughty; proud; conceited; full of self importance.

bòro, *m.* (*Chem.*) boron.

bórra, *f.* stuff, stuffing (*cushion*, &c.); shavings; hair; floss (*silk*); trash, rubbish.

borràccia (*pl.* -àcce), *f.* water-bottle.

bórro, *m.* gully, ravine.

bórsa, *f.* purse; bag; pouch; [Stock] Exchange, [']change; (*fig.*) money. ~ *valori*, stock exchange. ~ *di*

studio, bursary; scholarship, exhibition. ~ *d'acqua calda*, hot-water bottle. ~ *nera*, black market.
borsai[u]òlo, *m.* pick-pocket. **borsàta,** *f.* purseful. **borseggiàre,** *v.t.* to rob, pick pocket(s). **borséggio,** *m.* theft (*of purse*); pick-pocketing. **borsellíno,** *m.* small purse; fob. **borsétta,** *f.* bag; (*lady's*) hand-bag; work-bag; wallet. **borsísta,** *m.* stock-jobber; bursar.
borzacchíno, *m.* half-boot.
boscàglia, *f.* underwood; wood. **boscai[u]òlo,** *m.* wood-cutter; woodman. **boscàta,** *f.* wood; grove. **boscheréccio** (*pl.* -écci), *a.* woodland (*att.*); sylvan; rustic, rural. **boschétto,** *m.* grove; thicket. **boscimàne,** *a. & m.* Bushman (*S.A.*). **bòsco** (*pl.* **bòschi**), *m.* wood; forest. **boscóso,** *a.* wooded.
Bòsforo, *m.* Bosp[h]orus.
bòsso, *m.* box (*wood & tree*); box-wood. **bòssolo,** *m.* box, small box, dice-box; box-wood. ~ *della cartuccia*, cartridge case.
botànica, *f.* botany. **botànico** (*pl.* -ànici), *a.* botanic(al). ¶ *m.* botanist. **botanísta,** *m.* botanist.
bòtola, *f.* trap-door; manhole.
bòtta, *f.* blow; thrust; heavy fall; shot; (*fig.*) gibe, quip; toad.
bottaccíno, *m.* small barrel.
bottàccio, *m.* barrel; gutter; mill-pond.
bótte, *f.* cask; barrel; tun; culvert. *a mezza* ~, (*Arch.*) semi-circular.
bottéga (*pl.* -éghe), *f.* shop; store; warehouse, business premises; concern. **bottegàio,** *m.* -a, *f.* shop-keeper, tradesman, -woman. **botteghíno,** *m.* booth; lottery-office; box-office (*Theat.*); pedlar's box.
bottíglia, *f.* bottle, flask, jar. **bottiglicría,** *f.* wine-shop; cellar; bar.
bottíno, *m.* booty; prize; spoils; loot; sewage; cess-pool.
bòtto, *m.* blow; stroke, toll (*bell*). *di* ~, at once, suddenly.
bottonàio, *m.* -a, *f.* buttonmaker.
bottoncíno, *m.* little button; stud; bud. ~ *da camicia*, shirt stud. ~ *di rosa*, rosebud. **bottóne,** *m.* button; stud; knob, handle; bud; pimple. ~ *da collo*, collar stud. ~ *i gemelli*, ~ *i da polsino*, *m.pl.* cuff (or sleeve) links. ~ *di una manovella*, crank-pin (*Mech.*). **bottonièra,** *f.* row of buttons.

botulísmo, *m.* (*Med.*) botulism.
bovàro, See *boaro*.
bòve, *m.* ox (cf. *bue*). **bovína,** *f.* cow-dung. **bovíno,** *a.* bovine; cattle (*att.*). ¶ *m.pl.* **bovini,** cattle.
bòzza, *f.* swelling, tumour; sketch; rough copy; draft; corbel; boss; stopper (*Naut.*); proof, pull, proof sheet (*Typ.*). ~ *corretta*, clean proof. *fare le* ~*e*, to pull (*proof*) (*Typ.*).
bozzétto, *m.* sketch; outline; rough draft; rough model.
bòżżima, *f.* (cloth) dressing; size. **bożżimàre,** *v.t.* to dress; size.
bozzelàio, *m.* seller of cocoons. **bòzzolo,** *m.* cocoon.
bozzóne, *m.* galley [proof] (*Typ.*).
bràca, *f.* sling; tackle; trouser-leg; (*pl.*) **bràche,** trousers, breeches; drawers.
bracàre, *v.i.* (*aux.* avere) to gossip, tattle.
braccàre, *v.t.* to search; search for; scent out.
braccétto, *m.* small arm (*body*). *a* ~, arm in arm.
braccéggio, *m.* beating (*hunt.*); searching; scenting. **bracchière,** *m.* whipper-in, huntsman.
bracciàle, *m.* armlet; arm-rest (*car*).
braccialétto, *m.* bracelet.
bracciànte, *m.* day-worker; labourer. **bracciàre,** *v.t.* to brace, trim (*sails*). dim. *bracciatella*.
bracciatúra, *f.* measure; number of yards in a piece of cloth; sounding.
bràccio, *m.* (*pl.f.* **bràccia** (*human*), *pl.m.* **bràcci** (*in other senses*) arm; wing (*building*); neck (*land*); flight (*stairs*); yard, ell; fathom; (*Carp.*) brace. **bracci[u]òlo,** *m.* arm (*of chair*). *sedia a bracciuoli*, arm-chair, easy chair.
bràcco (*pl.* **bràcchi**), *m.* beagle; hound. ~ *da fermo*, setter.
bràce, bràcia & bràgia, *f.* live coal, burning coal. **bràge,** *f.pl.* embers.
bràche, *f.pl.* trousers.
brachicèfalo, *a.* brachycephalic, short-headed.
brachière, *m.* bandage; truss.
brachigrafía, *f.* shorthand.
bracière, *m.* brazier; warming-pan. **braci[u]òla,** *f.* cutlet; chop.
bràdo, *a.* wild, untamed.
bràge, see *brace*.
bràma, *f.* longing; ardent desire. **bramàre,** *v.t.* to long for; covet.
bramíno, *m.* brahmin.

bramíre (*pr.* -ísco, -ísci), *v.i.* (*aux.* avere) to roar; bell (*stag*). **bramíto,** *m.* roar, roaring; bell (*stag*).

bramosaménte, *ad.* eagerly, ardently. **bramosía,** *f.* eager desire; longing; covetousness, greed. **bramóso,** *a.* eager, desirous; covetous; greedy.

brànca (*pl.* **brànche**), *f.* branch; claw; paw; flight (*stairs*).

brancàta, *f.* handful; band; set.

brànchie, *f.pl.* (*fish*) gills.

brancicàre (*pr.* **bràncico, brànci-chi**), *v.t.* to handle (roughly), feel, finger.

brànco (*pl.* **brànchi**), *m.* herd; flock; drove; crowd; band.

brancolàre, *v.i.* (*aux.* avere) to grope, stumble, feel one's way. **branco-lóni,** *ad.* gropingly.

brànda, *f.* folding-bed; camp-bed.

brandèllo, *m.* rag; tatter; shred; slip.

brandíre (*pr.* -ísco, -ísci), *v.t.* to brandish.

bràndo, *m.* (*Poet.*) sword.

bràno, *m.* slip; fragment; shred; extract; passage; piece.

Brasíle (**il**), *m.* Brazil. *nocciole del B ~,* *f.pl.* Brazil nuts. **brasiliàno,** *a. & m.* Brazilian.

bravàccio, *m.* swaggerer, blusterer, bully. **bravaménte,** *ad.* bravely; stoutly; gallantly; cleverly. **bra-vàre,** *v.t.* to threaten. *v.i.* (*aux.* avere) to brag, bluster. **bravàta,** *f.* bravado, bluster, brag[ging]. **bràvo,** *a.* able; brave; clever; honest; capable; competent. ¶ *m.* bandit; cut-throat. ¶ *i.* bravo! hurrah, -ay! well done! hear! hear! **bravóne,** *m.* boaster. **bravúra,** *f.* bravery, skill, cleverness.

bréccia (*pl.* **brécce**), *f.* breach; gap; breccia. **brecciàme,** *m.* road metal.

brefotròfio, *m.* foundling-hospital.

Brèma, *f.* Bremen.

brénna, *f.* jade; hack; old horse (or mare).

brénta, *f.* measure of wine (100 litres).

brentína, *f.* measure of wine (50 litres).

Bretàgna (**la**), *f.* Brittany; Britain. *la Gran ~,* Great Britain.

bretèlle, *f.pl.* braces.

brètone, *a. & m.* Breton.

brève, *a.* short; brief. *fra ~,* shortly. ¶ *m.* brief (*pope's pastoral letter*). **breveménte,** *ad.* shortly; briefly.

brevettàre (*pr.* -étto, -étti), *v.t.* to patent; license. **brevétto,** *m.* brevet; patent; diploma, certificate; licence. *~ [d'invenzione],* [letters] patent.

breviàrio, *m.* breviary.

breviloquènza, *f.* concise eloquence.

brevità, *f.* brevity.

brézza, *f.* breeze. **brezzeggiàre,** *v.i.* (*aux.* essere) to blow a breeze.

briàco (*pl.* -àchi), *a.* drunk. **bria-cóne,** *m.* drunkard.

brícco (*pl.* **brícchi**), *m.* tankard, large jug.

bríccola, *f.* catapult.

briccónàta, *f.* low trick. **bric-cóne,** *m.* rogue; rascal. **bricco-neggiàre,** *v.i.* (*aux.* avere) to cheat; swindle. **bricconería,** *f.* roguery.

bríciola, *f.* crumb.

bríciolo, *m.* bit, tiny morsel.

bríga (*pl.* **bríghe**), *f.* care, trouble; vexation; strife. *attaccar ~ con,* to quarrel with, pick a quarrel.

brigadière, *m.* brigadier (*Mil.*); sergeant (*carabinieri*).

brigantàggio, *m.* brigandage. **bri-gànte,** *m.* brigand; sharper.

brigantíno, *m.* brigantine.

brigàre (*pr.* **brígo, bríghi**), *v.t.* to solicit. *v.i.* (*aux.* avere) to intrigue; strive.

brigàta, *f.* company; brigade; party of friends.

brigidíno, *m.* aniseed wafer biscuit.

bríglia, *f.* bridle; (*Naut.*) stay. *a ~ sciolta, a tutta ~,* at full speed. *~ di bompresso,* (*Naut.*), bob-stay.

brigóso, *a.* difficult, troublesome.

brillaménto, *m.* splendour; glitter; explosion, blowing up (*mine*).

brillantàre, *v.t.* to cut facets on, cut (*brilliant, diamond*).

brillànte, *a. & m.* brilliant, shining, glittering; sparkling.

brillàre, *v.i.* (*aux.* avere) to glitter; sparkle; shine (*lit. & fig.*). *far ~ una mina,* to blow up a mine.

bríllo, *a.* tipsy, half-drunk, half-seas over (*fig.*).

brína, *f.* hoar-frost.

brinàto, *a.* covered with hoar-frost; (*hair*) becoming grey, grizzled.

brindàre, *v.i.* (*aux.* avere) to toast; drink a health.

brindèllo, *m.* rag; tatter.

bríndisi, *m.inv.* toast (*to one's health*).

brío, *m.* animation; spirit, vivacity; sprightliness; (*Mus.*) brio.

briónia, *f.* bryony.

brióso, *a.* sprightly; vivacious; animated; spirited.

bríscola, *f.* briscola (*card-game*); trump (*card*).

Britannia (**la**), *f.* Britain. **bri-tànnico,** *a.* British; Britannic.

brívido, *m.* shiver; shudder.
brizzolàre, *v.i.* to speckle. **brizzolàto**, *p.a.* speckled, growing grey. **brizzolàrsi**, *v.refl.* to turn (grow) grey. **brizzolatúra**, *f.* speckling, becoming grey.
bròcca (*pl.* **bròcche**), *f.* pitcher; jug; ewer. **brocchétta**, *f.* small jug. **bròcco** (*pl.* **bròcchi**), *m.* shoot, sprout; curl.
bròccolo, *m.* broccoli.
bròda, *f.* weak broth; tasteless soup.
bròdo, *m.* broth; soup obtained from boiled meat; clear soup. ∼ *di bue*, beef tea. ∼ *lungo*, weak broth; (*fig.*) tedious discourse. *tutto fa* ∼, everything comes in handy.
brogliàre, *v.i.* (*aux.* avere) to stir, move; intrigue. *v.t.* embroil.
brogliàzzo, *m.* day-book.
bròglio, *m.* plot; intrigue.
bròlo, *m.* enclosure, garden, orchard.
bromúro, *m.* bromide.
bronchiàle, *a.* bronchial.
bronchíte, *f.* bronchitis.
bróncio (*pl.* **brónci**), *m.* grudge; ill-temper; sulkiness; pout, pouting. *fare il* ∼, to pout, sulk. **broncíre**, *v.i.* (*aux.* avere) to pout.
brónco, *m.* stump; stem; (*pl.*) **brónchi**, brushwood; (*Med.*) (the) bronchial tubes.
broncopolmoníte, *f.* (*Med.*) bronchial pneumonia.
brontolaménto, *m.* murmuring; complaint. **brontolàre**, *v.i.* (*aux.* avere) to mutter; grumble; groan; rumble. **brontolío**, *m.* (constant) grumbling; murmuring; muttering.
brontolóne, *m.* grumbler.
bronzàre, *v.t.* to bronze.
bronzína, *f.* (*Mach.*) bearing.
bronzíno, *a.* bronzed; sun-burnt; dark. *morbo* ∼, *m.* Addison's disease.
brónżo, *m.* bronze (*metal & work of art*).
brucàre (*pr.* **brúco**, **brúchi**), *v.t.* to strip off leaves from; browse on.
bruciacchiàre, *v.t.* to scorch; (*frost*) blacken.
bruciaménto, *m.* burning; scalding.
bruciapélo, *ad.* as in: *a* ∼, point-blank.
bruciàre (*pr.* **brúcio**, **brúci**), *v.t. & i.* (*aux.* essere) to burn, set on fire; be on fire; cauterize. **bruciàta**, *f.* roast chestnut. **bruciatíccio**, *m.* burnt material, thing burning, odour of burning. **bruciatúra**, *f.* burn;

burning; scald. **brucióre**, *m.* smart; burning sensation.
brúco (*pl.* **brúchi**), *m.* grub; caterpillar; worm. ¶ *a.* bare; wretched. *ignudo* ∼, stark naked.
brughièra, *f.* heath; moor; heather.
brulicàme, *m.* swarm; swarming.
brulicàre, *v.i.* to swarm, be crawling (with = *di*). **brulichío**, *m.* swarm, -ing; commotion.
brúllo, *a.* naked, bare.
brúm, *m.inv.* brougham; cab; carriage.
brúma, *f.* depth of winter; cold damp weather; ship-worm. **brumàle**, *a.* wintry, foggy.
brunétto, *a.* brownish (also *brunettino*, *brunastro*).
bruníre (*pr.* **-ísco**, **-ísci**), *v.t.* to burnish. **brunitóio**, *m.* burnisher (*inst.*); polishing stick. **brunitóre**, *m.* **-tóra**, *f.* burnisher (*pers.*). **brunitúra**, *f.* burnishing; polishing; burnish.
brúno, *a.* dark; brown. ¶ *m.* brown; mourning; crape; dark complexioned person; ∼**a**, *f.* brunette.
brunòtto, *a.* deep brown,
brúsca, *f.* horse-brush.
bruscaménte, *ad.* sharply, brusquely, bluntly.
bruschétto, *a.* tart, sourish. **bruschézza**, *f.* tartness; sourness.
bruschíno, *m.* dim. of *brusca*. (horse) brush; brush with strong bristles used by washerwomen, leather dressers, &c.
brúsco (*pl.* **brúschi**), *a.* sharp (*taste*); brusque (*manners*); cloudy (*weather*). (*fig.*) *tempi bruschi*, difficult times. *tra brusco e lusco*, at twilight. *con le brusche*, bluntly, brusquely. ∼*a svolta*, sharp turn (*road*).
brúscolo, *m.* mote, grain, tiny piece of straw or wood.
brusío, *m.* hubbub, noise, chatter; large quantity of things or persons.
brusíre (*pr.* **-ísco**, **-ísci**), *v.i.* (*aux.* avere) to hum; rumble.
Brussèlle, *f.* Brussels. *broccoletti di B*∼, *m.pl.* Brussels sprouts.
brúto, *m.* brute; wild animal; violent person. ¶ *a.* brutal, irrational, violent. *forza* ∼*a*, brute force.
bruttàre, *v.t.* to soil, dirty, stain; defile. **bruttézza**, *f.* ugliness.
brútto, *a.* ugly; unpleasant; repellant; bad; filthy; foul; sad; troubled; confused. *brutta notizia*, bad news. *alle brutte*, at the worst. *brutta copia*, foul copy. *venire alle brutte*, to begin quarrelling. **brut-**

túra, *f.* filth; something ugly or shameful; base or shameful action.

brúzzico, brúzzolo, *m.* (first light of) dawn.

buàccio (*pl.* -àcci), *m.* (*from* bue) (*fig.*) fool, dunce. dim. buacciuòlo, *m.* young fool.

buàggine, *f.* stupidity.

bùbbola, *f.* hoopoe; idle story; fable; nonsense.

bubbolàre, *v.i.* (*aux.* avere) to rumble; growl; roar; tremble. *v.t.* to hoax, pilfer, cheat; waste (*money*).

bubbolàta, *f.* nonsensical talk; story full of lies.

bubbolièra, *f.* collar with bells.

bubbolío, *m.* rumble (*as of thunder, &c.*).

bùbbolo, *m.* small bell for animal's collar. bubbolóne, *m.* -óna, *f.* great storyteller; hoaxer.

bubbóne, *m.* swelling (or tumour of the lymphatic glands) in the groin or armpit. bubbònico (*pl.* -ònici), *a.* bubonic, as in *peste ~a*, bubonic plague.

búca (*pl.* búche), *f.* hole; pit; pocket; cavity; cave; ditch; trench; grotto; underground chapel, oratory or restaurant (cf. *B ~ di s. Ruffillo* at Florence). *~ cieca*, pitfall, trap. *~ del suggeritore*, prompter's box. *~ delle lettere*, letter box. *~ del biliardo*, (billiard) pocket.

bucacchiàre, *v.t.* to bore (*holes*).

bucanéve, *m.* snow-drop.

bucàre (*pr.* búco, búchi), *v.t.* to bore, pierce; punch; prick; puncture; pit; broach; tap; lance (*tumour*); evade; get past. *~ la palla*, to miss the ball. bucàrsi, *v.refl.* to prick oneself.

bucàto, *a. & p.p.* bored, pierced, riddled. *aver le mani ~e*, to let money slip through one's hands (or one's fingers), spend lavishly. ¶ *m.* wash[ing]; bleaching; clean linen. *di ~*, clean, very white. *questa roba va in ~*, these things are going to the wash. *riportare il ~*, to bring back the wash[ing].

bucatúra, *f.* piercing, boring; hole.

bùccia (*pl.* búcce), *f.* peel; rind; bark; skin; shell; coating; crust; pod. *aver la ~ dura*, to be strong or tough (*pers*). *la ~ gli preme*, he is in fear of his life. *riveder le bucce a uno*, to give one a dressing down, criticize one severely.

búccina, *f.* (Roman) trumpet. bucci-

nàre, *v.t.* to proclaim, trumpet abroad. *v.i.* (*aux.* avere) sound the trumpet.

búccio, *m.* outer skin, outer layer of hide.

búccola, *f.* earing; curl; loop (*of letter*).

bucheràre, -erellàre, *v.t.* to riddle, pierce with many holes.

bucinàre, *v.t.* to murmur, whisper. bucinàrsi, *v.refl.* to be rumoured.

bucintòro, *m.* Bucentaur; state barge of Venice under the republic.

búco (*pl.* búchi), *m.* hole, aperture, orifice; cavity; hiding-place, retreat; dimple. *~ d'aria*, air-pocket. *fare un ~ nell'acqua*, to fail in an undertaking, have one's labour for nothing. *tappare dei buchi*, to pay one's debts. *dare nel ~*, to hit the nail on the head. *a ~*, exactly, precisely; nice(ly).

bucòlica, *f.* pastoral poetry. bucòlico (*pl.* -òlici), *a.* bucolic; pastoral.

buddísmo, *m.* Buddhism. buddísta (*pl.* -ísti), *m. & a.* Buddhist, Buddhistic(al).

budellàme, *m.* entrails, guts, bowels. budèllo, *m.* (*pl.* budella, *f.*; (*fig.*) budelli) bowel; gut; intestine.

budíno, *m.* pudding.

búe (*pl.* buoi), *m.* ox; (*fig.*) dunce, blockhead.

búfalo, *m.* buffalo.

bufàre, *v.i.* (*aux.* essere) to snow with gusts of wind.

bufèra, *f.* squall of rain, snow or hail; gust; storm. *~ di neve*, snowstorm, blizzard.

búffa, *f.* hood; visor; gust or blast (of wind).

buffàre, *v.t.* (*at draughts or chess*) to huff; *v.i.* (*aux.* avere) to blow, puff. buffàta, *f.* gust (*of wind*), puff (*of air*); (*draughts*) huff.

buffétto, *m.* fillip or flip of the finger. *pan ~*, very light bread.

búffo, *a.* comical; queer; ridiculous; amusing. *opera ~a, f.* comic opera. ¶ *m.* buffoon, comic actor or singer; puff of wind.

buffonàta, *f.* buffoonery; comical words or action.

buffóne, *m.* buffoon (*fig.*) untrustworthy person. buffoneggiàre, *v.i.* (*aux.* avere) to play the buffoon. buffonería, *f.* buffoonery.

buffonésco (*pl.* -éschi), *a.* comical.

bugía, *f.* lie, falsehood; flat candlestick or lamp of similar pattern. bugiàrdo, *a.* lying. ¶ *m.* liar.

bugigàttolo, *m.* small, dark room; stuffy hole.

bugióne, *m.* great lie; (*fam.*) great liar.

bugli[u]òlo, *m.* bucket; pail.

búgna, *f.* ashlar; (*Naut.*) clew (*of sail*).

búgno, *m.* bee-hive; (*pop.*) swelling.

búgnola, *f.* basket of plaited straw; tool-box; (*fig.*) pulpit, teacher's desk.

búgnolo, *m.* small straw basket.

bugràne, *f.* buckram.

búio (*pl.* **búi**), *a.* dark. ¶ *m.* darkness, dark; (*fig.*) prison. ~ *pesto,* pitch dark[ness].

búlbo, *m.* bulb.

Bulgaría (la), *f.* Bulgaria. **búlgaro,** *a. & m.* Bulgarian, Bulgar. ¶ *m.* Russia leather.

bulicàre (*pr.* **búlico, búlichi**), *v.i.* to seethe, bubble; boil up.

bulinàre, *v.t.* to engrave. **bulíno,** *m.* burin; graver; graving-tool.

bullétta, *f.* (*cf. bolletta*) small nail, tack; tin-tack; stud; ticket. **bullettàio** (*pl.* **-ài**), *m.* nail-maker, nail-merchant. **bullettàme,** *m.* collection of nails.

bullettíno, *m.* (*cf. bollettino*) bulletin; report; list.

bullóne, *m.* bolt.

buomprèsso, *see* bompresso.

b[u]ongustàio, *m.* connoisseur; gourmet. **b[u]ongústo,** *m.* taste, good taste.

buòno, *a.* good; sound; kind; nice; fine; boon (*companion*); palatable; fit; right; proper; safe. In compounds the diphthong **uo** may give place to the simple vowel **o** whenever the accent falls elsewhere, e.g. *bonalàna, bonamàno, bonsénso, boncuòre, bongustàio, &c. alla buona,* simply, without ceremony; plain, plainly. *di buon'ora,* early. *alla buon'ora* (*or alla bonora*), at last! (excl. of satisfaction). *far di buono,* to be in earnest. ~ *a nulla,* good-for-nothing. *con le buone,* gently, with kindness. *a buon diritto,* rightly. *Dio ce la mandi buona,* may we get out of this safely! *in buona,* at peace. ¶ *m.* good (person or thing); bond, commercial obligation; Treasury bill (~ *del Tesoro*); order for payment; warrant; debenture; written acknowledgement of indebtedness; coupon; cheque; relief-ticket, (~ *di beneficenza*) ~ *di consegna,* delivery note. ~ *di sbarco,* ~ *di scaricazione,* landing order or permit.

b[u]onuòmo, *m.* simple, good-natured man.

buràre, *v.t. & i.* to burn slowly; smoulder.

burattinàio, *m.* puppet-showman. **burattinàta,** *f.* puppet-show. **burattíno,** *m.* puppet; marionette; (*fig.*) light-headed person, trifler; buffoon.

burbànza, *f.* arrogance; ostentation. **burbanzóso,** *a.* haughty; ostentatious.

búrbera, *f.* windlass; capstan.

búrbero, *a.* cross, morose; scowling; surly.

búrchio, *m.* flat-bottomed canal boat.

burétta, *f.* graduated glass tube.

burèlio, *m.* drugget.

buriàna, *f.* squall; snow-storm; cold wind.

burína, *f.* (*cf. bolina*) bow-line. *andar di* ~, to go or sail swiftly.

búrla, *f.* jest; joke; fun; innocent trick. *da* ~, *per* ~, as a joke, in jest. *mettere in* ~, to treat as a joke. *pigliarsela in* ~, to take (something) as a joke. **burlàre,** *v.t.* to ridicule; make a fool of. *v.i.* (*aux.* avere) to jest; joke. **burlàrsi (di)** *v.refl.* to laugh at; make fun of.

burlésco (*pl.* **-éschi**), *a.* burlesque; comical; absurd.

burlétta, *f.* joke; farce; vaudeville.

burlévole, *a.* farcical, comical.

burlóne, *m.* joker, jester.

buròcrate, *m.* bureaucrat. **burocràtico** (*pl.* **-àtici**), *a.* bureaucratic. **burocrazía,** *f.* bureaucracy; (*fig.*) red-tape.

burràsca, *f.* storm. **burrascóso,** *a.* stormy.

búrro, *m.* butter.

burróne, *m.* deep ravine, gorge.

búsca, *f.* quest; search. **buscàre** (*pr.* **búsco, búschi**), *v.t.* to get; catch; procure; obtain by search or effort; fetch; gain. **buscàrsi,** *v.refl.* to earn; procure; incur; catch (*cold*).

buscheràre, *v.t.* to cheat, deceive, swindle. **buscheràta,** *f.* deception; error; nonsense.

buscherío, *m.* hubbub, noise, tumult; crowd.

busécca, *f.* (*Cook.*) highly spiced veal tripe.

busíllis, *m.* difficulty, as in *qui sta il* ~, here lies the difficulty. (From a misreading of *Lat. in diebus illis.*)

bússa, *f.* blow; slap; knock; (*pl.*) beating, thrashing. **bussàre,** *v.t.* to strike, slap. *v.i.* (*aux.* avere) to knock (at a door). **bussàta,** _f._ knocking; blow; damage.

bussétto, _m._ box-wood polisher used by shoe-makers.

bússola, _f._ mariner's compass; magnetic needle; compass-box; (_Mech._) bush; (_draught_) screen; inner door; (_fig._) reckoning, direction. ~ _giroscopica,_ gyro compass. _rilevamento_ ~, (_Naut._) _m._ compass bearing.

bussolàia, _f._ box-hedge.

bussolòtto, _m._ dice-box.

bústa, _f._ envelope; case for papers. ~ _affrancata,_ stamped envelope. ~ _paga,_ pay-packet.

bustàio, _m._ -a, _f._ stay-maker.

bústo, _m._ corset; bust.

butírro, _m._ butter.

buttafuòri, _m.inv._ call-boy.

buttalà, _m.inv._ clothes-horse.

buttàre, _v.t._ to throw, fling; throw away (also _buttar via_), squander; throw up, emit. _v.i._ (_aux._ avere) to shoot (_of plants_). **buttàrsi,** _v.refl._ to throw oneself down; lie down; settle, settle down (_of birds, rain, &c._).

buttasèlla, _m.inv._ (_Mil._) signal to saddle horse.

butteràto, _a._ pock-marked. **búttero,** _m._ pock-mark; mounted herdsman (of the Maremma).

buzzicàre, _v.i._ to stir, move.

búżżo, _m._ paunch; belly (_of animals_).

bużżúrro, _m._ (Swiss) hawker of roast chestnuts, &c.; rough fellow.

C

C, c (_ci_) _f._ the letter C.

ca', _f._ contr. of _casa,_ house.

càbala, _f._ cabal, clique, caucus; faction; intrigue; art of foretelling numbers in public lotteries. **cabalístico** (_pl._ -**ístici**), _a._ cabalistic.

cabalóne, _m._ intriguer.

càbbala, _f._ Cabbala; Jewish oral tradition; esoteric doctrine.

cabestàno, _m._ winch, capstan.

cabína, _f._ cabin; cab (_locomotive_); (_Aero._) cockpit; cage, car (_funicular_); box; hut. ~ _telefonica,_ telephone call-box. ~_di blocco_ or ~ _di manovra,_ signal-box (_Rly._). ~_da bagno,_ bathing-hut.

cablogràmma (_pl._ -**gràmmi**), _m._ cablegram, cable.

cabotàggio, _m._ coasting-trade. **cabotière,** _m._ captain of a coasting vessel. **cabotièro,** _a._ coasting. ¶ _m._ coasting vessel, coaster.

cacào, _m._ cocoa; cacao, cacao (tree).

càccia (_pl._ **càcce**), _f._ chase, hunt, hunting, shooting; game. ~ _riservata,_ game reserve. _aeroplano da_ ~, or _caccia,_ _m._ fighter (plane). ~ _a reazione,_ jet-fighter. _cane da_ ~, sporting dog. _licenza di_ ~, shooting licence, game-licence.

cacciabombardière, _m._ (_Aviat._) fighter-bomber.

cacciagióne, _f._ game; venison.

cacciamósche, _m.inv._ fly-flap.

cacciapàssere, _m.inv._ scarecrow (also **spaventapàsseri**).

cacciàre (_pr._ **càccio, càcci**), _v.t._ to chase, hunt, pursue; drive, drive in, drive out; utter (_cry, &c._); discharge; hurl; (_v.i._) (_aux._ avere) to hunt, go hunting; shoot, go shooting. **cacciàrsi,** _v.refl._ to plunge (in), drive (in), thrust (oneself) (in); hide oneself; intrude. ~ _in testa una cosa,_ to get something into one's head, to be obstinate.

cacciàta, _f._ hunting; hunt, hunting party; expulsion.

cacciatóra, _f._ shooting-jacket. **cacciatóre,** _m._ hunter; huntsman; sportsman; light infantryman (for reconnaissance. ~ _i a cavallo,_ light cavalry. **cacciatorpedinière,** _m._ _inv._ (_Nav._) destroyer. **cacciatríce,** _f._ huntress; sportswoman. **cacciavíte,** _m.inv._ screw-driver.

càchi, _m.inv._ khaki (_fruit & colour_). _divisa_ ~, khaki uniform.

cachínno, _m._ loud, empty laughter.

caciàio, _m._ -**àia,** _f._ cheese-maker. **càcio** (_pl._ **càci**), _m._ cheese. _andar d'accordo come pane e_ ~, _esser pane e_ ~, to be hand and glove, to be intimate, be in agreement. _cascare come il_ ~ _sui maccheroni,_ to turn up opportunely. **caciocavàllo,** _m._ a hard Sicilian cheese.

cacofonía, _f._ cacophony, discord.

càcto, _m._ cactus.

cadàvere, _m._ corpse, dead body. **cadavèrico** (_pl._ -**èrici**), _a._ cadaverous, corpse-like; ghastly, deadly pale.

cadènte, _p.a._ falling; declining, setting (_sun_); ending; enfeebled, decrepit. **cadènza,** _f._ cadence; rhythm, rhythmical movement; tune; fall (_voice_); time, step; pause; ending; (_Mus._) cadenza. **cadenzàto,** _p.a._

cadenced; rhythmical; in time.
cadére, *v.i.ir.* (*aux.* essere) to fall; tumble; drop; decline; sink; set; fail; flag; lapse; hang down.
cadétto, *a. & m.* younger (*son, brother*); cadet; junior, minor.
Càdice, *f.* Cadiz.
caducità, *f.* frailty; perishableness; transience, transiency; decay; (*Law*) loss of a right. **cadúco** (*pl.* **-úchi**), *a.* frail; perishable; fleeting, transient; short-lived; decrepit; (*Law*) lapsed, statute barred. *mal* ~, epilepsy.
cadúta, *f.* fall, drop; downfall, collapse. ~ *d'acqua,* water-fall. ~ *dei prezzi,* slump. **cadúto,** *p.a. & m.* fallen, dead (*in battle*); ruined; lost. *monumento ai* ~*i,* war memorial.
caffè, *m.inv.* coffee; coffee-house, café. *di color* ~, coffee-coloured. ~ *espresso,* cup of coffee made expressly for a customer (by machine and strainer*).* ~ *e latte* or *caffelatte,* coffee with milk, café au lait.
caffettièra, *f.* coffee-pot. **caffettière,** *m.* coffee-house keeper.
càffo, *a. & m.* odd (*number*); chance. *pari e* ~, odd & even (*game*).
cafóne, *m.* rude fellow, boor; peasant (*S. Italy*).
càfro, *a. & m.* Kaf[f]ir (*S. Africa*).
cagionàre, *v.t.* to cause; occasion; give rise to; produce. **cagióne** *f.* cause; reason; motive. *a* ~ *di,* on account of. **cagionévole,** *a.* weak, sickly, delicate; *salute* ~, poor health. **cagionevolézza,** *f.* weakness; sickliness.
cagliàre, *v.i.* (*aux.* essere) & **cagliàrsi,** *v.refl.* to curdle; clot. **càglio,** *m.* rennet.
càgna, *f.* bitch.
cagnàra, *f.* barking (*of dogs*), baying; bawling; uproar, hubbub; fuss; confusion. **cagnésco** (*pl.* **-éschi**), *a.* currish; snappish; surly. *guardare qualcuno in* ~, to scowl at someone. **cagnolíno,** *m.* pet dog, lap dog; puppy.
cagnòtto, *m.* dependant, hanger-on; (*formerly*) hired bully, spy.
Caìna, *f.* circle of hell reserved by Dante for traitors (*Inf. XXXII*).
Caíno, *m.* Cain; (*fig.*) fratricide; murderer.
Càiro (il), *m.* Cairo.
càla, *f.* cove, small bay.
calabrése. *a. & m.* Calabrian; native of Calabria. **Calàbria (la),** Calabria.
calabróne, *m.* hornet; bumble-bee.

calafatàre, *v.t.* to caulk. **calafàto,** *m.* caulker.
calamàio (*pl.* **-ài**), *m.* ink-pot; ink-well. **calamàro,** *m.* squid, cuttle-fish; dark ring round the eye.
calamístro, *m.* curling-tongs.
calamíta, *f.* magnet.
calamità, *f.* calamity; disaster. **calamitàre,** *v.t.* to magnetize. **calamitóso,** *a.* calamitous; disastrous.
càlamo, *m.* reed; Indian cane; reed-pipe; quill; arrow-shaft.
calàndra, *f.* wood-lark. **calandrino,** *m.* simpleton, naïve person (*from a character in Boccaccio*). **calàndro,** *m.* tawny pipit.
calànte, *p.a.* sinking, declining; setting; decreasing. *luna* ~, waning moon. *moneta* ~, light weight coin.
calàppio (*pl.* **-àppi**), *m.* snare; slip-knot.
calaprànzi, *m.inv.* service-lift, dumb-waiter.
calàre, *v.t.* to lower; let down; strike (*sails, &c.*). (*v.i.*) (*aux.* essere) to fall; sink; set; decline, droop; ebb; draw in, become shorter; decay. **calàta,** *f.* lowering, descent; fall; invasion; slope, declivity; inclined plane; quay, wharf. ~ *del sipario,* fall of the curtain (*Theat.*). ~ *del sole,* setting of the sun.
càlca, *f.* dense crowd, throng; press.
calcafógli, *m.inv.* paper-weight.
calcàgno, *m.* (*pl.f.* **-àgna,** *pl.m.* **-àgni**) heel. *menar le* ~*c,* to run away.
calcalèttere, *m.inv.* letter-weight.
calcàre, *v.t.* to tread; press down; trample; trace (*a drawing*); lay stress on, emphasize. ~ *le scene,* to tread the boards, go on the stage. ~ *la mano a,* to force one's hand.
càlcare, *m.* limestone. **calcàreo,** *a.* calcareous.
calcàta, *f.* trampling; tread; pressure.
càlce, *f.* lime. ~ *viva,* quicklime. *pietra di* ~, limestone.
càlce, *m.* lower part. *in* ~, at the foot of the page.
calcedònio, *m.* chalcedony.
calcestrúzzo, *m.* concrete, béton.
calciàre, *v.i.* (*aux.* avere) to kick. ~ *in porta,* to kick (or shoot) at goal. **calciatóre,** *m.* foot-baller, player.
calcína, *f.* mortar, lime. **calcinàccio,** *m.* bit of dry mortar or plaster. **calcinàio,** *m.* lime-pit. **calcinàre,** *v.t.* to calcine; dress with lime. **calcinóso,** *a.* chalky; full of lime.
càlcio, *m.* (*pl.* **càlci**) kick; foot-ball

(*the game*); butt-end; [rifle-]stock; tree-foot; calcium (*Chem.*). ~ *d'angolo*, corner kick. ~*d'inizio*, kick-off. ~ *di rigore*, penalty kick. ~ *di punizione*, free kick. *dare*, *menare*, *tirare un* ~ (or *calci*), to kick (*fig.*). *dare un* ~, to despise, insult. *fanno a calci tra loro* (*of things*), they clash. **calcístico** (*pl.* -ístici), *a.* football (*att.*). *società* ~*a*, football club.

càlco (*pl.* càlchi), *m.* cast; imprint; tracing, counter drawing.

calcografía, *f.* (*art of*) copper-plate printing. **calcògrafo,** *m.* copper-plate engraver.

càlcola, *f.* treadle.

calcolàbile, *a.* calculable. **calcolàre,** *v.t.* to calculate, reckon, estimate; compute; consider, reflect upon. **calcolatóre** (*f.* -tríce), *a.* & *n.* calculating; calculator. **calcolatríce,** *f.* calculating machine. **calcolazióne,** *f.* calculation. ~ *del manoscritto* (*Typ.*), casting-off copy, cast off. **càlcolo,** *m.* calculation, reckoning, estimate, computation; account; (*Math.*) calculus; (*Med.*) stone, calculus. ~*i biliari*, gall-stones.

caldàia, *f.* copper; boiler (*on engine*). **caldaménte,** *ad.* warmly. **caldàna,** *f.* warmth or heat (*of temper*); flush of rage.

caldarrostàio (*pl.* -ài), *m.* seller of roast chestnuts. **caldarròsta,** *f.inv.* roast chestnut.

caldeggiàre, *v.t.* to favour; support warmly, recommend. **calderàio,** *m.* boiler-maker; copper smith.

caldézza, *f.* warmth, heat. **càldo,** *a.* hot; eager; warm (all senses). ¶ *m.* heat, warmth. ~ ~, recent, up to date, quite new. *pigliarla* ~*a*, to take seriously; put one's best into. **caldúra,** *f.* heat (of summer); hot weather.

calendàrio, *m.* calendar, almanac. *avere nel* ~, to hold in esteem. **calendimàggio,** *m.* the first of May, May-day festivities.

calére, *v.i.* defect. (used only in 3rd sg., *cale*, *caleva*, &c.). *poco mi cale*, it matters little to me, I don't care. *mettere in non cale*, to disregard. *avere in non cale*, not to trouble about. **calèsse,** *m.* gig, one-horse carriage with two wheels.

calettàre, *v.t.* to put together, dove-tail; (*Mech.*) couple, connect, key on. *v.i.* (*aux.* avere) to tally, fit; close (*door*). **calettatúra,** *f.* fitting; fastening; (*Mech.*) coupling, keying on. ~ *a coda di rondine*, dove-tailing. ~ *a mortisa*, mortising; close joint.

calía, *f.* gold dust, gold filings; (*fig.*) old stuff.

calibràre, *v.t.* to gauge, calibrate. **càlibro,** *m.* calibre, bore; strength, standing (*fig.*); gauge, caliper[s].

càlice, *m.* cup, chalice; (*Bot.*) calyx.

calicò, *m.* calico.

califfo, *m.* caliph.

calígine, *f.* thick fog or mist; darkness. **caliginóso,** *a.* foggy; dark.

càlle, *m.* alley, lane; path.

callífugo, *m.* corn-plaster.

calligrafía, *f.* hand writing, calligraphy; penmanship.

callísta, *m.* chiropodist. **càllo,** *m.* corn; callus. **callóso,** *a.* hardened; hard; horny; callous.

càlma, *f.* calm; calmness; stillness; tranquillity; quiet; quietness; composure. **calmànte,** *a.* calming; soothing; appeasing. ¶ *m.* soothing drug; lenitive; sedative. **calmàre,** *v.t.* to calm; soothe; appease; lay (*storm*). **calmàrsi,** *v.refl.* to calm down; grow still; subside, abate; become smooth; become quiet. **càlmo,** *a.* calm; quiet; still; tranquill; composed, collected, cool; smooth (*sea*).

càlo, *m.* loss of bulk or weight; fall or drop in price; decline; waste; shrinkage; ullage (*Com.*). *prendere a* ~, to agree to pay for what one consumes.

calomelàno, *m.* calomel.

calóre, *m.* heat; warmth; glow; feverishness. **caloría,** *f.* calory. **calorífero,** *m.* heating apparatus. **caloróso,** *a.* warm; hot; cordial; hot-tempered.

calòscia (*pl.* -òsce), *f.* overshoe, galosh.

calòtta, *f.* skull-cap, calotte; (*Mech.*) cap; case (*watch*, &*c.*).

calpestàre, *v.t.* to trample down; tread upon. **calpestío** (*pl.* -íi), *m.* trampling; treading; tramp (*of feet*).

calúnnia, *f.* calumny; false charge; slanderous report. **calunniàre,** *v.t.* to calumniate, slander. **calunniatóre,** *m.* calumniator; slanderer. **calunnióso,** *a.* calumnious, slanderous.

calvàrio, *m.* calvary.

calvinismo, *m.* Calvinism. **calvinista** (*pl.* **-isti**), *a. & m.* calvinistic, Calvinist. **Calvino,** *m.* Calvin.

calvízie, *f.inv.* baldness. **càlvo,** *a. & m.* bald; bald(headed) person.

càlza, *f.* stocking; wick for a lamp. *far la* ~, to knit. **calzànte,** *a.* fitting; tight; suitable. **calzàre,** *v.t.* to put on (*shoes or stockings*); provide with boots or shoes; wedge up (*wheels, &c.*). *v.i.* (*aux.* avere or essere) to fit; be shod; suit. **calzàrsi,** *v.refl.* to put on one's shoes or stockings. **calzatóio,** *m.* shoe-horn.

calzatúra, *f.* (*also pl.*) foot-ware, boots & shoes; hose; hosiery. **calzettàio,** *m.* hosier. **calzetteria,** *f.* hosiery. **calzíno,** *m.* sock. *cigne* (*f.pl.*) *da* ~*i,* sock-suspenders. **calzolàio,** *m.* boot & shoemaker. **calzolería,** *f.* bootshop.

calzóni, *m.pl.* trousers; slacks.

camaleónte, *m.* chameleon.

camarílla, *f.* clique; cabal, camarilla.

camarlíngo & camerléngo, *m.* steward, treasurer; officer of the Papal court who deals with finance.

cambiàle, *f.* bill (of exchange); draft; promissory note. ~ *a breve scadenza,* ~ *a lunga scadenza,* short-dated, long-dated, bill. ~ *a vista,* bill payable at sight. *avallare una* ~, to back a bill. *emettere, tirare una* ~, to draw a bill. *girare una* ~, to endorse a bill.

cambiaménto, *m.* change, alteration. **cambiamonéte,** *m.inv.* money-changer.

cambiàre, *v.t. & i.* (*aux.* essere) to change; alter; shift; turn; exchange. **cambiàrio,** *a.* of exchange; exchange (*att.*). **cambiavalúte,** *m.inv.* money-changer. **càmbio,** *m.* change; exchange; rate of exchange. *in* ~ *di,* in exchange for; instead of; in place of. *agente di* ~, stockbroker. ~ *di velocità,* (*Motor*) change of gear; gear-box.

cambúsa, *f.* (*Naut.*) galley, caboose.

càmera, *f.* room; bed-room; chamber. ~ *ammobigliata,* furnished room. ~ *da affittare,* room to let. ~ *oscura,* (*Phot.*) dark room. *C*~ *dei Comuni, C*~ *Bassa,* House of Commons, Lower House (*Eng.*). *C*~ *dei Pari, C*~ *Alta,* House of Lords, Upper House. *C*~ *dei Deputati,* Chamber of Deputies (*Fr.*). ~ *di commercio,* Chamber of Commerce. *veste da* ~, dressing-

gown. **cameràta,** *f.* dormitory; group of pupils or associates; *m.* (*pl.* **-àti**), comrade; fellow-pupil; mate; chum; fellow-traveller, &c. **cameratismo,** *m.* comradeship.

camerièra, *f.* maid [servant]; chambermaid; housemaid; lady's maid; waitress; stewardess. **camerière,** *m.* waiter; man servant; valet; steward (*ship*).

cameríno, *m.* small room; (*actor's or athlete's*) dressing-room; box-office; cabin; closet; water-closet, lavatory.

càmice, *m.* alb; surplice; smock (*painter's, &c.*).

camícia (*pl.* **-ície**), *f.* shirt (*man's*); vest, chemise (*woman's*); jacket (*water, steam*); cover, lining, case, wrapper. ~ *da notte,* night shirt (*man's*); n.dress, n. gown (*woman's*). **camiciàio,** *m.* **-àia,** *f.* shirt-maker. **camiciòtto,** *m.* smock; blouse (*workman's*). **camici[u]òla,** *f.* vest, undervest.

caminétto, *m.* fireplace; small chimney. **camíno,** *m.* chimney; smoke-stack; fire-place; hearth. *gola di* ~, flue.

camióne, *m.* motor-truck; motor-lorry. **camionétta,** *f.* (*Mil.*) jeep.

camma, *f.* (*Mech.*) cam.

cammellière, *m.* camel-driver. **cammèllo,** *m.* camel.

cammèo, *m.* cameo.

camminaménto, *m.* (*Mil.*) communication trench; approach. **camminàre,** *v.i.* (*aux.* avere) to walk; go; move; proceed. **camminàta,** *f.* walk; walking; gait. **camminatóre,** *m.* **-tríce,** *f.* walker. **cammíno,** *m.* way, road; route; path; journey. *cammin facendo,* on the way. *far* ~, to progress. *mettersi in* ~, to set out, start.

camòrra, *f.* camorra, secret (criminal) society.

camóscio, *m.* chamois. *pelle di* ~, c. skin, c. leather.

campàgna, *f.* country, open country; country property; soil & its produce; campaign; long cruise. *artiglieria da* ~, field-artillery. *battere la* ~, to roam the country. *entrare in* ~, (*Mil.*) to take the field.

campagn[u]òlo, *a.* rustic; rural; country (*att.*). ¶ *m.* countryman; peasant.

campàle, *a.* (*Mil.*) pitched; hard; decisive. *battaglia* ~, pitched battle. *giornata* ~, hard day's work; decisive day.

campàna, *f.* bell; bell-glass; bell jar; cloche; cover; striking-mechanism of clock. *a forma di* ~, bell-shaped. *suonar le* ~*e,* to ring the bells. *suonar le* ~*e a morto,* to toll the knell. *esser di* ~*e grosse,* to be hard of hearing, to be deaf. ~ *martello,* alarm bell (*fire, &c.*). ~ *da palombaro,* diving bell. *boa a* ~, *f.* bell-buoy. *bronzo da* ~*e,* bell metal. **campanàccio,** *m.* cow-bell. **campanàro,** *m.* bellman, bell-ringer; bell-founder. **campanèlla,** *f.* small bell; metal ring; door-knocker; (*Bot.*) bluebell. **campanèllo,** *m.* door bell.

campanìle, *m.* bell-tower, steeple; belfry. *gare di* ~, *f.pl.* local rivalry, parish quarrels. **campanilìsmo,** *m.* parochialism, narrowness of outlook. **campàno,** *m.* cow-bell, cattle-bell.

campàre, *v.t.* to save (*from danger, &c.*); bring out the high lights (*in a picture, or the figures in a relief*). *v.i.* (*aux.* essere) to live, gain one's living. *si campa,* one (just) manages to live. *campare alla giornata,* to live from hand to mouth.

campeggiàre, *v.i.* (*aux.* avere) to camp, encamp; stand out, be conspicuous, catch the eye. **campéggio,** *m.* camping; camping place; logwood.

campèstre, *a.* rural, rustic.

Campidòglio, *m.* Capitol (*Rome*).

campionàrio, *m.* book of patterns; collection of samples; catalogue.

campionàto, *m.* championship; contest for championship.

campióne, *m.* champion; pattern; sample; ledger; register of taxes or fines. ~ *in erba,* (sport) coming man.

càmpo, *m.* field; ground; camp; court (*Ten.*); room; space; time; field of battle; background; subject, matter. ~*d'aviazione,* airfield. ~ *di golf,* golf course. ~ *d'onda,* (*Radio*) wave band. *dare* ~ *aperto,* to give free access. *mettere in* ~, to bring up, propose. *levare il* ~, to decamp. *correre i* ~ *i,* to roam about the country. *dar* ~ *di,* to give time for. ~ *franco,* liberty of action. *aiutante di* ~, adjutant. *sul* ~, at once.

camposànto, *m.* cemetery.

camuffàre, *v.t.* to disguise; mask.

camùso, *a.* snub-nosed.

can, *m.* Khan; medieval title in the Della Scala family of Verona.

Canadà (il), *m.* Canada. **canadése,** *a. & m.f.* Canadian.

canàglia, *f.* rabble, mob, riff-raff; blackguard, cad, scoundrel, rascal. **canagliàta,** *f.* mean or scoundrelly action; low trick. **canagliésco** (*pl. -éschi*), *a.* low, scoundrelly, rascally, vile. **canagliúme,** *m.* rabble, scum of the people, ragtag & bobtail.

canàle, *m.* canal, channel, duct, pipe, passage, groove, gutter, ditch, race, way. *il C* ~ *della Manica,* the English Channel. ~ *navigabile,* shipway, ship canal. ~ *di scolo,* drain; sewer. **canalétto,** *m.* small channel or canal; drain-pipe. **canalizzàre,** *v.t.* to canalize, pipe, drain; (*fig.*) concentrate, centralize.

cànapa, *f.* hemp. **canapàia,** *f.* hemp field. **canapàio** *or* **canapàro,** *m.* hemp-dresser; dealer in hemp.

canapè, *m.inv.* sofa, couch, settee.

canapificio, *m.* hemp-mill. **canapìno,** *a.* hempen; hemp (*att.*). ¶ *m.* hemp-dresser. **cànapo,** *m.* cable, hempen rope.

Canàrie (ísole), *f.pl.* Canary Islands, Canaries.

canarìno, *m.* canary. ¶ *a.* yellow, canary coloured.

canàsta, *f.* canasta (*card game*).

canavàccio, *m.* canvas.

cancàn, *m.inv.* cancan (*dance*); scandal, tattle; noise.

cancellàre, *v.t.* to cancel, cross out, rub out, wipe out; efface; erase; obliterate; annul.

cancellàta, *f.* railing.

cancellatúra, *f.* cancelling; erasure.

cancellería, *f.* chancellery; chancery; record-office; (office) stationery. **cancellieràto,** *m.* chancellorship. **cancellière,** *m.* chancellor; registrar. *C* ~ *dello Scacchiere,* Chancellor of the Exchequer (*Eng.*).

cancèllo, *m.* gate; railing; barrier; grating.

canceróso, *a.* cancerous. **cànchero,** *m.* canker, cancer; (*fig.*) bore.

cancrèna, *f.* gangrene.

càncro, *m.* cancer; Cancer. *il Tropico del C* ~, the Tropic of Cancer.

candeggiàre, *v.t.* to bleach; whiten. **candéggio,** *m.* bleaching.

candéla, *f.* candle; candle power; (*Motor.*) sparking-plug. *lampada da cento* ~ *e,* lamp (*Elec.*) of 100 candle power.

candelàbro, *m.* candelabrum; branched candle-stick.
Candelàia, -àra, (*pop.*) -òra, *f.* Candlemas (2 *Feb.*).
candelière, *m.* candle-stick; (*Naut.*) stanchion.
candidaménte, *ad.* candidly; ingenuously; frankly.
candidàto, *m.* candidate; aspirant.
candidatúra, *f.* candidature.
candidézza, *f.* whiteness; candidness; frankness. **càndido,** *a.* white; clean; pure; innocent; sincere; candid.
candíre (*pr,* -ísco, -ísci), *v.t.* (*of fruit*) to candy, crystallize; (*of sugar*) to refine, crystallize. **candíto,** *m.* candy, sugar candy. ¶ *a.* candied.
candóre, *m.* whiteness; purity; innocence; candour, frankness.
càne, *m.* dog; hound; hammer, cock (*of a gun*); (*Mech.*) pawl, catch; (*Astr.*) constellation of the Greater & Lesser Dog (*il C~ Maggiore & il C~ Minore*); (*pop.*) wretched singer or actor. ~ *barbone,* poodle. ~ *bastardo,* mongrel. ~ *da fermo,* setter. ~ *da punta,* pointer. ~ *da caccia,* hound, sporting dog. ~ *da guardia,* watch dog. ~ *da pastore,* sheep dog. ~ *poliziotto,* police dog. ~ *del S. Bernardo,* St. Bernard dog. ~ *di lusso,* fancy dog. *una muta di* ~*i,* a pack of hounds. *roba da* ~*i, f.* wretched stuff. *tempo da* ~*i, m.* horrid (beastly) weather.
canèstra, *f. &* **canèstro,** *m.* basket; hamper. **canestràio,** *m.* basket maker. **canestràta,** *f.* basketful.
cànfora, *f.* camphor.
cangévole, *&* **cangiàbile,** *a.* changeable, fickle. **cangiànte,** *a.* changing; variable; (*of colour*) iridescent. *seta* ~, *f.* shot silk. **cangiàre,** *v.t.* to change, alter. *v.i.* (*aux.* avere) & **cangiàrsi,** *v.refl.* to change, alter.
cangúro, *m.* kangaroo.
canícola, *f.* dog days; extreme (summer) heat; Sirius, dog-star. **canicolàre,** *a.* canicular. *i giorni* ~*i,* the dog-days.
caníle, *m.* dog kennel.
caníno, *m.* small dog, puppy. ¶ *a.* canine; (*fig.*) intense, persistent, furious. *dente* ~, eye tooth. *fame* ~*a,* ravenous hunger. *mosca* ~*a,* horse-fly; bore. *rosa* ~*a,* dog-rose; brier-rose. *tosse* ~*a,* whooping-cough.
canízie, *f.inv.* grey hairs, whiteness of hair; old age.

cànna, *f.* cane, reed; pipe; (*gun*) barrel; wind-pipe, gullet; rod (*measure,* about 2 metres); stick. ~ *da pesca,* fishing rod. ~ *da zucchero,* sugar-cane. ~ *d'India,* bamboo cane. *povero in* ~, extremely poor, as poor as a church mouse. *tremare come una* ~, to shake all over.
cannèlla, *f.* small tube; spout; spigot, tap; stick; cinnamon.
cannèllo, *m.* pipe; pipette; hollow rod; penholder; stick (*sealing wax*).
cannellóni, *m.pl.* (*Cook.*) tubes of pasta, filled with meat, &c.
cannéto, *m.* cane field, bed of reeds.
canníbale, *a. & m.* cannibal.
canníccio, *m.* reed-tray for drying fruit, rearing silk-worms, &c.
cannocchiàle, *m.* telescope; glass. ~ *da teatro,* opera-glass.
cannóne, *m.* gun, cannon; barrel, pipe, tube; raised frill or crease. ~ *antiaereo,* anti-aircraft gun. ~ *a retrocarica,* breech-loading gun. ~ *da campagna a tiro rapido,* quick-firing field gun. *affusto di* ~, *m.* gun-carriage. **cannoneggiaménto,** *m.* cannonade. **cannoneggiàre,** *v.t.* to cannonade, bombard, shell. **cannonièra,** *f.* gunboat. **cannonière,** *m.* gunner.
canòa, *f.* canoe.
canocchiale, *see* cannocchiale.
cànone, *m.* canon, rule (*Eccl.*); precept; ground rent. **canònica,** *f.* parsonage; rectory; house of parish priest. **canonicàto,** *m.* canonry; cathedral chapter; sinecure. **canònico** (*pl.* -ònici), *a.* canonical; correct; regular. *dritto* ~, canon law. *ore canoniche,* canonical hours. *libri canonici,* canonical books. ¶ *m.* canon (*pers.*). *canonici regolari,* those belonging to a monastic order.
canonísta (*pl.* -ísti), *m.* doctor or professor of canon law. **canonizzàre,** *v.t.* to canonize; (*fig.*) recognize as regular.
canòro, *a.* melodious; harmonious; resonant.
canottàggio, *m.* rowing; canoeing; **canottière,** *m.* canoeist; oarsman; rowing man. **canòtto,** *m.* canoe.
cànova, *f.* cellar; cave; wine or provision shop.
canovàccio (*pl.* -àcci), *m.* canvas; duster; plot; scenario of a *commedia dell' arte,* sometimes called *commedia a* ~.
cansàre, *v.t.* to remove; set aside;

save; shun; escape from. **cansàrsi,** *v.refl.* to make way; get out of the way.

cantàbile, *a.* suited for singing; musical, melodious. **cantafàvola,** *f.* fable; long unlikely tale. **cantai-[u]òlo,** *a.* singing, chirping. ¶ *m.* call-bird, decoy-bird.

cantambànco (*pl.* **-ànchi**), *m.* mountebank; street singer; strolling player.

cantànte, *a.* singing. ¶ *m.f.* singer. **cantàre,** *v.t. & i.* (*aux.* avere) to sing, chant; celebrate; write verses on; repeat over and over again; talk indiscreetly, reveal secrets. ~ *ad orecchio,* to sing by ear. ~ *da cane,* to bawl. *cantarla chiara,* to say something openly. ~ *sempre la stessa canzone,* to harp always on the same string. ¶ *m.* singing; song; strain; canto (*gen. of popular poem*).

cantàride, *f.* Spanish fly.

cantastòrie, *m.inv.* professional story-teller or ballad-singer. **cantàta,** *f.* cantata; singing. *Messa* ~, High Mass. **cantatóre,** *m.* **-tríce** *f.* singer; songster (*f.* songstress).

canteràno, *m.* chest of drawers.

canterellàre, *v.t. & i.* (*aux.* avere) to hum. **canteríno,** *a.* singing; warbling; chirping. *grillo* ~, chirping cricket. *uccello* ~, decoy-bird. ¶ *m.* popular or public singer.

càntica (*pl.* **càntiche**), *f.* poem; song; one of the three divisions of Dante's *Divine Comedy. La* ~ *di Salomone,* the Song of Solomon. **cantic-chiàre,** *v.t. & i.* (*aux.* avere) to sing softly; hum. **càntico** (*pl.* **càntici**), *m.* canticle, song, hymn. *Il* ~ *dei cantici,* the Song of Songs.

cantière, *m.* yard; shipyard; stocks (*Shipbldg.*); builder's yard. ~ *navale,* dockyard.

cantilèna, *f.* sing-song; monotonous chant. *sempre la stessa* ~, always the same old story!

cantína, *f.* cellar; canteen; wine (& provision) shop. ~ *sociale,* co-operative store for the sale of wine, &c. **cantinière,** *m.* butler; cellar-man; canteen-keeper.

cànto, *m.* singing; song; chant; lay. *canto* ~ *fermo,* plain song. ~ *gregoriano,* Gregorian chant. ~ *della cicala,* chirping of the cicada. ~ *del cigno,* swan song; (*fig.*) last effort. ~ *del gallo,* cock-crow, crowing of the cock.

cànto, *m.* corner; side, hand; part;

edge. *da un* ~, aside, apart. *dal* ~ *mio,* for my part. *da ogni* ~, on all sides. *dall'altro* ~, on the other hand. *per ogni* ~, everywhere, on every hand.

cantonàle, *a.* cantonal (*Switzerland*); ¶ *m.* angle-iron.

cantonàta, *f.* outer angle or side of a building; (street) corner; (*Typ.*) angular design on the outer corners of a book. *prendere una* ~, to put one's foot in it, say or do something stupid.

cantóne, *m.* corner (of a room); (*Geog.*) canton, district. *i C~i svizzeri,* the Swiss Cantons.

cantonièra, *f.* corner-cupboard; road-man's wife. ¶ as *a. casa* ~, road-man's house. **cantonière,** *m.* roadman, road-mender; railwayman in charge of a section of the line.

cantóre, *m.* singer; chorister; (*fig.*) poet. **cantoría,** *f.* choir, organ gallery; choir stalls. **cantoríno,** *m.* choir-book; manual of plain song.

cantùccio (*pl.* **-ùcci**), *m.* corner; nook; crust of bread or cheese.

canúto, *a.* hoary; white-haired.

canzonàre (*pr.* **-óno**), *v.t.* to make fun of, ridicule, mock; *v.i.* (*aux.* avere) to jest, joke, trifle.

canzóne, *f.* song; ode; elaborate lyric. *mettere in* ~, to mock (at), make fun of. *la stessa* ~! the same old story! **canzonétta,** *f.* short lyric or song; ballad. **canzonière,** *m.* collection of lyrical poems; song book.

caolíno, *m.* kaolin, porcelain clay.

càos, *m.* chaos; disorder, confusion. **caòtico** (*pl.* **-òtici**), *a.* chaotic.

capàce, *a.* capacious, roomy; able; fit; capable; expert; intelligent. **capacità,** *f.* capacity; capability; skill; skilfulness; cleverness, ability. ~ *giuridica,* legal position (*of individual*). **capacitàre,** *v.t.* to persuade; convince; enable; qualify.

capànna, *f.* hut, rustic shelter; cabin; shed; barn. **capànno,** *m.* bathing hut; bower; arbour. **capannóne,** *m.* large shed.

caparbiàggine & **caparbietà,** *f.* obstinacy, stubbornness, self-will. **capàrbio,** *a.* obstinate, self-willed. restive (*of horses*).

capàrra, *f.* earnest; pledge; caution-money.

capàta, *f.* blow with the head; *battere una* ~, *dare una* ~ *in,* to butt against, knock one's head against. **capatína,** *f.* call, brief visit. *dare.*

fare una ~ *a*, to call at, drop in at.

capécchio, *m.* tow; oakum.

capeggiàre, *v.t.* to head; lead.

capellíno, *m.* fine hair; (*pl.*) **capellíni,** fine vermicelli. **capéllo,** *m.* (*pl.* **capélli;** (*Poet.*) **capéi, capégli**) hair (a single human); hair's breadth. *a* ~, exactly, perfectly. *in capelli,* bare-headed. *essere a un* ~ *da,* to be within a hair's breadth of. *fare ai* ~*i,* to seize hold of one's hair; scuffle, fight. *fino ai* ~*i,* to the extreme limit (*of patience, &c.*). *ne ho fin sopra i* ~*i,* I have had quite enough of it. **capellúto,** *a.* hairy; long-haired.

capelvènere, *m.* maidenhair fern.

capèstro, *m.* rope, halter. *uomo da* ~, gallows-bird.

capezzàle, *m.* pillow, bolster.

capézzolo, *m.* nipple, teat; dug (*animal*).

capidòglio, *m.* sperm whale.

capiènza, *f.* capacity; size, content.

capigliatúra, *f.* head of hair.

capillàre, *a.* capillary.

capinéra, *f.* black-cap, great tit.

capíno, *m.* (dim. of *capo*) small head; scapegrace.

capíre (*pr.* **-ísco, -ísci**), *v.t.* to understand; make out; realize; *v.i.* (*aux.* essere) to be contained.

capitàle, *a.* capital; principal; chief; main; essential; great; fatal; deadly; mortal. *pena* ~, capital punishment. *peccato* ~, deadly sin. ¶ *m.* capital; principal; wealth; assets. ~ *azionario,* share capital. ~ *d'esercizio,* working c. ~ *di maneggio,* trading c. ~ *& lavoro,* capital & labour. ¶ *f.* capital [city, *letter*], metropolis. **capitalísmo,** *m.* capitalism. **capitalísta,** *m.* (*pl.* **-ísti**), capitalist. **capitalizzàre,** *v.t.* to capitalize.

capitàna, *f.* admiral's galley. *nave* ~, flag-ship. **capitanàre,** *v.t.* to captain, lead, command. **capitanería,** *f.* coastal district under command of a maritime authority. ~ *del porto,* harbour-master's office.

capitàno, *m.* captain; master; skipper. ~ *di lungo corso,* deep-sea captain, master of foreign-going vessel. ~ *di cabotaggio,* master of a coasting vessel. ~ *di nave mercantile,* master mariner. ~*di vascello,* captain (*Nav.*). ~ *di corvetta,* lieutenant-commander (*Nav.*) ~ *di fregata,* commander

(*Nav.*). ~ *di porto,* harbour master.

capitàre, *v.i.* (*aux.* essere) to arrive; turn up; happen; befall. ~ *bene,* to be lucky. ~ *male,* to be unlucky.

capitazióne, *f.* poll-tax (*Hist.*).

càpite (**in**), *ad.* (*Lat.*) in chief. *parola in* ~, word in large print at head of a page.

capitèllo, *m.* (*Arch.*) capital.

capitolàre, *v.i.* (*aux.* avere) to capitulate; surrender (on terms). ¶ *a.* capitular. ¶ *m.* capitulary. **capitolàto,** *m.* terms of a contract; specifications. **capitolazióne,** *f.* capitulation; terms of surrender. **capitolíno,** *a.* Capitoline, of the Capitol (*Rome*). **capìtolo,** *m.* chapter (*of a book*); cathedral chapter; facetious composition in *terza rima*; pact or convention, or one of its articles. *non aver voce in* ~, to have no authority, no voice in the matter.

capitomboràre, *v.i.* (*aux.* essere) to fall headlong; tumble down; turn a somersault. **capitómbolo,** *m.* tumble; headlong fall; somersault. **capitombolóni,** *ad.* head over heels.

capitóne, *m.* large eel.

càpo, *m.* head; chief; leader; commanding officer; principal; master; superior; superintendent; manager; foreman; top; heading; beginning; end; chapter; article; item; kind; object; point; thing; source; attention; inclination; (*Geog.*) cape, promontory. *da* ~, over again. *da* ~ *a piedi,* from top to bottom, from head to foot. *da* ~ *a fondo,* from end to end. *a* ~ *fitto,* upside down. *avere il* ~ *a,* to be fond of; be set on. *dare al* ~ *a,* to go to one's head, turn one's head. *far* ~, to end, come to an end; arrive. *far di suo* ~, to follow one's bent. *lavare il* ~ *a,* to scold. *lavata di* ~, scolding, reproof, dressing down. *mettersi in* ~, to take (it) into one's head. *mettersi col* ~ *a,* to give one's attention to. *rompere il* ~ *a,* to bore. *rompersi il* ~, to rack one's brain. ~ *ameno,* merry fellow. ~ *d'accusa,* count of indictment. ~ *d'anno,* New Year's Day. *la Provincia del C*~, Cape Province (S.A.). *il C*~ *di Buona Speranza,* the Cape of Good Hope. *la città del* ~, Capetown.

capobànda (*pl.* **capibànda**), *m.*

bandmaster; brigand chief; gang leader. **capocàccia** (*pl.* capicàccia*), *m.* head keeper. **capocàssa** (*pl.* capicàssa), *m.* chief cashier.

capòcchia, *f.* head (*of match, pin, nail, &c.*).

capòccia (*pl.* -òcci & -òccia), *m.* head of a peasant household; foreman; overseer.

capocòllo, *m.* (*Cook.*) smoked pork sliced thin (*as an hors d'œuvre*).

capocòmico (*pl.* capocòmici), *m.* chief comedian; head of a dramatic company. **capocuòco** (*pl.* capicuòchi), *m.* head cook, chef. **capòdanno**, see *capo*. **capofàbbrica** (*pl.* capifàbbrica), *m.* shop foreman. **capofìla** (*pl.* capifìla), *m.* file-leader (*Mil.*); leading file; leading vessel of a squadron. **capofìtto** (a), *ad.* head foremost (*dive*); with head down. **capogìro** (*pl.* capogìri), *m.* giddiness; fit of giddiness. **capolavóro** (*pl.* capolavóri), *m.* masterpiece. **capolìnea** (*pl.* capilìnea), *m.* (*Rly.*) terminus. **capolìno** (*pl.* capolìni), *m.* little head. *far* ~, to peep (out, in). **capolìsta** (*f'.* capilìsta), *m.* head of a list, first name on a list. **capoluògo** (*pl.* capoluòghi), *m.* chief town (*of province or district*). **capomàstro** (*pl.* capomàstri & capimàstri), *m.* master-builder.

caponàggine, *f.* stubbornness, obstinacy.

capopàgina (*pl.* capipàgina), *m.* (*Typ.*) head-piece. **capopàrte** (*pl.* capipàrte), *m.* party leader.

caporàle, *m.* corporal (*Mil.*). ~ *maggiore*, lance-corporal.

caporipàrto (*pl.* capiripàrto), *m.* head of a department. **caposàldo** (*pl.* capisàldi), *m.* fixed point of starting (*measurement, argument, &c.*) main point; basis; (*Mil.*) strong point. **caposcàlo** (*pl.* capiscàlo), *m.* (*Aviat.*) station commander. **caposcuòla** (*pl.* capiscuòla), *m.* founder of a school (*literary, artistic, scientific*). **caposquàdra** (*pl.* capisquàdra), *m.* group leader; foreman of a squad. **capostazióne** (*pl.* capistazióne), *m.* station-master. **capostìpite** (*pl.* capistìpiti), *m.* founder of a family. **capotambúro** (*pl.* capotambúri), *m.* drum major. **capotréno** (*pl.* capitréno), *m.* (*Rly.*) guard. **capovèrso** (*pl.* capovèrsi), *m.* beginning of a line of poetry or paragraph in prose; section; paragraph.

capovòlgere, *v.t. ir.* & **capovòlgersi**, *v.refl.* to upset; overturn; capsize; turn upside down. **capovòlta**, *f.* upset; capsizal, somersault.

càppa, *f.* cape; mantle; robe; tunic; cope; frock; hood; canvas covering (*for boats, hatchways, guns, &c.*); chimney piece; vault (*of sky*); letter K (*Gk., Eng., &c.*). ~ *del camino*, cowl (chimney). *vela di* ~, storm sail. *navigare alla* ~, to sail with everything lashed down; lie to in a storm. **cappamàgna**, *f.* state robe; prelate's cope. **cappeggiàre**, *v.i.* (*aux.* avere) to lie to (*Naut.*).

cappèlla, *f.* chapel; chaplaincy; simple benefice; choir; choral service. *musica a* ~, singing to the accompaniment of the organ alone. ~ *ardente*, funeral chamber & trappings. ~ *mortuaria*, mortuary chapel. *maestro di* ~, choir-master; precentor.

cappellàio, *m.* hatter. **cappellàno**, *m.* chaplain. **cappelleria**, *f.* hat shop. **cappellétto**, *m.* small hat; (*pl.*) stuffed hat-shaped portions of paste for soup. **cappellièra**, *f.* hatbox. **cappellinàio**, *m.* hat-stand. **cappèllo**, *m.* hat; bonnet; cover[ing]; lid; nail-head; preface, preamble; (*Mech.*) cap; crosshead. ~ *a due punte*, cocked hat. ~ *di paglia*, straw hat. ~ *a cilindro*, *a staio*, ~ *a tuba*, top-hat, silk h. ~ *a cilindro compressibile*, opera hat, gibus. ~ *duro di feltro*, bowler hat. ~ *floscio di feltro*, Trilby [h.]. ~ *morbido a tesa larga*, slouch h. *mettersi il* ~, to put on one's hat. *levarsi il* ~, to take off one's hat. *far di* ~, to bow. *giú i* ~*i!*, hats off! *amico di* ~, bowing acquaintance.

càppero, *m.* caper, caper-bush. *salsa di* ~*i*, caper sauce. **càpperi!** *i. excl. of surprise*, Good gracious!

càppio (*pl.* càppi), *m.* slip-knot.

cappóne, *m.* capon.

cappòtto, *m.* long cloak & hood; overcoat, greatcoat. *prender* ~, (cards) to lose the game without making a single point.

cappuccìno, *m.* Capuchin [friar]; coffee beaten up with a little milk (*resembling the colour of a Capuchin's gown*).

cappúccio, *m.* cowl; hood.

càpra, *f.* goat; she-goat; goat-skin;

trestle. **capràio** & **capràro**, *m.* goat-herd. **caprétta**, *f.* & **caprétto** *m.* kid.

capríccio, *m.* caprice; whim; freak; passing fancy; vagary. **capriccióso,** *a.* capricious; whimsical; freakish; wayward.

caprifico (*pl.* **-fichi**), *m.* wild fig tree. **caprifòglio**, *m.* honeysuckle.

caprino, *a.* goatish; goat's; goat (*att.*). *barba* ~*a*, goatee. *pelle* ~*a*, goat-skin. ¶ *m.* goat's dung; smell of a goat.

capri[u]òla, *f.* doe; roe-deer; somersault, caper. **capri[u]òlo**, *m.* roebuck. **càpro**, *m.* goat, billy-goat, he-goat. ~ *espiatorio*, (*fig.*) scapegoat.

càpsula, *f.* capsule; percussion cap.

captàre, *v.t.* to catch, collect; get; obtain by undue influence; (*Radio*) to get (*station*), dial, tune in; intercept. **captazióne**, *f.* use of undue influence (*to obtain legacy, &c.*); (*Radio*) getting (*a station*).

carabàttole, *f.pl.* trash, trifles. *pigliar* (*su*) *le* (*proprie*) ~, to pack up one's traps.

carabína, *f.* carbine, rifle. **carabinière**, *m.* carabineer; gendarme.

caràffa, *f.* water bottle; jug, decanter, carafe.

Caraíbico (*mare*), *m.* Caribbean Sea.

caràmbola, *f. or* **caràmbolo**, *m.* cannon (*billiards*). **carambolàre**, *v.i.* (*aux.* avere) to cannon.

caramèlla, *f.* caramel; monocle. **caramellàto**, *a.* & *m.* candied (fruit); *a.* monocled.

carapàce, *m.* carapace, shell (*of crustacean*).

caràto, *m.* carat; share in a commercial undertaking, *hence* **caratìsta**, *m.* (*pl.* **-ìsti**), part-owner.

caràttere, *m.* character, disposition; temper; nature, property, peculiarity, characteristic; style; mark; literary portrait; dramatic personage; letter; type of print or handwriting; (*pl.*) type (*col.*). *fonderia di* ~*i*, type-foundry. ~*i di testo*, (*Typ.*) book-face. ~ *gotico*, black letter (*Typ.*). ~ *grassetto*, bold-face (*Typ.*). ~ *schiacciato*, worn type (*Typ.*). **caratterìstica**, *f.* characteristic, feature, trait. **caratterístico** (*pl.* **-ístici**), *a.* characteristic. **caratterizzàre**, *v.t.* to characterize.

carbonàia, *f.* charcoal-pit; c. kiln; coal-cellar; bunker. **carbonàio**, *m.* charcoal-burner; coalman, coal-

seller. **carbonaménto**, *m.* coaling (*ship*), bunkerage. **carbonàro**, *m.* carbonaro. **i Carbonàri**, (*m.pl.*) & **la Carbonería**, *f.* the Carbonari.

carbonàto, *m.* (*Chem.*) carbonate. **carbònchio** (*pl.* **-ònchi**), *m.* carbuncle; smut (*Agric.*).

carboncíno, *m.* charcoal pencil.

carbóne, *m.* coal; charcoal; carbon. ~ *bianco*, hydraulic power. **carbonèlla**, *f.* charcoal in small sticks. **carbònico** (*pl.* **-ònici**), *a.* (*Chem.*) carbonic. **carbonièra**, *f.* coal-ship, collier; coal-cellar. **carbonífero**, *a.* carboniferous; coal (*att.*). **carbonìle**, *m.* coal-cellar; bunker. **carbònio**, *m.* carbon (*Chem.*). **carbonizzàre**, *v.t.* to carbonize.

carburànte, *m.* (*Aviat.*) fuel, aviation spirit. **carburatóre**, *m.* (*Motor.*) carburettor. **carbúro**, *m.* carbide.

carcàme, *m.* carcass. **carcàssa**, *f.* skeleton (**of** a ship); derelict vehicle; person of skin & bone; breast bones of a fowl; (*Elec.*) frame.

carceràre, *v.t.* to imprison. **carceràrio**, *a.* prison (*att.*). *guardia* ~*ia*, *f.* warder, jailor, prison guard. *vitto* ~*io*, *m.* prison fare. **càrcere**, *m.* (*pl.f.* **le càrceri**) prison; imprisonment; jail. **carcerière**, *m.* gaoler, jailor, warder.

carcinòma, *m.* carcinoma, cancer.

carciòfo, *m.* artichoke; (*fig.*) stupid person, simpleton; (*Theat.*) poor actor (*pop.*).

càrco, *a.* laden; burdened; weighed down. ¶ *m.* (*Poet.*) weight, burden.

cardàre, *v.t.* to card, comb (*cloth, wool, &c.*). **cardatóre**, *m.* **-trìce**, *f.* wool carder.

cardellíno, *m.* goldfinch.

cardíaco (*pl.* **-íaci**), *a.* cardiac. *male* ~, heart-disease.

cardinàle, *a.* cardinal (*virtues, numbers, &c.*); chief, principal; fundamental. ¶ *m.* cardinal. **cardinalízio,** *a.* belonging to or befitting a cardinal; (*fig.*) scarlet. *cappello* ~, cardinal's hat.

càrdine, *m.* hinge; *pl.* (*fig.*) poles, foundation, support(s).

cardiopàlmo, *m.* (*Med.*) palpitation of the heart.

càrdo, *m.* thistle; teasel, carding machine. ~ *mangereccio, or* **cardóne**, *m.* edible thistle, cardoon.

carèna, *f.* ship's bottom; submerged part of the hull; keel. **carenàre**, *v.t.* to careen, cause to heel over (*Naut.*).

carestía, *f.* scarcity, dearth, famine.
carézza, *f.* caress; affectionate touch; endearment; blandishment; costliness. **carezzàre** (*pr.* -**ézzo**), *v.t.* to caress; fondle; stroke; pat; cherish; flatter; indulge. *Cf.* **accarezzare**. **carezzévole**, *a.* caressing, fondling; coaxing; affectionate.
cariàrsi, *v.refl.* to decay (*of teeth, &c.*). *dente cariato*, decayed tooth.
cariàtide, *f.* caryatid.
càrica (*pl.* **cariche**), *f.* charge; office; appointment; situation; task, duties, instructions; care, custody; (*Mil.*) charge, attack; (*explosive or propelling*) charge; (*Elec.*) charging (*battery, accumulator*). *essere in* ~, to be in charge. *tornare alla* ~, (*fig.*) to persist, insist. *entrare in* ~, to take office. ~ *di scoppio*, blasting charge (*Min.*). **caricaménto**, *m.* loading; (*pump*) priming; (*watch*) winding. **caricàre** (*pr.* **càrico**, **càrichi**), *v.t.* to load, load up; lade, take on board; burden; overload, overdo, exaggerate; wind up (*clock, watch*); charge (*gun, mine, accumulator*); set (*trap, &c.*); fill; (*Mil.*) charge, attack impetuously. ~ *la dose*, to increase the dose. ~*le tinte*, to deepen the colours; (*fig.*) to exaggerate. *caricarla a qualcuno*, to play one a trick. ~ *qualcuno d'ingiurie*, to abuse someone. **caricàto**, *p.a.* charged; laden, &c.; (*fig.*) affected.
caricatúra, *f.* caricature; cartoon. *mettere in* ~, to caricature. **caricaturísta** (*pl.* -**ísti**), *m.* caricaturist.
càrico (*pl.* **càrichi**), *m.* load, burden; freight, cargo; loading, lading; shipment; charge, accusation; expense; weight (*of years, &c.*). *polizza di* ~, bill of lading, *f.* *nave da* ~, *f.* freighter, cargo boat. ¶ *a. & sync.pp.* (for **caricato**) loaded, laden; burdened; charged (*fig.*) full, strong, dark, deep (*colour*).
Caríddi, *m.* Charybdis.
càrie, *f.inv.* caries, decay (*teeth, &c.*).
cariglióne, *m.* chime, peal, carillon.
caríno, *a.* dear, darling; charming; nice (*dim. of* caro).
Carínzia (la), *f.* Carinthia.
carità, *f.* charity; love; benevolence; compassion, pity; alms; favour. *per* ~! for pity's sake!, for heaven's sake! ~ *di patria*, love of country. *dama di* ~, district visitor. *le suore della C*~, the Sisters of Charity.

ospizio di ~, alms-house; charitable institution. **caritatévole**, *a.* charitable, benevolent.
carlínga (*pl.* -**ínghe**), *f.* (*Aero.*) cockpit.
carlíno, *m.* early Neapolitan coin, named after Charles of Anjou. *il resto del* ~, (*fig.*) something into the bargain. *Il Resto del C*~, title of a famous journal of Bologna.
Carlomàgno, *m.* Charlemagne.
carlóna (alla), *ad. expr.* carelessly, thoughtlessly; haphazard.
càrme, *m.* (*Poet.*) dignified lyric; hymn; poem.
carmelitàno, *a. & m.* Carmelite; Carmelite friar, White Friar.
carmínio, *m.* carmine.
carnagióne, *f.* complexion.
carnàle, *a.* bodily, physical; carnal, sensual. *fratelli* ~*i*, brothers german.
carnascialésco (*pl.* -**éschi**), *a.* of carnival, carnival (*att.*). *canti* ~*eschi*, carnival songs (*of Lorenzo de' Medici & others*).
càrne, *f.* flesh; meat; pulp (*of fruit*). *in* ~, plump, prosperous. *rimettersi in* ~, to put on flesh. ~ *di bue*, beef. ~ *di castrato*, mutton. ~ *congelata*, frozen meat. ~ *del macellaio*, butcher['s] meat. ~ *di maiale*, pork. ~ *in scatola*, potted meat, canned m. ~ *stufata*, stewed meat, stew. ~ *tritata*, minced meat, mincemeat. ~ *di vitello*, veal. ~ *da cannone*, cannon fodder. *color di* ~, flesh-coloured. **carnéfice**, *m.* executioner; hangman. **carneficína**, *f.* carnage; slaughter.
carnevàle, *m.* carnival; merry-making, revel(s). **carnevalésco** (*pl.* -**éschi**), *a.* in the spirit of carnival; carnival (*att.*).
carnicíno, *m.* flesh colour. ¶ *a.* flesh-coloured.
carnièra, *f.* game-bag. **carnívoro**, *a. & m.* carnivorous; c. animal. **carnóso**, *a.* fleshy.
càro, *a.* dear, precious, well-loved; costly, expensive, high (-priced); *cara mia*, my dear. *caro mio*, my dear fellow. *i vostri* ~*i*, *i Suoi* ~*i*, your family, your dear ones, your relatives. *aver* ~, to love, value. *aver* ~ *di*, to be glad to. *tener(si)* ~, to like very much, be fond of. ¶ *ad.* dear, dearly. *gli costò* ~, it cost him dear[ly]. *pagar* ~*a* (*una cosa*), to pay dear (or dearly) for something (*lit. & fig.*).

carógna, *f.* carrion; carcass; worn-out animal; (*fig.*) sluggard, good-for-nothing.

caròla, *f.* round dance (*with song*); carol. **carolàre,** *v.i.* (*aux.* avere) to dance & sing; carol.

carolíngio, *a.* & *m.* Carlovingian; Carolingian. **Carónte,** *m.* Charon (*Myth.*).

carosèllo, *m.* tournament; military ride; merry-go-round.

caròta, *f.* carrot; idle story; hoax. *piantar* ~*e, vender* ~*e,* to tell idle stories; hoax.

caròtide, *f.* carotid artery.

carovàna, *f.* caravan; company of travellers; novitiate; dockers' union (*port of Genoa*). **carovanière,** *m.* caravan leader.

carovíveri, *m.inv.* high cost of living; cost of living bonus.

Carpàzi (**Monti**), *m.pl.* Carpathian Mountains.

carpentería, *f.* carpentry; carpenter's shop. **carpentière,** *m.* carpenter.

càrpine, *m.* hornbeam (tree).

carpíre (*pr.* -ísco, -ísci), *v.t.* to snatch; seize; grasp; steal; (*fig.*) screw out.

carpóne *or* **carpóni,** *ad.* on all fours. **carradóre** & **carràio,** *m.* cartwright: waggoner. **carràta,** *f.* cartload. **carreggiàbile,** *a.* passable for carts. *strada* ~, cart-road. **carreggiare,** *v.t.* to cart. *v.i.* (*aux.* avere) to drive a cart. **carreggiàta,** *f.* cart-road; cart-track; wheel-track.

carrèllo, *m.* (*Rly.*) trolley; (*Aviat.*) carriage. ~ *d'atterraggio,* under-carriage (*Aviat.*).

carrettière, *m.* carter. **carrétto,** *m.* hand-cart; child's cart.

carrièra, *f.* career, course; profession; walk of life; speed, swift pace, rapid progress. *a gran* ~, *a tutta* ~, at full speed. *andar di* ~, to career. *ufficiale di* ~, regular (professional) officer.

carri[u]òla, *f.* wheelbarrow.

càrro *m.* cart; car; waggon; truck; van; lorry; (*Typ.*) case. ~*armato,* ~ *blindato,* armoured car; tank (*Mil.*). ~ *bagagli,* luggage-van (*Rly.*). ~ *funebre,* hearse. ~ *matto,* trolley, lorry. ~ *merci,* goods waggon, truck (*Rly.*). ~ *rimorchiato,* trailer. ~ *di scorta,* tender (*Rly.*). ~ *di Tespi,* travelling-theatre. *C*~ (*di Boote*), Great Bear (*Astr.*).

carròccio, *m.* war-chariot (of the medieval Italian republics).

carròzza, *f.* carriage; car, railway-carriage; coach; cab. ~ *con buffet,* buffet car (*Rly.*). ~ *diretta,* (*Rly.*) through coach. ~ *letto,* sleeper, sleeping car. ~ *ristorante,* dining-car, restaurant-c. (*Rly.*). ~ *da nolo,* ~ *da noleggio.* cab; hackney-coach. *andare in* ~, to drive in a carriage. *marciare in* ~, (*fig.*) to lead a life of ease. **carrozzàbile,** *a.* passable for carriages. *strada* ~, carriage road. **carrozzàio,** *m.* coach-maker, carriage-builder. **carrozzería,** *f.* carriage-works; (*Motor*) body, body-work. **carrozzétta,** *f.* small car. ~ *laterale,* side-car. **carrozzína,** *f.* -**ino,** *m.* light carriage; perambulator.

carrúcola, *f.* pulley; wheel & axle; sheave.

càrta, *f.* paper; sheet of paper; map, chart; document; charter; card, ticket; page; (*pl.*) [playing] cards. ~ *bibbia,* India paper. ~ *bollata,* stamped paper (*for official documents*). ~ *carbone,* carbon p. (*duplicating*). ~ *da disegno,* drawing-paper. ~ *da giornali,* newsprint. ~ *da giuoco,* playing-card. ~ *da lettere* (in 8vo) note paper; (in 4to) letter-paper; writing p. ~ *a mano,* handmade paper. ~ *ministro,* foolscap. ~ *moneta,* [inconvertible] paper money. ~ *moschicida,* fly-paper. ~ *patinata,* art paper. ~ *lucida,* ~ *da ricalcare,* tracing paper. ~ *rigata,* ruled paper. ~ *senapata,* mustard plaster. ~ *straccia,* waste paper. ~ *sugante,* ~ *assorbente,* blotting-paper. ~ *velina,* tissue p. ~ *vetro,* ~ *vetrata,* sand p., glass p. ~ *igienica,* toilet-p. ~ *al tornasole,* (*Chem.*) litmus paper. *fabbricazione della* ~, *f.* paper-making, p. manufacture. *fabbisogno di* ~, *m.* paper consumption. **cartàccia** (*pl.* -àcce), *f.* coarse paper; waste-p.; (*cards*) card[s] of no value. **cartàceo,** *a.* papery; paper (*att.*). *moneta* ~*a,* paper-money.

Cartàgine, *f.* Carthage. **cartaginése,** *a.* & *m.* Carthaginian.

cartàio, *m.* paper-maker; manufacturer of playing-cards.

cartapècora, *f.* parchment; vellum. **cartapésta,** *f.* paper pulp; papier maché.

cartéggio (*pl.* -éggi), *m.* correspondence; collection of letters or papers.

cartèlla, *f.* label; printed form; tablet

(*for inscription*); notice; list; lottery ticket; share certificate or bond; satchel; portfolio; folder; scoring-frame. ~ *da scrittoio*, writing-pad. ~ *del debito pubblico*, Government bond. ~ *d'incanto*, conditions of sale (by auction). **cartellièra,** *f.* cabinet for keeping papers. **cartellíno,** *m.* ticket; label. **cartèllo,** *m.* placard; bill; shop-sign; mark of ownership (*on books, &c.*); cartel, syndicate, trust. *artista di* ~, artist of high repute. ~ *di sfida*, challenge. ~ *indicatore*, road sign, traffic s.

cartièra, *f.* paper-mill.

cartilàgine, *f.* cartilage, gristle.

cartína, *f.* small piece of paper; (*cards*) poor card; packet; dose. ~ *di aghi*, packet of needles.

cartòccio (*pl.* **-òcci**), *m.* paper-bag; cornet; scroll (*Arch.*); (*artil.*) cartridge; (*pl.*) dried maize leaves.

cartografía, *f.* cartography, map-making. **cartògrafo,** *m.* cartographer, map-maker.

cartolàio, *m.* stationer. **cartolería,** *f.* stationer's shop; stationery. **cartolína,** *f.* postcard, card. ~ *illustrata*, picture postcard.

cartomànte, *m.f.* fortune-teller (*by cards*). **cartomanzía,** *f.* fortune-telling.

cartóne, *m.* cardboard, pasteboard, millboard; cartoon. *scatola di* ~, cardboard box, carton. **cartoncíno,** *m.* (*dim.* of **cartone**), thin cardboard. ~ *patinato*, art-board, coated board.

cartúccia (*pl.* **-úcce**), *f.* cartridge, round of ammunition; scrap of paper. ~ *a palla*, ~ *a pallottole*, ball-cartridge. ~ *a salve*, ~ *a polvere sola*, blank c. **cartuccièra,** *f.* cartridge belt; c. pouch.

càsa, *f.* house; home; household; family; dynasty; hostel; establishment, institution; religious community, friary, convent; business firm. ~ *colonica*, farm-house. ~ *comunale*, municipality, city chambers. ~ *di correzione*, reformatory, approved school. ~ *di cura*, ~ *di salute*, nursing-home; mental home. ~ *editrice*, publishing house. ~*d'abitazione*, dwelling house. ~ *di commercio*, business h., firm. ~ *da giuoco*, gambling house, gaming h. ~ *dello studente*, students' Union. ~ *di pena*, prison, gaol; penitentiary. *in* ~, at home; indoors. *di* ~, intimate, familiar.

fatto in ~, home-made. *metter su* ~, to set up house. *stare di* ~, to live, reside. *donna di* ~, woman fond of her home, good housekeeper.

casàcca, *f.* coat, jacket, in the expr. *voltar* ~, to change sides; to turn one's coat (*fig.*).

casàle, *m.* hamlet, group of houses.

casalíngo (*pl.* **-ínghi**), *a.* homely, home (*att.*); domestic; plain; home-made. *alla* ~*a*, simply, in homely fashion.

casamàtta (*pl.* **casemàtte**), *f.* casemate.

casaménto, *m.* large building; tenement, block of flats.

casàto, *m.* family; family name; birth, origin.

cascàggine, *f.* drowsiness; weariness; weakness.

cascàme, *m.* (*often pl.*) remnants, refuse, waste.

cascamòrto, *m.* fop, dandy, hanger-on.

cascànte, *p.a.* falling; feeble; drooping. **cascàre,** *v.i.* (*aux.* essere) to fall, drop. *caschi il mondo*! happen what may! **cascàta,** *f.* fall; water-fall; hang (*of skirt or curtain*); necklace; festoon. **cascatèlla,** *f.* cascade; small waterfall.

cascatíccio (*pl.* **-ícci**), *a.* weak; frail; (*of fruit*) ready to drop; (*fig.*) susceptible, impressionable.

Cascemír (il), *m.* Kashmir.

cascína, *f.* dairy-farm; dairy. *le C*~*e*, *f.pl.* Cascine, public gardens in Florence. **cascinàio,** *m.* dairyman; owner of a dairy. **cascíno,** *m.* cheese mould.

càsco (*pl.* **càschi**), *m.* helmet; pith-helmet.

caseggiàto, *m.* group of houses.

caseifício, *m.* cheese-dairy; c. factory.

casèlla, *f.* pigeon-hole; small compartment; box; cell (*beehive*). ~ *postale*, (private) post-office box.

casellànte, *m.* (*Rly.*) level-crossing keeper; linesman.

casellàrio, *m.* set of pigeon-holes; filing-cabinet.

caseréccio (*pl.* **-écci**), *a.* homely.

casèrma, *f.* barrack[s].

casétta, *f.* little house; cottage.

casigliàno, *m.* fellow-lodger.

casimír & casimíro, *m.* cashmere.

casíno, *m.* country cottage; club-house; casino. **casípola,** *f.* hovel.

casísta (*pl.* **-ísti**), *m.* casuist. **casística,** *f.* casuistry.

càṣo, *m.* case; instance, occasion, circumstance; position; means; chance; possibility; (*Gram.*) case. *in ogni* ~, *in tutti i* ~*i*, *in qualunque* ~, in any case, at all events, at any rate. *a* ~, *per* ~, by chance, by any chance; casually, unthinkingly, at random. *a* ~ *pensato*, of set purpose. ~ *mai che*, *puta* ~ *che*, suppose that. *poniamo il* ~ *che*, let us suppose that . . . *non c'è* ~ *di*, there is no means of. *far* ~, to matter. *far* ~ *a*, to surprise; impress. *far* ~ *di*, to consider important; set store by.

casolàre, *m.* isolated dwelling; poor country-house.

casòtto, *m.* booth; hut; cabin. ~ *di rotta*, chart-house. ~ *del timone*, wheel-house.

Càspio (Mar), *m.* Caspian Sea.

càssa, *f.* case, chest, coffer, trunk; body (*of car*); cupboard; cashier's desk or window; cash; bony cavity; (*carriage*) interior; sounding-box; air-chamber (*life-boat*); water-tank (*submarine*). ~ *di fucile*, rifle-stock. ~ *da morto*, coffin. *gran* ~, big drum. ~ *di risparmio*, savings-bank. ~ *dei caratteri*, ~ *per composizione*, (*Typ.*) case. *avanzo di* ~, cash on hand, *m. bassa* ~, lower case (*Typ.*). ~ *per la spaziatura*, space & quad case (*Typ.*). *alta* ~, upper case (*Typ.*).

cassafòrte (*pl.* cassefòrti), *f.* safe; strong-room.

cassapànca (*pl.* cassapànche), *f.* settle; bench-locker; chest.

cassàre, *v.t.* to cancel, annul, squash; revoke, rescind.

cassàta, *f.* Neapolitan (or Sicilian) ice; cream-tart. cassatèlla, *f.* cream tartlet.

cassazióne, *f.* cassation, annulment; revocation. *Corte di C*~, Court of Cassation, C. of Criminal Appeal.

càssero, *m.* (*Naut.*) quarter-deck.

casseruòla, *f.* saucepan, stewpan; casserole.

cassétta, *f.* box; small case; drawer; coach-box. ~ *di sicurezza*, safe. ~ *da viaggio*, dressing-case. ~ *porta-utensili*, tool box.

cassétto, *m.* drawer; small case. cassettóne, *m.* chest of drawers.

cassière, *m.* -a, *f.* cashier.

cassinènse & cassinése, *a.* of Monte Cassino; Benedictine.

càssola, *f.* (*Cook.*) fish-soup.

cassóne, *m.* large case; large box; coffer; caisson; ammunition chest.

càsta, *f.* caste.

castàgna, *f.* chestnut. ~*e secche*, dried chestnuts. chestnut-cake, c.-tart. castagnàio, *m.* chestnut-gatherer; c.-seller. castagnéto, *m.* chestnut-grove. castagnétte, *f.pl.* castanets. castàgno, *m.* chestnut tree; chestnut wood. ¶ *a.* chestnut; brown. castagn[u]òla, *f.* cracker (*firework*).

castàldo, *m.* land-agent; factor.

castàno, *a.* chestnut-coloured; nut-brown.

castellàno, *m.* lord of the manor, squire. castellàna, *f.* lady of the manor. castèllo, *m.* castle; palace; manor house, country seat, mansion, hall; stronghold; group of buildings in an enclosure; builder's scaffold or tower; water-tower; mechanism of a watch; frame for breeding silk-worms; post from which puppets are manipulated in a puppet-show. ~ *di prua*, (*Naut.*) forecastle. ~ *di poppa*, (*Naut.*) quarterdeck. ~ *di carte*, house of cards.

castigàre (*pr.* ~*igo*, ~*ighi*), *v.t.* to chastise, punish; castigate; correct; chasten; prune; injure. castigatézza, *f.* correctness, purity (*of language or style*); moderation, continence; refinement (*of manners*). castigàto, *p.p.* & *a.* punished; corrected; polished; expurgated; pure; faultless; correct.

Castíglia (la), *f.* Castille.

castígo (*pl.* -ighi), *m.* punishment, chastisement.

castità, *f.* chastity. càsto, *a.* chaste, pure.

castóne, *m.* setting (*gem*), bezel.

Castòre, *m.* (*Myth.*) Castor. ~ *e Polluce*, (*Astr.*) Castor & Pollux.

castòro, *m.* beaver. *pelle di* ~, beaver [fur].

castràre, *v.t.* to castrate, geld; (*fig.*) prune, expurgate; prick, slit open (*chestnuts*). castràto, *m.* mutton; eunuch; gelding. castróne, *m.* wether; gelding. castronería, *f.* stupidity; nonsense.

casuàle, *a.* casual, fortuitous, accidental, *spese* ~*i*, sundry expenses. casualménte, *ad.* casually, accidentally, by chance.

casúccia, *f.* small house, cottage. casúpola, *f.* hovel; mean little house.

cataclísma (*pl.* -ísmi), *m.* cataclysm; inundation, deluge.

catacómba, *f.* catacomb.

catafàlco (*pl.* -àlchi), *m.* catafalque.

catafàscio (a), *ad. expr.* topsy-turvy; pell-mell.

catalèssi, *f.inv.* catalepsy. **catalèttico** (*pl.* -èttici), *a.* & *m.* cataleptic; (*Gram.*) catalectic.

catàlisi, *f.* (*Chem.*) catalysis. **catalizzatóre**, *m.* catalyst.

catalogàre (*pr.* -àlogo, -àloghi), *v.t.* to catalogue.

Catalógna (la), *f.* Catalonia.

catàlogo (*pl.* -àloghi), *m.* catalogue; list.

catapécchia, *f.* wretched hovel.

cataplàsma (*pl.* -àsmi), *m.* poultice; plaster; (*fig.*) bore.

catapúlta, *f.* catapult. **catapultàre**, *v.t.* to catapult; (*Aero*) launch by catapult.

catàrro, *m.* catarrh.

catàrsi, *f.* catharsis.

catàrtico (*pl.* -àrtici), *a.* & *m.* purgative; cathartic.

catàsta, *f.* pile, heap, stack. *legno da* ~, firewood. *a* ~*e*, in great quantity.

catàsto, *m.* register of lands; land office; land-tax.

catàstrofe, *f.* catastrophe.

catechísmo, *m.* catechism. **catechizzàre**, *v.t.* to catechize; reason with, try to persuade.

categoría, *f.* category, class. **categòrico** (*pl.* -òrici), *a.* categorical; precise, absolute; flat (*refusal*).

caténa, *f.* chain; (*fig.*) bond, tie, fetter, impediment; series, continuous succession; range (*mountains*). *pazzo da* ~, stark mad. *punto a* ~, chain-stitch. **catenàccio**, *m.* bolt (*door*). **catenèlla**, *f.* small chain, fine c. ~ *da orologio*, watch-chain.

cateràtta, *f.* cataract (*falls* & *Med.*); sluice, sluice-gate; downpour.

catetère, *m.* (*Med. instr.*) catheter.

catèrva, *f.* crowd, host, multitude, pack; large quantity; great number.

catinèlla, *f.* basin; wash-hand basin. *piovere a* ~*e*, to rain in torrents.

catíno, *m.* basin; wash-tub; (*Geog.*) basin.

càtodo, *m.* (*Elec.*) cathode.

Catóne, *m.* Cato; (*fig.*) man of severe manners.

catramàre, *v.t.* to tar. **catràme**, *m.* tar.

càttedra, *f.* desk; rostrum; chair

(*professorial or episcopal*); (*fig.*) professorship, teaching post. ~ *ambulante* (*di agricoltura*, &*c.*), travelling lectureship. **cattedràle**, *f.* cathedral. **cattedrànte**, *m.* professor, holder of a chair. **cattedràtico** (*pl.* -àtici), *a.* authoritative; professorial; pedantic.

cattivàre, *v.t.* & **cattivàrsi**, *v.refl.* to earn, win, gain; captivate, charm.

cattivèllo, *a.* naughty. ¶ *m.* naughty boy. **cattivería**, *f.* wickedness, naughtiness, spite; wicked action; misbehaviour.

cattività, *f.* captivity.

cattivo, *a.* bad, wicked, evil; ill-natured, malicious; mischievous, naughty; poor (*in quality*), paltry, sorry; nasty (*smell*, *taste*); wrong; faulty; wretched; worthless; harsh, rough, bitter (*fig.*).

cattolicésimo & **cattolicísmo**, *m.* catholicism, Roman Catholicism **cattòlico** (*pl.* -òlici), *a.* & *m.* catholic, Roman Catholic; orthodox.

cattúra, *f.* capture, arrest; seizure. *mandato di* ~, warrant for arrest. **catturàre** (*pr.* -úre), *v.t.* to capture, seize, take; arrest, catch.

Catúllo, *m.* Catullus. **Càucaso (il)**, *m.* the Caucasus.

caucciú, *m.* India-rubber, caoutchouc.

caudatàrio, *m.* train-bearer; (*fig.*) toady; hanger-on.

càusa, *f.* cause, occasion, ground[s]; reason, motive; fault; case, action (*Law*); lawsuit, proceedings (*Law*). *a* ~ *di*, on account of, owing to. *per* ~ *mia*, through my fault. *in* ~ *mia*, for my sake. *in* ~ *propria*, for oneself. *far* ~, *muovere* ~, to take legal action, *intentare una* ~ *a*, to bring a suit against. **causàle**, *a.* causal. ¶ *f.* (*Law*) motive. **causàre**, *v.t.* to cause, occasion, bring about, be the cause of, give rise to, produce.

causídico (*pl.* -ídici), *m.* lawyer (practising in the lower courts), attorney.

càustico (*pl.* càustici), *a.* caustic, biting, cutting, pungent. ¶ *m.* caustic (*Phar.*).

cautèla, *f.* caution; prudence; precaution. **cautelàre** (*pr.* -èlo), *v.t.* to defend; protect; make safe. **cautelàrsi**, *v.refl.* to take precautions.

cautèrio, *m.* cautery. **cauterizzàre**, *v.t.* to cauterize; sear.

càuto, *a.* cautious, prudent, wary, circumspect.

cauzióne, *f.* security, bail; caution money. *dare* ~, *prestare* ~, to give bail. *esser rilasciato dietro* ~, to be released on bail.

càva, *f.* quarry; pit, mine.

cavadènti, *m.inv.* tooth-drawer, dentist (*pop.*). **cavafàngo** (*pl.* -ànghi), *m.* dredger.

cavalcàre (*pr.* -àlco, -àlchi), *v.t. & i.* (*aux.* avere) to ride; bestride; go on horseback. **cavalcàta**, *f.* ride; riding; cavalcade; riding-party. **cavalcatúra**, *f.* mount, riding horse. **cavalcavía**, *f.* arch (*or* bridge) over a street, fly-over bridge. **cavalcióne, cavalcióni** (a), *ad.expr. & pr.* astride.

cavalieràto, *m.* knighthood. **cavalière**, *m.* rider, horseman; knight, chevalier; cavalier, gallant; gentleman; dance-partner (*male*); knight (*chess*). ~ *d'industria*, adventurer, swindler. ~ *di ventura*, fortune-hunter. ~ *servente*, lady's man, cavaliere servente. *a* ~ *di*, between. *essere a* ~ *di* (*of hill, &c.*), to command, overlook.

cavàlla, *f.* mare. **cavallàio**, *m.* horse-dealer. **cavallerésco** (*pl.* -éschi), *a.* chivalrous, knightly. *ordine* ~, order of knighthood. *romanzi* ~*eschi*, romances of chivalry. **cavallería**, *f.* cavalry; chivalry. **cavallerìzza**, *f.* riding-school; art of horsemanship. **cavallerìzzo**, *m.* riding-master; ring-master. **cavallétta**, *f.* grasshopper. **cavallétto**, *m.* easel; trestle; gantry. **cavallína**, *f.* filly, young mare. *correr la* ~, to sow one's wild oats. **cavallíno**, *a.* equine, horsy; horse (*species*). *mosca* ~*a*, horse-fly. *tosse* ~*a*, whooping-cough. ¶ *m.* small horse; pony; colt. **cavàllo**, *m.* horse. ~ *a dondolo*, rocking h. ~ *di legno*, ~*da giostra*, vaulting h.; hobby-h. ~ *di razza*, ~ (*di*) *puro sangue*, thoroughbred [h.]. ~*da corsa*, racehorse. ~ *di battaglia*, war-horse, charger; (*fig.*) favourite subject. ~ *da soma*, pack-horse. ~ *da tiro*, draught h., cart h. ~ *da caccia*, hunter. ~ *da noleggio*, hack. ~ *da sella*, saddle-horse. ~ *di San Francesco*, walking-stick. ~ *motore*, horse-power (*abb.* H.P.) (metric. 75 *chilogrammetri per second;* Eng. h.p. 550 foot pounds per second). *un'automobile di* 50 ~*i*, a 50 horse-power car. **cavallóne**, *m.* large horse; (*fig.*) big wave,

breaker, billow. **cavallúccio**, *m.* small horse, nag; honey-cake. *a* ~, astride one's shoulders.

cavapiètre, *m.inv.* quarryman. **cavàre**, *v.t.* to dig, extract; take out. pull out, draw out; remove, take off; wrest, worm out (*secret*); obtain; get, gain; derive. **cavàrsi**, *v.refl.* to free oneself (from), get out (of), get rid (of); quench, appease (*hunger, thirst*); satisfy (*a wish*). **cavàrsela**, *v.refl.* to get off. **cavastivàli**, *m.inv.* boot-jack. **cavàta**, *f.* extraction; excavation. ~ *di sangue*, blood-letting. **cavatàppi & cavaturàccioli**. *m.inv.* corkscrew. **cavatína**, *f.* (*Mus.*) cavatina; refrain; pretext, excuse. **cavatóre**, *m.* digger; miner.

cavèrna, *f.* cavern, cave; den. **cavernóso**, *a.* cavernous, hollow; deep.

cavèzza, *f.* halter.

caviàle, *m.* caviare.

cavícchio, *m.* peg; rung; dibble.

cavíglia, *f.* ankle; ankle-bone; (*Mech.*) plug; (*Naut.*) cleat, belaying pin.

cavillàre, *v.i.* (*aux.* avere) to quibble; raise captious objections. **cavillatóre**, *m.* quibbler. **cavillo**, *m.* quibble; cavil. **cavillóso**, *a.* quibbling; captious.

cavità, *f.inv.* cavity, hollow; hollowness. **càvo**, *a.* hollow, sunken; empty; deep. ¶ *m.* hollow; mould; cable. ~ *sottomarino*, submarine cable.

cavolàia, *f.* cabbage field, c. patch. **cavolfióre**, *m.* cauliflower. **càvolo** *m.* cabbage. ~ *riscaldato*, (*fig.*) old argument repeated as if it were new (*cf.* Scot. 'cauld kale het again'); broken friendship renewed, *&c.* *salvare capra e* ~ *i*, to eat one's cake and have it, to satisfy two contradictory conditions. *non me ne importa un* ~, it does not matter a straw to me, I don't care a fig.

cazzer[u]òla, *f.* saucepan.

cazzottàre, *v.t.* to punch. **cazzòtto**, *m.* punch, blow with the fist.

ce *ad. & conjunct. pn.* used for **ci** before **lo, li, gli, la, le & ne**. there; us, to us. *non* ~ *lo trovai*, I did not find him there. ~ *lo mostra*, he shows it to us.

cécca, *f.* magpie; (*fig.*) talkative woman. **Cécco**, *m. abb.* of Francesco.

cecità, *f.* blindness.

Cèco, *a. & m.* Czech. **Ceco-Slovàcchia** (la), *f.* Czecho-Slovakia. **Ceco-Slovàcco,** *a. & m.* Czecho-Slovak.

cedènte, *m.* (*Law*) assignor; transferrer.

cèdere, *v.i.* (*aux.* avere) to give way, give in, yield, submit, surrender, cave in; *v.t.* to give up, cede, surrender, yield; make over, assign, transfer, dispose of. ~ *il passo a uno,* to make way for someone. *cederla a,* to yield (the palm) to. **cedévole,** *a.* yielding; soft; flexible, supple; accommodating. **cedíbile,** *a.* transferable; assignable.

cedíglia, *f.* cedilla.

cediménto, *m.* yielding; sinking.

cèdola, *f.* coupon; counterfoil; slip; receipt-form; voucher.

cedràto, *a.* citron-flavoured. **cédro,** *m.* citron (*tree or fruit*); cedar. ~ *del Libano,* cedar of Lebanon.

ceffàta, *f.* slap in the face; box on the ear. **cèffo,** *m.* (*animal*) snout, muzzle; (*human*) face (*contemptuously*), as in *un brutto* ~, an ugly face; *far* ~, to make (ugly) faces. **ceffóne,** *m.* (*hard*) slap in the face or box on the ear.

celàre, *v.t.* to conceal, hide; hush up; receive (*stolen property*). **celataménte,** *ad.* secretly.

celebèrrimo, *a.* (*ir. superl. of* **celebre**) very famous; most celebrated. **celebràre** (*pr.* **cèlebro**), *v.t.* to celebrate; solemnize (*wedding, &c.*), keep (*festival*), hold; honour, exalt, sing the praises of. ~ *la messa,* to say mass. **cèlebre,** *a.* celebrated, famous. **celebrità,** *f.inv.* celebrity.

cèlere, *a.* rapid, swift, quick; fast. ¶ *m.* (**il**) ~, quick train; flying squad (*police*). **celerímetro,** *m.* speedometer. **celerità,** *f.* rapidity, swiftness, &c. **celerménte,** *ad.* swiftly, rapidly, quickly.

celèste, *a.* celestial, heavenly; light blue, sky-blue. *i C*~*i,* the Gods, the heavenly powers (*Poet.*). **celestíno,** *a.* pale blue.

cèlia, *f.* jest, joke. **celiàre,** *v.i.* (*aux.* avere) to jest, joke. **celiatore & celione,** *m.* jester, joker.

celibàto, *m.* celibacy, single life; bachelorhood. **cèlibe,** *a. & m.* bachelor, celibate, single, unmarried (*man*). For woman *see* **nubile.**

celidònia, *f.* celandine (*Bot.*).

cèlla, *f.* cell (*prison, monastery, hive*); store-room. **celleràrio,** *m.* cellarer. **cellière,** *m.* store-room; cellar.

cellofàne, *f.* cellophane.

cèllula, *f.* cell (*Biol., Elec., Pol.*). **cellulàre,** *a.* cellular. *segregazione* ~, *f.* close confinement. ¶ *m.* prison, jail. **cellulòide,** *f.* celluloid. **cellulósa,** *f.* cellulose.

Cèlta (*pl.* **Cèlti**), *m.* Celt, Kelt. **cèltico** (*pl.* **cèltici**), *a.* Celtic, Keltic.

cémbalo, *m.* tambourine; harpsichord, spinet.

cementàre (*pr.* **-énto**), *v.t.* to cement. **ceménto,** *m.* cement. ~ *armato,* reinforced concrete.

céna, *f.* supper. *far* ~, to take supper. *La C*~, *l'Ultima C*~, the Last Supper, the Lord's Supper. **cenàcolo,** *m.* supper-room; (*literary & artistic*) set, circle, coterie. *il C*~ *di Leonardo,* Leonardo's *Last Supper.* **cenàre,** *v.i.* (*aux.* avere) to sup, have (take) supper.

cenciàia, *f.* heap of rags. **cenciàio & cenciai[u]òlo,** *m.* -**a,** *f.* rag-picker; rag merchant. **céncio** (*pl.* **cénci**), *m.* rag, scrap (*of cloth, &c.*); duster; dish-cloth; (*pl.*) rags, tatters; tattered clothes; dirty linen (*fig.*); poverty, (the) weak (*fig.*). **cencióso,** *a.* ragged, tattered; in rags. ¶ *m.* ragamuffin.

cénere, *f.* ash[es]; embers; (*pl. fig.*) ashes, dust, remains. *Giorno delle C*~*i, mercoledi delle C . . . i,* or *Le C*~*i,* Ash-Wednesday. **Cenerèntola,** *f.* Cinderella. **ceneríno,** *a.* ash-coloured; ashen grey.

Cenísio (**Monte**), *m.* Mont Cenis.

cénno, *m.* sign, gesture, nod (*head*), wave (*hand*), wink (*eye*); hint; allusion; intimation; notice.

cenotàfio (*pl.* **-àfi**), *m.* cenotaph.

censiménto, *m.* census, taking of the c. *fare il* ~, to take the c. *modulo per il* ~, c. paper. **censire** (*pr.* **-ísco, -ísci**), *v.t.* to take the census of; assess, tax. **cènso,** *m.* patrimony; wealth; taxable income; national revenue; census.

censóre, *m.* censor; critic; examiner (*plays*). **censúra,** *f.* censorship; censure; board of censors. **censuràre,** *v.t.* to censure, criticize, find fault with, reprehend.

centàuro, *m.* centaur (*Myth.*); (*iron.*) motor-cyclist.

centellinàre, *v.t. & i.* (*aux.* avere) to sip. **centellíno,** *m.* sip.

centenàrio, *m.* centenary. ¶ *a. & m.* centenarian. centèŝimo, *a. & m.* hundredth, hundredth part; (*m.*) centesimo, centime, cent. centigrado, *a.* centigrade. centigràmmo, *m.* centigramme. centilitro, *m.* centilitre. centímetro, *m.* centimetre, $\frac{1}{100}$ metre or 0·3937 inch; tape measure (divided into cms., 1½ metres long). centinàio, *m.* (*pl.* centinàia, *f.*) hundred; about a hundred. *a* ~*a*, by hundreds, in hundreds.

centípede, *m.* centipede.

cènto, *a. card. num. inv. & m.* hundred. per ~, per cent. centomíla, *a. card. num. inv.* (a) hundred thousand. centomillèŝimo, *a. ord. num.* hundred thousandth.

centóne, *m.* cento; medley (*Lit. or musical*).

centràle, *a.* central. ¶ *f.* central office. ~ *elettrica,* power plant, power station. centralíno (*telefonico*), *m.* telephone exchange. centraliẑẑàre, *v.t.* to centralize. centràre, *v.t.* to centre. centrífugo (*pl.* -ifughi), *a.* centrifugal. centrípeto, *a.* centripetal. centrísta (*pl.* -ísti), *a.* (*Pol.*) belonging to the Centre. cèntro, *m.* centre; middle; (*fig.*) hub, heart, core; resort; point of concentration or dispersion; town; institute (*for special studies*); (*Foot*) centre. *il C*~, (*Pol.*) the Centre (party or parties of moderate opinions). ~ *avanti* or ~ *attacco,* (*Foot*) centre forward. ~*mediano* or ~ *sostegno,* (*Foot*) centre half-back. ~ *del bersaglio,* bull's-eye.

cèntuplo, *a. & m.* hundredfold, centuple.

céppo, *m.* (tree)stump; log; block; (*Mech.*) brake-block; alms-box; stock (*plough, anchor, family source*); (*pl.*) fetters, bonds, shackles. *C*~, or ~ *di Natale,* Christmas-box; C. log. *pasqua di C*~, or *C*~, Christmas-tide.

céra, *f.* wax, beeswax; aspect, air; face, look, complexion. ~ *da scarpe,* boot-polish. ~ *da calzolaio,* cobbler's wax. *avere una buona* ~, to look well. *far buona* ~ *a,* to welcome heartily. ceralàcca, *f.* sealing-wax.

ceràmica, *f.* ceramics, art of pottery; (*pl.* -àmiche) pieces of pottery.

ceràta (tela), *f.* oil-cloth; wax-cloth.

Cèrbero, *m.* Cerberus (*Myth.*).

cerbiàtto, *m.* fawn. cerbottàna, *f.* pea-shooter; ear-trumpet.

cérca, *f.* search, quest. cercàre (*pr.* cérco, cérchi), *v.t.* to seek, look for, want; ask; (*Radio*) dial; tune in to; *v.i.* (*aux.* avere) (*with* di) to try, endeavour, strive (to). ~ *briga,* to look for trouble. *cércasi* (in advertisements), wanted. cercàta, *f.* search. cercatóre, *m.* -trice, *f.* seeker, inquirer; also *att., e.g. frate* ~*ore,* mendicant friar.

cérchia, *f.* circle, circuit (*esp. of city-walls*); (*fig.*) range, sphere. cerchiàre (*pr.* cérchio, cérchi), *v.t.* to hoop (*casks, &c.*), encircle. cérchio (*pl.* cérchi), *m.* circle, ring; hoop; tyre; crinoline; halo. *far* ~, to stand in a circle. ~ *della morte,* looping the loop (*Aero.*). cerchióne, *m.* tyre, rim (*of a wheel*).

cereàle, *a. & m.* cereal.

cerebràle, *a.* cerebral, brain (*att.*). *febbre* ~, *f.* brain-fever.

cèreo, *a.* waxen; waxy; extremely pale.

Cèrere, *f.* Ceres (*Myth. & Astr.*). cereria,*f.* wax-chandler's shop; wax factory.

cerfòglio, *m.* chervil.

cerimònia, *f.* ceremony; pomp; formality; circumstance; fuss, ado, to-do. *far* ~, to stand on ceremony. *visita di* ~, formal visit. cerimoniàle, *a. & m.* ceremonial. cerimonióso, *a.* ceremonious, formal.

ceríno, *m.* wax match, vesta; taper. céro, *m.* large wax candle, church-c. ceróne, *m.* (*Theat.*) make-up.

cèrnita, *f.* choice, selection; grading.

cerosína, *f.* kerosene.

ceròtto, *m.* plaster; (*fig.*) bore; unsuccessful painting.

cerretàno, *m.* quack, charlatan; swindler.

cerréto, *m.* grove of Turkey oaks. cèrro, *m.* Turkey oak.

certaldése, *m.* native of Certaldo, *esp.* Boccaccio.

certàme, *m.* (*Poet.*) contest, competition.

certaménte, *ad.* certainly; of course. certéẑẑa, *f.* certainty, certitude. certificàre, (*pr.* -ífico, -ífichi) *v.t.* to certify, attest; witness; confirm; assure. certificàto, *m.* certificate, scrip; warrant, voucher; testimonial. ~ *d'azione* or *d'azioni,* share certificate. ~ *nominativo,* registered (share) certificate or scrip. ~*di nascita,* ~ *di morte,* birth, death certificate. **cèrto,** *a.* certain; sure; stated; some. ¶ *pl.m.* some, some people. ¶ *ad.* certainly. *ma* ~! certainly! of course! to be sure!

certósa, *f.* Carthusian monastery; chartreuse (*monastery & liqueur*); Charterhouse. **certosíno,** *m.* Carthusian [monk]; (*fig.*) solitary.

certúno, *pn.indef.* someone, somebody. **certúni,** *pn.pl.* some, some people.

cerúleo, *a.* cerulean, deep-blue.

cerússa, *f.* ceruse, white lead.

cèrva, *f.* hind, doe.

cervèllo (*pl.f.* **cervella,** *pl.m.* (*fig.*) **cervelli,** *m.* brain; brains, intellect, mind, head; sense, judgment; (*Cook.*) brains. ~ *balzano,* madcap, lightheaded fellow. ~*d'oca,* ~*di passero,* ~ *di fringuello,* block-head, empty-headed fellow. *stillarsi* (or *lambiccarsi) il* ~, to rack one's brains. *bruciarsi le* ~*a, farsi saltar le* ~*a,* to blow out one's brains. **cervellòtico** (*pl.* **-òtici),** *a.* queer, fantastic, capricious, unreasonable.

cervíce, *f.* nape of the neck; neck. *di dura* ~, stiff-necked, stubborn.

cervíno, *a.* of or belonging to the deer or stag. *il Monte C*~, the Matterhorn. **cèrvo,** *m.* deer, stag. ~ *volante,* stag-beetle; paper-kite. [*carne di*] ~, *f.* venison.

Cèsare, *m.* Caesar; emperor. *Giulio C*~, Julius Caesar. *i C*~*i,* the Caesars. **cesàreo,** *a.* Caesarean; imperial. *poeta* ~, *m.* poet of the imperial court (of Vienna). *taglio* ~, *m.* Caesarean operation.

cesellàre, *v.t.* to chisel; engrave (*gems*). **cesellatóre,** *m.* carver, sculptor; engraver. **cesèllo,** *m.* chisel; graver.

cesóie, *f.pl.* shears; scissors.

cèspite, *m.* (*Poet.*) tuft (*grass, &c.*); bush. **cèspo,** *m.* bush; shrub; tuft of grass, &c. **cespúglio,** *m.* bush; thicket, clump of bushes.

cessàre, *v.i.* (*aux.* avere) *&r.t.* to cease, leave off, break off, give up, discontinue, stop; *v.i.* (*aux.* essere) to subside, die down. **cessazióne,** *f.* cessation, discontinuance; suspension.

cessionàrio, *m.* assign, assignee; transferee (*Law*). **cessióne,** *f.* assignment; transfer; cession, surrender.

cèsso, *m.* closet, water-closet; lavatory.

césta, *f. & césto,* *m.* basket; hamper. **cestàio,** *m.* basket-maker. **cestinàre,** *v.t.* to throw into the waste-

paper basket. **cestíno,** *m.* small basket; waste-paper b.; (*child's*) go-cart. ~ *da viaggio,* lunch-basket. ~ *per la carta straccia,* waste-paper basket.

cetàceo, *a. & m.* cetacean.

cèto, *m.* class, order, rank.

cétra, *f.* zither; (*Poet.*) lyre.

cetri[u]òlo, *m.* cucumber; (*fig.*) fool, dolt.

Cevènne (**le**) *f.pl.* the Cevennes.

Ceylon (**il**) *m.* Ceylon.

che, ch', *c. & ad.* that; than; as; whether; how; but, only; when, as soon as; lest; let, may. *a meno* ~, unless. *appena* ~, *tosto* ~, as soon as. *di modo* ~, *in modo* ~, so that. *salvo* ~, unless. *se non* ~ (or *sennonché*), but. *senza* ~, without. ¶ *pn.rel.inv.* who, whom; that; which. ¶ *a. & pn.interr. & excl.* what, what? what a . . . ! what! ~ *ora e?* what o'clock is it? ~ *cosa fai?* what are you doing? ~ *c'e?* what is the matter? ~ *bella giornata!* what a fine day! ~*pazienza ci vuole!,* what patience is needed! *a* ~? for what purpose? of what use?

ché, *c.* (= **perché, poiché, affinché,** *&c.*) why, because, since, in order that.

chè, *i.* (*excl. of protest & astonishment*) what! no! never! *ma* ~! of course not! what nonsense! did you ever hear the like!

checché *& checchessía,* *pn.indef.* whatever; anything; everything.

chep[p]í, *m.inv.* képi, peaked cap (*Mil.*).

cherubíno, *m.* cherub.

chetaménte, *ad.* quietly; secretly. **chetàre,** *v.t.* to quiet; appease; silence. **cheticèlla** (**alla**), *ad.expr.* noiselessly; quietly; on the sly. **chéto,** *a.* quiet; still; silent.

chi, *pn.interr.* who? whom? ~*è?* who is it? ~ *c'e?* who is there? ¶ *pn.rel. with antecedent,* he who, him whom, she who, her whom, one who, one whom; whoever. *chi . . . chi . . . ,* some . . . others (*vb.sg.*), one . . . another . . . ~ *rompe paga,* he who calls the tune must pay the piper (*prov.*).

chiàcchiera, *f.* (*oft.pl.*), chatter, gossip, idle talk, false rumour, unfounded report; nonsense. *fare due* ~*e,* to have a chat. **chiac-chieràre** (*pr.* **-àcchiero),** *v.i.* (*aux.* avere) to talk; chat; chatter. **chiac-chieràta,** *f.* talk; chat; empty talk;

chatter. *fare una* ~, to have a talk.
chiacchieríno, *m*. chatterer, chatterbox. **chiacchieróne**, *m*. great
talker, chatterbox; tatler; backbiter.
chiàma, *f*. roll-call. **chiamare**, *v.t.*
to call; call for; hail; summon; name.
~ *al telefono*, to ring up. ~
un'imbarcazione, to hail a boat.
~ *sotto le armi*, to call up (*Mil.*).
~ *in disparte*, to call aside. ~*alla*
ribalta, to call to the footlights
(*Theat.*). *come vi chiamate?* what is
your name? **chiamàta**, *f*. call,
summons; call-up (*Mil.*); recall
(*Theat.*); cross-reference (*book or*
MS.). ~ *telefonica*, telephone call.
Chiànti, *m.inv.* district in Tuscany
famous for its wine; the wine itself.
chiappàre, *v.t.* to catch, seize;
surprise; trap.
chiàra, *f*. white of an egg. **chiara-**
ménte, *ad.* clearly; evidently;
plainly; distinctly, openly; bluntly;
frankly. **chiarézza**, *f*. clearness;
brightness; clarity; lucidity; perspicuity; fame. **chiarificàre**, *v.t.*
to clarify. **chiariménto**, *m*.
explanation. **chiaríre** (*pr.* -**ísco**,
-**ísci**), *v.t.* to make clear; explain;
clear up, remove (*doubt*, *&c.*);
illuminate, lighten up; put in the
high lights (*in picture*). **chiarírsi**,
v.refl. to become clear; make oneself
clear; assure oneself, ascertain; (*sky*,
weather) clear, clear up. **chiàro**, *a.*
clear, bright, light (*colour*); distinct,
plain, evident; intelligible; famous,
eminent, renowned. *giorno* ~, full
day-light. *vestir di* ~, to wear
light-coloured clothes. ¶ *m*. light;
brightness; clearness. ~ *di luna*,
moonlight. *mettere in* ~, to clear
up; explain; show clearly. ¶ *ad.*
clearly. ~ *e tondo*, frankly; openly.
chiaróre, *m*. light (*faint*), brightness;
gleam, glimmer; first light. ~ *del-*
l'alba, first light of dawn. **chiaro-**
scúro (*pl.* **chiaroscúri**), *m*. light
& shade; chiaroscuro.
chiaroveggènte, *a.* clear-sighted.
chiaroveggènza, *f*. clear-sighted-
ness.
chiassàta, *f*. hubbub, row, racket;
(noisy) scene. **chiàsso**, *m*. din,
noise, uproar; lane (*gen. in dim.*
chiassuòlo, chiassétto, chiassolíno).
far ~, to make a sensation, attract
attention. **chiassóne**, *m*. -**óna**, *f*.
noisy person; lover of noise.
chiassóso, *a.* noisy; loud (*of*
colour).

chiàtta, *f*. lighter, flat-bottomed boat;
pontoon. *ponte di* ~*e*, *m*. bridge of
boats.
chiavàccio, *m*. door bolt (*large*); bar.
chiavàio, *m*. locksmith. **chiàve**, *f*.
key; clue (*puzzle*); spanner, wrench;
plug, spigot; (*Mus.*) clef. ~ *dello*
scatto, latch-key. ~ *falsa*, skeleton
key. ~ *apritutto*, ~ *maestra*,
master-key. ~ *inglese*, monkey
wrench, coach w. *sotto* ~, locked
up, under lock & key. ~ *della*
volta, keystone (*lit. & fig.*). ~ *di*
sol, G (or treble) clef. ~ *di basso*,
F (or bass) c. **chiavétta**, *f*. small
key; cock, tap (*water*, *gas*). ~ *da*
orologio, watch-key. **chiavistèllo**,
m. bolt (*door or window*).
chiàzza, *f*. spot; stain. **chiazzàre**,
v.t. to spot, stain; mottle.
chícca, *f*. sweet, sweetmeat. **chíc-**
chera, *f*. small cup, coffee-c.
chicchessía (for **chi** *che* **sia**),
pn.indef.inv. anyone, anybody.
chicchirichí, *m*. cock-crow, cock-a-
doodle-doo.
chícco (*pl.* **chícchi**), *m*. grain, pip,
bean (*coffee*), stone (*grape*, *hail*);
grape (*c. d'uva*).
chiedènte, *m. & f*. applicant, plaintiff. **chiédere**, *v.t.ir.* to ask; ask for;
beg. ~ *un favore a qualcuno*, to ask
a favour of someone. ~ *qualcosa*
a qualcuno, to ask someone for
something. ~ *mille lire di qualcosa*,
to ask 1000 lire for something. *mi*
chiese del danaro, he asked me for
[some] money. ~ *perdono*, ~ *scusa*,
to ask (or beg) pardon.
chièrica, *f*. tonsure; (*fig.*) priesthood.
chiericàto, *m*. holy orders; priesthood, clergy. **chièrico** (*pl.* -**èrici**),
m. priest in minor orders; clerk,
cleric. **chierichétto**, *m*. chorister,
choir-boy; minor clerk.
chièsa, *f*. church. *la C*~ *anglicana*,
the Church of England. *la C*~
cattolica, the [Roman] Catholic c. ~
luterana, the Lutheran c. **chiesétta**,
f. small church. **chies[u]òla**, *f*.
small church; (*fig.*) group, set
(*literary*, *artistic*, *political*, *&c.*).
chíglia (*pl.* **chíglie**), *f*. keel.
chílo, *m*. chyle (*Med.*); abb. of chilo-
gramma. **chilocíclo**, *m*. kilocycle
(*Radio*). **chilogràmma** (*pl.* **chilo-**
grammi), *m*. kilogramme = 1000
grammes or 2.2046 lbs. **chílo-**
metro, *m*. kilometre = 1000 metres
or 0.62137 (about ⅝) mile. **chilo-**
mètrico (*pl.* -**mètrici**), *a.*

kilometric[al]. **chilowàtt**, *m.inv.*
(*Elec.*) kilowatt.
chimèra, *f.* chim[a]era. **chimèrico**
(*pl.* -**èrici**), *a.* chimerical; visionary,
fanciful, illusory.
chímica, *f.* chemistry. **chímico** (*pl.*
chímici), *a.* chemical. ¶ *m.* chemist
(*scientist*).
chimòno, *m.* kimono.
chína, *f.* slope, descent, declivity;
(*Bot.*) cinchona; Peruvian bark.
chinàre, *v.t.* to bend, bow, incline;
lower. **chinàrsi**, *v.refl.* to bend
down, stoop; submit.
chincaglière, *m.* ironmonger.
chincaglieria, *f.* hardware, ironmongery; ironmonger's shop.
chiníno, *m.* quinine.
chíno, *a. & sync. p.p.* of **chinare**,
bent, bowed, inclined.
chioccàre, *see* **schioccàre**.
chiòccia (*pl.* -**òcce**), *f.* brooding hen.
far la ~, to crouch. **chiocciàre**
(*pr.* -**òccio**, -**òcci**), *v.i.* (*aux.* avere)
to cluck. **chiocciàta**, *f.* brood of
chickens.
chiòcciola, *f.* snail; (*Anat.*) inner
portion of the ear; female screw.
scala a ~, spiral stair-case, winding
stair.
chioccolàre, *v.i.* (*aux.* avere) to
whistle (*like blackbird, &c.*); gurgle.
chioccolío, *m.* whistling (*of birds*);
gurgle (*water*). **chiòccolo**, *m.* bird-
whistle (*toy*); bird-call.
chiòdo, *m.* nail; (*fig.*) sharp pain;
neuralgic headache; fixed idea;
(*fam.*) debt. ~ *di garofano*, clove.
~ *da ribadire*, rivet. *passaggio
tracciato da* ~*i*, studded crossing.
piantare il ~, to be obstinate.
piantar ~*i*, to run into debt.
chiodóne, *m.* big nail, hob-nail.
chiòma, *f.* hair, head of hair; mane;
tail (*of comet*); (*Poet.*) foliage. **chio-
màto**, *a.* long-haired, with flowing
hair; (*Poet.*) leafy.
chiòsa, *f.* explanatory note, comment,
gloss. **chiosàre**, *v.t.* to annotate;
explain.
chiòsco (*pl.* -**òschi**), *m.* kiosk; stall;
bookstall.
chiòstro, *m.* cloister; convent; cell;
monastic life.
chiòtto, *a.* quiet, noiseless. ~ ~,
very still, perfectly silent.
chirografàrio, *a.* unsecured (*creditors, debts*); simple, naked (*deben-
tures*). *debitore* ~, book-debtor.
chirògrafo, *m.* written agreement;
bond under one's own hand.

chiromànte, *m. & f.* palmist, fortune-
teller. **chiromanzía**, *f.* palmistry.
chirurgía, *f.* surgery. **chirúrgico** (*pl.*
-**úrgici**), *a.* surgical. **chirúrgo**
(*pl.* -**úrgi** & -**úrghi**), *m.* surgeon.
Chisciòtte (**Don**), *m.* Don Quixote.
chisciottésco & **donchisciottésco**
(*pl.* -**éschi**), *a.* quixotic.
chitàrra, *f.* guitar. **chitarrísta** (*pl.*
-**ísti**), *m.* guitar-player.
chiú, *m.inv.* horned owl.
chiudènda, *f.* fence; paling; enclosure;
oven-door. **chiúdere**, *v.t. ir.* to
shut, close; shut off, turn off (*gas*);
shut up; stop (*hole*); clench (*fist*);
conclude, end, finish; enclose, confine; (*v.i.*) (*aux.* avere) to close, shut.
chiúdersi, *v.refl.* to close, end; shut
oneself up; (*of weather*) to be overcast.
chiúnque, *pn.indef.inv.* whoever,
whomsoever; any one who, anyone
whom; anyone, anybody.
chiúrlo, *m.* curlew.
chiúsa, *f.* barrier; dyke; dam, weir;
(*canal*) lock; enclosure; close, end,
conclusion. **chiúso**, *p.p.* of chiudere.
¶ *a.* close, closed, shut; enclosed;
secret; taciturn, reserved; (*weather*)
cloudy, overcast. ¶ *m.* enclosure;
pen; fold. **chiusúra**, *f.* closing,
closure; close; fastening; lock.
ci, *ad.* here; there (*unemphatic*; *for
emphasis* **qui** (here) & **là** (there).
~*siamo*, here we are. *c'è* . . ., *ci sono*,
there is . . ., there are . . . (*Fr. il y a*)
c'è chi dice, there are some who say.
¶ *pn. pers. conjunc.* us; to us; (*recipr.*)
each other, one another; (*refl.*) ourselves. ¶ *pn. demons.* (= Fr. **y**) of
it; about it; to it; at it; in it; by it; it;
that. *pensarci*, to think of it. *pensarci
su*, to think over it. *non ci badate*,
never mind that. *ci ho proprio gusto*,
I am very glad of it. *ci ho rimorso*,
I am sorry for it, I regret it.
N.B.—Before **lo, li, gli, la, le** &
ne, **ci** becomes **ce**. *ce lo disse*, he
told us so. *ce ne parlò*, he spoke to
us of it.
ciabàtta, *f.* slipper; down-at-heel
shoe. **ciabattíno**, *m.* cobbler.
ciàlda, *f.* sweet wafer; waffle.
cialdóne, *m.* wafer (*cornet*).
cialtróne, *m.* rascal, rogue, scoundrel;
shabby fellow (*in action or dress*).
cialtronería, *f.* rascality; roguery;
meanness (*of person and conduct*).
ciambèlla, *f.* ring-shaped cake; air-
cushion; (*child's*) teething-ring;
round pad.

ciambellàno, m. (court) chamberlain.
ciampicàre (pr. -àmpico, -àmpichi), v.i. (aux. avere) to stumble; shuffle (along). ciampicóne, m. shuffler; dawdler.
ciància (pl. ciànce), f. unfounded rumour; (pl.) gossip, tittle-tattle, idle talk; nonsense. cianciafrúscola, f. trifle, bagatelle. cianciàre (pr. -àncio, -ànci), v.i. (aux. avere) to chatter, talk nonsense. cianciatóre (f. -tríce), a. chattering. ¶ m.f. tatler, gossip.
cianfruśàglia, f. trash, rubbish.
cíano, m. cornflower. cianografía, f. cyanotype, blue-print. cianòśi, f. (Med.) cyanosis.
cianúro, m. cyanide.
ciào, i. (pop.) good-bye! so long!
ciàrla, f. idle rumour; false report; (pl.) gossip, idle talk; tittle-tattle. ciarlàre, v.i. (aux. avere) to chatter; gossip. ciarlataneria, f. quackery, charlatanism. ciarlatàno, m. charlatan; quack; cheap-jack. ciarlóne, m. -óna, f. great talker, idle t.; chatterbox.
ciarpàme, m. quantity of rubbish, rags, junk, &c.
ciascúno & ciaschedúno, a. each. ¶ pn.indef. each one, each person; everyone (individually).
cibàre, v.t. to feed. cibàrsi (di), v.refl. to feed (on), live (on). cibo, m. food, diet; dish, meal. cibòrio, m. ciborium, pyx.
cicàla, f. cicada. cicalàre (pr. -àlo), v.i. (aux. avere) to babble, chatter. cicalàta, f. long wearisome talk. cicalio (pl. -ii), m. continuous chatter (or chattering).
cicatríce, f. scar, mark. cicatriżżàre, v.t. v.i. (aux. essere) & cicatrizzàrsi, v.refl. to scar, mark; heal, skin over.
cícca (pl. cícche), f. stub, stump, cigar (or cigarette) end; quid (tobacco). ciccai[u]òlo, m. picker-up of cigar or cigarette-ends. ciccàre (pr. cícco, cícchi), v.i. (aux. avere) to chew tobacco.
cíccia, f. meat; flesh (human). cicciúto, a. plump.
cícero, m. (Typ.) pica. carattere ~, pica type.
ciceróne, m. guide, cicerone. C~, Cicero.
cicisbèo, m. lady's man; cicisbeo.
ciclamíno, m. cyclamen.
ciclíśmo, m. cycling. ciclísta (pl. -ísti), m.f. cyclist. ciclístico (pl.

-ístici), a. cycling (att.), cycle (att.) gara ~a, cycle-race. giro ~, cycling tour. See also bicicletta. cíclo, m. cycle (Math., Astr., Radio, legends); course (disease); [bi]cycle.
ciclóne, m. cyclone.
Ciclòpe, m. Cyclop[s] (Myth.).
ciclostíle, m. cyclostyle.
cicógna, f. stork.
cicòria, f. chicory.
cicúta, f. hemlock.
cièco (pl. cièchi), a. blind; dark; without exit; without doors or windows; unquestioning; inconsiderate. alla ~a, blindly, rashly. lanterna ~a, dark-lantern. mosca ~a, blindman's buff. vicolo ~, blind alley. ¶ m. blind man, -a, f. blind woman.
cièlo, m. heaven, heavens, sky; air; climate, clime; canopy; roof. a ~ aperto, in the open air. ~ coperto, overcast sky. per amor del ~, for heaven's sake. giusto C~! santo C~! Good Heavens!
cifra, f. figure, number, numeral (Arabic); cipher; amount; monogram. in ~ tonda, in round figures, in round numbers; approximately. ~ d'affari, turnover (Com.). ~ -indice, index number. cifràre, v.t. to write in cipher; mark (linen, &c.) with a monogram or initials.
cíglio (pl.f. cíglia, pl.m. cígli), m. eyelash; (fig.) eye(s), brow; look; edge, brink; verge, rim. aggrottare le ~a, to frown. in un batter di ~o, in the twinkling of an eye. ciglióne, m. bank, embankment; border, edge.
cignàle, m. wild boar.
cígno, m. swan; (fig.) poet, musician. canto del ~, swan-song.
cigolàre, v.i. (aux. avere) to creak; grate; squeak; hiss. cigolio (pl. -ii), m. (continuous) creaking, &c.
cilécca, f. failure; false hope, disappointment. far ~, to miss fire (lit. & fig.).
cilestríno & cilèstro, a. sky-blue, light-b.
cilício (pl. -íci), m. sackcloth; hair-shirt.
ciliegéto, m. cherry-orchard. ciliègia (pl. -ègie), f. cherry. ratafia di ~egie, f. cherry brandy. ciliègio (pl. -ègi), m. cherry-tree; c. wood.
cilindràre, v.t. to roll, press, smooth; mangle; calender. cilíndrico (pl. -índrici), a. cylindrical. cilíndro, m. cylinder; roller; roll; calender,

hot-press; barrel; drum. *cappello a ~* (*or ~*), top-hat.

címa, *f.* top, summit, peak; (*fig.*) highest point or degree; genius. *da ~ a fondo*, from top to bottom. *non è una ~*, he is not very bright. **cimàre**, *v.t.* to lop; poll; clip; shear; take the head off. **cimatúra**, *f.* clipping; clippings.

címbalo, *m.* cymbal. *essere in ~i*, to be merry, to be tipsy.

cimèlio (*pl.* -**èli**), *m.* curio; antique.

cimentàre (*pr.* -**énto**), *v.t.* to put to the test, try; risk; assay. **cimentàrsi**, *v.refl.* expose oneself to danger; strive, exert oneself. *~in*, to venture upon. **ciménto**, *m.* risky venture; trial, test.

címice, *f.* bug; drawing-pin.

cimièro, *m.* crest, heraldic ornament; (*Poet.*) helmet.

ciminièra, *f.* funnel; smoke-stack.

cimitèro, *m.* cemetery, burial ground, graveyard.

cimósa, *f.* selvage; rag for wiping a slate.

cimúrro, *m.* glanders.

Cína (la), *f.* China.

cinàbro, *m.* cinnabar; vermilion; red (*of lips or complexion*).

cíncia (*pl.* **cínce**) & **cinciallégra**, *f.* tit, tomtit.

cincílla, *f.* chinchilla (fur).

cíne & **cínema**, *m.abb. of* **cinematografo**. **cineàsta** (*pl.* -**àsti**), *m.* film-lover, film-fan; film-artist. **cinegiornàle** & **cinemagiornàle**, *m.* news-reel. **cinelàndia**, *f.* film-land, world of the films; film industry. **cinematografàre**, *v.t.* to film. **cinematografía**, *f.* cinematography. **cinematogràfico** (*pl.* -**àfici**), *a.* cinematographic; film (*att.*). *studio ~*, film studio. *attrice ~a*, film actress. **cinematògrafo**, *m.* cinematograph, cinema; picture-house, p. palace; pictures. *cinema a rilento*, slow-motion pictures.

cinerària, *f.* cineraria (*Bot.*). **cineràrio**, *a.* cinerary. **cinèreo**, *a.* ashy; ashen grey.

cinése, *a.* Chinese. *il ~*, Chinese (*language*). ¶ *m.f.* Chinese; China-man, Chinese woman.

cinètico (*pl.* -**ètici**), *a.* kinetic.

cingallègra, *see* cincia.

cíngere, *v.t. ir.* to surround, encompass, encircle; girdle; belt; wreathe; gird on (*sword*), put on; bind, clasp, embrace; border.

~d'assedio, to besiege. *~di una siepe*, to fence. **cínghia** (*pl.* **cínghie**), *f.* strap; thong; belt; (*pl.*) braces.

cinghiàle, *m.* wild boar.

cíngolo, *m.* girdle; belt (*Mech.*). *catena a ~i*, endless belt.

cinguettàre (*pr.* -**étto**), *v.i.* (*aux.* avere) to chirp, twitter; chatter, prattle. **cinguettío** (*pl.* -**ii**), *m.* (continual) chirping, twittering, &c.

cínico (*pl.* **cínici**), *a.* cynic, cynical. ¶ *m.* cynic. **cinísmo**, *m.* cynicism.

cínnamo & **cinnamòmo**, *m.* cinnamon.

cinquànta, *a. card. num.* & *m.inv.* fifty. **cinquantenàrio**, *m.* fiftieth anniversary. **cinquantènne**, *a.* fifty years old. ¶ *m.f.* man (or woman) of fifty. **cinquantènnio**, *m.* period of fifty years. **cinquantèsimo**, *a. num.ord.* fiftieth. **cinquantína**, *f.* fifty or so. *essere sulla ~*, to be about fifty years old.

cínque, *a.* & *m.inv.* five; fifth. **cinquecentésco** (*pl.* -**éschi**), *a.* of the 16th century; 16th century (*att.*). **cinquecentista** (*pl.* -**isti**), *m.* writer (or artist) of the 16th century. **cinquecènto**, *a.* & *m.inv.* five hundred. *il C~*, the 16th century; the Cinquecento. **cinquína**, *f.* set of five; five numbers (*lottery*, &c.); soldier's (five days') pay; actor's pay.

cínta, *f.* circuit; bounds; enclosure. **cínto**, *p.p.* of **cingere**. ¶ *m.* girdle; belt. *~ erniario*, truss. *il ~ di Venere*, the girdle of Venus. **cíntola**, *f.* waist; waistband. **cintúra**, *f.* belt, girdle; sash; waistband; waist, middle; waist lock (*Wrestling*); enclosure. *~ di salvataggio*, life-belt. *~ porta bretelle*, suspender b. *~ corazzata*, armour-plated belt (*warship*). **cinturóne**, *m.* belt (*sword*, &c.).

Cínzia, *f.* Cynthia (*Myth.*).

ciò, *pn.demons.inv.* that, this (*gen. referring to a fact or statement*). *a ~*, for this purpose, to that end. *con tutto ~*, for all that, nevertheless. *oltre a ~*, besides, moreover. *~ nonostante*, notwithstanding that, in spite of that. *essere da ~*, to be fit for that, to be capable of that.

ciòcca (*pl.* **ciòcche**), *f.* lock, tuft (*hair*); bunch, cluster (*flowers*, &c.). **ciòcco** (*pl.* **ciòcchi**), *m.* log, block (*wood*).

cioccolàta, *f.* chocolate; cocoa (*as a*

drink). ~ *al latte,* cocoa *(drink);*
milk chocolate. **cioccolatièra,** *f.*
chocolate-pot. **cioccolatière,** *m.*
chocolate manufacturer; c. seller.
cioccolatíno, *m.* chocolate *(sweet);*
(pl.) chocolates.
ciòcia *(pl.* **ciòcie),** *f.* rough shoe,
sandal *(worn by peasants of the
Roman campagna).* **ciociàro,** *m.*
-àra, *f.* peasant of the Roman
campagna.
cioè, *ad.* that is *(abb.* i.e.); namely
(abb. viz.).
ciémpo, *m.* wool-carder (in 14th
century Florence); plebeian. *i C~i,*
(Hist.) the Ciompi.
cioncàre *(pr.* **-ónco, ónchi),** *v.t.
& i.* to swill, tipple; drink to
excess.
ciondolàre *(pr.* **-óndolo),** *v.i.* *(aux.*
avere) to dangle; sway, totter; *(fig.)*
lounge; *(v.t.)* to swing *(arms),* roll
(head, &c.). **cióndolo,** *m.* trinket;
pendant. **ciondolóne,** *m.* dawdler;
lounger. **ciondolóni,** *ad.* dangling;
with a swaying movement.
ciòtola, *f.* bowl, cup.
ciottolàto, *m.* rough pavement;
pebbled path; crazy pavement.
ciòttolo, *m.* pebble; stone.
cipài, *m.inv.* sepoy.
cipíglio *(pl.* **-igli),** *m.* frown, scowl.
cipólla, *f.* onion; bulb; rose *(watering-
can).* **cipollàio** *(pl.* **-ài),** *m.* onion-
bed; o.-seller. **cipollína,** *f.* young
onion. ~*e sott'aceto,* pickled
onions.
cippo, *m.* column *(truncated);* pillar.
cipressàia, *f. &* **cipresseto,** *m.*
cypress-grove. **ciprèsso,** *m.* cypress
(tree & wood).
cipría, *f.* powder, toilet powder.
Cípro, *m.* Cyprus; C. wine.
circa, *ad.* about, approximately,
nearly. ¶ *pr. & ~ a,* about, as to,
concerning, regarding.
circàsso, *a. & m.* Circassian.
circo *(pl.* **circhi),** *m.* circus, *gen. in the
form ~ equestre.*
circolànte, *p.a.* circulating. **circo-
làre,** *v.i.* *(aux.* avere *&* essere) to
circulate, run, travel; move on;
(money) be current. *circolàte!* move
on! pass along! *far ~,* to put into
circulation, circulate, send round,
give currency to. ¶ *a. & f.* circular.
biglietto~, c. ticket, tourist ticket.
circolazióne, *f.* circulation,
running, travelling; traffic; currency;
turnover, sales. ~ *cartacea,* paper
currency. *vietata la ~,* no thorough-

fare *(vehicles).* ~ *in senso unico,*
one-way traffic.
círcolo, *m.* circle, circuit; club,
society; group; reception; district,
quarter, area, region.
circoncídere, *v.t. ir.* to circumcise.
circondàre *(pr.* **-óndo),** *v.t.* to
surround. **circondàrio,** *m.* district,
administrative sub-division of a
province. *tribunale di ~,* district
court, county court.
circonferènza, *f.* circumference,
girth.
circonflèsso, *a. & m.* circumflex.
circonlocuzióne, *f.* circumlocution.
circonvallazióne, *f.* outer circle
(walls, road, Rly., &c.); circular line
of defence.
circonveníre *(pr.* **-èngo,** *&c.,* like
venire), v.t. ir. to circumvent, outwit, overreach.
circoscrítto, *a.* circumscribed,
bounded, limited. **circoscrívere,**
v.t. ir. to circumscribe, limit; locate.
circoscrizióne, *f.* circumscription;
area. ~ *elettorale,* parliamentary
division, constituency.
circospètto, *a.* circumspect, cautious,
wary, guarded.
circostànza, *f.* circumstance, occasion;
opportunity. *alla ~,* according to
circumstances, if the opportunity
arises.
circuíre *(pr.* **-ísco, -ísci),** *v.t.* to
surround, encircle; circumvent, get
round; deceive, entrap. **circúito,**
m. circuit, round; round race.
~ *chiuso,* ~ *aperto,* ~ *corto,* close,
open, short circuit *(Elec.).*
Cirenàica (la), *f.* Cyrenaica.
círro, *m.* curl, lock of hair; *(Bot.)*
tendril; *(Meteor.)* cirrus cloud.
cirròsi, *f.* *(Med.)* cirrhosis.
cisalpíno, *a.* cisalpine, on the nearer
(S.) side of the Alps. **cispadàno,** *a.*
on the nearer *(S.)* side of the Po.
cispóso, *a.* rheumy, blear-eyed.
cistercènse, *a. & m.* Cistercian.
cistèrna, *f.* tank, cistern. *nave ~,*
tanker, tank steamer, *f. acqua di ~,*
rain-water, *f.*
cisti, *f.inv.* cyst, tumour. **cistíte,** *f.*
(Med.) cystitis.
citànte, *m.f.* plaintiff. **citàre,** *v.t.* to
cite, quote; mention; instance;
(Law) summon[s], sue. **citàto,** *m.*
defendant, person served with a
subpoena. **citazióne,** *f.* citation;
quotation; summons, subpoena.
Citerèa, *f.* Cytherea, Venus.
citerióre, *a.* hither *(Geog.).*

citíso or **cítiso**, *m.* laburnum.
citràto, *m.* citrate. **cítrico** (*pl.* **cítrici**), *a.* citric. **citríno**, *a.* citrine, lemon-coloured.
citrúllo, *a.* simple, stupid, silly. ¶ *m.* simpleton.
città, *f.inv.* city, town. ~ *giardino*, *f.* garden city. ~ *universitaria*, university centre, u. city. **citta-dèlla**, *f.* citadel; stronghold. **citta-dína**, *f.* small city. **cittadinànza**, *f.* citizenship, freedom of a city; body of citizens, population. **citta-dinésco** (*pl.* -**éschi**), *a.* citizen (*att.*) **cittadíno**, *m.* citizen, burgess; townsman. ¶ *a.* civic; city (*att.*).
cítto, *m.* (*pop. Tusc.*) boy. **cítta**, *f.* girl. *dim.* cittino, -a, cittolo, -a, cittolello, -a, &c.
ciúca (*pl.* **ciúche**), *f.* she-ass; donkey. **ciucàggine**, *f.* stupidity. **ciúco** (*pl.* **ciúchi**), *m.* ass, donkey. *With many dims.:* ciuchino, ciuchetto, ciuca-rello, ciucherello, &c.
ciúffo, *m.* tuft (*hair, feathers*); forelock; tassel; group of trees; bunch; cluster.
ciuffolòtto, *m.* bullfinch.
ciuffóne, *m.* big tuft; (*fig.*) shock-headed fellow, untidy person.
ciúrma, *f.* crew. **ciurmàglia**, *f.* mob; rabble. **ciurmàre**, *v.t.* to charm, cheat, inveigle.
civétta, *f.* owl; flirt, coquette. **civettàre** (*pr.* -**étto**), *v.i.* (*aux.* avere) to flirt. **civettería**, *f.* coquetry.
cívico (*pl.* **cívici**), *a.* civic; municipal.
civíle, *a.* civil; civilian (*att.*); civilized, refined. *abito* ~, plain clothes; (*Mil.*) mufti. *coraggio* ~, moral courage; public spirit. *diritto* ~, civil law. *parte* ~, *f.* plaintiff.
civilizzàre, *v.t.* to civilize. **civi-lizzatóre**, -**trice**, *a.* civilizing. **civiltà**, *f.* civilization; civility, good manners, courtesy.
clamóre, *m.* clamour, outcry; din, noise. **clamoróso**, *a.* clamorous; noisy.
clarino, *m.* clari[o]net.
clàsse, *f.* class, order; division, rank; rate; (*Sch.*) form, standard; (*Mil.*) levy, contingent (*of recruiting year*). *di* ~, of excellent quality. *fuori* ~, superlative, of s. quality. *le* ~*i medie*, the middle classes. *le* ~*i dirigenti*, the ruling classes. **classicismo**, *m.* classicism. **clàssico** (*pl.* **clàssici**), *a.* classic(al). **classificàre** (*pr.* -**ífico**, -**ífichi**), *v.t.* to classify; class. **classificazióne**, *f.* classifica-

tion; classing; rating; order, position (*Running, &c.*); also **classífica**, *f.* in the latter sense.
claudicàre, *v.i.* (*aux.* avere) to limp. **claudicazióne**, *f.* limping; lame-ness.
clàusola, *f.* clause; proviso, stipula-tion; close of a period or sentence.
claustràle, *a.* cloistral, claustral.
clàva, *f.* club, bludgeon.
clavicémbalo, *m.* harpsichord, spinet.
clemàtide, *f.* clematis, traveller's joy (*Bot.*).
clemènte, *a.* clement, mild, lenient; merciful. **clemènza**, *f.* clemency, mercy, leniency; mildness.
cleptòmane, *a.* & *m.* kleptomaniac. **cleptomanía**, *f.* kleptomania.
clericàle, *a.* & *m.* clerical. **clerical-ísmo**, *m.* clericalism. **clericàto**, *m.* clergy; priesthood. **clèro**, *m.* clergy.
cliché, (*Fr.*) *m.* stereotype; block; negative. ~ *a mezza tinta*, half-tone block. (Cf. *stereotipo* & *zincotipia*.)
cliènte, *m.f.* client, customer; patient. **clientèla**, *f.* clientele, public, con-nection; (*Med.*) practice; (*business*) custom; goodwill.
clíma (*pl.* **clími**), *m.* climate. **clima-tèrico** (*pl.* -**èrici**), *a.* climacteric (*Med.*); critical, dangerous. **climà-tico** (*pl.* -**àtici**), *a.* climatic.
clínica, *f.* clinic; nursing-home; surgery (*room*); clinical medicine. **clínico** (*pl.* **clínici**), *a.* clinical. ¶ *m.* clinician.
clistère, *m.* (*Med.*) enema.
clivo, *m.* (*Poet.*) low hill, declivity, slope.
cloàca, *f.* sewer, drain; (*fig.*) cesspool, sink.
cloràlio, *m.* chloral. **cloràto**, *m.* chlorate. **clorídrico** (*pl.* -**ídrici**), *a.* hydrochloric. **clòro**, *m.* chlor-ine. **cloroförmio**, *m.* chloroform. **cloroformizzàre**, *v.t.* to chloro-form. **cloròsi**, *f.* (*Med.*) chlorosis, green sickness. **clorúro**, *m.* chloride.
co' *pr.* & *art.* = **coi**, with the (*m.pl.*).
co-, com-, con-, *as prefix*; **co-** before a vowel or impure **s**; **com-** before a mute labial consonant; **con-** in all other cases.
coabitàre, *v.i.* (*aux.* avere) to cohabit. **coabitazióne**, *f.* cohabitation.
coaccusàto, *m.* fellow accused, fellow prisoner.
coadiutóre, -**trice**, *f.* coadjutor, assistant. **coadiuvàre**, *v.t.* to assist, support; co-operate with.

coagulàre, *v.t.* & coagulàrsi, *v.refl.* to coagulate.

coalizióne, *f.* coalition; alliance. coalizzàrsi, *v.refl.* to coalesce; combine; form an alliance.

coartàre, *v.t.* to coerce, constrain, force.

coàtto, *a.* forced, imposed by force. *domicilio ~,* forced residence in a given place.

cobàlto, *m.* cobalt.

cocaína, *f.* cocaine.

cócca (*pl.* cócche), *f.* notch (*arrow*); bow-string; corner (*sheet, apron, &c.*); (*pop.*) hen; pet child.

coccàrda, *f.* cockade, rosette.

cocchière, *m.* coachman, driver; cabman. còcchio (*pl.* cócchi), *m.* coach.

còccia (*pl.* còcce), *f.* swelling, pimple; shell, bark, pod; pipe-bowl; hilt, sword-guard; (*pop.*) head, pate.

coccinèlla, *f.* ladybird. cocciníglia, *f.* cochineal (*insect*). *carminio della ~,* cochineal (*dye*). Cf. *grana.*

còccio (*pl.* còcci), *m.* fragment of pottery; cracked pot; (*pers.*) crock, weakling; (*pl.*) earthenware, crockery.

cocciúto, *a.* obstinate, pig-headed.

còcco (*pl.* còcchi), *m.* coco-nut, coco-palm; (*child's language*) egg; (*pop.*) pet, darling.

coccodè, *m.inv.* (*hen*) cluck, clucking. *far ~,* to cluck.

coccodríllo, *m.* crocodile.

còccola, *f.* berry (*cypress, juniper, laurel, &c.*). coccolàrsi, *v.refl.* to nestle, lie at ease. coccolóni, *ad.* squatting.

cocènte, *p.a.* burning; (*fig.*) acute, bitter, vehement.

Cocincína (la), *f.* Cochin-China.

cocómero, *m.* water melon.

cocúzzolo, *m.* crown (*head, hat*); peak, summit.

códa, *f.* tail; brush (*fox*); train (*dress*); queue; file; rear, end, foot; *far ~,* to form a queue; await one's turn. *abito a ~ di rondine, m.* [swallow] tails (*dress coat*). *pianoforte a ~, m.* grand piano.

codardía, *f.* cowardice. codàrdo, *a.* cowardly. ¶ *m.* coward.

codésto, *a.* & *pn.* this; that. *Cf.* cotésto.

còdice, *m.* code; statute book; law; codex, manuscript in book form. *~ civile, ~ penale,* civil, penal code. *~ stradale,* highway code.

codicíllo, *m.* codicil.

codificàre (*pr.* -íficò, -ífichi), *v.t.* to codify.

codíno, *m.* small tail; pigtail; (*fig.*) Tory, reactionary.

coefficiènte, *m.* coefficient.

coerède, *m.f.* joint heir, -ess.

coerènte, *a.* coherent; consistent. coerènza, *f.* coherence; consistency. coesióne, *f.* cohesion.

coesístere, *v.i.* (*aux.* essere) to co-exist.

coetàneo, *a.* & *m.* contemporary.

coèvo, *a.* coeval.

cofanétto, *m.* small casket; jewel case. còfano, *m.* casket; chest; ammunition box; bonnet (*of a car*).

còffa, *f.* (*Naut.*) top. *~ di maestra,* maintop. *~ di mezzana,* mizzentop.

cogitabóndo, *a.* meditative, thoughtful.

cògliere & còrre (*pr.* còlgo, cògli, còglie, &c.*), *v.t. ir.* to pluck; pick; seize; catch; gather, collect; hit; surprise; overtake; understand.

cognàc, *m.* cognac, brandy.

cognàta, *f.* sister-in-law. cognàto, *m.* brother-in-law. ¶ *a.* cognate.

cognizióne, *f.* knowledge; cognition; (*pl.*) knowledge, learning, culture.

cognóme, *m.* surname, family name.

coiàio, *m.* leather dresser; dealer in leather & hides. coiàme, *m.* leather & hides.

coibènte, *m.* (*Phys.*) non-conductor. ¶ *a.* non-conducting.

coincidènza, *f.* coincidence; (*Rly.*) connection. coincídere, *v.i. ir.* (*aux.* avere) to coincide.

cointeressènza, *f.* profit-sharing.

coinvòlto, *p.p.* of *coinvolgere,* involved.

colà, *ad.* there.

colabròdo, *m.* colander. colàre, *v.t.* to strain, filter; colander; sieve; cast (*metal*); riddle; pour out drop by drop; (*v.i.*) (*aux.* essere) to flow, run, drain; drop, drip, trickle; leak; melt; gutter (*candle*); sink. colatíccio, *m.* drippings, dregs (*pl.*). colatóio, *m.* strainer, colander.

colazióne, *f.* breakfast; lunch[eon]; first or second meal of the day. *prima ~,* breakfast.

colèi, *demons. pn. f.* she, that woman.

coleòtteri, *m.pl.* coleoptera.

colèra, *m.* cholera.

colibrì, *m.inv.* humming-bird.

còlica, *f.* colic, gripes. còlico (*pl.* còlici), *a.* colic; griping.

colíno, *m.* strainer. *~ da tè,* tea strainer.

colite, f. colitis.

còlla, f. glue; paste. ~ di pesce, isinglass; fish glue.

collaboràre, v.i. (aux. avere) to collaborate. ~ a, to contribute to, write for (journal). collaboratóre, m. -tríce, f. collaborator, contributor.

collàna, f. necklace; series (of literary works).

collàre, m. collar (dog, horse, insignia of an order); (clerical) bands. collarétto, m. small collar; lace collar; shirt c., neckband.

collàsso, m. (Phys., Med.) collapse.

collateràle, a. collateral, side (att.).

collaudàre, v.t. to test, approve, pass (contractor's work, &c.).

collazionàre, v.t. to collate, compare (MSS., &c.). collazióne, f. collation; patronage, gift of a benefice; transfer of a personal legacy to one's fellow heirs.

còlle, m. hill (of moderate height).

collèga (pl. collèghi), m. colleague.

collegaménto, m. connection, junction; union. ufficiale di ~, liaison officer. collegàre (pr. -ègo, -èghi), v.t. to connect, join, link; unite.

collegiàle, a. collegiate. ¶ m. collegian; senior schoolboy. collègio (pl. -ègi), m. college; school; professional group or corps; body. [~] convitto, boarding-school. ~ elettorale, constituency (Pol.). Sacro C~, College of Cardinals. ~ degli avvocati, (the) Bar. ~ di difesa, advocates for the defence.

còllera, f. anger, rage, passion, temper. andare (montare, salire) in ~, to get angry, fly into a rage. accesso di ~, fit of anger. collèrico (pl. -èrici), a. choleric, irascible; quick-tempered.

collètta, f. collection (money); collect.

collettivísmo, m. collectivism. collettívo, a. collective, joint; common, general.

collétto, m. collar. ~ inamidato, starched collar. ~ morbido, soft c. (detached). ~ staccato, shirt c. (detached), cf. solino.

collettóre, m. collector; (Elec.) commutator. ~ delle imposte, taxcollector. collezióne, f. collection.

collimàre, v.i. (aux. avere) to have a common aim, tend to the same result; agree, coincide, tally.

collína, f. hill (fair-sized). collinóso, a. hilly.

collisióne, f. collision, clash; conflict.

còllo, m. neck; throat (anchor); turn of a rope; kink, hitch; bundle, parcel, package. ~ del piede, instep. al ~, (arm) in a sling. in ~, in one's arms. a rotta di ~, headlong, at breakneck speed. mezzo ~, half hitch (knot). rompersi il ~, to break one's neck.

collocaménto, m. placement; placing; disposal; giving (in marriage); appointment; employment. ~ a riposo, retirement, pensioning off. agenzia di ~, employment agency. ufficio di ~, registry office. collocàre (pr. còlloco, còllochi), v.t. to place, put; settle, arrange; give in marriage; invest (money); lay down; lay out. ~ a riposo, to pension off. collocàrsi, v.refl. to be placed, to be situated; take one's stand; settle; get married; obtain a post. collocazióne, f. arrangement; disposition; placing; classification (of creditors).

collòquio (pl. -òqui), m. colloquy, conversation.

collosità, f. stickiness, viscosity. collóso, a. gluey, sticky, viscous.

collotòrto (pl. collotòrti), m. hypocrite; wryneck (bird).

collòttola, f. nape of the neck.

collusióne, f. collusion.

colluttazióne, f. fray, scuffle.

colmàre (pr. cólmo), v.t. to fill up; fill to the brim; load (with honours, &c.); overwhelm; raise the level of (ground). colmàta, f. levelling up; silting up; bank; ridge; embankment. cólmo, a. full, brimful. ¶ m. top, summit, height, crown; depth, limit, extremity. al ~, to the utmost.

colofón, m.inv. (Typ.) colophon, imprint.

colómba, f. dove. colombàccio (pl. -àcci), m. woodpigeon. colombàia, f. dove-cot[e].

Colómbia (la), f. Columbia.

colómbo, m. pigeon. ~ viaggiatore, carrier pigeon. C~, m. Columbus.

còlon, m.inv. colon, large intestine.

colònia, f. colony; settlement. C~, f. Cologne.

colonía, f. farm contract (system of mezzadria). coloniàle, a. colonial. colònico (pl. -ònici), a. belonging to a tenant farmer (colono). casa ~a, farm-house. parte ~a, tenant's share.

colonizzàre, v.t. to colonize.

colónna, f. column, pillar; post; support. ~ sonora, sound track (films). ~ vertebrale, spinal column. colonnàto, m. colonnade.

colonnèllo, *m.* colonel.
colòno, *m.* tenant-farmer (under system of *mezzadria*); colonist, settler.
coloránte, *p.a.* colouring. *sostanza* ~, colouring matter. **coloràre** (*pr.* **-óro**), *v.t.* to colour; tinge; stain (*glass*); give colour (or plausibility) to; improve upon. **coloràto,** *p.a.* coloured; colourable. **colorazióne,** *f.* & **coloraménto,** *m.* colouring. **colóre,** *m.* colour, hue, colouring; paint, dye; complexion; appearance; pretext, show. *scatola di* ~*i*, box of paints. ~*i ad acquerello*, water-colours. ~*i ad olio*, oil-paints. *macinare i* ~*i*, to grind colours. ~*i nazionali*, national colours (*flags*). *sotto* ~ *di*, under pretext (colour, appearance) of. *diventare di mille* ~*i*, to show shame or embarrassment. *farne di tutti i* ~*i*, to commit every kind of folly. **coloríre** (*pr.* **-ísco, -ísci**), *v.t.* to colour, paint; enliven; heighten the colour of. **colorísta** (*pl.* **-ísti**), *m.* colourist. **coloríto,** *p.a.* coloured; rosy, ruddy. ¶ *m.* colouring; complexion.
colóro, *demons. pn. pl.* those; they, them.
colossàle, *a.* colossal. **Colossèo,** *m.* Coliseum. **colòsso,** *m.* colossus; giant.
cólpa, *f.* fault, offence, misdeed; error, mistake; guilt; blame. **colpabilità** & **colpevolézza,** *f.* culpability, guilt. **colpévole,** *a.* guilty, culpable; at fault. ¶ *m.* culprit; offender.
colpíre (*pr.* **-ísco, -ísci**), *v.t.* to hit; strike; smite; tap; knock; slap; stamp, impress; fall heavily [up]on. **cólpo,** *m.* blow; stroke; hit; chop; coup; knock; thrust; poke; cut, slash; slap; whack; dig; stab; shock; clap, peal; flap; rap; tap; wave, sweep; touch; shot, report; rush; beat; blast; gust; force; move; kick; prick; threw; pitch; cast; time, moment, instant; sudden turn; glance; sensation. ~ *diritto*, forehand drive (*Ten.*). ~ *schiacciato*, smash (*Ten.*). ~ *sbalzato*, lift (*Ten.*). ~ *sfalciato*, slice (*Ten.*). ~ *tagliato*, chop (*Ten.*). (~) *a volo*, volley (*Ten.*). (~) *a mezzovolo*, half volley (*Ten.*). (~) *smorzato*, drop shot (*Ten.*). (~) *vincente*, ace (*Ten.*). ~ *d'aria*, rush of air; draught; chill. ~ *di vento*, gust of

wind. ~ *di fortuna*, accident, sudden change of fortune (*good or bad*). ~ *fortunato*, lucky hit. ~ *di (da) maestro*, master stroke. ~ *di mare*, breaker, heavy sea. ~ *di grazia*, finishing stroke. ~*di mano*, sudden attack, lightning move. ~ *di scena*, stage effect. ~ *di sole*, sun-stroke. ~ *di stato*, coup d'état. ~ *di stantuffo*, thrust, stroke of the piston. ~ *di taglia*, undercut (*Box.*). ~*di teatro*, stage trick; sensation[al event]. ~ *di tamburo*, beat of drum. ~ *di fucile*, rifle-shot. [N.B.—Many expressions rendered in Fr. by prefixing the words *coup de* to a noun have their equivalent in Italian in words ending with the termination *-ata*. E.g. *manata*, (a) blow with the hand. *zampata*, a blow with the paw, &c.] *a un* ~, in an instant. *di* ~, at once. *sul* ~, there & then. **colpóso,** *a.* culpable; (*of crime*) unpremeditated. *omicidio* ~, manslaughter.
coltèlla, *f.* large knife, kitchen knife; ploughshare; cutler. **coltellàme,** *m.* cutlery. **coltellinàio,** *m.* cutler. **coltèllo,** *m.* knife; cutter; surgical knife. ~ *per trinciare, trinciante, m.* carving knife, carver. ~ *da tavola*, table-knife. ~*da frutta*, fruit k. ~ *per pane*, bread knife. ~ *a sega per pane*, bread saw. ~ *a doppio taglio*, two-edged knife. ~ *a manòla*, ~ *a cricco*, ~ *a serramanico*, clasp k.; jack k. *col* ~ *alla gola*, forced by threats, with a pistol at one's head (*fig.*). *a* ~, (*of bricks*) edgewise, edge to edge. *dim.* **coltellíno,** *m.* small knife; pocket k.; cheese k.
coltivàre, *v.t.* to cultivate, grow; raise; farm, till, work; improve; develop; promote; seek the society (or favour) of. **coltivatóre,** *m.* **-tríce,** *f.* cultivator, grower, agricultur[al]ist, farmer; husbandman. **coltivazióne,** *f.* cultivation; tillage; husbandry. ~ *del cotone*, cotton-growing.
còlto, *p.p.* of **cogliere.** ~ *sul fatto*, caught in the act. ~ *dalla notte*, overtaken by night.
cólto, *a.* cultivated; educated, cultured.
cóltre, *f.* coverlet; quilt; counterpane; pall; (*pl.*) bed-clothes. **cóltrice,** *f.* feather-bed, f. mattress; (*Poet.*) bed, couch.
cóltro, *m.* coulter, ploughshare.
coltúra, *f.* culture; cultivation, tillage, farming; rearing, production; colony

of bacteria; range of knowledge; intellectual life. ~ *dei bachi,* rearing of silkworms. ~ *di bacilli,* culture of bacilli. *gran* ~, high farming, large-scale farming.

colúbro, *m.* (*Poet.*) snake, adder, serpent.

colúi (*pl.* **colóro**), *demons. pn. 3rd sg.m.* he, that one, that person (*f.* **colèi**).

còlza, *f.* rape (*plant & seed*).

comandaménto, *m.* commandment, order, precept. *i dieci* ~*i*, the Ten Commandments (*O.T.*). **comandànte,** *m.* commander; commandant; commanding officer. ~ *in capo,* commander-in-chief. **comandàre,** *v.i.* (*aux.* avere) to give orders; command, order; ordain; bid; (*v.t.*) to command, be in command of; order; bespeak; prescribe; rule; control; direct. *comandi! comandate!* if you please! at your service! what can I do for you? **comandàta,** *f.* (*Nav. & Mil.*) fatigue party. **comàndo,** *m.* command, order; injunction; behest; (*Mech.*) driving; drive; driving gear; control; (*Mil.*) headquarters. *di* ~, (arranged) to order; feigned. *leva di* ~, gear lever; (*Aero.*) stick. ~ *superiore delle forze armate,* (*Mil.*) general headquarters. ~ *di corpo d'armata,* corps headquarters. ~ *battaglione,* ~ *compagnia,* battalion, company h.

comàre, *f.* god-mother; gossip, crony. *le Allegre* C~*i di Windsor,* the Merry Wives of Windsor.

comàsco (*pl.* **comàschi**), *a.* of Como and district. ¶ *m.* native of Como.

combaciaménto, *m.* tallying; fitting together; point of contact. **combaciàre** (*pr.* -**àcio,** -**àci**), *v.i.* (*aux.* avere) to fit closely together; tally.

combattènte, *m.* combatant; fighter. *ex*~, ex-service man. **combàttere,** *v.t. & i.* (*aux.* avere) to fight; oppose; combat; contend with; withstand; strive; vie. **combattiménto,** *m.* combat, fight, battle, action; war (*elements*); contest, bout, match.

combinàre (*pr.* -**íno**), *v.t.* to combine; contrive, devise; fix, settle; (*colours*) match; (*v.i.*) & **combinàrsi,** *v.refl.* to combine; unite; agree; come to terms; match. **combinazióne,** *f.* combination (*Chem., Phys.*); agreement; coincidence; chance. *per* ~, by chance.

combríccola, *f.* gang; coterie, set.

combustíbile, *a.* combustible. ¶ *m.* fuel, combustible material. **combustióne,** *f.* combustion; burning; conflagration, fire (*fig.*).

cóme, *ad.* as, like, such as; (*interrog.*) how, why, what. ¶ *c.* as, when, as soon as, since. *così . . .* ~, both . . . and. ~ *se,* as if. *ma* ~! what! (*excl. of surprise*). ¶ *m. il* ~, the reason, means, way. **comeché,** *c.* although.

comèta, *f.* comet; (*fig.*) (boy's) kite.

còmico (*pl.* **còmici**), *a.* comic; comical, funny, ludicrous, droll. ¶ *m.* comicality; comedy; comic writer; comic actor, comedian; funny man.

comígnolo, *m.* roof-ridge; chimney coping.

cominciaménto, *m.* beginning, start, commencement, outset, inception. **cominciàre** (*pr.* -**íncio,** -**ínci**), *v.t. & i.* (*aux.* essere & avere) to begin, commence, start. (When intrans., the aux. is *essere* if used without a complement, in other cases *avere*. It may be followed by the prepositions *a, con,* & *da.*)

comitàto, *m.* committee. *essere del* ~, to be on the committee. ~ *permanente,* standing c. **comitíva,** *f.* group, party, company. **comízio** (*pl.* -**ízi**), *m.* meeting; assembly; reunion; society. *indire un* ~, to call a meeting. *tenere un* ~, to hold a m. ~ *agrario,* agricultural society. ~ *elettorale,* meeting of electors.

còmma (*pl.* **còmmi**), *m.* parenthetic clause; paragraph; paragraph heading.

commèdia, *f.* comedy; comic action or situation; make-believe, sham. ~ *dell'arte,* ~*a soggetto,* (professional) improvised comedy of the 16th & 17th centuries. ~ *d'intreccio,* comedy of intrigue. **commediànte,** *m.f.* actor, actress; player; comedian, -ienne; playboy. **commediògrafo,** *m.* writer of comedies, comic dramatist; playwright.

commemoràre (*pr.* -**èmoro**), *v.t.* to commemorate. **commemorativo,** *a.* commemorative; memorial. *lapide* ~*a,* memorial tablet. *servizio* ~, memorial service.

commendatízia, *f.* letter of recommendation. **commendatóre,** *m.* holder of former It. grade of knighthood, *la commènda*. **commendévole**, *a.* praiseworthy, commendable. **commensàle**, *m.* table companion; messmate; fellow-boarder. **commentàre**, *v.t.* to comment on; annotate, expound. **comménto**, *m.* comment; commentary; exposition; remark. **commerciàle**, *a.* commercial; business, trade, trading (*att.*). **commerciànte**, *m.* trader, merchant; business man; dealer. **commerciàre** (*pr.* -**èrcio**, -**èrci**), *v.i.* (*aux.* avere) to trade, deal; hold intercourse. **commèrcio**, *m.* commerce, trade, trading; business; traders, commercial class; traffic, intercourse, dealings. *essere in* ~, to be on sale. *mettere in* ~, to put on the market. ~ *all'ingrosso*, wholesale trade. ~ *al minuto*, retail trade. ~ *bancario*, banking business. ~ *di esportazione*, export trade. *Camera di* ~, Chamber of Commerce. **commésso**, *m.* clerk; employé; messenger. *primo* ~, head clerk. ~ *di negozio*, shop-assistant; salesman. ~ *viaggiatore*, commercial traveller. **commestíbile**, *a.* edible; eatable. ¶ *m.pl.* food-stuffs; eatables; provisions. **comméttere** (*pr.* -**étto**), *v.t. ir.* to commit; perpetrate; order; entrust; expose; join together; (*Mech.*) assemble; (*Eccl.*) invest. **commiàto**, *m.* leave; discharge; dismissal; closing stanza of a canzone (*in form of farewell & dedication*). **commilitóne**, *m.* fellow-soldier; comrade. **commissariàto**, *m.* commissariat (*Mil.*); commissionership; status or office of a *commissario*. ~ *di polizia*, divisional police station. *corpo di* ~ *militare*, Army Service Corps. **commissàrio** (*pl.* -**àri**), *m.* commissioner; commissary; commissar; officer; purser (*ship*); paymaster (*Nav.*); steward (*sport*); superintendent (*police*). ~*per gli alloggi*, housing officer. ~ *del popolo*, People's Commissar (*U.S.S.R.*). ~ *di Pubblica Sicurezza*, Commissioner of Police. **commissionàrio**, *m.* agent, commission agent, factor. **commissióne**, *f.* commission; errand; order (*for goods*); committee. **commísto**, *a.* mixed.

commišuràre (*pr.* -**úro**), *v.t.* to measure one thing with another; compare; proportion; adapt. **committènte**, *m.* (*Com.*) consigner; buyer. **commodòro**, *m.* commodore. **commovènte**, *p.a.* moving, affecting, touching; pitiful. **commozióne**, *f.* commotion, upheaval; shock; shell shock; emotion, agitation. ~ *cerebrale*, concussion of the brain. **comm[u]òvere** (*pr.* -**uòvo**), *v.t. ir.* to move, touch, affect; agitate; disturb; excite. **commutàre**, *v.t.* to commute; change; reverse. **commutatóre**, *m.* commutator; switch (*Elec.*). **comò**, *m.inv.* chest of drawers. **Còmo**, *f.* Como. *Lago di C*~, *m.* lake of Como. **comodaménte**, *ad.* conveniently; comfortably, in comfort. **comodíno**, *m.* bedside table; (*Theat.*) drop-curtain. **comodità**, *f.inv.* convenience; comfort; opportunity. **còmodo**, *a.* convenient, handy; commodious, pleasant; comfortable; easy, easy-going, in easy circumstances; easy-fitting. *stia* ~, don't disturb yourself, don't get up. *luogo* ~, water-closet (*abb.* W.C.). ¶ *m.* convenience; comfort; opportunity; ease; leisure; use, service. **compaesàno**, *a.* belonging to the same country or district. ¶ ~-**ana**, *f.* fellow countryman, ~woman, person from the same district. **compàgine**, *f.* framework, structure; connection of parts; arrangement; close union. **compagnévole**, *a.* sociable; companionable. **compagnía**, *f.* company; companionship; bevy; covey. ~ *anonima*, joint-stock company. ~ *di assicurazione*, -*i*, insurance c. ~ *di disciplina*, (*Mil.*) disciplinary c. **compàgno**, *m.* companion; mate; fellow; associate; partner; husband. ~ *di giuoco*, *giuochi*, playmate. ~ *di scuola*, school-fellow. ~ *di viaggio*, fellow traveller, travelling companion. ¶ *a.* similar; exactly [a]like. **compagnóne**, *m.* good companion, boon c. **companàtico** (*pl.* -**àtici**), *m.* what is eaten with bread; (*fig.*) bread & butter, pittance. **comparàbile**, *a.* comparable. **comparàre**, *v.t.* to compare, liken. **comparatívo**, *a. & m.* comparative (*Gram.*, *&c.*). **comparàto**, *p.a.*

comparative. *anatomia ~a*, comparative anatomy. *letteratura ~a*, comparative literature. **comparazióne**, *f.* comparison; simile.
compàre, *m.* godfather; intimate; crony; accomplice.
comparíre (*pr.* -ísco, -ísci), *v.i.* (*aux.* essere) to appear; attend (in court). ~ *in giudizio*, ~ *dietro citazione*, (*Law*) to answer the summons. **comparizióne**, *f.* appearance (in court).
compàrsa, *f.* (*Theat.*) super; unimportant person, cipher (*pers.*); appearance; good appearance; (*Law*) appearance, answer to a summons.
compartecipàre, *v.i.* (*aux.* avere) to participate, share (in). **compartecipazióne**, *f.* participation, sharing. ~ *agli utili.* profit-sharing.
compartiménto, *m.* compartment; division; department (*flower*) bed. (*Rly.*) compartment, also *scompartimento.* ~ *delle macchine*, engine room. ~ *stagno*, water-tight compartment. **compartíre** (*pr.* -àrto, or -artísco, -artísci), *v.t.* to divide; distribute; share; (*of time*) arrange.
compassàre, *v.t.* to measure with compasses; do or say something deliberately or with precision. ~ *le parole*, to measure (or weigh) one's words. **compassàto**, *p.a.* measured, precise, regular. *uomo ~*, precisian.
compassióne, *f.* compassion, pity. *far ~*, to excite pity. *mi fa ~*, I am sorry for him, her.
compàsso, *m.* pair of compasses; compass. ~ *a balaustro*, bow compasses. ~ *dritto ad arco*, dividers. ~ *a punte regolabili*, scribing compasses. ~ *a verga*, beam compasses. *~curvo*, ~ *di cilindro*, cal[!]ipers. ~ *di via*, steering compass.
compatíbile, *a.* compatible, consistent. **compatiménto**, *m.* pity; forbearance, indulgence; sympathy. **compatíre** (*pr.* -ísco, -ísci), *v.t.* to pity; sympathize with; bear with; excuse.
compatriòt[t]a (*pl.* -òtti), *m. & f.* compatriot, fellow countryman, -woman.
compattézza, *f.* compactness; closeness; firmness, solidity. **compàtto**, *a.* compact, dense; concise, compendious. *una cipria compatta*, *f.* a compact [powder].
compendiàre, *v.t.* to summarize;

abridge, epitomize. **compèndio**, *m.* compendium; epitome.
compensàre (*pr.* -ènso), *v.t.* to compensate, offset; counterbalance; make up (for); requite; clear. *legno compensato*, *m.* plywood. **compensatóre**, -**trice**, *a.* compensating; counterbalancing; countervailing. **compensazióne**, *f.* compensation; set off, offset; quid pro quo; making up (*Stk. Ex.*); clearing (*Banking*). *pendolo a ~*, compensation pendulum. *stanza di ~*, clearing-house. **compènso**, *m.* compensation; remuneration; reward; indemnity.
cómpera, *f.* purchase. **comperàre**, *v.t.* to purchase, buy. *Cf.* **comprare**.
competènte, *a.* competent, qualified; sufficient; suitable, fair, adequate. **competènza**, *f.* competence; authority; province; jurisdiction; fee, remuneration.
competitóre, *m.* -**trice**, *f.* competitor, rival.
compiacènte, *a.* obliging; deferential, polite. **compiacènza**, *f.* kindness; politeness; deference; complaisance, obligingness; pleasure, satisfaction. **compiacére** (*pr.* -piàccio, -piàci), *v.t. ir.* to gratify; please; humour. **compiacérsi**, *v.refl.* to take pleasure; be willing, be so good as to; deign, condescend; be fond of (= *di*). ~ *con*, to congratulate. **compiaciménto**, *m.* pleasure, satisfaction; complacence, -cy.
compiàngere (*pr.* **compiàngo**, *&c.*, like *piangere*), *v.t. ir.* to pity, bewail, lament, deplore; *v.i.* (*aux.* avere), to lament, complain. **compiàngersi**, *v.refl.* to condole, lament. **compiànto**, *p.a.* regretted, lamented. ¶ *m.* pity, lament; grief; regret.
cómpiere (*pr.* **cómpio**, **cómpi**, *&c.*, like *empiere*; *p.p.* *compiuto*; other forms like **compire**), *v.t.* to accomplish, fulfil, perform; complete, finish; discharge, do (*duty*).
compièta, *f.* compline, last evening prayers.
compilàre (*pr.* -ílo), *v.t.* to compile, draw up, compose. **compilatóre**, *m.* -**trice**, *f.* compiler. **compilazione**, *f.* compilation.
compiménto, *m.* accomplishment; achievement; conclusion, completion; fulfilment. *dar ~*, to achieve. *a ~*, as a finish, or supplement. **compíre** (*pr.* -ísco,

-ísci), *v.t.* to complete, fulfil, perform, discharge; finish, bring to an end; perfect; gratify (*a wish*).
compitàre (*pr.* cómpito), *v.t.* to spell (out); pronounce separately each syllable with its letters.
compitézza, *f.* politeness, courtesy, refinement. compìto, *a.* accomplished, polite, well-mannered; finished.
cómpito, *m.* task, exercise; duty. *a* ∼, moderately; carefully.
compiúto, *a.* complete, perfect, finished. *fatto* ∼, accomplished fact.
compleànno, *m.* birthday.
complementàre, *a.* complementary, supplementary; additional. compleménto, *m.* complement; draft (*Mil.*).
complessióne, *f.* constitution, temperament.
complessità, *f.* complexity.
complessivaménte, *ad.* on the whole; altogether, in the aggregate. complessívo, *a.* comprehensive, total, aggregate, general. *entrata* ∼*a*, gross income. complèsso, *m.* whole; complex; combination. *in* ∼, on the whole, in general, altogether. ∼ *aggiunto*, (*Radio*) adaptor set. ¶ *a.* complex; robust, well built (*pers.*).
complèto, *a.* whole, entire, complete. ¶ *m.* (*man's*) suit.
complicàre (*pr.* còmplico, còmplichi), *v.t.* to complicate, [en]tangle, confuse. complicàrsi, *v.refl.* to become complicated; (*of illness*) to become worse, complications set in.
complicazióne, *f.* complication; intricacy.
còmplice, *m.* accomplice, accessory. ¶ *a.* accessory, privy, a party (to).
complicità, *f.* complicity.
complimentàre (*pr.* -énto), *v.t.* to compliment, congratulate. compliménto, *m.* compliment; (*pl.*) respects, kind regards; ceremony. *far*∼*i*, to pay compliments; stand on ceremony. *senza* ∼*i*, frankly, freely, without ceremony. *tanti*∼, kindest regards.
componènte, *a.* & *m.* component.
componiménto, *m.* composition, essay; settlement. compórre (*pr.* óngo, *&c.*, like *porre*), *v.t.* to compose; arrange, settle, adjust. compórsi, *v.refl.* to consist, be composed of.
comportàbile, *a.* tolerable, support-

able. comportaménto, *m.* action; behaviour. comportàre (*pr.* -òrto), *v.t.* to tolerate, support, endure; resist (*cold, &c.*); allow, permit; involve. comportàrsi, *v.refl.* to behave, act. ∼ *da*, to behave like.
compórto, *m.* tolerance; delay; respite; time of grace (*for payment*).
compòsito, *a.* (*Arch.*) composite.
compositóio (*pl.* -ói), *m.* (*Typ.*) composing-stick. compositóre, *m.* -tríce, *f.* composer; (*Typ.*) compositor. composizióne, *f.* composition; make up; type-setting; settlement, agreement, reconciliation; arrangement. *sala della* ∼, *f.* (*Typ.*) composing-room. ∼ *a mano*, (*Typ.*) hand-setting. ∼ *da conservare*, live matter, standing m. (*Typ.*). ∼ *interlineata*, leaded matter (*Typ.*). ∼ *stretta*, close spacing (*Typ.*).
compossessóre, *m.* compossedltríce, *f.* joint-owner.
compósta, *f.* mixture; compote; stewed fruit.
compostézza, *f.* composure, calm; modesty; grace, dignity, moderation.
compósto, *p.p.* of *compórre*. ¶ *a.* composed, grave, calm; modest; dignified; tidy, set in order; compound. *modi* ∼*i*, sedate manners. *interesse* ∼, compound interest. *proposizione* ∼*a*, compound sentence (*Gram.*).
cómpra, *f.* purchase. compràre (*pr.* cómpro), *v.t.* to buy, purchase; acquire. ∼ *a contanti*, to buy for cash. ∼ *a credito*. ∼*a respiro*, to buy on credit. compratóre, *m.* -tríce, *f.* buyer, purchaser.
comprèndere (*pr.* -èndo, *&c.*, like *prendere*), *v.t. ir.* to comprehend, understand, make out; comprise, include, cover.
comprensióne, *f.* comprehension, understanding. comprensívo, *a.* comprehensive. compréso, *p.p.* of *comprendere*, understood; included, including.
comprèssa, *f.* compress (*Med.*).
compressióne, *f.* compression. compressívo, *a.* compressory. comprèsso, *p.p.* of *comprimere*. ¶ *a.* compressed, compacted; oppressed; close; dense. compressóre, *m.* compressor. roller; air-pump. ∼ *stradale*, street-roller. ¶ *a.* compressing. comprímere (*pr.* -imo, -ìmi), *v.t. ir.* to compress; restrain.
compromésso, *p.p.* of *compromettere*.

¶ *m.* recourse to arbitration; compromise. *mettere in* ~, to hazard. **comprométtere** (*pr.* -étto, &c., like *mettere*), *v.t. ir.* to put to arbitration; expose to risk; hazard; compromise. **comprométtersi**, *v.refl.* to compromise oneself; promise; take on oneself; rely (or depend) on someone. *una persona da* ~, a person to be relied on. **compromissàrio** (*pl.* -àri), *m.* arbitrator.

comproprietà, *f.* joint ownership.

comprovàre (*pr.* -òvo), *v.t.* to prove (on evidence).

compulsàre (*pr.* -úlso), *v.t.* to examine, inspect (*papers, documents,* &c.); to summon to appear in court.

compúnto, *a.* regretful; consciencestricken; demure. **compunzióne,** *f.* regret; compunction.

computàbile, *a.* calculable. **computàre** (*pr.* còmputo), *v.t.* to compute, calculate, count. **computista** (*pl.* -ísti), *m.* accountant, bookkeeper. **computistería**, *f.* accountancy; book-keeping; accountant's office. **còmputo**, *m.* calculation; reckoning; account.

comunàle, *a.* communal; municipal; town, parish (*att.*). **comunànza**, *f.* community; society. *in*~, in common. ~ *d'interessi*, community of interests. **comúne**, *a.* common; usual, habitual, ordinary; general; in common, joint; trite, repeated many times, commonplace; vulgar, poor. *nome*~, common noun. *genere*~, common gender, *senso*~, popular opinion. ¶ *m.* commune; municipality; town, parish; administrative district; townspeople, citizens; majority or generality of people; town-hall. ¶ *f. La C*~, French revolutionary government of 1871 (and 1792); principal door (for *porta*~). **comuneménte,** *ad.* usually; generally; in common.

comunicàndo, *m.* -ànda, *f.* young communicant, (one who receives the Sacrament for the first time.) **comunicànte**, *m.* priest who administers the Sacrament. **comunicàre** (*pr.* -único, -únichi), *v.t.* to communicate, impart, inform; administer (*the Sacrament*); *v.i.* (*aux.* avere) to communicate (with); have connection (with). **comunicàrsi**, *v.refl.* to share with another; receive the Sacrament. **comunicatívo**, *a.* communicative; catching (*disease*), infectious. **comunicàto**, *p.p.* of

comunicare. ¶ *m.* bulletin (of official information). ~*di guerra*, war bulletin, w. communiqué.

comunicazióne, *f.* communication, connection. *mettere in* ~, (*Teleph.*) to put through. *togliere la* ~, (*Teleph.*) to cut off. *sono in* ~? (*Teleph.*) am I through? ~ *intercomunale*, (*Teleph.*) trunk call.

comunióne, *f.* communion, community, society; Sacrament. ~ *dei beni*, community of property. ~ *ereditaria*, community of heirs.

comunísmo, *m.* communism. **comunísta** (*pl.* -nísti), *m.f.* communist. **comunità**, *f.* community; inhabitants of a commune; municipality.

comúnque, *ad.* however, in whatever manner, no matter how, whatever, *non ci riuscirai, comunque tu faccia,* you won't succeed whatever you do.

cón, *pr.* with; at, against, towards. With the articles **il** & **i** takes the forms **col** & **coi** (**co'**), but should not be united with the other particles (hence *con lo, con la,* &c.). *levarsi* ~ *l'alba,* to rise at dawn. *combattere col nemico,* to fight against the enemy. *essere giusto con tutti,* to be just towards everyone.

conàto, *m.* effort, attempt.

cónca (*pl.* cónche), *f.* large earthenware basin; cavity, valley, hollow in the hills; shell; lock-basin in a canal. ~*dell'orecchio,* hollow of the outer ear. ~ *fessa*, person of a weak constitution or with weak health. *C*~ *d'oro,* the valley behind Palermo. **concàio** (*pl.* -ài), *m.* potter, dealer in earthenware.

concatenàre (*pr.* -éno), *v.t.* to link together (gen. fig. of an argument, ideas, &c.). **concatenazióne**, *f.* concatenation.

concàusa, *f.* contribution, cause, pre-existing cause, aggravation of guilt.

còncavo, *a.* concave, hollow; vaulted. ¶ *m.* hollow.

concèdere (*pr.* -èdo, -èdi, &c.), *v.t. ir.* to concede, grant, accord; admit.

concènto, *m.* harmony of voice and instrument (*Poet.*).

concentraménto, *m.* concentration. ~*di artiglieria,* artillery concentration. ~ *di tiro*, c. of fire. *campo di* ~, concentration camp. **concentràre**, *v.t.* to concentrate; centre (*fig.*); condense. **concentrazióne**, *f.* concentration (in more abstract sense); also for Chem. process.

concèntrico (*pl.* -èntrici), *a.* concentric.

concepíbile, *a.* conceivable, imaginable. concepíre (*pr.* -ísco, -ísci), *v.t.* to conceive; imagine; begin to form; form; formulate, draw up; entertain (*hopes, suspicions*). concepíto, *p.p.* of *concepire.* ¶ *a.* drawn up, worded. *una lettera cosi* ~*a*, a letter so worded.

conceria, *f.* tannery.

concèrnere, *v.t. defect.* (no pret. or p.p.) to concern, regard, be concerned with, relate to.

concertàre, *v.t.* to concert, plan together, hatch (*plot*); arrange, adjust; conduct (*concert or rehearsal*). concertàrsi, *v.refl.* to come to an understanding, act in concert. concertàto, *a.* concerted, arranged; agreed upon. *musica* ~ *a*, music accompanied by an orchestra. *pezzo* ~, concert piece. concertísta (*pl.m.* -ísti, *pl.f.* -íste), *m.f.* (professional) concert-artist. concèrto, *m.* concert; harmony; agreement. *agire di* ~, to act in concert. *di* ~, with common accord, unanimously.

concessionàrio (*pl.* -àri), *m.* holder of a concession, concession(n)aire, claim-holder; grant, claim, licence. concessióne, *f.* concession; permission; grant of land (*colonial*). concessívo, *a.* concessive. *proposizione* ~*a*, concessive clause (*Gram.*). concèsso, *p.p.* of *concedere. dato e non* ~, granting for the sake of argument.

concètto, *m.* conception; concept; plan, project, design; meaning; idea; opinion; fancy; conceit; reputation, esteem. concettóso, *a.* pithy; concise; sententious, full of conceits. concezióne, *f.* conception; idea. *l'Immacolata C* ~, the Immaculate Conception.

conchífero, *a.* shell-bearing (*mollusc*); full of shells (*ground*).

conchíglia, *f.* shell, sea-shell; baroque ornament in the shape of a sea-shell; (*Metall.*) chill mould, metal m.

conchiúdere, *see* concludere.

cóncia (*pl.* cónce), *f.* art of tanning; tan-field; tan. conciai[u]òlo, *m.* tanner.

concialàna, *f.* mattress-maker.

conciapèlli, *m.inv.* tanner (of hides).

conciàre (*pr.* cóncio, cónci), *v.t.* to dress, prepare, tan; adjust, arrange; preserve; repair; (*fig.*) to spoil, ill-treat, thrash.

conciatétti, *m.inv.* tiler, slater.

conciatóre, *m.* -tríce, *f.* tanner. conciatúra, *f.* tanning, dressing; mending.

conciliàbile, *a.* reconcilable. conciliàbolo, *m.* conventicle; secret meeting.

conciliàre (*pr.* -ílio, -íli), *v.t.* to reconcile, conciliate, pacify; win, win over, procure. conciliàrsi, *v.refl.* to become reconciled; win, gain. conciliatívo, *a.* conciliatory. *maniere* ~ *e*, engaging or conciliatory manners. conciliatóre, *m.* (-tríce, *f.*) *a. & m.f.* conciliatory; conciliator, peace-maker. conciliazióne, *f.* reconciliation, conciliation.

concílio (*pl.* -íli), *m.* general council (of the Church); (*fig.*) assembly.

concimàia, *f.* manure-pit, dung-heap. concimàre (*pr.* -ímo), *v.t.* to manure. concimatúra, *& concimazióne, f.* manuring. concíme, *m.* manure, dung; fertilizer.

concinnàre, *v.t.* render graceful and elegant. concinnità, *f.* grace, elegance, harmony of style. concínno, *a.* harmonious; elegant, appropriate.

concíno, *m.* tan, tanner's bark.

cóncio (*pl.* cónci), *sync.p.* for conciàto & *a.* tanned; dressed (*stone*), seasoned, set off; knocked about, spoilt; corrected. ¶ *m.* dressed stone; dung; filth.

concionàre (*pr.* -óno), *v.i.* (*aux.* avere) to declaim, harangue. concióne, *f.* declamation, harangue, discourse; assembly.

concisaménte, *ad.* concisely, briefly. concisióne, *f.* concision, conciseness. concíso, *a.* concise.

concistòro, *m.* consistory; Senate of Pope & Cardinals.

concitaménto, *m.* incitement; tumult, excitement, agitation. concitàre (*pr.* còncito), *v.t.* to stir up, incite, provoke.

concitataménte, *ad.* excitedly. concitàto, *p.p.* of *concitare.* ¶ *a.* excited, agitated.

concittadíno, *m.* -a, *f.* fellow-citizen. ¶ *a.* living in the same town.

conclàve, *m.* conclave. conclavísta, *m.* (*pl.* -ísti), member of a conclave.

concludènte, *a.* conclusive. conclúdere (*pr.* -údo, *&c.*, like *accludere*), *v.t. & i.ir.* (*aux.* avere) to conclude; be conclusive; clinch; carry out, effect. conclusionàle, *a.* (*Law*) concluding. *scrittura* ~, document containing the pleadings or conclusions in law, nisi prius record. **conclusióne**, *f.* conclusion, close, summing up. **conclusívo**, *a.* conclusive. **conclúso**, *p.p.* of *concludere*. ¶ *a.* closed.

concomitànte, *a.* concomitant, concurrent, simultaneous.

concordànza, *f.* concordance; agreement (*Gram.*). **concordàre** (*pr.* -òrdo), *v.t.* to reconcile, cause to agree, agree upon; *v.i.* (*aux.* avere) to agree. **concordàto**, *m.* concordat (*Eccl.*); agreement between a bankrupt and his creditors. ~ *preventivo*, agreement with creditors come to before bankruptcy is declared.

concòrde, *a.* in agreement, in accord; like-minded; consonant; similar; conformable. *di* ~ *parere*, of the same opinion. **concordeménte**, *ad.* unanimously, with one accord. **concòrdia**, *f.* concord; harmony; unanimity.

concorrènte, *a.* concurrent; convergent. *linee* ~ *i*, converging lines, *f.pl.* ¶ *m.* candidate, competitor, rival; applicant (for a situation). **concorrènza**, *f.* concourse; confluence; competition, rivalry. ~ *protetta*, (*Com.*) dumping. **concórrere** (*pr.* -órro, *&c.*, like *correre*), *v.i.* ir. (*aux.* avere) to assemble; run together; concur; co-operate; compete; share; agree; converge. ~*al successo*, to contribute to the success. **concórso**, *p.p.* of *concorrere*. ¶ *m.* concourse; confluence; competition, competitive examination; flow (*as of blood to the head*); co-operation, assistance; creditors' meeting. *mettere a* ~, to put up for competition; call for tenders. ~ *di circostanze*, combination of circumstances.

concretàre (*pr.* -èto), *v.t.* to make concrete (*what is abstract*); put into action. **concretézza**, *f.* concreteness, concrete form. **concrèto**, *a.* concrete, positive, decisive, substantial, real. **concrezióne**, *f.* concretion.

concubína, *f.* concubine. **concubinàto**, *m.* concubinage.

conculcàre (*pr.* -úlco, -úlchi), *v.t.* to oppress, trample upon; violate.

conc[u]òcere (*pr.* -uòcio, *&c.*, like *cuòcere*), *v.t.ir.* to concoct; digest.

concupíre (*pr.* -ísco, -ísci), *v.t.* to desire, lust after, covet. **concupiscènza**, *f.* concupiscence, lust.

concussionàrio (*pl.* -àri), *m.* extortioner, blackmailer. **concussióne**, *f.* extortion, exaction, blackmail.

condànna, *f.* condemnation, sentence; blame. **condannàbile**, *a.* worthy of condemnation, censurable. **condannàre**, *v.t.* to condemn. **condannàto**, *m.* condemned criminal (*not as in Eng. necessarily to death*).

condégno, *a.* adequate, suitable, proportionate.

condensàre (*pr.* -ènso), *v.t.* to condense. **condensatóre**, *m.* condenser. **condensazióne**, *f.* condensation.

condiménto, *m.* condiment, seasoning, sauce. **condíre** (*pr.* -ísco, -ísci), *v.t.* to flavour, season; dress (*vala* i); (*fig.*) supply; improve.

condirettóre, *m.* -tríce, *f.* co-director, -trix, joint-manager, -ess.

condiscendènza, *f.* acquiescence, compliance. **condiscéndere** (*pr.* -éndo, *&c.*, like *scendere*), *v.i. ir.* (*aux.* avere) to acquiesce, comply, yield to persuasion, give way (to).

condiscépolo, *m.* -épola, *f.* schoolfellow, fellow student.

condíto, *p.p.* of *condire*. ¶ *a.* tasty; full (of): prepared; crammed (with). ¶ *m.* condiment.

condivídere (*pr.* -ído, *&c.*, like *dividere*), *v.t. ir.* to divide between several persons; share.

condizionàle, *a.* conditional. ¶ *m.* conditional (mood) (*Gram.*).

condizionàre (*pr.* -óno), *v.t.* to qualify, impose a condition upon, make conditional; put into good condition; season, dress (food). ¶ **condizionàto**, *a.* fit, conditioned, qualified. *ben* ~, in good condition. **condizióne**, *f.* condition, proviso; quality; situation, state, position. *pongo per* ~ *che*, I must stipulate that. *a* ~ *che*, on condition that.

condogliànza, *f.* condolence, sympathy, expression of sympathy. **condolérsi** (*pr.* -olgo, *&c.*, like *dolere*), *v.refl. ir.* to condole (with), sympathize, express sympathy (with) *mi condolgo con lui della disgrazia che gli è successa*, I sympathize with him in the misfortune that has befallen him.

condomínio (*pl.* -íni), *m.* joint-rule, joint ownership, joint control. **condòmino**, *m.* (*Law*) joint owner. **condonàre** (*pr.* -óno), *v.t.* to condone, pardon, forgive; overlook; forego, remit. **condóno,** *m.* condonation, pardon, amnesty.

còndor *or* **condòre,** *m.* condor.

condótta, *f.* conduct, behaviour: management, driving (*a conveyance*); leadership; transport; method & system of water-supply; obligation of a *medico condotto* (see *condotto*) or panel doctor; district (or panel) served by the latter.

condottièro, *&* **condottière,** *m.* soldier of fortune, leader of mercenaries.

condótto, *p.p.* of **condurre.** ¶ *a.* in *medico* ~, doctor employed by a commune or municipality to give free treatment; *cf.* panel doctor. ¶ *m.* conduit, channel; pipe for conveying liquids or gas.

conducènte, *pr.p.* of condurre. ¶ *m.* driver; leader, conductor; manager. *proprietario* ~, owner-driver (*motor car*). ~ *di taxi,* taxi driver. ~ *sconsiderato,* road hog, careless driver. **condúrre** (*pr.* **-úco,** *&c.,* like *addurre*), *v.t. ir.* to conduct, guide, lead, drive, take, accompany, transport; bring, escort; manage, carry out, perform; transmit; induce, persuade. **condúrsi,** *v.refl.* to go; behave. **conduttività,** *f.* conductivity. **conduttóre,** *m.* **-tríce,** *f.* conductor, -tress, guard (*Rly.*); leader; tenant, manager; (*Elec.*) conductor.

confabulàre (*pr.* **-àbulo**), *v.i.* (*aux.* avere) to chat.

confacènte (*pr.p.* of *confare*). ¶ *a.* suitable, convenient. **confàrsi** (*pr.* **-fàccio,** *&c.,* like *fare*), *v.refl. ir.* to suit, agree with; fit.

confederàrsi, *v.refl.* to unite in a confederation or league, federate, band together. **confederazióne,** *f.* confederacy, confederation; league, union.

conferènza, *f.* conference; lecture. **conferenzière,** *m.* lecturer (*public*).

conferíre (*pr.* **-isco, -isci**), *v.t.* to confer, grant, give, bestow; compare; (*v.i.*) (*aux.* avere) to confer (with = *con*). ~ *a,* to benefit; contribute to.

conférma, *f.* confirmation. **confermàre** (*pr.* **-érmo**), *v.t.* to confirm, approve, attest; retain (*in employment*). **confermatívo,** *a.* confirmatory. **confermazióne,** *f.* confirmation.

confessàre (*pr.* **-èsso**), *v.t.* to confess, acknowledge, own; hear confession (*Eccl.*). **confessàrsi,** *v.refl.* to confess (*Eccl.*). **confessionàle,** *a.*

confessional. ¶ *m.* confessional (*box*). **confessióne,** *f.* confession; right of hearing confession (*Eccl.*); professed (*Protestant*) creed or belief; crypt containing relics (*Eccl.*); **confèsso,** *a.* confessed; convinced; acknowledged. **confessóre,** *m.* confessor.

confettàre (*pr.* **-ètto**), *v.t.* to candy; preserve; prepare; (*fig.*) to fawn upon. **confettièra,** *f.* sweet-meat box, bon-bon box. **confettière,** *m.* confectioner. **confètto,** *m.* sweet-meat; (*pl.*) sugar-almonds. *mangiare i* ~ *i,* (*fig.*) to celebrate a wedding. **confettúra,** *f.* sweet-meats; jam, preserves.

confezionàre (*pr.* **-óno**), *v.t.* to make up (*medical preparations, sweets or dress*); mix, compound, prepare; (*fig.*) finish well. **confezióne,** *f.* medical preparation; any made-up article (*dress, &c.*). ~*i in serie, f.pl.* ready-made clothing. ~*i su misura,* suits made to measure. ~*i uomini,* men's tailoring.

conficcàre (*pr.* **-ícco, -íchi**), *v.t.* to nail, drive in, hammer in (*nails, &c.*); (*fig.*) to fix; fix in one's memory. ~ *i cannoni,* to spike the guns.

confidàre (*pr.* **-ído**), *v.t.* to confide, impart (*secret*), entrust; (*v.i.*) (*aux.* avere) to trust. **confidàrsi,** *v.refl.* to confide in (= *con*); to rely upon (= *a*).

confidènte, *a.* confident, confiding. ¶ *m.* confidant; confidential agent; spy. **confidènza,** *f.* confidence; trust; intimacy; secret information; disclosure. **confidenziàle,** *a.* confidential.

configgere (*pr.* **-íggo,** *&c.,* like *figgere*), *v.t.* to nail, nail up; pierce; drive in; fix.

configuràre (*pr.* **-úro**), *v.t.* to shape, give another form to; (*fig.*) symbolize.

confinànte, *pr.p.* of *confinare.* ¶ *a.* adjacent, adjoining, contiguous, bordering. **confinàre** (*pr.* **-íno**), *v.t.* to confine; limit; banish to a prescribed domicile (*confino*); (*v.i.*) (*aux.* avere) to have the same boundary, adjoin, border on (= *con*). **confinazióne,** *f.* fixing of boundaries, demarcation of frontiers. **confíne,** *m.* boundary, frontier; boundary post; limit. **confíno,** *m.* sentence of prescribed domicile.

confísca, *f.* confiscation, forfeiture.

confiscàre (*pr.* -ísco, -íschi), *v.t.* to confiscate.

confitèmini (*Lat.*), *in expr. essere al* ∼, to be on (or at) the point of death.

confíteor, (*Lat.*) *m.* prayer beginning with this word.

confítto, *p.p.* of *configgere*. ¶ *a.* nailed, fixed. ∼ *in croce*, nailed on the cross.

conflagrazióne, *f.* conflagration.

conflítto, *m.* conflict, clash.

confluènte, *pr.p.* of *confluire*. ¶ *a. & m.* confluent. **confluènza**, *f.* confluence. **confluíre** (*pr.* -ísco, *&c.*, like *fluire*), *v.i.* (*aux.* essere *& avere*) to flow together, mix, meet.

confóndere (*pr.* -óndo, -óndi, *&c*), *v.t. ir.* to confound, confuse, perplex; mistake one for (= *con*). **confóndersi**, *v.refl.* to become confused, perplexed; to be needlessly troubled over someone or something.

conformàbile, *a.* conformable, adaptable; similar (to). **conformàre** (*pr.* -órmo), *v.t.* to conform; adapt, assimilate. **conformàrsi**, *v.refl.* to be adapted, conform (to) comply (with) (= *a.*). **conformazióne**, *f.* conformation, form, structure.

confórme, *a.* alike in form, similar, corresponding; in agreement. *per copia* ∼, certified as a correct copy. ¶ *ad.* conformably, in conformity. **confórme!** (for *conforme la circostanza*) that depends! **conformità**, *f.* conformity.

confortàbile, *a.* consolable, able to be comforted or encouraged (*not generally* comfortable *in the Eng. sense, which is rather* **comodo**, **agiato**, or **contento**). **confortàre** (*pr.* -òrto), *v.t.* to comfort, console, encourage; **confortatóre**, *m.* -tríce, *f.* comforter. **confortíno**, *m.* sweet cake; pick-me-up. **confòrto**, *m.* comfort (*mental & spiritual*), consolation, encouragement. *gli estremi* ∼ *i*, extreme unction (*Eccl.*).

confratèllo, *m.* member of a brotherhood or fraternity. **confraternità**, *f.* lay fraternity devoted to religion or good works.

confricàre (*pr.* -íco, -íchi), *v.t.* to rub, rub together.

confrontàre (*pr.* -ónto), *v.t.* to confront; compare. (*v.i.*) (*aux.* avere) to agree exactly. **confrónto**,

m. comparison; (*Law*) confrontation. *in* ∼ *di*, *a* ∼ *di*, in comparison with. *senza* ∼, incomparably. *stare a* ∼ *di*, to bear comparison with.

confucianísmo, *m.* Confucianism. **confuciàno**, *a. & m.* Confucian. **Confúcio**, *m.* Confucius.

confušaménte, *ad.* confusedly, in confusion, pell-mell. **confušióne**, *f.* confusion, embarrassment; medley, disorder. **confúšo**, *p.p.* of confondere. ¶ *a.* confused.

confutàre (*pr.* cònfuto), *v.t.* to confute, disprove. **confutazióne**, *f.* confutation.

congedàre (*pr.* -èdo), *v.t.* to discharge, dismiss, give leave to, suspend. **congedàrsi**, *v.refl.* to take leave. **congèdo**, *m.* discharge, leave (*of absence*); certificate of discharge. *dar* ∼, to dismiss. *prender* ∼, to take leave.

congegnàre (*pr.* -égno), *v.t.* to put together, mount, assemble (*pieces of machinery*); compose, arrange (*Lit. work*). **congégno**, *m.* apparatus, instrument, tool; assembly of parts, method of putting together.

congelaménto, *m.* freezing; congealing. *punto di* ∼, *m.* freezing point. **congelàre** (*pr.* -èlo), *v.t.* to congeal, freeze. **congelàrsi**, *v.refl.* to freeze, become congealed. **congelàto**, *p.p.* of *congelare*. ¶ *a.* frozen. *carni* ∼ *e*, frozen meat.

congènere, *a.* of the same kind, kindred.

congènito, *a.* congenital.

congèrie, *f.inv.* confused mass, heap, congeries.

congestionàre (*pr.* -óno), *v.t.* affect with congestion, cause blood to flow in excess to some organ of the body; (*fig.*) to overcrowd. **congestióne**, *f.* congestion, excessive accumulation of blood, or (*fig.*) of traffic, &c.

congettúra, *f.* supposition, conjecture, conjectural reading (*Lit.*). **congetturàre** (*pr.* -úro), *v.t.* to conjecture, surmise.

congioírsi (*pr.* -ísco, -ísci), *v.refl.* to rejoice together.

congiúngere *&* **congiúgnere** (*pr.* -úngo, -únghi, *&c.*, like *giungere*), *v.t.* to join together, unite. **congiúngersi**, *v.refl.* (*Mil.*) to link up. **congiungiménto**, *m.* (act of) joining, union; (*Mil.*) link-up. **congiuntaménte**, *ad.* jointly. **congiuntíva**, *f.* conjunctiva (*Med.*). **congiuntivíte**, *f.* conjunctivitis

(*Med.*). **congiuntívo**, *a.* conjunctive. ¶ *m.* subjunctive (*mood*) (*Gram.*). **congiúnto**, *p.p.* of *congiungere.* ¶ *m.* relative, relation. **congiuntúra**, *f.* point of junction; joint, seam; conjuncture, occasion, circumstance. **congiunzióne**, *f.* conjunction; connection, junction. **congiúra**, *f.* conspiracy, plot. **congiuràre** (*pr.* -**úro**), *v.i.* (*aux.* avere) to conspire, plot. **congiuràto**, *p.p.* of *congiurare.* ¶ *m.* conspirator.

conglobàre (*pr.* **cònglobo**), *v.t.* to roll into a ball.

conglomeràre (*pr.* -**òmero**), *v.t.* to gather into a mass, conglomerate. **conglomeràto**, *m.* conglomerate, pudding-stone (*Geol*); conglomeration.

conglutinàre (*pr.* -**útino**), *v.t.* to glue together.

congratulàrsi (con) (*pr.* -**àtulo**), *v.refl.* to congratulate.

congrèga, *f.* assembly, gathering (*often for questionable ends*); gang, set. **congregàre** (*pr.* -**ègo**, -**èghi**), *v.t.* to assemble. **congregazióne**, *f.* assembly; congregation; religious fraternity or reunion; institution. **congrèsso**, *m.* congress; conference.

congruaménte, *ad.* conveniently, suitably, consistently. **congruènza**, *f.* agreement, congruence, consistency. **còngruo**, *a.* congruous, suitable, adequate; convenient.

conguagliàre (*pr.* -**àglio**, -**àgli**), *v.t.* to equalize, balance; finish off (*art*). **conguàglio** (*pl.* -**àgli**), *m.* balancing, levelling, equalizing ;finishing off.

coniàre (*pr.* **cònio**, **còni**), *v.t.* to coin (*lit. & fig.*), mint, strike (*medal, &c.*). **coniatóre**, *m.* coiner (not in the sense of a maker of counterfeit coin, *falso monetario*). **coniatúra**, *f.* coining.

cònico (*pl.* **cònici**), *a.* conical. *tenda* ~*a*, *f.* bell tent.

conífero, *a.* coniferous. ¶ *m.* conifer. (*pl.f. le conifere.*)

coniglièra, *f.* rabbit-warren, r.-hutch. **coníglio** (*pl.* -**igli**), *m.* -**a**, *f.* rabbit.

cònio (*pl.* **còni**), *m.* wedge, die; imprint; stamp on coin; coinage; (*fig.*) brand, species, kind. *di nuovo* ~, brand new. *son tutti d'un*~, they are all alike.

coniugàle, *a.* conjugal, connubial, matrimonial, marriage (*tie*), married (*life*). **coniugàre** (*pr.* **còniugo**, **còniughi**), *v.t.* to conjugate (*Gram.*). **coniugàto**, *p.p.* of *coniugare.* ¶ *a.*

joined in marriage. **coniugazióne**, *f.* conjugation (*Gram.*). **còniuge**, *m.f.* consort, husband or wife; (*pl.*) *i coniugi*, the wedded pair, husband & wife.

conlegatàrio, *or* **collegatario**, *m.* joint legatee.

connaturàle, *a.* innate; of like nature; appropriate.

connazionàle, *m.* fellow-countryman.

connessióne, *f.* connexion. **connèsso**, *p.p.* of *connettere.* ¶ *m.* connexion (*thing connected*). **connèttere** (*pr.* -**ètto**, *&c.*, like *annettere*), *v.t. ir.* to connect, join, link.

connivènte, *a.* conniving. **connivènza**, *f.* connivance.

connotàto, *m.* external mark, personal characteristic.

connúbio (*pl.* -**úbi**), *m.* wedding; union.

connumeràre (*pr.* -**úmero**), *v.t.* to count together, number in a series.

còno, *m.* cone.

conòcchia, *f.* distaff; bunch of flax on the distaff.

conopèo, *m.* mosquito net; net placed over the ciborium or pyx in the service of the Mass (*Eccl.*).

conoscènte, *m.f.* acquaintance (*person*). **conoscènza**, *f.* knowledge, information, intelligence; acquaintance (*both senses*). **conóscere** (*pr.* **conósco**, **conósci**, *&c.*), *v.t. ir.* to know, discern, recognize; make the acquaintance of; take cognizance of. *darsi a* ~, *farsi* ~, to make oneself known. ~ *di vista*, ~ *di nome*, to know by sight, by reputation. ~ *alla voce*, to know by the voice. **conoscíbile**, *a.* recognizable, easily known. ¶ *m.* what can be known, (the) knowable.

conosciménto, *m.* cognition, discernment, judgment. **conoscitóre**, *m.* connoisseur, good judge (*paintings, vine, &c.*). **conosciutaménte**, *ad.* knowingly. **conosciúto**, *p.p.* of *conoscere.* ¶ *a.* well-known, famous.

conquassàre, *v.t.* to shake violently; smash. **conquàsso**, *m.* violent shock, crash, ruin. *mettere a* ~, *mandare in* ~, to break in pieces; (*fig.*) to ruin. *andare in* ~, to fall to ruin.

conquíbus (*Lat. cum quibus*), *m.inv.* (the) wherewithal, money.

conquídere (*pr.* -**ído**), *v.t. ir.* to disturb, subdue, destroy.

conquísta, *f.* conquest. **conquistàre**

(*pr.* **-ísto**), *v.t.* to conquer, win, acquire.

consacràre (*pr.* **-àcro**), *v.t.* to consecrate; ordain; dedicate; (*fig.*) devote, make valid or legitimate. **consacrazióne**, *f.* consecration; ordination; devotion (to).

consanguineità, *f.* blood-relationship. **consanguíneo**, *a.* related by blood, akin.

consapévole, *a.* aware, conscious, informed. *fare* ~, to inform. **consapevolézza**, *f.* knowledge, awareness, consciousness.

consapúto, *a.* well known. *fatto* ~, acknowledged fact.

cònscio (*pl.* **cònsci**), *a.* aware, conscious.

consecutívo, *a.* consecutive, following.

conségna, *f.* consignment, delivery; trust; (*Mil.*) confinement to barracks; (*pl.*) *consegne*, orders, daily orders (*Nav.*). ~ *a domicilio*, house delivery. *pagamento alla* ~, cash on delivery. **consegnàre** (*pr.* **-égno**), *v.t.* to deliver, consign; entrust, commit; confine to barracks; hand over, give in charge (*to police*). ~ *a memoria*, to commit to memory. **consegnatàrio** (*pl.* **-àri**), *m.* consignee. **consegnàto**, *p.p.* of *consegnare.* ¶ *a.* confined to barracks.

conseguènte, *a.* consequent. **conseguènza**, *f.* consequence. **conseguíre** (*pl.* **-éguo, -égui**, *&c.*), like *seguire*), *v.t.* to attain; obtain, win, achieve; (*v.i.*) (*aux.* essere) to result, follow. **conseguitàre** (*pl.* **-éguito**), *v.i.* (*aux.* essere) to result, happen.

consènso, *m.* consent, permission (*gen. written*).

consentàneo, *a.* in accord; unanimous; concurrent. **consentíre** (*pl.* **-ènto**), *v.i.* (*aux.* avere) to consent, agree; yield to (physical) pressure; (*v.t.*) to permit.

consertàre *v.t.* to intertwine; fold. **consèrto**, *sync. p.p.* of *consertare*, folded. *a braccia* ~*e*, with folded arms.

consèrva, *f.* store, storage, storeroom; reservoir; receptacle for preserving food, &c.; jam, preserved fruit; sauce; (*pl.*) tinned, canned or potted meats, &c.; preserves; (*Naut.*) convoy. *carne in* ~, tinned meat. ~ *di pomodoro*, tomato sauce. ~ *di piante*, hot-house. *andar di* ~, to sail in convoy; (*fig.*) act together. **conservàre** (*pr.* **-èrvo**), *v.t.* to

preserve, keep; retain; conserve. ~ *la composizione*, to keep the type standing. **conservàrsi**, *v.refl.* to keep, remain; take care of oneself. **conservatóre**, *m.* **-tríce**, *f.* conservator, keeper; warden; ranger; curator, -trix; conservative (*Pol.*); registrar (*mortgages*). ¶ *a.* preserving, preservative; (*Pol.*) conservative. **conservatòrio**, *m.* (*girls'*) school; academy (*music, &c.*). **conservazióne**, *f.* preservation; care; registry. ~ *in refrigeranti*, cold storage. *istinto di* ~, instinct of self-preservation.

consideràbile *&* **considerévole**, *a.* considerable; notable; eminent; large. **consideràndo**, *ad.* (*Law*) whereas, considering that. ¶ *m.inv.* preamble, recital; (*Law*) reasons for judgment. **consideràre** (*pr.* **-ídero**), *v.t.* to consider; examine; esteem; regard, deem. **considerazióne**, *f.* consideration; regard.

consigliàre (*pr.* **-íglio, -ígli**), *v.t.* to counsel, advise; recommend. **consigliàrsi** (*con*), *v.refl.* to take counsel with, ask advice of, consult. **consiglière**, *m.* adviser, counsellor; councillor. ~ *delegato*, managing director. ~ *privato*, privy councillor. ~ *comunale*, town-councillor. **consíglio** (*pl.* **-ígli**), *m.* advice, counsel; council. ~ *di amministrazione*, board of directors. *prender* ~ *di*, to consult. ~ *dei ministri*, cabinet (council).

consiliàre, *a.* of a council; council (*att.*); (*Eccl.*) conciliar.

consímile, *a.* alike, nearly alike; similar.

consistènte, *a.* consistent, firm, solid, durable. **consistènza**, *f.* consistence; substance; firmness; durability. **consístere** (*pr.* **-ísto**, *&c.*, like *assistere*), *v.i.* (*aux.* essere) to consist; be composed (of); lie, reside, consist (in); matter. *non consiste!* no matter!

consociàre (*pr.* **-òcio, -òci**), *v.t.* to associate, bring together. **consociazióne**, *f.* association, club. *C* ~ *Turistica Italiana*, Italian Touring Club. **consòcio** (*pl.* **-òci**), *m.* associate, partner, co-partner.

consolàbile, *a.* able to be consoled. **consolànte**, *a.* consoling, comforting, cheering. **consolàre** (*pr.* **-ólo**), *v.t.* to console, comfort; cheer, solace. **consolàrsi**, *v.refl.* to cheer up; take comfort; rejoice.

consolàre, *a.* consular.
consolàto, *a.* comforted, consoled.
¶ *m.* consulate.
consolatòrio (*pl.* -**òri**), *a.* consolatory. **consolazióne,** *f.* consolation, comfort, solace.
cònsole, *m.* consul.
consolidàre (*pr.* -**òlido**), *v.t.* to consolidate. **consolidàto,** *m.* Consolidated Fund, consols.
consólo, *m.* consolation, comfort; (*S. Italy*) food prepared by neighbours for a bereaved family.
consonànte, *a.* harmonious, corresponding, consonant. ¶ *f.* consonant (*Gram.*). **consonànza,** *f.* consonance, harmony; agreement of consonants in the ending of words.
consonàre (*pr.* -**uòno,** *&c.*, like *sonàre*), *v.i.* (*aux.* avere) to agree, correspond, harmonize. **cònsono,** *a.* consonant, agreeing (with).
consòrte, *m.f.* consort; husband or wife; associate. **consorterìa,** *f.* faction, clique; set.
consòrzio (*pl.* -**òrzi**), *m.* society, partnership, association, firm; syndicate; relationship. ~ *umano,* human society.
constàre (*pr.* -**cònsto**), *v.i.* (*aux.* essere) to consist, be composed (of); (*v.impers.*) to be known, to be proved. *non consta,* it is not proven, not certain. *a me consta che,* I am aware that.
constatàre, *v.t.* to remark, notice; ascertain; verify, establish. **constatazióne,** *f.* observation; ascertainment. Cf. *costatare, &c.*
consuèto, *a.* accustomed, usual, habitual. ¶ *m.* custom, habit. **consuetúdine,** *f.* custom, habit; intimacy.
consulènte, *a. & m.* consulting, consultant, adviser (*doctor or advocate*).
consùlta, *f.* consultation; consulting-room; council. ~ *municipale,* municipal council. *Sacra C*~, judicial & administrative Council of the Papal State. **consultàre** (*pr.* -**últo**), *v.t.* to consult; examine. **consultarsi** (**con**), *v.refl.* to take counsel with, seek advice from. **consùlto,** *m.* consultation (*medical, legal, &c.*).
consumàre (*pr.* -**úmo**), *v.t.* to consume, wear out, waste, spend, dissipate; commit; finish, complete, perfect, consummate. **consumàrsi,** *v.refl.* to waste away, pine away;

faint. **consumàto,** *a.* accomplished, perfect, consummate; lean; spare. ¶ *m.* strong soup, jelly broth.
consumatóre, *m.* -**tríce,** *f.* consumer. **consumazióne,** *f.* consumption; expense; drink [*in café*]; consummation, completion. ~ *dei secoli,* end of the world. **consúmo,** *m.* consumption, wear & tear, habitual use; quantity (of food, &c.) needed for habitual (or family) use. *pagare a* ~, to pay for what one consumes. *cooperativa di* ~, cooperative store. *dazio* ~, tax on articles of consumption. *per* ~, for everyday use, for practical use.
consuntívo, *a.* consumptive. *bilancio* ~, budget of income & expenditure for a fixed period. ¶ *m.* costing.
consúnto, *a.* worn out; wasted; consumed. **consunzióne,** *f.* consumption, waste; wasting disease, phthisis.
contàbile, *m.* accountant; book-keeper. **contabilità,** *f.* book-keeping.
contadinésco (*pl.* -**éschi**), *a.* of or like a peasant; rustic; peasant (*att.*).
contadíno, *m.* -**a,** *f.* peasant, peasant farmer. ¶ *a.* peasant (*att.*).
contàdo, *m.* district round a city (with farms, market-gardens, &c.); peasantry.
contàgio (*pl.* -**àgi**), *m.* contagion, infection; plague. **contagióso,** *a.* infectious, contagious.
contagócce, *m.inv.* dropping-glass.
contamináre (*pr.* -**àmino**), *v.t.* to contaminate, corrupt; infect; blend two pieces of writing together. **contaminazióne,** *f.* contamination, pollution, infection; literary fusion.
contànti, *m.pl.* ready money. *a* ~, *per* ~, for cash. **contàre** (*pr.* **cónto**), *v.t.* to count, reckon, calculate; value, esteem; propose, intend; relate; (*v.i.*) (*aux.* avere) to count, have credit or respect. ~*sopra,* ~ *su,* to rely upon. **contàta,** *f.* (rapid) counting (also *dim.*) **contatína. contatóre,** *m.* reckoner; narrator; meter (*gas, electricity, &c.*). ~ *a pagamento anticipato,* slot meter.
contàtto, *m.* contact, touch; relation.
cónte, *m.* count; Earl. **contèa,** *f.* county (*lit.* territory held by a count).
conteggiàre (*pr.* -**éggio,** -**éggi**), *v.t.* to keep accounts; include in an account. **conteggiàrsi,** *v.refl.* to make up their accounts (*as bet. two*

persons). **contéggio** (*pl.* **-éggi**), *m.* reckoning, fixing of prices, keeping of accounts.

contégno, *m.* demeanour, bearing, attitude; behaviour; dignity, reserve. *stare in* ~. to behave with dignity. **contegnóso,** *a.* staid, dignified, reserved.

contemperàre (*pr.* **-èmpero**), *v.t.* to temper, moderate, modify; blend in due proportion. **contemperàrsi,** *v.refl.* to sober down.

contemplàre (*pr.* **-èmplo**), *v.t.* to contemplate; consider; foresee. **contemplatívo,** *a.* contemplative. **contemplazióne,** *f.* contemplation.

contemporàneo, *a. & m.* contemporary.

contèndere (*pr.* **-èndo**, *&c.*, like *tendere*), *v.i. ir.* (*aux.* avere) to contend; (*v.t.*) contest, refuse, deny.

contenènte, *m.* container, holder. **contenére** (*pr.* **-èngo**, *&c.*, like *tenere*), *v.t. ir.* to contain, hold; comprise, include; restrain, control; repress. **contenérsi,** *v.refl.* to restrain oneself; forbear; behave.

contentàre (*pr.* **-ènto**), *v.t.* to content, satisfy; please, gratify. **contentatúra,** *f.* capacity of being satisfied. *di facile* ~, *di difficile* ~, easily satisfied, not easily s. **contentézza,** *f.* pleasure, satisfaction, contentment; joy, happiness. **contènto,** *a.* content; satisfied, pleased; glad. ¶ *m.* contentment.

contenúto, *p.p.* of *contenere.* ¶ *m.* content[s]; subject; tenor (*speech, letter, &c.*).

contería, *f.* fancy glass-ware, Venetian glass.

conterràneo, *a.* belonging to the same district or village. ¶ *m.* fellow-countryman.

contésa, *f.* contention, strife; controversy.

contéssa, *f.* countess.

contèssere (*pr.* **-èsso**, *&c.*, like *tessere*), *v.t.* to interweave, entwine; (*fig.*) to compose.

contestàbile, *a.* questionable, debatable, moot.

contestàre (*pr.* **-èsto**), *v.t.* to contest, oppose; dispute, challenge, question; deny; intimate, notify, declare. ~ *una contravvenzione,* to notify a breach of (*police*) regulations. **contestazióne,** *f.* dispute; objection; notification.

contèste, *m.* fellow-witness; (*pl.*) witnesses who agree in a deposition.

contèsto, *p.p.* of *contessere.* ¶ *m.* context; general argument (*book, writing or speech*); connexion; structure.

contestuàle, *a.* belonging to the context or general argument.

contézza, *f.* information, (*precise*) knowledge. *dar* ~, to inform. *aver* ~, to be informed.

contíguo, *a.* adjoining, neighbouring, contiguous.

continènte, *m.* continent; mainland. ¶ *a.* temperate, chaste. **continènza,** *f.* temperance, moderation, continence.

contingènte, *a.* contingent, incidental, accessory. ¶ *m.* contingent; share, quota. **contingènza,** *f.* contingency, chance event, circumstance.

continuàre (*pr.* **-ínuo**), *v.t.* to continue, keep on (or up); take up, resume; (*v.i.*) (*aux.* essere or avere, the latter of pers. only), to continue. **continuazióne,** *f.* continuation. **continuità,** *f.* continuity. **contínuo,** *a.* continuous, continual; unbroken; uninterrupted. *di* ~, continually.

cónto, *m.* account, bill; reckoning, calculation; reason, explanation; notice, information; store, value; interest; reputation, esteem; sake; business. *alla fin de'* ~ *i, a* ~ *i fatti,* after all, everything considered. *in fin dei* ~ *i,* finally, in conclusion. *a buon* ~ *o,* in any case, meanwhile. *per nessun* ~, on no account. *per* ~ *mio,* for my part, so far as I am concerned. *di* ~, *di gran* ~, much respected, highly esteemed. *far* ~ *di* (*with infin.*), to imagine, suppose; intend, *far* ~ *di* (or *sopra*) (*with noun or pron.*), to count upon, rely upon, propose. *fare i* ~*i,* to make up accounts. *far di* ~, to do sums, practise arithmetic. *metter* ~, *tornar* ~, (*impers.*), to be worth while, to be fitting. *render* ~ *di,* to give an account of. *rendersi* ~ *di,* to inform oneself about, to take into account. *tener di* ~, to take care of, treat with respect. ~ *aperto,* open (banking) account. ~ *corrente,* current account. ~ *preventivo,* budget. ~ *presuntivo,* estimate.

contòrcere (*pr.* **-òrco**, *&c.*, like *torcere*), *v.t. ir.* to contort, twist, distort. **contorcimènto,** *m.* contortion, twisting.

contornàre (*pr.* **-òrno**), *v.t.* to surround; trim or dress the cir-

cumference of; border; outline.
contórno, *m.* outline, rim, border; trimming, dressing.
contorsióne, *f.* contorsion. **contòrto,** *p.p.* of *contorcere.* ¶ *a.* contorted, twisted, distorted.
cóntra-, *prefix,* may indicate either opposition or (less commonly) reciprocity or symmetry. Before consonants other than impure s, z, gn, & ps, it requires the doubling of this letter. Not to be confused with *contro-,* which never requires this doubling.
contrabbandière, *m.* **-ièra,** *f.* smuggler. **contrabbàndo,** *m.* smuggling; smuggled goods, contraband. *di ~,* clandestinely, secretly.
contrabbàsso, *m.* double bass (*Mus.*).
contrabbilanciàre (*pr.* -**àncio**), *v.t.* to counterbalance, balance.
contraccambiàre (*pr.* -**àmbio**), *v.t.* to reciprocate; return, requite. *~ le gentilezze,* to return kindness for kindness. **contraccàmbio** (*pl.* -**càmbi**), *m.* return, exchange, requital. *rendere il ~,* to give like for like.
contraccólpo, *m.* counter-stroke; reaction, result; rebound; repercussion.
contràda, *f.* quarter of a town; wide street; stretch of country. *~ inglese,* country-dance.
contraddànza, *f.* square-dance, quadrille. *~ inglese,* country-dance.
contraddíre (*pr.* -**íco,** -**íci**), *&c.,* like *dire, v.t. ir.* to contradict. **contraddittòrio** (*pl.* -**òri**), *a.* contradictory; conflicting. **contraddizióne,** *f.* contradiction; discrepancy.
contraènte, *pr.p.* of *contrarre.* ¶ *a.* contracting. ¶ *m.* contracting party.
contraèrea, *f.* (*Mil.*) anti-aircraft defence. **contraèreo,** *a.* anti-aircraft.
contraffàre (*pr.* -**affò** *or* -**affàccio,** *&c.,* like *fare*), *v.t. ir.* to counterfeit, imitate, forge, falsify; adulterate. **contraffattóre,** *m.* -**trice,** *f.* forger, coiner, counterfeiter. **contraffàtto,** *a.* counterfeit, forged, adulterated. **contraffazióne,** *f.* counterfeiting, forgery; (*literary*) piracy.
contraffòrte, *m.* buttress; iron bar to secure doors or shutters.
contraggènio (*pl.* -**èni**), *m.* antipathy, aversion, disinclination. *a ~,* or *di ~,* unwillingly.
contràlto, *m.* contralto (*voice or singer*).
contrammàrcia (*pl.* -**màrce**), *f.*

counter-march, counter-movement (*Mil.*).
contrammiràglio (*pl.* -**àgli**), *m.* rear-admiral.
contrappàsso, *m.* retaliation.
contrappélo, *m.* wrong way (or contrary direction) of the hair or nap. *a ~,* or *di ~,* against the grain. *fare il ~,* to shave against the lie of the hair; (*fig.*) to speak ill of someone; criticize minutely.
contrappesàre (*pr.* -**éso**), *v.t.* to counterbalance; weigh one thing against another. **contrappéso,** *m.* counter-weight; counterpoise.
contrappórre (*pr.* -**óngo,** -**óni,** *&c.,* like *porre*), *v.t. ir.* to oppose; compare, set over against each other (*arguments, ideas, &c.*). **contrapposizióne,** *f.* contraposition, antithesis. **contrappósto,** *m.* antithesis, exact opposite.
contrappúnto, *m.* counterpoint (*Mus.*).
contrariàre (*pr.* -**àrio,** -**àri**), *v.t.* to thwart, oppose; baffle, counteract; vex, annoy. **contrarietà,** *f.* contrariness; opposition; adversity; misfortune; disagreement; disappointment; difficulty; obstacle. *~ del tempo,* unseasonable weather.
contràrio (*pl.* -**àri**), *a.* contrary, unfavourable; harmful; opposed. ¶ *m.* contrary, opposite.
contràrre (*pr.* -**àggo,** *&c.,* like *trarre*), *v.t.* to contract, make a contract of; form, conclude; incur. **contràrsi,** *v.refl.* to contract, shrink.
contrasségno, *m.* mark, sign, counter-sign; proof.
contrastàbile, *a.* disputable, open to question. **contrastàre** (*pr.* -**àsto**), *v.t.* to oppose, resist; dispute; contest, struggle for; (*v.i.*) *aux. avere,* to contend, struggle, conflict (with). **contrastàrsi,** *v.refl.* to quarrel, wrangle. **contràsto,** *m.* opposition; discord, strife, conflict (*of ideas, interests*); contrast (*of colours, &c.*). *senza ~,* without opposition.
contrattàbile, *a.* negotiable; ready to negotiate.
contrattàcco (*pl.* -**àcchi**), *m.* counter attack (*Mil.*).
contrattàre (*pr.* -**àtto**), *v.t. & i.* to negotiate (for sale or purchase); (*v.i.*) to bargain, haggle.
contrattémpo, *m.* brief interval; mishap, awkward incident, hitch *a ~, di ~,* inopportunely.

contràttile, *a.* contractile. **contràt-to**, *m.* contract; agreement; deed; indenture; articles; letter; bond. ~ *di noleggio*, (*Ship*) charter-party. ¶ *a.* contracted, shrunken. **contrat-túra**, *f.* contraction (*of the muscles*); shrinking.

contravveléno, *m.* antidote.

contravvenìre (*pr.* -èngo, &c., like *venìre*), *v.i.* (*aux.* avere) to be guilty of a contravention or infringement of the law. ~ *a*, to contravene, infringe. **contravvenzióne**, *f.* contravention; breach, infringement (or infraction) of the law; penalty paid for such offence.

contribuènte, *m.* contributor; tax-payer, rate-payer. **contribuíre** (*pr.* -ísco, &c., like *attribuíre*), *v.i.* (*aux.* avere) to contribute; (*fig.*) to help, aid, have part in (*a*). **contribúto**, *m.* contribution (*gen. voluntary*). **contribuzióne**, *f.* contribution (*gen. imposed*), tax, levy, &c.

contristàre (*pr.* -ísto), *v.t.* to grieve, afflict, sadden. **contristàrsi**, *v.refl.* to be (deeply) grieved.

contríto, *a.* contrite. **contrizióne**, *f.* contrition.

cóntro-, *prefix*, does not require doubling of following consonant.

cóntro, *pr.* against; opposite (to). *di* ~, facing, opposite. *dar* ~, to contradict.

controavvíso, *m.* contrary information.

controbilanciàre, *v.t.* to counter-balance.

controcàssa, *f.* outer casing, outer case (as of a watch).

controcólpo, *m.* return stroke; counter stroke.

controdichiarazióne, *f.* counter declaration.

controffensíva, *f.* counter-offensive.

controfinèstra, *f.* double window, outer window.

controfirmàre, *v.t.* to countersign.

controfòdera, *f.* inner lining.

controfóndo, *m.* false bottom, double bottom.

controllàre (*pr.* -òllo), *v.t.* to check, control, verify, inspect. **contròllo**, *m.* control, examination, inspection; register; place of inspection; inspector. ~*di volume*, volume control (*Radio*). *doppio* ~, dual control (*admin.*). **controllóre**, *m.* (*f.* -óra), inspector; ticket inspector.

controlúce, *f.* bad light. ¶ *ad.* in a bad light, against the light; with one's back to the light. **contro-lúme**, *m.* bad light (*artificial*).

contromàrca (*pl.* -marche), *f.* pass-out check (*Theat.*).

contromàrcia (*pl.* -àrce), *f.* counter-march.

contropàrte, *f.* opposite party (*Law*); opposite number (*pers. & Theat.*).

contropòrta, *f.* double door; inner door; screen-door.

contropropósta, *f.* counter-proposition.

contropròva, *f.* repetition of a test; recount (*votes*).

controquerèla, *f.* countercharge.

contrordinàre (*pr.*-órdino), *v.t.* to countermand.

controrifórma, *f.* Counter-Reformation.

controrivoluzióne, *f.* counter-revolution.

controscàrpa, *f.* overshoe; counter-scarp.

controscèna, *f.* appropriate action of a player on the stage to the words of his interlocutor.

controsènso, *m.* misconstruction; mis-translation; misinterpretation; wrong sense. *a* ~, in the wrong sense, or direction.

controspionàggio, *m.* counter-espionage.

controstimolànte, *m.* sedative (*Med.*). **controstímolo**, *m.* sedative action.

controstòmaco, *ad.* unwillingly.

controtorpedinièra, *f.* See *caccia-torpediniera*.

controvèrsia, *f.* controversy, disputation. **controversísta** (*pl.* -ísti), *m.* controversialist. **controvèrso**, *a.* debated, disputed, subject to controversy. **controvèrtere**, *v.t. def.* to controvert; dispute. **controvertíbile**, *a.* disputable, doubtful, controvertible.

contumàce, *a.* refractory, contumacious. ¶ *m.* defaulter who disobeys a judicial summons. **contumàcia**, *f.* contumacy; contempt of court; quarantine.

contúndere (*pr.* -úndo, -úndi), *v.t. ir.* to bruise; contuse.

conturbàre (*pr.* -úrbo), *v.t.* to disturb.

contusióne, *f.* bruise, contusion. **contúso**, *p.p.* of *contundere*. ¶ *a.* bruised.

contutóre, *m.* joint guardian.

contuttoché, *or* **con tutto che**, *c.* although. **contuttociò**, *ad.* nevertheless; however.

convalidàre (*pr.* -**àlido**), *v.t.* to render valid, validate, confirm.

convàlle, *f.* long wide valley; dale.

convégno, *m.* meeting, appointment, place of meeting.

convenévole, *a.* suitable, fit, fitting, proper; seemly, decorous; opportune. ¶ **convenévoli**, *m.pl.* compliments; greetings; ceremony. **convenevolézza**, *f.* propriety, decorum.

conveniènte, *pr.p.* of *convenire*. ¶ *a.* fitting, appropriate; expedient; moderate. **conveniènza**, *f.* convenience, suitability; conformity, agreement; harmonious adjustment; propriety; expedience,-cy, advantage.

conveníre (*pr.* -**èngo**, *&c.*, like *venire*), *v.i. ir.* (*aux.* essere) to come together, assemble; converge; (*v.i.*) (*aux.* avere) agree, grant, admit (that). *v.i. & impers.* (*aux.* essere) to be fitting, expedient, necessary; to be seemly, proper, in conformity with good manners; to fit, suit, become. *convien partire*, we had better go. *v.t.* to summon, convene.

conventícola, *f.* secret meeting.

convènto, *m.* convent, monastery. **conventuàle**, *a.* conventual.

convenúto, *p.p.* of *convenire*. ¶ *a.* agreed, settled. ¶ *m.* agreement, convention; (*Law*) defendant.

convenzionàle, *a.* conventional. **convenzióne**, *f.* convention; custom; constituent assembly.

convergènte, *a.* converging, convergent. **convergènza**, *f.* convergence. **convèrgere**, *v.i.* to converge.

conversàre (*pr.* -**èrso**), *v.i.* (*aux.* avere) to talk, converse. **conversazióne**, *f.* conversation, talk; evening party. **conversévole**, *a.* conversable, sociable.

conversióne, *f.* conversion; wheeling (movement) (*Mil.*).

convèrso, *m.* converse, opposite; lay brother (*Eccl.*).

convertíbie, *a.* convertible, exchangeable. **convertíre** (*pr.* -**èrto**, *&c.*, like *avvertire*), *v.t.* to convert; change, turn.

convèsso, *a.* convex.

convíncere (*pr.* -**ínco**, *&c.*, like *avvíncere*), *v.t. ir.* to convince; convict. **convínto**, *p.p.* of *convincere*. ¶ *a.* convinced; convicted. **convinzióne**, *f.* conviction; persuasion, belief.

convitàre (*pr.* -**íto**), *v.t.* to invite (to dinner). **convíto**, *m.* banquet.

convítto, *m.* boarding-school. **convittóre**, *m.* (*f.* -**tríce**), boarder (*Sch.*).

convivàle, *a.* convivial.

convivènza, *f.* life in common; society. *l'umana* ~, human society, humanity. **convívere** (*pr.* -**ivo**), *v.i.* (*aux.* essere) to live together, cohabit.

convocàre (*pr.* **cònvoco, cònvochi**), *v.t.* to convoke.

convogliàre (*pr.* -**òglio**), *v.t.* to convoy, escort. **convòglio** (*pl.* -**ògli**), *m.* cortège, procession; escort; convoy; train (*Rly.*). ~ *funebre*, funeral, funeral procession.

convolàre, *v.i.* (*aux.* essere) to fly together; to hasten.

convulsióne, *f.* convulsion, spasm; commotion. **convúlso**, *a.* convulsed; convulsive, agitated; (*fig.*) strange, confused, violent.

coonestàre (*pr.* -**èsto**), *v.t.* to gloss over, palliate, justify, find an excuse for.

cooperàre (*pr.* -**òpero**), *v.i.* (*aux.* avere) to cooperate. **cooperatívo**, *a.* cooperative. *società* ~*a*, or ~ *a, f.* cooperative society.

coordinàre (*pr.* -**órdino**), *v.t.* to coordinate, set in order, arrange.

coòrte, *f.* troop, cohort.

copèrchio (*pl.* -**èrchi**), *m.* cover. lid.

copernicàno, *a.* Copernican. *sistema* ~, Copernican system. **Copèrnico**, *m.* Copernicus.

copèrta, *f.* cover, covering; blanket, coverlet, rug, counterpane; upper deck; book cover or frontispiece; envelope. *soprac* ~, *f.* bed-spread. *alla* ~, covertly, secretly. **copertaménte**, *ad.* covertly, secretly, by stealth. **copertína**, *f.* small cover, wrapper; book-cover; cover over a picture. **copèrto**, *p.p.* of *coprire*. ¶ *a.* covered, closed, protected; heavily clothed; cloudy, overcast; sheltered; hidden, secret; masked. ¶ *m.* cover, covered place; shelter. *al* ~, under cover. **copertòio**, *m.* large rug. **copertóne**, *m.* tarpaulin. **copertúra**, *f.* covering; roof; roofing; plaster. *truppe di* ~, covering troops (*Mil.*). ~ *protettiva*, book-jacket.

còpia, *f.* abundance, plenty; copy; transcript; reproduction, imitation; model; example, specimen. *brutta* ~, rough copy, first draft. *bella* ~, fair (or clean) copy. ~ *conforme*, true copy. ~ *gratuita*, free copy

(*book*). *in* ~, in abundance.
copialèttere, *m.inv.* letter-book; copying press. **copiàre** (*pr.* **còpio, còpi**), *v.t.* to copy; transcribe; imitate. **copiatívo**, *a.* copying. *inchiostro* ~, copying ink. *lapis* ~, copying pencil. *carta* ~ *a*, carbon (paper). **copiatúra**, *f.* copying; cost of making copies. **copísta** (*pl.* -ísti), *m.* copyist. **copistería**, *f.* copying office, typing office, t. agency.

còppa, *f.* goblet, cup; scale of a balance; one of the four suits of Italian playing-cards (*denari, bastoni, spada e coppa*, Neapolitan); sporting trophy & the contest in which it is won, *e.g. correre la coppa Città di Milano*).

coppàle, *m.* copal (*resin, varnish*).

coppèlla, *f.* small crucible for refining & assaying precious metals. *oro* (*or argento*) *di* ~, purest gold (or silver), (*fig.*) person of the highest integrity.

coppétta, *f.* cupping-glass.

còppia, *f.* couple, pair. *a* ~, two by two.

coppière, *m.* cup-bearer.

coppiòla, *f.* discharge of both barrels of a double-barrelled gun.

còppo, *m.* earthenware oil-jar; hollow tile.

copribústo, *m.* bodice, undervest.

copricàpo, *m.* headgear.

coprif[u]òco, *m.* curfew.

copripiàtti, *m.inv.* dish-cover (of wire-gauze).

copripièdi, *m.inv.* coverlet for the feet.

coprìre (*pr.* **còpro**, &*c.*, like *aprire*), *v.t.* to cover; cover up; hide; protect; shelter; overpower, drown (*voice, noise*, &*c.*). **coprìrsi**, *v.refl.* to wrap oneself up; (*of sky*) to become overcast.

coprivivànde, *m.inv.* wire-gauze dish-cover.

còpto, *a. & m.* Coptic; Copt. *lingua* ~ *a*, Coptic (language).

còpula, *f.* copula (*Gram.* esp. of *vb. to be* in the sense of a predicate).

coràggio, *m.* courage; confidence; bravery, boldness; (*iron.*) effrontery. *far* ~, to encourage, cheer (up). *farsi* ~, to take courage. **coraggióso**, *a.* courageous.

coràle, *a.* choral. *libri* ~ *i*, (large) books of church-music. ¶ *m.* church-music; anthem-book; chorale.

coràllo, *m.* coral.

coràme, *m.* stamped leather.

coràno, *m.* Koran.

coratèlla, *f.* liver & lights.

coràzza, *f.* cuirass, breast-plate; fencer's protective vest; armour-plating of a ship; animal shell or carapace. **corazzàre** (*pr.* -àzzo), *v.t.* to armour (*lit. & fig.*). **corazzàta**, *f.* battleship.

corazzière, *m.* cuirassier; mounted carabinière.

còrba, *f.* wicker basket or hamper.

corbellàre (*pr.* -èllo), *v.t.* to make fun of, quiz, rally; ridicule; humbug. **corbellatóre**, *m.* jester, mocker. **corbellatúra**, *f.* mockery, ridicule, teasing, quizzing. **corbellería**, *f.* foolish or extravagant words or action, silliness, absurdity; joke, trifle.

corbèllo, *m.* round basket for fruit, made of strips of wood, with flat bottom; (*fig.*) blockhead.

corbézzolo, *m.* arbutus (tree). *corbezzoli!* exclamation of astonishment.

còrda, *f.* (*twisted*) cord of hemp (*by extens.* of *metal, silk*, or *straw*); string of a musical instrument, ~ *of a bow*; cord, rope, string; thread (*in cloth*); chord; sinew. *tenere uno sulla* ~, to keep one in suspense. *a* ~, perpendicularly; straightway, immediately. ~ *d'arco*, bow-string. *danzatore di* ~, rope-dancer. **cordàio**, *m.* rope-maker, rope-merchant. **cordàme**, *m.* cordage; rigging, ropes. **cordàta**, *f.* roping together of mountain-climbers; the party so roped. **cordellìna**, *f.* fine cord; braided silk or thread cord used as ornament on a uniform. **cordería**, *f.* rope-yard, rope-walk.

cordiàle, *a.* cordial, hearty, warm, sincere. ¶ *m.* cordial, comforting drink, aromatic spirit.

cordialóne, *m.* (*f.* -óna), good-natured person.

cordicèlla, *f.* small cord; pack-thread.

cordíglio (*pl.* -ígli), *m.* monk's girdle.

cordíte, *f.* inflammation of the vocal cords; cordite (*explos.*).

cordòglio (*pl.* -ògli), *m.* grief, sorrow, anguish, affliction.

cordoncíno, *m.dim.* of *cordone*; silk-twist, watch-guard, &c.

cordóne, *m.* cordon, ornamental cord or braid; ribbon (title & insignia) of some high knightly orders; string-course on a building (*Arch.*); guarded line or chain of military or police posts. ~ *sanitario*, sanitary cordon.

coréa, *f.* chorea, St. Vitus' dance. **C~** (la), *f.* Korea.

coreografía, *f.* choreography; art of ballet or of public spectacles. **coreògrafo**, *m.* designer of ballet, &c.

coriàceo, *a.* leathery.

coriàndolo, *m.* coriander (seed), used in confetti; also imitation confetti of paper or plaster.

coricàre (*pr.* **còrico, còrichi**), *v.t.* to lay down, put to bed. **coricarsi**, *v.refl.* to lie down; go to bed.

coricíno, *m.dim.* of *cuore*; darling.

corifèo, *m.* choir-leader, leading dancer; (*fig.*) leader (of party, enterprise, &c.).

corindóne, *m.* corundum.

Corínto, *f.* Corinth. **coríntio & corínzio** (*pl.* -ínzi), *a. & m.* Corinthian.

corísta (*pl.* -ísti), *m.* chorister, chorus-singer; musical pitch; tuning-fork. *f.* chorus-girl.

còrizza, *f.* rheum, catarrh, cold in the head.

cornàcchia, *f.* crow, rook; (*fig.*) chatterer, croaker. **cornacchiàia**, *f.* colony of rooks, flock of crows; (*fig.*) tiresome chatter. **cornacchiàre** (*pr.* -àcchio, -àcchi), *v.i.* (*aux.* avere) to caw; chatter.

cornalína, *f.* cornelian.

cornamúša, *f.* bagpipe.

cornàta, *f.* blow (or push) given by an animal with its horns. **còrneo**, *a.* horny. **cornétta**, *f.* cornet, horn, bugle; two-pointed pennon or pendant.

corníce, *f.* [picture] frame; cornice; narrow ledge on mountain side. ~ *lateràle*, (*Typ.*) box-rule. **corniciàre**, *v.t.* to frame, furnish with a cornice. **cornición̄e**, *m.* heavy (architectural) cornice; entablature, moulding.

corni[u]òla, *f.* cornelian (*stone & ring*).

còrno (*pl.f.* **còrna** (*animal*) *pl.m.* **còrni** (*moon*, *&c.*), *m.* horn; projection or excrescence; wing (*of an army*); point of a flame; mountain-peak; corn (*on the foot*); bump on the head; horn of the moon; Doge's cap; salient (*fortification*); figure in skating; arm of a river or point where road or river branches off; Little Bear (*Orsa minore* (*Astr.*); either alternative of a dilemma; (*fig.*) pride. *un* ~! nonsense! *non vale un* ~! it is not worth a fig! *alzar le* ~*a*, to become arrogant. *avere sulle* ~*a*, to hate, dislike. *darsi sulle* ~*a*, to come to blows. *dir* ~*a di*, to speak ill of, slander. *fiaccar* (or *spezzar*) *le* ~*a di*, to take down, humiliate. *ritirar le* ~ *a*, to draw in one's horns, restrain one's ardour, become humble. *rompersi le* ~*a*, to have the worst of it, be defeated. ~ *da scarpe*, shoe-horn. ~ *da caccia*, hunting horn. ~ *inglese*, cor anglais.

Cornovàglia (la), *f.* Cornwall.

cornucòpia, *f.* cornucopia, horn of plenty.

cornúto, *a.* horned.

còro, *m.* chorus, choir (*Mus. & Arch.*); troop of dancers.

Corógna, *f.* Corunna.

corollàrio (*pl.* -àri), *m.* corollary.

coróna, *f.* crown, coronet; wreath, garland; throne, monarch; rosary; sequence (*of poems, &c.*); highest part (*of building, fortress, &c.*); ring or circle (*fig.*); halo; circle of hair round the tonsure (*Eccl.*). *discorso della C~*, speech from the Throne. **coronàio** (*pl.* -ài), *m.* maker or seller of rosaries. **coronàle**, *m.* frontal bone (*Anat.*). **coronaménto**, *m.*crowning; completion; (*Naut.*) taffrail. **coronàre** (*pr.* -òno), *v.t.* to crown; reward; fulfil, accomplish. **coronazióne**, *f.* coronation. **coroncína**, *f.* small crown, coronet; chaplet; small rosary.

corpacciúto, *a.* corpulent, paunchy. **corpétto**, *m.* under-vest. **còrpo**, *m.* body; substance; material; staff; corps; mass; block; size; (*Typ.*) height of letters; hull (*of a ship*); belly. *a* ~, in a lump sum. *a* ~ *morto*, desperately. *a* ~ *a* ~, man to man; (*sport*) clinch. ~ *d'armata*, army corps. ~ *di guardia*, guard, guard-room. ~ *di reato*, ~ *del delitto*, material evidence (*crime*). ~ *insegnante*, teaching staff. **corporàle**, *a.* bodily, corporal. ¶ *m.* corporal (*Mil.*). **corporatúra**, *f.* bodily structure & appearance; figure, build, physique. **corporazióne**, *f.* corporation, company, association, g[u]ild. **corpòreo**, *a.* corporeal, bodily, material.

corpuscolàre, *a.* corpuscular. **corpú-scolo,** *m.* corpuscle.

Corpusdòmini, *m.inv.* (Feast of) Corpus Christi.

côrre, *see* cogliere.

corredàre (*pr.* **-èdo**), *v.t.* to furnish, provide, equip; furnish a bride's trousseau; accompany (*with documents*, *&c.*). **corredíno,** *m.* baby-linen, baby's layette. **corrèdo,** *m.* outfit; trousseau; (*fig.*) wealth, abundance; store; accompaniment.

corrèggere (*pr.* **-èggo**, *&c.*, like *reggere*), *v.t. ir.* to correct, rectify; reprove; revise; read (*proofs*); improve; clear, purify (*wines*, *&c.*).

corréggia & **coréggia** (*pl.* **-égge**), *f.* leather strap, girdle.

correità, *f.* complicity.

correligionàrio (*pl.* **-àri**), *a.* of the same religion. ¶ *m.* co-religionist.

corrènte, *pr.p.* of *correre*. ¶ *a.* current; running, flowing, easy, fluent; going (*pers.*); present; common, usual, general. *acqua* ~, running water. *conto* ~, current account (*bank*). *prezzo* ~, current price. *al* ~, informed, up to date. *il* ~[*mese*] ~, the current month. *al* 15 ~, on the 15th instant (*abb.* inst.). *a posta* ~, by return of post. ¶ *m.* small beam, joist; current month. (*f.*) current, stream; (*fig.*) fashion; trend of opinion; (*Typ.*) running headline. ~ *d' aria,* draught. *C*~ *del Golfc,* Gulf Stream. ~ *alternata,* alternating current (*Elec.*). **correteménte,** *ad.* fluently; currently.

corrèo, *m.* accomplice.

córrere (*pr.* **córro**), *v.i. ir.* (*aux.* avere, when the action is considered in itself, *essere,* when it indicates action towards a goal) to run; course; run about; hasten; flow; pass; go; circulate, be current; (*of distance*) intervene; (*v.t.*) to range, scour, travel rapidly over; race for (*a prize*); incur. ~ *la cavallina,* to sow one's wild oats. ~ *a,* to run after; (*fig.*) to covet. ~ *a rotta di collo,* to run at breakneck speed. *corre voce che,* there is a rumour that, they say that. *ci corre* [*molto*] *fra . . .,* there is a [great] difference between.

correspettívo, *a.* corresponding; reciprocal. ¶ *m.* compensation; thing given in exchange.

correttézza, *f.* correctness; honesty, fair-dealing. **correttívo,** *a. & m.*

corrective. **corrètto,** *p.p.* of *correggere.* ¶ *a.* correct, corrected; exact, right, true. **correttóre,** *m.* (*f.* **-tríce**) corrector -tress. ~ *di bozze,* proof-reader. **correzionàle,** *a.* correctional. ¶ *m.* reformatory. **correzióne,** *f.* correction, correcting; improvement, revision, reform. ~ *in piombo,* (*Typ.*) correction in type.

corrída, *f.* bull-fight.

corridóio (*pl.* **-ói**), *m.* corridor; passage[-way]; lobby. **corridóre,** *m.* runner; race-horse.

corrièra, *f.* mail-coach, postal-bus or motor. **corrière,** *m.* (*f.* **-èra**) messenger; carrier; postman, -woman; courier; passenger; diplomatic messenger, King's messenger; mail, post; daily correspondence; common title for newspapers. *a volta di* ~, by return of post.

corrigèndo, *a. & m.* juvenile offender under disciplinary training.

corrispettívo, *m.* equivalent amount; corresponding amount; compensation; consideration.

corrispondènte, *a.* corresponding, similar; analogous; proportionate. ¶ *m.* correspondent. **corrispondènza,** *f.* correspondence; agreement; mail, letters. ~ *in arrivo,* incoming mail. ~ *in partenza,* outgoing mail. ~ *di oltremare,* oversea[s] mail. ~ *per l'estero,* foreign mail.

corrispóndere (*pr.* **-óndo**, *&c.*, like *rispondere*), *v.i. ir.* (*aux.* avere) to correspond, agree; have the same meaning, shape, or appearance; match; look out on; be connected with (*con*); be in correspondence; respond to (*a*), repay with (*con.*); answer (*hope, expectation, &c.*). **corrispósto,** *p.p.* of *corrispondere.* ¶ *a.* returned, repaid; reciprocal, mutual. *amore* ~, mutual love.

corrivo, *a.* hasty, easy-going, careless, inconsiderate.

corroboràre (*pr.* **-òboro**), *v.t.* to strengthen, corroborate, support, confirm.

corródere (*pr.* **-ódo**, *&c.*, like *rodere*), *v.t. ir.* to corrode, wear away.

corrómpere (*pr.* **-ómpo**, *&c.*, like *rompere*), *v.t. ir.* to corrupt, deprave; contaminate, spoil; bribe, seduce. **corrosióne,** *f.* corrosion. **corro-sívo,** *a. & m.* corrosive.

corróso, *p.p.* of *corrodere.* ¶ *a.* worn away, corroded.

corròtto, *p.p.* of *corrompere.* ¶ *a.* corrupt, depraved; foul, contaminated. ¶ *m.* vicious or depraved person.

corrucciàre (*pr.* -úccio, -úcci), *v.t.* to anger, enrage; vex, torment. **corrucciàrsi,** *v.refl.* to be enraged; be vexed; get into a passion. **corrúccio** (*pl.* -úcci), *m.* anger, rage.

corrugaménto, *m.* wrinkling; knitting (*of the brows*). **corrugàre** (*pr.* -úgo, -úghi), *v.t.* to wrinkle; curl; knit (*the brows*).

corruscàre or **coruscàre,** *v.i.* (*aux.* avere*) to flash, sparkle, scintillate. **corrúsco** or **corúsco** (*pl.* -úschi), *a.* shining, sparkling.

corruttèla, *f.* moral corruption, depravity. **corruttíbile,** *a.* corruptible. **corruzióne,** *f.* corruption; decay; bribery.

córsa, *f.* race, run, running; course, journey, trip, route; fare; haste; hasty reading; piston-stroke; privateering. *di* ∼, hastily, in haste, running. *a tutta* ∼, *di gran* ∼, in great haste. *cavallo da* ∼, race-horse. ∼ *a piedi,* foot-race. ∼ *con ostacoli,* obstacle race. ∼ *nei sacchi,* sack-race. ∼ *compensata,* handicap. ∼ *di automobili,* motor-race, -racing. ∼ *agli armamenti,* arms (or armament) race. *perdere la* ∼, to lose (or miss) the train. *partire con la prima* ∼, to leave by the first train.

corsalétto, *m.* breast-plate, corselet.

corsàro, *m.* pirate, corsair.

corsèllo, *m.* space between two beds, or between a bed and the wall.

corsétto, *m.* corset (more com, busto).

corsía, *f.* gangway, narrow passage; hospital ward or school dormitory with one or more rows of beds.

corsívo, *a.* cursive, running (*hand*); (*pl.*) Italics, italic type.

córso, *p.p.* of *correre.* ¶ *a.* passed, elapsed; circulated; fallen due; sacked, plundered. ¶ *m.* course, progress; series, series of lectures; procession; (principal) street, passage; voyage; circulation; direction & flow of a river; space of time; currency rate; running, running-path. ∼ *del cambio,* rate of exchange. ∼ *legale,* legal tender. *aver* ∼, to be current; (*of a book*) to sell well. *anno in* ∼, (the) current year, present year. *mettere in* ∼, to put into circulation.

còrso, *a. & m.* Corsican.

corsóio, *a.* slipping, sliding, running. *nodo* ∼, running knot, slip-k.

córte, *f.* court, [law-] court; [court] yard; courtship, suit. *far(e) la* ∼ *a,* to pay court to. *tenere* ∼ *bandita,* to keep open house.

cortéccia (*pl.* -écce), *f.* bark, rind, crust.

corteggiàre (*pr.* -éggio, -éggi), *v.t.* to court, pay court to; flatter, woo. **cortéggio** (*pl.* -éggi), *m.* retinue, cortege, suite, train of attendants. **cortèo,** *m.* procession; group of friends attending a ceremony. ∼ *nuziale,* wedding party.

cortése, *a.* courteous; kind, polite, obliging. **cortesía,** *f.* courtesy, kindness.

còrtice, *m.* bark, rind; cortex, outer grey matter of the brain (*Anat.*).

cortigianería, *f.* courtier's art & manners; flattery, obsequiousness. **cortigianésco** (*pl.* -éschi), *a.* courtly, obsequious. **cortigiàno,** *m.* courtier; (*fig.*) flatterer.

cortíle, *m.* court-yard.

cortína, *f.* curtain; (*fig.*) screen. ∼*di fumo,* smoke-screen (*Mil.*). **cortinàggio** (*pl.* -àggi), *m.* bed-hang-ing[s], bed-curtain[s].

córto, *a.* short (*space, time*); brief; limited; poorly provided; deficient; insufficient. ∼ *a denaro, di denari,* short of money. ∼ *circuito,* short circuit (*Elec.*). *di* ∼*a vista,* short-sighted, near-sighted. *alle* ∼*e, per* (or *a*) *farla* ∼*a,* in short, to come to the point.

corvétta, *f.* curvet (*horse*); corvette (*Nav.*). **corvettàre** (*pr.* corvétto), *v.i.* (*aux.* avere) to curvet.

corvíno, *a.* (raven-)black, raven. **còrvo,** *m.* raven; crow. ∼*marino,* cormorant.

còsa, *f.* thing; matter; affair; business; event; fact; chattel; property; (*pl.*) compliments, regards; possessions; household goods; matters. *a* ∼ *fatta,* after the event. *qualche* ∼, *qualcosa,* something. *ogni* ∼, everything. *che* ∼? what? (*che*) ∼ *avete?* what's the matter with you? (*che*) *cos'ha?* what's the matter with him? ∼ *da nulla,* a mere trifle, a m. nothing. ∼ *da mangiare,* something to eat. ∼ *fatta capo ha,* once it's done it's done. *la* ∼ *pubblica,* the common weal, public welfare. dims. *cosetta, cosina, cosettina, coserella, coserellina.*

cosàccio (*pl.* -àcci), *m.* good-for-nothing fellow.

cosàcca (*pl.* -àcche), *f.* Cossack dance. **cosàcco** (*pl.* -àcchi), *a. & m.* Cossack.

còscia (*pl.* còsce), *f.* thigh; haunch; (*Cook.*) leg; (*Arch.*) abutment. ~ *di castrato*, ~ *di montone*, leg of mutton. ~ *di pollo*, l. of chicken. *calzoni a* ~, tights.

cosciènza, *f.* conscience; conscientiousness; consciousness. *senza* ~, unscrupulous. **coscienzióso**, *a.* conscientious; scrupulous.

cosciòtto, *m.* haunch. ~ *di selvaggina*, haunch of venison.

coscrìtto, *m.* conscript; recruit. **coscrizióne**, *f.* conscription.

coséno, *m.* (*Geom.*) cosine (*abb.* cos).

così, *ad.* so; as; thus; therefore; would that. ~ ~, so so. ~ *come*, as, just as. ~ ... *come* ..., both ... and, as well as. *proprio* ~, just so. ~ *che*, so that. ~ *da*, so as to. *e* ~ *via*, *e* ~ *di seguito*, and so on, and so forth. ~ *non fosse vero!* would that it were not true! *As a prefix, requires the doubling of the following consonant, e.g.* **cosiddétto**, *a.* so-called. **cosiffàtto**, *a.* such, similar, of this kind.

cosmètico (*pl.* -ètici), *a. & m.* cosmetic.

còsmico (*pl.* còsmici), *a.* cosmic. **còsmo**, *m.* cosmos, universe. **cosmopolìta** (*pl.* -ìti), *m. & a.* cosmopolite; cosmopolitan.

còso, *m.* (*pop.*) thing; fellow; what-d'you-call it, what's-his-name; indefinite sum, a matter of (*money*).

cospàrgere (*pr.* -àrgo, *&c.*, like *spargere*), *v.t. ir.* to strew; spread; sprinkle. **cospàrso**, *p.a.* strewn, &c. **cospèrso**, *p.a.* (from *cospergere*) wet, sprinkled.

cospètto, *m.* presence, view, sight.

cospìcuo, *a.* conspicuous, prominent, outstanding. *somma* ~*a*, considerable amount.

cospiràre (*pr.* -ìro), *v.i.* (*aux.* avere) to conspire, plot; tend. **cospiratóre**, *m.* -trìce, *f.* conspirator, plotter. **cospirazióne**, *f.* conspiracy, plot.

còsta, *f.* rib; (*gentle*) slope; hillside; coast, shore, seaboard. *a mezza* ~, halfway up (*hill*). *di* ~, sideways.

costà, *ad.* there (*near person spoken to*); in your place (*city, town*).

costànte, *a.* constant; firm, steady, invariable; steadfast, enduring.

Costantinòpoli, *f.* Constantinople.

costànza, *f.* constancy; steadfastness; persistence, perseverance; patience. *C*~, *f.* Constance. *Lago di* ~, *m.* Lake of C.

costàre (*pr.* còsto), *v.i.* (*aux.* essere) to cost. **costàta & costatèlla**, *f.* (*Cook.*) chop. **costàto**, *m.* ribs; (*pl.*) chest, side.

costeggiàre (*pr.* -èggio, -èggi), *v.t. & abs.* (*aux.* avere) to coast; skirt; run along; hug (*shore*); flank.

costèi, *demons. pn. f.s.* that woman, she.

costellàto, *a.* constellated; studded. **costellazióne**, *f.* constellation.

costernàre (*pr.* -èrno), *v.t.* to dismay, stagger. **costernazióne**, *f.* consternation, dismay.

costì, *ad.* there (*gen. less remote than* costà).

costièra, *f.* stretch of coast; southern slope. **costière**, *m.* coasting vessel, coaster; coastal pilot. **costièro**, *a.* coasting.

costipàre (*pr.* -ìpo), *v.t.* to heap up, condense; (*Med.*) to constipate, bind. **costipazióne**, *f.* constipation, costiveness; heavy cold.

costituènte, *p.a. & m.* constituent; component. ¶ *f.* constituent assembly. **costituire** (*pr.* -ìsco, -ìsci), *v.t.* to constitute; form, make up; establish, found; nominate; assign, settle (*dowry*); appoint. **costituìrsi**, *v.refl.* to form oneself, be formed; appoint oneself; give oneself up (*to justice*). ~ *parte civile*, to appear as a civil plaintiff. *l'Italia s'è costituita in nazione*, Italy has formed herself into a nation. **costitúto**, *m.* (*Law*) interrogation of the accused; shipmaster's report to the Office of Health. **costituzióne**, *f.* constitution, &c.; composition. ~ *della dote*, marriage settlement.

còsto, *m.* cost. *a qualunque* ~, at any cost; cost what it may. ~, *assicurazione, nolo* (*Com.*), cost, insurance, freight (*abb.* c.i.f.). ~ *e nolo*, cost & freight (*abb.* c.a.f.).

còstola, *f.* rib; back; spine (*book*). **costolétta**, *f.* cutlet; chop.

costóro, *demons. pn. m.f.* (*pl. of* costui, costei), those, those people; they

costóso, *a.* costly, expensive.

costrétto, *p.p.* of *costringere*. **costríngere** (*pr.* -ingo, -ingi, *&c.*, like *stringere*), *v.t. ir.* to force, constrain, compel; oblige; press,

compress. **costringiménto**, *m.* &
costrizióne, *f.* constraint; con-
striction; compulsion.
costruíre (*pr.* **-ísco, -ísci,** *p.p.*
costruito & *costrutto*), *v.t.* to build;
erect; construct; construe (*Gram.*).
costrútto, *m.* construction (*Gram.*);
meaning; profit; result. **costruttóre**
m. builder, maker, constructor.
costruzióne, *f.* construction; building; making; build; erection;
structure.
costúi, *demons. pn. m.sg.* that (or this)
man, that (or this) fellow (*deprec.*).
costumànza, *f.* custom, usage; politeness. **costumàre** (*pr.* **-úmo**), *v.i.*
(*aux.* essere) to be usual, customary;
to be in fashion; be in the habit of.
costumàto *a.* well-mannered, well-
bred. **costúme**, *m.* custom, usage,
habit; behaviour; costume, dress,
fancy dress; (*pl.*) manners, morals.
costúra, *f.* seam.
cotàle, *a.* & *pn. indef.* such; such **a**
one.
còte, *f.* whetstone; hone.
cotechíno, *m.* (*Cook.*) highly spiced
pork sausage.
coténna, *f.* pig-skin; thick skin; rind;
scalp; turf; (*fig.*) thick-skinned
(insensitive) person.
cotésto, *a.* & *demons. pn.* that, that
one (*near person addressed*). (*pl.*)
cotésti, *m.* **cotéste**, *f.* those, those
ones; such.
cotidiàno, *a.* daily. Cf. *quotidiano*.
cotógna or *mela* ~, *f.* quince.
cotógno, *m.* quince-tree.
cotolétta, *f.* cutlet. Cf. *costoletta*.
cotóne, *m.* cotton. *refe di* ~, cotton
thread, sewing c. *filato di* ~,
c. yarn. *tessuto di* ~, c. cloth. ~
idrofilo, cotton-wool. ~ *fulminante*,
gun-c. **cotonería**, *f.pl.* c. goods.
cotonière, *m.* cotton-spinner; c.
manufacturer. **cotonièro**, *a.* cotton
(*att.*). **cotonifício** (*pl.* **-íci**), *m.*
cotton-mill. **cotonóso**, *a.* cottony;
downy, fluffy.
còtta, *f.* surplice; cooking (*time* &
material); baking; (*bricks*) kilnful;
(*fig.*) infatuation; drunkenness.
cottíccio (*pl.* **-ícci**), *a.* half-done,
half-baked; (*fig.*) half-drunk, half-
seas over; half in love.
còttimo, *m.* job, contract. *lavoro a* ~,
piece-work; jobbing.
còtto, *p.a.* cooked, done; baked; (*fig.*)
drunk; deeply in love.
cottúra, *f.* cooking (*time, process,*
cost).

cotúrno, *m.* buskin. *calzare il* ~,
to compose tragedies; appear in
tragedy, tread the boards (*Theat.*).
cóva, *f.* brooding, sitting (*on eggs*);
brood; nest, nesting-place. **covàre**
(*pr.* **cóvo**), *v.t.* & *i.* (*aux.* avere) to
brood, sit brooding, (*fig.*) brood on
or over; cherish secretly; smoulder;
sicken for (*illness*); hatch. **covàta**, *f.*
brood; hatch[ing].
covíle, *m.* den, lair; hovel. **cóvo**, *m.*
den; lair; hole, burrow; (*hare*) form;
haunt, hiding-place.
covóne, *m.* sheaf, shock (*corn*);
bundle (*hay*).
Cózie (Alpi), *f.pl.* (the) Cottian Alps.
cozzàre (*pr.* **còzzo**), *v.t.* & *i.* (*aux.*
avere) to butt, b. at, b. against,
strike against; clash, collide with;
(*fig.*) run one's head against (*con*).
còzzo, *m.* clash; shock; collision;
conflict. *dar di* ~, ~ *in*, to butt;
b. against; (*fig.*) meet, knock up
against (*pop.*).
cozzóne, *m.* horse-dealer.
crac, *m.inv.* sound of cracking, crack;
collapse, downfall; bankruptcy.
Cracòvia, *f.* Cracow.
cràmpo, *m.* cramp.
crànio (*pl.* **cràni**), *m.* skull, cranium.
cràpula, *f.* excess (*eating* & *drinking*)
guzzling, debauch. **crapulóne**, *m.*
debauchee, glutton, heavy drinker.
cràsso, *a.* dense, gross, crass; coarse.
ignoranza ~*a*, crass (*or* gross)
ignorance.
cratère, *m.* crater; large bowl.
cravàtta, *f.* tie; cravat.
creànza, *f.* good breeding, politeness.
creàre (*pr.* **crèo, crèi, crèa,**
creàte, crèano; 1st *pl.pr. ind.* &
2nd *pl. subjunc. are not used*), *v.t.* to
create, make, produce; give rise to;
institute, appoint; interpret (part)
on the stage. **creàrsi**, *v.refl.* to
make oneself; gain, win for oneself;
arise, be formed; be founded.
creàto, *p.p.* of *creare.* ¶ *a.* formed.
ben ~, well-bred. *mal* ~, ill-bred.
¶ *m.* the universe; creature (*in sense*
of favourite). **creatúra**, *f.* creature;
infant, child; favourite.
crébbi, 1st. *sg. past def.* of *crescere.*
credènte, *m.* believer. **credènza**, *f.*
belief, faith; credit; sideboard; (*pl.*)
(religious) belief[s]. *compare a* ~,
to buy on credit. *lettere di* ~,
credentials. **credenziàle**, *a.* & *f.*
credential, letter of credit. **cre-**
denzière, *m.* butler. **credenzóne**,
m. (*f.* **óna**) credulous person.

crédere (*pr.* **crédo, crédi**, &c.) *v.t. & i.* (*aux.* avere) to believe; trust; think; consider, take for; please, think best. ¶ *m.* opinion; judgment; belief. **credíbile**, *a.* credible. **crédito**, *m.* credit; trust; standing; repute; belief. *saldo a* ~, credit balance. **creditóre**, *m.* (*f.* -**tríce**), creditor. **crèdo**, *m.* creed; Apostle's creed, also part of the Mass.
credulità, *f.* credulity. **crèdulo**, *a.* credulous.
crèma, *f.* custard; cream; fine flower (*fig.*); hair-cream, shoe polish.
cremaglièra, *f.* toothed rack.
cremàre (*pr.* **crèmo**), *v.t.* to cremate. **crematóio & forno crematòrio**, *m.* crematorium. **cremazióne**, *f.* cremation.
crèmisi, *m.inv.* crimson. **cremišíno**, *a.* crimson (coloured).
cremlíno, *m.* Kremlin.
cremóre, *m.* cream (*in the sense of* essence, extract). *cremore di tartaro*, cream of tartar.
creòlo, *n. & a.* creole.
creošòto, *m.* creosote.
crèpa, *f.* crack, fissure, crevice. **crepàccio** (*pl.* -**acci**), *m.* large fissure, crevice, crevasse.
crepacuòre, *m.* broken heart, heart-breaking grief.
crepàre (*pr.* **crèpo**), *v.i.* (*aux.* essere) to crack, split; do anything to excess, burst; (*fig.*) die. ~ *dalla risa*, to burst with laughter. ~ *dalla* (or *di*) *fatica*, to be thoroughly exhausted.
crepatúra, *f.* crack; crevice.
crepitàre (*pr.* **crèpito**), *v.i.* (*aux.* avere) to crackle. **crepitío** (*pl.* -**íi**), *m.* (continuous) crackling. **crèpito**, *m.* crackling.
crepuscolàre, *a.* of (the) twilight; twilight (*att.*); (*fig.*) dim, low-toned, shadowy. *poesia* ~, the poetry of the generation after Carducci, Pascoli & D'Annunzio, deliberately attuned to a minor key. Corazzini & Guido Gozzano were its leaders. **crepúscolo**, *m.* twilight, gloaming, dusk; decline.
crescèndo, *m.* crescendo (*Mus.*); (*fig.*) progress towards a climax. **crescènte**, *pr.p* of crescere. ¶ *a.* growing, increasing. *luna* ~, crescent moon. **crescènza**, *f.* growth; increase. *vestito a* ~, dressed to allow for growth. **créscere** (*pr.* **crésco, crésci**, &c.), *v.i. ir.* (*aux.* essere) to grow, increase, rise (*price, river*); (*v.t.*) to raise, increase, bring up. **crescimento**, *m.* growth, increase.
crescióne, *m.* cress. ~ *d'acqua*, water-cress. **crescionéto**, *m.* water-cress bed.
créscita, cresciúta, *f.* growth.
cresciúto, *p.p.* of *crescere*. ¶ *m.* widening or 'letting out' a stocking (*knitting*).
crèšima, *f.* confirmation, chrism (*Eccl.*). **crešimàndo**, *m.* -**a**, *f.* candidate for confirmation.
Crèšo, *m.* Croesus (*Myth.*).
créspa, *f.* wrinkle; curl; plait; crease. **créspo**, *a.* curled, curly, wrinkled; crisp; plaited, puckered. *capelli crespi*, woolly or fuzzy hair. ¶ *m.* crape.
crèsta, *f.* crest, ridge, top; lady's hat with many trimmings; (*fig.*) pride. **crestàia**, *f.* milliner.
crestomazía, *f.* collection of choice passages, anthology.
créta, *f.* clay, chalk. *C*~ (*la*), Crete. **cretàceo**, *m.* chalky. **cretése**, *a. & m.* Cretan.
cretiníšmo, *m.* cretinism; imbecillity; idiocy. **cretíno**, *m.* cretin; idiot; dunce.
cric *or* **crícche**, (*onomat*) sound of glass or ice breaking; or of a grasshopper's chirping. **cricchiàre**, *v.i.* (*aux.* avere) to creak, crack, crunch.
crícca (*pl.* **crícche**), *f.* set, clique; (*Com.*) ring.
crícco (*pl.* **crícchi**), *m.* jack, hand-j., lifting j. *coltello a* ~, jack-knife, clasp-k.
criccrí *or* **cri cri**, *m.inv.* chirp (*of cricket or other insect*).
Crimea (**la**), the Crimea.
criminàle, *a. & m.* criminal. **criminalità**, *f.* criminality; crime (gen. term). **crímine**, *m.* crime, felony.
crinàle, *m.* mountain ridge; comb.
críne, *m.* (*horse*) hair; (*vegetable*) fibre; (*Poet.*) (*human*) hair, locks. **crinièra**, *f.* mane; horsetail plume; abundant crop (*hair*).
crípta, *f.* crypt.
crišàlide, *f.* chrysalis. **crišantèmo**, *m.* chrysanthemum.
crìši, *f.* crisis; shortage, slump; attack, fit. ~ *delle abitazioni*, housing problem. ~ *ministeriale*. cabinet crisis.
crišòlito, *m.* chrysolite.
cristallàio (*pl.* -**ài**), *m.* glass worker, glass-blower; dealer in g. ware. **cristallàme**, *m.* glass-ware. **cristallería**, *f.* crystal glass(ware)

making or works; crystal ware. **cristallíno**, *a.* crystalline; crystal. ¶ *m.* crystalline lens (*eye*). **cristallizzàre**, *v.t.* to crystallize. **cristàllo**, *m.* crystal; (crystal) glass. ~ *a punta*, cut (crystal) glass. ~ *di rocca*, rock-crystal. **cristianésimo**, *m.* Christianity, (the) Christian religion. **cristianità**, *f.* Christendom; Christian faith. **cristianizzàre**, *v.t.* to christianize. **cristiàno**, *a. & m.* Christian; (*fig.*) *a.* decent, civilized. **Crísto**, *m.* Christ. *Gesú C~*, Jesus Christ. *un c~*, a crucifix.

critèrio (*pl.* **-èri**), *m.* criterion (*pl.* -eria), standard;‑ principle; judgment, opinion; (good) sense.

crítica (*pl.* **crítiche**), *f.* criticism, critique; review; critics (*col.*); censure, stricture. **criticàre** (*pr.* **crítico, crítichi**), *v.t.* to criticize, censure. **crítico** (*pl.* **crítici**), *a.* critical, censorious; crucial; ticklish. ¶ *m.* critic; reviewer.

crittogràmma (*pl.* **-gràmmi**), *m.* cryptogram.

crivellàre (*pr.* **-èllo**), *v.t.* to riddle (with holes); sift. **crivèllo**, *m.* sieve.

croàto, *a. & m.* Croatian, Croat. **Croàzia (la)**, *f.* Croatia.

croccànte, *a.* crisp; crackling. ¶ *m.* almond sweetmeat.

crocchétta, *f.* croquette.

cròcchia, *f.* chignon. **crocchiàre**, *v.i.* (*aux.* avere) to sound cracked, crackle; (*of joints*) crack; (*hen*) cluck. **cròcchio** (*pl.* **cròcchi**), *m.* group, circle; knot (*of persons*); crackling sound. *stare a* ~, to sit chatting.

cróce (*pl.* **cróci**), *f.* cross; rood; dagger, obelisk (*Typ.*); (*fig.*) trouble, suffering, trial. ~ *di Malta*, Maltese cross. *la C~ Rossa*, the Red Cross. *C~ del Sud*, Southern Cross. *a* ~, *in* ~, cross-wise; in the form of a cross. *punto in* ~, cross-stitch. *a occhio e* ~, at a rough guess, approximately.

cròceo, *a.* saffron-coloured.

crocevía, *m.* cross-roads.

crociàre (*pr.* **crócio, cróci**), *v.t.* to mark with a cross. **crociàrsi**, *v.refl.* to go on a crusade. **crociàta**, *f.* crusade. **crociàto**, *m.* crusader.

crocícchio (*pl.* **-ícchi**), *m.* cross-roads, crossing.

crocidàre (*pr.* **cròcido**), *v.i.* (*aux.* avere) to croak.

crocièra, *f.* cruise; arrangement in the form of a cross; cross bar (*Typ.*);

intersection; (*Aviat.*) long distance flight. *andare in* ~, to go on a cruise. *volta a* ~, cross-vaulting (*Arch.*).

crocífero, *m.* cross-bearer (*in a procession*). ¶ *a.* (*Bot.*) cruciferous. **crocifíggere** (*pr.* **-fíggo**, *&c.*, like *figgere*), *v.t. ir.* to crucify. **crocefissióne**, *f.* crucifixion. **crocifísso**, *p.p.* of *crocifiggere & a.* crucified. ¶ *m.* crucifix. *il C~*, the Crucified (Christ). **crocifórme**, *a.* cruciforme; cross-shaped.

cròco (*pl.* **cròchi**), *m.* crocus; saffron.

crogiolàre (*pl.* **cògiolo**), *v.t.* to cook on a slow fire. **crogiolàrsi**, *v.refl.* to make oneself comfortable, be snug, cuddle. **cògiolo**, *m.* cooking at a gentle heat. **crogi[u]òlo**, *m.* crucible; melting pot.

crollaménto, *m.* collapse, downfall. **crollàre** (*pl.* **cròllo**), *v.t.* to shake, toss (*head*) shrug (*shoulders*). *v.i.* (*aux.* essere) to totter; shake; collapse. **crollàta**, *f.* shake, toss, shrug. **cròllo**, *m.* shake; heavy blow, finishing blow; downfall, collapse, ruin, failure. *dare il* ~ *a*, to overthrow, upset. *dare il* ~*alla bilancia*, to turn the scale.

cromàtico (*pl.* **-àtici**), *a.* chromatic. **cromàto**, *a.* chromium-plated, chrome (*steel or leather*). **cromatúra**, *f.* chromium-plating.

cròmo, *m.* chrome; chromium. **cromolitografía**, *f.* chromolithography. **cromosòma** (*pl.* **-òmi**), *m.* chromosome. **cromotipía**, *f.* colour-printing, colour-print.

crònaca (*pl.* **crònache**), *f.* chronicle; news of the day; current gossip (*newspaper*). **crònico** (*pl.* **crònici**), *a.* chronic. ¶ *m.* incurable. **cronísta** (*pl.* **-ísti**), *m.* chronicler, reporter. **cronografía**, *f.* chronography. **cronògrafo**, *m.* chronograph; stop-watch. **cronología**, *f.* chronology. **cronològico** (*pl.* **-ògici**), *a.* chronological. **cronometrísta** (*pl.* **-ísti**), *m.* (*Sport*) time-keeper. **cronòmetro**, *m.* chronometer.

crosciàre (*pr.* **cròscio, cròsci**), *v.i.* (*aux.* avere) to pelt, pour; gurgle; hiss; roar (*water, applause*). *v.impers.* (*aux.* essere) to rain hard. **cròscio** (*pl.* **cròsci**), *m.* splash, hiss, gurgle; roar.

cròsta, *f.* crust; rind; shell; coating; incrustation; skin; scab; surface. **crostàceo**, *a. & m.* crustacean.

crostàta, f. [fruit] tart. ~di mele, apple-tart. crostíno, m. piece of toast. crostóso, a. crusty.

crucciàre (pr. crúccio, crúcci), v.t. to irritate, annoy; vex, torment. crucciàrsi, v.refl. to be vexed, troubled, irritated; get angry. crucciàto, a. angry, vexed. crúccio (pl. crúcci), m. anger, grief; vexation; irritation; worry. crucció-so, a. angry, quick-tempered, irritable.

cruciàle, a. crucial, decisive; (Anat.) cross-shaped. cruciàre, v.t. to torture, torment.

crucifórme, a. cruciform, cross-shaped.

crudaménte, ad. harshly, crudely, roughly.

crudèle, a. cruel; grievous; sore; bitter; painful. crudelménte, ad. cruelly. crudeltà, f. cruelty.

crudézza, f. crudity, harshness; rawness. crúdo, a. raw, immature, unripe; harsh, crude, rough; unbaked (pottery); cold; glaring (colour).

cruènto, a. blood-stained, bloody; (fig.) dreadful.

crumíro, m. black-leg (strike).

crúna, f. eye of a needle.

crup, crúppe, m. croup (Med.).

cruràle, a. of the leg or thigh, crural (Anat.). vene~ i, f.pl., crural veins.

crúsca, f. chaff, bran; freckle. La C~, the famous Florentine Accademia della Crusca, founded in 1583. cruscàio, m. dealer in bran; (fig.) purist, affected person.

cruschèlla, f. fine bran. crusche-rèlla, f. children's game of hunting for coins hidden in heaps of bran.

cruscòtto, m. instrument-panel (Aero., Motor car).

Cúba, f. Cuba. cubàno, a. & m. Cuban.

cubatúra, f. measurement of volume.

cubía, f. (Naut.) hawse-hole. (Also occhio di ~, di prua).

cúbico (pl. cúbici), a. cubical, cubic, cube (att.). radice ~a, cube root. equazione ~a, cubic equation. pollice ~, cubic inch. cubicolo, m. cubicle. cubísmo, m. cubism (Art.). cubísta (pl. -ísti), m. cubist. cúbo, m. cube. ¶ a. cubic.

cuccàgna, f. great abundance, plenty; unexpected good fortune, godsend. paese di C~, land of Cockaigne, imaginary country of plenty. albero della ~, giuoco della ~, (sport), climbing the greasy pole.

cuccétta, f. [sleeping] berth (ship, train); bunk.

cucchiaiàta, f. spoonful. cucchia-íno, m. small spoon; tea-spoon. cucchiàio (pl. -ài), m. spoon; spoonful. ~da tavola, tablespoon. ~ da frutta, ~da dessert, dessert spoon. cucchiaióne, m. ladle; large spoon.

cúccia (pl. cúcce), f. dog's bed; shake-down. cúcciolo, m. puppy; whelp.

cúcco (pl. cúcchi), m. pet, darling, favourite child; (pop.) cuckoo. vecchio ~, childish old man, dodderer.

cuc[c]ú, m.inv. cuckoo. orologio a ~, m. cuckoo clock.

cuccurucú, i. cock-a-doodle-doo.

cucína, f. kitchen; cooking, cookery, style of cooking; food; galley; caboose; cooking stove, range. ~a gas, gas cooking, g. cooker. cucinàre (pr. -íno, -íni), v.t. & i. to cook; prepare, dress (food); (fig.) to settle, deal with summarily. cucinière, m. (male) cook (professional); cookery book.

cucíre (pr. cúcio, cúci), v.t. & i. to sew; stitch; tack; (fig.) join together, attach; double-cross. macchina da ~, sewing-machine. ago da ~, sewing-needle. cucíto, m. sewing, needle-work. cucitríce, f. seamstress; sewing-machine (esp. for book-binding). cucitúra, f. seam; sewing, stitching.

cúculo, m. cuckoo.

cucúrbita, f. gourd, pumpkin; still, retort (Chem.).

cudú, m.inv. koodoo (African antilope).

cúffia, f. cap, baby's bonnet, coif; caul; cowl; covering; (Theat.) prompter's box; (Phot.) dark cloth; (Radio) head-phones, ear-phones. ~ da notte, nightcap. nascere con la ~, to be born with a silver spoon in one's mouth. cuffiòtto, m. child's cap; bonnet.

cugína, f. cugíno, m. cousin. ~ germano, m. first cousin, c. german. cuginànza, f. relationship between cousins.

cúi, rel. pn. inv. (after prep.) whom, which; (with def. art.) whose, of which.

culàtta, f. breech (gun, cannon); rump; seat of trousers.

culinàrio, a. culinary.

cúlla, f. cradle; cot. (fig.) birthplace; infancy. cullàre, v.t. to rock;

cradle; sway, dandle; lull; cherish; flatter; delude. **cullàrsi**, *v.refl.* (*fig.*) to delude oneself, cherish illusions.

cúlmine, *m.* top, summit.

cúlto, *m.* worship; cult; creed.

cultúra, *f.* culture; cultivation; farming; crop. **culturàle,** *a.* cultural.

cumulatívo, *a.* cumulative; joint, collective. *biglietto* ∼, joint ticket (*for party*). **cúmulo,** *m.* heap; store; lot; plurality (*of offices*); cumulus (*cloud*).

cúna, *f.* cradle.

cuneifórme, *a.* cuneiform. **cúneo,** *m.* wedge.

cuòca (*pl.* **cuòche**), *f.* (female) cook. **cuòcere** (*pr.* **cuòcio, cuòci, cuòce, cociàmo, cocéte, cuòciono**), *v.t. & i.ir.* to cook; roast; bake; stew; burn; boil; fire (*bricks*); smart; hurt, vex. **cuòco** (*pl.* **cuòchi**), *m.* (male) cook.

cuòio (*pl.m.* **cuòi,** *pl.f.* **cuòia**), *m.* leather; skin; (*f.pl.*) legs. *stender le* ∼*a,* to stretch one's legs, lie down, go to bed. *tirar le* ∼*a,* to die. *aver le* ∼*a dure,* to resist fatigue, be strong.

cuòre, *m.* heart; courage; love; generosity; feelings; core, centre, middle; height (*of summer*); depth (*of winter*); (*pl.*) hearts (*Cards*). *a* ∼, heart-shaped. *di* ∼, heartily. *asso di* ∼*i,* ace of hearts. *stare a* ∼, to be of concern, touch intimately. *farsi* ∼, to take courage. **c[u]oricíno,** *m.* (dim. of *cuore*) darling.

cupè, *m.inv.* coupé, brougham.

cupézza, *f.* gloom[iness]; sombre character.

cupidígia, *f.* greed; covetousness; cupidity. **cúpido,** *a.* eager; covetous; desirous; greedy; grasping.

Cupído, *m.* Cupid.

cúpo, *a.* dark; deep; sombre; obscure; sullen, taciturn.

cúpola, *f.* dome, cupola; (revolving) dome of observatory or gun-turret.

cúpreo, *a.* copper-coloured, cupreous.

cúra, *f.* care, diligence, attention; trouble, anxiety, solicitude; (*Med.*) treatment, cure; (*Eccl.*) spiritual charge, church, parish, parsonage; management; object of care. *a* ∼ *di,* edited by (*book*). *casa di* ∼, nursing-home. ∼ *d'anime,* cure of souls. **curàre,** *v.t.* to take care of; care for; pay heed to; be sensitive to; consider

important; (*Med.*) treat, nurse, cure; (*books*) edit, revise.

curatèla, *f.* guardianship, trusteeship. **curatívo,** *a.* curative. **curàto,** *m.* curate. **curatóre,** *m.* **-tríce,** *f.* guardian, trustee; administrator, -trix; curator; custodian; official receiver.

cúria, *f.* ecclesiastical court; tribunal, court of justice; legal profession. *la C*∼ *romana,* the Papal Court, the Holy See. ∼ *vescovile,* bishop's court. **curiàle,** *a.* curial; of the Papal Court; legal. ¶ *m.* lawyer.

currícolo, *m.* curriculum, course of study.

curiosàre, *v.i.* (*aux.* avere) to pry, eavesdrop; be inquisitive; look; listen. **curiosità,** *f.* curiosity; inquisitiveness; quaintness; curio; (*pl.*) sights (*of a city*). **curióso,** *a.* curious, strange. odd, quaint; inquisitive, prying. ¶ *m.* curious (*or* inquisitive) person; sight-seer; onlooker, bystander; collector (*art, books, &c.*).

cursóre, *m.* messenger; court messenger; (*Mech.*) sliding-rule, slide[r].

cúrva, *f.* curve, bend. ∼ *a forcella,* hairpin bend (*road*). ∼ *occulta,* concealed turning. **curvàre,** *v.t.* to curve, bend; bow. **curvàrsi,** *v.refl.* to bend; stoop; bow down.

curvatúra, *f.* curvature; convexity; curving, bending; camber, cambering (*Arch.*). *tetto a forte* ∼, high-arched roof. **curvilineo,** *a.* curvilinear. **cúrvo,** *a.* bent, curved; crooked; stooping. *spalle* ∼*e, s.pl.* round shoulders.

cuscinétto, *m.* small cushion; pad; pillion; (*Mech.*) bearing. ∼ *a sfere,* ball-bearing. *stato* ∼, buffer state (*Pol.*). **cuscíno,** *m.* cushion; pillow; bolster.

cúspide, *f.* (*Arch.*) cusp.

custòde, *m.f.* keeper; guardian; custodian; watchman; door-keeper; warder, wardress. *angelo* ∼, guardian angel. **custòdia,** *f.* custody; care; protection; case (*violin*). *camera di* ∼, strong room. **custodíre** (*pr.* **-ísco, -ísci**), *v.t.* to keep, guard, preserve; hold in custody; take care of.

cutàneo, *a.* cutaneous, skin (*att.*). **cúte,** *f.* skin (*human*) **cuticàgna,** *f.* nape; scalp. **cutícola,** *f.* cuticle.

cutrèttola, *f.* wagtail.

czèco (*pl.* **czèchi**), *a. & m.* Czech. See **ceco,** &c.

D

D, d, (*di*) *f.* the letter D.

da, *pr.* from; by (*with nouns & pronouns*); (= *Fr.* chez) at, to, in the house of; as; when (*to indicate age or condition*); like; for (*use or purpose*); in (*feature in which a person is defective*); with (*as a distinguishing mark*); of (*to indicate place of birth or origin*); (*with the infin.*) to indicate what is suitable, advisable, possible, or necessary. When combined with the *def. art.* it takes the forms **dal, dall', dallo, dalla** (*sg.*), **dai, dagli, dalle** (*pl.*). When used as a prefix, it requires the doubling of the initial consonant in the following word, *e.g.* **dabbene** from *da bene,* **daccanto** from *da canto,* **daffare** from *da fare,* &c. It is contracted to **d'** only in such adverbial phrases as *d'altronde,* on the other hand, *d'ora in poi,* from now onwards, &c. *da ciò,* as *a.* capable, suitable. *da poppa a prua,* (*Naut.*) fore and aft.

dabbàsso, *ad.* below.

dabbenàggine, *f.* honesty, simplicity, ingenuousness, probity, good nature.

dabbène, *a.inv.* honest, respectable, well-behaved, simple, good-natured. *uomo* ∼, honest man, respectable m. *dabben uomo,* simpleton.

daccànto, *pr. & ad.* near, close by, by the side of.

daccàpo, *ad.* over again, once more, from the beginning.

dacché *or* **da che,** *c.* since, as.

daddolíno, *m.* one who makes childish gestures & grimaces. **dàddolo,** *m.* grimace, face contortion; (*com.pl.* mincing ways, childish gestures). **daddolóne,** *m.* (*f.* -**ona**), one who is always making faces; affected person.

dàdo, *m.* die (*pl.* dice); point in the game of dice; cube, pedestal; (*Arch.*) dado; nut (*for screw*). *il* ∼ *è tratto,* the die is cast. *tessuto d* ∼*i,* cloth with a check (pattern).

daffàre, *m.* occupation, work.

dàga, *f.* dagger.

dagli, = **da gli** (*def. art. m.pl.*) from the, by the, &c. ¶ *i.* **dàgli!** go on! give it him!

dàino, *m.* deer, fallow-deer; buck; *f. pelle di* ∼, *f.* buckskin. **dàina,** doe.

dàlia, *f.* dahlia.

dallàto, *ad.* at one's side, near, nearby; sideways.

dalmàtica, *f.* wide-sleeved loose gown or vestment, dalmatic.

Dalmàzia (la), *f.* Dalmatia.

daltònico (*pl.* -**ònici**), *a. & m.* colour-blind (person). **daltonìsmo,** *m.* colour-blindness.

dàma, *f.* lady of rank; dame; partner (*Dance*); queen (*chess, cards*); (game of) draughts, king (*draughts*). *becca di* ∼, kind of sweet biscuit. ∼ *di compagnia,* lady companion. **damàre,** *v.t.* to crown (*draughts*); queen (*chess*).

damascàre (*pr.* -**àsco,** -**àschi**), *v.t.* to damask. **damascàto,** *m.* damask linen. **damascèno,** *a.* of Damascus. **damaschìna,** *f.* Damascus blade (or sword). **damàsco** (*pl.* -**àschi**), *m.* damask. **D**∼, *f.* Damascus.

dameríno, *m.* fop, dandy.

damière, *m.* draught-board.

damigèlla, *f.* young lady, maid-of-honour. **damigèllo,** *m.* squire, youth of noble family.

damigiàna, *f.* demijohn; (*Chem.*) carboy.

dàmo, *m.* wooer, gallant.

danàro, see *denaro.* **danaróso,** *a.* wealthy, rich, moneyed.

dànda, *f.* brace-band; (*pl.*) leading strings.

danése, *a.* Danish. ¶ *m.* Dane. *il* ∼, the Danish language. **Danimàrca** (la), *f.* Denmark.

dannàbile, *a.* damnable; blamable. **dannàre,** *v.t.* to damn, condemn. **dannàto,** *a. & n.* damned. **dannazióne,** *f.* damnation.

danneggiàre (*pr.* -**éggio,** -**éggi**), *v.t.* to injure, damage; impair. **danneggiàto,** *p.a.* injured, damaged. *merci* ∼ *e, f.pl.* damaged goods. ¶ *m.* injured person.

dànno, *m.* damage, harm, hurt, injury; loss; prejudice (*Law*); tort. *a mio* ∼, to my cost. **dannóso,** *a.* harmful, hurtful, injurious.

dannunzièno, *a.* in the style of D'Annunzio. ¶ *m.* follower of D'Annunzio.

dànte, *m.* in the expression *pelle di* ∼, buckskin.

Dànte, *m.* (no art.) Dante. *il D*∼, the copy of Dante, edition of Dante. **dantésco** (*pl.* -**éschi**), *a.* relating to Dante. *e.g. studi danteschi, stile dantesco, &c.* **dantista** (*pl.* -**isti**), *m.* Dante student or scholar.

Danúbio (il), *m.* the Danube.

dànza, *f.* dance. **danzàre,** *v.i.* (*aux.* avere) to dance. **danzatóre,** *m.* (*f.* **-tríce**) dancer.

dappertútto *or* **da per tutto,** *ad.* . everywhere.

dappiè, dappièdi, *ad.* at the foot; from the foot; downwards.

dappiú, *a.* greater, better, of more account (*quanto* ~, *&c.*).

dappocàggine, *f.* worthlessness, uselessness, ineptitude. **dappòco,** *a. & m.inv.* good for nothing, worthless.

dappòi, *ad.* afterwards. *e* ~? what then? **dappoiché,** *ad.* since.

dapprèsso, *a.* near, nearby, close at hand. **dappríma,** *ad.* at first.

dardeggiàre (*pr.* **-éggio, -éggi**), *v.t. & i.* to dart. **dàrdo,** *m.* dart.

dàre, *v.t. ir.* to give; bring, yield, produce; amount to (*of a total sum*); (*v.i.*) (*aux.* avere) to go (*fig.*); strike, stumble (against = *in*), cause irritation; break out, burst out; look out (upon), overlook (~*sopra* ~*su*). ~ *del tu,* to address familiarly (*in 2nd pers. sg.*). ~ *del ladro a qualcuno,* to call someone a thief. ~ *fuoco a.* to set fire to. ~ *gli esami,* to take examinations. ~ *luogo a.* to occasion, give rise to. ~ *in prestito,* to lend. ~ *motivo ài,* to afford ground for. ~ *torto a.* to blame, put the blame [up]on. *che età gli dareste?* how old would you take him to be? ~ *di piglio,* to seize, seize hold of. ~ *in ritirata,* to beat a retreat. *i rumori mi danno ai nervi,* (the) noises are getting on my nerves. *darla a gambe,* to take to one's heels. *darla per,* to rush off into (or across). ~ *nell'occhio,* to attract attention, stand out, strike the eye. ~ *in riso,* to burst out laughing. ~ *volta a,* (*Naut.*) to make fast; (*sail*) furl. **dàrsi,** *v.refl.* to give oneself up, surrender; devote oneself; be given (to) or addicted (to); happen. *può darsi,* it may be so, it is possible. ~ *intorno,* to look about, to look round. ~ *pensiero,* to take to heart. ~ *per vinto,* to give in, submit. *dàrsela,* to be alike (*in appearance, age, &c.*).

dàre, *m.* debt, debit, liability.

dàrsena, *f.* dock (*wet*), basin.

darvinísmo *&* **darwinísmo,** *m.* Darwinism.

dàta, *f.* date; church patronage; service (*tennis, &c.*); deal (at cards).

datàre, *v.t.* to date, put a date on.

datívo, *m.* dative (*Gram.*). ¶ *a.* in

tutore ~, guardian appointed by the court or by a father in his will.

dàto, *p.p.* of *dare.* ¶ *a.* addicted, inclined; determined; fixed; (*abs.*) granted, admitted. ~ *che,* seeing that, considering that, supposing that. ¶ *m.* datum, thing known or granted, assumption; premiss. (*pl.*)

dati, data.

datóre, *m.* (*f.* **-tríce**), giver. ~ *di lavoro,* employer, contractor. ~ *di una cambiale,* drawer of a bill.

dàttero, *m.* date (*fruit & palm*).

dattílico (*pl.* **-ílici**), *a.* dactylic (*pros.*). **dàttilo,** *m.* dactyl (*pros.*).

dattilografàre (*pr.* **-ògrafo**), *v.t.* to typewrite, type (also *scrivere a macchina*). **dattilografía,** *f.* typewriting. **dattilògrafo,** *m.* (*f.* **-ògrafa**), typist.

dattilología, *f.* art of speaking by the deaf and dumb language.

dattiloscopía, *f.* examination of finger-prints.

dattiloscrítto, *m.* type-script, typewritten document.

dattórno *&* **d'attorno,** *ad.* around, round about. *levarsi* ~, to get rid of; to go away. *qui* ~, here about[s].

davànti, *ad. & pr.* before, in front of (**a**), in the presence of. ¶ also as *a.inv.* e.g. *i denti* ~, the front teeth, *& m.* e.g. *il* ~ *della casa,* the front of the house.

davanzàle, *m.* sill, window-sill.

Davide, *m.* David.

davvéro, *ad.* really. *dire* ~, to be in earnest.

daziàre (*pr.* **-àzio, -àzi**), *v.t.* to impose a duty on, levy toll upon. **daziàrio** (*pl.* **-àri**), *a.* pertaining to custom duties or tolls; toll (*att.*). *tariffa* ~*a.* customs rates. *barriera* ~*a,* *f.* toll-bar, t.-gate. *cinta*~*a,* *f.* toll-gates, city boundaries. **dàzio,** *m.* duty, customs duty; customs office, toll, excise. ~ *d'entrata,* import duty. ~ *d'uscita,* export duty. ~ *consumo,* food-tax; excise.

de, *pr.* old form of **di,** revived by some mod. writers, such as Carducci, before the article.

de', *abb. of* **dei,** of the (*pl.m.*).

dèa, *f.* goddess.

debellàre, (*pr.* **-èllo**) *v.t.* to subdue.

debilitànte, *p.a.* debilitating, enfeebling, weakening. **debilitàre** (*pr.* **-ílito**), *v.t.* to weaken, enfecble, debilitate.

debitaménte, *ad.* duly, properly, justly, rightly. **dèbito,** *a.* due, proper. ¶ *m.* debt; due; (*fig.*) duty, obligation. ~ *pubblico*, national debt. **debitóre,** *m.* (*f.* **-tóra, -tríce**) debtor.

débole, *a.* weak; weakly; feeble; faint (*image*); slow (*pulse*). ¶ *m.* weak person; weak point; foible, weakness (*fig.*). **debolézza,** *f.* weakness. **debolménte,** *ad.* feebly, languidly, weakly.

debraiàre, (*Mech., Motor.*) to declutch.

dèca, *f.* decad[e], series of ten books (esp. of Livy).

decacòrdo, *m.* decachord, instrument of ten strings.

dècade, *f.* decade, space of ten years, or of ten days.

decadènte, *pr.p.* of **decadere.** ¶ *a.* decadent; declining. **decadènza,** *f.* decadence; decline. **decadére** (*pr.* **-àdo,** &c., like **cadere**), *v.i. ir.* (*aux.* essere) to decay, decline, become decadent; (*Law*) lose the exercise of a right. **decadúto,** *p.p.* of *decadere.* ¶ *a.* decayed, impoverished.

decàlitro, *m.* measure of ten litres (2.22009 gallons).

decàlogo, *m.* decalogue, (the) Ten Commandments.

decameróne, *m.* collection of tales like the D~ of Boccaccio (100 tales told by a company in ten days).

decàmetro, *m.* linear measure of ten metres (32.88992 feet).

decanàto, *m.* deanery. **decàno,** *m.* dean.

decantàre (*pr.* **-ànto**), *v.t.* to praise, extol; (*of liquor*) to decant.

decapitàre (*pr.* **-àpito**), *v.t.* to behead, decapitate.

decasíllabo, *a.* & *m.* decasyllabic, decasyllable, line of ten syllables.

decàstilo, *a.* ten-columned (*portico*).

decèdere, *v.i.* (*aux.* essere) to die, pass away. **decedúto,** *p.a.* & *m.* deceased.

decèmbre, *see* dicembre.

decennàle, *a.* recurring every ten years. ¶ *m.* recurrence or celebration of the tenth anniversary of some memorable date or event.

decènne, *a.* ten years old; [lasting] ten years (e.g. *decenne assedio di Troia*). **decènnio** (*pl.* **-ènni**), *m.* period of ten years.

decènte, *a.* decent, seemly, modest, becoming.

decentraménto, *m.* decentralization. **decentràre,** *v.t.* to decentralize.

decènza, *f.* decency, propriety.

decèsso, *m.* decease, death (*in bureaucratic terminology*).

decídere, *v.t. ir.* to decide, settle, resolve (*quarrels, controversies,* &c.). **decídersi,** *v.refl.* to resolve, make up one's mind.

decíduo, *a.* deciduous. *stella* ~*a,* falling star.

decifràre (*pr.* **-ífro**), *v.t.* to decipher.

decigràmma, *m.* decigramme = $\frac{1}{10}$ gramme or 1.543 grains.

decílitro, *m.* decilitre = $\frac{1}{10}$ litre or 0.176 pint.

dècima, *f.* tithe; tenth part.

decimàle, *a.* & *m.* decimal.

decimàre (*pr.* **dècimo**), *v.t.* to decimate; reduce; punish every tenth man with death; tithe.

decímetro, *m.* decimetre = $\frac{1}{10}$ metre or 3.937 inches. *doppio*~, 2 decimetre rule.

dècimo, *a. num. ord.* & *m.* tenth; tenth part. **decimoprímo, decimosecondo, decimoterzo,** &c. *a. num. ord.* eleventh, twelfth, thirteenth, &c.

decína, *f.* half-a-score, about ten.

decisióne, *f.* decision; conclusion; resolution; ruling, award. **decisivaménte,** *ad.* decisively, conclusively. **decisívo,** *a.* decisive, conclusive; critical; positive. *voto* ~, casting vote.

declamàre (*pr.* **-àmo**), *v.t.* & *i.* (*aux.* avere) to declame. **declamatorio,** *a.* declamatory.

declinàre (*pr.* **-íno**), *v.i.* (*aux.* avere) to go down, set, sink, slope, decline; decay, fall off (or away), come down, diminish; (*v.t.*) to refuse; decline (also *Gram.*); bend, bow. **declinazióne,** *f.* gradient, slope, decline, decrease, declension (*Gram.*); declination (*Astr.*).

declíve & **declívo,** *a.* sloping. **declívio** (*pl.* **-ívi**), *m.* declivity, slope. **declività,** *f.inv.* steepness.

decollàre (*pr.* **-òllo**), *v.t.* to behead, decapitate; (*v.i.*) (*aux.* avere) (*Aero.*) to take off. **decollazióne,** *f.* beheading, (*esp.* that of St. John the Baptist).

decòllo, *m.* (*Aero.*) take-off.

decomponènte, *a.* decomposing. **decompórre** (*pr.* **-óngo,** &c., like *porre*), *v.t. ir.* to decompose; disintegrate, dissolve. **decomposizióne,** *f.* decomposition. **decompósto,** *p.a.* decomposed.

decòro, *m.* dignity, decorum; ornament (*fig.*). decoróso, *a.* seemly, dignified.

decorrènza, *f.* course; term from which a contract has effect; falling due. decórrere (*pr.* -órro, &*c.*, like correre), *v.i. ir.* (*aux.* essere) to run down; pass, go by; run, have effect, count from (when a contract or interest on a deБt begins). decórso, *p.p.* of decorrere. ¶ *a.* past, last, elapsed. ¶ *m.* course, passage, passing.

decòtto, *a.* (*Law*) bankrupt. ¶ *m.* decoction. *partita* ~*a*, frozen credit. decozióne, *f.* decoction, preparation of the same; (*Law*) bankruptcy.

decrepitézza, *f.* decrepitude. decrèpito, *a.* decrepit.

descrescènte, *a.* decreasing, diminishing, abating. decréscere (*pr.* -ésco, &*c.*, like crescere), *v.i. ir.* (*aux.* essere) to decrease, diminish.

decretàle, *a.* of a (papal) decree. ¶ *f.pl.* le decretali, the Decretals, body of canon law. decretàre (*pr.* -éto), *v.t.* to decree. decréto, *m.* decree.

decúbito, *m.* position of one lying in bed. *i* ~ *i, m.pl.* or *piaghe da decubito, f.pl.* bed-sores.

dècuplo, *a.* tenfold, ten times greater.

dèdalo, *m.* labyrinth, maze (*fr.* Daedalus, who constructed the Cretan labyrinth).

dèdica, *f.* dedication; inscription (*in a book*). dedicàre (*pr.* dèdico, dèdichi), *v.t.* to dedicate. dedicàrsi, *v.refl.* to devote oneself. dedicatòria, *f.* letter of dedication.

dèdito, *a.* given up (to), engrossed (in). dedizióne, *f.* surrender; voluntary submission; devotion, (self) sacrifice.

dedótto, *p.p.* of dedurre.

dedúrre (*pr.* -úco, -úci, &*c.*, like addurre), *v.t. ir.* to derive; deduce; infer; deduct; draw forth (*music*); found (*colonies*); (*leg.*) state one's case in court. deduttívo, *a.* deductive. deduzióne, *f.* deduction; inference.

defalcàre (*pr.* -àlco, -àlchi), *v.t.* to deduct; diminish; withdraw. defàlco (*pl.* -àlchi), *m.* deduction.

defecàre (*pr.* -èco, -èchi), *v.t.* to defecate; (*Chem.*) to free (a liquid) from impurities.

defenestràre, *v.t.* to throw out of the window; (*fig.*) drive out of office.

defensionàle, *a.* (*Law*) for the defence.

deferènte, *pr.p.* of deferire. ¶ *a.* deferential; (*Physiol.*) deferent. deferènza, *f.* deference, respect. deferíre (*pr.* ísco, -ísci) *v.i.* (*aux.* avere) to defer; show deference (to); (*v.t.*) (*Law*) to administer (*an oath*); lodge (*accusation*); submit; remit (*case to court*). N.B. *not in the sense of* put off, postpone, *differire, rimandare, posporre.*

defettíbile, *a.* liable to fail; defective, faulty.

defezionàre, *v.i.* (*aux.* avere) to desert (*from party or cause*). defezióne, *f.* defection, desertion.

deficiènte, *a.* deficient; (*Sch.*) backward. ¶ *m.f.* mentally deficient person; idiot; half-wit. deficiènza, *f.* deficiency; lack, want. dèficit, *m.inv.* (*Com.*) deficit. *cf. disavanzo.*

defilàre, *v.i.* (*aux.* avere) to defile; file off; march past.

definíre (*pr.* -isco, -isci, like *finire*) *v.t.* to define; determine; resolve; settle (dispute). definitívo, *a.* definitive; decisive; absolute (*decree*); final; ultimate; standard (*edition*). definíto, *a.* definite; finite (*mood, Gram.*). definizióne, *f.* definition; decision.

deflazióne, *f.* deflation (*Fin.*).

deflessióne, *f.* deflection; deviation. deflèttere (*pr.* -ètto), *v.i.ir.* (*aux.* avere) to deflect; deviate; bend; alter course; withdraw. deflettóre, *m.* (*Aero.*) deflector.

defloràre, *v.t.* to deflower; strip of flowers; ravish. deflorazióne, *f.* defloration.

defluíre (*pr.* -ísco, -ísci), *v.i.* (*aux.* essere) to flow down. deflússo, *m.* downward flow.

deformàre (*pr.* -órmo), *v.t.* to disfigure, alter, deform; distort; warp; (*Mech.*) strain; spoil (*beauty of*). deformàrsi, *v.refl.* (*Mech.*) to warp, buckle. deformazióne, *f.* disfigurement (*action & result*); deformation. defórme, *a.* deformed; ugly; mis-shapen; mutilated. deformità, *f.inv.* deformity.

defraudàre (*pr.* -àudo), *v.t.* to defraud, cheat; deprive.

defúnto, *a. & m.* dead, defunct, deceased; (*a*) late.

degeneràre (*pr.* -ènero), *v.i.* (*aux.* avere) to degenerate; (*of illness*)

become critical. **degeneràto &
degènere**, *a.* degenerate.

degenerazióne, *f.* degeneration, degeneracy.

degènte, *a.* confined to bed, bedridden; in hospital. **degènza**, *f.* period of illness, stay (*in bed, in hospital*).

deglutíre (*pr.* **-ísco, -ísci**), *v.t.* to swallow.

degnaménte, *ad.* worthily. **degnàre** (*pr.* **dégno**), *v.t.* to deem worthy (of), think worth; grant; *v.i.* (*aux.* avere) & **degnàrsi**, *v.refl.* to deign, condescend. **degnazióne**, *f.* condescension. **dégno**, *a.* worthy, deserving; dignified.

degradaménto, *m.* degradation; deprivation of rank or dignity. **degradàre** (*pr.* **-àdo**), *v.t.* to degrade; reduce to the ranks. **degradazióne**, *f.* (the punishment of) degradation.

degustàre, *v.t.* to taste, sample (*wines, e.g.*). **degustazióne**, *f.* tasting; sipping.

deh!, *i.* (excl. of pain, compassion, prayer, &c.) ah! alas! for pity's sake!

dèi, *m.pl.* of **Dìo**, gods (*art.* **gli**).

deiezióne, *f.* evacuation (*bowels*); excrement; detritus.

deificàre (*pr.* **-ífico, -ífichi**), *v.t.* to deify.

deísmo, *m.* deism. **deísta** (*pl.* **-ísti**), *m.* deist. **deità**, *f.inv.* deity.

delatóre, *m.* (*f.* **-tríce**) informer, spy. **delazióne**, *f.* secret accusation. ~ *d'armi*, illicit bearing of arms. ~ *di giuramento*, administration of an oath.

dèlega & delegazióne, *f.* delegation. **delegàre** (*pr.* **dèlego, dèleghi**), *v.t.* to delegate; depute; appoint as representative; commit. **delegàto**, *m.* delegate; deputy. ~ *di pubblica sicurezza*, superintendent of police.

deletèrio, *a.* deleterious.

Delfinàto (il), *m.* (the) Dauphiné (*Geog.*).

delfíno, *m.* dolphin. **D~**, Dauphin.

delibàre (*pr.* **-íbo**), *v.t.* to taste, sample; (*Law*) touch in passing, allude to. **delibazióne**, *f.* (*Law*) consideration of a judgment passed in a foreign court.

deliberàre (*pr.* **-íbero**), *v.i.* (*aux.* avere) to deliberate, consult; (*v.t.*) decide, resolve on; adjudge; assign. **deliberàrsi**, *v.refl.* to decide, resolve. **deliberataménte**, *ad.* deliberately, after full consideration.

deliberatàrio, *m.* highest bidder; successful tenderer. **deliberatíva**, *f.* power of making decisions. **deliberatívo**, *a.* deliberative, able to make decisions. **deliberàto**, *a.* resolved, resolute, deliberate. **deliberazióne**, *f.* deliberation, resolution.

delicatézza, *f.* delicacy; refinement; softness; grace; tact; tactful action. **delicàto**, *a.* delicate; dainty; fastidious; refined; soft; elegant; pleasing; tactful; scrupulous. **delicatúra**, *f.* excessive delicacy; extreme elegance.

delimitàre (*pr.* **-ímito**), *v.t.* to delimit, determine or trace the limits of, define. **delimitazióne**, *f.* delimitation.

delineàre (*pr.* **-íneo, -ínei**), *v.t.* to delineate, trace, sketch, outline. **delineàrsi**, *v.refl.* to take shape. **delineazióne**, *f.* delineation.

delinquènte, *a. & m.* delinquent. **delinquènza**, *f.* delinquency; crime; criminality. **delínquere** (*pr.* **-ínquo**) (comp. tenses missing) *v.i. ir.* to commit a crime, or offence.

deliquescènte, *a.* (*Chem.*) deliquescent. **deliquescènza**, *f.* (*Chem.*) deliquescence; corruption (*fig.*).

delíquio (*pl.* **-íqui**), *m.* swoon; fainting-fit.

deliránte, *a.* raving, furious, delirious, frenzied. **deliràre** (*pr.* **-íro**), *v.i.* (*aux.* avere) to rave, be delirious. **delírio** (*pl.* **-iri**), *m.* raving, delirium, frenzy, unbridled passion.

delítto, *m.* crime. **delittuóso**, *a.* criminal.

delizia, *f.* delight. **deliziàre** (*pr.* **-ízio, -ízi**), *v.t.* to charm, delight; render delightful. **deliziàrsi**, *v.refl.* to take delight (in). **delizióso**, *a.* delightful, delicious.

dèlta, *m.* delta.

delúbro, *m.* (*Poet.*) temple, shrine.

delucidàre, *v.t.* to take the gloss from (new material).

delúdere, *v.t. ir.* to delude; frustrate; escape. **delusióne**, *f.* delusion, disappointment, deception.

demagògo (*pl.* **-òghi**), *m.* demagogue.

demandàre, *v.t.* to pass on, assign, delegate.

demànio (*pl.* **-àni**), *m.* demesne; crown lands; state property.

demarcazióne, *f.* demarcation.

demènte, *a. & m.* crazy, mad (person). **demènza**, *f.* insanity, madness, dementia.

demeritàre (*pr.* **-èrito**), *v.t.* to

forfeit (*esteem*, &c.); v.i. (*aux*. avere) to deserve censure; show oneself unworthy (of = *di*). **demèrito**, *m*. demerit, unworthiness.

democràtico (*pl*. -àtici), *a*. democratic. ¶ *m*. democrat. **democrazía**, *f*. democracy. **democristiàno**, *a*. & *m*. *abb*. of *democratico cristiano*, Christian-democratic, C.-democrat.

Demòcrito, *m*. Democritus.

demografía, *f*. demography, study of population.

demolíre (*pr*. -ísco, -ísci), v.t. to demolish, break up. **demolizióne**, *f*. demolition.

dèmone, *m*. demon; good or evil spirit; daemon, genius. **demoníaco** (*pl*. -íaci), *a*. demoniac[al]. ¶ *m*. demoniac. **demònio** (*pl*. -òni), *m*. devil; demon (*lit*. & *fig*.); imp (restless or mischievous child). **demonología**, *f*. demonology.

demopsicología, *f*. race psychology.

demoraliżżàre, v.t. to demoralize.

Demòstene, *m*. Demosthenes.

denàro, *m*. money; penny; one of the four suits in a pack of Ital. playing cards (*Neapolitan*).

denegàre (*pr*. dènego, dèneghi), v.t. to deny, disavow. **denegatóre**, *m*. one who denies; cynic; sceptic.

denaturàre, v.t. to denature; alter. *alcool denaturato*, methylated spirit.

denigràre (*pr*. -ígro), v.t. to blacken; (*fig*.), disparage, run down, defame. **denigratóre**, *a*. & *m*. (*f*. -tríce) defamatory; defamer, slanderer. **denigrazióne**, *f*. defamation; disparagement.

denominàre (*pr*. -òmino), v.t. to name, denominate. **denominatóre**, *m*. denominator (*Arith*.).

denotàre (*pr*. dènoto), v.t. to denote, signify, indicate.

densità, *f.inv*. density. **dènso**, *a*. dense, close; thick.

dentàle, *a*. dental. ¶ *m*. ploughshare. ¶ *f*. dental (consonant).

dentar[u]òlo, *m*. baby's ivory ring or coral (for biting on).

dentàta, *f*. bite; mark of a bite. **dentàto**, *a*. toothed; notched; cogged; dentate (*Bot*.). **dentatrice**, *f*. (*Mech*.) gear-cutting machine. **dentatúra**, *f*. set of teeth; cutting of teeth, teething; (*Mech*.) teeth; serration (*saw*, &c.). **dènte**, *m*. tooth; prong, protection; cog; tusk; notch; fluke (*anchor*); [jagged] peak. ~ *canino*, eye-tooth. ~ *di latte*, child's first tooth; milk-tooth. ~

superiore, upper tooth. ~ *del giudizio*, wisdom-tooth, eye-tooth. ~ *di leone*, dandelion (*Bot*.). *a* ~*i di sega*, serrate, saw-toothed. **dentellàre**, v.t. (*Mech*., *Carp*.) to notch, score, indent. **dentellatúra**, *f*. indentation; notching; serration. **dentèllo**, *m*. notch; dentil of a cornice (*Arch*.). **dentièra**, *f*. set of (artificial) teeth; denture, (dental) plate. **dentifrício** (*pl*. -ici), *m*. tooth-paste; t.-powder; mouth-wash. **dentísta** (*pl*. -ísti), *m*. dentist; dental surgeon. **dentizióne**, *f*. dentition, teething.

déntro, *ad*. within, inside; (*fig*.) in mind, in thought. ¶ *pr*. ~, ~*a*, ~*di*, in, inside (of); within; during, in the course of. With pers. pn. requires to be followed by *pr*. *di*. *darci*~, to guess, divine. *di* ~, from within.

denudàre, v.t. to denude; strip; despoil.

denúncia & **denúnzia**, *f*. report, announcement; notification; return; banns of marriage. **denunciàre** & **denunziàre** (*pr*. -úncio, -únci, & -únzio, -únzi), v.t. to announce, declare, report (*esp. to an authority*); denounce (*treaty*, &c.); inform against. ~ *una nascita*, to report a birth.

deperíbile, *a*. (*of goods or material*) perishable. **deperiménto**, *m*. wasting, pining away; decline, decay. ~ *nervoso*, nervous exhaustion. **deperíre** (*pr*. -ísco, ísci), v.i. (*aux*. essere) to waste away; dwindle, decline; lose strength; wither; perish.

depilàre, v.t. to remove hair, depilate, pluck. **depilatòrio**, *a*. & *m*. depilatory.

deploràre (*pr*. -òro), v.t. to deplore, lament, bewail. **deplorévole**, *a*. deplorable, pitiable.

deponènte, *pr.p*. of *deporre*. ¶ *a*. & *m*. deponent. **depórre** (*pr*. -óngo, &c.), like *porre*), v.t. *ir*. to lay down, put down, lay aside; take off (*clothes*); depose; give up, renounce, deposit; (*Law*) give evidence, testify, depose.

deportàre, v.t. to deport; transport (*convict*); remove. **deportazióne**, *f*. deportation.

depoŝitànte, *m.f*. depositor, customer (*bank*). **depoŝitàre** (*pr*. -òsito), v.t. to deposit; bank (*money*); consign; place; lodge; hand in. **depoŝitàrio** (*pl*. -àri), *m*. depositary,

trustee, confidant. **depòsito,** *m.*
deposit; [*act of*] depositing; store;
vault; cloak-room; depôt; sediment.
depoṣizióne, *f.* deposition; removal
(*fr.* office); testimony (*before a judge*).
la D~, the Descent from the Cross.
depósto, *p.p.* of *deporre.* ¶ *m.* legal
deposition; written evidence.
depravàre, *v.t.* to deprave, corrupt.
depravazióne, *f.* depravation;
depravity.
deprecàre (*pr.* -èco, -èchi), *v.t.* to
deprecate; pray that an evil be
averted; exorcise.
depredàre (*pr.* -èdo), *v.t.* to ravage,
despoil.
depressióne, *f.* depression. **deprèsso,**
p.p. of *deprimere.* ¶ *a.* dejected,
discouraged, dispirited; low-lying;
(*Poet.*) lowly. *polso*~, weak pulse.
deprezzàre (*pr.* -èzzo), *v.t.* to
depreciate, decry, undervalue, discredit.
deprimènte, *a.* depressing; tiresome.
deprímere (*pr.* -ímo, *&c.*, like
comprimere), *v.t. ir.* to depress;
press down, crush; dishearten,
discourage; humiliate.
depuràre (*pr.* -úro), *v.t.* to purify;
purge.
deputàre (*pr.* **dèputo**), *v.t.* to
depute; appoint; assign. **deputàto,**
m. deputy; M.P.; delegate. *Camera
dei* ~ *i,* Chamber of Deputies,
Parliament (*Fr.* or *Ital.*). **deputa-
zióne,** *f.* deputation; committee,
select committee.
deragliamento, *m.* derailment.
deragliàre (*pr.* -àglio, -àgli), *v.t.*
to derail; (*v.i.*) (*aux.* avere) to leave
the line (*Rly.*), go off the rails.
derelítto, *a.* derelict, abandoned,
forsaken. ¶ *m.* abandoned (*child,
&c.*). *ospizio dei* ~ *i, m.* home for
lost children. **derelizióne,** *f.*
dereliction.
derequiṣíre (*pr.* -ísco, -ísci), *v.t.* to
derequisition.
deretàno, *m.* hinder-part, bottom,
backside.
derídere (*pr.* -ído, *&c.*, like *ridere*),
v.t. ir. to mock, deride, laugh at.
deriṣíbile, *a.* laughable, ridiculous.
deríva, *f.* drift, lee-way. *andare
alla* ~, to drift, go adrift. **derivàre**
(*pr.* -ívo), *v.i.* (*aux.* essere) to spring,
rise (*of rivers*), originate; derive, be
derived; result, follow; (*Naut.*) make
leeway; (*v.t.*) to divert (*stream*),
deflect. **derivazióne,** *f.* derivation;
deflection.

dermatíte, *f.* (*Med.*) inflammation of
the skin. **dermatología,** *f.*
dermatology, study of skin diseases.
dèrno, *in ad. expr. in* ~, of a flag
rolled-up as a signal of distress.
dèroga, *f.* derogation. **derogàre** (*pr.*
dèrogo, dèroghi), *v.i.* (*aux.* avere)
to derogate, detract (from = *a*).
~*a*, to contravene.
derràta, *f.* merchandise; victuals;
agricultural produce (*when for sale*).
derubàre (*pr.* -úbo), *v.t.* to steal,
rob, plunder.
dèrvis (*pl.* **dervísci**), *m.* dervish.
deschétto, *m.* (*dim.* of *desco*) small
table, bench, stool. **désco** (*pl.*
déschi), *m.* (dinner) table; meal
upon the table; table laid for a meal;
board; butcher's block; bench; stool.
descrittívo, *a.* descriptive. **descrí-
vere** (*pr.* -ívo, *&c.*, like *scrivere*),
v.t. ir. to describe. **descrizióne,** *f.*
description.
deṣèrto, *a.* desert; wild; solitary; bare;
abandoned; deserted. ¶ *m.* desert,
wilderness.
deṣiàre *&* **diṣiàre** (*pr.* -ío, -íi), *v.t.*
(*Poet.*) to desire.
deṣideràbile, *a.* desirable. **deṣide-
ràre** (*pr.* -ídero), *v.t.* to desire;
wish; want. **deṣideràta,** *m.pl.*
desideràta, wants. **deṣidèrio** (*pl.*
-èri), *m.* desire, longing; regret. *ho
conseguito il mio* ~, I have attained
my desire. **deṣideróso,** *a.* desirous.
deṣignàre (*pr.* -ígno), *v.t.* to designate; indicate, point out; describe;
nominate; appoint. **deṣignazióne,**
f. designation, *&c.*
deṣinàre (*pr.* **déṣino**), *v.i.* (*aux.* avere)
to dine. ¶ *m.* dinner; dining.
deṣinènza, *f.* termination, ending
(*Gram.*).
deṣío, *m.* (*Poet.*) desire; thing longed
for.
deṣístere (*pr.* -ísto), *v.i. ir.* (*aux.*
avere) to desist, forbear, cease.
deṣolàre, *v.t.* to desolate, distress,
grieve. **deṣolàto,** *p.a.* desolate;
disconsolate, forlorn, distressed.
deṣolazióne, *f.* desolation.
dèṣpota (*pl.* **dèṣpoti**), *m.* despot.
dèsso (*f.* **déssa**), *pn.* that very one;
one's self; the same; his (or her)
(very) self.
destàre (*pr.* **dèsto**), *v.t.* to wake,
rouse, stir, awaken.
destinàre (*pr.* -íno), *v.t.* to destine,
design, intend, mean; allot; assign;
fate, doom; decree; decide; address
(*letters, &c.*). *destinato a,* bound for.

destinatàrio (*pl.* **-àri**), *m.* addressee; consignee; receiver, recipient; *a rischio e pericolo del*~, at owner's risk. **destinazióne**, *f.* destination; purpose. **destíno**, *m.* destiny, fate, lot, doom; destination; (*pl.*) fortunes, destinies.

destituíre (*pr.* **-ísco**, *&c.*, like *statuire*), *v.t.* to dismiss, remove. **destituíto**, *p.p.* of *destituire*. ¶ *a.* destitute, lacking, devoid (of). *un'accusa* ~*a di fondamento*, a groundless charge. **destituzióne**, *f.* dismissal; removal (*fr. office*).

désto, *sync. p.p.* of *destare*. ¶ *a.* awake, alert; ready, lively.

dèstra, *f.* right hand; right[-hand] side; Right (*in politics*) = conservatives. *a* ~, to the right.

destreggiàre (*pr.* **-éggio**, **-éggi**), *v.i.* (*aux.* avere) also **destreggiàrsi**, *v.refl.* to manage cleverly, contrive; juggle, finesse. **destrézza**, *f.* dexterity, agility; skill; sagacity. **destrière** & **destrièro**, *m.* (*Poet.*) steed, war-horse. **dèstro**, *a.* dexterous, skilful; alert, agile, accomplished, wide-awake; (*fig.*) right (*hand*, *side*, *eye*, *foot*). *mal*~, awkward. ¶ *m.* chance, opportunity; convenience. **destròrso**, *a.* & *ad.* from left to right; clock-wise (*circular movement*).

desuèto, *a.* obsolete; out of use; unusual.

desúmere (*pr.* **-úmo**, **-úmi**), *v.t. ir.* to derive; infer; deduce. **desúnto**, *p.p.* of *desumere*. ¶ *a.* derived, extracted.

detenére (*pr.* **-èngo**, *&c.*, like *tenere*), *v.t. ir.* to hold, keep; detain, hold under arrest. ~ *un record*, to hold a record (*sport*). ~ *un incarico*, to keep a post. **detentóre**, *m.* (*f.* **-tríce**)holder (*pers.*); receiver of stolen property. **detenúto**, *p.p.* of *detenere*. ¶ *a.* imprisoned, under arrest. **detenzióne**, *f.* detention; possession of stolen property.

detergènte, *a.* & *m.* detergent. **detèrgere** (*pr.* **-èrgo**, *&c.*, like *tergere*), *v.t. ir.* to cleanse.

deterioraménto, *m.* & **deteriorazióne**, *f.* deterioration. **deteriorársi**, *v.refl.* to deteriorate.

determinàre (*pr.* **-èrmino**), *v.t.* to determine, establish; define, specify; produce, cause; resolve. **determinàto**, *p.p.* of *determinare*. ¶ *a.* determinate, definite; determined, resolute; specific, particular. **deter-**

minazióne, *f.* determination; resolution; resolve. **determinísmo**, *m.* determinism.

detersívo, *a.* cleansing. **detèrso**, *p.p.* of *detergere*. ¶ *a.* cleansed, purified, clean, bright.

detettóre, *m.* (*Radio*) detector.

detonànte, *a.* detonating. **detonàre**, *v.i.* (*aux.* avere) to detonate. **detonatóre**, *m.* detonator.

detràrre (*pr.* **-àggo**, *&c.*, like *trarre*), *v.t. ir.* to deduct, take away; (*rarely*) to detract. **detrattóre**, *m.* (*f.* **-tríce**) detractor, slanderer. **detrazióne**, *f.* deduction; (*rarely*) detraction.

detríto, *m.* detritus; (*pl.*) rubble.

detronizzàre (*pr.* **-ízzo**), *v.t.* to dethrone.

détta, *f.* opinion, words, saying (in such expressions as *a* ~ *sua*, according to his opinion, according to what he says). *a* ~ *di tutti*, according to what everybody says.

dettàfono, *m.* dictaphone.

dettàglio *v.t.* to detail. **dettàglio**, *m.* detail; (*Com.*) retail. *vendere al* ~, to retail.

dettàme, *m.* dictate, precept; teaching[s].

dettàre (*pr.* **dètto**), *v.t.* to dictate; indicate; suggest; impose; (*Lit.*) to write or compose. **dettàto**, *m.* what is dictated, dictation (*exercise*); saying, proverb. **dettatúra**, *f.* dictation; what is dictated.

détto, *p.p.* of *dire*. ¶ *a.* named, nicknamed. ~ *fatto*, no sooner said than done. ¶ *m.* what is said, word, saying; witticism.

deturpàre (*pr.* **-úrpo**), *v.t.* to disfigure; spoil.

Deuteronòmio, *m.* Deuteronomy (*O.T.*).

devalutazióne, *f.* devaluation.

devastàre, *v.t.* to devastate, lay waste. **deveníre** (*pr.* **-èngo**, *&c.*, like *venire*), *v.i. ir.* (*aux.* essere) to arrive at a conclusion or judgment (*Law*).

deviaménto, *m.* deviation, deflection, aberration; leaving the line; shunting, derailment. **deviàre** (*pr.* **-ío**, **-íi**), *v.i.* (*aux.* avere), to deviate, digress; swerve; leave the line; run off the rails; (*v.t.*) to divert, turn aside. **deviatóre**, *m.* pointsman (*Rly.*), shunter. **deviazióne**, *f.* deviation (*Opt.*) deflection (*Elec.*, *etc.*). **dèvio**, *a.* devious.

devoluzióne, *f.* devolution, transfer.

devòlvere (*pr.* **-òlvo**), *v.t.* to transfer; assign, employ.

devotíssimo, *abb.* **dev(mo)**, most faithfully, most obediently. *Suo devmo*, yours faithfully (*in letters*).

devòto, *a.* devoted; devout; destined; consecrated. ¶ *m.* devotee, devout person. **devozióne**, *f.* devotion, reverence, piety.

di-, prefix.

di, *pr.* of, from, for, with, at, to (*with infin. after certain vbs.*), in, on, about, by, during; (*with def. art. in partitive constr.*) some, any; than (*with comparatives*). Combined with the def. art. takes the forms **del, dello, dell'** (*m.sg.*) **della** (*f.sg.*) **dei, de', degli** (*m.pl.*) **delle** (*f.pl.*). *dico ~ no*, I say no. *~ grazia*, please. *~ solito*, usually, generally. *~ sopra*, above, upstairs. *~ giorno*, by day. *d'inverno*, in winter. *~ passo*, at a walking pace. *uccello ~ passo*, bird of passage. *~ sbieco*, aslant, askew. *di male in peggio*, from bad to worse. *di gran lunga*, by far.

dí, *m.* day (*Poet.*). *al ~ d'oggi*, nowadays.

diabète, *m.* diabetes.

diacciàre (*pr.* **-àccio, -àcci**), *v.i.* (*aux.* essere) to freeze. **diàccio** (*pl.* **-àcci**), *m.* ice; clear white spot f und in some marbles. ¶ *a.* frozen, icy; chilly. **diacci[u]òlo**, *m.* icicle. ¶ *a.* brittle; sensitive to cold (*of tooth*).

diàcono, *m.* deacon.

diadèma (*pl.* **-èmi**), *m.* diadem.

diàfano, *a.* diaphanous, transparent.

diafràmma (*pl.* **-àmmi**), *m.* diaphragm; screen; stop (*Phot.*).

diagnoṡi, *f.* diagnosis. **diagnòstico** (*pl.* **-òstici**), *a.* diagnostic.

diagonàle, *a. & f.* diagonal.

diagràmma (*pl.* **-àmmi**), *m.* diagram.

dialettàle, *a.* dialectal.

dialèttica, *f.* dialectic[s]. **dialèttico** (*pl.* **-èttici**), *a.* dialectic.

dialettologìa, *f.* study of dialects.

diàlogo (*pl.* **-àloghi**), *m.* dialogue.

diamànte, *m.* diamond. **diamantífero**, *a.* containing diamonds, diamond-bearing (*rocks, strata, &c.*). **diamantíno**, *a.* adamantine.

diametralménte, *ad.* diametrically. **diàmetro**, *m.* diameter.

diàmine, *i.* (of surprise or impatience) good heavens! dash it all!

Diàna, *f.* Diana. **d** *~*, morning-star; reveillé; morning-watch (*Mar.*) *batter la ~*, to sound the reveillé; (*fig.*) to tremble from cold.

diànzi, *ad.* a short while ago, not long since.

diàpason, *m.inv.* (*Mus.*) octave; pitch; compass of voice or instrument; tuning-fork.

diària, *f.* daily travelling-allowance. **diàrio** (*pl.* **-àri**), *a.* daily, lasting a day. ¶ *m.* diary, journal. **diarísta** (*pl.* **-ísti**), *m.* diarist.

diarrèa, *f.* diarrhoea.

diàspro, *m.* jasper.

diatònico (*pl.* **-ònici**), *a.* (*Mus.*) diatonic.

diatríba, *f.* diatribe; dissertation.

diàvola, *f.* she-devil. **diavolàccio** (*pl.* **-àcci**), *m.* horrid devil. *buon ~*, good fellow. **diavolería**, *f.* devilment, devilry; malicious trick. **diavoléto**, *m.* devil of a row, noisy dispute, uproar. **diavolío**, *m.* pandemonium. **diàvolo**, *m.* devil.

dibàttere (*pr.* **-àtto**), *v.t.* to beat (*eggs, &c.*); flap, flutter (*wings*); discuss, debate. **dibàttersi**, *v.refl.* to struggle. **dibattiménto**, *m.* beating, shaking; struggling; discussion, legal debate. **dibàttito**, *m.* debate, discussion, controversy; flapping (*of wings*).

diboscàre (*pr.* **-òsco, -òschi**), *v.t.* to cut down (*trees*), clear, make a clearing of.

dibrucàre (*pr.* **-brúco, -brúchi**), *v.t.* to prune.

dicàce, *a.* sarcastic, satirical; loquacious. **dicacità**, *f.* sarcastic manner, causticity; garrulity.

dicastèro, *m.* each of the principal offices or departments of State; (*fig.*) department of a large office.

dicèmbre, *m.* December.

dicentràre *or* **decentràre**, *v.t.* to decentralize.

dicería, *f.* long tedious speech; (malicious) chatter; groundless rumour.

dicervellàre, *v.t.* to bewilder, confuse. **dicervellàrsi**, *v.refl.* to rack one's brains.

dicévole, *a.* suitable, becoming, decent, fitting.

dichiaràre, *v.t.* to declare, make known, explain, announce, judge, nominate. **dichiarazióne**, *f.* declaration. *~ giurata*, affidavit.

diciannòve, *a.inv.* (*card. num.*) nineteen. ¶ *m. il ~*, the nineteenth (*date*). **diciannovèsimo**, *a.* (*ord. num.*) nineteenth.

diciassètte, *a.inv.* (*card. num.*) seventeen. ¶ *m. il* ∼, the seventeenth (*date*). **diciassettèsimo**, *a.* (*ord. num.*) seventeenth.

dicíbile, *a.* that can be told or said; speakable.

dicimàre, *v.t.* to take off the top (of), lop.

dicioccàre (*pr.* -òcco, -òcchi), *v.t.* to thin the foliage of a tree, strip.

diciottènne, *a.* eighteen years old. **diciottèsimo**, *a.* (*ord. num.*) eighteenth. **diciòtto**, *a.inv.* (*card. num.*) eighteen. ¶ *m. il* ∼, the eighteenth (*date*).

dicitóre, *m.* (*f.* -**tríce**), reciter. **dicitúra**, *f.* manner of speaking, delivery; language, choice of words; diction, wording; (*Typ.*) subscription.

dicotomía, *f.* dichotomy.

didascalía, *f.* actor's cues in the dialogue of a play; running commentary on a film; note, caption. **didascàlica**, *f.* art of instruction; didactic poetry. **didascàlico** (*pl.* -àlici), *a.* instructive, didactic.

didàttico (*pl.* -àttici), *a.* didactic.

didéntro, *ad. & m.* inside.

Didóne, *f.* Dido (*Myth.*).

dièci, *a.inv.* (*card. num.*) ten. ¶ *m. il* ∼, the tenth (*date*). *le* ∼, ten o'clock. *alle* ∼ *di sera*, ten o'clock at night. **diecimíla**, *a.inv.* (*card. num.*) ten thousand. **diecimillèsimo**, *a.* (*ord. num.*) ten thousandth. **diecína**, see *decina*.

dièreši, *f.* dieresis (the separation into two syllables of the vowels of a diphthong and the sign (‥) which indicates this).

dièta, *f.* diet. **dietètica**, *f.* dietetics (*Med.*).

dietro, *ad.* back, backwards; behind, behind one's back. ¶ *pr.* or ∼ *a* (with pers. pronouns ∼ *di*) behind, after. ∼ *richiesta*, on application. ∼ *versamento di*, [up]on payment of.

dietrofrónt, *m.inv. & i.* (*Mil.*) right about turn.

difèndere (*pr.* -èndo), *v.t. ir.*, to defend, protect; prevent. **difensíbile**, *a.* defensible; tenable. **difensíva**, *f.* defensive. **difensívo**, *a.* defensive. **difensóre**, *m.* (*f.* **difenditríce**) defender. **difésa**, *f.* defence. **diféso**, *p.p.* of *difendere.* ¶ *a.* sheltered.

difettàre (*pr.* -étto), *v.i.* (*aux.* avere)

to lack, be lacking (in) (= *di*.)

difettivo *&* **difettóso**, *a.* defective, faulty. **difètto**, *m.* defect, blemish, flaw; failing, want.

diffamàre (*pr.* -àmo), *v.t.* to defame. **diffamatòrio**, *a.* defamatory. **diffamazióne**, *f.* defamation.

differènza, *f.* difference; dissension. *a* ∼ *di*, unlike. **differenziàle**, *a. & m.* differential. **differenziàre** (*pr.* -ènzio, -ènzi), *v.t.* to differentiate, discriminate.

differíre (*pr.* -ísco, -isci, *&c.*, like *ferire*), *v.i.* (*aux.* avere) to differ; (*v.t.*) to postpone, defer.

difficíle, *a.* difficult. **difficoltà**, *f.inv.* difficulty. **difficoltóso**, *a.* full of difficulties; (*pers.*) always looking for difficulties.

diffída, *f.* public notice; warning. **diffidàre** (*pr.* -ído), *v.i.* (*aux.* avere) ∼ *di*, to distrust, mistrust; (*v.t.*) (*Law*) to give public notice or warning. **diffidènte**, *a.* distrustful, suspicious. **diffidènza**, *f.* suspicion, distrust.

diffóndere (*pr.* -óndo, *&c.*, like *confondere*), *v.t. ir.* to diffuse; spread, pour out; shed; (*fig.*) propagate, give wide circulation to.

difformàre, *v.t.* to deform. **diffórme**, *a.* unlike, different.

diffrazióne, *f.* diffraction.

diffušióne, *f.* diffusion; diffuseness, prolixity. **diffúso**, *p.p.* of *diffondere.* ¶ *a.* diffuse, diffused.

difilàto, *ad.* (with *andare* or *venire*) straight, forthwith, immediately, directly.

difteríte, *f.* diphtheria.

díga (*pl.* **dighe**), *f.* dyke; dam; sea wall; barrier, (*fig.*) obstacle; defence.

digeríbile, *a.* digestible. **digeríre** (*pr.* -ísco, isci), *v.t.* to digest; (*fig.*) tolerate, endure, brook, stomach; (*study*) master. **digestióne**, *f.* digestion. **digestívo**, *a. & m.* digestive. **digèsto**, *m.* digest·(*Law*, *&c.*).

dighiacciàre (*pr.* -àccio, -àcci), *v.i.* (*aux.* avere) to thaw, melt.

Digióne, *f.* Dijon.

digitàle, *a.* of the finger[s]; finger (*att.*). *impronte* ∼*i*, *f.pl.* fingerprints. ¶ *f.* digitalis, fox-glove (*Bot.*). **digitazióne**, *f.* (*Mus.*) fingering.

digiunàre (*pr.* -úno), *v.i.* (*aux.* avere) to fast. **digiúno**, *a.* fasting, hungry; lacking (in), devoid (of = *di*), ignorant (of). ¶ *m.* fasting, fast.

dignità, *f.inv.* dignity; rank. **dignitóso,** *a.* dignified.

digradàre (*pr.* **-àdo**), *v.i.* (*aux.* essere) to slope (down); descend little by little, or step by step; fall gradually away; decline; diminish; (*of colours*) shade off; (*v.t.*) degrade; (*of colours*) soften.

digrassàre (*pr.* **-àsso**), *v.t.* to remove grease or fat from; scour; skim.

digressióne, *f.* digression.

digrignàre (*pr.* **-ígno**), *v.t.* to gnash (the teeth); (*animal*) show its teeth.

digrossàre (*pr.* **-òsso**), *v.t.* to reduce (in size), whittle down, rough-hew; (*fig.*) sharpen; teach the rudiments of a subject to.

digrumàre (*pr.* **-úmo**), *v.i.* (*aux.* avere) & *t.* to ruminate, chew the cud; eat greedily; (*fig.*) meditate, ponder.

diguazzàre (*pr.* **-àzzo**), *v.t.* to stir, shake, beat up; (*v.i.*) (*aux.* avere) to splash about; paddle, dabble.

dilaceràre (*pr.* **-àcero**), *v.t.* to lacerate; rend.

dilagàre (*pr.* **-àgo, -àghi**), *v.i.* (*aux.* essere) & **dilagàrsi,** *v.refl.* to flood, form a lake.

dilaniàre (*pr.* **-ànio, -àni**), *v.t.* to tear to pieces, rend (*lit.* & *fig.*).

dilapidàre (*pr.* **-àpido**), *v.t.* to squander, waste, dissipate.

dilatàre (*pr.* **-àto**), *v.t.* to dilate, extend. **dilatàrsi,** *v.refl.* to expand. **dilatazióne,** *f.* dilation, distension; expansion. *coefficiente di* ∼ *termica,* *m.* coefficient of thermal expansion.

dilavàre (*pr.* **-àvo**), *v.t.* to wash out, wash away.

dilazionàre, *v.t.* (*Com.*) to postpone, delay, defer. **dilazióne,** *f.* delay; respite.

dileggiàre (*pr.* **-éggio, -éggi**), *v.t.* to mock, scoff at. **diléggio** (*pl.* **-éggi**), *m.* derision, mockery; jeer, gibe.

dileguàre (*pr.* **-éguo**), *v.t.* to disperse, scatter, cause to disappear. **dileguàrsi,** *v.refl.* to disappear, vanish; dissolve (*mist,* &*c.*).

dilèmma (*pl.* **-èmmi**), *m.* dilemma.

dilettànte, *pr.p.* of *dilettare*. ¶ *m.* amateur, dilettante. **dilettantìsmo,** *m.* dilettantism. **dilettàre** (*pr.* **-étto**), *v.t.* & ∼ **a,** *v.i.* (*aux.* avere) to delight, give delight; please; amuse. **dilettàrsi,** *v.refl.* to take delight in (a, di, = in). **dilettévole** & **dilettóso,** *a.* delightful. **dilètto,**

m. pleasure, delight. ¶ *a.* beloved, much loved, dear. **dilezióne,** *f.* pure affection, spiritual love.

diligènte, *a.* diligent, careful, zealous. **diligenteménte,** *ad.* diligently. **diligènza,** *f.* diligence, care, assiduity; mail-coach.

dilombàrsi (*pr.* **-ómbo**), *v.refl.* to strain one's back. **dilombàto,** *p.a.* worn-out, enfeebled; (*of horses*) broken-backed.

dilucidàre (*pr.* **-úcido**), *v.t.* to clear up, explain, elucidate.

dilúcolo & **dilúculo,** *m.* day-break, first light of dawn.

diluíre (*pr.* **-ísco, -ísci**), *v.t.* to dissolve; dilute.

dilungàre, *v.t.* to prolong, remove farther off, keep at a distance. **dilungàrsi,** *v.refl.* to move away; digress, wander from the subject; expatiate.

dilúngo, *ad.* continuously; directly, straight on.

diluviàle, *a.* torrential, in a deluge. **diluviàre** (*pr.* **-úvio**), *v.i.* (*aux.* avere) & *v.impers.* (*aux.* essere) to rain in a deluge, or torrentially; (*fig.*) descend in floods; (*v.t.*) to eat voraciously, devour. **dilúvio** (*pl.* **-úvi**), *m.* deluge; abundance. **diluvióne,** *m.* (*f.* **-óna**) gross eater.

dimagràre (*pr.* **-àgro**) & **dimagríre** (*pr.* **-ísco, -ísci**), *v.t.* to make lean; *v.i.* (*aux.* essere), to become lean; lose weight.

dimandàre, see *domandare*.

dimàni, see *domani*.

dimenàre (*pr.* **-éno**), *v.t.* to shake, move back & forward, wag, swish (*tail*); beat [up] (*eggs*), knead (*paste,* &*c.*). ∼ *le ganasce,* to eat greedily. **dimenàrsi,** *v.refl.* to stir, move restlessly. **dimenío** (*pl.* **-íi,** *m.* agitation, constant shaking, &c.

dimenticànza, *f.* forgetfulness. **dimenticàre** (*pr.* **-éntico, -éntichi**), *v.t.* & **dimenticàrsi,** *v.refl.* to forget. **diméntico** (*pl.* **-éntichi**), *a.* forgetful.

dimessaménte, *ad.* humbly, modestly, submissively. **dimésso,** *p.p.* of *dimettere*. ¶ *a.* humble, modest, submissive; neglected, shabby.

dimestichézza, *f.* intimacy, familiarity. **dimèstico,** *a.* familiar, domestic.

diméttere (*pr.* **-étto,** &*c.*, like *mettere*), *v.t. ir.* to dismiss; remove; give up, renounce; condone. **diméttersi,** *v.refl.* to resign.

dimezzàre (*pr.* -èżżo), *v.t.* to divide in half, halve.
diminuíre (*pr.* -ísco, -ísci), *v.t.* to lessen, diminish, lower, reduce; *v.i.* (*aux.* essere) to grow less, diminish, decrease, decline, abate. **diminuíto**, *p.p.* of *diminuire.* ¶ *a.* reduced, shortened. **diminutívo**, *a. & m.* diminutive.
dimissionàrio (*pl.* -àri), *a.* resigned, retiring (*from office*). **dimissióne**, *f.* dismissal; resignation (*oft. pl.*). *offrire le sue* ∼*i*, to offer his resignation.
dimoiàre (*pr.* -òio), *v.i.* (*aux.* essere) to thaw. *neve dimoiata*, *f.* slush.
dimòra, *f.* stay; residence; dwelling; home; place of residence; delay. **dimoràre** (*pr.* -òro) *v.i.* (*aux.* avere) to reside, live, dwell; stay, remain, stop.
dimostrànte, *p.a.* demonstrating; proving. ¶ *m.* demonstrator. **dimostràre** (*pr.* -óstro), *v.t.* to show, display; demonstrate; prove, explain; *v.i.* (*aux.* avere) to show, give signs (of), appear. **dimostràrsi**, *v.refl.* to show oneself; prove oneself. **dimostrazióne**, *f.* demonstration, proof; sign, mark.
dimozzàre, see *smozzare.*
dína, *f.* (*Phys.*) dyne (*unit of force*).
dinàmica, *f.* dynamics. **dinàmico** (*pl.* -àmici), *a.* dynamic. **dinamísmo**, *m.* dynamic strength. **dinamíte**, *f.* dynamite. **dínamo**, *f.inv.* dynamo.
dinànzi, *ad.* in front, forward, before; (*of time*) formerly, before, ere now. ¶ *pr.* ∼ *&* ∼**a**, in front of, in the presence of, opposite; in comparison with. ¶ *m.* front, front portion; also *att. e.g. le ruote* ∼, the front wheels. *i denti* ∼, the front teeth.
dinastía, *f.* dynasty. **dinàsta** (*pl.* -àsti), *m.* dynast. **dinàstico** (*pl.* -àstici), *a.* dynastic.
dindín *or* **dindòn**, *onom.* ding-dong.
díndo *or* **díndio**, *m.* turkey.
dinegàre, *v.t.* to deny, refuse. **diniègo** (*pl.* -èghi), *m.* refusal, denial.
dinoccolàre (*pr.* -òccolo), *v.t.* to dislocate; break the neck of. **dinoccolàto**, *a.* listless, indifferent; feeble, tottering; awkward, clumsy.
dintórno *or* **d'intórno**, *ad.* around, round about, on every side, about. ¶ *pr.* ∼ a, [a]round. *levarsi* ∼, to get rid of. ¶ *m.pl. dintorni*, surroundings, neighbourhood.

Dío, *m.* God. *pl. gli dei*, the (pagan) gods. **dío**, *a.* (*Poet.*) divine.
diòcesi, *f.* diocese.
dioríte, *f.* (*Miner.*) diorite.
diottría, *f.* (*Opt.*) diopter. **diòttrico** (*pl.* -òttrici), *a.* dioptric(al).
dipanàre (*pr.* -àno), *v.t.* to unravel; disentangle; wind into a ball.
dipartiménto, *m.* department.
dipartírsi (*pr.* -àrto, -àrti), *v.refl.* to go away, depart; branch off, diverge; differ; digress. **dipartíta**, *f.* departure; (*fig.*) death.
dipendènte, *a.* depending. ¶ *m.* subordinate, dependant. **dipendènza**, *f.* dependence, dependency. **dipèndere** (*pr.* -èndo), *v.i. ir.* (*aux.* essere) to depend, derive, be contingent.
dipíngere (*pr.* -ingo, -íngi), *v.t. ir.* to paint, portray (*lit. & fig.*), depict. **dipíngersi**, *v.refl.* to paint oneself; be depicted. **dipínto**, *p.p.* of *dipingere.* ¶ *a.* painted; frescoed. ¶ *m.* painting (*often mural p.*).
diplòma (*pl.* -òmi), *m.* diploma, charter, certificate. **diplomàtica**, *f.* study of old charters and documents, palaeography. **diplomàtico** (*pl.* -àtici), *a.* diplomatic. ¶ *m.* diplomatist. **diplomazía**, *f.* diplomacy.
dipòi, *ad.* after, afterwards.
diportàrsi, *v.refl.* to behave. **dipòrto**, *m.* recreation, amusement.
diprèsso, *ad.* near, nearby. *a un* ∼, very nearly, approximately.
dipsòmane, *m. & f.* dipsomaniac. **dipsomanía**, *f.* dipsomania.
diradàre (*pr.* -àdo), *v.t.* to thin [out], space out, do (something) seldom. ∼ *le visite*, to be a rare visitor. *v.i.* (*aux.* essere) & **diradàrsi**, *v.refl.* to become thin or rare; dissolve, (*of weather*) clear.
diramàre (*pr.* -àmo), *v.t.* to cut away branches, prune, lop; send out, circulate (*notices, &c.*). **diramàrsi**, *v.rifl.* to branch out, branch off. **diramazióne**, *f.* lopping, pruning, thinning out; ramification, branching off.
dirazzàre, *v.i.* (*aux.* avere) to degenerate, lose the qualities of one's race or family.
díre (*pr.* díco, díci, díce, diciàmo, díte, dícono), *v.t. ir.* to say, tell; call; speak; suggest; bid (*adieu, auction*); attest; harmonize, suit. *si dice*, it is said. *dirsela con alcuno*, to agree (or be on good terms) with

someone. *dir la sua*, to give one's own opinion. *il giuoco mi dice*, the game is in my favour. *non c'è che dire*, it's a fact. *aver che dire con uno*, to have words, to quarrel with someone. *trovare a dire*, to find fault. *voler dire*, to mean. ¶ *m.* speech, words, saying; assertion; allegation. *arte del ~*, elocution. *ha un bel ~*, talk as he may. *oltre ogni ~*, beyond all description. *al~di tutti*, according to what everybody says. **dírsi**, *v.refl.* to style oneself.

direnàre, *v.t.* to fatigue; break the back of. **direnàrsi**, *v.refl.* to break one's back; be knocked up.

direttaménte, *ad.* directly, immediately, instantly. **direttíssimo**, *m.* express [train]. **direttíva**, *f.* direction, directive. **direttívo**, *a.* managing, leading; directive. *consiglio ~*, board of managers. **dirètto**, *p.p.* of dirigere. ¶ *a.* direct, straight; immediate; through (*carriage*), bound for (= *a*). ¶ *m.* quick train. **direttóre**, *m.* (*f.* -**tríce**) manager (*f.* manageress); editor; principal; head-master, h.-mistress; director; warden; leader. *~ delle poste*, Post Master. *~ dei lavori*, works manager. **dirigènte**, *p.a.* directing. ¶ *m.* director. *classi ~i, f.pl.* ruling classes. **direzióne**, *f.* direction; steering; management; director's office, editorial office (*newspaper, &c.*). **dirígere** (*pr.* -**ígo, ígi**), *v.t. ir.* to direct, manage, conduct; address. **dirigíbile**, *a.* dirigible. ¶ *m.* air-ship, dirigible.

dirímere (*pr.* -**imo, -ìmi**), *v.t.* to annul, invalidate; cut short, break off.

dirimpètto, *ad.* opposite. ¶ *~ a, pr.* opposite; in comparison with.

dirítta, *f.* right hand, right side, right. **dirítto**, *m.* right, law (*natural, moral, or written*), duty, reason; due, fee; study of law, giurisprudence; (*of medal, cloth, &c.*) face, right side. *a ~*, rightly. *a maggior ~*, with all the more reason. *di ~*, by right. *a ~ o a rovescio*, by hook or by crook. *~ di nascita*, *~ del sangue*, birthright. *~i d'autore*, copyright; royalties. *~i di riproduzione cinematografica*, film rights. *~ i di riproduzione giornalistica*, serial rights. *~ di ritenzione*, lien. *~ delle genti*, law of nations. *~ canonico*, canon law. *i ~ i dell' uomo*, the rights of man. *~ comune*,

common law. ¶ *~ or* **drítto**, *a.* straight; upright, erect; plumb; straight-forward, honest; right; right-hand[ed]. *nel ~ mezzo*, right in the middle, in the exact middle. ¶ *ad.* straight, straight on, straight ahead, straight forward; directly; rightly, honestly. *virare ~*, to aim straight. *andare ~, tirare ~*, to go straight ahead.

dirittúra, *f.* direction in a straight line; straightness; rectitude, honesty; (*race course*) straight. *a ~, or* **addirittúra**, *ad.* entirely, completely; absolutely; surely; forthwith.

dirizzàre (*pr.* -**ízzo**), *v.t.* to straighten; erect, hold up; direct, put right. *~ le orecchie*, to prick up one's ears. **dirizzàrsi**, *v.refl.* to draw oneself up, stand erect; address oneself; apply (to = *a*). **dirizzatúra**, *f.* [hair] parting. **dirizzóne**, *m.* thoughtless action or resolve; caprice; bad habit.

diro, *a.* dire, cruel.

diroccàre (*pr.* -**òcco, -òcchi**), *v.t.* to demolish, dismantle. **diroccàrsi**, *v.refl.* to fall with a crash.

dirómpere (*pr.* -**ómpo, &c.**, like rompere), *v.t. ir.* to soften, slacken, make supple; break, break in (*horses*); exercise, render agile, inure; (*v.i.*) *~ in*, to break into, burst into (*tears, laughter*). *bomba dirompente*, demolition bomb. **dirómpersi**, *v.refl.* to become soft or slack; become accustomed or inured.

dirottaménte, *ad.* abundantly, beyond measure; in torrents (*rain or tears*). **dirótto**, *p.p.* of dirompere. ¶ *a.* pouring, pelting, in torrents.

dirozzàre (*pr.* -**ózzo**), *v.t.* to rough-hew; refine, civilize.

dirugginíre (*pr.* -**ísco, -ísci**), *v.t.* to remove the rust from. *~ i denti*, to grind the teeth together.

dirupàre (*pr.* -**úpo**), *v.i.* (*aux.* essere) to plunge down; (*v.t.*) to hurl down. **dirupàto**, *a.* abrupt; rocky. **dirúpo**, *m.* rocky precipice, steep slope.

dirúto, *a.* (*Poet.*) ruined, fallen in ruins, dismantled.

disabbellíre (*pr.* -**ísco, -ísci**), *v.t.* to spoil the beauty of; disfigure. **disabbellírsi**, *v.refl.* to lose one's beauty.

disabitàto, *a.* uninhabited.

disaccóncio, *a.* unsuited.

disadàtto, *a.* unfitted, unfit; incapable;

untimely. **disadornàre** (*pr.* -**órno**), *v.t.* to disfigure; strip of ornament. **disadórno**, *a.* unadorned, bare.

disaffezionàre (*pr.* -**óno**), *v.t.* to alienate one's affection for, estrange. **disaffezionàrsi** (**da**), *v.refl.* to lose one's affection for. **disaffezióne**, *f.* loss of affection, want of sympathy, estrangement.

disagévole, *a.* uneasy, uncomfortable; difficult, hard.

disaggradévole, *a.* disagreeable, displeasing. **disaggradíre** (*pr.* -**ísco**, -**ísci**, *v.t.* to displease.

disagiàto, *a.* uncomfortable; needy. **disàgio** (*pl.* -**àgi**), *m.* discomfort; hardship; want. **a** ~, uncomfortable, ill at ease.

disalberàre (*pr.* -**àlbero**), *v.t.* to dismast.

disamàbile, *a.* unlovable. **disamàre**, *v.t.* to cease to love.

disamèno, *a.* unpleasant, disagreeable.

disàmina, *f.* close examination. **disaminàre** (*pr.* -**àmino**), *v.t.* to examine carefully or critically.

disamoràre (*pr.* -**óro**), *v.t.* to estrange. **disamóre**, *m.* indifference, dislike, estrangement. **disamoràrsi**, *v.refl.* to cease to love; lose interest in (with *pr.* **da**).

disanimàre (*pr.* -**ànimo**), *v.t.* to dishearten.

disappetènza, *f.* loss of appetite, disgust at food.

disapplicazióne, *f.* negligence, want of application.

disapprèndere (*pr.* -**èndo**, *&c.*, like *prendere*), *v.t. ir.* to unlearn.

disappúnto, *m.* disappointment; trouble, vexation.

disarmàre (*pr.* -**àrmo**), *v.t.* to disarm; dismantle. ~ **i** *remi*, to ship the oars. (*v.i.*) (*aux.* avere) to disarm. **disarmàto**, *p.a.* disarmed; (*ship*) out of commission. **disarmísta** (*pl.* -**ísti**), *m.* advocate of disarmament. **disàrmo**, *m.* disarmament.

disarticolàre (*pr.* -**ícolo**), *v.t.* to disjoint; untie.

disàstro, *m.* disaster. **disastróso**, *a.* disastrous, ruinous.

disattènto, *a.* inattentive, negligent.

disattitúdine, *f.* incapacity. **disattivàre**, *v.t.* (*Nav.*) to put out of action (*mine*, *&c.*).

disavànzo, *m.* deficit.

disavvedúto, *a.* heedless.

disavvenènte, *a.* unattractive, unprepossessing.

disavventúra, *a.* mishap, accident, misadventure. **disavventuràto**, *a.* unlucky, unfortunate.

disavvertènza, *f.* inadvertence; lack of attention.

disavvezzàre (*pr.* -**ézzo**), *v.t.* to disaccustom, dissuade, free from the habit of. **disavvezzàrsi**, *v.refl.* to lose the habit (of); neglect the attraction (of). **disavvézzo**, *a.* unaccustomed.

disbórso, *m.* disbursement; advance, laying out (*of money*). *essere* (*rimanere, trovarsi*) *in* ~, to be out of pocket.

disbramàre, *v.t.* to gratify (*a wish*), to satisfy (*a desire*).

disbrigàre (*pr.* -**ígo**, -**íghi**), *v.t.* to disentangle; d.spatch; clear off (*correspondence*, *&c.*); get (*someone*) out of a scrape. **disbrigàrsi**, *v.refl.* to get out of a difficulty, extricate oneself; get rid of; make haste. **disbrígo**, *m.* dispatch; prompt settlement.

discàrica, *f.* voucher. **discàrico**, *m.* discharge; excuse; easing; alleviation; justification, defence. *a* ~ *di coscienza*, to ease one's conscience.

discàro, *a.* disagreeable, unacceptable.

discendènte, *a.* descending. ¶ *m.* descendant. **discendènza**, *f.* lineage, stock, extraction; origin; descendants. **discéndere** (*pr.* -**éndo**, *&c.*, like *scendere*), *v.i. ir.* (*aux.* essere & avere) to descend, go down, lead down; sink, fall; spring (from); pass on; stay, put up.

discentràre (*pr.* -**èntro**), *v.t.* to decentralize.

discépolo, *m.* disciple, pupil, follower.

discèrnere (*pr.* -**èrno**, *&c.*, like *cernere*), *v.t. ir.* to discern, distinguish; choose; distribute. **discernimento**, *m.* discernment, judgment.

discervellàto, *a.* hare-brained, foolish, idiotic.

discésa, *f.* descent, declivity; fall; (*Radio*) lead-in; ~ *in picchiata*, (*Aviat.*) nose-dive.

dischiúdere, *v.t. ir.* to open; disclose, reveal.

discíngere (*pr.* -**ingo** -**íngi**), *v.t. ir.* to ungird, undo. **discínto**, *a.* ungirt.

disciògliere (*pr.* -**òlgo**, *&c.*, like *sciogliere*), *v.t. ir.* to loosen, unbind, undo, untie; pardon, release;

dissolve, melt. **disciòlto,** *p.p.* of *disciogliere.* ¶ *a.* loose; nimble; dissolved.

disciplina, *f.* discipline; instruction; subject of instruction; punishment; penance. **disciplinàre** (*pr.* **-íno, -íni**), *v.t.* to discipline. **disciplinatézza,** *f.* submission to discipline, habit of obedience.

dísco (*pl.* **díschi**), *m.* discus, quoit, disc; disk; railway signal; dial (*telephone*); record (*gramophone*). ~ *sul ghiaccio,* ice-hockey. ~ *volante,* 'flying saucer.'

díscolo, *a.* idle, dissolute, undisciplined, wild. ¶ *m.* rake; truant.

discólpa, *f.* exculpation; defence; excuse. **discolpàre** (*pr.* **-ólpo**), *v.t.* to exculpate, clear, free from blame. **discolpàrsi,** *v.refl.* to clear oneself, prove one's innocence.

disconoscènza, *f.* lack of appreciation; inability to recognize; ingratitude. **disconóscere** (*pr.* **-ósco,** &c., like *conoscere*), *v.t.* ir. to refuse to recognize, ignore, slight; be ungrateful for.

disconvenévole, *a.* inconvenient. **disconveníre** (*pr.* **-èngo,** &c., like *venire*), *v.i.* ir. (*aux.* essere) to be inconvenient or unsuitable; disagree.

discopèrto, *p.p.* of *discoprire.* ¶ *a.* open, unsheltered, unprotected. *a* ~, in the open, under the open sky. **discopríre,** *v.t.* to uncover.

discordàre (*pr.* **-òrdo**), *v.i.* (*aux.* avere) to be discordant, be out of tune; jar; disagree. **discòrde,** *a.* dissonant, discordant. **discòrdia,** *f.* discord, dissension, lack of harmony, variance. **discòrdo,** *m.* (*Poet.*) discord.

discórrere (*pr.* **-órro,** &c., like *correre*), *v.i.* ir. (*aux.* avere) to discourse, descant; talk; reason, hold forth. *e via discorrendo,* etcetera, and so forth. **discórso,** *m.* talk; discourse, speech, oration, address; commentary, treatise. ~ *della Corona,* speech from the Throne. *questo è un altro* ~, this is another story.

discòsto, *a.* distant, far; removed. ¶ *ad,* at some distance, far off.

discrédere (*pr.* **-édo**), *v.t.* to disbelieve. **discrédersi,** *v.refl.* to change one's mind.

discreditàre, *v.t.* to discredit. **discrédito,** *m.* discredit, disrepute.

discrepànza, *f.* discrepancy, difference; dissension.

discretaménte, *ad.* moderately tolerably, sufficiently, discreetly. **discretézza,** *f.* moderation, prudence, discretion. **discretíva,** *f.* power of discrimination or discernment. **discretívo** & **discrezionàle,** *a.* discretionary. **discréto,** *a.* moderate, fairly good; reasonable; discreet. **discrezióne,** *f.* discretion; moderation; judgment; will; free choice.

discussióne, *f.* discussion, debate; controversy. **discússo,** *p.p.* of *discutere,* discussed, examined. **discútere** (*pr.* **-úto**), *v.t.* ir. to discuss, debate, argue (over). **discutíbile,** *a.* disputable.

diśdegnàre, *v.t.* to disdain. **diśdégno,** *m.* disdain. **diśdegnóso,** *a.* disdainful.

diśdétta, *f.* notice to leave (either of landlord or tenant); termination of contract; withdrawal of subscription; calling in or settlement of a loan; forfeit; bad luck. **diśdétto,** *p.p.* of *disdire.* ¶ *a.* cancelled; withdrawn; revoked. **diśdíre** (*pr.* **-íco,** &c., like *dire*), *v.t.* ir. to cancel, discontinue, give up; withdraw; revoke, retract; take back (*words*), unsay; recant, disavow. (*v.i.*) (*aux.* avere) to be unbecoming, unfitting. **diśdírsi,** *v.refl.* to retract (one's words); contradict oneself; recant.

diśdòro, *m.* dishonour, shame.

diśegnàre (*pr.* **-égno**), *v.t.* to draw, sketch; design, describe, project; (*v.i.*) (*aux.* avere) to plan, resolve. **diśegnatóre,** *m.* (*f.* **-tríce**) designer, draughtsman. **diśégno,** *m.* design, drawing, illustration; art of design[ing]; sketch, sketching; draft; project, plan; intention, purpose. ~ *di legge,* bill (*parliamentary*). ~ *a mano libera,* free-hand drawing.

diśeguàle, *a.,* see *disuguale.*

diśeredàre (*pr.* **-édo**), *v.t.* to disinherit.

diśertàre (*pr.* **-èrto**), *v.t.* to lay waste, ravage, destroy, (*v.t.* & *i.*) (*aux.* avere) to desert; miss an appointment. **diśèrto,** *sync. p.p.* of *disertare.* ¶ *a.* spoiled, laid waste; (fr. Lat. *disertus*) eloquent. **diśertóre,** *m.* deserter. **diśerzióne,** *f.* desertion.

disfaciménto, *m.* dissolution, destruction, breaking up, decomposition. **disfàre** (*pr.* disfò or disfàccio, disfài, &c., like *fare*), *v.t.* ir. to undo; break up, take to pieces;

give up (*house*); destroy, rout, defeat; wear out. **disfàrsi**, *v.refl.* to dissolve, melt, decompose; fall to pieces, come undone. ~ *di*, to get rid of, dispose of. **disfàtta**, *f.* defeat, rout, overthrow. **disfattísta** (*pl.* -ísti), *a. & m.* defeatist. **disfàtto**, *a.* undone, defeated; worn out.

disfída, *f.* challenge; duel; contest.

disfioràre, *v.t.* to deflower, dishonour.

disfunzióne, *f.* (*Med.*) disorder, irregularity.

diśgiúngere (*pr.* -úngo, &*c.*, like *giungere*), *v.t. ir.* to separate. **diśgiuntívo**, *a.* (*Gram.*) disjunctive.

diśgradévole, *a.*, see *sgradevole*.

diśgràdo, *m.* dislike.   *a* ~, unwillingly. *avere a* ~, to dislike.

diśgràzia, *f.* misfortune, accident; disfavour; (*pl.*) casualties. *per* ~, & **diśgraziataménte**, *ad.* unfortunately. **diśgraziàto**, *a.* unfortunate, wretched; unhappy; awkward, ungraceful.

diśgregàre (*pr.* -égo, -éghi), *v.t. &* **diśgregàrsi**, *v.refl.* to break up, separate.

diśguído, *m.* miscarriage, loss (*letter, parcel,* &*c.*).

diśgustàre (*pr.* -ústo), *v.t.* to offend (*the senses*); shock, sicken; disgust; displease, vex. **diśgustàrsi**, *v.refl.* to take a dislike for (or to) (= *di*): be at variance; become less friendly. **diśgústo**, *m.* disgust, loathing; aversion, antipathy; distaste.

disíllabo, *a. & m.* (*Gram.*) disyllabic, disyllable.

diśimballàre, *v.t.* to unpack.

diśimpacciàre, *v.t.* to free from embarrassment; extricate from difficulties.

diśimparàre (*pr.* -àro), *v.t.* to unlearn, forget.

diśimpegnàre (*pr.* -égno), *v.t.* to release from an obligation; redeem an object given in pledge or in pawn; disengage; clear (e.g. *rigging, anchor or screw*). **diśimpégno**, *m.* what serves to free one from a pledge or promise, disengagement; fulfilment; release.

diśincantàre, *v.t.* to disenchant.

diśincatenàre, *v.t.* to unchain.

diśinfettànte, *a. & m.* disinfectant. **diśinfettàre** (*pr.* -étto), *v.t.* to disinfect.

diśingannàre, *v.t.* to undeceive, disabuse. **diśingànno**, *m.* disillusion; disappointment.

diśingranàre, *v.t.* to throw (put) out of gear.

diśinnamorare, *v.t.* to estrange, destroy one's love for, put out of conceit with.

diśinnestàre, *v.t.* (*Mech.*) to disconnect, disengage. ~ *la frizione*, (*Motor*) to declutch.

diśinseríre (*pr.* -ísco, -ísci) *v.t.* (*Elec.*) to disconnect.

diśintegràre, *v.t.* (*Phys.*) to disintegrate, split (*atom*).

diśinteressàre (*pr.* -èsso), *v.t.* to make one lose interest; to buy out (one's interest). **diśinteressàto**, *a.* disinterested. **diśinterèsse**, *m.* disinterestedness; indifference; unselfishness.

diśinvitàre, *v.t.* to ask not to come; withdraw an invitation.

diśinvòlto, *a.* self-possessed, frank, of easy manners. **diśinvoltúra**, *f.* coolness; ease; impudence.

diśistíma, *f.* disesteem, contempt. **diśistimàre**, *v.t.* to disesteem, slight.

dislivèllo, *m.* unevenness, difference of level.

dislocaménto, *m.* displacement. **dislocare** (*pr.* -òco, -òchi), *v.t.* to displace.

dislogàre, *v.t.* to dislocate.

diśmembràre, *v.t.* to dismember; forget.

diśméttere, *v.t. ir.* to leave off; cast off; dismantle.

diśmiśúra, *f.* excess, superfluity, redundance. *a* ~, excessively.

diśoccupàto, *a.* unoccupied, unemployed; idle, out of work. **diśoccupazióne**, *f.* unemployment.

diśonóre, *m.* dishonour, disgrace, shame. **diśonorévole**, *a.* dishonourable.

disópra, *ad.* above; upstairs. *al* ~ *di*, over, above. *per* ~, into the bargain. *prendere il* ~, to gain the upper hand.

diśordinàre (*pr.* -órdino), *v.t.* 'to throw into disorder, upset, disarrange; confuse; derange; (*v.i.*) (*aux.* avere) to go to excess. **diśordinàto**, *a.* confused, disorderly, wild; intemperate; extravagant. **diśórdine**, *m.* disorder, confusion, excess; malady, disease.

diśorientàre (*pr.* -ènto), *v.t.* to make one lose one's bearings or direction; (*fig.*) to disconcert; bewilder. confuse. **diśorientàrsi**, *v.refl.* to lose one's bearings; become bewildered or confused.

disormeggiàre, *v.t.* to unmoor.

disòssàre (*pr.* **-òsso**), *v.t.* to bone (*fowl, &c.*).

disótto, *ad.* below, underneath, downstairs. ¶ *pr.* below, under. *al ~ di,* below, under, lower than. *avere il ~,* to have the disadvantage, to have the worst of it.

dispàccio (*pl.* **-àcci**), *m.* dispatch, telegram.

disparàto, *a.* disparate, essentially different, incommensurable.

disparére, *m.* difference of opinion, disagreement.

dìspari, *a.inv.* odd (*number*); different, unequal. **disparità,** *f.inv.* disparity, difference, inequality.

dispàrte, *ad.* aside, apart. *in ~,* some way off, out of the way. *tirarsi in ~,* to keep aloof.

dispèndio (*pl.* **-èndi**), *m.* (heavy) expense, expenditure. **dispendióso,** *a.* expensive.

dispènsa, *f.* distribution; allotted portion; store-room; pantry; sideboard; part of a work published in parts; exemption; (*Eccl.*) licence for marriage between relations; (*Law*) dispensation.

dispensàre (*pr.* **-ènso**), *v.t.* to distribute, dispense; exempt; relax (*a rule*); remove (*an obstacle*). **dispensàrio,** *m.* dispensary. **dispensière,** *m.* distributor; steward.

dispepsía, *f.* dyspepsia. **dispèptico** (*pl.* **-pèptici**), *a. & m.* dyspeptic.

disperàre (*pr.* **-èro**), *v.i.* (*aux.* avere) to despair. **disperazióne,** *f.* desperation, despair.

dispèrdere (*pr.* **-èrdo,** *&c.,* like *perdere*), *v.t. ir.* to disperse, scatter; dispel; waste, squander. **dispersióne,** *f.* dispersion; loss; waste. **dispèrso,** *p.p.* of *disperdere.* ¶ *a.* dispersed, scattered, squandered; lost, missing.

dispètto, *m.* vexation, annoyance; ill-humour; spite; resentment. *a ~ di,* in spite of. *far ~ a,* to provoke. *avere a ~,* to despise. **dispettóso,** *a.* spiteful, scornful.

dispiacére (*pr.* **-iàccio,** *&c.,* like *piacere*), *v.i. ir.* (*aux.* essere) to displease. *me ne dispiace,* I am sorry for it. *se non vi dispiace,* if you please. ¶ *m.* displeasure; regret; annoyance.

dispnèa, *f.* (*Med.*) difficulty in breathing.

disponènte, *m.* (*Law*) testator. **disponìbile,** *a.* disposable. *posto ~,* vacant post. **disponibilità,** *f.inv.* availability; (*pl.*) available funds, liquid assets. *in ~* (*Mil.*) unattached.

dispórre (*pr.* **-óngo,** *&c.,* like *porre*), *v.t. ir.* to dispose, arrange, display, prepare; (*v.i.*) (*aux.* avere) to direct, provide, order. *~ di,* to dispose of, make testamentary disposition of; (*with inf.*) to arrange to. **dispórsi,** *v.refl.* to prepare; resolve. **dispositívo,** *m.* (*Mech.*) contrivance, appliance, device; (*Phot.*) adapter. *~ di comando,* (*Elec.*) control device. *~ di sicurezza,* safety appliance, safety catch. **disposizióne,** *f.* disposition, disposal; arrangement; natural bent, inclination; order, direction. **dispostézza,** *f.* orderly arrangement of (the) parts, shapeliness; composure; readiness, alertness. **dispósto,** *p.p.* of *disporre.* ¶ *a.* ready, prepared, inclined. *ben ~,* in good order; vigorous, active.

dispòtico (*pl.* **-òtici**), *a.* despotic. **dispotísmo,** *m.* despotism.

dispregévole, *a.* contemptible. **dispregiatívo,** *a.* contemptuous, disparaging; (*Gram.*) depreciatory (*suffixes*). **disprègio,** *m.* disparagement, contempt.

disprezzàbile, *a.* contemptible, despicable. **disprezzàre** (*pr.* **-èzzo**) or **dispregiàre** (*pr.* **-ègio**), *v.t.* to despise, scorn, disparage, undervalue. **disprèzzo,** *m.* scorn, disdain.

dìsputa, *f.* dispute, altercation, debate. **disputàre** (*pr.* **dìsputo**), *v.i. & t.* (*aux.* avere) to dispute, contest. **disputàrsi,** *v.refl.* to contend for. **disputazióne,** *f.* disputation, discussion.

dissanguàre (*pr.* **-ànguo, -àngui**), *v.t.* to bleed; impoverish; exhaust, ruin; (*fig.*) draw heavily on one's means.

dissapóre, *m.* disagreement (*between friends*), misunderstanding.

dissecàre (*pr.* **-éco, -échi**), *v.t.* to dissect.

disseccàre (*pr.* **-écco, -écchi**), *v.t.* to dry up, parch.

dissennàre (*pr.* **-énno**), *v.t.* to deprive of one's senses, drive one crazy.

dissènso, *m.* dissent, disagreement.

dissentería, *f.* (*Med.*) dysentery.

dissentíre (*pr.* **-ènto,** &*c.*, like *sentire*), *v.i.* (*aux.* avere) to dissent, disagree.

disseppellíre (*pr.* **-ísco,** &*c.*, like *seppellire*), *v.t.* to disinter, exhume; (*fig.*) unearth.

disserràre (*pr.* **-èrro**), *v.t.* to unlock, unfasten, open.

dissertàre (*pr.* **-èrto**), *v.i.* (*aux.* avere) to expatiate, hold forth, argue. **dissertazióne,** *f.* dissertation, thesis.

dissestàre (*pr.* **-èsto**), *v.t.* to unsettle; create difficulties for, embarrass (*financially & otherwise*). **dissestàto,** *a.* embarrassed; burdened with debt. **dissèsto,** *m.* embarrassment.

dissetàre (*pr.* **-éto**), *v.t.* to quench (*thirst*).

dissettóre, *m.* dissector. **dissezióne,** *f.* dissection.

dissidènte, *a.* & *m.* dissentient; dissenting, dissenter. **dissidènza,** *f.* dissent, disagreement. **dissídio** (*pl.* **-ídi**), *m.* dissension, discord.

dissigillàre (*pr.* **-íllo, -ílli**), *v.t.* to unseal.

dissímile, *a.* unlike.

dissimulàre (*pr.* **-ímulo**), *v.t.* to dissimulate; conceal.

dissipàre (*pr.* **díssipo**), *v.t.* to dissipate; squander.

dissociàre (*pr.* **-òcio, -òci**), *v.t.* to dissociate.

dissodàre (*pr.* **-òdo**), *v.t.* to break up (*hard ground*); clear; till.

dissolutézza, *f.* looseness, licentiousness; dissoluteness. **dissolúto,** *p.p.* of *dissolvere.* ¶ *a.* dissolute, licentious, irregular. **dissolvènte,** *a.* & *m.* dissolvent. **dissolvènza,** *f.* (*Cinema*) fade-out. **dissòlvere** (*pr.* **-òlvo,** &*c.*, like *assolvere*), *v.t.* to dissolve; separate; disperse, break up; annul.

dissomigliàre (*pr.* **-íglio, -ígli**), *v.i.* (*aux.* essere) to be unlike, differ.

dissonànte, *a.* dissonant, discordant. **dissonànza,** *f.* dissonance, discord. **dissonàre** (*pr.* **dissuòno,** &*c.*, like *sonare*), *v.i.* (*aux.* avere) to sound discordantly, to be out of tune; jar; (*fig.*) to disagree (with).

dissonnàre, *v.t.* to wake.

dissotterràre (*pr.* **-èrro**), *v.t.* to disinter, exhume; unearth (*lit. & fig.*).

dissuadére (*pr.* **-àdo**), *v.t. ir.* to dissuade.

dissuèto, *a.* unaccustomed. **dissuetúdine,** *f.* unfamiliarity; state of disuse.

dissuggellàre (*pr.* **-èllo**), *v.t.* to unseal.

distaccaménto, *m.* removal, separation; (*Mil.*) detachment. **distaccàre** (*pr.* **-àcco, -àcchi**), *v.t.* to detach, separate, pull apart; (*Mech.*) withdraw, disconnect; (*fig.*) alienate; (*v.i.*) (*aux.* essere) to stand out. **distàcco,** *m.* separation, detachment, (*Mech.*) disjunction; (*fig.*) indifference; parting, leave-taking.

distànte, *a.* distant, far; diverse, alien. ¶ *ad.* far, far off, far away. **distànza,** *f.* distance; length, range; way [off]. *mantenere le ~ e*, (*fig.*) to keep one's distance. *tenere alcuno a ~*, (*fig.*) to keep one at a distance. *~ focale,* (*Opt.*) focal length. **distanziàre,** *v.t.* to [out]-distance.

distàre (*pr.* **dísto**), *v.i. ir.* essere) to be distant or different; (*fig.*) to be at variance.

distèndere (*pr.* **-èndo,** &*c.*, like *stendere*), *v.t. ir.* to extend, stretch out; lay; spread; straighten; raise (*voice*); expound, develop (*argument*); draw up (*document*). ~ *un pugno,* to deliver a blow. **distèndersi,** *v.refl.* to stretch out, lie down; extend; expatiate. **distensióne,** *f.* extension, spreading, stretching; relaxation (*of tension*). **distésa,** *f.* expanse, expansion, range. *a ~,* continuously. **distesaménte,** *ad.* continuously. **distéso,** *p.p.* of *distendere. lungo disteso,* stretched at full length. ¶ *a.* extended; spacious; extensive, widespread; straight; flowing (*hair*). *per ~,* in full detail.

dístico (*pl.* **dístici**), *m.* couplet, distich.

distillàre (*pr.* **-íllo**), *v.t.* to distil; (*v.i.*) (*aux.* essere) to fall drop by drop. **distillatóio** (*pl.* **-ói**), *m.* still. **distillería,** *f.* distillery.

distínguere (*pr.* **-ínguo, -ínġui**), *v.t. ir.* to distinguish; divide; lend distinction to; signalize. **distínta,** *f.* note; list; schedule. ~ *di deposito,* ~ *di versamento,* pay-in slip. **distintívo,** *m.* badge, emblem; distinguishing mark, characteristic. ¶ *a.* distinctive. **distínto,** *p.p.* of distinguere. ¶ *a.* distinguished; prominent; distinct. *posto ~,* reserved seat.

distògliere (*pr.* **-òlgo,** &*c.*, like *togliere*), *v.t. ir.* to dissuade, deter;

distract, divert. **distòlto,** *p.p.* of *distogliere.*

distorsióne, *f.* distortion.

distràrre (*pr.* **-àggo,** *&c.,* like *trarre*), *v.t. ir.* distract, draw away, divert. **distràrsi,** *v.refl.* to take recreation; be distracted; divert one's attention. **distrattaménte,** *ad.* absentmindedly, carelessly. **distràtto,** *a.* absent-minded. **distrazióne,** *f.* distraction, inattention; absentmindedness; diversion, recreation.

distrétta, *f.* urgent need; imminent danger.

distrétto, *m.* district.

distribuíre (*pr.* **-isco, -ísci**), *v.t.* to distribute, give out; deal out; issue; dispense; arrange; assign, allot; deliver (*post*). **distributóre,** *m.* distributor. ~ *automatico,* automatic [delivery] machine, slot machine. ~ *di benzina,* petrol pump. **distribuzióne,** *f.* distribution; assignment, allotment; arrangement; layout; valve gear (*Mech.*); (*postal*) delivery. ~ *delle parti,* cast, casting (*Theat.*).

districàre *&* **distrigàre,** *v.t.* to extricate; disentangle. **distrigàrsi,** *v.refl.* to extricate oneself; get out (of).

distrúggere (*pr.* **-úggo,** *&c.,* like *struggere*) *v.t. ir.* to destroy; melt, consume. **distrúggersi,** *v.refl.* to pine away; wear oneself out. **distruggitóre,** *m.* (*f.* **-tríce**) destroyer. ¶ *a.* destructive. **distruttivo,** *a.* destructive. **distrútto,** *p.p.* of *distruggere.* ¶ *a.* ruined, wasted, consumed, melted.

disturbàre, *v.t.* to disturb, trouble; interrupt, annoy, vex. **disturbàrsi,** *v.refl.* to take trouble. **disturbo,** *m.* disturbance; trouble, inconvenience; disorder. ~*i atmosferici,* (*Radio*) atmospherics.

disubbidiènte, *a.* disobedient. **disubbidiènza,** *f.* disobedience. **disubbidíre** (*pr.* **-isco, -ísci**), *v.i.* (*aux.* avere) to disobey. ~ *a,* to disobey (*v.t.*).

disuguagliàre (*pr.* **-àglio, -àgli**), *v.t.* to make unequal. **disuguàle,** *a.* unequal; uneven; irregular.

disumanàre, *v.t.* to brutalize, render inhuman. **disumàno,** *a.* cruel, inhuman.

disumàre, *v.t.* to exhume.

disusàto, *a.* obsolete; disused; unaccustomed. **disúso,** *m.* disuse.

disútile, *a.* useless, harmful.

disvelàre, *v.t.* to unveil. Cf. *svelare.*

disvèllere, *v.t. ir.* to uproot; pluck out. Cf. *svellere.*

disviàre, *v.t.* to lead astray, mislead. Cf. *sviare.* **disvío,** *m.* leading astray; wandering; disservice; driving away (*of customers*).

ditàle, *m.* thimble; finger-stall. **ditàta,** *f.* finger-mark; tap of the finger.

Díte, *m.* Dis (*Myth.*).

díto, *m.* (*pl.m.* **díti,** *& f.* **díta**) finger, toe; inch; finger's breadth. ~ *grosso,* thumb, big toe. [~] *indice,* forefinger. *mostrare a ~,* to point at (or out) (*indicating scorn*).

dítta, *f.* firm, commercial house.

dittàfono, *m.* dictaphone.

dittatóre, *m.* dictator. **dittatòrio,** *a.* dictatorial. **dittatúra,** *f.* dictatorship.

díttico, *m.* diptych.

dittòngo (*pr.* **-ònghi**), *m.* diphthong. ~ *mobile,* **uo** or **ie,** where the diphthong becomes the simple vowel **o** or **e,** when unaccented or followed by two consonants, e.g. *giuòco, giocàva, piède, pedèstre.*

diúrno, *a.* diurnal, by day, daily, *albergo* ~, *m.* day-hostel. ¶ *m.* prayer-book with the canonical hours for use by day.

diutúrno, *a.* of long duration, lasting.

díva, *f.* goddess; popular actress or singer; prima donna. ~ *del cinema*[*tografo*], film star.

divagaménto, *m.* rambling, straying. **divagàre** (*pr.* **-àgo, -àghi**), *v.i.* (*aux.* avere) to wander (*from the subject*); stray. *v.t.* to distract. **divagàrsi,** *v.refl.* to seek recreation, amuse oneself.

divampaménto, *m.* blazing, burning. **divampàre,** *v.i.* (*aux.* essere) to blaze, flare up.

divàno, *m.* divan; settee.

divaricàre (*pr.* **-àrico, -àrichi**), *v.t.* to spread out; straddle.

divàrio (*pl.* **-àri**), *m.* variation, slight difference.

divedére, *v.i. ir.* to see clearly, used only in the expr. *dare a ~,* to show clearly, give to understand.

divèllere (*pr.* **-èllo**), *v.t. ir.* to uproot; (*fig.*) eradicate. **divèlto,** *p.a.* torn up, uprooted. ¶ *m.* trenching, breaking up ground (*Agr.*).

diveníre (*pr.* **-èngo,** *&c.,* like *venire*), *v.i. ir.* (*aux.* essere) to become, grow

(*gradual change*). ¶ *m.* (*Phil.*) becoming.
diventàre, *v.i.* (*aux.* essere) to become, turn (*sudden change*).
divèrbio (*pl.* -**èrbi**), *m.* altercation, lively dispute, 'words.'
divergènza, *f.* divergence, ~ency.
divèrgere (*pr.* -**èrgo**, *&c.*, like *convergere*), *v.i.* defect. (lacking compound tenses) to diverge, deviate.
diversificàre (*pr.* -**ífico**, -**ífichi**), *v.i.* (*aux.* essere) to vary, differ, be different; (*v.t.*) to diversify.
diversióne, *f.* deviation, digression; pastime, diversion. **diversità**, *f.inv.* diversity, variety, difference. **diversívo**, *a.* distracting; diverting. ¶ *m.* distraction, remedy, means of escape, diversion. **divèrso**, *a.* different, diverse; sundry, miscellaneous; various, many. *generi* ~ *i*, (*Com.*) sundries. ¶ *ad.* differently.
divertènte, *a.* amusing, diverting. **divertiménto**, *m.* amusement, diversion, source of amusement. **divertíre** (*pr.* -**èrto**, *&c.*, like *avvertire*), *v.t.* to divert, entertain, amuse; divert, turn aside. **divertírsi**, *v.refl.* to amuse, entertain oneself.
divestíre, see *svestire*.
divétta, *f.* variety actress; music-hall singer.
divezzàre (*pr.* -**ézzo**), *v.t.* to wean. **divezzàrsi**, *v.refl.* to wean oneself (from), get rid of (*a habit*). **divézzo**, *sync. p.p.* of *divezzare*, weaned.
diviàto, *a. & ad.* straight, straightway; quick, quickly.
dividèndo, *m.* dividend. **divídere** (*pr.* -**ído**), *v.t.* ir. to divide. **divídersi**, *v.refl.* to separate.
divietàre, *v.t.* to forbid, prohibit. **divièto**, *m.* prohibition. ~ *d'affissione*, stick no bills. ~ *di parcheggio*, no parking.
divinàre, *v.t.* to divine; foresee; predict. **divinatóre**, *m.* (*f.* -**trice**) diviner. **divinazióne**, *f.* divination, divining.
divincolàre (*pr.* -**íncolo**), *v.t.* to wriggle.
divinità, *f.inv.* divinity; (the) divine being, God. **diviniżżàre**, *v.t.* to deify; ennoble. **divíno**, *a.* divine, god-like.
divíṣa, *f.* device, motto, heraldic arms; uniform, livery; parting of the hair; (or ~*estera*) foreign currency or bills of exchange. ~ *di gala*, (*Nav.*, *Mil.*) full dress. ~ *ordinaria*, service dress. **diviṣaménto**, *m.*

project, plan; thought; design. **diviṣàre** (*pr.* -**íṣo**, -**íṣi**), *v.t.* to plan, conceive; design in heraldic colours; ornament. (*v.i.*) (*aux.* avere) to intend, propose; decide.
diviṣióne, *f.* division; department; separation, discord. **diviṣioniṡmo**, *m.* (*Art*) pointillism. **diviṣóre**, *m.* (*Arith.*) divisor. **diviṣòrio** (*pl.* -**òri**), *a.* dividing, separating. ¶ *m.* partition.
dívo, *a.* (*Poet.*) divine.
divoràre (*pr.* -**óro**), *v.t.* to devour, consume, lap up; swallow (*lit. & fig.*).
divorziàre, *v.i.* (*aux.* avere) & **divorziàrsi**, *v.refl.* to be divorced. ~ *da*, to divorce (*v.t.*). **divòrzio** (*pl.* -**òrzi**), *m.* divorce. *far* ~ *da*, to divorce.
divòto, *a.* devout, pious.
divulgàre (*pr.* -**úlgo**, -**úlghi**), *v.t.* to make known, divulge, spread [abroad]; popularize.
dizionàrio (*pl.* -**àri**), *m.* dictionary. ~ *geografico*, gazetteer. **dizióne**, *f.* diction; recital.
dò, *m.inv.* first note of the musical scale, *do*, *ut*, C.
doàrio (*pl.* -**àri**), *m.* widow's annual allowance.
dóccia (*pl.* **dócce**), *f.* water-pipe; spout; jet; mill-race; shower bath, douche. ~ *d'aria*, gas-jet. **docciàre** (*pr.* **dóccio**), *v.t.* to pour forth, shower, douche. **docciatúra**, *f.* douching, douche. **doccióne**, *m.* large pipe; gargoyle.
docènte, *m.* teacher. *libero* ~, qualified university lecturer not on the permanent staff.
dòcile, *a.* docile, obedient; (*of material*) easy to work. **docilità**, *f.* docility.
documentàre (*pr.* -**ènto**), *v.t.* to document; prove by means of documents, support by written evidence. **documentàrio**, *a.* documentary. ¶ *m.* documentary film. **documénto**, *m.* document, proof, voucher.
Dodecanèṣo (**il**), *m.* the Dodecanese.
dodicènne, *a.* twelve years old. **dodicèṣimo**, *a. num.ord.* twelfth. ¶ *m.* twelfth part, twelfth person. *in* ~, duodecimo (*volume*). **dódici**, *a.inv.* (*num.card.*) twelve. *il* ~, the twelfth, (*in dates*).
dóga (*pl.* **dóghe**), *f.* stave (*of a barrel*).
dogàle, *a.* belonging to the Doge.
dogàna, *f.* custom-house, customs. **doganàle**, *a.* belonging to the customs; customs (*att.*). *visita* ~,

customs inspection. **doganière,** *m.* customs officer.

dogàto, *m.* dogate, office & dignity of the Doge; period in which he held office; territory of Venice. **dòge** (*pl.* **dògi**), *m.* (*f.* **dogaréssa,** = wife of the Doge) doge of Venice or Genoa (*Hist.*).

dòglia, *f.* (acute) pain; ache; (*pl.*) **dòglie,** labour pains, pains of childbirth. **doglianza,** *f.* complaint, lament, lamentation.

dòglio, *m.* large jar, wine-jar; wooden barrel.

doglióso, *a.* sorrowful, sad; sorry.

dògma (*pl.* **dògmi**) or **dòmma** (*q.v.*) *m.* dogma. **dogmàtico** (*pl.* **-àtici**) *a.* dogmatic. **dogmatìsmo,** *m.* dogmatism.

dólce, *a.* sweet; soft; dulcet; gentle; mild; smooth; pleasant; easy; fresh (*water*). ¶ *m.* sweetness, sweet; (*pl.*) **dólci,** sweets, sweetmeats. **Dolcétto,** *m.* a Piedmontese table wine. **dolcézza,** *f.* sweetness; softness; mildness; gentleness; kindness; (*Poet.*) darling. **dolciàstro,** *a.* sickly sweet. **dolcificàre** (*pr.* **-ífico, -ifíchi**), *v.t.* to sweeten. **dolcígno,** *a.* rather sweet. **dolciúme,** *m.* sweet stuff; excessive sweetness; (*pl.*) **dolciúmi,** sweetmeats, sweets.

dólco (*pl.* **dólchi**), *a.* warm & moist. ¶ *m.* damp weather.

dolènte, *a.* sad, sorry, suffering, afflicted, painful. **dolére** (*pr.* **dòlgo, duòli, duòle**), *v.i. ir.* (*aux.* avere & essere—the latter when impers.) to cause pain or grief; to ache; (*impers.*) *mi duole,* &c., it grieves me, I regret, I am sorry. **dolérsi,** *v.refl.* to complain, grieve, mourn.

dolicocèfalo, *a.* (*Ethn.*) dolichocephalic, long-headed.

dòllaro, *m.* dollar.

dòlman, *m.inv.* dolman, loose Turkish (or Hungarian) jacket.

dòlo, *m.* fraudulent purpose; fraud, deceit.

dolomíte, *f.* dolomite; (*pl.*) (le) *D* ~ *i,* the Dolomites. **dolomítico** (*pl.* **-ítici**), *a.* dolomitic.

doloràre (*pr.* **-óro**), *v.i.* (*aux.* avere) to feel pain or grief. **dolóre,** *m.* pain, sorrow, grief. **doloróso,** *a.* painful, sorrowful.

dolóso, *a.* fraudulent, deceitful.

domànda, *f.* demand, request, petition, question, price asked for goods, or goods offered for sale. **domandàre,** *v.t. & i.* to ask, demand. ~ *di uno,* to ask news of someone. ~ *la parola,* to ask leave to speak. **domandàrsi,** *v.refl.* to be called; ask oneself (*reflectively*).

domàni, *ad.* to-morrow. *da oggi a* ~, immediately, instantly. *doman l'altro* (also *dopodomani, posdomani*), the day after to-morrow. ~ *a otto,* ~ *a quindici,* this day week, this day fortnight.

domàre (*pr.* **dómo**), *v.t.* to break in, tame; (*fig.*) to subdue. **domatóre,** *m.* (*f.* **-tríce**) tamer.

domattína, *f.* to-morrow morning.

doménica, *f.* Sunday. ~ *delle Palme,* Palm Sunday. ~ *di Pasqua,* Easter Sunday. ~ *in Albis,* Sunday after Easter. **domenicàle,** *a.* of Sunday; Sunday (*att.*); of the Lord or lord. *riposo* ~, Sunday rest. *orazione* ~, Lord's prayer. *parte* ~, landlord's share of farm produce (as contrasted with *parte colonica,* tenant's share). ¶ *m.* Sunday clothes, S. best.

domenicàno, *a. & m.* Dominican.

domèstica (*pl.* **-èstiche**), *f.* maid servant. **domesticaménte,** *ad.* familiarly. **domesticàre** (*pr.* **-èstico, -èstichi**), *v.t.* to tame; cultivate (*plants*). **domestichézza,** *f.* familiarity. **domèstico** (*pl.* **-èstici**), *a.* domestic; tame; cultivated (*plant*). *alla* ~*a,* familiarly. ¶ *m.* manservant.

domiciliàre, *a.* domiciliary. *perquisizione* ~, *f.* house search. **domiciliàrsi** (*pr.* **-ilio, -íli**), *v.refl.* to take up one's abode (residence). **domiciliàto,** *p.a.* residing, settled, living (at). **domicílio** (*pl.* **-íli**), *m.* domicile, place of residence.

dominànte, *a.* dominant, ruling; prevailing; commanding (*position*). ¶ *f.* (*Mus.*) dominant. **dominàre** (*pr.* **dòmino**), *v.t.* to dominate, overlook; tower above; control; command; rule, hold sway. (*v.i.*) (*aux.* avere) [hold] rule. domineer. **dominàrsi,** *v. refl.* to control oneself. **dominatóre,** *m.* (*f.* **-tríce**) ruler; (*att.*) ruling, commanding; domineering. **dominazióne,** *f.* domination, ascendancy; sway; control. **domínio** (*pl.* **íni**) *m.* dominion, authority, command; domain; ownership. *il D* ~ *del Canadà,* the Dominion of Canada.

dòmino, *m.* domino (*ball, costume,* or *wearer*); dominoes (*game*).

dòmma (*pl.* **dòmmi**), *m.* dogma.
dommàtica, *f.* dogmatics. **dommàtico** (*pl.* **-àtici**), *a.* dogmatic.
dommatiśmo, *m.* dogmatism.
dommatiżżàre, *v.i.* (*aux.* avere) to dogmatize.
dómo, *sync. p.p. of domare*, tamed.
dòmo, *m.* vault, cupola, dome; sky, house. *in ~ Petri*, in prison. See *duomo*.
dón, *m.* title of honour of priests & nobles. Cf. *don Rodrigo* & *don Abbondio*, in Manzoni's *Promessi Sposi*, *Don Giovanni*, Don Juan, *Don Chisciotte*, Don Quixote, &c.
donàre (*pr.* **dóno**), *v.t.* to bestow; (*v.i.*) (*aux.* avere) to suit; become.
donatàrio (*pl.* **-àri**), *m.* recipient of a gift or donation. **donatìvo**, *m.* gift of some value (*not made by deed*), donative. **donatóre**, *m.* (*f.* **-trìce**) donor. **donazióne**, *f.* donation, gift. *atto di ~*, deed of gift.
Don Chisciótte, *m.* Don Quixote.
donchisciottésco (*pl.* **-éschi**), *a.* Quixotic.
dónde *or* **d'ónde**, *ad.* whence, from where; wherefore. *averne ~*, to have good reason.
dóndola, *f.* rocking-chair. **dondolàre** (*pr.* **dóndolo**), *v.t. & v.i.* (*aux.* avere) to rock, swing. **dondolàrsi**, *v.refl.* to rock (oneself), swing, sway; (*fig.*) to lounge, loiter, idle about. *mi dondola la testa*, my head swims. **dondolío**, *m.* (continual) swinging, rocking. **dóndolo**, *m.* something swinging, or rocking; pendulum; plaything. *orologio a ~*, pendulum clock. *cavallo a ~*, rocking-horse. **dondolóne**, *m.* (*f.* **-óna**) idler, lounger.
dònna, *f.* woman; wife; lady; mistress; maid-servant; title of honour prefixed to the name of a noble lady, dame; queen (*cards*). *le mie ~e*, my women-folk (*wife, daughters, &c.*). *~ di casa*, housewife, one who lives wholly or mainly for the family. *Nostra D ~*, Our Lady, the Madonna. **donnàcchera**, **donnàccola**, *f.* low vulgar woman. **donnàccia**, *f.* horrid, disagreeable woman. **donnésco** (*pl.* **-éschi**), *a.* womanly, feminine.
dònnola, *f.* weasel.
dóno, *m.* gift.
donżèlla, *f.* maid, damsel (*Poet.*).
donżèllo, *m.* page, usher, messenger.
dópo, *pr.* after. ¶ *ad.* after, afterwards, later. *a ~*, for later, at a later time.

~ che, since. *dopodomani*, the day after to-morrow. *il giorno ~*, the next day. *e ~?* What next?
dopoprànzo, *m.* afternoon.
dopoguèrra, *m.* (the) post-war period.
dóppia, *f.* lining at the foot of a skirt; doubloon (*Com. Hist.*). **doppiaménte**, *ad.* doubly. **doppiàre** (*pr.* **dóppio**, **dóppi**), *v.t.* to double; to turn or double (*a promontory*). **doppiatúra**, *f.* doubling, folding.
doppieggiatúra, *f.* slur (*Typ.*).
doppière, *m.* candlestick (*orig. for two candles*). **doppiétta**, *f.* double-barrelled gun. **doppiézza**, *f.* duplicity. **dóppio**, *a.* double; dual; duplex (*Typ.*); (*fig.*) double-faced, insincere; ambiguous. *~ controllo*, *m.* (*Aero.*) dual control. *~ fondo*, *m.* (*ship*) false bottom. ¶ *m.* double, twice as much; sound of two or more bells at once. ¶ *ad.* veder ~, to see double. **doppióne**, *m.* duplicate; exact copy; (*Gram.*) doublet.
doràre (*pr.* **dòro**), *v.t.* to gild. **doratúra**, *f.* gilding.
dòrico (*pl.* **dòrici**), *a.* Doric.
dormicchiàre (*pr.* **-ícchio**, **-ícchi**), *v.i.* (*aux.* avere) to doze, drowse.
dormiènte, *a.* sleeping. ¶ *m.* sleeper; fixed end of a rope. *I sette ~ i*, the Seven Sleepers. **dormiglióne**, *m.* (*f.* **-óna**) late riser, sleepyhead. **dormíre** (*pr.* **dòrmo**, **dòrmi**), *v.i.* (*aux.* avere) to sleep; (*fig.*) be dormant, be in abeyance. ¶ *m.* sleep, sleeping. **dormíta**, *f.* sleep; lethargy. **dormitòrio** (*pl.* **-òri**), *m.* dormitory. **dormivéglia**, *m.* drowsiness; state between sleeping & waking.
dorsàle, *a.* of the back, back (*att.*). *spina ~*, spine, vertebral column, back-bone. **dòrso**, *m.* back; summit, ridge, crest (*mountain*); spine (*book*).
dosàggio, *m.* fixing the dose; proportion of ingredients. **dosàre** (*pr.* **dòso**), *v.t.* to fix the dose of; dose; distribute sparingly. **dosatúra**, *f.* dosage. **dòse** (*pl.* **dòsi**), *f.* dose.
dossàle, *m.* reredos, frontal for an altar; cover for a missal. **dossière**, *m.* back-rest. **dòsso**, *m.* back (*lit. & fig.*, *of persons*).
dossología, *f.* doxology.
dotàle, *a.* of a dowry. **dotàre** (*pr.* **dòto**), *v.t.* to endow. **dotazióne**, *f.* endowment; military or naval equipment; furnishings of a theatre. *~ della corona*, civil list. **dòte**, *f.*

dowry; money grant to a theatre or other public institution; natural gift or accomplishment, endowment.

dottaménte, *ad.* learnedly. **dòtto,** *a.* learned, expert. ¶ *m.* man of learning, learned man. **dottóra,** *f.* woman with title of doctor; bluestocking. **dottoràle,** *a.* doctoral.

dottoràto, *m.* doctorate. **dottóre,** *m.* (*f.* -óra, & -oréssa) doctor (*Law, Letters, Medicine, &c.*); medical man; learned man; father of the Church. ~ *angelico,* St. Thomas Aquinas. ~ *serafico,* St. Bonaventura. **dottoreggiàre** (*pr.* -éggio, -éggi), *v.i.* (*aux.* avere) to put on learned airs. **dottoréssa,** *f.* woman with a doctor's degree.

dottrína, *f.* doctrine; learning; teaching; catechism. **dottrinàle,** *a.* doctrinal.

dóve, *ad.* where, where? ~*che.* wherever. ~ *che sia,* somewhere or other. ¶ *m.* place, whereabouts. *in ogni* ~, *per ogni* ~, everywhere. **dovè,** 3rd s. past def. of *dovere.*

dòventàre, see diventare.

dovére (*pr.* dévo *or* débbo, dévi, déve), *v.i. ir.* (*aux.* avere *or* essere, the latter when the following infin. requires *essere*) to be obliged to; have to; should, ought; must; am to, &c. ¶ *v.t.* to owe. ¶ *m.* duty, task, what is right or necessary; (*pl.*) **dovéri,** respects, compliments. *più del* ~, more than is necessary. *è di* ~ *che,* it is right that. *a* ~, aright, as one should. *mettere a* ~, to make one obey orders, to keep one up to one's duties. **doveróso,** *a.* due, right, rightful, fitting.

dovízia, *f.* wealth, abundance, plenty. **dovizióso,** *a.* rich, abundant, plentiful.

dovúnque, *ad.* wherever.

dovutaménte, *ad.* duly, rightfully. **dovúto,** *p.p.* of dovere. ¶ *a.* due, fitting. ¶ *m.* due; debt.

dożżína, *f.* dozen; board & lodging[s]; price of board & lodging. *di* ~, *da* ~, common, second-rate, cheap. *stare a* ~, to board. *tenere a* ~, to take boarders. **dożżinàle,** *a.* common, ordinary, second-rate, cheap. **dożżinànte,** *m.* boarder.

draconiàno, *a.* draconian, harsh severe.

dràga (*pl.* dràghe), *f.* dredge, dredger. **dragàggio,** *m.* dredging, dragging, sweeping (*for mines*). **dragamíne,** *m.* mine-sweeper.

dragàre, *v.t.* to dredge, drag, sweep.

dràgo (*pl.* dràghi), *m.* dragon. ~ *or pallone* ~, kite-balloon. **dragomànno,** *m.* dragoman, interpreter. **dragóne,** *m.* dragon; dragoon (*Mil.*). **dragonéssa,** *f.* she-dragon.

dràmma (*pl.* dràmmi), *m.* drama. **dràmma,** *f.* dram (*measure of weight*); drachma (*Gk. coin*).

drammàtica, *f.* dramatic art. **drammàtico** (*pl.* -àtici), *a.* dramatic. **drammatiżżàre,** *v.t.* to dramatize. **drammatúrgo** (*pl.* -úrghi), *m.* playwright, dramatist, dramatic writer.

drappàre & **drappeggiàre** (*pr.* -éggio, -éggi), *v.t.* to drape (*Art.*). **drappèllo,** *m.* squad, platoon.

drappellóne, *m.* ornamental curtain; hanging for church festivals. **drappería,** *f.* drapery; drapery store, cloth warehouse. **dràppo,** *m.* cloth, silk cloth. ~ *mortuario,* pall. ~ *inglese* (or *d'Inghilterra*), court (sticking) plaster.

dràstico (*pl.* dràstici), *a.* drastic.

drenàggio (*pl.* -àggi), *m.* drainage; drain. *il* ~ *sulla sterlina,* the drain on sterling. *tubo di* ~, *m.* drain-pipe.

Drèsda, *f.* Dresden.

dríade, *f.* dryad.

dritta, *f.* right, right hand [side]; (*Naut.*) starboard.

dritto, *a.* straight, upright; right; honest; exact (*of time*); favourable, proper. ¶ *m.* right side, upper side; law.

drizza, *f.* halyard (*Mar.*). **drizzàre,** *v.t.* to straighten, make straight; hoist; direct, trim (*boat*); correct, put right; erect; (*v.i.*) (*aux.* avere) to veer off (*of wind*).

dròga (*pl.* dròghe), *f.* drug, spice. **drogàre** (*pr.* -ògo, -òghi), *v.t.* to spice. **droghería,** *f.* drysaltery, grocer's shop. **droghière,** *m.* grocer, drysalter. **droghísta** (*pl.* -ísti), *m.* druggist.

dromedàrio (*pl.* -àri), *m.* dromedary.

druídico (*pl.* -ídici), *a.* druidical, druid (*att.*). **drúido,** *m.* (*f.* -úida, -uidéssa) druid, *f.* druidess.

duàle, *a.* dual, two-fold. **dualìsmo,** *m.* dualism.

dubbiaménte, *ad.* doubtfully. **dubbiézza,** *f.* doubt, uncertainty. **dúbbio** (*pl.* dúbbi), *m.* doubt, hesitation, misgiving; uncertainty;

suspicion. ¶ *a.* doubtful, uncertain; dubious; questionable; suspicious. **dubbióso**, *a.* dubious, uncertain. **dubitàre** (*pr.* **dúbito**), *v.i.* (*aux.* avere) to doubt, waver, hesitate; be distrustful, suspect; be in doubt (about). ~ *di*, to distrust. **dubitóso**, *a.* doubtful; uncertain; irresolute.

Dublíno, *f.* Dublin.

dúca (*pl.* **dúchi**), *m.* duke. **ducàle**, *a.* ducal. **ducàto**, *m.* dukedom; duchy; ducat (*coin*).

dúce (*pl.* **dúci**), *m.* leader.

ducentísta (*pl.* **-ísti**), *m.* writer of the Duecento (13th century).

dúe, *a. inv. num. card. & m.*, two, the number two. ~ *su tre*, best of three (*Ten.*). **duecènto**, *a. inv. num. card.*, two hundred. ¶ *m.* il D ~, the 13th century.

duellànte, *m.* duellist. ¶ *a.* duelling. **duellàre** (*pr.* **-èllo**), *v.i.* (*aux.* avere) to fight a duel. **duellísta** (*pl.* **-ísti**), *m.* duellist. **duèllo**, *m.* duel.

duemíla, *a.inv.* (*num. card.*) two thousand.

duétto, *m.* duet.

dugènto, see *duecento*.

Duína, *f.* Dwina (*river*).

dulcinèa, *f.* sweetheart, lady-love (*fr. Don Quixote*).

dúna, *f.* [sand]dune, sand-hill, down.

Dunchèrche, *f.* Dunkirk.

dúnque, *c.* so, then.

dúo, *m.* duet (*Mus.*). **duodècimo**, *d. num. ord.* twelfth.

duodenàle, *a.* duodenal. **duodèno**, *m.* duodenum.

duòlo, *m.* (*Poet.*) sorrow, grief, pain.

duòmo, *m.* cathedral.

duplicàre (*pr.* **dúplico**, **dúplichi**), *v.t.* to double; duplicate. **duplicàto**, *m.* duplicate. **duplicatura**, *f.* (*Typ.*) double. **duplicazióne**, *f.* duplication.

dúplice, *a.* double, two-fold. **duplicità**, *f.inv.* duplicity, double-dealing.

dúplo, *a. & m.* double.

duràbile, *a.* durable, lasting, abiding.

duralumínio, *m.* duralumin.

duraménte, *ad.* harshly; hard, hardly; roughly. **dutànte**, *a.* lasting, continuing. ¶ *pr.* during, in the course of. **duràre** (*pr.* **dúro**), *v.i.* (*aux.* essere & avere) to last, continue; persist, persevere; hold out, wear (well). *perché la duri!* long may it last! ~ *in carica*, to remain in office. (*v.t.*) to endure, bear, stand, resist. ~ *fatica a*, to

have difficulty in. **duràstro**, *a.* rather hard, rather tough. **duràta**, *f.* duration, length (*time*). *essere di lunga* ~, to last long. **duratúro**, *a.* lasting. **durévole**, *a.* durable. **durézza**, *f.* hardness; (*fig.*) harshness, severity, insensibility. **duríccio**, *a.* rather hard. **dúro**, *a.* hard, firm, tough, stiff; (*fig.*) harsh, severe; insensible, deaf; stubborn; difficult; painful; stupid. *tener* ~, to hold out.

dúttile, *a.* ductile. **duttilità**, *f.* ductility.

E

E, e, *f.* the letter E. Has two sounds, close and open, here indicated by an acute & grave accent respectively, **é**, **è**. The former is found in the dim. termination **-étto**, in the abs. termination **-ézza**, in nouns & adjectives ending in **-énto**, **-éfice**, **-éto**, **-ése**, & **évole**, & in the ad. termination **-ménte**, &c.; the latter in diminutives in **-èllo**, in participles & adjectives in **-ènte**, and in nouns in **-ènza**.

¶ ~ or **ed** (for euphony, before vowels) *c.* and, &; then, very well; (*interrog.*) what about?; also; namely. *e . . . e . . .*, both . . . and. *tutti e due* both. *tutti e tre*, all three (here **e** is an old form of the *def. art. m.pl.* **i**).

e', *pn. abb.* of **ei**, **egli**, he.

è, *vb.* 3rd *sg. pres. indic. of* **essere**, to be.

ebanísta (*pl.* **-ísti**), *m.* cabinet-maker; *lit.* worker in ebony. **ebanistería**, *f.* cabinet-making; cabinet-maker's shop. **ebaníte**, *f.* ebonite. **èbano**, *m.* ebony (wood & tree).

ebbène, *c.* well; well then.

èbbi, *vb.* 1st *sg. past def. of* **avere**, to have.

eb[b]rézza, *f.* drunkenness, intoxication; (*fig.*) elation, exultation, rapture. **èb[b]ro**, *a.* drunk[en], intoxicated, inebriate[d], tipsy; (*fig.*) excited, mad, beside oneself.

ebdomadàrio (*pl.* **-àri**), *a.* weekly, appearing every week. ¶ *m.* weekly [journal], w. paper.

Èbe, *f.* Hebe (*Myth.*).

èbete, *a.* dull, dazed, stupid; feeble-minded. **ebetísmo**, *m.* feeble-mindedness; mental deficiency. **ebetúdine**, *f.* dullness, stupidity.

ebollizióne, *f.* ebullition; boiling. *punto di* ~, boiling point.

eboràrio (*pl.* -àri), *m.* worker in ivory.

ebràico (*pl.* -àici), *a.* Hebrew; Jewish, Hebraic. ¶ *m.* (the) Hebrew (language). *ristorante* ~, *m.* Jewish, kosher restaurant. **ebrèo,** *m.* Jew, Hebrew. ¶ *a.* Jewish, Hebrew.

Èbridi (le), *f.pl.* the Hebrides.

èbro, *see* ebbro. **Èbro**(l'), *m.* the Ebro.

ebúrneo, *a.* of ivory; as white as ivory; ivory (*att.*).

Écate, *f.* Hecate (*queen of Hell, Myth.*).

ecatómbe, *f.inv.* hecatomb; mass slaughter. **ecatòstilo,** *a.* (*Arch.*) with a hundred columns.

eccedènte, *p.a.* exceeding; excessive, in excess; surplus. ~ *il peso*, over-weight. ¶ *m.* & **eccedènza,** *f.* surplus; excess. **eccèdere** (*pr.* -cèdo, &*c.*, like *cedere*). *v.t.* to exceed; go beyond; surpass. *v.i.* (*aux* avere) to go too far; be immoderate. ~ *la velocità permessa*, to exceed the speed limit.

eccellènte, *a.* excellent. **eccellènza,** *f.* excellence; pre-eminence. *per* ~, pre-eminently. *E*~, Excellency (title abolished by legislative decree, 28 June, 1945). **eccèllere** (*pr.* -èllo), *v.i.* *ir.* (*aux.* essere) to excel; be pre-eminent; stand out (*above the rest*). **eccèlso,** *a.* lofty.

eccentricità, *f.* *inv.* eccentricity (*Geom., Astr.*). **eccèntrico** (*pl.* -èntrici), *a.* & *m.* eccentric (*Geom., Mech.*).

eccepíbile, *a.* (*Law*) exceptionable, objectionable. **eccepíre** (*pr.* -ísco, -ísci), *v.t.* to except, object (*Law*).

eccessívo, *a.* excessive, immoderate. **eccèsso,** *m.* excess. ~ *di peso*, excess weight.

eccètera (*abb.* ecc.), *ad.* etcetera (*abb.* etc.); and so on.

eccètto, *pr.* except, excepting, save, but; barring. ~ *che* (*non*), unless.

eccettuàre (*pr.* -èttuo, -èttui), *v.t.* to except.

eccezionàle, *a.* exceptional. **eccezióne,** *f.* exception; plea (*Law*). ~ *perentoria*, (*Law*) demurrer.

ecchímosi, *f.* (*Med.*) bruise.

eccídio (*pl.* -ídi), *m.* slaughter; massacre.

eccitàre (*pr.* èccito), *v.t.* to excite; incite; stir up; provoke; stimulate; rouse; fan. **eccitàrsi,** *v.refl.* to become excited; get angry. **eccitazióne,** *f.* excitation; incitement; excitement.

Ecclesìàste (l'), *m.* Ecclesiastes (*O.T.*). **ecclesìàstico** (*pl.* -àstici), *a.* ecclesiastic(al); clerical; church (*att.*). ¶ *m.* ecclesiastic, clergyman, cleric.

ècco, *ad.* here, here is, here are, &*c.* ~*mi*, ~*mi qui*, here I am. ~*ci*, ~*ci qui*, here we are. ~*li*, ~*là*, there. ~*lo la*, there he is. ~ *tutto*, that's all. ¶ *i.* see! look!

echeggiàre (*pr.* -éggio, -éggi), *v.i.* (*aux.* avere & essere) to echo; resound.

echíno, *m.* sea-urchin.

Ecla, *m.* Hecla (*Geog.*).

eclèttico (*pl.* -èttici), *a.* & *m.* eclectic. **eclettísmo,** *m.* eclecticism.

eclissàre, *v.t.* to eclipse (*lit.* & *fig.*); outshine, overshadow. **eclissàrsi,** *v.refl.* to become eclipsed; vanish. **eclíssi,** *f.* eclipse. **eclíttica,** *f.* ecliptic (*Astr.*).

ècloga, *see* egloga.

èco (*m.pl.* èchi), *m.* & *f.* echo. *fare* ~, to echo (*v.i.*). *farsi* ~ *di*, to echo (*v.t.*); repeat. ~ *della stampa*, press-cutting agency.

ecologìa, *f.* ecology.

economàto, *m.* stewardship, bursar-ship; steward's office, bursar's o. **economìa,** *f.* economy, thrift, saving; management; arrangement. economics. ~ *eccessiva*, ~ *gretta*, cheese-paring (*fig.*). ~ *domestica*, domestic economy, housekeeping. ~ *politica*, political economy. ~ *rurale*, husbandry. **econòmico** (*pl.* -òmici), *a.* economic; economical, thrifty; cheap. **economísta** (*pl.* -ísti), *m.* economist. **economiżżàre** (*pr.* -íżżo), *v.i.* (*aux.* avere) to economize, save. (*far(e) economia* is to be preferred.) **ecònomo,** *m.* steward; bursar. ¶ *a.* economical, thrifty, sparing.

ectoplàsma, *m.* ectoplasm.

Ècuador (l'), *m.* Ecuador. See *Equatore*.

Ècuba, *f.* Hecuba (*Myth.*).

ecumènico (*pl.* -ènici), *a.* ecumeni-cal, oecumenical.

edàce, *a.* (*Poet.*) devouring.

éden, *m.* Eden (*fig.*). *l'E*~ [the Garden of] Eden.

èdera, *f.* ivy.

edícola, *f.* news-stand, kiosk (*for sale of papers*); shelter; public con-venience.

edificànte, *p.a.* edifying. **edificàre** (*pr.* **-ífico, -ífichi**), *v.t.* to erect, build; b. up; edify; enlighten. **edifício** (*pl.* **-íci**) & **edifízio** (*pl.* **-ízi**), *m.* edifice, building, structure. **edíle,** *a.* building. **edilízia,** *f.* building trade; b. craft. *materiale per ∼, m.* building material. **edilízio** (*pl.* **-ízi**), *a.* building. *regolamento ∼,* building regulations.

Edimbúrgo, *f.* Edinburgh.

Édipo, *m.* Oedipus (*Myth.*).

èdito, *p.a.* published. **editóre,** *m.* (*f.* **-tríce**) publisher; editor, -tress. ¶ *a.* publishing. *casa editrice, f.* publishing house, publisher. **editoría,** *f.* book industry, publishing trade. **editoriàle,** *a.* & *m.* editorial.

editto, *m.* edict.

edizióne, *f.* edition; publishing, publication. *∼ a tiratura ristretta,* limited edition. *∼ tascabile,* pocket edition. *∼ economica,* cheap e. *∼ riveduta,* revised e.

edonísmo, *m.* hedonism. **edonísta** (*pl.* **-ísti**), *m.* hedonist.

educànda, *f.* boarding-school girl; g. at a convent school. **educàre** (*pr.* **èduco, èduchi**), *v.t.* to bring up, educate; train. **educàto,** *a.* well-bred, polite; educated. **educazióne,** *f.* education, training; upbringing; rearing; nurture; breeding, good breeding. *senza ∼,* ill-bred.

efèbo, *m.* (*Lit.*) youth, adolescent.

Efeso, *m.* Ephesus.

èffe, *f.* the letter F.

effeminàre (*pr.* **-émino**), *v.t.* to make effeminate. **effeminatézza,** *f.* effeminacy.

efferatézza, *f.* cruelty; brutality; act of cruelty. **efferàto,** *a.* barbarous; cruel.

efferènte, *a.* (*Med.*) efferent. *vasi ∼ i,* vessels carrying blood from the heart, &c.

effervescènte, *a.* sparkling, effervescent. **effervescènza,** *f.* effervescence, -ency; ferment; (*fig.*) unrest.

effettívo, *a.* effective; real; actual; active; **in cash, in coin; paid up** (*capital*). *socio ∼,* active member. ¶ *m.* (*Mil., oft.pl.*) effective; strength, complement, force (*men*). **effètto,** *m.* effect; consequence; result; action; purpose, avail; impression; appearance; screw, break, spin (*on ball*); bill; negotiable instrument. *in ∼, v.,* in fact, indeed. *per ∼ di,* in consequence of. **effettuàle,** *a.* real, effectual. **effettuàre** (*pr.*

-èttuo, -èttui), *v.t.* to effect, carry out, execute; make.

efficàce, *a.* efficient; efficacious; effectual; effective; able, adequate. **efficaceménte,** *ad.* efficiently, &c. **efficàcia,** *f.* efficacy; efficiency. **efficiènte,** *a.* efficient. **efficiènza,** *f.* efficiency; (*Mech.*) working order.

effigiàre (*pr.* **-ígio, -ígi**), *v.t.* to portray; represent. **effígie,** *f.inv.* effigy; portrait; image.

effímera, *f.* ephemera, May fly. **effímero,** *a.* ephemeral.

efflússo, *m.* efflux; discharge; outflow. **efflúvio** (*pl.* **-úvi**), *m.* effluvium (*pl.* **-uvia**).

effóndere (*pr.* **-óndo,** &c., like *fondere*), *v.t. ir.* to give out, effuse; pour forth; exhale; shed; give vent to; spread.

effrazióne, *f.* breaking; house-breaking. *furto con ∼, m.* burglary.

effúso, *p.p.* of *effondere.*

egemonía, *f.* hegemony.

Egèo (Mare) *m.* Aegean (Sea).

ègida, *f.* aegis; shield; protection.

Egídio (Sant'), *m.* Saint Giles.

Egína, *f.* Aegina (*Geog.*).

egíra, *f.* hegira.

Egítto (l'), *m.* Egypt. **egittología,** *f.* Egyptology. **egittòlogo** (*pl.* **-òlogi**), *m.* Egyptologist. **egiziàno,** *a.* & *m.* Egyptian. **egízio,** *a.* (*Hist.*) (ancient) Egyptian.

eglantína, *f.* eglantine; sweet briar.

égli, *pn.m.* he (*pl.* **essi**).

ègloga (*pl.* **ègloghe**), *f.* eclogue.

egoísmo, *m.* egoism; selfishness. **egoísta** (*pl.* **-ísti**), *m.* egoist. **egoístico** (*pl.* **-ístici**), *a.* egoistic(al).

egotísmo, *m.* egotism.

egrègio (*pl.* **-ègi**), *a.* remarkable, distinguished; high, noble; excellent, worthy. (In letters) *∼ signore,* Dear Sir, *∼a signora,* Dear Madam.

ègro, *a.* (*Poet.*) sick; weak, infirm; sad.

eguagliànza, *f.* equality. **eguagliàre** (*pr.* **-guàglio, -guàgli**), ·*v.t.* to equalize, make equal; equal; match; smooth, level. **equàle,** *a.* equal; even, level; alike; [all] the same, all one.

èh! *i.* ha! eh! **éhi!** *i.* hallo! **I** say! **èhm!** *i.* hem!

ei, *pn.m.* he (*abb.* of *egli*); they.

eia, *i.* hurrah! **Eia.** Employed by D'Annunzio in his aviator's cry of *eia eia, alalà!*

eiaculàre, *v.t.* to ejaculate (*fluid*). **eiaculazióne,** *f.* ejaculation (*fluid*).

Eidelbèrga, *f.* Heidelberg.

eiettóre, *m.* ejector (*Mech.*).
elaboràre (*pr.* **-àboro**), *v.t.* to elaborate; work out, evolve.
elargíre (*pr.* **-ísco, -ísci,** like *largire*), *v.t.* to grant; give liberally. **elargizióne,** *f.* gift, donation.
elasticità, *f.* elasticity, spring[iness]; resilience. **elàstico** (*pl.* **-àstici**), *a.* elastic, springy, resilient; supple; buoyant. ¶ *m.* elastic; rubber band; garter.
Èlba (**l'isola d'**), *f.* the Island of Elba.
élce, *f.* holm-oak; ilex.
elefànte, *m.* elephant.
elegànte, *a.* elegant, stylish, fashionable; graceful, polished (*speech, &c.*). **eleganteménte,** *ad.* elegantly; smartly. **elegantíre** (*pl.* **-ísco, -ísci**) *v.t.* to render elegant. **elegànza,** *f.* elegance, stylishness.
elèggere (*pr.* **-èggo,** *&c.*, like *leggere*), *v.t. ir.* to select, choose, prefer; elect; appoint. **eleggíbile,** *a.* eligible.
elegía, *f.* elegy. **elegíaco** (*pl.* **-íaci**), *a.* elegiac.
elementàre, *a.* elementary. **eleménto,** *m.* element; unit, fundamental part of an apparatus; cell (*Biol., Mech., Elec.*); congenial environment; (*pl.*) rudiments (*art or science*).
elemòsina, *f.* alms. *chieder l'* ~, to beg. *far(e) l'* ~, to bestow charity, give alms.
Èlena, *f.* Helen, Helena. *Sant'E* ~, St. Helena (*Geog.*).
elencàre (*pr.* **-ènco, -ènchi**), *v.t.* to [make a] list [of]; enumerate. **elènco** (*pl.* **-ènchi**), *m.* list; catalogue; inventory. ~ *telefonico,* telephone directory.
elettívo, *a.* elective. *affinità* ~*e, f.pl.* elective affinities. **elètto,** *p.p.* of *eleggere.* ¶ *a.* elect; select; choice.
elettoràle, *a.* electoral. *scheda* ~, *f.* ballot-paper. *urna* ~, *f.* ballot-box. **elettoràto,** *m.* franchise; electorate. **elettóre,** *m.* (*f.* **-tríce**) elector, constituent.
Elèttra, *f.* Electra (*Myth.*).
elettricísta (*pl.* **-ísti**), *m.* electrician. **elettricità,** *f.* electricity. **elèttrico** (*pl.* **-èttrici**), *a.* electric(al). **elettrificàre** (*pr.* **-ífico, -ífichi**), *v.t.* to electrify (*Rly., &c.*). **elettrificazióne,** *f.* electrification. **elettrizzàre** (*pr.* **-ízzo**), *v.t.* to electrify, electrize; thrill. **elèttro,** *m.* (yellow) amber; electrum.
elettrocalamíta, *f.* electro-magnet. **elettrochímica,** *f.* electro-chemistry. **elettrocuzióne,** *f.* electrocu-

tion. **elettrodinàmica,** *f.* electro-dynamics. **elèttrode,** *m.* electrode.
elettro-esecuzióne, *f.* electrocution. **elettròlisi,** *f.* electrolysis.
elettromagnètico (*pl.* **-ètici**), *a.* electro-magnetic. **elettróne,** *m.* electron. **elettrònico** (*pl.* **-ònici**), *a.* electronic. **elettroterapía,** *f.* electrotherapy. **elettrotipía,** *f.* electrotyping; electrotype.
Elèusi, *f.* Eleusis. **eleusíno,** *a.* Eleusinian.
elevàre (*pr.* **èlevo** & **elèvo**), *v.t.* to elevate, raise, lift; erect; exalt, extol. ~ *al quadrato,* (*Arith.*) to square. **elevàrsi,** *v.refl.* to rise; raise oneself. ~*a,* to reach; amount to. **elevatézza,** *f.* loftiness; dignity; nobility. **elevàto,** *a.* high, elevated; noble; lofty. **elevatóre,** *m.* elevator, lift. [*muscolo*] ~, (*Anat.*) elevator (muscle). **elevazióne,** *f.* elevation; raising; rise; increase; erection; height; altitude.
elezióne, *f.* election, polling; choice.
èlica (*pl.* **èliche**), *f.* (*Naut.*) propeller, screw; spiral, helix; (*Aero.*) air-screw.
Elicóna (**l'**), *m.* Helicon, Mt. H. (*Geog.*).
elicòttero, *m.* helicopter.
elídere (*pr.* **-ído**), *v.t. ir.* to elide (*Gram.*); neutralize; suppress.
eligíbile, *a.* eligible. **eligibilità,** *f.* eligibility.
eliminàre (*pr.* **-ímino**), *v.t.* to eliminate; weed out. **eliminatòria,** or *gara* ~, *f.* eliminating or trial heat; semi-final (*Sport*).
èlio, *m.* helium.
eliògrafo, *m.* heliograph, **elioterapía,** (*Med.*) sunlight treatment. **eliotròpio,** *m.* heliotrope.
Elisabétta, *f.* Elizabeth. **elisabettiàno,** *a.* & *m.* Elizabethan.
elísio, *a.* Elysian. *i Campi E* ~*i,* the Elysian Fields.
elisióne, *f.* elision (*Gram.*).
elisír & **elisíre,** *m.inv.* elixir.
elíso, *p.p.* of *elidere.* *E* ~, *m.* Elysium (*Myth.*).
élla, *pers. pn.f.* she (*pl.* **esse**). *E* ~, you.
èlle, *f.* the letter L.
ellènico (*pl.* **-ènici**), *a.* Hellenic, Greek. **ellenísmo,** *m.* Hellenism. **ellenísta** (*pl.* **-ísti**), *m.* Hellenist, Greek scholar.
èllera, *f.* (*pop.*) ivy.
Ellespónto (**l'**), *m.* the Hellespont (*Geog.*).
ellísse, *f.* ellipse (*Geom.*). **ellíssi,** *f.*

ellipsis (*Gram.*). **ellíttico** (*pl.* -íttici*), a. elliptic(al).
élmo, *m.* helmet. *dim.* elmétto.
elocuzióne, *f.* elocution; propriety & clearness of expression (*not confined, as in Eng., to oral delivery*).
elogiàre ⟨*pr.* -ògio, -ògi⟩, *v.t.* to eulogize; praise. commend. **elògio** (*pl.* -ògi*), *m.* eulogy, praise, encomium. **elogístico** (*pl.* -ístici*), *a.* eulogistic.
eloquènte, *a.* eloquent. **eloquènza**, *f.* eloquence; oratory.
elòquio (*pl.* -òqui*), *m.* mode of expression, speech, language.
èlsa, *f.* hilt.
Elsinóre, *f.* Elsinore.
elucidàre, *v.t.* to elucidate.
elucubrazióne, *f.* lucubration.
elúdere (*pr.* -údo*), *v.t. ir.* to elude, evade, shirk.
elvètico (*pl.* -ètici*), *a.* Swiss. *Confederazione* ~*a*, Swiss Confederation, Switzerland. **Elvèzia** (l'), *f.* Switzerland, Helvetia (*Hist.*).
elżeviriàno, *a.* Elzevir, from the press of the Elzevirs, the celebrated Dutch printers (17th century). **elżevíro**, *m.* book from the Elzevir press, or in E. type. *carattere* ~, Elzevir type; (*Typ.*) old style, old face.
emaciàto, *a.* emaciated.
emanàre (*pr.* -àno*), *v.t.* to issue; publish (*orders, decrees, &c.*); *v.i.* (*aux.* essere) to emanate, issue, proceed. **emanazióne**, *f.* emanation, efflux, effluence; issuing.
emancipàre (*pr.* -àncipo*), *v.t.* to emancipate. **emancipazióne**, *f.* emancipation.
Emanuèle, *m.* Emmanuel.
ematíte, *f.* haematite. **ematòsi**, *f.* (*Med.*) haematosis.
emazía (*pl.* -íe*), *f.* red blood corpuscle.
emblèma (*pl.* -èmi*), *m.* emblem, symbol; attribute. **emblemàtico** (*pl.* -àtici*), *a.* emblematic[al].
embolía, *f.* (*Med.*) embolism.
émbrice, *m.* roof-tile (*with raised edges*). *scoprire un* ~, to reveal a secret.
embriología, *f.* embryology. **embrióne**, *m.* embryo.
emendaménto, *m.* amendment. **emendàre** (*pr.* -èndo*), *v.t.* to amend, correct, improve. **emendatóre**, *m.* emender; corrector; censor. **emendazióne**, *f.* emendation, correction.
emergènte, *a.* consequent, resulting;

emergent. **emèrgere** (*pr.* -èrgo, -èrgi*), *v.i. ir.* (*aux.* essere) to emerge, rise out; issue; appear; stand out; loom; peep.
emèrito, *a.* emeritus, retired, honourably discharged.
emersióne, *f.* emersion; emerging, emergence.
emètico (*pl.* -ètici*), *a. & m.* emetic.
eméttere (*pr.* -étto, *&c.*, like *mettere*), *v.t. ir.* to emit, give out; utter; express; deliver (*judgement*); issue; put into circulation.
emicíclo, *m.* hemicycle. **emicrània**, *f.* (*Med.*) headache; hemicrania.
emigrànte, *a. & m.* emigrant. **emigràre** (*pr.* -ígro, -ígri*), *v.i.* (*aux.* avere, *if used abs.*, essere, *if to a specific place*) to emigrate; migrate (*birds, fishes*). **emigràto**, *m.* refugee, political exile. **emigrazióne**, *f.* emigration; migration.
eminènte, *a.* eminent, high; distinguished; prominent. **eminenteménte**, *ad.* eminently; highly. **eminènza**, *f.* eminence; height. *Sua E*~, His Eminence (*cardinal*).
emiplégia, *f.* (*Med.*) hemiplegia, paralysis of one side.
emíro, *m.* emir; ameer, amir.
emisfèro, *m.* hemisphere.
emissàrio (*pl.* -àri*), *m.* emissary; outlet of a lake or stream; effluent.
emissióne, *f.* emission; issue (*of currency*). *istituti d'* ~, banks authorized to issue paper money.
emistíchio (*pl.* -ichi*), *m.* hemistich, half-line of verse.
emittènte, *p.a.* emitting, issuing. ¶ *m.* issuer; *f.* (*Radio*) transmitting station.
emme, *f.* the letter M.
emofilía, *f.* (*Med.*) haemophilia. **emorragía**, *f.* (*Med.*) haemorrhage. **emorròidi**, *f.pl.* (*Med.*) piles, h[a]emorrhoids. **emotrasfusióne**, *f.* (*Med.*) blood-transfusion.
emoluménto, *m.* (*oft. pl.*) emolument. *percepire gli* ~*i*, to draw (receive) the emoluments.
emotività, *f.inv.* sensibility, emotionalism.
Empèdocle, *m.* Empedocles.
émpiere, *see* empire.
empietà, *f.* impiousness; impiety. **émpio** (*pl.* émpi*), *a.* impious, irreligious; pitiless; wicked.
empíre (*pr.* émpio, émpi, émpie*), *v.t. ir.* to fill; fill up; stuff, cram; crowd; load (*with benefits*); satisfy.
empíreo, *m.* (*Poet.*) Empyrean.

empiricaménte, *ad.* empirically, by rule of thumb.

empírico (*pl.* **-írici**), *a.* empiric[al], rule-of-thumb. ¶ *m.* empiric[ist]. *medico* ~, quack (doctor). **empi-rismo,** *m.* empiricism.

empìto, *p.p.* of *empire*. ¶ *a.* full; crammed.

émpito, *m.* (*Lit.*) rush, fury, violent motion.

empòrio (*pl.* **-òri**), *m.* emporium; trade centre; (*fig.*) vast collection.

emulàre (*pr.* **émulo**), *v.t.* to emulate; seek to rival. **emulatóre,** *m.* (*f.* **-trìce**) emulator; rival. **emula-zióne,** *f.* emulation. **èmulo,** *a.* emulous. ¶ *m.* emulator, rival.

emulsióne, *f.* emulsion.

encàustica, *f.* art of encaustic painting. **encàustico** (*pl.* **-àustici**), *a.* encaustic.

encíclica (*pl.* **-cícliche**), *f.* encyclical, Papal letter.

enciclopedìa, *f.* [en]cyclop[a]edia.

encomiàre (*pr.* **-òmio**, **-òmi**), *v.t.* to commend, praise. **encòmio** (*pl.* **-òmi**), *m.* encomium.

endecasíllabo, *a.* hendecasyllabic, of eleven syllables. ¶ *m.* hendeca-syllable, line of eleven syllables.

éndice, *m.* nest-egg.

endocardìte, *f.* (*Med.*) endocarditis.

Enèa, *m.* Aeneas. **Enèide,** *f.* Aeneid (of Virgil).

energìa, *f.* energy, power; vigour, resolution; efficacy (*remedy*). ~ *atomica,* atomic energy. **enèrgico** (*pl.* **-èrgici**), *a.* energetic, vigorous, powerful.

energúmeno, *m.* one possessed by a devil; enthusiast; fanatic.

enfàsi, *f.* bombast, pomposity; exag-geration; emphasis. **enfàtico** (*pl.* **-àtici**), *a.* bombastic, pompous; over-emphatic.

enfiagióne, *f.* swelling; tumour. **enfiàre** (*pr.* **énfio,** **énfi**), *v.i.* (*aux.* essere) & **enfiàrsi,** *v.refl.* to swell, inflate.

enfitèuśi, *f.* (*Law*) long lease at a ground rent.

enìgma & **enímma** (*pl.* **-ígmi** & **-ímmi**), *m.* riddle, conundrum, puzzle, enigma. **enigmàtico** & **enimmàtico** (*pl.* **-àtici**), *a.* enig-matic(al).

ènne, *f.* the letter N. **ennèśimo,** *a.* (*Math.*) nth (*term*).

ennè, *f.* henna (*dye*).

enòfilo, *a.* concerned with the produc-tion & improvement of wines.

circolo ~, wine-growers' club. **enologìa,** *f.* science of wine-growing.

enòrme, *a.* huge, enormous; (*fig.*) outrageous, absurd. **enormità,** *f.inv.* hugeness; enormity; out-rageous action; absurdity.

Enrico, *m.* Henry.

ènte, *m.* (*Phil.*) being; corporation, society. *E*~ *Supremo,* God. ~ *morale* (or *giuridico*), society or institution on which the law confers a legal personality, with rights & duties thereof. ~ *nazionale italiano turistico* (*abb.* ENIT), Italian tourist information bureau.

entelechìa, *f.* (*Phil.*) entelechy.

entèrico (*pl.* **-èrici**), *a.* intestinal, enteric. *febbre* ~*a,* f. enteric fever. **enterìte,** *f.* (*Med.*) enteritis.

entità, *f.inv.* entity.

entomologìa, *f.* entomology. **ento-mologísta** (*pl.* **-ísti**), & **ento-mòlogo** (*pl.* **-òlogi**), *m.* entomo-logist.

entràmbi, *pn.* *m.pl.* (*f.* **entràmbe**) both.

entràre (*pr.* **éntro**), *v.i.* (*aux.* essere) to enter; go in; come in; step in; walk in; get in; go; come. ~ *in,* to enter (*v.t.*), enter into, enter upon, begin. ~ *in carica,* to enter upon office. ~ *in gioco,* to come into play. ~ *in vigore,* to come into force. *il tre nel nove entra tre volte,* three into nine goes thrice. *che c'entra?* what has that got to do with it? *tu non c'entri,* this is no business of yours. *la settimana entrante,* the coming week, next week. **entràta,** *f.* entrance, entry; adit (*Min.*); admittance, admission; way in; income, revenue, receipt. *le* ~*e di favore,* the free list (*Theat.*). ~ *ed uscita,* debit & credit (*Bkkpg.*). **entratúra,** *f.* entrance, entry; entrance fee; familiarity, intimacy. *diritto d'* ~, right of entry; goodwill (*of a business*).

éntro, *pr.* & *ad.* within, in, in the course of. ¶ *sync. p.p.* of *entrare,* entered.

entropìa, *f.* entropy.

entuśiaśmàre, *v.t.* to enrapture, carry away. **entuśiaśmàrsi,** *v.refl.* to go into raptures. **entuśiàśmo,** *m.* enthusiasm; rapture. **entusi-àstico** (*pl.* **-àstici**), *a.* enthusiastic.

enumeràre (*pr.* **-úmero**), *v.t.* to enumerate; specify (*items*).

enunciàre & **enunziàre** (*pr.* **-úncio,**

-únci, & **-únzio, -únzi**), *v.t.* to enunciate; state definitely; pronounce.

enzíma (*pl.* **-zimi**), *m.* (*Biol.*, *Chem.*) enzym[e].

eòlio (*pl.* **-òli**), **eòlico** (*pl.* **eòlici**), *a.* Aeolian; Aeolic. *arpa eolia,* Aeolian harp. *dialetto eolico,* Aeolic dialect (*Gk.*).

epàtica, *f.* (*Bot.*) liverwort. **epàtico**, *a.* (*Med.*) hepatic. **epatíte**, *f.* hepatitis, inflammation of the liver.

eperlàno, *m.* smelt (*fish*).

èpica (*pl.* **èpiche**), *f.* epic; epic poetry.

epicèdio (*pl.* **-èdi**), *m.* epicedium; funeral ode or speech.

epicíclo, *m.* epicycle (*Astr.*).

èpico (*pl.* **èpici**), *a.* epic.

epicureísmo, *m.* epicurism; epicureanism. **epicurèo**, *a.* epicurean. ¶ *m.* epicure; Epicurean. **Epicúro**, *m.* Epicurus.

epidemía, *f.* epidemic, outbreak (*disease*). **epidèmico** (*pl.* **-èmici**), *a.* epidemic(al).

epidèrmide, *f.* (*anat.*) epidermis.

epidiascòpio, *m.* epidiascope.

epifanía, *f.* Epiphany. *La Notte dell'E~,* Twelfth Night (Shakespeare).

epiglòttide, *f.* (*Anat.*) epiglottis.

epigoni, *m.pl.* (*Lit.*) descendants; followers.

epígrafe, *f.* epigraph, inscription; quotation, motto (*prefixed to book or chapter*). **epigrafía**, *f.* study of ancient inscriptions.

epigràmma (*pl.* **-gràmmi**), *m.* epigram.

epilessía, *f.* epilepsy. **epilèttico** (*pl.* **-èttici**), *a.* & *m.* epileptic.

epilogàre (*pr.* **-ilogo, -iloghi**), *v.t.* to sum up. **epílogo** (*pl.* **-iloghi**), *m.* epilogue; summing up.

epiníco (*pl.* **-íci**), *m.* (*Lit.*) song of victory.

Epíro, *m.* Epirus (*Geog.*).

episcopàle, *a.* episcopal. **episcopàto**, *m.* episcopate; episcopacy.

episòdico (*pl.* **-òdici**), *a.* episodic[al]. **episòdio** (*pl.* **-òdi**), *m.* episode.

epistàssi, *f.* (*Med.*) epistaxis, nasal haemorrhage.

epistemología, *f.* epistemology (*Phil.*).

epístola, *f.* epistle. **epistolàre**, *a.* epistolary. **epistolàrio** (*pl.* **-àri**), *m.* letters, correspondence.

epitàffio (*pl.* **-àffi**), *m.* epitaph.

epitalàmio (*pl.* **-àmi**), *m.* epithalamium; nuptial ode.

epíteto, *m.* epithet.

epítome, *f.* epitome.

Epittéto, *m.* Epictetus.

època (*pl.* **èpoche**), *f.* epoch; era, age; time, period; notable point or stage in history.

epopèa, *f.* epic, epopee, epos.

eppúre, *c.* (*for* **e pure**) yet; and yet; nevertheless; however.

eptasillàbico (*pl.* **-àbici**), *a.* heptasyllabic, seven-syllabled (*line*).

epulóne, *m.* delicate liver; rich man in the Scripture parable.

epuraménto, *m.* & **epurazióne**, *f.* purifying, purification; refining. **epuràre** (*pr.* **-úro**), *v.t.* to purify; refine; free from impurities.

equaménte, *ad.* justly, fairly, equitably.

equànime, *a.* even-tempered, calm, serene; just. **equanimità**, *f.* equanimity, composure, serenity; patience; fair-mindedness.

equatóre, *m.* equator. *la Repubblica dell'E~,* *f.* Ecuador (*Geog.*). **equatoriàle**, *a.* equatorial. *regione delle calme ~i,* *f.* doldrums (*pl.*). ¶ *m.* equatorial (*telescope*). **equazióne**, *f.* equation.

equèstre, *a.* equestrian.

equilibràre (*pr.* **-íbro**), *v.t.* to equilibrate, poise, balance, counterbalance. **equilibrazióne**, *f.* balancing. **equilíbrio**, *m.* equilibrium; [equi]poise: balance; b. of power (*Pol.*). **equilibrísta** (*pl.* **ísti**), *m.* acrobat; rope-walker.

equinoziàle, *a.* equinoctial. **equinòzio** (*pl.* **-òzi**), *m.* equinox.

equipaggiàre (*pr.* **-àggio, -àggi**), *v.t.* to equip, fit out, rig (out). **equipàggio** (*pl.* **-àggi**), *m.* crew (*ship*); outfit, rig; train, equipage; turnout.

equiparàre (*pr.* **-àro, -àri**), *v.t.* to compare, parallel; equalize; make (or find) equal in merit.

equipollènte, *a.* of equal force or value.

equità, *f.* equity, fairness; justice; impartiality. **equitatívo**, *a.* equitable, &c.

equitazióne, *f.* riding; horsemanship. *scuola d'~,* *f.* riding-school.

equivalènte, *a.* & *m.* equivalent. **equivalére** (*pr.* **-vàlgo**, *&c.*, like *valere*), *v.i. ir.* (*aux.* avere & essere) to be equivalent (to); be tantamount (to); be the same (as). *Followed in each case by* a.

equivocàre (*pr.* **-ívoco, -ívochi**), *v.i.*

(*aux.* avere) to equivocate, use ambiguous words; misunderstand, be mistaken. **equívoco** (*pl.* **-ívoci**), *a.* equivocal; ambiguous, dubious, questionable. ¶ *m.* misunderstanding; ambiguity; equivocation.

èquo, *a.* equitable, fair, just.

èra, *f.* era, epoch.

Eràclito, *m.* Heraclitus.

erariàle, *a.* fiscal; of the Treasury. *avvocato* ~, Treasury counsel. **eràrio** (*pl.* **-àri**), *m.* Treasury; state finances.

Eràsmo, *m.* Erasmus.

èrba, *f.* grass; herb. *in* ~, immature; green; budding; in embryo. *filo d'*~, blade of grass. ~*bozzolina*, (*Bot.*) milkwort. ~ *cornetta*, (*Bot.*) larkspur. ~ *da febbre*, (*Bot.*) common centaury. **erbàccia** (*pl.* **-àcce**), *f.* weed. **erbàceo**, *a.* herbaceous. **erbàggio** (*pl.* **-àggi**), *m.* herb; (*pl.*) pot-herbs, vegetables, greens. **erbai(u)òlo**, *m.* streetseller of vegetables; costermonger. **erbàrio** (*pl.* **-àri**), *m.* herbarium. **erbétta**, *f.* short grass; thin g. **erbivèndolo**, *m.* green-grocer. **erbívoro**, *a. & m.* herbivorous (*animal*). **erbóso**, *a.* grassy; grass-grown. **erbúcce**, *f.pl.* sweet herbs.

Ercolàno, *f.* Herculaneum.

Èrcole, *m.* Hercules; (*fig.*) strong man. **ercúleo**, *a.* Herculean.

Èrebo (l'), *m.* Erebus (*Myth.*).

erède, *m.* heir, *f.* heiress. **eredità**, *f.inv.* heirship, inheritance (*right & property*); heirloom; heredity. *lasciare in*~, to bequeath. **ereditàre** (*pr.* **-èdito**), *v.t.* to inherit. **ereditàrio** (*pl.* **-ari**), *a.* hereditary. *principe* ~, Crown Prince, (*Eng.*) Prince of Wales.

eremíta (*pl.* **-íti**), *m.* hermit. **eremitàggio** (*pl.* **-àggi**), *m.* hermitage. **èremo**, *m.* solitary retreat; hermitage.

ereśía (*pl.* **ereśíe**), *f.* heresy. **erètico** (*pl.* **-ètici**), *a.* heretical. ¶ *m.* heretic.

erètto, *p.p.* of *erigere*. ¶ *a.* erect, upright; standing. **erezióne**, *f.* erection; raising, building; establishment, foundation.

èrg, *m.inv.* (*Phys.*) erg, ergon (*unit of work*).

ergastolàno, *m.* (*long-term*) convict. **ergàstolo**, *m.* convict prison; penal servitude.

èrica, *f.* heather.

Eriè (il lago d'), *m.* Lake Erie.

erígere (*pr.* **-ígo**, &*c.*, like *dirigere*), *v.t.* ir. to erect, put up, build; institute, set up, found; raise.

Erínni, *f.pl.* Erinyes, (the) Furies (*Myth.*).

erisìpèla, *f.* (*Med.*) erysipelas.

eritèma (*pl.* **-èmi**), *m.* (*Med.*) erythema; rash.

Eritrèa (l'), *f.* Eritrea (*Geog.*). **eritrèo**, *a. & m.* Eritrean, native of Eritrea. *Mare* ~, (the) Red Sea.

ermafrodíto, *a. & m.* hermaphrodite.

ermellíno, *m.* ermine.

Èrmes & Ermète, *m.* Hermes (*Myth.*). **ermeticaménte**, *ad.* hermetically (*sealed*). **ermètico** (*pl.* **-ètici**), *a.* hermetic; air-tight; (*fig.*) secret, close. **ermetíśmo**, *m.* secret doctrines associated with Hermes Trismegistus; (*fig.*) obscurity (*in poetry*, &*c.*).

èrmo, *a.* (*Poet.*) solitary.

èrnia, *f.* hernia; rupture. *cinto erniario*, *m.* truss.

Èro, *f.* Hero (*Myth.*). *E*~ *e Leandro*, Hero & Leander.

Eròde, *m.* Herod. **Eròdoto**, *m.* Herodotus.

eròe, *m.* hero. **eroíśmo**, *m.* heroism. **erogàre** (*pr.* **èrogo**, **èroghi**), *v.t.* (*Law*) to spend, distribute; bestow. **erogazióne**, *f.* bestowal; distribution.

eròico (*pl.* **-òici**), *a.* heroic. **eroicòmico** (*pl.* **-òmici**), *a.* mock-heroic.

eroína, *f.* heroine; (*Med.*) heroin.

erómpere (*pr.* **-ómpo**, &*c.*, like *rompere*) *v.i.* ir. (*aux.* avere) to break out, burst out.

eròtico (*pl.* **-òtici**), *a.* erotic; amatory.

èrpete, *m.* (*Med.*) herpes, shingles.

erpicàre (*pr.* **érpico**, **érpichi**), *v.t.* to harrow (*Agric.*). **èrpice**, *m.* harrow.

errabóndo, *a.* (*Lit.*) wandering, rambling.

errànte, *a.* wandering, roving; errant. **erràre** (*pr.* **èrro**), *v.i.* (*aux.* avere) to wander, roam, rove, stroll, stray; err.

erràta-còrrige, *m. or f.* (*Typ.*) errata, table of errata.

erràtico (*pl.* **-àtici**), *a.* erratic (*Geol.*, *Med.*, &*c.*); wandering, stray[ing]. **erràto**, *a.* wrong, mistaken.

èrre, *f.* the letter R.

erròneo, *a.* erroneous, false, mistaken. **erróre**, *m.* error, mistake, blunder; fallacy. ~ *d'ortografia*, misspelling. ~ *di stampa*, ~ *tipografico*, misprint, printer's error.

èrsᴄ, *m.* Erse.

èrta, *f.* (upward) slope; ascent; steep path. *stare all'* ∼, to be on the alert; be on one's guard. *all'erta!* look out! take care! **èrto**, *a.* steep.

erudíto, *a.* learned, scholarly, erudite. ¶ *m.* scholar, learned man. **erudizióne,** *f.* erudition, learning, scholarship.

eruttàre (*pr.* **-útto**), *v.t.* (*volcano*) to emit, eject (*lava, &c.*); *v.i.* (*aux.* avere) to eruct, belch; erupt. **eruttazióne,** *f.* eructation, belching. **eruttívo,** *a.* eruptive. **eruzióne,** *f.* eruption; rash.

erziàno, *a.* (*Elec.*) hertzian.

eśacerbàre (*pr.* **-èrbo**), *v.t.* to embitter, exacerbate; aggravate; irritate. **eśacerbazióne,** *f.* exacerbation; irritation; embitterment.

eśageràre (*pr.* **-àgero**), *v.t. & abs.* to exaggerate; overstate; overdo. **eśagerazióne,** *f.* exaggeration.

eśagonàle, *a.* (*Geom.*) hexagonal. **eśàgono,** *m.* hexagon.

eśalàre (*pr.* **-àlo**), *v.t. & i.* (*aux.* essere) to exhale; breathe forth; give out; reek (with *or* of). **eśalazióne,** *f.* exhalation (*act & vapour*); fume.

eśaltàre, *v.t.* to exalt; extol. **eśaltàrsi,** *v.refl.* to become excited, elated. **eśaltàto,** *a.* over-excited, heated; exalted. ¶ *m.* hot-head; fanatic. **eśaltazióne,** *f.* exaltation; elation; excitement.

eśàme, *m.* examination; inspection; scrutiny. *dare un* ∼, to sit (take) an examination.

eśàmetro, *m.* hexameter.

eśaminàre (*pr.* **-àmino**), *v.t.* to examine; inspect; overhaul; look into; interrogate. **eśaminatóre,** *m.* (*f.* **-tríce**) examiner.

eśàngue, *a.* bloodless; pale.

eśànime, *a.* exanimate, lifeless; dead.

eśattaménte, *ad.* exactly, precisely, correctly. **eśattézza,** *f.* exactness, exactitude; precision; accuracy; punctuality; correctness. **eśàtto,** *a.* exact, precise, accurate, correct; punctual. ¶ *p.p.* of *esigere*.

eśattóre, *m.* collector, tax-collector.

eśaudiménto, *m.* satisfaction, fulfilment; compliance. **eśaudíre** (*pr.* **-ísco, -ísci**). *v.t.* to grant, comply with (*a request*), hear, answer (*a prayer*); satisfy, fulfil (*a wish*).

eśauriènte, *a.* exhaustive. **eśauriménto,** *m.* exhaustion; depletion. **eśauríre** (*pr.* **-ísco, -ísci**) , *v.t.* to exhaust, wear out; drain empty;

deplete. **eśauríto,** *p.p.* of *esaurire*. ¶ *a.* exhausted, worn out; (*books*) out of print; (*goods*) sold out; (*dish*) off (*in restaurant*); spent; broken; finished. **eśàusto,** *p.a.* exhausted; effete.

eśautoràto, *p.a.* deprived of authority.

eśazióne, *f.* collection (*rates, taxes*); exaction.

ésca, *f.* bait (*lit. & fig.*); allurement; tinder (*lit. & fig.*); fuse (*expl.*).

escandescènza, *f.* outburst of rage. *dare in* ∼, to fire up, lose one's temper, go off the deep end (*pop.*).

escavatóre, *m.* digger, excavator; (*Mech.*) excavator.

eschilèo, *a.* Aeschylean, of Aeschylus. **Èschilo,** *m.* Aeschylus.

eschimése, *a. & m.* Eskimo.

esclamàre (*pr.* **-àmo**), *v.i.* (*aux.* avere) to exclaim; cry out. **esclamatívo,** *a.* exclamatory. *punto* ∼, mark of exclamation. **esclamazióne,** *f.* exclamation; ejaculation.

esclúdere (*pr.* **-údo,** *&c.*, like *accludere*), *v.t. ir.* to exclude; shut out; leave out; debar; (*Elec.*) cut out. **esclusióne,** *f.* exclusion. **esclusíva & esclusività,** *f.* exclusiveness; sole right; patent; monopoly. **esclusívo,** *a.* exclusive; sole. **esclúso,** *p.p.* of *escludere.*

escogitàre (*pr.* **-ògito**), *v.t.* to excogitate, think out; devise; contrive.

escreménto, *m.* excrement. **escrescènza,** *f.* excrescence.

Esculàpio, *m.* Aesculapius. **Escuriàle,** *m.* Escurial.

escursióne, *f.* excursion. ∼ *a piedi,* walking tour. **escursionísta** (*pl.* **-ísti**), *m.* excursionist, tripper.

escútere (*pr.* **escúto**), *v.t. ir.* (*Law*) to examine, interrogate (*witnesses*).

eśecràbile, *a.* execrable. **eśecràre** (*pr.* **-ècro**), *v.t.* to execrate.

eśecutívo, *a. & m.* executive. **eśecutóre,** *m.* executor; executioner; (*Mus.*) executant. **eśecutòria,** *f.* executory decree; writ of execution. **eśecutríce,** *f.* executrix. **eśecuzióne,** *f.* execution; performance, fulfilment; accomplishment; enforcement.

eśegèśi, *f.* exegesis.

eśeguíre (*pr.* **-ísco, -ísci**; also **-éguo,** *&c.*, like *seguire*), *v.t.* to execute, perform; accomplish, fulfil; carry out; make.

eśempigràzia, *ad.* for instance, for example, (*abb.*) e.g.

esémpio (*pl.* -émpi), *m.* example; instance; pattern; illustration (*fig.*); lead. esemplàre, *a.* exemplary, model. ¶ *m.* model; pattern; specimen; copy (*of a book*). esemplificàre (*pr.* -ífico, -ífichi), *v.t.* to exemplify.

esentàre (*pr.* -ènto, -ènti), *v.t.* to exempt. esènte, *a.* exempt; free; immune. esenzióne, *f.* exemption.

esèquie, *f.pl.* obsequies, funeral; funeral rites.

esercènte, *pr.p.* (of *esercire*) practising (*profession*); carrying on (*business*); plying (*trade*); keeping (*shop*). ¶ *m.* retail dealer. gli ~i, (*fam.*) the trade. esercire (*pr.* -ísco, -ísci) *v.t.* to practise, carry on, run (*a business*). esercitàre (*pr.* -èrcito), *v.t.* to exercise; train; drill; practise; ply (*trade*); exert. esercitazióne, *f.* (*oft.pl.*) exercise; training; drill. esèrcito, *m.* army. esercízio (*pl.* -ízi), *m.* exercise; practice; drill[ing]; activity; management; tenure (*of office*); (financial) year; (*accounting*) period. ~i di salvataggio, boat-drill.

esibíre (*pr.* -ísco, -ísci), *v.t.* to exhibit, display, produce (*oft. of documents in law*); offer. esibírsi, *v.refl.* to offer oneself; offer one's services. esibíta, *f.* exhibit.

esigènte, *a.* exigent, exacting; particular, hard to please. esigènza, *f.* exigence, -cy; requirement, demand. esígere (*pr.* -ígo, -ígi), *v.t. ir.* to exact, require, demand, call for; collect (*taxes, &c.*). esigíbile, *a.* due (*com., tax, &c.*).

esíguo, *a.* exiguous, scanty; small; slender.

esilaràre (*pr.* -ílaro), *v.t.* to exhilarate.

esíle, *a.* slender, thin.

esiliàre (*pr.* -illo, -íli), *v.t.* to exile, banish. esílio (*pl.* -íli), *m.* exile (*state*); place of exile.

esímere (*pr.* -ímo, -ími), *v.t. ir.* to exempt, free from an obligation.

esímio (*pl.* -ími), *a.* distinguished, eminent.

esistènte, *p.a.* existent, existing; extant; living. esistènza, *f.* existence; life; stock (*Com.*). esistenzialísmo, *m.* existentialism. esístere (*pr.* -ísto, &c., like *assistere*), *v.i.* (*aux.* essere) to exist, be; be extant.

esitàbile, *a.* saleable; marketable.

esitànte, *p.a.* hesitant, hesitating; doubtful; irresolute. esitànza, *f.* hesitancy, ~ce. esitàre (*pr.* èsito),

v.i. (*aux.* avere) to hesitate, waver; falter; (*v.t.*) to sell; dispose of. esitazióne, *f.* hesitation.

èsito, *m.* result, outcome, issue; success; denouement (*of a play*); sale.

esiziàle, *a.* ruinous, fatal.

èsodo, *m.* exodus, flight. *l'E*~, the Book of Exodus (*O.T.*).

esòfago (*pl.* -òfaghi), *m.* (*Anat.*) oesophagus; gullet.

esoneràre (*pr.* -ònero), *v.t.* to exonerate; exempt, release.

Esòpo, *m.* Aesop.

esorbitànte, *a.* exorbitant, extravagant, excessive. esorbitàre (*pr.* -òrbito), *v.i.* (*aux.* avere) to go to excess; exceed the just limit(s).

esorcísmo, *m.* exorcism. esorcizzàre, *v.t.* to exorcise.

esordiènte, *p.a.* beginning, starting. ¶ *m.f.* beginner, debutant (*f.* debutante). esòrdio (*pl.* -òrdi), *m.* exordium; beginning; debut, first appearance. esordíre (*pr.* -ísco, &c., like *ordire*), *v.i.* (*aux.* avere) to begin, start; begin speaking; make one's first appearance (*stage, &c.*).

esortàre (*pr.* -òrto), *v.t.* to exhort; urge.

esòso, *a.* hateful, odious.

esotèrico (*pl.* -èrici), *a.* esoteric. esòtico (*pl.* -òtici), *a.* exotic; foreign.

espàndere, *v.t.* to expand; spread, extend. espansióne, *f.* expansion. espansívo, *a.* expansive; effusive.

espatriàre (*pr.* -àtrio, -àtri), *v.i.* (*aux.* avere & essere) to emigrate, leave one's country, (*v.t.*) to expatriate, banish; expel.

espediènte, *a. & m.* expedient.

espèllere (*pr.* -èllo), *v.t. ir.* to expel, eject; drive out.

Espèridi (le), *f.pl.* (the) Hesperides.

esperiènza, *f.* experience; experiment. esperimentàre, see *sperimentare*. esperiménto, *m.* experiment, test, trial. esperíre (*pr.* -ísco, -ísci), *v.t.* (*Law*) to try, make trial of; use.

Èspero, *m.* Hesperus; evening star.

espèrto, *a.* expert, experienced; skilled. ~di, versed in. ¶ *m.* expert. See *perito*.

espettoràre (*pr.* -èttoro), *v.t. & abs.* to expectorate; spit.

espiàre (*pr.* -ío, -íi), *v.t.* to expiate, atone for. espiatòrio, *a.* expiatory. capro ~, scapegoat, innocent victim. espiazióne, *f.* expiation.

espiràre (*pr.* **-íro**), *v.i.* (*aux.* avere) to breathe out, exhale.

espletàre (*pr.* **-èto**), *v.t.* to fulfil, accomplish; dispatch. espletívo, *a.* & *m.* expletive.

esplicatívo, *a.* explanatory. esplícito, *a.* explicit, clear, definite.

esplòdere (*pr.* **-òdo**), *v.i. ir.* (*aux.* avere (*arms*) & essere (*mine*, &*c.*) to fire, explode, go off; (*fig.*) burst, burst out. *v.t.* & *far(e)* ~, to fire, explode, set off.

esploràre (*pr.* **-òro**), *v.t.* to explore; (*Mil.*) reconnoitre; (*fig.*) probe, sound. esploratóre, *m.* (*f.* **-tríce**) explorer; scout. *giovane* ~, boy-scout. ~ *-trice*, girl-guide. esplorazióne, *f.* exploration; (*Med.*, *Naut.*) sounding; (*Mil.*) scouting, reconnaissance.

esplošióne, *f.* explosion, report. esplošívo, *a.* & *m.* explosive.

esponènte, *m.* exponent. espórre (*pr.* **-óngo**, &*c.*, like *porre*), *v.t. ir.* to expose; show, display, exhibit; expound; explain; state.

esportàre (*pr.* **-òrto**), *v.t.* to export. esportatóre, *m.* exporter. ¶ *a.* exporting. esportazióne, *f.* export[ation]. ~ *protetta*, dumping (*Com.*).

espošitívo, *a.* explanatory. espošizióne, *f.* exposition; exposure; exhibition, show; aspect, frontage (*of house*). *tempo di* ~, (*Phot.*) exposure. espòsto, *p.p.* of esporre. ¶ *m.* statement, account, contents (*petition*, &*c.*); foundling. *ospizio degli* ~*i*, *m.* foundling hospital.

espressaménte, *ad.* expressly, on purpose. espressióne, *f.* expression; phrase. espressioníšmo, *m.* expressionism (*Art*). espressívo, *a.* expressive. esprèsso, *p.p.* of *esprimere.* ¶ *a.* express, clear, definite. [*caffe*] ~, coffee made separately for each customer with a coffee machine or pressure-filter. ¶ *m.* express delivery; express (*train*). [*lettera*] ~, express letter. esprímere (*pr.* **-ímo**), *v.t. ir.* to express; give expression to; voice; declare.

espropriàre (*pr.* **-òprio**, **-òpri**), *v.t.* to expropriate; dispossess. espropriazióne, *f.* (*Law*) expropriation.

espugnàre (*pr.* **-púgno**), *v.t.* to seize, take by storm; conquer.

espulšióne, *f.* expulsion. espúlšo, *p.p.* of *espellere*, expelled; ejected. espulšóre, *m.* ejector.

espúngere (*pr.* **-úngo**, &*c.*, like *pungere*), *v.t. ir.* to expunge, delete. espurgàre (*pr.* **-úrgo**, **-úrghi**), *v.t.* to expurgate; bowdlerize.

Esquilíno (l'), *m.* the Esquiline.

esquimése, *a.* & *m.* Eskimo.

éssa, *pn. pers. 3rd sg. f.* she; it. ésse, *pn. pers. 3rd pl. f.* they.

èsse, *f.* the letter S.

essènza, *f.* essence; spirit; (essential) oil; being, existence; objective character. ~ *di rose*, attar of roses. ~ *di bergamotto*, bergamot oil. essenziàle, *a.* & *m.* essential.

èssere (*pr.* **sóno**, **sèi**, **è**, **siàmo**, **siète**, **sóno**), *v.i. ir.* (*aux.* essere) to be, exist; consist; happen; become; have (*as aux.*); (*fut.*) to be possible, probable. ~ *di*, to belong to. ~ *in grado di*, to be able to. *non* ~ *da tanto da*, not to be capable of. ~ *per* (*with infin.*), to be about to. *sono venti anni che lavoro*, I have been working for twenty years. *che sarà di noi?* what will become of us? *sarà, ma non ci credo*, it may be so, but I don't think so. ¶ *m.* existence; state, condition; being; creature.

essiccàre (*pr.* **-ícco**, **-ícchi**), *v.t.* to dry; dry up; desiccate. ~*al forno*, to kiln-dry. essiccatóio (*pl.* **-ói**), *m.* drying-house, d.-room. essicazióne, *f.* drying, d. process.

ésso, *pn. pers. m.sg. 3rd pers.* he; it. (*pl.*) éssi, they.

essudàre (*pr.* **-súdo**), *v.t.* to exude.

èst, *m.* east. *verso* ~, eastward(s).

èstaši, *f.inv.* ecstasy; rapture. *mandare in* ~, to throw into ecstasies. estašiàrsi, *v.refl.* to go into ecstasies.

estàte, *f.* summer.

estàtico (*pl.* **-àtici**), *a.* ecstatic, enraptured.

estemporaneaménte, *ad.* extemporaneously, extemporarily; extempore. *parlare* ~, to speak extempore. estemporàneo, *a.* extemporaneous; extemporary; extempore. *un discorso* ~, an extempore speech.

estèndere (*pr.* **-èndo**, &*c.*, like *tendere*), *v.t. ir.* to extend; prolong; increase; enlarge. estendíbile, *a.* extensible.

estènse, *a.* of Este (ducal family of Ferrara & Modena).

estensióne, *f.* extension; extent; enlargement, increase; (*Mus.*) range, compass. estensívo, *a.* extensive.

estensóre, *m.* (*Law*) draftsman; chest expander. ¶ *a.* (*Anat.*) extensor (*muscle*).

estenuàre (*pr.* -**ènuo,** -**ènui**), *v.t.* to weaken; tire out, wear out; reduce; exhaust.

esterióre, *a. & m.* exterior.

esterminàre, see *sterminare.*

esternàre (*pr.* -**èrno**), *v.t.* (*of feelings*) to disclose, show openly; reveal; manifest. **esternàrsi,** *v.refl.* to open one's mind (or heart). **estèrno,** *a.* external, exterior; outer; outward; outside (*att.*). *per uso* ~, for external application, not to be taken (*Med.*). *alunno* (or *scolare*) ~, day-boy, day pupil. *posto* ~, outside seat (*bus, &c.*). *angolo*~, outer angle. ¶ *m.* outside; (*Sch.*) day-boy; non-resident assistant (*hospital*).

èstero, *a.* foreign. *affari* ~*i*, foreign affairs. *commercio* ~, foreign trade. *politica* ~*a*, foreign policy. ¶ *m.* foreign countries; (*pl.*) foreign affairs. *all'*~, abroad. *Ministero degli* (*affari*) *esteri*, Foreign Office, Ministry of Foreign Affairs. *Ministro degli* (*affari*) *esteri*, Minister of Foreign Affairs, Foreign Secretary (*Eng.*).

esterrefàtto, *a.* terrified.

estéso, *p.p.* of *estendere.* ¶ *a.* extensive; large, wide. *per* ~, in full.

estèta (*pl.* -**èti**), *m.* aesthete. **estètica,** *f.* aesthetics, **estètico** (*pl.* -**ètici**), *a.* aesthetic(al).

estimàre (*pr.* -**stímo**), *v.t.* to esteem; value; estimate. Cf. *stimare.* **estimatóre,** *m.* valuator; appraiser. **estimazióne,** *f.* estimation; esteem. **èstimo,** *m.* valuation; rating; land-tax.

estínguere (*pr.* -**íngui,** *&c.*, like *distinguere*), *v.t.* *ir.* to extinguish, put out; quench; slake; pay off (*debt*); soften. **estínguersi,** *v.refl.* to go out (*light*); pass away; die (out). **estínto,** *p.p.* of *estinguere.* ¶ *a. & m.* deceased. **estintóre** (*d'incendi*) *m.* (fire) extinguisher. **estinzióne,** *f.* extinction; slaking; quenching; paying off.

estirpàre, *v.t.* to extirpate, eradicate; root out; uproot.

estívo, *a.* summer (*att.*). *vacanze* ~ *e*, summer holidays, s. vacation. *ora* ~*a*, summer time. *semplice ora* ~*a*, single summer t. *doppia ora* ~*a*, double s.t. *stazione* ~*a*, summer resort.

estòllere (*pr.* -**òllo**), *v.t. ir.* to extol; exalt.

Estónia (**l'**), *f.* Esthonia.

estòrcere (*pr.* -**òrco,** *&c.*, like *torcere*), *v.t. ir.* to extort, wring. **estorsióne,** *f.* extortion.

estra- or **extra-,** prefix. ¶ *m.* extra, excess.

estradàre, *v.t.* to extradite. **estradizióne,** *f.* extradition.

estràneo, *a.* extraneous; foreign. ¶ *m.* stranger.

estràrre (*pr.* -**àggo,** *&c.*, like *trarre*), *v.t. ir.* to extract, take out; draw, draw out; excerpt; get; win; quarry. **estràtto,** *p.p.* of estrarre. ¶ *m.* extract; excerpt; off-print. ~ *dell' atto di nascita*, birth certificate. ~ *dell' atto di morte*, death c. **estrazióne,** *f.* extraction; digging, quarrying; drawing (*of lottery numbers*).

estremaménte, *ad.* extremely; exceedingly; intensely. **estremità,** *f.inv.* extremity; end; tip. **estrèmo,** *a. & m.* extreme (*a. & n.*); utmost; drastic; dire. ~*a unzione,* *f.* extreme unction. *l'e*~*a destra,* sinistra, the extreme right, left (*Pol.*). *l'*~*o Oriente,* the Far East.

estrinsecàre (*pr.* -**ínseco,** -**ínsechi**), *v.t.* to manifest, evince; express; show by outward signs. **estrinsecàrsi,** *v.refl.* to make known one's thoughts. **estrínseco** (*pl.* -**ínsechi** & -**ínseci**), *a.* extrinsic.

èstro, *m.* inspiration; ardour; fancy; caprice; gadfly. ~ *poetico,* poetic fire (or inspiration.) **estróso,** *a.* capricious, whimsical; animated.

estuàrio (*pl.* -**àri**), *m.* estuary; firth.

estuóso, *a.* stormy, tempestuous.

esuberànte, *a.* exuberant. **esuberànza,** *f.* exuberance.

esulàre (*pr.* **èsulo**), *v.i.* (*aux.* essere & avere) to go into exile; live in exile. **èsule,** *m. & f.* exile (*pers.*).

esulceràre, *v.t.* to exulcerate; exacerbate, irritate.

esultàre (*pr.* -**últo**), *v.i.* (*aux.* avere) to exult; rejoice.

esumàre (*pr.* -**úmo**), *v.t.* to exhume, unearth, disinter. **esumazióne,** *f.* exhumation.

età, *f.inv.* age. ~ *dell'oro,* golden age. *essere di* ~ *minore,* to be under age. *essere di* ~ *maggiore,* to be of age. **etàde,** *f.* (*Poet.*) age.

ètano, *m.* (*Chem.*) ethane.

etéra, *f.* hetaera, courtesan.

ètere, *m.* ether (*Chem.*, *Phys.*); sky (*Poet.*). **etèreo**, *a.* ethereal; heavenly.

eternàre (*pr.* -**èrno**), *v.t.* to make eternal, etern(al)ize; perpetuate. **eternità**, *f.inv.* eternity. **etèrno**, *a.* eternal; everlasting; never-ending.

eterodína, *f.* (*Radio*) heterodyne. **eterodossía**, *f.* heterodoxy. **eterodòsso**, *a.* heterodox. **eterogèneo**, *a.* heterogeneous.

ètica, *f.* ethics. **etichétta**, *f.* label; docket; tally; ticket; etiquette.

ètico (*pl.* **ètici**), *a.* ethical; ethic; hectic. ¶ *a. & m.* consumptive.

etíle, *m.* (*Chem.*) ethyl.

etimología, *f.* etymology. **etimològico** (*pl.* -**ògici**), *a.* etymological. **etimòlogo** (*pl.* -**òlogi**), *m.* etymologist.

etíope, *a. & m.* Ethiopian. **Etiòpia** (l'). *f.* Ethiopia. **etiòpico** (*pl.* -**òpici**), *a.* Ethiopic, Ethiopian. ¶ *m.* Ethiopian.

etisía, *f.* phthisis, consumption.

ètnico (*pl.* **ètnici**), *a.* ethnic, pagan. **etnografía**, *f.* ethnography. **etnògrafo**, *m.* ethnographer. **etnología**, *f.* ethnology.

ètra, *f.* (*Poet.*) air; sky.

etrúsco (*pl.* **etrúschi**), *a. & m.* Etruscan.

ettàgono, *m.* heptagon.

èttaro, *m.* hectare = 100 ares or 2.4711 acres.

ètte, *m.* trifle, tittle.

ètto, *abb.* of **ettogràmmo**, *m.* hectogram[me] = 100 gram[me]s or 3·527 ozs. avoirdupois. **ettòlitro**, *m.* hectolitre = 100 litres or 2·75 imperial bushels or 22·01 imperial gallons.

Èttore, *m.* Hector.

eucalípto, *m.* eucalyptus.

eucarestía, *f.* eucharist, holy communion. **eucarístico** (*pl.* -**ístici**), *a.* eucharistic.

Euclíde, *m.* Euclid.

eufemísmo, *m.* euphemism. **eufemístico** (*pl.* -**ístici**), *a.* euphemistic.

eufonía, *f.* euphony. **eufònico** (*pl.* -**ònici**), *a.* euphonic, euphonious.

Eufràte (l'), *m.* the Euphrates.

eufuísmo, *m.* euphuism. **eufuístico** (*pl.* -**ístici**), *a.* euphuistic.

Euganèo, *a.* Euganean. *i Colli Euganei*, the Euganean Hills.

eugenètica & **eugenía**, *f.* eugenics. **eugenètico** (*pl.* -**ètici**), *a.* eugenic.

Eumènidi (le), *f.pl.* the Eumenides, the Furies.

eunúco (*pl.* -**úchi**), *m.* eunuch.

Euridíce, *f.* Eurydice (*Myth.*).

Eurípide, *m.* Euripides.

Euròpa (l'), *f.* Europe. **europèo**, *a. & E~*, *m.* European.

eutanàsia, *f.* euthanasia.

Èva, *f.* Eve.

evacuàre (*pr.* -**àcuo**), *v.t. & abs.* to evacuate, void, clear out.

evàdere (*pr.* -**vàdo**), *v.i. ir.* (*aux.* essere) to escape, get away.

evanescènte, *a.* evanescent. **evanescènza**, *f.* evanescence; (*pl.*) fading (*Radio*).

evangèlico (*pl.* -**èlici**), *a.* evangelical. **evangelísta** (*pl.* -**ísti**), *m.* evangelist. **evangèlo** & *E~*, *m.* gospel.

evaporàre (*pr.* -**óro**), *v.i.* (*aux.* avere & essere) & **evaporàrsi**, *v.refl.* to evaporate. *v.t.* to vent. **evaporazióne**, *f.* evaporation.

evasióne, *f.* escape, flight. **evasívo**, *a.* evasive. **evàso**, *p.p.* of evadere. ¶ *m.* runaway, fugitive.

evenïènza, *f.* eventuality; contingency.

evènto, *m.* event; outcome, issue, result. *in ogni ~*, at all events, in any case. **eventuàle**, *a.* eventual; possible; contingent. **eventualità**, *f.inv.* eventuality, contingency, event. **eventualménte**, *ad.* eventually; in any case; according as things turn out.

evidènte, *a.* evident, obvious, plain. **evidenteménte**, *ad.* evidently, &c. **evidènza**, *f.* evidence.

evíncere (*pr.* -**vínco**, -**vínci**, &c., like *vincere*), *v.t.* (*Law*) to evict; oust, turn out.

eviràre, *v.t.* to emasculate. **eviràto**, *a.* unmanly, effeminate.

evitàbile, *a.* avoidable. **evitàre** (*pr.* **èvito**), *v.t.* to avoid, shun; eschew; evade, dodge, steer clear of; help (*with neg.*).

evizióne, *f.* (*Law*) eviction.

èvo, *m.* age; epoch; time(s). *medio ~*, Middle Age(s). *~ moderno*, modern times.

evocàre (*pr.* **èvoco**, **èvochi**), *v.t.* to evoke, call up, conjure up.

evoluzióne, *f.* evolution.

evvíva! *i.* hurrah! long live *~!* ¶ *m. inv.* cheer. *fare un ~*, to give a cheer.

ex-, *prefix*, *ex-*. *~ cancelliere*, ex-chancellor. *~ combattente*, ex-service man. *~ presidente*, ex-president.

ex-líbris, *m.inv.* book-plate. **ex-vóto**, *m.inv.* ex voto, votive offering.

extraterritorialità, *f. inv.* extra-territoriality.

Ezechía, *m.* Ezekias; Hezekiah (*O.T.*).

Ezechièllo, *m.* Ezekiel (*O.T.*).

eziandío, *ad.* even; also.

F

F, f, (*effe*) *f.* the letter F.

fa, *m.* (*Mus.*) fa. ¶ *ad.* ago, *poco tempo* ~, a short while ago. *dieci anni* ~, ten years ago. ¶ *v.* 3rd *sg. pres. ind.* of **fare**.

fabbisógno, *m.* what is necessary, requisite[s]; estimates of cost; (*Theat.*) property. ~ *di carta*, paper consumption.

fàbbrica (*pl.* **fàbbriche**), *f.* building; construction; fabric (*edifice*); factory, works, mill. *marca di* ~, trade-mark. *prezzo di* ~, cost price, prime cost. **fabbricànte**, *m.* manu-facturer; maker; builder. **fabbri-càre** (*pr.* **fàbbrico, fàbbrichi**), *v.t.* to build; manufacture; con-struct; make; fabricate; coin; invent; forge, trump up. **fabbricàto**, *m.* building. **fabbricatóre**, *m.* (*f.* -**tríce**) manufacturer; builder; fabricator (*of news, &c.*). **fabbrica-zióne**, *f.* manufacture, making, make. ~ *italiana*, made in Italy.

fàbbro, *m.* smith, blacksmith; (*fig.*) creator, inventor.

faccènda, *f.* business, matter, thing; duty. *una* ~ *seria*, a serious business, a serious matter. ~*e domestiche*, household duties. **faccendière** *m.* (*f.* -**èra**) busybody.

faccétta, *f.* small face; facet. **fac-cettàre** (also **sfaccettare**) (*pr.* **faccétto**), *v.t.* to cut a gem.

facchinàggio (*pl.* -**àggi**), *m.* porter-age; very heavy work. **facchíno**, *m.* porter.

fàccia, (*pl.* **fàcce**) *f.* face; cast of features; page; aspect; expression; (*Mech.*) side; pane. *di* ~ *a*, in front of, opposite. *visto di* ~, seen from the front. ~ *tosta*, effrontery; impudent fellow.

facciàta *f.* front, frontage; façade (*of a building*); (*written*) page.

fàce, *f.* torch.

facéto, *a.* facetious; witty; waggish; jocular. **facèzia**, *f.* joke, jest, witticism, humorous saying.

fachíro, *m.* fakir.

fàcile, *a.* easy; simple; fluent; facile, light; likely, probable; easily moved. liable (to); accommodating, easy-going. **facilità**, *f.inv.* facility, ease, easiness; fluency; aptitude. **facili-tàre** (*pr.* **facílito**), *v.t.* to facilitate, make easy.

facinoróso, *a.* lawless, violent, ruffianly.

facoltà, *f.inv.* faculty, authority, power; option, right, leave, liberty; [University] faculty; branch (*of study*); (*pl.*) property, wealth. **facoltatívo**, *a.* optional. **facoltóso**, *a.* wealthy.

facondaménte, *ad.* eloquently, fluently. **facóndia**, *f.* readiness of speech; eloquence, flow of language. **facóndo**, *a.* eloquent, fluent.

fàggio (*pl.* **fàggi**), *m.* beech (tree), beech-wood.

fagiàno, *m.* pheasant. **fagiàna**, *f.* hen-pheasant.

fagiolíno, *m.* French bean. ~ *nano*, kidney bean, green bean. **fagi[u]ò-lo**, *m.* bean; haricot bean; (*fig.*) blockhead.

fagliàre (*pr.* **fàglio, fàgli**), *v.i.* (*aux.* avere) to discard (*cards*). **fàglio** (*pl.* **fàgli**), *m.* discard.

fagocíta (*pl.* -**íti**), *m.* (*Biol.*) phago-cyte.

fagòtto, *m.* bundle; (*Mus.*) bassoon. *far* ~, to pack up; be gone.

fàida, *f.* feud, vendetta.

falànge, *f.* phalanx.

falanstèro (*pl.* -**èri**), *m.* phalanstery; socialist community of the type advocated by Fourier (1772–1837).

fàlbo, *a.* tawny.

falcàre, *v.i.* (*aux.* avere) to curvet (*horsemanship*).

fàlce, *f.* sickle; scythe. dim. *falcétto*. **falchétto**, *m.* hawk.

falciàre (*pr.* **fàlcio, fàlci**), *v.t.* to mow; cut down. **falciatóre**, *m.* (*f.* -**trice**) mower. **falciatríce**, *f.* mowing machine. **falciatúra**, *f.* mowing.

falcídia, *f.* reduction; cutting down (*of salaries, &c*).

falcióne, *m.* bill-hook; hay-cutter.

fàlco (*pl.* **fàlchi**), *m.* hawk. **falcóne**, *m.* falcon; derrick. **falconière**, *m.* falconer.

fàlda, *f.* flake; layer; slice; slab; plate; sheet; lower slope (*mountain*); brim (*hat*); skirt, flounce, flap, hem; (*pl.*) tail-coat. *a* ~ *a* ~, little by little. **faldàto**, *a.* flaky; stratified; pleated.

faldèlla, f. lint.

faldistòrio, m. faldstool.

falegnàme, m. carpenter, joiner. **falegnamería,** f. carpentry.

falèna, f. moth; light ash.

Falèrno, m. Falernian (wine) (Campania).

fàlla, f. leak. ~ di griglia, (Radio) grid leak.

fallàce, a. fallacious, misleading; deceitful, false. **fallàcia** (pl. -àcie), f. fallacy; fallaciousness.

fallàre, v.i. (aux. avere) to err, be mistaken.

fallíbile, a. fallible; liable to err.

falliménto, m. bankruptcy, insolvency; failure. **fallíre** (pr. -ísco, -isci, -isce), v.i. (aux. avere) to fail, be unsuccessful; go bankrupt, become insolvent; (v.t.) to miss.

fallíto, a. unsuccessful; unprofitable; bankrupt, insolvent.

fàllo, m. fault, error, slip. senza ~, without fail. essere in ~, to be at fault. ~ di piede, footfault (Ten.).

falò, m. bonfire.

falpalà, m. flounce.

falsamonéte, m.inv. coiner; forger (bank notes).

falsapòrta (pl. **falsepòrte**), f. secret door, blind door.

falsàre, v.t. to alter, distort; misrepresent; misconstrue; put insertions in a dress. ~ di rimbalzo, second (ball) (Ten.).

falsaríga (pl. **falsaríghe**), f. sheet ruled in lines placed under plain paper as a guide to writing straight; (fig.) model, example.

falsàrio (pl. -àri), m. forger, counterfeiter, coiner.

falsatóre, m. (f. -tríce) falsifier. **falsatúra,** f. insertion in a dress.

falsificàre (pr. -ífico, -ífichi), v.t. to falsify; forge; counterfeit; adulterate; debase; tamper with.

falsità, f.inv. falsity; falsehood; insincerity.

fàlso, a. false; wrong; untrue; base; counterfeit; forged; spurious; fictitious; bogus; disloyal; deceitful; unjust (weight); blank, blind (door, window). ~a partenza, f. false start. ~ponte, m. orlop (deck). ¶ m. falsehood; forgery; falsity; feint (fencing). essere nel ~, to be in error. testimoniare il ~, to bear false witness.

fàma, f. fame, renown, reputation; report. è ~, it is said, they say. esser in ~, to be in vogue.

fàme, f. hunger; starvation; dearth. aver ~, to be hungry.

famelicaménte, ad. greedily. **famèlico** (pl. -èlici), a. famishing, starving.

famigeràto, a. notorious, ill-famed.

famíglia, f. family; lineage; court, attendants; company. **famíglio** (pl. -ígli), m. manservant; usher, attendant.

familiàre, a. family (att.); familiar, intimate; domestic. ¶ m. intimate (friend); one of a [the] family.

famóso, a. famous; notorious; much talked of.

fanalàio (pl. -ài), & **fanalísta** (pl. -ísti), m. lighthouse-keeper; lamplighter. **fanàle,** m. lamp, lantern; headlight; ship's light; lighthouse; street or carriage lamp.

fanaticaménte, ad. fanatically. **fanàtico** (pl. -àtici), a. fanatic(al). **fanatíśmo,** m. fanaticism.

fanciúlla, f. girl, young girl. **fanciullàggine,** f. childishness; childish behaviour. **fanciullàta,** f. childish action; childish trick. **fanciullésco** (tl. -éschi), a. childish. **fanciullétto,** m. small boy, -a, f. s. girl. **fanciullézza,** f. childhood; boyhood, girlhood; infancy. **fanciúllo,** m. young boy; child. ¶ a. young, youthful.

fandònia, f. fib; made-up story; nonsense.

fanèllo, m. linnet.

fanfalúca, f. idle story; fantastic notion; trifle; nick-nack.

fanfàra, f. brass band; military music; flourish of trumpets, fanfare. **fanfaronàta,** f. brag, boastful talk or action. **fanfaróne,** m. braggart, boaster; (pop.) gasbag.

fangàia, f. muddy spot; m. road. **fangatúra,** f. (course of) mud baths. **fàngo** (pl. **fanghi**), m. mud, mire; (pl.) mud baths. **fangóso,** a. muddy.

fannullóne, m. (f. -óna) idler, lounger.

fantaccíno, m. foot-soldier, common soldier, ranker.

fantaśía, f. imagination; fancy; phantasy; caprice; whim; desire; fanciful object. articoli di ~, fancy articles. **fantàśima** or **fantàśma,** f. phantom, spectre, apparition. **fantaśmagoría,** f. series of fantastic illusions, dissolving view, phantasmagoria.

fantasticàre (*pr.* -àstico, -àstichi), *v.i.* (*aux.* avere) to fancy, indulge in fancies, day-dream. **fantasticheria**, *f.* reverie, day-dream, vain fancies. **fantàstico** (*pl.* -àstici), *a.* fantastic; fanciful; imaginary.

fànte, *m.* infantryman, foot-soldier; knave (or jack) at cards; boy, man-servant; *f.* maid-servant. **fantería**, *f.* infantry.

fantésca *f.* maid-servant. **fantíno**, *m.* jockey.

fantòccio (*pl.* -òcci), *m.* puppet; doll; (artist's) lay figure; scarecrow; simpleton. dim. *fantoccino.*

fantolíno, *m.* baby, little man.

farabolóne, *m.* (a) mere talker. **farabútto**, *m.* swindler, rascal, ne'er-do-well.

Faraóne, *m.* Pharaoh. **f~**, (*game of*) faro.

farcíre, *v.t.* to stuff (*cookery*). *pollo farcito*, stuffed fowl.

fardèllo, *m.* bundle; pack; burden.

fàre (*pr.* fò *or* fàccio, fài, fà), *v.t. & i.ir.* to do; make; create; form; build; perform; practise; effect; compose; write; play; commit; go; run; be; matter; have; get; keep; mind; get ready; get in; lay; set; (*Typ.*) pull (*proofs*); put; offer; offer up; give; take; take in (*provisions, &c.*); deal (*cards*); set up as; pretend to be; suit; cause; think; believe; take to be; grant; raise; rear; make up (*the cash*); amount to; contract (*a debt*); make out (*pretend*); wage (*war*); pay; ejaculate, say; charge; quote; accustom; call; turn. ¶ *m.* manner(s), behaviour; style; custom, habit; beginning; workmanship, construction. *sul far del giorno*, at daybreak. ~ *attenzione*, to pay attention, be careful. ~ *bel tempo*, ~ *cattivo tempo*, to be fine, to be bad weather. ~ *caldo*, ~ *freddo*, to be warm, cold (of weather). ~ *coda*, to queue [up]. ~ *colazione*, to breakfast; to [have] lunch. ~ *fare*, to have or get (something) done. ~ *male*, to hurt. ~ *omaggio*, to pay homage. ~ *progressi*, to make progress. ~ *il sarto*, *il calzolaio*, to be a tailor, a shoe-maker, &c. ~ *un bagno*, ~ *una passeggiata*, to take a bath, a walk. ~ *un brindisi*, to drink a toast. ~ *poco caso di*, to make light of. ~ *una visita*, to pay a visit (*doctor, tourist, &c.*). ~ *le veci di*, to replace; represent. ~ *naufragio*, to be (ship)-wrecked. ~ *vela*, to set sail. ~ *vista* (*di*), to pretend. ~ *da*, to act as. ~ *presto*, to make haste. ~ *a meno di*, to do without; to help, to refrain from. ~ *a metà*, to go halves, to share equally. *fa d'uopo*, it is necessary. **fàrsi**, *v.refl.* to become, grow; come, go; approach; do something to oneself or for one's own advantage; *farsi capire*, to make oneself understood (in such cases the *v.i.* is always active). *farsi la barba*, to shave (oneself). *fatevi avanti*, ~ *in qua*, come forward, c. nearer. *fatti in lì*, get out of my way, please. *f·rsi animo*, ~ *coraggio*, to take courage. *farsi beffe* (*di*), to ridicule, make fun (of).

farètra, *f.* quiver.

farfàlla, *f.* butterfly; (*Mech.*) throttle. **farfalleggiàre**, *v.i.* (*aux.* avere) to flutter about.

farfallíno, *m.* small butterfly or moth; (*fig.*) light-headed person, flibberti-gibbet. **farfallóne**, *m.* large moth or butterfly; lie; blunder.

farfugliàre, *v.i.* (*aux.* avere) to mumble; stutter.

farína, *f.* meal; flour. ~*di frumento*, wheaten meal. ~*d'avena*, oatmeal. ~ *gialla*, maize meal. ~ *di riso*, ground rice. **farinàceo**, *a.* farinaceous. **farinai[u]òlo**, *m.* flour-dealer. **farinàta**, *f.* pap; porridge. ~ *d'avena*, oatmeal porridge.

farínge, *f.* pharynx. **faringíte**, *f.* (*Med.*) pharyngitis; relaxed throat.

farinóso, *a.* floury.

farisàico (*pl.* -àici), *a.* pharisaic(al). **farisèo**, *m.* Pharisee; hypocrite.

farmacèutica, *f.* study of drugs. **farmacèutico** (*pl.* -èutici), *a.* pharmaceutical. **farmacía**, *f.* pharmacy; chemist's shop. **farmacísta** (*pl.* -ísti), *m.* (dispensing) chemist, pharmacist. **fàrmaco** (*pl.* fàrmachi), *m.* drug. **farmacología**, *f.* pharmacology. **farmacopèa**, *f.* pharmacopoeia.

farneticàre (*pr.* -ètico, -ètichi), *v.i.* (*aux.* avere) to rave, wander in one's talk; be crazy. **farnètico** (*pl.* -ètici), *a.* crazy; frantic. ¶ *m.* madman; madness.

fàro, *m.* lighthouse; beacon; headlight, headlamp. ~ *d'aeroporto*, airport beacon. ~ *di atterraggio*, (*Aviat.*) landing light. *nave* ~, lightship. ~ *galleggiante*, floating light. ~ *girante*, revolving light. *radio* ~, radio beacon.

farràgine, *f.* farrago; medley; hotch-potch. **farraginóso**, *a.* confused, mixed, ill-assorted.

fàrsa, *f.* farce. **farsésco** (*pl.* -éschi), *a.* farcical.

fascétta, *f.* corset; band; wrapper; medal-ribbon. *~da giornale*, news-paper-wrapper. **fascettàia**, *f.* corset-maker.

fàscia (*pl.* **fàsce**), band, bandage; belt; wrapper; cover; (*pl.*) swaddling clothes. *spedire sotto ~*, to send under cover. **fasciàme**, *m.* plating, sheathing; shell (*Ship*). **fasciàre** (*pr.* **fàscio, fàsci**), *v.t.* to bandage, swathe, wrap; bind up (*wound*). **fasciatúra**, *f.* bandaging, binding, swaddling; dressing (wound). **fasci-colo**, *m.* part or number of a perio-dical, or of book published in parts; group of documents relating to some particular person or object (Fr. *dossier*).

fascina, *f.* faggot, bundle of sticks; (*Mil.*) fascine.

fàscino, *m.* charm, fascination.

fàscio (*pl.* **fàsci**), *m.* bundle; (*fig.*) burden, weight; (*Rom.*) *fasces*, the lictor's rods; group. *~ di raggi*, *~ luminoso*, pencil of light. *andare* (or *mandare*) *in f~*, to go or send to ruin.

fàse, *f.* phase, period, stage, cycle.

fastèllo (*pl.m.* -èlli, *f.* -èlla), *m.* faggot, bundle of hay or wood.

fàsti, *m.pl.* records, annals.

fastídio, *m.* trouble, annoyance; anxiety; vexation; disgust. **fasti-dióso**, *a.* troublesome, tiresome, annoying, vexatious. **fastidíre** (*pr.* -ísco, -ísci), *v.t.* to annoy, trouble; weary, disgust.

fastígio (*pi.* -ígi), m. (*Arch.*) top, ridge; summit.

fàsto, *m.* pomp, magnificence; display, ostentation. **fastosaménte**, *ad.* ostentatiously, with pomp & display. **fastóso**, *a.* gorgeous, sumptuous; ostentatious; pompous.

fàta, *f.* fairy. *paese delle ~ e*, *m.* fairy-land. *racconto di ~e*, *m.* fairy tale. **fatàle**, *a.* fatal; destined. *uomo ~*, (the) man of destiny. **fatalísmo**, *m.* fatalism. **fatalísta**, *m.* fatalist. **fatalità**, *f.inv.* fate; destiny; fatality; mischance.

fatàto, *a.* bewitched, enchanted; fairy (*att.*).

fatíca (*pl.* **fatíche**), fatigue, labour; hard-work; trouble, difficulty. **fati-càre** (*pr.* -íco, -íchi), *v.i.* (*aux.*

avere) to toil, work hard. *~a*, to have difficulty in; be hardly able to. **faticóso**, *a.* laborious, hard, tiring; weary; painful, difficult.

fatídico (*pl.* -ídici), *a.* prophetic.

fàto, *m.* fate, lot, destiny.

fàtta, *f.* kind, sort; quality; action; (*animal's*) trail.

fattàccio (*pl.* -àcci), *m.* bad deed; crime. **fatterèllo**, *m.* trifling affair, unimportant event.

fattézze, *f.pl.* features.

fattíbile, *a.* feasible; practicable.

fattíccio (*pl.* -ícci), *a.* robust, stout.

fattispècie, *f.inv.* (*Law*) case in point; full particulars.

fattívo, *a.* active, busy; effective; useful. **fattízio** (*pl.* -ízi), *a.* factitious; artificial.

fàtto, *p.p.* of **fare**. ¶ *m.* fact; deed, feat; act, action; event; business, occurrence; affair, matter; subject. *in ~ di*, with regard to, in the matter of. *in linea di ~*, in point of fact. *il ~ sta*, the fact remains. *gran ~*, much. *il ~ mio*, what suits me, what I want. *sul ~*, in the act. *fatti diversi*, news items. ¶ *a.* complete, finished, ripe; ready-made. *uomo ~*, full-grown man. *giorno ~*, broad daylight.

fattóre, *m.* maker, creator; factor; element; steward, land agent; (*Math.*) factor. **fattoría**, *f.* farm (buildings); land-agency, steward-ship.

fattoríno, *m.* messenger; delivery man; office-boy; shop-man. *~ tele-grafico*, telegraph-messenger; t. boy.

fattucchière, *m.* (*f.* -èra) wizard, sorcerer, -ess; *f.* witch. **fattuc-chieria**, *f.* sorcery, witchcraft.

fattúra, *f.* make; making; work; workmanship; bill, invoice; sorcery, witchcraft. **fatturàre**, *v.t.* to adulterate, doctor (wine); to invoice.

fatuità, *f.inv.* fatuity, fatuousness; self-conceit. **fàtuo**, *a.* fatuous. *fuoco ~*, will-o'-the-wisp.

fàuci, *f.pl.* jaws.

fàuna, *f.* fauna.

fàuno, *m.* faun.

Fàusto, *m.* Faust. **fàusto**, *a.* propi-tious, happy, lucky.

fautóre, *m.*, **fautríce**, *f.* protector (*f.* protectress), supporter, pro-moter.

fàva, *f.* bean, broad bean. *pigliare due colombi a una ~*, to kill two birds with one stone (*fig.*).

favèlla, *f.* speech; language; tongue;

dialect. **favellàre** (*pr.* -**èllo**), *v.t. & abs.* to talk, speak; tell.

favilla, *f.* spark.

fàvo, *m.* honeycomb.

fàvola, *f.* fable; idle tale; untruth; plot (*drama or poem*); byword, laughing-stock, object of derision. **favoleggiàre** (*pr.* -**éggio**, -**éggi**), *v.i.* (*aux.* avere) to tell stories, esp. old tales. **favolóso**, *a.* fabulous, fabled.

favóre, *m.* favour, boon; kindness; goodwill; grace; approval. *per ~*, please. *biglietto di ~*, complimentary ticket. *cambiale di ~*, accommodation bill. *giorni di ~*, days of grace. **favoreggiàre** (*pr.* -**eggio**, -**eggi**), *v.t.* to aid, support; be an accomplice in; show favour to. **favorévole**, *a.* favourable; propitious. **favoríre** (*pr.* -**ísco**, -**ísci**), *v.t.* to favour, assist, support, encourage; promote; (*in terms of address*) be so kind as to . . . (*often with a verb understood*). *favorisca . . .*, please. **favoríta**, *f.* favourite; (*royal*) mistress. **favoritísmo**, *m.* favouritism. **favorito**, *p.p.* of **favorire.** ¶ *a.* favourite. ¶ *m.* favourite; darling, pet.

fazióne, *f.* faction. **fazióso**, *a.* factious.

fazzolétto, *m.* handkerchief.

fè, *f. abb.* of **féde**, faith. **fe'**, *3rd sg. past def.* of **fare**, abb. of **fece**.

febbràio (*pl.* -**ài**), *m.* February.

fèbbre, *f.* fever; (*fig.*) heat; excitement; violent desire. *~ del fieno*, hay fever. **febbricitànte**, *a.* feverish, in a feverish state. **febbrifugo** (*pl.* -**ifughi**), *m.* febrifuge, medicine to reduce fever. **febbrile**, *a.* feverish; restless. **febbrilménte**, *ad.* feverishly; restlessly. **febbróne**, *m.* violent fever. **febbróso**, *a.* feverish.

Fèbo, *m.* Phoebus (Apollo).

fèccia (*pl.* **fècce**), *f.* sediment, dregs; (*pl.*) lees; (*fig.*) rabble, mob. **fecciúme**, *m.* quantity of dregs or refuse; scum; rabble.

fèci, *f.pl.* (*Med.*) foeces; stools. **féci**, *1st sg. past def.* of **fare**.

fècola, *f.* fecula, starch (*Chem.*) *~ d'amone*, *~ indiana*, arrowroot.

fecondàre (*pr.* -**óndo**), *v.t.* to fertilize. **fecondità**, *f.* fertility. **fecóndo**, *a.* fertile, fruitful; prolific, productive.

feculènto, *a.* starchy (*food*).

féde, *f.* faith, belief, credit; honesty,

uprightness; trust, confidence; certificate. *~ di nascita*, birth certificate. *far ~*, to bear witness, attest. *prestar ~ a*, to credit, believe. *romper ~*, *venir meno alla ~*, to break one's word.

fedéle, *a.* faithful; true; exact; sincere. **fedeltà**, *f.inv.* faithfulness; fidelity; loyalty; (*Radio*) definition.

fèdra, *f.* pillow-case, p.-slip.

federàle, *a.* federal. **federalísmo**, *m.* federalism. **federàre**, *v.t. & federàrsi*, *v.refl.* to federate. **federazióne**, *f.* federation.

fedífrago (*pl.* -**ífraghi**), *a.* faithless, unfaithful, treacherous. ¶ *m.* one who breaks faith; traitor.

fedína, *f.* penal certificate; whisker.

Fèdra, *f.* Phaedra (*Myth.*).

fegatàccio, *m.* dare-devil. **fegatèlla**, *f.* (*Bot.*) liverwort, hepatica. **fegatèlli**, *m.pl.* slices of pig's liver. **fegatíno**, *m.* fowl's liver. **fégato**, *m.* liver; (*fig.*) courage. **fegatóso**, *a.* bilious, liverish, with the liver out of order.

fèlce, *f.* fern; bracken. **felcéto**, *m.* bed of ferns; fernery.

feldmarescìàllo, *m.* field-marshal.

feldispàto, *or* **feldspàto**, *m.* feldspar (*Min.*).

felíbro, *m.* félibre, mod. Provençal writer.

felíce, *a.* happy, fortunate, lucky; pleasant. **feliceménte**, *ad.* happily. **felicità**, *f.inv.* happiness; felicity; happy; bless. **felicitàrsi** (**con**), *v.refl.* to congratulate. **felicitazióne**, *f.* congratulation.

felíno, *a.* feline. **F~**, *m.* a dry white wine of Parma.

fellonía, *f.* treason, rebellion.

félpa, *f.* plush. **felpàto**, *a.* plushy, covered with plush.

feltràre (*pr.* **féltro**), *v.t.* to felt. **feltratúra**, *f.* felting. **féltro**, *m.* felt; piece of felt; felt hat.

felúca (*pl.* **felúche**), *f.* felucca, two-masted lateen vessel; (*fig.*) cocked hat.

fèlze, *m.* cabin of a gondola.

fémmina, *f.* female (*human or animal*); woman; girl. *vite ~*, female screw. *dim.* **femminélla**, **femminétta**. **femmíneo**, *a.* womanly; womanish, effeminate. **femminésco** (*pl.* -**éschi**), *a.* like a woman. **femminíle**, *a.* feminine; womanly; for women or girls; female. *genere ~*, feminine gender. ¶ *m. il ~*, feminine (noun). **femminíno**, *a.* feminine. **femminísmo**, *m.* feminism. **femminísta**, *a. & m.f.* feminist.

fèmore, *m.* femur; thigh-bone.

fenacetína, *f.* phenacetin[e] (*Med.*).

fendènte, *m.* downward cut of a sword, cutting blow. ¶ *p.a.* cleaving, cutting. **fèndere** (*pr.* **fèndo, fèndi, fènde**), *v.t.ir.* to cleave, split; cut. **fenditúra**, *f.* cleaving, splitting; cleft, split.

feníce, *f.* phoenix (*Myth.*).

Fenícia (la), *f.* Phoenicia. **fenício**, *a. & m.* Phoenician.

fènico (*pl.* **fènici**), *a.* carbolic. *acido* ~, *m.* carbolic acid.

fenicòttero, *m.* flamingo.

fenòlo, *m.* phenol (*Chem.*).

fenomenàle, *a.* phenomenal. **fenòmeno**, *m.* phenomenon (*pl.* -ena).

feràce, *a.* fertile. **feràle**, *a.* fatal, deadly.

fèretro, *m.* bier; hearse; catafalque.

fèria (*pl.* **fèrie**), *f.* (*gen.pl.*) (public) holiday(s); (*in Eccl. calendar*) all the days of the week, except Saturday & Sunday. *ferie pasquali, f.pl.* Easter holidays. ~ *estive*, Summer holidays, S. vacation. ~ *natalizie*, Christmas holidays. ~ *retribuite*, holidays with pay.

feriàle, *a.* ordinary, working. *giorni* ~ *i*, *m.pl.* working days, weekdays.

feríno, *a.* savage, wild, untamed.

feríre (*pr.* -**ísco**, -**ísci**, -**ísce**), *v.t.* to wound (*lit. & fig.*), strike; injure, offend. **feríta**, *f.* wound (*lit. & fig.*). **feríto**, *p.a. & m.* wounded; wounded man. *i* ~ *i*, the wounded.

feritóia, *f.* loophole, embrasure; (*Mech.*) vent.

férma, *f.* term of (voluntary) service (*Mil.*). **fermacàrte**, *m.inv.* paperweight. **fermàglio** (*pl.* -**àgli**), *m.* clasp; buckle; brooch. **fermapantalóne**, *m.inv.* trouser clip (*cycling*). **fermapiède**, *m.inv.* toeclip (*bicycle*). **fermàre** (*pr.* **férmo**), *v.t.* to stop, arrest; fix, fasten; close; keep steady; cook lightly. *v.i.* (*aux.* avere) to stop; point (*of a dog*). *cane da ferma, m.* pointer. **fermàrsi**, *v.refl.* to stop; stay, remain; (*Mech.*) stall. ~ *su*, to dwell upon, linger over. **fermàta**, *f.* stop, halt, pause; stopping place. ~ *facoltativa*, optional stop[ping-place], *s.* at request.

fermentàre, (*pr.* -**énto**), *v.i.* (*aux.*

avere) *&* **fermentàrsi**, *v.refl.* to ferment. **fermentazióne**, *f.* fermentation. **ferménto**, *m.* ferment; leaven.

fermézza, *f.* firmness; constancy; steadiness; spring-clasp. **férmo**, *a.* firm; fast; steady; settled; still; stagnant; immovable, resolved. *canto* ~, plain song. *punto* ~, full stop, period (*Gram.*). *ferma in posta*, to be called for, Poste-restante. ~! steady! *star* ~, to keep (stand) still. *tenere per* ~, to take for certain, to believe positively. ¶ *m.* distraint; seizure; arrest.

feróce, *a.* ferocious; fierce; savage; cruel. **feròcia** *&* **ferocità**, *f.* ferocity, savagery; cruelty.

Feròe (le), *f.pl.* the Faroes, F. islands.

ferràccio, *m.* scrap-iron, pig-iron; cast-iron. **ferraglio**, *m.* old iron; scrap-iron.

ferragósto, *m.* 1st of August; August holiday (Feast of the Assumption, Aug. 15).

ferràio (*pl.* -**ài**), *m.* blacksmith, smith.

ferrai(u)òlo, *m.* short wide cloak.

ferràme, *m.* quantity of iron; (*pl.*) iron ware, ironmongery. **ferraménta**, *f.pl. & ferramenti*, *m.pl.* hardware, ironmongery; iron fittings; i. tools. **ferràre** (*pr.* **fèrro**), *v.t.* to bind with iron; to shoe (a horse). **ferraréccia**, *f.* ironmongery; ironmonger's shop; (*pl.*) **ferrarécce**, iron ware, iron goods. **ferràta**, *f.* iron grating; iron railing. **ferràto**, *p.a.* shod; iron-bound; (*fig.*) strong (*in a subject*). ~ *a ghiaccio*, roughshod. *strada* ~ *a*, railway (track), railroad. **ferratúra**, *f.* shoeing (*horse*); horse-shoes. **ferravècchio** (*pl.* -**ècchi**), *m.* dealer in old iron. **fèrreo**, *a.* iron (*att.*); (*fig.*) strong, robust. **ferrétto**, *m.* (small) iron tool. **ferriàta**, *f.* grating, iron railing. **ferrièra**, *f.* iron-works; i. foundry; forge; iron-mine. **ferrígno**, *a.* iron-grey. **fèrro**, *m.* iron; sword (*Poet.*); (*pl.*) irons (*chains*); tools; instruments; horseshoes; shackles. ~ *da calza*, knitting-needle. ~ *da stirare*, flatiron. ~ *da ricci*, curling tongs. ~ *in barre*, bar iron. ~ *fucinato*, wrought i. ~ *grezzo*, pig i. ~ *laminato*, sheet i. *piccoli* ~ *i* (*Typ.*), florets. **ferróso**, *a.* ferrous (*Chem.*):

ferrovía, *f.* railway; railroad. ~ *aerea*, overhead (elevated) railway. **ferro-**

viàrio, *a.* railway (*att.*). **ferro-vière,** *m.* railwayman.

ferrugíneo & **ferruginóso,** *a.* ferruginous.

fèrtile, *a.* fertile, fruitful; prolific; fat (*land*). **fertilità,** *f.* fertility. **fertiliżżànte,** *m.* fertilizer. **fertiliżżàre,** *v.t.* to fertilize.

fèrula, *f.* rod.

fèrvere (*pr.* **fèrvo**), *v.i.* to be fervent; be ardent; be intense. *ferve il lavoro,* the work is going on assiduously. **fervóre,** *m.* fervour, ardour; (intense) heat. **fervoríno,** *m.* mild admonition or reproof; admonition.

fèrza, *f.* whip, scourge (*lit.* & *fig.*).

fésso, *p.a.* cloven; cleft; cracked. ¶ *m.* cleft, crack, division; silly fellow. **fessolíno,** *m.* small chink or crevice. **fessúra,** *f.* fissure; cleft; slit; crevice.

fèsta, *f.* feast, festivity; holiday; festival; fête; joy, rejoicing; saint's-day; birthday; entertainment, treat. *far ~,* to make merry; take a holiday. *mezza ~,* half-holiday. *far ~ a,* to welcome. *a ~,* in holiday attire. *abiti da ~,* Sunday clothes. *~del Corpus Domini,* Corpus Christi. **festai[u]òlo,** *m.* one who provides or arranges a festival. ¶ *a.* festival-loving. **festànte,** *a.* joyful, rejoicing. **festeggiàre** (*pr.* **-éggio, éggi**), *v.t.* to celebrate; keep (festival); welcome; applaud; *v.i.* (*aux.* avere) to feast; make merry. **festévole,** *a.* gay, joyous; festive. **festívo,** *a.* festive; festal. *biglietto ~,* week-end ticket.

festóne, *m.* festoon.

festóso, *a.* joyous, joyful; merry, gay.

festúca (*pl.* **festúche**), *f.* straw, bit of straw; mote.

fetènte, *a.* stinking (*lit.* & *fig.*).

fetíccio (*pl.* **-ícci**), *m.* fetish.

fètido, *a.* fetid; stinking; rank. **fetidúme,** *f.* stench; rottenness; rotten things.

Fetónte, *m.* Phaethon (*Myth.*).

fetóre, *m.* foul smell; stench.

fétta, *f.* slice; strip. *~ di pane,* slice of bread. *tagliare a ~ e,* to slice, cut into slices. **fettína,** *f.* small slice. **fettóne,** *m.* **-óna,** *f.* large slice. **fettúccia** (*pl.* **-úcce**), *f.* small slice; tape; ribbon. **fettuccíne,** *f.pl.* (*Cook.*) ribbon-shaped vermicelli.

feudàle, *a.* feudal. **feudalísmo,** *m.* feudalism. **feudatàrio,** *a.* & *m.* feudatory. **fèudo,** *m.* feud; fief.

fèż, *m.inv.* fez.

fía (*Poet.*) = *sia; sarà.*

fiàba, *f.* fairy story; fable; children's story; marvellous tale; dramatic fable.

fiàcca, *f.* lassitude; weakness; indolence. **fiaccaménte,** *ad.* languidly; weakly. **fiaccàre** (*pr.* **-àcco, -àcchi**), *v.t.* to weaken, weary, exhaust, wear out, tire out; break down; depress, dispirit. **fiaccheràio,** *m.* cabman. **fiacchézza,** *f.* weakness, weariness, lassitude. **fiàcco** (*pl.* **-àcchi**), *a.* weak, sluggish, tired; dull.

fiàccola, *f.* torch; blow lamp. **fiàccolàta,** *f.* torch-light procession.

fiaccóna, *f.* lazy woman; (*abs.*) extreme laziness. **fiaccóne,** *m.* sluggard.

fiàla, *f.* phial.

fiàmma, *f.* flame; (*Nav.*) pennon, pennant. *ritorno di ~ (Motor)* back-fire. *~ ossídrica* oxyhydrogen flame. **fiammànte,** *a.* flaming, blazing. *nuovo ~,* brand new. **fiammàta,** *f.* blaze. **fiammeggiàre** (*pr.* **-éggio, -éggi**), *v.i.* (*aux.* avere) to blaze, flame; shine. **fiammiferàio** (*pl.* **-ài**), *m.* (*f.* **-feràia**) maker or seller of matches. **fiammífero,** *m.* match. *scatola per ~ i,* *f.* match-box.

fiammíngo (*pl.* **-ínghi**), *m.* Fleming. ¶ *a.* Flemish. *il f~, la lingua fiamminga,* Flemish, the Flemish language.

fiancàre (*pr.* **-ànco, -ànchi**), *v.t.* to strengthen the sides of an arch or vault, &c. **fiancàta,** *f.* blow on the side or from the side; flank; spur; broadside (*Nav.*). **fiancheggiàre** (*pr.* **-eggio**), *v.t.* to flank; support. **fiànco** (*pl.* **-ànchi**), *m.* side; flank; abutment (*of a bridge*). *di ~,* sideways. *al ~ di,* by the side of. *~ destro! ~ sinistro!* right turn! left turn! (*Mil.*). *~ destro, ~ sinistro* (*Naut.*) starboard side, port s.

fiancúto, *a.* broad in the beam.

Fiàndra (**la**), *f.* & **Fiàndre** (**le**), *f.pl.* Flanders.

fiano & **fíeno** (*Poet.*) = *siano; saranno.*

fiàsca (*pl.* **fiàsche**), *f.* flask (*with flat sides*). **fiaschetteria,** *f.* wine-shop; bar. **fiaschetto,** *m.* small flask. **fiàsco** (*pl.* **-àschi**), *m.* flask, bottle (*Ital. wine-bottle, straw-covered, with narrow neck and bulging body*); fiasco, failure.

fiàta, *f.* (*Poet.*) time. *molte ~e, spesse ~e,* many times. **fiatàre,** *v.i.* (*aux.* avere) to breathe; speak softly, whisper. **fiàto,** *m.* breath; breathing; (*fig.*) strength. *~ grosso,* heavy breathing. *strumento a ~,* wind-instrument (*Mus.*).

fíbbia, *f.* buckle.

fíbra, *f.* fibre; constitution. **fibrílla,** *f.* fibril, small fibre. **fibróso,** *a.* fibrous.

ficcanàso, *m.* meddler, intruder; Paul Pry; Nosey Parker (*fam.*). **ficcàre** (*pr.* **fícco, fícchi**), *v.t.* to thrust; push (in), drive (in), poke (into); fix (upon). **ficcàrsi,** *v.refl.* to thrust in; push in; hide oneself; worm oneself (into); intrude. *~ in capo, ~ in testa,* to get into one's head, be determined.

fíco (*pl.* **fíchi**), *m.* fig; fig-tree. *~ d'India,* prickly pear. *non vale un ~ secco,* it is not worth a rap.

fidànza, *f.* confidence; trust. **fidanzaménto,** *m.* betrothal, engagement (*to marry*). **fidanzàre** (*pr.* **-ànzo**), *v.t.* to betroth. **fidanzàrsi,** *v.refl.* to become engaged. **fidanzàta,** *f.* fiancée, engaged girl. **fidanzàto,** *m.* fiancé, man engaged to be married. **fidàre,** *v.t.* to entrust; (*v.i.*) (*aux.* avere) to confide, trust, have confidence (in). **fidàrsi** (**di**), *v.refl.* to rely on. **fidatézza,** *f.* trustworthiness; fidelity. **fidàto,** *a.* trusted; trusty, trustworthy, faithful.

fidènte, *a.* confiding, trustful; confident.

Fídia, *m.* Phidias.

fído, *a.* faithful, trusty; devoted; trustful. ¶ *m.* (*Com.*) credit. *a ~,* on credit. *far ~,* to give credit.

fidúcia, *f.* confidence, trust. **fiduciàrio** (*pl.* **-àri**), *a. & m.* fiduciary; (*m.*) trustee. **fiducióso,** *a.* confident; hopeful.

fièle, *m.* gall, bile; jaundice; (*fig.*) hatred, rancour.

fienagióne, *f.* hay-making; time of hay-making; hay-harvest. **fieníle,** *m.* hay-loft; manger. **fièno,** *m.* hay. *febbre* (also *asma*) *del ~,* hay-fever. *~ serotino,* late crop of hay. *pagliaio di ~,* hay-rick.

fièra, *f.* wild beast; fair; exhibition, show. **fieraménte,** *ad.* fiercely; boldly; proudly. **fierézza,** *f.* fierceness; boldness, intrepidity; pride. **fièro,** *a.* fierce; bold; stern; severe; proud.

fiévole, *a.* feeble, weak. **fievolézza,** *f.* feebleness; weakness.

fifa, *f.* (*Mil. slang*) fear, terror; cowardice.

figgere (*pr.* **fíggo, fíggi**), *v.t. ir.* to fix. *figgersi in capo,* to get into one's head, be stubbornly of opinion.

fíglia, *f.* daughter; (*fig. Com.*) counter-foil. **figliàre** (*pr.* **fíglio, fígli**), *v.t. & i.* (*aux.* avere) to give birth to (of animals); (*cow*) calve; (*horse*) foal; (*sheep*) lamb, &c. **figliàstra,** *f.* step-daughter. **figliàstro,** *m.* step-son. **figliàta,** *f.* litter (of animals). **figliazióne,** *f.* progeny, offspring; branch, filiation.

fíglio (*pl.* **figli**), *m.* son; child. **figliòccia,** *f.* **figliòccio,** *m.* god-child. **figliolànza,** *f.* the relation of son to father, sonship; progeny, offspring; children.

figli[u]òla, *f.* daughter; girl. **figli[u]òlo,** *m.* son; boy.

fígnolo, *m.* boil.

figúra, *f.* figure; form, shape; face (*of pers.*), countenance; appearance, show(ing); court-card; character (*in novel, drama, &c.*); plate, illustration (*in a book*). *~ retorica,* figure of speech. *~ di prua,* figure-head (*ship*). *far ~,* to have a striking appearance; look well. **figuràccia,** *f.* bad or wretched figure. *fare una ~* (or *una brutta figura*), to cut a poor figure. **figurànte,** *m.f.* ballet-dancer; (*Theat.*) walker on, supernumerary. **figuràre** (*pr.* **-úro**), *v.t.* to represent; illustrate, symbolize. *v.i.* (*aux.* avere) to figure, appear; act, deal, behave; play a part; pretend; dress well. **figuràrsi,** *v.refl.* to imagine, fancy, think, suppose; figure to oneself. *si figuri!* just imagine! not at all! **figuratívo,** *a. & figuràto, p.a.,* figurative. **figurétta & figurína,** *f.* statuette; little figure; small illustration (*in a book*). **figurinàio** (*pl.* **-ài**), *m.* maker or seller of statuettes. **figuríno,** *m.* model, pattern; fashion-journal; dandy. **figurísta,** *m.* portrait-painter. **figúro,** *m.* cad; scoundrel.

fíla, *f.* row; line; file. *in ~,* (*Mil.*) in file. *per ~ a ~,* (*Mil.*) to the fix. *sinist(ra)!* (*Mil.*) right wheel! left wheel! *rompete le ~e!* (*Mil.*) dismiss! *in prima ~,* in the first row. *capo di ~,* leading file. *di ~, alla ~,* consecutively. *~ di stanze,* suite of rooms.

filàccia di cotóne, f. lint.
filaccióso, a. ragged; thready; frayed; stringy (meat).
filaménto, m. filament; thread.
filànda, f. silk-factory; spinning mill. **filandàia,** f. silk-spinner.
filantropía, f. philanthropy. **filantròpico** (pl. -òpici), a. philanthropic. **filàntropo,** m. philanthropist.
filàre, v.t. to spin; draw (into wire); pay out (cable); pour out (in a fine stream). v.i. (aux. avere) to spin; flow in a fine stream; run; be off; make off; file past; (of wine or syrup) rope; (of a lamp or candle) smoke; flirt. fila! off with you! get off! la nave fila dieci nodi l'ora, the ship is making ten knots an hour. far ~, to bring one to book, keep someone on the right path, put someone in his place. ¶ m. row (esp. of trees, posts, &c.). un ~ di pioppi, a row of poplars.
filarmònico (pl. -ònici), a. & m. philharmonic; lover of music.
filastròcca (pl. -stròcche), f. rigmarole, long & meaningless talk; children's nonsense rhyme[s].
filatelía & **filatèlica,** f. philately; stamp-collecting. **filatèlico** (pl. -èlici), a. philatelic. ¶ m. philatelist, stamp-collector.
filatíccio (pl. -ícci), m. coarse silk, floss-silk.
filàto, m. spun yarn. **filatóio** (pl. -ói), m. spinning-jenny; spinning roll. **filatóre,** m. (f. -tríce) spinner. **filatúra,** f. spinning.
filellènico (pl. -ènici), a. philhellenic. **filellèno,** m. philhellene.
filettàre (pr. -étto), v.t. to border (with ornament); thread (a screw). **filétto,** m. filament, fine thread; worm (screw); stripe (of rank); fine stroke (handwriting); ornamental border; fillet (Cook.); fraenum; snaffle (bit); bezel (gem, watch-glass).
filiàle, a. filial. casa ~ or ~, f. branch, branch establishment, branch office.
filiazióne, f. filiation; descent, derivation.
filibustière, m. filibuster; freebooter.
filièra, f. (Mech.) draw plate; die plate; screw plate; wire gauge. ~ per filettare, screw-cutting die.
filifórme, a. thread-like.
filigràna, f. filigree work; watermark (paper). **filigranàto,** a. filigreed; water-marked.

Filíppi, f. Philippi (Geog.).
filíppica, f. philippic.
Filippíne (le), f.pl. the Philippines, Philippine islands. **filippíno,** a. & m. native of the Philippines; priest of the oratory founded by San Filippo Neri.
filistéismo, m. philistinism. **filistèo,** a. & m. Philistine.
film, m. film (cinema). Cf. pellicola. girare un ~, to shoot a film. ~ al rallentatore, slow-motion film. ~ sonoro, sound film. ~di attualità, news f. [~] documentario, documentary, instructional f.
fillòssera, f. phylloxera.
fíio, m. thread (lit. & fig.); yarn; twine; wire; blade (of grass); edge (knife or sword); flow of current; tiny stream; (fig.) weak voice; what is slender or diminutive; clue. ~ di ordito, warp. ~ di trama, woof; yarn. ~ piombo, plumb-line, per ~ e per segno, accurately; in detail. di ~, fil ~, consecutively; continuously. essere appeso ad un ~, to hang by a thread.
fílobus, m.inv. trolley-bus.
filodrammàtico (pl. -àtici), a. & m. philodramatic; lover of the theatre; amateur player.
filología, f. philology. **filològico** (pl. -ògici), a. philological. **filòlogo,** (pl. -òlogi), m. philologist.
Filomèla, Filomèna, f. Philomel, Philomela (Myth.); (Poet.) nightingale.
filoncíno, m. small vein of mineral; (small) roll (of bread).
filóne, m. coarse thread; vein (of mineral); stream, flow (of current); big roll (of bread). ~ di lava, stream of lava. ~ di marea, tide-race.
filóso, a. stringy, thready.
filoṣofeggiàre (pr. -éggio, -éggi), v.i. (aux. avere) to philosophize.
filoṣofía, f. philosophy. **filoṣòfico** (pl. -òfici), a. philosophic(al). **filòṣofo,** m. philosopher.
Filottète, m. Philoctetes (Myth.)
filovía, f. electric car line, with overhead wire & no rails, trolley-[bus], line.
filtràre, v.t. & i. (aux. essere) to filter, strain; percolate. **filtrazióne,** f. filtration; filtering. **filtro,** m. filter; love potion, philtre.
filugèllo, m. silk-worm.
fílza, f. string; series of articles

strung together; file (*of papers*).
~ *di perle*, string of pearls. *punto a* ~, running stitch.
fímo, *m.* dung, manure.
finàle, *a.* final, ultimate, last. ¶ *m.* final (*sport*); finale (*Mus., Theat.*).
finalíno, *m.* (*Typ.*) tailpiece.
finalísta, *m.* finalist (*sport*). **finalità**, *f.* finality; end, purpose. **finalménte**, *ad.* finally; at last.
finaménte, *ad.* finely.
finànche & **finànco**, *ad.* even.
finànza, *f.* finance; (*pop.*) customs; (*pl.*) finances, cash, money, exchequer. *guardia di* ~, customs officer. **finanziàre**, *v.t.* to finance.
finanziàrio (*pl.* -àri), *a.* financial. *anno* ~, financial year. **finanzière**, *m.* financier; customs officer.
finché, *c.* till, until; as long as; while. ~ *non*, until.
fíne, *f.* end, close; conclusion. *volgere alla* ~, to draw to an end (*or* a close). ¶ *m.* end, purpose, object; intention; result. *a che* ~? to what end? for what purpose? *a* ~ *di*, in order to.
fíne, *a.* fine, thin, slender; delicate; refined; cunning.
finèstra, *f.* window. ~ *a saliscendi*, ~ *a ghigliottina*, sash-window. ~ *sporgente*, bay-w., bow w. ~ *a due battenti*, French w. Dim. *finestrella*, *finestrina*, *finestretta*; *finestrino*, *m.* (as in Rly. carriage, booking-office, &c.).
finestróne, *m.* large window.
finézza, *f.* fineness; subtlety, finesse; grace of manner; delicacy of expression.
fíngere (*pr.* **fíngo, fíngi, fínge**), *v.t.* & *i.ir.* (*aux. avere*) to feign, counterfeit, pretend; imagine, suppose.
finiménto, *m.* finishing, completion, accomplishment; ornament; set; (*pl.*) harness, trappings.
finimóndo, *m.* end of the world; (*fig.*) ruin, disaster.
finíre, (*pr.* -ísco, -ísci, -ísce), *v.t.* & *abs.* to finish, end, conclude; be done with, leave off; put an end to; (*fig.*) kill. *v.i.* (*aux. essere* & *avere*) to end, finish, come to an end; be over. ~ *con* (*with infin.*), to end by. ~ *di* (*with infin.*), to cease, leave off. *finiscila! finitela!* have done with it! give it up! *tutto è bene quel che finisce bene*, all's well that ends well.
finitaménte, *ad.* finitely; completely; perfectly; in a finished manner.
finitézza, *f.* high finish; perfection.

finítimo, *a.* adjoining; bordering; neighbouring.
finíto, *p.a.* finite; finished; perfect; settled; over, all over; utterly exhausted, done for.
finitúra, *f.* finish; finishing; finishing touches.
finlandése, *a.* Finnish. ¶ *m.* Finn, Finlander. *il* ~, the Finnish language, Finnish. **Finlàndia (la)**, *f.* Finland.
fíno, *a.* fine, thin, sharp; shrewd; subtle, cunning. ¶ *ad.* even.
fíno a, *pr.* till, until; (*of place*) as far as; to.
finòcchio (*pl.* -òcchi), *m.* fennel.
fíno da, *pr.* since, from; (*of place*) from.
finóra, *ad.* as yet, till now, up to this time; hitherto.
fínta, *f.* feint; pretence; false pocket; flap covering pocket or buttonholes; dribbling (*Foot.*). *far* ~, to pretend. **fintàggine**, *f.* duplicity; insincerity; pretence. **fintaménte**, *ad.* insincerely; feignedly; deceitfully. **fínto**, *p.a.* feigned, pretended; false; sham; artificial. ¶ *m.* hypocrite. **finzióne**, *f.* fiction; pretence; falsehood, sham, imposture.
fío, *m.* (*no pl.*) penalty, *in expr.* *pagare il* ~, to pay the penalty.
fioccàre (*pr.* -òcco, -òcchi), *v.i.* (*aux.* essere) to fall in flakes; to snow; (*fig.*) to shower; abound. **fiòcco** (*pl.* -òcchi), *m.* flake; flock; tuft; tassel; knot; (*powder*) puff.
fiochézza, *f.* hoarseness; weakness.
fiòcina, *f.* harpoon. **fiòcine**, *m.* grapestone; pip. **fiocinière**, *m.* harpooner. *also* (*more com.*) **fiociníno** *m.*
fiòco (*pl.* -òchi), *a.* hoarse, weak (*voice*); feeble; dim.
fiónda, *f.* sling; catapult.
fioràia, *f.* flower-girl, flower-seller. **fioràio** (*pl.* -ài), *m.* florist. **fioràme**, *m.* floral design; flower-pattern. **fioràto**, *a.* flowered. **fiordalíso**, *m.* lily; fleur-de-lis. **fióre**, *m.* flower; blossom, bloom; pick, choice; prime, heyday, blush, flush; surface; selection of poems or choice passages of prose; (*pl.f.*) clubs (*cards*). *fiori selvatici*, wild flowers. *vaso da fiore*, flower-pot. *mostra di fiori*, flower show. *a fior d'acqua*, on the surface of the water, level with the water. dim. *fiorellino*, *fioretto*, *fiorettino*, *m.*
fiòrdo, *m.* fiord.
fiorènte, *a.* blooming; flourishing.

fiorentíno, a. & m. Florentine. ¶ m. the dialect of Florence.

fiorétto, m. floweret; little flower; button of a foil; foil; choice passage (life or writing). i Fioretti di San Francesco, the Little Flowers of St. Francis. fioricultóre, m. flower-grower.

fiorífero, a. flowering. pianta ~a, flowering plant. fioríno, m. florin.

fioríre (pr. -ísco, -ísci), v.i. (aux. essere) to blossom, bloom, flower; (fig.) flourish, thrive, prosper; (v.t.) to adorn, strew with flowers (lit. & fig.). fiorísta, (pl. -ísti) m. & f. flower-lover; flower-painter; maker of artificial flowers. fioríta, f. flowers strewn on the ground (for procession, marriage, &c.); light coating (of snow, &c.); quantity of flowers; collection (of songs or lyrical poems); flowering. fioritaménte, ad. in a flowery style. fioríto, a. flowery; in flower. fioritúra, f. blossoming, flowering; flourishing; (pl.) grace-notes (Mus.). in piena ~, in full bloom.

fiorràncio, m. marigold.

fiottàre (pr. -òtto), v.i. (aux. avere) to gush, surge, flow; mutter, murmur; grumble. fiòtto, m. flood, large wave, surge; grumbling.

Firènze, f. Florence.

fírma, f. signature. apporre la (propria) ~, to affix one's signature. firmaménto, m. firmament. firmàre, v.t. to sign; subscribe. firmatàrio (pl. -àri), m. signatory.

fisaménte, ad. fixedly.

fisàrmònica, f. accordion.

fiscàle, a. fiscal; (inland) revenue (att.); (fig.) rigorous, inquisitorial. fiscalísmo, m. fiscal system; (fig.) inquisitorial proceedings. fiscalità, f. piling up of taxation; methods of [tax] collection.

fischiàre (pr. físchio, físchi), v.t. & i. (aux. avere) to hiss; whistle; (of ears) to sing, buzz. mi fischiano gli orecchi, my ears are singing or I have a singing in my ears. faceva fischiar lo staffile, he cracked his whip. fischiàta, f. hiss, hissing; whistle; (fig.) (a) mere song, very little. fischierèlla, f. bird-whistle. fischierellàre & fischiettàre, v.t. & i. to whistle softly. fischiettío (pl. -íi), m. whistling. fischiétto, m. child's whistle. físchio (pl. físchi), m. whistle (sound & instr.); whistling; hissing, buzzing.

físco (pl. físchi), m. public treasury; Treasury; [Inland] Revenue.

física, f. physics. físico (pl. (físici), a. physical. ¶ m. physicist; physique.

físima, f. whim; fancy; caprice.

fisiología, f. physiology. fisiòlogo (pl. -òlogi), m. physiologist.

fisionomía, f. physiognomy.

fisioterapía, f. (Med.) physiotherapy.

físo, a. fixed. ¶ ad. fixedly.

fissàggio (pl. -àggi), m. fixing; fixing-bath (Phot.).

fissaménte, ad. fixedly; steadily. fissàre, v.t. to fix; fasten; decide on; gaze at, look (or stare) at; engage (room, servant, &c.). fissàrsi, v.refl. to fix one's mind on; set one's heart on; take up one's residence. fissazióne, f. fixed idea; obsession; (Chem.) fixation.

físsi! i. (Mil.) eyes front!

fissità, f. fixity.

físso, a. fixed; firm, fast; steady; regular. ¶ m. fixed salary. ¶ ad. fixedly.

fístola, f. fistula (Med.); shepherd's pipe (consisting of seven reeds of unequal length, joined together).

fítta, f. acute pain, stitch; quantity, crowd; mark, bruise; (Mech.) dent; sinking ground, quagmire.

fittai[u]òlo, m. tenant farmer.

fittaménte, ad. thickly; closely.

fittízio (pl. -ízi), a. fictitious.

fítto, a. thick; dense; close; frequent. buio ~, notte ~a, pitch dark. nel più ~ inverno, in the depth of winter. ¶ p.p. of figgere. a capo ~, head downwards. ¶ m. thick, heart, centre; (= affitto) rent.

fiumàna, f. flooded river; flood; torrent; broad stream; (fig.) crowd. fiúme, m. river. dim. fiumicèllo, fiumicino. fiumiciàttolo, m. brook.

fiutafàtti, m.inv. eavesdropper; inquisitive person. fiutàre, v.t. to scent; smell; sniff; (fig.) pry into; suspect; divine; foresee. ~ tabacco, to take snuff. fiutàta, f. smelling; snuff(ing); (fig.) intuition. fiúto, m. scent, (sense of) smell; nose (fig.); acumen.

flabèllo, m. fan made of feathers.

flaccidézza, flaccidità, f. flabbiness; limpness; flaccidity. flàccido, a. limp, flabby.

flacóne, m. small bottle, phial.

flagellàre (pr. -èllo), v.t. to scourge; whip. flagèllo, m. scourge, whip;

(*fig.*) punishment; plague; ruin, calamity; abundance.

flanèlla, *f.* flannel.

flàngia (*pl.* **flànge**), *f.* flange.

flautàto, *a.* flute-like; musical; soft & clear. **flautèllo**, *m.* flageolet. **flautísta** (*pl.* -ísti), *m.* flute-player. **flàuto**, *m.* flute.

flàvo, *a.* yellow; tawny; fair.

flèbile, *a.* plaintive; mournful.

flebíte, *f.* phlebitis (*Med.*).

Flegetónte, *m.* Phlegethon (*Myth.*).

flèmma, *f.* phlegm; (*fig.*) coolness, calm[ness]; indifference. **flemmàtico** (*pl.* -àtici), *a.* phlegmatic; stolid.

flessíble, *a.* flexible; pliant, pliable. *rilegatura* ~, limp cover (*book*).

Flessínga, *f.* Flushing.

flessióne, *f.* flexion, flexure, bending; deflexion, -ction; inflexion, -ction; ending (*Gram.*). **flèsso**, *p.p.* of **flettere**. **flessuóso**, *a.* supple.

flèttere (*pr.* **flètto**), *v.t. ir.* to bend; flex (*Med.*).

flirtàre, *v.i.* (*aux.* avere), to flirt.

floreàle, *a.* floral.

flòrido, *a.* prosperous, flourishing; bright, florid.

florilègio (*pl.* -ègi), *m.* anthology.

floscézza, *f.* flabbiness; flaccidity. **flòscio** (*pl.* **flòsci**), *a.* flabby, flaccid; soft.

flòtta, *f.* fleet; navy. **flottàre**, *v.i.* (*aux.* avere), to float; taxi (*sea-plane*). **flottazióne**, *f.* floating; (*Min.*) flotation. **flottíglia**, *f.* flotilla; fleet of small vessels.

fluènte, *a.* fluent; flowing.

fluidità, *f.inv.* fluidity. **flúido**, *a.* & *m.* fluid. **fluíre** *pr.* -ísco, -ísci), *v.i.* (*aux.* essere) to flow.

fluorescènza, *f.* fluorescence.

fluòro, *m.* fluorine (*Chem.*).

flussióne, *f.* morbid flow or secretion (*Med.*); inflammation; catarrh; (*Math.*) fluxion. **flússo**, *m.* flow, effusion, discharge; dysentery; flux; flood-tide; flush (*at cards, four of one suit*). ~ *e riflusso*, flux & reflux, ebb & flow.

flútto, *m.* wave, surge, billow. **fluttuàre** (*pr.* **flúttuo**), *v.i.* (*aux.* avere) to rise & fall in waves, fluctuate, waver; float. **fluttuóso**, *a.* stormy, billowy; tempestuous; irresolute.

fluviàle, *a.* river (*att.*).

fobía, *f.* dread, fear; strong aversion.

fòca (*pl.* **fòche**), *f.* seal (*animal*).

focàccia, *f.* bun, cake.

focàia (pietra), *f.* flint (*for striking light*).

focàle, *a.* focal. *distanza* ~, focal length.

fóce, *f.* river mouth; valley opening; outlet, outfall.

focèna, *f.* porpoise.

focherèllo, *m.* little fire.

fochísta, *m.* fireman; stoker; maker of fire-works.

fòco, see *fuoco*.

focolaio (*pl.* -ài), *m.* centre of infection.

focolàre, *m.* hearth; fireplace; fireside; furnace (*boiler*); flue; (*fig.*) home; centre; source.

focóso, *a.* fiery, hot; impetuous, high-spirited.

fòdera, *f.* cover; lining; sheathing. **foderàre** (*pr.* **fòdero**), *v.t.* to line, sheathe; cover (*inside or out*). **foderatúra**, *f.* lining; sheathing.

fòdero, *m.* scabbard (*of sword*); sheath; case.

fòga, *f.* ardour, impetuosity; warmth, passion.

fòggia (*pl.* **fògge**), *f.* fashion, manner, mode; shape. *alla* ~ *di*, after the fashion of. *a* ~ *di*, shaped like. **foggiàre** (*pr.* **fòggio**, **fòggi**), *v.t.* to shape, fashion, form.

fòglia, *f.* leaf (*pl.* leaves); foil (*metal*). *metter le* ~*e*, (of trees) put on or bring forth leaves. ~ *d'acanto*, fig-leaf (*Art.*). ~ *di stagno*, tinfoil. **fogliàccio**, *m.* low-class newspaper, vile rag. **fogliàme**, *m.* foliage, leafage; leaves. **fogliétto**, *m.* small sheet (*of paper*); news sheet. ~ *volante*, handbill. **fòglio** (*pl.* -ògli), *m.* sheet (*of paper*); newspaper; receipt; licence. ~ *di guardia*, fly-leaf; end paper. ~ *di prova*, (*Typ.*) specimen page. ~*i aggiunti*, (*Typ.*) overs.

fógna, *f.* sewer; drain; culvert. **fognatúra**, *f.* drainage; sewerage. **fognóne**, *m.* main sewer.

fòla, *f.* idle tale; fable; fancy; (*pl.*) **fole!** nonsense!

fòlaga (*pl.* **fòlaghe**), *f.* coot (*bird*).

folàta, *f.* gust (of wind); flight (of birds). *lavorare a* ~*e*, to work by fits & starts.

folgorànte, *a.* shining, gleaming, flashing. **folgoràre** (*pr.* **fólgoro**), *v.i.* to shine, gleam, flash; lighten. **fólgore**, *m.* flash of lightning, thunderbolt.

fòlio, *m.* in-folio; work (edition) in folio, folio edition.

folklóre & **folclóre**, *m.* folklore.
fólla, *f.* crowd, throng; mass, multitude; crush.
follàre (*pr.* **fóllo**), *v.t.* to full (*cloth*); press (*grapes*).
fòlle, *a.* mad, crazy; foolish; (*Mech.*) free, loose. **folleggiàre** (*pr.* **-éggio**, **-éggi**), *v.i.* (*aux.* avere) to play the fool; be crazy; frolic.
foliétto, *m.* sprite, elf (*pl.* elves); goblin; imp.
follía, *f.* madness, insanity; folly, foolish act.
follicolàre, *a.* follicular. **follícolo**, *m.* follicle.
foltaménte, *ad.* thickly, closely. **fólto**, *a.* thick, close-set, crowded. ¶ *m.* thick, *nel* ~ *della mischia*, in the thick of the fray.
fomentàre (*pr.* **-énto**), *v.t.* to foment. **foménta**, *f.* fomentation (*Med.*). **fomentazióne**, *f.* fomentation (*process*). **foménto**, *m.* fomentation (*Med.* & *fig.*).
fòmite, *m.* tinder; (*fig.*) incitement, cause, incentive.
fónda, *f.* holster; anchorage. **fondàccio**, *m.* dregs, remnant, lees.
fóndaco (*pl.* **-fóndachi**), *m.* draper's shop; store, warehouse.
fondamentàle, *a.* fundamental, basic. **fondaménto**, *m.* (*pl.m.* **-énti** (*fig.*), *f.* **-énta**, *of a building*), foundation; basis, ground. **fondàre** (*pr.* **fóndo**), *v.t.* to found; establish; build; start. **fondàrsi**, *v.refl.* to be founded, rest; be based; take one's stand. **fondàta**, *f.* dregs. **fondataménte**, *ad.* justly, with good reason. **fondàto**, *p.a.* founded, well-founded, grounded, based. **fondatóre**, *m.* (*f.* **-tríce**) founder, -dress; promoter. ¶ *a.* founding. **fondazióne**, *f.* foundation; groundwork; establishment; building; institution.
fóndere (*pr.* **fóndo**), *v.t.* ir. to melt, dissolve; smelt; fuse; cast, found; merge; blend. **fondería**, *f.* foundry.
fondiàrio (*pl.* **-àri**), *a.* of real estate, land (*att.*), landed. *tassa* (or *imposta*) ~ *a*, *f.* land-tax. *credito* ~, *m.* loan secured upon land.
fondíglio, *m.* dregs; sediment.
fonditóre, *m.* (metal-)founder; -caster, smelter. ~ *di caratteri*, type-founder. **fonditúra**, *f.* melting, fusing; smelting. **fonditríce**, *f.* type-founding machine.
fóndo, *a.* deep. ¶ *m.* bottom; back; background; end; ground-floor or basement; piece of ground; holding;

fund; special section or endowment (*in library*). *articolo di* ~, *m.* leading article (*newspaper*). *fondi di caffè*, *m.pl.* coffee grounds. *vagoni da* (or *di*) ~, *m.pl.* rear carriages (*train*). *arrivare in* ~, to get to the end. *andare a* ~, to go to the bottom, sink (*lit.* & *fig.*). *mandare* (or *colare*) *a* ~, to send to the bottom, sink (*v.t.*). *corsa di* ~, *f.* endurance test (*sport*).
fonètica, *f.* phonetics. **fonètico** (*pl.* **-ètici**), *a.* phonetic.
fonogènico (*pl.* **-gènici**), *a.* suitable for recording (*sound, voice*).
fonogràfico (*pl.* **-àfici**), *a.* phonographic. *disco* ~, *m.* gramophone record. **fonògrafo**, *m.* phonograph; gramophone. **fonogràmma**, *m.* (*pl.* **-gràmmi**) telephone message (*in writing*). **fonología**, *f.* phonology. **fonòlogo** (*pl.* **-òlogi**), *m.* phonologist.
fontàna, *f.* fountain. **fónte**, *f.* spring, source (*lit.* & *fig.*); fountain. ¶ *m.* font. ~ *battesimale* (baptismal) font (*sarebbe*.
fòra (*Poet.*) = *sarebbe*.
forabòsco, *m.* wood-pecker. Cf. *picchio*.
foracchiàre, *v.t.* to bore; riddle with holes.
foraggiàre, *v.i.* (*aux.* avere) to forage. **foraggiàta**, *f.* foraging. **foràggio**, *m.* forage.
foramàcchie & **forasièpe**, *m.inv.* wren (*ornith.*).
foràme, *m.* small hole. **foraménto**, *m.* boring, drilling (*Mech.*). **foràre** (*pr.* **fóro**), *v.t.* to bore, drill; pierce; puncture (*tyre*); punch (*ticket*). **foratóio**, *m.* auger; gimlet. **foratríce**, *f.* boring machine. **foratúra**, *f.* boring, piercing, punching; puncture (*tyre*).
fòrbice, *f.* earwig.
fòrbici, *f.pl.* scissors, shears; (*crab, scorpion*) pincers, nippers, claws. *dim.* forbicétte, forbicine.
forbíre (*pr.* **-ísco**, **-ísci**), *v.t.* to wipe; polish; clean. **forbitézza**, *f.* polish, elegance; propriety (*of language*). **forbíto**, *a.* polished, elegant, neat. **forbitúra**, *f.* polishing, wiping, cleaning.
fórca (*pl.* **fórche**), *f.* (hay)-fork; pitch-f.; gallows.
forcai[u]òlo, *m.* reactionary, extreme Tory.
forcàta, *f.* as much hay, &c., as can be taken up by a fork; blow with a hay-fork.

for.cèlla, *f.* forked stick; fork (*of bicycle*); breast-bone; merry-thought (*of a chicken*); hair-pin.
forchétta, *f.* fork. ~ *da tavola*, table-fork. ~*da frutta*, dessert-fork.
forchettàta, *f.* food taken up by a fork, forkful. forchétto, *m.* two-pronged fork; pronged stick for hanging up or taking down goods in a shop. forchettóne, *m.* carving-fork. forcína, *f.* small fork; hairpin.
fòrcipe, *m.* forceps (*Surg.*).
forcóne, *m.* pitchfork.
forcúto, *a.* forked.
forènse, *a.* forensic, juridical. *i forensi*, *m.pl.* lawyers.
forése, *a.* rural; rustic. ¶ *m. f.* peasant.
forèsta, *f.* forest.   forestàle, *a.* forest (*att.*). *leggi ~ i, f.pl.* forest laws. *guardia ~, f.* forester.
foresterìa, *f.* guest-rooms in a monastery. forestière *or* -ièro, *m.* foreigner; visitor; guest; stranger. ¶ *a.* foreign. forestierúme, *m.* crowd of foreigners; foreign habits, f. ways.
forfécchia, *f.* earwig.   fórfora, *f.* dandruff; scurf.
fòrgia (*pl.* fòrge), *f.* forge, smithy.
forgiare, *v.t.* to forge; shape.
forièro, *m.* forerunner, precursor; portent. ¶ *a.* portending; preceding.
fórma, *f.* form; shape; mould; block (*hat*); last (*shoe*); briquette. ~ *di capello* (or *per capelli*) hat-block. ~ *di scarpe* (or *per scarpe*), shoe-last. ~ *di stampa,* forme (*Typ.*). ~ *di calzetta,* stocking-frame. *a ~ di V*, V-shaped.
formaggiàio (*pl.* -ài), *m.* cheese-maker; c.-monger. formaggièra, *f.* dish for grated cheese. formàggio (*pl.* -àggi), *m.* cheese.
formàle, *a.* formal, clear, solemn, precise.   formalína, *f.* (*Chem.*) formalin. formalità, *f.inv.* formality.
formalizzàre, *v.t.* to shock, scandalize, give offence to. formalizzàrsi, *v.refl.* to take offence, t. exception.
formàrc (*pr.* fórmo), *v.t.* to form; shape; fashion; mould; train; make, frame, draw; conceive. formàrsi, *v.refl.* to form, be formed; grow, improve. formataménte, *ad.* in due form. formàto, *p.a.* formed, shaped, moulded. ¶ *m.* shape; size; format (*of a book*) ~ *tascabile*, pocket size.   formatóre, *m.* moulder; maker of plaster-casts;

sculptor's assistant. formatúra, *f.* moulding. formazióne, *f.* formation; forming; training (*character, &c.*). *volo in ~,* mass flight (*Aviat.*).
formèlla, *f.* hole prepared for planting a tree; black; brick; briquette; imitation frame or painted panel.
formíca (*pl.* formíche), *f.* ant. ~ *bianca,* white ant. formicàio (*pl.* -ài), *m.* ant-hill; (*fig.*) swarm.
formicaleóne, *m.* ant-lion. formichière, *m.* ant-eater. formicolàre (*pr.* -ícolo), *v.i.* (*aux.* essere & avere) to swarm, be crowded; tingle; beat fast (*pulse*).   formicolío, *m.* swarming; swarm; tingling, feeling of pins & needles. formicóne, *m.* large ant.
formidàbile, *a.* formidable, dreadful.
formosità, *f.* beauty; handsomeness; shapeliness. formóso, *a.* (*Poet.*) beautiful, handsome; shapely.
fòrmula, *f.* formula.   formulàre (*pr.* fòrmulo), *v.t.* to formulate, draw up; express. formulàrio (*pl.* -ari), *m.* formulary.
fornàce, *f.* kiln, furnace; brickyard.
fornàio (*pl.* -ài), *m.* baker (*f.* fornàia, baker's wife).   dim. *fornarino, fornaino, fornarina, fornaretto.*
fornàta, *f.* batch of loaves for baking.
fornèllo, *m.* stove; (chemist's) furnace; bowl of a pipe. ~ *da cucina,* kitchen-stove. ~ *da campo,* camp stove.
forniménto, *m.* supply; equipment; requisites. forníre (*pr.* -ísco, -ísci), *v.t.* to furnish, provide, supply; (*Poet.*) finish. ~ *una impresa,* to carry out an undertaking. fornirsi (di), *v.refl.* to provide (furnish) oneself with. fornìto, *p.a.* supplied, furnished, provided; endowed. fornitóre, *m.* (*f.* -tríce) provider; contractor; purveyor; (recognized) tradesman. ~ *navale,* ship-chandler. ¶ *a.* providing, supplying, purveying.   fornitúra, *f.* supply; contract (for supplying the army & other public services).
fórno, *m.* oven; bake-house; baker's shop; furnace; kiln.
fóro, *m.* hole; tunnel; bore. ~ *della serratura,* key-hole.
fòro, *m.* forum, market-place, court of justice, law-courts; bar; lawyers. ~ *romano,* (the) Roman Forum. ~ *toscano,* Tuscan bar (or barristers).
forosèlla & forosétta, *f.* country-girl.

fórra, *f.* ravine, gorge.

fórse, *ad.* perhaps. ¶ *m.* doubt, question; in such phrases as *essere in ~,* to be in doubt, *lasciare in ~,* leave in d., *mettere in ~,* to question, throw doubt on. *senza ~,* without doubt, certainly.

forsennataménte, *ad.* madly, frantically. **forsennàto,** *a. & m.* mad, crazy, frantic; madman, &c.

fòrte, *a.* strong; sharp; severe; serious; bad; heavy; nigh; large; considerable; skilful, proficient; difficult; clever; loud; harsh; sour; hard; fast; well-up. *acqua ~,* aqua fortis, nitric acid. *a più ~ ragione,* all the more so, with better reason. *è troppo ~,* it's too bad; the affair is too serious. *dar man ~ a,* to assist, support, back up. ¶ *ad.* strongly, sharply, vehemently, loudly, aloud, forcibly, heavily; tightly; bitterly, harshly; hard, fast. ¶ *m.* fort; forte, strong point; bulk, larger part; sourness, acidity. **forteménte,** *ad.* strongly; highly; hard; loud[ly].

fortézza, *f.* fortitude; fortress (*Mil.*). *~ volante* (*Aviat.*), flying fortress.

forticcio (*pr.* -icci), *a.* rather sour.

fortificàre (*pr.* -ífico, -ífichi), *v.t.* to strengthen, brace, invigorate, fortify. **fortificativo & fortificatóre** (*f.* -tríce), *a.* fortifying, strengthening. **fortificazióne,** *f.* fortification.

fortíno, *m.* blockhouse; redoubt.

fortíssimo, *a.* very strong; v. loud. ¶ *ad. & m.* (*Mus.*) fortissimo.

fortúito, *a.* fortuitous, chance, casual, accidental.

fortúna, *f.* fortune, luck, chance; success; state, condition; storm at sea. *atterraggio di ~,* forced landing (*Aviat.*). *vela di ~,* storm sail. **fortunàle,** *m.* storm; tempest. **fortunàto,** *a.* fortunate, lucky; successful. **fortunóso,** *a.* eventful; risky; stormy, storm-tossed.

forúncolo, *m.* boil (*Med.*).

forviàre (*pr.* forvío, forvíi), *v.t.* to lead astray, mislead. *v.i.* (*aux.* avere) & **forviàrsi,** *v.refl.* to stray, go astray.

fòrza, *f.* strength; vigour; energy; force; power; compulsion; dint; (*pl.*) (*Mil.*) forces. *a ~ viva,* by main force. *a ~ di, per ~ di,* by dint of. *~ pubblica,* police. *~ maggiore,* force majeure, cause beyond control. *~ motrice,* motive power. *è ~,* it is necessary. *farsi ~,* to muster

up courage. **forzaménto,** *m.* forcing; picking (*lock*); running (*blockade*). **forzàre** (*pr.* fòrzo), *v.t.* to force, compel; strain; break open. *~ una serratura,* to pick a lock. *~ un blocco,* to run a blockade. **forzaménte,** *ad.* compulsorily; by force, by compulsion. **forzàto,** *p.a.* forced; strained; compulsory. *lavori ~ i,* penal servitude. ¶ *m.* convict.

forzière, *m.* coffer; strong-box.

forzóso, *a.* compulsory.

forzúto, *a.* powerful, strong, robust.

fósco (*pl.* fóschi), *a.* dark; gloomy; dull; hazy (*weather*).

fosfàto, *m.* phosphate. **fosfína,** *f.* phosphine.

fosforeggiàre (*pr.* -éggio, -éggi), *v.i.* (*aux.* avere) to phosphoresce. **fosfòreo & fosforescènte,** *a.* phosphorescent. **fosforescenza,** *f.* phosphorescence.

fòsforo, *m.* phosphorus. **fosfúro,** *m.* phosphide. **fosgène,** *m.* phosgene (*gas*).

fòssa, *f.* ditch; pit; hole; hollow; grave; den; cavity. **fossai[u]òlo,** *m.* ditcher.

fossàto, *m.* ditch; small stream, brook. dim. *fossatéllo.*

fossétta, *f.* dimple. **fossétto,** *m.* small ditch; gutter.

fòssile, *a. & m.* fossil. *carbon ~,* [pit] coal.

fòsso, *m.* (large) ditch; moat (*castle*). *~ macinante,* mill-stream.

fotogènico (*pl.* -gènici), *a.* photogenic. **fotografàre** (*pr.* -ògrafo), *v.t.* to photograph. **fotografía,** *f.* photography; photograph. *~ a colori,* colour photography. [~] *istantanea,* snapshot. *~ al lampo,* flashlight photograph. **fotògrafo,** *m.* photographer; camera-man. **fotoincisióne,** *f.* photogravure. **fotometría,** *f.* photometry.

fra, *pr.* between; among; in; within; to; amid. *~ poco,* in a short time. *~due giorni,* in (within) two days. *di ~,* from among. *parlare ~ sé,* to talk to oneself.

fra, *m.* (*contr. of* **frate**) friar, brother, father (*Eccl.*).

frac, *m.inv.* frock-coat.

fracàssa, *m.* also *capitan F~,* braggart, boaster.

fracassàre (*pr.* -àsso), *v.t.* to smash, break (up), shatter. **fracàsso,** *m.* crash; uproar; din; riot; bustle. **fracassóne,** *m.* (*f.* -óna) noisy person; blusterer.

fràcido, see *fradicio.*

fràdicio, *a. (pl.m.* **fràdici,** *f.* **fràdicie)** rotten, musty; wet. *bagnato* ~, wet through, wet to the skin. *[u]briaco* ~, dead drunk. **fradiciúme,** *m.* mass of wet (or rotten) things; wetness; rottenness.

fragile, *a.* frail, fragile; brittle; weak; *(glass)* with care. **fragilità,** *f.* fragility; weakness.

fràgola, *f.* strawberry. **fragolàia,** *f. &* **fragoléto,** *m.* strawberry-bed.

fragóre, *m.* crash, roar, great noise; clang. **fragoróso,** *a.* noisy; loud.

fraintèndere (*pr.* **-èndo,** *&c., like* **tendere**), *v.t. ir.* to misunderstand.

frale, *a. (Poet.)* frail; delicate. **fralézza,** *f.* frailty.

frammassóne, *m.* freemason. **frammassonería,** *f.* freemasonry.

frammentàrio, *a.* fragmentary. **framménto,** *m.* fragment.

frammescolàre (*pr.* **-éscolo**), *v.t.* to intermingle.

frammésso, *p.p.* of *frammettere,* inserted; interposed. **frammettènte,** *a.* interfering; intrusive. **framméttere** (*pr.* **-étto,** *&c., like* **mettere**), *v.t. ir.* to interpose; insert. **framméttersi,** *v.refl.* to interfere; meddle; intrude.

frammezzàre (*pr.* **-èżżo**), *v.t.* to interpose; intermingle.

frammischiàre (*pr.* **-íschio, -íschi**), *v.t.* to mix up; intermix.

frammísto, *a.* intermixed.

fràna, *f.* landslip, landslide. ~ *di ciotoli,* scree. **franàre,** *v.i. (aux.* essere) to fall in; slide down; cave in; collapse.

francaménte, *ad.* frankly; freely; openly. **francàre** (*pr.* **frànco, frànchi**), *v.t.* to stamp (*a letter*); prepay carriage; free, release. *non franca la spesa,* it is not worth while. **francatúra,** *f.* postage; prepayment (*letter or parcel*).

francescàno, *a. & m.* Franciscan. **Francésco,** *m.* Francis.

francéṡe, *a.* French. ¶ *m.* Frenchman; the French language. *f.* Frenchwoman. *i F* ~ *i,* the French.

franceṡíṡmo, *m.* Gallicism.

francheggiàre (*pr.* **-éggio, -éggi**), *v.t.* to reassure, give confidence to.

franchézza, *f.* frankness; freedom; candour; openness.

franchígia (*pl.* **-ígie**), *f.* exemption; legal privilege; franking (*Post*); immunity (*diplomatic*). *in* ~ *postale,*

post[age] free. ~ *doganale,* duty free (*Cust.*).

Frància (la), *f.* France.

frànco (*pl.* **frànchi**), *a.* free; frank, candid, outspoken; open, openhearted; above-board; fair (*field*); volunteer (*corps*). ~ *di porto,* carriage paid, c. free (*Com.*). *porto* ~, free port. ¶ *ad.* frankly. ¶ *m.* franc.

francobóllo, *m.* [postage] stamp.

francòfilo, *a. & m.* Francophil.

francòfobo, *a. & m.* Francophobe.

Francofòrte, *f.* Frankfort.

francolíno (di monte), *m.* ptarmigan.

frangènte, *m.* difficulty; difficult situation; emergency; breaker (*wave*).

fràngere (*pr.* **fràngo, fràngi**), *v.t. ir.* to break; crush; press (*olives*). **fràngersi,** *v.refl.* to break up, break in pieces.

fràngia (*pl.* **frànge**), *f.* fringe. dim. *frangetta, frangettina.* **frangiàre** (*pr.* **fràngio**), *v.t.* to fringe. **frangiatúra,** *f.* fringes; fringing.

frangíbile, *a.* breakable, easily broken. **frangiflútti,** *m.inv.* breakwater. **frangivènto,** *m.inv.* windscreen (*motor*).

franóso, *a.* precipitous; liable to sink or fall.

frànto, *p.p.* of **frangere,** broken, fractured, crushed.

frantóio (*pl.* **-ói**), *m.* oil-press; crusher. ~ *da pietra,* stone-crusher.

frantumàre (*pr.* **-úmo**), *v.t.* to break in pieces; crumble; crush; shatter. **frantumàrsi,** *v.refl.* to be shattered; to be shivered. **frantúmi,** *m.pl.* broken pieces, fragments, splinters.

fràppa, *f.* painted foliage; lappet, fringe.

frappórre (*pr.* **-óngo,** *&c., like* **porre**), *v.t. ir.* to interpose; insert. **frappórsi,** *v.refl.* to interfere. **frapposizióne,** *f.* interposition; interference. **frappósto,** *p.a.* interposed.

fraṡàrio (*pl.* **-àri**), *m.* phrase-book; collection of phrases; phrases.

fràsca (*pl.* **fràsche**), *f.,* bough, branch; bush; inn-signboard; idle story; (*pl.*) trifles, vanities. *il buon vino non ha bisogno di* ~, good wine needs no bush. **frascàme,** *m.* (green-) boughs, branches. **frascàto,** *m.* arbour, bower; shady place. *Festa de'* ~ *i,* (*Jewish*) Feast of Tabernacles.

frascheggiàre (*pr.* **-éggio, -éggi**), *v.i. (aux.* avere) to rustle; trifle, toy, dally. **frascheggío,** *m.* rustling (of leaves).

frascheria, *f.* trifle; nonsense.

fraschétta, *f.* small bough; twig; frivolous girl.

fràse, *f.* phrase; sentence. **fraseggiàre** (*pr.* **-éggio, -éggi),** *v.i.* (*aux.* avere) to form phrases; (*Mus.*) to mark the phrases. **fraseggiatóre,** *m.* phrase-maker. ¶ *a.* (*f.* **-tríce)** phrase-making. **fraséggio,** *m.* phrase-making; marking of phrases (*Mus.*). **fraseología,** *f.* phraseology.

frassinéto, *m.* ash-grove, ash plantation. **fràssino,** *m.* ash; ash-tree.

frastagliàre (*pr.* **-àglio, -àgli),** *v.t.* to slash; notch, indent; cut up, break. **frastagliàto,** *p.a.* indented; broken; intersected. **frastàglio,** *m.* indentation; cut; gash; fancy ornament.

frastornàre (*pr.* **-órno),** *v.t.* to interrupt; disturb; divert; derange; annoy, trouble.

frast[u]òno, *m.* din, uproar; confused noise.

fratacchióne, *m.* fat friar.

fràte, *m.* friar; monk; blot of ink. dim. *fraticéllo, fratino, fratùcolo.*

fratellànza, *f.* brotherhood.

fratellàstro, *m.* half-brother.

fratèllo, *m.* brother. **fratería,** *f.* friary. **fraternità,** *f.* fraternity; brotherhood; brotherliness. **fraternàre** & **fraternizzàre** (*pr.* **-ìzzo),** *v.i.* (*aux.* avere) to fraternize. **fratèrno,** *a.* brotherly, fraternal.

fratésco (*pl.* **-éschi),** *a.* monkish.

fratricída (*pl.* **-ìdi),** *a.* & *m.* fratricidal, fratricide (*agent*). **fratricídio,** *m.* fratricide (*act*).

fràtta, *f.* brake; thicket; bramble-bush.

frattàglie, *f.pl.* giblets, pluck, liver & lights; chitterlings.

frattànto, *ad.* meanwhile, meantime.

frattèmpo, *m.* interval; meantime, meanwhile. *nel* ~, in the meantime.

frattúra, *f.* fracture. ~ *composta,* compound fracture. **fratturàre** (*pr.* **-úro),** *v.t.* to fracture; break.

fraudolènto, *a.* fraudulent. **fraudolènza,** *f.* fraudulence.

frazionàre, *v.t.* to separate, divide; split; break into fractions. **frazióne,** *f.* fraction; breaking (*holy bread*); part of a commune or parish, ward; cluster of houses. ~ *commune,* (*Math.*) vulgar fraction. ~ *decimale,* decimal f. ~ *periodica,* recurring decimal.

fréccia (*pl.* **frécce),** *f.* arrow, dart; (*compass*) needle. **frecciàre** (*pr.* **fréccio, frécci),** *v.t.* to shoot an arrow at. **frecciàta,** *f.* arrow-shot; (*fig.*) taunt; gibe; sharp word; sudden stinging remark; request for a loan. **frecciatína,** *f.* rather cutting remark.

freddaménte, *ad.* coldly; coolly. **freddàre** (*pr.* **fréddo),** *v.t.* to chill; cool; (*fig.*) to kill. **freddézza,** *f.* coolness, coldness; indifference. **fréddo,** *a.* cold, cool. *a sangue* ~, in cold blood. ¶ *m.* cold. *prender* ~, to catch cold. *morire di* ~, to be frozen to death. *Dio manda il* ~ *secondo i panni,* God tempers the wind to the shorn lamb (*prov.*). **freddolóso,** *a.* chilly. **freddúra,** *f.* cold weather; cold (*complaint*); play on words; pun, pointless witticism. **freddurràio, freddurísta,** *m.* punster, maker of puns.

fregàccio, *m.* rough stroke (of pen or pencil). **fregàre** (*pr.* **frégo, frèghi),** *v.t.* to rub; underline; cheat or dupe. **fregàta,** *f.* rubbing. dim. *fregatina.*

fregàta, *f.* frigate.

fregiàre (*pr.* **frègio),** *v.t.* to decorate, adorn, embellish. **fregiatúra,** *f.* decoration. **frègio** (*pl.* **frègi),** *m.* decoration, ornament; frieze; (*pl.*) flourishes (*Typ.*).

frégo (*pl.* **frèghi),** *m.* line, stroke; dash, scrawl. *dar di* ~ *a,* to cross out, cancel.

frégola, *f.* excitement, strong desire; spawning (*fish*), rutting (*deer*).

fremebóndo, *a.* quivering, trembling; raging, passionate. **fremènte,** *p.a.* quivering, shuddering, &c. **frèmere** (*pr.* **frèmo),** *v.i.* (*aux.* avere) to quiver; shudder; throb; thrill; rage; roar; fume; fret. **frèmito,** *m.* thrill, quiver; shudder; roaring, raging.

frenàre (*pr.* **fréno),** *v.t.* to brake, apply the brake to; (*fig.*) curb, restrain, repress, check. **frenatóre,** *m.* brakesman.

frenastenía, *f.* (*Med.*) mental deficiency.

frenesía, *f.* frenzy; fury; rage; delirium. **frenètico** (*pl.* **-ètici),** *a.* frantic; frenzied; delirious.

fréno, *m.* brake; bit; curb; (bearing)-rein; (*fig.*) restraint, check; fr[a]enum (*Anat.*). ~ *a nastro,* band brake. ~ *sui cerchioni,* rim brake. ~ *sulle quattro rote,* four-wheel b. ~ *sul mozzo,* hub b. ~ *a mano,* hand brake. ~ *a pedale,* foot brake. ~ *a depressione,* vacuum b. ~ *di sicurezza,* emergency b. *bloccare i* ~*i,* to jam the brakes. *prova al* ~, brake test. *prova dei* ~*i,* braking test.

frenocòmio, *m.* [lunatic] asylum.

frequentàre (*pr.* **-énto**), *v.t.* to attend; frequent; resort to; associate with. **frequentatívo,** *a.* frequentative (*Gram.*). **frequentatóre,** *m.* (*f.* **-tríce**) frequenter; constant attender. **frequènte,** *a.* frequent; rapid (*pulse, &c.*). **frequènza,** *f.* frequency; attendance; concourse. *certificato di* ~, *m.* certificate of attendance.

fresàre (*pr.* **fréso**), *v.t.* (*Mech.*) to countersink; mill. **fresatríce,** *f.* milling machine, miller; (*Typ.*) block planer, leveller.

frescaménte, *ad.* coolly; freshly. **frescànte,** *m.* painter in fresco. **frescàre** (*pr.* **frésco**), *v.t.* to paint in fresco.

frescheggiàre (*pr.* **-éggio, -éggi**), *v.i.* (*aux.* avere) to take fresh air; go into the open air.

freschétto & **freschíno,** *a.* rather cool or fresh. **freschézza,** *f.* freshness; coolness. **frésco** (*pl.* **fréschi**), *a.* fresh; cool; chilly; new (*bread, &c.*); recent; new-laid; wet (*paint, &c.*). *di* ~, recently, just lately. *al* ~, in the open air; (*pop.*) in prison. *star* ~, to be in a fix, in a pickle. ¶ *m.* cool, coolness; cold; freshness. **frescúra,** *f.* coolness; chilliness; chill.

frétta, *f.* haste; hurry. *in* ~ *e furia,* in great haste; hurriedly. *darsi* ~, to seem in a great hurry. **frettolóso,** *a.* hasty; hurried.

freudismo, *m.* Freudism.

friàbile, *a.* friable, crumbling.

Fribúrgo, *f.* Freiburg.

fríggere (*pr.* **fríggo, fríggi**), *v.t. ir.* to fry; bake; *v.i.* (*aux.* avere) to frizzle; sputter; hiss; whine, whimper.

frigidézza & **frigidità,** *f.* coldness; frigidity. **frígido,** *a.* cold; frigid.

frígio, *a.* & *m.* Phrygian.

frignàre (*pr.* **frígno, frígni**), *v.i.* (*aux.* avere) to whimper; whine; cry. **frignóne,** *m.* (*f.* **-óna**) crying child; (*infant*) whimperer, whiner.

frigorífero, *a.* refrigerant, refrigerating. ¶ *m.* refrigerator.

Fríne, *f.* Phryne.

fringuèllo, *m.* finch; chaffinch.

friníre (*pr.* **-ísco, -ísci**), *v.i.* (*aux.* avere) to chirp.

frisàre, *v.t.* to make a grazing stroke at a ball (*billiards, &c.*).

Frísia (la), *f.* Friesland. **frisóne,** *a.* & *m.* Frisian, Frieslander.

frittàta, *f.* omelette. **frittèlla,** *f.* pancake; fritter. **fritto,** *p.p.* of **friggere,** fried. ~ *e rifritto,* (*fig.*) stale, *esser* ~, to be played out, done for. ¶ *m.* dish of fried food. **frittúra,** *f.* fry; frying; fried dish; fritter.

frivoleggiàre (*pr.* **-éggio, -éggi**), *v.i.* (*aux.* avere) to trifle; act or talk frivolously. **frivolézza** & **frivolità,** *f.* frivolity; frivolousness. **frívolo,** *a.* frivolous; trifling.

frizióne, *f.* friction; rubbing (*Med.*); dry shampoo; (*Mech.*) clutch.

frizzànte, *a.* piquant; cutting; sharp, pungent, sparkling (*wine*). **frizzàre,** *v.t.* to sting; prick; (*v.i.*) (*aux.* avere & *essere*) to sting; smart; itch. **frízzo,** *m.* jest; witticism; stinging; pricking.

frodàre (*pr.* **fròdo**), *v.t.* to cheat; defraud; swindle. **frodatóre,** *m.* (*f.* **-tríce**) swindler; defrauder. **fròde,** *f.* fraud; swindle; imposture. **fròdo,** *m.* smuggling. *merci di* ~, smuggled goods. *cacciare di* ~, to poach. *cacciatore di* ~, *m.* poacher. **frodolènto,** *a.* fraudulent. **frodolènza,** *f.* fraudulence; swindling.

fròge, *f.pl.* (sg. **frògia**) nostrils (*of a horse*).

frollàre (*pr.* **fròllo**), *v.t.* to soften, make tender; keep until it is high (*meat* ; (*v.i.*) (*aux.* essere) to become high or tainted. **fròllo,** *a.* soft; tender; high (*game, meat*); weak, tired out.

fròmbola, *f.* sling. **frombolàre** (*pr.* **fròmbolo**), *v.t.* to sling.

frónda, *f.* leafy branch; foliage; (the) Fronde (*Hist.*). **frondeggiànte,** *a.* leafy; covered with leaves. **frondeggiàre** (*pr.* **-éggio, -éggi**), *v.i.* (*aux.* avere) to come out in leaf, bear leaves. **frondóso,** *a.* leafy.

frontàle, *a.* frontal. ¶ *m.* frontal; frontlet; chimney-piece, mantelshelf. **frónte,** *f.* forehead; front (*of a building*); face; first part of the Petrarchan canzone stanza. ¶ *m.* front (*Mil.* & *Pol.*). *di* ~ *a,* opposite; in comparison with. *a* ~ *a* ~, face to face. *far* ~ *a,* to meet, face. *mettere a* ~, to compare.

fronteggiàre (*pr.* -éggio, -éggi), *v.t.* to face; meet; confront; defy.

frontespízio (*pl.* -ízi), *m.* frontispiece; title-page. ~ *morto*, fly-leaf preceding the title-page. *falso* ~, (*Typ.*) half-title.

frontièra, *f.* frontier; border.

frontóne, *m.* (*Arch.*) fronton; pediment.

frónzolo, *m.* useless ornament; trinket; trifle.

fronzúto, *a.* leafy.

fròtta, *f.* troop, band, flock, crowd.

fróttola, *f.* idle story, fable, rambling popular song; lie, fib; (*pl.*) **fróttole**, nonsense, humbug.

frottolóne, *m.* idle story teller, fibber.

frugàre (*pr.* frúgo, frúghi), *v.t.* to search; rummage; ransack; ferret out.

frúgolo, *m.* & **frúgola**, *f.* restless child; lively person.

fruíre (**di**), (*pr.* -ísco, -ísci), *v.t.* to enjoy; make use of; avail oneself of. **fruizióne**, *f.* fruition; enjoyment; use.

frullàna, *f.* scythe; hook; rustic dance.

frullàre, *v.t.* to beat up, whip; whisk (*eggs*); *v.i.* (*aux.* avere) to whirl; spin round, flutter. *far* ~ *il capo*, to get into one's head, to fancy (*impers.*). **frullíno**, *m.* (egg)-whisk. **frullío**, *m.* whirring, fluttering. **frúllo**, *m.* whirr, rustle; flutter; beating of wings. **frullóne**, *m.* bolter, sifting machine; device of the Accademia della Crusca (*Florence*).

frumentàceo, *a.* cereal. **fruménto**, *m.* wheat; corn; grain. **frumentóne**, *m.* Indian corn; maize.

frusciàre (*pr.* frúscio, frúsci), *v.i.* (*aux.* avere) to rustle. **fruscío** (*pl.* -íi), *m.* rustling, rustle; (*Radio*) background noise.

frústa, *f.* whip. **frustàre** *v.t.* to whip; (*fig.*) wear out (clothes, by hard usage); censure bitterly. **frustàta**, *f.* lash, cut with a whip. **frustatúra**, *f.* whipping. **frustíno**, *m.* riding-whip. **frústo**, *a.* worn-out; tattered. ¶ *m.* bit, morsel. **frustóne**, *m.* big whip.

frustràre, *v.t.* to frustrate.

frútice, *m.* shrub. **fruticéto**, *m.* shrubbery. **frútta**, *f.* fruit. *coltello da* ~, fruit-knife, dessert-knife. ~ *e dolci*, dessert. **fruttai[u]òlo**, *m.* fruiterer. **fruttáme**, *m.* fruitage;

painting of fruit. **fruttàre**, *v.t.* to produce, bear, yield; bring (forth); (*v.i.*) (*aux.* avere) to fructify; bear interest; pay; help. *è un commercio che frutta*, it is a paying business. **fruttéto**, *m.* orchard. **frutticultóre**, *m.* fruit-grower. **frutticultúra**, *f.* fruit-growing.

fruttièra, *f.* fruit-dish. **fruttífero**, *a.* fruit-bearing; (*fig.*) interest-bearing; profitable, useful. **fruttificàre** (*pr.* -ífico, -ífichi), *v.i.* (*aux.* avere) to fructify. **fruttífico**, *a.* fruitful. **fruttivéndolo**, *m.* (*f.* -a) fruiterer. **frútto**, *m.* (*pl.* **frutti** *m.* & **frutta** *f.*) fruit; (fruit-tree) produce; profit; result; interest, reward. **fruttuóso**, *a.* fruitful.

fu, *a.* late, deceased.

fucilàre (*pr.* -ílo), *v.t.* to shoot (*spy, deserter*). **fucilàta**, *f.* shot; fusillade. **fucilazióne**, *f.* [execution by] shooting. **fucíle**, *m.* gun, rifle. ~ *ad aria compressa*, air-gun. ~ *a doppia canna*, double-barrelled g. ~ *da caccia*, ~ *da pallini*, shot g. ~ *a retrocarica*, breech-loader. ~ *mitragliatore*, sub-machine gun, tommy-g. *a tiro di* ~, within gunshot. **fuciléría**, *f.* musketry. **fucilière**, *m.* rifleman; fusilier.

fucína, *f.* smithy; forge. **fucinàre**, *v.t.* to forge (*Metall.*).

fúco (*pl.* **fúchi**), *m.* drone (*bee*).

fúcsia, *f.* fuchsia. **fucsína**, *f.* aniline red (*dye*).

fúga (*pl.* **fúghe**), *f.* flight; escape; (*Mus.*) fugue. *mettere in* ~, to put to flight. **fugàce**, *a.* fleeting; transient. **fugàre** (*pr.* **fúgo**, **fúghi**), *v.t.* to put to flight.

fuggènte, *pr.p.* of **fuggire**. **fuggévole**, *a.* fleeting, transient. **fuggiasco** (*pl.* -àschi), *a.* & *m.* fugitive (*from justice*); runaway. **fuggifatíca**, *m.inv.* shirker; idler. **fúggi fúggi**, *m.inv.* headlong flight; panic flight. **fuggilòzio**, *m.* pastime. **fuggíre** (*pr.* **fúggo**, **fúggi**), *v.i.* (*aux.* essere) to flee; run away; fly, escape. elope. *v.t.* to shun; avoid. **fuggitivo**, *a.* & *m.* fugitive.

fúlcro, *m.* fulcrum.

fulgènte, *a.* bright; shining, brilliant, refulgent. **fúlgere** (*pr.* **fúlgo**, **fúlgi**), *v.i. ir.* (*aux.* essere & avere) (*Poet.*) to shine. **fúlgido**, *a.* bright, shining, refulgent. **fulgóre**, *m.* brightness; splendour; refulgence.

fulíggine, *f.* soot. **fuligginóso**, sooty.

fulmicotóne, *m.* gun-cotton.
fulminànte, *m.* lucifer match; percussion cap. **fulminàre** (*pr.* **fúlmino**), *v.t.* to strike (by lightning); (*fig.*) to denounce; confound; explode; dumbfound; crush; (*v.i.*) (*aux.* avere) to fulminate; thunder (against). **fulminàto**, *p.a.* struck by lightning; electrocuted; (*Elec.*) burnt out. **fúlmine**, *m.* thunderbolt; lightning. **fulmíneo**, *a.* swift, sudden, flashing, like lightning. **fulminío**, *m.* continual lightning.
fúlvo, *a.* tawny; yellow; golden; red.
fumàcchio, *m.* piece of smoky charcoal; smoke-plume; vapour, exhalation; fumarole (*volcano*).
fumai[u]òlo, *m.* chimney-stack; smoke-stack; funnel of a steamer; fumarole.
fumànte, *a.* smoking; reeking; fuming. **fumàre**, *v.t. & i.* to smoke. **fumàta**, *f.* smoke, smoking (*pipe*); puff of smoke; smoke signal. **fumatóio**, *m.* smoking-room. **fumatóre**, *m.* (*f.* **-tríce**) smoker. **fumicàre & fumigàre**, *v.i.* (*aux.* avere) to steam; emit fumes. **fumicóso**, *a.* steamy; fuming. **fúmido**, *a.* smoky; full of smoke. **fumísta**, *m.* heating engineer; **fumívoro**, *a.* smoke-consuming. **fúmo**, *m.* smoke; fume; vapour; (*fig.*) vanity. *andare in* ~, to end in smoke; come to nothing. *nero di* ~, *m.* lamp-black. **fumògeno**, *a.* smoke-producing. *bomba* ~*a*, *f.* smoke-bomb. *cortina* ~ *a*, *f.* smoke-screen (*Mil.*). **fumosità**, *f.* smokiness. **fumóso**, *a.* smoky.
funàio (*pl.* **-ài**), *m.* rope-maker. **funàmbolo**, *m.* rope-dancer, rope-walker; funambulist. **funàme**, *m.* cordage; collection of ropes; rigging. **fúne**, *f.* rope; cable.
fúnebre, *a.* funeral; funereal. *carro* ~, *m.* hearse. *discorso* ~, *m.* funeral oration. *marcia* ~, *f.* dead march. **funeràle**, *a. & m.* funeral. ¶ *m.pl.* *i funerali*, funeral, *f.* ceremonies, obsequies. **funèreo**, *a.* funereal; mournful; dismal; ghastly. **funestàre** (*pr.* **-èsto**), *v.t.* to afflict, vex, sadden; ruin. **funèsto**, *a.* deadly; baneful; baleful; fatal; lamentable; sorrowful.
fúnga, *f.* mould; mouldiness. **fungàia**, *f.* mushroom-bed; mouldy place.
fúngere (da) (*pr.* **fúngo, fúngi**), *v.i.*

ir. to act (as), perform the duties of, function as.
funghíre (*pr.* **funghísco, funghísci**), *v.i.* (*aux.* essere) to become mouldy; lie unused.
fúngo (*pl.* **fúnghi**), *m.* mushroom; fungus.
funicèlla, *f.* small rope; cord.
funicolàre, *a. & f.* funicular; funicular [railway]. **funícolo**, *m.* umbilical cord.
funivía, *f.* funicular (cable) railway (*passengers*).
funzionàle, *a.* functional. **funzionaménto**, *m.* (*Mech.*) working, running; operation. **funzionànte**, *p.a.* working; acting (as = *da*). **funzionàre** (*pr.* **-óno**), *v.i.* (*aux.* avere) to work; run (*Mech.*); function; act; operate. ~ *da*, to act as. **funzionàrio**, *m.* functionary; official. **funzióne**, *f.* function; office; service; ceremony. *in* ~ *di*, acting as.
fuochísta, see **fochísta**.
fuòco (*pl.* **fuòchi**), *m.* fire; flame; flare; flash; light; lamp; (*Opt.*) focus; firing (*Mil.*); heat (*fig.*); hearth. ~ *d'artifízio*, ~ *artificiale*, firework. ~ *di Bengala*, Bengal light. ~ *di bivacco*, watch fire. ~ *di paglia*, (*fig.*) flash in the pan. ~ *fatuo*, ignis fatuus, jack-o'-lantern, will-o'-the-wisp. ~ *di fucileria*, rifle-fire. ~ *di fila*, running fire. *mettere a*~, to focus (*Opt.*), *vigile del* ~, *m.* fireman.
fuorché, *c. & pr.* except, unless. **fuòri**, *ad. & pr.* out, outside, without; abroad; except. ~ *di*, out of; beyond. *di* ~, outside, out of doors; away. ~ *giuoco*, off-side (*football*). ~ *servizio*, out of use; off duty; (*Elec., Nav., &c.*), out of commission. ~! (*Theat.*) recall. ~ *di commercio*, for private circulation (*book*).
fuoribórdo, *m.* outboard (motor).
fuoruscíto, *m.* exile (*pers.*).
fuorviàre, fuorviàrsi, see forviare, &c.
furbacchiòlo, *m.* cunning little fellow. **furbacchióne**, *m.* cunning rascal. **furbàccio**, *a.* sly. **furbaménte**, *ad.* cunningly. **furbería**, *f.* cunning; slyness; astuteness. **furbésco** (*pl.* **-éschi**), *a.* cunning; artful. *lingua* ~ *a*, thieves' lingo. **furbétto**, *a.* rather cunning, r. sly. **furbízia**, *f.* cunning, artfulness. **fúrbo**, *a.* sly, cunning, artful. ¶ *m.* cunning fellow. *un* ~ *matri-*

colato, a thorough rogue. **furbóne,** *m.* great rogue.

furènte, *a.* furious; mad.

furería, *f.* quartermaster's office.

furétto, *m.* ferret.

furfantàccio, *m.* horrid rascal; scoundrel. **furfantàglia,** *f.* rabble; collection of rogues. **furfànte,** *m.* rascal, rogue, scoundrel. **furfantería,** *f.* rascality; roguery; rascally action. **furfantésco** (*pl.* **-éschi**), *a.* rascally, roguish.

furgóne, *m.* van; waggon; delivery van. *∼ per mobilia,* furniture van, pantechnicon. dim. *furgoncino.*

fúria, *f.* fury, rage; force, violence; haste, hurry. *a ∼ di,* by dint of; by force of; by means of. *in fretta e ∼,* in a violent hurry. *andare su tutte le ∼ ie,* to become furious, go into a violent rage. *andare a ∼,* to sell like hot cakes. *∼ composta,* restrained anger; (*driving*) steady pace, round p. **furibóndo,** *a.* furious, violent.

furière, *m.* quarter-master.

furiosétto, *a.* rather angry. **furióso,** *a.* furious, violent, fierce, angry; mad. **furóre,** *m.* fury, rage, passion; enthusiasm. **furoreggiàre** (*pr.* **-éggio, -éggi**), *v.i.* (*aux.* avere) to be the rage, make a hit, have great success (*singer, actor, play, &c.*).

furtívo, *a.* furtive, stealthy. **fúrto,** *m.* theft, robbery; plagiarism.

fusàio (*pl.* **-ài**), *m.* spindle-maker. **fusàto,** *a.* tapering, spindle-shaped.

fuscellíno, *m.* straw, small twig. hair-line (*Typ.*). **fuscèllo,** *m.* twig; small dry stick; (*fig.*) thin leg, thin person; (*pl.*) stilts.

fusciàcca, *f.* broad sash.

fusciàrra, *m.* scamp, mischievous boy.

fusellàto, *a.* tapering. **fusèllo,** *m.* axle-end; (*Mech.*) spindle.

fusíbile, *a.* fusible. ¶ *m.* (*Elec.*) fuse.

fusièra, *f.* spindle-holder.

fusióne, *f.* fusion; melting; casting. *punto di ∼,* melting-point.

fúso, *p.p.* of **fondere.** **fúso,** *m.* (*pl.m.* **fúsi** *&* *f.* **fúsa**) spindle; shaft; shank (*anchor*); post. *far le fusa,* to purr.

fusolièra, *f.* fuselage (*Aero.*).

fusòrio, *a.* melting, casting. *arte ∼ a,* *f.* (art of) metal-casting. *forno ∼,* *m.* blast-furnace.

fustàgno, *m.* fustian (*coarse cotton cloth*).

fustigàre (*pr.* **fústigo, fústighi**), *v.t.* to flog. **fustigazióne,** *f.* flogging.

fústo, *m.* stalk, stem, trunk; shaft (*of column*); frame; figure (*body*); butt (*gun*); drum, barrel, cask. *∼ del letto,* bedstead.

fútile, *a.* trifling, frivolous; vain, idle, futile; useless; nugatory. **futilità,** *f.inv.* futility; (*pl.*) trifles; trash.

futurísmo, *m.* futurism. **futurísta** (*pl.* **-ísti**), *a. & m.* futurist. **futúro,** *a.* future. ¶ *m.* future, futurity. *∼ anteriore,* future perfect (*Gram.*). *∼* [*semplice*], future [tense].

G

G, g, (*gi*), *f.* the letter G. Represents two sounds, one soft (or palatal) (as in Eng. *gem*) before *e* and *i,* the other hard (or guttural) as in Eng. *go*) before the other vowels, *h, l* and *r.*

gabàrra, *f.* barge, lighter; cargo-boat.

gabbacristiàni, *m.inv. &* **gabbadèo** (*pl.* **gabbadèi**) *m.* cheat; hypocrite.

gabbamóndo (*pl.* **gabbamóndi,** or *inv.*), *m.* cheat, swindler; imposter.

gabbanèlla, *f.* white hospital tunic worn by doctors & convalescents; any loose gown.

gabbàno, *m.* cloak; loose overcoat; gaberdine.

gabbàre, *v.t.* to cheat, deceive, impose upon. **gabbàrsi (di),** *v.refl.* to mock, make fun of.

gabbasànti, *m.inv.* hypocrite. **gabbatóre,** *m.* (*f.* **-tríce**) imposter.

gàbbia, *f.* cage; (*fig.*) prison, dock; hen-coop; crate; ox-muzzle; look-out post; top-sail. *∼ dell'ascensore,* [lift-] cage. dim. *gabbietta, gabbina, gabbiaccia, gabbiuola, gabbiolina, gabbiettina.*

gabbiàio (*pl.* **-ài**), *m.* bird-cage-maker.

gabbiàno, *m.* sea-gull.

gabbiàta, *f.* cageful (*of birds, &c.*).

gabbière, *m.* top-man, sailor who attends to the top-sails.

gabbióne, *m.* large cage.

gàbbo, *m.* jest, mockery, derision. *pigliare a ∼, prendere a ∼,* to make fun of; make light of.

gabèlla, *f.* duty, tax (*local or general, on articles of consumption*). **gabellàre** (*pr.* **-èllo**), *v.t.* to tax; rate for taxation; (*fig.*) *∼ per.* to pass off as, make . . . pass for, make . . . appear as. **gabellière, gabellòtto,** *m.* collector; exciseman.

gabinétto, *m.* cabinet; private room

study; closet; water-closet. ~ *di consultazione*, consulting room.

gaèlico (*pl.* -èlici), *a. & m.* Gaelic.

gàffa, *f.* boat-hook.

gaggìa, *f.* acacia, acacia-flower.

gagliàrda, *f.* galliard (*dance, Hist.*). **gagliardaménte**, *ad.* vigorously; boldly, strongly. **gagliardétto**, *m.* pennon. **gagliardía**, *f.* strength, vigour. **gagliàrdo**, *a.* strong, vigorous, hardy; powerful; brave; bold.

gagliòffo, *m.* lout. ¶ *a.* clumsy; loutish.

gagnolàre (*pr.* **gàgnolo**), *v.i.* (*aux.* avere) to yelp, howl; whine. **gagnolío**, *m.* continual yelping or whining.

gaiézza, *f.* gaiety, vivacity, sprightliness; brightness (*of dress or colour*). **gàio** (*pl.* **gài**), *a.* gay, sprightly, vivacious; gaudy.

gàla, *f.* gala; finery; frill (*lady's dress*). **galànte**, *a.* polite, courteous; gallant (*towards women*). **galantería**, *f.* politeness; courtesy; gallantry; delicacy, dainty (*of food*).

galantína, *f.* galantine.

galantuòmo (*pl.* -uòmini), *m.* gentleman; man of honour.

galàssia, *f.* galaxy; Milky Way (*Astr.*).

galatèo, *m.* book of manners; code of politeness; good breeding.

Gàlati, *m.pl.* Galatians. **Galàzia** (la), *f.* Galatia.

galèa, *f.* galley (*ship, Hist.*). **galeàzza**, *f.* large galley.

galèna, *f.* galena. *apparecchio a* ~, crystal-set (*Radio*).

galeóne, *m.* galleon (*Hist.*). **galeòtta**, *f.* galliot, small galley. **galeòtto**, *m.* galley slave; convict; (*pop.*) cunning fellow; (*Poet.*) go-between, pander. **galèra**, *f.* galley; convict prison, jail.

galèstro, *m.* marl.

Galilèa (la), *f.* Galilee. **galilèo**, *a. & m.* Galilean. *G*~, *m.* Galileo.

Galízia (la), *f.* Galicia.

gàlla, *f.* gall; oak-apple; blister; bubble; (*fig.*) inconstant person. *a* ~, afloat.

galleggiaménto, *m.* floating; floatage; buoyancy; flotation. *linea di* ~, *f.* water-line (*ship*).

galleggiànte, *a.* floating. ¶ *m.* float. **galleggiàre**, *v.i.* (*aux.* avere) to float, keep afloat; (*fig.*) lie on the top; (*of stomach*) rise.

galleria, *f.* gallery; tunnel; arcade; subway.

Gàlles, *m.* Wales, also *il paese di G*~,

gallése, *a.* Welsh. ¶ *m.* Welsh, the Welsh language; Welshman.

gallétta, *f.* ship's biscuit; cocoon. **gallétto**, *m.* cockerel, young cock.

Gàllia (la), *f.* Gaul.

gallicísmo, *m.* gallicism.

gallína, *f.* hen. ~ *di Faraone*, or ~ *faraona*, guinea-fowl. *carne di* ~, *f.* chicken. *latte di* ~, *m.* egg-flip. *morso di* ~, *m.* (*Bot.*) chickweed. *raspatura di* ~, *f.* scrawl, illegible writing.

gallinàccio, *m.* turkey-cock; type of mushroom. **gallinàceo**, *a.* gallinaceous, of the order of domestic fowls. **gallinèlla**, *f.* water-hen; young hen, pullet. *le sette G*~ *e*, the Pleiades (*Astr.*). **gàllo**, *m.* cock. *canto del* ~, cock-crow. ~ *d'India*, turkey-cock. ~ *di montagna*, black-cock; grouse. *peso* ~, bantam weight (*Box.*).

Gàllo, *a.* Gaul (*inhabitant of Gaul*).

gallonàre (*pr.* -óno), *v.t.* to decorate (with stripes); to trim with braid or lace. **gallóne**, *m.* chevron; stripe; gallon (= 4 quarts, or 4.5459631 litres).

gallòria, *f.* mirth, merriment; noisy merrymaking.

gallòzza *&* **gallòzzola**, *f.* blister; bubble.

galoppànte, *a.* galloping. *tisi* ~, galloping consumption. **galoppàre** (*pr.* -òppo), *v.i.* (*aux.* avere) to gallop. **galoppàta**, *f.* galloping; gallop. **galoppíno**, *m.* errand-boy; messenger. **galòppo**, *m.* gallop. *piccolo* ~, canter.

galòscia (*pl.* -òsce), *f.* galosh (or golosh).

galvànico (*pl.* -ànici), *a.* galvanic. **galvanísmo**, *m.* galvanism. **galvanizzàre**, *v.t.* to galvanize; (*fig.*) rouse (by shock or excitement). **galvanoplàstica**, *f.* galvanoplasty.

gàmba, *f.* leg. *essere in* ~, to be (or to feel) vigorous, active, brisk. *stare in* ~, to be careful. *darsela a gambe*, to take to one's heels, bolt. *mandare a gambe levate*, to trip up (by the heels). **gambacórta**, *m.* lame person. **gambàle**, *m.* legging; splint; boot-tree; stem of a plant. **gambàta**, *f.* blow with the leg; kick.

gamberettíno, *m.* shrimp.

gàmbero, *m.* cray-fish. ~ *di mare*, lobster.

gambétto, *m.* short stalk; gambit (*chess*). *dare il* ~, to trip.

gàmbo, *m.* stalk, stem; stroke; tail of a letter; shaft (*of a tool*).

gamèlla, *f.* mess-tin.

gàmma, *f.* gamut, range; musical scale; Greek G.

ganàscia (*pl.* -àsce), *f.* jaw. *stecca a* ~, fishplate (*Mech., Carp.*).
ganascíno, *m.* cheek.

gàncio (*pl.* gànci), *m.* hook. dim. *gancétto, gancino, gancettino.*

Gand, *f.* Ghent.

gànga (*pl.* gànghe), *f.* gangue, matrix (*of mineral ores*); veinstone.

Gànge (il), *m.* (the) Ganges.

gangheràre (*pr.* gànghero), *v.t.* to set on hinges; furnish with hinges; hinge; hook. **gangherèlla,** *f.* metallic eye for a hook. **gànghero,** *m.* hinge; hook; clasp. *fuori dei ganghri,* off the hinges; (*fig.*) in a bad temper.

gànglio (*pl.* gàngli), *m.* ganglion.

gàngola, *f.* swollen gland in the neck; swollen tonsil. **gangrèna,** *f.* gangrene.

Ganimède, *m.* Ganymede; (*fig.*) fop, dandy, beau.

gànza, *f.* mistress; paramour. **gànzo,** *m.* lover; paramour.

gàra, *f.* competition; contest; match; race. *a* ~, for a wager. *fare a* ~, *andare a* ~, to compete; vie. ~ *eliminatoria,* heat (*sport*). ~ *libera,* open event (*sport*). ~ *avantaggi.* handicap event.

garamoncíno & **garamóne,** *m.* (*Typ.*) bourgeois type, of 9 & 10 points respectively.

garànte, *p.a.* vouching, guaranteeing, warranting. ¶ *m.* surety, guarantor; **garantíre** (*pr.* -ísco, -ísci), *v.t.* to guarantee, warrant, go bail for; assure. **garanzía,** *f.* guarantee, surety; warrant(y).

garbàccio, *m.* rudeness, piece of rudeness; incivility; bad manners. **garbàre,** *v.i.* (*aux.* essere, *rar.* avere) to please, be pleasing; suit. **garbataménte,** *ad.* politely. **garbatézza,** *f.* politeness; grace; amiability. **garbàto,** *a.* polite; pleasing; well-mannered; graceful; kind. **garbíno,** *m.* south-west wind. **gàrbo,** *m.* politeness; courtesy; grace; tact; good manners; elegance, good cut (of clothes); gesture; pattern; habit, custom. *a* ~, pleasing, agreeable. *con* ~, politely; gracefully. ¶ *a.* (*of fruit, wine*) sour, bitter.

garbúglio, *m.* confusion, disorder,

mess; turmoil; agitation. **garbuglióne,** *m.* mischief-maker; intriguer.

gardènia, *f.* gardenia.

gareggiàre (*pr.* -éggio, -éggi), *v.i.* (*aux.* avere) to compete; vie; contend.

garènna, *f.* warren.

garétta, *or* **garítta,** *f.* sentry box; look-out post.

garétto, *m.* back of the heel; (*horse*) pastern, hock, fetlock.

garganèlla, in the expr. *bere a* ~, to gulp down.

gargarísmo, *m.* gargle. **gargarizzàre** (*pr.* -ízzo), *v.t.* & **gargarizzàrsi,** *v.refl.* to gargle. **gargaròzzo,** *m.* (*pop.*) throat, gullet.

gargòtta, *f.* cook-shop; cheap eating-house.

garibaldíno, *m.* one of Garibaldi's followers.

garofanàre (*pr.* -òfano), *v.t.* to season with cloves. **garofaníno,** *m.* (*Bot.*) sweet-william. **garòfano,** *m.* clove; [clove-]carnation; pink. *essenza di* ~, clove oil.

Garònna (la), *f.* the Garonne.

garrése, *m.* withers (*horse*).

garríre (*pr.* -ísco, -ísci), *v.i.* (*aux.* avere) (*of birds*) to chirp, twitter, cry; screech; (*flag., &c.*), flap; (*pers.*) scold; squabble. **garríto,** *m.* chirping, twittering (*of birds*); screech, screeching; scolding, chiding, squabbling.

garrulità, *f.* garrulousness; garrulity. **gàrrulo,** *a.* garrulous.

gàrza, *f.* heron; gauze. **garzàia,** *f.* heronry; place of difficult access.

garzàre, *v.t.* to card, tease [out]; teasel. **garzatríce,** *f.* carding machine. **garzatúra,** *f.* carding; teaseling. **garzèlla,** *f.* carding-comb. **gàrzo,** *m.* carding; teaseling. **garzòlo,** *m.* carded hemp; hemp fibre.

garzonàto, *m.* apprenticeship. **garzoncèllo,** *m.* lad. **garzóne,** *m.* shop-boy; farm-servant; apprentice.

gas, *m.inv.* gas. *becco del* ~, *m.* gas-burner. *contatore del* ~, *m.* gas-meter. *fornello a* ~, *m.* gas-cooker, gas-oven, gas-stove. *motore a* ~, *m.* gas engine, ~ *motor.* *radiatore a* ~ gas fire. *tubo del* ~, *m.* gas-pipe. *turbina a* ~, *f.* gas turbine. *officina del* ~, *f.* gas-works. *luce del* ~, *f.* g.-light, *illuminazione a* ~, *f.* gas-lighting, *maschera contro i* ~ *asfissianti,* or *m.* antigas, *f.* ~mask

(*war*). *bomba di gas tossici,f.* g.-shell.
gaśísta, *m.* gas-fitter.
gassògeno, *m.* gazogene; gas-generator (*motor, &c.*). **gassò-metro,** *m.* gasometer.
gassóso, *a.* gaseous; aerated.
gasteròpodo, *m.* gasteropod. **gàstri-co** (*pl.* **gàstrici**), *a.* gastric.
gastrite,*f.* gastritis. **gastronomía,** *f.* gastronomy. **gastronòmico** (*pl.* -**òmici**), *a.* gastronomic(al). gas-**trònomo,** *m.* gastronome[r].
gàtta, *f.* cat; tabby-cat; female cat; puss; pussy-cat. *far la ~ morta,* to pretend to be asleep. *~ ci cova,* there is something in the wind (*pop.*). *erba ~,* cat-mint.
gattabúia, *f.* (*pop.*) prison. **gatta-mòrta,** *f.* (*pop.*) hypocrite.
gattésco (*pl.* -**éschi**), *a.* cat-like; feline. **gàttice,** *m.* white poplar. **Gattinàra,** *m.* noted red wine of Piedmont (*prov. of Novara*). **gat-tíno,** *m.* kitten; small cat. **gàtto,** *m.* tom-cat; male cat. *~ selvatico,* wild cat. *~ d'Angora,* Persian cat. *~ soriano,* tortoise-shell cat. *~ siamese,* Siamese cat. *G~ cogli stivali,* Puss in Boots. **gattóne,** *m.* big cat; sly fellow, (*pl.*) mumps. **gattoni,** *ad.* stealthily; on all fours.
gattúccio, *m.* (*Carp.*) compass saw; key-hole s.
gaudènte, *a.* jolly, cheerful, merry. ¶ *m.* man of pleasure, Epicurean. **gàudio,** *m.* joy, cheerfulness. **gaudióso,** *a.* joyful, joyous.
gavazzàre (*pr.* -**àzzo**), *v.i.* (*aux.* avere) to revel, make merry.
gavétta, *f.* mess-tin.
gavitèllo, *m.* buoy.
gavòtta, *f.* gavotte.
gàżża, *f.* magpie.
gażżarra, *f.* uproar; rejoicings; discharge of guns or fireworks.
gażżèlla, *f.* gazelle.
gażżétta, *f.* gazette; newspaper. **gażżettière,** *m.* journalist; reporter. **gażżettíno,** *m.* gazette; news-sheet.
geènna, *f.* Gehenna, hell.
gelaménto, *m.* freezing. **gelàre** (*pr.* **gèlo**), *v.i.* (*aux.* essere), to freeze. **gelàta,** *f.* frost; hard-frost. **gela-tería,***f.* ice-cream shop. **gelatièra,** *f.* ice-cream freezer. **gelatière,** *m.* ice-cream merchant, -vendor. **gela-tína,** *f.* jelly; gelatine; isinglass; freezing mixture; (*Phot.*) emulsion. **gelatinóso,** *a.* gelatinous.
gelàto, *a.* frozen. ¶ *m.* ice, ice-cream (also *gelato alla panna*). *~ alle*

fragole, strawberry ice. *~ alla vainiglia,* vanilla i. **gèlido,** *a.* cold; icy. **gèlo,** *m.* frost; cold. *corroso dal ~,* frost-bitten. **gelóne,** *m.* chilblain.
gelosía, *f.* jealousy; venetian blind; movable portion of window, shutter. **gelóso,** *a.* jealous.
gèlso, *m.* mulberry; mulberry-tree. **gelsomíno,** *m.* jasmin[e], jessa-min[e].
gemebóndo, *a.* moaning; groaning.
gemèllo, *a. & m.* twin; (*pl.*) twins; sleeve-links. *nave ~a, f.* sister ship.
gèmere (*pr.* **gèmo**), *v.i.* (*aux.* avere) to moan, groan; weep; (*doves*) coo; (*aux.* essere) to ooze, to drip, leak, trickle (*of liquid*).
geminàre (*pr.* **gèmino**), *v.t.* to twin; arrange in pairs; double; repeat; damaskeen; geminate (*Biol.*). **gèmino,** *a.* (*Poet.*) double.
gèmito, *m.* groan; moan, moaning; cooing.
gèmma, *f.* gem; jewel; bud. *mettere le ~ e,* to bud, put forth buds. **gemmàre** (*pr.* **gèmmo**), *v.i.* (*aux.* avere) to bud. **gemmàrsi,** *v.refl.* to deck oneself with gems or jewels.
gendàrme, *m.* gendarme, policeman; (*pop.*) formidable woman.
genealogía, *f.* genealogy. **genea-lògico** (*pl.* -**ògici**), *a.* genealogical.
generalàto, *m.* generalship (*esp. of a religiovs order*). **generàle,** *a.* general. *sonare la ~,* to beat to quarters (*Mil.*). ¶ *m.* general. **generalíssimo,** *m.* generalissimo, commander-in-chief. **generalità,** *f.inv.* generality; majority; (*pl.*) often used incorrectly for particulars or personal details.
generàre (*pr.* **gènero**), *v.t.* to generate; produce; breed (*fig.*). **generatóre,** *m.* (*Mech., Elec.*) generator. **generazióne,** *f.* generation. **gènere,** *m.* kind; sort; type; style, fashion; gender; genus; genre (*pl.*) articles, products, merchandise. *il ~ umano,* the human race, mankind. *in ~,* in general. **genè-rico** (*pl.* -**èrici**), *a.* generic; general; indefinite, vague. *nome ~,* surname. ¶ *m.* actor playing various types of character. **generíno,** *m.* thing, article; creature (*in gen. sense*). **gènero,** *m.* son-in-law.
generosità, *f.* generosity. **generóso,** *a.* generous.
gèneśi, *f.* genesis. *la G~,* Book of Genesis (*O.T.*). **genètica,** *f.*

genetics. **genètico** (*pl.* **-ètici**), *a.* genetic. **genetlíaco** (*pl.* **-íaci**), *a. & m.* birthday.

gengíva, *f.* gum (*mouth*). **gengivíte,** *f.* inflammation of the gums.

genía, *f.* (low) set, (disreputable) crowd.

geniàle, *a.* clever, ingenious, endowed with genius; congenial, pleasing; sympathetic, genial. *letto* ~, nuptial bed. **genialità,** *f.* geniality; cleverness, genius. **gènio** (*pl.* **-gèni**), *m.* genius; talent; taste, inclination, liking; character, guardian spirit; [corps of] engineers.

genitívo, *a. & m.* genitive. **gènito,** *a.* born, begotten.

genitóre, *m.* genitríce, *f.* parent; father, mother. **genitúra,** *f.* birth; geniture.

gennàio (*pl.* **-ài**), *m.* January.

Gènova, *f.* Genoa. **genovése,** *a. & m.* Genoese.

gentàccia & **gentàglia,** *f.* rabble, mob; disagreeable people. **gènte,** *f.* people; folk[s], family; men; crew. ~ *di mare,* seamen, sea-faring folk. *diritto delle* ~*i, m.* law of nations.

gentildònna, *f.* gentlewoman; lady. **gentíle,** *a.* kind; polite; amiable, gentle; delicate, tender, soft (*meat*). *a. & m.* gentile; pagan. **gentilésco** (*pl.* **-éschi**), *a.* pagan. **gentilézza,** *f.* kindness, politeness, favour; good manners, refinement. **gentilísmo,** *m.* paganism. **gentilità,** *f.* heathendom. **gentilízio,** *a.* noble, ancestral. *stemma* ~, *m.* heraldic bearings. **gentiluòmo** (*pl.* **-uòmini**), *m.* gentleman; nobleman.

genuflessióne, *f.* genuflexion. **genuflèsso,** *a.* kneeling; on one's knees. **genuflèttersi,** *v.refl.* to kneel, kneel down.

genziàna, *f.* gentian.

geodesía, *f.* geodesy. **geodinàmica,** *f.* geodynamics. **geognosía,** *f.* geognosy. **geografía,** *f.* geography. **geogràfico** (*pl.* **-àfici**), *a.* geographic(al). **geògrafo,** *m.* geographer. **geología,** *f.* geology. **geològico** (*pl.* **-ògici**), *a.* geological. **geòlogo** (*pl.* **-òlogi**), *m.* geologist.

geòmetra (*pl.* **-òmetri**), *m.* geometer, geometrician; land-surveyor. **geometría,** *f.* geometry. **geomètrico** (*pl.* **-ètrici**), *a.* geometric(al).

Geórgia (**la**), *f.* Georgia (*U.S.A.,* Asia).

geòrgica (*pl.* **-òrgiche**), *f.* georgic, poem on husbandry. *le Georgiche di Virgilio,* Virgil's *Georgics.*

Gèova, *m.* Jehovah (*O.T.*).

gerànio (*pl.* **-àni**), *m.* geranium.

geràrca (*pl.* **-àrchi**), *m.* hierarch. **gerarchía,** *f.* hierarchy. **geràrchico** (*pl.* **-àrchici**), *a.* hierarchic(al).

Geremía, *m.* Jeremiah. **geremíade,** *f.* jeremiad; lamentation, doleful complaint.

gerènte, *m.* manager; agent; responsible editor (*newspaper,* &*c.*). **gerènza,** *f.* management; agency.

gèrgo (*pl.* **gèrghi**), *m.* slang; jargon.

Gèrico, *f.* Jericho.

gèria, *f.* basket (*for carrying bread on the back*).

Germània (**la**), *f.* Germany. **germànico** (*pl.* **-ànici**), *a.* Germanic; Teutonic. **germàno,** *a.* natural, full, german. *fratello* ~, brother german. *sorella* ~*a,* full-sister, sister german. ¶ *m.* own brother; wild duck. **germanòfilo,** *a. & m.* Germanophil. **germanòfobo,** *a. & m.* Germanophobe.

gèrme, *m.* germ (*lit. & fig.*). **germicída,** *a. & m.* germicide. **germiràre** (*pr.* **gèrmino**), *v.t. & i.* (*aux.* essere & avere) to germinate. **germogliàre** (*pr.* **-òglio,** **-ògli**), *v.i.* (*aux.* essere & avere) to bud, shoot; sprout. **germóglio** (*pl.* **-ògli**), *m.* bud; shoot; sprout.

gerofànte, *m.* hierophant. **geroglífico** (*pl.* **-ífici**), *m.* hieroglyph(ic).

Geròlamo, *m.* Jerome.

gerontocòmio, *m.* home for old people.

Gerošolimitàni, *m.pl.* Knights of St. John. **Gerošòlima,** *f.* (*Poet.*) Jerusalem.

gerúndio (*pl.* **-úndi**), *m.* gerund. **gerundívo,** *m.* gerundive.

Gerusalèmme, *f.* Jerusalem.

gessàia, *f.* chalk-pit. **gessàio, gessai[u]òlo,** & **gessinàio,** *m.* plasterer; plaster-cast maker; statuette-maker. **gessàre** (more com. *ingessare*), *v.t.* to plaster; adulterate wine with gypsum. **gessatúra,** *f.* plastering; treatment of wine with gypsum. **gessétto,** *m.* chalk (*for writing*); chalk-pencil. **gessíno,** *m.* small plaster figure. **gèsso,** *m.* chalk, piece of chalk; plaster; plaster-cast; gypsum, plaster of Paris. **gessóso,** *a.* chalky.

gèsta, gèste, *f.pl.* deeds, exploits,

memorable actions. *canzoni di* ~,
(*Fr.*) Chansons de geste; epic songs.
gestatòrio, *a.* in *sedia* ~ *a*, gestatorial
chair (*for carrying the Pope on certain
ceremonial occasions*).
gestióne, *f.* management; administration; conduct of affairs. **gestíre**
(*pr.* **-ísco, -ísci**), *v.i.* (*aux.* avere)
to make appropriate gestures (*in
speech, &c.*); *v.t.* to manage;
administer. **gèsto**, *m.* gesture; act;
action, deed. **gestóre**, *m.* manager;
traffic, goods superintendent (*Rly.*).
Gesú, *m.* Jesus.   *G~ Cristo*, Jesus
Christ.
gesúita (*pl.* **-íti**), *m.* Jesuit.
gettáre, *v.t.* to throw; cast; fling; hurl;
lay; sow.   ~ *via*, to throw away,
squander, waste.   **gettàrsi**, *v.refl.*
to throw oneself, fling oneself;
jump; fall. **gettàta**, *f.* throw; cast;
range (*gun*); shooting; shoots (*plant*);
jetty; pier. **gèttito**, *m.* yield (*tax*);
jettison; jetsam. **gètto**, *m.* jet; gush;
spout; throw; throwing; casting (*of
metal*); draft (*of letter, &c.*); shoot,
sprout (*Bot.*). **gettóne**, *m.* counter,
token.   ~ *di presenza*, attendance-
check (*indust.*).
ghèiscia, *f.* geisha (*Japan*).
ghéppio, *m.* kestrel.
gheríglio (*pl.* **-ígli**), *m.* kernel.
gherminèlla, *f.* trick.
ghermíre (*pr.* **-ísco, -ísci**), *v.t.* to
seize, snatch, clutch; carry off.
gheróne, *m.* gusset, harder (*skirt*).
ghétta, *f.* gaiter.
ghétto, *m.* ghetto, Jewish quarter.
ghía, *f.* (*Mech.*) whip-gin, tackle-
block with hoisting rope.
ghiacciàia, *f.* ice-house; ice-chest.
ghiacciàio, *m.* glacier. **ghiacciàre**,
v.t. & i. (*aux.* essere) & **ghiacciarsi**
v.refl. to freeze. **ghiacciàta**, *f.* iced
drink. **ghiacciàto**, *a.* frozen; icy;
iced. **ghiàccio**, *m.* ice. **ghiacci-
[u]òlo**, *m.* icicle; hailstone; flaw in
a precious stone.
ghiàia, *f.* gravel. **ghiaiàta**, *f.* gravel
path; strewing of gravel. **ghiaióso**,
a. gravelly, shingly.
ghiànda, *f.* acorn.
ghiandàia, *f.* jay.
ghiaréto, *m.* bank of shingle; gravelly
river-bed.
ghibellíno, *a. & m.* Ghibelline.
ghièra, *f.* ferrule (*of a walking stick,
&c.*); metal ring or cap.
ghigliottína, *f.* guillotine.
ghígna, *f.* ugly face; grimace; (*fig.*)
impudence. **ghignàre** (*pr.* **ghígno**),

v.i. (*aux.* avere) to sneer; grin
sarcastically. **ghignàta**, *f.* sneering;
sarcastic laughter. **ghignazzàre**
(*pr.* **ghignàzzo**), *v.i.* (*aux.* avere) to
sneer; laugh derisively. **ghígno**, *m.*
mocking, malicious, or ironic smile;
laugh; grin; sneer.
ghindàre, *v.t.* to hoist.
ghinèa, *f.* guinea.
ghíngheri (**in**), *ad. expr.* smartly
dressed; dressed (up) to the nines.
ghiótta, *f.* dripping-pan.
ghiottaménte, *ad.* greedily. **ghiótto**,
a. greedy, gluttonous; eager; dainty,
delicious (*of food*). **ghiottóne**, *m.*
glutton; gourmand. **ghiottonería,**
f. gluttony; delicious morsel, dainty
bit, tit-bit (*of food*).
ghiòżżo, *m.* gudgeon; blockhead.
ghiribízzo, *m.* whim; caprice.
ghiribiżżóso, *a.* capricious, whimsical.
ghirigòro, *m.* scroll; flourish (*in
writing*).   *a* ~, zig-zag.
ghirlànda, *f.* garland; wreath.   dim.
ghirlandetta, ghirlandina.   **ghir-
landàio** (*pl.* **-ài**), *m.* maker or seller
of wreaths.
ghiro, *m.* dormouse.   *dormire come
un* ~, to sleep like a top.
ghirónda, *f.* hurdy-gurdy, barrel-
organ.
ghísa, *f.* pig-iron; cast-iron.
già, *ad.* already; formerly; once; once
upon a time; yes, to be sure,
certainly; assuredly; indeed.   *abiti*
~ *fatti*, ready-made clothes.
giàcca (*pl.* **giàcche**), *f.* jacket; coat.
dim. *giacchetta, giacchettina, f.
giacchetto, giacchettino, m.*
giacché, *a.* since, as; now that;
in as much as.
giacènte, *p.a.* lying; situated; in
abeyance; (*letter*) unclaimed; dead;
(*of capital*) lying idle, uninvested.
giacènza, *f.* stay; (*Com. & Mar.*)
demurrage; stock; (*book-trade*) unsold copies. **giacére** (*pr.* **-àccio,
-àci, -àce**), *v.i. ir.* (*aux.* essere) to
lie; be situated; lie idle; be in
abeyance; be a dead letter.   **gia-
cíglio**, *m.* bed, couch, pallet.
giaciménto, *m.* bed, layer (*Geol.
Min.*).   ~ *di carbone*, coal-bed.
giacínto, *m.* hyacinth (*Bot.*); jacinth
(*Miner.*).
giacitóio, *m.* bed; couch; lair; lodging.
giacitúra, *f.* posture, position; way
of lying down.
giàco (*pl.* **-àchi**), *m.* coat of mail.
Giacóbbe, *m.* Jacob.

giacobíno, *m.* Jacobin. **giacobíta,** *a. & m.* Jacobite.

Giàcomo, *m.* James.

giaculatòria, *f.* ejaculatory prayer or curse. **giaculatòrio,** *a.* ejaculatory.

giàda, *f.* jade.

Giàffa, *f.* Jaffa.

giaggi[u]òlo, *m.* gladiolus.

giaguàro, *m.* jaguar.

giallàstro, **gialliccio, & giallò-gnolo,** *a.* yellowish. **gialletto & giallíno,** *a.* light yellow. **giàllo,** *a.* yellow. *farina* ~*a*, maize meal. ~ *di terra,* ~ *ocra,* yellow ochre. *libro* ~, yellow book (*gov. publication*); detective novel. **giallóre,** *m. & giallézza,* *f.* yellowness.

Giamàica (la), *f.* Jamaica.

giàmbico (*pl.* -àmbici), *a.* (*Pros.*) iambic. **giàmbo,** *m.* iambus, iamb.

giammài, *ad.* ever; never.

Gianícolo, *m.* Janiculum.

giannétta, *f.* walking cane.

Giànni, *m. contr.* of *Giovanni,* John, Johnny.

giannízzero, *m.* janissary.

Giàno, *m.* Janus (*Myth.*).

giansenísmo, *m.* Jansenism. **giansenísta** (*pl.* -ísti), *a. & m.* Jansenist.

Giapéto, *m.* Japheth (*O.T.*).

Giappóne (il), *m.* Japan. **giapponése,** *a. & m.* Japanese.

giàra, *f.* jar; drinking-cup.

giardinàggio, *m.* gardening. **giardinétto,** *m.* small garden. **giardinièra,** *f.* woman-gardener, gardener's wife; basket-carriage; coach; flower-stand; mixed salad. **giardinière,** *m.* gardener; nurseryman. **giardíno,** *m.* garden (usu. a flower garden, as distinct from **orto,** a kitchen-garden). ~ *pensile,* roof garden. ~ *zoologico,* zoological garden[s]; zoo. ~ *d' infanzia,* Kindergarten.

giarrettièra, *f.* garter. *l'Ordine della G*~, *m.* the Order of the Garter.

Giasóne, *m.* Jason (*Myth.*).

giaúrro, *m.* giaour, infidel.

Giàva, *f.* Java.

giavellòtto, *m.* javelin.

gibbosità, *f.inv.* gibbosity; convexity. **gibbóso,** *a.* gibbous; convex; humped, hunch-backed.

gibèrna, *f.* cartridge-box; c.-pouch.

gibétto, *m.* gibbet, gallows.

gibigiàna, *f.* reflected ray of sunlight.

Gibiltèrra, *f.* Gibraltar.

gíbus, *m.inv.* opera-hat, crush-hat; gibus.

giga (*pl.* gíghe), *f.* jig (*dance*).

gigànte, *a. & m.* giant. **giganteg-**

giàre (*pr.* -éggio, -éggi), *v.i.* (*aux.* avere) to tower; stand (or rise) like a giant. **gigantésco** (*pl.* -éschi), *a.* gigantic. **gigantéssa,** *f.* giantess.

gigliàceo, *a.* liliaceous. **gigliàto,** *a.* stamped with a lily; strewn or planted with lilies. **gíglio** (*pl.* gígli), *m.* lily; fleur-de-lis. ~ *delle convalli,* lily of the valley (*also* **mughetto**). ~ *tigrato,* tiger-lily. *La Città del G*~, *f.* Florence.

gílda, *f.* guild.

gilè, *m.* waistcoat.

gin, *m.inv.* gin.

ginecología, *f.* gynaecology. **ginecòlogo** (*pl.* -òlogi), *m.* gynaecologist. **ginecòmio,** *m.* hospital for women.

ginepràio (*pl.* -ài), *m.* juniper thicket; (*fig.*) labyrinth; difficult situation. **ginépro,** *m.* juniper.

ginèstra, *f.* broom (*Bot.*).

Ginévra, *f.* Geneva. **ginevríno,** *m.* inhabitant of Geneva.

gingillàre, *v.i.* (*aux.* avere) & **gingillàrsi,** *v.refl.* to trifle; linger. **gingillíno,** *m.* trifler; loiterer. **gingíllo,** *m.* toy; nick-nack; bauble; trifle. **gingillóne,** *m.* trifler; dawdler.

ginnasiàle, *a.* belonging to a gymnasium (*continental grammar-school*). *la prima* ~ (*sc.* classe), the first class in a grammar-school, or gymnasium. **ginnàsio** (*pl.* -àsi), *m.* gymnasium; classical school; grammar-school.

ginnàsta (*pl.* -àsti), *m.* gymnast; athlete. **ginnàstica,** *f.* gymnastics. **ginnàstico** (*pl.* -àstici), *a.* gymnastic.

ginnétto, *m.* jennet (*small horse*).

ginocchiàta, *f.* blow with, or on, the knee. **ginocchièllo,** *m.* knee-cap; shin-guard (*for protection*). **ginòcchio,** *m.* (*pl.m.* **ginòcchi,** *pl.f.* **ginòcchia**) knee. *rotella del* ~, knee-cap; (*Anat.*) knee-pan. *in* ~, on one's knees, or **ginocchióne, ginocchióni,** *ad.* on one's knees, kneeling.

Giòbbe, *m.* Job (*O.T.*).

giocàre (*pr.* -giuòco, giuòchi, &*c.*), *v.t. & i.* (*aux.* avere) to play; stake; bet; deceive; make fun of. **giocàrsi** (di) *v.refl.* to make sport of, make a fool of, deceive. **giocàta,** *f.* stake; play, manner of playing; turn to play; game. **giocatóre,** *m.* -**tríce,** *f.* player; speculator; gambler. ~ *di calcio,* football player, footballer. ~ *di Borsa,* stock-jobber. ~ *al* *rialzo,* bull (*Stk. Ex.*). ∼ *al ribasso,* bear (*Stk. Ex.*). **giocàttolo,** *m.* toy; plaything. **giocherellàre,** *v.i.* (*aux.* avere) to play, amuse oneself; play for small stakes; toy (with), trifle (with). **giòco,** see *giuoco.*

giocofòrza, *f.* necessity. *è* ∼, it is absolutely necessary. *mi fu* ∼, I was obliged.

giocolàre, *v.i.* (*aux.* avere) to play; juggle; perform on the tight rope. **giocolière,** *m.* (*f.* **-ièra**) juggler.

giocondità, *f.* mirth; gaiety; cheerfulness. **giocóndo,** *a.* gay; merry; joyous; (*Poet.*) jocund.

giocosità, *f.* facetiousness; mirth. **giocóso,** *a.* jocose, jocular; facetious, humorous.

giogàia, *f.* mountain range, chain of mountains; dewlap (*of oxen*). **giógo** (*pl.* **gióghi**), *m.* yoke; pair of oxen; summit, peak; mountain ridge.

giòia, *f.* joy; pleasure; delight; happiness; jewel, precious stone. *fuoco di* ∼, *m.* bonfire.

gioiellería, *f.* jewellery; jeweller's art; jeweller's shop. **gioiellière,** *m.* jeweller; goldsmith. **gioièllo,** *m.* jewel.

gioióso, *a.* joyful. **gioíre** (*pr.* **-ísco, -ísci**), *v.i.* (*aux.* avere) to rejoice. ∼ *di,* to enjoy, rejoice at, be glad of. **giòlito,** *m.* quiet pleasure, rest, enjoyment.

Giòna, *m.* Jonah (*O.T.*). **Giònata,** *m.* Jonathan (*O.T.*).

Giordàno, *m.* Jordan.

giorgína, *f.* dahlia.

giornalàccio, *m.* low-class [news-] paper; scurrilous rag. **giornalàio** (*pl.* **-ài**), newsagent; newsboy. **giornàle,** *m.* newspaper; journal; diary; day-book (*Com.*). ∼ *di bordo,* log-book. dim. *giornaletto, giornalino.* **giornalièro,** *a.* daily. ¶ *m.* day-labourer. **giornalísmo,** *m.* journalism. **giornalísta** (*pl.* **-ísti**), *m.* journalist. **giornalístico** (*pl.* **-ístici**), *a.* journalistic.

giornalménte, *ad.* daily; every day. **giornànte,** *f.* charwoman; daily help. **giornàta,** *f.* day (*duration*); day's work, d's pay, d's journey; march, stage, interval; battle. *lavorare a* ∼, or, *far la* ∼, to work by the day. ∼ *lavorativa,* working day. *vivere alla* ∼, to live from hand to mouth. *in* ∼, before the day is over, in the course of the day.

giórno, *m.* day. *in pieno* ∼, in broad day(light). *di* ∼ *in* ∼, day by day.

il ∼ *dopo,* next day, the day after. *il suo* ∼ *di ricevimento,* her day at-home. ∼ *delle Ceneri,* Ash Wednesday. *il* ∼ *dei morti,* All Souls' Day. ∼ *feriale,* working day. ∼ *di magro,* fast day. *ultimi* ∼*i di carnevale,* *m.pl.* Shrovetide.

Giòsafat, *m.* Jehoshaphat (*O.T.*).

Giosía, *m.* Josiah (*O.T.*).

giòstra, *f.* joust; tournament; merry-go-round. **giostràre** (*pr.* **giòstro**), *v.i.* (*aux.* avere) to joust; tilt; wrestle.

Giosuè, *m.* Joshua (*O.T.*).

giovaménto, *m.* benefit; advantage; avail.

giovanàccio & **giovanàstro,** *m.* young scamp; good-for-nothing. **gióvane,** *a.* young. ¶ *m.* young man; youth; *f.* young woman, girl. *il* ∼, the younger (of two). **giovanétta** & **giovinétta,** *f.* girl; young girl. **giovanétto** & **giovinétto,** *m.* boy, young boy; lad. **giovanézza,** *f.* youth; youthfulness. **giovaníle,** *a.* youthful; juvenile.

Giovànna, *f.* Jane; Joan.

Giovànni, *m.* John. *il bel San* ∼, the Baptistry at Florence.

giovanòtta, *f.* young woman. **giovanòtto,** *m.* young man; bachelor; apprentice (Merchant Navy).

giovàre (*pr.* **-óvo**), *v.i.* (*aux.* avere & essere) to avail; be of use; *v.t.* to help, favour. *mi giova credere,* I can well believe. **giovàrsi (di),** *v.refl.* to avail oneself of; utilize; profit by.

Giòve, *m.* Jove, Jupiter (*Myth.*).

giovedí, *m.inv.* Thursday.

Giovenàle, *m.* Juvenal.

giovènca, *f.* heifer. **giovènco** (*pl.* **-ènchi**), *m.* steer; young bullock.

gioventú, *f.inv.* youth (*the period; lit. & fig.*); young people; body of y. people.

gioveréccio (*pl.* **-écci**), *a.* ʼhelpful, useful; pleasant, agreeable.

giovévole, *a.* profitable; beneficial.

gioviàle, *a.* jovial; jolly. **giovialità,** *f.* joviality.

giovincèllo, *m.* stripling, young lad. **gióvine,** *a.* young. ¶ *m.* young man; *f.* young woman; girl. **giovinétta,** *f.* young girl; maiden (*Poet.*). **giovinetto,** *m.* young lad, youth. **giovinézza,** *f.* youth (*state*).

gipsotèca (*pl.* **-èche**), *f.* gallery of plaster casts.

giràbile, *a.* negotiable (*Com.*).

giracàpo, *m.* dizziness.

giràffa, *f.* giraffe.

giraménto, *m.* turning; turning round; circular motion. ~ *di testa*, dizziness.

giramóndo, *m.* wanderer; vagrant; globe-trotter; adventurer.

giràndola, *f.* Catherine-wheel; (*fig.*) fancy; caprice; flighty person. **girandolàre** (*pr.* **-àndolo**), *v.i.* (*aux.* avere) to stroll, ramble. **girandolíno,** *m.* weather-cock; inconstant person. **girandolóne,** *m.* lounger, loiterer.

gi ̀rante, *p.a.* turning, revolving. ¶ *m.* one who endorses a bill, endorser. **giràre,** *v.t.* to turn; turn round; slew; swing round; go round; travel over, round or through; surround; change; round off; get round; endorse (*bill*); shoot (*film*); *v.i.* (*aux.* avere) to turn, revolve; wheel; ramble; run; walk, circulate; be in circulation; measure round; (*of milk or wine*) turn sour, go bad. ~ *di bordo*, to tack (*Naut.*). ~ *al largo*, to sheer off. ~ *la palla*, to screw (*billiards*). *mi gira la testa*, my head swims. **giràrsi,** *v.refl.* to turn; turn round. **girarrósto,** *m.* spit; roasting-jack. **girasóle,** *m.* sun-flower. **giràta,** *f.* turn, turning, revolution; walk, stroll; deal, dealing (*cards*); time; endorsement (*bill*). **giratàrio** (*pl.* **-àri**), *m.* endorsee, one in whose favour a bill is endorsed. **giratína,** *f.* short walk; short turn (*e.g. of a key*); rounding off (*of a sentence*). **giratòrio,** *a.* gyratory; revolving. **giravòlta,** *f.* turning, turning round; (*fig.*) shift, change of front.

gíre (no *pr.*, *andare* takes its place), *v.i. ir. & defect.* (*aux.* essere) (*Poet.*) to go.

girèlla, *f.* pulley; small wheel; revolving disk; piece (*draughts or backgammon*); rowel (*spur*); round cheese; (*fig.*) political weather-cock. **girellàre** (*pr.* **-èllo**), *v.i.* (*aux.* avere) to stroll about; wander. **girèlio,** *m.* small ring or circle; bracelet; centre of an artichoke; steak from the back of the thigh. dim. *girellino, girelletto.*

girellonàre, *v.i.* (*aux.* avere) to saunter; stroll; loaf. **girellóne,** *m.* saunterer; loafer.

girétto, *m.* stroll, short walk.

girévole, *a.* turning; revolving; rotating; (*fig.*) fickle, capricious. *ponte* ~, *m.* revolving bridge.

girigògolo, *m.* scrawl; flourish; illegible scribble; nonsensical talk.

giríno, *m.* tadpole.

gíro, *m.* turn; round; tour; circumference; circuit; circle, rim; circulation; revolution; rotation; walk, stroll, drive, run, ride; lap (*sport*); trick. *mettere in* ~, to spread, put in circulation (*money, news, &c.*). *fare un giro*, to go for a turn. *pigliare in* ~, to tease. ~ *in automobile*, motor run.

girobússola, *f.* gyrocompass.

Giròlamo, *m.* Jerome.

girondíno, *m.* Girondist.

gironzàre & gironzolàre, *v.i.* (*aux.* avere) to saunter, ramble about; pry around.

giropilòta, *m.* (*Aero.*) automatic pilot, 'George.'

giroscòpio (*pl.* **-òpi**), *m.* gyroscope.

girotóndo, *m.* round dance.

girovagàre (*pr.* **-òvago**), *v.i.* (*aux.* avere) to ramble, wander about. **giròvago,** *a.* rambling, wandering, strolling. ¶ *m.* rambler, wanderer; hawker; tramp.

gíta, *f.* trip; tour; excursion; ramble. dim. *giterella.*

gitàno, *m.* (*f.* **-a**) Spanish gypsy.

gitànte, *m.f.* tripper. ~ *a piedi*, hiker.

gittare, *v.t.* (*Poet.*) to throw, cast.

giù, *ad.* down; below; downwards.

giùbba, *f.* jacket; coat; dress-coat; swallow-tail c.; mane (*lion*). dim. *giubbetta, giubbina, f. giubbetto, giubbino, giubbettino* (jumper) *m.* **giubbóne,** *m.* heavy coat. dim. *giubboncello, giubboncino m.*

giubilànte, *a.* jubilant; exultant. **giubilàre** (*pr.* **-úbilo**), *v.i* (*aux.* avere) to be jubilant; exult; rejoice; (*v.t.*) to pension off. **giubilàto,** *p.a.* pensioned [off]; retired. **giubilazióne,** *f.* retirement on pension.

giubilèo, *m.* jubilee. **giúbilo,** *m.* jubilation; rejoicing; joy.

giuccheria, *f.* foolishness; stupidity. **giúcco** (*pl.* **giúcchi**), *a.* stupid, silly; foolish. ¶ *m.* ass, silly fool. dim. *giuccarello* or *giuccherello.*

Giùda, *m.* Judas (*N.T.*); Judah (*O.T.*). *un g* ~, a Judas; infamous traitor.

giudàico (*pl.* **-àici**), *a.* Jewish. **giudaísmo,** *m.* Judaism. **Giudèa (la),** *f.* Judea. **giudèo,** *a.* Jewish. ¶ *m.* Jew.

giudicàre (*pr.* **-údico, -údichi**), *v.i.* (*aux.* avere) & *v.t.* to judge, think,

deem, consider; sentence. **giudi-
càto**, *p.a.* judged, deemed, thought;
sentenced. ¶ *m.* judgment; sentence.
giudicatóre, *m.* (*f.* **-trice**) judge
(*gen. sense*). **giudicatúra**, *f.*
judicature; judgeship; bench (or
body) of judges. **giúdice**, *m.* judge;
magistrate; justice (*pers.*). ~ *arbitro*,
referee (*Sport*).
Giudítta, *f.* Judith.
giudiziàle, *a.* judicial. **giudiziàrio**,
a. judiciary; judicial. **giudízio** (*pl.*
-ízi), *m.* judgment; opinion; trial;
verdict; decision; sentence; prudence;
good sense. *dente del* ~, wisdom-
tooth. *inviare a* ~, to commit for
trial. **giudizióso**, *a.* judicious;
sensible; wise.
giúggiola, *f.* jujube. **giúggiolo**, *m.*
jujube-tree. **giuggiolóne**, *m.* great
fool; dolt.
giúgno, *m.* June.
giugulàre, *a.* jugular.
giulebbàre (*pr.* **-èbbo**), *v.t.* to candy;
sweeten (*a drink*). **giulebbàrsi**,
v.refl. to cherish. **giulebbàto**, *p.a.*
candied. **giulèbbe**, *m.* julep.
Giúlia, *f.* Julia.
Giuliàno, *m.* Julian.
Giúlie (**Alpi**), *f.pl.* Julian Alps.
Giuliétta, *f.* Juliet.
Giúlio, *m.* Julius. *G* ~ *Cesare*, Julius
Caesar.
giulívo, *a.* merry; gay; joyful.
giullàre, *m.* jester; buffoon; strolling-
singer.
giumèlla, *m.* double handful.
giuménta, *f.* mare. **giuménto**, *m.*
beast of burden.
giúnca (*pl.* **giúnche**), *f.* (Chinese)
junk. **giuncàia**, *f. & **giunchéto**, *m.*
bed of rushes, reed-bed. **giuncàta**,
f. junket.
giunchíglia, *f.* jonquil.
giúnco (*pl.* **giúnchi**), *m.* rush;
reed.
giúngere (*pr.* **-úngo**, **-úngi**, **-únge**),
v.i. ir. (*aux.* essere) to arrive. (*v.t.*)
to join; combine; clasp (*hands*). ~ *a*,
to reach, overtake.
giúngla, *f.* jungle.
Giunóne, *f.* Juno (*Myth.*).
giúnta, *f.* addition; increase; surplus;
overweight; appendix; start; junta;
committee; council; board of
management; examination-board.
per ~, in addition, into the bargain.
a (or *di*) *prima* ~, at once, at first
sight.
giuntàre, *v.t.* to join; sew together;
(*fig.*) overreach, cheat, swindle.

giuntería, *f.* fraud, cheating,
swindling.
giuntína, *f.* edition of the Giunti press
(*Florence*).
giúnto, *p.a.* joined; clasped; arrived.
¶ *m.* joint; coupling; clutch (*Mech.*,
Motor). **giuntúra**, *f.* joint; juncture.
giunzióne, *f.* joint; junction.
giuocàre, see *giocare*.
giuòco & **giòco** (*pl.* **giuòchi**, **giòchi**),
m. game; play; sport; pastime;
set (articles for game); gaming;
gambling; speculation; trick; joke;
(*Mech.*) free play; action; clearance.
~ *di mano*, sleight of hand. ~ *di
parole*, play upon words, pun. ~ *d'*
azzardo, game of chance, game of
skill. ~ *leale*, fair play. ~ *sleale*,
foul play. *fuori* ~, off-side (*football*).
campo di ~, playground; playing
field.
Giúra, *m.* Jura.
giurabbàcco! giuraddio! *i.* by Jove!
giuraménto, *m.* (*solemn*) oath.
giuràre, *v.i.* (*aux.* avere) & *v.t.* to
swear, take an oath. **giuràto**, *p.a.*
sworn; declared. ¶ *m.* juryman.
banco dei ~ *i*, *m.* jury-box. **giura-
tòrio** (*pl.* **-òri**), *a.* on oath; sworn.
giúre, *m.* law; jurisprudence.
giureconsúlto, *m.* jurisconsult;
skilled lawyer.
giurése & **giuràssico**, *a.* jurassic
(*Geol.*).
giurí, *m.* jury (*in court of Assise or in
an affair of honour, giurì d'onore*).
giuría, *f.* jury (*in gen. sense & in
competitions, exhibitions, &c.*).
giurídico (*pl.* **-ídici**), *a.* juridical,
law (*att.*); legal. *condizione* ~ *a*,
legal position (*Pers.*).
giurisdizióne, *f.* jurisdiction. **giuri-
speríto**, *m.* skilled lawyer. **giuri-
sprudènza**, *f.* jurisprudence; law.
giurísta (*pl.* **-ísti**), *m.* jurist.
giúro, *m.* (*Poet.*) oath.
Giusèppe, *m.* Joseph.
giusquíamo, *m.* henbane.
giústa, *pr.* according to.
giustacuòre, *m.* close-fitting jacket.
giustaménte, *ad.* justly; rightly;
suitably; properly; exactly. **giu-
stappúnto**, *ad.* precisely, exactly.
giustézza, *f.* justness; propriety;
suitability; exactness; (*Typ.*) length
of the line. **giustificàre** (*pr.*
-ífico, **-ífichi**), *v.t.* to justify;
vindicate; make good. **giustifica-
tívo**, *a.* justificative. *documento* ~,
voucher. **giustificazióne**, *f.*
justification; vindication; excuse.

Giustiniàno, *m.* Justinian.

giustízia, *f.* justice. **giustiziàre** (*pr.* -ízio, -ízi), *v.t.* to execute; put to death. **giustizière,** *m.* executioner; hangman.

giùsto, *a.* just; right; proper; true; lawful; legitimate; equitable; fair; correct; accurate; exact; well-fitting; of reasonable size or shape. *il ~ mezzo,* the happy medium, the golden mean. *il ~ erede,* the rightful heir. ¶ *ad.* justly, rightly, exactly, just.

glaciàle, *a.* glacial, icy; frozen; frosty; frigid.

glàndola, *f.* gland. **glandulàre,** *a.* glandular.

glàuco (*pl.* **glàuchi**), *a.* sea-green; glaucous; greyish green; greyish-blue. **glaucòma,** *m.* (*Med.*) glaucoma.

glèba, *f.* glebe; soil; earth; clod; (*Poet.*) mould.

gli, *def. art. m.pl.* (before vowels, s impure, z and gn) the. ¶ *pers. pr.* [to] him; them; it (*nom.*).

glicerìna, *f.* glycerin(e).

glícine, *f.* wistaria.

glicosúria, *f.* (*Med.*) glycosuria.

gliéla, **gliélo,** *comp. pn. sg.* (*conjunctive*) it (to) him, it (to) her.

gliéle, **gliéli,** *comp. pn.* them (to) him, them (to) her.

gliéne, *comp. pn.* some to him, some to her; of it to him, of it to her.

glíttica, *f.* art of cutting gems.

globàle, *a.* total; inclusive; aggregate (*sum*); grand, sum (*total*). *somma ~, f.* lump sum. **globalménte,** *ad.* in gross, in the lump. **glòbo,** *m.* globe; ball; orb. *~ dell'occhio,* eye-ball. dim. *globetto, globulo* (globule), *globuletto, globettino.*

glòria, *f.* glory; fame; honour; splendour; pride; (*Art*) (accessory) group of angels or saints. ¶ *m.* part of the Mass wh. follows the Kyrie, beginning *Gloria in excelsis. farsi ~ di,* to glory in, be proud of. *s[u]onare a ~,* to ring the bells in honour of someone or for a festival. dim. *glorietta, gloriola, gloriuzza.* **gloriàrsi** (**di**), *v.refl.* to glory in, pride oneself on, take a pride in, **glorificàre** (*pr.* -ífico, -ífichi), *v.t.* to glorify. **glorióso,** *a.* glorious; proud.

glòssa, *f.* gloss; explanation; annotation. **glossàre** (*pr.* **glòsso**), *v.t.* to gloss; comment, annotate. **glossàrio** (*pl.* -àri), *m.* glossary. **glossatóre,**

m. commentator. **glossología,** *f.* glossology; science of language; linguistic[s].

glòttide, *f.* glottis. **glottología,** *f.* glossology; scientific study of languages.

glu glu, *m. & onomat. exp.* gurgle, gurgling; (*turkey*) gobbling.

glucòsio, *m.* glucose. **glútine,** *m.* gluten. **glutinóso,** *a.* glutinous; viscous; sticky.

gnàcchera, *f.* castanet.

gnào, gnàu, *m. & onomat. exp.* mew, mewing. **gnaulàre** (*pr.* gnàulo), *v.i.* (*aux.* avere) to mew; (*child*) cry, whine. **gnaulàta,** *f.* mewing, &c. **gnaulío,** *m.* continual mewing, &c.

gneiss, *m.inv.* gneiss (*Geol.*).

gnòcco (*pl.* **gnòcchi**), *m.* dumpling. dim. *gnocchetto, gnocchettino.*

gnòmico (*pl.* -òmici), *a.* gnomic. **gnòmo,** *m.* gnome; goblin.

gnorri (far lo), to feign ignorance.

gnòsi, *f.inv.* gnosis. **gnosticísmo,** *m.* gnosticism.

gòbba, *f.* hump. **gòbbo,** *a.* hump-backed, hunch-backed; humped; crooked, bent. ¶ *m.* hunch-back; hump. **gobbóni (andar),** to go bent.

gòccia (*pl.* **gócce**) & **gócciola,** *f.* drop. dim. *goccino m., gocciolina f. gocciolino m.* **gócce,** *f.pl.* earrings, ear-drops. **gocciàre** (*pr.* góccio, gócci*) & **gocciolàre** (*pr.* gócciolo), *v.i.* (*aux.* avere) to drip; trickle; fall in drops. **gocciolatúra,** *f.* dripping, trickling. **gocciolío,** *m.* constant dripping.

godére, *v.i.* (*aux.* avere) to rejoice; be glad; (*v.t.*) to enjoy; possess; profit from. **godérsi,** *v.refl.* to enjoy. **godérsela,** *v.refl.* to enjoy oneself; enjoy life.

goderéccio, *a.* delightful; agreeable. **godíbile,** *a.* enjoyable. **godiménto,** *m.* enjoyment, pleasure; possession, use.

godronàre, *v.t.* (*Mech.*) to knurl. **godronatúra,** *f.* knurling.

goffàggine, *f.* awkwardness; clumsiness; stupid action, blunder or saying. **goffaménte,** *ad.* awkwardly; clumsily. **gòffo,** *a.* awkward; clumsy.

Goffrédo, *m.* Godfrey; Geoffrey.

gógna, *f.* pillory.

góla, *f.* throat; (*fig.*) gorge; strait(s); (*Mech.*) groove; narrow opening; gluttony, desire. *far ~,* to tempt;

be a temptation. *mal di* ~, *m.* sore throat.

golétta, *f.* schooner; narrow gorge; collar. **gòlf**, *m.* golf. **gólfo**, *m.* gulf, bay, bight. *corrente del G*~, *f.* Gulf-stream.

Gòlgota, *m.* Golgotha (*N.T.*). **Golía**, *m.* Goliath (*O.T.*).

goliàrdico (*pl.* -àrdici), *a.* goliardic. *canti goliardici*, medieval student songs. **goliàrdo**, *m.* goliard; (wandering) student.

golosaménte, *ad.* greedily; gluttonously. **golosità**, *f.inv.* gluttony; greediness; tasty morsel. **golóso**, *a.* greedy; gluttonous.

golpàto, *a.* blighted; blasted; mildewed. **gólpe**, *f.* blight; mildew.

gómena, *f.* cable; hawser. ~ *da rimorchio*, tow rope.

gomitàta, *f.* blow (or shove) with the elbow. **gómito**, *m.* elbow; (*fig.*) sharp bend (*road or stream*); bent piece of tubing; crank. *albero a* ~, crank shaft. **gomítolo**, *m.* ball; skein; clew.

gómma, *f.* gum; resin; rubber; [rubber] tyre. ~ *arabica*, gum Arabic. ~ *da masticare*, chewing-gum. ~ (*per cancellare*), eraser. ~ (*elastica*), (india)rubber. **gommàto**, *a.* gummed. **gommóso**, *a.* gummy.

góndola, *f.* gondola. **gondolière**, *m.* gondolier.

gonfalóne, *m.* banner, standard. **gonfalonière**, *m.* standard-bearer.

gónfia, *f.* glass-blower. **gonfiàggine**, *f.* swelling; sense of repletion; (*fig.*) self-satisfaction, ridiculous pride. **gonfiagióne**, *f.* & **gonfiaménto** *m.* swelling; (*fig.*) exaggeration, bombast. **gonfianùvoli**, *m.inv.* boaster; braggart. **gonfiàre** (*pr.* **gónfio**, **gónfi**), *v.t.* to inflate, puff up, swell; pump up (*tyre*); exaggerate, magnify; exalt; flatter; bore; *v.i.* (*aux.* essere) & **gonfiàrsi**, *v.refl.* to swell, rise, swell up. **gonfiatóio**, *m.* inflator, tyre-pump. **gonfiatúra**, *f.* swelling; exaggeration; flattery; boasting; puffing up, puff (*excessive praise*). **gonfiézza**, *f.* swelling; inflation; distension; (*fig.*) pride. **gónfio** (*pl.* **gónfi**), *a.* swollen; inflated; distended; puffed up; proud; conceited; bombastic. **gonfióne**, *m.* corpulent person; one puffed up with conceit; chubby boy. **gonfióre**, *m.* (slight) swelling.

gónga (*pl.* **gónghe**), *f.* swollen gland; scrofula; scrofulous person.

gongolàre (*pr.* **góngolo**), *v.i.* (*aux* avere) to exult; be transported.

goniòmetro, *m.* goniometer; protractor.

gónna, *f.* gown; petticoat; skirt. ~ *calzoni*, divided skirt. **gonnèlla**, *f.* petticoat; slip. **gonnèllo**, *m.* child's petticoat; dim. *gonnellino*, *m.* **gonnellóna**, *f.* giddy woman, gadabout. **gonnellóne**, *m.* large petticoat; cassock.

gónzo, *m.* simpleton; blockhead; fool.

gòra, *f.* channel, conduit; [mill-] lade; irrigation canal; mill-pond; stagnant water; (*book*) stain. **goràta**, *f.* water of a conduit; mill-race. **gorgàta**, *f.* draught, drink.

gorgheggiàre (*pr.* **-éggio**, **-éggi**), *v.i.* (*aux.* avere) to trill, warble. **gorghéggio**, *m.* trilling; warbling; trill.

gòrgia, *f.* throat, guttural [pronunciation of] **r**.; burr.

gorgièra, *f.* frilled collar; ruff.

górgo (*pl.* **górghi**), *m.* whirlpool; abyss.

gorgogliàre (*pr.* **-óglio**, **-ógli**), *v.i.* (*aux.* avere) to gurgle; bubble. **gorgóglio**, *m.* gurgling, gurgle.

gorgóne, *m.* gorgon.

gorìlla, *m.* gorilla.

gòta, *f.* cheek.

Gòti, *m.pl.* Goths. **gòtico** (*pl.* **gòtici**), *a.* Gothic.

gótta, *f.* gout. **gottóso**, *a.* gouty.

governànte, *f.* governess. **governàre** (*pr.* **-èrno**), *v.t.* to govern; rule; guide; look after; steer; groom (*horse*); till; manure. **governativo**, *a.* government (*att.*); governmental. *palazzo* ~, *m.* government house. *scuola* ~*a*, *f.* State school. **governatoràto**, *m.* governorship. **governatóre**, *m.* governor. **governatríce**, *f.* governor's wife. **govèrno**, *m.* government; rule; administration; management; guidance; care; steering; helm.

gozzàta, *f.* cropful; gulp. **gózzo**, *m.* (*bird's*) crop; goitre.

gozzovíglia, *f.* debauch; revelry; merry-making.

gozzúto, *a.* affected with goitre.

gracchiàre (*pr.* **gràcchio**, **gràcchi**), *v.i.* (*aux.* avere) to croak. **gracchiàta** & **gracchiaménto**, *m.* croaking. **gràcchio**, *m.* jackdaw; crow; grackle.

Gràcco, *m.* Gracchus.

gracidàre (*pr.* **gràcido**), *v.i.* (*aux.* avere) to croak.

gràcile, *a.* slim; thin; weak; feeble, delicate. **gracilità**, *f.* slimness; slenderness; weakness.

gracimolàre, *v.t.* to glean (*grapes*). **gracímolo**, *m.* bunch of grapes left on vine after harvest; small portion.

gradàre, *v.t.* to gradate.

gradassàta, *f.* bluster; brag. **gradàsso**, *m.* blusterer; boaster, braggart.

gradataménte, *ad.* gradually; step by step; by degrees. **gradazióne**, *f.* gradation; grading; degree.

gradévole, *a.* pleasing, pleasant; agreeable. **gradevolézza**, *f.* agreeableness. **gradiménto**, *m.* enjoyment; pleasure; gratification; liking; acceptance, approval, approbation.

gradinàta, *f.* flight of steps; (*Theat.*) balcony. **gradíno**, *m.* step; degree, stage.

gradire (*pr.* **-ísco, -ísci**), *v.t.* to accept, receive with favour or pleasure, appreciate; like; find agreeable; be glad to (*or* that = *che*). **gradíto**, *a.* agreeable; pleasant; welcome.

gràdo, *m.* step; degree; rank; title; grade; condition; position; (good) will; pleasure; liking. *essere in ~*, to be able. *mettere in ~* (di), to enable. *di buon ~*, with pleasure; willingly. *di proprio ~*, of one's own accord. *a mal ~*, against one's will. *saper ~ di*, to be grateful for. *a ~ a ~*, step by step.

graduàle, *a.* gradual. **gradualménte**, *ad.* gradually; by degrees.

graduàre, *v.t.* to graduate, grade, mark out in degrees; confer a military rank on. **graduataménte**, *ad.* gradually; by degrees. **graduàto**, *p.a.* graduated; graded; progressive. ¶ *m.* graduate; non-commissioned officer. **graduatòria**, *f.* classification; class-list; graded list of creditors; pass-list. **graduazióne**, *f.* graduation; grading; preferment; promotion.

gràffa, *f.* clip; claw (*Mech.*); boat-hook.

graffiàre, *v.t.* to scratch. **graffiasànti**, *m.inv.* hypocrite. **graffiàta**, *f.* scratch; scratching. dim. *graffiatina*. **graffiatúra**, *f.* scratch. **gràffio**, *m.* scratch; grapnel; (*pl.*) grappling irons.

grafía, *f.* (hand) writing; spelling.

gràfico (*pl.* **-gràfici**), *a.* graphic. **grafíte**, *f.* graphite; blacklead.

grafología, *f.* graphology; study of handwriting. **grafomanía**, *f.* craze for writing.

gragn[u]òla, *f.* hail.

gramàglie, *f.pl.* mourning; mourning dress.

gramígna, *f.* weed; couch-grass. **gramignóso**, *a.* weedy; full of weeds.

grammàtica, *f.* grammar. **grammaticàle**, *a.* grammatical. **grammàtico** (*pl.* **-àtici**), *m.* grammarian. ¶ *a.* grammatical.

gràmmo, *m.* gram[me] = 15.432 grains.

grammòfono, *m.* gramophone.

gràmo, *a.* wretched; miserable; poor.

gràmola, *f.* kneading-trough. **gramolàre**, *v.t.* (*pr.* **gràmolo**) to knead; break; crush; bruise (*flax*).

gran, see **grande** or **grano**.

gràna, *f.* cochineal (*dye*); graining; grain; Parmesan (cheese), also *formaggio di ~*. *a.* (or *di*) *~ fine*; *a* (or *di*) *~ grossa*, fine-grained; coarse grained.

granadíglia, *f.* passion-flower, granadilla.

granàglie, *f.pl.* cereals; corn, grain. **granàio** (*pl.* **-ài**), *m.* barn; granary. **granai[u]òlo**, *m.* corn-dealer. ¶ *a.* grain-feeding, granivorous. **granàre**, *v.t.* to grain, granulate; *v.i.* (*aux.* essere) to seed, run to seed. Cf. *granire*.

granàta, *f.* broom; grenade (*projectile*). G ~ (la), Granada. **granatàio**, *m.* broom-seller. **granatière**, *m.* grenadier.

granàto, *m.* garnet. ¶ *a.* deep transparent red, wine-coloured.

grancancellería, *f.* chancellery; chancellor's residence. **grancancellière**, *m.* High chancellor.

grancàne, *m.* (great) Khan. **grancàssa**, *f.* big-drum, bass-drum.

granchiésco (*pl.* **-éschi**), *a.* crab-like. **grànchio** (*pl.* **grànchi**), *m.* crab; muscular cramp; claw (of a hammer); clamp; (*fig.*) mistake. dim. *grancella*, *f.* *granchietto*, *m.* **granchiolíno**, *m.* very small crab. **grancipòrro**, *m.* big crab; (*fig.*) bad blunder, mistake.

granconsiglio, *m.* Council of State.

grancordóne, *m.* high rank in an Order of Chivalry. **grancróce**, *m.* Grand Cross; highest rank in an order of chivalry (e.g. *Knight of Malta*).

grànde or (*contr.*) **gran**, *a.* great;
large; big; broad; wide; tall; high;
deep (*knowledge*, &c.); grand; noble;
grown up; full; loud; heavy; strong;
capital (*letter*); chief; general (*public*);
long (*time*); much, many. *a ~
velocità*, at full speed;   by fast
train.   *un gran che*, something
extraordinary (gen. in neg. expr.,
e.g. *non è un ~ che*, it is nothing
remarkable.   dim.   *grandétto,
grandino, grandicello*. ¶ *m.* grown-
up person; grandee, nobleman; (*pl.*)
great men.   *in ~*, on a large scale.
grandi e piccoli, old and young.
grandeggiàre (*pr.* **-éggio, -éggi**),
v.i. (*aux.* avere) to tower; rise
(*above*); soar; stand out; be ostentatious, show off, put on airs (*of
grandeur*).   **grandeménte**, *ad.*
greatly; deeply; highly. **grandézza**,
f. greatness; magnitude; size;
grandeur; display; (*phys.*) quantity.
Sua Grandezza, His Highness.
grandígia, *f.* pride; arrogance;
ostentation.
grandinàre (*pr.* **gràndino**), *v.i.* (*aux.
.ssere*) to hail. **grandinàta**, *f.*
hail-storm. **gràndine**, *f.* hail.
chicco di ~, *m.* hail-stone.
grandióso, *a.* grand, grandiose;
imposing; sumptuous.
grandúca (*pl.* **-úchi**), *m.* Grand
Duke.   **granducàto**, *m.* Grand
Duchy. **granduchéssa**, *f.* Grand
Duchess.
granèllo (*pl.m.* **-èlli**, *pl.f.* **-èlla**), *m.*
grain (*of corn*); stone or pip (*of
fruit*); seed; kernel; minute particle.
granèlla, *f.pl.* cereals.
granfàtto, *ad.* much; very; a great
deal. *non è ~*, it is not long since;
not long ago.
grànfia (*pl.* **grànfie**), *f.* claw; talon;
(*pl.* (*fig.*)) clutches. **granfiàre** (*pr.*
-ànfio, -ànfi), *v.t.* to clutch.
granigióne, *f.* seeding; formation of
the grain. **graníre** (*pr.* **-ísco,
-isci**), *v.i.* (*aux.* essere) to seed,
form grains; (*of child*) teethe; give
a grained or granulated surface.
granita, *f.* grated ice-drink.
graníto, *m.* granite. ¶ *a.* seeded;
grained;   firm,   robust,   well-
developed; (*Mus.*) with notes
separately heard or pronounced
(*note staccate*).
granitúra, *f.* seeding; milling; milled
edge (*of a coin*).
granivoro, *a.* granivorous, grain-
feeding.

granlàma, *m.* Grand Lama (*Tibet*).
granmaéstro, *m.* Grand Master
(*Masonry, Knights of St. John*).
granmercè, *ad.* many thanks.
gràno, *m.* corn; wheat; grain (*of sand,
&c.*); pip (*of fruit*); bead (*of rosary*);
grain (*weight*); minute particle.
granòcchia, *f.* frog.
granóne, & **grantúrco**, *m.* maize;
Indian corn.
granulàre, *a.* granular. ¶ *v.t.* to
granulate.
gràppa, *f.* clamp; cramp-iron; stalk;
(*Typ.*) bracket, brace; brandy
grappíno, *m.* small glass of brandy;
hook, grapnel.
grappolíno, *m.*   small   bunch.
gràppolo, *m.* bunch; cluster.
gràscia (*pl.* **gràsce**), *f.* fat; lard; (*pl.*)
victuals. **grascéta**, *f.* rich pasture.
gràspo, *m.* grape-stalk.
grassàccio, *a.* excessively fat.
grassaménte, *ad.* richly, abundantly; plentifully.
grassatóre, *m.* highwayman. **grassa-
zióne**, *f.* highway robbery.
grassèllo, *m.* piece of fat; suet;
slaked lime. **grassétto**, *m.* (*Typ.*)
heavy type. **grassézza**, *f.* fatness;
stoutness; richness (*of soil*); abundance.   **gràsso**, *a.* fat; stout;
plump; rich (*land, cooking, &c.*);
greasy; plentiful, abundant; loud;
lewd, licentious. *giorni ~ i*, days
when meat may be eaten. *giovedì ~*,
the last Thursday before Lent.
martedì   ~,   Shrove   Tuesday.
tempo ~, cloudy weather. *è andata
~a*, the thing has gone well.
a farla ~ a, at the most, at the best.
¶ *m.* fat; grease.   *~ di balena*,
blubber. **grassoccíno**, *a.* plump
(*child*). **grassòccio**, *a.* plump;
rather fat. **grassoccióne**, *a.* too fat.
grassóne, *m.* (**-óna**, *f.*) very fat
person. **grassòtto**, *a.* rather fat;
very fat.   **grassúme***, m.* fat
substance; manure.
gràta, *f.* grating.
grataménte, *ad.* gratefully, thank-
fully; agreeably.
gratèlla, *f.* gridiron; grill. *cotto
sulla ~*, grilled. *carne alla ~*, grill,
grilled meat. dim. *gratellina*, small
grating.
graticciàta, *f.* trellis-work; fence.
graticciàto, *m.* trellis, trellis-work.
graticcio (*pl.* **-icci**), *m.* trellis-
work; set of hurdles.
graticola, *f.* grating; grate; gridiron.
graticolàre (*pr.* **-ícolo**), *v.t.* to

divide (*a picture or drawing*) into squares (for copying); to close with a grating. **graticolàto**, *m.* railing; grating; trellis.

gratificàre (*pr.* **-ífico, -ífichi**), *v.t.* to bestow a gratuity on; remunerate; gratify. **gratificàrsi**, *v.refl.* to win one's favour. **gratificazióne**, *f.* bonus, gratuity; special fee; gratification.

gratitúdine, *f.* gratitude. **gràto**, *a.* grateful; pleasing; agreeable; gratifying; acceptable; kind.

grattacàpo, *m.* annoyance; trouble; worry; preoccupation.

grattacièlo, *m.* sky-scraper.

grattàre, *v.t.* to scratch; scrape; grate; scratch out, rub out, erase. **grattàta, grattatúra**, *f.* scratching; scraping; scratch; erasure. **gratta-tíccio**, *m.* (*mark of*) erasure. **grattíno**, *m.* scraper; ink-erasing knife.

grattúgia, *f.* grater. **grattugiàre**, *v.t.* to grate.

gratuitaménte, *ad.* free; free of charge; gratuitously. **gratúito**, *a.* gratuitous, free. *prestito* ~, loan without interest. **gratulatòrio**, *a.* congratulatory.

gravàbile, *a.* liable; taxable, dutiable. **gravafògli**, *m.inv.* letter-weight. **gravàme**, *m.* burden, encumbrance; gravamen; tax, duty. **gravàre**, *v.t.* to burden; load; serve an order of sequestration on; *v.i.* (~ **su**) (*aux.* avere) to weigh [up]on, lie heavy [up]on. **gràve**, *a.* heavy; grave; serious; stern; weighty; difficult; grievous; painful; deep; bad; dangerous; great. ~ *d' anni*, advanced in years. ¶ *m.* weight; heavy body. **graveménte**, *ad.* gravely, grievously; heavily; deeply. **graveolènte**, *a.* evil-smelling. **gravézza**, *f.* heaviness; hardship; imposition, tax; trouble, sadness, weariness.

gravidànza, *f.* pregnancy. **gràvido**, *a.* pregnant (*lit. & fig.*).

gravína, *f.* pick-axe; mason's pick.

gravità, *f.inv.* gravity (*Phys. & Moral*); weight; (*fig.*) seriousness; importance. **gravitazióne**, *f.* gravitation.

gravosaménte, *ad.* heavily; painfully. **gravóso**, *a.* heavy; burdensome, oppressive; hard, troublesome, vexatious; sad, painful.

gràzia (*pl.* **gràzie**), *f.* grace; favour; boon; permission, leave; pardon; mercy; kindness; charm; graceful-

ness. *di* ~*!* please! pray! *in* ~ *di*, on account of; with the help of; thanks to. *ogni* ~ *di Dio*, all sorts of good things. *domanda di* ~, petition for mercy. **graziàbile**, *a.* pardonable. **graziàre**, *v.t.* to pardon. **gràzie**, *f.pl. & i.* thanks; thanks! thank you! **grazióso**, *a.* gracious; graceful; dainty; elegant; pretty; gratuitous. *imprestito* ~, loan on easy terms.

grèca, *f.* zig-zag ornament or design (*in embroidery or on general's cap*). **grecàle**, *a.* north-east. ¶ *m.* north-east wind.

Grécia (la), *f.* Greece. **grecísta** (*pl.* **-ísti**), *m.* Greek scholar; Hellenist. **grèco** (*pl.* **grèci**), *a.* Greek; Grecian. ¶ *m.* Greek; Greek language; north-east wind.

grecolevànte, *m.* east-north-east wind.

gregàrio (*pl.* **-àri**), *m.* private (soldier); follower (*Pol.*, &*c.*). ¶ *a.* gregarious.

grègge, *m.* (*pl.f.* **le grèggi**) & **grèggia** (*pl.* **grègge**), *f.* flock; herd. **grèggio** & **grèzzo**, *a.* raw; rough; undressed; unbleached. *zucchero* ~, brown sugar.

gregoriàno, *a.* Gregorian. *canto* ~, Gregorian chant; plain-song. **Gregòrio**, *m.* Gregory.

grembialàta & **grembiulàta**, *f.* apronful. **grembiàle** & **grembi-úle**, *m.* apron. dim. **grembialíno** & **grembiulíno**, *m.* small apron; child's pinafore. **grèmbo**, *m.* lap; bosom; (*fig.*) womb; pale.

gremíre (*pr.* **-ísco, -ísci**), *v.t.* to fill; fill up; stuff full; crowd. **gremíto**, *p.a.* filled, full; stuffed; crowded.

gréppia, *f.* manger; crib; rack.

gréppo, *m.* steep rocky bank; cliff; crag; mound; edge of a ditch.

grès, *m.inv.* sandstone.

gréto, *m.* dry gravel-bed of a river; pebbly shore (*sea*). **grétola**, *f.* bar of a cage; pretext; one full of excuses. **gretóso**, *a.* gravelly.

grettaménte, *ad.* meanly; shabbily; stingily. **grettería** & **grettézza**, *f.* shabbiness, meanness, stinginess. **grétto**, *a.* mean, shabby, stingy; niggardly; feeble; narrow.

grève, *a.* heavy; grievous.

grída, *f.* proclamation; edict; ban. **gridàre**, *v.i.* (*aux.* avere) & *v.t.* to cry; cry out, shout, call; call for; proclaim; scream; bawl; clamour; scold. **gridàta**, *f.* shouting; bawling; scolding. **gridío**, (*pl.* **-ii**) *m.* incessant shouting.   **grído,** *m.* cry; shout; scream; fame; repute; rumour; report; outcry; tumult.

grifàgno, *a.* rapacious; fierce; hawk-like.

grifo, *m.* snout, muzzle; gryphon (*Myth.*).   **grifóne,** *m.* griffin, gryphon (*Myth.*); griffon (*vulture*).

grigiàstro, *a.* greyish.   **grígio,** *a.* grey, gray.   ~ *perla,* pearl grey. ~ *verde,* grey-green.

Grigióni (i), *m.pl.* the Grisons.

griglia, *f.* grating, grate; grille, grill; (*Radio*) grid.

Grignolíno, *m.* a delicate Piedmontese wine.

grillàre, *v.i.* (*aux.* avere) to simmer; begin to boil; hiss; ferment (*new wine*).   ~ *il cervello,* to take a fancy, to have a whim.

grillétto, *m.* trigger.   **gríllo,** *m.* cricket (*insect*); (*fig.*) whim, fancy, caprice.

grimaldèllo, *m.* picklock (*instr.*).

grínta, *f.* forbidding face; sulky expression; (*fig.*) insolence, impudence.   **grínza,** *f.* wrinkle; crease; fold.   **grinzóso,** *a.* wrinkled; creased.

gríppe, *f.* influenza.

grisòlito, *m.* chrysolite.

grissíni, *m.pl.* long Piedmontese bread rolls, in the shape of a wand (or *bastoncino*).

Groenlàndia (la), *f.* Greenland. **groenlandése,** *a. & m.* Greenland (*att.*). Greenlander.

grómma, *f.* incrustation; crust; tartar.   **grommàto,** *a.* crusted; encrusted with tartar, *&c.*

grónda, *f.* gutter; (*pl.*) eaves; slope; vertical folds in a skirt.   **grondàia,** *f.* gutter (*on a roof*).   **grondànte,** *p.a.* dripping; streaming.   **grondàre** (*pr.* **gróndo**), *v.i.* (*aux.* avere) to drip; flow; stream; gush; trickle; (*v.t.*) to pour out.

gróngo (*pl.* **grónghi**), *m.* conger-eel.

gròppa, *f.* back, rump, croup (*of horse*).   *in* ~, on the back.   **groppàta,** *f.* buck-jump.

gròppo, *m.* knot; tangle; lump (*in the throat*); squall (*at sea*).   **groppóne,** *m.* back.

gròssa, *f.* gross (*12 dozen*).   **grossàggine,** *f.* grossness; coarseness; ignorance.   **grossaménte,** *ad.* grossly; coarsely.   **grossézza,** *f.* size; bulk; thickness; bigness; volume; coarseness.   **grossísta** (*pl.* **-ísti**), *m.* wholesale dealer.   **gròsso,**

a. big; thick; coarse; rough (*sea*); swollen (*river*); harsh, loud (*voice*); excessive, too much; hard (*of hearing*); pregnant.   *caccia* ~*a,* *f.* big-game.   *dito* ~, thumb; big toe.   *pezzo* ~, important personage, big-wig.   *alla* ~ *a,* broadly.   *di* ~, *della* ~*a,* quite, deeply, much. *questa è* ~ *a,* this is (rather) too much!   *dormire della* ~ *a,* to sleep like a log.   *dirle* ~ *e,* to talk nonsense.   *raccontarle* ~ *e,* to tell tall tales.   ¶ *m.* bulk; main body; majority.

grossolanaménte, *ad.* coarsely; grossly; rudely.   **grossolanità,** *f.* coarseness; grossness; rudeness. **grossolàno,** *a.* coarse; gross; rough; rude; awkward.

gròtta, *f.* grotto, shallow cave; rocky wall or ridge.   *dim.* **grotticella,** **grotticina, grotterella,** *f.*

grottésco (*pl.* **-éschi**), *a. & m.* grotesque.

gròtto, *m.* grotto; steep place.

grovíglio, *m.* knot; kink; tangle; (*fig.*) entanglement; confusion.

gru, *f.inv.* crane (*bird & hoist*); (*Naut.*) davit.   ~*a vapore,* steam-crane.   ~ *a carroponte,* over-head travelling crane.

grúccia (*pl.* **grúcce**), *f.* crutch. **grucciàta,** *f.* blow with a crutch.

gruèra, *f.* gruyere (cheese).

grufolàre (*pr.* **grúfolo**), *v.i.* (*aux.* avere) to grub, poke about; root (*as pigs*).   **grufolàrsi,** *v.refl.* to wallow.

grugàre (*pr.* **grúgo, grúghi**), *v.i.* (*aux.* avere) to coo.

grugníre (*pr.* **-ísco, -ísci**), (*aux.* avere) to grunt.   **grugníto,** *m.* grunt; grunting.   **grúgno,** *m.* snout. *fare il* ~, to pout, sulk.

grullàggine, *f.* foolishness; stupidity. **grullería,** *f.* piece of stupidity; foolish words or action; foolishness. **grúllo,** *m.* foolish; silly; stupid. ¶ *m.* fool; simpleton.

grúmo, *m.* clot.   **grúmolo,** *m.* core; heart (*of a vegetable*); inside of a water-melon after seeds are removed. **grumóso,** *a.* clotted.

grúppe, *m.* croup (*Med.*)

grúppo, *m.* group; batch; cluster; knot; company, party, set; lump (*in throat*); squall (*of wind*).   ~ *di lunghezze d'onda,* (*Radio*) wave-band. *dim.* **gruppetto, gruppettino,** *m.*

grúzzolo, *m.* hoard.

guadàbile, *a.* fordable.

guadagnàre, *v.t.* to gain, get, earn

acquire; win; reach; catch; recover, make up for (*what is lost*). **guadàgno**, *m.* gain; profit; advantage; (*pl.*) earnings; winnings; profits. **guadàre**, *v.t.* to ford; wade across. **guàdo**, *m.* ford.

guài! *i.* woe! woe betide!

guaìna, *f.* sheath, scabbard; case.

guàio (*pl.* **guài**), *m.* misfortune, calamity, accident; failure (*Mech.*); trouble; difficulty, difficult situation; scrape; woe; wail[ing]. *il ~ è che*, the trouble is that . . .

guaíre (*pr.* **-ísco, -ísci**), *v.i.* (*aux.* avere) to yelp; whine; howl. **guaíto**, *m.* yelp, yelping; whine, whining.

gualcàre (*pr.* **-álco, -álchi**), *v.t.* to full (*cloth*). **gualchièra**, *f.* fulling-mill.

gualcíre (*pr.* **-ísco, -ísci**), *v.t.* to rumple; crumple.

guància (*pl.* **guànce**), *f.* cheek. **guanciàle**, *m.* pillow; cushion. *dim.* **guancialetto, guancialino, guancialuccio,** *m.*

guantàio (*pl.* **-ài**), *m.* glover; glove-maker. **guantería**, *f.* glove-shop; glove-[manu]factory. **guantièra**, *f.* glove box. **guànto**, *m.* glove; (*fig.*) gauntlet.

guardabarrière, *m.inv.* gate-keeper (*at level crossings*). **guardabòschi**, *m.inv.* woodman; forester. **guardacàccia**, *m.inv.* gamekeeper. **guardacòrpo**, *m.inv.* life-line. **guardacòste**, *m.inv.* coastguard. *nave ~*, *f.* coastal defence vessel. **guardafréni**, *m.inv.* brakesman. **guardalínee**, *m.inv.* linesman (*Sport*). **guardamagaẑẑíno**, *m.* store-keeper. **guardamàndrie**, *m.inv.* herdsman. **guardamàno**, *m.inv.* gauntlet; sword-guard; hand-rail. **guardapètto**, *m.inv.* breast-plate. **guardapòrto**, *m.inv.* guard-ship. **guardaportóne**, *m.inv.* door-keeper; liveried porter. **guardàre**, *v.t. & abs.* to look, look at, look on; consider, look into, examine; look after, protect, watch; regard, look upon; view. *~ fisso*, to gaze at. *~ con stupore*, to stare at. *~ per ogni verso*, to look (one) through & through. *~ uno dall, alto in basso*, to look one up & down. *v.i.* (*aux.* avere) to take care, mind; try. *~ in*, to look out on. **guardàrsi**, *v.refl.* to abstain, forbear; be careful, beware (foll. by *da*). *guardatevi dai borsaiuoli*, beware of pickpockets.

guardaròba, *f.* wardrobe; cloak-room; linen-room or cupboard. **guardarobièra**, *f.* cloak-room attendant; woman in charge of the linen-room. **guardarobière**, *m.* cloak-room attendant. **guardasigílli**, *m.inv.* keeper of the seals; Lord Chancellor; Lord Privy Seal (*Eng.*).

guardàta, *f.* look; glance. *dim.* *guardatina*, *f.* **guardatàccia**, *f.* evil look; scornful look. **guardatúra**, *f.* way of looking.

guàrdia, *f.* guard; guarding; watch; guardsman; watchman. *far la ~*, to keep guard, to k. watch. *stare in ~*, to be on one's guard¹ *guardie a piedi*, foot-guards; *~ a cavallo*, horse-guards; *~ del corpo*, life-guards. *corpo di guardia*, guard-room. *ufficiale di ~*, (*Nav.*) officer of the watch. *~ di finanza*, *~ doganale*, customs officer. *~ forestale*, forester. *foglio di ~*, fly-leaf.

guardiamarína, *m.inv.* acting sub-lieutenant (*Nav.*).

guardiàno, *m.* waiden; keeper; care-taker; watchman; herdsman. *padre ~*, father superior (*monast.*), *madre ~ a*, mother superior.

guardína, *f.* guardroom.

guardinfànte, *m.* crinoline.

guardíngo (*pl.* **-ínghi**); *a.* careful; cautious.

guardi[u]òlo, *m.* guard-house; guard-room.

guàrdo, (*Poet.*), see *sguardo*.

guarentígia (*pl.* **-ígie**), *f.* guarantee. **guarentíre**, see *garantire*.

guàri, *ad.* (*used only with neg.*) much, a long time; very. *non ha ~*, it is not long since, not long ago.

guaríbile, *a.* curable. **guarigióne**, *f.* recovery; cure. **guarire** (*pr.* **-ísco, -ísci**), *v.i.* (*aux.* essere) to recover; be cured. (*v.t.*) to cure; heal; free. **guaritóre**, *m.* healer.

guarnàcca, *f.* long cloak; robe.

guarnigióne, *f.* garrison. **guarniménto**, *m.* fitting (out); equipment; rigging; fortification; ornament; trimming; (*pl.*) fittings. **guarníre** (*pr.* **-ísco, -ísci**), *v.t.* to furnish; equip; fit out; rig; fortify; adorn; garnish (*food*). **guarníto**, *p.a.* equipped; trimmed; fortified; adorned; garnished. **guarnitúra**, *f.* fitting (out); trimming; lining; garniture. **guarnizióne**, *f.* trimming; lining; (*Cook*) garniture; (*Mech.*) gasket; packing.

Guascógna (la), *f.* Gascony. **guasconàta,** *f.* gasconade. **guascóne,** *m.* Gascon.
guastafèste, *m.inv.* spoil-sport, kill-joy. **guastaménto,** *m.* spoiling; marring; havoc; disfigurement. **guastamestièri,** *m.inv.* one who undercuts his fellow workers, scab; bungler. **guastàre,** *v.t.* to spoil; ruin; mar; make a mess of; taint, corrupt. **guastàrsi,** *v.refl.* to spoil; be spoiled; become tainted; change for the worse; decay. ~ *con qualcuno,* to fall out (quarrel) with someone. **guastastòmachi,** *m.inv.* bad food; indigestible dish. **guastatóre,** *m.* pioneer; sapper. **guàsto,** *a.* spoiled; spoilt; out of order; tainted; corrupt; vicious; depraved; rotten, decayed. ¶ *m.* damage; accident; breakdown; ruin.
guatàre, *v.t.* to gaze at; stare at; eye; pry into; look askance at.
guàttera, *f.* scullery-maid. **guàttero,** *m.* scullery-boy; scullion.
guattíre, *v.i.* (*aux.* avere) to yelp; to give tongue (*hounds*).
guàzza, *f.* heavy dew.
guazzabúglio (*pl.* -úgli), *m.* muddle, medley, mess; slush.
guazzàre, *v.t.* to ford; wade across; water (*animals*); *v.i.* (*aux.* avere) to wallow; welter; shake (*of liquids*). **guazzàta,** *f.* watering. **guazzatóio** (*pl.* -ói), *m.* horse-pond; watering place for animals. **guazzétto,** *m.* stew; hash. **guàzzo,** *m.* pool; ford; slush; liquid; (*Art.*) gouache. *passare a* ~, to wade across. *pittura a* ~, gouache [painting]. **guazzóso,** *a.* wet· dewy; slushy.
guèlfo, *m.* Guelf, Guelph.
guèrcio (*pl.m.* **guèrci,** *f.* **guèrce**), *a.* squint-eyed.
guerníre, see *guarnire.*
guèrra, *f.* war, warfare; strife, feud. ~ *di logoramento,* war of attrition. ~ *manovrata,* open warfare. ~ *di posizione,* ~ *di trincea,* trench warfare. **guerrafondàio** (*pl.* -ai), *m.* war-monger.
guerreggiàre (*pr.* -éggio, -éggi), *v.i.* (*aux.* avere) to (wage) war. **guerrésco** (*pl.* -éschi), *a.* warlike, martial, war (*att.*). **guerrièro,** *m.* warrior. ¶ *a.* warlike. **guerríglia,** *f.* guer[r]illa. **guerriglière,** *m.* guer[r]illa fighter; guer[r]illa; partisan.
gufàre, *v.i.* (*aux.* avere) to hoot; (*v.t.*) to mock. **gúfo,** *m.* owl.

gúglia, *f.* spire; pinnacle; obelisk. **gugliàta,** *f.* needleful (of thread).
Guglièlmo, *m.* William.
guida, *f.* guide; guidance; leadership; driving; steering; direction; guide (-book); directory; manual; rail; rut; wheel-track; (*Mech.*) slide; (*driving*) rein. *volante di* ~, steering wheel (*motor*). **guidàre,** *v.t.* to guide, lead, conduct; drive; steer; ride. ~ *una motocicletta,* to ride a motor cycle. **guidatóre,** *m.* (*f.* -tríce) driver.
guiderdóne, *m.* (*Lit.*) reward; recompense.
guidóne, *m.* pennant; mark flag.
guidoslitta, *f.* bob-sleigh.
guíndolo, *m.* reel.
guinzàglio (*pl.* -àgli), *m.* leash (*lit. & fig.*).
guísa, *f.* manner, way; mode; guise. *a* (*in*) ~ *di,* like, after the manner of. *di* (*in*) ~ *che,* so that.
guítto, *m.* strolling player. ¶ *a.* poor, low, beggarly.
guizzànte, *p.a.* quivering; darting; wriggling; flashing. **guizzàre,** *v.i.* (*aux.* avere) to dart; wriggle; flash; quiver; glide. **guízzo,** *m.* flash; wriggle; gliding.
gúscio (*pl.* gúsci), *m.* shell (*eggs, nuts, &c.,* & *fig.*); husk; cover; pod; hull; frame of a boat; scale-pan. *gusci della bilancia,* scales. ~ *di guanciale,* pillow-case.
gustàbile, *a.* enjoyable; agreeable; with a pleasant flavour. **gustàccio,** *m.* bad taste (or flavour). **gustàre,** *v.t.* to enjoy, relish; like; taste; try; (*v.i.*) to please. *non mi gusta questo vino,* I don't like this wine. **gustazióne,** *f.* tasting; gustation. **gustévole,** *a.* tasteful; palatable; appetizing; enjoyable. **gústo,** *m.* taste; flavour; relish; enjoyment; zest; gusto; liking. **gustóso,** *à.* tasty, savoury; agreeable; amusing.
guttapèrca, *f.* gutta-percha.
gutturàle, *a. & f.* guttural; guttural (*sound or letter*).

H

H, h, (*acca*) *f.* the letter H; nothing, nothing at all; jot, tittle. *non ci capisco un'acca,* I understand nothing about it.

The letter H remains in the Italian alphabet only as a convenient phonetic sign after *c* and *g* when these require to have a guttural sound before *e* and *i*, e.g. **che** as distinguished from **ce**, **chi** as distinguished from **ci**.

It is also preserved without any phonetic value (a) in four persons of the present indicative of *avere* (**ho, hai, ha, & hanno**) so that the eye may not confuse these with words of the same sound spelt without that letter; and (b) in exclamations such as **ah, ahi, ahimè, eh, ih, oh, ohi, & ohimè!**

It may also be found in foreign words, especially Latin, and in words derived from foreign proper names, such as *hegheliano* (Hegelian) & *hertziano* (Hertzian).

I

I, i, (*i*) the letter I, which now incorporates **J** (or I lunga), no longer used in Italian. When found, however, in such words as **iattanza, iucca, ièna, aiuola,** or any words in which it takes the place of I lunga, it retains a semi-consonantal sound approximating to Eng. y.

i, *def. art. m.pl.* (used before all consonants other than impure *s, z, x, gn, ps,*) the.

iacintèo & **iacintíno,** *a.* hyacinthine.

íadi, *f.pl.* Hyades (*Myth. & Astr.*).

iàfet, *m.* Japheth (*O.T.*).

ialíno, *a.* hyaline; translucent.

iàrda, *f.* yard (*Meas.* = 0.914399 metre).

iàto, *m.* hiatus (*Gram.*).

iattànza, *f.* boastfulness; boasting; bragging.

iattúra, *f.* misfortune; accident; loss.

Ibèri, *m.pl.* Iberians. **ibèrico** (*pl.* -èrici), *a.* Iberian.

ibernànte, *a.* hibernating; hibernant. **ibernazióne,** *f.* hibernation.

íbi & **íbis,** *m.* ibis.

ibridísmo, *m.* hybridism. **íbrido,** *a.* hybrid.

icàstica, *f.* art of representing reality. **icàstico** (*pl.* -àstici), *a.* figurative; pictorial.

ícchese, *f.* the letter X.

icneumóne, *m.* ichneumon.

icòna & **icòne,** *f.* icon. **iconoclàsta** & **iconoclàste** (*pl.* -àsti), *m.*

iconoclast. **iconoclàstico** (*pl.* -àstici), *a.* iconoclastic.

iconografía, *f.* iconography.

icóre *or* **ícore,** *m.* ichor.

ícs, *f.* the letter X. *i raggi* ∼, x-rays.

idàlgo (*pl.* **idàlghi**), *m.* hidalgo, Spanish grandee.

Iddío (*pl.* -íi), *m.* God. *Cf.* Dio.

idèa, *f.* idea; conception; plan; notion; opinion; vague belief; fancy; thought; intention; purpose. *neanche per* ∼, not at all, not in the least. **ideàbile,** *a.* imaginable; conceivable. **ideàle,** *a. & m.* ideal. **idealísmo,** *m.* idealism. **idealísta** (*pl.* -ísti), *m.* idealist. **idealístico** (*pl.* -ístici), *a.* idealistic. **idealità,** *f.* ideality; quality of being ideal; elevated feelings. **idealizzàre,** *v.t.* to idealize. **idealménte,** *ad.* ideally. **ideàre** (*pr.* -èo), *v.t.* to imagine; conceive; form the idea of.

identicità & **identità,** *f.* identity. **idèntico** (*pl.* -èntici), *a.* identical; (*diplom.*) identic. **identificàre** (*pr.* -ífico, -ífichi), *v.t.* to identify.

ideografía, *f.* ideography. **ideogràmma** (*pl.* -gràmmi), *m.* ideogram. **ideología,** *f.* ideology.

ídi, *m.pl.* Ides. *gl'idi di Marzo,* the Ides of March.

idillíaco (*pl.* -íaci), & **idíllico** (*pl.* -íllici), *a.* idyllic. **idíllio** (*pl.* -ílli), *m.* idyll.

idiòma (*pl.* -ómi), *m.* language; tongue; idiom; dialect. **idiomàtico** (*pl.* -àtici), *a.* idiomatic.

idiosincrasía, *f.* idiosyncrasy.

idiòta (*pl.* -òti), *a.* stupid; ignorant; untaught; imbecile. ¶ *m.* idiot; imbecile. **idiotàggine,** *f.* idiocy; ignorance; imbecility; idiotic words or action. **idiòtico** (*pl.* -òtici), *a.* idiotic; imbecile. **idiotísmo,** *m.* idiom, vulgar expression; idiocy. **idiozía,** *f.* idiocy.

idolàtra (*pl.* -àtri), *m.* idolator; *f.* idolatress. ¶ *a.* idolatrous. **idolatràre** (*pr.* -àtro), *v.t.* to worship (*idols*); idolize. **idolatría,** *f.* idolatry. **idolàtrico** (*pl.* -àtrici), *a.* idolatrous. **idoleggiàre** (*pr.* -éggio, -éggi), *v.t.* to make an idol of; idolize. **ídolo,** *m.* idol.

idoneaménte, *ad.* fitly; usefully; conveniently. **idoneità,** *f.* aptitude; fitness; ability. **idòneo,** *a.* fit; apt; serviceable; well fitted (for).

ídra, *f.* hydra (*Myth.*). **idrànte,** *m.* hydrant.

idràto, *m.* hydrate (*Chem.*).

idràulica, f. hydraulics. idràulico (pl. -àulici), a. hydraulic, water (att.). ¶ m. plumber.
idro, m. water-snake; contr. for idrovolante, sea-plane.
idro- as prefix corresponds to Eng. hydro-, and in many compounds is self-explanatory; but the following should be noted:—idrocefalìa, f. (Med.) water on the brain. idròfilo, a. absorbent. cotone ~, cotton-wool. idrofobìa, f. hydrophobia, rabies. idròfobo, a. hydrophobic; mad; rabid. cane ~, mad dog. idromànte, m. water-diviner, dowser. idromanzìa, f. water-divining, dowsing. idròpico (pl. -òpici), a. dropsical. idropisìa, f. & idrope, m. dropsy. idroplàno, m. sea-plane, cf. idrovolànte. idroscàlo, m. aeroport. idroscòpio (pl. -òpi), m. hydroscope (instrument for gauging specific gravity). idrostàtica, f. hydro-statics. idrovolànte, m. seaplane.
Ièfte, m. Jephtha (O.T.).
iemàle, a. (Poet.) wintry.
Iémen, m. Yemen (Geog.).
ièna, f. hy[a]ena.
Ièova, m. Jehovah (O.T.).
ieràtico (pl. -àtici), a. hieratic.
ièri, ad. yesterday. ier l'altro, & l'altro ieri, the day before yesterday. iermattina, yesterday morning.
ierofànte, m. hierophant.
ieroglìfico (pl. -glìfici), a. & m. hieroglyphic.
iettatúra, f. evil eye; malign influence; ill-luck.
Ifigenìa, f. Iphigenia (Myth.).
igiène, f. hygiene, hygienics, health, sanitation. igiènico (pl. -ènici), a. hygienic(al), healthy, sanitary; toilet (paper).
ignàro, a. ignorant (of = di); un-acquainted (with = di).
ignàvia, f. laziness; sloth; cowardice. ignàvo, a. lazy, cowardly.
ìgneo, a. fiery; igneous (Geol.). ignìto, a. burning, fiery, ignited. ignizióne, f. ignition.
ignòbile, a. ignoble.
ignomìnia, f. ignominy; dishonour; infamy; shameful action. ignominióso, a. ignominious; shameful.
ignorantàggine, f. ignorance; stupidity. ignorànte, a. ignorant; unlearned. ignorantèllo, a. rather ignorant. ignoranteménte, ad. ignorantly. ignorantóne, m. exceedingly ignorant fellow; dunce;

booby. ignorànza, f. ignorance.
ignoràre (pr. -òro), v.t. to be ignorant of; not to know; ignore. ignoràto, a. unknown; ignored.
ignotaménte, ad. secretly; in obscurity; incognito. ignòto, a. unknown. il Milite ~, the Unknown Soldier.
ignudaménte, ad. nakedly. ignudàre, v.t. & ignudàrsi, v.refl. to strip, undress. ignúdo, a. naked; bare.
ih! i. hullo! fie!
il, def. art. sg. m. the.
ilarànte (gas), m. laughing-gas. ilare, a. merry; hilarious; cheerful. ilarità, f. hilarity; good humour, mirth, merriment; laughter.
Ildebràndo, m. Hildebrand.
ìleo, m. ileum; part of the small intestine (Anat.). ilìaco (pl. -ìaci), a. iliac (Anat.); Trojan (of Ilium, i.e. Troy).
Ilìade, f. Iliad.
ìlice, f. ilex; holm oak.
ìlio, m. ilium (Anat.); I~, Ilion, m. Ilium; Troy.
illacrimàbile, a. (Poet.), not to be wept for; not worthy of tears. illacrimàto, a. unwept.
illagazióne, f. inundation.
illanguidìre (pr. -ìsco, -ìsci), v.i. (aux. essere) to languish; grow feeble; droop; (v.t.) to weaken; enfeeble. illanguidìto, a. languishing; enfeebled; drooping.
illatìvo, a. inferential.
illecitaménte, ad. illegitimately. illécito, a. illicit; unlawful; for-bidden.
illegàle, a. illegal. illegalità, f.inv. illegality.
illeggiadrìre (pr. -ìsco, -ìsci), v.t. to prettify; embellish.
illeggìbile, a. illegible; unreadable.
illegìttimo, a. illegitimate; unlaw-ful.
illéso, a. unhurt; unharmed; un-injured; intact; safe.
illetteràto, a. illiterate; unlettered.
illibàto, a. spotless; pure; chaste.
illico, ad. (Lat.) there; immediately; forthwith.
illimitataménte, ad. boundlessly; without limit. illimitàto, a. un-limited.
Illinése, m. Illinois (U.S.A.).
illiquidìre (pr. -isco, -isci), v.i. (aux. essere) to melt, soften.
Illíria (l'), f. Illyria. illírico (pl. -irici), a. Illyrian

illividíre (*pr.* -ísco, -ísci), *v.i.* (*aux.* essere) to turn pale or livid.

illògico (*pl.* -ògici), *a.* illogical.

illúdere (*pr.* -údo, &*c.*, like *alludere*), *v.t. ir.* to deceive; delude.

illumináre (*pr.* -úmino), *v.t.* to illuminate; light up; (*fig.*) enlighten. **illumináto**, *p.a.* lit up; illuminated; enlightened. ~ *a giorno*, flood-lit. **illuminazióne,** *f.* lighting; illumination. ~ *a giorno*, flood-lighting. *impianto di* ~, lighting installation.

illusióne, *f.* illusion; phantasm; dream; fond hope. ~ *ottica*, optical illusion. **illusionísta** (*pl.* -ísti), *m.* conjurer. **illúṣo**, *p.a.* deluded; deceived. **illuṣòrio** (*pl.* -òri), *a.* illusory, deceptive.

illustráre (*pr.* -ústro), *v.t.* to illustrate; render illustrious; illuminate; explain. **illustráto**, *p.a.* illustrated. *cartolina postale* ~*a*, picture post-card. **illustrazióne,** *f.* illustration; lustre (*fig.*); celebrity; explanation; plate, picture. **illústre**, *a.* illustrious; renowned. **illustríssimo**, *a.* most illustrious (*formal address or title of honour*).

illúvie, *f.inv.* filth.

illuvióne, *f.* inundation; flood.

ilòta (*pl.* -òti), *m.* helot.

imàgine, see *immagine*.

Imalàia, *m.* Himalaya (*Geog.*).

imbacchettoníre (*pr.* -ísco, -ísci), *v.i.* (*aux.* essere) to become a bigot; *v.t.* to make a bigot, render bigoted.

imbaccuccàre (*pr.* -cúcco, -úcchi), *v.t.* & **imbaccuccàrsi**, *v.refl.* to muffle up; wrap (oneself) up.

imbaldanzíre (*pr.* -ísco, -ísci), *v.t.* to embolden; make bold; *v.i.* (*aux.* essere) & **imbaldanzírsi**, *v.refl.* to become bold; be emboldened.

imballàggio, *m.* packing; packing material; cost of packing; *pl.* (*Com.*) empties. *carta da* ~, wrapping paper; brown paper. *gabbia da* ~, *f.* packing crate, crate. **imballàre**, *v.t.* to pack; wrap up. ~ *il motore*, (*Motor.*) to race the engine. **imballatóre**, *m.* (*f.* -tríce) packer. **imballatúra,** *f.* packing; cost of packing. **imbàllo**, *m.* packing.

imbalordíre (*pr.* -ísco, -ísci), *v.i.* (*aux.* essere) to be bewildered; become dizzy; *v.t.* to bewilder; make dizzy or stupid; stun.

imbalsamàre (*pr.* -àlsamo), *v.t.* to embalm; (*animals*) stuff. **imbalsamatóre**, *m.* embalmer.

imbambagiàre, *v.t.* to wrap in cotton-wool.

imbambolàre, *v.i.* (*aux.* essere) to soften; break into tears.

imbambolíre (*pr.* -ísco, -ísci), *v.i.* (*aux.* essere) to grow childish.

imbandieràre (*pr.* -èro), *v.t.* to deck with flags.

imbandigióne, *f.* preparation for a banquet or feast; dishes for a feast. *una ricca* ~, a rich table. **imbandíre** (*pr.* -ísco, -ísci), *v.t.* to lay the table for a banquet; (*fig.*) prepare, get ready.

imbarazzànte, *a.* embarrassing; perplexing; cumbersome; awkward. **imbarazzàre**, *v.t.* to embarrass; perplex; obstruct. **imbarazzàrsi** (di), *v.refl.* to meddle with; interfere in. **imbaràzzo**, *m.* embarrassment; perplexity; fix; trouble; straits; difficulty; bewilderment; quandary; inconvenience; obstacle; obstruction; impediment. ~ *di stomaco*, indigestion.

imbarbaríre (*pr.* -ísco, -ísci), *v.i.* (*aux.* essere) to become barbarous; (*of lang.*) grow corrupt; *v.t.* decivilize; corrupt.

imbarbogíre (*pr.* -ísco, -ísci), *v.i.* (*aux.* essere) to enter one's second childhood; grow old.

imbarcadèro & **imbarcatóio** (*pl.* -ói), *m.* landing-stage; pier. **imbarcàre** (*pr.* -àrco, -àrchi), *v.t.* to take on board; ship. **imbarcàrsi**, *v.refl.* to embark (*lit.* & *fig.*); sail. **imbarcazióne,** *f.* embarkation; taking on board; boat; ship. ~ *a vela*, sailing boat. ~ *a fondo piatto*, flat bottom[ed] boat. ~ *da diporto*, pleasure boat, yacht. ~ *di bordo*, pinnace. **imbàrco** (*pl.* -àrchi), *m.* embarkation; loading; shipping; landing-stage; wharf.

imbarilàre (*pr.* -ílo), *v.t.* to store (*wine*) in barrels; pack in a barrel (or barrels).

imbaṣaménto, *m.* groundwork; basis. **imbaṣàre**, *v.t.* to base. **imbaṣatúra,** *f.* base; basement; foundation.

imbastardiménto, *m.* degeneracy. **imbastardíre** (*pr.* -ísco, -ísci), *v.t.* to debase; corrupt; bastardize. *v.i.* (*aux.* essere) & **imbastardírsi**, *v.refl.* to degenerate; become degenerate.

imbastàre, *v.t.* to put a pack-saddle on.

imbastiménto, *m.* stitching (together), tacking, basting; (*fig.*)

rough sketch. **imbastíre** (*pr.* -ísco, -ísci), *v.t.* to stitch roughly; tack; baste; (*fig.*) put together; block out, make a rough sketch of. **imbastitúra**, *f.* stitching; tacking.

imbàttersi (**in**), *v.refl.* to meet; fall in with; run across (*without pr.*) to happen; as *s.m.* mere chance.

imbattíbile, *a.* invincible; unconquerable. **imbattúto**, *a.* unbeaten.

imbaulàre (*pr.* -aúlo), *v.t.* to pack in a trunk.

imbavagliàre (*pr.* -àglio, -àgli), *v.t.* to gag.

imbavàre, *v.t.* to drivel; to slaver (over).

imbeccàre (*pr.* -écco, -écchi), *v.t.* to feed (*birds*); (*fig.*) prompt, suggest. **imbeccàta**, *f.* prompting; suggestion.

imbecillàggine, *f.* foolishness; imbecility; act of folly. **imbecílle**, *a. & m.* imbecile. **imbecillíre** (*pr.* -ísco, -ísci), *v.i.* (*aux.* essere) to become imbecile or stupid. **imbecillità**, *f.inv.* imbecility.

imbèlle, *a.* unwarlike; cowardly.

imbellettàre (*pr.* -étto), *v.t.* to paint (*the face*). **imbellettàrsi**, *v.refl.* to paint one's face.

imbellíre (*pr.* -ísco, -ísci), *v.t.* to adorn; embellish; *v.i.* (*aux.* essere) to become prettier; grow beautiful.

imbèrbe, *a.* beardless.

imberciàre (*pr.* -ércio, -érci), *v.t.* to hit (*the mark*).

imbestialíre (*pr.* -ísco, -ísci), *& *imbestiàre**, *v.t.* to brutalize. **imbestialírsi** *& *imbestiàrsi**, *v.refl.* to become brutal; fly into a passion.

imbévere (*pr.* -èvo, &c., like bevere), *v.t. &* **imbéversi**, *v.refl.* to absorb; imbibe; be imbued with (*di*); assimilate. **imbevúto**, *p.a.* imbued; drenched; saturated (with = *di*).

imbiaccàre (*pr.* -àcco, -àcchi), *v.t.* to paint with white lead.

imbiadàto, *a.* sown with corn.

imbiancàre (*pr.* -ànco, -ànchi), *v.t.* to whiten; whitewash; bleach; (*fig.*) to reject; *v.i.* (*aux.* essere) to become white; dawn; (*of hair*) turn white (or grey). **imbiancatóre**, *m.* laundryman. **imbiancatríce**, *f.* laundress; washerwoman. **imbiancatúra**, *f.* whitewashing; bleaching. **imbianchíno**, *m.* house painter; (*fig.*) dauber, bad painter. **imbianchíre** (*pr.* -ísco, -ísci), *v.i.*

(*aux.* essere) to turn white; turn grey (*of hair*, &c.); grow pale.

imbiecàre, *v.t.* to warp.

imbietolíre (*pr.* -ísco, -ísci), *v.i.* (*aux.* essere) to become a dunce (*lit.* a beetroot); to go into ecstasies over little; be easily moved.

imbiettàre (*pr.* -étto), *v.t.* to wedge up, or in.

imbiondíre (*pr.* -ísco, -ísci), *v.t.* to make fair or blonde; *v.i.* (*aux.* essere) to become blonde (*of hair*, &c.); ripen (*of corn*).

imbirboníre (*pr.* -ísco, -ísci), *v.i.* (*aux.* essere) to become a rascal.

imbitumàre (*pr.* -úmo), *v.t.* to tar.

imbiżżarriménto, *m.* excitement; passion; fit of rage. **imbiżżarríre** (*pr.* -ísco, -ísci), *v.i.* (*aux.* essere) *& *imbiżżarrírsi**, *v.refl.* to become excited; fire up; get into a passion; (*of horses*) rear or bolt.

imbizzíre (*pr.* -ísco, -ísci), *v.i.* (*aux.* essere) *& *imbizzírsi**, *v.refl.* to fly into a rage.

imboccàre (*pr.* -ócco, -ócchi), *v.t.* to feed; prompt; suggest; put a trumpet (*or other wind instrument*) to one's mouth; enter; (*of horse*) receive the bit; (**in**) *v.i.* (*aux.* essere) to fit (into); work (into); flow (into); open (into). **imboccatúra**, *f.* mouthpiece (*mus. instr.*); mouth; outfall (*river*); entrance (*street or valley*); way of putting one's lips to a wind instrument; portion of bit within a horse's mouth.

imbocciàre (*pr.* -òccio, -òcci), *v.i.* (*aux.* essere) to come (or break) into bud. **imbócco** (*pl.* -ócchi), *m.* entrance.

imbolsíre (*pr.* -ísco, -ísci), *v.i.* (*aux.* essere) to become broken-winded.

imboniménto, *m.* showman's patter. **imboníre** (*pr.* -ísco) *v.t.* to quieten; allure.

imborghesíre (*pr.* -ísco, -ísci), *v.i.* (*aux.* essere) to become middle-class (in mind and habit), acquire middle-class ways.

imborsàre (*pr.* -órso), *v.t.* to pocket; put into a purse or bag.

imboscàre (*pr.* -òsco), *v.t.* to hide in a wood; place in ambush. **imboscàrsi**, *v.refl.* (*lit.*) to hide oneself in a wood; lie in ambush; shirk, esp. keep far from the front in wartime. **imboscàta**, *f.* ambush. **imboscàto**, *m.* shirker.

imboschiménto, *m.* afforestation. **imboschíre** (*pr.* -ísco, -ísci), *v.t.*

to afforest. *v.i.* (*aux.* essere) *&* **imboschírsi,** *v.refl.* to become covered with trees; run wild; thicken.

imbottàre (*pr.* -ótto), *v.t.* to put (*wine*) in casks. **imbottàto,** *m.* excise-duty on wine-making. **imbottatúra,** *f.* barrelling.

imbottigliàre (*pr.* -íglio, -ígli), *v.t.* to bottle; bottle up; (*fig.*) blockade.

imbottíre (*pr.* -ísco, -ísci), *v.t.* to stuff; fill; pad; quilt; upholster. **imbottíta,** *f.* (for **coperta** ∼) quilt. **imbottitúra,** *f.* stuffing; padding; quilting.

imbozżacchíre (*pr.* -ísco, -ísci), *v.i.* (*aux.* essere) to shrivel; become stunted; wither away.

imbozżimàre (*pr.* -òzżimo), *v.t.* to dress with size; smear; (*hum.*) paint (*the face*).

imbràca, *f.* breeching-strap (*of harness*); sling for supporting a workman. **imbracàre** (*pr.* -àco, -àchi), *v.t.* to fasten, tie up; sling; breech (*a child*); mend a torn page with gummed paper.

imbrattacàrte, *m.inv.* scribbler. **imbrattamúri** *&* **imbrattatéla,** *m. inv.* dauber. **imbrattàre,** *v.t.* to soil; stain; dirty. **imbràtto,** *m.* daub; badly written work; pig's wash; repellent dish.

imbrecciàre (*pr.* -éccio, -écci), *v.t.* to strew with gravel; ballast.

imbriacàre (*pr.* -àco, -àchi), *v.t.* to intoxicate.

imbrigliàre (*pr.* -íglio, -ígli), *v.t.* to bridle; curb; restrain.

imbroccàre (*pr.* -òcco, -òcchi), *v.t.* to hit (the mark); (*fig.*) guess right; find when required.

imbrodàre (*pr.* -òdo) *&* **imbrodolàre** (*pr.* -òdolo), *v.t.* to soil; stain; make a mess of.

imbrogliàre (*pr.* -òglio, -ògli), *v.t.* to entangle; tangle; confuse; muddle; embroil; mix up; clew up (*sail*); cheat; swindle. **imbrogliàrsi,** *v.refl.* to get confused or entangled. **imbrogliàto,** *a.* confused; [en]-tangled; intricate; perplexed; embroiled. **imbròglio** (*pl.* -ògli), *m.* tangle, confused situation; scrape; mess; difficulty; trick; fraud. **imbroglióne,** *m.* (*f.* -ona) cheat; swindler; meddler.

imbronciàre (*pr.* -óncio, -ónci), *v.i.* (*aux.* essere) *&* **imbronciàrsi,** *v.refl.* to become sulky; pout; take offence; (*sky*) grow dark. **im-**

bronciàto, *a.* sulky; surly; frowning; dark.

imbrunàre, *v.i.* (*aux.* essere) to grow dark, darken.

imbruníre (*pr.* -ísco, -ísci), *v.t.* to brown; tan (*with the sun*); *v.i.* (*aux.* essere) to grow dark. **sull'** ∼, at dusk, at night-fall.

imbrutíre (*pr.* -ísco, -ísci), *v.i.* *&* **imbrutírsi,** *v.refl.* to become brutalized.

imbruttíre (*pr.* -ísco, -ísci), *v.t.* to mar; disfigure; make ugly; *v.i.* (*aux.* essere) to grow ugly.

imbucàre (*pr.* -úco, -úchi), *v.t.* to put into a hole; put in the letter-box; post. **imbucàrsi,** *v.refl.* to creep into a hole; hide oneself.

imbuggeràrsi *&* **imbuscheràrsi,** *v.refl.* to be indifferent, not to care.

imburràre (*pr.* -úrro), *v.t.* to butter.

imbussolàre, *v.t.* to put into the ballot-box.

imbúto, *m.* funnel.

imbuzżàre, *v.t.* to cram; overfeed.

Imene *&* **Imenèo,** *m.* Hymen. **imenèo,** *a.* nuptial. **imenèi,** *m.pl.* nuptials; wedding. **imenòtteri,** *m.pl.* hymenoptera.

immacolàto, *a.* immaculate; spotless.

immagazżinàre (*pr.* -íno), *v.t.* to store.

immaginàbile, *a.* imaginable. **immaginàre** (*pr.* -àgino), *v.i.* (*aux.* avere) *&* **immaginàrsi,** *v.refl.* to imagine. **immaginatíva,** *f.* faculty of imagination. **immaginazióne,** *f.* imagination; fancy. **immàgine,** *f.* image.

immagríre (*pr.* -ísco, -ísci), *v.i.* (*aux.* essere) to grow thin.

immalinconíre (*pr.* -ísco, -ísci), *v.i.* (*aux.* essere) to become melancholy.

immancàbile, *a.* unfailing; certain; infallible.

immàne, *a.* monstrous; huge; cruel.

immaneggiàbile, *a.* unmanageable; intractable.

immanènte, *a.* immanent; inherent. **immanènza,** *f.* immanence.

immangiàbile, *a.* uneatable.

immantinénte, *ad.* at once; immediately.

immarcescíbile, *a.* incorruptible.

immarginàre (*pr.* -màrgino), *v.t.* to join at the edges. **immarginàrsi,** *v.refl.* to cicatrize; heal (up).

immascheràre (*pr.* -màschero), *v.t.* to mask. **immascheràrsi,** *v.refl.* to wear a mask.

immatricolàrsi (*pr.* -ícolo), *v.refl.* to matriculate. immatricolazióne, *f.* matriculation.

immaturaménte, *ad.* prematurely. immatúro, *a.* unripe; immature; premature.

immedesimàre (*pr.* -ésimo), *v.t.* to unite into one. immedesimàrsi (con), *v.refl.* to identify oneself with; become one with.

immedicàbile, *a.* incurable. immedicàto, *a.* uncured; (*Poet.*) cureless (*ills*).

immelensíre (*pr.* -ísco, -ísci), *v.i.* (*aux.* essere) to grow dull; become stupid.

immellettàre, *v.t.* to begrime; bemire.

immelmàrsi (*pr.* -èlmo), *v.refl.* to become muddy; soil one's clothes with mud.

immemoràbile, *a.* immemorial. immèmore, *a.* unmindful; forgetful.

immensuràbile, *a.* immeasurable.

immèrgere (*pr.* -èrgo, *&c.*, like *emergere*), *v.t. ir.* to dip; immerse; plunge; steep; soak. immèrgersi, *v.refl.* to plunge; immerse oneself; be absorbed (in).

immeritataménte, *ad.* undeservedly. immeritàto, *a.* undeserved, unmerited; unearned. immeritévole, *a.* undeserving.

immersióne, *f.* immersion; plunging; steeping. *linea d'* ∼, water-line. *fare un'* ∼, to take a dip.

immèttere (*pr.* -étto, *&c.*, like *mettere*), *v.t. ir.* to let in; introduce; induct.

immezzíre (*pr.* -ísco, -ísci), *v.i.* (*aux.* essere) to become overripe; go rotten (*of fruit*).

imminchionàre, *v.i.* (*aux.* essere) to become silly; grow stupid (in).

immischiàre (*pr.* -íschio, -íschi), *v.t.* to implicate; involve. immischiàrsi, *v.refl.* to meddle with; concern oneself with; be involved in; be mixed up in.

immiseríre (*pr.* -ísco, -ísci), *v.t.* to impoverish; make miserable. *v.i.* (*aux.* essere) to become poor; grow weak.

immissàrio (*pl.* -àri), *m.* affluent; tributary; intake.

immissióne, *f.* induction; letting in; breaking (or forcing) in.

immite, *a.* harsh; pitiless.

immòbile, *a.* immobile; set; immovable; motionless; still; station-

ary; fixed. *beni* ∼*i*, immovables; immovable property. immòbili, *m.pl.* premises. immobiliàre, *a.* immovable. *proprietà* ∼, real estate. immobilità, *f.* immobility. immobilitàre (*pr.* -ílito), *& *immobiliżżàre, *v.t.* to render immovable; immobilize; (*of capital*) lock up. immobilménte, *ad.* immovably.

immoderàto, *a.* immoderate; excessive; intemperate; unrestrained.

immolàre (*pr.* -òlo), *v.t.* to immolate; sacrifice; slay. immolazióne, *f.* immolation; sacrifice; holocaust.

immollàre (*pr.* -òllo), *v.t.* to wet; soak; drench.

immondézza, *f.* uncleanliness; foulness; impurity. immondízia, *f.* dirt; filth; (*pl.*) garbage; refuse; sweepings; trash. immóndo, *a.* dirty; filthy; unclean; foul.

immoràle, *a.* immoral. immoralità, *f.inv.* immorality.

immorbidíre (*pr.* -ísco, -ísci), *v.i.* (*aux.* essere) *& *immorbidírsi, *v.refl.* to soften.

immortalàre, *v.t.* to immortalize. immortàle, *a.* immortal. immortalità, *f.* immortality.

immòto, *a.* motionless; unmoved.

immucidíre (*pr.* -ísco, -ísci), *v.i.* (*aux.* essere) to grow musty; become tainted; go bad.

immúne, *a.* immune; exempt (from = *da*), free (from); safe; uninjured. immunità, *f.* immunity. immuniżżàre, *v.t.* to immunize.

immusíre (*pr.* -ísco, -ísci), *v.i.* (*aux.* essere) to sulk; pout.

immutàto, *a.* unchanged; unaltered.

imo, *a.* low; lowest. ¶ *m.* deepest part; bottom; humblest person.

impaccàre (*pr.* -àcco, -àcchi), *v.t.* to pack; wrap up. impacchettàre, *v.t.* to pack; make up in packets.

impacciàre (*pr.* -àccio, -àcci), *v.t.* to hinder; be in the way of; impede; embarrass; inconvenience; trouble. impacciàrsi, *v.refl.* to meddle; interfere; busy oneself with (= *con*). impacciàto, *a.* awkward; clumsy; embarrassed; ill at ease. impàccio (*pl.* -àcci), *m.* hindrance; impediment; encumbrance; obstacle; difficulty; embarrassment; trouble; scrape. *cavarsi d'* ∼, to get out of a scrape. impacciósu, *a.* tiresome, meddlesome.

impàcco (*pl.* -àcchi), *m.* compress (*Med.*).

impadronírsi (**di**), *v.refl.* (*pr.* -ísco, -ísci) to master; take possession of; seize; appropriate.

impagàbile, *a.* priceless; invaluable.

impaginàre (*pr.* -àgino), *v.t.* (*Typ.*) to make up; arrange in pages. **impaginatúra**, *f.* (*Typ.*) make-up; making-up.

impagliàre (*pr.* -àglio, -àgli), *v.t.* to pack in straw; cover with straw (*chairs, &c.*); stuff with straw. **impagliatóre**, *m.* (*f.* -tríce), chairmender; stuffer (*of animals*), taxidermist. **impagliatúra**, *f.* strawplaiting; packing in straw; chairmending; straw-bottoming.

impalancàto, *m.* palisade.

impalàre, *v.t.* to impale; stake (*vines*). **impalàto**, *a.* stiff; rigid.

impalcàre (*pr.* -àlco, -àlchi), *v.t.* to plank; floor; put a scaffold round. **impalcatúra**, *f.* scaffolding; planking; ceiling; flooring; hanging platform; point where a tree-stem branches out.

impaliidíre (*pr.* -ísco, -ísci), *v.i.* (*aux.* essere) to turn pale.

impalmàre, *v.t.* to marry (*lit.* to give one's hand in token of a promise to marry).

impaludàrsi, *v.refl.* to stagnate; turn into a swamp.

impampinàre, *v.t.* to wreathe (or cover) with vine-leaves.

impanàre (*pr.* -àno), *v.t.* to cover with bread crumbs; (*Mech.*) cut the thread of a screw. **cotoletta impanata**, dressed cutlet.

impancàrsi (*pr.* -àuco, -ànchi), *v.refl.* to set up as a judge or authority.

impaniàre (*pr.* -ànio, -àni), *v.t.* to smear with bird-lime; (*fig.*) entrap; ensnare. **impaniàrsi**, *v.refl.* to be caught or entangled; be deceived (*with flattery*).

impannàre, *v.t.* to cover with cloth (or paper).

impantanàre, *v.t.* to bemire. **impantanàrsi**, *v.refl.* to stick in the mud; sink in a swamp.

impaperàrsi, *v.refl.* to make a blunder in speech; get confused.

impappinàrsi, *v.refl.* to stammer; falter; lose the thread of one's discourse; get flustered.

imparacchiàre (*pr.* -àcchio, -àcchi), *v.t.* to learn badly.

imparagonàbile, *a.* incomparable.

imparàre, *v.t.* to learn. ~*a mente*, ~*a memoria*, to learn by heart.

imparatíccio (*pl.* -ícci), *m.* thing badly learned, beginner's work.

impareggiàbile, *a.* unparalleled; incomparable.

imparentàrsi, *v.refl.* to become related (to); marry into (= *con*).

ímpari, *a.* uneven; odd; unequal. **imparità**, *f.inv.* inequality.

impartíbile, *a.* indivisible.

impartíre (*pr.* -ísco, -ísci), *v.t.* to communicate; impart; assign; grant.

imparziàle, *a.* impartial. **imparzialità**, *f.* impartiality.

impassíbile, *a.* impassible; impassive. **impassibilità**, *f.* impassiveness.

impastàre, *v.t.* to knead; make into a paste; cover with paste; spread paste; fix with paste; (*Art.*) mix colours on a palette; impaste. **impastatríce**, *f.* kneading-trough. (*Mech.*) mixer. **impastatúra** *f.*, kneading; pasting.

impasticciàre (*pr.* -íccio, -ícci), *v.t.* to mix up, make a mess of; bungle; botch; daub. **impasticciàrsi**, *v.refl.* to get in(to) a mess.

impàsto, *m.* kneading; mixture; makeup; thick colour; impasto (*painting*).

impastoiàre (*pr.* -óio, -ói), *v.t.* to shackle; fetter; tether; clog; hinder; impede.

impatriàre, *v.t.* to repatriate.

impauríre (*pr.* -ísco, -ísci), *v.t.* to terrify; frighten; intimidate. *v.i.* (*aux.* essere) & **impaurírsi**, *v.refl.* to become afraid; be terrified. **impauríto**, *a.* frightened; fearful; terrified; afraid.

impavidaménte, *ad.* fearlessly. **impàvido**, *a.* fearless.

impazientàre (*pr.* -ènto), *v.i.* (*aux.* essere) & **impazientíre** (*pr.* -ísco, -ísci), *v.i.* (*aux.* essere) & -àrsi, -írsi, *v.refl.* to become impatient; lose one's patience. **impaziènte**, *a.* impatient. **impaziènza**, *f.* impatience.

impazzàre & **impazzíre** (*pr.* -ísco, -ísci), *v.i.* (*aux.* essere) to go mad; become insane; become crazy (for = *per* or *dietro*). *far* ~, to drive mad. **impazzàta** (**all'**), *ad. expr.* madly; rashly; inconsiderately. **impazziménto**, *m.* going mad; madness; insanity. **impazzíto**, *a.* mad; gone mad.

impeccàbile, *a.* faultless; impeccable.

impeciàre (*pr.* -écio, -éci), *v.t.* to coat with tar or pitch; tar.

impecoríre (*pr.* **-ísco, -ísci**), *v.i.* (*aux.* essere) to become like sheep.
impediménto, *m.* impediment; hindrance; obstacle; obstruction.
impedíre (*pr.* **-ísco, -ísci**), *v.t.* to impede; hinder; obstruct; stop. ~*di*, to prevent (from). **impeditívo**, *a.* obstructive.
impegnàre (*pr.* **-égno**), *v.t.* to engage; bind; pledge; pawn. **impegnàrsi**, *v.refl.* to undertake; engage (oneself); bind oneself; go bail; stand surety; get involved. **impegnatívo**, *a.* binding. **impegnàto**, *p.a.* engaged; bound; pledged; pawned; involved. **impègno**, *m.* pledge; promise; undertaking; engagement; care; diligence; zeal; duty; task.
impegolàre (*pr.* **-égolo**), *v.t.* to smear with pitch.
impelagàrsi (*pr.* **-èlago, -èlaghi**), *v.refl.* to get involved; get into trouble; (*lit.*) plunge into a sea (of troubles).
impèllere (*pr.* **-èllo**), *v.t. ir.* to impel; force; thrust; push.
impellicciàre (*pr.* **-íccio, -ícci**), *v.t.* to wrap up in furs; (*of furniture*) to veneer.
impenetràbile, *a.* impenetrable; impervious; (*fig.*) inscrutable. ~ *all'aria*, air-tight. ~ *all'acqua*, water-tight.
impenitènte, *a.* impenitent. **impenitènza**, *f.* impenitence; obduracy.
impennacchiàre (*pr.* **-àcchio, -àcchi**), *v.t.* to adorn with plumes.
impennàre (*pr.* **-énno**), *v.t.* to feather; (*fig.*) give wings to; (*abs.*) take up one's pen. **impennàrsi**, *v.refl.* to become fledged; (*Aero.*) climb; (*of horse*) prance; rear; (*fig.*) get angry; fire up. **impennàta**, *f.* rearing (*of horse*); penful (*of ink*). **impennàto**, *a.* (*of horse*) on its hind legs; prancing.
impensàbile, *a.* unthinkable. **impensàta (all'),** *ad. expr.* suddenly; unexpectedly; unawares. **impensataménte**, *ad.* unexpectedly. **impensàto**, *a.* unforeseen; unexpected.
impensieríre (*pr.* **-ísco, -ísci**), *v.t.* to preoccupy; make uneasy; cause anxiety to. **impensierírsi**, *v.refl.* to get uneasy; grow anxious (about = *di*). **impensieríto**, *a.* uneasy; preoccupied; anxious; thoughtful.
impepàre (*pr.* **-épo**), *v.t.* to pepper.

imperàre (*pr.* **-èro**), *v.i.* (*aux.* avere) to rule; reign; prevail. **imperatívo**, *a. & m.* imperative. **imperatóre**, *m.* emperor. **imperatríce**, *f.* empress.
impercettíbile, *a.* imperceptible.
imperciocché, *c.* since; inasmuch as; whereas; because.
imperdonàbile, *a.* unpardonable.
imperfètto, *a.* imperfect; faulty; incomplete. ¶ *m.* imperfect (tense).
imperfezióne, *f.* imperfection; flaw.
imperiàle, *a.* imperial. ¶ *m.* top, upper deck, outside (*bus or coach*). **imperialísmo**, *m.* imperialism. **imperialísta** (*pl.* **-ísti**), *a.* imperialistic. ¶ *m.* imperialist.
impèrio (*pl.* **-èri**), *m.* rule; command; (*fig.*) empire (*abs.*). **imperióso**, *a.* imperious; peremptory; authoritative.
imperíto, *a.* unskilled, unskilful; inexperienced; awkward.
imperitúro, *a.* imperishable.
imperízia, *f.* unskilfulness; lack of skill; awkwardness.
imperlàre (*pr.* **-èrlo**), *v.t.* to adorn with pearls; (*fig.*) cover with drops of dew or sweat, impearl (*Poet.*).
impermalíre (*pr.* **-ísco, -ísci**), *v.t.* to annoy; offend; give offence to; vex; make angry. *v.i.* (*aux.* essere) *&* **impermalírsi**, *v.refl.* to grow angry; take offence at (= *di*); take amiss.
impermeàbile, *a.* impermeable. ¶ *m.* waterproof; mackintosh; raincoat.
impermutàbile, *a.* that cannot be exchanged.
impernàre *&* **imperniàre** (*pr.* **-èrnio, -èrno**), *v.t. &* **imperniàrsi**, *v.refl.* to pivot; hinge (upon). **imperniatúra**, *f.* pivoting; pivot.
impèro, *m.* empire; dominion; rule.
imperocché, *c.* for; since; as; because.
imperscrutàbile, *a.* inscrutable.
impersonàle, *a.* impersonal. **impersonàre** (*pr.* **-óno**), *v.t.* to impersonate.
impertèrrito, *a.* undaunted; fearless.
impertinènte, *a.* impertinent; out of place. **impertinènza**, *f.* impertinence.
imperturbàto, *a.* unperturbed.
imperversàre (*pr.* **-èrso**), *v.i.* (*aux.* avere) to rage (*fig.*); storm; spread.
impèrvio (*pl.* **-èrvi**), *a.* impervious.
impetígine, *f.* (*Med.*) impetigo.
ímpeto, *m.* impetus; impetuosity; impulse; vehemence; outburst;

transport (*rage*, *&c.*); onset; rush; attack. **impetràre** (*pr.* -ètro), *v.t.* to ask for; obtain (by request).

impettìto, *a.* stiff; erect; straight.

impiagaménto, *m.* & **impiagatúra**, *f.* ulceration. **impiagàre** (*pr.* -àgo, -àghi), *v.t.* to ulcerate.

impiallacciàre (*pr.* -àccio, -àcci), *v.t.* to veneer. **impiallacciatúra**, *f.* veneering; veneer.

impianellàre, *v.t.* to lay (*flat*) tiles; pave with tiles.

impiantàre, *v.t.* to found; establish; set up; open (*account*, *&c.*).

impiantíre (*pr.* -ísco, -ísci), *v.t.* to floor; pave. **impiantíto**, *m.* floor (*tiled*); pavement.

impiànto, *m.* plant; system; installation; establishment. ~ *idrico*, water-works. ~ *di riscaldamento*, heating plant, h. system. ~ *del timone*, steering gear.

impiastracàrte, *m.inv.* & **impiastrafògli**, *m.inv.* scribbler. **impiastraménto**, *m.* plastering. **impiastràre** & **impiastricciàre** (*pr.* -íccio, -ícci), *v.t.* to plaster; daub. **impiastratéle**, *m.inv.* dauber. **impiàstro**, *m.* plaster; poultice; (*fig.*) tiresome person; bore.

impiccagióne, *f.* hanging. **impiccàre** (*pr.* -ícco, -ícchi), *v.t.* to hang. **impiccatóre**, *m.* hangman. **impiccatúra**, *f.* hanging.

impicciàre (*pr.* -íccio, -ícci), *v.t.* to embarrass. **impicciàrsi**, *v.refl.* to busy oneself with (*derogatory*).

impicciníre (*pr.* -ísco, -ísci), *v.t.* to diminish; lessen; make smaller; (*fig.*) depreciate. **impiccinírsi**, *v.refl.* to grow smaller.

impíccio (*pl.* -ícci), *m.* embarrassment; trouble; scrape; hindrance.

impicciolíre (*pr.* -ísco, -ísci), & **impiccolíre** (*pr.* -ísco, -ísci), *v.t.* to lessen; reduce; diminish in size. **impicciolírsi** & **impiccolírsi**, *v.refl.* to grow smaller; humble oneself.

impidocchiàre *or* -íre, *v.t.* to make lousy. **impidocchiàrsi**, *v.refl.* to become lousy; become covered with lice.

impiegàbile, *a.* employable; (*money*) that can be invested (or spent). **impiegàre** (*pr.* -égo, -éghi), *v.t.* to employ; use; utilize; take; spend; invest. **impiegàrsi**, *v.refl.* to be employed; employ oneself; find a

situation. **impiegàto**, *m.* employee; clerk. **impiegatúccio**, *m.* poor clerk; poor employee. **impiègo** (*pl.* -èghi), *m.* employment; employ; situation; office; appointment; investment. **impiegúccio**, *m.* small appointment, poor job.

impietosíre (*pr.* -ísco, -ísci), *v.t.* to move to pity; fill with pity; touch. **impietosírsi**, *v.refl.* to be moved to pity. ~ *di*, to pity.

impietriménto, *m.* petrifaction. **impietríre** (*pr.* -ísco, -ísci), *v.t.* & **impietrírsi**, *v.refl.* to petrify (*lit.* & *fig.*).

impigliàre (*pr.* -íglio, -ígli), *v.t.* to entangle; entrap.

impigríre (*pr.* -ísco, -ísci), *v.t.* to make lazy. *v.i.* (*aux.* essere) & **impigrírsi**, *v.refl.* to grow lazy. **ímpigro**, *a.* active; diligent; far from lazy.

impillaccheràre (*pr.* -àcchero), *v.t.* to splash with mud.

impinguaménto, *m.* fattening. **impinguàre** (*pr.* -ínguo), *v.t.* to fatten; (*fig.*) to manure; enrich.

impinzàre, *v.t.* to cram; stuff.

impiombàre (*pr.* -ómbo), *v.t.* to seal with lead; cover with lead; stop (*a tooth*); splice (*a cable*). **impiombatúra**, *f.* sealing; stopping (*for a tooth*); splicing (*a cable*).

impipàrsi, *v.refl.* to be indifferent; make light of; be unconcerned; not to care (about = *di*). *io me ne impipo*, I couldn't care less (*pop.*).

impiumàre, *v.t.* to feather; line with feathers. **impiumàrsi**, *v.refl.* to be fledged; (*fig.*) begin to grow a beard.

implacàbile, *a.* implacable. **implacàto**, *a.* inveterate; unrelenting.

implacidíre (*pr.* -ísco, -ísci), *v.t.* to appease.

implicàre (*pr.* ímplico, ímplichi), *v.t.* to implicate; involve; imply. **implicazióne**, *f.* implication.

imploràre (*pr.* -óro), *v.t.* to implore; entreat; beg or pray for. **implorazióne**, *f.* earnest prayer; entreaty.

implúme, *a.* unfledged; featherless.

impoliticaménte, *ad.* unwisely. **impolítico** (*pl.* -ítici), *a.* impolitic; imprudent.

impolpàre (*pr.* -ólpo), *v.i.* (*aux.* essere) to fatten, grow fat. *v.t.* (*fig.*) to stuff (e.g. *with quotations*).

impoltroníre (*pr.* -ísco, -ísci), *v.t.* to make lazy. **impoltronírsi**, *v.refl.* to become lazy.

impolveràre (*pr.* -ólvero), *v.t.* to

cover with dust; sprinkle with sand.
impolveràrsi, *v.refl.* to get dusty.
imponènte, *a.* imposing. **im-
ponènza**, *f.* grandeur; magnificence.
imponíbile, *a.* taxable. *reddito* ~,
t. income.
impopolàre, *a.* unpopular. **impopolarità**, *f.* unpopularity.
impoppàto, *a.* down by the stern
(*Mar.*).
imporporàre (*pr.* -órporo), *v.t.* to
stain purple; redden. **imporpor-
àrsi**, *v.refl.* to grow purple; redden;
blush.
impórre (*pr.* -óngo, *&c.*, like **porre**),
v.t. ir. to impose; inflict; lay; give;
order; command; enjoin. **impórsi**,
v.refl. to gain the upper hand;
dominate; be impressive; be
necessary; (*sport*) win.
importànte, *a.* important. ¶ *m.*
main thing; most important thing;
(main) point. **importànza**, *f.*
importance. **importàre** (*pr.* -òrto),
v.impers. (*aux.* essere) to matter; be
of importance; be necessary. *v.t.* to
import; mean; imply; signify; cause;
involve; require; amount to; cost.
importatóre, *m.* importer. **im-
portazióne**, *f.* importation; import.
impòrto, *m.* (total) amount.
importunàre (*pr.* -úno), *v.t.* to
annoy; trouble; importune. **importunità**, *f.imv.* importunity.
importúno, *a.* troublesome; tiresome; importunate.
imposizióne, *f.* tax; imposition.
impossessàrsi (*pr.* -èsso) *v.refl.* to
take possession (of = *di*); master.
impósta, *f.* tax; duty. ~ *sul reddito*,
income-tax. ~ *fondiaria*, land-tax.
impósta, *f.* shutter; leaf of a folding
door.
impostàre (*pr.* -ósto), *v.t.* to post
(*a letter*); place; define; set up;
enter (*in ledger*, *&c.*); lay down the
lines of; state (*a problem*, *&c.*); lay
down (*ship*); spring (*Arch.*). **im-
postàrsi**, *v.refl.* to take up one's
position. **impostazióne**, *f.* posting.
impósto, *p.p.* of **imporre**.
impostóre, *m.* (*f.* -óra) impostor.
impostúra, *f.* imposture; fraud.
impotàbile, *a.* undrinkable.
impoveriménto, *m.* impoverishment.
impoveríre (*pr.* -ísco, -ísci), *v.t.*
to impoverish. *v.i.* (*aux.* essere) *&*
-írsi *refl.* to become poor.
impraticàbile, *a.* impracticable;
(*road*) impassable.
impratichíre (*pr.* -ísco, -ísci), *v.t.*

to train; exercise; accustom; familiarize; make expert. **impratichírsi**,
v.refl. to practise; exercise oneself
(in); become master (of); become
familiar (with).
imprecàre (*pr.* -éco, -échi), *v.i.* (*aux.*
avere) to curse. **imprecatívo** *&*
imprecatòrio, *a.* imprecatory.
imprecazióne, *f.* curse; imprecation.
imprecisióne, *f.* inexactitude; inaccuracy; lack of precision. **im-
precíso**, *a.* vague; inexact; imprecise.
impregiudicàto, *a.* unprejudiced.
impregnàre (*pr.* -égno), *v.t.* to
impregnate; imbue.
impremeditàto, *a.* unpremeditated.
imprèndere (*pr.* -èndo, *&c.*, like
prendere), *v.t. ir.* to undertake;
initiate; begin. **imprendíbile**, *a.*
impregnable. **imprenditóre**, *m.*
contractor.
impreparàto, *a.* unprepared. **im-
preparazióne**, *f.* unpreparedness.
imprésa, *f.* undertaking; contract;
enterprise; management (*Theat.*);
exploit; deed; heraldic (or symbolic)
device or motto. **impresàrio** (*pr.*
-àri), *m.* undertaker; contractor;
manager, impresario (*Theat.*). ~ *di
pompe funebri*, (funeral) undertaker.
imprescindíbile, *a.* necessary; indispensable; absolute; that cannot
be set aside, omitted, or delayed.
impresciènza, *f.* want of foresight.
imprescrittíbile, *a.* indefeasible.
impressionànte, *a.* striking; impressive. **impressionàre** (*pr.*
-òno), *v.t.* to impress; make an
impression on; strike; affect; expose
(*Phot.*). **impressionàrsi**, *v.refl.* to
be deeply affected; be moved;
become discouraged. **impressióne**,
f. impression; impress; imprint;
printing, print; issue; sensation.
fa ~! how astonishing, shocking,
or disagreeable! **impressionísmo**,
m. impressionism.
impressóre, *m.* printer; (*Typ.*) press-
man.
imprestàre (*pr.* -èsto), *v.t.* to lend.
imprèstito, *m.* loan.
impreteríbile, *a.* indispensable;
absolute.
imprevedíbile, *a.* unforeseeable. **imprevedúto**, *ad.* unexpected-
ly. **imprevedúto** *&* **imprevísto**,
a. unforeseen.
imprevidènte, *a.* without foresight;

improvident. **imprevidènza,** *f.* lack of foresight; improvidence.

impreziosíre (*pr.* **-ísco, -ísci**), *v.t.* to render precious.

imprigionaménto, *m.* imprisonment. **imprigionàre** (*pr.* **-óno**), *v.t.* to imprison.

imprímere (*pr.* **-ímo,** *&c.,* like *comprimere*), *v.t.* *ir.* to impress; imprint; print; stamp; engrave (*fig.*).

improbità, *f.* wickedness; dishonesty. **ímprobo,** *a.* wicked, dishonest; (*of toil*) hard; laborious; continual; unendurable.

improduttívo, *a.* unproductive.

imprónta, *f.* mark; impression; stamp; impress; imprint; print; trace. *impronte digitali, f.pl.* finger-prints. ~ *del piede,* foot-print.

improntaménte, *ad.* impudently; importunately.

improntàre (*pr.* **-ónto**), *v.t.* to impress; imprint; mark; prepare.

improntitúdine, *f.* effrontery; impudence; importunity; rashness. **imprónto,** *a.* inopportune; impudent. *all* ~, at sight, at first sight.

impronunziàbile, *a.* unpronounceable.

impropèrio (*pl.* **-èri**), *m.* abuse; injury; insult; reproach.

impropízio, *a.* unfavourable; unpropitious.

improprietà, *f.* impropriety. **impròprio** (*pl.* **-òpri**), *a.* improper; unbecoming; unfit; unsuitable.

improrogàbile, *a.* that cannot be put off or postponed; pressing.

improvvidaménte, *ad.* improvidently; imprudently. **impròvvido,** *a.* improvident.

improvvišaménte, *ad.* suddenly; unexpectedly. **improvvišàre** (*pr.* **-íso**), *v.t.* & *i.* (*aux.* avere) to improvise; speak extempore or impromptu. **improvvišàta,** *f.* agreeable surprise. **improvvišatóre,** *m.* (*f.* **-tríce**) improviser; improvvisatore (*Ital.*). **improvvišazióne,** *f.* improvisation. **impròvvíso,** *a.* sudden; unexpected; unforeseen. *all'* ~, suddenly.

improvvísto, *a.* unprovided. *all'* ~, suddenly.

impúbe & **impúbere,** *a.* under the age of puberty.

impudicizia, *f.* immodesty. **impudíco** (*pl.* **-íchi**), *a.* immodest.

impugnàbile, *a.* disputable. **impugnàre** (*pr.* **-úgno**), *v.t.* to seize; grasp; grip; hold; take up (*arms*);

impugn; contest; deny. **impugnatúra,** *f.* grip; handle; hilt. **impugnazióne,** *f.* opposition; refutation; denial.

impulitézza, *f.* roughness; lack of polish; uncleanness. **impulíto,** *a.* rough; unpolished; unclean.

impulsióne, *f.* impulsion. **impulsívo,** *a.* impelling; propulsive. **impúlso,** *m.* impulse; push.

impúne, *a.* scatheless. **impuneménte** & **impunitaménte,** *ad.* with impunity. **impunità,** *f.* impunity. **impuníto,** *a.* unpunished.

impuntàre (*pr.* **-únto**), *v.i.* (*aux.* avere) to stumble; stutter; (*horse*) jib; come to a sudden stop. ~ *in,* to run against; stumble over. **impuntàrsi,** *v.refl.* to stop; settle; stumble in speech; be obstinate or stubborn in opinion. ~ *in,* to adhere, stick to. **impuntàto,** *a.* obstinate; unwilling to move.

impuntigliàrsi (*pr.* **-íglio, -ígli**), *v.refl.* to be stubborn; consider it a point of honour; take it into one's head.

impuntíre (*pr.* **-ísco, -ísci**), *v.t.* to sew; stitch; point; quilt. **impuntitúra,** *f.* quilting; back-stitch. **impuntúra,** *f.* pointed needlework; back-stitching.

imputàre (*pr.* **impúto**), *v.t.* to impute; ascribe; accuse; charge (with = *di*). **imputàto,** *m.* (the) accused; defendant. **imputazióne,** *f.* imputation; charge.

imputrescíbile, *a.* that cannot go bad, rot or decay. **imputridiménto,** *m.* putrefaction. **imputridíre** (*pr.* **-ísco, -ísci**), *v.i.* (*aux.* essere) to go bad; putrefy; rot.

impuzzàre (*pr.* **-úzzo, -úzzi**), *v.i.* (*aux.* essere) to stink. **impuzzíre** (*pr.* **-ísco, -ísci**), *v.t.* to infect; make foul or stinking. *v.i.* (*aux.* essere) to stink.

in, *pr.* in; in the place of; into; on; to; at; within; of; by; *essere* ~ *casa,* to be at home. *dottore* ~ *medicina,* doctor of medicine. *se io fossi* ~ *voi,* if I were in your place. ~ *isbaglio,* by mistake.

inàbile, *a.* unable; unfit; incapacitated; unqualified; ineligible. **inabilità,** *f.* inability. **inabilitàre** (*pt.* **-ílito**), *v.t.* to disable; disqualify. **inabilménte,** *ad.* unskilfully; awkwardly.

inabissàre (*pr.* **-ísso**), *v.t.* to engulf.

inabissàrsi, *v.refl.* to sink; be engulfed.

inabitàbile, *a.* uninhabitable. **inabitàto,** *a.* uninhabited.

inaccessíbile, *a.* inaccessible.

inaccèsso, *a.* unpenetrated; inaccessible.

inaccettàbile, *a.* unacceptable.

inaccordàbile, *a.* that cannot be granted, or allowed; impermissible; untunable; irreconcilable.

inaccòrto, *a.* unwary; unskilful.

inacerbíre (*pr.* -ísco, -ísci), *v.t.* to embitter. **inacerbírsi,** *v.refl.* to grow bitter.

inacetàre, *v.t.* to dress with vinegar.

inacetíre (*pr.* -ísco, -ísci), *v.i.* (*aux.* essere) to turn sour; turn into vinegar. **inacidíre** (*pr.* -ísco, -ísci), *v.i.* (*aux.* essere) to turn sour.

inacquàre, *v.t.* to water.

inacutíre (*pr.* -ísco, -ísci), *v.t.* to sharpen; make sharper. **inacutírsi,** *v.refl.* to become sharp[er].

inadattàbile, *a.* unadaptable. **inadàtto,** *a.* unfit (for); unsuitable; unbecoming; unqualified.

inadeguatézza, *f.* inadequacy.

inadeguàto, *a.* inadequate; insufficient.

inadempíbile, *a.* that cannot be fulfilled. **inadempiménto,** *m.* non-fulfilment. **inadempíto** & **inadempiúto,** *a.* unfulfilled.

inafferràbile, *a.* impossible to grasp.

inaffettàto, *a.* unaffected; without affectation.

inaffiàre, *v.t.* to water. **inaffiatóio,** *m.* watering-pot, w.-can.

inalàre, *v.t.* to inhale. **inalatóre,** *m.* (*Med.*) inhaler. **inalazióne,** *f.* inhalation.

inalbàre, *v.i.* (*aux.* essere) to turn white; *v.t.* to whiten.

inalberaménto, *m.* hoisting (*flag, &c.*); raising; rearing. **inalberàre** (*pr.* -àlbero), *v.t.* to hoist; raise; (*of land*) to plant trees on. **inalberàrsi,** *v.refl.* (*of horses*) to rear; (*fig.*) to lose one's temper.

inalidíre (*pr.* -ísco, -ísci), *v.i.* (*aux.* essere) & **inalidírsi,** *v.refl.* to dry up.

inalteràbile, *a.* unalterable. **inalteràto,** *a.* unaltered.

inalveàre (*pr.* -àlveo), *v.t.* to canalize; draw water into a channel.

inalzàre, see *innalzare*.

inamidàre (*pr.* -àmido), *v.t.* to starch. **inamidatúra,** *f.* starching.

inammendàbile, *a.* incorrigible; that cannot be improved or amended.

inammissíbile, *a.* inadmissible. **inamovíbile,** *a.* irremovable.

inàne, *a.* empty; vain; useless; inane.

inanellàre (*pr.* -èllo). *v.t.* to curl; form into rings; wed (with a ring). **inanellàto,** *a.* curly; adorned with rings.

inanimàre, see *inanimire*. **inanimàto,** *a.* inanimate.

inanimíre (*pr.* -ísco, -ísci), *v.t.* to animate; encourage; stir; excite. **inanimírsi,** *v.refl.* to take courage; take heart.

inanità, *f.* inanity. **inanizióne,** *f.* inanition.

inappagàbile, *a.* impossible to satisfy. **inappagàto,** *a.* unsatisfied.

inappellàbile, *a.* admitting of no appeal.

inappetènza, *f.* loss (or lack) of appetite.

inapprezzàbile, *a.* invaluable; inestimable; priceless; imperceptible; inappreciable.

inapprodàbile, *a.* unapproachable.

inappuntàbile, *a.* unexceptionable; irreproachable.

inappuràbile, *a.* that cannot be verified or cleared up. **inappuràto,** *a.* unverified; unsettled.

inaràbile, *a.* unploughable. **inaràto,** *a.* unploughed; untilled.

inarcaménto, *m.* bending; arching; curving; cambering. **inarcàre** (*pr.* -àrco, -àrchi), *v.t.* to bend; curve; arch; camber.

inargentàre (*pr.* -ènto,) *v.t.* to plate with silver.

inaridíre (*pr.* -ísco, -ísci), *v.t.* to parch; dry up. *v.i.* (*aux.* essere) & **inaridírsi,** *v.refl.* to become parched, dried up or exhausted.

inarmònico (*pl.* -ònici), *a.* inharmonious, discordant.

inarrendévole, *a.* unyielding; unbending; inflexible. **inarrendevolézza,** *f.* inflexibility.

inarrivàbile, *a.* unattainable; inimitable. **inarrivabilménte,** *ad.* inimitably; incomparably.

inarticolàto, *a.* inarticulate. **inascoltàto,** *a.* unheeded; unheard.

inasiníre (*pr.* -ísco, -ísci), *v.i.* (*aux.* essere) to grow dull; become stupid.

inaspettataménte, *ad.* unexpectedly. **inaspettàto,** *a.* unexpected; unlooked for.

inaspriménto, *m.* embitterment; exacerbation; sharpening; aggravation. **inaspríre** (*pr.* **-ísco, -ísci**), *v.t.* to embitter; exasperate; irritate; aggravate. *v.i.* (*aux.* essere) & **inasprírsi**, *v.refl.* to become embittered; become worse.

inastàre (*pr.* **-àsto**), *v.t.* to hoist (*flag, &c.*); to fix (*bayonets*).

inattaccàbile, *a.* unassailable.

inattendíbile, *a.* unfounded; unreliable; unworthy of consideration.

inattènto, *a.* inattentive. **inattenzióne**, *f.* inattention. **inattéso**, *a.* unexpected.

inattitúdine, *f.* inaptitude.

inattività, *f.inv.* inactivity. **inattívo**, *a.* inactive.

inàtto, *a.* unfitted; unsuited; unapt.

inattuàbile, *a.* impracticable.

inaudíbile, *a.* inaudible. **inaudíto**, *a.* unheard of; unprecedented.

inauguràre (*pr.* **-àuguro**), *v.t.* to inaugurate; to open (*exhibition, &c.*). **inaugurazióne**, *f.* inauguration; opening.

inauspicataménte, *ad.* inauspiciously; unpropitiously. **inauspicàto**, *a.* inauspicious.

inavvedutaménte, *ad.* inadvertently; carelessly. **inavvedutézza**, *f.* inadvertence; carelessness; inattention. **inavvedúto**, *a.* careless; thoughtless; inadvertent.

inavvertenteménte, *ad.* inadvertently. **inavvertènza**, *f.* inadvertence.

inavvertitaménte, *ad.* unthinkingly; inadvertently. **inavvertíto**, *a.* unnoticed; unobserved; uninformed; careless; inattentive.

inazióne, *f.* inaction.

inażżurràrsi, *v.refl.* to become blue; turn blue.

incagliaménto, *m.* (*ship*) stranding; running aground; stoppage; check; impediment. **incagliàre** (*pr.* **-àglio, -àgli**), *v.t.* to clog; hamper; bring to a standstill. *v.i.* (*aux.* essere) & **incagliàrsi**, *v.refl.* to strand; run aground; (*fig.*) to be hampered; come to a standstill. **incàglio** (*pl.* **-àgli**), *m.* stranding; hindrance; obstacle; stoppage.

incalappiàre, *v.t.* to ensnare.

incalcinàre (*pr.* **-íno**), *v.t.* to plaster (*with lime*); dress (*plants*) with lime.

incalcolàbile, *a.* incalculable.

incalliménto, *m.* hardening; callosity; callousness. **incallíre** (*pr.* **-ísco, -ísci**), *v.i.* (*aux.* essere) & **incallírsi**, *v.refl.* to harden; grow hard; become callous.

incaloriménto, *m.* heating; warming.

incaloríre (*pr.* **-ísco, -ísci**), *v.t.* to heat; warm. **incalorírsi**, *v.refl.* to become hot; become warm.

incalvíre (*pr.* **-ísco, -ísci**), *v.i.* (*aux.* essere) to become bald.

incalzaménto, *m.* pressing; following up; pursuit. **incalzànte**, *p.a.* pressing; pursuing. **incalzàre**, *v.t.* & *i.* (*aux.* avere) to press; pursue; chase; follow up closely. **incàlzo**, *m.* support; stiffening; reinforcement.

incameràre, *v.t.* to confiscate; to annex.

incamiciàre, *v.t.* to coat; plaster; cover. **incamiciatúra**, *f.* coating (*of paint, plaster, &c.*); plastering; lining; covering.

incamminàre (*pr.* **-íno**), *v.t.* to set going; start; direct; put on the right road. **incamminàrsi**, *v.refl.* to set out; make one's way (towards); make a start.

incanagliàrsi, *v.refl.* to keep low company; associate with rogues; become degraded.

incanalàre, *v.t.* to canalize; (*fig.*) to direct. **incanalatúra**, *f.* canalization; grooving; groove.

incancellàbile, *a.* indelible; ineffaceable.

incancreníre (*pr.* **-ísco, -ísci**), *v.i.* (*aux.* essere) (*Med.*) to become gangrenous.

incandescènte, *a.* incandescent. **incandescènza**, *f.* incandescence.

incannàggio, *m.* & **incannatúra**, *f.* reeling; winding (*thread, &c.*). **incannàre**, *v.t.* to reel; wind (*silk, &c.*). **incannatóio**, *m.* winder; spool. **incannatóre**, *m.* (*f.* **-tóra**) reeler; silk-winder (*pers.*).

incannucciàre, *v.t.* to trellis; support or protect a plant with canes. **incannucciàta**, *f.* trellis; trelliswork. **incannucciatúra**, *f.* trellising.

incantagióne, *f.* & **incantaménto**, *m.* charm; incantation; enchantment; spell. **incantàre**, *v.t.* to enchant; bewitch; put under a spell. **incantatóre**, *m.* charmer, enchanter. **incantatríce**, *f.* enchantress. **incantésimo**, *m.* enchantment; spell. **incantévole**, *a.* enchanting. **incànto**, *m.* charm; spell; enchantment; auction (sale). **d' ~**, marvellously well, excellently.

incantucciàrsi (*pr.* **-úccio, -úcci**), *v.refl.* to get into a corner; hide oneself (in a corner).

incanutíre (*pr.* -ísco, -ísci), *v.i.* (*aux.* essere) to grow grey; become grey-haired.

incapàce, *a.* incapable. **incapacità**, *f.* incapacity.

incaparbírsi & **incaponírsi**, *v.refl.* to become obstinate; be determined. **incaparbíto** & **incaponíto**, *a.* obstinate; stubborn.

incappàre (**in**), *v.i.* (*aux.* essere) to get (into), run (into); fall in (with); meet (with).

incappottàrsi, *v.refl.* to wrap oneself in a cloak; put on an overcoat.

incappucciàrsi, *v.refl.* to put on a hood.

incapriccírsi (*pr.* -íccio, -ícci), *v.refl.* to take a fancy (to); fall in love (with); become infatuated (with); (foll. by *di*).

incarbonírsi (*pr.* -ísco, -ísci), *v.refl.* to become carbonized.

incarceraménto, *m.* imprisonment; incarceration. **incarceràre** (*pr.* -àrcero), *v.t.* to imprison.

incardinàre, *v.t.* to hinge. **incardinàrsi**, *v.refl.* to hinge (upon); be hinged (upon).

incaricàre (*pr.* -àrico, -àrichi), *v.t.* to charge (with = *di*); entrust; ask. **incaricarsi** (**di**), *v.refl.* to take upon oneself; charge oneself with. **incaricàto**, *m.* deputy. ~ *d'affari*, chargé d'affaires. **incàrico** (*pl.* -àrichi), *m.* charge; commission; duty; office; appointment; task; assignment. *per* ~ *di*, on behalf of; on the part of.

incarnàre, *v.t.* to incarnate; embody; put into effect; wound, drive into the flesh. **incarnàto**, *p.a.* incarnate. ¶ *m.* rose-pink; flesh-colour. **incarnazióne**, *f.* incarnation.

incarníre (*pr.* -ísco, -ísci), *v.i.* (*aux.* essere) & **incarnírsi**, *v.refl.* to grow in (*toe-nail*). **incarníto**, *a;* in-grown, in-growing; ineradicable. *un'unghia* ~ *a*, an ingrowing nail.

incarogníre (*pr.* -ísco, -ísci), *v.i.* (*aux.* essere) to rot; (*fig.*) to become lazy or good for nothing.

incartaménto, *m.* set of papers; group of documents.

incartapecoríre (*pr.* -ísco, -ísci), *v.i.* (*aux.* essere) to wrinkle up; become dry and yellow (*like parchment*). **incartapecoríto**, *a.* dry and yellow; wrinkled with age.

incartàre, *v.t.* to wrap in paper; (*Mech.*) to planish.

incartocciàre (*pr.* -òccio, -òcci), *v.t.* to put in a paper bag; wrap in paper. **incartocciàrsi**, *v.refl.* to turn up; to curl; to become shrivelled up.

incartonàre (*pr.* -óno), *v.t.* to put between stiff paper covers.

incasellàre (*pr.* -èllo), *v.t.* to pigeon-hole.

incassàre, *v.t.* to put in a box; encase; set (*jewel*); cash, collect, receive. **incassàto**, *a.* enclosed; hollow, deep(ly) set (*eyes,* &c.). **incàsso**, *m.* amount collected; cash takings.

incastonàre, *v.t.* to set (*a gem*); mount; insert. **incastonatúra**, *f.* mounting; setting.

incastraménto, *m.* fitting; mortising; embedding. **incastràre**, *v.t.* to embed; let in; fit; mortise; drive; close. **incàstro**, *m.* recess, bezel; mortise; groove. ~ *a coda di rondine*, dovetailing.

incatarràrsi, *v.refl.* to catch cold.

incatenàre (*pr.* -èno), *v.t.* to chain; chain up; fetter; (*fig.*) captivate; enthral.

incatramàre, *v.t.* to tar.

incattivíre (*pr.* -ísco, -ísci), *v.t.* to make cross or wicked. *v.i.* (*aux.* essere) & **incattivírsi**, *v.refl.* to become cross or wicked.

incautaménte, *ad.* rashly; incautiously. **incàuto**, *a.* incautious; rash; imprudent.

incavalcàre (*pr.* -àlco, -àlchi), *v.t.* to superimpose; overlap; place astride; stagger (*pop.*). ~ *la maglia*, to slip one and knit one.

incavàre, *v.t.* to hollow out; excavate. **incavàto**, *a.* hollow. **incàvo**, *m.* cavity; hollow, hollowing [out]; notch.

incèdere (*pr.* -èdo, &c., like **cedere**), *v.i. ir.* (*aux.* avere) to stride; walk with a lofty gait.

incendiàre (*pr.* -èndio, -èndi), *v.t.* to set on fire; set fire to. **incendiàrsi**, *v.refl.* to catch fire. **incendiàrio** (*pl.* -àri), *a.* & *m.* incendiary. **incèndio** (*pl.* -èndi), *m.* (outbreak of) fire; conflagration; destruction by fire. ~ *doloso*, arson; fire-raising; incendiarism. *pompa da* ~, fire-engine; fire-pump.

inceneràre (*pr.* -énero), *v.t.* to strew with ashes. **inceneriménto**, *m.* incineration. **inceneríre** (*pr.* -ísco, -ísci), *v.t.* to reduce to ashes; incinerate.

incensàre (*pr.* -ènso), *v.t.* to fumigate

with incense; burn incense to; (*fig.*) flatter. **incensière,** *m.* censer; incense-burner. **incènso,** *m.* incense; (*fig.*) flattery; adulation.

incensuràbile, *a.* irreproachable. **incensuràto,** *a.* uncensured; blameless. *essere* ~, (*Law*) to be a first offender.

incentìvo, *m.* incentive.

incentràre, *v.t.* to centralize; concentrate.

inceppaménto, *m.* obstruction. **inceppàre,** *v.t.* to clog; fetter; impede; embarrass. **inceppàrsi,** *v.refl.* to jam; (*Aero.*) cut out.

incerallaccàre, *v.t.* to seal (*with sealing wax*).

inceràre, *v.t.* to wax. *tela-incerata,* *f.* oil-cloth; tarpaulin; oilskin.

incerchiàre (*pr.* -érchio, -érchi), *v.t.* to encircle; hoop.

incertaménte, *ad.* uncertainly; with no certainty. **incertézza,** *f.* uncertainty. **incèrto,** *a.* uncertain. ¶ *m.* uncertainty; (*pl.*) incidental profits; perquisites.

incespicàre (*pr.* -éspico, -éspichi), *v.i.* (*aux.* avere) to stumble.

incessàbile & **incessànte,** *a.* unceasing; incessant.

incèsso, *m.* stride; stately walk; gait; carriage.

incèsto, *m.* incest.

incètta, *f.* buying up; cornering; collecting; forestalling. **incettàre** (*pr.* -ètto), *v.t.* to buy up; corner; clear the market of; monopolize.

inchiavacciàre & **inchiavardàre,** *v.t.* to bolt, bar (*the door*).

inchiavàre, *v.t.* to lock.

inchiavistellàre, *v.t.* to padlock.

inchièsta, *f.* inquiry, investigation.

inchinàre (*pr.* -íno), *v.t.* to incline; bow (down). **inchinàrsi,** *v.refl.* to bow; stoop; submit. **inchinévole,** *a.* pliant; yielding; inclined; willing; disposed. **inchìno,** *m.* bow, curts[e]y.

inchiodàre (*pr.* -òdo), *v.t.* to nail; rivet; fix down. **inchiodàrsi,** *v.refl.* (*fig.*) to be nailed down; to get into debt. **inchiodatúra,** *f.* nailing (down); rivetting.

inchiostràre (*pr.* *ir.* -òstro), *v.t.* to stain with ink; (*Typ.*) to ink. **inchiòstro,** *m.* ink. ~ *copiativo,* copying ink. ~ *di China,* Indian ink. ~ *da stampa,* printing-i.

inchiúdere, *v.t. ir.* (*pr.* -chiúdo, &c., like chiudere) to shut in; enclose.

inciampàre, *v.i.* (*aux.* avere) to stumble. ¶ *m.* stumbling. **in-**

ciàmpo, *m.* hindrance; obstacle; stumbling-block.

incidentàle, *a.* accidental; incidental. **incidènte,** *m.* accident; incident; dispute. ~ *ferroviario,* railway accident. ~ *stradale,* road accident. street a. ~ *mortale,* fatal accident. **incidènza,** *f.* incidence. *per* ~, by chance; by the way; by the bye.

incìdere (*pr.* -ído), *v.t. ir.*, to engrave; incise; cut. ~ *ad acqua forte,* to etch.

incìnta, *a.f.* pregnant; with child; expectant (mother).

incipriàre (*pr.* -íprio, -ípri) *v.t.* & **incipriàrsi,** *v.refl.* to powder the face.

inciprigníre (*pr.* -ísco, -ísci), *v.t.* to irritate; inflame. *v.i.* (*aux.* essere) & **inciprignírsi,** *v.refl.* to fester.

incírca (all'), *ad. expr.* approximately; about.

incirconcíso, *a.* uncircumcized.

incirconscrìtto, *a.* uncircumscribed; unlimited; unconditioned.

incišióne, *f.* incision; cut; notch; engraving. ~ *in linoleum,* lino cut. **incišívo,** *a.* incisive. *dente* ~, incisor. **incíšo,** *a.* incised; engraved. **incišóre,** *m.* engraver.

incitaménto, *m.* incitement. **incitàre** (*pr.* -ìncito & ìncito), *v.t.* to incite; instigate.

incitrullìre (*pr.* -ísco, -ísci), *v.i.* (*aux.* essere) to become stupid or silly.

incivíle, *a.* uncivil; discourteous; barbarous; uncivilized. **inciviliménto,** *m.* (process of) civilization; refining (of manners). **incivilíre** (*pr.* -ísco, -ísci), *v.t.* to civilize; refine. **incivilménte,** *ad.* rudely; impolitely. **inciviltà,** *f.* incivility; want of manners; rudeness; barbarousness.

inclemènte, *a.* inclement. **inclemènza,** *f.* inclemency.

inclinàre, *v.t.* to incline; bend. *v.i.* (*aux.* avere) & **inclinàrsi,** *v.refl.* to incline; lean; (*ship*) heel, list; slope; tilt; dip (*magnetic needle*); ~ *in curva,* bank (*Aero.*). be disposed. **inclinàto,** *a.* inclined (*lit.* & *fig.*); leaning; slanting; sloping; bent; disposed; prone. **inclinazióne,** *f.* inclination; slope; slant; (*magnetic*) dip; propensity. **inclíne,** *a.* inclined; bent.

ínclito, *a.* famous; illustrious.

inclúdere (*pr.* -údo, &c., like accludere), *v.t. ir.* to include; enclose; comprise. **inclušióne,** *f.*

inclusion. **inclusívo,** *a.* inclusive.
inclúso, *p.a.* included; comprised; enclosed.
incoatívo, *a.* inchoative. **incoàto,** *a.* inchoate; just begun; undeveloped; (*Law*) instituted.
incoccàre (*pr.* **-òcco, -òcchi**), *v.t.* (*of arrow*) to fit to the notch, to the string.
incocciàre (*pr.* **-òccio, -òcci**), *v.i.* (*aux.* essere) & **incocciàrsi,** *v.refl.* to persist; remain obstinate.
incoerènte, *a.* incoherent. **incoerènza,** *f.* incoherence.
incògliere (*pr.* **-òlgo,** *&c.,* like *cogliere*), *v.i. ir.* (*aux.* essere) to happen; befall.
incògnita, *f.* (*Math.*) unknown quantity. **incògnito,** *a.* unknown. *in* ∼, *ad,* incognito.
incollaménto, *m.* sticking, pasting (together); jamming (*valve*). **incollàre,** *v.t.* to stick on; glue on; paste together; size. ∼ *manifesti,* to stick bills. **incollatóre,** *m.* sticker, poster. ∼ *d'affissi,* bill-sticker, bill-poster. **incollatúra,** *f.* sticking, pasting; neck (*sport*). *vincere per un'* ∼, to win by a neck.
incolleríre (*pr.* **-ísco, -ísci**), *v.i.* (*aux.* essere) & **incollerírsi,** *v.refl.* to get angry; fly into a passion.
incolonnàre (*pr.* **-ónno**), *v.t.* to draw up in columns (*Mil., Typ., &c.*).
incolóre & **incolóro,** *a.* colourless.
incolpàbile, *a.* chargeable, blamable; *also neg.* blameless, innocent. **incolpabilità** *f.* blamelessness; innocence. **incolpàre** (*pr.* **-ólpo**), *v.t.* to inculpate; accuse; charge. **incolpatóre,** *m.* accuser. **incolpazióne,** *f.* accusation, inculpation. **incolpévole,** *a.* innocent; blameless.
incoltaménte, *ad.* boorishly. **incoltézza,** *f.* boorishness; want of cultivation. ¶ **incólto,** *a.* uncultivated; neglected; unadorned; uncultured; unpolished; boorish; rough.
incòlto, *p.p.* of **incogliere,** befallen.
incòlume, *a.* unharmed; unhurt; uninjured; safe & sound. **incolumità,** *f.* safety; escape without injury.
incombènte, *a.* incumbent; impending. **incombènza,** *f.* charge; commission; task; errand. **incómbere,** *v.i.* (*without compound tenses*) to impend; weigh (upon); be incumbent (upon).

incombustíbile, *a.* incombustible; fire-proof.
incominciàre (*pr.* **-íncio, -ínci**), *v.t.* & *v.i.* (*aux.* essere) to begin; commence.
incomodaménte, *ad.* inconveniently; uncomfortably. **incomodàre** (*pr.* **-còmodo**), *v.t.* to incommode; put to trouble; disturb; annoy. **incomodàrsi,** *v.refl.* to trouble; put oneself to trouble. **incomodàto,** *a.* troubled; annoyed; indisposed; out of sorts. **incomodità,** *f.* inconvenience; trouble; annoyance. **incòmodo,** *a.* inconvenient; uncomfortable; troublesome. ¶ *m.* inconvenience; trouble; indisposition; ailment.
incomparàbile, *a.* matchless; incomparable.
incompartíbile, *a.* indivisible.
incompatíbile, *a.* incompatible. **incompatibilità,** *f.* incompatibility.
incompiúto, *a.* incomplete; unfinished.
incomplèto, *a.* incomplete; defective.
incomportàbile, *a.* insufferable; unbearable.
incompostaménte, *ad.* in a disorderly manner; unbecomingly. **incompostézza,** *f.* disorder; confusion; want of order. **incompósto,** *a.* disorderly; disordered; unbecoming.
incomprensíbile, *a.* incomprehensible. **incompréso,** *a.* not understood; misunderstood; unappreciated.
incomputàbile, *a.* incalculable.
inconcepíbile, *a.* inconceivable.
inconciliàbile, *a.* irreconcilable.
inconcludènte, *a.* inconclusive.
inconcússo, *a.* unshaken; unmoved; firm; stable.
incondizionàto, *a.* unconditional; absolute.
inconfessàbile, *a.* unavowable, that cannot be confessed.
inconfutàbile, *a.* irrefutable. **inconfutàto,** *a.* not disproved.
incongiungíbile, *a.* that cannot be united; incompatible.
incongruènte, *a.* inconsistent; not in conformity. **incongruènza,** *f.* incongruity; inconsistency. **incòngruo,** *a.* incongruous.
inconoscíbile, *a.* unknowable.
inconsapévole, *a.* unconscious; ignorant; uninformed. **inconsapevolézza,** *f.* ignorance; unconsciousness; want of information.
inconsciaménte, *ad.* unconsciously;

unawares. **incònscio** (*pl.* **-ònsci**), *a.* unconscious; unaware.

inconsequènte, *a.* inconsequent; incoherent.

inconsideratézza & **inconsiderazióne,** *f.* lack of consideration; inconsiderateness. **inconsideràto,** *a.* inconsiderate; rash; foolish.

inconsistènte, *a.* inconsistent, insubstantial, unreal; ill-grounded; fallacious. **inconsistènza,** *f.* inconsistency; lack of foundation.

inconsuèto, *a.* unusual; unaccustomed.

inconsultaménte, *ad.* unadvisedly; without reflection. **inconsúlto,** *a.* unadvised; unthinking; unreflecting.

incontaminàto, *a.* uncontaminated; unpolluted; undefiled.

incontanènte, *ad.* immediately; forthwith; at once.

incontentàbile, *a.* insatiable; exacting; hard to please. **incontentabilità,** *f.* inability to be satisfied.

incontestàbile, *a.* indisputable; incontestable. **incontestàto,** *a.* undisputed.

incontràre (*pr.* **-óntro**), *v.t.* to meet; meet with; fall in with. **incontràrsi,** *v.refl.* to meet; agree; coincide. ∼ *con,* to meet (in combat), to encounter.

incontrastàbile, *a.* indisputable; incontestable; unavoidable. **incontrastàto,** *a.* uncontested; unopposed.

incóntro, *m.* meeting; collision; encounter.

incóntro a, *pr.* towards; to; against; opposite. *all'* ∼ *di,* opposite. *all'* *incontro,* on the contrary. *andare* ∼ *a,* to meet; face; incur.

incontrovèrso, *a.* undisputed.

inconvenévole & **inconveniènte,** *a.* unbecoming; inconvenient. **inconveniènte,** *m.* inconvenience; drawback; defect; trouble; annoyance. **inconveniènza,** *f.* impropriety; inconvenience.

incoraggiaménto, *m.* encouragement. **incoraggiànte,** *p.a.* encouraging. **incoraggiàre** (*pr.* **-àggio, -àggi**), *v.t.* to encourage. **incoraggiàrsi,** *v.refl.* to take courage; take heart.

incordàre (*pr.* **-òrdo**), *v.t.* to rope, tie (up) with ropes; string (*Mus. instr.*). **incordàrsi,** *v.refl.* (*of muscle*) to become stiff; get a stiff neck.

incorniciàre (*pr.* **-ício, -íci**), *v.t.* to frame. **incorniciatúra,** *f.* framing.

incoronàre (*pr.* **-óno**), *v.t.* to crown. **incoronazióne,** *f.* coronation.

incorporàre (*pr.* **-òrporo**), *v.t.* to incorporate.

incorporeaménte, *ad.* incorporeally. **incorpòreo,** *a.* incorporeal.

incorreggíbile, *a.* incorrigible.

incórrere (*pr.* **-órro,** &*c.,* like *correre*), *v.i. ir.* (*aux.* essere) to incur; fall into (*fig.*). (*foll. by* in).

incorrettézza, *f.* incorrectness. **incorrètto,** *a.* incorrect.

incorròtto, *a.* incorrupted. **incorruttíbile,** *a.* incorruptible.

incórso, *p.p.* of **incorrere.**

incosciènte, *a.* unconscious; unconscientious. **incosciènza,** *f.* unconscious; lack of conscience.

incostànte, *a.* inconstant; fickle; changeable; unsettled. **incostànza,** *f.* inconstancy; fickleness; changeableness.

incostituzionàle, *a.* unconstitutional.

increànza, *f.* incivility; impoliteness; bad manners.

increàto, *a.* uncreated.

incredíbile, *a.* incredible; surprising. **incredulità,** *f.* incredulity. **incrèdulo,** *a.* incredulous. ¶ *m.* unbeliever.

increménto, *m.* increment; increase. *dare* ∼ *a,* (*Com.*) to favour; push.

incréscere (*pr.* **-ésco, -ésci,** &*c.,* like *crescere*), *v.i. ir.* (*aux.* essere) to annoy; be wearisome or unpleasant; (*gen. impers.*) *m'incresce,* I am sorry, I regret. **increscióso,** *a.* disagreeable; unpleasant; annoying.

increspaménto, *m.* & **increspatúra,** *f.* rippling; crinkling; curling. **increspàre** (*pr.* **-éspo**), *v.t.* & **increspàrsi,** *v.refl.* to ripple; wrinkle; curl (up).

incretiníre (*pr.* **-ísco, -ísci**), *v.i.* (*aux.* essere) to become an idiot.

incriminàbile, *a.* liable to prosecution; impeachable. **incriminàre** (*pr.* **-ímino**), *v.t.* to incriminate; prosecute; impeach. **incriminazióne,** *f.* accusation; charge; impeachment.

incrinàre (*pr.* **-íno**), *v.t.* & **incrinàrsi,** *v.refl.* to crack. **incrinatúra,** *f.* crack; flaw.

incriticàbile, *a.* not open to criticism.

incrociaménto, *m.* crossing; cross-breeding. **incrociàre** (*pr.* **-ócio, -óci**), *v.t.* & **incrociàrsi,** *v.refl.* to cross. **incrociàre,** *v.i.* (*aux.* avere) to cruise. **incrociatóre,** *m.* cruiser.

incrocicchiàre (*pr.* -ícchio, -ícchi), *v.t.* to interlace.

incrócio (*pl.* -óci), *m.* (*of roads, &c.*) crossing; intersection; (*of breeds*) cross.

incrollàbile, *a.* unshakable; firm; resolute.

incrostàre (*pr.* -òsto), *v.t.* to encrust; foul (*gun, ship's bottom*). **incrosta-zióne,** *f.* incrustation.

incrudelíre (*pr.* -ísco, -ísci), *v.i.* (*aux.* essere) to grow cruel; (*aux.* avere) to be pitiless; commit cruelties.

incrudíre (*pr.* -ísco, -ísci), *v.t.* to make worse; aggravate; embitter; *v.i.* (*aux.* essere) to become worse; grow worse.

incruènto, *a.* bloodless (*victory, &c.*).

incubatríce, *f.* incubator. **incuba-zióne,** *f.* incubation; hatching.

íncubo, *m.* incubus; nightmare.

incúdine, *f.* anvil.

inculcàre (*pr.* -úlco, -úlchi), *v.t.* to inculcate.

incúlto, *a.* rough; uncultivated.

incunàbolo, *m.* incunabulum (*pl.* -abula*).

incuneàre (*pr.* -úneo), *v.t.* to wedge.

incupíre (*pr.* -ísco, -ísci), *v.i.* (*aux.* essere) to become dark[er]; rouse one's gloomy. *v.t.* to darken; (*of colour*) deepen.

incuràbile, *a.* incurable. **incurànte,** *a.* careless; heedless; indifferent. **incurànza,** *f.* indifference; heedless-ness; negligence. **incúria,** *f.* indifference; negligence.

incuriosíre (*pr.* -ísco, -ísci), *v.t.* to excite one's curiosity; rouse one's interest. **incuriosírsi,** *v.refl.* to become curious. **incurióso,** *a.* uninterested; indifferent; incurious.

incursióne, *f.* incursion; inroad; raid. ~ *aerea,* air-raid.

incurvàbile, *a.* that cannot be bent. **incurvàre,** *v.t.* to bend. **incurvato,** *a.* bent; bowed (down); curved. **incurvíre** (*pr.* -ísco, -ísci), *v.i.* (*aux.* essere) to become bent.

incustodíto, *a.* unguarded.

incútere (*pr.* -úto), *v.t. ir.* to inspire (*fear, respect, &c.*); instil; strike.

índaco (*pl.* índachi), *m.* indigo.

indagàre (*pr.* -àgo, -àghi), *v.t. & i.* (*aux.* avere) to investigate; inquire (into); search (into). **indagatóre,** *m.* (*f.* -tríce) investigator. ¶ *a.* investigating; searching. **indàgine,** *f.* inquiry (or enquiry); investiga-tion. (*pl.*) researches, inquiries.

indàrno, *ad.* in vain.

indebitaménte, *ad.* unduly. **in-debitaménto,** *m.* running into debt; indebtedness, liabilities. **in-debitàre** (*pr.* -ébito), *v.t.* to cause (one) to run into debt. **indebitàrsi,** *v.refl.* to get into debt; run into debt. **indebitàto,** *a.* indebted; in debt. **indébito,** *a.* undue, unbecoming. *appropriazione* ~ *a, f.* embezzle-ment.

indebolíre (*pr.* -ísco, -ísci), *v.t.* to weaken; enfeeble; (*Phot.*) reduce. **indebolírsi,** *v.refl.* to become weak; become feeble or enfeebled; (*of sounds or colours*) become faint.

indecifràbile, *a.* indecipherable; illegible.

indecisióne, *f.* indecision; hesitation. **indecíso,** *a.* undecided; irresolute; hesitant.

indeclinàbile, *a.* indeclinable; in-variable; unavoidable; absolute.

indecoróso, *a.* indecorous; unseemly; indecent.

indefessaménte, *ad.* untiringly; in-defatigably; incessantly. **indefèsso,** *a.* indefatigable; unwearied; tire-less.

indefettíbile, *a.* unfailing.

indefiníbile, *a.* indefinable. **in-definíto,** *a.* indefinite.

indegnaménte, *ad.* unworthily. **indegnità,** *f.inv.* unworthiness; indignity; insult; mean action. **indégno,** *a.* unworthy; undeserving; worthless.

indelèbile, *a.* indelible; ineffaceable.

indelibàto, *a.* pure; spotless; intact.

indeliberàto, *a.* hasty; impulsive.

indelicatézza, *f.* indelicacy; lack of scruple(s).

indemaniàre (*pr.* -ànio, -àni), *v.t.* to hand over (*land*) to the State.

indemoniàrsi (*pr.* -ònio, -òni), *v.refl* to behave like one possessed **indemoniàto,** *a.* possessed (with a devil). ¶ *m.* demoniac; one possessed.

indènne, *a.* undamaged. **indennità,** *f.inv.* indemnity; allowance (*for expenses*). **indennizżàre,** *v.t.* to indemnify. **indennízżo,** *m.* in-demnification; indemnity.

indentàre (*pr.* -ènto), *v.t.* (*Mech.*) to cog, tooth (*wheel*); indent; engage; put into gear. **indentatúra,** *f.* toothing; indentation.

indentràrsi, *v.refl.* to penetrate (into). **indéntro,** *ad.* within; inside. *al-l' ~,* inwards.

indescrivíbile, *a.* indescribable.
indeterminatézza, *f.* imprecision; indefiniteness. **indeterminàto,** *a.* undetermined; imprecise; vague; indefinite.
indevòto, *a.* irreligious; undevout; irreverent.
índi, *ad.* thence; thereafter.
India (l'), *f.* India. *le ~ ie Orientali,* *f.pl.* the East Indies. *le ~ ie Occidentali,* the West Indies. *canna d'~,* *f.* bamboo cane. *castagno d' ~,* *m.* horse-chestnut (tree). *fico d' ~,* *m.* prickly pear. *pollo d' ~,* *m.* turkey. *porcellino d' ~,* *m.* guinea-pig. **indiàna,** *f.* print(ed cotton fabric); Indian woman. **I~ (l')** Indiana (*Geog.*). **indiàno,** *a. & m.* Indian. *far l' ~,* to feign ignorance.
indiavolàto, *a.* demoniac; devilish; fiendish; (*fig.*) fierce; furious; stormy; violent; difficult.
indicànte, *a.* indicative of. **indicàre** (*pr.* **índico, índichi**), *v.t.* to indicate; point out; point at; show; mark; mention; state; suggest; advise; mean. **indicatívo,** *a. & m.* indicative. **indicàto,** *a.* advisable; suitable; fit; right; proper. **indicatóre,** *m.* indicator; gauge; sign; guide[book] (*Rly., Street, Post.*), time-table; directory. *~ stradale,* traffic sign, road sign. *~ di pressione,* pressure gauge. *~telefonico,* telephone book, t. directory. *~della velocità,* speed indicator. ¶ *a.* (*f.* **-tríce**), indicating; indicative. **indicazióne,** *f.* indication; clue; information; direction(s).
índice (*pl.* **índici**), *m.* index; forefinger; hand (*clock, watch*); pointer; sign; mark; black list. *l'I~,* the Index [expurgatorius]. *~ di rifrazione,* refractive index (*Opt.*)
indicíbile, *a.* unspeakable; unutterable; inexpressible.
indietreggiaménto, *m.* withdrawal. **indietreggiàre,** *v.i.* (*aux.* avere & essere) to withdraw; draw back; give way; lose ground. **indiètro,** *ad.* back, backwards; behind, behindhand; slow (*of clock or watch*); (*Naut.*) abaft, aft.
indifendíbile, *a.* indefensible; untenable. **indiféso,** *a.* undefended, unprotected; unarmed.
indifferènte, *a.* indifferent; unconcerned. **indifferenteménte,** *ad.* indifferently; indiscriminately. **indifferentísmo,** *m.* attitude of

indifference. **indifferènza,** *f.* indifference; unconcern.
indifferíbile, *a.* that cannot be put off or deferred.
indígeno, *a.* native; indigenous. ¶ *m.* native.
indigènte, *a.* indigent, poor. ¶ *m.f.* pauper. **indigènza,** *f.* indigence; poverty; want.
indigeríbile, *a.* indigestible; (*fig.*) insupportable. **indigestióne,** *f.* indigestion. **indigèsto,** *a.* indigestible; undigested (*fig.*); crude, tedious, heavy, boring.
indignàre, *v.t.* to rouse to anger; shock. **indignàrsi,** *v.refl.* to become indignant; get angry; be shocked. **indignazióne,** *f.* indignation.
indimenticàbile, *a.* unforgettable.
indimostràbile, *a.* that cannot be proved. **indimostràto,** *a.* unproved.
indipendènte, *a.* independent. *~ da,* independent of. **indipendenza,** *f.* independence.
indíre (*pr.* **-íco,** *&c.,* like *dire*), *v.t.* *ir.* to announce; summon; call (*meeting*); fix; arrange; appoint.
indirettaménte, *ad.* indirectly. **indirètto,** *a.* indirect.
indirizzàre, *v.t.* to address; dedicate; direct. **indirizzàrsi,** *v.refl.* to address oneself (to); apply (to); set out (for); direct one's steps (towards). **indirízzo,** *m.* address; direction; guiding rule; course; domicile; petition; dedication.
indisciplinàto, *a.* undisciplined; unruly.
indiscretaménte, *ad.* indiscreetly. **indiscretézza,** & **indiscrezione,** *f.* indiscretion. **indiscréto,** *a.* indiscreet; forward; prying; inquisitive.
indiscutíbile, *a.* indisputable; unquestionable.
indispensàbile, *a.* indispensable; necessary. ¶ *m.* necessary; what is necessary.
indispettíre (*pr.* **-ísco, -ísci**), *v.t.* to vex; annoy; irritate. **indispettírsi,** *v.refl.* to be (or become) vexed, annoyed, irritated, piqued. **indispettíto,** *a.* vexed, annoyed, irritated, piqued.
indispórre (*pr.* **-óngo, -óni,** *&c.,* like *porre*), *v.t.* *ir.* to indispose; trouble; annoy; disgust. **indisposizióne,** *f.* indisposition. **indispósto,** *a.* indisposed; unwell, poorly, out of sorts.

indissolúbile, *a.* indissoluble.

indistinguíbile, *a.* indistinguishable.

indistintaménte, *ad.* indistinctly; indiscriminately.

indistínto, *a.* indistinct.

indistruttíbile, *a.* indestructible.

indívia, *f.* endive.

individuàle, *a.* individual; particular. **individuàre** (*pr.* **-íduo**), *v.t.* to specify; single out; locate; characterize accurately. **indivíduo**, *m.* individual; fellow.

indivišaménte, *ad.* jointly; without distinction. **indivišíbile**, *a.* indivisible; inseparable. **indivíšo**, *a.* undivided; joint.

indiziàre (*pr.* **-ízio**, **-ízi**), *v.t.* to point to; render suspect; throw suspicion on. **indiziàrio** (*pl.* **-àri**), *a.* presumptive, based on suspicion or inference. *prova ~a*, *f.* presumptive evidence; circumstantial evidence. **indízio** (*pl.* **-ízi**), *m.* token; sign; sympton; indication; clue; (*Law*) suspicious circumstance; circumʳ antial evidence.

Índo (l'), *m.* (the Indus (*river*).

indòcile, *a.* indocile; intractable; unruly. **indocilíre** (*pr.* **-ísco**, **-ísci**), *v.t.* to render docile.

Indo-cína (l'), *f.* Indo-China. **indo-cinése**, *a.* Indo-Chinese.

indolcíre (*pr.* **-ísco**, **-ísci**), *v.t.* to sweeten; soften.

índole, *f.* natural disposition; temperament; temper; character.

indolènte, *a.* indolent; slothful; apathetic; listless; indifferent; inert; painless (*Med.*). **indolenteménte**, *ad.* indolently; lazily; listlessly. **indolènza**, *f.* indolence; sloth; apathy; indifference.

indolenziménto, *m.* numbness; soreness; stiffness. **indolenzíre** (*pr.* **-ísco**, **-ísci**), *v.t.* to benumb; make stiff or painful. **indolenzírsi**, *v.refl.* to become benumbed, stiff or sore.

indomàbile, *a.* untamable; ungovernable; indomitable.

indomàni (l'), *m.* the next day; the following day; the day after.

indomàto & **indòmito**, *a.* unsubdued; indomitable; untamed.

indoraménto, *m.* & **indoratúra**, *f.* gilding. **indoràre** (*pr.* **-òro**), *v.t.* to gild.

indossàre (*pr.* **-òsso**), *v.t.* to put on (*clothes*); wear. **indossatríce**, *f.* mannequin. **indòsso**, *ad.* on, on one's person, on one's back.

Indostàn (l'), *m.* Hindustan. **indo-**

stànico & **indostàno**, *a.* & *m.* Hindustani.

indótto, *p.p.* of **indurre** & *a.* induced. ¶ *m.* (*Elec.*) armature.

indòtto, *a.* unlearned.

indovinàre (*pr.* **-íno**), *v.t.* to guess; divine; surmise; foresee; foretell; imagine. **indovinàrla**, to be right; succeed; hit the mark (*fig.*). **indo-vinèllo**, *m.* riddle; puzzle. **indo-víno**, *m.* (*f.* **-a**) soothsayer; fortune-teller; diviner. ¶ *a.* foreseeing; prophetic.

indubbiaménte & **indubitata-ménte**, *ad.* undoubtedly. **in-dúbbio** & **indubitàto**, *a.* undoubted.

indugiàre (*pr.* **-úgio**, **-úgi**), *v.i.* (*aux.* avere) & **indugiàrsi**, *v.refl.* to delay; linger; loiter. *~ su*, to linger over; dwell upon. **indugiatóre**, *m.* (*f.* **-tríce**) loiterer, dawdler. **indúgio**, *m.* delay.

indulgènte, *a.* indulgent; lenient. **indulgènza**, *f.* indulgence; forbearance; leniency. **indúlgere** (*pr.* **-úlgo**, **-úlgi**), *v.i. ir.* (*aux.* avere) to be indulgent (to), to indulge (in); *v.t.* to grant; allow; bestow as a favour. **indúlto**, *p.p.* of *indulgere.* ¶ *m.* (*Law*) free pardon; dispensation.

induménto, *m.* garment; article of clothing.

induriménto, *m.* hardening. **indu-ríre** (*pr.* **-ísco**, **-ísci**), *v.t.* to harden; inure.

indúrre (*pr.* **-úco**, **-úci**, &*c.*, like *addurre*), *v.t. ir.* to lead; induce; bring, persuade; infer. *~ in errore*, to mislead. *non c' ~ in tentazione*, lead us not into temptation (*N.T.*). **indúrsi**, *v.refl.* to resolve; decide; be induced (to); bring oneself (to).

indústre, *a.* industrious. **indústria**, *f.* ingenuity; diligence; industry; manufacture, trade. *cavaliere d' ~*, swindler; sharper. *~ essenziale*, *~ chiave*, key-industry. **indus-triàle**, *a.* industrial; manufacturing. ¶ *m.* industrialist; manufacturer; mill-owner. **industriàrsi**, *v.refl.* to strive; endeavour; work hard; do one's best. **industrióso**, *a.* industrious, busy.

induttànza, *f.* (*Elec.*) inductance. **induttívo**, *a.* inductive. **in-duttóre**, *m.* (*Elec.*) inductor. **induzióne**, *f.* (*Phil.* & *Elec.*) induction. *rocchetto d' ~*, induction-coil.

ineb[b]riaménto, *m.* inebriation; intoxication. **ineb[b]riàre,** *v.t.* to inebriate; make drunk; (*fig.*) fill with joy. **ineb[b]riàrsi,** *v.refl.* to get drunk; (*fig.*) go into raptures.

inebetíto, *a.* dull; stupid.

ineccepíbile & **ineccezionàbile,** *a.* unexceptionable.

inèdia, *f.* inanition; starvation; tedium; boredom.

inèdito, *a.* unpublished.

ineducàbile, *a.* that cannot be educated. **ineducàto,** *a.* ill-bred; impolite; uneducated.

ineffàbile, *a.* ineffable; unspeakable; unutterable.

ineffettuàbile, *a.* impossible to carry out; unrealizable.

inefficàce, *a.* inefficacious; ineffectual; fruit'ess. **inefficàcia,** *f.* ineffectiveness; inefficiency.

ineguaglIànza, *f.* inequality; unevenness; unlikeness; roughness. **ineguagliàto,** *a.* unequalled; unparalleled. **ineguàle,** *a.* unequal; uneven; unlike; irregular; changeable. **inegualità,** *f.inv.* inequality. **inegualménte,** *ad.* unequally.

inelegànte, *a.* inelegant; ungraceful; unpolished. **ineleganza,** *f.* inelegance.

ineleggíbile, *a.* ineligible.

ineluttàbile, *a.* inevitable; unavoidable; inescapable.

inenarràbile, *a.* unspeakable; that cannot be spoken of.

inerènte, *a.* inherent.

inèrme, *a.* unarmed.

inerpicàre (*pr.* -érpico, -érpichi), *v.i.* (*aux.* èssere) & **inerpicàrsi,** *v.refl.* to climb; clamber (up).

inèrte, *a.* inert; inactive; motionless; senseless. **inèrzia,** *f.* inertia; inertness; sluggishness; laziness.

inesàtto, *a.* inexact; incorrect; inaccurate; unpunctual. **inesaudíbile,** *a.* that cannot be granted or complied with. **inesaudíto,** *a.* unheard (*petition, &c.*); ungranted.

inesauríbile, *a.* inexhaustible. **inesàusto,** *a.* unexhausted.

inescusàbile, *a.* inexcusable.

ineseguíbile, *a.* impracticable; impossible of fulfilment.

inesercitàto, *a.* unpractised; untrained.

inesigíbile, *a.* (*of debt, taxes, &c*) which cannot be collected.

inesistènte, *a.* non-existent. **inesistènza,** *f.* non-existence.

inesoràbile, *a.* inexorable; unrelenting.

inesperiènza, *f.* inexperience. **inespertaménte,** *ad.* inexpertly; unskilfully. **inespèrto,** *a.* inexpert; unskilled; inexperienced.

inesplicàbile, *a.* inexplicable; unaccountable.

inesplòso, *a.* unexploded.

inesprimíbile, *a.* inexpressible.

inespugnàbile, *a.* impregnable.

inestinguíbile, *a.* inextinguishable; unquenchable.

inestirpàbile, *a.* ineradicable.

inestricàbile, *a.* inextricable.

inettaménte, *ad.* ineptly. **inettézza** & **inettitúdine,** *f.* ineptitude; unsuitability. **inètto,** *a.* inept; unfit; unsuitable.

inèzia, *f.* trifle; bagatelle; foolish remark.

infacóndia, *f.* unreadiness in speech.

infagottàre (*pr.* -òtto), *v.t.* to wrap up; make into a bundle. **infagottàrsi,** *v.refl.* to wrap oneself up; dress carelessly; dress like a guy.

infal'ibile, *a.* infallible; unfailing. **infallibilità,** *f.* infallibility.

infamàre (*pr.* -àmo), *v.t.* to defame; slander; render infamous; disgrace. **infamàrsi,** *v.refl.* to bring shame upon oneself; disgrace oneself. **infamatòrio** (*pl.* -òri), *a.* slanderous; defamatory; disgraceful. **infàme,** *a.* infamous, scandalous; of ill fame. **infàmia,** *f.* infamy; shame; disgrace; shameful action.

infangàre (*pr.* -àngo, -ànghi), *v.t.* to bespatter or stain with mud.

infànte, *m.* infant. **infantería,** *f.* infantry. **infanticída,** *m.* (*m.pl.* -cídi, *f.pl.* -cíde) child-murderer. ¶ *a.* infanticidal. **infanticidio,** *m.* infanticide; child-murder. **infantíle,** *a.* infantile; childish. *asilo* ~, kindergarten; children's shelter. **infànzia,** *f.* infancy; childhood; children.

infarcíre (*pr.* -ísco, -ísci), *v.t.* to stuff; cram.

infarinàre, *v.t.* to sprinkle with flour; powder; (*fig.*) give a smattering (of). **infarinàrsi,** *v.refl.* to become covered with flour; powder oneself; get a smattering (of). **infarinatúra,** *f.* sprinkling of flour; (*fig.*) smattering.

infastidíre (*pr.* -ísco, -ísci), *v.t.* to annoy; bore; disgust; molest.

infaticàbile, *a.* indefatigable; tireless.

infàtti, *ad.* in fact; indeed; really.

infattíbile, *a.* unfeasible; impracticable.

infatuàrsi, *v.refl.* to become infatuated. **infatuazióne**, *f.* infatuation.

infàusto, *a.* inauspicious; unlucky.

infecóndo, *a.* barren; unfruitful.

infedèle, *a.* unfaithful; faithless; infidel; inaccurate; dishonest; false. ¶ *m.* unfaithful person; infidel; unbeliever. **infedeltà**, *f.inv.* infidelity; unfaithfulness; faithlessness; breach of trust.

infelíce, *a.* unhappy; unfortunate; unsuccessful; unlucky; difficult; awkward. **infelicità**, *f.* unhappiness.

infemminíre (*pr.* **-ísco, -ísci**), *v.i.* (*aux.* essere) to become effeminate.

inferènza, *f.* inference.

inferióre, *a.* lower; bottom; under; nether; inferior; less. ¶ *m.* inferior (*pers.*). **inferiorità**, *f.* inferiority.

inferíre (*pr.* **-ísco, -ísci**), *v.i.* (*aux.* avere) to infer; deduce. *v.t.* to inflict.

infermàre (*pr.* **-érmo**), *v.t.* to weaken; to nullify. **infermàrsi**, *v.refl.* to become ill; fall ill. **infermería**, *f.* infirmary; hospital; sick-room (*Sch.*). ~ *di bordo*, sickbay (*Naut.*). **infermíccio** (*pl.* **-ícci**), *a.* sickly. **infermièra**, *f.* (sick-)nurse. **infermière**, *m.* hospital attendant; h. orderly; male-nurse. **infermità**, *f.inv.* infirmity; illness; sickness; disease. **inférmo**, *a.* infirm; ill; sick; weak. ¶ *m.* sick person; patient.

infernàle, *a.* infernal; hellish. **inférno**, *m.* hell; inferno.

inferocíre (*pr.* **-ísco, -ísci**), *v.t.* to make fierce or ferocious. *v.i* (*aux.* essere) & **inferocírsi**, *v.refl.* to become ferocious; *v.i.* (*aux.* avere) to commit acts of cruelty.

inferriàta, *f.* iron grating; grille.

infèrtile, *a.* unfertile. **infertilíre** (*pr.* **-ísco, -ísci**), *v.t.* to fertilize. **infertilità**, *f.* infertility; barrenness.

infervoràre, *v.t.* to fill with fervour; inspire with enthusiasm; animate.

infestàre (*pr.* **-èsto**), *v.t.* to infest; ravage; importune; molest. **infesto**, *a.* harmful; hurtful; obnoxious; tiresome; hostile.

infettàre (*pr.* **-ètto**), *v.t.* to infect; corrupt; taint. **infettívo**, *a.* infectious; contagious. **infezióne**, *f.* infection, contagion.

infiacchíre (*pr.* **-ísco, -ísci**), *v.t.* to weaken; enfeeble; enervate. *v.i.* (*aux.* essere) & **infiacchírsi**, *v.refl.*

to grow weak; lose one's strength; become enfeebled.

infiammàbile, *a.* inflammable. **infiammabilità**, *f.* inflammability. *punto di* ~, *m.* flash point. **infiammàre** (*pr.* **-àmmo**), *v.t.* to inflame; set on fire; kindle; excite. **infiammazióne**, *f.* inflammation. ~ *spontanea*, spontaneous combustion.

infiascàre (*pr.* **-àsco, -àschi**), *v.t.* to bottle; put in flasks.

infído, *a.* unfaithful; untrustworthy; faithless.

infieríre (*pr.* **-ísco, -ísci**), *v.i.* (*aux.* essere) to rage (*plague, fever, &c.*). *v.i.* (*aux.* avere) to be cruel or pitiless; become savage.

infievolíre (*pr.* **-ísco, -ísci**), *v.t.* to enfeeble; weaken. *v.i.* & **infievolírsi**, *v.refl.* to grow feeble; grow weak.

infíggere (*pr.* **-íggo, -íggi**, *&c.*, like *figgere*), *v.t.* *ir.* to drive in(to); fix (in); nail. **infíggersi**, *v.refl.* to penetrate; get driven in(to); go deep in(to); become impressed (*in memory &c.*).

infiguràbile, *a.* impossible to imagine.

infilacàppi & **infilaguaíne**, *m.inv.* bodkin.

infilàre, *v.t.* to thread (*needle*); string (*beads*); file (*documents, papers*); slip on; run through; transfix; push in; insert; go down, turn into (*street, road*); (*Mil.*) enfilade. *non ne infila mai una*, he never succeeds in anything. **infilàta**, *f.* series; row; suite; (*Mil.*) enfilade. **infilatúra**, *f.* threading; stringing; slipping on.

infiltraménto, *m.* & **infiltrazióne**, *f.* infiltration. **infiltràrsi**, *v.refl.* to infiltrate; percolate; seep; (*fig.*) creep (into).

infilzàre, *v.t.* to pierce; run through (*sword*); string together (*lit. & fig.*); file (*documents*). **infilzàta**, *f.* series; row; string; suite. **infilzatúra**, *f.* running through; stringing together; things strung together; unclassified items in a library.

infimaménte, *ad.* to the last degree; in the lowest place. **ínfimo**, *a.* lowest; very low; last. ¶ *m.* lowest place.

infíne, *ad.* at last; finally; after all.

infingardàggine, *f.* laziness; sloth-[fulness]. **infingardíre** (*pr.* **-ísco, -ísci**), *v.t.* to make lazy. *v.i.* (*aux.* essere) become lazy. **infingàrdo**, *a.* lazy; slothful; slack.

infíngersi, *v.refl. ir.* to feign; pretend.
infinità, *f.inv.* infinity; infinitude; vast number; great crowd. **infinitesìmàle**, *a.* infinitesimal. **infiníto**, *a.* infinite; boundless; limitless; numberless; (*Gram.*) infinitive. ¶ *m.* infinite; (*Gram.*) infinitive; (*Math.*) infinity.
infíno (a), *pr.* till; until; up to; as far as.
infinocchiàre, *v.t.* (*pop.*) to make a fool of; take in; deceive; impose upon.
infioccàto, *a.* tasselled.
infiochíre (*pr.* -ìsco, -ìsci), *v.i.* (*aux.* essere) to become hoarse.
infioràre (*pr.* -òro), *v.t.* to strew or deck with flowers.
infiorentírsi (*pr.* -ìsco, -ìsci), *v.refl.* to assume Florentine ways; became a Florentine; get a Florentine accent.
infiorescènza, *f.* inflorescence.
infirmàre, *v.t.* to invalidate; weaken; annul.
infischiàrsi (di), *v.refl.* to make light of; be indifferent to; not to care (for); laugh (at).
infísso, *p.p.* of *infiggere.* ¶ *m.* insertion; frame (*door, window*); (*pl.*) fixtures.
infittíre (*pr.* -ìsco, -ìsci), *v.i.* (*aux.* essere) to thicken; grow dense; become heavy (*rain, &c.*).
inflazióne, *f.* inflation (*Fin.*). **inflazionìsta**, *a.* inflationary; inflationist.
inflessíbile, *a.* inflexible. **inflessióne**, *f.* inflection.
inflèsso, *p.a.* inflected; bent. **inflèttere** (*pr.* -ètto), *v.t. ir.* to inflect; bend.
inflíggere (*pr.* -íggo, -íggi) like *affliggere*), *v.t. ir.* to inflict. **infliizióne**, *f.* infliction.
influènte, *a.* influential. ¶ *m.* affluent; tributary. **influènza**, *f.* influence; influenza. **influenzàre**, *v.t.* to influence; affect; sway; bias.
influíre (*pr.* -ìsco, -ìsci), *v.i.* (*aux.* avere) to have influence; exert influence. ~*su*, to influence (*v.t.*). **inflússo**, *m.* influx; influence; effect.
infocàre (*pr.* -uòco, -uòchi), *v.t.* to heat (up); make red hot; inflame; excite. **infocàrsi**, *v.refl.* to become hot; become red-hot (*lit. & fig.*). **infocàto**, *a.* burning; blazing; ardent; red-hot; flame-coloured.
infoderàre (*pr.* -òdero), *v.t.* to sheathe.

infognàrsi (*pr.* -ógno), *v.refl.* to sink; plunge deeply; get bogged.
in-fòlio, *m.* folio (*book*).
infoltíre (*pr.* -ìsco, -ìsci), *v.i.* (*aux.* essere) to thicken; become thick.
infondàto, *a.* unfounded; groundless.
infóndere (*pr.* -óndo, &c., like *fondere*), *v.t. ir.* to infuse; instil.
inforcàre (*pr.* -órco, -órchi), *v.t.* to take up on a pitch-fork; bestride; get on (*horse, bicycle*); put on (*spectacles*). **inforcàta**, *f.* quantity of hay taken up by a (pitch-)fork. **inforcatúra**, *f.* forking; bestriding; bifurcation.
informàre (*pr.* -órmo), *v.t.* to inform; notify; acquaint; pervade; permeate; spread through; inspire; imbue; give shape to; form; characterize. **informazióne**, *f.* (*often pl.*) information; piece of information. *ufficio* ~*i*, *m.* inquiry office. *servizio* ~*i*, *m.* intelligence service.
informe, *a.* shapeless.
informicolíre (*pr.* -ìsco, -ìsci), *v.t.* to cause to tingle; give one pins and needles. **informicolírsi**, *v.refl.* to tingle.
infornàre, *v.t.* to put in the oven. **infornàta**, *f.* batch of bread in the oven; (*fig.*) bunch, group.
infortíre (*pr.* -ìsco, -ìsci), *v.i.* (*aux.* essere) to turn sour.
infortúnio (*pl.* -úni), *m.* accident; casualty; misfortune; mischance.
infoscàre (*pr.* -ósco, -óschi), *v.t.* to darken; (*fig.*) confuse; perplex. *v.i.* (*aux.* essere) & **infoscàrsi**, *v.refl.* to become dark.
infossàre (*pr.* -òsso), *v.t.* to bury; excavate. **infossàrsi**, *v.refl.* to sink. **infossato**, *a.* sunken; fallen in; buried.
ínfra, *pr.* between; among.
infracidàre & **infradiciàre** (*pr.* -àdicio, -àdici), *v.t.* to wet; drench; soak. *v.i.* (*aux.* essere) to rot.
infracidíre & **infradicíre**, *v.i.* (*aux.* essere) to rot; decay; go bad.
infradiciàto, *a.* drenched; wet to the skin; wet through.
infralíre (*pr.* -ìsco, -ìsci), *v.t.* to weaken. *v.i.* (*aux.* essere) to grow weak.
inframmettènte, *a.* meddlesome. ¶ *m.* meddler; intruder. **inframméttere** (*pr.* -étto, &c., like *mettere*), *v.t. ir.* to interpose.

inframméttersi, *v.refl.* to meddle; intrude; interfere.

inframmischiàre, *v.t.* to intermingle; intermix. **inframmischiàrsi,** *v.refl.* to mingle (with); intermingle (with).

infranceśàre & **infranciośàre,** *v.t.* to Gallicize.

in ràngere (*pr.* **-ángo, -ángi,** &c., *like frangere*), *v.t. ir.* to break; shatter; crush; infringe; violate. **infrangíbile,** *a.* unbreakable. **infrànto,** *p.p.* of *infrangere.* **infrantóio,** *m.* olive-press; oil-press.

infrappórre (*pr.* **-póngo, -póni,** &c., *like porre*), *v.t. ir.* to interpose.

infrar[r]ósso, *a.* infra-red (*rays*).

infrascàre & **infrasconàre,** *v.t.* to cover with branches; (*fig.*) to overload with ornaments. **infrascàrsi,** *v.refl.* to hide under the branches or among the leaves.

infrascritto, *a.* undermentioned.

infrattànto, *ad.* meanwhile, in the meantime.

infrazióne, *f.* infringement; violation.

infreddàre (*pr.* **-éddo**), *v.t.* to cool. *v.i.* (*aux.* essere) & **infreddàrsi,** *v.refl.* to catch cold. **infreddatúra,** *f.* (a) cold. **infreddolíre** (*pr.* **-ísco, -ísci**), *v.i.* (*aux.* essere) & **infreddolírsi,** *v.refl.* to shiver with cold.

infrenàbile, *a.* unrestrainable. **infrenàre,** *v.t.* to restrain.

infrigidíre (*pr.* **-ísco, -ísci**), *v.t.* to chill. *v.i.* (*aux.* essere) to become chilled.

infrollíre (*pr.* **-ísco, -ísci**), *v.t.* to soften. *v.i.* (*aux.* essere) to become tender; become high (*of meat*); become weak or exhausted.

infrondíre (*pr.* **-ísco, -ísci**), *v.i.* (*aux.* essere) to become leafy; put on leaves.

infronzolàre, *v.t.* to deck out; trim up.

infruttífero & **infruttuóso,** *a.* unfruitful; unprofitable.

infuòri, *pr.* & *ad.* out; outwards. *all'* ~ *di,* with the exception of, except.

infurbíre (*pr.* **-ísco, -ísci**), *v.i.* (*aux.* essere) to grow cunning; become shrewd.

infuriàre, *v.t.* to enrage; infuriate; make angry. *v.i.* (*aux.* avere) to rage. *v.i.* (*aux.* essere) & **infuriarsi,** *v.refl.* to fly into a passion; lose one's temper.

infuśióne, *f.* infusion. **infúśo,** *p.p.* of *infondere.* ¶ *m.* infusion.

infuśòri, *m.pl.* infusoria.

ingabbanàrsi, *v.refl.* to wrap oneself in a cloak.

ingabbiàre, *v.t.* to cage; coop; set up the frame of a ship.

ingaggiàre, *v.t.* to engage; enlist; join (*battle*). **ingàggio** (*pl.* **-àggi**), *m.* enlistment; engagement.

ingagliardíre (*pr.* **-ísco, -ísci**), *v.t.* to strengthen. *v.i.* (*aux.* essere) & **ingagliardírsi,** *v.refl.* to grow strong; become stronger.

ingalluzírsi (*pr.* **-ísco, -ísci**), *v.refl.* to become elated; show off, give oneself airs.

ingangheràre, *v.t.* to hinge.

ingannàre (*pr.* **-ànno**), *v.t.* to deceive; cheat; beguile. **ingannàrsi,** *v.refl.* to be mistaken; to deceive oneself. **ingannatóre,** *m.* (*f.* **-tríce**) deceiver; cheat. ¶ *a.* deceiving.

ingannévole, *a.* deceitful; deceptive. **ingànno,** *m.* deceit; deception; trick; fraud; stratagem.

ingarbugliàre, *v.t.* to entangle; confuse; perplex; muddle; embroil. **ingarbuglióne,** *m.* muddler.

ingavonàrsi, *v.refl.* (*ship*) to heel (over), list.

ingegnàrsi, *v.refl.* to strive; exert oneself; endeavour; try.

ingegnère, *m.* engineer. **ingegnería,** *f.* engineering.

ingégno, *m.* talent; intelligence; understanding; ability; wit(s); genius; device; contrivance; tool; mechanism. **ingegnóso,** *a.* ingenious.

ingelosíre (*pr.* **-ísco, -ísci**), *v.t.* to make jealous. *v.i.* (*aux.* essere) & **ingelosírsi,** *v.refl.* to become jealous.

ingemmàre, *v.t.* to adorn with jewels. **ingemmàrsi,** *v.refl.* to deck oneself with jewels; bud.

ingeneràre, *v.t.* to engender; (*fig.*) produce.

ingeneróso, *a.* ungenerous.

ingènito, *a.* inborn; innate.

ingènte, *a.* huge; vast; enormous.

ingentiliménto, *m.* refinement; refining. **ingentilíre** (*pr.* **-ísco, -ísci**), *v.t.* to refine; civilize; ennoble. **ingentilírsi,** *v.refl.* to become refined; learn manners; become civilized.

ingenuaménte, *ad.* ingenuously; innocently. **ingenuità,** *f.* ingenuousness; simplicity; simple-

mindedness. **ingènuo**, *a.* ingenuous; frank; simple-minded.
ingerènza, *f.* interference. **ingeríre** (*pr.* -ísco, -ísci), *v.t.* to arouse; (*Med.*) ingest. **ingerírsi**, *v.refl.* to meddle; interfere.
ingessàre, *v.t.* to plaster; whitewash; chalk (*a cue*); set in plaster of Paris.
inghiaiàta, *f.* ballast (*Road, Rly.*).
Inghiltèrra (l'), *f.* England.
inghiottíre (*pr.* -ísco, -ísci), *v.t.* to swallow; swallow up; engulf.
inghirlandàre, *v.t.* to wreathe; engarland; encircle.
ingiallíre (*pr.* -ísco, -ísci), *v.t.* to yellow; make yellow. *v.i.* (*aux.* essere) to yellow; become yellow.
ingigantíre (*pr.* -ísco, -ísci), *v.t.* to magnify; exaggerate. *v.i.* (*aux.* essere) & **ingigantírsi**, *v.refl.* to become gigantic; be magnified or exaggerated.
inginocchiàrsi, *v.refl.* to kneel (down); go down on one's knees; fall on one's knees. **inginocchiàto**, *a.* kneeling; on one's knees. **inginocchiatóio**, *m.* kneeling stool; fald-stool. **inginocchióni**, *ad.* on one's knees.
ingioiàrsi & **ingioiellàrsi**, *v.refl.* to wear jewels; adorn oneself with jewels.
ingiú, *ad.* downwards; down.
ingiúngere (*pr.* -úngo, -úngi, &c., like *giungere*), *v.t. ir.* to enjoin; command; prescribe. **ingiunzióne**, *f.* injunction; order.
ingiúria (*pl.* -úrie), *f.* insult; affront; abuse; damage; outrage; wrong. **ingiuriàre**, *v.t.* to insult; abuse; revile; wrong. **ingiurióso**, *a.* insulting; offensive; abusive; outrageous.
ingiustificàto, *a.* unwarranted; unjustified. **ingiustízia**, *f.* injustice; wrong; injury. **ingiústo**, *a.* unjust; unfair; wrongful; unlawful.
inglése, *a.* English. ¶ *m.f.* Englishman; Englishwoman. *l'* ~, English, the English language. *gli Inglesi*, the English, the English people.
ingobbíre (*pr.* -ísco, -ísci), *v.i.* (*aux.* essere) to become hunchbacked.
ingoffíre (*pr.* -ísco, -ísci), *v.t.* to make awkward or clumsy. *v.i.* (*aux.* essere) & **ingoffírsi**, *v.refl.* to become awkward.
ingoiàre (*pr.* -óio, -ói), *v.t.* to swallow (up, down); engulf.

ingolfàrsi, *v.refl.* to plunge (into); be engulfed (in). **ingolfàto**, *a.* (*fig.*) engaged (in); absorbed (in). ~ *nei debiti*, deep in debt.
ingollàre, *v.t.* to gulp down; gobble up; bolt (*food*).
ingolosíre (*pr.* -ísco, -ísci), *v.t.* to make one's mouth water; excite one's greed. *v.i.* (*aux.* essere) & **ingolosírsi**, *v.refl.* to become greedy.
ingombrànte, *a.* cumbersome; encumbering. **ingombràre**, *v.t.* to encumber; be in one's way; obstruct; block up; crowd. **ingómbro**, *sync. p.p.* encumbered. ¶ *m.* encumbrance; obstruction, obstacle.
ingommàre, *v.t.* to gum.
ingordaménte, *ad.* greedily; eagerly. **ingordígia**, *f.* greed, greediness. **ingórdo**, *a.* greedy; gluttonous; covetous; eager; exorbitant. ¶ *m.* glutton.
ingorgàre (*pr.* -órgo, -órghi), *v.t.* to obstruct; choke (up). **ingorgàrsi**, *v.refl.* to be choked; become blocked. **ingórgo** (*pl.* -órghi), *m.* obstruction; blocking (up).
ingozzàre (*pr.* -ózzo), *v.t.* to swallow (*lit.* & *fig.*); gulp down; devour; cram. ~ *il cappello*, to pull one's hat down over one's eyes.
ingracilíre (*pr.* -ísco, -ísci), *v.i.* (*aux.* essere) & **ingracilírsi**, *v.refl.* to grow slim; become thin.
ingranàggio, *m.* (*Mech.*) gear; gearing; (*fig.*) mechanism; working. *scatola dell'* ~, gear-box. ~ *dello sterzo*, (*Motor*) steering gear. ~ *della prima velocità*, low gear (*Motor*). **ingranàre**, *v.t.* to put into gear. *v.i.* (*aux.* essere) to be in gear.
ingranchíre (*pr.* -ísco, -ísci), *v.t.* to benumb.
ingrandiménto, *m.* enlargement; increase; magnification. *lente d'* ~, *f.* magnifying-glass. **ingrandíre** (*pr.* -ísco, -ísci), *v.t.* to enlarge; magnify; increase; amplify; exaggerate. *v.i.* (*aux.* essere) & **ingrandírsi**, *v.refl.* to become larger; increase. **ingranditóre** (*f.* -tríce), *a.* magnifying; enlarging. ¶ *m.* enlarger; magnifier.
ingrassàggio, *m.* greasing, oiling. **ingrassaménto**, *m.* fattening. **ingrassàre**, *v.t.* to fatten; enrich; manure; grease; lubricate. *v.i.* (*aux.* essere) & **ingrassàrsi**, *v.refl.* to fatten; grow fat. **ingrassatóre**, *m.*

fattener; lubricator. **ingràsso,** m. fattening; manure.

ingratamente, ad. ungratefully; unpleasantly.

ingraticciàre, v.t. to trellis. **ingraticciàta,** f. trellis; trellis-work; lattice-work.

ingraticolàre, v.t. to close with a grating or fence. **ingraticolàto,** m. grating.

ingratitúdine, f. ingratitude; ungratefulness. **ingràto,** a. ungrateful; thankless; hard; difficult; unpleasant; unprofitable; (land) barren; sterile.

ingravidàre, v.t. to make pregnant. v.i. (aux. essere) to become pregnant.

ingraziàrsi, v.refl. to ingratiate oneself (with); to get into one's good graces.

ingrediènte, m. ingredient.

ingrèsso, m. entrance; entry; admittance. vietato l' ~, no admittance.

ingrinzíre (pr. -ísco, -ísci), v.t. to wrinkle. v.i. (aux. essere) & **ingrinzírsi,** v.refl. to become wrinkled.

ingrossaménto, m. enlargement; increase; swelling; thickening. **ingrossàre** (pr. -òsso), v.t. to swell; increase; make bigger; thicken; blunt; dull. v.i. (aux. essere) & **ingrossàrsi,** v.refl. to grow big[ger]; become stout; increase; swell; rise. **ingròsso (all')** ad. expr. wholesale.

ingrugníre (pr. -ísco, -ísci), v.i. (aux. essere) & **ingrugnírsi,** v.refl. to look sulky, pout.

ingrullíre (pr. -ísco, -ísci), v.i. (aux. essere) to become stupid.

inguadàbile, a. unfordable.

inguainàre (pr. -aíno), v.t. to sheath(e).

inguantàrsi, v.refl. to put on one's gloves. **inguantàto,** a. gloved; wearing gloves.

inguaríbile, a. incurable.

ínguine, m. groin.

inibíre (pr. -ísco, -ísci), v.t. to inhibit; prohibit; forbid; restrain.

iniettàre, v.t. to inject. **inezióne,** f. injection.

inimicàre, v.t. (pr. -íco, -íchi), v.t. to treat as an enemy; alienate; estrange; set at variance. **inimicàrsi,** v.refl. to quarrel; be at variance (with); make an enemy of. **inimicízia,** f. enmity; hostility. **inimíco** (pl. -íci), a. inimical; hostile.

ininterrótto, a. uninterrupted.

iniquaménte, ad. wrongly; wickedly; unjustly. **iniquità,** f.inv. wickedness; wrong; injustice. **iníquo,** a. wicked; iniquitous; unfair; unjust; wretched; abominable.

iniziàle, a. initial; commencing; opening; starting. ¶ f. initial; initial letter. **iniziàre,** v.t. to initiate; begin; commence; open; enter upon; enter into. **iniziatíva,** f. initiative; enterprise. **iniziàto,** m. initiate. **iniziazióne,** f. initiation. **inízio** (pl. -ízi), m. beginning; commencement. calcio d' ~, kick-off (football).

innacquàre (pr. -àcquo), v.t. to water down; dilute.

innaffiàre, v.t. to water; sprinkle. **innaffiatóio,** m. watering-pot, w.-can; sprinkler. **innaffiatríce,** f. watering cart.

innalzaménto, m. raising; heightening; elevation. **innalzàre,** v.t. to raise; erect; heighten. **innalzàrsi,** v. refl. to rise.

innamoraménto, m. falling in love; love; courtship. **innamoràre** (pr. -oro), v.t. to charm; attract; fascinate; inspire love in; win the love of. **innamoràrsi (di),** v.refl. to fall in love (with). **innamoràto,** a. in love (with), enamoured (of); fond (of). ¶ m. (f. -a) lover; sweetheart.

innànzi, pr. before; in the presence of; in preference to. ¶ ad. forward; on; in front. andare ~, tirare ~, to go on. piú ~, farther, further (on); at a later stage. essere ~ negli anni, to be [well] on in years.

innàrio (pl. -àri), m. hymnary.

innàto, a. innate; inborn. **innaturàle,** a. unnatural.

innavigàbile, a. unnavigable; unseaworthy. **innegàbile,** a. undeniable.

inneggiàre (pr. -éggio, -éggi), v.t. to extol; praise; hymn the praises of. v.i. (aux. avere) to sing hymns.

innescàre, v.t. to prime (blasting, artill.). **innésco,** m. priming.

innestaménto, m. & **innestatúra,** f. grafting.

innestàre (pr. -èsto), v.t. to graft; cross (in breeding); give an inoculation; (Mech.) insert; engage; plug. **innestatóio,** m. grafting-knife. **innèsto,** m. graft; shoot; inoculation; (Mech.) clutch.

ínno, m. hymn. ~ nazionale, national anthem.

innocènte, *a.* innocent. ¶ *m.* innocent (child); foundling. *dim. innocentino.*
innocènza, *f.* innocence; (*fig.*) infancy; childhood.
innocívo & **innòcuo,** *a.* harmless; inoffensive.
innodía, *f.* hymnody. **innògrafo,** *m.* hymn-writer; composer of hymns. **innología,** *f.* hymnology.
innominàbile, *a.* unnameable; unmentionable; shameful. **innominàto,** *a.* nameless; unnamed.
innovàre (*pr.* -**òvo**), *v.t.* to innovate; change, alter. **innovatóre,** *m.* (*f.* -**tríce**) innovator. ¶ *a.* innovating.
innumeràbile & **innumerévole,** *a.* innumerable; countless.
inoccupàto, *a.* unoccupied; at leisure, leisured.
inoculàre (*pr.* -**òculo**), *v.t.* to inoculate; give an inoculation of.
inodóro, *a.* inodorous; scentless; without smell.
inoffensíbile, *a.* invulnerable. **inoffensívo,** *a.* inoffensive; harmless. **inofféso,** *a.* unhurt.
inofficióso, *a.* (*Law*) of no effect; invalid.
inoltràre (*pr.* -**óltro**), *v.t.* to put forward; forward; send (on). **inoltràrsi,** *v.refl.* to advance; penetrate; enter (upon, into). **inoltràto,** *a.* late; advanced.
inóltre, *ad.* besides.
inondàre (*pr.* -**óndo**), *v.t.* to flood; inundate; overflow. **inondazióne,** *f.* flood, inundation.
inonestà, *f.* dishonesty. **inonèsto,** *a.* not honest; dishonest.
inonoràto, *a.* unhonoured.
inoperóso, *a.* idle; inactive.
inòpia, *f.* poverty; want; indigence.
inopinàbile, *a.* incredible; inconceivable; not to be foreseen. **inopinàto,** *a.* unexpected; unforeseen.
inopportúno, *a.* inopportune; unseasonable; untimely; awkward.
inoppugnàbile, *a.* incontestable; unobjectionable.
inordinàto, *a.* inordinate; excessive; disorderly.
inorgànico (*pl.* -**ànici**), *a.* inorganic.
inorgoglíre (*pr.* -**ísco,** -**ísci**), *v.t.* to make proud; puff up; elate. *v.i.* (*aux.* essere) & **inorgoglírsi,** *v.refl.* to grow proud; be puffed up; be elated.
inorpellàre (*pr.* -**èllo**), *v.t.* to tinsel.
inorridíre (*pr.* -**ísco,** -**ísci**), *v.i.* to terrify; frighten; strike with horror. *v.i.* (*aux.* essere) to be terrified; be struck with terror; be aghast.
inospitàle, *a.* inhospitable. **inòspite,** *a.* uninhabitable.
inosservànte, *a.* unobservant. **inosservànza,** *f.* non-observance; inattention. **inosservàto,** *a.* unobserved, unnoticed.
inossidàbile, *f.* rustless. *acciaio* ~, stainless steel.
in-ottàvo, *a.* & *m.* octavo.
inottusíre (*pr.* -**ísco,** -**ísci**), *v.i.* (*aux.* essere) to become blunt; (*fig.*) become dull.
inquadràre, *v.t.* to frame; distribute; arrange; enroll.
inqualificàbile, *a.* unspeakable; beyond words.
in-quàrto, *a.* & *m.* quarto.
inquietàre (*pr.* -**éto**), *v.t.* to disquiet; make uneasy; worry; harass. **inquiéto,** *a.* restless; uneasy; worried; anxious. **inquietúdine,** *f.* uneasiness; disquietude; restlessness; apprehension.
inquilíno, *m.* (*f.* -**a**) tenant; lodger.
inquirènte, *a.* investigating; examining. **inquisíre** (*pr.* -**ísco,** -**ísci**), *v.t.* to investigate; inquire into; search. *v.i.* (*aux.* avere) to inquire. **inquisitívo,** *a.* inquisitive. **inquisitóre,** *m.* inquisitor. **inquisizióne,** *f.* inquisition.
insabbiàre, *v.t.* to cover with sand.
insaccàre (*pr.* -**àcco,** -**àcchi**), *v.t.* to put in a sack; pack; stuff; fill (*sausage-skins,* &c.). **insaccàrsi,** *v.refl.* to pack oneself in(to); crowd (into); hide; dress like a guy. **insaccàto,** *p.a.* packed in[to] a sack; dressed in ill-fitting clothes. *corsa degli insaccati,* *f.* sack-race.
insalàta, *f.* salad. *condire l'* ~, to dress the salad. **insalatièra,** *f.* salad bowl.
insalúbre, *a.* unhealthy; insalubrious. **insalubrità,** *f.* insalubrity; unhealthiness.
insalvatichíre, *see* inselvatichire.
insanàbile, *a.* incurable.
insanguinàre (*pr.* -**ànguino**), *v.t.* to stain with blood. **insanguinàto,** *a.* blood-stained; bloody.
insània, *f.* madness; insanity; folly. **insaníre** (*pr.* -**ísco,** -**ísci**), *v.i.* (*aux.* essere) to go mad; become insane. **insàno,** *a.* insane; mad; foolish.
insaponàre (*pr.* -**óno**), *v.t.* to soap; lather; (*fig.*) flatter. **insaponàta** & **insaponatúra,** *f.* soaping; lathering.

insaporíre (*pr.* -**ísco**, -**ísci**), *v.t.* to flavour. **insaporíto**, *a.* tasty.

insapúta (**all'**), *ad. expr.* unknown (to); without the knowledge (of). *a mia* ~, unknown to me.

insaziàbile, *a.* insatiable. **insaziàto**, *a.* unsated; unappeased.

inscatolàre, *v.t.* to tin, can.

inscrívere (*pr.* -**ívo**, *&c.*, like *scrivere*), *v.t. ir.* to inscribe; enter; record. **inscríversi**, *v.refl.* to enter (for); enter one's name (for); subscribe. **inscrizióne**, *f.* inscription. Cf. **iscrivere**.

insecchíre (*pr.* -**ísco**, -**ísci**), *v.t.* to dry; dry up; shrivel. *v.i.* (*aux.* essere) to become dry; dry up; shrivel.

insediaménto, *m.* installation (*in office*); entering upon (*office*). **insediàre** (*pr.* -**èdio**, -**èdi**), *v.t.* to install. **insediàrsi**, *v.refl.* to enter upon office, be installed; settle.

in-sedicèsimo, *a. & m.* sextodecimo; *abb.* 16mo.

inségna, *f.* flag; standard; colours; coat of arms; sign-board; ensign; standard-bearer; badge; attribute.

insegnaménto, *m.* teaching; instruction; tuition; education; lesson; precept. **insegnànte**, *m.* teacher. ¶ *a.* teaching. **insegnàre**, *v.t.* to teach; show.

inseguiménto, *m.* pursuit. **inseguíre** (*pr.* -**ísco**, -**ísci**), *v.t.* to pursue; follow.

inselciàre (*pr.* -**élcio**, -**élci**), *v.t.* to pave.

insellàre (*pr.* -**èllo**), *v.t.* to saddle.

inselvatichíre (*pr.* -**ísco**, -**ísci**), to make wild. *v.i.* (*aux.* essere) & **inselvatichírsi**, *v.refl.* to become wild.

inseminàto, *a.* unsown; (*fig.*) desert[ed], abandoned, wild.

insenàrsi, *v.refl.* to form an inlet, small bay or harbour. **insenatúra**, *f.* inlet; creek; small bay; harbour; recess; loop.

insensatézza, *f.* senselessness; folly. **insensàto**, *a.* senseless; crazy; foolish. **insensíbile**, *a.* insensible; hard; unfeeling; dull; indifferent; imperceptible.

insepólto, *a.* unburied.

inseriménto, *m.* insertion. **inseríre** (*pr.* -**ísco**, -**ísci**), *v.t.* to insert, enclose; (*Elec.*) connect, plug in. **inserírsi**, *v.refl.* to be included; become part (of). **insèrta**, *f.* enclosure; enclosed document.

insèrto, *a.* inserted; grafted; united; enclosed. ¶ *m.* enclosure[s]; papers; file of documents; brief. **inserviènte**, *m.* attendant. **inserzióne**, *f.* insertion; advertisement.

insètto, *m.* insect. *polvere insetticida*, *f.* insect powder. **insettívoro**, *a.* insectivorous.

insídia, *f.* snare; trap; ambush; plot; deceit; danger. **insidiàre**, *v.t.* to lay traps for; ensnare; lie in wait for; try to seduce. ~ (**a,**) *v.i.* to make an attempt on (*life, honour, &c.*).

insiéme, *ad.* together; in company; at the same time. *mettere* ~, to accumulate; put together; assemble (*Mech.*). ¶ *m.* whole; complex; combination; total result; general effect. *nell'* ~, on the whole.

insiepàrsi, *v.refl.* to shelter or hide behind a hedge.

insígne, *a.* signal; famous; illustrious; arrant; notorious.

insignificànte, *a.* insignificant; meaningless; expressionless.

insigníre (*pr.* -**ísco**, -**ísci**), *v.t.* to decorate (*with a title or distinction*).

insignorírsi (*pr.* -**ísco**, -**ísci**), *v.refl.* to become master (of); take possession (of); become rich or powerful.

insíno, *pr.* till; until; to; as far as. ¶ *ad.* even. ~ (**a**) *che*, *c.* till; until; as long as.

insinuàre (*pr.* -**ínuo**), *v.t.* to insinuate; suggest; instil; infuse. **insinuàrsi**, *v.refl.* to insinuate oneself (into); creep, penetrate (into). **insinuazióne**, *f.* insinuation; hint; suggestion.

insípido, *a.* insipid; tasteless.

insipiènte, *a.* silly; foolish. **insipiènza**, *f.* silliness; foolishness; ignorance.

insístere (*pr.* -**ísto**), *v.i.* (*aux.* avere) to insist.

ínsito, *a.* innate; inborn.

insoàve, *a.* unpleasant; disagreeable.

insociévole & **insociàbile**, *a.* unsociable. **insociàle**, *a.* unsocial.

inso[d]disfàtto, *a.* unsatisfied; dissatisfied.

insofferènte, *a.* intolerant. **insoffríbile**, *a.* insufferable; unbearable; intolerable.

insolazióne, *f.* sun-stroke.

insolènte, *a.* insolent; impudent; saucy. **insolènza**, *f.* insolence; impertinence; piece of impertinence.

insolfàre (*pr.* -sólfo), *v.t.* to fumigate with sulphur.

insòlito, *a.* unwonted; unusual.

insolùbile, *a.* insoluble.

insolùto, *a.* unsolved; unpaid.

insolvènte, *a.* insolvent. insolvènza, *f.* insolvency. insolvíbile, *a.* (*of debt*) that cannot be paid.

insómma, *ad.* in short, in conclusion; in a word; on the whole; after all.

insommergíbile, *a.* unsinkable.

insondàbile, *a.* unfathomable.

insònne, *a.* sleepless. insònnia, *f.* sleeplessness; insomnia. insonníto & insonnolíto, *a.* sleepy; drowsy.

insordíre (*pr.* -ísco, -ísci), *v.i.* (*aux.* essere) to grow deaf.

insórgere (*pr.* -órgo, -órgi, &c., like sorgere), *v.i. ir.* (*aux.* essere) to rise; revolt; rebel. insorgiménto, *m.* rising; revolt; insurrection. insórto, *p.p.* of insorgere. ¶ *m.* rebel; insurgent; rioter.

insospettàto, *a.* unsuspected. insospettíre (*pr.* -ísco, -ísci), *v.t.* to rouse one's suspicions; make one suspicious. insospettírsi, *v.refl.* to grow suspicious; begin to suspect.

insostanziàle, *a.* unsubstantial.

insozzàre (*pr.* -ózzo), *v.t.* to soil; dirty; (*fig.*) sully.

insperàbile, *a.* not to be hoped for; beyond hope or expectation. insperàto, *a.* unhoped for; unexpected.

inspessíre (*pr.* -ísco, -ísci), *v.t.* & inspessírsi, *v.refl.* to thicken.

inspiegàbile, *a.* inexplicable. inspiegàto, *a.* unexplained.

instàbile, *a.* unstable; unsteady; unsettled; inconstant; insecure.

installàre, *v.t.* to install. installazióne, *f.* installation.

instancàbile, *a.* untiring; indefatigable, tireless.

instauràre (*pr.* -àuro), *v.t.* to set up; establish; install. instaurazióne, *f.* establishment, installation.

insterilíre (*pr.* -ísco, -ísci), *v.t.* to sterilize. Cf. *isterilire*.

instradàre, *v.t.* to set on the right road; send on. Cf. *istradare*.

insù, *ad.* up; upwards.

insuccèsso, *m.* failure.

insudiciàre (*pr.* -údicio, -údici), *v.t.* to soil; make dirty.

insufficiènte, *a.* insufficient, inadequate; incompetent. insufficiènza, *f.* insufficiency, shortage; weakness. insulàre, *a.* insular. insularità, *f.* insularity.

insulína, *f.* (*Med.*) insulin.

insulsàggine, *f.* dul[l]ness; stupidity; silliness. insúlso, *a.* silly; insipid; dull.

insúlto, *m.* insult; affront; attack (*of illness*); stroke.

insuperàto, *a.* unsurpassed.

insuperbíre (*pr.* -ísco, -ísci), *v.t.* to make proud. *v.i.* (*aux.* essere) & insuperbírsi, *v.refl.* to be proud; grow proud. ~ *di*, to take pride in; boast of.

insurrezióne, *f.* insurrection; rising.

insussistènte, *a.* unreal; unsubstantial; inexistent.

intaccàre (*pr.* -àcco, -àcchi), *v.t.* to notch; corrode; damage; reduce; cut into. ~ *il capitale*, to draw on one's capital. *v.i.* (*aux.* avere) to have an impediment in one's speech. intàcco, *m.* & intaccatúra, *f.* notch; score; impediment.

intagliàre, *v.t.* to carve; cut; incise; engrave. intagliatóre, *m.* carver; engraver. intàglio (*pl.* -àgli), *m.* engraved design; carving; incised gem.

intanàrsi, *v.refl.* to hide (oneself).

intànto, *ad.* meanwhile; in the meantime. ~ *che*, while; until, so that.

intarlàre, *v.i.* (*aux.* essere) to become worm-eaten.

intarmàre, *v.i.* & intarmàrsi, *v.refl.* to become moth-eaten.

intarsiàre (*pr.* -àrsio, -àrsi), *v.t.* to inlay. intàrsio & lavoro d' ~, *m.* inlaid work.

intasaménto, *m.* & intasatúra, *f.* obstruction; stoppage. intasàre, *v.t.* to obstruct, clog, choke; *v.i.* (*aux.* essere) & intasàrsi, *v.refl.* to be choked up; clogged; stuffed up (*nose, cold in the head*).

intascàre (*pr.* -àsco, -àschi), *v.t.* to pocket.

intàtto, *a.* intact; whole; uninjured; unblemished; unsullied.

intavolàre, *v.t.* to put on a board (e.g. *chess-men; baker's loaves, &c.*); board up; (*fig.*) begin; start; raise a subject for discussion. intavolàto, *m.* boarding; wainscoting; planking.

integèrrimo, *a.* (*superl.* of íntegro) most upright; strictly honest.

integràle, *a.* integral; whole; entire; (in) full; complete; unexpurgated. integràre (*pr.* -ègro), *v.t.* to complete; integrate; put right. integrità, *f.* integrity; honesty;

wholeness. **íntegro,** *a.* upright; honest; entire.

intelaiatúra, *f.* frame; framework; trestle; (*Motor*) chassis. ~ *di sostegno,* cradle (*ship*).

intellètto, *m.* intellect; understanding. **intellettuàle,** *a. & m.* intellectual; brain (*att.*).

intelligènte, *a.* intelligent. **intelligenteménte,** *ad.* intelligently. **intelligènza,** *f.* intelligence; intellect; understanding; knowledge; talent; (*on good*) terms; agreement. **intelligíbile,** *a.* intelligible; comprehensible; clear; audible.

intemeràta, *f.* reprimand; scolding; sharp reproof; tedious lecture. **intemeràto,** *a.* faultless; stainless; irreproachable.

intemperànte & intemperàto, *a.* intemperate. **intemperànza,** *f.* intemperance. **intempèrie,** *f.pl.* uncertain or inclement weather. **intempestívo,** *a.* untimely; ill-timed; inopportune; unseasonable.

intendènte, *pres. part.* of **intendere.** ¶ *m.* connoisseur; superintendent; manager; inspector. **intendènza,** *f.* superintendence; management; office. **intèndere** (*pr.* **-èndo,** &c., like *tendere*), *v.t. ir.* to understand; hear; listen to; intend; purpose; mean; require. **intèndersi,** *v.refl.* to be a (good) judge (of); agree; understand each other; come to an understanding; come to terms (with). *s'intende!* of course! naturally; to be sure! **intendiménto,** *m.* understanding; comprehension; intelligence; intention; purpose. **intenditóre,** *m.* connoisseur; judge; one quick to understand.

intenebràre, *v.t.* to obscure; darken.

inteneríre (*pr.* **-ísco, -ísci**), *v.t.* to soften; make tender; move (to pity, &c.).

intensificàre (*pr.* **-ífico, -ífichi**), *v.t.* to intensify; make more frequent; increase. **intensità,** *f.* intensity; force; strength; depth (*colour*).

intentaménte, *ad.* intently; attentively. **intentàre** (*pr.* **-ènto**), *v.t.* (*Law*) to bring (*an action*). **intentàto,** *a.* unattempted; unexplored. **intènto,** *a.* intent; tense; bent (on). ¶ *m.* intent; aim; purpose; intention; end; object.

intenzionàto, *a.* disposed; inclined; intentioned. **intenzióne,** *f.* intention; purpose; meaning; wish.

intepidíre (*pr.* **-ísco, -ísci**), *v.t.* make tepid; warm (up); cool down; (*fig.*) reduce; mitigate. *v.i.* (*aux.* essere) & **intepidírsi,** *v.refl.* to become tepid; warm up; cool down.

interaménte, *ad.* entirely; wholly; fully; completely; quite.

intercalàre (*pr.* **-àlo**), *v.t.* to insert; interpolate; intercalate. ¶ *a.* interpolated; intervening. *giorno* ~, 29th February in leap-years. ¶ *m.* refrain; repeated expression.

intercèdere (*pr.* **-èdo,** &c., like *cedere*), *v.i. ir.* (*aux.* avere) to intercede; intervene; exist, lie between (*of distance*); (*of time*) elapse. **intercessióne,** *f.* intercession. **intercessóre,** *m.* intercessor.

intercettàre (*pr.* **-ètto**), *v.t.* to intercept. **intercètto,** *sync. p.p.* of **intercettare.** **intercezióne,** *f.* interception.

interchiùdere (*pr.* **-chiúdo, -chiúdi** like *chiudere*), *v.t. ir.* to block; stop; obstruct; shut (in); enclose.

intercórrere (*pr.* **-órro,** &c., like *correre*), *v.i. ir.* (*aux.* essere) to elapse; pass; occur.

intercutàneo, *a.* subcutaneous.

interdétto, *p.p.* of **interdire.** ¶ *m.* interdict. **interdíre** (*pr.* **-íco, -íci,** &c., like *dire*), *v.t. ir.* to interdict; prohibit; forbid; (*Law*) disqualify.

interessaménto, *m.* interest; concern. **interessànte,** *a.* interesting. **interessàre,** *v.t. & abs.* to interest; concern; affect; touch; apply to; be of interest; matter. **interessàrsi** (*di or* a), *v.refl.* to take an interest (in); to care (for). **interessataménte,** *ad.* from interested motives; with interest. **interessàto,** *a.* interested; concerned; selfish; calculating; having an interest (in). ¶ *m.* **-a,** *f.* interested party. *tutti gli interessati,* all concerned. **interèsse,** *m.* interest; concern. ~ *composto,* compound interest (*Fin.*). ~ *semplice,* simple i.

interézza, *f.* entirety.

interferènza, *f.* (*Phys., Radio*) interference. **interferíre** (*pr.* **-ísco, -ísci**), *v.i.* (*aux.* avere) (*Phys.*) to interfere; produce interference.

interfogliàre, *v.t.* to interleave.

interiezióne, *f.* interjection.

interinàle, *a.* temporary; provisional; *ad interim.* **interinàto,** *m.* temporary office or tenure. **interíno,**

¶ *m.* one holding temporary office.
a. provisional; temporary; acting.
interìto, *a.* stock-still; bolt upright; stiff.
interlínea, *f.* space between the lines; (*Typ.*) lead. **interlineàre** (*pr.* -íneo), *v.t.* to interline; (*Typ.*) to lead.
interloquíre (*pr.* -ísco, -ísci), *v.i.* (*aux.* avere) to join in the conversation; intervene in a discussion; put in a word.
interlúnio (*pl.* -úni), *m.* period when moon is not visible.
intermediàrio, *a. & m.* intermediary; (*Com.*) middleman. **intermèdio** (*pl.* -èdi), *a.* intermediate; middle.
intermèżżo, *m.* interval; (*Mus.*) intermezzo.
interminàto, *a.* unfinished; (*Poet.*) limitless, boundless.
intermittènte, *a.* intermittent.
internaménto, *m.* internment. *campo d'* ~, internment camp. **internàre**, *v.t.* to intern (*war*, *&c.*); place under restraint (*lunatic*). **internàrsi**, *v.refl.* to enter into (*fig.*); identify oneself with (*a part*); throw oneself into (*fig.*); penetrate. **internàto**, *p.a.* interned. ¶ *m.* internee; inmate; boarding school.
internazionàle, *a.* international. ¶ *f.* international (*association*); internationale (*hymn*). **intèrno**, *a.* internal; interior; inner; inland; (*att.*) house; home. *alunno* ~, (*Sch.*) boarder. *medico* ~, house surgeon, house physician. ¶ *m.* interior; inside; (*sport*) inside [player]. *ministero degli I* ~*i*, Home Office. *ministro degli* ~, Home Secretary (England).
intèro & intièro, *a.* entire; whole; (*fig.*) honest; sincere.
interpellàre, *v.t.* to interpellate; ask; take a legal objection to.
interpolàre, *v.t.* to interpolate. **interpolazióne**, *f.* interpolation.
interpórre (*pr.* -óngo, *&c.*, like *porre*), *v.t.* ir. to interpose. **interpórsi**, *v.refl.* to interpose; intervene; mediate.
interpretàre, *v.t.* to interpret. **interpretazióne**, *f.* interpretation; construction; (*Mus.*) rendering, execution. **intèrprete**, *m.* interpreter; exponent.
interpunzióne, *f.* punctuation. *segni di* ~, punctuation marks.
interraménto, *m.* interment. **in-**

terràre (*pr.* -èrro), *v.t.* to inter; bury; earth up; build earthworks.
interrégno, *m.* interregnum.
interrogàre (*pr.* -èrrogo, -èrroghi), *v.t.* to interrogate; question; examine. **interrogatívo**, *a.* interrogative. **interrogatòrio** (*pl.* -òri), *m.* interrogatory; examination; cross-examination. **interrogazióne**, *f.* interrogation; question; query.
interrómpere (*pr.* -ómpo, *&c.*, like *rompere*), *v.t.* ir. to interrupt; break (off); discontinue; (*Elec.*) disconnect, switch off. **interrómpersi**, *v.refl.* to stop. **interrotto**, *p.a.* interrupted; broken off; cut off. **interruttóre**, *m.* (*f.* -trice) interrupter; (*Elec.*) switch. **interruzióne**, *f.* interruption.
intersecàre (*pr.* -èrseco, -èrsechi), *v.t.* to intersect. **intersecazióne & intersezióne**, *f.* intersection.
interstízio (*pl.* -ízi), *m.* interstice.
intervàllo, *m.* interval; space; gap.
interveníre (*pr.* -èngo, *&c.*, like *venire*), *v.i.* ir. (*aux.* essere) to intervene; happen; attend; be present. **interventísta**, *m.* interventionist (*Pol.*). **intervènto**, *m. & intervenzióne*, *f.* intervention; interference; presence.
intervísta, *f.* interview. **intervistàre**, *v.t.* to interview.
intésa, *f.* agreement; accord; understanding; entente. **intéso**, *p.p.* of *intendere & a.* understood; agreed; intent.
intèssere (*pr.* -èsso), *v.t.* ir. to weave, interweave. **intessúto**, *p.a.* woven, interwoven.
intestàre (*pr.* -èsto), *v.t.* to enter (*in an account*); register (*under a name*); (*Typ.*) to head (*a page*); (*Carp.*) join together by the head. **intestàrsi**, *v.refl.* to take it into one's head; be obstinate or determined. **intestàto**, *a.* intestate; stubborn; obstinate; entered; registered; inscribed; headed. **intestazióne**, *f.* heading; title.
intestíno, *m.* intestine. ¶ *a.* intestine; internal; domestic; civil.
intiepidíre, see *intepidire*.
intimàre, *v.t.* to intimate; give notice of; enjoin; order; summon; compel. **intimazióne**, *f.* order; injunction; summons; instruction; notification. **intimità**, *f.* intimacy.
íntimo, *a.* intimate; in[ner]most; inward; close; near; private. ¶ *m.* (*fig.*) heart; soul.

intimoríre (*pr.* -ísco, -ísci), *v.t.* to frighten; intimidate. *v.i.* (*aux.* essere) to be afraid.

intíngere (*pr.* -íngo, -íngi, *&c.*, like *tíngere*). *v.t. & i.ir.* to dip; moisten; wet; soak.

intíngolo, *m.* sauce; gravy; ragout; tasty dish. ~ *di lepre*, jugged hare (Cook.).

intínto, *p.a.* dipped; wet. ¶ *m.* sauce.

intirizzíre (*pr.* -ísco, -ísci), *v.t.* to benumb; numb; stiffen. intirizzíto, *a.* frozen stiff.

intisichíre (*pr.* -ísco, -ísci), *v.t.* to weaken; impoverish; throw into a consumption. *v.i.* (*aux.* essere) to become consumptive; pine away; languish.

intitolàre, *v.t.* to entitle; dedicate.

intoccàbile, *a.* untouchable.

intolleràbile, *a.* intolerable. intollerànte, *a.* intolerant. intollerànza, *f.* intolerance.

intonacàre (*pr.* -ònaco, -ònachi), *v.t.* to plaster; distemper; whitewash. intonacatúra, *f.* plastering. intònaco (*pl.* -ònachi), *m.* plaster.

intonàre (*pr.* -uòno), *v.t.* to intone; tune; strike up; begin (*a song, singing*). intonàrsi, *v.refl.* to be in tune (with); harmonize (with); tone (with). intonàto, *a.* in tune; in harmony. intonazióne, *f.* intonation; tuning; tone; opening bars or notes of a piece of music.

intònso, *a.* (*Typ.*) untrimmed, uncut; (*Poet.*) unshaven.

intontíre (*pr.* -ísco, -ísci), *v.t.* to stun; stupefy; astonish. intontírsi, *v.refl.* to be stunned; stupefied; astonished. intontíto, *a.* stunned; astonished; stupefied; stupid; dull.

intoppàre (*pr.* -òppo), *v.i.* (*aux.* essere & avere) to stumble. intòppo, *m.* obstacle; hindrance; stumbling-block; difficulty.

intorbidàre *&* intorbidíre (*pr.* -ísco, -ísci), *v.t.* to trouble; make turbid; foul; darken; obscure; confuse; confound.

intormentíre (*pr.* -ísco, -ísci), *v.t.* to benumb.

intorniàre (*pr.* -órnio, -órni), *v.t.* to surround.

intórno, *ad.* around; round; about. ¶ ~ **a**, *pr.* around; round; about; on the subject of; concerning; approximately. *guardarsi d'* ~, to look about. *levarsi d'* ~, to get rid of (*a person*). *darsi* ~, to trouble oneself about. *d'ogni* ~, on every side.

intorpidíre (*pr.* -ísco, -ísci), *v.t.* to render torpid. *v.i.* (*aux.* essere) *&* intorpidírsi, *v.refl.* to become torpid; grow benumbed; become enervated.

intossicàre (*pr.* -òssico, -òssichi), *v.t.* to poison.

intostíto, *a.* hardened; hard.

intraducíbile, *a.* untranslatable.

intralasciàre, *v.t.* to interrupt; leave off; neglect; omit.

intralciàre, *v.t.* to impede; interfere with; hamper; entangle; embarrass.

intramésso, *m.* side-dish. intraméttere (*pr.* -métto, -métti, *&c.*, like *mettere*), *v.t. ir.* to interpose; intermit. intraméttersi, *v.refl.* to intervene; interfere (with); meddle (with).

intramezzàre, *v.t.* to interpose; alternate.

intransigènte, *a.* uncompromising; intransigent. intransigènza, *f.* intransigence; severity; strictness.

intransitívo, *a. & m.* intransitive.

intrappolàre, *v.t.* to entrap.

intraprendènte, *a.* enterprising. intraprendènza, *f.* (spirit of) enterprise. intraprèndere (*pr.* -èndo, *&c.*, like *prendere*), *v.t. ir.* to undertake; enter upon; engage in; venture [up]on. intraprenditóre, *m.* contractor. intraprésa, *f.* undertaking; enterprise (usu. *impresa*).

intrattàbile, *a.* intractable.

intrattenére (*pr.* -èngo, *&c.*, like *tenere*), *v.t. ir.* to entertain; receive; cherish (a hope, &c.); carry on, keep on (correspondence); divert, amuse; keep waiting. intrattenérsi, *v.refl.* to linger; stop. ~ *su*, to dwell upon. intratteniménto, *m.* entertainment; diversion.

intra[v]vedére (*pr.* -védo, *&c.*, like *vedere*), *v.t. ir.* to catch a glimpse of; see dimly or indistinctly; have a vague idea of; foresee. intra[v]vedúto, *a.* dimly seen; foreseen.

intravveníre (*pr.* -vèngo, -vièni, *&c.*, like *venire*), *v.i. ir.* (*aux.* essere) to happen; intervene.

intrecciàre (*pr.* -tréccio, -trécci), *v.t.* to interlace; twine; plait; braid; twist; splice (*rope*); cross (*legs*); weave (*a pattern*). ~ *danze*, to dance. intréccio, (*pl.* -écci), *m.* intermingling; interlacing; complication; entanglement; knot; plot (*novel or play*).

intrepidézza, *f.* intrepidity; fearlessness; bravery. **intrèpido,** *a.* fearless; intrepid.

intricàre (*pr.* -íco, -íchi), *v.t.* to entangle. **intricàrsi,** *v.refl.* to get entangled. **intricàto,** *a.* entangled; intricate.

intrídere (*pr.* -ído), *v.t. ir.* to soak; moisten; form into a paste with water; knead; temper; imbrue.

intrigànte, *a.* intriguing. ¶ *m.* intriguer. **intrigàre** (*pr.* -ígo, -íghi), *v.t.* to entangle; confuse. *v.i.* (*aux.* avere) to intrigue. **intrigàrsi,** *v.refl.* to meddle (with); be mixed up (in). **intrígo** (*pl.* -íghi), *m.* intrigue.

intrinsecaménte, *ad.* intrinsically. **intrinsecàrsi** (*pr.* -ínseco, -ínsechi),) *v.refl.* to be intimately acquainted (with); penetrate; plunge deeply (into). **intrínseco** (*pl.* -ínsechi), *a.* intrinsic; intimate. **intrinsichézza,** *f.* intimacy.

intríso, *p.p.* of **intridere.** ¶ *m.* paste; dough; mixture; mash; mortar; (wet) plaster.

intristíre (*pr.* -ísco, -ísci), *v.i.* (*aux.* essere) to decay; droop; pine away; be sickly; grow melancholy.

introdótto, *p.p.* of **introdúrre.** **introdúrre** (*pr.* -úco, -úci, &*c.*, like *addurre*), *v.t. ir.* to introduce; import; bring in; bring up; move (*a resolution*); (*Mech.*) insert, drive in. **introdúrsi,** *v.refl.* to introduce oneself; get in; creep in; become current. **introduttívo,** *a.* introductory. **introduzione,** *f.* introduction.

introitàre (*pr.* -òito), *v.t.* to get in (*money*); receive in the form of cash. **intròito,** *m.* (*money*) receipts; revenue; returns; entry; beginning; (*Eccl.*) introit; introduction to the Mass.

introméssa & **intromissióne,** *f.* intervention; intrusion. **introméttere,** *v.t. ir.* to bring in; introduce; interpose. **introméttersi,** *v.refl.* to intervene; interfere; intrude.

intronàre (*pr.* -òno), *v.t.* to deafen; stun.

intronizzàre, *v.t.* to enthrone.

introvàbile, *a.* not to be found.

intrúdere (*pr.* -údo), *v.i. ir.* (*aux.* avere) & **intrúdersi,** *v.refl.* to intrude.

intrúglio, *m.* hotch-potch; mixture; horrid mess; confusion; intrigue.

intruppàrsi, *v.refl.* to flock together; join company with; troop.

intrusióne, *f.* intrusion. **intrusívo,** *a.* (*Geol.*) intrusive. **intrúso,** *p.p.* of **intrudere.** ¶ *m.* intruder; interloper.

intuffàre, *v.t.* to dip; steep; soak.

intuíre (*pr.* -ísco, -ísci), *v.t.* to perceive by intuition; guess; divine. **intuitívo,** *a.* intuitive; instant; clear; evident. **intúito,** *m.* & **intuizióne,** *f.* intuition.

intumescènza, *f.* swelling. **intumidíre** (*pr.* -ísco, -ísci), *v.i.* (*aux.* essere) to swell; swell up.

inuguàle, *a.* unequal. *Cf.* **ineguale.**

inumàno, *a.* inhuman; inhumane; barbarous.

inumàre (*pr.* -úmo), *v.t.* to bury; inter.

inumidíre (*pr.* -ísco, -ísci), *v.t.* to moisten; damp.

inurbàno, *a.* rude; unpolite; uncivil.

inusàto & **inusitàto,** *a.* obsolete; unusual.

inútile, *a.* useless; unnecessary.

invàdere (*pr.* -vàdo), *v.t. ir.* to invade; encroach [up]on; attack; break into.

invaghiménto, *m.* falling in love. **invaghíre** (*pr.* -ísco, -ísci), *v.t.* to attract; charm. **invaghírsi (di),** *v.refl.* to fall in love (with); become fond (of).

invalére (*pr.* -àlgo, &*c.*, like *valere*), *v.i. ir.* (*aux.* essere) to be introduced; come into fashion; become established.

invàlido, *a.* invalid; infirm; disabled; not valid.

invàlso, *p.p.* of **invalere.** ¶ *a.* prevalent; prevailing; established.

invaníre (*pr.* -ísco, -ísci), *v.t.* to make vain. *v.i.* (*aux.* essere) & **invanírsi,** *v.refl.* to become vain; grow conceited. **invàno,** *ad.* in vain.

invarcàbile, *a.* impassable.

invariàbile, *a.* invariable.

invasàre, *v.t.* to obsess; put in vases; put (*a ship*) on the (launching) cradle. **invasatúra,** *f.* launching-cradle.

invasióne, *f.* invasion. **invàso,** *p.p.* of *invadere.* **invasóre,** *m.* invader. ¶ *a.* invading.

invecchiaménto, *m.* ageing, growing old. **invecchiàre** (*pr.* -vècchio, -vècchi), *v.t.* to make old; age; make one look old. *v.i.* (*aux.*

essere) to grow old; age; get on in years; (*fig.*) become obsolete. **invecchiàrsi**, *v.refl.* to make oneself look old; to claim to be older than one is. **invecchiàto**, *a.* grown old; looking old[er]; obsolete.

invéce, *ad.* instead; on the contrary. *invéce di*, instead of.

inveíre (*pr.* **-ísco, -ísci**), *v.i.* (*aux.* avere) to inveigh (against); rail (at).

inveleníre (*pr.* **-isco, -ísci**), *v.t.* to envenom; embitter.

invendíbile, *a.* unsaleable. **invendicàto**, *a.* unpunished; unavenged. **invendúto**, *a.* unsold.

inventàre, *v.t.* to invent, find out, devise; contrive, make up, fabricate (*false story*). **inventariàre**, *v.t.* to inventory, to make an inventory of. **inventàrio** (*pl.* **-àri**), *m.* inventory. **inventíva**, *f.* inventiveness; inventive faculty. **inventívo**, *a.* inventive. **inventóre**, *m.* (*f.* **-tríce**) inventor. **invenzióne**, *f.* invention. *brevetto d'* ∼, patent.

inverdíre (*pr.* **-ísco, -ísci**), *v.i.* (*aux.* essere) to become green.

inverecóndia, *f.* immodesty; impudence. **inverecóndo**, *a.* impudent; immodest.

inverisímile, *a.* unlikely; improbable. Cf. *inverosimile*.

invermigliàre, *v.t.* to redden; to tinge with red. **invermigliàrsi**, *v.refl.* to redden; turn red; blush.

invernàle, *a.* winter (*att.*); wintry. **invernàta**, *f.* winter; duration of (the) winter.

inverniciàre, (*vt.* to varnish, paint. **invèrno**, *m.* winter.

invéro, *ad.* indeed; really; truly.

inverosímile, *a.* unlikely. **inverosimigliànza**, *f.* unlikelihood.

inversióne, *f.* inversion; (*Mech.*) reversal. **invèrso**, *a.* inverse; contrary; opposite; inverted. *all'inversa*, *ad.* backwards; (*fig.*) badly; wrong.

invertebràto, *a. & m.* invertebrate.

invertíre (*pr.* **-èrto** & **-ertísco** *like* avvertire), *v.t.* to invert; reverse.

investiménto, *m.* investment (*money*); siege; clash; collision.

investíre (*pr.* **-èsto, -èsti**), *v.t.* to invest; lay siege to; collide with; foul (*ship*); run over; knock against; run into; charge (*Mil.*); fall foul of. ∼ *di*, to invest with; appoint to (*office, title*). **investírsi**, *v.refl.* to enter thoroughly (*into a part*); become identified (with); collide;

run aground. **investitúra**, *f.* investiture.

invetriàre (*pr.* **-étrio, -étri**), *v.t.* to glaze. **invetriàta**, *f.* (*glass*) window, door, partition; sky-light. **invetriatúra**, *f.* glaze; glazing.

invettíva, *f.* invective.

inviàre (*pr.* **-ío, -íi**), *v.t.* to send; forward; dispatch; put on the way. **inviàto**, *m.* envoy.

invídia, *f.* envy. **invidiàbile**, *a.* enviable. **invidiàre**, *v.t.* to envy. **invidióso**, *a.* envious; (*Poet.*) invido.

invigilare (*pr.* **-ígilo**), *v.i.* (*aux.* avere) to invigilate; watch (over).

invigliacchíre (*pr.* **-isco, -ísci**), *v.i.* (*aux.* essere) to become a coward; become faint-hearted.

invigoríre (*pr.* **-ísco, -ísci**), *v.t.* to strengthen; invigorate. **invigorírsi**, *v.refl.* to become strong(er); gain strength.

invilíre (*pr.* **-ísco, -ísci**), *v.t.* to lower; depress; dishearten; debase; degrade. *v.i.* (*aux.* essere) to become of no account; be degraded; grow discouraged; lose heart.

inviluppàre (*pr.* **-úppo**), *v.t.* to wrap up; envelop; hide; (*fig.*) to confuse. **invilúppo**, *m.* wrapper; covering; confusion; intricacy.

invincíbile, *a.* invincible; unconquerable.

invío, *m.* despatch; sending; forwarding; shipment; (*of money*) remittance; final stanza of Petrarchan *canzone*.

inviperíre (*pr.* **-ísco, -ísci**), *v.i.* (*aux.* essere) & **inviperírsi**, *v.refl.* to become furious; become enraged.

invisceràrsi, *v.refl.* to penetrate deeply (into); go to the heart (of) (*a subject*).

invischiàre, *v.t.* to smear with birdlime; entice; entangle. **invischiàrsi**, *v.refl.* to get entangled (*lit. & fig.*).

inviscidíre (*pr.* **-ísco, -ísci**), *v.i.* (*aux.* essere) to become sticky or viscous.

invisíbile, *a.* invisible.

invíso, *a.* disliked; hated.

invitàre, *v.t.* to invite; ask; request; beg; challenge; screw up; attract; charm. **invitàto**, *m.* guest. **invíto**, *m.* invitation.

invítto, *a.* unconquered; invincible; indomitable.

invocàre (*pr.* **-òco, -òchi**), *v.t.* to invoke; appeal to; ask for; summon; cry for. **invocatívo**, *a.* invocatory. **invocazióne**, *f.* invocation; appeal.

invogliàre (*pr.* -òglio, -ògli), *v.t.* to induce; lead; tempt; create a wish or intention in someone.

involàre, *v.t.* to steal; carry off. **involàrsi**, *v.refl.* to steal away; fly away; disappear; elope.

invòlgere (*pr.* -òlgo, -òlgi, *&c.*, like *volgere*), *v.t. ir.* to wrap up; envelop; involve. **invòlgersi**, *v.refl.* to wrap oneself up; become involved.

involontàrio (*pl.* -àri), *a.* involuntary; unintentional.

involpíre (*pr.* -ísco, -ísci), *v.i.* (*aux.* essere) to grow cunning.

invòlto, *p.p.* of **involgere**. ¶ *m.* bundle; parcel; packet; scroll; roll (*of papers*).

invòlucro, *m.* covering; sheathe; case; pod; (*Anat.*) envelope.

inzaccheràre, *v.t.* to splash with mud.

inzavorràre, *v.t.* to ballast; load with ballast.

inzeppàre, *v.t.* to drive in a wedge; wedge; thrust in; cram; fill.

inzoccolàto, *a.* wearing clogs.

inzolfàre (*pr.* -ólfo), *v.t.* to dust (*vines*) with sulphur; to fumigate with sulphur.

inzotichíre (*pr.* -ísco, -ísci), *v.i.* (*aux.* essere) to become boorish or ill-mannered.

inzuccheràre, *v.t.* to sprinkle with sugar; sweeten; (*fig.*) flatter; cajole.

inzuppàre, *v.t.* to soak; drench; dip; steep. **inzuppàrsi**, *v.refl.* to be drenched; get wet through. **inzuppàto**, *p.a.* soaked, drenched; wet through; (*pop.*) drunk[en].

ío, *per. pn.* 1st *sg.* I. *son(o)* io, it is I. *non sono più io*, I am no longer myself.

iòdio, *m.* iodine. **iodofòrmio**, *m.* iodoform. **iodúro**, *m.* iodide.

Iokoàma, *f.* Yokohama.

iòle, *f.* (*Naut.*) gig; jolly boat.

iònico (*pl.* -ònici), *a.* Ionic. **Iònio**, *a. & m.* Ionian. *il Mar ~, m.* the Ionian Sea. *le Isole Ionie*, *f.pl.* the Ionian Islands. **iònio**, *m.* (*Chem.*) ionium.

ionizzàre, *v.t.* (*Chem.*) to ionize. **iòno** (*& iòne*), *m.* ion (*Elec.*).

iòsa (a), *ad. expr.* in abundance; abundantly; galore.

iosciamína, *f.* (*Chem.*) hyoscin.

iòta, *m.* iota; jot.

ipèrbole, *f.* hyperbole; (*Math.*) hyperbola. **iperboleggiàre** (*pr.* -éggio, -éggi), *v.i.* (*aux.* avere) to indulge in hyperbole(s).

ipercrítico (*pr.* -ítici), *a.* hypercritical.

ipnòsi, *f.* hypnosis. **ipnòtico** (*pl.* -òtici), *a.* hypnotic. **ipnotísmo**, *m.* hypnotism. **ipnotizzàre**, *v.t.* to hypnotize.

ipocondría, *f.* hypochondria. **ipocrisía**, *f.* hypocrisy. **ipòcrita** (*pl.* -òcriti), *m.* hypocrite. **ipòcrito**, *a.* hypocritical.

ipodèrmico (*pl.* -èrmici), *a.* hypodermic.

ipofosfíto, *m.* (*Chem.*) hypophosphate. **iposolfíto**, *m.* hyposulphite.

ipotèca, *f.* mortgage. **ipotecàre** (*pr.* -èco, -èchi), *v.t.* to mortgage. **ipotecàrio** (*pl.* -ari), *a.* mortgage (*att.*); on mortgage.

ipotenúsa, *f.* hypotenuse. **ipòteši**, *f.* hypothesis; supposition. *nella peggiore ~, if the worst comes to the worst.* **ipotètico** (*pl.* -ètici), *a.* hypothetic(al).

íppica, *f.* horse-racing. **íppico** (*pl.* íppici), *a.* horse (*att.*). *corse ippiche*, horse-races.

ippocastàno, *m.* horse-chestnut (tree).

Ippòcrate, *m.* Hippocrates. **Ippocrène**, *f.* Hippocrene.

ippòdromo, *m.* race-course; hippodrome.

Ippòlita, *f.* Hippolyta. **Ippòlito**, *m.* Hippolytus.

ippopòtamo, *m.* hippopotamus.

iprite, *f.* (*Chem.*) mustard gas, yperite.

íra, *f.* anger; rage; fury; passion; wrath. **iracóndo**, *a.* quick to anger; choleric; hot-tempered. **iràto**, *a.* angry; enraged; in a rage.

íre, *v.i. defect.* (*aux.* essere) (*Poet.*) to go.

íride, *f.* (*Bot. & Anat.*) iris; rainbow. **iridescènte**, *a.* iridescent. **iridescènza**, *f.* iridescence.

irídio, *m.* iridium (*Chem.*).

Irlànda (l'), *f.* Ireland. *Stato Libero d'I ~,* Irish Free State. **irlandése**, *a. & m.f.* Irish. *un I ~,* an Irishman. *una I ~,* an Irish woman. *gl(i) Irlandesi,* the Irish; the Irish people. *l'i ~,* Irish; the Irish language.

ironía, *f.* irony. **irònico** (*pl.* -ònici), *a.* ironic(al).

iróso, *a.* angry; wrathful.

irradiàre *& irraggiàre,* *v.t.* to shed light on; irradiate; shine on. *v.i.* (*aux.* avere) to radiate; shine.

irragionévole, *a.* unreasonable; unfair; irrational.

irrancidíre (*pr.* -ísco, -ísci), *v.i.* (*aux.* essere) to go, or become rancid.

irrazionàle, *a.* irrational.
irreàle, *a.* unreal. **irrealtà,** *f.* unreality.
irrecusàbile, *a.* undeniable; impossible to refuse.
irredentísmo, *m.* (*Pol.*) irredentism. **irredentísta** (*pl.* -isti), *m.* irredentist. **irredènto,** *a.* unredeemed (*territory, population*).
irrefragàbile, *a.* indisputable.
irrefrenàbile, *a.* impossible to curb. **irrefrenàto,** *a.* unrestrained.
irregolàre, *a.* irregular; abnormal; uneven; erratic. **irregolatirà,** *f.inv.* irregularity.
irreligióso, *a.* irreligious.
irreperíbile, *a.* that cannot be found [again].
irreprensíbile, *a.* irreproachable.
irrepugnàbile, *a.* unquestionable; irrefutable.
irrequietézza, *f.* restlessness. **irrequièto,** *a.* restless.
irretíre (*pr.* -ísco, -ísci), *v.t.* to snare; entrap.
irriconoscíbile, *a.* unrecognizable.
irrídere (*pr.* -ído, &c., like **ridere**), *v.t. ir.* to deride.
irriflessívo, *a.* thoughtless.
irrigàre (*pr.* -ígo, -íghi), *v.t.* to irrigate. **irrigazióne,** *f.* irrigation.
irrigidíre (*pr.* -ísco, -ísci), *v.t.* to stiffen, *v.i.* (*aux.* essere) & **irrigidírsi,** *v.refl.* to stiffen; become stiff. *irrigidirsi sull'attenti* (*Mil.*), to stand (stiffly) to attention.
irríguo, *a.* well-watered.
irrisióne, *f.* derision; railery; mockery. **irrisòrio,** *a.* derisory; paltry.
irritàre, *v.t.* to irritate; provoke; enrage; inflame. **irritazióne,** *f.* irritation; anger; inflammation.
írrito, *a.* (*Law*) null, void; of no effect.
irritrosíre (*pr.* -ísco, -ísci), *v.i.* (*aux.* essere) & **irritrosírsi,** *v.refl.* to grow stubborn.
irriverènte, *a.* irreverent. **irriverènza,** *f.* irreverence.
irrobustíre (*pr.* -ísco, -ísci), *v.t.* to strengthen.
irrómpere (*pr.* -ómpo, &c., like *rompere*). *v.i. ir.* (*aux.* essere) to burst in; break in.
irroràre, *v.t.* to bedew; besprinkle.
irruènte, *a.* rushing (in); impetuous; violent; rash.
irrugginíre (*pr.* -ísco, -ísci), *v.t.* to rust. *v.i.* (*aux.* essere) & **irruginírsi,** *v.refl.* to rust; become rusty. Cf. *arrugginire.*
irruvidíre (*pr.* -ísco, -ísci), *v.t.* to

roughen. *v.i.* (*aux.* essere) & **irruvidírsi,** *v.refl.* to become rough.
irruzióne, *f.* irruption; inroad; incursion; inrush.
irsúto, *a.* shaggy; hairy.
írto, *a.* bristling; erect; shaggy; bristly; thorny; full; crammed.
Isàcco, *m.* Isaac. **Isàia,** *m.* Isaiah (*O.T.*). **Isàra,** *f.* Isere (*river*).
isb-, isc-, isd-, &c., words beginning with impure *s*, when preceded by a word ending in a consonant, frequently have an I (i) prefixed for euphony, e.g. in Iscozia (Scozia); such words should be looked for under S.
iscrivere (*pr.* -ívo, &c., like **scrivere**), *v.t. ir.* to inscribe; enter; register; record. **iscríversi,** *v.refl.* to enter (for) (*an examination, e.g.*); to enter one's name (for); join. **iscrizióne,** *f.* inscription; entry (*competition, examination, club, school,* &c.). *domanda d'~,* application. *modulo per la domanda di ~,* application-form. *tassa di ~,* entrance fee.
Iside, *f.* Isis.
Ìslam, *m.* Islam. **islamíta,** *m* Islamite. ¶ *a.* Islamic.
Islànda (**l'**), Iceland. **islandése,** *a.* & (*language*) *m.* Icelandic. I~, *m.* Icelander.
Ismaèle, *m.* Ishmael.
isòbara, *f.* (*Meteor.*) isobar.
isòcrono, *a.* isochronous. **isògono,** *a.* with equal angles.
isoípsa, *f.* contour line (*Geog.*).
ísola, *f.* island; separate block of houses (also *isolato, m.*). **isolaménto,** *m.* isolation; insulation. *~ acustico,* sound-proofing. **isolàno;** *a.* insular. ¶ *m.* islander. **isolàre,** *v.t.* to isolate; separate; keep apart; insulate. **isolàto,** *p.a.* isolated; insulated. ¶ *m.* block (*of houses*). **isolatóre,** *m.* (*Elec.*) insulator. **isolétta,** *f.* & **isòlotto,** *m.* islet.
isòscele, *a.* isosceles (*Geom.*).
isotèrma, *f.* isotherm.
isòtopo, *m.* isotope. *~ radioattivo,* radio-active i.
ispànico (*pl.* -ànici), *a.* Hispanic.
ispettoràto, *m.* inspectorship; inspectorate; inspector's office. **ispettóre,** *m.* inspector. **ispettríce,** *f.* inspectress. **ispezionàre,** *v.t.* to inspect. **ispezióne,** *f.* inspection.
íspido, *a.* shaggy; bristly.
ispiràre, *v.t.* to inspire; infuse (into);

instil; breathe (*fig.*). **ispirazióne,** *f.* inspiration.

Iśraèle, *m.* Israel. **iśraelíta** (*pl.* **-íti**), *&* **iśraelítico** (*pl.* **-ítici**), *a.* Israelitic, Hebrew. **iśraelíta,** *m.* Israelite.

issàre, *v.t.* to hoist (*flag, &c.*).

issòpo, *m.* (*Bot.*) hyssop.

istantànea, *f.* snapshot (*phot.*). **istantàneo,** *a.* instantaneous. **istànte,** *m.* instant; moment; petitioner. ¶ *a.* instant; urgent; imminent. **istanteménte,** *ad.* pressingly; urgently; insistently.

istànza, *f.* application; petition; request; entreaty; insistence. *con* ∼, earnestly; urgently; insistently.

istèrico (*pl.* **-èrici**), *a.* hysterical. **isteríśmo,** *m.* hysteria.

istésso, *a.*, see **stesso.**

istigàre (*pr.* **-ígo,** **-íghi**), *v.t.* to instigate. **istigatóre,** *m.* (*f.* **-tríce**) instigator.

istillàre, see *instillare.*

istintívo, *a.* instinctive. **istínto,** *m.* instinct.

istituíre (*pr.* **-ísco,** **-ísci**), *v.t.* to institute; found; establish; appoint. **istitúto,** *m.* institute; institution. **istitutóre,** *m.* founder; tutor; instructor. **istitutríce,** *f.* governess. **istituzióne,** *f.* institution; establishment.

ístmo, *m.* isthmus.

istología, *f.* histology.

istoriògrafo, *m.* historiographer.

istradàre, *v.t.* to put on the right road; direct.

ístrice, *f.* porcupine.

istrióne, *m.* (comic) actor.

istruíre (*pr.* **-ísco -ísci**), *v.t.* to instruct; teach; educate; inform; direct. **istruírsi,** *v.refl.* to learn. **istruíto,** *a.* educated; learned.

istrumentàre, *v.t.* (*Mus.*) to instrument; write instrumental music; (*Law*) draw up a written contract. **istruménto,** *m.* instrument. Cf. *strumento.*

istruttívo, *a.* instructive. **istruttóre,** *m.* instructor; teacher. *giudice* ∼, examining magistrate. **istruttòria,** *f.* (*Law*) examination; investigation. **istruttòrio** (*pl.* **-òri**), *a.* (*Law*) preliminary. **istruzióne,** *f.* education; learning; teaching; instruction; tuition; direction; order.

istupidíre (*pr.* **-ísco,** **-ísci**), *v.t.* to make stupid or dull; *v.i.* (*aux.* essere) *&* **istupidírsi,** *v.refl.* to become stupid.

Ítaca, *f.* Ithaca.

Itàlia (**l'**), *f.* Italy. **italianaménte,** *ad.* in the Italian way; in the Italian spirit. **italianità,** *f.* Italian feelings; Italian spirit: Italian nationality. **italiàno,** *a.* *&* (*language*) *m.* Italian. *un I*∼, an Italian. *gli Italiani,* the Italians; the Italian people. **itàlico** (*pl.* **-àlici**), *a.* Italic; Italian. ¶ *m.* (*Typ.*) italic. **ítalo,** *a.* Italian (*arch.* *&* *poet.* except in compounds; *italo-britànnico, &c.*).

iteràre (*pr.* **ítero**), *v.t.* to repeat; iterate. **itertaménte,** *ad.* repeatedly.

itineràrio, *m.* itinerary; route.

íto, *p.p.* of *ire.*

ittèrico (*pl.* **-èrici**), *a.* jaundiced. ¶ *m.* person suffering from jaundice. **itterízia,** *f.* jaundice.

ittiòlo, *m.* (*Chem.*) ichthyol.

iúcca, *f.* yucca (*Bot.*).

iúgero, *m.* land-measure, about ¼ acre.

Iugoslàvia (**la**), *f.* Jugo-Slavia. **iugoslàvo,** *a.* *&* *m.* Jugo-Slav.

iugulàre, *a.* jugular.

iunióre, *a.* *&* *m.* junior.

iussióne, *f.* (*leg.*) command.

iúta, *f.* jute. **iutifício,** *m.* jute-factory, j. mill.

Iútland, *m.* Jutland.

ívi, *ad.* there.

J

J, j (*i lunga*), *f.* now used only in words of foreign origin, & elsewhere may always be replaced by **i.**

K

K, k (*cappa*), *f.* the letter K; is found only in words of foreign origin & gen. only as an initial letter. It tends to give place to *c* before the vowels *a, o, & u,* and to *ch* before *e* & *i,* but is kept in the abbs. *Kg., Km.,* & *Kl.* for *Kilogramme* (*It.* chilogramma), *Kilometre* (chilometro), & *Kilolitre* (chilolitro).

kàki, *a.* khaki.

kan (or *can*), *m.* khan.

kantiàno, *a.* Kantian.

kapòc (or *capòc*), *m.* kapok.

karakíri (or *carach'ri*), *m.* hara-kiri.
kedivàle, *a.* Khediv[i]al. **kedivè**, *m.* Khedive.
Kent, *m.* (*Geog.*) Kent. *del K~*, Kentish.
kepleriàno, *a.* of Kepler.
kimòno (or *chimòno*), *m.* kimono.
kodak, *m.* kodak.
kopeck (or *copeco*), *m.* copeck.
kreużer, *m.* kreutzer.
kummel, *m.* kummel.

L

L, 1 (*elle*), *f.* the letter L.
la, *def. art. f.sg.* (*pl.* **le**) the. With preps. *di*, *a*, *da*, *in*, & *su*, forms the compounds *della*, *alla*, *dalla*, *nella*, *sulla*. With *con*, on the other hand, it is usually kept separate, although the form *colla* is sometimes found. ¶ *conjunct. pn. 3rd sg.f.* her, it; also = ella (*nom.*) she, you. The pronominal *la* is sometimes equivalent to *quella cosa* or *questa cosa*, referring to something said or done, or to an antecedent understood, e.g. *l'ha fatta grossa*, he has blundered badly, he has made a mess of things; *smettila!* no more oi that! drop the subject! that's enough! *non bisogna prendersela*, there is no need to get angry, or to be offended. ¶ *m.inv.* (*musical note*) la; (*fig.*) tone, note, suggestion. *dare il ~*, to set the fashion, to give a suggestion. *dare il ~ a una conversazione*, to set the tone of a conversation.
là, *ad.* there; yonder. *al di ~ di*, *pr.* beyond; outside. With *su* & *giù* forms the compounds *lassù* (up there) & *laggiù* (down there); *là da*, close to, beside. *più ~*, over there; yonder; farther away. *~ oltre*, further on. *essere in ~ con gli anni*, to be well on (or advanced) in years.
làbbro, *m.* (*pl.m.* **labbri**, *f.* **labbra**), lip; edge. *~ leporino*, hare-lip. *mordersi le labbra*, to bite one's lips. **labbróne**, *n.* thick lip; thick-lipped person.
làbe, *f.* (*Poet.*) spot; stain.
labiàle, *a. & f.* labial.
làbile, *a.* unsteady; fleeting; ephemeral; transient; (*of memory*) weak.
labirínto, *m.* labyrinth; maze.
laboratòrio (*pl.* -**ori**), *m.* laboratory; workshop; work-room.

laborióso, *a.* laborious, hard-working; industrious; arduous; toilsome; hard; difficult.
laburísta (*pl.* -**isti**), *m.* labour man, member of the labour party. ¶ *a.* labour (*att.*).
làcca (*pl.* **làcche**), *f.* lacquer [*varnish*]. *cera ~*, sealing-wax. *~ in scaglia*, *gomma ~*, *f.* shellac. **laccàre**, *v.t.* to lacquer.
lacchè, *m.inv.* lackey; footman; man-servant.
làccio (*pl.* **làcci**), *m.* noose; knot; ambush; snare; trap; string. **lacci[u]òlo**, *m.* snare; gin; trap.
lacerànte, *a.* tearing; rending (*also fig.*). **laceràre**, *v.t.* to tear; tear up; rend; lacerate. **làcero**, *a.* torn; rent; in rags.
lacèrto, *m.* sinew; muscle & tendon.
lacònico (*pl.* -**ònici**), *a.* laconic.
làcrima & **làgrima**, *f.* tear; (*fig.*) drop. *~ Christi*, a sweet wine of Vesuvius & Sicily. *~ della Madonna*, snowdrop; lily of the valley. **lacrimàbile** & **lacrimévole**, *a.* pitiful; lamentable. **lacrimale**, *a.* lachrymal, tear (*att.*). **lacrimàre** & **lagrimàre**, *v.i.* (*aux. avere*) to weep; cry; shed tears; water, run (*eyes*). **lacrimògeno**, *a.* tear-producing. *gas ~*, tear-gas.
lacrimóso, *a.* tearful; lachrymose; weeping.
lacúna, *f.* gap; lacuna; hiatus; blank.
lacústre, *a.* lacustrine, lake (*att.*).
laddóve, *ad.* where; there where; while; whilst.
ladíno, *m.* Ladin, romance dialect spoken in the Engadine & the Grisons.
ladrería, *f.* theft, robbery; series of thefts. **ladrésco**, *a.* thievish. **làdro**, *m.* thief; robber. ¶ *a.* thievish; (*fig.*) seductive, bewitching; cruel; horrible. **ladronàia**, *f.* nest of thieves; band of thieves. **ladróne**, *m.* robber; highwayman. **ladronéccio**, *m.* larceny; theft; (*fig.*) unfair or excessive taxation; imposition. **ladronería**, *f.* theft; robbery; burglary. **ladronésco** (*pl.* -**éschi**), *a.* thievish; burglarious. **ladrúncolo**, *m.* petty thief; pilferer; young thief.
laggiú, *ad.* down there; there below; yonder.
laghétto, *m.* small lake; pond (*dim.* of *lago*).
lagnànza, *f.* complaint. **lagnàrsi**, *v.refl.* to complain. **làgno**, *m.*

lament; complaint. **làgo** (*pl.* **làghi**), *m.* lake; mere; (*Med.*) ventricle.

làgrima, &c., see *lacrima*.

lagúna, *f.* lagoon.

lài, *m.pl.* lays (*poems*); lamentations.

laicàto, *m.* laity. **làico** (*pl.* **làici**), *a.* lay. *frate* ~, lay brother. ¶ *m.* layman. *i laici,* the laity.

laidézza, *f.* foulness; obscenity; [act of] indecency. **làido,** *a.* foul; dirty; disgusting; loathsome; obscene. **laidúme,** *m.* dirt; filth.

làma, *f.* blade; [thin] sheet; plate; stretch of water, flooded ground; (*fig.*) swordsman. ¶ *m.* (*Zool.*) llama; (*Buddhist priest*) lama.

lambène, *p.a.* (*p.p.* of *lambire*) lapping; gliding over; skimming; touching lightly.

lambiccàre (*pr.* **-ícco, -ícchi**), *v.t.* to distil[l]. **lambiccàrsi,** *v.refl.* in the expr. ~ *il cervello,* to puzzle [one's head], rack one's brains. **lambiccàto,** *a.* strained; affected; far-fetched; artificial. **lambícco** (*pl.* **-ícchi**), *m.* retort; alembic.

lambíre (*pr.* **-ísco, -ísci**), *v.t.* to lap; lick; touch lightly; graze; skim [over]; glide over.

lambrúsca, *f.* wild vine. **lambrúsco** (*pl.* **-úschi**), *m.* a noted red wine from the province of Modena; grape from which this is made.

lamentàre (*pr.* **-énto**), *v.t.* to lament; mourn; regret. **lamentàrsi,** *v.refl.* to complain; moan; lament. **lamentazióne,** *f.* lamentation. **lamentévole,** *a.* plaintive; mournful; lamentable; regrettable; pitiable; pitiful. **lamentío** (*pl.* **-íi**), moaning; groaning; lamentation. **laménto,** *m.* lament; cry of grief or pain; complaint. **lamentóso,** *a.* plaintive; mournful; doleful.

lamièra, *f.* (*Metall.*) sheet; plate; sheet iron. ~*ondulata,* corrugated sheet iron.

làmina, *f.* thin plate; lamina. **laminàre** (*pr.* **làmino**), *v.t.* to roll (*metal*); laminate. **laminatóio** (*pl.* **-ói**), *m.* rolling-mill.

làmpada, *f.* lamp. ~ *a spirito,* spirit-lamp. ~*ad arco,* arc-lamp. ~*di sicurezza,* safety-lamp; ~ *chiusa,* hurricane lamp. **lampadàrio,** *m.* chandelier. **lampadína,** *f.* small lamp; bulb (*Elec.*). ~ *elettrica tascabile,* pocket flash-light.

lampànte, *a.* shining; brilliant; clear; evident.

lampeggiaménto, *m.* flashing; coruscation. **lampeggiàre** (*pr.* **-éggio**), *v.i.* (*aux.* avere) to flash; gleam; lighten. **lampeggío** (*pl.* **-íi**), *m.* continual flashing; coruscation.

lampionàio (*pl.* **-ai**), *m.* lamp-lighter (*pers.*). **lampioncíno,** *m.* small lamp; paper-lantern. **lampióne,** *m.* carriage-lamp; street-lamp. **lampísta** (*pl.* **-ísti**), *m.* lamp-trimmer. **lampistería,** *f.* lamp-room; lamp-store (*Rly.*).

làmpo, *m.* flash; lightning.

lampóne, *m.* raspberry.

lamprèda, *f.* lamprey.

làna, *f.* wool. ~ *filata, pettinato di* ~, or ~ *pettinata,* worsted. *calze di* ~, woollen stockings. **lanai[u]òlo,** *m.* wool-worker.

lancétta, *f.* (*dim.* of *lancia*) lancet; pointer; hand (*watch, clock*); small launch. **lància** (*pl.* **lance**), *f.* lance; spear; (*fig.*) lancer; launch, cutter; nozzle (*fire hose*). ~ *di salvataggio* (ship's) life-boat. *ponte delle* ~*ce,* *m.* boat-deck. **lanciabómbe,** *m.inv.* trench-mortar. **lanciafiàmme,** *m.inv.* flame-thrower. **lanciàre** (*pr.* **làncio, lànci**), *v.t.* to throw; cast; fling; hurl; shy; toss; pitch; fire; shoot; drop (*bombs*); launch; catapult (*aeroplane*); initiate; float; promote; issue; set (*fashion, dog on*); deliver (*ball,* Ten.*, &c.*); fly (*kite*). **lanciàrsi,** *v.refl.* to throw oneself, be thrown, &c. ~ *col paracadute,* (*Aviat.*) to parachute, bale out. **lanciasilúri,** *m.inv.* torpedo tube. **lanciàta,** *f.* thrust. **lancière,** *m.* lancer. *i lancieri,* the Lancers (*dance*).

lancinànte, *a.* (of pain) stabbing; shooting; piercing.

làncio (*pl.* **lànci**), *m.* throwing; throw (*distance thrown*); hurling, &c.; discharge (*torpedo, bomb, &c.*); leap; bound. *pista di* ~, *f.* (*Aero.*) runway.

lànda, *f.* heath; moor; sandy waste.

landò, *m.* landau.

lanería, *f.* (*oft. pl.* **-eríe**) woollen goods. **lanétta,** *f.* mixed wool; coarse wool.

languènte, *p.a.* languishing; drooping.

lànguido, *a.* languid; languishing; drooping; lackadaisical; flat; dull; weak. **languíre** (*pr.* **-lànguo** & **languísco, làngui** & **languísci**), *v.i.* (*aux.* avere) to languish; droop; pine; mope; long; weary; flag; drag; (*Com.*) to be slack or dull; wither;

fade. **languóre**, *m.* languor; listlessness; weakness; faintness.
lanièro, *a.* woollen; wool (*att.*).
lanifício (*pl.* -íci), *m.* wool factory; w. manufacture. **lanína**, *f.* fine wool[len] cloth; light wool (cloth).
lanitàl, *m.inv.* lanital, synthetic wool.
lanolína, *f.* lanolin.
lanóso, *a.* woolly.
lantèrna, *f.* lantern; lamp; harbour light [house]. ~ *cieca*, dark lantern; ~ *con lente sferica*, bull's eye [lantern]. ~ *magica*, magic lantern. *far vedere* (*mostrare*) *lucciole per lanterne*, to gull one, pretend the moon is made of green cheese.
lanternóne, *m.* big lantern; (*fig.*) tall thin man.
lanùgine, *f.* down. **lanuginóso**, *a.* downy.
lànzo, *m.* pikeman (*cf.* Loggia de' Lanzi at Florence).
Laocoónte, *m.* Laocoon (*Myth.*).
laparatomía, *f.* laparotomy (*Surg.*).
lapidàre (*pr.* làpido), *v.t.* to stone.
lapidària, *f.* science of inscriptions.
lapidàrio (*pl.* -ari), *a. & m.* lapidary. **lapidazióne**, *f.* stoning.
làpide, *f.* stone [slab]; tomb-stone; head stone; tablet.
làpis, *m.inv.* [lead] pencil; crayon. ~ *copiativo*, copying pencil. ~ *di gomma*, ink-eraser. **lapislàżżuli**, *m.* (*Miner.*) lapis-lazuli.
làppola, *f.* (*Bot.*) burdock, bur[r]; (*fig.*) importunate bore.
lappóne, *m.* Lapp; Laplander; language of Lapland. ¶ *a.* Lapp (*att.*). **Lappónia** (la), *f.* Lapland.
lardellàre (*pr.* -éllo), *v.t.* to lard (*lit. & fig.*); stuff with bacon; interlard.
lardèllo, *m.* piece of bacon.
lardíte, *f.* soap-stone; tailor's marker. **làrdo**, *m.* bacon; lard; fat.
lardóne, *m.* salt pork. **lardóso**, *a.* (*of meat*) fat.
largaménte, *ad.* widely; amply; abundantly; diffusely; broadly; largely. **largàre**, *v.t.* to widen; loosen; spread (*sail*); push off (*from shore*); get under way. **largheggiaménto**, *m.* profuseness; liberality.
largheggiàre (*pr.* -éggio, -éggi), *v.i.* (*aux.* avere) to be profuse; abound; be liberal; be open-handed.
largheggiatóre, *m.* (*f.* -tríce) liberal giver; open-handed person.
larghézza, *f.* width; breadth; amplitude; largeness; liberality; bounty.
largíre (*pr.* -ísco, -ísci), *v.t.* to

give liberally; bestow; grant. **largitóre**, *m.* (*f.* -tríce) liberal giver; bountiful person. **largizióne**, *f.* donation; gift. **làrgo** (*pl.* làrghi), *a.* wide; broad; large; ample; loose; easy; liberal; (*Mus.*) slow. ¶ *m.* width; breadth; space; room; (*Mar.*) offing. *fare* ~, to make room. *fu fatto* ~, a way was cleared. *prendere il* ~, to run away; put out to sea. *alla larga*, *ad.*, at a distance. *stare alla larga*, to stand off (*lit. & fig.*); keep at a distance. *alla* ~*!* away!
làri, *m.pl.* Lares (household gods); (*fig.*) home, family.
làrice, *m.* larch; larch [tree]; larchwood.
larínge, *f.* larynx. **laringíte**, *f.* laryngitis. **laringoscòpio**, *m.* (*Med.*) laryngoscope.
làrva, *f.* spectre; sham; appearance; larva. **larvàre**, *v.t.* to disguise; conceal. **larvataménte**, *ad.* in disguise. **larvàto**, *a.* masked; concealed.
lašàgne, *f.pl.* (broad) strips of macaroni. **lašagnóne**, *m.* (*fig.*) lubber; clumsy fellow.
làsca (*pl.* làsche), *f.* roach.
lasciapassàre, *m.inv.* pass; permit.
lasciàre (*pr.* làscio, làsci; *fut.* lascerò), *v.t.* to leave; quit; desert; abandon; give up; leave off; leave out; bequeath; let; allow; permit. ~ *cadere*, to drop, let fall. **làscito**, *m.* legacy; bequest.
lascívia, *f.* lasciviousness; lust.
lascívo, *a.* lascivious; lustful; wanton.
làssa, *f.* leash; slip; lead.
lassativo, *a. & m.* laxative; aperient.
lassézza, *f.* lassitude; weariness; fatigue. **làsso**, *a.* tired; weary; fatigued; unhappy. *me* ~*! ahi* ~*!* alas! ¶ *m.* lapse.
lassú, *ad.* up there; there above.
làstra, *f.* plate; sheet; slab; pane. *dim. lastrina*, *lastretta*. **lastricàre** (*pr.* làstrico, làstrichi), *v.t.* to pave. **lastricàto & làstrico** (*pl. lastrici & lastrichi*), *m.* pavement.
lastróne, *m.* large plate; slab.
latèbra, *f.* hiding-place; recess.
latènte, *a.* latent; hidden.
laterale, *a.* lateral; side (*att.*). *carrozzino* ~, side-car.
laterízio (*pl.* -ízi), *a.* brick (*att.*). ¶ *m.pl.* bricks; tiles; tiling.
làtice, *m.* (*Bot.*) latex.
latifondísta (*pl.* -ísti), *m.* owner of

large landed estate. **latifóndo**, *m.* large landed estate.

latinaménte, *ad.* in Latin; in the Latin fashion. **latinísta** (*pl.* -ísti), *m.* Latinist; Latin scholar. **latinità**, *f.* Latinity. *bassa* ~, popular Latin, Low Latin. **latino**, *a. & m.* Latin. *vela* ~*a*, lateen sail. **latinúccio**, *m.* simple Latin; elementary Latin.

latitànte, *a.* in hiding from justice.

latitúdine, *f.* latitude; scope; width.

làto, *m.* side. *a* ~ *di*, beside. *dal* ~ *mio*, for my part. *in ogni* ~, everywhere. ¶ *a.* wide.

latomía & **latòmia**, *f.* stone quarry; prison (esp. those of Syracuse, where the Greek prisoners were confined.

latóre, *m.* (*f.* **latríce**) bearer (*of a letter*).

latraménto, *m.* barking. **latràre**, *v.i.* (*aux.* avere) to bark. **latràto**, *m.* bark.

latrína, *f.* latrine.

latrocínio, *m.* larceny; theft.

làtta, *f.* tin; tin-plate; can. **lattàio**, *m.* tinsmith.

lattàio, *m.* milkman. **lattàia**, *f.* milkwoman; milk-maid; good milker (*cow*). **lattai[u]òlo**, *m.* milk-tooth (cf. *dente di latte*). **lattànte**, *m.* suckling. ¶ *a.* sucking. **lattare** for **allattare**, *v.t.* to suckle. **làtte**, *m.* milk. ~ *condensato*, ~ *concentrato*, condensed milk. ~ *in polvere*, powdered milk. ~ *scremato*, skim[med] milk. *dente di* ~, *m.* milk-tooth. **lattemièle**, *m.* whipped cream (Lombard for *panna montata*). **làtteo**, *a.* milky; milk (*att.*). *Via L* ~*a*, Milky Way. *dieta* ~*a*, milk diet. **lattería**, *f.* dairy; dairy-farm. **latticíni**, *m.pl.* dairy produce. **làttico** (*pl.* **làttici**), *a.* lactic. **lattièra**, *f.* milk-jug. **lattivéndolo**, *m.* (*itinerant*) milkman. ~ **véndola**, *f.* milkwoman.

lattúga, *f.* lettuce.

làuda & **làude** (*pl.* **laudi**), *f.* laud; hymn of praise; early religious lyric.

làudano, *m.* laudanum.

laudàre, *&c.*, see **lodare**. **laudatívo**, *a.* laudatory.

làurea, *f.* (*academic*) degree; laurel crown; diploma. **laureàndo**, *m.* undergraduate; candidate for a degree. **laureàre**, *v.t.* to confer a degree on. **laureàrsi**, *v.refl.* to graduate; take one's degree. **laureàto**, *m.* graduate. ¶ *a.* laureate.

Laurenziàna (**la**), *f.* the famous Laurentian Library at Florence, designed by Michael Angelo in the cloisters of San Lorenzo, to house the collections of Cosimo & Lorenzo de' Medici.

laurenziàno, *a.* Laurentian (*Geol. & Hist.*).

lauréto, *m.* laurel grove. **làuro**, *m.* laurel; bay; (*pl. fig.*) laurels.

lautaménte, *ad.* richly; sumptuously. **lautézza**, *f.* richness; sumptuousness. **làuto**, *a.* sumptuous; magnificent; big; handsome; rich.

làva, *f.* lava.

lavàbile, *a.* washable. **lavàbo**, *m.* wash-hand-basin; wash-stand; (*Eccl.*) lavabo. **lavacàpo**, *m.* scolding, dressing-down. **lavàcro**, *m.* bath; font. **lavàggio**, *m.* washing.

lavàgna, *f.* slate; blackboard.

lavamàno, *m.* wash-hand-basin; wash-stand.

lavànda, *f.* washing; lavender. **lavandàia**, *f.* washerwoman; laundress. **lavandàio**, *m.* laundryman. **lavandería**, *f.* laundry. **lavapiàtti**, *m.inv.* scullery-boy. **lavàre**, *v.t.* to wash. **lavàta**, *f.* washing; wash. ~ *di capo*, scolding; rebuke. dim. *lavatina*. **lavatívo**, *m.* enema. **lavatóio** (*pl.* -ói), *m.* wash-house; wash-tub. **lavatúra**, *f.* washing; wash; dish-water.

lavoracchiàre, *v.i.* (*aux.* avere) to work carelessly or indifferently. **lavoràccio**, *m.* bad work. **lavorànte**, *p.a.* working. ¶ *m.* worker; workman. **lavoràre**, *v.t. & i.* to work. **lavoratívo**, *a.* working; work (*att.*); (*Agr.*) ready for cultivation. *giorno* ~, working-day. **lavoratóre**, *m.* (*f.* -**tríce**) worker; workman, -woman. ¶ *a.* working. *le classi lavoratrici*, the working classes. **lavorazióne**, *f.* working; manufacture; make; (*Agr.*) cultivation, tillage. **lavorío**, *m.* intensive work; workmanship; constant activity; bustle. **lavóro**, *m.* work; labour; toil; task; workmanship. ~ *in legno*, woodwork. ~ *in pietra*, stonework. ~ *di fantasia*, fancy-work. ~ *d'ago*, needlework. *eccesso di* ~, overwork. *lavori forzati*, hard labour (*penal*). *camera del* ~, trade union. **lavoróne**, *m.* important work. **lavorúccio**, *m.* paltry job.

Làzio (**il**), *m.* Latium. (*Geog.*).

lazzarétto, *m.* lazaretto; fever-hospital. **Làzzaro**, *m.* Lazarus.

lażżaróne, *m.* (*Neapolitan*) beggar; rogue; vagabond.

làzzo, *m.* comic gesture or saying; gibe; jest; piece of buffoonery.

làzzo, *a.* sharp; tart; harsh in flavour.

le, *def. art. f.pl.* the. ¶ *pers. pn. f.pl. obj.* them. ¶ *pers. pn. f.sg. conjunct. indir. obj.* to her; her; to you.

leàle, *a.* loyal; faithful; fair; true; sincere. *poco* ∼, unfair. lealménte, *ad.* fair; fairly; loyally. lealtà, *f.* loyalty; faithfulness.

leàrdo, *a.* (*of horse*) grey.

lèbbra, *f.* leprosy. lebbróso, *a.* leprous. ¶ *m.* leper.

leccaménto, *m.* licking. leccapiàtti, *m.inv.* glutton; guzzler. leccapièdi, *m.inv.* flatterer. leccàrda, *f.* dripping-pan. leccàre (*pr.* lécco, lécchi), *v.t.* to lick; (*fig.*) flatter; polish; finish minutely (*writings, paintings, &c.*); graze. leccàta, *f.* lick; licking. dim. *leccatina.* leccàto, *a.* affected, laboured (*style*). leccatóre, *m.* (*f.* -tríce) & leccazàmpe, *m.inv.* (*fig.*) servile flatterer.

leccéto, *m.* grove of ilex trees (or holm-oaks). léccio (*pl.* lécci), *m.* ilex tree (holm-oak). ∼ *spinoso,* holly.

leccornía, *f.* dainty; tit-bit.

lécito, *a.* permissible; permitted; lawful; right.

lèdere (*pr.* lèdo, &c.), *v.t. ir.* to injure; hurt; harm; wound; offend.

léga (*pl.* léghe), *f.* league; union; society; alloy; temper; quality; class; league (*meas. of distance*). *di buona* ∼, of good quality; sound; genuine. *moneta di bassa* ∼, base coin.

legàccio (*pl.* -àcci), *m.* band; fastening; garter.

legàle, *a.* legal; statutory; law (*att.*); lawful. *studio* ∼, lawyer's office. ¶ *m.* lawyer. legalità, *f.* legality. legalizzàre, *v.t.* to legalize; satisfy; authenticate. legalizzazióne, *f.* legalization; ratification; authentication. legalménte, *ad.* legally; lawfully.

legàme, *m.* bond; tie; link; connection. legaménto, *m.* binding; fastening; tying; connection; ligament; liaison (*phonet.*); ligature (*Mus.*). legàre (*pr.* légo, léghi), *v.t.* to bind; tie; fasten; set, mount (*jewels*); tie up; bequeath. legatàrio (*pl.* -àri), *m.* legatee. legàto, *m.* legate; envoy; legacy; bequest. legatóre, *m.* [book]-binder; testator. legatúra, *f.* [book-]binding; tying; fastening;

attachment; ligature (*Mus. & Surg.*). ∼ *trequarti pelle,* half-binding. ∼ *in mezza pelle,* quarter binding (leather).

legazióne, *f.* legation.

légge, *f.* law; enactment; statute; act (of parliament). *di* ∼, perforce, of necessity. *proposta di* ∼, (parliamentary) bill.

leggènda, *f.* legend; (*Typ.*) caption; reference note, explanatory note, signs & symbols (*on map*). leggendàrio, *a.* legendary; fabled.

lèggere (*pr.* lèggo, lèggi, &c.), *v.t. ir.* to read; peruse.

leggerézza, *f.* lightness; levity; thoughtlessness. leggerménte, *ad.* lightly; slightly; thoughtlessly. leggèro, *a.* light; slight; frivolous; thoughtless; inconsiderate.

leggiadría, *f.* prettiness; grace; charm; gracefulness. leggiàdro, *a.* graceful; pretty; charming.

leggíbile, *a.* legible.

leggièri (di), *ad.* easily. leggièro, see *leggero.*

leggío, *m.* reading desk; lectern; music-stand.

leggitóre, *m.* (*f.* -tríce) reader.

legionàrio, *a. & m.* legionary. legióne, *f.* legion.

legislativo, *a.* legislative. legislatóre, *m.* (*f.* -tríce) legislator; lawgiver. ¶ *a.* legislative. legislatúra, *f.* legislature. legislazióne, *f.* legislation. legísta, *m.* (*pl.* -ísti) legist.

legìttima, *f.* legal share (*of property, irrespective of what is bequeathed by will*). legittimàre, *v.t.* to legitimate; legitimize. legìttimo, *a.* legitimate; lawful.

légna, *f.* (*s.* or *pl.*) (fire)wood; fuel. legnàceo, *a.* ligneous; woody. legnàia, *f.* wood-store; wood-pile. legnai[u]òlo, *m.* carpenter; joiner; cabinet-maker. legnàme, *m.* timber. legnàre, *v.t.* to beat; thrash; cane; cudgel. legnàta, *f.* blow with a stick; beating; caning. legnàtico, *m.* right of cutting firewood. légno, *m.* wood; log; club; cudgel; ship; carriage; wood-engraving. ∼ *stagionato,* seasoned timber. ∼ *compensato,* plywood. *pasta (polpa) di* ∼, *f.* wood-pulp. *rivestimento in* ∼, *m.* wainscot, wainscotting. legnóso, *a.* woody.

legulèio (*pl.* -èi), *m.* low-class lawyer.

legúme, *m.* vegetable. leguminóso, *a.* leguminous.

lèi, *pn. pers. 3 sg. f. (disjunct.)* she; her. **L ~,** you.

Lèida, *f.* Leyden.

Lemàno (Lagò), *m.* Lake Leman, Lake of Geneva.

lémbo, *m.* skirt; edge; border; margin; flange; side; strip.

lèmma, *m.* assumption; lemma *(phil. & math.).* **lemme lemme,** *ad.* very slowly, by slow degrees.

Lemosì, *f.* Limoges.

lèmure, *m.* lemur *(Zool.).*

léna, *f.* breath; wind; spirit; courage; vigour, effort. **L ~, Lena,** *dim.* of *Maddalena.*

lène, *a. (Poet.)* light; mild; soft; gentle. **leniménto,** *m.* softening; soothing; assuaging.

Leningràdo, *f.* Leningrad.

lenire *(pr. -ísco, ísci), v.t.* to soften; soothe; assuage. **lenitívo,** *a.* soothing; softening; lenitive. ¶ *m.* lenitive; soothing drug or appliance.

Lènno, *m.* Lemnos *(Geog.).*

lenocínio, *m.* blandishment; artifice; charm. **lenóne,** *m.* pander, procurer; pimp. **lenóna,** *f.* procuress.

lentaménte, *ad.* slowly.

lènte, *f.* lens; monocle; eye-glass; *(pl.)* glasses.

lentézza, *f.* slowness; sluggishness; dilatoriness; tardiness; delay.

lentícchia, *f.* lentil.

lentíggine, *f.* freckle. **lentigginóso,** *a.* freckled.

lènto, *a.* slow; sluggish; slothful; loose, slack.

lènza, *f.* fishing-line.

lenzuòlo, *m. (m.pl.* **lenzuoli,** *f.pl.* **lenzuola)** sheei; *(pl.)* bed-clothes. **~** *funebre,* **~** *mortuario,* winding-sheet, shroud.

leóne, *m.* lion. *dim. leoncèllo, leoncíno.*

Leóne, *m.* Leo. **leonéssa,** *f.* lioness. **leoníno,** *a.* leonine. *città* **~** *a,* the Vatican quarter of Rome, fortified by Pope Leo IV (9th cent.).

leopàrdo, *m.* leopard.

lepidézza, *f.* facetiousness; jocosity; witticism. **lèpido,** *a.* smart; witty; facetious.

lepidòtteri, *m.pl.* lepidoptera; moths.

leporíno, *a.* hare *(att.). labbro* **~,** hare-lip. **lèpre,** *f. (or m.)* hare.

lèrcio *(pl.* **lèrci),** *a.* filthy; foul. **lerciúme,** *m.* filth.

lèsbico, *a.* Lesbian. **Lèsbo,** *m.* Lesbos *(Geog.).*

lésina, *f.* awl; *(fig.)* miser; miserliness. **lesinàre,** *v.i. (aux.* avere) to be stingy; haggle; pinch; *(v.t.)* to grudge. **lesinería,** *f.* stinginess; meanness.

lesióne, *f.* injury; hurt; lesion *(Med.);* wound; damage; offence. **léso** *(p.p.* of *ledere), a.* injured; hurt; damaged; offended. *la parte* **~** *a,* *(Law)* the plaintiff.

lessàre *(pr.* **lésso),** *v.t.* to boil.

lèssico *(pl.* **lèssici),** *m.* lexicon; dictionary. **lessicografía,** *f.* lexicography. **lessicògrafo,** *m.* lexicographer.

lésso, *a. & sync. p.p.* of *lessare,* boiled. ¶ *m.* boiled meat.

lestaménte, *ad.* quickly; hastily; nimbly. **lestézza,** *f.* quickness; agility; dexterity. **lèsto,** *a.* quick; nimble; brisk; ready. **lestofànte,** *m.* swindler; cheap-jack.

letàle, *a.* lethal; deadly.

letamàio *(pl.* **-ài),** *m.* dunghill; manure heap. **letamàre,** *v.t.* to manure. **letàme,** *m.* litter; straw & dung; stable-manure.

letargía, *f. &* **letàrgo,** *m.* lethargy. **letàrgico** *(pl.* **-àrgici),** *a.* lethargic.

Léte, *m.* Lethe *(Myth.).*

leticàre *(pr.* **lético, létichi),** *v.i. (aux.* avere) *&* **leticàrsi,** *v.refl.* to quarrel; wrangle; litigate. Cf. *liticare, litigare.* **letichíno,** *m.* quarrelsome fellow. **letichío,** *m.* constant quarrelling.

letificàre, *v.t.* to gladden. **letízia,** *f.* joy; happiness. **letiziàre,** *v.t. &* **letiziàrsi,** *v.refl. (Poet.)* to rejoice.

lètta, *f.* hasty reading; glance; look.

lèttera, *f.* letter. **~** *per via aerea,* air [mail] letter. *carta* **~** letter-card. **~** *raccomandata,* registered letter. **~** *espresso,* express letter. **~** *di cambio,* bill of exchange. **~** *di credito,* letter of credit. **~** *d'avviso,* letter of advice. **~** *di presentazione,* **~** *di raccomandazione,* **~** *commendatizia,* letter of introduction. **~** *di vettura,* **~** *di porto,* consignment note, waybill. **~** *di procura,* power of attorney. **~** *missiva,* letter missive. **~** *maiuscola,* capital letter. **~** *minuscola,* small (lower case) letter. **~** *di scatola,* **~***cubitale,* block letter. *alla* **~,** literally. *in tutte* **~** *e,* in words at length; in full. *carta da* **~***e,* note-paper. letter paper. *uomo di* **~** *e,* man of letters. **letteràle,** *a.* literal. **letteràrio,** *a.* literary. *proprietà* **~** *a,* copyright. **letteràto,** *a.* lettered; cultured. ¶ *m.* literary man; man of letters. **letteratúra,** *f.* literature.

lèttico, *a. & m.* Latvian.

lettièra, *f.* bedstead; bedhead; (*animal*) bedding or straw. **lettíga** (*pl.* **lettíghe**), *f.* litter; stretcher (*on wheels*) (cf. *barella*).

lettíno, *m.* small bed; couch; crib; berth. **lètto,** *m.* bed; bedstead; (*river*) bed; marriage. ~ *da campo,* camp-bed. ~ *di ammalato,* ~ *di dolore,* sick-bed. *mettersi a* ~, to take to one's bed. *esser cos.ʃetto al* ~, to keep to one's bed. *c.mera da* ~, bedroom. ¶ *p.p.* of *leggere.*

lettoràto, *m.* readership (*Acad.*), lectureship. **lettóre, m. lettríce,** *f.* reader, lecture.~ **lettúra,** *f.* reading, perusal. *sala di* ~, reading-room. *libro di* ~, reading-book; reader.

lèva, *m.* lever (*lit. & fig.*). **lèva,** *f.* (*Mil.*) levy. **levàbile,** *a.* removable.

levànte, *m.* East. *il L* ~, the Levant. **levantíno,** *a. & m.* Levantine. **levàre** (*pr.* **lèvo**), *v.t.* to take [away], remove; quench; appease; except; take off; subtract; deduct; raise; rouse; lift; lift up; close (*a sitting of parliament, &c.*); levy; get; extract; **levàrsi,** *v.refl.* to rise; get up; get off; get out (of the way). ~ *d'attorno,* ~ *dinanzi,* to get rid of. **levàta,** *f.* rising; getting up; taking away; lifting; clearance; collection (*postal*); wholesale purchase. ~ *del sole,* sun-rise. ~ *di sangue,* letting of blood. **levàto,** *p.a.* removed; taken away; deducted; subtracted; excepted; raised; lifted [up]. *cadere a gambe* ~ *e,* to tumble down, fall on one's back. *fuggire a gambe* ~ *e,* to run off at full speed. *a bandiere* ~ *e,* with flying colours.

levatóio (ponte) (*pl.* **-ói**), *m.* draw-bridge.

levatríce, *f.* midwife.

levatúra, *f.* talent; [degree of] intelligence.

leviatàno, *m.* Leviathan.

levigàre, *v.t.* to smooth; polish. **levigatézza,** *f.* smoothness. **levigazióne,** *f.* polishing; smoothing.

levità, *f.* lightness; levity.

levíta (*pl.* **-íti**), *m.* Levite. **levítico** (*pl.* **-ítici**), *a.* Levitical. ¶ *m. il L* ~, Leviticus (*O.T.*).

levrière, *m.* greyhound.

lèzio (*pl.* **lèzi**), *m.* (often pl.) affectation; mincing way[s].

lezióne, *f.* lesson; lecture (*Univ.*); reprimand; reading (*variant*).

leziosàggine, *f.* affectedness. **leziosaménte,** *ad.* affectedly; lackadaisically. **lezióso,** *a.* affected; simpering; lackadaisical; mincing; effeminate.

léżżo, *m.* stink; bad smell; foul odour. **leżżóso,** *a.* stinking; foul; filthy; fetid. **leżżúme,** *m.* filth; stinking mass.

li, *pers. pn. 3 pl.m* (*conjunct.*) them.

lí, *ad.* there; here; now. *di* ~, from there; from here. *di* ~ *a un anno,* in a year from then.· *giù di* ~, thereabout[s]. ~ *per* ~, instantly, there & then; at first. *siamo sempre* ~, things remain as they were (or as before).

liàna, *f.* (*Bot.*) liana; liane. **lías, m.** lias (*Geol.*). **liàssico** (*pl.* **-àssici**), *a.* liassic. ¶ *m.* liassic period.

Líbano, *m.* Lebanon.

libàno, *m.* cable (of esparto fibre) (*Naut.*).

libàre (*pr.* **líbo**), *v.t.* to drink; to make libation[s]; taste lightly; sip; (for *allibare*) to lighten a ship. **libazióne,** *f.* libation; potation.

líbbra, *f.* pound (*avoirdupois weight* = 0·45359243 kilogramme).

libecciàta, *f.* south-westerly gale. **libèccio,** *m.* south-west wind.

libellísta (*pl.* **-ísti**), *m.* libeller; libellist. **libèllo,** *m.* libel; written declaration.

libèllula, *f.* dragon-fly.

liberàle, *a. & m.* liberal; open-handed; learned. **liberalísmo,** *m.* liberalism. **liberalità,** *f.* liberality; generosity; munificence.

liberalménte, *ad.* freely; liberally; frankly. **liberàre,** *v.t.* to free; set free; deliver; release. **liberatóre,** *m.* (**-tríce,** *f.*) liberator; deliverer. **liberazióne,** *f.* liberation; deliverance.

liberísmo, *m.* [theory of] free-trade. **liberísta** (*pl.* **-ísti**), *m.* free-trader. **líbero,** *a.* free; at liberty; disengaged; unoccupied; available; vacant; spare; open; welcome; clear (*way*); dissolute, licentious; unstamped (*paper*). ~ *arbitrio,* free will. ~ *scambio,* free trade. ~ *pensatore,* free-thinker. ~ *a pratica,* [free] pratique. *disegno a mano* ~ *a,* free-hand drawing. **libertà,** *f.* freedom; liberty. ~ *di parlare,* ~ *di parola,* freedom of speech, free speech; outspokenness. ~ *di stampa,* freedom of the press.

libertàrio, *m.* libertarian. **liberti-cída,** *m. & a.* liberticide; destroyer or destructive of liberty. **liberti-nàggio,** *m.* libertinage; licentiousness. **libertíno,** *a.* libertine, rakish. ¶ *m.* libertine, rake.

Líbia (la), *f.* Libya. **líbico,** *a. & m.* Libyan.

libídine, *f.* lust. **libidinóso,** *a.* lustful.

líbito, *m.* (*Poet.*) will; desire; pleasure; caprice.

líbra, *f.* balance; scales. *L~,* Libra (*constellation*).

libràio (*pl.* -ai), *m.* bookseller. *~ editore,* book-seller & publisher.

libràre, *v.t.* to poise; weigh (*fig.*). **libràrsi,** *v.refl.* to balance. *~a volo,* to soar.

libràrio, *a.* of books; book (*att.*). *il commercio ~,* the book-trade. **librería,** *f.* library; book-shop; book-case. **librésco** (*pl.* -éschi), *a.* bookish. **librettísta** (*pl.* -ísti), *m.* librettist. **librétto,** *m.* small book; notebook; libretto. *~ di banca,* bank-book; pass-book. *~ degli assegni,* cheque book. **libriccíno,** *m.* small book; booklet. **líbro,** *m.* book. *~ illustrato,* picture-book; illustrated b. *~ di preghiere,* prayer-book. *~ di lettura,* reading-book, reader. *~ di consultazione,* book of reference. *~ mastro,* ledger.

liceàle, *a.* pertaining to a *liceo* or high-school. **liceísta** (*pl.* -ísti), *m.* pupil of a *liceo.*

licènza, *f.* licence; permit; certificate; diploma; leave; leave of absence; furlough; (*tenants'*) notice to quit; dismissal; epilogue; (abuse of) liberty; licentiousness; irregularity. **licenziaménto,** *m.* dismissal; discharge. **licenziàre,** *v.t.* to dismiss; discharge; give up (*a tenancy*); pass (*proofs for the press*); grant a certificate to, confer a diploma on. **licenziàrsi,** *v.refl.* to resign; take one's leave; get one's diploma or certificate. *~ da,* to quit. **licenziàto,** *p.a.* dismissed; on leave; having a diploma. ¶ *m.* licentiate. **licenzióso,** *a.* licentious; dissolute; ribald.

licèo, *m.* high school; grammar-school; secondary s.; lycée (*Fr.*).

lichène, *m.* lichen (*Bot.*).

licitàre, *v.t.* (*leg.*) to put up for auction; to bid for (at auction). **licitazióne,** *f.* auction-sale; bid (*at auction*).

lído, *m.* shore, seashore; (*fig.*) land, country. *il L~,* the Lido (*Venice*).

Liègi, *f.* Liège.

lietaménte, *ad.* gladly; cheerfully; merrily. **lièto,** *a.* glad; happy; joyful; cheerful; merry.

lième, *a.* light; slight; easy; trifling.

lievitàre, *v.t.* to leaven; ferment. *v.i.* (*aux.* essere) to rise. Cf. *levitàre.* **lievitatúra,** *f.* fermentation; leavening. **lièvito,** *m.* yeast; leaven. *~ di birra,* yeast; barm. *~ in polvere,* yeast powder; baking p.

lígio (*pl.* lígi), *a.* faithful; true; loyal; obedient. [uomo]*~,* liegeman; sworn vassal (*Hist.*).

lignàggio, *m.* lineage.

lígneo, *a.* ligneous; woody. **lignite,** *f.* lignite.

ligure, *a. & m.* Ligurian. **Ligúria (la),** *f.* Liguria.

ligústro, *m.* (*Bot.*) privet.

Lílla, *f.* Lille.

lillà, *a. & m.* lilac.

lillipuziàno, *a. & m.* Lilliputian. ¶ *a.* (*fig.*) tiny.

líma, *f.* file.

limaccióso, *a.* miry; muddy; slimy.

limàre, *v.t.* to file; file away; gnaw; (*fig.* of style) to polish. **limatúra,** *f.* filing; filings.

límbo, *m.* limbo.

limitàre, *m.* threshold. ¶ *v.t.* to limit; keep within bounds; bound; confine; restrict; circumscribe. **limitàto,** *a.* limited; circumscribed; small; restricted. *responsabilità ~a,* limited liability. **limitazióne,** *f.* limitation. *~ delle nascite,* birth control. **límite,** *m.* limit; extent; bound; boundary. *~ di velocità,* speed limit. *~ delle nevi,* snow-line. **limítrofo,** *a.* bordering, adjacent; neighbouring.

límo, *m.* mud; mire; slime.

limonàio (*pl.* -ài), *m.* lemon-seller. **limonàta,** *f.* lemonade. **limóne,** *m.* lemon; lemon-tree. *succo di ~,* *m.* lemon-juice. *spremuta di ~, f.* lemon squash.

limòsina, *f.* alms. **limòsinàre,** *v.t. & i.* (*aux.* avere) to beg (for charity). **limòsinière,** *m.* almoner.

limóso, *a.* muddy.

limpidézza, *& ***limpidità,** *f.* clearness; limpidity; transparency. **límpido,** *a.* clear; limpid; transparent; pure.

linai[u]òlo, *m.* flax-dresser.

línce, *f.* lynx. **línceo,** *a.* lynx-like (*of eyes, &c.*).

lincèo, *m.* member of the (scientific) Academy 'dei Lincei', founded at Rome in 1603.
linciàggio, *m.* lynching. linciàre, *v.t.* to lynch.
lindézza, *f.* neatness; tidiness; spruceness; cleanliness. líndo, *a.* neat; clean; tidy. lindúra, *f.* neatness, &c.
línea, *f.* line; rank. ~ *retta*, straight line. ~ *ferroviaria*, railway line. ~ *aerea*, air line. ~ *di autobus*, bus line, bus-way. ~ *di carico*, load line. ~ *di galleggiamento*, water line (*ship*). ~ *di montaggio*, assembly l. ~ *di partenza*, starting l.; scratch l. ~ *maschile*, male line (of descent). lineàle, *a.* lineal. lineaménto, *m.* feature; lineament (*gen.* *pl.*). lineàre, *a.* linear. ¶ *v.t.* to draw lines on; delineate. lineétta, *f.* hyphen; short line; dash (*Teleg.*).
línfa, *f.* (*Physiol.*) lymph; (*Bot.*) sap.
linfaticaménte, *ad.* languidly; listlessly. linfàtico (*pl.* -àtici), *a.* lymphatic.
lingòtto, *m.* ingot.
língua, *f.* tongue; language; speech; strip. [~] *volgare*, vernacular. ~ *straniera*, foreign language. linguàccia, *f.* evil tongue; spiteful person. linguacciúto, *a.* talkative. ¶ *m.* sharp-tongued person.
Linguadòca (la), *f.* Languedoc (*Geog.*).
linguàggio, *m.* language (*gen. sense*); speech; parlance. linguàio *&* linguai[u]òlo, *m.* pedantic linguist. linguétta, *f.* tongue-shaped strip of leather, cardboard, &c.; clip. ~ *di una scarpa*, tongue of a shoe. linguísta (*pl.* -ísti), *m.* linguist. linguística, *f.* linguistics. linguístico (*pl.* -ístici), *a.* linguistic.
linifício, *m.* flax[-spinning] mill. líno, *m.* flax. *seme di* ~, linseed. *olio di* ~, linseed oil. *tela di* ~, *f.* linen. linòleum, *m.inv.* linoleum, *abb.* lino. *incisione in* ~, lino cut (*Typ.*). linóne, *m.* lawn (*linen*). linotipía, *f.* lino-typing. linotipísta, *m.* linotypist. linotípo, *m.* linotype. linséme, *m.* linseed; flax-seed.
liocòrno, *m.* unicorn.
lionàto, *a.* tawny; fawn-coloured.
Lióne, *f.* Lyons.
líppo, *a.* blear-eyed.
Lipsia, *f.* Leipzig.
liquefàre (*pr.* -faccio *&* -fo, like fare), *v.t. ir. &* liquefàrsi, *v.refl.* to

liquefy; melt. liquefazióne, *f.* liquefaction.
líquida, *f.* liquid [consonant]. liquidàre (*pr.* líquido), *v.t.* to liquidate; wind up; close; settle; pay [off]; sell off. liquidazióne, *f.* liquidation; winding-up (*society,* *company*); closing; settlement, account (*Ex.*); selling off. *vendita per* ~, clearance sale. líquido, *a.* liquid (*also fig.*); wet (*goods*); (*sounds*) clear, fluent, pure; bright, translucent (*eyes, sky, &c.*). *danaro* ~, cash. ¶ *m.* liquid; fluid.
liquirízia, *f.* liquorice. liquóre, *m.* liquor; liqueur; (*pl.*) spirits. liquorísta (*pl.* -ísti), *m.* dealer in spirits; publican.
líra, *f.* lira (*Ital.*); lyre (*mus. instr.*). ~ *sterlina*, (*Eng.*) pound [sterling]. L~, Lyra (*constell.*). lírica, *f.* lyric; lyric[al] poem; lyric[al] poetry. lírico (*pl.* lírici), *a.* lyric; lyrical. ¶ *m.* lyric poet. lirísta (*pl.* -ísti), *m.* player on the lyre.
Lisbóna, *f.* Lisbon.
lísca (*pl.* lísche), *f.* small fish bone; stalk of hemp; or flax; (*fig.*) morsel.
liscétto, *m.* rouge; paint; polish. liscézza, *f.* smoothness; softness. líscia (*pl.* lisce), *f.* smoothing-stone; flat-iron; polisher. lisciàre, *v.t.* to smooth; polish; (*Mech.*) burnish; (*fig.*) flatter; coax; lick (*animal with young*); clean; embellish. lisciàrsi, *v.refl.* to tidy oneself; dress with care. lisciàta, *f.* smooth[ing], rub[bing] down; polishing; (*fig.*) flattery, coaxing. lisciatúra, *f.* smoothing; burnishing. líscio (*pl.* lisci), *a.* smooth; glossy; sleek; easy; light; plain. *passarla* ~ *ia*, to get off lightly, go unpunished. *messa* ~ *ia*, low mass.
liscívia, *f.* lye. lisciviàre, *v.t.* to wash with lye, lixiviate (*Chem.*).
liscóso, *a.* bony; stalky.
líšo, *a.* worn-out; threadbare.
lísta, *f.* list; roll; panel (*jury*); bill; strip; stripe; band, streak. ~ *dei cibi*, bill of fare; menu. ~ *elettorale*, register of voters. listàre, *v.t.* to stripe, mark with stripes; border. listíno, *m.* list; note; table; price-list, time-table.
litania, *f.* (*gen.pl.* -íe) litany.
litantràce, *m.* anthracite. litargírio, *m.* litharge (*Chem.*).
líte, *f.* dispute; quarrel; law-suit. litichíno, *m.* quarrelsome person, disputant. litigànte, *m.* litigant;

suitor. **litigàre** (*pr.* **lítigo, lítighi**), *v.i.* (*aux.* avere) to quarrel; dispute. **litígio,** *m.* dispute; quarrel; altercation. **litigióso,** *a.* litigious; quarrelsome.

lítio, *m.* lithium (*Chem.*).

litocromía, *f.* chromolithography. **litografàre** (*pr.* **-ògrafo**), *v.t.* to lithograph. **litografía,** *f.* lithography. **litogràfico** (*pl.* **-àfici**), *a.* lithografic. **litògrafo,** *m.* lithographer.

lítro, *m.* litre.

littoràle, *m.* coast-line; sea-board. ¶ *a.* & **littoràneo,** coastal, coast (*att.*).

littóre, *m.* lictor (*Hist.*).

littorína, *f.* Diesel railway car.

Lituània (la), *f.* Lithuania. **lituàno,** *a.* & *m.* Lithuanian.

liturgía, *f.* liturgy. **litúrgico** (*pl.* **-úrgici**), *a.* liturgical.

liutàio, *m.* maker of stringed instruments. **liutísta** (*pl.* **-ísti**), *m.* lutanist, lute-player. **liúto,** *m.* lute.

livèlla, *f.* mason's level; plummet. ~ *a bolla d'aria,* spirit level. ~ *a cannocchiale,* surveyor's level. **livellaménto,** *m.* & **livellazióne,** *f.* levelling. **livellàre** (*pr.* **livèllo**), *v.t.* to level; set on a level. *v.i.* (*aux.* essere) to be on the same level; be on a level (with = con). **livèllo,** *m.* level; deed of lease; property held on lease. ~ *d'acqua,* water-level. *passaggio a* ~, level-crossing.

lividézza, *f.* lividness. **lívido,** *a.* livid; discoloured; (*fig.*) envious, spiteful. ¶ *m.* bruise. **lividóre,** *m.* pallor; lividity; envy, spite. **lividúra,** *f.* livid spot; discolouration; bruise. **livóre,** *m.* rancour; envy; bitterness; hatred; spite fulness.

Livórno, *f.* Leghorn.

livrèa, *f.* livery.

lízza, *f.* lists; tilt[ing]-yard. *la L* ~, public gardens at Siena.

lo (*pl.* **gli**), *def. art. m.sg.*; (before impure s, z, and gn) the. ¶ *pers. pron. m.* him; it (*obj.*)

lòbo, *m.* lobe.

locàle, *a.* local. ¶ *m.* place; room; (*pl.*) premises; rooms; seat (*of an institution*). ~ *equipaggio,* (*ship*) crew's quarters. **località,** *f.inv.* locality. **localizzàre,** *v.t.* to localize.

locànda, *f.* inn. **locandière,** *m.* (*f.* **locandièra**) inn-keeper.

locàre, *v.t.* to let; rent; (*for collocare*) to place. **locatàrio** (*pl.* **-àri**), *m.*

tenant; lodger, lessee. **locatívo,** *a.* (*Gram.*) locative; (*leg.*) for letting. *tassa sul valor* ~, *f.* house-tax. **locatóre,** *m.* (*f.* **-tríce**) landlord, (-lady); lessor. **locazióne,** *f.* lease; letting [out].

lòco, *m.* (*for* **luogo**) place. **locomòbile,** *f.* traction-engine. **locomotíva,** *f.* locomotive, [l.-] engine. **locomotívo,** *a.* locomotive. **locomotóre** (*f.* **-tríce**), *a.* & *m.* locomotor, -motive. **locomozióne,** *f.* locomotion.

locústa, *f.* locust.

locuzióne, *f.* locution; phrase; expression.

lodàbile, *a.* laudable, praiseworthy. **lodàre** (*pr.* **lòdo**), *v.t.* to praise; laud; extol; celebrate; commend; approve. **lodàrsi di** (*of pers.*), to be pleased with; to be fond of. **lodatívo,** *a.* laudatory. **lòde,** *f.* praise; commendation. **lodévole,** *a.* praiseworthy; laudable; commendable.

lodigiàno, *a.* & *m.* of Lodi, native of Lodi.

lòdo, *m.* award; expert opinion; arbiter's decision.

lòdola, *f.* lark; sky-lark.

logarítmo, *m.* logarithm.

loggétta, *f.* small open-sided gallery. **lòggia** (*pl.* **lògge**), *f.* loggia; open-sided gallery; masonic lodge. **loggiàto,** *m.* covered gallery; colonnade. **loggióne,** *m.* upper gallery (*Theat.*).

lògica, *f.* logic. **lògico** (*pl.* **lògici**), *a.* logical. ¶ *m.* logician.

logística, *f.* (*Mil.*) logistics; transport & supply.

lòglio, *m.* darnel.

logoraménto, *m.* attrition; wearing out; wearing down. **logoràre** (*pr.* **lógoro**), *v.t.* to wear out; wear down; exhaust; waste; spoil; ruin. **logorío,** *m.* wear; wear & tear. **lógoro,** *a.* worn out; threadbare; worn away.

lòlla, *f.* husk; chaff.

lombàggine, *f.* lumbago.

Lombardía (la), *f.* Lombardy. **lombàrdo,** *a.* & *m.* Lombard.

lombàta, *f.* loin (*of meat*). **lombatèllo,** *m.* fillet. **lómbo,** *m.* sirloin; loin; (*pl. fig.*) family; descent.

lombríco (*pl.* **-íchi**), *m.* earth-worm.

londinése, *a.* of London, London (*att.*). *L* ~, *m.* Londoner. **Lóndra,** *f.* London.

longànime, *a.* patient; forbearing. **longanimità,** *f.* forbearance.

longevità, *f.* longevity. longèvo, *a.* long-lived.
longitudinàle, *a.* longitudinal. longitúdine, *f.* longitude.
lontanaménte, *ad.* far away; afar; distantly; remotely; vaguely. lontanànza, *f.* distance; remoteness; absence. lontàno, *a.* distant; far [off]; remote. ¶ *ad.* far; far off; far away. lontanúccio, *a. & ad.* rather far.
lóntra, *f.* otter.
lónza, *f.* loin (*of meat*); panther (*the animal in Dante's Inf.*, I, 32–3).
loquàce, *a.* talkative; loquacious. loquacità, *f.* talkativeness.
loquèla, *f.* speech, manner of speaking; language; eloquence.
lordàre (*pr.* lórdo), *v.t.* to besmirch; bespatter; soil; dirty. lórdo, *a.* dirty; soiled; bespattered; gross. *peso* ~, gross weight. lordúme, *m.* quantity of filth. lordúra, *f.* filth; dirt.
Lorèna (la), *f.* Lorraine. lorenése, *a.* of Lorraine. ¶ *m.* native of Lorraine, Lorrainer.
loríca, *f.* cuirass.
lóro, *pers. pr. 3rd pl. m. f.* (*disjunct.*) they; them. ¶ *poss. a. & pn. inv. il* ~, *la* ~, *i* ~, *le* ~, their; theirs.
losànga, *f.* lozenge (*Her.*).
Losànna, *f.* Lausanne.
lósco (*pl.* lóschi), *a.* squint-eyed; one-eyed; (*fig.*) dubious, suspicious.
lòto, *m.* lotus (*Bot.*); mud. lotòfago (*pl.* -òfagi), *m.* lotus-eater.
lòtta, *f.* wrestling; struggle; fight, contest, tussle, fray. ~ *americana,* all-in wrestling. ~ *greco-romana,* Gr[a]eco-Roman wrestling. ~ *libera,* catch-[as-catch-]can. ~*di classe,* class war. lottàre (*pr.* lòtto), *v.i.* (*aux.* avere) to struggle; fight; contend; wrestle. lottatóre, *m.* wrestler.
lottería, *f.* lottery. lòtto, *m.* lot; portion; parcel; lottery; game of lotto.
Lovànio, *f.* Louvain.
lozióne, *f.* lotion.
lubbióne, *m.* upper gallery (*Theat.*).
lubricità, *f.* slipperiness; lubricity; lewdness; indecency. lúbrico (*pl.* lúbrici), *a.* slippery; lascivious; lewd; indecent.
lubrificànte, *a.* lubricating. ¶ *m.* lubricant. lubrificàre (*pr.* -ífico, -ífichi), *v.t.* to lubricate; oil, grease. lubrificatóre, *m.* lubricator.
Lúca, *m.* Luke.
lucchese, *a. & m.* of Lucca, native of L.

lucchétto, *m.* padlock; latch.
luccicànte, *a.* sparkling; shining. luccicàre (*pr.* lúccico, lúccichi), *v.i.* (*aux.* essere & avere) to shine; sparkle; gleam; glitter.
lúccio (*pl.* lúcci), *m.* pike (*fish*).
lúcciola, *f.* fire-fly; glow-worm.
lúce, *f.* light; luminary (*pers.*); aperture, port hole (*Mech.*); opening, span (*Arch.*); window; mirror; pupil (*eye*); (*pl.*) (*Poet.*) eyes. ~ *solare,* sunlight. ~ *elettrica,* electric l. ~*a gas,* gaslight. ~*al magnesio,* magnesium l. (*Phot.*). *filtro* ~, (*Phot.*) light filter. lucènte, *a.* shining; bright. lucentézza, *f.* brightness; brilliancy. lúcere (*pr.* lúce, lúcono). *v.i.* defect. (*Poet.*) to shine; gleam; be luminous.
lucèrna, *f.* lamp. L~, *f.* Lucerne. lucernàrio (*pl.* -àri), *m.* sky-light; dormer-window. lucernière, *m.* lampstand.
lucèrtola, *f.* lizard.
Lucía, *f.* Lucy.
lucidaménto, *m.* polishing; glazing; tracing. lucidàre (*pr.* lúcido), *v.t.* to polish; clean; glaze; gloss; copy by tracing. lucidézza, *f.* brightness; lustre; polish. lucidità, *f.* lucidity; clearness. lúcido, *a.* lucid; bright; clear; shining. ¶ *m.* brilliance; lustre; polish; tracing. ~ *da scarpe,* ~ *per le scarpe,* blacking, shoe-blacking.
Lucífero, *m.* Lucifer; (*fig.*) morning star.
lucígnolo, *m.* wick.
lucràre (*pr.* lúcro), *v.t.* to earn; gain. lucratívo, *a.* lucrative; profitable.
Lucrèzio, *m.* Lucretius.
lúcro, *m.* lucre; gain; profit. lucróso, *a.* profitable; lucrative.
luculènto, *a.* shining; gleaming; brilliant.
luculliàno, *a.* sumptuous (*feast, banquet*) (after Lucullus).
ludíbrio, *m.* mockery; scorn; ridicule; laughing-stock.
lúdo, *m.* game; public show.
lúe, *f.* contagion; infection.
luf, lúffa, *f.* loofah.
lúglio, *m.* July.
lúgubre, *a.* mournful; lugubrious; dismal.
lúi, *pers. pr. 3 sg. m.* (*disjunct.*) he; him. lui, *m.* wren.
Luígi, *m.* Louis. Luigiàna (la), *f.* Louisiana (U.S.A.).
lumàca, *f.* snail; slug; spiral curve. *scala a* ~, winding-stair. luma-

cóne, m. large snail; (fig.) sluggard,
slowcoach; worm of a screw.
lumàio (pl. -ai), m. lamp-lighter;
lamp-seller. lúme, m. light; lamp;
(pl. fig.) lights; knowledge; enlightenment; (Poet.) eyes. lumeggiàre
(pr. -éggio, -éggi), v.t. to shed light
on; illuminate; throw into (strong)
light; bring out the (high) lights in
(a picture). lumicíno, m. faint light;
small lamp. lumièra, f. chandelier;
bracket. luminàre, m. luminary.
luminària, f. (public) illumination.
luminèllo, m. wick-holder; candle-
socket. lumíno, m. small light.
~ da notte, night-light. luminóso,
a. luminous; clear; shining.
lúna, f. moon. ~ calante, waning
moon. ~ di miele, honeymoon.
lunàre, a. lunar. lunàrio (pl. -àri),
m. almanac; calendar. lunarísta
(pl. -ísti), m. almanac-maker;
weather-prophet; astrologer. lunà-
tico (pl. -àtici), a. crazy; capricious;
whimsical; eccentric. lunàto, a.
crescent-shaped.
lunedí, m. Monday.
lunétta, f. lunette (Arch.).
lungàggine, f. wearisome length;
tediousness; slowness; delay; rigmarole. lungagnàta, f. long tedious
speech or story. lungaménte, ad.
for a long time; at great length.
Lungàrno (pl. lungarni), m. street
alongside the Arno (Pisa, Florence).
lunghésso, pr. (Poet.) along. lunghét-
to, a. rather long. lunghézza, f.
length; duration; (sport) length.
~ d'onda, (Radio) wave length.
lúngi, ad. (Poet.) far; far off. da ~,
from afar. lungimirànte, a. far-
seeing. lúngo (pl. lúnghi), a. long;
slow; tall; thin; diluted. a lungo
(ad.), long, (for) a long time. per il
~, lengthwise; in length. alla ~a,
a ~ andare, in the long run. di gran
~a, far; by far. ¶ pr. along; during.
Lungotévere, m.inv. street alongside
the Tiber (Rome).
luògo (pl. luòghi), m. place; spot;
passage (in a book); room; time;
occasion; cause; (Math.) locus. aver
~, to take place; happen. in
qualche ~, somewhere. luogote-
nènte, m. lieutenant. luogotenènza,
f. lieutenancy.
lúpa, f. she-wolf. lupacchiòtto,
lupétto, lupicíno, m. wolf-cub;
young wolf. lupésco (pl. -éschi), a.
wolfish.
lupanàre, m. house of ill-fame; brothel.

lupinàio (pl. -ài), m. lupin-seller.
lupinèlla, f. (Bot.) sainfoin.
lupíno, m. (Bot.) lupin[e]. ¶ a.
wolfish.
lúpo, m. wolf (pl. wolves). ~ di mare,
sea-pike, sea-wolf; (fig.) old salt,
old sea-dog (sailor).
lúppolo, m. hop (plant).
lúrco (pl. lúrchi), a. greedy;
gluttonous.
luridézza, f. filthiness. lúrido, a.
dirty; filthy.
lusínga (pl. lusínghe), f. enticement;
flattery; false hope. lusingàre (pr.
-íngo, -ínghi), v.t. to entice; cajole;
flatter; deceive. lusingatóre, m.
(f. -tríce) flatterer; cajoler; wheedler;
deceiver. ¶ a. alluring; flattering;
&c. lusinghévole, a. flattering;
attractive; alluring. lusinghièro,
a. flattering; alluring; promising;
agreeable.
lussàre, v.t. to dislocate. lussazióne,
f. (Surg.) dislocation.
Lussembúrgo, m. Luxembourg.
lússo, m. luxury. lussuóso, a.
luxurious; sumptuous; rich; magnificent. lussureggiànte, a. luxuriant.
lussureggiàre (pr. -éggio, -éggi),
v.i. (aux. avere) to live in luxury;
grow luxuriantly. lussúria, f.
wantonness; sensuality; lust. lussu-
rióso, a. sensual; lustful.
lústra, f. appearance; pretence; pretext; shift. lustràle, a. lustral;
sacrificial; purifying. lustràre, v.t.
to polish; clean; (fig.) flatter. v.i.
(aux. avere) to shine. lustrascàrpe,
m.inv. shoeblack; boots (hotel).
lustríno, m. tinsel; sparkling ornament; glacé silk; shoeblack. lústro,
m. lustre; gloss; polish; lustrum
(period of 5 years). ¶ a. lustrous;
shiny; glittering; polished.
luteranésimo or luteranísmo, m.
Lutheranism. luteràno, a. & m.
Lutheran. Lutéro, m. Luther.
lútto, n. grief; mourning. luttuóso,
a. mournful.
lutulènto, a. muddy; miry.

M

M, m (emme), f. the letter M.
ma, c. & ad. but; why. ma che!
(excl. of surprise, ridicule or
disbelief), not at all! really? indeed!
you don't say so! did you ever hear
the like! what nonsense!

màcabro, *a.* macabre; grim; horrid; gruesome; ghastly. *danza* ~*a,* danse macabre, Dance of Death.
macadàm, *m.* macadam. **macadamiżżàre,** *v.t.* to macadamize.
màcca (a), *ad. expr.* in abundance.
Maccabèo, *a.* Maccabean. *Giuda* ~, Judas Maccabeus. *i Maccabei,* the Maccabees.
maccarèllo, *m.* mackerel.
maccheronàta, *f.* dish of macaroni; eating of m. **maccheróne,** *m.* (*gen. pl.*) macaroni; (*fig.*) blockhead. *pasticcio di* ~*i,* macaroni (&) cheese.
maccheronèa, *f.* macaronic poem.
maccherònico (*pl.* -ònici), *a.* macaronic.
màcchia (*pl.* **màcchie**), *f.* spot; stain; blot; speck; blemish; pointillist sketch or drawing; thicket; bush; scrub (Fr. *maquis*). ~ *solare,* sunspot. *darsi alla* ~, to take to the bush, become a highway robber. *alla* ~, secretly. *stampato alla* ~, printed clandestinely (with no name of place or printer, or under a false name). **macchiai[u]òlo,** *m.* impressionist painter; pointilliste. ¶ *a.* wild; shy. **macchiàre** (*pr.* **màcchio, màcchi**), *v.t.* to spot; stain; blot; soil; (be)spatter; (*fig.*) sully. **macchiétta,** *f.* (*dim.* of *macchia*) speck; sketch; caricature; odd character; (*Theat.*) vividly realized minor figure. **macchiettàre** (*pr.* -étto, -étti), *v.t.* to speckle. *grigio* ~ *ato,* dapple-grey. **macchiettista** (*pl.* -isti), *m.* caricaturist; (*Theat.*) actor who represents odd or comic types.
màcchina, *f.* machine; engine; apparatus; [motor-]car; bicycle; [printing-]press; (*fig.*) plot; machination; (*supernatural*) machinery (*in epic*). (N.B. **automobile** is the gen. name for a motor-car and **motore** for its engine). ~ *da cucire,* sewing-machine. ~ *da scrivere,* typewriter. *fatto a* ~, machine-made. ~ *a vapore,* steam-engine. *mettere in moto una* ~, to start a machine, an engine. *dare, fare* ~ *indietro,* to reverse the engine. ~ *rotativa,* rotary press (*Typ.*). *foglio di* ~ [*per la rivisione*], (*Typ.*) final proof. *dim. macchinetta, macchinina.* **macchinàle,** *a.* mechanical; automatic. **macchinàre,** *v.i.* (*aux.* avere) & *t,* to plot; contrive. **macchinàrio,** *m.* machin-

ery. **machinazióne,** *f.* machination; intrigue; plot. **macchinista** (*pl.* -isti), *m.* machinist; engineer; engine-driver; (*Typ.*) press-man.
macchinóso, *a.* complicated, complex; heavy; full of machinery.
macchióne, *m.* brushwood.
Macèdone, *a.* & *m.* Macedonian.
Macedònia (la), *f.* Macedonia. **m** ~, fruit-salad; type of cigarette.
macellàio (*pl.* -ài), *m.* butcher.
macellàre, *v.t.* to butcher; slaughter. **macellería,** *f.* butcher's shop. **macèllo,** *m.* slaughterhouse; (*fig.*) shambles, slaughter.
maceràre, *v.t.* to macerate; soak; steep; soften, ret (*flax, hemp*); (*fig.*) to waste (away), wear down. **maceratóio** & **màcero,** *m.* macerating-vat; retting-tank, rettery. *mandare al macero,* to sell as waste paper. **macerazióne,** *f.* maceration; mortification (*by fasting*).
macèrie, *f.pl.* ruins; debris; rubbish; remains.
machiavèllico (*pl.* -èllici), *a.* Machiavellian; crafty.
macía, *f.* heap of stones. **macigno,** *m.* hard stone; block of stone; flint.
macilènto, *a.* emaciated.
màcina, *f.* mill-stone. **macinàre,** *v.t.* to grind; mill; crush; pound. **macinàta,** *f.* grinding; milling. **macinatóio,** *m.* press; mill; corn-mill. **macinatóre,** *m.* & *a.* (*f.* -tríce) grinder; grinding. **macinatúra** & **macinazióne,** *f.* grinding; milling. **macinìno,** *m.* small mill. ~ *da caffe.* coffee-mill. **macinío** (*pl.* -ií), *m.* continual grinding.
maciúlla, *f.* brake (*for flax*). **maciullàre,** *v.t.* to break (*flax or hemp*); (*fig.*) chew.
macolàre & **maculàre,** *v.t.* to bruise; stain.
Maddaléna, *f.* Magdalen; bell of the Bargello tower at Florence, rung at executions (*Hist.*).
Madèra, *f.* Madeira (*Geog.*). *m.* Madeira (*wine*).
màdia, *f.* bread-bin; kneading-trough.
màdido, *a.* moist; damp; wet.
Madònna, *f.* Our Lady, the Virgin Mary; picture or statue of the Virgin. **madonnína,** *f.* small picture, shrine or statue of the Virgin. ~ *infilzata,* prude.
madóre, *m.* moisture; dampness.
madornàle, *a.* enormous; huge; gross.
màdre, *f.* mother; parent (*lit.* & *fig.*); dam; womb; source; mould; socket;

nun; head of convent or community of nuns; benefactress. *chiesa* ~, mother church. *idea* ~, main idea, original i. *lingua* ~, mother-tongue; source of a group of languages. *libro, registro* (or *bollettario*) *a* ~ *figlia*, book with counterfoils. **madreggiàre** (*pr.* **-éggio, -éggi**), *v.i.* (*aux.* avere) to take after one's mother; to be motherly. **madre-pàtria**, *f.* mother-country; motherland. **madrepêrla**, *f.* mother-of-pearl. **madrèpora** or **madrepòra**, *f.* madrepore. **madresélva**, *f.* honey-suckle; woodbine. **madre-víte**, *f.* female screw. **Madríd**, *f.* Madrid.
madrigàle, *m.* madrigal.
madrigna, *f.* stepmother.
madrilèno, *a. & m.* of Madrid; native of Madrid.
madrína, *f.* godmother.
maestà, *f.inv.* majesty. *Sua M*~, His Majesty, Her M. **maestóso**, *a.* majestic; stately; *& ad.* maestoso (*Mus.*).
maéstra, *f.* mistress (*Sch.*); teacher; (for *vela* ~) main-sail.
maestràle, *m.* north-west wind.
maestrànza, *f.* workmen; hands; mastery of a trade; freedom of a guild or corporation. **maestrévole**, *a.* masterly; skilful. **maestría**, *f.* skill; mastery; proficiency; control. **maéstro**, *m.* master; teacher. ~*di scuola*, schoolmaster. ~*di ballo*, dancing-master. ~*di scherma*, fencing-master. ~*d' equipaggio*, boatswain. ~ *compositore*, composer. ~ *di cappella*, choir master. ~ *di casa*, house steward. *colpo da* ~, master stroke. ¶ *a.* main; principal; master (*att.*); skilful. *albero* ~, main mast. *strada* ~ *a*, main road. *mano* ~ *a, f.* master hand.
màfia or **màffia**, *f.* mafia; secret (criminal) society (*Sicilian*).
màga (*pl.* **màghe**), *f.* witch; sorceress; enchantress.
magàgna, *f.* (hidden) fault or vice; blemish; defect. **magagnàre**, *v.t.* to spoil; damage; corrupt; impair.
magàri, *excl. & ad.* would to Heaven! even; maybe; perhaps.
magażżinàggio, *m.* storage; cost of storage. **magażżinière**, *m.* store-keeper; warehouseman. **magażżíno**, *m.* warehouse; store.
Magellàno, *m.* Magellan.
maggesàre (*pr.* **-éso**), *v.t.* to lay

fallow. **maggése**, *m.* fallow; fallow-land. ¶ *a.* of May, May (*att.*).
maggiai[u]òla, *f.* -**o**, *m.* (*Poet.*) May-singer. **màggio** (*pl.* **màggi**), *m.* May; festival of May; May-song; **maggiolàta**, *f.* May-song.
maggioràna, *f.* marjoram (*Bot.*).
maggiorànza, *f.* majority. *in* ~, for the most part, mostly. *a grande* ~, by a great majority. **maggiordòmo**, *m.* (house) steward; majordomo. **maggióre**, *a.* greater; larger; bigger; high(er); older; major. *età* ~, *f.* full age; majority. *stato* ~, *m.* (*Mil.*) staff, general staff. *altare* ~, *m.* high altar. *il* ~, (*superl.*) the greatest, largest, &c.; (*of two persons*) the elder, the older. *il* ~ *offerente*, the highest bidder (*auction*). ¶ *m.* major (*Mil.*); (*pl.*) ancestors; forefathers. **maggio-rènne**, *a.* of full age. **maggiorità**, *f.* (*Mil.*) majority. **maggiorménte**, *ad.* more; the more; all the more.
màgi (**i**), *m.pl.* the Magi.
magía, *f.* magic.
magiàro, *a. & m.* Magyar.
màgico (*pl.* **màgici**), *a.* magic; magical.
magistèro, *m.* mastery (*of an art, craft or profession*); teaching; teaching profession; doctor's degree; (*Chem.*) fine precipitate. *scuola di* ~, *f.* teachers' training college; department of Education (*Univ.*). **magi-stràle**, *a.* magistral; magisterial; professorial; masterly; haughty. **magistràto**, *m.* magistrate. **magi-stratúra**, *f.* magistracy.
màglia (*pl.* **màglie**), *f.* stitch; knot; mesh; link in a chain; mail; coat of mail; knitted vest; undervest; web (*spot in the eye*). *lavoro di* ~, knitting; net-work. *a* ~, knitted. **maglierìa**, *f.* hosiery; h. shop. **magliétta**, *f.* light vest; light knitted garment.
Magliabechiàna (**la**) (*Biblioteca Magliabechiana*), *f.* the library founded by A. Magliabechi (d. 1714), nucleus of the National Library of Florence.
màglio (*pl.* **màgli**), *m.* mallet; bat; sledge-hammer. *dim.* **maglietto**.
magli[u]òlo, *m.* shoot; sucker; vine-cutting.
magnànimo, *a.* magnanimous; generous.
magnàno, *m.* coppersmith; lock-smith.
magnàte (*pl.* **magnàti**), *m.* magnate; grandee. **magnatízio** (*pl.* **-ízi**), *a.* rich; noble.

magnèsia, *f.* magnesia. **magnèsio,** *m.* magnesium.

magnète, *m.* magnet; magneto. **magnètico** (*pl.* -ètici), *a.* magnetic; mesmeric. **magnetismo,** *m.* magnetism. **magnetíte,** *f.* lodestone. **magnetiżżàre,** *v.t.* to magnetize. **magneto-elettrico,** *a.* magneto-electric. **magnetiżżazióne,** *f.* magnetization (*Phys.*).

magnificaménte, *ad.* magnificently. **magnificàre** (*pr.* -ífico, -ífichi), *v.t.* to exalt; exaggerate. **magníficat,** *m.* magnificat; hymn to the Virgin. **magnificènza,** *f.* magnificence; grandeur. **magnífico** (*pl.* -ífici), *a.* magnificent; splendid; grand; fine; munificent; title of honour now reserved to the Rector (or Principal) of a University, *il* ~ *rettore.*

magniloquènte, *a.* grandiloquent; lofty in expression. **magniloquènza,** *f.* grandiloquence; lofty eloquence.

magnitúdine, *f.* magnitude. **màgno,** *a.* great; illustrious; wide; principal. *aula* ~*a,* *f.* main hall (*of Univ. or similar institution*).

magnòlia, *f.* magnolia.

màgo (*pl.* **màghi**), *m.* magician; wizard; sorcerer.

Magónza, *f.* Mainz. **magontíno,** *a.* of Mainz.

màgra, *f.* low-water. **magraménte,** *ad.* meagrely; scantily; poorly. **magrétto,** *a.* rather thin. **magrézza,** *f.* leanness; thinness; meagreness; scantiness. **màgro,** *a.* lean; thin; meagre; scanty; poor; paltry; spare; meatless (*meal*); fast (*day*); vegetable (*soup*). ¶ *m.* lean (meat); fish & vegetable diet; Lenten fare.

mài, *ad.* ever; (*negatively*) never. *se* ~, if ever; in case. *ora o* ~, now or never. *come* ~? how is that? how can that be? ~ *e poi* ~, not at all; on no account. ~ *più,* never again.

maiàla, *f.* sow. **maialàta,** *f.* dirty trick; foul action. **maiàle,** *m.* pig; swine. [*carne di*] ~, *f.* pork. dim. *maialino.* **maialésco** (*pl.* -éschi), *a.* swinish; foul; filthy.

mainò, *ad.* by no means; not at all; certainly not.

màio (*pl.* **mài**), *m.* (*Poet.*) green branch borne by youths for the festival of Calendimaggio; may flower. **maiòlica,** *f.* majolica.

maionése, *f.* mayonnaise [sauce].

Maiòrca, *f.* Majorca.

màis, *m.* maize; Indian corn.

maiuscolétti, *m.pl.* small capitals (*Typ.*). **maiúscolo,** *a.* & *m.* capital (letter). ~ *corsivo,* Italic capital.

Malàcca, *f.* Malacca. *stretto di* ~, Straits of M. *penisola di* ~, Malay Peninsula, Malaya.

malaccètto, *a.* unacceptable.

malàccio, *m.* serious ill; dangerous complaint; epilepsy.

malaccòlto, *a.* unwelcome; undesired. **malaccóncio,** *a.* unfit; unsuitable.

malaccòrto, *a.* awkward; unwise; rash, imprudent.

Malachía, *m.* Malachi (*O.T.*).

malachíte, *f.* malachite.

malacreànza (*pl.* **malacreànze**), *f.* bad manners; impoliteness; ill breeding. **malaféde** (*pl.* **malefédi**), *f.* bad faith; act of bad faith. **malaffàre,** *m.* evil living. **malaffètto,** *a.* ill disposed.

malafitta, *f.* quagmire; swampy ground.

malagévole, *a.* difficult; hard; uncomfortable; irksome; intricate. **malagevolézza,** *f.* difficulty; discomfort; fatigue.

malagiàto, *a.* uncomfortable; hard up; impecunious.

malagràzia, *f.* uncouthness; awkwardness; rudeness; bad grace, ungraciousness.

malalíngua (*pl.* **malelíngue**), *f.* slanderous tongue; slanderer; backbiter.

malaménte, *ad.* badly; awkwardly.

malandàre, *v.i.* (*aux.* essere) to go bad; go to ruin; take a bad turn. **malandàto,** *a.* in bad condition; in bad repair; in poor health, run down.

malandrinàggio, *m.* highway robbery. **malandríno,** *m.* robber; ruffian; scoundrel.

malànimo, *m.* malice; ill-will; malevolence; spite.

malànno, *m.* illness; infirmity; misfortune; calamity.

malapéna (a), *ad. expr.* hardly; scarcely; with difficulty.

malària, *f.* malaria. **malàrico** (*pl.* -àrici), *a.* malarial.

malarnése, *m.* rogue.

malarrivàto, *a.* unwelcome; unfortunate; unlucky. ¶ *m.* unlucky fellow.

malatíccio, *a.* sickly; delicate. **malàto,** *a.* sick; ill; unwell; sore.

¶ *m.* sick person; invalid; patient.
malattía, *f.* illness; sickness;
disease; ailment; malady; complaint.
malaugurataménte, *ad.* inauspiciously; under evil omens; unluckily; unfortunately. **malauguràto,** *a.* ill-omened; inauspicious; unlucky; unfortunate. **malaugúrio** (*pl.* -úri), *m.* ill omen.
malavíta, *f.* (*coll.*) gangsters; criminals.
malavòglia, *f.* ill-will; unwillingness; reluctance; sloth.
malavvedúto, *a.* unwise; imprudent. **malavventúra,** *f.* mischance. **malavvézzo,** *a.* ill-bred; unmannerly. **malavviàto,** *a.* straggling; loose; unruly. **malazzàto,** *a.* ailing; sickly. **malcadúco** (*pl.* -úchi), *m.* epilepsy. **malcapitàto,** *a.* unlucky; unfortunate. **malcàuto,** *a.* incautious; rash; imprudent. **malcèrto,** *a.* uncertain; dubious; irresolute. **malcollocàto,** *a.* ill-placed. **malcompósto,** *a.* ungraceful; awkward. **malcóncio** (*pl.* -ónci), *a.* knocked about; ill-used; damaged. **malcontènto,** *a.* dissatisfied; discontented. ¶ *m.* discontent; dissatisfaction; discontented person; malcontent. **malcopèrto,** *a.* half-naked. **malcorrispósto,** *a.* ill-requited. **malcostumàto,** *a.* ill-mannered; vicious; immoral; debauched. **malcreàto,** *a.* rude; churlish; ill-bred. **malcurànte,** *a.* careless; negligent.
maldèstro, *a.* awkward; blundering; unskilful. **maldicènte,** *a.* slanderous. ¶ *m.f.* slanderer. **maldicènza,** *f.* slander; scandal; malicious gossip.
màle, mal, *m.* evil; ill; pain; ache; sore; illness; disease; wrong; harm; hurt; injury; mischief; damage; trouble; discomfort; misfortune. *ho ~ a un dito,* I have a sore finger. *~ agli occhi,* sore eyes, eye trouble. *~ di testa, ~ di capo,* headache. *~ di denti,* toothache. *~ di gola,* sore throat. *~ di orecchi,* earache. *~ di cuore,* heart disease. *~ di mare,* seasickness. *~ di montagna,* mountain sickness. *~ sottile,* consumption. *far ~,* to hurt. *andare a ~,* to go bad. *mandar a ~,* to spoil. *metter ~,* to cause trouble; sow discord. *aversi a ~ di,* to take amiss; take offence at. *non c'è ~,* pretty well; pretty good. ¶ *ad.* ill; badly; wrong; amiss; mis-(*prefix*). *cavarsela ~,* to come off

badly. *riuscir ~,* to turn out badly. *star ~,* to be ill; be unbecoming; not to fit (*clothes*). *trovarsi ~,* to feel uneasy. *essere ~ in gambe,* to be in poor health; to be weak. *meno ~,* *manco ~,* fortunately; so much the better; I am so glad. *di ~ in peggio,* from bad to worse.
maledétto, *a.* cursed; accursed; *excl.* curse it! confound it! **malèdico** (*pl.* -èdici), *a.* slanderous. **maledíre** (*pr.* -íco, &c., like dire), *v.t. ir.* to curse. **maledizióne,** *f.* curse; cursing; malediction.
maleducàto, *a.* ill-bred. ¶ *m.* ill-bred person. **malefàtta,** *f.* blunder; **malefício, -fízio,** *m.* crime; wicked action; evil spell; witchcraft. **malèfico** (*pl.* -èfici), *a.* harmful; baleful; mischievous; pernicious. **malèrba,** *f.* noxious weed.
malése, *a. & m.* Malay. *il ~,* the Malay language. *Stati Federati ~ i,* Federated Malay States (F.M.S.). **Malèsia,** *f.* Malaya.
malèssere, *m.* indisposition; discomfort; uneasiness; difficulty (*financial,* &c.). **malèstro,** *m.* mischief. **malevolènte & malèvolo,** *a.* malevolent. **malevolènza,** *f.* ill-will; malevolence. **malfamàto,** *a.* ill-famed; disreputable. **malfàtto,** *m.* misdeed; crime. ¶ *a.* deformed; (*fam.*) difficult (*pers.*). **malfattóre,** *m.* evil-doer; criminal; malefactor. **malférmo,** *a.* unsteady; insecure; weak; tottering. **malfidàto,** *a.* distrustful; suspicious. **malfído,** *a.* unreliable; untrustworthy. **malfondàto,** *a.* ill-founded. **malgàrbo,** *m.* awkwardness; brusqueness; bad grace.
malgàscio, *a. & m.* (*lang.* or *native of Madagascar*) Malagasy.
malgiudicàre, *v.t.* to misjudge (*people or actions*).
malgovèrno, *m.* misgovernment; mismanagement; misuse.
malgradíto, *a.* unwelcome; disagreeable.
malgràdo, *or* **a malgrado di,** *pr. & ad.,* in spite of; notwithstanding. *mio ~,* in spite of myself; against my will.
malgrazióso, *a.* unattractive; ungracious.
malguardàto, *a.* unguarded; undefended; badly looked after.
malía, *f.* charm; enchantment; sorcery; witchcraft. **maliàrda,** *f.* sorceress; witch; enchantress.

malignità, *f.* malignity; malice; wickedness. **malígno,** *a.* evil, mischievous; malicious; malignant.
malinconía, *f.* melancholy; sadness. **malincònico** (*pl.* **-ònici**), *a.* melancholy; melancholic; sad; gloomy.
malincuòre (a), *ad. expr.* unwillingly; reluctantly.
malintenzionàto, *a.* evil-minded; ill-disposed. **malintéso,** *a.* wrong; misconceived; misunderstood; mistaken. ¶ *m.* misunderstanding.
malízia, *f.* mischievousness; cunning; artfulness; trick. **maliziétta,** *f.* trick. **malizióso,** *a.* mischievous, sly, cunning; artful.
malleàbile, *a.* malleable; pliant; adaptable.
mallèolo, *m.* ankle-bone.
mallevadóre, *m.* (*f.* **-dríce**) guarantor; surety; bail. *essere* ~, *stare* ~, *entrare* ~, to stand surety; go bail. **malleveria,** *f.* guarantee.
màllo, *m.* husk.
malmenàre (*pr.* **-éno, -éni**), *v.t.* to ill-treat; treat roughly; ill-use; mishandle. **malmenàto,** *p.a.* ill-treated; ill-used. **malmenío,** *m.* (*constant*) ill-usage.
malmésso, *a.* shabby; seedy. **malnàto,** *a.* ill-bred. **malnòto,** *a.* little known.
màlo, *a.* (*with nouns*) bad; evil; ill. **malòcchio** (*pl.* **-òcchi**), *m.* evil eye. *di* ~, askance; with ill-will. **malóra,** *f.* ruin, perdition. **malóre,** *m.* illness; misfortune.
malpensàto, *a.* ill-devised. **malpersuàso,** *a.* unpersuaded.
malpíglio, *m.* look of anger; disdain; scorn; contempt. **malpràtico** (*pl.* **-àtici**), *a.* inexperienced. **malpròprio,** *a.* improper. **malsàno,** *a.* unhealthy; unskilful; unwholesome; unsound. **malsicúro,** *a.* uncertain; insecure; unsteady. **malsoddisfàtto,** *a.* dissatisfied; discontented. **malsofferènte,** *a.* intolerant (of), impatient (of).
màlta, *f.* mortar. *riempimento con* ~, *m.* grouting. **M** ~, Malta.
maltalènto, *m.* evil disposition; bad frame of mind. **maltèmpo,** *m.* bad weather.
maltése, *a. & m.* Maltese.
màlto, *m.* malt.
maltollleràbile, *a.* intolerable; insupportable. **maltòlto,** *a. & m.* ill-gotten (*gains*). **maltratta-**

ménto, *m.* ill-treatment; ill-usage. **maltrattàre,** *v.t.* to ill-treat. **maltusiàno,** *a.* Malthusian.
malúccio, *ad.* rather badly. **malumóre,** *m.* ill-temper; spleen; ill-humour; discontent; discord.
màlva, *f.* mallow (*Bot.*). **malvàceo,** *a.* of (the) mallow.
malvàgio (*pl.* **-àgi,** *f.* **-àgie**), *a.* wicked; evil; noxious. **malvagità,** *f.* wickedness.
malvedúto, *a.* disliked; hated. **malvenúto,** *a.* unwelcome.
malversazióne, *f.* fraud; embezzlement.
malvissúto, *a.* dissolute. **malvísto,** *a.* disliked; hated; unwelcome. **malvivènte,** *m.* rogue; rascal; scamp; criminal. **malvívo,** *a.* half-dead. **malvolentièri,** *ad.* unwillingly; reluctantly. **malvolére,** *m.* ill-will; dislike. **malvolúto,** *a.* disliked; hated.
màmma, *f.* mother; mam[m]a (*fam.*); (*Poet.*) breast. ~ *mia!* (*excl.*) dear me! **mammalúcco** (*pl.* **-úcchi**), *m.* blockhead; (*lit.* Mameluk). **mammàrio,** *a.* mammary (*phys.*). **mammèlla,** *f.* teat, udder. **mammífero,** *m.* mammal. *i mammíferi,* mammals; mammalia.
màmmola, *f.* violet.
mammolíno *&* **màmmolo,** *m.* little child.
mammóne, *m.* mammon.
mammóso, *a.* big-breasted.
mammút, *m.inv.* mammoth.
manàta, *f.* handful; blow with the hand; cuff; slap.
mànca, *f.* left; left-hand; left[-hand] side.
mancaménto, *m.* deficiency; failing; defect; (*fault of*) omission; fainting-fit. **mancànte,** *a.* lacking; missing; failing; in need (of); in want (of); defective; deficient. **mancànza,** *f.* want; lack; deficiency; absence; default; fault. **mancàre** (*pr.* **mànco, mànchi**), *v.i.* (*aux.* essere *&* avere) to be lacking; be wanting; be missing; be in want (of = *di*); be in need (of); lack; want; run short (of = *di*); be absent; be away (from = *da*); die; die out; fail; neglect to act; do wrong; be at fault; turn faint. ~ *alla parola data,* to break one's word. *mi mancano le parole,* words fail me. *poco mancò che non cadesse,* he was within an ace of falling. *non mancava che questo!* this is the last straw! **man-**

càto, *a.* unsuccessful. **manchévole,** *a.* defective; faulty. **manchevolézza,** *f.* fault; defect.

mància (*pl.* **mànce**), *f.* gratuity; tip. dim. *mancétta.* **manciàta,** *f.* handful. **mancína,** *f.* left; left hand. **mancíno,** *a.* left-handed; (*fig.*) underhand; treacherous.

mancípio, *m.* (*Poet. & fig.*) slave. **Manciú,** *a. & m.* Manchu (China). **Manciúria** (la), *f.* Manchuria.

mànco (*pl.* **mànchi**), *a.* defective; left. [*mano*] *manca, f.* left hand. ¶ *m.* want; lack; defect. ¶ *ad.* less = meno. ~*male!* so much the better! better so!

mandaménto, *m.* borough; district; area of local administration. **mandànte,** *m.* (*Law*) principal (*as dist. from agent*); *pl.* (*Parl.*) constituents. **mandàre,** *v.t.* to send; forward; give out; emit; utter; put into circulation. ~ *ad effetto,* ~ *a buon fine,* to carry out; accomplish. ~ *a male, a monte, all'aria,* to ruin, spoil. ~ *al macero,* to sell as waste paper.

mandaríno, *m.* mandarin; mandarin(e) orange.

mandàta, *f.* series; sequence; turn (*cf key*); consignment. **mandatàrio,** *m.* (*Law*) agent as dist. from principal (*mandante*). **mandàto,** *m.* mandate; warrant; commission; order; command. ~ *in bianco,* blank cheque (*fig.*).

mandíbola, *f.* mandible.

mandolinàta, *f.* mandolin-concert. **mandolinísta** (*pl.* **-ísti**), *m.* mandolin player. **mandolíno,** *m.* mandolin.

màndorla, *f.* almond. **mandorlàto,** *m.* almond-cake; almond paste; nougat. ¶ *a.* almond-shaped. **mandorlo,** *m.* almond-tree.

mandra *&* **màndria,** *f.* herd; flock; drove; (*fig.*) troop; host. **mandràgola** *&* **mandràgora,** *f.* mandrake. **mandriàno,** *m.* herdsman; shepherd. ~ *a. f.* herdswoman; shepherdess.

mandríno, *m.* mandrel, -il; chuck (*lathe*).

mandrítta, *f.* right hand.

màne, *f.* morning (as in the expr. *da* ~ *a sera,* from morning to night, & in the *ad. stamane,* this morning.

maneggévole *&* **maneggiàbile,** *a.* manageable; easily handled; handy. **maneggiaménto,** *m.* handling; management. **maneggiàre,** *v.t.* to handle; manage; use; conduct; break in (*horses*). **manéggio,** *m.* handling; use; management; horsemanship, riding-school; riding-ground; intrigue; plot; trick.

manésco (*pl.* **-éschi**), *a.* ready with one's hand[s]; rough; brutal; aggressive.

manétte, *f.pl.* handcuffs. **manévole,** *a.* supple; pliable (*lit. & fig.*). **manfòrte,** *f.inv.* assistance; help; aid (*to police, &c.*).

mànga, *f.* mango (*fruit*).

manganàre, *v.t.* to calender; to mangle. **manganèllo,** *m.* small calender; cudgel. **manganatúra,** *f.* mangling; calendering.

manganése, *m.* manganese.

màngano, *m.* linen-press; calender; mangle.

mangeréccio (*pl.* **-écci**), *a.* edible; eatable; tasty. **mangería,** *f.* swindle; extortion. **màngia,** *m.* **il M**~, bell tower of the *Palazzo pubblico* of Siena, *Torre del Mangia.* **mangiàbile,** *a.* eatable. **mangiacapàrra,** *m.inv.* cheat; swindler. **mangiaformíche,** *m.inv.* ant-eater. **mangiaguadàgni,** *m.inv.* idle labourer; lazy workman. **mangiaménto,** *m.* eating; gnawing; (*fig.*) swindling. **mangiaminèstre,** *m.inv.* sponger. **mangiapagnòtte,** *m.inv.* lazy official. **mangiapàne,** **-polènta,** *m.inv.* lazy fellow; good for nothing. **mangiapòpolo,** *m.inv.* hater of the people. **mangiaprèti,** *m.inv.* hater of priests, anticlerical. **mangiàre,** *v.t. & i.* (*aux. avere*) to eat; have a meal; take one's meals; find the food (good, *bene,* or bad, *male*); (*fig.*) devour; squander; eat away; swallow, clip (*one's words*). ¶ *m.* eating; food (*eaten*). **mangiàta,** *f.* meal. *una buona* ~, a hearty meal. **mangiatóre,** *m.* (*f.* **-tríce**), eater. **mangiatútto,** *m.inv.* spendthrift. **mangíme,** *m.* animal food; bird-food; fodder. **mangióne,** *m.* great eater; glutton. **mangiucchiàre,** *v.i.* (*aux. avere*) *& t.* to eat poorly; eat without appetite; nibble.

mangòsta *&* **mangústa,** *f.* mongoose.

màni, *m.pl.* manes, shades of the departed.

manía, *f.* mania; passion; fad; hobby; whim; fancy. **maníaco** (*pl.* **-íaci**), *a. & m.* maniac; eccentric; faddy; passionate lover (*of music, &c.*).

mà_nica (_pl._ **màniche**), _f._ sleeve; hose [pipe]; channel; wing (_of a palace_). ~ _a vento_, wind-cone. **La M** ~, the (English) Channel. **manicarétto**, _m._ tit-bit; dainty.

manichèo, _a._ & _m._ Manichaean; Manichee. **manichíno**, _m._ wristband; cuff (_lady's_); lay-figure; mannequin. **mànico** (_pl._ **mànichi**), _m._ handle (_of knife_, &_c._); stick; helve; heft; neck (_violin_). ~ _di scopa_, broomstick.

manicòmio (_pl._ **-òmi**), _m._ lunatic asylum.

manicóne, _m._ large sleeve; large handle.

manicòtto, _m._ muff; (_Mech._) sleeve; coupling.

manicúre, _m._ & _f._ manicurist.

manièra, _f._ manner; way; wise; sort; kind; mannerism; style; (_pl._) manners. **manieràto**, _a._ affected; mannered; unnatural. **manierísmo** _m._ mannerism. **manieróso**, _a._ excessively polite.

manifattúra, _f._ manufacture; factory; workmanship. **manifatturièro**, _a._ manufacturing.

manifestaménte, _ad._ manifestly. **manifestàre**, _v.t._ to manifest; show; display; evince; declare; reveal. **manifestazióne**, _f._ manifestation; display; expression. **manifèsto**, _a._ manifest; apparent. ¶ _m._ poster; placard; bill; manifesto.

maníglia, _f._ handle (_door_, _drawer_, _trunk_, &_c._); bell-pull.

manigóldo, _m._ rascal; scoundrel; ruffian.

manilúvio, _m._ hand-bath.

manína, _f._ little hand.

manipolàre (_pr._ **-ípolo**), _v.t._ to manipulate; handle; work; (_fig._) to adulterate. **manipolatóre**, _m._ manipulator; (_fig._) intriguer, plotter. **manipolazióne**, _f._ manipulation; handling; working; adulteration; preparation. **manípolo**, _m._ handful; bundle; sheaf; company; maniple (third part of a Roman cohort).

maniscàlco (_pl._ **-àlchi**), _m._ farrier.

mànna, _f._ manna; (_fig._) blessing; delicacy. **mannàia**, _f._ axe; chopper; blade of the guillotine. **mannàro (lupo)**, _m._ were-wolf; (_fig._) bogey; person suffering from epilepsy. **mannèlla**, _f._ & **mannèllo**, _m._ sheaf.

màno (_pl._ **màni**), _f._ hand; hand-(writing); coat (of paint, varnish, &c.); lead, trick, or deal (_at cards_);

quire of paper (24 sheets); (_fig._) side; way; power; protection; (_woman's_) promise of marriage; aid; succour. _stretta di_ ~, _f._ handshake. ~_i in alto!_ hands up! _fatto a_ ~, handmade. _cucito a_ ~, hand-sewn. _carta a_ ~, hand-made paper. _torchio a_ ~, hand-press. _colpo di_ ~, sudden attack; sudden action. ~ _d'opera_, ! workmanship; labour. _giuoco di_ ~, legerdemain; sleight of hand. _di_ ~ _in_ ~, _a_ ~ _a_ ~, _man_ ~, successively, little by little; as, as soon as.

manodòpera, _or_ **man d'òpera**, _f._ labour; workmanship.

manomésso, _p.p._ of **manomettere** & _a._ opened (_letters_); violated; searched (_illegally_).

manòmetro, _m._ pressure-gauge.

manométtere (_pr._ **-étto**, &_c._, _like_ **mettere**), _v.t._ _ir._ to open (_letters_); violate; search (illegally); lay hands upon roughly; (_Hist._) set free. **manomissióne**, _f._ violation; illegal search; liberation (_of a slave_).

manomòrta, _f._ (_Law_) mortmain.

manòpola, _f._ gauntlet; arm-sling (_carriage_); knob (_Radio_, &_c._).

manoscrítto, _a._ & _m._ manuscript.

manovàle, _m._ builder's labourer.

manovèlla, _f._ handle; crank. ~ _d'avviamento_, starting-handle (_Motor_).

manòvra, _f._ manoeuvre; handling (_of ship_); shunting. **manovràre** (_pr._ **-òvro**), _v.t._ to manoeuvre; work (_machine_). **manovratóre**, _m._ driver. ~ _del tram_, tram-driver.

manrítto, _a._ right-handed. ¶ _m._ right-handed blow; right (_Box._). **manrovèscio**, _m._ back-handed blow; blow with the back of the hand; back-stroke. **mansàlva (a)**, _ad. expr._ with impunity.

mansionàrio, _m._ (_Eccl._) beneficed clergyman. **mansióne**, _f._ office; duty; function; permanent post; dwelling-place; fixed address.

mànso, _a._ (_Poet._) mild; tame; gentle.

mansuefàre (_pr._ **-àccio**, &_c._, _like_ **fare**), _v.t._ _ir._ to tame; soften; appease; pacify. **mansuèto**, _a._ mild; gentle; m^ek; tame. **mansuetúdine**, _f._ meekness; mildness; (_of animals_) tameness.

mantellàre (_pr._ **-èllo**), _v.t._ to cover with a mantle; (_fig._) cloak. **mantellétta**, _f._ cape; cloak; short mantle worn by prelates & court dignitaries. **mantellína**, _f._ short cloak; soldier's

cape; lady's mantle. **mantellíno,**
m. short cloak; christening-robe.
mantèllo, *m.* cloak; mantle;
(*animal*) coat, (*colour of*) hair.
mantenére (*pr.* **-èngo,** *&c.,* like
tenere), *v.t. ir.* to keep; maintain;
hold; support; keep up; perform.
manteníbile, *a.* maintainable;
possible to keep. **mantenimento,**
m. keeping; maintenance; preservation; support. **mantenúta,** *f.* kept
mistress.
màntice (*pl.* **màntici**), *m.* bellows;
hood (*of carriage*). **màntide,** *f.*
mantis (*insect*). **mantíglia,** *f.*
mantilla.
mànto, *m.* (rich) mantle; cloak. (*oft.*
fig.) ~ *di neve,* mantle of snow.
Màntova, *f.* Mantua. **mantovàno,**
a. & m. Mantuan.
manuàle, *a.* manual. ¶ *m.* handbook;
manual.
manúbrio (*pr.* **-úbri**), *m.* handle-bar;
dumb-bell.
manufàtto, *a.* hand-made; manu-
factured.
manutèngolo, *m.* resetter; receiver of
stolen goods; accomplice. **manu-
tenzióne,** *f.* maintenance (*buildings,*
&c.); preservation; care; keeping.
mànza, *f.* heifer. **mànzo,** *m.* steer;
beef. ~ *lesso,* boiled beef.
manzoniàno, *a.* of Manzoni. ¶ *m.*
follower of Manzoni.
maomettàno, *a. & m.* Mohammedan. **maomettismo,** *m.* Mo-
hammedanism. **Maométto,** *m.*
Mohammed.
màppa, *f.* map. **mappamóndo,** *m.*
map of the world in hemispheres;
geographical globe. ~ *celeste,* map
of the heavens.
marabútto, *m.* marabout.
marachèlla, *f.* trick; fraud; deceit;
fault.
maràme, *m.* refuse; rubbish.
marangóne, *m.* cormorant; joiner;
carpenter.
maràsca, *f.* morello cherry. **mara-
schíno,** *m.* maraschino, liqueur
made from morello cherry.
maràsma (*pl.* **-àsmi**), *m.* wasting
disease.
Maratóna, *f.* Marathon. **m~,** *f.*
marathon [race].
maràtta, *m.* Mahratta.
maravíglia, *f.* wonder; astonishment;
surprise; marvel. **maravigliàre,**
v.t. to astonish; surprise; amaze.
maravigliàrsi, *v.refl.* to wonder;
be surprised, astonished, amazed.

maraviglióso, *a.* wonderful; marvellous; amazing.
màrca (*pl.* **màrche**), *f.* mark; token;
counter; border district, march.
~ *di fabbrica,* trade-mark. ~*da
bollo,* revenue stamp (*on contract,*
poster or *receipt*). *Le Marche,* the
Marches (*Geog.*).
marcantònia, *f.* plump woman (*pop.*).
Marcantònio, *m.* Mark Antony.
marcàre (*pr.* **màrco, màrchi**),
v.t. to mark. ~ *i punti* (*sport*), to
keep the score. ~ *dei punti,* to
score; make points. **marcatóre,** *m.*
marker; scorer. **marcatúra,** *f.*
marking.
Marc'Aurèlio, *m.* Marcus Aurelius.
marcescíbile, *a.* perishable; corruptible.
marchésa, *f.* marchioness. **marchése,**
m. marquis; marquess.
Marchesi (Isole), *f.pl.* Marquesas
Islands.
marchiàno, *a.* huge; enormous;
gross.
marchigiàno, *a. & m.* of the Marches;
native of the Marches.
màrchio, *m.* mark; stamp; brand.
~ *di fabbrica,* trade mark.
marchionàle, *a.* of a marquis.
màrcia (*pl.* **màrce**), *f.* march (*Mil.*
& Mus.); festering matter; pus.
Marciàna (biblioteca), *f.* St. Mark's
Library (Venice).
marciapiède (*pl.* **-èdi**), *m.* side-walk;
pavement; (*station*) platform.
marciàre (*pr.* **màrcio, màrci**),
v.i. (*aux.* avere) to march. **marcià-
ta,** *f.* march; marching.
màrcido, *a.* rotting, withered; tainted;
(*fam.*) drunk. **màrcio** (*pl.* **màrci**),
a. rotten; tainted; putrid; festering;
spoiled; decayed; crumbling; far
gone. **marcióso,** *a.* purulent;
festering. (*fig.*) filthy. **marcíre** (*pr.*
-ísco, -ísci), *v.i.* (*aux.* essere) to
spoil, decay, rot, go bad; waste
away; fester. **marcíta,** *f.* flooded
meadow. **marcitúra,** *f.* maceration; soaking; rotting. **marciúme,**
m. corruption; rottenness; festering
sore; pus.
màrco (*pl.* **màrchi**), *m.* mark
(*money*). **M~,** Mark; Marcus.
màre, *m.* sea; ocean. *prometter ~i e
monti,* to make great promises.
uomo in ~! man overboard! *verde
~,* sea-green. **marèa,** *f.* tide; ebb
& flow. **mareggiàre,** *v.i.* (*aux.*
avere) to float; rise & fall in waves;
undulate; surge; swell. **mareggià-**

ta, *f.* surge; surging; swell; heavy sea.

marémma, *f.* maremma. **maremmàno,** *a.* of the Maremma.

maremóto, *m.* tidal wave due to an earthquake.

marèna, *f.* morello cherry & sweet drink made from it.

mareògrafo, mareòmetro, *m.* tide-gauge.

maresciàllo, *m.* marshal (*supreme mil. dignity*); highest grade of non-commissioned officer; (*Nav.*) chief petty officer.

marétta, *f.* slight swell; choppy sea.

marezżàre (*pr.* -éżżo), *v.t.* to water (*silk*); marble. **marezżatúra,** *f.* watering; watered effect; marbling.

Marfòrio, *m.* mutilated statue in Rome, to which pasquinades were attached.

margarína, *f.* margarine.

margheríta, *f.* pearl; daisy. **M~,** Margaret.

marginàle, *a.* marginal. **marginàre** (*pr.* màrgino), *v.t.* to leave a margin in printing (*Typ.*). **marginàto** & **marginóso,** *a.* with a [wide] margin. **marginatúra,** *f.* arrangement of the margin (*Typ.*); edging. **màrgine,** *m.* margin (*lit.* & *fig.*); edge; border. **~ di taglio,** (*Typ.*) fore-edge.

María, *f.* Mary; Maria. **mariàno,** *a.* of Mary; consecrated to the Virgin. *il mese* **~,** *m.* the month of May.

marína, *f.* navy; admiralty; sea; sea-coast; sea-piece (*painting*). **marinàio** (*pl.* -ài), *m.* sailor; seaman; mariner; marine. **~ di coperta,** deck hand; (*Nav.*) able. **~ scelto,** able [bodied] seaman. **marinàre,** *v.t.* to pickle; keep laid by. **~ la scuola,** to play truant. **marinarésco** (*pl.* -éschi), *a.* nautical; sailor-like; seamanlike. **marinàro,** *m.* (*pop.*) sailor. ¶ *a.* seafaring; seamanlike. *alla* **~a,** like a sailor; in sailor fashion. **marinería,** *f.* navigation; seamanship; ships & their personnel & equipment.

marinísmo, *m.* Marinism. **maríno,** *a.* marine; sea (*att.*).

mariolería, *f.* fraud; trick; swindle; roguery; swindling. **mari[u]òlo,** *m.* rogue; cheat; swindler.

marionétta, *f.* puppet; marionette. *spettacolo di* **~e,** *m.* puppet-show. **marionettísta** (*pl.* -ísti), *m.* puppet-master; p. showman.

maritàle, *a.* marital. **maritalménte,** *ad.* in the married relation. *convivere* **~,** to live as husband & wife. **maritàre,** *v.t.* to marry, give in marriage; join (*vines,* &*c.*), unite. **maritàrsi,** *v.refl.* (*of women*) to marry; get married. **maritàta,** *f.* married woman. **maríto,** *m.* husband. *da* **~,** (*of a girl*) marriageable; fit for marriage.

maríttimo, *a.* maritime; marine; sea (*att.*).

marmàglia, *f.* rabble.

marmellàta, *f.* marmalade (*with oranges*); jam.

marmièra, *f.* marble quarry. **marmífero,** *a.* abounding or dealing in marble. **marmísta** (*pl.* -ísto), *m.* worker in marble; marble-cutter; m.-polisher.

marnítta, *f.* pot; saucepan; camp-kettle.

màrmo, *m.* marble; (*pl.*) statues. *cava di* **~,** *f.* marble-quarry.

marmòcchio (*pl.* -òcchi), *m.* urchin; brat.

marmòreo, *a.* marble (*att.*); marmoreal; like marble. **marmorizżàre,** *v.t.* to vein like marble.

marmòtta, *f.* (*Zool.*) marmot; (*fig.*) stupid fellow; sleepyhead; idler; recluse; traveller's case of samples. **marmòtto,** *m.* small child; baby; cobbler's last.

màrna, *f.* marl. **M~ (la),** *f.* (the) Marne (river). **marnàre,** *v.t.* to dress with marl. **marnièra,** *f.* marl-pit. **marnóso,** *a.* rich in marl.

marocchíno, *a.* Moroccan. ¶ *m.* native of Morocco; morocco leather. **Maròcco (il),** *m.* Morocco. **marocchinàio,** *m.* morocco-dresser. **marocchinàre,** *v.t.* to dress morocco.

maróso, *m.* billow; breaker.

màrra, *f.* hoe; mattock; (*anchor*) fluke.

marràno, *m.* boor; ill-bred fellow; traitor; miscreant.

marràta, *f.* blow with a hoe. **marreggiàre,** *v.t.* to hoe.

marróne, *m.* (Spanish) chestnut; chestnut-colour; maroon; gross blunder; mattock. *marroni secchi,* dried chestnuts. *marroni canditi,* candied chestnuts (*Fr.* marrons glacés). **marronéto,** *m.* chestnut-grove.

Marsàla, *f.* Marsala (*W. Sicily*). *m.* Marsala (*famous wine of sherry-type*).

Marsíglia, *f.* Marseilles. **marsi-glíese,** *a.* of Marseilles. ¶ *f.* (the) Marseillaise.

marsína, *f.* dress-coat; evening dress (*men's*).

marsupiàle, *a. & m.* marsupial.

Màrta, *f.* Martha. **Màrte,** *m.* Mars.

martedí, *m.* Tuesday. ~ *grasso*, Shrove Tuesday.

martellaménto, *m. &* **martella-túra,** *f.* hammering. **martellàre,** *v.t.* to hammer; beat; strike. *v.i.* (*aux.* avere) to hammer; throb (*pulse or temples*). *martellarsi il cervello*, to rack one's brains. **martellàta,** *f.* blow with a hammer.

martelliàno, *a. & m.* verse of 14 syllables (called after P. I. Martelli, 1665–1727).

martèllio, *m.* constant hammering. **martèllo,** *m.* hammer; door-knocker. *campana* ~, alarm-bell (*fire, &c.*).

martinèlla, *f.* war-bell of the Florentine commune (*Hist.*). **martinèllo,** *m.* (*Mech.*) [lifting-] jack. *cf. binda*.

martingàla, *f.* martingale.

Martiníca (Isola), *f.* Martinique.

Martíno, *m.* Martin. *estate di San* ~, *f.* St. Martin's Summer; Indian Summer. *martin pescatore*, *m.* kingfisher.

màrtire, *m. f.* martyr. **martírio,** *m.* martyrdom; torture; torment. **martirizzàre,** *v.t.* to martyr; torment; torture. **martirològio,** *m.* martyrology; book of martyrs.

màrtora, *f.* marten (*Zool.*).

martoriàre, *v.t.* to torture; torment. **martoriatóre,** *m.* torturer. **mar-tòrio &** **martòro,** *m.* torture; torment.

Marucelliàna (la), *f.* Florentine library founded by F. Marucelli (d. 1703).

marxísmo, *m.* Marxism. **marxísta** (*pl.* **-ísti**), *a. & m.* Marxist; Marxian.

màrza, *f.* (*Bot.*) graft; scion.

marzaiuòlo, marzolíno, *or* **marzu-òlo,** *a.* of (the month of) March. **marzapàne,** *m.* marchpane; marzi-pan.

marziàle, *a.* martial; warlike. **M~,** *m.* Martial (*poet.*). **marziàno,** *m.* Martian (*inhab. of Mars*).

màrzio, *a.* of Mars. *campo* ~, drill-ground.

màrzo, *m.* March.

marzòcco, *m.* Marzocco, heraldic lion of Florence.

mas, *m.inv.*, E-boat.

mascalcía, *f.* farriery; horse-shoeing. **mascalzóne,** *m.* rascal; rogue; blackguard.

mascèlla, *f.* jaw. **mascellàre,** *a.* maxillary. *dente* ~, *m.* back-tooth.

màschera (*pl.* **màschere**), *f.* mask; masked figure; masker; (death) mask; disguise; masque. **maschera-ménto,** *m.* masking, disguise; camouflage. **mascheràre,** *v.t.* to mask; disguise; camouflage. **mascheràta,** *f.* masquerade. **mascheratúra,** *f.* masking; dis-guise; camouflage. **mascheróne,** *m.* (*Arch.*) mask; grotesque face.

maschiàccio, *m.* rough fellow; mannish-woman; virago; hoyden. **maschiétta,** *f.* mannish girl. *cap-pelli alla* ~, bob[bed hair]. **maschiétto,** *m.* (nice) little boy. **maschiézza,** *f.* masculinity; manli-ness; virility. **maschíle,** *a.* male; masculine; manly. *scuola* ~, boys' school. **màschio** (*pl.* **màschi**), *a.* male; manly; masculine; vigorous; virile. ¶ *m.* male; male child; boy; inner keep or tower (*fortress*); (*Mech.*) tenon, core, piston-shaft. **maschiótta,** *f.* tomboy; hoyden. **maschiòtto,** *m.* sturdy child; fine boy. **mascolíno,** *a.* masculine.

masnàda, *f.* set; gang; armed band. **masnadière,** *m.* highwayman; brigand.

màssa, *f.* mass; bulk; heap; pile; majority.

massacràre, *v.t.* to massacre. slaughter. **massàcro,** *m.* mas-sacre;

massaggiatóre, *m.* **-tríce,** *f.* masseur; masseuse. **massàggio,** *m.* massage.

massàia, *f.* housewife. **massàio,** *m.* householder; husband; husbandman; steward; manager.

massellàre, *v.t.* to hammer; beat (out) (*red-hot iron*). **massèllo,** *m.* block; lump; mass. *oro in* ~, gold ingot.

massería, *f.* farm; stock of cattle.

masserízia, *f.* furniture; house-keeping; (*pl.*) household goods.

massicciàre, *v.t.* to ballast; lay the foundation of a road. **massíccio** (*pl.* **-ícci**), *a.* massive; solid; stout. ¶ *m.* group of (mountain) peaks; massif.

màssima, *f.* maxim; rule; principle. **massimaménte,** *ad.* chiefly; especially; particularly; most. **màssimo,** *a.* greatest; highest;

utmost; maximum. ¶ *m.* most; maximum.
màsso, *m.* block; boulder.
massóne, *m.* mason; freemason. **massonería,** *f.* [free]masonry. **massònico** (*pl.* **-ònici**), *a.* masonic.
massóso, *a.* rocky; stony.
mastèllo, *m.* bucket; tub; vat.
masticaménto, *m. &* **masticazióne,** *f.* chewing; mastication. **masticàre,** *v.t.* to chew; masticate; (*fig.*) meditate (on); ponder (over); stammer (out); mangle (*words*); speak badly (*lang.*); grumble. *gomma da* ~, *f.* chewing-gum.
màstice, *m.* gum-mastic; putty.
mastíno, *m.* mastiff.
màstio, *m.* (*pop. for* **maschio**) keep; stronghold; donjon.
mastíte, *f.* (*Med.*) mastitis.
mastodónte, *m.* mastodon; elephant-[ine person]. **mastodòntico** (*pl.* **-òntici**), *a.* huge; enormous.
mastòide, *f.* mastoid (*bone, process*).
màstra, *f.* kneading-trough (*large*).
màstro, *m.* ledger (*libro* ~); master. ~ *muratore,* master-mason. ¶ *a.* principal; chief.
matàssa, *f.* skein; (*fig.*) tangle.
matemàtica, *f.* mathematics. **matemàtico** (*pl.* **-àtici**), *a.* mathematical. ¶ *m.* mathematician.
materassàio, *m.* mattress-maker. **materàsso,** *m.* mattress.
matèria, *f.* matter; material; substance; subject; ground; occasion. *indice delle* ~ *e*, table of contents. **materiàle,** *a.* material; physical; bodily; manual; sensual; clumsy; prosaic; unimaginative; matter-of-fact. ¶ *m.* material. **materialísmo,** *m.* materialism. **materialísta,** *m.* materialist. **materialístico** (*pl.* **-ístici**), *a.* materialistic. **materializzàre,** *v.t.* to materialize. **materialóne,** *m.* rough, uncouth fellow.
maternità, *f.* maternity; motherhood. *:asa di* ~, *f.* maternity hospital. **matèrno,** *a.* maternal; motherly; mother's (*side*); mother, native (*tongue*).
matíta, *f.* pencil; lead-pencil; crayon; chalk. **matitatóio,** *m.* pencil-holder, -case.
matriarcàto, *m.* matriarchy.
matríce, *f.* matrix; womb; (*Typ.*) matrix, mould; counterfoil. **matricída,** *m. & f.* matricide (*pers.*). **matricídio,** *m.* matricide (*crime*).
matrícola, *f.* register; roll; (*univ.*)

matriculation roll; matriculation number; freshman. **matricolàre,** *v.t.* to register; (*univ.*) enter on the matriculation roll. **matricolàrsi,** *v.refl.* to matriculate. **matricolàto,** *a.* thorough; arrant. *briccone* ~, arrant knave. **matricolazióne,** *f.* registration, matriculation. **matricolíno,** *m.* first year student; freshman.
matrígna, *f.* stepmother.
matrimoniàle, *a.* matrimonial; conjugal; nuptial; wedding (*att.*). *letto* ~, double bed. **matrimònio** (*pl.* **-òni**), *m.* marriage, matrimony, wedlock; match; wedding. ~ *d'amore,* ~ *d'inclinazione,* love match. ~ *di convenienza,* marriage of convenience. ~ *d'interesse,* money in.
matróna, *f.* matron.
mattacchióne, *m.* scatter-brain; gay companion. **mattaccíno,** *m.* jester; mimic; strolling player.
mattadóre, *m.* matador.
mattàna, *f.* whim, freak; fit of temper.
mattàre, *v.t.* (*chess*) to checkmate; (*fig.*) to conquer.
mattàta, *f.* foolery; act of folly.
matteggiàre (*pr.* **-éggio, -éggi**), *v.i.* (*aux.* avere) to play the fool.
Mattèo, *m.* Matthew.
matterèllo, *m.* rolling-pin. ¶ *a.* crazy; foolish. **matticcio,** *a.* light-headed; thoughtless.
mattína, *f.* morning. **mattinàle,** *a.* of (occurring in) the morning; matutinal; early; morning (*att.*). **mattinàta,** *f.* morning (*duration*); forenoon; morning music; (*Theat.*) matinée, afternoon performance. **mattinièro,** *a.* early-rising. **mattíno,** *m.* morning. *di buon* ~, early.
màtto, *a.* mad; crazy; insane; foolish; frantic; excessive; dull; weak; lustreless; mat. ¶ *m.* fool; madman; lunatic. **mattòide,** *a.* half-mad. ¶ *m. & att.* madcap.
mattonàia, *f.* brick-yard, brick-field. **mattonàio,** *m.* brick-maker. **mattonàme,** *m.* mass of (broken) bricks. **mattonàto,** *m.* tiled floor. **mattóne,** *m.* brick; tile. **mattonèlla,** *f.* small brick; flooring tile.
mattutíno, *a.* morning (*att.*); early. ¶ *m.* matins; morning.
maturaménte, *ad.* maturely. **maturàre,** *v.i.* (*aux.* essere) *& t.* to mature; ripen; become due. **maturàto,** *p.p.* of *maturare,* *a.* due (*of a*

bill). **maturazióne,** *f.* ripening; maturity; head. *venire a* ~ to come to a head. **maturità,** *f.* maturity; ripeness; completion (e.g. (*Sch.*) of the *corso secondario*). *esame di* ~, matriculation examination (*for university*). **matúro,** *a.* ripe; mature.

Matuŝalèmme, *m.* Methuselah (*O.T.*).

mauriziàno, *a.* of (the Order of) St. Maurice & St. Lazarus. **Maurízio,** *m.* Maurice. *l'isola Maurizio, f.* Mauritius.

mauŝolèo, *m.* mausoleum.

mazúrca (*pl.* **-úrche**), *f.* mazurka (*polka*).

màzza, *f.* club; cudgel; walking-stick (*or* cane); mace; mallet; sledge-hammer; (*painter's*) mahl-stick; (*printer's*) rounce (long handle by which one moves the screw of the press). **mazzapícchio,** *m.* beetle; mallet. **mazzàta,** *f.* blow with a club. **mazzière,** *m.* mace-bearer.

mazziniàno, *a.* of Mazzini. ¶ *m.* follower of Mazzini.

màzzo, *m.* bunch; bundle; bale; pack (*cards*); coil (*rope*); (*fig.*) class, category. **mazzolíno,** *m.* small bunch; nosegay.

mazz[u]òlo, *m.* mallet.

me' *contr. for* **mezzo** *or* **meglio** (q.v.).

me, *pn. disjunct.* me; I.

meàndro, *m.* meandering; winding.

meàto, *m.* (*phys.*) meatus; passage; channel.

meccànica, *f.* mechanics. **meccànico** (*pl.* **-ànici**), *a.* mechanical. ¶ *m.* mechanic; mechanician; chauffeur. **meccaníŝmo,** *m.* mechanism; works; gear. ~ *a orologeria,* clockwork. **meccaniżżàre,** *v.t.* to mechanize. **meccaniżżazióne,** *f.* mechanization.

mecenàte, *m.* Maecenas; patron (*Lit. & Art.*). M~, Maecenas.

méco, *pn. pers. & pr.* with me.

medàglia *f.* medal; coin (*Gk., Rom.*); badge. ~ *d'onore,* prize medal. **medaglière,** *m.* collection of medals (or coins). **medaglióne,** *m.* medallion, locket. **medaglísta** (*pl.* **-ísti**), *m.* collector of medals (or coins); medal-maker.

medeŝimàrsi, *v.refl.* to identify oneself (with). **medeŝimaménte,** *ad.* likewise; in the same way. **medéŝimo,** *a.* same; (*with pn.*) self. *io* ~, (I), myself, &c.

mèdia, *f.* average; mean. **mediàno,**

a. mean; middle. ¶ *m.* (*football*) half-back. **mediànte,** *pr.* by means of.

mediatóre, *m.* mediator; inter-mediary; (*Com.*) broker; middleman. **mediatríce,** *f.* mediatrix. **mediazióne,** *f.* mediation; brokerage; commission.

medicàbile, *a.* curable. **medicaménto,** *m.* treatment; medicament; remedy. **medicàre** (*pr.* **mèdico, mèdichi**), *v.t.* to doctor; treat; dress (*wound*). **medicàstro,** *m.* quack; ignorant doctor. **medicatóre,** *m.* (*f.* **-tríce**) healer. ¶ *a.* healing. **medicatúra & medicazióne,** *f.* treatment; (*wounds*) dressing. *posto di medicazione,* first-aid post. **medíceo,** *a.* Medicean; Medici (*att.*). **medichéssa,** *f.* lady doctor. **medicína,** *f.* medicine; remedy; physic. *studente in* ~, medical student. ~ *legale,* medical jurisprudence, forensic medicine. **medicinàle,** *a.* medicinal. ¶ *m.* medicine, drug. **mèdico** (*pl.* **mèdici**), *m.* doctor; physician; medical man, m. officer; (*of time*) healer. ~ *condotto,* parish doctor; panel d. ~ *chirurgo,* general practitioner. ~ *specialista,* specialist (*medical*).

medievàle, see *medioevàle.* **medievalísta** (*pl.* **-ísti**), *m.* mediaevalist.

mèdio (*pl.* **mèdi**), *a.* middle; middling; average. *il M*~ *Evo, m.* the Middle Ages. ~*a età, f.* middle age. ¶ *m.* mean; medium; middle finger. **mediòcre,** *a.* mediocre; middling; second rate. **mediocreménte,** *ad.* moderately. **mediocrità,** *f.* mediocrity. *l'aurea* ~, the golden mean.

medioevàle, *a.* medi[a]eval.

meditàbile, *a.* to be thought over, requiring meditation. **meditabóndo,** *a.* pensive; reflective; meditative; thoughtful. **meditàre** (*pr.* **mèdito**), *v.i.* (*aux.* avere) *& t.* to meditate; reflect (on); ponder; muse; plan; design. **meditazióne,** *f.* meditation.

mediterràneo, *a. & m.* Mediterranean. *il [mare] M*~, the Mediterranean [sea].

mèdium, *m.inv.* medium (*spiritualism*).

medúŝa, *f.* jelly-fish; medusa. M~, Medusa (*Myth.*).

Mefistòfele, *m.* Mephistopheles. **mefistofèlico** (*pl.* **-èlici**), *a.* Mephistophelian.

mefíte, *f.* foul air. **mefítico** (*pl.* -ítici*), *a.* mephitic.

megàfono, *m.* megaphone.

megalítico (*pl.* -ítici), *a.* megalithic.

megalòmane, *a. & m.* megalomaniac. **megalomanía,** *f.* megalomania.

megèra, *f.* old hag; witch.

mèglio, *ad. & a.* better. *tanto ~!* so much the better! ¶ *m. il ~,* the best, the best thing; the better part. *fare del suo ~,* to do his best. ¶ *f. la ~,* the better of it (*in struggle*); the best (*thing*). *alla ~,* as best one can, somehow.

méla, *f.* apple. **melacotógna,** *f.* quince. **melagràna,** *f.* pomegranate.

melanconía, *see* **malinconía,** &c.

Melanésia (la), *f.* Melanesia.

melarància, *f.* orange.

melàssa, *f.* molasses.

melàto, *a.* honeyed; flavoured with honey; honey-sweet.

Meleàgro, *m.* Meleager (*Myth.*).

melensàggine, *f.* silliness; stupidity. **melènso,** *a.* silly; stupid.

meléto, *m.* apple-orchard.

mèlico (*pl.* mèlici), *a.* lyrical.

meliníte, *f.* melinite.

melitènse, *a. & m.* Maltese.

mellífluo, *a.* mellifluous; honeyed; sweet.

mellonàia, *f.* melon-bed, patch of melons. **mellóne** *or* **melóne,** *m.* melon.

mélma, *f.* mud; mire. **melmóso,** *a.* muddy; miry.

mélo, *m.* apple-tree.

melodía, *f.* melody. **melòdico** (*pl.* -òdici), *a.* melodious.

melodràmma (*pl.* -àmmi), *m.* melodrama; opera; libretto. **melodrammàtico** (*pl.* -àtici), *a.* operatic; sentimental; melodramatic.

melogràno, *m.* pomegranate-tree.

melomanía, *f.* passion for music. **melopèa,** *f.* art of melody; blending of melodies; recitative chant.

Melpòmene, *f.* Melpomene (*Muse*).

membràna, *f.* membrane. **membranàceo,** *a.* membranaceous; (*manuscript*) parchment (*att.*).

membratúra, *f.* frame; limbs; structure. **mèmbro** (*pl.* **mèmbri, mèmbra,** *f.col.*), *m.* limb; member. **membrúto,** *a.* large-limbed; strong-limbed.

memènto, *m.* memento; intercessory prayer.

memoràbile, *a.* memorable. **memo-**

---

ràndo, *a.* worthy of memory; memorable. **memoràre,** *v.t.* to recall; recollect; commemorate. **mèmore,** *a.* mindful; grateful. **memòria** (*pl.* **memòrie**), *f.* memory; recollection; remembrance; memoir; record; memorial; souvenir; note (*of reminder*); (*pl.*) memoirs; recollections. *imparare a ~,* to learn by heart. **memoriàle,** *m.* memorial; memoir; catalogue; memorial tablet, &c.

mèna, *f.* (gen. *pl.*) underhand dealing; intrigue. **menàde,** *f.* maenad.

menabò, *m.inv.* (*Typ.*) dummy (*publisher's blank book*).

menadíto (a), *ad. expr.* exactly; perfectly; very well.

Menàndro, *m.* Menander.

menàre, *v.t.* to bring; lead; draw; strike; wield; wag. *~ le mani,* to fight.

menar[u]òla, *f.* (*Mech.*) borer; drill; brace & bit.

menàta, *f.* blow; toss; shake.

méncio, *a.* flabby; soft; feeble.

mènda, *f.* fault; blemish.

mendàce, *a.* lying; mendacious; untruthful; (*fig.*) deceitful; delusive. **mendàcio** (*pl.* -àci), *m.* falsehood; lie.

mendicànte, *m.* beggar; mendicant. ¶ *a.* begging; mendicant. **mendicàre** (*pr.* **mèndico, mèndichi**), *v.i.* (*aux.* avere) *& t.* to beg; to beg for; implore. **mendicità,** *f.* beggary; begging; beggars. **mendíco,** *m.* beggar; pauper. ¶ *a.* begging.

meneghino, *m.* (*pop.*) Milanese; Milanese dialect. **M~,** Meneghino, characteristic Milanese 'mask'.

Menelào, *m.* Menelaus.

menestrèllo, *m.* minstrel.

Mènfi, *f.* Memphis (*Geog.*).

menimpípo (for **me ne impípo,** lit. 'I fill my pipe with it' from impiparsi), *pop. expr.* I don't care (about it). *avere un'aria di ~,* to look indifferent.

meningíte, *f.* meningitis.

méno, *a. ad. & pr.* less; not so (much); fewer; under; minus; to (*of the hour*); except. *a ~, per ~,* cheaper. *a ~ che non,* unless. *il ~,* the least. *al ~, per lo ~,* at least. *fare a ~ di,* to abstain from, refrain from. *fare di ~ di,* to do without; go without. *venir ~,* to faint; fail.

Mèno, *m.* Main (river).

menomaménte, *ad.* by no means; not at all; nowise. **menomàre,** *v.t.*

to depreciate; belittle; diminish; impair. **mènomo**, *a.* least; smallest.

mènsa, *f.* table; board; (*fig.*) meal; (*Mil.*) mess; (*Eccl.*) income; revenue.

mensíle, *a.* monthly. ¶ *m.* wage; monthly wage; m. salary. **mensíl- ménte**, *ad.* monthly; once a month.

mènsola, *f.* bracket; corbel; console; console-table; window ledge. dim. *mensolina f.* & *mensolino, m.*

ménta, *f.* mint. ~ *de'gatti.* catmint. ~ *peperina*, peppermint.

mentàle, *a.* mental. **mentalità**, *f.* mentality.

mentàstro, *m.* wild mint; horsemint.

ménte, *f.* mind; intellect; intelligence; understanding; memory; attention.

mentecàtto, *a.* half-witted. ¶ *m.* fool; idiot.

mentíre (*pr.* -ísco -ísci, &*c.*, & **mento, menti**, &*c.*), *v.i.* (*aux.* avere) to lie; tell a lie; tell lies. *v.t.* to simulate; falsify; mis- represent. **mentitaménte**, *ad.* falsely; deceitfully. **mentíto**, *a.* false; falsified; disguised. **menti- tóre**, *m.* (*f.* -tríce) liar.

ménto, *m.* chin. dim. *mentino.*

mentòlo, *m.* menthol.

mèntore, *m.* mentor; counsellor; adviser.

mentòsto, *ad.* rather not.

mentovàre, *v.t.* to mention.

méntre, *ad.* & *c.* while; on the contrary. *in quel* ~, in the mean- time; meanwhile.

menzionàre, *v.t.* to mention. **men- zióne**, *f.* mention; mentioning.

menzógna, *f.* lie; falsehood; untruth. **menzognèro**, *a.* lying; false; untrue; mendacious; deceitful.

meraménte, *ad.* simply; merely; purely.

meravíglia, *f.* wonder; astonishment; amazement; surprise. **meravi- gliàre**, *v.t.* to astonish; amaze; surprise. **meravigliàrsi**, *v.refl.* to wonder; be surprised; be astonished. **meraviglióso**, *a.* wonderful; mar- vellous.

mercànte, *m.* merchant; trader; dealer. **mercanteggiàre** (*pr.* -éggio, -éggi), *v.i.* (*aux.* avere) to trade; deal; transact business; bargain. *v.t.* to sell; traffic in. **mercantésco** & **mercantíle**, *a.* mercantile. **mercantéssa**, *f.* trades- woman; merchant's wife. **mer- cantilísmo**, *m.* mercantilism. **mercantúccio** & **mercantuòlo**,

m. small trader; hawker. **mer- canzía**, *f.* merchandise; goods; wares. **mercàto**, *m.* market; dealing; traffic. *a buon* ~, cheap, cheaply. *per sopra* ~, into the bargain, in addition, besides.

mercatúra, *f.* commerce; trade; trading. **mèrce**, *f.* goods; mer- chandise; wares. *treno* ~*i*, *m.* goods train. *scalo* ~*i*, *m.* (*Rly.*) goods yard.

mercè, *f.* mercy; pity; grace; favour; help. ¶ *a.pr.* thanks (to), by virtue (of), by means (of). *la Dio* ~, thanks to God, by God's grace. ~ *vostra*, by your help, thanks to you.

mercéde, *f.* reward; recompense; pay; grace; pity.

mercenàrio, *a.* & *m.* mercenary.

mercería, *f.* haberdasher's (draper's) shop; (*pl.*) haberdashery; drapery. **merciàio** (*f.* -àia), *m.* haberdasher; draper; mercer. **merciai[u]òlo**, *m.* hawker; pedlar.

mercimònio, *m.* illicit trade.

mercoledí, *m.* Wednesday. *il* ~ *delle Ceneri*, Ash-Wednesday.

mercuriàle, *a.* mercurial. ¶ *m.* market report; (*pl.*) market-prices.

mercúrio, *m.* mercury; quicksilver. **M**~, Mercury (*Myth.* & *Astr.*).

mèrda, *f.* dirt; dung; excrement. **merdóso**, *a.* dirty; filthy.

merènda, *f.* light meal; light repast.

meretríce, *f.* prostitute.

meridiàna, *f.* sun-dial. **meridiàno**, *a.* & *m.* meridian. **meridionàle**, *a.* Southern; South. ¶ *m.* meridional; southerner.

meriggiàre, *v.i.* (*aux.* avere) to keep in the shade at noon; rest in the shade; take an afternoon nap. **meríggio**, *m.* midday; noon. **meriggióne**, *m.* lazy fellow.

merínga, *f.* meringue.

merino, *m.* merino; merino sheep.

meritataménte & **meritataménte** & **meritevolménte**, *ad.* deservedly; justly. **meritàre**, *v.t.* to deserve; merit; be worth; win; procure; require; want. **meritévole**, *a.* deserving; worthy. **mèrito**, *m.* merit; worth; reward; interest; good mark (*school*). *in* ~ *a*, as to; with regard to; about. **meritòrio**, *a.* meritorious.

merlàno, *m.* whiting (*fish*).

merlàto, *a.* battlemented; crenellated. **merlatúra**, *f.* battlements.

merlettàre (*pr.* -étto), *v.t.* to

ornament with lace. **merlétto,** *m.* & **merletti,** *m.pl.* lace.
Merlíno, *m.* Merlin. **m**~, *m.* marline (*Naut.*).
mèrlo, *m.* blackbird; (*fig.*) simpleton; sly fellow. dim. *merlotto.* **mèrli,** *m.pl.* battlements.
merlúzzo, *m.* cod; codfish. *olio di fegato di* ~, *m.* cod-liver oil.
mèro, *a.* mere; pure; simple; undiluted.
Merovíngio, *a.* & *m.* Merovingian.
mesàta, *f.* month (*duration*); month's pay.
méscere (*pr.* **mésco, mésci**), *v.t.* to pour out.
meschinaménte, *ad.* meanly; poorly; shabbily; stingily. **meschinéllo,** *a.* pitiable; poor; shabby; mean. **meschinería** & **meschinità,** *f.* meanness; wretchedness; misery; mean dealing; stinginess. **meschíno,** *a.* poor; miserable; wretched; mean; shabby; paltry; stingy; niggardly.
méscita, *f.* bar; tap-room; wine-shop; saloon for the sale of spirits. **mescitóra** & **mescitríce,** *f.* barmaid. **mescitóre,** *m.* barman.
mescolaménto, *m.* mixing; mixing up. **mescolànza,** *f.* mixture; blend. **mescolàre,** *v.t.* to mix; mix up; mingle; blend; shuffle (*cards*); stir. **mescolàrsi,** *v.refl.* to mix; mingle; blend; become involved (in); meddle. **mescolàta,** *f.* (*act of*) mixing; mixing up; shuffle; shuffling (*cards*). **mescolataménte,** *ad.* confusedly. **mescolío,** *m.* continual mixing; general mix-up.
mése, *m.* month; month's pay; monthly wages. *del corrente* ~, instant (*abb.* inst.). *del* ~ *scorso* (or *dello scorso* ~), ultimo (*abb.* ult.). *del* ~ *prossimo* (or *del prossimo* ~), proximo (*abb.* prox.). *quanti ne abbiamo del* ~? what day of the month is it?
meśmèrico (*pl.* **-èrici**), *a.* mesmeric. **meśmeríśmo,** *m.* mesmerism.
méssa, *f.* mass (*Eccl.*). ~ *alta,* ~ *grande,* ~ *cantata,* high mass. ~ *bassa,* ~*piana,* low mass. ~ *di requie,* requiem m. **méssa,** *f.* putting; putting forth (*buds*); putting up (*for sale*); stake (*game*); set; course (*at table*). ~ *in marcia,* starting. ~ *in scena,* staging (*play*). ~ *in macchina,* (*Typ.*) imposition.
messaggería, *f.* parcels office; forwarding-agency. **messagg[i]èro,** *m.* (*f.* **-èra**) messenger; (*fig.*) fore-

runner; harbinger. **messàggio** (*pl.* **-àggi**), *m.* message.
messale, *m.* missal; mass-book.
mèsse, *f.* harvest; crop.
messère, *m.* (*Hist.*) Sir; gentleman.
Messía, *m.* Messiah. **messiànico** (*pl.* **-ànici**), *a.* messianic.
messicàno, *a.* & *m.* Mexican. **Messico (il),** *m.* Mexico.
messitíccio, *m.* frail shoot (*Bot.*).
mésso, *p.p.* of *mettere.* ¶ *a.* situated; disposed. *ben* ~, well-dressed, well turned out; sturdy; stout. *mal* ~, badly turned out, badly dressed. ¶ *m.* messenger; (*Hist.*) legate. ambassador.
mestaménte, *ad.* sadly.
mestaménto, *m.* stirring. **mestàre,** *v.t.* to stir; mix. **mestatóio,** *m.* stirrer; ladle. **mestatóre,** *m.* mixer; (*fig.*) intriguer; agitator.
mèstica, *f.* priming (*for paint*); mixed colours (*on palette*). **mesticàre,** *v.t.* to prime; mix colours. **mestichería,** *f.* oil & colour shop.
mestierànte, *m.* journeyman. **mestière,** *m.* trade; occupation; employment; business; profession. *di* ~, by profession, professional. *ferri del* ~, tools of the trade. *mestieri* (*fare, essere*), (*Lit.*) to be necessary.
mestízia, *f.* sadness. **mèsto,** *a.* sad; sorrowful; gloomy.
méstola, *f.* or **méstolo,** *m.* ladle; trowel. **mestolàta,** *f.* ladleful; trowelful; blow with a ladle. **mestolóne,** *m.* large ladle; wild duck; lout; clumsy fellow.
mèta, *f.* goal; aim; end; purpose; object.
metà, *f.* half (*pl.* halves). *tagliare a* ~, to cut in half. *fare a* ~ *con,* to go halves with, share equally. *stare a* ~ *degli utili,* to have a half share in the profits.
metabolíśmo, *m.* metabolism. **metafíśica,** *f.* metaphysics. **metafíśico** (*pl.* **-íśici**), *a.* metaphysical. ¶ *m.* metaphysician.
metàfora, *f.* metaphor. **metaforeggiàre** & **metaforiźźàre,** *v.i.* (*aux.* avere) to indulge in metaphor(s); speak metaphorically. **metafòrico** (*pl.* **-òrici**), *a.* metaphorical.
metàfrasi, *f.* word for word translation.
metàllico (*pl.* **-àllici**), *a.* metallic. **metallífero,** *a.* metalliferous. **metàllo,** *m.* metal; (*fig.*) tone; sound. **metallurgía,** *f.* metallurgy.

metallúrgico (*pl.* -úrgici), *a.* metallurgic(al). **metallúrgo** (*pl.* -úrgi), *m.* metallurgist.

metamòrfico (*pl.* -òrfici), *a.* meta-, morphic. **metamòrfoṣi**, *f.inv.* metamorphosis.

metàteṣi, *f.* transposition; meta-thesis. **metempsicòṣi**, *f.* metempsychosis.

metèora, *f.* meteor. **meteòrico** (*pl.* -òrici), *a.* meteoric. **meteoríte**, *f.* meteorite.

meteorología, *f.* meteorology. **meteorològico** (*pl.* -ògici), *m.* meteorological. *previṣioni meteorologiche*, *f.pl.* weather forecast. **meteoròlogo** (*pl.* -òlogi), *m.* meteorologist.

metíccio (*pl.* -ícci), *a.* half-bred; cross-bred; hybrid. ¶ *m.* half-breed, half-caste; cross.

meticoloṣità, *f.* meticulousness. **meticolóṣo**, *a.* meticulous; over-scrupulous; fastidious.

metíle, *m.* methyl (*Chem.*). **metílico**, *a.* methylic.

metodicità, *f.* orderliness; regularity. **metòdico** (*pl.* -òdici), *a.* methodical. **metodíṣmo**, *m.* methodism. **metodíṣta** (*pl.* -íṣti), *a. & m.* methodist. **mètodo**, *m.* method; way; custom; practical handbook or grammar.

metonimía, *f.* metonymy.

metonomàṣia, *f.* change of name.

mètopa (*pl.* **mètope**), *f.* metope (*Arch.*).

metràggio, *m. &* **metratúra**, *f.* measurement, measuring; length (*in metres*); [quantity] surveying.

mètrica, *f.* metrics, prosody; science of versification. **mètrico** (*pl.* **mètrici**), *a.* metric; metrical. **mètro**, *m.* metre (*verse*); metre = 39·370113 inches; metre measure or tape or stick (1 metre long). ~ *quadrato*, square metre = 10.7639 sq. feet. ~ *cubico*, cubic metre = 35.3148 cu. feet. **metrònomo**, *m.* metronome. **metròpoli**, *f.inv.* metropolis. **metropolíta**, *m.* Metropolitan (*Gk. church*). **metropolitàno**, *a.* metropolitan.

méttere, *v.t. ir.* to put; place; lay; set; stake; put on; cause; compare; charge; draw; thrust; turn; put forth (*leaves, &c.*); lead. (*v.i.*); suppose (*v.i.*). **méttersi**, *v.refl.* to put oneself; get into; enter (into); begin; start; set in; set out.

mettibócca. *m.inv.* meddler; meddle-some talker. **mettilòro**, *m.* gilder. **mettimàle**, *m.inv. &* **mettiscàndali**, *m.inv.* mischief-maker; scandal-monger.

mettitóre, *m.* putter; placer; gamester, punter (*cf. scommettitore*).

mèżża, *f.* half; half-hour; half share; short cue (*billiards*). **meżżadría**, *f.* metayage (*Fr.*), crop-sharing system. **meżżàdro** *&* **meżżaiuòlo**, *m.* tenant who farms his land on the crop-sharing system; metayer. **meżżalàna** (*pl.* **meżżelàne**), *f.* linsey-wolsey; material half-wool & half-cotton. **meżżalúna** (*pl.* **meżżelúne**), *f.* crescent; half-moon; cleaver; curved (*sausage*) knife; lunette (*Arch.*).

meżżàna, *f.* flat tile or flooring-brick; side of bacon; mizzen (*sail*); go-between; procuress.

meżżaníno, *m.* entresol; mezzanine (*floor*).

meżżàno, *a.* mean; middle; middle-sized; middle-class (*att.*). ¶ *m.* go-between; procurer. **meżżanòtte** (*pl.* **meżżenòtti**), *f.* midnight. **meżżatínta** (*pl.* **meżżetínte**), *f.* half-tint. **meżżavía** (a), *ad. expr.* half-way. **meżżería**, *f.* (*cf. mezzadria*) letting of a farm on the crop-sharing system. **meżżétta**, *f.* vessel holding half a litre or half a pint. **meżżína**, *f.* jug; pitcher.

mèżżo, *a.* half. *una mezz'ora*, half an hour. *a mezz'asta*, at half mast. *mezze misure*, half measures. *a mezza via*, half-way. *una mezza verità*, a half truth. *un ritratto a mezzo busto*, a half-length portrait. *mezzo lutto*, half mourning. *legatura in* ~*a tela*, quarter cloth binding. *in* ~*a pelle*, q. leather binding. ¶ *ad.* half. ~ *morto*, half dead. ~ *vestito*, half dressed, h. clad. ¶ *m.* half; means; medium; middle. *due* ~*i fanno un int*[*i*]*ero*, two halves make a whole. *a* (or *per*) ~ *di*, by means of. *il bel* ~, the very middle.

meżżobústo, *m.* bust; head & shoulders; half-length portrait. **meżżocolóre**, *m.* neutral colour. **meżżodí** *&* **meżżogiórno**, *m.* noon; midday; south. **meżżolàno**, *a.* mediocre; middling.

meżżómbra, *f.* half-tone (*painting*). **meżżorilièvo**, *m.* demi-relief (*Art.*). **meżżotèrmine**, *m.* expedient; make-shift; compromise; subterfuge; evasion. **meżżovíno**, *m.* thin wine; wine & water.

meżżúccio, _m._ makeshift; mean device.

mi, _pers. pr. Ist. sg. (conjunct. form)_ me; to me; _(with refl. vb.)_ myself. **mi,** _m._ _(musical note)_ mi; E.

miagolaménto, _m. &_ **miagolàta,** _f._ mewing. **miagolàre,** _v.i._ _(aux._ avere) to mew. **miagolío,** _m._ constant mewing. **miào,** _m._ _(onomat.)_ miaow. _fare ~, &_ **miaulàre,** _v.i._ to miaow.

míca, _f._ mica _(Min.);_ crumb; particle. ¶ _ad._ not; not at all; not in the least. **micàceo,** _a._ micaceous; containing mica. **micasc[h]ísto,** _m._ mica-schist.

micàdo, _m._ mikado.

míccia _(pl._ **mícce),** _f._ fuse _(explos.)._

Micène, _f._ Mycenae _(Geog.)._

michelàccio, _m._ lounger; loafer.

Michelàngelo, _m._ Michael Angelo. **michelangiolésco** _(pl._ **-éschi),** _a._ in the style of Michael Angelo; _(fig.)_ grandiose, majestic.

Michèle, _m._ Michael. _giorno di San ~,_ Michaelmas.

michétta, michettína, _f._ small loaf; roll.

mícia, _f._ puss[y], pussy cat.

micidiàle, _a._ deadly; killing.

micíno, _m._ kitten. **mício** _(pl._ **míci),** _m._ cat; tom-cat; tailor's chalk.

micròbio _&_ **micròbo,** _m._ microbe. **microcòsmo,** _m._ microcosm. **micròfono,** _m._ microphone. **microfotografía,** _f._ micro-photography; microphotograph. **microscòpico** _(pl._ **-òpici),** _a._ microscopic(al). **microscòpio,** _m._ microscope. **microzoàri,** _m.pl._ infusoria.

Mída, _m._ Midas _(Myth.)._

midólla, _f._ marrow; medulla _(Anat.);_ crumb. **midóllo,** _m._ marrow; pith. _~ spinale,_ spinal cord. **midollóne,** _m._ crustless bread; _(fig.)_ flabby person. **midollóso,** _a._ marrowy; pithy; crumbly.

mièle, _m._ honey. _luna di ~,_ honey-moon.

mielíte, _f._ _(Med.)_ inflammation of the spinal cord.

mlètere _(pr._ **mièto, mièti),** _v.t._ to reap; mow. **mietitóre,** _m._ _(f._ **-tríce)** reaper; mower; harvester; _(f.)_ reaping machine. **mietitúra,** _f._ mowing; reaping; harvesting.

migliàio, _m._ _(pl.f._ **-ìaia)** (a) thousand. **migliaríno,** _m._ chaffinch; bunting _(ornith.);_ rifle bullet. **migliar[u]òla,** _f._ small shot.

míglio, _m._ _(pl.f._ **míglia)** mile; millet.

miglioràbile, _a._ capable of improvement. **miglioraménto,** _m._ improvement. **miglioràre,** _v.t. & i._ _(aux._ essere) to improve; get better. **miglioratívo,** _a._ ameliorative. **miglióre,** _a._ better. _il (la) ~,_ the best; the better. **miglioría,** _f._ amelioration.

mignàtta, _f._ leech; _(fig.)_ importunate person; usurer.

mígnolo, _a._ little. ¶ _m._ little finger; little toe; _(&_ **mígnola)** olive-blossom.

mignóne, _m._ favourite; armlet; _(Typ.)_ minion.

migràre, _v.i._ _(aux._ avere _&_ essere) to migrate. **migratóre,** _a. & m._ migrant. **migratòrio,** _a._ migratory. **migrazióne,** _f._ migration.

míla, _a._ num., _pl._ of **mille** _(q.v.)._

milanése, _a. & m._ Milanese. **Milàno,** _f._ Milan.

miliardàrio, _m._ multimillionaire; fabulously rich man. **miliàrdo,** _m._ milliard, a thousand millions.

miliàre, _a._ _(Path.)_ miliary; marking miles; mile _(att.). colonna ~_ (Rom.), _pietra ~,_ milestone.

milionàrio, _m._ millionaire. **milióne,** _m._ million. **milionèsimo,** _a._ millionth.

militànte, _a._ militant. **militàre,** _a._ military; soldierly. ¶ _m._ military man; soldier. ¶ _v.i._ _(aux._ avere) to militate, tell; serve _(in the army)._ **militarésco** _(pl._ **-éschi),** _a._ military; like a soldier _(but with a shade of disapproval)._ **militarísmo,** _m._ militarism. **militarizzàre,** _v.t._ to militarize. **mílite,** _m._ militiaman; soldier. _il M~ Ignoto,_ the Unknown Warrior (or Soldier). **milízia,** _f._ militia; army; force.

millànta, _a._ num. indef. a great many; ever so many; a thousand _(fig.)._ **millantàre** _v.t._ to boast of; exaggerate. **millantàrsi,** _v.refl._ to be proud (of); brag, boast; **millantatóre,** _m._ _(f._ **-tríce)** boaster; braggart; swaggerer. **millantería,** _f._ boast; boasting; swagger.

mílle _(pl._ **mila),** _m. & a.inv._ (a or one) thousand. _I e ~ e una Notte,_ The Arabian Nights. _mi par mill'anni di ~,_ I long to, am anxious to. **millècuplo,** _a._ thousandfold. **millefòglie,** _m.inv._ milfoil; yarrow; Genoese pastry. **millenàrio,** _a._ millenary; lasting for a thousand years. **millènnio,**

m. millennium. **millèsimo,** *a.* thousandth. ¶ *m.* thousandth part; date, year. **milligràmma** & **-gràmmo,** *m.* milligram[me] = 0.015 grain. **millítro,** *m.* thousandth (part) of a litre. **millímetro,** *m.* millimetre = 0.03937 inch.

mílza, *f.* spleen; milt.

míma, *f.* mime; (*pantomime*) dancer. **mimètico** (*pl.* -ètici), *a.* mimetic. **mímica,** *f.* gesticulation; mimicry. **mímico** (*pl.* **mímici**), *a.* mimic.

mímmo, *m.* (*pop.*) baby.

mímo, *m.* mime; buffoon; clown; (*pantomime*) dancer. **mimògrafo,** *m.* writer of mimes or pantomimes. **mína,** *f.* mine (*explos.*); bushel (*meas. of capacity*). ~ *galleggiante,* ~ *alla deriva,* drifting (floating) mine. **minàbile,** *a.* capable of being mined.

minaccévole, *a.* threatening; menacing. **minàccia** (*pl.* -àcce), *f.* threat; menace. **minacciànte,** *a.* threatening. **minacciàre,** *v.t.* & *abs.* to threaten; menace. **minaccióso,** *a.* threatening.

minàre, *v.t.* to mine; undermine; injure. *zona* ~*ata,* *f.* minefield.

minaréto, *m.* minaret.

minatóre, *m.* miner; pitman; collier. **minatòrio,** *a.* threatening; minatory.

minchionàggine, *f.* foolishness; silliness. **minchionàre,** *v.t.* to ridicule; jeer at; quiz; banter; 'rag'. **minchionatóre,** *m.* scoffer; jester; mocker. **minchionatòrio,** *a.* mocking; bantering; jeering. **minchionatúra,** *f.* mockery; raillery; banter; trick; deception. **minchióne,** *m.* simpleton; fool; ninny. **minchionéria,** *f.* foolishness; silliness; piece of stupidity; foolish joke; nonsense.

mineràle, *a.* & *m.* mineral. **mineralista** & **mineralogísta** (*pl.* -ísti), *m.* mineralogist. **mineralogía,** *f.* mineralogy. **mineràrio,** *a.* mining.

minèstra, *f.* soup. **minestrína,** *f.* thin soup. **minestróne,** *m.* vegetable soup; large bowl of soup; (*fig.*) medley.

mingherlíno, *a.* slim; lean; slender.

miniàre, *v.t.* to illuminate (*with miniatures*); (*fig.*) to heighten; embellish; describe in minute detail. **miniatóre,** *m.* illuminator; miniaturist. **miniatúra,** *f.* miniature.

minièra, *f.* mine (*lit.* & *fig.*); quarry. ~ *di carbone,* coal-mine; colliery.

mínima, *f.* (*Mus.*) minim. **minimaménte,** *ad.* (not) at all, (not) in the least. **mínimo,** *a.* least; lowest; smallest; very small. ¶ *m.* minimum.

mínio, *m.* red lead.

ministeriàle, *a.* ministerial. **ministèro,** *m.* ministry; office; secretaryship; board; agency, services, good offices; ministration. *M*~ *degli Affari Esteri,* Foreign Office (*Eng.*). *M*~ *dell'Agricoltura e delle Foreste,* Ministry of Agriculture & Forests. *M*~ *del Commercio Estero,* M. of Foreign Trade. *M*~ *della Difesa,* M. of Defence. *M*~ *delle Finanze,* Treasury Board (*Eng.*). *M*~ *di Grazia e Giustizia,* M. of Justice. *M*~ *dell'Industria e del Commercio,* M. of Industry & Commerce. *M*~ *dell'Interno,* Home Office (*Eng.*). *M*~ *del Lavoro e della Previdenza Sociale,* M. of Labour & Social Security. *M*~ *delle Poste e Telecomunicazioni,* M. of Posts & Telecommunications. *M*~ *della Pubblica Istruzione,* M. of Education (*Eng.*). *M*~ *del Tesoro,* Treasury (*Eng.*). *Pubblico* ~, Public Prosecutor. **minístro,** *m.* minister; Secretary [of State]; ambassador; clergyman. *carta* ~, foolscap (*paper*). ~ *di Stato,* cabinet minister. *Consiglio dei* ~*i,* cabinet council, Cabinet. *Primo* ~, *Presidente del Consiglio* [*dei* ~*i*], Premier, Prime Minister. ~ *dell'Interno,* Home Secretary, Secretary of State for Home Affairs. ~ *degli Affari Esteri,* Foreign Secretary, Secretary of State for Foreign Affairs. ~ *delle Finanze,* Chancellor of the Exchequer. ~ *senza portafoglio,* Minister without portfolio (*not in the Cabinet*).

minorànza, *f.* minority. **minoràre,** *v.t.* to lessen; impair; attenuate; diminish. **minoràsco,** *m.* trust in favour of a younger son. **minoràto,** *a.* disabled. **minorazióne,** *f.* diminution; disablement. **minóre,** *a.* less; minor; lesser; smaller; younger; shorter; lower. **minorènne,** *a.* under age. ¶ *m.* minor. **minorità,** *f.* minority (*age*).

Minòsse, *m.* Minos (*Myth.*).

minuétto, *m.* minuet.

minúgia, *f.* cat-gut; violin-string.

minúscola, *f.* small (lower case) letter. **minúscolo,** *a.* minute, tiny,

,diminutive; (*fig.*) paltry. *lettera* ∼ *a*, small letter.

minúta, *f.* minute; note; rough copy; draft; bill of fare; menu. **minu-tàglia** & **minuzzàglia**, *f.* [quantity of] small articles; minutiae; rabble; mob; small fry (*fish*). **minuta-ménte**, *ad.* minutely; accurately; in detail. **minutàre**, *v.t.* to draw up (*document*); minute. **minu-teríe**, *f.pl.* trinkets; trifles. **minu-tézza**, *f.* minuteness; smallness; thinness; (*pl.*) trifles. **minúto**, *m.* minute (*time*). ¶ *a.* minute; small; fine; detailed; precise; over-precise; common; unimportant. *al* ∼, retail. **minúzia**, *f.* trifle; small detail. **minuziosaménte**, *ad.* minutely; precisely; over-precisely; in detail. **minuziosità**, *f.* excessive attention to detail(s); pedantry; subtlety. **minúzzolo**, *m.* scrap; shred; tiny portion.

mío (*pl.m.* **mìei**, *pl.f.* **mie**), *poss. a.* my; mine. *i miei*, my parents; my family.

míope, *a.* & *m.* short-sighted; s.-sighted person. **miopía**, *f.* & **miopísmo**, *m.* shortsightedness.

miosòtide, *f.* myosotis; forget-me-not.

míra, *f.* sight (*gun*); aim; object; purpose. *prendere di* ∼, to aim at. **miràbile**, *a.* admirable; wonderful. **mirabília**, *f.pl.* wonders; wonderful things. **mirabilménte**, *ad.* admirably; wonderfully.

miràcolo, *m.* miracle; wonder; miracle-play. *dim.* **miracolíno**, *m.* little wonder; infant prodigy. **mira-colóso**, *a.* miraculous; wonderful.

miràggio, *m.* mirage; illusion; (false) hope.

mirallégro, *m.* congratulation.

miràndo, *a.* wonderful; admirable. **miràre**, *v.t.* to look at; gaze at; admire. *v.i.* (*aux.* avere) to aim.

miríade, *f.* myriad.

miríca, *f.* tamarisk (*tree*).

mirífico (*pl.* **-ifici**), *a.* magnificent; wonderful.

miríno, *m.* (gun-)sight; (*phot.*) view-finder.

mírmica, *f.* red-ant. **mirmi-coleóne**, *m.* ant-lion.

mírra, *f.* myrrh. **mirròlo**, *m.* (volatile) oil of myrrh.

mirtéto, *m.* myrtle-grove. **mirtíllo**, *m.* bilberry; myrtle-berry; whortle-berry. **mírto**, *m.* myrtle.

mišantropía, *f.* misanthropy. **miš-antròpico** (*pl.* **-òpici**), *a.* mis-

anthropic(al). **mišàntropo**, *m.* misanthrope. **misavventúra**, *f.* misadventure.

miscèla, *f.* blend; mixture. **miscel-lànea**, *f.* miscellany. **miscellàneo**, *a.* miscellaneous.

míschia (*pl.* **míschie**), *f.* fight; scuffle; fray; melée. **mischiànza** & **mischiatúra**, *f.* mixture. **mischiàre** (*pr.* **míschio**, **míschi**), *v.t.* to mix; shuffle (cards). **míschio** (*pl.* **-míschi**), *a.* mixed. ¶ *m.* mixture.

misconóscere (*pr.* **-ósco**, &c., *like* conoscere), *v.t. ir.* not to recognize; to refuse recognition to; disregard; slight.

miscredènte, *m.* unbeliever. ¶ *a.* unbelieving. **miscredènza**, *f.* unbelief; disbelief.

miscúglio, *m.* medley; sorry mixture.

mišeràbile, *a.* miserable; wretched. **mišerabilità**, *f.* indigence; poverty; destitution. **mišeràndo**, *a.* pitiable; wretched.

mišerère, *m.* miserere (*Ps. LI in the Vulgate*); cry for mercy; (*fig.*) sad or tiresome person. *essere al* ∼, to be in extremity. **mišerévole**, *a.* pitiable; wretched; miserable. **mišèria** (*pl.* **mišérie**), *f.* great poverty; scarcity; wretchedness; meanness; distress; trifle; wretched business; (*pl.*) troubles, defects. **mišericòrde**, *a.* merciful. **mišeri-còrdia**, *f.* mercy; pity. *La M*∼, lay association for succour in accident, illness, or at funerals. ¶ *i.* mercy on us! good gracious! **míšero**, *a.* miserable; wretched; unhappy; poor; mean; paltry. **mišèrrimo**, *a.* (*ir. superl.* of misero) very miserable; wretched.

misfàtto, *m.* misdeed; crime.

mišogàllo, *m.* hater of the French. *il M*∼, title of a work by Alfieri (1798). **mišogamía**, *f.* misogamy; hatred of marriage. **mišoginía**, *f.* misogyny; hatred of women. **mišò-gino**, *m.* misogynist.

missionàrio, *m.* missionary. **mis-sióne**, *f.* mission.

missíva, *f.* missive; letter.

mistaménte, *ad.* in mixed order; promiscuously.

misterióšo, *a.* mysterious. **mistèro**, *m.* mystery; mystery-play.

misticísmo, *m.* mysticism. **místico** (*pl.* **místici**), *a.* & *m.* mystic. **mistificàre** (*pr.* **-ífico**, **-ífichi**), *v.t.* to mystify.

mistióne, *f.* mixture. **místo,** *a.* mixed; variegated. ¶ *m.* mixture. **mistúra,** *f.* mixture.

misúra, *f.* measure; size; measurement; moderation; means; aim; cadence. *pesi e* ~*e,* weights & measures. **misurapióggia,** *m.inv.* rain-gauge. **misuràbile,** *a.* measurable. **misuràre,** *v.t.* to measure; gauge; (*v.i.*) to measure. **misuràrsi,** *v.refl.* to measure oneself; try one's strength; contend. **misurataménte,** *ad.* moderately; in measure. **misuratézza,** *f.* moderation; measure. **misuràto,** *a.* measured; moderate; careful; cautious; scanty. **misuratóre,** *m.* measurer; surveyor; gauger; meter. ~ *del gas,* gas-meter. **misurazióne,** *f.* measurement; measuring; surveying. **misuríno,** *m.* small measure; small gauge.

míte, *a.* mild; gentle; moderate. **mitézza,** *f.* mildness; gentleness; moderateness; cheapness.

mítico (*pl.* **mítici**), *a.* mythical.

mitigàre (*pr.* **mítigo, mítighi**), *v.t.* to mitigate; temper; allay; appease; assuage; alleviate. **mitigazióne,** *f.* mitigation; alleviation.

míto, *m.* myth. **mitología,** *f.* mythology. **mitològico** (*pl.* -**ògici**), *a.* mythological.

mítra & **mítria,** *f.* mitre.

mitràglia, *f.* grape-shot. **mitragliàre,** *v.t.* to machine-gun. **mitragliatríce,** *f.* machine-gun. **mitraglière,** *m.* machine-gunner.

mitriàto, *a.* mitred.

Mitridàte, *m.* Mithridates. **mitridàtico** (*pl.* -**àtici**), *m.* antidote (*to poison*).

mittènte, *a.* sending; forwarding. ¶ *m.* sender.

mnemònica, *f.* mnemonics (*pl.*).

Mnemòsine, *f.* Mnemosyne (*Myth.*).

mo' (*for* **modo**), *m.* way. *a* ~ *di,* by way of; like. ¶ **mò,** *ad.* just now; a moment ago.

moarè, *m.* watered silk; moire.

mòbile, *a.* movable; portable; flying (*column*); sliding (*scale, roof*); mobile; inconstant; fickle; capricious; changeable. *beni* ~*i,* personal property; movable property; movables. *caratteri* ~*i,* movable type. *tassa sulla ricchezza* ~, income-tax. ¶ *m.* piece of furniture; (*pl.*) furniture. **mobília,** *f.* furniture. **mobiliàre,** *a.* movable. *proprietà* ~, *or* ~, personal

property; movable property. ¶ *v.t.* to furnish. **mobilità,** *f.* mobility; (*fig.*) fickleness; inconstancy. **mobilitàre** & **mobilizzàre,** *v.t.* to mobilize (*troops, capital, &c.*). **mobilitazióne** & **mobilizzazióne,** *f.* mobilization. **mobilménte,** *ad.* with mobility; capriciously.

mòca, *m.* mocha (*coffee*).

mocchétto, *m.* moquette.

mocchíno, *m.* (pocket) handkerchief.

moccicóne, *m.* sniveller; idiot; dunce; child with a running nose. **moccicóso,** *a.* snivelling. **móccio** (*pl.* **mócci**), *m.* running mucus; nasal discharge; slime. **moccióso,** *a.* slimy; snivelling.

moccolàia, *f.* candle-snuff.

moccolétto & **moccolíno,** *m.* small taper; bit of candle; mild oath. **mòccolo,** *m.* taper; candle (end); oath; curse. *tirar* ~*i,* to swear. **moccolóne,** *m.* sniveller.

mòda, *f.* fashion; vogue; mode (*dress*); (*pl.*) millinery. *di* ~, in [the] fashion, fashionable, modish, stylish.

modàle, *a.* modal. **modalità,** *f.* modality; way; method; detail.

modanàre, *v.t.* to mould. **modanatúra,** *f.* moulding. **mòdano,** *m.* mould; (*Arch.*) module; netting-needle, crochet-n.

modèlla, *f.* artist's model. **modellaménto,** *m.* & **modellatúra,** *f.* modelling. **modellàre,** *v.t.* to model; mould; fashion; design; shape; form. **modellatóre,** *m.* (*f.* -**tríce**) modeller. **modèllo,** *m.* model; pattern; specimen; perfect type; paragon; sampler (*Need.*).

modenése, *a.* & *m.* Modenese; native of Modena. *pozzo* ~, artesian well.

moderàre, *v.t.* to moderate; check; curb; mitigate; allay; slacken. **moderatézza,** *f.* moderation. **moderàto,** *a.* moderate. **i moderati,** the moderates (*Pol.*). **moderazióne,** *f.* moderation.

modernísmo, *m.* modernism. **modernísta** (*pl.* -**isti**), *m.* modernist. **modernità,** *f.* modernity. **modernizzàre,** *v.t.* to modernize. **modèrno,** *a.* modern; up-to-date; new (*woman*). **i moderni,** *m.pl.* the moderns.

modestaménte, *ad.* modestly; simply; plainly. **modèstia,** *f.* modesty; humility; simplicity.

modèsto, *a.* modest; plain; simple; moderate; quiet (*dress*).

modicità, *f.* moderateness; cheapness; lowness (*of price*). **mòdico** (*pl.* **mòdici**), *a.* moderate, low, small (*price, means*).

modífica, *f.* modification; alteration. **modificàre**, *v.t.* to modify; alter; vary. **modificazióne**, *f.* modification; alteration; change, variation.

modigliòne, *m.* modillion (*Arch.*).

modíno (a), *ad. expr.* carefully; neatly; accurately; properly.

modísta, *f.* dressmaker; milliner. **modistería**, *f.* milliner's shop.

mòdo, *m.* way; manner; mode; method; means; measure; mood (*Gram.*); key (*Mus.*); (*pl.*) manners. ~ *di dire*, expression. ~ *di vedere*, opinion. *in che* ~? how? *in qualsiasi* ~, anyhow. *ad ogni* ~, at any rate. *di* ~ *che*, so that. *in* ~ *da*, so as (to). *a* ~ (*with noun*) well-mannered, well-bred. *a* ~ (*with vb.*), carefully, properly, well.

modulàre (*pr.* **mòdulo**), *v.t.* to modulate. **modulazióne**, *f.* modulation. **mòdulo**, *m.* form (*for filing up or in*). ~ *stampato*, printed form. ~ *per telegramma*, telegram form. *riempire un* ~, to fill up (in) a form.

moèrre *or* **moèrro**, *m.* moire (*silk*).

moffétta, *f.* skunk.

mògano, *m.* mahogany.

mòggio (*pl.m.* **mòggi**, *f.* **mòggia**), *m.* bushel. *a moggia*, in great quantity. *lucerna sotto il* ~, light under a bushel.

mògio (*pl.* **mògi**), *a.* quiet; dull; dejected; crestfallen; abashed. ~ ~, very quiet.

móglie (*pl.* **mógli**), *f.* wife. dim. *moglietta, moglina.*

moína, *f.* simper; smirk; (*oft. pl.*) blandishments; mincing ways.

mòla, *f.* mill-stone; grindstone. **molàre**, *a. & m.* molar (*tooth*). ¶ *v.t.* (*pr.* **mòlo**) to grind.

mólcere (*pr.* **mólce**, *3rd sg.*), *v.t. defect.* to soothe; mollify; caress.

móle, *f.* mass; bulk; size; pile; (massive) building; mausoleum. *un lavoro di gran* ~, a heavy job.

molècola, *f.* molecule; small particle.

molènda, *f.* charge for grinding corn, olives, &c.

molestàre (*pr.* -**èsto**), *v.t.* to vex; annoy; tease; molest; trouble. **molèstia**, *f.* trouble; annoyance; molestation. **molèsto**, *a.* trouble-some; annoying; vexatious; grievous.

molinàio, **molíno**, see *mulino.*

molinàre, *v.i.* (*aux.* avere) to whirl; turn rapidly. **molinèllo**, *m.* winch; windlass; whirl.

mòlla, *f.* (elastic) spring; (*pl.*) tongs. **mollàre**, *v.t. & abs.* to let go; slacken; relax; release; loose[n]; give up. **mòlla** (*excl.*) (*Naut.*) let go!

mòlle, *a.* soft; mellow; flabby; flexible; limp; loose; weak; wet; moist; effeminate; lascivious.

molleggiaménto, *m.* springiness; elasticity. **molleggiàre** (*pr.* -**éggio**, -**éggi**), *v.i.* (*aux.* avere) to be elastic, spring, be flexible; sway up & down. **mollétta**, *f.* small spring, watch-spring; (*pl.*) small tongs, sugar-tongs. **mollettièra**, *f.* puttee (*gen. pl.*). **mollettòne**, *m.* swansdown; soft thick flannel. **mollézza**, *f.* softness; ripeness (*fruit*); feebleness; effeminacy.

mollíca, *f.* crumb (of bread).

mollícchio (*pl.* -**ícchi**), *m.* morass. **mollíccio** (*pl.* -**ícci**), *a.* rather soft; damp; humid. **mollificàre** (*pr.* -**ífico**, -**ífichi**), *v.t.* to soften; mollify.

mollúsco (*pl.* **mollúschi**), *m.* mollusc.

mòlo, *m.* mole; breakwater; pier; quay; wharf.

molòsso, *m.* mastiff.

moltéplice, *a.* numerous; manifold; complex. **molticolóre**, *a.* many-coloured. **moltifórme**, *a.* multiform. **moltilàtero**, *a.* multi-lateral; many-sided. **moltilòquio**, *m.* gabbling; chatter.

moltíplica, *f.* (*Mech.*) gear [ratio]. **moltiplicàndo**, *m.* multiplicand. **moltiplicazióne**, *f.* multiplication; reproduction; increase. **moltiplicàre** (*pr.* -**íplico**, -**íplichi**), *v.t. & moltiplicàrsi**, *v.refl.* to multiply. **moltiplicatóre**, *m.* multiplier. **moltiplicatríce**, *f.* multiplying-machine. **moltiplicità**, *f.* multiplicity.

moltisonànte, *a.* loud; high-sounding. **moltíssimo**, *a. pn. & ad.* very much; a great deal; (*pl.*) **moltíssimi**, *a. & pn.* very many, a great many.

moltitúdine, *f.* multitude; crowd.

mólto, *a.* much; long (*time*); (*pl.*) **molti**, many. ¶ *ad.* very; much; greatly; widely; well. *a dir* ~, at most, at the most. *fra non* ~, in a short time. *ci corre* ~, there is a great difference. *di* ~, by far.

Molúcche (le), *f.pl.* the Moluccas (*Geog.*).

momentaneaménte, *ad.* for the moment; temporarily; momentarily. **momentàneo,** *a.* momentary. **moménto,** *m.* moment (*time, importance*); instant. dim. *momentino,* little bit.

mònaca (*pl.* **mònache**), *f.* nun. dim. *monachella, monachina.* **monacàle,** *a.* conventual. **monacànda,** *f.* novice. **monacàre** (*pr.* **mònaco, mònachi**), *v.t.* to make a nun. **monacàrsi,** *v.refl.* to become a nun; take the veil. **monacazióne,** *f.* taking the veil; entry into an Order.

mònaco (*pl.* **mònaci**), *m.* monk; friar. **M~,** *f.* Monaco; Munich.

mònade, *f.* monad.

monàrca (*pl.* **-àrchi**), *m.* monarch. **monarchía,** *f.* monarchy. **monàrchico** (*pl.* **-àrchici**), *a.* monarchic(al). ¶ *m.* monarchist; royalist.

monastèro, *m.* monastery. **monàstico** (*pl.* **-àstici**), *a.* monastic. **monasticísmo,** *m.* monasticism.

Moncenísio, *m.* Mont Cenis.

moncheríno, *m.* stump (*arm without hand*). **mónco** (*pl.* **mónchi**), *a.* maimed; mutilated; defective; incomplete. **moncóne,** *m.* stump.

mónda, *f.* cleaning; winnowing.

mondanità, *f. inv.* worldliness; (*pl.*) vanities. **mondàno,** *a.* worldly; mundane; earthly; worldly-minded; (*of woman*) fast; fashionable.

mondàre (*pr.* **móndo**), *v.t.* to peel; strip; weed; winnow; clean; cleanse, purify. **mondatúra,** *f.* cleaning; winnowing; peeling; weeding. **mondézza,** *f.* cleanliness; purity. **mondezzàio,** *m.* dust bin; rubbish-heap; heap of dirt.

mondiàle, *a.* world-wide; world (*att.*); universal.

mondíglia, *f.* refuse; siftings; chaff; dross; alloy.

móndo, *a.* clean; cleansed; pure; free (from); stripped (of); peeled; bald; winnowed. ¶ *m.* world.

monegàsco (*pl.* **-àschi**), *a. & m.* of Monaco, native of Monaco.

monèlla, *f.* saucy girl, tomboy; romp; hussy. **monellería,** *f.* (childish) trick; prank. **monellésco** (*pl.* **-éschi**), *a.* roguish; rascally. **monèllo,** *m.* urchin; gamin.

monéta, *f.* coin; piece (*of money*). ~ *spicciola,* change; small change. **monetàggio,** *m. &* **monetazióne,**

f. mintage; minting. **monetàre** (*pl.* **-éto**), *v.t.* to coin; mint. **monetàrio,** *a.* monetary; money (*att.*).

Mongòlia (la), *f.* Mongolia. **Mòngolo,** *a. & m.* Mongol.

moníle, *m.* necklace.

monísmo, *m.* monism.

mònito, *m.* warning; admonition; reproof. **monitóre,** *m.* adviser; instructor; gazette; monitor. **monizióne,** *f.* admonition.

monòcolo, *m.* monocle; eye-glass. ¶ *a.* one-eyed. **monocòrdo,** *m.* monochord (*Mus.*), single-stringed instrument. **monodía,** *f.* monody. **monogamía,** *f.* monogamy. **monògamo** *a.* monogamous. ¶ *m.* monogamist. **monografía,** *f.* monograph. **monogràmma** (*pl.* **-àmmi**), *m.* monogram. **monolítico** (*pl.* **-ítici**), *a.* monolithic. **monòlito,** *m.* monolith. **monòlogo** (*pl.* **-òloghi**), *m.* monologue. **monoplàno,** *m.* monoplane (*Aviat.*). **monopòlio** (*pl.* **-òli**), *m.* monopoly. **monopolísta** (*pl.* **-ísti**), *m.* monopolist. **monopolizzàre,** *v.t.* to monopolize. **monosillàbico** (*pl.* **-àbici**), *a.* monosyllabic. **monosíllabo,** *m.* monosyllable. **monoteísmo,** *m* monotheism. **monotonía,** *f.* monotony. **monòtono,** *a.* monotonous. **monotipía,** *f.* (*Typ.*) monotype.

Monreàle, *f.* Montreal (*Canada*); Monreale (*Sicily*).

monsignoràto, *m.* dignity or office of a monsignore. **monsignóre,** *m.* monsignor(e); title of a bishop or other prelate; My Lord, Your Lordship.

monsóne, *m.* monsoon.

mónta, *f.* (*of animals*) covering; breeding-season; stud; (*turf*) mount; jockey.

montacàrichi, *m.* (goods) lift; hoist; elevator. **montachiàra,** *f.* creamwhisk.

montàggio, *m.* (*Mech.*) raising; mounting; setting; assembling; erection.

montàgna, *f.* mountain. *dim.* **montagnòla,** hillock, mound. **montagnóso,** *a.* mountainous. **montanàro,** *m.* mountaineer; highlander. ¶ *a.* mountain (*att.*), living in the mountains. **montaníno,** *a.* mountain (*att.*); of the mountains. *aria* ~*a,* mountain air. *usi* ~*i,* mountain customs. **montàno,** *a.* mountain (*att.*); on the mountains.

villaggio ~, mountain village. *erta* ~*a*, mountain-slope.

montànte, *a.* mounting; rising. ¶ *m.* step; support; strut (*Aero*); amount; total.

montàre (*pr.* **mónto**), *v.i.* (*aux.* essere & avere) to mount; ascend; climb; come up; go up. *v.t.* to mount (*guard, gem, gun, &c.*); assemble, put together (*Mech.*); raise, hoist; elevate; wind (up) (*watch, spring*); set up; furnish (*house*); organize (*plot*); whip (*cream, &c.*); excite; cover (*mare, cow*). *v.i.* (*aux.* essere) to rise; grow; increase; fly (into a passion); amount (to); (*v.impers.*) to matter. **montàta,** *f.* ascent; rise. **montàtóio** (*pl.* -ói), *m.* step, running-board. **montatóre,** *m.* (*Mech.*) setter, mounter; fitter; erector. **montatúra,** *f.* assembling, putting together (*Mech.*); organizing; getting up; (*fig.*) (a) put up job, (a) got up affair.

montavivànde, *m.inv.* service-lift, dinner l.

mónte, *m.* mount; mountain; heap; bulk; quantity; great deal; failure (in such phrases as *andare a* ~, to fail; *mandare a* ~, to cause to fail). *per monti e per valli*, up hill and down dale. ~ *di pietà*, (municipal) pawn-shop.

Montecitòrio, *m.* parliament-house at Rome.

Montepulciàno, *m.* small town in Tuscany; wine produced there.

monticèllo, *m.* hillock; mound.

montóne, *m.* ram.

montuóso, *a.* mountainous; hilly.

montúra, *f.* uniform.

monumentàle, *a.* monumental, huge.

monuménto, *m.* monument; memorial; building (*public or historic*).

mòra, *f.* mulberry; negress; Moorish woman; game of *mora* (or *morra*); (*Law*) delay, arrears (*of payment*); cairn; heap of stones.

moràle, *a.* moral. ¶ *f.* moral (*of story, event, &c.*); morals; morality. ¶ *m.* morale; moral condition. **moraleggiàre,** *v.i.* (*aux.* avere) & **moralizzàre,** *v.t.* to moralize. **moralísta** (*pl.* -ísti), *m.* moralist. **moralità,** *f.* morality; moral sense. **moralizzatóre,** *m.* (*f.* -tríce) moralizer. ¶ *a.* moralizing, edifying. **moralménte,** *ad.* morally.

moratòria, *f.* (*Law*) moratorium. **moratòrio,** *a.* dilatory.

moràvo, *a.* & *m.* Moravian.

morbidaménte, *ad.* softly; delicately; tenderly; weakly. **morbidétto,** *a.* rather soft. **morbidézza,** *f.* softness; delicacy; tenderness; mellowness; weakness, effeminacy; sensuality. **morbidità,** *f.* morbidness.

mòrbido, *a.* soft; delicate; tender; mellow; weak; effeminate; sensual; morbid.

morbíllo, *m.* measles.

mòrbo, *m.* disease; illness; plague; contagion. ~ *asiatico*, cholera. **morbóso,** *a.* morbid; contagious; unhealthy.

mordàce, *a.* sharp; biting; pungent; sarcastic; satirical. **mordacità,** *f.* pungency; sarcasm. **mordènte,** *a.* caustic; biting; pungent. ¶ *m.* (*acid*) mordant; (*Mus.*) mordent. **mòrdere** (*pr.* **mòrdo**), *v.t. ir.* to bite (*lit. & fig.*). *mordersi le labbra*, to bite one's lips. **mordicchiàre,** *v.t.* to nibble (at). **morditóre,** *m.* (*f.* -tríce) biter. **morditúra,** *f.* bite; sting.

morèllo, *a.* almost black.

morèna, *f.* (*Geol.*) moraine.

morènte, *a.* dying; fading. ¶ *m.f.* dying man, woman.

morésco (*pl.* -éschi), *a.* Moorish. (*danza*) ~ *a*, Moorish dance.

morétta, *f.* brunette; Moorish girl; negro-girl. dim. *morettina*. **morétto,** *m.* dark-skinned boy; Moorish boy; young negro. ¶ *a.* dark; black.

Morfèo, *m.* Morpheus.

morfína, *f.* morphia; morphine.

morfología, *f.* morphology.

morganàtico (*pl.* -àtici), *a.* morganatic.

moría, *f.* pestilence; contagious disease; high mortality.

moribóndo, *a.* dying; moribund.

morigeratézza, *f.* good behaviour; honesty & simplicity of life; orderly ways; temperance; sobriety. **morigeràto,** *a.* orderly; temperate; of simple habits; of good morals.

morìre (*pr.* **muòio** & **mòro, muòri, muòre, moriàmo, morìte, muòiono**), *v.i. ir.* (*aux.* essere) to die; be dying; die away; die out; d. down. **moritúro,** *a.* about to die; doomed to die.

mormóne, *m.* Mormon. **mormonísmo,** *m.* Mormonism.

mormoracchiàre (*pr.* -àcchio, -àcchi), *v.i.* (*aux.* avere) to murmur under one's voice; grumble; complain. **mormoraménto,** *m.* murmuring; whispering; grumbling.

mormoràre (*pr.* mórmoro), *v.i.*
(*aux.* avere) *&* *t.* to murmur,
whisper; grumble; mutter. mor-
moratóre, *a.* *& m.* (*f.* -tríce)
murmuring, murmurer, grumbler.
mormorazióne, *f.* murmuring;
grumbling. mormoreggiàre (*pr.*
-éggio, -éggi), *v.i.* (*aux.* avere) to
murmur; whisper. mormorío (*pl.*
íi), *m.* constant murmur[ing]; grumbling; whisper[ing]; rustling.

mòro, *m.* mulberry-tree; Moor; negro;
dark-skinned person or animal. ¶ *a.*
dark; black; dark-skinned; Moorish.

morosità, *f.* slowness; tardiness;
delay. moróso, *a.* tardy; in arrears.
¶ *m.* (*pop.* for amoroso) lover.

mòrra, *f.* game of mor(r)a.

mòrsa, *f.* (*Mech.*) vice; nose-ring
(*bull*); projecting stone or brick in
an unfinished wall.

morsèllo, *m.* morsel; mouthful.

morsicàre (*pr.* mòrsico, mòrsichi),
v.t. to bite. morsicatúra, *f.* bite;
sting. morsicchiàre (*pr.* -icchio,
-ícchi), *v.t.* to nibble (at). mòrso,
m. bite; morsel; bit (*bridle*); jaw
(*vice*).

mortadèlla, *f.* (Bologna) sausage.

mortàio (*pl.* -ài), *m.* mortar;
furnace for fusing metals.

mortàle, *a.* mortal; deadly; fatal.
salto ~ (complete) somersault. ¶ *m.*
mortal, mortal man.

mortalétto, *m.* small mortar; cracker.

mortalità, *f.* mortality. mortal-
ménte, *ad.* mortally; deadly.
mòrte, *f.* death. *a* ~, to death;
to the death; mortal (*strife*);
mortally; deadly. *la pena di* ~,
capital punishment.

mortèlla, *f.* myrtle.

morticíno, *m.* -a, *f.* dead child.

mortífero, *a.* death-dealing; deadly.

mortificànte, *a.* vexing; grievous;
mortifying; humiliating. morti-
ficàre (*pr.* -ífico, -ífichi), *v.t.* to
mortify (*lit. & fig.*); vex; grieve;
humiliate; (*Med.*) to anæsthetize
locally. mortificazióne, *f.* mortification (*lit. & fig.*); vexation;
humiliation.

mòrto, *a.* dead (*lit. & fig.*); killed;
dull; blunt; still; stagnant. *peso* ~,
deadweight. ¶ *m.* dead man;
dummy (*whist*). *i* ~ *i*, the dead.
il giorno dei ~ *i*, All Souls' Day
(Nov. 2).

mortòrio (*pl.* -òri), *m.* funeral;
funeral procession.

mortuàrio (*pl.* -àri), *a.* mortuary;

death (*att.*). *fede* ~*a*, *f.* death
certificate. *annunzio* ~, announcement of death. *carro* ~, hearse.

mòrva, *f.* glanders.

Mòsa, *f.* Meuse (*Geog.*).

mosàicista (*pl.* -ísti), *m.* worker in
mosaic. mosàico (*pl.* -àici), *m.*
mosaic. ¶ *a.* mosaic; Mosaic (of
Moses).

mósca (*pl.* mósche), *f.* fly; patch;
beauty spot; tuft (*on chin*), imperial,
goatee (*beard*). ~ *cieca*, blind-man's
buff. M~, *f.* Moscow.

moscadèllo, *a.* see moscatello.
moscàdo, *a.* see moscato.

moscàio, *m.* swarm of flies. moscai-
[u]òla, *f.* fly-net; fly-trap; dish-
cover of wire-gauze to keep off flies.

moscardíno, *m.* dandy; young fop;
species of dormouse.

moscatèllo, *a.* with a muscat flavour.
uva ~ *a*, muscatel grape. moscàto,
a. muscat; with an odour of musk.
noce ~ *a*, nutmeg. ¶ *m.* muscat
(*wine*).

mosceríno, *m.* gnat; midge.

moschèa, *f.* mosque.

moschettería, *f.* musketry.
moschettiere, *m.* musketeer.
moschétto, *m.* musket. moschet-
tóne, *m.* spring-hook or clasp
(*watch-chain, &c.*); blunderbuss.

moschicída (*pl.* -ídi), *a.* fly-killing.
carta ~, fly-paper.

móscio (*pl.* mósci), *a.* flabby; soft;
muffled (*sound*); empty (*pockets*).

moscóne, *m.* big fly; blue-bottle.

Mosè, *m.* Moses.

Mosèlla, *f.* Moselle (*Geog.*); moselle
(*wine*).

mòssa, *f.* movement; move (*game,
war*); gesture; manœuvre. (*pl.*) le
mosse, start; starting-place. *prender
le* ~ *e*, to start. *essere sulle* ~*e*,
to be on the move, to be about to
start. mossàccia, *f.* bad move.
mossière, *m.* starter (*running*).
mòsso, *p.p.* of muovere *& a.*
moved, impelled, prompted; stirred;
agitated; troubled; rough (*sea*);
(*Mus.*) lively, animated.

mostàccio *m.* (ugly) face; mug.
mostaio, *a.* juicy.

mostàrda, *f.* (French) mustard.
mostardièra, *f.* mustard-pot.

mósto, *m.* must; grape-juice; new
wine. mostóso, *a.* full of must.

móstra, *f.* show; exhibition; display;
ostentation; pretence; sample; dial-
plate. *sala di* ~, show-room. ~ *di
bottega*, show-case. *vetrina di* ~,

show-window. *far* ~ *di*, to feign; pretend. *mettersi in* ~, to attract notice; make oneself conspicuous. **mostràbile**, *a.* demonstrable; presentable; that may be shown. **mostràre** (*pr.* **móstro**), *v.t.* to show; exhibit; display; give signs of; demonstrate, give proof of; (*v.i.*) to seem. **mostràrsi**, *v.refl.* to show oneself; appear; be seen; prove to be. **mostricína**, *f.* small sample. **mostricíno**, *m.* little monster; huge child. **mostríno**, *m.* second-dial on a watch. **móstro**, *m.* monster; prodigy. **mostruóso**, *a.* monstrous; enormous; prodigious.

mòta, *f.* (liquid) mud; mire.

motivàre, *v.t.* to account for, state the motive of; give the reason(s) for; justify; furnish a motive for; cause. **motívo**, *m.* motive; reason; cause; motif (*Art.*). ¶ *a.* motive; impelling; moving.

mòto, *m.* motion; impulse; movement; agitation; emotion; stir. *in* ~, in motion; on the move. *le leggi del* ~, the laws of motion. **motocarrozzétta**, *f.* motor-cycle with side-car. **motociclétta**, *f.* motor-cycle. **motociclísmo**, *m.* motor-cycling. **motociclísta** (*pl.* -**isti**), *m.* motorcyclist. **motociclístico**, *a.* motorcycling (*att.*). **motocultúra**, *f.* tractor farming, mechanized f. **motonàve**, *f.* motor-ship. **motopattíno**, *m.* m.-scooter. **motopescheréccio**, *m.* motor fishing-boat.

motóre, *m.* engine; motor; motor engine. ~ *a benzina*, petrol-engine. ~ *Diesel*, Diesel-engine. *mettere in moto il* ~, to start (up) the engine. *spegnere il* ~, to shut off the engine. *un* ~ *fuori bordo*, an outboard motor. ¶ *a.* propelling; driving; (*Anat.*) motor. **motorísta** (*pl.* -**isti**), *m.* motor-man; mechanician. **motorístico** (*pl.* -**istici**), *a.* motor (*att.*). *gare* ~ *istiche*, motor-races. **motorizzàre**, *v.t.* to motorize. **motoscàfo**, *m.* motor-boat.

motóso, *a.* muddy, miry.

motríce, *f.* driving-car (*Rly.*, tram-*way*). ¶ *a. f.* motive; propelling; driving.

motteggévole, *a.* jesting; jocular; facetious. **motteggiaménto**, *m.* pleasantry; jest; joke. **motteggiàre**, *v.i.* (*aux.* avere) to jest; joke. (*v.t.*) to banter; make fun of; mock. **motteggiatóre** (*f.* -**tríce**), *m.*

jester; joker; banterer; mocker. ¶ *a.* jesting. **mottéggio**, *m.* banter; raillery; witty saying.

mottétto, *m.* (*Mus.*) motet. **mòtto**, *m.* motto; saying; device; maxim; word.

motupròprio (**di**), *ad. expr.* spontaneously, of one's own free will. **motupròpri**, *m.pl.* decrees of a sovereign.

movènte, *m.* motive; cause; reason; incentive. ¶ *a.* moving. **movènza**, *f.* (graceful) movement; gesture; (*pl.*) carriage; gait. **movíbile**, *a.* movable.

movimentàto, *a.* busy; lively, stirring; eventful. **movimentísta** (*pl.* -**isti**), *m.* (*Rly.*) traffic superintendent. **moviménto**, *m.* movement; motion; traffic; gesture.

Mozambíco, *m.* Mozambique.

moziόne, *f.* motion (*debate*).

mozzaménto, *m.* cutting off; docking; cropping; mutilation. **mozzàre** (*pr.* **mòzzo**), *v.t.* to cut off; cut away; dock (*tail*); crop (*ears*); lop; cut short; take away (*breath*). **mozzatóre**, *m.* mutilator. **mozzatúra**, *f.* cutting off; docking; cropping; part cut off.

mozzicàre (*pr.* **mózzico**), *v.t.* to break in pieces; lop off; clip (*one's words*). **mozzicóne**, *m.* stump. **mózzo**, *sync. p.p. of* **mozzare** *& a.* docked; cropped; truncated; mutilated. ¶ *m.* (*Mar.*) apprentice, cabin-boy; stable-boy, groom; (*Typ.*) incomplete page.

mòzzo, *m.* hub; boss.

mozzorécchi, *m.inv.* pettifogger.

múcca (*pl.* **múcche**), *f.* (milch) cow. **múcchio** (*pl.* **múcchi**), *m.* heap; stack; pile; great quantity; large number. *a múcchi*, in abundance. *dim. mucchietto*, small heap.

múcido, *a.* musty; mouldy; half-rotten.

mucillàggine, *f.* mucilage; gum. **mucillagginóso**, *a.* mucilaginous; gummy.

múco *&* **múcco** (*pl.* **múchi**, **múcchi**), *m.* mucus. **mucósa**, *f.* mucous membrane. **mucosità**, *f.* sliminess. **mucóso**, *a.* mucous; slimy.

múda, *f.* moulting; moulting season; mew, cage for moulting birds.

muezzíno, *m.* muezzin.

múffa, *f.* mould; must. **muffíre** (*pr.* -**isco**, -**isci**), *v.i.* (*aux.* essere) to grow mouldy or musty. **muffíto** *&*

muffóso, *a.* mouldy; musty.
muffosità, *f.* mouldiness; mustiness; (*fig.*) haughtiness, pride.
mugghiàre (*pr.* múgghio, múgghi) & muggíre (*pr.* -ísco, -ísci, *or* muggo), *v.i.* (*aux.* avere) (*of oxen*) to bellow, low; (*fig.*) to roar; howl. múgghio & muggíto, *m.* bellowing, lowing; roar, roaring; howling.
múggine, *m.* mullet.
mughétto, *m.* lily of the valley.
mugíc, *m.inv.* moujik; Russian peasant.
mugnàio (*pl.* -ài), *m.* miller. mugnàia, *f.* miller's wife.
mugolàre, *v.i.* (*aux.* avere) to yelp; whine; whimper; moan; howl; roar (*as of the wind*). mugolío, *m.* (constant) howling; whining; moaning; yelping. mugolóne, *m.* one who whines or whimpers.
mulàggine, *f.* mulishness; stubbornness. mulattièra, *f.* or *strada* ~, mule-track. mulattière, *m.* muleteer.
mulàtto, *m.* mulatto; half-breed.
mulésco (*pl.* -éschi), *a.* mulish. mulétto, *m.* young mule.
mulièbre, *a.* (*Lit.*) feminine; womanly.
mulinàia, *f.* blizzard; whirlwind of snow. mulinàre (*pr.* -íno), *v.t.* to whirl round; (*fig.*) indulge in idle fancies; muse. mulinèllo, *m.* windlass; capstan; whirlpool; whirlwind; whirl; whirling motion; hand-mill; ventilation fan; swivel; reel; (*fig.*) intrigue. mulinío, *m.* (constant) whirling. mulíno, *m.* mill. ~ *a vento*, windmill. ~ *ad acqua*, water-mill.
múlo, *m.* mule.
múlta, *f.* fine; penalty. multàre, *v.t.* to fine.
multicolóre, *a.* many-coloured. multifórme, *a.* multiform. multilateràle, *a.* many-sided.
múltiplo, *a.* & *m.* multiple.
múmmia, *f.* mummy. mummificàre (*pr.* -ífico, -ífichi), *v.t.* to mummify.
múngere (*pr.* múngo, múngi, *like* ungere), *v.t. ir.* to milk; (*fig.*) squeeze; exploit, extract money from. mungitóre, *m.* -tríce, *f.* milker; (*fig.*) sponger. mungitúra, *f.* milking.
municipàle, *a.* municipal; town (*att.*).
município (*pl.* -ipi), *m.* municipality; town-hall.
munificènte, *a.* munificent. munificènza, *f.* munificence; liberality;

bounty. munífico (*pl.* -ífici), *a.* munificent; bountiful; generous.
muníre (*pr.* -ísco, -ísci), *v.t.* to supply; provide; furnish; fortify. munizióne, *f.* munition; ammunition; (*gen. pl.*) munitions. munizionière, *m.* munitions officer; navy contractor.
múnto, *p.p. of* mungere & *a.* pale; exhausted.
muòvere & mòvere (*pr.* muòvo, muòvi, muòve, moviàmo, movéte, muòvono), *v.t. ir.* to move; stir (up); rouse; excite; induce; incite; impel; bring (*a suit*); wage (*war*). *v.i.* (*aux.* essere) to start; set out; advance; go. muòversi, *v.refl.* to move; stir.
múra, *f.pl.* (*col.*) walls; walls of a city. muràglia, *f.* (high) wall; barrier. muraglióne, *m.* thick high wall. muràle, *a.* mural; wall (*att.*). muràre, *v.t.* to wall; build a wall; wall up, immure, shut up. muràrio, *a.* building (*att.*). muràta, *f.* ship's side; bulwark. muratóre, *m.* mason; bricklayer. muratúra, *f.* building; masonry. muràzzo, *m.* sea-wall; dyke. murétto & muricci[u]òlo, *m.* low wall.
múria, *f.* brine.
múrice, *m.* murex.
múro, *m.* (*m.pl.* múri, *f.pl.* (*col.*) múra) wall.
mùsa, *f.* Muse; (*fig.*) poetry. musagète, *m.* epithet of Apollo, leader of the Muses.
musàccio, *m.* ugly face. musàre, *v.i.* (*aux.* avere) to stare; sniff.
muschiàto, *a.* musky. *rosa* ~*a*, musk-rose. múschio, *m.* musk; musk-deer; moss.
músco *or* múschio (*pl.* múschi), *m.* moss.
muscolàre, *a.* muscular. muscolatúra, *f.* muscular system. múscolo, *m.* muscle; mussel. muscolóso, *a.* muscular.
muscóso, *a.* mossy.
musèo, *m.* museum.
musèr[u]òla, *f.* muzzle; nose-band.
música, *f.* music. musicàbile, *a.* that can be set to music. musicàle, *a.* musical. musicalità, *f.* taste for music; melodiousness. musicànte, *m.* professional musician; executant, performer. musicàre (*pr.* músico, músichi), *v.t.* to set to music; play or sing. musichétta, *f.* light music. musicísta (*pl.* -ísti), *m.* musician; composer. músico (*pl.* músici), *a.* musical. ¶ *m.* musician.

múśo, *m.* muzzle (*animal nose & mouth*), snout; face; mug. **mušolièra,** *f.* muzzle. **mušóne,** *m.* **-óna,** *f.* sulky person; pouter. **mušonería,** *f.* sulkiness; sullenness. **mušorno,** *a.* (*Poet.*) sulky; stupid; dark, lowering (*sky*).

mussolína, *f.* muslin.

mus[s]ulmàno, *a. & m.* Mussulman; Mohammedan.

mustàcchio (*pl.* -àcchi *or* -àcci), *m.* moustache.

múta, *f.* change (*act & substitute*); team, relay (*horses*); pack (*hounds*); relief (*guard*); set (*sails, studs, jewels*); moult; moulting (*feathers*). *a ~ a ~*, by turns. **mutàbile,** *a.* mutable; changeable; inconstant. **mutabilità,** *f.* mutability; inconstancy.

mutaménte, *ad.* mutely, silently; noiselessly.

mutaménto, *m.* change; alteration; variation. **mutànde, mutandíne,** *f.pl.* drawers. *~ da bagno,* bathing-drawers. **mutàre,** *v.t.* to change; alter; vary; (*animals*) shed; (*birds*) moult. *v.i.* (*aux.* essere & avere) & **mutàrsi,** *v.refl.* to change. **mutazióne,** *f.* change; alteration; mutation; variation. **mutévole,** *a.* changeable; variable; inconstant. **mutevolézza,** *f.* changeableness; inconstancy.

mutézza, *f.* silence.

mutilàre (*pr.* **mútilo**), *v.t.* to mutilate. **mutilàto & mútilo,** *a.* mutilated; disabled. **mutilazióne,** *f.* mutilation.

mutiśmo, *m.* dumbness; obstinate silence. **múto,** *a.* dumb; mute; silent; speechless. *sordo e ~,* deaf & dumb. *scena ~ a,* dumb show. **mútolo,** *a.* dumb.

mútria, *f.* haughty demeanour; boldness; audacity.

mutualità, *f.* mutuality; mutual association (*for charity, &c.*); reciprocity. **mutualménte,** *ad.* mutually; reciprocally. **mutuànte,** *a.* lending. ¶ *m.* lender; mortgagee. **mutuàre,** *v.t.* to lend; borrow; mortgage. **mutuatàrio** (*pl.* -àri), *m.* borrower; mortgager. **mútuo,** *a.* mutual; reciprocal. *società di ~ soccorso,* benefit society, friendly society. ¶ *m.* loan. *dare a ~,* to lend. *prendere a ~,* to borrow. *atti di ~,* documentary evidence of borrowing or loans.

N

N, n, (*enne*) *f.* the letter N.

nabàbbo, *m.* nabob.

nabísso, *m.* imp, little devil.

Nabucodònosor, *m.* Nebuchadnezzar (*O.T.*).

nàcchera, *f.* kettledrum; (*pl.*) castanets.

nàchero, *m.* dwarf. ¶ *a.* dwarfish, crooked.

nàfta, *f.* naphtha. **naftalína,** *f.* naphthalene. **naftòlo,** *m.* naphthol.

nàiade, *f.* naiad; water-nymph.

nàja, *f.* (*Mil. slang*) army discipline; army.

Nanchíno, *f.* Nankin(g). **n~, m.** nankeen.

nànna, *f.* nurses' word for hushing babies to sleep; hushaby; sleep. *far la ~* (*of child*) to go to sleep, *andare a ~,* to go to bed. **nínna nànna,** *f.* lullaby; cradle-song.

nànnoli, *m.pl.* toys.

nàno, *a. & m.* dwarf.

Nànte, *f.* Nantes.

Napoleóne, *m.* Napoleon. **napoleònico** (*pl.* -ònici), *a.* Napoleonic. **napoleoníśmo,** *m.* Napoleonic system.

napoletàno, *a. & m.* Neapolitan. **Nàpoli,** *f.* Naples.

nàppa, *f.* tassel; tuft. *dim.* **nappína,** *f.* tuft; pompon; top-knot.

nàppo, *m.* (*Poet.*) goblet; cup.

Narbòna, *f.* Narbonne.

Narcíśo, *m.* Narcissus (*Myth.*). **n~,** (*Bot.*) narcissus; daffodil.

narcòtico (*pl.* -òtici), *a. & m.* narcotic; opiate.

nàrdo, *m.* nard; spikenard.

naríce, *f.* nostril; (*pl.*). *le~ i,* nostrils.

narràbile, *a.* that can be told. **narràre,** *v.t.* to tell; relate; narrate; recount. **narratívo,** *a.* narrative. **narratóre,** *m.* (*f.* -tríce) narrator; story-teller. **narrazióne,** *f.* narration; narrative; tale; story; recital (*of facts*).

narvàlo, *m.* narwhal.

nasàle, *a.* nasal. **nasàta,** *f.* blow with or on the nose.

nascènte, *p.a.* rising; dawning; nascent; springing (*buds*); shooting; growing. **nàscere** (*pr.* **nàsco, nàsci,** *&c.*), *v.i. ir.* (*aux.* essere) to be born; originate; rise; spring up; shoot (up); come up; bud; be hatched; grow. *far~,* to give rise to, cause, occasion. **nàscita,** *f.* birth; origin; family. **nascitúro,** *a.* about to be born; yet to be born, rise, spring up, &c.; future.

nascóndere, *v.t. ir.* to hide; conceal, disguise; dissemble. **nascóndersi,** *v.refl.* to hide (oneself), be hidden. **nascondíglio,** *m.* hiding-place; lair. **nascondiménto,** *m.* hiding; concealing; concealment. **nasconditóre,** *m.* (*f.* **-tríce**) concealer; dissembler. **nascostaménte,** *ad.* secretly; stealthily, by stealth. **nascósto,** *a. & p.p.* hidden; concealed, secret, underhand. *di~,* secretly, by stealth.

naseggiàre, *v.i.* (*aux.* avere) to have a nasal sound.

nasèllo, *m.* door-catch; hake, whiting (*fish*).

nasièra, *f.* nose-band; nose-ring; nose-piece. **nàso,** *m.* nose, (*fig.*) face. *~a~,* face to face. dim. *nasetto, nasino, nasettino, nasicchio* (funny little nose), *nasuccio.*

nàspo, *m.* reel.

nàssa, *f.* eel-pot; lobster-pot; net; trap. **nàsso,** *m.* (*Poet.*) yew. **N~,** *f.* Naxos.

nastrifórme, *a.* ribbon-like; ribbon-shaped. **nastríno,** *m.* ribbon; small ribbon; book-mark; tape (*telegr.*). **nàstro,** *m.* ribbon; band; tape.

nastúrzio, *m.* nasturtium; cress.

nasúto, *a.* big-nosed; (*fig.*) sharp; alert.

natàle, *a.* native; natal; birth (*att.*). **N~,** *m.* Christmas. *m.* (*often pl.*) birth; birthday; birthplace. *avere i~i,* to be born. *dare i~i a,* to be the birth-place of. **natalízio** (*pl.* **-ízi**), *a.* Christmas (*att.*); natal; birth (*att.*). *giorno ~,* or *~,* birthday.

natànte, *a.* floating; swimming. **natatóia,** *f.* fin; web of duck's foot; swimming bladder. **natatòrio,** *a.* swimming. *vasca, piscina ~a,* *f.* swimming-pool, swimming-bath.

nàtica (*pl.* **nàtiche**), *f.* buttock.

natío (*pl.* **-íi**), *a.* native. **natività,** *f.* nativity. **natívo,** *a.* native, innate, natural. ¶ *m.* native. **nàto,** *a. & p.p.* of *nascere,* born; risen. ¶ *m.* child.

nàtta, *f.* wen.

natúra, *f.* nature; life (*Art*). *~ morta,* still life. *pagare in ~,* to pay in kind. **naturàle,** *a.* natural. *al~,* life-sized; life-like. ¶ *m.* nature; character; disposition; constitution (*phys.*). **naturalézza,** *f.* natural-

ness. **naturalísmo,** *m.* naturalism. **naturalísta** (*pl.* **-ísti**), *m.* naturalist. **naturalità,** *f.* citizenship; political status; naturalization. **naturalizzàre,** *v.t.* to naturalize. **naturalizzàrsi,** *v.refl.* to become naturalized. **naturalizzazióne,** *f.* naturalization.

naufragàre (*pr.* **nàufrago, nàufraghi**), *v.i.* (*aux.* essere & avere) to be (ship)wrecked, to shipwreck; (*fig.*) fail; be disappointed; come to nought (nothing). **naufràgio** (*pl.* **-àgi**), *m.* shipwreck, wreck. **nàufrago** (*pl.* **nàufraghi**), *a.* (ship-)wrecked. ¶ *m.* shipwrecked man, s. person; castaway.

naumachìa, *f.* sea-fight (*spectacle*).

nàusea, *f.* nausea; disgust, loathing. **nauseabóndo,** *a.* nauseous; loathsome; foul; sickening. **nauseànte,** *a.* nauseating, nauseous. **nauseàre,** *v.t.* to nauseate; sicken; disgust; make sick.

nàutica, *f.* nautical science; (art of) navigation. **nàutico** (*pl.* **nàutici**), *a.* nautical.

nàutilo, *m.* nautilus.

navàle, *a.* naval; navy (*att.*); sea (*att.*). **navalèstro,** *m.* boatman; ferryman; bargee.

Navàrra, *f.* Navarre.

navàta, *f.* nave; aisle (*Arch.*).

nàve, *f.* ship; vessel; craft; boat; bottom; navy. *~a vapore,* steamship; steamer. *~ cisterna, ~ petroliera,* tank-ship, tanker. *~ da carico,* cargo boat. *~ capofila,* (*Nav.*) leading ship. *~ serrafila,* rear ship. *~ prodiera,* ship next ahead. *~ poppiera,* ship next astern. *~ gemella,* sister ship. *~ da battàglia,* battleship. *~ ammiràglia,* flag-ship. *~ di pattúglia,* patrol ship. *~officina,* repair ship. [*~*] *posamine,* mine-layer. [*~*]*spazzamine,* mine-sweeper. dim. *navicella, navicello.*

navigàbile, *a.* navigable. **navigabilità,** *f.* navigability; seaworthiness. **navigàre** (*pr.* **nàvigo, nàvighi**), *v.i.* (*aux.* avere) to navigate; sail; steer one's course; (*fig.*) behave. *v.t.* to sail. **navigatóre,** *m.* navigator; sailor. ¶ *a.* (*f.* **-tríce**) seafaring. **navigazióne,** *f.* navigation; voyage; cruise. **navíglio,** *m.* ship; craft; fleet; navy. *canale~,* ship-canal. *~mercantile,* merchant navy. *~ peschereccio,* fishing fleet.

Naż[ż]arèno, *a. & m.* Nazarene.

Nàż[ż]aret, *f.* Nazareth.

nazionàle, *a.* national. **naziona-**
lísmo, *m.* nationalism. **naziona-**
lísta (*pl.* -ísti), *a. & m.* nationalist.
nazionalità, *f.* nationality. **na-**
zionalizzàre, *v.t.* to nationalize.
nazióne, *f.* nation; people. *Società*
delle N~i, League of Nations.
nazísmo, *m.* nazism. **nazísta,** *a.*
& m. nazi.

ne, *pn. & ad. conjunct.* of it, its, of
him, or her; of them; their; about it,
about them, &c.; (*partitive*) some;
any; (*Poet.*) us.

ne', for *nei,* in the (*m.pl.*).

né, *c.* neither; nor.

neànche, *c.* not even.

nébbia, *f.* fog; haze; mist. **nebbi-**
àccia, *f.* **nebbióne,** *m.* dense
fog; heavy mist. **nebbiolína,**
f. light mist. **Nebbiòlo,** *m.* a
red wine of Piedmont. **nebbió-**
sità, *f.* fogginess, haziness; mistiness. **nebbióso,** *a.* foggy, hazy;
misty.

nebulósa, *f.* nebula (*Astr.*). **nebulo-**
sità, *f.* mistiness; haziness; nebulo-
sity (*lit. & fig.*). **nebulóso,** *a.*
nebulous; cloudy; clouded (*lit. &*
fig.).

néccio, *m.* (for *castagneccio*) chestnut-
meal cake.

necessariaménte, *ad.* necessarily.
necessàrio, *a.* necessary; needful.
¶ *m. il ~,* what is necessary; the
needful. **necessità,** *f.* necessity;
need; poverty. **necessitàre,** *v.t.*
to necessitate. (*v.i.*) be in want
(of = *di*).

necrología, *f.* obituary, o. notice;
funeral oration. **necrologio,**
obituary. **necromanzía,** *f.* necromancy; black art. *Cf.* **negro-**
manzía (more com.). **necròpoli,**
f.inv. necropolis. **necroscopía,** *f.*
autopsy. **necroscòpico** (*pl.* -òpici),
a. post-mortem. **necròsi,** *f.inv.*
necrosis; gangrene.

neerlandése, *m.* Dutchman, Nether-
lander. ¶ *a.* Dutch, Netherlandish.
Neerlàndia (la), *f.* the Netherlands
(*pl.*).

nefandézza, *f.* infamy. **nefàndo,** *a.*
infamous; abominable. **nefàrio,** *a.*
nefarious. **nefàsto,** *a.* luckless;
ill-fated; ill-omened; disastrous;
fatal.

nefríte, *f.* nephritis.

negàbile, *a.* deniable. **negàre** (*pr.*
nègo, nèghi), *v.t.* to deny; refuse;
disown. **negativa,** *f.* denial; refusal;
negative (*Phot., Gram.*). **negatívo,**

a. negative. **negàto,** *a.* unfit;
unsuited; not granted. **negazióne,**
f. negation; denial; disavowal.

neghittóso, *a.* slothful; slack; lazy.

neglettaménte, *ad.* carelessly;
neglectfully. **neglètto,** *a.* neglected;
uncared for; untidy.

négli, *pr. & def. art. m. pl.* in the.

negligènte, *a.* negligent; careless;
neglectful; remiss. **negligènza,** *f.*
negligence; neglect; carelessness;
default. **negligere** (*pr.* **neglígo,**
neglígi), *v.t. defect.* to neglect; slight.

negoziàbile, *a.* negotiable; marketable. **negoziànte,** *m.* tradesman;
trader; merchant; dealer. **negoziàre**
(*pr.* -òzio, -òzi), *v.i.* (*aux. avere*) to
deal; trade; carry on a trade;
negotiate; bargain; (*v.t.*) to negotiate.
negoziàto, *m.* (*gen. pl.*) negotiation;
agreement. **negoziatóre,** *m.* (*f.*
-tríce) negotiator, -tress *or* -trix.
negoziazióne, *f.* negotiation; transaction. **negòzio** (*pl.* -òzi), *m.* shop;
trade; business; transaction.

négra, *f.* negress. **negrétto,** *m.* young
negro. **negrézza,** *f.* blackness.
negrière, -ièro, *m.* slave-dealer;
slave-trader. ¶ *a.* slave (*att.*).
nave ~ a, slave-ship. **négro,** *m.*
negro; blackamoor. ¶ *a.* black;
negro. **negròide,** *a. & m.* negroid.

negromànte, *m.* (*f.* -mantéssa)
necromancer; sorcerer (*f.* -ess).
negromanzía, *f.* necromancy; black
art; sorcery.

nègus, *m.inv.* Negus (*Abyssinia*).

nèh? (*non è vero*) *excl. interrog.* isn't it?

nel, nello, nella, *&c.,* *pr. & art,* in
the.

némbo, *m.* cloud; rain-cloud; cloud-
burst. **nembóso,** *a.* stormy.

Nembròtte, *m.* Nimrod (*O.T.*).

nèmeši, *f.inv.* nemesis.

nemíco (*pl.* -íci), *a.* hostile; inimical.
¶ *m.* enemy; foe; adversary; enemy
(*att.*).

nemmànco & nemméno, *c.* not
even.

nènia, *f.* dirge; lamentation; funeral
song.

nenufàr, *m.inv.* nenuphar; water-lily.

nèo, *m.* mole (*on the skin*); patch;
slight defect. dim. *neino.*

neoclassicísmo, *m.* neo-classicism.

neòfito, (*pl.* -òfiti), *m.* neophyte.

neolatíno, *a.* neo-Latin, Romance.
le lingue ~e, the Romance languages.

neolítico (*pl.* -ítici), *a.* neolithic
(*Geol.*).

neologísmo, *m.* neologism.

nèon, *m.* neon. *luce di* ~, neon light.
neonàto, *a.* new-born. ¶ *m.* -a, *f.*
new-born child, infant, baby.
nepènte, *m.* nepenthe.
nepotísmo, *m.* nepotism.
neppúre, *c.* not even.
nequízia, *f.* wickedness; iniquity.
neràstro, *a.* blackish.
nerbàre, *v.t.* to flog, beat; drub.
nerbàta, *f.* vigorous blow. **nerba-**
túra, *f.* beating; drubbing; flogging.
nèrbo, *m.* sinew; muscle; whip;
(*fig.*) force; strength; best part,
flower (*army, &c.*). **nerborúto &**
nerbúto, *a.* muscular; sinewy.
nereggiaménto, *m.* blackening.
nereggiàre, *v.i.* (*aux.* avere) to
turn black; be nearly black; appear
black.
nerèide, *f.* nereid; sea-nymph. **Nèreo,**
m. Nereus (*Myth.*).
nerétto, *a.* blackish. ¶ *m.* (*Typ.*)
thick type; heavy type. **nerézza,** *f.*
blackness. **neríccio,** *a.* blackish.
néro, *a.* black; dark; swarthy;
brown (*bread*); gloomy. *il mar N* ~,
the Black Sea. ¶ *m.* black; b. (man,
boy); man of colour. **nerofúmo,** *m.*
lamp-black. **nerógnolo,** *a.* blackish.
Neróne, *m.* Nero.
nerúme, *m.* quantity of black; black
things.
nervatúra, *f.* (*Anat.*) nervous system;
(*Bot.*) nervation; ribbing (*Arch. &*
book-binding). **nèrveo,** *a.* nerve
(*att.*); of the nerves. **nervíno,** *a. &*
m. nervine. **nèrvo,** *m.* nerve; sinew;
vein (*leaf*); rib (*Arch.*); (*fig.*) energy;
vigour. **nervosità,** *f.* nervousness.
nervóso, *a.* nervous; (*style*) vigorous.
nèsci (**fare il**) to feign ignorance.
nescieménte, *ad.* unknowingly;
unwittingly.
nèspola, *f.* medlar. **nèspolo,** *m.*
medlar-tree.
nèsso, *m.* connection; link; (*Mus.*) tie;
nexus. **N** ~, *m.* Nessus (*Myth.*).
nessúno, *pn. inv.* nobody, no one;
anybody; anyone. ¶ *a.* no.
Nèstore, *m.* Nestor.
nettadènti, *m.inv.* tooth-pick. **netta-**
ménte, *ad.* cleanly; clearly; sharply;
openly; distinctly; entirely. **netta-**
ménto, *m.* cleaning; cleansing.
nettapénne, *m.inv.* pen-wiper.
nettàre (*pr.* **nétto**), *v.t.* to clean;
cleanse.
nèttare, *m.* nectar.
nettatóre, *m.* (*f.* -**tríce**) cleaner.
nettatúra, *f.* cleaning; cleansing.

nettézza, *f.* cleanness; clearness;
sharpness; neatness; tidiness.
nétto, *a.* clean; clear; distinct;
sharp; neat; net.
nettúnio, *m.* neptunium (*element*).
Nettúno, *m.* Neptune.
neurastenía, *f. & nevrastenía,** *f.*
neurasthenia. **neuròlogo,** *m.*
neurologist; nerve-specialist. **neu-**
ròsi & nevròsi, *f.* neurosis.
neuròtico & nevròtico (*pl.* -**òtici**),
a. & m. neurotic.
neutràle, *a. & m.* neutral. **neutralísta**
(*pl.* -**ísti**), *m.* advocate of neutrality.
neutralità, *f.* neutrality. **neutral-**
iżżàre, *v.t.* to neutralize (*Pol.,*
Chem.). **nèutro,** *a.* neuter; neutral,
indefinite. ¶ *m.* neuter (*Gram.*).
neutróne, *m.* (*Phys.*) neutron.
nevàio (*pl.* -**ài**), *m.* snow-field.
nevàta, *f.* fall of snow, snow-fall.
nevàto, *a.* snowy; snow-white.
néve, *f.* snow. ~**i** *perpetue,*
perpetual s. *falda di* ~, snow-flake.
nevicàre (*pr.* **névico, névichi**), *v.i.*
(*aux.* essere) to snow. **nevicàta,** *f.*
snow-fall; snow-storm. **nevíschio**
(*pl.* -**íschi**), *m.* sleet; drizzling snow;
thick fine snow. **nevosità,** *f.*
snowiness. **nevóso,** *a.* snowy.
nevralgía, *f.* neuralgia. **nevràlgico**
(*pl.* -**àlgici**), *a.* neuralgic. **nevra-**
stenía, *f.* neurasthenia. **nevra-**
stènico (*pl.* -**ènici**), *a. & m.*
neurasthenic. **nevròsi,** *f.inv.*
neurosis. **nevròtico** (*pl.* -**òtici**),
a. & m. neurotic.
nevvéro, *excl. interrog.* isn't it? isn't
it true? isn't it so?
níbbio (*pl.* **níbbi**), *m.* kite (*bird*).
nícchia (*pl.* **nícchie**), *f.* shell; niche;
recess; nook; (*fig.*) post, situation.
nicchiàre (*pr.* **nícchio, nícchi**),
v.i. (*aux.* avere) to hesitate. **nícchio**
(*pl.* **nícchi**), *m.* shell; conch; priest's
three-cornered hat; shell-shaped
lamp.
níchel, *m.inv. & nichèlio,** *m.* nickel.
nichelíno, *m.* nickel coin. **nichel-**
[**l**]**àre,** *v.t.* to nickel; nickel-plate.
nichel[**l**]**atúra,** *f.* nickel-plating.
nichilísmo, *m.* nihilism. **nichilísta**
(*pl.* -**ísti**), *m.* nihilist.
nicotína, *f.* nicotine.
nidiàce, *a.* unfledged. ¶ *m.* fledg[e]-
ling. **nidiàta,** *f.* brood; nestful.
nidificàre (*pr.* -**ifico, ífichi**), *v.i.*
(*aux.* avere) to build a nest; to nest.
nidificazióne, *f.* nest-building;
nesting. **nido,** *m.* nest; roost; aerie;
(*fig.*) home; haunt.

niègo (*pl.* **nièghi**), *m.* (*Poet.*) denial; refusal.

niellàre, *v.t.* to inlay with niello.

nièllo, *m.* niello (*inlaid enamelwork*).

niènte, *pn.indef.* nothing; (*interrog.*) anything. ¶ *m.* trifle; mere nothing. ¶ *a.* no. ¶ *ad* ~, *per* ~, ~*affatto*, not at all. **nientediméno**, *ad. & c.* nevertheless. **nienteméno**, *ad.* no less (than); nothing less (than).

Nilo (**il**), *m.* (the) Nile.

nímbo, *m.* nimbus; aureole; halo; cloud; rain-cloud.

nínfa, *f.* nymph; chrysalis. **ninfàle**, *a.* nymphean. ¶ *m.* tale or poem of the nymphs, cf. *il N* ~ *Fiesolano* (Boccaccio). **ninfèa**, *f.* water-lily.

Nínive, *f.* Nineveh.

nínna nànna, *f.* lullaby; cradle-song. **ninnàre**, *v.t.* to lull; sing to sleep. **ninnolàre**, *v.t.* to amuse (a child). *v.i.* (*aux.* avere) to trifle. **nínnolo**, *m.* trifle; trinket; nick-nack. **ninnolóne**, *m.* trifler.

níno, *m.* pet; dear; darling (*child*).

nipóte, *m.* nephew; grandson. *f.* niece; granddaughter. *i nipoti* (*m.pl.*) grandchildren; descendants. **nipotíno**, *m.* little nephew; grandson. **nipotína**, *f.* little niece; granddaughter.

nippònico (*f.l.* **-ònici**), *a.* Japanese.

nitidaménte, *ad.* clearly; distinctly. **nitidézza**, *f.* clearness; brightness. **nítido**, *a.* clear; shining; distinct; concise. **nitóre**, *m.* (*Poet.*) brightness.

nitràto, *m.* nitrate. **nítrico** (*pl.* **nítrici**), *a.* nitric.

nitríre (*pr.* **-ísco, -ísci**), *v.i.* (*aux.* avere) to neigh. **nitríto**, *m.* neigh; neighing.

nitro, *m.* nitre; saltpetre. **nitroglicerína**, *f.* nitroglycerin(e). **nitróso**, *a.* nitrous.

niúno, *pn.indef.* no one. ¶ *a.* no.

niutoniàno, *a. & m.* Newtonian.

níveo, *a.* snowy; snow-white.

Nízza, *f.* Nice. **nizzàrdo**, *a.* of Nice. ¶ *m.* native of Nice. *il gran* ~, Garibaldi.

no, *neg. particle*, no; not. ~*e poi* ~, a thousand times no. *credo di* ~, I think not. *dire di* ~, to say no. ¶ *m.inv.* no, nay.

nòbile, *a. & m.* noble. **nobilésco**, *a.* haughty. **nobiliàre**, *a.* of the nobility. **nobilitàre**, *v.t.* to ennoble; dignify. **nobiltà**, *f.* nobility. **nobilúccio**, *m.* lordling.

nòcca, (*pl.* **nòcche**) ,*f.* knuckle.

nocchière, -ièro, *m.* steersman; pilot. **nocchierúto**, *a.* knotty.

nocchíno, *m.* blow with the knuckles. **nòcchio** (*pl.* **nòcchi**), *m.* knot (*wood*). **nocchióso** *&* **nocchiúto**, *a.* knotty; knobby; gnarled; full of knots.

nocci[u]òla, *f.* nut; hazel-nut. *color* ~, hazel. **nocciolàio**, *m.* nut-seller; nut-cracker (*bird*). **nocci-[u]òlo**, *m.* hazel; hazel-tree. **nocciòlo**, *m.* fruit-stone; (*fig.*) kernel, heart (*of question, &c.*).

noccolúto, *a.* with big knuckles.

nóce, *f.* walnut; nut. ~*di cocco*, coco[a]-nut. ~*moscata*, nutmeg. ~*del piede*, ankle-bone. ~*del collo*, Adam's apple. ¶ *m.* walnut-tree.

nocèlla, *f.* nut; filbert; ball & socket joint. ~ *del piede*, ankle-bone. ~ *della mano*, wrist-bones.

nocènte, *a.* noxious; hurtful; injurious.

nocepèsca (*pl.* **-pèsche**), *f.* nectarine. **nocepèsco** (*pl.* **-pèschi**), *m.* nectarine-tree.

nocéto, *m.* walnut-grove.

nocévole, *a.* hurtful; harmful; noxious. **nocevolézza**, *f.* hurtfulness; harmfulness.

nocívo, *a.* harmful; noxious; unwholesome; injurious. **nocuménto**, *m.* harm; injury; damage.

nodèllo, *m.* joint (*plant, hand, finger,* or *wrist*).

nòdo, *m.* knot; node; cluster; crux; rub; tie, bond (*fig.*); bow (*ribbon*). *lì è il* ~, that's the rub. ~*scorsoio*, slip-knot; running noose. ~*piano*, reef knot. ~*gordiano*, Gordian knot. ~*parlato*, clove hitch. **nodosità**, *f.* knottiness. **nodóso**, *a.* knotty; gnarled.

Noè, *m.* Noah (*O.T.*).

nói, *pn.* we; us. *noi stessi*, ourselves. *noi altri*, people like ourselves, us.

nòia, *f.* tedium, tediousness; ennui; boredom; weariness; trouble; annoyance. *avere a* ~, to dislike. *venire a* ~ *a*, to weary. **noióso**, *a.* tedious; tiresome; boring; irksome; annoying.

noleggiaménto, *m.* hiring. **noleggiàre**, *v.t.* to hire; charter, freight (*ship*); let or hire out. **noleggiatóre**, *m.* hirer; charterer; freighter. **nolèggio**, *m.* hire; freight. *vettura da* ~, hackney-coach. *contratto di* ~, charter-party.

nolènte, *a.* unwilling. *me* ~, against my will. ¶ *ad.* unwillingly. *volente o* ~, willy-nilly.

nòlo, *m.* hire; [cost of] freight. *a ~, da ~,* on hire. *dare a ~,* to hire out. *prendere a ~,* to hire. *costo, assicurazione, ~,* cost, insurance, freight (*abb. c.i.f.*).

nòmade, *a.* nomad(ic). ¶ *m.* nomad; wanderer.

nomàre, *v.t.* (*Poet.*) to name. **nóme,** *m.* name; style; reputation; stock, family; noun. *~di battesimo,* Christian name. *~ e cognome* (Christian) name & surname. *~ di fanciulla,* maiden name. *~ di battaglia, ~d'arte,* nom de guerre, assumed name, alias; pseudonym. *~ e prenome,* full name. *~ d'arte,* stage-name. *conoscere di ~,* to know by name. *chiamare per ~,* to call by name. *senza ~,* nameless.

nomèa, *f.* renown; celebrity; reputation.

nomenclatúra, *f.* nomenclature. **nomígnolo,** *m.* nickname.

nòmina, *f.* nomination; appointment; reputation; card of admission. **nominàbile,** *a.* mentionable; eligible; suitable for nomination or appointment. **nominàle,** *a.* nominal. **nominalísmo,** *m.* nominalism. **nominàre,** *v.t.* to nominate; appoint; choose; mention; name. **nominàrsi,** *v.refl.* to be called; to be named. **nominataménte,** *ad.* by name; particularly. **nominatívo,** *a.* nominative; registered; inscribed. *titoli ~ i,* registered bonds, inscribed b. ¶ *m.* nominative, nominative case. **nominatóre,** *m.* (*f.* **-tríce**) nominator; patron, patroness. ¶ *a.* nominating. **nominazióne,** *f.* nomination.

non, *ad.* not. *~che,* not only. *non ... che,* but, only. *~ piú,* no more, no longer. *non combattente,* non-combatant.

nonagenàrio (*pl.* **-àri**), *a. & m.* nonagenarian. **nonagèsimo,** *a.* ninetieth.

noncurànte, *a.* careless; indifferent; heedless. **noncurànza,** *f.* carelessness; heedlessness; indifference.

nondimànco & nondiméno, *ad.* nevertheless; however; still; yet.

non-intervènto, *m.* non-intervention; non-interference.

nònna, *f.* grandmother. **nònno,** *m.* grandfather. **nònni,** *m.pl.* grandparents; ancestors.

nonnúlla, *m.* mere nothing; trifle.

nòno, *a. num. ord.* ninth.

nonostànte, *pr.* notwithstanding; in spite of. ¶ *ad.* notwithstanding; nevertheless. *~che,* although.

non-paríglia, *m.* (*Typ.*) non-pareil.

nonpertànto, *ad.* nevertheless; however; still; yet.

nonsènso, *m.* nonsense.

non-ti-scordar-di-mé, *m.inv.* forget-me-not (*flower*).

nònuplo, *a.* ninefold.

norcíno, *m.* pork-butcher.

nòrd, *m.* north; (*att.*) north(ern). *America del N~,* North America. *mare del N~,* North Sea. *latitudine ~,* north latitude. **nord-est,** *m.* north-east. *vento di ~,* north-east wind. **nord-nord-ovest,** n.n.w. **nòrdico** (*pl.* **nòrdici**), *a.* north; northern; Nordic. ¶ *m.* northerner; northman. **nord-ovèst,** *m.* north-west.

nòria, *f.* irrigation-wheel.

Norimbèrga, *f.* Nuremberg.

nòrma, *f.* rule; regulation; norm; standard. **normàle,** *a.* normal; standard; ordinary. **normalísta** (*pl.* **-ísti**), *m.* pupil of a normal school. **normalità,** *f.* normality.

Normandía (la), *f.* Normandy. **normànno,** *a. & m.* Norman.

norvegése, *a. & m.* Norwegian. **Norvègia** (la), *f.* Norway.

nosocòmio (*pl.* **-òmi**), *m.* hospital.

nossignóra! *ad.* no, Madam! **nossignóre!** *ad.* no, Sir!

nostalgía, *f.* home-sickness; nostalgia. **nostàlgico** (*pl.* **-àlgici**), *a.* nostalgic; homesick.

nostràle, nostràno, *a.* of our (own) country; home (*att.*); home-grown; domestic.

nòstro, *poss. a.* our; ¶ *poss. pr.* ours. *i ~i,* our people, our relatives; our party.

nostròmo, *m.* boatswain.

nòta, *f.* note; list; bill; invoice; mark. *~ del bucato,* washing-list. *~delle vivande,* bill of fare. **notàbile,** *a.* notable; remarkable; worthy of note. ¶ *m.* person of distinction, notable; notability (*pers.*). **notabilità,** *f.* remarkableness; distinction.

notàio, *m.* notary; n. public; conveyancer. **notàre** (*pr.* **nòto**), *v.t.* to note; take note of; notice; remark; observe. *farsi ~,* to attract attention; make oneself conspicuous. **notariàto,** *m.* profession of a notary. **notaríle,** *a.* notarial. **notàro,** *m.* notary. **notazióne,** *f.* notation. **notévole,** *a.* remarkable; notable; considerable. **note-**

volménte, *ad.* notably; remarkably; considerably. **notífica** (*pl.* **-ifiche**), *f.* notification; communication. **notificàbile**, *a.* notifiable. **notificàre** (*pr.* **-ífico, -ifici**), *v.t.* to notify. **notificazióne**, *f.* notification; notice. **notízia**, *f.* news; piece of news; notice; report; account; note; knowledge. **notiziàrio**, *m.* news (*col.*); news bulletin. **nòto**, *a.* known; well-known. ¶ *m.* south-wind. **notorietà**, *f.* notoriety. **notòrio** (*pl.* **-òri**), *a.* notorious; well-known. **nottambulísmo**, *m.* night-wandering; somnambulism; sleep-walking. **nottàmbulo**, *a. & m.* night-wandering; night-wanderer; somnambulist; sleep-walker. **nottànte**, *m. & f.* night-nurse. **nottàta**, *f.* night (*duration*). **nòtte**, *f.* night. *di* ~, by night. *questa* ~, to-night; last night. *sul far della* ~, *al cader della* ~, at night-fall. **nottetèmpo** *& di* ~, *ad.* in the night-[time]. **nottívago** (*pl.* **-ívaghi**), *a. & m.* night-wandering; night wanderer. **nòttola**, *f.* night-jar (*bird*); bat; wooden latch. ~*di sicurezza*, safety catch. **nottolíno**, *m.* door-latch; cam; Adam's apple (*throat*). **nottolóne**, *m.* large bat; (*fig.*) big clumsy fellow. **nottúrno**, *a.* nocturnal; nightly; night (*att.*). *guardiano* ~, night-watchman. *ritrovo* ~, night-club. ¶ *m.* (*Mus.*) nocturne. **novànta**, *a. card. num. inv.* ninety. **novantènne**, *a.* ninety years old. *a. & m.f.* nonagenarian. **novantèsimo**, *a. ord. num.* ninetieth. **novantína**, *f.* series of ninety or thereabouts. **novantúno**, *card. num.* ninety-one. **novatóre**, *m.* (*f.* **-tríce**) innovator. **novazióne**, *f.* innovation; alteration (*contract, &c.*); renewal, conversion (*loan*). **nòve**, *a. & m.* nine; ninth. **novecentésco** (*pl.* **-éschi**), *a.* twentieth century (*att.*). **novecentísmo**, *m.* (spirit of) 20th century art, literature, &c. **novecènto**, *a. card. num. inv.* nine hundred. *il* N~, *m.* the twentieth century. **novèlla**, *f.* short story; story; tale; (*piece of*) news. **novellaménte**, *ad.* again; afresh; in a new way; newly; recently. **novellàre** (*pr.* **-èllo**), *v.i.* (*aux.* avere) to tell stories. **novella-**

tóre, *m.* (*f.* **-tríce**) story-teller. **novellétta**, *f.* short tale; novelette. **novellière**, *m.* story-writer; gossip-monger. **novellína**, *f.* short tale; children's story. **novellíno**, *a.* early; tender; new; unskilled. ¶ *m.* beginner; inexperienced person. **novellísta**, *m.* story-writer; (political) gossip-monger. **novellística**, *f.* story telling; art of the short story; writing of stories; (*col.*) tales, stories. **novèllo**, *a.* new; early; fresh; (*fig.*) tender; newly-married; newly-appointed. **novèmbre**, *m.* November. **novèna**, *f.* (*Eccl.*) nine days' devotions. **novenàrio**, *m.* (*prosod.*) line of nine syllables. **novennàle**, *a.* recurring every nine years; lasting nine years. **novènne**, *a.* nine years old. **novènnio** (*pl.* **-ènni**), *m.* period of nine years. **noveràre** (*pr.* **nòvero**), *v.t.* to enumerate; count; reckon; number. **nòvero**, *m.* number; category; class. **novilúnio** (*pl.* **-úni**), *m.* (*day, period of*) new moon. **novíssimo**, *a.* quite new; last. **novità**, *f. inv.* novelty; originality; innovation; something new; news. ~ *editoriale*, (*of book*) just published. **novízia**, *f.* novice. **noviziàto**, *m.* novitiate; apprenticeship. **novízio** (*pl.* **-ízi**), *m.* novice; beginner; apprentice. ¶ *a.* inexperienced; unskilled. **nòvo**, see *nuovo*. **nozióne**, *f.* notion; idea; principle. **nòzze**, *f.pl.* wedding; nuptials; marriage. **núbe**, *f.* cloud. **nubifràgio** (*pl.* **-àgi**), *m.* heavy shower; cloud-burst; down-pour. **núbile**, *a. & f.* unmarried; marriageable; unmarried girl. **núca**, *f.* nape (of the neck). **núcleo**, *n.* nucleus. **nucleàre**, *a.* nuclear. *scissione* ~, *f.* nuclear fission. **nudaménte**, *ad.* nakedly; barely; simply; bluntly; plainly. **nudità**, *f.* nakedness; nudity. **núdo**, *a.* naked; nude; bare; barren. **nudríre** (*pr.* **núdro, núdri**, *& nudrísco, nudrísci*), *v.t.* to nourish (*cf. nutrire*). **núgolo**, *m.* cloud; swarm. **núlla**, *indef. pn.* nothing. **nulladiméno**, *ad.* none the less, nevertheless; however. **nullàggine**, *f.* nothingness. **nullatenènte**, *m.* one who owns nothing. **nullità,** *f.* nullity; worthlessness; thing (or person) of no worth. **núllo,** *a.* null; null & void; invalid; of no effect, no.

núme, *m.* divinity; god; deity.

numeràbile, *a.* numerable; that can be counted. **numeràle,** *a. & m.* numeral. **numeràre,** *v.t.* to number; count. **numeràrio,** *m.* specie. ∼*di cassa,* cash on hand. **numerataménte,** *ad.* by number; one by one. **numeratóre,** *m.* numerator. **numeratríce,** *f.* calculating machine. **numerazióne,** *f.* numeration; numbering. **numèrico** (*pl.* -**èrici**), *a.* numerical. **numeríno,** *m.* number (*esp. lottery n.*). **número,** *m.* number; numeral; rhythm. *di* ∼, precisely. ∼ *-i pari,* ∼ *-i dispari,* even, odd number(s). **numeróso,** *a.* numerous; large; rhythmic(al); harmonious.

numišmàtica, *f.* numismatics. **numišmàtico** (*pl.* -**àtici**), *a.* numismatic. ¶ *m.* numismatist.

núncio, see *nunzio.*

nuncupatívo, *a.* nuncupative. *testamento* ∼, will made orally before witnesses, not in writing.

Nunziàta, *f.* short for *Annunziata* (*prop. n.*). **nunziatúra,** *f.* nunciature; nuncio's residence. **núnzio** (*pl.* **núnzi**), *m.* messenger; nuncio. ∼ *apostolico,* ∼ *pontificio,* papal nuncio.

nuòcere (*pr.* **nòccio, nuòci, nuòce**), *v.i. ir.* (*aux.* avere). to be hurtful, harmful, injurious. *v.t.* to hurt; harm; injure; damage; prejudice.

nuòra, *f.* daughter-in-law.

nuotàre (*pr.* **nuòto**), *v.i.* (*aux.* avere) to swim; (*fig.*) to roll; wallow. **nuotàta,** *f.* swimming; swim; method of s. **nuotatóre,** *m.* (*f.* -**tríce**), swimmer. **nuòto,** *m.* swimming.

nuòva, *f.* news. **n[u]ovaménte,** *ad.* again; once more. **nuòvo,** *a.* new; novel; strange; fresh; inexperienced. *di* ∼, again. *di bel* ∼, over again. ∼ *venuto,* *m.* newcomer. *la Nuova Zelanda,* *f.* New Zealand.

nuràghe (*pl.* **nuràghi**), *m.* conical prehistoric monument(s) of Sardinia.

nutricàre (*pr.* -**íco,** -**íchi**), *v.t.* (*Poet.*) to nourish; foster. **nutríce,** *f.* nurse; wet-nurse. **nutriménto,** *m.* nourishment; nutriment; food; feeding.

nutríre (*pr.* **nútro, nútri,** *&* -**ísco,**

-**ísci**), *v.t.* to nourish; nurture; feed; suckle; (*fig.*) foster; cherish; entertain; harbour; bear. **nutritívo,** *a.* nutritious; nutritive. **nutritóre,** *m.* (*f.* -**tríce**) nourisher; fosterer. ¶ *a.* nourishing. **nutrizióne,** *f.* nutrition; nourishment.

núvola, *f.* cloud. **nuvolàglia,** *f.* mass of clouds. **nuvolàta,** *f.* cloud-burst; shower of rain; mass of cloud. **nuvolàto,** *a.* overcast; cloudy. **núvolo,** *a.* cloudy. ¶ *m.* cloud; swarm. **nuvolóne,** *m.* large cloud; heavy cloud. **nuvolosità,** *f.* cloudiness. **nuvolóso,** *a.* cloudy.

nuziàle, *a.* nuptial; wedding (*att.*); bridal. **nuzialménte,** *ad.* befitting a wedding; in wedding garb.

O

O, o, *f.* the letter O. Has two sounds, close and open, here distinguished respectively by an acute & a grave accent. Unaccented o is close.

o, od, *c.* or. *o . . . o,* either . . . or, whether . . . or . . . ¶ *i.* O! oh!

òaši, *f.inv.* oasis (*lit. & fig.*).

obbediènte, *a.* obedient; dutiful; submissive. **obbediènza,** *f.* obedience. **obbedíre** (*pr.* -**ísco,** -**ísci**), *v.i.* (*aux.* avere) *& ∼ a* (*v.t.*), to obey; submit (to); be subject (to); yield (to); comply (with); respond (to). Cf. *ubbidire.*

obbligànte, *p.a.* obliging, binding. **obbligàre** (*pr.* **òbbligo, òbblighi**), *v.t.* to oblige, compel, bind. **obbligàrsi,** *v.refl.* to bind oneself; undertake; be surety (for). **obbligàto,** *p.a.* obliged; indebted; bound; obbligato (*Mus.*). **obbligatòrio** (*pl.* -**òri**), *a.* compulsory; obligatory; binding. **obbligazióne,** *f.* obligation; (*Com.*) bond, debenture. **obbligazionísta** (*pl.* -**ísti**), *m.* bond-holder, debenture-h. **òbbligo** (*pl.* **òbblighi**), *m.* obligation; duty.

obblìo, *&c.,* see *oblio.*

obbròbrio, *m.* shame; infamy; disgrace; opprobrium. **obbrobrióso,** *a.* shameful, infamous; opprobrious.

obelísco (*pl.* -**íschi**), *m.* obelisk.

oberàre, *v.t.* to encumber *with debts, &c.),* burden, load.

obešità, *f.* obesity, fatness, corpulence. **obèšo,** *a.* obese, fat, corpulent.

òbice (*pl.* **òbici**), *m.* howitzer; shell; grenade.

obiettàre (*pr.* **-ètto**), *v.t. & abs.* to object (*che* = that); o. to, o. against; allege. **obiettività**, *f.* objectivity; objectiveness. **obiettívo**, *a. & m.* objective (*Phil. & Gram.*). ¶ *m.* objective; object glass; lens; aim, object. **obiètto**, *m.* object; aim, purpose (see *oggetto*). **obiezióne**, *f.* objection; demur.

obituàrio, *m.* obituary; register of deaths.

obiurgazióne, *f.* objurgation.

oblàta, *f.* **-o**, *f.* oblate; lay-sister, l.-brother. **oblatóre**, *m.* **-tríce**, *f.* donor; founder; donator, offerer. **oblazióne**, *f.* oblation; offering; donation; presenting of bread & wine in the Eucharist.

obliàre (*pr.* **-ío**, **-ii**), *v.t.* (*Poet.*) to forget. **oblío** (*pl.* **-oblíi**), *m.* forgetfulness; oblivion. **oblióso**, *a.* (*Poet.*) oblivious, forgetful.

obliquità, *f.* obliquity; crookedness. **oblíquo**, *a.* oblique, slanting, skew; indirect; side (*glance*); crooked (*fig.*), underhand.

oblò, *m.inv.* port-hole.

oblúngo (*pl.* **oblúnghi**), *a.* oblong.

òboe, *m.inv.* hautboy; oboe. **oboísta** (*pl.* **-ísti**), *m.* oboist.

òbolo, *m.* small coin, mite. *l' ~ di S. Pietro*, Peter's penny, P's pence.

òc (**língua d'**), *f.* langue d'oc, (old) Provençal.

òca (*pl.* **òche**), *f.* goose. *pelle d' ~*, gooseflesh. *far andare in pelle d' ~*, to give one the creeps. *maschio dell' ~*, gander.

occasionàle, *a.* occasional; incidental; fortuitous; chance (*att.*). **occasionalménte**, *ad.* occasionally; casually; by chance. **occasionàre** (*pr.* **-óno**), *v.t.* to occasion; cause. **occasióne**, *f.* occasion; opportunity; opening; chance. *all' ~*, on occasion. *alla prima ~*, at the first opportunity. *d' ~*, second-hand, used; occasional (*occupation*).

occàso, *m.* (*Poet.*) setting; decline; sunset; west.

occhiàia, *f.* eye-socket; (dark) ring under the eye. **occhialàio** (*pl.* **-ài**), *m.* optician (*trade*). **occhialétto & occhialíno**, *m.* eye-glass, monocle. **occhiàli**, *m.pl.* spectacles; glasses; eye-glasses. *~ da sole*, sun-glasses; goggles. **occhiàta**, *f.* glance; look. **occhiàto**, *a.* ocellated; full of eyes (*like peacock's tail*). **occhieggiàre**,

v.t. to eye; ogle; cast glances at; (*v.i.*) (*aux.* avere) to glance.

occhièllo, *m.* button-hole; eye, eyelet; fly-leaf. **occhiétto**, *m.* small eye. *far l' ~ a*, to wink at. **òcchio** (*pl.* **òcchi**), *m.* eye; look; sight; port-hole; eye-hole; bud; face (*Typ.*). *~ di bue*, bull's eye (*window*). *~ di gatto*, cat's eye (*jewel*). *a ~ nudo*, with the naked eye. *a perdita d' ~*, out of sight. *a quattr' ~ i*, tête-à-tête. *in un batter d' ~*, in the twinkling of an eye, in an instant. **occhiúto**, *a.* full of eyes, or buds; (*fig.*) watchful, vigilant; attentive.

occidentàle, *a.* west; western; westerly. **occidènte**, *m.* west, occident. **occíduo**, *a.* (*Poet.*) setting; western.

occípite, *m.* back of the head.

occitànico (*pl.* **-ànici**), *a.* Provençal.

occlúdere, *v.t. ir.* to stop up; close; obstruct. **occlusióne**, *f.* stoppage (*Med.*).

occorrèndo, *ger.* of *occorrere*, in case of need. **occorrènte**, *a. & m.* necessary; needful; requisite. **occorrènza**, *f.* circumstance, occasion, incident, occurrence, event; requirement. *all' ~*, in case of need; according to circumstances. **occórrere** (*pr.* **occórro**, *&c.*, like *correre*; gen. in 3rd pers.) *v.i. ir.* (*aux.* essere) to be necessary; be required; be wanting; happen, occur. *mi occorre*, I require, I want. *non occorre* (with infin.), there is no occasion to, one need not.

occultaménto, *m.* concealment. **occultàre**, *v.t.* to hide; conceal; keep secret. **occultazióne**, *f.* concealment; (*Astr.*) occultation. **occultíssmo**, *m.* occultism; (the) occult. **occúlto**, *a.* occult; hidden, concealed; (*Astr.*) occulted. *socio ~*, sleeping partner.

occupànte, *a.* occupying. ¶ *m.* occupant; occupier. **occupàre** (*pr.* **òccupo**) *v.t.* to occupy; hold (*post, place*); keep busy. **occupàrsi**, *v.refl.* to occupy oneself, busy oneself (with = *di*). **occupàto**, *p.a.* engaged; busy; occupied. **occupatóre**, *m.* **-tríce**, *f.* occupier. ¶ *a.* occupying. **occupazióne**, *f.* occupation; business; pursuit.

Oceània (**l'**), *f.* Oceania. **oceànico** (*pl.* **-ànici**), *a.* oceanic. **oceàno**, *m.* ocean, sea. *l'O ~ Atlantico. Pacifico, Indiano*, the Atlantic, Pacific, Indian

o. *l'o~ Àrtico, Àntartico,* the Arctic, Antarctic, o. **oceanografía,** *f.* oceanography. **oceanògrafo,** *m.* oceanographer.

òcra, *f.* ochre.

oculàre, *a.* ocular; eye (*att.*). (*lente*) ~, *f.* eye-piece. *testimone* ~, eye-witness (*pers.*). **oculataménte,** *ad.* warily; cautiously; shrewdly. **oculatézza,** *f.* wariness; cautiousness; circumspection; discernment. **oculàto,** *a.* prudent; wary. **oculísta** (*pl.* -ísti), *m.* oculist, eye-doctor.

od, *c.* See *o.*

odalísca (*pl.* -ísche), *f.* odalisque.

òde, *f.* ode.

odiàre, *v.t.* to hate; detest; dislike. **odiatóre,** *m.* -tríce, *f.* hater.

odicína, *f.* short ode.

odiernaménte, *ad.* nowadays; at present. **odièrno,** *a.* of to-day, to-day's; present day (*att.*).

òdio, *m.* hatred; dislike. **odiosità,** *f.* odiousness; hatefulness. **odióso,** *a.* hateful; odious.

Odissèa, *f.* Odyssey (*lit. & fig.*).

odontoiatría, *f.* odontology; dentistry.

odoràccio (*pl.* -àcci), *m.* bad smell. **odorànte,** *a.* smelling. **odoràre,** *v.t.* to smell; scent; (*v.i.*) (*aux. avere*) to smell. **odoràto,** *m.* (sense of) smell; scent (*faculty*). ¶ *a.* (*Poet.*) odorous, sweet-scented. **odóre,** *m.* smell; odour; perfume, scent. **odorífero,** *a.* odoriferous. **odoróso,** *a.* sweet-smelling; scented; odorous; fragrant.

oè, *i.* hullo! hulloa!

Ofèlia, *f.* Ophelia.

òffa, *f.* cake; biscuit (of rye); (*fig.*) sop.

offèndere (*pr.* -èndo, &c., like *difendere*). *v.t. ir.* to offend; hurt. **offèndersi,** *v.refl.* to be offended, take offence. **offenditóre,** *m.* -tríce, *f. &* **offensóre,** *m.* -óra, *f.* offender. **offensíva,** *f.* (*Mil.*) offensive. **offensívo,** *a.* offensive.

offerènte, *p.a.* offering. ¶ *m.* offerer; bidder (*auction*). *il maggior(e)* ~, the highest bidder. **offeríre,** see *offrire.* **offèrta,** *f.* offer; offering; bid; tender. **offertòrio** (*pl.* -òri), *m.* offertory.

offésa, *f.* offence, injury; hurt. **offéso,** *p.p.* of *offendere.*

officiàre (*pr.* -ício, -íci), *v.i.* (*aux. avere*) to officiate. (*v.t.*) to apply to; address. **officína,** *f.* workshop; works; laboratory. **officinàle,** *a.* prepared to a standard recipe or

prescription. **officio,** see *ufficio.* **officióso,** *a.* obliging; serviceable; semi-official.

offríre (*pr.* òffro, òffri), *v.t. ir.* to offer; proffer, tender; bid (*auction*); afford; present. **offrírsi,** *v.refl.* to offer; present itself (or oneself). **offrènte,** *m.* bidder.

offuscaménto, *m.* darkening; dimming; dimness (*light, sight, &c.*). **offuscàre** (*pr.* -úsco, -úschi), *v.t.* to darken; obscure; dim. **offuscàrsi,** *v.refl.* to grow dark; grow dim.

oftalmía, *f.* ophthalmia. **oftàlmico** (*pl.* -àlmici), *a.* ophthalmic.

oggettivaménte, *ad.* objectively. **oggettivàre,** *v.t.* to objectify. **oggettivàrsi,** *v.refl.* to assume concrete shape. **oggettività,** *f.* objectivity; objectiveness. **oggettívo,** *a. & m.* objective. **oggètto,** *m.* object; theme; subject; thing, article; purpose, aim.

òggi, *ad. & m.* to-day. ~ *a otto,* ~ *a quindici,* to-day (or this day) week, fortnight. *a tutt'* ~, right up to to-day. **oggidí** *&* **oggigiórno,** *ad.* nowadays.

ogíva, *f.* ogive, pointed arch. **ogivàle,** *a.* ogival.

ógni, *indef. a.inv.* every; each; (*with superlative*) even the. ~ *giorno,* every day. ~ *tre giorni,* every three days; every third day. *in* ~ *luogo,* everywhere. *in* ~ *modo,* (in) every way; anyway; in any case; anyhow. *sotto* ~ *rispetto,* (in) every way; in every respect. **ogniqualvòlta,** *ad.* whenever; every time that. **Ognissànti,** *m.* All Saints' Day (*Nov.* 1). **ognóra,** *ad.* always. ~ *che,* whenever; every time that. **ognúno,** *indef. pn. inv.* everyone; each (one).

oh!, *i.* oh! O! **ohè!** *i.* hallo, hullo! **òhi!** *i.* ah! **ohimè!** *i.* alas! **oibò,** *i.* fie! for shame! ah!

oïl (**lingua d'**), *f.* langue d'oïl, old French.

olà! *i.* hullo, look out!

Olànda (**l'**), *f.* Holland. **olandése,** *a.* Dutch. ¶ *m.* Dutchman, *f.* Dutch woman. *gli O* ~*i,* the Dutch.

oleàceo *&* **oleaginóso,** *a.* oleaginous; oily.

oleàndro, *m.* oleander.

oleàrio, *a.* of oil; oil (*att.*).

oleàstro, *m.* wild olive.

oleàto, *a.* oiled. *carta* ~*a,* oil-paper.

oleífero, *a.* oil-bearing. **oleifício,** *m.* oil-works. **oleodótto,** *m.* oil pipe-

line. **oleografía,** *f.* oleograph.
oleosità, *f.* oiliness. **oleóso,** *a.*
oily.
oleżżànte, *a.* fragrant; sweet-smelling;
s.-scented. **olezzàre** (*pr.* **-éżżo**),
v.i. (*aux.* avere) to smell sweet; be
fragrant. **oléżżo,** *m.* fragrance;
sweet smell; s. scent; perfume.
olfattívo & **olfattòrio,** *a.* olfactory. **olfàtto,** *m.* sense of smell;
scent.
oliàndolo, *m.* oilman; oil merchant.
oliàre, *v.t.* to oil. **oliatóre,** *m.*
oil-can (*with nozzle*).
olíbano, *m.* [frank]incense.
olièra, *f.* cruet-stand.
oligàrca (*pl.* **-àrchi**), *m.* oligarch.
oligarchía, *f.* oligarchy. **oli-
gàrchico** (*pl.* **-àrchici**), *a.* oli-
garchic(al).
Olímpia, *f.* Olympia. **olimpíaco**
(*pl.* **-píaci**), *a.* Olympic. *giuochi* ~*i*,
Olympic games. *periodo* ~, (an)
Olympiad. **olimpíade,** *f.* Olympiad.
olímpico (*pl.* **-ímpici**), *a.* Olympic;
Olympian. *feste olimpiche*, Olympics;
Olympic Games. **olímpio** (*pl.*
-ímpi), *a.* Olympian (*Myth.*).
olimpioníco (*pl.* **-oníci**), *m.*
Olympian winner. **Olímpo,** *m.*
Olympus.
òlio (*pl.* **òli**), *m.* oil. ~ *lubrificante,*
machine o., lubricating o. ~ *da
ardere,* lamp oil. ~ *di (fegato di)
merluzzo,* cod-liver oil. ~ *di (semi
di) lino,* linseed oil. ~ *di paraffina,*
liquid paraffin (*Phar.*). ~ *di spermaceti,* sperm-(aceti) oil. ~ *da
tavola,* ~ *commestibile,* salad oil. ~
di ricino, castor oil. ~ *d'oliva,* olive
oil. *bidone per* ~, *m.* oil-can
(*storage*). *serbatoio d'* ~, *m.* oil-tank.
lampada ad ~, oil lamp. *pittura ad*
~, oil painting.
olíva, *f.* olive. *verde* ~, olive-green.
olivàstro, *a.* olive (*complexion*).
olivàto, *a.* planted with olive [tree]s.
olivéto, *m.* olive grove. **olivígno,**
a. olive (coloured). **olívo** & **ulívo,**
m. olive (-tree); o.(-wood).
olmàia, *f.* row of elms. **olméto,** *m.*
grove of elms. **olmétto,** *m.* young
elm. **ólmo,** *m.* elm (-tree). ~ *di
montagna,* wych-elm.
olocàusto, *m.* holocaust; sacrifice.
Olofèrne, *m.* Holophernes.
ològrafo, *a.* holograph.
olóna, *f.* sail-cloth.
oltracciò, *ad.* besides that (or this).
oltracotànte, *a.* arrogant; overbearing; overweening. **oltra-**

cotànza, *f.* arrogance; insolence;
presumption.
oltraggiàre, *v.t.* to outrage; insult;
abuse; violate. **oltraggiatóre,** *m.*
-tríce, *f.* perpetrator of an outrage;
insulter; violator. **oltràggio** (*pl.*
-àggi), *m.* outrage; insult; abuse;
offence; violation; crime. **oltrag-
gióso,** *a.* outrageous; scurrilous;
offensive; insulting.
oltr'àlpe, *ad.* beyond the Alps.
oltramontàno, *a.* ultramontane;
foreign.
oltrànza, *f.* extreme; excess. *ad* ~,
to the death; mortal; internecine;
desperately; to the bitter end; out
& out.
óltre, *pr.* & *ad.* beyond; besides; more
than; far; further. *passar* ~, to pass
on, go on. *piu* ~, farther; further.
oltreché, *pr.* & *ad.* besides (being);
apart from the fact that. **oltre-
màre,** *ad.* & **d'** ~ **-mare,** *a.*
oversea[s]. *commercio d'* ~, overseas
trade. **oltremaríno,** *a.* oversea.
¶ *m.* (*azzurro*) ~, *m.* ultramarine
(*pigment*).
oltremisúra & **oltremòdo,** *ad.*
beyond measure; exceedingly;
excessively.
oltrepassàre, *v.t.* to go beyond,
overstep; exceed, surpass; pass, overtake (*vehicles*).
oltretómba, *m.inv.* under-world;
other world; (the) Beyond.
omaccíno, *m.* little man; manikin.
omàccio, *m.* coarse fellow. **omac-
cióne,** *m.* big man (*lit.* & *fig.*).
omàggio (*pl.* **-àggi**), *m.* homage.
copia (or *esemplare*) *in* ~, presentation copy (*book*).
omài, *ad.* (*Poet.*) now; now &
henceforth.
ombelicàle, *a.* umbilical. *cordone* ~,
umbilical cord. **ombelíco** (*pl.*
-íchi), *m.* navel.
ómbra, *f.* shade; shadow; ghost;
suspicion; umbrage; offence. *terra
d'* ~, umber. **ombràre** (*pr.*
ómbro), *v.t.* to shade (*Art.*).
ombràrsi, *v.refl.* to withdraw into
the shade; conceal oneself; (*of
horse*) shy. **ombràtile,** *a.* retiring;
in the shade; shady (*lit.* & *fig.*).
ombratúra & **ombreggiatúra,** *f.*
shading. **ombreggiàre,** *v.t.* to
shade, overshadow. **ombreggiàto,**
p.a. shaded; (*Typ.*) hand-tooled.
ombrèlla, *f.* (*Bot.*) umbel. **ombrellí-
fero,** *a.* umbelliferous (*Bot.*).
ombrellàio, *m.* umbrella-maker; u.-

seller. **ombrellàta**, *f.* blow with an umbrella. **ombrellíno**, *m.* parasol. **ombrèllo**, *m.* umbrella; sunshade. **ombrellóne**, *m.* large umbrella.

ombròmetro, *m.* rain-gauge.

ombrosità, *f.* shadiness; suspiciousness; nervousness; (*horse*) skittishness. **ombróso**, *a.* shady; suspicious; touchy; (*horse*) skittish.

Ombúrgo, *f.* Homburg (*Geog.*).

omèga, *m.* omega. *alfa ed ~*, alpha & omega, beginning & end.

omèi, *m.pl.* lamentations; cries of grief.

omelía, *f.* homily.

omeopatía, *f.* homeopathy. **omeopàtico** (*pl.* -àtici), *a.* homeopathic. **omeopatísta** (*pl.* -ísti), *m.* homeopath[ist].

Oméro, *m.* Homer. **omèrico** (*pl.* -èrici), *a.* Homeric.

òmero, *m.* (*Anat.*) humerus; shoulder.

omertà, *f.* solidarity among criminals.

omésso, *p.p.* of *omettere*. **ométtere** (*pr.* -étto, *&c.*, like *mettere*). *v.t. ir.* to omit, leave out.

ométto *&* **omíno**, *m.* little man, manikin.

omicída (*pl.* -ídi), *m.* homicide (*pers.*); murderer. ¶ *a.* homicidal; murderous. **omicídio** (*pl.* -ídi), *m.* homicide (*act*); murder.

òmicron, *m.* omicron

omilètico (*pl.* -ètici), *a.* homiletic.

omissióne, *f.* omission.

òmnibus, *m.inv.* omnibus. *treno ~*, slow train (stopping at all stations).

omofonía, *f.* homophony; identity of sound. **omòfono**, *a.* homophonous; identical in sound. *parola ~a*, homophone.

omogeneità, *f.* homogeneity; homogeneousness. **omogèneo**, *a.* homogeneous.

omologàre (*pr.* -òlogo, -òloghi), *v.t.* (*leg.*) to approve; ratify. **omologazióne**, *f.* ratification.

omóne, *m.* big man; stout man.

omónimo, *m.* homonym; namesake.

omosessuàle, *a.* homosexual.

onàgro, *m.* wild ass.

óncia (*pl.* ónce), *f.* ounce (*avoirdupois* = 28.35 grammes; *troy & apothecaries' weight* = 31.1035 grammes).

ónda, *f.* wave; billow (*Poet.*) sea, main; water; stream. *a ~e*, wavy; in waves. *lunghezza d' ~*, wave-length. dim. *ondetta*, *ondicina*. **ondàta**, *f.* wave; blow from a wave. *~ di caldo*, heat wave.

ónde, *ad.* whence; from where. ¶ *pn.*

rel. from which, by w., with w. ¶ *c.* so that, in order that.

ondeggiànte, *a.* waving; wavering; wavy. **ondeggiàre** (*pr.* -éggio, -éggi), *v.i.* (*aux.* avere) to wave; undulate; (*fig.*) waver; fluctuate. **ondóso**, *a.* full of waves; wavy; waving; undulatory; stormy. **ondulàre** (*pr.* òndulo), *v.i.* (*aux.* avere) to undulate; wave; (*v.t.*) wave. *farsi ~ i capelli*, to have one's hair waved. **ondulàto**, *a.* undulating, wavy; corrugated (*iron*). **ondulatòrio**, *a.* undulatory. **ondulazióne**, *f.* waving. *~ dei capelli*, hair-waving. *una ~ permanente*, a perm[anent wave].

oneràre (*pr.* ònero), *v.t.* to burden; load. **oneràrio**, *a.* bearing a burden; freight-carrying. *nave ~a*, cargo-boat. **ònere**, *m.* burden; (*fig.*) tax; duty; obligation. **oneróso**, *a.* onerous; burdensome.

onestà, *f.* uprightness; honourable conduct; modesty; decency; honesty. **onèsto**, *a.* honourable; upright; respectable, straight, decent; well-bred, civil, courteous; fair, reasonable. *giuoco ~*, fair play.

ònice, *f.* onyx.

onnipotènte, *a.* omnipotent; almighty. **onnipotènza**, *f.* omnipotence. **onnipresènte**, *a.* omnipresent; ubiquitous. **onnisciènte**, *a.* omniscient. **onnisciènza**, *f.* omniscience. **onniveggènte**, *a.* all-seeing. **onnívoro**, *a.* omnivorous.

onomàstico (*pl.* -àstici), *m.* patron saint's day; dictionary of proper names.

onomatopèa, *f.* onomatopoeia. **onomatopèico** (*pl.* -èici), *a.* onomatopoeic; onomatopoetic.

onoràbile, **onoràndo**, *&* **onorévole**, *a.* honourable. **onorànza**, *f.* honour, mark of public esteem; (*pl.*) solemnity; celebration. **onoràre** (*pr.* -óro), *v.t.* to honour; be an honour to; confer honour upon. **onoràrsi** (*di*), *v.refl.* to hold in honour; be proud of. **onoràrio**, *a.* honorary. ¶ *m.* honorarium; fee; salary. **onóre**, *m.* honour; respect; fame; dignity; distinction. *serata d' ~*, benefit performance, b. night. **onorificènza**, *f.* honour; dignity; title; decoration. **onorífico** (*pl.* -ífici), *a.* honorific; implying respect.

ónta, *f.* shame; disgrace; ignominy; affront; insult. *ad ~ di*, in spite of.

ontàno, *m.* alder (tree).

onústo, *a.* (*Poet.*) laden; loaded; full.

opacità, *f.* opacity; opaqueness. **opàco** (*pl.* **-àchi**), *a.* opaque.

opàle, *m.* opal. **opalìno**, *a.* opaline.

òpera, *f.* work; labour; action; deed; (*literary or artistic*) work, composition; opera; office of works. ~ *buffa*, ~ *comica*, comic opera; musical comedy. ~ *lirica*, grand opera. *teatro dell'* ~, opera-house. **operàbile**, *a.* workable; practicable; (*Surg.*) operable. **operàia**, *f.* workwoman; worker. **operàio**, *m.* workman; hand. ¶ *a.* working. **operànte**, *a.* acting; working. **operàre** (*pr.* **òpero**), *v.i.* (*aux.* avere) to operate, work, act; (*v.t.*) operate upon (*Surg.*). **operatìvo**, *a.* operative. **operàto**, *m.* conduct; behaviour; action. ¶ *p.a.* wrought; diapered. **operatóre**, *m.* **-tríce**, *f.* operator (*Surg. & Cine.*). ¶ *a.* working; operating. **operatòrio**, *a.* operative; operating. *sala* ~*a*, operating theatre. **operazióne**, *f.* operation; (*Com.*) transaction.

operétta, *f.* operetta; vaudeville; musical comedy. **operettísta**, (*pl.* **-ísti**), *m.* writer of musical comedies. **operísta** (*pl.* **-ísti**), *m.* composer of operas.

operosità, *f.* industry; industriousness. **operóso**, *a.* industrious; hard-working.

opifício (*pl.* **-ici**), *m.* works; factory.

opìmo, *a.* fertile; rich; abundant.

opinàbile, *a.* conceivable; thinkable.

opinàre (*pr.* **-íno**), *v.i.* (*aux.* avere) to think; be of opinion; opine.

opinióne, *f.* opinion; view.

oppiàto, *m.* opiate. **òppio**, *m.* opium. **oppiòmane**, *m.* opium addict.

opponènte, *m.* opponent; opposer; adversary. ¶ *p.a.* opposing.

oppórre (*pr.* **-óngo**, *&c.*, like *porre*), *v.t. ir.* to oppose; set over against; offer (*resistance*); object; give (*refusal*). **oppórsi** (a), *v.refl.* to oppose; be opposed to; object (to); appeal against.

opportunaménte, *ad.* opportunely, fortunately, appropriately, suitably, at the right moment. **opportunísta** (*pl.* **-ísti**), *m.* opportunist, time-server. **opportunità**, *f. inv.* opportunity, occasion; opportuneness; expediency; appropriateness. **opportúno**, *a.* opportune, timely, well-timed; suitable, appropriate, proper; expedient, advisable.

opposizióne, *f.* opposition; contrast; contradistinction; objection. **oppósto**, *p.p.* of *opporre*. ¶ *a. & m.* opposite; contrary. *all'* ~, on the contrary.

oppressióne, *f.* oppression; (*fig.*) weight. **opprèsso**, *p.p.* of *opprimere*. ¶ *a.* oppressed; weighed down. **oppressóre**, *m.* oppressor. **opprimènte**, *a.* (*fig.*) suffocating; sultry; cruel; crushing; grinding. **opprímere** (*pr.* **-ímo**, *&c.*, like *comprimere*), *v.t. ir.* to oppress; crush; lie heavy on; overpower; overwhelm.

oppugnàbile, *a.* disputable; assailable. **oppugnàre**, *v.t.* to oppugn; oppose; confute; refute; assail, attack.

oppúre, *c.* or; or else.

òpra, *f.* (*Poet.* for *opera*) work; one day's work; day-labourer.

optàre (*pr.* **òpto**), *v.i.* (*aux.* avere) to choose; (followed by *per*) opt.

opulènto, *a.* opulent; rich. **opulènza**, *f.* opulence.

opuscolétto, *m.* small pamphlet. **opúscolo**, *m.* pamphlet.

opzióne, *f.* option.

óra, *f.* hour; time; moment; present; o'clock. *l'* ~ *d'accendere le luci*, lighting-up time. ~ *di chiusura*, closing time. (~) *per i piccoli*, children's hour (*Radio*). ~ *d'andare a letto*, bedtime. ~ *ufficiale*, standard time. ~ *media di Greenwich*, Greenwich mean time. ~ *locale*, local time. ~ *estiva*, ~ *legale*, summer time. ~ *di mangiare*, ~ *dei pasti*, meal t. *ultima* ~ *per impostare le lettere*, latest time for posting. ~*e d'ufficio*, business hours. ~*e di punta*, ~ *di affluenza*, ~*e di maggior traffico*, rush hours, peak hours. ~*e straordinarie*, overtime. *alla buon'* ~, well & good, all right. *di buon'* ~, early, betimes, in good time. ¶ *ad.* now; at present. *fino ad* ~, till now; so far. *fino da* ~, from now on. *da* ~ *in avanti*, *da* ~ *in poi*, henceforth; from this time forward. *or* ~, just; just now. ~ *per sempre*, once for all.

oracoleggiàre (*pr.* **-éggio**, **-éggi**), *v.i.* (*aux.* avere) to speak like an oracle; prophesy. **oràcolo**, *m.* oracle.

oràle, *a.* oral; viva voce; verbal. **oralménte**, *ad.* orally; by word of mouth.

oramài, *ad.* now; by this time; from now onwards.

oràrio, *m.* time-table. *in* ~, punctually; up to time. ¶ *a.* hourly; per hour. *velocita* ~*a*, speed per hour. *segnale* ~, time signal (*Radio*).

oratóre, *m.* orator, speaker. **oratòria,** *f.* oratory; eloquence. **oratòrio** (*pl.* -òri), *m.* oratory (*chapel*); oratorio (*Mus.*). ¶ *a.* oratorical.

oraziàno, *a.* Horatian. **Oràzio,** *m.* Horace.

orazióne, *f.* oration; speech; prayer.

orbàre (*pr.* òrbo), *v.t.* to bereave; deprive.

òrbe, *m.* orb; sphere; globe; world.

orbène, *ad.* well; well now.

òrbita, *f.* orbit; limit; (*eye*) socket.

òrbo, *a.* bereft; deprived; blind; squinting.

òrca (*pl.* òrche), *f.* grampus; (*Myth.*) , orc (*cf.* Ariosto, *O.F.*).

Orcadi (le), *f.pl.* the Orkney Islands; Orkney.

orchèstra, *f.* orchestra. **orchestràle,** *a.* orchestral. **orchestràre** (*pr.* -èstro), *v.t.* to orchestrate.

orchidèa, *f.* orchid.

órcio (*pl.* órci), *m.* pitcher; jar. **orci(u)òlo,** *m.* small jar.

órco (*pl.* órchi), *m.* ogre. **O**~, (*Myth.*) Orcus.

òrda, *f.* horde.

ordígno, *m.* tool; implement; instrument; (*pl.*) gear; implements.

ordinàbile, *a.* possible to order or arrange. **ordinàle,** *a. & m.* ordinal. **ordinaménto,** *m.* ordering (arrangement); order; disposition; organization; ordinance; decree. **ordinànza,** *f.* ordinance; decree; regulation; order; orderly; batman. *ufficiale d'*~, orderly officer; staff-o. **ordinàre** (*pr.* órdino), *v.t.* to order, arrange, set in order; ordain; prescribe. **ordinàrio,** *a.* ordinary; common; customary; usual. ¶ *m.* ordinary; wont; usual meal; (*Eccl.*) confessor to a nunnery. **ordinàta,** *f.* ordinate (*Geom.*). **ordinataménte,** *ad.* duly; methodically; in order. **ordinativo,** *m.* order. ~ *di consegna,* delivery order. **ordinazióne,** *f.* order; decree; ordination (*Eccl.*); prescription (*Med.*). *fatto su* ~, made to order.

órdine, *m.* order; disposition; succession; series; grade; rank; rule; command. *all'* ~, ready. *di prim'* ~, first-rate, of the highest order. ~ *del giorno,* agenda, business (before the meeting); order of the day. ~*i sacri,* holy orders. ~

pubblico, law & order, peace; public policy. ~ *sparso,* ~ *chiuso,* open, close order (*Mil.*). *presentare* ~*i di servizio,* to report for duty (*Nav., Mil.*).

ordíre (*pr.* -ísco, -ísci), *v.t.* to weave; (*fig.*) plot. **ordíto,** *m.* warp; (*fig.*) web; tissue; plot. **orditúra,** *f.* (*fig.*) weaving; contriving; plotting; structure.

orèade, *f.* (*Myth.*) oread; mountain nymph.

orécchia, *f.* ear; dog's ear (*page*). **orecchiànte,** *m.f.* one who plays or sings by ear. **orecchiàre** (*pr.* -écchio, -écchi), *v.i.* (*aux.* avere) to listen; eavesdrop. **orecchiàta,** *f.* box on the ear. **orecchiétta,** *f.* (*Anat.*) auricle. **orecchíno,** *m.* earring. **orécchio** (*pl.* orécchi), *m.* ear. *a portata d'* ~, within ear-shot. *stare ad* ~*i tesi,* to prick up one's ears. *dolore all'* ~, ear-ache. *esser(e) duro d'* ~, to be hard of hearing. **orecchióne,** *m.* large ear; bat; (*pl.*) mumps. **orecchiúto,** *a.* long-eared.

oréfice, *m.* goldsmith. **oreficería,** *f.* goldsmith's shop; goldsmith's art or wares.

orétta, *f.* (short) hour; nearly an h.

òrfana & **orfanèlla,** *f.* orphan-girl. **òrfano,** *a. & m.* orphan. ~ *di padre,* fatherless. **orfanèllo,** *m.* little o.; orphan-boy. **orfanèlli** *m.pl.* orphan children. **orfanotròfio,** *m.* orphanage.

Orfèo, *m.* Orpheus (*Myth.*). **òrfico** (*pl.* òrfici), *a.* Orphic.

organàio, *m.* organ-builder. **organétto** (*a manovella* or *di Barberia*) *m.* barrel-organ, street-organ. *sonatore d'* ~, organ-grinder. **orgànico** (*pl.* -ànici), *a.* organic. **organísmo,** *m.* organism. **organísta** (*pl.* -ísti), *m.* organist. **organiżżàre** (*pr.* -iżżo), *v.t.* to organize. **organiżżatóre,** *m.* organizer. **òrgano,** *m.* organ.

orgàsmo, *m.* orgasm; violent excitement.

òrgia (*pl.* òrge), *f.* orgy; riot (*fig.*).

orgóglio, *m.* pride. **orgoglióso,** *a.* proud; haughty.

orientàle, *a.* oriental; eastern; east. *vento* ~, East wind. *Indie O*~*i,* East Indies. ¶ *m.* Oriental. **orientaménto,** *m.* orientation; bearings, direction; aspect; trend; tendency; (*Naut.*) trimming (*sails, yards*). *senso d'* ~, bump of locality. **orientàre** (*pr.* -ènto), *v.t.* to orient[ate]; turn, direct; point, set;

trim (*sails*, *&c.*). **orientàrsi**, *v.refl.*
to find (take, get) one's bearings.
oriènte, *m.* east, East; Orient.
il vicino O~, *l'estremo O~*, the
near East, the far East. *il Grande
O~*, the Grand Lodge (*Masonic*).
orifiàmma, *f.* oriflamme; banner.
orifízio (*pl.* -ízi), *m.* orifice; aperture;
mouth (*fig.*).
Origéne, *m.* Origen.
originàle, *a.* original; first (*edition*);
inventive; odd, queer, eccentric.
¶ *m.* original; original character,
eccentric person. **originalità**, *f.*
originality. **originàre** (*pr.* -ígino),
v.t. & i. (*aux.* essere) to originate.
originàrio, *a.* original; primary;
first. *essere ~ di*, to come from, be
a native of. ¶ *m.* native. **orígine**,
f. origin; beginning; outset; cause;
source; birth; family; descent.
origliàre (*pr.* -íglio, -ígli), *v.i.* (*aux.*
avere) to eavesdrop; spy.
origlière, *m.* pillow.
orína, *f.* urine. **orinàle**, *m.* chamber-
pot. **orinàre** (*pr.* -íno), *v.i.* (*aux.*
avere) to urinate; pass water.
orinàrio, *a.* urinary. **orinatóio**, *m.*
, urinal.
Orióne, *m.* (*Myth. & Astr.*) Orion.
oriúndo, *a.* native. *essere ~ di*, to be
a native of, be born at.
orizzontàle, *a.* horizontal. **oriz-
zónte**, *m.* horizon.
Orlàndo, *m.* Roland.
orlàre (*pr.* órlo), *v.t.* to border; edge;
hem; rim. *~ a giorno*, to hem-
stitch. **orlatúra**, *f.* edging; bordering; hemming. **orlíccio**, *m.* kissing-
crust; edge of a broken surface.
órlo, *m.* border; edge; hem; rim;
brink; verge. *~ vivo*, sharp edge.
~ sfilato, open-work hem. *~ a
punto, a strega*, herring-bone hem.
órma, *f.* foot-print; trace; track;
mark. **ormàre** (*pr.* órmo), *v.t.* to
follow (in) the track of.
ormài, *ad.* now; at this moment; by
now; henceforth.
ormeggiàre (*pr.* -éggio, -éggi), *v.t.*
to moor. **orméggio**, *m.* mooring;
moorings; hawser.
ormóne, *m.* (*Physiol.*) hormone.
ornaménto, *m.* o̓rnament; decoration.
ornàre (*pr.* órno), *v.t.* to adorn;
decorate; beautify; ornament.
ornatézza, *f.* ornateness. **ornàto**,
p.a. ornate; ornamented; decorated;
adorned. ¶ *m.* ornamentation;
decoration; art of design. **ornatúra**,
f. ornamenting; ornamentation.

ornitología, *f.* ornithology. **ornito-
lògico** (*pl.* -ògici), *a.* ornithological.
ornitòlogo (*pl.* -òloghi), *m.*
ornithologist.
òro, *m.* gold. *~ laminato*, rolled g.
~ greggio, *~ grezzo*, unrefined g.
~ di coppella, *~ di zecchino*, pure
g., refined g. *~ di 24 carati*,
24-carat g. *d'~*, gold; golden.
orologería, *f.* clock & watch making;
watchmaker's shop. **orologiàio** (*pl.*
-ài), *m.* watch-maker; clock-maker.
orològio (*pl.* -ògi), *m.* watch; clock;
time-piece. *~ a pesi*, *~ di torre*,
grandfather['s] clock. *~ a ripetizione*, repeater; repeating watch.
~ a cariglione, chiming clock,
musical c. *~ solare*, sun-dial.
~ a polvere, hour-glass. *~ da polso*,
wrist-watch.
oròscopo, *m.* horoscope. *trarre un ~*,
to cast a h.
orpellàre, *v.t.* to deck or cover with
tinsel. **orpèllo**, *m.* tinsel.
orrèndo & orríbile, *a.* horrible;
repellent; fearful; dreadful; awful.
òrrido, *a.* horrid; frightful; terrifying; dreary; bristly. ¶ *m.* precipice;
ravine.
orróre, *m.* horror; dread; fear;
loathing.
órsa, *f.* she-bear. *l'O~ maggiore*,
l'O~ minore, the Great, the Little
Bear (*Astr.*). **orsacchiòtto &
orsacchíno**, *m.* bear-cub. **orsíno**,
a. ursine; bearish. **òrso**, *m.* bear.
~ bianco, *~ polare*, polar b.
, ~ grigio, grizzly b.
Orsola, *f.* Ursula. **orsolína**, *a. & f.*
Ursuline (belonging to order óf
nuns founded in 1537 for nursing
the sick & teaching girls).
orsú, *i.* come now! come on!
ortàggi, *m.pl.* pot-herbs; vegetables;
greens. **ortàglia**, *f.* vegetable;
vegetable garden, market g.; (*pl.*)
garden produce.
ortènsia, *f.* hydrangea.
ortíca (*pl.* ortíche), *f.* nettle. **orti-
càio & ortichéto**, *m.* bed of
nettles. **orticària**, *f.* nettle-rash.
orticultóre, *m.* horticulturist. **orti-
cultúra**, *f.* horticulture; gardening.
òrto, *m.* garden, kitchen-garden;
orchard. *~ botanico*, botanical
garden. *~ secco*, herbarium. **òrto**,
m. (*Poet.*) rise; sun-rise; east.
ortodossía, *f.* orthodoxy. **orto-
dòsso**, *a.* orthodox.
ortografía, *f.* spelling; correct
spelling; orthography. **ortogràfico**

(pl. -àfici), *a.* orthographical; correct *(spelling)*.

ortolàno, *m.* market gardener.

ortopedìa, *f.* orthopaedic surgery. **ortopèdico** *(pl. -èdici)*, *a.* orthopaedic. ¶ *m.* orthopaedic surgeon.

Orvièto, *f.* Orvieto. *m.* (white) wine of O.

òrza, *f.* bowline; weather halyard. *andare, stare ad ~*, to sail close to the wind. *mettersi ad ~*, to haul to windward.

orżai[u]òlo, *m.* sty[e] *(in the eye)*.

orżàre *(pr. órzo)*, *v.i. (aux.* avere) to luff; sail near the wind.

orżàta, *f.* barley-water. **òrżo**, *m.* barley.

ošànna, *m.inv.* hosanna.

ošàre *(pr. òso)*, *v.t. & i. (aux.* avere) to dare, d. to, venture, v. to.

oscenità, *f.inv.* obscenity; indecency; filthy language. **oscèno**, *a.* obscene; indecent.

oscillàre *(pr. -illo)*, *v.i. (aux.* avere) to oscillate; sway (about); swing; *(fig.)* fluctuate; waver; hesitate; vary. **oscillatòrio**, *a.* oscillatory. **oscillazióne**, *f.* oscillation; swaying; &c.

oscuraménto, *m.* darkening; black-out. **oscurantìšmo**, *m.* obscurantism. **oscuràre** *(pr. -úro)*, *v.t.* to darken; dim; obscure; overcast; overshadow; *(Mil.)* black-out. **oscuràrsi**, *v.refl.* to grow dark; grow dim; be overcast. **oscurità**, *f.* darkness; obscurity. **oscúro**, *a.* dark; dim; murky; obscure; *(fig.)* doubtful; humble; unknown.

Osìride, *m.* Osiris *(Myth.)*.

òsmoši, *f.* osmosis.

ospedàle, *m.* hospital. dim. *ospedalétto. ~ da campo*, field dressing-station.

ospitàle, *a.* hospitable. **ospitalière**, *a.* hospital *(att.)*. *gli O ~ i*, the Knights of Malta. **ospitalità**, *f.* hospitality. **ospitaménte**, *ad.* hospitably. **ospitàre** *(pr. òspito)*, *v.t.* to entertain; shelter; give hospitality to. **òspite**, *m.f.* guest; *m.* host, *f.* hostess. **ospizio** *(pl. -ìzi)*, *m.* hospice; hostel; almshouse; asylum; home.

ossàlico *(pl. -àlici)*, *a.* oxalic. *acido ~*, oxalic acid.

ossàme, *m.* heap of bones. **ossàrio**, *m.* ossuary; charnel-house. **ossatúra**, *f.* bony structure; skeleton; *(fig.)* framework; firm foundation; hull *(ship)*. **òsseo**, *a.* osseous; bony.

ossequènte, *a.* respectful; deferential; obedient. **ossequiàre** *(pr. -èquio, -èqui)*, *v.t.* to pay one's respects to; treat with respect; pay homage to. **ossèquio**, *m.* homage; respect; obedience; *(pl.)* **ossèqui**, respects, regards. **ossequióso**, *a.* respectful; obsequious.

osservàbile, *a.* noticeable; perceptible. **osservànte**, *a.* observant. ¶ *m.* member of the stricter branch of the Franciscan order, *i minori Osservanti*. **osservànza**, *f.* observance *(Eccl.)*; respect; obedience. *l'O~*, church & convent of the Osservanti near Siena, founded 1423 by San Bernardino. **osservàre** *(pr. -èrvo)*, *v.t.* to observe; notice; remark; watch; keep; comply with. **osservatóre**, *m. -tríce, f.* observer. **osservatòrio** *(pl. -òri)*, *m.* observatory; observation post *(Mil.)*. **osservazióne**, *f.* observation; remark.

ossessionànte, *a.* haunting; worrying. **ossessionàre**, *v.t.* to obsess; pre-occupy; worry; haunt. **ossessióne**, *f.* obsession. **ossèsso**, *a.* obsessed; haunted; possessed. ¶ *m.* man possessed, one suffering from obsessions.

ossétto, ossicèllo, & **ossicíno**, *m.* small bone.

οssía, *c.* or; or rather

Òssian, *m.* Ossian. **ossiànico** *(pl. -ànici)*, *a.* Ossianic.

ossidàre *(pr. òssido)*, *v.t.* to oxidize. **ossidazióne**, *f.* oxidation. **òssido**, *m.* oxide. **ossídrico** *(pl. -ídrici)*, *a.* oxyhydrogen *(att.)*. *cannello ~*, o. blowpipe.

ossificàre *(pr. -ífico, -ífichi)*, *v.t.* to ossify. **ossificazióne**, *f.* ossification.

ossigenàre *(pr. -ígeno)*, *v.t.* to oxygenate; *(of hair)* to peroxide. **ossígeno**, *m.* oxygen.

ossìtono, *a.* oxytone, accented on the last syllable.

òsso *(pl.m. òssi, pl.f. òssa)*, bone; *(fruit)* stone. *~ buco*, marrow-bone. *~di balena*, whalebone. *~ di seppia*, cuttle-fish bone. **ossúto**, *a.* bony; big-boned; *(fig.)* strong.

ostacolàre *(pr. -àcolo)*, *v.t.* to hinder; obstruct; oppose; interfere with. **ostàcolo**, *m.* obstacle; obstruction; hindrance. *corsa sugli ~i, f.* obstacle-race.

ostàggio *(pl. -àggi)*, *m.* hostage.

ostàre *(pr. òsto)*, *v.i. (aux.* avere) to be opposed; form an obstacle. *~ a,* to hinder; prevent. *il nulla osta,* permission.

òste, *m.* inn-keeper; host. **òste,** *f.* (*Poet.*) army; host.

osteggiàre (*pr.* **-éggio, -éggi**), *v.t.* to oppose; be hostile to.

ostèllo, *m.* (*Poet.*) dwelling; abode.

ostensíbile, *a.* ostensible.

ostensòrio, *m.* monstrance (*Eccl.*).

ostentàre (*pr.* **-énto**), *v.t.* to parade; show off; exhibit; feign.

ostentatóre, *m.* **-tríce,** *f.* boaster; ostentatious person. ¶ *a.* boastful; ostentatious. **ostentazióne,** *f.* ostentation; parade; pretence; affectation.

ostería, *f.* inn; public house.

ostéssa, *f.* landlady (*of an inn*); hostess.

ostètrica (*pl.* **-ètriche**), *f.* midwife. **ostetrícia,** *f.* midwifery; obstetrics. **ostètrico** (*pl.* **-ètrici**), *a.* obstetric(al). ¶ *m.* obstetrician.

òstia, *f.* Host, consecrated wafer (*Eccl.*); wafer (*for sealing letters or wrapping up powders*); sacrificial victim.

òstico (*pl.* **òstici**), *a.* hard; harsh; unpleasant; difficult.

ostíle, *a.* hostile; adverse; opposed. **ostilità,** *f.* hostility; opposition; aversion.

ostinàrsi (*pr.* **-íno**), *v.refl.* to persist; insist. **ostinatézza** & **ostinazióne,** *f.* obstinacy; stubbornness; persistence. **ostinàto,** *a.* obstinate; stubborn; persistent.

ostracísmo, *m.* ostracism.

òstrica (*pl.* **òstriche**), *f.* oyster. **ostricàio,** *m.* oyster-bed; oyster-seller. **ostricultúra,** *f.* oyster culture.

òstro, *m.* (*Poet.*) purple; south wind.

ostruíre (*pr.* **-ísco, -isci**), *v.t.* to obstruct; block (up); stop. **ostruttívo,** *a.* obstructive. **ostruzióne,** *f.* obstruction; stoppage.

otalgía, *f.* (*Med.*) ear-ache.

Otèllo, *m.* Othello.

ótre, *m.* wine-skin; goat-skin bottle.

ottàgono, *m.* octagon.

ottàno, *m.* (*Chem.*) octane.

ottànta, *card. num. inv.* eighty. **ottantésimo,** *a. ord. num.* eightieth. **ottantína,** *f.* eighty; four score. *ha passato l'~,* he is over eighty.

ot[t]àrda, *f.* bustard.

ottatívo, *a.* & *m.* optative.

ottàva, *f.* octave. **ottavíno,** *m.* octave-flute; piccolo (*Mus.*).

ottàvio, *m.* Octavius.

ottàvo, *a. ord. num.* eighth. ¶ *m.* eighth (part). *in-ottavo* (*book*), octavo (*abb.* 8vo). *~a rima,* octave, stanza of 8 lines.

ottemperàre (a), *v.t.* to obey; comply with.

ottenebraménto, *m.* & **ottenebrazióne,** *f.* darkening. **ottenebràre** (*pr.* **-énebro**), *v.t.* to darken; obscure; (*fig.*) cloud.

ottenére (*pr.* **-èngo,** &*c.,* like *tenere*), *v.t. ir.* to obtain; get; gain; reach. **otteníbile,** *a.* obtainable.

ottènne, *a.* eight years old; for eight years. **ottènnio,** *m.* period of eight years.

Ottentòtto, *m.* Hottentot.

ottenúto, *p.p.* of *ottenere.*

ottétto, *m.* (*Mus.*) octet[te].

òttica, *f.* optics. **òttico** (*pl.* **òttici**), *a.* optic(al). ¶ *m.* optician.

ottimaménte, *ad.* very well; extremely well; admirably. **ottimísmo,** *m.* optimism. **ottimista** (*pl.* **-ísti**), *m.* optimist. **ottimístico** (*pl.* **-ístici**), *a.* optimistic. **òttimo,** *a.* very good; excellent. ¶ *m.* best.

òtto, *a.* & *m.* eight; eighth.

ottòbre, *m.* October. **ottobríno,** *a.* October (*att.*); ripening in O.

ottocentésimo, *a. ord. num.* eight-hundredth. **ottocènto,** *card. num. inv.* eight hundred. *l'O~,* the 19th century.

ottomàna, *f.* ottoman (*sofa*). **ottomàno,** *a.* & *m.* Ottoman; Turk(ish).

ottomíla, *card. num. inv.* eight thousand.

ottonàio (*pl.* **-ài**), *m.* brass-worker. **ottonàme,** *m.* brass-ware.

ottonàrio (*pl.* **-àri**), *m.* verse (line) of eight syllables.

ottóne, *m.* brass; (*pl.*) brass instruments, brasses (*Mus.*). *O~, m.* Otho.

ottòpode, *m.* octopus.

ottuagenàrio, *a.* & *m.* octogenarian.

ottúndere (*pr.* **-úndo**), *v.t. ir.* to blunt (*lit.* & *fig.*); (*fig.*) weaken; deaden (*sense or faculty*); soften, enfeeble, make obtuse.

otturàre, *v.t.* to block (up); close; seal; obstruct; choke; stop (*tooth,* &*c.*). **otturatóre,** *m.* (*Phot.*) shutter; breech-block (*Artil.*); obturator, plug.

ottusaménte, *ad.* obtusely. **ottusità,** *f.* obtuseness; bluntness; dullness. **ottúso,** *a.* obtuse; blunt; dull.

ovàia, *f.* ovary. **ovai[u]òlo,** *m.* egg-cup.

ovàle, *a. & m.* oval. *palla ~, f.* Rugby (football).

ovàrio, *m.* ovary (*Bot. & Anat.*). **ovariotomìa,** *f.* (*Surg.*) ovariotomy.

ovàto, *a.* egg-shaped; ovate.

ovàtta, *f.* wadding. **ovattàre,** *v.t.* to wad, stuff or line with wadding.

ovazióne, *f.* ovation.

óve, *ad.* where; when. ¶ *c.* if; in case.

òvest, *m.* west.

Ovìdio, *m.* Ovid.

ovìle, *m.* fold; sheep-fold.

ovìno, *a.* ovine. ¶ *m.* small egg; sheep. **ovìparo,** *a.* oviparous.

òvo, see *uovo.*

òvolo, *m.* (*Arch.*) ovolo, convex egg-shaped moulding; species of mushroom.

ovúnque, *ad.* anywhere, everywhere; wherever.

ovvéro, *c.* or; or indeed; otherwise.

ovviaménte, *ad.* obviously. **ovviàre** (a) (*pr.* **-io, -ìi**), *v.t.* to obviate; avoid. **òvvio** (*pl.* **òvvi**), *a.* obvious.

oziàre (*pr.* **òzio, òzi**), *v.i.* (*aux.* avere) to idle; idle about; lounge. **òzio** (*pl.* **òzi**), *m.* idleness; leisure; indolence; spare time. **oziosàggine,** *f.* laziness; indolence. **oziosità,** *f.inv.* idleness; idle talk; useless trifle. **ozióso,** *a.* idle; lazy; indolent; useless; (*capital*) uninvested.

ożòno, *m.* ozone.

P

P, p (*pi*), *f.* the letter P.

pacataménte, *ad.* quietly; peacefully; placidly. **pacatézza,** *f.* quiet[ness]; calm[ness]; peacefulness. **pacàto,** *a.* calm; quiet; peaceful; placid.

pàcca (*pl.* **pàcche**), *f.* slap.

pacchétto, *m.* packet; small parcel.

pàcchia, *f.* food (*animal*); hearty meal; good living.

pacchiàna, *f.* countrywoman. **pacchiàno,** *m.* countryman. ¶ *a.* rustic, countrified.

pacchieróne, *m.* stout fellow. **pacchieróna,** *f.* plump girl.

pacchìna, *f.* blow on the back of the head.

pacciàme, *m.* litter of leaves, sticks, &c.

pàcco (*pl.* **pàcchi**), *m.* parcel; package.

paccottìglia, *f.* barter goods; trash; parcel carelessly made up.

pàce, *f.* peace; pax (*Eccl.*). *con vostra buona ~,* by your leave. *darsi ~,* to calm down, be resigned.

pachidèrma, *m.* pachyderm; (*fig.*) thick-skinned person.

pacière, *m.* peacemaker.

pacificàre (*pr.* **-ìfico, -ìfichi**), *v.t.* to pacify; appease. **pacificatóre,** *m.* (*f.* **-trìce**) peacemaker. ¶ *a.* pacifying. **pacìfico** (*pl.* **-ìfici**), *a.* pacific, peaceable; peaceful; peace-loving. *l'Oceano P~, il P~,* the Pacific Ocean. *the P.* **pacificóne** *& pacioccóne,* *m.*(*f.* **-óna**) placid, easy-going person. **pacifìsmo,** *m.* pacifism; pacificism. **pacifìsta** (*pl.* **-ìsti**), *m.* pacifist; pacificist.

padèlla, *f.* frying-pan; bed-pan; warming-pan. **padellàta,** *f.* panful; blow with a frying pan.

padiglióne, *m.* pavilion; tent; canopy; hangings for church festival; (*Anat.*) outer ear; section of exhibition buildings, &c.

Pàdova, *f.* Padua. **padovàno,** *a. & m.* Paduan.

pàdre, *m.* father; parent; sire (*Poet.*); friar. **padreggiàre,** *v.i.* (*aux.* avere) to resemble one's father; take after one's father. **padrìgno,** *m.* stepfather (also *patrigno*). **padrìno,** *m.* god-father; second (*duel*).

padróna, *f.* mistress; landlady; proprietress. **padronàle,** *a.* belonging to the master; private. **padronànza,** *f.* mastery; ownership; command. *~di sé,* self-possession, self-control. **padronàto,** *m.* possession; ownership. **padroncìna,** *f.* young mistress; master's daughter. **-cíno,** *m.* young master, master's son. **padróne,** *m.* master; landlord; owner; proprietor. **padroneggiàre,** *v.t.* to master; rule; command; control. *v.i.* (*aux.* avere) to act as master. **padronésco** (*pl.* **-éschi**), *a.* masterful; patronizing.

padùle, *m.* marsh; swamp.

paesàggio (*pl.* **-àggi**), *m.* landscape; l. painting; description of scenery; (*pl.*) scenery. **paesàno,** *a.* native; of the country; of the (same) district; provincial; homely; home (*att.*). ¶ *m.* countryman. **-ana,** *f.* countrywoman. **paése,** *m.* country, land; native place; district; region; town; small town; village. dim. *paesello, paesetto, paesettino; paesino.* **paesì-**

sta (*pl.* **-ísti**), *m.f.* landscape-painter.

paf! paffe! *i.* sound of· a slap or smack. **pàffete!** *i.* sound of (child's) fall.

paffutézza, *f.* plumpness. **paffúto**, *a.* plump; chubby.

Pàfo, *f.* Paphos.

pàga, *f.* pay, wages. *busta* ~, pay-packet. *foglio di* ~, pay-roll, p.-sheet. **pagàbile**, *a.* payable. **pagaménto**, *m.* payment. ~ *alla consegna*, cash on delivery (*abb.* C.O.D.).

paganaménte, *ad.* in pagan fashion. **paganeggiàre**, *v.i.* (*aux.* avere) to act or think in a pagan fashion. **paganésimo**, *m.* paganism. **paganizzàre**, *v.t.* to paganize; make a pagan of. **pagàno**, *a.* pagan; heathen.

pagàre (*pr.* **pàgo**, **pàghi**), *v.t.* to pay; p. for; p. out; cash (*cheque*); stand (*drink, &c.*). ~ *in contanti*, to pay cash. **pagàto**, *a.* paid; settled. **pagatóre**, *m.* payer; paymaster.

pagèlla, *f.* (school) report.

pàggio (*pl.* **pàggi**), *m.* page (*pers.*). **pagherò** (*cambiario*), *m.inv.* promissory note.

pàgina, *f.* page (*book*); leaf. ~ *pari*, (*Typ.*) left hand page, verso. ~ *dispari*, right-hand p., recto. **paginatúra**, *f.* paging; pagination. *paginetta*, *-ina*, *-uccia*, dims. of *pagina*.

pàglia, *f.* straw. *capello di* ~, straw hat.

pagliaccésco (*pl.* **-céschi**), *a.* clownish; foolish; nonsensical. **pagliàccia**, *f.* poor straw, inferior s. **pagliacciàta**, *f.* clowning, buffoonery. **pagliàccio**, *m.* clown; buffoon.

pagliàio, *m.* heap of straw; hay stack. **pagliàto** & **paglieríno**, *a.* straw-coloured. **pagliíccio**, *m.* chopped straw. **paglieríccio**, *m.* palliasse; straw-mattress; sack full of straw.

pagliéto, *m.* reed-bed.

pagliétta, *f.* low straw hat with broad brim.

paglietta, *m.* straw-mat; chair-seat; (*Naut.*) fender.

pagliúca & **pagliúzza**, *f.* bit of straw; speck; mote.

pagnòtta, *f.* loaf; (*fig.*) living; pay. dim. *pagnottina*, *pagnottella*. **pagnottísta** (*pl.* **-ísti**), *m.* one who works only for· pay; timeserver; hireling.

pàgo (*pl.* **pàghi**), *a.* satisfied; content(ed); pleased.

pagúro, *m.* hermit crab (*also called* Bernardo l'Eremita).

pàio, *m.* (*f.pl.* **paia**) pair; couple; brace.

paiolàta, *f.* potful; cauldronful. **pai[u]òlo**, *m.* (*metal*) pot; cauldron; kettle; platform for artillery. dim. *paiolino*, *paioletto*.

pàla, *f.* shovel; blade (*oar or screw*); altar-piece. *ruota a* ~*e*, *f.* paddle-wheel.

paladíno, *m.* paladin; knight-errant; (*fig.*) defender, champion.

palafítta, *f.* embankment of piles; pile-dwelling. **palafittàre**, *v.t.* to strengthen with piles, palisade. **palafittícolo**, *m.* (*ancient*) lake-dweller.

palafrenière, *m.* groom; footman.

palafréno, *m.* (*Poet.*) palfrey.

palàgio, *m.* (*Poet.*) palace.

palaménto, *m.* oars of a boat (*coll.*).

palànca, *f.* stake; plank (bridge); copper (coin), half-penny. *le palanche*, money.

palanchíno, *m.* palanquin.

palànco, *m.* tackle; roller for launching ships or moving heavy weights.

palàta, *f.* shovelful; stroke with an oar; blow with a shovel. **palatàle**, *a.* palatal. **palatína**, *f.* fur tippet. **palatíno**, *a.* palatine. *guardie* ~ *e*, papal guards. *il P*~, the Palatine. **palàto**, *m.* palate.

palazzína, *f.* small palace; villa. **palàzzo**, *m.* palace; mansion; palatial house.

palchétto, *m.* (*Theat.*) box; shelf. **palchettóne**, *m.* stage box.

pàlco (*pl.* **pàlchi**), *m.* platform; flooring; stand; scaffold; (*Theat.*) box, stall. ~*di proscenio*, stage-box. ~*di platea*, pit-stall. ~*morto*, lumber-room.

palcoscènico, *m.* stage (*Theat.*); boards.

palèo, *m.* [peg-] top.

paleografía, *f.* palaeography. **paleògrafo**, *m.* palaeographer.

palešaménto, *m.* disclosure. **palešàre**, *v.t.* to make public; disclose; reveal. **palešàrsi**, *v.refl.* to show oneself; reveal oneself (as). **paléše**, *a.* clear; manifest; obvious.

Palestína (la), *f.* Palestine.

palèstra, *f.* gymnasium; (*fig.*) exercise; training-ground.

palétta, *f.* (small) shovel; palette. **palettàta**, *f.* shovelful.

palétto, *m.* small pole; bolt.

palinodía, *f.* palinode; recantation.

palinsèsto, *m.* palimpsest.

pàlio, *m.* (*pl.* **pàlii**) cloak; piece of rich cloth (*given as prize in a race*); (*fig.*) race (*esp. that of Siena*); race-course; prize.

palischérmo, *m.* skiff; pinnace.

palissàndro, *m.* rosewood.

palizzàta, *f.* fence; paling; palisade.

pàlla, *f.* ball; bullet; shot. ~*da biliardo,* billiard-ball. ~*a nuoto,* water-polo. ~*di neve,* snow-ball. (*pl.*) *palle,* the arms of the Medici (6 balls on a gold field).

pallacanèstro, *f.* basket-ball.

pallacòrda, *f.* tennis; lawn-t., t. court.

Pàllade, *f.* Pallas (*Myth.*).

pallàdio (*pl.* -àdi), *m.* palladium (*statue of Pallas*); (*fig.*) shield, safeguard.

pallàio, *m.* (*pl.* -ài) maker or seller of balls; billiard-marker.

pallàta, *f.* blow from a ball. *fare a* ~*e di neve,* to snowball.

palleggiàre, *v.t. & i.* (*aux.* avere) to toss; shift; dribble (*football*); play ball. **palléggio,** *m.* (*sport*) dribbling; tossing.

pallésco (*pl.* -éschi), *m.* a follower of the Medici (see *palla*). **pallétta,** *f.* dim. of *palla,* grape-shot.

palliàre, *v.t.* to palliate; cloak; disguise. **palliatìvo,** *a. & m.* palliative.

pallidétto, pallidíno & pallidúccio, *a.* rather pale. **pallidézza,** *f.* paleness; pallor; (*fig.*) faintness. **pàllido,** *a.* pale; pallid; faint.

pallína, *f.* little ball; marble (*toy*); small shot.

pallíno, *m.* little ball; jack (*bowls*); small shot, pellet; knob; pommel.

pàllio (*pl.* **pàlli**), *m.* (*Eccl.*) pallium.

palloncíno, *m.* child's balloon; Chinese lantern.

pallóne, *m.* balloon; large ball; game of *pallone* (played in a court with a high retaining wall, and a ball struck with an armlet of wood). ~ *frenato,* ~*drago,* captive-balloon. ~*di sbarramento,* barrage-balloon. ~*di assaggio,* kite balloon.

pallóre, *m.* pallor; paleness.

pallòttola, *f.* little ball; pellet; bullet.

pallottolière, *m.* abacus.

pàlma, *f.* palm (*hand, branch of tree & symbol of victory*). *Domenica delle P ~ e,* Palm Sunday.

palmàre, *a.* clear; evident; (*Anat.*) palmar. **palmàta,** *f.* slap with the hand.

palmàto, *a.* (*Bot.*) palmate; (*Zool.*) webbed.

palméto, *m.* palm-grove.

palmípede, *a.* web-footed.

palmízio, *m.* palm-tree; p.-branch.

pàlmo, *m.* palm (*hand*); hand's breadth; span. ~ *a* ~, little by little, foot by foot.

pàlo, *m.* pole; stake; post. ~*di partenza,* ~ *di arrivo,* starting post, winning p. ~*della porta,* goal-post (*Foot.*).

palombàro, *m.* diver.

palombèlla, *f.* wood-pigeon. **palómbo,** *m.* ring-dove; dog-fish.

palpàbile, *a.* palpable. **palpaménto,** *m.* handling; feeling; (*Med.*) palpation. **palpàre,** *v.t.* to feel; handle; touch. **palpatína,** *f.* light touch.

pàlpebra, *f.* eyelid.

palpeggiaménto, *m.* feeling; handling; fingering. **palpeggiàre,** *v.t.* to keep on handling or touching; feel; finger.

palpitànte, *a.* palpitating; throbbing. **palpitàre,** *v.i.* (*aux.* avere) to palpitate; throb; tremble. **palpitazióne,** *f.* palpitation; throbbing. **pàlpito,** *f.* throb; beat.

paludaménto, *m.* (*Hist.*) military cloak.

palúde, *f.* marsh; swamp; fen; morass. **paludóso,** *a.* marshy. **palústre,** *a.* marsh (*att.*). *febbre* ~, *f.* marsh-fever.

pambollíto & panbollíto, *m.* pap.

pàmpino, *m.* vine-branch; v. tendril; v.-leaf. **pampinóso,** *a.* covered with vine-leaves.

pànama, *m.inv.* panama (*hat*). **P~,** Panama (*Geog.*).

panàre, *v.t.* to cover with bread-crumbs. **panàta,** *f.* panada; bread-soup. **panattièra,** *f.* bread-basket.

pànca (*pl.* **pànche**), *f.* bench; form. **pancàccio,** *m.* plank-bed, camp-bed. **pancàta,** *f.* benchful. **panchétta,** *f. & **panchétto,** *m.* small bench; footstool. *panchetto piegatore,* camp-stool. **panchína,** *f.* small bench; low platform.

pància (*pl.* **pànce**), *f.* belly; paunch. **panciàta,** *f.* bellyful. **panciòlle (stare in),** to lounge on a chair or sofa, take one's ease, with waistcoat unbuttoned. **pancióne,** *m.* big belly. **panciòtto,** *m.* waistcoat.

panciúto, *a.* paunchy; corpulent.

pancóne, *m.* large bench; plank; carpenter's bench. **panconcèllo,** *m.* lath; narrow plank.

pancòtto, *m.* pap; bread-soup.

pàncreas, *m.inv.* pancreas. **pancreàtico** (*pl.* -àtici), *a.* pancreatic.

pancreatíte, f. (Med.) inflammation of the pancreas.

pandemònio, m. pandemonium.

pàne, m. bread; loaf (bread, sugar); lump; ingot; pat (butter). ~ raffermo, stale bread.

Pan[e], m. Pan (Myth.).

panegírico (pl. -írici), m. panegyric. **panegirísta** (pl. -ísti), m. panegyrist.

panellènico (pl. -ènici), a. pan-hellenic.

panèllo, m. oil-cake. **paneréccio,** m. whitlow.

panettería, f. bakery; baker's shop. **panètto,** m. small loaf. **panettóne,** m. large (Milanese) cake. **panfílo,** m. yacht. **panfòrte,** m. Sienese ginger-bread. **pangrattàto,** m. fried bread-crumbs; soup with grated bread in it.

pània, f. bird-lime; (fig.) trap; snare; entanglement.

pànico (pl. pànici), a. & m. panic.

panièra, f. panier; open basket; basket-carriage. **panieràio,** m. basket-maker. **panieràta,** f. basketful. **panière,** m. (deep) basket. **panieríno,** m. small basket; work-basket.

panificàre (pr. -ífico, -ífichi), v.i. (aux. avere) & t. to make bread; bake; (v.t.) turn into bread. **panificazióne,** f. bread making; baking. **panifício,** m. bake-house; bakery.

panino, m. roll (bread); bun. ~ ripieno, ~ imbottito, sandwich.

panióne, m. lime[d]-twig. **panióso,** a. sticky; gluey.

pànna, f. cream; (motor) accident; breakdown. ~ montata, whipped cream.

pannai[u]òlo, m. draper.

panneggiaménto, m. drapery (Art.). **panneggiàre,** v.t. to drape.

pannèllo, m. panel (Arch.); linen cloth. **pannicèllo,** m. piece of cloth; (pl.) rags; (fig.) ~ i caldi, useless remedies. **pannína,** f. woollen cloth. **pànno,** m. cloth; woollen cloth; (fig.) film, layer; (pl.) clothes.

pannòcchia, f. cob (of maize or millet). **pannolàno,** m. (pl. pannilàni) woollen cloth. **pannolíno,** m. (pl. pannilíni) linen cloth.

panòplia, f. panoply.

panoràma (pl. -àmi), m. panorama. **panslavísmo,** m. pan-Slavism.

Pantalóne, m. Pantaloon. **pantalóni,** m.pl. trousers.

pantàno, m. bog; swamp. **pantanóso,** a. boggy; miry.

panteísmo, m. pantheism. **panteísta** (pl. -ísti), m. pantheist.

Pànteon, m. Pantheon; temple.

pantèra, f. panther.

pantòfola, f. slipper.

pantògrafo, m. pantograph.

pantomíma, f. pantomime.

panzàna, f. idle story; nonsense.

Pàolo, m. Paul. **paolòtto,** a. devout; pious; bigoted (after St. Vincent de Paul).

paonàzzo, a. violet; purple; peacock-blue.

papà, m. inv. papa; dad; daddy; father. **Pàpa,** m. (pl. pàpi), Pope.

papàbile, a. eligible as pope. **papàle,** a. papal. **papalína,** f. skull-cap. **papalíno,** a. of the Pope's party or household; attached to the Pope. **papàto,** m. papacy (office).

papàvero, a. poppy.

pàpera, f. goose; (fig.) silly woman; blunder; error in pronunciation. **pàpero,** m. gander; gosling. dim. paperello, -ino, -ottolo.

papésco (pl. -éschi), a. popish; papistical.

papíro, m. papyrus.

papísmo, m. papacy (system); popery. **papísta** (pl. -ísti), m. papist.

pàppa, f. pap, soaked bread.

pappafíco (pl. -íchi), m. hood, diver's helmet; top gallant sail; imperial (beard).

pappagallescaménte, ad. in parrot fashion. **pappagalésco** (pl. -éschi), a. parrot-like. **pappagàllo,** m. parrot.

pappagòrgia, f. double-chin.

pappàre, v.t. to gulp down; gobble up; gorge. **pappàta,** f. hearty meal. **pappatóre,** m. (f. -tríce) guzzler; huge eater. **pappatòria,** f. feast; feasting. **pappína,** f. pap; poultice; (fig.) scolding. **pappolàta,** f. thin soup; over-cooked food; (fig.) tedious talk. **pappolóne,** m. great chatterer. **pappóne,** m. great eater.

pàpula, f. pimple.

paràbola, f. parable; parabola (Geom.).

parabórdo, m. fender (Naut.). **parabrézza,** m. wind-screen (Aviat. & motor.). **paracadúte,** m.inv. parachute. **paracadutísta** (pl. -ísti), m. parachutist. (reparti di) paracadutisti, paratroops. **paracamíno,** m. fire-screen. **paracàrro,** m. kerbstone. **paracènere,** m. fire-guard:

tender paracièlo, *m.* root; canopy; ceiling.

Paraclèto, *m.* Paracle Ghost.

paracólpi, *m.inv.* buffer paradigma (*pl.* -igmi), *m.* paradigm.

paradišèa, *f.* bird of paradise. **paradišíaco** (*pl.* -íaci), *a.* heavenly; paradisaic(al). **paradíšo,** *m.* paradise; heaven.

paradossàle, *a.* paradoxical **paradòsso,** *m.* paradox.

parafàngo (*pl.* -anghi), *m.* mud-guard.

paràf[f]a, *f.* flourish (*after a signature*).

paraffína, *f.* paraffin[e].

parafòco, *m.* fire-guard.

parafrašàre (*pr.* -àfraso), *v.t.* to paraphrase. **paràfraši,** *f.* paraphrase. **parafràstico** (*pl.* -àstici), *a.* paraphrastic.

parafúlmine, *m.* lightning conductor.

parafuoco, see *parafoco*.

paràggio, *m.* coastal district; (*pl.*) quarter; parts; neighbourhood.

paragonàbile, *a.* comparable. **paragonàre** (*pr.* -óno), *v.t.* to compare. **paragóne,** *m.* comparison. *pietra di ~, f.* touchstone.

paragrafàre (*pr.* -àgrafo), *v.t.* to paragraph; divide into paragraphs. **paràgrafo,** *m.* paragraph; section mark (§).

paraguài, *m.* (*pop.*) overcoat; cloak; overall.

paràliši, *f.* paralysis. **paralítico** (*pl.* -ítici), *a.* & *m.* paralytic. **paralizzàre,** *v.t.* to paralyse (*lit. & fig.*).

parallàsse, *f.* parallax (*Astr.*).

parallèla, *f.* parallel; parallel line; (*pl.*) parallels; parallel bars (*gym.*). **parallelíšmo,** *m.* parallelism. **parallèlo,** *a.* & *m.* parallel. **parallelogràmmo,** *m.* parallelogram.

paralogíšmo, *m.* paralogism; illogical reasoning; fallacy.

paralúme, *m.* lamp-shade; eye-shade.

paramàno, *m.* wrist-band.

paraménto, *m.* vestment; (*church*) hanging.

paramíne, *m.inv.* (*Nav.*) paravane.

paramósche, *m.inv.* fly-flap; fly-net; dish-cover of metallic gauze.

parancàre, *v.t.* to hoist by tackle. **parànco** (*pl.* -ànchi), *m.* tackle.

parànza & **paranzèlla,** *f.* small lateen craft; fishing boat.

paraòcchi, *m.pl.* goggles; blinkers (*horse*).

parapètto, *m.* parapet; sill.

parapíglia, *f.* turmoil; bustle; confusion.

paràre, *v.t. & i.* (*aux.* avere) to adorn; deck; decorate (*with hangings*); prepare; stretch out; offer; hoist (*sails*); drive; catch; shelter; avoid; prevent; stop; avert; parry; ward off; keep off; keep out (*light*); succeed; lead up to. *andare a ~,* to drive at (*fam.*). **paràrsi,** *v.refl.* to dress up; protect oneself; shelter; appear; present oneself.

parasóle, *m.* parasol; sunshade.

parassíta (*pl.* -íti), *m.* parasite. **parassitàrio** & **parassítico** (*pl.* -ítici), *a.* parasitic(al).

paràta, *f.* parade; display; defence; parry; parade-ground; defence-work. *abito di ~,* full dress.

paratàsche, *m.inv.* pocket-flap.

paratía, *f.* bulkhead. *~ stagna,* water-tight b.

paràto, *m.* ornament; hangings (*Eccl.*); curtains (*bed*). *carta da ~ i,* wall paper. ¶ *a.* ornamental; decorated; hung. **paratóre,** *m.* decorator. **paratúra,** *f.* decoration.

paraúrti, *m.inv.* shock-absorber; bumper (*motor*). **paravèste,** *m.* dress-guard (*Cyc.*).

paravènto, *m.* screen (*lit. & fig.*); (*motor*) wind-screen.

Pàrca, *f.* Fate (*Myth.*). *pl. le Parche.*

parcaménte, *ad.* sparingly; moderately; frugally.

parcàre (*pr.* pàrco, pàrchi), *v.t.* to park (*car, artillery*).

parcèlla, *f.* bill; note of expenses; portion.

parchéggio, *m.* parking, parking place. **pàrco** (*pl.* pàrchi), *m.* park; enclosure; yard; paddock; (car) park. ¶ *a.* frugal; moderate; sparing.

pàrdo, *m.* leopard.

parécchio (*pl.* parécchi), *a.* a good deal, a good many; some, considerable (*time, distance*); (*pl.*) several; many. ¶ *ad.* much; very much.

pareggiàbile, *a.* comparable; fit to equal. **pareggiaménto,** *m.* levelling; balancing; putting on an equality. **pareggiàre,** *v.t.* to equal; be equal to; equalize; put on the same footing; level; balance; gain official recognition for. **pareggiàrsi,** *v.refl.* to be equal; compare oneself with; square accounts. **paréggio,** *m.* equalization; balance; balancing.

parèlio, *m.* parhelion.

paregòrico, *m.* paregoric.
parentàdo, *m.* relationship; kinship; stock; lineage; relatives; link by marriage; marriage.   **parentàli,** *m.pl.* celebration (*in honour of the illustrious dead*). **parènte,** *m.* kinsman; relation.   **parentèla,** *f.* relationship; relatives.
parèntesi, *f.inv.* parenthesis; bracket(s)(,).   *tra* ~, incidentally; by the by.   ~ *quadre,* square brackets.   **parentètico** (*pl.* -ètici), *a.* parenthetic(al).
parére (*pr.* pàio, pàri, pàre, pariàmo, paréte, pàiono), *v.i. ir. oft. impers.* (*aux.* essere) to seem; appear; look; look like.   *che ve ne pare?* what do you think of it? *fate come vi pare,* do as you please (or as you like).   *mi pare di sì,* I think so.   *mi par mill' anni che,* I long to.   ¶ *m.* opinion, judgment; advice.
paréssa, *f.* peeress (*Eng.*).
paréte, *f.* wall (*inner wall of a house*); internal surface.
pargoleggiàre, *v.i.* (*aux.* avere) to talk or behave like a child.   **pargolétto** & **pàrgolo,** *m.* (*Poet.*) little child; baby;   ¶ *a.* tiny, small.
pàri, *a.* equal; like; same; even (*number*).   *andar* ~, to match. *siamo* ~, we are quits.   *in* ~ *tempo,* at the same time.   *del* ~, as well; likewise; also.   *quaranta* ~, deuce (*Ten.*).   ¶ *m.* peer; equal; like; level. *a un* ~, on the same level.   ¶ *f.* par (*Stk. Ex.*); equality.   *alla* ~, at par. *sopra la* ~, above p.   *sotto la* ~, below p.   *portarsi alla* ~ *di,* to catch up with.
pària, *m.* pariah; outcast; untouchable.
parificàre, see *pareggiare.*
Parìgi, *f.* Paris (*Geog.*).   **parigìno,** *a.* & *m.* Parisian.
parìglia, *f.* pair, couple.   *render la* ~, to give tit for tat.
pariménte & **-ménti,** *ad.* likewise; also.
pàrio, *a.* Parian (*marble*).
parità, *f.* parity; equality.   *a* ~ *di condizioni,* conditions being equal.
parlamentàre, *ad.* parliamentary.   ¶ *v.i.* (*aux.* avere) to discuss; parley. **parlamentàrio,** *m.* parliamentarian; bearer of a flag of truce.   **parlaménto,** *m.* parliament; parley.
parlànte, *a.* speaking; talking; (*fig.*) lifelike (*portrait*).
parlantìna, *f.* talkativeness; loquacity; indiscreet talk.   **parlàre,** *v.i.* (*aux.*

avere) & *t.* to speak; talk.   ~ *pel naso,* to speak through the nose. ~ *alla muta,* to speak by signs. ¶ *m.* talk; way of speaking; speech; dialect.   **parlàta,** *f.* conversation; way of speaking; dia.ec. .arlatóre, *m.* (*f.* -tríce) speaker; ta.ker. **parlatòrio,** *m.* parlour (*convent, school*).
parmigiàno, *a.* & *m.* Parmesan (of Parma), native of P. (*formaggio*) ~, Parmesan [cheese].
Parnàso, *m.* Parnassus; (*fig.*) poetry; poets. **parnassiàno,** *a.* Parnassian.
pàro, *m.* (= paio) pair.   *mettere a* ~, to compare.   P ~, *f.* Paros (*Geog.*).
parodìa, *f.* parody.   **parodiàre,** *v.t.* to parody. **parodìsta** (*pl.* ísti), *m.* parodist.
paròla, *f.* word; term; speech; doctrine; maxim, promise; parole. *gi[u]oco di* ~ *e,* pun; play upon words.   ~ *e incrociate,* cross-words, cross-word puzzle. **parolàccia,** *f.* bad word; coarse word. **parolàio,** *m.* wordy speaker; proser; talkative person.   ¶ *a.* loquacious; long-winded. **parolìna,** *f.* nice word. **parolóna,** *f.* big word; long word. **parolóne,** *m.* bombastic word.
parossìsmo, *m.* paroxysm.
parricìda (*pl.* -ídi), *m.f.* parricide (*pers.*).   ¶ *a.* parricidal. **parricídio,** *m.* parricide (*crime*).
parrocchétto, *m.* parakeet; paroquet; fore-topmast.
parròcchia, *f.* parish; parish church. **parrocchiàle,** *a.* parochial; parish (*att.*).   *chiesa* ~, parish church. **parrocchiàno,** *m.* parishioner. **pàrroco** (*pl.* pàrroci), *m.* parish priest.
parrùcca, *f.* wig; periwig; (*fig.*) severe scolding. **parrucchière,** *m.* hair-dresser; wig-maker. **parruccóne,** *m.* large wig; (*fig.*) big-wig, reactionary.
parsimònia, *f.* parsimony; frugality.
pàrso, *p.p.* of *parere.*
partàccia (*pl.* -àcce), *f.* shameful action; bitter reproof. **pàrte,** *f.* part; portion; share; place; direction; quarter; side, hand; day; party; rôle; character (*Theat.*) & actor playing the part.   ~ *del leone,* lion's share. *a* ~, separately; apart.   *a* ~ *a* ~, bit by bit.   *da* ~, aside; out of the way.   *da* ~ *mia,* on my behalf; on my part; from me.   *d'altra* ~, on the other hand; besides.   *di* ~ *in* ~, everywhere.   *dell'altra* ~, on the other side.   *da* ~ *a* ~, through,

right through. ~*i di ricambio,*
(*Mech.*) spare parts. *spirito di* ~,
party spirit. ~*civile,* plaintiff
(*Law*). *fare una* ~, to play a part.
partecipànte, *m.* participant; person
taking part; partaker; sharer. **par-
tecipàre** (*pr.* **-écipo**), *v.i.* (*aux.*
avere) to partake; participate; take (a)
part; share; attend; be present; (*v.t.*)
to communicate; notify; announce;
impart; bestow; grant. **partecipa-
tóre,** *m.* (*f.* **-tríce**) sharer; informant. **partecipazióne,** *f.*
participation; sharing; announcement; confirmation. **partécipe,** *a.*
partaking; participating; acquainted;
informed. *esser* ~ *di,* to share.
parteggiàre, *v.i.* (*aux.* avere) to take
sides. ~ *per,* to side with.
Partenóne, *m.* Parthenon.
partenopèo, *a.* (*Poet.*) Neapolitan.
partènte, *a.* departing; leaving;
starting. ¶ *m.* person leaving;
(*horse*) starter. **partènza,** *f.*
departure; start[ing]; (*ship*) sailing.
partíbile, *a.* divisible. **particèlla,** *a.*
particle. **particípio** (*pl.* **-ípi**), *m.*
participle. **partícola,** *f.* consecrated
wafer (*Eccl.*).
particolàre, *a.* particular; peculiar;
[e]special; private. ¶ *m.* particular;
detail; (private) individual. **parti-
colareggiàre,** *v.i.* (*aux.* avere) to
go into details; to give minute
details. **particolarménte,** *ad.*
particularly; [e]specially; in particular.
partigiàna, *f.* halberd; female partisan. **partigianería,** *f.* partisanship.
partigiàno, *m.* partisan; follower;
supporter; guer[r]illa (fighter). ¶ *a.*
partisan; partial; factious.
partíre (*pr.* **-ísco, -ísci**), *v.t.* to
divide; separate. *v.i.* (*pr.* **pàrto,
pàrti**) (*aux.* essere) to leave; start;
set out; (*ship*) sail. **partírsi,** *v.refl.*
to leave, depart. ~ *da,* to give up;
depart from. **partíta,** *f.* (*sport*)
game; match; round; rubber; party;
(*Com.*) quantity; lot (*goods*); entry
(*ledger*). ~ *a buche,* match-play
(*Golf*). ~*d'onore,* duel. ~ *semplice.*
~*doppia,* single, double entry
(*Bkkpg.*). **partitaménte,** *a.*
separately; distinctly; point by
point. **partitivo,** *a. & m.* partitive.
partíto, *m.* party (*polit.,* &c.);
decision, course (of action); proposal;
terms; match (*marriage, m. partner*);
advantage; profit, benefit; purpose;
resolve; vote; condition, situation;

odds (*in a game*). *prendere* ~, to
take sides. *prendere un* ~, to make
up one's mind, decide. *mal* ~,
[sorry] plight, predicament. ¶ *a.*
divided, separated. **partitúra,** *f.*
(*musical*) score. **partizióne,** *f.*
partition; division.
pàrto, *m.* childbirth; birth; delivery;
new-born baby. **partoriènte,** *f.*
woman in childbed. **partoríre** (*pr.*
-ísco, -ísci), *v.t.* to give birth to;
bear; (*of animals*) foal; litter, &c.;
(*fig.*) produce; originate. *v.i.* (*aux.*
avere) to be in labour; be delivered.
parvènte, *a.* seeming; apparent;
visible. **parvènza,** *f.* appearance,
aspect; show; pretence.
pàrvolo, *m.* (*Poet.*) baby; small child.
parziàle, *a.* partial; biased; one-sided.
parzialità, *f.* partiality; favouritism;
parzialménte, *ad.* partially; partly;
unfairly.
pàscere (*pr.* **pàsco, pàsci**), *v.i.* (*aux.*
avere) to graze; & *v.t.* to feed on;
feed. **pàscersi** (**di**), *v.refl.* to feed
on; (*fig.*) to cherish.
pascià, *m.* pasha.
pascimento, *m.* feeding, grazing.
pascióna, *f.* rich pasture land;
(*fig.*) prosperity.
pasciúto, *p.p.* of *pascere.* ¶ *a.* plump,
well-fed.
pascolàre, *v.i.* (*aux.* avere) to graze;
pasture. **pàscolo,** *m.* pasture; food
(*lit. & fig.*).
Pàsqua, *f.* Easter. ~*di rose,* Whit-
sunday; Pentecost. ~*de'morti,* All
Souls' Day, Nov. 2. ~*degli Ebrei,*
Passover. **pasquàle,** *a.* Easter
(*att.*); paschal.
pasquinàta, *f.* lampoon; pasquinade.
passàbile, *a.* passable; tolerable; fair;
pretty good. **passabilménte,** *ad.*
passably, &c.
passàggio (*pl.* **-àggi**), *m.* passage;
passing; crossing; transit; transition;
passage way; gangway; way;
thoroughfare; traffic. *diritto di* ~,
right of way. *dim. passaggetto.*
~ *a livello,* level crossing. ~*sotterraneo,* subway. ~ *tracciato da
chiodi,* studded crossing (pedestrian
crossing); *vietato il* ~, no thoroughfare. ~ *interdetto,* no entry (traffic
sign). *di* ~, in passing.
passaiòla, *f.* stepping-stone.
passamàno, *m.* lace, braid, ribbon
(trimming). **passamantería,** *f.*
passementerie (*Fr.*); trimmings;
factory or shop for trimmings.
passànte, *m.* passer-by; guard or

keeper through which the end of a belt or strap is passed.

passapòrto, *m.* passport.

passàre, *v.i.* (*aux.* essere) & *v.t.* to pass; pass along; pass through; pass by; pass on; pass in; pass over; go; cross; spend; call, look in; ferry over; slip on; exceed; overstep; rank; give; hand over; (*Bkkpg.*) enter; post; transfer; (*coin, &c.*) place, put; cease (*fire*); happen; exist. ~ *a un esame,* to pass an examination. *passarsi di,* to abstain from; dispense with. *passarsela bene,* to get on well, be well off; *10 libbre e passa,* ten pounds and over. **passàta,** *f.* passage; (*fenc.*) lunge, pass; look; glance; shower of rain; (*Agr.*) ridge; strip; (*cook*) mash, purée.

passatèmpo, *m.* pastime, amusement.

passatína, *f.* brief glance.

passatísta (*pl.* -ísti), *m.* traditionalist.

passàto, *a.* past; faded; (*Cook.*) over-done; gone (bad). ¶ *m.* past; past time(s). **passatóia,** *f.* strip of carpet; stair-c. **passatóio,** *m.* foot-bridge; stile; stepping stone.

passatóre, *m.* ferryman.

passeggèro, *a.* passing; transient; fleeting. ¶ *m.* passenger; traveller.

passeggiàre, *v.i.* (*aux.* avere) to walk; take a w., go for a w. ~*a cavallo,* to ride, go for a r. ~ *in carrozza,* to take a drive; go for a drive. **passeggiàta,** *f.* walk, drive; ride. **passeggièro,** see *passeggero.* **passéggio,** *m.* (*public*) walk; promenade; walk; walking.

passeràio & **passerío,** *m.* twittering (*of sparrows, &c.*); chirping; (*fig.*) chattering.

passerèlla, *f.* gangway; footbridge.

pàssero, *m.* (*pl.* **pàssera**) sparrow. **passeròtto,** *m.* young sparrow.

passettíno, *m.* baby's step. **passétto,** *m.* short step.

passíbile, *a.* liable; susceptible.

passibilità, *f.* liability; suscepti-bility.

passíccio, *a.* rather withered. **passi-flòra,** *f.* passion-flower.

passionàle, *m.* (*Eccl.*) book of martyrs.

passionataménte, *ad.* passionately. **passionàto,** *a.* passionate; im-passioned. **passióne,** *f.* passion; suffering; love; sorrow; keen desire; anxiety. **passionísta** (*pl.* -ísti), *m.* Passionist (*monk*).

passivaménte, *ad.* passively. **passi-vità,** *f.inv.* passivity; indebtedness,

liabilities. **passívo,** *a.* passive. ¶ *m.* passive (*Gram.*); debts, liabilities.

pàsso, *m.* step; pace; stride; gait; walk; march; footfall; footprint; progress; procedure; speed; rate; passage; entrance; inlet; pass (*Geog.*); straits (*Geog.*); pitch, tread (*screw*). ~ *accelerato,* quick march. *P ~ di Calais,* Straits of Dover. *a ~ di lumaca,* at a snail's pace. *a ~ di carica,* at the double (*Mil.*). (*andare*)*al* ~, drive slowly, dead slow (*traffic sign*). *andar di pari ~ con,* to keep pace with. *uccello di* ~, bird of passage. ¶ *a.* faded, shrivelled; dried. *uva* ~*a,* raisins (also *uva secca*).

pàsta, *f.* paste; dough; pulp; sausage-meat; piece of pastry; sweet; bonbon; macaroni; (*fig.*) nature; temper-[ament]; constitution. ~ *asciutta,* dish of macaroni made with cheese. ~*spoglia,* puff paste. ~ *dentifricia,* tooth paste. *avere le mani in* ~, to have a finger in the pie (*fig.*). *mettere le mani in* ~, to meddle in other people's affairs. *un uomo di buona* ~, a good-natured man.

pastàio, *m.* macaroni-maker or seller.

pasteggiàre, *v.i.* (*aux.* avere) to have one's meals; eat at table.

pastèllo, *m.* pastel; coloured crayon. **pastèlla,** *f.* batter; (*fig.*) trickery; (electoral) fraud.

pasticca, *f.* lozenge; tablet; pastille.

pasticcería, *f.* pastry; confectioner's shop. **pasticétto,** *m.* small pie; (*fig.*) mess; muddle. **pasticciàre,** *v.i.* (*aux.* avere) & *v.t.* to mingle; make a mess of. **pasticcière,** *m.* pastry-cook; confectioner. **pasticc-cíno,** *m.* tartlet; sweetmeat; bonbon. **pasticcio,** *m.* pie; (*fig.*) mess; scrape; embarrassment; botched work; (*Art*) imitation, copy. *trovarsi nei pasticci,* to be in a fix. *bel* ~*!* a nice mess! **pasticcióne,** *m.* busybody; meddler.

pastíglia, *f.* pastille; lozenge. **pasti-nàca,** *f.* parsnip.

pàsto, *m.* meal; repast; food; fruit-pulp; lights (*offal*); (*fig.*) affair; bargain. *vino da* ~, table wine. *a tutto* ~, freely, abundantly.

pastòcchia, *f.* idle story; (*pl.*) non-sense, humbug.

pastóia, *f.* clog; tether; shackle; (*horse*) pastern.

pastóne, *m.* dough; thick soup; horse-food; chicken feed.

pastóra, *f.* shepherdess. dim. *pasto-*

rella. **pastoràle**, *a.* pastoral. ¶ *m.* crozier, pastoral staff. *f.* pastoral, pastoral letter. **pastóre**, *m.* shepherd; pastor; clergyman (*Protest.*). dim. *pastorello.*

pastorizżàre, *v.t.* to pasteurize (*milk*).

pastosità, *f.* softness; stickiness. **pastóso**, *a.* soft; sticky; mellow.

pastranàio, *m.* cloakroom attendant.

pastràno, *m.* overcoat; loose cloak.

pastricciàno, *m.* simple good-natured fellow.

pastúra, *f.* pasture; pasturage. **pasturàre** (*pr.* -úro), *v.t. & i.* (*aux.* avere) to pasture; graze.

patàcca, *f.* worthless coin; large stain; thing of no value; meaningless decoration.

patagóne, *a. & m.* Patagonian.

patapúm, *onomat. excl.* bang, clap, thud.

patàta, *f.* potato (*pl.* potatoes). dim. *patatina.* ~*e tenere*, new potatoes. **patatàio**, *m.* potato merchant.

patatràc! *onomat. excl.* crash!

patavíno, *a.* of Padua, Paduan.

patèlla, *f.* limpet.

patèma (*pl.* -èmi), *m.* pain; anxiety; chagrin.

patènte, *f.* licence; certificate; diploma. ~*di sanità,* [clean] bill of health. ~*di circolazione,* car licence. ~ *di autista,* ~ *di abilitazione,* driving licence. ~*per la vendita degli alcoolici,* licence for the sale of drink. ¶ *a.* patent; obvious; clear; evident.

pateràcchio (*pl.* -àcchi), *m.* friendly agreement; (*pop.*) marriage.

pateréccio (*pl.* -écci), *m.* whitlow.

paternàle, *f.* reprimand; scolding; rebuke. ¶ *a.* (*Poet.*) paternal. **paternità**, *f.* paternity; fatherhood. **patèrno**, *a.* paternal; fatherly; father's. **paternòstro**, *m.* paternoster; Lord's Prayer.

patètico (*pl.* -ètici), *a.* pathetic.

patíbile, *a.* endurable.

patibolàre, *a.* of the gallows; hangdog (*look*). **patíbolo**, *m.* gallows; scaffold; place of execution.

patiménto, *m.* suffering.

pàtina, *f.* patina; varnish; dubbin[g] (*for leather*); coating. **patinàre**, *v.t.* to varnish; dub (*leather*). **patinatúra,** *f.* varnishing; dubbing. **patinóso**, *a.* (*of bronzes*) showing a patina; (*of tongue*) coated, furred.

patíre (*pr.* -ísco, -ísci), *v.i.* (*aux.* avere) *& t.* to suffer; bear; endure; permit. **patíto**, *a.* sickly; suffering; run down (*from illness*).

patología, *f.* pathology. **patològico** (*pl.* -ògici), *a.* pathological. **patòlogo** (*pl.* -òlogi), *m.* pathologist.

Patràsso, *f.* Patras.

pàtria, *f.* native land; country; fatherland; home.

patriàrca (*pl.* -àrchi), *m.* patriarch. **patriarcàle**, *a.* patriarchal; (*fig.*) venerable.

patrígno, *m.* step-father.

patrimònio (*pl.* -òni), *m.* patrimony; inheritance; heritage; estate.

pàtrio, *a.* native; domestic; of one's own country; of one's own home. **patriò[t]ta** (*pl.* -òti *&* -òtti), *m.* patriot. **patriòttico** (*pl.* -òttici), *a.* patriotic. **patriottísmo**, *m.* patriotism.

patrízio (*pl.* -ízi), *a. & m.* patrician.

patrizżàre, *v.i.* (*aux.* avere) to resemble (or take after) one's father.

patrocinàre (*pr.* -ino, -ini), *v.t.* to defend; support; protect; plead (*a cause*); champion. *avvocato patrocinante,* counsel for the defence. **patrocinàto**, *m.* client. **patrocinatóre**, *m.* protector; defender; supporter. **patrocínio**, *m.* patronage; protection; defence; support.

patròna *&* **patronéssa,** *f.* patroness. **patronàto**, *m.* patronage; charitable institution (*esp. for the protection of children*). **patronímico** (*pl.* -ímici), *a. & m.* patronymic. **patròno**, *m.* patron; protector; patron saint; (*Mar.*) skipper.

pàtta (**pari e**), *a. & ad.* quits; all square.

patteggiàbile, *a.* negotiable; that can be arranged. **patteggiaménto**, *m.* arrangement, bargaining; compromise. **patteggiàre**, *v.i.* (*aux.* avere) *& t.* to negotiate; bargain; come to terms. **patteggiatóre**, *m.* (*f.* -tríce) bargainer; negotiator; party to a bargain. ¶ *a.* bargaining; negotiating.

pattinàggio, *m.* skating. ~ *a rotelle,* roller-skating.

pattinàre (*pr.* **pàttino**), *v.i.* (*aux.* avere) to skate. **pattinatóre**, *m.* (*f.* -tríce) skater. **pàttino**, *m.* skate; (*Aviat.*) skid.

pàtto, *m.* pact; agreement; compact; (*pl.*) terms; understanding. *a* ~ *che,* on condition that. *a nessun* ~, by no means. *a qualunque* ~, *a tutti i* ~ *i,* at any cost. *P* ~ *atlantico,* Atlantic Pact.

pattúglia, *f.* patrol. **pattugliàre**, *v.i.* (*aux.* avere) to patrol.

pattuíre (*pr.* **-ísco, -ísci**), *v.i.* (*aux.* avere) & *t.* to strike a bargain; agree upon; fix; settle.

pattúme, *m.* litter; refuse; dust-heap. **pattumièra,** *f.* dust-bin.

patúrne, *f.pl.* low spirits; melancholy. *avere le* ~, to be in the dumps.

pauperísmo, *m.* pauperism.

paúra, *f.* fear; dread. **pauràccia,** *f.* horrid fright. **paurétta** & **pauríccia,** *f.* slight alarm; apprehension. **paurosaménte,** *ad.* fearfully; dreadfully; timidly. **pauróso,** *a.* timorous; timid; (*horse*) shy, skittish; fearful; alarming; dreadful; frightful.

pàusa, *f.* pause; stop; (*Mus.*) rest. **pausàre,** *v.i.* (*aux.* avere) to pause; stop; show deliberation.

paventàre (*pr.* **-ènto**), *v.i.* (*aux.* avere) & *t.* to be afraid; fear.

pavesàre, *v.t.* to dress (*ship*); deck with flags. **pavesàto** *a.* dressed with flags.

pavése, *a.* of Pavia. ¶ *m.* native of Pavia.

pavidaménte, *ad.* fearfully; timidly; in alarm. **pàvido,** *a.* timid; frightened.

pavimentàre (*pr.* **-énto**), *v.t.* to pave; floor. **paviménto,** *m.* pavement; floor.

pavóna & **pavonéssa,** *f.* pea-hen. **pavonàzzo,** *a.* & *m.* peacock-blue; violet; purple. **pavoncèlla,** *f.* lapwing. **pavoncèllo** & **pavoncíno,** *m.* young peacock. **pavóne,** *m.* peacock. **pavoneggiàrsi,** *v.refl.* to strut (*like a peacock*); show off; be as proud as a peacock.

pazientàre, *v.i.* (*aux.* avere) to wait; be patient; have patience. **paziènte,** *a.* patient; enduring; forbearing. ¶ *m.* patient; sufferer. **paziènza,** *f.* patience; forbearance; endurance; friar's sleeveless gown; scapular; game of patience.

pazzacchióne, *m.* hare-brained fellow; madcap. **pazzàccio,** *m.* arrant fool. **pazzaménte,** *ad.* madly; excessively. **pazzarèllo** & **pazzerèllo,** *a.* rather mad. ¶ *m.* fool; silly fellow. **pazzeggiàre,** *v.i.* (*aux.* avere) to play the fool. **pazzescaménte,** *ad.* wildly; foolishly; like a lunatic. **pazzésco** (*pl.* **-éschi**), *a.* crazy; wild; foolish. **pazzía,** *f.* madness; lunacy; insanity; frenzy; folly; foolish act; mad idea. **pàzzo,** *a.* mad; insane; lunatic; wild; foolish; frenzied. ¶ *m.* madman; lunatic.

pe', *pr.* & *art.* = *pei, per i.*

peàna (*pl.* **-àni** & **-àna**), *m.* paean.

pècca, *f.* fault; error; blemish; defect. **peccàbile,** *a.* liable to err. **peccaminóso,** *a.* sinful. **peccàre** (*pr.* **pècco, pècchi**), *v.i.* (*aux.* avere) to sin; err; offend; be faulty or defective. **peccàto,** *m.* sin; fault. *che* ~! what a pity! **peccatóre,** *m.* (*f.* **-tríce**) sinner. **peccatúccio,** *m.* peccadillo; slight fault; slip; trifling offence.

pécchia, *f.* bee. **pecchióne,** *m.* bumble-bee; drone.

péce, *f.* pitch. ~ *liquida*, tar. ~*da calzolai*, cobbler's wax.

Pechíno, *f.* Peking. **pechinése,** *a.* & *m.* Pekingese.

pecióso, *a.* smeared with pitch.

pècora, *f.* sheep; ewe. ~ *segnata*, (*fig.*) black sheep. **pecoràggine,** *f.* sheepishness; stupidity. **pecoràia,** *f.* shepherdess. **pecoràio,** *m.* shepherd. **pecoràme,** *m.* flock of sheep (*lit.* & *fig.*). **pecoréccio,** *a.* sheepish. ¶ *m.* maze; confusion. **pecorèlla,** *f.* small sheep; (*pl.*) sea-foam; fleecy clouds. **pecorésco** (*pl.* **-éschi**), *a.* sheepish. **pecoríle,** *m.* sheepfold. ¶ *a.* sheepish. **pecoríno,** *a.* sheep's; sheepish. *cacio* ~, or ~, sheep's milk cheese. **pècoro,** *m.* ram; wether. **pecoróna,** *f.* big ewe. **pecoróne,** *m.* big sheep; (*fig.*) blockhead; poor-spirited creature. **pecorúme,** *m.* (*fig.*) servile flock (*of imitators*, &*c.*).

peculàto, *m.* embezzlement (*public funds*). **peculiàre,** *a.* peculiar; special; particular. **pecúlio** (*pr.* **-úli**), *m.* savings; nest-egg; earnings (*of convict*); gratuity (*on discharge, Mil.* & *Navy*). **pecúnia,** *f.* money. **pecuniàrio,** *a.* pecuniary. **pecunióso,** *a.* wealthy; avaricious.

pedàggio (*pl.* **-àggi**), *m.* toll. **pedàgna,** *f.* stretcher (*in rowing boat*).

pedagogía, *f.* pedagogy; education. **pedagògico** (*pl.* **-ògici**), *a.* pedagogic(al). **pedagògo** (*pl.* **-òghi**), *m.* pedagogue.

pedalàre & **pedaleggiàre,** *v.i.* (*aux.* avere) & *t.* to pedal. **pedàle,** *m.* pedal; treadle. ~*a sega*, rat-trap pedal. ~ *d'innesto*, clutch p. ~ *forte*, loud p. ~ *sordo*, soft p. **pedalièra,** *f.* pedal (key) board. **pedalísta,** *m.* pedaller; cyclist. ~ *audace*, scorcher.

pedàna, *f.* foot-rest; bedside rug; platform; jumping-off board.

pedànte, *m.* pedant. **pedantería**, *f.* pedantry. **pedantésco** (*pl.* **-éschi**), *a.* pedantic.

pedàta, *f.* kick; footprint; stair step.

pedèstre, *a.* pedestrian; (*fig.*) dull, monotonous.

pediatría, *f.* cure of sick children. **pediàtrico** (*pl.* **-àtrici**), *a.* for sick children.

pedicúre, *m. & f.* chiropodist.

pedignóne, *m.* chilblain (*on foot*). **pedilúvio** (*pl.* **-úvi**), *m.* foot-bath.

pedína, *f.* man (*draughts*); pawn (*chess*). **pedináre** (*pr.* **-íno**), *v.t.* to follow; dog the steps of; spy upon.

pedíssequo, *a.* servile; clumsy; over-literal.

pedòmetro, *m.* pedometer. **pedonàle**, *a.* (reserved) for foot-passengers. *traffico* ~, foot-traffic. **pedóne**, *m.* pedestrian; foot-soldier; pawn (*chess*).

pedúccio, *m.* small pedestal; bracket; (*Arch.*) corbel; (*pl.*) (*animal*) trotters.

pedúle, *m.* stocking foot.

pedúncolo, *m.* stalk (*Bot.*).

pegamòide, *f.* pegamoid.

Pègaso, *m.* Pegasus.

pèggio, *ad.* worse. *alla* ~, at the worst; somehow or other; very badly. *il* ~, the worst. **peggioraménto**, *m.* worsening: deteriorating, -ion. **peggioràre**, *v.i.* (*aux. essere*) to become worse; grow w. ¶ *v.t.* to make worse. **peggiorativo**, *a. & m.* pejorative; depreciatory (*word or suffix, e.g.* -accio). **peggióre**, *a.* worse. *il* ~, *la* ~, *i* ~ *i*, *le* ~ *i*, the worst.

pégno, *m.* pledge; token. *giuoco dei pegni*, forfeits.

pégola, *f.* (*melted*) pitch.

pèlago (*pl.* **pèlaghi**), *m.* sea (*lit. & fig.*).

pelàme, *m.* hair (*animal*); plumage; (*horse's*) coat.

pelàre (*pr.* **pélo**), *v.t.* to peel; strip; pluck (*fowl*); pare; (*fig.*) fleece. **pelàrsi**, *v.refl.* to lose one's hair; become bald; fall (*leaves*); (*fig.*) to tear one's hair. **pelàta**, *f.* plucking; stripping; (*hum.*) baldness; bald head. **pelatúra**, *f.* peeling; paring; stripping.

pellàgra, *f.* pellagra (*skin disease*). **pellàio** (*pl.* **-ài**), *m.* leather-dresser; l. merchant. **pellàme**, *m.* skins; hides. **pèlle**, *f.* skin; hide; leather; peel, rind.

pellegrína, *f.* female pilgrim; pelerine;

tippet. **pellegrinàggio** (*pl.* **-àggi**), *m.* pilgrimage. **pellegrinàre**, *v.i.* (*aux. avere*) to travel; wander; go on pilgrimage. **pellegríno**, *a.* vagrant; foreign; rare; exquisite. ¶ *m.* pilgrim; traveller.

pellicàno, *m.* pelican.

pelliccería, *f.* furs; furrier's shop. fur-trade. **pellíccia** (*pl.* **-ícce**), *f.* fur; fur coat. **pellicciàio** (*pl.* **-ài**), *m.* furrier. **pelliccióne**, *m.* heavy fur coat.

pellícola, *f.* film; pellicle; membrane. ~ *cinematografica*, cinematograph film. ~*su rocchetto*, roll film (*Phot.*).

pelliróssa (*pl.* **-ósse**), *m.f.* red-skin; North American Indian.

pellúcido, *a.* pellucid; transparent.

pélo, *m.* hair; fur; coat (*animal*); pile, nap; surface (*water*); crack (*in a wall*). ~ *di capra d'Angora*, mohair. *a* ~, bare-back[ed] (*Riding*). *dal* ~ *raso*, short-haired, smooth-haired (*dog*). *con* ~ *ruvido*, ~ *rigido*, rough-haired, wire-haired (*dog*). **pelosità**, *f.* hairiness; shagginess. **pelóso**, *a.* hairy; shaggy.

péltro, *m.* pewter.

péluria, *f.* down; soft hair. **pelúzzo**, *m.* short soft hair; fine cloth.

pèlvi, *f.inv.* pelvis (*Anat.*).

péna, *f.* penalty; punishment; pain; suffering; trouble, distress; sorrow; pity, difficulty. *a mala* ~, hardly, scarcely, barely; with difficulty. *valere la* ~ *di* (with infin.), to be worth . . . *non ne vale la pena*, it is not worth while. **penàle**, *a.* penal; criminal. ¶ *f.* penalty. **penalísta** (*pl.* **-ísti**), *m.* criminal jurist; barrister. **penalità**, *f.* penalty. **penàre**, *v.i.* (*aux. avere*) to suffer; find it difficult; take pains; be hardly able.

penàti, *m.pl.* household gods (*fig.*).

pencolàre (*pr.* **pèncolo**), *v.i.* (*aux. avere*) to hang down; dangle; totter; waver; hesitate; be unsteady.

pendàglio (*pl.* **-àgli**), *m.* pendant; frog (*sword*); (bed)curtain or hanging(s). *pendagli da forca*, gallows-birds.

pendènte, *a.* hanging (down); dangling; drooping; leaning; pending; unsettled; outstanding. *torre* ~, *f.* leaning tower (*Pisa, Bologna*). ¶ *m.* pendant, ear-drop. **pendènza**, *f.* gradient, declivity; slope; affair pending; outstanding balance (*debt*). **pèndere**, *v.i.* (*aux. avere*) to hang,

hang down; lean; incline; slope; be inclined; (*fig.*) be pending. **pendíce,** *f.* declivity, slope. **pendío** (*pl.* -íi), *m.* slant; incline; slope.

pèndola, *f.* pendulum clock. **pendolàre,** *see* penzolare. **pèndolo,** *m.* pendulum. ¶ ~ *or* **pèndulo,** *a.* hanging.

penetràbile, *a.* penetrable. **penetràle,** *m.* innermost recess. **penetrànte,** *a.* penetrating; acute; searching. **penetràre,** *v.i.* (*aux.* essere) *& t.* to penetrate; pierce; break into; permeate; pervade; sink in; fathom; see through. **penetratíva,** *f.* insight; intelligence. **penetrazióne,** *f.* penetration; (*fig.*) insight.

penicillína, *f.* penicillin (*Chem.*). **peninsulàre,** *a.* peninsular. **penísola,** *f.* peninsula.

penitènte, *a. & m.* penitent. **penitènza,** *f.* penitence; penance. **penitenziàle,** *a.* penitential. **penitenziàrio** (*pl.* -àri), *a.* penitentiary. ¶ *m.* penitentiary, reformatory; convict prison.

pénna, *f.* feather; pen; (*fig.*) writer. (*Poet.*) wing. ~ *d'oca,* quill (pen). ~*stilografica,* ~ *a serbatoio,* fountain pen. *scorso di* ~, slip of the pen. ~ *di struzzo,* ostrich feather; **pennacchièra,** *f.* plume on a helmet or horse's head. **pennacchiétto,** *m.* small bunch of feathers, small plume. **pennàcchio** (*pl.* -àcchi), *m.* plume; bunch of feathers; cloud of smoke. **pennacchiúto,** *a.* plumed; adorned with feathers. **pennàccia,** *f.* bad pen. **pennai[u]òlo,** *m.* scribbler; penny-a-liner; pen dealer. **pennàta,** *f.* penful (*of ink*); stroke of a pen.

pennàto, *m.* bill-hook. ¶ *a.* feathered.
pennécchio, *m.* bunch of flax on the distaff.

pennellàre *& ***pennellaggiàre,** *v.i.* (*aux.* avere) *& t.* to paint; work with a brush. **pennellàta,** *f.* brush-stroke; touch of the brush. **pennallatúra,** *f.* brush-work; painting. **pennèllo,** *m.* brush; paint-brush; (*fig.*) painter. *dim.* pennelletto, pennellino.

penníno, *m.* nib; steel-pen. **pennivéndolo,** *m.* scribbler; hack.
pennoncèllo, *m.* small flag; s. plume; streamer. **pennoncíno,** *m.* small yard (*ship*). **pennóne,** *m.* pennon; flag; yard (*of a ship*).
pennúto, *a.* feathered; fledged. ¶ *m.* bird; feathered creature.

penómbra, *f.* twilight; half-light; shade (*fig.*).
penosaménte, *ad.* painfully; with difficulty. **penóso,** *a.* painful; troublesome; difficult.
pensàbile, *a.* thinkable. **pensànte,** *a.* thinking; -minded (*ben(e)* = right). **pensàre,** *v.i.* (*aux.* avere) *& t.* to think; t. out; t. over; imagine; contrive. ~*a,* to think of (persons). ~ *di,* to think of (things); resolve; mean. **pensàta,** *f.* thought; idea. **pensataménte,** *ad.* designedly; intentionally; on purpose. **pensatóio** (*pl.* -ói), *m.* (*hum.*). place where one thinks. *entrare nel* ~, to put on one's thinking-cap. **pensatóre,** *m.* (*f.* -tríce) thinker.
pensièro, *m.* thought; way of thinking; idea, intention; trouble; anxiety. **pensieróso,** *a.* thoughtful; pensive.
pènsile, *a.* hanging. **pensilína,** *f.* projecting roof.
Pensilvània (la), *f.* Pennsylvania.
pensionàre (*pr.* -óno), *v.t.* to pension; p. off. **pensionàrio,** *m.* pensioner; boarder; paying guest. **pensionàto,** *p.a.* pensioned. ¶ *m.* pensioner; boarding-school. **pensióne,** *f.* pension; boarding-house; board [& lodging].
pènso, *m.* (*Sch.*) imposition; lines.
pensóso, *a.* pensive; thoughtful; anxious.
pentàgono, *m.* pentagon. **pentàmetro,** *m.* pentameter.
pentatèuco, *m.inv.* Pentateuch (*O.T.*).
Pentecòste, *f.* Whitsun[tide]; Pentecost.
pentiménto, *m.* repentance. **pentírsi** (*pr.* **pènto**), *v.refl.* to repent; regret.
péntola, *f.* (two-handed) earthenware pot; pot. **pentolàio,** *m.* seller of earthenware; potter. **pentolàta,** *f.* potful. **pentolíno** *o* **péntolo,** *m.* small pot. **pentolóne,** *m.* large pot.
penúltimo, *a. & m.* last but one; penultimate.
penúria, *f.* penury; scarcity; dearth; lack.
penżolàre, *v.i.* (*aux.* avere) to dangle; hang down. **pènżolo,** *a.* hanging down. ¶ *m.* hanging cluster (*of grapes,* &*c.*). **penżolóne** *& ***penżolóni,** *ad. & a.* dangling; drooping.
peònia, *f.* peony (*Bot.*).
pepaiòla, *f.* pepper-pot; p. box, castor. **pepàto,** *a.* peppered; spiced; (*fig.*) spicy; peppery; pungent;

witty. *pan* ~, ginger-bread. **pépe,** *m.* pepper. ~*di Caienna,* ~ *rosso,* Cayenne p., red p. **peperíno,** *a.* pepper-coloured. ¶ *m.* lava; tufa. **peperóne,** *m.* capsicum (*Bot.*); chilli; chilly (*relish*).

pepíta, *f.* nugget (*Min.*).

pepolíno, *m.* thyme (*Bot.*).

pepsína, *f.* pepsin. **pèptico** (*pl.* **pèptici**)*, a.* peptic.

per, *pr.* for; through; by; by way of; on account of; owing to; in return for; by means of; in order to (with infin.). ~ *l'addietro,* ~*l'innanzi,* heretofore, in the past, formerly. ~*l'appunto,* just so! precisely. ~*lo piú,* for the most part; generally. ~ *modo che,* so that. ~*modo di dire,* ~ *cosí dire,* so to speak; as it were. ~ *tempo,* early. *stare* ~ (*with infin.*), to be about to. ~ *cento,* per cent.

péra, *f.* pear; (*fig.*) head.

peránco, *ad.* yet.

perbacco! *i.* by Jove!

percàlle, *m.* cotton cambric. **percallína,** *f.* glazed cotton.

percentuàle, *f.* percentage.

percepíbile, *a.* perceptible; discernable; noticeable. **percepíre** (*pr.* -**ísco, -ísci**)*, v.t. & i.* (*aux.* avere) to perceive; notice; collect; receive, get (*taxes, salary, &c.*). **percettíbile,** *a.* perceptible; noticeable. **percettívo,** *a.* perceptive. **percettóre,** *m.* collector (*taxes. &c.*). **percezióne,** *f.* perception.

perché, *c. & ad.* why; because; since, for; as; that, in order that; so that. ¶ *m. il* ~, the reason.

perciò, *c.* therefore; so; for that reason.

perciocché, *c.* for; as; since.

percórrere (*pr.* -**órro**, *&c.,* like *correre*)*, v.t. ir.* to traverse; travel through (or over); pass through; run through; scour; cover (*distance*); glance through (*book or writing*). **percórso,** *m.* distance; stretch; run; way; course; journey; passage (*by sea*), voyage.

percòssa, *f.* blow; stroke. **percòsso,** *p.p.* of *percuotere.* **perc[u]otere** (*pr.* -**uòto**)*, v.t. ir.* to strike; beat; hit. **percussióne,** *f.* percussion.

perdènte, *a.* losing. ¶ *m. f.* loser. **pèrdere** (*pr.* **pèrdo**)*, v.i.* (*aux.* avere) *& t.* to lose; miss; waste; ruin; (*abs.*) leak. **pèrdersi,** *v.refl.* to lose oneself; get lost; disappear; miscarry; go to ruin. **perdifiàto (a),** at the top (*or* pitch) of one's

voice; with all one's strength. **perdigiórno,** *m.* idler. **pèrdita,** *f.* loss; waste (*time*). **perditèmpo,** *m.* waste of time; time lost. **perditóre,** *m.* (*f.* -**tríce**) loser. **perdizióne,** *f.* perdition; ruin; destruction.

perdonàbile, *a.* pardonable; excusable. **perdonàre** (*pr.* -**óno**)*, v.t. & * ~ **a,** to pardon; forgive; excuse; spare. **perdóno,** *m.* pardon; forgiveness.

perduràre, *v.i.* (*aux.* avere *&* essere) to last; persist; persevere; continue. **perdurévole,** *a.* durable; lasting.

perdutaménte, *ad.* desperately; hopelessly; madly.

peregrinàre, *v.i.* (*aux.* avere) to travel; wander; go abroad. **peregrinazióne,** *f.* peregrination. **peregrinità,** *f.* singularity; rarity. **peregríno,** *a.* rare; precious; uncommon.

perènne, *a.* perennial; perpetual; inexhaustible.

perènto, *p.p.* of *perimere.* ¶ *a.* (*Law*) expired; lapsed; out of date; annulled. **perenzióne,** *f.* (*Law*) annulment; expiry; lapse.

perentòrio (*pl.* -**òri**)*, a.* peremptory.

perequàre (*pr.* **pèrequo**)*, v.t.* to equalize. **perequazióne,** *f.* equalization; equal distribution.

perfettaménte, *ad.* perfectly; completely. **perfettíbile,** *a.* perfectible. **perfètto,** *a.* perfect; full; complete. ¶ *m.* perfect (*tense*).

perfezionàbile, *a.* capable of being perfected, completed or improved. **perfezionaménto,** *m.* improvement; perfecting; specialization; completion. *studi di* ~, advanced studies. **perfezionàre** (*pr.* -**óno**)*, v.t.* to perfect; improve; complete; bring to perfection. **perfezionàrsi,** *v.refl.* to become perfect; acquire a perfect knowledge of (= *in*). **perfezióne,** *f.* perfection; excellence finish, completion.

perfídia, *f.* perfidiousness; treachery; perfidy. **pèrfido,** *a. & m.* treacherous, perfidious (person). *a.* malignant (*disease, &c.*).

perfíne (alla), *ad.* at last; at length. **perfíno,** *ad.* even.

perforàre (*pr.* -**óro**)*, v.t.* to perforate; pierce; drill; punch; bore. ~ *un biglietto,* to punch a ticket. **perforatríce,** *f.* drill (*rock, &c.*).

pergamèna, *f.* parchment. **pergamenàto,** *a.* parchment-like. *carta* ~, **a,** parchment paper.

pèrgola, *f.* pergola; arbour; vine-trellis.

Pèricle, *m.* Pericles.

pericolànte, *a.* tottering; unsafe; unsteady; in danger. **pericolàre** (*pr.* -ícolo), *v.i.* (*aux.* avere) to be in danger; threaten to fall. **perícolo,** *m.* danger; peril. **pericolóso,** *a.* dangerous; risky; perilous.

perièlio (*pl.* -èli), *m.* perihelion (*Astr.*). **perifería,** *f.* periphery; boundary; outskirts.

perifrasi, *f.* periphrasis; roundabout phrase or way of speaking.

períglio, *m.* (*Poet.*) danger; peril.

perimetro, *m.* perimeter.

periòdico (*pl.* -òdici), *a. & m.* periodical; *a.* periodic; recurrent, recurring. **período,** *m.* period, stage; spell; sentence. dim. *periodetto, periodino, perioduccio.*

peripatètico (*pl.* -ètici), *a.* peripatetic. **peripezía,** *f.* vicissitude; change of fortune; (*pl.*) ups and downs.

períre (*pr.* -ísco, -ísci), *v.i.* (*aux.* essere) to perish; be lost; die.

periscòpio (*pl.* -òpi), *m.* periscope.

peristílio (*pl.* -ili), *m.* peristyle (*Arch.*).

peritànza, *f.* hesitation; shyness. **peritàrsi,** *v.refl.* to hesitate; be shy or backward (in *or* about = *a*); have scruples.

perìto, *a.* expert; skilled; skilful. ¶ *m.* expert.

peritonite, *f.* peritonitis.

peritóso, *a.* hesitant; shy.

peritúro, *a.* perishable.

perízia, *f.* skill; expert skill; expert's report; valuation; survey. **periziàre** (*pr.* -ízio, -izi), *v.t.* to estimate; appraise. *corsa periziata, f.* handicap (*horse racing*).

pèrla, *f.* pearl (*lit. & fig.*). dim. *perlina, perletto, perlettina.* **perlàceo,** *a.* pearly. **perlàio,** *m.* worker in pearl; dealer in pearls. **perlàto,** *a.* pearly; adorned with pearls. *orzo ~,* pearl barley.

perlustràre, *v.t.* to reconnoitre; search; patrol (*police*). **perlustrazióne,** *f.* reconnaissance; reconnoitring; patrol.

permalóso, *a.* irritable; touchy.

permanènte, *a.* permanent; lasting; standing. **permanènza,** *f.* permanence, -ency; stay; residence. **permanére** (*pr.* -àngo, &c., like *rimanere*), *v.i. ir.* (*aux.* essere) to remain; stay; last; persist.

permeàbile, *a.* permeable. **permeàre,** *v.t.* to permeate.

permésso, *m.* permission; leave; leave of absence; licence; permit. *~! i,* excuse me, allow me. **perméttere** (*pr.* -étto, &c., like *mettere*), *v.t. ir.* to allow, permit; may. **permissíbile,** *a.* allowable; permissible.

pèrmuta, *f.* exchange; barter. **permutàbile,** *a.* exchangeable. **permutàre** (*pr.* pèrmuto), *v.t.* to exchange; barter; remove; rearrange; permute. **permutazióne,** *f.* permutation; transposition; exchange.

perníce, *f.* partridge. **perniciósa,** *f.* (for *febbre ~a*) malignant fever.

pèrnio & pèrno, *m.* pivot; axis, hinge; support; stud, stud-bolt; (*fig.*) turning point. dim. *pernetto, pernietto.*

pernottaménto, *m.* stay during the night; passing the night. **pernottàre** (*pr.* -òtto), *v.i.* (*aux.* avere) to pass the night.

péro, *m.* pear tree.

però, *c.* however; but; yet; therefore; on that account. **perocché,** *c.* because; for; as, since.

peroràre (*pr.* -òro), *v.i.* (*aux.* avere) *& t.* to plead; defend (*a case*); perorate, close a speech. **perorazióne,** *f.* peroration; pleading; defence.

peròssido, *m.* peroxide.

perpendicolàre, *a. & f.* perpendicular. **perpendícolo (a),** *ad. expr.* perpendicularly.

perpetràre (*pr.* pèrpetro), *v.t.* to perpetrate; commit (*crime, offence*).

perpètua, *f.* (priest's) housekeeper (after Perpetua, a character in Manzoni's *I Promessi Sposi*). **perpetuàre** (*pr.* -ètuo), *v.t.* to perpetuate. **perpetuità,** *f.* perpetuity. **perpètuo,** *a.* perpetual, permanent; constant; for life; everlasting. *in ~,* perpetually; for ever; in perpetuity.

perplessità, *f.* perplexity. **perplèsso,** *a.* perplexed, uneasy; puzzled; baffled.

perquisíre (*pr.* -ísco, -ísci), *v.t.* (*Law*) to search. **perquisizióne,** *f.* perquisition; search. *mandato di ~,* search-warrant.

perscrutàre (*pr.* -úto), *v.t.* to investigate; search.

persecutóre, *m.* (*f.* -tríce) persecutor. **persecuzióne,** *f.* persecution.

perseguíre (*pr.* -séguo, -ségui, *&c.*, like *seguire*), *v.t.* to pursue (*lit. & fig.*); follow; continue; (*Law*) prosecute.

perseguitàre (*pr.* -éguito), *v.t.* pursue; persecute.

perseveràute, *a.* persevering. **perseverànza**, *f.* perseverance. **perseveràre** (*pr.* -èvero), *v.i.* (*aux.* avere) to persevere.

persiàna, *f.* shutter; sun-shutter; Venetian blind.

persiàno, *a. & m.* Persian. *il ~, la lingua ~ a*, Persian, the Persian language.

pèrsico (*pl.* pèrsici), Persian. *pesce ~*, perch (*fish*). *il Golfo ~*, the Persian Gulf.

persíno, *ad.* even.

persistènte, *a.* persisting; persistent. **persistènza**, *f.* persistence, -cy. **persístere** (*pr.* -ísto, *&c.*, like *assistere*), *v.i.* (*aux.* avere) to persist.

pèrso, *p.p.* of *perdere.* ¶ *a.* (*Poet.*) deep purple (verging on black).

persóna, *f.* person; body; figure; self. *di ~, in ~*, personally. *per ~*, per head, apiece. **personàggio** (*pl.* -àggi), *m.* personage; character (*Theat.*); (*pl.*) dramatis personae. **personàle**, *a.* personal. ¶ *m.* staff; personnel; figure (*bodily shape*). **personalità**, *f.inv.* personality; (*pl.*) well-known people. **personificàre** (*pr.* -ífico, -ífichi), *v.t.* to personify; impersonate.

perspicàce, *a.* perspicacious, discerning, shrewd. **perspicàcia**, *f.* perspicacity.

perspicuità, *f.* perspicuity. **perspícuo**, *a.* perspicuous; clear; clear in expression.

persuadére (*pr.* -uàdo, *&c.*, like *dissuadere*), *v.t. ir.* to persuade; convince. **persuasióne**, *f.* persuasion; conviction. **persuasíva**, *f.* persuasiveness.

pertànto, *c.* on that account, therefore, consequently. *non~*, nevertheless.

pèrtica (*pl.* pèrtiche), *f.* pole; rod; perch (*Meas.*) (Eng. 5½ yds.; square p. 30¼ sq. yds. Milanese *c.* 6½ are). **perticàta**, *f.* blow with a pole. **perticóne**, *m.* long pole; (*fig.*) tall thin fellow.

pertinàce, *a.* pertinacious. **pertinàcia**, *f.* pertinacity.

pertinénza, *f.* pertinence, -cy; competence.

pertòsse, *f.* whooping-cough.

pertúgio (*pl.* -úgi), *m.* aperture; hole; opening.

perturbàre, *v.t.* to perturb; agitate; upset (*fig.*). **perturbazióne**, *f.* perturbation, disturbance.

Perú (il), *m.* Peru.

perugíno, *a.* of Perugia. ¶ *m.* native of P.

peruviàno, *a. & m.* Peruvian.

pervàdere, *v.t. ir.* to pervade; penetrate; permeate.

perveníre (*pr.* -èngo, *&c.*, like *venire*), *v.i. ir.* (*aux.* essere) to arrive (*with effort*). ~*a*, reach, attain (to).

perversióne, *f. & pervertiménto*, *m.* perversion. **perversità**, *f.* perverseness; perversity; wickedness. **pervèrso**, *a.* perverse; wicked; bad. **pervertíre** (*pr.* -ísco, -ísci), *v.t.* to pervert; lead astray. **pervertíto**, *m.* pervert; apostate.

pervicàce, *a.* obstinate. **pervicàcia**, *f.* obstinacy.

pervínca (*pl.* -vínche), *f.* periwinkle (*Bot.*).

pésa, *f.* weighing-machine; weigh-house. **pesàggio**, *m.* weighing; (*Turf*) w.-in; w.-in room. **pesalèttere**, *m.inv.* letter-balance, l. scales. **pesànte**, *a.* heavy; weighty; ponderous; wearisome. **pesanteménte**, *ad.* heavily; ponderously; weightily. **pesantézza**, *f.* heaviness; weight; dullness; tiresomeness. **pesàre** (*pr.* péso), *v.t.* to weigh (*lit. & fig.*); ponder. *v.i.* (*aux.* avere & essere) to weigh; lie heavy; bear; press. **pesàta** *& pesatúra*, *f.* weighing.

pèsca (*pl.* pèsche), *f.* peach.

pésca, *f.* fishing; fishery; catch (*fish*). ~*con la lenza*, angling. ~*della balena*, whale-fishery; w.-fishing. *barca da ~*, fishing boat. **pescàggio**, *m.* draught (*ship*). **pescagióne**, *f.* fishing; draught (*ship*). **pescàia**, *f.* dam; weir. **pescàre** (*pr.* pésco, péschi), *v.i.* (*aux.* avere) *& t.* to fish; (*fig.*) fish up; pick up; fish out; find; catch; draw (*of ship*). **pescàta**, *f.* catch; draught (*of fishes*). **pescatóre**, *m.* (*f.* -tríce) fisherman, fisher. *martin ~*, kingfisher (*bird*). **pésce** (*pl.* pésci), *m.* fish. *giocare ad uno un ~d'aprile*, to make an April fool of one. ~ *d'acqua dolce*, freshwater fish. ~ *di mare*, salt-water fish, sea-fish. [~] *persico*, perch. ~*rosso*, gold-fish. **pescecàne** (*pl.* -àni), *m.* shark; dog-fish; (*fig.*) (war) profiteer.

pescheréccio (*pl.* -écci), *a.* fishing;

engaged in fishing. *barca* ~*ia, f.*
fishing boat. **peschería,** *f.* fish-
market; f. shop. **peschièra,** *f.*
fish-pond; fishery. **pesciai[u]òla,** *f.*
fish-kettle. **pesciai[u]òlo,** *m.* fish-
monger. **pescicoltúra,** *f.* fish-
culture. **pesciolíno,** *m.* small fish;
(*pl.*) fry; whitebait. **pescivéndola,**
f. fish-woman; fish-wife. **pesci-**
véndolo, *m.* fish-hawker.
pèsco (*pl.* **pèschi**), *m.* peach tree.
pescóso, *a.* abounding in fish, full of
fish.
péso, *m.* weight (*lit. & fig.*), burden;
load. *a* ~, by weight. *di* ~, of full
weight. *pigliar di* ~, *levare di* ~, to
lift up, carry away bodily. ~*netto*,
net weight. ~*lordo*, gross weight.
~*morto*, dead w. (*lit. & fig.*).
~*specifico*, specific gravity. (*Sport*)
~*mosca*, fly-weight. ~ *piuma*,
feather-weight. ~*leggiero*, light w.
~*medio*, middle w. ~ *massimo*,
heavy w.
pessimaménte, *ad.* very badly.
pessimísmo, *m.* pessimism. **pessi-**
místa (*pl.* **-ísti**), *m.* pessimist.
pessimístico (*pl.* **-ístici**), *a.* pessi-
mistic. **pèssimo,** *a.* very bad;
wicked; foul. *il* ~, *la* ~*a*; (*pl.*)
i ~ *i, le* ~ *e,* the worst.
pésta, *f.* [beaten] track; trace; foot-
print; footstep. *sulle peste di,* on the
track of. *trovarsi nelle peste,* to find
oneself in difficulties. **pestaménto,**
m. pounding; crushing; treading;
stamping (*feet*). **pestàre** (*pr.*
pésto), *v.t.* to pound; stamp (*feet*);
tread [up]on; trample (on). **pestàta**
*& ***pestatúra,** *f.* pounding; crushing;
trampling.
pèste, *f.* plague; pestilence; pest (*lit.*
& fig.); stench. ~ *bovina,* cattle
plague, rinderpest.
pestèllo, *m.* pestle.
pestilènte, *a.* pestilent. **pestilènza,**
f. pestilence; plague; foul odour.
pestilenziàle, *a.* pestilential.
pestío, *m.* (constant) pounding;
trampling; stamping (*feet*).
pésto, *sync. p.* of *pestare.* ¶ *a.* crushed,
trampled; (*fig.*) black and blue;
aching. *carta* ~*a,* papier-maché.
¶ *m.* pulped rags for paper making;
strong sauce with basil and much
garlic, characteristic of the Genoese
cookery. **Pésto,** *f.* Paestum (*Geog.*).
pestóne, *m.* rammer.
pètalo, *m.* petal.
petàrdo, *m.* petard; cracker (*firework*);
fog-signal.

petènte, *m.f.* petitioner. **petizióne,** *f.*
petition. ~*di principio,* begging the
question.
petràia, *f.* stone quarry; heap of
stones.
Petràrca, *m.* Petrarch. **petrarcheg-**
giàre, *v.i.* (*aux.* avere) to imitate
Petrarch; write in the Petrarchan
manner. **petrarchésco** (*pl.* **-éschi**),
a. Petrarchan; Petrarch's. **petrifi-**
care, see *pietrificare.*
petrolièra (**nave**), *f.* tanker; tank-
steamer. **petrolière,** *m.* incendiary.
petrolífero, *a.* rich in petroleum;
oil-bearing. *pozzo* ~, oil-well.
azioni ~ *e, f.pl., valori* ~ *i, m.pl.*
oil-shares.
petróso, *a.* stony. Cf. *pietroso.*
pettégola, *f.* gossiping woman; gossip.
pettegolare *& ***pettegoleggiàre,**
v.i. (*aux.* avere) to gossip. **pettego-**
làta, *f.* gossip (*talk*). **pettegolézzo,**
m. trivial gossip, tittle-tattle; petty
wrangling. **pettegolío,** *m.* gossiping.
pettégolo, *m.* (*pers.*) gossiper;
gossip; tattler. ¶ *a.* talkative;
gossiping; tale-bearing.
pettinàre (*pr.* **pèttino**), *v.t.* to comb;
scratch; card; dress (*wool*); (*fig.*)
scold; find fault with. **pettinàta,** *f.*
combing; (*fig.*) scolding, dressing
down.
pettinatóre, *m.* *& ***pettinatríce,** *f.*
hair-dresser. **pettinatúra,** *f.*
combing; carding; dressing (*hair,*
wool); coiffure. **pèttine,** *m.* comb.
pèttina, *f.* small comb, pocket-
comb. **pettinèlla,** *f.* fine-tooth
comb. **pettinièra,** *f.* comb-case.
pettirósso, *m.* robin [redbreast].
pètto, *m.* breast; chest; (*fig.*) heart.
malattie di ~, pulmonary or chest
diseases. *mal di* ~, consumption.
a~ *a*~, face to face. **pettoràle,** *m.*
breastplate; breast-band (*horse*);
pectoral (*Eccl.*). ¶ *a.* breast (*att.*)
pectoral (*Anat.*). **pettorúto,** *m.*
proud; haughty; with the chest
thrown out.
petulànte, *a.* arrogant; overbearing;
impertinent. **petulànza,** *f.* arrogance; impertinence.
pèzza, *f.* piece (or roll) (*paper or cloth,*
ribbon, &c.); cloth; piece of cloth;
cutting; patch; (*child's*) wrapper;
dressing (*wound*); (*fig.*) time. *gran*
~, *buona* ~, *lunga* ~, long time.
pezzàto, *a.* speckled; spotted;
dappled; pied. **pezzatúra,** *f.*
dappled effect; speckling; spotting.
pezzènte, *m.* ragamuffin; mendicant.

pezzentería, *f.* beggary; crowd of beggars.

pezzettíno, *m.* tiny bit; very small piece. **pezzétto,** *m.* bit; small piece; scrap. **pèzzo,** *m.* piece; portion; fragment; coin; cannon; literary or musical composition; man (*chess*, *draughts*); space of time; short article (*journal*). *tutto d'un* ~, all of a piece; (*fig.*) of sterling character. ~ *a* ~, piece by piece. ~ *grosso*, important person, bigwig. ~ *di ricambio*, ~ *di rispetto*, spare part, s. piece.

pezz[u]òla, *f.* handkerchief.

piacènte, *a.* pleasing; pleasant; agreeable.

piacentíno, *a.* of Piacenza. **¶** *m.* native of P. **piacére** (*pr.* **piàccio, piàci**), *v.i. ir.* (*aux.* essere) to please; be pleasing. *fate come vi piace*, do as you like. **piacere (a)** to please (*v.t.*). *vi piace la musica?* do you like music? *piacesse a Dio che fosse così!* would to God it were so! **¶** *m.* pleasure; delight; convenience; favour; kindness; amusement; enjoyment. *per* ~, please; if you please. **piacévole,** *a.* pleasant; agreeable; graceful; pretty. **piacevoleggiàre,** *v.i.* (*aux.* avere) to joke; jest; indulge in pleasantries. **piacevolézza,** *f.* charm; agreeableness; pleasantness; gracefulness. **piaciménto,** *m.* pleasure; liking.

piàga (*pl.* **piàghe**), *f.* sore; wound; (*fig.*) evil; calamity; bore (*pers.*). dim. *piaghetta.* **piagàre** (*pr.* **-àgo, -àghi**), *v.t.* to produce a sore; ulcerate.

piaggería, *f.* flattery.

piàggia (*pl.* **-piàgge**), *f.* declivity; slope; (*Poet.*) (sea) shore.

piaggiàre, *v.t.* to flatter; coax. **piaggiatóre,** *m.* (*f.* **-tríce**) flatterer.

piagnistèo, *m.* whining; crying.

piagnolóso, *a.* mournful; tearful. **piagnóne,** *m.* (*f.* **-óna**) hired mourner; mute at a funeral; tearful person. **piagnucolàre,** *v.i.* (*aux.* avere) to whimper; whine; cry (*child*). **piagnucolío,** *m.* constant whimpering. **piagnucolóne,** *m.* (*f.* **-óna**) whiner; whimperer. **piagnucolóso,** *a.* whining; whimpering; tearful.

piagóso, *a.* full of sores.

piàlla, *f.* plane (*tool*). **piallàccio,** *m.* veneer. **piallàre,** *v.t.* to plane. **piallàta,** *f.* planing; stroke with a plane. **piallatríce,** *f.* planing-

machine. **piallatúra,** *f.* planing; (*wood*) shavings. **piallóne,** *m.* jack-plane.

piaménte, *ad.* piously; devoutly.

piàna, *f.* plain; level ground; plank. **pianaménte,** *ad.* quietly; softly; gently; smoothly; simply. **pianàre,** *v.t.* to smooth; flatten (*metal*); level. **pianeggiàre,** *v.i.* (*aux.* avere) to be nearly flat; be level; be even.

pianèlla, *f.* slipper; flat tile.

pianeròttolo, *m.* staircase landing.

pianéta (*pl.* **-éti**), *m.* planet. **¶** *f.* chasuble (*Eccl.*).

pianézza, *f.* smoothness; flatness; clearness; easiness; ease.

piangènte, *p.a.* weeping; in tears. **piàngere,** *v.i. ir.* (*aux.* avere) to weep; mourn; cry. *v.t.* to lament; bewail; mourn for; weep over; shed (*tears*). **piangolóso,** *a.* whining; whimpering.

pianificàre, *v.t.* to plan. **pianificazióne,** *f.* (*oft. pl.*) planning. ~*i postbelliche, f.pl.* post-war planning.

pianigiàno, *a.* lowland, inhabiting the plain(s). **¶** *m.* inhabitant of the plain[s], lowlander.

pianíno, *ad.* slowly; softly. **pianíssimo,** *ad.* very slowly, v. softly. **pianísta** (*pl.* **-isti**), *m. f.* pianist.

piàno, *a.* level; flat; smooth; even; (*Geom.*) plane; clear; plain; easy; simple; unassuming; low (*voice*); (*Gram.*) accented on the last syllable but one. *corsa* ~*a*, flat race. **¶** *ad.* softly; gently; slowly; quietly; in a low voice. *pian* ~, very gently; v. softly. **¶** *m.* plane; level; floor, stor[e]y; plan; project; scheme; (*for* pianoforte) piano. *in* ~, horizontally. *a* ~, on the ground floor. *al primo* ~, on the first floor. ~*di guerra*, plan of campaign. *primo* ~, (*cinema*) close-up. **pianofòrte** (*pl.* **pianofòrti**), *m.* piano; pianoforte. ~*a coda*, grand piano. ~*verticale*, upright p.

piànta, *f.* plant; tree; plan, ground plan; map (*town, &c.*); list; sole (*foot*). *di prima* ~, in the first sketch. *di sana* ~, completely; anew; afresh; from the beginning. ~ *stradale*, road map. dim. *pianticella, pianticina, piantina.* **piantagióne,** *f.* plantation. **piantàre,** *v.t.* to plant, place; put, fix, plunge, thrust; pitch (*tent, lit. & fig.*); set up; leave (in the lurch); quit, abandon. ~*gli occhi addosso a*, to stare at. ~*una casa lussuosa*, to set up an expensive establishment. **piantàta,** *f.* planting; row of plants. **piantatóre,** *m.* planter.

pianterréno, *m.* ground floor.

piànto, *m.* weeping; tears; plaint.

piantonàia, *f.* nursery (*plants*). **piantonàre,** *v.t.* to mount guard over. **piantóne,** *m.* (*plant*) cutting; shoot; watchman; soldier on guard.

pianúra, *f.* (wide) plain; open plain.

piàstra, *f.* slab; metal plate; breastplate; piastre (*coin*). ∼ *su ghiaccio,* curling (*Sport*). dim. **piastrella,** *f.* quoit.

piastríccio, *m.* medley; hotch-potch. **piastricciàno,** *m.* blockhead. **piastróne,** *m.* large metal plate; flag-stone; breastplate; (*fencing*) plastron; front (*shirt, &c.*).

piàtta, *f.* pontoon. **piattafórma,** *f.* platform.

piattàia, *f.* plate-rack. **piattàio,** *m.* crockery-seller.

piattíno, *m.* small plate; saucer. **piàtto,** *a.* flat (*lit. & fig.*) dull; uninspired. ¶ *m.* plate; dish (*of food*); scale-pan; cymbal (*Mus.*).

piàttola, *f.* black-beetle; cockroach; crab-louse; (*fig.*) bore (*pers.*). **piattalóso,** *a.* lousy.

piattonàre, *v.t.* to strike with the flat of the sword.

piàzza, *f.* square; market (place); mob, rabble; clearing (*in forest*); bald patch. ∼ *d'arrivo,* putting green (*Golf*). far ∼ *pulita,* to make a clean sweep. ∼ *d'armi,* parade ground; drill ground. *vettura di* ∼, cab. *prezzo di* ∼, market price. dim. *piazzetta, piazzettina, piazzuola.* **piazzafòrte,** *f.* fortified town; fortress; stronghold. **piazzaiolàta & piazzàta,** *f.* street squabble; scene; row. **piazzaiòlo,** *m.* street loafer; cad. **piazzàle,** *m.* large square; open space, esplanade. **piazzàrsi,** *v.refl.* (*Sport*) to be placed. **piazzísta,** *m.* commercial traveller; canvasser. **piazzuòla,** *f.* small square. ∼*di partenza,* tee (*Golf*).

píca, *f.* magpie.

Pic[c]ardía (la), *f.* Picardy.

pícca (*pl.* **pícche**), *f.* pike (*weapon*); pique, spite; tiff; (*pl.*) spades (*cards*). *mettere a* ∼, to provoke; irritate.

piccànte, *a.* stinging; cutting; pointed; pungent; racy; piquant. **piccàre,** *v.t.* to prick; sting; pique; nettle; irritate. **piccàrsi,** *v.refl.* to be

piqued; to be offended. ∼ *di,* to plume oneself on.

picchettàre, *v.t.* to picket; mark out with stakes; spot, speckle. **picchétto,** *m.* picket (*Mil.*); stake; piquet (*game*). ∼ *d'onore,* guard of honour.

picchiaménto, *m.* knocking; hitting; striking. **picchiapètto,** *m.* hypocrite. **picchiàre,** *v.t.* to knock; strike; hit; beat; tap. **picchiàta,** *f.* knock; stroke; blow; (*Aviat.*) dive. **picchierellàre,** *v.t. & i.* (*aux.* avere) to tap (*with hammer*). **picchierèllo,** *m.* sculptor's hammer. **picchiettàre,** *v.t. & i.* (*aux.* avere) to tap; drum; spot, speckle. **picchiettàto,** *a.* speckled, spotted. **picchiettío,** *m.* (constant) tapping; drumming. **pícchio,** *m.* woodpecker; knock; knocker. *di* ∼, all of a sudden. **picchiòtto,** *m.* (door) knocker.

piccinería, *f.* meanness; pettiness; mean action. **piccíno,** *a.* small; tiny. *vino* ∼, light wine. ¶ *m.* little boy, child, little one.

piccíolo, *a.* (*Poet.*) small; little. ¶ *m.* small coin; farthing.

piccionàia, *f.* pigeon-house; dovecote; gallery (*Theat.*). **piccióne,** *m.* pigeon. ∼ *viaggiatore,* carrierpigeon. dim. *piccioncino.*

picci[u]òlo, *m.* stalk (*Bot.*).

pícco, *m.* peak; gaff (*Naut.*). *a* ∼, vertically. *andare, mandare a* ∼, to go, send, to the bottom.

piccolézza, *f.* smallness; pettiness; meanness; mean act; trifle. **piccolíno,** *a.* small; tiny; young. **píccolo,** *a.* little; small; short; diminutive; young; scanty; slight; low; slow; petty; light; mean; narrow. ∼ *borghese,* person of modest means. ∼*possidente,* small landowner. ∼*e spese, f.pl.* petty expenses. *a* ∼*a velocità,* by slow train, by goods train. ¶ *m.* boy, little boy. *i piccoli,* the children, the little ones; the young (*of an animal*).

picconàta, *f.* blow with a pick-axe. **piccóne,** *m.* pick-axe; mattock; stone-mason's hammer. **picconière,** *m.* sapper; miner.

piccosità, *f.* touchiness; peevishness. **piccóso,** *a.* touchy; peevish.

piccòzza, *f.* hatchet; ice-axe.

píceo, *a.* pitch black; pitchy.

pidocchiería, *f.* stinginess; meanness; mean action. **pidòcchio,** *m.* louse.

pidocchióso, *a.* lousy; (*fig.*) mean, dirty, miserly.

piède, *m.* foot (*lit. & fig.*), trotter; base; bottom; leg (*chair, &c.*,); stalk (*glass*); ground; footing; foothold; stand; standard. *a ~ i*, on foot. *corsa a ~ i*, foot-race. *salto a ~ i giunti*, standing jump. *posti in ~ i*, standing room (*Theat.*). *avere il ~ marino*, to have (get) one's sea-legs. **piedilúvi**, *m.inv.* foot-bath. **piedistàllo**, *m.* pedestal.

pièga (*pl.* **pièghe**), *f.* fold; crease; plait, pleat; wrinkle; bend; (*fig.*) turn. **piegàbile**, *a.* flexible; pliable. **piegaménto**, *m.* folding; bending; flexion (*Anat.*). **piegàre** (*pr.* **piègo**, **pièghi**), *v.t.* to fold; fold up; bend; *v.i.* (*aux.* avere) turn; give way; lean; submit. **piegàrsi**, *v.refl.* to submit; yield; bow; bend; crease; fold up. **piegàta**, *f.* bend, folding. **piegatóre**, *m.* (*f.* -**tríce**) folder (*pers.*); -**tríce**, *f.* (*Typ.*) folding-machine. **piegatúra**, *f.* folding; bending. **pieghettàre**, *v.t.* to plait. **pieghévole**, *a.* pliable; pliant; flexible; supple; folding; yielding; submissive. *sedia ~*, folding chair. **pieghevolézza**, *f.* pliability; flexibility; submissiveness. **pieghevolménte**, *ad.* flexibly; submissively. **piègo** (*pl.* **pièghi**), *m.* cover; wrapper; envelope; packet (*papers*).

Piemónte (il), *m.* Piedmont. **piemontése**, *a. & m.* Piedmontese.

pièna, *f.* flood; overflow; spate; crowd. **pienaménte**, *ad.* fully; completely; quite. **pienézza**, *f.* fullness; abundance. **pièno**, *a.* full. ¶ *m.* fullness; perfection; height; depth (*fig.*). **pienòtto**, *a.* plump.

pietà, *f.* pity; mercy; piety; (*Art*) the dead Christ. *per ~!* for pity's sake! *senza ~*, (*a.*) pitiless, (*ad.*) pitilessly. *monte di ~*, pawnbroker's shop. **pietànza**, *f.* dish, portion, plate (*of meat*).

pietosaménte, *ad.* compassionately; mercifully; piteously; pitiably. **pietóso**, *a.* compassionate; merciful; piteous; pitiable; pitiful, sorry.

piètra, *f.* stone. *~per affilare*, whet-stone; grindstone. *~focaia*, flint. *~calcare*, limestone. *~del focolare*, hearth-stone. *~da taglio*, freestone. *~dello scandalo*, stumbling block, rock of offence. *~lunare*, moon-stone. *~miliare*, milestone. *~da mulino*, millstone (or, *macina di~*).

~ sepolcrale, tombstone. *~di paragone*, touchstone (*lit. & fig.*). *~ filosofale*, philosopher's stone. *~preziosa*, precious stone; gem. **pietràme**, *m.* heap of stones. **pietrificàre**, *v.t.* to petrify.

Piètro, *m.* Peter.

pietróso, *a.* see *petroso*.

pievàno, *m.* rector; parish-priest. **pième**, *f.* parish; p. church.

pifferàio & **pifferàro**, *m.* piper. **piffero**, *m.* pipe (*instr.*); piper.

pigiàma, *m.inv.* pyjama[s].

pigiaménto, *m.* pressing; squeezing; crushing. **pigia pigia**, *m.* crush; press; dense crowd. **pigiàre**, *v.t.* to press (*grapes, &c.*). squeeze; crush. **pigiàrsi**, *v.refl.* to crowd, crush. **pigiàta**, *f.* squeeze. **pigiatóre**, *m.* (*wine*) presser; squeezer. **pigiatríce**, *f.* wine-press. **pigiatúra**, *f.* pressing; crushing.

pigionàle, *m.* tenant; lodger. **pigióne**, *f.* rent.

pigliàre, *v.t.* to take; catch; seize. *pigliarla per uno*, to take one's part. *pigliarsela con uno*, to throw the blame on one; get angry with one. **pigliàrsi**, *v.refl.* to take; catch (*cold, &c.*); come to an understanding; marry. **píglio**, *m.* hold; catch; look; bearing. *dar di ~ a*, to seize hold of.

Pigmalióne, *m.* Pygmalion.

pigménto, *m.* pigment.

pigmèo, *m.* pigmy.

pignàtta, *f.* pot; cooking-pot; kitchen-pot.

pignoràre, *v.t.* (*Law*) to distrain.

pigolaménto, *m.* chirping; cheeping; chirruping. **pigolàre**, *v.i.* (*aux.* avere) to chirp; cheep; chirrup; pipe (*birds*), &c. **pigolío** (*pr.* -**ii**), *m.* constant chirping, &c.

pigrézza, *f.* sluggishness.

pigraménte, *ad.* lazily; sluggishly. **pigrízia**, *f.* laziness; sloth; idleness. **pígro**, *a.* lazy; indolent; slothful; sluggish.

píla, *f.* heap, pile; (*Elec.*) battery, cell, pile; pier (*bridge*), buttress; basin, font. *~ di ricambio*, refill (*Elec. torch*).

pilastràta, *f.* row of (small) pillars. **pilastríno**, *m.* small pillar; post. **pilàstro**, *m.* pillar; pilaster; square column.

Pilàto, *m.* Pilate. *mandar da Erode a ~*, to send from pillar to post.

pillàcchera, *f.* splash (of mud). **pillaccheróso**, *a.* splashed with mud.

pillàre, *v.t.* to tread; ram; ram down.
píllo, *m.* rammer.
píllela, *f.* pill.   dim.   *pilloletta,*
pillolina.
pillottàre, *v.t.* to baste (*meat*).
pillòtto, *m.* basting-ladle; dripping-
pan.
pílo, *m.* javelin.   **pilóne,** *m.* pillar;
pylon; pier (*bridge*); tower; rammer.
~d'ormeggio, mooring-mast.
pilòta (*pl.* -òti), *m.* pilot.   **pilotàggio,**
m. pilotage.   *scuola di ~,* *f.* flying
school.   **pilotàre,** *v.t.* to pilot (*lit.*
& *fig.*); (*Aero.*) fly.
piluccàre (*pr.* -úcco, -úcchi), *v.t.*
to pluck; pick; pick out; p. up.
piluccàrsi, *v.refl.* to tear out one's
hair.   **piluccatóre** (*f.* -tríce), *m.*
picker.   ¶ *a.* picking.   **piluccóne,** *n.*
confirmed beggar.
piménto, *m.* allspice; Jamaica pepper,
red pepper.   **pimpinèlla,** *f.*
pimpernel.
pína, *f.* pine-cone.
pinacotèca (*pl.* -èche), *f.* picture-
gallery.
pindàrico (*pl.* -àrici), *a.* Pindaric.
Píndaro, *m.* Pindar.
pinéta, *f.* & **pinéto,** *m.* pine wood;
pine forest.
pingere (*pr.* -ingo, -íngi), *v.t.* & *i.ir.*
(*aux.* avere) to paint; push.
píngue, *a.* fat, corpulent; rich; large.
pinguèdine, *f.* fatness; corpulence.
pinguíno, *m.* penguin.
pinífero, *a.* pine-bearing.
pínna, *f.* fin; (*pl.*) outer walls of the
nose.
pinnàcolo, *m.* pinnacle.
píno, *m.* pine (*tree, wood*); (*Poet.*) ship.
pinòcchio, *m.* pine-seed.   **P~,**
Pinocchio, title of a work by Collodi
(Carlo Lorenzini).
pínta, *f.* pint; (measure of capacity
varying from Eng. p. of (approx.)
½ litre to that of Modena, 2¼
litres.)
pínza, *f.* pliers.   **pínze,** *f.pl.* pincers;
forceps;   (*Typ.*) gripper.   dim.
pinzètte, small pincers, tweezers.
pío, *a.* pious, devout; obedient;
dutiful; compassionate; charitable.
P~, *m.* Pius.
pioggerèlla, *f.* drizzle; fine rain.
pióggia (*pl.* piógge), *f.* rain.   *una*
~ dirotta, heavy rain; a downpour.
scroscio di ~, shower.
piombàggine, *f.* plumbago; blacklead;
graphite.   **piombàre,** *v.t.* to plumb;
to affix a leaden seal to; cover with
lead; stop (*tooth*); *v.i.* (*aux.* essere)

to fall (suddenly or heavily); plunge;
pounce; sink like lead.   *~ su,*
~ addosso, to assail.   **piombatúra,**
f. sealing; soldering; plumbing;
leading.   **piombífero,** *a.* lead-
bearing.   **piombíno,** *m.* plummet;
plumb-line; leaden seal.   **piómbo,**
m. lead; shot; plummet; plumb-line.
a ~, perpendicularly.   *di ~,*
violently.
pionière, *m.* sapper; pioneer.
pioppàia, *f.* & **pioppéto,** *m.* poplar-
grove.   **pióppo,** *m.* poplar.
pióta, *f.* sod; sole of the foot.   **piotàre,**
v.t. to turf.
piovàna (**acqua**), *f.* rain-water.
piovàno, *m.* parson; curate.
piovènte, *m.* pitch or slope of a roof.
piòvere (*pr.* **piòvo, piòvi, piòve**),
v.i. ir. (*aux.* essere & avere) to rain
(*lit.* & *fig.*); drip; descend; slope
(*mountain or roof*).   *v.t.* to rain; let
fall; pour out.   **piovigginàre,** *v.i.*
(*aux.* avere & essere) to drizzle.
piovigginóso, *a.* rainy; drizzling.
piovórno, *a.* (*sky*) full of watery
clouds; of rain.   **piovóso,** *a.* rainy;
wet.
piòvra, *f.* octopus; (*fig.*) blood-
sucker.   **piovúta,** *f.* rainfall.
pípa, *f.* pipe; tobacco-pipe.   **pipàre,**
v.i. (*aux.* avere) to smoke a pipe.
pipàta, *f.* pipeful; smoke.   dim.
pipatina.   **pipétta,** *f.* small pipe;
(*Chem.*) pipette.
pipistrèllo, *m.* bat (*Zool.*); sleeveless
cloak.
pipíta, *f.* pip (*fowls*); agnail (*loose skin*
at the base of the human nail).
pira, *f.* pyre; funeral pile.
piramidàle, *a.* pyramidal.   **pirà-**
mide, *f.* pyramid.
piràta (*pl.* -àti), *m.* pirate.   **pirateg-**
giàre, *v.i.* (*aux.* avere) to pirate;
practise piracy.   **piratería,** *f.*
piracy.   **piratésco** (*pl.* -éschi) &
piràtico (*pl.* -àtici), *a.* piratic(al).
Pirenèi (**i**), *m.pl.* the Pyrenees.
Pirèo (**il**), *m.* the Piraeus.
pirite, *f.* pyrites.
piroétta, *f.* pirouette.   **piroettàre,**
v.i. (*aux.* avere) to pirouette.
piròga, *f.* (native) canoe.
piròscafo, *m.* steamer; steamship;
steamboat.
pirotecnía & **pirotècnica,** *f.* pyrotechnics; fireworks.   **pirotècnico**
(*pl.* -tècnici), *a.* pyrotechnic; firework (*att.*).
pisciatóio, *m.* urinal.
piscína, *f.* fish-pond; swimming pool

pisellàta, *f.* dish of peas. **pisèllo,** *m.* pea. *zuppa di* ~ *i,* *f.* pea soup.

pisolàre, *v.i.* (*aux.* avere) to snooze; doze. **pisolíno, písolo,** *m.* snooze; doze; nap.

pispigliàre, *v.i.* (*aux.* avere) to whisper. **pispíglio,** *m.* whisper, whispering. **-ío,** *m.* (continual) whispering.

písside, *f.* pyx.

písta, *f.* track (*running, racing*); run (*toboggan*); race-course, course; track, trail; scent; clue. ~ *di lancio,* ~*di decollo* (*Aviat.*) runway.

pistàcchio, *m.* pistachio [nut].

pistàgna, *f.* coat-collar; facings.

pistíllo, *m.* pistil (*Bot.*).

pistòla, *f.* pistol. **pistolettàta,** *f.* pistol-shot.

pistóne, *m.* piston.

Pitàgora, *m.* Pythagoras. **pitagòrico** (*pl.* -òrici), *a.* Pythagorean. *tavola* ~*a, f.* multiplication table(s).

pitòcca, *f.* beggar woman. **pitoccàre** (*pr.* pitòcco, pitòcchi), *v.i.* (*aux.* avere) to beg. **pitocchería,** *f.* beggary; meanness; beggarly action. **pitòcco** (*pl.* -òcchi), *m.* beggar; miser; mean person.

pitóne, *m.* python (*serpent*). **pitonéssa,** *f.* pythoness; witch.

píttima, *f.* plaster; (*fig.*) bore.

pittóre, *m.* (**pittríce,** *f.*) painter. **pittorèllo,** *m.* bad painter; dauber. **pittòrico** (*pl.* -òrici), *a.* pictorial. **pittorésco** (*pl.* -éschi), *a.* picturesque. **pittúra,** *f.* painting (*art & product*); picture. **pitturàccia,** *f.* daub. **pitturàre,** *v.i.* (*aux.* avere) & *t.* to paint.

pitúita, *f.* phlegm; mucus. **pituitàrio,** *a.* pituitary. *glandola* ~ *a,* pituitary gland.

piú, *ad.* more; -er (*suffix forming comparatives*); longer; any l., any more. *il* ~, most. *mai* ~, never again; certainly not. *per lo* ~, for the most part; mostly. *sempre* ~, more & more. ¶ *a.inv.* many, several. *i* ~, most; most people; the majority.

piúma, *f.* feather; plume; pen. *peso* ~, feather-weight (*Box.*). **piumàccio,** *m.* feather bolster, pillow, or cushion. **piumàggio,** *m.* plumage. **piumíno,** *m.* eider-down quilt; plume of feathers, aigrette; powder-puff. **piumóso,** *a.* downy; feathery.

pi[u]òlo, *m.* low stone column; peg; post; rung (*ladder*).

piuttòsto, *ad.* rather; sooner, instead.

píva, *f.* pipe; bagpipe.

piviàle, *m.* cope (*Eccl.*).

pivière, *m.* plover.

pizzaguèrra, *f.* mischief-maker.

pizzicàgnolo, *m.* pork-butcher; cheesemonger; Italian warehouse-man.

pizzicàre (*pr.* pízzico, pízzichi), *v.t.* to pinch; nip; sting; bite; (*mus. instr.*) twang, pluck (*strings*); play 'pizzicato'; (*fig.*) to extort; catch. *v.i.* (*aux.* avere) to itch; tingle; smart. **pizzicàta,** *f.* pinching, plucking, &c.; tiny sweets. **pizzicàto,** *a. ad. & m.* (*Mus.*) pizzicato.

pizzichería, *f.* Italian warehouse; pork-butcher's shop.

pízzico, *m.* pinch (*salt,* &c.); (*fig.*) tingling. **pizzicóre,** *m.* smart; sting; itch. **pizzicòtto,** *m.* pinch; nip; flick (*whip*).

pízzo, *m.* peak (*mountain*); imperial, goatee [beard]; (*pl.*) lace; whiskers.

placàbile, *a.* placable, easily appeased; mild; forgiving. **placàre** (*pr.* plàco, plàchi), *v.t.* to appease; allay; alleviate. **placàrsi,** *v.refl.* to subside; become appeased.

plàcca (*pl.* plàcche), *f.* plate; metal badge; spot. **placcàre** (*pr.* plàcco, plàcchi), *v.t.* to plate.

placidézza & placidità, *f.* placidity; serenity. **plàcido,** *a.* mild; peaceful; serene; placid.

plàcito, *m.* (*Lit.,* Hist.) decree; judgement; approval; assembly.

plàga, (*pl.* plàghe) *f.* region; stretch of land or sky.

plagiàrio, *m.* plagiarist. **plàgio,** *m.* plagiarism; plagiary.

planàre, *v.i.* (*aux.* avere) (*Aviat.*) to plane; glide down; vol-plane.

planetàrio, *a.* planetary. ¶ *m.* planetarium; orrery. **planimetría,** *f.* plane geometry. **planisfèro,** *m.* planisphere; star-map.

plàsma, *m.* plasma. **plasmàre,** *v.t.* to mould; form.

plàstica, *f.* plastic art; modelling. ~*chirurgica,* plastic surgery. **plasticità,** *f.* plasticity. **plàstico** (*pl.* -àstici), *a.* plastic; pliant; supple. ¶ *m.* modeller; model.

plàtano, *m.* plane-tree.

platèa, *f.* (*Theat.*) pit. **plateàle,** *a.* low; vulgar.

plàtino, *m.* platinum. **platinotipía,** *f.* platinotype.

Platóne, *m.* Plato. **platònico** (*pl.* -ònici), *a.* Platonic.

plaudíre (*pr.* plàudo, &c., like

applaudire), *v.i.* (*aux.* avere) to applaud.
plauśíbile, *a.* praisewcrthy; acceptable; reasonable; plausible. **plàuśo**, *m.* applause; approbation; praise; distinction (*exam.*).
plàustro, *m.* ox-cart. *il P* ~, (*Astr.*) the Plough; Charles's Wain.
plautíno, *a.* Plautine. **Plàuto**, *m.* Plautus.
plebàccia & **plebàglia**, *f.* mob; rabble. **plèbe**, *f.* common people. **plebèo**, *a.* & *m.* plebeian. **plebiscíto**, *m.* plebiscite.
plèiade, *f.* pleiad. *le P* ~ *i*, (*Astr.*) the Pleiades.
plenàrio, *a.* plenary. **plenilúnio** (*pl.* **plenilúni**), *m.* full moon. **plenipotènza**, *f.* full power. **plenipotenziàrio**, *a.* & *m.* plenipotentiary. **plentitúdine**, *f.* plenitude; fulness.
pleonàśmo, *m.* pleonasm. **pleonàstico** (*pl.* **-àstici**), *a.* pleonastic.
plèsso, *m.* (*Anat.*) plexus.
plètora, *f.* plethora; super-abundance; glut.
plèttro, *m.* (*Mus.*) plectrum; (*fig.*) lyre, poetry.
plèura, *f.* (*Anat.*) pleura. **pleuríte**, *f.* pleurisy.
plíco (*pl.* **plíchi**), *m.* cover; envelope; packet. dim. *plichetto*.
Plínio, *m.* Pliny.
plínto, *m.* plinth.
ploràre (*pr.* **plòro**), *v.i.* (*aux.* avere) (*Poet.*) to weep; (*fig.*) rain.
plotóne, *m.* squad; platoon.
plúmbeo, *a.* leaden; lead (*att.*); (*fig.*) heavy; dull; livid.
pluràle, *a.* & *m.* plural. **pluralità**, *f.* plurality. **pluraliźźàre**, *v.t.* to put in the plural.
Plutàrco, *m.* Plutarch.
plúteo, *m.* book-case; b. shelves.
Plúto, *m.* Plutus. **plutòcrate**, *m.* plutocrat. **plutocràtico** (*pl.* **-àtici**), *a.* plutocratic. **plutocrazía**, *f.* plutocracy.
plutónio, *m.* plutonium (*Min.*).
pluviàle (**acqua**), *f.* rain-water. **pluviòmetro**, *m.* rain-gauge.
pneumàtico (*pl.* **-àtici**), *a.* pneumatic. ¶ *m.* [pneumatic] tyre.
pneumonìte, *f.* pneumonia.
Po (**il**), *m.* the Po.
po' *contr.* of **poco** *or* **poi** (*q.v.*).
poc'anzi, *ad.* a short time ago; only just now; a short time before.
pochettíno, pochétto, pochíno & **pocolíno** (*dims.* of **poco**), *ad.* ever

so little; very little; rather; a little while. ¶ *a.* & *indef. pn.* little; very little; (*pl.*) few; very few. **pochézza**, *f.* smallness; scantiness; narrowness; lack; insufficiency. **pochíssimo**, *a. ad.* & *indef. pn.* very little; (*pl.*) very few. **pòco**, *ad.* little; not much; not very; a short time, a little while. (Oft. has nearly the force of a negative, Eng. *non-* or *un-*. *E.g. poco simpatico*, unattractive (*pers.*).) *a* ~ *a* ~, little by little. ~ *fa*, a short time ago. *fra* ~, in a short time; before long; shortly. *a ogni* ~, every now & then. *per* ~ (*non*), ~ *manca che* . . . (*non*), all but, nearly, almost. ¶ *a.* & *indef. pn.* (*pl.m.* **pochi**, *f.* **poche**) little; (*pl.*) few, a few.
podàgra, *f.* gout in the feet.
podére, *m.* farm; holding; estate. dim. *poderetto, poderino*. **poderóso**, *a.* powerful; mighty.
podestà, *m.* podestà (administrative head of a commune). *f.* power; authority. **podestariàto**, *m.* office of podestà. **podestería**, *f.* jurisdiction & offices of the podestà.
podíśmo, *m.* foot-racing. **podista** (*pl.* **-isti**), *m.* runner (*professional*). **podístico**, *a.* foot-racing (*att.*). *gara* ~ *a*, *f.* foot-race.
poèma (*pl.* **poèmi**), *m.* poem (*gen. long narrative p.*). dim. *poemétto*.
poeśía, *f.* poetry; poem (*gen. short lyrical poem*). dim. *poesi*[*u*]*ola*.
poèta (*pl.* **poèti**), *m.* poet. **poetàre**, *v.i.* (*aux.* avere) to write poetry; be a poet. **poeteggiàre**, *v.i.* (*aux.* avere) to play the poet; tend towards poetry (*of prose, &c.*). **poetàstro**, *m.* poetaster. **poetéssa**, *f.* woman poet; poetess. **poètica**, *f.* poetics; art of poetry. **poètico** (*pl.* **-ètici**), *a.* poetic[al].
poffàre, poffarbàcco, poffare il Cielo! *excl.* good heavens!
poggiacàpo, *m.inv.* head-rest. **poggiapièdi**, *m.inv.* foot-rest.
poggiàre, *v.t.* to put; place; rest. *v.i.* (*aux.* avere) to rise; climb; move; rest; steer before the wind. **poggiarsi**, *v.refl.* to lean (against).
poggiàta, *f.* slope; declivity. **pòggio**, *m.* hill; hillock; knoll. **poggi**[*u*]*òlo*, *m.* balcony; parapet; low hill.
pòi, *ad.* then; afterwards; next; after all. *e* ~? what next? *da ora in* ~, from now onwards. *prima o* ~, sooner or later.
poiàna, *f.* buzzard.

poiché, *c.* since; when; after; for; as.
polàcca, *f.* polonaise (*Mus. & dress*).
polàcco (*pl.* **-àcchi**), *a.* Polish.
¶ *m.* Pole; Polish, the Polish language.
polàre, *a.* polar; pole (*att.*). **stella** ~, *f.* pole star; North star. **polarità,** *f.* polarity. **polarizzàre,** *v.t.* to polarize.
pòlca, *f.* polka.
polèmica, *f.* polemic; polemics. **polèmico** (*pl.* **-èmici**), *a.* polemic-[al]; controversial.
polènta, *f.* polenta.
policlínica, *f. &* **policlínico,** *m.* general hospital. **políctomo,** *a.* polychrome. **polièdro,** *m.* polyhedron. **poligamía,** *f.* polygamy. **polígamo,** *a.* polygamous. ¶ *m.* polygamist. **poliglòtta,** *a. & m.* polyglot. **polígono,** *m.* polygon. **Polinèsia** (la), *f.* Polynesia. **pòlipo,** *m.* polyp. **polisíllabo,** *a.* polysyllabic. ¶ *m.* polysyllable.
politeàma, *m.* theatre for various types of spectacle. **politècnico** (*pl.* **-ècnici**), *a.* polytechnic. ¶ *m.* polytechnic (*institution*); technical school; school of engineering. **politeísmo,** *m.* polytheism. **politeísta** (*pl.* **-ísti**), *m.* polytheist.
política, *f.* politics; policy. **político** (*pl.* **-ítici**), *a.* political; politic; crafty. ¶ *m.* politician; politic person; schemer. **politicóne,** *m.* schemer.
polizía, *f.* policing; police (*force*); p. regulations; p. station. ~ **di circolazione,** traffic police. ~ **stradale,** traffic regulations. **poliziésco** (*pl.* **-éschi**), *a.* police (*att.*). **romanzo** ~, detective novel. **poliziòtto,** *m.* policeman; detective.
pòlizza, *f.* policy (*Insce.*); voucher; receipt-form; note; bill; lottery-ticket. ~ **di carico,** bill of lading. ~ **di cambio,** bill of exchange. ~ **di pegno,** ~ **del Monte di Pietà,** pawn-ticket.
pólla, *f.* spring (*of water*).
pollàio, *m.* poultry-yard; fowl-house; hen-coop. **pollai[u]òlo,** *m.* poulterer. **pollàme,** *m.* poultry. **pollàstra,** *f.* young hen; pullet; (*fig.*) simple girl. **pollàstro,** *m.* young fowl; cockerel; (*fig.*) stripling. **pollería,** *f.* poultry market; poulterer's shop.
pòllice, *m.* thumb; big toe; inch.
pollicultúra, *f.* poultry-farming.
pòlline, *m.* pollen.

póllo, *m.* fowl; chicken. ~*d'India,* turkey.
pollóne, *m.* (*Bot.*) sucker; shoot.
polmonàre, *a.* pulmonary. **polmóne,** *m.* lung. **polmoníte,** *f.* pneumonia; inflammation of the lung(s).
pòlo, *m.* pole (*Astr., Phys., &c.*); polo.
Polònia (la), *f.* Poland.
pólpa, *f.* pulp (*fruit, &c.*); flesh (*animal*). **polpàccio,** *m.* calf (of the leg). **polpacciúto,** *a.* plump; fleshy. **polpastrèllo,** *m.* fleshy tip of finger or thumb. **polpétta,** *f.* croquette, rissole; meat-ball. **polpettóne,** *m.* hash; hashed meat. **pólpo.** *m.* octopus. **polpóso,** *a.* pulpy. **polpúto,** *a.* fleshy.
polsíno, *m.* cuff; wristband. ~*i alla moschettiera,* double cuffs. **pólso,** *m.* wrist; pulse; (*fig.*) energy, strength; skill. **orologio da** ~, wrist-watch.
poltíglia, *f.* mush; pulp; mud; slush.
poltríre (*pr.* **péltro &** **poltrísco**), *v.i.* (*aux.* avere) to live in idleness; lie lazily in bed. **poltróna,** *f.* arm-chair; easy chair; (*Theat.*) stall. **poltronàggine &** **poltronería,** *f.* laziness: indolence. **poltróne,** *m.* lazy fellow; slacker; coward; poltroon. **poltronésco** (*pl.* **-éschi**), *a.* lazy; indolent. **poltroneggiàre,** *v.i.* (*aux.* avere) to loiter; idle.
poiveràio, *a.* dusty & gusty; dust-raising, as in the prov. *gennaio* ~ *empie il granaio.*
pólvere, *f.* dust; powder. *caffè in* ~, ground coffee. *zucchero in* ~, powdered sugar. **polverièra,** *f.* powder-magazine. **polverifício,** *m.* powder-factory. **polverína,** *f.* powder (*Med.*). **polveríno,** *m.* sand-box (*for drying ink*). **polverío,** *m.* dust; cloud of dust. **polverizzàre,** *v.t.* to pulverize. **polveróne,** *m.* great cloud of dust. **polveróso,** *a.* dusty. **polverúme,** *m.* dust; heap of dust. **polvíscolo,** *m.* see *pulviscolo.*
pomàta, *f.* pomade; pomatum; salve.
pomellàto, *a.* dapple[d]. **pomèllo,** *m.* pommel; cheek-bone.
pomeridiàno, *a.* afternoon (*att.*); (*contr.*) p.m. **pomeríggio,** *m.* afternoon.
pométo, *m.* fruit-garden; apple-orchard.
pómice, *f.* pumice; p.-stone.
pomicultúra, *f.* fruit-growing.
pómo, *m.* fruit (*esp. apple*); fruit-tree; apple-tree; pommel; knob; rounded top; head (*of a stick*); rose

(can). ~*d'Adamo*, Adam's apple. ~*d'albero*, masthead truck. **pomodòro** (*pl.* **pomidòro**), *m.* tomato (*pl.* tomatoes).

pómpa, *f.* pomp; ostentation; display; pump. ~*da incendio*, fire-engine. ~*per* (or ~*da*) *bicicletta*, bicycle pump. ~*aspirante*, suction pump. ~*premente*, force-pump. ~*e funebri*, funeral; funeral ceremonies; undertaking. **pompàre**, *v.t.* to pump; p. up. **pompàta**, *f.* pumping. **pompeggiàre**, *v.i.* (*aux.* avere) to make a display; strike the eye. **pompeggiàrsi**, *v.refl.* to flaunt; strut; deck oneself out.

Pompèi, *f.* Pompeii. **Pompèo**, *m.* Pompey.

pompière, *m.* fireman.

pompóso, *a.* pompous; stately; ostentatious.

pònce, *m.inv.* & **poncíno**, *m.* punch. ~*al rum*, rum punch.

póncio, *m.* poncho, S. Amer. cloak popularized by Garibaldi.

ponderàbile, *a.* deserving consideration; having appreciable weight (*lit. & fig.*). **ponderàre**, *v.t.* to ponder; think on; t. over; weigh (*fig.*). *v.i.* (*aux.* avere) to muse; meditate; ponder. **ponderataménte**, *ad.* deliberately; thoughtfully; with due consideration. **ponderatézza**, *f.* circumspection; deliberation; (habitual) caution. **ponderàto**, *a.* considered; careful; deliberate. **ponderazióne**, *f.* pondering; reflection. **ponderóso**, *a.* ponderous; heavy. **pòndo**, *m.* weight (*lit. & fig.*) load; burden.

ponènte, *m.* west; west wind. **ponentíno**, *m.* light west wind. **poniménto**, *m.* placing; laying (*of hands*).

pónte, *m.* bridge; platform; scaffolding; deck (*ship*). ~*di barche*, bridge of boats. ~*girevole*, swing br. ~*levatoio*, draw-bridge. ~*pensile*, ~*sospeso*, suspension b. ~*sospeso da catene*, chain-bridge. ~*dell' asino*, pons asinorum. ~ *di manovra*, hurricane deck. ~ *superiore*, upper deck. ~ *di stiva*, lower deck. *giuoco del* ~, *m.* Bridge (*cards*).

pontéfice, *m.* pontiff; pope.

ponticèllo, *m.* (*dim.* of **ponte**) small bridge; light b.; bow (*violin*). **pon'icíno**, *m.* (*dim.* of **ponte**) rest (*billiards*).

pontificàle, *a.* pontifical. **pontificàre** (*pr.* **-íﬁco**, **-íﬁchi**), *v.i.* (*aux.*

avere) to officiate (as pontiff); to pontify. **pontificàto**, *m.* pontificate. **pontiﬁcio**, *a.* Papal.

pontíle, *m.* landing-stage.

Pontíne (**paludi**), *f.pl.* Pontine marshes.

pontóne, *m.* pontoon; (*flat-bottomed*) ferry-boat.

ponzàre, *v.i.* (*aux.* avere) to strain; make an effort; (*fig.*) to meditate; ponder.

Pònzio (**Pilàto**), *m.* Pontius Pilate (*N.T.*).

popolàccio, *m.* populace; rabble; mob. **popolàno**, *a.* of the people. ¶ *m.* man of the people. **popolàre**, *a.* popular. ¶ *v.t.* to populate; people. **popolarésca**, *f.* folk-lore; study of popular traditions and customs. **popolarésco** (*pl.* **-éschi**), *a.* popular; vulgar. **popolarità**, *f.* popularity. **popolazióne**, *f.* population; people. **popolíno**, *m.* common people; humble folk. **pòpolo**, *m.* people; nation; tribe; population; crowd; (*Hist.*) medieval Florentine republic; popular government. ~ *grasso*, rich bourgeoisie. ~ *minuto*, workmen; artisans. **popolóso**, *a.* populous.

poponàia, *f.* melon-bed. **popóne**, *m.* melon.

póppa, *f.* breast (*woman's*); poop, stern. **poppaiòla**, *f.* feeding-bottle. **poppànte**, *m.* sucking child, suckling; baby. **poppàre**, *v.i.* (*aux.* avere) & *t.* to suck; s. up. **poppàt**, *f.* sucking. **poppatóio**, *m.* artificial nipple; teat. **poppière**, *m.* rower (or gondolier) nearest the stern. **poppúta**, *a.f.* big-breasted; b.-b. woman.

pòr, *contr.* of **porta**.

pòrca (*pl.* **pòrche**), *f.* sow; ridge between two furrows. **porcàio**, **porcàro**, *m.* swineherd. *porcaio* also = dirty place, pigsty (*fig.*).

porcellàna, *f.* porcelain; china (*ware*). **porcellíno**, *m.* little pig; (*fig.*) dirty child. ~ *d'India*, guinea-pig. **porcèllo**, *m.* young pig. **porchería**, *f.* dirt; dirty trick; obscenity; filth. **porchétta**, *f.* roast pig; young sow. **porchétto**, *m.* sucking pig. **porcíle**, *m.* pigsty. **porcíno**, *a.* porcine; pig (*att.*). *carne* ~*a*, *f.* pork. **pòrco** (*pl.* **-òrci**), *m.* pig; swine; pork.

pòrfido, *m.* porphyry.

pòrgere (*pr.* **pòrgo**, **pòrgi**), *v.t. ir.* to hold out; reach out; stretch out; stick out; give; offer; hand; bear;

bring. *~d'ascolto,* ~ *l'orecchio,* to listen. **porgitóre,** *m.* (*f.* **-tríce**) bearer (*letter, greetings, &c.*).

pornografía, *f.* pornography.

pòro, *m.* pore. **poróso,** *a.* porous.

pórpora, *f.* purple; (*fig.*) cardinalship. **porporàto,** *a.* clothed in purple. ¶ *m.* cardinal. **porporíno,** *a.* rosy (*lips*); purple.

pórre (*pr.* **póngo, póni,** *&c.*), *v.t. ir.* to put; set; place; lay; (*fig.*) to suppose.

pòrro, *m.* leek; wart. **porróso,** *a.* warty.

pòrta, *f.* door, doorway; gate; gateway; goal (*football*) *~a due battenti,* double door. ~ *secondaria,* ~ *di servizio,* back door; tradesmen's entrance. ~ *volante,* swing door. ~ *imbottita,* padded door.

porta-, *prefix,* comps. so formed are very numerous, and are almost all *m.sg.inv.* whether they end with a sg. or pl. termination. **portaaèrei,** *m.inv.* aircraft carrier (*ship*). **portabagàgli,** *m.inv.* luggage carrier; porter. **portabigliétti,** *m.inv.* card-case; note-case. **portacappèlli,** *m.inv.* hat-box. **portacàrte,** *m.inv.* paper-holder; mapcase. **portacatíno,** *m.inv.* washstand. **portacénere,** *m.inv.* ashtray. **portacrostíni,** *m.inv.* toastrack. **portafiammíferi,** *m.inv.* match-box. **portafiàschi,** *m.inv.* bottle-rack; bin. **portafióri,** *m.inv.* flower-stand. **portafògli** *&* **portafòglio,** *m.inv.* pocket-book; notecase; letter-case; wallet; (*Pol.*) portfolio; (*fig.*) ministry; ministerial office. **portafortúna,** *m.inv.* mascot. **portagiòie** *&* **portagioièlli,** *m.inv.* jewel-box. **portalàpis,** *m.inv.* pencil holder. **portalèttere,** *m.inv.* postman. **portamonéte,** *m.inv.* purse. **portampólle,** *m.inv.* cruet-stand. **portamúsica,** *m.inv.* music stand. **portaombrèlli** *&* **portombrèlli,** *m.inv.* umbrella-stand. **portaórdini,** *m.inv.* messenger. **portaorològio,** *m.inv.* watch-stand; w. pocket. **portapàcchi,** *m.inv.* message boy; (*bicycle*) carrier. **portapénne,** *m.inv.* penholder. **portaprànzi,** *m.inv.* tray. **portaritràtti,** *m.inv.* portrait-frame; photograph f. **portasapóne,** *m.inv.* soap-dish. **portasigarétte,** *m.inv.* cigarette case; c. holder. **portasígari,** *m.inv.* cigar-case. **porta-**

spazzatúre, *m.inv.* dustpan. **portaspílli,** *m. inv.* pin-cushion. **porta-**[u]**òvo,** *m.* (*pl.* -**uòva**) egg-cup. **portavivànde** *&* *carrello* ~, *m.inv.* dinner-wagon. **portavóce,** *m.inv.* speaking-trumpet; megaphone; s.-tube; (*fig.*) mouthpiece (*pers.*).

portàbile, *a.* portable. **portàle,** *m.* portal.

portaménto, *m.* carriage; bearing; conduct. **portànte,** *a.* as in *ben* ~, very active; well preserved. **portantína,** *f.* sedan-chair; carrying chair. **portàre,** *v.t. & i.* (*aux.* avere) to bear; carry; take; bring; wear, have on; cause, bring about; yield; produce; have; show; adduce; bring forward; allege; prompt; lead, incline; turn (*discussion*); set; praise; post (*Bkkpg.*). **portàrsi,** *v.refl.* to go; be; do; stand; behave. **portàta,** *f.* reach; range; span; scope; compass; capacity; importance; significance; purport; tonnage (*ship*); dish, course (*meal*). *a* ~ *di voce,* within call. *a* ~ *d'orecchio,* within hearing. *a* ~ *di mano,* within reach. *di prima* ~, of the first importance. **portàtile,** *a.* portable; small (*arms*). **portàto,** *a.* inclined; disposed; given. ¶ *m.* outcome; result; issue; effect. **portatóre,** *m.* (*f.* **-tríce**) bearer. *azione al* ~, share to bearer (*Fin.*).

portèllo, *m.* small door; port-hole. **portellíno,** *m.* port-hole.

portènto, *m.* marvel; prodigy; omen; portent. **portentóso,** *a.* marvellous; prodigious; astonishing; portentous.

porticàto, *m.* colonnade; arcade. **pòrtico** (*pl.* **pòrtici**), *m.* portico; porch; (*pl.*) colonnade. **portièra,** *f.* door-curtain; portress. **portière,** *m.* door-keeper; porter; janitor; concierge; (*football*) goal-keeper. **portinàia,** *f.* portress; door-keeper (*f.*); concierge. **portinàio,** *m.* doorkeeper; concierge; janitor. **portinería,** *f.* porter's lodge.

pòrto, *m.* harbour; port; haven; carrying; wearing; carriage; postage; post (horse). *~affrancato,* postage prepaid. *~assegnato,* carriage payable on delivery. *franco di* ~, carriage free *~franco,* free port; bonded warehouse. *in* ~ *franco,* in bond. *diritti di* ~, harbour dues. ¶ *p.p.* of *porgere;* syncop. *p.p.* of *portare = portato.*

Portogàllo (il), *m.* Portugal. **porto-**

ghése, *a. & m.* Portuguese; *il ~,
la lingua ~*, Portuguese (*language*).
portolàno, *m.* portolano (book of
sailing directions).
portóne, *m.* gate; large door; carriage
entrance.
portòvo, *m.* egg-cup.
portuàle & portuàrio, *a.* of a port
or harbour. **portuàle,** *m.* docker.
porzioncèlla & porzioncína, *f.*
small part; tiny portion. **porz, ine,**
f. portion; part; share.
pòsa, *f*, laying; placing; pause; rest;
accent; stress; posture; attitude;
pose; (*Phot.*) exposure. **posa-
cénere,** *m.inv.* ash-tray. **posa-
fèrro,** *m.inv.* rest for a hot-iron.
posalúme, *m.inv.* lamp-stand.
posamíne, *m.inv.* mine-layer (*ship*).
posapiàno, *m.inv.* 'handle with care';
(*label*) with care, fragile; sluggard;
slowcoach (*pers.*). **posapiède** *or*
posapièdi, *m.inv.* foot-stool.
posàre, *v.t.* to place; put; lay; set.
v.i. (*aux.* avere) rest; stand; pose;
sit (*portrait*). **posàrsi,** *v.refl.* to
settle; alight; rest; sit; perch.
posàta, *f.* cover (*knife, fork &
spoon*). **posataménte,** *ad.* calmly;
quietly; sedately. **posatézza,** *f.*
staidness; composure; calm[ness];
quietness. **posatóre,** *m.* poseur;
affected person.
posbèllico (*pl.* **-èllici**), *a.* post-war.
pòscia, *ad.* then; afterwards.
poscrítto, *m.* postscript.
posdatare, *v.t.* to post-date. **posdomani,** *ad.* the day after to-morrow.
positíva, *f.* (*Photo.*) positive. **posi-
tivaménte,** *ad.* positively. **posi-
tívo,** *a.* positive; real; certain;
practical; matter of fact. **positúra,**
f. attitude; posture; place; position.
posizióne, *f.* situation; position.
posponiménto, *m. & posposizióne,*
f. postponement. **pospórre** (*pr.*
-óngo, &c., like *porre*), *v.t.* ir. to
postpone.
pòssa, *f.* power; strength; vigour.
possànza, *f.* strength; power;
puissance.
possedére (*pr.* **possièdo** *or* **possèggo,
possièdi, possiède**), *v.t.* ir. to own;
possess; have; hold; be master of
(*language, &c.*). **possediménto,** *m.*
possession; colony; estate; property.
posseditóre, *m.* (*f.* **-trice**) owner;
possessor; master (mistress) (*of a
language*, etc.). **possessióne,** *f.*
possession; ownership; property.
possèsso, *m.* possession; tenure;

occupation; ownership. **possessóre,**
m. possessor; owner; holder.
possíbile, *a.* possible. **possibilità,** *f.*
possibility. **possibilménte,** *ad.*
possibly.
possidènte, *m.f.* owner of real estate;
landowner. **possidènza,** *f.* right to
possession; proprietors, owners
(*col.*).
pòsta, *f.* post; post-office; mail, mails;
stake (*wager*); stall (*animal*). *~aerea,*
air-mail. *direttore delle ~ e*, post-
master. *fermo in ~*, poste restante,
to be called for. *ministro delle ~e,*
Postmaster-General. *ufficio centrale
delle ~e*, General Post-Office. *a ~*,
a bella ~, on purpose; expressly
(for the purpose). *a sua ~*, as he
pleases. *di ~*, quickly; directly.
di questa ~, of this size (or shape).
stare alla ~, to watch. **postàle,** *a.*
postal; post, mail (*att.*). *cartolina ~,*
f. postcard. *vaglia ~*, *m.inv.* postal
order; money-order. *timbro ~,*
postmark. *furgone ~*, mail-van.
postàre, *v.t.* to place; station; post.
posteggiàre, *v.t.* to lie in wait for;
watch for; park (car). **postéggio,**
m. stand, cab-rank; parking-place;
parking.
postèma, *f.* abscess.
postergàre, *v.t.* to reject; throw
away; (*fig.*) postpone, defer.
pòsteri, *m.pl.* descendants; posterity.
posterióre, *a.* posterior; subsequent;
later; hind[er], back. **posterior-
ménte,** *ad.* subsequently, later,
later on; at the back; from behind.
posterità, *f.* posterity; issue.
postíccio, *a.* artificial; false; sham;
fictitious.
posticíno, *m.* (*dim.* of *posto*) pleasant
little spot; small post.
posticipàre, *v.t.* to defer; postpone.
posticipataménte, *ad.* after the
proper time; when the work is
finished. **posticipàto,** *a.* delayed;
deferred; after the event. *pagamento ~*, deferred payment.
postiglióne, *m.* postilion.
postílla, *f.* note; marginal note.
postillàre, *v.t.* to annotate.
postíno, *m.* postman.
pósto, *m.* place; spot; position; site;
station; seat; situation; post; appointment; space, room. *~riservато,*
reserved seat. *~d'angolo,* corner
seat. *~d'insegnante,* teaching post.
~di medicazione, dressing-station.
~di primo soccorso, first-aid post.
¶ *p.p.* of *porre*.

postoché or **posto che**, c. assuming that, supposing that.

post-operatòrio, a. post-operative.

postrèmo, a. last.

postulànte, m. applicant; petitioner; (*Eccl.*) postulant. **postulàre**, v.t. to demand; claim; require; postulate.

pòstumo, a. posthumous.

postúra, f. place; situation (*Geog.*), posture.

postútto (al), ad. expr. after all.

potàbile, a. drinkable; fit for drinking.

potai[u]òlo & **potatóio**, m. pruning-knife; p. hook. **potaménto**, m. & **potatúra**, f. pruning; lopping. **potàre**, v.t. to prune; lop.

potàssa, f. potash. **potàssio**, m. potassium.

potènte, a. powerful; mighty; strong; potent. **potènza**, f. power; strength; authority; force; faculty. **potenziàle**, a. & m. potential.

potére (*pr.* **pòsso, puòi, può**), v.i. ir. (*aux.* avere & essere if the following infin. requires it), to have power; be able; can (*pres.*); can do; be allowed; may (*pres.*); could (*imperf. pret. & condit.*); might (*imperf. pret. & condit.*). può darsi, può essere, it may be. non ne posso piú, I am at the end of my strength, I am done up. ¶ m. power; authority; ability.

potestà, f.inv. power; authority.

poveràccio, m. poor fellow; poor devil. **poveràglia**, f. poor people; beggars (*col.*), mendicants. **poverèllo**, m. poor man. il ~ d'Assisi, St. Francis. **poverétto** & **poveríno**, m. poor little fellow. **pòvero**, a. poor; needy; unfortunate; humble; scanty. ¶ m. poor man; pauper; beggar; mendicant. **povertà**, f.inv. poverty; want; scarcity.

pozióne, f. potion; draught.

pózza, f. puddle; pool. **pozzànghera**, f. puddle; dirty pool; duck-pond. **pozzétta**, f. small pool; dimple. **pozzétto**, m. small well; tank; reservoir. **pózzo**, m. well; (*mine*) shaft; tank; fount (*fig.*).

Pràga, f. Prague.

pragmatísmo or **prammatísmo**, m. pragmatism.

prammàtica, f. custom; rescript. essere di ~, to be customary. risposta di ~, regulation answer.

pranzàre, v.i. (*aux.* avere) to dine. **pranzétto**, m. light dinner; plain d. **prànzo**, m. dinner; dinner-party.

Prassítele, m. Praxiteles.

pratai[u]òlo & **pratènse**, a. of the fields or meadows; field (*att.*). **pratellína**, f. daisy. **pratería**, f. meadow[s]; grassland, prairie.

pràtica (*pl.* **pràtiche**), f. practice; experience; training; practical knowledge; familiarity, intercourse; business; matter; affair; (*pl.*) dealings, arrangements, steps (*fig.*); pratique (*Naut.*); custom; customers; observances (*Eccl.*). **praticàbile**, a. practicable. **praticàccia**, f. empirical skill or knowledge; person whose company is to be avoided. **praticaménte**, ad. practically. **praticànte**, a. practising. ¶ m. apprentice; church-goer, practising churchman. **praticàre**, v.t. to practise; carry out, exercise; frequent; associate with; make; open; execute. **pràtico** (*pl.* **-àtici**), a. practical; experienced. ¶ m. practitioner; expert. ~di, familiar with; experienced in.

pràto, m. meadow. regina dei ~i, meadow-sweet. dims. pratellino, pratello, praticello. **pratolína**, f. daisy. **pratolíno**, m. mushroom.

pravità, f. wickedness. **pràvo**, a. wicked.

pre, abb. of **prete**. **pre-**, in comps. before(hand).

preaccennàto, a. aforesaid.

preàlpi, f.pl. foot-hills of the Alps.

preàmbolo, m. preface; preamble.

preavvertíre (*pr.* **-èrto, -èrti**, like avvertire) & **preavvisàre**, v.t. to inform in advance. **preavvíso**, m. notice; forewarning.

prebènda, f. prebend; stipend (*Eccl.*). **prebendàrio**, m. prebendary.

precarietà, f. precariousness. **precàrio**, a. precarious.

precauzióne, f. precaution.

prèce, f. (*Poet.*) prayer.

precedènte, a. preceding; previous; former. ¶ m. precedent. **precedènza**, f. precedence; priority. in ~, in advance. **precèdere**, v.t. to precede.

precettàre, v.t. to summon; cite. **precettísta** (*pl.* **-ísti**), m. author of precepts. **precètto**, m. precept; maxim; order. **precettóre**, m. tutor; teacher; preceptor.

precídere, v.t. ir. to cut short; c. off.

precíngere (*pr.* **-íngo, -íngi**), like cingere), v.t. ir. to surround; girdle.

precipitàre, v.t. to precipitate; hasten; throw down; fling headlong. v.i. (*aux.* essere) to fall; precipitate; crash (*Aero.*); rush on; hasten.

precipitàrsi, *v.refl.* to rush; throw oneself down. **precipitàto,** *a.* rash, hasty, precipitate. ¶ *m.* precipitate (*Chem.*). **precipitazióne,** *f.* precipitancy, haste; precipitation, fall. **precípite,** *a.* headlong; precipitous. **precipitévole** *a.* impetuous; hasty; steep. **precipitóso,** *a.* precipitous; precipitate, hasty. **precipízio,** *m.* precipice. *a* ~, headlong.

precipuaménte, *ad.* chiefly; mainly. **precípuo,** *a.* chief; principal.

precisàre, *v.t.* to state precisely; specify. **precisióne,** *f.* precision; accuracy; exactness. **precíso,** *a.* precise; exact; punctual; sharp (*hour*); definite; accurate.

preclàro, *a.* prominent; illustrious; noble.

preclúdere, *v.t. ir.* to block; preclude.

precòce, *a.* precocious; early; premature. **precocità,** *f.* precociousness; precocity, &c.

preconcètto, *a.* preconceived. ¶ *m.* preconception.

preconóscere, *v.t. ir.* to foreknow; know beforehand.

precórrere, *v.t. ir.* to anticipate; be in advance of; outrun. **precursóre,** *m.* precursor; forerunner; harbinger; (*att.*) precursory, premonitory.

prèda, *f.* booty; prey. **predàce,** *a.* predatory. **predàre,** *v.t.* to plunder; pillage; prey upon.

predèlla, *f.* altar-step; dais; carriage-step; footboard. **predellíno,** *m.* foot-stool; child's (high) chair; (folding) carriage step.

predestinazióne, *f.* predestination.

predétto, *a.* aforesaid; above-mentioned. ¶ *p.p.* of *predire,* foretold.

prèdica (*pl.* **prèdiche**), *f.* sermon. **predicàre,** *v.i.* (*aux.* avere) *& t.* to preach; proclaim; praise; predicate. **predicàto,** *m.* predicate (*Gram.*). **predicatóre,** *m.* preacher. **predicatòrio,** *a.* predicatory. **predicazióne,** *f.* preaching. **predichétta,** *f. &* **predicòzzo,** *m.* (*fig.*) admonition; scolding.

predilètto, *a. & m.* favourite. **predilezióne,** *f.* predilection. **prediligere** (*pr.* **-diligo, -diligi**), *v.t. ir.* to prefer; have a liking for; hold dear, dearer or dearest.

predíre (*pr.* **-díco, -díci,** &c., like *dire*), *v.t. ir.* to foretell; predict; forecast.

predispórre (*pr.* **-óngo, -óni,** &c., like *porre*), *v.t. ir.* to predispose; arrange in advance.

predizióne, *f.* prediction.

predominàre, *v.i.* (*aux.* avere) to predominate; prevail; take the first place. **predomínio,** *m.* supremacy; predominance.

predóne, *m.* robber; plunderer; marauder.

prefabbricàto, *a.* prefabricated.

prefàto, *a.* aforesaid.

prefazióne, *f.* preface; introduction. dim. *prefazioncella.*

preferènza, *f.* preference. *di* ~, preferably; mostly. *a* ~ *di, in* ~ *di,* rather than; in preference to. **preferenziàle,** *a.* preferential; preference (*att.*). *titoli* ~*i, azioni* ~*i,* preference stock; p. sharcs. **preferíbile,** *a.* preferable. **preferíre** (*pr.* **-ísco, -ísci**), *v.t.* to prefer. **preferíto,** *a.* favourite.

prefètto, *a.* prefect. **prefettúra,** *f.* prefecture.

prèfica, *f.* hired female mourner (*Hist.*).

prefíggere (*pr.* **prefiggo, prefíggi**), *v.t. ir.* to prefix; fix beforehand. **prefíggersi,** *v.refl.* to purpose, intend; set before one. **prefísso,** *m.* prefix. ¶ *a.* prefixed; fixed; appointed.

pregàre (*pr.* **prègo, prèghi**), *v.t.* to pray; request; ask; beg; invite. *prego!* don't mention it! (*expr. of politeness*).

pregévole, *a.* valuable.

preghièra, *f.* prayer; request; entreaty. *libro di* ~*e,* prayer-book.

pregiàbile, *a.* estimable; valuable. **pregiàre,** *v.t.* to esteem; value; appreciate; prize. **pregiàrsi,** *v.refl.* to have the honour to; to beg to (*in letters,* &c.).

prègio, *m.* value; good quality; excellence; merit; esteem.

pregiudicàre, *v.t.* to prejudge; prejudice; injure; harm. **pregiudicàto,** *a.* suspected, suspect. ¶ *m.* previously convicted person; suspect. **pregiudiziàle,** *a.* prejudicial; (*leg.*) before judgement; previous. **pregiudízio,** *m.* prejudice; previous conviction.

pregnànte, *a.* pregnant (*lit. & fig.*). **pregnànza,** *f.* pregnancy. **prégno,** *a.* full; saturated; impregnated; rich (in); teeming (with); pregnant.

pregustàre, *v.t.* to have a foretaste of; anticipate.

pregustazióne, *f.* foretaste; anticipation. **preistòrico** (*pl.* **-òrici**), *a.* prehistoric.

prelàto, *m.* prelate; church dignitary.

prelazióne, *f.* pre-emption. **prelevaménto,** *m.* deduction; drawing (*money out*). **prelevàre,** *v.t.* to take away; draw (out); deduct.

prelezióne, *f.* introductory lecture. **prelibàre,** *v.t.* to have a foretaste of; try in advance. **prelibàto,** *a.* excellent; choice; delicious.

preliminàre, *a. & m.* preliminary.

prelúdio, *m.* prelude.

premeditàto, *m.* premeditated. *assassinio* ~, wilful murder.

premènte, *a.* pressing; urgent. *pompa* ~, force-pump. **prèmere,** *v.t. & i.* (aux. avere *& essere*) to press; weigh upon; concern, interest; matter. Oft. impers., e.g. *mi preme di*, I am anxious to (*with infin.*).

preméssa, *f.* premiss; premise; previous statement. **preméttere,** *v.t. ir.* to premise; say first of all; put forward; give preference to. ~ *a*, place before.

premiàbile, *a.* deserving a prize; worthy of reward. **premiàre,** *v.t.* to give (or award) a prize to; reward. **premiàto,** *m.* prize-winner. **premiatóre,** *m.* (*f.* -**trìce**) prize-giver. **premiazióne,** *f.* prize-giving; distribution of prizes.

preminènte, *a.* pre-eminent. **preminènza,** *f.* pre-eminence.

prèmio, *m.* prize; premium (*Insce. & Fire*); bounty; subsidy; reward.

premitúra, *f.* pressing.

premoríre (a), *v.t. ir.* to predecease; die before.

premunìre (*pr.* -**ísco,** -**ísci**), *v.t.* to strengthen beforehand; forearm; forewarn. **premunìrsi,** *v.refl.* to be forearmed; protect oneself. ~ *di* to provide oneself with (*means of defence*).

premúra, *f.* care; solicitude; attention; kindness; eagerness; haste; urgency. **premurosaménte,** *ad.* attentively; solicitously; thoughtfully; kindly; readily; politely. **premuróso,** *a.* eager; careful; solicitous; attentive; kind.

prèndere, *v.t. ir.* to take, t. up; t. over; catch; seize; capture; surprise; lay hold of; pick up; acquire; get; win; charge; earn; adopt; assume; engage; regard; consider; deal with; strike; keep; observe (*Easter*); *v.i.* (aux. avere) to turn; go (*right or left, &c.*); to set; congeal; curdle; take root. ~ *a*, to begin, set about. ~ *di mira*, to gaze at, stare at. ~ *quota*, to take off

(*Aero*), gain height. **prèndersi,** *v.refl.* to take; seize hold of each other; get married; come to an agreement; congeal, coagulate. ~ *a pugni*, ~ *a botte*, ~ *a schiaffi*, to come to blows. *prendersela con*, to get angry with, to lay the blame on. *prendersela calda*, to feel anger or enthusiasm about something. *prendersela comoda*, to take it (things) easy. **prenditóre,** *m.* receiver; (*manager*) of a lottery; payee, acceptor of a bill.

prenóme, *m.* Christian name. **prenominàto,** *a.* above-mentioned; aforesaid.

prenotàre, *v.t.* to book; engage. ~ *posti*, to book seats. **prenotazióne,** *f.* booking (in advance).

prènsile, *a.* prehensile.

preoccupàre, *v.t.* to pre-occupy (*lit. & fig.*); trouble; worry; make anxious. **preoccupàrsi,** *v.refl.* to be pre-occupied, anxious, worried. **preoccupazióne,** *f.* preoccupation; care; worry; anxiety.

preopinànte, *m.* previous speaker.

preparàre, *v.t.* to prepare; make ready; lay (*fire*); coach (*pupil*); read for (*exam.*). **preparàrsi,** *v.refl.* to prepare, get ready; brew (*storm*). **preparatìvo,** *m.* preparation. **preparàto,** *m.* preparation (*Med. & Anat.*); (*pl.*) advance arrangements. **preparatòrio,** *a.* preparatory. **preparazióne,** *f.* preparation.

preponderànte, *a.* preponderant; predominant. **preponderànza,** *f.* preponderance. **preponderàre,** *v.i.* (aux. avere) to preponderate; prevail.

prepórre (*pr.* -**póngo,** -**póni,** *&c.*, like *porre*), *v.t. ir.* to prefix; place in front; place over; set above; prefer. **preposizióne,** *f.* preposition. **prepósto,** *m.* provost (*Eccl.*); rector.

prepotènte, *a.* arrogant; overbearing; insolent; powerful; irrepressible. **prepotènza,** *f.* abuse of power; arrogance; insolence; overbearing action or behaviour.

preraffaelìta, *a. & m.* Pre-Raphaelite.

prerogatìva, *f.* prerogative.

présa, *f.* seizure; capture; taking; grasp; grip; hold; pinch (*salt, snuff*); point to catch hold of; terminal (*Elec., Radio*); inlet; intake. *alle* ~*e*, at grips. *far* ~, to set; coagulate. *cane da* ~, *m.* setter.

preságio, *m.* presage; omen; portent; presentiment; foreboding; premoni-

tion. **preśagíre** (*pr.* -ísco, -ísci),
v.t. & i. (*aux.* avere) to presage;
portend; [fore]bode; augur; predict;
foresee. **preśàgo** (*pl.* -àghi), *a.*
presaging; foreboding; foreseeing.
prèsbite, *a. & m.* long-sighted; l.-s.
person.
preśbiteriàno, *a. & m.* Presbyterian.
preśbitèrio, *m.* presbytery (*Arch.*);
rectory, vicarage, parsonage.
presciènte, *a.* prescient. **presciènza**,
f. prescience, foreknowledge.
prescíndere, (**da**), *v.t.* to put aside;
leave out of consideration.
prescrítto, *a.* prescribed; fixed;
obligatory; (*Law*) barred by Statute.
¶ *m.* prescript; ordinance. **pre-
scrívere**, *v.t. ir.* to prescribe;
ordain; fix; establish. **prescrizióne**,
f. prescription (*Law & Med.*);
ordinance; directions.
preśentàbile, *a.* presentable. **pre-
śentàre**, *v.t.* to present; offer; pay
(*respects*); produce; show; introduce.
preśentàrsi, *v.refl.* to appear; occur;
arise; present oneself; sit (*for an
examination*). **preśentazióne**, *f.*
presentation; introduction. **pre-
śènte**, *a.* present; this (*letter, &c.*).
¶ *m.* present, present time; present
tense. ¶ *f.* this [letter]; gift, present.
preśenteménte, *ad.* at present;
now.
presentiménto, *m.* presentiment;
foreboding; misgiving. **presentíre**
(*pr.* presènto, -ènti), *v.t.* to have
a presentiment of; anticipate; forebode.
preśènza, *f.* presence; attendance;
appearance, sight. **preśenziàre**,
v.t. & i. (*aux.* avere) to be present
(at), attend. **preśèpio & preśèpe**
(*Poet.*), *m.* manger; crib; painting or
model of the group in the Manger,
(*infant Jesus, Mary, Joseph, the ox,
the ass, and the shepherds.*)
prèside, *m.* principal (*school*); head-
master; dean; presiding judge. **preśi-
dènte**, *m.* president; chairman.
~ *del consiglio* (*dei ministri*), premier;
prime minister. **presidènza**, *f.*
presidency; chairmanship. **presi-
denziàle**, *a.* presidential.
presidiàre, *v.t.* to garrison. **presídio**,
m. garrison.
presièdere (*pr.* -sièdo), *v.i. ir.* (*aux.*
avere) to preside, act as chairman;
be at the head of.
préso, *p.p.* of *prendere*.
prèssa, *f.* press; crowd, crowding;
throng, crush; pressure; haste; press

(*Mech.*).   **pressacàrte**,   *m.inv.*
paper-weight.
pressànte, *a.* pressing; urgent.
press'a póco, *ad.* about; nearly.
pressàre, *v.t.* to press (*lit. & fig.*).
prèssi, *m.pl.* neighbourhood; vicinity;
environs.
pressióne, *f.* pressure. *perdita di* ~,
f. pressure drop (*Mech.*).
prèsso, *pr.* near, by, beside; with; to;
among; care of (*abb.* c/o). ~ *a*, in
comparison with. ¶ *ad.* near,
nearby; near at hand. *a un di* ~,
very nearly. ~ *a*, (*with infin.*) about
to, on the point of. **pressoché**, *ad.*
almost, nearly.
pressóio, *m.* press (*Mech.*). **pressúra**,
f. pressure; oppression.
prestabilíre (*pr.* -ísco, -ísci, like
stabilire), *v.t.* to fix beforehand;
establish in advance.
prestaménte, *ad.* quickly; readily.
prestanóme, *m.* (*fig.*) dummy;
man of straw.
prestànte, *a.* excellent; eminent; of
noble presence. **prestànza**, *f.* excellence; eminence; dignity of bearing.
prestàre, *v.t.* to lend; give, render
(*obedience*); take (*oath*); attribute.
farsi ~, to borrow. **prestàrsi** (**a**),
v.refl. to countenance; be fit for; be
useful; consent; indulge in; give way
to. **prestatóre**, *m.* (*f.* -tríce)
lender. **prestazióne**, *f.* lending;
loan; service; tax; impost.
prestézza, *f.* quickness; rapidity;
alertness; address.
prestigiatóre, *m.* (*f.* -tríce) conjuror;
juggler. **prestígio**, *m.* prestige;
authority; illusion; conjuring; sleight
of hand.
prestíno, *ad.* rather early; rather
quickly.
prèstito, *m.* loan. *dare a* ~, to lend.
prendere, *pigliar in* ~, to borrow.
affitti e ~*i*, lend-lease (*Pol.*).
prèsto, *a.* quick; prompt. ¶ *ad.* soon;
early; quickly. *piú* ~, earlier,
sooner. ~ *o tardi*, sooner or later.
al piú ~ *possibile*, as soon as possible.
far ~, to be quick; make haste.
presto! quick! be quick!
preśúmere, *v.i. ir.* (*aux.* avere) to
presume; think; believe; guess;
jecture, imagine. ~ *di*, to rely on.
preśumíbile, *a.* presumable. **pre-
śuntívo**, *a.* presumptive. **pre-
śúnto**, *p.p.* of *presumere*; *a.* supposed;
apparent; presumptive. **pre-
śuntuóso**, *a.* presumptuous. **pre-
śunzióne**, *f.* presumption.

presuppórre (*pr.* -óngo, -óni, *&c.*, like *porre*), *v.i. ir.* (*aux.* avere) *& t.* to pre-suppose; suppose.

prète, *m.* priest; clergyman (*Angl.*). *dim. pretino.*

pretendènte, *m.* pretender; claimant; applicant; suitor; wooer. **pretèndere,** *v.i. ir.* (*aux.* avere) to claim; profess; pretend; contend, assert. (*v.t.*) to want; claim; pretend to; require; exact. **pretensióne,** *f.* claim, pretension. **pretenzióso,** *a.* pretentious.

preteríre (*pr.* -ísco, -ísci), *v.t.* to omit; break off (*an engagement*); disobey (*orders*). **pretèrito,** *a. & m.* preterit; past, past time.

pretermèttere, *v.t. ir.* to pass over; omit.

pretésa, *f.* pretension; claim; pretence. **pretésco** (*pl.* -éschi), *a.* priestly.

pretèsto, *m.* pretext, pretence, plea, excuse.

pretóre, *m.* judge; police magistrate.

prettaménte, *ad.* merely; simply; purely; really. **prètto,** *a.* mere; pure; real; good; correct.

pretúra, *f.* office of police-magistrate; district-court; court of first instance.

prevalènte, *a.* prevalent; prevailing. **prevalére** (*pr.* -vàlgo, -vàli), *v.i. ir.* (*aux.* essere *&* avere) to prevail. *su* ~, prevail over. **prevalérsi,** *v.refl.* to avail oneself, take advantage (of).

prevaricàre (*pr.* -àrico, -àrichi), *v.i.* to betray one's trust; act dishonourably; embezzle. **prevaricatóre,** *m.* (*f.* -tríce) defaulter; embezzler. **prevaricazióne,** *f.* breach of trust; default.

prevedére (*pr.* -védo, *&c.*, like *vedere*), *v.t. ir.* to foresee; forecast; provide for. **prevedíbile,** *a.* foreseeable; to be foreseen. **prevedúto,** *a. & p.p.* of *prevedere*, foreseen, forecast. **preveggènte,** *a.* foreseeing; prescient; provident. **preveggènza,** *f.* foresight.

preveníre (*pr.* -engo, *&c.*, like *venire*), *v.t. ir.* to precede; forestall; anticipate; meet (*wish, &c.*), provide against (*loss, &c.*); prevent; avoid; forewarn; ward off.

preventivaménte, *ad.* beforehand; in anticipation, preventively. **preventivàre,** *v.t.* to estimate; allocate (*expenditure*). **preventívo,** *a.* preventive; anticipated; estimated. *bilancio* ~, estimated budget.

carcere ~, imprisonment on suspicion. ¶ *m.* estimate (*Fin.*). **prevenúto,** *a. & p.p.* of *prevenire*. ¶ *m.* suspect. **prevenzióne,** *f.* prepossession; prejudice; bias; prevention; precautionary measure[s].

previaménte, *ad.* previously.

previdènte, *a.* provident; foreseeing. **previdènza,** *f.* foresight; prudence.

prèvio, *a.* previous. **previsióne,** *f.* prevision; forecast; expectation. ~ *i meteorologiche,* weather forecast. **previsto,** *a. & p.p.* of *prevedere.*

prevòsto, *m.* see *preposto.*

preziosísmo, *m.* artificial style (*Lit.*); affectation. **preziosità,** *f.* preciousness; costliness; preciosity. **prezióso,** *a.* precious; valuable; costly; (*style*) artificial, elaborate; affected.

prezzàbile, *a.* valuable; estimable. **prezzàre,** *v.t.* to value; appraise. **prezzatóre,** *m.* valuer.

prezzémolo, *m.* parsley.

prèzzo, *m.* price; value, worth, cost; terms; rate; charge; fare. ~ *di costo,* cost price. ~*all' ingrosso,* wholesale p. ~ *al minuto,* retail p. *listino dei* ~*i,* price list.

prezzolàre, *v.t.* to hire.

pría, *ad.* (*Poet.*) before.

Príamo, *m.* Priam.

prigióne, *f.* prison. ¶ *m.* prisoner. **prigionía,** *f.* imprisonment. **prigionièro,** *m.* prisoner.

prillàre, *v.t.* to twirl. *v.i.* (*aux.* avere) to whirl. **príllo,** *m.* swift turn; whirl; whirling; spinning (*spindle, top, dancer*).

príma, *ad.* before; formerly; beforehand; once; earlier; first; rather. ~ *o poi,* sooner or later. *quanto* ~, as soon as possible. *come* ~, as soon as ever. ¶ ~ *di, pr.* before. ¶ ~ *che, ad.* before. ¶ *f.* first class (*Rly.*); first form (*Sch.*); first performance; f. night (*Theat.*). ~ *di cambio,* first of exchange.

primaménte, *ad.* at first; in the first place; chiefly. **primariaménte,** *ad.* primarily. ' **primàrio,** *a.* primary. **primàte,** *m.* primate. **primatíccio,** *a.* early (*fruit, vegetables*). **primàto,** *m.* primacy; pre-eminence. **primavèra,** *f.* spring. **primaveríle,** *a.* vernal; spring (*att.*). **primazía,** *f.* primacy. **primeggiàre,** *v.i.* (*aux.* avere) to excel; take the lead. **primèvo,** *a.* primeval.

primièra, *f.* primero (*card game*). **primieraménte,** *ad.* in the first place; above all. **primièro**, *a.* first; former.

primigènio, *a.* original. **primitívo**, *a.* primitive, original; primeval; pristine; primary; crude. **primízia**, *f.* early fruit; novelty; (*pl.*) first fruits. **prímo**, *a.* first; prime; former. *di ~a mano*, first-hand. *di prim'ordine*, first rate, f.-class. ¶ *ad.* first[ly]. **primogènito**, *a.* first-born. **primogenitóre**, *m.* progenitor. **primogenitúra**, *f.* primogeniture; birth-right. **primordiàle**, *a.* primordial, primary; primeval. **primòrdio**, *m.* beginning; **prímula**, *f.* primrose.

principàle, *a.* principal; chief; main. ¶ *m.* principal; manager; chief; senior partner. **principàto**, *m.* principality. **príncipe**, *m.* prince. dim. *principino.* **principésco** (*pl.* -**éschi**), *a.* princely. **principéssa**, *f.* princess. dim. *principessina.* **principiànte**, *a.* beginning. ¶ *m.f.* beginner. **principiàre**, *v.i.* (*aux.* essere *&* avere) *& t.* begin; commence; start. **princípio**, *m.* beginning; principle.

prióra, *f.* prioress. **prioràto**, *m.* priorate; priorship. **prióre**, *m.* prior. **prioría**, *f.* priory. **priorità**, *f.* priority.

prísco (*pl.* **príschi**), *a.* ancient; early (*times*).

prísma, *m.* prism. **prismàtico** (*pl.* -**àtici**), *a.* prismatic.

pristíno, *a.* former; ancient; primitive.

privàre, *v.t.* to deprive; strip; deny.

privataménte, *ad.* privately; in private (life).

privatíva, *f.* patent; monopoly; tobacconist's shop; (*pl.*) letters patent. *generi di ~*, (State) monopolies.

privatívo, *a.* privative; exclusive. **privàto**, *a. & m.* private, private person.

privazióne, *f.* privation; loss; deprivation. **prívo**, *a.* devoid; destitute. *~ di*, lacking in, without.

prò, *m.* advantage; benefit; profit. **pro'**, *abb.* of *prode.*

proàva, *f. & proàvo*, *m.* great grandmother; great grandfather.

probàbile, *a.* probable; likely. **probabilità**, *f.* probability; likelihood; chance.

probaménte, *ad.* honestly; uprightly. **probità**, *f.* probity; uprightness; honesty.

problèma (*pl.* -**èmi**), *m.* problem;

question. **problemàtico** (*pl.* -**àtici**), *a.* problematic[al]; uncertain.

pròbo, *a.* upright; honest; just.

probòscide, *f.* proboscis; trunk.

procaccévole, *a.* industrious. **procàccia**, *m.* letter carrier; rural postman. dim. *procaccino*, *m.* (*fig.*) factotum. **procacciànte**, *a.* meddlesome. ¶ *m.* busy-body; meddler. **procacciàre**, *v.t.* to get by effort; procure; try. **procacciàrsi**, *v.refl.* *~ da vivere*, to earn one's living. **procàce**, *a.* saucy; impudent; provoking. **procacità**, *f.* impudence; impertinence; sauciness.

procèdere (*pr.* -**èdo**), *v.i.* ir (*aux.* essere) to proceed; act; go on. ¶ *m.* conduct; behaviour; process (*of time*). **procediménto**, *m.* proceeding[s]; course; conduct; dealing. **procedúra**, *f.* procedure.

procèlla, *f.* storm; tempest. **procellària**, *f.* stormy petrel. **procellóso**, *a.* stormy.

processàbile, *a.* indictable; liable to be prosecuted. **processàccio**, *m.* unfair trial. **processàre**, *v.t.* to bring to trial; try; prosecute. **processióne**, *f.* procession. **procèsso**, *m.* trial; process.

procínto (**essere in**), *loc.* to be on the point (of); to be going (to).

proclàma (*pl.* -**àmi**), *m.* proclamation (*written*); (*pl.*) banns of marriage. **proclamàre**, *v.t.* to proclaim.

proclíve, *a.* inclined. **proclività**, *f.* tendency; inclination; proclivity.

procómbere, *v.i. defect.* (*aux.* essere) to fall (face foremost).

procrastinàre, *v.i.* (*aux.* avere) *& t.* to procrastinate; put off; defer.

procreàre (*pr.* **procrèo**), *v.t. & abs.* to procreate; generate.

procúra, *f.* procuration; power of attorney; proxy. **procuràre**, *v.t.* to procure; get; cause. *~di*, to try; take care; manage. **procuratóre**, *m.* attorney; proxy. *~generale*, Attorney General. *~ della Repubblica*, public prosecutor.

pròda, *f.* edge; border; bank; shore; side.

pròde, *a.* valiant; brave; bold. ¶ *m.* valiant man, *&c.* **prodézza**, *f.* prowess; gallantry; bravery; act of gallantry; brave deed.

prodigàre, *v.t.* to lavish; squander; pour out; be prodigal of. **prodígio** (*pl.* **prodígi**), *m.* prodigy; marvel. **pròdigo** (*pl.* **pròdighi**), *a.* prodigal; lavish.

prodigióso, *a.* prodigious; marvellous.

proditòrio, *a.* treacherous.

prodótto, *p.p.* of *produrre.* ¶ *m.* product.

pròdromo, *m.* (*oft. pl.*) premonitory sign, symptom.

prodúrre (*pr.* **-úco, -úci**), *v.t. ir.* to produce; bring forth; bear; yield, show; cause; give rise to; manufacture. **produttività,** *f.* productivity. **produttívo,** *a.* productive. **produttóre,** *m.* (*f.* **-tríce**) producer; manufacturer. ¶ *a.* producing. **produzióne,** *f.* production; output; manufacture.

proemiàle, *a.* prefatory; introductory. **proèmio,** *m.* preface; introduction.

profanàre, *v.t.* to profane; desecrate; pollute. **profanazióne,** *f.* profanation, &c. **profanità,** *f.* profanity. **profàno,** *a.* profane; secular; ignorant; unskilled. ¶ *m.* layman; outsider; bad judge; (*pl.*) (the) profane, &c.

profènda, *f.* provender, fodder.

proferíre (*pr.* **-ísco, -ísci**), *v.t.* to utter; pronounce (*judgment*); proffer. **proferírsi,** *v.refl.* to offer (one's services).

professàre, *v.t.* to profess; practise. **professióne,** *f.* profession. **professionísta,** *m.* professional man; professional (*sport*). **professo,** *sync. p.p.* of *professare,* professed. **professoráto,** *m.* professorship. **professóre,** *m.* professor; teacher; master; lecturer; instructor. **professoréssa,** *f.* professor (*fem.*); mistress.

profèta (*pl.* **-èti**), *m.* prophet. **profetàre,** *v.i. & t.* to prophesy; predict. **profetéssa,** *f.* prophetess. **profètico** (*pl.* **-ètici**), *a.* prophetic. **profetizzàre,** *v.i. & t.* to predict; prophesy; foretell. **profezía,** *f.* prophecy.

profícuo, *a.* useful; profitable.

profilàre, *v.t.* to draw in profile. **profilo,** *m.* profile, side face; contour, outline, section; (*Lit.*) sketch. **profilàssi,** *f.* prophylaxis.

profittàre, *v.i.* (*aux.* avere) to profit; progress, make progress. *~ di, mettere a ~,* to profit by. **profittévole,** *a.* profitable. **profítto,** *m.* profit; benefit; advantage; progress. *a ~ di,* for the benefit of. *partecipazione ai ~ i, f.* profit-sharing.

proflúvio, *m.* flow; flood; abundance; (*Med.*) discharge.

profondaménte, *ad.* deeply; profoundly; (*sleep*) soundly. **profondaménto,** *m.* sinking; sounding; deepening. **profondàre,** *v.i.* (*aux.* essere) to sink; *v.t.* to deepen. **profondàrsi,** *v.refl.* to sink (*fig.*); become absorbed, be immersed; penetrate. **profóndere** (*pr.* **-fóndo**) *v.t. ir.* to lavish; squander; waste. **profóndersi,** *v.refl.* to be lavish. **profondità,** *f.* depth; profundity. **profóndo,** *a.* deep; profound.

pròfugo (*pl.* **pròfughi**), *a. & m.* refugee.

profumàre, *v.t.* to perfume; scent. **profumataménte,** *ad.* largely; generously; handsomely; dearly (*usu. of spending or paying*). **profumàto,** *a.* scented, sweet-smelling; (*fig.*) dear, expensive. **profumería,** *f.* perfumery; perfume shop. **profumière,** *m.* perfumer; distiller of perfumes. **profúmo,** *m.* perfume; fragrance; scent. dim. *profumino.*

profuṡaménte, *ad.* profusely; abundantly; at great length. **profuṡióne,** *f.* profusion; abundance.

progènie, *f.* progeny; issue. **progenitóre,** *m.* (*f.* **-tríce**) ancestor, -tress, progenitor, -tress.

progettàre, *v.t.* to plan; project; design. **progettísta,** *m.* planner; schemer. **progètto,** *m.* project; plan; scheme; (*Typ.*) lay-out. *~ di legge,* bill (*parl.*).

progràmma, *m.* programme; syllabus; prospectus; platform (*Pol.*). *~delle corse,* race-card.

progredíre (*pr.* **-ísco, -ísci**), *v.i.* (*aux.* avere & essere) to progress, advance. **progressióne,** *f.* progression. **progressívo,** *a.* progressive. **progrèsso,** *m.* progress.

proibíre (*pr.* **-ísco, -ísci**), *v.t.* to forbid; prohibit. **proibitívo,** *a.* prohibitory; prohibitive. **proibizióne,** *f.* prohibition. **proibizionísta,** *m.* prohibitionist.

proiettàre, *v.t.* to cast; throw; project. **proièttile,** *m.* projectile; missile. **proiettóre,** *m.* searchlight; head-lamp; projector. **proiezióne,** *f.* projection; lantern-slide.

pròle, *f.* issue, offspring, progeny. **proletariàto,** *m.* proletariat[e]. **proletàrio,** *a. & m.* proletarian.

prolífico (*pl.* **-ífici**), *a.* prolific. **prolissità,** *f.* prolixity. **prolísso,** *a.* prolix; long-winded.

pròlogo (*pl.* **pròloghi**), *m.* prologue. **prolungaménto,** *m.* prolongation; extension; continuation. **pro-**

lungàre, v.t. to prolong; protract; extend, lengthen. **prolungàrsi,** v.refl. to continue; extend. **prolungataménte,** ad. at great length.

prolusióne, f. opening lecture.

promemòria, f.inv. memorandum.

proméssa, f. promise.

Promèteo, m. Prometheus.

promettènte, a. promising. **prométtere** (pr. **prométto**), v.i. ir. (aux. avere) & t. to promise.

prominénte, a. prominent. **prominènza,** f. prominence.

promiscuità, f. promiscuity. **promíscuo,** a. promiscuous. **promissívo,** a. promissory.

promontòrio, m. promontory; headland.

promòsso, p.p. of promuovere. ¶ a. promoted; passed (exam), successful (candidate). **promotóre,** m. promoter. **promozióne,** f. promotion; preferment.

promulgàre, v.t. to promulgate. **promulgazióne,** f. promulgation; publication. **prom[u]òvere** (pr. -uòvo & c. like muovere), v.t. ir. to promote; induce; cause.

pronipóte, m. & f. grand nephew or g. niece; great grandchild; (m.pl.) descendants.

pròno, a. prone; prostrate.

pronóme, m. pronoun. **pronominàle,** a. pronominal.

pronosticàre, v.t. to prognosticate; forecast; foretell. **pronòstico** (pl. -òstici), m. prognostic; omen; forecast; prediction.

prontaménte, ad. promptly; quickly; readily. **prontézza,** f. readiness; quickness; promptitude; animation; ease. **prónti (a),** ad. expr. ready-money, (for) cash. **prónti!** i, (Mil.) ready! (Teleph.) hallo! **prónto,** a. ready; prompt; quick; alert. **prontuàrio,** m. hand-book; book of reference.

prònubo, m. bridesman; best man (wedding).

pronúncia & **pronúnzia,** f. pronunciation. **pronunciàre** & **pronunziàre,** v.t. to pronounce; utter; deliver (judgement; speech). **pronunziàto,** a. pronounced; marked; notable; decided.

propagànda, f. propaganda. **propagàre,** v.t. to propagate.

propalàre, v.t. to spread (news); publish abroad.

propèndere (pr. -èndo, &c., like pèndere), v.i. (aux. avere) to incline; lean; be inclined. **propensióne,** f. propensity; inclination. **propènso,** a. inclined; ready.

Propèrzio, m. Propertius.

propína, f. examiner's fee.

propinquità, f. propinquity; relationship. **propínquo,** a. near; akin; related.

propiziàre, v.t. to propitiate. **propiziazióne,** f. propitiation. **propízio,** a. propitious.

proponiménto, m. purpose; resolution. **propórre** (pr. -póngo, -póni, like porre), v.t. ir. to propose; propound. **propórsi,** v.refl. to purpose; intend; resolve.

proporzionàle, a. proportional. **proporzionàre,** v.t. to proportion. **proporzionàto,** a. proportionate. **proporzióne,** f. proportion.

propòsito, m. purpose; object; aim; intention; design; subject. di ~, on purpose, intentionally; seriously, in earnest. a ~, a. & ad. to the point; apposite(ly); pertinent(ly); suitable, -ably, appropriate(ly); by design. a ~ di, with reference to. **propòsta,** f. proposal. **propósto,** m. provost (Eccl.). **proposizióne,** f. proposition; sentence.

própriaménte, ad. properly; really; exactly. **proprietà,** f.inv. property; estate, holding; ownership; rights; propriety. ~ letteraria, copyright. **proprietàrio,** m. proprietor. **pròprio,** a. proper; peculiar; characteristic; appropriate; inherent; literal; own; actual; right; true; exact; neat; clean. ¶ ad. just; really; exactly.

propugnàcolo, m. bulwark; outwork.

propugnàre, v.t. to plead for; advocate; champion; support; fight for. **propugnatóre,** m. champion; defender; supporter.

propulsióne, f. propulsion. ~ a reazione, jet propulsion. **propulsívo,** a. propellent; propelling. **propulsóre,** m. propeller.

pròra, f. prow; bow (ship).

pròroga, f. delay; respite; adjournment, prorogation. **prorogàre,** v.t. to delay; put off; extend; prorogue.

prorómpere (pr. -rómpo, &c., like rompere), v.i. ir. (aux. avere) to burst out; break out.

pròsa, f. prose; piece of prose. compagnia di ~, dramatic company (as disting. fr. an operatic c.). **prosàico** (pl. -àici), a. prosaic. **prosàpia,** f. race; stock; lineage.

prosàstico (*pl.* -àstici), *a.* prose (*att.*). **prosatóre**, *m.* prose-writer.

proscènio, *m.* proscenium.

prosciògliere (*pr.* -òlgo, -òlgi, *&c.*), *v.t. ir.* to acquit; release; absolve; set free. **prosciogliménto**, *m.* acquittal; absolution; release.

prosciugàbile, *a.* capable of being drained or dried up; reclaimable. **prosciugaménto**, *m.* draining (*land*); drying up; reclamation. **prosciugàre**, *v.t.* to dry (up); drain; reclaim.

prosciùtto, *m.* ham.

proscrìtto, *a.* proscribed; outlawed; banished; exiled. ¶ *m.* outlaw; exile; banished man. **proscrìvere**, *v.t. ir.* to proscribe; outlaw; banish (*lit. & fig.*). **proscrizióne**, *f.* proscription; banishment.

prosecutóre, *m.* continuator. **prosecuzióne**, *f. & proseguiménto**, *m.* continuation; prosecution (*studies*, *&c.*). **proseguíre** (*pr.* -séguo, *&c.*, like *seguire*), *v.t. & i.* (*aux.* avere, *with persons*, essere *or* avere *with things*) to continue; push on with; pursue; go on; persist.

proselitísmo, *m.* proselytism. **prosèlito**, *m.* proselyte.

prosíndaco, *m.* acting mayor.

prosodìa, *f.* prosody. **prosòdico** (*pl.* -òdici), *a.* prosodic.

prosperàre, *v.i.* (*aux.* avere) to thrive; prosper. **prosperità**, *f.* prosperity; wealth. **pròspero**, *a.* prosperous; prospering; thriving; flourishing; happy; favourable. **prosperóso**, *a.* healthy; sturdy; (*fig.*) prosperous.

prospettàre, *v.t.* to look out [up]on; show. **prospettìva**, *f.* perspective; prospect; view. **prospètto**, *m.* prospect; view; prospectus; table, summary. **prospiciènte**, *a.* overlooking; with a view of.

prossenèta (*pl.* -èti), *m.* intermediary; go-between.

prossimaménte, *ad.* very soon; in a short time; presently. **prossimità**, *f.* proximity. **pròssimo**, *a.* very near; nearest; next; immediate (*cause*). ¶ *m.* neighbour, fellow creature.

pròstata, *f.* prostate (gland).

prostèndere, *v.t. ir.* to stretch (out); extend. **prostèndersi**, *v.refl.* to spread; stretch; lie down.

prosternàre, *v.t.* to prostrate; lay low. **prosternàrsi**, *v.refl.* to prostrate oneself; bow down. **prosternazióne**, *f.* prostration.

prostituíre (*pr.* -ísco, -ísci), *v.t.* to prostitute. **prostituzióne**, *f.* prostitution.

prostràre, *v.t.* to prostrate; throw down; exhaust; pull down (*fig.*). **prostrazióne**, *f.* prostration; exhaustion; depression.

protagonìsta (*pl.* -ísti), *m.* protagonist.

protèggere (*pr.* -tèggo, -tèggi), *v.t. ir.* to protect; shelter; defend; encourage; favour; patronize. **proteggitóre**, *m.* (*f.* -tríce) protector; protectress; (*att.*) protecting.

proteìne, *f.pl.* proteins.

protèndere, *v.t. ir.* to stretch (out); extend.

Pròteo, *m.* Proteus.

protèrvia, *f.* impudence; arrogance; obstinacy. **protèrvo**, *a.* impudent; obstinate; arrogant; rash; impetuous.

protèso, *a.* outstretched.

protèsta, *f.* protest; remonstrance; protestation. **protestànte**, *a. & m.* Protestant. **protestantésimo**, *m.* Protestantism. **protestàre**, *v.i.* (*aux.* avere) *& t.* to protest. **protestàto**, *a.* (*Com.*) dishonoured (*bill*). **protestatóre**, *m.* (*f.* -tríce) protester. **protestazióne**, *f.* protestation. **protèsto**, *m.* (*Com.*) protest (*bill of exchange*).

protettìvo, *a.* protective. **protètto**, *p.p.* of proteggere. esportazione ~a, *f.* dumping. **protettoràto**, *m.* protectorate; protectorship. **protettóre**, *m.* protector. **protettrìce**, *f.* protectress. **protezióne**, *f.* protection; patronage. misure di ~ antiaerea, air-raid precautions (*abb.* A.R.P.). **protezionìsmo**, *m.* protectionism. **protezionìsta**, *m.* protectionist.

pròto, *m.* overseer (*Typ.*).

protocòllo, *m.* protocol; record; register.

protoplàsma, *m.* protoplasm.

protòtipo, *m.* prototype.

protràrre (*pr.* -àggo, -ài), *v.t. ir.* to protract; defer; prolong. **protrazióne**, *f.* protraction.

protuberànza, *f.* protuberance.

pròva, *f.* proof; trial; test; ordeal; examination; evidence; token; pledge; experience; rehearsal. a ~, on trial. a ~ di bomba, bomb-proof; shell-proof. ~ generale, dress rehearsal. foglio di ~, (*Typ.*) specimen page. **provàbile**, *a.* demonstrable. **provàre**, *v.t. & i.* (*aux.* avere) to prove;

show; demonstrate; try; test; feel (*pain*, *pleasure*); taste; experience; rehearse; try on (*dress*). **provataménte,** *ad.* assuredly; decidedly. **provàto,** *a.* tried; experienced.

proveniènte, *a.* coming (from); originating (from). **provenienza,** *f.* origin; provenance; source. **provenire** (*pr.* -**vèngo,** -**vièni,** *like venire*), *v.i. ir.* (*aux.* essere) to come (from); originate (from); derive (from); arise (from); be caused (by).

provènto, *m.* proceeds; income.

Provènza (la), *f.* Provence. **provenzàle,** *a.* Provençal. **provenzaleggiàre,** *v.i.* (*aux.* avere) to imitate Provençal literature.

proverbiàle, *a.* proverbial. **proverbiàre,** *v.t.* to scold; jeer at. **provèrbio,** *m.* proverb.

provétta, *f.* test-tube.

provétto, *a.* experienced; advanced in years.

provincia (*pl.* -**ínce**), *f.* province; district. **provinciàle,** *a.* provincial. *strada* ∼, main road (of a province). **provincialismo,** *m.* provincialism.

províno, *m.* sample; rehearsal (*ballet*, *cinema*).

provocànte, *a.* provoking; provocative. **provocàre,** (*pr.* **pròvoco,** **pròvochi**), *v.t.* to provoke; rouse; stir up; cause. **provocatívo,** *a.* provocative. **provocazióne,** *f.* provocation.

provvedére (*pr.* **provvédo,** *&c.*, *like vedere*), *v.t. ir.* to provide; supply; furnish. *v.i.* (*aux.* avere) to make provision. **provvediménto,** *m.* provision; precaution; measure. **provveditóre,** *m.* steward; manager; (*Educ.*) supervisor; superintendent. **provvedúto,** *p.p.* of *provvedere.*

provvidènte, *a.* provident. **provvidènza,** *f.* providence; good angel; godsend. **provvidenziàle,** *a.* providential. **pròvvido,** *a.* provident. foreseeing; thrifty. **provvigióne,** *f.* provision; commission. **provvisòrio,** *a.* temporary; provisional. **provvísta,** *f.* supply; provision. **provvísto,** *p.p.* of *provvedere.*

prozía, *f.*, **prozío,** *m.* great-aunt; great-uncle.

prúa, *f.* prow; bow(s) (*ship*).

prudènte, *a.* prudent; careful, cautious. **prudènza,** *f.* prudence. **prudenziàle,** *a.* prudential.

prúdere, *v.i. defect.* to itch. **prudóre,** *m.* itching.

prúgna, *f.* plum; prune. **prúgno,** *m.* plum-tree.

pruína, *f.* (*Poet.*) hoar-frost.

prunàio & **prunéto,** *m.* thorn-bush; thicket. **prúno,** *m.* thorn.

prurígine, *f.* itching. **pruriginóso,** *a.* itching; itchy. **pruríto,** *m.* itch (*lit.* & *fig.*), itching.

pseudònimo, *m.* pseudonym.

psichiàtra (*pl.* -**àtri**), *m.* psychiatrist. **psichiatría,** *f.* psychiatry. **psíchico** (*pl.* -**íchici**), *a.* psychic(al). **psicoanàliśi,** *f.* psycho-analysis. **psicología,** *f.* psychology. **psicològico** (*pl.* -**ògici**), *a.* psychological. **psicòlogo** (*pl.* -**òglogi**), *m.* psychologist. **psicopàtico** (*pl.* -**àtici**), *a.* psychopathic. ¶ *m.* psychopath. **psicòśi,** *f.* psychosis.

pst! *i.* hush!

pubblicàbile, *a.* fit for publication. **pubblicàre** (*pr.* **púbblico,** **púbblichi**), *v.t.* to publish; bring out; issue; edit. **pubblicazióne,** *f.* publication; publishing; issue. **pubblicísta,** *m.* publicist. **pubblicità,** *f.* publicity; advertising. *piccola* ∼, miscellaneous advertisements (*newspapers*). **pubblicitàrio,** *a.* advertising. **púbblico,** *a.* public; national (*debt*). ¶ *m.* public; audience.

pubertà, *f.* puberty.

pudibóndo, *a.* modest; bashful; prudish. **pudicízia,** *f.* modesty; bashfulness. **pudíco** (*pl.* -**íchi**), *a.* modest; chaste. **pudóre,** *m.* modesty; decency.

pueríle, *a.* childish; puerile. **puerilità,** *f.* childishness; puerility. **puerízia,** *f.* childhood; boyhood. **puerpèrio,** *m.* confinement, lying-in.

pugilàto, *m.* boxing, pugilism. **pugilàtore,** *m.* boxer.

púglia, *f.* counter; pool (*cards*). **Púglia** (la), *f.* Apulia. **pugliése,** *a.* & *m.* belonging to Apulia; native of Apulia.

púgna, *f.* fight; battle (*Poet.*). **pugnàce,** *a.* pugnacious. **pugnalàre,** *v.t.* to stab. **pugnalàta,** *f.* stab. **pugnàle,** *m.* dagger. **pugnàre,** *v.i.* (*aux.* avere) to fight (*Poet.*).

pugnèllo & **pugnétto,** *m.* handful. **pugnitòpo,** *m.* butcher's broom (*Bot.*). **púgno,** *m.* fist; punch; blow; hand(writing); handful. *dim.* *pugnino,* baby's fist. *fare a* ∼*i,* to box; fight; (*fig.*) to clash; contradict.

púla, *f.* chaff.

púlce, *f.* flea. *color* ~, puce. **pulciàio,** *m.* nest of fleas. **pulcióso,** *a.* full of fleas.

Pulcinèlla, *m.* Punch; Punchinello. ~*di mare,* puffin. **pulcinellàta,** *f.* piece of buffoonery; Punch & Judy show.

pulcíno, *m.* chick; chicken.

pulédra, *f.* filly. **pulédro,** *m.* colt; foal.

puléggia, *f.* pulley.

puliménto, *m.* polish; polishing; cleaning. **pulíre** (*pr.* -isco, -isci), *v.t.* to clean; polish. **pulìrsi,** *v.refl.* to clean oneself; wash oneself. **puliscipénne,** *m.inv.* pen-wiper. **puliscipièdi** & **pulisciscàrpe,** *m.inv.* door-mat; scraper. **pulíta,** *f.* clean[ing]. *dare una* ~ *a,* to clean. **pulitaménte,** *ad.* properly; neatly; smoothly; quietly; politely. **pulitézza,** *f.* cleanliness; cleanness; neatness; polish; propriety. **pulíto,** *a.* clean; neat; well-kept; tidy; smooth; well-mannered. ¶ *m.* clean copy. **pulizía,** *f.* cleaning; cleanliness; tidiness. *fare una bella* ~, to make a clean sweep.

pullulàre, *v.i.* (*aux.* avere) to spring up; spread; swarm.

púlpito, *m.* pulpit.

pulsàre, *v.i.* (*aux.* avere) to pulsate; beat; throb. **pulsazióne,** *f.* pulsation; beat; throb; throbbing.

pulvíscolo, *m.* fine dust; fine spray.

pulzellóna, *f.* old maid.

pum! *i. onomat.* bang!

pungènte, *a.* pungent; stinging; prickly; (*fig.*) biting; sharp; poignant.

púngere (*pr.* púngo, púngi), *v.t. ir.* to sting; prick (*lit.* & *fig.*). **pungiglióne,** *m.* sting. **pungolàre,** *v.t.* to goad (*lit.* & *fig.*). **púngolo,** *m.* goad; (*fig.*) prick, spur.

punìbile, *a.* punishable. **punìre** (*pr.* -isco, -isci), *v.t.* to punish; chastise. **punitivo,** *a.* punitive. **punitóre,** *m.* (*f.* -**tríce**) punisher. ¶ *a.* punishing; punitive. **punizióne,** *f.* punishment.

púnta, *f.* point; tip; end; top; peak; headland, promontory; (*pen*) nib; (*fig.*) sharp pain; stab; stitch (*in the side*); small amount, slight tinge or trace; touch; flying visit. *in* ~ *dei piedi,* on tiptoe. *cane da* ~, pointer (*dog*). *ore di* ~, rush hours. **puntàle,** *m.* metal point; ferrule; tag **puntaménto,** *m.* pointing; aiming; (*artil.*) levelling; laying. **puntàre,** *v.t.* to point; level (*gun*);

fix, direct (*eyes, gaze*); lay, put; bet, wager; prick (*chart*); *v.i.* (*aux.* avere) to push, press. **puntàta,** *f.* thrust; part, instalment (*of serial work*); stake, bet. **puntatóre,** *m.* gun layer; punter; gambler.

punteggiaménto, *m.* dotting. **punteggiàre,** *v.i.* (*aux.* avere) & *t.* to dot; punctuate. **punteggiatúra,** *f.* dotting; punctuation.

puntellàre, *v.t.* to prop; buttress; shore up; support. **puntello,** *m.* prop; support.

punter[u]òlo, *m.* punch; awl; bodkin; weevil (*insect*).

puntíglio, *m.* punctilio; obstinacy.

puntína, *f.* drawing pin. **puntíno,** *m.* dot. *cotto a* ~, cooked to a turn. **puntiscrítto,** *m.* laundry mark.

púnto, *m.* point; spot; place; dot; stitch; mark; moment; detail, particular; particle. ~ *fermo,* full stop. *due* ~*i.* colon. ~ *e vírgola,* semi-colon. ~ *interrogativo,* mark of interrogation. ~ *esclamativo,* mark of exclamation. ~*di ebollizione,* boiling point. ~*di congelamento,* freezing point. ~*in croce,* cross-stitch. ¶ *a.* & *ad. with neg. non . . . punto,* no, none, not at all. ¶ *p.p.* of *pungere.* **puntolíno,** *m.* dot. **puntóne,** *m.* rafter; strut; (*Mil.*) salient; wedge-shaped formation in battle.

puntuàle, *a.* punctual. **puntualità,** *f.* punctuality.

puntuazióne, *f.* punctuation.

puntúra, *f.* puncture; sting; bite (*insect*); prick; hypodermic injection; shooting pain.

punzecchiàre, *v.t.* to prick (*lightly* & *repeatedly*); sting; bite; goad; (*fig.*) to tease; pin-prick.

punzonàre, *v.t.* to punch; p. out. **punzóne,** *m.* punch; die-stamp; punch with the fist; tool for stamping ornament on back or cover of books (*leather bound*).

pupàttola & **pupàzzola,** *f.* doll; tiny child. **pupazzétto,** *m.* caricature. **pupàzzo,** *m.* puppet.

pupílla, *f.* pupil (*eye*); female ward. **pupíllo,** *m.* ward; pupil (*Law*).

puraménte, *ad.* purely; simply; merely; only. **purché,** *c.* provided [that], on condition that. **purchessía,** *a.* any; any whatever; of any kind.

púre, *ad.* & *c.* also, too; yet, still; however; even; somehow; anyhow; really; (*sometimes has the effect of an*

elliptical clause understood). *non* ~,
not only; not even. *senza* ~,
without even.
purè, *m.* purée; mash; [thick] soup.
purézza, *f.* purity; clearness (*air, sky*).
púrga, *f.* purge. **purgànte,** *a. & m.*
purgative; laxative; aperient. **pur-gàre** (*pr.* **púrgo, púrghi**), *v.t.* to
purge; purify; cleanse; clear;
expurgate. **purgatívo,** *a. & m.*
purgative; laxative; aperient.
purgatòrio, *m.* purgatory. ¶ *a.*
purgatorial. **purgatúra,** *f.* purga-tion; disinfection; cleansing. **purga-zióne,** *f.* purgation; purification;
expiation; acquittal. **purificàre,**
v.t. to purify, cleanse. **purifica-zióne,** *f.* purification.
puríśmo, *m.* purism. **purísta,** *m.*
purist. **purità,** *f.* purity; chastity.
puritaníśmo, *m.* puritanism. **puri-tàno,** *m. & a.* Puritan; puritanical.
púro, *a.* pure; unalloyed; un-adulterated; plain; mere; sheer;
clear; neat (*not diluted*). **puro-sàngue,** *m.inv.* thoroughbred
(*horse*).
purpúreo, *a.* purple; crimson; deep
red.
purtròppo, *ad.* unfortunately.
purulènto, *a.* purulent.
pús, *m.* pus, matter.
pusillànime, *a.* pusillanimous; faint-hearted. ¶ *m.* coward. **pusillani-mità,** *f.* pusillanimity. **puśillo,** *a.*
weak; feeble; of no account.
pústola, *f.* pustule, pimple.
putacàso, *c.* supposing; let us
suppose.
putatívo, *a.* putative; reputed.
Putifàrre, *m.* Potiphar (*O.T.*).
putifèrio, *m.* stench; mess; shindy;
scandalous row. **putíre** (*pr.* -**ísco,**
-**ísci**), *v.i.* (*aux.* avere) to stink.
putrèdine, *f.* corruption; rottenness;
putridity. **putrefàre** (*pr.* -**faccio,**
&c., like *fare*), *v.i. ir. &* **putrefàrsi,**
v.refl. to putrefy; rot; go bad.
putrefazióne, *f.* putrefaction.
putrescènte, *a.* putrescent, begin-ning to putrefy. **pútrido,** *a.* putrid;
rotten. **putridúme,** *m.* rottenness;
filth; garbage; mass of filth. **putríre**
(*pr.* -**ísco, -ísci**), *v.i.* to putrefy; rot.
pútto, *m.* child's figure (*Art.*).
púzza, *f.* stench. **puzzàre,** *v.i.* to
stink. **púzzo,** *m.* stench; bad smell.
púzzola, *f.* pole-cat. **puzzolènte,**
a. stinking; fetid.
puzzóne, *m.* evil-smelling person;
(*fig.*) skunk.

Q

Q, q, (*cu*) *f.* the letter Q.
qua, *ad.* here; hither. ~ *& là,* here
& there. *il mondo di* ~, this world,
the present world. *di* ~ *delle Alpi,*
on this side of the Alps. *più* ~,
later, later on.
quacqueríśmo, *m.* Quakerism.
quàcquero, *a. & m.* Quaker.
quadèrna, *f.* set of four numbers.
quadernétto, *m.* note book.
quadèrno, *m.* copy-book; exercise
book.
quàdra, *f.* square sail.
quadragèsimo, *a. ord. num.* fortieth.
Quadragèsima, *f.* Lent; Quadra-gesima.
quadrangolàre, *a.* quadrangular.
quadràngolo, *m.* quadrangle.
quadrànte, *m.* quadrant; clock-face;
dial. ~ *solare,* sun-dial (*portable*).
quadràre *v.t.* to square; adjust.
v.i. (*aux.* essere *&* avere) to fit; suit.
quadràto, *a.* square; (*fig.*) strong;
sound; sensible; shrewd; firm. ¶ *m.*
square. ~ *ufficiali,* (*Nav.*) ward-room. *dim. quadratino.* **quadra-túra,** *f.* squaring (*Math. & Astr.*)
quadrature. **quadrèlla,** *f.* four-sided file; square tile. **quadrèllo,**
m. square tile; (*pl.f.*) **quadrèlla,**
(*Poet.*) arrows.
quadrettàre, *v.t.* to divide into
squares; chequer. **quadrétto,** *m.*
small picture; small square (*chess-board, check-pattern, &c.*).
quàdri, *m.pl.* diamonds (*cards*);
pictures.
quadriènnio, *m.* period of four years.
quadrifogliàto, *a.* four-leaved.
quadrifòglio, *m.* four-leaved sham-rock.
quadríglia, *f.* quadrille.
quadrilàtero, *a. & m.* four-sided;
quadrilateral. **quadrimèstre,** *m.*
period of four months. **quadri-motóre,** *m.* (*Aviat.*) four-engined
plane. **quadrívio** (*pl.* -**ívi**), *m.*
cross-roads; meeting of four roads.
quàdro, *a.* square; (*fig.*) strong;
sensible. ¶ *m.* picture (*lit. & fig.*);
description; sight; square (*pattern*);
table; summary; cadre (*Mil.*).
quadrúpede, *a. & m.* four-footed;
quadruped. **quadruplicàre,** (*pr.*
-**úplico, -úplichi**), *v.t.* to multiply
by four; quadruple. **quadrúplice**
& **quàdruplo** *a.* quadruple; four-fold.

quaggiú, *ad.* here below; in this
world.

quàglia, *f.* quail. dim. *quagliotto,
quagliétta, quagliettina.*

quagliàre, *v.t. & i. (aux.* essere) &
quagliàrsi, *v.refl.* to curdle. *Cf.
cagliare.* **quagliàta,** *f.* curds;
junket. **quàglio,** *m.* rennet.

quàlche, *a. indef. inv.* some; any.
(*Sg. in form & in agreement, even
when pl. in meaning.*) ~ *cosa,
qualcosa,* something; anything. *in
~ luogo,* somewhere; anywhere.
~ *volta,* sometimes.

qualchedúno, see *qualcuno.*

qualcòsa, *pn. indef.* something; anything.

qualcúno, *pn. indef.* some one; any
one; somebody, anybody; (*sg. in
form, pl. in meaning*) some; any.

quàle, *a. & pn. interrog.* what? which?
¶ *a.indef.* what; what a; as, just as.
tale ~, ~, such as, just as. ~ *e
quale,* the same. ¶ *il* **quàle,** *pn. rel.*
(*f.* **la** ~, *m.pl.* **i quali,** *f.pl.* **le quali**)
who; whom; which. *del q., della q.,
dei* ~*i, delle* ~*i,* of whom, whose.
So *al* ~, *col* ~, *dal* ~, &c., (*with
pers.*) to whom, with w., by w.,
from w.; (*with things*) to which,
with w., &c. *la qual cosa,* which,
a fact which (*ref. to a preceding
clause*).

qualífica (*pl.* -**ífiche**)~*f.* qualification;
designation; title. **qualificàre** (*pr.*
-**ífico,** -**ífichi**), to qualify; designate,
style; call; describe. **qualificatívo,**
a. qualifying.

qualità, *f.* quality; property; profession; capacity; status; kind.

qualménte, *ad.* how; as.

qualóra, *ad. & c.* when; whenever; if.

qualsíasi, qualsisía, & **qualsi-
vòglia** (*pl.* **qualsíansi** *or* **qualsi-
síano** & **qualsivògliano**), any;
whatever. **qualúnque,** *a. indef. inv.*
any; whatever. **qualvòlta** (**ógni**),
ad. whenever.

quàndo, *ad. & c.* when; whenever; if.
di ~ in ~, now & then, from time
to time. ~ . . . ~, sometimes . . .
sometimes. *da* ~, since, ever since.

quantità, *f.* quantity; amount. *una
grande* ~, a great deal, a lot, lots.

quànto, *ad.* how, how much; as.
~ *a,* as for, as to, as regards, for.
per ~, as far as, however (much).
~ *prima,* as soon as possible. ¶ *a.
& pn.* how much; as much as; what,
all that. *tanto . . . quanto,* as much
as, so much . . . as **quànti,** *m.pl.,*

quànte, *f.pl.* how many; as. *tanti
. . . quanti, tante . . . e,* as many
as.

quantúnque, *c.* though, although.

quarànta, *card. num. inv.* forty.

quarantèna, *f.* quarantine.

quarantènne, *a.* forty years old.
quarantèsimo, *a. ord. num.*
fortieth. **quarantína,** *f.* about
forty; some forty; quarantine. *essere
sulla* ~, to be about forty (years of
age). **quarantottàta,** *f.* rash
venture. **quarantòtto,** *card. num.
inv.* forty-eight. *il Q~,* the rising(s)
of 1848, esp. that of Milan.

quarésima, *f.* Lent. **quaresimàle,**
a. Lenten.

quartàle, *m.* (*Theat.*) quarter of an
actor's salary.

quartàna, *f.* quartan ague; q. fever.

quartétto, *m.* (*Mus.*) quartet(te).
quarticèllo, *m.* quarter; quarter of
an hour.

quartière, *m.* (*Mil.*) quarters;
barracks; quarter (*in war*); quarter
(*city*); ward, district; neighbourhood;
flat; lodging(s). ~ *generale,* (*Mil.*)
headquarters. dim. **quartierino,** *m.*
small flat.

quartina, *f.* quatrain (*verse*).
quartíno, *m.* quarter of a litre,
pint; (*Mus.*) small clarinet. **quàrto,**
a. ord. num. fourth. ¶ *m.* quarter;
fourth (part); (*Typ.*) quarto.
edizione in ~, quarto edition.
quartogènito, *a. & m.* fourth born;
fourth child.

quàrzo, *m.* quartz.

quàsi, *ad.* almost; quasi-; nearly; as if;
about.

quàssia, *f.* quassia.

quassú, *ad.* up here.

quaternàrio, *m.* line of four syllables.
¶ *a.* (*Geol.*) quaternary.

quàtto, *a.* squat; crouching; cowering.
~ ~, quietly, very q.

quattordicènne, *a.* fourteen years
old. **quattordicèsimo,** *a. ord. num.*
fourteenth. **quattòrdici,** *card. num.
inv. & m.* fourteen; 14th.

quattrinàio, *m.* rich man; miser.
quattríno, *m.* farthing; (*pl.*) money.

quàttro, *card. num. inv. & m.* four;
4th. *a quattr'occhi,* in private.
tête-à-tête. fare ~ passi, to take a
stroll. *il Lago dei Q~ Cantoni,*
the Lake of Lucerne.

quattrocentèsimo, *a. ord. num.* four
hundredth. **quattrocentísta** (*pl.*
-**ísti**), *m.* artist or writer of the 15th
century. **quattrocènto,** *card. num.*

inv. four hundred. *il Q* ~, *m.* the 15th century, the Quattrocento.
quattromíla, *card. num. inv.* four thousand.

quégli, quéi, *&* **quéllo,** *demons. pn. m.sg.* he; the one. **quél, quéllo,** *m.* **quélla,** *f. demons. a.sg.* that; **quéi, quégli,** *m. pl.,* **quélle,** *f.pl. demons. a.* those. ¶ **quéllo,** *m.sg.,* **quélla,** *f.sg. demons. pn.* that; that one; the one; he; she. **quelli, quégli, quéi,** *m.pl.,* **quélle,** *f.pl. demons. pn.* those; the ones; those ones; they. *quello . . . questo, quelli . . . questi,* the former . . . the latter.

quercéta, *f.* & **quercéto,** *m.* oak-plantation; grove of oaks. **quèrcia** *(pl.* **quèrce),** *f.* oak; oak-tree.
quercíno, *a.* oaken; oak *(att.).*
querèla, *f.* complaint; action *(at law).*
querelànte, *m.* plaintiff. **querelàre** *(pr.* **-èlo),** *v.t.* to bring an action against; prosecute. **querelàrsi,** *v.refl.* to complain; take legal proceedings.
querimònia, *f.* complaint; lament. **quèrulo,** *a.* querulous; complaining.
quesíto, *m.* question; query; examination question; problem. *proporre un* ~, to put a question.
quésti, *demons. pn. 3 sg. m.* this man; this person *(used only in nom.).*
questionàre *(pr.* **-óno),** *v.i. (aux.* avere) to quarrel; dispute. **questionàrio,** *m.* set of questions; questionnaire. **questióne,** *f.* question; problem; matter; issue; quarrel, dispute; action at law.
quésto, *demons. a. m.sg.,* **quésta,** *f.sg.* this; **quésti,** *m.pl.,* **quéste,** *f.pl.* these. ¶ *demons. pn.* this, this one; *(pl.)* these, these ones; the latter *(sg. & pl.).*
questóre, *m.* commissioner of police.
quèstua, *f.* begging *(for charity);* collection of alms. **questuàre** *(pr.* **quèsto),** *v.i. (aux.* avere) to beg; seek for alms.
questúra, *f.* police-headquarters. **questuríno,** *m.* policeman; police officer.
quèto, quetàre, *&c.,* see *quieto, quietare.*
qui, *ad.* here; *(Poet.)* hither. ~ *vicino,* near here, near by. ~ *intorno,* hereabout(s). *di* ~, hence. *da* ~, from here; from now.
quiescènte, *a.* quiescent. **quie-scènza,** *f.* quiescence; retirement.
quietànza, *f.* receipt. **quietanzàre,** *v.t.* to receipt; give a receipt for.

quietàre *(pr.* **-ièto),** *v.t.* to quiet, quieten; soothe, calm. **quietàrsi,** *v.refl.* to quiet, quieten down; become quiet. **quiète,** *f.* quiet, quietness; calm; stillness; rest; peace. **quietísmo,** *m.* quietism.
quièto, *a.* quiet; still; calm; tranquil; peaceful.
quinàrio, *m.* line of five syllables.
quinci, *ad.* hence; from here; on this side.
quíndi, *ad.* & *c.* hence; from here; thence; on that side; therefore; then; afterwards. ~ *innanzi,* henceforth.
quindicènne, *a.* fifteen years old.
quindicèsimo, *a. ord. num.* fifteenth. **quíndici,** *card. num. inv.* fifteen. **quindicína,** *f.* about fifteen; fifteen days' pay, fortnight's wages. *una* ~ *(di giorni),* a fortnight. **quindicinale,** *a.* fortnightly.
quinquagenàrio, *a.* & *m.* fifty years old; man of fifty. **quinquagèsimo,** *a. ord. num.* fiftieth.
quinquennàle, *a.* quinquennial; five-year *(plan).* **quinquènnio,** *m.* period of five years.
quínta, *f.* fifth *(Mus.);* fifth class, f. form; *(pl.)* wings, flies *(Theat.). dietro le* ~*e,* behind the scenes *(lit. & fig.).*
quintàle, *m. (metric)* quintal = 100 kilos. ~ *inglese,* hundredweight *(abb.* cwt.) = 112 lbs.
quintèrno, *m. (lit.)* five sheets *(paper);* quire (24 *or* 25 *sheets);* copy-book. **quintessènza,** *f.* quintessence. **quintétto,** *m.* quintet(te). **quintíno,** *m.* fifth part of a litre. **quintogènito,** *a. num. ord.* & *m.* fifth. **quintogènito,** *m.* fifth child. **quintúplice,** *a.* five-fold.
Quirinàle, *m.* Quirinal (formerly the royal palace at Rome); now seat of the Republican Government.
quisquílie, *f.pl.* trifles; idle disputes.
quistióne, &c., see *questione,* &c.
quitànza, *f.* see *quietanza.*
quíví, *ad.* here; there.
quòndam *(Lat.),* *ad.* formerly; at one time. ¶ *a.* former; late, deceased.
quòta, *f.* part; share; quota; hill *(on* map); *(Aviat.)* height. *volare a bassa* ~, *(Aviat.)* to fly low. *prendere* ~, to climb, gain height. **quotàre,** *v.t.* to assess; quote *(Stk. Ex.).* **quotazióne,** *f.* quotation *(Stk. Ex.).*
quotidiàno, *a.* daily; everyday. ¶ *m.* daily (paper).
quòto & **quoziènte,** *m.* quotient.

R

R, r (*erre*), *f.* the letter R.
rabàrbaro, *m.* rhubarb.
rabattíno, *a. & m.* industrious; toiling; toiler.
raballinàre, *v.t.* to wrap up; pack in; roll up.
rabbaruffàre, *v.t.* to ruffle; pull about. **rabbaruffàrsi**, *v.refl.* to scuffle; become dishevelled.
rabbassàre, *v.t.* to lower again.
rabbàttere, *v.t.* to pull to; half-close (*door or shutter*).
rabbellíre (*pr.* **-ellísco**), *v.t. &* **rabbellírsi**, *v.refl.* to beautify; adorn (oneself); improve.
rabberciàre, *v.t.* to botch; patch up. **rabberciatóre**, *m.* mender; patcher; botcher. **rabberciatúra**, *f.* mending; patching.
ràbbi, *m.inv.* rabbi.
ràbbia, *f.* rage; anger; fury; (*dogs*) rabies; hydrophobia.
rabbínico (*pl.* **-ínici**), *a.* rabbinical. **rabbíno**, *m.* rabbin; master of Hebrew law; rabbi. *il Gran R~*, the Chief Rabbi.
rabbiosaménte, *ad.* furiously; madly; in a fit of rage. **rabbióso**, *a.* furious; choleric; rabid.
rabboccàre (*pr.* **-ócco, -ócchi**), *v.t.* to fill up; f. to the brim; refill. **rabboccatúra**, *f.* refilling.
rabbonacciàre, *v.i.* (*aux.* avere) *&* **rabbonacciàrsi**, *v.refl.* to become calm (again); to quiet(en) down; become reconciled. **rabboníre** (*pr.* **-isco, -isci**), *v.t.* to pacify; calm (down).
rabbottonàre, *v.t.* to button (up) again.
rabbracciàre, *v.t.* to re-embrace.
rabbriccicàre, *v.t.* to patch up.
rabbrividíre (*pr.* **-ísco, -ísci**), *v.i.* (*aux.* essere *&* avere) to shudder; shiver.
rabbruscàre, *v.i.* (*aux.* essere) to darken; become overcast; grow threatening (*sky, weather*). **rabbruscàrsi**, *v.refl.* to grow gloomy; become morose.
rabbruscolàre, *v.t.* to save up.
rabbuffàre, *v.t.* to ruffle; disorder; reprove; reprimand. **rabbuffàrsi**, *v.refl.* to become ruffled; lower; grow stormy. **rabbúffo**, *m.* stern rebuke.
rabbuiàre, *v.i.* (*aux.* essere) *&* **rabbuiàrsi**, *v.refl.* to grow dark.
rabdomànte, *m.* water-diviner;

dowser. **rabdomanzía**, *f.* water-divining, dowsing.
rabelesiàno, *a.* Rabelaisian.
rabescàme, *m.* arabesques (*pl.*).
rabescàre, *v.t.* to adorn with arabesques. **rabésco** (*pl.* **-éschi**), *m.* arabesque.
ràbido, *a.* rabid.
raccapezzàre, *v.t.* to put together; collect; understand; find out. **raccapezzàrsi**, *v.refl.* to understand, make out; see one's way.
raccapricciànte, *a.* horrifying; terrifying. **raccapricciàre**, *v.i.* (*aux.* essere *&* avere) *&* **raccapricciàrsi**, *v.refl.* to feel horror; shudder; shake with fear. **raccapríccio**, *m.* horror; terror; disgust.
raccattacénere, *m.inv.* ash-pan. **raccattàre**, *v.t.* to pick up; collect (*scraps, trifles*). **raccattatíccio**, *m.* rubbish. **raccattatóre**, *m.* picker-up.
raccenciàre, *v.t.* to mend; patch (up). **raccenciàrsi**, *v.refl.* to improve one's position; put on better clothes.
raccèndere, see *riaccendere*.
raccertàre, *v.t. &* **raccertàrsi**, *v.refl.* to make certain; reassure (oneself).
racchetàre, *v.t.* to quiet; soothe; console.
racchétta, *f.* racquet.
racchiocciolàrsi, *v.refl.* to curl up; huddle; cower.
racchiúdere, *v.t. ir.* to contain; hold.
racciabattàre, *v.t.* to patch up; cobble.
raccògliere (*pr.* **-òlgo, -ògli**, like *cogliere*), *v.t. ir.* to gather; pick up; collect; assemble; (*fig.*) reap. **raccògliersi**, *v.refl.* to assemble; collect one's thoughts; pull oneself together; concentrate (*mentally*); retire. **raccoglimento**, *m.* gathering; concentration; absorption; meditation; retirement. **raccoglitíccio**, *a.* picked up here & there. ¶ *m.* haphazard collection. **raccoglitóre**, *m.* (*f.* **-tríce**) gatherer; collector; compiler. **raccòlta**, *f.* collection; harvest; crop. *chiamare a ~*, to rally. *sonare a ~*, to sound the retreat. **raccòlto**, *p.p.* of *raccogliere*. ¶ *m.* crop; harvest.
raccomandàre, *v.t.* to recommend; fasten up; attach; commit; entrust; register (*in post*). **raccomandàrsi**, *v.refl.* to implore, entreat, beg; to commend oneself; recommend oneself. *mi raccomando* (*polite depreca-*

tory expr.), please; allow me; if I may. **raccomandàta**, *f.* registered letter. **raccomandàto**, *p.a.* recommended; registered. **raccomandazióne**, *f.* recommendation; registration.

raccomodaménto, *m.* & **raccomodatúra**, *f.* mending; repairing. **raccomodàre**, *v.t.* to mend; repair; put in order; readjust. **raccomodatóre**, *m.* (*f.* **-tóra**, **-tríce**) mender; repairer.

racconciàre, *v.t.* to mend; repair; amend; improve. **racconciàrsi**, *v.refl.* to make it up; be reconciled; tidy oneself; recover (*health, beauty*); (*weather*) clear. **racconciatúra**, *f.* mending; repairing. **raccóncio**, *sync. p.p.* of *racconciare*, mended; repaired; amended; improved.

raccontàbile, *a.* worth recounting; fit to tell. **raccontafàvole**, *m.inv.* story-teller; liar. **raccontàre**, *v.t.* to tell; relate; recount; narrate. *si racconta*, they say, it is said. **raccontatóre**, *m.* (*f.* **-tríce**) teller; narrator. **raccónto**, *m.* story; tale; narrative; report.

raccoppiàre, *v.t.* to re-unite.

raccorciàre & **raccorcíre** (*pr.* **-ísco**, **-ísci**), *v.t.* to shorten. **raccorciàrsi**, *v.refl.* to grow shorter; shrink.

raccordàre, *v.t.* to connect; link (together). **raccòrdo**, *m.* connection; link line (*Rly.*). *binario di* ∼, (*Rly.*) siding.

raccostaménto, *m.* bringing together; comparison. **raccostàre**, *v.t.* to bring near; push close; compare.

raccozzàre, *v.t.* to bring together. **raccozzàrsi**, *v.refl.* to re-assemble; meet.

rachítico (*pl.* **-ítici**), *a.* rickety (*child*); stunted (*plant*); blighted. **rachítide**, *f.* rickets.

racimolàre, *v.i.* (*aux.* avere) to glean (*grapes*). *v.t.* (*fig.*) to pick up, scrape together. **racimolatóre**, *m.* (*f.* **-tríce**) picker; collector; gleaner. **racímolo**, *m.* small bunch of grapes.

racquistaménto, *m.* recovery. **racquistàre**, *v.t.* to regain; recover. **racquísto**, *m.* recovery.

ràda, *f.* roadstead, road(s) (*Naut.*).

radaménte, *ad.* sparsely; rarely; seldom.

radàzza, *f.* mop; (*Naut.*) swab. **radazzàre**, *v.t.* to swab (*decks*).

raddensàre, *v.t.* to thicken; condense

further. **raddensàrsi**, *v.refl.* to become thicker.

raddirizzàre, *v.t.* to put straight again; correct. **raddirizzatúra**, *f.* correction; re-straightening.

raddobbàre, *v.t.* (*Naut.*) to refit; repair. **raddòbbo**, *m.* refitting; repair; repairing (*ships*).

raddolciménto, *m.* sweetening; softening (*fig.*). **raddolcíre** (*pr.* **-ísco**, **-ísci**), *v.t.* to sweeten; (*fig.*) to soften; soothe; allay. *v.i.* (*aux.* essere) & **raddolcírsi**, *v.refl.* to become milder (*weather*); be allayed, soothed, softened.

raddoppiaménto, *m.* doubling; reduplication. **raddoppiàre**, *v.t.* to double; redouble.

raddrizzaménto *m.* & **raddrizzatúra**, *f.* straightening.

raddrizzàre, see *raddirizzare*.

radènte, *p.a.* grazing; skimming (past). **ràdere**, *v.t. ir.* to shave; erase, scratch out; raze; graze; rake (*artil.*). *il* ∼, *radersi*, shaving.

radézza, *f.* thinness; space between two rows (*trees*, &*c.*); scarcity; rarity.

radiàle, *a.* radial. **radiante**, *a.* radiant; beaming.

radiàre, *v.t.* to cancel; erase. *v.i.* (*aux.* avere) to radiate; emit rays; beam. **radiàto**, *p.a.* erased; struck off; cancelled; radiate; surrounded by rays; radiated. **radiatóre**, *m.* radiator. **radiazióne**, *f.* radiation; cancellation.

ràdica (*pl.* **ràdiche**), *f.* root; briarwood. **radicàle**, *a.* & *m.* radical; (*f.*) root (*Gram.*). **radicalísmo**, *m.* radicalism. **radicaménto**, *m.* striking root. **radicàre**, *v.t.* & *i.* (*aux.* essere) to root. **radicàrsi**, *v.refl.* to root; take root. **radicàto**, *a.* rooted; deep-seated. **radicazióne**, *f.* taking root.

radícchia & **radicchièlla**, *f.* dandelion. **radícchio**, *m.* radish.

radíce, *f.* root (*lit.* & *fig.*); origin; cause; source; radish.

ràdio, *m.* radium. ¶ *f.* wireless; radio. *trasmettere per* ∼, to broadcast. *ascoltare la* ∼, to listen in.

radioattívo, *a.* radio-active. **radiocrònaca**, *f.* broadcast news, b. description. **radiodiffusióne**, *f.* broadcasting. **radiofònico** (*pl.* **-ònici**), *a.* wireless, radio (*att.*). *apparecchio* ∼, *m.* wireless set. *stazione* ∼*a*, *f.* wireless station. *licenza* ∼*a*, *f.* wireless licence.

programma ~ *d'oggi, m.* to-day's broadcast programme. **radiogoniòmetro,** *m.* radio direction-finder. *un faro radiogoniometrico,* a radio beacon. **radiografía,** *f.* radiography. **radiogràmma,** *m.* radiogram.

radióso, *a.* radiant; bright; shining.

radiotelegrafía, *f.* radiotelegraphy. **radiotelegrafísta,** *m.* wireless operator. **radioterapía,** *f.* radiotherapy. **radiotrašméttere,** *v.t. ir.* to broadcast. *stazione radiotrasmettente, f.* broadcasting station. **radiotrasmissióne,** *f.* broadcasting.

raditúra, *f.* erasing; scratching out.

ràdo, *a.* rare, sparse; thin; scattered; infrequent; occasional; slow (*steps*). *di* ~, *rade volte,* seldom, rarely.

radunàre, *v.t. &* **radunàrsi,** *v.refl.* to assemble; gather; collect. **radunàta,** *f.* assembly; gathering, rally.

radúra, *f.* glade; bare patch.

Raffaèllo, *m.* Raphael.

raffazzonaménto, *m.* patching up; re-arrangement; recasting. **raffazzonàre,** *v.t.* to patch up; re-arrange; re-cast; correct.

rafférma, *f.* confirmation; renewal; re-enlistment; extension of term of military service. **raffermàre,** *v.t.* to renew (*contract*); strengthen; confirm; solidify. **rafférmo,** *a.* firm; hard; (*bread*) stale.

ràffica (*pl.* **ràffiche**), *f.* squall; violent gust of wind; (*fig.*) shower, hail.

raffiguràre, *v.t.* to recognize; represent; symbolize.

raffilàre, *v.t.* to sharpen; whet; pare; trim. **raffilatóre,** *m.* sharpener; clipper; trimmer. **raffilatúra,** *f.* sharpening, &c.

raffinaménto, *m.* refining. **raffinàre,** *v.t.* to refine. **raffinatézza,** *f.* refinement. **raffinàto,** *a.* refined (*sugar, manners, &c.*); subtle; ingenious. **raffinería,** *f.* refinery.

ràffio, *m.* hook; grappling-iron. *di riffi o di raffi,* by hook or by crook.

raflittíre (*pr.* **-ísco, -ísci**), *v.t.* to thicken.

rafforzaménto, *m.* strengthening; reinforcement. **rafforzàre,** *v.t.* to strengthen; reinforce. **rafforzàrsi,** *v.refl.* to be strengthened; become stronger.

raffreddaménto, *m.* cooling. **raffreddàre,** *v.t.* to cool. **raffreddàrsi,** *v.refl.* to cool, c. down; grow cold; catch cold. **raffreddóre,** *m.* cold; chill.

raffrenàre, *v.t.* to restrain; check; curb.

raffrescaménto, *m.* cooling. **raffrescàre** (*pr.* **-ésco**), *v.i.* (*aux.* essere) *&* **raffrescàrsi,** *v.refl.* to grow cool; turn cooler. **raffrescàta,** *f.* cooling; fall in temperature.

raffrontaménto, *m.* comparison. **raffrontàre,** *v.t.* to compare; confront; bring together, unite. **raffrònto,** *m.* comparison.

raganèlla, *f.* tree-frog; rattle; clapper.

ragàzza, *f.* girl. dim. *ragazétta, ragazzina.* **ragazzàglia,** *f.* host of children; noisy crowd of boys. **ragazzàta,** *f.* childish action; boyish trick. **ragàzzo,** *m.* boy. dim. *ragazzétto, ragazzino.*

raggentilíre (*pr.* **-ísco, -ísci**), *v.t.* to refine; educate; civilize; teach good manners (to). **raggentilírsi,** *v.refl.* to improve one's manners.

raggiànte, *a.* radiant. **raggiàre,** *v.i.* (*aux.* avere) to radiate; shine. **ràggio** (*pl.* **ràggi**), *m.* ray (*of light*); beam; gleam; radius (*Geom.*); spoke (*wheel*); (*Poet.*) fame, glory; (*pl.*) (*Poet.*) rai, eyes.

raggiornàre, *v.i. impers.* (*aux.* essere) to dawn; be daylight again.

raggiraménto, *m.* trick; swindle. **raggiràre,** *v.t.* to cheat; trick; swindle. **raggiràrsi,** *v.refl.* to turn about; go round; beat about the bush. **raggiratóre,** *m.* (*f.* **-tríce**) trickster; swindler. **raggíro,** *m.* trick; subterfuge.

raggiúngere, *v.t. ir.* to reach; overtake; rejoin; attain; hit (*target*); amount to. **raggiungiménto,** *m.* attainment; achievement.

raggiustàre, *v.t.* to re-adjust; repair; set in order; reconcile.

raggomitolàre, *v.t.* to roll up; make into a ball. **raggomitolàrsi,** *v.refl.* to curl up; roll oneself up.

raggranchíto, *a.* benumbed.

raggranellàre, *v.t.* to gather; scrape together; glean.

raggrinzàre *&* **raggrinzíre** (*pr.* **-ísco, -ísci**), *v.t.* to wrinkle, w. up; shrivel. (*v.i.*) (*aux.* essere) to become wrinkled.

raggrottàre, *v.t.* to wrinkle. ~ *la ciglia,* to frown, knit the brows.

raggrumàre, *v.t. &* **raggrumàrsi,** *v.refl.* to clot.

raggruppaménto, *m.* grouping;

group, cluster. **raggruppàre**, *v.t.* to assemble; group; arrange in groups. **raggruppàrsi**, *v.refl.* to form a group (groups); cluster.
raggruzzolàre, *v.t.* to put together; save (up).
ragguagliàbile, *a.* comparable. **ragguagliaménto**, *m.* equalization. **ragguagliàre**, *v.t.* to compare; balance; equalize, level; inform. **ragguàglio**, *m.* information; report; comparison; equalization; rate; (*pl.*) news.
ragguardévole, *a.* considerable; notable; important. **ragguardevolézza**, *f.* importance.
ràgia, *f.* rosin; resin.
ragionaménto, *m.* reasoning; argument; discussion. **ragionàre**, *v.i.* (*aux.* avere) to reason; argue; discuss; discourse; talk. **ragionàto**, *a.* reasoned; logical. **ragionatóre**, *m.* reasoner. **ragióne**, *f.* reason; law, right; justice; ownership; rate; ratio; price; style (*of a firm*). *avere* ~, to be right. *farsi* ~, to assure oneself. *render* ~, to render account. **ragionería**, *f.* book-keeping; accountancy.
ragionévole, *a.* reasonable. **ragionevolézza**, *f.* reasonableness. **ragionière**, *m.* accountant; book-keeper.
ragliaménto, *m.* braying. **ragliàre**, *v.i.* (*aux.* avere) to bray. **ragliàta**, *f.* & **ràglio**, *m.* braying; bray.
ràgna, *f.* cobweb; web; spider's web; (*cloth*) threadbare patch. **ragnàre**, *v.i.* (*aux.* avere & essere) (*cloth*) to become threadbare; (*sky*) to be covered with thin fleecy clouds. **ragnatéla**, *f.* & **ragnatélo**, *m.* cobweb, web, spider's w. **ragnàto**, *a.* threadbare. **ragnatúra**, *f.* (*cloth*) bare patch; (*sky*) thin clouds.
ràgno, *m.* spider.
ragú, *m.* ragout.
ràia, *m.* rajah.
ràion, *m.inv.* rayon, artificial silk.
rallacciàre, *v.t.* to tie up again.
rallargàre, *v.t.* to widen; expand. **rallargàrsi**, *v.refl.* (*of sky*) to clear.
rallegraménto, *m.* joy; rejoicing; (*pl.*) congratulations. **rallegràre**, *v.t.* to gladden; cheer. **rallegràrsi**, *v.refl.* to rejoice; be glad; cheer up. ~ *con*, to congratulate.
rallentàre, *v.t.* to slacken; relax; lessen. *v.i.* (*aux.* essere) & **rallentàrsi**, *v.refl.* to slow down;

to become slack. *un film rallentato*, a slow-motion picture (*Cinema*).
rallignàre, *v.i.* (*aux.* avere) to take root again.
ràma, *f.* branch; twig.
ramàio, *m.* copper-smith.
ramàrro, *m.* green lizard.
ràme, *m.* copper.
ramétto, **ramicèllo**, *m.* small branch; twig.
ramificàre, *v.i.* (*aux.* avere) & **ramificàrsi**, *v.refl.* to branch, branch out, ramify.
ramingàre, *v.i.* (*aux.* avere) to wander; roam. **ramíngo** (*pl.* -ínghi), *a.* wandering; roving; solitary.
ramíno, *m.* copper pot or kettle.
rammaricàrsi, *v.refl.* to grieve; regret; complain. **rammàrico** (*pl.* -àrichi), *m.* regret; grief; sorrow.
rammendàre, *v.t.* to darn; mend. **rammendatríce**, *f.* darner; mender. **rammendatúra**, *f.* darning; mending. **ramméndo**, *m.* darn; mending; repair.
rammentàre, *v.t.* to call to mind; recall; remind. **rammentàrsi**, *v.refl.* to remember; recollect.
rammodernàre, *v.t.* to modernize; bring up to date; remodel.
rammolliménto, *m.* softening. **rammollíre** (*pr.* -ísco, -ísci), *v.t.* to soften; mollify. **rammollírsi**, *v.refl.* to soften; grow soft; become effeminate.
ràmo, *m.* branch (*lit.* & *fig.*); bough; antler. **ramoscèllo**, *m.* small branch; twig. **ramóso**, *a.* branched; branching; branchy.
ràmpa, *f.* flight of steps; ramp; steep slope. **rampàta**, *f.* slope; blow from a paw.
rampicànte, *a.* climbing; creeping (*plant*). ¶ *m.* climber (*Zool.*); creeper (*plant*). **rampicàre**, *v.i.* (*aux.* avere & essere) & **rampicàrsi**, *v.refl.* to climb; scramble up.
rampicóne, *m.* harpoon; grappling-iron.
rampíno, *m.* hook; prong; pot-hook; (*fig.*) pretext.
rampógna, *f.* rebuke; reproof. **rampognàre**, *v.t.* to rebuke; reprove; reproach.
rampollàre, *v.i.* (*aux.* essere) to spring, rise; shoot (up) (*plant*). **rampóllo**, *m.* spring (*water*); shoot (*plant*); (*fig.*) scion, offspring.
rampóne, *m.* harpoon.
ràna, *f.* frog.

ranciàto, a. orange (coloured).
rancidézza & **rancidità**, f. rancidness, rancidity. **rancidíre** (pr. -isco, -isci), v.i. (aux. essere) to go (or become) rancid. **ràncido**, a. rancid; rank. **rancidúme**, m. rancid stuff; rancidity ;(fig.) what is stale or out of date.
rancière, m. mess-cook. **ràncio**, m. ration (army); mess. ¶ a. orange (coloured).
rancóre, m. grudge; bitterness; rancour.
randàgio, a. stray; wandering. ¶ m. wanderer.
randellàre, v.t. to club; cudgel; beat. **randellàta**, f. blow with a club. **randèllo**, m. club; cudgel.
ranèlla, f. washer (for bolt & nut).
ràngo (pl. rànghi), m. rank; degree; station.
rannicchiàrsi, v.refl. to crouch; cuddle; curl (oneself) up.
rànno, m. lye.
rannobilíre (pr. -ìsco, -ìsci), v.t. to ennoble; redeem.
rannodàre, v.t. to re-tie; (fig.) renew (friendship, &c.). **rannodàrsi**, v.refl. to re-unite; re-assemble.
rannuvolàre, v.t. to cloud. **rannuvolàrsi**, v.refl. to cloud over (lit. & fig.); to become gloomy; darken.
ranòcchia, f., **ranòcchio**, m. frog (often used of small boys). dim. ranocchiétto, ranocchino.
rantolàre, v.i. (aux. avere) to breathe heavily; have the death rattle (in one's throat). **ràntolo**, m. heavy breathing; death-rattle.
ranúncolo, m. buttercup; crowfoot; ranunculus.
ràpa, f. turnip; (fig.) stupid fellow; dunce.
rapàce, a. rapacious. uccello ∼, bird of prey. **rapacità**, f. rapacity; greed.
rapàre, v.t. to crop the hair close.
rapidità, f. swiftness; quickness; rapidity. **ràpido**, a. swift; rapid; quick. ¶ m. express; express train.
rapiménto, m. rapture; ecstasy; ravishment; abduction.
rapína, f. robbery; rapine; fury. uccello di ∼, bird of prey.
rapíre (pr. -ìsco, -ìsci), v.t. to carry off; steal; seize; abduct; kidnap; ravish, enrapture.
rapaciàre & **rappacificàre**, v.t. to reconcile; pacify; restore peace to.
rappezzàre, v.t. to patch up; piece

together; mend. **rappezzatúra**, f. patching up; piecing together; mending; patch. **rappèzzo**, m. patch; patched place; (fig.) poor excuse.
rappiccàre, v.t. to refasten; hang up again; start again; renew.
rappicciníre (pr. -ìsco, -ìsci) & **rappicciolíre** (pr. -ìsco, -ìsci), v.t. to diminish; reduce; shorten; (fig.) belittle. **rappicciolíre**, v.i. (aux. essere) & **rappicciolírsi**, v.refl. to become smaller, diminish.
rappigliàrsi, v.refl. to set, thicken; curdle; coagulate.
rapportàre, v.t. to report; relate; tell; inform; ascribe; bring in, introduce; transfer; transport; reproduce. **rapportàrsi** (a), v.refl. to have reference to, relate to; to be advised by, take the advice of.
rappòrto, m. report; statement; relation; link, connection; intercourse; reference; ratio; proportion.
rapprèndere, v.i. (aux. essere) & **rapprèndersi**, v.refl. to set, thicken; curdle; coagulate; to be benumbed.
rappresàglia, f. reprisal.
rappresèntànte, m. representative; agent. **rappresèntànza**, f. agency (Com.); representation (Pol.); deputation. ∼ proporzionale, proportional representation. **rappresèntàre**, v.t. to represent; perform (play); play (a part). **rappresèntativo**, a. representative. **rappresèntazióne**, f. representation; performance (Theat.); description.
rapsodía, f. rhapsody.
raraménte, ad. seldom; rarely **rarefàre** (pr. -fàccio, -fài, -fà, &c., like fare), v.t. ir. to rarefy. **rarefazióne**, f. rarefaction. **rarézza**, f. rareness, rarity. **rarità**, f. rarity, rareness; curiosity; valuable specimen. **ràro**, a. rare; exceptional; uncommon.
rasàre, v.t. to smooth; polish; clip (hedge); shave bare.
raschiaménto, m. scraping; scratching. **raschiàre**, v.t. to scrape; scratch out; erase. ∼via, to scrape off. v.i. (aux. avere) & **raschiàrsi**, v.refl. (in gola) to clear one's throat. **raschiatóio**, m. scraper. **raschiatúra**, f. scraping; scratching; erasure; (pl.) scrapings. **raschiétto**, m. scraper; eraser. **ràschio**, m. scraping; scratching; slight cough; irritation (in the throat).

rasciugàre, *v.t.* to dry up; (*fig.*) finish, exhaust.

raśentàre, *v.t.* to graze; shave past, pass close to; skim; be near (to), border upon. **raśènte,** *pr.* close to, very near.

ràso, *a.* close-cropped, c. shaven; bare, naked, open; smooth. *a* ~ *di*, level with, flush with. *pieno* ~, or ~, full to the brim. ~ *al suolo*, razed to the ground. ¶ *m.* satin.

rasoiàta, *f.* cut with a razor. **rasóio,** *m.* razor. ~*di sicurezza*, safety razor.

ràspa, *f.* rasping-file. **raspànte,** *a.* rasping; (*fig.*) sour. **raspàre,** *v.t.* to rasp; scrape; scratch about (for); paw, stamp (*horses*). **raspatíccio,** *m.* piece of bad workmanship; scrawl; scratch. **raspatúra,** *f.* rasping; grating; (*pl.*) filings, raspings. **raspíno,** *m.* smoothing-file; small bunch (*of grapes or grape-stalks*).

ràspo, *m.* mange (*dog*); grape-stalk; sour taste.

rasségna, *f.* review (*Mil.*, *Lit.*, *&c.*); parade; muster; detailed description; registration. **rassegnàre,** *v.t.* to resign; pass in review; submit (*documents*). **rassegnàrsi,** *v.refl.* to resign oneself; submit; (*ending a letter*) to be, remain. **rassegna-zióne,** *f.* resignation; submission.

rassetaménto, *m.* arrangement; re-arrangement; correction. **rasset-tàre,** *v.t.* to arrange; re-arrange; set in order; repair; correct; tidy up.

rassicurànte, *a.* reassuring. **rassi-curàre,** *v.t.* to assure; reassure. **rassicuràrsi,** *v.refl.* to make sure; be reassured; recover confidence.

rassodaménto, *m.* consolidation; strengthening; hardening; drying (up). **rassodàre,** *v.t. & v.i.* (*aux.* essere) to consolidate, make firm; harden; dry, &c., *&* **rassodàrsi,** *v.refl.* to become firm; consolidate; harden; dry (up).

rassomigliànte, *a.* like. **rassomi-gliànza,** *f.* likeness; resemblance. **rassomigliàre,** *v.i.* (*aux.* essere) to be like; resemble. **rassomigliàrsi,** *v.refl.* to be like; resemble (*each other*).

rastrellàre, *v.t.* to rake; search; ransack; (*Mil.*) mop up. **rastrel-lièra,** *f.* hay-rack, crib; dish-rack; arms-stand. **rastrèllo,** *m.* rake.

rasúra, *f.* scraping; slight cut; erasure.

ràta, *f.* instalment. **rateàle,** *a.* by instalments; partial; periodic(al).

ratafià, *m.* ratafia. ~ *di ciliege*, cherry-brandy.

ratífica *&* **ratificazióne,** *f.* ratification. **ratificàre** (*pr.* -**ífico,** -**ífichi**), *v.t.* to ratify, confirm.

rattaccàre, *v.t.* to refasten; re-attach, re-unite. **rattacconàre,** *v.t.* to patch, repair or heel (shoes).

rattaménte, *ad.* quickly; swiftly, rapidly.

rattenére (*pr.* -**tèngo,** -**tièni,** *&c.*, like *tenere*), *v.t. ir.* to keep back; check; restrain; detain. **rattenérsi,** *v.refl.* to restrain oneself. **rattenúta,** *f.* restraint; detention; keeping back (*payment, salary, &c.*).

rattepidíre (*pr.* -**ísco,** -**ísci**), *v.t.* to cool. *v.i.* (*aux.* essere) *&* **rattepi-dìrsi,** *v.refl.* to become cool, cool down.

rattézza, *f.* swiftness.

rattizzàre, *v.t.* to stir up (*fire*); (*fig.*) to excite; kindle.

ràtto, *m.* abduction; kidnapping; rape; (*sewer*) rat. ¶ *a.* swift, quick, rapid. ¶ *ad.* swiftly, *&c.*

rattoppàre, *v.t.* to patch; mend.

rattrappíre (*pr.* -**ísco,** -**ísci**), *v.t. & i.* (*aux.* essere) to contract; shrink. **rattrappírsi,** *v.refl.* to become paralysed. **rattràrre** (*pr.* -**àggo,** *&c.*, like *trarre*) *v.i.* (*aux.* essere) *&* **rattràrsi,** *v.refl.ir.* to contract.

rattristàre, *v.t.* to grieve; sadden. **rattristíre** (*pr.* -**ísco,** -**ísci**), *v.t.* to depress; weaken; enfeeble. *v.i.* (*aux.* essere) *&* **rattristírsi,** *v.refl.* to grow feeble; droop.

raucaménte, *ad.* hoarsely. **raucè-dine,** *f.* hoarseness. **ràuco** (*pl.* **ràuchi**), *a.* hoarse. Cf. *roco.*

ravennàte, *a.* of Ravenna. ¶ *m.* inhabitant of Ravenna.

raviòli, *m.pl.* (*Cook.*) pockets of stuffed pasta. **ravizzóne,** *m.* (*Bot.*) rape.

ravvaloràre, *v.t.* to strengthen; give value to.

ravvedérsi, *v.refl.* to see one's error; acknowledge one's faults; repent; reform. **ravvediménto,** *m.* repentance; reformation; amendment. **ravvedúto,** *a.* repentant; reformed.

ravvìare, *v.t.* to put in order; arrange;

adjust; set going again; put on the right way. **ravviàrsi**, *v.refl.* to start again; reform; tidy oneself (*hair, dress, &c.*).

ravvicinàre, *v.t.* to bring closer; reconcile; compare. **ravvicinàrsi**, *v.refl.* to draw closer; become reconciled. *una visuale ravvicinata*, a close-up (*Cinema*).

ravvisàre, *v.t.* to recognize; perceive.

ravvivàre, *v.t.* to revive; revivify; animate; enliven; stir (*fire*).

ravvòlgere (*pr.* -òlgo, -òlgi, *&c.*, like *volgere*), *v.t.* to wrap up; envelop; involve. **ravvòlgersi**, *v.refl.* to become enveloped; curl up; get involved; become confused (*in speech*).

rayon, *m.* see *raion*.

raziocinàre, *v.i.* (*aux.* avere) to reason. **raziocinativo**, *a.* reasoning. **raziocínio**, *m.* reason; reasoning; thinking.

razionàle, *a.* rational; pure (*mechanics*). **razionalísmo**, *m.* rationalism.

razionaménto, *m.* rationing. **razionàre**, *v.t.* to ration. **razióne**, *f.* ration; allowance; portion.

ràzza, *f.* race; breed; kind. *di* ∼ *pura*, thoroughbred (*horse*). *di* ∼ *incrociata*, cross-bred. **razzamàglia**, *f.* rabble; riff-raff; mob.

razzia, *f.* raid; foray; insect-powder, insecticide. **razziàre**, *v.t. & i.* (*aux.* avere) to raid; plunder. **razziatóre**, *m.* raider.

razzísmo, *m.* racialism.

ràzzo, *m.* rocket; flare; ray; beam; spoke (*wheel*). ∼*luminoso*, star-shell; flash-bomb.

razzolàre, *v.i.* (*aux.* avere) to scrape; scratch about; rummage; weed, hoe; stir (*fire*). ∼*il cervello*, to puzzle one's brains.

ré (*e* close), *m.inv.* king. **rè** (*e* open), *m.* D (*Mus.*), re.

reagíre (*pr.* -ísco, -ísci), *v.i.* (*aux.* avere) to react.

reàle, *a.* real; royal. **realísmo**, *m.* realism. **realísta** (*pl.* -ísti), *m.* realist; royalist. **realístico** (*pl.* -ístici), *a.* realistic. **realiżżare**, *v.t.* to realize; obtain, fetch (*price*). **realiżżarsi**, *v.refl.* to come true, be realized. **realiżżazióne**, *f.* realization.

realménte, *ad.* really, in reality. **realtà**, *f.* reality.

reàme, *m.* (*Poet.*) realm; kingdom.

reàto, *m.* punishable offence; crime.

reattívo, *a.* reactive. **reazionàrio**,

a. & m. reactionary. **reazióne**, *f.* reaction. (*Aviat.*) *apparecchio a* ∼, jet [propelled] plane. *propulsione a* ∼, jet-propulsion. ∼ *a catena*, chain-reaction.

rébbio, *m.* prong.

reboànte, *a.* bombastic; high-sounding.

rèbus, *m.inv.* rebus; picture puzzle; riddle.

recalcitrànte, *a. & m.* recalcitrant.

recanatése, *a. & m.* native of Recanati. *il* [*grande*] ∼, Leopardi, b. there 1798.

recapitàre, *v.t.* to deliver; hand over (*letters, &c.*). **recàpito**, *m.* delivery; address; destination (*letter, parcel*); office; place of call.

recàre, *v.t.* to bring; fetch; carry; take; give; turn, render, translate; bring about, cause; ascribe. **recàrsi**, *v.refl.* to go; betake oneself; put oneself; take; bring. ∼ *a mente*, to bring to mind, recollect. ∼*a cuore*, to take to heart.

recèdere (*pr.* -cèdo, *&c.*, like *cedere*), *v.i. ir.* (*aux.* essere *&* avere) to recede; withdraw.

recensióne, *f.* review (*of a book*). **recensíre** (*pr.* -ísco, -ísci), *v.t.* to review. **recensóre**, *m.* reviewer.

recènte, *a.* recent; late; new. **recentíssime**, *f.pl.* latest news.

rècere (*pr.* rècio, rèci, rèce), *v.i.* to vomit; retch.

recèsso, *m.* recess; recession; (*Law*) renouncement; withdrawal.

recettività, *f.* receptivity. **recettívo**, *a.* receptive. **recezióne**, *f.* reception; admission (to office).

recídere, *v.t. ir.* to cut; cut off; c. down; excise; replough. **recídersi**, *v.refl.* to split; rip.

recidíva, *f.* relapse. **recidivàre**, *v.i.* (*aux.* essere) to relapse. **recidívo**, *a.* relapsing. ¶ *m.* one who relapses into crime; old offender; habitual criminal.

recíngere (*pr.* -íngo, -íngi, like *cingere*), *v.t. ir.* to enclose; surround; fence (in). **recínto**, *m.* enclosure; enclosed place.

recipiènte, *a.* suitable; adequate. ¶ *m.* vessel.

recíproca, *f.* (*Math.*) reciprocal. **reciprocaménte**, *ad.* reciprocally; mutually. **recíproco** (*pl.* -íproci), *a.* reciprocal; mutual; inverse; converse.

recisaménte, *ad.* decidedly; sharply; resolutely. **recisióne**, *f.* cutting off;

excision. **recíso,** *a.* short; curt; determined; resolute; uncompromising.

rècita, *f.* performance; recital; recitation. **recitànte,** *m.* performer; actor (*amateur*). **recitàre,** *v.t.* to recite; repeat; say; act; play; perform. **recitativo,** *m.* recitative (*Mus.*). **recitatóre,** *m.* (*f.* -tríce) reciter. **recitazióne,** *f.* recitation; recital; performance; acting.

reclamàre, *v.t.* to claim; demand, ask for. *v.i.* (*aux.* avere) to complain; protest; raise objections; lodge a complaint.

réclame, *f.* (*Fr.*) advertisement; advertising. **reclamístico** (*pl.* -ístici*),* *a.* advertisement, advertising (*att.*).

reclàmo, *m.* complaint.

reclinàre, *v.t.* & **reclinàrsi,** *v.refl.* to rest; recline.

reclusióne, *f.* imprisonment, confinement; seclusion. **reclúso,** *m.* prisoner; convict; recluse. **reclusòrio,** *m.* prison; penitentiary.

rècluta (more correctly, *reclúta*)*,* *f.* recruit; (*fig.*) novice. **reclutaménto,** *m.* recruitment; recruiting. **reclutàre,** *v.t.* to recruit.

recòndito, *a.* hidden; concealed; recondite.

record, *m.* (*sport*) record. ~*di velocità,* speed record.

recriminazióne, *f.* recrimination; complaint.

recrudescènza, *f.* recrudescence.

redarguíbile, *a.* questionable. **redarguíre** (*pr.* -uísco, -uísci*),* *v.t.* to challenge (or question) (*a statement*); find fault with; scold; reproach.

redattóre, *m.* member of the editorial staff of a newspaper; journalist; compiler. **redazióne,** *f.* editing; compiling; drawing up; editorial office or staff.

redditízio, *a.* profitable; paying. **rèddito,** *m.* income; revenue. *imposta sul* ~*, f.* income-tax.

redentóre, *m.* -tríce, *f.* redeemer. ¶ *a.* redeeming. **redenzióne,** *f.* redemption.

redigere (*pr.* **redígo, redígi**)*,* *v.t.* ir. to draw up; draft, redraft; compile; edit (a newspaper); write; compose.

redimere (*pr.* **redímo**)*,* *v.t.* ir. to redeem; ransom; set free. **redimíbile,** *a.* redeemable.

rèdine, *f.* rein. *le redini,* the reins (*lit.* & *fig.*).

redivívo, *a.* returned to life.

rèduce, *a.* returning; returned; come back. ¶ *m.* veteran; ex-service man.

reduplicàre, *v.t.* to redouble; reduplicate.

réfe, *m.* thread.

referèndum, *m.* referendum. **referènza,** *f.* reference; information; testimonial. **refèrto,** *m.* medical report; report made to a superior.

refettòrio, *m.* refectory. **refezióne,** *f.* refection; light meal; repast.

refrattàrio, *a.* refractory; stubborn; unmanageable; fire-proof. ¶ *m.* persistent law-breaker; (*Mil.*) defaulter.

refrigerànte, *a.* refrigerant. ¶ *m.* refrigerator. **refrigeràre,** *v.t.* to cool; refresh. **refrigèrio,** *m.* relief; comfort; solace; cooling refreshment.

refurtíva, *f.* stolen property; s. goods.

refúso, *m.* (*Typ.*) wrong letter.

regalàre, *v.t.* to present; make a present of. **regalàto,** *a.* (*fig.*) cheap, dirt cheap, given away.

regàle, *a.* royal; regal; kingly. **regalía,** *f.* gratuity; (*pl.*) produce (*eggs, poultry* &*c.*) given by a tenant-farmer to his landlord.

regàlo, *m.* present; gift. dim. *regalíno, regalétto, regalúccio.*

regàta, *f.* regatta.

regèsto, *m.* chronological list of documents.

reggènte, *m.* regent. **reggènza,** *f.* regency. **règgere** (*pr.* **règgo, règgi,** &*c.*)*,* *v.t.* ir. to support; hold up; bear; carry; hold; keep; govern, rule; beat (*cards*). *v.i.* (*aux.* avere) to bear (*ice*); stand; last; hold out. **règgersi,** *v.refl.* to stand; last; keep going.

règgia (*pl.* **règge**)*,* *f.* (royal) palace.

reggiàno, *a.* of Reggio Emilia. ¶ *m.* native of Reggio.

reggi-, (*fr.* *reggere*) forms numerous comps. all *m.* & *inv.,* e.g. *reggicatinèlle,* wash-stand; *reggilúme,* lamp-stand; *reggipància,* body-belt; belly-band (*horses*); *reggipètto,* breast-band; brassiere, &*c.*

reggiménto, *m.* regiment; government. **reggitóre,** *m.* (*f.* -tríce) administrator; ruler; manager, -ess.

regía, *f.* state monopoly (*of Salt* & *Tobacco*); shop for sale of excisable goods; (*Theat., Cinema*) work of the producer.

regicída (*pl.* -ídi)*,* *m.* regicide (*pers.*). ¶ *a.* regicidal. **regicídio,** *m.* regicide (*crime*).

regíme, m. regime; government; regimen, diet.

regína, f. queen. **règio,** a. royal. ¶ m. king (cards).

regionàle, a. regional; provincial. **regionalísmo,** m. regionalism; provincialism; local partisanship. **regióne,** f. region; district.

regísta (pl. -ísti), m. (Theat., Cinema) producer.

registràre, v.t. to register; record; (Com.) enter; regulate (watch); (Typ.) adjust. **registratóre,** m. registrar; recorder; register. ~di cassa, cash-register. ~di velocità, speed-register. **registrazióne,** f. registration; sorting. **regístro,** m. register; record. ~di classe, class register. tassa di ~, stamp duty. mutar ~, to change one's tone; alter one's conduct.

regnànte, a. reigning; ruling; prevailing. ¶ n. sovereign; ruler. **regnàre,** v.i. (aux. avere) to reign; rule; prevail; predominate. **régno,** m. reign; kingdom.

règola, f. rule; order; regulation; guidance; moderation. di ~, as a rule. in ~, in order. **regolamentàre,** a. regulation (att.); regular, prescribed. **regolaménto,** m. regulation; settlement. **regolàre,** a. regular. ¶ v.t. (pr. règolo, règoli), to regulate; control; settle (account). **regolarità,** f. regularity. **regolarizzàre,** v.t. to regularize. **regolarménte,** ad. regularly; duly; in order. **regolatézza,** f. orderliness; moderation. **regolàto,** a. orderly; well regulated; regular; moderate; temperate. **regolatóre,** m. (f. -tríce) regulator; governor (Mech.). ¶ a. regulating.

regolízia, f. liquorice.

règolo, m. ruler (for drawing lines); wood or metal bar (of cage, railings, &c.); golden-crested wren. ~ calcolatore, slide-rule.

regredíre (pr. -dísco, -dísci), v.i. (aux. essere & avere) to lose ground; go back. **regressióne,** f. regression. **regrèsso,** m. regress; regression; decline.

reiètto, a. rejected; outcast; forsaken. ¶ m. outcast. **reiezióne,** f. rejection.

reìna, f. (Poet.) queen.

reintegràre, v.t. to reinstate; restore; compensate; indemnify.

reità, f. guilt.

relativaménte, ad. relatively; comparatively. ~ a, with regard to.

relatività, f. relativity. **relatívo,** a. relative; proportionate. **relatóre,** m. reporter. **relazióne,** f. report; relation; connection, connexion; acquaintance(ship).

relegare (pr. rèlego, rèleghi), v.t. to relegate; banish; confine. **relegazióne,** f. banishment; confinement.

religióne, f. religion; religious order. **religióso,** a. religious; sacred (song, &c.); scrupulous. ¶ m. monk, friar. **religiósa,** f, nun.

relíquia, f. relic. **reliquiàrio,** m. reliquary; shrine.

relítto, m. spit of land left high & dry by the waves; (pl.) wreckage.

remàre & remigàre, v.i. (aux. avere) to row. **remàta,** f. rowing; row; stroke [of the oar]. **rematóre,** m. rower; oarsman. **rematríce,** f. rower; oarswoman. **remeggiàre,** v.i. (aux. avere) to flap (wings); row. **reméggio,** m. rowing; flapping; oars (coll.).

remissíbile, a. pardonable; excusable. **remissióne,** f. remission; forgiveness (injury or debt).

remissivaménte, ad. humbly, submissively. **remissívo,** a. submissive; yielding; meek; humble.

rèmo, m. oar.

remolíno & rèmolo, m. eddy; gust of wind; whirlwind; whirlpool.

rèmora, f. impediment; delay (fr. remora, the sucking-fish supposed to delay ships).

remòto, a. remote; distant; secluded. passato ~, (Gram.) past indefinite.

réna, f. sand; sands. **renàio,** m. sand-pit; sandy ground. **renai-[u]òlo,** m. sand-digger.

renàno, a. of the Rhine; Rhenish; Rhine (att.).

rèndere, v.t. ir. to give back, return, restore; surrender; give up; make do; pay; repay; render; give, yield; produce; represent, play, create, render (character, in acting); translate. **rèndersi,** v.refl. to make oneself . . .; become; go; surrender; yield.

rendicónto, m. report; rendering of accounts. **rendiménto,** m. rendering; returning (thanks); yield; product; efficiency. **rèndita,** f. income; revenue; stock. ~ vitalizia, life annuity.

rène, m. kidney. **renèlla,** f. (Med.) gravel. **renétta,** f. rennet (apple).

réni (le), f.pl. loins; back. dare le~, voltar le ~, to turn one's back.

renitènte, *a.* unwilling; stubborn; recalcitrant.   *essere* ∼ *alla leva*, (*Mil.*) to fail to appear at the call-up. **renitènza**, *f.* stubbornness; recalcitrance; resistance.

rènna, *f.* reindeer.

Rèno, *m.* (the) Rhine; (the) Reno (*tributary of the Po*).

renóso, *a.* sandy.

rèo, *a.* guilty; wicked, evil. ¶ *m.* convict; delinquent; accused.

repàrto, *m.* department (*hospital, store, &c.*); (*Mil.*) party; detachment.

repentàglio, *m.* danger; risk.

repènte, *a.* sudden; rapid; very steep. ¶ *ad.* ∼, & *di* ∼, suddenly. **repentíno**, *a.* sudden; unexpected.

reperíbile, *a.* to be found. **reperíre** (*pr.* **-ísco, -ísci**), *v.t.* to find; f. again; discover.

repertòrio, *m.* repertory; inventory; collection.

rèplica(*pl.* **rèpliche**),*f.* reply; repartee; repetition; (*pl.*) run of a play. **replicàre** (*pr.* **rèplico**), *v.t.* to reply, retort; repeat. **replicataménte**, *ad.* repeatedly.

reprensióne, *f.* rebuke. **repressióne**, *f.* repression. **reprímere**, *v.t. ir.* to repress; quell; put down; restrain; check.

rèprobo, *a. & m.* reprobate.

repúbblica, *f.* republic; commonwealth. **repubblicàno**, *a. & m.* republican.

repulísti (fare [un]), *fam. expr.* to make a clean sweep (of).

repulsióne, *f.* repulsion, aversion. **repulsóre**, *m.* buffer (*Rly.*).

reputàre, *v.t. & i.* (*aux.* avere) consider; deem; think. **reputàto**, *a.* esteemed. **reputazióne**, *f.* reputation. Cf. *riputare*, &c.

rèquie, *f.* rest; peace; pause; requiem.

requisíre (*pr.* **-ísco, -ísci**), *v.t.* to requisition, commandeer, impress. **requisíto**, *m.* requisite; qualification. **requisitòria**, *f.* charge; indictment.

résa, *f.* surrender; rendering (*of accounts*); delivery; return.

rescíndere, *v.t. ir.* to rescind; cancel; annul.

rescrítto, *m.* rescript.

resèda, *f.* mignonette.

residènte, *a. & m.* resident. **residènza**, *f.* residence; residency. **residuo**, *m.* residue; balance.

rèsina, *f.* resin. **resinóso**, *a.* resinous.

resipiscènza, *f.* recognition of error.

resistènte, *a.* resistant; strong, tough; hard-wearing; (*colour*) fast. ∼ *a,* proof against.   **resistènza**, *f.* resistance; opposition; strength; toughness; endurance; stamina. **resístere**, *v.i.* (*aux.* avere) to hold out. ∼ *a,* to resist; withstand; endure, put up with; stand (*test*); be proof against.

réso, *p.p.* of rendere.

resocontísta (*pr.* **-ísti**), *m.* reporter. **resocónto**, *m.* report; account; (*ban't*) return.

respingènte, *m.* buffer (*Rly.*). **respíngere** (*pr.* **-íngo, -íngi**), *v.t. ir.* to push back, drive back, repel; reject; refuse; return, send back; (*exam.*) plough, pluck. **respingiménto**, *m.* rejection. **respínto**, *p.p.* of respingere.

respiràre, *v.i.* (*aux.* avere) & *t.* to breathe; respire; inhale; exhale. **respirazióne**, *f.* respiration; breathing. **respíro**, *m.* breath; breathing; delay, respite; breathing-space; (*fig.*) small instalment.

responsàbile, *a.* responsible. **responsabilità**, *f.* responsibility. **responsívo**, *a.* responsive; in reply (*Law*). **respònso**, *m.* response; answer, reply; decision.

rèssa,*f.* crowd; throng; (*fig.*) pressure, importunity.

rèsta, *f.* string (*onions*); beard of corn; (fish) bone.

restànte, *a.* remaining. ¶ *m.* remainder. **restàre**, *v.i.* (*aux.* essere) to remain; stay; stop; be left; (*with p.p.*) to be.

restauràre, *v.t.* to restore; re-establish. **restauratóre**, *m.* restorer. **restaurazióne**, *f.* restoration; re-establishment. **restàuro**, *m.* restoration; repair.

restío, *a.* restive, restless; stubborn, unmanageable; reluctant; loath; jibbing (*horse*). ¶ *m.* restiveness.

restituíre (*pr.* **-ísco, -ísci**), *v.t.* to return; give back; pay (to); restore; make good. **restituzióne**, *f.* restitution; return; restoration.

rèsto, *m.* rest, remainder; residue; change (*money*); (*pl.*) remains. *del* ∼, however; besides; for the rest. (

restríngere (*pr.* **-íngo, -íngi**, *&c.*, like *stringere*), *v.t. ir.* to tighten; squeeze; narrow; restrict; take in (*dress*); lessen; contract. **restríngersi**, *v.refl.* to shrink; decrease; contract; narrow. **restringiménto**, *m.* tightening;

narrowing; contracting, &c. **re-strizióne**, f. restriction.

retàggio, m. inheritance; heritage; property. **retàta**, f. catch, haul (lit. & fig.). **réte**, f. net; network; system (Rly., &c.); goal (football); dress-guard (cycling). dim. retina, reticèlla, reticina, reticola.

reticènte, a. reticent. **reticènza**, f. reticence; concealment.

reticolàto, m. wire entanglement; (pl.) barbed-wire (defences).

rètina, f. retina. **retìna**, f. hair-net.

rètore, m. rhetorician; writer on rhetoric. **retòrica**, f. rhetoric. **retòrico** (pl. -òrici), a. rhetorical.

retribuíre (pr. -uísco, -uísci), v.t. to reward; recompense; pay; repay. **retribuzióne**, f. remuneration; pay; reward; retribution.

retrívo, a. backward; reactionary; behind the times.

rètro, ad. behind. ¶ m. back; verso (coin or medal); back room. **retrobottéga**, f. back-shop. **retrocàrica**, f. breech-loading. fucile a ~, breech-loader, b.-loading gun. **retrocèdere**, v.i. ir. (aux. avere & essere) to step back; draw b.; turn b.; recede, retreat. (v.t.) to degrade; reduce in rank. **retrocessióne**, f. retrocession; degradation; retreat. **retrocucína**, f. back-kitchen; scullery. **retrogradazióne**, f. retrograde motion (Astr.). **retrògrado**, a. retrograde; backward; reactionary. **retroguàrdia** (pl. guàrdie), f. rear-guard. **retroscèna**, f. back-stage, behind the scenes; (fig.) underhand work, intrigue. **retroscrítto**, a. written on the back. **retrospettívo**, a. retrospective. **retrostànza**, f. back-room, closet; recess. **retroversióne**, f. retranslation; (Surg.) retroversion. **retrovíe**, f.pl. (Mil.) lines of communication; zone behind the front

rètta, f. straight line; terms, charge (board, &c.); attention; wear, resistance. dar ~, to pay attention. ~ d'arrivo, home stretch (racing).

rettaménte, ad. right, rightly; honestly; correctly.

rettangolàre, a. rectangular. **rettàngolo**, m. rectangle.

rettífica & **rettificazióne**, f. rectification; correction; purification. **rettificàre** (pr. -ífico, -ífichi), v.t. to rectify; correct; repair; make straight.

rèttile, m. reptile.

rettilíneo, a. rectilinear; (fig.) right; correct. ¶ m. straight; straight road.

rettitúdine, f. rectitude. **rètto**, a. upright; straightforward; correct; straight; right (way, angle, &c.). ¶ m. rectum.

rettoràto, m. rectorship. **rettóre**, m. rector; principal (college or university). **rettríce**, f. directress; head-mistress.

rettorica, see retorica.

reúccio, m. kinglet, petty ruler.

rèuma, m. rheumatic pain; rheumatism. **reumàtico** (pl. -àtici), a. rheumatic. **reumatísmo**, m. rheumatism. **reumatizzàto**, a. afflicted with rheumatism.

reverèndo, a. reverend. ¶ m. priest; clergyman. **reverènte**, a. reverent, respectful. **reverènza**, f. reverence. **reverenziàle**, a. reverential. **reveríre**, see riverire.

revišióne, f. revision; audit. **revišóre**, m. reviser; auditor. ~ di bozze, proof-reader.

rèvoca & **revocazióne**, f. revocation; repeal. **revocàre** (pr. rèvoco), v.t. to revoke; repeal; recall.

revòlver, m.inv. revolver. **revolveràta**, f. revolver shot.

revulsióne, f. (Med.) revulsion.

rézzo, m. shade; coolness; light breeze.

ri-, prefix, again, Eng. re-, with numerous compound verbs, the sense of which can be generally deduced from the simple form.

riabilitàre, v.t. to rehabilitate. **riabilitazióne**, f. rehabilitation.

riacquistàre, v.t. to recover; buy back. **riacquísto**, m. recovery; repurchase.

riàlto, m. rise (in the ground); knoll; embankment; steps in front of a building; embroidery in relief; addition to a meal.

rialzàre, v.t. to heighten; raise; raise up again. **rialzàrsi**, v.refl. to rise; get up (again); improve (weather). **rialzísta**, m. bull (Stk. Ex.). **riàlzo**, m. rise (in price; Stk. Ex.); raising; lifting up; prominence, hump.

riandàre, v.i. ir. (aux. **rivàdo** or **rivò**, &c., like andare) to return; go back again. v.t. to recall; go over again; revise.

riapertúra, f. re-opening. **riapríre**, v.t. & **riaprírsi**, v.refl. to re-open.

riarmàre, v.t. & i. (aux. avere) to rearm; refit. **riàrmo**, m. rearmament.

riàrso, *a.* dry; parched.

riassètto, *m.* re-arrangement; re-adjustment.

riassúmere, *v.t. ir.* to sum up; recapitulate; summarize; resume; take up again; re-employ. **ri-assúnto,** *m.* summary; summing up; recapitulation. **riassunzióne,** *f.* resumption; re-employment.

riattàre, *v.t.* to repair; rearrange; restore.

riattivàre, *v.t.* to renew; re-establish; bring into use again; restore.

riavére (*pr.* **riò, riài, rià,** like *avere*), *v.t. ir.* to get back, recover. **riavérsi,** *v.refl.* to recover (*one's strength, one's senses*); revive. **riavúta,** *f.* (*sport*) revenge; return match.

riav[v]àllo, *m.* renewal (*bill of exchange*).

ribadiménto, *m.* riveting; clinching; confirmation. **ribadire** (*pr.* **-ísco, -íscì**), *v.t.* to clinch; nail down; confirm; fix; rivet (*lit.* & *fig.*). **ribaditóre,** *m.* riveter. ¶ *a.* (**-trice,** *f.*) clinching; riveting.

ribaldería, *f.* ruffianly conduct; scoundrelism; rascality; shameful performance. **ribàldo,** *m.* scoundrel; ruffian; rogue.

ribàlta, *f.* flap; trap-door; (*Theat.*) footlights (*lit.* screen before the footlights); front of the stage. **ribaltàre,** *v.t.* to upset; capsize (*v.i.*) (*aux.* essere & avere) to overturn, be upset.

ribassàre, *v.t.* to lower; reduce; (*v.i.*) (*aux.* essere) to fall; drop; go down. **ribassísta** (*pl.* **-ísti**), *m.* bear (*Stk. Ex.*). **ribàsso,** *m.* fall (*in price*); discount; reduction.

ribàttere, *v.t.* to hammer; beat again; knock again at (*door*); strike again; clinch; repel; confute; (*sport*) return (*the ball*). *v.i.* (*aux.* avere) reply; retort. **ribattiménto,** *m.* clinching, riveting; confutation; return. **ri-battitóre,** *m.* riveter; one who returns the service (*Ten.,* &c.). **ribattitúra,** *f.* clinching; riveting. **ribattúta,** *f.* return of the service (*at ball games*).

ribellàre, *v.t.* to cause to rebel; rouse; incite (to revolt). **ribellàrsi,** *v.refl.* to rebel; rise (against). **ribèlle,** *m.* rebel. ¶ *a.* rebel (*att.*); rebellious. **ribellióne,** *f.* rebellion.

ríbes, *m.inv.* gooseberry.

riboccàre (*pr.* **-òcco, -òcchi**), *v.t.* & **v.i.** (*aux.* essere), to grout, point

(*brickwork*); to be full to over-flowing; overflow. **ribócco,** *m.* overflow; super-abundance.

ribolliménto, *m.* ebullition; agitation. **ribollíre** (*pr.* **-bóllo, -bólli**), *v.i.* (*aux.* avere) to boil; boil again; to be overheated; ferment; be agitated; (*v.t.*) to reboil. **ribollitúra,** *f.* reboiling.

ribòtta, *f.* junketing; spree; debauch.

ribrézzo, *m.* shudder; horror; disgust; feverish chill.

ributtànte, *a.* shocking; hideous; disgusting. **ributtàre,** *v.t.* & *i.* (*aux.* avere) to hurl back, reject, repel; disgust.

ricadére, *v.i. ir.* (*aux.* essere) to fall back; fall down again; relapse. **ricadúta,** *f.* relapse.

ricalcàre, *v.t.* to press down; tread (down); retrace (*one's own steps*); follow (*the footsteps of someone*); transfer (*drawing*).

ricalcitrànte, *a.* recalcitrant.

ricamàre, *v.t.* to embroider. **ricama-trice,** *f.* embroiderer. **ricamatúra,** *f.* embroidery.

ricambiàre, *v.t.* to return; recipro-cate; repay, requite. **ricàmbio,** *m.* return; exchange; requital; replace-ment. *pezzo di* ~, spare, spare part.

ricàmo, *m.* embroidery (*lit.* & *fig.*).

ricattàre, *v.t.* to blackmail. **ricatta-tóre,** *m.* (*f.* **-trice**) blackmailer. **ricàtto,** *m.* blackmail; blackmailing.

ricavàre, *v.t.* to draw (out); extract; derive (*profit,* &c.). **ricavàto** & **ricàvo,** *m.* proceeds, gain.

riccaménte, *ad.* richly. **ricchézza,** *f.* wealth, riches; richness.

ríccio (*pl.* **rícci**), *m.* hedgehog; curl. ¶ *a.* curly. **rícciolo,** *m.* curl; lock (*hair*). **ricciolúto** & **ricciúto,** *a.* curly; curly-headed.

rícco (*pl.* **ríchi**), *a.* rich; wealthy. **riccóne,** *m.* very rich man.

ricérca (*pl.* **ricérche**), *f.* research; investigation; inquiry; demand. **ricercàre** (*pr.* **-cérco, -cérchi**), *v.t.* to seek out; search for; investi-gate; inquire into; (*Poet.*) touch, try. **ricercatézza,** *f.* preciosity; studied refinement (*dress, manners, style*). **ricercàto,** *a.* affected; far-fetched; studied; sought after, (much) in demand. **ricercatóre,** *m.* (*f.* **-trice**) investigator; researcher; seeker.

ricètta, *f.* prescription; recipe.

ricettàcolo, *m.* receptacle; repository. **ricettaménto,** *m.* harbouring; re-setting, fencing (*stolen goods*).

ricettàre, *v.t.* to conceal; harbour (*criminal*); shelter; receive (*stolen goods*). ricettàrio, *m.* book of prescriptions; book of recipes. ricettatóre, *m.* (*f.* -tríce) receiver, resetter; fence. ricettazióne, *f.* receiving stolen goods; resetting. ricettività, *f.* receptivity. ricettívo, *a.* receptive. ricètto, *m.* refuge; shelter.

ricévere, *v.t. & abs.* to receive; admit; get; meet with; accept; welcome; take in (*boarders*); be at home (*to visitors*); give audience. riceviménto, *m.* reception; receipt. ricevitóre, *m.* receiver (*pers. & Teleph.*). ricevitoría, *f.* receiving-office. ricevúta, *f.* receipt. ricezióne, *f.* reception (*Radio*).

richiamàre, *v.t.* to call back; (*Mil.*) call up; recall; call; call again; summon; bring together; attract (*attention*); rebuke; refer to. richiamàrsi, *v.refl.* to lodge a complaint (or appeal); refer, apply to. richiamàto, *m.* man (soldier) called-up. richiàmo, *m.* call; summons; decoy; admonition; signal (*by sound*); recall; cross-reference mark; catch-word.

richiedènte, *m.* applicant; petitioner. richièdere, *v.t. ir.* to ask again for; ask back; ask; demand; require; necessitate; summon, send for. richièsta, *f.* request; demand. richièsto, *a.* sought after; in demand.

ricíngere, see *recingere*.
rícino (òlio di), *m.* castor-oil.
ricognizióne, *f.* recognition; verification; (*Mil.*) reconnaissance.
ricollocaménto, *m.* replacement. ricollocàre (*pr.* -òlloco, -òllochi), *v.t.* to replace; put back; place again. ricolmàre, *v.t.* to fill to the brim. ricólmo, *a.* full; brim-full.
ricominciàre, *v.t. & i.* (*aux.* essere) to begin again.
ricomparíre (*pr.* -parísco *or* -pàio, *&c.*, like *apparire*), *v.i. ir.* (*aux.* essere) to reappear. ricompàrsa, *f.* reappearance.
ricompènsa, *f.* compensation; reward; recompense. ricompensàre, *v.t.* to compensate; reward; recompense.
ricompórre (*pr.* -óngo, *&c.*, like *compórre*), *v.t. ir.* to recompose; reassemble (*machine, &c.*). ricompórsi, *v.refl.* to recover oneself; regain composure; settle down.
riconciliàre, *v.t.* to reconcile. riconciliazióne, *f.* reconciliation.

ricondúrre (*pr.* -úco, -úci, *&c.*, like *condurre*), *v.t. ir.* to bring back; lead back (*or* again).
riconférma, *f.* confirmation; fresh confirmation.
riconoscènte, *a.* grateful; thankful. riconoscènza, *f.* gratitude; thankfulness. riconóscere (*pr.* -ósco, -ósci, *&c.*, like *conoscere*), *v.t. ir.* to recognize; acknowledge; identify; confess. riconoscíble, *a.* recognizable. riconosciménto, *m.* recognition; acknowledgment; avowal; identification. *targa di* ~, *f.* number plate (*Motor*).
riconquísta, *f.* reconquest; recovery. riconquistàre, *v.t.* to reconquer; recover; regain.
riconségna, *f.* redelivery; reconsignment; handing back.
riconversióne, *f.* reconversion. riconvertíre (*pr.* -èrto, -èrti, *&c.*, like *avvertire*), *v.t.* to reconvert.
ricopèrto, *p.a.* covered, covered up. ricopríre (*pr.* -còpro, *&c.*, like *coprire*), *v.t. ir.* to cover; cover up; hide.
ricordàbile, *a.* memorable; notable; worth recording. ricordànza, *f.* remembrance; memory; recollection. ricordàre, *v.t. & i.* (*aux.* avere) to remember; call to mind; recollect; recall; mention. ~ *a*, to remind. ricordàrsi, *v.refl.* to remember; recollect. ricordévole, *a.* mindful; memorable. ricòrdo, *m.* remembrance; memory; tradition; recollection; warning; souvenir; record; note; memorandum; reminder; (*pl.*) memoirs.
ricorrènte, *a.* recurrent; recurring; occurring. ricorrènza, *f.* recurrence; occasion; anniversary. ricórrere (*pr.* -órro, -órri, *&c.*, like *córrere*), *v.i. ir.* (*aux.* avere *&* essere) to run again; have recourse; resort; appeal; apply; recur; return; appear again. ricórso, *m.* appeal; complaint; return; recurrence.
ricostituíre (*pr.* -ísco, -ísci), *v.t.* to reconstitute; re-establish; re-form.
ricostruíre (*pr.* -ísco, -ísci), *v.t.* to rebuild; reconstruct.
ricòtta, *f.* buttermilk curd. *uomo di* ~, (*fig.*) weakling; spiritless person. ricòtto, *p.p.* of *ricuocere*.
ricoveràre, *v.t.* to shelter; give shelter to; receive. ricoveràrsi, *v.refl.* to take refuge; seek shelter. ricoveràto, *m.* inmate (*of a charitable institution*); refugee. ricóvero,

m. refuge; shelter; dug-out; cab (*locomotive*).

ricreàre, *v.t.* to re-create; re-appoint; relieve; refresh; amuse. **ricreàrsi,** *v.refl.* to find (*or* take) recreation; amuse oneself. **ricreatívo,** *a.* recreative; pleasant; amusing; light (*reading*). **ricreatóre** (*f.* **-tríce**), *a.* refreshing; restorative. **ricreazióne,** *f.* recreation; play; pastime; amusement; refreshment.

ricrédersi, *v.refl.* to change one's mind; recant; be undeceived.

ricuòcere (*pr.* **-cuòcio, -cuòci,** *&c.*, like *cuocere*), *v.t. ir.* to recook, cook again; rebake; reheat; anneal.

ricuperàre, *v.t.* to recover. **ricúpero,** *m.* recovery; rescue; salvage.

ricúsa, *f.* refusal; objection. **ricusàre,** *v.t.* to refuse; reject; deny; (*Law*) challenge (*witness*).

ridacchiàre, *v.i.* (*aux.* avere) to giggle; laugh ironically.

rídda, *f.* whirling dance; crowd; confusion.

ridènte, *a.* laughing; (*fig.*) bright, smiling. **rídere,** *v.i. ir.* (*aux.* avere) to laugh. **rídersi** (**di**), *v.refl.* to laugh (at), deride.

ridestàre, *v.t. &* **ridestàrsi,** *v.refl.* to re-awaken, arouse (again); wake; wake up.

ridicolàggine, *f.* absurdity; nonsense. **ridícolo,** *a.* ridiculous; absurd; paltry. ¶ *m.* ridicule; ridiculousness.

ridondànte, *a.* redundant. **ridondànza,** *f.* redundance; redundancy. **ridondàre,** *v.i.* (*aux.* essere *&* avere) to redound; overflow.

ridosso (**a**), *ad. expr.* (*Naut.*) in shelter; close by, very near, close at hand; behind, above, at its back; on one's back (*fig.*).

ridótta, *f.* (*Mil.*) redoubt.

ridótto, *p.p.* of *ridurre.* **mal ~,** in a bad way, in a sorry plight. ¶ *m.* resort, retreat; (*Theat.*) foyer; clubhouse. **ridúrre** (*pr.* **-dúco, -dúci**), *v.t. ir.* to reduce; blight; bring back; drive (*to despair*); restrict; (*Mus.*) arrange, adapt. **riduzióne,** *f.* reduction; discount; arrangement; adaptation.

riècco , *x·l.* here is (*or* are) again.

riecheggiàre, *v.i.* (*aux.* avere) to re-echo.

riêdere, *v.i.* (*Poet.*) to return.

riedificàre, *v.t. & i.* (*aux.* avere) to rebuild.

riémpiere (*pr.* **-émpio, -émpi,** *&c.*)

& **riempíre** (*pr.* **riémpio** *or* **riempísco** like *empire*), *v.t.* to fill; fill up; fill in (forms); cram; stuff. ~ *di nuovo,* refill. **riempiménto,** *m.* filling; filling up. **riempitívo,** *a.* filling; superfluous; pleonastic. ¶ *m.* pleonasm; expletive; stop-gap.

rientrànte, *a.* receding; (*fortif.*) re-entrant. **rientràre,** *v.i.* (*aux.* essere) to re-enter; return (*home*); be reinstated; recede; withdraw; contract; be included. **rientràta,** *f.* re-entrance, re-entry; reappearance. **riéntro,** *m.* shrinking; shrinkage.

riepilogàre, *v.t.* to ₋ecapitulate. **riepílogo** (*pl.* **-íloghi**), *m.* recapitulation; résumé.

rievocàre, *v.t.* to recall; conjure up again.

rifaciménto, *m.* remaking; recasting; remodelling; remodelled form of a literary work; compensation; adaptation. **rifàre** (*pr.* **rifò** *or* **rifàccio,** *&c.*, like *fare*), *v.t. ir.* to remake; do (over) again; do up; repair; rebuild; renew; make good; return (*invitation, &c.*); set off; imitate; give back; (*cards*) deal again. ~ *la strada,* to retrace one's steps. **rifàrsi,** *v.refl.* to begin again; recover one's health (*strength, losses, &c.*); get even, be revenged; have a fresh helping of food; clear (up) (*weather*).

rifàscio (**a**), *ad. expr.* in disorder, in confusion; pell-mell.

rifàtto, *p.p.* of *rifare.* **villano ~,** *m.* upstart; nouveau riche.

riferiménto, *m.* reference. **riferíre** (*pr.* **-erísco, -erísci**), *v.t.* to report; relate; tell; refer; attribute; return (*thanks*). **riferírsi,** *v.refl.* to refer; relate.

riférma, *f.* re-engagement. **rifermàre,** *v.t.* to stop again; (re-)confirm; re-engage.

riffa, *f.* violence; raffle, lottery. **riffóso,** *a.* rowdy; insolent.

rifiatàre, *v.i.* (*aux.* avere) to breathe again; take a deep breath; (*with neg.*) speak one word.

rifilàre, *v.t.* to spin again; str.ke, deal (*blow*); trim.

rifiniménto, *m.* finish; finishing; exhaustion. **rifiníre** (*pr.* **-ísco, -ísci**), *v.t.* to finish; finish off; exhaust, wear down; w. out. *v.i.* to stop, leave off. **rifinírsi,** *v.refl.* to wear oneself out. **rifinitézza,** *f.* exhaustion, utter weariness. **rifi-**

níto, *a.* exhausted, worn out.
rifinitúra, *f.* finish, final touches.
rifioriménto, *m.* flourishing; reflourishing; revival. **rifioríre** (*pr.* -fiorísco, -fiorísci, *&c.*), *v.i.* (*aux.* avere *&* essere) to flourish; reflourish; regain strength; bloom again; re-appear; (*v.t.*) to adorn; retouch; (*Mus.*) add flourishes to; strew with fresh gravel. **rifioríto,** *a.* reflourishing; blooming again. **rifioritúra,** *f.* reflorescence; efflorescence; embellishment; (*Mus.*) added flourish; fresh gravel for a path; re-appearance of a stain.
rifiutàre, *v.t.* to refuse; decline; reject; deny. *v.i. &* **rifiutàrsi,** *v.refl.* to refuse. **rifiúto,** *m.* refusal; (*cards*) revoke, renounce; decline; (*pl.*) refuse; escaped steam or liquid; waste; scum (*fig.*). ~ *i di carta,* waste paper.
riflessaménte, *ad.* by reflection; indirectly. **riflessióne,** *f.* reflection; reflexion; deliberation; meditation. **riflessívo,** *a.* thoughtful; reflective; (*Gram.*) reflexive. **riflèsso,** *p.a.* reflected; (*physiol.*) reflex. **¶** *m.* reflection; reflex. **riflessóre,** *m.* reflector (*as in telescope*). **riflèttere,** *v.t. ir.* to reflect; concern. *v.i.* (*aux.* avere) to reflect; think; ponder. **riflettóre,** *m.* searchlight; reflector.
rifluíre (*pr.* -fluísco, -fluísci), *v.i.* (*aux.* avere *&* essere) to flow back; ebb. **riflússo,** *m.* ebb; ebbing; reflux; refluence.
rifocillàre, *v.t.* to refresh; revive; comfort; cheer up.
rifóndere (*pr.* -óndo, -óndi, *&c.*, like *fondere*), *v.t. ir.* to remelt; make good; refund; reimburse. **rifondíbile,** *a.* that can be recast, or refunded.
rifórma, *f.* reform; (*Mil.*) discharge. *la R~,* the Reformation. **riformàre,** *v.t.* to reform; form anew; amend; (*Mil.*) discharge, put upon half-pay. **riformatóre,** *m.* (*f.* -tríce*) reformer. **riformatòrio,** *m.* reformatory.
rifornimento, *m.* refurnishing; supply. **riforníre** (*pr.* -ísco, -ísci, *&c.*), *v.t.* to refurnish; supply; provide.
rifràngere, *v.t. ir.* to refract. **rifrangiménto,** *m.* refraction. **rifrattóre,** *m.* refractor. **¶** *a.* refracting. **rifrazióne,** *f.* refraction.
rifréddo, *m.* cold dish.
rifríggere, *v.t.* to fry again; warm up

again; (*fig.*) keep touching up repeat many times. **rifrítto,** *p.p.* of *rifriggere.* **¶** *a.* rifrittúme, *m.* (*fig.*) re-hash. **rifrittúra,** *f.* (*fig.*) tedious repetition.
rifuggíre (*pr.* -fúggo, -fúggi, *&c.*, like *fuggire*), *v.i.* (*aux.* essere) to flee, flee again, take refuge; (*aux.* avere) shrink; be averse (from, to); (*v.t.*) to shun.
rifugiàrsi, *v.refl.* to take refuge.
rifugiàto, *m.* refugee. **rifúgio,** *m.* refuge; shelter.
rifulgènte, *a.* refulgent. **rifúlgere,** *v.i. ir.* (*aux.* essere *&* avere) to shine; be resplendent; become apparent.
rifusíbile, *a.* that can be remelted or recast; that may be refunded. **rifusióne,** *f.* remelting; recasting; refunding. **rifúso,** *p.p.* of *rifondere.*
ríga (*pl.* **ríghe**), *f.* line; row; streak; stripe; parting (*hair*); (*Mus.*) stave. *in ~!* (*Mil.*) fall in! *rompete le righe!* fall out! dismiss!
rigàglie, *f.pl.* giblets.
rigàgnolo, *m.* runnel; rivulet; brook.
rigàre, *v.t.* to rule (*lines*); furrow; rifle (*gun*). ~ *diritto,* to act straightforwardly; go straight. **rigatíno,** *m.* striped cloth. **rigàto,** *a.* striped; ruled; furrowed; (*Arch.*) fluted.
rigattière, *m.* second-hand dealer.
rigatúra, *f.* ruling, *&c.*, see *rigare.*
rigettàre, *v.t. & i.* to throw back, out, or again; reject; put out fresh shoots.
rigidézza *&* **rigidità,** *f.* rigidity; stiffness; rigour; strictness; austerity.
rígido, *a.* rigid; stiff; strict; rigorous; austere; severe; very cold.
rigiraménto, *m.* turning round.
rigiràre, *v.t.* to turn round (again); *t.* about; go round; surround; manage; turn, round off (*phrase*); trick, dupe, deceive, cajole; re-indorse (*bill*); employ (*capital*); **rigiràrsi,** *v.refl.* turn, *t.* round; walk about. *rigirarsela bene,* to manage one's affairs well. **rigiratóre,** *m.* (*f.* -tríce) trickster.
rigíro, *m.* turning; twisting; winding; (*fig.*) trick; subterfuge; intrigue; movement (of capital); (*pl.*) windings (*of a river*).
rígo (*pl.* **ríghi**), *m.* line; boundary line; watercourse; (*Mus.*) stave.
rigóglio, *m.* luxuriance; exuberance; bloom; rankness (*of growth*). **rigoglióso,** *a.* luxuriant; flourishing; rank. **rigolétto,** *m.* circle of dancers holding hands. **rigolíno,** *m.* groove.
rigonfiaménto *m.* swelling; rising.

rigonfiàre, *v.t.* to inflate (again), swell, puff up. **rigónfio**, *a.* swollen; full; puffed up.

rigóre, *m.* rigour; severity; strictness. *a~ di termine*, in the strict sense. **rigorísta** (*pl.* **-ísti**), *m.* severe moralist. **rigoróso**, *a.* rigorous; strict; severe.

rigovernàre, *v.t. & i.* to wash up; clean; groom, curry (*horse*); apply fresh manure; re-govern. **rigovernatúra**, *f.* cleaning; washing up; dishwater.

riguadagnàre, *v.t.* to regain; win back; recover.

riguardàre, *v.t.* to look at again; look closely at; examine; look over, revise; concern, regard; consider; take care of; be concerned with. *v.i.* (*aux.* avere) to consider; look out. **riguardàrsi**, *v.refl.* to take care of oneself; be on one's guard; abstain; beware (of). **riguardàta**, *f.* look; glance. *dim.* **riguardatina**, hasty glance. **riguardàto**, *a.* prudent; wary; circumspect. **riguardévole**, *a.* considerable; remarkable. **riguàrdo**, *m.* regard; respect; consideration; attention; care. **riguardóso**, *a.* respectful; considerate.

rigurgitànte, *a.* overflowing; swarming. **rigurgitàre**, *v.i.* (*aux.* avere) to gush back; pour up again; regurgitate; (*fig.*) overflow, swarm.

rilasciaménto, *m.* release; weakening. **rilasciàre**, *v.t.* to leave . . . again; release; grant, give; give up; relinquish. **rilasciàrsi**, *v.refl.* to relax; slacken; weaken. **rilàscio**, *m.* release; granting; surrender; giving up; deduction.

rilassaménto, *m.* slackening; relaxation. **rilassàre**, *v.t.* to slacken; relax; let go; loosen; weaken. **rilassatézza**, *f.* laxity; looseness; slackness. **rilassàto**, *a.* lax; loose; relaxed; slack.

rilegàre, *v.t.* to bind; rebind; fasten up again. **rilegatóre**, *m.* bookbinder. **rilegatúra**, *f.* binding; bookbinding; rebinding. *~ flessibile*, limp cover.

rilènto, (a), *ad.* slowly, cautiously.

rilevaménto, *m.* drawing (*a plan*); (*Naut.*) bearing; raising (up); bringing up; reviving; relieving (*guard*); projection; prominence. **rilevànte**, *a.* important; considerable; prominent. **rilevàre**, *v.t.* to take away; take over; take off again;

draw; relieve (*guard*, *sentry*, *&c.*); point out; notice. **rilevàrsi**, *v.refl.* to rise again; stand up again; recover. **rilevataménte**, *ad.* in relief. **rilevatàrio**, *m.* lessee, transferee; successor, purchaser. **rilevàto**, *p.p.* of *rilevare*. ¶ *a.* in relief; projecting; protruding.

rilièvo, *m.* relief; projection; slight rise (*ground*); remark; (*pl.*) leavings, crumbs, gleanings.

rilucènte, *a.* shining; glittering. **rilucentézza**, *f.* brillancy; glitter. **rilúcere** (*pr.* **-lúco**, **-lúci**), *v.i.* to shine; glitter; (*no compound tenses*).

riluttànte, *a.* reluctant. **riluttànza**, *f.* reluctance.

ríma, *f.* rhyme; rime; poetry; (*pl.*) lyrical poems. *terza ~*, the linked stanzas of three lines (*terzine*) employed by Dante in the *Divine Comedy*. *ottava ~*, stanza of eight lines commonly used in Italian romantic narrative poems (Boccaccio, Ariosto, &c.). *~ al mezzo*, middle-rhyme.

rimandàre, *v.t.* to send again; send back; put off; defer; postpone; refer (*reader*) (to another page); reject. **rimàndo**, *m.* return; postponement; reference.

rimaneggiaménto, *m.* re-handling; remodelling; re-arrangement; alteration. **rimaneggiàre**, *v.t.* to rehandle; remodel; rearrange; alter; reform.

rimanènte, *a.* remaining. ¶ *m.* remainder. **rimanènza**, *f.* residue; remainder; stay. **rimanére** (*pr.* **rimàngo**, **rimàni**, **rimàne**), *v.i. ir.* (*aux.* essere) to remain; stay; stop; stick; rest; agree; be left; leave off; to be (*as aux. with p.p.*); be situated; die. *~ a* (*impers.*), to depend on, rest with.

rimangiàre, *v.t.* to eat again; (*fig.*) break (*promise*); retract; unsay.

rimarcàre, *v.t.* to remark; notice. **rimarchévole**, *a.* remarkable.

rimàre, *v.i. & t.* to rhyme; versify. **rimarginàre**, *v.t.* to draw the edges together; close up; heal. **rimàrio**, *m.* book of rhymes; rhyming dictionary.

rimasto, *p.p.* of *rimanere*.

rimasúglio, *m.* remains; residue.

rimatóre, *m.* (*f.* **-trìce**) rhymer; rhymster.

rimbacuccàrsi, *v.refl.* to muffle oneself up; wrap oneself up (again).

rimbalzàre, *v.i.* to rebound. **rimbal-**

zèllo, *m.* (*game*) ducks & drakes.
rimbàlzo, *m.* rebound.
rimbambiménto, *m.* dotage; second childhood. **rimbambinire** & **rimbambíre** (*pr.* -ísco, -ísci), *v.i.* (*aux.* essere) to grow childish; be in one's dotage.
rimbarcàre, *v.t.* & **rimbarcàrsi,** *v.refl.* to re-embark. **rimbàrco,** *m.* re-embarkation.
rimbeccàre, *v.t.* & *i.* (*aux.* avere) to retort; to peck; answer rudely. **rimbeccàrsi,** *v.refl.* to quarrel. **rimbécco,** *m.* retort; repartee; sharp answer.
rimboccàre, *v.t.* to tuck up (*sleeves*); turn up (*trousers*); turn down (*sheets*). **rimboccatúra,** *f.* & **rimbócco,** *m.* tucking up, turning down.
rimbombàre, *v.i.* (*aux.* assere & avere) to resound; thunder; roar. **rimbombío,** *m.* reverberation. **rimbómbo,** *m.* loud noise; roar; reverberation.
rimborsàbile, *a.* repayable. **rimborsàre,** *v.t.* to repay; reimburse. **rimbórso,** *m.* repayment; reimbursement.
rimboscaménto & **rimboschiménto,** *m.* reafforestation. **rimboscàre** & **rimboschíre** (*pr.* -ísco), *v.t.* to reafforest.
rimbrottàre, *v.t.* to scold; rebuke. **rimbròtto,** *m.* reproof; (harsh) rebuke.
rimbucàre, *v.t.* to put in a hole; hide; put in the wash (again).
rimediàbile, *a.* remediable. **rimediàre,** *v.t.* & *i.* (*aux.* avere) to remedy. ~ *a,* find a remedy for; make up for; earn. **rimèdio,** *m.* remedy; cure.
rimembrànza, *f.* remembrance. **rimembràre,** *v.t.* to call to mind, remember.
rimenàre, *v.t.* to bring back; handle; stir; shake; roll. **rimenàta,** *f.* handling; (*fig.*) scolding. **rimenío,** *m.* shaking up.
rimeritàre, *v.t.* to requite; recompense; compensate. **rimèrito,** *m.* recompense.
rimescolaménto, *m.* mixing; medley; confusion; (*cards*) shuffling; sudden shock. **rimescolàre,** *v.t.* to mix up; (*cards*) shuffle; rummage among; rake up. **rimescolàrsi,** *v.refl.* to mix oneself up (with); receive a sudden shock; be upset (*fig.*). **rimescolàta,** *f.* mixing; (*cards*) shuffle, shuffling. **rimescolío,** *m.*

constant mixing or changing about; confusion; prolonged shock.
riméssa, *f.* coach-house; shed; garage; replacement; remittance(s); return (*ball*); store; provision; crop; sprout; shoot(ing) (*plant*). vendere *a* ~, to sell at a loss.
rimessaménte, *ad.* submissively. **rimésso,** *p.p.* of *rimettere.* ¶ *a.* submissive; cowed; mild.
rimestàre, *v.t.* to stir up; agitate; raise again. **rimestatóre,** *m.* agitator.
riméttere (*pr.* -métto, &*c.,* like *mettere*), *v.t.* ir. to put back; replace; put again; make up; set again; put off; refer; submit; pardon; send; send in (*account*); remit; repay (*loan*); lose; do up; bring up; vomit; restore; put right; cut (*teeth*); develop (*feathers*); throw out (*shoots*). **riméttersi,** *v.refl.* set (put) oneself again; recover; (*weather*) improve. ~*a,* ~*in,* to continue, resume.
rimiràre, *v.t.* to gaze at (attentively, or with admiration); stare at.
rimodernaménto, *m.* modernization; modernizing. **rimodernàre,** *v.t.* to modernize; remodel. **rimodernàrsi,** *v.refl.* to become up-to-date.
rimontàre, *v.i.* & *t.* to remount; go up (*stream*); go back (to); date (*from*); repair; re-assemble (*machinery*). **rimontatúra,** *f.* (*Mech.*) reassembling.
rimorchiàre, *v.t.* to tow. *carro rimorchiato,* m. trailer (*Motor*). **rimorchiatóre,** *m.* tug; tow-boat. **rimorchiatúra,** *f.* towing. **rimòrchio,** *m.* tow; towing; trailer. *prendere a* ~, to take in tow. *corda da* ~, *f.* tow rope. *un* ~ *caravana,* a trailer caravan.
rimòrdere, *v.t.* ir. (*of conscience*) to prick); cause pain (*fig.*). **rimòrso,** *m.* remorse.
rimostrànza, *f.* remonstrance; protest. **rimostràre,** *v.i.* (*aux.* avere) to remonstrate,, *v.t.* to show again.
rimoviménto, *m.* & **rimozióne,** *f.* removal.
rimpagliàre, *v.t.* to cover again with straw; re-seat (*straw-seated chair*).
rimpannucciàrsi, *v.refl.* to be better off (*lit.* wear better clothes).
rimpastàre, *v.t.* to re-knead; re-mix; recast; re-arrange. **rimpàsto,** *m.* remixing; rearrangement; shuffle.
rimpatriàre, *v.t.* to repatriate. **rimpàtrio,** *m.* repatriation.

rimpettíre (*pr.* **-ísco, -ísci**), *v.i.* (*aux.* essere) & **rimpettírsi**, *v.refl.* to swell with pride; carry one's head high.

rimpiàngere, *v.t.* to lament (over); regret. **rimpiànto**, *m.* regret.

rimpiattàre, *v.t.* to hide; hide away; conceal. **rimpiattíno**, *m.* hide-and-seek.

rimpiazzàre, *v.t.* to replace.

rimpicciolíre (*pr.* **-ísco, -ísci**), *v.t.* to lessen; diminish; make smaller. *v.i.* (*aux.* essere) to grow smaller; decrease.

rimpiegàre, *v.t.* to re-employ.

rimpinzàre, *v.t.* to cram; stuff.

rimpolpàre, *v.t.* to fatten; (*fig.*) to enrich.

rimproveràre, *v.t.* to reprove; reproach; scold; rebuke; reprimand. **rimproveràrsi**, *v.refl.* to reproach oneself (with); repent (of). **rimpròvero**, *m.* reproach; reproof; rebuke; reprimand.

rimuginàre, *v.t.* & *abs.* to rummage (for); turn over in one's mind.

rim[u]òvere (*pr.* **-muòvo, -muòvi**, like *muovere*), *v.t. ir.* to remove; dissuade; deter.

rinascènte, *a.* renascent; reviving; returning. **rinascènza**, see *rinascimento*, **rinàscere** (*pr.* **-àsco, -àsci**, like *nascere*), *v.i. ir.* (*aux.* essere) to be born again; spring up again; revive. **rinasciménto**, *m.* & **rinàscita**, *f.* rebirth; revival; renaissance. **rinàto**, *p.a.* reborn.

rincacciàre, *v.t.* to drive back. **rincagnàrsi**, *v.refl.* to scowl. **rincagnàto**, *a.* snub(-nosed). **rincalzàre**, *v.t.* to pull down (*hat*); tuck in (*bedclothes*); follow up closely; force (*growth*); press; urge; prop. **rincàlzo**, *m.* reinforcement; support. **rincantucciàre**, *v.t.* to drive into a corner. **rincantucciàrsi**, *v.refl.* to creep into a corner; hide (oneself).

rincaràre, *v.t.* to raise (*the price of*); increase (*quantity, dose*). *v.i.* (*aux.* essere) to grow dearer; become more expensive; rise (in price). **rincàro**, *m.* rise in prices; rising cost.

rincasàre, *v.i.* (*aux.* essere) to return home.

rinchiúdere (*pr.* **-údo, -údi**, &*c.*, like *chiúdere*), *v.t. ir.* to shut up; shut in; enclose. **rinchiúso**, *m.* enclosure; enclosed place. *saper di* ~, to have a close (or musty) smell.

rincontràre, *v.t.* & **rincontràrsi**, *v.refl.* to meet, meet again. **rincóntro**, *m.* meeting; comparison. ¶ *ad.* & *pr.* opposite.

rincoràre, *v.t.* to encourage; cheer (up). **rincoràrsi**, *v.refl.* to be encouraged; take heart again.

rincorniciàre, *v.t.* to reframe.

rincórrere (*pr.* **-órro**, &*c.*, like *correre*), *v.t. ir.* to pursue; chase; run after. **rincórsa**, *f.* short run. *prendere la* ~, to dart off.

rincréscere, *v.i.* (*aux.* essere) (used only in 3rd pers.) to displease; cause regret. *mi rincresce*, I am sorry. *me ne rincresce*, I regret it. *sono cose che rincrescono*, they are things which are displeasing. **rincrescévole**, *a.* regrettable; unpleasant; annoying. **rincresciménto**, *m.* regret.

rincrudiménto, *m.* worsening; aggravation. **rincrudíre** (*pr.* **-ísco, -ísci**), *v.t.* to aggravate; embitter. *v.i.* (*aux.* essere) & **rincrudírsi**, *v.refl.* to grow worse; become more severe.

rinculàre, *v.i.* (*aux.* essere & avere) to recoil; draw back; shrink. **rincúlo**, *m.* recoil.

rinfacciàre, *v.t.* to fling in one's face; cast in one's teeth; reproach with; taunt with.

rinfagottàre, *v.t.* to make up in a bundle; dress badly.

rinfiancàre, *v.t.* to prop; support. **rinfiànco**, *m.* prop; support.

rinfocolàre, *v.t.* to rekindle; revive.

rinforzaménto, *m.* strengthening; reinforcement. **rinforzàre**, *v.t.* to strengthen; reinforce; prop up. **rinfòrzo**, *m.* reinforcement.

rinfrancàre, *v.t.* to re-animate; re-invigorate; encourage.

rinfranchírsi (*pr.* **-ísco, -ísci**), *v.refl.* to become more skilful; improve (in).

rinfrescaménto, *m.* & **rinfrescatúra**, *f.* cooling; refreshing; freshening. **rinfrescànte**, *p.a.* cooling; refreshing. ¶ *m.* gentle laxative. **rinfrescàre**, *v.t.* to cool, refresh; freshen up; restore (*painting*). **rinfrescàrsi**, *v.refl.* to become cooler; cool down; take refreshments. **rinfrescàta**, *f.* refreshing coolness; refreshing shower. **rinfrésco** (*pl.* **-éschi**), *m.* light refreshment[s]; (*pl.*) fresh provisions (*ship*).

rinfronzíre (*pr.* **-ísco, -ísci**), *v.i.* (*aux.* essere & avere) to put on (out) new leaves. **rinfronzírsi**, v.refl. to deck oneself out; smarten oneself.

rinfúśa (alla), ad. expr. in confusion; anyhow; higgledy-piggledy; (of cargo) in bulk.

ringalluzzàre & **ringalluzzíre** (pr. -ísco, -ísci), v.t. to inspirit; elate. **ringalluzàrsi** & **ringalluzzírsi**, v.refl. to become elated; look proud as Punch. **ringalluzzíto**, a. elated; proud.

ringhiàre, v.i. (aux. avere) to snarl; growl. **ringhièra**, f. rail; railing, banisters; parapet. **rínghio**, m. snarl; growl. **ringhióso**, a. snarling.

ringiovaniménto, m. rejuvenation. **ringiovaníre** (pr. -ísco, -ísci), v.t. to rejuvenate; make look younger. v.i. (aux. essere) to grow young again; recover vigour; look younger.

ringraziaménto, m. thanks; thanksgiving; (pl.) thanks. **ringraziàre**, v.t. to thank; decline with thanks.

rinnegàre, v.t. to deny; disown; repudiate. **rinnegàto**, a. & m. renegade.

rinnovàbile, a. renewable. **rinnovaménto**, m. renewal; revival. **rinnovàre**, v.t. to renew; revive; renovate; put on (something) new; repeat. **rinnovazióne**, f. renovation; renewal.

rinnovellàre, v.t. to renew; renovate. **rinn[u]òvo**, m. renewal (of bill, &c.).

rinocerónte, m. rhinoceros.

rinomànza, f. renown; fame. **rinomàto**, a. renowned; famous.

rinsaldàre, v.t. to restarch; resolder; (fig.) to strengthen; consolidate.

rinsanguàre, v.t. to give new life (or strength) to. **rinsanguàrsi**, v.refl. to recover; become prosperous again.

rinsaníre (pr. -ísco, -ísci), v.i (aux. essere) to recover; recover one's health.

rinsaviménto, m. return to reason. **rinsavíre** (pr. -ísco, -ísci), v.i. (aux. essere) to recover one's wits; become sensible again.

rinserràre, v.t. to shut up; shut in; catch (shut) (one's finger in a door).

rintoccàre, v.i. (aux. essere & avere) to toll (bell); strike (clock). **rintócco** (pl. **rintócchi**), m. stroke (clock, bell); knell; toll; (pl.) tolling.

rintracciàbile, a. traceable. **rintracciàre**, v.t. to trace; follow up; find; find out.

rintrecciàre, v.t. to intertwine; interlace.

rintronaménto, m. booming; deafening; stunning. **rintronàre**, v.t. to deafen; stun; shake; v.i. (aux. essere & avere) to boom; resound.

rintuzzàre, v.t. to blunt; (fig.) dull; abate; repress; fling back (accusation).

rinúncia or **rinúnzia**, f. renunciation; renouncement; (cards) renounce. **rinunciàre** or **rinunziàre**, v.t. & i. (aux. avere) to renounce; give up; relinquish; resign; refuse.

rinvelenire (pr. -ísco, -ísci), v.t. to envenom still more; embitter; aggravate; exasperate. v.i. (aux. essere) & **rinvelenírsi**, v.refl. to become embittered.

rinveniménto, m. discovery; recovery; coming to one's senses; (Metall.) annealing. **rinveníre** (pr. -vèngo, -vièni, &c., like venire), v.t. ir. to find; discover; re-discover; anneal. v.i. (aux. essere) to recover one's senses; come to oneself; soften; swell out. **rinvenírsi**, v.refl. to find a way out.

rinverdíre (pr. -ísco, -ísci), v.t. to make green again; revive. v.i. (aux. essere) to grow green again; freshen up; revive.

rinvestiménto, m. re-investment (Fin., siege). **rinvestíre** (pr. -èsto, -èsti), v.t. to reinvest (Fin.); invest more closely (siege); strengthen (wall); cover (gen. bottle with straw); reinstate.

rinviàre, v.t. to adjourn; put off; defer; postpone; send back; remit (to another court).

rinvilio, m. depreciation; decline, fall (in prices). **rinvilíre** (pr. -ísco, -ísci), v.t. to lower; bring down. v.i. (aux. essere) to fall in price; become cheaper.

rinvío, m. adjournment; postponement; (Mech.) transmission.

río, a. (Poet.) wicked; cruel; guilty. ¶ m. (Poet.) brook; rivulet; canal (Venice).

rionàle, a. of a (city) ward. **rióne**, m. ward; quarter; part of a city.

riordinaménto, m. re-arrangement; restoration of order. **riordinàre**, v.t. to re-arrange; put in order (again); reorganize; give a fresh order for. **riordinatóre**, m. (f. -tríce) reorganizer. ¶ a. re-organizing.

riottóso, a. quarrelsome; riotous; sulky; sullen.

rípa, f. bank; shore; steep place.

riparàbile, *a.* reparable. **riparàre,** *v.t.* to repair; mend; protect; shelter; ward off; parry; keep off; keep out; retrieve; make good; provide for; meet (*requirements*); re-sit (*exam.*). ∼ *a,* to remedy; redress. *v.i.* (*aux.* essere) & **riparàrsi,** *v.refl.* to take shelter; find refuge. **riparatóre,** *m.* (*f.* **-tríce**) mender; protector; guardian. ¶ *a.* reparative. **riparazióne,** *f.* repair; reparation. *esami di* ∼, *m.pl.* second (autumn) session of examinations.

ripàro, *m.* shelter; screen; cover; defence; remedy; means of protection.

ripartíbile, *a.* divisible (into shares). **ripartiménto,** *m.* & **ripartizióne,** *f.* division; distribution. **ripartíre** (*pr.* **-ísco, -ísci**), *v.t.* to share; divide; distribute; parcel out. *v.i.* (*pr.* **-àrto, -àrti**) (*aux.* essere) to go away again; leave again; start again. **ripàrto,** *m.* distribution; division; department.

ripassàre, *v.i.* (*aux.* essere) to pass again; call again. *v.t.* to cross again; look over, run over again, re-read; revise; strop (*razor*); grind; (*tool*); (*Mech.*) overhaul; adjust. **ripassàta,** *f.* revision; look over; rub; polish; stropping. dim. *ripassatina.* **ripàsso,** *m.* return; repetition; revision.

ripensàre, *v.i.* (*aux.* avere) to think over; think again (of) = *a*); (*v.t.*) to recall to mind.

ripentiménto, *m.* repentance. **ripentírsi** (*pr.* **-ènto, -ènti**), *v.refl.* to repent; change one's mind; think better of it.

ripercòssa, *f.* & **ripercotiménto,** *m.* repercussion; reflection.

ripercuòtere (*pr.* **-cuòto, -cuòti,** *&c.,* like *scuotere*), *v.t.* ir. to strike again; beat back, give back, send back, throw back; reflect; echo back. *v.i.* (*aux.* essere) & **ripercuòtersi,** *v.refl.* rebound; re-echo. **ripercussióne,** *f.* repercussion.

ripescàre, *v.t.* to fish up; pick up; get hold of; find again.

ripetènte, *m.* pupil attending the same class for a second year. **ripètere,** *v.t.* to repeat, rehearse; (*Law*) claim (*damages, &c.*); derive. **ripetitóre,** *m.* (*f.* **-tríce**) private teacher; tutor, coach. **ripetizióne,** *f.* repetition, recurrence; revision; rehearsal; private lesson, coaching. *ucile a* ∼, *m.* repeating rifle. *orologio*

a ∼, *m.* repeating watch, repeater. **ripetutaménte,** *ad.* repeatedly. **ripetúto,** *a.* repeated, reiterated.

ripiàno, *m.* flat part; piece of level ground; terrace; plateau; (*stair*) landing.

ripícco, *m.* pique; spite.

ripidézza, *f.* steepness. **rípido, a.** steep.

ripiegaménto, *m.* folding; bending back; (*Mil.*) withdrawal, retreat. **ripiegàre,** *v.t.* to bend back; fold; fold up again; *v.i.* (*aux.* avere) give way; g. ground, withdraw, retire; shift, makeshift. **ripiegàrsi,** *v.refl.* to bend down; crouch; become bent with age. ∼*in sé stesso,* to retire into oneself, become reserved. **ripiegàta,** *f.* sudden bending; bend (*river*). **ripiegatúra,** *f.* fold; folding; bending. **ripiègo** (*pl.* **-èghi**), *m.* expedient; shift; substitute; remedy.

ripienézza, *f.* ful[l]ness; surfeit; repletion. **ripièno,** *a.* full; chockfull; replete (with); stuffed (with). ¶ *m.* filling; stuffing (*Cook.*).

ripigliàre, *v.t.* to resume; reprimand. **ripigliàrsi,** *v.refl.* to recover; correct oneself. **ripiglíno,** *m.* (*game*) cat's cradle.

ripiombàre, *v.i.* (*aux.* essere) to fall down again; sink down again; fall back (again); plunge back; (*wall*) fall sheer; (*v.t.*) to throw down again; plunge back.

ripórre (*pr.* **-óngo, -óni,** *&c.,* like *porre*), *v.t.* ir. to put back; replace; set (again); lay (again); put away; hide; conceal.

riportàre, *v.t.* to bring back (or again); take back; carry back; relate; report; receive, get; carry off; win; reproduce (*drawing*); (*Bkkpg.*) carry forward; c. over; bring forward. **riportàrsi,** *v.refl.* to refer; appeal; go back. **riportatóre,** *m.* (*f.* **-tríce**) reporter. **ripòrto,** *m.* (*Bkkpg.*) amount to be carried forward; (*Stk. Ex.*) contango.

riposànte, *a.* restful; pleasant; soothing; agreeable. **riposàre,** *v.t.* to rest; refresh; relieve; lay down. *v.i.* to rest; stand; lie down; sleep; repose, be buried. ∼ *in,* to rely on. **riposàta,** *f.* rest; halt; pause. **riposataménte,** *ad.* quietly; peacefully. **riposàto,** *a.* quiet; peaceful. **ripòso,** *m.* rest; repose; retirement; (*Theat.*) no performance.

ripostaménte, *ad.* secretly. **ripostí-**

glio, *m.* nook; lumber-room; recess; place to put things. **ripósto,** *a.* secret; hidden.

riprèndere (*pr.* -**èndo, -èndi,** *&c.,* like *prendere*), *v.t. ir.* to take back; get back; recover; retake; recapture; resume; take up again; take in (*dress*); pick up (*stitch*); reprove; find fault with. *v.i.* (*aux.* avere) to begin again; start again; recover; reply; retort; rejoin. **riprèndersi,** *v.refl.* to recover; correct oneself (*speaking*). **riprensibile,** *a.* reprehensible. **riprensióne,** *f.* reproof; reprehension.

riprésa, *f.* retaking, recapture; recovery; resumption; renewal; revival; repetition; round (*Box*); bout (*Fenc.*).

ripréso, *p.p.* of *riprendere.*

ripristinàre, *v.t.* restore; re-establish, renew.

riprodúrre (*pr.* -**dúco, -dúci,** *&c.,* like *produrre*), *v.t. ir.* to reproduce. **riprodúrsi,** *v.refl.* to recur; reproduce, breed. **riproduttívo,** *a.* reproductive. **riproduzióne,** *f.* reproduction.

ripromèttere (*pr.* -**métto,** *&c.,* like *mettere*), *v.t. ir.* to promise again. **ripromèttersi,** *v.refl.* to hope; hope for; expect.

ripròva, *f.* fresh proof; new evidence; confirmation; proof. **riprovàre,** *v.t. & i.* to reprove; censure; reject; refute; try again; experience again. **riprovàto,** *a.* unsuccessful; rejected. **riprovazióne,** *f.* reprobation. **riprovévole,** *a.* blameworthy; despicable; shameful.

ripudiàre, *v.t.* to repudiate; reject. **ripúdio,** *m.* repudiation; rejection.

ripugnànte, *a.* repugnant; disgusting; contrary. **ripugnànza,** *f.* repugnance; aversion; reluctance. **ripugnàre,** *v.i.* (*aux.* avere) to be repugnant; be contrary; disgust.

ripulíre (*pr.* -**ísco, -ísci**), *v.t.* to clean, clean up; clear; sweep away; weed; (*fig.*) make a clean sweep of; (*cards*) sweep the board; correct. **ripulírsi,** *v.refl.* to tidy oneself; make oneself smart. **ripulíta,** *f.* clean; cleaning; (*fig.*) cleaning up. **ripulitúra,** *f.* cleaning.

ripúlsa, *f.* refusal; repulse. **ripulsióne,** *f.* repulsion; aversion. **ripulsívo,** *a.* repulsive; repellent; disgusting.

riquadràre, *v.t.* to square (*number*); make square (*shape*); paint &

decorate (*the walls of a room*). *v.i.* (*aux.* avere) to measure in area. **riquadratóre,** *m.* decorator. **riquadratúra,** *f.* squaring; decoration.

rísa, *f.pl.* of *riso.*

risàcca, *f.* surf.

risàia, *f.* rice-field. **risai[u]òlo,** *m.* **risai[u]òla,** *f.* worker in the rice-field.

risaldàre, *v.t.* to resolder; solder. **risaldatúra,** *f.* resoldering.

risalíre (*pr.* -**àlgo, -àli,** *&c.,* like *salire*), *v.i. ir.* (*aux.* essere) to go up again; rise (*price*); go back; rise again; remount. *v.t.* to ascend, re-ascend. ~ *la corrente,* to stem the current.

risaltàre, *v.t.* to jump over (again). *v.i.* (*aux.* avere) to stand out; show up, catch the eye. *v.i.* (*aux.* avere & essere) to rebound; project; emerge. *far* ~, to enhance, bring out strongly, make (more) conspicuous. **risàlto,** *m.* prominence; relief; emphasis; vividness; (*Mech.*) projection, projecting part.

risanaménto, *m.* healing; (*fig.*) reformation; reclamation. **risanàre,** *v.t.* to heal; cure; reform; reclaim (*land*). *v.i.* (*aux.* essere) & **risanàrsi,** *v.refl.* to recover; become healthy. **risanatóre,** *m.* (*f.* -**trice**) healer. ¶ *a.* healing.

risapére (*pr.* -**sò, -sài, -sà,** like *sapere*), *v.t. ir.* to know; come to know; get to know (or hear of). **risapúto,** *p.a.* well known; known.

risarcíbile, *a.* reparable. **risarciménto,** *m.* compensation; reparation. **risarcíre** (*pr.* -**ísco, -ísci**), *v.t.* to compensate; indemnify; repair.

risàta, *f.* laughter; burst of laughter; hearty laugh. *dim. risatina.*

risàzio, *a.* fully satisfied; sated (with).

riscaldaménto, *m.* heating; (*fig.*) warmth (*of feeling*); excitement; irritation. **riscaldàre,** *v.t.* to heat; warm; warm up; (*fig.*) excite. **riscaldàrsi,** *v.refl.* to warm oneself; get warm; become excited. **riscaldàta,** *f.* warming; warm; warming up. **riscaldatóre,** *m.* heater; heating-apparatus. **riscàldo,** *m.* (*Med.*) inflammation; irritation; heat-spot; feverishness.

riscattàre, *v.t.* to ransom; (*Law*) redeem. **riscattàrsi,** *v.refl.* (*cards*) to recover one's losses. **riscàtto,** *m.* ransom; redemption.

rischiaménto, *m.* illumination; brightening; (*lit.* & *fig.*) lighting up. **rischiaràre,** *v.t.* to light up; illuminate; clear up; enlighten. *v.i.* (*aux.* essere) & **rischiararsi,** *v.refl.* to become clear; light up. **rischiaríre,** *v.i.* (*aux.* essere) & **rischiarìrsi,** *v.refl.* to brighten, become clear, or clearer. **rischiàre,** *v.t.* to risk, expose to risk; venture. *v.i.* to run the risk (of = *di*). **ríschio,** *m.* risk. **rischióso,** *a.* risky; dangerous. **risciacquaménto,** *m.* rinsing. **risciacquàre,** *v.t.* to rinse; rinse out. **risciacquàta,** *f.* rinse; rinsing; (*fig.*) scolding. dim. *risciacquatina.* **risciacquatúra,** *f.* rinsing; dish-water. **risciò,** *m.* ricksha(w). **riscontàre,** *v.t.* to re-discount. **riscónto,** *m.* rediscount; rediscounting. **riscontràbile,** *a.* that may be found; that may be checked. **riscontràre,** *v.t.* to find; meet with; notice; check; collate; compare; verify. **riscontràrsi,** *v.refl.* to meet; cross; tally; match. **riscóntro,** *m.* meeting; examination; checking; verification; comparison; control; collation; reply; acknowledgement; counterpart; support; draught (*air*). *far ~,* to tally. *~ di cassa,* verification of cash. *ufficio del ~,* controller's office. **riscopríre** (*pr.* **-còpro, -còpri,** &c., like *coprire*), *v.t. ir.* to re-discover; uncover again; reveal in turn. **riscòssa,** *f.* shaking; shock; start; insurrection; revolt; (*Mil.*) recovery of a lost position; support; redress; redemption. **riscossióne,** *f.* collection (*debts*). **riscòsso,** *p.p.* of *riscuotere.* ¶ *m.* cash collected. **riscotíbile,** *a.* recoverable. **riscotiménto,** *m.* collection; recovery (*money*); starting (*shock*). **risc[u]òtere** (*pr.* **-scuòto,** &c., like *scuotere*), *v.t. ir.* to shake; rouse; startle; (*money*) receive, draw; get in; collect; (*praise*) win, earn; take out of pawn; make good (*loss*). **risc[u]òtersi,** *v.refl.* to start; be alarmed; come to (*after fainting*). **risecàre** (*pr.* **-sèco, -sèchi,**) *v.t.* to cut down (*expenses*); cut off; cut out; cut away. **riseccàre** (*pr.* **-sécco, -sécchi**), *v.t.* & *i.* (*aux.* essere) & **riseccarsi,** *v.refl.* to dry (up). **risécco** (*pl.* **-écchi**), *a.* dry; withered; dried up.

risedére (*pr.* **-siédo** *or* **-séggo,** &c., like *sedere*), *v.i. ir.* (*aux.* avere) to sit down again; be situated; reside. **risentiménto,** *m.* resentment. **risentíre** (*pr.* **-ènto,** &c., like *sentire*), *v.t.* to hear again; feel again; feel; experience; suffer. *v.i.* (*aux.* avere) show traces (of); feel the effects (of). **risentírsi,** *v.refl.* to wake up; show signs of life; (*of buildings*) show signs of decay; recover one's senses; feel offended; get angry; show one's resentment. **risentitaménte,** *ad.* angrily; resentfully. **risentíto,** *a.* resentful; angry. **riserbàre,** &c., see *riservare.* **risèrbo,** *m.* discretion; reserve; self-restraint. **riserràre,** *v.t.* to close again; shut tighter. **risèrva,** *f.* reserve; reservation. **riservàre,** *v.t.* to keep; reserve; set aside; put off. **riservàrsi,** *v.refl.* to reserve oneself; reserve to oneself; claim. **riservataménte,** *ad.* with reservation(s); under reserve. **riservatézza,** *f.* reserved manners; reserve; prudence, circumspection. **riservàto,** *a.* reserved; private, confidential. **riservíre** (*pr.* **-sèrvo, sèrvi,** &c., like *servire*), *v.t.* to serve again; return a favour. **riservìsta** (*pl.* **-ìsti**), *m.* reservist. **risìbile,** *a.* laughable; ridiculous. **risicàre,** *v.t.* & *i.* (*aux.* avere) to risk. **rísico,** *m.* risk. **risicoltúra,** *f.* rice-growing. **risièdere** (*pr.* **-sièdo, sièdi**), *v.i.* (*aux.* avere) to reside. **risìpola,** *f.* erysipelas. **rísma,** *f.* ream (*paper*); quality; sort, kind. **ríso,** *m.* (*pl.f.* **risa**) laugh; laughter; (*Poet.*) smile; laughing; (*pl.*) laughter. ¶ *m.* (*pl.* **risi**) rice. **risolàre,** *v.t.* to re-sole (*boots*). **risolatúra,** *f.* resoling. **risolíno,** *m.* little laugh; smile. **risollevàre,** *v.t.* to raise again; lift up again; elevate; bring up again. **risòlto,** *p.p.* of *risolvere,* solved, settled. **risolutaménte,** *ad.* resolutely. **risolutézza,** *f.* resoluteness; resolution. **risolutívo,** *a.* (*Med.*) resolutive; laxative; efficacious. *patto ~,* (*Law*) agreement which terminates a contract. **risolúto,** *p.p.* of *risolvere.* ¶ *a.* resolute; determined; resolved; free (*style*). **risoluzióne,** *f.* resolution; solution (*problem*);

(*Law*) dissolution (of contract); (*Art*) freedom of touch. **risòlvere,** *v.t.* to resolve; solve; settle; dissolve; end; annul. *v.i.* (*aux.* avere) & **risòlversi,** *v.refl.* to resolve; decide; dissolve; be reduced (to); be transformed.

risonànte, *a.* resonant; resounding. **risonànza,** *f.* resonance; sound. **risonàre** (*pr.* -suòno, -suòni), *v.i.* (*aux.* essere & avere) to resound; ring (out); echo; (*v.t.*) ring again; play again (*Mus.*); echo, utter.

risóne, *m.* unpolished rice.

risórgere (*pr.* -órgo, -órgi, &c., like *sorgere*), *v.i. ir.* (*aux.* essere) to rise again; revive; return. **risorgiménto,** *m.* revival; awakening; rebirth. *il R* ~, the Risorgimento, Italian national revival of the 19th century, esp. 1831–70.

risórsa, *f.* resource; expedient, shift.

risortíre (*pr.* -sorto, -sorti), *v.i.* (*aux.* essere) to go out again. *v.t.* (*pr.* -sortísco, -sortísci) to re-allot.

risórto, *p.p.* of *risorgere.*

risòtto, *m.* savoury dish of rice.

risovveniménto, *m.* remembrance. **risovvenírsi** (di), *v.refl.* to remember; recollect.

risparmiàre, *v.t.* to save (up); spare. **risparmiatóre,** *m.* (*f.* -tríce) saver; thrifty person. **rispàrmio,** *m.* saving. *cassa di* ~, *f.* savings bank.

rispecchiàre, *v.t.* to reflect; (*fig.*) mirror.

rispedíre (*pr.* -ísco, -ísci), *v.t.* to send again; s. back; forward. **rispedizióne,** *f.* sending back; reshipping; forwarding.

rispettàbile, *a.* respectable; worthy of respect; considerable. **rispettàre,** *v.t.* to respect. **rispettivaménte,** *ad.* respectively. ~ *a*, in comparison with; considering. **rispettívo,** *a.* respective. **rispètto,** *m.* respect; regard; Italian folk-lyric, gen. of 6 or 8 lines. ~ *a, per* ~ *a, a* ~ *a, in* ~ *a*, compared with, in comparison with. *di* ~, in reserve. *àncora di* ~, *ruota di* ~, *f.* spare anchor, s. wheel (*Naut.*). **rispettóso,** *a.* respectful.

risplendènte, *a.* shining; glittering; aglow; glorious. **risplèndere,** *v.i.* (*aux.* essere & avere) to shine; s. brightly; glitter; be famous or glorious.

rispondènte (a), answering (to); in keeping (with); in harmony (with).

rispondènza, *f.* correspondence; harmony; agreement; relation. **rispóndere,** *v.i. ir.* (*aux.* avere) & *t.* to answer, reply, respond; say in reply; write back; correspond (to); agree (with); (*cards*) follow suit. ~ *di*, to answer for. **rispósta,** *f.* answer; reply; response. *con* ~ *pagata*, reply paid.

rispostàccia, *f.* rude answer.

ríssa, *f.* scuffle; brawl; conflict; quarrel. **rissàre,** *v.i.* (*aux.* avere) to quarrel; begin a fight; fight. **rissóso,** *a.* quarrelsome.

ristabiliménto, *m.* re-establishment; restoration; re-instatement. **ristabilíre** (*pr.* -ísco, -ísci), *v.t.* to re-establish; restore; return; retrieve; reinstate.

ristagnaménto, *m.* stagnation; stanching; stopping the flow (*of blood, &c.*). **ristagnàre,** *v.t.* to re-solder; reline with tin; stanch; render stagnant. *v.i.* (*aux.* avere) to stagnate. **ristagnatúra,** *f.* soldering; retinning. **ristàgno,** *m.* stagnation; slackness (*business, &c.*); dul[l]ness.

ristàmpa, *f.* (*Typ.*) reprint; reprinting; new impression. **ristampare,** *v.t.* to reprint.

ristàre (*pr.* ristò, ristài, &c., like *stare*), *v.i. ir.* (*aux.* essere) to stay again; stop; cease for a moment. **ristàrsi,** *v.refl.* to refrain.

ristorànte, *m.* restaurant; (*station*) refreshment room. **ristoràre,** *v.t.* to restore; refresh; compensate; console. **ristoratóre,** *m.* restorer; restaurant. ¶ *a.* (*f.* -tríce) refreshing. **ristòro,** *m.* refreshment; rest; solace; comfort; relief; amends.

ristrettaménte, *ad.* narrowly; in straitened circumstances. **ristrettèzza,** *f.* narrowness; shortness; lack; (*pl.*) narrow (*or* straitened) circumstances. **ristrétto,** *a.* narrow; limited; mean; restricted; shrunken; tight; compressed; concentrated. *prezzo* ~, reduced price, lowest price. ¶ *m.* summary; epitome; reduced price.

ristuccàre, *v.t.* to re-plaster; plaster up; (*fig.*) cloy; weary; nauseate. **ristucchévole,** *a.* cloying; tiring. **ristúcco** (*pl.* -úcchi), *a.* sick; (*fig.*) tired.

risúcchio, *m.* whirlpool; eddy.

risultànte, *a.* resultant; resulting. **risultànza,** *f.* result; issue; outcome. **risultàre,** *v.i.* (*aux.* essere) to result; follow; appear; transpire; become known; emerge; spring; prove to be; turn out to be. **risuitàto**, *m.* result.

risuonàre, see *risonare.*

risurrezióne, *f.* resurrection.

risuscitàre, *v.t.* to resuscitate, revive; bring back; bring to life again. *v.i.* (*aux.* essere) to rise again; revive.

risvegliaménto, *m.* awakening. **risvegliàre**, *v.t.* to wake (up); rouse; awaken; stir (up); revive; excite. **risvegliàrsi**, *v.refl.* to wake up; wake again. **risvegliatóre**, *m.* (*f.* -tríce) awakener. ¶ *a.* awakening. **risvéglio**, *m.* awakening; revival.

risvòlta, *f. & risvòlto**, *m.* sharp turn; cuff; lapel.

ritagliàre, *v.t.* to cut out; clip (off); re-cut. **ritàglio**, *m.* clipping; cutting; snippet; (*time*) odd moment.

ritardaménto, *m.* delay, delaying; deferment; postponement. **ritardàre**, *v.t.* to delay; defer; put off; retard. *v.i.* (*aux.* avere (*pers.*) essere (*things*) to delay; wait; be late; be slow (*watch*). **ritàrdo**, *m.* delay. *essere in ~*, to be late.

ritégno, *m.* restraint; reserve; moderation; reluctance; hesitation; barrier; support.

ritemperàre, *v.t.* to re-sharpen; temper anew. **ritempràre**, *v.t.* to strengthen; give new strength to.

ritenére (*pr.* -éngo, -ièni, *&c.*, like *tenere*), *v.t. ir.* to hold back; detain; repress; stop; retain; keep; hold; withhold; deduct. *v.t. & i.* (*aux.* avere) to consider; regard; maintain; think; hold; remember. **ritenérsi**, *v.refl.* to restrain oneself; refrain; consider oneself. **ritenitíva & ritentiva**, *f.* retentiveness; strength of memory.

ritentàre, *v.t.* to tempt again. *v.i.* (*aux.* avere) to try again; make a fresh attempt.

ritentívo, *a.* retentive.

ritenúta, *f.* deduction; stoppage (*from pay*); retention. **ritenutaménte**, *ad.* with reserve; reservedly; moderately. **ritenutézza**, *f.* reserve; moderation. **ritenúto**, *a.* reserved; self-possessed. **ritenzióne**, *f.* retention.

ritíngere (*pr.* -íngo, -íngi, *&c.*, like *tingere*), *v.t. ir.* to dye again; re-paint. **ritínto**, *a.* dyed, re-dyed; painted.

ritiràre, *v.t.* withdraw; retract; draw back; take back; draw in; draw (*salary*); cash (*money-order*); reprint; throw again; fire again. ~ *da*, take after, resemble. **ritiràrsi**, *v.refl.* to retire; withdraw; retreat; shrink (*cloth*); contract. **ritiràta**, *f.* retreat; water-closet (*abb.* W.C.). **ritirataménte**, *ad.* in a retired way; in retirement. **ritiratézza**, *f.* seclusion. **ritiràto**, *a.* retired; secluded. **ritíro**, *m.* withdrawal; retirement; retreat. *in ~*, (*Mil.*) on the retired list.

rítmico (*pl.* **rítmici**), *a.* rhythmic(al); measured. **rítmo**, *m.* rhythm.

ríto, *m.* rite; ceremony; custom.

ritoccaménto, *m. & ritoccatúra**, *f.* retouching. **ritoccàre** (*pr.* -òcco, -òcchi**), *v.t.* to retouch; touch up; revise; touch upon again; have a second helping of. ~ *a*, to be one's turn again. **ritocchíno**, *m.* snack between meals; additional helping. **ritócco** (*pl.* -òcchi**), *m.* additional touch, final touch.

ritògliere (*pl.* -tòlgo, -tògli**, *&c.*, like *togliere*), *v.t. ir.* to take back; take away again.

ritòrcere (*pr.* -tòrso, -tòrci**, *&c.*, like *torcere*), *v.t. ir.* to twist; retwist; twist back; retort; turn . . . against. **ritòrcersi**, *v.refl.* to become twisted.

ritornàre, *v.i.* (*aux.* essere) to return; come back; go back; recur. *v.t.* to return; give back. **ritornàta**, *f. & ritórno**, *m.* return. *biglietto di andata e ritorno*, *m.* return ticket. *partita di ritorno*, *f.* return game, return match. *ritorno di fiamma*, back fire (*Mech.*). **ritornèllo**, *m.* refrain.

ritorsióne, *f.* retort; retaliation. **ritòrta**, *f.* withy; (*fig.*) chain; bond. **ritòrto**, *a.* twisted.

ritraènte, *p.a.* representing; reproducing. **ritràrre** (*pr.* -àggo, -ài**, *&c.*, like *trarre*), *v.t. ir.* to draw back; withdraw; turn away; pull again; p. harder; get, obtain; draw; derive; portray; reproduce; represent; prevent; hold back. ~ *da*, take after, resemble. **ritràrsi**, *v.refl.* to draw back; withdraw; take shelter.

ritrattàre, *v.t.* to rehandle; treat again (of); retract; recant; withdraw; portray. **ritrattazióne**, *f.* rehandling; retraction; recantation; withdrawal. **ritràttile**, *a.* retractile; retractable. *carello ~*, *m.* (*Aero.*)

retractable (under)carriage. **ritrat-tíno**, *m.* small portrait. **ritrattísta** (*pl.* **-ísti**), *m.* portrait-painter. **ritràtto**, *p.p.* of *ritrarre*. ¶ *m.* portrait; picture. ~ *in piedi*, full-length portrait.

ritríto, *a.* stale.

ritrósa, *f.* bag-net.

ritrosàggine, *f.* backwardness; awkward rusticity; stubbornness; shyness. **ritrosaménte**, *ad.* reluctantly; shyly; with aversion. **ritrosía**, *f.* bashfulness; shyness; reluctance; aversion. **ritróso**, *a.* backward; bashful; shy; moving backwards; wayward; reluctant. *a* ~, backwards; the wrong way about. *a* ~ *della corrente*, against the stream. ¶ *m.* eddy; whirlpool; reversed mouth of trap or net.

ritrovaménto, *m.* discovery; re-discovery; recovery. **ritrovàre**, *v.t.* to find again; meet again; re-discover; recover; invent; call upon, visit. **ritrovàrsi**, *v.refl.* to find oneself; be present; meet again. **ritrovatóre**, *m.* inventor; dis-coverer. **ritròvo**, *m.* meeting place; rendez-vous; place of resort; haunt; circle; society; gathering; party.

ritto, *a.* straight; upright; erect; right (*direction*). *man* ~*a* or ~*a*, right hand. ¶ *m.* right side; upright; support.

rittorovèscio, *ad.* upside down.

rituàle, *a.* ritual; customary. **ritua-lìsmo**, *m.* ritualism. **ritualménte**, *ad.* according to ritual or custom.

rituffàre, *v.t. &* **rituffàrsi**, *v.refl.* to plunge again. **ritúffo**, *m.* fresh plunge.

riunióne, *f.* meeting; gathering; reunion. **riuníre** (*pr.* **-ísco**, **-ísci**, *&c.*, like *unire*), *v.t.* to assemble; gather; unite; reunite; bring to-gether again; combine; reconcile. **riunírsi**, *v.refl.* to meet; be united; come together again. **riuníto**, *p.a.* united; reunited; gathered; assembled; combined; amalgamated.

riuscíbile, *a.* likely to succeed. **riuscíre** (*pr.* **rièsco**, **rièsci**), *v.i. ir.* (*aux.* essere) to succeed; prosper; be successful; be able (to); result; turn out, prove (to be); end by being; produce the effect of; go out again; give access to; arrive (at). **riuscíta**, *f.* success; issue; exit; way out (*fig.*); result. **riuscíto**, *a.* successful.

riva, *f.* bank; shore.

rivagheggiàre, *v.t.* to long for again; court again; (*fig.*) pursue further.

rivàle, *a. & m.* rival. **rivaleggiàre**, *v.i.* to vie, compete. ~ *con*, to rival.

rivalérsi (*pr.* **-àlgo**, **-àli**, *&c.*, like *valere*), *v.refl.. ir.* to make use (of) again; make good one's losses.

rivalicàre, *v.t.* to cross again; recross.

rivalità, *f.* rivalry.

rivàlsa, *f.* revenge; (*Com.*) redraft. *cambiale di* ~, *f.* bill of exchange given for one that was not met.

rivalutàre, *v.t.* to revalue; restore the value of.

rivarcàre, *v.t.* to recross.

rivedére (*pr.* **édo**, *&c.*, like *vedere*), *v.t. ir.* to see again; meet again; revisit; review; revise; touch up; read (proof). *a rivederci!, a riveder-La!* goodbye! au revoir. **rivedíbile**, *a.* subject to revision; (*Mil.*) tempo-rarily unfit. **riveditóre**, *m.* reviser; (*proof*) reader. **rivedúta**, *f.* revision; review. **rivedúto**, *p.a.* revised.

rivelàre, *v.t.* to reveal; disclose; display. **rivelatóre**, *m.* (*f.* **-tríce**) revealer; detector (*Radio*). ¶ *a.* revealing. **rivelazióne**, *f.* revela-tion; disclosure.

rivéndere, *v.t.* to resell; retail. **rivendíbile**, *a.* resalable.

rivendicàre, *v.t.* to vindicate (com-pletely); claim; recover possession of.

rivéndita, *f.* resale; retail selling; shop. ~ *di sale e tabacchi*, shop for sale of government monopolies (*salt, tobacco, stamps*). **rivenditóre**, *m.* retailer; small shopkeeper. **rivendúgliola**, *f. &* **rivendúgliolo**, *m.* hawker; costermonger.

riverberaménto, *m. &* **riverbera-zióne**, *f.* reverberation; reflection. **riverberàre**, *v.t.* to reverberate; throw back; reflect; dazzle. **riverberàrsi**, *v.refl.* to reverberate; be reflected. **rivèrbero**, *m.* reverberation; reflection; excessive heat or light.

riverènte, *a.* reverent; respectful. **riverènza**, *f.* reverence; bow; curtsey. **riveríre** (*pr.* **-ísco**, **-ísci**), *v.t.* to respect; pay one's respects to; honour; revere.

riversaménto, *m.* outpouring. **riversàre**, *v.t.* to pour; p. out; p. out again; turn; (*fig.*) throw. **riversàrsi**, *v.refl.* to pour, flow, rush.

riversíbile, *a.* (*Law*) subject to reversion. **riversióne**, *f.* (*Law*) reversion. **rivèrso**, *a.* reversed, upset; on one's back. ¶ *m.* reverse; back, wrong side; overflow; misfortune.

rivestiménto, *m.* covering; lining; facing (*wall*); revetment. **rivestire** (*pr.* -èsto, -èsti), *v.t.* to re-clothe; dress (again]; cover; sheath; line; hold, take up (*post*). **rivestírsi**, *v.refl.* to dress oneself again; (*fig.*) be clothed. **rivestitúra**, *f.* (material) covering; lining.

riviéra, *f.* coast. *la R~*, the Riviera (French & Ital.). **rivieràsco** (*pl.* -àschi), *a.* of the Riviera. ¶ *m.* inhabitant of the Riviera.

rivíncere (*pr.* -vínco, -vínci, -vínce, &c.), like *vincere*), *v.i.* (*aux.* avere) & *t. ir.* to win again; w. back; defeat again. **rivíncita**, *f.* return match, return game; revenge.

rivíšita, *f.* return visit. **riviśitàre**, *v.t.* to revisit.

rivísta, *f.* review, inspection; magazine; review; revue.

rivívere (*pr.* -vívo, &c., like *vivere*), *v.t. ir.* to live again (one's life). *v.i.* (*aux.* avere & essere) to live again; come to life again; revive.

rivivìfcàre, *v.t.* to revivify; revive.

rivo, *m.* stream. dim. *rivolo, rivoletto*.

rivocàre, &c., see *revocare*.

rivolàre, *v.i.* to fly again; fly back. **rivolére** (*pr.* vòglio, &c., like *volere*), *v.t. ir.* to want again; want back.

rivòlgere (*pr.* -òlgo, -òlgi, &c., like *volgere*), *v.t. ir.* to turn; direct; address; turn round; revolve (*in one's mind*); overturn; turn away; dissuade. **rivòlgersi**, *v.refl.* turn round; t. back; turn, apply (to); address oneself (to); set out (for); change one's mind. **rivolgiménto**, *m.* disturbance; change; upheaval; turning; upsetting.

rivòlta, *f.* revolt, rebellion; mutiny; sharp turn; turning. **rivoltànte**, *a.* revolting, disgusting. **rivoltàre**, *v.t.* to turn over; turn; turn inside out; cause to revolt; direct. **rivoltàrsi**, *v.refl.* to turn round; turn over (*as in bed*); turn; be turned; revolt; rebel; mutiny. **rivoltàto**, *p.a.* turned; turned over; turned inside out. **rivoltèlla**, *f.* revolver. *~ a sei colpi*, six-chambered r. **rivòlto** *p.p.* of *rivolgere*. ¶ *m.* reverse side (of a dress).

rivoltolàre, *v.t.* to turn; t. over; roil; r. over. **rivoltolàrsi**, *v.refl.* to roil; roll about; wallow. **rivoltolío**, *m.* constant turning. **rivoltolóne**, *m.* somersault. **rivoltolóni**, *ad.* turning over and over. **rivoltóso**, *a.* rebellious.

rivoluzionàre, *v.t.* incite to revolt; revolutionize. **rivoluzionàrio**, *a.* & *m.* revolutionary. **rivoluzióne**, *f.* revolution.

rivulsióne, *f.* revulsion.

rizzaménto, *m.* straightening; erection; bristling (*of hair*). **rizzàre**, &c., see *drizzare*.

roàno, *a.* & *m.* roan. **R~**, *f.* Rouen.

ròba, *f.* things; goods; stuff; material; cloth. **robàccia**, *f.* rubbish; poor stuff.

róbbia, *f.* madder.

robinétto, *m.* cock; tap.

robustézza, *f.* strength; sturdiness; robustness. **robùsto**, *a.* strong; sturdy; robust; vigorous.

rocàggine, *f.* hoarseness. **rocaménte**, *ad.* hoarsely.

ròcca, *f.* rock; fortress; stronghold. *cristallo di ~*, rock crystal, *m.* *~ di camino*, chimney-pot, *f.* **rócca**, *f.* distaff.

roccétto, *m.* rochet; surplice.

rocchétto, *m.* reel; bobbin; ratchet-(wheel); (*Elec.*) coil. *~ d'induzione*, induction coil.

ròccia (*pl.* **ròcce**), *f.* rock, cliff; crag. **rocciatóre**, *m.* cragsman; rock-climber. **roccióso**, *a.* rocky.

ròcco (*pl.* **ròcchi**), *m.* (*chess*) castle; rook.

rochézza, *f.* hoarseness. **ròco** (*pl.* **ròchi**), *a.* hoarse.

rococò, *a.* & *m.* rococo.

Ròdano, *m.* Rhone.

ródere, *v.t. ir.* to gnaw; nibble; eat (away, into); consume; corrode; fret; (*fig.*) torture. **ródersi**, *v.refl.* to chafe (with rage); to be worried; to be consumed.

Rodésia (la), *f.* Rhodesia. **rodesiàno**, *a.* & *m.* Rhodesian.

Ròdi, *f.* Rhodes (*Geog.*).

rodiménto, *m.* gnawing; (*fig.*) anxiety; worry. **roditóre**, *m.* rodent. ¶ *a.* (*f.* **roditríce**) gnawing; corroding.

rododèndro, *m.* rhododendron.

rodomontàta, *f.* rodomontade; boastful talk. **rodomónte**, *m.* braggart (after Rodomonte, a character in Ariosto's O.F.).

rogàre (*pr.* **rògo**, **ròghi**), *v.t.* (*Law*)

to draw up (a deed). **rogatóre,** *m.*
draftsman. **rògito,** *m.* (*Law*) deed;
instrument; attestation.
rógna, *f.* mange; scab; itch. **rognóso,**
a. mangy; scabby; itchy.
rognóne, *m.* kidney (*butcher's meat*).
rògo, *m.* stake; (funeral) pyre;
fire.
Rolàndo, *m.* Roland. **Róma,** *f.*
Rome.
Romàgna (la), *f.* Romagna. **ro-
magn[u]òlo,** *a. & m.* of (the)
Romagna; inhabitant of R.
romàico (*pl.* -àici), *m.* Romaic (*mod.
Gk. vernacular*).
romanaménte, *ad.* in the Roman
way; in the Roman style. **romàncio,**
a. & m. Romansch (dialect of the
Grisons). **romanésco** (*pl.* -éschi),
a. & m. mod. Roman dialect.
Romania (la), *f.* Roumania.
romànico (*pl.* -ànici), *a.* Romance
(*lang.*); Romanesque (*Arch.*). **ro-
manísta** (*pl.* -ísti), *m.* specialist in
Roman law. **romanità,** *f.* spirit of
ancient Rome, her character &
civilization. **romàno,** *a. & m.*
Roman.
romanticaménte, *ad.* romantically.
romantichería, *f.* romantic sentiment; (*pl.*) romantic ideas; *¶*
nonsense. **romanticísmo,** *m.*
romanticism. **romàntico** (*pl.*
-àntici), *a.* romantic.
romànza, *f.* (*Mus.*) ballad; romance;
song. **romanzatóre,** *m.* romancer.
romanzésco (*pl.* -éschi), *a.* romantic;
adventurous. **romanzière,** *m.*
novelist. **romànzo,** *a.* Romance
(*lang.*). *¶ m.* novel; romance.
rómba, *f.* roar; rumble; confused din;
thunder (*fig.*). **rombàre,** *v.i.* (*aux.*
avere) to roar; rumble.
rómbo, *m.* rhomb (*Geom.*); turbot;
booming sound. **rombòide,** *m.*
rhomboid.
romèno, *a. & m.* Roumanian.
romèo, *m.* pilgrim.
romitàggio & romitòrio, *m.* hermitage. **romíto,** *a.* lonely; solitary.
¶ m. hermit.
Ròmolo, *m.* Romulus.
rompènti, *m.pl.* reefs just under
water. **rómpere,** *v.t.* ir. &
rómpersi, *v.refl.* to break; b. up;
b. in; b. off; snap; rupture; disrupt;
burst; interrupt; cut off; infringe;
upset; cancel. *rompersi la testa,* to
rack one's brains. *v.i.* (*aux.* avere)
to break; be wrecked; burst (*into
tears*); clear (*sky*). **rompíbile,** *a.*

breakable. **rompicàpo** (*pl.* -àpi),
m. trouble; worry; puzzle. **rompi-
còllo** (*pl.* -còlli), *m.* dangerous spot;
precipice; perilous affair; dare-devil.
a ~, headlong. **rompighiàccio,**
m.inv. ice-breaker. **rompiménto,**
m. breaking; (*fig.*) trouble, nuisance.
rompinóci, *m.inv.* nut-crackers.
rompiónde, *m.inv.* breakwater.
rompiscàtole & rompistivàli,
m.inv. tiresome person; bore.
rompitèsta, *m.* puzzle; riddle.
rompitóre, *a. & m.* (*f.* -tríce),
breaker; breaking. **rompitútto,**
m. destructive person.
rónca & róncola, *f.* pruning-hook.
ronchétto, *m.* pruning knife.
ronchióne, *m.* big rock; crag.
roncíglio, *m.* hook.
rónda, *f.* round, rounds; patrol;
watch.
róndine, *f.* swallow. **rondinèlla,** *f.*
house-martin.
rondò, *m.* rondeau; (*Mus.*) rondo.
rondóne, *m.* swift (*bird*).
ronzàre, *v.i.* (*aux.* avere) to buzz; hum.
ronzíno, *m.* nag; jade; worn-out horse.
ronzío (*pl.* -íi), *m.* continuous hum;
low murmur.
ronzóne, *m.* blue-bottle (*fly*); (*fig.*)
admirer, hanger-on.
ròrido, *a.* dewy.
ròsa, *f.* rose; rose-window; rose
diamond. ~ *dei venti,* compass-card.
~ *muschiosa,* ~ *muscosa,* moss-rose.
~ *muschiata,* musk-r. ~ *tea,* tea
rose. ~*canina,* bush rose, dog r.
rosàceo, *a.* rosaceous. **rosàio,** *m.*
rose-bush; rose-tree. **rosàrio,** *m.*
rosary (*beads*). **rosàto,** *a.* rosy;
rose-scented; made from roses.
ròseo, *a.* rosy; rose-coloured.
rosbíf, rosbíffe, *m.* roast beef.
roséto, *m.* rose-garden, rosary.
rosétta, *f.* rosette.
rosicànte, *a. & m.* rodent. **rosicàre**
(*pr.* rósico, rósichi), *v.t.* to nibble;
(*fig.*) gain a little.
rosicchiàre, *v.t.* to nibble lightly.
rosícchio, *m.* dry crust (of bread).
rosign[u]òlo, *m.* nightingale.
róso, *p.p.* of *rodere.*
rosolàccio, *m.* poppy.
rosolàre, *v.t.* (*cook*) to brown.
rosolía, *f.* German measles.
rosòlio, *m.* rosolio.
rosóne, *m.* (*Arch.*) rose-window;
(*Typ. & Arch.*) rose ornament.
ròspo, *m.* toad; (*fig.*) unsociable
person.
rossàstro & rosseggiànte, *a.*

reddish. **rosseggiàre**, *v.i.* (*aux.* avere) to redden, grow red. **rossétto**, *a.* reddish. ¶ *m.* rouge. **rossézza**, *f.* redness. **rossíccio** & **rossígno**, *a.* reddish. **rósso**, *a.* red. ¶ *m.* red (*colour*). *pl. i rossi*, followers of an extreme party of the Left. **Mar**(e) ~, Red Sea. *la Croce R* ~*a*, the Red Cross. *camicie* ~ *e*, *f.pl.* red-shirts, Garibaldians. **rossóre**, *m.* redness; flush; blush; (*fig.*) shame.

rosticceria, *f.* cook shop.

rostràto, *a.* beaked. **róstro**, *m.* rostrum; platform; beak of a hawk.

ròta, *f.* see *ruota*. **rotàbile**, *a.* suitable for wheeled traffic. *strada* ~, carriage road. **rotàia**, *f.* rail; wheel-track. **rotàre** (*pr.* **ruòto**, **ruòti**), *v.i.* to rotate; revolve; wheel. **rotativa**, *f.* (*Typ.*) rotary machine. **rotatòrio**, *a.* rotatory; rotary. **rotazióne**, *f.* rotation.

roteaménto, *m.* rotating; wheeling; rolling. **roteàre**, *v.i.* (*aux.* avere) to rotate; wheel; roll.

rotèlla, *f.* small wheel; castor; roller. *pattino a* ~*e*, *m.* roller-skate. **rotína**, *f.* & **rotíno**, *m.* small wheel.

rotocalcografía, *f.* offset process (*printing*).

rotolaménto, *m.* rolling. **rotolàre**, *v.t.* to roll; r. up. **rotolàrsi**, *v.refl.* to roll; wallow. **ròtolo**, *m.* roll; bundle. **rotolóne**, *m.* tumble, fall. **rotolóni** (a), **ròtoli** (a), *ad.expr.* (*fig.*) to grief, to rack & ruin.

rotónda, *f.* round building (*church*, &c.); rotunda. **rotondàre**, *v.t.* to make round; reduce to round figures, &c. **rotondità, rotondézza**, *f.* rotundity; roundness. **rotóndo**, *a.* round; rotund; plump.

rótta, *f.* course; route; rout; disorderly retreat. **rottàme**, *m.* fragment; (*t.l.*) **rottámi**, broken rubbish; scraps; bits; lumber; wreckage. **rottaménte** *ad.* jerkily. **rótto**, *p.p.* of *rompere*. ¶ *a.* broken. ¶ *m.* break, fracture; (*pl.*) small change. **rottúra**, *f.* break, rupture; breaking off; breach; breakage.

ròtula, *f.* knee-cap.

rovàio, *m.* north wind.

rovènte, *a.* red-hot; scorching.

róvere, *m.* oak. **roveréto**, *m.* oak plantation; grove of oaks.

rovèscia, *f.* lap(p)el; facing of a sleeve. **rovesciaménto**, *m.* upsetting; overturning; capsizing. **rovesciàre**, *v.t.* to upset; overturn;

overthrow; pour; throw. **rovesciàrsi**, *v.refl.* to overturn; be upset; capsize; (*Cycl.*) have a spill. **rovèsci**~, *a.* reversed; turned upside down. *a* ~, *alla* ~*a*, inside out, upside down; badly. ¶ *m.* reverse (*coin*, *medal*); wrong side; opposite; set-back; reverse; disaster; violent shower; (*tennis*) backhand stroke. **rovescióne**, *m.* blow; slap; box on the ear. *a* ~ & ~*i*, *ad.* on one's back; backward[s].

rovéto, *m.* bramble bush; briar patch.

rovína, *f.* ruin; crashing fall; violence; fury (*of nature*). *a* ~, abundantly; in torrents. **rovinànte**, *a.* crumbling; falling in ruin. **rovinàre**, *v.t.* to ruin; throw down; *v.i.* (*aux.* essere) to crash; fall with a crash; collapse; go to ruin; crumble. **rovinatíccio**, *a.* shaky. **rovinàto**, *a.* ruined; wasted; spoilt. **rovinatóre**, *m.* destroyer; ravager. **rovinío** (*pl.* -*ii*), *m.* succession of crashes. **rovinóso**, *a.* ruinous; violent; impetuous.

rovistàre, *v.t.* & *i.* to ransack; rummage; search minutely. **rovistatóre**, *m.* (*f.* -**trice**) rummager; searcher.

róvo, *m.* briar; bramble.

różża, *f.* jade; broken-down horse. **rożżaménte**, *ad.* roughly; rudely; clumsily. **rożżézza**, *a.* roughness; rawness. **różżo**, *a.* rough; raw; unpolished; uncouth.

rúba, *f.* plunder; robbery. *andare a* ~, to sell rapidly; meet with a ready sale. *mettere a* ~, to pillage.

rubacchiàre, *v.t.* & *i.* to pilfer.

rubacuòri, *m.* & *f.inv.* lady-killer; attractive woman.

rubaménto, *m.* robbery; theft; burglary.

rubapàgo & **rubapàglie**, *m.inv.* one not worth his wages; idle servant. **rubàre**, *v.t.* to steal. **rubatóre**, *m.* (*f.* -**trice**) thief; robber. **rubería**, *f.* theft; robbery.

rubicànte, *a.* reddish.

rubicóndo, *a.* ruddy; rubicund; rosy.

Rubicóne, *m.* Rubicon.

rubídio, *m.* rubidium (*metal*).

rubinétto, *m.* tap; cock. **rubíno**, *m.* ruby.

rubíżżo, *a.* healthy; hale; ruddy-complexioned.

rúblo, *m.* rouble.

rubríca (*pl.* **rubríche**), *f.* rubric; heading; column (*newspaper*); set of regulations; address-book. **rubri-càre**, *v.t.* to enter; write in the address book.

rúde, *a.* rude; rough; coarse; harsh.

rúderi, *m.pl.* ruins; remains.

rudimentàle, *a.* rudimentary. **rudiménto**, *m.* rudiment (*gen. pl.*).

rúffa, *f.* scramble. *fare la* ~, to throw coppers to the crowd. *fare a* ~ *raffa*, to catch what one can.

ruffiàno, *m.* pander, pimp.

rúga (*pl.* **rúghe**), *f.* wrinkle.

rúggine, *f.* rust; blight; mildew; (*fig.*) ill-feeling; bad blood. **rugginóso**, *a.* rusty; rust-coloured.

ruggíre (*pr.* **-ísco**, **-ísci** *&* **rúggi**, **rúgge**), *v.i.* (*aux.* avere) to roar. **ruggíto**, *m.* roar; roaring.

rugiàda, *f.* dew (*lit. & fig.*). **rugiadóso**, *a.* dewy.

rugliàre, *v.i.* (*aux.* avere) to rumble; roar; growl.

rugosità, *f.* roughness; ruggedness; unevenness. **rugóso**, *a.* wrinkled.

ruína, *&c.*, see *rovina*.

rulétta, *f.* roulette (*game*).

rullàggio, *m.* (*Aviat.*) taxi-ing. **rulla-ménto**, *n.* roll; rolling. **rullàre**, *v.i.* to roll (*ship or drum*); (*Aviat.*) to taxi; *v.t.* to roll (*street, &c.*). **rullío**, *m.* roll, rolling. **rúllo**, *m.* roll (*drum, &c.*); (*Mech.*) drum; roller; cylinder. *scrittoio a* ~, *m.* roll-top desk.

rum, *m.* rum.

Rumanía (la), *f.* R[o]umania. **rumèno**, *a. & m.* R[o]umanian.

ruminànte, *a. & m.* ruminant. **ruminàre**, *v.t. & i.* to ruminate; chew the cud; (*fig.*) ponder; ruminate. **ruminazióne**, *f.* rumination; chewing the cud.

rumóre, *m.* noise; uproar; din; hum; rumour. **rumoreggiaménto**, *m.* rumbling noise. **rumoreggiànte**, *a.* noisy; restless; rumbling; muttering. **rumoreggiàre**, *v.i.* (*aux.* avere) to make a noise; rumble; talk loudly. **rumorío** (*pl.* **-íi**), *m.* continual noise. **rumoróso**, *a.* noisy; loud; much talked of.

rúna, *f.* rune; runic inscription. **rúnico** (*pl.* **rúnici**), *a.* runic.

ruòlo, *m.* roll; list. *di* ~, on the regular staff.

r[u]òta, *f.* wheel. ~*dentata*, cogwheel. ~ *d'ingranaggio*, gear wheel. ~ *di ricambio*, spare w. *far la* ~, to spread its tail (*peacock*).

rúpe, *f.* rock; cliff. **rupèstre**, *a.* rocky; rock (*att.*).

rupía, *f.* rupee.

ruràle, *a.* rural. ¶ *m.* countryman. *i* ~*i*, country people.

ruscèllo, *m.* brook; streamlet. dim. *ruscellétto*.

russaménto, *m.* snoring. **russàre**, *v.i.* (*aux.* avere) to snore.

Rússia (la), *f.* Russia. **rússo**, *a. & m.* Russian. **russòfilo**, *a. & m.* Russophil. **russòfobo**, *a. & m.* Russophobe.

rusticàggine, **rustichézza**, *&* **rusticità**, *f.* rusticity. **rústico** (*pl.* **rústici**), *a.* rustic.

rúta, *f.* rue (*Bot.*).

rutèno, *a. & m.* Ruthenian.

rutilànte, *a.* (*Poet.*) shining; sparkling.

ruttàre, *v.i.* (*aux.* avere) to belch. **rútto**, *m.* belching.

ruvidétto, *a.* rather rough. **ruvidézza** *&* **ruvidità**, *f.* roughness. **rúvido**, *a.* rough; rude; unpolished; boorish.

ruzzàre, *v.i.* (*aux.* avere) to romp; play; prance.

ruzzolàre, *v.i.* (*aux.* essere *&* avere) to roll; r. down; tumble. **ruzzolío**, *m.* continued rolling. **ruzzolóne**, *m.* tumble; heavy fall. **ruzzolóni**, *ad.* headlong.

S

S, s, (*esse*) *f.* the letter S.

Sàba, *f.* Sheba (*O.T.*).

sàbato, *m.* Saturday; sabbath (*Jewish*).

sabàudo, *a.* of Savoy; of the house of Savoy.

sàbbia, *f.* sand. **sabbiàia**, *f.* sand-pit. **sabbiàre**, *v.t.* to sand. **sabbióne**, *m.* gravel; sandy soil. **sabbióso**, *a.* sandy.

sabotàggio, *m.* sabotage, foul play. **sabotàre**, *v.t.* to sabotage, damage, wilfully wreck; thwart; botch.

sàcca (*pl.* **sàcche**), *f.* bag; satchel; wallet; (*Mil.*) pocket. ~ *da viaggio*, travelling-bag, kit-bag. dim. *sacchetta*. **saccapàne**, *m.* haversack.

saccarína, *f.* saccharin[e].

saccàta, *f.* sackful; bagful.

saccènte, *m.* sciolist; wiseacre; pedant; *f.* bluestocking. **saccentería**, *f.* sciolism, smattering (of learning). **saccentóne**, *m.* wiseacre, pedant.

saccheggiaménto, *m.* sacking; pillaging; pillage; plundering; plunder. **saccheggiàre**, *v.t.* to sack; pillage;

plunder. **saccheggiatóre,** m.
plunderer; pillager. **sàcco** (pl.
sàcchi), m. sack; bag; pouch; sackcloth (Theol.); sac; sack[ing] (of a
city); pillage. ~ postale, mail bag;
~ a terra, sand-bag. ~ a pelo,
sleeping bag. ~ da montagna,
rucksack. **saccòccia** (pl. saccòcce),
f. pocket. **saccóne,** m. palliasse,
straw mattress.
sacèllo, m. (Poet.) chapel.
sacerdotàle, a. priestly, sacerdotal.
sacerdòte, m. priest. **sacerdo-**
téssa, f. priestess. **sacerdòzio,** m.
priesthood; ministry.
sacramentàle, a. sacramental;
solemn; binding. **sacramentàre,**
v.t. to administer the sacrament to
(the dying); v.i. to take an oath.
sacramentarsi, v.refl. to communicate (Relig.). **sacramento,** m.
sacrament; oath.
sacràre, v.t. to consecrate; dedicate.
sacràrio, m. shrine; sanctuary.
sacrestía, see sagrestia.
sacrificàre (pr. -ífico, -ífichi), v.t. &
abs. to sacrifice. **sacrifício,** m.
sacrifice; offering.
sacrilègio, m. sacrilege. **sacrílego**
(pl. -íleghi), a. sacrilegious.
sacripànte, m. blusterer; bully;
rascal.
sàcro, a. sacred; holy. **sacrosànto,**
a. sacrosanct; sacred; indisputable.
saétta, f. arrow; dart; thunderbolt;
flash (lightning); hand (watch);
sculptor's tool; (fam.) restless child;
imp. **saettàre,** v.t. to shoot; dart.
saettaménto, m. archery. **saetta-**
tóre, m. (f. -tríce) archer. ¶ a.
shooting, darting.
sàffico (pl. sàffici), a. Sapphic.
Sàffo, f. Sappho.
sagàce, a. sagacious; shrewd. **sagàcia,**
& sagacità, f. sagacity; shrewdness.
saggézza, f. wisdom; prudence.
saggiaménte, ad. wisely; prudently;
judiciously.
saggiàre, v.t. to try; test; assay; taste;
sample. **saggiatóre,** m. assayer;
tester. **saggiatúra,** f. testing;
assaying; sampling.
sàggio, a. wise; sage; sapient;
judicious, prudent; sensible; well-
behaved; good (child). ¶ m. essay;
trial; test; sample; specimen; rate
(interest). **saggísta** (pl. -ísti), m.
essayist.
sagittàrio, m. archer. S~, (Astr.)
Sagittarius.
sàgoma, f. mould; moulding; shape;

architectural section. **sagomàre,**
v.t. to mould, shape. fogli sagomati
per imballo uova, moulded paper for
packing eggs.
sàgra, f. consecration (church);
celebration; (annual) festival.
sagràre, v.i. to swear; curse.
sagràto, m. consecrated ground;
churchyard; church square; oath.
sagrestàno, m. sacristan; sexton.
sagrestía, f. sacristy; vestry.
sagri[no], m. shagreen.
sagú, m. sago.
saia, f. serge; twill. **sàio** (pl. sai), m.
monastic gown.
sàla, f. hall; lounge; room; ward
(hospital); house (theatre, &c.);
auditorium; office. ~ da pranzo,
dining-room. ~ da tè, tea room.
~ d'aspetto, waiting-room (Rly.).
~ caldaie, boiler room. ~da ballo,
ball-room, dancing hall. ~
macchine, engine room. ~ dei
modelli, pattern-shop.
salacca (pl. salàcche), f. pilchard.
salàce, a. lascivious; pungent; spicy.
salacità, f. lasciviousness; pungency; spiciness.
salagióne, salatúra, f. salting; curing.
salamàndra, f. salamander.
salàme, m. (spiced) sausage; (fig.)
lout; blockhead.
salamelècco & **salamelècche,** m.
salaam; low bow.
salamòia, f. brine; pickle. **salàre,**
v.t. to salt.
salariàre, v.t. to hire; pay (wages or
salary) to. **salàrio,** m. wages; pay;
salary.
salassàre, v.t. to bleed; let blood
from; (fig.) extort money from.
salàsso, m. blood-letting; (fig.)
extortion.
salàto, p.a. salted. ¶ a. salt; briny;
(fig.) pungent. bue ~, m. corned
manzo ~ a, f. corned beef. pagar ~,
to pay dear; pay through the nose.
salato, m. salted meat; salt pork.
salatúra, f. salting.
sàlce, salcéto, sàlcio, see salice,
saliceto.
salcígno, a. knotty; tough; stodgy;
stubborn; cross-grained.
salcràutte, m. sauerkraut.
sàlda, f. starch-water. **saldaménte,**
ad. firmly; solidly; steadily. **saldàre,**
v.t. to solder; weld; (fig.) strengthen;
settle (account). ~ a ottone, to braze.
saldàrsi, v.refl. to heal [up]
(wound). **saldató'e,** m. soldering-
iron. **saldatóre,** m. solderer;

welder. **saldatúra,** *f.* soldering;
welding; solder (*material*); healing
up. ~ *a ottone*, brazing. ~ *ossidrica*,
oxy-hydrogen welding.
saldézza, *f.* firmness; steadiness; (*fig.*)
constancy; resolution. **sàldo,** *a.*
firm; steady; steadfast; staunch;
stiff; strong. ¶ *m.* (*account*) balance;
settlement.
sàle, *m.* salt; (*fig.*) mother-wit;
judgement; good sense; piquancy;
pungency. ~ *inglese*, Epsom salts.
salgèmma, *m.* rock-salt.
sàlice, *m.* willow (tree). **salicéto,** *m.*
willow-bed; group of willows.
salicilàto, *m.* salicylate. **salicílico**
(**-ílici**), *a.* salicylic.
saliènte, *a.* salient; projecting; rising;
prominent; conspicuous. ¶ *m.*
(*Mil.*) salient.
salièra, *f.* salt-cellar. **salína,** *f.* salt-
pond; salt-works. **salíno,** *a.* saline,
salty.
salíre (*pr.* **sàlgo, sàli, sàle**), *v.i.* ir.
(*aux.* essere) & *v.t.* to rise; go up;
mount; increase; climb; ascend.
saliscéndi, *m.inv.* going up and down;
alternation; (*door*) latch. *i* ~ *della
fortuna*, the ups and downs of
fortune.
salíta, *f.* ascent; ascension; rise;
increase; slope.
salíva, *f.* saliva. **salivàle** & **saliva-
tòrio,** *a.* salivary.
sàlma, *f.* corpse; dead body; remains;
burden.
salmàstro, *a.* rather salt; brackish.
salmeggiaménto, *m.* psalm-singing.
salmeggiàre, *v.i.* (*aux.* avere) to
sing psalms.
salmería, *f.* baggage-train.
salmí, *m. inv.* stew, salmi.
salmísta (*pl.* **-ísti**), *m.* psalmist.
sàlmo, *m.* psalm. **salmodía,** *f.*
psalmody. **salmodiàre,** *v.i.* (*aux.*
avere) to sing psalms.
salmóne, *m.* salmon.
salnítro, *m.* saltpetre; nitre.
Salomóne, *m.* Solomon.
salóne, *m.* hall; large hall; saloon.
Salonícco, *f.* Salonika.
salottíno, *m.* sitting-room; parlour.
salòtto, *m.* drawing-room; parlour;
reception-room.
salpàre, *v.i.* (*aux.* avere) to weigh
anchor; sail; set out. *salpa!* (*Naut.*)
up anchor!
sàlsa, *f.* sauce.
salsamentàrio, *m.* pork-butcher;
dealer in salted provisions.
salsaparíglia, *f.* salsaparilla.

salsèdine, *f.* saltness; saltiness.
salsíccia, *f.* sausage; sausage-meat.
salsicciàio, *m.* sausage-maker.
salsièra, *f.* sauce-boat.
sàlso, *a.* salt; salty. **salsúme,** *m.*
saltness; salted meat.
saltabécca (*pl.* **-bécche**), *f.* grasshopper. **saltabeccàre,** *v.i.* (*aux.*
avere) to hop; skip.
saltaleóne, *m.* (*Mech.*) spring.
saltamartíno, *m.* jumping toy; jack-
in-the-box; (*pop.*) cricket; grasshopper; lively child.
saltàre, *v.t.* & *i.* to jump; jump over;
leap; leap over; clear; skip; spring,
vault. **saltatóio,** *m.* perch (*bird*).
saltatóre, *m.* (*f.* **-tríce**) jumper;
dancer; rope-dancer; hurdler.
saltellàre, *v.i.* (*aux.* avere) to skip;
hop. **salterellàre,** *v.i.* to skip
about; hop about. **salterèllo,** *m.*
little jump; hop; cracker (*firework*).
saltèrio, *m.* psalm-book; psalter
saltimbànco (*pl.* **-ànchi**), *m.* mountebank; tumbler; acrobat.
sàlto, *m.* jump; leap; vault; spring;
hop.
saltuariaménte, *ad.* desultorily; at
intervals; by fits and starts. **saltu-
àrio,** *a.* desultory; intermittent,
irregular.
salubèrrimo, *a.* (*superl.* of *salúbre*)
very healthy, wholesome, or
salubrious. **salúbre,** *a.* salubrious;
healthy; wholesome. **salubrità,** *f.*
salubrity; healthiness; wholesome-
ness.
salumàio, *m.* salt-provision dealer;
pork butcher. **salúme,** *m.* salt
meat; salt provisions. **salumería,** *f.*
pork-butcher's shop; salt-provision
shop.
salutàre, *v.t.* to salute; greet; bow to;
welcome; send regards to; say
good-bye to. ¶ *a.* salutary; beneficial;
healthful; wholesome. **salutazióne,**
f. salutation; greeting.
salúte, *f.* health; safety; well-being;
welfare; salvation. *casa di* ~, *f.*
nursing-home. *Esercito della S* ~,
m. Salvation Army. **salutísta** (*pl.*
-ísti), *m.* Salvationist (member of
Salvation Army).
salúto, *m.* salute; salutation; greeting;
bow.
sàlva, *f.* salvo; salute (*guns*); volley;
round (*of applause*). **salvacondótto**
(*pl.* **-ótti**), *m.* safe-conduct. **salva-
danàio** *or* **salvadanàro,** *m.* money-
box. **salvagènte,** *m.* life-belt; life-

buoy; (traffic) island, street refuge. ~ *a sacco*, breeches-buoy. **salvaguardàre**, *v.t.* to safeguard; protect. **salvaguàrdia**, *f.* safeguard. **salvaménto**, *m.* safety; rescue; deliverance; saving. **salvàre**, *v.t.* to save; rescue; deliver; preserve; reserve. **salvàrsi**, *v.refl.* to save oneself, to take refuge. **salvàndo**, *ger.* of *salvare*, as *pr.* saving; barring; but for. **salvatàggio**, *m.* rescue; salvage. *apparecchio di* ~, life-saving apparatus. *battello, barca di* ~, life-boat. *cintura di* ~, life-belt. *gli esercizi di* ~, boat drill (*Naut.*). **salvàtico**, *&c.*, see *selvatico*. **salvatóre**, *m.* (*f.* **-tríce**) saviour; rescuer; deliverer. *S* ~, Redeemer. ¶ *a.* saving; redeeming. **salvazióne**, *f.* salvation. **sàlve!** *i.* hail! *Salve Regina*, *f.* prayer to the Virgin. **salvézza**, *f.* safety; salvation. **sàlvia**, *f.* sage (*Bot.*). **salviétta**, *f.* napkin. **sàlvo**, *a.* safe; secure. ¶ *m.* safety; safe place; condition; reservation. ¶ *pr.* except; excepting; save; barring. **sambúco** (*pl.* **-úchi**), *m.* elder (tree). **Sàmo**, *f.* Samos (*Geog.*). **San**, *abb.* of **Santo**, Saint. **sanàbile**, *a.* curable; that can be healed. **sanàre**, *v.t.* to cure; heal; (*fig.*) to rectify; (*of place*) to make healthy. **sanatívo**, *a.* healing; sanative; curative. **sanatóre**, *m.* (*f.* **-trice**) healer. ¶ *a.* healing. **sanatòria**, *f.* act of indemnity; decree of legitimization. **sanatòrio**, *m.* sanatorium. **sancíre** (*pr.* **-ísco**, **-ísci**), *v.t.* to decree; confirm; ratify; sanction. **sàndalo**, *m.* sandal; sandalwood; punt; lighter. **sanése**, *a.* Sienese. **sàngue**, *m.* blood; gore; family; stock; race; lineage; origin; extraction; kinship. *analisi del* ~, *f.* blood test. ~ *di drago*, dragon's blood. ~ *freddo*, coolness; composure; self-possession. **sanguígna**, *f.* blood-stone; red crayon; drawing in red chalk. **sanguígno**, *a.* sanguine; full-blooded; blood (*att.*); containing blood. *vasi* ~ *i*, *m.pl.* blood-vessels. *diaspro* ~, *m.* (*Min.*) blood-stone. **sanguinàre**, *v.i.* to bleed. **sanguinàrio**, *a.* sanguinary; blood-thirsty. **sànguina**, *m.* or **sanguinèlla**, *f.* dog-wood. **sangu-**

íneo, *a.* blood-stained. **sanguinolènte** *&* **sanguinolènto**, *a.* dripping blood; bloodstained; mixed with blood. **sanguinóso**, *a.* bloody; sanguinary; ferocious. **sanguisúga**, *f.* leech; (*fig.*) blood-sucker; extortioner. **sanità**, *f.* soundness (*of body and mind*); health; sanity. **sanitàrio**, *a.* sanitary; concerning public health. *corpo* ~, (army) medical corps. *ufficiale* ~, health officer. **sàno**, *a.* sound; healthy; wholesome; sane. **sànscrito**, *m.* Sanskrit. **Sansóne**, *m.* Samson. **santabàrbara**, *f.* powder-magazine (*Nav.*). **santèlmo**, *m.* Saint Elmo's fire. **santarèllo**, *m.*, ~*a*, *f.* young devotee; sanctimonious young person. **santificàre**, *v.t.* to sanctify; consecrate; canonize; observe (*Holy days*). **santificazione**, *f.* sanctification; observance (*of Holy days*). **santimònia**, *f.* sanctimoniousness. **santíno**, *m.* young saint; small image of a Saint. **Santíppe**, *f.* Xantippe (*wife of Socrates*); (*fig.*) scold. **santíssimo**, *a.* most sacred; most holy. ¶ *m. il S* ~, the Blessed Sacrament. **santità**, *f.* holiness; saintliness; sanctity. *Sua S* ~, His Holiness (*the Pope*). **sànto**, *a.* holy; sainted; saintly; godly; consecrated; hallowed. ¶ *m.* saint; patron s. **santocchiería**, *f.* bigotry; sanctimoniousness. **santòcchio**, *m.*, **santòcchia**, *f.* devotee; bigot; hypocrite. **sàntolo**, *m.* godfather. **sàntola**, *f.* godmother. **santóne**, *m.* hermit; great saint. **santuàrio**, *m.* sanctuary; shrine. **sanzionàre**, *v.t.* to sanction; ratify; approve; authorize. **sanzióne**, *f.* sanction; approval; authorization; penalty. **sapére** (*pr.* **so**, **sai**, **sa**), *v.t.* *& i.ir.* to know; be aware of; be acquainted with; learn; know of; understand; know how to; be able to; can; taste (of); smell (of). ~ *grado a*, to be grateful to. ~ *di lettere*, to have some education. ~ *male*, to displease. *mi sa male che*, I am sorry, I regret (that). ~ *mill'anni*, to desire ardently. ¶ *m.* knowledge; learning; scholarship. **sàpido**, *a.* (*Lit.*) well-flavoured. **sapiènte**, *a.* wise; learned; well-informed. ¶ *m. & f.* learned man,

l. woman; scholar; well-informed person. **sapientóne,** *m.* great scholar; (*iron.*) wiseacre. **sapiènza,** *f.* wisdom; knowledge; learning.

saponàceo, *a.* soapy; saponaceous. **saponàio,** *m.* soap-maker. **saponàta,** *f.* lather; soap-suds; soaping. **sapóne,** *m.* soap. *bolla di* ~, soap-bubble (*lit. & fig.*). ~ *per barba* (*in bastoncino*), shaving-stick. **saponétta,** *f.* cake of soap; soap ball; toilet soap; hunter (*watch*). **saponièra,** *f.* soap-dish. **saponifício,** *m.* soap-works. **saponóso,** *a.* soapy.

sapóre, *m.* flavour; taste; relish; savour. **saporíno,** *m.* delicate flavour. **saporíre** (*pr.* -ísco, -ísci), *v.t.* to impart flavour; to relish. **saporitaménte,** *ad.* deliciously; with relish; with zest. *dormire* ~, to sleep soundly. **saporíto,** *a.* savoury; tasty; delicious; witty; lively; piquant; expensive. **saporóso,** *a.* tasty; well-flavoured.

sapúta, *f.* knowledge (*of a fact*). *per* ~, by hearsay. **saputaménte,** *ad.* knowingly; consciously; with a pretence of knowledge. **saputèllo,** *m.* wiseacre; pretended scholar; sciolist. **sapúto,** *a.* learned.

saracinésca, *f.* portcullis; sluice-[gate]; door-catch; rolling shutter. **saracíno,** *m.* quintain, wooden figure for tilting at; (*fig.*) butt, object of ridicule.

Saragózza, *f.* Saragossa.

sarcàsmo, *m.* sarcasm. **sarcàstico** (*pl.* -àstici), *a.* sarcastic.

sarchiaménto, *m. &* **sarchiatúra,** *f.* weeding. **sarchiàre,** *v.t.* to weed. **sarchiatóre,** *m.* (*f.* -tríce) weeder (*pers.*); also -trice, *f.* weeder (*Mech.*). **sàrchio,** *m.* hoe; weeding hook.

sarcòfago (*pl.* -òfaghi), *m.* sarcophagus.

Sardégna (la), *f.* Sardinia. **sardèlla,** *f.* pilchard. **sardína,** *f.* sardine. **sardo,** *a. & m.* Sardinian. **sardònico** (*pl.* -ònici), sardonic.

sargàsso, *m.* sargasso; gulf-weed. *Mare dei Sargassi,* *m.* Sargasso Sea. **sàrgia,** *f.* coverlet; flowered stuff for curtains.

sarménto, *m.* vine-shoot; vine-branch. **sàrta,** *f.* dressmaker; tailoress. **sàrtia** (*pl.* **sàrtie**), *f.* (*Naut.*) shroud. **sartiàme,** *m.* rigging; cordage. **sàrto,** *m.* tailor. **sartoría,** *f.* tai'or's shop; tailoring; dressmaking.

sassàia, *f.* dam; barrier of stones; stony ground; heap of stones. **sassai[u]òla,** *f.* volley of stones; fight with stones. **sassai[u]òlo,** *m.* wood-pigeon, rock-dove. **sassàta,** *f.* blow from a stone. **sassétto,** *m.* pebble; small stone. **sassífraga,** *f.* saxifrage (*Bot.*). **sàsso,** *m.* stone; pebble; rock; tombstone. *Gran S* ~ *d'Italia,* Monte Corno, the highest peak of the Apennines, 9,560 ft. **sassòfono,** *m.* saxophone. **sassóne,** *m.* large stone. ¶ *a. & m.* Saxon. **Sassònia (la),** *f.* Saxony. **sassóso,** *a.* stony.

Sàtana, *m.* Satan. **satànico** (*pl.* -ànici), *a.* Satanic; diabolical.

satèllite, *m.* satellite.

sàtira, *f.* satire. **satireggiàre,** *v.t.* to satirize. **satirésco** (*pl.* -éschi), *a.* satyr-like. **satírico** (*pl.* -írico), *a.* satiric(al). ¶ *m.* satirist. **sàtiro,** *m.* satyr.

satólla, *f.* fill; full meal; bellyful (*fig.*). **satollàre,** *v.t.* to sate; satiate; fill (up). **satóllo,** *a.* satiated; sated; overfed.

saturàre, *v.t.* to saturate; glut. **saturazióne,** *f.* saturation. **saturnàli,** *m.pl.* saturnalia. **saturníno,** *a.* saturnine, sombre; (*Chem.*) saturnine. **satúrnio,** *a.* Saturnian. **saturnísmo,** *m.* lead-poisoning. **Satúrno,** *m.* Saturn.

sàturo, *a.* saturated.

sàuro, *a.* sorrel; chestnut (*horse*); saurian. ¶ *m.* chestnut horse.

sàvio, *a.* wise; sage; judicious; good (*child*). ¶ *m.* sage.

Savòia (la), *f.* Savoy. **savoiàrdo,** *a. & m.* Savoyard.

saziàre, *v.t.* to satisfy fully; satiate. **saziàrsi,** *v.refl.* to be satiated; to be tired of (*di*). **sazietà,** *f.* satiety. **saziévole,** *a.* cloying; stodgy; (*fig.*) tiresome. **sàzio,** *a.* sated; satiated; full (up); wearied; tired; sick.

śbaccellàre, *v.t.* to shell (*peas*). **śbacchettàre,** *v.t.* to beat (*rugs, &c.*); flap; dust.

śbacchiàre, *v.t. & i.* to bang. **śbacchío,** *m.* constant banging.

śbadatàggine, *f.* carelessness; heedlessness; inattention. **śbadataménte,** *ad.* carelessly; heedlessly, inattentively. **śbadàto,** *a.* careless; heedless; inattentive.

śbadigliaménto, *m.* yawning. **śbadigliàre,** *v.t.* (*aux.* avere) to yawn. **śbadíglio,** *m.* yawn; yawning.

śbafère, *v.t.* to scrounge. **śbafatóre,**

m. scrounger. **sbàfo,** *m.* scrounging.

sbagliàre, *v.i.* *(aux.* avere) *&* **sbagliàrsi,** *v.refl.* to blunder; be mistaken; be wrong; make a mistake; err. **sbagliàre,** *v.t.* to miss; miscalculate. **sbagliàto,** *a.* wrong; mistaken; erroneous; incorrect. **sbàglio,** *m.* mistake; error; blunder; fault.

sbalestraménto, *m.* missing the mark; erratic movement. **sbalestràre,** *v.i.* *(aux.* avere) to miss the mark; go wrong; wander *(fig.).* *v.t.* to drive; thrust; remove; send from pillar to post. **sbalestràto,** *a.* unbalanced; rash; wild.

sballàre, *v.t.* to unpack. *sballarle grosse,* to talk big; tell tall stories. **sballatúra,** *f.* unpacking. **sballàto,** *a.* *(fig.)* unsettled. **sballonàta,** *f.* tall story. **sballóne,** *m.* teller of tall stories; romancer; boaster.

sballottàre, *v.t.* to toss; toss about; push about.

sbalordiménto, *m.* amazement; bewilderment. **sbalordíre** *(pl.* -ísco, -ísci), *v.t.* to bewilder; stun; strike dumb with astonishment; amaze; dumbfound. **sbalorditàggine,** *f.* bewilderment; awkwardness; confusion. **sbalorditívo,** *a.* amazing; astonishing; bewildering; incredible. **sbalordíto,** *a.* amazed; dumbfounded; astounded.

sbalzaménto, *m.* hurling down; casting out; overthrow; dismissal; removal. **sbalzàre,** *v.t.* to overthrow; cast out; fling (down); remove; dismiss; *(v.i.)* spring; dart; leap.

sbalzellàre, *v.t.* to jerk; jolt; *v.i.* *(aux.* avere) bounce; jolt. **sbalzellío,** *m.* jolting; bouncing. **sbalzellóne,** *m.* jolt; jerk. *a ~i,* with sudden jerks.

sbàlzo, *m.* bound; spring; leap; rush; dash; start; sudden change.

sbancàre *(pr.* -ànco, -ànchi), *v.t.* to break the bank *(cards).*

sbandaménto, *m.* disbanding; dispersal; *(ship)* listing; list; heeling (over). **sbandàre,** *v.t.* to disband; disperse; break up; *(Naut.)* cause to heel over; throw on her beam-ends *(ship).* *v.i.* *(aux.* avere) *&* **sbandàrsi,** *v.refl.* *(Naut.)* to heel; list; *(motor)* skid.

sbandieraménto, *m.* display (or waving) of flags. **sbandieràre,** *v.i.* to display flags; wave flags.

sbandiménto, *m.* banishment.

sbandíre *(pr.* -ísco, -ísci), *v.t.* to banish.

sbaragliaménto, *m.* routing; dispersing; rout; dispersal. **sbaragliàre,** *v.t.* to throw into confusion; rout; disperse. **sbaraglíno,** *m.* backgammon. **sbaràglio,** *m.* rout; confusion; turmoil; risk; danger; jeopardy.

sbarazzàre, *v.t.* to clear; free from obstruction(s). **sbarazzàrsi** *(di),* *v.refl.* to get rid of. **sbarazzinàta,** *f.* prank; dirty trick. **sbarazzíno,** *m.* scamp; street urchin.

sbarbàre, *v.t.* to shave; uproot; get to the root of. **sbarbatèllo,** *m.* youngster; lad; beardless boy.

sbarbicàre, *v.t.* to uproot.

sbarcàre, *v.t.* to disembark; put ashore; land; unload; discharge; *(v.i.)* *(aux.* essere) to land. *~ il pilota,* to drop the pilot. **sbarcatóio,** *m.* quay; landing stage; wharf. **sbàrco** *(pl.* **sbàrchi),** *m.* disembarkation; landing; unloading. *ponticello di ~,* *m.* gangway *(shore to ship).*

sbàrra, *f.* bar, barrier; cross-bar *(Gym);* tiller (also *s~ del timone).* **sbarraménto,** *m.* barrage *(Mil.);* obstruction; barring; barricading. *tiro di ~,* barrage-fire. **sbarràre,** *v.t.* to bar; bar up; block up; unbar; open wide. **sbarràto,** *p.p.* of *sbarrare.* *¶ a.* *(eye)* wide open; *(Cheque)* crossed.

sbatacchiaménto, *m.* banging; slamming **sbatacchiàre,** *v.t.* *&* *i.* to knock; knock about; bang; slam. **sbatacchío,** *m.* constant banging.

sbàttere, *(pr.* **sbàtto,** *&c.*, like *battere),* *v.t.* to shake; toss, fling; flap; bang, slam *(door);* whip *(eggs);* stamp *(feet).* *v.i.* *(aux.* avere) *&* **sbàttersi,** *v.refl.* to bang; slam; toss; toss about. **sbattiménto,** *m.* beating; shaking, *&c.* **sbattúto,** *p.p.* of *sbattere.* *¶ a.* depressed; worn out; harassed.

sbavaménto, *m.* slobbering; slavering. **sbavàre,** *v.i.* *(aux.* avere) to slobber; slaver. **sbavatúra,** *f.* slobber; slaver; slime *(snail);* blur; *(Typ.)* indistinct impression; uncut edge *(paper).* **sbavóne,** *m.* slobberer.

sbèffa, *&c.,* see *beffa.*

sbellicàrsi (dalle risa), *v.refl.* to split one's sides with laughter.

sbendàre, *v.t.* to unbandage; unbind.

sberlèffo, *m.* grimace.

sberrettàrsi, *v.refl.* to take off one's cap.

sbevazzàre, *v.i.* to tipple; drink immoderately.

sbiadíre (*pr.* -ísco, -ísci), *v.i.* (*aux.* essere) to fade; turn pale; become pale.

sbiancàre (*pr.* -ànco, -ànchi), *v.t.* to whitewash; bleach. *v.i.* (*aux.* essere) & **sbiancàrsi**, *v.refl.* to turn white; fade; grow pale. **sbiancatúra**, *f.* whitewashing; bleaching.

sbiasciàre & **sbiascicàre**, *v.t.* & *i.* (*aux.* avere) to mumble.

sbiecaménte, *ad.* aslant; askew; obliquely; askance. **sbiecàre**, *v.t.* to distort; look askance at; straighten; (*v.i.*) (*aux.* avere & essere) to slant; lie obliquely. **sbièco** (*pl.* -èchi), *a.* oblique; awry. *di* ∼, askew; askance.

sbigottiménto, *m.* dismay; consternation; discouragement. **sbigottíre** (*pr.* -ísco, -ísci), *v.t.* to terrify; dismay; (*v.i.*) (*aux.* essere) & **sbigottirsi**, *v.refl.* to be dismayed, terrified. **sbigottíto**, *a.* downcast; dismayed.

sbilanciaménto, *m.* loss of balance; derangement; unsettling. **sbilanciàre**, *v.t.* to unbalance; unsettle; derange. **sbilanciàrsi**, *v.refl.* to lose one's balance; (*fig.*) spend beyond one's means. **sbilàncio**, *m.* want of balance; disproportion; excess; deficit.

sbilènco (*pl.* -ènchi), *a.* crooked; bandy-legged; bow-legged.

sbirciàre, *v.t.* & *i.* (*aux.* avere) to eye closely; cast sidelong glances at. **sbirciàta**, *f.* close inspection; sidelong glance.

sbirichinàre, *v.i.* (*aux.* avere) to play childish tricks.

sbirràglia, *f.* police; police-spies. **sbírro**, *m.* constable (*deprec.*).

sbiżżarrírsi (*pr.* -ísco, -ísci), *v.refl.* to indulge one's whims; have one's own way; amuse oneself. **sbiżżírsi** (*pr.* -ísco, -ísci), *v.refl.* to show one's temper.

sbloccàre, *v.t.* to raise the blockade of.

sboccaménto, *m.* outfall, outflow; mouth. **sboccàre**, *v.i.* (*aux.* essere) (*river*) to flow (into); fall (into); (*street*) open (into); debouch; emerge; overflow; (*v.t.*) to break the mouth (or rim) of; to pour a few drops from (or the oil from the top of a flask). **sboccàto**, *a.* foul; foul-mouthed.

sbocciàre, *v.i.* (*aux.* essere) (*of flowers*) to open; blow; blossom.

sbòccio, *m.* blossoming; bloom.

sbócco (*pl.* **sbócchi**), *m.* outlet; opening; river-mouth; market.

sbocconcellàre, *v.t.* to nibble; eat slowly; cut in small pieces; break the edge of (*plate*, &*c.*).

sbollíre (*pr.* -ísco, -ísci), *v.i.* (*aux.* essere & avere) to go off the boil; (*passion*) die down.

sbombàre, *v.t.* to boast of; disclose indiscreetly; tell tall stories. **sbombolóne**, *m.* boaster.

sbòrnia, *f.* intoxication, drunkenness; infatuation. **sborniàrsi**, *v.refl.* to become intoxicated; get drunk. **sbornióne**, *m.* drunkard.

sborsàre, *v.t.* to disburse; lay out; pay [out]. **sbórso**, *m.* disbursement; outlay.

sbottonàre, *v.t.* to unbutton. **sbottonàrsi**, *v.refl.* (*fig.*) to unbosom oneself.

sbozzàre, *v.t.* to sketch (out); outline; rough-hew. **sbozzíno**, *m.* jack-plane. **sbòzzo**, *m.* rough sketch.

sbozzolàre, *v.i.* to take the cocoons from the branches; emerge from the cocoon (*silk-worm*, *moth*).

sbracàre, *v.t.* to unbreech. **sbracàrsi**, *v.refl.* to take off one's breeches. ∼ *dalle risa*, to burst with laughter.

sbracciàrsi, *v.refl.* to tuck up one's sleeves; (*fig.*) busy oneself; strive; use every effort. **sbràccio**, *m.* elbow-room; swing of the arm.

sbraciàre, *v.t.* to poke; stir (*the fire*). *v.i.* (*aux.* avere) swagger, make a display. **sbraciatóio**, *m.* poker.

sbraitàre, *v.i.* to shout; bawl. **sbraitío**, *m.* uproar; constant shouting. **sbraitóne**, *m.* shouter; bawler.

sbranàre, *v.t.* to tear to pieces.

sbrancàre, *v.t.* to detach; separate; take from the flock. **sbrancàrsi**, *v.refl.* to scatter; stray from the flock. **sbrandellàre**, *v.t.* to tear into shreds (or strips).

sbrattàre, *v.t.* to clean; clear; put in order.

sbravazzàre, *v.i.* (*aux.* avere) to brag; bluster.

sbréndolo, *m.* shred; rag; tatter. **sbrendolóne**, *m.* ragamuffin; tatterdemalion.

sbriciolàre, *v.t.* & **sbriciolàrsi**, *v.refl.* to crumble.

sbrigaménto, *m.* dispatch; haste; expedition. **sbrigàre**, *v.t.* to dispatch; finish off. **śbrigàrsi,** *v.refl.* to make haste. ~ *di,* to get rid off. **śbrigatívo,** *a.* expeditious, quick.

śbrigliàre, *v.t.* to unbridle; (*fig.*) relieve; loosen. **śbrigliataménte,** *ad.* freely; in sprightly fashion; without restraint. **śbrigliatézza,** *f.* unruliness; sprightliness. **śprigliàto,** *a.* unbridled; unchecked; unruly; lively; spirited; brilliant.

śbrogliàre, *v.t.* to disentangle; extricate.

śbruffàre, *v.t.* to squirt (upon); besprinkle. **śbruffàta,** *f.* sprinkling. **śbrúffo,** *m.* sprinkle; (*fig.*) bribe; hush-money.

śbucàre, *v.i.* (*aux.* essere) to emerge, issue; come out (of). *v.t.* to draw out; dislodge; start (*fox, &c.*).

śbucciàre, *v.t.* to skin; peel; pare; shell; husk; (*fig.*) have a superficial knowledge of. **śbucciàrsi,** *v.refl.* to scrape one's skin; cast the skin; slough the skin. **śbucciatúra,** *f.* peeling; paring; shelling, *&c.*; scratch.

śbudellàre, *v.t.* to disembowel; (*fish*) gut; stab.

śbuffàre, *v.i.* (*aux.* avere) to puff; snort; pant; fume (*with rage*). **śbuffàta,** *f.* & **śbùffo,** *m.* puff; snort; gust of wind.

śbugiardàre, *v.t.* to give the lie to; convict of lying.

scàbbia, *f.* scab, scabies; itch; (*sheep*) rot. **scabbiósa,** *f.* scabious (*Bot.*). **scabbióso,** *a.* scabby; scabbed.

scàbro, *a.* rough, rugged. **scabrosità,** *f.* roughness; ruggedness; (*of style*) hardness; inequality; scabrousness. **scabróso,** *a.* rough; rugged; difficult; scabrous.

scàcchi, *m.pl.* chess. **scacchièra,** *f.* chess-board; draught-board. **scacchière,** *m.* chess-board; Exchequer. *il Cancelliere dello S~,* the Chancellor of the Exchequer. **scacchísta** (*pl.* -ísti), *m.* chess-player. **scacchístico** (*pl.* -ístici), *a.* of chess; chess (*att.*).

scàccia, *f.* beater.

scacciamósche, *m.inv.* fly-flap. **scacciapensièri,** *m.inv.* pastime; distraction; jew's-harp. **scacciàre,** *v.t.* to drive; drive away; drive out; expel; dispel.

scaccíno, *m.* verger; sexton.

scàcco (*pl.* scàcchi), *m.* square; check; (*pl.*) chess. ~! check! (*chess*). ~ *matto,* checkmate. *a* ~*i,*

chequered. *tenere in iscacco,* to keep (hold) at bay.

scadènte, *a.* falling; declining; poor (*in quality*); (*bill*) falling due. **scadènza,** *f.* (*of bills*) maturity. *a breve* ~, short-dated. **scadére,** *v.i.* ir. (*aux.* avere) to fall off; decline; sink; decrease; devolve; (*of bills*) fall due; expire. **scadiménto,** *m.* decline; decay. **scadúto,** *a.* due; fallen due; expired; decayed.

scafàndro, *m.* diver's dress; diving apparatus.

scaffàle, *m.* book-case; set of book-shelves; what-not; (*Typ.*) composing-frame. **scaffalatúra,** *f.* shelving.

scàfo, *m.* hull; (*Aero.*) body.

scagionàre, *v.t.* to acquit; exculpate; excuse; justify.

scàglia (*pl.* scàglie), *f.* scale (*fish*); flake; chip; fragment. **scagliàre,** *v.t.* to hurl; fling; throw. **scagliàrsi,** *v.refl.* to rush; hurl oneself (at).

scaglionàre, *v.t.* to echelon, form in echelon. **scaglióne,** *m.* echelon; large step; mountain terrace.

scaglióso, *a.* scaly.

scagnòzzo, *a.* poor, sorry. ¶ *m.* bungler; poor priest.

scàla, *f.* staircase; stairs; ladder; (*Mus., &c.*) scale; order; sequence; extent; proposition. ~ *mobile,* escalator.

scalabríno, *a.* sly (*lit.* Calabrian).

scalaménto, *m.* scaling; escalade.

scalaffiàre, *v.t.* & *i.* (*aux.* essere) to free; escape from a snare.

scalàre, *v.t.* to scale; scale down; reduce by degrees; graduate (*payments, colours*); arrange according to scale. ¶ *a.* graduated; proportional. **scalàta,** *f.* climbing; scaling; escalade.

scalcagnàto, *a.* down at heel; shabby. **scalcinàto,** *a.* (*fig.*) shabby; seedy (*lit.* unplastered).

scàlco (*pl.* scalchi), *m.* steward; carver.

scaldabàgno, *m.inv.* geyser. **scaldalètto,** *m.inv.* warming-pan. **scaldamàno** & **scaldamàni,** *m.inv.* hand-warmer; children's game of hand upon hand. **scaldaménto,** *m.* heating; warming. **scaldapiàtti,** *m.inv* plate-warmer. **scaldapièdi,** *m.inv.* footwarmer; portable warming-pan. **scaldàre,** *v.t.* to heat; warm. **scaldàrsi,** *v.refl.* to warm oneself; get warm; become excited. **scaldàta,** *f.* warming. **scaldavivànde,** *m.inv.* chafing-dish; dish-warmer. **scaldíno**, *m.* foot-warmer; portable warming-pan.

scalèa, *f.* flight of steps. **scalétta**, *f.* stairway; short ladder. **scalettàto**, *a.* arranged in steps.

scalfíre (*pr.* -ísco, -ísci), *v.t.* to graze; scratch. **scalfittúra**, *f.* scratch; graze.

scalinata, *f.* steps; flight of steps. **scalíno**, *m.* step (*stair*, *door*); (*fig.*) stage.

scalmàna, *f.* chill, cold. **scalmanàrsi**, *v.refl.* to catch a chill, take a chill; (*fig.*) worry (*oneself*); tire oneself out. **scalmanàto**, *a.* flustered; out of breath.

scalmièra, *f.* (*set of*) rowlocks; rowlock. **scàlmo**, *m.* stanchion; thole-pin.

scàlo, *m.* wharf; landing-place; landing; port of call; goods platform; goods yard (*Rly.*); slip; stocks (*ship-building*); ∼ *di alaggio*, slipway. ∼ *ferroviario*, marshalling-yard. *porto di* ∼, port of call. *volo senza* ∼, non-stop flight (*Aviat.*).

scalógno, *m.* shallot.

scalóna, *f.* long staircase. **scalóne**, *m.* grand staircase.

scalpellàre, *v.t.* to chisel; engrave. **scalpellatura**, *f.* chiselling. **scalpellíno**, *m.* stone-cutter; small chisel. **scalpèllo**, *m.* chisel; scalpel. ∼ *a freddo*, cold chisel.

scalpicciàre, *v.i.* to tramp; scrape with the feet. **scalpíccio**, *m.* constant tramping or scraping of feet.

scalpitàre, *v.i.* to paw the ground.

scalpóre, *m.* bustle; fuss; noise; noisy complaint[s].

scaltrézza, *f.* cunning; craftiness; sharpness; shrewdness; slyness; artfulness. **scaltríre** (*pr.* -ísco, -ísci), *v.t.* to sharpen (*wits*); make knowing; smarten. **scaltríto**, *a.* shrewd; cunning; experienced. **scàltro**, *a.* smart; sharp; shrewd; crafty; cunning; artful.

scalzàrsi, *v.refl.* to take off one's shoes & stockings. **scàlzo**, *a.* barefoot, bare-footed.

scambiàre, *v.t.* to exchange; mistake (*one person or thing for another*); transfer; fill the place of; change into smaller money. **scambiétto**, *m.* caper; frequent change; quick movement of the feet (*dancing*). **scambiévole**, *a.* reciprocal. **scambievolézza**, *f.* reciprocity. **scàmbio**, *m.* exchange; substitute;

mistake (in identification); (*Rly.*) switch; points. *libero* ∼, free trade. **scambista** (*pl.* -ísti), *m.* pointsman, shunter. *libero* ∼, free trader (*Pol.*).

scamiciàrsi, *v.refl.* to take off one's shirt; (or, coat & waistcoat). **scamiciàto**, *a.* in shirt sleeves; shirtless; (*fig.*) plebeian.

scamosciatóre, *m.* dresser of chamois skins.

scampafórca, *m.inv.* gallows-bird.

scampagnàre, *v.i.* (*aux.* avere) to go for a trip in the country. **scampagnàta**, *f.* trip in the country; picnic.

scampaménto, *m.* escape; safety.

scampanàre, *v.i.* (*aux.* avere) to ring out; chime; peal. **scampanàta**, *f.* peal; ringing of bells.

scampanellàre, *v.i.* (*aux.* avere) to ring the (door) bell. **scampanellàta**, *f.* ring; loud ring (of door-bell). **scampanellío**, *m.* prolonged ringing (of door-bell). **scampanío**, *m.* continuous ringing; chiming; pealing of bells.

scampàre, *v.t.* to save; rescue; avoid; escape. *v.i.* (*aux.* essere) to escape; get away. **scàmpo**, *m.* safety; escape.

scàmpolo, *m.* remnant.

scanagliàrsi, *v.refl.* to abuse one another.

scanalàre, *v.t.* to channel; groove. **scanalatúra**, *f.* channelling; slot; groove; (*Arch.*) fluting; (*Carp.*) rabbet.

scancellare, &c., see *cancellare*.

scandagliàre, *v.t.* to sound (*Naut.* & *fig.*). **scandagliatóre**, *m.* leadsman. **scandàglio**, *m.* sounding-line; lead; sounding-rod; sounding. *lanciare lo* ∼, to heave the lead (*Naut.*).

scandalizzàre, *v.t.* to scandalize; shock. **scàndalo**, *m.* scandal. **scandalóso**, *a.* scandalous; shocking.

scàndere & **scandíre** (*pr.* -ísco, -ísci), *v.t.* to scan (*verse*) pronounce clearly; articulate deliberately.

Scandinàvia (la), *f.* Scandinavia. **scandinàvo**, *a.* & *m.* Scandinavian.

scannàre, *v.t.* to cut the throat of; butcher; (*fig.*) ruin; unroil; unwind. **scannatóre**, *m.* cut-throat.

scannaménto, *m.* channelling; grooving; fluting (*Arch.*); unwinding. **scannellàre**, *v.t.* to groove; flute; unwind; thin out (*weeds*). **scannellatúra**, *f.* unwinding; fluting, &c. **scannèllo**, *m.* writing-cabinet;

movable writing desk; steak from the thigh.

scànno, *m.* bench; seat; sand-bank.

scansafatíche, *m.inv.* loafer; idler.

scansàre, *v.t.* to avoid; shun; escape from; remove; move away; parry; ward off (*blow*). **scansàrsi,** *v.refl.* to stand aside; withdraw; get out of the way.

scansía, *f.* bookcase; set of shelves.

scansióne, *f.* scansion.

scànso, *m.* avoidance. *a* ~ *di,* to avoid, in order to avoid.

scantonaménto, *m.* turning the corner; removing corners; dog's-earing (*page, book*). **scantonàre,** *v.t.* to round off; remove corners; (*page*) dog's-ear; avoid (*by turning a corner*). *v.i.* (*aux.* avere) to turn the corner. **scantonatúra,** *f.* wearing off the corners; dog's-earing; corner broken off.

scantucciàre, *v.t.* to cut off the edges (*esp. of a loaf*).

scanzonàto, *a.* free and easy. **scanzonatúra,** *f.* ease of manners.

scapaccióne, *m.* slap; smack.

scapàre, *v.t.* to cut off the head (*of fish*).

scapatàggine, *f.* heedlessness; recklessness; thoughtless action. **scapàto,** *a.* thoughtless; reckless; heedless. **scapatóna,** *f.* **-one,** *m.* thoughtless young person.

scapecchiatóio, *m.* flax-comb.

scapestràto, *a.* wild; dissolute; licentious. ¶ *m.* scapegrace; dissolute fellow; libertine.

scapezzàre, *v.t.* to prune; lop.

scapigliàre, *v.t.* to ruffle, rumple. **scapigliàrsi,** *v.refl.* to undo one's hair; become dishevelled; (*fig.*) lead a dissolute life. **scapigliatúra,** *f.* free and easy habits; loose living; unconventional manners; bohemianism.

scapitàre, *v.i.* (*aux.* avere) to suffer loss; lose; sink (*fig.*). **scàpito,** *m.* detriment; damage; loss.

scapitozzàre, *v.t.* to lop off; cut off; pollard.

scàpola, *f.* shoulder-blade.

scapolàre, *m.* scapular[y]; monastic scarf. ¶ *v.t.* to rescue. *v.i.* (*aux.* avere) & **scapolàrsi,** *v.refl.* to escape; slip away; make off. **scàpolo,** *a.* single; unmarried. ¶ *m.* bachelor.

scappaménto, *m.* escapement (*spring*); escape (*gas*); exhaust (*Mech.*). **scappàre,** *v.i.* (*aux.* essere) to

escape; run away; flee; take to flight. **scappàta,** *f.* flight; escape; escapade; excursion; short call; outburst. **scappatèlla** & **scappatína,** *f.* minor escapade; short excursion. **scappatóia,** *f.* evasion; subterfuge; pretext; bluff.

scapellàre, *v.t.* to remove the hat; knock the hat off. **scapellàrsi,** *v.refl.* to raise one's hat. **scapellàta,** *f.* salutation (*by raising one's hat*), bow.

scappellottàre, *v.t.* to give a rap on the head; cuff; slap. **scappellòtto,** *m.* rap on the head; slap. *entrare a* ~*i,* to enter without paying. *passare a* ~*i,* to be treated leniently by an examiner (*Sch.*).

scappucciàre, *v.t.* & **scappucciàrsi,** *v.refl.* to take off one's hood. *v.i.* (*aux.* avere) to stumble; blunder; go astray. **scappúccio,** *m.* blunder; stumble.

scarabàttola, *f.* show-case; snow-shoe; (*pop.*) thing of no value.

scarabèo, *m.* scarab; beetle.

scarabocchiàre, *v.t.* & *i.* to scrawl; scribble; blot. **scarabocchiatóre,** *m.* (*f.* **-tríce**) scribbler; scrawler. **scarabòcchio,** *m.* scrawl; blot.

scarafàggio, *m.* beetle; cockchafer.

scaramúccia (*pl.* **-úcce**), *f.* skirmish. **scaramucciàre,** *v.i.* (*aux.* avere) to skirmish.

scaraventàre, *v.t.* to hurl; fling.

scarceraménto, *m.* & **scarcerazióne,** *f.* release (from prison). **scarceràre,** *v.t.* to release from prison; set free. **scàrco,** *a.* for scarico, discharged.

scardàre, *v.t.* to husk (*chestnuts*). **scardassàre,** *v.t.* to card (*wool*).

scàrica, *f.* discharge; volley; shower. **scaricaménto,** *m.* unloading; discharging. **scaricàre** (*pr.* **scàrico, scàrichi**), *v.t.* to discharge; unload; lighten (*a colour*). **scaricàrsi,** *v.refl.* (*pers.*) to relieve oneself; acquit oneself (of); (*river*) discharge; flow (into); (*clock*) run down; (*watch*) be unwound. **scaricatóio,** *m.* wharf; place of discharge; outfall; exhaust-pipe; waste-pipe. **scaricatóre,** *m.* unloader; docker. **scàrico** (*pl.* **scàrichi**), *a.* unloaded; discharged; run down; not wound up. ¶ *m.* discharge; unloading; refuse-tip; dump. *tubo di* ~, exhaust pipe.

scarificàre, *v.t.* to scarify.

scarlattína, *f.* scarlet-fever. **scarlàtto,** *a.* & *m.* scarlet.

scarmigliàre, *v.t.* to ruffle.

scarnaménto, *m.* loss of flesh. **scarnàre**, *v.t.* to remove superfluous flesh from. **scarnàrsi**, *v.refl.* to grow thin. **scarnàto**, *a.* thin; flesh-coloured. **scarnificàre**, *v.t.* to scrape or tear off flesh from; lacerate. ~ *un'unghia incarnata*, to relieve an ingrowing-nail. **scarníre** (*pr.* **-ísco, -ísci**), *v.t.* to make lean. **scarnírsi**, *v.refl.* to grow lean. **scarníto**, *a.* emaciated; lean; scanty. **scàrno**, *a.* thin; lean; meagre.

scàrpa, *f.* shoe; scarp; skid (*wheel*), drag (*carriage*). **scarpàccia**, *f.* old shoe; poor shoe. **scarpàio** & **scarpàro**, *m.* pedlar of shoes & slippers.

scarpàta, *f.* scarp; escarp; escarpment.

scarpétta & **scarpína**, *f.* small shoe; light shoe; baby's shoe. ~ *da ballo*, dancing shoe; pump.

scarrozzàre, *v.i.* (*aux.* avere) to go out for a drive, take a drive; (*v.t.*) take for a drive. **scarrozzàta**, *f.* drive (in a carriage).

scarsaménte, *ad.* insufficiently; slightly; barely. **scarseggiàre**, *v.i.* (*aux.* essere) to be lacking (in = *di*); to be scarce.

scarsèlla, *f.* purse; pocket; hollow in a wall.

scarsézza & **scarsità**, *f.* scarcity; scarceness; lack. **scàrso**, *a.* scanty; scarce; poor; lean; short.

scartabellàre, *v.t.* to turn over the pages (*or leaves*) rapidly (*of a book*); skim through.

scartafàccio, *m.* scribbling-book; waste-paper.

scartaménto, *m.* elimination; rejection; (*Rly.*) gauge. *ferrovia a ~ ridotto*, narrow-gauge railway. **scartàre**, *v.t.* to discard; reject. *v.i.* (*aux.* avere) to swerve; dribble (*Foot.*). **scartàta**, *f.* rejection; reproof; (*horse*) swerve. **scàrto**, *m.* putting aside, discarding; dribbling (*Foot.*); what is discarded; discard (*cards*); person rejected for military service.

scartocciàre, *v.t.* to strip (*maize*); unwrap, unpack.

scasàre, *v.t.* to turn out (*tenant, lodger*). *v.i.* (*aux.* avere) to change lodgings.

scassàre, *v.t.* to unpack; break in; force open; break up (*ground*). **scassatóre**, *m.* housebreaker.

scassinàre, *v.t.* to pick the lock of; force. **scassinatóre**, *m.* picklock.

scàsso, *m.* house-breaking; burglary.

scatenàre, *v.t.* to unchain; (*fig.*) let loose; cause. **scatenàrsi**, *v.refl.* to break loose; break out.

scàtola, *f.* box (*light*); tin. ~ *armonica*, musical box. *lettere di ~*, *f.pl.* block letters. *carne in ~e*, *f.* canned meat.

scattàre, *v.i.* (*aux.* essere *or* avere) to spring up; go off (*gun*); differ; diverge; (*fig.*) fly into a passion; lose one's temper. ~ *in piedi*, to spring to one's feet. **scàtto**, *m.* release (*spring*); sudden movement; jerk; click; spring-catch (*lock*); (*fig.*) wide divergence; outburst; explosion.

scaturìgine, *f.* spring; source. **scaturíre** (*pr.* **-ísco, -ísci**), *v.i.* (*aux.* essere) to spring; gush; gush forth; spout; rise; (*fig.*) ensue, follow.

scavalcàre, *v.t.* to unhorse; (*fig.*) oust, displace; supplant; climb over; step over; skip (*in reading*); slip (*stitch*).

scavaménto, *m.* & **scavazióne**, *f.* excavation; digging (out). **scavapózzi**, *m.inv.* well-sinker. **scavàre**, *v.t.* to excavate; dig out; hollow out; sink (*well*). **scavatóre**, *m.* excavator; digger; miner. **scavatúra**, *f.* hole; cavity.

scavezzacòllo, *m.* reckless fellow; daredevil; scamp; headlong fall; rash venture.

scàvo, *m.* excavation (*gen. pl. for archaeological research*); hollow; work of excavation; material excavated. ~ *di galleria*, driving (piercing) of a tunnel.

scégliere (*pr.* **scélgo, scégli, scéglie**), *v.t. ir.* to choose; select; pick (out). **sceglitóre**, *m.* (*f.* **-tríce**) chooser; selector.

sceícco (*pl.* **-ícchi**), *m.* sheik[h].

scelleratézza & **scelleratàggine**, *f.* wickedness; villainy. **scelleràto**, *a.* wicked; villainous. ¶ *m.* villain, scoundrel, miscreant.

scellíno, *m.* shilling.

scélta, *f.* choice; selection; pick; option; quality. **sceltézza**, *f.* choiceness; exquisiteness. **scélto**, *a.* choice; exquisite; carefully chosen; picked; select(ed).

scemaménto, *m.* diminution; reduction; abatement. **scemàre**, *v.t.* to diminish; lessen; abate; reduce; lower. *v.i.* (*aux.* essere) to fall; decrease; grow less; drop; decline; (*moon*) wane. **scémo**, *a.* diminished; reduced; half-empty; not full;

foolish; half-witted. ¶ *m.* diminution; half-witted person.

scempiàggine *&* **scempiatàggine,** *f.* foolishness; stupidity; folly. **scémpio,** *a.* simple; single (*letter, flower, &c.*); silly. ¶ *m.* simpleton; havoc; slaughter.

scèna, *f.* scene; stage. **scenàrio,** *m.* scenario (*Theat.*) scenery (*painted*). **scenàta,** *f.* scene; row; commotion.

scéndere, *v.i.* ir. (*aux.* essere *&* avere) to descend; go down; come down; run (down); fall; sink; drop; finish up. ~ *a,* to go to; put up at (*hotel*). *v.t.* to take down. **scendilètto,** *m.inv.* bedside mat or carpet.

sceneggiaménto, *m.* staging (*Theat.*). **sceneggiàre,** *v.t.* to stage; put on the stage; dramatize; produce. **sceneggiatúra,** *f.* staging; arrangement of scenes. **scènico** (*pl.* **scènici**), *a.* scenic; theatrical; stage (*att.*). **scenografía,** *f.* scene-painting. **scenògrafo,** *m.* scene-painter.

sceríffo, *m.* sheriff.

scèrnere, *v.t.* to discern; distinguish; choose; select; separate (out).

scervellàre, *v.t.* to drive to distraction. **scervellàrsi,** *v.refl.* to rack one's brains. **scervellàto,** *a.* harebrained.

scésa, *f.* (down-hill) slope. **scéso,** *p.p.* of *scendere.*

scetticísmo, *m.* scepticism. **scèttico** (*pl.* **scèttici**), *a.* sceptical. ¶ *m.* sceptic.

scettràto, *a.* sceptred. **scèttro,** *m.* sceptre.

sceveràre (*pr.* **scévero**), *v.t.* (*Lit.*) to sever; separate; divide; part.

scévro, *a.* free (from); exempt (from).

schèda, *f.* slip of paper; card; form; application form; slip. ~ *per votazione,* voting-paper, ballot-paper. **schedàrio,** *m.* card-index.

schéggia (*pl.* **schégge**), *f.* splinter; flake; chip. dim. *scheggiola, scheggiolina.* **scheggiàre,** *v.t.* *&* **scheggiàrsi,** *v.refl.* to splinter.

schelètrico (*pl.* **-ètrici**), *a.* skeleton-like. **scheletríto,** *a.* reduced to a skeleton. **schèletro,** *m.* skeleton; (*fig.*) frame; carcass.

schèma (*pl.* **schèmi**), *m.* scheme; outline; project; plan.

schérma, *f.* fencing; swordsmanship; (*fig.*) polemic.

schermàglia, *f.* scuffle; scrimmage; skirmish; (*fig.*) discussion; debate.

schermitóre, *m.* -**trice,** *f.* fencer.

schermíre (*pr.* -**ísco,** -**ísci**), *v.i.* (*aux.* avere) to fence. **schermirsi,** *v.refl.* to defend oneself. ~ *da,* to parry; ward off. **schérmo,** *m.* screen (*Cinema, Lantern, Phot.*); protection; defence; shelter.

schernévole, *a.* scornful; contemptuous; scoffing; sneering. **scherníre** (*pr.* -**ísco,** -**ísci**), *v.t.* to scoff at; sneer at; jeer at; scorn; despise. **schernitóre,** *m.* (*f.* -**tríce**) scoffer; sneerer. ¶ *a.* sneering; derisory. **schérno,** *m.* sneer; taunt; mockery; derision.

scherzàre, *v.i.* to joke; jest; trifle; play. **scherzévole** *&* **scherzóso,** *a.* playful; facetious; jesting; joking. **schérzo,** *m.* joke; jest; trick; fun; freak.

schiàccia (*pl.* **schiàcce**), *f.* weighted trap; (*pl.*) curling-tongs.

schiacciaménto, *m.* crushing; squashing; cracking; flattening; collapse. **schiaccianóci,** *m.inv.* nut-cracker-[s]. **schiacciànte,** *p.a.* crushing; overwhelming; decisive. **schiacciàre,** *v.t.* to crush; squash; squeeze; crack; flatten; (*fig.*) pluck (*exam.*); settle completely; tread on. **schiacciàta,** *f.* crushing; squeezing; squeeze; flat cake.

schiaffeggiàre, *v.t.* to slap; cuff; smack; box on the ear. **schiàffo,** *m.* slap; smack; box on the ear; (*fig.*) insult; affront.

schiamazzàre, *v.i.* (*aux.* avere) to make a din; shout; (*geese*) cackle; (*hen*) cluck; (*bird*) squawk. **schiamàzzo,** *m.* noise; uproar; shouting; cackling, &c.

schiantàre, *v.t.* to break; tear up; wrench away; shatter; snap off; burst open. **schiànto,** *m.* crash; clap; burst; noise of breaking or tearing; (*fig.*) pang; sudden blow; affliction. *di* ~, on a sudden; suddenly.

schiàppa, *f.* *&* **schiappíno,** *m.* booby; duffer (*esp. at games*); inexpert player.

schiariménto, *m.* clearing up; explanation; elucidation. **schiaríre** (*pr.* -**ísco,** -**ísci**), *v.t.* to clear; make clear; clarify; illuminate; elucidate; throw light upon; explain. *v.i.* (*aux.* essere) to become light; clear; break (*day*); (*of colour*) fade. **schiarírsi,** *v.refl.* to clear; become clear; brighten; light up; (*of hair, or trees*) grow thin; be thinned out.

schiàtta, *f.* race; stock; family.

schiattàre, *v.i.* (*aux.* essere) to burst.

schiattíre (*pr.* -isco, -isci), *v.i.* (*aux.* avere) to yelp.

schiavitú, *f.* slavery. **schiàvo**, *m.* (*f.* schiava) slave. ¶ *a.* slave (*att.*); enslaved; subject; subjugated.

schiavóne, *a. & m.* Slavonian.

schiccheracàrte *&* **schiccherafògli**, *m.inv.* scribbler. **schiccheràre**, *v.t.* to scribble; tell; blab.

schidionàre, *v.t.* to spit, put on the spit. **schidionàta**, *f.* row of birds, &c., on a spit. **schidióne**, *m.* (*roasting*) spit; broach.

schièna, *f.* back; backbone. **schienàle**, *m.* spine; back; (chair) back.

schièra, *f.* band; troop; rank; company; group. **schieraménto**, *m.* marshalling. **schieràre**, *v.t. &* **schieràrsi**, *v.refl.* (*Mil.*) to marshall; draw up; be drawn up; (*fig.*) array oneself; take sides.

schiettaménte, *ad.* frankly; openly; sincerely; simply; purely. **schiettézza**, *f.* frankness; openness; sincerity. **schiètto**, *a.* frank; open; sincere; plain; pure; genuine; undiluted.

schifàre, *v.t.* to shun; dislike; loathe. **schifàrsi**, *v.refl.* to feel reluctance (to). **schifiltà**, *f.* fastidiousness. **schifiltóso**, *a.* fastidious; hard to please. **schifo**, *m.* disgust; loathing; skiff (*Naut.*). **schifosità**, *f.* loathsomeness; disgusting character; disgusting thing; horror. **schifóso**, *a.* loathsome; filthy; disgusting; revolting.

schioccàre (*pr.* -òcco, -òcchi), *v.t. & i.* to crack (*whip*); snap (*fingers*); smack. **schioccàta**, *f.* crack of a whip. **schiòcco** (*pl.* -òcchi), *m.* crack; snap; smack, &c.

schioppettàta, *f.* shot; gunshot. **schiòppo**, *m.* gun.

schiribízzo, *m.* whim.

Schíro, *f.* Scyros.

schísto, *m.* schist (*Geol.*).

schiúdere, *v.t. & i. ir. &* **schiúdersi**, *v.refl.* to open.

schiúma, *f.* foam; froth; lather; scum; dross. ~ *di mare*, meerschaum. **schiumàre**, *v.t.* to skim; remove the scum or dross from. *v.i.* (*aux.* avere) to froth; foam. **schiumóso**, *a.* frothy; foaming.

schivàbile, *a.* avoidable. **schivafatíche**, *m.inv.* shirker. **schivàre**, *v.t.* to avoid; shun; protect from.

schívo, *a.* shy; bashful; retiring; coy; averse (to, from = *di*).

schizofrenía, *f.* schizophrenia.

schizzàre, *v.t.* to sketch; emit; send out; eject; squirt; splash; bespatter; squirt out; (*v.i.*) (*aux.* essere) gush; squirt. **schizzàta**, *f.* splash. **schizzatóio**, *m.* syringe. **schizzétto**, *m.* squirt; small syringe. **schizzinóso**, *a.* fastidious; squeamish; hard to please. **schizzo**, *m.* sketch; splash; squirt; jet; drop.

sci, *m.inv.* ski.

scia, *f.* wake (*of ship*); track.

scià, *m.* Shah.

sciàbola, *f.* sabre. **sciabolàta**, *f.* sabre-cut.

sciacàllo, *m.* jackal.

sciacquàre, *v.t.* to rinse; rinse out. **sciacquatúra**, *f.* rinsing(s); slops.

sciagúra, *f.* calamity; misfortune; mishap; disaster. **sciaguràto**, *a.* unfortunate; unlucky; ill-starred; wretched; wicked. ¶ *m.* wretch.

scialacquàre, *v.t.* to squander; waste; dissipate. **scialacquatóre**, *m.* squanderer; spendthrift.

scialaménto, *m.* dissipation. **scialàre**, *v.i. &* **scialàrsi**, *v.refl.* to enjoy oneself; be wasteful or self-indulgent; dissipate.

scialbo, *a.* pale; wan; faint; faded; vague; dim. **scialbóre**, *m.* drabness.

scialle, *m.* shawl.

scialo, *m.* luxury; display; show; lavishness; waste. **scialóne**, *m.* spendthrift; riotous liver.

scialúppa, *f.* shallop; sloop; launch.

sciamannàto, *a.* slovenly; careless; clumsy.

sciamàre, *v.i.* (*aux.* avere *&* essere) to swarm; emigrate. **sciamatúra**, *f.* swarming (*bees*). **sciàme**, *m.* swarm; (*fig.*) crowd; host.

sciampàgna, *m.* champagne (*wine*).

sciancàrsi, *v.refl.* to lame oneself; become lame; dislocate one's hip. **sciancàto**, *a.* lop-sided; crippled; lame. ¶ *m.* cripple.

sciaràda, *f.* charade.

sciàre, *v.i.* to ski.

sciàrpa, *f.* (*Mil.*) sash; scarf.

sciàtica, *f.* sciatica.

sciatóre, *m.* (*f.* -tríce) skier.

sciattàgine, **sciattería**, *&* **sciattézza**, *f.* slovenliness; untidiness; awkwardness. **sciattàre**, *v.t.* to spoil; mar. **sciàtto**, *a.* slovenly; untidy; careless; clumsy. **sciattóna**, *f.* slut; slattern. **sciattóne**, *m.* slovenly fellow; sloven.

scíbile, *a.* knowable. ¶ *m.* knowledge.

scib[b]olet, *m.inv.* shibboleth.

sciènte, *a.* knowing; aware (of); conscious (of). **scienteménte,** *ad.* knowingly; wittingly. **scientífico** (*pl.* **-ífici**), *a.* scientific. **sciènza,** *f.* science; knowledge; learning; lore. **scienziàto,** *m.* scientist; man of science; learned person.

scilinguàgnolo, *m.* (*Anat.*) fraenum, ligament of the tongue; (*fig.*) tongue; speech. **con lo ~ bene sciolto,** very talkative. **avere lo ~ sciolto,** to have a ready tongue.

scilinguàre, *v.i.* (*aux.* avere) to stutter; stammer. **scilinguatúra,** *f.* stuttering; inability to pronounce clearly.

scílla, *f.* (*Bot.*) squill. **S~** (*Geog.* & *Myth.*) Scylla.

scimitàrra, *f.* scimitar.

scímmia, *f.* ape; monkey. **scimmieggiàre** & **scimmiottàre,** *v.t.* to ape; mimic. **scimmiésco** (*pl.* **-éschi**), *a.* ape-like. **scimmiòtto,** *m.* young monkey. **scimpanzè,** *m.inv.* chimpanzee.

scimunitàggine, *f.* silliness; foolishness. **scimuníto,** *a.* silly; foolish.

scíndere, *v.t.* *ir.* to split; divide; sever; separate.

scintílla, *f.* spark; sparkle. **scintillàre,** *v.i.* (*aux.* avere) to sparkle; twinkle; scintillate. **scintillío,** *m.* sparkling; twinkling.

sciocchería, & **sciocchézza,** *f.* foolishness; stupidity; nonsense; foolish action; piece of stupidity; mistake. **scioccaménte,** *ad.* foolishly; stupidly. **sciòcco** (*pl.* **sciòcchi**), *a.* foolish; silly; (*of food*) insipid, tasteless. **scioccóne,** *m.* utter fool; simpleton.

sciògliere (*pr.* **sciòlgo, sciògli, sciòglie**), *v.t.* *ir.* to undo; untie; loose; loosen; let loose; unleash; unfurl; set free; release (*from vow or obligation*); solve; dissolve (*alliance, marriage,* &c.); melt; resolve (*doubt*); fulfil (*vow, promise*); raise (*hymn, song*). **sciògliersi,** *v.refl.* to free oneself; melt; dissolve; (*meeting*) break up; (*joint or muscle*) lose its stiffness. **scioglilíngua,** *m.inv.* tongue-twister; play of words. **sciogliménto,** *m.* dissolution (*marriage, partnership, parliament, contract*); melting; termination; breaking up (*meeting*), end.

scioltaménte, *ad.* freely; easily; nimbly; fluently. **scioltézza,** *f.*

ease; fluency; freedom (of movement); agility; nimbleness. **sciòlto,** *p.p.* of *sciogliere.* ¶ *a.* loose; easy; free; nimble; disengaged; unbound (*book*). **burro ~,** melted butter. **versi ~ i,** unrhymed verse, blank verse. **a briglia ~a,** headlong, at full speed.

scioperàggine, *f.* idleness. **scioperànte,** *a.* striking; on strike. ¶ *m.* striker. **scioperàre,** *v.i.* (*aux.* avere) to strike, go on strike. **scioperatàggine,** *f.* idleness due to a strike; strike mentality. **scioperatézza,** *f.* unemployment. **scioperàto,** *a.* out of work; on strike. ¶ *m.* striker. **sciòpero,** *m.* strike. **~ bianco,** stay-in strike, sit-down strike. **~ della fame,** hunger-strike.

sciorinaménto, *m.* airing (*of clothes*); disclosure; display. **sciorinàre,** *v.t.* to air; hang out (*clothes*); display; spread out; (*fig.*) pour out; rattle off; disclose.

sciovinísmo, *m.* chauvinism. **sciovinísta** (*pl.* **-ísti**), *m.* chauvinist. ¶ *a.* chauvinistic.

scipitàggine & **scipitézza,** *f.* silliness; insipidity; fatuity; dul[l]ness. **scipíto,** *a.* insipid; tasteless; dull; silly.

sciròcco (*pl.* **-òcchi**), *m.* s[c]irocco; warm south-east wind of the Mediterranean.

sciroppàre, *v.t.* to sweeten; candy with syrup. **sciròppo,** *m.* syrup.

scísma, *m.* schism. **scismàtico** (*pl.* **-àtici**), *a.* schismatic.

scissióne, *f.* splitting; split; division; secession. **scísso,** *p.p.* of *scindere.* **scissúra,** *f.* cleft; furrow; dissension; disagreement; break.

scíta, *a.* & *m.* Scythian.

sciupàre, *v.t.* to spoil; damage; ruin; waste; consume; squander. **sciupàrsi,** *v.refl.* to spoil; be spoiled; be run down in health. **sciupàto,** *a.* wasted; spoiled; run down (in health). **sciupío,** *m.* constant waste; waste; wastage. **sciupóne,** *m.* waster; squanderer; spendthrift.

scivolàre, *v.i.* (*aux.* essere & avere) to slip; slide; glide. **scivolàta,** *f.* slide. **scívolo,** *m.* (*Aviat.*) runway, slip (*for sea-planes*); (*Mus.*) trill. **scivolóne,** *m.* slip (*in walking*).

sclerósi, *f.* sclerosis (*Med.*).

scoccàre, *v.t.* to shoot; shoot off; let fly; throw; fling; dart. *v.i.* (*aux.* essere) to go off; dart; fly; spring (*catch*); stroke (*hours*).

scocciànte, *a.* boring. scocciàre, *v.t.* to break; harass; bore.

scòcco, *m.* shooting off; letting fly; twang (*of a bow*); smack (*kiss*); striking (*clock*); stroke (*hour*).

scodàre, *v.t.* to dock the tail of.

scodèlla, *f.* bowl; soup-plate. scodellàre, *v.t.* to dish up; serve out; (*fig.*) pour out. scodellàta, *f.* helping (*food*). scodellíno, *m.* small bowl; (*Mech.*) sump.

scodinzolàre, *v.i.* to wag the tail.

scoglièra, *f.* reef of rocks; rocky cliff. scòglio, *m.* rock; reef; (*fig.*) difficulty; stumbling-block. scoglióso, *a.* rocky; difficult; dangerous.

scoiàttolo, *m.* squirrel.

scolàre, *v.t. & i.* to drain off; drip; run off; pass through a strainer. scolarésca, *f.* pupils; school-children (*col.*); students; student-body. scolarésco (*pl.* -éschi), *a.* school (*att.*); schoolboy (*att.*). scolàro, *m.* schoolboy; pupil. scolàstica, *f.* scholasticism; scholastic philosophy. scolàstico (*pl.* -àstici) *a.* scholastic.

scolatóio, *m.* drain-pipe; strainer; sink. scolatúra, *f.* draining; dripping; dregs.

scollacciàto & scollàto, *a.* low-necked (*dress*); wearing low-necked dress; (*fig.*) immodest. scollàre, *v.t.* to cut away (neck of garment); unglue. scollatúra, *f.* neck-hole; opening.

scollaménto, *m.* disconnection; untying; uncoupling; lack of continuity. scollegàre, *v.t.* to disconnect. scollegàrsi, *v.refl.* to come undone.

scólo, *m.* drain; drain-pipe; drainage; (*Med.*) discharge.

scoloraménto, *m.* discoloration. scoloràre, *v.t.* to discolour; deprive of colour. scoloríre (*pr.* -ísco, -ísci), *v.i.* (*aux.* essere) & scolorírsi, *v.refl.* to lose colour; grow pale. scoloríto, *a.* colourless; pale; faded.

scolpàre, *v.t.* to exculpate; excuse; justify.

scolpíre (*pr.* -ísco, -ísci), *v.t.* to sculpture; chisel; carve; cut; engrave; (*fig.*) pronounce distinctly. scolpitaménte, *ad.* clearly; distinctly.

scólta, *f.* sentry; sentinel; watch.

scombiccheràre, *v.t.* to scribble.

scombinàre, *v.t.* to disarrange; (*Typ.*) distribute (*type*).

scombussolàre, *v.t.* to upset; disturb; derange.

scomméssa, *f.* bet; wager; stake. scomméttere, *v.t. ir.* to bet; wager; stake; disconnect; undo. scométtersi, *v.refl.* to come apart.

scomodàre, *v.t.* to trouble; inconvenience; disturb. scòmodo, *a.* uncomfortable; inconvenient; troublesome. ¶ *m.* discomfort; annoyance.

scompaginàre, *v.t.* to disarrange; upset; (*Typ.*) break up.

scompagnàto, *a.* odd; not matching.

scomparíre (*pr.* scompàio & scomparísco, -pàri & -parísci, *&c.*). *v.i. ir.* (*aux.* essere) to disappear; vanish; retire; cut a poor figure. scompàrsa, *f.* disappearance.

scompartiménto, *m.* compartment (*Rly.*); division; sharing. scompartíre (*pr.* -ísco, -ísci), *v.t.* to divide (up) separate; share; allot; sharing; allotting.

scompigliàre, *v.t.* to upset; throw into disorder; ruffle; discompose; trouble; confound. scompíglio, *m.* disorder; confusion; upset[ing]; perturbation; fuss & discord.

scomplèto, *a.* incomplete.

scompórre (*pr.* -óngo, -óni, -óne, like *porre*), *v.t. ir.* to break up; take to pieces; analyse; decompose; disarrange; trouble; worry; agitate; discompose; (*Math.*) resolve; (*Typ.*) distribute. scompórsi, *v.refl.* to decompose; be troubled; worried; upset; lose one's temper (*or* composure). scomposizióne, *f.* decomposition; perturbation; disorder; (*Typ.*) distribution of type; dead matter. scompostézza, *f.* disorder; confusion; discomposure.

scomúnica, *f.* excommunication. scomunicàre, *v.t.* to excommunicate.

sconcatenàre, *v.t.* to disconnect; unchain.

sconcertànte, *a.* disconcerting; baffling. sconcertàre, *v.t.* to disconcert; baffle; perturb. sconcèrto, *m.* confusion; discord; disagreement; lack of harmony.

sconcézza, *f.* indecency; obscenity.

sconciàre, *v.t.* to spoil; mar. sconciàrsi, *v.refl.* to miscarry; strain, sprain. sconciatúra, *f.* miscarriage. scóncio, *a.* indecent; obscene; ill-shaped, deformed. ¶ *m.* shame.

sconclusionàto, *a.* inconclusive; rambling; inconsequent.

sconfacènte, *a.* unsuiteble; unbecoming.

sconfessàre, *v.t.* to disavow; disown.

sconficcàre, *v.t.* to pull out (*nail*); undo; unfasten; take to pieces.

sconfíggere, *v.t. ir.* to defeat; discomfit. **sconfiggiménto,** *m.* discomfiture.

sconfinaménto, *m.* breaking of bounds; escape; trespass[ing]. **sconfinàre,** *v.i.* to quit the confine (*prescribed domicile*); break bounds; cross the frontier; (*fig.*) digress widely; exceed the limits (of). **sconfinàto,** *a.* boundless; unlimited.

sconfítta, *f.* defeat; rout; discomfiture.

sconfortànte, *a.* discouraging; disheartening; distressing. **sconfortàre,** *v.t.* to dishearten; discourage; distress. **sconfòrto,** *m.* discouragement; depression; distress.

scongiuràre, *v.t.* to entreat; implore; exorcise; avert; remove. **scongiúro,** *m.* exorcism; entreaty.

sconnessióne, *f.* disconnectedness; want of connection; desultoriness. **sconnèttere,** *v.t. ir.* to disconnect.

sconoscènte, *a.* ungrateful; thankless. **sconoscènza,** *f.* ingratitude; ungratefulness. **sconóscere** (*pr.* -nósco, -nósci*),* *v.t. ir.* to fail to recognize; be ignorant of; slight; disregard; *v.t. & i.* (*aux.* avere) to be ungrateful (for); fail to appreciate. **sconosciúto,** *a.* unknown; disregarded; unappreciated. ¶ *m.* stranger.

sconquassàre, *v.t.* to smash; shatter; destroy.

sconsideratézza, *f.* thoughtlessness; inconsiderateness; rashness. **sconsideràto,** *a.* thoughtless; heedless; inconsiderate; rash.

sconsigliàre, *v.t.* to dissuade; deter; discourage. **sconsigliatézza,** *f.* rashness; inconsiderateness. **sconsigliàto,** *a.* rash; foolish; indiscreet; ill-advised.

sconsolàto, *a.* disconsolate.

scontàre, *v.t.* to discount (*bill of exchange*); deduct; take off discount from; expiate; atone for; pay for.

scontentàre, *v.t.* to dissatisfy; displease; disappoint. **scontentézza,** *f.* discontent; dissatisfaction; disappointment. **scontènto,** *a.* discontented; dissatisfied; disappointed. ¶ *m.* discontent; dissatisfaction.

scontísta (*pl.* -ísti)*,* *m.* (*bill*) discounter. **scónto,** *m.* discount; reduction; allowance. *tasso* (*ufficiale*) *di* ~, bank-rate.

scontràre, *v.t.* to meet (with); encounter. **scontràrsi,** *v.refl.* to encounter; meet; collide. **scontríno,** *m.* check; ticket; receipt; voucher. **scóntro,** *m.* collision; encounter.

scontróso, *a.* cantankerous; illtempered; peevish; touchy; irritable.

sconvenévole, *a.* unseemly; indecorous; improper. **sconvenevolézza,** *f.* unseemliness; indecorum; breach of good manners. **sconveniènte,** *a.* unbecoming; unsuitable; unseemly. **sconvenienza,** *f.* unsuitableness; impropriety. **sconveníre** (*pr.* -vèngo, -vièni, &c., like *venire*). *v.i. ir.* (*aux.* essere) to be unbecoming; to be unsuitable.

sconvòlgere, *v.t. ir.* to upset; overturn; turn upside down; throw into confusion; derange. **sconvolgiménto,** *m.* confusion; upsetting; overturning. **sconvòlto,** *p.p.* of *sconvolgere.* ¶ *a.* perturbed; convulsed. *mare* ~, troubled sea.

scòpa, *f.* broom; scopa (*card game*). **scopàre,** *v.t.* to sweep.

scoperchiàre, *v.t.* to uncover; take off the lid (of); unroof.

scopèrta, *f.* discovery; revelation; disclosure; (*Mil.*) reconnaissance. **scopertaménte,** *ad.* openly. **scopèrto,** *a.* open; exposed; unprotected; bare; uncovered; undecked (*boat*); overdrawn (*account*); clear; manifest.

scopéto, *m.* heath. **scopétta,** *f.* brush; small broom.

scòpo, *m.* purpose; object; aim; end; target; design.

scoppiaménto, *m.* uncoupling; explosion. **scoppiàre,** *v.i.* (*aux.* essere) to burst (*lit. & fig.*); explode; break out; (*v.t.*) to uncouple. **scoppiettàre,** *v.i.* (*aux.* avere) to crackle. **scoppiettío,** *m.* crackling. **scòppio,** *m.* burst; bursting; explosion; outbreak; crack (*whip*). ~ *del carro,* the traditional firework display outside the Duomo of Florence on Easter Eve, when a spark is carried to the High Altar from a waggon in the square.

scopríre (*pr.* scòpro, scòpri, &c., like *coprire*), *v.t. ir.* to discover; find out; detect; descry; sight (*land*); reveal; disclose; uncover; lay bare; unveil; expose; show. **scoprírsi,**

v.refl. to expose oneself; take off one's hat. **scopritóre,** *m.* discoverer.

scoraggiaménto, *m.* discouragement. **scoraggiàre,** *v.t.* to discourage; dishearten.

scoràre, *v.t.* to dishearten; depress.

scorbúto, *m.* scurvy.

scorciàre, *v.t.* to shorten; foreshorten (*Art.*). *v.i.* (*aux.* essere) & **scorciàrsi,** *v.refl.* to shorten; grow shorter. **scorciatóia,** *f.* short cut. **scórcio,** *m.* end; close; foreshortening; grimace.

scordàre, *v.t.* & **scordàrsi,** *v.refl.* to forget. *non-ti-scordar-di-mé,* forget-me-not (*flower*). **scordàre,** *v.t.* to untune; put out of tune. **scordàrsi,** *v.refl.* to get out of tune; (*fig.*) disagree. **scordataménte,** *ad.* discordantly.

scòrgere (*pr.* scòrgo, scòrgi), *v.t. ir.* to perceive; descry; discern; notice.

scòria, *f.* dross; slag; scoria; skimmings.

scornàre, *v.t.* (*fig.*) to put to shame; hold up to ridicule. **scòrno,** *m.* shame; ignominy; disgrace. *avere a ~,* to scorn, hold in contempt. *avere ~ di,* to be disgraced by.

scoronàre, *v.t.* to uncrown; dethrone; lop off the top (*of a tree*); break the crown (*of a tooth*).

scorpacciàta, *f.* bellyful.

scorpióne, *m.* scorpion.

scorporàre, *v.t.* to separate, disincorporate; spend out of capital.

scorrazzaménto, *m.* roving; raiding. **scorrazzàre,** *v.i.* (*aux.* avere) to rove (about); run about; (*v.t.*) (*Mil.*) to raid; overrun.

scórrere, *v.t. ir.* to scour; raid; run through; glance over. *v.i.* (*aux.* essere) to run; glide; roll; flow; fly (*time*); elapse. **scorrería,** *f.* raid.

scorrettaménte, *ad.* incorrectly; improperly. **scorrettézza,** *f.* incorrectness; (*fig.*) impropriety. **scorretto,** *a.* incorrect; improper.

scorrévole, *a.* easily flowing; fluent; gliding. **scorrevolézza,** *f.* fluency.

scorrezióne, *f.* incorrectness; error, slip.

scorribànda, *f.* incursion; raid.

scórsa, *f.* glance; rapid examination. **scórso,** *m.* slip; oversight; involuntary error in speaking or writing. ¶ *p.p.* of *scorrere.* *a.* last; past. *il mese ~,* last month.

scorsóio (*nodo*), *m.* running knot.

scòrta, *f.* escort: convoy; provision;

subvention. **scortàre,** *v.t.* to escort; convoy.

scortecciàre, *v.t.* to peel; strip; bark.

scortése, *a.* rude; impolite; uncivil; discourteous; unkind. **scortesía,** *f.* rudeness; incivility; discourtesy; unkindness.

scorticàre, *v.t.* to skin; flay; (*fig.*) fleece. **scorticatúra,** *f.* abrasion; scratch. **scortichíno,** *m.* skinning knife; (*fig.*) extortioner, usurer.

scòrza, *f.* bark; rind; (*fig.*) outside; exterior. **scorzàre,** *v.t.* to peel; strip; bark. **scorzóne,** *m.* adder; boor; stubborn fellow.

scoscéndere, *v.t. ir.* (like *scéndere*) to break; split; cleave. *v.i.* (*aux.* essere) & **scoscéndersi,** *v.refl.* to fall; crash down; collapse; slide down. **scoscéso,** *p.p.* of *scoscendere.* ¶ *a.* rugged; precipitous; steep.

scòssa, *f.* shock; shake; jerk; sharp shower; sudden loss or damage. *~ elcttrica,* electric shock. *~ di terremoto,* earthquake s. **scòsso,** *p.p.* of *scuotere.* *cavallo ~,* riderless horse. **scossóne,** *m.* severe shock; violent shake; heavy shower.

scostaménto, *m.* removal; separation; distance apart. **scostàre,** *v.t.* to remove; put aside; put out of the way. **scostàrsi,** *v.refl.* to stand aside; get out of the way; make way; wander (*from the subject*); swerve.

scostumatézza, *f.* coarse manners; evil living; dissoluteness; licentiousness. **scostumàto,** *a.* dissolute; licentious; low; ill-mannered.

scotennàre, *v.t.* to skin; scalp.

scotiménto, *m.* shaking; jolting.

scòtta, *f.* (*Naut.*) sheet; whey.

scottaménto, *m.* scorching; burning; scalding. **scottànte,** *a.* scorching; scalding; burning (*lit.* & *fig.*); stinging (*fig.*). **scottàre,** *v.i.* & *t.* to scorch; burn; scald; (*fig.*) to sting; nettle. **scottàta,** *f.* scalding; light cooking. **scottatúra,** *f.* burn; burning; scald.

scòtto, *m.* bill; score; reckoning; share (*of a bill*).

scovàre, *v.t.* to drive out; dislodge; rouse (*game*); find; discover.

Scòzia (la), *f.* Scotland.

scozzàre, *v.t.* (*cards*) to shuffle. **scozzàta,** *f.* snuffle (*cards*).

scozzése, *a.* Scottish. ¶ *m. S~,* Scot; Scotsman; *f.* Scotswoman.

scozzonàre, *v.t.* to train; break in (*horse*). **scozzonatóre** & **scozzóne,** *m.* trainer; horse-breaker.

scozzonatúra, f. training; breaking-in.

scrànna, f. high-backed chair.

screanzàto, a. unmannerly; ill-bred.

screditàre, v.t. to discredit. scrédito, m. discredit; disgrace.

scremàre, v.t. to skim; cream off.

screpolàre, v.i. & screpolàrsi, v.refl. to split; crack. screpolàto, a. cracked; chapped (hands). screpolatúra, f. & scrèpolo, m. crack; fissure.

screziàto, a. variegated; speckled. scrèzio, m. variegation; (fig.) variance; difference; disagreement.

scríba (pl. scríbi), m. scribe; copyist. scribacchiàre, v.t. to scribble. scribacchiatóre & scribacchíno, m. scribbler.

scricchiolàre, v.i. to creak; grate.

scrícciolo, m. wren (bird).

scrígno, m. strong-box; money-box; jewel-case.

scriminatúra, f. parting (of the hair).

scrímolo, m. (extreme) edge.

scrítta, f. writing; inscription; notice; poster; written contract. scrítto, p.p. of scrivere. ¶ m. [piece of] writing; written document; hand-writing; (pl.) literary works; writings. scrittóio, m. writing-desk; study. scrittóre, m. scrittríce, f. writer; author; authoress. scrittorèllo, m. scribbler. scrittúra, f. writing; hand(writing); deed; entry (Bkkpg.); engagement (Theat.). ~ a macchina, typewriting. scritturàbile, a. (Bkkpg.) suitable for entry. (Theat.) suitable for engagement. scritturàle, m. clerk; bookkeeper; copyist. ¶ a. scriptural. scritturàre, v.t. (Bkkpg.) to enter; (Theat.) to engage.

scrivanía, f. writing-desk. scrivàno, m. clerk; copyist.

scrívere, v.t. & abs. ir. to write.

scroccàre, v.t. to scrounge. scroccatóre & scroccóne, m. sponger; scrounger.

scrocchiàre, v.i. (aux. avere) to creak.

scròcco, m. sponging; scrounging; creaking.

scròfa, f. sow. scròfola, f. scrofula. scrofolóso, a. scrofulous.

scrollaménto, m. shaking; tossing; shrugging. scrollàre, v.t. to shake; toss; shrug (shoulders). scrollàta, f. shake; toss; shrug. scròllo, m. shake; shaking; vibration.

scrosciàre, v.i. (aux. essere & avere) to pelt (rain); roar; hiss; pioggia

scrosciante, f. pelting rain. scròscio, m. heavy shower (rain); roar; storm (fig.); (out)burst; clap; thunder (fig.).

scrostàre, v.t. to remove the crust from; peel; strip; chip off (plaster, &c.).

scrúpolo, m. scruple; qualm. scrupolóso, a. scrupulous.

scrutaménto, m. scrutiny; search; investigation. scrutàre, v.t. to scrutinize; search; pry into; peer into; investigate. scrutatóre, m. investigator; scrutineer (of votes). ¶ a. (f. -tríce) inquisitive, searching, closely observant.

scrutinàre, v.t. to scrutinize. scrutinatóre, m. scrutinizer. scrutínio, m. poll; ballot; voting; vote; (Sch.) addition of marks.

scucíre (pr. scúcio, scúci), v.t. ir. to unstitch; take down (piece of sewing, &c.).

scudería, f. stable (esp. racing & royal). scudière & scudièro, m. groom. scudisciàre, v.t. to whip; lash. scudisciàta, f. whipping. scudíscio, m. switch, whip (riding).

scúdo, m. shield; (fig.) defence; defender; (Her.) escutcheon.

scúffia, f. cap.

scuiacciàre, v.t. to spank.

scultóre, m. sculptor; carver. scultrice, f. sculptress; woman sculptor. scultúra, f. sculpture; carving.

sc[u]oiàre, v.t. to skin; flay.

scuòla, f.d. school; schoolroom; class-room; class.

scuòtere, v.t. ir. to shake; shake off; shake up; shrug (shoulders); agitate; stir; move; assail; rouse; excite; disregard; weaken; impair. scuotiménto, see scotimento.

scúre, f. axe; hatchet. scurétto, a. rather dark. ¶ m. small axe; small shutter; inner shutter.

scuríre (pr. -íscc, -ísci), v.t. to darken; obscure; tone down; (v.i.) (aux. essere) & scurirsi, v.refl. to grow dark. scúro, a. dark; deep (colour); dim; obscure; gloomy. ¶ m. dark; darkness; shaded part of a picture; (window) shutter.

scurríle, a. scurrilous. scurrilità, f. scurrility.

scúsa, f. apology; excuse; pretext. scusàbile, a. excusable. scusàre, v.t. to excuse; pardon; forgive; justify. scusàrsi, v.refl. to apologize; excuse oneself; justify oneself.

scússo, *a.* plain; bare.

sdaziaménto, *m.* clearing (*customs*). sdaziàre, *v.t.* to clear (*or* pass) through the customs.

sdebitàrsi, *v.refl.* to get out of debt; pay off one's debt[s]; discharge one's obligations.

sdegnàre, *v.t.* to disdain; scorn; refuse; take a loathing for (*food*); irritate; enrage. sdegnàrsi, *v.refl.* to get angry; be offended; refuse. sdégno, *m.* indignation; anger; scorn; disdain; contempt; (*pl.*) moments of irritation; bursts of scorn or indignation. sdegnóso, *a.* scornful; haughty; indignant.

sdentàto, *a.* toothless.

sdiacciàre, *v.t.* to thaw.

sdilinquiménto, *m.* swoon; fainting-fit; (*fig.*) lackadaisicalness; false sentiment. sdilinquíre (*pr.* -ísco, -ísci), *v.t.* to weaken. *v.i.* (*aux.* essere) & sdilinquírsi, *v.refl.* to swoon; faint; droop; (*fig.*) become foolishly sentimental.

sdoganàre, *v.t.* to clear through the customs.

sdolcinàto, *a.* mawkish; sickly-sweet; affected. ¶ *m.* mealy-mouthed person.

sdoppiàre, *v.t.* to uncouple. ~ le *consonanti*, to use one consonant in place of two.

sdraiàre, *v.t.* to stretch out (or lay out) at full length. sdraiàrsi, *v.refl.* to lie down; stretch oneself out. sdràio, *m.* lying down; relaxed position. *sedia a* ~, *f.* deck-chair.

sdrucciolàre, *v.i.* (*aux.* essere & avere) to slip; slide. sdrucciolévole, *a.* slippery; sliding. *verso* ~, line accented on the third last syllable. *parola* ~*a*, word accented on third last syllable. ¶ *m.* slippery spot; slide; steep slope.

sdrúcio, *m.* tear, rent, rip. sdrucíre (*pr.* sdrucísco & sdrúcio, sdrucísci, sdrucísce & sdrúce), *v.t.* to tear, rend; rip (up); unstitch. sdrucíto, *a.* worn out; rent; thread-bare; unstitched. *barca* ~*a*, crazy boat. sdrucitúra, *f.* unstitching; rent; rip.

se, *c.* if, whether; what if, suppose. ~ *il tempo lo permetterà*, weather permitting. *anche* ~, even if, even though. *come* ~, as if. ~ *no*, otherwise; or else; if not. ~ *non altro*, at least.

sé, *pn. refl. disjunct.* (gen. after a preposition) oneself; himself; her-

self; itself; themselves. *L'Italia farà da* ~, Italy will act by herself. *ognuno per* ~, everyone for himself.

se, *pn. refl. conjunct.* (for *si*, before *lo*, *la*, *li*, *le*, *ne*) E.g. *si dice*, but *se la dice*, &c.

sebbène, *c.* though; although.

secàre, *v.t.* to cut.

sécca (*pl.* sécche), *f.* shoal; sandbank; (*fig. oft. pl.*) difficulty; embarrassment.

seccàggine, *f.* dryness; (*fig.*) weariness; trouble; annoyance. seccaménte, *ad.* drily; (*fig.*) abruptly; bluntly. seccaménto, *m.* drying (up); (*fig.*) annoyance. seccànte, *a.* tiresome; boring; troublesome. seccàre, *v.t.* to dry; dry up; wither; weary; bore; annoy. seccatóio, *m.* drying-room. seccatóre, *m.* (*f.* -tríce) bore. seccatúra, *f.* drying (*esp. of chestnuts*); annoyance; nuisance. secchézza, *f.* dryness; (*fig.*) thinness; stiffness.

sécchia (*pl.* sécchie), *f.* pail; bucket. secchiàta, *f.* bucketful. sécchio (*pl.* sécchi), *m.* pail, bucket. ~ *per carbone*, coal scuttle. dims. *secchiello, secchierella, secchietto, secchina, secchiolina, secchiolino*, &c.

sécco (*pl.* sécchi), *a.* dry; dried; withered; wizened; parched; thin; spare; gaunt; lean; curt; bald (*style*, &c.); stiff. ¶ *m.* dryness; dry portion; dry place; dry ground; dry weather. ¶ *ad.* drily; (*answer*) coldly. *dare in* ~, to run aground. *lasciare in* ~, to leave in the lurch. *rimanere al* ~, to be left penniless. seccúme, *m.* dry things (*coll., esp. branches and leaves*).

scentèsimo, *a. num. ord.* six-hundredth. scentísmo, *m.* 17th century mannerism of style. scentísta, *m.* writer or artist of the 17th century.

secèrnere, *v.t. ir.* to secrete.

secessióne, *f.* secession.

séco, *pr. comp.* (*Lat.* secum) with him; with her; with them.

secolàre, *a.* secular (*clergy,* &c.); age-long; time-honoured; lay; laic; worldly (*life*). ¶ *m.* layman; (*pl.*) laity. secolarésco (*pl.* -éschi), *a.* secular; worldly. secolarizzàre, *v.t.* to secularize. sècolo, *m.* century; age; era; secular life; world.

secónda, *f.* after-birth; (*Mus.*) second; (*Rly.*) second class. ¶ *ad.* well, favourably. *andare a* ~, to go well.

secondàre, *v.t.* to support; back-up;

gratify; favour; follow; indulge. **secondàrio**, *a.* secondary; minor; side *(att.).* *linea* ~*a*, branch line *(Rly.).* **secóndo**, *a.* second *(ord. num.)*; favourable; propitious. ~*a galleria*, upper circle *(Theat.).* ¶ *m.* second *(time, duel, &c.).* ¶ *ad.* in the second place. ¶ *pr.* according to. [è] ~*!* it depends (on circumstances)! **secondogènito**, *a.* secondborn. ¶ *m.* second son.

secrèto, *p.p.* of *secernere.* ¶ *m.* *(Physiol.)* secretion.

secrezióne, *f.* secretion.

sèdano, *m.* celery.

sedàre, *v.t.* to assuage; allay; appease; calm; put down *(rebellion, &c.).* **sedatívo**, *a. & m.* sedative.

sède, *f.* seat *(lit. & fig.)* residence; office. *Santa S*~, Holy See. ~ *sociale*, office of a company.

sedentàrio, *a.* sedentary.

sedére *(pr.* **sièdo** *&* **sèggo**, **sièdi**, **sième**), *v.i. ir. (aux.* avere) to sit; sit down; be situated. ¶ *m.* sitting (down); backside; posterior; seat *(of chair).* **sedérsi**, *v.refl.* to sit down; take a seat. **sederíno**, *m.* small folding seat *(carriage, &c.).* **sèdia**, *f.* chair; seat. ~ *a dondolo*, rockingchair. ~ *a sdraio*, deck chair. ~ *pieghevole*, camp stool.

sedicènne, *a.* sixteen years old.

sedicènte, *a.* self-styled; would-be.

sedicèsimo, *a. num. ord.* sixteenth.

sédici, *a. & m.* sixteen; 16th.

sedíle, *m.* seat; chair; bench.

sediménto, *m.* sediment, deposit.

sedizióne, *f.* sedition. **sedizióso**, *a.* seditious.

sedótto, *p.p.* of *sedurre.* **sedúrre** *(pr.* **-dúco**, **-dúci**, *&c.),* *v.t. ir.* to seduce; entice; please; (al)lure; corrupt; charm.

sedúta, *f.* sitting; meeting. ~ *segreta*, *(Parl.)* secret session.

seduttóre, *m.(f.* **-tríce)**;tempter (-tress, *f.);* seducer. **seduzióne**, *f.* seduction; temptation; allurement; charm.

séga *(pl.* **séghe***), f.* saw. ~ *per metalli*, hack saw. ~ *a nastra*, ~ *a lama continua*, belt saw, band s. ~ *a macchina*, frame s. ~ *da traforo*, fret s.

ségala, *or* **ségale**, *f.* rye.

segantíno, *m.* sawyer. **segàre**, *v.t.* to saw; saw off; mow; reap; cut; cut off; *(Math.)* intersect; open *(vein).* **segatóre**, *m.* mower. **segatúra**, *f.* mowing; mowing time; sawing; sawdust.

sèggio, *m.* seat; chair *(official);* *(Eccl.)* see; *(cathedral)* stall; *(fig.)* place; office; authority. **sèggiola**, *f.* chair. **seggiolàio**, *m.* chair-maker or mender. **seggiolína**, *f.*, *-íno*, *m.* child's chair. **seggiolóne**, *m.* large chair; arm-chair; easy chair.

seghería, *f.* saw-mill. **seghétta**, *f.* small saw; fret(work)-saw. **seghettàto**, *a.* notched; serrated.

segnacàrte, *m.inv. &* **segnalibro** *(pl.* **-líbri)**, *m.* book-marker; bookmark.

segnàcolo, *m.* mark; sign.

segnalàre, *v.t.* to signalize; point out; notify; signal. **segnalàrsi**, *v.refl.* to distinguish oneself. **segnalataménte**, *ad.* markedly; notably; eminently. **segnalatóre**, *m.* *(Nav.)* signaller; *(Rly.)* signalman. **segnalazióne**, *f.* signalling; signal. *cabina di* ~, signal-box. ~*i luminose*, traffic lights. **segnàle**, *m.* signal; sign; token; omen. ~ *orario*, time signal *(Radio).* ~ *indicatore*, sign post; fingerpost. ~ *di traffico*, traffic sign[al].

segnàre, *v.t.* to mark; note; note down; enter *(on a register);* indicate; show; trace; mark out; draw; sign; scratch; *(game)* score. ~ *il passo*, *(Mil.)* to mark time. **segnàrsi**, *v.refl.* to cross oneself; make the sign of the cross. **segnataménte**, *ad.* especially; chiefly. **segnatàsse**, *m.inv.* post-office mark on unstamped or insufficiently stamped letter. **segnatàrio**, *a. & m.* signatory. **segnatóre**, *m.* marker; scorer; indicator. **segnatúra**, *f.* marking; stamp; *(Typ.)* signature.

ségno, *m.* sign; mark; token; target; motion; wave *(hand);* bull's eye; aim; trace; track; vestige; signal; standard; degree; measure; spot; symbol.

ségo *(pl.* **séghi***), m.* tallow; suet. **segóso**, *a.* fatty, rich.

segóne, *m.* large saw; pit-saw.

segregàre *(pr.* **sègrego**, **sègreghi***),* *v.t.* to segregate; isolate. **segregàrsi**, *v.refl.* to withdraw. **segregazióne**, *f.* segregation; seclusion. ~ *cellulare*, solitary confinement.

segretariàto, *m.* secretariat(e); secretaryship. **segretàrio**, *m.* secretary; amanuensis; secretary bird. ~ *comunale*, town clerk. ~ *particolare*, private secretary. **segretària**, *f.* lady secretary. **segretería**, *f.* secretary's office; secretarial staff.

segretézza, *f.* secrecy. **segréto,** *a.* & *m.* secret.

seguàce, *m.f.* follower; adherent; supporter.

seguènte, *a.* following; next; ensuing. **seguènza,** *f.* sequence.

segúgio, *m.* bloodhound.

seguíre (*pr.* séguo, ségui), *v.t.* & *abs.* to follow; accompany; imitate; obey; keep; continue; ensue; result.

seguitaménte, *ad.* consecutively. **seguitàre,** *v.i.* to go on; keep on; continue.

seguito, *p.p.* of *seguire.* **séguito,** *m.* sequence; series; succession; run; sequel; continuation; consequence; suite; train; attendants; retinue; set. *andare in ~,* to run on (*in series*). *il ~ al prossimo numero,* to be continued in our next.

sèi, *a.* & *m.* six; 6th. **seicènto,** *a. num. card. inv.* six hundred. *il S~,* the 17th century. **seimíla,** *a. num. inv.* six thousand.

sélce (*pl.* sélci), *f.* flint. **selciàio** & **selciatóre,** *m.* paver; pavior. **selciàre,** *v.t.* to pave. **selciàto,** *m.* pavement, paved street.

seleníte, *f.* selenite.

selettívo, *a.* selective. **selezionàre,** *v.t.* to select (*sport,* &*c.*). **selezióne,** *f.* selection.

sèlla, *f.* saddle. **sellàio,** *m.* saddler. **sellàre,** *v.t.* to saddle. **sellàto,** *a.* saddle-backed. **sellería,** *f.* saddlery; harness-room; saddler's shop.

sèltz (acqua di), *f.* seltzer-water; soda-water.

sélva, *f.* wood; forest.

selvaggiaménte, *ad.* rudely; furiously; savagely. **selvaggína,** *f.* game (*hunt*). **selvàggio,** *a.* wild; savage; brutal; uncivilized. ¶ *m.* savage.

selvàtico (*pl.* -àtici), *a.* wild; uncultivated; untamed; unsociable.

selvóso, *a.* wooded; woody.

semàforo, *m.* traffic-lights; semaphore.

semàntica, *f.* semantics.

sembiànte, *m.* semblance; appearance; aspect; mien. *far ~ di,* to pretend. **sembiànza,** *f.* look; countenance; aspect; (*pl.*) features. **sembràre,** *v.t.* & *i.* (*aux.* essere) to seem; appear; look like; sound like; taste like; feel like.

séme, *m.* seed (*lit.* & *fig.*); germ; origin; cause; source; race; breed; suit (*cards*). **seménta,** *f.* sowing; seed-time; seed. **sementàre,** *v.t.* to sow. **seménte,** *f.* seed (*for sowing*). **semènza,** *f.* seed; (*fig.*) origin; descent; race; progeny; offspring. **semenzàio,** *m.* seed-plot (*lit.* & *fig.*); seed-merchant.

semenzíre & **sementíre** (*pr.* -ísco, -ísci), *v.i.* (*aux.* essere) to run to seed; go to seed.

semestràle, *a.* half-yearly. **semèstre,** *m.* half-year, six months.

semi, *prefix. compounds with* semi-half-, semi-, demi-, *are numerous but are self-explanatory, except in a few cases, most of which are given below.* **semibiscròma,** *f.* (*Mus.*) demisemiquaver. **semicròma,** *f.* semiquaver. **semicúpio,** *m.* hipbath. **semidiàpason,** *m.* (*Mus.*) diminished octave. **semidiapènte,** *m.* (*Mus.*) minor fifth. **semidío** (*pl.* semidèi), *m.* demigod. **semidítono,** *m.* (*Mus.*) minor third. **semifinàle,** *a.* & *f.* (*Sport*) semifinal. **semifinalísta** (*pl.* -ísti), *m.* semifinalist. **semiminíma,** *f.* (*Mus.*) crotchet.

sémina, *f.* sowing; seed; seed-time. **seminagióne,** *f.* sowing; seed-time. **seminàre,** *v.t.* to sow (*lit.* & *fig.*); scatter; spread; disseminate.

semínario, *m.* seminary. **seminaríssta** (*pl.* -ísti), *m.* seminarist.

seminàto, *m.* ground that has been sown. *uscire dal ~,* to digress; wander from the subject. **seminatòio,** *m.* seed-drill. **seminatóre,** *m.* sower. **seminatríce,** *f.* sower; (*Mech.*) seeding-machine. **seminatúra,** *f.* sowing.

semisfèra, *f.* hemisphere.

semíta (*pl.* -iti), *m.* Semite. **semítico** (*pl.* -ítici), *a.* Semitic.

semivívo, *a.* half-dead, between life and death.

semivólo, *m.* (*Ten.*) half-volley.

sémola, *f.* bran; fine flour; (*pl.*) freckles.

semovènte, *a.* self-moving; self-propelled; automatic. *cannone ~, m.* self-propelled gun.

Sempióne (il), *m.* the Simplon Pass.

sempitèrno, *a.* everlasting.

sémplice, *a.* simple; single; ordinary; private (*soldier*); plain; homely; mere; simple(-minded); unsophisticated. **sémplici,** *m.pl.* medicinal herbs; simples. **sempliscióne,** *m.* simple good-natured man. **sempliciòtto,** *m.* simpleton. **semplicísta,** *m.* herbalist. **semplicità,** *f.* simplicity. **semplificàre,** *v.t.* to simplify. **semplificazióne,** *f.* simplification.

sèmpre, *ad.* always. *per ~,* for ever; for good and all. *~ che & sempreché,* provided that. *~ più,* more and more. **semprevérde,** *a. & m.* evergreen. **sempreviva,** *f.* everlasting (*plant* or *flower*).

sèna or **sènna,** *f.* senna (*Bot.*).

sènapa & **sènape,** *f.* mustard. **senapièra,** *f.* mustard-pot. **senapismo,** *m.* mustard plaster; mustard poultice.

senàrio, *m.* (verse) line of six syllables.

senàto, *m.* senate. **senatoràto,** *m.* senatorship. **senatóre,** *m.* senator.

senése, *a. m. f.* Sienese, of Siena.

senile, *a.* senile. **senilità,** *f.* senility.

senióre, *a. & m.* senior; elder; older.

Sènna, *f.* Seine.

sénno, *m.* (good) sense; judgement; wisdom.

séno, *m.* bosom; breast; (*Geog.*) inlet; bay; cove; (*Math.*) sine.

Senofónte, *m.* Xenophon.

senofobía, *f.* xenophobia, hatred of foreigners. **senòfobo,** *m.* xenophobe.

sensàle, *m.* broker; middleman. *~ di effetti, ~ di cambiali,* bill-broker. *~ di fondi pubblici e titoli di credito,* stock & share broker. *~ marittimo,* ship-broker.

sensataménte, *ad.* sensibly; judiciously. **sensatézza,** *f.* good sense; prudence; judgement. **sensàto,** *a.* sensible; prudent; judicious.

sensazionàle, *a.* sensational; thrilling; exciting. **sensazióne,** *f.* sensation; feel(ing); sense.

sensería, *f.* brokerage; agency.

sensibile, *a.* sensitive; susceptible; responsive; sensible; alive; sentient; sensitized (*Phot.*); tender; sore; appreciable; palpable; perceptible. **sensibilità,** *f.* sensitiveness; feeling; sensitivity (*Phot. Chem. &c.*). **sensibilizzàre,** *v.t.* (*Phot.*) to sensitize. **sensibilménte,** *ad.* appreciably; considerably. **sensitiva,** *f.* sensitiveness; (*Bot.*) sensitive plant. **sensitívo,** *a.* sensitive; sensory. **sènso,** *m.* sense; sensation; feeling; sentiment; judgement; understanding; meaning; import; direction; way. *buon ~,* good sense, common s.; sense. *in ~ giusto,* in the right direction. *in ogni ~,* in every direction. *una strada a ~*

unico, a one-way street. *circolazione in ~ unico,* one-way traffic.

sensòrio, *a.* sensory. **sensuàle,** *a.* sensual. **sensualità,** *f.* sensuality; voluptuousness.

sentènza, *f.* opinion; maxim; pronouncement; (*Law*) sentence; judg[e]ment ; award; decree; decision. **sentenziàre,** *v.t.* to judge; sentence; decide. *v.i.* (*aux.* avere) to talk sententiously. **sentenzióso,** *a.* sententious.

sentièro, *m.* footpath; path; track.

sentimentàle, *a.* sentimental. **sentimentalità,** *f.* sentimentality.

sentiménto, *m.* feeling; sentiment; opinion.

sentína, *f.* bilge; (*fig.*) sink.

sentinèlla, *f.* sentry; sentinel; guard; watch.

sentíre (*pr.* **sènto, sènti**), *v.t. & abs.* to feel; hear; learn; be conscious of; smell; scent; taste; taste of; smell of; smack of; be redolent of. **sentirsi,** *v.refl.* to feel. **sentitaménte,** *ad.* cordially; heartily; deeply. **sentíto,** *a.* heartfelt; cordial; sincere; strong; deep. *per ~ dire,* by hearsay.

sentóre, *m.* smell; scent; odour; sense; feeling; inkling; sign.

sènza, *pr.* without.

senziènte, *a.* sentient.

separàre (*pr.* **separo, separi**), *v.t.* to separate; sever; divide. **separàrsi** *v.refl.* to separate; part; part company. **separazióne,** *f.* separation; parting; severance.

sepolcràle, *a.* sepulchral. **sepolcréto,** *m.* cemetery. **sepólcro,** *m.* sepulchre; tomb; grave. **sepoltúra,** *f.* burial; burial-place; tomb.

seppelliménto, *m.* interment; burial. **seppellíre** (*pr.* **-ísco, -ísci**), *v.t.* to bury; inter; (*fig.*) to cover; hide. **seppellitóre,** *m.* grave-digger.

séppia, *f.* cuttle-fish; sepia.

sèpsi, *f.* sepsis (*Med.*).

sequèla, *f.* succession; sequence. **sequènza,** *f.* sequence; run (*cards, &c.*).

sequestraménto, *m.* (*Law*) distraining; seizing. **sequestràre,** *v.t.* (*Law*) to distrain; seize; attach; sequestrate; (*fig.*) isolate; seclude. **sequèstro,** *m.* (*Law*) distraint; sequestration; embargo.

séra, *f.* evening; night.

seràfico (*pl.* **-àfici**), *a.* seraphic. **serafíno,** *m.* seraph. **seràle,** *a.* evening (*att.*). **seralménte,** *ad.* every evening. **seràta,** *f.* evening;

evening-party; (*Theat.*) evening performance. ~ *di onore*, benefit night.

serbàre, *v.t.* to keep; put aside; reserve; save up; preserve. **serbatóio**, *m.* reservoir; tank. **sèrbo**, *m.* keeping; custody; reserve. *mettere in* ~, to put by.

serenàta, *f.* serenade. **seneníssimo**, *a. & m.* (*title*) Serene Highness. **serenità**, *f.* calm[ness], serenity. **seréno**, *a.* bright; clear; unclouded; calm; tranquil; dispassionate. ¶ *m.* clear sky. *al* ~, in the open air.

sergènte, *m.* sergeant. *allievo* ~, lance-sergeant.

seriaménte, *ad.* seriously; earnestly; gravely; heavily.

sèrico (*pl.* **sèrici**), *a.* silk (*att.*); silky. **sericultóre**, *m.* breeder of silk-worms. **sericultúra**, *f.* silk-worm breeding; silk industry.

sèrie, *f.inv.* series; succession; range; set; chapter (*accidents*).

serietà, *f.* seriousness; gravity; trust-worthiness. **sèrio**, *a.* serious; grave; responsible; genuine; bonafide. **seriocòmico** (*pl.* **-còmici**), *a.* serio-comic.

sermoncíno, *m.* short sermon; (*fig.*) rebuke; reprimand. **sermóne**, *m.* weighty discourse; sermon; (*fig.*) admonition; lecture (*scolding*). **sermoneggiàre**, *v.i.* (*aux.* avere) to sermonize; preach.

seròtino, *a.* (*Lit.*) late; tardy.

serpàro, *m.* snake-charmer. **sèrpe**, *m.* serpent; snake. **serpeggiànte**, *a.* winding; meandering. **serpeggiàre**, *v.i.* (*aux.* avere) to wind; creep; meander. **serpènte**, *m.* serpent; snake. dim. *serpentello.*

serpentína, *f.* serpentine (*Geol.*). **serpentíno**, *a.* serpentine; snake-like; tortuous; sinuous. ¶ worm (*still*, *&c.*).

serpígine, *f.* (*Med.*) ringworm.

sérqua, *f.* dozen (*eggs, nuts, &c.*); lot, lots.

sèrra, *f.* greenhouse, glass-house, conservatory; dyke; mountain chain (*Sp. Sierra*); waistband; crowd. *fiore di* ~, *m.* hothouse plant (*fig.*). ~ *per viti*, vinery. ~ *per palme*, palm house.

serràglio, *m.* wild beasts' cage; menagerie; harem; seraglio; (*Arch.*) keystone.

serràme, *m.* lock; fastening. **serraménto**, *m.* locking; tightening; clenching (*fist*). **serràre**, *v.t.* to

lock; lock up; shut; close; close up; squeeze; clench (*fist*); hold tightly. **serràrsi**, *v.refl.* to stand close; close up. **serràta**, *f.* lock-out. **serràto**, *a.* close; compact; concise; serried; swift. **serratúra**, *f.* lock. ~ *di sicurezza*, safety lock. ~ *a doppia mandata*, double lock.

Sèrse, *m.* Xerxes.

sèrto, *m.* (*Lit.*) garland; wreath.

sèrva, *f.* maid-servant. **servàggio**, *m.* bondage; serfdom; slavery. **servènte**, *a.* serving; (in-)waiting. ¶ *m.* servent; lay brother; gunner; server (*Ten.*). **servígio**, sec *servizio*.

servíle, *a.* servile. **servilità**, *f.* servility.

servíre (*pr.* **sèrvo, sèrvi**), *v.t. & abs.* to serve; be of use; wait (on); attend to; serve up. **servirsi (di)**, *v.refl.* to use; make use (of); help oneself (*at table*). ~ *da*, to deal with (*tradesman*). **servitóre**, *m.* servant. **servitú**, *f.* servitude; slavery; servants (*col.*); easement (*Law*). ~ *di passaggio*, right of way (*Law*).

serviziàle, *m.* enema (*Med.*). **serviziévole**, *a.* serviceable; obliging. **servízio**, *m.* service; favour; kindness; worship; serve, service (*tennis*); employ[ment]; supply; running; department; duty; attendance, waiting (*hotel*, *&c.*); set (*dishes, utensils*). ~ *da tavola*, dinner-service, dinner-set. ~ *da tè*, tea service, tea-set. *scala di* ~, back stairs. ~ *diretto*, through service (*Rly.*).

sèrvo, *m.* servant; man-servant; slave. ~ *muto*, dumb-waiter.

sèsamo, *m.* sesame (*Bot.*). *apriti, s~!* open sesame!

sessagenàrio, *a.* sixty years old. ¶ *m.* sexagenarian.

sessagèsima, *f.* Sexagesima Sunday. **sessagèsimo**, *a. num. ord.* sixtieth.

sessànta, *num. card. inv.* sixty. **sessantènne**, *a.* sixty years old. ¶ *m.* sexagenarian. **sessantèsimo**, *a. num. ord.* sixtieth. **sessantína**, *f.* three score, about sixty. **sessènne**, *a.* six years old. **sessènnio**, *m.* (*period*) six years.

sessióne, *f.* session.

sèsso, *m.* sex. **sessuàle**, *a.* sexual.

sèsta, *f.* (*Mus.*) sixth; (*fencing*) sixte; leg of a compass. *f.pl.* pair of compasses.

sestànte, *m.* sextant.

sestétto, *m.* (*Mus.*) sextet. **sestína**, *f.* six line stanza. **sèsto**, *a. num. ord.*

sixth. ¶ *m.* good order; right size (or shape); sixth part; (*Typ.*) format; (*Arch.*) rib of vault, curvature of an arch. **sestodècimo**, *a. num. ord.* sixteenth. **sèstuplo**, *a.* sixfold.

séta, *f.* silk. ~ *greggia*, raw silk. ~ *vegetale*, artificial silk. *commercio della* ~, silk trade. **setàccio**, *m.* sieve. **setàceo**, *a.* silky. **setai[u]òlo**, *m.* silk merchant; silk weaver.

séte, *f.* thirst (*lit. & fig.*); drought.

seteria, *f.* silk(s); silk factory; silk mill; (*pl.*) silk-goods. **setifício**, *m.* silk-mill; silk-factory.

sétola, *f.* bristle; coarse hair; chap; crack in the skin. **setolíno**, *m.* hat-brush; whisk. **setolóso**, *a.* bristly.

sètta, *f.* sect; faction.

settàgono, *m.* heptagon.

settànta, *a. & m. inv.* seventy. **settantènne**, *a.* seventy years old. ¶ *m.f.* septuagenarian. **settantèsimo**, *a. num. ord.* seventieth. **settantína**, *f.* (number of) about seventy; age of seventy.

settàrio, *a. & m.* sectarian. **settatóre**, *m.* (*Lit.*) partisan; follower.

sètte, *a. & m. inv.* seven; 7th. **settecentèsimo**, *a. num. ord.* seven hundredth. **settecènto**, *num. card. inv.* seven hundred. *il S* ~, the 18th century. **settecentésco** (*pl.* -éschi), *a.* 18th century (*att.*).

settèmbre, *m.* September. **settembríno**, *a.* of September; September (*att.*). *vino* ~, poor wine.

settèmplice, *a.* sevenfold.

settenàrio, *m.* verse (line) of seven syllables; period of seven days or seven years. **settennàle**, *a.* septennial. **settènne**, *a.* seven years old. **settènnio**, *m.* period of seven years.

settentrionàle, *a.* north; northern; northerly. ¶ *m.* northerner. **settentrióne**, *m.* north.

setticemía, *f.* (*Med.*) septicaemia.

sèttico (*pl.* **sèttici**), *a.* septic.

settimàna, *f.* week. **settimanàle**, *a.* weekly. ¶ *m.* weekly, weekly journal; week's pay. **settimanálménte**, *ad.* weekly; by the week.

sèttimo, *a. num. ord.* seventh.

sètto, *m.* (*Anat.*) septum.

settóre, *m.* sector; area.

settuagenàrio, *a. & m.* septuagenarian. **settuagèsimo**, *a. num. ord.* seventieth.

sèttuplo, *a.* sevenfold.

severità, *f.* severity; harshness.

sevèro, *a.* severe; strict; austere; stern; rigid; harsh; rough.

sevízia, *f.* (*oft. pl.* **sevízie**) cruelty.

sezionaménto, *m.* (*Anat.*) dissection.

sezionàre, *v.t.* (*Anat.*) to dissect.

sezióne, *f.* section; division; department; side (*school*); group; (*Anat.*) dissection.

sfaccendàre, *v.i.* (*aux.* avere) to be busy; bustle about. **sfaccendàto**, *a.* idle; unoccupied. ¶ *m.* loafer; idler.

sfaccettàre, *v.t.* to facet; cut facets on.

sfacchinàre, *v.i.* (*aux.* avere) to drudge; toil; work hard. **sfacchinàta**, *f.* heavy piece of work.

sfacciatàggine, *f.* impudence; effrontery. **sfacciàto**, *a.* impudent; shameless; loud (*colour*); dazzling (*light*).

sfacèlo, *m.* breakdown; ruin; collapse.

sfaciménto, *m.* decay; ruin; weakening; undoing.

sfàlda, *f.* flake; layer; scale. **sfaldàre**, *v.t.* to cut into slices; scale. **sfaldàrsi**, *v.refl.* to flake off; come off in flakes or layers; exfoliate. **sfaldatúra**, *f.* flaking (off); scaling.

sfamàre, *v.t.* to appease (*hunger*); satisfy. **sfamàrsi**, *v.refl.* to appease one's hunger.

sfangàre, *v.i.* (*aux.* avere) to tramp through mud. *v.t.* to clean the mud off; get out of the mud; (*fig.*) get out of difficulties.

sfàre (*pr.* **sfàccio** *cr* **sfò**, *&c.*, like *fare*), *v.t. ir.* to undo; dissolve; melt; take apart. **sfàrsi**, *v.refl.* to weaken; decompose. ~ *di*, to get rid of.

sfarfallàre, *v.i.* to emerge from the cocoon; burst from the bud; (*fig.*) flutter about; talk nonsense.

sfarinàrsi, *v.refl.* to crumble.

sfàrzo, *m.* pomp; magnificence; idle display. **sfarzosità**, *f.* ostentation; foolish pomp. **sfarzóso**, *a.* sumptuous; gorgeous; pompous.

sfasciaménto, *m.* unwrapping; dismantling; unbinding; ruin; collapse. **sfasciàre**, *v.t.* to unbind; undo; dismantle; demolish. **sfasciàrsi**, *v.refl.* to break down; collapse; become undone.

sfasciúme, *m.* litter; rubbish; ruin(s); wreck (*fig.*).

sfataménto, *m.* discrediting; exposure. **sfatàre**, *v.t.* to discredit; expose; unmask; deprive of charm or prestige.

sfàtto, *a.* undone; unmade; ruined; flabby; overcooked.

sfavillaménto, *m.* sparkle; glitter; brilliance. **sfavillàre**, *v.i.* (*aux.*

avere *or* essère) to sparkle; glitter.
sfavillío, *m.* sparkling; glittering; flashing.
sfavóre, *m.* disfavour; disapproval.
sfavorévole, *a.* unfavourable; adverse; contrary. **sfavoríre** (*pr.* -ísco, -ísci), *v.t.* to disapprove; discourage; oppose; treat unfairly.
sfebbràto, *a.* free from fever.
sfegatàrsi, *v.refl.* to bawl; shout; get in(to) a rage; wear oneself out. **sfegatàto**, *a.* passionate; devoted. ¶ *m.* hothead.
sfèra, *f.* sphere; orb; globe; circle. *un cuscinetto a* ～*e*, ball bearings (*Mech.*). **sfèrico** (*pl.* **sferici**), *a.* spherical.
sferràre, *v.t.* to unshoe (*horse*); free a prisoner from irons; draw a weapon from a wound; deliver (*attack*); plant (*kick*).
sfèrza, *f.* whip; lash; scourge. **sferzàre**, *v.t.* to whip; lash; thrash; flog; scourge. **sferzàta**, *f.* cut with a whip; thrashing; (*fig.*) sharp rebuke.
sfiaccolàto, *a.* worn out; jaded; feeble.
sfiancàre, *v.t.* to wear out; overwork; knock up. *v.i.* to give way; cave in; (*Anat.*) burst. **sfiancàrsi**, *v.refl.* to overwork oneself; tire oneself (out).
sfiatàre, *v.i.* (*aux.* avere) to exhale. *v.i.* (*aux.* essere) escape; leak (*gas, air*). **sfiatàrsi**, *v.refl.* to become breathless (*by shouting, talking*). **sfiatàto**, *a.* breathless; out of breath. **sfiatotóio**, *m.* vent; air-hole.
sfibbiàre, *v.t.* to unclasp; unbuckle; unfasten; (*fig.*) let fly (*insults, &c.*).
sfibràre, *v.t.* to weaken; enervate; unnerve.
sfída, *f.* challenge; defiance. **sfidànte** & **sfidatóre**, *m.* challenger. **sfidàre**, *v.t.* to defy; challenge; dare; face; brave; (*abs.*) be confident. *Sfido io!* to be sure! of course!
sfidúcia, *f.* mistrust; distrust; lack of confidence. **sfiduciàre**, *v.t.* to discourage; dishearten.
sfiguràre, *v.t.* to disfigure. *v.i.* (*aux.* avere) to cut a poor figure.
sfilacciàre, *v.t.* to fray out; unravel.
sfilàre, *v.t.* to unthread; unstring; unhitch; slip off. *v.i.* (*aux.* essere & avere) to march past; file off. **sfilàta**, *f.* march past; row (*vehicles*).
sfínge, *f.* sphinx.
sfiniménto, *m.* great weakness; exhaustion. **sfiníre** (*pr.* -ísco, -ísci), *v.t.* to exhaust; wear out.

v.i. (*aux.* essere) swoon; faint.
sfinírsi, *v.refl.* to become exhausted; swoon; faint.
sfintère, *m.* (*Anat.*) sphincter.
sfioràre, *v.t.* to graze; touch lightly; caress; touch upon; skim over.
sfioríre (*pr.* -ísco, -ísci), *v.i.* (*aux.* essere) to fade.
sfissàre, *v.t.* to cancel (*an agreement*).
sfoderàre, *v.t.* to unsheath; (*fig.*) display.
sfogàre, *v.t.* to vent; give vent to; give free play to; disclose. **sfogàrsi**, *v.refl.* to relieve (give vent to) one's feelings.
sfoggiàre, *v.t.* & *i.* to show off; flaunt; be ostentatious. **sfòggio**, *m.* show; parade; ostentation; display; luxury; abundance.
sfòglia, *f.* foil (*metal*); flake. *pasta* ～, puff-paste. **sfogliàre**, *v.t.* to strip off (*leaves*); turn over the pages of (*book*); glance through; draw one by one from a pack (*cards*). **sfogliàrsi**, *v.refl.* to shed leaves or petals; flake off. **sfogliàta**, *f.* thin pastry; rapid glance (*through a book*). **sfogliatúra**, *f.* shedding of leaves; exfoliation.
sfógo (*pl.* **sfóghi**), *m.* vent; outlet; free play; relief; effect; development; outburst; (*Med.*) eruption.
sfolgoràre, *v.i.* (*aux.* essere & avere) to blaze; flash. **sfolgorío**, *m.* blaze; flashing; glitter.
sfollaménto, *m.* dispersal; break up (*crowd, meeting*); reduction of staff; (*Mil.*) evacuation. **sfollàre**, *v.t.* & *i.* (*aux.* essere & avere) to disperse; break up; evacuate. **sfollàto**, *m.* evacuee.
sfondaménto, *m.* breaking; breaking open, &c. See *sfondare*. **sfondàre**, *v.t.* to break; break down; break open; stave in; burst open; wear a hole in; knock the bottom out of. *v.i.* (*aux.* avere) to progress, succeed. *v.i.* (*aux.* essere) to sink. **sfondàto**, *a.* bottomless; boundless; worn out; worn in[to] holes. **sfóndo**, *m.* background; recess in a wall or ceiling (*intended for a painting*).
sformàre, *v.t.* to destroy the shape of; pull out of shape; take out of the mould; deform; disfigure. *v.i.* (*fam.*) lose patience. **sformàto**, *a.* shapeless; huge; ugly.
sforníre (*pr.* -ísco, -ísci), *v.t.* to strip; deprive of furniture or provisions. **sforníto**, *a.* destitute; unprovided.

sfortúna, *f.* ill luck; misfortune. **sfortunàto,** *a.* unlucky; unfortunate.

sforzaménto, *m.* compulsion. **sforzàre,** *v.t.* to compel; force; urge; strain. **sforzàrsi,** *v.refl.* to exert oneself; strive. **sfòrzo,** *m.* effort; endeavour; exertion; strain; stress.

sfossàre, *v.t.* to dig up. **sfossàto,** *a.* deep-set; sunken (*eyes*).

sfracassàre *&* **sfracellàre,** *v.t.* to shatter; smash.

sfrancesàre, *v.t.* *&* **sfrancesàrsi,** *v.refl.* to free from French habits (*speech or dress*); (*fam.*) speak French badly.

sfranchíre (*pr.* **-ísco, -ísci**), *v.t.* to give free play to; give confidence to. **sfranchírsi,** *v.refl.* to acquire facility or confidence.

sfratàre, *v.t.* to unfrock (*priest*).

sfrattàre, *v.t.* to dismiss; turn out; expel. **sfràtto,** *m.* expulsion; dismissal; notice to quit.

sfregàre (*pr.* **sfrégo, sfréghi**), *v.t.* to rub.

sfregiàre, *v.t.* to disfigure; deface; slash; (*fig.*) disgrace; tarnish. **sfrégio,** *m.* disfigurement; gash; cut; scar; slur; affront; disgrace.

sfrenàre, *v.t.* to unbridle; let loose. **sfrenataménte,** *ad* wildly; immoderately; without restraint; dissolutely; licentiously. **sfrenatézza,** *f.* wildness; profligacy; licentiousness. **sfrenàto,** *a.* unbridled; unrestrained; excessive; dissolute; licentious.

sfríggere (*pr.* **sfríggo,** *&c.,* like *friggere*), *v.i. ir.* (*aux.* avere) to hiss. **sfrig[g]olàre,** *v.i.* (*aux.* avere) to sputter. **sfringuellàre,** *v.i.* (*aux.* avere) to twitter; warble; (*fig.*) chatter.

sfrondàre, *v.t.* to strip of leaves; (*fig.*) curtail; reduce what is superfluous.

sfrontatézza, *f.* effrontery; impudence; shamelessness. **sfrontàto,** *a.* shameless; impudent.

sfruttaménto, *m.* exploitation. **sfruttàre,** *v.t.* to exploit; work (*mines, &c.*) exhaust; make the most of; profit by; abuse; take advantage of; sweat (*labour*); misuse; sterilize. **sfruttatóre,** *m.* exploiter; profiteer; sweater.

sfuggévole, *a.* fleeting; transitory. **sfuggíre** (*pr.* **sfúggo, sfúggi, sfúgge**), *v.i.* (*aux.* essere) to escape;

slip; slip out; pass unnoticed. *~ a una promessa,* to break a promise. *v.t.* avoid; shun. **sfuggíta** (**alla**), *ad. expr.* hastily; stealthily; incidentally.

sfumàre, *v.i.* (*aux.* essere) to disappear; vanish; evaporate; end in smoke; come to nothing. *v.t.* (*colour*) to tone down; (*line, shadow*) soften; (*sound*) diminish gradually. **sfumatézza,** *f.* delicacy of shading or gradation. **sfumatúra,** *f.* shade; shading; nuance; light wash of colour.

sfuriàre, *v.i.* (*aux.* avere) to rage; fly into a passion. **sfuriàta,** *f.* outburst (*of passion*); scolding.

ṡgabellàre, *v.t.* to clear; take out of bond. **ṡgabellàrsi** (*di*), *v.refl.* to get rid of; shirk.

ṡgabèllo, *m.* stool; bench.

ṡgabuzzíno, *m.* closet; lumber-room.

ṡgambàre, *v.i.* (*aux.* avere) to stride; walk fast. *v.t.* to break the stalk (*of a flower*). **ṡgambàta,** *f.* walk; long walk; run.

ṡgambettàre, *v.i.* (*aux.* avere) to kick the legs about; take short quick steps; frisk; trip; (*child*) toddle; caper. **ṡgambétto,** *m.* caper; jump. *dare lo ~ a,* to trip (up).

ṡganasciàrsi, *v.refl.* to dislocate one's jaw. *~ dalle risa,* to split one's sides with laughing.

ṡganciàre, *v.t.* uncouple; unhook; (*Aviat.*) to release; drop (*bombs, &c.*). **ṡganciàrsi,** *v.refl.* (*Mil.*) to disengage.

ṡgangheràre, *v.t.* to unhinge; dislocate. **ṡgangherataménte,** *ad.* rudely; boisterously; awkwardly; immoderately. **ṡgangheràto,** *a.* unhinged; loose; disjointed; awkward; ramshackle; rickety; worn-out; coarse; immoderate.

ṡgarbatézza, *f.* rudeness; unmannerliness; roughness; awkwardness; clumsiness. **ṡgarbàto,** *a.* rude; rough; unmannerly; awkward; clumsy. **ṡgàrbo,** *m.* piece of rudeness; offence; bad grace.

ṡgargiànte, *a.* gorgeous; showy; stylish.

ṡgarràre, *v.i.* (*aux.* avere) to go wrong.

ṡgattaiolàre, *v.i.* (*aux.* essere) to wriggle out; slip away.

ṡgelàre, *v.i.* (*aux.* essere *&* avere) *& t.* to melt; thaw. **ṡgèlo,** *m.* thaw.

ṡghémbo, *a.* crooked; oblique; slant. *a ~,* crookedly; obliquely; aslant.

ṡghèrro, *m.* hired ruffian or assassin.

ṡghignazzàre, *v.i.* (*aux.* avere) to laugh scornfully; guffaw. **ṡghignazzàta,** *f.* coarse laugh; guffaw.

ṡgobbàre, *v.i.* (*aux.* avere) to work hard; drudge; toil.

ṡgocciolàre, *v.i.* (*aux.* essere) to drip; trickle. *v.t.* to pour out in drops; drain to the last drop. **ṡgocciolatóio,** *m.* eaves; cornice over a window. **ṡgocciolatúra,** *f.* dripping. **ṡgocciolío,** *m.* constant dripping. **ṡgócciolo,** *m.* last drop; dripping.

ṡgolàrsi, *v.refl.* to shout oneself hoarse.

ṡgomberàre & **ṡgombràre,** *v.t.* to clear; remove; sweep away; (*Mil.*) give up; abandon (*position*); free; release. *v.i.* (*aux.* avere) to remove; go away; clear out. **ṡgómbro,** *a.* clear; free; empty. ¶ *m.* removal; clearing away; mackerel.

ṡgomentàre, *v.t.* to terrify; dismay; alarm. **ṡgoménto,** *m.* alarm; dismay; fright. ¶ *a.* alarmed; dismayed; frightened.

ṡgomìnàre, *v.t.* to throw into disorder; disperse; rout. **ṡgominío,** *m.* utter confusion.

ṡgomitolàre, *v.t.* to unwind.

ṡgonfiaménto, *m.* deflation (*tyre,* &c.); emptying; collapse. **ṡgonfiàre,** *v.t.* to deflate; reduce; empty; bring down; flatten (out). *v.i.* & **ṡgonfiàrsi,** *v.refl.* to become deflated; go down (*of swelling*). **ṡgónfio,** *a.* deflated; reduced; flattened; empty; emptied.

ṡgonellàre, *v.i.* (*aux.* avere) to gad about. **ṡgonnellóna,** *f.* gad-about.

ṡgórbia, *f.* gouge.

ṡgorbiàre, *v.t.* to blot; stain; scrawl. **ṡgòrbio,** *m.* scrawl; blot; daub.

ṡgorgàre, *v.i.* (*aux.* essere) to gush; gush out; spout; pour; spring; well; flow; disgorge.

ṡgovernàre, *v.t.* to misgovern; mismanage. **ṡgoverno,** *m.* misgovernment; mismanagement.

ṡgozzàre, *v.t.* to cut the throat of; (*fig.*) to bleed (*by usury*). **ṡgozzíno,** *m.* usurer.

ṡgradévole, *a.* unpleasant; disagreeable. **ṡgradíto,** *a.* unpleasant; unwelcome; undesirable.

ṡgraffiàre, *v.t.* to scratch; pilfer; steal.

ṡgrammaticàre, *v.i.* (*aux.* avere) to make mistakes in grammar. **ṡgrammaticatúra,** *f.* mistake in grammar.

ṡgranàre, *v.t.* to shell; hull; husk.

~*gli occhi,* to open the eyes wide.

ṡgranàrsi, *v.refl.* to crumble.

ṡgranchíre (*pr.* -ísco, -ísci), to stretch. **ṡgranchírsi,** *v.refl.* to wake up; stretch oneself; rouse oneself to action.

ṡgranocchiàre, *v.t.* to crunch; munch; devour.

ṡgravaménto, *m.* lightening; alleviation; relief. **ṡgravàre,** *v.t.* to lighten; unload; (*fig.*) relieve. **ṡgravàrsi,** *v.refl.* to relieve oneself; unburden oneself. **ṡgràvio,** *m.* relief, alleviation; lightening. ~ *delle imposte,* reduction in taxation.

ṡgraziatàggine, *f.* clumsiness; awkwardness. **ṡgraziàto,** *a.* awkward; clumsy; ungainly; ungraceful.

ṡgretolàre, *v.t.* to grind (down); pound; gnash (*teeth*). **ṡgretolàrsi,** *v.refl.* to crumble; fall to pieces.

ṡgridàre, *v.t.* to scold; rebuke. **ṡgridàta,** *f.* scolding; rebuke.

ṡgrondàre, *v.i.* (*aux.* essere) to trickle; drip.

ṡgrovigliàre, *v.t.* to disentangle.

ṡgrugnàta, *f.* blow in the face.

ṡguaiatàggine, *f.* awkwardness; clumsiness; coarseness; stupidity. **ṡguaiàto,** *a.* awkward; slovenly; ill-mannered. ¶ *m.* rough, ill-mannered fellow.

ṡguainàre, *v.t.* to unsheathe.

ṡgualcíre (*pr.* -ísco, -ísci), *v.t.* to rumple.

ṡgualdrína, *f.* strumpet; trollop.

ṡguàrdo, *m.* look; glance.

ṡguarníre & **ṡguerníre** (*pr.* -ísco, -ísci), *v.t.* to strip, dismantle.

ṡguàttera, *f.* scullery maid. **ṡguàttero,** *m.* scullery boy.

ṡguazzàre, *v.t.* to forá; lead cattle into the water. *v.i.* (*aux.* avere) to wade; flounder; wallow; shake (*of liquid in a vessel*).

ṡguinzagliàre, *v.t.* to unleash; let loose; let loose on.

ṡgusciàre, *v.t.* to shell; hull; husk. *v.i.* (*aux.* essere) to slip off; steal away.

si, *pn. refl.* oneself; himself; herself; itself; themselves. ¶ **si,** *pn. indef.* one; people; they; we. ¶ **si,** *pn. recipr.* each other; one another. ¶ **si,** *m.* (*Mus.*) si, B.

sí, *ad.* yes. *abb.* of *cosí,* so; thus.

sia . . . sia, *c.* whether . . . or.

Siam (il), *m.* Siam. **siamése,** *a.* & *m.* Siamese. *il* ~, Siamese (*language*).

sibaríta (*pl.* -íti), *m.* sybarite.

Sibèria (la), *f.* Siberia. siberiàno, *a. & m.* Siberian.

sibilànte, *f.* (*Gram.*) sibilant. sibilàre, *v.i.* (*aux.* avere) to hiss; whistle; whizz; wheeze.

sibílla, *f.* Sibyl. sibillíno, *a.* sibylline.

síbilo, *m.* hiss; hissing sound; whizz; whizzing; whistle; wheezing.

sicàrio, *m.* cut-throat; hired assassin.

sicché, *c.* so that.

siccità, *f.* drought; dryness; dry weather.

siccóme, *ad. & c.* as; since.

Sicília (la), *f.* Sicily. siciliàno, *a. & m.* Sicilian.

sicofànte, *m.* spy; informer.

sicomòro, *m.* sycamore.

sicumèra, *f.* self-sufficiency; pompousness.

sicúra, *f.* safety-bolt; safety-catch. sicurézza, *f.* safety; security; certainty; assurance. *agente di Pubblica S~*, policeman. *cassetta di ~*, safe. *rasoio di ~*, safety razor. *uscita di ~*, emergency door. sicúro, *a.* safe; secure; sure; confident; assured; reliable. ¶ *ad.* certainly. ¶ *m.* safety. sicurtà, *f.* guarantee; security (*Law, Com.*).

sideràle, *a.* sidereal. sidèreo, *a.* starry.

sideríte, *f.* loadstone. siderurgía, *f.* iron-working. siderúrgico (*pl.* -úrgici), *a.* iron-working; iron (*att.*). *stabilimento ~*, iron-works.

sídro, *m.* cider.

sièpe, *f.* hedge; wall; barrier; hurdle. *corsa su ~i, f.* hurdle-race, steeplechase.

sièro, *m.* whey; (*Med.*) serum. sieroterapía, *f.* serum therapy.

sièsta, *f.* siesta; afternoon nap.

siffàtto, *a.* such; of such a nature.

sifílide, *f.* syphilis.

sifóne, *m.* sifon; waterspout.

sigaràia, *f.*, sigaràio, *m.* cigarmaker; itinerant cigar & cigarette seller. sigarétta, *f.* cigarette. sígaro, *m.* cigar.

sigillàre, *v.t.* to seal. sigíllo, *m.* seal (*lit. & fig.*) stamp (*fig.*); impression.

sígla, *f.* initials; monogram; abbreviation.

significàre, *v.t.* to mean; signify; symbolize; imply; indicate; intimate; notify. significatívo, *a.* significant; expressive; full of significance; meaning(ful). significàto, *m.* meaning; signification; sense; import.

signóra, *f.* lady; Mrs. Madam.

Nostra S~, Our Lady; the Madonna. signóre, *m.* gentleman; Mr.; Sir!; lord. signoreggiàre, *v.t. & i.* to rule; master; dominate (*lit. & fig.*); sway; lord it over; domineer.

signoría, *f.* (*title*) Lordship; lordship; dominion, rule; (*Hist.*) governing body of a medieval comune. signoríle, *a.* gentlemanlike; courtly; aristocratic. signoralità, *f.* distinction of manners; courtly behaviour. signorína, *f.* young lady; Miss. signoríno, *m.* young gentlemen; Master. signoròtto, *m.* country squire.

silènte, *a.* silent. silenziatóre, *m.* silencer. silènzio, *m.* silence. silenzióso, *a.* silent; noiseless; quiet.

silfíde, *f.* Sylph.

sílice, *f.* silex; flint. silíceo, *a.* flinty.

síllaba, *f.* syllable. sillabàre, *v.t.* to spell out; pronounce by syllables. sillabàrio, *m.* spelling-book. sillàbico (*pl.* -àbici), *a.* syllabic. síllabo, *m.* syllabus; index.

sillogísmo, *m.* syllogism.

sílo, *m.* silo. *conservazione nei sili, f.* ensilage.

silografía, *f.* wood-engraving. silògrafo, *m.* wood-engraver.

siluétta, *f.* silhouette.

silu?ànte, *a.* torpedo boat. siluràre, *v.t.* to torpedo; (*fig.*) to cashier. *aerosilurante, m.* torpedo-carrying plane. silúro, *m.* torpedo.

silvàno, *a.* silvan; sylvan; rural. silvèstre, *a.* wild; rustic. silvicultóre, *m.* forester. silvicultúra, *f.* forestry.

simboleggiàre *&* simbolizzàre, *v.t.* to symbolize. simbòlico (*pl.* -òlici), *a.* symbolic(al). simbolísmo, *m.* symbolism. símbolo, *m.* symbol.

similàre, *a.* similar; homogeneous. similarità, *f.inv.* similarity; homogeneity. símile, *a.* like; alike; such; similar. similitúdine, *f.* likeness; similitude; simile. similménte, *ad.* likewise; similarly. similòro, *m.* pinchbeck.

simmetría, *f.* symmetry. simmètrico (*pl.* -ètrici), *a.* symmetric(al).

simonía, *f.* simony.

simpatía, *f.* liking; like; common feeling; sympathy. simpàtico (*pl.* -àtici), *a.* nice; pleasant; agreeable; congenial. simpatizzàre, *v.i.* (*aux.* avere) to take a liking (to); take a liking to each other.

simulácro, *m.* simulacrum; image; shadow; shadowy likeness; mere pretence; sham.

simuláre, *v.t.* to feign; simulate; sham.

simultàneo, *a.* simultaneous.

simún, *m.inv.* simoom; simoon.

sinagòga, *f.* synagogue.

sinceraménte, *ad.* sincerely; truly; candidly; honestly; really. **sinceràre,** *v.t.* to convince; persuade; assure; absolve; acquit. **sincerità,** *f.* sincerity; truth; candour. **sincèro,** *a.* true; genuine; sincere; unfeigned; frank; candid.

sincopáre, *v.t.* to syncopate. **sincopàto,** *a.* syncopated. *musica ~a,* ragtime. **sincopatúra,** *f.* syncopation. **síncope,** *f.* syncope.

sincronizzàre, *v.t. & i.* to synchronize. **síncrono,** *a.* synchronous.

sindacalísmo, *m.* syndicalism. **sindacalísta** (*pl.* **-ísti**), *m.* syndicalist. **sindacàre,** *v.t.* to audit; inspect; censure. **sindacàto,** *m.* syndicate; trade union; control; inspection. **síndaco** (*pl.* **síndaci**), *m.* mayor; Lord Mayor; syndic; auditor.

sinecúra, *f.* sinecure.

sinèddoche, *f.* synecdoche. **sinèreśi,** *f.* syneresis.

sinfonía, *f.* symphony. **sinfònico** (*pl.* **-ònici**), *a.* symphonic.

singhiozzàre, *v.i.* (*aux.* avere) to sob; hiccup. **singhiózzo & singúlto,** *m.* sob; hiccup.

singolàre, *a.* singular; peculiar; odd; queer; quaint; single (*combat*). ¶ *m.* (*Ten.*) single; (*Gram.*) singular. **singolarità,** *f.* singularity, &c. **singolareggiàre,** *v.i.* (*aux.* avere) to stand out; excel. **síngolo,** *a.* single; individual.

sinístra, *f.* left (*position & politics*); left hand. **sinistraménte,** *ad.* ominously; disastrously. **sinistràre,** *v.t.* to damage. **sinístro,** *a.* left; left-hand (*att.*); sinister; ominous; grim; lurid; inauspicious; contrary; unfavourable. ¶ *m.* accident; mishap; (*Box.*) left.

síno (a), *pr.* till; until; up to; as far as.

sínodo, *m.* synod.

sinòlogo (*pl.* **-òlogi**), *m.* Chinese scholar; sinologue.

sinònimo, *a.* synonymous. ¶ *m.* synonym

sinòssi, *f.* synopsis. **sinòttico** (*pl.* **-òttici**), *a.* synoptic(al).

sintàssi, *f.* syntax. **sintàttico** (*pl.* **-àttici**), *a.* syntactic.

sínteśi, *f.* synthesis. **sintètico** (pl.). **-ètici**), *a.* synthetic(al).

sintomàtico (*pl.* **-àtici**), *a.* symptomatic(al). **síntomo,** *m.* symptom; sign; token.

sintonizzàre, *v.t.* (*Radio*) to syntonize.

sinuosità, *f.inv.* sinuosity; bend. **sinuóso,** *a.* sinuous; winding.

sioníśmo, *m.* Zionism. **sionísta** (*pl.* **-ísti**), *m.* Zionist.

sipàrio, *m.* (*Theat.*) curtain; drop-curtain.

Siracúśa, *f.* Syracuse.

Síre, *m.* Sire (form of address to King).

sirèna, *f.* siren; hooter; siren (*Myth*).

Síria (la), *f.* Syria. **siríaco,** *a. & m.* Syriac. **siriàno,** *a. & m.* Syrian.

sirínga, *f.* syringe; (*Bot.*) syringa. **siringàre,** *v.t.* to syringe.

Sírio, *m.* Sirius; dog-star.

siròppo, *m.* syrup.

Sísifo, *m.* Sisyphus (*Myth*).

síśmico (*pl.* **síśmici**), *a.* seismic. **sismografía,** *f.* seismography. **sismògrafo,** *m.* seismograph. **sismòlogo** (*pl.* **-òlogi**), *m.* seismologist.

sistèma (*pl.* **-èmi**), *m.* system. **sistemàre,** *v.t.* to arrange; regulate; settle. **sistemàtico** (*pl.* **-àtici**), *a.* systematic. **sistemazióne,** *f.* regularization; arrangement; settlement; lay-out; set-up.

sistíno, *a.* Sistine; Sixtine (*after Pope Sixtus IV*). *Capella S ~ a,* Sistine Chapel.

sitibóndo, *a.* thirsty; (*fig.*) thirsting; eager.

síto, *m.* place; site; spot. ¶ *a.* situated; placed.

situàre, *v.t.* to place. **situazióne,** *f.* situation; position; condition.

Sivíglia, *f.* Seville.

ślabbràre, *v.t.* to cut off the lips; break the mouth or rim (*of a bottle or vase*) open; widen. *v.i.* (*aux.* essere) overflow; brim over; gape (*wound*).

ślacciàre, *v.t.* to undo, unlace; untie.

ślanciàre, *v.t.* to hurl; fling; throw. **ślanciàrsi,** *v.refl.* to rush; hurl oneself (upon); (*fig.*) be bold or daring. **ślanciato,** *a.* slim; slender. **ślancio,** *m.* rush; dash; onset; jump; start; impulse; outburst.

ślargàre, *v.t.* to enlarge; widen.

ślattàre, *v.t.* to wean.

ślavàto, *a.* pale; colourless; washed out.

ślàvo, *a. & m.* Slav. **ślavòfilo** *a. &*

m. Slavophil. **šlavòfobo,** *a. & m.* Slavophobe.

šleale, *a.* unfaithful; disloyal. **šlealtà,** *f.* disloyalty.

šlegàre, *v.t.* to unbind; untie; undo; loosen; unfasten. **šlegàto,** *a.* loose; unbound (*book*); unconnected.

Slésia (la), *f.* Silesia.

šlítta, *f.* sledge; sleigh; (*Mach.*) slide. **šlittaménto,** *m.* sliding; skidding. **šlittàre,** *v.i.* (*aux.* essere & avere) to sledge; slide; slip; skid (*motor*). **slittàta,** *f.* (*Motor.*) skid.

šlogaménto, *m. &* **šlogatura,** *f.* dislocation. **šlogàre,** *v.t.* to dislocate.

šloggiàre, *v.t.* to dislodge. *v.i.* (*aux.* avere) to decamp; clear out; retire.

šlombàre, *v.t.* to break the back of; wear out; exhaust. **šlombàrsi,** *v.refl.* to knock oneself up (*fig.*).

Slovàcchia (la), *f.* Slovakia. **Slovàcco** (*pl.* -àcchi), *a. & m.* Slovak. **Slovèno,** *a. & m.* Slovene.

šlungàre, *v.t.* to prolong.

šmaccàto, *a.* sickeningly sweet; nauseous; excessive.

šmacchiàre, *v.t.* to remove stains from; clean; scour.

šmacco, (*pl.* **šmàcchi**) *m.* affront; shame; disgrace.

šmagàrsi, *v.refl.* to lose courage; be dismayed; get confused. **šmagàto,** *a.* confounded; dismayed.

šmagliànte, *a.* dazzling; gaudy. **šmagliàre,** *v.i.* (*aux.* avere) to shine brightly; sparkle. *v.t.* to undo the meshes (*of a net*); take (*fish*) out of a net; take down (*a piece of knitting*); break the links (*of a chain*).

šmagnetizzàre, *v.t.* to demagnetize.

šmaltàre, *v.t.* to enamel; glaze. **šmaltatóre,** *m.* enameller. **šmaltatúra,** *f.* enamelling.

šmaltíre (*pr.* -ísco, -ísci), *v.t.* to sell off; get rid of; sleep off; digest; swallow (*affront*).

šmaltitóio, *m.* drain; sewer.

šmàlto, *m.* enamel; enamel-work; glaze; artificial stone. *cuore di* ∼, heart of stone.

šmammolàrsi, *v.refl.* to be extremely happy. ∼ *dalle risa,* to laugh heartily.

šmanceria, *f.* affectation; simpering; mincing manner. **šmanceróso,** *a.* affected; mincing.

šmangiàre, *v.t.* to eat away; corrode; wear down.

šmània, *f.* morbid restlessness; (*eager*) desire; impatience; frenzy. **šmaniàre,** *v.i.* (*aux.* avere) to rave; dote; toss about. *smaniarsi di,* to be crazy for. **šmanióso,** *a.* eager; madly desirous.

šmantellàre, *v.t.* to dismantle.

šmargiassàre, *v.i.* (*aux.* avere), to bluster; brag; hector; play the bully. **smargiassàta,** *f.* bluster; brag[ging]; bullying. **šmargiàsso,** *m.* bully; blusterer; braggart.

šmàrra, *f.* hoe.

šmarriménto, *m.* bewilderment; loss; error; miscarriage. **šmarríre** (*pr.* -ísco, -ísci), *v.t.* to lose; mislay; mislead; bewilder; confuse. **šmarrírsi,** *v.refl.* to lose one's way; go astray; be bewildered or confused. **šmarríto,** *a.* bewildered; frightened; lost; stray(ed); miscarried. *ufficio di oggetti* ∼*i,* lost property office.

šmascellaménto, *m.* dislocation of the jaw(s). **šmascellàrsi,** *v.refl.* to dislocate one's jaws. ∼ *dalle risa,* to split one's sides with laughing.

šmascheràre, *v.t.* to unmask.

šmembràre, *v.t.* to dismember.

šmemoratàggine, forgetfulness; absence of memory. **šmemoràto,** *a.* forgetful; absent-minded.

šmentíre (*pr.* -ísco, -ísci), *v.t.* to deny; give the lie to; contradict; belie. **šmentíta,** *f.* denial; contradiction.

šmeraldíno, *a.* emerald green. **šmeràldo,** *m.* emerald.

šmerciàre, *v.t.* to sell; sell off; dispose of. **smèrcio,** *m.* sale; selling off.

šmerigliàre, *v.t.* to polish with emery; (*of glass*) to grind. *carta smerigliato,* emery-paper. **šmeríglio,** *m.* emery.

šmerlàre, *v.t.* to trim with purl or picot edging; embroider the edges of. **šmèrlo,** *m.* purl; picot edging.

šmésso, *p.p. of* **šmetterè.** ¶ *a.* cast-off (*clothes*). **šméttere,** *v.i.* (*aux.* avere) (*with di. & inf.*), to leave off; stop; give up. *v.t.* to leave off; cast off; give up; drop; cease.

šmezzàre, *v.t.* to halve; cut in half.

šmidollàre, *v.t.* to draw out the pith or marrow of. **šmidollàrsi,** *v.refl.* to grow weak; lose one's strength.

šmilàce, *f.* smilax (*Bot.*).

šmílzo, *a.* slim; slender (*lit. & fig.*); thin; poor; spare; empty.

šminuíre (*pr.* -ísco, -ísci), *v.t.* to diminish; lessen. **šminuzzàre,** *v.t.* to mince; hash; hew; cut up.

Smírne, *f.* Smyrna.

šmistaménto, *m.* sorting; (*Rly.*) shunting. *posto di* ∼, *m.* (*Mil.*)

clearing-station. *spedale di* ~, *m.* casualty clearing-station. **śmistàre,** *v.t.* to sort; (*Rly.*) shunt; switch.

śmiśuràto, *a.* immense; boundless.

śmobiliàre, *v.t.* to unfurnish; remove the furniture from. **śmobilitàre,** *v.t.* to demobilize.

śmoccolàre, *v.t.* to snuff (*candle*). *v.i.* (*aux.* avere) to swear; curse. **śmoccolatóio,** *m.* (*candle*) snuffers.

śmodàto & **śmoderàto,** *a.* immoderate; excessive; intemperate. **śmoderatézza,** *f.* excess; lack of moderation; intémperance; exaggeration.

śmontàggio, *m.* (*Mech.*) dismounting; disassembling. **śmontàre,** *v.i.* (*aux.* essere) to dismount; alight; (*colours*) fade; (*prices*) drop; go down. *v.t.* to take to pieces; (*Mech.*) dismantle; bring down; upset (*plot*); relieve (*guard*).

śmòrfia, *f.* wry face; grimace; coaxing smile or gesture. **śmorfióso,** *a.* affected; mincing; insinuating; wheedling. ¶ *m.* wheedler.

śmòrto, *a.* pale; wan; sallow; (*metal*) dull; (*colour*) dead.

śmorzàre, *v.t.* to extinguish (*light*); shade (*lamp*) tone down (*colours*); damp (*sound*); slake (*lime*); quench (*thirst*); (*fig.*) appease; abate. **śmorzàrsi,** *v.refl.* to grow faint[er]; die away; go out; be extinguished. **śmorzatóre,** *m.* ~ *di scosse,* shock absorber.

śmòsso, *p.p.* of *smuovere.*

śmozzàre, *v.t.* to lop off; chip off; curtail. **śmozzicàre,** *v.t.* to maim; mutilate; cut to pieces; cut short.

śmúngere, *v.t. ir.* to drain; dry up; milk; exhaust; (*fig.*) fleece. **śmúnto,** *a.* pale; wan; emaciated; exhausted; lean; thin; scraggy.

śm[u]òvere, *v.t. ir.* to shift; displace; move; stir; affect; excite; deter; dissuade. **śm[u]òversi,** *v.refl.* to move; be moved (*lit.* & *fig.*).

śmussàre, *v.t.* to blunt; bevel; chamfer; round off the angles of; (*fig.*) smooth; soften. *pialla da* ~, bevelling machine (*Typ.*). **śmussatúra,** *f.* bevelling; chamfered edge. **śmusso,** *m.* bevel; chamfering chisel, chamfer. ¶ *a.* bevelled.

śnaturaménto, *m.* change of nature; denaturalization; perversion. **śnaturàre,** *v.t.* to alter the nature of; change; misrepresent. **śnaturatézza,** *f.* unnaturalness. **śnaturàto,** *a.* unnatural; cruel; monstrous.

śnebbiàre, *v.t.* to dispel the mist from; clear. *v.i.* (*aux.* essere) & **śnebbiàrsi,** *v.refl.* to become clear.

śnellézza, *f.* nimbleness; agility; slimness; slenderness. **śnèllo,** *a.* nimble; brisk; active; swift; slim; slender.

śnervànte, *a.* enervating; exhausting. **śnervàre,** *v.t.* to enervate; exhaust; enfeeble; unnerve. **śnervatézza,** *f.* debility; weakness.

śnicchiàre & **śnidàre,** *v.t.* to dislodge; drive out; find out.

snòb, *m.f.inv.* snob. **śnobiśmo,** *m.* snobbery.

śnocciolàre, *v.t.* to remove the kernel from; (*fig.*) to explain; tell (*beads, money*); rattle off (*stories*).

śnodàre, *v.t.* to untie; loosen; unravel; undo; stretch; make supple; exercise (*stiff joint*). **śnodàrsi,** *v.refl.* to become unwound; untied, &c.; (*road*) wind. **śnodàto,** *a.* flexible; supple; articulate.

śnudàre, *v.t.* to lay bare; bare; unsheathe.

śoàve, *a.* sweet; soft; mild; gentle. **soavità,** *f.* sweetness; softness; gentleness.

sobbalzàre, *v.i.* to start; jolt; jump (up); throb. **sobbàlzo,** *m.* start; jolt.

sobbollíre (*pr.* **sobbóllo**), *v.i.* (*aux.* avere) to simmer; boil gently.

sobbórgo (*pl.* **sobbórghi**), *m.* suburb.

sobrietà, *f.* temperance; moderation; sobriety. **sòbrio,** *a.* temperate; moderate; sober.

socchiúdere, *v.t. ir.* to half-shut; leave ajar. **socchiúso,** *a.* ajar; half-open.

soccómbere, *v.i.* (*aux.* essere) to succumb; be overcome; give way; yield; die.

soccórrere, *v.t. ir.* to succour; help; assist; relieve. *v.i.* (*aux.* essere & avere) occur; come to mind. **soccorrévole,** *a.* helpful; charitable. **soccórso,** *m.* help; aid; succour; assistance; relief. *posto di primo* ~, first-aid station. *società di mutuo* ~, benefit society. *uscita di* ~, emergency exit.

sociàle, *a.* social; corporate; registered (*capital, offices*); of the firm; company's. *statuto* ~, *m.* articles of association. **socialíśmo,** *m.* socialism. **socialista** (*pl.* -**ísti**), *m.* socialist. **socializżazióne,** *f.* socialization. **società,** *f.* society; community; companionship; fellowship; club; company; firm; partnership. ~ *anonima,* joint stock

company. ~ *di mutuo soccorso,*
friendly society; benefit s. *S~ delle
Nazioni,* League of Nations. ~
edilizia, building society. **sociévole,**
a. sociable; companionable. **sòcio**
(pl. **sòci**), *m.* associate; member;
fellow; partner. **sociología,** *f.*
sociology.
Sòcrate, *m.* Socrates. **socràtico** *(pl.*
-àtici), *a.* Socratic.
sodalízio, *m.* association; brotherhood;
confraternity; guild.
sodaménte, *ad.* firmly; solidly; com-
pactly. **sodàre,** *v.t.* to consolidate;
strengthen; make solid.
soddisfacènte, *a.* satisfactory. **sod-
disfaciménto,** *m.* satisfaction;
compliance; fulfilment; discharge
(debt or obligation). **soddisfàre** *(pr.*
-fàccio *or* **-fò, -fai, -fa,** like *fare*),
v.t. ir. to satisfy; fulfil; gratify; comply with; meet; answer; discharge.
soddisfazióne, *f.* satisfaction;
gratification; reparation; approval.
sodézza, *f.* solidity; firmness; compactness.
sòdio, *m.* sodium.
sòdo, *a.* solid; firm; substantial;
strong; compact; hard; hard-boiled
(egg); heavy; untilled *(land).* ¶ *m.*
firm ground; solid block; foundation,
&c.
sofà, *f.* sofa.
sofferènte, *a.* suffering; ailing; unwell;
patient; enduring. **sofferènza,** *f.*
suffering; pain; patience; endurance.
soffermàrsi, *v.refl.* to stop a little;
pause for a moment; linger *(over a
point or argument).* **soffermàta,** *f.*
short stay; stop; pause.
soffiaménto, *m.* blowing; puffing.
soffiàre, *v.t. & i.* (aux. avere) to
blow; blow up; blow out; spit *(cat);*
fan *(flames)* breathe; puff; pant;
prompt; prime; huff *(draughts).*
soffiarsi il naso, to blow one's nose.
soffiàta, *f.* puff; breath *(of wind).*
soffiatóre, *m.* blower *(glass, &c.);*
inciter, prompter.
sòffice, *a.* soft.
soffiétto, *m.* bellows; *(carriage)* hood;
puff *(journalistic).* ~ *editoriale,*
blurb. **sóffio,** *m.* puff; whiff; breath;
breathing; blowing. **soffióne,** *m.*
bellows-pipe; forge-blower; *(Geol.)*
jet of steam or gas; *(Bot.)* dandelion.
soffítta, *f.* garret; attic; lumber-room.
soffítto, *m.* ceiling.
soffocaménto, *m.* choking; stifling;
suffocation. **soffocànte,** *a.* suffocating; stifling; oppressive. **soffocàre,**

v.t. & i. to stifle; choke; suffocate;
smother; extinguish; hush up.
soffocazióne, *f.* suffocation.
soffreddàre, *v.t. & i.* to cool; cool
down.
soffregàre, *v.t.* to rub gently.
soffribile, *a.* endurable; bearable;
supportable. **soffríre** *(pr.* **sòffro,**
sòffri, *&c.*), *v.t. & i. ir.* to suffer;
endure; bear; stand; put up with.
soffrítto, *m.* onion sauce.
sofísma *(pl.* **-íśmi**), *m.* sophism.
sofística, *f.* sophistry. **sofisticàre,**
v.i. (aux. avere) to argue sophistic-
ally. *v.t.* to adulterate; sophisticate.
Sòfocle, *m.* Sophocles.
soggettàre, *v.t.* to subdue; subject.
soggettívo. *a.* subjective. **soggètto,**
m. subject; subject matter; topic;
fellow; individual. ¶ *a.* subject;
subjected; subordinate; liable. ~*a
modificazione,* subject to alterations
(time-table, &c.). **soggezióne,** *f.*
subjection; awe; timidity; embarrassment; uneasiness; constraint.
sogghignàre, *v.i.* to smile com-
placently; laugh in one's sleeve;
sneer; jeer. **sogghígno,** *m.* sneer;
mocking laugh.
soggiacére *(pr.* **-giàccio, -giàci,
-giàce),** *v.i. ir.* (aux. avere) to be
subject to); be liable; succumb.
soggiaciménto, *m.* subjection.
soggiogaménto, *m.* subjugation;
subjection. **soggiogàre,** *v.t.* to
subjugate; subdue; bring into
subjection.
soggiornàre, *v.i.* (aux. avere) to
sojourn; stay; reside. **soggiórno,** *m.*
stay; sojourn; resort; residence.
permesso di ~, permission to stay.
tassa di ~, visitors' tax.
soggiúngere, *v.t. ir.* to add; append;
subjoin. *v.i.* (aux. avere) to answer;
remark. **soggiuntívo,** *a. & m.*
subjunctive.
sòglia, *f.* threshold; sill; (door)step.
sòglio, *m.* throne.
sògliola, *f.* sole *(fish).*
sognàre, *v.t.* to dream; dream of;
imagine; conceive; long for. *v.i.*
(aux. avere) to dream; fancy; muse;
wander *(in mind).* **sognàrsi,** *v.refl.*
to fancy. **sognatóre,** *m.* (*f.* **-tríce**)
dreamer; visionary. ¶ *a.* dreaming.
sógno, *m.* dream; reverie; fancy;
vision.
sòia, *f.* soya-bean; soy-bean.
sòl, *m.* (*Mus.*) sol; G.
solàio, *m.* attic; garret; loft; frame of
a ceiling.

solaménte, *ad.* only; merely; solely.
solàre, *a.* solar; sun (*att.*); sunlight (*treatment*). **solàta**, *f.* sunstroke. **solatío**, *a.* sunny. ¶ *m.* sunny spot.
solatúra, *f.* soling (*boots & shoes*).
solcàre, *v.t.* to furrow; plough (*lit. & fig.*). **solcàta**, *f.* furrow; drawing a furrow. **sólco** (*pl.* **sólchi**), *m.* furrow; water-furrow; track; wrinkle. **solcòmetro**, *m.* (*Naut.*) log.
soldatésca, *f.* soldiery; (*undisciplined*) soldiers. **soldatescaménte**, *ad.* in soldierly fashion. **soldatésco** (*pl.* **-éschi**), *a.* soldierly; soldierlike (*sometimes with a depreciatory sense*). **soldatíno**, *m.* young soldier; toy-soldier. **soldàto**, *m.* soldier.
sòldo, *m.* soldo (*coin of low value*); (*fig.*) copper; penny; pay (*Mil. Nav., &c.*), wages; (*pl.*) money.
sóle, *m.* sun; sunshine.
solecísmo, *m.* solecism.
soleggiàre, *v.t.* to sun; expose to the sun. *v.i.* (*aux.* avere) to bask (or lie) in the sun.
solènne, *a.* solemn; formal; impressive; eminent; thorough; arrant; terrific. **solennità**, *f.* solemnity; celebration. **solennizzàre**, *v.t.* to solemnize.
solére (*pr.* **sòglio**, **suòli**, **suòle**), *v.i. ir.* (*aux.* essere) to be in the habit of; be wont; be accustomed; use (*in the past tense*).
solèrte, *a.* diligent; industrious; active; enterprising; careful; attentive. **solèrzia**, *f.* diligence; industriousness, &c.
solétta, *f.* stocking sole; stocking-foot; loose sole (*cork, &c.*), for boot or shoe. **solétto**, *a.* alone; all alone.
sòlfa, *f.* gamut; sol-fa; music; musical scale.
solfanèllo, *m.* (sulphur) match.
solfàra & **solfatàra**, *f.* sulphur-mine. **solfàto**, *m.* sulphate.
solfeggiàre, *v.t. & abs.* to sol-fa. **solféggio**, *m.* sol-fa; solfeggio.
solfíto, *m.* sulphite. **sólfo**, *m.* sulphur; (*cf.* zolfo (more com.)) brimstone. **solforàto**, *a.* sulphuretted. **solfòrico** (*pl.* **-òrici**), *a.* sulphuric. **solforóso**, *a.* sulphurous. **solfúro**, *m.* sulphide.
solicèllo, *m.* faint wintry sun.
solidàle, *a.* joint; joint & several. **solidàre**, *v.t.* to solidify. **solidariaménte**, *ad.* jointly & severally; jointly. **solidarietà**, *f.* solidarity; joint liability. **solidàrio**, *a.* joint & several. **solidézza** & **solidità**,

f. solidity. **sòlido**, *a.* solid; firm; compact; substantial; strong; (*colour*) fast. ¶ *m.* solid. *in* ~ (*Law*), conjointly with others.
solilòquio, *m.* soliloquy.
solíngo (*pl.* **solínghi**), *a.* lonely; solitary.
solíno, *m.* (*starched*) collar or cuff.
solísta (*pl.* **solísti**), *m. f.* soloist.
solitaménte, *ad.* usually; as a rule.
solitàrio, *a.* solitary; lonely; alone; secluded. ¶ *m.* hermit; solitaire (*gem & game*); patience (*game*).
sòlito, *a.* usual; customary; accustomed. *al* ~, *di* ~, as a rule; as usual.
solitúdine, *f.* solitude; loneliness; wilderness; wild (*Poet.*). **solívago** (*pl.* **-ívaghi**), *a.* wandering alone.
sollazzàre, *v.t.* to amuse; entertain; divert; provide with recreation. **sollazzévole**, *a.* amusing; entertaining; pleasant. **sollàzzo**, *m.* amusement; entertainment; recreation; pastime.
sollecitaménte, *ad.* quickly; readily; eagerly. **sollecitàre**, *v.t.* to hasten; urge; solicit; request; entreat. **sollecitazióne**, *f.* solicitation; entreaty. **sollécito**, *a.* prompt; speedy; ready; eager; solicitous. **sollecitúdine**, *f.* solicitude; care; diligence; promptitude; readiness; despatch.
solleóne, *m.* dog-days.
solleticaménto & **sollético** (*pl.* **-étichi**), *m.* tickling; (*fig.*) stimulus; excitement. **solleticànte**, *a.* (*fig.*) appetising; flattering. **solleticàre**, *v.t.* to tickle; (*fig.*) to excite; flatter; tempt (*appetite*).
sollevàre, *v.t.* to lift; raise; stir up; comfort; relieve. **sollevàrsi**, *v.refl.* to rise; rebel; get up (*after illness*). **sollevatóre**, *m.* (*f.* -tríce) agitator; leader of revolt. ¶ *a.* lifting; raising. **sollevazióne**, *f.* rising; rebellion; sedition.
sollièvo, *m.* relief; alleviation; comfort.
sollúchero, *m.* thrill. *andare in* ~, to go into raptures (*or* ecstasies).
sólo, *a.* alone; only; unique; sole. ¶ *ad.* only. ¶ *m.* solo (*Mus.*).
sòlo, see *suolo*.
solstízio, *m.* solstice.
soltànto, *ad.* only.
solúbile, *a.* soluble. **solutivo**, *a.* laxative. **soluzióne**, *f.* solution; break (*in continuity*); decision; discharge (*Law*). ~ *madre*, ~ *di*

riserva, stock solution (*Phot.*).
solvènte, *a. & m.* solvent.
solvènza & solvibilità, *f.* solvency.
sòlvere, *v.t.* to dissolve; solve; liquefy; perform; settle (*debt*).
sòma, *f.* burden; load; weight.
Somàlia (la), *f.* Somaliland.
somàro, *m.* ass; donkey (*lit. & fig.*). dim. **somarello.**
somigliànte, *a.* resembling; like. **somiglianza,** *f.* resemblance; likeness. **somigliàre,** *v.i.* (*aux.* essere & avere) to resemble; be like.
sómma, *f.* sum; amount; addition; conclusion; gist.
sommaménte, *ad.* in the highest degree; extremely; exceedingly. **sommàre,** *v.t.* to add up. *v.i.* to amount to. **sommàrio,** *a.* summary; compendious; brief; scant; done with dispatch. ¶ *m.* summary; synopsis; epitome.
sommèrgere, *v.t. ir.* to submerge; flood; swamp; overwhelm. **sommèrgersi,** *v.refl.* to sink; (*submarine*) submerge; dive. **sommergíbile,** *a.* submergible. ¶ *m.* submarine. **sommergiménto,** *m.* & **sommersióne,** *f.* submergence; submersion.
sommessaménte, *ad.* in a subdued tone; humbly; softly. **sommésso,** *a.* subdued; humble; low; soft.
somministràre, *v.t.* to provide; supply; administer.
sommissióne, *f.* submission.
sommità, *f.* summit (*lit. & fig.*); top. **sómmo,** *a.* very great; highest; topmost; supreme. ¶ *m.* summit; top.
sommòssa, *f.* rising; riot. **sommòsso,** *a.* troubled; excited. **somm[u]òvere,** *v.t. ir.* to stir up; incite; rouse; excite.
sonacchiàre & sonicchiàre, *v.t.* to strum. **sonaglièra,** *f.* collar with bells. **sonàglio,** *m.* harness bell; rattle; (*fig.*) fool. *serpente a ~i, m.* rattlesnake. **sonagliàre,** *v.i.* (*aux.* avere) to tinkle.
sonànte, *a.* ringing; sounding; sonorous. *denaro ~,* ready cash. **sonàre,** see *suonare.* **sonàta,** *f.* ring; ringing (*bell*); (*Mus.*) sonata. **sonatóre,** *m.* (*f.* -**tríce**) (*Mus.*) player; performer; executant.
sónda, *f.* sounding line; sounding rod; (*Med.*) sound, probe. **sondàggio,** *m.* sounding. **sondàre,** *v.t.* to sound; gauge; probe.
sonería, *f.* striking-mechanism (*clock*); alarm.

sonettísta (*pl.* -**ísti**), *m.f.* sonneteer, writer of sonnets. **sonétto,** *m.* sonnet.
sonnacchióso, *a.* drowsy; sleepy. **sonnambulísmo,** *m.* somnambulism; sleep-walking. **sonnàmbulo,** *m.* -**a,** *f.* somnambulist; sleepwalker. **sonnecchiàre,** *v.i.* (*aux.* avere) to doze; slumber. **sonnelíno,** *m.* short sleep; nap. **sonnilòquio,** *m.* talking in one's sleep. **sónno,** *m.* sleep; slumber. **sonnolènto,** *a.* drowsy; sleepy; somnolent. **sonnolènza,** *f.* drowsiness; sleepiness; somnolence.
sonorità, *f.* sonority; sonorousness. **sonòro,** *a.* sonorous; resonant; high-sounding; sounding; sound (*att.*); (*phonetics*) sonant. *film ~,* sound-film. *onda ~ a,* sound-wave.
sontuóso, *a.* sumptuous.
soperchiàre. *See soverchiare, &c.*
soperchiería, *f.* overbearing conduct; insolence; outrage; imposition.
sopiménto, *m.* soothing; alleviation. **sopíre** (*pr.* -**ísco, -ísci**), *v.t.* to calm; appease; allay; lull. **sopóre,** *m.* drowsiness; light sleep; torpor; lethargy. **soporífero,** *a. & m.* soporific.
sopperíre (a) (*pr.* -**ísco, -ísci**), *v.i* to provide (for); make up (for).
soppesàre, *v.t.* to weigh in one's hand.
soppiantàre, *v.t.* to supplant; oust.
soppiàtto (di), *ad. expr.* stealthily; secretly.
sopportàbile, *a.* endurable; bearable.
sopportàre, *v.t.* to bear; endure; tolerate; suffer; support; stand; put up with. **soppòrto,** *m.* support; toleration. *~ a rulli,* roller bearings (*Mech.*).
soppressióne, *f.* suppression; abolition. **sopprímere,** *v.t. ir.* to suppress; abolish.
sópra, *pr.* on; upon; over; above; beyond. *as prefix =* Eng. super-; sur-; above-; extra-; over-. *If followed by a consonant, this is generally doubled e.g.* sopraccarico, *sopraddetto,* sopraffare, *&c. With this clue, the meaning of such compounds can generally be deduced from the parent root.*
soprabbondànte *or* **sovrabbondànte,** *a.* superabundant.
soprabbústo, *m.* bodice.
sopràbito, *m.* overcoat.
sopraccàpo, *m.* anxiety; trouble; care.

sopraccàrico or **sovraccarico**, m. surcharge; supercargo; excessive load; additional burden. ¶ a. overloaded.

sopraccàrta, f. envelope; cover; address on envelope.

sopraccennàto & **sovraccennàto**, a. above-mentioned.

sopraccíglio, m. eyebrow.

sopraccitàto, a. above-quoted.

sopraccopèrta, f. counterpane; coverlet; (book)cover; outer envelope.

sopraddétto, a. aforesaid; above-mentioned.

sopraffàre (pr. -affò or -affàccio, -affài, -affà), v.t. ir. to overcome; overpower; overwhelm. **sopraffazióne**, f. oppression; tyranny.

sopraffíno, a. superfine; extreme; first-rate; clever; cunning.

sopraggiúngere (pr. like giungere), v.i. (aux. essere) to arrive; turn up; happen; occur; ensue. (v.t.) to overtake. **sopraggiúnta**, f. unexpected arrival. per ~, into the bargain; besides.

sopraintendènte & **soprintendènte**, m. superintendent. ¶ a. superintending. **sopraintendènza**, f. superintendence. **soprintèndere** (a), v.i. ir. (aux. avere) to superintend.

sopra[l]luògo, ad. on the spot. ¶ m. (pl. -òghi) investigation on the spot.

soprammercàto, m. surplus. per ~, into the bargain, in addition; besides.

soprammòdo, ad. exceedingly; extremely.

soprammontàre, v.i. (aux. essere) to superabound; be excessive; (collar) stand up.

soprannaturàle, a. supernatural.

soprannóme, m. nickname. **soprannomináre**, v.t. to nickname.

soprannumeràrio, a. supernumerary.

sopràno, m. soprano (Mus.). ¶ a. (Poet.) sovereign; highest.

soprappensièro, ad. absent-mindedly.

soprappiú, m. extra; addition.

soprascàrpa, f. overshoe; galosh.

soprascrìtta, f. superscription; address (on envelope).

soprasensìbile, a. super-sensible.

soprassàlto, m. start; sudden movement. di ~, on a sudden; with a start.

soprassedére, v.i. (aux. avere) to wait; suspend action. ~ a, to defer; put off.

soprastàlli, m.pl. & **soprastallíe**, f.pl. demurrage.

soprastànte, a. overhanging; impending. ¶ m. watchman; overseer; superintendent. **soprastàre**, see sovrastare.

soprattàssa, f. surtax; supertax.

soprattútto, ad. above all; especially; principally.

sopravanzàre, v.t. to pass; surpass. v.i. (aux. essere) to project; jut out; remain over. **sopravànzo**, m. surplus; remainder; balance; residue.

sopravveníre (pr. -vèngo, -vièni, &c., like venire), v.i. ir. (aux. essere) to happen; occur; supervene; arrive; come up. **sopravvènto**, m. advantage; superiority; upper hand (fig.). ¶ ad. windward. le Isole ~ e sottovento, the Windward & Leeward Islands. **sopravvenúta**, f. unexpected arrival.

sopravvèste, f. overall.

sopravvissúto & **sopravvivènte**, a. surviving. ¶ m. survivor. **sopravvivènza**, f. survival. **sopravvívere**, v.i. ir. (aux. essere) survive; continue to exist. ~ a, to survive; outlive.

soprintèndere, see sopraintendere.

soprúso, m. abuse of power; act of tyranny; insult; injury; outrage.

soqquadràre, v.t. to turn upside down. **soqquàdro**, m. confusion; disorder.

sor-, prefix, abb. of sopra.

sòrba, f. sorb; sorb-apple.

sorbettièra, f. ice-box. **sorbettière**, m. ice-cream vendor. **sorbétto**, m. ice-cream.

sorbíre (pr. -ísco, -ísci), v.t. to sip; swallow; suck.

Sorbóna, f. Sorbonne (University of Paris).

sórcio (pl. **sórci**), m. mouse (pl. mice). dim. sorcetto, sorcino.

sordàggine, f. deafness (slight). **sordaménte**, ad. with a dull sound; (fig.) secretly, by underhand means. **sordézza** & **sordità**, f. deafness.

sordidézza, f. meanness; sordidness. **sòrdido**, a. sordid; mean; dirty.

sordína, f. & **sordíno**, m. (Mus.) mute; sordine. alla ~a, stealthily; noiselessly. in ~a, in a minor key.

sórdo, a. deaf (lit. & fig.); dull; hollow (voice); mute[d]; muffled; underhand. ¶ m. deaf person. **sordomúto** (pr. **sordomúti**), a. deaf & dumb. ¶ m. deaf-mute.

sorèlla, *f.* sister. **sorellàstra,** *f.* step-sister.

sorgènte, *f.* spring; source; fountain; origin; cause.

sórgere, *v.i. ir. (aux.* essere) to rise; get up; stand up; rise up; arise; proceed; spring (from).

soriàno, *a.* Syrian. *gatto* ~, tabby cat.

sormontàre, *v.t.* to surmount; (over-) top; overcome.

sornióne, *a.* surly; sneaking; sly.

sorpassàre, *v.t.* to surpass; outdo; excel; pass, overtake. **sorpassàto,** *a.* out of date; old-fashioned.

sorprendènte, *a.* surprising; astonishing. **sorprèndere,** *v.t. ir.* to surprise; astonish; take advantage of. **sorprésa,** *f.* surprise; astonishment; stratagem.

sorrèggere (*pr.* **-règgo, -règgi,** *&c.,* like *reggere*) *v.t. ir.* to hold up; support; sustain.

sorridènte, *a.* smiling. **sorrídere,** *v.i. ir. (aux.* avere) to smile. *v.t.* to smile upon; please; attract. **sorríso,** *m.* smile. dim. *sorrisétto, sorrisino.*

sorsàta, *f.* gulp; draught. **sorseggiàre,** *v.t. & i.* to sip. **sórso,** *m.* drink; drop (*fig.*) draught.

sòrta, *f.* kind; sort.

sòrte, *f.* lot; fate; destiny; fortune; chance; luck; augury. **sorteggiàre,** *v.t.* to draw by lot; assign by lot. **sortéggio,** *m.* drawing (*of lots*).

sortilègio, *m.* witchcraft; sorcery; spell.

sortíre (*pr.* **sòrto, sòrti**), *v.i. (aux.* essere) to go out; come out; leave; emerge; issue; spring; sally forth; stand out. *v.t.* (*pr.* **sortísco, sortísci**) to have; get (by nature or fortune); draw (by lot); assign; allot.

sortíta, *f.* sortie; sally; (*actor's*) entry; (*fig.*) sally; witty remark.

sorvegliàntc, *m.* watchman; caretaker; keeper; overseer; inspector; superintendent. **sorvegliànza,** *f.* surveillance; watchful care; supervision; superintendence. **sorvegliàre,** *v.t.* to watch; watch over; superintend.

sorvolàre, *v.t. & i.* to fly over; pass over; rise above.

sòsia, *m.* double (*pers.*).

sospèndere, *v.t. ir.* to hang (up); suspend; stop; put a stop to; adjourn; defer; put off. **sospensióne,** *f.* suspension; adjournment; temporary stoppage; springing (*Motor.*). *molla di* ~, suspension spring. **sospensíva,** *f.* delay.

sospensòrio, *a.* suspensory. ¶ *m.* suspensory bandage. **sospéso,** *a.* hanging; (*fig.*) uncertain; in suspense. ¶ *m.* suspense. *ponte* ~, suspension bridge. in expr. *in* ~, in suspense

sospettàbile, *a.* liable to suspicion. **sospettàre,** *v.t. & i. (aux.* avere) to suspect, question. **sospètto,** *m.* suspicion; (*pers.*) suspect. ¶ *a.* suspect; suspicious. **sospettóso,** *a.* suspicious; full of suspicion; cautious.

sospíngere, *v.t. ir.* to drive; drive on; push; push forward; urge.

sospiràre, *v.i. (aux.* avere) to sigh. *v.t.* to sigh for; regret; lament. **sospíro,** *m.* sigh. **sospiróne,** *m.* deep sigh; heavy sigh; long drawn sigh. **sospiróso,** *a.* sighing; full of sighs.

sossópra, *ad.* upside down; topsy-turvy.

sòsta, *f.* halt; stay; rest; pause; cessation; truce; respite. *divieto di* ~, *m. proibizione di* ~, *f.* no parking.

sostantívo, *a. & m.* substantive.

sostànza, *f.* substance; matter; essence; property; patrimony. **sostanziàle,** *a.* substantial; well-founded. **sostanzióso,** *a.* substantial; nourishing; nutritious; (*wine*) full-bodied.

sostàre, *v.i. (aux.* avere) *&* **sostàrsi,** *v.refl.* to stop; halt; stay; pause; desist.

sostégno, *m.* support; prop. **sostenére** (*pr.* **-engo,** *&c.,* like **tenére**), *v.t.* to sustain; support, hold up; uphold; keep; maintain; back (up); stand; bear; afford; (*Theat.*) act, perform (*a part*).

sostentaménto, *m.* support; sustenance. **sostentàre,** *v.t.* to support; sustain; maintain.

sostenutézza, *f.* gravity; reserve; stiffness; haughtiness. **sostenúto,** *a.* stiff; reserved; distant (*in manner*); haughty.

sostituíre (*pr.* **-ísco, -ísci**), *v.t.* to take the place of; replace; deputize for. **sostitúto,** *m.* deputy; substitute. **sostituzióne,** *f.* change; substitution; replacement. *in* ~ *di,* in place of.

sostràto, *m.* substratum.

sottacéti, *m.pl.* pickles. **sottàcqua,** *ad.* underwater.

sottàna, *f.* petticoat; (*Eccl.*) cassock. **sottanína,** *f.* underpetticoat.

sottécchi, *ad.* stealthily; by stealth.

sottèndere, *v.t. ir.* (*Geom.*) to subtend.

sottentràre, *v.i.* (*aux.* essere) to creep in; slip in. ~ *a,* to take the place of.

sotterfúgio, *m.* subterfuge.

sottèrra, *ad.* underground. **sotterràneo,** *a.* underground; subterranean. ¶ *m.* cave; vault; dungeon. **sotterràre,** *v.t.* to bury; hide; spend, consume (*fig.*).

sottigliézza, *f.* fineness, thinness; (*fig.*) subtlety; acuteness; ingenuity. **sottíle,** *a.* thin; fine; slender; (*fig.*) subtle; sharp; sly. *mal* ~, consumption.

sottintendènte, *m.* sub-manager. **sottintèndere,** *v.t. ir.* to understand (*what is implied, not expressed*); guess, divine.

sótto, *pr. & ad.* under; beneath; underneath; below. **sotto-** as prefix = *under-; assistant-; sub-.*

sottoascèlle, *m.inv.* dress-shield.

sottocàpo, *m.* assistant chief.

sottòcchio, *ad.* before one; under one's eyes.

sottocóda, *m.* crupper (*horse*).

sottocommissióne, *f. & sotto-comitàto,* *m.* sub-committee.

sottocopèrta, *f.* under-cover *or* coverlet; (*Naut.*) lower deck.

sottocóppa, *f.* saucer.

sottocutàneo, *a.* subcutaneous.

sottofàscia, *m.inv.* printed matter posted open, under a wrapper.

sottogàmba, *ad.* carelessly; without effort; in one's stride.

sottogóla, *f.* chin-strap.

sottolineàre, *v.t.* to underline; (*fig.*) emphasize.

sottolunàre, *a.* sublunary.

sottomaríno, *a. & m.* submarine.

sottomésso, *a.* submissive, obedient; respectful. **sottométtere,** *v.t. ir.* to subdue, subject; vanquish. **sottométtersi,** *v.refl.* to submit; acquiesce; yield; give in. **sottomissióne,** *f.* submission; subjection; subjugation; submissiveness; humility; resignation.

sottomuràta, *f.* substructure.

sottopància, *m.* girth-strap; belly-band.

sottopassàggio, *m.* subway; underground passage.

sottopiède, *m.* cork sole.

sottopórre (*pr.* **-óngo, -óni,** *&c.,* like *porre*), *v.t. ir.* to submit; subject; expose. ~ *a,* to place under, put under. **sottopórsi,** *v.refl.* to submit. **sottoposizióne,** *f.* subjection; submission.

sottoprefètto, *m.* sub-prefect. **sotto-**

prióra, *f.* sub-prioress. **sottoscrítto,** *a. & m.* undersigned. **sottoscrittóre,** *m.* signatory; subscriber. **sottoscrívere,** *v.t. ir.* to subscribe; sign; underwrite. *v.i.* (*aux.* avere) to assent; agree; adhere. **sottoscrizióne,** *f.* subscription; signature.

sottosópra, *ad.* upside down; topsy-turvy.

sottospècie, *f.inv.* sub-species.

sottostàre (*pr.* **-stò, stài,** *&c.,* like *stare*), *v.i. ir.* (*aux.* essere) to lie below; occupy a subordinate position; submit; give in. ~ *a,* to be subject(ed) to; endure; experience; obey.

sottosuòlo, *m.* subsoil. **sottotenènte.** *m.* second lieutenant. ~ *di vascello,* sub-lieutenant (*Nav.*). **sottotítolo** *m.* sub-title. **sottovàso,** *m.* saucer (*for flower-pot*). **sottoventàto,** *a.* driven to leeward. **sottovènto,** *m.* (*Naut.*) lee. ¶ *ad.* leeward. **sottovèste,** *f.* waist-coat; undergarment. **sottovóce,** *ad.* in a low voice; in an undertone.

sottràrre (*pr.* **-tràggo, -trài,** *&c.,* like *trarre*), *v.t.* to subtract; deduct; withdraw; draw out; steal (*from*); embezzle. ~ *a,* conceal from; deliver from; rescue from. **sottràrsi** (a), *v.refl.* to get out of; escape from; evade; withdraw (from). **sottrazióne,** *f.* subtraction; deduction; theft.

sottufficiàle, *m.* non-commissioned officer; warrant officer (*Nav.*).

sovènte, *ad.* often.

soverchiaménte, *ad.* excessively; immoderately. **soverchiànte,** *a.* overwhelming; crushing. **soverchiàre,** *v.t.* to surpass; overcome; overflow; overwhelm; browbeat. *v.i.* (*aux.* avere) to be in excess; rise in flood. **soverchiatóre,** *m.*(*f.* **-tríce**), overbearing person. ¶ *a.* overbearing. **soverchiería,** see *soperchieria.* **sovèrchio,** *a.* excessive; immoderate; superfluous. ¶ *m.* excess; superabundance.

sóvra, see *sopra.*

sovrabbondànte, *&c.,* see *soprabbondante.*

sovràna, *f.* sovereign (*Eng. gold coin*); female ruler. **sovraneggiàre,** *v.i. & t.* (*aux.* avere) to exercise sovereign sway; to rule; domineer (over). **sovranità,** *f.* sovereignty; supremacy. **sovràno,** *a.* sovereign; supreme. ¶ *m.* sovereign (*ruler*).

sovrappórre (*pr.* **-póngo, -póni,** *&c.*, like *porre*), *v.t. ir.* to lay (things) on or upon another; place above; superimpose. **sovrappórsi** (a), *v.refl.* to place oneself above; get the better of; make oneself master of.

sovraproduzióne, *f.* over-production.

sovrastàre (a) (*pr.* **-àsto, -àsti**), *v.i.* (*aux.* avere) to hang over; dominate; surpass; impend; threaten.

sovrimpórre (*pr.* **-óngo, -óni,** *&c.*, like *porre*), *v.t. ir.* to superimpose. **sovrimpósta,** *f.* super-tax; additional tax.

sovrumàno, *a.* superhuman.

sovveníre (*pr.* **-vèngo, -vièni,** *&c.*, like *venire*), *v.t. ir.* to help; assist. *v.i.* (*aux.* essere) to occur; come to mind. ¶ *m.* memory; remembrance. **sovvenirsi,** *v.refl.* to come to mind; come back (*fig.*). ~ *di*, to remember; recall. **sovvenzióne,** *f.* subvention; subsidy.

sovversióne, *f.* overthrow; destruction; subversion. **sovversívo,** *a.* subversive. **sovvertiménto,** *m.* overturning; upsetting; overthrow; revolt. **sovvertíre** (*pr.* **-verto**), *v.t.* to subvert; overthrow; upset.

sozzaménte, *ad.* filthily; foully. **sozzàre,** *v.t.* to make filthy (usu. *insozzare*). **sozzézza,** *f.* dirtiness; filthiness. **sózzo,** *a.* filthy; foul; loathsome; polluted. **sozzúra,** *f. & * **sozzúme,** *m.* filth; foulness; loathsomeness; pollution.

spaccalégna, *m.inv.* wood-cutter. **spaccaménto,** *m.* splitting; cleaving. **spaccamontàgne & spaccamónti,** *m.inv.* braggart; boaster. **spaccapiètre,** *m.inv.* stone-breaker. **spaccàre** (*pr.* **spàcco, spàcchi**), **spaccàrsi,** *v.refl.* to split; crack; burst. **spaccatúra,** *f.* split; cleft; crack.

spacchettàre, *v.t.* to undo (*a parcel*). **spacchíno,** *m.* stone-breaker.

spacciàbile, *a.* readily saleable. **spacciàre,** *v.t.* to sell; sell out; sell off; get rid of; give out (*fig.*); spread (*reports*); dispatch; kill. **spacciàto,** *a.* done for. *è bell'e s ~!* it's all over with him! **spacciatóre,** *m.* seller; (*fig.*) distributor; one who gives currency to (*false money, news, &c.*). **spàccio,** *m.* sale; shop. **spàcco** (*pl.* **-àcchi**), *m.* split; crack; cleft. **spacconàta,** *f.* brag; braggadocio. **spaccóne,** *m.* braggart; boaster.

spàda, *f.* sword. **spadaccíno,** *m.* swordsman. **spadíno,** *m.* dirk; short sword. **spadóne,** *m.* broadsword; big sword.

spadroneggiàre, *v.i.* (*aux.* avere) to lord it; domineer.

spaesàto, *m.* displaced person.

spaghétti, *m.pl.* spaghetti, thin strings of macaroni. dim. *spaghettini*.

spaginàre, *v.t.* (*Typ.*) to alter the paging of.

spagliàre, *v.t.* to remove the straw from (*bottle, chair, &c.*).

Spàgna (la), *f.* Spain.

spagnolétta, *f.* sash-bolt (*window*); spool (*silk, &c.*); (type of) cigarette.

spagn[u]olo, *a.* Spanish. ¶ *m.* Spaniard. *lo s ~*, Spanish, the Spanish language.

spàgo (*pl.* **spàghi**), *m.* string; twine; packthread.

spaiàre, *v.t.* to separate a pair. **spaiàto,** *a.* odd; unmatched.

spalancàre (*pr.* **-ànco, -ànchi**), *v.t.* to open wide; throw open. **spalancàto,** *a.* wide open.

spalàre, *v.t.* to shovel away; sweep away; (*rowing*) feather. **spalàta &** **spalatúra,** *f.* shovelling; sweeping away.

spàlla, *f.* shoulder; (*pl.*) back; (*pl. fig.*) strength; courage; aid; expense. **spall'armi!** (*Mil.*) shoulder arms! **spallàre,** *v.t.* to sprain or dislocate the shoulder of. **spallàta,** *f.* push (or heave) of the shoulder(s); shrug of the shoulder(s).

spalleggiàre, *v.t.* to back; support.

spallétta, *f.* parapet; embankment; retaining-wall.

spallièra, *f.* back (*chair, sofa*); bedhead (or -foot); espalier; row of plants trained up a wall or espalier.

spallína, *f.* epaulet[te]. **spallúccia** (*pl.* **-úcce**), *f.* narrow shoulder. *far spalucce*, to shrug one's shoulders. **spallucciàta,** *f.* shrug of the shoulders.

spalmàre, *v.t.* to smear.

spàlto, *m.* glacis.

spampanàre, *v.t.* to strip a vine of its leaves. **spampanàrsi,** *v.refl.* to shed leaves or petals; (*fig.*) spread; expand; boast.

spàndere, *v.t.* to spread; scatter; shed; spill. **spandiménto,** *m.* spreading; scattering; shedding.

spànna, *f.* span (*width of the open hand*). **spannàre,** *v.t.* to skim (*milk*).

spannocchiàre, *v.t.* to husk; strip (*maize cobs*).

spappagallàre, *v.i.* (*aux.* avere) to chatter (*lit.* talk like a parrot).

spappolàre, *v.t.* to pulp. **spappolàrsi,** *v.refl.* to become soft or mushy.

spàragio, *m.* (*pop.* for *asparago*) asparagus.

sparàre, *v.t. & i.* to shoot; fire; discharge; rip open. **sparàta,** *f.* discharge; volley. **sparatòria,** *f.* shooting; shooting affair; exchange of shots.

sparecchiàre, *v.t.* to clear (away).

sparéggio, *m.* inequality; disparity; difference; deficit.

spàrgere, *v.t. ir.* to spread; scatter; strew; shed. **spargimento di sangue,** *m.* shedding of blood, bloodshed.

sparíre (*pr.* -ísco, -ísci, &c.), *v.i.* (*aux.* essere) to disappear; vanish. **sparizióne,** *f.* disappearance.

sparlàre, *v.i.* to speak ill (of). **sparlatóre,** *m.* (*f.* -**trice**) slanderer; backbiter.

spàro, *m.* shot; report (*gun*).

sparpagliàre, *v.t.* to scatter; disperse; squander.

sparsaménte, *ad.* sparsely; here and there; disconnectedly. **spàrso,** *p.p.* of *spargere*. ¶ *a.* scattered; loose. *in ordine* ~, (*Mil.*) in open order.

spartiàcque, *m.inv.* watershed.

spartíbile, *a.* divisible. **spartíre** (*pr.* -ísco, -ísci), *v.t.* to divide [up]; separate; share; distribute. **spartitaménte,** *ad.* separately; one by one. **spartíto,** *m.* (part of a) musical score. **spartizióne,** *f.* division; partition; distribution.

spàrto, *m.* esparto grass.

sparúto, *a.* lean; thin; spare; wan; meagre.

sparvière *or* **sparvièro,** *m.* hawk.

spasimànte, *m.* (*fig.*) ardent lover; wooer. **spasimàre,** *v.i.* (*aux.* avere) to suffer agonies; be racked with pain; long ardently. **spàs[i]mo,** *m.* pang; spasm. **spasmòdico** (*pl.* -òdici), *a.* spasmodic.

spassàrsi, *v.refl.* to amuse oneself; enjoy oneself.

spasseggiàre, &c., see *passeggiare*.

spassionàrsi, *v.rcfl.* to calm oneself; give vent to one's feelings; unbosom oneself. **spassionataménte,** *ad.* dispassionately; impartially.

spàsso, *m.* amusement; recreation; pastime. *andare a* ~, to go for a walk.

spastoiàre, *v.t.* unshackle. **spastoiàrsi** (di), *v.refl.* to get rid of.

spàto, *m.* (*Min.*) spar.

spàtola, *f.* spatula; harlequin's wooden sword. ~ *d'Arlecchino*, slap-stick.

spatriaménto, *m.* expatriation.

spauràcchio, *m.* scarecrow.

spauríre (*pr.* -ísco, -ísci), *v.t.* to frighten; terrify; alarm.

spavaldería, *f.* effrontery; impudence; defiance; boastfulness; boast. **spavàldo,** *a.* bold, arrogant; insolent; boastful; defiant.

spaventàre, *v.t.* to terrify; frighten; scare; appal. **spaventataménte,** *ad.* timorously; fearfully; in terror. **spaventàto,** *a.* frightened; fearful. **spaventévole,** *a.* frightful; terrible; appalling; huge; enormous. **spavènto,** *m.* fright; terror; fear.

spaziàre, *v.i.* (*aux.* avere) to range; rove; soar; move freely; wander about. *v.t. &* **spazieggiàre,** to space; space out. **spazieggiatúra,** *f.* (*Typ.*) spacing.

spazientírsi, *v.refl.* (*pr.* -ísco, -ísci, &c.), to lose patience.

spàzio, *m.* space; room; space of time; interval; distance. **spaziosità,** *f.* spaciousness. **spazióso,** *a.* spacious; ample; wide; large; broad.

spazzacamíno (*pl.* -íni), *m.* chimney-sweep. **spazzaménto,** *m.* sweeping.

spazzamíne, *m.inv.* mine-sweeper.

spazzanéve, *m.inv.* snow-plough.

spazzàre, *v.t.* to sweep; sweep away. **spazzàta,** *f.* (a) sweeping. **spazzatína,** *f.* light sweeping; dusting. **spazzatúra,** *f.* sweeping; (*pl.*) sweepings, refuse. **spazzaturàio** *&* **spazzíno,** *m.* sweeper; dustman; scavenger.

spàzzola, *f.* brush. **spazzolàio,** *m.* brush-maker. **spazzolàre,** *v.t.* to brush; dust. **spazzolàta,** *f.* (a) brushing. **spazzolíno,** *m.* small brush. ~ *per i denti*, tooth-brush. ~ *per le unghie*, nail-brush.

specchiàio, *m.* mirror-maker or dealer. **specchiàrsi,** *v.refl.* to look at oneself in a mirror; to be reflected (or mirrored). ~ *in*, (*fig.*) to mirror oneself on; take example from. **specchiàto,** *a.* flawless; spotless; blameless; upright. **specchièra,** *f.* looking-glass; dressing-table. **specchiétto,** *m.* hand-mirror; small looking-glass; piece of quartz placed behind a precious stone to intensify its brightness; (*fig.*) synopsis. **spècchio** (*pl.* **spècchi**), *m.* mirror;

looking-glass; pattern. ~ *retro-spettivo*, driving mirror. ~ *ustorio*, burning-glass. ~ *d'acqua*, sheet of wa:er.

speciàle, *a.* special; particular; singular. specialista (*pl.* -ísti), *m.* specialist. specialità, *f.* specialty; (*Com.*) special line. specializzàrsi, *v.refl.* to specialize.

spècie, *f.inv.* species; kind; sort; variety; description.

specífica, *f.* detailed list, bill or note. specificaménto, *m.* & specifica-zióne, *f.* specification. specificàre, *v.t.* to specify. specífico (*pl.* -ífici), *a.* & *m.* specific.

specíllo, *m.* (*Surg.*) probe.

speciosità, *f.* speciousness. specióso, *a.* specious.

spèco (*pl.* spèchi), *m.* cave; den; cavern.

spècola, *f.* observatory. spècolo, *m.* (*Surg.*) speculum. speculàre, *v.t.* & *i.* (*aux.* avere) to speculate; observe; meditate. speculatíva, *f.* speculative faculty. speculatóre, *m.* (*f.* -tríce) speculator (*trade* & *philosophy*). speculatívo, *a.* speculative. speculazióne, *f.* speculation.

spedàle, *m.* hospital. spedalità, *f.* hospital treatment.

spediènte, *m.* expedient; contrivance; makeshift.

spedíre (*pr.* -ísco, -ísci), *v.t.* to hasten; expedite; send; dispatch; forward; ship; dispatch (*goods, letters, parcels*); draw up; settle; arrange (finally); (*Med.*) make up (*prescription*); give up (*patient*); sped[isce], (*on letters*) sender, sent by. spedírsi, *v.refl.* to be quick; make haste. speditaménte, *ad.* expedi-tiously; quickly; readily; fluently. speditézza, *f.* quickness; expedition; readiness; dispatch. speditívo, *a.* expeditious; prompt. spedíto, *a.* quick; prompt; easy; fluent. ¶ *ad.* quickly; fluently. speditóre, *m.* (*f.* -tríce) sender; (*m.*) shipper; consignor. spedizióne, *f.* expedi-tion; (*goods*) shipment; shipping; forwarding; consignment; (*letters* & *parcels*) dispatch. spedizionière, *m.* forwarding-agent.

spégnere, *v.t. ir.* to extinguish; put out; blow out; (*gas*) turn out (*or* off); (*elec. light*) switch off; (*fig.*) quench; slake; allay; dilute. ~ *il motore*, to shut off the engine (*Motor*). spégnersi, *v.refl.* to be extinguished; go

out; vanish; pass away, &c. spegni-tóio, *m.* extinguisher, fire-e.

spelacchiàre & spelàre, *v.t.* to strip of hair. spelacchiàrsi & spelàrsi, *v.refl.* to lose one's hair. spelacchiàto, *a.* nearly bald; stripped of leaves; mangy; shabby.

spellàre, *v.t.* to skin; excoriate; (*fig.*) extort money from.

spelónca (*pl.* -ónche), *f.* cave; den; cavern.

spème, *f.* (*Poet.*) hope.

spendaccióne, *m.* spendthrift. spèndere, *v.t.* & *abs. ir.* (*aux.* avere) to spend; lay out; expend; employ; use; make use of. spenderéccio, *a.* lavish; prodigal; liberal. spèndita, *f.* spending. spenditóre, *m.* spender; spend-thrift.

spennacchiàre & spennàre, *v.t.* to strip of feathers; pluck; (*fig.*) fleece.

spensieratàggine & spensieratézza, *f.* thoughtlessness. spensierata-ménte, *ad.* thoughtlessly. spensi-eràto, *a.* thoughtless; careless.

spénto, *p.p.* of *spegnere*. ¶ *a.* extinguished; extinct; lifeless; dead.

spenzolàre, *v.i.* (*aux.* avere) to dangle. spenzolóne & spenzolúni, *ad.* dangling; hanging down.

spèra, *f.* sphere; (*Poet.*) sky; small round mirror; beam.

speràbile, *a.* to be hoped (for). sperànza, *f.* hope. speranzóso, *a.* hopeful. speràre, *v.t.* to hope; hope for; expect; rely (on).

spèrdere, *v.t.* to disperse; scatter; drive away; remove; lose; nullify. spèrdersi, *v.refl.* to disperse; be scattered; get lost; go astray; disappear; vanish.

sperdúto & spèrso, *a.* lost; un-comfortable; ill at ease.

spergiuràre, *v.t.* & *i.* (*aux.* avere) to swear falsely; perjure oneself. spergiúro, *a.* perjured. ¶ *m.* perjurer; perjury.

sperimentàle, *a.* experimental. sperimentàre, *v.t.* to make trial of; try; test; essay. speriménto, *m.* experiment.

spèrma, *m.* sperm.

spermacèti, *m.* spermaceti. sperma-tozòo, *m.* spermatozoon (*pl.* sperma-tozoa).

speronàre, *v.t.* to ram (*ship*). speróne, *m.* spur; abutment (*wall*); ram (*ship*).

sperperàre, *v.t.* to squander; dissi-

pate; waste. **sperperatóre,** *m.*
waster; wastrel; squanderer. **spèr-**
pero, *m.* waste; dissipation; squandering.

sperticàto, *a.* exaggerated; excessive;
overdone; (*tree*) grown too tall.

spésa, *f.* expense; cost; (*pl.*) expenses;
expenditure. **spesàre,** *v.t.* to pay
(someone's) expenses; pay the keep
of. **spesàto,** *a.* with all expenses
paid.

spesseggiàre, *v.t.* to repeat; reiterate,
v.i. (*aux.* essere *&* avere) to happen
often; be frequent; become frequent.
spessézza, *f.* density; thickness.
spésso, *a.* thick; dense; compact;
frequent. ¶ *ad.* often; frequently.
spessóre, *m.* thickness.

spettàbile, *a.* worthy of respect.
spettabilità, *f.* importance; eminence.

spettàcolo, *m.* spectacle; sight; scene;
play; entertainment; show; performance. **spettacolóso,** *a.*
spectacular; showy; sensational;
imposing.

spettànte, *a.* due. **spettànza,** *f.*
concern; business. essere di ~ (*di*),
to be one's duty. **spettàre,** *v.i.*
(*aux.* essere) to belong (to); be one's
turn; be one's duty; concern.

spettatóre, *m.* (*f.* **-tríce**) spectator;
onlooker; bystander; (*m.pl.*) audience
(*Theat.*, *&c.*).

spettegolàre, *v.i.* (*aux.* avere) to
gossip.

spettinàre, *v.t.* to ruffle the hair of.
spettinàrsi, *v.refl.* to ruffle one's
hair; take down one's hair. **spetti-**
nàto, *a.* unkempt; dishevelled;
uncombed.

spettràle, *a.* spectral; ghostly; un-
earthly; eerie, -ry; weird. **spèttro,**
m. spectre; ghost; apparition;
spectrum. **spettroscòpio,** *m.*
spectroscope.

speziàle, *m.* druggist; grocer. **spèzie,**
f.inv. spice. **spezierìa,** *f.* spices;
spicery; druggist's shop; grocer's
shop.

spezzàbile, *a.* breakable; fragile.
spezzaménto, *m.* breaking; fractur-
ing. **spezzàre,** *v.t.* to break; break
into pieces; fracture. **spezzata-**
ménte, *ad.* brokenly; spasmodically;
bit by bit; by fits and starts.
spezzatíno di vitello, *m.* veal cut
small and stewed. **spezzatúra,** *f.*
breaking; breakage; odd volume.
spezzettàre, *v.t.* to cut in(to) small
pieces; mince; hash.

spezzóne, *m.* bomb-stick; incendiary
bomb.

spìa, *f.* spy; informer; (*Sch.*) tell-tale;
sneak.

spiacènte, *a.* sorry; unpleasant.
spiacére, see *dispiacere.* **spiacé-**
vole, *a.* unpleasant; disagreeable.
spiacevolézza, *f.* unpleasantness;
disagreeableness.

spiàggia (*pl.* **spiàgge**), *f.* shore;
beach.

spianàre, *v.t.* to level; make level;
smooth; smooth out; raze to the
ground; roll out (*pastry*); (*fig.*)
elucidate. **spianàta,** *f.* levelling;
flat space; esplanade. **spianatóio,**
m. rolling-pin. **spiàno** (**a tutto**),
ad. abundantly; profusely; continuously.

spiantàre, *v.t.* to uproot; root up;
demolish; destroy. **spiantatóre,** *m.*
gardener's trowel. **spiànto,** *m.* ruin;
destruction.

spiàre, *v.t. & abs.* to spy upon; spy
into; pry into; watch; inquire into.
spiaréla, *f.* peep-hole.

spiattellàre, *v.t.* to declare openly;
speak plainly; tell flatly. **spiattella-**
taménte, *ad.* openly; plainly;
flatly; without disguise.

spiàzzo, *m.* open space; clearing (*in a*
wood).

spiccànte, *a.* bright (*colour*); striking,
spiccàre, *v.t.* to detach; cut off;
pluck (off); articulate; pronounce
distinctly; bring out clearly (*meaning,*
sense); (*Law*) issue. ~ *un salto,* to
take a leap. ~ *il volo,* to fly up;
(*fig.*) take to flight. ~ *il bollore.*
to begin to boil. *v.i.* (*aux.* avere)
to stand out; be conspicuous; excel.
spiccatamente, *ad.* distinctly;
notably; conspicuously. **spiccàto,**
a. prominent; striking; clear; distinct; strong; notable; remarkable.

spicchio, *m.* (*fruit*) segment; (*orange,*
lemon, &c.) quarter; (*apple, pear,*
&c.) slice.

spicciàre, *v.t.* to dispatch (*business*);
attend to the requirements of
(*customers, &c.*). *v.i.* (*aux.* essere)
to gush out; spurt out; dash away.
spicciàrsi, *v.refl.* to make haste.

spiccicàre, *v.t.* to detach; articulate;
pronounce clearly. **spiccio,** *a.*
expeditious; quick; prompt.

spicciolàre, *v.t.* to pluck; pick off;
change into smaller money.
spicciolàta (alla) *&* **spicciolata-**
ménte, *ad.* little by little; (a) few
at a time. **spícciolo,** *a.* small.

¶ *m.* small coin; (*pl.*) small change; coppers.

spícco, *m.* vividness; relief. *fare* ~, to stand out; catch the eye.

spicilègio, *m.* scrap-book; selection (*Lit.*); gleaning.

spidocchiàre, *v.t.* to delouse; clean from lice.

spièdo, *m.* (*kitchen*) spit.

spiegàbile, *a.* explicable. **spiegaménto**, *m.* explanation; unfolding; spreading out; (*Mil.*) deployment. **spiegàre**, *v.t.* to spread (out); lay out; display; unfold; unfurl; deploy (*troops*); raise (*voice*); explain; justify; interpret. **spiegàrsi**, *v.refl.* to explain oneself; make oneself understood; open; be unfurled. **spiegataménte**, *ad.* openly; clearly. **spiegatívo**, *a.* explanatory. **spiegatúra**, *f.* unfolding. **spiegazióne**, *f.* explanation.

spiegazzàre, *v.t.* to crumple (up); crease; rumple.

spietàto, *a.* pitiless; ruthless; implacable.

spifferàre, *v.i.* (*aux.* avere) to play the pipe. *v.t.* (*of wind*) to blow through a narrow aperture; to repeat all that one has seen or heard. **spifferàta**, *f.* playing of pipes. **spiffero**, *m.* draught of air. **spifferóne**, *m.* telltale.

spíga (*pl.* **spíghe**), *f.* ear of corn. *mattonato a* ~, herring-boned brickwork. *tessuto a* ~, twill; twilled cloth. **spighétta**, *f.* trimming; braid.

spigliataménte, *ad.* freely; easily. **spigliatézza**, *f.* ease; agility; nimbleness; self-possession. **spigliàto**, *a.* easy; graceful; accomplished; self-possessed.

spígo, *m.* lavender.

spigolàre, *v.t.* to glean. **spigolatóre**, *m.* (*f.* **-tríce**) gleaner. **spigolatúra**, *f.* gleaning.

spígolo, *m.* sharp corner.

spigríre (*pr.* **-ísco**, **-ísci**), *v.i.* & **spigrírsi**, *v.refl.* to shake off laziness.

spílla, *f.* tie-pin; brooch.

spillaccheràre, *v.t.* to brush off mud from.

spillàio, *m.* pin-maker. **spillàre**, *v.t.* to broach; pierce; tap (*cask*). **spillàtico** (*pl.* **-àtici**), *m.* pin-money. **spillatúra**, *f.* tapping; broaching; piercing. **spíllo**, *m.* pin; hair-pin; jet of water; piercer; gimlet. **spillóne**, *m.* hat-pin.

spilorcería, *f.* niggardliness; stinginess; meanness; tight-fistedness. **spilòrcio**, *a.* stingy; mean; miserly; close-fisted. ¶ *m.* miser; niggard.

spiluccàre, *v.t.* to pluck off.

spilungóne, *a.* very tall and thin. ¶ *m.* (*f.* **-óna**) lanky fellow; very tall girl.

spína, *f.* thorn [bush]; thorn; spine (*Bot.*); fish-bone; bung-hole (*cask*); (*Elec.*) plug; pin of a lock. ~ *dorsale*, spine; backbone.

spinàce, *m.* spinach. *pl.* *gli spinaci*, spinach (*Cook.*).

spinàio, *m.* thicket.

spinàle, *a.* spinal.

spinàto, *a.* thorny; barbed; twilled. **spinéto**, *m.* brier-bush; thicket.

spíngere, *v.t.* *ir.* to push; shove; drive; thrust; (*fig.*) to induce.

spiníte, *f.* spinal meningitis; inflammation of the membrane(s) of the spinal cord.

spíno, *m.* thorn-tree. **spinosità**, *f.* spinosity; thorniness; (*fig.*) difficulty; ticklishness. **spinóso**, *a.* full of spines; prickly; thorny (*lit.* & *fig.*); (*fig.*) perplexing; troublesome; ticklish; knotty.

spínta, *f.* push; shove; thrust.

spínte o spónte, *ad.* *exp.* by hook or [by] crook.

spínto, *p.p.* of *spingere*. ¶ *a.* high; ambitious (*gen.* *with* *troppo*). **spintóne**, *m.* violent shove.

spiombàre, *v.t.* to raise the lead (*Naut.*); *v.i.* (*aux.* essere & avere) to weigh as heavy as lead.

spionàggio, *m.* espionage; spying. **spioncíno**, *m.* peep-hole. **spióne**, *m.* (*important*) spy; master-spy. **spiovènte**, *a.* falling; drooping. **spiòvere**, *v.i.* (*aux.* essere) to stop raining; run off (*water*); flow; fall (*of hair*, . . . *over the shoulders*).

spippolàre, *v.t.* to pick off; (*fig.*) rattle off.

spíra, *f.* spiral; coil.

spiràbile, *a.* fit to be breathed; breathable. **spiràglio**, *m.* air-hole; vent[-hole]; sky-light; small opening; (*fig.*) gleam.

spiràle, *a.* & *f.* spiral.

spiràre, *v.i.* (*aux.* avere) to blow softly; breathe. *v.i.* (*aux.* essere) (*fig.*) breathe one's last, expire, pass away; die; end; expire (*period set*). *v.t.* to breathe out; give off; exhale; inspire.

spiritàre, *v.i.* (*aux.* essere) to shiver; be possessed (*by an evil spirit*);

tremble with fear. **spiritàto,** *a.* possessed; crazy; mad; terrified. **spiritèllo,** *m.* sprite.

spiritísmo, *m.* spiritualism.

spírito, *m.* spirit; ghost; mind; soul; sense; wit; courage; temper; boldness; humour; head; leader; inspiration; alcohol; alcoholic spirit (*oft. pl.*); (*Gram.*) breathing. lo S~ Santo, the Holy Ghost; the Holy Spirit. **spiritosàggine,** *f.* effort at wit. **spiritosità,** *f.* wit; wittiness; witticism; vivacity; alcoholic strength. **spiritóso,** *a.* witty; vivacious; (*wine*) strong; spirituous; alcoholic. **spirituàle,** *a.* spiritual. **spiritualísmo,** *m.* spiritualism (*Phil.*).

spíro, *m.* (*Poet.*) spirit; breath; soul.

spirtàle, *a.* (*Poet.* for *spirituale*) spiritual.

spiumacciàre, *v.t.* to shake up (*bed, esp.*). **spiumàre,** *v.t.* to pluck; strip of feathers; (*fig.*) to fleece. **spiumàrsi,** *v.refl.* to lose one's feathers.

spizzicàre, *v.t.* to pinch; nibble; take a little of. **spizzicatúra,** *f.* (*Typ.*) faulty impression.

splendènte, *a.* bright; shining; resplendent. **splèndere,** *v.i.* (*aux.* essere & avere) to shine; be resplendent. **splendidézza,** *f.* magnificence. **splèndido,** *a.* splendid; gorgeous; magnificent. **splendóre,** *m.* brightness; splendour; magnificence.

splenètico (*pl.* -ètici), *a.* splenetic.

Splúga (Passo dello), *m.* Splügen Pass.

spodestàre, *v.t.* to dispossess; deprive of power or property; dethrone.

spoetizżàre, *v.t.* to deprive of one's illusions; shock. **spoetizżàrsi,** *v.refl.* to become coarse; lose one's ideals.

spòglia, *f.* slough (*serpent, worm*); skin (*wild beast*); spoil; booty; remains (*mortal*); fallen leaves.

spogliaménto, *m.* & **spogliatúra,** *f.* spoliation; plundering; stripping; divesting; undressing. **spogliàre,** *v.t.* to undress; strip; divest; despoil; plunder; cast (*skin*). **spogliàrsi,** *v.refl.* to undress (*oneself*); divest oneself (of). **spogliatóio,** *m.* dressing-room. **spogliatóre,** *m.* despoiler; plunderer. **spogliazióne,** *f.* spoliation; plundering. **spòglio,** *a.* bare; uncovered; undressed. ¶ *m.* scrutiny; examination; perusal;

selection; stripping; undressing; counting (*of votes*); (*pl.*) cast-off clothes.

spòla, *f.* shuttle. **spolétta,** *f.* fuse.

spolmonàrsi, *v.refl.* to shout oneself hoarse; (*lit.*) tire one's lungs.

spolpàre, *v.t.* to strip the flesh off; (*fig.*) to despoil; fleece; bleed white.

spoltríre (*pr.* spóltro & **spoltrísco**) & **spoltroníre** (*pr.* -ísco), *v.t.* to cure of laziness.

spolveràre, *v.t.* to dust; brush; (*Art*) pounce; (*fig.*) make a clean sweep of; eat greedily. **spolveratóre,** *m.* duster. ~ elettrico, vacuum cleaner. **spolverína,** *f.* dust-cloak. **spolveríno,** *m.* pounce-box. **spolverío,** *m.* cloud of dust. **spolverizżàre,** *v.t.* to powder; sprinkle with powder; pulverize; (*Art*) to pounce. **spólvero,** *m.* dusting; dust raised by dusting; fine flour; pounce; (*fig.*) smattering; show[iness].

spónda, *f.* bank; edge; border; side of a cart; parapet.

sponsàli, *m.pl.* nuptials; wedding.

spontaneità, *f.* spontaneity; spontaneousness. **spontàneo,** *a.* spontaneous; voluntary.

spònte o spínte, *ad. expr.* willy-nilly.

spopolàre, *v.t.* to depopulate.

spoppàre, *v.t.* to wean.

spòra, *f.* (*Bot.*) spore. **sporàdico** (*pl.* -àdici), *a.* sporadic.

sporcacciàre, *v.t.* to make filthy. **sporcaccióne,** *m.* filthy person. **sporcàre,** *v.t.* to dirty; soil; foul; besmirch. **sporchézza,** *f.* dirtiness; filth[iness]. **sporcheria** & **sporcízia,** *f.* dirt; filth. **spòrco** (*pl.* spòrchi), *a.* dirty; foul; filthy.

sporgènte, *a.* jutting; protruding; projecting. **sporgènza,** *f.* protrusion; projection; jutting point. **spòrgere,** *v.i. ir.* (*aux.* essere) to project; jut out. *v.t.* to stretch out; hold out; put out; put forward; present; hand out. ~ querela, to lodge a complaint. **spòrgersi,** *v.refl.* to lean out; jut out; stand out; protrude.

spòrta, *f.* basket; shopping basket; hamper; wide-brimmed straw-hat.

sportèllo, *m.* wicket [gate]; shutter; counter (*cashier's*); booking-office; ticket-window; carriage-door.

sportívo, *a.* sporting; sportsmanlike. ¶ *m.* sporting man.

spòrto, *p.p.* of *sporgere.* ¶ *a.* outstretched. ¶ *m.* projection; stall for display of goods in front of a shop.

spòsa, *f.* bride; betrothed [bride]; spouse, wife. sposalízio, *m.* wedding. sposàre, *v.t.* to marry; give in marriage; betroth; (*fig.*) to embrace; espouse: adopt. sposàrsi, *v.refl.* to get married; marry. sposína & sposétta, *f.* young bride; young wife. sposíno, *m.* young husband. spòso, *m.* bridegroom; husband. *pl. gli sposi,* the married couple. *i promessi ~ i,* the betrothed.

spossaménto, *m.* & spossatézza, *f.* exhaustion; weakness; prostration. spossàre, *v.t.* to exhaust. spossataménte, *ad.* wearily.

spostaménto, *m* displacement; change; shift[ing]. spostàre, *v.t.* to move; shift; displace; change; alter.

sprànga, *f.* bar; cross-bar; bolt. sprangàre, *v.t.* to bar; bolt.

spràzzo, *m.* splash; flash; spot of light; beam; gleam.

sprecaménto & sprèco (*pl.* sprèchi), *m.* squandering; dissipation; waste. sprecàre, *v.t.* to waste; squander; dissipate; use up. sprecóne & sprecatóre, *m.* squanderer; waster; wastrel.

spregévole, *a.* contemptible; despicable; mean. spregiàre, *v.t.* to despise; disdain. spregiatívo, *a.* disdainful; disparaging. spregiatóre, *m.* scorner; despiser. sprègio, *m.* contempt; scorn; disdain.

spregiudicàre, *v.t.* to free from prejudice. spregiudicàrsi, *v.refl.* to get rid of one's prejudices. spregiudicatézza, *f.* open-mindedness, freedom from prejudice. spregiudicàto, *a.* unprejudiced; open-minded.

sprèmere, *v.t. ir.* to squeeze; press (out); wring. spremilimóni, *m.inv.,* & spremitóio, *m.* lemonsqueezer. spremitura, *f.* squeezing; pressing (out); wringing. spremúta, *f.* squash. *~ di limone,* lemon-squash. spremúto, *p.p.* of *spremere.*

spretàre, *v.t.* to unfrock (*priest*).

sprezzàbile, *a.* contemptible; despicable. sprezzànte, *a.* contemptuous; haughty; disdainful. sprezzàre, *v.t.* to despise; scorn; slight; disdain. sprezzatóre, *m.* (*f.* -tríce) scorner; despiser. ¶ *a.* scornful; con-

temptuous. sprèzzo, *m.* contempt; scorn; disdain.

sprigionàre, *v.t.* to release; set free; (*fig.*) emit; give off; exhale.

sprillàre, *v.i.* (*aux.* essere) to spout; spirt out. spríllo, *m.* spout; jet.

sprimacciàre, *v.t.* to shake up.

sprizzàre, *v.i.* (*aux.* essere) to spout; spurt out. *v.t.* to sprinkle; spray.

spròcco (*pl.* spròcchi), *m.* shoot; twig.

sprofondaménto, *m.* sinking; foundering. sprofondàre, *v.t.* to sink; send to the bottom. *v.i.* (*aux.* essere) to sink; founder; go to the bottom; give way. sprofondàrsi, *v.refl.* to sink (*lit.* & *fig.*); sink back; be absorbed.

sprolòquio, *m.* long rambling speech; nonsensical tirade.

spronaménto, *m.* spurring; incitement. spronàre, *v.t.* to spur; goad; (*fig.*) incite; urge. spróne, *m.* spur; (*battleship*) ram; (*fig.*) stimulus.

sproporzionàle & sproporzionàto, *a.* disproportionate. sproporzionalità & sproporzióne, *f.* want of proportion; disproportion.

spropositàre, *v.i.* to blunder; talk nonsense. spropòsito, *m.* mistake; blunder; absurdity; excessive amount.

spropriàre, *v.t.* to expropriate. spropriàrsi, *v.refl.* to sell one's property.

sprovvedére (*pr.* -édo, -édi, -éde, &c., like *vedere*), *v.t. ir.* to deprive; leave unprovided. sprovvista (alla), *ad. expr.* unawares; unexpectedly. sprovvedúto & sprovvísto, *a.* unprovided; destitute.

spruzzàglia, *f.* spray; fine rain; drizzle. spruzzàre, *v.t.* to spray; sprinkle; splash. *v.i.* (*aux.* essere & avere) to drizzle. spruzzàta, *f.* sprinkling, spraying; light shower. sprúzzo, *m.* spray, splash.

spudoràto, *a.* shameless; impudent.

spúgna, *f.* sponge. spugnàta & spugnatúra, *f.* sponge (*action*); sponging; sponge down. spugnóso, *a.* spongy.

spulàre, *v.t.* to winnow; fan. spulatúra, *f.* winnowing; fanning.

spulciàre, *v.t.* to rid of fleas; (*fig.*) to scrutinize; examine minutely. spulciatúra, *f.* (*fig.*) scrutiny; close inspection.

spuleżżàre, *v.i.* (*aux.* essere) to run away; make off. spuléżżo, *m.* flight.

spúma, *f.* foam; froth. spumànte, *a.* foaming; (*wine*) sparkling. spumàre & spumeggiàre, *v.i.* (*aux.* avere) to foam; froth; sparkle. spumóso, *a.* frothy; foamy.

spuntàre, *v.t.* to blunt; break the point of; cut (off) the tip of; trim; undo; unpin; (*fig.*) overcome; remove; erase; strike out. *v.i.* (*aux.* essere) to appear; (*sun*) rise; (*day*) break; dawn; peep out; begin to be visible; (*tears*) start; well up. spuntatúra, *f.* blunting; cutting off the tip; tip; stump; end.

spuntellàre, *v.t.* to unprop.

spuntino, *m.* snack; light refreshment; snack bar.

spúnto, *m.* acidity; sourness; (*prompter's*) cue; starting point; rise; origin; impulse; (*sport*) spurt.

spunzecchiàre, *v.t.* to prick. spunzonàre, *v.t.* to prod.

spurgàre, *v.t.* to purge; clean; clear one's throat; expectorate. spúrgo (*pl.* spúrghi), *m.* purging; cleansing; expectoration; (*Med.*) discharge; (*pl.*) remnants, residue.

spúrio, *a.* spurious; illegitimate.

sputacchiàre, *v.i.* (*aux.* avere) to spit (repeatedly). sputacchièra, *f.* spittoon. sputapépe, *m.inv.* irritable person; witty talker. sputàre, *v.t.* & *i.* to spit. sputasénno & sputasentènze, *m.inv.* wiseacre. spúto, *m.* spit; spittle; spitting.

squadernàre, *v.t.* to turn over the leaves of (*book*); open wide; examine; exhibit.

squàdra, *f.* (carpenter's) square; (*Mil.*) squad; (*naval*) squadron; detachment; group; team. doppia ~, T-square. essere a ~, to be at right angles. ~ di soccorso, breakdown gang. ~ mobile, ~ volante, flying squad. squadràre, *v.t.* to square; look one squarely in the face; look one up and down. squadríglia, *f.* small square; squadron (*Aviat.*, *Naut.*, & *light craft*). squàdro, *m.* squaring; (engineer's) square.

squagliàre, *v.t.* to melt; melt down; liquefy. squagliàrsi, *v.refl.* to melt down; (*fig.*) make off; steal away.

squalífica *f.* disqualification.

squàllido, *a.* dismal; dreary; cheerless; gloomy; grim. squalióre, *m.* dreariness; cheerlessness; gloom.

squàlo, *m.* shark; dog-fish.

squàma, *f.* scale (*fish or snake*); flake (*metal*). squamàre, *v.t.* to scale;

remove scales. squamóso, *a.* scaly; flaky.

squarciagola (a), *ad. expr.* at the top (or pitch) of one's voice. squarciaménto, *m.* tearing; rending; ripping up. squarciàre, *v.t.* to tear; rend; rip up. squàrcio, *m.* rent; gash; piece torn off; extract from a book.

squartaménto, *m.* quartering. squartàre, *v.t.* to cut up; quarter; chop. squartatóio, *m.* chopper; butcher's cleaver.

squassaménto, *m.* violent shaking. squassàre, *v.t.* to shake violently; rock; brandish. squàsso, *m.* violent shock.

squattrinàre, *v.t.* to leave penniless. *v.i.* (*aux.* avere) to spend largely. squattrinàrsi, *v.refl.* to be left penniless. squattrinàto, *a.* penniless.

squilibràre, *v.t.* to throw out of balance; unbalance. squilibràrsi, *v.refl.* to lose one's balance; (*fig.*) get into difficulties. squilibràto, *a.* unbalanced; deranged; mad. ¶ *m.* unbalanced person; one mentally deranged. squilíbrio, *m.* lack of balance; difference; inequality.

squilla, *f.* bell; small bell; harness-bell; cow-bell; sound of the Ave Maria. squillànte, *a.* shrill; ringing sharp and clear; pealing; blaring (*trumpet*). squillàre, *v.i.* (*aux.* avere) to ring; peal; blare; sound; resound. squillo, *m.* blast (*horn*, *trumpet*); peal (*bell*); any sharp and resonant sound.

squinànzia, *f.* quinsy.

squinternàre, *v.t.* to take (a book) to pieces; turn over the leaves of (a book); (*fig.*) ruffle; confuse; scrutinize.

squisitézza, *f.* rare quality; excellence; delicacy; perfection. squisíto, *a.* delicious; delicate; exquisite; of rare quality.

squittínio, *m.* balloting; scrutiny of votes.

squittíre (*pr.* -ísco, -ísci), *v.i.* (*aux.* avere) to yelp.

sradicàre, *v.t.* to uproot; eradicate; extirpate.

sragionaménto, *m.* irrational talk; false reasoning. sragionàre, *v.i.* (*aux.* avere) to talk irrationally; reason falsely. sragionévole, *a.* unreasonable; irrational; senseless; preposterous.

sregolatézza, *f.* disorder; intemperance; dissipation; excess. sregolàto,

a. disordered; intemperate; immoderate; dissolute.
stabbi[u]òlo, *m.* sty; pig-sty.
stàbile, *a.* stable; fixed; firm; steady; settled; durable; lasting; permanent. *beni ∼ i*, real estate. ¶ *m.* landed property; building; house. **stabiliménto**, *m.* establishment; settlement; works; factory. **stabilíre** (*pr.* -ísco, -ísci), *v.t.* to establish; fix; settle; determine upon; ascertain; state. **stabilírsi**, *v.refl.* to establish oneself; settle. **stabilità**, *f.* stability; steadiness; firmness. **stabilizzàre**, *v.t.* to stabilize.
staccàbile, *a.* detachable. *foglio ∼*, loose leaf. **staccaménto**, *m.* detachment; separation; unfastening, &c. **staccàre**, *v.t.* to detach; separate; remove; pull off; unhook; take down (*pictures*); unyoke; pronounce each word distinctly; play a note *staccato*. *v.i.* (*aux.* avere) to stand out prominently. **staccàrsi**, *v.refl.* to become detached, &c.; withdraw (from); retire (from); break off; break away from.
stacciàre, *v.t.* to sift; sieve; bolt. **stacciatúra**, *f.* sifting; siftings; bran. **stàccio**, *m.* sieve; hair-sieve.
stàcco (*pl.* **stàcchi**), *m.* separation; detachment; difference; piece detached; ticket.
stadèra, *f.* steelyard.
stàdio, *m.* stadium; sports ground; stage; degree of progress.
stàffa, *f.* stirrup; foot-board (*carriage*). **staffétta**, *f.* small stirrup; courier; despatch-rider. *macchina ∼*, pilot-engine. *corsa ∼*, relay race. **staffière**, *m.* groom; footman.
staffilaménto, *m.* & **staffilàta**, **staffilatúra**, *f.* whipping; thrashing. **staffilàre**, *v.t.* to whip; thrash; flog. **staffíle**, *m.* whip (*leather*); strap; thong; stirrup-strap.
staggiàre, *v.t.* to prop (*fruit-trees*). **stàggio**, *m.* prop; stay; stay-rod; one of the two shafts of a ladder; back leg (or high back) of a chair; upright bar of a cage.
stagionàre, *v.t.* & *i.* (*aux.* essere) to season; ripen; mature. **stagionàto**, *a.* seasoned; ripe; mature; elderly. **stagióne**, *f.* season, time (*of year*). *i prezzi di ∼*, high-season charges. *i prezzi fuori ∼*, off-season c.
stagnàio, *m.* tin-smith; tinman. **stagnaménto**, *m.* soldering; stagnation. **stagnàre**, *v.t.* to tin; cover or line with tin; solder; stanch

(*blood*, &*c.*). *v.i.* (*aux.* avere) to stagnate. **stagnàta**, *f.* tinning; tin-pan; packet (*of tobacco*, &*c.*) wrapped in tin-foil. **stagníno**, *m.* tin-smith; tinman. **stàgno**, *m.* tin; pond. ¶ *a.* water-tight. **stagn[u]òla**, *f.* tin-foil.
stàio (*pl.m.* **stài**, & *f.* **stàia**), *m.* bushel.
stalagmíte (*pl.* -íti), *f.* stalagmite. **stalattíte** (*pl.* -íti), *f.* stalactite.
stàlla, *f.* stable; cow-shed. **stallàggio**, *m.* stabling. **stallière**, *m.* stableman; stable-boy. **stàllo**, *m.* stall (*church*); seat (*of honour*); (chess) stalemate. **stallóne**, *m.* stallion.
stamàne, **stamàni** & **stamattìna**, *ad.* this morning.
stambécco (*pl.* -écchi), *m.* wild goat. **stambèrga**, *f.* den; garret; hovel. **stambúgio**, *m.* small dark room. **stamburàre**, *v.i.* (*aux.* avere) to beat the drum; (*v.t.*) to sing the praises of. **stamburàta**, *f.* drumming.
stàme, *m.* thread; fine carded wool; (*Bot.*) stamen.
stàmpa, *f.* impress; impression; stamp; stamping; mould; print; printing; press; press work; machining (*Typ.*); engraving; sort; class; (*pl.*) printed matter. *∼ in rilievo a secco*, blind blocking (*Typ.*). *∼ con matrice di acciaio*, die stamping. *errore di ∼*, misprint. *ritagli di ∼*, press cuttings. **stampàre**, *v.t.* to print; stamp; impress; strike (*coins*); punch. **stampatèllo**, *m.* print-like characters; block letters. **stampàto**, *m.* printed form; (*pl.*) printed matter. **stampatóre**, *m.* printer. *nome dello ∼*, imprint.
stampèlla, *f.* crutch.
stamperìa, *f.* printing-works; printing office. **stampíglia**, *f.* board with movable numbers (*lottery*, &*c.*); rubber or metal stamp; fly-sheet; printed form. **stampíno**, *m.* stencil. **stàmpo**, *m.* stamp; mould; (*fig.*) kind, sort, type, class.
stanàre, *v.t.* to drive out; find out.
stancaménte, *ad.* wearily. **stancàre**, *v.t.* to tire; fatigue; weary; exhaust; bore. **stanchévole**, *a.* tiring; tiresome; wearisome. **stanchézza**, *f.* tiredness; weariness; fatigue. **stànco** (*pl.* **stànchi**), *a.* tired; weary; annoyed; sick (of); fatigued; (*land*) exhausted.
stànga, *f.* bar; (*cart*) shaft. **stangàre**, *v.t.* to bar. **stanghétta**, *f.* small bar;

bolt (*lock*); vertical line of division in writing or print; (curved) arm of spectacles.

stanòtte, *ad.* to-night; this night; last night.

stànte (*pres. part.* of *stare*), *a.* this; present; existing; current. ¶ *pr.* owing to; on account of; considering. *poco* ~, a short time ago. *seduta* ~, during (the sitting). ~ *che*, as; since; seeing that.

stantío, *a.* stale.

stantúffo, *m.* piston; (*pump*) plunger.

stànza, *f.* room; apartment; (place of) residence; (*verse*) stanza. ~ *di compensazione* (Banking), clearing-house. **stanziàle**, *a.* permanent.

stanziaménto, *m.* deliberation; decree; (*of funds*) setting apart; appropriation. **stanziàre**, *v.t.* to set apart (funds) for a special purpose; appropriate. *v.i.* (*aux.* avere) to deliberate; decree; (*Mil.*) to be quartered.

stanzíno, *m.* small room; closet.

stappàre, *v.t.* to uncork.

stàre (*pr.* stò, stài, stà, &*c.*), *v.i. ir.* (*aux.* essere) to stay; stand; lie; sit; be situated; remain; keep; stop; wait; be; live; consist; depend; fit; suit. ~*bene*, ~ *male*, to be well, unwell. ~ *fermo*, to stand still. ~ *ritto*, to stand upright, s. straight. ~ *saldo*, to stand firm, s. fast. ~ *a vedere*, to wait & see. ~ *a sentire*, to wait to hear. ~ *ad ascoltare*, to listen. ~ *a sedere*, to be seated, remain seated. ~ *allo scherzo*, to take a joke. ~ *per* (*with infin.*) to be about to; (*with n.* or *pn.*) to side with, support. ~ *sulle generali*, to keep to generalities. ~ *in forse*, to be in doubt. ~ *al viso*, to suit the complexion.

stàrna, *f.* partridge. **starnazzàre**, *v.i.* to flutter; flap the wing on the ground; (*birds*) dust.

starnutaménto, *m.* sneezing. **starnutàre** & **starnutíre** (*pr.* -ísco, -ísci), *v.i.* (*aux.* avere) to sneeze. **starnúto**, *m.* sneeze; sneezing.

staséra, *ad.* this evening, to-night.

stàsi, *f.* (*Med.*) stasis; inactivity; stoppage; standstill.

statàle, *a.* of the state; state (*att.*). ¶ *n.* state employé; civil servant.

statàre, *v.i.* (*aux.* avere) to summer; pass the summer.

statàrio, *a.* steady; (*Law*) summary.

stàte, *f.* (*pop.* for *estate*) summer.

staterèllo, *m.* small state. **stàtica**, *f.* statics. **stàtico** (*pl.* -àtici), *a.* static. **statísta** (*pl.* -ísti), *m.* statesman. **statística**, *f.* statistics.

stàto, *m.* state; condition; situation; frame (of mind); plight; repair; order; fettle; trim; status; position; posture; profession; occupation; record; account; return; list. *S* ~, *m.* State; government. *gli* ~ *i balcanici*, the Balkan States. *lo S* ~ *Libero d'Irlanda*, the Irish Free State. *gli S* ~ *i Uniti*, the United States (of America).

stàtua, *f.* statue. **statuària**, *f.* statuary; sculpture. **statuàrio**, *m.* statuary (*pers.*). ¶ *a.* statuary.

statuétta, *f.* statuette.

statuíre (*pr.* -ísco, -ísci), *v.t.* to decree; ordain.

statúra, *f.* stature; height (*of pers.*), size.

statutàle & **statutàrio**, *a.* statutory. **statúto**, *m.* statute; constitution; articles of association.

stavòlta, *ad.* (for *questa v.*) this time.

stazionàre, *v.i.* (*aux.* avere) to stay; stop. **stazionàrio**, *a.* stationary. **stazióne**, *f.* station. ~ *balneare*, watering place. ~ *climatica*, health resort.

stàzza, *f.* tonnage (of ship); gauging-rod. **stazzàre**, *v.t.* to gauge; measure; have a tonnage of.

stearína, *f.* stearin. **steatíte**, *f.* steatite.

stécca (*pl.* stécche), *f.* small stick; slat; rib (of fan or umbrella); splint; [billiard] cue; paper-knife; piece of whalebone (in corsets); (*Rly.*) fish-plate; (*Mus.*) false note. **steccàre**, *v.t.* to fence in; rail off; put in splints; cut with a paper-knife. **steccàto**, *m.* paling; palisade; rails (*racecourse*). **stecchétto**, *m.* small stick; (*fig.*) short rations; short allowance. **stecchíno**, *m.* toothpick. **stecchíre** (*pr.* -ísco, -ísci, &*c.*), *v.t.* to kill (instantly); *v.i.* (*aux.* essere) & **stecchírsi**, *v.refl.* to become stiff; dry up; grow lean. **stecchíto**, *a.* dead; dried up; parched; extremely thin. *morto* ~, stone dead. **stécco** (*pl.* stécchi), *m.* stick; dry twig; thorn; tooth-pick.

stecconàre, *v.t.* to fence in. **stecconàta**, *f.* & **stecconàto**, *m.* enclosure; stockade. **steccóne**, *m.* stake.

stèla & **stèle**, *f.* pillar.

stélla, *f.* star (lit. & fig.); rowel (of spur); asterisk. ~ *di mare*, starfish.

~ *del mattino*, morning-star. ~ *cadente,* ~ *filante,* shooting-star, falling star. **stellàre,** *a.* stellar. **stellàto,** *a.* starry; starred; starli[gh]t; (*Bot.*) stellate[d]. **stellétta,** *f.* small star; asterisk; star (*on uniform*).

stèlo, *m.* stem; stalk.

stèmma (*pl.* **stèmmi**), *m.* coat of arms; escutcheon; crest; armorial bearings.

stemperàre, *v.t.* to dilute; dissolve; mix. **stemperàrsi,** *v.refl.* to melt.

stemperataménte, *ad.* immoderately; excessively.

stendàrdo, *m.* standard; banner.

stèndere, *v.t.* *ir.* to spread (out); stretch (out); lay out; extend; knock down; draw up (*a report*); smooth out (*wrinkles*). **stèndersi,** *v.refl.* to stretch oneself; spread; extend.

stenebràre, *v.t.* (*fig.*) to enlighten.

stenodattilògrafa, *f.* **stenodattilògrafo,** *m.* shorthand typist. **stenografàre,** *v.t.* to write in shorthand; take down (in shorthand). **stenografía,** *f.* shorthand; stenography. **stenògrafo,** *m.* shorthand writer; stenographer.

stentàre, *v.i.* (*aux.* avere) to be in need; be hardly able; find it hard to; have difficulty (in, over). **stentatézza,** *f.* difficulty; narrow circumstances; poverty. **stentàto,** *a.* hard; difficult; straitened; stunted; laboured (*style*). **stentíno,** *m.* stunted child. **stènto,** *m.* hardship; suffering; privation; difficulty; effort; toil. ¶ *a.* stunted.

stentòreo, *a.* stentorian.

stéppa, *f.* steppe (*Geog.*).

stèrco (*pl.* **stèrchi**), *m.* excrement; dung.

stereometría, *f.* solid geometry.

stereoscòpio, *m.* stereoscope. **stereotipàre,** *v.t.* to stereotype. **stereotipía,** *f.* stereotyping; stereotype.

stèrile, *a.* sterile; barren; unfruitful; useless; vain. **sterilità,** *f.* sterility; barrenness; unproductiveness. **sterilizzàre,** *v.t.* to sterilize.

sterlína, *f.* (*Eng.*) pound; pound sterling.

sterminaménto, *m.* extermination; destruction. **sterminàre,** *v.t.* to destroy; ravage; exterminate. **sterminatézza,** *f.* boundlessness; immensity. **sterminàto,** *a.* limitless; boundless; endless; immense; enormous. **sterminatóre,** *m.* (*f.* **-tríce**) destroyer. ¶ *a.* destroying.

stermínio, *m.* destruction; extermination.

stèrno, *m.* breast-bone.

sternutàre & **sternutíre** (*pr.* **-ísco,** **-ísci**), *v.i.* (*aux.* avere) to sneeze. **sternúto,** *m.* sneeze; sneezing.

sterpàglia, *f.* weeds; brushwood; undergrowth. **sterpàio,** *m.* thicket. **sterpàme,** *m.* heap of brushwood. **stèrpo,** *m.* stump; stub; decaying shoot.

sterràre, *v.t.* to dig up; dig out; excavate; level. **stèrro,** *m.* digging up; excavation; earth dug up.

stertóre, *m.* stertorous breathing.

sterzàre, *v.t.* to divide (*lit. into three parts*); divide proportionately; thin out (*a wood*). *v.t.* & *i.* (*aux.* avere) (*of a carriage*) to turn. **sterzàrsi,** *v.refl.* to take turns at work; share out one's work or income. **stèrzo,** *m.* transom; pruning; thinning.

stéso, *p.p.* of *stendere.* ¶ *a.* smeared; spread.

stèssere, *v.t.* to unweave; (*fig.*) unravel.

stésso, *a.* & *pn.* same; self.

stesúra, *f.* drawing up; drafting; draft.

stetoscòpio, *m.* stethoscope.

stía, *f.* hen-coop.

stíge, *m.* Styx (*Myth.*).

stigma, (*pl.f.* **le stigmate**) *m.* stigma; stamp; brand.

stíle & **stílo,** *m.* style; beam (*balance*); dagger. **stilettàre,** *v.t.* to stab. **stilettàta,** *f.* stab. **stilétto,** *m.* small dagger; stiletto. **stilísta** (*pl.* **-ísti**), *m.* stylist. **stilística,** *f.* rhetoric; precepts of literary style.

stílla, *f.* drop. **stillàre,** *v.t.* & *i.* (*aux.* essere) to exude; drip; ooze; distil. *stillarsi il cervello,* to rack one's brains. **stillicídio,** *m.* dripping.

stílio, *m.* still.

stílo, *m.* stylus; arm of a steelyard; shaft of a column; axis of a spiral staircase; stiletto. **stilogràfica** (**penna**), *f.* fountain pen; stylograph.

stíma, *f.* esteem; estimation; respect; consideration; valuation; dead reckoning. **stimàbile,** *a.* estimable; respectable. **stimàre,** *v.t.* to esteem; appreciate; reckon; judge; consider; think; deem; value; estimate; appraise. **stimatóre,** *m.* valuer; appraiser.

stímmate, *f.pl.* stigmata (*of St. Francis,* &c.).

stimolàre, *v.t.* to stimulate; urge on; goad; whet; (*fig.*) drive; encourage;

excite. **stimolo,** *m.* stimulus; incentive; incitement; goad; spur.

stincàta, *f.* blow on the shin. **stínco** (*pl.* stinchi), *m.* shin; shin-bone.

stíngere, *v.t. ir.* to discolour; fade; (*fig.*) obscure; deface. *v.i.* (*aux. essere*) & **stíngersi,** *v.refl.* to lose colour; fade; (*fig.*) to change character. **stinto,** *a.* faded.

stipa, *f.* brushwood. **stipàre,** *v.t.* to clear of undergrowth; pack closely. **stipàto,** *a.* crowded.

stipendiàre, *v.t.* to pay a salary to; engage for a salary; hire; employ. **stipendiàto,** *m.* stipendiary. ¶ *a.* salaried. **stipèndio,** *m.* salary.

stipettàio, *m.* cabinet-maker. **stípite,** *m.* [door-]post; jamb; stem (*plant, or tree, without branches*); (*family*) stock. **stípo,** *m.* cabinet (*for coins, &c.*); chiffonier.

stipulàre, *v.t.* to stipulate; draw up; lay down; contract; arrange; settle.

stiracalzóni, *m.inv.* trouser-stretcher.

stiracchiàre, *v.t.* to pull; tug; (*fig.*) force; distort; wrench; quibble; haggle (*over pence*). **stiracchiàto,** *a.* forced; distorted.

stiraménto, *m.* stretching; pulling; contraction. **stiràre,** *v.t.* to stretch out; iron (*linen*). **stiràrsi,** *v.refl.* to stretch; stretch oneself. **stiratóio,** *m.* ironing-board; ironing blanket. **stiratóra** & **stiratríce,** *f.* laundress. **stiratúra,** *f.* ironing. **stíro** (**ferro da**), *m.* iron.

stírpe, *f.* race; stock; extraction; birth; issue; descent.

stitichézza, *f.* costiveness; constipation. **stítico** (*pl.* stítici), *a.* costive; constipated.

stíva, *f.* (*ship's*) hold; plough-handle. **stivàggio,** *m.* stowage.

stivàle, *m.* boot. **stivalétto,** *m.* boot; half-boot. **stivalóne,** *m.* top-boot; jack-boot; fishing-boot.

stivàre, *v.t.* to stow; stow away; cram; pack; heap up. **stivatóre,** *m.* stevedore.

stizza, *f.* anger; vexation; ill-humour; irritation. dims. *stizzina, stizzetta, stizzarella.* **stizzíre** (*pr.* -isco, -isci), *v.t.* to vex; irritate. **stizzírsi,** *v.refl.* to get angry; fly into a rage. **stizzíto,** *a.* angry; cross. **stizzóso,** *a.* irritable; petulant; spiteful.

stoccafisso, *m.* dried cod; stockfish.

Stoccàrda, *f.* Stuttgart.

stoccàta, *f.* thrust (*with dagger or rapier*); stab; (*fig.*) sudden application for money. **stòcco** (*pl.* stòcchi),

m. dagger; rapier. *bastone a* ~, *m.* sword-stick.

Stoccòlma, *f.* Stockholm.

stòffa, *f.* cloth; material; stuff; (*fig.*) character; nature; quality.

stòia, *f.* mat; hassock (*of straw or cane*); sun-blind or roof of matting or reeds.

stoicísmo, *m.* Stoicism. **stòico** (*pl.* stòici), *a.* stoical. ¶ *m.* Stoic.

stòla, *f.* (*Eccl.*) stole; surplice.

stòlido, *a.* stolid, stupid.

stoltaménte, *ad.* foolishly; stupidly. **stoltézza,** *f.* foolishness; folly; stupidity. **stólto,** *a.* foolish; silly; stupid. ¶ *m.* fool.

stomacàre, *v.t.* & *abs.* to sicken; nauseate; disgust. **stomacàrsi,** *v.refl.* to be sickened or disgusted (with, by = *di*); become sick of. **stomachévole,** *a.* disgusting; loathsome; revolting. **stomàchico** (*pl.* -màchici), *a.* & *m.* stomachic. **stòmaco** (*pl.* stòmachi), *m.* stomach.

stonàre, *v.i.* (*aux.* avere) to be out of tune; (*fig.*) to disagree; be out of place; (*colour*) not to harmonize. *v.t.* to disconcert; disturb. **stonàto,** *a.* out of tune; false (*note*); (*fig.*) out of place. **stonatúra,** *f.* dissonance; false note.

stóppa, *f.* tow; oakum. **stoppabúchi,** *m.inv.* wad (*of tow, &c.*); (*fig.*) stop-gap. **stoppàccio,** *m.* wad; wadding. **stoppàre,** *v.t.* to stop with tow; plug.

stóppia, *f.* stubble.

stoppíno, *m.* wick; taper.

stòrcere, *v.t. ir.* to twist; untwist; distort; wrench; wrest; dislocate; unravel; (*fig.*) alter; misrepresent. **stòrcersi,** *v.refl.* to twist; writhe.

stordiménto, *m.* dizziness; dullness; stupefaction. **stordíre** (*pr.* -ísco, -ísci), *v.t.* to stun; daze; bewilder; stupefy. **stordtàggine** & **stordtézza,** *f.* folly, stupidity; foolish action or mistake; bewilderment. **stordíto,** *a.* foolish; thoughtless; bewildered; giddy; scatterbrained.

stòria, *f.* history; story; tale. **stòrico** (*pl.* stòrici), *a.* historical; (*Gram.*) historic. ¶ *m.* historian. **storièlla,** *f.* little story; fanciful story; fib; lie. **storiògrafo,** *m.* historiographer.

storióne, *m.* sturgeon.

stormíre (*pr.* -ísco, -ísci), *v.i.* (*aux.* avere) to rustle. **stórmo,** *m.* swarm; flock; crowd; host.

stornàre, *v.t.* to avert; turn aside;

ward off; deter; dissuade; (*Bkkg.*) transfer.

stornellàre, *v.i.* (*aux.* avere) to sing folk-songs, such as the *stornello*.

stornèllo, *m.* *stornello* or *fiore*, a folk-lyric of three lines, generally beginning with an invocation to a flower. **stórno**, *m.* turning aside; turning off; (*Bkkpg.*) transfer. ¶ *a.* grey; grizzled.

storpiaménto, *m.* & **storpiatúra**, *f.* crippling; maiming; marring; bungling. **storpiàre**, *v.t.* to cripple; maim; mar; spoil; mangle; bungle. **storpiàto**, *a.* & **storpio**, *a.* crippled; maimed, &c. ¶ *m.* cripple.

stòrta, *f.* wrenching; twisting; distortion; (*river*) bend; sprain; wrick; (*Chem.*) retort. **stortézza**, *f.* crookedness; (*fig.*) falseness. **stòrto**, *p.p.* of *storcere.* ¶ *a.* crooked; twisted; deformed; (*eyes*) squinting; (*legs*) bandy; (*fig.*) false; erroneous. **stortúra**, *f.* deformity; (*fig.*) false idea; mistake.

stovigliàio, *m.* dealer in earthenware & crockery. **stoviglie**, *f.pl.* crockery; household utensils.

stra-, *prefix*, corruption of Lat. *extra*, indicates intensity, superiority or excess. *Eng.* very, extremely, super-, extra, over-. e.g. **strabèllo**, extremely beautiful. **strafíne**, superfine.

strabalzàre, *v.i.* (*aux.* essere) to jump about; jolt; toss up and down.

strabastàre, *v.i.* (*aux.* essere) to be more than enough; to suffice perfectly.

stràbico (*pl.* **stràbici**), *a.* squint; squinting. ¶ *m.* person with a squint; squinter.

strabiliànte, *a.* astonishing; amazing. **strabiliàre**, *v.i.* (*aux.* avere) & **strabiliarsi**, *v.refl.* to marvel greatly; be astonished, amazed.

strabismo, *m.* squinting; squint. **straboccàre**, *v.i.* (*aux.* essere & avere) to overflow; superabound. **strabocchévole**, *a.* overflowing; superabundant; excessive.

stracantàre, *v.i.* (*aux.* avere) to sing too loudly or out of tune.

stracàrico (*pl.* **-càrichi**), *a.* overloaded; overladen; overburdened.

stràcca, *f.* fatigue. *alla* ~, wearily; indifferently. **straccàggine**, *f.* weariness; slackness. **straccàre**, *v.t.* to tire (out).

straccería, *f.* rags. **stracchíno**, *m.* a Lombard cheese. **stracciàio** &

stracciaiuòlo, *m.* rag-merchant. **stracciàre**, *v.t.* to tear; rend; comb (*silk from cocoon*). **stracciàto**, *a.* in rags. ¶ *p.p.* of *stracciare.* **straccína**, *f.* rag-picker. **stràccio** (*pl.* **stràcci**), *m.* rag; tatter; rent; tear; scrap. ¶ *a.* torn, in rags. *carta* ~ *a*, waste paper. **straccióne**, *m.* ragged fellow; tatterdemalion. **stràcco** (*pl.* **stràcchi**), *a.* tired out; worn out; (*fig.*) poor; weak; stale; tepid, &c.

stracollàre, *v.i.* to fall over. **stracollàrsi**, *v.refl.* to sprain; strain; dislocate.

stracontènto, *a.* extremely happy; overjoyed. **stracòtto**, *a.* (*Cook.*) overdone. ¶ *m.* stew.

stràda, *f.* street; road; way. ~ *nazionale*, arterial road. ~ *laterale*, by-pass [road]. ~ *maestra*, main road. ~ *carrozzabile*, carriage road. **stradale**, *a.* of the road(s); road (*att.*). *codice* ~, highway code. *incidenti* ~*i*, road accidents. *manutenzione* ~, upkeep of the roads. *pianta* ~, road map. *regolamento* ~, rule of the road.

stradivàrio, *m.* stradivarius (*violin by Antonio Stradivari, of Cremona, 1644–1737*).

stradúccia & **stradúcola**, *f.* lane; alley.

strafalciàre, *v.i.* (*aux.* avere) to act thoughtlessly. **strafalcióne**, *m.* gross blunder; careless person.

strafàre (*pr.* **-fàccio** *or* **-fò**, *&c.*, like *fare*), *v.i. ir.* (*aux.* avere) to do too much; take unnecessary pains; overdo it. **strafàtto**, *a.* over-ripe; overlaboured.

strafelàto, *a.* thoroughly tired out; panting.

strafíne, *a.* superfine; of extra quality.

strafóro (**di**), *ad. expr.* secretly; stealthily.

strafottènte, *a.* regardless of other's feelings; indifferent; careless of convention. **strafottènza**, *f.* disregard for others' feelings; indifference. **strafòttersi**, *v.refl.* not to care a rap (for); to be indifferent (to).

stràge, *f.* slaughter; havoc; massacre; mass; abundance.

stràglio, *m.* (*Naut.*) stay.

stralciàre, *v.t.* to prune; lop off; slash; (*fig.*) remove; take off; settle; clear up; balance (*accounts*); come to a compromise (over). **stralciatúra**, *f.* pruning, &c. **stràlcio,** *m.* pruning; compromise.

stràle, *m.* (*Poet.*) arrow; dart.

stralunàre, *v.t.* (*eyes*) to open wide; roll. **stralunàto,** *a.* staring; wide-open.

stramazzàre, *v.t.* to fell; knock (down) senseless. *v.i.* (*aux.* essere) to fall heavily. **stramazzàta,** *f.* & **stramazzóne,** *m.* heavy fall; violent blow.

strambería, *f.* oddity; eccentricity. **stràmbo,** *a.* crooked; odd; queer; eccentric. **strambòtto,** *m.* strambotto, folk-lyric of 8 or 6 lines.

stràme, *m.* straw; litter.

strampalàto, *a.* odd; queer; extravagant; illogical.

stranaménte, *ad.* strangely; oddly. **stranézza,** *f.* strangeness; oddity.

strangolaménto, *m.* strangling; strangulation; choking. **strangolàre,** *v.t.* to strangle; throttle; choke.

straniàre, *v.t.* to alienate; estrange; draw away (from). **straniàrsi,** *v.refl.* to become estranged; drift apart. **stranièro,** *a.* foreign. ¶ *m.* foreigner. **stràno,** *a.* strange; queer; odd; eccentric; funny.

straordinariaménte, *ad.* extraordinarily; uncommonly; immensely. **straordinàrio,** *a.* extraordinary; unusual; uncommon; exceptional; enormous.

strapagàre, *v.t.* to over-pay.

strapazzàre, *v.t.* to ill-use; ill-treat; mishandle; bungle; botch; overwork; abuse; scold; swear at. **strapazzàta,** *f.* scolding; reprimand; rebuke. **strapazzàto,** *a.* ill-used; over-worked, &c. *uova ~ e,* scrambled eggs. **strapàzzo,** *m.* fatigue; excess; rough usage; common use. ¶ *a.* stark mad.

strapiombàre, *v.i.* (*aux.* essere & avere) to be out of the perpendicular; lean out; overhang; weigh heavily. **strapontíno,** *m.* tip-up seat.

strappàre, *v.t.* to snatch; tear; pull away; pluck; wrench; wring; extort; tear up; tear out; tear away. **strappàta,** *f.* sharp tug; pull; wrench. *dim.* strappatella, strappatina. **stràppo,** *m.* tear; rent; pull; wrench; (*fig.*) exception; infraction.

strapúnta, *f.* or **strapúnto,** *m.* quilt. **strapuntíno,** *m.* tip-up seat.

straripàre, *v.i.* (*aux.* essere & avere) to overflow.

strascicaménto, *m.* trailing; dragging;

(*of words*) drawling. **strascicàre,** *v.t.* to trail; drag; shuffle; drawl. **strascicàrsi,** *v.refl.* to drag oneself; shuffle. **stràscico** (*pl.* **stràscichi**), *m.* trailing; dragging; train (*dress* & *fig.*); sequel; (*pl.*) after-effects.

strascinàre, *v.t.* to drag; drag along the ground. **stràscino,** *m.* drag-net; trammel-[net].

strasecolàre, *v.i.* (*aux.* essere & avere) to be amazed.

strat[t]agèmma (*pl.* **-èmmi**), *m.* stratagem. **stratèga** (*pl.* **-èghi**), *m.* strategist. **strategía,** *f.* strategy. **stratègico** (*pl.* **-ègici**), *a.* strategic.

stratificàre, *v.t.* to stratify. **stratificazióne,** *f.* stratification. **stràto,** *m.* stratum (*pl.* strata); layer; coating. **stratosfèra,** *f.* stratosphere.

stràtta, *f.* pull; jerk. **strattóne,** *m.* violent pull; wrench.

stravagànte, *a.* queer; odd; fantastic; extravagant. **stravagànza,** *f.* oddness; eccentricity; queer behaviour.

stravècchio, *a.* very old.

straviziàre, *v.i.* (*aux.* avere) to be intemperate. **stravízio,** *m.* excess; intemperance; dissipation.

stravòlgere, *v.t. ir.* to roll; twist (*lit.* & *fig.*) distort. **stravòlto,** *a.* twisted; contorted; crooked; convulsed; agitated; troubled; upset; overturned.

straziànte, *a.* atrocious; heartrending. **straziàre,** *v.t.* to torture; tear to pieces; lacerate; spoil; ruin. **stràzio,** *m.* torment; torture; laceration; destruction.

stréga (*pl.* **stréghe**), *f.* witch; sorceress. **stregàre,** *v.t.* to bewitch. **stregóne,** *m.* wizard; sorcerer. **stregonería,** *f.* witchcraft; sorcery.

strégua, *f.* standard; rate; way.

stremàre, *v.t.* to exhaust; reduce to extremities.

strènna, *f.* gift; present; esp. Christmas or New Year's gift (~ *di* Natale, ~ *di capo d'anno*).

strenuaménte, *ad.* strenuously; vigorously. **strènuo,** *a.* strenuous; vigorous.

strepitàre, *v.i.* (*aux.* avere) to make a noise; make a din; make an uproar. **strèpito,** *m.* uproar; noise; din; clamour. **strepitóso,** *a.* noisy; uproarious; loud; clamorous.

streptòmicina, *f.* (*Med.*) streptomycine.

strétta, *f.* grasp; grip; hold; clasp; embrace; squeeze; (*olives*) pressing; pressure; pang; narrow space; pass;

(*Mus.*) finale. ∼ *di mano*, handshake. **strettaménte**, *ad.* tightly; strictly. **strettézza**, *f.* narrowness; scarcity; (*pl.*) straits; straitened circumstances. **strétto**, *a.* narrow; tight; strict; fast; close; near; intimate. ¶ *m.* strait[s]. ¶ *ad.* strictly; narrowly. **strettóio**, *m.* press.

stría, *f.* furrow; fluting; stripe; streak. **striàre**, *v.t.* to streak; stripe.

stricnína, *f.* strychnine.

stridènte, *a.* shrill; sharp; jarring; (*colours*) clashing; strident; striking; violent. **strídere**, *v.i. defect.* (*aux.* avere) to creak; jar; scrape (*sound*); screech; shriek; squeak; chirp; (*colours*) jar; clash. **stridío**, *m.* (continuous) creaking; screeching; shrieking. **strído**, *m.* shrill cry; shriek; screech. **stridóre**, *m.* creaking; shrieking; (*teeth*) gnashing; scraping. **strídulo**, *a.* shrill; piercing.

strigàre, *v.t.* to unravel; disentangle.

strìge, *f.* screech owl.

strìglia, *f.* curry comb. **strigliàre**, *v.t.* to groom; curry; (*fig.*). scold; rebuke.

strillàre, *v.i.* (*aux.* avere) & *t.* to shriek; scream; shout; cry (*newspapers*, *&c.*). **stríllo**, *m.* shriek; scream; cry. **strillóne**, *m.* newsboy.

strimpellàre, *v.t.* to strum; thrum; scrape (*violin*).

strinàre, *v.t.* to singe. **strinàto**, *m.* & **strinatúra**, *f.* singeing; smell of singeing.

strínga, *f.* shoe-lace. **stringàre**, *v.t.* to lace tightly; (*fig.*) restrict; make concise. **stringàto**, *a.* concise; terse; close-fitting.

stringènte, *a.* pressing; urgent; cogent; compelling. **stríngere**, *v.t. ir.* to tighten; press; squeeze; grasp; clasp; clench (*fists*); bind together; form (*alliance*, *friendship*); constrain; compel; besiege; stipulate, close (*discussion*). **stríngersi**, *v.refl.* to draw near; get close; squeeze closer together. **stringiménto**, *m.* tightening; pressing; squeezing; contraction.

stríscia (*pl.* **stríscie**), *f.* strip; stripe; streak; (razor-)strop. ∼ *di scorrimento*, tread (*tyre*). **strisciaménto**, *m.* dragging; trailing; shuffling; stroking; grazing; skimming; creeping; crawling; (*fig.*) flattery; fawning. **strisciànte**, *a.* creeping; (*fig.*)

cringing; fawning; obsequious. **strisciàre**, *v.t.* to drag; trail; shuffle (*feet*); creep along by; graze; skim; stroke (*animal*); slur; (*fig.*) grovel before; flatter. *v.i.* (*aux.* avere) to creep; crawl; glide; slide; slip; cringe. **strisciàta** & **strisciatúra**, *f.* rub; rubbing; stroking; sliding, &c.; (*fig.*) flattery; compliment. **striscióne**, *m.* flatterer. **striscióni**, *ad.* with a shuffling movement.

stritolàre, *v.t.* to crush; grind down; break into small pieces; destroy.

strizzalimóni, *m.inv.* lemon-squeezer.

strizzàre, *v.t.* to squeeze; press; wring; wring out. ∼ *l'occhio*, to wink. **strizzàta**, *f.* squeeze; wring; wringing. ∼*d'occhio*, wink.

stròfa & **stròfe**, *f.* strophe; stanza.

strofinàccio, *m.* duster. **strofinàre**, *v.t.* to rub; wipe.

strologàre, *v.t.* & *i.* (*aux.* avere) to study; think (of); muse (upon); (*lit.* to tell fortunes, cast horoscopes, read the stars).

strombazzàre, *v.t.* to trumpet; trumpet abroad; puff.

stroncàre, *v.t.* to break; cut off; maim; criticize savagely. **stroncatúra**, *f.* destructive criticism; savage review. **strónco** (*pl.* **stronchi**), *a.* broken; maimed; worn out. ¶ *m.* cripple.

stropicciàre, *v.t.* to rub; scrape; scrub; (*feet*) drag; shuffle.

stròzza, *f.* throat; throttle; gullet; windpipe. **strozzaménto**, *m.* strangling; throttling; choking. **strozzàre**, *v.t.* to strangle; throttle; choke; (*fig.*) fleece, rob. **strozzàto**, *a.* & *p.p.* strangled; throttled; choked. *ernia* ∼ *a*, (*Med.*) strangulated hernia. **strozzatúra**, *f.* choking; narrowing. **strozzíno**, *m.* money-lender; usurer.

strúggere, *v.t. ir.* to melt; consume; waste; destroy. **strúggersi**, *v.refl.* to melt; be consumed (*with desire*, envy, *&c.*); long (for); be afflicted or distressed. **struggiménto**, *m.* melting; liquefaction; tender feeling; longing; torment; boredom; destruction. **struggitóre**, *m.* (*f.* **-trice**) destroyer. ¶ *a.* destroying.

strumentàle, *a.* instrumental. **strumentàre**, *v.t.* (*Mus.*) to instrument; (*Law*) to draw up (*documents*). **struménto**, *m.* tool; implement; instrument (*Mus.*, *Science*, *Law*).

strusciàre, *v.t.* to wear out; rub;

waste. **strusciàrsi,** *v.refl.* to cringe; fawn (upon).
strútto, *m.* lard. ¶ *p.p.* of *struggere.*
struttúra, *a.* structure.
strúzzo, *m.* ostrich.
Stuàrdo, *m.* **Stuàrda,** *f.* Stuart.
stuccàre, *v.t.* to plaster; stucco; coat with stucco; surfeit; disgust. **stuccatóre,** *m.* plasterer. **stuccatúra,** *f.* plastering. **stucchévole,** *a.* tedious; tiresome; boring; disgusting. **stucchevolézza,** *f.* tiresomeness; affectation; insipidity; artificiality. **stucchinàio,** *m.* seller (or maker) of plaster statuettes. **stucchíno,** *m.* plaster statuette. **stúcco** (*pl.* **stúcchi**), *m.* plaster; stucco; plaster figure. ¶ *a.* (*sync. p.p.* of *stuccare*) disgusted; sick (of).
studènte, *m.* student. **studentésca,** *f.* students (*body*); student community. **studentésco** (*pl.* **-éschi**), *a.* student's; students'; student (*att.*). **studentéssa,** *f.* woman student. **studiacchiàre,** *v.t.* to study listlessly; make a pretence of studying. **studiàre,** *v.t. & abs.* to study; read; survey; examine. **studiàrsi,** *v.refl.* to try; endeavour; do one's best. **studiataménte,** *ad.* affectedly; designedly; on purpose. **stúdio,** *m.* study; preparation (*Sch.*); survey; examination; care; pains; (lawyer's) office; chambers; (*artist's, photographer's*) studio. **studióso,** *a.* studious; desirous (of). ¶ *m.* scholar; (disinterested) student.
stúfa, *f.* stove; (*fig.*) oven; hot-house. ~ *a petrolio,* oil stove. **stufàre,** *v.t.* to stew; (*fig.*) to bore; weary; disgust. **stufàrsi,** *v.refl.* to grow weary; get bored; get sick (of). **stufàto,** *m.* stewed meat; stew. ¶ *a.* stewed, braised. **stúfo,** *a.* tired; sick; fed up.
stuòia, *f.* mat; matting. **stuoíno,** *m.* door-mat.
stuòlo, *m.* troop; group; band.
stupefacènte, *a.* stupefying; astonishing. ¶ *m.* narcotic [drug]. **stupefàre** (*pr.* **fàccio, -fài, -fà,** like *fare*), *v.t. ir.* to stupefy; surprise; astonish. **stupefazióne,** *f.* stupefaction; insensibility; astonishment.
stupèndo, *a.* wonderful; marvellous; magnificent.
stupidàggine, *f.* imbecility; foolishness; silliness; piece of stupidity. **stupidaménte,** *ad.* stupidly; foolishly. **stupidíre** (*pr.* **-disco, -disci**), *v.t.* to make stupid. *v.i.*

(*aux.* essere) to become stupid. **stupidità,** *f.* stupidity; foolishness; dullness. **stúpido,** *a.* idiotic; imbecile; obtuse; dull; foolish. ¶ *m.* fool; blockhead.
stupíre (*pr.* **-ísco, -ísci,** *&c.*), *v.i.* (*aux.* essere) to be astonished; amazed, surprised. **stupóre,** *m.* amazement; astonishment; stupor.
stupràre, *v.t.* to violate; ravish. **stúpro,** *m.* violation; rape.
stúra, *f.* uncorking; (*fig.*) lead; beginning. **sturàre,** *v.t.* to uncork.
sturbaménto, *m.* disturbance; trouble. **sturbàre,** *v.t.* to disturb.
stuzzicadènti, *m.inv.* toothpick. **stuzzicaménto,** *m.* prodding; stirring up; irritation. **stuzzicàre,** *v.t.* to stir (up); poke; prod; whet (*appetite, curiosity*); excite; provoke; tease. **stuzzichíno,** *m.* (*fam.*) irritating person.
su, *pr.* on, upon; over; above; about; after. ¶ *ad.* up. ~ *per,* up (*pr.*). ~ *per giù & suppergiú,* *ad.* approximately; almost, nearly; roughly [speaking].
suaccennàto, *a.* above-mentioned; aforesaid.
suadènte, suasívo, *a.* persuasive.
subaffittàre, *v.t.* to sub-let. **subaffítto,** *m.* sublet; sub-letting. **subalpíno,** *a.* sub-alpine; Piedmontese. **subaltèrno,** *m.* dependant; subordinate. **subappaltatóre,** *m.* sub-contractor. **subappàlto,** *m.* sub-contract.
subàsta, *f.* auction, forced sale.
súbbia, *f.* stone-mason's chisel.
súbbio, *m.* weaver's beam.
subbúglio, *m.* hubbub; turmoil; confusion; upheaval.
subcosciènte, *m.* (*Psych.*) (the) subconscious.
súbdolo, *a.* cunning; crafty; deceitful; shifty; underhand.
subentràre (a), *v.i.* (*aux* essere) to take the place (of); succeed; replace.
subíre (*pr.* **-ísco, -ísci**), *v.t.* to undergo; suffer; endure.
subissàre, *v.t.* to ruin; overthrow. **subísso,** *m.* ruin; outburst; shower (*fig.*).
subitaménte, *ad.* immediately; suddenly; unexpectedly. **subitaneaménte,** *ad.* suddenly; unawares. **subitaneità,** *f.* suddenness. **subitàneo,** *a.* sudden.
súbito, *a.* sudden. ¶ *ad.* immediately; quickly; at once; directly; soon. **subíto,** *p.p.* of *subire.*

sublimàre, *v.t.* (*Chem.*) to sublimate; raise up; exalt. **sublimàto,** *m.* (*Chem.*) sublimate. **sublimazióne,** *f.* sublimation.

sublìme, *a.* sublime. **sublimità,** *f.* sublimity.

suboderàre, *v.t.* to suspect; get wind of.

subordinàre, *v.t.* to subordinate. **subordinàto,** *a. & m.* subordinate.

subornàre, *v.t.* to suborn.

suburbàno, *a.* suburban. **subúrbio,** *m.* suburb(s); more com. *sobborgo.*

succedàneo, *a.* as a substitute for. ¶ *m.* substitute (*product*).

succèdere, *v.i. ir.* (*aux.* essere) to succeed; follow; happen; occur; befall. **successióne,** *f.* succession. **successìvo,** *a.* successive; next; following. **succèsso,** *m.* success; course (*of time*). **successóre,** *m.* (*f.* -óra) successor.

succhiaménto, *m.* sucking; suction. **succhiàre,** *v.t.* to suck; suck in; suck up; absorb. **succhiàta,** *f.* suck. **succhiellàre,** *v.t.* to bore. **succhièllo,** *m.* gimlet; auger.

succhióne, *m.* (*Bot.*) sucker; parasite.

succìnto, *a.* succinct; brief; concise.

súcco (*pl.* súcchi), *m.* juice; sap (*fig.*) essence; spirit; substance. **succosaménte,** *ad.* pithily; concisely; substantially. **succosità,** *f.* juiciness. **succóso,** *a.* juicy. **succulènto,** *a.* succulent; juicy.

succursàle, *f.* branch, branch-office; branch-house.

succutàneo, *a.* subcutaneous.

sud, *m.* south; (*att.*) south[ern]. *l'Africa del Sud,* South Africa. *l'America del Sud,* South America. *Croce del Sud, f.* Southern Cross. *sud-africano,* South African. *sud-americano,* South American. *~ est, m.* south east. *~ ovest, m.* south west. *il S~ Ovest africano,* South West Africa.

sudàre, *v.i.* (*aux.* avere) *& t.* to sweat, perspire, ooze; exude; exude moisture; (*fig.*) toil; drudge. **sudàrio,** *m.* shroud; winding-sheet. **sudàta,** *f.* sweat; sweating.

suddétto, *a.* aforesaid; above-mentioned.

suddìtanza, *f.* subjection; citizenship. **súddito,** *m.* subject (*pers.*).

suddividere, *v.t. ir.* to sub-divide; divide. **suddivisióne,** *f.* sub-division.

sud-est, *m.* see *sud.*

sudicerìa, *f.* dirtiness; dirty trick;

filthiness; indecency; (*pl.*) foul language. **súdicio,** *a.* dirty; foul; filthy. **sudicìume,** *m.* (quantity of) dirt; filth.

sudóre, *m.* sweat; perspiration.

sud-ovest, see *sud.*

suespòsto, *a.* above-stated.

sufficiènte, *a.* sufficient; enough. **sufficiènza,** *f.* sufficiency; sufficient amount; sufficient quantity; (*Sch.*) pass-mark.

suffisso, *m.* suffix.

suffragàre, *v.t.* to support; assist; (*Eccl.*) pray for the dead. **suffragétta,** *f.* suffragette. **suffràgio,** *m.* suffrage; vote; approval; prayer (*for the souls of the dead*).

suffumicàre, *v.t.* to fumigate. **suffusióne,** *f.* suffusion (*Med.*).

suga (**carta**), *f. pop.* for *carta sugante,* blotting-paper. **sugàre,** *v.t.* to manure; absorb (*ink*).

suggellàre, *v.t.* to seal; seal up; stamp. **suggèllo,** *m.* seal.

suggeriménto, *m.* suggestion. **suggeríre** (*pr.* -ìsci, -ìsci), *v.t.* to suggest; prompt. **suggeritóre,** *m.* (*Theat.*) prompter. **suggestionàre,** *v.t.* to hypnotize. **suggestióne,** *f.* (hypnotic) suggestion; (*Law*) undue influence. **suggestìvo,** *a.* suggestive; stimulating; interesting. *interrogazione ~ a,* leading question.

súghero, *m.* cork; cork-tree.

sìgna, *f.* lard; lubricating grease.

súgo (*pl.* súghi), *m.* sap; juice; gravy; (*fig.*) substance; purpose; rich manure. **sugóso,** *a.* juicy.

suicìda, *a.* suicidal. ¶ *m.* suicide (*pers.*). **suicidàrsi,** *v.refl.* to commit suicide; kill oneself. **suicìdio,** *m.* suicide (*act*).

suindicàto, *a.* above-mentioned; above-stated.

suìno, *a.* of swine; swine (*att.*). *carne ~ a,* pork. ¶ *m.* swine.

sulfúreo, *a.* sulphureous.

sultanìna, *f.* sultana raisin. **sultàno,** *m.* Sultan.

summentovàto, *a.* above-mentioned. **sunnominàto,** *a.* above-named.

súnto, *m.* summary; résumé; recapitulation. **suntuóso,** *a.* sumptuous.

súo, *a. & pn. poss.* his; her; hers; its; (*pop. & poet.*) their.

suòcera, *f.* mother-in-law. **suòcero,** *m.* father-in-law.

suòla, *f.* sole (*boot, shoe*). **suòlo,** *m.* soil; ground; floor; standing-room; sole-leather.

s[u]onàre, *v.i.* (*aux.* avere) *& t.* to

sound; ring; play; blow; strike; mean. **suonatóre,** see *sonatore*. **suòno,** *m.* sound.

suòra, *f.* nun; sister (*Eccl.*).

superàbile, *a.* surmountable; possible to overcome. **superàre,** *v.t.* to surpass; excel; overcome; exceed.

supèrbia, *f.* pride; arrogance. **supèrbo,** proud; arrogant; haughty; splendid; superb.

superficiàle, *a.* superficial; hasty. **superfície,** *f.* (*pl.* **superficie** & **superfici**), surface; area; outside.

superfluità, *f.* superfluity. **supèrfluo,** *a.* superfluous; unnecessary; redundant. ¶ *m.* surplus.

superióre, *a.* superior; upper; higher. **superiorità,** *f.* superiority. **superiorménte,** *ad.* in a higher degree; on the upper side.

superlatívo, *a.* & *m.* superlative.

supèrno, *a.* celestial; divine; supreme.

supèrstite, *a.* surviving. ¶ *m.* survivor.

superstizióne, *f.* superstition. **superstizióso,** *a.* superstitious.

superuòmo, *m.* superman.

supinaménte, *ad.* carelessly; indolently; in servile fashion; supinely. **supíno,** *a.* supine; lying face upward; lying on one's back; servile. ¶ *m.* supine (*Gram.*).

suppellèttile, *f.* furniture; furnishings; fittings; equipment.

suppergiú, *ad.* approximately; nearly; roughly (speaking).

supplementàre, *a.* supplementary; additional. *treno* ~, relief train. **suppleménto,** *m.* supplement; addition; extra; supplementary volume; or part of a journal. ~ [*di tassa*], excess [fare].

supplènte, *m.* & *f.* substitute; deputy; (*Sch.*) temporary teacher; locum tenens. **supplènza,** *f.* substitution; temporary post; supply [work] (*Sch.*).

suppletívo, *a.* supplementary.

súpplica (*pl.* **súppliche**), *f.* petition; supplication; entreaty. **supplicànte,** *a.* suppliant. ¶ *m.* & *f.* petitioner; suppliant. **supplicàre,** *v.t.* to beg; implore; entreat; supplicate. **supplicazióne,** *f.* supplication. **súpplice** & **supplichévole,** *a.* suppliant; imploring; supplicating.

supplíre (a) (*pr.* **-ísco, -ísci**), *v.i.* (*aux.* avere) to take the place of; meet (a need); make up for.

suppliziàre, *v.t.* to execute. **supplí-**

zio, *m.* punishment; torture; torment; (extreme) penalty; execution.

supponíbile, *a.* possible to suppose.

suppórre (*pr.* **-póngo, -póni, -póne,** like *porre*), *v.t.* & *i.* ir. (*aux.* avere) to suppose; assume; infer; take. **supposizióne,** *f.* supposition. **suppósta,** *f.* suppository (*Med.*). **suppósto,** *a.* & *p.p.* of *supporre*, supposed; substituted. ¶ *m.* supposition. ~ *che,* *c.* supposing.

suppuraménto, *m.* & **suppurazióne** *f.* suppuration. **suppuràre,** *v.i.* (*aux.* essere & avere) to suppurate.

supremazía, *f.* supremacy. **suprèmo,** *a.* supreme; highest; crowning; paramount; last (*consolation, rites,* &*c.*).

surrealísmo, *m.* surrealism.

surrettízio, *m.* surreptitious.

surriferíto, *a.* above mentioned.

surriscaldaménto, *m.* overheating. **surriscaldàre,** *v.t.* to overheat.

surrogàre (*pr.* **surrògo**), *v.t.* to take the place of; replace. **surrogàto,** *m.* substitute.

suscettíbile, *a.* susceptible; easily offended; touchy.

suscitàre, *v.t.* to rouse; provoke; stir up; arouse; give rise to.

susína, *f.* plum. **susíno,** *m.* plum-tree. **súso,** *ad.* (*Poet.*) up.

suspicióne, *f.* (*Law*) suspicion.

susseguènte, *a.* subsequent; next following; successive. **susseguènza,** *f.* succession. **susseguíre** (*pr.* **-sèguo, -ségui**), *v.t.* to follow (next); succeed.

sussidiàre, *v.t.* to subsidize; aid; assist. **sussidiàrio,** *a.* subsidiary; auxiliary. *cappella* ~ a, *f.* chapel of ease. **sussídio,** *m.* subsidy; grant; subvention; aid; dole.

sussiègo (*pl.* **-èghi**), *m.* stiff attitude; imposing air; exaggerated dignity; haughtiness.

sussistènza, *f.* subsistence; existence; (*Mil.*) supply service, (*pl.*) army provisions. **sussístere,** *v.i.* (*aux.* essere & avere) to exist; subsist.

sussultàre, *v.i.* (*aux.* avere) to start; jump; tremble; (*heart*) beat violently. **sussúlto,** *m.* start; tremor. **sussultòrio,** *a.* jerky.

sus[s]urràre, *v.i.* (*aux.* avere) & *t.* to whisper; murmur. **sus[s]urra-tóre,** *m.* (*f.* **-tríce**) whisperer; murmurer; grumbler. ¶ *a.* murmuring. **sus[s]urrío,** *m.* (constant) murmuring; rustling. **sus[s]úrro,** *m.* murmur; rustle.

sutúra, *f.* suture.

súvvi, *ad.* up there; up aloft.

švagaménto, *m.* recreation; diversion; distraction. **švagàre,** *v.t.* to amuse; divert; distract one's thoughts or attention. **švagàrsi,** *v.refl.* to divert one's thoughts; while away the time; amuse oneself. **švagàto,** *a.* absent-minded; inattentive. **švágo** (*pl.* **švághi**), *m.* amusement; recreation.

švaligiaménto, *m.* wholesale robbery; large scale burglary. **švaligiàre,** *v.t.* to steal everything from; rifle; plunder; rob.

švalutàre, *v.t.* to depreciate; devalue. **švalutazióne,** *f.* depreciation; devaluation.

švampàre, *v.i.* (*aux.* essere & avere) of *flame, heat, steam, &c.*) to burst out; escape. *v.i.* (*aux.* essere) (*of passion*), quieten down; evaporate.

švaniménto, *m.* fading away; vanishing; enfeeblement. **švaníre** (*pr.* -**ísco, -ísci,** &*c.*), *v.i.* (*aux.* essere) to vanish; disappear; come to nothing; lose flavour, quality or strength. **švaníto,** *a.* vanished; enfeebled.

švàno, *m.* recess in a wall.

švantàggio, *m.* disadvantage; drawback; detriment. **švantaggióso,** *a.* unfavourable; detrimental; disadvantageous; prejudicial.

švaporàre, *v.i.* (*aux.* essere) to evaporate.

švariaménto, *m.* variation. **švariàre,** *v.t.* divert; distract (*attention*); vary; change; (*v.i.*) (*aux.* avere *with persons*, essere *with things*) to vary; change; wander; waver; change colour; be different. **švariàto,** *a.* varied; various. **švarióne,** *m.* blunder.

švašàre, *v.t.* to re-pot; plant out.

švecchiaménto, *m.* modernization; pruning. **švecchiàre,** *v.t.* to renew; modernize; freshen up; prune. **švecchiatúra,** *f.* renewal of worn-out parts.

švedése, *a.* Swedish. ¶ *m.* Swede. *lo* ~, Swedish, the Swedish language.

švéglia, *f.* waking (up); alarm-clock; alarm-signal; reveillé. **švegliàre,** *v.t.* to wake; wake-up; awaken; (*fig.*) rouse; animate. **švegliàrsi,** *v.refl.* to wake; wake-up; be awakened. **švegliàta,** *f.* awakening.

švegliatézza, *f.* wakefulness; (*fig.*) quickness; readiness; vivacity. **švéglio,** *a.* (wide) awake; (*fig.*) alert; quick-witted.

švelàre, *v.t.* to unveil; reveal; disclose. **švelataménte,** *ad.* openly.

švelenàrsi, & **švelenírsi** (*pr.* -**ísco**), *v.refl.* (*fig.*) to give vent to one's anger or malice.

švèllere, *v.t. ir.* to up-root; pluck out.

šveltézza, *f.* quickness; agility; nimbleness; slimness. **šveltíre** (*pr.* -**ísco, -ísci**), *v.t.* to make quick; make slender; make supple; make livelier; smarten (up). **šveltírsi,** *v.refl.* to become quick, &c. **švèlto,** *a.* slim; slender; quick; nimble; smart; quick-witted. ¶ also *p.p.* of *svellere.*

švenàre, *v.t.* to kill by opening the veins; bleed; (*fig.*) extort money from.

švenévole, *a.* languishing; lackadaisical; sentimental; affected. **švenevolézza,** *f.* mawkishness; lackadaisicalness; false sentiment; affectation.

šveniménto, *m.* swoon; fainting-fit; faint. **šveníre** (*pr.* **švèngo, švièni,** &*c.*, like *venire*), *v.i. ir.* (*aux.* essere) to faint; swoon.

šventagliàre, *v.t.* to fan.

šventàre, *v.t.* to foil; frustrate; baffle; thwart; ventilate; air (*bedding*). **šventatàggine** & **šventatézza,** *f.* thoughtlessness; heedlessness; carelessness; lightheadedness. **šventàto,** *a.* careless; thoughtless; light-headed.

šventola, *f.* fan; fire-fan. **šventolaménto,** *m.* waving; fluttering; flapping; fanning. **šventolàre,** *v.t.* to unfurl; wave; flutter; flap; fan. (*v.i.*) (*aux.* avere) (*of flag*) to fly; flutter; wave. **šventolàrsi,** *v.refl.* to fan oneself.

šventràre, *v.t.* to disembowel (*fish*) gut; rip up; (*fig.*) open up; demolish (*for reconstruction*); widen.

šventúra, *f.* misfortune; mishap; bad luck. **šventuràto,** *a.* unfortunate; unlucky. **švenúto,** *p.p.* of *švenire.* ¶ *a.* unconscious; in a faint.

švergognàre, *v.t.* to disgrace; humiliate; shame; put to shame. **švergognatézza,** *f.* shamelessness; impudence. **švergognàto,** *a.* shameless; impudent; abashed, put to shame.

švernaménto, *m.* wintering. **švernàre,** *v.i.* (*aux.* avere) to winter; pass (*or* spend) the winter.

śvèrża, *f.* stick; splinter.

śvesciàre, *v.t.* to blab (out); blurt out.

śvestíre (*pr.* śvèsto, *&c.*), *v.t.* to undress.

śvettàre, *v.t.* to cut off the top of . (*trees*); pollard.

Śvèvo, *a. & m.* Swabian.

Śvèzia (la), *f.* Sweden.

śviaménto, *m.* deviation; running off the lines; leading (or going) astray. śviàre, *v.t.* to turn aside; lead astray; switch (*Rly.*). *v.i.* (*aux.* avere) *&* śviàrsi, *v.refl.* to go astray; run off the lines. śviàto, *a.* misguided. śviatóre, *m.* (*Rly.*) pointsman.

śvicolàre, *v.i.* (*aux.* essere *&* avere) to turn the corner; slink away.

śvignàre, *v.i.* (*aux.* essere) to slip away; make off; decamp.

śvigoriménto, *m.* enfeeblement; weakening; loss of vigour. śvigoríre (*pr.* -ísco, -ísci), *v.t.* to enfeeble; weaken.

śviliménto, *m.* depreciation; debasement. śvilíre (*pr.* -ísco, -ísci), *v.t.* to debase; depreciate.

śvillaneggiàre, *v.t.* to insult; abuse; revile.

śviluppaménto, *m.* development. śviluppàre, *v.t.* to develop. śvilupàrsi, *v.refl.* to develop; grow; increase; make off; decamp. śvilúppo, *m.* development; expansion; opening out; spread; growth; increase.

śvinàre, *v.i.* (*aux.* avere) to draw the wine from the vat.

śvincolàre, *v.t.* to release; free; disengage; redeem (*from pawn*); clear (*from customs*). śvíncolo, *m.* release; liberation; clearance; bill of clearance.

śvisaménto, *m.* disfigurement; misrepresentation; distortion (*of facts*). śvisàre, *v.t.* to disfigure; (*fig.*) misrepresent; distort; alter.

śvisceraménto, *m.* (*fig.*) thorough examination; exhaustive research. śvisceràre, *v.t.* to eviscerate; (*fig.*) to exhaust; examine thoroughly. śvisceraménte, *ad.* ardently; passionately. śvisceratézza, *f.* ardent love; deep affection; devoted attachment. śvisceràto, *a.* ardent; passionate; deep; tender; heartfelt; devoted; sincere. amìco ∼, bosom friend.

śvísta, *f.* oversight.

śvitàre, *v.t.* to unscrew. śvitatúra, *f.* unscrewing.

śviticchiàre, *v.t.* to disentangle; . disentwine.

Śvízzera (la), *f.* Switzerland. śvízzero, *a. & m.* Swiss.

śvogliaménto, *m.* disinclination. śvogliàre, *v.t.* to disincline; distract (from). śvogliàrsi (di), *v.refl.* to be disinclined for; take a dislike to. śvogliatàggine *&* śvogliatézza, *f.* listlessness, indifference; laziness. śvogliàto, *a.* listless; lazy; unwilling; loath. śvogliatóne, *m.* slacker; shirker.

śvolàre, *v.i.* (*aux.* avere) to fly; flutter.

śvolazzàre, *v.i.* (*aux.* avere) to flutter; flit; fly here and there; hover. śvolazzío, *m.* constant fluttering. śvolàzzo, *m.* flutter; flourish (*handwriting*); ornamental initial (*MS. & Typ.*); (*pl.*) excessive ornamentation.

śvòlgere, *v.t. ir.* to unroll; unwind; unfold; develop; work out; complete; display; set forth; compose. śvòlgersi, *v.refl.* to take place; go on; happen; occur. śvolgiménto, *m.* development; expansion; course; treatment; working out (*argument, &c.*).

śvòlta, *f.* turn; turning; turning point; winding; direction. śvoltàre, *v.i.* (*aux.* avere) to turn. *v.t.* to unroll. śvoltèta, *f.* turn; turning. śvòlto, *p.p.* of *svolgere* or *syncop. p.p.* of *svoltare.* ¶ *m.* turn.

śvoltolàre, *v.t.* to roll. śvoltolàrsi, *v.refl.* to roll about; wallow.

śvotàre (*pr.* śvuòto, śvuòti), *v.t.* to empty.

T

T, t (*ti*), *f.* the letter T. *fatto a T*, T-shaped. *ferro a T*, T-iron.

tabaccàia, *f.* tabaccàio, *m.* tobacconist. tabaccàre, *v.i.* (*aux.* avere) to take snuff. tabacchièra, *f.* snuffbox. tabàcco (*pl.* -àcchi), *m.* tobacco. ∼ *da naso*, or ∼, snuff. tabaccóso, *a.* snuffy; smelling of tobacco.

tabàrro, *m.* loose cloak.

tàbe, *f.* (*Med.*) tabes.

tabèlla, *f.* table, list; schedule; votive tablet.

tabernàcolo, *m.* shrine; tabernacle; ciborium.

tablòide, *m.* tabloid.
tabú, *m.* taboo.
tàcca (*pl.* **tàcche**), *f.* notch; nick; dint; (*fig.*) size; height; quality; blemish; defect.
taccagnería, *f.* stinginess; meanness; miserliness. **taccàgno,** *a.* stingy; mean; miserly.
taccherèlla, *f.* slight blemish or fault.
tacchíno, *m.* turkey[-cock]. **tacchína,** *f.* turkey[-hen].
tàccia, *f.* blemish; fault; imputation; charge. **tacciàbile** (**di**), *a.* chargeable (with); liable to the imputation (of). **tacciàre** (**di**), *v.t.* to accuse (of); charge (with); tax (with); impute.
tàcco (*pl.* **tàcchi**), *m.* heel (*of shoe*).
tàccola, *f.* slight fault; flaw; trifle; mere nothing.
taccuíno, *m.* note-book; memorandum-book.
tacére (*pr.* **tàccio, tàci, tàce,** *&c.*), *v.i. ir.* (*aux.* avere) to be silent; keep silent. (*v.t.*) to be silent about; keep silent (or silence) about; pass over in silence; keep secret; leave out; omit; say nothing about; leave unsaid; conceal. *far* ~, to silence; hush. **tacitaménte,** *ad.* silently; noiselessly; tacitly. **tacitàre,** *v.t.* to silence; bribe; pay off (*creditor*). **tacitàrsi** (*con.*), *v.refl.* to come to terms with. **tàcito,** *a.* silent; tacit. *socio* ~, sleeping partner. **Tàcito,** *m.* Tacitus.
taciturnltà, *f.* taciturnity. **tacitúrno,** *a.* taciturn; sulky.
tafàno, *m.* horse-fly; gad-fly.
tafferúglio, *m.* brawl; scuffle; scrimmage.
taffetà, *m.* taffeta; sticking-plaster. ~ *inglese,* court-plaster.
tàglia, *f.* ransom; tribute; blood-money; price (on one's head); levy; war-indemnity; tally[-stick]; tackle; size. **tagliabórse,** *m.inv.* cut-purse.
tagliabòschi *&* **taglialégna,** *m.inv.* wood-cutter; wood-chopper.
tagliacàrte, *m.inv.* paper-knife.
tagliafíli, *m.inv.* wire-cutter.
tagliamàre, *m.inv.* cut-water (*bow*).
tagliaménto, *m.* cutting. **tagliàndo,** *m.* coupon. **tagliapésce,** *m.inv.* fish-slice. **tagliapiètre,** *m.inv.* stonecutter. **tagliàre,** *v.t.* to cut; cut down; cut off; cut out; carve; hew; trim; clip. **tagliàta** *&* **tagliatúra,** *f.* cutting; cut. **tagliatèlli** *&* **taglieríni,** *m.pl.* ribbon vermicelli. **tagliatóre,** *m.* cutter.

taglieggiàre, *v.t.* to assess; levy contributions from; extort money from.
tagliènte, *a.* cutting (*lit. & fig.*); sharp; bitter (*cold*).
taglière, *m.* trencher (*platter*).
tàglio, *m.* cut; cutting; cutting-out (*tailor's*); edge (*knife, sword*); shape; size; dress-length; piece of cloth for a suit. ~ *di capelli,* hair-cut. ~ *di capelli alla garçonne,* shingle; shingled-hair. ~ *dorato,* gilt edges (*book*).
taglióne, *m.* talion; retaliation; eye for an eye.
tagliuzzàre, *v.t.* to cut into small pieces; mince; shred; hash.
Tàgo (**il**), *m.* (the) Tagus (*Geog.*).
tàlamo, *m.* (*Poet.*) nuptial bed.
talàre, *a.* reaching to the ankles. *veste* ~, *f. abito* ~; *m.* priest's gown; cassock.
talché, *ad.* so that; such that.
tàlco, *m.* talc.
tàle, *a.* such; like; similar; as, so; so great; so big. *il signor Tal dei Tali,* Mr. So & So.
talentàre, *v.i.* (*aux.* essere) to please; be pleasing; be to one's liking (or taste). **talènto,** *m.* talent; ability; gift (for); wish. *mal* ~, spite; ill-will.
Talète, *m.* Thales.
talismàno, *m.* talisman.
tallíre (*pr.* **-ísco, -ísci,** *&c.*), *v.i.* (*aux.* essere *&* avere) to run to seed.
tallóne, *m.* heel.
talménte, *ad.* so; so much; to such an extent; in such a way. **talòra** *&* **talvòlta,** *ad.* sometimes.
tèlpa, *f.* mole (*animal*).
talúno, *pn. indef.* somebody; someone; (*pl.*) some; certain people.
tamaríndo, *m.* tamarind. **tamarísco** (*pl.* **-íschi**) *&* **tameríce** (*pl.* **-ici**), *m.* tamarisk. **tamburàre,** *v.t.* to beat. **tambureggiàre,** *v.i.* (*aux.* avere) to drum. **tamburèllo,** *m.* small drum; tambourine; timbrel. **tamburinàre,** *v.i.* (*aux.* avere) *&* **tamburinàrsi,** *v.refl.* to drum with the fingers; thrum. **tamburíno,** *m.* drummer; drummer-boy; small drum; tambourine. **tambúro,** *m.* drum; drummer; barrel (*watch, winch*); cylinder. *capo* ~, drum-major.
Tamígi (**il**), *m.* the Thames.
tamponàre, *v.t.* to plug; stop; bung; pad; dab; collide with; (*Med.*) tampon. **tampóne,** *m.* plug;

stopper; tampion; bung; wad; pad; (*Med.*) tampon.

tàna, *f.* den; hole; lair.

tanagliàre, *v.t.* to torture with pincers. **tanàglie** *or* **tenàglie,** *f.pl.* pincers; nippers.

tanè, *a.* tawny; tan. ¶ *m.* tan-colour.

tanfàta, *f.* whiff of foul air. **tànfo,** *m.* musty smell; bad smell; stench.

tangènte, *a.* tangent(ial). ¶ *f.* tangent (*Geom.*); share. **tàngere,** *v.t.* (*Poet.*) to touch.

Tàngeri, *f.* Tangier.

tànghero, *m.* boor; bumpkin; lout.

tangíbile, *a.* tangible.

tàngo (*pl.* **tànghi**), *m.* tango.

tanníno, *m.* tannin; tannic acid.

tantafèra, *f.* rigmarole; long-winded story.

Tàntalo, *m.* Tantalus (*Myth.*). **t ~,** tantalus (*spirit stand*); (*Min.*) tantalum.

tantíno (**un**), *ad. expr.* a little bit; somewhat; rather. **tànto,** *a.* so much; so great; (*pl.*) so many; as many. ¶ *ad.* so; so much; so long; such; as well (as); as long; as far. ogni ~, every now and then. *di ~ in ~,* from time to time. ~ *quanto,* as much as. *tanti ~ quanti,* as many as.

tapinàre, *v.i.* (*aux.* avere) to lead a wretched life. **tapíno,** *a.* wretched; miserable.

tàppa, *f.* stage; halting-place. **tappa-búchi,** *m.inv.* (*fig.*) stop-gap. **tappàre,** *v.t.* to stop; stop-up; plug; cork; bung; muffle (up). **tappàrsi,** *v.refl.* to shut oneself up; muffle oneself (up).

tappetàre, *v.t.* to carpet. **tappetíno,** *m.* small carpet; rug. **tappéto,** *m.* carpet; rug; mat; cloth; cover; tapis. ~ *erboso,* (green)sward. ~ *verde,* green baize; gaming-table.

tappezzàre, *v.t.* to hang with tapestry; paper (*wall*); cover; line; carpet (*with flowers*); upholster. **tappezzería,** *f.* tapestry; hangings; arras; tapestry-work; wall-paper; upholstery; upholsterer's shop. **tappezzière,** *m.* tapestry maker; upholsterer; decorator; paper-hanger.

tàppo. *m.* plug; stopper; cork; cap; bung. ~ *di assale,* axle cap (*Mech.*). ~ *di valvola,* valve cap (*tyre*). **tàra,** *f.* defect; weakness; taint; tare (*Com.*).

tarabúso, *m.* bittern.

tarantèlla, *f.* tarantella.

taràntola, *f.* tarantula.

taràto, *a.* weak, sickly; defective.

tarchiàto, *a.* sturdy; thick-set.

tardaménte, *ad.* slowly; tardily; late. **tardànza,** *f.* delay. **tardàre,** *v.i.* (*aux.* avere) to delay; be late; be long (in); loiter; linger. *v.t.* to delay; retard. **tardézza,** *f.* slowness; tardiness. **tàrdi,** *ad.* late. **tardità,** *f.* slowness; backwardness. **tardívo,** *a.* tardy; belated; late; slow; sluggish; backward. **tàrdo,** *a.* late; slow; sluggish; tardy; lazy; slow-witted.

tàrga (*pl.* **tàrghe**), *f.* name-plate; number-plate (*car*); shield. **targhétta,** *f.* small plate; big slice.

tariffa, *f.* tariff, rate, rates, scale (*of charges*); price-list; fare.

tarlàre, *v.i.* (*aux.* essere) & **tarlàrsi,** *v.refl.* to be worm-eaten. **tarlàto,** *a.* worm-eaten. **tarlatúra,** *f.* worm-hole; dust of worm-eaten wood. **tàrlo,** *m.* wood-worm; boring-worm; (*fig.*) gnawing of conscience, remorse.

tàrma, *f.* grub of the clothes moth; moth. **tarmàre,** *v.i.* (*aux.* essere) & **tarmàrsi,** *v.refl.* to be moth-eaten.

taroccàre, *v.i.* (*aux.* avere) to play a trump-card or 'tarot' at the game of tarocchi; *more gen.* to play a trump-card; get angry; grumble. **taròcco,** *m.* *usu. pl.* **taròcchi,** taroc; tarot (It. card-game). **taroccóne,** *m.* grumbler.

tarpàre, *v.t.* to clip (*the wings of*); pare.

tarsía, *f.* inlaid (wood) work; tarsia; marquetry. **tarsiàre,** *v.t.* to inlay. **tartagliàre,** *v.i.* (*aux.* avere) to stutter; stammer. **tartaglióne,** *m.* (*f.* -óna*), stutterer; stammerer.

tartàna, *f.* tartan (one-masted lateen vessel).

tartàrico (*pl.* **-àrici**), *a.* tartaric. **tàrtaro,** *m.* (*Chem.* & *Dent.*) tartar. **T ~,** Tartarus; hell; inhabitant of Tartary.

tartarúga (*pl.* **-úghe**), *f.* tortoise; turtle; tortoise-shell; (*fig.*) sluggard; slow-coach.

tartassàre, *v.t.* to harass; vex; bully.

tartína, *f.* slice of bread & butter (or with jam, fish or meat paste).

tartúfo, *m.* truffle.

tàsca (*pl.* **tàsche**), *f.* pocket; satchel; case. **tascàbile,** *a.* suitable for the pocket; pocket (*att.*). **tascapàne,** *m.inv.* haversack; pouch. **tascàta,** *f.*

pocketful.   **taschíno,** *m.* small pocket; waistcoat pocket; fob.

tàssa, *f.* tax; rate; duty; due; charge; fee.   ~ *di soggiorno,* visitors' tax. ~ *sullo spettacolo,* entertainment tax. **tassàbile,** *a.* taxable. **tassàmetro,** *m.* taximeter. **tassàre,** *v.t.* to tax; rate; assess; charge with duty; charge [for].

tassativaménte, *ad.* definitely; precisely; positively. **tassatívo,** *a.* positive; precise; definite; specific. **tassatóre,** *m.* assessor. **tassazióne,** *f.* taxation; rating; assessment; charges.

tassí, *m.inv.* taxi [cab]. **tassidermía,** *f.* taxidermy.

tàsso, *m.* yew [-tree]; (*Zool.*) badger. ~ *di sconto,* (*Fin.*) discount, rate.

tastàre, *v.t.* to touch; try; feel carefully; sound; probe. **tastàta,** *f.* touching; feeling; sounding.

tasteggiàre, *v.t.* to touch the keys (of a piano). **tastièra,** *f.* keyboard. **tàsto,** *m.* key; tapper (*Teleg.*); touch; feel(ing). **tastoni** *&* **a tastóni,** *ad.* by feeling or groping; gropingly.

tàttica, *f.* tactics.   **tàttico** (*pl.* **tàttici**)**,** *a.* tactical.   ¶ *m.* tactician.

tàttile, *a.* tactile.

tàtto, *m.* touch; feeling; tact.

tatuàggio, *m.* tattooing; tattoo. **tatuàre,** *v.t.* to tattoo.

taumaturgía, *f.* thaumaturgy. **taumatúrgo** (*pl.* **-úrghi**)**,** *a.* wonderworking.   ¶ *m.* wonder-worker.

tauríno, *a.* taurine. **tauromachía,** *f.* bull-fight.

tautología, *f.* tautology. **tautològico** (*pl.* **-ògici**)**,** *a.* tautological.

tavèrna, *f.* public-house; tavern. **tavernière,** *m.* publican; tavern-keeper.

tàvola, *f.* table; board; slab; tablet; plank; list; index; plate (*illustration*); (page) illustration. *biancheria da* ~**,** table linen.   ~ *allungabile,* draw leaf t.   ~ *pitagorica,* multiplication table.   ~ *da giuoco,* gaming table. ~ *da pranzo,* dining table.   ~ *reale,* backgammon. *la T* ~ *Rotonda,* the Round Table (*Arthurian*).   *t* ~ *rotonda, t* ~ *comune,* table d'hôte. **tavolàccio,** *m.* plank-bed. **tavolàta,** *f.* table spread for dinner; guests round the table; table (in this sense). **tavolàto,** *m.* wainscotting; hoarding; wooden floor. **tavolétta,** *f.* small table; tablet. **tavolière,** *m.* chess-board; draught-board; backgammon-board; card-table. **tavolíno,** *m.* small table; desk.   ~ *da*

notte, bed-side table; night table. **tàvolo,** *m.* table.   ~ *da toletta,* dressing table. **tavolòzza,** *f.* palette.

tàzza, *f.* cup; mug; basin (*of fountain*).

te, *pn. pers. disjunct. 2nd sg.* thee (*Poet.*); you. **tè,** *m.* tea.

teatràle, *a.* theatrical; dramatic. **teàtro,** *m.* theatre; playhouse; stage; drama; scene; seat (*as of war*); dim. *teatrino. il* ~ *di Pulcinella,* Punch & Judy Show.

Tèbe, *f.* Thebes.

tècnica, *f.* technique. **tècnico** (*pl.* **tècnici**)**,** *a.* technical.   ¶ *m.* technician. **tecnicolóre,** *n.* technicolour. **tecnología,** *f.* technology.

téco, *pn. pers.* with thee; with you.

tedescaménte, *ad.* in the German way. **tedeschería,** *f.* German ways; Germans (*coll.*).   **tedésco** (*pl.* **tedéschi**)**,** *a. & m.* German.

tediàre, *v.t.* to weary; bore; tire. **tèdio,** *m.* tedium; tediousness; weariness. **tedióso,** *a.* tedious; tiresome; weary; wearisome.

tegàme, *m.* pan, deep pan. **téglia,** *f.* pan; saucepan; baking pan.

tégola, *f. &* **tégolo,** *m.* tile. **tegolàia,** *f.* tile-works.

teièra, *f.* tea-pot.

teísmo, *m.* theism. **teísta** (*pl.* **teísti,** *m.* theist.

téla, *f.* cloth; linen; calico; canvas; painting; picture; plot; web; curtain (*Theat.*). **teiàio,** *m.* loom; frame; chassis; sash (*window*).

telefèrica, *f.* overhead cable-way. **telefonàre,** *v.t. & abs.* to telephone; 'phone. **telefonàta,** *f.* telephone call; telephone message. **telefònico** (*pl.* **-ònici**)**,** *a.* telephonic, telephone (*att.*). **telefonísta** (*pl.* **-ísti,** *f.* **-íste**)**,** *m.f.* telephonist; telephone operator. **teléfono,** *m.* telephone. **telefotografía,** *f.* telephotography. **telegrafàre,** *v.t. & abs.* to telegraph; wire. **telegrafía,** *f.* telegraphy.   ~ *senza fili,* wireless telegraphy. **telegràfico** (*pl.* **-àfici**)**,** *a.* telegraphic; telegraph (*att.*). **telegrafísta** (*pl.* **-ísti**)**,** *m.* telegraphist; telegraphic operator. **telègrafo,** *m.* telegraph; telegraph office. **telegràmma** (*pl.* **-gràmmi**) *m.* telegram; wire.

telèmetro, *m.* range-finder.

telepatía, *f.* telepathy; thought-reading.

telería, *f.* linen (cloth); soft-goods.

telescòpico (*pl.* **-òpici**)**,** *a.* telescopic(al). **telescòpio,** *m.* telescope.

televisióne, *f.* television. *trasmettere per ~,* to televise.

télo, *m.* breadth of cloth; piece of cloth. **télo,** *m.* (*Poet.*) dart; javelin.

teloslítta, *f.* tire-escape.

téma, *f.* fear. **tènia** (*pl.* **tèmi**), *m.* theme; topic; subject; exercise; composition (*Sch.*); stem (*Gram.*).

temènza, *f.* fear; dread; awe.

temerário, *a.* rash; reckless; foolhardy. **temére,** *v.t. & abs.* to fear; be afraid of; dread; hesitate; shrink from; cannot stand. **temerità,** *f.* temerity; rashness, &c.

Tèmi & Tèmide, *f.* Themis.

temibile, *a.* to be feared; inspiring fear; to be dreaded.

tempáccio, *m.* nasty weather.

tèmpera, *f.* temper (*metal*); distemper; tempera (*painting*); timbre (*sound*). **temperalàpis & temperamatíte,** *m.inv.* pencil-sharpener. **temperaménto,** *m.* temperament; temper; disposition; just proportion; arrangement; compromise; expedient; mitigation. **temperànte,** *a.* temperate; soothing; (*Med.*) sedative. **temperànza,** *f.* temperance; moderation. **temperàre,** *v.t.* to temper; mitigate; moderate; adjust; sharpen (*pencil*); distemper. **temperatúra,** *f.* temperature; tempering; sharpening. **tempèrie,** *f.* mild or seasonable weather; settled state of the atmosphere. **temperíno,** *m.* pen-knife; pocket-knife.

tempèsta, *f.* storm; tempest. **tempestàre,** *v.i.* (*aux.* avere) to storm; rage; hail. *v.t.* to vex; annoy; harass; importune; knock; shake; toss about; pull about. **tempestàto,** *a.* beaten; (*fig.*) richly adorned; decked. **tempestío,** *m.* (*fig.*) flood; outburst. **tempestívo,** *a.* opportune; timely; seasonable. **tempestóso,** *a.* tempestuous; stormy; boisterous.

tèmpia, *f.* temple (*forehead*). **tèmpio** (*pl.* **tèmpli**), *m.* temple; church. dim. *tempietto.*

tempíssimo, *a ~,* in the nick of time. *per ~,* very early. **tèmpo,** *m.* time; while; times; days; age; season; weather; tense (*Gram.*); beat; measure (*Mus.*); phase. **tèmpora,** *f.pl.* Ember days. **temporàle,** *a.* temporal; secular. ¶ *m.* storm. **temporaneità,** *f.* temporary character. **temporàneo,** *a.* temporary; transitory.

temporeggiàre, *v.i.* (*aux.* avere) to temporize; procrastinate. **temporeggiatóre,** *m.* temporizer; procrastinator.

tèmpra, *f.* temper; disposition; temperament; moral fibre. **tempràre,** *v.t.* to temper; inure; whet (*appetite*).

tenàce, *a.* tenacious; adhesive; tough; stiff; stubborn; retentive. **tenàcia & tenacità,** *f.* tenacity, &c.

tenàglie, see *tanaglie.*

tènda, *f.* tent; curtain; awning. bell tent. *~ da bagno,* bathing tent. *grande ~ (da campo),* marquee.

tendènza, *f.* tendency; trend; bent; inclination; leaning; propensity; liking. **tèndere,** *v.t. ir.* to stretch; stretch out; hold out (*hand, &c.*); strain; crane (*neck*); bend (*bow*); lay; spread; set (*trap, &c.*); tighten. *v.i.* (*aux.* avere) to tend; aim (*at*); turn; be inclined; lead; conduce.

tendína, *f.* blind; shutter; eye-shade. **tèndine,** *m.* tendon; sinew.

tènebre, *f.pl.* dark(ness); gloom. **tenebróso,** *a.* dark; murky; gloomy; obscure.

tenènte, *m.* lieutenant. *~ di vascello,* lieutenant (*Nav.*).

tenére (*pr.* **tèngo, tièni, tiène**), *v.t. ir.* to hold; hold on; restrain (*tears*); keep; have; gain; win; obtain; contain; take; take up (*space*); consider, regard. *v.i.* (*aux.* avere) to hold; last; cling; border on; owe; partake; savour; be like; take after; be owing to; rest; lie; be anxious; sit. **tenérsi,** *v.refl.* to keep; stand; sit; stick; contain oneself; refrain; regard oneself.

tenerézza, *f.* tenderness; softness; fondness; love. **tènero,** *a.* tender; soft; sensitive; new; early (*youth*); fond; loving; affectionate. ¶ *m.* tender part; (*fig.*) weak side. **tenerúme,** *m.* soft part; soft things; (*fig.*) mawkishness; sentimentality.

tènia, *f.* tape-worm.

tenibile, *a.* tenable.

teniménto, *m.* holding. **tenitóre,** *m.* holder.

tenóre, *m.* tenor; purport; content(s); terms; bearing; manner; system; grade; standard; (*Mus.*) tenor (*voice, singer*). **tenoreggiàre,** *v.i.* (*aux.* avere), to sing tenor. **tenoríle,** *a.* (*Mus.*) tenor (*att.*).

tensíle, *a.* tensile. **tensióne,** *f.* tension; tightness; pressure; strain. **tensóre,** *m.* (*Anat.*) tensor.

tènta, *f.* (*Surg.*) probe. **tentàbile,** *a.* open to trial or temptation.

tentàcolo, *m*. tentacle; feeler.
tentàre, *v.t.* to attempt; try; test; feel; tempt; (*Surg.*) sound, probe. **tentatívo**, *m*. attempt; trial. **tentatóre**, *m*. **tentatríce**, *f*. tempter; temptress. ¶ *a*. tempting. **tentazióne**, *f*. temptation.
tentènna, *m*. waverer; irresolute person. **tentennaménto**, *m*. shaking; waggling; wavering; vacillation. **tentennàre**, *v.t.* to shake; waggle. *v.i.* (*aux.* avere) to oscillate; swing; hesitate; waver; totter; stagger; be unsteady. **tentennóne**, *m*. waverer.
tentoni (a), *ad. expr.* gropingly; hesitatingly.
tènue, *a*. thin; fine; tenuous; small; slight; slender; watery (*fluid*). **tenuità**, *f*. thinness, &c.
tenúta, *f*. estate, farm; holding (*of land*); (*cubic*) capacity; uniform. ~ *di fatica*, working clothes. ~ *dei libri*, book-keeping. **tenutàrio**, *m*. landed proprietor; land-holder. **tenúto**, *a*. obliged; bound; also *p.p.* of *tenere*.
tenzonàre, *v.i.* (*aux.* avere) to dispute; contend; be at strife. **tenzóne**, *f*. combat; contest; *esp.* poetic contest.
teocrazia, *f*. theocracy.
Teòcrito, *m*. Theocritus.
teodolíto, *m*. theodolite.
teología, *f*. theology. **teològico** (*pl.* -**ògici**), *a*. theological. **teòlogo** (*pl.* -**òlogi**), *m*. theologian.
teorèma (*pl.* -**èmi**), *m*. theorem. **teorètico** (*pl.* -**ètici**), *a*. theoretic(al). **teoría**, *f*. theory. **teòrico** (*pl.* -**òrici**), *a*. theoretical. ¶ *m*. theorist. **teorizzàre**, *v.i.* to theorize.
teosofía, *f*. theosophy.
tepidézza, *f*. tepidness; tepidity; lukewarmness. **tèpido**, *a*. tepid; lukewarm. **tepóre**, *m*. warmth, pleasant warmth.
téppa, *f*. mob; band (of roughs). **teppísmo**, *m*. hooliganism; ruffianism. **teppísta** (*pl.* -**ísti**), *m*. hooligan; rough; ruffian.
terapèutica, *f*. therapeutics. **terapèutico** (*pl.* -**èutici**), *a*. therapeutic(al).
terapía, *f*. therapy.
terebentína, *f*. turpentine.
Terènzio, *m*. Terence.
tèrgere, *v.t. ir.* to wipe; wipe off; wipe away; scour; clean; polish; dry (*tears*). **tergicristàllo**, *m.inv.* (*motor*) screen-wiper.
tergiversàre, *v.i.* to hesitate; answer

evasively; beat about the bush. **tergiversazióne**, *f*. evasiveness; hesitation.
tèrgo, *m*. back. *a* ~, on the back; overleaf. *da* ~, from behind.
termàle, *a*. thermal; hot. *sorgente* ~, *f*. hot spring. **tèrme**, *f.pl.* thermal baths; hot baths; hot springs.
terminàbile, *a*. terminable. **terminàle**, *a*. terminal; boundary (*att.*). **terminàre**, *v.t. & i.* (*aux.* essere) to terminate; end; wind up; finish. **terminazióne**, *f*. termination; ending. **tèrmine**, *m*. boundary; bound; limit; space; term; end; time; date; aim; object; (*pl.*) terms, condition(s). **terminología**, *f*. terminology.
tèrmite, *m*. termite; white ant; (*Chem.*) thermit; incendiary bomb.
termodinàmica, *f*. thermodynamics.
termoelèttrico (*pl.* -**ettrici**), *a*. thermoelectric.
termòmetro, *m*. thermometer. ~ *clinico*, clinical thermometer.
Termòpili, *f.pl.* Thermopylae.
tèrmos, *m.inv.* thermos (flask). **termosifóne**, *m*. heating-installation. *riscaldamento centrale a* ~, central heating. **termòstato**, *m*. thermostat.
ternàrio, *a*. ternary. **tèrno**, *m*. winning draw of three numbers out of five in the public lottery; (*fig.*) stroke of luck; winning card.
tèrra, *f*. earth; ground; land; soil; estate; property; clay; shore (*Naut.*); world; country; village; locality. **terracòtta** (*pl.* **terrecòtte**), *f*. figure in terracotta. **terràglia**, *f*. crockery; pottery; earthenware. **Terranòva** (la), *f*. Newfoundland. *m.inv.* Newfoundland [dog]. **terrapièno**, *m*. platform; terrace; embankment; level surface; open space; (*Mil.*) terreplain. *Terra Santa*, *f*. Holy Land.
terràzza, *f. & terràzzo*, *m*. balcony; terraced roof; terrace; flat roof. *dim. terrazzino*.
terremòto, *m*. earthquake.
terréno, *m*. ground; soil; land; field; site. ¶ *a*. earthly. **tèrreo**, *a*. earthy; earth-coloured; dull; yellowish; wan.
terríbile, *a*. terrible; terrific; dreadful; formidable. **terribilità**, *f*. awe-inspiring quality; awesomeness; formidableness.
terríccio, *m*. mould; loam.
terrière, *a*. land-owning; landed.

terrificàre. *v.t.* to terrify; frighten; appal.

terrígno, *a.* (*of colour*) dull; yellowish; wan; underground.

terrína, *f.* earthenware pot; tureen.

territoriàle, *a.* territorial. **territòrio,** *m.* territory.

terróre, *m.* terror; dread.

terróso, *a.* earthy; muddy. **terrúcola,** *f.* barren soil; hamlet, small village.

Tersícore, *f.* Terpsichore (*Myth.*).

tèrso, *a.* terse.

tèrza, *f.* (*Eccl. & fencing*) tierce; (*Rly.*) third class; (*Sch.*) third form, third class. **terzàna,** *f.* tertian fever; tertian ague. **terzétto,** *m.* triplet; trio. **terziàrio,** *a. & m.* tertiary. **terzína,** *f.* tercet; group of three lines forming the unit of *terza rima*. **terzíno,** *m.* bottle holding ⅓ of a *fiasco*; (*football*) full back. **tèrzo,** *a. num. ord.* third. *terza rima,* arrangement of 11-syllabled lines in interlocked groups of three (*terzine*) as in Dante's *Divina Commedia.* ¶ *ad.* thirdly.

tésa, *f.* brim (*hat*); bird-net, -netting.

tèschio, *m.* skull.

tèsi, *f.* thesis; proposition. **téso,** *p.p.* of *tendere.* ¶ *a.* taut, tight; (*fig.*) overstrung (*nerves*).

tesoreggiàre, *v.t.* to hoard; treasure up.

tesorería, *f.* treasury. **tesorière,** *m.* treasurer. **tesòro,** *m.* treasure.

Tèspi, *f.* Thespis. *il carro di T~,* travelling theatre.

Tessàlia (la), *f.* Thessaly.

tèssera, *f.* card; ticket; tally; pass. *~ annonaria,* ration-card. *~ di riconoscimento,* identification card. **tesseraménto,** *m.* rationing; distribution of membership cards (*society & party*). **tesseràre,** *v.t.* to ration; distribute cards of membership. **tesseràto,** *a.* rationed. ¶ *m.* member (of a party).

tèssere, *v.t.* to weave (*lit. & fig.*).

tèssile, *a.* textile. **tessitóre,** *m.* **tessitríce,** *f.* weaver. **tessitúra,** *f.* weaving. **tessúto,** *m.* cloth; fabric; (*Biol.*) tissue; (*fig.*) web.

tèsta, *f.* head; top; face; person; lead; brains; wits. *~ quadra,* good head, clever, well-balanced man. *~ carica,* war-head (*torpedo*). *~ di Turco,* Aunt Sally. *~ di ponte,* bridge-head. *~ di sbarco,* (*Mil.*) beach-head.

testàbile, *a.* that can be bequeathed.

testàceo, *a. & m.* testacean.

testamentàrio, *a.* testamentary. **testaménto,** *m.* will; testament. *il Vecchio, il Nuovo T~,* the Old, the New Testament.

testardàggine, *f.* obstinacy; stubbornness. **testàrdo,** *a.* obstinate, stubborn; headstrong.

testàre, *v.t. & abs.* to bequeath; make one's will.

testàta, *f.* head; top; heading; blow with the head. **testàtico** (*pl.* **-àtici**), *m.* poll-tax; head-tax.

testatóre, *m.* **testatríce,** *f.* testator; testatrix.

testé, *ad.* lately; a short time ago; just now.

testícolo, *m.* testicle.

testificàre, *v.t. & abs.* to testify; declare. **testimóne,** *m. & f.* witness. *~ di accusa,* witness for the prosecution. *~ di difesa,* witness for the defence. *~ oculare,* eye-witness. **testimoniàle,** *a.* of the witness(es); given in evidence. **testimoniànza,** *f.* testimony; evidence; witness; mark; token. **testimoniàre,** *v.t. & i.* (*aux.* avere) to witness; bear witness; testify; give evidence. **testimònio,** *m.* witness (*pers.*); evidence.

tèsto, *m.* text.

testolína, *f.* little head; pretty little head; (*fig.*) girl. **testóne,** *m.* big head; (*fig.*) obstinate fellow; block-head.

testuàle, *a.* textual.

testúggine, *f.* tortoise; turtle.

tètano, *m.* tetanus, lock-jaw.

tetràggine, *f.* gloom; sadness.

tetràgono, *a.* four-sided; (*fig.*) four-square; firm; steadfast; unflinching.

tètro, *a.* gloomy; dismal; sad.

tétta, *f.* nipple; teat; (*fig.*) breast. **tettàre,** *v.i. & abs.* to suck (*of child*).

tétto, *m.* roof; house top; (*fig.*) house; home. *~ mobile,* sliding roof (*motor, &c.*). **tettóia,** *f.* shed; penthouse; (*station*) roof.

Tèutone, *m.* Teuton. **teutònico** (*pl.* **-ònici**), *a.* Teutonic.

Tévere (il), *m.* the Tiber.

ti, *pn. pers. conjunc.* you; to you; thee; to thee.

tiberíno, *a.* of the Tiber.

Tibúllo, *m.* Tibullus.

tíc, *m.* tick (*clock*); tic; twitching; (*fig.*) habit; mannerism; trick. **ticchettàre,** *v.i.* to tick. **ticchettío,** *m.* ticking.

tícchio, *m.* tic; whim; fancy; caprice.

tiepidézza & **tiepidità,** f. tepidness;
tepidity; lukewarmness. **tièpido,** a.
tepid; lukewarm.

tifo, m. typhus. **tifòide** & **tifoidèa,**
f. typhoid fever.

tifóne, m. typhoon; hurricane. **tifóso,**
m. typhus patient; (fig.) fan; fanatic.
un ~ del calcio, a football fan.

tíglio, m. lime; lime-tree; fibre; bast;
vein (in stone). **tiglióso,** a. tough
(meat); fibrous.

tígna, f. ring-worm, or other eruption
on the head. **tign[u]òla,** f. (clothes)-
moth; worm; weevil. **tignóso,** a.
scabby; scurfy. ¶ m. person affected
with ring-worm, &c.

tigràto, a. striped, streaked, tabby.
tígre, m. tiger; f. tigress. **tigrésco**
(pl. -éschi), a. tigerish.

Tígri (il), m. the Tigris. **tigròtto,** m.
young tiger.

timbàllo, m. kettle-drum.

timbràre, v.t. to stamp; postmark.
timbratúra, f. stamping. **tímbro,**
m. stamp; timbre. ~ postale,
postmark. ~ in gomma, rubber
stamp.

timidézza, f. timidity; shyness,
diffidence. **tímido,** a. timid;
nervous; shy; bashful, diffident.

tímo, m. thyme.

timóne, m. rudder; helm; handle-bar
(bicycle); shaft; pole (cart). **ti-
moneggiàre,** v.t. to steer. **timoni-
èra,** f. wheel-house. **timonière,** m.
helmsman; steersman.

timoràto, a. respectful; scrupulous;
devout. **timóre,** m. fear; awe.
timoróso, a. timorous; fearful.

tímpano, m. ear-drum; kettle-drum;
(Anat. & Arch.) tympanum; (Arch.)
spandrel.

tinàia, f. vat-room; cellar. **tinèllo,** m.
small cask; s. tub; servants' hall;
small dining room.

tíngere, v.t. ir. to dye; paint; stain;
tincture; tinge; colour.

tíno, m. vat; tub. **tinòzza,** f. tub;
wash-tub; bath-tub.

tínta, f. dye; colour; complexion;
colouring; tint; shade; hue; tinge;
touch; strain. **tinteggiàre,** v.t. to
tint; tinge; tincture.

tintinnàre & **tintinníre** (pr. -ísco,
-ísci), v.i. (aux. essere & avere) to
tinkle; jingle; clink; chink; tingle.
tintín & **tintínno,** m. tinkling;
jingling, &c.

tínto, a. & p.p. of tingere, dyed;
stained, &c. **tintóre,** m. dyer.
tintoría, f. dyeworks; (art of)

dyeing. **tintúra,** f. dyeing; dye;
(Chem.) tincture.

típico (pl. típici), a. typical.

típo, m. type (model & Typ.);
standard; specimen. un bel ~,
a queer fellow, character, funny
chap. **tipografía,** f. typography;
printing-works; printing office.
tipogràfico (pl. -àfiici), a. typo-
graphic(al); letterpress (att.). **tipò-
grafo,** m. printer; typographer.

tiralínee, m.inv. drawing-pen. **tira-
màntici,** m.inv. organ-blower.
tiramólla & **tiremmòlla,** m.inv.
rope part taut and part slack; ferry
rope; (fig.) indecision; waverer.

tiranneggiàre, v.t. to tyrannize (over);
oppress. v.i. (aux. avere) to play the
tyrant; rule despotically; tyrannize.
tirannèllo, m. petty tyrant.
tirannésco (pl. -éschi), a. tyrannous, despotic. **tirannía,** f.
tyranny. **tirannícida** (pl. -ídi), m.
tyrannicide (pers.). **tirannicídio,**
m. tyrannicide (act). **tirànnico** (pl.
-ànnici), a. tyrannic(al); arbitrary;
high-handed; despotic. **tirànnide,**
f. despotism. **tirànno,** m. tyrant.
¶ a. tyrannous; tyrannical.

tirànte, m. connecting-rod; tie-rod;
(Arch.) tie-beam. ~ del freno,
brake-rod (Mech.).

tiràre, v.t. & i. (aux. avere) to draw;
pull; drag; tug; haul; get; derive;
attract; bring about; entail; extract;
deliver (blow); fire; shoot; let off;
blow (wind); go; push (on); incline;
verge; print; print off; machine.
tirastivàli, m.inv. boot-jack.
tiràta, f. pull; draw; tirade.
tiratàppi, m.inv. cork-screw.

tiràto, a. stingy; close-fisted. **tira-
tóre,** m. drawer; marksman; shot.
franco ~, sniper. ~ di scherma,
fencer. **tiratúra,** f. drawing;
pull(ing). printing; impression;
circulation (book, paper).

tirchiería, f. meanness; stinginess;
niggardliness. **tírchio,** a. mean;
stingy; niggardly; miserly. ¶ m.
miser.

tirèlia, f. trace (harness). **tirétto,** m.
drawer.

tiritèra, f. long-winded story; endless
tirade; rigmarole.

tiro, m. shooting; shot; firing; fire;
range (of fire); draught; cast; throw;
stroke (billiards); trick. ~ con l'arco,
archery. ~ di sbarramento, barrage-
fire. un ~ (a segno), a shooting
gallery.

tirocinànte, *m.* apprentice; beginner; tyro. **tirocìnio**, *m.* apprenticeship; novitiate.

tiròide, *a. & f.* thyroid. **tiroidèo**, *a.* thyroid.

tirolése, *a. & n..* Tyrolese. **Tiròlo**, *m.* Tyrol.

tirréno, *a.* Tyrrhene; Tyrrhenian.

tiṣàna, *f.* infusion; (herb) tea.

tiṣi, *f.* !phthisis, consumption. **tíṣico** (*pl.* tìṣici), *a. & m.* consumptive.

titànico (*pl.* -ànici), *a.* titanic. **Titàno**, *m.* Titan.

titillàre, *v.t.* to titillate; tickle.

titolàre, *a.* titular; regular; rightful. ¶ *m.* (regular) holder; occupant; incumbent. **tìtolo**, *m.* title; (title) deed; muniment; document; proof; evidence, qualification; right; status; title page; heading; certificate; scrip; warrant; bond; security; stock; share; holding; claim; fineness (*coins*); precious metal in alloy; grade; strength (*solution*). a ~ di, in virtue of, by right of, as.

Titóne, *m.* Tithonus (*Myth.*).

titubànte, *a.* hesitant; irresolute; faltering. **titubànza**, *a.* irresoluteness; hesitancy; perplexity. **titubàre** (*pr.* tìtubo), *v.i.* (*aux.* avere) to falter; hesitate; waver. **titubazióne**, *f.* hesitation; perplexity.

Tiziàno, *m.* Titian.

tìzio (un), *m.* some fellow or other.

tizzo *&* **tizzóne**, *m.* brand; firebrand.

to' *&* **toh!** *i.* I say! (surprise); look here! hallo!

toccànte, *a.* touching, regarding.

toccàre (*pr.* tòcco, tòcchi), *v.t.* to touch; feel; taste; finger; tap; hit; strike; play (*piano, &c.*); move, affect, concern; injure; offend; touch on, allude to; meddle with; adjoin; call at, touch at (*ship*); reach; draw (*salary*). *v.i.* (*aux.* essere) to befall; fall to the lot of; be the duty of; be the turn of. **toccàrsi**, *v.refl.* to meet. **toccàta**, *f.* touch; (*Mus.*). toccata. **toccheggiàre**, *v.i.* (*aux.* avere) to toll (*bell*). **tóccé** (*pl.* tócchi), *sync. p.p.* of *toccare*. ¶ *m.* touch; stroke; toll (*bell*). al ~, at one o'clock; at the stroke of one. **tòcco**, *m.* piece; figure (*pers.*); toque.

toelétte, *f.* see *toletta*.

tòga (*pl.* tòghe), *f.* toga, professor's gown. **togàto**, *a.* wearing a gown.

tògliere *&* **tòrre** (*pr.* tòlgo, tògli, tòglie, &c.), *v.t. ir.* to take, take

away; remove; carry away; carry off; seize; steal; free; prevent, hinder.

tolemàico (*pl.* -àici), *a.* Ptolemaic.

tolétta, *f.* toilet; toilette; toilet-table, dressing-table; dressing-room.

tolleràbile, *a.* tolerable. **tollerànte**, *a.* tolerant. **tollerànza**, *f.* tolerance; toleration; endurance. **tolleràre**, *v.t.* to tolerate; bear, suffer, endure.

Tolornèo, *m.* Ptolemy.

Tolóne, *f.* Toulon. **Tolóṣa**, *f.* Toulouse.

tomàio, *m.* (*shoe*) upper; vamp.

tómba, *f.* tomb; grave; (*fig.*) death.

tómbola, *f.* tombola (lottery game); (*fig.*) fall. **tombolàre**, *v.i.* (*aux.* essere) to fall headlong; tumble.

tomíṣmo, *m.* Thomism. **tomìsta** (*pl.* -ísti), *m.* Thomist.

tòmo, *m.* tome; volume. dim. *tometto.*

tònaco, *f.* tunic; (*Eccl.*) cassock; frock; cowl.

tonàre *or* **tuonàre** (*pr.* tuòno, tuòni), *v.i.* (*aux.* avere *&* essere) to thunder; boom.

tondàre, *v.t.* to round, round off; trim. **tondeggiàre**, *v.t.* to round, make round. *v.i.* (*aux.* essere) to be somewhat round.

tondíno, *m.* small plate; (*Arch.*) astragal. **tóndo**, *a.* round; in relief; full; stupid. ¶ *ad. in expr. chiaro e ~*, roundly, plainly, frankly. ¶ *m.* ring, circle; plate; (*Art.*) tondo, round picture; globe, sphere.

tónfo, *m.* splash; heavy fall; plunge.

tònica, *f.* tonic (*Mus.*); keynote. **tònico** (*pl.* tònici), *a. & m.* tonic.

tonnellàggio, *m.* tonnage; burden (*ship*). **tonnellàta**, *f.* ton (*Eng.* ton (2240 lbs.) = 1016 kilos; U.S. or short ton (2000 lbs.) = 907 kilos; metric ton, 1000 kilos).

tonnína, *f.* pickled tunny. **tónno**, *m.* tunny.

tòno, *m.* tone, accent, stress; tune (*fig.*); style; manner; keeping; (*Mus.*) tone; key; (= **tuono**) thunder.

tonsília, *f.* tonsil. **tonsillíte**, *f.* tonsillitis.

tonsúra, *f.* tonsure. **tonsuràre**, *v.t.* to tonsure.

tónto, *a.* dull; silly; dense; stupid.

topàzio, *m.* topaz.

tòpico (*pl.* tòpici), *a.* topical; external (*Med.*); local; to the point.

tòpo, *m.* mouse; rat.

topografía, *f.* topography. **topo-**

gràfico (*pl.* **-àfici**), *a.* topographical. **topògrafo**, *m.* topographer.
topolíno, *m.* mouselet, small mouse; baby (motor) car. *T* ~, Mickey Mouse. **toporàgno**, *m.* shrewmouse.
tòppa, *f.* door-lock; patch; piece let in. **tòppo**, *m.* block; log.
toràce, *m.* thorax (*Anat.*).
tórba, *f.* peat.
tórbido, *a.* turbid; muddy; gloomy; cloudy; troubled. ¶ *m.* trouble; disorder; disturbance.
torbièra, *f.* peat-bog, peat-moss. **torbóso**, *a.* peaty.
tòrcere (*pr.* **tòrco, -tòrci**), *v.t.* *ir.* to twist; wring.
torchiàre, *v.t.* to press. **tòrchio**, *m.* press, hand-press (*Typ.*). *essere sotto i torchi*, to be in the press.
tòrcia (*pl.* **tòrce**), *f.* torch; taper.
torcicòllo, *m.* crick, stiff neck; wryneck (*bird*); (*fig.*) hypocrite, bigot.
tor ci mént o, *m.* & **torcitúra**, *f.* twist, twisting.
tórdo, *m.* thrush; (*fig.*) simpleton; ninny.
torèllo, *m.* young bull.
torinése, *a.* of Turin. ¶ *m.* native of Turin. **Toríno**, *f.* Turin.
tórlo, *m.* yolk (*of an egg*).
tórma, *f.* crowd, swarm; herd.
torménta, *f.* snow-storm; blizzard.
tormentàre, *v.t.* to torment, torture; rack; worry; plague.
tormentatóre, *m.* tormentor.
torménto, *m.* torment, torture; pain. **tormentóso**, *a.* tormenting; troublesome; vexing.
tornacónto, *m.* profit; benefit; utility.
tornàre, *v.i.* (*aux.* essere) to return; turn; come back; go back; recur; reappear; turn out; prove to be; become; be correct; be worth while. **tornasóle**, *m.* sunflower; (*Chem.*) litmus. **tornàta**, *f.* return; sitting (of an assembly).
torneàre, *v.i.* (*aux.* avere) to joust; tilt; wheel round. **tornèo**, *m.* tournament.
tórnio, *m.* lathe; turning lathe.
tornìre (*pr.* **-ísco, -ísci**), *v.t.* to turn; (*fig.*) shape; polish. **tornitóre**, *m.* turner.
tórno, *m.* period. *in quel* ~, thereabouts; about. ¶ *pr.* & *ad.* round, about. ~ ~, round about, all round.
tòro, *m.* bull.
torpedinàre, *v.t.* to torpedo. **torpèdine**, *f.* torpedo; torpedo-fish.

torpedinièra, *f.* torpedo-boat.
torpedóne, *m.* motor-bus.
tòrpido, *a.* torpid, sluggish. **torpóre**, *m.* torpor, lethargy; stiffness.
tórre, *f.* tower; castle, rook (*chess*). ~ *d'avorio*, ivory tower (*fig.*).
torreggiàre, *v.i.* (*aux.* avere) to tower.
torrènte, *m.* torrent; stream; (*fig.*) flood. **torrenziàle**, *a.* torrential.
torrétta, *f.* turret.
tòrso, *m.* trunk, torso. **tórso** & **tórsolo**, *m.* stump; core (*apple*, &c.).
tórta, *f.* tart; cake, pastry; pie, pudding. ~ *di mele*, apple pie. **tòrta**, *f.* twist, twisting. **tortèllo**, *m.* fritter. **tortièra**, *f.* pie-dish; baking pan.
tòrto, *p.p.* of torcere. ¶ *a.* crooked. ¶ *m.* wrong; injury; injustice; fault; crooked timber. *a* ~, wrongly, wrongfully. *aver(e)* ~, to be wrong.
tórtora, *f.* turtle-dove. **tortoreggiàre**, *v.i.* (*aux.* avere) to coo.
tortuóso, *a.* tortuous; crooked; winding; wriggling, twisting; underhand.
tortùra, *f.* torture; rack. **torturàre**, *v.t.* to torture. *torturarsi il cervello*, to rack one's brains.
tòrvo, *a.* grim; surly.
tosaménto, *m.* & **tosatúra**, *f.* shearing. ~ *delle pecore*, sheepshearing. **tosàre**, *v.t.* to shear; clip. **tosatóre**, *m.* shearer.
Toscàna (la), *f.* Tuscany. **toscaneggiàre**, *v.i.* (*aux.* avere) to affect the Tuscan style in writing and speaking. **toscàno**, *a.* & *m.* Tuscan.
tòsco (*pl.* **tòschi**), *m.* poison.
tosóne, *m.* fleece.
tósse, *f.* cough.
tòssico (*pl.* **tòssici**), *m.* poison. ¶ *a.* toxic, poisonous. **tossicologìa**, *f.* toxicology.
tossìre (*pr.* **tósso** & **tossísco**), *v.i.* (*aux.* avere) to cough.
tostaménte, *ad.* speedily.
tostàre, *v.t.* to roast (*coffee*); toast. **tostíno**, *m.* coffee-roaster.
tòsto, *ad.* soon. ~*che*, as soon as. **tòsto**, *a.* toasted; hard; hardboiled. *faccia* ~ *a*, cheek, impudence.
totàle, *a.* total, whole; absolute. ¶ *m.* total. **totalità**, *f.* totality; entirety; mass, whole body. **totalizzatóre**, *m.* totalizator (*races*). **totalménte**, *ad.* totally; entirely; wholly; utterly. **totocàlcio**, *m.* football pool(s).
tovàglia, *f.* [table]-cloth. **tova-**

gliolíno, *m.* bib; small napkin.

tovagliòlo, *m.* napkin, serviette; tray-cloth.

tòzzo, *a.* squat; stocky; stumpy; thick-set. ¶ *m.* piece; morsel (*esp. of bread*).

tra, *pr.* among; between. ~ *me,* to myself.

trabàccolo, *m.* small (*Adriatic*) fishing boat; lugger; (*fig.*) ramshackle thing.

traballàre, *v.i.* (*aux.* avere) to stagger, totter, reel; lurch; jolt; shake. **traballío,** *m.* staggering, tottering; reeling; shaking, jolting. **traballóne,** *m.* stagger, lurch, heavy jolt.

trabalzàre, *v.i.* (*aux.* essere) to jolt; jerk; rebound; (*v.t.*) shift, remove.

trabíccolo, *m.* warming-pan; rickety vehicle.

traboccàre, *v.i.* (*aux.* avere & essere) to brim over, overflow (*avere* is used esp. of the vessel, or source, *essere* of what is poured out). **trabocchétto,** *m.* pitfall; snare. **trabocchévole,** *a.* overflowing; superabundant. **trabócco** (*pl.* **-ócchi**), *m.* overflow, overflowing.

tracannàre, *v.t.* to gulp down, drink at one draught.

traccagnòtto, *a.* sturdy, stocky; squat, dumpy.

traccheggiàre, *v.i.* (*aux.* avere) to dally, delay.

tràccia (*pl.* **tràcce**), *f.* trace; trail; track; spoor; (foot) step; foot-print; mark; vestige; outline, general plan. **tracciàre,** *v.t.* to trace, lay out, mark out; map out; draw; sketch; outline. **tracciatóre,** *m.* tracer.

trachèa, *f.* windpipe; (*Anat.*) trachea. **tracheotomía,** *f.* tracheotomy.

Tràcia (la), *f.* Thrace.

tracòlla, *f.* shoulder-belt. **tracollàre,** *v.i.* (*aux.* essere) to stagger; fall; overbalance; collapse. **tracòllo,** *m.* collapse; breakdown.

tracòma, *m.* (*Med.*) trachoma.

tracotànte, *a.* overbearing, over-weening; arrogant. **tracotànza,** *f.* arrogance.

tradiménto, *m.* treason; betrayal; treachery. **tradíre** (*pr.* **-ísco, -ísci**), *v.t.* to betray; reveal; deceive; be unfaithful to. **traditóre,** *m.* traitor, traitress; betrayer. ¶ *a.* treacherous.

tradizionàle, *a.* traditional. **tradizióne,** *f.* tradition; delivery (*Law*).

tradòtta, *f.* troop-train; leave-train.

traducíbile, *a.* translatable. **tradúrre** (*pr.* **-dúco, -dúci**), *v.t. ir.* to translate; turn; express, interpret;

summon; take, bring. **traduttóre,** *m.* **traduttrice,** *f.* translator. **traduzióne,** *f.* translation.

traènte, *m.* drawer (*of a bill*).

trafelàre, *v.i.* (*aux.* avere) to breathe heavily; pant; be tired out. **trafelàto,** *a.* panting; breathless; exhausted.

trafficànte, *m.* trader, dealer, trafficker. **trafficàre,** *v.i.* to traffic. trade, deal. **tràffico,** *m.* traffic; trading; trade.

trafíggere, *v.t. ir.* to transfix; pierce.

trafila, *f.* draw-plate; wire-gauge; (*fig.*) series. **trafilàre,** *v.t.* to draw (wire).

trafilétto, *m.* (*newspaper*) paragraph; satirical notice.

trafitta & **trafittúra,** *f.* pang; stabbing pain. **trafitto,** *p.a.* transfixed.

traforàre, *v.t.* to bore; pierce; perforate. **traforo,** *m.* piercing, boring; tunnel(ling); perforation. *lavoro in ~,* fretwork. *lavoro di ~,* filigree work.

trafugàre, *v.t.* to carry off secretly; purloin; steal. **trafugataménte,** *ad.* stealthily, by stealth.

tragèdia, *f.* tragedy.

traghettàre & **tragittàre,** *v.t.* to ferry across. **traghétto,** *m.* ferry.

tràgico (*pl.* **tràgici**), *a.* tragic[al]. ¶ *m.* tragedian. **tragicòmico** (*pl.* **-òmici**), *a.* tragicomic. **tragicommèdia,** *f.* tragicomedy.

tragìtto, *m.* journey; trip; crossing; passage (*by sea*).

traguàrdo, *m.* winning post; level, sight-vane.

Traiàno, *m.* Trajan.

traiettòria, *f.* trajectory.

trainàre, *v.t.* to drag, draw, haul. **tràino,** *m.* drawing, dragging, haulage; truck; sledge; waggon-load; baggage-train.

tralasciàre, *v.t.* to leave out, omit; put aside; leave off; discontinue; break off; give up.

tràlcio, *m.* vine-shoot, vine branch; shoot (of any climbing plant).

tralíccio, *m.* sacking, ticking; trellis, trellis-work.

tralignàre, *v.i.* (*aux.* essere & avere) to degenerate.

tralúcere, *v.i. defect.* (no comp. tenses) to shine through, shine forth; be transparent. **tralucènte,** *a.* translucent; transparent.

tràm, tramvài, *m. inv.* tram, tram-car (*cf.* **tranvai,** the more accepted form).

tràma, *f.* woof; weft; (*fig.*) plot.

tramandàre, *v.t.* to hand down, hand on, transmit.

tramàre, *v.t. & i.* (*aux.* avere) to plot.

trambústo, *m.* turmoil, confusion; bustle. tramenío, *m.* (continual) stir; fuss; bustle.

tramescolàre, *v.t.* to mix up; blend. tramestàre, *v.t.* to jumble [up].

tramezzàre, *v.t.* to partition [off]; interpose; insert. tramèżżo, *m.* partition; bulkhead; interval. ∼ *tra navata e coro*, rood screen. ¶ *pr.* between, among.

tramischiàre, *v.t.* to mix, mingle.

tràmite, *m.* path; way; course; means.

tramòggia, *f.* hopper.

tramontàna, *f.* north wind; north. tramontàre, *v.i.* (*aux.* essere) to set, go down; fade.

tramónto, *m.* setting; sunset; (*fig.*) end, decline.

tramortíre (*pr.* -ísco, -ísci), *v.i.* (*aux.* essere) to faint; swoon. *v.t.* to stun.

tràmpoli, *m.pl.* stilts. trampolíno, *m.* spring-board, diving board.

tramutàre, *v.t.* to change, shift, alter; transform; transmute; re-bottle. tramutatóre, *m.* transmuter.

tranèllo, *m.* snare, trap; plot.

trangugiàre & tranghiottíre (*pr.* -ísco, -ísci), *v.t.* to gulp down.

trànne, *pr.* except, save, but.

tranquillàre & tranquilliżżàre, *v.t.* to calm, soothe, quiet, tranquillize. tranquillità, *f.* tranquillity, calm; peace, peacefulness. tranquíllo, *a.* tranquil, quiet, calm, peaceful, still; undisturbed; easy.

transalpíno, *a.* transalpine. trans-atlàntico (*pl.* -àntici), *a.* trans-atlantic. ¶ *m.* liner.

transàtto, *p.p.* of *transigere.* transazióne, *f.* transaction; deal[ing]; arrangement; compromise, composition (*debtor*).

transétto, *m.* (*Arch.*) transept.

transìgere (*pr.* -sígo, -sígi), *v.i. ir.* (*aux.* avere) to come to terms, reach an agreement; yield; compound; compromise.

transitàre, *v.i.* (*aux.* avere) to pass (across, through, over). transitívo, *a.* transitive. trànsito, *m.* transit. *vietato il* ∼, no thoroughfare. transitòrio, *a.* transitory; transient. transizióne, *f.* transition.

transpadàno, *a.* beyond the Po; (on the left bank of the Po).

transúnto, *m.* summary; extract; certified copy.

transustanziazióne, *f.* transubstantiation.

tranvài, *m.inv.* tram-[car]. tranvía, *f.* tramway; tramline. tranviàrio, *a.* tram, tramway (*att.*). tranvière, *m.* tramway-man.

trapanàre, *v.t.* to drill; (*Surg.*) trepan. trapanatríce, *f.* drilling machine, mechanical drill. trapanatúra & trapanazióne, *f.* drilling; (*Surg.*) trepanning. tràpano, *m.* drill; auger; trepanning-saw.

trapassàre, *v.t.* to pierce, pass through, transfix; overstep; pass over; pass by; neglect. *v.i.* (*aux.* essere) to pass; pass on; pass away, die. trapassàto, *a.* dead, deceased. ¶ *m.* (*Gram.*) past perfect, pluperfect (*tense*). trapàsso, *m.* passage; transition, passing; death, decease; (*Law*) transfer.

trapelàre, *v.i.* (*aux.* essere) to trickle (out), ooze out; leak out (*lit. & fig.*); come to be known.

trapestío, *m.* trampling. trapèzio, *m.* trapeze; (*Geom.*) trapezium.

trapiantàre, *v.t.* to transplant. trapiantàrsi, *v.refl.* (*fig.*) to emigrate, settle.

trappísta (*pl.* -ísti), *a. & m.* Trappist.

trappòco, *ad.* shortly, in a short time.

tràppola, *f.* pitfall; trap; snare; (*fig.*) piece of deception. trappolàre, *v.t.* to entrap; dupe, deceive. trappolería, *f.* trickery, deception. trappolíno, *m.* springboard. trappolóne, *m.* trickster.

trapuntàre, *v.t.* to embroider; quilt. trapúnto, *m.* embroidery; quilting.

tràrre (*pr.* -tràggo, -trài, -tràe, &*c.*), *v.t. ir.* to draw; pull, drag; attract; get; lead; fling; throw; heave (*sigh*); spin (*silk*). *v.i.* (*aux.* essere) to go, approach, run (up). tràrsi, *v.refl.* to draw.

trasalíre (*pr.* -ísco, -ísci), *v.i.* (*aux.* avere & essere) to start. *far* ∼, to startle.

trasandàre (*pr.* trasàndo, trasàndi, *reg.*), *v.t.* to neglect. trasandàto, *a.* slovenly; careless; neglected.

trasbordàre, *v.t.* to tran[s]ship, trasbórdo, *m.* tran[s]shipment.

trascégliere (*pr.* -scélgo, -scégli, &*c.*), like *scegliere*), *v.t. ir.* to pick (out); choose; select.

trascendènte, *a.* transcendent, surpassing. trascendènza, *f.* transcendence, -cy. trascèndere, *v.t.t. ir.*

to transcend; surpass; be beyond.
v.i. (*aux.* avere) to go to excess;
(*aux.* essere) to descend, stoop (*fig.*).
trascinàre, *v.t.* to drag; drag along;
trail; carry; bear; (*fig.*) carry away,
fascinate.
trascoloraménto, *m.* discolouration;
change of colour. **trascoloràre**, *v.t.*
to change the colour of; discolour.
trascoloràrsi, *v.refl.* to change
one's colour, blush; grow pale.
trascórrere, *v.t. ir.* to spend, pass
(*time*); run over, run through, skim
(*book, pages, &c.*); travel through;
go about, wander about, roam
(*country*); pass over; leave aside;
omit to mention. *v.i.* (*aux.* essere)
pass, elapse (*time*). *v.i.* (*aux.* avere)
go too far (*fig.*), run to excess.
trascorrévole, *a.* transient. **tra-
scórso**, *m.* lapse (*of time*); fault,
slip; waywardness. ¶ *a. & p.p.* of
trascorrere, spent, passed; passed
over; travelled, elapsed, &c.
trascrittóre, *m.* -**trice**, *f.* transcriber;
copyist. **trascrívere**, *v.t. ir.* to
transcribe. **trascrizióne**, *f.* transcript[ion]; copy.
trascuràbile, *a.* negligible. **tra-
scuràggine**, *f.* indifference. **tra-
scurànza**, *f.* carelessness, thoughtlessness; neglect. **trascuràre**, *v.t.*
to neglect; disregard, slight; be
indifferent (to, about); omit. **tra-
scuratézza**, *f.* negligence; carelessness, slovenliness. **trascuràto**, *a.*
careless; negligent, slovenly.
trasecolàre, *v.i.* (*aux.* essere & avere)
to be amazed, startled, astonished;
start, show surprise.
trasentíre (*pr.* -**ènto**), *v.t.* to hear
vaguely; learn by hearsay.
trasferíbile, *a.* transferable. **tras-
feriménto**, *m.* removal; change;
transfer; transference. **trasferíre**
(*pr.* -ísco, -ísci), *v.t.* to move,
remove; transfer; translate (*bishop*)
shift; change. **trasfèrta**, *f.* transfer.
trasfiguràre, *v.t.* to transfigure.
trasfigurazióne, *f.* transfiguration.
trasformísta (*pl.* -ísti), *m.f.* quick-
change artiste.
trasfóndere, *v.t. ir.* to transfuse.
trasfusióne, *f.* transfusion.
trasgredíre (*pr.* -ísco, -ísci), *v.t. & i.*
(*aux.* avere) to transgress; infringe;
break; violate; disobey. **trasgres-
sióne**, *f.* transgression; infringement.
traslataménte, *ad.* figuratively;
metaphorically. **traslatàre**, *v.t.* to

transfer, remove; transport. **tra-
slàto**, *a.* figurative; metaphorical.
¶ *m.* metaphor. **traslazióne**, *f.*
removal, transfer; conveyance;
translation (*bishop*).
traslocaménto & **traslòco**, *m.*
removal. **traslocàre**, *v.t.* to move;
transfer. *v.i.* to move, remove,
change one's address.
trasméttere, *v.t. ir.* to transmit;
pass on; hand on; send; convey.
~ *per radio*, to broadcast.
trasmissióne, *f.* transmission;
(*Mech.*) shafting; (*radio*) broadcasting. *cinghia di* (*per*) ~, *f.*
conveyor belt, transmission b.
trasmodàre, *v.i.* to go to excess;
overstep proper bounds; exaggerate.
trasmodàto, *a.* immoderate;
excessive.
trasmutàre, *v.t.* to transmute; transform.
trasognàre, *v.i.* (*aux.* avere) to dream;
be day-dreaming; be lost in reverie.
trasognàto, *a.* dreamy, dreaming,
day-dreaming; lost in reverie;
bewildered, far away (*fig.*).
traspadàno, *a.* across the Po (north
of the Po).
trasparènte, *a.* transparent. ¶ *m.*
transparency (*picture*). **trasparèn-
za**, *f.* transparence, -cy. **trasparíre**
(*pr.* -pàio & -parísco), *v.i.* (*aux.*
essere) to appear (through); shine
(through); be transparent; (*fig.*) be
obvious.
traspiràre, *v.i.* (*aux.* avere) to
perspire; (*Bot.*) transpire. **traspira-
zióne**, *f.* perspiration; (*Bot.*)
transpiration.
traspórre (*pr.* -óngo, &c., like *porre*),
v.t. ir. to transpose.
trasportàre, *v.t.* to transport; convey;
carry; transfer; (*Mus. & Math.*)
transpose. *lasciarsi* ~ (*dall'ira*) to
fly into a rage. **traspòrto**, *m.*
transport, conveyance, carriage;
(*Bkkg.*) transfer; rapture. *nave* ~,
f. troopship, transport. ~ *funebre*,
funeral.
Trastévere, *m.* popular quarter of
Rome, lying 'across the Tiber'.
trastullàre, *v.t.* to amuse. **trastul-
làrsi**, *v.refl.* to play; amuse oneself;
toy (with), trifle (with). **trastúllo**,
m. play; toy; game; amusement;
(*fig.*) sport, plaything; laughing
stock.
trasudàre, *v.i.* (*aux.* avere) to
transude; perspire excessively.
trasumanàre, *v.i.* (*aux.* essere) to be

transfigured; become more than human.

traśversàle, *a. & f.* transversal; transverse.

traśvolàre, *v.t.* to fly (across). **traśvolàta,** *f.* flight. *t~ atlantica,* flight across the Atlantic.

tràtta, *f.* tug, pull; (*Com.*) bill, draft; drawing (*lots, &c.*); distance, stretch, section (*Rly.* or *road*); interval, period; train; throng. *~ dei negri,* slave trade. *~ dei bianchi,* sweating system. **trattàbile,** *a.* tractable; manageable. **trattaménto,** *m.* treatment, usage; reception; entertainment; salary, emoluments; allowance of food, table. **trattàre,** *v.t.* to treat, handle, employ; work, play; deal with; deal in; discuss; have relations with. *v.i.* to deal (with = *con*); treat (of = *di*); speak, write (of = *di*). **trattàrsi,** *v.refl. impers.* to be a question (of = *di*); have to do (with = *di*). **trattàrio,** *m.* drawee (*of bill*). **trattatísta** (*pl.* -ísti), *m.* writer of treatises. **trattatíva,** *f.* negotiation (*us. pl.*). **trattàto,** *m.* treaty; treatise; tract.

tratteggiàre, *v.t.* to draw (in outline), sketch, delineate; describe; crosshatch. **trattéggio,** *m.* outlining, sketching, delineating; sketch, outline.

trattenére (*pr.* -èngo, *&c.*, like *tenere*), *v.t. ir.* to keep, keep back; detain; hold, hold back, keep waiting; restrain; entertain; amuse. **trattenérsi,** *v.refl.* to stay, remain, stop, restrain oneself. *~da,* help, avoid. **tratteniménto,** *m.* detention, delay; stay, sojourn; party, entertainment.

trattíno, *m.* hyphen; dash.

tràtto, *m.* distance, stretch, reach (*river*); space; period (*of time*); moment, instant; stroke, line; dash; difference; feature, trait, gesture; manner, bearing; pull, tug; twitch; touch; reference, relation; passage (*in a book*). *~d'unione,* hyphen. ¶ *p.p.* of *trarre & a.* led, pulled, drawn, &c. **trattóre,** *m.* inn-keeper, restaurant-keeper; silk spinner; tractor. **trattoría,** *f.* eating-house, inn, restaurant. **tratríce,** *f.* tractor.

travagliàre, *v.t.* to trouble; torment; harass; afflict. *v.i.* (*aux.* avere) to toil, labour. **travàglio,** *m.* toil, labour; trouble; pain; travail; distress.

travalicàre, *v.t.* to cross, pass(over).

travaśàre, *v.t.* to pour off, decant.

tràve, *f.* beam; rafter; girder.

travedére (*pr.* -védo, *&c.,* like *vedere*), *v.t. ir.* to catch a glimpse of; see dimly or indistinctly. *v.i.* (*aux.* avere) to be mistaken (in seeing).

travéggole, *f.pl.* distorted vision. *avere le ~,* not to see straight or correctly, mistake one thing for another.

travèrsa, *f.* cross-bar; cross-piece; cross-head (*piston*); (*Rly.*) sleeper; (*Mil.*) traverse; cross street; sideturning. **traversàre,** *v.t.* to cross. **traversàta,** *f.* crossing. **traversía,** *f.* mishap, misfortune, accident; trial, trying experience. **traversína,** *f.* (*Rly.*) sleeper. **travèrso,** *a.* transverse; cross; oblique; (*fig.*) wrong; underhand; untoward; adverse; rough (*sea*). ¶ *m.* breadth; beam (*ship*). *a~,* across. *di ~,* askew, awry, amiss, wrong; askance. **travertíno,** *m.* (*Geol.*) travertine.

travestíre (*pr.* -vèsto, -vèsti), *v.t.* to disguise; travesty, burlesque; misrepresent; transform.

traviaménto, *m.* deviation; aberration; perversion. **traviàre,** *v.t.* to mislead, lead astray; pervert. **traviàrsi,** *v.refl.* to go astray; stray.

travicèllo, *m.* joist; small beam.

traviśàre, *v.t.* to distort, falsify, misrepresent; alter; disguise; conceal.

travolgiménto, *m.* overturning; overthrow; confusion. **travòlgere,** *v.t. ir.* to sweep away; carry away; overwhelm; overturn, upset; throw into confusion. *~gli occhi,* to roll the eyes. **travòlto,** *a.* overturned, upside down.

traziòne, *f.* traction.

tre, *a. num. card. & m.* three; 3rd. *~ volte,* three times, thrice. *regola del ~,* rule of three. *~alberi,* m.inv. three-masted ship, three-master.

trébbia, *f.* flail; (*Poet.*) threshing. **Trebbiàno,** *m.* a white wine of Romagna. **trebbiàre,** *v.t.* to thresh. **trebbiatóre,** *m.* thresher. **trebbiatríce,** *f.* threshing machine **trebbiatúra,** *f.* threshing.

tréccia (*pl.* **trécce**), *f.* plait, tress; pigtail; string (*onions, &c.*). **trecciàio,** *m.,* -a, *f. &* **trecciài- [u]òlo,** *m.,* -a, *f.* straw-plait worker. **trecentèsimo,** *a. num. ord.* three hundredth. **trecentísta** (*pl.* -ísti), *m.* 14th century writer or artist. **trecènto,** *num. ord.* three hundred.

¶ m. il T~, the 14th century, the Trecento.

tredicènne, a. thirteen years old. **tredicèsimo,** a. num. ord. thirteenth. **trédici,** num. card. & m. thirteen; thirteenth.

trèggia, f. sledge.

trégua, f. truce; (fig.) respite; rest.

tremac[u]òre, m. palpitation; trepidation; anxiety. **tremàre** (pr. **trèmo**), v.i. to tremble, shake, quake; quiver; shiver. **tremarèlla,** f. nervous anxiety; (slang) funk; trembling. **tremebóndo,** a. trembling.

tremèndo, a. awful; fearful; tremendous.

trementína, f. turpentine.

tremíla, num. card. three thousand. **tremillèsimo,** a. num. ord. three thousandth.

trèmito, m. trembling; quiver[ing]. **tremolàre,** v.i. (aux. avere) to tremble; quiver. **tremolío,** m. constant trembling; quaking. **trèmolo,** a. quivering; trembling; tremulous. ¶ m. (Mus.) tremolo. **tremóre,** m. tremor; shaking; quivering; quaking.

tremòto, m. (pop. for terremoto) earthquake. **trèmula,** f. asp[en] (tree).

trèno, m. train (Rly.); train, retinue; manner, way (life); pace, rate; routine; threnody, lamentation.

trenodía, f. threnody.

trénta, num. card. thirty. ¶ m. thirty; 30th. **trentènne,** a. thirty years old. **trentènnio,** m. period of thirty years. **trentèsimo,** a. num. ord., thirtieth. **trentína,** f. about thirty. Trentíno (il), m. the Trentino.

Trénto, f. Trent, Trento.

trentunèsimo, a. num. ord. thirty-first. **trentúno,** num. card. thirty-one.

trepidànza & **trepidazióne,** f. trepidation; flurry; anxiety. **trepidàre,** v.i. (aux. avere) to tremble; be in a flutter; be anxious. **trèpido,** a. trembling; timorous; anxious; fluttering.

treppiède & **treppièdi,** m. tripod; three-legged stool; trivet.

trésca, f. intrigue; flirtation; rough country dance. **trescàre,** v.i. to intrigue; prance about.

tréspolo, m. trestle; broken down vehicle.

trevigiàno, a. & m. of Treviso, native of Treviso.

Trèviri, f. Trier, Treves (Geog.).

triàca, f. theriac (supposed antidote to bites of poisonous animals (Hist.).

tríade, f. triad.

triangolàre, a. triangular. **triàngolo,** m. triangle.

tribolàre, v.t. to vex; trouble; afflict; worry. v.i. (aux. avere) to toil, labour; suffer; be in need. **tribolazióne,** f. tribulation; suffering. **tríbolo,** m. trouble; trial, suffering. **tribórdo,** m. (Naut.) starboard.

tribú, f.inv. tribe.

tribúna, f. tribune; rostrum; platform; stand; gallery; loft (organ). ~ centrale, grand-stand. **tribunale,** m. tribunal; bench; court. **tribúno,** m. tribune (magistrate); demagogue.

tributàre, v.t. to give, offer, pay, render, bestow (homage, honour, &c.). **tributàrio,** a. & m. tributary. sistema ~, system of taxation. **tribúto,** m. tribute; tax; debt (fig.).

tricíclo, m. tricycle. **tricolóre,** a. & m. tricolour. **tricòrne,** a. three-horned. **tricòrno,** m. three-cornered hat.

tríc tràc, m. backgammon.

tricromía, f. three-colour printing.

tridènte, m. trident; hayfork. **tridentíno,** a. of Trent. il Concilio~, the Council of Trent.

triennàle, a. triennial. **triènne,** a. three years old; of three years' duration. **triènnio,** m. period of three years.

trifòglio, m. trefoil; clover; shamrock. **trífora,** f. (Arch.) window divided into three sections. **trifòrio,** m. (Arch.) triforium.

trigèmino, m. triplet. parto ~, birth of triplets. **trigèsimo,** a. num. ord. thirtieth.

tríglia, f. mullet. **tríglifo,** m. (Arch.) triglyph, three-grooved tablet.

trigonometría, f. trigonometry.

trillàre, v.i. (aux. avere) to trill. **tríllo,** m. trill, shake (Mus.).

trilogía, f. trilogy. **trilústre,** a. fifteen years old (see **lustro**). **trimestràle,** a. quarterly. **trimèstre,** m. quarter; three months; term (Sch.); quarter's rent, salary, &c. **trimotóre,** m. (Aviat.) three-engined plane.

trína, f. [point-] lace.

trinàcrio, a. (Poet.) Sicilian.

trincàre, v.t. to drink hard; swill; toss off. **trincàta,** f. draught, deep drink. **trincàto,** a. (fig.) deep, subtle.

trincèa, f. trench. trinceraménto, m. entrenchment. trinceràre, v.t. to entrench. trinceràrsi, v.refl. to entrench oneself; become entrenched.

trinciànte, m. carving-knife. trinciapàglia, m.inv. hay-cutter. trinciaradíci & trinciaràpe, m.inv. turnip-cutter, slicing-knife. trinciàre, v.t. to cut up; carve. trinciàrsi, v.refl. to tear; split. trinciàto, m. cut tobacco, pipe-tobacco.

trincóne, m. heavy drinker.

trinità, f. trinity. la Santissima T~, the Trinity. T~ (la), Trinidad.

trionfàle, a. triumphal. trionfàre, v.i. (aux. avere) to triumph, be triumphant. ~ di, to triumph over. triónfo, m. triumph; trump (card); epergne.

Trióni, m.pl. (Astr.) Great & Little Bear, Charles's Wain.

tripartíre (pr. -ísco, -ísci), v.t. to divide in[to] three. tripartíto, a. tripartite.

triplicàre, v.t. to treble; triplicate. tríplice, a. threefold, treble, triple. tríplo, a. triple.

trípode, m. tripod.

trípoli, m. (Min.) rotten-stone. Trípoli, f. Tripoli.

tríppa, f. tripe. trippería, f. tripe-shop. trippóne, a. & m. pot-bellied (person).

tripudiàre, v.i. (aux. avere) to exult; jump for joy. tripúdio, m. exaltation; jumping for joy; jubilation.

trirégno, m. (Pope's) tiara, or triple crown.

trisàvolo, m., trisavola, f. great-great-great-grandfather; g.-g.-grandmother.

trisillàbico (pl. -àbici), a. trisyllabic. trisíllabo, m. trisyllable.

tristàccio, m. scoundrel, evil-doer. tristaménte, ad. wickedly.

Tristàno, m. Tristram.

tríste, a. sad, sorrowful, woeful; dreary, gloomy, dismal; bleak, depressing. tristézza, f. sadness, &c.

tristízia, f. wickedness; wretchedness; wicked deed. trísto, a. bad, wicked, evil; sorry, wretched; deplorable.

tritacàrne, m.inv. mincer. tritaménte, ad. finely, minutely. tritàre, v.t. to mince, hash; pound; rub down; (fig.) treat in too great detail, over-refine. tríto, a. minced, pounded, beaten; worn out; rubbed

down; fine; trite, commonplace; mincing, finikin.

tritolàre, v.t. to crush, pound. trítolo, m. scrap, little bit.

tritóne, m. triton. T~, Triton (Myth.).

tríttico (pl. tríttici), m. triptych (Art.).

tritúme, m. (gen.) tritúmi, m.pl. bits, scraps; crumbs.

triúmviro, m. triumvir.

trivèlla, f. auger. trivellàre, v.t. to drill, bore.

triviàle, a. low, coarse, vulgar. trivialità, f. vulgarity; coarseness; coarse expression.

trivio, m. cross-roads.

trofèo, m. trophy.

troglodíta (pl. -íti), m. troglodyte, cave-dweller. trògolo, m. trough.

tròia, f. sow. T~, f. Troy. troiàno, a. & m. Trojan.

Tròilo, m. Troilus.

trómba, f. trumpet; trump (last, of doom); bugle; horn (motor); pump siphon (for drawing off wine); (Anat.) tube; trunk (elephant); water-spout; (fig.) public auction; well (of staircase). m.f. trumpeter. trombàre, v.t. to draw off wine with a siphon; sell by auction; (pop.) reject. trombétta, f. bugle; (child's) trumpet; m.inv. bugler, trumpeter. trombettàre, v.i. (aux. avere) to trumpet. trombettiére, m. trumpeter; bugler. trombóne, m. trombone; blunderbuss.

trombòsi, f.inv. (Med.) thrombosis.

troncàre, v.t. to cut off, cut short; break off, interrupt; truncate; break, break in two; clip (end of a word). trónco (pl. trónchi), a. maimed, mutilated; truncated; broken off short. parola ~ a, word accented on last syllable. ¶ m. trunk (tree); (Rly.) trunk-line. troncóne, m. stump; (fig.) lineage, stock.

troneggiàre, v.i. (aux. avere) to sit (as) on a throne.

tronfiàre, v.i. (aux. avere) to strut proudly, spread its feathers (peacock, turkey); puff, pout. trónfio, a. puffed up, conceited.

tròno, m. throne.

tropicàle, a. tropical. tròpico (pl. tròpici), m. tropic. ~ del Cancro, tropic of Cancer. ~ del Capricorno, tropic of Capricorn.

tròpo, m. trope.

tròppo, ad. too, too much. pur ~, unfortunately; only too well. ¶ a.

& *pn.* too much. *pl.* **tròppi,** too many.

tròta, *f.* trout.

trottapiàno, *m.* slowcoach. **trottàre,** *v.i.* (*aux.* avere) to trot. **trottàta,** *f.* trot; run. **trottatóre,** *m.* trotter.

trotterellàre, *v.i.* (*aux.* avere) to trot along; toddle (*child*). **trotterèllo,** *m.* jog-trot. **tròtto,** *m.* trot.

tròttola, *f.* top, spinning-top. **trottolàre,** *v.i.* (*aux.* avere) to spin, whirl round. **trottolíno,** *m.,* **-ína,** *f.* toddler, small child.

trovàbile, *a.* possible to find. **trovadóre** & **trovatóre,** *m.* troubadour, Provençal poet; minstrel. **trovàre,** *v.t.* to find, find out, discover; get; think; like; spare (*the time*). **trovàrsi,** *v.refl.* to be; feel; happen to be. **trova-ròbe,** *m.inv.* (*Theat.*) property man; costumier. **trovàta,** *f.* [lucky] find; invention; contrivance; trick; expedient. **trovatèllo,** *m.* foundling. **trovàto,** *m.* invention; discovery; contrivance. **trovatóre,** *m.* finder; inventor; troubadour.

truccàre, *v.t.* to cheat; (*Theat.*) make up. **truccàrsi,** *v.refl.* (*Theat.*) to make (oneself) up. **truccatóre,** *m.* dresser (*Theat.*). **truccatúra,** *f.* (*Theat.*) make up, making up. **trúcco** (*pl.* **trúcchi**) *m.* trick.

trúce, *a.* cruel, savage, fierce; threatening; grim. **truceménte,** *ad.* fiercely; cruelly; savagely; threateningly.

trucidàre, *v.t.* to kill, murder; cut up.

trúciolo, *m.* chip, shaving (*wood*).

truculènto, *a.* truculent.

trúffa, *f.* cheat, swindle, swindling. **truffàre,** *v.t.* to cheat, swindle. **truffatóre,** *m.* (*f.* **-tríce**) cheat (*pers.*), swindler. ~ *di carte,* card-sharper. **trufferìa,** *f.* cheating, swindling; trick.

trullàggine & **trullerìa,** *f.* silliness. **trúllo,** *a.* silly. ¶ *m.* simpleton, nincompoop.

trúppa, *f.* troop, band; host; set, gang; (*Theat.*) troupe; flock.

tu, *pn. pers.* 2nd *sg.* thou, you.

túba, *f.* trumpet; organ reed; (*Anat.*) tube; tall hat. **tubàre,** *v.i.* (*aux.* avere) to coo. **tubatúra** & **tubazióne,** *f.* piping; system of pipes.

tubercolàre, *a.* tubercular. **tubèrcolo,** *m.* tubercle. **tubercolòsi,** *f.* tuberculosis. **tubercolóso,** *a.* tuberculous. ¶ *m.* consumptive.

túbero, *m.* tuber. **tuberósa,** *f.* tuberose.

túbo, *m.* pipe; tube. ~ *di scarico,* exhaust pipe (*Mech.*). *caldaia a* ~*i, f.* tubular boiler. **tubolàre,** *a.* tubular.

Tucídide, *m.* Thucydides.

tufàto, *a.* stuffy.

tuffàre, *v.t.* to plunge. **tuffàrsi,** *v.refl.* to plunge; dive. **tuffàta,** *f.* plunge; dive; dip. **túffo,** *m.* dip, dive, plunge, plump, sudden heavy fall (*rain*); throb; sudden emotion.

túfo, *m.* tufa.

tugúrio, *m.* hovel.

tulipàno, *m.* tulip.

túlle, *m.* tulle.

tumefàre (*pr.* **-fàccio** & **-fò, -fài, -fà,** &*c.,* like *fare*), *v.t. ir.* & **tumefàrsi,** *v.refl.* to swell. **tumidézza,** *f.* tumidity, inflation. **túmido,** *a.* tumid; swollen; inflated (*lit.* & *fig.*). **tumóre,** *m.* tumour.

tumulàre, *v.t.* to bury. **túmulo,** *m.* tumulus; cairn; grave; barrow.

tumúlto, *m.* tumult, uproar, turmoil, riot. **tumultuànte,** *a.* riotous. ¶ *m.* rioter. **tumultuàre,** *v.i.* (*aux.* avere) to start a riot or tumult. **tumultuario,** *a.* tumultuary. **tumultuóso,** *a.* tumultuous, riotous.

tungstèno, *m.* (*Chem.*) tungsten.

túnica, *f.* tunic.

Túnisi, *f.* Tunis (*capital*). **Tunisia (la),** *f.* Tunis (*state*), Tunisia. **tunisíno,** *a.* & *m.* Tunisian.

túo, *a. poss. m. sg.;* tua, *f. sg.;* tuoi, *m.pl.;* tue, *f.pl.;* thy, your. ¶ *pr. poss.* thine; yours.

t[u]onàre (*pr.* **tuòno, tuòni**), *v.i.* (*aux.* avere & essere) to thunder; roar. **tuòno,** *m.* thunder; roar.

tuórlo, *m.* yolk (of an egg).

turabúchi, *m.inv.* stop-gap (*fig.*). **turàcciolo,** *m.* cork; stopper.

turàre, *v.t.* to plug; stop; cork; bung.

túrba, *f.* crowd; mob, rabble.

turbàbile, *a.* easily disturbed. **turbaménto,** *m.* perturbation; uneasiness; excitement; confusion, commotion.

turbànte, *m.* turban.

turbàre, *v.t.* to trouble; disturb; confuse. **turbàrsi,** *v.refl.* to become agitated, uneasy, or perturbed; grow murky or gloomy. **turbàto,** *a.* troubled; uneasy; agitated, disturbed.

turbína, *f.* turbine. ~ *a vapore,* steam t. **turbinàre,** *v.i.* (*aux.* avere) to whirl; eddy. **túrbine,** *m.* whirlwind, hurricane. **turbínio,** *m.* whirling; eddying; turmoil; storm; restless throng. **turbinóso,** *a.* stormy, tumultuous; eddying; whirling.

turbolènte, *a.* turbulent, unruly, restless; troubled; boisterous. **turbolènza,** *f.* turbulence.

turcàsso, *m.* quiver (*arrows*).

turchése, *f.* turquoise.

Turchía (la), *f.* Turkey.

turchinétto, *m.* washerwoman's blue. **turchiníccio,** *a.* bluish. **turchíno,** *a. & m.* deep blue, dark blue.

túrco (*pl.* **túrchi**), *a.* Turkish. ¶ *m.* Turk; Turkish, (the) T. language. **turcòfilo,** *a. & m.* Turcophil. **turcòfobo,** *a. & m.* Turcophobe. **Turcomànno,** *m.* Turkoman.

Turèna (la), *f.* Touraine.

turgescènte, *a.* turgescent, turgid; swollen. **turgidézza,** *f.* turgidity; (*fig.*) pompousness. **túrgido,** *a.* turgid; (*fig.*) pompous, bombastic, inflated.

turíbolo, *m.* thurible; censer.

turísmo, *m.* touring. **turísta** (*pl.* **-ísti**), *m.* tourist. **turístico** (*pl.* **-ístici**), *a.* touring; tourist (*att.*).

turlupinàre, *v.t.* to fool, swindle; cheat.

túrno, *m.* turn, rotation.

túrpe, *a.* disgraceful, base; filthy; indecent. **turpilòquio,** *m.* coarse language; filthy conversation. **turpitúdine,** *f.* turpitude; baseness.

turrito, *a.* turreted.

túta, *f.* (*workman's*) overall.

tutèla, *f.* tutelage, guardianship, wardship, protection. **tutelàre,** *v.t.* to protect, defend. ¶ *a.* tutelar(y), guardian (*att.*).

tutóre, *m.* **tutríce,** *f.* guardian. **tutòrio,** *a.* tutelar; tutorial. *autorità* ~ *a,* superior authority.

tuttavía, *ad. & c.* still, yet; nevertheless, all the same (*colloquial*).

tútto, *pn. sg.* all; everything. *pl.* **tutti,** all; everybody, everyone. *il* ~, the whole, the lot. ¶ *a.* (*m. pl.* **tutti,** *f.pl.* **tutte**) all, the whole (of); every; any; full; only; sole. *a* ~ *andare,* at full speed. *a* ~ *a prova,* perfectly safe. *a* ~ *spiano,* without interruption; profusely, abundantly. *tutt'e due, tutt'e tre,* both, all three. ¶ *ad.* quite; very; thoroughly; entirely; wholly; all; completely; fully; wide;

stark (*naked*); bolt (*upright*); just. *tutt'al più,* at the most. *tutt'altro che,* all but. ~ *d'un tratto,* all of a sudden, all at once. *del* ~, quite. *a tutt'oggi,* up to the present. **tuttoché,** *c.* though, although. **tuttodí,** *ad.* always, continually. **tuttóra,** *ad.* still, always.

tzigàno, *a. & m.* gipsy, Tzigane.

U

U, u, *f.* the letter U.

uàdi, *m.* wadi, wady (*African watercourse*).

ubbía (*pl.* **ubbíe**), *f.* delusion, prejudice, groundless fear, foolish superstition.

ubbidiènte, *a.* obedient. **ubbidíre** (*pr.* **-ísco, -ísci**), *v.i.* (*aux.* avere) *& t.,* to obey. ~ *a,* to obey (*v.t.*) cf. **obbedire.**

ubbióso, *a.* superstitious; full of foolish fears & prejudices. **ubbriàco,** *&c.,* see **ubriàco,** *&c.*

ubertà, *f.* fertility; abundance. **ubertóso,** *a.* fruitful; fertile.

ubicazióne, *f.* whereabouts, position, situation.

ubiquità, *f.* ubiquity.

ubriacàre (*pr.* **-àco, -àchi**), *v.t.* to intoxicate; make drunk. **ubriacàrsi,** *v.refl.* to get drunk; become intoxicated. **ubriacatúra,** *f.* intoxication. **ubriachézza,** *f.* drunkenness. **ubriàco** (*pl.* **-àchi**), *a.* drunk, drunken; intoxicated; tipsy. **ubriacóne,** *m.* (*f.* **-óna**) drunkard.

uccellagióne, *f.* feathered game. **uccellàre,** *v.i.* (*aux.* avere) to snare birds, go fowling. *v.t.* (*fig.*) to dupe, gull. **uccellatóre,** *m.* bird-catcher, fowler; (*fig.*) deceiver, trickster. **uccellatúra,** *f.* (*fig.*) trickery, deceit. **uccellièra,** *f.* aviary. **uccèllo,** *m.* bird, fowl. ~ *di mal augurio,* bird of ill omen. ~ *da gabbia,* cage bird. ~ *mosca,* humming bird. *veduta a volo d'* ~, bird's eye view.

uccídere (*pr.* **-ído, -ídi**), *v.t. ir.* to kill, slay; slaughter. **uccisióne,** *f.* killing; slaughter. **uccíso,** *p.p.* of *uccidere & a.* killed, slain, dead (*in battle*). **uccisóre,** *m.* killer, slayer; murderer.

Ucraina (l'), *f.* (the) Ukraine.
udibile, *a.* audible. **udiènza**, *f.*
audience; hearing (*court*). **udire**
(*pr.* **òdo, òdi, òde, udiàmo,
udite, òdono**), *v.t. ir.* to hear;
listen to. **udìta**, *f.* hearsay. **udìto**,
m. (sense of) hearing. **uditóre**, *m.*
(*f.* **-trice**) hearer; listener; auditor,
-tress. **uditòrio**, *a.* auditory.
¶ *m.* audience, hearers.
uff! *i.* what a bore! what a nuisance!
ufficiàle, *a.* official. ¶ *m.* officer;
official. ~ *dello stato civile*, registrar
(*Births, &c.*). ~ *di marina*, naval
officer. ~ *di giornata*, orderly.
~ *del genio*, engineer (*Mil.*).
ufficiàre, *v.i.* (*aux.* avere) to
officiate. **ufficio**, *m.* office; department; service; duty. *d'* ~, official
(ly); in virtue of one's office.
ufficióso, *a.* officious (*Diplomacy*),
informal, semi-official, unofficial;
obliging. **uffizio**, *m.* office; service;
worship.
ùfo (**a**), *ad. expr.* gratis, gratuitously;
uselessly.
ùggia, *f.* deep shade, gloom; (*fig.*)
dislike; annoyance; boredom.
uggiolàre, *v.i.* (*aux.* avere) to howl;
whine. **uggiolìo**, *m.* constant
whining; howling. **uggióso**, *a.*
tiresome; troublesome; dull; boring;
gloomy.
ùgna, *&c.*, see **unghia**, *&c.*
ùgola, *f.* (*Anat.*) uvula.
Ugonòtto, *m.* Huguenot.
uguagliaménto, *m.* equalization;
equalizing. **uguagliànza**, *f.*
equality; similarity. **uguagliàre**,
v.t. to equal; be equal to; equalize,
make equal; balance; level. **uguàle**,
a. equal; same; [a]like; uniform,
balanced; level. **ugualità**, *f.*
equality. **ugualménte**, *ad.* equally;
all the same, nevertheless.
uh! *i.* ah! oh! **uhm!** *i.* hum! h'm!
ulàno, *m.* uhlan.
ùlcera, *f.* ulcer. **ulceraménto**, *m.*
& **ulcerazióne**, *f.* ulceration.
ulceràre, *v.t.* to ulcerate.
ulceràrsi, *v.refl.* to become
ulcerated. **ulceróso**, *a.* ulcerous.
uliginóso, *a.* damp; moist.
Ulìsse, *m.* Ulysses.
ulìva, *f.* olive. **ulìvo**, *m.* olive-tree;
, olive branch.
Ulma, *f.* Ulm (*Geog.*).
ulterióre, *a.* further; ulterior; subsequent. **ulteriorménte**, *ad.*
further on; later on.
ultimaménte, *ad.* lately, of late;

recently; at last. **ultimàre**, *v.t.* to
finish; bring to an end; complete.
ultimàtum, *m.* ultimatum. **ulti-
mazióne**, *f.* completion; termination; finishing. **ùltimo**, *a.* last,
latest, newest; utmost; ultimate.
ultimogènito, *a.* last-born, latest
born. ¶ *m.* last-born child.
ultóre, *m.* **ultrìce**, *f.* avenger.
ùltra-, *prefix, as in Eng.* ultra-, in the
highest degree; extremely. *non plus
ultra*, *m.* height; highest pitch;
perfect specimen. **ultraviolétto**,
a. ultra-violet. *raggi* ~ *i*, ultra-
violet rays.
ululàre, *v.i.* (*aux.* avere) to howl.
ululàto *&* **ùlulo**, *m.* howl[ing].
umanaménte, *ad.* humanly; humane-
ly. **umanàre**, *v.t.* to make human;
humanize; render humane. **uma-
nàrsi**, *v.refl.* to become human;
become man; become humane.
umanésimo, *m.* humanism. **uma-
nìsta** (*pl.* **-isti**), *m.* humanist.
umanità, *f.* humanity; mankind.
umanitàrio, *a. & m.* humanitarian.
umanizzàre, *v.t.* to humanize.
umàno, *a.* human; humane; natural.
umane lettere, belles-lettres, polite
letters, literature.
umbràtile, *a.* (*Poet.*) shady; dark;
, imaginary.
Umbria (l'), *f.* Umbria. **ùmbro**,
a. & m. Umbrian.
umettaménto, *m. &* **umettazióne**,
f. moistening; wetting. **umettàre**,
v.t. to moisten; damp; wet.
umidézza, *f.* dampness. **umidità**,
f. humidity; damp[ness]; moisture. **ùmido**, *a.* damp, moist,
wet, humid. ¶ *m.* stew, stewed
meat.
ùmile, *a.* humble, lowly; modest;
simple. **umiliànte**, *a.* humiliating;
mortifying. **umiliàre**, *v.t.* to
humiliate, humble. **umiliazióne**, *f.*
humiliation; mortification. **umil-
ménte**, *ad.* humbly, &c. **umiltà**,
f. humility.
umóre, *m.* humour, mood, temper;
moisture; humour (*Physiol. &
Med.*). *buon* ~, good humour,
good temper. *cattivo* ~, ill humour,
ill temper. **umorìsmo**, *m.* humour;
humorousness. **umorìsta** (*pl.*
-isti), *m.* humorist. **umorìstico**
(*pl.* **ìstici**), *a.* humorous; facetious;
funny; comic.
un, ùna, see *uno*.
unànime, *a.* unanimous. **unanime-
ménte**, *ad.* unanimously. **unani-**

mità, *f.* unanimity, consensus. *all'* ~, unanimously.

uncinàre, *v.t.* to hook; seize with a h.; grapple. *croce uncinata*, swastika. uncinétto, *m.* small hook; crochet-hook. *lavoro all'* ~, crochet work. uncíno, *m.* hook.

undècimo & undicèsimo, *a. num. ord.* eleventh. undicènne, *a.* eleven years old. úndici, *num. card. inv.* eleven. *l'* ~ *del mese*, the eleventh of the month.

úngere (*pr.* úngo, úngi), *v.t. ir.* to grease; smear; anoint; (*fig.*) flatter.

ungherése, *a.* & *m.* Hungarian. Ungheria (l'), *f.* Hungary.

únghia (*pl.* únghie), *f.* nail; claw; hoof. unghiàta, *f.* scratch. unghiàto & unghiúto, *a.* furnished with nails or claws. unghióne, *m.* big claw. unghi[u]òlo, *m.* small (sharp) claw (*bird or cat*, &c.).

unguènto, *m.* ointment; unguent.

ungulàto, *a.* hoofed, furnished with hoofs or claws; (*Zool.*) ungulate.

unicaménte, *ad.* solely, uniquely; only. unicameralísmo, *m.* single chamber system (*Parl.*). unicità, *f.* uniqueness. único, (*pl.* únici), *a.* only; sole; single; one; unique.

unicolóre, *a.* of one colour. unicòrno, *m.* unicorn.

unificàre (*pr.* -ífico, -ífichi), *v.t.* to unify, consolidate, standardize. unificazióne, *f.* unification.

uniformàre, *v.t.* to render uniform, bring into line. uniformàrsi, *v.refl.* to conform; comply. unifórme, *a.* uniform; even; regular. ¶ *f.* uniform; regimentals. uniformeménte, *ad.* uniformly, evenly. uniformità, *f.* uniformity.

unigènito, *a.* only-begotten (*Eccl.*). ¶ *m.* only son.

unilateràle, *a.* unilateral; one-sided.

unióne, *f.* union; unity. *U*~ *Sudafricana*, Union of South Africa. *U*~ *delle Repubbliche Socialiste Sovietiche*, Union of Soviet Socialist Republics (*abb.* U.S.S.R.).

uníre (*pr.* -ísco, -ísci), *v.t.* to unite; join; enclose (*in letter*).

unísono, *a.* in unison. ¶ *m.* unison; harmony; concord.

unità, *f.* unity; unit. unitaménte, *ad.* unitedly; conjointly. ~*a*, with, in company with. unitàrio, *a.* unitary; unitarian. *prezzo* ~, one price only. unitarísmo, *m.* unitarianism. unitézza, *f.* compactness; firmness; smoothness; uni-

formity. uníto, *p.p.* of *unire*, *a.* united, uniform.

universàle, *a.* universal; general. *erede* ~, sole heir. *il giudizio* ~, the last judgment. universalità, *f.* universality; whole. universaleggiàre & universaliżżàre, *v.t.* to make general or universal.

università, *f.* university. universitàrio, *a.* university (*att.*). ¶ *m.* university man.

univèrso, *m.* universe.

univoco (*pl.* -ívoci), *a.* alike in name; , with a single meaning.

Unni, *m.pl.* Huns.

ún(o), *m.*, una, un', *f. indef. art.* a, an. ¶ uno, *m.*, una, *f.*; *indef. pr.* one. ¶ uno, *m.*, una, *f. num. card.* one. *ad* ~ *ad* ~, one by one; one after another. *l'* ~, each (*price of articles*). *l'* ~ *l'altro*, *gli uni gli altri*, one another, each other. *l'* ~ *e l'altro*, both. *l'* ~ *o l'altro*, either. *né l'* ~ *né l'altro*, neither. *un giorno o l'altro*, some day or other. *una volta*, once. *una volta per tutte*, once for all. *c'era una volta*, upon a time. *dieci contro uno*, ten to one.

únto, *p.p.* of *ungere* & ¶ *a.* greasy; dirty. ¶ *m.* grease; fat; (*fig.*) flattery. untúme, *m.* grease; fat; greasy stuff; (*fig.*) flattery. untuosità, *f.* greasiness; oiliness; (*fig.*) unctuousness. untuóso, *a.* greasy; oily; unctuous.

unzióne, *f.* unction.

uòmo (*pl.* uòmini), *m.* man (*pl.* men). ~ *qualunque*, ~ *medio*, man in the street; common man.

uòpo, *m.* need, necessity. *essere, avere, fare* ~, or *d'*~, to be necessary, have need (of).

uòse, *f.pl.* leggings.

uòvo & òvo (*pl.* gli uòvi, more com. le uòva, *f.pl.*), *m.* egg.

úpupa, *f.* hoopoe (*bird*).

uragàno, *m.* hurricane (*lit.* & *fig.*). Uràli (Montì), *m.pl.* Ural Mountains.

uràngo, *m.* orang-outang.

urànio, *m.* uranium.

urbanésimo, *m.* growth of towns; movement of population into cities. urbanística, *f.* town-planning. urbanità, *f.* urbanity; courtesy; civility. urbàno, *a.* urban; city (*att.*); urbane, civil, courteous, polite.

Urbe (l'), *f.* 'the city', *for* Rome, the Eternal City.

uremía, *f.* (*Path.*) uraemia. uretère,

m. (*Anat.*) ureter. **úretra,** *f.* (*Anat.*) urethra.

urgènte, *a.* urgent; pressing. **urgènza,** *f.* urgency; emergency. *d'~,* urgent, urgently; in an emergency. **úrgere** (*pr.* **úrge, úrgono**), *v.t.* (*defect.*) to urge, press; (*fig.*) incite. *v.i.* (*compound tenses missing*) to be urgent, be pressing. *urgono aiuti,* help is urgently required.

úri, *f.inv.* houri.

úrico (*pl.* **úrici**), *a.* uric. **urinàrio,** *a.* urinary.

urlàre, *v.i.* (*aux.* avere) to howl; shout; bawl; shriek. **urlàta,** *f.* howl; shout (*oft. of derision*), hoot. **urlío,** *m.* prolonged shouting or howling. **úrlo** (*pl.* **gli urli,** *also* (*of pers.*) le **úrla,** *f.*), *m.* howl; shout; cry; shriek; yell.

úrna, *f.* urn; ballot-box; (*Poet.*) tomb.

urrà! *i.* hurrah!

urtànte, *a.* (*fig.*) irritating; annoying. **urtàre,** *v.t.* to knock against; stumble against; collide with; shove; push; (*fig.*) annoy, jar upon. *v.i.* (*aux.* avere) to knock; strike; clash. **urtàrsi,** *v.refl.* to clash, collide, quarrel. **urtàta,** *f.* push; shove. dim. *urtatina.* **úrto,** *m.* push, shove; knock; clash; collision; attack, onset. **urtóne,** *m.* shove, violent shove.

uṣàbile, *a.* usable. **uṣànza,** *f.* usage, custom. **uṣàre,** *v.t.* to use, make use of, employ; wear, w. out; show, display, practise. *v.i.* (*aux.* avere) to be accustomed; be fashionable; be worn. *~ di,* to make use of. *~ con,* to frequent (the company of). **uṣàto,** *a.* worn out; second-hand; usual.

uṣbèrgo, *m.* (*Hist.*) hauberk, coat of mail; (*fig.*) defence, shield.

uscènte, *pr.p* of *uscire.* ¶ *a.* retiring (*from office*). **uscière,** *m.* usher; doorkeeper. **úscio,** *m.* door; door of a room. **usciolíno** & **usciòlo,** *m.* small door; wicket, w.-gate. **uscíre** (*pr.* **èsco, èsci, èsce, usciàmo, uscíte, èscono**), *v.i. ir.* (*aux.* essere) to go out; come out; come (from); issue; be published; appear; get out; escape; be finished; end (in); result. **uscíta,** *f.* exit, way out; egress; coming out, going out; withdrawal; outlet; outlay, expenditure; export; outcome, upshot; word ending. *giornata di ~,*

f. (servant's) day out. *all' ~ di,* ad. at the end of, on leaving. **uscíto,** *a.* descended, born, sprung; (*of book*) just out.

uṣign[u]òlo, *m.* nightingale.

uṣitàto, *a.* used, in (common) use; usual. *poco ~* (*of words*), rare.

úṣo, *m.* use; power of using; usage, custom, practice. *~ e costume,* use & wont. ¶ *a.* accustomed, in the habit of, used (to).

ússaro & **ússero,** *m.* hussar.

Ussíti, *m.pl.* Hussites.

ussoricída, &*c.*, see *uxoricida,* &*c.*

ustionàre, *v.t.* to burn; scorch. **ustióne,** *f.* burn. **ustòrio,** *a.* burning. *specchio ~,* or *~,* burning glass.

uṣuàle, *a.* usual; customary; ordinary.

uṣufruíre (*pr.* -**ísco,** -**ísci,** &*c.*), *v.i.* (*aux.* avere) to take advantage (of); benefit (by, from). **uṣufrútto,** *m.* usufruct.

uṣúra, *f.* usury. **uṣuràio,** *m.* usurer. **uṣureggiàre,** *v.i.* (*aux.* avere) to practise usury; be a usurer.

uṣurpàre, *v.t.* to usurp. **uṣurpatóre,** *m.* (*f.* -**tríce**) usurper. **uṣurpazióne,** *f.* usurpation.

utensíle, *m.* utensil; implement; tool.

utènte, *m.f.* user. **utènza,** *f.* use; (*coll.*) those who use, users (*Gas,* &*c.*).

uteríno, *a.* uterine. **útero,** *m.* uterus.

útile, *a.* useful, serviceable; effective; due, good (*time*). ¶ *m.* profit; utility; benefit; interest (*on a loan*). **utilità,** *f.* utility, use[fulness]; profit, benefit. **utilitàrio,** *a.* utilitarian. **utilitaríṣmo,** *m.* utilitarianism. **utiliẓẓàbile,** *a.* utilizable, that can be made use of. **utiliẓẓàre,** *v.t.* to utilize, make use of, turn to account. **utiliẓẓazióne,** *f.* utilization. **utilménte,** *ad.* usefully; profitably.

utopía, *f.* utopia. **utopìsta** (*pl.* -**ísti**), *m.* utopian. **utopístico** (*pl.* -**ístici**), *a.* utopian.

úva, *f.* grape, grapes. *~ passa,* raisin(s). *~ spina,* gooseberry. **uvàggio,** *m.* grapes of different kinds.

uvizzolo, *m.* wild vine.

uxoricída (*pl.* -**ídi**), *m.* wife-murderer. **uxoricídio,** *m.* wife-murder.

úẓẓa, *f.* sharpness in the air; light breeze. **úẓẓo,** *m.* bulge; bulging side (*cask,* &*c.*).

úẓẓolo, *m.* whim, caprice; fancy, passion (for).

V

V, v, (*vi*) *f.* the letter V.
vacànte, *a.* vacant, unoccupied.
vacànza, *f.* vacancy; holiday; (*pl.*)
holidays; vacation; recess. **vacàre,**
v.i. (*aux.* essere) to be vacant.
vàcca (*pl.* **vàcche**), *f.* cow. ~ *da*
latte, milch cow. **vaccàio** *or*
vaccàro, *m.* cowherd, neatherd.
vaccherèlla, *f.* heifer. **vaccherìa,**
f. cow-house, byre; dairy (farm).
vacchétta, *f.* cow-hide. **vaccinàre,**
v.t. to vaccinate. **vaccinazióne,** *f.*
vaccination. **vaccìno,** *m.* vaccine,
lymph.
vacillàre, *v.i.* (*aux.* avere) to be
unsteady, totter, wobble; vacillate,
be irresolute; waver; flicker.
vacuità, *f.* vacuity, emptiness. **vàcuo,**
a. vacuous, empty.
va-e-vièni, *m.* going & coming.
vagabondàggio, *m.* vagrancy;
truancy. **vagabondàre,** *v.i.* (*aux.*
avere) to rove, wander (about).
vagabóndo, *a.* vagabond; vagrant;
roving; truant. ¶ *m.* vagabond;
vagrant; tramp.
vagaménte, *ad.* vaguely; prettily;
gracefully. **vagàre,** *v.i.* (*aux.* avere)
to wander; ramble.
vagheggiàre, *v.t.* to gaze fondly at;
view with delight; long for; woo;
cherish (*hope, &c.*). **vagheggíno,**
m. beau; fop; dandy.
vaghézza, *f.* beauty; gracefulness;
delight; longing; desire; vagueness.
vagína, *f.* (*Anat.*) vagina; sheath.
vagíre (*pr.* **-ísco, -ísci**), *v.i.* (*aux.*
avere) to whimper; cry (*baby*).
vagíto, *m.* whimper; (*child's*) cry;
crying.
vàglia, *m.inv.* postal order; money
order; cheque (*v. bancario*); *f.*
ability; worth; merit.
vagliàre, *v.t.* to sift (*lit. & fig.*);
(*fig.*) consider; examine; weigh.
vàglio, *m.* sieve.
vàgo (*pl.* **vàghi**), *a.* vague; desirous;
beautiful; wandering; fond; eager;
handsome; charming; seductive.
(The third is the commonest meaning, but the first is nearest to the
etymological sense, from *vagare*, to
wander (Lat. *vagus,* wandering). In
poetry, sometimes two or more
meanings blend in the word).
vagóne, *m.* (*Rly.*) carriage; coach; car;
wagon; truck.

vai[u]òlo, *m.* smallpox. **vaiolóso,** *a.*
suffering from small-pox. ¶ *m.*
smallpox patient.
Valachìa (la), *f.* Walachia.
valànga (*pl.* **valànghe**), *f.* avalanche.
Valchiúsa, *f.* Vaucluse.
Valdàrno, *m.* Valdarno, valley of the
Arno.
valdése, *a. & m.* Waldensian.
i Valdesi, the Waldenses.
vàle! *i. & m.* (*Lat.*) farewell!
valènte, *a.* skilful; capable; clever.
valentía, *f.* skill; capacity; ability;
worth. **valentuòmo** (*pl.* **-uòmini**),
m. honest man; man of ability.
Valènza, *f.* Valencia (*Spain*).
valére (*pr.* **vàlgo, vàli, vàle**), *v.i. ir.*
to be worth; avail; count; profit; be
effective; be available; be valid; be
of use. **valérsi** (**di**), *v.refl.* to avail
oneself of; make use of; employ.
Valésia, *f.* Valois.
valetudinàrio, *a. & m.* valetudinarian.
valévole, *a.* available; valid; efficacious.
valicàbile, *a.* that can be crossed or
forded. **valicàre,** *v.t.* to cross; ford.
vàlico (*pl.* **vàlichi**), *m.* pass;
passage; gap; ford.
validaménte, *ad.* effectually; effec-
tively; fitly; ably; strongly; strenuously. **validità,** *f.* validity; worth;
(*fig.*) strength; force; ability. **vàlido,**
a. valid; sound; good (*reasons*);
effective; able.
valigería, *f.* portmanteau-shop.
valigétta, *f.* small suit-case; attaché-
case. **valígia** (*pl.* **-ígie**), *f.* suitcase;
portmanteau; bag. **valigiàio,** *m.*
maker of trunks & portmanteaus;
trunk & bagmaker.
vallàta, *f.* (wide) valley. **vàlle,** *f.*
valley.
Vallèsia, *f.* Vaud (Switzerland).
vallétta, *f.* small valley; dell. **vallétto,**
m. valet. **valligiàno,** *m.* inhabitant
of the valley(s); valley-dweller;
dalesman.
vàllo, *m.* rampart; wall.
vallonàta, *f.* broad valley. **valloncèl-
lo,** *m.* narrow valley; glen. **vallóne,**
m. deep valley. ¶ *a. & m.* Walloon.
valóre, *m.* value; worth; meaning;
valour; gallantry; courage; value
[date], as at (*Com.*); security (*Fin.*);
stock; share; investment; holding;
asset; bill; paper; money. ~
assegnato, declared value. ~ *locativo,* house tax. ~*i mobili,* stocks &
shares, transferable securities.

oggetto di ~, valuable [article], a. of value. **valorizzàre,** *v.t.* to turn to account; employ to advantage. cf. *avvalorare.* **valoróso,** *a.* valorous, brave, valiant; (*fig.*) excellent; great.

Valpolicèlla, *m.* noted red wine (prov. of Verona).

valsènte, *m.* value; price.

valúta, *f.* market value; price; monetary value; money; currency. ~ *estera,* foreign money, f. currency. ~ *intesa,* agreed net value. ~ *in conto,* value on account. **valutàre,** *v.t.* to value; appraise. **valutazióne,** *f.* valuation.

valva, *f.* (*Zool. & Bot.*) valve. **valvola,** *f.* (*Mech. & Radio*) valve. ~*di sicurezza,* safety valve. *apparecchio a cinque* ~*e,* (*Radio*) five-valve set.

valzer, *m.inv.* waltz. *ballare il* ~, to waltz.

vàmpa, *f.* flame; blaze; heat of flame or fire; blush. **vampàta,** *f.* burst of flame; flush; rush (*hot air*).

vampeggiàre, *v.i.* (*aux.* avere) to blaze; flame.

vampíro, *m.* vampire.

vanaglòria, *f.* vainglory; boastfulness; empty pride. **vanagloriàrsi,** *v.refl.* to boast; brag; be proud (of). **vanaglorióso,** *a.* vainglorious; boastful; arrogant.

vanaménte, *ad.* vainly; ineffectually; uselessly; with vanity or conceit.

vandalísmo, *m.* vandalism; wanton destruction. **vàndalo,** *a. & m.* vandal.

vaneggiaménto, *m.* wild talk; raving. **vaneggiàre,** *v.i.* (*aux.* avere) to talk incoherently; be delirious; rave; wander (*in speech & thought*).

vanerèllo, *a.* rather vain. **vanèsio,** *a.* foppish; vain. ¶ *m.* fop.

vànga (*pl.* **vanghe**), *f.* spade. **vangàre,** *v.t.* to dig. **vangatóre,** *m.* digger. **vangatúra,** *f.* digging.

vangèlo, *m.* gospel.

vaníglia, *f.* vanilla.

vanilòquio, *m.* empty talk; random t.

vanità, *f.* vanity; conceit. **vanitóso,** *a.* vain; conceited.

vànni, *m.pl.* (*Poet.*) pinions; wings.

vàno, *a.* vain; ineffectual; useless; empty. ¶ *m.* what is useless; room; door or window space; opening.

vantaggiàre, *v.t.* to benefit; help. **vantaggiàrsi,** *v.refl.* to profit (by). **vantaggióso,** *m.* superabundant; (*added to numbers*) and over. **vantaggíno,** *m.* little extra; some-

thing over. **vantàggio,** *m.* advantage; odds, start (*allowed in a race*); (*Typ.*) galley. ~ *per colonne,* (*Typ.*) slip galley. **vantaggióso,** *a.* advantageous; profitable; favourable.

vantàre, *v.t.* to boast of; vaunt; praise; extol; cry up. **vantàrsi,** *v.refl.* to boast; brag; vaunt. **vantatóre,** *m.* (*f.* -**trice**) boaster. **vantería,** *f.* boast[ing]; brag[ging]. **vànto,** *m.* boast; honour; name; title.

vànvera (a), *ad. expr.* at random, loosely, without reflexion.

vapóre, *m.* vapour; fume; mist; steam; (*by extens.*) steamer, steamship, steam engine. *a* ~, steam (*att.*). **vaporizzàre,** *v.t.* to vaporize; spray. **vaporizzatóre,** *m.* spray[er]; atomizer. **vaporóso,** *a.* vaporous; misty; hazy; filmy; gauzy.

varàre, *v.t.* to launch.

varcàbile, *a.* passable. **varcàre,** *v.t.* to cross, pass, overstep. **vàrco** (*pl.* **vàrchi**), *m.* passage; way; pass; ford.

variàbile, *a.* variable; changeable; unsettled. **variànte,** *a.* varying. ¶ *f.* variant. **variàre,** *v.t. & abs.* to vary, change, variegate; diversify, differ. **variazióne,** *f.* variation, change.

varicèlla, *f.* chicken-pox.

varicóso, *a.* varicose. *vena* ~*a,* varicose vein.

variegàto, *a.* variegated. **varieggiàre,** *v.i.* (*aux.* avere) to vary constantly. **varietà,** *f.inv.* variety; diversity; (*pl.*) miscellany, miscellaneous news. *spettacolo di* ~, variety show. *teatro di* ~, variety theatre; music-hall. **vàrio,** *a.* various; varied; different; several. **variopìnto,** *a.* many-coloured; variegated; speckled.

vàro, *m.* launch, launching.

Varsàvia, *f.* Warsaw.

vasàio, *m.* potter. **vasàme,** *m.* pottery.

vàsca (*pl.* **vàsche**), *f.* basin; tub; pool; pond; reservoir. *dim. vaschetta.*

vascèllo, *m.* vessel, ship.

vascolàre, *a.* vascular.

vaselína, *f.* vaseline. **vasellàme,** *m.* earthenware; crockery. ~*d'argento,* silver-plate.

vàso, *m.* pot; vase; vessel. ~ *da fiori,* flower-pot. ~ *sanguigno,* blood-vessel. ~ *da notte,* chamber-pot.

vassàilo, *m.* vassal.

vassóio, *m.* tray. ~*da tè,* tea-tray.

vastità, *f.* great extent; wide expanse. **vàsto,** *a.* wide, ample, extensive.

vàte, m. (Poet.) bard; prophet.
Vaticàno, m. Vatican.
vaticinàre, v.t. to prophesy. vaticínio, m. prophecy, prediction.
ve, pn. pers. conjunct. for vi (before lo la, li, le, ne) you, to you. ¶ ad. there (before the same particles).
ve'! i. (for vedi) look! see!
vècchia (pl. vècchie), f. old woman. vecchiàia, f. [old-] age. vecchierèlla & vecchiétta, f. poor old woman; good old woman. vecchierèllo & vecchiétto, m. poor old man; good old man. ¶ a. rather old. vecchiézza, f. age, old age. vècchio (pl. vècchi), a. old, aged; of long standing; in long use; mellow; decayed; ancient. il ~, the old (opp. the new). i vecchi, the old, old people (either sex).
véccia (pl. vécce), f. (Bot.) vetch; tare.
véce, f. stead; place; change; vicissitude; (pl.) functions, office. in sua ~, in his stead. fare le ~i di, to act as.
vedére (pr. védo & véggo, védi, véde, &c.), v.t. & abs. ir., to see; look (at, on); behold; sight; regard; understand; examine; see to it; meet; visit. stare a ~, to wait & see.
vedétta, f. look-out (place); watch; sentinel; look-out man. stare in ~, stare alle ~ e, to be on the look-out.
védova, f. widow. vedovànza, f. widowhood. vedovàto, p.a. widowed, bereaved. vedovíle, a. widower's; widow's. ¶ m. (widow's) dower. védovo, m. widower; relict.
vedúta, f. sight; view.
vedúto, p.a. seen; regarded. ~ di buon occhio, liked, loved; favourably regarded. ~ di mal occhio, disliked; unfavourably regarded.
veeménte, a. vehement. veemènza, f. vehemence.
vegetàle, a. & m. plant (life); vegetable. vegetàre, v.i. (aux. avere) to vegetate. vegetarianísmo, m. vegetarianism. vegetariàno, a. & m. vegetarian. vegetazióne, f. vegetation.
vègeto, a. vigorous, strong; flourishing, thriving; luxuriant.
veggènte, p.a. seeing. ¶ m. seer.
véglia (pl. véglie), f. waking; watch; vigil; sitting up; staying up; wakeful night; evening gathering; wake.
vegliànte, a. watching; waking.
vegliàrdo, m. old man.

vegliàre, v.i. (aux. avere) to be awake; to sit up (late); stay up; watch; be on the look-out. v.t. to watch by (sick pers. at night); attend. ~ su, watch over, keep an eye on. vegliatóre, m. watchman; watcher. vegliatríce, f. night nurse. vèglio, m. (Poet.) old man. veglióne, m. masked ball.
veícolo, m. vehicle; (fig.) medium, carrier (infection).
véla, f. sail, canvas. velàio, m. sailmaker. velàme, m. sails (coll.). velaménto, m. covering; veiling. velàre, v.t. to veil; cover; conceal; dim. velàrio, m. awning; curtain; disguise. velatúra, f. (Naut.) sails (coll.); veiling; (Phot.) clouding; coating; glazing.
veleggiàre, v.i. (aux. avere) & t. to sail.
veléno, m. poison; venom. velenóso, a. poisonous; venomous.
velería, f. sail-room, sail-loft.
velétta, f. (lady's) veil.
velière & velièro, m. sailing-ship; sailing-boat.
velína (carta), f. tissue-paper.
velívolo, m. aeroplane; glider.
velleità, f. vague intention, impulse, whim.
vellicaménto, m. & vellicazióne, f. tickling. vellicàre, v.t. to tickle.
vèllo, m. fleece. vellóso, a. hairy, shaggy.
vellutàto, a. velvety. vellutíno, m. fine velvet; velvet ribbon. vellúto, m. velvet. [di cotone] ~ a grosse coste, corduroy. ~ di cotone, velveteen.
vélo, m. veil; velum; thin tissue; muslin; gauze; voile; mist; fog; mask; blind.
velóce, a. swift, quick, rapid. velocípede, m. velocipede; cycle. velocísta, m. sprinter. velocità, f. swiftness, speed, velocity. velòdromo, m. cycle-track.
véltro, m. greyhound.
véna, f. vein; (fig.) trickle; streak; mood; luck.
venàle, a. venal; market[able], sale (value). venalità, f. venality.
venàre, v.t. to vein. venatúra, f. veining; (Bot.) venation.
vendémmia, f. vintage; vintage-time; grape-gathering. vendemmiàre, v.i. to gather grapes. v.t. (fig.) to gather, reap. vendemmiatóre, m. (f. -tríce) vintager; grape-gatherer.
véndere, v.t. to sell; sell at; sell for; sell up. venderéccio, a. salable.

vendétta, *f.* revenge; vengeance; feud.

vendíbile, *a.* salable, marketable; venal.

vendicàre, *v.t.* to avenge; revenge; vindicate. **vendicatívo,** *a.* revengeful; vindictive. **vendicatóre,** *m.* (*f.* -**tríce**) avenger; vindicator.

véndita, *f.* sale, selling. ~*all'asta,* auction (sale). ~ *all'ingrosso,* wholesale (selling). ~ *al minuto,* retail. ~ *a rate,* instalment plan, hire purchase. **venditóre,** *m.* (*f.* -**tríce**) seller, vendor. **vendúto,** *a. & p.p.* of *vendere,* sold.

venefício, *m.* poisoning. **venèfico** (*pl.* -**èfici**), *a.* poisonous; venomous.

veneràbile *&* **veneràndo,** *a.* venerable. **veneràre,** *v.t.* to venerate, worship. **venerazióne,** *f.* veneration; worship.

venerdì, *m.* Friday. *il V* ~ *santo,* Good Friday.

Vènere, *f.* Venus. **venèreo,** *a.* venereal.

Vèneto (il), *m.* Venetia. **Venèzia,** *f.* Venice. **veneziano,** *a. & m.* Venetian.

vènia, *f.* pardon. **veniàle,** *a.* venial.

veniènte, *p.a.* coming; next. **veníre** (*pr.* **vèngo, vièni, viène,** *&c.*), *v.i. ir.* (*aux.* essere) to come; strike (*idea*); get; occur; be; happen; fall; hail (*da* = from). ~*alle mani,* to come to blows. ~*a parole,* to have words. ~ *meno,* to faint; fail.

venóso, *a.* venous.

ventagliàrsi, *v.refl.* to fan oneself. **ventàglio,** *m.* fan. *coda a* ~, fan-tail.

ventàre, *v.i.* (*aux.* avere) to blow (hard); be windy. **ventar[u]òla,** *f.* weather-cock; ventilator; fire-fan. **ventàta,** *f.* gust of wind.

ventènne, *a.* twenty years old. **ventènnio,** *m.* period of twenty years. **ventèsimo,** *a. num. ord.* twentieth. **vénti,** *num. card. inv.* twenty. *¶ m.* twenty; 20th.

venticèllo, *m.* light wind, breeze.

venticínque, *num. card. inv.* twenty-five. **venticinquèsimo,** *a. num. ord.* twenty-fifth.

ventilàbro, *m.* winnowing-fan.

ventilàre, *v.t.* to ventilate (*lit. & fig.*); winnow. **ventilatóre,** *m.* fan; ventilator. **ventilazióne,** *f.* ventilation; airing.

ventína, *f.* score; about twenty.

vènto, *m.* wind. **vèntola,** *f.* fire-fan; fire-screen; lamp-shade. **ventolàre,** *v.t.* to fan; winnow; (*v.i.*) (*aux.*

avere) to wave; flutter. **ventósa,** *f.* cupping-glass; air-hole; sucker. **ventosàre,** *v.t.* (*Med.*) to cup. **ventosità,** *f.* flatulence. **ventóso,** *a.* windy.

ventràle, *a.* ventral. **vèntre,** *m.* belly, abdomen; paunch; womb; bilge (*cask*).

ventrícolo, *m.* ventricle.

ventrièra, *f.* body-belt.

ventrilòquio, *m.* ventriloquism, -quy. **ventríloquo,** *m.* ventriloquist.

ventunèsimo, *a. num. ord.* twenty-first. **ventúno,** *num. card. inv.* twenty-one.

ventúra, *f.* fortune; luck; chance. **venturière, -ièro,** *m.* adventurer, soldier of fortune.

ventúro, *a.* next; coming; to come; future. *i* ~ *i,* posterity. **venturóso,** *a.* lucky, fortunate.

venustà, *f.* beauty; loveliness. **venústo,** *a.* beautiful, charming, lovely.

venúta, *f.* coming; arrival.

veràce, *a.* true; veracious; real. **veracità,** *f.* truthfulness, veracity.

veraménte, *ad.* truly; really; indeed.

verànda, *f.* veranda(h).

verbàle, *a.* verbal. *¶ m.* minutes (*meeting*). *mettere a* ~, to minute, enter in the minutes.

verbèna, *f.* vervain (*Bot.*).

verbigràzia, *ad.* for instance, for example, *abb.* e.g.

vèrbo, *m.* verb; word. **verbosità,** *f.* verbosity, wordiness; prolixity. **verbóso,** *a.* verbose, wordy; prolix.

verdàstro, *a.* greenish. **verdazzúrro,** *a.* bluish green; sea-green.

vérde, *a. & m.* green. *essere al* ~, to be penniless.

verdechiàro, *a.* light green. **verdebrúno, verdecúpo,** *&* **verdescúro,** *a.* dark green.

verdeggiànte, *a.* verdant. **verdeggiàre,** *v.i.* (*aux.* avere) to appear green; turn green. **verdegiàllo,** *a.* apple-green. **verdemàre,** *a.* sea-green. **verderàme,** *m.* verdigris.

verdétto, *m.* verdict.

verdézza, *f.* greenness. **verdíccio** *&* **verdògnolo,** *a.* greenish. **verdóne,** *m.* greenfinch; green linnet. **verdúra,** *f.* verdure, greenery; greenness; green vegetables, green stuff, greens. *minestra con* ~, vegetable soup.

verecóndia, *f.* modesty, bashfulness. **verecóndo,** *a.* modest, bashful.

vérga (*pl.* **vérghe**), *f.* rod; wand;

verge; (*symbol of office*) staff; bar (*precious metal*). ~ *pastorale*, crozier. **vergàre**, *v.t.* to flog; stripe, mark with stripes, rule, draw lines on; write. **vergàta**, *f.* stroke with a rod. **vergatíno**, *m.* striped cloth. **vergàto**, *a.* striped; ruled. *carta* ~*a*, ruled paper.

verginàle, *a.* virgin, virginal, maidenly. **vérgine**, *f.* virgin. *la* (*Beata*) *V.* ~, the Virgin Mary, the Blessed V. ¶ *a.* virgin; free. **verginèlla**, *f.* young maiden. **verginità**, *f.* virginity; maidenhood.

vergógna, *f.* shame; modesty; infamy, dishonour. **vergognàrsi**, *v.refl.* to be ashamed. **vergognóso**, *a.* ashamed; bashful, shame-faced; sheepish; shameful, disgraceful, inglorious.

veridicità, *f.* veracity, truthfulness. **verídico** (*pl.* **-ídici**), *a.* veracious, truthful.

verífica, *f.* inspection; examination; verification. **verificàre** (*pr.* **-ífico, -ífichi**), *v.t.* to verify; check; examine. **verificàrsi**, *v.refl.* to happen; come true. **verificatóre**, *m.* examiner; inspector. **verificazióne**, *f.* verification; examination; checking; vouching; auditing.

verisimigliànte, *&c.*, see **verosimigliante**, *&c.*

verísmo, *m.* realism. **verísta**, *a.* realistic. ¶ *m.* realist, realistic writer.

verità, *f.* truth, verity; fact. **veritièro**, *a.* truthful, veracious.

vèrme, *m.* worm.

vermicèlli, *m.pl.* vermicelli.

vermicolàre, *a.* vermicular. **vermifórme**, *a.* vermiform. **vermífugo** (*pl.* **-ífughi**), *a. & m.* vermifuge.

vermíglio, *a. & m.* vermilion.

verminóso, *a.* verminous.

vèrmut, *m.inv.* vermouth.

vernàccia, *f.* strong white wine.

vernàcolo, *a. & m.* vernacular.

vernàle, *a.* (*Poet.*) wintry. **vernàre**, *v.i.* (*aux.* avere) to winter.

verníce, *f.* varnish; paint; glaze; polish; varnishing day; (*fig.*) veneer, smattering. ~*per mobili*, French polish. ~*ad olio*, oil-varnish; oil-paint. ~ *antiumida*, damp-resisting varnish. ~ *antiruggine*, rust-resisting v. **verniciàre**, *v.t.* to varnish; paint; glaze; polish. **verniciàto**, *p.a.* varnished, glazed, polished. *scarpe* ~*e*, patent-leather shoes. **verniciatóre**, *m.* varnisher;

polisher. **verniciatúra**, *f.* varnishing; glazing.

vèrno, *m.* (for *inverno*) winter.

véro, *a.* true; real; genuine; right; downright, thorough, arrant. ¶ *m.* truth; (*Art.*) life, nature.

veróne, *m.* balcony.

verònica, *f.* (*Bot.*) veronica.

verosimigliànte, *a.* likely. **verosimiglìànza**, *f.* likelihood; verisimilitude. **verosímile**, *a.* likely; probable.

verricèllo, *m.* small windlass, winch.

vèrro, *m.* boar.

verrúca (*pl.* **verrúche**), *f.* wart. **verrucóso**, *a.* warty.

versàccio, *m.* bad line, bad verse (*poetry*); horrible cry; scornful gesture.

Versàgiia, *f.* Versailles.

versaménto, *m.* out-pouring; payment; paying in; p. out; remittance; instalment; deposit (*Bank*). *distinta di* ~, pay-in slip.

versànte, *m.* side, slope (*hill, &c.*); drainage area, watershed; payer; depositor. **versàre**, *v.t.* to pour (out); shed, spill; tip; overturn; upset; pay; p. in; p. out; deposit. *v.i.* to spill; leak; live; be; turn (upon); treat (of).

versàtile, *a.* versatile; changeable, fickle. **versatilità**, *f.* versatility; changeableness.

versàto, *a.* versed, skilled, proficient (in); conversant (with).

verseggiàre (*pr.* **-éggio, -éggi**), *v.t.* to versify, turn into verse. *v.i.* (*aux.* avere) to versify, write verse(s). **verseggiatóre**, *m.* **verseggiatríce**, *f.* versifier.

versétto, *m.* verse (*Bible*); versicle; short line; short verse. **versificàre** (*pr.* **-ífico, -ífichi**), *v.t.* to versify, turn into verse.

versióne, *f.* version; translation; unseen [translation].

versipèlle, *a.* wily, astute, cunning, crafty. ¶ *m.* cunning fellow.

vèrso, *m.* verse, line (*poetry*); note, song (*birds*); sense; means; way; direction, side; gesture; proceeding; verso, reverse (*coin, page*). ~ *sciolto* (*gen. pl.*), unrhymed verse; blank verse. *al* ~, overleaf. ¶ *pr.* towards; to; against; about (*time*). ~ *casa*, homeward(s). ~ *di*, in comparison with.

vèrsta, *f.* verst (*Russian measure of length*) = 1067 *metres*).

vèrtebra, *f.* vertebra (*pl.* vertebrae).

vertebràle, *a.* vertebral; spinal (*column*). **vertebràto**, *a. & m.* vertebrate.

vertènte, *a.* (*Law*) pending; undecided. **vertènza**, *f.* dispute, quarrel; question, difference. **vèrtere**, *v.i. defect.* to be (about). ~ *su*, to turn (on); regard.

verticàle, *a.* vertical, upright. ¶ *f.* vertical. **verticalménte**, *ad.* vertically.

vèrtice, *m.* (*Geom.*) vertex; top; height.

vertígine, *f.* dizziness; giddiness; vertigo. **vertiginóso**, *a.* dizzy; giddy.

verúno, *a.* any; (*with neg.*) none. ¶ *pn.* anyone, anybody; no one, nobody.

verżicàre, *v.i.* (*aux.* avere) to turn green. **verżière**, *m.* kitchen-garden, market-garden; fruit & vegetable market. **verżúra**, *f.* greenery, verdure; greens, green plants.

véscia (*pl.* **vésce**), *f.* puff-ball (*fungus*).

vescíca (*pl.* **-scíche**), *f.* bladder; (*Anat., Bot.*) vesica. **vescicànte**, *m.* blistering ointment. **vescichétta**, *f.* small bladder; vesicle; blister.

vescovàdo, *m.* bishop's palace. **vescovàto**, *m.* episcopate; bishop's see; episcopal revenue. **vescovíle**, *a.* episcopal. **véscovo**, *m.* bishop.

vèspa, *f.* wasp. **vespàio**, *m.* wasp's nest; (*fig.*) hornet's nest; (*Med.*) mass of boils.

Vespașiàno, *m.* Vespasian. *v*~, urinal (*street*).

vèspero, *m.* (*Poet.*) evening. *V*~, the evening star, Vesper, Hesperus. **vespertíno**, *a.* evening (*att.*). **vèspro**, *m.* vespers, evensong; evening.

vessàre, *v.t.* to vex, oppress; (*fig.*) grind. **vessatóre**, *m.* oppressor. ¶ *a.* (*f.* **-trice**) oppressive. **vessatòrio**, *a.* oppressive; vexatious. **vessazióne**, *f.* oppression; cruel injustice.

vessíllo, *m.* (*Poet.*) standard; flag.

vestàglia, *f.* dressing-gown. **vestàle**, *f.* vestal (virgin). **vèste**, *f.* dress, gown; garment; suit of clothes; covering, (*straw*) casing for a bottle; (*fig.*) guise, pretext; appearance; quality, right, authority; (*pl.*) clothes, attire.

Vestfàlia (la), *f.* Westphalia.

vestiàrio, *m.* clothes; outfit; (*Theat.*) wardrobe. **vestiarísta**, *m.* (*Theat.*) costumier.

vestíbolo, *m.* vestibule (entrance) hall, lobby.

vestígio (*pl.m.* **-ígi**, *f.* **-ígia**), *m.* footprint, track, trace; vestige; (*pl.*) footprints, vestiges, remains.

vestiménto, *m.* (*pl.* **-énti**, *f.* **-énta**), garment; vestment; (*f.pl.*) clothes, clothing. **vestíre** (*pr.* **vèsto**, **vèsti**), *v.t.* to dress; clothe; wear. *v.i.* (*aux.* avere) & **vestírsi**, *v.refl.* to dress, be dressed; dress oneself. **vestíto**, *m.* dress; coat; suit of clothes; (*pl.*) clothes. **vestitúra**, *f.* dressing. **vestizióne**, *f.* (*Eccl.*) (ceremony of) taking the habit (of an Order); (*nun*) taking the veil.

Vesúvio, *m.* Vesuvius.

veteràno, *m.* veteran; ex-service man (*Mil.*).

veterinària, *f.* veterinary science. **veterinàrio**, *a.* veterinary. ¶ *m.* veterinary surgeon.

vèto, *m.* veto.

vetràio, *m.* glass-blower; g. manufacturer; glazier. **vetràme**, *m.* glass ware. **vetràta**, *f.* glass door; g. partition; (*large*) window. **vetrería**, *f.* glass-works; (*pl.*) glass ware. **vetrificàre** (*pr.* **-ífico**, **-ífichi**), *v.t.* to vitrify. **vetrína**, *f.* glass-case; show-case; glass-cupboard; show-window; shop-window. **vetríno**, *a.* brittle; glassy. ¶ *m.* microscopic slide.

vetriolico, *a.* vitriolic. **vetri[u]òlo**, *m.* vitriol.

vétro, *m.* glass; pane (of glass). **vetróso**, *a.* vitreous, glassy.

vétta, *f.* top; summit.

vettóre, *m.* vector (*Math. & Astr.*); carrier.

vettovagliaménto, *m.* provisioning; victualling. **vettovagliàre**, *v.t.* to provision; victual. **vettovàglie**, *f.pl.* provisions; victuals.

vettúra, *f.* carriage; coach; cab; car. *signori, in* ~! (*Rly.*) take your seats, please! ~ *di piazza*, hackney cab. *stazione di* ~*e*, cab rank. ~ *da corsa*, racing car. ~ *a due posti*, two-seater. ~ *da turismo*, touring car. **vetturétta**, *f.* small [motor-] car, runabout. **vetturíno**, *m.* driver; coachman; cabman.

vetustà, *f.* (*Lit.*) antiquity; decay; (old) age. **vetústo**, *a.* ancient, old.

vezzeggiaménto, *m.* fondling, caressing. **vezzeggiàre**, *v.t.* to fondle; caress; coax. **vezzeggiativo**, *a.* coaxing; caressing; (*Gram.*) diminutive (*of endings that indicate* *endearment*, &c.). ¶ *m.* pet-name.

vézzo, *m.* habit; bad habit; trick; endearment; ornament; necklace; toy, plaything; (*pl.*) charms, attractions. **vezzóso**, *a.* graceful, pretty, charming.

vì, *ad.* there. ¶ *pn. pers. conjunct.* you, to you.

vía, *f.* street; road; way; route, track; means, measure; channels. *a metà* ~, halfway, midway. *la V* ~ *lattea*, the Milky Way, galaxy. ~*e di fatto*, assault (& battery); blows, violence, force. ~*e di mezzo*, half-measures. ¶ *ad.* away; off. ¶ *i.* come now! that's enough! well! *e così* ~, and so on; and so forth. ~ *che*, as, as soon as.

viabilità, *f.* (good) condition (*of roads*); viability.

viadótto, *m.* viaduct.

viaggiàre, *v.i.* (*aux.* avere) to travel; journey; voyage; (*goods*) to be carried. **viaggiatóre**, *m.* (*f.* -**tríce**) traveller; passenger. **viàggio**, *m.* journey, voyage, trip; tour; (*pl.*) travels. dim. *viaggétto*.

viàle, *m.* avenue.

viandànte, *m.* passer-by; pedestrian; traveller.

viàtico (*pl.* -**àtici**), *m.* provision for journey; viaticum.

viavài, *m.* going & coming; bustling, bustle.

vibràre, *v.i.* (*aux.* avere) to vibrate, quiver. *v.t.* to shake; brandish; hurl; strike, deal, deliver (*a blow*), lash (*tail*). **vibràto**, *a.* vigorous, energetic; concise. **vibrazióne**, *f.* vibration; quivering.

vicariàto, *m.* vicariate; curacy; living. **vicàrio**, *m.* vicar; curate.

vice-, (*prefix.*) vice-, assistant, deputy.

vicecancellière, *m.* vice-chancellor. **vicedirettóre**, *m.* (*business*) assistant manager; (*Sch.*) deputy headmaster; (*journalism*) assistant editor. **vice-presidènte**, *m.* vice-president; vice-chairman. **viceré**, *m.* viceroy. **vicereàle**, *a.* viceregal. **viceregína**, *f.* vice-reine.

vicènda, *f.* vicissitude; change; turn (*of service*); event. *a* ~, in turn; mutually, reciprocally. **vicendévole**, *a.* alternate; mutual; reciprocal. **vicendevolézza**, *f.* reciprocity. **vicendevolménte**, *ad.* mutually; reciprocally; in turn; by turns.

vicevèrsa, *ad.* viceversa.

vicinàle, *a.* parish (*att.*), local. *strada* ~, road between villages, country road.

vicinànte, *a.* neighbouring. ¶ *m.* neighbour. **vicinànza**, *f.* nearness; closeness; vicinity; proximity; (*pl.*) neighbourhood, surroundings. **vicinàto**, *m.* neighbourhood; neighbours (*coll.*). **vicíno**, *a.* near, n. at hand; neighbouring. ~ *a*, near; beside; by; close to. ¶ *m.* neighbour.

vicissitúdine, *f.* vicissitude.

víco (*pl.* **vichi**), *m.* hamlet; village.

vícolo, *m.* lane; alley. dim. *vicoletto*.

vidimàre, *v.t.* to stamp as correct; visé; indorse; authenticate.

Viènna, *f.* Vienna. **viennése**, *a.* & *m.* Viennese.

vieppiú, *ad.* much more, far more; more & more.

vietàre, *v.t.* to forbid; prohibit. **vietàto**, *p.a.* forbidden, prohibited. ~*a l'affissione*, stick no bills. *rigorosamente* ~ *fumare*, smoking is strictly forbidden.

vièto, *a.* (*Lit.*) old, antiquated; obsolete; stale; musty.

vigènte, *a.* (*Law*) in force. **vígere** (*pr.* **víge, vígono**), *v.i. defect.* to be in force; be in use.

vigèsimo, *a. num. ord.* twentieth.

vigilànte, *a.* vigilant, watchful. **vigilànza**, *f.* vigilance; watchfulness. **vigilàre**, *v.t.* to watch (over), keep a watch on. *v.i.* (*aux.* avere) to be on the alert, keep watch, be on one's guard. **vígile**, *a.* watchful; alert; wakeful. ¶ *m.* watchman; policeman; fireman.

vigília, *f.* vigil; eve (*Eccl.*, &c.). *la* ~ *di Natale*, Christmas Eve. *la* ~ *di Pasqua*, Easter Eve.

vigliaccherìa, *f.* cowardice, cowardliness; meanness. **vigliàcco** (*pl.* -**àcchi**), *a.* cowardly. ¶ *m.* coward.

vígna, *f.* vineyard; (*pl.*) vines. **vignai[u]òlo**, *m.* vine-dresser. **vignéto**, *m.* vineyard.

vignétta, *f.* vignette; cut.

vigógna, *f.* vicuna, vicugna.

vigóre, *m.* vigour; strength; (*Law*) force. **vigoreggiàre**, *v.i.* (*aux.* avere) to thrive; acquire vigour. **vigoría**, *f.* energy; vigour. **vigoróso**, *a.* strong; vigorous.

víle, *a.* vile; low; mean; cheap; base; cowardly. ¶ *m.* coward; dastard. **vilificàre** (*pr.* -**ífico**, -**ífichi**), *v.t.* to vilify. **vilipèndere**, *v.t. ir.* to

despise. **vilipèndio,** *m.* contempt.
vilipéso, *p.a.* despised; scorned.
villa, *f.* country-house, country-seat;
villa. **villàggio,** *m.* village. **villa-
nàccio,** *m.* ill-bred fellow; boor.
villanàta, *f.* rude action, act of
a boor; rude words. **villanèllo,** *m.*
villanèlla, *f.* country-lad, country-
girl. **villanésco** (*pl.* -**éschi**)*, a.*
boorish; rude. **villanía,** *f.* abuse;
rudeness; bad manners; (*pl.*) insults.
villàno, *a.* rude; rough. ¶ *m.*
rustic; countryman; boor. ~ *rifatto,*
parvenu. **villàna,** *f.* countrywoman;
ill-bred woman.
villeggiànte, *m.* summer visitor;
holiday-maker. **villeggiàre,** *v.i.*
(*aux.* avere) to spend one's (summer)
holidays in the country. **villeggia-
túra,** *f.* country-holiday(s).
villeréccio (*pl.* -**écci**)*, a.* rustic, rural.
víllico (*pl.* **víllici**)*, m.* (*Lit.*)
villager; countryman; peasant.
villíno, *m.* small country house;
cottage.
villóso, *a.* hairy; shaggy.
viltà, *f.* cowardice; meanness.
vilúppo, *m.* tangle; (*fig.*) confusion.
vimináta, *f.* wicker-work. **vímine,**
m. osier; withy.
vinàccia (*pl.* **vinàcce**)*, f.* dregs of
pressed grapes. **vinàccio,** *m.* bad
wine. **vinacci[u]òlo,** *m.* grape-
stone. **vinàio** (*pl.* -**ài**)*, m.* wine
merchant; vintner. **vinàrio,** *a.*
wine (*att.*); relating to wine.
vínca (*pl.* **vínche**)*, f.* periwinkle
(*Bot.*). **vincàstro,** *m.* shepherd's
crook; crook.
vincènte, *p. & a.* winning. ¶ *m.*
winner. **víncere** (*pr.* **vínco, vìnci,
vínce, &c.**)*. v.t. & i. ir.* to win;
carry off (prize); conquer; vanquish;
beat; overcome; master.
vinchéto, *m.* osier-bed. **vincibòsco,**
m. honeysuckle. **vincíglio** (*pl.*
-**igli**)*, m.* withy.
víncita, *f.* winning; winnings. **vinci-
tóre,** *m.* (*f.* -**tríce**) winner; victor;
conqueror. ¶ *a.* winning, conquering.
vínco (*pl.* **vínchi**)*, m.* osier; withy.
vincolàre, *v.t.* to bind. **víncolo,** *m.*
tie, bond.
víndice, *m.* avenger. ¶ *a.* avenging.
vinèllo, *m.* thin wine. **vinícolo,** *a.*
wine-growing; w.-producing. **vini-
coltúra,** *f.* cultivation of vines.
vinífero, *a.* wine-producing. **vini-
ficazióne,** *f.* wine-making. **víno,**
m. wine. **vinosità,** *f.* vinosity.
vinóso, *a.* vinous.

vínto, *a. & p.p.* of *vincere.*
viòla, *f.* violet; viola (*Mus.*). ~ *del
pensiero,* pansy, heartsease.
violàceo, *a.* violaceous; of violet
colour; of (the) violet family (*Bot.*).
violàre, *v.t.* to violate, transgress,
break; contaminate; desecrate.
violentàre, *v.t.* to do violence to;
force, compel; violate. **violènto,** *a.*
violent. **violènza,** *f.* violence;
duress; stress.
violétta, *f.* violet. **violétto,** *a. & m.*
violet (colour).
violinísta (*pl.m.* -**isti**, *pl.f.* -**íste**)*,
m.f.* violinist. **violíno,** *m.* violin,
fiddle. *il primo* ~, the first violin
(*pers.*). **violoncèllo,** *m.* violoncello,
'cello.
viòttola, *f.* (foot-) path. **viòttolo,** *m.*
path; lane; narrow street.
vípera, *f.* viper, adder. **vipèreo &
viperíno,** *a.* viperous (*tongue, &c.*).
viràggio, *m.* turning; tacking (*Naut.*);
toning (*Phot.*).
viràgo (*pl.* -**àgini**)*, f.* virago; amazon.
viràre, *v.t. & abs.* to turn; bank
(*Aero.*); heave (*Naut.*); transfer; tone
(*Phot.*). ~ *di bordo,* to tack (*Naut.*);
put about; turn about.
Virgílio, *m.* Virgil.
virginàle & virgíneo, *a.* virginal,
virgin (*att.*); maidenly.
vírgola, *f.* comma. *punto e* ~, semi-
colon. **virgolàre,** *v.t.* to mark with
commas. **virgolétte,** *f.pl.* inverted
commas, quotation marks.
virgúlto, *m.* young shoot; shrub.
viríle, *a.* manly; virile. **virilità,** *f.*
manliness; virility; manhood.
virtú, *f.* virtue; power; faculty; property; strength; courage; characteristic quality. **virtuàle,** *a.* virtual.
virtualità, *f.* potentiality. **virtuosità,** *f.* virtuousness; (*Art*) virtuosity.
virtuóso, *a.* virtuous; strong; skilled.
¶ *m.* virtuous man; (*Art*) virtuoso.
virulènto, *a.* virulent. **virulènza,** *f.*
virulence.
visàccio, *m.* ugly face.
visceràle, *a.* visceral. **víscere,** *m.*
vital organ, internal organ. **vísceri,**
m.pl. viscera. **víscere,** *f.pl.* bowels
(*fig.*); heart (*fig.*).
víschio (*pl.* **víschi**)*, m.* bird-lime;
mistletoe. **viscidézza & viscidità,**
f. stickiness. **víscido,** *a.* viscid;
sticky. **viscidúme,** *m.* (mass of)
sticky stuff.
vísciola, *f.* wild cherry. **vísciolo, m.**
wild cherry tree.
viscóso, *a.* viscous; sticky.

visíbile, *a.* visible. **visibílio,** *m.* profusion, great number. *andare, mandare, in* ~, to go, throw, into ecstasies (or raptures).

visièra. *f.* visor; fencing-mask; peak *(cap).* **visionàrio,** *a. & m.* visionary. **visióne,** *f.* vision; sight; seeing; fantasy, phantasy; hallucination.

visír, *m.inv.* vizi[e]r.

vísita, *f.* visit; call; inspection; examination. *biglietto di* ~, visiting card. ~ *doganale,* customs' examination. **visitàre,** *v.t.* to visit *(rarely in the social sense);* examine; inspect. **visitatóre,** *m.* (*f.* -**tríce**) visitor; examiner. **visitazióne,** *f.* visitation (*Eccl.*).

visívo, *a.* visual; of sight. **víso,** *m.* face. *a* ~ *aperto,* openly. *far buon* ~ *a,* to look favourably on.

vispézza, *f.* liveliness; briskness. **víspo,** *a.* lively; brisk.

vissúto, *p.p.* of *vivere.*

vísta, *f.* sight, faculty of s.; view; prospect; appearance. **vistàre,** *v.t.* to visé *(passport).* **visto,** *p.p.* of *vedere.* ¶ *m.* visé, visa.

Vístola (la), *f.* the Vistula.

vistosità, *f.* gaudiness; showiness. **vistóso,** *a.* gaudy, showy; pretty; large; considerable.

visuàle, *a.* visual.

víta, *f.* life; lifetime; living; livelihood; biography; waist. **vitàccia,** *f.* wretched life.

vitàlba, *f.* traveller's joy, clematis (*Bot.*).

vitàle, *a.* vital. **vitalità,** *f.* vitality. **vitalízio,** *a.* lasting for life. ¶ *m.* life annuity.

vitamína, *f.* vitamin.

vitàto, *a.* planted with vines. **víte,** *f.* vine; (*Mech.*) screw.

vitèllo, *m.* calf; veal. dim. *vitellino.*

vitíccio (*pl.* -**icci**), *m.* vine-tendril. **viticultúra,** *f.* vine growing.

vitína, *f. & vitino,* *m.* small waist; small screw.

vítreo, *a.* vitreous; glassy.

víttima, *f.* victim.

vítto, *m.* food; board; living. ~ *e alloggio,* board & lodging.

vittòria, *f.* victory. **V** ~, Victoria. **vittoriàle,** *a.* triumphal. *il V* ~, D'Annunzio's villa at Gardone Riviera (on Lake Garda). **Vittorio,** *m.* Victor. **vittorióso,** *a.* victorious. **vittríce,** *a.f.* (*Poet.*) victorious.

vituperàndo, *a.* ignominious; contemptible. **vituperàre,** *v.t.* to

vituperate; abuse; disgrace. **vituperatívo,** *a.* vituperative. **vituperévole,** *a.* blameworthy, contemptible. **vitupèrio,** *m.* shame; infamy; abuse; (*pl.*) insults. **vituperóso,** *a.* shameful, despicable.

viúzza, *f.* narrow street; lane.

víva! *i.* hurrah! long live —!

vivacchiàre, *v.i.* (*aux.* avere) to get a bare living; rub along.

vivàce, *a.* lively, vivacious, sprightly; quick; gay; (*colour*) bright. **vivacità,** *f.* liveliness; brightness; vivacity; sprightliness; quickness (*mind*).

vivaddío! *i.* good heavens! yes.

vivàgno, *m.* selvage, selvedge; border.

vivàio, *m.* nursery (*plants*); fish-pond.

vivaménte, *ad.* keenly; deeply; strongly; warmly; heartily. **vivànda,** *f.* dish of food; (*pl.*) food, viands.

vivandière, *m.* butler; canteen-keeper.

vivènte. *a.* living. **vívere** (*pr.* **vívo, vívi**), *v.i.* (*aux.* essere) & *t. ir.* to live; be alive; subsist; endure; behave. ¶ *m.* living, livelihood. **víveri,** *m.pl.* provisions; victuals; supplies.

vivézza, *f.* liveliness; sprightliness; brightness; splendour. **vívido,** *a.* vivid; lively. **vivificàre** (*pr.* -**ífico**, -**ífichi**), *v.t.* to vivify, quicken; vitalize; invigorate; enliven, cheer. **vivificatívo** & **vivificatóre** (*f.* -**tríce**), *a.* vivifying.

vivíparo, *a.* viviparous. **vivisezióne,** *f.* vivisection. *fare la* ~ *di,* to vivisect.

vívo, *a.* alive; live; living; quick; lively; sprightly; brisk; smart; sharp; vital; keen; crisp; hasty; spirited; vivid; clear; bright. *a* ~ *a forza,* by main (or sheer) force. *a viva voce,* by word of mouth, orally. *argento* ~, quick-silver. *calcina* ~ *a,* quicklime. ¶ *il* ~, *m.* the quick (flesh); the heart (*of a matter*); life (*Art*). *i vivi,* the living. *al* ~, to the life.

viziàre, *v.t.* to vitiate; spoil (*child*). **viziaménte,** *ad.* faultily; imperfectly. **viziàto,** *a.* vitiated; defective; spoilt. **vízio** (*pl.* **vízi**), *m.* vice; defect; fault; bad habit. **vizióso,** *a.* vicious; defective; dissipated.

vízzo, *a.* withered, faded; flabby.

vocabolàrio, *m.* vocabulary; dictionary. **vocàbolo,** *m.* word; term.

vocàle, *a.* vocal. ¶ *f.* vowel. **vocaliz-**

żàre, *v.t.* to vocalize. *v.i.* (*aux.* avere) (*Mus.*) to sing by vowels only. **vocatívo**, *m.* vocative (*Gram.*). **vocazióne**, *f.* vocation; calling; call (*divine*).

vóce, *f.* voice; register; speech; word; dictate(s); opinion; rumour; say; vote; item. *dim.* *vocína*, *f.* *vocíno*, *m.* *vocerèlla*, *f.* *vocétta*, *f.*, &c. **vociàre**, *v.i.* (*aux.* avere) to bawl. **vociferàre**, *v.i.* (*aux.* avere) to vociferate; shout; rumour, report. **vocío**, *m.* constant shouting, bawling. **vocióna**, *f.* **vocióne**, *m.* loud voice; loud talker.

vòga, *f.* rowing; fashion, vogue; ardour. **vogàre** (*pr.* vògo, vòghi), *v.i.* (*aux.* avere) to row. ~ *a coda*, to scull. **vogàta**, *f.* row, rowing. **vogatóre**, *m.* rower, oarsman.

vòglia (*pl.* vòglie), *f.* wish; desire; will; intention; birthmark. **voglióso**, *a.* desirous; capricious. **vogliúzza**, *f.* caprice, foolish wish.

vói, *pn. pers. disjunct.* you.

volàno, *m.* shuttlecock.

volànte, *p.a.* flying. *colonna* ~, flying column. *squadra* ~, flying squad. *foglio* ~, fly-sheet. *cervo* ~, kite. ¶ *m.* fly-wheel; wheel (*Motor*). **volàre** (*pr.* vólo), *v.i.* (*aux.* essere & avere) to fly.

volantíno, *m.* leaflet; wheel (*Mech.*). **volàta**, *f.* flight.

volàtile, *a.* winged; volatile. ¶ *m.* winged creature (*gen. pl.*). **volatilizzàre**, *v.t.* & *i.* to volatilize. **volatilizzàrsi**, *v.refl.* to volatilize; evaporate; vanish (*into the air*). **volatívo**, *a.* (*Aviat.*) suitable for flying, flying (*weather*).

volatóre, *m.* (*f.* **-tríce**) flyer. ¶ *a.* flying.

volènte, *a.* willing. **volentièri**, *ad.* willingly, gladly.

volére, (*pr.* vòglio, vuòi, vuòle, &c.) *v.t.* & *i. ir.* to will; want; wish; like; (be) please(d to); mean; intend; require; need; should (be), is (to be).

volgàre, *a.* vulgar; common; low; everyday; vernacular. *lingua* ~, vernacular. ¶ *m.* vulgar tongue, vernacular. **volgarità**, *f.* vulgarity. **volgarizzàre**, *v.t.* to popularize; translate into the vernacular.

vòlgere (*pr.* vòlgo, vòlgi, vòlge), *v.t. ir.* to turn; t. round; direct; draw; put; translate. *v.i.* (*aux.* essere & avere) & **vòlgersi**, *v.refl.* to turn; t. round; revolve. **volgíbile**, *a.*

that can turn or be turned. **volgiménto**, *m.* turning.

vólgo (*pl.* vólghi), *m.* common people; crowd; vulgar herd.

volicchiàre & **volitàre**, *v.i.* (*aux.* avere) to flit; flutter.

volizióne, *f.* volition.

vólo, *m.* flight; flying.

volontà, *f.inv.* will; (*pl.*) wishes. **volontàrio**, *a.* voluntary; self-willed, wilful, wayward. ¶ *m.* volunteer. **volonteróso**, *a.* willing, eager, full of good will.

volpacchiòtto, *m.* fox-cub, young fox. **volpàia**, *f.* fox's den, fox-hole. **vólpe**, *f.* fox. **volpíno**, *a.* crafty, foxy; fox-coloured. ¶ *m.* fox-cub. **volpóne**, *m.* old fox.

vòlt & **vòlta**, *m.inv.* volt (*Elec.*).

vòlta, *f.* time; turn; turning; vault. *una* ~, once, *due* ~*e*, twice. *c'era una* ~, once upon a time. *qualche* ~, sometimes. *a sua* ~, in his turn.

voltàbile, *a.* that can turn or be turned; inconstant. **voltafàccia**, *m.inv.* turning about; change of front; volte-face.

voltàggio (*pl.* -àggi), *m.* voltage. **voltàico** (*pl.* -àici), *a.* voltaic. **voltàmetro**, *m.* voltameter.

voltàre, *v.t.* & *i.* (*aux.* avere) to turn; t. round; t. over; change; translate. **voltàrsi**, *v.refl.* to turn. **voltàta**, *f.* turn, turning; change of direction.

volteggiàre (*pr.* -éggio, -éggi), *v.i.* (*aux.* avere) to turn about; fly about, flit, hover; flutter; flap; perform feats of horsemanship or gymnastics; vault; shuffle; wriggle. **voltéggio**, *m.* turning; vaulting; trick-riding & similar circus gymnastics.

volterriàno, *a.* Voltairian.

voltímetro, *m.* voltmeter.

vólto, *m.* face; countenance, aspect. **vòlto**, *p.p.* of *volgere*. ¶ *a.* turned; given (to), devoted. ¶ *m.* arch, vault.

voltolàre, (*pr.* vòltolo) *v.t.* to roll, r. about. **voltolóni**, *ad.* rolling, tumbling.

voltúra, *f.* (*Law*) transfer, assignment.

volúbile, *a.* fickle, inconstant; glib, voluble; (*Bot.*) climbing (*plant*); twining; (*Poet*) circling, rolling. **volubilità**, *f.* fickleness, inconstancy; volubility.

volúme, *m.* volume, tome; quantity, mass, bulk, measurement. **voluminóso**, *a.* voluminous; bulky.

volúta, *f.* (*Arch.*) volute; spiral curve; **voluttà**, *f.* delight; sensual pleasure.

voluptuousness. **voluttuàrio** (*pl.* **-àri**), *a.* voluptuary; unnecessary (*expense*, *&c.*). **voluttuóso**, *a.* voluptuous.

vòlvere, see *volgere*.

vòmere *&* **vòmero**, *m.* ploughshare.

vómico (*pl.* **vòmici**), *a.* emetic; vomitory. *noce* ~*a*, nux vomica (*Med.*).

vomitàre (*pr.* **vòmito**), *v.t. & i.* to vomit, spew, belch (out). **vomitatívo**, *a. & m.* emetic. **vòmito**, *m.* vomiting, vomit.

voràce, *a.* voracious; greedy. **voracità**, *f.* voracity, voraciousness, greed(iness).

voràgine, *f.* gulf, deep hollow.

vòrtice, *m.* vortex; whirlpool; whirl, swirl. **vorticóso**, *a*, whirling, swirling.

Vosgi (i), *m.pl.* (the) Vosges.

Vossignoria, *f.* Your Lordship; Your Ladyship.

vòstro, *a.poss.* your. ¶ *pn. poss.* yours. *i vostri*, your family, your people.

votànte, *p.a.* voting. ¶ *m.f.* voter. **votàre**, *v.i.* (*aux.* avere) to vote; (*v.t.*) pass; carry (*motion*); offer; consecrate. **votàrsi**, *v.refl.* to devote oneself.

votatúra, *f.* emptying.

votazióne, *f.* voting; vote (*coll.*).

votàzza, *f.* scoop; ladle; baler.

votívo, *a.* votive. **vóto**, *m.* vow; votive offering; desire; prayer; vote.

vulcànico (*pl.* **-ànici**), *a.* volcanic. **vulcaníte**, *f.* vulcanite. **vulcanizzàre**, *v.t.* to vulcanize.

vulcàno, *m.* volcano (*pl.* volcanoes). **V** ~, Vulcan (*Myth.*).

Vulgàta, *f.* (the) Vulgate (*bible*).

vúlgo, see *volgo*.

vulneràbile, *a.* vulnerable. **vulneràre**, *v.t.* to wound; injure; offend.

v[u]otàggine *&* **v[u]otézza**, *f.* emptiness; vacuity. **v[u]otaménto**, *m.* emptying. **vuotàre**, *v.t.* to empty; vacate. **v[u]otatúra**, *f.* emptying. **v[u]òto**, *a.* empty; void; vacant; idle; aimless; silly. ~ *di*, devoid of. ¶ *m.* void; vacuum; space; gap; vacancy; empty (*case*, *&c.*).

W

W, w, (*doppio vu*) *f.* the letter W, used only in a few foreign words such as **watt**, **chilowatt** (*Elec.*); forms no real part of the Italian alphabet.

X

X, x, (*ics*, *icchese*) *f.* the letter X, is used only at the beginning of a few foreign words, and tends to be replaced in these by initial s, as it has been already by double s in the middle of words. *raggi* X, X rays.

xenofobia (*also* senofobía), *f.* hatred of foreigners, xenophobia. **xenòfobo**, *m.* hater of foreigners.

xeres, *m.* sherry.

xilofonísta (*also* silofonísta), *m.* xylophone player. **xilòfono** (*also* silòfono), *m.* xylophone.

xilografía, *f.* (*also* silografía) wood-engraving. **xilogràfico** (*pl.* -àfici), *a.* of wood-engraving. **xilògrafo** (*also* silògrafo), *m.* wood-engraver.

Y

Y, y, (*ipsilon*, *ipsilonne*) *f.* the letter Y is generally replaced by i (e.g. *ciclo*) but may be found in a few foreign words which have not become fully italianized. It is also used as a mathematical & algebraic symbol.

Z

Z, z, (*zèta*) *f.* the letter Z.

żabaióne, *m.* egg-flip.

zàcchera, *f.* splash, splash of mud. **zaccheróna**, *f.* slattern. **zaccheróne**, *m.* slovenly fellow, one careless of appearance(s). **zaccheróso**, *a.* bespattered with mud, &c.

zaffàta, *f.* whiff (*of foul air*, *&c.*); stench.

żafferàno, *m.* saffron.

żaffíro, *m.* sapphire.

żagàglia, *f.* assegai, (*native*) spear.

żàino, *m.* knapsack; pack.

zàmpa, *f.* paw; claw; leg; foot (*lit. & fig.*). ~*e di gallina*, crow's-feet; ~*e di maiale*, pigs' trotters. **zampàre**, *v.i.* (*aux.* avere) to paw the ground. **zampàta**, *f.* blow with the paw. **zampettàre**, *v.i.* (*aux.* avere) to toddle; totter.

zampillàre, *v.i.* (*aux.* essere *&* avere) to gush; spirt out; spring. **zampíllo**, *m.* jet; spirt; squirt; stream.

zampíno, *m.* little paw; (*fig.*) finger.

zampógna, *f.* [reed-]pipe; bag-pipe. **zampognàro,** *m.* piper.

zampóne, *m.* big paw; (pig's) trotter.

zàna, *f.* basket; cradle; niche, recess; (*fig.*) cheat, fraud.

zàngola, *f.* churn.

zànna, *f.* tusk; fang. **zannàta,** *f.* blow with the tusk.

zànni, *m.* clown; zany; buffoon.

zannúto, *a.* tusked; fanged.

zanzàra, *f.* mosquito. **zanzarièra,** *f.* mosquito-net.

zàppa, *f.* hoe; mattock. **zappàre,** *v.t. & abs.* to hoe; dig. **zappatóre,** *m.* (*f.* -**trìce**) hoer; digger; (*Mil.*) sapper. *Genio ~ i,* corps of sappers.

zar, *m.inv.* Czar. **zarìna,** *f.* Czarina.

zàttera, *f.* raft; lighter.

zavòrra, *f.* ballast. **zavorràre,** *v.t.* to ballast.

zazzera, *f.* shock of hair; mane; long hair. **zazzerúto,** *a.* wearing one's hair long, or in a shock.

zèbra, *f.* zebra.

zécca, *f.* mint. *nuova di ~,* brand-new.

zecchíno, *m.* sequin.

zèffiro, *m.* zephyr; light breeze.

Zelànda & Zeelàndia (la), *f.* Zealand. *Nuova Zelanda (la),* New Zealand.

zelànte, *a.* zealous. **zelantería,** *f.* zealotry; excess of zeal. **zelatóre,** *m.* (*f.* -**trìce**) zealot. **zèlo,** *m.* zeal.

zènit, *m.inv.* zenith.

zènzero, *m.* ginger.

zéppo. *a.* full; crammed; crowded.

zerbíno, *m.* dandy; coxcomb; door-mat.

zèro, *m.* cipher; zero, nought (*as in telephone numbers*); nothing. *uno ~,* a mere nothing.

zèta, *f.inv.* the letter Z. *dall' A alla Z,* from A to Z, from beginning to end.

zèugma, *m.* (*Gram., Rhet.*) zeugma.

Zeus, *m.* Zeus.

zía, *f.* aunt.

zibaldóne, *m.* medley; collection of notes or reflections (e.g. Leopardi's).

zibellíno, *m.* sable (*Zool., fur*).

zibétto, *m.* civet (*animal & scent*); civet-cat.

zígomo, *m.* cheek-bone.

zigríno, *m.* shagreen.

zigzàg, *m.inv.* zigzag.

zimàrra, *f.* robe; cassock.

zimbèllo, *m.* decoy; decoy-bird; lure; laughing-stock.

zinàle, *m.* apron.

zincàre, *v.t.* to zinc, cover with zinc. **zínco,** *m.* zinc, spelter. **zinco-**

grafía, *f.* zincography. **zincògrafo,** *m.* zincographer; (*Typ.*) block-maker; process engraver.

zincotipía, *f.* zincotype; zinco-typing.

zingarésca, *f.* gipsy song. **zingarésco** (*pl.* -**éschi**), *a.* gipsy (*att.*). **zíngaro,** *m.* **zíngara,** *f.* gipsy (m.f.).

zínnia, *f.* zinnia (*Bot.*).

zinzíno, *m.* little bit; small quantity.

zío (*pl.* **zìi**), *m.* uncle.

zípolo, *m.* spigot.

zirlàre, *v.i.* (*aux.* avere) to whistle (*thrush*); whistle, cry; sing like a thrush. **zírlo,** *m.* thrush's cry.

zitèlla, *f.* maid; unmarried girl. **zitellóna,** *f.* old maid; spinster. **zitellóne,** *m.* old bachelor.

zittíre (*pr.* -**ísco,** -**ísci**), *v.i.* (*aux.* avere) & *t.* to hiss. **zítto,** *a.* silent. *star ~,* to keep silence, silent. **~ [~]!** silence! quiet! hold your tongue!

zizzània, *f.* darnel; (*fig.*) discord, dissension.

zoccolàio, *m.* maker of wooden shoes, or clogs. **zoccolànte,** *m.* Franciscan friar. **zoccolàre,** *v.i.* (*aux.* avere) to clatter; tramp about in clogs. **zòccolo,** *m.* clog; sabot; wooden shoe; hoof (*pl.* hooves); (*Arch.*) plinth, socle; dado; skirting board.

zodiacàle, *a.* zodiacal. **zodíaco** (*pl.* -**íachi**), *m.* zodiac.

zolfanèllo & zolfíno, *m.* (sulphur) match. **zolfàra & zolfatàra,** *f.* sulphur-mine. **zolfatúra,** *f.* sulphuration. **zólfo,** *m.* sulphur. **zolforàto,** *a.* sulphurated; sulphur-ized.

zòlla, *f.* clod; sod; turf; lump. **zollétta,** *f.* (small) lump (*sugar, &c.*).

zombàre, *v.t. & i.* (*aux.* avere) to thump.

zòna, *f.* zone; belt; area; girdle; (*Med.*) shingles. *~ [equatoriale] delle calme,* doldrums (*Naut.*).

zònzo (a), *ad. expr. andare a ~,* to saunter about; loaf, loiter.

zoología, *f.* zoology. **zoològico** (*pl.* -**ògici**), *a.* zoological. **zoòlogo** (*pl.* -**òlogi**), *m.* zoologist. **zoologísta** (*pl.* -**ísti**), *m.* dealer in foreign animals.

zoppàggine, *f.* limp; lameness.

zoppicànte, *a.* limping; halting; shaky. **zoppicàre,** *v.i.* (*aux.* avere) to limp; (*fig.*) halt; walk lame; stand unsteadily; be shaky. **zoppicóne & zoppicóni,** *ad.* limping[ly], halting-

ly, unsteadily. zòppo, a. lame;
limping; halting; unsteady; wob-
bling.
żoticàggine & żotichézza, f.
boorishness, roughness; rusticity.
żòtico (pl. żòtici), a. boorish,
rough; coarse (cloth); hard (soil).
żoticóne, m. utter boor; rude
fellow.
żuàvo, m. zouave.
zúcca (pl. zúcche), f. pumpkin,
gourd; (fig.) head; pate. zuccàta,
f. knock on the head; blow with the
head. fare alle ~e con, to butt
against.
zuccheràre, v.t. to sugar, sweeten.
zuccherièra, f. sugar-basin. zuc-
cherifício, m. sugar-refinery, s.
works. zuccheríno, a. sugary;
sweet. ¶ m. sweet, sweetmeat;
sugar-plum. zúcchero, m. sugar.
~d'orzo, barley s. ~ in pezzi,
~ a zollette, lump s. ~ in pani,
loaf s. (whole). zuccheróso, a.
sugary.

zucchétto, m. scull-cap.
zucchíno, m. vegetable marrow.
zuccóne, m. large pumpkin; (fig.)
bald head; dunce; blockhead.
zúffa, f. scuffle, scrummage, tussle.
zufolaménto, m. whistling; buzzing,
singing (in the ears). zufolàre, v.i.
(aux. avere) to whistle; (of ears) to
sing, buzz. zufolíno, m. whistle.
zufolío, m. constant whistling,
singing, buzzing. zúfolo, m.
whistle; pipe; flageolet.
zuingliàno, a. Zwinglian.
Żulú, m.inv. Zulu. il paese dei Z~
Zululand.
zúppa, f. soup; sop; (fig.) confusion,
mess; job; trouble; scolding. ~ di
verdura, vegetable soup. zuppièra,
f. soup-tureen. zúppo, a. wet;
drenched, soaked.
Zurígo, f. Zurich.
zurlàre, v.i. (aux. avere) to romp,
be skittish. żużżurullóna, f.
romping girl, tomboy. żużżurul-
lóne, m. rollicking fellow.

A

A, *letter*, a, *f.* *From A to Z*, dall'a alla zeta. *capital* ~, A maiuscola, *small* (*lower case*) ~, a minuscola. ¶ **a, an**, *indefinite art*, un, uno, *m.* un', una, *f.* 2 *or* 3 *times* ~ *day*, 2 o 3 volte al giorno.

aback, *ad.* *taken* ~, sconcertato, preso all'impensata, alla sprovvista.

abacus, *n.* abaco (*Arch.*); abbaco, *m.*

abaft, *ad.* (*Naut.*) all'indietro. ¶ *pr.* dietro di.

abandon, *v.t.* abbandonare. ¶ *n.* disinvoltura, *f.*, brio, *m.*, vivezza, *f.* ~*ed* (*woman*), (donna) perduta, sregolata, sfacciata. ~**ment**, *n.* abbandono, *m.*

abase, *v.t.* abbassare, umiliare.

abash, *v.t.* sconcertare, confondere, svergognare.

abate, *v.t.* scemare, ridurre a meno, diminuire. *v.t. & i.* cedere (di), subire una riduzione. *v.i.* (*of storm, anger, &c.*) calmarsi, abbonacciarsi. ~**ment**, *n.* ribasso, sconto, scemamento, *m.* bonificazione, *f.*

abattoir, *n.* ammazzatoio, macello, *m.*

abbess, *n.* badessa, *f.* **abbey**, badia, *f.* **abbot**, *n.* abate, *m.*

abbreviate, *v.t.* abbreviare, accorciare, compendiare. **abbreviation**, *n.* abbreviatura, abbreviazione, *f.*; abbreviamento, *m.*

ABC, *n.* abbiccì, alfabeto, *m.*

abdicate, *v.t. & i.* abdicare, rinunziare (al trono, &c.). **abdication**, *n.* abdicazione, rinunzia, *f.*

abdomen, *n.* addome, ventre, *m.* *lower part of the* ~, basso ventre, *m.* **abdominal**, *a.* addominale. ~ *belt*, ventriera, *f.*

abduct, *v.t.* rapire, trafugare, levar via. ~**ion**, *n.* ratto, *m.* sottrazione, *f.*

abeam, *ad.* (*Naut.*) per traverso.

abed, *ad.* a letto, in letto, coricato.

aberration, *n.* aberrazione, *f.*, sviamento, *m.*

abet, *v.t.* sostenere, appoggiare, incoraggiare, far buon viso a, aver parte in, rendersi complice di.

abeyance, *n.* *in* ~, giacente (*Leg.*); sospeso, interrotto; pendente.

abhor, *v.t.* aborrire, detestare, aver in orrore. **abhorrence**, *n.* ripugnanza, avversione, *f.*, aborrimento, *m.* **abhorrent**, *a.* ripugnante, aborrevole.

abide, *v.i. & t. ir.* restare, stare, rimanere; soffrire, sopportare, tollerare. *to* ~ *by*, mantenere (una promessa), attenersi a, tener fermo. **abiding**, *a.* costante, durevole, permanente.

ability, *n.* abilità, capacità, *f.*, ingegno, talento, *m.*

abject, *a.* abbietto, spregevole, vile. ~**ion**, *n.* abbiezione, *f.*, avvilimento, *m.*

abjure, *v.t.* abiurare, ritrattare, rinunziare.

ablative [**case**] *n.* ablativo, *m.*

able, *a.* abile, capace; destro, valente. ~ *bodied*, sano, robusto. ~ [*bodied*] *seaman*, marinaio scelto, *m.* *to be* ~ *to*, potere, sapere, esser in grado di. **ably**, *ad.* abilmente, destramente, valentemente.

abnegation, *n.* abnegazione, rinunzia, *f.*, sacrificio, *m.*

abnormal, *a.* anormale, irregolare. ~**ity**, *n.* anormalità, *f.*

aboard, *ad.* (*Naut.*) a bordo. ¶ *pr.* a bordo di.

abode, *n.* abitazione, casa, stanza, dimora, *f.*, domicilio, soggiorno, *m.* *to take up one's* ~, stabilirsi. ¶ *pret. of* abide.

abolish, *v.t.* abolire, sopprimere, abrogare, annullare. **abolition**, *n.* abolizione, soppressione, *f.*, annullamento, *m.*

abominable, *a.* abominevole, infame. **abominate**, *v.t.* abominare, detestare, aborrire. **abomination**, *n.* abominazione, *f.* a borrimento, *m.* infamia, *f.*

aboriginal, *a. & n.* aborigeno, -e, *a. & m.* **aborigines**, *n.pl.* aborigeni, *m. & f.pl.*

abortion, *n.* aborto, *m.*, sconciatura, *f.* **abortive**, *a.* abortito; (*fig.*) fallito.

abound, *v.i.* abbondare, pullulare.

about, *pr.* intorno a; attorno a, presso, presso a, presso di, vicino a; a proposito di, in fatto di, al soggetto di, circa, riguardo a, in riguardo di; verso, su, sopra; sul conto di, di. ¶ *ad.* intorno, attorno, all'intorno,

d'intorno; circa, all'incirca; quasi,
press'a poco, a un dipresso. *to be*
~ *to*, stare per, essere sul punto di,
essere in procinto di. *what is it all*
~? di che si tratta? *what are you
thinking* ~? a che pensate? *what do
you think* ~ *it?* che ne pensate?
to bring ~, cagionare.

above, *pr.* su, sopra, al di sopra di.
¶ *ad.* su, sopra, di sopra; in alto,
verso l'alto; più di, superiore a.
from ~, dall'alto. ~*all*, soprattutto,
prima di tutto. ~ *board*, franco,
schietto; carte in tavola. ~
mentioned, suddetto, predetto, suac-
cennato. ~ *named*, sunnominato.

abrade, *v.t.* raspare, grattare; *(skin)*
graffiare, scorticare. **abrasion**, *n.*
(*Phys.*) attrito, tritamento, logorio,
m.; raschiatura, raspatura, *f.*; *(skin)*
graffiatura, scorticatura, *f.*

abreast, *ad.* di fronte, in fila. ~ *of*,
all'altezza di.

abridge, *v.t.* accorciare, abbreviare,
riassumere, compendiare. **abridg[e]-
ment**, *m.* sunto, riassunto, compendio, *m.* ~*ed edition*, edizione
ridotta.

abroad, *ad.* all'estero; fuori. *from* ~,
dall'estero, di fuori. *there is a
rumour* ~ *that*, corre voce che.
to spread ~, spargere (la voce, la
notizia, &c.), divulgare, disseminare.

abrogate, *v.t.* abrogare, annullare.
abrogation, *n.* abrogazione, *f.*

abrupt, *a.* scosceso, precipitoso; *(of
manners)* brusco, impulsivo. ~*ly*,
ad. di botto, di scatto, bruscamente.
to treat ~*ly*, trattare con sgarbo,
sgarbatamente, senza pazienza.
~*ness*, *n.* asprezza; scortesia;
subitaneità.

abscess, *n.* ascesso, postema, *m.*

abscond, *v.i.* scappare, evadere,
sfuggire, sottrarsi alla giustizia,
rendersi contumace.

absence, *n.* assenza; mancanza,
omissione, *f.* ~ *of mind*, distrazione,
disattenzione, sbadataggine, *f.*
absent, *a.* assente. ~*-minded*,
distratto. ¶ ~ *oneself*, assentarsi,
andarsene. **absentee**, *n.* assente;
(Mil.) disertore, *m.* **absently**, *ad.*
distrattamente, disattentamente.

absinth, *n.* assenzio, liquore
d'assenzio, *m.*

absolute, *a.* assoluto. ~*ly*, *ad.*
assolutamente.

absolution, *n.* assoluzione, *f.*
absolve, *v.t.* assolvere, rilasciare.

absorb, *v.t.* assorbire. **absorbent,**

a. assorbente. **absorbing**, *a.*
interessantissimo. *absorbent cotton*
wool, *n.* cotone idrofilo, *m.* **absorption**, *n.* assorbimento, *m.*

abstain, *v.i.* astenersi. ~*er*, *n.*
astinente, astemio, *m.* **abstemious**,
a. astemio. **abstention**, *n.* astensione, *f.* **abstinence**, *n.* astinenza, *f.*,
digiuno, *m.*

abstract, *a.* astratto. ¶ *n.* sommario,
sunto, ristretto, riassunto, compendio, *m.* *the* ~ *(opp. concrete)*
l'astratto, *m.* ¶ *v.t.* astrarre,
staccare, rimuovere; *(steal)* rapire,
involare, appropriarsi. **abstraction**, *n.* astrazione, distrazione, *f.*

abstruse, *a.* astruso, recondito, oscuro.

absurd, *a.* assurdo. **the** ~, **an
absurdity**, l'assurdo, *m.*, un'assurdità, *f.*

abundance, *n.* abbondanza, copia,
dovizia, *f.* **abundant**, *a.* abbondante, fertile, copioso. ~*ly*, *ad.*
abbondantemente, ampiamente, profusamente.

abuse, *n.* abuso, eccesso, *m.*; ingiurie,
f.pl., insulto, oltraggio, *m.* ¶ *v.t.*
abusare; ingiuriare, oltraggiare,
svillaneggiare; malmenare, maltrattare. **abusive**, *a.* ingiurioso,
offensivo.

abutment (*Arch.*), *n.* rinfianco *(flying-
buttress)*, fianco, *m.*, coscia (di ponte,
&c.), *f.*

abyss, *n.* abisso, baratro, *m.*, voragine,
f., profondità, *f.*

Abyssinia, *n.* l'Abissinia, *f.* **Abyssinian**, *a.* & *n.* abissino.

acacia, *n.* acacia, *f.*

academic[al], *a.* accademico (*pl.*-ici);
(year) scolastico, accademico. **academician**, *n.* accademico, *m.*
academy, *n.* accademia, *f.*

acanthus, *n.* acanto, *m.*

accede, *v.i.* accedere, acconsentire.

accelerate, *v.t.* accelerare. **acceleration**, *n.* accelerazione, *f.* **accelerator**, *n.* acceleratore, *m.*

accent, *n.* accento, *m.* ¶ *v.t.* &
accentuate, accentare, accentuare.

accept, *v.t.* accettare, accogliere,
aggradire; *(sport record, &c.)* ammettere, riconoscere valido. ~**able**,
a. accettabile, gradevole. ~**ance**,
n. accettazione, accoglienza, *f.*
~**ation**, *n.* accettazione, *f.*; significato, *m.* ~**ed term**, frase consacrata, *f.* ~**or**, *n.* accettante, *m.*
~ *for honour* (*Com.*), a per
intervento, *m.*

access, *n.* accesso, abbordo, aditu, *m.*,

entrata, *f.* **~ible,** *a.* accessibile, abbordabile. **~ion,** *n.* accessione, aggiunta; venuta (salita) al trono, *f.* *list of* ~s (*Lib.*), registro d'ingresso. **accessory,** *a.* accessorio. ¶ *n.* accessorio, *m.*; (*Law.*) complice, *m. & f.*

accidence, (*Gram.*) *n.* morfologia.

accident, *n.* accidente, incidente, caso, *m.*; disgrazia, *f.* *street* ~, incidente stradale, *m.* *personal* ~ *insurance,* assicurazione contro gl'infortuni, *f.* **accidental,** *a.* accidentale, accessorio, fortuito. ¶ (*Mus.*) *n.* segno accidentale.

acclaim, *v.t.* acclamare. **acclamation,** *n.* acclamazione, *f.*

acclimatization, *n.* acclimatazione, acclimazione, *f.* **acclimatize,** *v.t.* acclimatare, acclimare.

acclivity, *n.* erta, salita, *f.*

accommodate, *v.t.* accomodare, adattare, aggiustare; ospitare, alloggiare; prestare, venire in aiuto a. ~ *oneself to,* accomodarsi, acconciarsi a. **accommodating,** *a.* compiacente, soccorrevole. **accommodation,** *n.* accomodamento, accordo, *m.,* conciliazione, *f.;* alloggio, *m.;* prestito, *m.* ~ *bill* (*Com.*) cambiale di comodo, *f.*

accompaniment, *n.* accompagnamento, *m.* **accompan[y]ist,** *n.* accompagnatore, -trice, *m.f.* **accompany,** *v.t.* accompagnare.

accomplice, *n.* complice, *m.f.*

accomplish, *v.t.* compire, compiere, condurre a fine; adempire, adempiere; eseguire, effettuare. **~ed,** *a.* compito, perfetto; garbato, colto, bene educato. **~ment,** *n.* adempimento, *m.,* esecuzione, *f.;* talento, *m.,* dote, cognizione, *f.*

accord, *n.* accordo, *m.* *of one's own* ~, di sua propria volontà, spontaneamente, di spontanea volontà. *with one* ~, di comune accordo, unanimemente, concordemente. ¶ *v.t.* accordare; concedere. *v.i.* accordarsi, confarsi. **~ance,** *n.* accordo, *m.,* conformità, *f.* *in* ~ *with,* conforme a, d'accordo con, di concerto con. **according as,** come, secondo che, a misura che. **according to,** secondo, conforme a. **accordingly,** *ad.* perciò, in (di *or* per) conseguenza, quindi, dunque.

accordion, *n.* fisarmonica, *f.*

account, *n.* conto, calcolo; valore, pregio, *m.*; racconto, *m.,* relazione, esposizione, notizia, *f.* **~s,** *pl.*

conti. (*Stk. Ex.*) lettera. *of no* ~, da nulla, da poco. *on no* ~, per nulla al mondo. *by all* ~s, al dire di tutti. *on* ~ (*Com.*), in acconto. *on* ~ *of,* a cagione di; (*Com.*) per conto di. ~ *book,* libro di conti. *current* ~, conto corrente. *interest* ~, conto interesse. *to open an* ~ *with,* accendere, aprire un conto a. *to settle an* ~, aggiustare, liquidare, saldare un conto. ~ *rendered,* conto rimesso. *to take into* ~, tenere conto di, prendere in considerazione, far conto di. ~ *sales,* conto di vendita. ~ *day* (*Stk. Ex.*), giorno di liquidazione, *m.* ¶ *v.t.* considerare, tenere per, stimare, reputare. ~ *for,* rendere conto di, rendere ragione di; spiegare. **~able,** responsabile; da ascriversi (a), da attribuirsi (a), dovuto (a). **~ancy,** *n.* contabilità, *f.* **~ant,** *n.* contabile, ragioniere, *m.* **~ing,** *n.* contabilità, *f.* ~ *machine,* macchina calcolatrice, *f.* ~ *period,* esercizio, *m.*; revisione dei conti, *f.*

accoutre, *v.t.* vestire, arredare, guarnire, fornire, equipaggiare. **~ment,** *n.* apparecchio, corredo, guarnimento, equipaggiamento, *m.*

accredit, *v.t.* accreditare. **~ed,** *p.a.* accreditato, approvato, autorizzato, fornito di lettere credenziali (di autorizzazione).

accrue, *v.i.* provenire, derivare; accrescere, maturare. **~d** *interest,* interessi maturati ed aggiunti al capitale.

accumulate, *v.t.* accumulare. *v.i.* accumularsi. **accumulation,** *n.* accumulazione, *f.,* accumulamento, *m.*; massa, *f.,* monte, mucchio, *m.* **accumulator,** *n.* accumulatore, *m.*

accuracy, *n.* accuratezza, esattezza, giustizia, precisione, *f.* **accurate,** *a.* esatto, giusto.

accursed, *a.* maledetto.

accusation, *n.* accusa; incolpazione, imputazione, *f.* **accusative [case],** *n.* accusativo, *m.* **accuse,** *v.t.* accusare, incolpare. *the* ~*d,* l'accusato, l'incolpato. **accuser,** *n.* accusatore, *m.* **accusing,** *a.* accusante.

accustom, *v.t.* abituare, assuefare, avvezzare. **~ed,** *p.a.* abituato, assuefato; avvezzo, solito. *to be* ~*ed,* solere.

ace, *n.* asso, *m.* (*cards, aviation, &c.*). *within an* ~ *of,* vicinissimo-a, a un dito di.

acerbity, *n.* acerbità, asprezza, *f.*
acetate, *n.* acetato, *m.* **acetic,** *a.* acetico.
acetylene, *n.* acetilene, *m.* ~ *lamp,* lampada ad a., *f.* ~ *burner,* becco da a., *m.*
ache, *n.* dolore, male, *m.* ¶ *v.i.* dolere. *my head aches,* mi duole la testa (il capo).
achieve, *v.t.* compiere, effettuare, conseguire, pervenire a. ~**ment,** *n.* compimento, conseguimento; fatto, trionfo, *m.* ~**s,** gesta, *f.pl.*
aching, *s.* doloroso, palpitante.
achromatic, *a.* acromatico.
acid, *a.* & *n.* acido, *a.* & *m.*, agro, *a.* ~**ity,** *n.* acidità, agrezza. **acidulate,** *v.t.* acidulare.
acknowledge, *v.t.* ammettere, riconoscere, accettare, confessare. ~ *receipt of,* accusare ricevimento di, ricevuta di. **acknowledg[e]ment,** *n.* riconoscimento, *m.*, ammissione, *f.*; ricevuta, *f.*; (*pl.*) ringraziamenti, *m.pl.*
acme, *n.* colmo, cima, apogeo, *m.*
acne, *n.* (*Med.*) acne, *m.*
acolyte, *n.* acolito, *m.*
acorn, *n.* ghianda, *f.* ~ *crop,* raccolto di ghiande, *m.*
acoustic, *a.* acustico. ~**s,** *n.pl.* acustica, *f.sg.* (*Science*); proprietà acustiche, *f.pl.*
acquaint, *v.t.* avvertire, avvisare, far sapere. *to* ~ *oneself with,* mettersi al corrente di, prendere informazioni su, prendere conoscenza di, informarsi di. *to be* ~*d with,* conoscere, intendersi di. ~**ance,** *n.* conoscenza, *f.*, relazioni personali, *f.pl.*
acquiesce, *v.i.* contentarsi, restar soddisfatto, acconsentire, acquiescere; sottomettersi; dichiararsi soddisfatto. **acquiescence,** *n.* acquiescenza, *f.*
acquire, *v.t.* acquistare, ottenere, conseguire, conquistare; imparare. ~**ments,** *n.pl.* cognizioni, *f.pl.* **acquisition,** *n.* acquisto, *m.*
acquit, *v.t.* assolvere, discolpare. *to* ~ *oneself,* comportarsi. **acquittal,** *n.* assoluzione, discolpa, *f.*
acrid, *a.* acre, pungente, aspro, mordace. ~**ity,** *n.* agrezza, mordacità, *f.*
acrimonious, *a.* acrimonioso. **acrimony,** *n.* acrimonia, asprezza, *f.*
acrobat, *n.* acrobata, funambolo, *m.* **acrobatic,** *a.* acrobatico. ~**s,** *n.pl.* acrobatismo, funambolismo, *m.*

across, *ad.* a traverso, di traverso, per traverso; obliquamente; (*cross-word clues*) orizzontalmente. ¶ *pr.* attraverso a; dall'altra parte di, di là da. *our neighbours* ~ *the Channel,* i nostri vicini d'oltre Manica.
acrostic, *n.* acrostico, *m.*
act, *n.* atto, *m.*, azione, *f.*, fatto, *m.*, operazione, *f.*, esercizio, *m.* ~ *of parliament,* legge, *f.*, *pl.* atti, *m.pl.* *taken in the* [*very*] ~, colto (proprio) sul fatto; (*Leg.*) in flagrante. ¶ *v.t.* fare; rappresentare, dare, recitare; (*v.i.*) agire, funzionare, operare. ~ *as,* (*Dram.*) far la parte di; fare le veci di, agire come sostituto di. ~ *for* (*Leg.*), agire per conto di, nell'interesse di, in vece di. *to* ~ *up to,* conformarsi a. **acting** (*Theat.*), *n.* arte del recitare, recitazione, rappresentazione, arte teatrale, *f.* ~ *manager* (*Bus.*), gerente responsabile, *m.* ~ *partner,* socio attivo, socio accomandante, *m.*
actinic rays, raggi attinici, *m.pl.*
action, *n.* azione, *f.*, fatto, *m.*, operazione, *f.*; efficacia, *f.*; battaglia, *f.*; causa, *J.*, processo, *m.*, lite, *f.*; carato (*share, Com.*), *m.*; gesto, *m.*; movimento, *m.*; (*Mech.*) meccanismo, funzionamento, *m.* *to bring an* ~ *against,* muovere causa a, intentare un processo contro.
active, *a.* attivo, operoso, energico; agile, snello, lesto, svelto. *in* (*on*) ~ *service,* in servizio attivo. ~ *voice,* voce attiva, *f.* **activity,** *n.* attività, *f.*; moto, movimento, *m.*, mossa, *f.*; agilità; operosità, *f.*
actor, -tress, *n.* attore, *m.*, attrice, *f.*
actual, *a.* reale, vero, effettivo; attuale, presente. ~**ity,** *n.* attualità, realtà, *f.* ~**ly,** *ad.* realmente, addirittura, di fatto, in effetto.
actuary, *n.* attuario, *m.*
actuate, *v.t.* attuare, effettuare; mettere in atto; muovere, spingere, animare, ispirare.
acumen, *n.* acume, *m.*, acutezza, *f.*
acute, *a.* acuto, aguzzo; penetrante, vivo, intenso, pungente; accorto, perspicace, sottile. ~ *angled,* *a.* acutangolo. ~**ly,** *ad.* acutamente, sottilmente. ~**ness,** *n.* acutezza, sagacità, penetrazione, sottilità, *f.*
A.D. (**Anno Domini**), anno di grazia, di Cristo, dell'era volgare.
adage, *n.* adagio, proverbio, *m.*
adamant, to be, essere adamantino, duro, inflessibile.

Adam's ale, acqua, *f.*

Adam's apple, pomo d'Adamo, *m.*

adapt, *v.t.* adattare, accomodare, aggiustare; acconciare. **~ation,** *n.* adattamento, *m.* **~er,** *n.* (*Phot.*) adattatore, *m.*; (*pers. fig.*) montatore, *m.*

add, *v.t.* aggiungere, attaccare, unire; addizionare, sommare; soggiungere. (*part*) **added** (*to a building*), annesso.

adder, *n.* vipera, *f.*

addict oneself to (**to**), darsi a, abbandonarsi a.

addition, *n.* aggiunta, giunta, *f.*, aumento, supplemento, *m.*; addizione, somma, *f.*; annesso, *m.* *in* ~, inoltre, per giunta, di piú. **~al,** *a.* addizionale, supplementare.

addled, *a.* vuoto; putrido. **addle-headed,** con cervello di stoppa, testa di stoppa. scervellato, capo scarico.

address, *n.* (*of letters, &c.*) indirizzo, recapito, *m.*; (*speech, &c.*) discorso, *m.*, conferenza, lezione, lettura, predica, petizione, *f.*; (*skill*) destrezza, prontezza, speditezza, *f. sender's* ~, indirizzo del mittente. *to pay one's* ~ *es to,* far la corte a. ¶ *v.t.* indirizzare, dirigere, rivolgere; indirizzarsi a. **~ee,** *n.* destinatario, *m.*, -a, *f.*

adduce, *v.t.* addurre, arrecare, fornire, metter innanzi, citare, allegare.

adenoids, *n.pl.* adenoidi, *f.pl.*

adept, *a.* esperto, abile, perito. ¶ *n.* esperto, perito, *m.*

adequate, *a.* bastante, sufficiente, adeguato; capace, comodo, atto; efficace, ragionevole. **~ly,** *ad.* adeguatamente, bastevolmente, a sufficienza, abbastanza; comodomente.

adhere, *v.i.* aderire, attaccarsi, unirsi, attenersi. *to* ~ *to* (*promise, &c.*), mantenere. **adherence,** *n.* aderenza, *f.* **adhesion,** *n.* adesione, *f.* **adhesiveness,** *n.* tenacità, viscosità, *f.* **adhesive,** *a.* tenace, viscoso. ~(*stamp*) *paper,* carta gommata, *f.* ~ *tape,* tela gommata, *f.*

adieu, *i. & n.* addio, *i. & m.*

ad infinitum, *ad.* all'infinito.

adipose, *a.* adiposo, grasso.

adit, *n.* adito, accesso, *m.*, entrata, *f.*

adjacent, *a.* contiguo, vicino, adiacente, limitrofo.

adjectival, *a.* aggettivale, di aggettivo. **adjective,** *n.* aggettivo, *m.*

adjoin, *v.i.* esser contiguo, confinare

(con). ~**ing,** *a.* contiguo, confinante, attiguo, vicino, adiacente.

adjourn, *v.t.* aggiornare, rimandare, rimettere, rinviare. ~**ment,** *n.* aggiornamento, rinvio, *m.*

adjudge, adjudicate, *v.t.* aggiudicare. **adjudication,** *n.* aggiudicazione, *f.*

adjunct, *n.* aggiunta, giunta, appendice, *f.*, accessorio, *m.*; (*pers.*) aggiunto, *m.*

adjure, *v.t.* scongiurare; supplicare, pregare.

adjust, *v.t.* aggiustare, adattare, applicare; ordinare, sistemare; (*of accounts*) pareggiare, bilanciare. ~**able spanner,** chiave inglese, *f.* ~**ment,** aggiustamento, saldamento, regolazione, *m.*, liquidazione, *f.*; messa in punto, *f.* ~ *of average* (*Insce.*), liquidazione d'avaria, *f.*

adjutant, *n.* aiutante maggiore, *m.*

ad libitum, *ad.* ad libitum; a volontà, a piacere.

administer, *v.t.* amministrare; somministrare (*Med., Eccl., &c.*); dare, deferire (*oath*). **administration,** *n.* amministrazione; somministrazione, *f.*, governo, *m.*, gestione, *f.* **administrator, -trix,** *n.* amministratore, -trice; curatore, -trice, *m. & f.*; gerente, *m.f.*

admirable, *a.* ammirabile.

admiral, *n.* ammiraglio, *m.* ~ *of the fleet,* comandante di squadra. *vice* ~, vice-ammiraglio. *rear* ~, contrammiraglio. **Admiralty,** *n.* (*Eng.*) Ammiragliato. ~ [*Office*], Ministero della Marina, *m.*

admiration, *n.* ammirazione, *f.* **admire,** *v.t.* ammirare. **admirer,** *n.* ammiratore, -trice, *m.f.* **admiringly,** *ad.* con meraviglia.

admissible, *a.* ammissibile; accettabile. **admission,** *n.* ammissione, *f.* ricevimento, *m.*; accesso, ingresso, *m.*, entrata, *f.*; confessione, *f. ticket of* ~, biglietto d'ingresso, *m.* ~ *free,* entrata libera.

admit, *v.t.* ammettere, accogliere, introdurre; concedere, permettere; riconoscere (valido); (*as member*) ricevere. ~ *bearer,* lasciar entrare. **admittance,** *n.* ammissione, *f.*, accesso, *m.*, entrata, *f. no* ~, vietato l'ingresso, è proibito l'ingresso.

admixture, *n.* mescolanza, *f.*, mescolamento, *m.*, miscela, *f.*, commistione, *f.*

admonish, *v.t.* ammonire, riprendere,

esortare. **admonition**, *n*. ammonizione, *f*., consiglio, *m*., avvertimento, *m*., riprensione, *f*.

ado, *n*. affaccendamento, *m*., chiacchiera, -e, *f. & pl.*, ciancia, -ce, *f. & pl.*; scalpore, *m*., storie, *f.pl.* *to make no ~ about it*, non farsene caso, non stare sulle cerimonie. *much ~ about nothing*, un gran da fare per niente, molto rumore per nulla.

adolescence, *n*. adolescenza, *f*. **adolescent**, *a. & n*. adolescente.

Adonis, *n*. adone, giovane molto bello, *m*.

adopt, *v.t.* adottare; prendere, accettare. **adopted**, **adoptive** (*of pers.*), adottato, adottivo. **adoption**, *n*. adottamento, *m*., adottazione, *f*.

adorable, *a*. adorabile. **adoration**, *n*. adorazione, *f*. **adore**, *v.t.* adorare. **adorer**, *n*. adoratore, -trice, *m.f.*

adorn, *v.t.* ornare, abbellire; decorare, guarnire, parare, adornare. **~ment**, *n*. ornamento, abbellimento, paramento, *m*.

Adriatic, *a. & n*. Adriatico, *a. & m*.

adrift, *ad. & a*. alla deriva, in deriva, abbandonato.

adroit, *a*. destro, scaltro, lesto, accorto, astuto. **~ness**, *n*. destrezza, sveltezza, scaltrezza, *f*.

adulate, *v.t.* adulare, lusingare. **adulation**, *n*. adulazione, lusinga, *f*. **adulatory**, *a*. adulatorio, lusinghiero.

adult, *a. & n*. adulto, maturo; uomo fatto, *m*.

adulterate, *v.t.* adulterare, contaminare, contraffare, falsificare. **adulteration**, *n*. adulterazione, contaminazione, falsificazione, *f*.

adulterer, **-ess**, *n*. adultero, -a, *m.f.* **adulterous**, *a*. adultero. **adultery**, *n*. adulterio, *m*.

ad valorem, ad valorem, computato in base al valore dichiarato.

advance, *n*. progresso, avanzamento, *m*.; (*Mil*.) avanzata, *f*.; aumento, rialzo, *m*.; anticipazione, *f*.; prestito, *m*.; (*glacier*) movimento, *m*., discesa, *f*. *payment in ~*, contro pagamento anticipato. *in ~ of*, avanti, davanti, innanzi, prima, in faccia a. ¶ *v.t.* avanzare, mettere avanti, mettere innanzi, promuovere; presentare (una domanda, una proposta); aumentare; prestare. *v.i.* avanzarsi, andare innanzi, farsi innanzi, inoltrarsi. **~ment**, *n*. avanzamento, *m*., promozione, *f*.

advantage, *n*. vantaggio, beneficio, profitto, *m*.; giovamento, *m*., utilità, *f*. *gain the ~*, prendere, ottenere il vantaggio, il sopravvento. *~ [game]* (*Ten*.), vantaggio. *~ in*, vantaggio alla battuta. *~ out*, vantaggio alla rimessa. **~ous**, *a*. vantaggioso.

advent, *n*. venuta, apparizione, *f*.; (*of Christ*) avvento, *m*.; (*Eccl*.) avvento, *m*.

adventitious, *a*. avventizio.

adventure, *n*. avventura, impresa, *f*. ¶ *v.t.* avventurare, arrischiare. *v.i.* avventurarsi. **adventurer**, *n*. avventuriere; truffatore, imbroglione, *m*. **adventuress**, *n*. avventuriera; truffatrice, imbrogliona, *f*. **adventurous**, *a*. avventuroso.

adverb, *n*. avverbio, *m*. *~ of number*, *a*. di quantità. **adverbial**, *a*. avverbiale.

adversary, *n*. avversario, *m*. **adverse**, *a*. avverso; contrario, opposto; sbilanciato. **adversity**, *n*. avversità, sventura, miseria, *f*.

advert, *v.i.* alludere, volgere il discorso (a).

advertise, *v.t.* avvisare, pubblicare, raccomandare, render noto; (*v.i.*) far fare degli annunzi, fare la pubblicità. *~ for*, domandare per via di annunzi. **advertisement**, *n*. avviso, annunzio; cartello, affisso, *m*., inserzione, *f*. *~ hoardings*, quadri di affissione, *m.pl.* **advertiser**, *n*. chi fa degli annunzi; inserzionista, *m.f.* **advertising**, *n*. pubblicità, *f*. *~ agent*, *~ consultant*, consulente per la pubblicità, *m*.

advice, *n*. consiglio, avviso, *m*.; informazioni, *f.pl.* **advisable**, *a*. consigliabile, conveniente, opportuno. **advise**, *v.t.* consigliare; avvisare; avvertire; persuadere. **advisedly**, *ad*. apposta, a bella posta; intenzionalmente; deliberatamente, a bello studio. **adviser**, *n*. consigliere, *m*. **advisory**, *a*. consultativo.

advocate, *n*. avvocato patrocinante, avvocato (*in It. both advocate and solicitor*); difensore; partigiano, *m*. ¶ *v.t.* consigliare, proporre; patrocinare, difendere.

advowson, *n*. patronato, *m*.

adze, *n*. ascia, *f*.

Aegean sea (**the**), il mare Egeo, l'Egeo, *m*.

aegis, *n*. egida, *f*.

Aeolian, *a.* eolio (*harp*, *Mus.*, *&c.*).
Aeolic, *a.* eolico (*dialect*).
aerate, *v.t.* aerare. ~*d drinks*, bibite
gassose, *f.pl.* ~*d lemonade*, *water*,
limonata, acqua gassosa. **aeration,**
n. aerazione, *f.*
aerial, *a.* aereo. ¶ (*Radio*) *n.* antenna,
f.
aerie, aery (*cyrie*), *n.* nido (*eagle*,
&c.), *m.*
aerodromo, *n.* aerodromo, campo
d'aviazione, *m.*
aerodynamic, *a.* aerodinamico. ~*s*,
n. aerodinamica, *f.*
aerolite, *n.* aerolito, *m.*, meteorite, *f.*
aeronaut, *n.* aeronauta, *m.* ~**ic(al)**,
a. aeronautico. ~**ics,** *n.pl.* aeronautica, *f.*
aeroplane, *n.* aeroplano, velivolo, *m.*
Aesop, *n.* Esopo, *m.*
aesthete, *n.* esteta, *m.* **aesthetics,**
n.pl. estetica, *f.sg.*
afar, *ad.* lontano, lungi, lontana-
mente. *from* ~, da lontano,
affability, *n.* affabilità, *f.* **affable,** *a.*
affabile, di facile abbordo. **affably,**
ad. affabilmente, con affabilità.
affair, *n.* affare, *m.*, faccenda, *f.*;
amoruccio, *m. a nice* ~ (*iron.*),
un bell'imbroglio.
affect, *v.t.* affettare, riguardare,
influire su, interessare, commuovere;
(*for the worse*) nuocere, indebolire,
danneggiare; fingere, pretendere.
~**ation,** *n.* affettazione, *f.* ~**ed,** *a.*
affettato, lezioso, manierato, smorfioso, artifizioso; commosso; affetto,
ammalato (di). ~**edly,** *ad.* leziosa-
mente, in modo affettato. ~**ing,**
p.a. commovente. **affection,** *n.*
affetto, *m.*, affezione, *f.*, amore, *m.*;
malattia, *f.* ~**ate,** *a.* affezionato,
affettuoso, amorevole.
affiance, *n.* confidenza, fede, fiducia,
f.; fidanzamento, *m.*, promessa di
matrimonio, *f.* ¶ *v.t.* fidanzare.
affidavit, *n.* affidavit, *m.*, deposizione
giurata, dichiarazione giurata, *f.*
affiliate, *v.t.* affiliare.
affinity, *n.* affinità; parentela, *f.*
affirm, *v.t.* affermare, (*Leg.*)
confermare, convalidare, ratificare;
sanzionare; asserire; attestare.
~**ation,** *n.* affermazione; ratifica, *f.*
~**ative,** *a.* affermativo. ¶ *n.*
affermativa, *f.*
affix, *n.* affisso, *m.* ¶ *v.t.* apporre
(*signature*, *&c.*); attaccare (*postage
stamp*, *&c.*). ~**ture,** *n.* affissione, *f.*
afflict, *v.t.* affliggere, abbattere,
travagliare, contristare. ~**ion,** *n.*

afflizione, *f.*, dolore, *m.*; flagello
(*war*, *plague*, *&c.*), *m.*
affluence, *n.* opulenza, ricchezza;
affluenza, abbondanza, *f.* **affluent,**
a. ricco, opulento, benestante,
abbondante; affluente, tributario.
¶ *n.* affluente, *m.*
afford, *v.t.* fornire, provvedere;
permettere. *can* ~ *to*, potere,
avere i mezzi di.
afforest, *v.t.* imboschire. ~**ation,** *n.*
imboschimento, *m.*
affray, *n.* rissa, zuffa, mischia, baruffa,
scaramuccia, avvisaglia, *f.*
affreightment, *n.* noleggio, trasporto
per mare, *m.*
affront, *n.* affronto, *m.*, ingiuria,
offesa, *f.*, oltraggio, *m.* ¶ *v.t.*
offendere.
Afghan, *a.* afghano. ¶ *n.* Afghano.
Afghanistan, *n.* l'Afghanistan.
afield, *ad: far* ~, molto lontano.
afire, aflame, *ad.* a (in) fuoco, in
fiamma, acceso.
afloat, *ad. & a.* a galla, galleggiante;
(*fig.*) a piedi, in circolazione,
divulgato.
aforesaid, *a.* predetto, suddetto,
come sopra. ¶ *n.* suddetto, *m.*
afraid, *a.* pauroso, impaurito. *to be*
~ *of*, aver paura di, temere.
afresh, *ad.* di nuovo, da capo.
Africa, *n.* l'Africa, *f.* **African,** *a.*
africano. ¶ *n.* africano, *m.*
aft, after, *a.* retro, di poppa. ~**hold,**
stiva di poppa, *f.* ¶ *ad.* all'indietro,
dietro.
after, *ad.* dopo, di poi, appresso, in
seguito. ¶ *c.* dopo che, posciaché,
una volta che. ¶ *pr.* dopo, appresso;
dietro, in capo a; alla moda di.
~*all*, dopo tutto, insomma, in
conclusione, alla fin dei conti, in
sostanza, alla fine delle fini. ~ *the
event*, a cose fatte, a fatto avvenuto.
day ~ *day*, di giorno in giorno.
aftermath, *n.* seconda falciatura, *f.*,
secondo raccolto; fieno serotino,
fieno settembrino, *m.*; (*fig.*) seguito,
m., effetti susseguenti, *m.pl.*
afternoon, *n.* pomeriggio, *m.* ¶ *a.*
pomeridiano, dopo mezzogiorno.
after-taste (*unpleasant*), *n.* sapore
(*nauseante*) che ritorna a gola, *m.*
after-thought, *n.* riflessione (*dopo
compiuto l'atto*) *f.*, secondo
pensiero, *m.*
afterwards, *ad.* dopo, poi, poscia,
piú tardi, in appresso, in seguito.
again, *ad.* ancora, ancora una volta,
di nuovo; di piú, altresí, pure;

d'altra parte, d'altronde, parimente. ~ & ~, *time* & ~, molte volte, tante e tante volte, ripetutamente. **again** *after a verb is often expressed by the prefix* ri-; *e.g.* to put back again, rimettere, *to set out again*, ripartire, &c.

against, *pr.* contro, incontro, contrario a; (*over* ~) dirimpetto a, di fronte a, in faccia a. ~ *the grain*, ~ *one's will*, a malincuore, di mala voglia. *it goes* ~ *the grain*, non gli va a genio. ~ *the light*, controluce, controlume. *to lean* ~, *v.t.* appoggiare a; *v.i.* appoggiarsi a.

agate, *n.* agata, *f.*

age, *n.* età, *f.*; secolo, *m.*; tempo, *m.*; epoca, *f.*; evo, *m.*; (*old age*) vecchiezza, vecchiaia, *f.* *to be* 10 years *of age* or *aged* 10, avere dieci anni. *he is not of* ~ (or *is under*) ~, è minorenne. *to come of full* ~, essere maggiorenne, raggiungere l'età maggiore (*or* maggiorenne). ~ *of retirement*, età pel collocamento a riposo. *it is* ~s *since* . . . , è un secolo che non . . .

aged (*of an advanced age*), *a.* attempato, vecchio vecchio. *he has* ~ *considerably*, è invecchiato di molto. *the* ~ (*either sex*), i vecchi, *m.pl.*

agency, *n.* azione, *f.*; mediazione, *f.*; agenzia, *f.*; ufficio, *m.*, rappresentanza, *f.* *advertising* ~, ufficio di pubblicità, *m.* *news* ~, agenzia di informazioni, *f.* *employment* ~, ufficio di collocamento, *m.* *sole* ~, rappresentanza esclusiva, *f.*

agenda, *n.* ordine del giorno, *m.*

agent, *n.* agente, rappresentante; fattore, *m.*; sostanza (*Chem.*). *commission* ~, commissionario, *m.* *shipping* ~, agente di trasporti marittimi. *to act as* ~, agire in qualità di intermediario.

agglomerate, *v.t.* agglomerare. **agglomeration,** *n.* agglomerato, *m.*, massa, agglomerazione, *f.*

agglutinate, *v.t.* agglutinare.

aggravate, *v.t.* aggravare, accrescere, aumentare; peggiorare, inacerbire; irritare, stuzzicare, esasperare.

aggregate, *a.* totale, complessivo, intero, compiuto. ¶ *n.* totale, *m.*, somma, *f.*; tutto l'insieme, *m.*, totalità, *f.*, complesso, *m.* **aggregation,** *n.* aggregazione, *f.*

aggression, *n.* aggressione, *f.* **aggressive,** *a.* aggressivo. **aggressor,** *n.* aggressore, *m.*

aggrieved party, offeso, malcontento, *m.*, -a, *f.*

aghast, *a.* spaventato, atterrito, stordito, stupefatto, sbalordito.

agile, *a.* agile, leggiero, svelto, destro. **agility,** *n.* agilità, destrezza, prestezza, *f.*

agio, *n.* ag[g]io, *m.*

agitate, *v.t.* agitare. **agitation,** *n.* agitazione, *f.* **agitator,** *n.* agitatore, *m.*

aglow, *a.* cocente, fervente, incandescente, arroventato.

agnail, *n.* patereccio, giradito, *m.*

ago, *ad.* fa, or sono, ora è, addietro; prima. *a short time* ~, poco fa.

agog, *a.* impaziente, in piedi, curioso, sollecito.

agonizing, *a.* straziante, dolorosissimo. **agony,** *n.* strazio, tormento, *m.*, angoscia, *f.*; (*death pangs*) agonia, *f.*

agrarian, *a.* agrario.

agree, *v.i.* accordarsi, convenire, intendersi, andare (essere, mettersi) d'accordo; (*Gram.*) concordare. *v.t.* accordare, bilanciare, pareggiare, stabilire. *to* ~ *to*, acconsentire, approvare, aderire. *quite* ~ *with*, essere (trovarsi) perfettamente d'accordo, in perfetto accordo. *meat does not* ~ *with me*, la carne mi fa male, non posso digerire la carne. *the climate does not* ~ *with him*, l'aria gli si confà poco. ~**able**, *a.* gradevole, piacevole, grato, ameno; favorevole, conforme (a). *to be* ~ *to*, essere disposto a, essere contento di. ~**d price**, prezzo convenuto, *m.* **agreement,** *n.* accordo, *m.*, concordanza, combinazione, conformità, *f.*; consenso, *m.*; patto, *m.*, convenzione, intesa, *f.*; contratto, mercato, *m.*

agricultural, *a.* agricolo, agrario. ~ *engine*, locomobile, *f.* ~ *implements*, macchine agrarie, *f.pl.* ~ *show*, esposizione agricola, *f.* ~ *association*, comizio agrario, *m.* **agricultur[al]ist,** *n.* agricoltore, coltivatore, *m.* **agriculture,** *n.* agricoltura, *f.*

agronomist, *n.* agronomo, *m.* **agronomy,** *n.* agronomia, *f.*

aground, *ad.* & *a.* a secco, in secco, incagliato. *to run* ~, *v.i.* & *t.* incagliarsi, incagliare, arrenare, dare in secco.

ague, *n.* febbre intermittente (palustre, malarica), *f.*

ahead, *ad.* avanti, in avanti, davanti, innanzi. *go* ~, avanti!

ahoy, *i.* ohe, olà! *ship* ~. ohe! della nave.

aid, *n.* aiuto, soccorso, sussidio, *m.*; assistenza, *f.* ¶ *v.t.* aiutare, soccorrere, assistere,

aide-de-camp, *n.* aiutante di campo, *m.*

ail, *v.t. & i.* avere, soffrire. *what* ~*s him?* che cosa ha? con chi l'ha? ~*ing, a.* malaticcio. ~*ment, n.* malattia, infermità, indisposizione, *f.*

aim, *n.* mira, *f.*, scopo, intento, fine, *m.*; meta, intenzione, *f.*, oggetto, disegno, *m.*; puntamento *(rifle, &c.),* *m.* ¶ *v.t.* appuntare, puntare, drizzare, tendere *(bow, &c.).* ~*at,* mirare, prender di mira; avere per fine (oggetto, scopo, &c.). ~*less, a.* senza scopo, inutile.

air, *n.* aria, *f.*; cielo, *m.*; brezza, brezzolina, *f.*, venticello, *m.*; aspetto, *m.*, cera, apparenza, sembianza, *f.*; fare, *m.*, maniera, *f.*, contegno, *m.* *to give oneself* ~*s,* fare l'importante, credersi persona d'importanza, darsi importanza, pavoneggiarsi. ~*borne,* sostenuto dall'aria; aerotrasportato. ~*craft,* aereo, aeromobile, apparecchio (aereo), *m.*; aerei, velivoli, *m.pl.*; ~*craft carrier,* nave portaerei, *f.* ~*craft exhibition,* esposizione (mostra) aeronautica, *f.* ~ *current,* corrente d'aria, *f.* ~ *cushion,* cuscino pneumatico, *m.* ~ *cylinder,* cilindro ad aria, *m.* ~ *defence,* difesa antiaerea, *f.* ~*field,* campo d'aviazione, aerodromo, *m.* ~*gun,* fucile pneumatico, f. ad aria compressa, *m.* ~*hole,* spiraglio, *m.* ~ *lighthouse,* faro aereo, *m.* ~ *line,* linea aerea, rotta aerea, *f.* ~*liner,* aeroplano di linea (civile), *m.* ~*mail,* posta aerea, *f. by* ~*mail,* per posta aerea, per via aerea. ~*mail fee,* sopratassa per posta aerea, *f.* ~*mail letter,* lettera per via aerea, *f.* ~*man,* aviatore, *m.* ~ *mechanic,* motorista, *m.* *A* ~ *Ministry,* Ministero dell'aeronautica. ~*mail packet,* pacco per via aerea, *m.* ~ *pilot,* pilota aereo, pilota di velivolo. ~*plane,* aeroplano, velivolo, *m.*; ~*fighter,* apparecchio da caccia, caccia, *m.*; *bomber,* aeroplano da bombardamento, *m.* ~ *pocket,* buco d'aria, *m.* ~*pump,* macchina pneumatica *(Phys.)*; pompa a vuoto, *f.* ~ *race,*

corsa aerea, *f.* ~ *raid,* incursione aerea, *f.* ~ *shaft (Min.),* pozzo di ventilazione, *m.* ~*ship,* aeronave, *f.*, dirigibile, *m.* ~ *station,* aeroporto, *m.* ~*tight,* impermeabile all'aria, ermetico. ~*way,* rotta aerea, *f.*; *(Min.)* ventilatore, *m.*, condotta d'aria, *f.* ~*woman,* aviatrice, *f.* ~*worthy,* atto alla navigazione aerea. ¶ *v.t.* ventilare, sventolare, dare aria, far vento a; *(fig.)* discutere, divulgare. ~*ing,* aeraggio, sventolamento, *m.*; passeggiata (col fresco) *f.*, giro, *m.* ~*less,* senz'aria. ~*y, a.* arioso, leggiero; *(idle)* ozioso, capriccioso

aisle, *n.* navata, *f. side* ~, *n.* laterale.

ajar, *a.* socchiuso. *be* ~, star socchiuso.

akimbo, *ad.: to set one's arms* ~, mettersi le mani alle anche. *with arms* ~, colle mani alle anche.

akin, *a.* congiunto, parente, affine.

alabaster, *n.* alabastro, *m.* ¶ *a.* alabastrino.

alacrity, *n.* alacrità, *f.*

alarm, *n.* allarme, avvertimento, *m.*; spavento, *m.* ~ *bell,* campana martello, *f.*, campanello d'allarme, *m.* *alar[u]m clock,* sveglia, *f.* ¶ *v.t.* allarmare; impaurire, spaventare. ~*ing, a.* allarmante; impressionante; spaventevole.

alas, *i.* ohimè, ahimè.

alb, *n.* camice, *m.*

albatross, *n.* albatro, *m.*

albino, *n.* albino, *m.*, **a,** *f.*

album, *n.* album, *m.*

aibumen, *n.* albume, *f.* **albumin,** *n.* albumina, *f.*

alchemist, *n.* alchimista, *m.* **alchemy,** *n.* alchimia, *f.*

alcohol, *n.* alcool, *m.* ~*ic, a.* alcoolico.

alcove, *n.* alcova, *f.*

alder, *n.* ontano, *m.*

alert, *a.* vigilante, attento. *on the* ~, all'erta.

Alexandria, *n.* Alessandria d'Egitto, *f.* **Alexandrian & Alexandrine,** *a.* alessandrino.

alfresco, *ad. & a.* al fresco, arioso.

algebra, *n.* algebra, *f.*

Algeria, *n.* l'Algeria, *f.* **Algerian,** *a.* algerino. ¶ *n.* algerino. **Algiers,** *n.* Algeri, *m.*

alias, *ad.* detto, altrimenti detto. ¶ *n.* nome assunto, pseudonimo, *m.*

alibi, *n.* alibi, *m.*

alien, *a.* alieno, altro, contrario; estraneo, straniero, forestiero;

esotico. ¶ *n.* straniero, forestiere, *m.*

alienate, *v.t.* alienare.

alight, *a.* acceso, illuminato. ¶ *v.i.* scendere, atterrare, posarsi. ~ *on the water (seaplane)* ammarare.

align, *v.t.* allineare. ~**ment,** *n.* allineamento, *m.*

alike, *a.* simile, pari, uguale. ¶ *ad.* parimente, similmente, allo stesso modo. *to be* ~, rassomigliarsi.

alimentary, *a.* alimentario. **alimony,** *n.* pensione alimentaria, *f.*, assegnamento alimentario, *m.*

alive, *a.* vivo, vivente, in vita, vitale; desto, sveglio, vivace; sensibile, vegeto, rigoglioso. *no man* ~, nessuno al mondo. *to be* ~ *with vermin,* brulicare di vermini.

alkali, *n.* alcali, *m.*

all, *a.* tutto, intero, totale. ~ *the year round,* per tutto l'anno. ~ *those who,* tutti quelli che, quanti. *at* ~ *hours,* a tutte le ore, fuor di tempo; circa mezzanotte. *on* ~ *occasions,* ad ogni occasione. *on* ~ *fours,* carponi. ¶ *ad.* tutto, del tutto, interamente. ~ *at once,* tutto a un tratto, tutto d'un tratto. *once for* ~, una volta per sempre. ~ *but, ad.* quasi, poco meno che, press'a poco, poco manca che; *pr.* fuori, meno, eccetto. ~ *but he,* tutti meno lui. ~*right,* va bene, benissimo. ~ *the better,* tanto meglio. ~ *the same,* nondimeno, con tutto ciò, pure, tuttavia. *it is* ~ *the same to me,* per me fa lo stesso, è tutt'una per me. ¶ *n.* tutto. ~ *of us,* noi tutti, tutti i nostri. *that is* ~, ecco tutto, è tutto dire. *that is not* ~, questo non è tutto, c'è dell'altro. *is that* ~? non c'è altro? *one's* ~, tutte le proprie sostanze, tutti i suoi averi. 2, 3 ~ (*Ten.*), 2, 3 per parte. Cf. *love* ~, ~ *change!,* si cambia! ~ *clear,* (*Mil.*) cessato l'allarme. ~ *in,* tutto compreso. ~*in wrestling,* lotta americana, *f.* ~ *told* or ~ *in* ~, tutto sommato, tutto quanto, in tutto.

allay, *v.t.* reprimere; calmare, alleviare; scemare, diminuire.

allegation, *n.* allegazione, *f.* **allege,** *v.t.* allegare, addurre, citare.

allegiance, *n.* lealtà, fedeltà, *f.*

allegoric[al], *a.* allegorico. **allegory,** *n.* allegoria, *f.*

alleviate, *v.t.* alleviare, alleggerire. **alleviation,** *n.* alleviazione, *f.*

alley, *n.* vicolo, viale, *m.*; chiassuolo.

alliance, *n.* alleanza, lega, unione, *f.*

alligator, *n.* alligatore, *m.*

allocate, *v.t.* assegnare, stanziare. **allocation,** *n.* assegnamento, *m.*

allot, *v.t.* assegnare; distribuire; destinare. ~**ment,** *n.* assegnazione; ripartizione, *f.*; pezzo di terra, *m.*

allow, *v.t.* permettere, autorizzare; ammettere; soffrire, lasciare; concedere; fare. ~**ance,** *n.* permesso, *m.*; tolleranza; gratifica, *f.*; assegno; sconto, *m.*; indennità, *f.*

alloy, *n.* lega, *f.* ¶ *v.t.* mescolare (con bassi metalli); ridurre.

all-round, *a.* compiuto, perfetto.

allspice, *n.* pimento, *m.*

allude to (*to*), *v.i.* alludere (a), riferirsi (a).

allure, *v.t.* allettare, attrarre, attirare. ~**ment,** *n.* allettamento, *m.*

allusion, *n.* allusione, *f.*

alluvion, alluvium, *n.* alluvione, *f.*

ally, *n.* alleato, *m.* ¶ *v.t.* alleare, apparentare; collegare, congiungere. *v.i.* allearsi, apparentarsi, imparentarsi (con.).

almanac, *n.* almanacco; lunario, calendario, *m.*

almighty, *a.* onnipotente. *the Almighty,* l'Onnipotente, Dio onni potente, *m.*

almond, *n.* mandorla, *f.* ~ *eyes,* occhi a mandorla. ~ *tree,* mandorlo, *m.*

almost, *ad.* quasi, presso che, press'a poco, poco meno che, poco manca che, vicino a.

alms, *n.s. & pl.* elemosina, limosina; carità, *f.* ~*giving,* il fare l'elemosina, *m.* ~*house,* ospizio de' poveri, *m.*

aloe, *n.* aloe, *m.*; (*pl.*) succo d'aloe, *m.*

aloft, *ad.* su, sopra, in alto.

alone, *a.* solo, solitario, solingo. *to let* (or *leave*) ~, lasciar stare, lasciar tranquillo, lasciar in pace, non toccare. ¶ *ad.* solo, soltanto, solamente.

along, *pr. & ad.* lungo, per. ~*side of* (*pers.*), accanto a, accosto di. ~*side* [*the ship*], bordo a bordo. *to come* ~ *side,* abbordare. ~ *the road,* per la strada, per la via. *all* ~ *the road,* per tutta la strada. *come* ~ *with me,* venga con me, venga insieme con me. *come* ~! via, andiamo! su via! presto! *all* ~, tutto il tempo. *to get* ~, fare progressi.

aloof, *ad.* da banda, da parte, a distanza. ¶ *a.* lontano, rifuggente, alieno. *to stand* ~, starsene da banda, *to keep* ~, tenersi a distanza.

aloud, *ad.* a voce alta.

alpaca, *n.* alpaca, *m.*

alpha, *n.* alfa, *m.* **alphabet,** *n.*

alfabeto; abbiccí, *m.* ~ical, *a.* alfabetico.

Alpine, *a.* alpestre, alpino. **the Alps,** le Alpi, *f.pl.*

already, *ad.* già, di già.

Alsace, *n.* l'Alsazia, *f.* **Alsatian,** *a.* alsaziano. ¶ *n.* (*pers.*) alsaziano; (*dog*). cane-lupo, *m.*

also, *ad.* anche, pure, altresí, parimente.

altar, *n.* altare, *m.* ~cloth, paliotto, *m.*; tovaglia da altare, *f.* ~piece, ancona, pala d'altare, *f.*

alter, *v.t.* alterare, cangiare, mutare, cambiare; trasformare, variare. *v.i.* alterarsi, cangiarsi, cambiare, cambiarsi, trasformarsi, mutarsi. ~ *the date of* (*function, &c.*), trasferire. ~ation, *n.* alterazione, *f.*, cambiamento, mutamento, *m.*; trasformazione, *f.*

altercation, *n.* altercazione, *f.*, diverbio, battibecco, *m.*

alternate, *a.* alterno, vicendevole, scambievole. ~ *months* (*newspaper appearing*), bimestrale. ¶ *v.t. & i.* alternare; alternarsi, avvicendarsi. **alternating,** *p.a.* alternante; (*current, Elec.*) alternato. **alternative,** *a.* alternativo, vicendevole. ¶ *n.* alternativa, *f.*

although, *ad. & c.* benché, sebbene, quantunque, ancorché, malgrado che.

altitude, *n.* altezza, altitudine, *f.*

alto, *n. & ~saxhorn,* alto, *m.* ~clef, chiave di do, *f.*

altogether, *ad.* tutt'insieme, affatto, totalmente, interamente, in tutto, in totale.

altruist, *n.* altruista, *m.* ~ic, *a.* altruistico. **altruism,** *n.* altruismo, *m.*

alum, *n.* allume, *m.*

aluminium, *n.* alluminio, *m.*

always, *ad.* sempre.

amalgam, *n.* amalgama, *m.* ~ate, *v.t.* amalgamare. **amalgamation,** *n.* amalgamazione, *f.*

amanuensis, *n.* amanuense, copista, segretario, *m.*

amass, *v.t.* ammassare, adunare.

amateur, *n.* amatore, dilettante, *m.* ~ *status,* qualità di dilettante, *f.* **amatory,** *a.* amatorio, erotico.

amaze, *v.t.* stupire, stordire, sbalordire; impressionare, sorprendere, meravigliare. ~ment, *n.* stupore, *m.*, meraviglia, *f.*

Amazon (*woman*), *n.* amazzone, *f.* **the ~** (*river*), le Amazzoni, *f.pl.*, fiume delle Amazzoni, *m.*

ambassador, -dress, *n.* ambasciatore, *m.*, -trice, *f.*

amber, *n.* ambra, *f.* ~gris, *n.* ambra grigia, *f.*

ambiguity, *n.* ambiguità, *f.*, equivoco, *m.* **ambiguous,** *a.* ambiguo, dubbioso, equivoco.

ambition, *n.* ambizione, *f.* **ambitious,** *a.* ambizioso.

amble along (to), ambiare, andare al passo.

ambrosia, *n.* ambrosia, *f.*

ambulance, *n.* ambulanza, *f.*

ambuscade, ambush, *n.* imboscata, *f.*, agguato, *m.* **to ambush,** *v.t.* mettere in imboscata, in agguato; fare, tendere un'imboscata a, per. *to lie in ambush,* imboscarsi, mettersi in agguato.

ameer, *n.* emiro, *m.*

ameliorate, *v.t.* migliorare. **amelioration,** *n.* miglioramento, *m.*

amen, *i. & n.* amen, *i. & m.*

amenable, *a.* responsivo, trattabile, docile; responsabile; esposto, soggetto (a), passibile. ~ *to a fine,* passibile di multa.

amend, *v.t.* emendare, correggere, rettificare, migliorare. *v.i.* riformarsi ~s, *n.* ammenda, compensa, *f.* *make ~ for,* riparare, fare ammenda di, risarcire.

amenity, *n.* amenità, *f.* **amenities,** *n.pl.* comodità, *f.pl.*

America, *n.* l'America, *f.* **American,** *a.* americano. ~ *cloth,* tela cerata, *f.* ¶ *n.* americano.

amethyst, *n.* ametista, *f.* ¶ *a. &* ~ine, d'ametista, ametistino.

amiability, *n.* amabilità, gentilezza, *f.* **amiable,** *a.* amabile, gentile. **amiably,** *ad.* gentilmente.

amicable, *a.* amichevole.

amid, amidst, *pr.* a mezzo a, in mezzo a, fra, tra; dentro, nel corso di. **amidships,** *ad.* a mezza nave.

amiss, *ad. & a.* male. *something ~,* qualche guaio, qualche cosa di male. *come ~,* far male. *nothing comes ~ to him,* tutto gli va per il suo verso. *take ~,* aver a male.

ammonia, *n.* ammoniaca, *f.*

ammunition, *n.* munizioni, *f.pl.* ~ *wagon,* vettura-cassone, *f.*, carro di munizioni, retrotreno di cassone, *m.*

amnesty, *n.* amnistia, *f.*

among, amongst, *pr.* fra, tra; in; in mezzo a; nel numero di, del n. di; presso, da. ~ *strangers,* spaesato.

amorous, *a.* amoroso, innamorato.

amorphous, *a.* amorfo, informe.
amortization, *n.* ammortizzazione, *f.*
amortize, *v.t.* ammortizzare.
amount, *n.* montante, *m.* somma, quantità, *f.* ¶ *v.i.* ammontare, montare, sommare; valere (*amount to*), venire a, ridursi a ~*ing to*, ammontare a.
ampere, *n.* ampere, *f.* **ampersand,** *n.* il segno &; congiunzione commerciale (*Typ.*).
amphibian, *n.* anfibio, *m.* **amphibious,** *a.* anfibio.
amphitheatre, *n.* anfiteatro, *m.*
ample, *a.* ampio. ~**ness,** *n.* ampiezza, *f.* **amplifier** (*Radio*), *n.* amplificatore, *m.* **amplify,** *v.t.* & *i.* amplificare. **amplitude,** *n.* ampiezza; (*Phys., Astr.*) amplitudine, *f.*
amputate, *v.t.* amputare. **amputation,** *n.* amputazione, *f.*
amulet, *n.* amuleto, *m.*
amuse, *v.t.* divertire, distrarre, svagare, ricreare. ~**ment,** *n.* divertimento, diporto, passatempo, spasso, svago.
an, *indef. art. or a.* un, uno, *m.*, un', una, *f.*
Anacreon, *n.* Anacreonte, *m.*
anachronism, *n.* anacronismo, *m.*
anaemia, *n.* anemia, *f.* **anaemic,** *a.* anemico.
anaesthetic, *a.* & *n.* anestetico, *a.* & *m.* **anaesthesia,** *n.* anestesia, *f.*
anagram, *n.* anagramma, *m.*
analogous, *a.* analogo. **analogy,** *n.* analogia, *f.*
analyse, *v.t.* analizzare; (*Bkkpg.*) fare lo spoglio di. **analysis,** *n.* analisi, *f.* **analyst,** *n.* (*Chem.*) analizzatore; (*Math.*) analista, *m.* **analytic(al),** *a.* analitico.
anarchic(al), *a.* anarchico. **anarchist,** *n.* anarchista, *m.* **anarchy,** *n.* anarchia, *f.*
anatomical, *a.* anatomico. **anatomy,** *n.* anatomia, *f.*
ancestor, *n.* avo, antenato, progenitore. **ancestral,** *a.* avito, ereditario, degli antenati, degli avi. **ancestry,** *n.* stirpe, schiatta, prosapia, razza; famiglia, *f.*
anchor, *n.* àncora, *f.* ¶ *v.t.* & *i.* ancorare, ancorarsi. **anchorage,** *n.* ancoraggio, *m.*
anchoret, anchorite, *n.* anacoreta, *m.*
anchovy, *n.* acciuga, *f.* ~ *paste,* acciugata, *f.*
ancient, *a.* antico. ¶ *n.* anziano. ~**ness,** *n.* antichità, *f.*

and, *c.* (*abb.* &), e, ed, &. ~ *even,* anzi, eppure (~ yet). ~ *so on* or ~ *so forth,* e via dicendo, e così di seguito. *to go* ~ *see,* andare a vedere. *Mr. so-*~*-so,* il signor tal-dei tali. *more* ~ *more,* di più in più. *two* ~ *two,* a due a due. *steak* ~ *potatoes,* bistecca con patate.
andiron, *n.* alare, *m.* (*com.* -i, *pl.*).
anecdote, *n.* aneddoto, *m.*, storiella, *f.*, raccontino, *m.*
anemone, *n.* anemone, *m.*
aneroid [barometer], barometro aneroide, *m.*
anew, *ad.* di nuovo, da capo.
angel, *n.* angelo. ~ *skin,* pelle delicata, fine, morbida. ~**ic(al),** *a.* angelico. **angelica** (*Bot.*), *n.* angelica, *f.* **angelus** [bell], Ave Maria, avemaria *or* avemmaria, *f.*
anger, *n.* collera, stizza, *f.*, sdegno, *m.*, ira, rabbia, *f.*, furore, *m.* ¶ *v.t.* mettere in collera, adirare, muovere ad ira, irritare, provocare a sdegno.
angina, *n.* angina, *f.* ~ *pectoris,* a. pectoris.
angle, *n.* angolo, canto; cantone, cantonata (*of building or street*). ~ *iron,* cantonale, ferro d'angolo, *m.*
angle, *v.i.* pescare coll'amo. ~ *for,* pescare, pescare per (*lit. & fig.*). **angler,** *n.* pescatore, *m.*
Anglican, *a.* anglicano. **Anglicanism,** *n.* anglicanismo, *m.*
angling, *n.* pesca coll'amo, arte del pescare, *f.*; il pigliar pesci coll'amo, *m.*
Anglomania, *n.* anglomania, *f.* **Anglophil(e),** *a.* & *n.* anglofilo, *a.* & *m.* **Anglophobia,** *n.* anglofobia, *f.* **Anglo-Saxon,** *a.* & *n.* anglo-sassone, *a.* & *m.f.*
angrily, *ad.* stizzosamente, crucciatamente. **angry,** *a.* incollerito, adirato, stizzito, irato, crucciato. *to get* (or *be*) ~, adirarsi, sdegnarsi, impermalirsi. *to be* ~ *with oneself for,* rimproverarsi di, rinfacciarsi di.
anguish, *n.* angoscia, *f.*
angular, *a.* angolare.
aniline, *n.* anilina, *f.* ~ *dye,* tinta d'anilina, *f.*
animal, *a.* animale. ¶ *n.* animale, *m.*
animate, *a.* vivo, vivente. ¶ *v.t.* animare. **animation,** *n.* animazione, *f.*
animosity, animus, *n.* animosità, ostilità, *f.*, malanimo, *m.*
aniseed, *n.* anici, *m.pl.,* liquore d'anici, *m.*
ankle, *n.* caviglia, *f.,* malleolo, *m.;*

stinco (*shin*). ~*sock*, calzino, *m.*,
calzettina, *f.*
annals, *n.pl.* annali, fasti, *m.pl.*
anneal, *v.t.* ricuocere, rinvenire,
~**ing,** ricottura, *f.*, rinvenimento, *m.*
annex, *v.t.* annettere, attaccare,
aggiungere. ~**ation,** *n.* annessione,
f. **annex[e],** *n.* annesso, *m.*
annihilate, *v.t.* annientare, annichilare, distruggere. **annihilation,** *n.*
annientamento, annichilamento, *m.*
anniversary, *a. & n.* anniversario,
a. & m.
annotate, *v.t.* annotare, chiosare,
postillare. **annotation,** *n.* annotazione, chiosa, postilla (*marginal a.*), *f.*
announce, *v.t.* annunziare. ~**ment,**
n. annunzio, *m.*, annunziamento,
avviso, *m.* **announcer** (*Radio*), *n.*
annunciatore, *m.*
annoy, *v.t.* annoiare, seccare, infastidire, incomodare, disturbare. *to be*
~*ed with,* avere a noia. ~**ance,** *n.*
noia, seccatura, *f.*, disturbo, *m.*
~**ing,** *a.* noioso, fastidioso, seccante,
importuno.
annual, *a.* annuo, annuale. ¶ *n.*
annuale; (*book*) annuario, *m.*
annuitant, *n.* chi gode d'un assegno
annuale, d'un vitalizio annuale.
annuity, *n.*
annualità, *f.*, assegno annuale, *m.*,
pensione annuale, *f. life* ~, vitalizio,
m.
annul, *v.t.* annullare. ~**ment,** *n.*
annullamento, *m.*; cassazione, *f.*
annum, *n.: per* ~, all'anno, ogni anno.
Annunciation (**the**), (l')Annunzia-
zione, *f.*
anode, *n.* (*Elec.*) anodo, *m.*
anodyne, *a.* anodino. ¶ *n.* anodino,
lenitivo, *m.*
anoint, *v.t.* ungere, unguentare;
sacrare. ~**ed,** *a. & n.* unto,
unguentato; spalmato; sacrato.
anomalous, *a.* anomalo. **anomaly,**
n. anomalia, *f.*
anon, *ad.* fra poco, all'istante, subito
subito. *ever and* ~, ogni tanto.
anonymous, *a.* anonimo.
another, *a. & pn.* altro, *m.*, -a, *f.*;
un altro, *m.*, un'altra, *f.*; nuovo,
secondo. *one* ~, l'un l'altro.
answer, *n.* risposta, *f.*, riscontro, *m.*;
(*acknowledgment*), replica, *f.* ~*s to
correspondents,* piccola posta, *f.*
~ *to the riddle,* soluzione del-
l'enigma, della sciarada. ¶ *v.t.*
rispondere a; corrispondere; servire
a. ~ [*back*], replicare. *it will never
answer* (*it won't do*), così non va,
non può stare. ~ *for,* rispondere,

essere responsabile (per, di), essere
(entrare) mallevadore (per), rendersi
(stare) garante di. ~**able,** *a.*
responsabile.
ant, *n.* formica, *f.* ~ *eater,* *n.*
formichiere, *m.* ~*hill,* *n.* formi-
colaio, *m.* ~*lion,* *n.* formicaleone,
m. ~*'s nest,* *n.* formicaio, *m.*
antagonism, *n.* antagonismo, *m.*,
ostilità, *f* **antagonist,** *n.* antagoni-
sta, *m.* **antagonize,** *v.t.* rendere
ostile.
antarctic, *a.* antartico. *the A* ~ *ocean,*
l'oceano Glaciale Antartico, *m.*
antecedent, *a. & n.* antecedente,
a. & m.
antechamber, *n.* anticamera, *f.*
antedate, *v.t.* antidatare.
antediluvian, *a.* antidiluviano.
antelope, *n.* antilopa, -e, *f.*
ante meridiem (*abb.* a.m.), *ad.* prima
di mezzogiorno, avanti mezzodì.
¶ *a.* antimeridiano.
antenna, *n.* antenna, *f.*
anterior, *a.* anteriore.
anteroom, *n.* anticamera, *f.*
anthem, *n.* salmo, *m.*, antifona, *f.*;
(*national*) inno, *m.*
anther, *n.* antera, *f.*
anthology, *n.* antologia, *f.*, florilegio,
m., crestomazia, *f.*
anthracite, *n.* antracite, *f.* ~ *stove,*
n. stufa ad antracite, a carbone
incombustibile, *f.*
anthrax, *n.* antrace, *m.*
anti-aircraft, *a.* antiaereo.
antic, *n.* (*pl.*) capriole, sgambettate,
scimmiottate, stravaganze, *f.pl.*,
eccessi, *m.pl.*
antichrist, *n.* anticristo, *m.* *the A* ~,
l'A.
anticipate, *v.t.* anticipare, precedere,
prevenire. **anticipation,** *n.* anticipazione, previsione, *f.*
anticlimax, *n.* (figura per la quale si
scende da un concetto o argomento
più forte ad uno più debole).
anticyclone, *n.* anticiclone, *m.*
anti-dazzle lamp *or* **light,** faro
anti-abbagliante, *m.*
antidote, *n.* antidoto, contravveleno,
m.
anti-French, *a.* gallofobo.
antimony, *n.* antimonio, *m.*
antipathetic, *a.* antipatico. **antipathy,** *n.* antipatia, avversione, *f.*
antipodes, *n.pl.* antipodi, *m.pl.* (*lit. &
fig.*).
antiquary, antiquarian, *n.* anti-
quario, *m.* **antiquated,** *a.* antiquato, di moda passata, di foggia

antica. **antique,** *a.* antico. ¶ *n.*
(*style*) antico, *m.*; (*relic*) antichità, *f.*,
oggetto antico, *m.*, anticaglia, *f.*
antiquity, *n.* antichità, *f.*, evo
antico, *m.*

antirrhinum, *n.* antirrino, *m.*, bocca
di leone, *f.*

antiseptic, *a. & n.* antisettico, *a. &
m.*

antithesis, *n.* antitesi, *f.* **anti-
thetic(al),** *a.* antitetico, *pl.* ci.

anti-toxin, *n.* anti-tossina, *f.*

antler, *n.* corno di cervo, *m.* ~s, *n.pl.*
palchi, *m.pl.*

Antwerp, *n.* Anversa, *f.*

anus, *n.* ano, *m.*

anvil, *n.* ancudine, *f.*

anxiety, *n.* ansia, ansietà, *f.*, affanno,
m., ambascia, *f.*; sollecitudine,
premura, *f.* **anxious,** *a.* ansio,
ansioso, inquieto; sollecito, premuroso. *to be ~ about,* disturbarsi
per; essere sollecito di. ~ly, *ad.*
ansiosamente.

any, *a. ad. & pn.* qualche, qualunque,
qualsiasi; del, dello, della, dei, degli,
delle, ne; alcuno, piú. *has he ~?*
ne ha? ~ *farther,* ~ *further,* piú
lontano. ~ *more,* ancora; (*neg.*) piú.

anybody, anyone, *n. & pn.* qualcuno,
taluno, chiunque, alcuno; gente, *n.f.*;
chichessia.

anyhow, *ad.* in ogni caso, in qualsiasi
modo; alla rinfusa, senza distinzione.

anything, *pn. & n.* qualcosa, qualche
cosa, alcuna cosa; chechessia, (*neg.*)
niente, nulla. ~ *but,* tutt'altro che.

anywhere, *ad.* dovunque, in qualche
luogo, dove che sia; (*neg.*) da
nessuna parte.

aorta, *n.* aorta, *f.*

apace, *ad.* presto, speditamente, a
gran passo.

apart, *ad.* da parte, in disparte, da
banda. ~ *from,* eccezione fatta di;
separato da.

apartment, *n.* stanza, camera, *f.*
~s, alloggio, appartamento, *m.*

apathetic, *a.* apatico. **apathy,** *n.*
apatia, *f.*

ape, *n.* scimmia, *f.*, scimmiotto, *m.*,
bertuccia, *f.* ¶ *v.t.* scimmiottare.

aperient, *n.* aperitivo, aperiente, *m*

aperture, *n.* forame, buco, *m.*,
apertura, *f.*

apex, *n.* apice, *m.*, cima, *f.*

aphorism, *n.* aforismo, *m*

apiary, *n.* apiario, *m.*

apiece, *ad.* a testa, per ciascuno.

apish, *a.* scimmiesco.

apogee, *n.* apogeo, *m.*

apologetic, *a.* apologetico. ~s, *n.pl.*
apologetica, *f.* **apologize,** *v.i.*
apologizzare, scusarsi. *I beg to ~,*
La prego di scusarmi. ~ *to her,*
le faccia le sue scuse. **apology,** *n.*
apologia, scusa, *f.*

apoplectic, *a. & n.* apoplettico, *a. &
m.* ~ *fit,* colpo apoplettico, colpo
di apoplessia, *m.* **apoplexy,** *n.*
apoplessia, *f.*

apostasy, *n.* apostasia, *f.* **apostate,**
n. apostata, *m.* ¶ *a.* apostatico,
pl. -ci.

apostle, *n.* apostolo, *m.* *the A~s'
Creed,* credo apostolico, *m.* **aposto-
late, apostleship,** *n.* apostolato, *m.*
apostolic(al), *a.* apostolico.

apostrophe, *n.* (*address*) apostrofe, *f.*;
(*punct.*) apostrofo, *m.* **apostrophize,** *v.t.* apostrofare.

apothecaries' measure, misura
farmaceutica, *f.*

apothecary, *n.* farmacista, *m.*

apotheosis, *n.* apoteosi, *f.*

appal[l], *v.t.* spaventare, impaurire,
atterrire. **appalling,** *a.* spaventevole.

apparatus, *n.* apparato, apparecchio;
(*notes, &c.*) corredo, *m.*

apparel, *n.* vestimenti, abiti, *m.pl.*,
vestiario, *m.* *wearing ~,* oggetti di
vestiario, *m.pl.*

apparent, *a.* apparente, evidente,
visibile; illusorio; (*heir*) presuntivo.
~ly, *ad.* apparentemente, a (*or* per)
ciò che pare, a quanto pare.

apparition, *n.* apparizione, *f.*, fantasma, spettro, *m.*

appeal, *n.* appello, ricorso, richiamo,
m.; supplicazione, preghiera, *f.*;
attrattiva, *f.*, fascino, *m.*, incanto, *m.*
¶ *v.i.* appellare, fare appello,
richiamarsi, ricorrere (a); supplicare,
pregare. *I ~ to you,* me ne appello
a Lei.

appear, *v.i.* apparire, mostrarsi,
comparire, presentarsi; (*seem*)
sembrare, parere. *it would ~ that
. . . ,* a quanto pare . . . ~ance,
n. apparenza, comparsa, venuta, *f.*;
aspetto, *m.*, sembianza, parvenza,
aria, *f.* ~s, apparenza, *f.*, convenienze esteriori, *f.pl. to keep up ~s,*
salvar l'apparenza.

appease, *v.t.* calmare, placare,
acquietare, mitigare, tranquillizzare.

appellation, *n.* denominazione, *f.*,
nome, titolo, *m.*

append, *v.t.* appendere, apporre,
attaccare, aggiungere. ~age,
appendix, *n.* appendice, aggiunta, *f.*;

annesso, *m.* **appendicitis,** *n.* appendicite, *f.*

appertain, *v.i.* appartenere, spettare, riferirsi (a), essere proprio (di).

appetite, *n.* appetito, gusto, *m.*, inclinazione, *f.* **appetizer,** *n.* aperitivo, *m.* **appetizing,** *a.* appetitoso, piacente, gustoso.

applaud, *v.t.* applaudire, approvare; gridare (viva). **applause,** *n.* plauso, applauso, *m.*, lode, approvazione, *f.*

apple, *n.* mela, *f.*, pomo, *m.*; (*eye*) globo (dell'occhio), *m.* ~ **orchard,** *n.* meleto, *m.* ~ **tree,** melo, *m.*

appliance, *n.* apparecchio, mezzo, ordigno, arnese, *m.*

applicant, *n.* postulante, candidato, aspirante, *m.* **application,** *n.* applicazione, domanda, richiesta, *f.*; rapporto, *m.*, relazione, *f.*; messa in opera, *f.*; diligenza, cura, *f.*; (*brake*) frenaggio, *m.* ~ **form** (*for shares*) bollettino di sottoscrizione, *m.*

applied (*of sciences*), *a.* applicato, **appliqué lace,** [trina d'] applicazione, *f.* **appliqué [work]** (metal), applicato, *m.* **appliqué** (*or* **applied**) **work** (*Emb.*), ricamo applicato, *m.*

apply, *v.t.* applicare, adattare, apporre; (*brake*) mettere. ~ **for,** chiedere, cercare, domandare, richiedere, sollecitare; sottoscrivere. (*to*) ~ *oneself,* dedicarsi, darsi, mettercisi (con impegno), attendere a. ~ **to,** rivolgersi a, indirizzarsi a.

appoint, *v.t.* nominare, assegnare; fissare, stabilire. ~**ment,** *n.* appuntamento, fissato, *m.*; nomina, *f.*, impiego, posto, *m. he missed his* ~, mancò all'appuntamento. ~*s & promotions,* nomine e promozioni. *by* ~ (*official*), per ordine, per decreto.

apportion, *v.t.* distribuire, dispensare; compartire, scompartire, spartire.

apposite, *a.* apposito, acconcio, adatto.

apposition, *n.* apposizione, *f.*

appraise, *v.t.* valutare, stimare, periziare. ~**ment,** *n.* valutazione, *f.* apprezzamento, *m.*, stima, perizia (*expert skill*), *f.* **appraiser,** *n.* stimatore, esperto, perito; ammiratore, *m.*

appreciable, *a.* sensibile, percettibile; considerevole. **appreciably,** *ad.* sensibilmente.

appreciate, *v.t.* apprezzare, pregiare, stimare, riconoscere; (*v.i.*) aumentare, aumentare di valore. *I do not appreciate it, it does not suit me,*

it is not to my taste, non mi va a genio. **appreciation,** *n.* apprezzamento, *m.*; stima, riconoscenza, *f.*; aumento di valore, *m.*

apprehend, *v.t.* apprendere, capire, intendere, comprendere; credere, supporre; temere; prendere, arrestare, cogliere. **apprehension,** *n.* apprendimento, *m.*; comprensione, intelligenza, *f.*; apprensione, preoccupazione, *f.*, timore, *m.*; presa, *f.*, arresto, *m.*

apprentice, *n.* apprendista, allievo, novizio, *m.*; (*Naut.*) mozzo, *m.* ¶ *v.t.* collocare. ~**ship,** *n.* noviziato, tirocinio, *m.*

apprise, *v.t.* avvertire, avvisare, informare, ragguagliare.

approach, *n.* accostamento, avvicinamento; accesso, abbordo. ¶ *v.t.* avvicinarsi a, accostarsi a, appressarsi a; approssimarsi a; (*v.i.*) avvicinarsi, accostarsi, appressarsi. ~**able,** *a.* accessibile, di facile abbordo.

approbation, *n.* approvazione, *f.*

appropriate, *a.* convenevole, proprio, acconcio, adatto. ¶ *v.t.* appropriarsi; afferrare, rubare.

approval, *n.* approvazione, *f. on* ~, *a prova.* **approve,** *v.t.* approvare, assentire a, ratificare, sanzionare; lodare. ~*d school,* casa di correzione, *f.*

approximate, *a.* approssimativo. ~**ly,** *ad.* circa, quasi, all'incirca. **approximation,** *n.* approssimazione, *f.*

apricot, *n.* albicocca, *f.* ~ **tree,** *n.* albicocco, *m.*

April, *n.* aprile, *m. to make an* ~ *fool of,* giocare un pesce d'aprile a.

apron, *n.* grembiale, grembiule, *m.*

apropos, *ad.* a proposito.

apse, *n.* abside, *f.*

apt, *a.* atto, adatto, acconcio; pronto, intelligente; disposto, proclive. ~**ly,** *ad.* giustamente, bene a proposito. ~**ness,** *n.* giustezza, prontezza, *f.* **aptitude,** *n.* attitudine, disposizione, *f.*

aqua fortis, *n.* acqua forte, *f.* **aquamarine,** *n.* acquamarina, *f.* **aqua regis,** *n.* acqua regia, *f.*

aquarium, *n.* aquario, *m.*

aquatic, *a.* (*plant*) acquatico, (*sport*) nautico.

aqueduct, *n.* acquedotto, *m.*

aqueous, *a.* acqueo, acquoso.

aquiline, *a.* aquilino.

Arab, *a.* arabo. ¶ *n.* arabo, *m.*

arabesque, *n.* arabesco, rabesco (*com. pl.* -eschi). **Arabia,** *n.* (l')Arabia, *f.* **Arabian,** *a.* arabo, arabico, *pl.* -ci. ~ *gulf*, Golfo arabico, *m.* *the* ~ *nights*, le Mille e una notte. ¶ *n.* arabo, *m.* **Arabic** (*language*), *n.* l'arabo, *m.* **Arabic numerals,** cifre arabiche, *f.pl.*

arable, *a.* arabile.

arbiter, *n.* arbitro, *m.* **arbitrage** & **arbitrament,** *n.* arbitrato, arbitramento, *m.* **arbitrary,** *a.* arbitrario. **arbitrate,** *v.t.* arbitrare. **arbitration,** *n.* arbitrato, *m.*, sentenza arbitrale, *f.* ~ *clause*, clausola compromissoria, *f.* **arbitrator,** *n.* arbitro, *m.*

arbor, *n.* (*Mech.*) albero, *m.*, coppaia, *f.*, asse, *m.*

arbour, *n.* frascato, pergolato, *m.*

arc, *n.* arco, *m.* ~ *lamp*, *n.* lampada ad arco, *f.*

arcade, *n.* arcata, *f.*, colonnato, *m.*

arch, *a.* furbo, furbetto, maliziosetto. ¶ *n.* arco, *m.* ¶ *v.t.* inarcare, curvare, piegare; (*v.i.*) incurvarsi.

archaeologic(al), *a.* archeologico. **archaeologist,** *n.* archeclogo, *m.* **archaeology,** *n.* archeologia, *f.*

archaic, *a.* arcaico.

archangel, *n.* arcangelo, *m.*

archbishop, *n.* arcivescovo, *m.* **archbishopric,** *n.* arcivescovado, -ato, *m.*

archdeacon, *n.* arcidiacono, *m.*

archer, *n.* arciere, *m.* ~y, *n.* tiro all'arco, *m.*

Archimedean screw, *n.* vite d'Archimede, *f.*

archipelago, *n.* arcipelago, *m.*

architect, *n.* architetto, *m.* **architectural,** *a.* architettonico. **architecture,** *n.* architettura, *f.*

archives, *n.pl.* archivio, *m.s.*

archly, *ad.* furbamente, da maliziosetta. **archness,** *n.* astuzia, finezza, *f.*

archway, *n.* arcata, *f.*, arcale, *m.*, passaggio arcato, *m.*, volta, *f.*

arctic, *a.* artico. *the* A~ *Ocean*, l'oceano [Glaciale] Artico, *m.*

ardent, *a.* ardente. ~ly, *ad.* ardentemente. **ardour,** *n.* ardore, *m.*

arduous, *a.* arduo.

are, see *be.* ~ *you there?* (*Teleph.*) olà! chi parla?

area, *n.* area, circoscrizione, *f.*, spazio, *m.*; (*Theat.*) platea, *f.*

arena, *n.* arena, *f.*, circo, teatro, anfiteatro, *m.*

argentine, *a.* argentino. A~ (*Geog.*),

a. argentino. ¶ *n.* argentino, *m.* *the* A~, *n.* l'Argentina, *f.*

argue, *v.i.* & *t.* argomentare, discutere, disputare, ragionare; arguire. **argument,** *n.* argomento, *m.*, discussione, *f.*; dibattimento, *m.*; dibattito, *m.*, sunto, sommario, *m.* ~ation, *n.* disputa, *f.*, disputazione, *f.*, ragionamento, *m.* ~ative, *a.* disputativo.

aria (*Mus.*), *n.* aria, *f.*

arid, *a.* arido. ~ity, *n.* aridità, *f.*

aright, *ad.* correttamente, rettamente, bene, giustamente.

arise, *v.i.* *ir.* alzarsi, levarsi; nascere, sorgere, crescere; accadere, avvenire, succedere, sopravvenire; provenire, derivare, procedere.

aristocracy, *n.* aristocrazia, *f.* **aristocrat,** *n.* aristocratico, *m.* **aristocratic(al),** *a.* aristocratico.

arithmetic, *n.* aritmetica, *f.* ~al, *a.* aritmetico. ~ian, *n.* aritmetico, *m.*

ark, *n.* arca, *f.* *the* A~ *of the Covenant*, l'arca dell'Alleanza, *f.* *Noah's* ~, arca di Noe, *f.*

arm, *n.* (*limb*) braccio, *m.* (*f.pl.*) -cia; (*of cross*, *sea*, *river*, &*c.*), *m.pl.* -ci; (*weapon*), arma, arme, *f.* (*pl.* -i); (*pl. Her.*) scudo gentilizio, *m.*, armi gentilizie, *f.pl.*, stemma, *m.*; (*of chair*, &*c.*) bracciuolo, *m.* ~ *in* ~, a braccetto. *to be up in* ~s, incollerirsi, montare in collera; essere alle prese (con), essere in rivolta. ~ *chair*, sedia a bracciuoli, poltrona, *f.* ~*hole*, giro della manica, *m.* ~*pit*, ascella, *f.* ¶ *v.t.* armare, munire, fortificare; (*v.i.*) armarsi, vestirsi l'armatura, prendere le armi.

armadillo, *n.* armadillo, *m.*

armament, *n.* armamento, *m.*, armatura, *f.*

armature, *n.* (*Phys.*) armatura, *f.*; (*dynamo*) indotto, *m.*

Armenia, *n.* l'Armenia, *f.* **Armenian,** *a.* armeno. ¶ *n.* armeno, *m.*

armful, *n.* bracciata, *f.*

armistice, *n.* armistizio, *m.* A~ *Day*, giorno dell'armistizio, anniversario dell'armistizio, *m.*

armlet, *n.* braccialetto, *m.*

armorial, *a.* & *n.* araldico, *a.*, araldica, *f.*, libro d'araldica, *m.* ~ *bearings*, stemma gentilizio, *m.*, armi gentilizie, *f.pl.*

armour, *n.* armatura, *f.*; (*sheathing*) blindaggio, *m.* ~ *plate*, corazza, *f.* ~ *plating*, corazzatura, *f.* ~ed, *a.* corazzato, blindato. ~ *car*, carro

armato, *m.*, carro blindato, *m.* **~er,** *n.* armaiuolo, *m.* **~y,** *n.* armeria; galleria d'armi. *f.*

army, *n.* esercito, *m.*, armata, *f.* ~ *contractor*, fornitore dell'esercito, *m.* ~ *service corps*, commissariato, *m.* *in the* ~, sotto le armi. *to join the* ~, andar soldato.

arnica, *n.* arnica, *f.*

aroma, *n.* aroma, *m.* **aromatic,** *a.* aromatico.

around, *ad.* attorno, intorno, in giro. ¶ *pr.* attorno a, intorno a.

arouse, *v.t.* destare, svegliare, risvegliare; stimolare, ravvivare, far sorgere, far nascere.

arpeggio, *n.* arpeggio, *m.*

arraign, *v.t.* citare (chiamare) in giudizio, accusare, riprendere.

arrange, *v.t.* disporre, aggiustare, sistemare; stabilire, fissare; accomodare, assettare; (*Mus.*) ridurre. **~ment,** *n.* disposizione, *f.*, accomodamento, assetto, *m.*; (*Mus.*) riduzione, *f.*

arrant, *a.* notorio, perfetto, matricolato; (*but rendered gen. by aug.* arci-, *e.g.* arcibriccone, *a. rogue*, arcifanfano, *a. boaster, braggart, or* -one, *e.g.* scioccone, *a. fool*).

arras, *n.* arazzo, *m.*

array, *n.* ordine, *m.*, schiera, *f.*; abbigliamento, *m.* ¶ *v.t.* schierare, disporre; costituire; abbigliare (*of dress*).

arrears, *n.pl.* arretrato, *m.* gli arretrati, *m.pl. in arrear[s]*, [in] arretrato.

arrest, *n.* arresto, *m.*; sosta, sospensione, *f. under* ~, (*Civil*) in stato d'arresto; (*Mil.*) agli arresti. ¶ *v.t.* arrestare, mettere in arresto, prendere; impedire. **~er,** (*Elec., &c.*), scaricatore, *m.*

arris, *n.* spigolo, *m.*

arrival, *n.* arrivo, *m.*, venuta, *f.*

arrive, *v.i.* arrivare, giungere. ~ *unexpectedly*, sopravvenire.

arrogance, *n.* arroganza, *f.* **arrogant,** *a.* arrogante. **~ly,** *ad.* arrogantemente. **to arrogate** [**to oneself**], arrogarsi.

arrow, *n.* freccia, saetta, *f.*

arsenal, *n.* arsenale, *m.*

arsenic, *n.* arsenico, *m.* **~al,** *a.* arsenicale.

arson, *n.* incendio doloso, *m.*

art, *n.* arte, *f.*; tecnica, *f.*; artificio, *m.* astuzia, *f.* ~ *needlework*, lavori d'ago fino, *m.pl.* ~ *school*, scuola (accademia) delle Belle Arti, *f.*

arterial (*Anat.*), *a.* arteriale, arterioso. ~ *road* (*Eng.*), strada nazionale, *f.*

artery, *n.* arteria, *f.*

Artesian, *a.* artesiano.

artful, *a.* astuto, furbo, scaltro, artificioso. ~ *dodger*, furbo matricolato, briccone, furfante, *m.* **~ness,** *n.* astuzia, scaltrezza, *f.*

arthritis, *n.* artrite, *f.*

artichoke, *n.* carciofo, *m.*

article, *n.* articolo, oggetto; capo, *m.*; (*pl.*) articoli, *m.pl.*; statuto, *m.*; (*pl. ship's*) ruolo d'equipaggio. **~s of association,** statuto (della società anonima). ~ [*of luggage*], collo, *m.* **~d clerk,** apprendista, *m.* **leading** ~, articolo di fondo, *m.*

articulate, *a.* articolato. ¶ *v.t.* articolare, pronunziare (distintamente), staccare; (*v.i.*) articolarsi; esprimersi. **articulation,** *n.* articolazione, *f.*

artifice, *n.* artificio, artifizio, *m.* ordigno, *m.*; stratagemma, *m.*

artificer, *n.* artefice, artigiano, *m.*

artificial, *a.* artificiale.

artillery, *n.* artiglieria, *f.* **~man,** *n.* artigliere, *m.*

artisan, *n.* artigiano.

artist & **artiste**, *n.* artista, *m.f.* **artistic,** *a.* artistico. ~ *novelties*, articoli di novità, *m.pl.* **~ally,** *ad.* artisticamente.

artless, *a.* ingenuo, semplice, innocente.

Aryan, *a.* ariano.

as, *ad.* & *c.* come, siccome, mentre, poiché, che; quale, per quanto; (= *what*) ciò che, quello che; da, per, a titolo di, in via di. ~ . . . ~, così . . . come, tanto . . . quanto, tanto . . . da (*with inf.*). ~ *also*, come pure. ~ [& *when*], ~ [& *when*] *required*, secondo le esigenze del caso. ~ *before*, come prima. ~ *far* ~, *pr.* fino a, sino a; (*ad.*) per quanto, in quanto, fin che non. ~ *for*, ~ *to*, ~ *regards*, quanto a, in quanto a, intorno a, per quanto riguarda, su. ~ *it were*, per così dire. ~ *long* ~, *c.* finché, fin tanto che. ~ *per*, secondo. ~ *well* ~, *c.* non che (nonché), tanto . . . che, nello stesso tempo che. ~ *soon* ~ *possible*, quanto prima. ; ~ *much* ~ *possible*, per quanto è possibile. ~ *well* ~ *possible*, il meglio possibile.

asbestos, *n.* amianto, asbesto, *m.*

ascend, *v.t. & i.* ascendere, salire, montare, risalire; crescere. **~ancy, ~ency,** & **~ant, ~ent,** *n.*

influenza, autorità morale, superiorità, f. **ascension**, n. ascensione, salita, f. A~ Day, festa dell'Ascensione, f. **ascent**, n. salita; erta, f., pendio, m.

ascertain, v.t. accertarsi, stabilire, determinare; scoprire, accorgersi.

ascetic, a. ascetico. ¶ n. asceta, m.

ascribe, v.t. ascrivere, attribuire; imputare.

ash, n. oft. pl. cenere, f., oft. pl. ceneri. ~ blonde (colour) biondo cenerino m. ~ pan, n. cassetto della cenere, m. ~ pit, n. ceneraio, m. ~ tray, n. portacenere, m.inv. ~ tree, n. frassino, m. ~ Wednesday, giorno delle Ceneri, le Ceneri.

ashamed, a. vergognoso, confuso. to be ~, vergognarsi, aver vergogna.

ashen, **ashy** (ash-coloured), a. cenerino, cenerognolo.

ashlar, n. pietra da taglio, bugna, f.

ashore, ad. a terra, a secco. to run ~, andare in secco, tirare a secco.

Asia, n. l'Asia, f. ~ Minor, l'A~ minore. **Asiatic**, a. asiatico. ¶ n. asiatico, m.

aside, ad. a parte, in disparte, da parte, da banda. ¶ n. to put ~, mettere da parte, riserbare; eccettuare, rigettare. to set ~, mettere da parte; (Law) annullare (giudizio). to turn ~, v.t. stornare, distrarre; (v.i.) deviare, voltarsi da parte. to step ~, farsi da parte.

ask, v.t. domandare, chiedere; invitare, pregare; interrogare, sollecitare, richiedere. to ~ a question, fare (rivolgere) una domanda. ~ not to come (guests), disinvitare, rivocar l'invito.

askance, ad. a traverso, a sbieco. look ~ at, guardare di traverso, guardare di sbieco; guardare di mal'occhio.

askew, ad. a traverso, stortamente.

aslant, ad. obliquamente, in modo sghembo, a sghimbescio.

asleep, a. addormentato. to fall ~, addormentarsi.

asp, n. (serpent) aspide, m.; (tree) tremula, f.

asparagus, n. asparago, sparagio, m. ~ tongs, pinze da asparagi, f.pl.

aspect, n. aspetto, m., apparenza, vista, figura, f.; lato, m.

aspen, n. tremula, f.

asperity, n. asperità, f.

asperse, v.t. aspergere, spruzzare; calunniare. **aspersion**, n. calunnia, f.

asphalt, n. asfalto, m. ¶ v.t. asfaltare.

asphyxia, n. asfissia, f. **asphyxiate**, v.t. asfissiare.

aspirant, n. aspirante, m.f. **aspirate**, v.t. aspirare. **aspiration**, n. aspirazione, f. to aspire to, aspirare a.

aspirin, n. aspirina, f.

ass, n. asino, ciuco, m.; (she) asina, f. ass's foal, asinello, m. ass's (or asses') milk, latte d'asina, m.

assail, v.t. assalire. **assailant**, n. assalitore, m., -trice, f.

assassin, n. assassino, m. ~ate, v.t. assassinare, uccidere, ammazzare. ~ation, n. assassinio, m., omicidio, m.

assault, n. assalto, m. ~ & battery, percosse e ferite, vie di fatto, f.pl. take by ~, prendere d'assalto. ¶ v.t. assalire.

assay, n. saggio, assaggio, m., prova, f. ¶ v.t. assaggiare. ~er, n. saggiatore, assaggiatore, m.

assemblage, n. concorso, m.; calca (di gente), folla, f.; adunamento, m. **assemble**, v.t. adunare, radunare, convocare, raccogliere, riunire; ammassare; (v.i.) adunarsi, radunarsi, raccogliersi, riunirsi. **assembly**, n. assemblea, adunanza, f.

assent, n. consenso, assenso, m., approvazione, f. to ~ to, assentire a, consentire a, dare l'assenso a, approvare.

assert, v.t. asserire, affermare, sostenere; rivendicare (right[s], &c.). **assertion**, n. asserzione, affermazione; rivendicazione, f.

assess, v.t. tassare, censire; fissare. ~ment, n. tassa, f., censo, m., imposta, f.

asset, n. articolo dell'attivo. ~s, (pl.) attivo, m., attività, f.pl., fondi, m.pl., beni mobili ed immobili, m.pl., proprietà disponibile, f.

assiduity, n. assiduità, f. **assiduous**, a. assiduo. ~ly, ad. assiduamente.

assign, n. ¶ v.t. assegnare, designare, delegare. ~ation, n. assegnazione, f., attribuzione, f., appunto (promissory note); convegno, m. ~ee, n. cessionario, curatore, mandatario, m. ~ment, n. assegno, assegnamento, m., cessione, f.

assimilate, v.t. assimilarsi, assimilare, assist, v.t. aiutare, dare aiuto, soccorrere, assistere; dare man forte. ~ance, n. aiuto, soccorso; (to police) man forte. ~ant, n. assistente, aggiunto. ~ master, sottomaestro, *m.* ~ *mistress*, sottomaestra, *f.* ~ *station-master*, sotto capo-stazione, *m.*

assize, *n.* **assizes,** *n.pl.* assise, *f.pl.*

associate, *n.* socio, compagno; (*professor*) aggiunto; straordinario. ¶ *v.t.* associare, unire; (*v.i.*) associarsi (con), praticare (con), frequentare. **association,** *n.* associazione, unione, compagnia, *f.*, comizio, consorzio, *m.* A ~ *football*, giuoco del calcio, *m.*

assort, *v.t.* assortire, scompartire. ~**ment,** *n.* assortimento, scompartimento, *m.*, scelta, *f.*

assuage, *v.t.* calmare, placare, sedare, mitigare, quietare.

assume, *v.t.* assumere, arrogarsi; sopporre, congetturare. ~*d name*, nome di guerra, *m.* **assuming,** *a.* presuntuoso. **assumption,** *n.* assunto, *m.*, assunzione, *f.* A ~ (*Eccl.*), *n.* Assunzione, festa dell'Assunzione, *f.*

assurance, *n.* assicurazione, certezza; arditezza, sfrontatezza, *f.* *life* ~ (*insurance*), assicurazione sulla vita. **assure,** *v.t.* assicurare, accertare, stabilire. **assuredly,** *ad.* sicuramente.

Assyria, *n.* l'Assiria, *f.* **Assyrian,** *a.* assiro. ¶ *n.* assiro, *m.*

aster, *n.* astero, *m.*

asterisk, *n.* asterisco, *m.*

astern, *ad.* a poppa, indietro.

asteroid, *n.* asteroide, *m.*

asthma, *n.* asma, *f.* **asthmatic,** *a.* asmatico, *pl.* -ci.

astigmatic, *a.* astigmatico.

astigmatism, *n.* astigmatismo, *m.*

astir, *ad. & a.* in piedi, in moto, desto.

astonish, *v.t.* stupire, sbalordire, stordire, maravigliare. ~**ing,** *a.* stupendo, meraviglioso, sorprendente. ~**ingly,** *ad.* da fare stupire, stupendamente. ~**ment,** *n.* stupore, *m.*, meraviglia, *f.*

astound, *v.t.* see **astonish.**

astray, *ad. & a.* fuor di via, smarrito, traviato. *go* ~, smarrirsi. *lead* ~, sviare, traviare.

astride, astraddle, *ad. & a.* a cavalcioni.

astringent, *a.* astringente.

astrologer, *n.* astrologo, *m.* **astrology,** *n.* astrologia, *f.*

astronomer, *n.* astronomo, *m.* **astronomic(al),** *a.* astronomico. **astronomy,** *n.* astronomia, *f.*

astute, *a.* astuto.

asunder, to tear, *v.t.* squarciare.

asylum, *n.* asilo, ricovero, rifugio, ricetto, *m.* *lunatic* ~, manicomio, *m.* *orphan* ~, orfanotrofio, *m.*

at, *pr.* a, ad, contro, in, da, di, in casa da, in casa di, presso, su. ~ *a loss, a profit*, in perdita, con una perdita, con profitto. ~ *all*, alquanto, in certo grado, in alcun grado. *not* ~ *all*, niente affatto, punto, in nessun modo. ~ *first*, da prima (dapprima), sulle prime, al principio, all'inizio. ~ *hand*, vicino, sotto mano. ~ *home*, in casa, a casa, da (me, te, lui, &c.), presso (di). ~ *last*, finalmente, alla fin fine, dopo tutto. ~ *least*, al meno. ~ *length*, (*time*) finalmente; (*space*) disteso. ~ *once*, subito, all'istante. ~ *owner's risk*, a rischio e pericolo del destinatario. ~ *sea*, sul mare, in mare; (*fig.*) smarrito. ~ *the same time*, allo stesso tempo, simultaneamente; nondimeno. ~ *war*, in guerra.

Athanasian Creed (the), il simbolo attribuito a sant'Atanasio, *m.*

atheism, *n.* ateismo, *m.* **atheist,** *n.* ateo, ateista, *m.* **atheistic,** *a.* ateo, ateistico.

Athenian, *a.* ateniese. ¶ *n.* ateniese, *m.f.* **Athens,** *n.* Atene, *f.*

athirst, *pred. a.* assetato.

athlete, *n.* atleta, *m.* **athletic,** *a.* atletico, *pl.* -ci. ~ *meeting,* ~ *sports,* riunione sportiva, gara atletica, *f.*, giuochi atletici, *m.pl.* **athletics,** *n.pl.* atletica, *f.*, esercizi atletici, *m.pl.*

at home, *ad.* in casa, a casa, da (me, te, lui, &c.). ¶ *n.* ricevimento, *m.* *her day* ~, il suo giorno di ricevimento, *m.*

athwart, *ad.* a, di *or* per traverso; obliquamente. ¶ *pr.* attraverso.

Atlantic, *a.* atlantico. ~ *liner,* transatlantico, *m.* *the* A ~ *Ocean,* l'oceano Atlantico, l'Atlantico, *m.*

atlas, *n.* atlante, *m.*

atmosphere, *n.* atmosfera, *f.* **atmospheric(al),** *a.* atmosferico, *pl.* -ci. **atmospherics** (*Radio*), *n.pl.* disturbi atmosferici, *m.pl.*

atom, *n.* atomo, *m.* ~ *bomb,* bomba atomica, *f.* ~**ic(al),** *a.* atomico, *pl.* -ci. ~**izer,** *n.* vaporizzatore, *m.*

atone for (to), *v.t.* espiare, lavare, risarcire, riparare. **atonement,** *n.* espiazione, *f.*, risarcimento, *m.*, riparazione, *f.*

atonic, a. atono.

atrocious, a. atroce. atrocity, n. atrocità, f.

atrophy, n. atrofia, f.

attach, v.t. attaccare, unire, congiungere; affezionare; (Law) staggire. attaché, n. addetto, m. ~ case, valigetta, f. attachment. n. attaccamento, m.; inclinazione, f.; affetto, m.; legame, m.; (Law) sequestro, staggimento, m.

attack, n. attacco, assalto, m. ¶ v.t. attaccare, assalire, investire; (of disease) comunicarsi, attaccarsi.

attain, v.t. conseguire, raggiungere, pervenire a, ottenere, acquistare. ~ment, n. conseguimento, raggiungimento, acquisto, m.; (pl.) cognizioni, f.pl., doti, f.pl., doni, talenti, m.pl.

attar, n. essenza (di rose), f.

attempt, n. tentativo, m.; prova, f.; saggio, sforzo, m.; (criminal) tentativo, m. to make an ~ on, fare un tentativo contro. ¶ v.t. tentare (di), cercare (di), provare (di), sforzarsi (di or per). ~ed murder, tentativo d'omicidio, m. ~ed suicide, tentativo di suicidio, m.

attend, v.t. attendere (a), assistere (a), intervenire (a), partecipare (a); accompagnare; recarsi (a). may success ~ you, che possiate riuscire. ~ to, badare (a), far attenzione (a); provvedere (a), occuparsi (di). ~ance, n. assistenza, f., intervento, servizio, m.; corteggio, m. is ~ included? è compreso il servizio? ~ant, n. servitore, custode, m., guardia, f.; (pl.) seguito, corteggio, m.; (Theat.) maschera, f., (Theat. box) maschera, f. attention, n. attenzione; cura, f., riguardo; accorgimento, m.; premura, f. to pay ~, fare attenzione, badare (a), ascoltare. attentive, a. attento; sollecito, premuroso.

attenuate, v.t. attenuare, assottigliare, scemare, diminuire.

attest, v.t. attestare, affermare. ~ation, n. attestazione, testimonianza, f.

Attic, a. attico.

attic, n. soffitta, f.

attire, v.t. abbigliamento, vestiario, m., abiti, m.pl., vestimenta, f.pl. ¶ v.t. abbigliare, vestire.

attitude, n. attitudine, f., atteggiamento, m., posa, f., postura, f., posizione, f.

attorney, n. avvocato, procuratore

legale, m. power of ~, mandato di procura, m.

attract, v.t. attrarre, attirare; cattivarsi, allettare. attraction, n. attrazione, attrattiva, f., fascino, m.; (pl.) cose interessanti, f.pl.; vezzi, m.pl. attractive, a. attraente, attrattivo, seducente; (Phys.) attrattivo.

attributable, a. attribuibile. attribute, n. attributo, m. ¶ v.t. attribuire, ascrivere; addossare, assegnare. attributive, a. attributivo. attributively (Gram.), ad. aggettivamente; in apposizione.

attrition, n. attrizione, f., tritamento, logoramento, m.

attune, v.t. accordare.

auburn hair, capelli di color castagno.

auction, n. asta, asta pubblica, f., incanto, m. ~ mart, ~ rooms, sala di vendita, f. ~eer, n. banditore, m.

audacious, a. audace. audacity, n. audacia, f.

audible, a. udibile.

audience, n. (hearing) udienza, f.; (pers.) uditorio, m.

audit, v.t. sindacare, controllare, verificare. ~[ing], n. verificazione, revisione, f.; riscontro, m., verifica, f. audition, n. udienza, f. auditor, n. revisore dei conti, verificatore, m. auditor, -tress, n. uditore, m., -trice, f., ascoltatore, m., -trice, f. auditorium, n. sala (del teatro, dei concerti, &c.), f.

auger, n. trapano, m.

aught, n. chechessia. for ~ I know, per quanto io sappia.

augment, v.t. aumentare, accrescere.

augur, n. auguro, m. ¶ v.t. presagire, pronosticare, augurare. ~y, n. augurio, m.

august, a. augusto. A~, n. agosto, m.

auk, n. alca, f.

aunt, n. zia, f. A~ Sally, testa di Turco, f.

aureole, n. aureola, f.

auricle (heart), n. auricola, orecchietta (del cuore), f. auricula, n. orecchio d'orso, m. auricular, a. auricolare.

auriferous, a. aurifero.

aurora, n. aurora, f. ~ borealis, aurora boreale.

auspice, n. auspizio, m. ~s, auspizi, m.pl. auspicious, a. auspicale, favorevole, di buon augurio.

austere, a. austero. austerity, n. austerità, f.

austral, a. australe. Australasia, n. l'Australasia, f. Australia, n.

l'Australia, *f.* **Australian,** *a.* australiano. ¶ *n.* australiano, *m.*

Austria, *n.* l'Austria, *f.* **Austrian,** *a.* austriaco, *pl.* -ci. ¶ *n.* austriaco, *m.*

authentic, *a.* autentico. ~**ity,** *n.* autenticità, *f.*

author, *n.* (*lit. & fig.*) autore, *m.*; (*fig. only*) padre, inventore, creatore, *m.* ~**ess,** *n.* autrice, *f.*

authoritative, *a.* autorevole. ~**ly,** *ad.* autorevolmente. **authority,** *n.* autorità, competenza, *f.*, diritto, *m.*, reputazione, *f.*, potere, *m.*, esempio, *m.*, influenza, *f.*, gravità, *f.*; garanzia, testimonianza, *f.* *on good* ~, di buona fonte. *to be regarded as an* ~, fare autorità. *on his* ~~~~ ~, di propria autorità, di proprio arbitrio. **the authorities,** le autorità, *f.pl.*, l'amministrazione, *f.*, il governo, *m.*

authorization, *n.* autorizzazione, *f.* **authorize,** *v.t.* autorizzare.

authorship, *n.* arte dello scrivere, *f.*, mestiere di scrittore, *m.*, professione d'autore, *f.*; letteratura, *f.*; (*fig.*) fonte, paternità, *f.*

autobiography, *n.* autobiografia, *f.*

autocracy, *n.* autocrazia, *f.* **autocrat,** *n.* autocrata, *m.* **autocratic(al),** *a.* autocratico.

autogenous, *a.* autogeno.

autograph, *n. & a.* autografo, *m. & a.* ~ *book,* albo per la raccolta di firme o di scritti autografi, *m.*

automatic(al), *a.* automatico. ~ [*delivery*] *machine,* distributore automatico, *m.* **automaton,** *n.* automa, *m.*

autonomous, *a.* autonomo. **autonomy,** *n.* autonomia, *f.*

autopsy, *n.* autopsia, *f.*

autumn, *n.* autunno, *m.* ~**al,** *a.* autunnale.

auxiliary, *a. & n.* ausiliare. *a. & m.f.*

avail, *n.* efficacia, *f.*, effetto, *m.*, utilità, *f.* *his efforts were of no* ~, i suoi sforzi furon vani. *to* ~ *oneself of,* profittare di, servirsi di, valersi di, utilizzare. *to* ~ *oneself of the services of,* servirsi, giovarsi. ~ **able,** *a.* disponibile, libero, alla mano, sotto mano; (*ticket*) valido. *this ticket is* ~ *till the end of the month,* questo biglietto vale sino alla fine del mese.

avalanche, *n.* valanga, *f.*

avarice, *n.* avarizia, *f.* **avaricious,** *a.* avaro.

avenge, *v.t.* vendicare. **avenger,** *n.*

vendicatore, *m.*, -trice, *f.* **avenging,** *a.* vendicatore, -trice.

avenue, *n.* viale, *m.*; (*fig.*) accesso, *m.*

aver, *v.t.* affermare.

average, *a.* medio. ¶ *n.* media, *f.*, comune, *m.*, avaria, *f.*; (*Marine Law*) avaria. (*Fire Insce.*) *on an* ~, in media. ~ *adjustment,* liquidazione (d'avaria). ¶ *v.t.* fare in media, ammontare in media a.

averse to, from, avverso a, contrario a. *I am averse to,* sono avverso a . . . *I am not averse to it,* non ho nulla in contrario. **aversion,** *n.* avversione, *f.*

avert, *v.t.* sviare, schermire, deviare, allontanare.

aviary, *n.* uccelliera, *f.*

aviation, *n.* aviazione, *f.* ~ *ground,* campo d'aviazione, *m.m.* **aviator,** *n.* aviatore, -trice, *m.f.*

avid, *a.* avido. ~**ity,** *n.* avidità, *f.*

avocation, *n.* mestiere, *m.*

avoid, *v.t.* evitare, scansare, schivare, sfuggire. ~**able,** *a.* evitabile, scansabile.

avow, *v.t.* confessare, dichiarare. ~**al,** *n.* dichiarazione, confessione, *f.*

await, *v.t.* attendere, aspettare.

awake, *a.* sveglio, desto. ¶ *v.t. ir.* svegliare, destare; (*v.i.*) svegliarsi, destarsi. **awaken,** *v.t.* svegliare, risvegliare, destare. ~**er,** *n.* svegliatore, *m.* trice, *f.*; (*alarm-clock*) sveglia, *f.* ~**ing,** *n.* risveglio, *m.*

award, *n.* sentenza, *f.*, giudizio, *m.*; (*at a show, &c.*) premio, *m.* ~ *of contract,* aggiudicazione, *f.* ¶ *v.t.* aggiudicare, assegnare. ~ *a medal to,* assegnare una medaglia a, decorare con una m. ~ *a prize to,* assegnare, premiare con, incoronare di. ~ *the contract for,* aggiudicare.

aware, *a., to be* ~ *of,* sapere, accorgersi di. *not to be* ~ *of,* ignorare.

away, *ad.* via, fuori; (*from home*) assente. ~ *on holiday,* in villeggiatura. *to get* ~, scampare. *to go* ~, andarsene, partire. *to make* ~ *with,* distruggere. ~ *with you!,* va via! via!

awe, *n.* timore, *m.*, paura riverente, *f.* ~**struck,** colpito di timore e d'ammirazione, impaurito. ¶ *v.t.* ispirare timore e riverenza, impaurire. **awful,** *a.* terribile, spaventevole.

awhile, *ad.* un pezzo, qualche tempo.

awkward, *a.* goffo, impacciato, malaccorto; imbarazzato, maldestro.

an ~ *position, an* ~ *question,* una posizione imbarazzante, una domanda imbarazzante. *the* ~ *age,* l'età ingrata, *f.* ~ *incident,* incidente imprevisto (inconveniente), contrattempo, *m.*

awl, *n.* lesina, *f.*

awn, *n.* resta, *f.*

awning, *n.* tenda, *f.* ~ *deck,* ponte tenda, *m.*

awry, *ad. & a.* a sghembo, storto.

axe, *n.* scure, *f.,* ascia, *f.,* accetta, *f.;* (*butcher's, executioner's*) mannaia, *f.*

axiom, *n.* assioma, *m.* ~**atic,** *a.* assiomatico.

axis, *n.* asse, *m.*

axle, *n.* asse, albero, *m.,* sala, *f.* **axle [tree],** *n.* sala della ruota, *f.,* asse della r., *m.*

ay, *i. & n.* sì, *i. & m.*

azalea, *n.* azalea, *f.*

Azores (the), le Azzorre, *f.pl.*

azure, *a.* azzurro. ¶ *n.* azzurro, *m.*

B

B, b, (bi) *f.;* (*Mus.*) *letter* si, *m.*

baa, *v.i.* belare. **baa[ing],** *n.* belamento, belato, *m.*

babble, *n.* balbettamento, *m.;* chiacchiera, ciarla, *f.;* cicaleccio, *m.* ¶ *v.i.* balbettare; chiacchierare, ciarlare, cicalare; (*stream*) mormorare; (*of hound*) abbaiare. **babbler,** *n.* ciarlone, *m.,* -a, *f.*

babel, (*fig.*) *n.* babele, frastuono, *m.,* confusione, *f.*

baboon, *n.* babbuino, *m.*

baby, *n.* neonato, infante; bambino, bimbo, bambolino, fantolino, piccino, putto, pargolo, *m.* ~ *car* (motor), topolino, *m.* ~ *carriage,* carrozzino, *m.* ~ *clothes,* fasce, *f.pl.* ~ *doll,* pupattola, bambola, *f.* ~ *face,* viso infantile, *m.* ~ *grand,* pianoforte a mezzacoda, *m.* ~ *linen,* pannolini, *m.pl.,* corredino, *m.* ~ *square,* pannolino, *m.* ~ **hood,** infanzia, *f.* ~**ish,** *a.* infantile, bambinesco.

Babylon, *n.* Babilonia, *f.* **Babylonian,** *a.* babilonese.

Bacchanalia, *n.pl.* baccanali, *m.pl.* **Bacchic,** *a.* bacchico, *pl.* -ci.

bachelor, *n.* scapolo, celibe, *m.;* (*science, &c.*) baccelliere, *m.* ~ *flat,* appartamento da scapolo, *m.* ~ *girl,* maschietta, *f.* ~**hood,** celibato, *m.*

back, *ad.* dietro, indietro, a ritroso, addietro; di ritorno. *With verbs it is often expressed by the prefix* ri-; *e.g.* ricascare, *to fall back, to relapse;* rivenire, *to come back.* ¶ *n.* dorso, dosso, *m.;* schiena, *f.,* reni, *f.pl.;* tergo, *m.,* spalle, *f.pl.,* (*book*) dorso; (*Foot.*) terzino, *m. from front to* ~, dal dinanzi al di dietro, da petto a reni. *seat with* ~ *to the engine,* posto di spalle alla macchina, *m. to travel with one's* ~ *to the engine,* viaggiare con le spalle alla macchina. *with one's* ~ *to the light,* (stare) controluce. ¶ *v.t.* appoggiare, secondare, sostenere, sussidiare; (*bill of exchange*) controfirmare, avallare (una cambiale); (*Betting*) puntare su, scommettere (su); (*v.i.*) andare (tirarsi, farsi) indietro, indietreggiare, rinculare; (*of wind*) girare (contro il sole).

back-bite, *v.i.* sparlare; (*v.t.*) diffamare, denigrare. **backbiting,** *n.* diffamazione, denigrazione, *f.,* sparlamento, *m.*

backbone, *n.* spina, *f.,* dorsale, *m.,* fil delle reni, *m.;* (*fig.*) forza, energia, *f.,* nerbo, *m.,* fermezza, decisione, *f.*

back door, porta di servizio, porta di dietro, *f.,* porta posteriore; entrata riservata, *f.*

back edge (*book*), margine di cucitura, *m.*

backer, *n.* partigiano, *m.,* protettore, *m.;* (*Betting*) scommettitore, *m.*

back fire, ritorno di fiamma, *m.*

backgammon, *n.* trictrac, *m.,* tavola reale, *f.,* sbaraglino, *m.*

background, *n.* fondo, sfondo, *m.*

backhand[ed], *a.* di rovescio, indiretto, inaspettato. ~**er,** *n.* (*Ten.*) colpo di rovescio, *m.*

backing, *n.* (*support*) sostegno, appoggio, rinforzo, *m.;* (*going back*) rinculare, ritiro, *m.,* ritirata, *f.*

back margin (*book*), margine di cucitura, *m.*

back number (*periodical*), vecchio numero, numero arretrato; (*fig.*) di moda passata.

back-pedal, *v.i.* contropedalare.

back room, retrocamera, retrostanza, stanza interna, *f.*

backsight (*gun*), *n.* alzo, *m.,* tacca di mira, *f.*

backslider, *n.* recidivo, *m.* **backsliding,** *n.* ricaduta, recidiva, *f.*

backstays (*Naut.*), *n.pl.* paterassi, paterazzi, *m.pl.*

backstitch, *n.* punto indietro, *m*

back tooth, dente mascellare, molare, *m.*

backward, *a.* tardivo, poco avanzato, arretrato, ritardato, retrogrado; (*child*) che ha progredito poco. ¶ ~, ~s, *ad,* indietro, addietro, all'indietro, a ritroso, in senso inverso. ~**ness,** *n.* tardezza, *f.,* stato arretrato, sviluppo tardivo, *m.*; svogliatezza, *f.*; esitazione, timidezza, *f.*

backwash, *n.* risacca, *f.*

back water (to), sciare [coi remi].

back-water, *n.* acqua cheta fuori della corrente principale, *f.*

bacon, *n.* lardo, *m.*; pancetta, *f.*

bacteria, *n.pl.* batteri, *m.pl.*

bad, *a.* cattivo, reo, malo, malvagio; forte, grande, grave, brutto, grosso, serio; irregolare; falso; guasto. *to go* ~ (*meat, &c.*), guastarsi, imputr:dire. ~ *debt(s),* credito inesigibile, *m.*; *pl.* -i. ~ *form,* sgarbo, *m.,* sgarbatezza, *f.*; cattivo gusto, *m.,* mal costume, scostumatezza, *f.* ~ *language,* parole grossolane, indecenti, *f.pl.,* bestemmia, *f.*; *pl.* ie. ~ *lot,* ~ *boy,* cattivo soggetto, briccone, bricconcello, *m.* ~ *time [of it],* (passare) un brutto quarto d'ora. *in a* ~ *way,* impacciato, imbarazzato; ammalato. ~ *workmanship,* rozza fattura, *f.* *piece of* ~ *workmanship,* lavoro mal fatto. *too* ~! peccato! *I am on* ~ *terms with him.* non sono nelle sue grazie. *trade is* ~, gli affari non vanno. ¶ *n.* male, *m.* *from* ~ *to worse,* di male in peggio. *to the* ~ (*out of pocket*), in perdita, scapitato. *to go to the* ~, andare a male, andare in rovina.

bade, *pass. rem. di* bid, *v.t.*

badge, *n.* distintivo, *m.,* insegna, *f.,* segno, *m.*; placca, medaglia, *f.*; emblema, simbolo, *m.*; livrea, assisa, *f.*

badger, *n.* tasso, *m.* ¶ *v.t.* annoiare, tormentare, stuzzicare, infastidire.

badinage, *n.* scherzo, *m.,* canzonatura, *f.,* motteggio, *m.,* burletta, *f.*

badly, *ad.* male, gravemente, malamente; assai, molto.

badminton, *n.* badminton, *m.*

badness, *n.* cattiveria; imperfezione, cattiva qualità; malvagità, nequizia, *f.*; (*argument, &c.*) debolezza, *f.*

baffle, *v.t.* sconcertare, frustrare; sventare (*plot, &c.*). ~ [**plate**], *n.* parafiamme, *m.*; lamiera di diaframma, *f.*; (*Radio*) schermo acustico, *m.*

bag, *n.* sacco, sacchetto, *m.*; borsa, saccoccia, valigia, *f.*; (*of game*) presa, *f.,* selvaggina, *f.* *saddle-* ~, bisaccia, *f.* ~ *snatcher,* borsaiuolo, *m.* ¶ *v.i.* insaccare, imborsare; prendere; (*v.i. trousers*) gonfiarsi. ~**ful,** *n.* saccata, *f.*

bagatelle (*trifle*), *n.* inezia, *f.*; (*game*) bagattella, *f.*

baggage, *n.* bagaglio, *m.*; (*saucy girl*) cattivella, ragazzaccia, impertinente, *f.*; (*Mil.*) bagaglie, *f.pl.*

baggy, *a.* gonfio.

bagpipe(s), *n.* cornamusa, piva, *f.*

bail, *n.* cauzione, garanzia, malleveria, sicurtà, *f.* **bail[sman]** *n.* garante, mallevadore, consegnatario, *m.* *to give* ~, *go* ~, dare (prestare, versare) cauzione, star mallevadore; portarsi garante pel rilascio sotto cauzione. *to release on* ~, rilasciare sotto cauzione. ¶ *v.t.* prestare cauzione. ~ *out,* far rilasciare sotto cauzione. ~ (*or* **bale**) [**out**] (*boat*), *v.t.* aggottare, sgottare; (*Aero.*) *v.i.* lanciarsi col paracadute. **baler,** *n.* sessola, gottazza, votazza, *f.*

bailiff, *n.* usciere addetto a un tribunale, ufficiale giudiziario; agente di polizia; fattore, *m.*

bait, *n.* esca, *f.*; (*fig.*) esca, *f.,* allettamento, inganno, *m.,* lusinga, *f.* ¶ *v.t.* inescare, adescare; stuzzicare, irritare; (*horses, &c.*) rinfrescare, alimentare, abbeverare.

baize, *n.* sargia, baietta, *f.* ~ *door,* controporta (coperta, foderata di baietta).

bake, *v.t.* (far) cuocere (al forno), infornare; cucinare, (*v.i.*) cuocersi. ~*house* *n.* forno, *m.*; (*Mil.*) panificio, *m.* **baker,** *n.* fornaio, panettiere, *m.* ~**y,** *n.* fornaio, panificio, *m.* **baking,** *n.* (*process*) cottura, panificazione, *f.*; (*batch of loaves*) fornata. ~ *powder,* *n.* lievito, *m.* ~ *tin,* teglia, *f.*

balance, *n.* bilancia, *f.*; bilancio, *m.*; saldo, *m.,* differenza, *f.*; pareggio, equilibrio, *m.* ~ *of power* (*Pol.*), equilibrio (europeo, &c.) politico, *m.* ~ *sheet,* *n.* bilancio, rendiconto, *m.* ~ *sheet & schedules,* prospetto, inventario, *m.* ~ *of trade,* bilancia del commercio, *f.* ~ *weight,* *m.* contrappeso, *m.* ~ *wheel* (*Horol.*) bilanciere, *m.* ¶ *v.t.* bilanciare, pesare; saldare, pareggiare; (*v.i.*) bilanciarsi, preggiarsi. *to* ~ *an account* (*at close of financial year*), chiudere un conto con un saldo

(di . . .). ~*d lever*, basculla, *f.*
balancing, *n.* bilanciamento, *m.*
~ *pole* (*tight rope*), bilanciere, *m.*
balcony, *n.* balcone, terrazzino, *m.*,
loggia, balconata, *f.*
bald, *a.* calvo, spelato; (*fig.*) nudo,
secco.
balderdash, *n.* ciance, fole, frottole,
f.pl., filastrocca, *f.*
baldness, *n.* calvizie, *f.*; (*fig.*) nudità.
povertà, *f.*
bale, *n.* balla, *f.* ¶ *v.t.* formare
(ridurre) in balle, imballare. ~ [*out*]
(*boat*), *v.t. see* bail.
Balearic islands, le Baleari, *f.pl.*
baleful, *a.* funesto, maligno, nocivo,
calamitoso.
balk, *n.* trave, *f.*; inciampo, *m.* ¶ *v.t.*
frustrare, sventare, impedire; evitare.
(*v.i.*) impuntarsi. *to* ~ *oneself of,*
privarsi di.
Balkan, *a.* balcanico; (*States, Peninsula*) dei Balcani. **the** ~s, i Balcani,
m.pl., la Balcania, *f.*
ball, *n.* palla, *f.*, pallone, *m.*, pallotta,
pallottola, ballotta, sfera, *f.*; (*eye,
lightning*) globo, *m.*; (*thumb*) polpa-
strello, *m.*; (*pendulum*) disco, *m.*
(*wool, string*) gomitolo, *m.*; (*Danc.*)
ballo, *m.* ~ *& socket* [*joint*],
articolazione sferica, snodatura
sferica, *f.* ~ *bearings,* cuscinetti
a sfere, *m.pl.* ~ *cartridge,* cartuccia
a pallottole, *f.* ~ *cock,* chiave a
galleggiante, *f.* ~ *frame,* abbaco, *m.*
~ *room,* sala da ballo, *f.* ¶ *v.t.*
appallottolare.
ballad, *n.* (*poem*) ballata, *f.*; (*song*)
canzone, canzonetta, romanza, *f.*
ballast, *n.* (*road, Rly.*) zavorra,
ghiaia, *f.*; (*Build.*) zavorra di
muratura, *f.*; (*Naut., Aero.*) zavorra,
f.; (*fig.*) fermezza, saldezza, *f.*
¶ *v.t.* zavorrare, caricar di zavorra.
ship in ~, bastimento in zavorra.
ballet, *n.* balletto, *m.* ~ *dancer,*
ballerino, -a, *m.f.* ~ *skirt,* gonnellino, *m.*
balloon, *n.* pallone, aerostato, *m.*
~ *fabric,* tela da pallone, *f.* ~ed,
(*dress*) gonfio. ~ing, *n.* aerostazione, *f.* ~ist, *n.* aeronauta, *m.*
ballot, *n.* scrutinio, *m.*, votazione, *f.*;
estrazione, *f.*, sorteggio, *m.* ~ *box,*
urna, *f.* ~ *paper,* scheda di votazione, *f.* ¶ *v.i.* votare a scrutinio
segreto. ~ *for* (*pers.*) votare a s.s.
per una persona; eleggere a sorte,
a scrutinio segreto; (*place*) tirare
a sorte; (*precedence*) tirare a sorte.
balm, *n.* balsamo, *m.*; (*fig.*) conforto,

m. ~y, *a.* balsamico, *pl.* -ci,
odoroso.
balsam, *n.* balsamo, *m.*; (*garden plant*)
balsamina, *f.* ~ [*tree*], balsamino,
m. ~ic, *a.* balsamico.
Baltic sea (**the**), il mare Baltico, *m.*
baluster, *n.* balaustro, *m.* **balustrade,** *n.* balaustrata, *f.*
bamboo, *n.* bambù, *m.*
bamboozle, *v.t.* corbellare, canzonare,
mistificare.
ban, *n.* bando, *m.*, interdizione,
scomunica, *f.* ¶ *v.t.* bandire,
interdire.
banana, *n.* banana, *f.* ~ [*plant* or
tree], banano, *m.*
band, *n.* benda, striscia, fascia, *f.*;
lista, *f.*, nastro, *m.*, (*Bookb.*) legatura,
f.; (*hat*) cordone, *m.*; banda, musica,
f.; compagnia, mano, *f.* ~ *box,*
cappelliera, *f.* ~ *brake,* freno a
nastro, *m.* ~ *saw,* sega a nastro, *f.*
~ *master,* capobanda, *m.* ~ *stand,*
palco (per bande), *m.* ¶ *v.t.* fasciare;
listare; collegare; (*v.i.*) collegarsi,
unirsi.
bandage, *n.* benda, fascia, fasciatura,
f. ¶ *v.t.* fasciare. **bandeau,** *n.*
benda, *f.*
bandit, *n.* bandito, brigante, *m.*
bandoleer, *n.* bandoliera, *f.*
bandsman, *n.* bandista, *m.*
bandy, *v.t.* rimandare, ribattere.
~ *words with,* scambiare parole con,
disputare, dibattere. ~[-legged], *a.*
storto, dalle gambe storte.
bane, *n.* guaio, flagello, *m.*, sventura,
f., danno, *m.* ~ful, *a.* funesto,
nocivo, dannoso.
bang, *n.* colpo, scoppio, gran rumore,
rimbombo, *m.* ¶ *i.* pum! paf!
¶ *v.t. & i.* sbattere, sbacchiare;
scoppiare, rimbombare; (*door*) chiudere violentemente; sbattere con
fracasso.
bangle, *n.* anello da polso, braccialetto, *m.*
banish, *v.t.* bandire. ~ment, *n.*
bando, esilio, *m.*
banister, *n.* balaustro, *m.*
bank, *n.* riva, sponda, *f.*, argine, *m.*,
alzata, *f.*; (*Fin.*) banca, cassa, *f.*;
banco, *m.* ~ *draft,* vaglia bancario,
m. ~ *holiday,* festa civile, *f.* ~ *note,*
banconota, *f.*, biglietto di banca, *m.*
~ *paper* (*writing*), carta da banca, *f.*
~ [*pass*] *book,* libretto di deposito,
m. ~ *rate,* tasso di sconto, *m.*
~ *transfer,* storno, *m.* *saving*[s] ~,
cassa di risparmio, *f.* ¶ *a.* bancario.
¶ *v.t.* arginare; deporre nella banca;

(v.i.) (*Aero.*) virare, inclinarsi in curva; (*Cards*) tener banco. ~ *on*, far assegnamento sopra. ~**er**, *n.* banchiere, *m.* ~**ing**, *n.* professione bancaria, *f.*

bankrupt, *a. & n.* fallito, *a. & m. to go* ~, far bancarotta, essere dichiarato fallito. ~**cy**, *n.* bancarotta, *f.*, fallimento, *m.*

banner, *n.* bandiera, *f.*, gonfalone, vessillo, stendardo, *m.*

banns, *n.pl.* bandi del matrimonio, *m.pl.*, publicazioni di matrimonio,*f.pl.*

banquet, *n.* banchetto, convito, *m.* ~*ing hall*, sala da banchetto, *f.*

bantam weight (*Box.*), peso gallo, *m.*

banter, *n.* motteggio, *m.*, beffa, burla, *f.* ¶ *v.t.* motteggiare, canzonare, beffeggiare.

baptism, *n.* battesimo, *m.* ~**al**, *a.* battesimale. **baptist[e]ry**, *n.* battistero, *m.* **baptize**, *v.t.* battezzare.

bar, *n.* barra, sbarra, verga, stanga, barriera, *f.*; mescita, *f.*, bar, *m.*, taverna, liquoreria, *f.*; (*Law*) foro, *m.*, professione forense, *f.*; (*Mus.*) battuta, *f.*; (*window*) spranga, traversa, sbarra, *f.*; (*counter*) banco, *m.* ~*bell*, manubrio, *m.* ~ *of the statute of limitations*, prescrizione, *f.* ~*iron*, ferro in verghe, *m.* ¶ *v.t.* sbarrare, impedire; escludere; eccettuare.

barb, *n.* punta, spina, *f.* ~[*ed*] *wire*, ferro spinato, reticolato, *m.*

Barbado[e]s, *n.* Barbados, *f.*

barbarian, *a. & n.* barbaro, *a. & m.* **barbaric**, **barbarous**, *a.* barbaro, barbaresco. **barbarism**,*n.* barbarie, *f.*; (*Gram.*) barbarismo, *m.* **barbarity**, *n.* crudeltà, selvatichezza, barbarie, *f.*

Barbary ape, scimmia di Barberia, *f.*

barber, *n.* barbiere, *m.*

barber[r]y, *n.* berbero, crespino, *m.*

Barcelona, *n.* Barcellona, *f.*

bard, *n.* (*Poet.*) bardo, vate, *m. The Bard of Avon* (Shakespeare), il cantore d'Avon, *m.*

bare, *a.* nudo, spogliato, scoperto, svestito, spolpato; semplice, solo, schietto; magro, scarso, povero; mero; (*majority*) esiguo, scarso, debole. ~*back[ed]* (*Riding*), a nudo, a pelo. ~ *back horse*, dorso nudo. ~*faced*, sfacciato, sfrontato. ~*facedly*, sfacciatamente. ~*fist boxing*, pugilato a pugni nudi, *m.* ~*foot[ed]*, scalzo, a piedi nudi. ~ *ground*, nuda terra, *f.* ~ *headed*, a capo scoperto. ¶ *v.t.* mettere a nudo,

nudare; denudare, spogliare, spolpare; (*sword, &c.*) sfoderare, sguainare. *to lay* ~ (*fig.*), rivelare, smascherare. ~**ly**, *ad.* appena, scarsamente. ~**ness**, *n.* nudità, povertà, scarsezza, *f.*

bargain, *n.* affare, accordo, patto, mercato, cambio, *m.*, convenzione, condizione, *f.* *into the* ~, di soprappiú, per giunta. ¶ *v.i.* contrattare, mercanteggiare, negoziare, patteggiare, pattuire; (*haggle*) stiracchiare. ~**er**, *n.* patteggiatore, *m.*

barge, *n.* chiatta, barca, *f.* **bargee**, **bargeman**, *n.* chiattaiuolo, barcaiuolo, *m.*

bark, *n.* (*tree*) scorza, corteccia, *f.*; (*dog*) abbaiare, abbaiamento, abbaio, *m.*; (*ship*) brigantino a palo, *m.*, (*Poet.*) nave, barca, *f.* ¶ *v.t.* scortecciare, scorzare; (*v.i.*) abbaiare. ~**ing**, *n.* (*tree*) scortecciamento, *m.*, scortecciatura,*f.*; (*dog*) abbaiamento, *m.*, abbaiata, *f.*

barley, *n.* orzo, *m.* ~ *sugar*, zucchero d'orzo, *m.* ~ *water*, tisana d'orzo, *f.*

barm, *n.* lievito, *m.*

barn, *n.* granaio, *m.* ~ *owl*, *n.* barbagianni, *m.* ~*yard*, *n.* corte del pollame, *f.*

barnacle, *n.* (*Crust.*) dattero di mare, *m.*; (*pl. spectacles*) occhiali, *m.pl.*

barometer, *n.* barometro, *m.* **barometric(al)**, *a.* barometrico.

baron, **-ess**, *n.* barone, -essa, *m.f.*

barque, *n.* brigantino a palo, *m.*

barrack, *n. oft. pl.* caserma, *f.* ~ *room*, caserma, *f.* ¶ *v.t.* alloggiare in caserma.; (*boo*) fischiare, applaudire ironicamente.

barrage, *n.* sbarramento, *m.* ~*balloon*, pallone di sbarramento, *m.*

barratry, *n.* baratteria, *f.*

barrel, *n.* barile, *m.*, botte, *f.*, fusto, *m.*; (*gun*) canna, *f.*; tubo, cilindro, *m.*, cannetta, *f.*; (*pipe, pen*) cannuccia,*f.*; (*Arch., Horol.*) tamburo, *m.* ~ *organ*, organetto a cilindro, *m.* ¶ *v.t.* imbarilare, mettere in barile, imbottare, mettere in botte.

barren, *a.* sterile. ~**ness**, *n.* sterilità, *f.*

barricade, *n.* barricata, *f.* ¶ *v.t.* barricare.

barrier, *n.* barriera, *f.*, cancello, steccato; confine, limite, *m.*

barring, *pr.* eccetto, eccettuando, eccettuato, eccezione fatta di, fuorché, salvo, tranne, non compreso.

barrister [at law], *n.* avvocato [patrocinante], *m.*

barrow, *n.* cariola, barella, *f.*; (*coster's*) carretto, *m.*; (*mound*) tumulo, *m.*

barter, *n.* baratto, cambio, *m.* ~ *goods*, merci da barattare, *f.pl.* ¶ *v.t.* barattare, cambiare, scambiare.

barytone, *n.* baritono, *m.*

basal, *a.* basico, *pl.* -ci, fondamentale.

basalt, *n.* basalto, *m.*

bascule bridge, ponte a basculla, *m.*; bilancia a ponte, *f.*

base, *a.* vile, basso, ignobile, sordido. ~ *coin*, moneta falsa, *f.* ~ *metal*, basso metallo, *m.* ¶ *n.* base, *f.*, fondamento, zoccolo, imbasamento, *m.*; principio, *m.* ~ *line* (*Ten.*), barra, *f.* ¶ *v.t.* basare, fondare, imbasare. ~**less**, infondato, senza fondamento, senza base. ~**ly**, *ad.* vilmente, in modo infame, spregevolmente. ~**ment**, *n.* fondo, sotterraneo, *m.*; sottoscala, bugigattolo, *m.* ~**ness**, *n.* bassezza, viltà, *f.*

bashful, *a.* vergognoso, timido, verecondo, modesto. ~**ness**, *n.* vergogna, modestia, timidezza, verecondia, *f.*

basic, *a.* fondamentale; (*Chem.*, *&c.*) basico, *pl.* -ci.

basil, *n.* (*Bot.*) basilico, *m.*; (*hide*) bazzana, *f.*

basilica, *n.* basilica, *f.*

basilisk, *n.* basilisco, *m.*

basin, *n.* bacino, *m.*, vasca, *f.*, catino, bacile, *m.*, catinella, bacinella, scodella, *f.*; lavabo, lavamani, *m.*

basis, *n.* base, *f.*, fondamento, *m.*

bask, *v.i.* scaldarsi; sdraiarsi (al sole, &c.).

basket, *n.* paniere, *m.*, cesta, *f.*, canestro, *m.*; bugnola, cestina, sporta, *f.*; gerla (*concal basket for bread, charcoal, &c.*), zana (*oval basket of plaited wood, for grapes, cheese, bread, &c.*), *f.* ~ *ball*, pallacanestro, *m.* ~**maker**, panieraio, cestaio, canestraio, *m.* ~**making**, ~ *work*, viminata, *f.* ~**ful**, *n.* panierata, *f.*

Basque, *a. & m.* basco. *il b*~, the Basque language.

bas-relief, *n.* bassorilievo, *m.*

bass, *n.* (*fish*) pesce persico, *m.*; (*bast*) tiglio, *m.* ~ [*voice, singer, string, tuba*], basso, *m.* ~ *clef*, chiave di fa, *f.* ~ *drum*, gran cassa, *f*

bassinet, *n.* culla, *f.*

bassoon, *n.* fagotto, *m.*

bast, *n.* tiglio, *m.*

bastard, *a.* bastardo; (*fig.*) spurio,

falso, contraffatto. ¶ *n.* bastardo, *m.* ~**y**, *n.* bastardaggine, *f.*

baste, *v.t.* (*Need.*) imbastire; (*meat*) spruzzare (l'arrosto); (*beat*) bastonare.

bat, *n.* maglio, *m.*, mazza, racchetta, *f.*; (*Zool.*) pipistrello, *m.*

batch, *n.* gruppo, *m.*, piccola schiera, *f.*, mano, *f.*; (*of loaves*) fornata, infornata, *f.*

bate, *v.t.* abbattere, ridurre, far ribassare. *with* ~*ed breath,* a voce bassa.

bath, *n.* bagno, *m.*, vasca, bagnarola, *f.*; (*tub*) tinozza, vasca da bagno, *f.* ~*s*, stabilimento di bagni, stabilimento balneare, *m.* *shower* ~, doccia, *f.*, bagno a doccia, *m.* ~ *attendant*, bagnaiuolo, *m.*, -a, *f.*, bagnino, *m.* *B* ~ *chair*, poltrona a ruote, *f.*, carrozzella da malati, *f.* ~ *gloves*, guanti di toletta, *m.pl.* ~ *gown*, accappatoio da bagno, *m.* ~*man*, bagnaiuolo, *m.* ~ *mat*, stoia da bagno, *f.* ~*room*, stanza da bagno, *f.* ~ *salts*, i sali per bagno, *m.pl.* ~ *tub*, tinozza, vasca da bagno, *f.* ~ *wrap*, accappatoio da bagno, *m.* **bathe,** *n.* bagnata, *f.* ¶ *v.t.* bagnare; (*v.i.*) bagnarsi, fare un bagno, prendere un bagno.

bather, *n.* bagnante, *m.f.* **bathing,** *n.* bagnare, bagno, *m.*, bagni, *m.pl.* ~ *box*, cabina da bagno, *f.* ~ *cap*, cuffia da bagno, *f.* ~ *costume*, ~ *suit*, ~ *dress*, costume da bagno, *m.* ~ *drawers*, mutandine da bagno, *f.pl.* ~ *machine*, cabina da bagno (a ruote), *f.* ~ *place*, posto adatto per fare un bagno, *m.* ~ *resort*, stazione balneare, *f.* ~ *slip*, calzoncino, *m.* ~ *tent*, tenda da spiaggia, *f.*

bathos, *n.* sentimento falso, *m.*; inezie, *f.pl.*

batman, *n.* ordinanza, *f.*

baton, *n.* bastone, *m.*; bacchetta, *f.*; (*relay race*) bastoncino, *m.*; (*bread*) bastoncello, *m.*

battalion, *n.* battaglione, *m.*

batten, *n.* asse, tavoletta, *f.* ¶ *v.t.* ~ *down* (*Naut.*) chiudere i boccaporti. ~ *on*, ingrassarsi di, arricchirsi di.

batter, *n.* (*cookery*) pasta, farinata, *f.*; (*Build.*) muro inclinato, declivio, *m.* ¶ *v.t.* battere, rompere, sfondare. ~**ing-ram,** ariete, *m.* ~**y,** *n.* batteria, *f.*

battle, *n.* battaglia, *f.*, combattimento, *m.* ~ **axe,** azza, *f.* ~ *cruiser,* incrociatore corazzato, *m.* ~ *field*, campo di battaglia, *m.* ~ *ship*, nave da battaglia, *f.* ¶ *v.i.* combattere, battersi, lottare, pugnare; dibattersi, sforzarsi.

battledore, *n.* racchetta, *f.* ~ *& shuttlecock*, giuoco del volano, *m.*

battlement, *n.* merlo, *m.* ~*ed*, *a.* merlato.

bauble, *n.* bazzecola, *f.*, ciondolino, *m.*; (*fool's*) scettro di follia, *m.*, balocco con sonaglio, *m.*

baulk, *n. & v.t.* Same as *balk*.

bauxite (*Min.*), *n.* bauxite, *f.*

Bavaria, *n.* la Baviera, *f.* **Bavarian**, *a.* bavarese. ¶ *n.* bavarese, *m.f.*

bawl, *v.i.* gridare, vociare, sbraitare, urlare.

bay, *a.* baio. ¶ *n.* (*horse*) cavallo baio, *m.*; (*Geog.*) baia, *f.*, seno, golfo, *m.*, insenatura, *f.*; (*Arch.*) vano, *m.*; (*tree*) lauro, *m.* *B* ~ *of Biscay*, golfo della Biscaglia, *m.* ~ *rum*, lozione aromatica per capelli, *f.* ~ *tree*, lauro, *m.* ~ *window*, finestra sporgente, *f.* *at* ~, a bada, a guardia, alle strette. *to hold at* ~, tenere a bada, tenere lontano, respingere. ¶ *v.i.* abbaiare. ~*ing*, *n.* abbaiamento, *m.*

bayonet, *n.* baionetta, *f.*

bazaar, *n.* bazar, *m.*

B.C. (*before Christ*), a.C. (avanti Cristo).

be, *v.i.* ir. essere, esistere, stare; avere, fare, farsi; andare, darsi, trovarsi. ~ *that as it may*, comunque sia. *it is . . . since*, è (sono) . . . che. *it may* ~ (*so*), può darsi. *it might* ~ *so*, potrebbe darsi. *there is* (*are*) *some*, ce n'è, ce ne sono, ve n'ha. *there is none left*, non ce n'è più. *I am leaving*, me ne vado, parto. *a · man to* ~ *feared*, un uomo da temere. *not to* ~ *confused with*, non da confondere con. *to* ~ *after*, perseguire, perseguitare. *to* ~ *hungry, thirsty, &c.*, aver fame, sete, &c. *to* ~ *off*, andarsene, partire. *be off with you!* via da qui! Fuori! andatevene! *to* ~ *well*, star bene. *for the time being*, nel frattempo, temporaneamente.

beach, *n.* lido, *m.*, riva, spiaggia, piaggia, marina, *f.*, littorale, *m.* ~*comber*, *n.* (*pers.*) girellone di spiaggia, *m.* (*wave*) cavallone, *m.* ~ *fishing*, pesca rivierasca, *f.* ~ *tent*, tenda da spiaggia, *f.* ¶ *v.t. & i.* arrenare, arrenarsi.

beacon, *n.* faro, fanale, segnale, *m.* ¶ *v.t. & i.* guidare; far lume a.

bead, *n.* grano, *m.*, perla, perlina, *f.*; (*in yarn*) bozzolino, *m.* *glass* ~*s*, perline di vetro, *f.pl. string of* ~*s*, filo di perle, rosario, *m.* *tell one's* ~*s*, recitare (dire) il rosario.

beadle, *n.* bidello, *m.*

beak, *n.* becco; sperone di nave, *m.* ~*er*, *n.* coppa, tazza, *f.*

beam, *n.* (*timber*, *&c.*) trave, *f.*; baglio; subbio, *m.*; (*plough*) stanga, *f.* (*Mach.*) bilanciere, *m.*; (*scale*) asta (di bilancia); (*ship's timber*) baglio, *m.*; (*ship's breadth*) larghezza, *f.*; (*ray*) raggio, *m.* (*rays*) raggi, *m.pl.*, fascio luminoso, fascio di raggi, *m.*; (*compasses*) asta, gamba (del compasso), *f.* *on her* ~ *ends*, ingavonato, incaponito. *to see the mote in another's eye and not the* ~ *in one's own* (Matt. vii, 3), vedere i bruscoli altrui e non le sue travi, notare il fuscello nell'occhio altrui e non veder la trave nel proprio. ¶ *v.i.* brillare, risplendere, rifulgere; raggiare, irradiare, irradiarsi.

bean, *n.* fava, *f.*, fagiuolo, fagiolino, *m. coffee* ~, chicco, *m.*, bacca di caffè, *f.*

bear, *n.* orso, *m.*, -a, *f.*; (*B*~, *Astr.*) Orsa, *f.*; (*pers.*) orso, burbero, *m.*; (*Mach.*) punzone, *m.*; (*Stk. Ex.*) ribassista, *m.* ~ *account or* ~*s* (*Fin.*), scoperto, *m.* ~ *garden* (*fig.*) tumulto, *m.*, baraonda, *f.* ~ *leader*, esibitore di orsi, *m.* ~*'s cub*, orsetto, orsacchio, orsacchino, orsacchiotto, *m.* ~*'s ear*, orecchia d'orso, *f.* ~ *skin*, pelle d'orso, *f.* ¶ *v.t.* sostenere, sopportare, reggere, portare; soffrire, tollerare, comportare, ammettere, patire, subire; rapportare, riferire; (*give birth to*) partorire. ~ (*to right*, *left*), appoggiare (poggiare), inclinarsi, a destra, a sinistra. *to* ~ *comparison with*, reggere al confronto con. *to* ~ *in mind*, tenere in mente. *to* ~ *interest*, produrre interesse. *to* ~ *witness*, attestare. ~*able*, *a.* sopportabile, tollerabile.

beard, *n.* barba, *f.*; (*Bot.*) resta, *f.*; (*Typ.*) bianco alla base, *m.* ~*ed*, *a.* barbuto. ~*less*, *a.* imberbe.

bearer, *n.* portatore, latore, *m.*; (*Fin.*) latore. ~ *cheque, share*(*s*), assegno al latore, azione, -i, al latore. ~ *of a flag of truce*, parlamentario, *m.*

bearing, *n.* portamento, contegno, piglio, aspetto, *m.*; (*Naut.*) rilevamento, *m.*; (*gait*) andatura, *f.*, portamento, *m.*, (*Mech.*, *oft. pl.*) cuscinetto, -i, *m.* & *pl.*; (*pl. Her.*) stemma, *m.*, armi gentilizie, *f.pl.* ~*rein*, imbrigliatura, *f.* ~ *surface*, superficie portante, *f.* *I have lost my* ~*s*, son disorientato, ho perduto la bussola. ¶ *p.a. bearing on*, relativo a.

beast, *n.* bestia, *f.*, animale, *m.* ~ *of burden*, bestia da soma, *f.* ~*ly*, *a.* bestiale; sporco.

beat, *n.* colpo, *m.*, battuta, *f.*; (*heart*, *pulse*, *watch*) battito, *m.*; corso, giro, *m.*, ronda, *f.*; (*Hunt.*) battuta, *f.* ¶ *v.t.* & *i.* battere, percuotere; bastonare, frustare, sferzare; (*eggs*, &*c.*) sbattere; vincere, sorpassare, superare, eccedere. (*Hunt.*) scacciare. *to* ~ *about the bush*, prenderla larga, menare il cane per l'aia; raggirarsi, battere la campagna; tergiversare. ~ *back*, ~ *off*, respingere. ~*en path*, strada battuta, *f.* *off the beaten track*, fuori di mano, isolato, appartato. ~ *a retreat*, battere in ritirata. ~*er*, *n.* battitore, *m.*; (*game*) scaccia, *m.*

beatify, *v.t.* beatificare.

beating, *n.* battimento, bastonamento, *m.*, bastonata, bastonatura, frustata, *f.*; sconfitta, *f.*; (*Hunt.*) battuta, *f.*; (*heart*, *pulse*, &*c.*) battito, *m.* ~ *rain*, pioggia battente, pioggia dirotta, *f.*

beau, *v.t.* bellimbusto, vagheggino, *m.*

beautiful, *a.* bello, vago, grazioso, avvenente, leggiadro, piacente. ¶ *n.* bello, *m.* **beautify,** *v.t.* abbellire, ornare. **beauty,** *n.* bellezza, vaghezza, *f.* *B*~ & *the Beast*, la bella e la bestia. ~ *parlour*, istituto di bellezza, *m.* ~ *spot*, luogo pittoresco, *m.*, (*mole*) neo, *m.*; (*patch on the face*) neo posticcio, *m.*

beaver, *n.* castoro, castorino, *m.*

becalmed, *a.* abbonacciato, restato in bonaccia.

because, *c.* perché, però che, perciocché, ché; a causa che, per causa che. ~ *of*, a cagione di, a causa di.

beck, *n.* ruscello, ruscelletto, *m.* *at the* ~ & *call of*, a disposizione di, agli ordini di. **beckon,** *v.i.* accennare, far segno.

become, *v.i. ir.* diventare, divenire; farsi, riuscire. *with a.* & *p.p. often rendered by pronominal form of vb.*, *as to become accustomed*, abituarsi. (*v.t. ir.*) convenire addirsi a, *what has* ~ *of him!* che ne è stato? **becoming,** *a.* convenevole, dicevole, adatto, conveniente. *this is very* ~ *to you*, questo le sta molto bene.

bed, *n.* letto; giaciglio; (*sea*) fondo; (*river*) letto, alveo; (*Geol.*) strato, giacimento, *m.*; (*Hort.*) aiuola, *f.*; (*oyster*) banco [d'ostriche], ostricaio, *m.* *camp* ~, letto da campo, *m.* *folding* ~, letto portatile, letto a ribalta, *m.* *to go to* ~, coricarsi, andare a letto. ~ *clothes*, lenzuola, *f.pl.*, lenzuoli e coperte, *m.pl.* ~ *fellow*, compagno di letto, *m.*; moglie, concubina, *f.* ~ *head*, testa, estremità del letto, *f.* ~ *jacket*, giacchettina da letto, *f.* ~ *pan*, scaldaletto; bacino da letto, *m.* ~ *plate*, lastra di fondazione, *f.* ~ *post*, colonna di letto, *f.* ~*ridden*, costretto a letto. ~*room*, camera da letto, *f.* ~*room slippers*, pantofole, ciabatte, *f.pl.* ~ *settee*, canapé, *m.* ~ *side*, sponda del letto, *f.* *at the* ~ *side*, al capezzale. ~ *side carpet*, tappetino, *m.* *a good* ~*side manner*, buone maniere professionali, *f.pl.* ~*side table*, comodino, *m.* ~ *socks*, calzette da notte, *f.pl.* ~ *sores*, decubiti, *m.pl.*, piaghe da decubito, *f.pl.* ~*spread*, coperta da letto, *f.* ~*stead*, lettiera, *f.* ~ *stone*, macina inferiore, *f.* ~*time*, ora di coricarsi, *f.* ¶ *v.t.* mettere a letto; piantare.

bedding, *n.* biancheria da letto; giacitura, stratificazione, *f.*

bedeck, *v.t.* abbellire, ornare.

bedew, *v.t.* irrorare; umettare, aspergere di rugiada.

bedizen, *v.t.* rinfronzolire, azzimare.

bedlam, *n.* manicomio, *m.*; (*fig.*) baccano, chiasso, *m.*

bedraggle, *v.t.* inzaccherare, infangare.

bee, *n.* ape, pecchia, *f.* ~ *eater*, *n.* gruccione, grottaione, *m.* ~*hive*, *n.* alveare, *m.*, arnia, *f.*, bugno, *m.* ~*keeping*, *n.* apicultura, *f.* *swarm of* ~*s*, gomitolo di pecchie, *m.* *a* ~ *in one's bonnet*, grillo, *m.*, smania, *f.*

beech [tree], *n.* faggio, *m.* ~*marten*, *n.* faina, *f.* ~*mast*, *n.* faggina, faggiuola, *f.* ~*nut*, *n.* faggiuola, *f.*

beef, *n.* manzo, *m.*, carne di bove, di bue, *f.* ~*steak*, *n.* bistecca, *f.* ~*tea*, *n.* brodo di manzo, *m.*

beer, *n.* birra, *f.* ~ *engine*, *n.* pompa da birra, *f.* ~ *shop*, *n.* birreria, bettola, *f.*

beet, *n.* bietola, *f.* ~ *sugar*, *n.* zucchero di barbabietola, *m.* *beetroot*, *n.* barbabietola, *f.*

beetle, *n.* scarafaggio, coleottero, *m.*; (*rammer*) mazzuolo; pillo. *beetling* *brows*, ciglia folte, *f.pl. beetling crag*, roccia strapiombante, *f.*

befall, *v. i. ir.* accadere, avvenire, succedere.

befit, *v.t.* addirsi a, convenire a. **befitting**, *a.* convenevole.

before, *ad.* prima, per l'addietro, per l'innanzi; avanti, davanti, innanzi. ¶ *c.* prima che, innanzi che, anziché, ¶ *pr.* prima di, innanzi, innanzi a; al cospetto di. ~ *you could say Jack Robinson* or *say knife*, in men che non si dice. ~**hand**, *ad.* in anticipo, anticipatamente, prima del tempo.

befriend, *v.t.* favorire, trattare da amico, proteggere, dare prove di amicizia a, aiutare.

beg, *v.t. & i.* mendicare, accattare; pregare, domandare, chiedere, cercare; (*Com.*) avere l'onore di. (*dog*) ~ *for*, chiedere, sollecitare; mendicare, domandare, pregare. ~ *the question*, fare una petizione di principio.

beget, *v.t. ir.* generare, procreare; cagionare, far sorgere, ingenerare.

beggar, *n.* mendicante, *m.f.*, mendico, *m.*, -a, *f.*, accattone, *m.*, -a, *f.*; (*fig.*) diavolo, *m.* ¶ *v.t.* impoverire, ridurre al verde, alla miseria. ~**ly**, *a.* gretto, meschino, ristretto, angusto. ~**y**, *n.* mendicità, *f.*, accattonaggio, *m.*; inopia, miseria, indigenza, *f. reduced to* ~, ridotto alla mendicità, alla miseria.

begin, *v.t. & i.ir.* cominciare, incominciare, iniziare, principiare, esordire, mettersi a. ~ *again*, ricominciare. **beginner**, *n.* principiante, esordiente, novizio. **beginning**, *n.* principio, inizio, cominciamento; esordio, primo passo, *m.*, prime mosse, *f.pl.*, primo tratto, *m.*; capo, *m.*, origine, causa, *f.*

begone, *i.* va via! via! andatevene!

begonia, *n.* begonia, *f.*

begrudge, *v.t.* invidiare, mostrar invidia per; lesinare.

beguile, *v.t.* ingannare, tentare, sedurre; (*charm, amuse*) divertire, distrarre.

behalf of (**on**), nell'interesse di, a favore di, a vantaggio di; dalla parte di, in nome di.

behave, *v.i. & reflexive*, comportarsi, portarsi, condursi, agire. ~ [*properly*]! (to child) sta buono! **behaviour**, *n.* comportamento, *m.*, condotta, *f.*, contegno, *m.*

behead, *v.t.* decapitare, decollare,

tagliare la testa a. ~**ing**, *n.* decapitazione, decollazione, *f.*

behest, *n.* carico, comando, *m.*

behind, *ad.* dietro, indietro, addietro, a tergo; (*horse's back*) in groppa; (*time*) in ritardo. ¶ *pr.* dietro, dietro a, dietro di; indietro di, dall'altro lato di; in groppa a. *from* ~, per di dietro, dal di dietro, da tergo. ~**hand**, *ad.* in ritardo, indietro.

behold, *v.t. & i.ir.* mirare, vedere, scorgere, rimirare, guardare. ¶ *i.* ecco! guardate! ~*en to*, grato, obbligato. ~**er**, *n.* spettatore, *m.*

behoof, *n.* interesse, vantaggio, *m.* **beho[o]ve**, *v.t. imp.* convenire a.

being, *n.* essere, *m.*, esistenza, *f.*; creatura, *f. for the time* ~, pel momento. *in* ~, vigente; in esistenza, in vita. *the Supreme B*~, l'Essere Supremo.

belabour, *v.t.* bastonare, battere.

belated, *a.* tardato, ritardato, tardivo.

belay, *v.t.* attaccare, assicurare (una fune, un cavo). *belaying-pin*, *n.* caviglia, *f.*

belch[ing], *n.* rutto, *m.* **belch**, *v.i.* ruttare; (*v.t. fig.*) eruttare, vomitare.

beldam(e), *n.* vecchiaccia, vecchia strega, *f.*

beleaguer, *v.t.* assediare, investire.

belfry, *n.* campanile, *m.*, cella campanaria, *f.*

Belgian, *a. & n.* belga, *a. & m.f.* **Belgium**, *n.* il Belgio, *m.*

Belgrade, *n.* Belgrado, *f.*

belie, *v.t.* smentire; travestire.

belief, *n.* fede, credenza, *f.*; fiducia, *f.*, credito, *m.*; opinione, *f.*, convincimento, *m.* **believable**, *a.* credibile, degno di fede. *beyond* ~, oltre ogni credere, incredibile. *to the best of my* ~, per quanto io sappia.

believe, *v.t. & i.* credere, aver fiducia in, prestar fede (a), ritenere per vero. *to make* ~, far credere, far finta, dare ad intendere. **believer**, *n.* credente, fedele, *m.f.*

belittle, *v.t.* rimpicciolire, impiccinire, impiccolire, svalutare.

bell, *n.* campana, *f.*, campanello, *m.*; (*sheep, cattle*) campanaccio, sonaglio, *m.* ~[*flower*], campanella, *f.* ~ *glass & jar*, campana di vetro, campana di giardino, *f.* ~ *mouth[ed]*, allargato, in forma di campana. ~*pull*, ~*rope*, cordone di campanello, *m.* ~*push*, bottone di suoneria, *m.* ~ *ringer*, suonatore di campane, campanaro, *m.* ~ *tent*, tenda conica, t. da campo, f. ~ *tower*, campanile, m. ~ *turret*, piccolo campanile, m. ~*wether*, montone del campanaccio, m. ¶ (*of deer*) *v.i.* bramire, muggire, gridare.

belladonna, *n.* belladonna, f.

belle, *n.* bella donna, f.

bellicose, *a.* bellicoso. **belligerent,** *a. & n.* belligerante, *a. & m.*

bellow, *v.i.* muggire, mugghiare, ruggire.

bellows, *n.pl.* soffietto, mantice, m.

belly, *n.* ventre, m., pancia, f., stomaco, m. ~*band*, sottopancia, m. ¶ *v.i.* gonfiarsi.

belong, *v.i.* appartenere (a), essere (di), spettare (a). ~*ings*, *n.pl.* beni, effetti personali, *m.pl.*

beloved, *a. & n.* caro, amato, diletto, prediletto.

below, *ad.* giú, di sotto, a basso. *here* ~, quaggiú, in terra. ¶ *pr.* sotto, al disotto di, piú in basso di; inferiore a.

belt, *n.* cintura; cinghia, f.; cinturino; cinturone, m.; fascia, f.; zona, f. ¶ *v.t.* cingere, munire di cintura, circondare. ~*ing*, *n.* cinghia, f., *pl.* -ie.

belvedere, *n.* belvedere, m.

bemoan, *v.t.* lamentare, piangere.

bench, *n.* banco; sedile, m.; panca, f.; scranna, f.; banco del giudice, m.; magistratura, f. ~ *lathe*, tornio da banco, m. ~ *mark*, segno dell'agrimensura, m. ~ *vice*, morsa da banco, f.

bend, *n.* curva, curvatura, f.; angolo, m.; svolto; giro, m.; piegata, f.; (*knot*) nodo, m. ~ *of the arm*, gomito, m. ¶ *v.t.* curvare; piegare; chinare, inchinare; (*thoughts, &c.*) dirigere, rivolgere, applicare; (*bow*) tendere; (*eye*) fissare; (*v.i.*) curvarsi, piegarsi, inchinarsi. *on* ~*ed knee[s]*, in ginocchio, sulle ginocchia, inginocchiato. ~*ing*, *n.* piegamento, m., flessione, f. ~ *of the knee*, flessione del ginocchio, f.

beneath, *ad.* di sotto, a basso, giú, al di sotto. ¶ *pr.* sotto, al di sotto di; inferiore a.

benediction, *n.* benedizione, f.

benefaction, *n.* beneficenza, f. **benefactor, -tress,** *n.* benefattore, m., -trice, f.

benefice, *n.* benefizio, m.

beneficence, *n.* beneficenza, carità, f. **beneficent,** *a.* caritatevole, generoso.

beneficial, *a.* benefico, salutare, utile. **beneficiary,** *n.* beneficiario, m.,

-a, f. **benefit,** *n.* beneficio, profitto, vantaggio, giovamento, m.; (*Theat.*) recita di beneficenza, serata d'onore, f. *margin of* ~ (*Com.*), margine di utile, m. ~ *society*, società di beneficenza, società di mutuo soccorso, f. ¶ *v.t.* giovare, beneficare, fare del bene a.

benevolence, *n.* benevolenza, f. **benevolent,** *a.* benevolo.

Bengal, *n.* il Bengala, m. ~ *light*, bengala, fuoco del Bengala, m. **Bengali, -lee,** *a. & n.* bengalese, *a. & m.*

benighted, *a.* sorpreso dalla notte; (*fig.*) avvolto nell'oscurità, ignorante.

benign, benignant, *a.* benigno. **benignly, benignantly,** *ad.* benignamente.

benjamin, *n.* benzoino, m. B~, *n.* Beniamino; (*fig.*) figlio minore, favorito.

bent, *a.* curvo, curvato, piegato, chinato, inchinato; torto, ricurvo. ~ *lever*, leva a gomito, f. ~*wood furniture*, mobili in legno curvato, *m.pl.* ¶ *n.* disposizione, inclinazione, tendenza, f., indirizzo, m. ¶ *to be* ~ *on*, essere deciso a, determinato a, portato a; fissato sopra.

benumb, *v.t.* intorpidire, intirizzire.

benzine, benzoline, *n.* benzina, f.

benzoin, *n.* benzoino, m.

benzol[e], benzene, *n.* benzolo, m.

bequeath, *v.t.* testare, disporre (legare, lasciare) per testamento; (*fig.*) trasmettere. **bequest,** *n.* legato, lascito, m., disposizione testamentaria, f.

berber[r]y, *n.* berbero, crespino, m.

bereave, *v.t. ir.* privare, spogliare; orbare. ~*ment,* *n.* perdita (di persona cara); lutto.

beret, *n.* berretto, m.

bergamot, *n.* (*orange, pear*) bergamotto, m.; (*pear*) pera bergamotta, f. ~*oil*, olio di bergamotto, m. ~*tree* (*orange*), bergamotto, m.

Bermudas (the), le Bermude, *f.pl.*

berry, *n.* bacca, f.; (*coffee*) grano, m.

berth, *n.* cuccetta, f.; posto, impiego; ancoraggio, m. *to give a wide* ~ *to*, tenersi a distanza da, evitare.

beryl, *n.* berillo, m.

beseech, *v.t. ir.* implorare, scongiurare, supplicare.

beset, *v.t. ir.* assediare, circondare, serrare; ossessionare. *besetting sin*, difetto abituale, peccato favorito, m.

beside, *pr.* accanto a, accosto a, a lato di, vicino a, presso. *he was* ~

himself with rage, era fuori di sé dalla rabbia. ~ *the mark*, fuori di proposito, male a proposito. **besides,** *ad.* inoltre, d'altronde, di piú, ancora, del resto, d'altra parte, non che. ¶ *pr.* oltre che, eccettuato.

besiege, *v.t.* assediare. **besieger,** *n.* assediante, *m.*

besmear, *v.t.* cospargere (di), ungere (di); (*fig.*) imbrattare (di).

besmirch, *v.t.* insudiciare, macchiare, sporcare, insozzare, scolorare.

besom, *n.* scopa, granata, *f.*

besotted, *a.* abbrutito, istupidito.

bespangle, *v.t.* cospargere di lustrini, stellare.

bespatter, *v.t.* spruzzare (con, di, fango, &c.), inzaccherare.

bespeak, *v.t. ir.* ordinare; sollecitare; farsi promettere. **bespoke,** *p.a.* (*su.it,* &c.) fatto (confezionato) su misura, su ordinazione; (*tailor, bootmaker*) su misura.

besprinkle, *v.t.* aspergere, cospargere, spruzzare (di).

best, *a.* il migliore, il piú perfetto, l'ottimo. ~ *man* (*wedding*), paggio d'onore, *m.* ~ *quality*, qualità scelta, *f.* ~ *seller*, libro a gran tiratura, *m.* ¶ *ad.* meglio. ¶ *the* ~, il meglio, la miglior cosa. *to make the* ~ *of it*, trarre il miglior partito da. *to have the* ~ *of it*, averne la meglio. *in one's* [*Sunday*] ~, con gli abiti migliori. *to do one's* ~, *the* ~ *one can*, fare del proprio meglio, fare il possibile.

bestial, *a.* bestiale, brutale.

bestir oneself (to), muoversi, affrettarsi; ingegnarsi, darsi da fare.

bestow, *v.t.* accordare, conferire, dare, dispensare.

bestride, *v.t. ir.* accavalciare, montare, essere a cavalcioni.

bet, *n.* scommessa, *f.* ¶ *v.t.* scommettere, fare una scommessa.

betake oneself (to), *v.refl. ir.* recarsi (a), rendersi (a), ricorrere (a), darsi (a), rifugiarsi (in, presso).

bethink oneself (to), *v.refl. ir.* ricordarsi (di); riflettere (su), considerare, mettersi a pensare.

Bethlehem, *n.* Betlemme, *f.*

betide, *v.t.* accadere (a). *whate'er* ~, qualunque cosa avvenga, comunque vada la cosa.

betimes, *ad.* presto, di buon'ora, per tempo.

betoken, *v.t.* significare, esser segno di, presagire, preannunziare.

betray, *v.t.* tradire, ingannare;

denunciare; far vedere, lasciar trasparire. ~ *one's trust*, abusare della fiducia di qualcuno. ~**al,** *n.* tradimento, *m.* ~**er,** *n.* traditore, *m.*, -trice, *f.*

betroth, *v.t.* fidanzare, promettere. ~**al,** *n.* fidanzamento, *m.* ~**ed,** *a.* & *n.* fidanzato, *m.*, -a, *f.*; promessi sposi, *m.pl.*

better, *a.* migliore, superiore; preferibile. *my* ~ *half* (*wife*), la mia metà, *f.* ~ *looking*, piú bello, piú grazioso, meglio fatto. *to be* ~ (*health*), star meglio, andar meglio. *it is* ~ *to*, è meglio, vale meglio. ¶ *ad.* meglio. *so much the* ~, tanto meglio. *to get the* ~ *of*, superare, avere la meglio di. ¶ *n.* (*pers.*), superiore, *m.f.* ¶ *v.t.* migliorare. ~**ment,** *n.* miglioramento, *m.*

better *or* **bettor,** *n.* scommettitore, *m.*, -trice, *f.* **betting,** *n.* lo scommettere, *m.*, scommesse, *f.pl.*; (*odds*) punti di vantaggio, *m.pl.*, quota, *f.*

between, *pr.* fra, tra, in mezzo a. ~ *now* & *then*, da questo momento fino a . . . ~ [*times*], ad intervalli, di tempo in tempo. ~ *decks*, corridoio, *m.*

bevel, *n.* ugnatura, *f.*, angolo, *m.*; (*Typ.*) smussatura; faccettatura, *f.* ~ [*square*], squadra falsa, *f.* ~ *wheel*, ruota ad angolo, *f.* ¶ *v.t.* tagliare ad angolo, tagliare a sbieco, ugnare; smussare.

beverage, *n.* bevanda, *f.*, beveraggio, *m.*

bevy, *n.* gruppo, stuolo, *m.*, brigata, compagnia, *f.*; (*birds*) stormo, *m.*; (*animals*) branco, *m.*

bewail, *v.t.* piangere, rimpiangere, lamentare, deplorare.

beware, *v.t.* stare in guardia (contro), stare all'erta, guardarsi (da), non fidarsi (di). ~ *of pickpockets*, attenti ai borsaiuoli! ~ *of the trains*, attenti ai treni!

bewilder, *v.t.* sbalordire, confondere, sgomentare, sconcertare, sviare.

bewitch, *v.t.* affascinare, ammaliare, incantare. ~**ing,** *a.* affascinante, incantevole. ~**ingly,** *ad.* d'incanto, incantevolmente, irresistibilmente.

beyond, *ad.* oltre, al di là, piú lungi, lontano. ¶ *pr.* oltre, al di là di, piú lungi di, dall'altro lato di. *the* ~ (*future life*), l'al di là, *m.*

bezel, *n.* castone, filo, taglio, *m.*

bias, *n.* linea obliqua, obliquità, *f.*, sbieco, *m.*; (*fig.*) parzialità, *f.*, pregiudizio, *m.*, prevenzione, *f.*

¶ *v.t.* fare inclinare da un lato; influire (su). **bias[s]ed,** *p.a.* obliquo, parziale, ingiusto.

bib, *n.* bavaglino, *m.*

Bible, *n.* Bibbia, *f.* ~ *Society*, Società per la diffusione della Bibbia, *f.* **biblical,** *a.* biblico.

bibliography, *n.* bibliografia, *f.* **bibliophil[e],** *n.* bibliofilo, *m.*

bibulous, *a.* assorbente; (*pers.*) dedito al bere.

biceps, *n.* bicipite, *m.*

bicker, *v.i.* altercare, leticare, disputare.

bicycle, *n.* (*safety*) bicicletta, *f.*; (*high*) biciclo, *m.* **bicyclist,** *n.* ciclista, biciclista, *m.f.*

bid, *n.* (*Stk. Ex.*) domanda, *f.*; (*auction*) offerta, *f.* *to make a* ~ *for,* fare un'offerta; voler cattivare (*sympathy, &c.*). ¶ *v.t. & i.ir.* comandare, ordinare; invitare; offrire; (*adieu*) dire; (*welcome*) dare; (*Stk. Ex.*) domandare. ~ *higher than,* fare un'offerta migliore di. **bidder,** *n.* offerente, concorrente (all'asta pubblica), *m.f.*

bide one's time (to), aspettare il tempo propizio, l'occasione favorevole.

biennial, *a.* biennale, bienne.

bier, *n.* bara, *f.*

bifurcation, *n.* biforcazione, *f.*

big, *a.* grosso, grande; (*tall*) alto, grande; forte; (*pregnant*) incinta; (*animals*) pregna. ~ *boned,* dalle ossa grosse. ~ *game hunting,* caccia grossa, *f.* ~ *stores,* grandi magazzini, *m.pl.* [*the*] ~ *traders,* il gran[de] commercio, *m.*

bigamist, *n.* bigamo, *m.,* -a, *f.* **bigamous,** *a.* bigamo. **bigamy,** *n.* bigamia, *f.*

bight, *n.* golfo, *m.,* insenatura, baia, *f.*; (*rope*) doppino, *m.*

bigness, *n.* grossezza, grandezza, *f.*

bigot, *n. &* ~ed, *a.* bigotto, *m.,* -a, *f.,* bacchettone, *m.,* -a, *f.* ~ry, *n.* bigottismo, *m.,* bigotteria, *f.*

bigwig, *n.* pezzo grosso, cane grosso, *m.*

bike, *n.* bicicletta, *f.*

bilberry, *n.* mortella, *f.,* mirtillo, *m.*

bile, *n.* bile, *f.*; (*fig.*) bile, stizza, *f.*

bilge, *n.* (*ship*) sentina, *f.*; (*cask*) rigonfio, *m.* ~*water,* acqua della sentina, *f.*

bilious, *a.* bilioso.

bilk, *v.t.* ingannare, truffare, evadere, scroccare.

bill, *n.* (*bird*) becco, *m.*; (*notice, &c.*) affisso, foglio, annunzio, programma, cartello, cartellone, *m.*; (*parliament*) progetto di legge, *m.*; (*account*) conto, *m.,* nota, fattura, *f.*; (*Fin.*) cambiale, *f.,* effetto, *m.,* bolletta, lettera, *f.*; mandato, *m.*; (*pl.*) cambiali, carte, *f.pl.,* effetti, *m.pl.* ~ *file,* cartella, *f.* ~ *head[ing],* intestazione di fattura, *f.* ~*hook,* roncola, *f.* ~ *of costs,* parcella, *f.* ~ *of exchange,* cambiale, lettera di cambio, *f.* ~ *of fare,* carta dei piatti, lista delle vivande, *f.* ~ *of health,* patente di sanità, *f.* ~ *of indictment* (*Law*), atto di accusa, *m.* ~ *of lading,* polizza di carico, *f.* ~ *payable, receivable,* cambiale passiva, cambiale attiva, *f.* ~ *poster,* ~ *sticker,* attacchino, *m.* stick no ~s, divieto d'affissione. ¶ *v.t.* affiggere; annunziare mediante affisso; compilare una lista di; (*v.i.*) beccarsi. ~ *& coo,* accarezzarsi.

billet, *n.* biglietto, *m.,* lettera, *f.*; posto, impiego, *m.*; alloggio, *m.*; (*Mil.*) biglietto d'alloggio, *m.*; (*pl.*) accantonamento, alloggiamento, *m.*; (*log*) ceppo (da ardere, bruciare), *m.* ¶ *v.t.* alloggiare, accantonare (presso).

billiard: ~ *ball,* palla da biliardo, *f.* ~ *cue,* stecca da biliardo, *f.* ~ *marker,* segnapunti, *m.* ~ *room,* [sala da] biliardo, *f.* ~ *table,* [tavola da] biliardo, *f.* ~s, *n.pl.* biliardo, *m.*

billingsgate, *n.* linguaggio triviale, gergo di pescivendoli, *m.*

billion (*a million millions*), bilione, *m.*

billow, *n.* onda, ondata, *f.,* maroso, *m.* ¶ *v.i.* formare marosi, ondeggiare, spumare. ~y, *a.* ondoso, tempestoso.

billy goat, caprone, *m.*

bimonthly, *a.* (*in alternate months*) bimestrale; (½ *monthly*) bimensile.

bin, *n.* madia, cantina, cassetta, *f.* *corn* ~, arca da grano, *f.*

bind, *v.t. ir.* legare, attaccare, bendare, fasciare; avvolgere, cingere; stringere, vincolare; obbligare, impegnare, far promettere; (*sheaves*) fare i covoni; (*books*) rilegare; (*paper covers*) cartonare; (*with metal*) ferrare; (*Med.*) costipare, generare stitichezza, rendere stitico. *I'll be bound,* scommetterei. *a ship* (*steamer*) *bound for* . . . , un bastimento (piroscafo) destinato a, diretto per, in partenza per . . . ~er, *n.* (*sheaf,* *pers.*) legatore, *m.*; (*Mach.*) macchina per legare i covoni, *f.*; (*book*) legatore, rilegatore, *m.*; (*tie*) legame, *m.*; (*papers*) cartella, *f.* ~ing, *a.* obbligatorio, impegnativo, valido; attaccante, stringente. *It is ~ upon me,* ho l'obbligo (di), sono obbligato (a). ¶ *n.* ri legatura, copertina, *f.*; bordo, *m.*; bordura, orlatura, *f.*; gallone, *m.*

bindweed, *n.* vilucchio, convolvolo, *m.*

bine, *n.* stelo (di pianta rampicante, del luppolo).

binnacle, *n.* abitacolo, *m.*, chiesola, *f.*

binocular, *n.* binocolo, *m.*

biographer, *n.* biografo, *m.* **biography,** *n.* biografia, vita, *f.*

biologist, *n.* biologo, *m.*, *pl.* -gi. **biology,** *n.* biologia, *f.*

biped, *n.* bipede, *m.* ~[al], *a.* bipede. **biplane,** *n.* biplano, *m.*

birch, *n.* (*tree*) betulla, *f.*; (*rod*) verghe, *f.pl.* ~ *bark,* scorza di betulla, *f.* ~ *bark canoe,* piroga, *f.* ~ *broom,* scopa di betulla, *f.* ¶ *v.t.* sferzare, staffilare. ~ing, *n.* staffilamento, *m.*, bastonatura, *f.*

bird, *n.* uccello, *m.*; (*small*) uccellino, uccelletto, *m.* ~ *call,* fischio, richiamo, *m.* ~ *catcher,* uccellatore, *m.* ~ *catching,* *n.* uccellagione, *f.*, uccellamento, *m.* ~ *fancier,* amatore d'uccelli; venditore d'uccelli, *m.* ~ *lime,* *n.* vischio, *m.*, pania, *f.*; (*v.t.*) invischiare, impaniare. ~ *of ill omen,* uccello di cattivo augurio, *m.* ~ *of paradise,* uccello paradiso, *m.* ~ *seed,* semi per gli uccelli, *m.pl.* ~'*s-eye maple,* acero macchiettato, *m.* ~'*s-eye view,* veduta a volo d'uccello, *f.* ~ *shot,* piccolo piombo da sparo, *m.* ~[*s*'] *nester,* chi va a caccia di nidi (di nidiate). ~ [*s*'] *nesting,* caccia di nidi (di nidiate), *f.*

birth, *n.* nascita, *f.*; nascimento, *m.*; origine, stirpe, *f.*; (*childbed*) parto, *m.* ~ *certificate,* certificato di nascita. ~ *control,* limitazione delle nascite, *f.* ~day, compleanno, giorno natalizio, giorno di nascita, *m.* ~mark, voglia, *f.* ~place, luogo natio, luogo di nascita, *m.* ~rate, media delle nascite, natalità, *f.* ~right, diritto di nascita, di primogenitura, *m.*

bis, *ad.* due volte; (*encore*) bis.

Biscay, *n.* Biscaglia, *f.*

biscuit, *n.* biscotto, biscottino, *m.* ~ *barrel,* ~ *box,* scatola da biscotti, *f.* ~ [*ware*], biscuit, *m.*

bisect, *v.t.* bisecare, dividere (tagliare) in due. **bisection,** *n.* bisezione, *f.*

bishop, *n.* vescovo, *m.*; (*Chess*) alfiere, *m.* ~'*s house & bishopric,* vescovado, vescovato, *m.*

bismuth, *n.* bismuto, *m.*

bison, *n.* bisonte, *m.*

bit, *n.* pezzo, pezzetto, pezzettino, *m.*; un poco, *m.*, piccola porzione, *f.* bricciolo, frammento, straccio, *m.*; pezza, *f.*; (*bread*) tozzo; (*crumb*) bricciola, *f.*; (*other food*) boccone, *m.*; (*bridle*) morso, freno, *m.*; (*borer*) chiocciola, trivella, *f.*; (*key*) ingegno della chiave, *m.*; (*iron of plane, &c.*) ferro a scalpello, *m.* ~ *of stuff* (*old or new*), pezza di stoffa, di tessuto, *f.* ~stock, trapano a mambrio, *m.*

bitch, *n.* cagna, *f.* ~ *fox,* volpe femina, *f.* ~ *wolf,* lupa, *f.*

bite, *n.* morso, *m.*, morsicatura, *f.*; (*sting*) puntura, *f.*; (*to eat*) boccone, *m.*, qualche cosa da mangiare. *I have a ~!* (*Fish.*), abbocca! ¶ *v.t. & i.ir.* mordere, morsicare; pungere.

biting, *a.* mordente; (*fig.*) piccante, pungente, sarcastico. ~ *cold,* freddo mordente, *m.*

bitter, *a.* amaro, agro, piccante, acido, pungente; (*fig.*) accanito, aspro, crudele, violento, profondo; doloroso. ~ *pill* (*fig.*) boccone amaro, *m.* ~ *sweet,* *a.* agrodolce; (*n. Bot.*) morella, *f.* ~ly, *ad.* amaramente, agramente, acerbamente; accanitamente, profondamente; (*cold*) estremamente. *it is ~ cold,* fa un freddo cane. *cry ~,* piangere amaramente, dirottamente, come una Maddalena. ~ness, *n.* amarezza, acredine, *f.*; rancore, *m.*; severità, *f.*, odio, *m.* ~s, *n.* amaro, *m.*

bittern, *n.* tarabuso, *m.*

bitumen, *n.* bitume. *m.* **bituminous,** *a.* bituminoso.

bivalve, *a. & n.* bivalve, mollusco bivalve, *m.*

bivouac, *n.* bivacco, *m.* ¶ *v.i.* bivaccare.

blab, *v.t.* divulgare; (*v.i.*) chiacchierare, ciarlare.

black, *a.* nero, scuro, tetro; negro, moro; (*fig.*) sinistro, triste, perfido, funesto, minaccioso. ~ *& blue,* ammaccato, livido. [*down*] *in ~ & white,* per iscritto. ~ball (*Voting*), palla nera, *f.*, voto contrario, *m.* ~ *beetle,* scarafaggio, *m.* ~berry, mora selvatica, *f.* ~berry bush, rovo, *m.* ~bird, merlo, *m.*; (*hen*) merla, *f.* ~*board*, tavola nera, lavagna, *f.* ~*bordered envelope*, busta listata a lutto, a nero, *f.* ~*cap* (*bird*), capinera, *f.* ~*-cock*, fagiano di monte, *m.* ~*currant(s)*, ~*currant bush*, ~*currant cordial*, ribes nero, *m.* ~*eye*, occhio pesto, *m.* *to give someone a* ~ *eye*, pestare (ammaccare) gli occhi a qualcuno. *B*~ *Forest*, Foresta Nera, *f.* ~*frost*, gelata nera, *f.* ~*guard*, mascalzone, furfante, *m.*, canaglia, *f.* ~*head*, (varietà di) gabbiano. ~*lead*, piombaggine, *f.* ~*leg*, scroccone, *m.*; (*in strikes*) crumiro, *m.* ~ *letter*, carattere gotico (*Typ.*). ~ *lines* (*under paper*), falsariga, *f.* ~ *list*, indice, *m.*; (*v.t.*) mettere all'i. ~ *magic*, ~ *art*, magia nera, *f.* ~*mail*, *n.* estorsione, *f.*, ricatto, *m.*; (*v.t.*) ricattare. ~*mailer*, ricattatore, *m.*, -trice, *f.* ~ *mark* (*bruise*) ammaccatura, contusione, *f.* ~*out*, oscuramento, *m.* ~ *pudding*, sanguinaccio, *m.* *B*~ *Sea*, Mar Nero, *m.* ~*sheep* (*fig.*), scellerato, ribaldo, *m.* ~*smith*, fabbro, maniscalco, *m.* ~*smith's shop*, smithy, officina da fabbro, maniscalcia, *f.* ~*thorn*, prugnolo, prugno salvatico, *m.* ¶ *n.* (*colour*, *man*) nero, negro, *m.*; (*ball*—*Gaming*) nero, *m.* ¶ *v.t.* annerire; (*boots*) lustrare, lucidare, dare il nero alle calzature.

blackamoor, *n.* negro, *m.*, -a, *f.*

blacken, *v.t.* annerire; (*fig.*) denigrare.

blacking, *n.* annerimento, *m.*; (*boots*) lucido, lustro, *m.* ~ *brush*, spazzola da lustrare, per dare il lucido. **blackish,** *a.* nerastro, nericcio, nerigno. **blackness,** *n.* nerezza, oscurità, *f.*

bladder, *n.* vescica, *f.* ~*wort*, *n.* otricolare, *f.* ~*wrack*, *n.* sargasso, *m.*

blade, *n.* (*grass*) filo (d'erba), *m.*; (*knife, &c.*) lama, *f.*; (*vane*) ala, *f.*, (*oar, screw, &c.*) pala, *f.*

blame, *n.* biasimo, *m.*, colpa, *f.*, responsabilità, *f.*; rimprovero, *m.* ¶ *v.t.* biasimare, rimproverare. *am I to* ~?, è colpa mia? *he has himself to* ~, deve prendersela con sé stesso. ~*less, a.* irreprensibile, senza colpa, innocente. ~**worthy,** *a.* biasimevole.

blanch, *v.t. & i.* imbiancare, fare impallidire; impallidire.

bland, *a.* blando, dolce, addolcito; (*fig.*) sdolcinato, melato. ~**ish-**

ment, *n.* blandizia, *f.*, *pl.* -ie, moina, *f.*, *gen. pl.*, -e.

blank, *a.* bianco, vuoto; confuso, sconcertato. ~ *cartridge*, cartuccia a polvere, *f.* ~ *cheque*, assegno in bianco, *m.* ~ *darkness*, ~ *silence*, profonda oscurità, *f.*, profondo silenzio, *m.* ~ *space*, spazio in bianco, *m.* ~ *verse*, versi sciolti, *m.pl.* ¶ *n.* lacuna, *f.*, spazio in bianco, *m.*; (*Com.*) modulo, *m.*; (*lottery*) biglietto rimasto senza premio; (*for coin*) piastrino, *m.*

blanket, *n.* coperta (di lana, da letto), *f.*

blare, *n.* suono (di tromba). ¶ *v.i.* risuonare; ruggire.

blarney, *n.* adulazione, *f.*, moine, *f.pl.*

blaspheme, *v.i. & t.* bestemmiare.
blasphemer, *n.* bestemmiatore, *m.*
blasphemous, *a.* bestemmiante.
blasphemy, *n.* bestemmia, *f.*

blast, *n.* vento, colpo di vento, *m.*; (*trumpet*) suono (di tromba), *m.*, strombettata, *f.*; (*bellows*) soffio, *m.*; (*explosion*) esplosione, *f.*, scoppio, *m.* ~ *furnace*, alto forno, *m.* ~*hole*, buco di mina, *m.* ¶ *v.t.* distruggere, rovinare, annientare; far saltare; far scoppiare; minare, spaccare; confondere, maledire; (*blight*) far appassire. ~*ing*, *n.* esplosione, *f.*, azione di far saltare; distruzione, rovina, *f.* ~*powder*, polvere da mina, *f.*

blatant, *a.* rumoroso, clamoroso, chiassoso, forte.

blaze, *n.* vampa, fiamma, *f.*, fuoco, *m.*, luce, *f.*, splendore, *m.* *in a* ~, in fiamme. ¶ *v.i.* avvampare, fiammeggiare; brillare, splendere, risplendere; (*v.t.*) far risplendere. ~ *a trail*, segnare una pista. ~ *abroad*, bandire, divulgare; pubblicare, far conoscere. ~ *away*, tirare senza interruzione. ~ *up*, prender fuoco, scoppiare. **blazing,** *a.* ardente, risplendente, acceso, avvampante, in fiamme.

blazon, *v.t.* blasonare; (*fig.*) propalare, pubblicare; vantarsi di. ~**ry,** *n.* araldica, *f.*

bleach, *v.t.* imbiancare, imbianchire, candeggiare. ~**er,** *n.* imbiancatore, *m.*, -trice, *f.* ~**ery,** *n.* imbiancatoio, *m.* ~**ing,** *n.* imbiancamento, candeggio, *m.* ~*ing powder*, cloruro di calcio, *m.*

bleak, *a.* nudo, esposto al vento; lugubre, triste.

blear-eyed, *a.* cisposo, dagli occhi infiammati.

bleat, *v.i.* belare. **bleat[ing],** *n.* belato, belamento, *m.*

bleed, *v.i. ir.* sanguinare, far sangue, perder sangue, versar sangue; (*v.t.*) salassare, cavar sangue. ~**ing,** *n.* emorragia, perdita di sangue, *f.*; salasso, *m.*

blemish, *n.* difetto, *m.*, macchia, magagna, *f.* ¶ *v.t.* danneggiare, macchiare, sfigurare.

blend, *n.* miscela, mescolanza, *f.* ¶ *v.t. ir.* mescolare; mischiare, confondere; (*wines*) mescolare; (*v.i. ir.*) mescolarsi; fondersi; armonizzare. ~**ing,** (*wines*), *n.* mescolamento, *m.*, mescolata, *f.*

bless, *v.t.* benedire, santificare; (*bell, &c.*) dedicare. **blessed, blest,** *a.* benedetto, santo, beato. *the Blessed Virgin* [*Mary*], la Santa Vergine, *f.* *to be* ~ *with,* essere dotato di. **blessedness,** *n.* beatitudine, *f.* **blessing,** *n.* benedizione, *f.*; bene, dono, *m.*; (*grace*) grazia, *f.* *to say a* ~ *before meals,* recitare il benedicite.

blight, *n.* golpe, ruggine, *f.*; soffio funesto, *m.*; (*fig.*) maledizione, *f.* ¶ *v.t.* ingolpare, riardere; danneggiare, guastare.

blind, *a.* cieco. ~ *alley,* vicolo cieco, *m.* ~ *blocking* (*Bookb.*), doratura a freddo, *f.* ~ *senza* colori; stampa in rilievo a secco, *f.* ~ *man, woman,* cieco, cieca, *m.f.* *the* ~, i ciechi, *m.pl.* ~*man's buff,* mosca cieca, *f.* ~ *tooling* (*Bookb.*), ferri a freddo, *m.pl.* ~*worm,* cecilia, *f.* ¶ *n.* tendina, cortina, *f.*; (*Venetian* ~*s*) gelosie, persiane, *f.pl.*; (*shop*) copertone, *m.*; (*fig.*) finta, *f.*; pretesto, velo, *m.* ¶ *v.t.* accecare; oscurare; (*dazzle*) abbagliare. ~*fold, v.t.* bendare gli occhi a. ~**ly,** *ad.* ciecamente; temerariamente. ~**ness,** *n.* cecità, *f.*, (*fig.*) accecamento, *m.* *colour* ~, daltonismo, *m.*

blink, *n.* occhiata, *f.*; (*glimmer*) barlume, *m.* ¶ *v.i.* battere le palpebre; vacillare; (*v.t.*) evitare. ~ *at,* socchiudere gli occhi a. ~**ers,** *n.pl.* paraocchi, *m.pl.*

bliss, *n.* beatitudine, gioia, felicità, *f.* ~**ful,** *a.* beato, beatifico, felicissimo.

blister, *n.* vescichetta, bolla, *f.*; (*plaster*) vescicante, *m.* ¶ *v.t.* produrre (far venire) vescichette su.

blithe, *a.* gaio, allegro, giocondo.

blizzard, *n.* tempesta di neve, *f.*, uragano, *m.*, tormenta, *f.*

bloat, *v.t.* affumicare. ~**ed,** *p.a.* gonfiato. **bloater,** *n.* or **bloated herring,** aringa affumicata, *f.*

block, *n.* blocco, *m.*, massa, *f.*; (*chopping*) ceppo, *m.*; (*shape*) forma, *f.*; (*houses*) gruppo, *m.*, isola, *f.*; (*pulley*) bozzello, *m.*; (*Typ.*) matrice, *f.*; (*stoppage*) ingombro, ostacolo, *m.* ~ *calendar,* calendario in blocco, *m.* ~ *letters* (e.g. child's writing) lettere di scatola, *f.pl.* *in* ~ *letters* (*as on coupon*), in caratteri di stampa. ~*making* (*Typ.*), stereotipia, *f.* ~ *of flats,* casamento, *m.* ~ *tin,* stagno in pani, *m.* ~ *writing,* scrivere in lettere di scatola. ¶ *v.t.* bloccare, ingombrare, ostruire; (*Bookb.*) dorare. ~*up* (*door*), murare.

blockade, *n.* blocco, *m.* ¶ *v.t.* bloccare.

blockhead, *n.* zuccone, scioccone, *m.*

blockhouse, *n.* fortino, *m.*

blocking (*Bookb.*), *n.* doratura, *f.*; (*blind*) stampa in rilievo a secco, *f.*

blockmaker (*process engraver*), *n.* zincografo, *m.*

blond, *as applied to a woman.* **blonde,** *a.* biondo, *m.*, -a, *f.* ¶ *n.* (*colour*) biondo, *m.* (*pers.*) biondo, *m.*, -a, *f.*

blood, *n.* sangue, *m.*; (*dandy*) bellimbusto, *m.* ~ *heat,* calore (normale) del sangue, *m.* ~*hound,* segugio, cane poliziotto, *m.* ~ *letting,* salasso, *m.* ~ *orange,* arancia maltese, *f.* ~ *poisoning,* avvelenamento del sangue, *m.* ~ *pressure,* tensione arteriale, pressione del sangue, *f.* ~ *red,* rosso come il sangue. ~ *relationship,* consanguineità, *f.* ~*shed,* effusione (spargimento, *m.*) di sangue, *f.* ~*shot, a.* iniettato di sangue. ~*stained,* insanguinato. ~*stone,* ematite, *f.* ~*sucker,* sanguisuga, mignatta, *f.* ~ *test,* esame del sangue, *m.* ~*thirsty,* sanguinario, assetato di sangue. ~ *transfusion,* trasfusione del sangue, *f.* ~ *vessel,* vaso sanguigno, *m.* ~*less, a.* esangue, anemico; senza spargimento di sangue. ~**y,** *a.* sanguinoso, sanguinario, insanguinato.

bloom, *n.* fiore, *m.*; fioritura, *f.* ¶ *v.i.* fiorire. ~**ing,** *a.* in fiore, fiorito; (*fig.*) fiorente. ¶ *n.* fioritura, *f.*

blossom, *n.* fiore, *m.* ¶ *v.i.* fiorire; sbocciare. ~**ing,** *n.* fioritura, *f.*

blot, *n.* macchia, *f.*, sgorbio, *m.*; difetto, *m.* ¶ *v.t.* macchiare, sgorbiare; insozzare; (*paper with useless writing*) sgorbiare; (*with blotting paper*) asciugare (con carta sugante). ~ *out*, cancellare, fare sparire.

blotch, *n.* pustola, bolla, *f.*, enfiatello, *m.*; macchia, zacchera, *f.*; pittura mal fatta, *f.*

blotting: ~ *case*, ~ *pad*, *blotter*, *n.* cartella di carta sugante, *f.* ~ *paper*, carta sugante, *f.*

blouse, *n.* blusa, *f.* ~ *front*, pettino, *m.*

blow, *n.* colpo, *m.*, botta, *f.*; urto, *m.*; (*pl.*) colpi, *m.pl.* *to come to* ~*s*, venire alle mani. ~*fly*, mosca della carne, *f.* ~*gun*, ~*pipe*, ~*tube* (*dart tube*), cerbottana, *f.* ~ *hole*, sfiatatoio, *m.* ~*pipe*, tubo, cannello, *m.* ¶ *v.t.* ir. soffiare (sopra, dentro, in); (*wind instrument*) suonare; soffiare in; (*to puff, to wind*) sfiatare, (*v.i.* ir.) soffiare, tirare (vento); (*flower*) fiorire, aprirsi, sbocciare; (*fuse*) fondersi. ~ *a horn*, suonare il corno. ~ *in*, sfondare. ~ *one's brains out*, far saltare le cervella. ~ *one's nose*, soffiarsi il naso. ~*out*, spegnere. ~*up*, gonfiare; far saltare, far scoppiare; (*v.i.*) scoppiare; gonfiarsi. ~*er*, *n.* soffiatore, *m.*; (*furnace*) valvola, *f.*, sfiatatoio, soffione, *m.*

blubber, *n.* grasso di balena, *m.* ¶ *v.i.* singhiozzare, piangere come un vitello.

bludgeon, *n.* randello, *m.*, mazza piombata, *f.*

blue, *a.* azzurro, turchino; (*sky-blue*) celeste, ceruleo. *Bluebeard*, Barbablu, *m.* ~*bell*, campanula, *f.*, giacinto salvatico, *m.* ~*bottle*, mosca della carne, *f.*, moscone, *m.* ~ *devils*, abbattimento dello spirito; delirium tremens, delirio, *m.* ~-*eyed*, dagli occhi azzurri. ~ *gum*, eucalipto, *m.* ~ *jacket*, marinaio, *m.* ~ *mark* (*bruise*), lividura, *f.* ~ *mouldy* (*cheese*), verdognolo. ~ *pencil*, *v.t.* segnare a matita azzurra; cancellare. B~ *Peter*, bandiera di partenza, *f.* ~*pill*, pillola mercuriale, *f.* ~*print*, disegno di officina, *m.*; cianografia, *f.* ~*stocking*, saccente, donna saccente, *f.* ~*tit*, cincia azzurra, *f.* ¶ *n.* azzurro, turchino, *m.*; cielo, *m.*; (*pl.*) ipocondria, *f.*, nervi, *m.pl.* ¶ *v.t.* tingere in azzurro.

bluff, *a.* brusco, franco. ¶ *n.* inganno, pretesto, *m.*; millanteria, montatura,

f.; promontorio a picco, *m.* ¶ *v.t.* ingannare, adescare; far credere. ~*er*, *n.* millantatore, *m.*

bluish, *a.* bluastro, azzurrognolo.

blunder, *n.* errore, sbaglio, fallo, *m.*, svista, *f.* ¶ *v.i.* sbagliare, sviare, commettere un errore; pigliar un granchio, prendere una cantonata; agire goffamente.

blunt, *a.* spuntato, non affilato, smussato; brusco, franco, rude. ¶ *v.t.* smussare, spuntare, ottundere. ~*ly*, *ad.* bruscamente, rudemente; improvvisamente. ~*ness*, *n.* rudezza, franchezza, *f.*; essere senza taglio (filo, punta).

blur, *n.* macchia, imbrattatura, *f.*; (*mirror*) alito, *m.* ¶ *v.t.* macchiare, confondere, sfigurare, turbare, offuscare.

blurb, *n.* soffietto editoriale, *m.*

blurred, *p.a.* indistinto, confuso, macchiato, turbato, offuscato. **blurry**, *a.* indistinto.

blurt out, *v.t.* lasciar sfuggire, scattar su a dire.

blush, *n.* rossore, rosso, *m.* *at the first* ~, a bella prima, a prima vista. ¶ *v.i.* arrossire. ~*ing*, *p.a.* arrossendo, vergognoso, rosso.

bluster, *n.* fanfaronata, millanteria, *f.* ¶ *v.i.* strepitare, smargiassare, tempestare. ~*er*, *n.* fanfarone, spaccone, rodomonte, *m.*

boa, (*wrap*) *n.* boa, *m.* ~*constrictor*, boa, *m.*

boar, *n.* verro, *m.*; (*wild*) cinghiale, *m.*; (*young wild*) cinghiale di latte, cinghialetto, *m.* ~*hound*, veltro, alano, *m.* ~*hunt[ing]*, caccia al cinghiale, *f.* ~ *spear*, spiedo da caccia, *m.*

board, *n.* asse, *f.*, tavola, *f.*; vitto, *m.*, dozzina, pensione, *f.*; (*notice*) cartello, *m.*, insegna, *f.*; (*Naut.*) bordo, *m.* *in* ~*s* (*book*), cartonato. *on* ~, a bordo. ~ *& lodging*, ~-*residence*, vitto ed alloggio, *m.*, pensione, *f.* *full* ~, pensione completa, *f.* ~ *of directors*, *f.* consiglio d'amministrazione, comitato, *m.*, giunta, *f.* ~ *of examiners*, commissione d'esame, *f.* B~ *of Trade* (*England*), Ministero del Commercio (*Italy*). ¶ *v.t.* impalcare, intavolare; prendere a dozzina (a pensione), tenere a dozzina; (*ship*) abbordare, accostare, salire a bordo di; (*train, car*) salire in; (*v.i.*) (*feed*) prendere i pasti, stare a dozzina (presso). ~ *up* (*window*,

&c.), intavolare, coprire con assi.
~er, *n.* pensionario, convittore,
dozzinante, *m.* **~ing**, *n.* intavolato,
m.; pensione, *f.*, vitto, *m.*; (*Naut.*)
abbordaggio, *m.* **~** *house*, *n.*
pensione, *f.* **~** *-in*, internato.
~ *school*, pensionato, collegio,
convitto, *m.*

boast, *n.* vanto, *m.*; (& **boasting**)
vanteria, *f.* ¶ *v.t.* vantare; (*v.i.*)
vantarsi (di). **~er**, *n.* millantatore,
vantatore, *m.*, -trice, *f.* **~ful**, *a.*
millantatore, *m.*, -trice, *f.*, vantatore,
m., -trice, *f.*, vanaglorioso, *m.*, -a, *f.*

boat, *n.* barca, *f.*, battello, *m.*; canotto,
m., lancia, *f.*; imbarcazione, *f.* **~**
deck, ponte [delle] lance, *m.* **~**
fishing, pesca a barca, *f.* **~hook**,
gancio d'accosto, *m.* **~house**, tettoia
per imbarcazioni, *f.* **~load**, barca
piena, barcata, *f.* **~man**, barcaiuolo,
battelliere, *m.* ¶ *v.i.* andare in
barca, andare in canotto. **~ing**, *n.*
canottaggio, *m.* **boatswain**, *n.*
nostromo, *m.*

bob, *n.* pendente, peso (disco) d'un
pendolo, *m.*; piccolo inchino, *m.*;
ritornello, *m.* ¶ *v.i.* muoversi a
scatti, fare un inchino brusco.
bob[*bed hair*], i capelli corti; (*French*)
i capelli corti alla Giovanna d'Arco,
m.pl.

bobbin, *n.* rocchetto, fuso, *m.*,
bobina, *f.*, cannello, *m.*

bobsleigh, *n.* guidoslitta, *f.*

bobtail, *n.* coda mozza, *f.* *tag-rag* &
~, plebaglia, canaglia, marmaglia,
f.

bode, *v.t.* presagire, predire, annunziare. **~** *ill*, **~** *well*, esser di cattivo
(buono) augurio.

bodice, *n.* busto, giubbetto, *m.*

bodily, *a.* corporeo, fisico; materiale,
reale. *to be in* **~** *fear*, temere per
la vita. ¶ *ad.* corporeamente,
fisicamente, di peso.

bodkin, *n.* punteruolo, infilacappi, *m.*

body, *n.* corpo, *m.*; sostanza, *f.*;
massa, *f.*, raccolta, *f.*; gruppo, *m.*,
classe, compagnia, *f.*, collegio, *m.*,
brigata, *f.*; grosso, *m.*; (*dead*)
cadavere, *m.*; (*water*) specchio, *m.*;
(*vehicle*) cassa, *f.*; guscio, *m.* **~** &
~work (*motor*), carrozzeria, *f.*,
scocca, *f.* **~belt**, ventriera, *f.* **~**
builder (*motor*). fabbricante di
carrozze d'automobili. **~** *corporate*, ente morale, *m.*

bog, *n.* pantano, *m.*, palude, *f.*,
acquitrino, *m.* ¶ *v.t.* impantanare.

bogey (*Golf*), *n.* norma, *f.*

bog[**e**]**y** [**man**], *n.* orco, *m.*, babao, *m.*,
diavolo, *m.*

boggle, *v.i.* trasalire, tentennare;
esitare, equivocare.

boggy, *a.* paludoso, acquitrinoso.

bogie (*Rly.*), *n.* carrello, *m.*

bogus, *a.* falso, finto, contraffatto.

Bohemia, *n.* la Boemia, *f.*; (*fig.*)
scapigliatura, vita zingaresca, *f.*
Bohemian, *a.* boemo; (*fig.*) zingaresco. ¶ *n.* Boemo, *m.*, -a, *f.*

boil (*Path.*), *n.* foruncolo, fignolo, *m.*

boil, *v.t.* far bollire, lessare; (*v.i.*)
bollire. **~** *down*, condensare,
ridurre. **~** *over*, traboccare; (*fig.*)
andare in furia. **~ed**, *p.a.*; **~** *beef*,
lesso di manzo, *m.* **~** *egg*, (*soft*)
uovo da bere, (*hard*) uovo sodo, *m.*
~ *potatoes*, patate bollite, *f.pl.* **~er**,
n. (*steam*) caldaia, *f.*; (*kitchener*)
bagnomaria, *m.*; (*pot*) marmitta,
pignatta, *f.*, casseruola, *f.* **~maker**,
calderaio, *m.* **~making** & **~works**,
fabbrica di caldaie, *f.* **~plate**,
lamiera di caldaie, *f.* **~room**, sala
delle caldaie, *f.* **~ing**, *n.* ebollizione, *f.* **~** *point*, punto d'ebollizione, *m.* (212°F. or 100°C.).

boisterous, *a.* agitato, tempestoso,
violento; rumoroso, turbolento.

bold, *a.* ardito, audace, prode,
coraggioso; sfrenato, sfacciato; netto,
rilevato, sporgente; (*Typ.*) neretto.
~-faced (*type*), [carattere] grassetto.
~ly, *ad.* arditamente, coraggiosamente; sfacciatamente; nettamente.
~ness, *n.* arditamento, coraggio, *m.*;
temerità, *f.*; vigoria, *f.*

Bolivia, *n.* la Bolivia, *f.* **Bolivian**, *a.*
boliviano. ¶ *n.* boliviano, *m.*, -a, *f.*

bollard, *n.* palo d'ormeggio, *m.*

Bologna, *n.* Bologna, *f.* *inhabitant
of* **~**, bolognese, *m.f.*

bolster, *n.* capezzale, *m.* **~** *up*, *v.t.*
sostenere, dare (prestare) appoggio
avventizio a.

bolt, *n.* dardo, *m.*, freccia, *f.*; bollone,
m.; (*door*) catenaccio, chiavistello,
paletto, *m.*; (*lock*) stanghetta, *f.*;
(*thunder*) fulmine, *m.*; (*flight*) fuga, *f.*,
volo, *m.* ¶ *v.t.* chiudere con catenaccio, mettere il chiavistello a; (*sift*)
stacciare; (*food*) inghiottire senza
masticare, ingollare; (*v.i.*) (*horse*)
prendere la mano; (*pers.*) prendere
il volo, partire come una freccia.

bolt upright, tutto dritto.

bolus, *n.* grossa pillola, *f.*

bomb, *n.* bomba, *f.* **~-proof**, a prova
di bomba. **~shell** (*fig.*), colpo di
sorpresa, momento di stordimento,

m. ~*thrower*, lanciabombe, *m.*
atom[ic] ~, bomba atomica, *f.*
delayed action ~, bomba a scoppio
ritardato. ¶ *v.t.* (*Aero.*) gettare,
lanciare [*bombe*]. (*Mil.*) bombardare.
bombard, *v.t.* bombardare. ~**ier**,
n. bombardiere, *m.* ~**ment**, *n.*
bombardamento, *m.*
bombast, *n.* linguaggio ampolloso,
stile gonfio, *m.* ~**ic**, *a.* ampolloso,
enfatico.
bomber, *n.* (*Aero.*) apparecchio da
bombardamento, *m.*; (*pers.*) bombardiere, *m.*
bona fide, *a. & ad.* di buona fede,
in buona fede.
bond, *n.* legame, vincolo, *m.*; unione,
f.; (*Fin.*) obbligazione, *f.*, titolo,
buono, *m.*; (*Law*) cauzione, *f.*
bond[*ed warehouse*], deposito (magazzino) doganale, punto franco. *in*
bond[*ed warehouse*], in deposito
doganale, sotto vincolo doganale.
bond note, bolletta di transito, *f.*
¶ **bond**, *v.t.* mettere (depositare) in
un magazzino doganale, mettere in
deposito; ipotecare; (*masonry*) connettere. **bondage**, *n.* servaggio, *m.*,
servitù, schiavitù, *f.* **bonded**
storekeeper, magazziniere, *m.*
bondholder, *n.* portatore d'obbligazione, proprietario di titoli, *m.*,
obbligazionista, *m.f.*
bone, *n.* osso, *m.* (*m.pl.* ossi, *f.pl.* ossa);
(*fish*) lisca, spina, *f.*; (*pl. dead*) ossa,
f.pl.; (*castanets*) nacchere, castagnette
f.pl. ~ *of contention*, pomo della
discordia, *m.* ¶ *v.t.* disossare; (*steal*)
rubare.
bonfire, *n.* falò, *m.*
bonnet, *n.* (*woman's*) cappello, *m.*;
(*man's*) berretto, *m.*; (*cover*) cofano
(dell'automobile), *m.*
bonny, *a.* bello, vezzoso, grazioso,
leggiadro.
bonus, *n.* avanzo, buono, soprassoldo,
m. ~ *shares*, azioni di godimento,
f.pl.
bony, *a.* ossuto, osseo, scarno; (*fish*)
pieno di lische, di spine; (*big-boned*)
che ha le ossa grosse. ~ *palate*,
parte anteriore (ossea) del palato,
p. duro.
boo, *v.t.* fischiare.
booby, *n.* stupido, balordo, sciocco,
baloccone, scioccone, *m.*; (*games*)
schiappa, *f.* ~ *prize*, indennizzo, *m.*
~ *trap*, acchiappatoio, *m.*
book, *n.* libro; libretto; registro, *m.*;
(*day*) libro giornale; (*log-book*)
giornale di bordo, *m.*; (*old & of little*

value), libraccio; libercolo, *m.* ~*bin-*
der, legatore di libri, *m.* ~*binding*,
legatura, *f.* ~*case*, scaffale, *m.*,
libreria, *f.*, armadio, *m.* ~ *debt*, articolo dell'attivo, debito non estinto,
credito chirografario, *m.* ~*ends*,
serralibri, *m.inv.* ~ *hunter*, raccoglitore di libri, collezionista di libri,
m. ~*keeper*, contabile, *m.f.* ~*-*
keeping, *n.* contabilità, *f.* ~ *lover*,
amatore di libri, bibliofilo, *m.*
~*maker*, compilatore di libri; (*races*)
allibratore, *m.* ~*mark*[*er*], segnalibro, *m.* ~*-matches*, fiammiferi
staccabili, *m.pl.* ~*muslin*, organdisse,
m. ~ *of stamps*, libretto di francobolli, *m.* ~ *of travel coupons*,
libretto di tagliandi, *m.* ~*plate*,
ex libris. ~*rest*, leggio, *m.*, scansia,
f. ~*seller*, libraio, *m.* ~*seller*
& publisher, libraio-editore, *m.*
~*seller's shop*, libreria, *f.* ~*shelf*,
palchetto, *m.*; (*pl.*) scaffale, *m.*
scansia, *f.* ~*stall*, banco, chiosco,
m., edicola, *f.* (per la vendita di
libri). ~*trade*, commercio librario,
m. ~ *trough*, portalibri, *m.inv.*
~ *value*, valore contabile, *m.*
~*worm* (*pers.*), topo di biblioteca,
m. to make a ~ (*Betting*), accettare
scommesse. ¶ *v.t.* registrare, iscrivere, prenotare; (*v.i.*) registrarsi,
iscriversi; prendere un biglietto
per . . . **booking**, *n.* registrazione,
f.; posto prenotato, *m.*, prenotazione,
f. ~ *clerk* (*Rly.*), bigliettinaio, *m.*
~ *hall*, (*Rly.*), sala per la vendita
biglietti, *f.* ~ *office*, ufficio (dei)
biglietti, *m.* **booklet**, *n.* libretto,
opuscolo, libriccino, *m.*
boom, *n.* (*harbour*) catena di porto, *f.*;
(*crane*) braccio (della gru), *m.*;
(*prices*) rapido rialzo, *m.*, attività
negli affari, *f.* ¶ *v.i.* rimbombare,
tuonare; prosperare, aumentare
rapidamente.
boon, *a.* gaio, gioioso. ~ *companion*,
compagno ameno, compagno
d'osteria, compagnone, *m.* ¶ *n.*
favore, beneficio, *m.*
boor, *n.* villano, rusticone. ~**ish**, *a.*
rozzo, zotico. ~**ishness**, *n.*
rustichezza, grossolanità, *f.*
boot, *n.* stivale, stivaletto, stivalone,
m.; (*pl.*) calzatura, *f.*; (*pl. pers.*)
lustrino d'albergo, garzone d'albergo,
m. ~ *& shoe repairer*, ciabattino, *m.*
~ *& shoe trade*, commercio delle
calzature, *m.* ~*jack*, cavastivali,
tirastivali, *m.inv.* ~*lace*, stringa da
stivale, *f.* ~*maker*, calzolaio, *m.*

~*tree*, gambale, *m.*, forma per calzature, *f.* ¶ *v.t.* calzare. ~*ee*, *n.* calzatura di media altezza per signore, scarpetta per bambini, *f.*

booth, *n.* baracca, *f.*, baraccone, *m.*

bootless, *a.* vano, inutile.

booty, *n.* bottino, *m.*

booze, *v.i.* sbevazzare, ubriacarsi.

bo-peep (*to play at*), far capolino, far cucu.

boracic, *a.* boracico.   **borax**, *n.* borace, *m.*

border, *n.* orlo, margine, bordo, *m.*; confine, *m.*, frontiera, *f.*; (*garden*) bordura, *f.*; (*Typ. ornament*) listello, *m.* ~*land*, paese limitrofo, *m.* ~*line case*, caso limite, *m.* ¶ *v.t.* orlare; bordare. ~ [*up*]*on*, confinare con, essere limitrofo di, estendersi lungo, rasentare.

bore, *n.* buco, foro; alesaggio, *m.*; (*gun*) anima, *f.*; calibro, *m.*; (*Min.*) sondaggio, *m.*; (*tidal*) riflusso, mascaretto, *m.*; (*nuisance*) noia, seccatura, *f.*; (*pers.*) seccatore, *m.*, -trice, *f.*, seccante, *m.f.*, individuo noioso, *m.* ~ *core*, anima, *f.* ~*hole*, buca, *f.*, pozzo, foro alesato, *m.* ¶ *v.t.* bucare, forare, perforare; alesare, barenare; sondare; (*fig.*) annoiare, seccare; tediare. ~**dom**, *n.* noia, *f.*, tedio, *m.*

boric, *a.* borico.

boring machine, (*Min.*) macchina perforatrice; (*Mech. Engin.*) alesatrice, *f.*

born, *p.p. & a.* nato; partorito; generato; di nascita; nativo (di). oriundo (di). ~ *blind*, cieco dalla nascita, cieco nato. *to be* ~, nascere; (*fig.*) venire al mondo, vedere la luce.

boron (*Chem.*), *n.* boro, *m.*

borrow, *v.t.* prendere a prestito, in prestito, farsi prestare; accattare; (*fig.*) adottare, derivare. ~**er**, *n.* chi prende a prestito; accattatore, *m.*, -trice, *f.* ~**ing**, *n.* prestito, (il) prendere a prestito, *m.*

borzoi, *n.* levriere russo, *m.*

bosom, *n.* seno; grembo; petto, *m.*; (*church*) grembo. ~ *friend*, amico del cuore, *m.* ~ *sin*, peccato segreto, *m.*

Bosphorus (**the**), il Bosforo, *m.*

boss, *n.* bernoccolo, *m.*, bugna, protuberanza, *f.*; mozzo, *m.*; (*Arch.*) ornamento in rilievo, rosone, *m.*; (*pers.*) padrone, capo, *m.* *propeller* ~, mozzo dell'elica.

botanic(al), *a.* botanico. ~ *gardens*, orto botanico, *m.*   **botanist**, *n.* botanico, *m.*, botanista, *m.f.* **botanize**, *v.i.* raccogliere piante, erborizzare. **botany**, *n.* botanica, *f.*

botch, *n.* rappezzo, rattoppo, lavoro mal fatto, *m.* ¶ *v.t.* rappezzare, rattoppare; acciabattare, abborracciare; rabberciare.

both, *a. & ad.* ambedue, entrambi, ambo; tutt'e due, l'uno e l'altro. ~ . . . *and*, e . . . e . . . , tanto . . . quanto . . . , tanto . . . che . . . , così . . . come, sia . . . che . . . ; (*at the same time*) insieme, ad un tempo. ~ *of us*, noi due.

bother, *n.* fastidio, cruccio, *m.*; importunità, *f.* ¶ *i.* che seccatura! al diavolo! ¶ *v.t.* importunare; infastidire, seccare. ~**ation**, *i.* diamine!

bottle, *n.* bottiglia, *f.*; fiasco, *m.*; boccetta, *f.*; (*feeding*) biberon, *m.*; (*gas, &c.*) bombola, *f.* ~ *brush*, spazzolino per bottiglie, *m.* ~ *rack*, portabottiglie, portafiaschi, *m.inv.* ¶ *v.t.* imbottigliare, infiascare; mettere in bottiglie. ~ *up* (*block, of fleet, &c.*), imbottigliare.

bottom, *n.* fondo, *m.*; base, *f.*, fondamento, piede, *m.*; part più bassa, *f.*; deretano, culo, *m.*; (*of chair, &c.*) fondo, sedile, *m.*; (*lowland*) bassopiano, *m.*; (*ship*) nave, *f.*, scafo, naviglio, *m.*; (*of ship*) carena, *f.* *from top to* ~, dall'alto in basso, da cima a fondo. ¶ *a.* inferiore; del fondo, del basso; il più basso. ~ *fishing*, pesca di fondo, *f.* ~ *margin* (*book, page*), bianco di piede, *m.* ¶ *v.t.* (*a cask, &c.*) mettere il fondo a; (*v.i.*) toccare il fondo. ~**less**, *a.* senza fondo, insondabile; smisurato.

bough, *n.* ramo, ramoscello, *m.*

bought book, libro (registro) degli acquisti, *m.*

boulder, *n.* masso, sasso, *m.*

bounce, *n.* balzo, rimbalzo, *m.*; vanteria, millanteria, bravata, fanfaronata, *f.* ¶ *v.i.* rimbalzare; vantarsi, fare il fanfarone. **bouncing girl**, grassoccia; maschietta, *f.*

bound, *n.* balzo, salto; limite, termine, confine, *m.* *to exceed all* ~*s*, oltrepassare ogni limite. ¶ *v.t.* limitare, confinare; (*v.i.*) balzare, saltare. ~ *for* (*ship*), diretto a, destinato a, in partenza per. *to be* ~ *to*, essere costretto a, essere obbligato a (verso), **essere impegnato verso**;

dovere. ¶ *p.a.* (*book*) legato, rilegato. ~ *in paper boards,* cartonato. **boundary,** *n.* limite, confine, *m.,* frontiera, *f.* ~ *line,* linea di demarcazione, *f.* **bounden duty,** sacro dovere, dovere imperativo, *m.* **boundless,** *a.* illimitato, sconfinato.

bounteous, *a.* abbondante, largo, generoso. **bounty,** *n.* bontà, generosità, munificenza, *f.;* premio, *m.* ~-*fed,* premiato.

bouquet, *n.* mazzo, *m.;* (*wine*) fragranza, *f.*

bourgeois, *a. & n.* borghese, *a. & m.f.*

bourn, *n.* ruscello, ruscelietto, corso d'acqua, *m.*

bourn[e], *n.* limite; segno, *m.,* mira, *f.*

bout, *n.* assalto, *m.,* lotta, partita, *f.;* accesso, colpo; periodo, *m.*

bovine, *a.* bovino; (*fig.*) stupido.

bow, *n.* (*knot*) nodo, *m.,* rosetta, *f.;* (*neck-tie*) nodo, *m.,* cravatta, *f.,* (*curve*) curvo, arco, *m.;* (*fiddle, &c.*) archetto, *m.;* (*saddle*) arcione, *m.;* (*padlock, &c.*) ansa, *f.* ~ *compasses,* compasso a balaustro, *m.* ~ *window,* finestra ad arco, *f.*

bow, *n.* inchino, saluto, *m.,* riverenza, *f.;* (*ship*) prora, prua, *f.* ¶ *v.t.* inchinare, piegare, curvare; (*v.i.*) inchinarsi, piegarsi. ~ *& scrape,* prosternarsi, fare dei profondi inchini. ~ *to,* cedere, sottomettersi a; salutare, fare un inchino a, fare una riverenza a.

bowdlerize, *v.t.* espurgare.

bowels, *n.pl.* budella, *f.pl.,* intestini, *m.pl.;* (*fig.*) viscere, *f.pl.* *to have a motion of the* ~, andar di corpo.

bower, *n.* pergola, *f.,* frascato, *m.*

bowing & scraping, prosternazione, *f.*

bowl, *n.* coppa, scodella, *f.,* bacino, *m.,* vaschetta, *f.;* (*pipe*) fornello, *m.,* (*game*) boccia, *f.* *game of* ~*s,* giuoco delle bocce, *m.* ¶ *v.i.* (*cricket*) servire la palla; (*bowls*) giuocare alle bocce. ~**ful,** *n.* scodellata, *f.*

bow-legged, *a.* sbilenco, con le gambe ricurve, dalle gambe arcuate.

bowler [**hat**], *n.* cappello duro, *m.*

bowline, *n.* bolina, *f.*

bowling: ~ *alley,* pallottolaio, *m.* ~ *green,* giuoco delle bocce, *m.*

bowman, *n.* arciere, *m.;* (*boat*) prodiere, *m.*

bowsprit, *n.* bompresso, *m.*

bow-wow, *n.* abbaiamento, *m.;* (*child's lang.*) bau-bau, teté, totó, cane, *m.*

box, *n.* scatola, cassa, cassetta, *f.,* bossolo, *m.;* (*ballot*) urna, *f.;* (*cardboard*) scatola di cartone, *f.;* (*driver's*) cassetta, *f.;* (*horse*) stallo, scompartimento, *m.;* (*jury*) banco, *m.;* (*sentry*) garitta, *f.;* (*Theat.*) palco, *m.* ~ *camera, n.* camera a forma rigida, *f.* ~**maker,** *n.* bossolaio, cassettaio, *m.* ~ *of paints,* scatola di colori, *f.* ~ *office,* ufficio biglietti, (*Theat.*) botteghino, *m.* ~ *on the ear*[*s*], schiaffo, *m.* ~**room,** deposito, stanzino, ripostiglio, *m.* ~ *rule* (*Typ.*), cornice laterale, *f.* ~ *spanner,* chiave per dadi, *f.* ~ *spring mattress,* letto a molle, *m.* *money* ~, salvadanaio, *m.* ~ [*tree*] *& ~ wood,* bosso, bossolo, *m.* ¶ *v.t.* incassare, mettere in una cassetta; (*some one's ears*) schiaffare, schiaffeggiare; (*fight*) fare a pugni, battersi; (*v.i.*) pugilare. *to ~ the compass,* fare il giro della bussola. ~**er,** *n.* pugilatore, *m.* ~**ing,** *n.* pugilato, *m.* ~ *glove,* guanto da pugilato, *m.* ~ *match,* partita di pugilato, *f.*

boy, *n.* ragazzo, fanciullo, giovanetto, *m.* *cabin* ~, mozzo, *m.* *choir* ~, corista, *m.* ~ *scout,* giovane esploratore, *m.* ~**hood,** *n.* (*early*) puerizia, fanciullezza, *f.;* (*late*) adolescenza, *f.* ~**ish,** *a.* fanciullesco, puerile.

boycott, *n.* boicottaggio, *m.* ¶ *v.t.* boicottare.

brace, *n.* (*strut, stay*) attacco, puntello, sostegno, *m.,* staffa, grappa, *f.;* (*tool*) girabecchino, trapano, *m.,* menarola, *f.;* (*pair*) coppia, *f.,* paio, *m.;* (*Typ.*) or {}, grappa, *f.;* (*pl. Dress*) bretelle, *f.pl.* (*child's*) cigne, *f.pl.* ¶ *v.t.* attaccare, legare; serrare, stringere; rinvigorire, dare del tono (a); (*Mar.*) bracciare.

bracelet, *n.* braccialetto, *m.*

bracing, *a.* invigorante, salubre, fortificante.

bracken, *n.* felce ramosa, *f.*

bracket, *n.* mensola, *f.,* braccio, *m.;* (*Typ.*) [] parentesi quadra, *f.;* () parentesi rotonda, *f.;* {} grappa, *f.* ¶ *v.t.* mettere fra parentesi; accoppiare; pareggiare. *to be* ~*ed* (*exams*), essere classificato *ex aequo* (*or* alla pari).

brackish, *a.* salmastro.

brad, *n.* chiodo, *m.* ~**awl,** *n.* punteruolo, *m.,* lesina, *f.*

brag, *n.* vanto, *m.,* vanteria, millanteria, *f.* ¶ *v.i.* vantarsi (di). **braggart,** *n.* millantatore, fanfarone, spaccone, *m.*

brahmin, *n.* bramino, *m.*

braid, *n.* treccia, *f.*; cordone, cordoncino, passamano, gallone, *m.* ¶ *v.t.* intrecciare, guarnire di treccia, di gallone, ornare con treccia, con gallone.

brain, *n.*, & ~s, *pl.* cervello, *m.*; testa, *f.*, giudizio, senno, intelletto, *m.*; (*pl. Cook.*) cervella, *f.pl.* ~*fag*, esaurimento nervoso, *m.* ~*fever*, febbre cerebrale, *f.* ~*wave*, idea spontanea, *f.*, lampo di genio, *m.* ~*work*, lavoro intellettuale, *m.* ~**less**, *a.* senza cervello, scervellato, stupido, stordito.

braise, *v.t.* stufare (con lardo, &c.).

brake, *n.* (*on wheel*) freno, *m.*; (*waggonette*) carrozzetta, *f.*, (*bracken*) felce ramosa, *f.*; (*thicket*) macchia, *f.*, cespuglio, *m.* ~ [*gear*], organi di frenaggio, *m.pl.*; (*carriage*) meccanismo, *m.* ~ *van* (*Rly.*) furgone, *m.* ¶ *v.t.* frenare. *to put on* (*or apply*) *the* ~, applicare il freno, serrare il freno. **brakesman,** *n.* frenatore, *m.*

bramble, *n.* rovo (*plant*), *m.*; mora (*berry*), *f.*

bran, *n.* crusca, *f.*

branch, *n.* ramo, *m.*; frasca, fronda, *f.*; braccio, *m.*; diramazione, *f.*; reparto, *m.* ~ *line* (*Rly.*) linea secondaria, *f.*, ~ *office*, succursale, filiale; agenzia, *f. root* & ~, *a.* completo; radicale. ¶ *v.i.* metter rami; ramificare; diramarsi. ~ *off*, *v.i.* biforcarsi. ~ *out* (*fig.*), espandersi, svilupparsi.

brand, *n.* (*fire*) tizzone, *m.*; (*fig.*) macchia, *f.*, stigma, *m.*; (*Poet.*) brando, *m.*; (*Com. & hot iron*) marca, *f.*, marchio, *m.* **bran[d] new,** nuovo di zecca. ¶ *v.t.* marcare con ferro rovente; segnare con un marchio; lacciare, stigmatizzare.

brandish, *v.t.* brandire.

brandy, *n.* acquavite, *f.*, cognac, *m.* ~ & *soda*, c. con acqua di Seltz.

brass, *n.* ottone; (*Poet.*) bronzo; (*bearing*) cuscinetto, *m.*, bronzina, *f.*, (*cheek*) sfrontatezza, impudenza, *f. the* ~ (*Mus.*), gli ottoni. ~ *band*, fanfara, *f.* ~ *farthing*, quattrino, centesimo, *m. I don't care a* ~ *farthing*, non m'importa proprio nulla. ~ *foundry*, fonderia di ottone, *f.* ~ *wares*, ottoname, *m.*

brassière, *n.* reggipetto, *m.inv.*

brassy, *a.* che somiglia all'ottone.

brat, *n.* marmocchio, birichino, monello, *m.*; monella, ragazzaccia, *f.*; (*pl. col.*) ragazzaglia, *f.*

bravado, *n.* bravata, *f.* **brave,** *a.*

coraggioso, bravo, ardito, animoso, prode, intrepido; onesto, fermo; bello, eccellente. ~ *man*, [uomo] coraggioso, &c. *a* ~ *show*, un bell'effetto. ¶ *v.t.* sfidare, affrontare, resistere a. ~**ry**, *n.* coraggio, ercismo, *m.*; bravura, *f.* **bravo**, *i.* bravo! bene!

brawl, *n.* zuffa, rissa, lite rumorosa, *f.* ¶ *v.i.* azzuffarsi, rissare, altercare rumorosamente; (*stream*) mormorare, gorgogliare. ~**er**, *n.* sbraitone, schiamazzatore, attaccabrighe, *m.*

brawn, *n.* carne di verro, *f.*; (*fig.*) forza muscolare, *f.* ~**y**, *a.* forte, muscoloso.

bray, *v.i.* ragliare. ~[**ing**], *n.* raglio, *m.*

braze, *v.t.* saldare (in ottone & zinco); coprire d'ottone. **braze** (*joint*) & **brazing,** *n.* saldatura, *f.*

brazen, *a.* d'ottone; ottonato. ~**faced**, sfrontato, sfacciato, con una faccia di bronzo. *to* ~ *it out*, far lo sfacciato.

brazier, *n.* (*pers.*) ottonaio; (*pan*) braciere, *m.*

Brazil, *n.* il Brasile, *m.* **Brazilian,** *a.* brasiliano. ¶ *n.* brasiliano, *m.*, -a, *f.*

breach, *n.* breccia; rottura, interruzione; infrazione, violazione, contravvenzione, *f.* ~ *of faith*, mancanza di fede, *f.*, abuso di confidenza, *m.* ~ *of promise*, rottura (violazione) di promessa di matrimonio, *f.* ~ *of trust*, infedeltà, *f.*, abuso di fiducia, *m.*

bread, *n.* pane, *m.* ~ *crumbs* (*Cook.*), pan grattato, *m.* ~ *knife*, coltello per pane, *m.* ~ *saw*, coltello a sega per pane, *m.* ~ *winner*, sostegno della famiglia, *m.*

breadth, *n.* larghezza; ampiezza; distesa; (*of stuffs*) altezza, *f.*

break, *n.* rottura, frattura, spaccatura; interruzione; cessazione; soluzione di continuità; pausa; (*gap*) apertura; breccia; lacuna, *f.*; (*day*) spuntare, fare; (*voice*) mutamento; (*prices*) ribasso, scarto, *m.*, caduta, *f.*; (*on ball*) effetto; (*Bil.*) tiro, seguito di punti, *m.*; (*waggonette*) carrozzetta; vettura di piacere, *f.*; (*Typ.*) righino, *m.* ~ *of journey*, fermata, interruzione di viaggio, *f.* ¶ *v.t. ir.* rompere; spezzare; spaccare; schiantare; fracassare; frangere; infrangere; sciogliere; violare; interrompere; dirompere; metter fine a; distruggere; (*the bank, Gaming*) fare saltare il banco; (*a set*) sparigliare, scompagnare, spaiare; (*news*) rivelare; (See also *broken*); (*v.i.* *ir.*) rompersi, spezzarsi, &c.; (*voice*) mutarsi; (*dawn*) spuntare, apparire; (*waves*) frangersi, infrangersi, spezzarsi. ¶ ~ *bulk* (*Ship.*) incominciare a scaricare. ~ *cover* (*Hunt.*) scovarsi. ~ *down*, *v.t.* abbattere; (*v.i.*) accasciarsi; (*Motor.*) avere una panna, rimanere in p. ~ *into*, irrompere in, invadere; forzare; penetrare; interrompere. ~ *loose*, liberarsi, sciogliersi, svincolarsi. ~ *of the habit*, disabituare, divezzare. ~ *one's arm*, rompersi il braccio. ~ *one's heart*, *v.t.* spezzare il cuore. ~ *one's back*, rompersi la schiena. ~ *one's word*, mancare di parola. ~ *open*, sforzare, scassinare. ~ *out*, (*fire*, *war*, *&c.*) scoppiare; dichiararsi; (*fig.*) apparire; traboccare, stripare; evadere. ~ *their engagement* (*marriage*), disaccordarsi. ~ *through*, penetrare, aprirsi un passaggio attraverso. ~ *up*, (*school*) andare in vacanza; (*weather*) cambiare, guastarsi. (*ice*) sciogliersi; dighiacciare, sgelare. ~ *upon the wheel*, mettere alla ruota; sottoporre alla tortura della r. **breakable**, *a.* fragile; (*notice*, *with care*) posa piano. **breakage**, *n.* rottura, spezzatura, frattura; interruzione. **breakaway**, *n.* dislocazione; deriva; evasione, fuga, *f.* **breakdown**, *n.* (*failure*) fiasco; (*collapse*) sfacelo, crollo, disfacimento, *m.*; (*car*, *&c.*) panna, *f.*; (*health*) prostrazione, *f.*; indebolimento, abbattimento, *m.* ~ *gang*, squadra di soccorso, *f.* **breaker**, *n.* (*pers.*) rompitore; demolitore, distruttore; (*wave*) frangente, *m.* **breakfast**, *n.* prima colazione, *f.* ~ *cup*, tazza da colazione, *f.* ~ *service*, ~ *set*, servizio da c, *m.* ¶ *v.i.* fare la prima colazione. **breaking**, *n.* rottura, frattura; infrazione, violazione; (*holy bread*) frazione, *f.*; (*voice*) mutamento, *m.* **breakneck**, *n.* rompicollo, *m.* *a* rompicollo, headlong. *a* ~ *pace*, un passo massacrante, *m.* **breakwater**, *n.* diga, *f.*; frangiflutti, *m.inv.*

breast, *n.* seno; petto. *at the* ~, alla mammella, alla poppa. ~ *bone*, sterno, *m.* ~ *high*, all'altezza del petto. ~*plate*, piastrone, *m.* ~ *pocket*, tasca di fianco, *f.* ~ *strap*, *n.* (*horse*) pettorale, *m.* ~ *stroke* (*Swim.*), nuotata a rana, *f.*

breath, *n.* respiro; soffio; fiato, *m.*; lena, *f.* **breathe**, *v.i.* & *t.* respirare, prendere fiato; spirare; sussurrare. **breathing**, *n.* respirazione, *f.*, respiro, *m.* ~ *space*, spazio vitale, *m.* **breathless**, *a.* senza fiato; sfiatato; esanime.

breech, *n.* deretano, *m.*; (*gun*) culatta, *f.* ~ *block*, otturatore, *m.* ~*loading*, a retrocarica. **breeches**, *n.pl.* calzoni, *m.pl.*, brache, *f.pl.* *knee* ~, calzoncini, *m.pl.* ~ *buoy*, salvagente a brache, *m.*

breed, *n.* razza, schiatta, *f.* ¶ *v.t. ir.* allevare; generare; (*v.i. ir.*) moltiplicarsi, riprodursi. ~*er*, (*stock*), *n.* allevatore, *m.* ~*ing*, *n.* (*animals*) allevamento, *m.*; (*pers.*) educazione, costumatezza, *f.*

breeze, *n.* (*wind*) brezza, (*light*, *gentle*) brezzolina, (*Poet.*) aura, *f.*; (*gadfly*) tafano, *m.*; (*cinders*) rifiuti di coke, *m.pl.* **breezy**, *a.* arioso; fresco, vivace.

Bremen, *n.* Brema, *f.*

Breslau, *n.* Breslavia, *f.*

brethren, *n.pl.* fratelli, confratelli, *m.pl.*

breviary, *n.* breviario, *m.*

brevier, *n.* (*Typ.*) garamoncino, *m.*

brevity, *n.* concisione; brevità, *f.*

brew, *v.t.* (*beer*) fabbricare, fare; (*tea*) preparare; (*v.i.*) fare la birra; essere in fermentazione; (*storm*) levarsi, prepararsi; (*fig.*) covare, tramarsi. ~*er*, *n.* birraio, fabbricante di birra, *m.* ~*ery*, *n.* fabbrica di birra, *f.* ~*ing*, *n.* fabbricazione della birra, *f.*

briar, *n.* rovo; pruno, *m.*; erica bianca; (*pipe wood*) radica, *f.* ~ *rose*, rosa canina, *f.*

bribe, *n.* dono, *m.*, offerta (fatta per corrompere); (*fig.*) offa, *f.* ¶ *v.t.* corrompere, sedurre, influenzare, ungere la mano a. ~*ry*, *n.* corruzione, *f.*

brick, *n.* mattone, *m.*; (*pl. child's game*) giuoco di costruzione in legno, *m.* ~*field*, mattonaia, *f.* ~*kiln*, fornace a mattoni, *f.* ~*layer*, muratore, *m.* ~*maker*, mattonaio, fabbricante di mattoni, *m.* ~ *paving*, pavimentare in mattoni, pavimento di m~i, *m.* ~ *work*, muratura in mattoni, *f.* *fire* ~, mattone refrattario, *m.*

bridal, *a.* nuziale, di nozze; di sposa.

bride, *n.* sposa, sposa novella, *f.* ~ & ~*groom*, sposi novelli, *m.pl.* ~ *cake*, torta nuziale, *f.* ~*groom* sposo, *m.* *bridesmaid,* damigella d'onore, *f.* *bridesman* (best man), amico dello sposo, paggio d'onore, *m.*

bridge, *n.* ponte, *m.*; (*foot*) passerella, *f.*; (*ship*) ponte di commando, *m.*; (*violin*) ponticello; (*nose*) rialto; (*Cards*) giuoco del ponte, *m.* ¶ *v.t.* gettar un ponte su; (*fig.*) saltare; (*gap*) colmare. ~*head,* testa di ponte, *f.*

bridle, *n.* briglia, *f.*; freno, *m.* ~*path,* sentiero da cavallo, *m.* ¶ *v.t.* imbrigliare; mettere la briglia a; (*curb*) raffrenare; (*v.i.*) stizzirsi, insuperbirsi.

brief, *a.* breve, corto, conciso. ¶ *n.* causa, *f.*; incartamento, *m.* ~ *bag,* borsa, saccoccia (d'avvocato). ¶ *v.t.* affidare una causa a, costituire. ~**less,** *a.* senza causa, senza clienti. ~**ly,** *ad.* brevemente, alla breve, in b.

brier, *n.* rovo; pruno, *m.*; erica bianca, *f.*; (*pipe wood*) radica, *f.*

brig, *n.* brigantino, *m.*

brigade, *n.* brigata, *f.* ¶ *v.t.* costituire in brigata, -e.

brigand, *n.* brigante, *m.* ~**age,** *n.* brigantaggio, *m.*

bright, *a.* brillante, chiaro, lucido, lucente, luminoso, illuminato, risplendente; gaio, vivace, vivo, intelligente. ~**en,** *v.t.* far brillare, illuminare, rischiarare; (*polish*) lucidare; animare, rallegrare. ~**ly,** *ad.* brillantemente, luminosamente, chiaramente; lucidamente; gaiamente, &c. ~**ness,** *n.* lucentezza, *f.*, splendore, lustro, *m.*; vivacità, intelligenza, *f.*

Bright's disease, nefrite cronica, *f.*

brill, *n.* rombo liscio, *m.*

brilliance, brilliancy, *n.* splendore, lustro, *m.* **brilliant,** *a.* brillante, splendido, risplendente; insigne. ¶ *n.* brillante, *m.* ~**ine,** *n.* brillantina, *f.* ~**ly,** *ad.* brillantemente.

brim, *n.* orlo; bordo, *m.*; (*hat*) tesa, falda, ala, *f.* ¶ ~ *over,* traboccare. ~**-full** *or* ~**ful,** *a.* ricolmo, pieno fino all'orlo.

brimstone, *n.* zolfo, *m.*

brindled, *a.* tigrato, chiazzato.

brine, *n.* salamoia (*pickle*); acqua salata, *f.*; (*Poet.*) mare, *m.*; lagrime, *f.pl.*

bring, *v.t.* *ir.* portare, rpportare; recare; condurre, menare; fruttare; fare; mettere. ~ *about,* produrre, causare, **cagionare,** condurre a,

effettuare; determinare. ~ *an action against,* intentare un processo contro, far causa contro. ~ *back,* ricondurre, rimenare, riportare; richiamare; far ritornare; rimettere. ~ *forth,* mettere al mondo; produrre; dare alla luce. ~ *forward,* recare, produrre; metter innanzi; (*new arguments*) rimettere in ballo, in discussione; (*Bkkpg.*) riportare. ~ *in* (*house*), introdurre, far entrare. ~ *out,* fare uscire; portar fuori; far vedere, far mostrarsi; (*colours, &c.*) far risaltare; sviluppare; pubblicare; (*Theat.*) far rappresentare; (*into society*) introdurre in società. ~ *up,* allevare, educare; evocare, richiamare alla mente; far salire; (*for discussion*) intavolare, metter in tavola, mettere in discussione. ~ *up the rear,* chiudere la marcia. ~**er of ill luck,** chi porta sfortuna. ~**ing up,** educazione, *f.*

brink, *n.* orlo; bordo, *m.*; vigilia, *f.*

briny, *a.* salmastro; marino.

briquet[te], *n.* mattonella, formella di carbone, *f.*

brisk, *a.* vivace, attivo, vispo, svelto, rapido; acuto. ~ *fire* (*Mil.*) fuoco accelerato, *m.*

brisket, *n.* petto, *m.*

briskness, *n.* attività. animazione, vivacità, *f.*

bristle, *n.* setola, *f.*; pelo, *m.* ¶ *v.t.* far rizzare; (*v.i.*) rizzarsi; irrigidirsi. *bristling with difficulties,* spinosissimo.

bristly, *a.* setoloso; irto.

Bristol Channel (the), il canale di Bristol.

Britain, *n.* la Gran Bretagna, *f.* *Britannia metal,* metallo inglese, *m.* **British,** *a.* britannico; inglese. ~ *ambassador,* ambasciatore d'Inghilterra, *m.* ~ *consul,* console britannico, *m.* ~ *Isles,* Isole Britanniche, *f.pl.*

Brittany, *n.* la Bretagna.

brittle, *a.* fragile, vetrino. ~**ness,** *n.* fragilità, *f.*

broach, *n.* (*spit*) spiedo, *m.*; (*Mech.*) ◀ alesatrice; fresa a spina, broccia, *f.* ¶ *v.t.* (*cask*) spillare; (*bore*) alesare; brocciare; (*fig.*) abbordare, intavolare.

broad, *a.* largo; ampio; esteso; aperto; grande; pieno; (*accent*) marcato; (*ribald*) volgare, indelicato, osceno; (*hint*) chiaro, non equivoco. ~ *bean,* fava, *f.* ~**-brimmed hat,** cappello a larghe tese, *m.* ~**cast,** *a.* sparso; disseminato; divulgato; (*Radio*) radiodiffuso. ¶ *n.* trasmissione [radiofonica],*f.* ¶ *ad.* largamente, a caso. ¶ *v.t.* disseminare, spargere, divulgare; diffondere; (*Radio*) trasmettere per radio, radiodiffondere. ~*casting*, radiodiffusione, *f.* ~*casting station*, posto di radiodiffusione, *m.* *in* ~ *daylight*, a giorno chiaro, a pieno giorno. ~*-minded*, dalle vedute larghe, tollerante. ~*-shouldered*, dalle spalle larghe. ~*side*, (*Naut.*) fianco, *m.*, banda, *f.*; (*guns, fire*) bordata, *f.*; (*fig.*) manifesto, *m.* ~*sword*, spadone, *m.* ~*en*, *v.t.* allargare, estendere. ~*ly*, *ad.* largamente, ampiamente, in termini generali, nell'insieme. ~*ness*, *n.* larghezza, ampiezza; volgarità, indelicatezza, *f.*; accento marcato, *m.*

brocade, *n.* broccato, *m.*

brochure, *n.* opuscolo, *m.*

broil, *n.* rissa, *f.*; tafferuglio, *m.* ¶ *v.t.* arrostire sulla graticola. **broiling**, *a.* bruciante, ardente.

broke (*hard up*), *a.* al verde, alle strette.

broken, *a.* (*country*) ineguale, frastagliato, tormentato, accidentato; (*health*) acciaccato, deperito, malandato; (*speech, sleep, &c.*) interrotto, rotto; (*English, Italian, &c.*) incerto, imperfetto, imbastardito, cattivo. *to be* ~ *down* (*car*), avere una panna, rimanere in p. *to be* ~*-hearted*, essere affranto dal dolore, avere il cuore spezzato. ~ *reed* (*fig.*), persona (o cosa) su cui non si può fare assegnamento. ~ *water*, frangenti, *m.pl.* ~*-winded*, bolso.

broker, *n.* mediatore, sensale; agente, commissionario; banchiere, *m.* ~ **age**, *n.* mediazione, senseria, *f.*

bromide, *n.* bromuro, *m.* **bromine**, *n.* bromo, *m.*

bronchia, *n.pl.* bronchi, *m.pl.* **bronchitis**, *n.* bronchite, *f.*

bronze, *n.* bronzo, *m.* ¶ *v.t.* bronzare, abbronzare.

brooch, *n.* cammeo, fermaglio, *m.*; spilla, *f.*, spillone, *m.*

brood, *n.* covata, nidiata; famiglia, *f.*; bambini, *m.pl.* ~ *hen*, chioccia, *f.* ~ *mare*, cavalla da monta, c. di razza, *f.* ¶ *v.i.* covare; ruminare. ~*ing time*, covatura, stagione della c., *f.*

brook, *n.* ruscello, *m.* ¶ *v.t.* sopportare, tollerare, soffrire. ~*let*, *n.* ruscelletto, *m.*

broom, *n.* scopa, granata; (*Bot.*) ginestra, *f.* ~*stick*, manico della scopa, *m.*

broth, *n.* brodo, *m.*; zuppa, *f.*

brother, *n.* fratello; confratello; collega; (*Eccl.*) frate., *m.* ~*-in-arms*, camerata, compagno d'armi, commilitone, *m.* ~*-in-law*, cognato, *m.* *step-*~, fratellastro, *m.* ~*hood*, fraternità, fratellanza; confraternità, *f.* ~*ly*, *a.* fraterno.

brougham, *n.* carrozza, *f.*, brum, *m.*

brow, *n.* fronte, *f.*, sopracciglio; (*forehead & cliff*) ciglio, *m.*; (*hill*) sommità, *f.* ~*beat*, *v.t.* intimidire, ingiuriare, minacciare.

brown, *a.* bruno; (*boots—yellowish*) giallo; (*boots—tan*) avana; (*paper*) giallo, bruno, marrone; da pacchi, da imballaggio; (*bread—light*) bigio; (*bread—dark*) bruno, intero; (*sunburnt*) abbronzato. ~ *hair*, capelli castagni, *m.pl.* ~ *owl*, allocco, *m.* ~ *study*, fantasticheria, meditazione, *f.* *in a* ~ *study*, impensierito, nelle nuvole. ~ *sugar*, zucchero greggio, *m.* ¶ *n.* bruno, color bruno, c. marrone, *m.* ¶ *v.t.* brunire, abbrunire; abbronzare; (*meat*) rosolare. ~*ish*, *a.* bruniccio, brunetto.

brownie, *n.* folletto, spirito benigno, *m.*

browse, *n.* germogli, *m.pl.*, verdura, *f.*; pascolo, *m.* ¶ *v.i. & t.* brucare, pascolare.

bruise, *n.* ammaccatura, contusione, *f.*; bernoccolo, *m.*; (*dent*) tacca, intaccatura, *f.* ¶ *v.t.* ammaccare, contundere; fare una tacca, un'intaccatura (in). ~*d*, *p.a.* ammaccato, contuso.

brunt, *n.* peso; urto, *m.*; forza, *f.*

brush, *n.* spazzola, *f.*; pennello, *m.*; spazzolata, *f.*; (*Elec.*) spazzola, *f.*; (*fox*) coda, *f.*; (*affray*) scaramuccia, *f.* ~*head* (*of hair*), capelli a spazzola, *m.pl.* ~*maker*, setolinaio, spazzolaio, *m.* ~*wood*, macchia; fratta, *f.*, sterpeto, *m.*; frasche tagliate, *f.pl.* ¶ *v.t.* spazzolare; scopare; (*mud off*) sfangare, pulire; (*graze*) sfiorare. ~ *one's hair, teeth*, spazzolarsi i capelli, i denti. ~ *up* (*fig.*) ripassare, rivedere.

Brussels, *n.* Brusselle, *f.* ~ *carpet*, tappeto di Brusselle, *m.* ~ *sprouts*, cavoli di B., *m.pl.*

brutal, *a.* brutale. ~*ity*, *n.* brutalità, *f.* ~*ize*, *v.t.* abbrutire. **brute**, *n.* bruto, *m.* ~ *beast*, bestia, *f.*, animale, *m.* *the* ~ *creation*, regno

animale, *m.*, gli animali, *m.pl.*
~ *force*, forza bruta, mera forza, *f.*
brutish, *a.* brutale, bestiale.
bubble, *n.* bolla, bollicina; (*fig.*)
chimera, fantasia, *f.*, progetto vano
m. ¶ *v.i.* far bolle, sollevarsi in
bolle; bollire, sibilare. ~ *over*,
traboccare.
buccaneer, *n.* pirata, *m.*
buck, *n.* (*deer*) daino, *m.*; (*jump*)
capriola, *f.*; (*pers.*) damerino, *m.*
~ *rabbit*, coniglio (maschio), *m.*
~*skin*, pelle di daino, *f.* ~*shot*,
pallini da caccia, p. da lepre, *m.pl.*
bucket, *n.* secchia, *f.*, secchio,
secchione, *m.*; (*water-wheel*) cassetto;
(*elevator*) scompartimento, *m.*;
(*Mech.*) pistone (di pompa); (*ship*)
bugliolo, *m.* ~ *shop*, agenzia di
cambio irregolare, *f.* ~*ful*, secchia
piena, secchiata, *f.*
buckle, *n.* fibbia, *f.* ¶ *v.t.* affibbiare;
piegare; storcere; (*v.i.*) piegarsi,
curvarsi, storcersi. ~ *to*, applicarsi
a. **buckler**, *n.* scudo, *m.*
buckram, *n.* garza rigida; tela da
fusto, *f.*
buckthorn, *n.* spino cervino, *m.*
buckwheat, *n.* grano saraceno, *m.*
bucolic, *a.* bucolico.
bud, *n.* germoglio, bottone, bocciuolo,
m., boccia, gemma, *f.*; (*fig.*) germe,
m. ¶ *v.i.* germogliare, sbocciare,
metter le gemme; nascere.
buddhist, *a. & n.* buddista, *a. & m.f.*
budding, (*fig.*) *a.* nascente; in erba.
budge, *v.i.* muoversi, cedere terreno.
budget, *n.* bilancio pubblico, b.
preventivo, *m.* ~ *of news*, fascio di
notizie, di nuove, *m.* ~ *for*, portare
al bilancio, stanziare una somma in
b. per.
buff (*colour*), *a. & n.* fulvo, bruno-
giallastro, color camoscio, *a. & m.*
~ *leather*, pelle di bufalo, *f.* blind
man's ~, mosca cieca, *f.* ¶ *v.t.*
lucidare (con pelle); rendere liscio.
buffalo, *n.* bufalo, *m.*
buffer, *n.* paracolpi, reggiscosse,
m.inv.; respingente, tampone, *m.*
~ *state*, stato cuscinetto, *m.*
buffet, *n.* (*blow*) schiaffo, *m.*; (*sideboard*) credenza, *f.*; (*at a ball*) (cf.
running buffet, buffet, *m.* ~ *car*,
carrozza ristorante, *f.* ¶ *v.t.* schiaffeggiare.
buffoon, *n.* buffone, *m.* ~*ery*, *n.*
buffonata, buffoneria, *f.*
bug, *n.* cimice, *f.* ~*bear*, *n.* spauracchio, lupo mannaro; seccatore, *m.*
bugle, *n.* tromba, cornetta, *f.*, corno

da segnali, *m.*; (*Bot.*) bugola, *f.*
~ *call*, chiamata di tromba, di
corno, *f.* **bugler**, *n.* trombettiere,
sonatore di corno, *m.*
buhl[*work*], *n.* lavoro d'intarsio in
ottone o tartaruga, *m.*
build, *n.* costruzione, struttura;
corporatura, *f.* *of sturdy* ~ or *well
built* (man), ben piantato. ¶ *v.t. tr.*
costruire, fabbricare, edificare, fare.
~ *up*, costruire, edificare; elevare,
erigere; fondare, stabilire. ~*er*, *n.*
costruttore, impresario di costruzioni, fabbricante; (*workman*) muratore, *m.* ~*ing*, *n.* costruzione, *f.*;
edificio, *m.*, fabbrica, *f.*; stabile, *m.*;
casa, *f.*; monumento, *m.* ~*line*,
allineamento, *m.* ~ *materials*,
materiali da costruzione, *m.pl.*
~ *site*, terreno da costruzione, *m.*
~ *industry*, edilizia, industria edilizia, *f.* ~ *society*, società immobiliare,
f. *ship* ~, costruzione navale, *f.*
built-over carriage entrance, portone,
m.
bulb, *n.* (*Bot.*) bulbo, *m.*; cipolla, *f.*;
(*Anat.*) bulbo; globo, *m.*; ampolla, *f.*;
(*Elec.*) bulbo; (*Thermometer, Barom.*)
bulbo, *m.*, vaschetta, *f.*; (*Chem.*)
bolla; ampolla, *f.*; (*Phot.*) pera, *f.*
~ *exposure*, esposizione a pera, *f.*
~ *shade* (*Elec.*), paralume, *m.*
bulbous, *a.* bulboso.
Bulgaria, *n.* la Bulgaria, *f.* **Bulgarian**, *a. & m.* bulgaro.
bulge, *n.* gonfio, gonfiore, *m.*, protuberanza, escrescenza, convessità;
pancia, *f.* ¶ *v.i. & t.* gonfiarsi,
gonfiare; far pancia.
bulk, *n.* volume, *m.*, massa, *f.*; grosso,
m.; parte maggiore, *f.*; carico, *m.*
in ~ (*Ship.*), alla rinfusa, all'ingrosso;
sciolto, senza imballaggio. ~*head*,
paratia, *f.*; tramezzo, *m.* *to* ~ *large*,
essere d'importanza, sembrare
(grande, difficile, &c.). ~*y*, *a.*
voluminoso, massiccio, grosso;
ingombrante.
bull, *n.* toro, *m.*; (*Pope's*) bolla, *f.*;
(*incongruity*) sproposito, contro-
senso, *m.*; (*Stk. Ex.*) rialzista, *m.*;
(*shot*) barilozzo, *m.* ~ *calf*, torello,
m. ~ *dog*, molosso, *m.* ~ *elephant*,
elefante maschio, *m.* ~ *fight*, corrida
di tori, corsa di t., *f.* ~ *fighter*,
toreadore, *m.* ~*'s-eye*, (*target*)
barilozzo, centro del bersaglio, *m.*;
(*window*) occhio di bue, *m.* ~*'s-eye
lantern*, lanterna cieca, l. con lente
sferica, *f.*
bullet, *n.* palla, pallottola, *f.* ~*-proof*

shield, scudo a prova di pallottole, *m.*

bulletin, *n.* bollettino; avviso, *m.*

bullfinch, *n.* ciuffolotto, *m.*

bullion, *n.* oro (argento) in verghe, *m.*; moneta fuori corso, *f.*; *(fringe)* pesante frangia d'oro o d'argento, *f.*

bullock, *n.* bue, *m.*

bully, *n.* bravaccio, prepotente, tiranno, *m.* ¶ *v.t.* tormentare, intimidire, malmenare, fare il bravaccio con.

bulrush, *n.* giunco, *m.*; *(reed mace)* biodo da capanne, *m.*

bulwark, *n.* baluardo; bastione, *m.*; *(ship's)* murata, *f.*

bumble-bee, *n.* calabrone, *m.*

bump, *n.* urto, colpo, *m.,* collisione, *f.*; bernoccolo, *m.,* protuberanza, *f.* ¶ *v.t. & i.* urtare, urtarsi (contro), battere (contro); scontrarsi (con).

bumper, *n. (brim-full glass)* bicchiere colmo; *(motor)* reggiscosse, para-colpi, *m.inv.* ~ *crop,* raccolta eccezionale, abbondante, *f.* ~ *house,* sala gremita, *f.*

bumpkin, *n.* rusticone, villano, zotico, *m.*

bumptious, *a.* presuntuoso, arrogante. ~**ness,** *n.* arroganza, presunzione, *f.*

bun, *n.* panetto, panino; pasticcino, *m.*; ciambella, piccola focaccia, *f.*; *(hair)* crocchia, *f.*

bunch *n.* mazzo; fascetto; fastello; *(grapes, bananas)* grappolo; ciuffo; nodo, mucchietto, gruppo. ¶ *v.t.* fare un mazzo di, legare in fascio, raccogliere in pieghe; raggomitolare.

bundle, *n.* fagotto; fascio; fastello; fardello; pacco, pacchetto; manipolo, *m.*; *(papers)* filza, *f.*, incartamento, *m.* ¶ *v.t.* affastellare, impacchettare; raccogliere; mettere in filza; far fagotto.

bung, *n.* tappo, zaffo; turacciolo, tampone, *m.* ~*[hole],* cocchiume, *m.* ¶ *v.t.* tappare, turare.

bungalow, *n.* casetta, piccola villetta, *f.*; *(Indian type)* capanna, *f.*

bungle, *n.* guazzabuglio, lavoro mal fatto, pasticcio, *m.* ¶ *v.t.* guastare, eseguire maldestramente, abborracciare. **bungler,** *n.* guastamestiere, *m. & f.,* abborracciatore, *m.,* -trice, *f.*

bunion, *n.* gonfiore infiammato (soprosso) al pollice del piede, *m.*

bunk, *n.* cuccetta, *f.*

bunker, *n.* cassone, *m.*; carbonaia, *f.*, carbonile, *m.*; *(Golf)* ostacolo, *m.* ~ *coal,* carbone per la macchina, *m.*

bunkum, *n.* frottole, sciocchezze, *f.pl.,* paroloni, *m.pl.*

bunting, *n. (stuff)* stamigna, *f.*; *(flags)* bandiere, *f.pl.*; *(bird)* crociere, *m.*

buoy, *n.* boa, *f.,* gavitello, *m.* *life-*~, salvagente, *m.* ¶ *v.t.* segnare con boe. ~ *up,* tenere a galla; incorraggiare, sostenere. ~**ancy,** *n.* leggerezza; facoltà di stare a galla; *(fig.)* elasticità, *f.,* brio, *m.,* vivacità, *f.* ~**ant,** *a.* leggero, capace di stare a galla; elastico; vivo, animato.

bur[r], *n. (Bot.)* lappola, bardana, *f.*; involucro di semi che s'attaccai panni; *(burdock)* bardana, *f.*; *(fig.)* persona attaccaticcia, *f.*

burden, *n.* fardello, carico, peso, *m.,* soma, *f.*; onere, *m.*; *(ship)* portata, *f.,* tonnellaggio, *m.*; *(song)* ritornello, *m.* ¶ *v.t.* caricare; gravare; imbarazzare, tassare. ~**some,** *a.* oneroso, pesante, gravoso.

burdock, *n.* bardana, *f.*

bureaucracy, *n.* burocrazia, *f.* **bureaucrat,** *n.* burocrate, *m.* ~**ic,** *a.* burocratico.

burglar, *n.* ladro con effrazione, scassinatore, *m.* ~ *alarm,* apparecchio avvisatore contro il furto, *m.* ~**y,** *n.* furto con effrazione, scasso, *m.* ~ *insurance,* assicurazione contro i furti, *f.* **burgle,** *v.t.* rubare mediante effrazione, scassinare.

Burgundy, *n.* la Borgogna, *f.*; *(wine)* vino di B., *m.*

burial, *n.* sepoltura, *f.*; interramento, *m.*; inumazione, *f.* ~ *fees,* tasse di sepoltura, *f.pl.,* diritti mortuari, *m.pl.* ~ *ground,* cimitero, *m.* ~ *place,* luogo di sepoltura, *m.*; tomba, sepoltura, *f.* ~ *service,* ufficio dei morti, *m.*

burlesque, *a. & m.* burlesco. ¶ *v.t.* parodiare; burlare, burlarsi di.

burly, *a.* robusto, corpacciuto, corpulento.

Burma, *n.* la Birmania, *f.* **Burmese,** *a. & n.* birmano.

burn, *n.* bruciatura, scottatura, *f.*; ruscello, ruscelletto, *m.* ¶ *v.t. & i.ir.* bruciare, scottare; *(bricks)* cuocere; incendiare; calcinare; *(of sun)* abbronzare; ardere. *I have burnt my arm,* mi sono bruciato il braccio. *to burn one's fingers (fig.),* rimanere scottato. ~**er,** *n. (gas, &c.)* becco, *m.* ~**ing,** *a.* bruciante, infiammato, ardente; scottante; vivo, acuto. ~ *glass,* specchio ustorio, *m.* ¶ *n.* arsione, combustione, *f.*; incendio, *m.*; cottura *(bricks, &c.),* *f.*;

(*smell*) bruciaticcio, odore di bruciato, *m.*

burnish, *v.t.* (*metal, &c.*), brunire; (*paper, &c.*) satinare. ~**ing,** *n.* brunitura, *f.*; satinare, *m.*

burnt, *p.a.*: ~ *almond,* mandorla tostata, *f.* ~ *brick,* mattone cotto, *m.* ~ *offering,* olocausto, *m.* ~ *Sienna,* terra di Siena, *f.*

burr, *n.* pronuncia enfatica delle R; cote, *f.*; (*metal, &c.*) superficie rozza, pietra da macina, *f.*; (*moon, star*) anello nebuloso, *m.* See also *bur*[r].

burrow, *n.* tana, *f.*, covile, buco, *m.* ¶ *v.i.* rintanarsi; fare un buco, una galleria, covare sotterra.

bursar, *n.* economo, tesoriere; studente che gode di una borsa di studio, *m.* ~'s *office & * ~**ship,** *n.* economato, *m.* **bursary,** *n.* borsa di studio, *f.*

burst, *n.* scoppio, *m.*, esplosione; rottura, *f.*; (*light*) lampo, baleno, *m.*; (*speed*) impeto, slancio, *m.*; (*eloquence*) foga, *f.*, slancio, movimento, *m.*; (*passion, &c.*) trasporto, accesso, scoppio, parossismo, *m.* ¶ *v.t. ir.* far scoppiare, far crepare; rompere; (*v.i. ir.*) scoppiare; crepare; precipitarsi; (*bud*) sbocciare. ~**ing,** *n.* scoppio, *m.*, esplosione; rottura, *f.*

burthen (*ship*), *n.* portata, *f.*, tonnellaggio, *m.*

bury, *v.t.* seppellire; interrare, sotterrare.

[']**bus,** *n.* omnibus; autobus, *m.inv.* ~*way,* linea d'autobus, *f.*

bush, *n.* cespuglio, arbusto, *m.*; frasca, *f.*; (*scrub*) boscaglia, macchia; (*Mach.*) bronzina, fodera di bronzo; presa di corrente a spina, *f.* *to beat about the* ~, divagare, menare il cane per l'aia.

bushel, *n.* staio, *m.* Imperial measure = 8 gallons or 3.637 decalitres.

bushy, *a.* folto; fronzuto, cespuglioso.

busily, *ad.* energicamente, attivamente.

business, *n.* affare, negozio; commercio, *m.*; faccenda; bisogna; impresa, *f.*; mestiere, *m.*; questione [da esaminare], *f.*; ordine del giorno, *m.*; argomento, *f.* (*fuss*) strepito, *m.* ~ *as usual during alterations,* la casa rimane aperta durante i lavori. ~ *card,* biglietto da visita, *m.* ~ *day,* giorno di lavoro, *m.* ~ *hours,* ore d'affari, *f.pl.* ~*like,* pratico, intendente, perito; metodico, serio. ~ *man,* uomo d'affari, *m.*

~ *premises,* locali commerciali, *m.pl.* ~ *quarter,* parte commerciale, *f.*, quartiere commerciale, *m.* ~ *world,* mondo degli affari, *m.*

buskin, *n.* borzacchino, stivaletto; coturno, *m.*

bust, *n.* busto; petto, *m.* ~ *bodice,* reggipetto, *m.*, sottovita, *f.* ~ *measurement,* misura del busto, *f.*

bustard, *n.* ottarda, *f.*

bustle, *n.* scompiglio, movimento, trambusto, andirivieni; (*dress*) puf, *m.* ¶ *v.i.* agitarsi, industriarsi, affaccendarsi.

busy, *a.* occupato, affaccendato; attivo; diligente. ~ *bee,* ape industriosa, *f.* ~ *man, woman,* attivo, -a.; laborioso, -a. ~*body,* ficcanaso, imbroglione, intrigante, *m.*; pettegola, *f.*

but, *c.* ma; però; se non che, sen[n]onché, che. ~ *for,* se non fosse, senza. ¶ *ad. & pr.* fuorché, eccetto, soltanto. non . . . che. ¶ *n.* ma, *m.*; obbiezione, *f.*

butcher, *n.* macellaio, beccaio, *m.* ~'s *meat,* carne macellata, *f.* ~'s *shop,* macelleria, beccheria, *f.* ¶ *v.t.* macellare; massacrare; far strage di. ~*y,* *n.* macellazione, *f.*; macello, *m.*; strage, *f.*

butler, *n.* maggiordomo, *m.*

butt, *n.* (*cask*) botte, *f.*; (*pl. behind target*) terrapieno; (*rifle*) calcio; (*cue*) manico; (*pers.*) bersaglio, zimbello; (*ram, &c.*) cozzo, *m.* ¶ *v.i. & t.,* cozzare.

butter, *n.* burro, *m.* ~ *cooler,* vaso pel burro, *m.* ~ *dish,* piatto pel burro, *m.* ~ *milk,* siero di latte, *m.* ¶ *v.t.* imburrare. ~*ed toast,* crostino al burro, *m.*

buttercup, *n.* bottone d'oro, *m.*

butterfly, *n.* farfalla, *f.*

buttock, *n.* natica, chiappa; (*beef*) coscia di manzo, *f.*

button, *n.* bottone; (*pl. boy*) paggio, *m.* ~*hole,* occhiello, *m.* ~*hole scissors,* forbici da occhiello, *f.pl.* ~*hole stitch,* punto a occhiello, *m.* ~*hole (detain),* trattenere [colle ciance]. ~*hook,* allacciabottoni, *m.* ¶ *v.t.* abbottonare. ~ *oneself up,* abbottonarsi.

buttress, *n.* contrafforte; sostegno, appoggio; (*flying*) arco a sprone, arco d'appoggio, arco rampante, *m.* ¶ *v.t.* appoggiare, sostenere, rinforzare.

buxom, *a.* grassoccio, rotondetto; giocondo, spigliato. ~*ness,* rotondezza; spigliatezza, *f.*

buy, *v.t. ir.* comprare, acquistare. ~ *back,* ricomprare. ~ *in,* ricomprare. ~ *out,* rilevare la parte di. ~ *up,* acquistare, accaparrare. ~**er,** *n.* compratore, -trice; acquirente, *m.f.* ~**ing,** *n.* compra, *f.,* acquisto, *m.*

buzz, *v.i.* ronzare, rombare.

by, *pr.* da; per; con; a; accanto a, presso di. ¶ *ad.* vicino, accanto. ~ & ~, fra poco. ~ *the* ~, ~ *the way,* a proposito; di sfuggita; cammin facendo.

bye (*odd man*), *n.* esente, *m.*

by[e-]law, *n.* regolamento, *m.*

by-election, *n.* elezione parziale, *f.*

bygone, *a.* passato, trascorso; antico, d'altri tempi.

by-pass, *n.* strada di scansamento, *f.;* (*gas*) tubetto, *m.*

bypath, *n.* sentiero, *m.;* traversa, *f.*

by-product, *n.* prodotto secondario; sottoprodotto, *m.*

bystander, *n.* assistente, astante, *m. & f.;* spettatore, -trice, *m.f.*

byway, *n.* stradicciola; traversa, *f.*

byword, *n.* proverbio; zimbello, *m.*

C

C. (*Mus.*) *letter,* do, *m.* ~ *clef,* chiave di do, *f.*

cab, *n.* vettura, carrozza, *f.;* (*locomotive*) ricovero, *m.* ~*man,* vetturino, *m.* ~ *rank,* stazione delle vetture da nolo, *f.*

cabal, *n.* cabala, *f.*

cabaret show, *n.* caffè concerto; spettacolo di varietà, *m.*

cabbage, *n.* cavolo, *m.* ~ *lettuce,* lattuga cappuccia, *f.* ~ *tree,* palmisto, *m.*

cabin, *n.* cabina, camera; capanna, *f.* ~ *boy,* camerotto, *m.* ~ *passenger,* passagero, (-a) di cabina, *m.f.* ~ *trunk,* baule da cabina, *m.*

cabinet, *n.* gabinetto; armadio; stipo, *m.* ~ *council,* Consiglio dei Ministri, *m.* ~ *gramophone,* fonografo a stipo, *m.* ~ *maker,* ebanista, *m.* ~ *making & work,* ebanisteria, *f.* ~ *minister,* Ministro di Stato, *m.*

cable, *n.* cavo, *m.* ~ *railway,* funicolare, *f.* ~ *release,* (*Phot.*) otturatore metallico, *m.* ¶ (*Teleg.*) *v.t.* telegrafare.

caboose *n.* (*Naut.*) cucina, *f.;* (*U.S.A.*) furgone, *m.*

ca' canny strike, *n.* sciopero bianco, *m.*

cacao, *n.* cacao, *m.* ~ *tree,* albero del cacao, *m.*

cachet, *n.* sigillo, *m.;* impronta, *f.*

cachou, *n.* casciú, *m.*

cackle, *n.* grido, cicalio; chiacchierio, *m.* ¶ *v.i.* (*hens*) chiocciare; (*geese*) gridare.

cacoethes, *n.* prurito, *m.*

cactus, *n.* cacto, fico d'India, *m.*

cad, *n.* canaglia, *f.,* figuro, *m.*

caddie, (*golf*) *n.* ragazzo, *m.,* portabastoni, *m.inv.*

caddy, *n.* scatola da tè, *f.*

cadence, *n.* cadenza, *f.*

cadet, *n.* cadetto; allievo [della scuola navale], *m.*

cadge, *v.i.* guadagnucchiare; mendicare. **cadger,** *n.* rigattiere; mendicante, *m.*

Cadiz, *n.* Cadice, *f.*

cage, *n.* gabbia, *f.* ~ *bird,* uccello da gabbia, *m.* ¶ *v.t.* mettere in gabbia, ingabbiare.

cairn, *n.* tumulo; mucchio di pietre, *m.*

Cairo, *n.* il Cairo, *m.*

caisson, *n.* cassone, *m.*

cajole, *v.t.* lusingare, piaggiare. ~**ry,** *n.* moine, lusinghe, *f.pl.*

cake, *n.* pasta, torta; focaccia, *f.;* dolce, *m.;* (*soap, &c.*) pezzo. ~*stand,* servitore muto, *m.* ¶ *v.i.* indurirsi.

calabash, *n.* zucca vuota, *f.*

calamitous, *a.* calamitoso. **calamity,** *n.* calamità, *f.*

calcareous, *a.* calcareo.

calcine, *v.t.* calcinare.

calcium, *n.* calcio, *m.*

calculate, *v.t. & i.* calcolare. ~*ed to,* atto a, capace di. **calculating machine,** *n.* calcolatrice meccanica, *f.* **calculation & calculus,** *n.* calcolo, *m.*

caldron, *n.* caldaia, *f.*

calendar, *n.* calendario, almanacco, *m.;* (*prisoners for trial*), lista, *f.* ~ *year,* anno solare, *m.*

calender, *n.* cilindro, *m.* ¶ *v.t.* cilindrare.

calf, *n.* vitello, *m.;* (*leg*) polpa, *f.* polpaccio, *m.* ~*skin,* pelle di vitello, *f.*

calibrate, *v.t.* calibrare. **calibre,** *n.* calibro, *m.*

calico, *n.* tessuto di cotone, calico, *m.*

Californian, *n. & a.* californiano, *a.*

caliph, *n.* califfo, *m.*

call, *n.* chiamata, *f.*, grido; appello, richiamo, *m.*; voce, *f.*; (*trumpet, bugle*) squillo, *m.*; visita; telefonata; (*Religion*) vocazione, *f.*; (*of a ship*) fermata, *f.*; scalo, rilascio, *m.*; (*Fin.*) domanda, chiamata; richiesta, *f.*; (*cards*) invito, accenno, *m.* ∼ *bird*, uccello di richiamo, *m.* ∼ *boy*, avvisatore, *m.* ∼ *of the blood* (*fig.*), vincolo del sangue, *m.* ∼ *box*, cabina telefonica, *f.* ∼ *over* [*of names*], appello nominale, *m.*, chiama, *f.* ∼ *to arms*, chiamata alle armi, *f.* ¶ *v.t. & i.* chiamare, gridare; richiamare; citare; convocare, riunire; svegliare; nominare, intitolare; visitare; toccare, fare scalo. ∼ *back*, richiamare. ∼ *for*, domandare, richiedere; venire a prendere; (*trumps*) invitare, esigere. ∼ *off*, richiamare, distrarre; annullare, contromandare, disdire; (*hounds*) richiamare. ∼ *out*, gridare; sfidare; chiamare alle armi. ∼ *upon*, invocare, rivolgersi a; visitare. **caller**, *n.* visitatore, -trice, *m.f.* **calling**, *n.* appello, *m.*; chiamata; convocazione; vocazione, professione, *f.*, mestiere, *m.* *Radio-Rome* ∼, parla Radio-Roma.

cal[l]iper, *n.* calibro; (*pl.*) compasso a grossezze, calibro, *m.* ¶ *v.t.* calibrare.

callosity & callus, *n.* callo, *m.*, callosità, *f.* **callous**, *a.* calloso, insensibile.

callow, *a.* senza piume; (*fig.*) in erba, di primo pelo, giovane. ∼ *youth*, giovane imberbe.

calm, *a.* calmo, tranquillo. ¶ *v.t.* calmare, tranquillizzare. ∼**ness**, *n.* calma, tranquillità; bonaccia, *f*

calorie, *n.* caloria, *f.*

calumniate, *v.t.* calunniare. **calumny**, *n.* calunnia, *f.*

Calvary, *n.* (*place*) Calvario, *m.*; (*representation*) calvario, *m.*

calve, *v.i.* figliare, partorire.

calyx, *n.* calice, *m.*

cam, *n.* camma, eccentrico, *m.* ∼**shaft**, albero a eccentrico, *m.*

camber, *n.* curvatura, convessità, *f.*; inarcamento, *m.*

cambric, *n.* tela batista, *f.*

came, *n.* piombo, *m.*

camel, *n.* cammello, *m.* ∼ *driver* cammelliere, *m.*

camellia, *n.* camelia, *f.*

cameo, *n.* cammeo, *m.*

camera, *n.* macchina fotografica, *f.* ∼**man**, fotografo, *m.* ∼ *obscura*

(*opt.*) camera oscura, *f.* *in* ∼, in sessione segreta.

cami-knickers, *n.* camicetta-mutandine, *f.*

camisole, *n.* camiciuola, *f.*, giubbetto, *m.*

camomile, *n.* camomilla, *f.*

camouflage, *n.* mascheramento, *m.* ¶ *v.t.* mascherare, camuffare.

camp, *n.* campo, *m.* ∼ *bed*, letto-da campo, *m.* ∼ *stool*, sedia pieghevole, *f.*; sedile da campo, *m.* ¶ *v.i. & t.* accampare. ∼ *out*, accamparsi [all' aperto].

campaign, *n.* campagna, *f.* ∼**er**, *n.* soldato, veterano, *m.*

campanula, *n.* campanula, *f.*

camphor, *n.* canfora, *f.* ∼**ate**, *v.t.* canforare.

camping out, *n.* accamparsi, accampamento, campeggio, *m.*

can, *n.* scatola di latta, *f.*; secchiello, *m.* ¶ *v.t.* mettere in iscatola, conservare [in iscatola]. *canned salmon*, conserva di salmone in iscatola; scatola di salmone, *f.*

can, *v. aux. ir.* potere, sapere.

Canada, *n.* (il) Canadà, *m.* **Canadian**, *n. & a.* canadese.

canal, *n.* canale, *m.* ∼**ize**, *v.t.* canalizzare.

canary, *n.* canarino; (*wine*) vino delle Canarie, *m.* ∼ *seed*, canaria, *f.* *the C* ∼ *Islands*, le Canarie, *f.pl.*

cancel, *n.* (*Typ.*) pagina cassata, *f.*; cartone; (*Mus.*) bequadro, *m.* ¶ *v.t.* cassare, cancellare, annullare; contrordinare, rievocare.

cancer (*Med.*), *n.* cancro, *m.* ∼**ous**, *a.* cancheroso, canceroso.

candelabrum, *n.* candelabro, *m.*

candid, *a.* sincero, franco; schietto, candido.

candidate, *n.* candidato, pretendente, *m.*

candied peel, *n.* scorza di cedro candita, *f.*

candle, *n.* candela, *f.* ∼ *grease*, sego, *m.* ∼ *power*, candela, *f.* ·a 60 *c.p. lamp*, una lampada elettrica da 60 candele. ∼*stick*, candeliere, *m.*; bugia, *f.* ¶ (*eggs*) *v.t.* mirare in trasparenza. **candling**, *n.* esame in trasparenza, *m.*

candour, *n.* sincerità, franchezza, *f.*

candy, *v.t.* candire. **sugar** ∼, *n.* zucchero candito, *m.*

cane, *n.* canna, *f.*, giunco, *m.*; mazza, (*Sch.*) bastone. ∼ **sugar**, zucchero di canna, *m.* ¶ *v.t.* bastonare; (*chair*) impagliare.

canine, *n.* canino.
canister, *n.* scatola, *f.*
canker, *n.* (*lit. & fig.*) canchero, *m.*
~ *worm,* bruco, *m.* ¶ *v.t.* corrompere, corrodere; incancrenire.
canned goods, *n.* conserve in iscatole, *f.pl.*
cannibal, *n. & a.* cannibale, antropofago, *m.*
cannon, *n.* cannone; (*Bil.*) carambolo, *m.* ~*ball,* palla di cannone, *f.* ~ *shot,* cannonata, *f.* ~ade, *n.* cannoneggiamento, *m.* ¶ *v.t.* cannoneggiare.
canny, *a.* astuto, fino, malizioso, furbo.
canoe, *n.* (*Canadian, &c.*) canotto; (*Rob Roy*) sandolino, *m.*; (*dugout*) canoa, piroga, *f.*
canon, *n.* (*Eccl. rule*) canone, *m.*; (*pl. taste*) norme, *f.pl.*; (*pers.*) canonico, *m.* ~ *law,* diritto canonico. **canonicate, canonry,** *n.* canonicato, *m.* **canonize,** *v.t.* canonizzare.
canopy, *n.* baldacchino, *m.*, tenda, volta; (*Arch.*) pensilina, *f.*
cant, *n.* gergo, *m.*; bacchettoneria; (*slope*) pendenza, inclinazione, *f.* ¶ *v.t.* chinare.
cantankerous, *a.* bisbetico, burbero.
cantata, *n.* cantata, *f.*
canteen, *n.* cantina; (*bottle*) bidone, *m.* ~-*keeper,* cantiniere, *m.*
canter, *n.* galoppo sciolto, piccolo galoppo; (*pers.*) bacchettone, *m.*
Canterbury Bell, *n.* campanula, *f.*
canticle, *n.* cantico, *m.*
cantilever, *n.* modiglione, *m.*, mensola, *f.* ~ *bridge,* ponte a sbalzo, *m.*
canto, *n.* canto, *m.* **cantor,** *n.* cantore, *m.*
canvas, *n.* canavaccio, *m.*, tela; vela, *f.*
canvass, *v.t.* discutere; sollecitare, brigare. ~er, *n.* sollecitatore, agente, *m.*
canyon, cañon, *n.* burrone, *m.*
cap, *n.* berretta, *f.*; (*peaked*) berretto, *m.*; cuffia, *f.*; copertura, *f.*; bottone, *m.*; capsula, *f.* ~ & *bells,* berretto a sonagli, *m.* ¶ *v.t.* coprire il capo; completare, coronare. *to* ~ *all,* per render la cosa completa.
capability, *n.* capacità, *f.* **capable,** *a.* capace, atto; abile. **capacious,** *a.* spazioso. **capacitate,** *v.t.* abilitare.
capacity, *n.* capacità, *f.*
caparison, *v.t.* ingualdrappare; drappeggiare.
cape, *n.* (*Geog.*) capo; (*Dress*) mantello,

m. the ~ *of Good Hope,* il Capo di Buona Speranza.
caper, *n.* capriola, *f.*, salto, *m.*; (*Bot.*) cappero, *m.* ¶ *v.i.* capriolare, saltellare.
capillary, *a.* capillare.
capital, *a.* capitale; ammirabile, famoso, ottimo; (*letter*) maiuscolo. ¶ *n.* (*country*) capitale, *f.*; (*county, province, &c.*) capoluogo; (*Arch.*) capitello; (*Fin.*) capitale, *m.*; (*letter*) maiuscola, *f.* ~ & *Labour,* il Capitale e il Lavoro. ~ *expenditure,* spese d'impianto, *f.pl.* ~ *stock* & ~ *sum,* capitale, *m.* ~ *value,* valore del capitale, *m.* ~ist, *n.* capitalista, *m.* ~ize, *v.t.* capitalizzare.
capitulate, *v.i.* capitolare. **capitulation,** *n.* capitulazione, *f.*
capon, *n.* cappone, *m.*
caprice, *n.* capriccio, ghiribizzo, *m.* **capricious,** *a.* capriccioso, bizzarro.
capsicum, *n.* peperone, *m.*
capsize, *v.t.* capovolgere, ribaltare; (*v.i.*) capovolgersi, ribaltarsi.
capstan, *n.* argano, *m.*; (*lathe*) revolver, *m.*
capsule, *n.* capsula, *f.*
captain, *n.* capitano; (*Nav.*) capitano di vascello; (*of merchant ship*), capitano marittimo, *m.*
caption, *n.* intestazione, leggenda, *f.*
captious, *a.* difficile, cavilloso.
captivate, *v.t.* cattivarsi. **captive,** *a. & n.* prigioniero, -a, *a. & m.f.* **captivity,** *n.* prigionia, *f.* **capture,** *n.* presa. ¶ *v.t.* prendere.
Capuchin friar, nun, *n.* cappuccino, -a, *m.f.*
car, *n.* carro; vagone, *m.*; carretta, carrozza, *f.*; (*Aero.*) gondola, navicella, *f.* *motor* ~, automobile, *f.* ~ *bandit,* brigante in automobile, *m.* ~ *park,* parco automobilistico, *m.*
caracol[e], *n.* caracollo, *m.*
caramel, *n.* caramella, *f.*
carapace, *n.* carapace, *m.*
carat, *n.* carato, *m.*
caravan, *n.* carovana, *f.*; (*house on wheels*) carrozzone di zingari, carro-carovana, *m.* **caravanserai,** *n.* caravanserraglio, *m.*
caraway, *n.* caro, carvi, *m.*
carbide, *n.* carburo, *m.*
carbine, *n.* carabina, *f.*
carbolic acid, *n.* acido fenico, *m.*
carbon, *n.* (*Chem.*) carbonio, *m.*; (*Elec.*) carbone, *m.* ~ *copy,* copia da carta al carbone, *f.* ~ *monoxide,* monossido di carbone, *m.* ~ *paper,*

carta [al] carbone, *f.* **carbonate,** *n.*
carbonato, *m.* **carbonic,** *a.*
carbonico. **carboniferous,** *a.*
carbonifero. **carbonize,** *v.t.*
carbonizzare; (*v.i.*) carbonizzarsi.
carboy, *n.* fiascone, *m.*
carbuncle, *n.* (*jewel & Med.*)
carbonchio, *m.*
carburettor, *n.* carburatore, *m.*
carcase *or* **carcass,** *n.* carcame, *m.*;
(*ship, &c.*) carcassa, *f.*
card, *n.* carta; (*loose index*) scheda, *f.*;
(*textiles*) cardo, *m.*; (*golf*) scheda dei
punti, *f.* ~*board,* cartone, *m.*
~*board maker,* fabbricante di
cartone, *m.* ~ *case,* portacarte, *m.inv.*
~ *index & ~ index cabinet,*
schedario, *m.* ~ *sharper,* baro,
truffatore di carte, *m.* ~ *table,*
tavola da giuoco, *f.* ~ *trick,* giuoco
di prestigio colle carte, *m.* ¶ *v.t.*
cardare.
cardigan [jacket], *n.* panciotto a
maglia, *m.*
cardinal, *a. & n.* cardinale, *a. & m.*
care, *n.* cura, attenzione; premura;
accuratezza; precauzione; inquietudine, ansietà; custodia, *f.* ~ *of,*
c/o, presso. ~*taker,* guardiano, -a,
m.f. guardaporte, *m.* ~*worn,*
abbattuto, prostrato. ¶ *v.i.* curarsi,
badare.
careen, *v.t.* carenare.
career, *n.* carriera; corsa, *f.* ¶ *v.i.*
slanciarsi, galoppare.
careful, *a.* accurato, attento, premuroso; prudente. ~**ness,** *n.*
attenzione, premura; prudenza, *f.*
careless, *a.* negligente, spensierato.
~**ness,** *n.* negligenza, trascuranza,
f.
caress, *n.* carezza, *f.* ¶ *v.t.* accarezzare.
caret, *n.* segno di mancanza, *m.*
cargo, *n.* carico, *m.* ~ *boat, steamer,*
nave da carico, *f.*; bastimento,
battello, piroscafo da carico, *m.*
Caribbean Sea, Mare dei Caraibi, *m.*
caricature, *n.* caricatura, *f.* ¶ *v.t.*
mettere in caricatura.
carman, *n.* carrettiere, *m.*
Carmelite, *n.* (*friar, nun*) Carmelita,
m.f.
carmine, *n.* carminio, *m.* ¶ *a.*
carminiato.
carnage, *n.* strage, *f.*
carnal, *a.* carnale.
carnation, *n.* garofano; (*colour*)
incarnato, rosso, *m.*
carnelian, *n.* corniola, *f.*
carnival, *n.* carnevale, *m.*
carnivora, *n.pl.* carnivori, *m.pl.*

carnivorous, *a. & * **carnivore,** *n.*
carnivoro, *a. & m.*
carob [bean], *n.* carruba, *f.*
carol, *n.* cantico, canto, *m.* *Christmas*
~, cantico di Natale, *m.* ¶ *v.i.*
cantare; (*lark*) gorgheggiare, trillare.
carousal, *n.* gozzoviglia, orgia, *f.*
carouse, *v.i.* gozzovigliare.
carp, *n.* carpione, *m.* ¶ *v.i.* cavillare.
~ *at,* censurare.
Carpathians [the], *n.* (i) Carpazi, *m.pl.*
carpenter, *n.* legnaiuolo, falegname,
m. ¶ *v.i.* fare il legnaiuolo.
carpentry, *n.* lavoro di legname, *m.*
carpet, *n.* tappeto, *m.* ~ *broom,*
scopa, *f.* ~ *knight,* cavaliere da
salotto, *m.* ~ *slippers,* pantofole,
f.pl. ~ *sweeper,* macchina spazzatrice [per pulire i tappeti], *f.* ¶ *v.t.*
tappetare.
carriage, *n.* vettura, carrozza, *f.*;
vagone; (*gun*) affusto, *m.*; (*Mach.*)
slitta, *f.*; portamento, *m.,* andatura,
f.; porto, trasporto, *m.*; spese di
trasporto, *f.pl.* ~ & *pair,* carrozza
con due cavalli, *f.* ~ *attendant*
(*hotel, &c.*) portiere, *m.* ~ *entrance,*
entrata per carrozze, *f.* ~ *forward,*
porto assegnato. ~ *jack,* cricco, *m.*
~ *paid,* ~ *free,* franco di porto.
carrier, *n.* portatore; carrettiere;
spedizioniere, corriere, *m.*; (*Mach.*)
slitta, *f.* *luggage* ~, portabagaglio,
m. ~ *pigeon,* piccione viaggiatore, *m.*
~ *tricycle,* triciclo portamerci, *m.*
carrion, *n.* carogna, *f.*
carrot, *n.* carota, *f.* ~*y hair,* capelli
color carota, *m.pl.*
carry, *n.* portata, *f.,* (*Arith.*) riporto,
m. ¶ *v.t.* portare; trasportare;
recare; menare; condurre; spedire;
(*Arith.*) riportare; votare. ~ *away,*
portar via, strappare, togliere; (*fig.*)
trasportare. ~ *forward* (*Book-
keeping*), riportare. ~ *on,* condurre,
proseguire; continuare; lamentarsi;
condursi male. ~ *out,* eseguire,
effettuare, realizzar e; portar fuori.
cart, *n.* carro, *m.*; carretta, *f.*; barroccio, *m.* ~ *grease,* sugna, *f.* ~*horse,*
cavallo da carretta, *m.* ~*load,*
carrettata, *f.* ~*note* (*Cust.*), lasciapassare, *m.* ¶ *v.t.* trasportare,
carreggiare, portare. ~**age,** *n.*
trasporto, porto, *m.*; spese di
trasporto, *f.pl.* ~**er,** *n.* carrettiere,
carrettaio, *m.*
Carthusian [monk], *n.* certosino, *m.*
~ *monastery,* certosa, *f.*
cartilage, *n.* cartilagine, *f.*
cartoon, *n.* cartone, *m.*; caricatura, *f.*

~ist, *n.* artista, disegnatore, caricaturista, *m.*

cartouche, *n.* cartoccio, *m.* cartridge, *n.* cartuccia, *f.*; (*cannon*) cartoccio, *m.* ~ belt, cartucciera, *f.* ~ pouch, giberna, *f.*

carve, *v.t.* scolpire, intagliare; (*meat*) trinciare, tagliare. carver (*pers.*), *n.* scultore, intagliatore; trinciatore, tagliatore, *m.* carving, *n.* scultura, *f.*, intaglio; trinciare, taglio, *m.* ~ knife or [*meat*] carver, trinciante, *m.* ~ tool, scalpello, *m.*

cascade, *n.* cascata, cascatella, *f.*

case, *n.* caso; stato, *m.*; questione; causa, *f.*, affare, processo, *m.*; cassa, scatola; valigia, sacca, *f.*; sacco, *m.*; busta, copertina, *f.*; astuccio, fodero; scrigno; portafogli, *m.*; (*sausage*) sacco, *m.*, budella, *f.pl.*; (*precision balance*) cassa, vetrina; (*piano*) cassa; (*Typ.*) cassa, *f. suit* ~, valigia, *f.* ~ ending (*Gram.*), desinenza [del caso], *f. in* ~ *of need*, all'uopo, in caso di bisogno. ~ *opener*, arnese per aprire, *m.* ¶ *v.t.* rivestire, rinchiudere; (*Min.*) incamiciare.

caseharden, *v.t.* cementare; (*fig.*) indurire.

casemate, *n.* casamatta, *f.*

casement, *n.* battente, *m.*, imposta, *f.* ~ window, finestra a gangheri, *f.* ~ cloth, tessuto per imposta, *m.* ~ stay, gancio del battente, *m.*

cash, *n.* contanti, *m.pl.*, numerario, denaro, *m.*; cassa, *f.*; fondi, *m.pl.* ~ in hand, pronti contanti, *m.pl.* ~book, libro di cassa, *m.* ~box, cassetta, *f.* ~ desk, cassa, *f.* ~ discount, sconto, *m.* ~ down, a pronta cassa. *in* ~ & *for* ~, a contanti. ~ *on delivery*, spedizione contro pagamento, *f.* ~ *register*, registratore di cassa, *m.* ~ *with order*, pagamento coll'ordinazione. ¶ *v.t.* incassare; cambiare, pagare. ~ier, *n.* cassiere, *m.* ~ & *bookkeeper*, cassiere-contabile, *m.* ¶ *v.t.* cassare, destituire.

cashmere, *n.* casimirra, *f.*

casing, *n.* rivestimento, *m.*, custodia, copertura, *f.*; stipite, *m.*; gabbia, *f.*

cask, *n.* botte, *f.*; barile, *m.*

casket, *n.* scrigno, *m.*

Caspian Sea (The), il mare Caspio, *m.*

casserole, *n.* casseruola, *f.*

cassia, *n.* senna d'Egitto, *f.* ~ tree, cassia, *f.*

cassock, *n.* sottana, *f.*

cast, *n.* getto, lancio; gesso; pezzo fuso, *m.*; giacchiata, *f.*; minugia da pesca, *f.*; sommare, *m.*, addizione, *f.*; (*Theat.*) distribuzione delle parti, *f.*; (*worm*) deposito, *m.*, deiezione, *f.* ~ of features, fisonomia, aria, *f.* ~ of mind, tendenza, *f.*, temperamento, *m.* ¶ *v.t. ir.* gettare, lanciare, buttare; fondere, colare; sommare, calcolare; distribuire. ~ iron, ghisa, *f.*; ferro fuso, *m.*; (*fig.*, *a*) rigido. ~ its skin, cambiar di pelle. ~net, giacchio, *m.* ~ off, (*Typ.*) valutare; (*Naut.*) mollare; abbandonare. ~off clothing, vecchi abiti, abiti smessi, *m.pl.* ~ on (*Knit.*), avviare. ~ out, scacciare, rigettare, buttar via. ~ shadow, ombra gettata, *f.* ~ steel, acciaio fuso, *m.* [*crucible*] ~ steel, acciaio fuso [in crogiuolo], *m.*

castanet, *n.* castagnetta, *f.*

castaway, *n.* naufrago, *m.*; (*fig.*) reprobo, *m.*

caste, *n.* casta, *f.*; ceto, *m.*

castellated, *a.* merlato.

caster, *n.* gettatore, fonditore, calcolatore, *m.*; (see *castor*).

castigate, *v.t.* gastigare. castigation, *n.* gastigo, *m.*

casting, *n.* getto; pezzo fuso; giacchiare, *m.*; sommazione; pesca a getto, *f.* ~ off (*Typ.*), valutazione, *f.*; (*Knit.*) terminamento, *m.* ~ on, avviamento, *m.* ~ rod, canna da pesca, *f.* ~ vote, voto decisorio, *m.*

castle, *n.* castello, *m.*; rocca; (*Chess*) torre, *f.* ¶ *v.i.* (*chess*) arroccare.

castor or caster, *n.* (*bottle*) ampollina, pepaiola; (*roller*) rotella, *f.* ~ oil, olio di ricino, *m.* ~ oil plant, ricino, *m.* castor (or caster) sugar, polvere di zucchero, *f.*

castrate, *v.t.* castrare. castration, *n.* castrazione, *f.*

casual, *a.* casuale, fortuito; (*remark*) di passaggio. ~ labourer, lavorante giornaliero, *m.* ~ profit, tornaconto casuale, *m.* ~ water (*golf*), pozza fortuita, *f.* ¶ *n.* disgraziato di passaggio, vagabondo, *m.* ~ty, *n.* disgrazia; vittima, *f.*; (*pl. Mil.*) perdite, *f.pl.*

casuistry, *n.* casuistica, *f.*

cat, *n.* gatto, *m.*; (*whip*) frusta, *f.*; (*tipcat*) bastoncino, *m.* ~ burglar, ladro gatto, *m.* ~call, fischio, fischietto, *m.* ~calling, fischiare, *m.* ~'s cradle, giuoco del ripiglino, *m.* ~'s eye (*jewel*), occhio di gatto, *m.* ~'s paw (*fig.*), minchione, strumento, *m.* ~ tribe, razza dei gatti, *f.*

cataclysm, *n.* cataclismo, *m.*

catacomb, *n.* catacomba, *f.*
catafalque, *n.* catafalco, *m.*
catalepsy, *n.* catalessia, *f.* cataleptic,
   a. catalettico.
catalogue, *n.* catalogo, *m.* ¶ *v.t.*
   catalogare.
catapult, *n.* catapulta, *f.*; (*boy's*)
   fionda, frombola, *f.* ¶ *v.t. & abs.*,
   scagliare, frombolare; (*Aero.*) lanciare.
cataract, *n.* (*Med.*) cateratta; (*falls*)
   cascata, *f.*
catarrh, *n.* catarro, *m.*
catastrophe, *n.* catastrofe, *f.*
catch, *n.* presa; (*fish*) pescata, retata;
   (*trick*) trappola, *f.*, inganno; (*Mech.*)
   dente d'arresto, scatto; (*window
   catch*, *&c.*) nottolino, gancio, uncino,
   m. ~*phrase*, grido popolare, motto,
   m. ~*word*, richiamo, *m.* ¶ *v.t. &
   i.tr.* cogliere, acchiappare, pigliare,
   afferrare, prendere; attaccarsi;
   sorprendere; (*cold*) buscarsi. ~ *as
   ~ can*, lotta libera, *f.* ~ *fire*,
   accendersi, prender fuoco; (*cook.*)
   abbruciare. ~ *on*, venire in voga;
   capire. ~*er*, *n.* prenditore, *m.*
   ~*ing*, *a.* contagioso; seducente,
   attraente.
catechism, *n.* catechismo, *m.*
   catechize, *v.t.* catechizzare.
categorical, *a.* categorico. category,
   n. categoria.
cater, *v.i.* provvedere. ~ *for*,
   provvedere; indirizzarsi a, mirare.
caterer, *n.* provveditore, -trice;
   trattore; ristoratore, *m.*
caterpillar, *n.* bruco, *m.* ~ *tractor*,
   trattore a cingoli, *m.*
caterwaul, *v.i.* miagolare.
catgut, *n.* corda di minugia, *f.*
cathead, *n.* grua di capone, *m.*
cathedral, *n.* duomo, *m.*; cattedrale, *f.*
catherine wheel, *n.* girandola, *f.*
   to turn ~ ~*s*, fare la ruota.
cathode, *n.* catodo, *m.*
catholic, *a. & n.* cattolico, *a. & m.*
   ~*ism*, *n.* cattolicismo, *m.*
catkin, *n.* (*Bot.*), amento, *m.*
cattle, *n.* bestiame, *m.* ~*bell*,
   campanaccio, *m.* ~ *market*,
   mercato del bestiame, *m.* ~ *plague*,
   peste bovina, *f.* ~ *show*, esposizione
   dei bovini, *f.* ~ *truck*, vagone
   bestiame, *m.*
Caucasian, *a.* caucasico. ¶ *n.*
   caucasico, -a, *m.f.* the Caucasus,
   il Caucaso, *m.*
caucus, *n.* riunione del partito,
   adunanza del partito; cabala, *f.*
caul, *n.* cuffia, *f.*; (*Anat.*) amnio, *m.*

cauldron, *n.* caldaia, *f.*
cauliflower, *n.* cavolfiore, *m.*
caulk, *v.t.* calafatare.
causative, *a.* causativo. cause, *n.*
   cagione, causa, *f.*; motivo; processo,
   m., lite, *f.* ~ *list*, ruolo delle cause,
   m. ¶ *v.t.* cagionare, causare,
   provocare, produrre; fare, *e.g. to* ~
   to vary, far variare.
causeway, *n.* terrapieno, *m.*, diga, *f.*
caustic, *a. & n.* caustico, *a. & m.*
   cauterize, *v.t.* cauterizzare.
   cautery, *n.* cauterio, *m.*
caution, *n.* prudenza, cautela, *f.*;
   avvertimento, *m.* ~! attenti!
   ¶ *v.t.* avvertire, premunire.
cautious, *a.* cauto, prudente.
   ~*ness*, *n.* prudenza, circospezione,
   f.
cavalcade, *n.* cavalcata, *f.*
cavalier, *a.* brusco, scortese, alterigio.
   ¶ *n.* cavaliere, *m.*
cavalry, *n.* cavalleria, *f.*
cave, *n.* caverna, spelonca, grotta, *f.*,
   antro, *m.* ~ *dweller*, abitatore di
   caverne, troglodita, *m.* ~ *in*, *v.t.*
   scassare; (*v.i.*) cedere.
cave! *i.* attenti!
cavern, *n.* caverna, *f.* ~*ous*, *a.*
   cavernoso.
caviar[e], *n.* caviale, *m.*
cavil, *n.* cavillo, *m.* ¶ *v.i.* cavillare,
   criticare.
cavity, *n.* cavità, *f.*, buco, *m.*
caw, *v.i.* gracchiare.
Cayenne pepper, *n.* pepe di Caienna,
   m.
cease, *v.i. & t.* cessare. *without* ~,
   senza tregua. ~*less*, *a.* continuo,
   incessante. ~*lessness*, *n.* continuità, *f.*
cedar, *n.* cedro, *m.*
cede, *v.t.* cedere.
ceil, *v.t.* soffittare. ~*ing*, *n.* soffitto,
   m.
celebrate, *v.t. & i.* celebrare,
   solennizzare. ~*d*, *a.* celebre,
   famoso, rinomato. celebrity, *n.*
   celebrità, *f.*
celery, *n.* sedano, appio. *m.*
celestial, *a.* celeste.
celibacy, *n.* celibato, *m.* celibate, *n.*
   celibe, *m.*
cell, *n.* cella, cellula, *f.*; alveolo, *m.*;
   (*pl. Mil.*) prigione, *f.*; (*Phys.*)
   elemento, *m.* *dry* ~, pila a secco, *f.*
cellar, *n.* cantina, *f.* ¶ *v.t.* mettere in
   cantina. ~*er*, *n.* cantiniere, *m.*
'cellist, *n.* violoncellista, *m.* 'cello, *n.*
   violoncello, *m.*
cellular, *a.* cellulare. celluloid, *n.*

celluloide, *f.* **cellulose**, *n.* cellulosa, *f.*
Celt, *n.* Celto, *m.* **Celtic**, *a. & (language)* *n.* celtico, *a. & m.*
cement, *n.* cemento; smalto, *m.* ¶ *v.t.* cementare.
cemetery, *n.* cimitero, *m.*
cenotaph, *n.* cenotafio, *m.*
cense, *v.t.* incensare. **censer**, *n.* turibolo, incensiere, *m.*
censor, *n.* censore, *m.* **~ious**, *a.* censorio. **~ship** & **vote of censure**, *n. &* [**board of**] **censors**, censura, *f.* **censure**, *v.t.* censurare; biasimare.
census, *n* censimento, censo, *m.*
centaur, *n.* centauro, *m.*
centenarian, *n.* centenario, *m.* **centenary**, *n.* centenario, *m.*
centigrade, *a.* centigrado.
centipede, *n.* millepiedi, *m.*
central, *a.* centrale. *C~ America,* l'America Centrale, *f.* **~ heating**, termosifone, *m.* **~ize**, *v.t.* accentrare, centralizzare. **centre**, *n.* centro; punto, *m.* ~ *bit,* succhiello, *m.* ~ *board,* chiglia di deriva, *f.* ~ *forward* (Foot.), centro d'attacco, *m.* ~ *half,* c. mediano, *m.* **~piece**, trionfo da tavola, *m.* **~punch**, punzone, *m.* ~ *service line* (Ten.), linea mediana, *f.* ¶ *v.t.* concentrare.
centrifugal, *a.* centrifugo. **centripetal**, *a.* centripeto.
century, *n.* secolo, *m.*
ceramic, *a.* ceramico. **~s**, *n.* ceramica, *f.*
cereal, *a. & n.* cereale, *a. & m.*
ceremonial, *n.* cerimoniale, *m.* ¶ *a.* cerimoniale, rituale. **ceremonious**, *a.* cerimonioso. **~ness**, *n.* cerimoniosità, *f.* **ceremony**, *n.* cerimonia, *f.*, rito, *m.*
certain, *a.* certo. **~ty**, *n.* certezza; cosa certa, *f. for a ~,* per certo.
certificate, *n.* fede, *f.*, attestato, atto, certificato, *m.* ¶ *v.t.* attestare, certificare. **certify**, *v.t.* attestare, certificare; dichiarare.
cesspool, *n.* bottino, pozzo nero, *m.*
Ceylon, *n.* il Ceylon, *m.*
Chadband, *n.* santocchio, bacchettone, *m.*
chafe, *v.t.* fregare, stropicciare; (*v.i.*) logorarsi; (*fig.*) irritarsi, riscaldarsi.
chaff, *n.* pagliola, lolla, gluma, *f.*; motteggio, *m.* **~-cutter**, trinciapaglia, tritapaglia, *m.* ¶ *v.t.* motteggiare, canzonare, beffare.
chaffinch, *n.* fringuello, *m.*
chafing dish, *n.* scaldavivande, *m.*

chain, *n.* catena; catenella, *f.*; (*fig.*) concatenamento, *m.*, cintura, *f.* (Imperial linear meas.) = 22 yards or 20.1168 metres. ~ *bridge,* ponte sospeso, *m.* ~ *stitch,* punto a catenella. ~ *store,* negozio a catena, *m.* ¶ ~ & ~ *up, v.t.* incatenare.
chair, *n.* sedia, seggiola; (Univ.) cattedra; (at meeting) presidenza, *f.*; (Rail.) cuscinetto, *m.* ~ *attendant,* noleggiatore di carrozzelle; noleggiatore di sedie, *m.* **~back** (Need.), poggiacapo, *m.* [*loose*] ~ *cover,* copertella, *f.* ¶ **~!** all'ordine! ¶ *v.t.* portare in trionfo.
chairman, *n.* presidente, *m.* **~ship**, *n.* presidenza, *f.*
chalcedony, *n.* calcedonia, *f.*
chalice, *n.* calice, *m.*, coppa, *f.*
chalk, *n.* calcare; gesso, *m.*; creta, *f.*; (Bil.) bianco, *m.* **~line**, (cord) cordella, *f.*; (mark) segno, *m.*, linea, *f.* ~ *pit,* cava di gesso, *f.* ¶ *v.t.* segnare col gesso. **~y**, *a.* cretoso, gessoso.
challenge, *n.* sfida, *f.*; cartello, *m.*; (Mil.) chi-va-là, *m.* ~ *cup,* coppa challenge, *f.* ~ *match,* campionato, *m.* ¶ *v.t.* sfidare, provocare; contestare; ricusare; fermare.
chalybeate, *a.* ferruginoso.
chamber, *n.* camera, stanza, *f.*; (pl.) gabinetto, *m.* ~ *counsel,* avvocato consulente, avvocato consultore, *m.* **~maid**, cameriera, *f.* ~ *music,* musica da camera, *f.* ~ *pot,* orinale, *m.* *six* **~ed** *revolver,* revolver a sei colpi, *m.*, rivoltella, *f.*
chameleon, *n.* camaleonte, *m.*
chamfer, *n.* smusso, *m.* ¶ *v.t.* smussare; scanalare.
chamois, *n.* camoscio, *m.* ~ *leather,* pelle di camoscio, *f.*
champ, *v.t.* rodere, masticare.
champagne, *n.* sciampagna, *f.* ~ *glass,* bicchiere da sciampagna, *m.*
champion, *n.* campione, difensore, *m.* *lady* ~, campionessa, *f.* ~ *idiot,* solenne bestia, *f.* ~ *turnip,* re delle rape, *m.* **~ship**, *n.* campionato, *m.*
chance, *a.* casuale, fortuito; d'occasione. ¶ *n.* caso, *m.*, sorte; ventura; occasione, *f. to ~ it,* arrischiarla, prendere il rischio. ~ *shot,* colpo riuscito a caso, *m.*
chancel, *n.* coro, *m.*
chancellery, *n.* cancelleria, *f.* **chancellor**, *n.* cancelliere, *m.* *C~ of the Exchequer* (Eng.), Ministro delle Finanze (Ital.), *m.*
chancre, *n.* ulcera venerea, *f.*

chandelier, *n.* lampadario, candelabro, *m.*

chandler, *n.* ceraiuolo; droghiere, *m.*

change, *n.* cambiamento, *m.*, vicenda; alterazione; mutazione; variazione, *f.*; movimento, *m.*; (*money*) spiccioli, *m.pl.*; (*exchange*) borsa, *f. at* ∼ (*barometer*), al variabile. ∼ *of clothes,* muta di panni, *f.* ∼ *of front,* voltafaccia, *m.*; conversione, *f.* ∼ *speed* [*gear*], cambio di velocità, *m.* ¶ *v.t. & i.* cambiare; cambiar di; cambiarsi, mutare, cangiare, scambiare. ∼ *here for* . . . , si cambia qui per . . . ∼ *one's mind, one's linen,* cambiar d'avviso, mutarsi i panni. ∼ *the subject,* cambiar discorso, cambiare argomento. ∼ *step,* cambiar il passo. ∼**able,** *a.* incostante, variabile, mutabile, cangiante.

channel, *n.* canale, stretto, *m.*; (*fig.*) via, *f. the English C*∼, la Manica. *the C*∼ *Islands,* le Isole Normanne, *f.pl.* ¶ *v.t.* solcare, scannellare, scanalare. **channelling,** *n.* scanalatura, *f.*

chant, *n.* canto fermo, *m.* ¶ *v.i. & t.* cantare, salmeggiare. **chanty,** *n.* cantilena, *f.*, canto, *m.*

chaos, *n.* caos, *m.* **chaotic,** *a.* confuso, caotico.

chap, *n.* ragazzo; bravo, *m.*; (*pl.*) (*on the skin*) screpolature; (*animal*) gote; (*vice*) mascelle, *f.pl.* ¶ *v.t. & i.* screpolare, screpolarsi.

chapel, *n.* cappella, chiesetta, *f.* ∼ *of ease,* chiesetta succursale, *f.*

chaperon, *n.* guardiana, *f.* ¶ *v.t.* accompagnare.

chaplain, *n.* cappellano, *m.* ∼**cy,** *n.* cappellanato, *m.*

chaplet, *n.* corona, ghirlanda, *f.*; rosario, *m.*

chapter, *n.* capitolo, *m.*

char, *n.* (*fish*) salmarino, *m.* ¶ *v.t.* abbruciacchiare; carbonizzare; (*v.i.*) abbruciacchiarsi; lavorare a giornata.

charabanc, *n.* carrozzone a panche trasversali; autobus, *m.*

character, *n.* carattere, *m.*, indole, *f.*, naturale, *m.*; riputazione; lettera; parte, *f.*; personaggio; certificato, *m.* **characteristic,** *a.* caratteristico. ¶ *n.* caratteristica, *f.*; sintomo, *m.* **characterize,** *v.t.* caratterizzare.

charade, *n.* sciarada, *f.*

charcoal, *n.* carbone di legna; carboncino, *m.* ∼ *burner,* carbonaio, *m.* ∼ *drawing,* disegno al carboncino, *m.* ∼ *pencil,* carboncino, *m.*

chare, *v.i.* lavorare a giornata.

charge, *n.* carico, *m.*, carica, *f.*; incarico, *m.*; custodia; guardia; accusa, *f.*; comandamento, *m.*; incombenza, *f.*; (*bishop's*) mandamento; prezzo, *m.*; spese, *f.pl.* ¶ *v.t.* caricare; domandare; ordinare; prescrivere; affidare, incaricare; incolpare, accusare. ∼**able,** *a.* imputabile; responsabile; applicabile; da pagare.

charger, *n.* (*horse*) cavallo di battaglio; (*Poet.*) destriero; (*dish*) piatto, tagliere, *m.*

charily, *ad.* parcamente, prudentemente.

chariot, *n.* carro, *m.* **charioteer,** *n.* conduttore di carro, *m.*

charitable, *a.* caritatevole, elemosiniere; pietoso. **charity,** *n.* carità; elemosina; compassione, *f.*

charlatan, *n.* ciarlatano, cerretano, saltimbanco, *m.*

charm, *n.* incanto; fascino, *m.*; vaghezza, *f.*; (*trinket*) ciondolo; talismano, amuleto, portafortuna, *m.* ¶ *v.t.* incantare, affascinare, ammaliare; invaghire. ∼**er,** *n.* incantatore, -trice; mago, -a. ∼**ing,** *a.* grazioso, incantevole, affascinante.

charnel house, *n.* ossario, *m.*

chart, *n.* carta nautica, *f.*; grafico; diagramma, *m.* ¶ *v.t.* fare la carta di . . . , portare sulla carta geografica; tracciare.

charter, *n.* statuto; privilegio, *m.*, patente, *f.* ∼ *party,* contratto di noleggio, *m.* ¶ *v.t.* noleggiare; privilegiare. ∼**er,** *n.* noleggiatore, *m.* ∼**ing,** *n.* noleggio, *m.*

charwoman, *n.* giornante, *f.*

chary, *a.* cauto, prudente; gretto; avaro. ∼ *of,* poco disposto a.

chase, *n.* caccia; (*gun*) scarica, volata, *f.*; (*Typ.*) telaio, *m.* ¶ *v.t.* scacciare, inseguire; (*Hawking*) cacciare; (*metals*) cesellare. **chaser** (*Nav.*), *n.* cacciatore, *m.* ∼ *plane,* aeroplano da caccia, *m.*

chasm, *n.* abisso, gorgo, vuoto, *m.*

chassé, *n.* chassé, *m.* ¶ *v.t.* far chassé. ∼**-croisé,** *n.* chassé-croisé, *m.*

chassis, *n.* telaio, *m.*, intelaiatura, *f.*

chaste, *a.* casto; (*fig.*) di buon gusto. **chasten** & **chastise,** *v.t.* castigare. **chastisement,** *n.* castigo, *m.*

chastity, *n.* castità, *f.*

chasuble, *n.* pianeta, *f.*

chat, *n.* chiacchiera; chiacchierata, *f.* ¶ *v.i.* chiacchierare.

chattel, *n.* mobile, *m.*; (*pl.*) effetti, beni mobili, *m.pl.*

chatter, *n.* ciarle, *f.pl.*, cicaleccio, *m.* ¶ *v.i.* ciarlare; cicalare; (*teeth*) battere; (*tool*) tintinnare. **~box,** *n.* ciarlone, *a*, chiacchierone, *a.*

chauffeur, *n.* conduttore, meccanico; autista, *m.*

cheap, *a.* (*article*, &*c.*) a buon mercato, a buon prezzo, poco costoso; (*ticket*, &*c.*) a prezzo ridotto; (*price*) buono, basso, vile. **~** *edition,* edizione economica, *f.* **~*jack*,** mercaiuolo ambulante, *m.* **~er,** *a.* a miglior mercato, meno costoso, a prezzo piú basso. **~ly,** *ad.* a buon mercato, a buon prezzo. **~ness,** *n.* buon prezzo, prezzo basso, *m.*; i prezzi bassi, *m.pl.*

cheat, *n.* (*pers.*) truffatore, -trice, scroccone, -a; baro, *m.* ¶ *v.t.* & *i.* truffare, frodare, ingannare, defraudare. **~ing,** *n.* truffa, fraude, *f.*, inganno, *m.*

check, *n.* scacco; freno; controllo, ritegno, arresto; bollettino di bagaglio; (*design*) disegno quadrettato, *m.*; (*stuff*) tela quadrettata, *f.*; (*att.*) di controllo, di riscontro, verificatore, trice. ¶ *v.t.* ritenere, frenare, moderare; controllare, riscontrare, verificare; disegnare a quadretti. ¶ (*Chess*) *i.* scacco! **~mate,** scacco matto! *v.t.* dare scacco matto a; (*fig.*) impedire, ostacolare.

cheek, *n.* guancia, gota; impudenza, sfacciataggine, *f.* **~bone,** zigomo, *m.* **~y,** *a.* impudente, sfacciato, sfrontato.

cheep, *v.i.* pigolare. **~ing,** *n.* pigolio, *m.*

cheer, *n.* (*food*) tavola, *f.*, trattamento, *m.*; consolazione, *f.*; applauso, evviva, *m.*; (*face*) cera, *f.* ¶ *v.t.* rallegrare, rincorare, incoraggiare; applaudire. **~** *up,* consolare, rallegrare. **~** *up!* coraggio! animo! **~ful,** *a.* contento, gaio, lieto, allegro. **~fulness,** *n.* allegrezza, *f.*, buon umore, *m.*, contentezza, letizia, *f.* **~less,** *a.* triste, malinconico.

cheese, *n.* formaggio, cacio, *m.* **~** *cover,* coperchio, *m.* **~** *dairy,* fabbrica di formaggi, cascina, *f.* **~** *industry,* l'industria dei formaggi, *f.* **~** *knife,* coltello da formaggio, *m.* **~mite,** acaro del formaggio, *m.* **~monger,** formaggiaio, caciaiuolo, *m.* **~paring,** spilorceria, *f.*; (*a.*) spilorcio. **~plate,** portaformaggio, *m.*

cheetah, *n.* ghepardo, *m.*

chemical, *a.* chimico. ¶ *n.* composizione chimica, *f.*

chemise, *n.* camicia, *f.*

chemist, *n.* (*scientist*) chimico; (*druggist*) farmacista, *m.* **~'s** *shop,* farmacia, *f.* **~ry,** *n.* chimica, *f.*

cheque, *n.* assegno bancario, mandato, *m.* **~** *book,* libretto degli assegni, *m.*

chequer, *v.t.* disegnare a scacchi, screziare. **~ed,** (*fig.*) *p.a.* equivoco.

cherish, *v.t.* curare, favorire, proteggere; tener caro, avere a cuore; accarezzare; nutrire.

cherry, *n.* ciliegia, *f.* **~** *orchard,* ciliegeto, *m.* **~** *pie,* (*Bot.*) eliotropio, *m.* **~red,** *a.* & *n.* color ciliegia, *a.* & *m.* **~stone,** nocciolo di ciliegia, *m.* **~** *tree,* ciliegio; (*wild*) visciolo, *m.*

cherub, *n.* cherubino, *m.* **cherubic,** *a.* cherubico.

chervil, *n.* cerfoglio, *m.*

chess, *n.* scacchi, *m.pl.* **~board,** scacchiere, *m.* **~men,** pezzi, *m.pl.*

Cheshire cheese, *n.* formaggio di Chester, *m.*

chest, *n.* (*Anat.*) petto, torace, *m.*; (*box*) cassa, *f.*, forziere, scrigno, *m.* **~** *expander,* apparecchio estensore, *m.* **~** *handle,* maniglia, *f.* **~** *measurement,* misura del torace, *f.* **~** *of drawers,* cassettone, *m.* **~** *register* or *voice,* voce di petto, *f.*

chesterfield, *n.* (*overcoat*) soprabito chesterfield; (*couch*) sofà, *m.*

chestnut, *n.* castagna, *f.*, marrone, *m.* **~** *brown,* castagno. **~** *tree,* castagno, marrone, *m.*

cheval dressing table, *n.* toletta psiche, *f.* **cheval glass,** *n.* psiche, *f.*

chevy, *v.t.* cacciare, inseguire.

chew, *v.t.* & *i.* masticare; (*tobacco*) ciccare; (*fig.*) ruminare. **~** *the cud,* ruminare. **~ing,** *n.* masticazione; (*fig.*) ruminazione, *f.* **~gum,** gomma da masticare, *f.*

chiaroscuro, *n.* chiaroscuro, *m.*

chicane, *v.t.* & *i.* rigirare, cavillare. **~ry,** *n.* cavillamento, *m.*, trufferia, *f.*

chick, *n.* pulcino, pollastro, *m.* **chickabiddy,** *n.* gallinella, *f.* **chicken,** *n.* pollo, pollastro, *m.*, pollastra, *f.* **~heart** (*pers.*), pauroso, poltrone. **~pox,** morbiglione, *m.*, varicella, *f.*

chickweed, *n.* centonchio, *m.*, gallinella, *f.*

chicory, *n.* cicoria; endivia, *f.*

chide, *v.t.* & *i.ir.* rimproverare, riprendere, sgridare.

chief, *a.* primo, principale, sommo.

~ *attraction*, piú bello, spettacolo piú bello, *m.* *to be* ~ *mourner*, guidare il corteo funebre. ~ *rabbi*, rabbino maggiore, *m.* ~ *town*, capoluogo, *m.* ¶ *n.* capo, principale, superiore, *m.* ~*ly*, *ad.* principalménte, soprattutto. **chieftain**, *n.* capó, cɔpitano, *m.*

chiffon, *n.* chiffon, *m.* **chiffonier**, *n.* stipo, *m.*

chilblain, *n.* gelone, *m.*

child, *n.* bambino, fanciullo; figlio, *m.* *from a* ~, da bambino, dalla culla. *with* ~, incinta. ~*bed*, parto, *m.* ~*birth*, partorire, *m.* ~*'s play*, trastullo, *m.*; fanciullaggine, *f.*; un giuoco di bambini, *m.* ~ *welfare*, puericoltura, *f.* *the* ~ *world*, il mondo dei bambini, *m.* ~*hood*, *n.* fanciullezza, infanzia, *f.* ~*ish*, *a.* fanciullesco, infantile; puerile. ~*ishness*, *n.* fanciullaggine, puerilità, *f.* ~*less*, *a.* senza figli. ~*like*, *a.* fanciullesco, da bambino. **children**, *n.pl.* bambini, fanciulli, *m.pl.* ~*'s hour* (*Radio*), ora dei bambini, o. dei piccoli, *f.*

Chile, -li, *n.* il Cile, il Chile, *m.* **Chilean, -lian**, *a.* cileno. ¶ *n.* cileno, -a; chileno, -a, *m.f.*;

chill, *a.* freddo, glaciale; gelato, ghiacciato. ¶ *n.* freddo, *m.*, freddura, *f.*, raffreddamento, brivido, *m.*; freddezza; (*Metal.*) conchiglia; (*fig., of age*) frigidità, *f.* *to take the* ~ *off* (*water*), fare intiepidire; (*wine*) riscaldare leggermente. ¶ *v.t.* raffreddare, agghiacciare; intirizzire, far rabbrividire; scoraggiare. **chilliness**, *n.* freddezza, freddura, *f.*; freddo, *m.* **chilly**, *a.* freddo, freddiccio; (*pers.*) freddoloso.

chime[s], *n.pl.* cariglione; scampanio, *m.* ¶ *v.i.* suonare, risuonare. ~ *in with*, armonizzare con, accordarsi con. *chiming clock*, orologio a cariglione, *m.*

chim[a]era, *n.* chimèra, *f.* **chimerical**, *a.* chimerico.

chimney, *n.* fumaiuolo, camino, *m.*, gola del camino, *f.*; (*lamp*) scartoccio, *m.* ~ *corner*, canto del camino, *m.* ~ *on fire*, fuoco nella gola del camino, *m.* ~*piece*, caminetto, *m.* ~*pot*, rocca di camino, *f.* ~*sweep*, spazzacamino, *m.*

chimpanzee, *n.* scimpanzè, *m.*

chin, *n.* mento, *m.* ~*strap*, sottogola, *m.*

china & ~*ware*, *n.* porcellana, ceramica, *f.* ~ *cabinet*, vetrina,

scansia, *f.* ~ *clay*, caolino, *m.* ~ *manufacturer* & ~ *dealer*, fabbricante & negoziante di porcellane, *m.* ~ *shop*, negozio di porcellane, *m.*

China, *n.* (*Geog.*) la Cina, *f.* ~*aster*, pratolina doppia, *f.*

chine, *n.* schiena, *f.*

Chinese, *a.* cinese. ~ *lantern*, palloncino cinese, *m.* ~ *puzzle*, (*fig.*) rompicapo cinese, *m.* ¶ *n.* (*language*) cinese, *m.*, (*pers.*) cinese, *m. & f.*

chink, *n.* fessura, crepatura, *f.*, fesso, spacco, *m.* ¶ *v.t.* fendere; (*v.i.*) tintinnare.

chintz, *n.* indiana; tela dipinta, *f.*

chip, *n.* scheggia, *f.*, truciolo; pezzetto, frammento, *m.* *to be a* ~ *of the old block*, ritrarre dal ceppo. ~ *potatoes*, patate fritte, *f.pl.* ¶ *v.t.* truciolare, tagliare, scheggiare; (*v.i.*) scheggiarsi.

chiropodist, *n.* pedicure, *m.* **chiropody**, *n.* pedicura, *f.*

chirp, *n.* pigolio, cinguettio; (*insect*) canto, *m.* ¶ *v.i.* pigolare, cinguettare; cantare.

chisel, *n.* cesello, scalpello, *m.* ¶ *v.t.* cesellare, scalpellare, intagliare.

chit, *n.* bambina, *f.*; ragazzina, ragazzaccia, *f.*; (*note*) biglietto, *m.*, nota, *f.*; (*servant's*) benservito, *m.* **chit-chat**, *n.* ciarle, chiacchiere, *f.pl.*

chivalrous, *a.* cavalleresco. **chivalry**, *n.* cavalleria; cortesia, *f.*

chive, *n.* cipollina, *f.*

chivy, *v.t.* cacciare, inseguire.

chlorate, *n.* clorato, *m.* **chloride**, *n.* cloruro, *m.* ~ *of lime*, cloruro di calce, *m.* **chlorine**, *n.* cloro, *m.* **chloroform**, *n.* cloroformio, *m.* ¶ *v.t.* cloroformizzare.

chocolate, *n.* cioccolata, *f.*; (*pl.*) cioccolatini, *m.pl.*, chicche, *f.pl.* ~ *box*, scatola da chicche, confettiera, *f.* ~ *cream*, cioccolatino alla crema, *m.* ~ *eclair*, pasta alla cioccolata, *f.* ~ *manufacturer* or *seller*, cioccolatiere, *m.* ~ *pot*, cioccolattiera, *f.*

choice, *a.* scelto, squisito; eletto, raro. ¶ *n.* scelta, elezione, *f.*; fióre, fior fiore, *m.* ~*ness*, *n.* eccellenza, rarità, *f.*

choir, *n.* coro, *m.* ~*boy*, corista, *m.* ~*master*, maestro di cappella, *m.*

choke, *v.t.* soffocare, strangolare, strozzare; ingombrare, ostruire, turare. ~*full*, *a.* pieno zeppo, pieno come un uovo.

cholera, *n.* colèra, *m.*

choose, *v.t. ir.* scegliere, eleggere, preferire; (*v.i. ir.*) scegliere.

chop, *n.* taglio, colpo, *m.*; costoletta; (*pork*) braciola di maiale, *f.*; (*pl.*) mascelle, *f.pl.* ¶ *v.t.* (*meat*, &c.) sminuzzare; (*wood*) tagliare. ~ *off*, troncare, mozzare, staccare. **chopper**, *n.* mannaia, *f.* **chopping-block**, *n.* ceppo, *m.* **chopping-board**, *n.* tagliere, *m.* **choppy sea**, *n.* maretta, *f.*

chopstick, *n.* bacchetta [per mangiare alla cinese], *f.*

choral, *a.* corale. ~ *society*, società corale, *f.*

chord, *n.* corda, *f.*; (*Mus.*) accordo, *m.*

choreography, *n.* coreografia, *f.*

chorister, *n.* corista, *m.*, *f.* **chorus**, *n.* coro, *m.*; ripresa, *f.*, ritornello, *m.* ~ *singer* (*opera*), corista, *m.f.* *to repeat in* ~, cantare in coro. *to join in the* ~, far coro.

Christ, *n.* Cristo, *m.* **christen**, *v.t.* battezzare. **Christendom**, *n.* cristianità, *f.* **christening**, *n.* battesimo, *m.* **Christian**, *a.* cristiano. ~ *name*, nome di battesimo, prenome, *m.* ~ *Science*, il culto dei scientisti cristiani, *m.*; Scienza cristiana, *f.* ¶ *n.* cristiano, -a. **Christianity**, *n.* cristianesimo, *m.* **christianize**, *v.t.* cristianizzare.

Christmas & ~**tide**, *n.* Natale, *m. at* ~, alla festa di Natale, a Natale. ~ *box*, ~ *present*, strenna di Natale, strenna natalizia, *f.* ~ *pudding*, budino all'inglese, *m.* ~ *tree*, albero di Natale, *m.*

chromate, *n.* cromato, *m.*

chromatic, *a.* cromatico.

chrome, *n.* cromo, *m.*; (*att.*, *steel*, *leather*) cromato; (*yellow*) color cromato. **chromium**, *n.* cromo, *m.*; (*att.*, *steel*) al cromo. ~*plated*, al cromo.

chronic, *a.* cronico.

chronicle, *n.* cronaca, *f.* C~*s* (*Bible*), Paralipomeni, *m.pl.* ¶ *v.t.* registrare, raccontare. **chronicler**, *n.* cronista, *m.*

chronological, *a.* cronologico. **chronology**, *n.* cronologia, *f.*

chronometer, *n.* cronometro, *m.*

chrysalis, *n.* crisalide, *f.*

chrysanthemum, *n.* crisantemo, *m.*

chub, *n.* cefalo, *m.*

chubby, *a.* paffuto. ~ *umbrella*, ombrellino, *m.*

chuck, *n.* (*lathe*) mandrino, *m.* ¶ *v.t.* (*throw*) buttare, gettare, lanciare, tirare. ~ *farthing*, buttar soldi, *m.*

~ *out*, scacciare, metter fuori. ~ *under the chin*, accarezzare sotto il mento.

chuckle, *v.i.* gongolare; ridere sotto i baffi.

chum, *n.* camerata, compagno, *m.*

chump, *n.* ciocco, ceppo, tronco, *m.* ~ *chop*, costoletta di montone, *f.*

chunk, *n.* ceppo, pezzo, *m.*

church, *n.* chiesa, *f.*; tempio, *m. the* C~ *of England*, la Chiesa Anglicana. ~ *service*, ufficio divino, *m.* ~ *warden*, fabbriciere, *m.* ~*yard*, camposanto, *m.*; (*public square surrounding a church*, as St. Paul's Churchyard,) piazza, *f.*, *e.g. la Piazza di* S. Pietro.

churching, *n.* purificazione, *n.*

churl, *n.* villano, zoticone, *m.* ~**ish**, *a.* burbero, aspro.

churn, *n.* zangola, *f.* ~ *dash*[*er*], mestola, *f.*; sbattiburro, *m.* ¶ *v.t.* zangolare; agitare, sbattere.

cider, *n.* sidro, *m.*

cigar, *n.* sigaro, *m.* ~ *case*, porta-sigari, *m.* ~ *cutter*, tagliasigari, *m.* ~ *holder*, bocchino, *m.*

cigarette, *n.* sigaretta, *f.* ~ *box*, scatola da sigarette, *f.*, porta-sigarette, *m.* ~ *case*, porta-sigarette, *m.* ~ *holder*, bocchino, *m.* ~ *end*, ~ *stub*, mozzicone [di sigaretta], *m.*

cinder, *n.* cenere, brace; (*Metall.*) scoria, *f. burnt to a* ~, carbonizzato. ~ *sifter*, crivello da cenere, *m.* ~ *track*, pista di cenerume, *f.*

Cinderella, *n.* Cenerentola, *f.*

cinema, **cinematograph**, *n.* cinema, cinematografo, *m.* ~ *star*, divo dei film, *m.*, diva dei film, *f.*

cineraria (*Bot.*), *n.* ceneraria, *f.*

cinerary, *a.* cenerario.

Cingalese, *a.* & *n.* cingalese, *m.f.*

cinnabar, *n.* cinabro, *m.*

cinnamon, *n.* cannella, *f.*

cipher, *n.* cifra, *f.*; zero, nulla, *n. word in* ~, parola in cifra, *f.* ¶ *v.t. & i.* calcolare, conteggiare.

circle, *n.* cerchio; circolo; ambiente, *m.*; (*Theat.*) prima galleria, *f.* ¶ *v.t.* circondare, accerchiare; (*v.i.*) girare, circolare. **circlet**, *n.* cerchietto, *m.*; corona, *f.*; anello, *m.* **circuit**, *n.* circuito; giro, *m.*; (*district*) circoscrizione, *f.* ~*ous*, *a.* tortuoso; scostato, indiretto. **circular**, *a.* & *n.* circolare, *a.* & *f.* **circulate**, *v.t.* far circolare, diffondere; (*v.i.*) circolare. **circulating**, *a.* circolante. ~ *decimal*, decimale periodica, *f.* ~ *library*, biblioteca circolante, *f.*

circulation, *n.* circolazione; diffusione; (*newspaper*) tiratura, *f.*
circumcise, *v.t.* circoncidere. **circumcision,** *n.* circoncisione, *f.*
circumference, *n.* circonferenza, *f.*
circumflex, *a.* & *n.* circonflesso, *a.* & *m.*
circumlocution, *n.* circonlocuzione, *f.*; giro di parole, *m.*
circumscribe, *v.t.* circoscrivere.
circumspect, *a.* circospetto, cauto.
circumstance, *n.* circostanza, particolarità, *f.*, dettaglio, *m.*; condizione, *f.*; stato, *m.*; ceremonia, *f.* *in easy* ~s, benestante. *in straitened* (or *reduced*) ~s, nelle strettezze, nella miseria. ~s *permitting,* per quanto le circostanze lo permetteranno, secondo le circostanze, possibilmente. **circumstantial,** *a.* circostanziale. ~ *account,* relazione particolare, *f.* ~ *evidence,* prova indiretta, *f.*
circumvent, *v.t.* circonvenire, prevenire, impedire.
circus, *n.* circo; (*in city*) girone, cerchio, *m.*; (*traffic*) circolazione giratoria, *f.*
cirrhosis, *n.* cirrosi, *f.*
cirrus, *n.* cirro, *m.*
Cistercian, *a.* cistercense.
cistern, *n.* cisterna, *f.*, serbatoio, *m.*; (*barometer*) vaschetta, *f.*
citadel, *n.* cittadella, rocca, *f.*
cite, *v.t.* citare; ingiungere.
citizen, *n.* cittadino, *a.* ~*ship,* *n.* cittadinanza; nazionalità, *f.*
citric, *a.* citrico. **citron,** *n.* cedro, *m.*
city, *n.* città, *f.*
civet [**cat**], *n.* zibetto, *m.*
civic, *a.* civico.
civil, *a.* civile; cortese. ~ *commotion,* movimento popolare, *m.* ~ *engineering,* ingegneria civile, *f.* ~ *servant,* impiegato governativo, ufficiale civile, *m.* ~ *service,* amministrazione civile, *f.* ~*ian,* *n.* borghese, *m.* ~*ity,* *n.* cortesia, gentilezza, *f.*
civilization, *n.* civilizzazione, *f.*; incivilimento, *m.*; civiltà, *f.* **civilize,** *v.t.* incivilire. **civilizing,** *a.* civilizzatore.
clack, *n.* schioccare, battere, *m.* schioccata, *f.* ~ *valve,* valvola ad animella, *f.*
claim, *n.* reclamo, *m.*, rivendicazione; pretensione, pretesa, *f.*; diritto; titolo, *m.*; domanda, *f.* ¶ *v.t.* rivendicare, domandare; pretendere; attribuirsi, arrogarsi. ~*ant,* *n.*

pretendente; reclamante, *m.* ~-**holder,** *n.* concessionario, *m.*
clairvoyance, *n.* chiaroveggenza, *f.* **clairvoyant,** *n.* chiaroveggente, *m.f.*
clam, *n.* ostrica americana, *f.*
clamber [**up**], *v.i.* & *t.* arrampicarsi su; salire.
clamminess, *n.* pastosità, *f.*, mollore, *m.* **clammy,** *a.* pastoso, molliccio.
clamorous, *a.* clamoroso; strepitoso.
clamour, *n.* clamore; strepito, *m.* ¶ *v.i.* gridare, strepitare, vociferare. ~ *for,* strepitare per avere, domandare a gran voce.
clamp, *n.* strettoio, rampone, *m.*; grappa, *f.* ¶ *v.t.* assicurare, fermare con grappe.
clan, *n.* clan, *m.*; casata, *f.*
clandestine, *a.* clandestino.
clang, *n.* tintinnio, suono, *m.* ¶ *v.i.* tintinnare, suonare, strepitare.
clank, *n.* strepito, suono metallico, *m.* ¶ *v.i.* suonare, strepitare.
clap, *n.* colpo, scoppio; battimano, *m.* ~*trap,* discorso demagogico, *m.* ¶ *v.t.* & *i.* batter le mani, mettere.
clapper, *n.* applauditore; battente; (*bell*) battaglio, battacchio, *m.*
clapping, *n.* applauso, battimano, battimento delle mani, *m.*
claret, *n.* bordò, *m.inv.*
clarify, *v.t.* clarificare.
clarion, *n.* chiarina, trombetta, *f.* **clarionet,** *n.* clarinetto, *m.*
clash, *n.* cozzo, urto; incontro; fracasso; conflitto, *m.*, opposizione, *f.* ¶ *v.i.* cozzarsi, urtarsi; incontrarsi; opporsi, contrastare.
clasp, *n.* fermaglio, *m.*, fibbia; stretta, *f.*, amplesso, *m.* ~ *knife,* coltello a scatto, c. a serramanico, *m.* ¶ *v.t.* stringere; abbracciare; serrare; (*one's hands*) giungere.
class, *n.* classe; categoria, *f.*; ceto, *m.*, ordine, *f.* ~ *book,* libro scolastico, *m.* ~ *consciousness,* spirito del ceto, *m.* ~*mate,* compagno di classe, *m.* ~ *prize,* premio al merito, *m.* ~*room,* aula, *f.* ~ *war,* guerra sociale, *f.* ¶ *v.t.* classare, qualificare.
classic & **classical,** *a.* classico. **classic,** *n.* classico, *m.* **classification,** *n.* classificazione, *f.* **classify,** *v.t.* classificare. **classing,** *n.* classificazione, *f.*
clatter, *n.* rumore, strepito, chiasso, fracasso, *m.* ¶ *v.i.* strepitare, risuonare, far chiasso.
clause, *n.* clausola, *f.*; articolo, paragrafo, comma, *m.*; (*Gram.*) proposizione.

claustral, *n.* claustrale.
claw, *n.* artiglio, *m.*, unghia, *f.*; graffio, uncino, *m.* ¶ *v.t.* graffiare, aggraffare, uncinare.
clay, *n.* argilla, creta, terra, *f.* ~ *pigeon,* piccione artificiale, *m.* ~ *pipe,* pipa di terra, *f.* ~ *pit,* cava d'argilla, *f.* **clayey,** *a.* cretaceo, argilloso.
clean, *a.* pulito, terso, netto, mondo; schietto; puro; sano; (*Typ.* *proof*) pulito, senza correzioni; (*jump*) schietto. ~ *shaven,* sbarbuto. ~ *slate* (*fig.*), colpo di spugna, *m.* *to make a* ~ *sweep,* fare piazza pulita. ¶ *v.t.* pulire, nettare, purgare, mondare. ~**er,** *n.* pulitore, -trice; nettatore, -trice, *m.f.*; giornante, *f.* ~**ing,** *n.* ripulitura, *f.*, nettamento, *m.* **cleanliness,** *n.* pulizia, nettezza, *f.* **cleanse,** *v.t.* purgare, purificare, lavare, nettare.
clear, *a.* chiaro, limpido, puro, nitido; certo, evidente, manifesto; libero. ~ *soup,* consumè, brodo ristretto, *m.* ~ *sighted,* perspicace. ¶ *v.t.* chiarire, rischiarare; sgombrare, liberare; saltare; attraversare; vuotare, levare; liberare, sbarazzare; assolvere, esonerare; (*table*) sparecchiare; (*letter-box*) fare la levata; (*cheque*) compensare; (*shop goods*) liquidare, (*Cust.* ~ *goods*) sdoganare, svincolare; (*ship*) partire; dichiarare il carico (in dogana. *to* ~! (*shop*) liquidazione! ~ *up, v.t.,* rischiarare; (*doubt*) dissipare; spiegare; rassettare, sgombrare; (*v.i.*) rasserenarsi, rischiarirsi. ~**ance,** *n.* (*Mech.*) gioco; (*goods through Cust.*) sdoganamento, sdaziamento, *m.*; (*ship*) partenza, *f.* ~ *papers,* patente doganale, *f.* ~ *sale,* vendita per liquidazione, *f.* ~**ing,** *n.* (*glade*) radura; liquidazione; levata, *f.*; sgombro, *m.*, (*of land*) dissodamento, *m.*; liberazione; assoluzione, *f.*; chiarimento, rischiaramento, *m.* ~ *house,* stanza di compensazione, *f.* ~**ness,** *n.* chiarezza, nettezza, purezza, *f.*
cleat, *n.* gattello, *m.*
cleavage, *n.* sfaldamento; fendimento, *m.* **cleave,** *v.t. ir.* fendere, spaccare; (*v.i. ir.*) fendersi; attaccarsi, appicciarsi, aderire. **cleaver,** *n.* mannaia, scure, *f.*
clef, *n.* chiave, *f.*
cleft, *n.* fessura, spaccatura, *f.* *to be in a* ~ *stick,* essere nel ronco; essere molto impacciato.

clematis, *n.* vitalba, clematide, *f.*
clemency, *n.* clemenza, *f.* **clement,** *a.* clemente.
clench, *v.t.* stringere; chiudere.
clergy, *n.* clero, *m.* ~*man,* *n.* chierico, prete, *m.* **cleric,** *n.* ecclesiastico, *m.* ~*al,* *a.* da impiegato, da scrivano; da scrivano; (*of clergy*) ecclesiastico, clericale. ~ *error,* sbaglio della penna; (*Law*) errore di cancelleria, *m.* ¶ *n.* ecclesiastico, clericale, *m.*
clerk, *n.* impiegato, contabile, commesso; scrivano, copista; (*court*) cancelliere; segretario, *m.* ~ *of the weather,* ufficio meteorologico, *m.* ~ *of the works,* sorvegliante ai lavori, *m.*
clever, *a.* abile; destro; capace. ~ *move,* destrezza, *f.* ~**ness,** *n.* abilità, destrezza, *f.*
clew, *n.* bugna, *f.*; filo, gomitolo, indizio, *m.*, chiave, *f.*
click, *n.* schiocco, tic-tac, *m.*; (*Mech.*) molla, *f.*, scatto; rampone, *m.*
client, *n.* cliente, *m.* **clientele,** *n.* clientela, *f.*
cliff, *n.* balza, rupe, *f.*, dirupo, precipizio, *m.*
climacteric, *n.* climaterico, *m.*
climate, *n.* clima, *m.* **climatic,** *a.* climatico.
climax, *n.* (*Rhet.*) gradazione, *f.*; colmo, apice, *m.*
climb, *n.* salita, *f.* ¶ *v.t.* salire; (*v.i.*) arrampicarsi, ascendere, poggiare, innalzarsi. ~ *over,* scavalcare. ~**er,** *n.* alpinista, *m.f.*; pianta rampicante, *f.* ~**ing boots,** *n.pl.* scarpe da alpinisti, scarpe coi chiodi, *f.pl.*
clime (*Poet.*), *n.* cielo, *m.*; regione, *f.*
clinch (*Box.*), *n.* strette, *f.pl.* ¶ *v.t.* ribadire; stringere; (*fig.*) ribadire; (*Box.*) venire alle strette. ~**er,** *n.* rampone, *m.*
cling, *v.i. ir.* aggrapparsi, attaccarsi, avviticchiarsi, agganciarsi, aderire, tenere. ~*stone,* duracino, *m.*
clinic, *n.* clinica, *f.* ~*al,* *a.* clinico. ~*ian,* *n.* clinico, *m.*
clink, *n.* (*glasses*) toccare, *m.*; (*lock-up*) stinche, *f.pl.*, carcere, *m. v.t.* toccare (i bicchieri), far tintinnare; (*v.i.*) tintinnare.
clinker, *n.* scoria, *f.*
clip, *n.* fermaglio; fermacarte; ritenitore, *m.*; tosatura, *f.* ¶ *v.t.* ritagliare; tosare; (*ticket*) bucare; (*words*) mangiare, storpiare. **clippers,** *n.pl.* forbici, *f.pl.* **clippings,** *n.pl.* ritagli, *m.pl.*

clique, *n.* consorteria; combriccola, *f.*; sindacato, *m.*

cloak, *n.* mantello, *m.*, cappa, *f.*, gabbano, *m.*; (*fig.*) velo, *m.*, maschera, *f.* **~room,** vestiario; deposito, *m.* ¶ *v.t.* velare, mascherare.

clock, *n.* orologio, *m.*; pendola, *f.*; (*taximeter*) tassametro, *m.*; (*on stocking*) mandorla, *f.* ~ & *watch maker,* orologiaio, *m.* ~*work* (*movement*), meccanismo d'orologio, *m.* ~*work train,* trenino meccanico, *m.*

clod, *n.* zolla, *f.* ~ *crusher,* mazzeranga, *f.* ~(*hopper*), villano, tanghero, *m.*

clog, *n.* zoccolo, *m.*; (*fig.*) intoppo, *m.* ~ *dance,* ballo di zoccolanti, *m.* ¶ *v.t.* ingombrare, incagliare; ostruire; inceppare.

cloister, *n.* chiostro, *m.* ¶ *v.t.* chiudere nel chiostro, chiudere in convento, inclaustrare. **cloistral,** *a.* claustrale.

close, *a.* chiuso; stretto; serrato; denso; pesante, afoso; minuzioso; assiduo; intimo; vicino, contiguo; fedele, esatto; attento. ~*fitting,* attillato. ~ *season,* stagione del risparmio, stagione quando la caccia è proibita, *f.* ~ *shaven,* bene sbarbato. ¶ *ad.* vicino, di vicino; presso, d'accosto. ~ *up,* in primo piano. ¶ *n.* fine, conclusione, *f.*; (*precincts*) recinto, chiuso, *m.* the ~ *of the day,* tramonto, *m.* ¶ *v.t.* chiudere; concludere; finire; sciogliere; liquidare; serrare; turare, otturare; (*v.i.*) chiudersi; concludere, finire, terminare; sciogliersi; venire alle mani. ~*ly,* *ad.* da vicino; attentamente; strettamente. **~ness,** *n.* solidità; intimità; vicinanza; afa; pesantezza, *f.* **closet,** *n.* gabinetto, armadio, *m.* ¶ *v.t.* rinchiudere. **close-up,** *n.* (*Cinema*) visuale ravvicinata, *f.*

closing, *n.* chiusura; fine; liquidazione, *f.* ~*down sale,* liquidazione, *f.* ~ *price,* prezzo di chiusura, *m.* **closure,** *n.* chiusura, *f.*

clot, *n.* grumo, *m.* ¶ *v.i.* raggrumarsi, coagularsi.

cloth, *n.* panno, tessuto, *m.*, stoffa, tela, *f.*; tovaglia, coperta, *f.*; (*clergy,* &*c.*) abito, *m.* ~ *manufacturer* & ~ *merchant,* pannaiuolo, *m.* ~ *trade,* commercio di tessuti, *m.* **clothe,** *v.t.* vestire, rivestire; coprire. **clothes,** *n.pl.* vestiti, abiti;

panni, *m.pl.*; vestiario, *m.*; (*worn*) abiti vecchi, *m.pl.* ~ *basket,* cesta dei panni sudici, *f.* ~ *brush,* spazzola da panni, *f.* ~ *hanger,* attaccapanni, *m.* ~ *horse,* cavalletto, *m.* ~ *line,* corda per stendere il bucato, *f.* ~ *peg,* attaccapanni, *m.* ~ *prop,* pertica da tenditoio, *f.* **clothier,** *n.* pannaiolo; sarto, *m.* **clothing,** *n.* vestiti, *m.pl.*; vestiario, *m.*

cloud, *n.* nuvola; (*fig.*) macchia; (*Poet.*) nube, *f.* ~*burst,* acquazzone, *m.* in the ~*s,* (*fig.*) nelle nubi, fuori della realtà. under a ~, (*fig.*) mal veduto, screditato; disgraziato. ¶ *v.t.* annuvolare; (*fig.*) offuscare, rattristare. ~**less,** *a,* senza nuvole, sereno. ~**y,** *a.* nuvoloso, coperto di nuvole; torbido; oscuro, tenebroso.

clout, *n.* pezza, *f.*, straccio; (*blow*) pugno, schiaffo, *m.*

clove, *n.* chiodo di garofano, *m.* ~ *of garlic,* spicchio d'aglio, *m.* ~ *tree,* garofano, *m.*

cloven hoof, *n.* piede biforcuto, piede caprino, *m.*

clover, *n.* trifoglio, *m.* to be in ~, (*fig.*) stare come un papa.

clown, *n.* pagliaccio, zanni, buffone; villano, zotico, *m.* ~**ery,** *n.* pagliacciata, zanneria, buffonata; grossolanità, *f.* ~**ish,** *a.* zannesco, buffonesco; zotico.

clox, *n.pl.* mandorle, *f.pl.*

cloy, *v.t.* satollare, stuccare (*with =* di).

club, *n.* clava, mazza, *f.*, randello; (*golf*) bastone, *m.*, spatola, *f.*; (*people*) circolo, casino, *m.*, società, *f.*; (*cards*) fiori, *m.pl.* ~*foot,* piede storto, piede grosso, *m.* ~ *together,* unirsi, associarsi, fare una borsa.

cluck, *n.* chioccio, *m.* ¶ *v.i.* chiocciare.

clue, *n.* indicazione, chiave, *f.*; indizio, *m.*

clump, *n.* massa, *f.*, blocco, gruppo, *m.*; zolla, *f.*

clumsiness, *n.* goffaggine, malaccortezza, ineleganza, *f.* **clumsy,** *a.* goffo, maldestro, malaccorto, sgraziato, incomodo, pesante. ~ *fellow,* goffo, *m.*

cluster, *n.* gruppo, grappolo, raggruppamento, ammasso; mazzo; (*bees,* &*c.*) sciame, *m.* ¶ *v.t.* raggrupparsi, riunirsi.

clutch, *n.* presa, stretta; (*eggs*) covata, *f.*; (*Mech.*) innesto, *m.* ¶ *v.t.* & *i.* impugnare, afferrare, agguantare.

coach, *n.* cocchio, *m.*; diligenza;

carrozza, *f.*; vagone; (*tutor*) ripetitore, maestro; (*sport*) istruttore, allenatore, *m.* ~ *builder*, carrozziere, *m.* ~ *building*, carrozzeria, *f.* ~ *horse*, cavallo da tiro, *m.* ~ *house*, rimessa, *f.* ~*man*, cocchiere, *m.* ~ *screw*, tirafondi, *m.* ~ *wrench*, chiave inglese, *f.* ¶ *v.t.* ammaestrare; imboccare, indettare.

coadventurer, *n.* compagno d'avventura, cointeressato, *m.*

coagulate, *v.t.* coagulare; (*v.i.*) coagularsi.

coal, *n.* carbone; litantrace, *m.* ~ *cellar*, carbonaia, *f.* ~*field*, bacino carbonifero, *m.* ~ *heaver*, facchino carbonario, *m.* ~ *merchant*, negoziante di carbone, *m.* ~ *mine*, miniera di carbone, *f.* ~ *miner*, minatore di carbone. ~ *mining*, sfruttamento delle miniere di carbone, *m.* ~ *scuttle*, secchia da carbone, *f.* ~ *strike*, sciopero dei minatori di carbone, *m.* ~ *tar*, catrame minerale, *m.* ~ *yard*, deposito di carbone, *m.* ¶ *v.i.* rifornirsi di carbone.

coalesce, *v.i.* unirsi, congiungersi, confluire. **coalition**, *n.* coalizione, *f.*, blocco, *m.*

coarse, *a.* grossolano, ruvido, grosso; rozzo; sgarbato. ~*fish*, pesce bianco, *m.* ~**ness**, *n.* grossolanità, grossezza; rozzezza; zoticheria, *f.*

coast, *n.* costa, costiera, *f.*, litorale, lido, *m.* ~ *defence ship*, nave guardacosta, *f.* ~*guard*, guardacoste, *m.* ~ *station*, stazione costiera, *f.* ¶ *v.i.* costeggiare; (*bicycling*) scendere a ruota libera. ~**er**, *n.* nave di cabotaggio, *f.*, bastimento costiero; cabottiere, *m.* ~ *hub*, ruota libera con freno a contropedalata. ~**ing**, *n.* navigazione costiera, *f.*; cabotaggio; (*bicycling*) scendere a ruota libera, *m.* ~ *trade*, cabotaggio, *m.*

coat, *n.* abito; soprabito, *m.*; giacca, giubba, giacchetta; (*Mil.*) tunica, *f.*, (*animal's*) pelame, pelo, vello, *m.*; (*Anat., &c.*) parete; tunica, *f.*; (*layer*) strato, mano, *m.* ~ *of arms*, stemma, *m.*, armi, *f.pl.*, scudo, *m.* ~ *of mail*, lorica di maglia, *f.* ¶ *v.t.* rivestire, ricoprire, spalmare. ~**ee**, *n.* giacca a falde corte, *f.*

coax, *v.t.* blandire, accarezzare.

cob, *n.* (*horse*) cavalotto, *f.* (*Build.*) miscuglio di paglia ed argilla per murare, stucco, *m.*; (*corn*) spiga, *f.* ~ *nut*, avellana, *f.*

cobalt, *n.* cobalto, *m.*

cobble stone, *n.* ciottolo, *m.* ~*s* (*coal*), *pl.* carbone fossile a pezzi alquanto piccoli. ¶ *v.t.* rattoppare, acciabattare.

cobbler, *n.* ciabattino, *m.* ~*'s wax*, pece da calzolaio, *f.*

cobra, *n.* cobra, *f.*

coburg loaf, *n.* pagnotta cornuta, *f.*

cobweb, *n.* ragnatelo, *m.*, ragnatela, *f.*

cocaine, *n.* cocaina, *f.*

Cochin-China, *n.* la Cocincina, *f.* **Cochin-Chinese**, *a.* cocincinese. ¶ *n.* cocincinese, *m.f.*

cochineal, *n.* cocciniglia, *f.*

cock, *n.* gallo, *m.*; (*tap*) rubinetto, *m.*, chiave, *f.*; (*hay*) bica, *f.*; (*of a gun*) cane, *m.* ~*a doodle-doo*, chicchirricchi, *m.* ~*-&-bull story*, fandonia, fantasticaggine, fantasticheria, *f.* ~ *bird*, uccello maschio, *m.* ~*crow*, canto del gallo, *m.* ~ *of the walk*, primasso; gallo della cecca, *m.* ~ *pheasant*, fagiano maschio, *m.* ¶ *v.t.* alzare, drizzare; (*gun*) armare. ~*ed hat*, cappello a due punte, *m.*

cockade, *n.* coccarda, *f.*

cockatoo, *n.* cacatua, *m. inv.*

cockchafer, *n.* scarafaggio, *m.*

cockerel, *n.* galletto, *m.*

cockle, *n.* (*Mol.*) cardio; (*Bot.*) loglio, *m.* ¶ *v.t.* raggrinzare; (*v.i.*) raggrinzarsi.

cockpit, *n.* arena, *f.*; (*ship*) cassero; (*Aero.*) carlinga, *f.*

cockroach, *n.* blatta, *f.*

cockscomb, *n.* cresta di gallo, *f.*; (*Bot.*) amaranto, *m.*

cocktail, *n.* (*drink*) cocktail, bicchierino, *m.* ~ *bar*, bar-cocktail, *m.* ~ *shaker*, shaker, *m.* ~ *table*, tavolina, *f.*

cocoa, *n.* (*bean*) cacao, *m.*; (*drink*) cioccolata, *f.*

coco nut, *n.* cocco, *m.*; noce di cocco, *f.* ~ *palm*, cocco, *m.*

cocoon, *n.* bozzolo, *m.*

cod fish, *n.* merluzzo, *m.*, (*dried*) baccalà, *m.* ~*fisher*, pescatore di merluzzo, *m.* ~*liver oil*, olio di fegato di merluzzo, *m.*

coddle, *v.t.* vezzeggiare, carezzare; cuocere a fuoco lento. ~ *oneself*, crogiolarsi.

code, *n.* codice, *m.*; cifra, *f.* ~ *word*, parola in cifra, *f.* ¶ *v.t.* cifrare, tradurre in cifra. **codicil**, *n.* codicillo, *m.* **codify**, *v.t.* codificare.

coefficient, *n.* coefficiente, *m.*

coerce, *v.t.* costringere.

coffee, *n.* caffè, *m.inv.* ~ *cup*, tazza da

caffè, *f.* ~ *pot,* caffettiera, *f.*
~ *room,* salotto, *m.* ~ *spoon,*
cucchiaino, *m.* ~ *table,* tavolina, *f.*
~ *tree,* pianta del caffè, *f.* ~
planter, piantatore di caffè, *m.*
coffer, *n.* cofano; scrigno, *m.*; cassa, *f.*
coffin, *n.* cassa da morto, *f.*
cog, *n.* dente, *m.* ~*wheel,* ruota
dentata, *f.* ¶ *v.t.* dentare; (*dice*)
truffare coi dadi.
cogency, *n.* forza, *f.* **cogent,** *a.*
potente, convincente.
cogitate, *v.i.* meditare, riflettere.
cogitation, *n.* meditazione, *f.*
cognate, *a.* congiunto, analogo, della
stessa origine.
cognisance, *n.* conoscenza, *f.*
cognisant of, informato di.
cognomen, *n.* cognome, *m.*
cohabit, *v.i.* coabitare.
cohere, *v.i.* aderire insieme. **co-**
herence, *n.* coerenza, *f.* **coherent,**
a. coerente, conseguente. ~*ly,* di
modo coerente. **cohesion,** *n.*
coesione, *f.* **cohesive,** *a.* aderente,
attaccaticcio.
cohort, *n.* coorte, *f.*
coil, *n.* rotolo, *m.*; aduglia, *f.*; gomitolo,
viluppo, *m.*; (*snake*) spira; (*Elec.*)
bobina, *f.* ¶ *v.t.* ravvolgere,
adugliare, ripiegare; (*rope*) cogliere.
~ *up,* ripiegare; ripiegarsi.
coin, *n.* moneta, *f.*; (*corner*) angolo, *m.*
~ *cabinet,* gabinetto numismatico,
m. ~ *machine,* distributore automatico, *m.* ~ *v.t.* battere, coniare,
monetare; (*fig.*) inventare, fabbricare. ~**age,** *n.* monetazione, *f.*,
conio, *m.*; (*fig.*) fabbricazione, *f.*;
denaro. *m.*, monete, *f.pl.*
coincide, *v.i.* coincidere; combinarsi.
coincidence, *n.* combinazione, *f.*
coiner, *n.* falso monetario; (*fig.*)
inventore, *m.* *coining press,* zecca, *f.*
coir, *n.* borra di cocco, *f.*
coke, *n.* cok, *m.*
colander, *n.* colatoio, *m.*
cold, *a.* freddo. *in* ~ *blood,* a sangue
freddo. ~ *blooded,* freddo, insensibile, flemmatico. ~ *chisel,* scalpello,
m. ~ *cream,* colcrem, *m.* ~ *snap,*
colpo di freddo, *m.* ~ *steel,*
arma bianca, *f.* ~ *storage,* conservazione a freddo, *f.* ~ *store,* frigidario,
m. ¶ *n.* freddo, *m.*; freddura, *f.*;
(*Path.*) raffreddore, *m.* ~ *on the*
chest, raffreddore di petto, *m.* ~ *in*
the head, raffreddore di testa, *m.*
~**ness,** *n.* freddezza, *f.*, freddo, *m.*
coleoptera, *n.* coleottero, *m.* **cole-**
opterous, *a.* coleottero.

colic, *n.* colica, *f.*
collaborate, *v.i.* collaborare. **col-**
laborator, *n.* collaboratore, -trice,
m.f. **collaboration,** *n.* collabora-
zione, *f.*
collapse, *n.* crollo, *m.*, caduta;
rovina; fallita, *f.* ¶ *v.i.* crollare,
cadere; (*fig.*) fallire. **collapsible,** *a.*
pieghevole.
collar, *n.* (*of Order, etc.*) collare;
collaretto, colletto; bavero, *m. shirt*
~ (*detached*), solino, *m.* ~ *bone,*
clavicola, *f.* ~ *stud,* bottone di
colletto, *m.* ¶ *v.t.* afferrare;
impugnare.
collate, *v.t.* collazionare; confrontare.
collateral, *a.* collaterale, accessorio,
sussidiario. ~ *security,* cauzione, *f.*
collation, *n.* collazionamento;
riscontro, confronto, *m.*; (*snack*)
merenda, *f.*
colleague, *n.* collega, consocio, *m.*
collect, *n.* colletta, *f.* ¶ *v.t.* raccogliere, riunire; ritirare, levare,
prendere; far collezione; riscuotere,
incassare, ritirare; accattare. ~**ed,**
p.a. raccolto; calmo. ~**ion,** *n,*
collezione, raccolta, riunione, *f.*;
incasso, *m.*; esazione; questua;
levata; presa, *f.*; ammasso, *m.*
~ *of coins or medals,* collezione
numismatica, *f.* ~**ive,** *a.* collettivo.
~**or,** *n.* raccoglitore; compilatore;
ricevitore; esattore; questuante;
collezionista, *m.* ~**orship,** *n.*
ricevitoria, *f.*
college, *n.* collegio, convitto, liceo,
m.; università, *f.*; seminario; conservatorio, *m.*; accademia, *f.*
collegian, *n.* collegiale, *m.* **col-**
legiate, *a.* collegiato.
collide, *v.i.* incontrarsi, urtarsi.
~ *with,* incontrare, urtare.
collier, *n.* (*pers.*) minatore di carbone
fossile; (*ship*) bastimento carboniero,
m. ~**y,** *n.* miniera di carbone
fossile, *f.*
collision, *n.* incontro, urto, *m.*;
collisione, *f.*; abbordo, abbordaggio,
investimento, *m.* ~ *mat,* guardalato,
m.
colloquial, *a.* familiare. ~**ism,** *n.*
espressione familiare, *f.* **colloquy,**
n. colloquio, *m.*
collusion, *n.* collusione, *f.*
colon, *n.* due punti, *m.pl.*; (*Anat.*)
colon, *m.*
colonel, *m.* colonnello, *m.* C~ *Bogey*
(*Golf*) norma, *f.* ~ *commandant,*
brigadiere, *m.*
colonial, *a.* coloniale. C~ *Office*

Ministero delle Colonie, *m.*
colonist, *n.* colono, *m.* **colonize,**
v.t. colonizzare.
colonnade, *n.* colonnato, *m.*
colony, *n.* colonia, *f.*
colophon, *n.* sottoscrizione, *f.*
colossal, *a.* colossale. **colossus,** *n.*
colosso, *m.*
colour, *n.* colore; colorito, *m.*;
(*complexion*) carnagione, *f.*; (*pl.*)
bandiera, *f.* under ~ of (*fig.*), sotto
colore di. ~ *bar*, distinzione sociale
o legale tra i negri ed i bianchi, *f.*
~ *blind*, affetto da daltonismo,
incapace di distinguere i colori.
~ *blindness*, daltonismo, *m.* ~
photography, fotografia a colori, *f.*
¶ *v.t.* colorare, colorire; tingere;
miniare; (*pipe*) annerire. ~**able,** *a.*
specioso, plausibile. ~ *imitation*,
contraffattura; contraffazione, *f.*
~**ed,** *p.a. & p.p.* ~ *dress*, abito
di colore, *m.* *flame-*~ *ribbon*, nastro
color di fuoco, *m.* *rose-*~ *shoes*,
scarpe di color rosa, *f.pl.* ~**ing,** *n.*
colorito, *m.*; coloratura, colorazione,
f. ~**less,** *a.* senza colore; pallido,
incolore.
colt, *n.* puledro, *m.* **coltsfoot** (*Bot.*),
n. farfaro, *m.*
Columbia, *n.* la Colombia, *f.*
columbine (*Bot.*), *n.* aquilegia, *f.*
column, *n.* colonna, *f.*; pilastro, *m.*;
(*news on special subject*) rubrica, .
colza, *n.* colza, *f.*
coma, *n.* (*Med.*) coma, *m.*; (*Bot. &*
comet) chioma, *f.*
comb, *n.* pettine, *m.*; pettinata, *f.*;
(*crest*) cresta, *f.*; (*honey*) favo, *m.*
curry~, striglia, *f.* ~*maker*,
pettinaio, *m.* ¶ *v.t.* pettinare;
(*curry*) strigliare. ~ *out* (*fig.*),
eliminare.
combat, *n.* combattimento, *m.*;
tenzone, lotta, *f.* ¶ *v.t.* combattere.
~**ant,** *a. & n.* combattente, *a. &*
m.f. ~**ive,** *a.* battagliero, combattivo. ~**iveness,** combattività, *f.*
combination, *n. &* ~**s** (*dress*), *n.pl.*
combinazione, *f.* **combine,** *n.*
coalizione, *f.* ¶ *v.t.* combinare,
riunire, congiungere; (*v.i.*) combinarsi, coalizzarsi; cooperare.
combing, *n.* pettinatura, *f.*
combustible, *a.* combustibile.
combustion, *n.* combustione, *f.*
~ *chamber* (*motor*), camera di
scoppio, *f.*
come, *v.i. ir.* venire; provenire;
arrivare, giungere; presentarsi; farsi;
mettersi; entrare; essere. ~! ~!

ma che! andiamo! ~! ~ *along!*
vieni! suvvia! andiamo! sbrigatevi!
fate presto! ~ *about*, accadere,
avvenire, succedere. ~ *across*,
incontrarsi con; trovare per caso.
~ *back*, ritornare, rivenire. ~ *down*,
scendere, discendere; derivare;
decadere. ~ *for*, venire a cercare,
a trovare, a prendere. ~ *from* (*be*
a native of), essere di, essere
originario di, oriundo di. ~
home, ritornare (a casa), rientrare.
~ *home to* (*fig.*), toccare al vivo.
~ *in*, entrare, passare. ~ *in!*
avanti! passate! ~ *now!* andiamo!
via! badate! ma che! ~ *off*,
staccarsi; (*ink, &c.*) venir via.; aver
luogo; (*well, badly*) riuscire bene,
male. ~ *off on* (*dye*), stingere.
~ *on!* su! avanti! coraggio! ~ *out*,
uscire; sortire; debuttare; (*book,*
&c.) uscire, pubblicarsi. ~ *to*,
venire a, finire in, esser ridotto a;
ammontare a; (*decision*) prendere;
(*one's senses*) riprendere (i sensi),
rinvenire. ~ *to an agreement*,
mettersi d'accordo. ~ *to blows*,
venire alle mani. ~ *to light*, venire
in luce, scoprirsi. ~ *to pass*,
accadere, avvenire. ~ *to terms*,
venire a patti. ~ *true*, avverarsi;
realizzarsi. ~ *undone*, ~ *unsewed*,
disfarsi; scucirsi. ~ *up* (*sprout*),
spuntare, germogliare. ~ *upon*,
incontrare; sorprendere; scoprire.
~ *what may*, avvenga che può.
~ *nearer!* fatti più in qua!
come- &-go (**the**), l'andare e il
venire, il viavai; l'andirivieni, *m.*
comedian, *n.* commediante, attore
comico; buffone, *m.* **comedy,** *n.*
commedia, *f.*; comico, *m.* ~ *writer*,
autore, scrittore di commedie, *m.*
comeliness, *n.* bellezza, grazia, *f.*,
bell'aspetto, *m.* **comely,** *a.* bello,
grazioso, di bell'aspetto.
comer, *n.* veniente; chi viene; venuto,
-a, *m.f.* *the first* ~, il primo venuto.
comet, *n.* cometa, *f.*
comfort, *n.* conforto, *m.*, consolazione, *f.*, sollievo, *m.*; comodità, *f.*,
comodo, *m.*, agiatezza, *f.*, agio (*oft.*
pl. agi), benessere, *m.* ¶ *v.t.*
consolare, confortare. ~**able,** *a.*
comodo, agiato; di conforto.
~**ably,** *ad.* comodamente, a suo
comodo, a bell'agio. ~**er,** *n.*
consolatore, *m.*, -trice, *f.*; (*scarf*)
sciarpa di lana, *f.*
comic & comical, *a.* comico,

umoristico; buffo, burlesco; ridicolo. ~ *actor*, comico, buffo, comediante, *m.* ~ *opera*, opera buffa, *f.* ~ *song*, canzone burlesca, c. comica, c. umoristica; canzonetta, *f.* ~ *turn*, numero comico, *m.*

coming, *p.a.* da venire; futuro; prossimo. ¶ *n.* venuta, *f.*; arrivo, *m.*; (*of Christ*) avvento, *m.* [*I am*] ~! vengo! subito! eccomi! ~ & *going*, andirivieni, *m.* ~ *out* (*in society*), debutto, *m.*

comma, *n.* virgola, *f.*; (*Mus.*) comma, *m.*

command, *n.* comando, *m.*, ordine, -i, *m. & pl.*; padronanza, *f.* ¶ *v.t.* comandare; ordinare; disporre di, avére a disposizione; (*a view of*) dare su; (*respect, &c.*) ispirare. ~ant, *n.* comandante, capo, *m.*

commandeer, *v.t.* requisire.

commander, *n.* comandante, capo; (*Nav.*) capitano di fregata, *m.* ~-*in-chief*, comandante in capo, generalissimo, *m.* *commanding officer*, comandante, capo.

commandment, *n.* comandamento, *m.*

commemorate, *v.t.* commemorare.

commence, *v.t. & i.* cominciare, incominciare, iniziare, esordire. ~ment, *n.* principio, incominciamento, inizio, esordio; debutto, *m.*; origine, *f.*

commend, *v.t.* commendare, lodare; applaudire; raccomandare. ~able, *a.* lodevole, degno di lode. ~ation, *n.* elogio, *m.*; lode, *f.*

commensurate, *a.* proporzionato, commisurato.

comment, & **commentary,** *n.* commento, commentario, *m.* **to comment on,** commentare; fare commenti su; annotare, chiosare; illustrare. **commentator,** *n.* commentatore; chiosatore; (*Radio*) cronista radiofonico, *m.*

commerce, *n.* commercio; traffico; negozio, *m.*; affari, *m.pl.* **commercial,** *a.* commerciale; commerciante, mercantile, di commercio, d'affari. ~ *sale rooms*, borsa di commercio, b. di mercanzie, *f.* ~ *traveller*, viaggiatore di commercio, commesso viaggiatore, *m.* ~ism, *n.* mercantilismo, *m.* ~ize, *v.t.* mettere sul mercato; estendere la clientela di. ~ly, *ad.* commercialmente.

commiserate, *v.t.* commiserare, provare (dimostrare) pietà per.

commissariat, *n.* commissariato, *m.*; intendenza militare, *f.*

commission, *n.* commissione; mediazione, provvigione, senseria, *f.*; incarico, mandato, *m.*; (*officer's*) brevetto, *m.* ~ *agent*, commissionario, *m.* ¶ *v.t.* incaricare, autorizzare; ordinare, commissionare; (*officer*) nominare; (*ship*) armare. ~ed *work*, lavoro fatto su commissione, *n.* **commissionaire,** *n.* fattorino, *m.* **commissioner,** *n.* commissario; membro di commissione, *m.*

commit, *v.t.* commettere, fare; consegnare; affidare; rinviare. ~ *for trial*, rinviare a giudizio, mettere in stato d'accusa. ~ *no nuisance*, è proibito di deporre immondizie. ~ *oneself*, impegnarsi; compromettersi. ~ *to prison*, mandare in prigione. ~ *to writing*, mettere in iscritto. ~ment (*Com.*), *n.* impegno. *committal order*, mandato d'arresto.

committee, *n.* commissione, *f.*, comitato, *m.*

commode, *n.* cassettone, canterano, *m.*; seggetta, *f.*

commodious, *a.* spazioso, comodo, conveniente. ~ly, *ad.* convenientemente, spaziosamente. ~ness, *n.* comodità, *f.*

commodity, *n.* derrata, merce, *f.*; genere di prima necessità; articolo, *m.*; risorsa, *f.*

common, *a.* comune; generale; usuale; consueto; ordinario, normale; frequente; volgare, banale; semplice; popolare; tipico; pubblico. ~ *knowledge*, notizia pubblica, *f.* ~ *land*, terre comunali, *f.pl.*; pascolo comune, *m.* ~ *law*, diritto comune, d. convenzionale, *m.* *the* ~ *people*, la gente comune, la plebe, *f.*, il volgo, il popolino, *m.* ~ *sense*, senso comune, buon senso, *m.* ~ *snake*, colubro, *m.* *the* ~ *weal*, la cosa pubblica, *f.*, lo Stato, *m.* *in, out of the* ~, in, fuori del, comune. *to be on short commons*, essere a stecchetto, a razioni ridotte. ~ly, *ad.* comunemente, abitualmente. ~ness, *n.* banalità; volgarità; frequenza, *f.* ~place, *a.* banale, comune; (*n.*) banalità, *f.*; luogo comune, *m.* ~wealth, *n.* stato, *m.*; comunità, *f.* *the C*~ *of Australia*, la Federazione Australiana, *f.*

commonalty, *n.* comunità, *f.*, popolo, *m.*, plebe, *f.* **commoner,** *n.* borghese, *m.*

commotion, *n.* commozione, agitazione, *f.*; movimento, *m.*
communal, *a.* comunale. **commune,** *v.i.* conversare, conferire, intrattenersi. **communicant,** *n.* comunicante; (*Eccl.*) comunicando, *m.* **communicate,** *v.t. & i.* comunicare, far sapere; aver corrispondenza; (*Eccl.*) ricevere la Santa Comunione. **communication,** *n.* comunicazione, *f.* ~ *cord*, segnale d'allarme, *m.* ~ *trench*, ramo di trincea, *m.* **communicative,** *a.* comunicativo. **communion,** *n.* comunione; (*Eccl.*) Santa Comunione, Eucarestia, *f.* ~ *cup*, calice, *m.* ~ *service*, ufficio della comunione, *m.* ~ *table*, altare, *m.*, mensa sacra, *f.* **communism,** *n.* comunismo, *m.* **communist,** *n.* comunista, *m.f.* **community,** *n.* comunità, *f.*
commutator, *n.* commutatore, *m.*
commute, *v.t.* commutare.
Como (Lake), il lago di Como, *m.*
compact, *a.* compatto. ~ [*powder.*] cipria compatta, *f.* ¶ *n.* patto, accordo, *m.* ~**ness,** *n.* compattezza, *f.*
companion, *n.* compagno, *m.*, -a, *f.*, camerata, *m.f.*; (*thing*) pendente, *m.* *lady* ~, dama di compagnia, *f.* ~**able,** *a.* socievole. ~**ship,** *n.* compagnia, società, *f.*, cameratismo, *m.*
company, *n.* compagnia; società; associazione; banda; truppa; frotta; partita, *f.*; gruppo; (*ship*) equipaggio, *m.*, ciurma, *f.*; mondo, *m.*; gente, *f.*
comparable, *a.* comparabile, paragonabile. **comparative,** *a.* comparativo; (*sciences*) comparato. ¶ (*Gram.*) *n.* comparativo, *m.* **compare,** *v.t.* comparare, assomigliare; paragonare; confrontare ; collazionare. **comparison,** *n.* comparazione, *f.*; confronto, paragone, raffronto, *m.*
compartment, *n.* compartimento, scompartimento, *m.*; cassa, casella, *f.*
compass, *n.* circonferenza, *f.*; circolo, *m.*; area, *f.*, spazio, *m.*, limiti, *m.pl.*; estensione, portata, *f.*; (*magnetic*) bussola, *f.*; (*voice*) diapason, *m.inv.*, estensione, *f.*; (*musical*) estensione, *f.*, registro, *m.* ~ *card*, rosa dei venti, *f.* **compass[es],** *n.*[*pl.*] compasso, *m.* *compasses with pen point, with pencil point,* compasso

a tiralinee, a portalapis. **compass,** *v.t.* circondare, recingere; ottenere, realizzare; (*evil design*) complottare.
compassion, *n.* compassione, pietà, *f.* ~**ate,** *a.* pieno di compassione.
compatible, *a.* compatibile.
compatriot, *n.* compatriota, *m.f.*
compeer, *n.* uguale, pari, *m.*
compel, *v.t.* costringere, forzare, obbligare.
compendious, *a.* sommario. **compendium,** *n.* compendio, *m.*, epitome, *f.*
compensate, *v.t.* compensare, indennizzare, risarcire. **compensation,** *n.* compensazione, indennità, *f.*, risarcimento, *m.*
compete for, concorrere a. ~ **with,** fare concorrenza a. sostenere la concorrenza con.
competence, -cy, *n.* agiatezza; competenza; abilità, capacità, *f.* **competent,** *a.* competente, adatto, atto.
competition, *n.* concorrenza; competizione; gara, *f.*, concorso, *m.*
competitor, *n.* concorrente, *m.f.*, competitore, *m.*, -trice, *f.*
compile, *v.t.* compilare.
complacence, -cy, *n.* compiacimento, *m.* **complacent,** *a.* compiaciuto. ~**ly,** *ad.* con compiacimento.
complain, *v.i.* lamentarsi; lagnarsi. ~ *of* (*medically*), accusare. ~**ant,** *n.* (*Law*) parte civile, *f.* **complaint,** *n.* lamento, *m.*, lagnanza; protesta; querela; accusa, *f.*; (*Med.*) affezione, malattia, *f.*
complaisance, *n.* compiacenza; cortesia, *f.* **complaisant,** *a.* compiacente; cortese.
complement, *n.* complemento, *m.* ~**ary,** *a.* complementare.
complete, *a.* completo, intero; finito, perfetto. ¶ *v.t.* completare. ~**d** (*time, age*), *p.p.* compiuto. **completion,** *n.* completamento, perfezionamento, *m.*
complex, *a. & n.* complesso, *a. & m.*
complexion, *n.* (*of face*) colorito, *m.*, carnagione, *f.*; (*fig.*) carattere, aspetto, *m.*
complexity, *n.* complessità, *f.*
compliance, *n.* condiscendenza, conformità, *f.*; adempimento, *m.*, osservanza, *f.* **compliant,** *a.* accomodante, compiacente, accondiscente.
complicate, *v.t.* complicare. **complication,** *n.* complicazione, *f.*
complicity, *n.* complicità, *f.*

compliment, n. (oft. pl.) complimento, saluto, ossequio, omaggio,
m.; (pl.) cose, f.pl. ~s of the season,
i migliori auguri di Natale, di
buon'anno, &c., m.pl. ¶ v.t.
complimentare, congratularsi con,
felicitarsi con. ~ary, a. laudativo,
di complimento, di felicitazione;
(dinner, &c.) d'onore; (ticket) di
favore; (copy) in omaggio.
complin[e] (Eccl.), n. compieta, f.
comply, v.i. abs. sottomettersi,
acconsentire, ubbidire. ~ with,
conformarsi a, condiscendere a;
rispettare, ubbidire a, soddisfare,
compiere. not complied with (rule),
inosservato, non eseguito.
component, a. costituente; componente. ¶ n. componente, m. ~ part,
pezzo staccato, m.
compose, v.t. comporre; calmare. to
be ~d of, comporsi di. ~ oneself,
ricomporsi, calmarsi. ~d, p.p.
composto, calmo. **composer** (Mus.)
n. compositore, m., -trice, f., autore,
m. composing stick (Typ.), compositoio, m. **composite,** a. composto,
misto; (Arch., Bot.) composito.
composition, n. composizione;
costituzione, f.; tema, m.; (to
creditors) accomodamento, concorda-
to, m. **compositor** (Typ.), n.
compositore, m., -trice, f.
composure, n. compostezza, calma,
f., sangue freddo, m.
compound, a. composto; (Mech.)
composito; (steam) compound. ~
interest, interesse composto, m. (oft.
pl.). ¶ n. composto; recinto; campo
di concentramento, m. ¶ v.t. comporre; mischiare; combinare; transigere con. (v.i.) transigere, venire
ad un accordo, una transazione.
comprehend, v.t. comprendere;
capire; includere. **comprehension,**
n. comprensione, f. **comprehensive,** a. comprensivo.
compress, n. compressa, f. ¶ v.t.
comprimere, restringere. ~ion, n.
compressione, f. ~or, n. compres-
sore, m.
comprise, v.t. comprendere, contenere, includere.
compromise, n. compromesso, accomodamento, m., transazione, f.
¶ v.t. & i. compromettere, transigere; capitolare. ~ oneself, compromettersi.
comptroller, n. controllore, m. ~ of
the Royal Household, maggiordomo,
m.

compulsion, n. costrizione, f. com-
pulsorily, ad. forzatamente, per
forza. **compulsory,** a. forzato,
obbligatorio.
compunction, n. compunzione, f.
computation, n. computo, calcolo, m.
compute, v.t. computare, contare,
calcolare.
comrade, n. camerata, m.f. ~ship,
n. cameratismo, m.
con, v.t. ripassare, rivedere, studiare
attentamente.
concave, a. concavo. **concavity,** n.
concavità, f.
conceal, v.t. nascondere, celare;
dissimulare; sopprimere; tacere;
ricettare. ~ment, n. reticenza;
dissimulazione; soppressione, f.;
nascondimento, m.
concede, v.t. accordare, abbandonare;
(grant) concedere, ammettere.
conceit, n. boria, affettazione, f.
~ed, a. vanitoso; vanesio; borioso;
affettato; presunzioso. to be ~,
essere vanitoso, essere pieno di sé.
conceivable, a. concepibile. **conceive,** v.t. & i. concepire.
concentrate, v.t. concentrare. **concentration,** n. concentrazione, f.,
concentramento, m.
concentric, a. concentrico.
conception, n. concezione, f.
concern, n. affare, m., faccenda;
sollecitudine, ansietà, preoccupazione, f.; interesse, m.; relazione;
azienda, ditta, impresa, f., negozio,
m. ¶ v.t. concernere, interessare,
riguardare; toccare; appartenere a;
importare a. to be ~ed about,
inquietarsi per.. to be ~ed in,
ingerirsi in. ~ing, pr. in riguardo
a, circa, intorno.
concert, n. concerto; accordo, m.
~ grand [piano], pianoforte a coda,
m. ~ pitch, diapason normale, m.
¶ v.t. concertare. **concerto,** n.
concerto, m.
concession, n. concessione, f. con-
cession[n]aire, n. concessionario,
m.
conch, n. conca; conchiglia, f.
~ology, n. conchiliologia, f.
conciliate, v.t. conciliare. **conciliation,** n. conciliazione, f.
concise, a. conciso; (edition) compatto.
~ness, n. concisione, f.
conclave, n. conclave, m.; assemblea,
f.
conclude, v.t. & i. concludere;
arrestare, chiudere. ~d (serial),
seguito e fine.

conclusion, *n.* conclusione; decisione, *f.* to *try* ~*s with,* misurarsi con. **conclusive,** *a.* conclusivo.

concoct, *v.t.* mettere insieme; confezionare; concuocere; (*fig.*) ordire, tramare, macchinare. ~**ion,** *n.* concozione; mescolanza; macchinazione; panzana, *f.*

concomitant, *n.* accompagnamento, *m.*

concord, *n.* concordia; armonia, *f.*; (*Mus.*) accordo, *m.*; (*Gram.*) concordanza, *f.* ~**ance,** *n.* concordanza, *f.*; indice alfabetico, *m.*

concourse, *n.* concorso, *m.*, affluenza, *f.*

concrete, *a.* concreto. **the concrete** (*opp. abstract*), il concreto. ¶ *n.* calcestruzzo, cemento, *m. reinforced* ~, cemento armato.

concubine, *n.* concubina, *f.*

concupiscence, *n.* concupiscenza, *f.*

concur, *v.i.* concurrere; aderire; esser d'accordo. **concurrence,** *n.* concorso, consenso, *m.*; adesione, *f.*

concussion, *n.* scossa, *f.*; urto, *m.* ~ *of the brain,* commozione cerebrale, *f.*

condemn, *v.t.* condannare. ~*ed man, woman,* condannato, -a, a morte, *m.f.* **condemnation,** *n.* condanna, *f.*; biasimo, *m.*

condensation, *n.* condensazione, *f.* **condense,** *v.t.* condensare. ~*d milk,* latte condensato, l. concentrato, *m.* **condenser,** *n.* (*Phys., Elec., Opt.*) condensatore, *m.*

condescend, *v.i.* condiscendere, accondiscendere, degnarsi. **condescension,** *n.* condiscenza, *f.*

condign, *a.* giusto, adeguato.

condiment, *n.* condimento, *m.*

condition, *n.* condizione, *f.*; stato; grado; patto, *m.*; (*col. pl.*) regime, *m.*, condizioni, *f.pl.* ~*s of sale,* cartella d'incanto, *f. on* ~ *that,* a condizione che. ¶ *v.t.* condizionare. ~**al,** *a.* condizionale.

condole with, condolersi con, esprimere le sue condoglianze a. **condolence,** *n.* condoglianza, *f.*

condone, *v.t.* condonare; scusare, perdonare.

conduce, *v.t.* contribuire, condurre, tendere.

conduct, *n.* condotta, *f.*; maneggiamento, *m.*, direzione, *f.* ¶ *v.t.* condurre, guidare, dirigere, maneggiare, menare. ~*ed tour,* escursione accompagnata, *f.* **conductor.**

-**tress,** *n.* conduttore, *m.*, -trice, *f.*; guida, *f.*, capo, direttore, *m.*; (*tram, bus*) bigliettario, *m.*

conduit, *n.* condotto, tubo, *m.*

cone, *n.* (*Geom.*) cono, *m.*; (*fir, pine*) pina, pigna, *f.*; (*ice cream wafer*) cialdone, *m.*

confectioner, *n.* ~*'s* confettiere, pasticciere, *m.* ~*'s shop,* confetteria, pasticceria, *f.* ~**y,** *n.* confetteria, pasticceria, *f.*; dolci, confetti, *m.pl.* ~ *box,* scatola di dolci, *f.*

confederacy, *n.* confederazione, *f.* **confederate,** *n.* confederato, *m.*; complice, *m.f.* ¶ *v.i.* confederarsi. **confederation,** *n.* confederazione, *f.*

confer, *v.t. & i.* conferire. **conference,** *n.* conferenza, *f.*

confess, *v.t.* confessare, riconoscere, ammettere; accusarsi di; (*v.i.*) confessarsi. ~**edly,** *ad.* per propria confessione, per propria ammissione.

confession, *n.* confessione, ammissione; (*faith*) professione, *f.* ~**al,** *n.* confessionale, *m.* **confessor,** *n.* confessore, *m.*

confidant, -e, *n.* confidente, *m.f.* **confide,** *v.t.* confidare; affidare; (*v.i.*) confidare, fidarsi. **confidence,** *n.* confidenza; fiducia; (*secret*) confidenza, *f.* ~ *trick,* truffa all'americana, *f.* **confident,** *a.* confidente, sicuro. **confidential,** *a.* confidenziale. ~**ly,** *ad.* confidenzialmente. **confiding,** *p.a.* fiducioso, confidente.

confine, *v.t.* confinare; rinchiudere; limitare; restringere; chiudere; imprigionare. ~ *oneself to, within,* limitarsi a, non uscir fuori di. ~ *to barracks,* consegnare. *to be* ~ *d* (*woman*), partorire. ~*d to bed,* obbligato a letto. ~**ment,** *n.* detenzione; prigionia, prigione, reclusione, *f.*; confino, *m.*; (*woman*) parto, partorire, *m.* ~ *to barracks,* consegna, *f. solitary* ~, segregazione cellulare, *f.* **confines,** *n.pl.* confini, *m.pl.*

confirm, *v.t.* confermare; ratificare; rafforzare; stabilire; approvare; (*Eccl.*) cresimare. ~**ation,** *n.* conferma; ratificazione; approvazione, *f.*; rafforzamento, *m.*; (*Eccl.*) cresima; confermazione, *f.* ~**ed,** *p.a.* inveterato, ostinato, convinto; matricolato. ~ *invalid,* inguaribile, incurabile.

confiscate, *v.t.* confiscare. **confiscation,** *n.* confisca, *f.*

conflagration, *n.* conflagrazione, *f.*, incendio, *m.*

conflict, *n.* conflitto, *m.*, lotta, *f.*; urto; contrasto, *m.* ¶ *v.i. & abs.* contraddirsi, non accordarsi. ~**ing,** *p.a.* contrario, opposto, in conflitto, in contrasto.

confluence, *n.* confluenza, *f.*, concorso, *m.*; affluenza, *f.*

conform, *v.t.* conformare; (*v.i.*) conformarsi. ~**able,** *a.* conforme. ~**ably,** *ad.* conformemente, conforme. ~**ation,** *n.* conformazione, *f.* ~**ity,** *n.* conformità, *f.*, accordo, *m.*

confound, *v.t.* confondere. ~**ed,** *p.a.* maledetto.

confraternity, *n.* confraternità; (*pers.*) fraternità, *f.*

confront, *v.t.* affrontare, confrontare.

confuse, *v.t.* confondere; mischiare; scompigliare; sconcertare. **confused,** *a.* confuso; disordinato; sconcertato. ~**ly,** *ad.* confusamente, alla rinfusa. **confusion,** *n.* confusione, *f.*, disordine, scompiglio; imbarazzo, *m.*

confute, *v.t.* confutare.

congeal, *v.t.* congelare; coagulare; (*v.i.*) congelarsi; coagularsi.

congenial, *a.* simpatico.

congenital, *a.* congenito.

conger [eel], *n.* grongo, *m.*

congest, (*Med.*), *v.t.* congestionare, ingorgare. ~**ion,** *n.* (*Med.*) congestione, *f.*, ingorgamento, *m.*; (*traffic, &c.*) congestione, *f.* ~ *of the blood, of the lungs,* congestione sanguigna, cerebrale, polmonare, *f.* ~ *of the liver,* congestione del fegato, *f.*

conglomerate, *n.* conglomerato, *m.*

congratulate, *v.t.* congratularsi con, felicitare, rallegrarsi con, complimentare. ~ *oneself,* felicitarsi. **congratulation,** *n.* felicitazione, *f.*, complimento, mirallegro, *m.*

congregate, *v.t.* congregare, riunire; (*v.i.*) congregarsi, radunarsi, riunirsi. **congregation,** *n .*congregazione, *f.*, assembramento, radunamento, *m.*; (*of pers.*) assemblea, *f.*

congress, *n.* congresso, *m.* **member of the** (*or* a) ~, congressista, *m.f.*

congruity, *n.* congruità, *f.* **congruous,** *a.* congruo; conveniente. ~**ly,** *ad.* congruamente.

conic(al), *a.* conico.

conifer, *n.* conifero, *m.* ~**ous,** *a.* conifero.

conjectural, *a.* congetturale. **con-**

jecture, *n.* congettura, *f.* ¶ *v.t.* congetturare.

conjoin, *v.t.* congiungere. **conjoint,** *a.* congiunto.

conjugal, *a.* coniugale.

conjugate, *v.t.* coniugare. **conjugation,** *n.* coniugazione, *f.*

conjunction, *n.* congiunzione, *f.* **conjuncture,** *n.* congiuntura, *f.*

conjure, *v.t.* (*adjure*) scongiurare; (*enchant*) stregare, ammaliare; (*v.i.*) fare il prestigiatore. ~ *away,* esorcizzare. ~ *up,* evocare. **conjurer, -or,** *n.* prestigiatore, *m.*, -trice, *f.* **conjuring,** *n.* prestidigitazione, *f.*, prestigio, *m.* ~ *trick,* giuoco di prestigio, *m.*

connect, *v.t.* connettere, collegare, congiungere, unire; (*Elec.*) accoppiare. ~**ed,** *p.a.* congiunto; apparentato. **connecting rod,** biella, *f.* **connexion, -nection,** *n.* connessione, *f.*; collegamento, *m.*; relazione; congiunzione, *f.*; contatto; rapporto, *m.*; (*Rly.*) corrispondenza, *f.*; parente, *m.f.*, congiunto, *m.*; clientela, *f.*

conning tower, torre di manovra, *f.*

connivance, *n.* connivenza, *f.* **connive at,** essere connivente a.

connoisseur, *n.* conoscitore, *m.*, -trice, *f.*, perito, *m.*; buongustaio, *m.*

connote, *v.t.* implicare, significare in più.

connubial, *a.* coniugale, matrimoniale.

conquer, *v.t.* vincere, conquistare. **conqueror, conqueress,** *n.* vincitore, *m.*, -trice, *f.*, conquistatore, *m. William the Conqueror,* Guglielmo il Conquistatore. **conquest,** *n.* conquista, *f.*

consanguinity, *n.* consanguineità, *f.*

conscience, *n.* coscienza, *f* ~ *money,* restituzione anonima, *f. to be* ~*-stricken,* essere punto (morso) dalla coscienza. **conscientious,** *a.* coscienzioso. ~**ness,** *n.* coscienza, *f.*

conscious, *a. to be* ~, aver conoscenza. *to be* ~ *of,* avere coscienza di, esser conscio di, essere consapevole di, sentire. ~**ly,** *ad.* consapevolmente, coscientemente. ~**ness,** *n.* coscienza; conoscenza, *f.*

conscript, *n.* coscritto, *m.* ~**ion,** *n.* coscrizione, *f.*

consecrate, *v.t.* consacrare; benedire; dedicare; sacrare. ~**d,** *p.a.* benedetto; consacrato; santo. **consecra-**

tion, *n.* consacrazione; benedizione; sagra, *f.*

consecutive, *a.* consecutivo.

consensus, *n.* unanimità, *f.*

consent, *n.* consenso, accordo, *m.* ¶ *v.i.* acconsentire; assentire, andare d'accordo.

consequence, *n.* conseguenza, *f.*; seguito; effetto, *m.*; importanza, *f.* **consequent,** *a.* conseguente. *consequential damages,* danni indiretti, *m.pl.* **consequently,** *ad.* conseguentemente, per conseguenza, perciò.

conservative, *a.* conservatore; conservativo. ¶ *n. &* **conservator,** conservatore, *m.*, -trice, *f.* **conservatory,** *n.* serra, *f.*

consider, *v.t.* considerare, riguardare, tenere; deliberare su; (*v.i. & abs.*) meditare, riflettere. ~**able,** *a.* considerevole. ~**ate,** *a.* premuroso, gentile, simpatico. ~**ation,** *n.* considerazione, riflessione, deliberazione, *f.*; riguardo, *m.*, deferenza, *f.*; motivo, *m.*, ragione; premura; importanza; (*Law*) causa, garanzia, provvigione, *f.* ~ [*money*], prezzo, compenso, *m.*, rimunerazione, indennità, *f. in ~ of* (value received), in considerazione di, per compenso di. (matter) *under* ~, in corso d'esame. *without due* ~, alla leggera. ~**ing,** *pr.* atteso, visto, considerando.

consign, *v.t.* consegnare; affidare; rimettere, spedire; relegare; (*goods*) consegnare, inviare, spedire. ~**ee,** *n.* consegnatario, destinatario, *m.* ~**ment,** *n.* consegna, spedizione, *f.*, invio, *m.* ~ *note* (*Rly.*), nota di spedizione, *f.* (*goods*) *on* ~, in consegna. ~**or,** *n.* consegnatore, *m.*

consist, *v.i.* consistere, comporsi. ~**ence,** -**cy,** *n.* consistenza; coerenza, *f.* ~**ent,** *a.* coerente; costante; compatibile. ~**ently with,** in conformità con, in accordo con. ~**ory,** *n.* concistoro, *m.*

consolation, *n.* consolazione, *f.* ~ *prize,* premio di consolazione, indennizzo, *m.* **console,** *v.t.* consolare. ¶ *n. &* ~**table,** mensola, *f.*

consolidate, *v.t.* consolidare; unificare. **consolidation,** *n.* consolidazione, *f.*

consonance, *n.* consonanza, *f.* **consonant,** *a.* (*Mus., words*) consonante. ~ *with,* in accordo con. ¶ *n.* consonante, *f.*

consort, *n.* sposo, *m.*, sposa, *f.*;

(*Naut.*) conserva, *f.*; (*Nav.*) nave di scorta, *f.* ¶ *v.i.* associarsi. ~ *with,* frequentare.

conspicuous, *a.* cospicuo, prominente, vistoso; insigne, eccezionale. *to make oneself* ~, farsi notare, far mostra di sé, pavoneggiarsi.

conspiracy, *n.* cospirazione, congiurazione, *f.* **conspirator,** *n.* cospiratore, *m.*, -trice, *f.*, congiuratore, *m.*, -trice, *f.*, congiurato, -a, *m.f.* **conspire,** *v.i. & t.* cospirare, congiurare.

constable, *n.* agente di polizia, poliziotto, *m.*, guardia di pubblica sicurezza, *f.* **constabulary,** *n.* polizia, *f.*, carabinieri, *m.pl.*

constancy, *n.* costanza, *f.* **constant,** *a.* costante. ¶ *n.* costante, *f.* ~**ly,** *ad.* costantemente.

constellation, *n.* costellazione, *f.*

consternation, *n.* costernazione, *f.*

constipate, *v.t.* costipare. **constipation,** *n.* costipazione; stitichezza, *f.*

constituency, *n.* circoscrizione elettorale, *f.*, collegio elettorale, *m.*; elettori, *m.pl.* **constituent,** *a.* costituente, componente. ¶ *n.* componente; ingrediente, *m.*; (*pl.*) elettori, *m.pl.* **constitute,** *v.t.* costituire; stabilire. **constitution,** *n.* costituzione, *f.*; temperamento, *m.*; (*written*) statuto, *m.* ~**al,** *a.* costituzionale.

constrain, *v.t.* costringere, forzare, obbligare. **constraint,** *n.* costrizione; forza; soggezione, *f.*

construct, *v.t.* costruire, fare, fabbricare; stabilire; comporre. ~**ion,** *n.* costruzione; fabbrica; interpretazione, *f.* ~**ional,** *a.* di costruzione. ~ *outfit* (*boy's*), giuoco di costruzione meccanica, *m.* ~**or,** *n.* costruttore, *m.*

construe, *v.t.* costruire, tradurre; spiegare.

consul, *n.* console, *m.* ~**ar,** *a.* consolare. ~**ate &** ~**ship,** *n.* consolato, *m.*

consult, *v.t.* consultare. ~**ation,** *n.* consulto, *m.*, consultazione, *f.* **consulting,** *p.a.:* ~ *physician,* medico consulente, *m.* ~ *room,* gabinetto di consultazione, *m.*, sala di c., *f.*

consume, *v.t.* consumare, divorare; (use) consumare. **consumer,** *n.* consumatore, *m.*, -trice, *f.* (*town gas, elec.*) abbonato, *m.*

consummate, *a.* consumato, perfetto, finito. ¶ *v.t.* consumare, finire.

consummation, *n.* consumazione, perfezione, fine, *f.*
consumption, *n.* (*destruction*) consunzione; (*Med.*) consunzione, tisi, tubercolosi, *f.*; (*use*) consumo, *m.*, consumazione, *f.* **consumptive,** *a. & n.* tisico, *a. & m.*, tubercoloso, *a. & m.*, -a, *f.*
contact, *n.* contatto; toccamento, *m.*
contagion, *n.* contagio, *m.* **contagious,** *a.* contagioso. ~ness, *n.* contagio, *m.*
contain, *v.t.* contenere, includere, tenere; comprendere; trattenere; reprimere. ~er, *n.* contenente, recipiente, *m.*
contaminate, *v.t.* contaminare, infettare. **contamination,** *n.* contaminazione, *f.*
contango, *n.* riporto, *m.* ¶ *v.t.* riportare.
contemplate, *v.t.* contemplare; meditare; divisare, progettare; considerare; (*v.i.*) meditare. **contemplation,** *n.* contemplazione, meditazione, *f. in* ~, in vista, in progetto. **contemplative,** *a.* contemplativo; meditativo.
contemporaneous & contemporary, *a.* contemporaneo. **contemporary,** *n.* contemporaneo; (*newspaper*) collega, *m.*
contempt, *n.* disprezzo, sprezzo, dispregio, sdegno, *m.* ~ *of court*, offesa alla corte, *f.* ~ible, *a.* sprezzabile; spregevole. **contemptuous,** *a.* sprezzante, sdegnoso.
contend, *v.t. & i.* ~ *that*, pretendere che. ~ *with*, combattere; lottare contro; disputare.
content, *a.* contento; pago, soddisfatto. ¶ *n.* contentamento, contento; (*holding*) contenenza, *f.*; tenore; titolo, *m.*; volume, *m.*, capacità, *f.*; (*pl.*) contenuto, tenore, *m.*; indice [di materie], *m.* ¶ *v.t.* accontentare, appagare, soddisfare. ~ed with, soddisfatto di. *easily* ~ed, di facile contentamento. ~edly, *ad.* felicemente, tranquillamente; con soddisfazione, senza lagnarsi.
contention, *n.* discordia; disputa; contesa, *f. my* ~ *is that,* io sostengo che. **contentious,** *a.* litigioso; contenzioso.
contentment, *n.* contentamento, *m.*, contentezza, *f.*
contest, *n.* contesa, lotta, *f.*, combattimento, *m.*; gara, *f.*, concorso, *m.*; giostra, *f.* ¶ *v.t.* contestare, contrastare; disputare.

context, *n.* contesto, *m.*
contexture, *n.* contestura, *f.*
contiguity, *n.* contiguità, *f.* **contiguous,** *a.* contiguo.
continence, *n.* continenza, *f.* **continent,** *a.* continente. ¶ *n.* continente, *m.*; terra ferma, *f. the C* ~ (*Europe*), il continente. ~al, *a.* continentale.
contingency, *n.* contingenza, eventualità, *f.,* imprevisto, *m.*; (*pl.*) spese impreviste, *f.pl.* ~ *fund*, fondo di previdenza, *m.* **contingent,** *a.* contingente, aleatorio, eventuale. ¶ *n.* contingente, *m.*; (*of recruiting year*) classe, *f.*
continual, *a.* continuo, incessante; ripetuto. **continuance,** *n.* continuazione; durata, *f.* **continuation,** *n.* continuazione, *f.,* seguito, *m.*; (*Stk. Ex.*) riporto, *m.* **continue,** *v.t. & i.* continuare, proseguire, seguire; prolungare; durare; persistere; rimanere; conservare; (*carry forward*) riportare. *to be* ~d (*serial*), a seguire. ~ *in our next*, segue al prossimo numero. **continuity,** *n.* continuità, *f.* **continuous,** *a.* continuo. ~ *performance* (*cinema*), spettacolo permanente, *m.* ~ly, *ad.* continuamente, senza interruzione.
contort, *v.t.* contorcere. ~ed, *p.a.* contorto, storto. **contortion,** *n.* contorsione, *f.* ~ist, *n.* contorsionista, *m.f.*
contour, *n.* contorno; profilo, tracciato, *m.* ~ *line*, isoipsa, *f.* ~ *map*, piano quotato con isoipse, *m.*
contra, *n.* contropartita, *f.* ¶ *v.t.* annullare, cancellare. ~ *account*, conto in contropartita, *m.* ~ *entry*, contropartita, *f.*
contraband, *n.* contrabbando, *m.*; (*att.*) di contrabbando.
contrabasso, *n.* contrabbasso, *m.*
contract, *n.* impresa, *f.*; appalto; contratto, patto, *m.*, convenzione, *f.*; atto, trattato, *m. on* ~ *or by* ~ *or* ~ (*att.*), in appalto, a contratto. ~ *note*, distinta, *f.* ~ *price*, prezzo d'appalto, *m.* ¶ *v.t.* (*shrink*) restringere, far restringere, contrarre, far c. (*Law*) contrarre, contrattare, imprendere, appaltare; (*v.i. or abs.*) contrarsi, restringersi; (*Law*) contrattare, trattare. ~ant (*pers.*) *or* **contracting party,** *n.* contraente, *m.f.* ~ing, *a* contraente. ~ion, *n.* contrazione; diminuzione, *f.*; restringimento, *m.*; abbreviazione, *f.*

~or, *n.* imprenditore, *m.*, -trice, *f.*; fornitore, *m.*, -trice, *f.*; appaltatore, *m.*; impresario, *m.* **contractual,** *a.* contrattuale.

contradict, *v.t.* contraddire. ~ion, *n.* contraddizione, *f.* ~ory, *a.* contradditorio.

contradistinction, *n.* opposizione, *f.*, contrasto, *m.*

contralto, *n.* contralto, *m.*

contrariety, *n.* contrarietà, *f.* **contrarily** & **contrary,** *ad.* contrariamente. **contrary,** *a.* contrario; opposto; inverso. ¶ *n.* contrario, opposto, *m.* *on the* ~, al contrario.

contrast, *n.* contrasto, *m.*, opposizione, *f.* ¶ *v.t.* & *i.* mettere in contrasto; contrastare, far contrasto. ~ing, *a.* in contrasto (con).

contravene, *v.t.* contravvenire a, infrangere. **contravention,** *n.* contravvenzione, infrazione, *f.*

contribute, *v.t.* contribuire con; dare, pagare; (*v.i.*) contribuire, provvedere. ~ *to* (*journal*), collaborare a. **contribution,** *n.* contribuzione, *f.*, contributo; apporto, *m.*; quota, *f.* *to lay under* ~, mettere a contribuzione. **contributor** (*to journal*), *n.* collaboratore, *m.*, -trice, *f.*

contrite, *a.* contrito. **contrition,** *n.* contrizione, *f.*

contrivance, *n.* congegno, *m.*; invenzione, *f.*; artificio, *m.*; combinazione, *f.*; espediente, *m.* **contrive,** *v.t.* combinare, inventare macchinare. ~ *to*, trovar mezzo di, riuscire a.

control, *n.* controllo; posto di controllo; freno; comando, *m.*; autorità; padronanza, *f.* ¶ *v.t.* controllare; contenere; frenare, reprimere; dominare; dirigere, amministrare; verificare. **controller,** *n.* controllore, *m.*

controversial, *a.* polemico, di controversia. **controversy,** *n.* controversia, *f.* **controvert,** *v.t.* disputare, controvertere, contestare.

contumacy, *n.* contumacia, *f.*

contumely, *n.* contumelia, ingiuria (*oft. pl.*), *f.*; obbrobrio, *m.*

contuse, *v.t.* contundere, ammaccare. **contusion,** *n.* contusione, *f.*

conundrum, *n.* indovinello, *m.*; sciarade, *f.*; enimma, *m.*

convalesce, *v.i.* rimettersi in salute, entrare in convalescenza. **convalescence,** *n.* convalescenza, *f.*

convalescent, *a.* & *n.* convalescente, *a.* & *m.f.*

convene, *v.t.* convocare.

convenience, *n.* comodità, convenienza, *f.*; comodo, agio, *m.*; (*w.c.*) luogo comodo, *m.* **convenient,** *a.* comodo, conveniente, convenevole. ~ly, *ad.* comodamente, convenientemente.

convent, *n.* convento, monastero, *m.*; casa, *f.* ~ *school*, convento, *m.*

convention, *n.* convenzione, *f.* ~al, *a.* convenzionale. ~alism & ~ality, *n.* convenzionalismo, *m.* ~alist, *n.* convenzionalista, *m.f.*

converge, *v.i.* convergere. **convergent,** *a.* convergente.

conversant, *a.* versato (in), pratico (di), competente (in).

conversation, *n.* conversazione, *f.*, colloquio; discorso, *m.*; chiacchierata, *f.* ~al, *a.* di conversazione. ~[al]ist, *n.* conversatore, *m.*, -trice, *f.*, (bel) parlatore, *m.* **conversazione,** *f.* riunione, *f.*

converse, *a.* & *n.* contrario; converso, *a.* & *m.*; reciproco, *a.* ¶ *v.i.* conversare; discorrere, chiacchierare insieme.

conversion, *n.* conversione, *f.*, convertimento, *m.*; trasformazione, *f.*; (*Fin.*) conversione, *f.* ~ *loan*, prestito di conversione, *m.* **convert,** *n.* convertito, *m.*, -a, *f.* ¶ *v.t.* convertire, trasformare, trasmutare. *to become* ~ed (*Relig.*), convertirsi. ~er, *n.* convertitore, *m.* ~ible, *a.* convertibile.

convex, *a.* convesso. ~ity, *n.* convessità, *f.*

convey, *v.t.* [tras]portare; condurre; spedire; mandare; comunicare, esprimere; (*Law*, &c.) trasferire, traslatare, trasmettere, cedere. ~ance, *n.* trasporto, mezzo di trasporto; veicolo, *m.*, vettura, *f.*; (*Law*) traslazione, trasmissione, *f.*, trasferimento, trapasso, *m.*, cessione, *f.*; (*deed*) atto traslativo, atto di trasmissione, *m.* **conveyor,** *n.* (*Mech.*) convogliatore, trasportatore, *m.* ~ *belt*, c. a cinghia.

convict, *n.* condannato, *m.*, -a, *f.*, forzato, *m.* ~ *prison*, bagno, ergastolo, penitenziario, *m.* ¶ *v.t.* convincere; condannare. ~ion, *n.* convinzione; condanna, *f.* *person with previous* ~s, recidivo, *m.*, -a, *f.*

convince, *v.t.* convincere. **convincing,** *p.a.* convincente.

convivial, *a.*, ~ *gathering*, allegra

compagnia, *f.* ~ *person*, persona gioviale, *f.*, allegro convitato, *m.*

convocation, *n.* convocazione, *f.* **convoke,** *v.t.* convocare.

convolvulus, *n.* convolvolo, vilucchio, *m.*

convoy, *n.* convoglio, *m.*; scorta, *f.* ¶ *v.t.* convogliare, scortare.

convulse, *v.t.* scuotere, agitare violentemente, mettere in convulsioni. *to be* ~*d* (laughing), torcersi. **convulsion,** *n.* convulsione, *f.* **convulsive,** *a.* convulsive.

cony, -ney, *n.* coniglio, *m.*

coo, *v.i.* tubare.

cook, *n.* cuoco, *m.*, -a, *f.*; (*ship's*) cuoco di bordo, *m.* ~*'s boy*, sguattero, *m.* ~ *shop*, rosticceria, *f.* ¶ *v.t.* far cuocere, cucinare; (*fig.*) cucinare, manipolare, falsificare; (*v.i.*) cuocere, cuocersi. **cooker,** *n.* cucina economica, *f.*; fornello di cucina, *m.* **cookery,** *n.* cucina, arte culinaria, *f.* ~ *book*, libro (manuale) di cucina, *m.* **cooking,** *n.* cucina; cocitura, *f.* ~ *apples*, mele da cucinare, *f.pl.*

cool, *a.* fresco; freddo; calmo; disinvolto, indifferente; impudente, sfacciato. ~*-headed*, calmo, equilibrato. ¶ *n.* fresco, *m.*, frescura, *f.* *in the* ~, al fresco, frescamente. ¶ *v.t.* rinfrescare; attiepidire; raffreddare; (*v.i.*) attiepidirsi; raffreddarsi, rinfrescarsi. ~ *down*, calmarsi; rinfrescarsi. ~ *one's heels*, stare ad aspettare. ~**er,** *n.* vaso refrigerante, *m.* ~**ness,** fresco, *m.*, frescura, *f.*; freddezza; calma, *f.*; sangue freddo, *m.*, flemma, *f.*; indifferenza, *f.*

coomb, *n.* valletta, *f.*

coop, *n.* stia, *f.* ~ [*up*], *v.t.* rinchiudere, chiudere in gabbia; mettere nella stia.

cooper, *n.* bottaio, *m.* ~**age,** *n.* mestiere di bottaio, *m.*; bottega di b., *f.*

cooperate, *v.i.* cooperare. **cooperation,** *n.* cooperazione, *f.* **cooperative,** *a.* cooperativo. ~ *society*, [società] cooperativa, *f.*

coordinate, *v.t.* coordinare.

coot, *n.* folaga, *f.*

cope, *n.* cappuccio, *m.*; pianeta, *f.* ¶ *v.t.* ricoprire; coronare. ~ *with*, tener testa a, lottare contro, tener fronte a.

Copenhagen, *n.* Copenaghen, *f.*

coping, *n.* comignolo, colmo, coronamento, *m.*

copious, *a.* copioso, ricco, abbondante.

copper, *n.* rame, *m.*; (*vessel*) caldaia, *f.*, paiuolo, calderone, *m.* ~ [*coin*], soldo, *m.*, moneta di rame, *f.*; (*pl.*) soldi, *m.pl.* ~ *beech*, faggio rosso, *m.* ~ *bit* (*soldering*), saldatoio, *m.* ~*-coloured*, color [di] rame. ~ *plate*, lastra di rame, *f.* ~ *plate engraving*, incisione su rame, stampa in r., *f.*; taglio dolce *m.* ~ *plate* [*hand*] *writing*, bella scrittura, calligrafia, *f.* ~*smith*, ramaio, calderaio, *m.* ~*smith's* [*& brazier's*] *trade*, mestiere di calderaio, *m.* ¶ *v.t.* ramare, rivestire di rame.

copperas, *n.* copparosa, *f.*, vetriolo verde, *m.*

coppice, copse, *n.* boschetto, *m.*; macchia, *f.*

copulation, *n.* copulazione, *f.*

copy, *n.* copia; trascrizione, *f.*; calco; esemplare; esempio, modello; (*newspaper*) numero, *m.*; (*Law*) copia, trascrizione; spedizione, *f.* ~ *book*, quaderno, *m.* ~*cat*, scimmia, *f.* ¶ *v.t.* copiare; trascrivere; riprodurre; ricalcare. **copying,** *n.* trascrizione, *f.* ~ *ink*, inchiostro copiativo, *m.* **copyist,** *n.* copista, *m.f.*

copyright, *n.* proprietà letteraria, *f.*, diritti d'autore, *m.pl.* ~ *by So-&-So*, i diritti di riproduzione e di traduzione sono riservati per tutti i paesi.

coquet, *v.i.* civettare. ~**ry,** *n.* civetteria, *f.* **coquettish,** *a.* civettuolo, da civetta.

coral, *n.* corallo; (*baby's*) sonaglio di corallo, *m.* ~ *fisher*, pescatore di coralli, *m.* ~ *reef*, banco di corallo, -i, *m.*

corbel, *n.* modiglione, *m.*

cord, *n.* corda, *f.*; cordoncino; spago, *m.*; funicella, *f.*; cordone, *m.* (*braided*). ¶ *v.t.* legare con corde, con una corda, con una funicella. ~**age,** *n.* cordame; *m.*

cordial, *a.* cordiale, caloroso. ¶ *n.* cordiale, *m.* ~**ity,** *n.* cordialità, *f.*

corduroy, *n.* velluto di cotone a grosse coste, *m.*

core, *n.* cuore; torsolo; midollo, *m.*; anima, *f.* ¶ *v.t.* (*of fruit*) togliere il torsolo da.

Corea or Korea, *n.* la Corea, *f.*

co-respondent, *n.* coimputato, ~a (*in action for divorce*); complice in adulterio, *m.f.*

Corinth, *n.* Corinto, *f.* **Corinthian,** *a.* corinzio, di Corinto. ¶ *n.* corinzio, *m.*, -a, *f.*

cork, n. sughero; (*stopper*) turacciolo, tappo, m. ~ *jacket*, corsetto di sughero, m., giacchetta di salvataggio, f. ~*screw*, cavatappi, tiratappi, m.inv. ~*screw*, v.i. attorcigliarsi. ~*screw staircase*, scala a chiocciola, f. ~*-tipped* (*cigarettes*), con bocchino di sughero. ~ *tree*, sughero, m. ¶ v.t. turare, tappare. ~y, a. sugheroso; che sa di sughero.

cormorant, n. cormorano, m.

corn, n. grano, m.; grani, m.pl.; biada, f.; cereali, m.pl.; (*Indian*) granturco, m.; (*on feet*) callo, (*soft*) occhio di pernice, m. ~ *chandler*, venditore al minuto di cereali, m. ~ *cob*, pannocchia del granturco, f. ~*cure*, ~*plaster*, callifugo, m. ~ *exchange*, borsa dei grani, f. ~*field*, campo di grano, m. ~*flour*, farina di grano, f. ~*flower*, fioraliso, m.

corned beef, carne di bue salata, di manzo salata, f.

cornelian, n. cornalina, f.

corner, n. angolo, canto; cantone; cantuccio, m.; (*street*) cantonata, f.; (*Com.*) accaparramento, m.; incetta, f.; (*att.*) d'angolo, di cantone. ~ *cupboard*, cantoniera, f. ~ *kick* (*Foot.*), calcio d'angolo, m. ~*stone*, pietra angolare, p. di cantone, f. ¶ v.t. mettere in angolo, rincantucciare, acculare; (*monopolize*) accaparrare, incettare.

cornet, n. (*cone*) cornetto, cartoccio, m.; (*Mus.*) cornetta, f.; (*ice cream wafer*) cono, cialdone, m.

cornice, n. cornice, f.; cornicione, m. ~ *pole*, portatende, m.inv.

Cornish, a. di Cornovaglia.

cornucopia, n. cornucopia, f.

Cornwall, n. la Cornovaglia, f.

corolla, n. corolla, f.

corollary, n. corollario, m.

corona, n. corona, f. **coronation,** n. incoronazione, f. **coronet,** n. corona (nobiliare), f.

corporal & **corporeal,** a. corporale; corporeo. **corporal,** n. caporale; (*cavalry*) brigadiere, m. **corporate,** a. corporato. costituito, sociale. ~ *body*, ente morale, civile, giuridico, m. ¶ v.i. costituirsi, far corpo. **corporation,** n. corporazione; (*municipal*) municipalità, f.; (*fam.*) pancione, m.

corps, n. corpo; equipaggio, m.

corpse, n. cadavere, m. ~*like,* a. cadaverico.

corpulence, -ency, n. corpulenza, f. **corpulent,** a. corpulento, panciuto.

Corpus Christi, Corpus Domini, m.

corpuscle, n. corpuscolo, m.

correct, a. corretto; esatto, giusto. ¶ v.t. correggere; rettificare; raddrizzare; emendare; castigare. ~*ed copy*, bella copia, f. ~*ion,* n. correzione; rettificazione; emendazione, f.; raddrizzamento, m.; riprensione, f. ~*al,* a. correzionale. ~*ive,* n. correttivo, m. ~*ness,* n. correttezza, esattezza, giustezza, f. ~*or,* n. correttore, m., -trice, f.

correlative, a. correlativo.

correspond, v.i. corrispondere; rispondere. ~*ence,* n. corrispondenza; raccolta di lettere, f.; epistolario, m. ~*ent,* n. corrispondente, m.f. ~*ing,* p.a. corrispondente.

corridor, n. corridoio; andito, m. ~ *carriage*, vagone con corridoio laterale, vagone a corridoio, m.

corrie (*Geol.*), n. cavità, buca, f.

corroborate, v.t. corroborare; confermare.

corrode, v.t. corrodere. **corrosion,** n. corrosione, f. **corrosive,** a. & n. corrosivo, a. & m.

corrugate, v.t. corrugare. ~*d* [*sheet*] *iron* & ~*d iron sheet*, lamiera di ferro ondulata, f.

corrupt, v.t. corrompere, viziare, guastare. ~*ible,* a. corruttibile. ~*ion,* n. corruzione; corruttela, f.

corsair, n. corsaro, m.

corset, n. busto, m., fascetta, f. ~*-maker*, bustaia, fascettaia, f. ¶ v.t. mettere il busto a . . .

Corsica, n. la Corsica, f. **Corsican,** a. corso. ¶ n. corso, a.

corundum, n. corindone, m.

coruscate, v.i. scintillare, brillare.

cos, n. or **Cos lettuce,** n. lattuga romana, f.

cosily, ad. comodamente, a tutt'agio, comodo comodo.

cosmetic, a. & n. cosmetico, a. & m.

cosmic(al), a. cosmico.

cosmopolitan & **cosmopolite,** a. & n. cosmopolitico; cosmopolita, m.

cost, n. costo, prezzo, m., spesa, f. *at all* ~*s,* ad ogni costo, a qualunque prezzo, avvenga che può. ~ *of living bonus*, indennità del caro vivere, f. ~ *of living figure*, indice del costo della vita, m. ~ *price*, prezzo di costo, prezzo d'acquisto, m. ¶ v.i. ir. costare.

costermonger, n. fruttivendolo, m.

costive, *a.* stitico. **~ness**, *n.* stitichezza, *f.*

costliness, *n.* costo alto, *m.*; sontuosità, *f.* **costly**, *a.* costoso; sontuoso.

costume, *n.* vestito; costume, *m.* ~ *piece*, ~ *play*, dramma storico, *m.*

costumier, *n.* vestiarista, *n.*; sarta, *f.*

cosy, *a.* comodo, gradevole; ad agio. ~ *corner*, cantuccio comodo, *m. to make oneself* ~, crogiolarsi.

cot, *n.* culla, *f.*, lettino, *m.*; capanna, *f.*

coterie, *n.* cricca, combriccola, *f.* ~ *of wits*, circolo spiritoso, *m.*

cottage, *n.* capanna, casa contadinesca; villetta, *f.*

cottar, -er, *n.* contadino, *m.*

cotter, *n.* (*Mech.*) bietta, chiavetta, *f.* ~ *pin*, chiavetta, *f.*

cotton, *n.* cotone, *m.* ~ *cloth*, tessuto di cotone, *m.* ~ *goods*, cotonerie *f.pl.* ~ *industry*, industria cotoniera, *f.* ~ *mill*, cotonificio, *m.* ~ *plant*, pianta del cotone, *f.* ~ *waste*, stoppaccio, *m.* ~ *wool*, bambagia, *f.* ~y, *a.* cotonato; cotonoso.

couch, *n.* canapè, *m. inv.*, poltrona a sdraio, *f.* ¶ *v.t.* mettere in resta; (*v.i.*) coricarsi, acquattarsi. ~*ed in these terms*, redatto cosí. ~ *grass*, *n.* gramigna, *f.*

cough, *n.* tosse, *f.* ~ *mixture*, sciroppo per la tosse, *m.* ~ *lozenge*, pastiglia per la tosse, *f.* ¶*v.i.* tossire. ~ *up*, espettorare.

council, *n.* consiglio; (*Eccl.*) concilio, *m.* **councillor**, *n.* consigliere, *m. Privy C*~, *n.* consigliere di Stato, *m.*

counsel, *n.* consiglio; (*pers.*) avvocato, *m.* ¶ *v.t.* consigliare. **counsellor**, *n.* consigliatore, consigliere, *m.*

count, *n.* conto; (*pers.*) conte, *m.* ~ *of indictment*, capo d'accusa, *m.* ¶ *v.t.* contare, numerare; (*votes*) scrutinare. ~ *upon*, far assegnamento su, contare su.

countenance, *n.* viso, volto, *m.*; faccia, fisonomia, *f.*; appoggio, favore, *m.* ¶ *v.t.* tollerare, appoggiare, incoraggiare.

counter, *n.* ricambio, opposto, contrario; (*play*) gettone, *m.*; (*meter*) calcolatore, contatore, *m.*, macchina calcolatrice, *f.*; (*shop*) banco, *m.*; (*cashier's*) cassa, *f.*, sportello, *m.* ¶ *v.t.* reagire a, ricambiare, contrariare. *to run* ~ *to*, opporsi a.

counteract, *v.t.* neutralizzare, contrariare.

counter attack, *n.* contrattacco, *m.*

counterbalance, *n.* contrappeso, *m.* ¶ *v.t.* controbilanciare, contrappesare.

counterclaim, *n.* riconvenzione, *f.*

counterfeit, *a.* contraffatto, falso. ¶ *n.* contraffazione, *f.* ¶ *v.t.* contraffare, falsare. ~**er**, *n.* contraffattore, falsario, *m.*

counterfoil, *n.* matrice, *f.*

counter instructions, *n.* contrordine, *m.*

countermand, *v.t.* contrordinare, contromandare.

counterpane, *n.* sopraccoperta, *f.*

counterpart, *n.* controscritta, *f.*; (*pers.*) controparte, *f.*, doppio, *m.*; (*deed*) doppio, duplicato, *m.*

counterpoint, *n.* contrappunto, *m.*

counterpoise, *n.* contrappeso, *m.* ¶ *v.t.* controbilanciare, contrappesare.

countershaft, *n.* albero secondario, *m.*; ~ *& accessories*, trasmissione secondaria, *f.*

countersign, *n.* parola d'ordine, *f.* contrassegno, *m.* ¶ *v.t.* controfirmare. *counter signature*, controfirma, *f.*

countersink, *n.* fresatura, *f.* ~ *bit*, fresa, fresatrice, *f.* ¶ *v.t.* fresare, accecare.

counterstroke, *n.* contraccolpo, *m.*, risposta, *f.*

countervailing duty, *n.* imposta compensatrice, *f.*

counterweight, *n.* contrappeso, *m.*

countess, *n.* contessa, *f.*

counting, *n.* conto, computo, *m.* ~ *house*, cassa, *f.* **countless**, *a.* innumerabile, innumerevole.

country, *n.* paese, *m.*; canipagna; provincia; regione; patria, *f.*; (*politics*) corpo elettorale, *m.*, elettori, *m.pl.*, pubblico, *m.* ~ *club*, circolo di golf, circolo dei villeggianti, *m.* ~ *cottage*, villina, *f.* ~ *dance*, contraddanza, *f.* ~ *house*, villa, *f.* ~ *life*, vita campestre, *f.* ~*man*, ~ *woman*, contadino, -a.; paesano, -a. *fellow* ~*man*, *-woman*, compaesano, -a; compatriotta, *m.*, *f.* ~ *seat*, castello, *m.*, villa, *f.* ~*side*, campagna, *f.* ~ *town*, città di provincia, *f.*

county, *n.* contea, *f.*; (*in Italy*) provincia, *f.* ~ *town*, capoluogo di provincia, *m.*

couple, *n.* coppia, catena, *f.* ¶ *v.t.* accoppiare; attaccare. **couplet**, *n.* distico, *m.* **coupling**, *n.* accoppiamento; manicotto; attacco, *m.*

coupon, *n.* cedola, *f.*, tagliando, *m.*, polizza, *f.*

courage, *n.* coraggio, *m.* **~eous,** *a.* coraggioso.

courier, *n.* corriere, *m.*

course, *n.* corso, corrente, *m.*; carriera; via, *f.*; andamento, progresso, *m.*, successione, ordine, *f.*; *(meal)* piatto, *m.*, portata, *f.*; *(Build.)* strato, *m.*, fila, *f.*; *(ground)* campo, terreno, *m.*; *(pl., Med.)* regole, *f.pl. in due* ~, a tempo debito. *of* ~, naturalmente, senza dubbio, ben inteso, certamente, s'intende. *why, of* ~! si figuri! ¶ *v.t.* & *i.* correre, cacciare. **courser** *(Poet.), n.* destriere, *m.*

coursing, *n.* caccia coi levrieri, *f.*

court, *n.* cortile, *m.*; corte, *f.*; commissione, *f.*; tribunale, *m.*, giustizia; udienza, *f.*; *(Ten.)* campo da tennis, *m.* ~ *card,* carta figurata, figura, *f.* ~ *of inquiry,* commissione d'inchiesta, *f.* *prize* ~ *(Nav.),* commissione delle prede, *f.* ~ *martial,* consiglio di guerra, *m.*, tribunale militare, *f.* ~*s of justice,* palazzo di giustizia, *m.*; Giustizia, *f.* ~ *plaster,* drappo inglese, taffeta inglese, *m.* ~ *shoes,* scarpe scollate, *f.pl.* ~ *train,* veste di corte, veste con strascico, *f.* ~*yard,* cortile, *m.* ¶ *v.t.* fare la corte a, corteggiare; *(disaster)* invitare. *to* ~ *favour,* brigare. *to* ~ *the favour of,* corteggiare.

courteous, *a.* cortese. **courtesan,** *n.* cortigiana, etera, *f.* **courtesy,** *n.* cortesia, *f.* **courtier,** *n.* cortigiano, gentiluomo di corte, *m.* **courtly,** *a.* cortese, distinto. **courtship,** *n.* corte, *f.*, corteggiamento, *m.*

cousin, *n.* cugino, -a, *m.f.*

cove, *n.* ansa, cala, *f.*

covenant, *n.* convenzione, *f.*, patto, *m.* ¶ *v.i.* convenire, impegnarsi, pattuire.

Coventry (to send to) *(fig.),* scansare, mettere in quarantena, boicottare.

cover, *n.* busta, *f.*; tappeto; coperchio, *m.*; campana; fodera, *f.*; involucro, *m.*; copertina, *f.*; riparo, ricovero, asilo, *m.*, macchia, *f.*; pretesto, velo; deposito, *m.*, garanzia; provvisione, *f.*, indennizzo, *m.* ¶ *v.t.* coprire, ricoprire; involgere; apparecchiare; nascondere, celare; dissimulare; comprendere; provvedere a; *(of animals)* montare, coprire. ~*ed walk,* andito coperto, *m.*, galleria, *f.* ~**ing,** *n.* copertura, *f.*; vestiti, *m.pl.*; *(of animals)* monta, *f.*, accoppia-

mento, *m.* ~ *card,* carta piú alta, *f.* ~**let,** *n.* coperta, *f.*

covert, *a.* coperto, nascosto. ¶ *n.* macchia, *f.*; bosco, *m.* ~ *coat,* paltò, *m.inv.* ~**ly,** *ad.* di nascosto.

covet, *v.t.* brameggiare, bramare, desiderare. ~**ous,** *a.* cupido. ~**ousness,** *n.* cupidigia, *f.*

covey, *n.* branco, stormo, *m.*

cow, *n.* vacca, *f.*; *(of elephants, &c.)* femmina. ~*bell,* campanaccio, *m.* ~*herd,* vaccaio, *m.* ~ *hide,* pelle di vacca, *f.* ~*house,* ~ *shed,* vaccheria, stalla, *f.* ~ *keeper,* allevatore di bovine, *m.* ~*lick,* zazzera, *f.* ~*pox,* vaccino, *m.* ¶ *v.t.* intimidire, intimorire.

coward, *n.* vile, *m.*, codardo, -a, *m.f.* ~**ice,** *n.* vigliaccheria, codardia, *f.* ~**ly,** *a.* vile, vigliacco, codardo.

cower, *v.i.* rannicchiarsi; rabbassarsi.

cowl, *n.* cappuccio; fumaiuolo, *m.*; mitra del camino, *f.*

cowrie, *n.* cauri, *m.*

cowslip, *n.* primula, primavera, *f.*

coxcomb, *n.* vanesio, fatuo, *m.*

coxswain, *n.* padrone, timoniere, *m.*

coy, *a.* ritroso, timido. ~**ness,** *n.* ritrosia, timidezza, *f.*

cozen, *v.t.* gabbare, ingannare, sedurre.

crab, *n. (Crust.)* granchio; *(Hoisting)* verricello, *m.* ~ *apple,* mela selvatica; *(tree)* melo selvatico. ~ *louse,* piattola, *f. to catch a* ~ *(Boat.),* pigliare un granchio.

crabbed, *a.* arcigno, aspro, burbero. ~ *handwriting,* scritturaccia, *f.*

crack, *a.* di prim' ordine, ottimo, famoso. ~*-brained,* pazzo, scervellato. ~*-jaw name,* nomaccione, *m.* ¶ *n.* fessura, crepa, *f.*, spacco, *m.*; screpolatura, *f.*; *(noise)* schiocco, crac, cric, scricchiare, *m.* ~ *of doom,* giudizio finale, *m.* ¶ *v.t.* fendere, spaccare, screpolare; far schioccare; *(nuts)* rompere; *(open a bottle)* sturare; *(voice)* cambiare. ~**ed,** *a. (daft)* scervellato. **cracker,** *n. (firework)* salterello, *m.*, *(Christmas)* petardo di carta; *(whip)* sferzino, *m.*

crackle, *v.i.* scoppiettare, crepitare. **crackling,** *n. (Teleph.)* scoppiettìo, *m.*; *(pork)* rosolato, *m.* **cracknel,** *n.* croccante, *m.*

cracksman, *n.* ladro, *m.*

Cracow, *n.* Cracovia, *f.*

cradle, *n.* culla, *f.*; *(Surg.)* archetto, letto, *m.* ¶ *v.t.* cullare.

craft, *n.* furberia, *f.*; artifizio, *m.*;

scaltrezza, astuzia, *f.*; mestiere, *m.*; (*Naut.*) naviglio, *m.*; barca, *f.*
craftsman, *n.* artigiano, artefice, *m.* ~*ship,* *n.* maestria d'arte, *f.* **crafty,** *a.* furbo, scaltro, astuto, fino.
crag, *n.* roccia, rupe, *f.*, scoglio, *m.* **craggy,** *a.* scosceso, roccioso.
cram, *v.t.* riempire; infarcire; rimpinzare; (*poultry*) ingrassare; (*exam.*) indettare, dar l'imbeccata a; (*v.i.*) rimpinzarsi; prepararsi alla lesta, farsi indettare. ~ *full,* pieno come un uovo, pieno zeppo.
cramp, *n.* (*Path.*) crampo, granchio, *m.*; (G *or* C) granchio, arpione; gancio, *m.* ~ *iron,* ferro, arpione, *m.* ¶ *v.t.* comprimere, impedire; intirizzire; indolenzire. assicurare con ramponi.
cranberry, *n.* mortella, *f.*
crane, *n.* gru, *f.* ~*fly,* tipula, *f.* ¶ *v.t.* distendere il collo; (*v.i.*) spingersi avanti.
cranium, *n.* cranio, *m.*
crank, *n.* (*Mech.*) manovella, *f.*; gomito, *m.*; (*pers.*) originale, *m.f.*, fantastico, -a; (*whim*) ghiribizzo, *m.* ~ *gear,* (*cycle*) pedali, *m.pl.* ~ *pin,* bietta della manovella, *f.* ~*shaft,* albero a gomito, albero a manovella, *m.* ~ *tool,* ferro a gomito, gancio, *m.* ¶ *v.t.* girare la manovella. ~ *up,* mettere in azione il motore (*Motor.*).
cranny, *n.* fessura, *f.*
crape, *n.* crespo, *m.*
crash, *n.* fracasso, *m.*; rovina, *f.*; crac; crollo, fallimento, *m.* ¶ *i.* patatrac! ¶ *v.i.* precipitarsi; rovinarsi; (*v.t.*) fracassare.
crass, *a.* crasso, grossolano.
crate, *n.* cesta, gabbia, *f.*
crater, *n.* cratere, *m.*
crave, *v.t.* implorare. ~ *for,* bramare.
craven, *a.* vigliacco, codardo, vile.
craving, *n.* brama, smania, *f.*
crawl, *n.* strisciamento; (*Swim.*) crawl, *m.* ¶ *v.i.* strisciare, trascinarsi. ~ *with,* brulicare di. ~*ers,* child's, *n.pl.*, combinazioni, *f.pl.*
crawfish, crayfish, *n.* gambero, *m.*
crayon, *n.* pastello, *m.*
craze, *n.* smania, follia, *f.* ¶ *v.t.* fare impazzire. **crazy,** *a.* folle, pazzo, demente; decrepito, bislacco. *to drive someone* ~, rompere il capo a, fare impazzire. ~ *pavement,* lastricato rustico, *m.*
creak, *v.i.* stridere, scricchiolare, cigolare.
cream, *n.* panna, *f.*, fior di latte, *m.*; (*artificial*) crema, *f.*; (*of story*) bello,

m. ~ *cheese,* formaggio alla crema, *m.* ~ *coloured,* color crema. ~ *ice,* gelato alla crema, *m.* ~ *jug,* vasetto da panna, *m.* ~ *laid,* carta liscia, *f.* ~**ery,** *n.* latteria, *f.*
crease, *n.* piega; grinza, *f.* ¶ *v.t.* spiegazzare; stirare.
create, *v.t.* creare; fare; produrre; provocare. **creation,** *n.* creazione, *f.* **creative,** *a.* creatore. **creator, -tress,** *n.* creatore, -trice. **creature,** *n.* creatura, *f.*, essere; animale, *m.*, bestia, *f.* ~ *comforts,* comodi, *m.pl.*
crèche, *n.* asilo infantile, *m.*
credence, *n.* credenza, *f.* **credentials,** *n.pl.* lettera credenziale, *f.*; credenziali, *m.pl.* **credibility,** *n.* credibilità, *f.* **credible,** *a.* credibile. **credibly,** *ad.* da chi sa.
credit, *n.* credenza, fede; riputazione; fiducia, *f.*; onore; credito; avere, *m.* *do* ~ *to,* fare onore s. ~ *balance,* saldo creditore, *m.* ~ *note,* nota di accreditamento, *f.* ¶ *v.t.* credere, accreditare una somma ad una persona. ~**able,** *a.* lodevole. ~**or,** *n.* creditore, *m.*
credo, *n.* credo, *m.*, professione di fede, *f.*
credulity, *n.* credulità, semplicità, *f.* **credulous,** *a.* credulo.
creed, *n.* credo, *m.*; professione di fede; credenza, fede, *f.*
creek, *n.* cala, *f.*; fiumicino, *m.*
creel, *n.* paniere da pesca, *m.*
creep, *v i.ir.* strisciarsi, trascinarsi, insinuarsi. *it makes one's flesh* ~, fa venire la pelle d'oca. ~*ing paralysis,* paralisi progressiva, *f.* ~**er,** *n.* rampicante, *f.*; (*grapnel*) grappino, *m.*
cremate, *v.t.* cremare. **cremation,** *n.* cremazione, *f.* **crematorium,** *n.* crematoio, *m.*
crenellate, *v.t.* merlare.
creole, *n.* creolo, -a, *m.f.*
creosote, *n.* creosoto, *m.*
crepitate, *v.i.* crepitare.
crescendo, *ad. & n.* crescendo, *ad. & m.*
crescent, *n.* mezzaluna, *f.*
cress, *n.* crescione, *m.* ~ *bed,* crescionato, *m.*
cresset, *n.* torciere, *m.*
crest, *n.* cresta, *f.*, ciuffo, *m.*; cima, *f.*; cimiero, *m.* ~*fallen,* mortificato, abbattuto. ~**ed,** *a.* crestato, col ciuffo; (*sea*) spumante.
Crete, *n.* la Creta, *f.*
cretonne, *n.* cotonina, *f.*

crevasse, *n.* crepaccio, *m.* **crevice,** *n.*
crepacciolo, *m.*, fessura, *f.*

crew, *n.* (*ship*) equipaggio, personale,
m.; (*gun*) armamento, *m.*; (*set, gang*)
ciurma, *f.*

crewel stitch, *n.* ricamo, *m.*

crib, *n.* mangiatoia, *f.*; lettino, *m.*,
culla; chiave, traduzione, *f.*; plagio,
m. ¶ *v.t.* copiare; ingabbiare.

cribbage, *n.* cribbage, *m.*

crick (*in neck*), *n.* torcicollo, *m.*

cricket, *n.* grillo, *m.*, cavalletta, *f.*;
(*game*) cricket, *m.*

crier, *n.* banditore, *m.*

crime, *n.* delitto, *m.*

Crimea, *n.* la Crimea, *f.*

criminal, *a.* criminale, delittuoso.
the C~ *Investigation Department*
(*C.I.D.*), la polizia segreta. ~ *law,*
diritto penale, *m.* ¶ *n.* delinquente,
m.f. **criminate,** *v.t.* incriminare.

crimp, *v.t.* arricciare, increspare,
pieghettare; arruolare forzatamente.

crimson, *n.* chermisi, *m.*, porpora, *f.*
¶ *a.* chermisino, purpureo, porporino. ¶ *v.t.* imporporare.

cringe, *v.i.* umiliarsi, strisciarsi.
cringing. *a.* servile.

crinkle, *n.* piega, ruga, *f.* ¶ *v.t.*
piegare, corrugare.

cripple, *n.* zoppo, storpiato, sciancato,
m. ¶ *v.t.* storpiare; (*fig.*) paralizzare.
~**d,** *a.* storpiato, zoppo, zoppicante;
(*ship*) avariato, disarmato.

crisis, *n.* crisi, *f.*

crisp, *a.* duretto, croccante; (*air*)
frizzante; (*hair*) crespo; (*style*) nitido,
spiccato. ¶ *v.t.* increspare.

criss-cross, *v.i.* incrociarsi.

criterion, *n.* criterio, *m.*

critic, *n.* critico, -a, *m.f.* ~**al,** *a.*
critico; pericoloso, decisivo. **criticism,** *n.* critica, *f.* **criticizable,** *a.*
censurabile, biasimevole. **criticize,**
v.t. critica e, riprendere.

croak, *v.i.* (*raven*) gracchiare; (*frog*)
gracidare.

crochet, *n. & ~ hook,* uncinetto, *m.*

crockery, *n.* stoviglie, *f.pl.*, vasellame,
m.; maiolica, *f.*

crocodile, *n.* coccodrillo, *m.*; fila (di
ragazze), coda, *f.* ~ *tears,* lagrime
di coccodrilo, *f.pl.*

crocus, *n.* croco, zafferano, *m.*

Croesus, *n.* Creso, *m.*

crone, *n.* vecchiaccia, *f.* **crony,** *n.*
compare, *m.*; comare, *f.*

crook, *n.* uncino; vincastro; pastorale;
(*pers.*) scroccone, *m.* ¶ *v.t.* curvare,
piegare. ~**ed,** *a.* adunco; storto;
curvo, ricurvo; (*legs*) storto; (*fig.*)

perverso, indiretto. ~**edly,** *ad.* di
traverso, di sbieco. ~**edness,** *n.*
obliquità; deformità; perversità, *f.*

crop, *n.* raccolta, messe, *f.*; (*bird*)
gozzo, *m.*; (*whip*) frustino, *m.* ¶ *v.t.*
tosare; raccogliere; brucare; (*ears*)
mozzare, tagliare. ~ *up,* sopravvenire, sorgere. ~ *up again,*
riapparire.

croquet, *n.* croquet, *m.* ~ *court,*
campo da croquet, *m.*

crosier, crozier, *n.* pastorale, *m.*

cross, *a.* bisbetico, burbero, di
cattivo umore. ¶ comps; ~*bar,*
~*beam,* traversa, trave, *f.* ~*belt,*
bandoliera, *f.* ~*bred,* meticcio.
~*breed,* incrocio, *m.*, razza incrociata, *f.* ~*-breeding,* incrociamento,
m. ~ *country running race,* cross-
country, *m.* ~ *examine,* interrogare,
rinterrogare. ~*-eyed,* strabico,
guercio. ~ *hatch,* contrattagliare,
tratteggiare. ~*-patch,* borbottona,
f. ~*piece,* traversa, *f.* be at ~ *purposes,* fraintendersi, imbrogliarsi. ~
reference, richiamo, *m.* ~ *road,* via
trasversale, *f.* ~ *roads,* crocicchio,
m., crocevia, *f.* ~ *section,* taglio
trasversale, *m.*; sezione t., *f.* ~
stitch, punto incrociato, *m.* ~*wise,* di
traverso. ~*word (puzzle),* parole incrociate, *f.pl.* ¶ *n.* croce, *f.*; incrociamento, *m.*; incrocio, *m.*; (*on a letter
T*) taglio, *m.* ¶ *v.t.* incrociare; traversare; tagliare; passare; (*a cheque*)
sbarrare; contrariare, impedire. ~
oneself, segnarsi. ~ *out,* cancellare,
cessare.

crosse, (Lacrosse), *n.* bastone, *m.*

crossing, *n.* incrociamento, *m.*;
traversata, *f.*; passaggio, *m.*; (*cheque*)
sbarramento, *m.* ~ *the line ducking,*
battesimo della linea, *m.*

crotchet, *n.* (*Mus.*) seminima, *f.*;
(*whim*) ghiribizzo, capriccio, *m.*
~ *rest* (*Mus.*), pausa di seminima,
f. ~**y,** *a.* ubbioso, capriccioso.

crouch, *v.i.* accovacciarsi, rannicchiarsi, accoccolarsi.

croup, *n.* (*Med.*) cruppe, *m.*; (*rump*)
groppone, *m.*

crow, *n.* cornacchia, *f.*, corvo, *m.*;
(*cock's*) canto, *m.* ~*bar,* palanchino,
m. ~*foot* (*Bot.*) ranuncolo, *m.* ~*'s
foot,* (*wrinkle*) ruga, grinza, *f.* ~*'s
nest* (*Naut.*), gabbia, coffa, *f.* as the
~ *flies,* a volo d'uccello. ¶ *v.i.* ir.
cantare. ~ *over,* millantarsi,
vantarsi sopra.

crowd, *n.* folla, calca, serra, *f.*;
affollamento, *m.* ¶ *v.t.* affollare,

serrare, imgombrare; (*v.i.*) affollarsi, accalcarsi. ~ *round*, affollarsi intorno a. ~**ed**, *p.a.* affollato, ingombro, serrato; pieno.

crown, *n.* corona, *f.*; (*arch*) volta; (*head*) sommità, *f.*; (*Hat*) fondo, *m.*, forma, *f.*, cocuzzolo, *m.* C~ *Colony*, colonia imperiale, *f.* ¶ *v.t.* coronare; (*draughts*) damare. ~**ing**, *n.* incoronazione, *f.* ¶ *a.* supremo, sommo. ~ *piece*, il piú bello, *m.*

crucial, *a.* decisivo, critico.

crucible, *n.* crogiuolo, *m.* ~ *cast steel*, acciaio al crogiuolo, *m.*

crucifix, *n.* crocifisso, *m.* ~**ion**, *n.* crocifissione, *f.* **crucify,** *v.t.* crocifiggere.

crude, *a.* crudo, greggio; rozzo, grossolano. ~**ness**, *n.* crudità, rozzezza, *f.*

cruel, *a.* crudele. ~**ty**, *n.* crudeltà; (*in Law*) sevizie, *f.pl.*

cruet, *n.* oliera; (*Eccl.*) ampollina, *f.*

cruise, *n.* crociera, *f.* ¶ *v.i.* incrociare. **cruiser,** *n.* incrociatore, *m.* **cruising,** *n.* incrociamento, *m.* ¶ *a.* d'incrociamento, di crociera. ~ *taxicab*, taxi vagante, *m.*

crumb, *n.* briciola; (*opp. crust*) midolla, *f.* ~ *brush*, spazzola per le briciole, *f.* ~ *scoop*, mestola da briciole, *f.* ~ *tray*, raccogli-briciole, *m.inv.* ¶ (*Cook.*) *v.t.* panare.

crumble, *v.t.* sminuzzare, sbriciolare; (*v.i.*) sbriciolarsi, sgretolarsi. **crumbly,** *a.* sgretoloso, friabile.

crumple, *v.t.* raggrinzare; spiegazzare; acciaccare; (*v.i.*) raggrinzarsi. ~ *up*, schiacciarsi.

crunch, *v.t.* sgretolare, schiacciare.

crupper, *n.* groppa, *f.*; (*harness*) posolino, *m.*

crusade, *n.* crociata, *f.* **crusader,** *n.* crociato, *m.*

crush, *n.* serra, calca, *f.* ~ *hat*, gibus, *m.* ~ *room*, ridotto, *m.* ¶ *v.t.* schiacciare; pestare, frantumare; schiantare; sopprimere, annientare. ~*ed-strawberry* (*colour*), color fragole peste. ~**er**, *n.* frantoio; pestello, *m.*

crust, *n.* crosta, *f.*; (*earth's*) crosta, corteccia, *f.*

crustacean, *a. & n.* crostaceo, *a. & m.*

crusted, *a.* incrostato. **crusty,** *a.* (*bread*) crostoso, duro; (*fig.*) burbero, irritabile.

crutch, *n.* gruccia, stampella, *f.*

crux, *n.* perno, nodo, *m.*

cry, *n.* grido, *m*, *in full* ~, in piena corsa. ¶ *v.i.* gridare; piangere; (*v.t.*) gridare. ~ *out*, gridare, esclamare. ~ *up*, vantare, esaltare. ~**ing**, *a.* gridante. ¶ *n.* gridare; pianto, *m.*, lagrime, *f.pl.*

crypt, *n.* critta, *f.*

crystal, *n.* cristallo, *m.* ¶ *a.* di cristallo, cristallino. ~ *gazing*, cristalloscopia, *f.* ~ *glass*, cristallo, *m.* ~ *glassware, making, or works*, cristalleria, *f.* ~ *set* (*Radio*), radio a galena, *f.* **crystalline,** *a.* cristallino. ~ *lens* (*eye*), cristallino, *m.* **crystallize,** *v.t.* cristallizzare; (*v.i.*) cristallizzarsi. *crystallized fruits*, frutta candita, *f.*

cub, *n.* piccolo, *m.*

Cuban, *a.* cubano. ¶ *n.* cubano, -a, *m.f.*

cube, *n.* cubo, *m.* ~ *root*, radice cubica, *f.* ~ *sugar*, zucchero in pezzi, *m.* ¶ *v.t.* cubare. **cubic,** *a.* cubico. ~ *foot*, piede cubico, *m.* = 0.028317 cubic metre. ~ *inch*, pollice cubico, *m.* = 16.387 cubic centimetres. ~ *yard*, iarda cubica, *f.* = .764553 cubic metre. ~**al**, *a.* cubico.

cubicle, *n.* camerella, *f.*, cubicolo, *m.*

cubism, *n.* cubismo, *m.* **cubist,** *n.* cubista, *m.f.*

cuckoo, *n.* cuculo, *m.* ~ *clock*, oriuolo col cuculo, *m.*

cucumber, *m.* cetriolo, *m.*

cud, *n.* ruminatura, *f.* *chew the* ~, ruminare.

cuddle, *v.t.* accarezzare, stringere, serrare. ~ *up*, crogiolarsi, raggomitolarsi.

cudgel, *n.* bastone, randello, *m.* ¶ *v.t.* bastonare. ~ *one's brains*, lambiccarsi il cervello. **cudgelling,** *n.* bastonatura, *f.*

cue, *n.* parola, *f.*; (*Theat.*) suggerimento, *m.*; (*Bil.*) stecca, *f.*

cuff, *n.* (*blow*) schiaffo, pugno, *m.*; (*shirt*) polsino, manichino, *m.*; (*coat*) paramano, *m.* ~**links**, bottoni gemelli, *m.pl.* ¶ *v.t.* schiaffeggiare.

cuirass, *n.* corazza, *f.* ~**ier**, *n.* corazziere, *m.*

culinary, *a.* culinario.

cull, *v.t.* cogliere, raccogliere; scegliere.

cullender, *n.* colatoio, *m.*

culm, *n.* (*Bot.*) culmo, gambo, *m.*

culminate, *v.i.* culminare; colmare. **culminating,** *a.* culminante.

culpability, *n.* colpevolezza, *f.* **culpable,** *a.* colpevole. **culprit,** *n.* colpevole, *m.f.*

cultivate, *v.t.* coltivare. **cultivation,** *n.* coltivazione, *f.* **cultivator,** *n.* coltivatore, -trice, *m.f.* **culture,** *n.* coltura, cultura, *f.* ~d, *p.a.* colto, culto.

culvert, *n.* condotto sotterraneo, *m.*

cum, (*Lat.*) *pr.* con.

cumber, *v.t.* imbarazzare, ingombrare. ~some, **cumbrous,** *a.* incomodo, ingombrante.

cumulative, *a.* cumulativo.

cumulus, *n.* cumulo, *m.*

cuneiform, *a.* cuneiforme.

cunning, *a.* scaltro, accorto, fine, astuto, abile. ¶ *n.* scaltrezza, accortezza, finezza, abilità, *f.*

cup, *n.* tazza; coppa, *f.,* calice; bussolotto, *m.*; (*barometer*) vaschetta, *f.*; (*thimblerigger's*) bussolotto, *m.* ~ & ball, bilboquet, *m.* ~ bearer, coppiere, *m.* ~board, armadio, *m.*; credenza, *f.* ~board love, amore interessato, *m.* ¶ *v.t.* (*Surg.*) applicar le ventose a.

cupel, *n.* coppella, *f.* ¶ *v.t.* coppellare.

Cupid, *n.* Cupido, *m.*

cupidity, *n.* cupidigia, *f.*

cupola, *n.* cupola, *f.* ~ furnace, forno a cupola, *m.*

cupping-glass, *n.* ventosa, *f.*

cur, *n.* botolo, *m.*

curable, *a.* guaribile.

curacy, *n.* cura, *f.*; vicariato, *m.* **curate,** *n.* curato, *m.*

curative, *a.* curativo.

curator, **-trix,** *n.* conservatore, -trice, *m.f.*

curb, *n.* (*harness*) barbazzale, *m.*; (*street*) orlo del marciapiede, *m.*; (*fig.*) freno, *m.* ¶ *v.t.* (*horse*) frenare; (*street*) bordare; (*fig.*) frenare, moderare.

curd(s), *n.* latte rappreso, *m.*; giuncata, *f.* **curdle,** *v.t.* cagliare; (*fig.*) ghiacciare.

cure, *n.* guarigione; cura, *f.*; rimedio, *m.*; (*souls*) cura, *f.* water, grape ~, cura delle acque, dell'uva, *f.* ¶ *v.t.* guarire; rimediare a; (*salt*) salare; (*smoke*) affumicare; (*herrings*) marinare.

curfew, *n.* coprifuoco, *m.*

curio, *n.* rarità, anticaglia, *f.* ~ cabinet, vetrina, *f.*

curiosity, *n.* curiosità, *f.* **curious,** *a.* curioso. the ~ thing, lo strano, *m.* ~ person, curioso, -a, *m.f.*

curl, *n.* ricciolo, riccio, *m.* ~ paper, diavolino dei capelli, *m.* ¶ *v.t.* arricciare, inanellare; avvolgere. ~ up, ripiegarsi, raggrinzare; aggrovig-

liarsi. **curler,** *n.* (*hair*) diavolino, *m.* curling iron, ferro da ricci, *m.*

curlew, *n.* chiurlo, *m.*

curliness, *n.* ricciutezza, *f.* **curling,** *n.* arricciare; (*Sport*) piastra su ghiaccio, *f.* ~ tongs, ferro da ricci, *m.* **curly,** *a.* ricciuto, inanellato.

curmudgeon, *n.* burbero; spilorcio, *m.*

currant, *n.* (*red, white, black*) ribes rosso, bianco, nero, *m.*; (*dried*) uva passa, *f.* ~ bush, ribes, *m.*

currency, *n.* corso, *m.*; circolazione, *f.*; denaro, *m.* foreign ~, denaro straniero, *m.* **current,** *a.* corrente, in corso, in voga. ~ events, attualità, *f.pl.* ~ liabilities, esigibilità, *f.pl.* ¶ *n.* corrente, *f.*

curriculum, *n.* corso, curricolo, *m.*

curry, *n.* cari, riso all'indiana, *m.* ¶ *v.t.* (*leather*) conciare; (*horse*) strigliare. ~ favour with, corteggiare, adulare. ~comb, striglia, *f.* ~ing, *n.* conciatura, *f.*, strigliare, *m.*

curse, *n.* maledizione, imprecazione, bestemmia, *f.*; flagello, *m.* ¶ *v.t.* maledire; affliggere; (*v.i.*) bestemmiare, imprecare. **cursed,** *a.* maledetto.

cursory, *a.* frettoloso, superficiale.

curt, *a.* breve, secco, reciso, corto, brusco.

curtail, *v.t.* raccorciare, abbreviare, troncare; (*output*) limitare, ridurre.

curtain, *n.* tenda, cortina; tela, *f.*, sipario, *m.* ~ holder, laccio di tenda, *m.* ~ lecture, lavata di capo coniugale, *f.* ~ raiser, commedietta, *f.* ~ rod, portatende, *m.*

curtly, *ad.* bruscamente, recisamente.

curtsy, **-sey,** *n.* riverenza, *f.*

curvature, *n.* curvatura, *f.* ~ of the spine, deviazione della colonna vertebrale, *f.*

curve, *n.* curva, *f.* ¶ *v.t.* curvare, piegare. **curvet,** *n.* capriola, corvetta, *f.* ¶ *v.i.* corvettare. **curvilinear,** *a.* curvilineo.

cushion, *n.* cuscino, guanciale; cuscinetto, *m.*; (*Bil.*) mattonella, *f.* ~ cover, coperta di cuscino, *f.*, copriguanciale, *m.*

custard, *n.* crema, *f.*

custodian, *n.* guardiano, conservatore, *m.* **custody,** *n.* custodia; guardia, *f.*; arresto, *m.* take into ~, arrestare.

custom, *n.* costume; uso, *m.*; costumanza, usanza; consuetudine; clientela, *f.* ~ary, *a.* consueto, abituale, dell'uso; solito, usuale;

ordinario. **~er**, *n.* cliente; avventore; (*at cafe*) consumatore; (*at
bank*) depositante, *m.*
customs, *n.pl. & custom house,*
dogana, *f.* ~ *duty,* dazio [doganale],
m., dogana, *f.* ~ *agent,* agente di
dogana, *m.* ~ *officer,* ufficiale di
dogana, doganiere, *m.*
cut, *n.* taglio; colpo, *m.*; staffilata;
tacca, incisione, *f.*; squarcio, sfregio;
pezzo, *m.*, fetta, *f.*; fessura, *f.*, canale,
m.; riduzione, *f.*, ribasso, *m.*;
affronto, insulto, *m.*; vignetta,
incisione (*engraving*). ~ *off the joint,*
taglio di carne, *m.*, fetta d'arrosto, *f.*
~-out, interruttore, *m.* ¶ *v.t.* *ir.*
tagliare; dividere; trinciare; secare;
falciare, mietere; incidere, scolpire;
intagliare; tosare; tagliuzzare,
sminuzzare; (*cards*) alzare; ridurre,
restringere; ferire; togliere il saluto
a; (*teeth*) mettere, spuntare (*v.i.*).
have one's hair ~, farsi tagliare
i capelli. ~ *& dried* or *dry,* bell'e
fatto. **~-away** (neck of garment),
scollare. ~ *back* (*Hort.*), recidere.
~ [*crystal*] *glass,* cristallo molato, *m.*
~ *down,* abbattere; tagliare; mietere;
ridurre; sciabolare. ~ *edges* (*book*),
margini tagliati, *m.pl.* ~ *in* (*on road*),
tagliare. ~ *off,* tagliare; troncare;
recidere; amputare; falciare; intercettare; interrompere; distruggere;
isolare. ~ *open-work stitch,* punto a
giorno, *m.* ~ *out,* tagliare; frastagliare; separare; escludere. ~ *short,*
tagliar corto, interrompere; troncare.
~-throat, assassino, scannatore, *m.*
~ *up,* trinciare; spezzare; tagliare
in pezzi.
cutaneous, *a.* cutaneo.
cute, *a.* fino, astuto, ingegnoso.
cuticle, *n.* cuticola; epidermide, *f.*
cutlass, *n.* arma da taglio (usata da
marinai), *f.*
cutler, *n.* coltellinaio, *m.* **cutlery**, *n.*
& ~ works & ~ shop, coltelleria, *f.*
cutlet, *n.* costoletta, *f.*
cutter, *n.* (*clothes, &c.*) tagliatore, *m.*,
-trice, -tora, *f.*; (*gems, &c.*) incisore,
intagliatore, cesellatore, *m.*; (*trade,
price*) guastamestieri, *m.inv.*; (*tool*)
lama, *f.*, coltello, *m.*; fresa; mola, *f.*;
(*boat*), cottro, canotto a vela, *m.* ~
wheel, mola, *f.* *stone* ~, tagliapietre,
m.inv., scalpellino, *m.* **cutting**, *p.a.*
tagliente; affilato; sarcastico,
mordente. ~ *board,* tagliere, *m.*
~ *edge,* taglio, filo tagliente, *m.*;
lama, *f.* ~ *knife,* (*straw*) trinciapaglia, *m.inv.*; (*Typ.*) tagliatore, *m.*

¶ *n.* taglio, *m.*, tagliata, *f.*; incisione,
f.; trinciamento, *m.*, trinciatura, *f.*;
(*teeth*) spuntare, *m.*; (*newspaper*)
ritaglio, *m.*; escavazione, trincea, *f.*;
traforamento, traforo, *m.*; tosatura,
f.; (*snip of cloth*) pezzettino, *m.*;
ritaglio, *m.*; (*plant*) rampollo,
pollone, *m.* ~ *out* (*clothes*), taglio,
m. **~-out** *scissors,* forbici per
tagliare, *f.pl.* ,
cuttle fish, seppia, *f.* ~ *bones,* ossi
di seppia, *m.pl.*
cutty (**pipe**), *n.* pipa corta d'argilla, *f.*
cutwater, *n.* (*bow*) tagliamare; (*bridge*)
becco, *m.*
cyanide, *n.* cianuro, *m.*
cyclamen, *n.* ciclamino, *m.*
cycle, *n.* ciclo, *m.*; *abb.* for *bicycle,*
bicicletta, *f.* *motor cycle,* motocicletta, *f.* ~ *car,* vetturetta a
motore, *f.* ~ *race,* corsa ciclistica, *f.*
~ *show,* mostra di biciclette, *f.* ~
track, velodromo, *m.* ¶ *v.i.* andare in
bicicletta, pedalare. *to ride a motor*
~, guidare una motocicletta. **cycling**, *n.* ciclismo, *m.* **cyclist**, *n.*
ciclista, *m.f.* **cyclometer**, *n.* contagiri, *m.inv.*
cyclone, *n.* ciclone, *m.*
cyclop[a]edia, *n.* enciclopedia, *f.*
cygnet, *n.* piccolo cigno, *m.*
cylinder, *n.* cilindro; rullo, *m.*
cylindrical, *a.* cilindrico.
cymbals, *n.pl.* cimbali, *m.pl.*
cynic, *n.* cinico, *m.* ¶ ~ *& cynical,*
a. cinico. **cynicism**, *n.* cinismo, *m.*
cynosure (*fig.*), *n.* centro d'attrazione,
m.
Cynthia, *n.* Cinzia, *f.*
cypher, *n.* same as *cipher.*
cypress, *n.* cipresso, *m.*
Cyprus, *n.* Cipro, *m.* **Cyprian,
Cypriot**, *n.* cipriota (*m.*); abitante di
Cipro, *m.f.*
cyst (*Med.*), *n.* ciste, *f.*
Czech, *a. & (language)* *n.* ceco, *a. &
m.* ¶ (*pers.*) *n.* ceco, -a, *m.f.*
Czecho-Slovak, *a. & n.* ceco-
slovacco, *a. & m.*
Czecho-Slovakia, *n.* la Cecoslovac-
chia, *f.*

D

D (*Mus.*) *letter,* ré, *m.*
dab, *n.* colpo leggero; pezzetto,
pezzettino, *m.*; macchietta; (*mud*)
zacchera, *f.*, schizzo, *m.*; (*paint*)

leggera mano di colore; (*painting*—*see daub*) imbratto, *m.*; (*fish*) lima, *f.* ¶ *v.t.* picchiettare; macchiettare; ~ *on*, applicare. **dabber,** *n.* tampone, *m.*

dabble, *v.i.* guazzare; immischiarsi (in). ~ *on the stock exchange*, speculare in borsa. **dabbler,** *n.* guastamestiere; dilettante, *m.*

dace, *n.* lasca, *f.*

dachshund, *n.* (cane) bassotto tedesco, *m.*

dad(dy), *n.* babbo, *m.*

daddy-longlegs, *n.* tipula, *f.*

dado, *n.* dado, zoccolo, *m.*

daemon, *n.* demone, *m.*

daffodil, *n.* asfodelo, narciso dei prati, *m.*

daft, *a.* sciocco; matto.

dagger, *n.* daga, *f.*, pugnale, *m.*; (*Typ.*) croce, *f.* *at* ~*s drawn*, a coltello, in aperta inimicizia. *to look* ~*s* (*at*), lanciare sguardi furiosi, fare gli occhiacci.

dahlia, *n.* dalia, *f.*

daily, *a.* giornaliero; quotidiano; (*Astr.*) diurno. ~ *help*, giornante, donna a ore, *f.* ~ (*paper*), (giornale) quotidiano. ¶ *ad.* giornalmente; quotidianamente.

dainties, *n.pl.* delicatezze, *f.pl.*, bocconi, *m.pl.*; ghiottonerie, leccornie, *f.pl.* **daintily,** *ad.* delicatamente. **daintiness,** *n.* delicatezza, *f.* **dainty,** *a.* delicato, grazioso, graziosetto, elegante.

dairy, *n.* latteria, cremeria, *f.* ~ (*farm*), *n.* vaccheria, *f.* ~*maid*, *n.* lattaia, lattivendola, *f.* ~*man*, *n.* garzone di latteria, lattivendolo, *m.*

dais, *n.* impalcatura, *f.*; palco, baldacchino, *m.*

daisy, *n.* margherita, *f.*

dale, *n.* valle, vallata, *f.*

dally, *v.i.* indugiare, tardare; frivoleggiare, amoreggiare.

Dalmatia, *n.* (la) Dalmazia, *f.* **Dalmatian,** *a.& n.* dalmata *a.& m.f.*

dam, *n.* diga, *f.*, sbarramento, *m.*; (*Animal*) madre, *f.* ¶ *v.t.* arginare, fornire di diga; (*fig.*) contenere.

damage, *n.* danno, guasto, *m.*; avaria; (*pl. Law*) danni, *pl.* ¶ *v.t.* danneggiare, guastare; nuocere a; avariare. ~ *wilfully*, sabotare.

damascene, *v.t.* damaschinare. **Damascus,** *n.* Damasco, *f.* **damask,** *n.* damasco, *m.*

dame, *n.* dama, donna, *f.*

damn, *v.t.* dannare, mandare al diavolo; (*a play*) fischiare. ~**able,**

a. maledetto. ~**ation,** *n.* dannazione, *f.* ~**ed,** *a.* dannato, maledetto; fischiato. *the* ~, i dannati. ~**ing,** *p.a.* condannatorio, che condanna; (*proof*) schiacciante.

damp, *a.* umido, madido, molle; ~*mark* (*in books*), macchia d'umidità. ~*proof*, impermeabile. ¶ *n.* umidità. ¶ *v.t.* inumidire, bagnare; umettare; (*fig*) abbattere, scoraggiare, turbare; (*shock*) (*deaden*) ammortire, smorzare. ~**er,** *n.* (*piano*) sordina, *f.*; (*furnace*) regolatore, *m.* (*Radio*) sordina, *f.*; (*stamps, label*) spugna francobolli, *f.*; (*pers.*) guastafeste, *m.* ~**ness,** umidità, *f.*

damsel, *n.* damigella, zitella, *f.*

damson, *n.* prugna damaschina, *f.* ~ (*tree*), *n.* prugno di Damasco, *m.*

dance, *n.* danza, *f.*, ballo, *m.*; festa da ballo, *f.* ~ *frock*, veste da ballo, *f.* ~ *hall*, sala da ballo, *f.* *D*~ *of Death*, Danza macabra, *f.* ~ *partner*, cavaliere, *m.*, dama, *f.* ~ *tea*, thé dansant, *Fr.* ¶ *v.i. & t.* ballare, danzare. ~ *attendance* (*on*), fare anticamera. **dancer,** *n.* ballerino, *m.*, -a, *f.* **dancing,** *n.* ballo, *m.*, danza, *f.* ~ *man*, amante del ballo, *m.* ~ *master*, maestro di ballo, *m.*

dandelion, *n.* dente di leone, *m.*; radicchiella, *f.*

dandle, *v.t.* dondolare, far ballare, cullare.

dandruff, -iff, *n.* forfora, *f.*

dandy, *n.* bellimbusto, damerino; elegante, *m.*

Dane, *n.* danese, *m.f.*

danger, *n.* pericolo, rischio, *m.* *this patient is out of danger*, questo paziente è fuori pericolo. ~**ous,** *a.* pericoloso.

dangle, *v.i.* penzolare; (*v.t.*) far penzolare.

Danish, *a.* danese. ¶ (*language*) il danese, *m.*

dank, *a.* umido, umidiccio.

dapper, *a.* attillato, elegante.

dappled, *p.a.* macchiettato, pomellato.

dare, *v.i. ir.* osare, arrischiarsi; (*v.t. ir.*) sfidare, provocare. *I* ~ *say*, credo bene, oso dire. *How* ~ *you*, non so come abbia l'ardire. ~*devil*, *n.* [uomo] audace. **daring,** *a.* ardito, audace, intrepido. ¶ *n.* audacia, *f.*, ardimento, *m.*

dark, *a.* oscuro, buio, fosco, bruno; cupo, nero, tenebroso; triste, sinistro. *the* ~ *ages*, il medioevo, *m.*, i secoli dell'ignoranza, *m.pl.* ~ *horse*, outsider, *m. to be a* ~ *horse*, (*fig.*) esser un'acqua cheta. ~ *lager*, birra nera, scura, *f.* ~ *lantern*, lanterna cieca, *f.* ~ *man*, ~ *boy*, bruno, brunetto, *m.* ~ *room* (*Phot.*), camera oscura, *f.* ~ *slide*, negativa, *f.* ~ *woman*, ~ *girl*, bruna, brunetta, *f.* ¶ *n.* oscurità, *f.*, tenebre, *f.pl. after* ~, dopo che è caduta la sera, di notte tempo. *in the* ~, (*fig.*) alla cieca, nell'ignoranza. *it is getting* ~, si fa buio. *pitch* ~, buio pesto. ~**en**, *v.t.* oscurare, abbuiare, offuscare; (*paint.*) smorzare; (*v.i.*) oscurarsi, abbuiarsi. ~**ish**, *a.* piuttosto scuro, nerastro; ~**ly**, *ad.* oscuramente. ~**ness**, *n.* oscurità, *f.*, tenebre, *f.pl.*, buio, *m.* **dark[e]y**, *n.* negro, *m.*

darling, *a.* carino, favorito, prediletto. ¶ *n.* carino, *m.*, -a, *f.*; favorito, *m.*, -a, *f.*

darn, *n.* rammendo, *m.* ¶ *v.t.* rammendare. ~**ing**, *n.* rammendatura, *f.* ~ *needle*, *n.* ago da rammendare, *m.*

darnel, *n.* loglio, *m.*, zizzania, *f.*

dart, *n.* dardo, *m.*; (*Poet.*) strale, *m.*; (*pl.*) dardi, *m.pl.*, giuoco dei dardi, *m.* ¶ *v.t.* scagliare, lanciare, dardeggiare (*oft. fig.*). (*v.i.*) balzare, scattare, lanciarsi, precipitarsi, lanciarsi, (contro, su).

dash, *n.* slancio, impeto, *m.*; foga, *f.*; ardimento, *m.*; goccia, *f.*; tantino, *m.*; (*Teleg.*) punto, *m.*; (*Typ.*) lineetta, *f. to make a dash at, for*, precipitarsi su, lanciarsi su (sopra). ~**board**, *n.* parafango, *m.* ¶ *v.t.* lanciare, gettare; schiacciare, rompere; urtare; (*hopes*) annientare. ~ *to pieces*, ridurre in pezzi, in frantumi, spezzare, schiantare. ~**ing**, *a.* focoso, ardito; brillante.

dastard, *n.* vigliacco, codardo, vile, *m.* ~**ly**, *a.* vigliacco. ¶ *ad.* vigliaccamente.

data, *n.pl.* dati, *m.pl.*

date, *n.* data, *f.*; periodo, termine, *m.*; epoca, scadenza, *f.*; (*fruit*) dattero, *m. to* ~, a questo giorno. *up* (*or down*) *to* ~, al corrente, aggiornato; nuovo, di moda. ~ *palm*, *n.* dattero, *m.* ~ *stamp*, *n.* timbro mobile, *m.* ¶ *v.t.* datare.

dative [case], *n.* dativo, *m.*

datum, *n.* dato, *m.*

daub, *n.* imbratto; scarabocchio, *m.*; (*for walls*) intonaco, *m.* ¶ *v.t.* imbrattare; intonacare.

daughter, *n.* figlia, *f.*; figliola. *step* ~, figliastra, *f.* ~*-in-law*, nuora, *f.*

daunt, *v.t.* intimidire, scoraggiare. ~**less**, *a.* impavido, intrepido.

davit, *n.* gru, *f.*

dawdle, *v.i.* indugiare, gingillare, gironzare; bighellonare, cincischiare.

dawn, *n.* alba, punta del giorno; aurora, *f. the* ~ *will soon be here*, sarà tosto giorno. ¶ *v.i.* spuntare, albeggiare. ~**ing**, *a.* albeggiante, (*fig.*) nascente.

day, *n.* giorno, *m.*; giornata, *f. the* ~ *after*, il giorno dopo, il giorno seguente, l'indomani, *m. a* ~ *after the fair*, un po' troppo tardi, un' occasione sfuggita. *the* ~ *after to-morrow*, dopodomani, posdomani. *the* ~ *before*, il giorno prima, il giorno innanzi, la vigilia. *the* ~ *before yesterday*, *ad.* avantieri, l'altrieri. *the* ~ *after the morrow*, l'indomani. *one of these fine* ~s, un giorno o l'altro. ~ *book*, giornale, *m.* ~ *boarder*, mezzo convitto, *m.* ~*break*, spuntare del giorno, *m.*, alba, *f.*; *at* ~, al far del giorno, sul far del giorno, allo spuntar del giorno. ~*dream*, fantasticheria, *f.* ~ *labourer*, giornaliero, *m.* ~*light*, giorno, *m.*; luce, *f. broad* ~, pieno giorno, giorno chiaro, piena luce. ~*light-loading roll-film camera*, macchina fotografica per pellicole su rocchetti da cambiarsi in pieno giorno, *f.* ~ *nursery*, asilo per bambini, *m.* ~ *of atonement*, giorno di propiziazione, *m.* ~ *of the month*, giorno del mese, *m. what is the* ~ *of the month?* quanti ne abbiamo del mese? ai quanti siamo del mese? ~ *scholar*, alunno esterno, allievo esterno, *m.*, -a, *f.* ~ *school*, scuola esterni, *f.* ~*'s journey*, giornata (di viaggio), *f.* ~*time*, ore del giorno, *f.pl.*, giorno, *m. in the* ~*time*, durante il giorno. *at the present* ~, oggigiorno, al tempo che corre. *from* ~ *to* ~, di giorno in giorno, da un giorno all'altro. *the good old* ~s, il tempo che Berta filava, (*prov.*).

daze, *v.t.* stupefare, sbalordire; abbagliare.

dazzle, *n.* abbagliamento, *m.* ~ *lamp*, *light*, faro abbagliante, *m.* ¶ *v.t.* abbagliare; (*v.i.*) brillare, risplendere.

deacon, *n.* diacono, *m.*

dead, *a. & ad.* morto; spento; inanimato, insensibile; (*liquor*) guasto. ~ *beat*, ~ *tired*, stanco morto, spossato, stracco morto. ~ *calm*, calma piatta, bonaccia, *f.* ~ *centre*, punto morto, *m.* ~ *drunk*, ubriaco marcio. ~ *end*, vicolo cieco; binario cieco, *m.*; incaglio, *m.* ~ *fall*, trabocchetto, ~ *heat*, corsa indecisa, prova nulla, *f.* ~ *letter*. (*Post*) lettera giacente, *f.*; (*fig.*) lettera morta, *f.* ~ *office*, ufficio delle lettere giacenti, in giacenza. ~*lock*, incaglio, *m.*, situazione senza uscita, *f.* ~ *loss*, perdita totale, p. completa. ~ *march*, marcia funebre, *f.* ~ *reckoning* (*Naut.*), rombo stimato, *m.* D~ *Sea*, Mar Morto, *m.* ~ *season*, stagione morta, *f.* ~ *slow* (*traffic sign*), al passo. ~ *wire*, filo tagliato, *m. the* ~, i morti, i defunti, *m.pl.* ~**en**, *v.t.* ammortire, ammorzare, (*sound*) attutire, assordare. ~**ly**, *a.* mortale, fatale, implacabile; (*aim*) senza fallo. ~ *nightshade*, belladonna, *f.* ~ *sin*, peccato mortale, *m.*

deaf, *a.* sordo. ~ *& dumb*, sordomuto. ~ *& dumb alphabet*, alfabeto dei sordomuti, *m.* ~ *as a post*, sordo come una campana. ~ *mute*, sordomuto, *m.*, sordomuta, *f.* ~**en**, *v.t.* assordare, stordire. ~**ness**, *n.* sordità, *f.*

deal, *n.* (*cards*) dare, *m.*, mano, *f.*; (*wood*) abete, legno di abete, *m.*; (*business*) affare, partito, patto, scambio, *m. a great* ~, *a good* ~, una gran quantità, molto, assai. *whose deal is it?* a chi tocca fare le carte? ¶ *v.t. ir.* (*cards*) dare, fare, distribuire; (*blow*) assestare, dare, vibrare; (*v.i. ir.*) agire, comportarsi, condursi; trattare, commerciare (in). ~ *out*, distribuire, ripartire. ~ *with* (*shop*), servirsi da, fornirsi presso (da). *to have to* ~ *with*, avere a che fare con, avere da fare con. ~**er**, *n.* esercente, *m.f.*; negoziante, *m.f.*; venditore, *m.*, -trice, *f.*; fornitore, *m.*, -trice, *f.*; (*cards*) distributore. ~**ing**, *n.* azione, maniera di agire, condotta, *f.*; (*pl.*) relazioni, *f.pl.*; rapporti, *m.pl.*; pratiche, *f.pl.*; trattative, *f.pl. double* ~, contegno equivoco. *underhand* ~s, mene, *f.pl.*

dean, *n.* decano, *m.* ~**ery**, *n.* (*office*) decanato, *m.*

dear, *a. & ad.* caro, carino; prezioso, grazioso; costoso, a prezzo elevato. *my* ~, cara mia, cara amica, *f. my* ~ *fellow*, caro mio, caro amico, *m. O* ~*!* Dio mio! là! là! che mai!

O dear no! niente affatto, mainò! mai e poi mai. ~**est** (*pers.*), caro, carissimo, *m.*, -a, *f.* ~**ly**, *ad.* caramente, teneramente, ~**ness** (*price*), *n.* caro prezzo, *m.*

dearth, *n.* carestia, *f.*

death, *n.* morte, *f.*; decesso, trapasso, *m.*; (*pl. obituary*), necrologia, *f.*, registro delle morti, *m.* ~ *bed*, letto di morte, *m.* ~ *blow*, colpo mortale, colpo di grazia, *m.* ~ *certificate*, atto di decesso, estratto mortuario, *m.*, fede di decesso, *f.* ~ *duties*, imposte di successione, *f.pl.* ~ *knell*, rintocco funebre, *m.* ~ *rate*, media della mortalità, *f.*, tasso di mortalità, *m.* ~ *trap*, inciampo, pericolo mortale, *m.* ~ *warrant*, ordine di esecuzione, mandato di morte, *m.*; (*fig.*) sentenza di morte, *f.* ~ *watch* [*beetle*], anobio, oriuolo della morte, *m.* ~**less**, *a.* immortale, imperituro.

debar, *v.t.* escludere (da), vietare (a). ~ *by time* (*Law*), prescrivere, interdire (a). ~*ment by time*, decadenza, prescrizione, *f.*

debase, *v.t.* avvilire; alterare, falsificare, ridurre il fino di (una moneta).

debatable, *a.* discutibile, contestabile.

debate, *n.* dibattito, *m.*, discussione, controversia, *f.* ¶ *v.t.* dibattere, discutere; contestare. *debating society*, circolo di conferenze, *m.*

debauch, *v.t.* corrompere, pervertire, debosciare. ~**ee**, *n.* libertino, debosciato; discolo, *m.* ~[**ery**], *n.* crapula, deboscia, *f.*

debenture, *n.* obbligazione, *f.* ~ *holder*, portatore di obbligazioni, *m.*, -trice, *f.*

debilitated, *p.a.* debilitato. **debility**, *n.* debolezza, debilità, *f.*

debit, *n.* debito, *m.* ¶ *v.t.* addebitare. **debt** [*due by the trader*], debito (passivo), *m.* **debt** [*due to the trader*], debito (attivo), *m. in debt*, indebitato. *involve in debt*, indebitare. *run into* ~, indebitarsi, ingolfarsi nei debiti. *get out of* ~, sdebitarsi, pagare i debiti. **debtor**, *n.* debitore, *m.*, -trice, *f.* ~ [*side*], lato del debito, *m.*

decad[e], *n.* decade, *f.*

decadence, *n.* decadenza, *f.* **decadent**, *a.* decadente.

decagon, *n.* decagono, *m.*

decamp, *v.i.* svignarsela.

decant, *v.t.* travasare. ~**er**, *n.* caraffa, *f.*; (*small*) caraffino, *m.*

decapitate, *v.t.* decapitare.

decay, *n.* decadenza, rovina, *f.*; scadimento; deperimento; sfacelo, *m.*; (*teeth*) caria, *f.* ¶ *v.i.* decadere, declinare, deperire; corrompersi, guastarsi; indebolirsi, logorarsi; marcire; (*teeth*) cariarsi.

decease, *n.* decesso, trapasso, *m.*; morte, *f.* ¶ *v.i.* decedere, morire. ∼ed, *n.* morto, defunto, deceduto.

deceit, *n.* inganno, *m.*; frode, truffa, *f.* ∼ful, *a.* ingannevole, perfido, falso. **deceive,** *v.t.* ingannare. **deceiver,** *n.* ingannatore *m.*, -trice, *f.*

December, *n.* dicembre, *m.*

decency, *n.* decenza, convenienza, *f.*

decennial, *a.* decennale.

decent, *a.* decente, conveniente. *not in* ∼ *use* (*words*), triviale. ∼ly, *ad.* decentemente, convenientemente, onestamente.

decentralize, *v.t.* decentrare. **decentralization,** *n.* decentramento, *m.*

deception, *n.* inganno, *m.*; illusione, menzogna, *f.* **deceptive,** *a.* ingannevole, fallace, illusorio.

decibel (*Phys.*), *n.* decibel, *m.inv.*

decide, *v.t.* decidere; (*v.i.*) decidersi, pronunciarsi. **decided,** *a.* deciso, risoluto. ∼ly, *ad.* decisamente, in modo risoluto, certamente; assai, sensibilmente.

deciduous, *a.* cadente, caduco; (*Bot.*) deciduo.

decimal, *a. & m.* decimale. ∼ *point,* punto decimale, *m.*

decimate, *v.t.* decimare.

decipher, *v.t.* decifrare.

decision, *n.* decisione, sentenza, *f.* ∼ *in one's favour,* decisione in proprio favore. **decisive,** *a.* decisivo.

deck, *n.* ponte, *m.*; coperta, *f.*; (*of bridge*) ponte del cassero centrale. ∼ *cabin,* cabina di coperta, *f.* ∼ *chair,* sedia a sdraio, *f.* ∼hand, marinaio di ponte, *m.* ∼ *tennis,* deck-tennis, *m.* ¶ *v.t.* adornare, ornare, parare; (*ship*) fornire di ponte. ∼ *with flags,* pavesare. ∼·*witn flowers,* decorare.

declaim, *v.i.* declamare. ∼ *against,* inveire contro. **declamatory,** *a.* (*bad sense*) declamatorio, (*good sense*) recitativo.

declaration, *n.* dichiarazione, *f.*, proclama, *m.* **declare,** *v.t.* dichiarare, manifestare, proclamare, annunziare; denunziare. *well, I declare!* veramente? questa, poi!

declension, (*Gram.*) *n.* declinazione, *f.*

decline, *n.* scesa, *f.*; declivio, *m.*, pendio, *m.*; decadenza, *f.*; decadimento, *m.*; (*day*) cadere, declinare, *m.*; (*price*) ribasso, *m.* ¶ *v.t.* inclinare, abbassare, declinare; rifiutare; (*v.i.*) inclinarsi, abbassarsi, pendere, declinare, scemare.

declivity, *n.* declivio, *m.*

decoction, *n.* decotto, *m.*

decode, *v.t.* decifrare.

decompose, *v.t.* decomporre, sciogliere, scomporre; (*v.i.*) decomporsi, sciogliersi, scomporsi.

decorate, *v.t.* decorare, ornare, parare. **decoration,** *n.* decorazione, *f.* **decorative,** *a.* decorativo. **decorator,** *n.* decoratore.

decorous, *a.* decoroso, decente; **decorum,** *n.* decoro, *m.*

decoy, *n.* (*bait*) esca, *f.*; (*place*) capannuccia, *f.*; (*pers.*) allettatore, *m.*, -trice, *f.*; lusingatore, *m.*, -trice, *f.* ∼ *bird,* uccello di richiamo, zimbello, *m.* ¶ *v.t.* allettare, adescare; attirare in un insidia.

decrease, *n.* diminuzione, *f.*; decrescimento, scemamento, *m.* ¶ *v.i.* diminuire, decrescere; *v.t.* diminuire, scemare, ridurre.

decree, *n.* decreto, *m.*; sentenza, *f.* ∼ *absolute,* sentenza definitiva, *f.* ∼ *nisi,* sentenza interlocutoria, *f.* ¶ *v.t.* decretare.

decrepit, *a.* decrepito. **decrepitude,** *n.* decrepitezza, *f.*

decry, *v.t.* disprezzare, discreditare, screditare; denigrare.

dedicate, *v.t.* dedicare. **dedication,** *n.* dedica, *f.*, omaggio, *m.*

deduce, *v.t.* dedurre.

deduct, *v.t.* sotrarre, dedurre, detrarre; diffalcare. **deduction,** *n.* deduzione, sottrazione, ritenuta, trattenuta, *f.*; diffalco, *m.*

deed, *n.* atto, *m.*; azione, *f.*; impresa, *f.*; affare, *m.*; documento, certificato, titolo, *m.*; (*pl.*) fatti, *m.pl.*; gesta, *f.pl.*

deem, *v.t.* stimare, ritenere; giudicare. ∼ed, *p.p.* ritenuto, giudicato.

deep, *a.* profondo, alto, lungo; segreto; astuto, furbo; vivo; (*in depth*), in profondità; (*colours*) scuro, vivo, carico, cupo, bruno; (*mourning*) grave, stretto; (*sound*) grave, profondo. ∼-*sea captain,* capitano a (di) lungo corso, *m.* ∼-*sea fishing,* pesca al largo, *f.* ∼-*sea navigation* & ∼-*sea voyage,* lungo corso, *m.*; ∼-*seated,* profondo, intimo, riposto. ∼-*water harbour,* porto di marea, *m.* ¶ *n.* (alto) mare, oceano; abisso, *m.*

~en, *v.t.* approfondire; aumentare; incavare; (*colour*) caricare. ~[ly], *ad.* profondamente, estremamente, gravemente.

deer, *n.* cervo, *m.*; daino, *m.*; (*col.*). i cervi, *m.pl.* ~ *stalking*, caccia al cervo, *f.*

deface, *v.t.* sfigurare, guastare; cancellare, sfregiare. ~ed, *p.a.* sfigurato, guastato, sfregiato.

de facto, *ad.* infatti.

defalcate, *v.i.* truffare, malversare. **defalcation,** *n.* diffalco, *m.* truffa; malversazione, *f.*

defamation, *n.* diffamazione, *f.* **defamatory,** *a.* diffamatorio. **defame,** *v.t.* diffamare.

default, *n.* difetto, *m.*; assenza, mancanza, contumacia, *f. by* ~, in contumacia. *in* ~ *of*, in mancanza di. ¶ *v.t.* mancare al dovere; essere contumace; non comparire; essere reo di malversazione di fondi. ~er, *n.* chi viene meno ai propri obblighi, ai propri impegni; (*Mil.*) consegnato, *m.*; (*debtor*) moroso, contumace. ~ *on parade,* (*Mil.*) renitente, *m.*

defeat, *n.* sconfitta, disfatta, *f.* ¶ *v.t.* sconfiggere, vincere; frustrare, sventare; eludere.

defecate, *v.t. & i.* defecare.

defect, *n.* difetto, vizio, *m.* ~ion, *n.* defezione, *f.* ~ive, *a.* difettoso, deficente, (*child*) tarato; anormale; (*Gram.*) difettivo.

defence, *n.* difesa, *f.*; (*leg.*) eccezione. ~less, *a.* indifeso, inerme, senza difesa. **defend,** *v.t.* difendere. ~ant, *n.* convenuto, prevenuto, citato, *m.* ~er, *n.* difensore, *m.*

defensible, *a.* difendibile, sostenibile, giustificabile. **defensive,** *a.* difensivo. ¶ *n.* difensiva, *f.*

defer, *v.t.* (*put off*) differire, rimandare; ritardare; (*submit*) deferire, sottomettere (a); (*v.i.*) essere deferente, sottomettersi. ~ence, *n.* deferenza, *f.*; riguardo, rispetto, *m.* **deferential,** *a.* deferente, rispettoso.

defiance, *n.* sfida, disfida; noncuranza, *f.*; disprezzo, *m.* **defiant,** *a.* provocatore, insolente, ardito.

deficiency, *n.* deficenza, mancanza, scarsezza, *f.*; difetto, *m.* **deficient,** *a.* deficente, scarso, debole. *to be deficient in,* mancare in, essere deficente in. **deficit,** *n.* ammanco, deficit, disavanzo, *m. cash* ~, ammanco di cassa. *to make good*

(*refund*) *a* ~, colmare un deficit, un ammanco.

defile, *n.* gola, *f.*; passo stretto, *m.* ¶ *v.i* sfilare, defilarsi; (*v.t.*) insozzare, corrompere, imbrattare. ~ment, *n.* insozzamento, *m.*; imbrattatura, *f.*; corruzione, *f.*

definable, *a.* definibile. **define,** *v.t.* definire, dare la definizione di. **definite,** *a.* definito. ~ly, *ad.* definitamente. **definition,** *n.* definizione, *f.* **definitive,** *a.* definitivo.

deflate, *v.t.* (*tyre*) sgonfiare; (*Fin.*) deflazionare. **deflation,** *n.* sgonfiamento, *m.*; (*Fin.*) deflazione, *f.*

deflect, *v.t.* deflettere, far deviare. **deflection, -xion,** *n.* deviazione, deflessione, *f.*

defloration, *n.* (*ravishment*) deflorazione, *f.*; (*stripping of flowers*) sfiorare, *m.* **deflower,** *v.t.* (*ravish*) deflorare, violare; (*strip of flowers*) sfiorare, spogliare.

deforest, *v.t.* disboscare. ~ation, *n.* disboscamento, *m.*

deform, *v.t.* deformare. ~ed, *a.* deforme, deformato. ~ity, *n.* deformità, *f.*

defraud, *v.t.* frodare, truffare, defraudare.

defray, *v.t.* pagare; (*expenses, of, for*) fare le spese di, coprire le spese di.

deft, *a.* abile, accorto, desto, lesto. ~ness, *n.* accortezza, abilità, grazia, *f.*

defunct, *a.* defunto, deceduto. ¶ *n.* defunto, *m.*, -a, *f.*

defy, *v.t.* sfidare.

degeneracy & degeneration, *n.* degenerazione, *f.* **degenerate,** *v.i.* degenerare.

degradation, *n.* degradazione, *f.* **degrade,** *v.t.* degradare; avvilire.

degree, *n.* grado, rango, stato, *m.*, classe, condizione, *f.*; ordine, *m.*; (*Univ.*) laurea. *by* ~s, a poco a poco; gradatamente. *not in the slightest* ~, neppur per sogno, neanche per idea. *to a certain* ~, *in some* ~, fino ad un certo punto. *to such a* ~, a tal punto, a tal grado.

deify, *v.t.* deificare.

deign, to degnarsi (di).

deity, *n.* divinità, *f.*; (*chiefly Poet.*) deità, *f.*

deject, *v.t.* abbattere; deprimere. ~ion, *n.* abbattimento, *m.*, deiezione, *f.* ~ed, *a.* abbattuto, scoraggiato.

de jure, *ad.* di diritto.

delay, *n.* indugio, ritardo, *m.* ¶ *v.t.*

rimandare, ritardare, differire; (v.i.) indugiare.

del credere, del credere, m.

dele, printing direction, da omettersi.

delectation, n. diletto, m.

delegate, n. delegato, m., -a, f. ¶ v.t. delegare. **delegation**, n. delegazione, f.

delete, v.t. cancellare, omettere.

deleterious, a. deleterio, nocivo.

deliberate, a. deliberato, premeditato, ponderato, determinato, stabilito, fermo, risoluto, lento. ¶ v.i. deliberare, ponderare, risolversi; riflettere, discutere. ~ly, deliberatamente, apposta. **deliberation**, n. deliberazione, f., riflessione, f.

delicacy, n. delicatezza, f.; (food) leccornia, ghiottoneria, f. **delicate**, a. delicato, squisito.

delicious, a. delizioso, squisito.

delight, m. piacere, piacer, m.; delizia, f. ¶ v.t. dilettare, piacere (a); (v.i.) dilettarsi, provare diletto. ~ful, a. dilettevole, delizioso, incantevole. ~fully, ad. dilettevolmente, deliziosamente.

delimit[ate], v.t. delimitare.

delineate, v.t. delineare, disegnare. **delineation**, n. delineazione, f.; delineamento, m.

delinquency, n. delinquenza, f. **delinquent**, n. delinquente, m.

deliquescence, n. deliquescenza, f.

delirious, a. delirante, in delirio. to be ~, delirare. **delirium**, n. delirio, m. ~ tremens, delirium tremens.

deliver, v.t. liberare; consegnare, rimettere; distribuire; (blow) dare, vibrare; (Med.) partorire; (judgement), emettere; (ball, Ten.) lanciare; (lecture) fare, tenere; (speech) pronunciare; (pump) avviare. to be ~ed of, partorire di; (fig.) sgravarsi (da). ~ance, n. liberazione, f.; rilascio, pronunziamento, m. ~er, n. liberatore, m., -trice, f. ~y, n. consegna; distribuzione, rimessa, f.; modo di parlare, eloquio, m.; (judgement) pronuncia, emissione, f.; (birth) parto, m. to take ~, prendere la consegna. on ~, all'atto della consegna. cash on ~, payment on ~, consegna contro assegno, rimborso alla consegna. ~man, ~boy, fattorino, m. ~ van, furgone, furgoncino, m.

dell, n. valletta, f.

delphinium, n. piede di allodola, m.

delta, n. delta, m.

delude, v.t. deludere, ingannare; illudere.

deluge, n. diluvio, m. ¶ v.t. inondare.

delusion, n. delusione, f., inganno, m., illusione, f. **delusive**, a. ingannevole, illusorio.

delve, v.t. vangare, zappare; (fig.) frugare, penetrare, sondare.

demagogue, n. demagogo, m.

demand, n. domanda, richiesta, f.; reclamo, m. ~ note (taxes), intimazione, f. on ~, su domanda; (Com.) a presentazione, a vista. ¶ v.t. domandare, reclamare; richiedere, esigere; (Com.) ricercare.

demarcation, n. demarcazione, f.

demean oneself (to) (behave), comportarsi. **demeanour**, n. contegno, comportamento, atteggiamento, m.

demented, p.a. demente, pazzo. **dementia**, n. demenza, f.

demerit, n. demerito, m.

demesn, n. demanio, m.

demigod, n. semidio, m.

demijohn, n. damigiana, f.

demise, n. decesso, m.; (leg.) cessione, f., trasferimento, m.; affittanza, f. ¶ v.t. cedere, trasferire, affittare.

demisemiquaver, n. semibiscroma, f.

demobilize, v.t. smobilitare, smobilizzare. **demobilization**, n. smobilitazione, f.

democracy, n. democrazia, f. **democrat**, n. & **democratic**, a. democratico, m. & a.

demolish, v.t. demolire. **demolition**, n. demolizione, f.; (pl.) demolizioni, f.pl.; sventramento, m.

demon, n. demonio, demone, m.

demonetize, v.t. demonetizzare.

demoniac, n. indemoniato, m., -a, f.

demonstrate, v.t. dimostrare, manifestare, esporre, spiegare, provare (v.i.). **demonstration**, n. dimostrazione, spiegazione, f.; prova, f.; (political, &c.) riunione, f. **demonstrative**, a. dimostrativo. **demonstrator**, n. (Sch., Univ.) dimostratore, m., -trice, f.

demoralize, v.t. demoralizzare.

Demosthenes, n. Demostene, m.

demulcent, a. emolliente.

demur, n. esitazione, f.; dubbio, m.; temporeggiamento, m.; (Law) eccezione, f. ¶ v.i. esitare, temporeggiare; (Law) essere in mora; opporre eccezione a. to ~ to, non ammettere; opporsi a.

demure, a. modestino, fino, furbo;

affettatamente modesto; (*woman*) gatta morta, santarella, *f.*

demurrage, *n.* controstallia, *f.* (*gen. pl.* -ie); giacenza, scorta, *f.*; mora, *f.*

demurrer, *n.* (*Law*) eccezione perentoria, *f.*; (*pers.*) oppositore, temporeggiatore, moroso, *m.*

demy, *n.* (*paper*) formato di carta di centimetri 56 × 44 (per la stampa), di centimetri 51 × 38 (per disegno); (*pers.*) titolare di una borsa di Magdalen College, Oxford.

den, *n.* tana, *f.*; covile, *m.*, gabbia, *f.*, fossa, *f.*; antro, nido, gabinetto, *m.*; (*robbers*) covo, nascondiglio, *m.*

denature, *v.t.* denaturare.

denial, *n.* diniego, *m.*; negazione; rinnegazione, *f.*; rifiuto, *m.*; smentita, *f.* *I gave him a flat* ~, gli dissi un bel no. *self* ~, abnegazione, *f.*

denizen, *n.* abitante; cittadino (naturalizzato), *m.*; ospite, *m.f.*

Denmark, *n.* la Danimarca, *f.*

denominate, *v.t.* denominare, chiamare. **denomination,** *n.* denominazione, *f.*; (*sect*) setta religiosa, *f.*; (*unit*) taglio, valore, *m.* ~al, *a.* particolare, settario. **denominator,** *n.* denominatore, *m.*

denote, *v.t.* denotare, significare, indicare.

denounce, *v.t.* denunciare; dichiarare.

dense, *a.* denso, spesso, fitto, folto.

dent, *n.* tacca, ammaccatura; impronta, *f.* ¶ *v.t.* ammaccare, intaccare, fare una tacca a.

dental, *a.* (*Anat.*) dentario; (*Gram.*) dentale. ~ *surgeon*, dentista, chirurgo odontoiatra, *m.* ¶ (*Gram.*) *n.* dentale, *f.* **dentate,** *a.* dentato. **dentist,** *n.* dentista. ~**ry,** *n.* chirurgia dentaria, *f.* **dentition,** *n.* dentizione, *f.* **denture,** *n.* dentiera, *f.*

denude, *v.t.* denudare.

denunciation, *n.* denunzia, *f.*

deny, *v.t.* negare, smentire; rinnegare; rifiutare; contraddire, opporre. *to* ~ *it*, negare.

deodorize, *v.t.* deodorare.

depart, *v.i.* partire, andarsene, ritirarsi; allontanarsi, scostarsi; (*fig.*) rinunziare (a) venir meno (a). ~ *this life*, lasciare questo mondo, morire. ~**ed,** *n.* defunto, trapassato, morto, *m.f.*

department, *n.* dipartimento, reparto, *m.*, divisione, *f.*, ramo, servizio, ufficio, *m.* ~**al,** *a.* dipartimentale. ~(*al*) *store(s)*, magazzino in grande stile.

departure, *n.* partenza, *f.*; rinunzia, *f.*;

(*lapse*) abbandono, *m.* *new* ~, innovazione, *f.* ~ *platform*, piattaforma partenze, *f.*

depend, *v.i.* dipendere (da), contare (su o sopra), fare assegnamento (su o sopra). ~**ant,** ~**ent,** *n.* dipendente, *m.f.* ~**ence,** *n.* dipendenza, *f.* ~**ency,** *n.* dipendenza, *f.*; (*country*) colonia, *f.*; territorio dipendente, *m.* ~**ent,** *a.* dipendente. *to be dependent on,* dipendere da.

depict, *v.t.* dipingere.

deplete, *v.t.* esaurire, vuotare.

deplorable, *a.* deplorevole. **deplore,** *v.t.* deplorare; rimpiangere.

deploy, *v.t.* spiegare. ~**ment,** *n.* spiegamento, *m.*

deponent, (*pers.*) *n.* deponente, *m.f.*

depopulate, *v.t.* depopolare, spopolare. **depopulation,** *n.* (*action*) spopolamento. (*state*) depopolazione, *f.*

deport, *v.t.* deportare. ~**ation,** *n.* deportazione, *f.*

deportment, *n.* comportamento, portamento, contegno, *m.*

depose, *v.t.* deporre; detronizzare; testificare.

deposit, *n.* deposito; sedimento, *m.*; consegna, *f.*; versamento; pegno, *m.*; caparra, *f.*; (*Geol.*) deposito, giacimento, *m.* ~ *account* (*bank*), conto dei depositi a termine, *m.* ~ *book* (*savings*), libretto (di risparmio), *m.* ~ *receipt*, ricevuta di deposito, *f.* ¶ *v.t.* depositare, deporre. ~**ary,** *n.* depositario, *m.* ~**ion,** *n.* deposizione, *f.* ~**or,** *n.* depositante, *m.f.* ~**ory,** *n.* deposito, *m.* **depot,** *n.* deposito; (*fig.*) repertorio, *m.* ~ *supply* ~**s,** depositi di rifornimenti, *m.pl.*

depravation & **depravity,** *n.* depravazione, malvagità, *f.* **deprave,** *v.t.* depravare. ~**d,** *p.a.* depravato, malvagio, corrotto.

deprecate, *v.t.* deprecare.

depreciate, *v.t.* deprezzare, dispregiare; (*v.i.*) deprezzarsi, subire un deprezzamento. **depreciation,** *n.* deprezzamento, *m.* **depreciatory,** *a.* deprezzativo.

depredation, *n.* depredazione, *f.*

depress, *v.t.* deprimere, abbassare, abbattere; rattristare; diminuire, ridurre, (*prices*) abbassare. ~**ing,** *p.a.* deprimente, rattristante. ~**ion,** *n.* depressione, *f.*, abbattimento, languore, abbassamento, *m.*

deprivation, *n.* privazione, *f.*; (*Eccl.*)

deposizione. **deprive**, *v.t.* privare; (*Eccl.*) deporre.

depth, *n.* profondità, altezza, *f.*; fondo, abisso, *m.*; (*winter*) cuore, (*colour*) vigore, *m.*; (*earth*) viscere, *f.pl.*; (*night*) colmo, bel mezzo, *m.*; (*sound*) gravità. ~ *charge*, bomba di profondità, *f.*

deputation, *n.* deputazione, delegazione, *f.* **depute**, *v.t.* deputare, delegare. **deputize for**, sostituire.

deputy, *n.* deputato, delegato; sostituto, supplente, aggiunto, *m.* ~ *chairman*, vice-presidente, *m.* ~ *governor*, vice governatore, *m.* ~ *professor*, professore aggiunto, *m.*

derail, *v.t.* far deragliare; sviare; (*v.i.*) deragliare, uscire dalle rotaie. ~**ment**, *n.* deragliamento, sviamento, *m.*

derange, *v.t.* disordinare, scompigliare, disorganizzare, turbare.

derelict, *a.* derelitto, abbandonato. ¶ *n.* relitto, *m.* ~**ion**, *n.* abbandono, *m.* omissione, negligenza, *f.*

deride, *v.t.* deridere, beffare, farsi beffe di. **derision**, *n.* derisione, *f.* **derisive**, *a.* derisorio. **derisory**, *a.* derisorio.

derivation, *n.* derivazione, *f.* **derivative**, *n.* derivativo, *m.* **derive**, *v.t.* derivare; ottenere; trarre, raccogliere. *to be derived from*, derivare da; provenire (da).

derogate, *v.i.* derogare. **derogatory**, (*disparaging*), *a.* denigratorio, disprezzante.

derrick, *n.* falcone, *m.*; (*crane*) gru, falcone con taglia, *m.*; (*ship's*) albero di carico, *m.*

dervish, *n.* dervis, dervigio, *m.*

descant, *v.i.* discorrere, dissertare (su); (*Mus.*) comporre.

descend, *v.i.* & *t.* scendere, discendere, cadere; abbassarsi; passare, trasmettersi (a). ~*ed*, *from*, disceso da, trasmesso da. ~**ant**, *n.* discendente, *m.f.*, (*pl.*) posteri, *m.pl.* **descent**, *n.* scesa, discesa, *f.*; pendio, *m.*; (*lineage*) discendenza, nascita, *f.*, lignaggio, *m.*; genealogia, *f.* ~ *from the Cross*, Deposizione dalla Croce, *f.*

describe, *v.t.* descrivere. **description**, *n.* descrizione, denominazione; specie, *f.*; genere, *m.* **descriptive**, *a.* descrittivo; (*catalogue*) ragionato.

descry, *v.t.* scoprire, scorgere, percepire.

desecrate, *v.t.* profanare.

desert, *a.* deserto. ¶ *n.* deserto, *m.*; solitudine, *f.*; merito, *m.* ¶ *v.t.* & *i.* disertare, abbandonare, passare (1). ~*ed*, *a.* deserto; disertato, abbandonato. ~**er**, *n.* disertore, *m.* ~**ion**, *n.* diserzione, *f.*

deserve, *v.t.* meritare. **deservedly**, *ad.* meritatamente. **deserving**, *a.* (*pers.*) meritevole, benemerito, degno; (*of action*) meritorio, degno. ~ *of praise*, lodevole. ~ *of blame*, biasimevole.

desiccate, *v.t.* disseccare. **desiccation**, *n.* disseccamento, *m.*

desideratum, *n.* desideratum, *m.*

design, *n.* disegno, piano; proposito, progetto, modello, *m.*; intenzione, *f.*, intento, scopo, *m.*; portata, *f.* ¶ *v.t.* disegnare, proporsi; divisare, progettare; avere l'intenzione (di).

designate, *v.t.* designare, indicare; nominare; destinare. **designation**, *n.* designazione.

designedly, *ad.* apposta, intenzionalmente. **designer**, *n.* disegnatore; costruttore; autore; inventore, progettista, *m.*; intrigante, *m.f.* **designing**, *a.* intrigante, maleintenzionato.

desirable, *a.* desiderabile, gradevole, vantaggioso. **desire**, *n.* desiderio, *m.*, voglia, brama, *f.*; domanda, *f.* ¶ *v.t.* desiderare, augurarsi, volere, pregare, richiedere, bramare. **desirous**, *a.* desideroso, vago, bramoso. *to be* ~ *of*, desiderare, essere desiderosi di.

desist, *v.i.* desistere (da); rinunziare (a); cessare (di).

desk, *n.* tavolo, scrittoio, *m.*, scrivania, *f.*; leggio, *m.*; cattedra, *f.*; (*cashier's*) cassa, *f.*

desolate, *a.* desolato, devastato, spopolato. ¶ *v.t.* desolare, devastare, spopolare. **desolation**, *n.* desolazione, devastazione, *f.*; spopolamento, *m.*; afflizione, *f.*

despair, *n.* disperazione, *f.* ¶ *v.i.* disperare. *to drive to* ~, spingere, ridurre alla disperazione. *his life is* ~*d of*, si dispera della sua vita. ~**ing**, & **in** ~, disperato.

despatch, *n.* & *v.t.* same as *dispatch*.

desperado, *n.* bandito, sgherro, bravaccione; disperato, forsennato. **desperate**, *a.* disperato; furioso; accanito, funesto, terribile; (*illness*) inguaribile. ~**ly**, *ad.* disperatamente, furiosamente, accanitamente; ad oltranza, a corpo morto, pazzamente, perdutamente, follemente. **desperation**, *n.* disperazione,

esasperazione, *f.*, furore, accanimento, *m.*
despicable, *a.* disprezzabile, basso, meschino. **despise,** *v.t.* sprezzare, disprezzare, sdegnare, disdegnare; trascurare.
despite, *n.* dispetto, *m.* ¶ *pr.* malgrado, a dispetto di.
despoil, *v.t.* spogliare.
despond, *v.i.* scoraggiarsi, lasciarsi abbattere, disperare. ~**ency,** *n.* abbattimento, scoraggiamento, *m.*; disperazione, *f.* ~**ent,** *a.* scoraggiato, abbattuto, disperato.
despot, *n.* despota, tiranno, *m.* ~**ic,** *a.* dispotico. ~**ism,** *n.* dispotismo, *m.*, tirannide, *f.*
dessert, *n.* frutta, *f.*; frutta e dolci, *m.pl.* ~ *grapes,* uva da tavola, *f.* ~ *spoon,* cucchiaio da dolci, da dessert, *m.* (*sweet*) ~ *wine,* vino [dolce] da tavola, *m.*
destination, *n.* destinazione, *f.* **destine,** *v.t.* destinare, assegnare; designare. **destiny,** *n.* destino, fato, *m.*, sorte, *f.* man of ~, uomo fatale, *m.*
destitute, *a.* indigente. ~ *of,* privo di, sprovvisto di. the ~, gl'indigenti, *m.pl.* **destitution,** *n.* indigenza, miseria; destituzione, *f.*
destroy, *v.t.* distruggere, rovinare. ~**er,** *n.* distruttore, *m.*; demolitore; sterminatore, *m.*, -trice, *f.*; rovinatore, *m.*, -trice, *f.*; (*torpedo-boat*) ~, *n.* cacciatorpediniere, *m.* **destruction,** *n.* distruzione, rovina, *f.*, sterminio, *m.* **destructible,** *a.* distruttibile, fragile. **destructive,** *a.* distruttivo, nocivo. ~ *person,* rompitutto, *m.* **destructor,** *n.* forno per bruciare i rifiuti, *m.*
desultorily, *ad.* ad intervalli; a salti; senza metodo, sconnessamente, oziosamente, pigramente. **desultory,** *a.* sconnesso, senza metodo, a sbalzi; indolente, ozioso.
detach, *v.t.* staccare, isolare. ~**able,** *a.* staccabile. ~**ed house,** casa staccata, c. isolata. ~**ment,** *n.* distacco, isolamento, *m.*; (*Mil.*) distaccamento, *m.*
detail, *n.* dettaglio, particolare, *m.* ¶ *v.t.* dettagliare, esporre in dettaglio, raccontare punto per punto; (*Mil.*) distaccare.
detain, *v.t.* detenere, trattenere; ritardare, fare attendere; arrestare, custodire.
detect, *v.t.* scoprire, scorgere; sorprendere. ~**ion,** *n.* scoperta,

sorpresa, *f.* ~**ive,** *n.* agente segreto di polizia. ~ *story,* romanzo poliziesco, *m.* ~**or** (*Radio, &c.*) *n.* rivelatore, *m.*
detent, *n.* scatto, dente d'arresto, *m.* ~**ion,** *n.* detenzione; prigionia; (*Sch.*) punizione, *f.*
deter, *v.t.* dissuadere, distogliere, scoraggiare. to be ~**red from,** astenersi da, essere distolto da.
deteriorate, *v.i.* deteriorarsi; peggiorare, aggravarsi.
determinate, *a.* determinato, fissato, stabilito. **determination,** *n.* determinazione, decisione, risoluzione, *f.* **determine,** *v.t.* determinare, decidere, precisare, fissare; stabilire; terminare, mettere fine a; (*v.i.*) decidersi; risolversi; deliberare. ~ **d,** *p.a.* deciso, risoluto, accanito; determinato, fissato, stabilito.
detest, *v.t.* detestare. ~**able,** *a.* detestabile.
dethrone, *v.t.* detronizzare, deporre dal trono.
detonate, *v.i.* scoppiare, detonare; (*v.t.*) fare scoppiare, far detonare. **detonation,** *n.* scoppio, *m.*, detonazione, *f.* **detonator,** *n.* detonatore, *m.*
detour, *n.* giravolta, rigirata, *f.*; giro, *m.*
detract from, *v.t.* detrarre da, togliere, derogare a; denigrare, diffamare. **detractor,** *n.* detrattore, calunniatore, diffamatore, *m.*
detrain, *v.i.* scendere dal treno.
detriment, *n.* detrimento, danno, pregiudizio, *m.* ~**al,** *a.* pregiudizievole, nocivo, dannoso. to be ~ to, essere pregiudizievole per, tornare a detrimento di.
detritus, *n.* detrito, *m.*
deuce, *n.* diavolo, diamine, *m.*; (*cards*) due; (*Ten.*) 40 pari. to play the ~ with, rovinare completamente.
Deuteronomy, *n.* Deuteronomio, *m.*
devaluation, *n.* deprezzamento, svalutamento, *m.*
devastate, *v.t.* devastare. **devastation,** *n.* devastazione, *f.* **devastator,** *n.* devastatore.
develop, *v.t.* sviluppare; (*Min.*) aprire, sfruttare; (*v.i.*) svilupparsi. ~**er,** (*Phot.*) sviluppatore; (*mixture*) rivelatore, *m.* ~**ing bath,** bagno sviluppatore, b. rivelatore, *m.* ~**ment,** *n.* sviluppo, svolgimento, *m.*
deviate, *v.t.* deviare. **deviation,** *n.* deviazione, *f.*; errore, scostamento, *m.*
device, *n.* espediente, mezzo, piano,

progetto, disegno, *m.*; (*emblem*) divisa, *f.*, emblema, stemma, *m.*

devil, *n.* diavolo, *m. the* ~*!* diamine! che diavolo! ~**ish,** *a.* diabolico. ~**ment,** *n.* cattiveria; diavoleria, *f.* ~**ry,** *n.* azione diabolica, *f.*

devious, *a.* deviato, tortuoso; errante, vagante; falso.

devise, *v.t.* escogitare, immaginare; progettare, inventare; tramare; (*Law*) legare per testamento.

devoid, *a.* (*chi.*) privo, sprovvisto, vuoto (di); digiuno (di).

devolve, *v.i.* devolvere (a), spettare (a), toccare (a), passare (a).

devote, *v.t.* dedicare, dare, consacrare. **devotee,** *n.* devoto, *m.*, -a, *f.*, bigotto, *m.*, -a, *f.* **devotion,** (*Relig.*) *n.* devozione, *f.*; (*pl.*) devozioni, preghiere, *f.pl.*; (*zeal*) devozione, premura, *f.* ~**al,** *a.* pio, religioso, di devozione.

devour, *v.t.* divorare, ingoiare, inghiottire.

devout, *a.* devoto, pio. ~**ness,** *n.* devozione, pietà, *f.*

dew, *n.* rugiada, *f.* ~*drop,* *n.* goccia di rugiada, *f.*

dewlap, *n.* giogaia, *f.*

dewy, *a.* rugiadoso.

dexterity, *n.* destrezza, sveltezza, agilità, *f.* **dextrous, dexterous,** *a.* destro, accorto, attivo, acconcio, lesto.

dextrin, *n.* destrina, *f.*

diabetes, *n.* diabete, *m.*

diabolic(al), *a.* diabolico.

diacritical, *a.* diacritico.

diadem, *n.* diadema, *m.*

diaeresis, *n.* dieresi, *f.*

diagnose, *v.t.* diagnosticare. **diagnosis,** *n.* diagnosi, *f.*

diagonal, *a.* diagonale. ¶ *n.* diagonale, *f.*

diagram, *n.* diagramma, *m.*

dial, *n.* (*plate*) quadrante, *m.*; (*calculating mach.*) mirino; (*Teleph.*) disco, *m.*; (*compass*) bussola. ¶ *v.t.* (*Teleph.*) formare il numero sul disco.

dialect, *n.* dialetto, *m.*

dialectics, *n.* dialettica, *f.*

dialogue, *n.* dialogo, *m.*

diameter, *n.* diametro, *m.* **diametric,** *a.* diametrale.

diamond, *n.* diamante, *m.*; (*Geom.*) rombo, *m.*; (*pl. cards*) quadri, *m.pl.* ~ *ring,* anello di brillanti, *m.* ~ *wedding,* nozze di diamante, *f.pl.* ~ *cutter,* diamantaio, *m.* ~ *cutting,* taglio di diamanti, *m.*

diaper, *n.* tela operata, biancheria confezionata, *f.* ¶ *v.t.* operare, screziare.

diaphanous, *a.* diafano.

diaphragm, *n.* diaframma, *m.*

diarrhoea, *n.* diarrea, *f.*

diary, *n.* diario, *m.*; (*of one's life*) giornale, *m.*

diatonic, *a.* diatonico.

diatribe, *n.* diatriba, *f.*

dibble, *n.* piuolo, *m.*

dibs, *n.pl.* (*child's game*) ossetti, *m.pl.*

dice, *m.pl.* dadi, *m.pl.* ~ *box,* bossolo da dadi, *m.*

dickens (the), diamine, diavolo, *m.*

dictate, *v.t. & i.* dettare. ~ *to,* dare ordini a, signoreggiare, tiranneggiare. ~[s], *n.*[*pl.*] dettami, *m.pl.*; voce, *f.* **dictation,** *n.* dettatura, *f.* ordini, *m.pl.* (*Sch.*) dettato, *m.*

dictator, *n.* dittatore, *m.* ~**ial,** *a.* dittatorio, imperioso, assoluto. ~**ship,** *n.* dittatura, *f.*

diction, *n.* dizione, *f.* ~**ary,** *n.* dizionario, vocabolario, lessico, *m.*

dictum, *n.* detto, *m.*

didactic, *a.* didattico.

die, *n.* dado, *m.*; (*Mech.*) conio, stampo, *m.* ~ *sinker,* medagliaio, *m.*

die, *v.i. ir.* morire, decedere; (*fig.*) crepare, cessare, perire, sparire; spegnersi; (*of laughing, &c.*) morire, crepare. ~ *away,* morire, svanire, sparire, cessare. ~ *down,* estinguersi, spegnersi; (*storm, anger, &c.*) abbonacciarsi. ~*-hard,* intransigente, *m.f.*

diet, *n.* dieta, *f.*, regime, *m.*, regime alimentare, *m.*; alimento, vitto, *m.*, viveri, *m.pl.* ¶ *v.t.* mettere a dieta, *m.*, a regime; (*v.i.*) esser a dieta, stare a dieta, a regime. ~**ary,** *n.* regime, vitto dietetico, *m.* ~ *tread,* pane di regime.

differ, *v.i.* differire, essere diverso, non essere d'accordo, litigare. ~**ence,** *n.* differenza, diversità, divergenza, *f.*; disaccordo, diverbio, contrasto, *m.*; controversia, contestazione, disputa, *f.*; questione; vertenza, *f.*; (*payment*) resto, supplemento, *m.* ~**ent,** *a.* differente, diverso, differenziale. ~**ential,** *a.* differenziale. ~*al calculus,* calcolo d. ~ (*gear*) differenziale. **differentiate,** *v.t.* differenziare. **differently,** *ad.* differentemente, altrimenti.

difficult, *a.* difficile. ~ *to catch,* inafferrabile. **difficulty,** *n.* difficoltà, pena, *f.*; imbarazzo, *m.* (*pl.*) strette, *f.pl. with* ~, difficilmente, *(ship in)* **difficulties** *(Navigation)*, in pericolo; avariato.

diffidence, *n.* timidezza; modestia, *f.* **diffident**, *a.* timido, esitante.

diffuse, *v.t.* diffondere. ¶ *a.* diffuso. ~ed, *a.* diffuso. **diffusion**, *n.* diffusione, *f.*

dig, *n.* colpo, *m.*; vangata, zappata, *f.*; *(fig.)* puntata, spinta, *f.* ¶ *v.t. & i. ir.* vangare, zappare. ~ *up*, estrarre, scavare, sradicare.

digest, *n.* digesto, *m.* ¶ *v.t. & i.* digerire, assimilare. ~**ible**, *a.* digeribile. ~**ion**, *n.* digestione, *f.* ~**ive**, *a. & n.* digestivo, *a. & m.*

digger *(pers., gold)* cercatore; *(gen.)* scavatore, minatore. **digging**, *n.* *(action)* vangatura, *f.* ~**s**, *pl.* miniere (d'oro), *f.pl.*

digit, *n.* dito, *m.* *a* ~ (o–9) una [sola] cifra. **digitalis** *(Phar.)*, *n.* digitale, *f.*

dignified, *a.* dignitoso, solenne. **dignitary**, *n.* dignitario, *m.* **dignify**, *v.t.* onorare, decorare, nobilitare, elevare a dignità. **dignity**, *n.* dignità, *f.*

digress, *v.i.* digredire, fare una digressione, deviare. ~**ion**, *n.* digressione, *f.* **digressive**, *a.* digressivo.

dike, *n.* diga, *f.*; *(Geol. & Min.)* vena, *f.*, filone, *m.* ¶ *v.t.* digare.

dilapidate, *v.t.* dilapidare. ~*d state* *(building)*, caduto in rovina, crollante, *a.*

dilate, *v.t.* dilatare. *v.i.* dilatarsi; tirare in lungo.

dilatoriness, *n.* lentezza, *f.*, ritardo, *m.* **dilatory**, *a.* *(pers.)* tardo, tardivo, procrastinante; *(policy)* *(Law)* dilatorio.

dilemma, *n.* dilemma, *m.*

dilettante, *n.* dilettante, *m.f.*

diligence, *n.* diligenza, *f.* **diligent**, *a.* diligente, industrioso. ~**ly**, *ad.* diligentemente.

dilly-dally, *v.i.* gingillarsi, indugiarsi, tentennare, vacillare.

dilute, *v.t.* diluire, stemperare, annacquare. **dilution**, *n.* dilluimento, stemperamento, annacquamento, *m.*; diluzione, *f.*

diluvial, *a.* diluviale.

dim, *a.* oscuro, indistinto; torbido, appannato; debole, scialbo. ¶ *v.t.* oscurare, offuscare, appannare; *(motor lights)* abbassare. *dimmed* *lights*, le luci abbassate, i fari abbassati.

dimension, *n.* dimensione, grandezza, mole, misura, *f.*; calibro, *m.*, formato *(book)*; grado, *m.* ~*ed* *sketch*, schizzo quotato, *m.*

diminish, *v.t.* diminuire, ridurre, impiccolire, abbassare; *(v.i.)* diminuire, ridursi, abbassarsi. **diminution**, *n.* diminuzione, riduzione, *f.*, abbassamento, *m.* **diminutive**, *a.* diminutivo, piccolissimo; *(Gram.)* diminutivo. ¶ *(Gram.)* *n.* diminutivo, *m.*

dimness, *n.* oscurità, debolezza, *f.*

dimple, *n.* fossetta, *f.* **dimpled**, *a.* a fossette.

din, *n.* baccano, rumore, fracasso, *m.* ¶ *v.t.* stordire.

dine, *v.i.* pranzare, desinare. ~ *out*, pranzare, desinare fuori, fuori di casa. **diner**, *n.* commensale, convitato, *m.*

dinghy *or* **dingey**, *n.* piccolo battello, *m.*

dingy, *a.* scolorito, sbiadito, scuro.

dining: ~ *car*, vagone ristorante, *m.* ~ *room & ~ saloon*, sala da pranzo, *f.* ~ *table*, tavola da pranzo, *f.* **dinner**, *n.* pranzo, desinare, *m.* *at* ~, a pranzo. ~ *jacket*, smoking (da pranzo), *m.* ~ *lift*, calapranzi, *m.* *give a* ~ *(party)*, dare, offrire un pranzo. ~ *plate*, piatto, *m.* ~ *service*, servizio da tavola, *m.* ~ *time*, ora del pranzo, *f.* ~ *wagon*, portavivande, *m.inv*

dint, *n.* tacca, ammaccatura, impressione, *f. by* ~ *of*, a forza di.

diocesan, *a.* diocesano. **diocese**, *n.* diocesi, *f.*

diopter, *n.* diottra, *f.* **dioptric**, *a.* diottrico.

dip, *n.* tuffo, *m.*, immersione, *f.*; inclinazione, depressione, *f.*, avvallamento, *m.*; *(ink)* pennata, *f.* ¶ *v.t.* tuffare, immergere; abbassare, inclinare; *(motor headlights)* abbassare (i fari) *(v.i.)* immergersi, tuffarsi; abbassarsi; inclinarsi.

diphtheria, *n.* difterite, *f.*

diphthong, *n.* dittongo, *m.*

diploma, *n.* diploma, *m.*

diplomacy, *n.* diplomazia, *f.* **diplomatic**, *a.* diplomatico. **diplomat[ist]**, *n.* diplomatico, *m.*

diptych, *n.* dittico, *m.*

dire, *a.* *(distress)* estremo, terribile, orrendo; *(necessity)* crudele.

direct, *a.* diretto, diritto, immediato; *(fig.)* franco, schietto. ~ *current* *(Elec.)*, corrente continua, *f.* ~ *trade*, commercio diretto, *m.* ¶ *ad.*

direttamente. ¶ *v.t.* dirigere, indirizzare, rivolgere, applicare; amministrare, condurre; sopraintendere a; comandare, ordinare, dare istruzioni a. ∼ *me to*, indicarmi. ∼**ion**, *n.* direzione, *f.*; senso, ordine, *m.*; istruzione, *f.*; (*address*) indirizzo, recapito, *m.*; (*pl.*) direzioni, *f.pl.*; istruzioni, *f.pl.*; sensi, lati, *m.pl.*; indicazioni, *f.pl.* ∼*s for use*, indicazioni (istruzioni) per l'uso. **directly,** *ad.* direttamente; immediatamente; tosto, subito; difilato; appena che; subito che.

director, *n.* (*of company*) amministratore, *m.*, -trice, *f.*, (di società anonima); (*managing*) ∼, amministratore delegato, (*manager*) direttore, *m.*, -trice, *f.*; gerente, *m.f.* ∼**ate**, *n.* direttorato, *m.*, amministrazione, *f.*

directory, *n.* indicatore, annuario, *m.*; guida, *f.*; (*Fr. hist.*) Direttorio, *m.*

direful, *a.* pauroso, terribile, orrendo.

dirge, *n.* canto funebre, *m.*; trenodia, *f.*

dirigible, *a. & n.* dirigibile, *a. & m.*; aeronave, *f.*

dirk, *n.* daga, *f.*; pugnale, spadino, *m.*

dirt, *n.* sudiciume, *m.*, sporcizia, sozzura, *f.*; (*mud*) fango, *m.* ∼ *cheap*, a prezzo vile. ∼*track*, pista, *f.* **dirtily,** *ad.* sporcamente, sozzamente. **dirtiness,** *n.* sozzura, sporcizia, *f.* **dirty,** *a.* sporco, sudicio, sucido, sozzo, infangato. ∼ *pig*, porco, sporcaccione, sozzone. ∼ *proof*, bozza piena di correzioni. ∼ *trick*, tiro birbone, *m.*, villania, *f.* ∼ *work* (*fig.*) porcheria, cattiveria, *f.*; inganno, tradimento, *m.* ¶ *v.t.* insozzare, sporcare, infangare.

disable, *v.t.* rendere incapace, inabilitare; storpiare; (*ship*) avariare. ∼*ed soldier*, ∼ *sailor*, invalido, mutilato di guerra, *m.* ∼**ment** (*disability*), *n.* incapacità, impotenza, invalidità, *f.*

disabuse, *v.t.* disingannare.

disadvantage, *n.* svantaggio, *m.* *place at a* ∼, mettere in una situazione svantaggiosa. ∼**ous,** *a.* svantaggioso.

disaffection, *n.* malvoglia, *f.*, alienamento, spirito di ribellione, *m.*

disagree, *v.i.* differire, discordare, non essere d'accordo; discutere con; (*food*) fare male a, nuocere a; non confarsi (a). ∼**able,** *a.* sgradevole, spiacevole. ∼**ment,** *n.* disaccordo, *m.*, dissidenza, *f.*, litigio, *m.*; (*figures*) discordanza, differenza, *f.*

disallow, *v.t.* non ammettere, disapprovare, proibire.

disappear, *v.i.* sparire, svanire, scomparire. ∼**ance,** *n.* scomparsa, sparizione, *f.*

disappoint, *v.t.* deludere, sconcertare, contrariare, mandare a vuoto, sventare, frustrare, mancare di parola (con qualcuno). *don't* ∼ *me*, non mancare di parola con me, non venir meno alla tua promessa. ∼**ment,** *n.* disappunto, disinganno, *m.*, disillusione, *f.* ∼ *in love*, disillusione amorosa, *f.*

disapprobation & **disapproval,** *n.* disapprovazione, *f.* **disapprove,** *v.t.* disapprovare.

disarm, *v.t.* disarmare. **disarmament,** *n.* disarmo, *m.*

disarrange, *v.t.* disordinare, guastare; (*someone's*) *hair*, scomporre, scompigliare.

disarray, *n.* disordine, scompiglio, *m.*

disaster, *n.* disastro, *m.*, catastrofe, *f.*

disastrous, *a.* disastroso.

disavow, *v.t.* ritrattare, rinnegare, smentire, sconfessare. ∼**al,** *n.* ritrattazione, sconfessione, *f.*

disband, *v.t.* sbandare, licenziare; (*v.i.*) sbandarsi, separarsi.

disbelief, *n.* incredulità, *f.* **disbelieve,** *v.t.* non credere, non prestar fede a.

disbud, *v.t.* spollonare.

disburden, *v.t.* sgravare, scaricare, liberare da un peso. ∼ *oneself*, sgravarsi.

disburse, *v.t.* sborsare. ∼**ment,** *n.* sborso, *m.*

disc, *n.* disco, *m.*, placca, *f.*

discard, *v.t.* congedare, rigettare, mettere da parte; (*cards*) scartare.

discern, *v.t.* discernere, distinguere. ∼**ible,** *a.* discernibile. ∼**ing,** *a.* giudizioso, assennato. ∼**ment,** *n.* discernimento, giudizio, *m.*, assennatezza, penetrazione, *f.*

discharge, *n.* scarico, sparo, *m.*; scarica, *f.*; pagamento, *m.*; quietanza, *f.*, (*duty*) adempimento, *m.*; (*acquittal*) assoluzione, liberazione, *f.*; (*Med.*) flusso, *m.*, suppurazione, *f.*, (*Mil., navy*) congedo, *m.*; (*bankrupt*) riabilitazione, *f.*, (*document*) fede di congedo, *f.* ¶ *v.t.* scaricare, (*firearm*) sparare; emettere; pagare, saldare; soddisfare; adempiere; assolvere; riabilitare; rilasciare, mettere in libertà; licenziare, congedare; (*v.i.*) scaricarsi; suppurare. *to get* (*obligation*) *discharged,* togliere, cancellare; scaricarsi.

disciple, *n.* discepolo, *m.* **disciplinarian,** *n.* chi sa mantenere la disciplina; maestro severo, *m.* **disciplinary,** *a.* disciplinare. **discipline,** *n.* disciplina, *f.* ¶ *v.t.* disciplinare.

disclaim, *v.t.* sconfessare, rinnegare, rinunciare a. **~er,** *n.* sconfessione, *f.*

disclose, *v.t.* scoprire, rivelare, divulgare, palesare. **disclosure,** *n.* rivelazione, scoperta, *f.*, palesamento, *m.*

discoloration, *n.* scoloramento, *m.* **discolour,** *v.t.* scolorare.

discomfit, *v.t.* confondere, sconfiggere, sconcertare. **~ure,** *n.* sconfitta, *f.*

discomfort, *n.* sconforto, disagio, incomodo, *m.*

discompose, *v.t.* scomporre, turbare, alterare. **discomposure,** *n.* scomposizione, *f.*, turbamento, *m.*, alterazione, *f.*

disconcert, *v.t.* sconcertare.

disconnect, *v.t.* sconnettere, disgiungere; (*Mech.*) disinnestare; (*Elec.*) interrompere; (*switch*) disinserire.

disconsolate, *a.* sconsolato.

discontented, *a.* scontento, malcontento. **discontent[ment],** *n.* scontento, *m.* scontentezza, *f.*

discontinuance, *n.* cessazione, sospensione, soppressione, *f.* **discontinue,** *v.t.* cessare, sospendere, (*a train*) sopprimere. **~** *one's subscription,* or *season ticket,* disabbonarsi, disdire l'abbonamento.

discord, *n.* discordia, *f.*, disaccordo, *m.*, dissenso, dissidio, *m.*, (*Mus.*) dissonanza, *f.* **discordance,** *n.* discordanza, *f.* **~ant,** *a.* discordante.

discount, *n.* sconto, ribasso, *m.*, (opp. *premium*) perdita, *f.* *to be at a* **~,** essere sotto la pari, (*fig.*) essere poco stimato, screditato. **~** *broker,* scontista, *m.* **~** *charges,* rata, *f.*, saggio dello sconto, *m.*; aggio, *m.* ¶ *v.t.* scontare; (*fig.*) far la tara a.

discountenance, *v.t.* disapprovare, opporsi a; vedere male.

discounter, *n.* scontista, *m.* **discounting,** *n.* sconto, *m.*

discourage, *v.t.* scoraggiare, dissuadere. **~ment,** *n.* scoraggiamento, *m.*

discourse, *n.* discorso, ragionamento,

m., discussione, *f.* ¶ *v.i.* discorrere (di), ragionare (di), intrattenersi (su).

discourteous, *a.* scortese. **discourtesy,** *n.* scortesia, *f.*

discover, *v.t.* scoprire, accorgersi di; far vedere. **~er,** *n.* scopritore, *-trice, m.f.* **~y,** *n.* scoperta, *f.*

discredit, *n.* scredito, discredito, *m.* ¶ *v.t.* screditare. **~able,** *a.* disonorevole; che porta discredito.

discreet, *a.* prudente, discreto.

discrepancy, *n.* contraddizione, *f.*

discrete, *a.* distinto, separato.

discretion, *n.* discrezione, *f.* **~ary,** *a.* discrezionale. *full* **~** *power,* carta bianca, *f.*

discriminate, *v.t.* & *i.* distinguere, discriminare. **discrimination,** *n.* discriminazione, distinzione, *f.*; giudizio, discernimento, *m.*

discursive, *a.* discorsivo, sconnesso, prolisso.

discus, *n.* disco, *m.*

discuss, *v.t.* discutere, dibattere. **~ion,** *n.* discussione, *f.*

disdain, *n.* sdegno, disdegno, disprezzo, *m.* ¶ *v.t.* sdegnare, disdegnare. **~ful,** *a.* sdegnoso.

disease, *n.* malattia, *f.*, male, *m.* **~ed,** *a.* ammalato, malato; (*meat*) infetto.

disembark, *v.t.* & *i.* sbarcare. **~ation,** *n.* sbarco, *m.*

disembody, *v.t.* disincarnare; sciogliere.

disembowel, *v.t.* sventrare, sbudellare.

disenchant, *v.t.* disincantare, rompere, togliere l'illusione (a).

disencumber, *v.t.* sbarazzare, sgombrare; (*Fin.*) sgravare.

disengage, *v.t.* disimpegnare, disimpacciare, liberare, sciogliere. **~d,** *a.* disimpegnato, libero, sciolto.

disentangle, *v.t.* disimpacciare, sbarazzare; (*fig.*) chiarire.

disestablishment, [of the Church] *n.* cessazione di rapporti tra la Chiesa e lo Stato, *f.*

disfavour, *n.* sfavore, *m.*

disfigure, *v.t.* sfigurare, deformare. **~ment,** *n.* sfiguramento, *m.*, deformazione, *f.*

disforest, *v.t.* diboscare.

disgorge, *v.t.* emettere, riversare; rilasciare possesso di.

disgrace, *n.* onta, vergogna, *f.*; disonore, obbrobrio, *m.* *in* **~,** in disgrazia. ¶ *v.t* (*dismiss*) destituire, licenziare; (*shame*) disonorare. **~ful,** *a.* vergognoso, disonorante.

disgruntled, *a.* malcontento, cupo, di malumore.

disguise, *n.* travestimento, mascheramento, *m.*, maschera, *f.* ¶ *v.t.* travestire, mascherare; celare, nascondere.

disgust, *n.* disgusto, *m.*, nausea, *f.*, schifo, fastidio, *m.* ¶ *v.t.* disgustare, spiacere, offendere. ~**ing,** *a.* disgustoso, stomachevole, schifoso, nauseabondo.

dish, *n.* piatto, *m.*, scodella, *f.*, terrina, *f.*; (*Phot.*) bacinella, *f.*; (*food*) piatto, *m.*, pietanza *f.* ~*cloth,* strofinaccio, *m.* ~ *cover,* *n* copripiatto, *m.* ~ *warmer,* scaldavivande, *m.inv.* ~*washer,* lavapiatti, *m.inv.* ~ *up,* *v.t.* servire; scodellare. ~**ed,** servito; scodellato. ~**ful,** *n.* piattopieno, *m.*, scodellata, *f.*

dishabille, *n.* veste da camera, *f.*

dishearten, *v.t.* scoraggiare, abbattere, disanimare.

dishevelled, *a.* scapigliato, arruffato, scompigliato.

dishonest, *a.* disonesto. ~**y,** *n.* disonestà, *f.*

dishonour, *n.* disonore, *m.*, infamia, *f.* ¶ *v.t.* disonorare. ~**able,** *a.* (*pers.*) disonorato, disonesto; (*action*) disonorevole. ~*ed bill,* cambiale in sofferenza, c. insoluta, *f.* ~*ed cheque,* assegno a vuoto, *m.*

disillusion, *n.* disillusione, *f.* ¶ *v.t.* disilludere.

disinclination, *n.* avversione, ripugnaza, svogliatezza, *f.* **disincline,** *v.t.* rendere avverso a, indisporre.

disincorporate, *v.t.* sciogliere (una corporazione); staccare (da una c.).

disinfect, *v.t.* disinfettare. ~**ant,** *n.* disinfettante, *m.* ~**ion,** *n.* disinfezione, *f.*

disingenuous, *a.* simulato, finto, falso, poco sincero.

disinherit, *v.t.* diseredare.

disintegrate, *v.t.* disintegrare; (*v.i.*) disintegrarsi.

disinter, *v.t.* esumare.

disinterested, *a.* disinteressato; imparziale. ~**ness,** *n.* disinteresse, *m.*

disinterment, *n.* esumazione, *f.*

disjoin, *v.t.* disgiungere, disunire.

disjoint, *v.t.* disarticolare, slogare, smontare. ~**ed,** *a.* disarticolato, slogato, sconnesso, smontato.

disk, *n.* disco, *m.*

dislike, *n.* antipatia, avversione, ripugnanza, *f.* ¶ *v.t.* provare antipatia per; sentire avversione per; non amare; detestare, prendere in uggia. *I* ~, mi spiace, non mi va. *she took a* ~ *to him,* ella lo prese a noia.

dislocate, *v.t.* slogare. **dislocation,** *n.* slogatura, lussazione, *f.*; (*of industries, troops, &c.*) dislocazione, *f.*

dislodge, *v.t.* sloggiare, scacciare.

disloyal, *a.* sleale, infedele, ribelle. ~**ty,** *n.* slealtà, infedeltà; ribellione, *f.*

dismal, *a.* lugubre, triste, tetro, funesto, melanconico.

dismantle, *v.t.* smantellare.

dismast, *v.t.* disalberare.

dismay, *n.* spavento, sgomento, *m.*, costernazione, *f.* ¶ *v.t.* spaventare, sgomentare.

dismember, *v.t.* smembrare.

dismiss, *v.t.* congedare, licenziare; destituire, esonorare (da servizio); bandire, scacciare; deporre; scartare, mettere da parte; sciogliere; rigettare, respingere, rinviare. ~**al,** *n.* congedo, licenziamento, *m.*, destituzione, *f.*, rigetto, rinvio, scioglimento, *m.*

dismount, *v.i.* smontare; scendere (da cavallo); (*v.t.*) smontare.

disobedience, *n.* disobbedienza, *f.* **disobedient,** *a.* disobbediente. **disobey,** *v.t.* disobbedire a; (*v.i.*) disobbedire.

disoblige, *v.t.* usare scortesia a; far displacere a; agire in modo scortese verso. **disobliging,** *a.* scortese, sgarbato, incivile. ~**ness,** *n.* scortesia, sgarbatezza, *f.*

disorder, *n.* disordine, *m.*, sregolatezza, confusione, *f.*; (*Med.*) disturbo, *m.*, malattia, *f.*, male, *m.* ¶ *v.t.* disordinare, turbare, scompigliare. ~**ly,** *a.* disordinato, in disordine, irregolare, mal regolato.

disorganize, *v.t.* disorganizzare.

disown, *v.t.* sconfessare, rinnegare, ripudiare.

disparage, *v.t.* deprezzare, screditare, denigrare, detrarre da. ~**ment,** *n.* deprezzamento, disprezzo, *m.*, denigrazione, *f.* *it is no* ~ *to,* non è fare ingiustizia a. **disparaging,** *a.* deprezzante. **disparate,** *a.* disparato. **disparity,** *n.* disparità, *f.*

dispassionate, *a.* & ~**ly,** *ad.* spassionato, *a.*, spassionatamente, *ad.*

dispatch, *n.* speditezza, celerità, sollecitudine, prontezza, *f.*; disbrigo, *m.*; invio, *m.*, spedizione, *f.*; (*message*) dispaccio, *m.* ~ *boat*, battello staffetta, *m.* ~ *case*, cartella da viaggio, *f.* ~ *clerk*, spedizioniere, *m.* ~ *rider*, staffetta, *f.* ¶ *v.t.* spedire, inviare; sbrigare; spacciare; condurre a termine; uccidere.

dispel, *v.t.* dissipare, disperdere, scacciare.

dispensary, *n.* farmacia, *f.*; (*charitable*) dispensario, *m.* **dispensation,** *n.* (*of Providence*) grazia, *f.*; afflizione mandata dal cielo; (*exemption*) dispensa; esecuzione, *f.*, esonero, *m.* **dispense,** *v.t.* dispensare, distribuire, (*Med.*) somministrare. ~ *with*, fare a meno di; destituire. **dispenser,** *n.* dispensatore, *m.*, -trice, *f.*; (*Med.*) farmacista, *m.f.*

dispeople, *v.t.* spopolare.

dispersal & **dispersion,** *n.* dispersione, *f.* **disperse,** *v.t.* disperdere; spargere.

dispirit, *v.t.* scoraggiare, abbattere, demoralizzare, deprimere, disanimare.

displace, *v.t.* spostare; (*from office*) destituire, cambiare di posto; sostituire (*securities, Fin.*). ~**ment,** *n.* spostamento, *m.*, (*Naut.*) (*ship's*) dislocamento, *m.*

display, *n.* mostra, *f.*, spettacolo, *m.*; pompa, *f.*, sfoggio, *m.*, ostentazione, *f.*; spiegamento, *m.*, manifestazione, *f.* ~ *advertisement*, annunzio, *m.*; grande pubblicità, *f.* ~ *cabinet*, vetrina, mostra di bottega, *f.* ~ *figure*, ~ *model*, modella, *f.*, manichino, *m.* ¶ *v.t.* spiegare, mostrare, far mostra di, esibire; far vedere; dar prova di. ~*ed in bold type*, esposto in grandi caratteri.

displease, *v.t.* dispiacere a, scontentare. **displeasure,** *n.* dispiacere, *m.*

disposable, *a.* disponibile. **disposal,** *n.* disposizione, *f.*, (*sale*) vendita, *f.* **dispose,** *v.t.* disporre, collocare, inclinare. ~ *of*, disporre di, disfarsi di; vendere; sbrigare; regolare. *well, ill* ~*ed towards*, ben disposto, mal disposto. (a, verso). **disposition,** *n.* disposizione, *f.*, indole, *f.*, carattere, *m.*, inclinazione, *f.*

dispossess, *v.t.* spossessare, spodestare, spogliare, (*Law*) espropriare.

disproof, *n.* confutazione, *f.*

disproportion, *n.* sproporzione, *f.* ~**ate,** *a.* sproporzionato.

disprove, *v.t.* confutare.

dispute, *n.* disputa, controversia, contestazione, vertenza, *f.*, altercazione, *f.*, litigio, *m.* *v.t.* & *i.* contestare, disputare, contrastare; altercare, litigare. ~ *every inch of the ground*, (*Mil.*) contestare ogni pollice di terreno.

disqualification, *n.* squalifica, incapacità, interdizione, *f.* **disqualified,** (*Law*) *p.p.* & *a.* interdetto. **disqualify,** *v.t.* squalificare, rendere incapace, inabilitare; (*Law*) interdire.

disquiet, *v.t.* inquietare. ~[**ude**], *n.* inquietudine, *f.*

disquisition, *n.* disquisizione, *f.*

disrate, *v.t.* abbassare di classe, di grado.

disregard, *n.* noncuranza, indifferenza, trascuranza, *f.*, sprezzo, *m.* ¶ *v.t.* disconoscere, negligere, non fare caso di, (*instructions*) trasgredire.

disrelish, *n.* disgusto, *m.*, ripugnanza, *f.*

disreputable, *a.* malfamato, screditato, **disrepute,** *n.* cattiva reputazione, *f.*, discredito, *m.*

disrespect, *n.* mancanza di rispetto, *f.* ~**ful,** *a.* poco rispettoso, irriverente.

disrobe, *v.t.* svestire.

disrupt, *v.t.* rompere. ~**ion,** *n.* rottura, *f.*, scisma, *m.*

diss, (*Typ.*) *v.t.* distribuire.

dissatisfaction, *n.* scontento, malcontento, *m.*, scontentezza, *f.* **dissatisfied,** *a.* insoddisfatto (di), poco soddisfatto, malcontento (di).

dissect, *v.t.* dissecare, sezionare. ~**ion,** *n.* dissezione, *f.*

dissemble, *v.t.* & *i.* dissimulare, fingere. **dissembler,** *n.* dissimulatore, -trice, *m.f.*, ipocrita, *m.f.*

disseminate, *v.t.* disseminare.

dissension, *n.* dissenso, *m.*, discordia, *f.*, dissidio, *m.* **dissent,** *n.* dissenso, *m.*, (*Eccl.*) dissidenza, *f.* ¶ *v.t.* dissentire. ~**er** & **dissentient,** *n.* dissidente, *m.f.* *without a* ~, all'unanimità. ~**ing,** & **dissentient,** *a.* dissidente, dissenziente.

dissertation, *n.* dissertazione, *f.*

disservice, *n.* disservizio, discapito, torto, danno, detrimento, *m.*

dissidence, *n.* dissidenza, *f.* **dissident,** *a.* dissidente.

dissimilar, *a.* dissimile. ~**ity,** *n.* dissomiglianza, *f.*

dissimulate, *v.t.* & *i.* dissimulare, fingere.

dissipate, *v.t.* dissipare, dileguare; (*v.i.*) dispersersi. **dissipation,**

n. dissipazione; intemperanza, *f.*; vizio, *m.*; dispersione, *f.*

dissociate, *v.t.* dissociare, disunire, separare.

dissolute, *a.* dissoluto, corrotto, vizioso. ~**ness,** *n.* dissolutezza, corruzione, *f.*

dissolution, *n.* dissoluzione, *f.*, scioglimento, *m.*, (*Chem.*) decomposizione, *f.* **dissolve,** *v.t.* sciogliere, dissolvere. (*v.i.*) sciogliersi. **dissolvent,** *a.* & *n.* dissolvente, solvente, *a.* & *m.* *dissolving views,* quadri, visioni dileguantisi, *m.* & *f.pl.*

dissonance, *n.* dissonanza, *f.* **dissonant,** *a.* dissonante; contrario.

dissuade, *v.t.* dissuadere, sconsigliare.

dissyllable, *n.* disillabo, *m.* **dissyllabic,** *a.* disillabico.

distaff, *n.* rocca, conocchia, *f.*

distance, *n.* distanza, lontananza, *f.* *what is the* ~ *to?* quanto c'è di qui a . . .? *to keep one's distance.* mantenere la distanza; portar rispetto. *keep yout* ~, stia al suo posto. ~ *apart* or *between,* intervallo, *m.* ~ *glasses,* occhiali per vedere a lunga distanza, *m.pl.* ~ *swim,* nuotata di lunga distanza, *f.* ¶ *v.t.* distanziare, oltrepassare.

distant, *a.* distante, lontano, discosto, (*fig.*) riservato, contegnoso; superficiale; vago. ~ *signal,* (*Rly.*) segnale a distanza, *m.*

distaste, *n.* disgusto, *m.* avversione, *f.* svogliatezza, *f.* ~**ful,** *a.* disgustoso, sgradevole, fastidioso, spiacevole.

distemper, *n.* malattia (di cani), indisposizione, *f.*, (*paint*) tempera, *f.*, intonaco, *m.* ¶ *v.t.* fare a tempera, intonacare.

distend, *v.t.* distendere, dilatare, gonfiare. **distension,** *n.* distensione, dilatazione, *f.*, gonfiamento, *m.*

distich, *n.* distico, *m.*

distil, *v.t.* distillare, estrarre. **distillate** & **distillation,** *n.* distillato, *m.*, distillazione, *f.* **distiller,** *n.* distillatore, *m.* ~**y,** *n.* distilleria, *f.*

distinct, *a.* distinto, chiaro, netto, ~**ion,** *a.* distinzione, *f.* ~**ive,** *a.* distintivo. ~**ness,** *n.* chiarezza, nettezza, *f.* **distinguish,** *v.t.* distinguere. *to be* ~*able from,* distinguersi da. ~**ed,** *a.* distinto, insigne.

distort, *v.t.* tordere, storcere, deformare, alterare, svisare. ~*ing mirror,* specchio deformante, *m.* ~**ion,** *n.* distorsione, deformazione, *f.*, (*fig.*) travestimento, *m.*

distract, *v.t.* distrarre, distogliere; fare impazzire. ~**ed,** *p.a.* distratto, demente. ~**ion,** *n.* distrazione, *f.*, divertimento, *m.*; follia, pazzia, disperazione, *f.*

distrain upon, (*pers.*) sfrattare, eseguire un'azione forzata a carico di, dare lo sfratto a; (*goods*) espropriare, pignorare, sequestrare. ~**able,** *a.* soggetto ad espropriazione, ad azione forzata, espropriabile. *not* ~, non soggetto ad espropriazione. **distraint,** *n.* espropriazione, azione forzata, *f.* pignoramento, sequestro, sfratto, *m.*

distress, *n.* afflizione, miseria, angoscia, angustia, *f.*, (*Law*) sequestro, *m.*, confisca, *f.* ¶ *v.t.* affliggere, contristare, dar dolore a, angustiare. ~**ing,** *a.* affliggente, penoso, doloroso.

distribute, *v.t.* distribuire, ripartire. **distribution,** *n.* distribuzione, *f.*

district, *n.* distretto, circondario, quartiere, *m.*, circoscrizione, zona, *f.* ~ *manager,* n. direttore regionale, *m.* ~ *visitor,* n. dama di carità, *f.*

distrust, *n.* diffidenza, sfiducia, *f.*, sospetto, *m.* ¶ *v.t.* diffidare di, sospettare di. ~**ful,** *a.* diffidente, sospettoso.

disturb, *v.t.* disturbare, turbare, incomodare, dare incomodo a. ~**ance,** *n.* disturbo, disordine, *m.*, sommossa, *f.*

disunion, *n.* disunione, *f.* **disunite,** *v.t.* disunire, separare.

disuse, *n.* disuso, *m.* ~**d,** *p.a.* disusato, fuori uso, caduto in disuso.

ditch, *n.* fossa, *f.*, fosso, *m.*

ditto, *n.* detto, idem (*ad.*). *to say nothing but* ~ *to everything,* essere sempre d'accordo.

ditty, *n.* canzone, canzonetta, *f.*

divan, *n.* divano, *m.*; sala da fumare, *f.*

dive, *n.* tuffo, sbalzo, *m.*; (*Aero.*) picchiata, *f.* *nose* ~, discesa in picchiata, *f.* ~ *bomber,* n. aereo da bombardamento in picchiata; bombardiere in picchiata, *m.*; picchiatello, *m.* ¶ *v.i.* tuffarsi, immergersi, precipitarsi. ~ *bombing,* bombardamento in picchiata, *m.* **diver,** *m.* (*swim.*) tuffatore, *m.*; (*in diving dress*) palombaro, *m.*; (*bird*) marangone, tuffetto, *m.*

diverge, *v.i.* divergere. **divergence,** *n.* divergenza, *f.* **divergent,** *a.* divergente.

diverse, *a.* diverso, differente, disparato. **diversify,** *v.t.* diversifi-

care, variare. **diversion,** *n.*
diversione, distrazione, *f.*, divertimento, *m.* **diversity,** *n.* diversità, *f.*
divert, *v.t.* sviare, stornare; *(amuse)*
divertire, distrarre.
Dives, *n.* ricco, *m.*, *(Bible)* il ricco
epulone, *m.*
divest, *v.t.* spogliare, svestire.
divide, *v.t.* dividere, ripartire,
disunire, separare; spartire, distribuire; *(Parl.)* fare votare, mettere
ai voti. ~*d skirt,* gonna-pantaloni,
f. **dividend,** *n.* dividendo; *(of
estate)* riparto, *m.* ~ *warrant,*
mandato per la riscossione del
dividendo, ordine di pagmento del
dividendo, *m.*; cedola di d., *f.*
dividers, *n.pl.* compassi, *m.pl.*
divination, *n.* divinazione, *f.* **divine,**
a. divino. ¶ *n.* ecclesiastico, teologo,
m. ¶ *v.t.* indovinare, presentire.
diviner, *n.* indovino, mago, *m.*
diving: ~ *bell,* *n.* campana da
palombaro, *f.* ~ *board,* trampolino,
m. ~ *dress,* scafandro, *m.*
divining rod, bacchetta divinatoria, *f.*
divinity, *n.* divinità, *f.*; *(science)*
teologia, *f.*, *(D.D.)* dottore in
teologia, *m.*
divisible, *a.* divisibile. **division,** *n.*
divisione, *f.*, spartimento, *m.*;
discordia, disunione, *f.*; voto, *m.*,
votazione, *f.*; sezione *(electoral, &c.).*
divisor, *n.* divisore, *m.*
divorce, *n.* divorzio, *m.* ¶ *v.t.*
divorziare, separare. *to be* ~*d,*
divorziarsi, essere divorziato.
divot, *n.* *(Golf)* piota, *f.*
divulge, *v.t.* divulgare, rivelare,
svelare, palesare.
dizziness, *n.* vertigine, *f.*, stordimento,
m. **dizzy,** *a.* vertiginoso, stordito.
do, *v.t. ir.* fare, compiere, commettere,
rendere, causare, *(cooking)* far
cuocere; *(distance)* percorrere. *v.i. ir.*
agire, fare; stare, andare, convenire,
bastare, riuscire. ~ *away with,*
abolire, sopprimere, fare sparire.
[please] do not touch, vietato toccare;
non toccare. ~ *nothing, n.* fannullone, *m.*, -a, *f.*; perdigiorno, *m.*
~ *one's hair,* pettinarsi. ~ *one's
utmost to,* fare tutto il possibile per.
~ *over again,* rifare. ~ *up,*
rimettere a nuovo; piegare, avvolgere
imballare, impacchettare; *(repair)*
riparare. ~ *without,* fare a meno di.
I have done, ho finito.
docile, *a.* docile. **docility,** *n.*
docilità, *f.*
dock, *n.* *(tail)* troncone, *m.*; sottocoda,

f.; *(Bot.)* romice, erba pazienza, *f.*,
lapazio, *m.*; *(court)* banco degli
accusati, degli imputati; *(Naut.)*
bacino, *m.*, darsena, *f.* ~ *company,*
compagnia, società dei bacini, *f.*
~ *strike,* sciopero dei lavoratori dei
bacini, dei portuali, *m.* ~ *warehouse,* magazzino doganale, *m.*
naval ~*yard,* arsenale; cantiere
navale, *m.* ¶ *v.t.* mozzare, tagliare;
fare entrare in bacino. *v.i.* entrare in
bacino. ~*er,* *n.* lavoratore dei
bacini, scaricatore, portuale, *m.*
docket, *n.* etichetta, *f.*, listino, *m.*
¶ *v.t.* fare un estratto (o sommario)
di, contrassegnare; munire di
etichetta.
doctor, *n.* dottore, medico, *m.* ¶ *v.t.*
curare, medicare, somministrare
medicina a; *(falsify)* adulterare,
falsificare. *(patch up)* raccomandare,
aggiustare, riparare. ~**ate,** *n.*
dottorato, *m.*
doctrinaire, *n. & a.* dottrinario,
m. & a. **doctrine,** *n.* dottrina, *f.*
document, *n.* documento, scritto, *m.*
~**s,** *n.pl.* documenti, *m.pl.*, carteg-
gio, *m.* ~ *cabinet,* casellario, *m.*
~ *case,* portafogli, *m.*, cartella, *f.*
¶ *v.t.* documentare. ~**ary,** *a.*
documentario.
dodder, *n.* *(Bot.)* cuscuta, *f.* ¶ *v.i.*
barcollare, vacillare, tremare.
dodge, *n.* gherminella, *f.*, raggiro,
gioco, artifizio, stratagemma,
sotterfugio, tiro, *m.* ¶ *v.t.* eludere,
schivare, raggirare; *(v.i.)* muoversi,
spostarsi rapidamente, cambiare di
posto, agire con sotterfugi, con
scaltrezza, saltare qua e là. **dodger,**
n. furbo, raggiratore, *m.* *artful* ~,
furbacchione, *m.*
doe, *n.* *(deer)* daina, *f.*; *(hare)* lepre
femmina, *f.*, *(rabbit)* coniglia, *f.*
~ *skin,* pelle di daina, *f.*
doer, *n.* fattore, chi fa, *m.*
doff, *v.t.* levarsi, togliere.
dog, *n.* cane, *m.*; *(fox, wolf)* (volpe)
maschio, cane lupo, *m.*; *(fire)*
alare, *m.* ~ *biscuit,* biscotto per
cani, *m.* ~ *cart,* biroccino, *m.*
~ *days,* *m.pl.* canicola, *f.*, giorni
canicolari, *m.pl.* ~*fish,* pescecane,
m. ~ *latin,* latino di sacrestia,
latino maccheronico, *m.* ~ *racing,*
or dogs, corse di levrieri, *f.pl.* ~
rose, rosa canina, eglantina, *f.* ~['s]
ear, angolo di pagina ripiegato.
v.t. ripiegare, fare l'orecchio ad
una pagina. ~ *show,* esposizione
canina, *f.* ~ *violet,* violetta dei

boschi, violetta canina, *f.* ¶ *v.t.*
seguire (come un cane), spiare.
to ~ one's steps, seguire la pista di.
dogged, *a.* ostinato, accanito,
violento, determinato. ~**ly,** *ad.*
ostinatamente, accanitamente, &c.
~**ness,** *n.* ostinazione, risolutezza,
tenacia, *f.,* accanimento, *m.*
doggerel, *n.* cattivi versi, versi
irregolari, *m.pl.*
doggy *or* **doggie,** *n.* canino, *m.*
dogma, *n.* dogma, domma, *m.*
dogmatic, *a.* dogmatico. **dogmatize,** *v.i.* dogmatizzare.
doily, *n.* salviettina, *f.*
doings, *n.pl.* fatti, *m.pl.,* faccende,
f.pl.; (*underhand*) modi clandestini
d'agire, *m.pl. your doing,* (*fig.*)
colpa tua, sua, &c. *those are fine
doings,* Lei ne fa delle belle.
doldrums, (*Naut.*) calme equatoriali,
f.pl. to be in the ~, (*fig.*) essere
malinconico, essere d'umor nero.
dole, *n.* carità, elemosina; piccola
quantità, *f.* ~ *out,* distribuire in
piccole quantità. ~**ful,** *a.* lugubre.
doll *&* **dolly,** *n.* bambola, bambolina,
f., fantoccio, *m.* ~*-faced,* paffuto.
~*'s house,* casa di bambola, *f.*
dollar, *n.* dollaro, *m.*
dolomite, *n.* dolomite, *f.* *the
Dolomites,* le Dolomiti, *f.pl.*
dolphin, *n.* (*porpoise*) delfino, *m.;*
(*dorado*) dorata, *f.;* (*mooring*) palo
d'ormeggio, *m.*
dolt, *n.* balordo, minchione, stupido,
m.
domain, *n.* demanio, *m.* (*fig.*) dominio,
m.
dome, *n.* cupola, *f.*
domestic, *a.* domestico, casalingo;
(*coal or like*) di casa, casalingo;
(*trade*) interno, nazionale. ~
training, scuola per massaie, *f.*
¶ *n.* domestico, *m.,* -a, *f.;* servo, *m.,*
-a, *f.* **domesticate,** *v.t.* rendere
casalingo, domestico; (*animals*)
addomesticare. **domesticated,** *a.*
(*pers.*) casalingo. **domesticity,** *n.*
domesticità, *f.*
domicile, *n.* domicilio, *m.* ¶ *v.t.*
domiciliare. *domiciliary visit,* perquisizione domiciliare, *f.*
dominant, *a.* dominante. **dominate,**
v.t. & i. dominare. **domination,** *n.,*
dominazione, *f.* **domineer,** *v.t.*
dominare. *v.i.* spadroneggiare.
~**ing,** *a.* prepotente, imperioso,
dominatore.
Dominican, *n.* domenicano, *m.*
dominion, *n.* dominio, *m.;* impero,

m.; padronanza, *f.* *D~ of Canada,
of New Zealand,* Dominio del
Canadà, della Nuova Zelanda, *m.*
domino, *n.* domino, *m.inv. game of
~oes,* partita a domino, *f.*
don, *v.t.* indossare, mettere, vestire.
don, *n.* insegnante universitario,
dotto, *m.*
donation, *n.* dono, *m.;* (*Law*) donazione, *f.;* (*pl.*) carità, elemosina, *f.*
done, *p.p.* fatto; (*Cook*) cotto.
donee, *n.* donatario, *m.*
donkey, *n.* asino, asinello, ciuco, *m.*
~ *driver,* asinaio, *m.* ~ *engine,*
cavallino, *m.* ~ *pump,* pompa di
alimentazione, *f.*
donor, *n.* donatore, *m.,* -trice, *f.;*
(*Law*) donante, *m.f.*
doom, *n.* condanna; sorte funesta, *f.*
¶ *v.t.* condannare; destinare
fatalmente. **doomsday,** *n.* giudizio
universale, *m.;* (*fig.*) le calende
greche.
door, *n.* porta, *f.;* uscio, ingresso, *m.;*
(*carriage, car*) sportello, *m. revolving
~,* porta girevole. *swing ~,* porta
volante, *f.,* (*peephole*) spioncino, *m.*
~ *bell,* campanello, *m.* ~ *curtain,*
portiera, *f.* ~*keeper,* portinaio, *m.*
-a, *f.* ~ *mat,* stuoia, *f.* ~*step,*
soglia, *f.* ~*way,* vano (della porta),
m.
dorado, *n.* dorata, *f.*
Dorcas, *n.* ~ *society,* società di
beneficenza, *f.*
Doric, *a. & n.* dorico, *a. & m.*
dormant, *a.* addormentato, latente,
inattivo; caduto in disuso, giacente.
~ (*or sleeping*) *partner,* socio
accomandante, socio occulto, *m.*
dormer [window], *n.* abbaino, *m.*
dormitory, *n.* dormitorio, *m.*
dormouse, *n.* ghiro, *m.*
dory, *n.* orada, *f.;* pesce S. Pietro, *m.*
dose, *n.* dose, *f.* ¶ *v.t.* dosare.
dot, *n.* punto, *m.;* (*child*) piccolino,
piccino, *m.* ¶ *v.t.* punteggiare,
(*Mus.*) puntare. *dotted line,* linea
punteggiata, *f.*
dotage, *n.* imbecillità, *f.,* rimbambi-
mento, *m.* **dotard,** *n.* vecchio
rimbambito; (*of comedy*) pantalone,
m. **dote** *or* **doat,** *v.i.* rimbambire.
~ *on,* innamorarsi follemente di;
essere infatuato di.
double, *a.* doppio; (*bent*) curvo.
~ *n. s. &c.* (*spelling*), doppia n. s., *&c.*
~ *oh, five, six, sev-en,* ate (*Teleph.*),
doppio zero, cinque, sei, sette, otto.
~ *acting,* a doppio effetto. ~
barrelled gun, fucile a due canne, *m.*

~ *bass*, contrabbasso, *m.* ~ *bed*, letto matrimoniale, *m.* ~[-*bedded*] *room*, camera a due letti, *f.* ~ *breasted*, a doppio petto. ~ *collar*, collo rovesciato. ~ *cream cheese*, formaggio di latte non scremato. ~ *cuffs*, *m.*, polsini alla moschettiera, *m.pl.* ~ *dealing*, doppiezza, malafede, *f.* ~ *edged*, a due tagli; (*fig.*) ambiguo. ~ *entry book-keeping*, tenuta dei libri in partita doppia. ~ *faced*, doppio in malafede. ~-*fronted* (*house*), a due facciate. ~ *meaning* or ~ *entendre*, frase, locuzione o parola a doppio senso, senso equivoco. ~ *saucepan*, bagnomaria, *m.* ~ *width* (*cloth*), doppia larghezza, doppia altezza. ¶ *ad.* doppio. ¶ *n.* doppio, *m.*, (*Turf*) doppia vittoria, colpo di due; (*counterpart*) controparte, *f.* *at the* ~ (*Mil.*), a passo di corsa, a passo ginnico. ~*s game* (*Ten.*), partita doppia, *f.* ¶ *v.t.* & *i.* doppiare, raddoppiare; moltiplicare per due; raddoppiarsi; piegare in due; serrare; (*dodge*) fare una giravolta.

doubt, *n.* dubbio, *m.* ¶ *v.t.* dubitare di, sospettare, (*v.i.*) dubitare, stare in dubbio. *no doubt*, senza dubbio. ~*ful*, *a.* dubbio, dubbioso, incerto. ~*less*, *a.* senza dubbio.

douceur, *n.* mancia, *f.*

douche, *n.* doccia, *f.*

dough, *n.* pasta, *f.*

doughty, *a.* valoroso, prode, eroico. ~ *deeds*, azioni eroiche, *f.pl.*, atti d'eroismo, *m.pl.*

dour, *a.* ostinato.

douse, *v.t.* immergere, tuffare; abbassare, spegnere, estinguere.

dove, *n.* colomba, *f.* ~*cot*[*e*], colombaia, *f.* ~*tail*, *n.* coda di rondine, *f.* ¶ *v.t.* incastrare a coda di rondine, calettare a c. di r.

dowager, *n.* vedova nobile (che gode di un doario), *f.* *queen* ~, regina madre, *f.*

dowdy, *a.* sciatto, disordinato, negletto (*dress* or *person*).

dowel, *n.* piolo, *m.*, cavicchio, *m.*, caviglia, *f.* ¶ *v.t.* incavigliare.

dower, *n.* doario, *m.* ¶ *v.t.* dotare.

down, *a.* abbassato, basso; caduto; discendente; disceso; tramontato. ~*grade*, discesa, *f.* *on the* ~*grade*, in discesa. ~ *line*, ~ *train*, linea discendente, treno discendente. *on the* ~ *journey*, all'andata.

down, *ad.* giú, abbasso, a terra; (*prices*) in ribasso; (*crossword clues*)

verticalmente. (*sun*, *moon*) tramontato. *at the going* ~ *of the sun*, *of the moon*, al tramonto del sole, della luna. *to walk with the head* ~, *the hands* ~, camminare con la testa bassa, le mani in giú. ~ *at heel*, scalcagnato. ~ *there*, laggiú. ~ *below*, giú ,di sotto. ~ *to*, fino a.

down- (*comps*), ~*cast*, abbattuto, accasciato, triste. ~*fall*, caduta, rovina, *f.* ~*hearted*, scoraggiato, abbattuto. ~*hill*, in discesa, discendente. ~*pour*, acquazzone, rovescio di pioggia, *m.*, forte pioggia, *f.* ~*right*, *a.* franco, schietto, positivo; (*deprec.*) matricolato; (*ad.*) affatto. ~*stairs*, *ad.* giú per le scale; al pian terreno. ~*stream*, *ad.* a filo dell'acqua, con la corrente, secondo corrente. ~*stroke*, *n.* (*piston*) colpo discendente (dello stantuffo); (*writing*) asta grossa, *f.* ~*trodden*, calpestato, oppresso. ~*ward*, *a.* discendente. ~*ward*[*s*], *ad.* in basso, in discesa, in giú, all'in giú.

down, *i.* giú! discendete! sedete! ~ *with* . . ., abbasso . . .

down, *n.* lanugine, peluria, *f.*; primo pelo, *m.*; collina bassa, collina erbosa, *f.*; (*sand-hill*) duna, *f.* ~ *quilt*, piumino, *m.*

down, *pr.* lungo, discendendo, secondo.

down, *v.t.* deporre, abbassare, abbattere. ~ *tools* (*strike*), scioperare.

downy, *a.* (coperto) di lanugine, di peluria; lanuginoso; (*fig.*) dolce, soffice.

dowral, *a.* dotale. **dowry**, *n.* dote, *f.*; doario, *m.*

dowser, *n.* rabdomante, *m.f.* **dowsing**, *n.* rabdomanzia, *f.* ~ *rod*, bacchetta divinatoria (d'un rabdomante), *f.*

doyley, *n.* salviettina, *f.*

doze, *v.i.* assopirsi, sonnecchiare. *to have a* ~, fare una dormita; schiacciare un sonnellino.

dozen, *n.* dozzina, *f.* *by the dozen*, per dozzina, alla dozzina.

drab, *a.* sbiadito, scolorito, monotono, grigio bruno; comune, ordinario.

drachm, *n.* (*apothecaries' measure*) = 3.552 millilitres. *a* ~*'s weight* = 3.888 grammes.

drachma, *n.* dracma, *f.*

draff, *n.* (*Brewing*) rifiuti di malto, *m.pl.*; feccia dell'orzo, *f.*

draft, *n.* (*men*) distaccamento; (*outline*) abbozzo, *m.*; bozza, *f.*; (*drawing bill* *or cheque*), tratta, *f.*; (*bill, cheque*) vaglia (cambiario), assegno circolare, *m.* ¶ *v.t.* stendere, abbozzare, disegnare; (*writings*) redigere; (*Mil.*) arruolare. **draftsman,** *n.* disegnatore; estensore; compositore; (*writings*) redattore.

drag, *n.* impedimento, ostacolo, *m.*; (*dredger*) draga, *f.*; (*wheel*) scarpa, *f.*; zoccolo, *m.*; (*carriage*) carrozza (a quattro cavalli); carrozzone; (*net*) rete a strascico; tramaglio; trascino, *m.*; scorticaria, *f.* ¶ *v.t.* tirare, trascinare per forza, strascinare; (*wheel*) frenare; (*pond*) dragare; (*anchor*) arare. *v.i.* trascinarsi, avanzare con difficoltà. ~ *about, v.t.* trascinare, stiracchiare.

draggle, *v.t.* strascicare, inzaccherare; (*v.i.*) trascinarsi.

dragoman, *n.* dragomanno, *m.*

dragon, *n.* drago, *m.* ~*fly,* libellula, *f.* ~*'s blood,* sangue di drago, *m.*

dragoon, *n.* dragone, *m.* ¶ ~ *into,* costringere a, intimidire.

drain, *n.* fogna, *f.*, scolatoio, canale di scolo, *m.*, (*demand*) drenaggio, *m.* ~*pipe,* tubo di drenaggio; tubo di scolo, tubo di scarico, *m.* ¶ *v.t.* fare scolare, drenare, fognare; prosciugare; vuotare; (*fig.*) esaurire, lasciare a secco. ~ *away,* far colare (l'acqua) da . . . ~**age,** *n.* scolo, drenaggio, *m.*; fognatura, *f.* (*surplus water*), scolatura, *f.* ~**er,** *n.* scolatoio, *m.* ~**ing,** *n.* (*land*) prosciugamento, *m.* ~*ing rack, n.* scolapiatti, *m.inv.*

drake, *n.* papero, anitra (maschio), *m.*

dram, *n.* (*avoirdupois*) = 1.772 grammes; (*draught*) goccia, *f.*; bicchierino, *m.* ~*shop,* spaccio di liquori, *m.*

drama, *n.* dramma, *m.* the ~, il teatro. **dramatic,** *-a.* drammatico. *dramatis personae,* personaggi, *m.pl.*

dramatist, *n.* autore, -trice, drammatico, -a., *m.f.*; drammaturgo, *m.* **dramatize,** *v.t.* drammatizzare.

drape, *v.t.* coprire di panno; panneggiare; parare. **draper,** *n.* (*cloth*) pannaiuolo, *m.*; (*general*) negoziante di tessuti; merciaio; mercante di pannine, *m.* ~**y,** *n.* drapperia, *f.*; (*Art*) panneggiamento, *m.*

drastic, *a.* drastico.

draught, *n.* (*drink*) sorso, *m.*, sorsata, *f.*; pozione, bibita, bevanda, *f.*; (*air*) corrente d'aria, *f.*; (*fire*) tiraggio, *m.*; (*design*) disegno,

tracciato, schizzo, piano, progetto; (*writing*) brutta copia, *f.*; (*fish*) retata, *f.*; prodotto della pesca, *m.*; (*ships*) pescaggio, *m.*; immersione, *f.*; (*pl., game*) giuoco della dama, *m.* ~ *horse,* ~ *ox,* cavallo, bue da tiro, *m.* ~ *beer,* birra da barile, *f.* ~ *board,* tavoliere, *m.* ¶ *v.t.* (see *draft*) disegnare, redigere. **draughtsman,** *n.* disegnatore, *n.*, (*writings*) redattore, *m.* **draughty,** *a.* esposto a correnti d'aria.

draw, *n.* tirata, *f.*; sorteggio, *m.*, estrazione (di lotteria); attrazione, lusinga, *f.*; (*game*) partita nulla, *f.*

draw, *v.t.* *ir.* tirare, attirare, trarre, trascinare; attingere, spillare; disegnare; estrarre; (*Fin.*) trarre, prelevare; (*Metal*) trafilare; (*so much water—ship*) pescare; (*wages*) riscuotere, percepire; *v.i. ir.* tirare, trarsi, muoversi, dirigersi; (*tea*) farsi. ~ *a game,* fare partita nulla. ~ *aside,* farsi da parte. ~*back,* farsi indietro, rinculare, indietreggiare, ritirarsi; (*curtains*) aprire (le tendine). ~ *down,* tirar giù, abbassare, far discendere. ~ *in* (days), accorciarsi, abbreviarsi. ~ *near,* accostarsi, avvicinarsi. ~ *off, v.t.* tirare, (*water*) attingere, (*wine*) spillare; vuotare; ritirare. *v.i.* ritirarsi, allontanarsi. ~ *on,* tirare innanzi; indossare; infilare; (*Com.*) trarre su; (*time*) avvicinarsi. ~ *the long bow,* esagerare. ~ *out, v.t.* cavar fuori, farsi pagare, levare; prolungare; estrarre. *v.i.* allungarsi; prolungarsi; distendersi. ~ *up, v.t.* tirare su; tirare in alto; (*boat*) tirare a terra; alzare; (*writing*) redigere; stendere; (*Mil.*) disporre in fila, allineare. *v.i.* (*carriage*) fermarsi.

drawback, *n.* (*Cust.*) rimborso di dazio; dazio di ritorno; (*fig.*) inconveniente, svantaggio, *m.*

drawbridge, *n.* ponte levatoio, *m.*

drawee, *n.* trattario, *m.*

drawer, *n.* (*wire, &c.*) tenditore; (*tavern*) garzone, *m.*; (*of bill, cheque*) traente. *m.f. refer to* ~, rivolgetevi al traente; (*receptacle*) cassetto, tiretto, *m.*; (*pl. chest*) cassettone, comò, *m.*; (*pl. dress*) mutande, *f.pl.*

drawing, *n.* disegno, *m.*, (*lottery*) estrazione, *f.*; (*lots*) sorteggio, *m.* ~ *board,* tavola da disegno, *f.* ~ *knife,* coltello a due manichi, c. da bottaio, *m.* ~ *pen,* tiralinee; *m.inv.* ~ *pin,* puntina da disegno, *f.* ~ *room,* salotto, salone, *m.*; (*court*) ricevimento, *m.*

drawl, *v.t.* strascicare (le parole).
draw-leaf-table. tavola da allungare, *f.*
drawn: ~ *battle,* battaglia indecisa, *f.* ~ *face,* viso contratto, sparuto, sofferente, *m.* ~ *game,* partita nulla, *f.* ~ *number,* numero estratto, *m.* ~ *sword.* spada nuda s. sguainata, *f.*
drawplate, *n.* filiera, *f.*
dray, *n.* carromatto, *m.*; camion, *m.* ~ *horse,* cavallo da carromatto, da traino, *m.* ~*man,* carrettiere, *m.*
dread, *a.* terribile, pauroso. ¶ *n.* timore, *m.* paura, *f.,* terrore, spavento, *m.* ¶ *v.t.* temere, aver paura. ~**ful,** *a.* pauroso, terribile, spaventevole, potente. *Dreadnought,* (*Nav.*) nave da battaglia, *f.*
dream, *n.* sogno, *m.* ¶ *v.i. & t. ir.* sognare, fare un sogno; immaginarsi. ~ *of,* sognare, concepire. ~**er,** *n.* sognatore, -trice, *m.f.*; visionario, -a, *m.f.* ~**y,** *a.* da sognatore; vago; vano; pieno di sogni.
drear[y]. *a.* triste, tetro, lugubre, desolato. **dreariness,** *n.* desolazione; tristezza; tetraggine, *f.*
dredge, *n.* draga, *f.* ¶ *v.t.* dragare; (*sprinkle*) cospargere. **dredger,** *n.* draga, *f.* **dredging,** *n.* dragaggio; cospargimento, *m.*
dregs, *n.pl.* feccia, *f.*
drench, *v.t.* bagnare, inzuppare, inondare. ~*ing rain,* pioggia penetrante, dirotta.
Dresden, *n.* Dresda, *f.* ~ *china,* porcellana di Sassonia, *f.*
dress, *n.* abito, vestito, abbigliamento, *m.,* veste, *f.*; vestiti, *m.pl.*; vestiario, *m.* ~ *bow,* cravatta da società, *f.* ~ *circle,* prima galleria, *f.* ~ *circle seat,* posto nella prima galleria, *m.* ~ *coat,* abito da sera, *m.,* giubba, *f.* abito da cerimonia, *m.* ~ *guard* (*cycle*), paraveste, *m.* ~*maker,* sarta, *f.* ~*making,* confezione di vesti, *f.,* sartoria, *f.* ~ *protector,* sotto-ascelle, *m.f. inv.* ~ *rehearsal,* prova generale, *f.* ~ *shirt,* camicia da sera, *f.* ~ *shoes,* scarpe di vernice, *f.pl.* ~ *boots,* stivaletti di vernice, *m.pl.* ~ *stand,* manichino, *m.* ~ [*suit*], ~ *clothes,* abito da sera, da cerimonia, *m.,* gran tenuta, *f.* ¶ *v.t.* vestire, abbigliare; (*in fancy dress*) vestire in abito da maschera; (*ship with flags*) pavesare; (*wound*) medicare; (*food*) apprestare; preparare; (*salad*) condire; (*materials*) preparare, trattare; (*stone*) conciare;

(*Mil.*) allineare. ~ *oneself,* vestirsi, abbigliarsi. ~ *one's hair,* pettinarsi. ~ ~ *for dinner,* vestirsi, abbigliarsi per pranzo. ~ *like a guy,* infagottarsi, vestire come uno spauracchio. ~ *the window*(*s*); fare la vetrina. ~ *up,* ~ *out,* abbellire, adornare; parare; camuffare. **dresser,** *n.* (*Theat.*) vestiarista, *m.f.*; abbigliatore, -trice, *m.f.*; (*Med.*) assistente, *m.f.*; (*kitchen*) tavola da cucina, *f.,* scaffale da cucina, *m.* **dressing,** *n.* abbigliamento, *m.*; (*of wound*) medicazione, *f.*; (*on wound*) medicamento, *m.*; (*food*) preparazione, *f.*; (*salad*) condimento, *m.* ~ *case,* astuccio da toletta, *m.* ~ *comb,* pettine da toletta, *m.* ~ *gown,* veste da camera; vestaglia; accappatoio, *m.* ~ *jacket,* camicino, *m.* ~ *room,* gabinetto da toletta, *m.*; toletta, *f.*; (*Theat.*) camerino, spogliatoio, *m.* ~ *table,* toletta, *f.,* tavolo da toletta, *m.*
dribble, *n.* goccia, *f.*; (*slaver*) bava; saliva, *f.* ¶ *v.i.* (*aux.* avere) gocciolare; fare bava. *v.t.* (*Foot.*) palleggiare. **dribbling,** (*Foot.*) palleggio, *m.* *in drib*[*b*]*lets,* a pezzettini.
dried, *p.a.* secco, seccato, messo a secco; prosciugato, asciugato; (*raisins, fruit, fish, &c.*) uva secca, frutta secca, pesce secco; (*apples, &c., in rings*) mele secche, *f.pl.* **drier,** *n.* essiccatoio, stenditoio, *m.* (*s. or pl. for paint.*) seccativo, *m.*
drift, *n.* mira, tendenza, portata; direzione, *f.*; scopo, *m.*; mucchio, ammasso, *m.*; (*snow*) turbine, *m.*; falda, *f.*; cumulo, *m.*; (*Naut. & fig.*) deriva, *f.*; (*Min.*) galleria, *f.*; (*Geol.*) deposito alluionale, *m.* (*net*) strascino, traino, *m.* ~[*pin*], spina, *f.* ~*wood,* legname portato dalla corrente, *m.* ¶ *v.t.* portare, trascinare; accumulare, bloccare; (*v.i.*) portarsi, lasciarsi portare, trascinarsi; (*Naut.*) derivare, andare alla deriva; accumularsi, ammonticchiarsi. ~**er** (*boat*), *n.* motopeschereccio, *m.*
drill, *n.* trapano, succhiello, trivello, *m.*; punta di trapano, *f.*; (*Min.*) perforatrice, *f.*; (*furrow*) solco, *m.*; (*agric. mach.*) seminatoio, *m.,* seminatrice, *f.*; (*Mil.*) esercitazione, *f.*; (*fabric*) traliccio, *m.* ~ *bow,* archetto, *m.* ~ *ground,* piazza d'armi, *f.,* campo di manovra, *m.* ~ [*holder*], trapano, portasucchiello, *m.* ~ *sergeant,* sergente istruttore, *m.* ¶ *v.t.* forare,

perforare, bucare; seminare in solchi; (*Mil.*) esercitare; (*v.i.*) esercitarsi, fare un corso di esercitazioni. **drilling,** *n.* perforamento, *m.*; perforazione, *m.*; semina a solchi, *f.*; (*Mil.*) esercitazione, *f.* ~ *machine,* perforatrice, *f.*

drily, *ad.* (*answer coldly*) seccamente, freddamente; (*with dry sarcasm*) causticamente, sarcasticamente.

drink, *n.* bibita, bevanda, *f.*; beveraggio, *m.*; bevuta, sorsata, *f.* *to have a* ~, bere qualche cosa. ~ *money,* mancia, *f.* ¶ *v.t. & i. ir.* bere. ~ *in* (*fig.*), assorbire, imbeversi di. ~ *off,* bere d'un fiato, tracannare, (bere) in un sol sorso. ~**able,** *a.* potabile. ~**er,** *n.* bevitore, -trice, *m.f.* ~**ing,** *att.*: ~ *fountain,* fontana pubblica, *f.* ~ *song,* canzone bacchica, *f.* ~ *straw,* paglia, cannuccia, *f.* ~ *trough,* abbeveratoio, *m.* ~ *water,* acqua potabile, *f.*

drip, *n.* goccia, *f.*, gocciolamento, *m.*, stillicidio, *m.* ~ (*stone*), pietra da filtro, *f.* ¶ *v.i.* stillare, gocciolare; gemere, trapelare. **dripping,** *n.* gocciolamento, stillicidio, *m.*; grasso d'arrosto, *m.* ~ *pan,* leccarda, *f.* ~ *wet,* tutto bagnato, bagnato fradicio, tutto inzuppato.

drive, *n.* passeggiata in carrozza, corsa in carrozza, scarrozzata, *f.*; viale, corso, *m.*; passeggiata per le carrozze, *f.*; energia, forza, *f.*, sforzo, *m.*; (*hunt.*) caccia, *f.*; (*Mach.*) trasmissione, *f.*; (*golf*) colpo, *m.*; (*Ten.*) volata diritta, *f.*; (*Min.*) galleria, *f.* ¶ *v.t. ir.* spingere, cacciare; sospingere; costringere, forzare; ridurre; fare; far marciare; (*horse, car, &c.*) guidare, condurre; (*nail*) conficcare; (*golf*) tirare (il colpo); (*screw*) girare (una vite), avvitare, torcere; (*Mach.*) far marciare, governare; (*Min.*) scavare, perforare. ~ *one mad,* far perdere la testa a, rendere furioso, far impazzire. *v.i. ir.* andare in carrozza; affrettarsi, balzare, precipitarsi; (*of snow, rain*) battere, sferzare; (*fig.*) mirare a, tendere a. ~ *ashore,* (*ship*) essere gettato sulla costa, arenarsi. ~ *away, v.t.* scacciare, cacciare; (*v.i.*) partire (in carrozza). ~ *back, v.t.* respingere; (*v.i.*) ritornare in carrozza. ~ *into a corner,* cacciare (ricacciare) in un angolo. ~ *out,* ~ *off, v.t.* espellere, cacciar fuori, spinger fuori, far uscire; (*v.i.*)

uscire in carrozza. ~ *slowly,* (*traffic sign*) adagio, al passo.

drivel, *n.* bava; sciocchezza, stupidaggine, *f.* ¶ *v.i.* far bava; (*fig.*) farneticare.

driver, *n.* cocchiere, carrettiere, conduttore, vetturino, *m.*; autista (*motor*), (*Rly.*) macchinista, *m.*; (*golf*) mazza, *f.*, bastone, *m.* ~'*s licence,* patente di abilitazione, *f.*

driving, *n.* maniera di condurre, di guidare, *f.* azione di spingere, di cacciare, *f.*; (*Mech.*) azionamento, comando, *m.*; trasmissione, *f.*; (*nails, piles*) conficcamento, *m.*; (*piles*) infissione, *f.* ~ *mirror,* specchio retrospettivo, *m.* ~ *rain,* pioggia con raffiche, p. sferzante, *f.* ~ *shaft,* albero di trasmissione, albero motore, *m.* ~ *wheel,* ruota motrice, *f.*

drizzle, *n.* pioggia fine, pioggerella, *f.* ¶ *v.i.* piovigginare.

droll, *a.* bizzarro, burlone, comico, faceto. ~**ery,** *n.* buffoneria, *f.*, scherzo, *m.*; modi scherzevoli, *m.pl.* **drolly,** *ad.* in modo bizzarro, scherzevole; burlescamente, comicamente.

dromedary, *n.* dromedario, *m.*

drone, *n.* ronzio, *m.*; pigrone, fannullone, *m.*; (*Mus.*) bordone, *m.* ~ (*bee*), calabrone, *m.*, fuco, *m.* ¶ *v.i.* ronzare; salmodire.

droop, *v.i.* pendere, curvarsi, lasciar cader la testa; (*wilt*) languire. ~**ing,** *a.* pendente, languente. ~ *looks,* aria languida, *f.*, sguardi languidi, *m.pl.* ~ *spirits,* spirito abbattuto, morale abbattuto, *m.*, depressione di spirito, *f.*

drop, *n.* goccia, gocciola, gocciolina, *f.* (*sweet*) pastiglia, *f.*; (*fall*) caduta, *f.*, ribasso, *m.*; (*gallows*) botola, *f.*, trabocchetto, *m.*; (*ear-ring*) pendente, ciondolo, *m.*; (*drink*) sorso, gocciolino, *m.*, goccia, *f.* ~ *bottle,* contagocce, *m.inv.* ~ *curtain,* sipario, *m.* ~ *forged,* impresso. ~ *kick,* (*Rugby*) calcio di rimbalzo, *m.* ~ *stamp,* maglio a caduta, *m.* ¶ *v.t.* lasciar cadere; abbandonare, rinunziare a; abbassare; trascurare, smettere, lasciar sfuggire, insinuare; (*anchor*) gettare; (*curtain, Theat., &c.*) calare; (*pers. at door*) deporre, lasciare alla porta; (*letter in post*) gettare; (*a line*) scrivere, inviare; (*a stitch*) lasciar cadere; (*tear*) versare; (*her young*) partorire. *v.i.* cadere, cascare; calare; gocciolare; cessare;

abbattersi. *dropped stitch* (*Knit.*), maglia caduta, *f.* **dropper,** *n.* or *dropping-tube,* contagocce, *m.inv.*
droppings (*dung*), *n.pl.* sterco, *m.*
dropsical, *a.* idropico. **dropsy,** *n.* idropisia, *f.*
dross, *n.* scoria, *f.*; (*fig.*) rifiuto, *m*
drought, *n.* siccità, secchezza, *f.*
drove, *n.* branco, gregge, *m.*; mandra, *f.* **drover,** *n.* bovaro, mandriano, conducente di bestiame, *m.*
drown, *v.t.* annegare, affogare; (*sounds*) soffocare, dominare, coprire. *v.i.* annegare, affogare. ~ *oneself,* annegarsi, affogarsi. *the* [*apparently*] ~*ed,* gli annegati, *m.pl.* ~**ing,** *n.* sommersione, *f.*; (*fatality*) annegamento, affogamento, *m.* *a* ~ *man,* un annegato.
drowsiness, *n.* sonnolenza, *f.*, assopimento, *m.* **drowsy,** *a.* assopito, addormentato, sonnacchioso. *to make* ~, assopire, addormentare.
drub, *v.t.* bastonare. **drubbing,** *n.* bastonatura, *f.*
drudge, *n.* schiavo, uomo di fatica, chi attende ad un lavoro ingrato, *m.*, schiava, donna di servizio indefesso, *f.* ¶ *v.i.* sfacchinare, lavorare come un negro. ~**ry,** *n.* lavoro ingrato, lavoro penoso, *m.*; miseria, *f.*
drug, *n.* droga, *f.*, medicamento, *m.*; narcotico, *m.* ~ *traffic,* commercio dei narcotici, *m.* ~*store,* drogheria, farmacia, *f.* ¶ *v.t.* narcotizzare.
drugget, *n.* droghetto, *m.*
druggist, *n.* farmacista, *m.*; (*wholesale*) droghiere, *m.*
Druid, *n.* Druido, *m.*
drum, *n.* tamburo, *m.*; (*ear*) timpano, *m.*; cilindro, *m.* ~*head,* pelle del tamburo, *f.*, rondo del tamburo, *m.* ~*head court martial,* tribunale militare, *m.* ~ *major,* tamburo maggiore, *m.* ~ *stick,* bacchetta da tamburo, *f.*; (*fowl*) gamba di pollo, *f.* ¶ *v.i.* battere il tamburo; tamburreggiare. ~ *into,* fare entrare in mente a forza di ripetere. **drummer,** *n.* tamburo, tamburino, *m.*
drunk, *a.* ub[b]riaco, briaco; ebbro; avvinato; sborniato; cotto; alticcio. *to get* ~, ub[b]riacarsi. ~**ard,** *n.* ub[b]riacone, -a, *m.f.* ~**en,** *a.* ub[b]riaco, ebbro. ~ *bout,* orgia, *f.* ~ *brawl,* disputa violenta di ub[b]riachi, *f.* ~**enness,** *n.* ub[b]riachezza, sbornia, *f.*; (*habitual*) ub[b]riachezza, *f.*, alcoolismo, *m.*
dry, *a.* secco, arido, asciutto, prosciugato, a secco; assetato, sitibondo;

sarcastico, caustico, mordace; insipido, uggioso. ~ *dock,* bacino di carenaggio, *m.* ~ *fly fishing,* pesca alla mosca secca, *f.* ~*land,* (*opp. sea*), ~ *place,* secco, *m.*, terraferma, *f.* ~ *goods,* cereali; tessuti, *m.pl.*; stoffe, *f.pl.* ~ *measure,* misura per cereali, *f.* ~ *nurse,* balia asciutta, *f.* ~ *point,* incisione a secco, *f.* ~ *rot,* fungo del legno, tarlo del legno, *m.* ~ *salter,* droghiere, *m.* ~ *saltery,* drogheria, *f.* ~ *shampoo,* frizione, *f.* ~ *shod,* *a. & ad.* a piedi asciutti, senza bagnarsi i piedi. ¶ *v.t. & i.* seccare, prosciugare, asciugare, essiccare, mettere a secco; (*v.i.*) asciugare, asciugarsi, essiccarsi. ~ *up,* asciugare, seccarsi, inaridirsi. ~*-clean,* pulire a secco.
dryad, *n.* driade, *f.*
dryer[s] (*for paint.*), seccativo, *m.*
drying, *n.* essiccamento, disseccamento, prosciugamento, *m.* ~ *room,* essiccatoio, *m.*, camera d'essiccamento, *f.* ~ *stove,* apparecchio essiccatore, *m.* ~ *yard,* seccatoio, tenditoio, *m.* **dryly,** *ad.* same as *drily.* **dryness,** *n.* secchezza, aridità, siccità, *f.*
dual, *a.* doppio; (*Gram.*) duale.
dub, *v.t.* (*knight*) armare, creare cavaliere, rivestire del titolo di . . . ; (*nickname*) soprannominare; battezzare; qualificare.
dubbin[g], *n.* grasso (per stivali), *m.*
dubious, *a.* dubbio, incerto, indeciso, dubbioso.
ducal, *a.* ducale. **duchess,** *n.* duchessa, *f.* **duchy,** *n.* ducato, *m.*
duck, *n.* anitra, *f.*; (*dip*) tuffo, *m.*; (*Box, &c.*) schivata, *f.*; (*cloth*) traliccio, *m.*, tela olona, *f.* ~*s & drakes* (*game*), giuoco di rimbalzella, *m.* ~**s,** *pl.* calzoni di traliccio, vestito di traliccio. ~ *pond,* pozzanghera, *f.* ~*'s egg,* uovo d'anitra, *m.*; (*cricket*) zero. ~*weed,* lente palustre, *f.* ¶ *v.t.* tuffare, immergere, sommergere; (*v.i.*) abbassare il capo, curvare il capo, chinare. ~**ling,** *n.* anitroccolo, *m.* ~[y] (*pers.*), carino, -a, coricino, -a, *m.f.*
duct, *n.* condotto, tubo, canale, *m.*; (*Zool., Bot.*) vaso, *m.*
ductile, *a.* (*metals*) duttile; (*pers.*) docile.
dudgeon (*in*), in collera.
due, *a.* dovuto, debito, esigibile, pagabile; doveroso, regolare, giusto,

prescritto; accaduto; maturato; legittimo, meritato. *the train is due at*, il treno arriva a . . . *ir ~ course*, a tempo (debito), a tempo e luogo; regolarmente. *~ date*, scadenza, *f*. *over~*, scaduto; tardi, in ritardo. ¶ *ad*. direttamente, in pieno. ¶ *n*. dovuto, *m*.; quota, *f*.; (*duty*) imposta, tassa, *f*., diritto, *m*. *customs' ~s*, dazio doganale, *m*., gabella, *f*. *to give everyone his ~*, dare ad ognuno il suo.

duel, *n*. duello, *m*. *to fight a ~*. battersi in duello. **duellist**, *n*, duellante, duellista, *m*.

duenna, *n*. donna attempata, governante, *f*.

duet[t], *n*. duetto, *m*.

duffer, *n*. minchione, sciocco, *m*.; (*at a game*) schiappa, *f*.; schiappino, *m*.

dug, *n*. mammela, poppa, *f*.

dug-out, *n*. ricovero, *m*.

duke, *n*. duca, *m*. *~dom*, *n*. ducato, *m*.

dulcet, *a*. dolce.

dulcimer, *n*. dolcemele, *m*.

dull, *a*. (*of colour*) fosco, smorto, scuro; (*of sound*) sordo, senza risonanza; (*of light*) debole; (*edge*) smussato; (*opp. of bright*) appannato; insipido, scipito, ottuso, pesante, triste, uggioso, stupido. *the weather is ~*, fa un tempo uggioso (coperto). *~ of hearing*, duro d'orecchi. *~ of sight*, miope. *~ season*, stagione morta. ¶ *v.t.* offuscare, ammorzare; (*sound*) attenuare, soffocare; (*edge*) smussare; (*senses*) indebolire, istupidire, inebetire; intorpidire. *~ard*, *n*. stupido, balordo. **dul[l]ness**, *n*. (*mental*) noia; tardità di mente; (*bodily*) pesantezza, stanchezza, *f*.; intorpidimento, torpore, *m*., assopimento; (*material*) appannamento, offuscamento, *m*.; (*sound*) sordità; (*hearing*) durezza d'udito, *f*.; (*Com.*) ristagno (del mercato), *m*.

duly, *ad*. debitamente, dovutamente, regolarmente, come richiesto, come prescritto. *~ authorized representative*, rappresentante accreditato, *m*.

dumb, *a*. muto; silenzioso. *~ animals*, animali, *m.pl.*, bestie, *f.pl*. *~bell*, manubrio, *m*. *~ show*, mimica, pantomima, scena muta, *f*.

dumbfound, *v.t.* confondere, sbalordire, stordire. *I was ~ed*, restai di sasso.

dumbness, *n*. mutismo, *m*.

dummy, *a*. finto, falso. *~ book* (*for*

bookshelf), libro finto, *m*. ¶ *n*. fantoccio, manichino, *m*.; (*fig*.) prestanome; uomo di paglia, *m*.; (*Mil.*) simulacro, *m*.; (*cards*) morto, *m*.

dump, *n*. catasta, *f*.; mucchio; scarico, *m*. *to be in the ~s*, essere d'umor nero, essere malinconico. ¶ *v.t.* buttare giù, scaricare; (*Econ.*) vendere a prezzo di rifiuto. *~ing*, *n*. esportazione protetta, concorrenza protetta, *f*. *~y*, *a*. corto e grosso, tozzo.

dun, *a*. bruno, cupo. ¶ *n*. creditore importuno, *m*. ¶ *v.t.* importunare, perseguire, chiedere denari importunamente.

dunce, *n*. ignorante, stupido.

dunderhead, *n*. balordo, stupido.

dune, *n*. duna, *f*.

dung, *n*. letame, sterco, *m*. *~ beetle*, scarabeo stercorario, *m*. *~hill*, letamaio, mucchio di letame, *m*. ¶ *v.t.* concimare con letame; (*fig.*)

dungeon, *n*. prigione sotterranea, *f*.

Dunkirk, *n*. Dunkerque, *f*.

dunnage, *n*. pagliolato, *m*.

duodecimal, *a*. duodecimale. **duodecimo**, *a*. & *n*. (*abb*. 12mo) dodicesimo, in-dodicesimo (*abb*. in 12mo.).

duodenal, *a*. del duodeno. **duodenum**, *n*. duodeno, *m*.

dupe, *n*. gonzo, *m*., vittima di un inganno, *f*. ¶ *v.t.* ingannare, gabbare. *~ry*, *n*. inganno, *m*.

duplicate, *a*. doppio, duplicato; (*tools, parts*) di ricambio. *~ train*, treno supplemento, treno bis, *m*. ¶ *n*. duplicato, *m*. ¶ *v.t.* duplicare; raddoppiare. **duplication**, *n*. duplicazione, *f*. **duplicity**, *n*. duplicità; doppiezza, *f*.

durable, *a*. durevole. **duration**, *n*. durata, *f*.

duress[e], *n*. costrizione; prigionia, *f*.; imprigionamento, *m*.

during, *pr*. durante.

dusk, *n*. crepuscolo, *m*. *at ~*, sull'imbrunire, al cader della notte, sul far della notte. *~y*, *a*. bruno, nerastro, oscuro.

dust, *n*. polvere, *f*.; (*of the dead*) ceneri, *f.pl*. *~bin*, cassetta della spazzatura, *f*. *~coat*, spolverino, *m*. *~cover*, copertina, *f*. *~man*, spazzino, spazzaturaio, *m*. *~pan*, paletta per le spazzature, *f*. *~sheet*, fodera, *f*., lenzuolo per coprire i mobili, *m*. ¶ *v.t.* spolverare (*remove dust*); (*sprinkle*) cospargere, impolverare. ~**er**, *n.* strofinaccio, *m.* ~**y**, *a.* polveroso, coperto di polvere.

Dutch, *a.* olandese; all'olandese. ~ *auction*, incanto, *m.* ~ *cheese*, formaggio olandese, *m.* ~ *courage*, finto coraggio, coraggio dato da stimolanti, *m.* ~ *East Indies*, Indie Orientali olandesi, *f.pl.* ~*man*, ~*woman*, olandese, *m.f.* ~ *oven*, forno olandese, forno portatile, *m.* ¶ (*language*) *n.* l'olandese, *m.*, lingua olandese, *f.*

dutiable, *a.* soggetto a dazio; tassabile.

dutiful & **duteous**, *a.* obbediente, rispettoso, deferente, ossequioso.

duty, *n.* dovere, *m.*; funzione, *f.*, servizio, *m.*; imposta, tassa, *f.*, gabella, *f.*, dazio, *m.*, diritto, *m.*; omaggi, rispetti, *m.pl.* on ~, di servizio, in servizio, in funzione. *off* ~, libero, fuori servizio. ~ *free*, *a.* franco di dazio, esente da dazio, esente da tasse; (*ad.*) in franchigia [di diritti]. ~ *paid*, *a.* sdoganato, dazio compreso.

dwarf, *n.* & *a.* nano, -a, *m.f.* ¶ *v.t* rimpicciolire.

dwell, *v.i. ir.* abitare, dimorare, stare. ~ [*up*]*on*, fermarsi su, insistere su, indugiare su. ~**er**, *n.* abitante, *m.f.* ~**ing**, *n.* abitazione, dimora, residenza, *f.* ~ *place*, dimora, *f.*, domicilio, *m.* ~ *house*, casa, casa abitata, *f.*

dwindle, *v.i.* diminuire, deperire, scemare. **dwindling**, *n.* deperimento, *m.*, diminuzione, *f.*

dye, *n.* tintura, tinta, *f.*, colore, *m.* ~ *stuffs*, materie coloranti, *f.pl.* ~*works*, tintoria, *f.* of the deepest ~, (*fig.*) del più atroce. ¶ *v.t.* tingere. ~**ing**, *n.* tintura; tintoria, *f.* ~**er** [& **cleaner**], *n.* tintore, *m.*

dying, *a.* morente, moribondo, agonizzante; ultimo, estremo, supremo. *the* ~, i moribondi, *m.pl.*; gli agonizzanti, *m.pl.* *to be* ~, essere morente, in punto dì morte, in agonia. ~ *words*, ultime parole, estreme parole, *f.pl.*

dyke, *n.* & *v.t.* same as *dike*.

dynamic(**al**), *a.* dinamico. **dynamics**, *n.* dinamica, *f.*

dynamite, *n.* dinamite, *f.*

dynamo, *n.* dinamo, *f.* ~*-electric*(*al*), dinamo-elettrico.

dynasty, *n.* dinastia, *f.*

dysentery, *n.* dissenteria, *f.*

dyspepsia, *n.* dispepsia, *f.* **dyspeptic**, *a.* & *n.* dispeptico, *a.* & *m.*

E

E (*Mus.*) *letter*, mi, *m.*

each, *a.* & *pn.* ciascuno, *m.*, -a, *f.* ~ *one*, ciascuno. ~ *other*, l'un l'altro, gli uni gli altri, a vicenda, reciprocamente, . . . si, . . . ci.

eager, *a.* ardente, avido, impaziente, desideroso; sollecito, premuroso. *to be* ~ *for*, essere avido di, desideroso di, impaziente di. ~**ly**, *ad.* avidamente, ardentemente. ~**ness**, *n.* ardore, *m.*; avidità, vivacità, impazienza, *f.*

eagle, *n.* (*bird*) aquila, *f.*; (*standard*) aquila, *f.*

eaglet, *n.* aquilotto, *m.*

ear, *n.* orecchio, *m.*; (*corn*) spiga, *f.* ~*ache*, mal d'orecchio, *m.* ~*drum*, timpano, *m.* ~*flap*, orecchietta, *f.* ~*mark*, contrassegno, *m.*; (*v.t.*) contrassegnare. ~*phones*, cuffia, *f.* ~*piece* (*teleph.*), telefono. ~*ring*, orecchino, *m.* *within* ~*shot*, a portata d'orecchio. ~ *trumpet*, cornetto acustico, *m.*

earliness, *n.* l'esser presto, *m.*; ora poco avanzata; precocità, *f.*

early, *a.* poco avanzato; prematuro; precoce; primo, prossimo; mattutino; antico, anziano; (*youth*) tenero. ~ *fruits*, frutti primaticci, *m.pl.* ~ *vegetables*, primizie, *f.pl.* ~ *morning tea*, il tè del mattino, *m.* *to be* (*up*) ~, *to be an* ~ *riser*, levarsi presto, di buon'ora, di buon mattino, essere mattiniero. *at the earliest*, al più presto. *not earlier than*, non prima di. ¶ *ad.* di buon'ora, presto, prima, per tempo, a tempo.

earn, *v.t.* guadagnare, acquistare; meritare.

earnest, *a.* serio, sincero; premuroso, zelante; ardente, caloroso. ¶ *n.* pegno, *m.*; (*fig.*) prenotazione, *f.* ~ *money*, caparra, *f.* *in* ~, sul serio, in buona fede; (*a.*) commosso. ~**ly**, *ad.* seriamente, sinceramente, calorosamente, ardentemente. ~*ness*, *n.* serietà, diligenza, *f.*; ardore, zelo, *m.*; premure, *f.pl.*

earning, *n.* guadagno, *m.*; (*pl.*) guadagni, *m.pl.*

earth, *n.* terra, *f.*; terreno, suolo, *m.*; (*of fox*) tana, *f.* ~ *connection*, (*Elec.*) *n.* presa di terra, *f.* ~*quake*, terremoto, *m.* ~*work*, lavoro di terra, terrapiena, *m.* ~**s**, (*Mil.*) lavoro di sterro, *m.* ¶ *v.t.* (*Hort.*)

rincalzare; (*Elec.*) mettere a terra.
~**en,** *a.* di terra cotta. ~*enware,*
vasellame, *m.*; terraglie, maioliche,
f.pl. ~**ly,** *a.* terrestre, della terra; di
quaggiú; mondano. ~**y,** *a.* di terra,
terroso; (*fig.*) grossolano.
earwig, *n.* forfecchia, *f.*
ease, *n.* agio, riposo, conforto, *m.*;
tranquillità, agiatezza; disinvoltura,
facilità, *f.* *to be at* ~, star comodo,
trovarsi a proprio agio.   ¶ *v.t.*
sollevare, alleviare; addolcire, lenire;
sgravare,   alleggerire;   (*Naut.*)
allentare; (*v.i.*) mollare.
easel, *n.* cavalletto, *m.*
easement, *n.* (*Law*) servitú, *f.*
easily, *ad.* facilmente, agevolmente,
senza sforzo, senza fatica, adagio.
not ~, malagevolmente, con
difficoltà.   *he takes things* ~,
prende il mondo come viene.
easing, *n.* sollievo, alleviamento, *m.*
east, *n.* est, oriente, levante, *m.*
from ~ *to west,* dall'oriente all'occidente. *the E* ~ (*Geog.*), l'Oriente, *m.*
¶ *a.* d'est, d'oriente, di levante,
orientale.   *E* ~ *Africa,* l'Africa
orientale, *f.* *the E* ~ *Indies,* le Indie
orientali, *f.pl.*
Easter, *n.* Pasqua, *f.*   ~ *egg,* uovo
pasquale, *m.*
easterly, *a.* d'est, dell'est. **eastern,**
a. dell'est, situato ad est; orientale;
(*question, &c.*) d'Oriente.
easy, *a.* facile, agevole; disinvolto,
spigliato,   naturale;   a   suo   agio,
tranquillo, comodo; liberale. *in* ~
circumstances,   benestante,   agiato.
~ *chair,* *n.* poltrona, *f.*   ~*going
person,*   spensierato,   *m.*,   persona
disinvolta, *f.*   ~ *to get on with*
(*pers.*), simpatico, affabile, di facile
abbordo. *not* ~, malagevole.
eat, *v.t. & v.i. ir.* mangiare.   ~ *away,*
~ *into,* rodere, rosicchiare. ~ *up,*
divorare,   consumare.   ~**able,**   *a.*
commestibile, mangiabile. ~**ables,**
n.pl. generi alimentari; viveri, *m.pl.*
~**er,** mangiatore, *m.*, -tricé, *f.*
~**ing:** ~ *apples,* mele da tavola, *f.pl.*
~ *house,* trattoria, *f.*, ristorante, *m.*
eaves, *n.pl.* grondaia, *f.*
eavesdrop, *v.i.* ascoltare segretamente.
eavesdropper, *n.* spione, chi ascolta
di nascosto.
ebb, *n.* riflusso, *m.*   ~ *tide,* marea
calante, bassa marea, *f.*   ¶ *v.i.*
rifluire, abbassarsi; (*fig.*) declinare,
decadere.
ebonite, *n.* ebanite, *f.*

ebony, *n.* (*wood, tree*) ebano, *m.*
ebullition, *n.* ebollizione, *f.*
eccentric, *a. & n.* eccentrico, *a. & m.*
eccentricity, *n.* eccentricità, *f.*
Ecclesiastes, *n.* L'Ecclesiaste, *m.*
ecclesiastic, *n. & -al,* *a.* ecclesiastico,
m. & a.
Ecclesiasticus, *n.* l'Ecclesiastico, *m.*
echo, *n.* eco, *f.*   ¶ *v.t.* fare eco, echeggiare; (*v.t.*) farsi eco di.
eclectic, *a.* eclettico.
eclecticism, *n.* ecletticismo, *m.*
eclipse, *n.* eclisse, *m.*   ¶ *v.t.* eclissare.
to become ~*d,* eclissarsi.
ecliptic, *a.* eclittico.   ¶ *n.* eclittica,
f.
eclogue, *n.* egloga, *f.*
economic, *a.* economico.   ~(**al**), *a.*
economico; (*pers.*) economo, frugale.
~**s,** *n.pl.* scienza economica,
economia, *f.*
economist, *n.* economista, *m.*
economize, *v.t. & i.* economizzare.
economy, *n.* economia, *f.*
ecstasy, *n.* estasi, *f.*   *to go into
ecstasies,* andare in estasi, estasiarsi.
ecstatic, *a.* estatico.
Ecuador, *n.* l'Ecuador, *m.*, la repubblica dell'Equatore, *f.*
ecumenical, *a.* ecumenico.
eczema, *n.* eczema, *m.*
eddy, *n.* vortice, turbine, risucchio, *m.*
¶ *v.i.* turbinare, girare a mò di
vortice.
edelweiss, *n.* stella delle Alpi, *f.*
Eden (*fig.*), *n.* eden, *m.inv.* [*the
Garden of*] ~, l'Eden, il paradiso
terrestre, *m.*
edge, *n.* orlo, bordo, margine, *m.*;
sponda, *f.*; filo, taglio, *m.* ~ *tools,*
strumenti taglienti, arnesi da taglio,
m.pl. *give an* ~ *to* (*sharpen*),
affilare. ~**ways,** ~**wise,** *ad.* di
fianco, di lato, da canto. **on** ~,
impaziente, inquieto, sulle spine.
¶ *v.t.* bordare, orlare.   ~ *away,*
allontanarsi poco a poco.   ~ *up to,*
avvicinarsi di soppiatto a.
edging, *n.* bordo, *m.*, bordatura;
frangia, *f.*
edible, *a.* commestibile, mangiabile.
edict, *n.* editto, *m.*
edifice, *n.* edificio, edifizio, *m.*
edify, *v.t.* edificare.
Edinburgh, *n.* Edimburgo, *f.*
edit, *v.t.* redigere, dirigere, pubblicare.
~*ed by* (book), a cura di.   ~**ion,**
edizione, *f.*   ~ *binding,* rilegatura di
biblioteca, *f.*
editor, -tress, *n.* redattore, *m.*;
-trice, *f.*; direttore, *m.*; -trice, *f.*

editorial, *a.* del redattore, della redazione; editoriale. ¶ *n.* articolo di fondo, *m.* ~ *staff,* redazione, *f.*

educate, *v.t.* istruire; educare; allevare.

education, *n.* istruzione, *f.*; insegnamento, *m.* ~*al, a.* di istruzione, di educazione. ~ *establishment,* istituto d'insegnamento, d'educazione, *m.*

educator, *n.* istitutore, *m.*; -trice, *f.*; maestro, *m.*, -a, *f.*; educatore, *m.*; -trice, *f.*

educe, *v.t.* estrarre, fare uscire.

eel, *n.* anguilla, *f.* ~ *pot,* nassa, *f.*

eerie, ~y, *a.* lugubre, fantastico.

efface, *v.t.* cancellare, fare sparire.

effaceable, *a.* cancellabile.

effect, *n.* effetto, risultato, scopo, intento, *m.*; efficacia, *f.*; *(pl.)* beni, *m.pl.*; roba, *f.* ¶ *v.t.* effettuare, produrre, compiere.

effective, *a.* effettivo, efficace. ¶ *n.* effettivo, *m.*

effectual, *a.* efficace.

effeminacy, *n.* effeminatezza.

effeminate, *a. & m.* effeminato. *to (make)* ~, effeminare.

effervesce, *v.i.* spumare, spumeggiare, essere in effervescenza. **effervescence, -ency,** *n.* effervescenza, *f.* **effervescent,** *a.* effervescente. **effervescing** *(drink),* *a.* effervescente, spumeggiante.

effete, *a.* indebolito, esausto, logoro, stracco; usato, vecchio, fuori moda.

efficacious, *a.* efficace.

efficiency, *n.* efficienza, capacità, *f.*

efficient, *a.* efficace, capace.

effigy, *n.* effigie, *f.*

effloresce, *v.i.* essere efflorescente.

efflorescence, *n.* efflorescenza, *f.*

effluence, *n.* emanazione, *f.*; efflusso, *m.*

effluvium, *n.* effluvio, *m.*

efflux, *n.* efflusso, *m.*

effort, *n.* sforzo, *m.*

effrontery, *n.* sfrontatezza, *f.*

effulgence, *n.* splendore, *m.* **effulgent,** *a.* splendente, risplendente.

effusion, *n.* effusione, *f.*

effusive, *a.* espansivo. **effusiveness,** *n.* espansività, *f.*

eft, *n.* salamandra acquatica, *f.*; tritone, *m.*

egg, *n.* uovo, *m.* (uova, *pl.f.*); *(silkworm)* seme, *m.* ~*cup,* portauovo, *m.* ~ *merchant,* ovaio, *m.* ~*shell,* guscio d'uovo, *m.* ~ *on, v.t.* incitare, istigare, spingere innanzi.

eglantine, *n.* rosa canina, *f.*

ego, *n.* io, *m.* **egoism,** *n.* egoismo, *m.*

egoist, *n.* egoista, *m.f.* **egoistic(al),** *a.* egoistico. **egotism,** *n.* egotismo, *m.* **egotist,** *n.* egoista, *m.f.*, chi esalta il proprio io. **egotistic(al),** *a.* egoistico.

egregious, *a.* insigne, matricolato, enorme.

egress, *n.* uscita, *f.*; egresso, *m.*

egret, *n.* *(bird)* garzetta, *f.*; *(tuft)* piumino, pennacchio, ciuffo, ciuffetto, *m.*; fantasia, *f.*

Egypt, *n.* l'Egitto, *m.* **Egyptian,** *a.* egiziano. ¶ *n.* egiziano, *m.* **Egyptologist,** *n.* egittologo, *m.* **Egyptology,** *n.* egittologia, *f.*

eh, *i.* ch! dunque!

eider [duck], *n.* anitra, *f.* ~*down,* peluria, *f.*, piumino, *m.*

eight, *a. & n.* otto, *a. & m.*

eighteen, *a. & n.* diciotto, *a. & n.* *18 hole course (Golf),* percorso di 18 buche, *m.*

eighteenth, *a. & n.* diciottesimo, decimottavo, *a. & m.*; diciotto, *m.*

eighth, *a. & n.* ottavo, *a. & m.*; otto, *n.* ~*ly, ad.* in ottavo luogo.

eightieth, *a. & n.* ottantesimo, *a. & m.*

eighty, *a. & n.* ottanta, *a. & m.* 81, *&c.,* ottantuno, ottanta due, &c.

either, *pn. & a.* l'uno o l'altro; l'una o l'altra; uno dei due, una delle due; uno, una. ¶ *c. o.* ~ *or,* o . . . o, sia . . . sia. ¶ *ad. with neg.* neanche, nemmeno, neppure. *nor I* ~, nemmeno io, neanche io. ~ *way,* in ogni modo; per l'una o per l'altra via.

ejaculate, *v.t. & abs.* gridare, esclamare; *(fluid)* emettere.

ejaculation, *n.* esclamazione, *f.*; grido, *m.*; *(fluid)* emissione, *f.*

eject, *v.t.* espellere, gettar fuori, scacciare; *(Mech., Phys.)* eiettare. **ejection,** *n.* espulsione, *(Med.)* eiezione, *f.*

eke out, *v.t.* supplire a . . .; prolungare.

elaborate, *a.* elaborato. ¶ *v.t.* elaborare.

elapse, *v.i.* passare, trascorrere, decorrere.

elastic, *a.* elastico. ¶ *n.* elastico, *m.*; gomma, *f.* ~ *band,* fascia elastica, fascia di gomma, *f.*

elasticity, *n.* elasticità, *f.*

elate, *v.t.* esaltare, sollevare, insuperbire. **elated,** *a.* esaltato, allegro, inorgoglito. **elation,** *n.* esaltazione, *f.*; allegria, *f.*

Elba (the **Island of**), Elba (l'isola d'Elba), *f.*

Elbe (the) (*river*), *n.* l'Elba, *f.*

elbow, *n.* gomito, *m.* *to rest one's* ~(*s*) *on*, poggiare il gomito su, stare coi gomiti su . . . *to rest on one's* ~, appoggiarsi al (sul) gomito. ~ *grease* (*fig.*), olio di gomito. ~ *room*, agio, spazio, *m.*; libertà d'azione. *f.* ¶ *v.t.* dare gomitate a. urtare col gomito. *to* ~ *one's way*, farsi largo a colpi di gomito, a forza di gomitate.

elder, *a.* maggiore, piú vecchio, piú anziano. ¶ *n.* maggiore; anziano (*Eccl.*); (*Bot.*) sambuco, *m.* ~ *s*, i nostri maggiori, *m.pl.* ~*berry*, bacca di sambuco, *f.*

elderly, *a.* attempato, d'una certa età.

eldest, *n. & a.* il maggiore, il piú vecchio, il primogenito, *m. & a.*

El Dorado, *n.* Eldorado, *m.*

elect, *v.t.* eleggere, scegliere; decidersi a. *the* ~ (*Relig.*), gli eletti, *m.pl.* ~*ed member*, eletto, *m.*, -a, *f.*

election, *n.* elezione, *f.* ~ *agent*, agente elettorale, *m.* **election-eering,** *n.* manovre elettorali, *f.pl.*

elector, *n.* elettore, *m.*, -trice, *f.* **electorate,** *n.* elettorato, *m.*; gli elettori, *m.pl.*

electric, *a.* elettrico. ~ *bowl fire*, radiatore elettrico parabolico, *m.* ~ *eel*, ginnoto, *m.* ~ *sign*, insegna luminosa, *f.* ~ *torch*, lampada a torcia, l. tascabile. *f.*

electrical, *a.* elettrico. ~ *engineer*, ingegnere elettrotecnico, *m.* ~*fitter*, elettricista, *m.*

electrically, *ad.* elettricamente.

electrician, *n.* elettricista, *m.*

electricity, *n.* elettricità, *f.*

electrify, *v.t.* elettrizzare; (*Rly., &c.*) elettrificare.

electrize, *v.t.* elettrizzare.

electrocute, *v.t.* giustiziare mediante elettroesecuzione.

electrode, *n.* elettrodo, *m.*

electrolier, *n.* lampadario a luce elettrica, *m.*

electrolysis, *n.* elettrolisi, *f.*

electromagnet, *n.* elettrocalamita, *f.*

electron, *n.* elettrone, *m.*

electroplate, *n.* placcato, *m.* **electroplating,** *n.* galvanoplastica, *f.*; galvanostegia, *f.* ¶ *v.t.* placcare (*in argento, &c.*).

electrotype, *n.* elettrotipo, *m.*

elegance, *n.* eleganza, *f.* **elegant,** *a.* elegante. **elegantly,** *ad.* elegantemente.

elegy, *n.* elegia, *f.* **elegiac,** *a.* elegiaco. ¶ ~*s*, *n.pl.* verso elegiaco, *ri.*

element, *n.* elemento, fattore, *m.*; (*Chem.*) elemento, corpo semplice. ~*al*, *a.* fondamentale.

elementary, *a.* elementare; (*Sch.*) primario. *Elementary Physics, &c.* (*book*). Elementi, Rudimenti d⁞... Fisica, &c., *m.pl.*

elephant, *n.* elefante, *m.* ~[*ine person*], mastodonte, *m.*

elevate, *v.t.* elevare, esaltare.

elevation, *n.* elevazione, altezza, altitudine, altura, *f.*

elevator, *n.* elevatore, montacarico, ascensore, *m.*; (*Surg.*) muscolo elevatorio, *m.* (*in shoe*), alzata, *f.*

eleven, *a. & n.* undici, *a. & m.*

eleventh, *a. & n.* undecimo, undicesimo, decimo primo, *a. & m.*; undici, *m.*

elf, *n.* folletto, *m.*; fata, *f.* **elfin,** *a.* di folletto, di fata, incantato. **elfish,** *a.* di folletto, di fata.

elicit, *v.t.* evocare, cavare, fare uscire, fare dire, fare confessare.

elide, *v.t.* elidere.

eligible, *a.* eleggibile, conveniente.

eliminate, *v.t.* eliminare. *eliminating heat*, prova eliminatoria, *f.*

elision, *n.* elisione, *f.*

elixir, *n.* elisir, *m.*

Elizabethan, *a.* elisabettiano, d'Elisabetta, del tempo d'Elisabetta.

elk, *n.* alce, *m.*

ellipse & ellipsis, *n.* elisse, *f.*; (*Gram.*) ellisse, *f.*

elliptic(al), *a.* ellittico.

elm [*tree*], *n.* olmo, *m.* ~ *grove*, olmeto, *m.* ~ *row*, olmaia, *f.*

elocution, *n.* elocuzione, declamazione, *f.*

elongate, *v.t.* allungare.

elope, *v.i.* fuggire. **elopement,** *n.* fuga, *f.*

eloquence, *n.* eloquenza, *f.* **eloquent,** *a.* eloquente. **eloquently,** *ad.* eloquentemente.

else, *ad.* altro; altrimenti; se non; inoltre, di piú. ~*where*, *ad.* altrove, in altra parte, in altro luogo. *anybody* ~, qualsiasi altro, qualunque altro. *no one* ~, nessun altro. *someone* ~, qualche altro. *who* ~? chi altro, chi altri? *where* ~? dove ancora? *nothing* ~, nient'altro, niente di piú.

Elsinore, *n.* Elsinore, *f.*

elucidate, *v.t.* elucidare, chiarire, spiegare.

elude, *v.t.* eludere.

elusive, *a.* fuggevole, ingannevole.

Elysian, *a.* elisio.

Elysium, *n.* Elisio, Eliso, *m.*; (*Myth*) Elisio, *m.*

emaciated, *a.* emaciato, dimagrato.

emanate, *v.i.* emanare, provenire, derivare.

emancipate, *v.t.* emancipare.

emasculate, *v.t.* castrare; (*fig.*) effeminare, snervare.

embalm, *v.t.* imbalsamare.

embank, *v.t.* arginare, munire di argine, digare. **embankment,** *n.* argine, *m.*; argini, *m.pl.*; diga, *f.*; terrapieno, *m.*

embargo, *n.* embargo; divieto, *m.*; proibizione, *f.*

embark, *v.t.* imbarcare; (*v.i.*) imbarcarsi. **embarkation,** *n.* imbarco, *m.*

embarrass, *v.t.* imbarazzare. ~ment, *n.* imbarazzo, *m.*

embassy, *n.* ambasciata, *f.*

embattle (*v.t.*) (*Arch.*), munire di parapetti merlati. **embattled,** *p.a.* schierato in ordine di battaglia.

embed, *v.t.* incassare, incastonare, fissare, piantare.

embellish, *v.t.* abbellire.

ember days, Quattro Tempora, *f.pl.*

embers, *n.pl.* ceneri, *f.pl.*; brace, *f.*

embezzle, *v.t. & i.* commettere un'appropriazione indebita, sottrarre, malversare; appropriarsi indebitamente di. **embezzlement,** *n.* appropriazione indebita, sottrazione, *f.*

embitter, *v.t.* inasprire, amareggiare.

emblazon, *v.t.* blasonare.

emblem, *n.* emblema, *m.* **emblematic(al),** *a.* emblematico, simbolico.

embodiment, *n.* incorporamento, *m.*; incorporazione, *f.* **embody,** *v.t.* incorporare, incarnare.

embolden, *v.t.* incoraggiare, rincorare, imbaldanzire.

embolism, *n.* embolismo, *m.*

emboss, *v.t.* lavorare di rilievo (d'incavo); stampare. ~ed stamp, francobollo ad impressione, *m.*

embrace, *n.* abbraccio, *m.*; stretta, *f.* ¶ *v.t.* abbracciare, stringere; (*fig.*) comprendere.

embrasure, *n.* (*Arch.*) svasatura muraria, *f.*; (*Mil.*) feritoia, *f.*

embrocation, *n.* embrocazione, embrocca, *f.*

embroider, *v.t.* ricamare. **embroiderer, -ess,** *n.* ricamatore, *m.*; ricamatrice, *f.* **embroidery,** *n.* ricamo, *m.* ~ cotton, tela di cotone da ricamo, *f.* ~ hoops, telaio da ricamo, *m.*

embroil, *v.t.* imbrogliare.

embryo, *n.* embrione, *m.* in ~ (*fig.*), in erba.

embryonic, *a.* embrionale, in embrione.

emend, *v.t.* emendare, correggere. **emendation,** *n.* emendazione, correzione, *f.*

emerald, *n.* smeraldo, *m.*

emerge, *v.i.* emergere, apparire, sorgere. **emergence,** *n.* apparizione, contingenza, *f.*

emergency, *n.* emergenza, *f.*; caso imprevisto, *m.* in case of ~, in caso urgente. ~ brake, freno di soccorso, *m.* ~ exit, uscita di sicurezza, *f.*

emeritus, *a.* emerito.

emery, *n.* smeriglio, *m.* ~ cloth, tela smeriglio, tela smerigliata, *f.* ~ paper, carta smeriglio, *f.*

emetic, *a. & n.* emetico, *a. & m.*

emigrant, *n.* emigrante, *m.f.* **emigrate,** *v.i.* emigrare. **emigration,** *n.* emigrazione. ~ officer, agente d'emigrazione, *m.*

eminence, *n.* eminenza, *f.* His E~ (*cardinal*), Sua Eminenza. **eminent,** *a.* eminente. **eminently,** *ad.* eminentemente.

emir, *n.* emiro, *m.*

emissary, *n.* emissario, *m.*

emission, *n.* emissione, *f.*

emit, *v.t.* emettere, esalare.

emollient, *a. & n.* emolliente, *a. & m.*

emoluments, *n.pl.* emolumenti, *m.pl.*

emotion, *n.* emozione, commozione, *f.*

emotional, *a.* emozionante, facile all'emozione, impressionabile.

empanel a jury, formare la lista dei giurati.

emperor, *n.* imperatore, *m.*

emphasis, *n.* enfasi, energia, *f.* to lay ~ upon or **emphasize,** *v.t.* dare enfasi a, incalzare su; mettere in rilievo; accentuare; sottolineare.

emphatic, *a.* enfatico.

empire, *n.* impero, *m.*

empiric(al), *a.* empirico. **empiricism,** *n.* empirismo, *m.* **empiric[ist],** *n.* empirico, *m.*

employ, *v.t.* impiegare, usare, servirsi di, adoperare. he is in my ~, è al mio servizio, in mio servizio. **employee,** *n.* impiegato, *m.*, -a, *f.* **employer,** *n.* padrone, *m.*; padrona, *f.*; principale, *m. & f.* **employment,** *n.* impiego, lavoro, *m.*; occupazione, *f.* ~ agency, ufficio di collocamento, *m.*

emporium, *n.* emporio, *m.*

empower, *v.t.* autorizzare, conferire i poteri a, abilitare.

empress, *n.* imperatrice, *f.*

emptiness, *n.* vacuità, inanità, *f.*; vuoto, *m.*

empty, *a.* vuoto, vacante; vacuo, inane, vano. ~ *handed,* a mani vuote. *to be* ~ *headed,* essere senza cervello. *on an* ~ *stomach,* a stomaco vuoto. ¶ (*case, &c.*) *n.* vuoto, *m.* ¶ *v.t.* vuotare, scaricare, sgombrare.

empyrean, *n.* empireo, *m.*

emulate, *v.t.* emulare.

emulation, *n.* emulazione, gara, *f.* **emulator,** *n.* emulo, *m.*

emulsion, *n.* emulsione, *f.*

enable, *v.t.* mettere in grado di, permettere di; (*Law*) abilitare.

enact, *v.t.* decretare, ordinare, stabilire, promulgare. **enactment,** *n.* decreto, statuto, *m.*; ordinanza, *f.*

enamel, *n.* & ~*ware,* smalto, *m.* ¶ *v.t.* smaltare. *enamelled iron,* lamiera di ferro smaltata, *f.* **enamelling,** *n.* smaltatura, *f.*

enamoured, *p.p.* innamorato.

encage, *v.t.* mettere in gabbia.

encamp, *v.i.* & *t.* accamparsi, accampare. **encampment,** *n.* accampamento, *m.*

encase, *v.t.* incassare, rinchiudere.

encash, *v.t.* incassare.

encaustic, *a.* & *n.* encaustico, *a.* & *m.*

enceinte, *a.* incinta.

enchain, *v.t.* incatenare.

enchant, *v.t.* incantare. **enchanter, -ress,** *n.* incantatore, *m.*; incantatrice, *f.* **enchanting,** *p.a.* incantevole, incantatore. **enchantment,** *n.* incanto, incantesimo, *m.*

enchase, *v.t.* cesellare, intagliare.

encircle, *v.t.* circondare, cingere, abbracciare.

enclave, *n.* recinto, *m.*

enclose, *v.t.* chiudere, cingere, circondare; (*in letter*) accludere, inchiudere, compiegare.

enclosed, *p.p.* chiuso, cinto, circondato; accluso, incluso, compiegato, annesso.

enclosure, *n.* recinto, *m.*; (*in letter*) allegato, *m.*

encomium, *n.* encomio, elogio, *m.*

encompass, *v.t.* circondare, abbracciare.

encore, *i.* & *n.* bis, *m.* ¶ *v.t.* bissare.

encounter, *n.* incontro, scontro, urto, cozzo, *m.*; zuffa, *f.* ¶ *v.t.* incontrare, affrontare.

encourage, *v.t.* incoraggiare, inanimare; incitare, stimolare.

encroach on (**to**), usurpare, invadere, estendersi sopra; abusare di. **encroachment,** *n.* usurpazione, *f.*; abuso, *m.*; l'estendersi, *m.*

encumber, *v.t.* ingombrare. **encumbrance,** *n.* ingombro, carico, debito, *m.*; ipoteca, *f.*

encyclic(al), *a.* & *n.* enciclico, *a.* & *m.*

encyclop[a]edia, *n.* enciclopedia, *f.*

end, *n.* fine, *f.*; capo, *m.*; termine, *m.*; estremità, *f.*; fine, scopo, intento, *m.*; mira, *f.*; oggetto, *m.*; risultato, *m.*; conclusione, *f.* *no* ~ *of,* una infinità di. *on* ~, ritto, rizzato; (*hair*) drizzato; (*fig.*) sotto sopra, rovesciato. ~ *paper,* foglio di guardia, *m.* ~ *in smoke,* andare in fumo. *make both* ~*s meet,* coprire le spese. ¶ *v.t.* finire, compiere, metter fine a, terminare; (*v.i.*) finire, cessare, ridursi a.

endanger, *v.t.* esporre a pericolo, arrischiare; compromettere.

endear, *v.t.* rendere caro.

endearment, *n.* parola amorevole, carezza, *f.*

endeavour, *n.* tentativo, sforzo, *m.* ¶ *v.i.* sforzarsi di, tentare di.

ending, *n.* fine, conclusione, *f.*; (*Gram.*) desinenza, terminazione, *f.*

endive, *n.* indivia, *f.*

endless, *a.* & **-ly,** *ad.* senza fine, interminabilmente; interminabile.

endorse, *v.t.* scrivere sul rovescio, vistare, attergare; (*fig.*) approvare, appoggiare, sottoscrivere; (*Com.*) girare, munire di girata, trasformare. ~ *back,* rigirare. ~ *over to,* girare in favore di. **endorsement,** *n.* (*bill, cheque, &c.*) girata, *f.*; (*Insce.*) legittima, *f.*

endow, *v.t.* dotare.

endowment, *n.* dotazione, *f.*; dono, talento, *m.*

endue, *v.t.* rivestire (di); dotare.

endurable, *a.* sopportabile, tollerabile. **endurance,** *n.* pazienza, tolleranza; (forza di) resistenza, *f.* ~ *test,* prova di resistenza, *f.* **endure,** *v.t.* sopportare, tollerare, soffrire, subire; (*v.i.*) durare.

enema, *n.* lavatura, *f.*; clistere, *m.*

enemy, *n.* & *a.* nemico, *a.* & *m.*

energetic, *a.* energico. ~*s* (*Phys.*), *n.pl.* energetica, *f.* **energize,** *v.t.* infondere energia a; (*Elec.*) caricare.

energy, *n.* energia, *f.*

enervate, *v.t.* snervare.

enfeeble, *v.t.* indebolire.

enfilade, *n.* infilata, *f.* ¶ *v.t.* infilare, prendere l'infilata.

enfold, *v.t.* avviluppare, avvolgere; serrare.

enforce, *v.t.* rafforzare, imporre, applicare, far eseguire, esercitare, far valere.

enforceable, *a.* eseguibile, che si può imporre, applicare, porre in effetto.

enfranchise, *v.t.* affrancare; conferire il diritto elettorale a, dare il voto a.

engage, *v.t.* impegnare, obbligare; prendere a servizio, ingaggiare; prenotare; noleggiare; attaccare; occupare; attrarre, cattivare; (*Mech.*) ingranare; (*v.i.*) prender parte (a), entrare (in), occuparsi (di); (*Mil.*) dare battaglia. **engaged,** *p.p.* occupato; impegnato; prenotato; noleggiato; fidanzato, promesso; (*dance*) invitata. (*Teleph.*) (linea) occupata. *have you ~d a servant?* ha fissato una serva? **engagement,** *n.* impegno, obbligo; fidanzamento, *m.*, promessa di matrimonio, *f.* *~ ring,* anello di fidanzamento, *m.* **engaging,** *p.a.* attraente, simpatico.

engender, *v.t.* ingenerare, far nascere, produrre.

engine, *n.* macchina, *f.*, motore, *m.*; (*Rly.*) locomotiva, *f.*; (*of war*) strumento, ordigno, *m.* *~ driver,* *~man,* macchinista, *m.* *~ turning* arabescatura, *f.*

engineer, *n.* ingegnere, meccanico, *m.*; (*maker*) costruttore di macchine, *m.*; (*ship*) macchinista; (*Mil.*) ufficiale del genio, soldato del genio, *m.* ¶ *v.t.* macchinare.

engineering, *n.* ingegneria, *f.*; genio, *m.*

engine-less, *a.* senza motore.

England, *n.* l'Inghilterra, *f.* **English,** *a.* inglese. *the ~ Channel,* la Manica, *f.* *the ~ Church,* la Chiesa anglicana, *f.* *~man,* *~woman,* inglese, *m.f.* ¶ (*language*) *n.* l'inglese, *m.*; lingua inglese, *f.*

engraft, *v.t.* innestare.

engrave, *v.t.* incidere, intagliare, scolpire. **engraver,** *n.* incisore, intagliatore, *m.* **engraving,** *n.* incisione, *f.*

engross, *v.t.* monopolizzare, incettare, accaparrare; (*Law*) far copia autentica. **engrossment** (*Law*), *n.* copia autentica.

engulf, *v.t.* inghiottire, ingoiare, divorare.

enhance, *v.t.* aumentare, intensificare, far risaltare.

enigma, *n.* enigma, *m.* **enigmatic(al),** *a.* enigmatico.

enjoin, *v.t.* ingiungere; ordinare.

enjoy, *v.t.* godere, gustare, assaporare. *~ oneself,* divertirsi, godersela, rallegrarsi. **enjoyable,** *a.* gradevole, piacente. **enjoyment,** *n.* godimento; uso, *m.*

enlarge, *v.t.* ingrandire, estendere, allargare. *~ upon,* dilungarsi sopra. **enlargement,** *n.* ingrandimento, *m.*; estensione, *f.* **enlarger** (*Phot.*), *n.* ingranditore, *m.*

enlighten, *v.t.* illuminare, rischiarare, (*fig.*) istruire. **enlightenment,** *n.* lume, *m.*; sapere, *m.*; schiarimenti, *m:pl.*

enlist, *v.t.* arruolare, iscrivere, (*fig.*) cattivarsi. **enlistment,** *n.* arruolamento, *m.*

enliven, *v.t.* vivificare, animare.

enmity, *n.* inimicizia, *f.*

ennoble, *v.t.* nobilitare, annobilire; (*fig.*) elevare.

enormity, *n.* enormità, *f.* **enormous,** *a.* enorme. **enormously,** *ad.* enormemente. **enormousness,** *n.* enormità, *f.*

enough, *a.* abbastanza, sufficiente, a sufficienza. ¶ *ad.* abbastanza, bastantemente. ¶ *n.* abbastanza, *f.*; il necessario, *m.*; sufficienza, *f.* *to be ~,* bastare. *~ of that!* basta così! finiamola! *to have ~ & to spare,* avere più che abbastanza, avere più che il sufficiente.

enquire, &c., same as *inquire,* &c.

enrage, *v.t.* rendere furioso, far arrabbiare, irritare.

enrapture, *v.t.* incantare, colmar di gioia, entusiasmare. *to be ~d,* estasiarsi, infervorarsi.

enrich, *v.t.* arricchire.

enrol, -ll, *v.t.* inscrivere, registrare; arruolare. **enrolment,** *n.* inscrizione, registrazione, *f.*; arruolamento, *m.*

ensconce, *v.t.* mettere al coperto, avviluppare (in), rimpiattare.

enshrine, *v.t.* rinchiudere, custodire come cosa sacra.

enshroud, *v.t.* avvolgere, velare; nascondere; seppellire.

ensign, *n.* (*banner, flag*) bandiera, insegna, *f.*; (*Naut.*) bandiera di poppa, *f.*

enslave, *v.t.* rendere schiavo, ridurre in servitù, assoggettare.

ensnare, *v.t.* prendere al laccio; *(fig.)* ingannare, insidiare, sedurre.

ensue, *v.i.* seguire, risultare.

ensuing, *p.a.* seguente, successivo, prossimo, futuro.

ensure, *v.t.* assicurare.

entablature, *n.* cornicione, *m.*; trabeazione, *f.*

entail, *n.* assegnazione, sostituzione, *f.* ¶ *v.t.* cagionare, imporre, richiedere, portare con sé; *(Law)* intestare a, assegnare, sostituire a limitazioni.

entangle, *v.t.* imbrogliare, aggrovigliare, arruffare, avviluppare.

enter, *v.t.* entrare (in, dentro), penetrare; inscrivere, registrare; *(law action)*; intentare; *(claim)* avanzare; *(protest)* fare presentare; *(v.i.)* entrare, penetrare. ~ *into* (bargain, contract, *&c.*), fare, addivenire a, concludere, contrarre, intavolare. ~ *into possession,* prendere possesso (di). ~X *(Theat.)*, entra X.

enteric, *a.* enterico.

enterprise, *n.* impresa, *f.* **enterprising,** *a.* intraprendente.

entertain, *v.t.* accogliere, intrattenere, ospitare, ricevere; *(abs.)* trattare; divertire; *(hopes)* nutrire, *(doubts, opinions)* avere, concepire; *(ideas)* ammettere. **entertainer,** *n.* canzonettista, *m.f.*; buffone, *m.* **entertainment,** *m.* trattenimento, ricevimento, *m.*; accoglienza, *f.*; festa, serata, partita di piacere, *f.*; divertimento, passatempo; spettacolo, *m.*; recita, *f.* ~ *tax,* tassa sullo spettacolo, *f.*

enthral(l), *v.t.* asservire.

enthrone, *v.t.* mettere sul trono; *(bishop)* intronizzare. **enthronement,** *n.* intronizzazione, *f.*

enthusiasm, *n.* entusiasmo, *m.* **enthusiast,** *n.* entusiasta, *m.f.* **enthusiastic,** *a.* entusiastico. **enthusiastically,** *ad.* entusiasticamente.

entice, *v.t.* allettare, sedurre. **enticement,** *n.* incitamento, allettamento, *m.*; lusinga, attrazione, *f.* **enticing,** *p.a.* seducente, attraente.

entire, *a.* intero, tutto, completo, assoluto.

entirety, *n.* interezza, totalità, *f.*

entitle, *v.t.* intitolare; dare diritto a, conferire il diritto a. *I am ~d to it,* ci ho diritto, ne ho diritto.

entity, *n.* entità, *f.*

entomb, *v.t.* mettere nella tomba, seppellire.

entomologist, *n.* entomologo, *m.*

entomology, *n.* entomologia, *f.*

entr'acte *(Theat.)*, *n.* intervallo, *m.*; musica eseguita tra un atto e l'altro.

entrails, *n.pl.* viscere, *f.pl.*; intestini, *m.pl.*

entrain, *v.t.* imbarcare (sul treno).

entrance, *n.* entrata, *f.*; ingresso, *m.* ~ [*fee*], prezzo di entrata, *m.*

entrance, *v.t.* incantare, estasiare.

entrap, *v.t.* trappolare, accalappiare, prendere in trappola.

entreat, *v.t.* supplicare, pregare, insistere, importunare.

entreaty, *n.* supplica, *f.*; suppliche, *f.pl.*

entrench, *v.t.* trincerare. **entrenchment,** *n.* trinceramento, *m.*

entrust, *v.t.* affidare, confidare.

entry, *n.* ingresso, *m.*; entrata, *f.*; accesso, *m.*; *(Bkpg.)* partita; scrittura, tenuta, *f.*; registrazione, *f.*; registro, *m.*; *(Cust.)* dichiarazione, *f.*; *(Law)* presa di possesso. *single* ~, partita, *f.* (partita semplice). *double* ~, partita doppia. ~ *in register of births, of marriages, of deaths,* atto di nascita, atto di matrimonio, atto di morte, di decesso, *m.* ~ *only (one way street),* senso unico.

entwine, *v.t.* intrecciare, allacciare.

enumerate, *v.t.* enumerare.

enunciate, *v.t.* enunciare.

envelope, *n.* busta, *f.*; involucro *(Bot., &c.),* *m.* ¶ *v.t.* avviluppare, avvolgere; *(Mil.)* accerchiare.

envenom, *v.t.* avvelenare.

enviable, *a.* invidiabile.

envious, *a.* invidioso.

environ, *v.t.* circondare.

environment, *n.* ambiente, *m.*

environs, *n.pl.* dintorni, *m.pl.*

envisage, *v.t.* contemplare.

envoy, *n.* inviato; legato, *m.*; [ministro] plenipotenziario, *m.*

envy, *n.* invidia, *f.*; oggetto d'invidia, *m.* ¶ *v.t.* invidiare.

epaulet[te], *n.* spallina, *f.*

epergne, *n.* centro (da tavola), trionfo da tavola, *m.*

ephemera, -ron, *n.* effimera, *f.* **ephemeral,** *a.* effimero.

epic, *a.* epico. ¶ *n.* epopea, *f.*; poema epico, *m.*

epicure, *n.* epicureo. **epicurean,** *a. & n.* epicureo, *a. & n.*

epidemic, *n.* epidemia, *f.* **epidemic(al),** *a.* epidemico.

epidermis, *n.* epidermide, *f.*

epiglottis, *n.* epiglotta; epiglottide, *f.*

epigram, *n.* epigramma, *m.*

epigraph, *n.* (*prefixed to book or*

chapter) epigrafe, *f.*; (*on stone*) iscrizione, *f.*
epilepsy, *n.* epilepsia, *f.*
epileptic, *a. & n.* epilettico, *a. & m.*
epilogue, *n.* epilogo, *m.*
Epiphany, *n.* Epifania, Befana, *f.*
episcopal, *a.* episcopale, vescovile.
episcopate & episcopacy, *n.* episcopato, vescovato, *m.*
episode, *n.* episodio, *m.*
epistle, *n.* epistola, *f.* **epistolary,** *a.* epistolare.
epitaph, *n.* epitaffio, *m.*
epithet, *n.* epiteto, *m.*
epitome, *n.* epitome, sunto, compendio, *m.*
epitomize, *v.t.* epitomare, abbreviare.
epoch, *n.* epoca, *f.* ~ *making,* *a.* che fa epoca.
epopee & epos, *n.* epopea, *f.*
Epsom salt[s], sal d'Inghilterra, *m.*
equable, *a.* equabile.
equal, *a.* eguale, uguale; pari. ~ *to* (task), capace di, pari a, all'altezza di. ¶ *n.* eguale, *m.f.* ¶ *v.t.* eguagliare, uguagliare. *other things being* ~, a parità di condizioni. *on* ~ *terms,* sopra un piede d'eguaglianza.
equality, *n.* uguaglianza, ugualità, *f.*; (*rights*) (*votes*) parità, *f.*
equalize, *v.t.* eguagliare; egualizzare; rendere uguale.
equanimity, *n.* equanimità, *f.*
equation, *n.* equazione, *f.*
equator, *n.* equatore, *m.* ~**ial,** *a.* equatoriale. [*telescope*], telescopio equatoriale, *m.*
equerry, *n.* scudiero, *m.*
equestrian, *a.* equestre. ¶ *n.* cavaliere, *m.*; cavallerizzo, *m.*
equilibrate, *v.t.* equilibrare. **equilibrium,** *n.* equilibrio, *m.*
equine, *a.* equino; ippico.
equinoctial, *a.* equinoziale. ~ *gales,* burrasche equinoziali, *f.pl.* **equinox,** *n.* equinozio, *m.*
equip, *v.t.* fornire, allestire, armare.
equipage, *n.* equipaggio, *m.*; attrezzi, *m.pl.* **equipment,** *n.* allestimento, corredo, armamento, *m.*
equipoise, *n.* equilibrio, *m.*
equitable, *a.* equo. **equity,** *n.* equità, *f.*
equivalent, *a. & n.* equivalente, *a. & m.* *to be* ~, equivalere (a).
equivocal, *a.* equivoco, ambiguo. **equivocate,** *v.i.* equivocare. **equivocation,** *n.* equivoco, *m.*
era, *n.* era, epoca, *f.*
erase, *v.t.* cancellare, raschiare.

eraser, *n.* (*knife*) raschino, *m.*; (*rubber*) gomma per cancellare.
erasure, *n.* cancellatura, raschiatura, *f.*
ere, *pr.* prima di. ¶ *c.* prima che. ~ *long,* fra breve, fra poco, presto.
Erebus, *n.* Erebo, *m.*
erect, *a.* dritto, ritto. ¶ *ad.* in piedi, con la testa alta. ¶ *v.t.* erigere, innalzare; (*Mech.*) montare; (*fig.*) fondare, stabilire. **erection,** *n.* erezione; costruzione; installazione, montatura, *f.* **erector** (*of machinery*) costruttore, montatore, *m.*
Erie (Lake), il lago Erie, *m.*
ermine, *n.* ermellino, *m.*
erode, *v.t.* erodere, rodere. **erosion,** *n.* erosione, *f.*
erotic, *a.* erotico.
err, *v.i.* sbagliare, sviare, errare.
errand, *n.* messaggio, *m.*; commissione, *f.* ~ *boy,* commesso, fattorino, *m.* ~ *girl,* commessa, *f.*
errant, *a.* errante, ramingo, girovago.
erratic, *a.* irregolare, eccentrico; (*Geol., Med., &c.*) erratico.
erratum, *n.* errore di stampa, *m.*
erroneous, *a.* erroneo, falso. ~**ly,** *ad.* erroneamente.
error, *n.* errore, fallo, sbaglio, *m.*; colpa, *f.*
eructation, *n.* eruttazione, *f.*
erudite, *a.* erudito. **erudition,** *n.* erudizione, *f.*
erupt, *v.i. & t.* eruttare. **eruption,** *n.* eruzione, *f.*
erysipelas, *n.* risipola, *f.*
escalator, *n.* scala mobile, *f.*
escallop, *n.* petonchio, *m.*
escapade, *n.* scappata, *f.*
escape, *n.* fuga, evasione, scappata, *f.*; scampo; scappamento; apparecchio di salvataggio, *m.* ~ *pipe,* tubo di scappamento, *m.* ~ *valve,* valvola di scappamento, *f.* ¶ *v.i.* scampare, fuggire, sfuggire, evadere, scappare; sottrarsi, salvarsi, rifugiarsi; (*v.t.*) sfuggire a, sottrarsi a; schivare, evitare. *escaped prisoner,* evaso, fuggiasco, *m.* ~**ment,** *n.* scappamento, *m.*
escarpment, *n.* scarpata, erta, *f.*
escheat, *n.* eredità devoluta allo Stato, *f.* ¶ *v.i.* decadere, essere devoluto (allo Stato); (*v.t.*) confiscare, toccare; devolvere (allo Stato).
eschew, *v.t.* evitare, schivare.
escort, *n.* scorta, *f.* ¶ *v.t.* scortare, accompagnare.
escutcheon, *n.* stemma, scudo, blasone, *m.*

espagnolette, *n.* spagnoletta, *f.*
espalier, *n.* spalliera, *f.*
esparto [grass], *n.* sparto, *m.*
especial, *a.* speciale, notabile. **especially,** *ad.* specialmente, soprattutto. ~ *as,* tanto piú che.
espionage, *n.* spionaggio, *m.*
esplanade, *n.* spianata, *f.*
espousal, *n.* sposalizio, *m.*; (*fig.*) adesione; adozione, *f.* ~**s,** *n.pl.* sponsali, *m.pl.* **espouse,** *v.t.* sposare; (*fig.*) abbracciare.
espy, *v.t.* scorgere.
esquire (*Hist.*), *n.* scudiero, *m.* **Esquire,** *n.* (*abb. Esq.*) Signore, *m.*
essay, *n.* saggio, *m.*; prova, *f.*; sforzo, tentativo, *m.* ¶ *v.t.* tentare, cercare, provare. **essayist,** *n.* scrittore, *m.* (scrittrice, *f.*) di saggi, saggista, *m.f.*
essence, *n.* essenza, *f.*
essential, *a.* essenziale. ~ *oil,* olio essenziale, *m.* ¶ *n.* essenziale, *m.*
establish, *v.t.* stabilire, fondare, istituire, creare; confermare, constatare. *the* ~*ed Church,* la Chiesa nazionale, *f.*
establishment, *n.* stabilimento, *m.*; fondazione, *f.*; istituzione; conferma, *f.*; accertamento, *m.*; casa di commercio, ditta, *f. peace* ~ (*Mil.*), piede di pace, *m. war* ~, piede di guerra.
estate, *n.* proprietà, *f.*, patrimonio, *m.*; beni, *m.pl.*; terre, *f.pl. personal* ~, beni mobili. *real* ~, beni immobili. ~ *agency,* agenzia immobiliare, *f.* ~ *agent,* (*private*) fattore, intendente *m.*, (*public*) agente di beni statali, *m.* ~ *duty,* imposta sul patrimonio, *f. mortgaged* ~, proprietà ipotecata, *f.*
esteem, *n.* stima, considerazione, *f.*; conto, *m.* ¶ *v.t.* stimare.
Esthonia, *n.* l'Estonia, *f.*
estimate, *n.* stima, valutazione, perizia, *f.*; preventivo, apprezzamento, giudizio, *m.*; opinione, *f.*; (*pl.*), bilancio preventivo, *m.* ¶ *v.t.* stimare, valutare, periziare, apprezzare. ~**d,** *p.a.* stimato, valutato, periziato. **estimation,** *a.* giudizio, *m.*; stima, valutazione, *f.*
estop (*Law*), *v.t.* eccepire; impedire.
estrange, *v.t.* alienare. ~**ment,** *n.* alienazione, *f.*
estuary, *n.* estuario, *m.*
et cetera, *phrase & n.* (*abb.* etc., &c.) eccetera, *abb.* ecc., *phrase & m.*
etch, *v.t.* incidere all'acquaforte.
etcher, *n.* acquafortista, *m.*

etching, *n.* incisione all'acquaforte, *f.* ~ *needle,* bulino, stilo, *m.*
eternal, *a.* eterno. *the* ~ *triangle,* l'eterno triangolo. **etern[al]ize,** *v.t.* eternare, rendere eterno. **eternity,** *n.* eternità, *f.*
ether, *n.* etere, *m.* **ethereal,** *a.* etereo, celeste.
ethical, *a.* etico. **ethics,** *n.pl.* etica, *f.*
Ethiopia, *n.* l'Etiopia, *f.* **Ethiopian,** *a.* etiopico, etiope. ¶ *n.* etiope, *m.f.*
ethnography, *n.* etnografia, *f.*
ethnologic(al), *a.* etnologico. **ethnologist,** *n.* etnologo, *m.* **ethnology,** *n.* etnologia, *f.*
ethyl, *n.* etile, *m.*
etiolate, *v.t.* far(e) intristire, far impallidire.
etiquette, *n.* etichetta, *f.*; decoro, *m.*; convenienze, *f.pl.*
Eton crop, *n.* taglio dei capelli alla maschietta, *m.*
etymologic(al), *a.* etimologico. **etymology,** *n.* etimologia, *f.*
eucalyptus, *n.* eucalipto, *m.*
Eucharist, *n.* Eucaristia, *f.*
eugenic, *a.* eugenico. **eugenics,** *n.pl.* eugenia, eugenica, *f.*
eulogistic, *a.* elogistico. **eulogize,** *v.t.* elogiare. **eulogy,** *n.* elogio, *m.*
Eumenides, *n.pl.* Eumenidi, *f.pl.*
eunuch, *n.* eunuco, *m.*
euphemism, *n.* eufemismo, *m.* **euphemistic,** *a.* eufemistico.
euphonic & euphonious, *a.* eufonico. **euphony,** *n.* eufonia, *f.*
Euphrates (the), l'Eufrate, *m.*
Europe, *n.* l'Europa, *f.* **European,** *a.* europeo. ¶ *n.* europeo, *m.*
Eustachian tube, tromba d'Eustachio, *f.*
evacuate, *v.t. & i.* evacuare.
evade, *v.t.* evadere, eludere, schivare, sottrarsi a.
evanescent, *a.* evanescente.
evangelic(al), *a.* evangelico. **evangelist,** *n.* evangelista, *m.*
evaporate, *v.t.* fare evaporare (*v.i.*), evaporare. **evaporation,** *n.* evaporazione, *f.*
evasion, *n.* evasione, *f.* ~ *of tax,* evasione dei tributi, evasione d'una tassa, *f.*
evasive, *a.* evasivo.
even (*Poet.*), *n.* sera, *f.* ~*song,* inno della sera, *m.*, preghiera della **s.** ~*tide,* cadere del giorno, imbrunire, *m.*; serata, *f.*

even, *a.* eguale, uguale; liscio; unito; piano; pari. ~ *number,* numero pari. ~ *with (ground, &c.),* a livello di. ¶ *v.t.* appianare, livellare; rendere liscio; unire, equalizzare. *to be* ~ *with (someone),* essere pari, al pari con; rivaleggiare con. ~ *handed,* imparziale. ¶ *ad.* anche, fino, perfino, pure. ~ *if,* ~ *though,* anche se, quand'anche. *not* ~, neanche, neppure. ~ *so,* proprio così, appunto, precisamente.

evening, *n.* sera, serata, *f.*; *(fig.)* declinare, *m.*, fine, *f.* ~ *dew,* ~ *damp,* serena, *f.* ~ *dress (man),* abito da cerimonia, *m.*; frac con le falde, *m.*; marsina, *f.*; abito a coda, *m.*; *(woman)* toletta da sera, *f.* ~ *gown,* veste da sera; abito da sera, da ricevimento. ¶ *a.* serale, di sera, della sera.

evenly, *ad.* ugualmente; lisciamente; parimenti.

evenness, *n.* uguaglianza; levigatezza; calma, *f.*

event, *n.* avvenimento, caso, evento, *m.*; esito, risultato, *m.*; *(sport)* prova, *f.* *at all* ~s, in ogni caso. *in the* ~ *of,* in caso di. **eventful,** *a.* pieno di avvenimenti, pieno di incidenti, memorabile.

eventual, *a.* eventuale. **eventuality,** *n.* eventualità, *f.*

eventuate, *v.i.* risultare, riuscire.

ever, *ad.* mai, sempre. *for* ~, per sempre. ~ *after,* d'allora in poi, dopo. ~ *so little,* per quanto piccolo, poco. *once and for* ~, una volta per sempre. ~ *since,* da che, dal tempo che, da quel tempo in qua.

everlasting, *a.* sempiterno, eterno; *(Bot.) a. & n.* semprevivo, *a.* -a, *f.*

evermore, *ad.* sempre, eternamente. *for* ~, in eterno.

every, *a.* ogni; tutti i, tutte le. ~*body, everyone, every one (every person),* ognuno, tutti. ~*day, a.* di ogni giorno, di tutti i giorni; comune, ordinario. ~*day clothes,* abito civile. ~*one (each),* ciascuno. ~*thing, n.* ogni cosa, tutto, tutto ciò (che). ~*where, ad.* dappertutto, ogni dove, in ogni luogo, ovunque.

evict, *v.t.* evincere, espellere, espropriare. **eviction,** *n.* evizione, espulsione, *f.*

evidence, *n.* testimonianza, evidenza, prova, *f.*; rilievo, *m.* *to be* ~, fare fede. *to give* ~, testimoniare, rendere testimonianza. ¶ *v.t.* dimostrare, provare. **evident,** *a.* evidente, manifesto. **evidently,** *ad.* evidentemente.

evil, *a.* cattivo, malvagio, perverso. ~ *days,* avversità, miseria, *f.* ~ *disposed (person), a. & n.* maldisposto, malintenzionato, *a. & m.* ~*doer,* malfattore, *m.* ~ *eye,* malocchio. *m.* *The E*~ *One,* il Diavolo, *m.* ~ *speaking, a.* maldicente; *(n.)* maldicenza, *f.* ~ *spirit,* spirito maligno, *m.* ¶ *ad.* male, mal- *(prefix),* malamente. ¶ *n.* male, *m.*; cattiveria, perversità; disgrazia; malattia, *f.*

evince, *v.t.* manifestare, mostrare.

eviscerate, *v.t.* sviscerare.

evocation, *n.* evocazione, *f.* **evoke,** *v.t.* evocare.

evolution, *n.* evoluzione, *f.*; sviluppo, svolgimento, *m.*, *(Biol., &c.)* evoluzione, *f.*; *(Geom.)* estrazione di radice; *(Chem.)* esalazione, *f.* **evolve,** *v.t.* evolvere; sviluppare, svolgere; *(v.i.)* evolversi, svilupparsi.

ewe, *n.* pecora, *f.* ~ *lamb,* agnella, *f.*

ewer, *n.* brocca, *f.*; boccale, *m.*

ex-, *prefix.* ~*professor,* ex-professore, professore a riposo. ~*service man,* ex-combattente, *m.*

ex, *pr.*: ~ *bond,* sdoganato. ~ *dividend,* senza dividendo. ~ *ship,* ~ *steamer* (sales), fuori della nave, del vapore. ~ *steamer* (transhipment), trasbordato. ~ *store,* ~ *warehouse,* fuori magazzino, alla porta del magazzino. ~ *wharf,* sulla calata, sulla banchina.

exacerbate, *v.t.* esacerbare.

exact, *a.* esatto, preciso, rigoroso. ¶ *v.t.* esigere, estorcere. **exacting,** *p.a.* esigente. **exaction,** *n.* esazione, estorsione, *f.* **exactly,** *ad.* esattamente; appunto; giustamente. **exactness, exactitude,** *n.* esattezza, *f.*

exaggerate, *v.t. & abs.* esagerare.

exalt, *v.t.* esaltare.

examination, *n.* esame; interrogatorio, *m.*; ispezione; visita; investigazione, *f.*; scrutinio; concorso, *m.* ~ *paper,* tema d'esame, *m.* ~ *fee,* tassa d'esame, *f.* *degree* ~, *(Univ.),* esame di laurea. *entrance* ~, esame d'ammissione. **examine,** *v.t.* esaminare, interrogare; visitare, ispezionare, perquisire. **examinee,** *n.* candidato, -a, *m.f.* **examiner,** *n.* esaminatore, -trice, *f.*; ispettore,

-trice, *f.*; (*plays*) censore teatrale, *m.*
board *of* ~**s,** commissione d'esame, *f.*
example, *n.* esempio, esemplare, modello, *m.*
exasperate, *v.t.* esasperare.
excavate, *v.t.* scavare. **excavation,** *n.* scavo, scavamento, sterro, *m.*; escavazione, *f.* **excavator,** *n.* (*Mach.*) escavatore, *m.*
exceed, *v.t.* eccedere, oltrepassare. **exceedingly,** *ad.* eccessivamente, estremamente, stra- (*prefix*).
excel, *v.i.* primeggiare, eccellere; (*v.t.*) superare, sorpassare. **excellence,** *n.* eccellenza, *f.* His Excellency, Sua Eccellenza. **excellent,** *a.* eccellente. **excellently,** *ad.* eccellentemente, benissimo.
except, *c.* senonché, a meno che. ~ *&* ~**ing,** *pr.* eccetto, salvo, ad eccezione di, fuori di, eccettuato. ¶ *v.t.* eccettuare. **exception,** *n.* eccezione, *f.* to take ~ to, trovare a ridire, aversi a male, mettere in questione, fare obbiezione a. **exceptionable,** *a.* riprensibile, criticabile. **exceptional,** *a.* eccezionale.
excerpt, *n.* brano, squarcio, estratto, *m.*; citazione, *f.* ¶ *v.t.* fare un estratto di, scegliere brani, &c.
excess, *n.* eccesso, troppo, *m.*; eccedenza, *f.*; eccedente, *m.*; soprappiù, *m.*; prodigalità, stravaganza, intemperanza, smoderatezza, *f.* ~ (*fare*), supplemento, prezzo supplementare, *m.* ~ *profits,* sopraprofitto, *m.* ~ *weight,* soprappeso, *m.* **excessive,** *a.* eccessivo, soperchio, smoderato.
exchange, *n.* cambio, scambio, *m.*; permuta, *f.*, baratto, *m.*; (*Stk. Ex.*) borsa, *f.*; (*Teleph.*) posto (telefonico) centrale, *m.* ~ *business,* aggiotaggio, *m.* bill *of* ~, cambiale, *f.*; ~ [*premium*], aggio, *m.* rate *of* ~, ~ *rates,* corso del cambio, *m.* ¶ *v.t.* scambiare, cambiare, permutare, barattare.
exchequer, *n.* tesoro, *m.*; tesoreria, *f.*; Ministero delle finanze, *m.*, (*Eng.*) Scacchiere, *m.*, (*of pers.*) mezzi, *m.pl.*; risorse, finanze, *f.pl.*
excise, *n.* imposte indirette, *f.pl.*; dazio interno, *m.*; regia, *f.* ~*man,* agente delle imposte, impiegato della Regia, *m.*
excite, *v.t.* eccitare, stimolare, provocare, aizzare. **excitement,** *n.* eccitamento, stimolo, *m.*; febbre,

emozione, esaltazione, eccitazione, agitazione, *f.*
exclaim, *v.i.* esclamare, gridare. ~ *against,* gridare contro, inveire contro. **exclamation,** *n.* esclamazione, *f.*; grido, *m.*
exclude, *v.t.* escludere. **exclusion,** *n.* esclusione, *f.* **exclusive,** *a.* exclusivo. ~ *right(s),* diritti esclusivi, *m.pl.*; esclusività, *f.*
excommunicate, *v.t.* scomunicare. **excommunication,** *n.* scomunica, *f.*
excrement, *n.* escremento; sterco, *m.*
excrescence, *n.* escrescenza, *f.*
excruciating, *p.a.* crucciante, torturante, atr ce. ~ *pains,* dolori atroci, *m.pl.*
exculpate, *v.t.* scolpare. **exculpation,** *n.* discolpa, *f.*
excursion, *n.* escursione, gita; digressione, *f.* ~ *ticket,* biglietto d'escursione, *m.* ~ *train,* treno escursionista, treno di piacere, *m.*
excursionist, *n.* escursionista, *m.f.*
excuse, *n.* scusa, *f.*; pretesto, *m.* ¶ *v.t.* scusare, perdonare; esentare, esonerare. ~ *me,* scusi, scusate! [con] permesso!
execrable, *a.* esecrabile. **execrate,** *v.t.* esecrare.
executant, *n.* esecutore, -trice, *m.f.*
execute, *v.t.* eseguire, mettere in esecuzione; fare, compiere; adempiere, esercitare; giustiziare; (*document*) eseguire, firmare. **execution,** *n.* esecuzione, *f.*; eseguimento, adempimento, *m.*; compimento, *m.*; azione forzata, *f.*; sequestro, *m.*; supplizio capitale, *m.* **executioner,** *n.* boia, carnefice, giustiziere, *m.*
executive, *n.* potere esecutivo, *m.*; direzione, *f.*; Stato Maggiore, *m.*
executor, *m.f.s.* *trice,* *n.* esecutore, -trice, *m.f.* **executory,** *a.* esecutivo.
exemplary, *a.* esemplare.
exemplify, *v.t.* esemplificare; servire d'esempio a, dare un esempio di.
exempt, *a.* esente. ¶ *v.t.* esentare, dispensare. **exemption,** *n.* esenzione, *f.*
exequies, *n.pl.* esequie, *f.pl.*
exercise, *n.* esercizio; (*Sch.*) compito, lavoro, *m.* ~ *book,* *n.* quaderno, *m.* ¶ *v.t.* esercitare; (*Stk. Ex. option*) riservarsi (il diritto di opzione; (*v.i.*) esercitarsi.
exergue, *n.* esergo, *m.*
exert, *v.t.* esercitare, fare uso di, impiegare. ~ *oneself,* sforzarsi (di), adoperarsi (per), fare tutto il possibile.
exertion, *n.* sforzo; impiego, uso, *m.*

exfoliate, *v.i.* esfogliarsi, sfaldarsi.
exhalation, *n.* esalazione, *f.* **exhale**, *v.t.* esalare.
exhaust, *n.* scarico, *m.*; aspirazione, *f.* ¶ *v.t.* esaurire; (*Phys.*) aspirare. **exhaustion**, *n.* esaurimento, *m.*; aspirazione, *f.* **exhaustive**, *a.* esauriente; completo. **exhaustively**, *ad.* esaurientemente, completamente; a fondo.
exhibit, *n.* esibita, *f.*; documento, *m.*; (*Law, Civil*) pezza giustificativa, (*Criminal*) p. d'appoggio, *f.* ¶ *v.t.* esibire, esporre, manifestare, mostrare, produrre. **exhibition**, *n.* esposizione, mostra, *f.*; salone, *m.*; esibizione, *f.*, (*college*) borsa (di studio), *f.* **exhibitioner**, *n.* borsista, titolare di una borsa di studio, *m.f.* **exhibitor**, *n.* esibitore, espositore, *m.*
exhilarate, *v.t.* esilarare.
exhort, *v.t.* esortare.
exhume, *v.t.* esumare.
exigence, -cy, *n.* esigenza, *f.*
exiguous, *a.* esiguo.
exile, *n.* esilio, bando, *m.*; (*pers.*) esule, esiliato, -a, *m.f.* ¶ *v.t.* esiliare.
exist, *v.i.* esistere. **existence**, *n.* esistenza, *f.*
exit, *n.* uscita, *f.* *to make one's ~*, uscire. *~X* (*Theat.*), esce X, via X.
ex-libris, *n.* ex libris, *m.*
exodus, *n.* esodo, *m.*; partenza, *f.* *E ~* (*Bible*), Esodo, *m.*
ex officio, ex officio, a titolo d'ufficio.
exonerate, *v.t.* esonerare, discolpare, scolpare.
exorbitance, *n.* esorbitanza, *f.*; eccesso, *m.* **exorbitant**, *a.* esorbitante, eccessivo. **exorbitantly**, *ad.* esorbitantemente, eccessivamente.
exorcise, *v.t.* esorcizzare.
exordium, *n.* esordio, *m.*
exotic, *a.* esotico. ¶ *n.* pianta esotica, *f.*
expand, *v.t.* espandere, diffondere, dilatare, sviluppare; (*v.i.*) espandersi, &c. **expanse**, *n.* distesa, espansione, *f.*; (*wing*) apertura, larghezza, *f.* **expansion**, *n.* espansione, estensione, *f.*; sviluppo, *m.* **expansive**, *a.* espansivo.
expatiate, *v.i.* dilungarsi (sopra).
expatriate, *v.t.* espatriare, spatriare.
expect, *v.t.* aspettare, attendere, contare (di, che); sperare, pensare, credere; promettersi, attendersi; esigere, volere. **expectancy**, *n.* attesa, aspettativa, *f.* **expectant**, *a.*

aspettante, aspirante, speranzoso. *~ mother*, donna incinta, *f.*
expectation, *n.* aspettazione, previsione, speranza, *f.*
expectorate, *v.t. & abs.* espettorare.
expedience, -cy, *n.* convenienza, *f.*; vantaggio, *m.* **expedient**, *a.* conveniente, opportuno, a proposito. ¶ *n.* espediente, mezzo, *m.*
expedite, *v.t.* accelerare, facilitare, sbrigare. **expedition**, *n.* spedizione, *f.*; prontezza, speditezza, *f.* **expeditionary**, *a.* spedizionario. **expeditious**, *a.* spedito, sbrigativo.
expel, *v.t.* espellere, scacciare.
expend, *v.t.* spendere, consumare; esaurire. **expenditure**, *n.* spesa, *f.*; spese, *f.pl.*; sborso, dispendio, *m.* **expense**, *n.* spesa, *f.*; spese, *f.pl.* *at the ~ of*, alle spese di. *at one's own ~*, a proprie spese. **expensive**, *a.* dispendioso, costoso.
experience, *n.* esperienza, pratica, *f.* ¶ *v.t.* esperimentare, provare, fare l'esperienza di.
experiment, *n.* esperimento, *m.*; prova, *f.* ¶ *v.i.* fare un esperimento, sperimentare. *~ on*, fare esperimenti su. **experimental**, *a.* sperimentale.
expert, *a. & n.* esperto, *a. & m.*; perito, *m.* **expertness**, *n.* abilità, capacità, perizia, *f.*
expiate, *v.t.* espiare, fare espiazione di.
expiration & **expiry**, *n.* scadenza, *f.*; fine, cessazione, *f.* **expire**, *v.i.* decorrere, scadere, cessare; morire, (*v.t.*) espirare. **expiring**, *a.* morente.
explain, *v.t.* spiegare, esporre. **explainable**, *a.* spiegabile. **explanation**, *n.* spiegazione, *f.* **explanatory**, *a.* spiegativo, esplicativo. *~ note* (*on map*), leggenda, *f.*
expletive (*Gram.*), *a.* espletivo. ¶ *n.* parola espletiva, *f.*; pleonasmo, *m.*; (*in verse*) parola inutile; (*oath*) bestemmia, *f.*
explicit, *a.* esplicito.
explode, *v.t.* fare scoppiare, fare esplodere, fare saltare; brillare (una mina); (*fig.*) distruggere, screditare; (*v.i.*) scoppiare, esplodere, saltare. *~d theory*, teoria abbandonata, screditata, *f.*
exploit, *n.* bel fatto, fatto d'armi, impresa gloriosa; gesta, *f.pl.* ¶ *v.t.* sfruttare, utilizzare, trarre partito da. **exploitation**, *n.* sfruttamento, *m.*
explore, *v.t.* esplorare. **explorer**, *n.*

esploratore, *m.*; esploratrice, *f.* **exploration,** *n.* esplorazione, *f.* **explosion,** *n.* esplosione, *f.*; scoppio, *m.* **explosive,** *a.* esplosivo. ¶ *n.* esplosivo, *m.*; (*Gram.*) esplosiva, *f.*

exponent, *n.* esponente, espositore; interprete, *m.*; (*Math.*) esponente, *m.*

export, *v.t.* esportare. **export-[ation],** *n.* esportazione, *f.* **exporter,** *n.* esportatore, *m.*

expose, *v.t.* esporre, scoprire, svelare, smascherare; (*Phot.*) esporre. ∼ *for sale,* esporre per la vendita. **exposition,** *n.* esposizione, *f.*; commentario, *m.*

expostulate, *v.i.* fare (rivolgere) delle rimostranze (con, contro). **expostulation,** *n.* rimostranza, *f.*

exposure, *n.* smascheramento, *m.*; (*Phot.*) fotografia a posa (breve, lunga, &c.), esposizione, posa, *f.*

expound, *v.t.* spiegare, chiarire, commentare, interpretare.

express, *a.* espresso, formale. ¶ (*Post., &c.*) *n.* espresso, *m.* ∼ *letter,* lettera (inviata) per espresso, l. espresso, *f.* ∼ *messenger,* corriere (espresso). ∼ *parcel,* (*Post*) pacco espresso, servizio espresso dei pacchi postali. ∼ (*train*), (*Rly.*) [treno] direttissimo, *m.* ¶ *v.t.* esprimere. **expression,** *n.* espressione, *f.* **expressive,** *a.* espressivo. **expressly,** *ad.* apposta, appunto, espressamente, esplicitamente.

expropriate, *v.t.* espropriare.

expulsion, *n.* espulsione, *f.*

expunge, *v.t.* cancellare; radiare.

expurgate, *v.t.* espurgare.

exquisite, *a.* squisito. **exquisitely,** *ad.* squisitamente. **exquisiteness,** *n.* squisitezza, *f.*

extant (to be), esistere.

extempore, *a.* estemporaneo, improvvisato. ¶ *ad.* estemporaneamente, ex tempore. **extemporize,** *v.t. & i.* improvvisare.

extend, *v.t.* estendere, prolungare, allargare, allungare; tendere; dilatare. ∼*ed order* (*Mil.*), ordine sparso, *m.* **extension,** *n.* estensione, *f.*; prolungamento, *m.*; allungamento; (*Teleph.*) posto supplementare, *m.* ∼ *ladder,* scala estensibile, allungabile, *f.* ∼ *tripod,* treppiede estensibile, *m.* **extensive,** *a.* estensivo, esteso, largo. **extensively,** *ad.* estesamente, estensivamente.

extensor (*muscle*), *n.* (muscolo) estensore, *m.*

extent, *n.* estensione, *f.*; grado, punto, limite, *m.*; portata; mole, *f.* *to a certain* ∼, fino ad un certo punto. *to a great* ∼, in alto grado, in gran parte. *to what* ∼? fin dove? fino a qual grado?

extenuate, *v.t.* estenuare, attenuare.

exterior, *a.* esteriore, esterno. ¶ *n.* esteriore, esterno, *m.*

exterminate, *v.t.* sterminare.

external, *a.* esterno, esteriore. **externally,** *ad.* all'esterno, esternamente.

exterritoriality, *n.* estraterritorialità, *f.*

extinct, *a.* estinto. **extinction,** *n.* estinzione, *f.*

extinguish, *v.t.* estinguere, spegnere, smorzare. **extinguisher,** *n.* (*light*) spegnitoio, *m.*; (*fire*) estintore, smorzatore, *m.*

extirpate, *v.t.* estirpare.

extol, *v.t.* estollere, esaltare, lodare.

extort, *v.t.* estorcere. **extortion,** *n.* estorsione, *f.* **extortionate,** *a.* esorbitante, oppressivo, eccessivo. **extortioner,** *n.* concussionario, chi è colpevole di estorsione, *m.*

extra, *a.* addizionale, extra, supplementare, eccedente, di più. ∼ *binding,* rilegatura di lusso, *f.* ∼ *fare,* prezzo supplementare, supplemento, *m.* ∼ *postage,* sopratassa postale, *f.* ¶ *ad.* fuori, in aggiunta, inoltre. ¶ *n.* supplemento, *m.*; aggiunta, *f.*; il di più, soprappiú, *m.*

extract, *n.* estratto; brano, *m.* ¶ *v.t.* estrarre. **extraction,** *n.* estrazione, *f.*; origine, *m.*; nascita, *f.*

extradite, *v.t.* estradare, consegnare per estradizione. **extradition,** *n.* estradizione, *f.*

extramural, *a.* estramurale, fuori le mura.

extraneous, *a.* estraneo.

extraordinary, *a.* straordinario. ¶ *n.* inviato straordinario, *m.*; cosa insolita, cosa straordinaria, *f.*

extraterritoriality, *n.* estraterritorialità, *f.*

extravagance, *n.* stravaganza, *f.*; (*money*) prodigalità, *f.* **extravagant,** *a.* stravagante; (*of pers.*) prodigo, spendereccio; (*price*) esorbitante. **extravagantly,** *ad.* prodigalmente; stravagantemente.

extreme, *a. & n.* estremo, *a. & m.* ∼ *penalty,* pena capitale, pena di morte, *f.* ∼ *unction,* *n.* estrema unzione, *f.* **extremist,** *n.* estremista, *m.f.*; (*att.*) esagerato, violento. **extremity,** *n.* estremità, situazione critica, *f.*; imbarazzo, *m.*

extricate, *v.t.* distrigare, sbarazzare, sbrogliare. ~ *oneself,* cavarsi, sbarazzarsi.

extrinsic, *a.* estrinseco.

exuberance, *n.* esuberanza, *f.* **exuberant,** *a.* esuberante.

exude, *v.i.* essudare, trasudare, (*v.t.*) essudare.

exult, *v.i.* esultare.

ex voto, *n.* ex-voto, *m.*

eye, *n.* occhio, *m.*; (*needle*) cruna, *f.*; occhio dell'ago, *m.*; (*fruit*) occhio; (*potato*) occhio della patata, *m.* ~*ball,* globo dell'occhio, *m.* ~*bath,* bacinetto oculare, *m.* ~*bolt,* bullone ad occhio, *m.* ~*brow,* sopracciglio, *m.* ~*brow pencil,* lapis per le sopracciglia, lapis nero, *m.* ~*brow tweezers,* pinzette per le sopracciglia, *f.pl.* ~ *doctor,* oculista, *m.f.* ~*s front!* (*Mil.*) (occhi) fissi! ~*glass,* monocolo, *m.*; (*pl.*) occhiali, *m.pl.* ~*lash,* ciglio, *m.*; ciglia, *f.pl.* ~*lid,* palpebra, *f.* ~*-opener,* rivelazione, *f.* ~*piece,* oculare, *m.* ~*shade,* paralume, *m.* ~*sight,* vista, *f.* ~*sore,* oggetto sgradevole all'occhio, alla vista. ~*tooth,* dente canino, *m.* ~ *trouble,* mal d'occhi. ~ *-witness,* testimone oculare, *m.f.* ¶ *v.t.* guardare, adocchiare, sorvegliare, occhieggiare.

eyelet, *n. &* ~*hole,* occhiello, *m.*

eyot, *n.* isolotto (di fiume), *m.*

eyrie, *n.* nido d'uccello da preda, *m.*

F

F (*Mus.*) *letter,* fa, *m.* ~*clef,* chiave di fa, *f.*

fable, *n.* favola, *f.* ~*d,* *p.p.* finto, favoloso.

fabric, *n.* tessuto, *m.*; stoffa, *f.*; (*edifice*) fabbrica, *f.*; edificio, *m.* (*fig.*) struttura, *f.* ~ *gloves,* guanti di tessuto, *m.pl.*

fabricate, *v.t.* fabbricare, costruire.

fabrication, *n.* fabbricazione, *f.*

fabricator, *n.* fabbricante, *m.*

fabulist, *n.* favoleggiatore, *m.*

fabulous, *a.* favoloso.

facade, *n.* facciata, *f.*

face, *n.* faccia, *f.*; viso, volto, *m.*, figura, fisionomia, *f.*; (*wry*) smorfia, *f.*; (*clock*) quadrante, *m.*; (*cloth*) diritto, *m.*; (*Cards*) figura, *f.*; (*of type*) occhio, *m.* ~ *ache,* nevralgia facciale. ~ *cream, white,* crema per la faccia, *f.* ~ *lifting,* chirurgia estetica del viso, *f.* ~ *massage,* massaggio della faccia, *m.* ~ *plate* (*dial*), quadrante, *m.* ~ *plate* (*lathe*) mandrino, *m.* ~ *powder,* cipria, *f.* ~ *to* ~, a quattr'occhi, faccia a faccia, fronte a fronte. ~ *value* (*Fin.*) valore nominale. ¶ *v.t.* far fronte a, fronteggiare, affrontare, resistere a; essere di fronte, essere esposto a; essere in faccia a; coprire, rivestire. ~*d with* (*silk, &c.*) con rivolte di (seta ecc.).

facet, *n.* faccetta, *f.* ¶ *v.t.* faccettare.

facetious, *a.* faceto.

facia [**board**], *n.* piattaforma, *f.*; insegna (di negozio), *f.*

facial, *a.* facciale.

facies, *n.* aspetto, *m.*; faccia, *f.*

facile, *a.* facile. **facilitate,** *v.t.* facilitare. **facility,** *n.* facilità, *f.*

facing, *n.* (*dress*) mostreggiatura, risvolta, *f.*; (*building*) rivestimento; *m.* ¶ *ad. & pr.* di fronte, dirimpetto. ~ *the engine* (*to travel*), viaggiare nel senso della macchina; (*seat*) posto che guardi la macchina.

facsimile, *n.* facsimile, *m.* ~ *signature &* ~ *stamp,* firma in facsimile, *f.*, timbro, *m.*

fact, *n.* fatto, *m.*

faction, *n.* fazione, *f.*

factious, *a.* fazioso.

factitious, *a.* fittizio.

factor, *n.* fattore, *m.*; (*pers.*) fattore, agente, commissionario, *m.*

factory, *n.* fabbrica, officina, *f.*; stabilimento, opificio, *m.* ~ *hand,* *n.* operaio di fabbrica, *m.* ~ *inspector,* *n.* ispettore delle fabbriche (di lavoro), *m.*

factotum, *n.* factotum, *m.*

faculty, *n.* facoltà, capacità, *f.*; potere, talento, *m.*, (*Univ.*) Facoltà.

fad, *n.* fantasia, ubbia, smania, *f.*; grillo, *m.*

faddist, *n.* persona capricciosa, piena di ubbie, *f.*

fade, *v.i.* appassire, avvizzire, deperire, languire, sbiadire, impallidire, svanire; (*v.t.*) fare appassire, scolorire. ~ *away,* appassire, deperire, svanire. ~ *out,* perire, svanire, estinguersi, morire. ~*d,* *p.a.* sbiadito, scolorito, appassito.

fag, *n.* lavoro ingrato, *m.*; fatica, *f.* ¶ *v.t.* esaurire, vessare; (*v.i.*) sgobbare, faticarsi. ~ *end, n.* pezzo stracco, *m.*

fag[g]ot, *n.* fascina, *f.* ¶ *v.t.* affagottare.

Fahrenheit, *a.* Fahrenheit.

fail, *v.i.* fallire, non riuscire, riuscire male, fare fiasco; mancare; fallire, fare fallimento, fare bancarotta; (*fig.*) naufragare, deperire, languire; (*v.t.*) mancare, venir meno a, tradire, abbandonare. ~ *in one's duty,* mancare, venir meno all'adempimento del proprio dovere. *without* ~, senza fallo.

failing, *n.* difetto, debole, *m.*; colpa, *f.* ¶ *pr.* in mancanza di, in difetto di.

failure, *n.* insuccesso, fiasco, *m.*; indebolimento, *m.*; caduta, *f.*; (*Com.*) bancarotta, *f.*; fallimento, *m.* *a* ~ *as a barrister,* &c., un avvocato mancato, &c.

fain, *a.* & *adv.* *to be* ~ *to,* essere disposto a, essere contento, essere soddisfatto in mancanza di meglio. *I would* ~ *be,* sarei volentieri, mi piacerebbe essere. *I would* ~ *have,* avrei volentieri, vorrei avere.

faint, *a.* debole, esaurito, languente; fiacco. ~ *hearted,* timido, pusillanime, scoraggiato. ~ *ruled* (*paper*), carta rigata, *f.* ¶ *v.i.* venir meno, svenire, indebolirsi, tramortire.

fainting (fit), *n.* svenimento, deliquio, *m.*

fair, *a.* bello, chiaro; favorevole; conveniente; leale, equo, giusto, onesto; modico, mediocre; ragionevole, sufficiente; (*skin*) bianco; (*hair*) biondo. *at* ~ (*barometer*) al bello. ~ *copy,* bella copia, copia pulita, *f.*; (*Sch.*) copia corretta, copia fedele, *f.* ~ *haired,* dai capelli biondi. ~ *haired person,* biondo, -a. *by* ~ *means or foul,* colle buone o colle cattive. ~ *play,* buon giuoco, *m.*; onestà, *f.* *not* ~, ingiusto, disonesto, non del giuoco. ~ *promises,* belle promesse. ~ *sex,* bel sesso, *m.* ~ *spoken,* affabile, dalla parola melata, sdolcinato. ~*way,* canale, passo navigabile, *m.* ¶ *n.* fiera, *f.*; mercato, *m.*

fairly, *ad.* bene; cosí cosí; favorevolmente, onestamente; con giustizia.

fairness, *n.* equità, giustizia; buona fede, imparzialità, *f.*; bellezza, bianchezza, *f.*

fairy, *n.* fata, *f.* ~ *cycle,* bicicletta da bambini, *f.* ~ *lamp,* ~ *light,* lampada cinese, *f.* *Fairyland, n.*

mondo (regno) delle fate, *m.* ~*like,* *a.* magico, incantevole. ~ *ring,* cerchio magico, *m.* ~*tale,* fiaba, racconto di fate, novella delle fate, *f.*

faith, *n.* fede; fiducia; confidenza; religione, *f.* **faithful,** *a.* fedele. *the* ~, i fedeli, i credenti, *m.pl.* **faithfulness,** *n.* fedeltà, *f.* **faithless,** *a.* senza fede, infedele, perfido. **faithlessness,** *n.* infedeltà, mancanza di fede, perfidia, *f.*

fake, *n.* cosa finta, contraffazione, truffa, *f.* ¶ *v.t.* contraffare, truffare, mascherare i difetti di.

fakir, *n.* fachiro, *m.*

falcon, *n.* falcone, *m.* **falconer,** *n.* falconiere, *m.* **falconry,** *n.* falconiera, *f.*

fall, *n.* caduta, discesa, *f.*; declivio; abbassamento, decrescimento, *m.*; diminuzione, *f.*, ribasso, *m.*; cadenza, decadenza; presa, cattura; rovina, *f.*; velo, *m.*; veletta, *f.*; (*pl.*) cascata, cateratta, *f.*; salto, *m.* (*tackle*) catena di comando, c. di manovra, *f.* ¶ *v.i.* ir. cadere, cascare; abbassarsi, diminuire, discendere; morire, perire, soccombere. ~ *back,* ricadere, indietreggiare, rinculare, darsi indietro. ~ *down,* cadere giú, prostrarsi, crollare. ~ *due,* maturare, scadere. ~ *in* (*cave in*), affondare, crollare, rovinare, scadere; (*Mil.*) mettersi in fila, formare le file. ~ *in love,* innamorarsi. ~ *in with* (*opinion*), accordarsi con, mettersi d'accordo con, accedere a. ~ *off,* staccarsi, distaccarsi; cascare da, cadere; abbassarsi, diminuire, scemare. ~ *out with,* litigare, venire a parola (con), venire ad una rottura. ~ *foul of,* incollerirsi con. *fall out,* cadere fuori; accadere; (*Mil.*) rompere le file. ~ *through* (*fail*), fallire, andare a monte. ~ *to,* mettersi a, cominciare; toccarsi a, spettare a.

fallacious, *a.* fallace. **fallacy,** *n.* illusione, falsità, fallacia, *f.*

fallals, *n.pl.* & **failalery,** *n.* ninnoli, *m.pl.*; balocchi, *m.pl.*

fallen angel, angelo decaduto, *m.* **fallen leaves,** foglie cadute, *f.pl.*

fallibility, *n.* fallibilità, *f.* **fallible,** *a.* fallibile.

falling star, stella cadente, *f.*

fallow, *a.* (*colour of deer*) fulvo; (*land*) incolto, a maggese. ~ *deer,* daino, *m.* *to lie* ~, essere incolto. ¶ *v.t.* coltivare a maggese, lasciare incolto.

false, *a.* falso; insincero; perfido; bugiardo, menzognero; artificiale, posticcio, finto. ~ *bottom*, doppio fondo, *m*. ~ *shame*, falsa vergogna, *f*. ¶ *ad*. falsamente. ~**hood**, *n*. menzogna, *f*. **falsely**, *ad*. falsamente. **falseness**, *n*. falsità, perfidia, *f*. **falsetto**, *n*. falsetto, *m*. **falsify**, *v.t*. falsificare, contraffare.

falter, *v.i*. vacillare, esitare, titubare, balbettare.

fame, *n*. fama, rinomanza, riputazione, *f*.; nome, *m*. ~**d**, *a*. rinomato, famoso.

familiar, *a*. familiare, intimo. ~ *face*, volto familiare, faccia conosciuta, aspetto noto. ~ (*spirit*), genio familiare. ¶ *n*. familiare, intimo, *m*. **familiarity**, *n*. familiarità, *f*. **familiarize**, *v.t*. familiarizzare.

family, *n*. famiglia, casa, *f*.; casato, *m*. ~ *likeness*, aria di famiglia, *f*. ~ *life*, vita di famiglia, *f*. *friend of the* ~, amico di casa. ~ *man*, padre di famiglia, *m*. ~ *tree*, albero genealogico, *m*.

famine, *n*. carestia, *f*. ~ *price*, prezzo di carestia.

famish, *v.t*. affamare. *to be* ~*ing*, essere affamato, morire di fame.

famous, *a*. famoso, rinomato, celebre. ~ *case* (*Law*), processo famoso, *m*.

fan, *n*. ventaglio; ventilatore, *m*. ~*light*, lunetta, imposta, *f*. ~*tail*, coda a ventaglio, *f*. ¶ *v.t*. fare vento su, ventilare, sventolare, fare aria (a) (*corn*) vagliare; (*fire*, &c., *fig*.) attirare, soffiare. *to* ~ *oneself*, farsi vento.

fanatic, *n*. fanatico, *m*. **fanatical**, *a*. fanatico. **fanaticism**, *n*, fanatismo, *m*. **fanaticize**, *v.t*. infanatichire, destare fanatismo in.

fancied, *p.a*. immaginato.

fancier, *n*. amatore, *m*.; (*dealer*) negoziante, *m*.

fanciful, *a*. fantastico, capriccioso, bizzarro.

fancy, *n*. fantasia, *f*.; capriccio, ghiribizzo, *m*.; bizzarria, *f*.; gusto, *m*.; voglia, *f*.; idea, immaginazione, *f*. ~ (*article*), oggetto di fantasia; articolo di fantasia, *m*. ~ *bread*, pasticceria, *f*.; pasticcini, *n.pl*. ~ *dog*, cane di lusso, *m*. ~ *draper*, negoziante di tessuti, *m*. ~ *drapery*, biancheria ricamata, biancheria con ricami di fantasia. ~ *dress*, costume, *m*.; abito da maschera, *m*. ~ *dress ball*, ballo in costume, *m*.; ballo in maschera, *m*. ~ *goods*, articoli di lusso, *m.pl*. ~ *leather goods* or *shop*, articoli di marocchino. ~ *needle-*

work, ricamo, *m*.; lavoro di fantasia. ~ *roll*, pane molle, *m*. ~*work*, lavoro di fantasia, *m*. ¶ *v.t*. immaginare, immaginarsi, supporre, figurarsi; aver gusto per. ~ *oneself*, figurarsi, immaginarsi. *I fancy I see*, mi sembra di vedere.

fang, *n*. dente, *m*.; zanna, *f*.

fantasia, *n*. fantasia, *f*. **fantastic**, *a*. fantastico. **fantasy**, *n*. fantasia, *f*.

far, *ad*. lontano, lungi, da lontano; molto, assai, di gran lunga. *from* ~, da lontano. *how* ~ *is it to . . .?* quanto c'è da qui a . . .? ~ *& wide*, da tutti i lati, da tutte le parti, in lungo ed in largo. *as* ~ *as*, per quanto, fino a. *as* ~ *as the eye can reach*, a portata dell'occhio, della vista. ~ *be it from me!* il cielo me ne guardi! ~ *from it!* tutt'altro! ~ *-fetched*, ricercato, affettato, forzato; troppo spinto, stiracchiato. ~ *into the night*, fino a notte tarda, fino a notte inoltrata; fino alle ore piccole. ~ *off*, molto lontano. ~ *-reaching*, di lunga portata, che si stende lontano. ~*-seeing*, previdente, chiaroveggente. ~*-sighted*, lungimirante. *go too far*, passare i limiti. *too* ~, troppo in là. ¶ *a*. lontano, distante, discosto, remoto. *The F* ~ *East*, l'Estremo Oriente.

farce, *n*. farsa, *f*. **farcical**, *a*. burlesco, illusorio.

fare, *n*. prezzo (del biglietto, della corsa, &c.), *m*.; vitto, *m*.; tavola, *f*.; viaggiatore, *m*.; viaggiatrice, *f*. *bill of* ~, lista delle vivande, *f*. ~ *stage* (*bus*, &c.), corsa, *f*. ¶ *v.i*. stare, trovarsi; mangiare, vivere; riuscire. *to* ~ (*feed*) *well*, mangiare bene, vivere lautamente. ~ *well*, *i*. & *n*. addio; arrivederla, arrivederci. *to bid* ~, *to take* ~ *of*, dire addio a, accomiatarsi da.

farina, *n*. farina, *f*. **farinaceous**, *a*. farinaceo.

farm, *n*. podere, *m*.; tenuta, masseria, *f*. ~ *hand*, contadino giornaliero, *m*. ~*stead*, fattoria, *f*. ~*house*, casa colonica, casa contadina, *f*. ~*yard*, cortile, *m*.; corte del pollame, bassa corte, *f*. ¶ *v.t*. coltivare; (*lease*) affittare, prendere in affitto. ~ *out*, dare in affitto, affittare. **farmer**, *n*. coltivatore, agricoltore, colono fittaiolo, *m*. **farming**, *n*. coltivazione, agricoltura; affitto, *m*.; (*att*.) agricolo, colonico.

faro (*Cards*), *n*. faraone, *m*.

farrago, *n*. faraggine, *f*.

farrier, *n.* maniscalco, *m.* **farriery,** *n.* mascalcia, *f.*

farrow, *n.* figliata (di una scrofa), *f.* ¶ *v.i.* figliare.

farther, *ad.* piú lontano, piú al di là, piú oltre, piú in là.

farthest, *a.* il piú lontano. ¶ *ad.* piú lontano. *at the ~,* al piú, al massimo, al piú tardi.

farthing, *n.* quattrino, *m.,* ¼ penny; *(fig.)* soldo, centesimo, *m.*

fasces, *n.pl.* *(Hist.)* fasci, *m.pl.*

fascinate, *v.t.* affascinare. **fascinating,** *a.* affascinante. **fascination,** *n.* fascino, *m.*

fascine, *n.* fascina, *f.*

fascism, *n.* fascismo, *m.* **fascist,** *n.* fascista, *m.f.*

fashion, *n.* moda, usanza, voga, *f.;* maniera, guisa, *f.;* modo, stile, *m.;* foggia, *f.;* genere, *m.* *~ book,* giornale di mode, *m.* *~ plate,* figurino, *m.* ¶ *v.t.* foggiare, formare, fare, modellare. *fully fashioned (stocking),* (calza) velatissima. *~ able,* *a.* alla moda, di moda, in voga, elegante. *~ society,* bel mondo, gran mondo. *~ably, ad.* alla moda, elegantemente, distintamente.

fast, *a.* rapido, veloce; fermo, solido, saldo; fisso, aderente a, stretto, attaccato a; *(ship-moored)* ormeggiato; *(friend)* fedele; *(dissipated),* gaudente; libero; scostumato; *(of clock)* in anticipo, avanti; *(on clock)* anticipo. *~ asleep,* profondamente addormentato. *~ colour,* forte. *~ cruiser (speed boot),* motoscafo, *m.* *~ sailer (ship),* nave rapida, *f.* *~ sleep,* sonno profondo. ¶ *ad.* rapidamente, a grande velocità; fermamente, saldamente, fortemente, bene; *(rain)* forte. *to hold ~,* tenere fermo, tener saldo, attaccarsi fortemente a. *to make ~,* fissare, legare, serrare, assicurare; ormeggiare. ¶ *n.* digiuno, *m.;* *(Naut.)* ormeggio, *m.* ¶ *v.i.* digiunare.

fasting, *n.* digiuno, *m.* *~[ing] day,* giorno di magro, *m.*

fasten, *v.t.* fissare, attaccare, legare, serrare, sbarrare. *~ on (fig.),* imputare a. *~ off (Need.),* fermare.

fastener & **-ing,** *n.* attacco, *m.;* legame, *m.;* fermaglio, *m.;* *(door)* chiusura, *f.;* *(window)* spagnoletta, *f.*

fasti, *n.pl.* fasti, *m.pl.*

fastidious (to be), essere fastidioso, fare il difficile, f. il delicato.

fastness, *n.* rapidità; solidità; fedeltà; fortezza, *f.*

fat, *a.* grasso, pingue, corpulento, ben pasciuto; *(land)* fertile. *~head,* *n.* minchione, scioccone, grullo. ¶ *n.* grasso, *m.;* adipe, *m.* *to live on the ~ of the land,* vivere grassamente.

fatal, *a.* fatale, funesto, mortale.

fatalism, *n.* fatalismo, *m.* **fatalist,** *n.* fatalista, *m.f.* **fatality,** *n.* fatalità, morte violenta, *f.*

fate, *n.* fato, destino, *m.;* sorte, *f.* *the Fates (Myth.),* le Parche, *f.pl.* *to be ~d to,* essere destinato a, condannato a.

fateful, *a.* fatale.

father, *n.* padre, *m.* *F~ Christmas,* il vecchio Natale. *~-in-law,* suocero, *m.* *~land,* *n.* patria, *f.* *~'s side (family),* da lato di padre. ¶ *v.t.* adottare. *~ upon,* attribuire a, imputare a. *~hood,* *n.* paternità, *f.* *~less,* *a.* senza padre, orfano. *~ly,* *a.* paterno.

fathom, *n.* braccio, *m.* (Eng. fathom = 6 feet = metre 1.83 approx.). ¶ *v.t.* sondare, scandagliare.

fathomless, *a.* senza fondo, insondabile.

fatigue, *n.* fatica, *f.,* *(Mil.)* lavoro di fatica, *m.* *~ dress,* *(Mil.)* jacket *(Mil.),* tenuta di fatica, *f.* ¶ *v.t.* affaticare, stancare.

fatiguing, *a.* affaticante, faticoso.

fatness, *n.* grassezza, pinguedine, corpulenza, *f.* *fatted calf,* vitello grasso, *m.* **fatten,** *v.t.* ingrassare. **fattish,** *a.* grassoccio. **fatty,** *a.* grasso, adiposo; untuoso, grassotto. *~ degeneration,* degenerazione adiposa, *f.*

fatuity, *n.* fatuità, *f.* **fatuous,** *a.* fatuo.

fauces, *n.pl.* gola, *f.*

faucet, *n.* cannello, *m.*

fault, *n.* colpa, *f.;* errore, difetto, *m.;* *(Geol.)* spostamento, *m.* *to a ~* *(ad. phrase),* all'eccesso. *to find ~ with,* criticare, trovare a ridire, biasimare, censurare. *~ finder,* *n.* censore, critico, *m.* **faultless,** *a.* senza colpa, irreprensibile. **faulty,** *a.* difettoso, imperfetto.

faun, *n.* fauno, *m.*

fauna, *n.* fauna, *f.*

favour, *n.* favore, *m.;* grazia, *f.;* piacere, *m.;* benevolenza, *f.;* ordine, *m.;* commissione, *f.;* colori, *m.pl.;* nodo (di nastri), *m.;* *(Com. letter)* gradita, stimata, *f.* ¶ *v.t.* favorire.

ill ~*d*, brutto, malfatto. **favourable,** *a.* favorevole. **favourite,** *a.* favorito, prediletto. ~ *author,* autore prediletto. ~ *book,* libro favorito, prediletto. ¶ *n.* favorito, *m.f.* *the* ~, cavallo preferito. **favouritism,** *n.* favoritismo, *m.*

fawn, *n.* cerbiatto, caprioletto, *m.*; (*colour*) fulvo. ~[-*coloured*], (color) fulvo, rossiccio. ¶ (*of deer*) *v.i.* figliare. ~ [*up*]*on*, accarezzare, lisciare, adulare.

fear, *n.* paura, tema, *f.*; timore, *m.* ¶ *v.t. & i.* temere, avere paura di (che). **fearful,** *a.* spaventoso; pauroso, timido. **fearless,** *a.* intrepido, senza paura. **fearlessness,** *n.* intrepidezza, intrepidità, *f.*

feasibility, *n.* praticabilità, *f.* **feasible,** *a.* praticabile, fattibile.

feast, *n.* festa, *f.*; festino, banchetto, convito, *m.* ¶ *v.t.* festeggiare, far festa a; (*v.i.*) far festa, banchettare; (*fig.*) dilettarsi, godere. **feasting,** *n.* festeggiamento, *m.*; baldoria, *f.*

feat, *n.* fatto, *m.*; azione straordinaria, *f.*; (*pl.*) gesta, *f.pl.*

feather, *n.* penna, piuma, *f.*; (*pl.*) piume, penne, *f.pl.*; (*Carp. & Mach.*) linguetta, *f.* ~ *bed,* letto (materasso) di piume, *m.* ~*brained person,* spensierato, uomo senza cervello, *m.* ~ *dealer,* ~ *dresser,* piumaio, *m.* ~ *duster,* spazzolino di piume, pennacchio, *m.* ~ *stitch,* punto di piuma, *m.* ~ *trade,* commercio in piume, *m.* ~*weight* (*Box.*) [pugilatore del] peso piuma. ¶ (*Rowing*) *v.i.* spalare il remo. ~*ed,* *p.a.* piumato; pennuto. ~ *game,* uccelli selvatici, *m.pl.* ~ *hat,* cappello piumato, cappello guarnito di piume, *m.* *the* ~ *tribe,* gli uccelli, *m.pl.* **feathery,** *a* piumoso.

feature, *n.* lineamento, tratto, aspetto, *m.* ~*s,* *pl.* fisionomia, *f.*; fattezze, sembianze, *f.pl.*

February, *n.* febbraio, *m.*

fecund, *a.* fecondo. **fecundate,** *v.t.* fecondare. **fecundity,** *n.* fecondità, *f.*

federal, *a.* federale. **federate,** *v.t.* federare. **federation,** *n.* federazione, confederazione, *f.*

fee, *n.* onorario, *m.*; diritto, *m.*; tassa, *f.*

feeble, *a.* debole, fiacco.

feed, *n.* cibo, nutrimento, *m.*; pascolo, *m.*; alimentazione, *f.*; (*of oats*) avena, *f.*; (*Mach.*) rifornimento, *m.* ~ *pump,* pompa di alimentazione, *f.*

¶ *v.t. ir.* nutrire, alimentare, dare da mangiare, pascolare; (*Typ.*) marginare; (*v.i. ir.*) mangiare, nutrirsi. ~ *forcibly,* ingozzare. **feeder,** *n.* alimentatore, mangiatore, *m.*; (*bib*) bavaglino, *m.*; (*stream, Rly.*) affluente; (*Elec.*) linea d'alimentazione, *f.* ~*ing bottle,* biberon, poppatoio, *m.*

feel, *n.* tatto, tasto, tocco, *m.* ¶ *v.t. & i. ir.* sentire; palpare, tastare, frugare; sentirsi, risentirsi, provare, subire, passare, avere. **feeler,** *n.* antenna, *f.*; tentacolo, *m.*; (*fig.*) sondaggio, *m.* **feeling,** *a.* sensibile, commovente. ¶ *n.* sentimento, *m.*, sensibilità, emozione, commozione, simpatia, *f.*, tasto, tatto, *m.*; sensazione, *f.*; (*pl.*) sentimento, *m.* **feelingly,** *ad.* sentitamente, con simpatia.

feign, *v.t. & i.* fingere, simulare.

feint, *n.* finta, *f.* ~ *ruled,* rigato. ¶ *v.i.* fingere, simulare.

felicitous, *a.* felice. **felicity,** *n.* felicità, *f.*

Felidae, *n.pl.* felini, *m.pl.*

feline, *a. & n.* felino.

fell, *n.* pelle, *f.*; vello, *m.* ¶ *v.t.* abbattere. **feller,** *n.* abbattitore, *m.* **felling,** *n.* abbattimento, taglio, *m.*

felloe, *n.* quarto (di ruota), *m.*

fellow, *n.* compagno, socio, *m.*; collega, *m.f.*, camerata, *m.f.*; membro, aggregato; uomo, individuo, soggetto, tipo, diavolo; complice, compare, *m.* ~ *boarder,* *n.* commensale, *m.f.* ~ *citizen,* concittadino, -a, *m.f.* ~ *countryman,* -*woman,* compatriota, connazionale, *m.f.* ~ *creature,* simile, *m.f.* ~ *man,* simile, *m.* ~ *feeling,* *n.* simpatia, *f.* ~ *passenger,* ~ *traveller,* compagno di viaggio, *m.*, compagna di viaggio, *f.* ~ *sponsor,* compare, *m.*; comare, *f.* ~ *student,* compagno, -a, di studi; condiscepolo, -a, *m.f.* ~ *sufferer,* compagno, -a, di sventure, di sfortuna, *m.f.* *workman,* compagno di lavoro, *m.*

fellowship, *n.* società, *f.*; consorzio, *m.*; cameratismo, *m.*; amicizia, *f.*

felo de se, *n.* suicidio, *m.*; (*pers.*) suicida, *m.f.*

felon, *n.* malfattore, criminale, fellone, *m.* **felonious,** *a.* malvagio, criminale, fellone. **felony,** *n.* fellonia, *f.*; delitto grave, *m.*

fel[d]spar, *n.* feldspato, *m.*

felt, *n.* feltro, *m.* ~ *(hat),* cappello di feltro, *m.* ¶ *v.t.* feltrare.

female, *a.* femminilo. ¶ *n.* femmina, *f.*

feminine, *a. & n.* femminile, *a. & n.f.* femminino, muliebre, *a.* **feminism,** *n.* femminismo, *m.* **feminist,** *a. & n.* femminista. **feminize,** *v.t.* femminizzare.

femur, *n.* femore, *m.*

fen, *n.* palude, *f.*; pantano, *m.*; maremma, *f.*

fence, *n.* siepe, *f.*; stecco, steccato, *m.*; palizzata, cinta, barriera, *f.*; scherma, difesa, *m.*; *(Mach.)* guida, *f.*; *(pers.)* ricettatore (di oggetti rubati), *m.*; ricettatrice, *f.* ¶ *v.t.* assiepare, chiudere (circondare) con siepe, palizzata, barriera, &c.; *(v.i.)* schermire, tirare di scherma; difendersi, proteggersi argomentando abilmente. ~ *in,* cingere, chiudere, riparare. ~ *off,* barrare, sbarrare.

fencer, *n.* schermitore, *m.*; schermitrice, *f.*; *(horse)* saltatore, *m.*

fencing, *n.* scherma; *f.*; *(foils)* schermare con fioretto, *m.* ~ *master,* maestro di scherma, maestro d'armi. ~ *school,* sala di scherma, sala d'armi, scuola di scherma, *f.*

fend [**off**], *v.t.* riparare, parare. ~ *for oneself,* arrangiarsi, provvedersi.

fender, *n.* paracenere, parafuoco, *m.*; *(Naut.)* parabordo, *m.*

fennel, *n. & ~ seed,* finocchio, *m.*

ferment, *n.* fermento, *m.*; *(fig.)* fermentazione, *f.*; agitazione, *f.*; movimento, *m.* ¶ *v.i.* fermentare; *(v.t.)* fare fermentare. **fermentation,** *n.* fermentazione, *f.*; lievito, *m.*

fern, *n.* felce, *f.*

ferocious, *a.* feroce. **ferocity,** *n.* ferocia, *f.*

ferret, *n.* furetto, *m.* ¶ *v.t.* cacciare col furetto. ~ *about,* frugare. ~ *out,* snidare, scovare.

ferro-concrete, *n.* cemento armato, *m.*

ferrous, *a.* ferroso.

ferruginous, *a.* ferruginoso.

ferrule, *n.* ghiera, *f.*; puntale, *m.* ¶ *v.t.* mettere una ghiera a.

ferry, *n.* passaggio, tragitto, traghetto, *m.* ~ *(boat).* barca di traghetto; battello, *m.* ~*man,* barcaiuolo di traghetto, batteliere, *m.* ~ *over,* traghettare.

fertile, *a.* fertile, fecondo, fruttifero, fruttuoso. **fertility,** *n.* fertilità, fecondità, *f.* **fertilize,** *v.t.* fertilizzare. **fertilizer,** *n.* fertilizzatore, ingrasso, concime, *m.*

fervent & **fervid,** *a.* fervido, fervente. **fervently** & **fervidly,** *ad.* ardentemente, fervidamente. **fervour** & **fervency,** *n.* ardore, fervore, *m.*

fester, *v.i.* ulcerarsi; infettarsi; corrompersi.

festival, *n.* festa, *f.*; *(musical)* festival, *m.*; gran festa con musica, *f.* **festive,** *a.* festivo, di festa, gaio, allegro. **festivity,** *n.* festa, *f.*; giubilo, *m.*; allegrezza, *f.*

festoon, *n.* festone, *m.* ¶ *v.t.* festonare, ornare di festoni.

fetch, *v.t.* andare a cercare; portare; condurre; prendere, riprendere; *(sigh)* mandare, trarre; *(price)* dare, produrre, rendere, valere. ~ *it!* *(to dog)* piglia!

fête, *n.* festa, *f.* *(at a fair)* festa (ambulante), *f.* ¶ *v.t.* fare festa a.

fetid, *a.* fetido. **fetidness,** *n.* fetidezza, *f.*; fetore, *m.*

fetish, -ich[**e**]**,** *n.* feticcio, *m.* **fetishism,** *n.* feticismo, *m.*

fetlock, *n.* garretto, *m.*; barbetta, *f.*

fetter, *n.* catena, *f.*; ferro, *m.* ¶ *v.t.* incatenare, mettere i ferri (le catene, i ceppi) a.

fettle, *n.* ordine, *m.*

feud, *n.* querela, disputa, contesa, *f.*; *(Hist.)* feudo, *m.* **feudal,** *a.* feudale. **feudalism** & **feudality,** *n.* feudalismo, *m.* *the Feudal System,* il sistema feudale, *m.*

fever, *n.* febbre, *f.* ~ *case* *(pers.),* febbricitante, *m.f.* **feverish,** *a.* *(pers.)* febbricitante; *(fig.)* febbrile.

few, *a. & n.* poco, *m.*; pochi, *m.pl.*; poche, *f.pl.*; alcuni, *m.pl.*; alcune, *f.pl.* ~ *& far between,* pochi ed a rari intervalli. *a ~ more people,* poche altre persone, poca altra gente. *the chosen ~,* i pochi eletti, *m.pl.* *a ~ weeks ago,* poche settimane fa, alcune settimane fa.

fewer, *a.* meno, in minor numero. *the ~ the better,* in meno si è, e meglio si sta.

fez, *n.* fez, *m.*

fiasco, *n.* fiasco, *m.*

fiat, *n.* decreto, ordine, *m.*

fib, *n.* fandonia, bugia innocua, *f.*; frottola, *f.* ¶ *v.i.* contare fandonie. **fibber,** *n.* contastorie, bugiardo, contatore di frottole, *m.*

fibre, *n.* fibra, *f.*; tiglio, *m.* **fibril,** *n.* fibrilla, *f.* **fibrous,** *a.* fibroso.

fibula, *n.* fìbula, *f.*

fickle, *a.* incostante, mutabile. **fickleness**, *n.* incostanza, mutabilità, *f.*

fiction, *n.* finzione, menzogna, *f.*; (*prose*) romanzo, *m.* **fictitious**, *a.* fittizio, finto. **fictive**, *a.* immaginario.

fiddle, *n.* violino, *m.* ~ *stick*, archetto (di violino), *m.*; (*pl.*, *i.*) sciocchezze! eh via! frottole! ¶ *v.i.* suonare il violino; (*fig.*) baloccarsi, gingillarsi, tentennare. **fiddler**, *n.* violinista, *m.f.*; suonatore di violino, *m.*, suonatrice di violino, *f.* **fiddling**, *a.* frivolo.

fidelity, *n.* fedeltà, *f.*

fidget, *v.i.* agitarsi, essere irrequieto, impazientirsi. ~s, *n.pl.* agitazione, irrequietezza, *f.* **fidgety**, *a.* agitato, irrequieto, impaziente.

fiduciary, *a.* fiduciario.

fie, *i.* ohibò! vergogna!

fief (*Hist.*), *n.* feudo, *m.*

field, *n.* campo, prato, terreno, *m.*; (*pl.*) campagna, *f.*, prati, *m.pl.*; (*ice*) banco, *m.*; (*pl. Poet.*) campi, *m.pl.*; (*Mil.*) campo (di battaglia), *m.*; campagna, *f.*; (*Min.*) giacimento, *m.*; (*hunt*) caccia, *f.*; (*Turf*) campo, *m.*; (*Her.*) campo, *m.* ~ *artillery*, artiglieria da campo, da campagna, *f.* ~ *camera*, camera a piede, *f.* ~*day*, giorno di manovra, *m.*, manovre, *f.pl.*; (*fig.*) discussione importante, giornata campale, *f.* ~ *fare*, tordella, *f.* ~ *geology*, geologia, *f.* ~*glass[es]*, binocolo (da campagna), *m.* ~*lark*, allodola dei campi, *f.* F~ *Marshal*, Maresciallo, *m.* ~*mouse*, topo campagnolo, *m.* ~ *sports*, esercizi all'aria aperta, *m.pl.* ~*works*, opere campali, *f.pl.*

fiend, *n.* demonio, *m.*; spirito maligno, *m.* **fiendish**, *a.* diabolico, infernale.

fierce, *a.* feroce, violento. **fiercely**, *ad.* ferocemente, furiosamente, impetuosamente. **fierceness**, *n.* ferocia, furia, violenza, *f.*

fiery, *a.* di fuoco, ardente, bollente, bruciante, focoso, infiammato.

fife & **fifer**, *n.* piffero, *m.*

fifteen, *a.* & *n.* quindici, *a.* & *m.*

fifteenth, *a.* & *n.* quindicesimo, *a.* & *m.*; (*date*) quindici, *m.*

fifth, *a.* quinto. ¶ *n.* quinto, cinque, *m.*; (*Mus.*) quinta, *f.*

fiftieth, *a.* & *n.* cinquantesimo, *a.* & *n.* ~ *anniversary*, cinquantenario, *m.*

fifty, *a.* & *n.* cinquanta, *a.* & *m.* ~ (*or so*), cinquantina, *f.* *to be on the verge of* ~, *to be almost* ~, essere sulla cinquantina.

fig, *n.* fico, *m.*; (*fig.*) *not to be worth a* ~, non avere alcun valore. *I don't care a* ~ *for it*, non me n'importa niente, un fico. ~*leaf*, foglia di fico, *f.*; (*Art.*) foglia d'acanto, *f.* ~ *tree*, fico, *m.*

fight, *n.* combattimento, *m.*; lotta, battaglia, scaramuccia, *f.* ¶ *v.i. ir.* battersi, lottare, fare a pugni, battagliare; (*v.t. ir.*) battersi con, combattere; (*a battle*) combattere, dare battaglia; (*one's way*) aprirsi un passaggio combattendo.

fighter, *n.* combattente, guerriero. ~*ing plane*, apparecchio da caccia, caccia, *m.*

figment, *n.* finzione, invenzione, *f.*

figurative, *a.* figurativo, allegorico, simbolico. ~ *sense*, senso figurativo, *m.*

figuratively, *ad.* figurativamente; (*sense*) metaforicamente.

figure, *n.* figura, forma, *f.*; aria, *f.*; busto; aspetto, *m.*, disegno; prezzo, *m.*; persona, *f.*; (*Arith.*) cifra, *f.*; (*bodily shape*) figura. ~ *of speech*, figura retorica, *f.* *in round* ~s, in cifra tonda. ~ *dance*, danza figurata, *f.* ~*head* (*ship*), figura di prua, *f.* ~ *skating*, figure sul ghiaccio, *f.pl.*; pattinaggio a figure, *m.* ¶ *v.t.* & *i.* figurare, figurarsi, immaginare; (*Mus.*) cifrare; rappresentare, formare, calcolare; operare, stampare. ~d (*textiles*), *p.a.* operato; improntato; fiorato.

Fiji, *n.* le isole Figi, *f.pl.*

filament, *n.* filamento, *m.*

filbert, *n.* avellana, *f.* ~ (*tree*), avellano, *m.*

filch, *v.t.* rubacchiare, carpire, involare.

file, *n.* (*rank*) fila, *f.*; (*of people*) fila, coda, *f.*; (*for letters*) schedario, *m.*; (*bundle*) fascio, *m.*; collezione, *f.*; (*tool*) lima, *f.* ~ *leader*, capofila, *m.* ¶ *v.t.* mettere in fila; fare raccolta di; conservare; limare. ~ *off*, andarsene in fila. ~ *past*, sfilare.

filial, *a.* filiale.

filiation, *n.* figliazione, *f.*

filibuster, *n.* filibustiere, *m.*

filigree [work], *n.* filigrana, *f.* ~d, *a.* ornato con filigrana.

filing, *n.* messa in fila, messa in fascio, *f.*; deposito, *m.*; collezione, *f.*; trasmissione; limatura, *f.*; (*pl.*)

limatura, *f*. ~ *cabinet*, casellario, schedario, *m*.

fill, *n*. sufficienza, sazietà, quantità sufficiente, *f*.; (*pipe*) pipata, *f*. ¶ *v.t*. empire, riempire, colmare, completare, occupare; coprire; imbottire; caricare; (*tooth*) riempire, impiombare. ~ *in*, empire, riempire. ~ *in time*, servire a passare il tempo. ~ *up*, empire, occupare, completare, colmare; (*ullaged cask*) sondare.

fillet, *n*. benda, *f*.; filetto, *m*.; (*Arch*.) cordone, *m*., cordonata, *f*. ~ *of veal*, filetto di vitello. ~*ed sole*, filetto di sogliola, *m*.

filling, *n*. riempimento, *m*.; imbottitura, *f*.; (*tooth*) impiombatura, *f*. ~ *station*, posto di rifornimento di benzina, *m*.

fillip, *n*. colpo col dito, *m*.; (*fig*.) stimolo, incitamento, *m*.

fillister, *n*. incorzatoio, *m*.

filly, *n*. puledra, *f*.

film, *n*. pellicola, *f*., film, *m*.; membrana; patina, *f*.; (*fig*.) velo, *m*. ~ *camera*, macchina fotografica per pellicola, *f*. ~ *fan*, tifoso del cinema, *m*. ~ *rights*, diritto d'adattazione cinematografica, *m*. ~ *star*, stella del cinematografo, *f*., divo, diva dello schermo, *m.f*. ~ *world*, regno del cinema, *m*. ¶ *v.t*. rappresentare in un film, adattare per il cinema.

filmy, *a*. tenue, vaporoso, velato.

filter, *n*. filtro, *m*. (*Phot*.) filtro luce, *m*. ¶ *v.t. & i*. filtrare.

filth, *n*. sporcizia, *f*.; immondizie, *f.pl*.; sozzume, *m*. **filthiness**, *n*. sozzura, *f*. **filthy**, *a*. sporco, sozzo.

fin, *n*. pinna, aletta, natatoia, *f*.

final, *a*. finale; ultimo; definitivo; decisivo. ~ *dividend*, dividendo finale, *m*. ~ (*heat*), prova decisiva, *f*.; prova finale, *f*. **finale** (*Mus*.), *n*. finale, *m*. **finalist**, *n*. (*Sport*) finalista, *m.f*. **finality**, *n*. finalità, *f*.

finance, *n*. finanza, *f*.; (*pl*.) finanze, *f.pl*. ¶ *v.i*. (*v.t*.) finanziare. **financial**, *a*. finanziario. ~ *year*, esercizio finanziario; anno finanziario, *m*.

finch, *n*. fringuello, cardellino, *m*.

find, *n*. scoperta, *f*.; oggetto trovato, oggetto rinvenuto, *m*. ¶ *v.t*. ir. trovare, scoprire, rinvenire; provare; apprendere; sorprendere; giudicare; ritenere; pronunziare, emettere; dichiarare; aggiudicare. ~ *out*, trovare, scoprire, risolvere; prendere, sorprendere.

finder, *n*. inventore, trovatore, *m*.; (*camera*) mirino, *m*.; (*telescope*) cercatore, *m*.

finding (*jury*), *n*. sentenza, *f*.; verdetto, *m*.

fine, *a*. bello, elegante, ben fatto; fine; delicato; sottile; buono; eccellente; prezioso; magnifico. ~ *arts*, arti belle, belle arti, *f.pl*. *one of these* ~ *days*, *one* ~ *day*, un giorno o l'altro; uno di questi giorni; un bel giorno. ~ -*draw*, rammendare. ~ *metal*, fino. *gold 22 carats* ~, di fino oro a 22 carate. ~ *speaking*, *n*. eloquio, bell'eloquio, *m*.; facondia, eloquenza, *f*. ~ *things*, cose belle, *f.pl*.; oggetti magnifici, *m.pl*. ¶ *n*. multa, ammenda, *f*. *in* ~, finalmente, alla fine, infine. ¶ *v.t*. multare, colpire d'ammenda; (*wine*) chiarificare, chiarire.

finely, *ad*. finemente; delicatamente; sottilmente.

fineness, *n*. bellezza, delicatezza, *f*.; sottigliezza; purezza, distinzione; bontà, *f*.; (*gold*, &c.) fino, *m*.

finery, *n*. lusso, sfarzo, *m*.; abiti belli, fronzoli, *m.pl*.

finesse, *n*. finezza, *f*. ¶ *v.t. & i*. (*card*) ricorrere all'astuzia, giuocare una carta d'inganno. *finest quality*, prima qualità, qualità scelta.

finger, *n*. dito, *m*. ~ *board*, tastiera, *f*. ~ *bowl*, sciacquadita, *m.inv*. ~*mark*, ditata, *f*.; segno del dito, *m*. ~*plate*, placca, *f*. ~*post*, palo indicatore, *m*. ~*print*, impronta digitale, *f*. ~*stall*, ditale, *m*. ¶ *v.t*. maneggiare, palpare, tastare, toccare; (*Mus*.) digitare.

fingering (*Mus*.), *n*. digitazione, *f*.

finical, **finikin[g]**, *a*. affettato; cavilloso; sofistico.

finis, *n*. fine, *f*.

finish, *n*. finitura, ultima mano, *f*.; (*end*) fine, *f*. ¶ *v.t. & abs. & i*. finire, completare, dare l'ultima mano (a), terminare, cessare, compiere. *to* ~ *speaking*, finire di parlare. ~*ing stroke*, ultimo tocco, *m*.; ultima mano, *f*.; (*fig*.) colpo di grazia, *m*. ~*ing touches*, ultimo tocco, ultima mano.

finite, *a*. limitato, delimitato; (*Gram*.) finito.

Finland, *n*. la Finlandia, *f*. **Fin[n]**, **Finlander**, *n*. finlandese, *m*. **Finnish**, *a*. finlandese. ¶ (*language*) *n*. il finlandese, *m*.; la lingua finlandese, *f*.

fir [*tree*], *n*. abete, *m*. ~ *plantation*, abetaia, *f*.

fire, *n.* fuoco, incendio, *m.*; *(gun)* tiro, *m. (house, &c., on)* al fuoco! ~ *alarm,* segnalatore di incendio, *m.* ~*arms,* armi da fuoco, *f.pl.* ~*box,* focolare, *m.*; camera di combustione, *f.* ~*brand,* tizzone, *m.*; *(fig.)* mettimale, *m.f.* ~*brick,* mattone refrattario, *m.* ~ *brigade,* corpo dei pompieri, *m.*; i pompieri, *m.pl.* ~*clay,* argilla refrattaria, *f.* ~*damp,* grisú, gas esplosivo, *m.* ~ *dog,* alare, *m.* ~ *eater (fig.),* bravaccio, smargiasso, *m.* ~ *engine,* pompa da incendio, *f.* ~ *escape,* uscita di sicurezza, *f.*; apparecchio di salvataggio, *m.* ~ *extinguisher,* estintore, *m.* ~*fly,* lucciola, *f.* ~*guard,* parafuoco, *m.* ~ *hydrant,* ~ *plug,* bocca da incendio, *f.* ~ *insurance,* assicurazione contro gli incendi, *f.* ~ *irons,* ferri (arnesi) del focolare, accessori da caminetto, *m.pl.* ~*lighter,* accendifuoco, *m.inv.* ~*man,* pompiere, vigile del fuoco, *m. (stoker)* fuochista, *m.* ~*place,* caminetto, focolare, *m.* ~*proof,* a prova di fuoco; incombustibile; resistente al fuoco; refrattario; *(v.t.)* rendere i. ~*raising,* incendio doloso, *m.* ~ *screen,* parafuoco, *m.* ~*side,* focolare domestico, *m.* ~*side chair,* sedia accanto al focolare, *f.* ~ *station,* stazione (posto) di pompieri, *f.* ~*wood,* legna da ardere. ~*work(s),* fuochi d'artificio, *m.pl.* ¶ *v.t.* incendiare, mettere fuoco a, accendere, infiammare; *(shot)* tirare, sparare; *(v.i.)* incendiarsi, infiammarsi, prendere fuoco; *(gun)* far fuoco, tirare. ~*!* *(Mil.),* fuoco!

firing, *n.* accensione, combustione, *f.,* l'incendiare, *m.*; *(Mil.)* sparo, fuoco, tiro, *m.*; ~*scarica,* cannonata, *f.* ~*party,* ~ *squad,* plotone d'esecuzione, *m.*

firkin, *n.* bariletto, *m.*; tinozza, *f.* *Meas.* = 9 *or* 8 *gallons.*

firm, *a.* fermo, saldo, stabile, costante. ¶ *n.* ditta, casa (commerciale). ~ *(name),* ragione sociale, *f. publishing* ~, casa editrice, *f.* ~'*s capital,* capitale sociale, *m,*

firmament, *n.* firmamento, *m.*

firmness, *n.* fermezza, saldezza, solidità, costanza, *f.*

first, *a.* primo; *(after 20, 30, &c.)* unesimo; *(cousin)* germano. ~ *aid,* primo soccorso, *m. appearance & ~ work, or ~ book,* debutto, esordio, *m. to make one's ~ appearance,* esordire. ~ *attempt,*

primo tentativo, primo getto, *m.* ~*born,* primogenito, primo nato, maggiore. ~ *class,* prima classe, *f. the ~comer,* il primo venuto, *m. F~ Commissioner of Works (Eng.),* Ministro dei Lavori pubblici, *m.* ~ *cut,* prima fetta, *f.* ~ *edition,* edizione originale, *f.*; prima edizione. ~ *finger,* indice, *m.* ~ *floor,* primo piano, *m.* ~ *fruits,* primizie, *f.pl. F~ Lord of the Admiralty (Eng.),* Ministro della Marina, *m.* ~ *match (opp. return match),* gara, partita, *f.* ~*-rate,* di primo ordine. ¶ *ad.* primieramente, in primo luogo, all'inizio, per la prima volta, in prima fila. ~, *at* ~, ~ *of all,* prima, sulle prime, da prima, prima di tutto, innanzi tutto. ~ & *foremost,* a bella prima, anzitutto. *the first,* il primo, la prima. *the ~ January,* il primo gennaio. ~ *of exchange,* prima di cambio.

firstly, *ad.* in primo luogo.

firth, *n.* estuario, golfo, *m.*

fiscal, *a.* fiscale. ~ *system,* fiscalismo, *m.*

fish, *n.* pesce, *m.* ~*bone,* resta, lisca, *f.* ~*bowl,* boccale, *m.* ~ *glue,* colla di pesce, *f.* ~ *hook,* amo, *m.* ~*kettle,* pesciaiuola, *f.* ~ *market,* mercato del pesce, pescheria, *f. (wet) ~ merchant & salesman,* pesciaiuolo, negoziante di pesce (all'ingrosso), *m.* ~*monger,* pescivendolo, *m. neither fish nor fowl,* né carne né pesce. ~ *out of water (pers.),* pesce fuor d'acqua, *m.* ~*plate (Rly.),* stecca a ganascia, *f.* ~*pond,* vivaio, *m.*; peschiera, *f.* ~ *shop,* ~ *stall,* banco da pesce. ~ *slice,* tagliapesce, *m.inv.* ~ *spear,* fiocina, *f.* ~ *wife,* pescivendola, *f.* ¶ *v.i. & t. & ~ for,* pescare. ~ *out,* ~ *up,* pescare; ripescare. ~ *(plate),* *v.t.* adattare le stecche (ad una frattura). ~*erman,* *n.* pescatore, *m.*

fishery, *n.* pesca, *f.*; *(ground)* pescheria, *f.*

fishing, *n.* pesca, *f.* ~ *boat,* barca da pesca, barca pescherccia, *f.* ~ *rod,* canna da pesca, *f.* ~ *tackle,* articoli da pesca, *m.pl.*; attrezzi pescherecci, *m.pl.*

fishy, *a.* di pesce, *(fig.)* dubbio, equivoco, sospetto.

fissure, *n.* fessura, crepatura, *f.* ¶ *v.t.* fare una fessura (a, in . . .).

fist, *n.* pugno, *m.*

fisticuffs, *n.pl.* pugni, *m.pl.*; combattimento a pugni, *m.*

fistula, *n.* fistola, *f.*

fit, *a.* atto, capace, buono a; a proposito, convenevole; degno; opportuno, idoneo; giusto, ragionevole. ~ *for service,* atto al servizio. *to keep* ~ *(athletics),* mantenersi addestrato, tenersi in esercizio. ¶ *n.* accesso, attacco, *m.*; convulsione, crisi, *f.*, forma, *f.*; taglio, *m.*; *(Mech.)* montaggio, *m.* ~ *of coughing,* accesso di tosse, *m.* *by* ~*s & starts,* a scatti, a sbalzi, saltuariamente. ¶ *v.t.* adattare, accomodare, aggiustare; abbigliare; calzare; montare; *(v.i.)* convenire; adattarsi; andare bene. ~ *in,* entrare in; incastrarsi in; accordarsi con; quadrare con. ~ *out,* fornire, provvedere, corredare, armare. ~ *tightly,* aderire; *(dress)* essere (venire) attillato. ~ *up,* preparare, arredare, allestire, montare.

fitful, *a.* incerto, irregolare, a scatti.

fitly, *ad.* convenevolmente, giustamente, a proposito.

fitness, *n.* convenienza, capacità, *f.*; adattamento, *m.*; buona salute, *f.* *fitted case, dressing c.,* valigia con necessari di toletta, *f.*

fitter, *n.* aggiustatore, montatore, apparecchiatore, *m.*; *(clothes)* sarto, *m.*, sarta, *f.*

fitting, *a.* convenevole, idoneo, appropriato, giusto, a proposito. ~s, *n.pl.* accessori, mobili, arredi, *m.pl.*; *[& fixtures]* attrezzatura, *f.*

five, *a. & n.* cinque, *a. & m.* ~ *finger exercise,* esercizio delle cinque dita, *m.* ~ *year plan,* piano quinquennale, *m.* ~s, *n.* giuoco della palla, *m.*; pallacorda, *f.*

fix, *n.* difficoltà, situazione senza uscita, *f.*; imbarazzo, *m.* ¶ *v.t.* fissare; stabilire, sistemare, assicurare. ~ed, *a.* fisso, fissato, stabile, stabilito, assicurato. ~ *(rate of) exchange,* corso del cambio fissato, convenuto. ~ *focus camera,* camera a foco fisso, *f.* ~ *salary,* stipendio fisso, *m.* ~ing, *n.* fissaggio, *m.* ~ *& toning bath,* bagno di viraggio e di fissaggio, *m.* ~ *[solution]* (*Phot.*), fissatore, *m.* **fixture,** *n.* infisso, *m.*; *(Sport)* data fissata, *f.* ~s *& fittings,* attrezzatura, *f.*

fizz[le], *v.i.* fischiare, sibilare; spumeggiare. *fizzle out,* fare fiasco, non riuscire, andare in aria.

flabbergast, *v.t.* stupire, sbalordire.

flabbiness & flaccidity, *n.* mollezza, fiacchezza, floscezza, *f.* **flabby & flaccid,** *a.* molle, fiacco, floscio.

flag, *n.* bandiera; *(pl.)* pavese, *m.*; *(Bot.)* 'iride, *m.* ~ *of truce (Mil.),* bandiera di parlamentare; *(Nav.)* *to dress (a ship) with* ~s, pavesare; ~ *ship,* nave ammiraglia, *f.* ~*staff,* asta (di bandiera). ~ *[stone],* pietra, da lastrico, *f.* ¶ *v.t.* lastricare; *(v.i.)* affievolirsi, languire, rallentarsi.

flagellate, *v.t.* flagellare.

flageolet, *n.* zufolo, *m.*

flagitious, *a.* scellerato, atroce.

flagon, *n.* giara, *f.*, boccale, *m.*, fiasco, *m.*

flagrant, *a.* flagrante.

flail, *n.* correggiato, *m.*

flair, *n.* disposizione naturale, attitudine, *f.*

flake, *n.* flocco, *m.*, falda, scaglia, lamina, sfoglia, *f.* ¶ *v.i.* formarsi in fiocchi, scagliarsi, squamarsi. **flaky,** *a.* scaglioso, laminoso, fioccoso; *(pastry)* sfogliato.

flame, *n.* fiamma, vampa, *f.* ~*thrower,* n. lanciafiamme, *m.inv.* ¶ *v.i.* fiammeggiare, mandare fiamme, avvampare, *(fig.)* infiammarsi; *(v.t.)* infiammare.

flamingo, *n.* fenicottero, *m.*

Flanders, *n.* la Fiandra, *f.*

flange, *n.* flangia; ala, *f.*, rialzo, risalto, bordino, *m.* ¶ *v.t.* munire di flangia di bordino.

flank, *n.* fianco, lato, *m.*; *(meat)* pancia, *f.*, petto, *m.* ¶ *v.t.* fiancheggiare.

flannel, *n.* flanella, *f.* ~ette, *n.* flanella di cotone, *f.*

flap, *n.* falda, tesa, linguetta, orecchietta, tavoletta, *f.*, abbattibile, *f.*, scacciamosche, *m.*; colpo (d'ala, &c.), *m.*, lembo, *m.* ¶ *v.t. & i.* battere (le ali), aleggiare, scuotere, penzolare, dare colpi (di coda).

flare, *n.* luce chiara, *f.*, vivo chiarore, *m.*, fiamma, fiaccolata, *f.*; *(signal)* razzo, segnale luminoso, *m.* ¶ *v.i.* fiammeggiare, avvampare; *(lamp)* filare.

flash, *a.* falso, di bassa lega. ¶ *n.* lampo, baleno *(lightning)*; getto, splendore, *m.*, vampa, *f.* *(fig.),* barlume, *m.* ~ *in the pan (fig.),* colpo fallito, fiasco. ~*lamp (elec. torch),* lampada elettrica portatile, *f.* ~*light (Phot.),* lampo al magnesio, *m.* ~ *of light & * ~ *of lightning,* baleno, *m.* ~*[ing] point,* punto d'infiammabilità, *m.* ¶ *v.i.* lampeggiare, balenare, sfolgorare, sfavillare; *(v.t.)* gettare, lanciare, schizzare; *(fig.)* passare come un baleno, apparire improvvisamente.

flask, *n.* fiaschetta, fiasca, *f.*, fiasco, *m.*

flat, *a.* piatto, piano, appianato; unito, disteso; positivo, reciso, netto; insipido, senza gusto, guasto, (*colour*) ammortito, smorzato; (*sound*) stonato; (*nose*) camuso, (*Mus.*) bemolle. ~ **iron,** ferro da stirare. ~ **bottomed,** a fondo piatto. ~ **race,** corsa piana, corsa senza ostacoli, *f.* ~ **roof,** tetto a terrazza, *m.*, terrazza, *f.* ¶ *ad.* nettamente. ~ **on one's face,** (cader) bocconi. **to sing** ~, stonare. ¶ *n.* superficie unita, piana, spianata, *f;* (*rooms*) appartamento, piano di una casa; *m;* (*plain, shoal*) pianura, *f.*, piano, bassopiano; bassofondo, *m.* (*Mus.*) bemolle, *m.* ~**ly,** *ad.* piattamente; nettamente. ~**ness,** *n.* pianezza; (*liquor*) scipitezza, *f.*

flatten, *v.t.* appiattire, appianare, spianare, laminare (*metals*); guastare (*liquors*).

flatter, *v.t.* adulare, lusingare; abbellire. ~**er,** *n.* adulatore, *m.*, -trice, *f.* ~**ing,** *a.* lusinghiero, adulatorio. ~**y,** *n.* adulazione, lusinga, *f.*

flatulence, -**cy,** *n.* flatulenza, *f.* **flatus,** *n.* flato, *m.*

flaunt, *v.t.* ostentare, sfoggiare, fare pompa di.

flautist, *n.* flautista, *m.*

flavour, *n.* sapore, gusto, *m.* ¶ *v.t.* dare sapore a; condire. ~**ing,** *n.* condimento, *m.*

flaw, *n.* difetto, *m.*, tacca, magagna, *f.*, vizio, *m.*; incrinatura (*crack*) *f.* ~**less,** *a.* senza difetto, senza macchia. ~**y,** *a.* ventoso, tempestoso.

flax, *n.* lino, *m.* ~ **field,** campo di lino, *m.* ~**en,** *a. & n.* biondo; *a.* di lino.

flay, *v.t.* scorticare, scuoiare.

flea, *n.* pulce, *f.* ~**bite,** morso di pulce, *m.*; (*fig.*) bagatella, *f.*

fledged (to be), impiumarsi, mettere le ali. **fledg[e]ling,** *n.* uccelletto, *m.*

flee, *v.i. & t.ir.* fuggire, scappare, rifugiarsi.

fleece, *n.* vello, *m.* ¶ *v.t.* tosare, (*fig.*) scorticare, derubare. **fleecy,** *a.* velloso, lanuto, lanoso; biancheggiante. ~ **clouds,** *sky fleeced with clouds,* cumuli, *m.pl.*

fleet, *n.* flotta, *f.* ~ **of foot,** rapido, veloce, lesto di piede, dal piede veloce. ~**ing,** *a.* fugace, passeggero fuggevole.

Fleming, *n.* fiammingo, *m.* -a, *f.* **Flemish,** *a. & (language) n.*

fiammingo, *a. & m.* la lingua fiamminga, *f.*

flesh, *n.* carne, *f.*, polpa, *f.*; (*meat*) carne, *f.* ~ **brush,** spazzola per frizioni, *f.* ¶ (*Hunt.*) *v.t.* aizzare. ~**y,** *a.* carnoso, polputo, corpulento.

flexible, *a.* flessibile, pieghevole; (*fig.*) trattabile. **to make** ~, rendere flessibile, r. pieghevole, piegare. **flex-[ible wire],** filo flessibile, cordone, *m.* **flexor,** *a. & n.* flessore, muscolo flessore, *a. & m.*

flick, *n.* buffetto, colpetto, *m.*; (*sound*) schiocco, *m.*; (*brush*) colpetto. ¶ *v.t.* dare un buffetto a; toccare con la frusta.

flicker, *n.* guizzo, tremolio. ¶ *v.i.* guizzare, tremolare.

flier, *n.* aviatore, *m.*, -trice, *f.*

flight, *n.* fuga, *f.*, volo, *m.*, volata, *f.*, (*time*) corso; (*projectile*) traietto, *m.*; (*birds*) stormo, *m.* ~ **of stairs,** branca di scale, *f.* ~ **of steps,** scalinata, gradinata, *f.* ~**y,** *a.* leggero, incostante, volubile, stordito.

flimsy, *a.* leggero, debole, tenue; (*fig. excuse, &c.*) frivolo.

flinch, *v.i.* esitare, trasalire, ritirarsi (per dolore o paura).

fling, *n.* getto, lancio, *m.* ¶ *v.t. ir.* gettare, lanciare. **to have one's** ~, godersela, scialare. ~ **away &** ~ **off,** rigettare, respingere, disfarsi di, sbarazzarsi di, scuotere il giogo di.

flint, *n.* selce, silice, *f.*, ciottolo, *m.*, (*pietra*) focaia, *f.* ~ **& steel,** acciarino e focaia. ~ **glass,** vetro di rocca, cristallo inglese. ~**y,** *a.* siliceo, di sasso, duro.

flip, *see* flick.

flippant, *a.* disinvolto, impertinente, petulante; (*tongue*) sciolto.

flipper, *n.* natatoia, *f.*

flirt (*pers.*), *n.* bellimbusto, damerino, *m.*, civetta, civettuola, vanerella, *f.* ¶ *v.i.* civettare, amoreggiare. ~**ation,** *n.* civetteria, *f.*, amoreggiamento, *m.*

flit, *v.i.* svolazzare, volteggiare; sloggiare, sgombrare. ~ **about,** svolazzare, volteggiare. ~**ting,** *a.* fugace, passeggero. ¶ *n.* sloggiamento, sgombro, *m.*

flitch, *n.* lardone, fianco di lardo, *m.*

float & ~**er,** *n.* galleggiante; sughero, *m.* ~ (*board*), galleggiante. ~ **plane,** idrocorsa, *f.* ¶ *v.t.* fare galleggiare, tenere a galla; (*Fin.*) lanciare; (*v.i.*) galleggiare, stare a galla; (*Swim.*) fare la plancia, *f.* il morto. ~**ation** (*Fin.*), *n.* lanciamento, *m.*, costituzione, *f.* ~ing, *a.* galleggiante; (*Mech.*) flottante; (*debt*) fluttuante.

flock, *n.* gregge, branco, stormo, *m.*, mandra, *f.*; (*wool*, *&c.*) fiocco, *m.*, borra (di lana), *f.* ¶ *v.i.* affollarsi, adunarsi, accorrere, affluire; (*birds*) andare a stormi.

floe, *n.* lastra, lastrone di ghiaccio ~*ice*, ghiaccio galleggiante, *m.*

flog, *v.t.* frustare, sferzare, bastonare, fustigare. *a flogging*, frusta, fustigazione, bastonatura, *f.*

flong (*Typ.*), *n.* carta preparata per le matrici della stereotipia.

flood, *n.* alluvione, inondazione, piena, *f.*, flusso, torrente, *m.*; (*of the tide*) flusso, *m.* ~*gate*, chiusa, *f.* ~*lighting*, illuminazione con proiettori. ~*tide*, marea montante, *f.*, flusso, *m.* ¶ *v.t.* inondare, sommergere.

floor, *n.* pavimento, (*of wood*), impiantito, tavolato, palchetto, *m.*; (*storey*) piano. *on one* ~ (*rooms*), allo stesso livello, alla pari. ~*cloth*, tela cerata, *f.* ~ *lamp*, torciere. *floor-polish*, cera da lustrare, *f.* ~ *polisher*, (*pers.*) lucidatore di pavimenti, *m.* ~ *space*, area, *f.* spazio per ballare, *m.* ¶ *v.t.* pavimentare, impiantire, palchettare; atterrare, gettare per terra; sconcertare.

flora, *n.* flora, *f.* **floral,** *a.* florale. ~ *design*, fiorame, *m.* **Florence,** *n.* Firenze, *f.* **Florentine,** *a. & n.* fiorentino, *a. & m.* **florid,** *a.* florido, fiorito. **Florida,** *n.* la Florida, *f.* **florist,** *n.* fioraio, *m.*, -a, *f.*, fiorista, *m.f.*

florin, *n.* fiorino, *m.*

floss, *n.* borra, *f.* ~ *silk*, borra di seta, *f.*, filaticcio, *m.*

flotation (*Fin.*), *n.* lanciamento, *m.*, promozione, costituzione, *f.*

flotilla, *n.* flottiglia, *f.*

flotsam, *n.* relitto, rigetto del mare, *m.*

flounce, *n.* balza, balzana, piega, *f.*, volante, *m.* ¶ *v.t.* guarnire con volanti. ~ *about*, agitarsi, dimenarsi.

flounder (*fish*), *n.* passerino, *m.* ¶ *v.i.* dibattersi, dimenarsi; impappinarsi.

flour, *n.* farina, *f.* ~ *dealer*, negoziante di farina, *m.* ~ *merchant*, farinaiolo, *m.* ~ *mill*,

flourish, *n.* paraffa, *f.*; tratto di penna, svolazzo, ghirigoro; (*with stick*) mulinello; (*of hand*) gesto; (*Mus.*) fioritura, *f.*, preludio, *m.* ¶ *v.t.* brandire, ostentare; (*v.i.*) fiorire,

prosperare; fare il mulinello (*stick or sword*). ~ing, *a.* fiorente, prospero.

floury, *a.* farinoso, coperto di farina.

flout, *v.t.* schernire, beffarsi di, burlarsi di. ~ *at*, farsi giuoco di.

flow, *n.* flusso, corso, *m.*, corrente, *f.*, torrente, *m.*, abbondanza, profusione, affluenza, *f.* ~ *of words*, facilità. ¶ *v.i.* scorrere, colare, fluire; seguire, emanare, traboccare; circolare; (*tide*) montare, salire.

flower, *n.* fiore, *m.* ~ *bed*, aiuola, *f.* ~ *garden*, giardino, *m.* ~ *girl*, fioraia, *f.* ~ *holder*, portafiori, *m.inv.* ~ *market*, mercato dei fiori, *m.* ~*pot*, vaso da fiori, *m.* ~ *show*, esposizione dei fiori, esposizione floreale, *f.* ~ *stand*, portavasi, *m.inv.* canestra da fiori, *f.* ~ *work*, lavoro a fiori. ¶ *v.i.* fiorire. ~*et*, *n.* fiorellino, *m.* ~ing, *a.* a fiori, fiorito. ¶ *n.* fioritura, *f.* ~y, *a.* fiorito, in fiore, a fiori.

flowing, *a.* corrente, scorrevole, volubile; (*tide*) montante.

fluctuate, *v.i.* fluttuare. **fluctuation,** *n.* fluttuazione, *f.*, oscillazione, *f.*, movimento, *m.*

flue, *n.* tubo, condotto, passaggio, *m.*, gola di camino, *f.*

fluency, *n.* scorrevolezza, speditezza, facilità, *f.* **fluent,** *a.* scorrevole, fluente, facile, copioso, fecondo. ~ly, *ad.* correntemente, speditamente, scorrevolmente, facilmente.

fluff, *n.* borra, *f.*; (*under furniture*) lanugine, *f.*; (*hair*) lanugine, peluria, *f.*, peluzzo, *m.* *to* ~ *up*, scuotere le penne. ~y, *a.* piumoso, lanuginoso, peloso.

fluid, *a.* fluido. ¶ *n.* (*imponderable*) fluido, *m.*; (*ponderable*) liquido, *m.* ~ity, *n.* fluidità, *f.*

fluke, *n.* (*anchor*) marra, *f.*; (*chance*) colpo di fortuna, caso inaspettato, *m.*; (*animal parasite*) linguattola, *f.*

flummery, *n.* tiritera, sciocchezza, *f.*

flunkey, *n.* servitore (in livrea), lacchè, *m.* ~dom, *n.* servitorame, *m.*

fluorescent, *a.* fluorescente. **fluorine,** *n.* fluorina, *f.* **fluor spar,** spato, *m.*, fluorite di calcio, *f.*

flurry, *n.* agitazione, *f.*, trambusto, *m.* ¶ *v.t.* agitare, trambustare.

flush, *a.* abbondante, copioso, ben munito (di contanti); piano. ~ *with*, a fior di, allo stesso livello di. ¶ *n.* rossore, *m.*, rossezza, *f.*, arrossimento, accesso (d'ira), *&c.*), *m.*; accensione, *f.*; (*Cards*) flusso, goffo, *m.* ¶ *v.t.* fare arrossire; lavare, inondare; (*Hunt.*) levare, fare levare; (*v.i.*) arrossire, imporporarsi, coprirsi di rossore. ~*ed face*, viso rosso. *he* ~*d deeply*, arrossí vivamente.

Flushing, *n.* Flessinga, *f.*

fluster, *v.t.* agitare, confondere, perturbare; (*with drink*) ubbriacare.

flute, *n.* flauto, *m.*; (*groove or fluting*) scanalatura, scannellatura, *f.* **flutist,** *n.* flautista, *m.f.*

flutter, *n.* battito (d'ali), volteggiamento, *m.*, agitazione, *f.*, turbamento, *m.* ¶ *v.i.* agitarsi, dibattersi, volteggiarsi, svolazzare, palpitare, (*v.t.*) agitare, battere (le ali); turbare, sconcertare.

fluty, *a.* flautato, di flauto.

fluvial, fluviatile, *a.* fluviale.

flux, *n.* flusso, *m.*; (*Chem. & Metall.*) fondente, *m.*

fly, *n.* mosca, *f.*; (*trouser*) sparato, *m.* ~*blown*, infetto con cacchioni, sporcato. ~*catcher* (*bird*), pigliamosche, *m.inv.* ~*dirt*, cacata di mosca, *f.* ~*fishing*, pesca con mosche artificiali, *f.* ~*leaf*, foglietto di guardia, *m.* ~*line*, lenza per la pesca con mosche artificiali, *f.* ~*net*, moscaiuola, *f.* ~*paper*, carta moschicida, *f.* ~*press*, bilanciere, *m.* ~*rod* (*Fish.*), canna da pesca[re] con mosche artificiali. ~*speck*, cacata di mosca, *f.* ~*swat*[*ter*], *m.*; cacciamosche, *m.inv.* ~*flap*, *m.inv.* ~*trap* (*plant*), pigliamosche, *m.inv.* ~*weight* (*Box.*), peso mosca. ~*wheel*, volano, *m.* ~*whisk*, cacciamosche, *m.inv.* ¶ *v.i. ir.* volare; fuggire, involarsi; saltare; montare; (*v.t. ir.*) fare volare; (*flag*) battere, sventolare; (*kite*) lanciare. ~*about*, svolazzare, volteggiare, diffondersi. ~ *at*, slanciarsi su, assalire, avventarsi su. ~ *away*, involarsi, pigliare il volo. ~ (*spring*) *back*, saltare indietro, rimbalzare. ~ *open*, aprirsi di scatto. ~*er*, *n. see* flier. ~*ing*, *n.* volo, volare, *m.*, l'aviazione, *f.* ~ *ace*, asso (d'aviazione), *m.* ~ *boat*, idroplano, idrovolante, *m.* ~ *buttress*, arco a sprone, contrafforte ad arco. *m.* ~ *colours*, bandiere spiegate, *f.pl.* ~ *column*, colonna leggera, *f.* ~ *fish*, pesce volante. ~ *ground*, campo d'aviazione, *m.* ~ *squad*, squadra mobile, *f.*, celere, *m.* ~ *squadron*, squadriglia, leggera, *f.* ~ *visit*, breve visita, v. di volata.

foal, *n.* puledro, *m.*, -a, *f.*, cavallino,

m., -a, *f.*; (*ass's*) asinello, *m.*, -a, *f.* ¶ *v.i.* figliare.

foam, *n.* schiuma, spuma, *f.* ¶ *v.i.* spumare, spumeggiare. ~*y*, *a.* spumoso.

fob, *n.* taschino da orologio, *m.* ~ *off*, dilazionare, rimandare.

focal, *a.* focale. **focus,** *n.* foco, fuoco, *m.*; *in* ~, a foco. ¶ *v.t.* mettere a foco. **focussing,** *n.* messa a foco, *f.*

fodder, *n.* foraggio, *m.*

foe, *n.* nemico, avversario, *m.*, -a, *f.*

foetus, *n.* feto, *m.*

fog, *n.* nebbia, bruma, *f.*; (*Phot.*) velo, *m.* ~ *horn*, corno da nebbia, megafono, *m.* ~ *signal*, segnale da nebbia, *m.*, petardo, *m.* ¶ *v.t.* annebbiare; oscurare; appannare; (*Phot.*) velare. **foggy,** *a.* nebbioso, brumoso.

fog[**e**]**y,** *n. or old* ~, vecchiotto, *m.*, vecchio barbogio. **fogyish,** *a.* da vecchiotto.

foible, *n.* debole, *m.* ~*s*, *n.pl.* debolezze, *f.pl.*

foil, *n.* (*tinsel*) foglio (di metallo), orpello, *m.*; (*Fenc.*) fioretto, *m.*; (*fig.*) contrasto, *m.*, ombra, *f.* ¶ *v.t.* sventare, mandare a vuoto, frustrare.

foist, *v.t.* fare passare, interpolare. ~ *upon*, insinuare.

fold, *n.* piega, ripiegatura, *f.*, addiaccio, ovile, *m.*; (*in compounds*) volte, *f.pl.* (*Relig.*) gregge, *m.* ¶ *v.t.* piegare, stringere; (*arms*) incrociare; (*hands*) congiungere, incrociare; (*sheep*) addiacciare, stabbiare. ~ *up*, *v.t.* ripiegare, avvolgere; (*v.i.*) ripiegarsi. ~*er*, *n.* piegatore, *m.*, -trice, *f.*; (*publicity*) stampiglia; cartella; ~*ing*, *p.a.:* ~ *camera*, apparecchio fotografico pieghevole, *m.* ~ *door*, porta a battenti, *f.* ~ *machine*, macchina piegatrice, *f.* ~ *seat*, strapuntino, *m.*

foliaceous, *a.* fogliaceo. **foliage,** *n.* fogliame, *m.* **foliate,** *a.* fogliato, foggiato come una foglia. **foliation,** *n.* fogliazione, *f.*

folio, *n.* foglio, *m.*; (*book*) *n. & a.* in-foglio, *m. & a.*

folklore, *n.* folklore, *m.*

folk[**s**]**,** *n.pl.* gente, *f. the old* ~, i vecchi, *m.pl.*

follicle, *n.* follicolo, *m.*

follow, *v.t.* seguire, inseguire; proseguire, tenere dietro; (*v.i.*) seguire, seguirne, risultare, derivare, susseguire. ~ *suit* (*Cards*), rispondere al colore. *as* ~*s*, come segue, come appresso. *it does not* ~ *that*, non ne viene per conseguenza che. ~ *through*, proseguire, inseguire. ~ *up*, seguire un pista; completare. ~**er**, *n.* seguace, discepolo, partigiano, aderente, (*pl.*) seguito, *m.*; ammiratori, innamorati, *m.pl.* ~**ing** (*day*, *&c.*), *a.* seguente, appresso. *in the* ~ *manner*, nel modo seguente, *come segue.* *the* ~ [*persons*], i sottoscritti, *m.pl.* ¶ *n.* seguito, *m.*

folly, *n.* follia, sciocchezza, stoltezza, *f.* l'assurdo, *m.*

foment, *v.t.* fomentare. ~**ation**, *n.* fomentazione, *f.* (*Med.*). fomento, *m.*

fond, *a.* vago, affezionato, invaghito, appassionato, amante, tenero, carezzevole; folle. *to be* ~ *of*, amare, essere affezionato a, essere invaghito di. *she is very* ~ *of music*, ha molta passione per la musica, è appassionata per la musica.

fondle, *v.t.* accarezzare.

fondness, *n.* tenerezza, affezione, inclinazione, *f.*, gusto, *m.*

font, *n.* (*Eccl.*) fonte, fonte battesimale, *m.* (*Typ.*). corpo, *m.*

food, *n.* cibo, alimento, *m.*, viveri, *m.pl.*, vitto, mangiare, nutrimento, *m.*, (*animals*) pastura, *f.*, pascolo, *m.*; (*fig.*) materia, *f.*, soggetto, argomento, *m.* ~ *& drink*, il bere e il mangiare. *give* ~ *for thought*, dare da pensare. ~*stuff*, genere alimentare, *m.*

fool, *n.* sciocco, stolto, imbecille, stupido, insensato, idiota, testardo, minchione, semplicione, babbeo, scempio, scimunito, zimbello, *m.*; (*Hist.*, *court*) buffone, *m.* *to play the* ~, fare lo sciocco, l'imbecille, &c. ~*hardiness*, temerità, *f.* ~*hardy*, temerario. ~*proof*, *a.* a prova delle sciocchezze, a tutta prova, a prova di bomba. ~*'s cap*, scettro della follia, *m.* *foolscap* (*paper*), carta ministro, carta di rispetto, carta protocollo, *f.* ¶ *v.t.* ingannare, prendersi giuoco di, gabbare. ~ (*about*), *v.i.* fare l'imbecille, &c., scherzare, burlare. ~**ery**, *n.* sciocchezza, stoltezza, stravaganza, buffonata, burletta, *f.* ~**ish**, *a.* sciocco, stolto, ridicolo, insensato, imprudente. ~**ishness**, *n.* stoltezza, insensatezza, imprudenza, *f.*

foot, *n.* piede, *m.*, (*animal*) zampa, *f.*; zoccolo, *m.*, base, parte inferiore; infanteria, *f.*; (*Meas.*) piede = 0.30480 metre. ~ *& mouth disease*, stomatite aftosa (epizootica), *f.* ~*ball*, pallone, *m.*, palla, *f.*; (*game*)

calcio, *m.* ~*baller*, calciatore, *m.* ~*bath*, bagno di piedi, pediluvio, *m.* ~*board*, predella, *f.*, predellino, *m.* ~*bridge*, passarella, *f.*, ponticello, *m.* ~*fall*, passo, *m.* ~*fault* (*Ten*). fallo del piede, *m.* ~*hold*, presa del piede, *f.*, punto d'appoggio, *m.*, (*fig.*) piede, *m.* ~*lights*, lumi della ribalta, *m.pl.*, ribalta, *f.* ~*man*, lacchè, servo, staffiere, *m.* ~*note*, nota a piè di pagina, *f.*, postilla, *f.* ~*pad*, ladrone, grassatore, *m.* ~ *passenger*, pedone, *m.*, -a, *f.* ~*path*, sentiero, *m.*; (*street*) marciapiede, *m.* ~*plate* (*Rly.*), piattaforma, *f.* ~*print*, passo, *m.*, impronta del piede, *f.*; (*fig.*) orma, *f.* ~ *race*, corsa podistica, *f.*, corsa pedestre, c. a piedi. ~*sore*, che ha male ai piedi, zoppicante. ~*step*, passo, *m.*, pedata, *f.*; (*fig.*) orma, *f.*, orme, *f.pl.*, vestigia, *f.pl.* ~*stool*, sgabello, *m.*, poggiapiedi, *m.inv.* ~*warmer*, scaldapiedi, scaldaletto, *m.inv.* ~*wear*, calzatura, *f.* ~*work*, giuoco del piede, *m.* *on* ~, *a piedi*, in piedi, in cammino. ~**ing**, *n.* piede, posto, sostegno, *m.*, posizione, *f.*, condizione, livello, *m.*; (*Build.*) base, *f.*, basamento, *m.*, fondazione, *f.* *on an equal* ~, allo stesso livello, a parità di condizione. *on a war* ~, *peace* ~, sul piede di guerra, sul piede di pace. *to pay for one's* ~, pagare la matricola.

fop, *n.* bellimbusto, damerino, *m.*

foppish, *a.* attillato, affettato, elegante, vano.

for, *pr.* per, a favore di, in cambio di; a causa di; a dispetto di; verso di, a, da, durante, malgrado. ~ *all that*, malgrado tutto ciò, nondimeno, tuttavia. ~ *oneself*, per proprio conto. ~ *& against*, pro e contro. *the pros & cons*, gli argomenti pro e contro. ¶ *c.* perché, imperocché, per la ragione che.

forage, *n.* foraggio, *m.* ~ *cap*, berretto di fatica, *m.*, berretto di bassa tenuta. ¶ *v.t.* & *i.* foraggiare, fare incetta di foraggio, andare in cerca di foraggio, raccolta di foraggio; (*bird*) beccarsi, raccogliere foraggio. **forager,** *n.* foraggiere, *m.*

forasmuch as, *c.* giacché, visto che, considerato che.

foray, *n.* incursione, razzia, scorreria, *f.*

forbear, *v.i. ir.* astenersi da, trattenersi da, fare a meno di, non volere. ~**ance**, *n.* indulgenza, pazienza, tollerazione, *f.*

for[e]bears, *n.pl.* antenati, *m.pl.*

forbid, *v.t. ir.* proibire, vietare, interdire, impedire. *God* ~! Dio non vogiia! Dio ci liberi! **forbidding,** *a.* ripugnante, repulsivo, ributtante; aspro, severo.

force, *n.* forza, *f.*, vigore, *m.*, validità, energia, *f.* ~ *of circumstances,* forza delle circostanze. *by* ~, per forza. *by* ~ *of,* a forza di. *in* ~, in forza; vigente, in vigore. ~ *pump,* pompa premente, *f.* ¶ *v.t.* forzare, obbligare, costringere, imporre; violare, prendere con la forza, aprire con forza; (*meat*) infarcire; (*plants*) maturare in serra. **forced,** *p.a.* costretto, obbligato, forzato; affettato. *by* ~ *marches,* a marce forzate. **forcedly,** *ad.* forzatamente. **forceful,** *a.* forte, vigoroso, possente, potente. **forcemeat,** *n.* ripieno, *m.*

forceps, *n.s. & pl.* (*Surg.*) pinze, *f.pl.* (*dental*) cane, *m.*; (*obstetrical*) forcipe *m.*

forcible, *a.* forte, energico; forzato. **forcibly,** *ad.* fortemente, energicamente. *forcing bed, forcing frame.*

ford, *n.* guado, *m.* ¶ *v.t.* guadare, passare a guado. ~**able,** *a.* guadabile.

fore, *a.* d'innanzi, davanti, di fronte, frontale, anteriore; (*Naut.*) di prua, di trinchetto. ~*paw,* zampa anteriore (davanti). ¶ *ad.* prima, in anticipo, anteriormente, pre-. ~ *& aft,* da prua a poppa. ~ *& aft sails,* auriche, *f.pl.* ¶ (*Golf*) *i.* attenti! ¶ *n.* davanti, *m.* (*Naut.*) prua, *f.*

forearm, *n.* avambraccio, *m.* ¶ *v.t.* (*fig.*) premunire, avvertire. *forewarned, forearmed,* uomo avvisato è mezzo salvato.

forebode, *v.t.* presagire, presentire. **foreboding,** *n.* presentimento, presagio, *m.*

forecast, *n.* previsione, *f.*, prevedimento, progetto, *m.* ¶ *v.t. ir.* prevedere.

forecastle *or* **foc's'le,** *n.* castello di prua, *m.*

foreclose, *v.t.* ipotecare. **foreclosure,** *n.* ipoteca, *f.*

forecourt, *n.* (*house*) anticorte, *f.*; (*castle, palace*) primo cortile.

fore edge *or* **foredge** (*book*), *n.* margine di taglio, *m.*

forefathers, *n.pl.* antenati, *m.pl.*

forefinger, *n.* indice, *m.*

foregoing, *p.a.* precedente. *the* ~, ciò che precede. *foregone con-*

clusion, partito preso, cosa certa. ~ *decision,* decisione già fatta, esito previsto.

foreground, *n.* primo piano, *m.*

forehand [stroke] (*Ten.*), *n.* colpo diritto, *m.*

forehead, *n.* fronte, *f.*

foreign, *a.* straniero, forestiero, estero; (*fig.*) estraneo, alieno, esotico. ~ *exchange rates,* corso del cambio sull'estero. ~ *affairs,* affari esteri, *m.pl.* ~ *body,* corpo estraneo. ~*-going ship,* nave di lungo corso, *f.* ~ *note paper,* carta da lettere per l'estero, *f.* F~ *Office* (*Eng.*), Ministero degli Affari Esteri. ~**er,** *n.* straniero, *m.*, -a, *f.*; forestiere.

foreknowledge, *n.* prescienza, *f.*

foreland, *n.* promontorio, *m.*

forelock (*hair*), *n.* ciuffo (sulla fronte), *m.*

foreman, *n.* capo-squadra, capo-mastro, capo. ~ *of job* (*Build.*), capo-lavorante, primo operaio. ~ *of the jury,* capo dei giurati.

foremast, *n.* albero di trinchetto, *m.*

foremost (the), il primo. *to be* ~, essere in prima linea fra . . . *first & ~,* a bella prima, anzitutto.

forenoon, *n.* mattino, *m.*, mattinata, *f.*

forensic, *a.* forense; (*medicine*) legale.

forerunner, *n.* precursore, *m.*

foresee, *v.t. ir.* prevedere, antivedere.

foreshadow, *v.t.* adombrare, preannunziare, far presentire.

foreshore, *n.* spiaggia, *f.*

foreshorten, *v.t.* raccorciare.

foresight, *n.* previsione, previdenza, prescienza, *f.*

forest, *n.* foresta, selva, *f.*, bosco, *m.*; (*att.*) forestale.

forestall, *v.t.* prevenire, anticipare.

forester, *n.* (*officer*) guardia forestale, *f.* **forestry,** *n.* silvicultura, *f.*

foretaste, *n.* pregustamento, *m.*

foretell, *v.t. ir.* predire, presagire, annunziare.

forethought, *n.* previdenza, premeditazione, *f.*

forewarn, *v.t.* preavvertire, preavvisare, prevenire.

forewoman, *n.* prima operaia, prima lavorante, maestra, *f.*

foreword, *n.* prefazione, *f.*, premio, *m.*

forfeit, *n.* multa, pena, ammenda, *f.*, pegno, *m.*; (*at play*) posta, *f.*; (*pl.*) giuochi di società, *m.pl.* ¶ *v.:* confiscare, perdere per confisca, demeritare; (*honour*) perdere (l'onore), essere disonorato. *I have done* *nothing to ~ your esteem*, non ho demeritato di voi. **~ure**, *n.* perdita, confiscazione, *f.*

forgather, *v.i.* adunarsi.

forge, *n.* fucina, *f.* ¶ *v.t.* fucinare; fabbricare; contraffare, falsificare. *to ~ ahead*, tirare avanti. **~d**, *p.a.* contraffatto. **forgeman**, *n.* fabbro, *m.* **forger**, *n.* falsario, contraffatore, *m.*, -trice, *f.*, falsamonete, *m.* **forgery**, *n.* falso, *m.*, contraffazione, falsificazione, *f.* *crime of ~*, reato di falso, *m.*

forget, *v.t. ir.* dimenticare, scordare. **~-me-not**, miosotide, non-ti-scordar-di-mé, *m.* *~ oneself*, agire (comportarsi) indecorosamente. **~-ful**, *a.* dimentico, scordevole, negligente. **~fulness**, *n.* dimenticanza, negligenza, *f.*, oblio, *m.*

forgive, *v.t. ir.* perdonare; (*pers.*) perdonare a . . . **~ness**, *n.* perdono, *m.*, remissione, *f.*

forgo, *v.t. ir.* rinunziare a, astenersi da.

fork, *n.* forca, forcella, *f.*; (*table, &c.*) forchetta, *f.*; (*tree*) forcella, *f.*, ramo biforcato, *m.*; (*road, &c.*) biforcazione, *f.*, biforcamento, *m.* ¶ *v.i.* biforcarsi. **~ed**, *a.* forcuto, biforcato. *~ lightning*, fulmine a zig-zag, *m.*

forlorn, *a.* abbandonato, perduto; sconsolato. *~ hope*, vana speranza, impresa, disperata, *f.*

form, *n.* forma, guisa, foggia, *f.*, tipo, *m.*, formalità, *f.*; (*paper*) modulo, *m.*; (*school*) classe, *f.*; (*seat*) banco, *m.*; (*hare*) covo (di lepre), *m.* ¶ *v.t.* formare, costituire, farsi, formarsi. *~ fours*, mettersi per quattro. *~ single file*, (andare) in file per uno. *~ two deep*, mettersi in due file. **~al**, *a.* formale, convenzionale, di cerimonia. **~ality**, *n.* formalità, *f.* **~ation**, *n.* formazione, *f.* **form[e]** (*Typ.*), *n.* forma, *f.*

former, *a.* primo, antico, precedente, passato. *the ~*, *the latter*, quello, questo, quegli, questi, il primo, il secondo; i primi, i secondi. **~ly**, *ad.* già, altre volte; un tempo, in altri tempi, anticamente.

formidable, *a.* formidabile.

Formosa, *n.* Formosa, *f.*

formula, *n.* formula, *f.* **~ry**, *n.* formulario, *m.* **formulate**, *v.t.* formulare. **formulism**, *n.*, formulismo, *m.* **formulist**, *n.* & **~ic**, *a.* convenzionalista, *m.* & *att.*

fornication, *n.* fornicazione, *f.*

forsake, *v.t. ir.* abbandonare.

forsooth, *ad.* davvero, veramente, in verità.

forswear, *v.t. ir.* abiurare, rinnegare, rinunciare a. *~ oneself*, spergiurare.

fort, *n.* fortezza, *f.*, forte, *m.*; (*small*) fortino, *m.* **forte** (*Mus.*), *ad.* forte. ¶ (*strong point*) *n.* forte, *m.*

forth, *ad.* fuori; in avanti. *~coming*, *a.* prossimo, presso a venire, che sta per uscire, presso a comparire, &c. *and so ~*, e cosí di seguito, e cosí via. *~right*, franco, schietto, esplicito, onesto. *~with*, *ad.* subito, immediatamente, incontanente, difilato.

fortieth, *a. & n.* quarantesimo, *a. & m.*

fortification, *n.* fortificazione, *f.*; (*wine*) alcoolizzazione (dei vini), *f.* **fortify**, *v.t.* fortificare. *fortified place*, piazzaforte, *f.* **fortitude**, *n.* forza d'animo, *f.*, coraggio, *m.*

fortnight, *n.* quindicina, *f.*, quindici giorni, *m.pl.* **~ly**, *a.* quindicinale. ¶ *ad.* ogni quindici giorni, quindicinalmente.

fortress, *n.* fortezza, *f.*

fortuitous, *a.* fortuito.

fortunate, *a.* fortunato. **~ly**, *ad.* fortunatamente, per buona fortuna.

fortune, *n.* fortuna, sorte, *f.*, oroscopo, *m.*, caso, *m.*, beni, *m.pl.*, dote, *f.*, patrimonio, *m.* *to tell ~s*, predire la fortuna. *~teller*, indovino, *m.*, -a, *f.*, chi dice la fortuna, chi pretende di predire la fortuna. *~telling*, sortilegio, *m.*, predizione della fortuna, *f.*

forty, *a. & n.* quaranta, *a. & m.*

forum, *n.* foro, *m.*, aula magna, *f.*

forward, *a.* avanzato; forte, progredito, precoce; ardente, impudente, sfacciato; (*Com.*) futuro, a termine. *~ delivery*, a futura consegna. **~[s]**, *ad.* avanti, innanzi. ¶ *n.* (*Foot.*) avanti, attaccante, *m.* ¶ *v.t.* spedire; far[e] proseguire (*letters*); promuovere, inoltrare, assecondare, aiutare. *to be ~d*, da rispedirsi. *please ~*, (*letters*) pregasi far proseguire. **~ing agent**, spedizioniere, *m.* **~ness**, *n.* impudenza, sfacciataggine; precocità, *f.*

fossil, *a. & n.* fossile, *a. & m.*

foster, *v.t.* allevare, nutrire; favorire, promuovere, incoraggiare, sostentare. *~ brother*, fratello di latte, *m.* *~ child*, bambino lattante (a balia). *~ mother*, balia, nutrice, *f.*

foul, *a.* sporco, sudicio, sozzo; schifoso, viziato, fetido, immondo; brutto, osceno; cattivo, disonesto, vergognoso, infame; perfido, sleale; (*words*) sconcio, grossolano, ingiurioso. ~*-breathed*, che ha l' alito pesante. ~*-mouthed*, sboccato, che usa parole sconce (grossolane, oscene), ~ *play*, trucco, modo d'agire disonesto, tranello, *m.* ¶ *n.* fallo (*Football*), *m.* ¶ *v.t.* sporcare, imbrattare, insudiciare, insozzare; (*Naut., rope, &c.*) imbarazzare; (*ship*) investire. ~*ness, n.* sporcizia, sozzura, immondezza, *f.*

found, *v.t.* stabilire, fondare, mettere su, creare; (*Metal*) fondere.

foundation, *n.* fondazione, istituzione, costituzione, *f.*, base, *f.*, fondamento, *m.* (*f. pl. -a*); creazione, borsa, *f.*, stabilimento, *m.* ~ *scholar*, titolare di una borsa di studio, borsista, *m. m.f.* ~ *stone*, prima pietra, *f.*, (*fig.*) pietra fondamentale.

founder, *n.* fondatore, *m.*, creatore, fattore, *m.*; (*race*) autore; (*family*) progenitore; promotore, *m.*; (*metal*) fonditore, *m.* ~*s' shares*, azioni devolute ai promotori di società anonima. ¶ *v.i.* andare a picco (a fondo), colare a picco, affondare.

foundered (*Vet.*), *p.a.* attrappato, storpiato.

foundling, *n.* trovatello, *m.*, -a, *f.* ~ *hospital*, ospizio dei trovatelli, degli innocenti, *m.*

foundress, *n.* fondatrice, *f.*

foundry, *n.* fonderia, *f.*

fount, *n.* fonte, sorgente, *f.*; (*Typ.*) fondita, *f.*, corpo (di caratteri), *m.*

fountain, *n.* fontana, sorgente, *f.*, getto (d'acqua), *m.* ~*head*, sorgente, *f.* ~ *of youth*, fontana di gioventù. ~*pen*, penna stilografica, *f.* ~ *pen ink*, inchiostro per penna stilografica, *m.*

four, *a. & n.* quattro, *a. & m.* ~*fold*, quadruplo; quadruplice; quattro volte (*ad.*). ~*footed*, quadrupede. ~*poster*, letto a colonne, *m.* ~ *score*, *a. & n.* ottanta, *a. & m.* ~*some* (*Golf*), partita giuocata da due coppie. ~*wheeler*, veicolo a quattro ruote. ~*wheel brake*, freno sulle quattro ruote, *m.* ~*wheeled*, a quattro ruote. *on all* ~*s*, *ad.* carpone, carponi.

fourteen, *a. & n.* quattordici, *a. & m.* ~*th*, *a. & n.* quattordicesimo, *a. & m.*, decimo quarto, il quattordici, *m.* **fourth,** *a. & n.*

quarto, *a. & m.* ~*finger*, dito mignolo, mignolo, *m.* ¶ *n.* quarto, *m.*, -a, *f.*; il quattro, *m.*; (*part*) quarto, *m.*, quarta parte, *f.*; (*Mus.*) quarta, *f.*

fowl, *n.* pollo, uccello; volatile, *m.* (*gen. pl. -i*). ~*house*, pollaio, *m.* ~*er, n.* uccellatore, *m.* ~*ing, n.* uccellagione, *f.* ~*piece*, fucile da caccia, *m.*

fox, *n.* volpe, *f.*; volpone, *m.* ~*cub*, volpicino, *m.* ~*earth*, ~*'s hole*, volpaia, tana da volpe, *f.* ~*glove*, digitale, *f.* ~*hound*, cane da volpe, bracco, *m.* ~*hunting*, caccia alla volpe, *f.* ~ *terrier*, fox-terrier, *m.* ~*trot*, fox-trot, *m.* ~*y* (*fig.*), *a.* astuto, scaltro.

foyer, *n.* ridotto, *m.*

fracas, *n.* fracasso, *m.*

fraction, *n.* frazione, *f.* ~*al*, *a.* frazionario.

fractious, *a.* dispettoso, litigioso, stizzoso, permaloso.

fracture, *n.* frattura; rottura, *f.* ¶ *v.t.* fratturare.

fr[a]enum, *n.* (*Anat.*) frenulo, *m.*

fragile, *a.* fragile. **fragility,** *n.* fragilità, *f.*

fragment, *n.* frammento. ~*ary*, *a.* frammentario.

fragrance, *n.* fragranza, *f.* **fragrant,** *a.* fragrante.

frail, *a.* fragile, debole. ¶ *n.* cesto, *m.*, sporta, *f.* ~*ty*, *n.* fragilità, debolezza, *f.*

frame, *& ~work*, *n.* cornice, *f.*; telaio, *m.*, intelaiatura, *f.*; castello, *m.*, incastellatura, impalcatura, armatura; ossatura, carcassa; taglia, statura, *f.*; (*Need.*) telaio, *m.*; (*Typ.*) scaffale, *m.* ~ *aerial*, antenna a gabbia, *f.* ~ *of mind*, stato d'animo, *m.*, disposizione, *f.* ¶ *v.t.* formare, comporre, costruire, concepire, redigere, tramare; (*picture*) incorniciare, mettere in cornice, inquadrare. **framing** (*act*), *n.* inquadramento, *m.*, messa in cornice, *f.*; composizione, costruzione, *f.*

France, *n.* la Francia, *f.*

franchise, *n.* franchigia, *f.*, diritto di voto, *m.*

Franciscan, *n.* francescano, *m.*, -a, *f.* ~ *nun*, francescana, *f.*

Francophil[e], *a. & n.* francofilo, *a. & n.* **Francophobe,** *a. & n.* francofobo, *a. & m.*

frank, *a.* franco, sincero, schietto.

~ness, *n.* franchezza, sincerità, schiettezza, *f.*

Frankfort, *n.* Francoforte, *f.*

frankincense, *n.* incenso, *m.*

frantic, *a.* frenetico.

fraternal, *a.* fraterno. **fraternity,** *n.* fraternità, fratellanza, *f.* **fraternize,** *v.i.* fraternizzare. **fratricide** (*pers.*), *n.* & **fratricidal,** *a.* fratricida, *a.* & *m.f.*

fraud, *n.* frode, *f.*, inganno, dolo, *m.* **fraudulent,** *a.* fraudolento, doloso.

fraught with, pieno di, carico di, destinato a recare.

fray, *n.* rissa, mischia, *f.*, combattimento, *m.*

fray, *v.i.* & *t.* ragnare, logorare.

freak, *n.* capriccio, ghiribizzo, *m.*, fantasia, *f.* ~ *of nature,* aborto di natura, *m.* ~**ish,** *a.* capriccioso, bizzarro.

freckle, *n.* lentiggine, *f.* ¶ *v.t.* macchiettare (di lentiggini). ~**d,** *a.* lentigginoso.

free, *a.* libero, franco, aperto, generoso; gratuito; volontario; disinvolto, familiare, largo. *free from,* esente da; scevro di. ~ *with,* prodigo di. ~ *allowance of luggage or weight allowed,* franchigia di bagaglio, *f.* ~ & *bonded warehouses,* depositi doganali, depositi franchi, magazzini doganali. ~ & *easy,* familiare, disinvolto, spigliato. ~ & *easy manner,* disinvoltura, *f.* *in a* ~ & *easy way,* alla buona, senza cerimonie. ~ *board,* capo di banda, opera morta, bordo libero. ~ *competition,* libertà di concorrenza. ~*booter,* filibustiere, *m.* ~ *copy,* copia gratuita, copia in esame, *f.* ~ *fight,* mischia (battaglia) generale, *f.* ~ *gift* (*Relig.*), dono gratuito, *m.* ~*hand,* (*fig.*) carta bianca, *f.* ~*hand drawing,* disegno a mano libera, disegnare a mano libera. ~*lance,* soldato mercenario; (*fig.*) chi non appartiene ad alcun partito, o giornale. *the* ~ *list* (*Theat.*), le entrate di favore, *f.pl.* ~*mason,* [fra]massone, *m.* ~*masonry,* [fra]-massoneria, *f.* ~ *pass,* lasciapassare; (*Rly.*) biglietto di libera circolazione. ~ *stone,* pietra da taglio. ~*thinker,* libero pensatore, *m.* ~ *thinking,* ~ *thought,* libertà di pensiero, *f.* ~ *trade,* libero scambio, *m.* ~ *trader,* libero-scambista, liberista, *m.* ~ *verse,* versi liberi, *m.pl.* ~ *warehouse,* deposito franco. ~*wheel,* ruota libera, *f.* ~*will,*

spontanea volontà, *f.*; (*Phil.*) libero arbitrio, *m.* ¶ *ad.* franco, gratuitamente. ~ *on board,* franco a bordo. ~ *on rail,* franco vagone. ¶ *v.t.* liberare, affrancare, sbarazzare, sciogliere, esonerare. **freedom,** *n.* libertà, esenzione, franchigia, scioltezza, *f.* *free[dom of] speech,* libertà di parlare, libera parola, *f.* **freely,** *ad.* liberamente, francamente, volentieri, apertamente; prodigamente; gratuitamente.

freeze, *v.t. ir.* agghiacciare, gelare, far gelare; (*v.i. ir.*) gelare, ghiacciare, ghiacciarsi. **freezer,** *n.* ghiacciaia, *f.*, apparecchio congelatore, *m.* *freezing point,* punto di congelamento (*thermometer*), *m. at freezing,* a zero.

Freiburg (*Baden*), *n.* Friburgo in Brisgovia, *f.*

freight, *n.* porto; nolo, noleggio; carico, *m.* ¶ *v.t.* noleggiare.

French, *a.* francese. ~ *ambassador, consul,* ambasciatore francese, ambasciatore di Francia, console francese. ~ *beans,* fagiolini, *m.pl.*; (*unripe*) fagioli verdi. ~ *chalk,* steatite, *f. to take* ~ *leave,* partire all'inglese, andarsene *or* filare all'inglese, non chiedere permesso!. ~ *lesson, master,* lezione di francese, *f.*, insegnante di francese, *m.* ~*man,* ~*woman,* francese, *m.f.* ~ *nail,* ~ *polish,* vernice francese, *f.* ~*-speaking Switzerland,* la Svizzera francese. ~ *window,* porta-finestra. ¶ (*language*) *n.* francese, *m.*, la lingua francese, *f. the* ~ (*pl.*), i francesi, *m.pl.*, il popolo francese, *m.* **Frenchify,** *v.t.* infrancesare.

frenzied, *p.a.* frenetico, forsennato, delirante. **frenzy,** *n.* frenesia, *f.*; delirio, *m.*

frequency, *n.* frequenza, *f.* **frequent,** *a.* frequente. ¶ *v.t.* frequentare, praticare. ~**er,** *n.* frequentatore, *m.*; -trice, *f.* **frequently,** *ad.* spesso, spesse volte, frequentemente.

fresco, *n.* affresco, *m.*

fresh, *a.* fresco, recente, nuovo; inesperto, novizio; riposato; lindo; imbiancato. ~ *from school,* appena uscito dalla scuola. ~ *from the wash,* fresco di bucato. ~*man,* studente d'università novamente iscritto, matricolino, *m.* ~ *paragraph,* alinea, *m.* ~*water,* acqua fresca, *f.*; (*not salt*) acqua dolce, *f.* ~*water fishing,* pesca d'acqua dolce, *f.* ~**en,** *v.t.* & *i.* rinfrescare, rinfres-

carsi; crescere. ~et, *n.* piena, *f.*
~ly, *&* ~, *ad.* frescamente, di
fresco, recentemente, di nuovo, di
bel nuovo; (*with p.p.*) di fresco, *e.g.*
fresh[*ly*]-*gathered roses*, rose colte di
fresco, appena colte. ~ness, *n.*
freschezza, novità, *f.*
fret, *n.* (*on guitar. &c.*) sbarretta
rilevata, *f.* (*Arch.*, *Her.*) greca, *f.*
~saw, *n.* sega da traforo, *f.* ~work,
lavoro d'incavo (in legno), *m.* ¶ *v.i.*
agitarsi, dimenarsi, irritarsi; (*v.t.*)
agitare, vessare; rodere, logorare,
strofinare; lavorare d'incavo, cesellare. ~ful, *a.* irritabile, stizzoso,
permaloso.
friable, *a.* friabile.
friar, *n.* frate, monaco, *m.* *Black* ~,
domenicano. *Grey* ~, francescano,
White ~, carmelitano. ~y, *n.*
convento, monastero, *m.*
friction, *n.* (*Mech.*) attrito, *m.*,
frizione, *f.*
Friday, *n.* venerdì, *m.* *Good* ~,
Venerdì Santo.
fried fish, pesce fritto, *m.*
friend, *n.* amico, *m.*, -a, *f.*; partigiano,
m. ~less, *a.* senza amici. ~liness,
n. disposizione amichevole, benevolenza, *f.* ~ly, *a.* amichevole, ben
disposto, benevolo. ~ *society*,
società (associazione) di mutuo
soccorso, *f.* ~ship, *n.* amicizia, *f.*
Friesland, *n.* la Frisia, *f.*
frieze, *n.* fregio, *m.*; tela di Frisia, *f.*
frigate, *n.* fregata, *f.*
fright, *n.* spavento, orrore, *m.*,
paura, *f.*, timore, *m.* ~en, *v.t.*
impaurire, spaventare, intimorire,
intimidire, terrorizzare, fare orrore
a. ~ful, *a.* terribile, spaventevole,
orribile.
frigid, *a.* frigido, glaciale, freddo;
impotente. ~ity, *n.* frigidità,
freddezza, *f.*
frill, *n.* trina increspata (striscia di);
gala, increspata, *f.* ~s *& furbelows*,
ninnoli, *m.pl.*, cianfruscole, *f.pl.*
¶ *v.t.* increspare.
fringe, *n.* frangia, *f.*; bordo, orlo, *m.*
¶ *v.t.* orlare, ornare con (di) frangia.
frippery, *n.* roba usata, *f.*
Frisian, *a.* frisone, della Frisia.
¶ *n.* frisone, *m.*
frisk, *n.* sgambetto, salto, *m.* ¶ *v.i.*
sgambettare, saltellare.
frisket, (*Typ.*) *n.* fraschetta, *f.*
frisky, *a.* vispo, vivace, irrequieto.
fritter (*Cook.*), *n.* frittella, *f.* ~ *away*,
scialacquare, sperdere, ridurre a
niente.

frivolity, *n.* frivolezza, *f.* frivolous,
a. frivolo.
friz[z], frizzle, *v.t.* arricciare.
frizzle (*bacon, &c.*), *v.t.* friggere,
grillare.
frock, *n.* veste, vestina, *f.*, costume, *m.*;
(*smock*) camiciotto, *m.*, blusa, *f.*;
(*monk's*) tonaca, *f.* ~ *coat*, finan-
ziera, *f.*, doppio petto, *m.*
frog, *n.* rana, *f.*, ranocchio, *m.*; (*coat*)
alamaro, passamano, *m.*; (*horse*)
fettone, *m.*; (*Rly.*) incrocia, *m.*;
(*sword*) dragona, *f.* froggery, *n.*
ranocchiaia, *f.*
frolic, *v.i.* scherzare, folleggiare,
sgambettare, saltellare. ¶ *n.*
trastullo, scherzo, *m.*, scappata,
biricchinata, *f.* ~some, *a.* scherzevole, scherzoso, pazzerello, giocoso.
from, *pr.* da, dopo, di, a, per; fino da,
sino da; a causa di; a contare da,
a cominciare da, a decorrere da,
a partire da; da parte di, a nome di.
where are you from? di dove
siete?
frond, *n.* fronda, *f.*
front, *a.* anteriore, dal davanti, sul
davanti; di faccia; primo; frontale.
¶ *n.* fronte, facciata, *f.*, davanti, *m.*,
parte anteriore, *f.*; (*shirt*) davanti,
petto, pettino; (*lady's hat*) tesa, ala
anteriore, *f.*; (*hair*) ciuffo, *m.*
~ [*line*] (*Mil.*), fronte, *m.*, prima
linea, *f.* ~ *margin* (book page),
margine di taglio, *m.* ~ *room*,
stanza sul davanti, di facciata,
stanza che dà sulla strada, *f.*
(*shirt*) petto (della camicia). *in* ~
& in ~ *of.* davanti, in faccia, in
faccia a, dirimpetto a, dirimpetto,
di fronte a. *on the* [*sea*] ~, sul mare.
(*hotel*). ¶ *v.t.* affrontare, fronteggiare,
fare faccia a, essere di fronte a, dare
su. ~age, *n.* facciata, *f.*, davanti,
m.; (*extent*) lunghezza della facciata. ~al, *a.* frontale, di fronte
(*Anat.*).
frontier, *n.* frontiera, *f.*, confine, *m.*;
(*att.*) di frontiera, limitrofo,
confinante.
frontispiece, *n.* (*book*) frontespizio
m.; illustrazione in capo ad un libro,
f.; (*Arch.*) frontespizio, *m.*
frontsman, *n.* chi fa (prepara) la
vetrina.
frost, *n.* gelo, *m.*, gelata, *f.*; (*degrees of*)
freddo, *m.*; (*fig.*) ghiaccio, *m.*
~bite, congelamento, *m.* ~bitten,
congelato. ~ed glass, vetro appannato, vetro smerigliato; ~y, *a.* di
gelo, ghiacciato, glaciale.

froth, *n.* schiuma, spuma, *f.* ¶ *v.i.* spumeggiare, far spumare. ~y, *a.* spumoso; (*fig.*) frivolo, leggero, vuoto.

frown, *n.* aggrottamento delle ciglia, cipiglio, viso arcigno, *m.* ¶ *v.i.* accigliarsi, increspare le ciglia. ~ [up]on, guardare corrucciata-mente, con viso arcigno; (*fig.*) essere contrario a.

frowzy, *a.* ammuffito, sporco, sciatto

frozen, *p.a.* agghiacciato, gelato; (*meat*, &c.) (carne) congelata; (*credits*) crediti congelati, *m.pl.* [*as if*] ~ *stiff*, agghiacciato (d'orrore, &c.).

fructify, *v.i.* fruttificare; (*v.t.*) fecondare, fertilizzare.

frugal, *a.* frugale. ~ity, *n.* frugalità, *f.*

fruit, *n.* frutto, *m.*, (*table*) frutta, *f.* ~ *bowl*, fruttiera, *f.* ~ *press*, strettoio, *m.* ~ *salad*, insalata di frutta, *f.* ~ *shop & trade*, bottega di frutta, *f.*; commercio delle frutta, *m.* ~ *tree*, albero fruttifero, *m.* **fruiterer**, *n.* fruttaiuolo, frutti-vendolo, *m.* **fruitful**, *a.* fruttifero; (*fig. & poet.*) fecondo, fertile. ~ness, *n.* fertilità, fecondità, *f.* **fruition**, *n.* fruizione, *f.*; (*fig.*) godimento, uso, *m.* **fruitless**, *a.* senza frutto; (*fig.*) infruttuoso, vano. ~ly, *ad.* infruttuosamente, inutil-mente, vanamente.

frump, *n.* vecchia sciattona, *f.*

frustrate, *v.t.* frustrare. **frustration**, *n.* (il) frustrare, scacco, insuccesso, *m.*

frustum, *n.* tronco, *m*

fry, *n.* (*fish*) (*small*) pesciolini, *m.pl.* (*fig.*) oggetti di poco conto; (*Cook.*) frittura, *f.* ¶ *v.t.* friggere, far friggere; (*v.i.*) friggere. ~ing, *n.* & ~ *oil* or *fat*) frittura, *f.* ~ *pan*, *n.* padella, *f.* *to fall out of the* ~ *into the fire*, cadere dalla padella nella brace.

fuchsia, *n.* fucsia, *f.*

fuddle, *v.t.* far ubbriacare, istupidire (coll'alcool). ~d, *p.a.* ubbriaco, brillo.

fudge, *i.* frottole, sciocchezze, *f.pl.* ¶ *v.t.* falsificare.

fuel, *n.* combustibile, *m.*; (*Aviat.*) carburante, *m.*; (*fig.*) alimento, *m.*, esca, *f.* ~ *oil*, petrolio da ardere, *m.* ¶ *v.t.* riscaldare.

fugitive, *a.* fuggitivo, fuggiasco, passeggero, errante. ¶ *n.* fuggitivo, fuggiasco.

fugleman, *n.* capofila, *m.*

fugue, *n.* fuga, *f.*

fulcrum, *n.* fulcro, *m.*; (*fig.*) punto d'appoggio, *m.*

fulfil, *v.t.* compiere, adempiere, appagare, realizzare, colmare; (*expectations*) corrispondere a, disimpegnare. ~ment, *n.* adempi-mento, compimento, soddisfaci-mento, *m.*, realizzazione, *f.*

full, *a.* pieno, ripieno, completo; colmo, sazio; intero, ampio, abbondante, grande; maturo; grosso; integrale; carico, sovraccarico. ~ *back* (*Foot.*) terzino, *m.* ~ *binding*, legatura intera, *f.*, rilegatura. ~ *blooded*, sanguigno. ~ *bodied* (*wine*), generoso. *in* ~ *discharge*, a saldo. ~ *dress*, tenuta da sera, abito da cerimonia, *f.* ~ *face* (*type*), caratteri grassi, *m.pl.*, (*ladies*) abito da sera, *m.*, gran toletta. ~grown, fatto, grande, pienamente cresciuto. ~*-length mirror*, psiche, *f.* ~*length portrait*, ritratto in piedi, r. di grandezza naturale. ~ *moon*, plenilunio, *m.* ~ *name* (*pers.*), nome (di battesimo) e cognome, *m.* ~ *of fish* (*river*, *lake*), pescoso. ~ *orchestra*, grande orchestra. ~point, ~stop, punto fermo, *m.* ~ *price*, prezzo forte, *m.* ~size, grandezza naturale, *f.* *in* ~, in pieno, pienamente, integralmente; (*words*) in tutte lettere, per disteso; *Also* = *fully*. ¶ *n.* pieno, colmo, *m.*, misura completa, *f.* *to the* ~, del tutto, interamente.

full, *v.t.* gualcare, follare. ~er, *n.* gualchieraio, follatore, *m.* ~'s *earth*, terra da purgo, *f.* *fulling mill*, gualchiera, *f.*

fully, *ad.* pienamente, interamente; tutto, bene, completamente. ~paid *share*, azione versata per intero, interamente versata, azione liberata, *f.*

fulminate, *v.i. & t.* fulminare.

ful[l]ness, *n.* abbondanza, copia, sazietà, ampiezza, *f.*, volume, *m.*

fulsome, *a.* stomachevole, ser-vile.

fumble, *v.i.* tastare maldestramente; brancolare, andare a tastoni.

fume, *n.* fumo, vapore, *m.*, esalazione, stizza, collera, *f.* ¶ *v.i. & t.* emettere esalazioni, vapori, &c., fumicare; irritarsi, andare in collera. ~d (*oak*), *a.* patinato, tinto.

fumigate, *v.t.* affumicare, suffumi-care.

fun, *n.* divertimento, *m.*, gaiezza, *f.*, giuochi, *m.pl.*, bel tempo, *m.*, baia, burla, celia, giocosità, *f.*, scherzo, *m.* to make ~ *of*, beffarsi di, volgere in ridicolo, dare la baia a.

function, *n.* funzione, cerimonia, mansione, *f.*, ufficio, *m.*; pranzo, ricevimento ufficiale. ~al, *a.* funzionale. ~ary, *n.* funzionario, *m.*

fund, *n.* fondo, capitale, *m.*, cassa, *f.*; (*pl.*) titoli, *m.pl.*, rendita, *f.*, denaro, *m.* ~ *holder*, portatore di titoli (del debito consolidato). ~ed debt, debito consolidato, *m.* ¶ *v.t.* investire in fondi pubblici, consolidare.

fundament, *n.* sedere, deretano, *m.* ~al, *a.* fondamentale.

funeral, *n.* funerale, sotterramento; convoglio funebre, corteo funebre, *m.*, (*elaborate*) funerali, *m.pl.*, esequie, *f.pl.* ¶ *a.* funebre, mortorio. ~ *oration*, orazione funebre, elogio funebre. ~ *service*, ufficio dei morti, *m.* **funereal,** *a.* funereo, lugubre.

fungous, *a.* fungoso. **fungus,** *n.* fungo, *m.*

funicular, *a. & n.* funicolare, *a. & f.*

funnel, *n.* fumaiolo; imbuto, *m.*; (*wooden*) pevera, *f.*

funny, *a.* divertente, comico, buffonesco. ~ *bone*, nervo cubitale, *m.* ~ *little* (*pers.*), ometto bizzarro, buffoncello, *m.* ~ *man*, comico (della compagnia d'attori). *a* ~ (*queer*) *man*, tipo bizzarro, bell'originale, *m.* the ~ *part*, il comico, *m.*

fur, *n.* pelliccia, *f.*; deposito, *m.*, incrostazione, patina, *f.* ~ *coat*, ~ *lined*, foderato di (con) pelliccia. ~ *lining*, fodera di pelliccia. ~-*trade*, commercio delle pellicce, *m.*

furbelows, *n.pl.* falpalà, *m.*, balzane, *f.pl.*

furbish, *v.t.* forbire.

furious, *a.* furioso, infuriato, accanito.

furl, *v.t.* ammainare, serrare, piegare.

furlong, *n.* misura di lunghezza, stadio, *m.* = ⅛ *mile or* 201.168 *metres.*

furlough, *n.* congedo, *m.*, licenza, *f.* on ~, in congedo.

furnace, *n.* fornace, *f.*, forno, focolare, *m.*

furnish, *v.t.* fornire, provvedere; ammobiliare, mobiliare; guarnire; offrire. ~ed *apartments or rooms*, stanze ammobiliate, *f.pl.* ~ing

fabrics, tessuti d'ammobiliamento.

furniture, *n.* mobili, *m.pl.*, mobilia, *f.*; (*piece*) mobile, *m.*, guarnitura, *f.*; (*church*) arredo, *m.* ~ *polish*, ~ *dealer*, negoziante di mobili. ~ *remover*, agenzia di trasporti. ~ *van*, furgone (pel trasporto dei mobili), *m.* ~ *warehouse*, deposito per mobili, magazzino, &c., *m.*

furore, *n.* furore, *m.*

furred (*tongue*), *p.a.* carica.

furrier, *n.* pellicciaio, *m.* ~y, *n.* pelliccería, *f.*

furrow, *n.* solco, *m.* ¶ *v.t.* solcare.

furry, *a.* di pelliccia, coperto di pelliccia; (*tongue*) carica, patinosa.

further, *a.* ulteriore, più lontano, altro, nuovo. ¶ *ad.* più lontano, al di là; inoltre, ancora, di più, più in là. ¶ *v.t.* promuovere, avanzare, appoggiare, favorire, facilitare. ~ance, *n.* promozione, *f.*, appoggio, avanzamento, *m.* ~more, *ad.* di più, inoltre, oltre a ciò. **furthest,** *a.* (il) più lontano, ultimo, estremo. ¶ *ad.* più lontano.

furtive, *a.* furtivo.

fury, *n.* furia, *f.*, furore, accanimento, *m.*, (*pers.*) furiosa, furia, *f.*, matta, virago, *f.* F~ (*Myth.*), Furia, *f.*

furze, *n.* ginestra spinosa, *f.*

fuse, *n.* spoletta, miccia, *f.* (*powder*); (*Elec.*) piombo fusibile, *m.* ¶ *v.t. & i.* fondere, fondersi.

fusee (*Horol.*), *n.* piramide, *f.*

fuselage, *n.* fusoliera, *f.*

fusible, *a.* fusibile.

fusillade, *n.* fucilata, *f.*

fusion, *n.* fusione, *f.*

fuss, *n.* chiasso, rumore; affaccendamento, *m.*, cerimonie, *f.pl.* ¶ *v.i.* fare del chiasso, menar scalpore; inquietarsi, affaccendarsi. ~y, *a.* chiassoso, affaccendato, agitato; cerimonioso.

fustian, *n.* fustagno, *m.*; (*fig.*) stile ampolloso, *m.*

fusty, *a.* che puzza di rinchiuso, ammuffito. ~ *smell*, odore di rinchiuso, *m.*

futile, *a.* futile. **futility,** *n.* futilità, *f.*

future, *a.* futuro, venturo, da venire; (*Com.*) a termine. ¶ *n.* futuro, avvenire, *m.*; (*pl.*, *Com.*) operazioni a termine. ~ (*tense*), futuro [semplice], *m.* ~ *perfect*, futuro anteriore. **futurity,** *n.* l'avvenire, *m.*

fuzzy, *a.* (*hair*) arricciato, increspato; (*image*) impalpabile, indistinto.

G

G (*Mus.*) *letter*, sol *m*. ~ *clef*, chiave
di sol, *f*.
gabble, *v.t.* pronunziare rapidamente
ed incoerentemente; (*v.i.*) cicalare,
chiacchierare.
gable, *n.* frontone, *m*.; parte triangolare d'una muraglia all'estremità.
~*roof*, tetto a due pioventi, a due
falde.
gad about, *v.i.* vagare, vagabondare,
gironzare, correre qua e là. **gad-
about**, *n.* giramondo, vagabondo, *m*.
gad-fly, *n.* tafano, *m*.
gadget, *n.* (piccolo) congegno,
artifizio, ordigno, *m*.; macchina, *f*.
gaff, *n.* (*spear*) uncino, *m*.; fiocina, *f*.;
(*spar*) picco (di randa), *m*.
gaffer, *n.* compare, *m*.; capo lavorante,
m.
gag, *n.* bavaglio, *r*.; apribocca, *m.inv.*;
(*actor's*) frizzo improvvisato, *m*.;
trovata, *f*.; interpolazione, *f*. ¶ *v.t.*
mettere il bavaglio; (*v.i.*) fare inter-
polazioni o aggiunte.
gage, *n.* pegno, *m*. See also ga[u]ge.
gaiety, *n.* gaiezza, giocondità, *f*.
gaily, *ad.* gaiamente, allegramente.
gain, *n.* guadagno, profitto, vantaggio;
lucro, *m*. ¶ *v.t.* guadagnare;
(*victory*) riportare; (*one's end*) raggiungere, ottenere; (*v.i.*) progredire,
profittare, fare progressi; (*Clock*)
andare avanti. ~ *admittance*,
ottenere l'accesso, introdursi. *to be
the gainer* (*by*), guadagnare a, (con).
gainsay, *v.t.* contraddire, negare.
gait, *n.* andatura, *f*.; portamento, *m*.
gaiter, *n.* ghetta, uosa, *f*.
gala, *n.* gala, *f*.; (*att.*, *day*, *night*,
dress, *performance*) di gala. ~ *night*
(*at dance hall*), serata di gala, *f*.
galanty show, ombre cinesi, *f.pl.*
galaxy, *n.* (*Astr.*) galassia, Via
Lattea; (*fig.*) costellazione, *f*.
gale, *n.* vento da burrasca, *m*.; procella,
f.; bufera, *f*.; uragano, *m*.; tempesta,
f.
galena, *n.* galena, *f*.; solfuro di
piombo, *m*.
gall, *n.* bile, *f*.; fiele, *m*. ~ (*nut*),
galla, noce di galla. ~*fly*, mosca
galla, *f*. ~ *bladder*, vescicola del
fiele, della bile, *f*. ~*stone*, calcolo
biliare, *m*. ¶ *v.t.* fregare, scorticare,
infastidire, irritare.
gallant, *a.* coraggioso, valoroso;
galante, bravo; vistoso; (*to women*)
galante, cavalleresco, cortese. ¶ *n.*

galante, cicisbeo, cavaliere, *m*.
~**ly**, *ad.* coraggiosamente, valorosa-
mente, con galanteria, cavalleresca-
mente; vistosamente. ~**ry**, *n.* prodezza, *f*.; coraggio, *m*.; galanteria, *f*.
galleon (*Hist.*), *n.* galeone, *m*.
gallery, *n.* galleria, loggia, tribuna, *f*.;
anfiteatro, *m*.; (*Theat.*) loggione, *m*.
galley, *n.* (*boat*) galea, galera, *f*.;
imbarcazione a remi, *f*.; (*Cook's*)
cucina, *f*.; (*Typ.*) vantaggio, *m*.
~ (*proof*), bozza (di composizione)
non ancora impaginata, *f*. ~ *slave*,
galeotto, *m*.
Gallic, *a.* gallico, francese. **Gallican**,
a. & n., gallicano, *a. & m.* **gallicism**, *n.* gallicismo, *m*.; francesismo.
gallicize, *v.t.* gallicizzare, francesiz-
zare.
gallinaceae, *n.pl.* gallinacei, *m.pl.*
galling, *a.* irritante.
gallipot, *n.* barattolo, vaso di terra
verniciato (per medicinali), *m*.
gallon (*imperial*), *n.* gallone, *m*.;
== 4 quarts or 4.5459631 litres; 3.78
litres in U.S.A.
galloon, *n.* gallone, *m*. (distintivo
degli ufficiali).
gallop, *n.* galoppo, *m*. ¶ *v.i.* galoppare.
~*ing consumption*, tisi galoppante, *f*.
Gallophil(e), *a. & n.* gallofilo,
francofilo, *a. & m.* **Gallophobe**,
a. & n. gallofobo, francofobo, *a. & m.*
gallows, *n.pl. & s.* forca, *f*.; patibolo,
m. ~ *bird*, avanzo di forca, uomo da
forca, *m*.; persona da capestro, *f*.;
arnese da galera, *m*.
galop (*dance*), *n.* galoppo, *m*.
galore, *ad.* in abbondanza, a bizzeffe,
a iosa, a profusione.
galosh, *n.* galoscia, soprascarpa di
gomma, *f*.
galvanic, *a.* galvanico. **galvanism**,
n. galvanismo, *m*. **galvanize**, *v.t.*
galvanizzare. **galvanoplasty**, *n.*
galvanoplastica, *f*.
Gambia, *n.* la Gambia, *f*.
gambit, *n.* gambitto, *m*.
gamble, *n.* giuoco d'azzardo, *m*.;
speculazione; scommessa; impresa
arrischiata, *f*. *to be on the* ~,
giuocare, darsi al giuoco. *to have
a* ~, abbandonarsi alla speculazione.
¶ *v.i.* giuocare; (*wager*) scommettere; speculare. ~ *away*,
dissipare, perdere al giuoco.
gambler, *n.* giuocatore, bisciaiuolo;
speculatore, *m*. **gambling**, *n.*
giuoco (d'azzardo), *m*.; speculazione,
f. ~ *den*, casa da giuoco, bisca,
biscazza, *f*.

gamboge, *n.* gomma gutta, *f.*

gambol, *n.* capriola, *f.*; salto, sgambetto; trastullo, *m.*; scappata, *f.* ¶ *v.i.* saltellare, sgambettare, fare le capriole.

game, *n.* giuoco, *m.*; partita, *f.*; (*dodge*) sotterfugio, trucco, *m.*; astuzia, *f.*; (*Hunt.*) selvaggina, *f.* ~*s all* (*Ten.*), pari a cinque. ~ *bag,* carniere, *m.* ~*cock,* gallo da combattimento, *m.* ~*keeper,* guardacaccia, *m.* ~ *licence* (*to kill*), licenza di caccia, *f.* ~ *of skill,* giuoco di bravura, giuoco di destrezza, *m. big* ~ *shooting,* caccia grossa, *f.* ¶ *a.* coraggioso; volonteroso; pronto, sportivo. *to have a* ~ *leg,* avere una gamba zoppa, andare a gamba zoppa. ¶ *v.i.* giuocare (d'azzardo). ~**ster,** *n.* giocatore, *m.* **gaming,** *n.* giuoco, *m.*; giocare, *m.* ~ *house,* casa da giuoco, *f.* ~ *table,* tavola da giuoco, *f.*

gammon, *n.* (*bacon*) quartiere salato (del porco), prosciutto salato, *m.*; (*fig.*) vanteria, mistificazione, *f.*; frottole, *f.pl.*

gamp, *n.* ombrellaccio, *m.*

gamut, *n.* (*colour & Music*) gamma, *f.*; (*fig.*) scala, serie, *f.*

gamy, *a.* che abbonda di selvaggina; (*Cook.*) avente il gusto o l'odore della selvaggina. ~ *flavour,* sapore di fagiano, *m.*

gander, *n.* papero, maschio dell'oca, *m.*

gang, *n.* gruppo, *m.*; banda, brigata, squadra, *f.* ~ *plough,* aratrice, *f.* ~**er,** *n.* caposquadra, *m.*

Ganges (the), il Gange, *m.*

ganglion, *n.* ganglio, *m.*

gangrene, *n.* cancrena, *f.* ¶ *v.t.* fare incancrenire.

gangue, *n.* ganga, *f.*

gangway, *n.* andito, corridoio, *m.*; (*on ship*) barcarizzo, passavanti, *m.*; (*to shore*) passerella, *f.*; plancia da sbarco, *f.*

gannet, *n.* corvo di mare bianco, *m.*, sula, *f.*

gantry, *n.* (*gantry-crane*) gru a cavalletto, *f.*; (*for cask*) cavalletto, *m.*

gaol, *n.* carcere, *m.*; prigione, *f.* ~*bird,* galeotto, *m.* **gaoler, gaoleress,** carceriere, *m.*, carceriera, *f.*

gap, *n.* apertura, breccia, lacuna, *f.*; vuoto, buco, passaggio, intervallo, interstizio, varco, *m.*

gape, *v.i.* sbadigliare; spalancarsi;

rimanere a bocca aperta (per meraviglia, &c.). ~ (*at the moon*), baloccarsi. **gaper,** *n.* chi sbadiglia.

garage, *n.* autorimessa, *f.* ¶ *v.t.* mettere in rimessa.

garb, *n.* vestito, costume, abbigliamento, *m.*

garbage, *n.* rifiuti, *m.pl.*; immondizie, *f.pl.*; spazzatura, *f.* ~ *heap,* mondezzaio, *m.*

garble, *v.t.* alterare, falsificare.

garden, *n.* (*flowers*) giardino, *m.*; (*vegetables*) orto, *m.*; (*small*) giardinetto, *m.* ~ *city,* città giardino, *f.* ~ *cress,* crescione, *m.* ~ *engine,* irrigatore, *m.* ~ *flower,* fiore di giardino, *m.* ~ *hose,* tubo dell'acqua (per innaffiamento), *m.* ~ *mint,* menta verde, *f. the G* ~ *of Eden,* Eden, paradiso terrestre, *m.* ~ *party,* merenda in giardino, festa campestre, *f.* ~ *plant,* pianta del giardino, dell'orto, pianta coltivata, *f.* ~ *plots,* aiuole, *f.pl.* ~ *roller,* rulla da giardino, *m.* ~ *stuff,* legumi, *m.pl.*; erbe, *f.pl.*; ortaggi, *m.pl.* ~ *tools,* utensili per giardinieri, *m.pl.* ¶ *v.i.* coltivare (lavorare) un giardino, lavorare nel giardino, fare il giardiniere. ~**er,** *n.* giardiniere, *m.*, -a, *f.*; ortolano, *m.*, -a, *f.*

gardenia, *n.* gardenia, *f.*

gardening, *n.* giardinaggio, *m.*; orticultura, *f.*

garfish, *n.* aguglia, *f.*; luccio, *m.*

gargle, *n.* gargarismo, *m.* ¶ *v.i.* gargarizzare, fare i gargarismi.

gargoyle, *n.* gronda sporgente (foggiata come una testa umana o d'animale), *f.*

garish, *a.* sfarzoso, appariscente, vistoso.

garland, *n.* ghirlanda, *f.*; serto, *m.*

garlic, *n.* aglio, *m.*

garment, *n.* abito, vestito, oggetto di vestiario, *m.*

garner, *n.* granaio, *m.* ¶ *v.t.* mettere nel granaio; (*fig.*) ammassare, raccogliere.

garnet, *n.* granato, *m.*

garnish, *n.* ornamento, abbellimento, *m.*; (*Cook.*) contorno, *m.* ¶ *v.t.* adornare, guarnire, abbellire.

garret, *n.* soffitta, *f.*; solaio, soppalco, *m.*

garrison, *n.* guarnigione, *f.*; presidio, *m.* ~ *artillery,* artiglieria da piazza, *f.* ¶ *v.t.* presidiare, fornire di guarnigione.

garrulous, *a.* garrulo, loquace.

garter, *n.* giarrettiera, *f.*; legaccio, *m.*

Order of the G~, Ordine della Giarrettiera, *m.* ~s, elastici, *m.pl.*

gas, *n.* gas, *m.inv.* ~ *bracket,* braccio (della lampada) a gas, *m.* ~ *burner,* becco a gas, *m.* ~ *cooker,* ~ *oven,* cucina, stufa, fornello a gas. ~ *engine,* ~ *motor,* motore a gas, *m.* ~ *fire,* radiatore a gas, *m.* ~ *fitter,* gasista, *m.* ~ *fittings,* impianto del gas, apparecchio del gas, *m.* ~ *light,* illuminazione a gas, *f.*; lume a gas, *m.* ~*light paper* (*Phot.*), carta lenta ad impressionarsi con luce artificiale, *f.* ~ *lighting,* illuminazione a gas, *f.* ~ *man,* gasista, *m.* ~ *mask,* (*war*) maschera antigas, *f.*; (*fire*) casco respiratore, *m.* ~ *meter,* contatore del gas, *m.* ~ *pipe,* tubo del gas, *m.* ~ *producer,* gasogeno, *m.* ~ *ring,* fornello, *m.* ~ *shell,* granata chimica, bomba di gas tossici, *f.* ~ *worker,* gassaiuolo, *m.* ~*works,* officina del gas, *f.* ¶ *v.t.* sottoporre all'azione del gas; (*War*) attaccare con gas. ~**eous,** *a.* gassoso.

gash, *n.* incisione, *f.*; taglio, sfregio, *m.*; squarcio, *m.*; ferita, *f.* ¶ *v.t.* incidere, tagliare, sfregiare.

gasify, *v.t.* convertire in gas.

gasket, *n.* guernizione, *f.*; (*Naut.*) gerlo, *m.*

gasogene, *n.* gasogeno, *m.* **gasometer,** *n.* gasometro, *m.*

gasp, *n.* sforzo per respirare, anelito, respiro affannoso o difficile, *m.* *to* ~ *for breath,* ansare, fare degli sforzi per respirare. **gasping,** *a.* ansimante, trafelato.

gassy, *a.* gassoso; verboso.

gast[e]ropod, *n.* gasteropodo, *m.* **gastric,** *a.* gastrico. **gastritis,** *n.* gastrite, *f.* **gastronome[r],** *n.* gastronomo, *m.* **gastronomic[al],** *a.* gastronomico. **gastronomy,** *n.* gastronomia, *f.*

gate, *n.* porta, *f.*; portone, *m.*; (*dock*) chiusa, *f.*; (*park*) cancello, *m.*; barriera, *f.*; (*sluice*) cateratta, *f.* ~ *crasher,* *n.* intruso, ospite non invitato, *m.* ~ *keeper,* *n.* portinaio, guardaportone, *m.*; (*level crossing*) guardabarriere, *m.f.* ~ *money,* incasso, *m.*; ricetta, *f.*; entrata, *f.*; prezzo d'ingresso, *m.* ~*way,* portone, passaggio, ingresso, *m.*

gather, *n.* crespa, piega, *f.* ¶ *v.t.* raccogliere, cogliere; acquistare, ricavare; radunare, riunire; accumulare, ammassare; (*breath,* &*c.*) riprendere; (*grapes*) vendemmiare; (*infer*) desumere, dedurre, giudicare,

capire, comprendere, rilevare (*Need.*) pieghettare; (*v.i.*) raccogliersi, riunirsi, adunarsi, formarsi, prepararsi, aumentare; (*Med.*) fare postema, andare in suppurazione. ~**er,** *n.* raccoglitore, *m.*, -trice, *f.* ~**ing,** *n.* raccolta, collezione, riunione, adunata, adunanza, assemblea, *f.*; (*Med.*) ascesso, postema, *m.*; suppurazione, *f.*

gating (*Hyd.*), *n.* vagliatura, *f.*

gaudy, *a.* sfarzoso, fastoso, vistoso.

ga[u]ge, *n.* misura, stazza, norma, *f.*; calibro, indicatore, manometro, livello, *m.*; (*Rly. track*) larghezza, *f.*; scartamento, *m.* ¶ *v.t.* misurare, stazzare, stimare, assaggiare. *gauging rod,* asta di sonda, *f.*

gaunt, *a.* scarno, magro, attenuato, macilento.

gauntlet, *n.* guanto lungo, *m.*; (*fig.*) guanto di sfida, *m.*; sfida, *f.* *to take up the* ~, accettare la sfida. *to run the* ~, passare sotto il fuoco, passare per le picche.

gauze, *n.* garza, *f.*; velo, *m.* **gauzy,** *a.* simile a garza, leggero o trasparente come un velo.

gavotte, *n.* gavotta, *f.*

gawky, *a.* goffo, balordo, sguaiato.

gay, *a.* gaio, allegro, vivace. ~ *man,* gaudente, *m.*

gaze, *n.* sguardo, sguardo fisso, *m.*; contemplazione, *f.* *to* ~ *at,* fissare, contemplare, guardare fissamente, mirare.

gazelle, *n.* gazzella, *f.*

gazette, *n.* gazzetta, *f.*; giornale ufficiale, *m.*

gazetteer, *n.* dizionario geografico, *m.*

gear, *n.* arredo, *m.*; arnesi, *m.pl.*; bardatura, *f.*; corredo, *m.*; dispositivo, meccanismo; ingranaggio, *m.*; masserizie, *m.pl.*; roba, *f.*; (*toothed rack and pinion*) ingranaggio ad asta dentata, *m.*; (*ratio*) moltiplica, *f.*; (*bicycle*) sviluppo di velocità, *m.* ~*box,* scatola del cambio di velocità, *f.* ~*case,* carter, *m.* ~ *ratio,* rapporto di trasmissione, *m.* ~*wheel,* ruota d' ingranaggio, *f.* ¶ *v.t.* ~ [*up*], *put in* ~, ingranare; congegnare; avviare, mettere in moto.

gee-gee, *n.* (*child's speech*) cavallo, *m.* **gee up,** *i.* ih!

gehenna, *n.* inferno, *m.*

gelatin[e], *n.* gelatina, *f.* **gelatinous,** *a.* gelatinoso.

geld, *v.t.* castrare. ~**ing,** *n.* castrone, *m.*; castrazione, *f.*

gem, *n.* gemma, *f.*; (*pl.*) pietre preziose, *f.pl.*

gender, *n.* genere, *m.*

genealogical, *a.* genealogico. **genealogy,** *n.* genealogia, *f.*

general, *a.* generale, l'insieme di, comune, collettivo. ~ *cargo,* carico a colletta, *m.* ~ *effect,* insieme, *m.* ~ *expenses,* spese generali, *f.pl.* ~ *post office,* ufficio postale centrale, *m.*; posta centrale, *f.*, direzione generale delle Poste, *f.* the ~ *public,* il pubblico in generale, la generalità del pubblico, la gran massa del pubblico. ~ *servant,* donna a tutto servizio, *f.* to become ~, generalizzarsi, farsi (diventare) generale, comune. ¶ *n.* generale, *m.*; (*roll of the drum*) generale, *f.* the ~ (*fig.*), il generale, *m.* ~**issimo,** *n.* generalissimo, *m.* ~**ity,** *n.* generalità, *f.* ~**ize,** *v.t. & i.* generalizzare. ~**ly,** *ad.* generalmente, in genere, in linea generale. ~**ship,** *n.* generalato, *m.*, grado di generale, *m.*; strategia, abilità militare, *f.*

generate, *v.t.* generare, causare, produrre. **generating,** *p.a.* generatore, generativo. ~ *station* (*Elec.*), centrale elettrica, *f.* **generation,** *n.* generazione, *f.*; **generator,** *n.* generatore, *m.*

generic, *a.* generico.

generosity, *n.* generosità, *f.* **generous,** *a.* generoso, liberale, munifico.

genesis, *n.* genesi, *f.*; (*fig.*) origine, *f.* G~ (*Bible*), la Genesi, *f.*

genet, *n.* (*civet*) genetta, *f.*

geneva (*gin*), *n.* ginepro, spirito di ginepro, *m.* G~ (*Geog.*), Ginevra, *f.* Lake of G~, Lago di Ginevra, Lago Lemano, *m.* **Genevan,** *a.* di Ginevra, ginevrino.

genial, *a.* mite, dolce, caldo; di buon umore, cordiale, socievole. ~**ity,** *n.* genialità, cordialità, *f.*

genital, *a.* genitale.

genius, *n.* genio, *m.*; demone, *m.*

Genoa, *n.* Genova, *f.* **Genoese,** *a.* genovese. ¶ *n.* genovese, *m.f.*

genteel, *a.* (*iron*) snob, pretendente a modi raffinati.

gentian, *n.* genziana, *f.*

gentile, *n.* chi non appartiene alla religione ebraica.

gentility, *n.* distinzione, raffinatezza; nascita elevata; gentilezza, *f.*

gentle, *a.* dolce, mansueto, soffice, tenero. of ~ *birth,* di qualità, ~*folk*(s), gente di qualità, *f.* ~*man,*

gentiluomo, galantuomo, signore, *m.* ~*man farmer,* gentiluomo di campagna, *m.* ~*manliness,* *n.* signorilità, *f.*, maniere gentili, *f.pl.*; modi gentili, *m.pl.* ~*manly,* da gentiluomo; signorile. ~*men of the robe* (*lawyers*), gente della toga, *f.* ~*woman,* gentildonna, dama, signora, *f.* ¶ *n.* verme della carne, bruco, *m.* ~**ness,** *n.* dolcezza, soavità, tenerezza, *f.* **gently,** *ad.* dolcemente, soavemente. **gentry,** *n.* piccola nobiltà, *f.*; gente, *f.*

genuflexion, *n.* genuflessione, *f.*

genuine, *a.* genuino, autentico. ~**ness,** *n.* autenticità, *f.*

genus, *n.* genere, *m.*

geodesy, *n.* geodesia, *f.* **geognosy,** *n.* geognosia, *f.* **geographer,** *n.* geografo, *m.* **geographic(al),** *a.* geografico. **geography,** *n.* geografia, *f.* **geologic(al),** *a.* geologico. **geologist,** *n.* geologo. **geology,** *n.* geologia, *f.* **geometer** & **geometrician,** *n.* geometra, *m.* **geometric(al),** *a.* geometrico. **geometry,** *n.* geometria, *f.*

Georgia, *n.* (*U.S.A.*) la Georgia, *f.* (*Asia*) la Georgia, *f.*

geranium, *n.* geranio, *m.*

germ, *n.* germe, *m.*; (*fig.*) germe, germoglio, embrione, *m.*

german, *a.* germano.

German, *a.* tedesco, germanico. ~ *measles,* rosolia, *f.* ~ *Ocean,* Mare del Nord, *m.* ~ *silver,* argentone, *m.* ¶ *n.* (*pers.*) tedesco, *m.*, -a, *f.*; (*language*) il tedesco, *m.*; la lingua tedesca, *f.*

germander, *n.* (*Bot.*) camedrio, *m.*

germane to, pertinente a, a proposito, appropriato a, che riguarda.

Germany, *n.* la Germania, *f.*

germinate, *v.i.* germinare. **germination,** *n.* germinazione, *f.*

gerund, *n.* gerundio, *m.*

gestation, *n.* gestazione, *f.*

gesticulate, *v.i.* gesticolare.

gesture, *n.* gesto, *m.*

get, *v.t. ir.* ottenere, acquistare, procurare, guadagnare; apprendere, cogliere, raccogliere; pigliare, beccarsi, buscarsi; ricevere, trovare, avere, andare a prendere; fare, farsi; persuadere; (*v.i. ir.*) andare, arrivare, pervenire; diventare, riuscire, farsi, cominciare a. Often rendered by si (the reflexive), e.g. ~ *away,* (*v.i.*) salvarsi, allontanarsi, scampare, fuggire; (*v.t.*) fare allontanare. ~ *back, v.t.* riavere;

(v.i.) rivenire, ritornare. ~ down, scendere. ~ hold of, afferrare, impadronirsi di. ~ in, entrare, introdursi; (corn) mettere (il grano) nel granaio. ~ married, sposarsi, prender moglie, prender marito. ~ on, andare avanti, far strada, riuscire. ~ out, sortire, scappare, evadere. ~ out of the way, uscire fuori di strada, trarsi da parte, tenersi alla larga. ~ over, sormontare, rimettersi da. ~ ready, preparare; prepararsi. ~ rid of, sbrigarsi di, levarsi d'attorno, disfarsi di, sbarazzarsi di. ~ round (someone), ingannare con le moine. ~ up, alzarsi. ~ up steam, riscaldare. **get-up,** n. abbigliamento, modo di vestirsi, m.

gewgaw, n. ninnolo, m., cianfrusaglia, f.

geyser, n. (spring) geyser, m., sorgente calda, f.; stufa da bagno, f.

ghastly, a. orribile, spaventevole, pallidissimo, pallido come la morte.

Ghent, n. Gand, f.

gherkin, n. cetriolino, m. pickled ~, cetriolino nell'aceto.

ghetto, n. ghetto, m.

ghost, n. spettro, spirito, fantasma, m.; anima, f. ~ story, racconto di spiriti, di fantasmi, di spettri, m. to give up the ~, rendere l'anima. the Holy G~, lo Spirito Santo. ~ly, a. spettrale.

ghoul, n. demonio che divora i cadaveri (secondo la fantasia orientale).

giant, a. gigantesco, da gigante. **giant, -ess,** n. gigante, m., gigantessa, f. giant['s] strides, passi da gigante, m.pl.

gibber, v.i. parlare rapidamente ed incoerentemente, borbottare. ~ish, n. parole intelligibili, f.pl.; gergo incomprensibile, m.; suono inarticolato, m.

gibbet, n. forca, f., patibolo, m. ¶ v.t. (fig.) mettere alla berlina.

gibe, n. beffa, f., scherno, m., burla mordace, f. ¶ v.t. ~, ~ at, beffare, beffarsi di.

giblets, n.pl. frattaglie, rigaglie, f.pl.

Gibraltar, n. Gibilterra, f.

giddiness, n. vertigine, f., capogiro, m., stordimento, m. **giddy,** a. (height) vertiginoso; (flighty) scervellato, spensierato; stordito. it makes me feel ~, mi fa girare la testa. ~ head, stordito, m., -a, f.; persona spensierata, f.

gift, n. dono, regalo, donativo, m.; donazione, f.; (Christmas or New Year) strenna, f.; (for coupons) premio, m.; (of an office) nominazione, f.; talento, m. the ~ of the gab, dono della favella, m. ~ed, a. dotato d'ingegno.

gig, n. baroccino, calessino, m.; (boat) iole, f.

gigantic, a. gigantesco.

giggle, v.i. ridere per niente, ridere stupidamente.

gild, n. See g[u]ild. ¶ v.t. ir. indorare. ~er, n. doratore, indoratore, m. ~ing, n. doratura, f.

gill, n. (fish) branchia, f.; (imperia measure) = ¼ pint or 0·142 litre.

gilt, n. doratura, indoratura, f. ¶ p.a. dorato, indorato. ~-edged, (book) a taglio dorato; (investment, security) (titoli) di primissimo ordine.

gimcrack, n. ninnolo, gingillo, m.; cianciafruscola, f. ¶ a. vistoso ma senza valore.

gimlet, n. succhiello, m.

gimp, n. filato di seta o di cotone intrecciato con filo metallico; cordoncino, m.; passamano, m. ~ nail, chiodetto, m.

gin, n. (snare) trappola, f.; (hoist) gru, f.; (cotton) macchina per sgranare il cotone, f.; (spirit) gin, liquore di ginepro, m. ~ shop, debito di liquori, m. ¶ v.t. mondare, sgranare (il cotone).

ginger, n. zenzero, m. ~ bread, panforte, panpepato, m. ~ hair, capelli rossicci, color rosso carota, rossaccio. ~ nut, dolce di panpepato, confortino, m. ~ly, ad. delicatamente, pian piano.

gingham, n. (fabric) tessuto di cotone tinto in filato; ombrellaccio, m.

gipsy, n. zingaro, m., -a, f.

giraffe, n. giraffa, f.

girandole, n. girandola, f.; doppiere, m.; candeliere a bracci, m.

girasol[e] (opal), n. girasole, m.

gird, v.t. ir. cingere. ~ at, schernire, beffarsi di. ~er, n. trave, f., traversa, f. ~le, n. cintura, f.; cinturino, m. ¶ v.t. circondare, cingere.

girl, n. ragazza, fanciulla, giovinetta, signorina, zitella, f. ~ guide, giovine esploratrice, f. ~hood, n. fanciullezza, giovinezza, adolescenza, f. ~ish, a. di ragazza, di fanciulla.

girth, n. cinghia; circonferenza, f.; giro, m.

gist, *n.* sostanza, *f.*; punto essenziale, *m.*; essenziale, *m.*

give, *v.t. ir.* dare; fare; fornire; apportare; produrre; rendere, offrire, presentare; arrecare, procurare; prestare, donare, proferire. ~ *& take,* reciproca concessione, *f.*; compromesso, *m.* ~ *back,* rendere, restituire. ~ *one's name,* dare il (proprio) nome, declinare il proprio nome. ~ *in,* rinunciare alla lotta, cedere. ~ *oneself away,* tradirsi, esporsi al ridicolo, ad essere scoperto. ~ *out,* distribuire; diffondere; rilasciare; esalare; annunziare, pubblicare, proclamare; far credere, dare ad intendere; (*lamp, &c.*) estinguersi, spegnersi, essere esaurito. ~ *someone a piece of one's mind,* lavare il capo a qualcuno, dire a qualcuno il fatto suo. ~ *up,* abbandonare, rinunciare a, cedere, desistere da; (*patient*) condannare. ~ *oneself up* (*to police*), costituirsi. ~ *way,* cedere, piegare. **given to,** dedito a, incline a. **giver,** *n.* datore, *m.*, -trice, *f.*; donatore, *m.*, -trice, *f.* law ~, legislatore, *m.*

gizzard, *n.* ventriglio, *m.*

glacé kid gloves, guanti glacés, *m.pl.*

glacial, *a.* glaciale; (*Geol.*) glaciale. **glacier,** *n.* ghiacciaio, *m.* ~ *snow,* nevato, *m.*

glad, *a.* lieto, contento, felice. **gladden,** *v.t.* rallegrare, accontentare, allietare, rendere felice.

glade, *n.* radura, *f.*

gladiator, *n.* gladiatore, *m.*

gladiolus, *n.* gladiolo, *m.*

gladly, *ad.* volentieri, con piacere, di buon grado. **gladness,** *n.* contentezza, gioia, *f.*

glamour, *n.* fascino, incanto, incantesimo, *m.*; malia, *f.*

glance, *n.* sguardo, colpo d'occhio, *m.*; occhiata, *f.*; occhiatina, *f.*; (*loving*) dolce sguardo, *m.*; occhiata civettuola. ¶ *v.i.* gettare (lanciare) uno sguardo, dare un'occhiata, balenare. ~ *at,* adocchiare, guardare; accennare brevemente a. ~ *off,* deviare, scivolare, andare a finire (in . . . a . . .).

gland, *n.* glandola, *f.*

glanders, *n.pl.* cimurro, *m.*

glare, *n.* bagliore, *m.*; luce abbagliante, *f.*; splendore, *m.*; sguardo feroce, sguardo penetrante, *m.* ¶ *v.i.* brillare di luce intensa. ~ *at* (*pers.*), guardare con occhio torvo, guardare di traverso, guardare fissamente.

glaring, *a.* abbagliante, accecante, manifesto, patente; (*eyes*) torvo, fiero, sporgente.

Glasgow, *n.* Glasgovia, *f.*

glass, *n.* vetro; cristallo; bicchiere; specchio; barometro; telescopio, *m.*; (*pl.*) occhiali, *m.pl.*; lenti, *f.pl.* ~ (*with care*), fragile, posa piano. ~ *beads,* perline, *f.pl.* (di vetro). ~ *bowl,* tazza di cristallo, coppa di cristallo, *f.* ~ *case,* vetrina, *f.* ~ *cloth,* tessuto di vetro, *m.*; (*duster*) canovaccio, strofinaccio, *m.* ~ *cutter,* tagliatore di cristalli, *m.*; diamante di vetraio, *m.* ~ *door,* porta a vetri, *f.*; porta a invetriate, *f.* ~*house,* serra, *f.* ~*maker,* vetraio, *m.* ~ *making, & ~works,* fabbricazione del vetro, vetreria, *f.* ~ *of beer,* bicchiere di birra, *m.* ~*paper,* carta vetrata, *f.* ~ *shade,* campana, *f.*, globo (di vetro), *m.* ~(*ware*), vetrame, *m.*; vetrerie, *f.pl.*) articoli di vetro, *m.pl.* ~*y,* *a.* di vetro, vitreo; (*fig.*) (*eye*) vetrino.

glaucous, *a.* glauco.

glaze, *n.* smalto, *m.*; vernice, *f.* ¶ *v.t.* (*window*) fornire di vetri, di finestre, invetriare; smaltare, verniciare, inverniciare; polire, cilindrare; candire, crostare. ~ *frost,* nevischio, *m.* **glazier,** *n.* vetraio, *m.*

gleam, *n.* barlume, raggio, *m.*; lucentezza, *f.* ¶ *v.i.* brillare, rilucere, risplendere.

glean, *n.* spigolare, raccogliere; (*grapes*) racimolare, spicciolare. ~*er,* *n.* spigolatore, *m.*, -trice, *f.*; racimolatore, *m.* ~*ing,* *n.* spigolatura, *f.*, spigolamento, *m.*; racimolatura, *f.*; (*pl.*) spigolatura, *f.*

glebe, *n.* gleba, *f.*; podere annesso ad una canonica, *m.*

glee, *n.* allegria, gioia, gaiezza, *f.*; canzone a parecchie voci, composizione vocale d'insieme, *f.*

gleet, *n.* scolo dall'uretra, *m.*

glen, *n.* valletta, *f.*

glib, *a.* (*pers.*) volubile; (*tongue*) sciolto.

glide, *n.* scivolamento, *m.*; scivolata, *f.*; (*Danc.*) valzer strisciato, *m.* ¶ *v.i.* scivolare, sdrucciolare. **glider** (*Aero.*), *n.* aliante. **gliding** (*Aero.*), *n.* volo a vela, *m.*

glimmer, *n.* luce debole, luce fioca, *f.*; barlume, *m.* ¶ *v.i.* gettare (emettere) una luce fioca.

glimpse, *n.* sguardo passeggero, *m.*,

occhiata momentanea, *f.* *catch a* ~
of, intravvedere, vedere alla sfuggita.
glint, *n.* riflesso, *m.;* scintilla, *f.;*
barlume, *m.* ¶ *v.i.* scintillare,
brillare.
glister,   glitter, *v.i.* brillare,
risplendere. **glitter,** *n.* lustro, scintil-
lio, *m.*
gloaming, *n.* crepuscolo, *m.*
gloat over, divorare (covare) con gli
occhi, guardare con piacere crudele,
trionfare di.
globe, *n.* globo, *m.,* sfera, *f.;* (*fish
bowl*) vaschetta, *f.* **globular,** *a.*
globulare. **globule,** *n.* globulo, *m.,*
corpuscolo, *m.*
gloom, *v.t.* oscurare,   rattristare.
~(**iness**), *m.* oscurità, *f.,* tenebre,
f.pl.; buio, *m.;* tristezza, *f.;* malinconia, *f.* ~**y,** *a.* cupo, fosco, oscuro,
lugubre, malinconico, triste.
glorify, *v.t.* glorificare, esaltare,
celebrare. **glorious,** *a.* glorioso.
glory, *n.* gloria, fama, *f.* ~ *in,*
gloriarsi di, vantarsi di.
gloss, *n.* lustro, *m.;* vernice, *f.;*
(*comment*), chiosa, glossa, *f.* ¶ *v.t.*
lucidare, verniciare; (*text*) chiosare,
annotare. ~ (*over*) mascherare,
dissimulare. ~**ary,** *n.* glossario, *m.*
~**y,** *a.* lucido, lucente, liscio;
(*phot. paper*) brillante, lucido.
glottis, *n.* glottide, *f.*
glove, *n.* guanto, *m.* ~ *stretcher,*
allarga-guanti, *m.* ~ *trade,* commercio di guanti, del guantaio.
¶ *v.t.* inguantare. *to put on one's* ~*s,*
mettere i guanti. **glover,** *n.*
guantaio, *m.*
glow, *n.* incandescenza, *f.;* rossore,
calore, splendore, *m.;* ardore,
entusiasmo, *m.;* riflessi rossi, *m.pl*
(del cielo, &c.); (*pleasant in the body*)
sentire un calore per tutto il corpo.
~ *lamp,* lampada incandescente, *f.*
~*worm,* lucciola, *f.* ¶ *v.i.* rosseg-
giare, essere incandescente, ardere.
~*ing with health,* con una bella
carnagione.
glower at, guardare torvamente.
gloze over, mascherare, dissimulare.
glucose, *n.* glucosio, *m.*
glue, *n.* colla, *f.,* colla forte, *f.;*
(*Marine*) c. da marina. ~ *pot,* vaso
da colla, *m.* ¶ *v.t.* incollare. ~**y,** *a.*
colloso, viscoso, gelatinoso.
glum, *a.* arcigno, cupo, cagnesco,
ritroso.
glume, *n.* gluma, *f.*
glut, *n.* sovrabbondanza, sazietà, *f.;*

eccesso, ingombro, *m.* ¶ *v.t.*
saziare, ingombrare.
gluten, *n.* glutine, *m.* **glutinous,** *a.*
glutinoso.
glutton, *n.* ghiotto, ghiottone, goloso,
mangione, *m.* ~**ous,** *a.* ghiotto,
goloso. ~**y,** *n.* ghiottoneria,
golosità, *f.*
glycerin[e], *n.* glicerina, *f.*
gnarl, *n.* nodo, nocchio, *m.* ~**ed,** *a.*
nodoso, nocchieroso, nocchieruto.
gnash   one's   teeth,   digrignare
(battere) i denti.
gnat, *n.* culice, moscerino, *m.*
gnaw, *v.t. & i.* rodere, rosicchiare.
~**ing,** rodimento, rosicchio, *m.,*
rosicatura, *f.*
gneiss, *n.* gneiss, *m.*
gnome, *n.* gnomo, *m.*
gnostic, *a. & n.* gnostico, *a. & m.*
go, *n. pop.* moda, voga; forza, *f.;* brio,
vigore, *m.;* energia, *f.;* affare, *m.,*
disinvoltura, *f.;* moto, movimento,
m.; prova, *f.;* tentativo, *m.* (*with
neg.*) utilità, *f.;* valore, *m.* *it was
no* ~, non vi fu modo di riuscire.
it's no ~, non va, non può stare.
¶ *v.i. & t.ir.* andare; camminare;
recarsi, portarsi, rendersi; partire,
andarsene; fare, tornare; riuscire,
diventare. *are you ready? go!*
Siete pronti? *who goes there? go! va*
là? ~ *ahead,* andare innanzi,
proseguire, progredire, tirar via.
~*-ahead,* attivo, intraprendente. ~
astray, smarrirsi, deviare. ~ *away,*
andar via, allontanarsi, partire,
andarsene. ~ *back,* tornare indietro,
rifare la strada, indietreggiare,
retrocedere. ~*-between,* intermediario, mediatore, mezzano. ~ *by,*
passare; seguire, riferirsi a, regolarsi
sopra. ~ *cart,* carriola, carrozzella
per bambini, *f.* ~ *down,* scendere,
discendere; declinare, decadere; (*sun,
moon*) tramontare; (*ship*) affondare,
colare a picco; (*swelling*) diminuire,
sgonfiarsi. ~ *for,* andare a cercare,
andare a prendere, fare, valere,
contare, assalire. ~ *in,* entrare,
salire, concorrere. ~ *off,* andar via,
allontanarsi, partire, andarsene;
esplodere, scoppiare. ~ *on,*
continuare, andare avanti, procedere.
on! Avanti! Coraggio! Andiamo!
~ *on board a ship, an aeroplane,*
imbarcarsi, salire a bordo. ~ *out,*
uscire; (*light*) spegnersi. ~ *over,*
attraversare, percorrere, esaminare,
ripetere, scorrere; (*jump*) saltare;
(*the mark*) passare il segno. ~*-slow*

strike, sciopero bianco, *m.* ~
through, passare attraverso, passare per, attraversare, percorrere;
penetrare, fendere, forare; adempiere, compiere; soffrire, sopportare,
subire. ~ *through with*, finire,
venire a capo di, condurre a buon
fine. ~ *to press*, andare in stampa.
~ *to sleep*, addormentarsi, cadere in
sonno, essere colto dal sonno. ~ *to
sleep again*, riaddormentarsi. ~ *up*,
montare, salire, innalzarsi, rimontare, risalire, presentarsi (a).
~ *with*, accompagnare, andare con,
seguire. ~ *without*, andare senza,
fare senza, fare a meno di, passarsi
di, non ottenere.

goad, *n.* pungolo, *m.*; *(fig.)* stimolo,
eccitamento, *m.* ¶ *v.t.* pungere,
pungolare, spronare.

goal, *n.* termine, *m.*; meta, mira, *f.*;
fine, scopo, *m.*; *(football)* porta, rete,
f. ~ *area, line*, area della porta, linea
di fondo, *f.* ~ *keeper, kick, post*,
portiere, *m.*; rimessa del portiere, *f.*;
palo della porta, *m.* ~ *averages*,
quoziente reti, *m.*

goat, *n.* capra, *f.*; *(he)* capro, caprone,
m. ~ *herd*, capraio, *m.*, -a, *f.* ~ *ee*,
n. barbetta a punta, *f.*, pizzo, *m.*

gobble, *v.t.* ingoiare, (in fretta o
avidamente); *(v.i. of turkey)* chiocciare.

goblet, *n.* coppa, tazza, *f.*; bicchiere,
m.

goblin, *n.* spirito maligno, fantasma,
folletto, *m.*

God, *n.* Dio, *m.* *God's acre*, camposanto, *m.* **god,** *n.* dio, *m.*; *pl.* dei;
(pl. Theat.) loggione, *m.* ~ *child*,
figlioccio, *m.* ~ *daughter*, figlioccia,
f. ~ *father*, padrino, *m.* ~ *head*,
divinità, *f.* ~ *mother*, madrina, *f.*
~ *send*, provvidenza, *f.*; fortuna
impensata, *f.*; guadagno inaspettato,
m.; bazza, *f.* ~ *son*, figlioccio, *m.*
goddess, *n.* dea, *f.* **godless,** *a.*
ateo, empio. **godlike,** *a.* divino,
deiforme. **godliness,** *n.* santità, *f.*;
pietà. **godly,** *a.* pio, religioso.

goffer, *n.* *(goffering iron)* ferro da
arricciare, *m.* ¶ *v.t.* increspare,
arricciare.

goggles, *n.pl.* occhiali di protezione,
m.pl.

going, *n.* andata, *f.*; andare, *m.*;
partenza, *f.* ~ *& coming*, andata
e ritorno; viavai, *m.* ~ *back to
school*, ritorno alla scuola, *m.* ~
concern, azienda in piena efficienza,
in attività. *value as a* ~ *concern*,

valore dell'utile netto (di un'azienda
in attività). ~, ~, *gone!* uno due
e tre, aggiudicato! ~ *s on*, *(iron.)*
sconcezze, *f.pl.*

goitre, *n.* gozzo, *m.*

gold, *n.* oro, *m.* ~ *beater*, battiloro, *m.*
~ *beater's skin*, buccio, sottile
pergamena fatta con intestini di bue.
the G ~ *Coast*, la Costa d'Oro, *f.*
~ *digger*, cercatore d'oro, *m.*
~ *field*, campo aurifero, terreno
aurifero, *m.* ~ *finch*, cardellino, *m.*
~ *fish*, orata, *f.* ~ *lace*, gallone
d'oro, *m.* ~ *leaf*, foglia d'oro, *f.*
~ *mine*, miniera d'oro, *f.* ~ *smith*,
orefice, *m.* ~ *(smith's) work*,
oreficeria, *f.* ~ *tipped (cigarettes)*,
sigarette con bocchino d'oro, *f.pl.*
~ *washer*, *(pers.)* lavatore d'oro, *m.*
¶ *a.* d'oro, aureo. ~ *blocking*
(Bookb.), doratura in oro,*f.* ~ *francs*,
franchi oro, *m.pl.* ~ *en*, *a.* d'oro,
dell'oro, dorato; *(fig.)* felice, prezioso.
~ *hair*, capelli biondi, *m.pl.* ~ *calf*,
vitello d'oro, *m.* ~ *mean*, giusto
mezzo, *m.* ~ *rain*, pioggia d'oro, *f.*
~ *syrup*, melassa raffinata, *f.* ~
wedding, nozze d'oro, *f.pl.*

golf, *n.* golf, *m.* ~ *club*, bastone
m. ~ *course, links*, campo di golf, *m.*
~ *er*, *n.* giuocatore di golf, *m.*

golosh, *n.* galoscia, *f.*

gondola, *n.* gondola, *f.*; *(Aero.)*
navicella, *f.* **gondolier,** *n.* gondo-
liere, *m.*

gong, *n.* gong, tam-tam, *m.inv.*

good, *a.* buono; bello; bravo; onesto;
saggio; virtuoso; dabbene; favorevole, propizio; vantaggioso; utile;
ben fatto, solido; di valore; *(of a
child)* buono, saggio; ~ *angel*,
angelo custode, *m.* ~ *breeding*,
buone maniere, maniere educate,
f.pl.; buona educazione, *f.* ~ *bye*,
i. & n. addio, *i. & m.*, arrivederci, *i.*
~ *conduct prize*, premio di buona
condotta, *m.* *a* ~ *deal, a* ~ *many*,
una grande quantità, molto, parecchio. *a* ~ *ear (for music)*, buon
orecchio, orecchio delicato, orecchio
musicale, *m.* ~ *evening*, ~ *night*,
buona sera, buona notte. *a* ~ *for-
nothing*, *n. & a.* (un) buono a nulla,
che vale nulla, un cattivo soggetto,
m. *G* ~ *Friday*, Venerdí Santo, *m.*;
~ *gracious!* Dio mio!í bontà de
Cielo! ~ *looking*, bello, leggiadro!
ben fatto. *my* ~ *man*, amico mio,
caro mio. ~ *morning!* ~ *afternoon!*
~ *day!* buongiorno! ~ *nature*,
bontà, bonomia, *f.*; buon umore,

buon cuore, *m.* ~ *natured (pers.)*;
di buon cuore, bonario, benigno,
(*laugh*) gioviale, allegro. ~ *offices*;
servizio, ministero, *m.*; servigi, *m.pl.*,
buoni uffici, *m.pl.* the ~ *old days*,
i bei tempi antichi, il tempo che
Berta filava. *a* ~ *way*, abbastanza
lontano, un bel pezzo (di cammino).
a ~ *while*, molto tempo, un pezzo,
un buon pezzo. ~*will*, buon
volere, *m.*; benevolenza, *f.*; favore,
m.; simpatia, *f.*; avviamento, *m.*;
(*Com.*) clientela, *f.* ¶ *i.* bene! ben
fatto! va bene, d'accordo. ¶ *n.*
bene, buono, vantaggio, *m.*; utilità, *f.*
for ~, per sempre, per davvero.
it's no ~*!* è inutile! *it's no* ~,
non vale niente, non serve a nulla.
to the ~, profitto netto. **goodies,**
n.pl. chicche, *f.pl.*; dolci, *m.pl.*
goodness, *n.* bontà, benevolenza,
probità, virtù, *f.* *for* ~' *sake*, per
pietà, in grazia, per l'amor di Dio,
per carità.
goods, *n.pl.* beni, effetti, *m.pl.*; merci,
f.pl. ~ *train*, treno merci, *m.*
by ~ *train*, a piccola velocità.
goose, *n.* oca, *f.* ~*flesh,* (*fig.*) pelle
d'oca, *f.* ~*step,* passo da parata,
passo cadenzato, *m.*
gooseberry, *n.* ribes, *m.*; uva spina, *f.*
~ *bush*, ribes spinoso, arbusto d'uva
spina, *m.*
Gordian knot, nodo gordiano, *m.*
gore, *n.* sangue, *m.*; (*gusset*) gherone,
m.f. ¶ *v.t.* ferire con le corna,
trafiggere.
gorge, *n.* (*Geog.*) burrone, *m.*; stretta,
valle, *f.*; (*throat*) gola, strozza, *f.*
¶ *v.t* satollare, impinzare.
gorgeous, *a.* sfarzoso, sontuoso, ricco,
sgargiante, magnifico.
gorilla, *n.* gorilla, *m.*
gormandize, *v.i.* impinzarsi, mangiare golosamente, satollarsi.
gorse, *n.* ginestra spinosa, *f.*
gory, *a.* insanguinato.
goshawk, *n.* astore, *m.*
gosling, *n.* paperetto, *m.*
gospel, *n.* vangelo, *m.* ~ (*truth*),
verità sacrosanta, *f.*
gossamer, *n.* garza sottilissima, *f.*;
filamenti di S. Maria, *m.pl.*
gossip, *n.* ciarla, chiacchiera, *f.*;
pettegolezzi, *m.pl.*; diceria, *f.*; (*pers.*)
pettegolo, *m.*, -a, *f.*; comare, *f.*
¶ *v.i.* pettegolare, chiacchierare.
goth (*fig.*), *n.* barbaro. **Gothic,** *a.*
gotico.
gouache (*Art.*), *n.* guazzo, lavoro a
guazzo, *m.*

gouge, *n.* sgorbia, *f.* ¶ *v.i.* sgorbiare.
gourd, *n.* zucca, *f.*
gourmand, *a. & n.* ghiotto, ghiottone.
a. & m.
gourmet, *n.* b[u]ongustaio, *m.*
gout, *n.* gotta, *f.*; (*feet*) podagra, *f.*
~*y,* *a.* gottoso, podagroso.
govern, *v.t.* governare, reggere;
(*Gram.*) reggere. ~*ess,* *n.* istitutrice, governante, *f.* ~*car[t]*, veicolo
leggero con due sedili. ~*ment,*
governo, *m.*; amministrazione,
direzione, *f.* ~ *in power*, governanti,
m.pl. ~ *organ*, giornale ufficiale, *m.*
~*or,* *n.* governatore, *m.*; (*Mach.*)
regolatore, *m.* ~*orship,* *n.*
governatorato, *m.*; direzione, *f.*
gown, *n.* vestito, *m.*; veste, *f.*; abito, *m.*;
(*cassock*) zimarra, *f.*; (*acad.*) toga,
cappa, *f.*
grab, *v.t.* agguantare, afferrare,
impadronirsi (violentemente) di.
grace, *n.* grazia, *f.*; favore, *m.*;
eleganza, leggiadria, *f.*; (*before meal*)
benedicite, *m.*; (*after*) grazie, *f.pl.*
~*note,* fioritura, *f.* the *G*~*s*, le
Grazie, *f.pl.* his *G*~, Sua Grazia.
your G~, Vostra Grazia. ¶ *v.t.*
adornare, abbellire; favorire, onorare.
~*ful,* *a.* grazioso, leggiadro,
elegante.
gracious, *a.* grazioso; clemente,
condiscendente. ~*ness,* *n.* cortesia,
grazia; clemenza, condiscendenza, *f.*
gradation, *n.* gradazione, *f.* **grade,**
n. grado, *m.* ¶ *v.t.* graduare;
classificare. **gradient,** *n.* (*up*)
salita, *f.*; (*down*) pendenza, china, *f.*;
declivio, *m.*; (*up or down*) inclinazione, *f.* **gradual,** *a.* graduale.
graduate, *v.t.* graduare; (*v.i.*)
ottenere un grado accademico;
laurearsi. ¶ *n.* laureato, *m.*, -a, *f.*
Gr[a]eco-Roman wrestling, lotta
greco-romana, *f.*
graft, *n.* (*Hort.*) innesto, *m.*; (*Surg.*)
trapianto, *m.*; (*spoils*) donativo
corruttore, *m.* ¶ *v.t.* innestare,
trapiantare. ~*ing,* (*Knit.*) ricuci-
tura, *f.*; (*Hort.*) innestamento, *m.*
grail, *n.* (*Poet.*) coppa, *f.*; calice, *m.*
grain, *n.* grano, granello, *m.*; grana-
glie, *f.pl.*; chicco, *m.*; cereali, *m.pl.*;
(*wood, &c.*) grana, vena, *f.*; filo, *m.*;
(*precious stones*) acqua, *f.*; (*weight*)
= 0.0648 gramme; (*pl. brewer's*)
residui di semi, *m.pl.* *against the* ~,
a malavoglia. ¶ *v.t.* granire,
granulare; marmorare, venare. ~*ed,*
p.a. (*leather, &c.*) conciato, (col
pelo rimosso); (*wood*) venato.

coarse-~, fine-~, (*Metall.*) a grana grossa, fine. ~ing, *n.* venatura, *f.*; concia delle pelli, *f.*

grains (*fish spear*), *n.* arpione, *m.*

grammalogue, *n.* stenogramma, *m.*

grammar, *n.* grammatica, *f.* ~ian, *n.* grammatico, *m.* **grammatical**, *a.* grammatico.

gramophone, *n.* grammofono, fonografo, *m.* ~ needle, puntina da grammofono, *f.* ~ record, disco, *m.*

grampus, *n.* orca, *f.*

Granada, *n.* (*Spain*) Granata, *f.*

granadilla, (*Bot.*) *n.* granadiglia, *f.*

granary, *n.* granaio, *m.*

grand, *a.* grande; grandioso, imponente, magnifico. ~child, ~son, ~daughter, nipote, *m. & f.* ~children, nipoti, *m.pl.* ~father, nonno, *m.*; avo, *m.* ~father's clock, orologio a pendolo, *m.* ~mamma, nonna, avola, *f.* ~mother, nonna, ava, *f.* ~ piano, pianoforte a coda, *m.* ~ staircase, scalone, *m.*; scala d'onore, *f.* ~stand, tribuna (principale), *f.* ~ total, somma, *f.*; totale, *m.* **grandee**, *n.* gran signore; Grande di Spagna, *m.* **grandeur**, *n.* grandezza, *f.*; magnificenza, *f.* (*feeling*) elevatezza, *f.*

grandiloquence, *n.* grandiloquenza, magniloquenza, *f.* **grandiloquent**, *a.* grandiloquente, magniloquente.

grandiose, *a.* grandioso.

granite, *n.* granito, *m.*

granny, *n.* avola, nonna, *f.*

grant, *n.* concessione, *f.*; dono, *m.* ¶ *v.t.* accordare, concedere, rendere, assegnare; accogliere, esaudire. granted! sia pure! granted that it be so, ammesso che sia così. God ~ it! Dio lo voglia, Dio voglia che. to take for ~ed, presupporre, tenere per fermo, ammettere per vero. ~ee, *n.* concessionario, *m.* ~or, *n.* concedente, *m.f.*

granulate, *v.t.* granulare. ~d sugar, zucchero cristallizzato, *m.* **granule**, *n.* granulo, granello, *m.*

grape, *n.* uva, *f.*; acino (*berry or stone of the ~*), *m.*; (*pl.*) uva, *f.*; uve, *f.pl.* ~fruit, pampelimosa, *f.* ~shot, mitraglia, *f.* ~stone, acino, chicco, vinacciuolo, *m.*

graph, *n.* grafico, *m.* ~ic, *a.* grafico.

graphite, *n.* grafite, *f.*

grapnel, *n.* grappino, ancorotto, *m.* **grapple**, *v.t.* aggrappare. ~ with. afferrare, venire alle prese con, aggrapparsi a; (*fig.*) trattare.

grasp, *n.* presa, stretta, *f.*; (*fig.*) potere, *m.*; comprensiona, *f.* ¶ *v.t.* afferrare, impugnare, agguantare, stringere. within one's ~, a portata di mano. to loose one's ~, allentare la stretta. ~ round the body, cingere. ~ing, *p.a.* avido, cupido, avaro.

grass, *n.* erba, erbetta, *f.*; (*Min.*) superficie, *f.* a ~ (*plant*), una graminacea, *f.* ~ court (*Ten.*) l'erba. ~hopper, cavalletta, *f.* ~land, prateria, *f.*; terreno erboso, *m.* ~ plot, tappeto verde, *m.* ~ snake, biscia, *f.* ~ widow, vedova a titolo temporaneo, *f.* ~y, *a.* erboso.

grate, *n.* grata, *f.* ¶ *v.t.* grattugiare; (*teeth*) digrignare, far stridere i denti; (*ears*) lacerare, straziare. ~d bread crumbs, pangrattato, *m.*

grateful, *a.* grato, riconoscente; gradito. to be ~ to, for, essere riconoscente a; mostrarsi grato per. ~ness, *n.* riconoscenza, *f.*

grater, *n.* grattugia, raspa, *f.*

gratification, *n.* gratificazione, *f.*; soddisfacimento, godimento, *m.*

gratify, *v.t.* appagare, gratificare, soddisfare, piacere a, contentare; (*request*) esaudire.

gratin, *n.* crosta, *f.* ~ate, *v.t.* crostare.

grating, *n.* grata, griglia, *f.*; graticolato, cancello, *m.*; inferriata; *f.* ¶ *p.a.* aspro, stridente, discordante, irritante. ~ sound, stridore, *m.*

gratis, *ad.* gratis, gratuitamente, a ufo.

gratitude, *n.* gratitudine, riconoscenza, *f.*; riconoscimento, *m.*

gratuitous, *a.* gratuito; senza motivo. ~ness, *n.* gratuità, *f.* **gratuity**, *n.* dono, *m.*; mancia, *f.*, gratificazione, *f.* (*on discharge*) indennità, *f.*

gravamen, *n.* gravame, torto, *m.*; motivo (di un'accusa), *m.*

grave, *a.* grave, serio, austero. ¶ *n.* tomba, fossa, *f.*; sepolcro, *m.* ~clothes, lenzuolo mortuario, sudario, *m.* ~digger, becchino, *m.* ~stone, pietra sepolcrale, lapide, *f.* ~yard, cimitero, camposanto, *m.* ¶ *v.t.* (*ship*) riparare; raddobbare; (*v.t. ir.*) (*fig.*) imprimere, scolpire.

gravel, *n.* ghiaia, *f.*; (*Med.*) renella, *f.*; calcoli, *m.pl.* ~ path, ~ walk, viale ghiaiato, coperto di sabbia, *m.* ~ pit, cava di ghiaia, di rena, *f.* ¶ *v.t.* (*fig.*) imbarazzare. ~ly, *a.* ghiaiato, ghiaioso.

graver, *n.* incisore, *m.*; (*tool*) bulino, *m.*

graving dock, bacino di raddobbo, *m.*
gravitate, *v.i.* gravitare. **gravitation,** *n.* gravitazione, *f.* **gravity,** *n.* (*Phys.*) gravità, *f.*; peso, *m.*; (*fig.*) gravità, austerità, serietà, *f.*

gravy, *n.* sugo, *m.*; salsa, *f.* ~ *boat,* salsiera, *f.*; vaso da salsa, *m.* ~ *spoon,* cucchiaio per la salsa, *m.*

gray. See *grey.* **grayling,** *n.* ombrina, *f.*

graze, *n.* escoriazione, *f.* ¶ *v.t.* & *i.* sfiorare, radere, rasentare, escoriare; (*sea bottom*) dragare; (*cattle*) pascere, pascersi, pascolare, fare pascolare.

grazier, *n.* allevatore di bestiame, *m.* *grazing land,* pascolo, *m.*

grease, *n.* grasso, unto, *m.*; (*in wool*) grasso animale, *m.* ~ *box,* scatola lubrificatrice, *f.* ~*paint,* belletto, *m.* ~*proof paper,* carta impermeabile al grasso. ¶ *v.t.* ingrassare, ungere, lubrificare. **greasiness,** *n.* untuosità, oleosità, *f.* **greasy,** *a.* grasso, unto, untuoso, oleoso, macchiato di grasso. ~ *pole,* albero della cuccagna, *m.*

great, *a.* grande, forte, alto, lungo; grosso, molto. ~ *aunt,* prozia, *f.* ~ *bell,* campanone, *m.* G ~ *Britain,* la Gran Bretagna, *f.* ~*coat,* soprabito, *m.*; (*Mil.*) cappotto, *m.* ~ *Dane,* cane danese, *m.* a ~ *deal,* a ~ *many,* una gran quantità, molto, molti. ~-*grandchildren,* pronipoti, *m.pl.* ~-*granddaughter,* -*son,* prosnipote, *m.f.* ~-*grandfather,* -*mother,* bisnonno, *m.*; bisnonna, *f.* ~ ~-*grandfather,* -*mother,* trisavolo, *m.*; trisavola, *f.* ~ *toe,* pollice (del piede), alluce, *m.* ~ *uncle,* prozio, *m.* *the* ~ (*fig.*), il grande. *the* ~ *ones,* i grandi, *m.pl.* ~*ly,* *ad.* molto, assai, grandemente, fortemente. ~*ness,* *n.* grandezza, *f.*

grebe, *n.* colimbo, *m.*

Grecian, *a.* greco. **Greece,** *n.* la Grecia, *f.*

greediness, *n.* golosità, ghiottoneria, *f.*; (*fig.*) cupidigia, *f.* **greedy,** *a.* ghiotto, goloso, ingordo, avido.

Greek, *a.* greco. ~ *fret* (*Arch.*), greca, *f.* ¶ *n.* (*pers.*) greco, *m.*; (*language*) il greco, *m.*; la lingua greca, *f.*; (*fig.*) arabo, linguaggio incomprensibile, *m.* (*to me* = per me).

green, *a.* verde; (*fig.*) in erba, inesperto, novizio; (*fruit*) immaturo, acerbo. ~ *baize,* tappeto verde, *m.* ~*finch,* verdone, *m.* ~*fly,* àfide, *m.* ~*gage,* susina claudia, *f.* ~*grocer,* fruttaiolo, fruttivendolo, *m.* ~*horn,*

pecorone, sbarbatello, babbeo, *m.* ~*house,* serra, *f.* ~ *peas,* piselli verdi, *m.pl.* ~ *room,* ridotto, *m.* ~*stuff* or *greens,* ortaggio, *m.*; verdura, *f.*; erbe, *f.pl.* ~*sward,* tappeto verde, *m.*; (*roadside*) margine erboso, *m.* ~ *wood,* foresta, *f.*; fogliame, *m.* ~ *yard,* chiuso, *m.* ¶ *n.* verde, *m.*; verzura, *f.*; (*grass plot* & *Golf*) praticello, *m.* ¶ *v.t.* & *i.* rendere verde, inverdire. ~*ery,* *n.* verdura, *f.* ~*ish,* *a.* verdastro.

Greenland, *n.* la Groenlandia, *f.* ~*er,* *n.* groenlandese, *m.f.*

greenness, *n.* color verde, *m.*; verdezza, verdura, *f.*; (*fig.*) inesperienza, ingenuità, *f.*

greet, *v.t.* salutare, accogliere, dare il benvenuto a, felicitare. ~*ing,* *n.* saluto, *m.*, accoglienza, salutazione, *f.*

gregarious, *a.* gregario.

Gregorian, *a.* gregoriano.

Grenada (*W. Indies*), *n.* la Granata, *f.* **grenade,** *n.* granata, *f.* **grenadier,** *n.* granatiere, *m.* **grenadine,** *n.* (*cordial, fabric*) granatina, *f.*

grey, gray, *a.* & *n.* grigio, bigio, *a.* & *m.* ~ *friar,* francescano, *m.* ~ *matter of the brain,* sostanza grigia del cervello, materia grigia, *f.* ~ *mullet,* muggine, *f.* ¶ *v.t.* colorire in grigio. ~*ish,* *a.* grigiastro. ~*ness,* *n.* color grigio, *m.*

greyhound, *n.* levriere, *m.* ~ *racing,* corse di levrieri, *f.pl.*

grid, *n.* inferriata, grata, *f.*; (*Radio*) griglia (di valvola). ~ *iron,* graticola, gratella, *f.*

grief, *n.* dolore, dispiacere, rammarico, *m.*; afflizione, pena, *f.*

grievance, *n.* torto, danno, *m.*; doglianza, *f.*; gravame, reclamo, *m.*

grieve, *v.t.* affliggere, rattristare, accorare; (*v.i.*) affliggersi, rattristarsi, lamentarsi. **grievous,** *a.* doloroso, penoso, grave, triste.

griffin, griffon, *n.* griffone, *m.*

grill, *n.* gratella, graticola, *f.*; (*meat*) arrosto sulla gratella, sulla graticola. ~*room,* rosticceria, *f.* ¶ *v.t.* cuocere (arrostire) sulla gratella.

grill[e], *n.* inferriata, *f.*; cancello, *m.*

grim, *a.* torvo, truce, orrendo, feroce, arcigno. ~ *death,* la Morte.

grimace, *n.* smorfia, *f.* ¶ *v.i.* fare le smorfie.

grime, *n.* sporcizia, *f.*, sudiciume, *m.* ¶ *v.t.* sporcare. **grimy,** *a.* sporco sudicio, imbrattato.

grin, *n.* sogghigno, *m.*, smorfia, *f.*
¶ *v.i.* sogghignare.

grind, *v.t.* ir. macinare, tritare,
sgretolare; (*glass*) levigare, smerigliare; (*knives*) affilare, arrotare;
(*teeth*) digrignare, sgretolare; (*fig.
work*) (*v.i.*) sgobbare. ~ *at,*
sgobbare. ~*stone,* mola, macina, *f.*
~ *down,* opprimere, schiacciare,
logorare, ridurre in polvere, tri-
turare. ~*ery,* *n.* arnesi da calzolaio,
m.pl. ~*ing* (*corn*), *n.* macinamento,
m., macinatura, macinazione, *f.*

grip, *n.* presa, stretta, impugnatura, *f.*
¶ *v.t.* afferrare, impugnare,
stringere.

gripes, *n.pl.* dolori colici, *m.pl.*

grisly, *a.* orribile, spaventevole,
brutto.

Grisons (the), *n.pl.* i Grigioni, *m.pl.*

grist, *n.* grano da macinare, frumento,
m. *to bring* ~ *to the mill* (*prov.*),
far venire l'acqua al mulino. *all is*
~ *to his mill,* tutto è buono per
lui.

gristle, *n.* cartilagine, *f.* **gristly,** *a.*
cartilaginoso.

grit, *n.* sabbia, arenaria, *f.*; (*fig.*)
fermezza, risoluzione, *f.* **gritty,** *a.*
sabbioso, renoso, pieno di ghiaia.

grizzled, *a.* (*hair*) brizzolato. *grizzly
bear,* orso grigio, *m.*

groan, *n.* gemito, lamento, *m.* ¶ *v.i.*
gemere, lamentarsi.

groats, *n.pl.* farina d'avena, *f.*;
tritello d'avena, *m.*

grocer, *n.* droghiere, *m.* ~*'s shop*
& *grocery,* drogheria, *f.*

grog, *n.* grog, *m.*, (specie di ponce).

groggy, *a.* vacillante, titubante;
brillo.

groin, *n.* inguine, *m.*; (*Arch.*) lunetta,
f.

groom, *n.* staffiere, mozzo di stalla,
palafreniere, *m.* ¶ *v.t.* strigliare.
well ~*ed,* elegante, pulito, lindo,
forbito.

groomsman, *n.* paggio d'onore,
amico dello sposo, *m.*

groove, *n.* scanalatura, *f.*; canale,
incastro, *m.*; (*fig.*) vecchia abitudine,
abitudine fissa, *f.* ¶ *v.t.* scanalare.

grope, *v.t.* & *i.* tastare, brancolare,
andare a tastoni, a tentoni.

grosbeak, *n.* frusone, *m.*

gross, *a.* grossolano; rozzo, ruvido;
ripugnante. (*Com.*) lordo, complessivo. ~ *income,* entrata lorda,
f. ~ *weight,* peso lordo, *m.* ¶
(144) *n.* grossa, *f.* ~*ness,* *n.*
grossolanità, rozzezza; enormità, *f.*

grotesque, *a.* & *n.* & ~(**ness**), *n.*
grottesco, *a.* & *m.*

grotto, *n.* grotta, *f.*

ground, *n.* terra, *f.*; terreno, suolo, *m.*;
area, *f.*; territorio, *m.*; campo, fondo,
fondamento, sfondo, *m.*; causa,
ragione, *f.*; motivo, *m.*; (*pl.*) ragioni,
f.pl., motivo, *m.*; (*pl. Law*) motivo,
m.; (*pl. dregs*) deposito, sedimento,
m.; (*coffee,* &*c.*) fondi, *m.pl.*; feccia,
posatura, *f.*; (*of mansion*) parco, *m.*;
giardini, *m.pl.*; (*fishing, cruising*)
località pescosa, *f.*; paraggi dove si
sta in crociera, *m.pl.* ~ *angling,*
pesca senza galleggiante, pesca di
fondo, *f.* ~ *floor,* piano terreno,
fondo, *m.* ~ *game,* cacciagione col
pelo (lepri, conigli, &c.), *f.* ~ *ivy,*
edera terrestre, *f.* ~ *landlord,*
proprietario fondiario, *m.* ~ *line*
(*Fish.*), lenza senza galleggiante,
lenza di fondo, *f.* ~ *man,* guardiano
del terreno, *m.* ~*nut,* arachide, *f.*
~ *rent,* rendita fondiaria, *f.*; livello,
m. ~ *swell,* mare lungo, mare di
fondo, *m.* ~ *work,* fondamento, *m.*,
base, *f.* ¶ *p.p.* macinato, in polvere;
(*rice,* &*c.*) farina di . . .; (*glass*)
(vetro) smerigliato; (*stopper*) turacciolo smerigliato. ¶ *v.t.* & *i.* porre
a terra, metter giú, basare, fondare;
basarsi, fondarsi; (*Elec.*) mettere
a terra; (*ship*) fare incagliare,
amenare; dare in secco, incagliare.
~*less,* *a.* malfondato, infondato.
~*lessly,* *ad.* senza ragione.

groundsel, *n.* senecione, *m.*

group, *n.* gruppo, crocchio, *m.*;
brigata, *f.* ~ *firing,* (*Artil.*) tiro
concentrato, *m.* ¶ *v.t.* aggruppare,
radunare, raggruppare.

grouse, *n.* gallo di montagna, *m.*;
¶ *v.i.* brontolare.

grout[ing], (*Build.*) *n.* colamento,
riempimento, *m.*; malta, *f.*

grove, *n.* boschetto, *m.*; piantagione,
f.

grovel, *v.i.* avvilirsi, strisciare, strasci-
carsi per terra, abbassarsi.

grow, *v.i.* ir. crescere, aumentare;
svilupparsi, moltiplicarsi; allignare,
spuntare; ingrandire; farsi, divenire.
often expressed by refl., e.g. *to grow
alarmed,* allarmarsi; *to grow cold,*
raffreddarsi, &c.; (*v.t.* ir.) far
crescere; coltivare; produrre. ~
green again & ~ *young again,*
rinverdire. ~*er,* *n.* coltivatore,
produttore, *m.*, -trice, *f.*

growl, *n.* ringhio, grugnito, *m.* ¶ *v.i.*
grugnire, ringhiare.

grown up, *a. & n.* adulto, *a. & m.*;
uomo fatto, grande, *m.* **growth**, *n.*
crescimento, *m.*, crescenza, crescita,
f.; aumento, *m.*; estensione, *f.*;
progresso, sviluppo, frutto, prodotto,
m.; vegetazione, *f.*; ascesso, tumore,
m.; (*vintage*) vendemmia, *f.*

groyne, *n.* paraonde, *m.inv.*; riparo
(contro i guasti della marea),
m.

grub, *n.* larva, *f.*; bruco, verme, *m.*
~ [up], *v.t.* sradicare, estirpare,
sterpare. **grubber**, *n.* sterpatore,
raccoglitore, *m.* **grubby**, *a.*
(*wormy*) verminoso, bacato; (*dirty*)
sudicetto.

grudge, *n.* rancore, malvolere, *m.*;
animosità, *f.* ¶ *v.t.* invidiare, dare
di mala voglia. *have (bear) a ~
against*, avere rancore con, serbare
rancore a. *I have a ~ against you*,
io l'ho con Lei.

gruel, *n.* brodo lungo fatto d'orzo
o d'avena. ~**ling**, *a.* duro, faticoso.

gruesome, *a.* orribile, raccapricciante,
spaventoso.

gruff, *a.* burbero, aspro.

grumble, *v.i.* borbottare, brontolare,
lagnarsi. ~ *at*, ~ *about*, lagnarsi di.
~**r**, *n.* brontolone, *m.*, -a, *f.*

grunt, *n.* grugnito, *m.* ¶ *v.i.* grugnire.

guano, *n.* guano, *m.*

guarantee, **-ty**, *n.* garanzia, *f.* ¶ *v.t.*
garantire. **guarantor**, *n.* garante,
mallevadore, *m.*

guard, *n.* guardia, *f.*; (*pers.*) guardia,
f., custode, *m.*; (*train*) capotreno,
conduttore, *m. on ~*, in guardia, di
guardia, all'erta. ~*house*, ~*room*,
corpo di guardia, *m.* ~'*s room*, furgone del conduttore, *m.* ¶ *v.t. & i.*
custodire, difendere, proteggere;
stare in guardia; premunirsi, guardarsi. ~**ed**, *p.a.* cauto, circospetto.

guardian, *n.* custode, *m.*, tu ore,
m., -trice, *f.*; guardia, *f.*; guardiano,
m., -a, *f.*; (*att.*) custode, tutelare.
~*ship*, *n.* tutela, *f.*; (*Law*) autorità
tutoria, curatela, *f.*

guava, *n.* guiava, *f.*; (*tree*) guiavo, *m.*

gudgeon, *n.* ghiozzo, *m.*

guelder rose, pallone di neve, *m.*

guerdon, *n.* guiderdone, *m.*

guer[r]illa, *n.* guerriglia, *f.*, partigiano, *m.* ~*war[fare]*, guerriglia,
guerra di scaramucce, *f.*

Guernsey, *n.* Guernsey, *f.* **g**~, *n.*
camiciotto di lana, *m.*

guess, *n.* congettura, cosa indovinata,
supposizione, *f.* ¶ *v.t. & i.* indovinare, congetturare, supporre.

guest, *n.* ospite, *m.f.*; invitato, *m.*,
-a, *f.*; convitato, *m.*, -a, *f.* ~
chamber, camera degli ospiti, *f.*
~ *of honour*, convitato d'onore, *m.*

guffaw, *v.i.* scoppiare (dare) in una
grossa risata.

Guiana, *n.* la Guiana, *f.*

guidance, *n.* condotta, direzione, *f.*;
governo, *m.*; norma, *f.* **guide**, *n.*
guida, *f.*; cicerone, *m.*; scorta, *f.*
~[*book*], guida, *f.*; indicatore, *m.*
~ *post*, palo indicatore, *m.* ~ *rope*,
fune di sicurezza, *f.*; (*Aero.*), stabi-
lizzatore, *m.* ¶ *v.t.* guidare, condurre,
dirigere; scortare; governare. *guiding
principle*, principio governante, *m.*;
regola, norma, *f.* ~*d missile*, siluro
volante, *m.*

g[u]ild, *n.* corporazione, associazione,
maestranza, *f.*; consorzio, *m.*;
(*church*) circolo, *m.* **guildhall**,
n. palazzo municipale, *m.*

guile, *n.* astuzia, furberia, *f.* ~**less**,
a. senz'artificio, semplice, ingenuo.

guillotine, *n.* ghigliottina, *f.*; (*for
paper-cutting*) cesoia a ghigliottina,
f. ¶ *v.t.* ghigliottinare.

guilt, *n.* colpa, colpabilità, reità,
colpevolezza, *f.* ~**less**, *a.* senza
colpa, innocente. ~**y**, *a.* colpevole,
reo.

guinea, (21/-) *n.* ghinea, *f.* ~*fowl*,
gallina faraona, gallina di Faraone, *f.*
~*pig*, porcellino d'India, *m.*; (*pers.*)
persona che si preoccupa dell'emolumento e non del proprio ufficio.
G~ (*Geog.*), la Guinea, *f.*

guise, *n.* apparenza; maschera, *f.*

guitar, *n.* chitarra, *f.*

gules (*Her.*), *n.* color rosso, *m.*

gulf, *n.* golfo; abisso; vortice, *m.*;
(*fig.*) grande intervallo, *m.* **G**~ *of
the Lion*, Golfo del Leone. **G**~
Stream, Corrente del Golfo, *f.*

gull, *n.* (*sea*) gabbiano, *m.*; (*pers.*)
minchione, semplicione, *m.* ¶ *v.t.*
ingannare, minchionare, gabbare.

gullet, *n.* gola, *f.*; esofago, *m.*

gullible, *a.* credulo, ingannabile.

gully, *n.* borro; fosso, *m.*; gola, *f.*;
(*gutter*) fossetto di scolo, canale di
scolo, *m.* ~*hole*, buca di scarico,
f.

gulp, *n.* sorso, tratto, *m.*; boccata,
sorsata, *f. at a ~*, d'un tratto.
to ~ down, inghiottire, tranguggiare,
tracannare, ingozzare.

gum, *n.* gomma, *f.*; (*Anat.*) gengiva, *f.*
~ *arabic*, gomma arabica. ~ *boil*,
ascesso alle gengive, *m.* ~ *tree*,
albero da gomma, *m.* ¶ *v.t.* in

gommare. **gummy**, *a*. gommoso, aderente.

gumption, *n*. senno, *m*.; accortezza, praticità, *f*.

gun, *n*. fucile, schioppo; cannone, pezzo (d'artiglieria), *m*.; bocca da fuoco, *f*. ∼*boat*, cannoniera, *f*. ∼ *captain*, capo pezzo. ∼ *carriage*, affusto (del cannone), *m*. ∼ *cotton*, fulmicotone, *m*. ∼ *licence*, licenza di porto d'armi, *f*. ∼ *layer*, puntatore, *m*. ∼ *metal*, bronzo rosso, *m*. ∼*-powder*, polvere da cannone, da sparo, p. nera, *f*.; ∼ *runner*, contrabbandiere di armi, *m*. ∼ *running*, contrabbando di armi, *m*. ∼*shot*, colpo di fucile, colpo di cannone, *m*. *within* ∼, a portata di fucile, di cannone. ∼*shot wound*, ferita d'arma da fuoco, *f*. ∼*smith*, armaiuolo, *m*. **gunner**, *n*. artigliere, (*Naut*.) cannoniere, *m*. ∼*y*, *n*. tiro d'artiglieria, *m*.; scienza dell'artiglieria, *f*.

gunwale, **gunnel**, *n*. capo di banda, *m*.

gurgle, *n*. gorgoglio, *m*. ¶ *v.i.* gorgogliare.

gurnard, **gurnet**, *n*. capone, *m*.

gush, *n*. getto, scoppio, sgorgo, zampillo, *m*.; effusione, affettazione, *f*. ¶ *v.i.* sgorgare, scaturire, scoppiare, schizzare, effondersi, zampillare; parlare con espansività sentimentale.

gusset, *n*. gherone, *m*.; (*Mech*.) bazzoletto, *m*.

gust, *n*. colpo (di vento), *m*.; raffica, *f*.

gusto, *n*. gusto, piacere, godimento, *m*.

gusty, *a*. (*wind*) impetuoso; (*day*) ventoso, (con un vento che viene a raffiche).

gut, *n*. budello, intestino, *m*.; (*Fish.*) crine di Firenze, *m*.; (*Naut.*) gola, *f*. ¶ *v.t.* sventrare, sviscerare, (*fig.*) saccheggiare.

gutta-percha, *n*. guttaperca, *f*.

gutter, *n*. (*roof*) gronda, grondaia; (*street*) cunetta, zanella, *f*. (*conduit*) fossetto di scolo, canale; (*fig.*) trivio, fango, *m*.; mota, *f*. ∼*language*, linguaggio triviale (da trivio), *m*. ∼*snipe*, monello, *m*. ¶ *v.i.* (*candle*) colare.

guttural, *a*. gutturale. ¶ *n*. suono gutturale, *m*.

guy, *n*. (*rope*) ritenuta, *f*.; (*pers.*) caricatura, *f*.; figura fantastica, *f*.; spauracchio, *m*.

guzzle, *v.i.* mangiare (o bere) ghiottamente, satollarsi, mangiare a crepapelle.

gymnasium, *n*. scuola di ginnastica, *f*.; palestra, *f*. **gymnast**, *n*. ginnasta, *m*. ∼**ic**, *a*. ginnastico. ∼**ics**, *n.pl.* ginnastica, *f*.

gynaecology, *n*. ginecologia, *f*.

gypseous, *a*. gessoso. **gypsum**, *n*. gesso, *m*. ∼ *quarry*, gessaia, cava di gesso, *f*.

gyrate, *v.i.* girare. **gyration**, *n*. giramento, *m*. **gyratory**, *a*. giratorio. **gyroscope**, *n*. giroscopio, *m*.

H

H, h, (acca), *f*.

haberdasher, *n*. merciaio, *m*., -a, *f*. ∼*y*, merceria, *f*.; articoli di merceria, *m.pl.*

habiliment, *n*. abbigliamento, vestiario, *m*.; (*pl.*) abbigliamenti, vestiti, abiti, *m.pl.*

habit, *n*. abitudine, consuetudine, *f*.; vezzo, uso; stato, temperamento, *m*.; (*pl.*) abitudini, *f.pl.*; modi, *m.pl.*; (*dress*) abito, costume, *m*. *to be in the ∼ of doing so*, avere l'abitudine di fare così, di farlo. *I got into the ∼ of*, mi sono avvezzato a . . . *riding ∼*, amazzone, *f*. ∼**able**, *a*. abitabile. **habitat**, *n*., **habitation**, *n*. abitazione, dimora, *f*. **habitual**, *a*. abituale, solito, familiare. ∼ *criminal*, recidivo, pregiudicato. **habituate**, *v.t.* abituare.

hack, *n*. taglio irregolare, *m*.; cavallo da nolo, *m*.; (*jade*) cavallaccio, *m*. ∼ *saw*, seghetto, *m*. ∼ (*writer*) scrittoruccio, imbrattacarte, *m*. ¶ *v.t.* tagliuzzare, frastagliare; colpire con un calcio agli stinchi.

hackney carriage, carrozza da nolo, *f*. **hackneyed**, *p.p.* banale, trito, ripetuto a sazietà, fritto e rifritto. ∼ *phrase*, frase stereotipata, *f*.; luogo comune, *m*., espressione bell'e fatta, *f*. ∼ *refrain*, ritornello, *m*.

haddock, *n*. specie di merluzzo, merluzzo fresco, *m*.

Hades, *n*. Ade, *m*.

haematite, *n*. ematite, *f*.

haemorrhage, *n*. emorragia, *f*. **haemorrhoids**, *n.pl.* emorroidi, *f.pl.*

haft, *n*. manico, *m*.

hag, *n*. strega, vecchiaccia, *f*.

haggard, *a*. magro, sparuto, smunto, intristito, sofferente.

haggle, *v.i.* mercanteggiare, stare a stiracchiare, tirare sul prezzo.

Hague, (the), l'Aia, *f.*

ha-ha (*sunk fence*), *n.* salto di lupo, fosso di cinto, *m.*

hail, *n.* grandine; gragnuola, *f.*; appello, saluto, *m.*; accoglienza, *f.* *to damage by* ∼, devastare di grandine. *within* ∼, a portata di voce. ∼*stone*, chicco di grandine, *m.*; (*fig.*) grossa grandine. ∼*storm*, grandinata, *f.*, tempesta di grandine, *f.* ¶ *i.* salute! salve! ave (Maria, &c.). ∼ *fellow well met*, da familiare, compagnone allegro, *m.* ¶ *v.i.* imp. grandinare; (*v.t.*) salutare, chiamare, accogliere. ∼ *from*, essere di, venire da.

hair, *n.* (un) capello, *m.*; (dei) capelli, *m.pl.*; capigliatura, *f.*; crine, *m.*; crini, *m.pl.*; chioma, *f.*; pelo, *m.*; crini, *m.pl.* ∼ *brush*, spazzola da capelli, *f.* ∼ *comb*, pettine, *m.* ∼ *curler*, ferro da ricci, *m.* ∼*cutting*, taglio di capelli, *m.* ∼*dresser*, parrucchiere, barbiere, *m.* ∼*dresser's head*, modello, *m.*, testa di cera (da parrucchiere), *f.* ∼ *drier*, macchina per asciugare i capelli. ∼ *mattress*, materasso di crine, *m.* ∼ *net*, rete per capelli, reticella per capelli, *f.* ∼ *oil*, olio profumato, olio per capelli, *m.* ∼*pin*, forcina (da capelli), *f.* ∼*pin bend*, brusca svolta, curva a forcella, *f.* ∼ *shirt*, cilicio, *m.* ∼ *slide*, ferma-capelli, *m.inv.* to split a ∼, cercare il pelo nell'uovo, cavillare. ∼ *splitting*, cavillosità, sottigliezza eccessiva, *f.* ∼*spring*, molla a spirale, *f.* ∼ *waver*, ferro per l'ondulazione, *m.* ∼**less,** *a.* senza capelli, calvo, imberbe. ∼**y,** *a.* peloso; capelluto; crinito.

hake, *n.* nasello, *m.*

halation (*Phot.*), *n.*, alone, *m.*

halberd, *n.* alabarda, *f.*

halcyon days, giorni sereni, giorni di pace e felicità, *m.pl.*

hale, *a.* sano, robusto, ben portante. *to be* ∼ *& hearty,* essere in gamba.

half, *n.* metà, mezzo, *m.*; (*Rly. ticket*) tagliando, *m.* by ∼, per metà, a metà. to go halves with, fare a metà con. *he never does things by halves,* non fa mai le cose a mezzo. *No. 29½* (*house*), N° 29 bis. ¶ *a.* mezzo. on ∼ *profit,* a metà. ¶ *ad.* a metà, a mezzo. ∼ *a crown,* una mezza corona. ∼ *a cup,* una mezza tazza. ∼ *an hour,* una

mezz'ora, *f.* ∼*-back* (*Foot.*), mediano, sostegno, *m.* ∼ *binding,* rilegatura in mezza pelle, *f.* ∼ *bound,* mezzo rilegato. ∼*bred,* di razza mista. ∼*breed,* meticcio, *m.*, -a, *f.* ∼ *brother,* fratellastro, fratello uterino, *m.* ∼ *caste,* di sangue misto, mulatto. ∼ *cock,* tacca di riposo. ∼ *fare,* ∼ *price,* metà prezzo, *f.* ∼ *holiday,* mezza festa, *f.* ∼ *hose,* calzine, *f.pl.* ∼ *length portrait,* ritratto a mezzo busto, *m.* ∼ *light,* mezza luce, penombra, *f.* *at* ∼ *mast* (*flag*), a mezz'asta, a mezz'albero. ∼ *open,* *a.* aperto a metà; socchiuso. ∼ *past twelve,* mezzogiorno e mezza, mezzanotte e mezza. ∼ *past two,* due ore e mezza. *on* ∼ *pay,* a mezza paga, a metà stipendio (pensionato). ∼*penny,* soldo, *m.* ∼ *sister,* sorellastra, sorella uterina, *f* ∼*-time* (*Foot.*), intervallo, *m.* ∼*-title,* falso frontespizio, occhiello, *m.* ∼*tone block,* cliché a mezza tinta, *m.* ∼*way,* a mezza strada. ∼ *track* (*vehicle*), autocarro a ruote e cingoli, *m.* ∼*way house,* casa a mezza strada. ∼*way up* (*the hill*), a mezza salita. ∼ *witted,* scemo, cretino, sciocco, stupido. ∼*-year,* semestre, *m.* ∼*yearly,* *a.* semestrale; (*ad.*) semestralmente, a semestri.

halibut, *n.* rombo, *m.*, pianuzza, *f.*

hall, *n.* sala, *f.*; salone, *m.*; aula, *f.*; atrio, vestibolo, *m.* ∼*mark,* *n.* bollo, *m.*; (*v.t.*) bollare, controllare. ∼ *porter,* portinaio, *m.* ∼*-stand,* attaccapanni, *m.inv.* town ∼, palazzo municipale, *m.*

hallelujah, *n.* alleluia, *m.*

hallo[a], *i.* ehi, ohè; (*Teleph.*) pronto! ∼ *there!* olà! **halloo,** grido di caccia, hallalì. ¶ *v.i.* gridare, vociare; (*v.t. dogs*) incitare con la voce. ∼ *to,* chiamare ad alta voce.

hallow, *v.t.* consacrare, dedicare. ∼**ed,** *p.a.* santo, sacro, benedetto.

hallucination, *n.* allucinazione, *f.*

halo, *n.* alone, *m.*; aureola, gloria, *f.*

halt, *n.* sosta, *f.*; alto, *m.*; fermata, *f.*, tappa, *f.* ¶ *i.* alto! alto là! ¶ *v.i.* fermarsi, arrestarsi, fare alt; (*waver*) esitare; (*limp*) zoppicare; (*v.t.*) fermare; (*Mil.*) far fermare, dare l'alta.

halter, *n.* (*Harness*) cavezza, *f.*; (*hanging*) capestro, *m.*; forca, *f.*

halting, *a.* esitante, zoppicante.

halve, *v.t.* dividere per metà, dividere in due parti uguali, dimezzare, smezzare.

halyard, n. drizza; sagola, f.
ham, n. (in man) coscia, f.; poplite, m.; (hog, boar) prosciutto, m. ~ & eggs, prosciutto e uova.
Hamburg, n. Amburgo, f.
hamlet, n. casale, piccolo villaggio, m.; frazione, f. **Hamlet,** n. Amleto, m.
hammer, n. martello, m.; (power) pilone, m.; (gun) cane, m.; (auction) asta, f.; incanto, m. ~ cloth, gualdrappa, f., coperta del seggiolino del cocchiere, f. sledge ~, mazza, mazzetta, f. steam ~, maglio a vapore, m. ¶ v.t. martellare, battere. ~ away, battere e ribattere sullo stesso argomento, perseverare.
hammock, n. amaca, f.
hamper, n. paniere, cesto, canestro, m. top ~, (Naut.) attrezzatura ingombrante, f. ¶ v.t. imbarazzare, inceppare, intralciare.
hand, n. mano, f.; pugno, m.; (pointer) lancetta, sfera, f.; (writing) scrittura, calligrafia, firma, f.; (side) parte, direzione, f.; canto, m.; (Cards) mano, f.; carte, f.pl.; (horse) = 4 inches or 10·16 centimetres; (pl. men) operai, impiegati, braccianti; (att.) manuale, a mano, di mano, portatile. at ~, sottomano, a portata di mano, vicino, disponibile. on ~, in corso, in magazzino. on the other ~, dall'altra parte, d'altra parte, dall'altro canto, invece, al contrario. ~bag (lady's, &c.), borsetta a mano, f. ~bill, annunzio, avviso, m.; (political, &c.) programma, prospetto, m. ~book, manuale, libretto, m.; guida, f. ~cuff, v.t. ammanettare; (n.pl.) manette, f.pl. ~kerchief, fazzoletto, m.; (silk) pezzuola di seta, f. ~s off! non toccate! giù le mani! ~rail, ringhiera, f.; corrimano, appoggiatoio, guidamano, m. ~shake, stretta di mano, f. ~spike, leva, f.; palanchino, m. ~ tooled (Bookb.) ombreggiato. ~ to ~ (fight), corpo a corpo. from ~ to mouth, alla giornata. ~s up! mani in alto! ~writing, scrittura a mano, calligrafia, f. ¶ v.t. porgere. ~ down (fig.), trasmettere. ~ in, consegnare, rimettere. ~ [over], rimettere, deferire. ~ over (to justice), consegnare. ~ round, far circolare, passare (far passare) di mano in mano. ~ful, n. pugno, m.; manata, f.; manipolo, m.
handicap, n. (Sport) handicap, abbuono, m.; corsa periziata, f.;

(fig.) impiccio, svantaggio, m. ¶ v.t
handicapper, n. periziatore, m.
handicraft, n. mestiere, m.; arte, f.
handicraftsman, n. artigiano, artefice, m.
handle, n. manico, m.; maniglia, f.; manovella, impugnatura, f.; (umbrella) manico, m. ~bar (cycle), manubrio, m. ¶ v.t. maneggiare; manipolare; toccare, trattare; governare; servirsi di. to ~ roughly, malmenare. **handling,** n maneggiamento, m.; manipolazione, f.; maneggio, uso, m.
handsel, n. caparra, strenna, f.; primo uso, m. ¶ v.t. dare una strenna a; usare per la prima volta.
handsome, a. bello, grazioso; generoso: ben fatto, elegante. ~ly, ad. generosamente, liberalmente; graziosamente, bellamente. ~ness, n. bellezza, grazia; liberalità, generosità, f.
handy, a. (pers.) abile, destro; (things) comodo, maneggevole, alla mano, a portata di mano; (man) fasservizi, m. ~-pandy (hand, Nursery talk), giuoco in cui uno deve indovinare in quale mano l'altro tiene un oggetto.
hang, v.t. ir. appendere, sospendere; attaccare; (gallows) impiccare; (head) abbassare, chinare, lasciar cadere. (v.i.) pendere, penzolare, esser sospeso. ~ about, gironzare, dondolarsi. ~back, esitare, rinculare, restare indietro. ~ heavy (time), tardare. ~ out (washing), stendere; (flags) issare. ~dog, a. basso, abbattuto, da scampaforca. ~man, boia, m. ~nail, manereccio, m.
hangar, n. tettoia, aviorimessa, f.
hanger, n. uncino, m.; (Mach.) staffa, f. ~ on, scroccone, parassita, ciondolone, m. **hanging,** p.a. sospeso, pensile, pendente, pendolo, penzolante. ~ committee (Art.), giuria d'ammissione, f. ~ garden, giardino pensile, m. ~ lamp, lampada a sospensione, f. (death by) ~, impiccagione, f.
hangings, n.pl. (bed) cortinaggio, pendaglio, parato, m.; tappezzerie, f.pl.
hank, n. matassa, f.
hanker after, agognare a, bramare.
Hanover, n. Annover, f.; (province) l'Annover, m.
haphazard, ad. a caso, per caso.

hapless, *a.* sfortunato, infelice.

happen, *v.i.* accadere, avvenire, succedere; verificarsi, darsi. **~ing,** *n.* avvenimento, evento, fatto, *m.*

happiness, *n.* felicità, *f.* **happy,** *a.* felice, lieto, fortunato, propizio. **~-go-lucky** *person,* spensierato, imprevidente, *m.* **to a ~ issue,** ad un buon risultato, con un esito favorevole. **~ medium,** giusto mezzo, *m.* **a ~ new year,** buon Capodanno.

harangue, *n.* arringa, *f.* ¶ *v.t. & i.* arringare.

harass, *v.t.* irritare, molestare, disturbare, tormentare, frustrare, contrariare, intralciare.

harbinger, *n.* precursore, foriere, messaggero, *m.*

harbour, *n.* porto, *m.*; (*fig.*) asilo, rifugio, *m.* **~ master,** capitano di porto, *m.* **~ station,** stazione marittima, *f.* ¶ *v t.* albergare, ricettare, dare asilo a, trattenere; (*criminal*) proteggere, ricevere.

hard, *a.* duro, aspro, forte, saldo, difficile, arduo, gravoso, penoso, rigoroso; (*water*) crudo. **~ & fast,** saldo, assoluto. **~ bitten,** risoluto, tenace. **~-bitten sailor,** lupo di mare, *m.* **~-boiled egg,** uovo sodo (*pl.* uova sode). **~ brush,** spazzola rude, *f.* **~ cash,** denaro contante, *m.*; moneta sonante, *f.* **~ court** (*Ten.*), terra battuta, *f.* **~ labour,** lavori forzati, *m.pl.* **~ palate,** palato duro, *m.* **~ roe,** uova, *f.pl.* **~ roed,** pieno d'uova. **~ solder,** saldatura forte, *f.* **~ tack,** biscotto da marinaio, *m.* **~ to please,** esigente, incontentabile. **~ware,** chincaglieria, *f.* (*or pl.* -ie); (*builder's*) serrame, *m.*; ferramenta, *f.pl.*; ferrami, *m.pl.* **~ wearing & for ~ wear,** duraturo, durevole; resistente. **~ working,** laborioso, instancabile. ¶ *ad.* a forza, per forza; duro, duramente? molto, vigorosamente; rapidamente; male; (*drink*) secco; (*look*) fissamente; (*raining*) a dirotto, dirottamente. **~ up,** a secco, al verde, alle strette. **harden,** *v.t.* indurire; assodare; indurare; (*to temper metal*) temperare. **hardihood,** *n.* ardimento, *m.*, audacia, sfrontatezza, *f.* **hardly,** *ad.* appena, a stento; duramente, difficilmente, con difficoltà. **hardness,** *n.* durezza, severità, *f.*; rigore, *m.*; (*water*) crudezza, *f.* **~ of hearing,** durezza, *f.*; essere

duro d'orecchio. **hardship,** *n.* fatica, pena, privazione, ingiustizia, *f.* **hardy,** *a.* robusto, forte, vigoroso, indurito alla fatica, ardito; (*plant*) selvatico, di piena terra.

hare, *n.* lepre, *f.*; (*young*) leprotto, *m.* **~ & hounds,** caccia alla lepre, *f.* **~ bell,** campanula, *f.* **~ brained,** scervellato, sventato, stordito. **~lip,** labbro fesso, labbro leporino, *m.*

harem, *n.* arem, *m.*

haricot beans (*dried*), fagiuoli secchi, *m.pl.*

hark, *i.* ascolta! ascolti! ascoltate! **to ~ back to,** ritornare su.

harlequin, *n.* arlecchino, *m.* **~ade,** arlecchinata, *f.*

harm, *n.* danno, male, torto, pregiudizio, malfatto, *m.* ¶ *v.t.* nuocere a, danneggiare, far torto a, pregiudiziare. *bodily* **~,** vie di fatto, *f.pl. he means no* **~,** non ci mette malizia. **~ful,** *a.* nocivo, nocevole, dannoso. **~less,** *a.* innocuo, inoffensivo, innocente. **~lessness,** *n.* innocuità, innocenza, *f.*

harmonic, *a. & n.* armonico, *a. & m.* (*pl.* = onici). **harmonica,** *n.* armonica, *f.* **harmonious,** *a.* armonioso; (*fig.*) concorde, simmetrico. **harmonium,** *n.* armonio, *m.* **harmonize,** *v.t. & i.* armonizzare. **harmony,** *n.* armonia, *f.*

harness, *n.* bardatura, *f.*; finimenti, *m.pl. die in* **~,** morire sul lavoro. **~ maker,** sellaio, *m.* **~ room,** *n.* selleria, *f.* ¶ *v.t.* bardare; (*waterfall*) usare per la forza motrice.

harp, *n.* arpa, *f. to be always* **~ing** *on the same string,** ripetere sempre la stessa cosa, tornare sempre sullo stesso argomento. **~ist,** *n.* arpista, *m.f.*

harpoon, *n.* rampone, *m.*; fiocina, *f.* ¶ *v.t.* ramponare.

harpsichord, *n.* clavicembalo, *m.*

harpy, *n.* arpia, *f.*

harrow, *n.* erpice, *m.* ¶ *v.t.* erpicare; (*fig.*) straziare, lacerare, tormentare.

harry, *v.t.* depredare, devastare, saccheggiare; imbarazzare.

harsh, *a.* aspro, ruvido, duro, severo; (*taste*) acre; (*voice*) rauco, sgradevole all'orecchio. **~ness,** *n.* asprezza, durezza, severità; acredine, *f.*

hart, *n.* cervo, *m.* **hartshorn,** *n.* ammoniaca liquida, *f.*

harum-scarum, *n.* storditaggine, storditezza, *f.* ¶ *a.* scervellato, stordito, sventato.

harvest, *n.* raccolto, *m.*; messe, *f.*

~ *festival*, festa del raccolto, *f.*
~ *man* (*insect*), falangio, *m.* ¶ *v.t.*
mietere, raccogliere, fare il raccolto.
~**er**, *n.* mietitore, *m.*, -trice, *f.*;
(*Mach.*) mietitrice, *f.*

hash, *n.* guazzabuglio, *m.*; carne
trita, *f.*; guazzetto, ragù, *m.* ¶ *v.t.*
tritare, sminuzzare. *to make a* ~ *of*
(*fig.*), impasticciare.

hasp, *n.* fermaglio, *m.*

hassock, *n.* inginocchiatoio, cuscino, *m.*

haste, *n.* fretta; precipitazione;
prestezza, *f. to* [*make*] ~ & **hasten**,
v.i. affrettarsi, darsi fretta, far
presto. **hasten**, *v.t.* affrettare,
accelerare; precipitare; sollecitare.
hasty, *a.* frettoloso; rapido, pronto,
precipitato; (*temper*) irritabile,
collerico.

hat, *n.* cappello, *m.* ~ & *coat stand*,
attaccapanni, *m.inv.* ~ *box*, cappelliera, *f.* ~ *brush*, setolino, *m.*;
spazzola da cappelli, *f.* ~ *peg*,
portacappelli, *m.inv.* ~ *shop* &
~ *trade*, cappelleria, *f.* ~*s off!*
giú i cappelli!

hatch (*brood*), *n.* covata, *f.* ~[*way*],
n. boccaporto, *m.* ¶ *v.i.* (*eggs*)
uscire dall'uovo; (*v.t.*) covare; (*fig.*)
ordire, macchinare, complottare;
(*engrave*) tratteggiare.

hatchet, *n.* accetta, *f.* ~ *face*, faccia
con lineamenti sporgenti.

hatching, *n.* covatura, *f.*; (*engraving*)
tratteggio, *m.*; ombreggiatura, *f.*

hatchment, *n.* stemma, *m.*

hate, *n.* odio, *m.* ¶ *v.t.* odiare, avere
in odio. ~**ful**, *a.* odioso. **hater**, *n.*
odiatore, *m.*, -trice, *f.* **hatred**, *n.*
odio, *m. full of* ~, pieno di odio.

hatter, *n.* cappellaio, *m.*

haughtily, *ad.* .eramente, altezzosa-
mente. **haughtiness**, *n.* fierezza,
alterigia, *f.* **haughty**, *a.* altero,
fiero, superbo.

haul, *n.* (*fish*) retata, *f.* ¶ *v.t.* tirare,
alare, trascinare. ~ *down*, (*flag*,
sails) ammainare. ~*age contractor*,
imprenditore di trasporti, *m.*

haunch, *n.* anca, coscia, *f.*; (*meat*)
quarto, *m.*; (*Arch.*) braccio, *m.*

haunt, *n.* soggiorno, ritiro, ridotto, *m.*
¶ *v.t.* frequentare; ossessionare;
infestare. ~**ed**, infestato dagli spiriti.

hautboy (*Mus.*), *n.* oboe, *m.*

Havana, *n.* l'Avana, *f.* ~ [*cigar*],
avana, sigaro avana, *m.*

have, *v.t. ir.* avere; tenere; possedere;
prendere; fare. ~ *on* (*wear*), indossare, portare, vestirsi di. ~ *you
finished?* (*Teleph.*) avete finito di

parlare?

haven, *n.* porto, *m.*; (*fig.*) asilo,
rifugio, riparo, *m.*

haversack, *n.* bisaccia, *f.* tascapane,
m.inv.

havoc, *n.* strage, *f.*; guasto, *m.*;
devastazione, rovina, *f.*

Havre, *n.* Havre, *f.*

haw, (*Bot.*) *a.* bacca del biancospino, *f.*
~*finch*, becco duro, *m.* ~*thorn*,
biancospino, *m.* ¶ *v.i.* biascicare.

Hawaii, *n.* le isole Havai, *f.pl.*
~**an**, *a.* havaiano.

hawk, *n.* falco, sparviere, *m.* ¶ *v.i.*
cacciare col falco; (*throat*) liberare
la gola dalla flemma tossendo; (*v.t.*)
portare in giro per la vendita.
~**er**, *n.* merciaiuolo ambulante, *m.*
~**ing**, (*Falconry*) *n.* caccia col
falco, falconeria, *f.*

hawser, *n.* gherlino, *m.*; alza a,
gomena, *f.*

hay, *n.* fieno, *m.* ~*cock*, mucchio di
fieno, *m.* ~ *fever*, febbre da fieno,
f., catarro estivo, *m.* ~ *loft*, fienile,
m. ~*maker*, falciatore, *m.* ~*making*,
fienagione, *f.* ~*rick*, ~*stack*,
pagliaio di fieno, *m.*

Hayti, *n.* Haiti, *f.*

hazard, *n.* azzardo, rischio; caso, *m.*;
(*Golf*) ostacolo, *m.* ¶ *v.t.* arrischiare,
rischiare, azzardare. ~**ous**, *a.*
rischioso, arrischiato, temerario.

haze, *n.* nebbia, nebbiosità, bruma, *f.*

hazel, *n.* avellano, nocciuolo; (*att.*,
colour, *eyes*) bruno, chiaro, nocciuolo. ~ *nut*, avellana, nocciuola, *f.*

hazy, *a.* nebbioso, nebuloso, brumoso.

he, *pn.* egli, ei, esso; lui; quegli, colui.
¶ *n.* & *att.* maschio, *a.* & *m.*
~ *goat*, caprone, *m.*

head, *n.* testa, *f.*; capo, *m.*; cervello,
m.; titolo, *m.*; rubrica; sorgente,
origine, *f.*; termine, *m.*; estremità, *f.*;
fondo, *m.*; testata; cima, *f.*; pomo;
rostro, *m.*; (*of hair*) capigliatura,
capellatura, *f.*; (*bed*) capezzale, *m.*;
(*on glass of beer*) schiuma, *f.*; (*coin*)
faccia, *f.*; (*book page*), testa, *f.*,
taglio superiore, *m.* (*ship*) prua,
prora, *f.* (*spear*, &*c.*) ferro, *m.*;
punta, (*steam*) pressione, *f.*
~*s or tails?* faccia o pila? ~*ache*,
mal di capo, *m.*; emicrania, *f.*
~ *band*, benda, *f.*; (*bookb.*) capitello,
m. ~ *clerk*, capo-commesso, *m.*
~ *cook*, capo-cuoco, *m.* ~*dress*,
~*gear*, pettinatura, acconciatura del
capo; cuffia, *f.* ~*land*, capo,
promontorio, *m.* ~*light*, fanale di
prora, *m.*; (*motor*) faro, fanale, *m.*

~*line* (*book*), intestazione, *f.*; titolo corrente, *m.* (*news*) rubrica, *f.* ~*long*, *a.* precipitato, avventato; (*ad.*) a capo fitto, precipitosamente. ~ *master*, principale, rettore, direttore, *m.* ~ *of a family*, capo [di una] famiglia, capoccia, *m.* ~ *mastership*, direttorato, *m.* ~ *mistress*, direttrice, *f.* ~ *of shoots*, ceppo, *m.* ~ *office*, ufficio principale, *m.*; sede primaria, *f.* ~-*on collision*, urto frontale, *m.* ~*phones*, cuffia, *f.* ~*quarters*, amministrazione centrale, *f.*; ufficio centrale, *m.*; (*staff*) stato maggiore, quartiere generale, *m.* ~ *register* or *voice*, voce di testa, *f.* ~*room*, spazio per muoversi, *m.* ~*sman*, boia, carnefice, giustiziere, *m.* ~ *stall*, capestro, *m.*; cavezza, testiera, *f.* ~*stone*, pietra angolare; pietra sepolcrale, *f.* ~*strong*, testardo, ostinato, pertinace. ~ *waiter*, capocameriere, *m.* ~*waters*, sorgente, *f.* ~*way*, progresso, cammino, *m.*; (*Naut.*) abbrivo, *m.* ~*wind*, vento di prua, *m.* ¶ *v.t.* capeggiare; capitanare; condurre, dirigere; essere a capo di, mettersi alla testa di; intestare, intitolare, dare il titolo a. ~ *the procession*, essere a capo di. ~*ed* (*paper*), *p.a.* intestato, intitolato. ~*ing*, *n.* intestazione, rubrica, *f.*; titolo, *m.* ~*y*, (*liquor*) *a.* forte, che dà alla testa, inebriante.

heal, *v.t.* guarire, risanare; (*fig.*) rimediare a; (*v.i.*) guarire; cicatrizzarsi. ~*er*, *n.* risanatore, guaritore, *m.*; (*of time*) medicina, *f.* ~*ing*, *n.* guarigione, *f.*; risanamento, *m.* ¶ *a.* risanatore, *m.*, -trice, *f.*; curativo.

health, *n.* salute, *f.*; (*toast*) brindisi *m.* ~ *officer*, medico dell'ufficio sanitario. bill of ~, patente di sanità, *f.* ~ *resort*, stazione climatica, *f.*; luogo di cura, *m.* ~*y*, *a.* sano, in buona salute, salubre.

heap, *n.* mucchio, monte, *m.*; catasta, massa, *f.*; ammasso, *m.* ¶ *v.t.* or ~ up, ammucchiare, accatastare, ammassare.

hear, *v.t.* & *t.ir.* sentire, udire, ascoltare, intendere; (*witness, Law*) esaminare; (*learn*) apprendere; (*prayer*) esaudire. ~ *from*, ricevere notizie da. ~*er*, *n.* uditore, ascoltatore, *m.*, -trice, *f.* ~*ing*, *n.* udito, *m.*; udienza, *f.*; esame di

testimoni, *m.* *to be hard of* ~, essere duro d'orecchio, avere l'udito grosso. ~ *say*, sentita dire, diceria, voce, informazione di seconda mano, *f.*

hearken, *v.i.* ascoltare, stare attento, prestare attenzione.

hearse, *n.* carro funebre, *m.*

heart, *n.* cuore; centro, punto centrale; affetto, coraggio, *m.*; anima, *f.*; fondo, *m.*; (*cabbage, &c.*) grumolo, *m.* *by* ~, a mente, a memoria. ~ & *soul* (*fig.*), anima e corpo. ~*break*, crepacuore, *m.* ~*breaking*, ~*rending*, straziante. ~*burn*, bruciori di stomaco, *m.pl.* ~ *case*, (*pers.*) cardiaco, *m.*, -a, *f.* ~ *disease*, malattia di cuore, *f.* *in one's* ~ *of* ~*s*, nel fondo del cuore, in fondo all'anima. ~*en*, *v.t.* animare, incoraggiare, rassicurare. ~*felt*, vivo, di cuore, profondamente sentito. *to be* ~*less*, essere senza cuore. ~*less person*, inumano, chi ha il cuore duro, insensibile. **heartsease** (*Bot.*), viola del pensiero, *f.*

hearth, *n.* focolare, camino, *m.* ~ *brush*, granata per caminetti, *f.* ~*rug*, tappeto, *m.* (stuoia, *f.*), pel focolare. ~*stone*, pietra del focolare *f.*; (*whitening*), pietra arenaria, *f.*

heartily, *ad.* cordialmente, di cuore; francamente; profondamente; di buon appetito. **hearty**, *a.* cordiale, di cuore, forte, sano, robusto; (*fit*) disposto; (*laugh*) grossa risata, risata di cuore, *f.*; (*meal*) buono, abbondante, copioso. *hale* & ~, sano e rubizzo.

heat, *n.* calore, caldo, *m.*; afa, *f.*; temperatura (elevata), *f.*; (*fig.*) ardore, calore, fuoco, *m.*; foga, animosità, collera, *f.*; (*Sport*) prova, *f.*; (*animals*) eccitamento sessuale, *m.* ~ *lightning*, baleno secco, *m.*, lampi estivi, *m.pl.* ~ *stroke*, colpo di sole, *m.* ~*wave*, ondata di calore, *f.* ¶ *v.t.* riscaldare; infiammare. ~*er*, *n.* riscaldatore, *m.*; (*bath*) scaldabagno, *m.inv.*; (*feet*) scaldino, *m.*; scaldapiedi, *m.inv.*; (*food*) scaldavivande, scaldapiatti, *m.inv.* *immersion* ~ (*Elec.*), resistenza corazzata, *f.*

heath, *n.* (*land*) brughiera, landa, *f.*; (*shrub*) erica, scopa, *f.* ~ *cock*, gallo di brughiera, *m.*

heathen, *n.* pagano, *m.*, -a, *f.* ~[*ish*], *a.* pagano. ~*ism*, *n.* paganesimo, *m.*

heather, *n.* erica, scopa, *f.*

heating, *n.* riscaldamento, *m.* *central* ~, r. centrale, *m.* ~ *apparatus,* calorifero, termosifone, *m.*

heave, *v.t.* *ir.* sollevare; gettare; (*anchor*) levare; (*lead*) gettare; spingere; tirare; (*sigh*) emettere, mandare; (*v.i.*) sollevarsi, gonfiarsi; palpitare; (*retch*) recere. ~ *to* (*Naut.*), mettere in panna, fermare.

heaven, *n.* cielo, *m.*; cieli, *m.pl.* ~ly, *a.* celeste, divino.

heavier than air machine, apparecchio piú pesante dell'aria, aeroplano, *m.* **heavily,** *ad.* pesantemente, di peso, con difficoltà. **heaviness,** *n.* pesantezza, *f.* **heavy,** *a.* pesante, grave, carico; forte, grosso, rilevante. ~ *cheeked,* con guancia paffuta. ~ *fish,* pesce grosso, *m.* ~ *fishing,* pesca del pesce grosso, *f.* ~ *shell* (*Artil.*), proiettile pesante, *m.*; (*armour piercing*) granata perforante, *f.* ~*weight* (*for lifting or throwing*), peso, *m.* (*Box.*) peso massimo, *m.*

Hebraic & **Hebrew,** *a.* ebraico, ebreo. **Hebrew** (*language*), *n.* l'ebraico, *m.*, lingua ebraica, *f.*

Hebrides, *n.pl.* Ebridi, *f.pl.*

hecatomb, *n.* ecatombe, *f.*

heckle, *v.t.* rivolgere domande imbarazzanti ad un candidato alle elezioni.

hectic (*fever*), *a.* etico, tisico.

hector, *n.* millantatore, bravaccione, smargiassone, *m.* ¶ *v.t.* insolentire, malmenare; (*v.i.*) fare lo spaccone.

hedge, *n.* siepe, *f.*; (*fig.*) barriera, protezione, *f.* ~*hog,* riccio, *m.* ~*row,* siepe, *f.*; filare di alberelli, *m.* ~*sparrow,* passera scopaiola, *f.* ¶ *v.t.* piantare (una siepe); cingere di siepe; (*v.i.*) evadere una domanda, mettersi al coperto. ~ *in,* assiepare.

heed, *n.* attenzione, cura, retta; precauzione, *f.* ¶ *v.t.* badare a, dare retta a, prestare attenzione a. ~*less,* *a.* disattento, negligente, sbadato.

heel, *n.* calcagno; tallone; tacco, *m.*; (*rubber*) tacco di gomma; (*Naut.*) piede, calcagnolo, *m.* *at the* ~*s of,* alle calcagna di. *down at* ~*s,* scalcagnato; (*fig.*) d'apparenza sciatta; *head over* ~*s,* sottosopra, sossopra, a capitombolo. *to turn head over* ~*s,* fare i capitomboli.

hefty, *a.* forte, gagliardo, robusto.

hegemony, *n.* egemonia, *f.*

heifer, *n.* giovenca, *f.*

height, *n.* altezza; altura, elevazione; sommità; piena; cima, *f.*; colmo, apogeo, *m.*; (*star*) altitudine, *f.*; (*stature*) statura, *f.*; (*of summer*) colmo dell'estate, cuore dell'estate, *m.* ~**en,** *v.t.* accrescere, aumentare, intensificare; fare spiccare, mettere in rilievo; innalzare.

heinous, *a.* enorme, atroce.

heir, *n.* erede, *m.*; erede, ereditiera, *f.* ~*loom,* mobile inalienabile, *m.* ~*ship,* eredità, *f.*

helianthus, *n.* elianto, *m.*

helical, *a.* ad elica, a spirale.

helicopter, *n.* elicottero, *m.*

heliotrope, *n.* eliotropio, *m.*

helium, *n.* elio, *m.*

helix, *n.* elica, spirale, *f.*; (*ear*) elice, *f.*

hell, *n.* inferno, *m.*; (*gambling*) bisca, *f.* ~*cat,* furia, stregonaccia, *f.*

Hellenism, *n.* ellenismo, *m.*

hellish, *a.* diabolico, infernale.

hello (*Teleph.*), *i.* pronto!

helm, *n.* timone, *m.*; (*fig.*) timone, *m.* guida, *f.* **helmsman,** timoniere, *m.*

helmet, *n.* elmo, elmetto; casco, *m.*

helot, *n.* ilota, *m.* ~*ism,* *n.* ilotismo, *m.*

help, *n.* aiuto, soccorso, *m.*; assistenza, *f.*; servo, *m.*, -a, *f.*; domestico, *m.*, -a, *f.* ¶ *v.t.* & *i.* aiutare, soccorrere, assistere; servire; rimediare a; evitare. ~ *one another,* aiutarsi (l'un l'altro). ~*!* aiuto! al soccorso! ~ *it,* non posso farci nulla. *I cannot not* ~ *it,* non potevo fare altrimenti. *it cannot be* ~*ed,* non c'è da farci nulla. *one cannot* ~ *admiring him,* non si può fare a meno di ammirarlo. ~**er,** *n.* aiutatore, *m.,* -trice, *f.*; aiutante, *m.f.* ~*ful* & ~*ing,* *a.* soccorrevole, d'aiuto, utile. ~*ing* (*food*), porzione, *f.* ~*less,* *a.* senza soccorso, impotente, incapace. ~*mate,* *n.* socio, *m.*; consorte, *m.f.*

helter-skelter, *ad.* alla rinfusa.

helve, *n.* manico, *m.*

hem, *n.* orlo, *m.*; bordura, *f.* ¶ *v.t.* orlare; fregiare; (*v.i.*) schiarirsi la voce, esitare nel parlare. ~ *in,* cingere, circondare, investire.

hematite, *n.* ematite, *f.*

hemisphere, *n.* emisfero, *m.*

hemlock, *n.* cicuta, *f.*

hemorrhage, *n.* emorragia, *f.*

hemorrhoids, *n.pl.* emorroidi, *f.pl.*

hemming, *n.* orlatura, *f.*

hemp, n. canapa, f. ~ seed, seme di canapa, m. ~[en], a. di canapa.
hemstitch, n. punto d'orlo, m. ¶ v.t. orlare a giorno.
hen, n. gallina, f.; chioccia, f. ~coop, stia, gabbia, f. ~house, pollaio, m. ~ partridge, pernice, f. ~pecked, malmenato dalla moglie, (uno) di cui la moglie porta i calzoni. ~ pheasant, fagiana, f. ~roost, pollaio, posatoio, m.
hence, ad. di qua, di qui; donde, per conseguenza; quindi, perciò. six months ~, di qui a sei mesi. ~forth, ~ forward, ad. d'ora innanzi, per l'avvenire, ormai.
henchman, n. paggio, partigiano, seguace, m.
henna, n. ennè, m.
her, pn. & a. la, lei; di lei, suo, (sua, sue, suoi). to ~, le, a lei.
herald, n. (Hist.) araldo, m.; (fig.) messaggero, m. ¶ v.t. annunciare, proclamare. ~ic, a. araldico. ~ry, n. araldica, f.; blasone, m.
herb, n. erba, f. ~aceous, a. erbaceo. ~ border, bordura di fiori vivaci, f. ~age, n. erbaggio, m. ~al, n. elenco di erbe medicinali, m. ~alist, n. erborista, m.f. ~arium, n. erbario, m. ~ivorous, a. & ~ animal, erbivoro, a. & m. **herborize,** v.i. erborizzare.
Herculean, a. erculeo. a Hercules, un ercole, un colosso, un gigante.
herd, n. gregge, m.; mandra, f.; (deer) branco, m. ~ book, libro genealogico, m. the (common) ~, il volgo, m. the ~ instinct, il sentimento gregario, m. ~ together, associarsi, mescolarsi, vivere in gregge. ~ed together, ammucchiato. **herdsman,** n. mandriano, pastore, m.
here, ad. ci, qui, qua, di qui, di qua; presente! neither ~ nor there, né qui né altrove; di poca importanza. ~ below, quaggiù. ~ I am, eccomi. ~ is, ~ are, ecco. ~ lies (grave), qui giace. [look] ~! guardate, ascoltate! **hereabout[s],** ad. qui presso, qui vicino; all'intorno. **hereafter,** ad. d'ora innanzi, per l'avvenire; nell'altro mondo. **hereby** (Law), ad. col presente atto.
hereditament, n. bene stabile, m.; eredità, f. **hereditary,** a. ereditario. **heredity,** n. eredità, f.
herein (Law), ad. qui accluso, qui allegato. **hereinafter,** ad. dopo, più sotto.

heresy, n. eresia, f. **heretic,** n. eretico, m. ~al, a. eretico.
hereunder, ad. qui sotto. **hereupon,** ad. su questo, su ciò, allora, in quella, lassù. **herewith,** ad. con ciò, con questo; qui accluso, qui allegato, qui unito, con la presente.
heritage, n. eredità, f.
hermaphrodite, n. ermafrodito, m.
hermetic, a. ermetico.
hermit, n. eremita, romito, m. ~ crab, paguro bernardo, m. ~age, n. eremitaggio, romitorio, m.
hernia, n. ernia, f.
hero, n. eroe, m.; (fig. drama) protagonista, m. ~ worship, culto degli eroi, m. ~ic, a. eroico. ~icomic, a. eroicomico. ~ine, n. eroina, f. ~ism, n. eroismo, m.
heron, n. airone, m. ~ry, n. luogo dove si allevano gli aironi.
herpes, n. erpete, m.
herring, n. aringa, f. ~ boat, barca da pesca per le aringhe. ~boning (Need.), punto incrociato, m. ~ fishery (& ~ season), pesca delle aringhe, f.
hers, pn. il suo, la sua, i suoi, le sue; di lei. **herself,** pn. ella medesima, lei medesima, essa medesima, lei stessa, essa stessa; sé.
hesitate, v.i. esitare; essere incerto, essere in dubbio; titubare. **hesitation,** n. esitazione, f.
heterodox, a. eterodosso.
hew, v.t. ir. (tree) tagliare, abbattere; (stone) tagliare.
hexagon, n. esagono, m. ~al, a. esagonale. ~ nut, dado esagonale, m. **hexameter,** n. esametro, m.
heyday of life, i più bei giorni della vita, m.pl.; il fiore dell'età, m.
hi, i. olà!
hiatus, n. lacuna, fessura, f.; (Gram.) iato, m.
hibernate (Zool.), v.i. fare l'ibernante.
hiccup, n. singulto, singhiozzo, m. ¶ v.i. avere il singulto.
hidden, p.a. nascosto, celato; latente; misterioso, occulto. ~ from sight, sottratto alla vista. **hide,** v.t. ir. nascondere, celare. ~ [oneself], nascondersi. ~-&-seek, moscacieca. ~ bound (fig.), intrattabile, ostinato.
hide, n. pelle, f.
hideous, a. bruttissimo, ripulsivo, orribile.
hiding (thrashing), n. bastonatura, f.; legnate, f.pl.
hiding place, nascondiglio, m.
hierarchy, n. gerarchia, f.

hieroglyph, *n.* geroglifico, *m.*

higgle, *v.i.* lesinare sul prezzo, stiracchiare.

higgledy-piggledy, *ad.* a catafascio, alla rinfusa.

high, *a.* alto, elevato, superiore; illustre, importante, grande; forte, violento; (*dear*) caro; (*meat*) passato; (*game*) guastato; (*in height*) grande, alto, dell'altezza di. ~ *altar,* altare maggiore, *m.* ~ *& dry* (*Naut.*), a secco, sulla spiaggia. ~*-born,* nobile, di alta nascita. ~*-class,* distinto, superiore, d'alta classe; (*wine*) di prima qualità. ~ *collar,* colletto rigido, *m.* ~ *coloured,* di carnagione viva, di colore vivace. ~ *dive,* tuffo da una grande altezza, *m.* ~ *flown,* ampolloso, altosonante. ~ *flying,* ambizioso. ~ *gear* (*Motor*) quarta velocità, presa diretta, *f.* ~*-handed,* prepotente, arbitrario. ~ *hat,* cappello alto, cappello a cilindro. ~ *heeled,* a tacco alto, coi tacchi alti. ~ *jump,* salto in altezza, *m.* ~*lights* (*Art.*), lumi, lumeggiamenti, *m.pl.* ~ *mass,* messa grande, messa cantata, *f.* ~ *priest,* gran sacerdote, *m.* ~ *society,* ~ *life,* alta società, *f.*; gran mondo, *m.* ~*-speed steel,* acciaio rapido, *m.* ~ *tide,* ~ *water,* alta marea, piena marea, *f.* ~*-water mark,* livello dell'alta marea, *m.*; (*fig.*) apogeo, *m.* ~*way,* strada pubblica, strada maestra, *f.* ~*way code,* codice stradale, *m.* ~*wayman,* bandito, grassatore, *m.* ~*way robbery,* grassazione, *f.* *to come to* ~ *words,* bisticciare, venire a parolacce. ¶ *ad.* alto, forte, altamente, fòrtemente, in alto. ~ *pitched* (*roof*), a pendenza ripida. ~*er,* *a.* più alto, superiore. ~ *bid,* maggiore offerta, *f.* ~ *education,* insegnamento superiore, *m.* ~ *mathematics,* matematica superiore, *f.* ~ *notes* (*Mus.*), note più alte, *f.pl.*, (*voice*) strillante, acuto. *the* ~*est bidder,* il (la) miglior offerente, il (la) maggior offerente, *m.f.* ~*ly,* *ad.* altamente; grandemente; molto; eminentemente; caldamente; potentemente; vivamente. ~ *amusing,* bizzarro, impagabile. ~ *strung,* eccitabile, pieno d'ardore. ~*ness,* *n.* altezza; intensità, *f.*; (*title*) Altezza, *f.*

highland, *a.* dell'altipiano, di paese di montagna. ¶ *n.* H~s, *pl.* paese di montagna, *m.*; altipiani, *m.pl.* ~*er,* montanaro, *m.*

hiker, *n.* escursionista a piedi, *m.f.*

hilarious, *a.* ilare. **hilarity,** *n.* ilarità, *f.*

hill, *n.* colle, *m.*; collina, *f.*; poggio, *m.*; altura, *f.*; (*reference map*) quota, *f.* ~ *climb,* ascensione, scalata (d'un colle, d'una montagna), *f.* *up* ~ *& down dale,* per monti e per valli. ¶ (*Hort.*) *v.t.* rincalzare, coprire di terra. **hillock,** *n.* monticello, *m.*; collinetta, *f.* **hilly,** *a.* collinoso, montuoso, accidentato.

hilt, *n.* elsa, impugnatura, guardia (di spada), *f.*

him, *pn.* lo, lui, quello, colui. **himself,** *pn.* egli stesso, lui stesso, lui medesimo; sé stesso, sé medesimo; sé, si; *to* ~, gli, a lui.

Himalaya, *n.* Imalaia, *f.*

hind (*deer*), *n.* cerva, *f.*

hind[er], *a.* posteriore, di dietro.

hinder, *v.t.* impedire, ostacolare; intralciare; ritardare.

hindmost, *a.* ultimo, il più indietro.

hindrance, *n.* ostacolo, impedimento, inciampo, intoppo, ingombro, *m.* *without* ~, senza ostacoli, senz'ingombro.

Hindu, -doo, *a.* indiano. ¶ *n.* Indù, *m.f.* **Hindustani,** *n.* l'indostano, *m.*

hinge, *n.* cardine, *m.*; cerniera, *f.*; ganghero, *m.*; perno, *m.*; (*fig.*) perno, *m.* ¶ *v.i.* imperniarsi, incardinarsi, girare su; (*fig.*) dipendere, volgersi su. ~*d,* *p.a.* incardinato, imperniato.

hinny, *n.* mulo, muletto, bardotto, *m.* ¶ *v.i.* nitrire.

hint, *n.* accenno, cenno, avviso, *m.*; insinuazione, idea, *f.* ¶ *v.t.* accennare, dare cenno, dare ad intendere. ~ *at,* suggerire, insinuare, fare intravedere.

hip, *n.* anca, *f.*; fianco, *m.*; (*Arch.*) padiglione, *m.* ~ *bath,* semicupio, *m.* ~ *pocket,* tasca dei calzoni, *f.* ~ *measurement,* misura delle anche, *f.*

hippodrome, *n.* ippodromo, *m.*

hippopotamus, *n.* ippopotamo, *m.*

hire, *n.* nolo, noleggio; affitto, fitto, *m.*; pigione, locazione, *f.* ~ *purchase,* ~ *system,* vendita a rate, *f.* ¶ *v.t.* noleggiare, prendere (dare) a nolo; affittare, prendere (dare) in affitto, appigionare, locare; (*assassin, &c.*) corrompere, comprare. ~*d,* *p.p.* noleggiato, affittato, locato, appigionato; mercenario. ~ *carriage,* carrozza da nolo, vettura da nolo, *f.*

~ling, *n.* mercenario, *m.* hirer, *n.* noleggiatore, *m.*, -trice, *f.*

hirsute, *a.* irsuto, peloso.

his, *pn. & a.* (il) suo, (la) sua, (i) suoi, (le) sue; di lui.

hiss, *v.t. & i.* fischiare, sibilare. ~[ing], *n.* fischio, *m.*; fischiata, *f.*; sibilo, sibilio, *m.*

historian, *n.* storico, *m.*, -a, *f.* historiated, *a.* istoriato. historic & historical, *a.* storico. history, *n.* storia, *f.*

histrion, *n.* istrione, *m.* ~ic, *a.* istrionico, del teatro.

hit, *n.* (*lit. & fig.*) colpo, *m.* a ~! (*fencing*) toccato! *lucky* ~, buon colpo, colpo felice, successo, *m.*, trovata, *f.* ~ *or miss*, checchè avvenga. ¶ *v.t. ir.* colpire, percuotere, battere. ~ *the mark*, cogliere nel segno, dare nel segno, raggiungere il segno. ~ *it off* (*with*), accordarsi, essere d'accordo (con). ~ *out*, menare colpi forti, diventare aggressivo. ~ *upon*, rincontrare, imbattersi in, scoprire.

hitch, *n.* ostacolo, intoppo, nodo, *m.* ¶ *v.t.* attaccare, appendere.

hither, (*Geog.*) *a.* citeriore. ~ & *thither*, qua e là. ~to, *ad.* finora, fin qui, fino al presente, fino ad ora.

hive, *n.* alveare, *m.*; arnia, *f.*; bugno, *m.*

hoard, *n.* gruzzolo, tesoro, ammasso, *m.* ¶ *v.t.* accumulare, ammassare; (*v.i.*) fare il gruzzolo. ~er, *n.* incettatore, *m.*, -trice, *f.*; avaro, *m.*, -a, *f.*

hoarding, *n.* (*scaffolding*) impalancato, assito, *m.*; (*saving*) accumulazione, economia, *f.*

hoar frost, brina, *f.*

hoarhound, *n.* (*Bot.*) marrubio, *m.*

hoarse, *a.* rauco, fioco. ~ness, *n.* raucedine, fiocaggine, *f.*

hoary, *a.* bianco, canuto, vecchio; dai capelli bianchi.

hoax, *n.* canzonatura, mistificazione, *f.*; inganno, scherzo di cattivo genere, *m.* ¶ *v.t.* mistificare, ingannare, canzonare. (*v.i.*) piantar carote. ~er, *n.* mistificatore, ingannatore, *m.*

hobble, *v.i.* zoppicare; (*v.t.*) impastoiare, far zoppicare. hobbledehoy, *n.* giovanotto (adolescente) goffo, *m.* hobbling along, zoppicante, zoppicando.

hobby, *n.* (*bird*) falco, *m. an art. collecting, gardening*). is his ~, è amatore di . . . , è la sua distrazione; (*a sport*) is his ~, è la sua

passione. ~ *horse*, cavallo di legno; (*fig.*) ticchio, *m.*, fissazione, *f.*

hobgoblin, *n.* demonietto, folletto, *m.*

hobnail, *n.* chiodo grosso da stivale, *m.* ~ed, *p.a.* ferrato, dalle scarpe chiodate, fornito di bullette.

hob-nob with, dare del tu a; trincare con.

Hobson's choice (it is), (è una) scelta forzata.

hock, *n.* vino bianco del Reno; (*horse*) garretto, *m.*

hockey, *n.* hockey, *m.*; palla al maglio, *f.* ~ *skates*, pattini da'hockey'sul ghiaccio. ~ *stick*, bastone da 'hockey'. ice ~, disco sul ghiaccio, *m.*

hocus, *v.t.* ingannare; narcotizzare. ~ pocus, *n.* gherminelle, *f.pl.*; giuoco di prestigio, *m.*

hod, *n.* vassoio da muratore, trogolo portatile da calcina, *m.*

Hodge (*Eng.*), *n.* campagnuolo, *m.*

hoe, *n.* zappa, zappetta, *f.*; (*mattock*) marra, *f.* ¶ *v.t.* zappare.

hog, *n.* maiale, porco, *m.* ~backed, a schiena d'asino, inarcato. hoggish, *a.* da porco, bestiale.

hogshead, *n.* botte (della capacità di 54 galloni o di 238 litri), *f.* hogwash, risciacquatura di porci, *f.*

hoist, *n.* paranco, *m.*; montacarichi, *m.inv.*; ascensore, *m.* ¶ *v.t.*inalzare, ghindare, sollevare; (*flag*) issare, inalberare.

hold, *n.* presa, stretta, *f.*; impugnatura, abbracciatura, *f.*; sostegno, *m.*; influenza, *f.*; potere, *m.*; rocca, fortezza, *f.*; (*Box.*) presa, *f.*; (*ship*) stiva, *f.* ¶ *v.t.* tenere; contenere; possedere, avere; occupare; arrestare, trattenere; custodire; celebrare; reggere; tenere per, riguardare come; ritenere, pensare, stimare. ~all, portamantelli, *m.* ~ *back*, ~ *in*, ritenere, tenere per sé, tenersi (starsene) indietro. ~ *fast*, tenere fermo, tener saldo, tener duro, attaccarsi a. ~ *forth*, discorrere, perorare. ~ *on*, perseverare, tenersi fermo, continuare a resistere. ~ *on!* ~ *the line!* (*Teleph.*) rimanete all'apparecchio! tenete la comunicazione! ~ *one's own*, mantenere la propria posizione, continuare a resistere. ~ *one's nose*, turarsi il naso. ~ *one's tongue*, tacere, star zitto, tenere la lingua a freno. ~ *out*, resistere, tener fermo; durare; porgere, dare, offrire. ~ *up*, alzare, sollevare;

sopportare, sostenere; esporre;
arrestare, ostruire; (*v.i.*) (*pop.*) non
piovere, restar chiaro. ~**er**, *n.*
astuccio, *m.*; asticciuola, *f.*; fodero,
m.; guaina, *f.*; ricettacolo, *m.*;
in compounds *porta-*, always, *m.*,
e.g. *paper*~, portacarte; *pencil*~,
portalapis, *pen*~, portapenne,
m.inv.; (*pers.*) possessore, *m.*, -a,
f.; portatore, *m.*, -trice, *f.*;
detentore, *m.*, -trice, *f.*; latore, *m.*,
-trice, *f.* ~**ing**, *n.* tenuta, *f.*;
possesso, *m.*; cosa posseduta, *f.*

hole, *n.* buca, *f.*; buco, *m.*; apertura,
f.; orifizio, *m.*; foro, *m.*; (*fox's*) tana,
volpaia, *f.*; (*Golf*) buca, *f.* ~ *-&-
corner*, clandestino, segreto, di
soppiatto. ¶ *v.t.* bucare, perforare,
forare; scavare; (*Golf*) fare entrare
nella buca.

holiday, *n.* festa, *f.*; giorno festivo,
giorno di festa, *m.*; vacanza, villeggiatura, *f.*; (*pl.*) ferie, vacanze, *f.pl.*
~ *camp*, colonia di vacanze, *f.*
~ *resort*, luogo di villeggiatura, *m.*
holily, *ad.* santamente. **holiness**, *n.*
santità, *f.* *His H*~, Sua Santità.
Holland, (*Geog.*), *n.* l'Olanda, *f.*
~**s** [*gin*], *n.* ginepro olandese, *m.*
h~, *n.* tela d'Olanda, *f.*
hollo, *v.t.* gridare, vociare.
hollow, *a.* cavo, vuoto, cavernoso,
infossato; (*voice*) sordo. ~ *cheeked*,
dalle guancie infossate. ~ *ground*,
escavato, scanalato, cavernoso. *to
beat* ~, vincere del tutto. ¶ *n.*
cavo, *m.*; cavità, *f.*; depressione, *f.*;
(*Top.*) conca, *f.* ~ [*out*], *v.t.*
incavare, scanalare, scavare.
holly, *n.* agrifoglio, *m.* ~*berry*, bacca
dell'agrifoglio, dell'alloro spinoso, *f.*
hollyhock, *n.* malvarosa, *f.*
holm-oak, *n.* leccio, *m.*
holocaust, *n.* olocausto, *m.*; (*fig.*)
immolazione, *f.*; massacro, *m.*
holster, *n.* fonda, fondina, *f.*
holy, *a.* santo, sacro, consacrato;
(*bread, water*) benedetto; (*day*)
giorno santo, *m.*; festa, *f.* *Holy
Ghost, Holy Spirit*, Spirito Santo, *m.*
H~ *Land*, Terra Santa, *f.* ~
orders, ordini sacri, *m.pl.* *H*~ *See*,
Santa Sede, *f.* ~ *water basin*,
acquasantiera, *f.* ~ *water sprinkler*,
aspersorio, *m.* *H*~ *Writ*, Sacra
Scrittura, *f.* ~ *year*, Anno Santo, *m.*
homage, *n.* omaggio, *m.*
home, *n.* casa, dimora, *f.*; domicilio,
focolare, tetto domestico, *m.*; famiglia, patria, *f.*; asilo, ospizio, rifugio,
paese, *m.*; lari, penati, *m.pl.*;

(*Running*) meta, *f.*; punto d'arrivo,
m. ~ *for the aged*, ospizio per i
vecchi, *m.* *at* ~, see under *at*. ¶ *ad.*
a casa, verso casa, ritornato, di
ritorno, rientrato; all'interno, nel
paese; al vivo, direttamente. ¶ *a.*
domestico, casalingo, della casa,
della famiglia; paesano, del paese;
nostrano; nazionale, interno, indigeno. ~ *country*, patria, *f.*;
(*a*) paesano, indigeno. ~ *life*,
vita di famiglia, *f.* ~ *made wine*, vino
fatto in casa, *m.* *H*~ *Office* (*Eng.*),
Ministero dell'Interno, *m.* ~ *port*,
porto d'iscrizione, *m.* *H*~ *Rule*,
autonomia, *f.*; indipendenza legisla-
tiva, *f.* *H*~ *Secretary*, Ministro
dell'Interno, *m.* ~*sick*, nostalgico.
~*sickness*, nostalgia, *f.* ~ *trade*,
commercio interno, *m.*; (*ship*) grande
cabotaggio, *m.* ~ *truths*, fatti
spiacevoli circa sé stesso. ~*work*
(*Sch.*), compito fatto (scritto) a casa.
(*trade*) lavoro fatto a casa, articoli
fatti a casa. ~**less**, *a.* senza casa,
senza tetto. ~**liness**, *n.* modi
casalinghi, *m.pl.*; abitudini casa-
linghe, *f.pl.* **homely**, *a.* casalingo,
domestico, semplice.
homeopath, &c. Same as *homoeopath*, &c.
Homeric, *a.* omerico, d'Omero.
homespun, *n.* tela filata in casa, *f.*
homestead, *n.* casa colonica, *f.*
homeward, *a. & ad.* verso casa,
verso il proprio paese. ~ *bound*,
di ritorno. ~**s**, *ad.* verso casa,
verso il proprio paese.
homicidal, *a.* omicida, micidiale.
homicide, *n.* (*pers.*) omicida, *m.f.*;
(*act*) omicidio, *m.*
homily, *n.* omelia, *f.*; discorso, *m.*
homing pigeon, colombo messaggero
m.
homoeopath[**ist**], *n.* omeopatista;
medico omeopatico, *m.* **homoeo-
pathic**, *a.* omeopatico. **homoeo-
pathy**, *n.* omeopatia, *f.*
homogeneous, *a.* omogeneo.
homonym, *n.* omonimo, *m.*
hone, *n.* cote, *f.*
honest, *a.* probo, onesto, integro, leale,
franco, retto, diritto, giusto, sincero,
di buona fede. ~**y**, *n.* probità,
onestà, integrità, lealtà, sincerità,
buona fede, *f.*; (*Bot.*) lunaria, *f.*
honey, *n.* miele, *m.*; (*pers.*) carino, *m.*,
-a, *f.* coricino, *m.* ~ *bee*, ape
domestica, ape operaia, *f.* ~*comb*,
n. favo, *m.*; (*v.t.*) crivellare. ~*moon*,
luna di miele, *f.* ~*suckle*, capri-

foglio, *m.* **~ed,** *a.* addolcito, dolce (come il miele), melato.

honorarium, *n.* onorario, *m.*

honorary, *a.* onorario, onorifico, senza stipendio. ~ *membership,* iscrizione onoraria, *f.* **honour,** *n.* onore, *m.*; (*Com.*) accettazione, *f.*; (*Com.*) intervento, *m.* ~*s list,* lista di onorificenze, *f.* ¶ *v.t.* onorare, fare onore a; (*Com.*) accettare. ~**able,** *a.* onorevole, spettabile. ~ **mention,** accessit, *m.* ~**ed,** *p.a.* onorato, rispettato; (*Com.*) accetto.

hood, *n.* cappuccio, *m.*; (*carriage, motor*) mantice, *m.* ~**wink,** bendare (gli occhi a); (*fig.*) ingannare.

hoof, *n.* zoccolo, *m.*; unghia, *f.* ~**ed,** *a.* che ha (gli) zoccoli.

hook, *n.* uncino, gancio, rampino, *m.*; roncola, *f.*; (*sickle*) falce, *f.*; (*bill*~) ronca, *f.* roncone, *m.*; (*fish*) amo, *m.*; (*Box.*) hook, *m.* ~ *& eye,* gancio ad occhio. ~ *stick,* vincastro, *m.* *by* ~ *or by crook,* per amore o per forza, di ruffa o di raffa. ¶ *v.t.* agganciare, uncinare, aggraffare; prendere all'amo. ~[**ed**] (*nose*), *a.* aquilino.

hookah, *n.* narghilè, *m.*

hooligan, *n.* teppista, *m.* ~**ism,** *n.* teppismo, *m.*

hoop, *n.* cerchio, *m.* ~ *iron,* reggetta, *f.* ~ *skirt,* guardinfante, *m.*; crinolina, *f.* ¶ *v.t.* cerchiare, accerchiare.

hooping cough, tosse canina, ipertosse, *f.*

hoopoe, *n.* upupa, *f.*

hoot, *v.t.* fischiare; (*v.i.*) (*owl*) ululare; (*Motor*) suonare il corno. ~**er,** *n.* sirena, *f.*; corno, *m.* ~[**ing**] (*booing*), *n.* fischiata, baiata, *f.*

hop, *n.* salto su una gamba, piccolo salto, saltello, *m.*; capriola, danza, *f.* ~ (*plant*), luppolo, *m.* ~**field,** luppoliera, *f.* ~ *picking,* raccolto del luppolo, *m.* ~ *pole,* palo da luppoli, *m.* ¶ *v.t.* conciare (una bevanda) col luppolo; (*v.i.*) saltellare, fare piccoli salti; fare il raccolto del luppolo.

hope, *n.* speranza, *f.* ¶ *v.t. & i.* sperare. ~**ful,** *a.* pieno di speranza, speranzoso; fiducioso, incoraggiante. (*lad*) che promette bene. ~**less,** *a.* senza speranza, disperato.

hopper, *n.* (*Mach.*) tramoggia, *f.*

horde, *n.* orda, moltitudine, *f.*

horehound, *n.* marrubio, *m.*

horizon, *n.* orizzonte, *m.* **horizontal,** *a.* orizzontale.

horn, *n.* corno, cornetto, *m.*; (*pl. deer*) cornatura, *f.*; (*insect*) antenna, *f.*; (*gramophone*) braccio acustico, *m.* ~*beam,* carpino, *m.* ~ *of plenty,* cornucopia, *f.*; corno dell'abbondanza, *m.* ~*-rimmed spectacles,* occhiali cerchiati in corno, *m.pl.* *horned cattle,* bovini, *m.pl.*; grosso bestiame, *m.*

hornet, *n.* calabrone, *m.* ~*'s nest* (*fig.*), vespaio, *m.*

horny, *a.* di corno; (*hands*), calloso.

horology, *n.* orologeria, *f.*

horoscope, *n.* oroscopo, *m.*

horrible *&* **horrid,** *a.* orribile, orrido. **horror,** *n.* orrore, *m.*

hors-d'oeuvres, antipasto, *m.*

horse, *n.* cavallo, *m.*; (*pl.*) cavalleria, *f.*; cavalli, *m.pl.*; (*trestle*) cavalletto, *m.* ~ *artillery,* artiglieria a cavallo, *f.* *on* ~*back,* a cavallo. ~ *bean,* fava da foraggio, *f.* ~ *block,* montatoio, *m.* ~ *box,* vagone-scuderia. ~ *breaker,* domatore di cavalli, *m.* ~ *chestnut,* (*tree*) ippocastano, *m.* ~ *dealer,* negoziante di cavalli, *m.* ~ *flesh,* carne di cavallo, *f.* ~*fly,* mosca cavallina, *f.* ~ *gear,* finimenti (di cavallo), *m.pl.* ~*hair,* crine, *m.* ~*man,* cavaliere, cavalcatore, *m.* ~*manship,* equitazione, *f.*; maneggio, *m.* ~*play,* giuoco grossolano, *m.*; scherzo rozzo, *m.* ~ *pond,* abbeveratoio, *m.* ~*power,* cavallo-vapore (*Eng. h.p.* = 550 foot pounds per second; *It. h.p.* = 75 kilogrammetres per sec., or ·9863 of Eng. *h.p. a* 10 ~*-(power) car,* un auto a dieci cavalli. ~ *race,* corsa di cavalli, *f.* ~ *racing,* corse [di cavalli], *f.pl.* ~*-radish,* rafano, *m.*; barba forte, *f.* ~*shoe,* ferro di cavallo, *m.* ~ *show,* concorso ippico, *m.* ~ *species,* razza cavallina, *f.* ~ *tail plume,* criniera, *f.* ~*whip,* frusta, *f.*, frustino, *m.*, sferza, *f.*; (*v.t.*) frustare, sferzare. ~*woman,* cavalcatrice, cavallerizza, *f.*; amazzone, *f.* **horsy,** *a.* di cavallo, ippomane, amatore di cavalli.

horticultural, *a.* d'orticoltura. **horticulture,** *n.* orticultura, *f.* **horticulturalist,** *n.* orticoltore, *m.*

hosanna, *n.* osanna, *m.*

hose, *n.* (*Dress, col. as pl.*) calze, calzette, *f.pl.*; (*pipe*) tubo flessibile, *m.*, manichetta, *f.* **hosier,** *n.* calzettaio, *m.* ~**y,** *n.* maglieria, *f.*; calze, *f.pl.*, *&c.*

hospitable, *a.* ospitale. **hospital,** *n.* ospedale, *m.* ~ *attendant,* ~ *nurse,*

infermiere, *m.*, infermiera, *f.* ~
service, servizio ospitaliere, *m.*
~ *ship*, nave ospedale, *f.* **hospitality**, *n.* ospitalità, *f.*
host, *n.* (*pers.*) ospite, (*Lit.*) anfitrione;
oste, albergatore, *m.*; (*crowd, army*)
folla, moltitudine, *f.*; esercito, *m.*;
(*Eccl.*) ostia, *f.* ~**ess**, *n.* ospite,
ostessa, *f.*
hostage, *n.* ostaggio, *m.*; (*fig.*) pegno,
m.
hostel, *n.* ospizio, *m.*; casa (dello
studente, ecc.), *f.* ~**ry** (*archaic*), *n.*
osteria, *f.*; albergo, *m.*
hostile, *a.* ostile, nemico. **hostility**,
n. ostilità, *f.*
hostler, *n.* stalliere, *m.*
hot, *a.* caldo, ardente; focoso,
scottante, bruciante. *to get* ~ &
to run ~, riscaldarsi. *I gave it him*
~, gli ho dato una bella lavata di
capo. ~*bed*, (*Hort.*), concimaia, *f.*;
(*fig.*) officina, sorgente, *f.* ~ *cockles*,
(child's game) guancialino d'oro, *m.*
in ~ *haste*, in fretta e furia. ~*head*,
testa calda, *f.*, individuo impulsivo,
n. ~*headed*, impetuoso, impulsivo,
di cervello caldo, eccitabile,
violento, fiero. ~-*house*, serra, *f.*
~ *spring*, sorgente termale, *f.*
~*water bottle*, scaldapiedi, *m.inv.*,
borsa d'acqua calda, *f.*
hotchpotch, *n.* (*Cook.*) carne in
umido con cavoli, orzo, ecc.;
guazzabuglio, *m.*
hotel, *n.* albergo, *m.* ~ *keeper*,
albergatore, *m.*
hotly, *ad.* caldamente, vivamente,
violentemente.
hough, *n.* garretto, *m.*
hound, *n.* cane da caccia, bracco,
seguio, levriere, *m.*; (*bitch*) femmina
di un cane da caccia, *f.* ~ *on*,
incitare. ~ *out*, scacciare.
hour, *n.* ora, *f.* ~ *glass*, orologio a
polvere, *m.* ~ *hand*, lancetta (delle
ore), *f.* ~*ly*, *a.* che accade ogni ora;
(*ad.*) d'ora in ora, ad ogni ora.
house, *n.* casa, *f.*; dimora, *f.*; abitazione, *f.*; domicilio, *m.*; famiglia, *f.*;
camera, *f.*; ditta, *f.*; (*Theat.*) sala,
f.; (*with*) *neither* ~ *nor home*, senza
tetto. ~ *agency*, ~ *agent*, agenzia
di locazione, *f.* ~ *coal*, carbone di
casa, *m.* ~ *dog*, cane da guardia, *m.*
~ *flannel*, strofinaccio, *m.* ~*fly*,
mosca domestica, *f.* ~ *full* (*Theat.*),
sala al completo, *f.* ~*hold*, casa,
famiglia, *f.*; (*staff*) domestici, *m.pl.*
~*hold bread*, pane casalingo, *m.*
~*hold gods*, lari, penati, *m.pl.*

~*hold goods*, mobili domestici,
utensili domestici, *m.pl.* ~*hold
linen*, biancheria domestica, *f.*
~*holder*, capo di casa, capofamiglia,
m. ~*keeper*, massaia, governante, *f.*
~*keeping*, faccende domestiche, *f.pl.*
economia domestica; gestione della
casa, *f.* ~ *leek*, sempre-vivo dei
tetti. ~*maid*, serva, domestica;
donna di servizio, *f.* ~ *martin*,
rondinella, *f.* ~ *number*, numero, *m.*
H~ *of Commons*, ~ *of Lords*,
Camera dei Comuni, Camera dei
Lordi, *f.* ~ *of the deceased*, casa
mortuaria, *f.* ~ *painter*, decoratore
d'abitazioni, *m.* ~ *property*,
proprietà immobiliare, *f.*; beni
immobili, *m.pl.* ~ *sparrow*,
passero, *m.* ~ *tax*, tassa sul valor
locativo, *f.* ~*top*, tetto, *m.* *to give
a* ~ *warming*, inaugurare la casa
nuova con un ricevimento. ~*wife*,
padrona di casa, massaia, *f.* ~-
wifery, economia domestica, *f.*
~*work*, faccende domestiche, *f.pl.*
¶ *v.t.* alloggiare, albergare, mettere
al coperto; (*Carp.*, *&c.*) incassare;
(*harvest*) portare dentro il raccolto;
(*carriage*) mettere nella rimessa,
portare in rimessa. **housing**, *n.*
alloggio, *m.* ~ *problem*, crisi degli
alloggi, *f.*
hovel, *n.* casupola, *f.*, tugurio, *m.*
hover, *v.i.* volteggiare, librarsi sulle
ali; esitare.
how, *ad.* come, in che modo. ~ *is
that?* come mai? ~ *long?* quanto
a lungo? per quanto tempo? ~ *far?*
quanto lontano? fin dove? ~ *much*,
~ *many*, quanto, quanti, *m.pl.*,
quante, *f.pl.*
however, *c.* & *ad.*, comunque, tuttavia, però, del resto, eppure, per
altro, per quanto, nondimeno, in
qualunque modo.
howitzer, *n.* obice, *m.*
howl, *n.* urlo, ululato, *m.* ¶ *v.i.*
urlare, ululare; (*wind*) lamentare.
~*er*, *n.* (*fam.*) strafalcione; errore
grossolano, *m.*
hoyden, *n.* chiassona, *f.*
hub, *n.* mozzo (di ruota), *m.*; (*fig.*)
centro, *m.* ~ *brake*, freno sul mozzo,
m.
hubbub, *n.* baccano, chiasso, fracasso,
m.; baraonda, *f.*
huckaback, *n.* tela operata, *f.* ~
towel, salvietta a nido d'api, *f.*
huckster, *n.* rigattiere, rivendugliolo,
m.
huddle, *v.t.* affrettare, pigiare, gettare

alla rinfusa; (v.i.) affollarsi, accalcarsi.

hue, n. tinta, gradazione di tinta,
sfumatura, f.
hue & cry, clamore dell'inseguimento,
gridio, m.
huff (draughts), v.t. soffiare. to take
the ~, prendersela a male, saltare
la mosca al naso. he is in a ~,
si è stizzito.
hug, n. abbraccio, m.; stretta, f.
¶ v.t. stringere, abbracciare; (the
wind, Naut.) stringere il vento;
(the shore) serrare la terra, costeggiare; (an error) mantenere, accarezzare.
huge, a. enorme, smisurato. ~ly, ad.
enormemente, estremamente.
hulk, n. carcassa, nave disattrez-
zata, f. ~ing, a. grosso, goffo.
hull, n. (husk) guscio, m.; (ship) scafo,
m. ¶ v.t. sbricciare.
hullabaloo, n. baccano, schiamazzo,
m.
hullo[a], i. olà; (Teleph.) pronto!
hum, v.i. & t. (bee, &c.) ronzare;
(top) trottolare, frullare; (tune)
canterellare. ¶ i. uhm! ~ & haw,
balbettare, titubare, fare uhm!
human, a. umano. **humane,** a.
umano. **humanist,** n. umanista, m.
humanitarian, a. & n. umani-
tario, a. & m. **humanity,** n.
umanità, f. **humanize,** v.t.
umanizzare.
humble, a. umile. ¶ v.t. umiliare.
~ bee, calabrone, m. ~ness, n.
umiltà, f.; (birth) umile nascita, f.;
umili natali, m.pl. the humbler
classes, il popolo minuto, m.
humbug, n. frottola, fandonia,
mistificazione, f.; (pers.) ciarlatano,
m.; impostore, m., -a, f. ¶ i.
frottole! sciocchezze! ¶ v.t.
corbellare, canzonare, mistificare,
ingannare.
humdrum, a. monotono, banale,
ordinario, triste.
humerus, n. omero, m.
humid, a. umido. ~ity, n. umidità,
umidezza, f.
humiliate, v.t. umiliare. **humility,**
n. umiltà.
humming bird, colibri, m.
humming top, trottola, f.
hummock, n. poggio; monticello, m.
humorist, n. umorista, m.; (entertainer) comico, commediante, m.
humorous, a. umoristico, faceto,
spiritoso. ~ly, ad. con umore,
facetamente. **humour,** n. (mood)

umore, m., disposizione, f.; (jocosity)
giocosità, giovialità, f.; umorismo,
m. ¶ v.t. compiacere, cercare di
piacere a, lasciar fare a.
hump, n. bernoccolo, m.; gobba,
protuberanza, enfiagione, f. ~back,
n., & ~backed, a. gobbo, a. & m.,
-a, f.
hundred, a. & n. cento, a. & m.
~ (or so), centinaio, m. (-aia, f.pl.).
~weight, n. (imperial measure)
= 112 pounds or 50·80 kilo-
grammes. ~fold, a. & n. centuplo,
a. & m. ~th, a. & n. centesimo,
a. & m.
Hungarian, a. ungherese. ¶ n.
ungherese, m.f.; (language) l'ungherese, m.; lingua ungherese, f.
Hungary, n. l'Ungheria, f.
hunger, n. fame, f. ~strike, sciopero
della fame, m. ~ striker, scioperante
della fame, m.f. ~ after, agognare,
bramare, aver sete di. **hungrily,**
ad. ingordamente, famelicamente.
hungry, a. affamato, famelico.
to be ~, very ~, aver fame, aver
gran fame.
hunk, n. grosso pezzo, m.; (pl. miser)
avaro, spilorcio, m.
hunt, n. caccia, f.; inseguimento, m.;
ricerca, f.; (riding to hounds) caccia
alla volpe, f. ¶ v.t. & i. cacciare,
inseguire, andare alla caccia di.
~ for, cercare, ricercare. ~ out,
scovare, cavar fuori. ~er, n.
cacciatore, m.; cavallo di caccia, m.;
(curios) cercatore, m.; (watch)
saponetta, f.; orologio da tasca con
doppia cassa, m. **hunting,** n.
caccia, f.; (science) arte venatoria, f.
~ box, padiglione di caccia, m.
huntress, n. cacciatrice, f. **huntsman,** n. cacciatore, m.; (man in
charge) capocaccia, m.
hurdle, n. graticcio, m. ~ fence,
barriera portatile, f. ~ race, corsa
con ostacoli, f. ~r, n. ostacolista,
m.
hurdy-gurdy, organetto a mano
vella, m.; ghironda, f.
hurl, v.t. scagliare, lanciare.
hurly-burly, n. chiasso, baccano,
tumulto, tafferuglio, m.
hurrah, -ray, n. acclamazione, f.
¶ i. urrah! evviva! viva!
hurricane, n. uragano, m. ~ deck,
ponte di passeggiata, ponte di
manovra, m. ~ lamp, lampada
chiusa, f.
hurry, n. fretta, furia, precipitazione,
premura, f. ¶ v.t. affrettare,

precipitare; (*v.i.*) affrettarsi. ~ *up*, far presto.

hurt, *n.* danno, male; torto; pregiudizio, *m.*; ferita, lesione, *f.* ¶ *v.t. ir.* fare male a, danneggiare, ledere, nuocere a; ferire, far torto a.

husband, *n.* marito, sposo, *m.* ¶ *v.t.* usare con frugalità, risparmiare.

husbandman, *n.* agricoltore, lavoratore dei campi, *m.* **husbandry**, *n.* agricoltura, *f.*; lavoro dei campi, *m.*; economia, frugalità, *f.*

hush, *n.* silenzio, *m.*; calma, *f.* ~ *money*, prezzo del silenzio, *m.* ¶ *i.* zitto! silenzio! ¶ *v.t.* far tacere; calmare. ~ *up*, nascondere, tenere celato, far passare sotto silenzio.

husk, *n.* guscio, baccello, *m.*; (*walnut*) mallo, *m.*; (*grain*) loppa, *f.* ~y, (*hoarse*) *a.* rauco, velato.

hussy, **-zzy**, *n.* briccona, civetta, sgualdrina, *f.*

hustle, *v.t.* spingere, investire, cozzare, urtare.

hut, *n.* baracca, cabina, *f.*; tugurio, *m.*

hutch, *n.* casotto, *m.*; gabbia, *f.*; vagoncino, *m.* *rabbit's* ~, conigliera, *f.*

hyacinth, *n.* giacinto, *m.*

hyaena, *n.* iena, *f.*

hybrid, *a.* ibrido, meticcio. ¶ *n.* ibrido, *m.*

hydra, *n.* idra, *f.*

hydrangea, *n.* idrangea, ortensia, *f.*

hydrant, *n.* idrante, *m.*; bocca d'acqua, *f.*

hydrate, *n.* idrato, *m.*

hydraulic, *a. &* ~s, *n.pl.* idraulico, *a.*; idraulica, *f.*

hydrocarbon, *n.* idrocarburo, *m.* **hydrochloric**, *a.* idroclorico. **hydrogen**, *n.* idrogeno, *m.* **hydropathic**, *a.* idropatico. ¶ **hydropathy**, *n.* idropatia, *f.* **hydrophobia**, *n.* idrofobia, *f.* **hydroplane**, *n.* idrovolante, *m.*

hyena, *n.* iena, *f.*

hygiene, *n. &* **hygienics**, *n.* igiene, *f.* **hygienic[al]**, *a.* igienico.

hymen, *n.* imene, *f.*

hymenoptera, *n.pl.* imenotteri, *m.pl.*

hymn, *n.* inno, carme, *m.*; canzone, *f.*; (*in church*) inno, canto spirituale, *m.*; laude, *f.* ~ *book*, libro d'inni, *m.*; raccolta d'inni, *f.*; innario, *m.*

hyperbola *&* **hyperbole**, *n.* iperbole, *f.*

hyphen, *n.* lineetta, *f.*; (*end of line*) tratto d'unione, *m.*

hypnotism, *n.* ipnotismo, *m.* **hypnotize**, *v.t.* ipnotizzare.

hypochondriac, *a. & n.* ipocondriaco, *a. & m.*, -a, *f.* **hypocrisy**, *n.* ipocrisia, *f.* **hypocrite**, *n.* ipocrita, *m.f.* **hypocritical**, *a.* ipocrito. **hypodermic**, *a.* ipodermico. ~ *syringe*, siringa ipodermica, *f.* **hyposulphite**, *n.* iposolfito, *m.* **hypothecation**, *n.* ipoteca, *f.*; atto di ipotecare, *m.* **hypothesis**, *n.* ipotesi, *f.* **hypothetic[al]**, *a.* ipotetico.

hyssop, *n.* issopo, *m.*

hysteria, *n.* isteria, *f.*; isterismo, *m.* **hysteric[al]**, *a.* isterico. **hysterics**, *n.pl.* attacco d'isteria, *m.*; accesso di isterismo, *m.*

I

I, *pn.* io; mi, me. *It is* ~, sono io. *he speaks more than* ~, egli parla piú di me. *Here* ~ *am*, eccomi.

iambic, *a.* giambico. ¶ *n.* giambo, *m.*

ibex, *n.* stambecco, *m.*

ibis, *n.* ibi, *m.*

ice, *n.* ghiaccio, *m.*; gelato, *m.* ~ *age*, era glaciale, *f.* ~ *axe*, piccozza, *f.* ~*berg*, montagna (galleggiante) di ghiaccio, *f.* ~ *blink*, riflesso del ghiaccio, *m.* ~*box &* ~*house*, ghiacciaia, *f.* ~ *chamber*, frigorifero, *m.* ~ *cream*, gelato, sorbetto alla panna, *m.* ~ *cream freezer*, sorbettiera, *f.* ~ *cream vendor*, gelatiere, *m.*, -a, *f.* ~ *hockey*, disco sul ghiaccio, *m.* ~ *pack*, agglomerazione di campi di ghiaccio, *f.* ~ *pail*, sorbettiera, *f.*; rinfrescatoio, *m.* ~ *skates*, pattini da ghiaccio, *m.pl.* ¶ *v.t.* ghiacciare, congelare; (*wine, &c.*) mettere in ghiaccio; (*cakes, &c.*) glassare.

Iceland, *n.* l'Islanda, *f.* ~*er*, *n.* islandese, *m.f.* ~*ic*, *a. & (language) n.* islandese, *m.*, lingua islandese, *f.*

ichthyology, *n.* ittiologia, *f.*

icicle, *n.* ghiacciuolo, *m.* **icing** (*sugar*), *n.* zucchero a velo, *m.*

icon, *n.* icona, *f.* **iconoclast**, *n.* iconoclasta, *m.*

icy, *a.* glaciale, di ghiaccio, gelato, diaccio.

idea, *n.* idea, *f.* **ideal**, *a. & n.* ideale, *a. & m.* ~*ist*, *n.* idealista, *m.f.*

identical, *a.* identico. **identification**, *n.* identificazione, *f.* ~ *number* (*motor car*), numero di circolazione, *m.* **identify**, *v.t.*

identificare. **identity**, *n.* identità, *f.*
~ *card*, carta d'identità, *f.*, documento di legittimazione, *m.* ~ *disc*, disco d'identità, *m.*, targa di riconoscimento (*car*), *f.*
idiocy, *n.* imbecillità, *f.*, ebetismo, cretinismo, *m.*
idiom, *n.* (*dialect*) idioma, *m.*; (*phrase*) idiotismo, *m.*
idiosyncrasy, *n.* idiosincrasia, *f.*
idiot, *n.* & ~**ic**, *a.* idiota, ebete, imbecille, *a.* & *m.f.*
idle, *a.* ozioso, pigro, indolente, infingardo; inutile, vano; disoccupato, inattivo, scioperato, sospeso. ~ *fancy*, chimera, fantasia, *f.* ¶ *v.i.* passare il tempo nell'ozio, oziare; metter tempo in mezzo, indugiare, star con le mani in mano. ~**ness**, *n.* ozio, *m.*, pigrizia, *f.*, infingardaggine, *f.* **idler**, *n.* pigro, ozioso, infingardo, *m.* **idly**, *ad.* pigramente, oziosamente, infingardamente.
idol, *n.* idolo, *m.* **idolater**, **-tress**, idolatra, *m.f.* **idolatrous**, *a.* idolatra. **idolatry**, *n.* idolatria, *f.* **idolize**, *v.t.* idolatrare; idoleggiare.
idyl[l], *n.* idillio, *m.* **idyllic**, *a.* idillico (*pl.* -ici), idilliaco (*pl.* -iaci).
if, *c.* se. ~ *not*, se non.
igneous, *a.* igneo. **ignis fatuus**, *n.* fuoco fatuo, *m.* **ignite**, *v.t.* accendere, infiammare; (*v.i.*) infiammarsi, prendere fuoco. **ignition**, *n.* accensione, *f.*
ignoble, *a.* ignobile.
ignominious, *a.* ignominioso. **ignominy**, *n.* ignominia, *f.*
ignoramus, *n.* ignorante, *m.f.*
ignorance, *n.* ignoranza, *f.* **ignorant**, *a.* ignorante. *to be* ~ *of*, ignorare.
ignore, *v.t.* passare sotto silenzio, trascurare, far vista di non conoscere.
iguana, *n.* iguana, *f.*
ill, *n.* male, danno, *m.* ~*s*, *n.pl.* mali, *m.pl.*; disgrazie, *f.pl.* *speak* ~ *of*, parlar male di, dir male di, parlare sfavorevolmente di. ¶ *a.* malato, ammalato; cattivo, malo; infelice, sfortunato. ¶ *ad.* male, poco, malamente. ~*-advised*, malaccorto, imprudente, sconsigliato. ~*-assorted*, poco adatto, sconveniente, disparato; (*pair*) mal maritato, mal accoppiato. ~*-famed*, malfamato. ~*-fated*, ~ *starred*, malaugurato, disgraziato, nato sotto cattiva stella. ~*-favoured*, brutto, sgraziato, deforme. ~ *feeling*, malumore,

rancore, *m.*, inimicizia, malevolenza, *f.* ~*-gotten gains*, beni mal acquistati, *m.pl.* ~ *humour*, malumore, malanimo, *m.* ~ *luck*, mala fortuna, mala sorte, *f.* ~*-mannered*, scostumato, grossolano. ~*-natured* (*person*), cattivo, malizioso, malvagio. ~*-omened*, di cattivo augurio, nefasto, sinistro. ~*-temper*, mal talento, *m.*, malizia, *f.*, cattivo carattere, *m.* ~*-tempered*, malizioso, malintenzionato, astioso. ~*-timed*, inopportuno, intempestivo, fuor di proposito. ~*-treat*, ~*-use*, malmenare, trattar male, usar male. ~ *will*, malanimo, rancore, *m.*, malevolenza, *f.* *to bear* ~ *will*, voler male a, serbar rancore a.
illegal, *a.* illegale, illecito.
illegible, *a.* illeggibile.
illegitimacy, *n.* illegittimità, *f.* **illegitimate**, *a.* illegittimo.
illicit, *a.* illecito.
illiterate, *a.* & *n.* analfabeta, illeterato.
illness, *n.* malattia, indisposizione, *f.*; male, *m.*
illogical, *a.* illogico. ~**ity**, *n.* illogicità, *f.*
illuminate, *v.t.* illuminare, rischiarare; (*festively*) illuminare; (*MS.*) illuminare, miniare. **illumination**, *n.* illuminazione; miniatura, *f.* **illumine**, *v.t.* rischiarare.
illusion, *n.* illusione, *f.* **illusive**, **illusory**, *a.* illusorio.
illustrate, *v.t.* illustrare; (*fig.*) spiegare, interpretare. ~*d price list*, catalogo illustrato, *m.* **illustration**, *n.* illustrazione, incisione, immagine, tavola, *f.*; esempio, *m.* ~ *in text*, illustrazione nel testo. ~ *outside text*, fuori testo. **illustrious**, *a.* illustre. *to make* ~, rendere illustre, illustrare.
image, *n.* immagine, *f.* ~**ry**, *n.* immagini, figure retoriche, *f. l.* **imaginary**, *a.* immaginario. **imagination**, *n.* immaginazione, fantasia, *f.* **imagine**, *v.t.* & *i.* immaginare, avere un'idea di, immaginarsi, figurarsi, farsi un'idea di.
imbecile, *a.* imbecille. ¶ *n.* imbecille, *m.f.*
imbibe, *v.t.* bere, assorbire; assimilare.
imbricate, *v.t.* sovrapporre, coprire di embrici.
imbroglio, *n.* imbroglio, *m.*
imbrue, *v.t.* immergere, intridere, bagnare.
imbue, *v.t.* imbevere, impregnare di.

~**d,** *p.p.* imbevuto, ispirato, possesso, impregnato.

imitate, *v.t.* imitare; contraffare. **imitation,** *n.* imitazione, contraffazione, *f.*; (*att.*) contraffatto, falso, artificiale. **imitator,** *n.* imitatore, *m.*, -trice, *f.*

immaculate, *a.* immacolato, senza macchia. *the I~ Conception,* l'Immacolata Concezione, *f.*

immanent, *a.* immanente.

immaterial, *a.* immateriale, indifferente, poco importante. *to be ~,* non importare, essere indifferente.

immature, *a.* immaturo.

immeasurable, *a.* smisurato, oltre misura.

immediate, *a.* immediato; (*on letters*) urgente. ~**ly,** *ad.* subito, immediatamente, all'istante, d'un tratto.

immemorial, *a.* immemorabile.

immense, *a.* immenso. ~**ly,** *ad.* immensamente. **immensity,** *n.* immensità, *f.*

immerse, *v.t.* immergere, tuffare. **immersion,** *n.* immersione, *f.*

immigrate, *v.i.* immigrare.

imminence, *n.* imminenza, *f.* **imminent,** *a.* imminente.

immoderate, *a.* immoderato, smodato, eccessivo.

immodest, *a.* immodesto, impudico, sfacciato.

immolate, *v.t.* immolare, sacrificare.

immoral, *a.* immorale. ~**ity,** *n.* immoralità, *f.*

immortal, *a. & n.* immortale, *a. & m.f.* ~**ity,** *n.* immortalità, *f.* ~**ize,** *v.t.* immortalare, rendere immortale.

immortelle, *n.* sempreviva, *f.*

immovable, *a.* immobile, fermo.

immunity, *n.* immunità, *f.*

immure, *v.t.* rinchiudere, incarcerare.

immutable, *a.* immutabile.

imp, *n.* folletto, demonio; (*fam.*) diavoletto, demonietto, *m.*

impact, *n.* urto, *m.*, collisione, *f.*

impair, *v.t.* indebolire, menomare, intaccare.

impale, *v.t.* trafiggere, infilzare; (*Hist.*) impalare.

impalpable, *a.* impalpabile.

impanel a jury, formare la lista dei giurati.

impart, *v.t.* impartire, comunicare, far sapere.

impartial, *a.* imparziale, equo. ~**ity,** *n.* imparzialità, *f.*

impassable, *a.* (*road*) i mpraticabile; (*river*) inguadabile.

impassible & impassive, *a.* impassibile.

impassioned, *p.p.* appassionato, infiammato.

impasto, *n.* impasto, *m.*

impatience, *n.* impazienza, *f.* **impatient,** *a.* impaziente. *to grow ~,* impazientirsi. ~**ly,** *ad.* impazientemente, con impazienza.

impeach, *v.t.* accusare (di reato contro lo Stato); imputare.

impecunious, *a.* indigente, povero, bisognoso.

impede, *v.t.* impedire, ostacolare, ritardare. **impediment,** *n.* impedimento, ostacolo, *m.* ~ *of speech,* ~ *in one's speech,* difetto di pronuncia, *m.*, articolazione indistinta, *f.* **impedimenta,** *n.pl.* bagagli, *m.pl.*

impel, *v.t.* muovere, spingere.

impending, *p.a.* imminente, sovrastante.

impenetrable, *a.* impenetrabile.

impenitence, *n.* impenitenza, *f.* **impenitent,** *a.* impenitente.

imperative, *a. & n.* imperativo, *a. & m.*; modo imperativo, *m.*

imperceptible, *a.* impercettibile.

imperfect, *a. & ~* [*tense*], *n.* imperfetto, *a. & m.*; tempo imperfetto, *m.* ~**ion,** *n.* imperfezione, *f.*

imperial, *a.* imperiale; (*weights & measures*) inglese. ~ *& foreign* (*postal system*), internazionale; (*mails*) marittimo. ¶ (*beard*) *n.* pizzo, *m.*; imperiale, *m.* ~**ist,** *n. & ~istic,* a. imperialista, *m.f.*; imperialistico, *a.*

imperil, *v.t.* rischiare, esporre a pericolo; compromettere.

imperious, *a.* imperioso, fiero, altero.

imperishable, *a.* imperituro.

impermeable, *a.* impermeabile.

impersonal, *a.* impersonale.

impersonate, *v.t.* impersonare; fare (una parte). **impersonation,** *n.;* personificazione, *f.*; (*Theat.*) rappresentazione, *f.* (*Law*) supposizione di persona, *f.*

impertinence, *n.* impertinenza, *f.* **impertinent,** *a.* impertinente. ~**ly,** *ad.* impertinentemente.

imperturbable, *a.* imperturbabile.

impervious, *a.* impervio, impermeabile, impenetrabile.

impetuous, *a.* impetuoso.

impetus, *n.* impeto, *m.*

impiety, *n.* empietà, *f.*

impinge [up]on, battere contro, urtare contro.

impious, *a.* empio.

impish, *a.* malizioso, di folletto.

implacable, *a.* implacabile.

implant, *v.t.* impiantare; inculcare; infondere.

implement, *n.* ordigno, strumento, utensile, arnese, *m.* ¶ *v.t.* effettuare; adempiere; completare.

implicate, *v.t.* implicare, compromettere. *not* ~*d,* disinteressato, non implicato. **implication,** *n.* implicazione; induzione,*f.* **implicit,** *a. &* **implied,** *p.a.* implicito, tacito.

implore, *v.t.* implorare.

imply, *v.t.* implicare, importare, voler dire; insinuare.

impolite, *a.* sgarbato, scortese. ~**ness,** *n.* scortesia, sgarbatezza, *f.*

impolitic, *a.* impolitico, imprudeten.

imponderable, *a. & n.* imponderabile, *a. & m.*

import, *n.* (*meaning*) significato, senso, rilievo, *m.* (*importance*) importanza, *f.*; (*Com., &c.*) importazione, *f.* ~ *duty,* dazio d'importazione, *m.* ¶ *v.t.* significare, indicare, importare; (*Com., &c.*) importare, introdurre.

importance, *n.* importanza, *f.* **important,** *a.* importante.

importation, *n.* importazione, *f.* **importer,** *n.* importatore.

importunate, *a.* importuno, indiscreto, insistente. **importune,** *v.t.* importunare. **importunity,** *n.* importunità, insistenza, *f.*

impose, *v.t.* imporre. ~ (*upon*) *someone,* ingannare, gabbare, truffare. (*person*) *of imposing appearance,* d'aspetto imponente. *imposing stone,* marmo, *m.* **imposition,** *n.* imposizione, *f.*; impostura, *f.,* trucco, inganno, *m.*; (*Sch.*) penso, lavoro punitivo, *m.*

impossibility, *n.* impossibilità, *f.* **impossible,** *a.* impossibile.

impost (*Arch.*), *n.* concio d'imposta, *m.*; pietra di spalla, *f.*

impostor, *n.* impostore, *m.*, -a, *f.* **imposture,** *n.* impostura, *f.,* inganno, *m.*

impotence, -cy, *n.* impotenza, *f.* **impotent,** *a.* impotente.

impound, *v.t.* staggire, sequestrare, confiscare; mettere al sicuro.

impoverish, *v.t.* impoverire.

impracticable, *a.* impraticabile.

imprecation, *n.* imprecazione, bestemmia, *f.*

impregnable, *a.* imprendibile, inespugnabile.

impregnate, *v.t.* impregnare, fecondare. ~**d** (*wood*), *p.a.* iniettato.

impresario, *n.* impresario, *m.*

impress, *n.* impronta, impressione, *f.* ¶ *v.t.* imprimere, impressionare, fare impressione a; inculcare, infondere; commuovere. ~*ed stamp,* francobollo ad impressione, timbro a secco, *m.* ~*ion* (*Typ.*) impressione, impronta, *f.*; (*Typ.*) impressione, *f. to be under the* ~, essere sotto l'impressione (di), avere l'idea (che). ~**ionism,** *n.* impressionismo, *m.* **impressive,** *a.* commovente, impressionante, solenne.

imprint, *n.* impronta, *f.* See also *printer's* ~ *& publisher's* ~. ¶ *v.t.* imprimere.

imprison, *v.t.* imprigionare, incarcerare. ~**ment,** *n.* prigionia, *f.,* incarceramento, *m.*

improbability, *n.* improbabilità, *f.* **improbable,** *a.* improbabile, inverosimile. **improbably,** *ad.* improbabilmente.

impromptu, *ad. & a.* all'improvviso, improvvisato. ¶ *n.* improvvisazione, *f.*

improper, *a.* sconvenevole, sconveniente, sconcio; inadatto, improprio. ~**ly,** *ad.* impropriamente, incorrettamente. **impropriety,** *n.* sconvenienza, sconvenevolezza; improprietà, *f.*

improve, *v.t.* migliorare, abbellire; mettere in valore; (*land*) bonificare. ~ *on,* perfezionare, fare meglio di. ~ *on acquaintance,* guadagnare ad essere conosciuto. ~**ment,** *n.* miglioramento, progresso, *m.*; (*land*) bonificazione, *f.* ~**s,** migliorie, *f.pl.*

improvidence, *n.* imprevidenza, *f.* **improvident,** *a.* imprevidente.

improvise, *v.t.* improvvisare. (*Theat.*) recitare a soggetto.

imprudence, *n.* imprudenza, *f.* **imprudent,** *a.* imprudente. ~**ly,** *ad.* imprudentemente.

impudence, *n.* impudenza, sfacciataggine, sfrontataggine, *f.* **impudent,** *a.* impudente, sfacciato, sfrontato. ~**ly,** *ad.* impudentemente, sfacciatamente. **impudicity,** *n.* impudicizia, *f.*

impugn, *v.t.* impugnare, attaccare, accusare.

impulse *&* **impulsion,** *n.* impulso, *m.*; impulsione. spinta, *f.,* slancio,

impeto; istinto, desiderio, *m.*
impulsive, *a.* impulsivo.
impunity, *n.* impunità, *f.* with ~,
impunemente.
impure, *a.* impuro; immondo;
impudico. **impurity,** *n.* impurità;
impudicizia, oscenità, *f.*
imputation, *n.* imputazione, attribuzione, *f.*, addebito, *m.* **impute,** *v.t.*
imputare, ascrivere, attribuire.
in, *pr.* in, a; di, da; fra, entro; per, con;
sotto, su, durante, in capo a. ¶ *ad.*
dentro, a casa, in casa; al potere;
(*light, fire*) acceso, vivo, non spento.
~ *a month,* fra un mese. ~ *a
fortnight,* fra quindici giorni. ~
a week from today, oggi a otto. ~
the day, ~ *the night,* di giorno,
di notte. *ninety-nine times* ~ *a
hundred,* novantanove su cento.
~ *between,* fra. ~ *demand,* ricercato.
~ *fashion,* alla moda, di moda, in
voga. ~ *print,* a stampa, stampato;
in vendita, in circolazione. ~ *the
press,* in corso di stampa, sotto
stampa. ~ *there,* là dentro. *ins &
outs,* tutti i dettagli, *m.pl.*; tutte le
particolarità, *f.pl.*
inability, *n.* incapacità, inabilità, *f.*
inaccessible, *a.* inaccessibile.
inaccuracy, *n.* inesattezza, *f.*
inaccurate, *a.* inesatto, poco esatto.
inaction, *n.* inattività, *f.* **inactive,** *a.*
inattivo.
inadequate, *a.* insufficiente, sproporzionato, impari, inadeguato.
~**ly,** *ad.* insufficientemente.
inadmissible, *a.* inammissibile.
inadvertently, *ad.* inavvertente-
mente, per svista.
inalienable, *a.* inalienabile.
inane, *a.* vano, futile, vacuo.
inanimate, *a.* inanimato, senza vita.
~ *nature,* natura morta, *f.*
inanition, *n.* inanizione, *f.*
inanity, *n.* futilità, vacuità, inanità, *f.*
inapplicable, *a.* inapplicabile.
inapposite, *a.* poco a proposito, non
pertinente.
inappreciable, *a.* trascurabile, di
nessun conto.
inappropriate, *a.* improprio, disadatto, inappropriato, poco adatto.
inapt, *a.* inetto, poco acconcio.
inaptitude, *n.* incapacità, inettitudine, *f.*
inarticulate, *a.* inarticolato, indistinto.
inasmuch (as), *ad.* dacché, poiché,
visto che.
inattentive, *a.* disattento, distratto.

inaudible, *a.* inaudibile, basso, che
non si fa sentire, che non può udirsi.
inaugurate, *v.t.* inaugurare.
inauspicious, *a.* inauspicato, infausto,
malaugurato.
inborn & **inbred,** *a.* innato,
congenito.
incalculable, *a.* incalcolabile, incommensurabile.
incandescence, *n.* incandescenza, *f.*
incandescent, *a.* incandescente;
(*lamp,* &*c.*) lampada ad incandescenza, *f.*
incantation, *n.* incantesimo, incanto,
m.
incapable, *a.* incapace, inabile.
incapably, *ad.* inabilmente. **in-
capacitate,** *v.t.* rendere incapace
(a . . . di . . .), inabilitare. **incapacity,** *n.* incapacità, inabilità, *f.*
incarcerate, *v.t.* incarcerare.
incarnate, *a.* incarnato; roseo.
incarnation, *n.* incarnazione, *f.*
incautious, *a.* incauto, imprudente.
incendiarism, *n.* incendio doloso, *m.*
incendiary, *a.* & *n.,* incendiario,
a. & *m.*
incense, *n.* incenso, *m.*; (*fig.*) adulazione, *f.* ~ *box,* navicella, *f.,* vaso
per l'incenso, *m.* ~ *burner,*
incensiere, turibolo, *m.* ¶ *v.t.*
(*perfume*) incensare; (*enrage*) esasperare, infiammare, stizzire.
incentive, *n.* incentivo, stimolo, *m.*
inception, *n.* inizio, principio,
cominciamento, *m.*
incertitude, *n.* incertezza, *f.*
incessant, *a.* incessante. ~**ly,** *ad.*
incessantemente.
incest, *n.* incesto, *m.* **incestuous,** *a.*
incestuoso.
inch, *n.* dito, pollice, *m.* = 2.54
(about 2½) centimetres. ~ *by* ~,
palmo a palmo, grado a grado.
incidence, *n.* incidenza, *f.* **incident,**
n. incidente, *m.* ¶ *a.* incidentale,
inerente. ~**al,** *a.* incidentale,
accidentale, fortuito. ~ *expenses,*
spese eventuali, *f.pl.* ~**ally,** *ad.*
incidentalmente.
incinerate, *v.t.* incenerire. **incinera-
tor,** *n.* forno crematorio, *m.*
incipient, *a.* incipiente, nascente.
incise, *v.t.* incidere. **incision,** *n.*
incisione, *f.* **incisive,** *a.* incisivo.
incisor, *n.* [dente] incisivo, *m.*
incite, *v.t.* incitare, stimolare, incoraggiare. ~**ment,** *n.* incitamento,
m.
incivility, *n.* scortesia, inciviltà, *f.*;
atto incivile, *m.*

inclemency, *n.* inclemenza, *f.*; rigore, *m.* **inclement,** *a.* inclemente.

inclination, *n.* inclinazione, disposizione, propensità; pendenza, *f.* **incline,** *n.* piano inclinato, *m.*, costa, *f.*; (*down*) pendio, declivio, *m.*; declività, china, *f.*; (*up*) salita, rampa, *f.* ¶ *v.t.* & *i.* inclinare, chinare; rendere disposto, volgere; tirare, essere disposto, essere proclive; (*colour*) tendere a. **inclined,** *p.a.* & *p.p.* (*plane*) inclinato; (*fig.*) disposto, propenso, proclive.

include, *v.t.* includere, accludere, abbracciare, comprendere, contenere. **including,** *participle,* compreso. *not* ~, non compreso; escluso, senza contare. **inclusive,** *a.* tutto compreso, inclusivo; (*sum*) globale; (*dates*) inclusivamente. *our terms are* ~, è tutto compreso nel prezzo. ~ *charge,* prezzo inclusivo; compreso tutte le spese. ~ *of,* compreso. ~**ly,** *ad.* inclusivamente.

incognito, *n.* incognito, *m.* ¶ *ad.* in incognito.

incoherence, *n.* incoerenza, *f.* **incoherent,** *a.* incoerente.

incombustible, *a.* incombustibile.

income, *n.* rendita, *f.*, reddito, *m.*, entrate, *f.pl.* ~ *tax,* imposta sul reddito, i. sulla rendita, *f.* ~ *tax return,* dichiarazione del reddito, *f.*

incoming, *a.* entrante; (*mail, letter*) in arrivo; (*tide*) montante.

incommensurable, *a.* incommensurabile. **incommensurate with,** senza proporzione con, non c'è proporzione fra.

incommode, *v.t.* incomodare, recare incomodo a, disturbare.

incomparable, *a.* incomparabile.

incompatibility, *n.* incompatibilità, *f.* ~ *of temper,* incompatibilità di carattere, *f.* **incompatible,** *a.* incompatibile.

incompetence, *n.* incompetenza, *f.* **incompetent,** *a.* incompetente.

incomplete, *a.* incompleto, incompiuto. **incompletion,** *n.* l'essere incompleto, *m.*, imperfezione, *f.*

incomprehensible, *a.* incomprensibile.

inconceivable, *a.* inconcepibile.

inconclusive, *a.* inconcludente.

incongruity, *n.* incongruità, *f.* **incongruous,** *a.* incongruo. ~**ly,** *ad.* incongruamente.

inconsequent[ial], *a.* inconseguente.

inconsiderable, *a.* inconsiderabile.

inconsiderate, *a.* senza considerazione, senza riguardi, inconsiderato, incauto.

inconsistency, *n.* inconsistenza, *f.* **inconsistent,** *a.* inconsistente.

inconsolable, *a.* inconsolabile.

inconspicuous, *a.* incospicuo, poco cospicuo; minuto, impercettibile.

inconstancy, *n.* incostanza, *f.* **inconstant,** *a.* incostante.

incontinent, *a.* incontinente.

incontrovertible, *a.* incontrovertibile.

inconvenience, *n.* inconveniente, incomodo, disturbo, contrattempo, *m.* ¶ *v.t.* incomodare, disturbare, scomodare, dare noia a. **inconvenient,** *a.* incomodo, inconveniente, molesto.

incorporate, *v.t.* incorporare; (*a limited company*) erigere in ente morale.

incorrect, *a.* scorretto, inesatto, erroneo. ~**ness,** *n.* inesattezza, *f.*

incorrigible, *a.* incorreggibile.

incorruptible, *a.* incorruttibile.

increase, *n.* aumento, accrescimento, incremento, rialzo, *m.*; crescenza, *f.*, frutto, *m.* ¶ *v.t.* aumentare, accrescere, ingrandire; (*v.i.*) aumentare, crescere, ingrandirsi, subire un aumento, un rialzo. **increasing,** *p.a.* crescente, che aumenta, in aumento.

incredibility, *n.* incredibilità, *f.* **incredible,** *a.* incredibile. **incredulity,** *n.* incredulità, *f.* **incredulous,** *a.* incredulo.

increment, *n.* incremento, plus-valore, *m.*

incriminate, *v.t.* incriminare.

incrust, *v.t.* incrostare.

incubate, *v.t.* & *i.* covare. **incubation,** *n.* incubazione, *f.* **incubator,** *n.* incubatrice, *f.*, chioccia meccanica, *f.*

incubus, *n.* incubo, *m.*

inculcate, *v.t.* inculcare.

inculpate, *v.t.* incolpare.

incumbent, *n.* titolare (d'un benefizio ecclesiastico). *m.* *to be* ~ *on,* incombere.

incur, *v.t.* incorrere in, attirarsi addosso, esporsi a.

incurable, *a.* & *n.* incurabile, *a.* & *m.f.*; insanabile, *a.*

incursion, *n.* incursione, *f.*

indebted, *a.* indebitato, obbligato, tenuto. ~**ness,** *n.* debiti, *m.pl.*; stato di debito, *m.*; l'essere indebitato, *m.*

indecency, *v.* indecenza, *f.* **indecent,** *a.* indecente. ~**ly,** *ad.* indecentemente.

indecipherable, *a.* indecifrabile.

indecision, *n.* indecisione, *f.*

indecorous, *a.* indecoroso.

indeed, *ad.* difatti, in verità, a dire il vero, veramente, davvero, in effetto, in realtà, già. ¶ *i.* davvero?

indefatigable, *a.* infaticabile, instancabile, persistente.

indefensible, *a.* indifendibile, indifensibile.

indefinable, *a.* indefinibile. **indefinite,** *a.* indefinito; (*leave*) illimitato.

indelible, *a.* indelebile, incancellabile.

indelicacy, *n.* indelicatezza, *f.* **indelicate,** *a.* indelicato.

indemnify, *v.t.* indennizzare, risarcire.

indemnity, *n.* indennizzo, risarcimento, *m.,* indennità, *f.*

indent, *n.* requisizione ufficiale; ordinazione data a mezzo di commissionario, *f.* ¶ *v.t.* dentellare, intaccare; (*Typ.*) comporre una linea piú in dentro delle altre. ~ *for,* requisire, fare una domanda di. **indentation,** *n.* dentellatura, tacca, *f.* **indention,** *n.* recesso, *m.* **indenture,** *n.* controscritta, *f.*; (*Law*) atto contenente un contratto bilaterale.

independence, *n.* indipendenza, *f.* **independent,** *a.* indipendente. *to te* ~, vivere di rendita; essere indipendente (da). *person of* ~ *means,* reddituario, *m.,* -a, *f.*; proprietario, *m.,* -a, *f.* ~**ly,** *ad.* indipendentemente.

indescribable, *a.* indescrivibile.

indestructible, *a.* indistruttibile.

indeterminate, *a.* indeterminato.

index, *n.* indice; repertorio; indicatore; segno, indizio, *m.;* indicazione, *f.;* ago, *m.;* lancetta, *f.* ~ *expurgatorius,* indice dei libri condannati e proibiti, *m.* ¶ *v.t.* fare indice (a . . . di . . .), disporre in indice.

India, *n.* l'India, *f.* ~ *paper,* carta bibbia, *f.* **Indian,** *a.* indiano. ~ *Archipelago,* arcipelago delle Indie, *m.* ~ *club,* clava, *f.* ~ *corn,* granturco, *m.* ~ *ink,* inchiostro della Cina, *m.* ~ *mail,* valigia delle Indie, *f.* ~ *Ocean,* Oceano Indiano, Mare delle Indie, *m.* ~ *summer,* estate di San Martino, *f.* ¶ *n.* indiano, *m.,* -a, *f.*

indiarubber, *n.* cauccíú, *m.,* gomma

elastica, *f.* ~ *stamp,* bollo (timbro) a cauccíú, *m.*

indicate, *v.t.* indicare, accennare.

indication, *n.* segno, sintomo, indizio, *m.,* indicazione, *f.* **indicative,** *a.* indicativo. ~ [*mood*], *n.* [modo] indicativo, *m.* *to be* ~ *of,* indicare. **indicator,** *n.* indicatore, *m.*

indict, *v.t.* accusare, mettere in (stato d') accusa, processare, imputare. ~**ment,** *n.* atto d'accusa, *m.*

Indies (the), *n.pl.* le Indie, *f.pl.*

indifference, *n.* indifferenza, *f.* **indifferent,** *a.* indifferente. ~**ly,** *ad.* indifferentemente.

indigence, *n.* indigenza, *f.*

indigenous, *a.* indigeno.

indigent, *a.* indigente.

indigestible, *a.* indigesto. **indigestion,** *n.* indigestione, *f.*

indignant, *a.* sdegnoso, indignato. ~**ly,** *ad.* con indignazione. **indignation,** *n.* indignazione, *f.* **indignity,** *n.* indegnità, offesa, *f.*

indigo, *n.* indaco, *m.* ~ *blue,* azzurro d'indaco, indaco. ~ *plant,* indigofera, *f.,* anile, *m.*

indirect, *a.* indiretto.

indiscreet, *a.* indiscreto. **indiscretion,** *n.* indiscrezione, *f.*

indiscriminate, *a.* che non fa distinzioni, cieco, confuso, generale. ~**ly,** *ad.* senza distinzione, alla cieca, a caso.

indispensable, *a.* indispensabile.

indisposed, *p.p.* indisposto, malaticcio; mal disposto. **indisposition,** *n.* indisposizione, leggera malattia, *f.*

indisputable, *a.* indisputabile, incontestabile.

indissoluble, *a.* indissolubile.

indistinct, *a.* indistinto.

indite, *v.t.* redigere, comporre.

individual, *a.* individuale. ¶ *n.* individuo, *m.* ~**ity,** *n.* individualità, *f.*

indivisible, *a.* indivisibile.

Indo-China, *n.* l'Indocina, *f.*

indolence, *n.* indolenza, *f.* **indolent,** *a.* indolente. ~**ly,** *ad.* indolentemente.

indomitable, *a.* indomabile; (*will*) ferreo, forte, fermo.

indoor, *a.* di casa, interno, domestico; al coperto; a domicilio; (*staff*) di casa; (*games*) di sala. ~**s,** *ad.* in casa, dentro alla casa, al coperto, all'interno.

indubitable, *a.* indubitabile.

induce, *v.t.* indurre; portare a, fare, dare a. ~ *to strike,* far scioperare. ~**ment,** *n.* persuasione, lusinga, esca, *f.*; allettamento, motivo, stimolo, *m.*

induct, *v.t.* installare, insediare, investire. ~**ion,** *n.* induzione, *f.*; (*Eccl.*) investitura, *f.*

indulge, *v.t.* indulgere, concedere; (*pers.*) essere indulgente verso, compiacere. ~ *in,* abbandonarsi a, indulgere in; soddisfare; accarezzare (un'idea). **indulgence,** *n.* indulgenza; compiacenza, licenza, *f.*; eccesso, *m.* **indulgent,** *a.* indulgente.

indurate, *v.t.* indurire, rendere duro.

industrial, *a.* industriale. ~ *disease,* malattia professionale, *f.* ~**ism,** *n.* industrialismo, *m.* ~**ize,** *v.t.* industrializzare. **industrious,** *a.* industrioso; laborioso, diligente, assiduo. **industriously,** *ad.* industriosamente, laboriosamente, &c.

industry, *n.* industria, *f.*

inebriate, *a.* inebbriato, ebbro. ¶ *n.* briacone, ubriacone, *m.* ¶ *v.t.* inebbriare.

ineffable, *a.* ineffabile.

ineffaceable, *a.* incancellabile.

ineffective & **ineffectual** & **inefficacious,** *a.* inefficace, inutile, vano. ~**ly,** *ad.* senza risultato.

inefficient, *a.* inefficiente, poco capace.

inelastic (*Phys.*), *a.* senza elasticità, molle.

inelegant, *a.* inelegante.

ineligible, *a.* ineleggibile; inabile.

inept, *a.* inetto. **ineptitude,** *n.* inettitudine, dappocaggine, *f.*

inequality, *n.* ineguaglianza, *f.*

inequitable, *a.* ingiusto, non equo, poco equo.

ineradicable, *a.* inestirpabile.

inert, *a.* inerte. **inertia,** *n.* inerzia, *f.*

inestimable, *a.* inestimabile.

inevitable, *a.* inevitabile.

inexact, *a.* inesatto. **inexactitude,** *n.* inesattezza, *f.*

inexcusable, *a.* inescusabile, imperdonabile.

inexecutable, *a.* ineseguibile.

inexhaustible, *a.* inesauribile.

inexorable, *a.* inesorabile.

inexpedient, *a.* inopportuno.

inexpensive, *a.* poco costoso, a buon mercato.

inexperience, *n.* inesperienza, imperizia, *f.* ~**d,** *a.* inesperto.

inexplicable, *a.* inesplicabile.

inexplicit, *a.* non esplicito, poco chiaro.

inexpressible, *a.* inesprimibile.

in extenso, *ad.* in extenso.

inextinguishable, *a.* inestinguibile.

in extremis, *ad.* in extremis, agli estremi.

inextricable, *a.* inestricabile.

infallible, *a.* infallibile.

infamous, *a.* infame; (*Law*) infamante. **infamy,** *n.* infamia, *f.*

infancy, *n.* infanzia, *f.*; (*Law*) età minore, *f.* **infant,** *n.* neonato, *m.*, -a, *f.*; bambino, piccolo, *m.*, -a, *f.* (*Law*) minorenne, *m.f.* ~ *colony,* colonia nascente, *f.* ~ *mortality,* mortalità infantile, *f.* ~ *prodigy,* prodigio infantile, fanciullo miracoloso, *m.* ~ *school,* asilo infantile, giardino d'infanzia, *m.* **infanticide,** *n.* infanticidio, *m.* (*act*); (*pers.*) infanticida, *m.f.* **infantile,** *a.* infantile, d'infanzia; (*Med.*) infantile.

infantry, *n.* fanteria, *f.* ~**man,** fante, fantaccino, soldato di fanteria, *m.*

infatuate, *v.t.* infatuare. *to become* ~*d,* infatuarsi (di). **infatuation,** *n.* infatuazione, *f.*

infect, *v.t.* infettare; corrompere. ~**ion,** *n.* infezione, *f.* ~**ious,** *a.* infettivo; contagioso.

infer, *v.t.* inferire, dedurre, desumere. ~**ence,** *n.* inferenza; deduzione, conclusione, *f.* **inferential,** *a.* deduttivo. ~**ly,** *ad.* per via d'inferenza.

inferior, *a.* & *n.* inferiore, *a.* & *m.f.* ~**ity,** *n.* inferiorità, *f.* ~ *complex,* complesso d'inferiorità, *m.*

infernal, *a.* infernale. **inferno,** *n.* inferno, *m.*

infertile, *a.* infertile, sterile.

infest, *v.t.* infestare; molestare.

infidel, *a.* & *n.* infedele, *a.* & *m.f.* ~**ity,** *n.* infedeltà, *f.*

in-fighting (*Box.*), combattimento corpo a corpo, *m.*

infiltrate, *v.i.* infiltrarsi.

infinite, *a.* infinito. *the* ~, l'Infinito, Dio, *m.* **infinitesimal,** *a.* infinitesimale. **infinitive** [**mood**], *n.* [modo] infinito, *m.* **infinitude** & **infinity,** *n.* infinità, *f.* **infinity** (*Math., Phot.*), l'infinito, *m.*

infirm, *a.* infermo. ~**ary,** *n.* infermeria, *f.* ~**ity,** *n.* infermità, *f.*

inflame, *v.t.* infiammare; accendere; eccitare. **inflammable,** *a.* infiammabile. **inflammation,** *n.* infiammazione, *f.*

inflate, *v.t.* gonfiare; (*fig.*) enfiare, ingrandire, ingrossare. ~**d**, (*fig.*), *p.p.* ampolloso, tumido, turgido.
inflation, *n.* gonfiamento, *m.*; (*Fin.*) inflazione, *f.*
inflect, *v.t.* (*Gram.*) inflettere; (*voice*) modulare. **inflexible**, *a.* inflessibile. **inflexion**, -**ction**, *n.* inflessione; modulazione, *f.*
inflict, *v.t.* infliggere. ~**ion**, *n.* inflizione, *f.*
inflow, *n.* afflusso, *m.*
influence, *n.* influenza, *f.*, ascendente, *m.* ¶ *v.t.* influire su, influenzare.
influential, *a.* influente, autorevole, che ha grande influenza.
influenza, *n.* influenza, *f.*
influx, *n.* afflusso, *m.*; affluenza, *f.*
inform, *v.t.* informare; annunziare, comunicare, avvisare, ragguagliare, far sapere, mettere al corrente. ~ *against*, denunziare, deferire un'accusa contro. ~**al**, senza cerimonia; (*Law*) che non è nelle forme prescritte, non conforme alle norme ufficiali. ~ *gathering*, piccola riunione, riunione in famiglia, r. alla buona, r. senza cerimonie. ~**ality**, *n.* mancanza di formalità, *f.* ~**ant**, *n.* informatore, *m.*, -trice, *f.* ~**ation**, *n.* informazione, *f.*; avviso, *m.*, notizia, *f.* (*oft. pl.*); ragguagli, *m.pl.*; (*Law*) delazione, denunzia, *f.* ~**er**, *n.* (*Law*) delatore, *m.*, -trice, *f.*
infraction, *n.* infrazione, contravvenzione, *f.*
infrequent, *a.* infrequente, poco frequente, raro.
infringe, *v.t.* contravvenire, trasgredire, infrangere, violare. ~**ment**, *n.* contravvenzione, infrazione, violazione, contraffazione, *f.* ~ *of copyright*, contraffazione letteraria, violazione dei diritti d'autore, *f.*
infuriate, *v.t.* far infuriare, far arrabbiare.
infuse, *v.t.* infondere, instillare; fare un'infusione (di); ispirare. **infusible**, *a.* infusibile. **infusion**, *n.* infusione, *f.* **infusoria**, *n.pl.* infusori, *m.pl.*
ingathering, *n.* raccolta, *f.*
ingenious, *a.* ingegnoso, inventivo, abile. **ingenuity**, *n.* ingegnosità, destrezza, inventiva, astuzia, *f.*
ingenuous, *a.* ingenuo. ~**ness**, *n.* ingenuità, *f.*
ingle nook, angolo del focolare, *m.*
inglorious, *a.* inglorioso; ignominioso.

ingoing, *a.* entrante, che entra; (*mail, letters*) in arrivo.
ingot, *n.* lingotto, *m.*
ingrained, *a.* radicato, inveterato.
ingratiate oneself with, insinuarsi nelle buone grazie di.
ingratitude, *n.* ingratitudine, *f.*
ingredient, *n.* ingrediente, *m.*
ingress, *n.* accesso, ingresso, *m.*; entrata, *f.*
ingrowing, (*nail*) *a.* (unghia) incarnata.
inhabit, *v.t.* abitare. ~**able**, *a.* abitabile. ~**ant**, *n.* abitante, *m.f.*
inhale, *v.t.* inalare.
inherent, *a.* inerente.
inherit, *v.t.* & *abs.* ereditare. ~**ance**, *n.* eredità, successione, *f.*, patrimonio, retaggio, *m.*; (*right*) eredità, successione, *f.* ~**or**, ~**ress**, ~**rix**, *n.* erede, *m.f.*
inhibit, *v.t.* inibire, impedire.
inhospitable, *a.* inospitale.
inhuman, *a.* inumano. ~**ity**, *n.* inumanità, *f.*
inimical, *a.* ostile, avverso, contrario, nemico.
inimitable, *a.* inimitabile.
iniquitous, *a.* iniquo. **iniquity**, *n.* iniquità, *f.*
initial, *a.* iniziale, primo. ¶ *n.* iniziale, *f.*; (*pl.*) iniziali, *f.pl.* ¶ *v.t.* apporre le proprie iniziali.
initiate, *n.* iniziato, *m.*, -a, *f.* ¶ *v.t.* incominciare, prendere l'iniziativa per, iniziare; (*pers.*) iniziare. **initiation**, *n.* iniziazione, *f.* **initiative**, *n.* iniziativa, *f.*
inject, *v.t.* iniettare. ~**ion**, *n.* iniezione, *f.* ~**or**, *n.* iniettore, *m.*
injudicious, *a.* poco giudizioso, imprudente, indiscreto.
injunction, *n.* ingiunzione, *f.*
injure, *v.t.* nuocere a, danneggiare, ledere, ferire. fare torto a. ~ *fatally*, ferire mortalmente. **injurious**, *a.* nocivo (a), dannoso (per), lesivo (di). **injury**, *n.* male, danno, torto, *m.*; offesa, ferita, lesione, *f.*; (*fig.*) ingiuria, *f.*
injustice, *n.* ingiustizia, *f.*
ink, *n.* inchiostro, *m.* ~ *bottle*, bottiglia da inchiostro, *f.* ~ *eraser*, raschietto, raschino, *m.* ~*pot*, calamaio, *m.* ~*stand*, portacalamaio, *m.* *copying* ~, inchiostro copiativo, *m.* ~*well*, calamaio, *m.* *fountain pen* ~, inchiostro per penna stilografica, *m.* *printer's* ~, inchiostro da stampa, *m.* ¶ *v.t.* inchiostrare, tingere d'inchiostro.

~ *in*, mettere all'inchiostro. ~ *up*
(*Typ.*), inchiostrare.
inkling, *n.* sentore, sospetto, accenno,
m.
inlaid, *p.a.*; ~ *linoleum*, linoleo
incrostato, *m.* ~ *work*, intarsio,
lavoro d'intarsio, *m.*
inland, *n.* interno; (*Post*) servizio
postale interno, l'interno, *m.* ~
revenue, fisco, *m.*, entrate fiscali,
f.pl. ¶ *ad.* nell'interno, verso
l'interno.
inlay, *v.t. ir.* intarsiare; incrostare.
inlet, *n.* baia, insenatura, *f.*; (*Mach.*)
immissione, *f.*
inmate, *n.* abitante, *m.f.*; ospite, *m.f.*;
(*paying*) pensionante, *m.f.*; (*asylum*)
interno, *m.*, -a, *f.*
inmost, *a.* il piú profondo, il piú
intimo, il piú recondito.
inn, *n.* albergo, *m.*, locanda, osteria, *f.*
~ *keeper*, albergatore, *m.*, -trice, *f.*;
locandiere, *m.*, -a, *f.*
innate, *a.* innato, ingenito. ~ **ness,**
n. l'essere innato.
inner, *a.* interiore, interno, intimo,
segreto. ~ *harbour*, porto interno,
m. *the* ~ *man*, spirito dell'uomo;
(*fam.*) stomaco, appetito, *m.* ~ *tube*
(*tyre*), camera d'aria, *f.* ~ *room*,
retro-stanza, stanza interna, *f.*
innermost, *a.* il piú profondo, il piú
intimo, il piú recondito.
innings, *n.* (*Cricket*) turno, *m.*; (*fig.*)
volta, *f.*, periodo, *m.*
innocence, *n.* innocenza, *f.* **innocent,**
a. & n. innocente, *a. & m.f.*
~ **ly,** *ad.* innocentemente.
innocuous, innoxious, *a.* innocuo.
innovation, *n.* innovazione, *f.*
innovator, *n.* innovatore, *m.*
innuendo, *n.* insinuazione, *f.*
innumerable, *a.* innumerevole, innumerabile.
inobservance, *n.* inosservanza, *f.*
inoculate, *v.t.* inoculare. **inoculation,** *n.* inoculazione, *f.*
inodorous, *a.* inodoro.
inoffensive, *a.* inoffensivo.
inoperative, *a.* inefficace, senza
effetto, senza risultato.
inopportune, *a.* inopportuno. ~ **ly,**
ad. inopportunamente.
inordinate, *a.* eccessivo, smisurato.
inorganic, *a.* (*matter, body*) inorga-
nico; (*chemistry*) chimica inorganica,
f.
in-patient, *n.* interno, ammalato
ricoverato all'ospedale, *m.*
inquest, *n.* inchiesta, *f.*
inquire, *v.t. & i.* domandare,

chiedere (cercare) informazioni (di,
da); prendere notizie, informarsi;
indagare, ricercare. ~ *within*,
rivolgersi qui. **inquirer,** *n.* indagatore, *m.*, -trice, *f.*; chi domanda
informazioni, *m.f.* *inquiring mind,*
[spirito] indagatore, *m.* **inquiry,** *n.*
domanda, richiesta, inchiesta,
indagine, interrogazione, ricerca, *f.*;
esame, *m.*, informazioni, indagini,
f.pl. ~ *form*, modulo, *m.*, scheda, *f.*
~ *office*, ufficio informazioni, *m.*
~ *operator* (*Teleph.*), operatrice
d'informazioni, *f.*
inquisition, *n.* inquisizione, *f.* **inquisitive,** *a.* curioso, indagatore;
indiscreto.
inroad *&* **inrush,** *n.* incursione,
irruzione, *f.*
insane, *a.* insano, demente, alienato,
matto, pazzo. **insanity,** *n.* insania,
demenza, *f.*; (*folly*) pazzia, stoltezza,
f.
insanitary, *a.* insalubre, malsano.
insatiable, *a.* insaziabile.
inscribe, *v.t.* iscrivere, inscrivere,
incidere; dedicare. ~ *d stock*, titoli
nominativi, *m.pl.* **inscription,** *n.*
iscrizione, soprascritta; dedica, *f.*
inscrutable, *a.* inscrutabile.
insect, *n.* insetto, *m.* ~ *powder*,
polvere insetticida, *f.* **insectivora,**
n.pl. insettivori, *m.pl.* **insectivorous,** *a.* insettivoro.
insecure, *a.* malsicuro, incerto, poco
sicuro. **insecurity,** *n.* pericolo, *m.*,
incertezza, mancanza di sicurezza,
f.
insensate, *a.* insensato. **insensible,**
a. insensibile.
inseparable, *a. & n.* inseparabile.
a. & m.f.
insert (*Typ.*) *n.* aggiunta, *f.*, allegato,
m. ¶ *v.t.* inserire, introdurre.
~ **ion,** *n.* inserzione, *f.*
inset, *n.* pezzo riportato, *m.* ¶ *v.t. ir.*
aggiungere; inserire; (*Typ.*) acca-
vallare.
inshore, *a.* costiero. ~ *fishing*, pesca
costiera, *f.*
inside, *n.* interno, *m.*, parte interna, *f.*,
il di dentro, *m.* ¶ *a.* interno,
dell'interno, interiore. ~ *edge*,
(*Skating*) curva interna, *f.* ¶ *ad.*
dentro, all'interno. ~ *out*, a
rovescio. *turn* ~ *out*, mettere a
rovescio, rovesciare.
insidious, *a.* insidioso.
insight, *n.* penetrazione, conoscenza
intima, *f.*, discernimento, *m.*
insignia, *n.pl.* insegne, *f.pl.*

insignificant, *a.* insignificante.
insincere, *a.* poco sincero, finto, falso. **insincerity,** *n.* insincerità, mancanza di sincerità, *f.*
insinuate, *v.t.* insinuare.
insipid, *a.* insipido, scipito, (*fig.*) insulso.
insist, *v.i.* insistere. ~ence, *n.* insistenza, *f.*
insobriety, *n.* intemperanza, *f.*
insolation, *n.* insolazione, *f.*, colpo di sole, *m.*
insolence, *n.* insolenza, *f.* **insolent,** *a.* insolente. ~ly, *ad.* insolentemente.
insoluble, *a.* insolubile.
insolvency, *n.* insolvenza, *f.*, fallimento, *m.* **insolvent,** *a.* insolvente, fallito. *to become* ~, fallire.
insomnia, *f.* insonnia, *f.*
insomuch, *ad.* a tal punto (che), al punto (che).
inspect, *v.t.* ispezionare, esaminare; visitare, controllare, verificare; perquisire; riguardare; (*Mach.*) collaudare. ~ion, *n.* ispezione, verifica; (*Customs*) visita, *f.*; esame, collaudo, *m.* ~ *committee,* commissione di vigilanza, *f.* ~or, *n.* ispettore, *m.*; (*weights, &c.*) verificatore, *m.* ~orship, ispettorato, *m.*
inspiration, *n.* ispirazione, *f.* **inspire,** *v.t.* ispirare.
inspirit, *v.t.* animare, incoraggiare. ~ing, *a.* ispirante, incoraggiante.
instability, *n.* instabilità, *f.*
install, *v.t.* installare, insediare. ~ation, *n.* instaurazione, *f.*, insediamento, *m.*; impianto, *m.*
instalment, *n.* acconto, versamento, *m.*, rata, *f.*, pagamento rateale, *m.*; fascicolo, *m.* ~ *plan,* vendita a rate, con pagamenti rateali, *f.*
instance, *n.* esempio, caso, *m.*, occasione, *f.*; (*Law*) istanza, *f.* *for* ~, per esempio. ¶ *v.t.* citare ad esempio. **instant,** *a.* immediato, istantaneo; (*month*) corrente. ¶ *n.* istante, momento, attimo, *m.* *in an* ~, in un batter d'occhio. **instantaneous,** *a.* istantaneo. ~ly, *ad.* subito, all'istante.
instead, *ad.* invece, anziché. ~ *of,* invece di, in luogo di, al posto di.
instep, *n.* collo del piede, *m.*
instigate, *v.t.* istigare, incitare; promuovere. **instigation,** *n.* istigazione, *f.*
instil[l], *v.t.* instillare; (*fig.*) inculcare, infondere.

instinct, *n.* istinto, *m.* ¶ *a.* animato (di), pieno (di), imbevuto (di). ~ive, *a.* istintivo.
institute, *n.* istituto, *m.* ¶ *v.t.* istituire, fondare; (*Law*) intentare (una causa). **institution,** *n.* istituzione, *f.*, istituto, *m.*
instruct, *v.t.* istruire, insegnare; prescrivere, ordinare; (*counsel*) costituire, nominare. ~ion, *n.* istruzione, *f.*, insegnamento, *m.*; (*pl.*) istruzioni, disposizioni, *f.pl.*; ordini, *m.pl.* ~ional film, film educativo, *m.* ~ive, *a.* istruttivo. **instructor,** *n.* insegnante, professore; (*Mil.*) istruttore, *m.* **instructress,** *n.* istruttrice, insegnante, *f.*
instrument, *n.* strumento, arnese, ordigno, *m.*; (*Law*) atto, documento, *m.* ~al, *a.* strumentale. *to be* ~ *in,* contribuire a, servire a, concorrere a. ~alist, *n.* strumentista, *m.f.* ~ality, *n.* mezzo; concorso, *m.*, opera, *f.*
insubordinate, *a.* insubordinato.
insufferable, *a.* insopportabile, intollerabile.
insufficiency, *n.* insufficienza, *f.* **insufficient,** *a.* insufficiente. ~ly, *ad.* insufficientemente.
insular, *a.* insulare. ~ity, *n.* insularità, *f.* **insulation,** *n.* isolamento, *m.* **insulator,** *n.* isolatore, *m.* **insulate,** *v.t.* isolare.
insulin, *n.* insulina, *f.*
insult, *n.* insulto, affronto, oltraggio, *m.*, ingiuria, *f.* ¶ *v.t.* insultare, oltraggiare. ~ing, *a.* insultante, ingiurioso.
insuperable, *a.* insuperabile, insormontabile.
insupportable, *a.* insopportabile, intollerabile.
insurance, *n.* assicurazione, *f.*; (*Post*) raccomandazione, *f.* ~ *agent,* agente d'assicurazione, *m.* ~ *company,* compagnia d'assicurazione, società d'assicurazione, *f.* **insure,** *v.t.* assicurare; (*Post*) raccomandare, dichiarare il valore; (*v.i.*) assicurarsi. ~d (*pers.*), assicurato, *m.*, -a, *f.* ~d *for £*— (*Post*), valore dichiarato L. ~d *for £*— (*Post*), valore dichiarato L. ~d *parcel,* pacco con valore dichiarato, pacco raccomandato, *m.* **insurer,** *n.* assicuratore, *m.*
insurgent, *a. & n.* insorto, ribelle, *m.*; insorgente, ribelle, *a.*
insurmountable, *a.* insormontabile.
insurrection, *n.* insurrezione, sommossa, *f.*
intact, *a.* intatto.

intaglio, *n.* intaglio, *m.*

intake, *n.* immissione; presa d'acqua; (*Mech.*) energia assorbita; (*pump,* &c.) aspirazione, *f.*

intangible, *a.* intangibile.

integer, *n.* numero intero, *m.* **integral,** *a.* integrale. **integrity,** *n.* integrità, *f.*

intellect, *n.* intelletto, *m.* **intellectual,** *a. & n.* intellettuale, *a. & m.f.*

intelligence, *n.* intelligenza, *f.*; informazioni, *f.pl.*; avviso, *m.*, notizia, *f.*; accordo, *m.* ~ *department,* ufficio informazioni, *m.* **intelligencer,** *n.* informatore, *m.* **intelligent,** *a.* intelligente. ~**ly,** *ad.* intelligentemente. **intelligible,** *a.* intelligibile.

intemperance, *n.* intemperanza, *f.* **intemperate,** *a.* intemperante, intemperato, eccessivo.

intend, *v.t.* destinare, designare; (*v.i.*) intendere, avere l'intenzione (di), proporsi (di). ~**ed,** *a.* intenzionale, deliberato, volontario.

intense, *a.* intenso. ~**ly,** *ad.* intensamente. **intensify,** *v.t.* intensificare; (*Phot.*) rinforzare. **intensity,** *n.* intensità, *f.*

intent, *a.* intento, attento; assorto; fissato. ~ *on,* intento a, assorto in. ¶ *n.* intento, fine, scopo, disegno, *m.* *to all* ~*s & purposes,* sotto ogni riguardo pratico, virtualmente. ~**ion,** *n.* intenzione, *f.*; scopo, fine, *m.*; (*pl. matrimonial*) motivo, *m.* ~**al,** *a.* intenzionale; premeditato. **intentioned,** *a.* intenzionato. **intentness,** *n.* attenzione concentrata; intensa applicazione, *f.*

inter, *v.t.* seppellire, sotterrare.

intercalate, *v.t.* intercalare.

intercede, *v.i.* intercedere.

intercept, *v.t.* intercettare.

intercession, *n.* intercessione, *f.* **intercessor,** *n.* intercessore, *m.*

interchange, *n.* scambio reciproco, *m.* ~ *station* (*Rly.*), stazione di corrispondenza, *f.* ~**able,** *a.* scambievole l'uno per l'altro, alternativo.

intercourse, *n.* rapporti, *m.pl.*, relazioni, *f.pl.*; commercio, traffico, *m.*

interdict, *n.* interdetto, *m.* ¶ *v.t.* interdire, proibire. ~**ion,** *n.* interdizione, *f.*

interest, *n.* interesse, *m.*; interessi, *m.pl.*; attrattiva; attenzione; parte, partecipazione, *f.* *to take no further* ~ *in,* non interessarsi piú di. ~ *on overdue payments,* interessi moratori, *m.pl.* *principal & ~,* capitale ed

interessi. *rate of* ~, saggio d'interesse, *m.* *simple* ~, *compound* ~, interesse semplice, i. composto, *m.* ¶ *v.t.* interessare, importare. ~**ed,** *p.a.* interessato. ~ *party,* parte (persona) interessata, *f.* ~**ing,** *p.a.* interessante. *in an* ~ *condition* (*pregnant*), incinta, in istato interessante.

interfere, *v.i.* intervenire (in), immischiarsi (in), intromettersi (in). ~ *with* (*hinder*), opporsi a, ostacolare; impicciarsi di, intralciare. **interference,** *n.* intervento, *m.*, intromissione, *f.*, ingerenza, *f.*; intralcio, *m.*; (*Phys.*) interferenza, *f.*

interim, *n.* frattempo, intervallo, *m.* ~ *dividend,* dividendo interinale, d. provisorio, *m.*

interior, *a. & n.* interiore, interno, *a. & m.*

interject, *v.t.* interporre, inserire, inframmettere. ~**ion,** *n.* interiezione, *f.*

interlace, *v.t.* intrecciare, intessere.

interlard, *v.t.* lardellare; infiorare.

interleave, *v.t.* interfogliare.

interline, *v.t.* interlineare. **interlinear,** *a.* interlineare. **interlineation,** *n.* interlineazione, *f.*

interlocutor, -tress, *or* **-trix,** *n.* interlocutore, *m.*, -trice, *f.*

interloper, *n.* intruso, *m.*

interlude, *n.* intervallo, *m.*; (*Mus.*) intermezzo, interludio, *m.*

intermarriage, *n.* matrimonio tra diversi ceti, diverse famiglie, o diverse razze, o fra stretti parenti. **intermarry,** *v.i.* contrarre matrimonio fra parenti o con una persona di diversa razza o famiglia o condizione.

intermeddle, *v.i.* immischiarsi, ingerirsi.

intermediary, *n. & a.* intermediario, *a. & m.* **intermediate,** *a.* intermedio. ~*course* (*Sch.*), corso medio, *m.*

interment, *n.* seppellimento, *m.*, inumazione, *f.*

intermezzo, *n.* intermezzo, *m.*

interminable, *a.* interminabile.

intermingle, *v.t.* mescolare, frammischiare.

intermission, *n.* intermissione, interruzione, *f.* **intermittent,** *a.* intermittente. ~*light* (*Naut.*), luce i., *f.*, faro [a luce] i., *m.*

intermix, *v.t.* mescolare, frammischiare.

intern, *v.t.* internare.

internal, *a.* interno. ~ *combustion engine,* motore a combustione interna, *m.* ~**ly,** *ad.* internamente, all' interno.

international, *a.* internazionale. ~ (*association*) & ~**e** (*hymn*), *n.* internazionale, *f.* ~**ist,** *n. & a.* internazionalista, *m.f. & a.*

internecine, *a.* micidiale, ad oltranza.

internment, *n.* internamento, l'internare, *m.* ~ *camp,* campo di concentramento, *m.*

interpolate, *v.t.* interpolare.

interpose, *v.t.* interporre; (*v.i.*) interporsi.

interpret, *v.t.* interpretare. ~**ation,** *n.* interpretazione, *f.* ~**er,** *n.* interprete, *m.f.*

interregnum, *n.* interregno, *m.*

interrogate, *v.t.* interrogare. **interrogation,** *n.* interrogazione, *f.* ~ *mark,* punto interrogativo, *m.* **interrogative,** *a. & n.* interrogativo, *a. & m.* **interrogatory,** *n.* interrogatorio, questionario, *m.*

interrupt, *v.t.* interrompere. ~**er,** *n.* (*pers.*) interruttore, *m.,* -trice, *f.;* (*switch*) interruttore, *m.* **interruption,** *n.* interruzione, *f.*

intersect, *v.t.* intersecare, tagliare. ~**ion,** *n.* intersecazione; intersezione, *f.*

intersperse, *v.t.* disseminare, spargere qua a là, cospargere; alternare con.

interstice, *n.* interstizio, *m.*

intertwine, *v.t.* intrecciare, intessere.

interval, *n.* intervallo, *m.;* (*Theat.*) intervallo, *m.*

intervene, *v.i.* intervenire, frapporsi; (*time*) trascorrere. **intervention,** *n.* intervento, *m.*

interview, *n.* intervista, *f.,* abboccamento, colloquio, *m.,* udienza, *f.;* ¶ *v.t.* intervistare, abboccarsi con.

inter vivos, fra i vivi.

interweave, *v.t. ir.* intessere, intrecciare.

intestate, *a.* intestato, senza disposizioni testamentarie.

intestinal, *a.* intestinale. **intestine,** *a. & n.* intestino, *a. & m.;* interno, domestico *a.*

intimacy, *n.* intimità, *f.* **intimate,** *a. & n.* intimo, familiare, *a. & m.* ¶ *v.t.* far sapere, dare ad intendere, annunziare, avvisare, dichiarare, accennare. **intimation,** *n.* avviso, cenno, indizio, *m.;* intimazione, *f.*

intimidate, *v.t.* intimidire.

into, *pr.* in, dentro.

intolerable, *a.* intollerabile. **intolerance,** *n.* intolleranza, *f.* **intolerant,** *a.* intollerante.

intonation, *n.* intonazione, *f.* **intonate, intone,** *v.t.* intonare.

intoxicate, *v.t.* ubbriacare, inebriare; (*poison*) intossicare. ~**d,** *a.* ubbriaco, inebriato, ebbro. **intoxication,** *n.* ubbriachezza, ebbrezza; intossicazione, *f.*

intractable, *a.* intrattabile, indocile.

intrados, *n.* intradosso, *m.*

intransitive, *a.* intransitivo.

intrench, *v.t.* trincerare.

intrepid, *a.* intrepido. ~**ity,** *n.* intrepidità, *f.*

intricacy, *n.* complicazione, *f.,* imbroglio, carattere intricato, *m.* **intricate,** *a.* complicato, intricato.

intrigue, *n.* intrigo, *m.;* tresca, *f.;* intreccio, *m.* ¶ *v.i.* intrigare, tramare, brigare, complottare; (*v.t.*) intrigare, brigare. **intriguer,** *n. &* **intriguing,** *a.* intrigante, *a. & m.f.*

intrinsic, *a.* intrinseco, essenziale, proprio, vero.

introduce, *v.t.* introdurre, fare entrare, presentare, far conoscere; cominciare, iniziare. ~ *oneself,* introdursi, presentarsi. **introducer,** *n.* introduttore, *m.,* -trice, *f.* **introduction,** *n.* introduzione, presentazione; prefazione, *f.*

introit, *n.* introito, *m.*

introspection, *n.* introspezione, *f.*

intrude, *v.i.* intrudere, insinuarsi, interporsi. **intruder,** *n.* intruso, *m.,* -a, *f.* **intrusion,** *n.* intrusione, *f.*

intuition, *n.* intuito, *m.,* intuizione, *f.* **intuitive,** *a.* intuitivo. ~**ly,** *ad.* intuitivamente.

inundate, *v.t.* inondare. **inundation,** *n.* inondazione, *f.*

inure, *v.t.* indurire, abituare, avvezzare.

invade, *v.t.* invadere. **invader,** *n.* invasore, *m.*

invalid, *a.* invalido, infermo, ammalato; (*Law*) invalido, nullo. ¶ *n.* ammalato, *m.,* -a, *f.,* invalido, *m.,* -a, *f.,* infermo, *m.,* -a, *f.* ¶ *v.t.* (*Mil.*) riformare (*declare unfit*). ~**ate,** *v.t.* rendere nullo; invalidare. **invalided,** *p.a.* invalido; riformato (*Mil.*). **invalidity,** *n.* invalidità, *f.*

invaluable, *a.* inestimabile, impagabile.

invariable, *a.* invariabile.

invasion, *n.* invasione.

invective, *n.* invettiva, ingiuria, *f.* **inveigh,** *v.i.* inveire. ~ *against,* declamare contro, scagliarsi contro, inveire contro.

inveigle, *v.t.* adescare, attirare, sedurre.
invent, *v.t.* inventare. ~**ion,** *n.* invenzione, *f.*; inganno, *m.*, frode, *f.*; *(fiction)* fantasia, immaginazione, *f.* ~**ive,** *a.* inventivo.
inventor, -tress, *n.* inventore, *m.*, -trice, *f.*
inventory, *n.* inventario, *m.* ¶ *v.t.* fare l'inventario di, inventariare.
inverse, *a.* inverso. **inversion,** *n.* inversione, *f.* **invert,** *v.t.* invertire. ~*ed commas,* virgolette, *f.pl.* *to put in* ~*ed commas,* mettere fra virgolette.
invertebrate, *a. & n.* invertebrato, *a. & m.*
invest, *v.t.* investire; circondare, mettere l'assedio a.; *(money)* investire, collocare, impiegare.
investigate, *v.t.* investigare, indagare. **investigation,** *n.* investigazione, indagine, *f.* **investigator,** *n.* investigatore, *m.*
investiture, *n.* investitura, *f.*
investment, *n.* investimento, collocamento, impiego, *m.*; *(Mil.)* investimento, *m.* **investor,** *n.* chi ha danari da investire, chi investe capitali. *small* ~, piccolo risparmiatore, *m.*
inveterate, *a.* inveterato; incorreggibile, ostinato; inguaribile.
invidious, *a.* sgradevole, offensivo; scabroso. ~ *distinction,* distinzione che provoca invidia, distinzione sgradita, *f.*
invigilate, *v.i.* invigilare.
invigorate, *v.t.* invigorire, rinforzare.
invincible, *a.* invincibile.
inviolable, *a.* inviolabile. **inviolate,** *a.* inviolato, intatto.
invisible, *a.* invisibile. ~ *ink,* inchiostro simpatico, *m.* ~ *mending,* rammendo invisibile, *m.*
invitation, *n.* invito, *m.* **invite,** *v.t.* invitare, fare (rivolgere) un invito a; allettare, attrarre. **inviting,** *p.a.* attraente, attrattivo, seducente.
invocation, *n.* invocazione, *f.*
invoice, *n.* fattura, *f.* ¶ *v.t.* fatturare.
invoke, *v.t.* invocare.
involuntary, *a.* involontario.
involve, *v.t.* implicare, coinvolgere; compromettere; cagionare, causare; portare con sé, rendere necessario. ~**d,** *p.a.* implicato, coinvolto, compromesso. ~ *language,* stile involuto, discorso abbindolato.
invulnerable, *a.* invulnerabile.
inward, *a.* interiore, interno, intimo.

~*bound,* di ritorno. ~[s], verso l'interno, all'interno. ~**ly,** *ad.* internamente, intimamente. fra se.
~**s,** *n.pl.* visceri, *m.pl.*; interiora, *f.pl.*
iodine, *n.* iodio, *m.*
ion, *n.* iono, *m.*
Ionian, Ionic, *a.* Ionio, ionico.
iota, *n.* iota, *f.*
ipecacuanha, *n.* ipecacuana, *f.*
irascible, *a.* irascibile, irritabile, collerico. **irate,** *a.* adirato, iroso.
ire, *n.* ira, collera, *f.*; sdegno, *m.*
Ireland, *n.* l'Irlanda, *f.*
iridescence, *n.* iridescenza, *f.* **iridescent,** *a.* iridescente.
iridium, *n.* iridio, *m.*
iris, *n.* iride, *f.*
Irish, *a.* irlandese. *the* ~ *Free State,* lo Stato Libero d'Irlanda, *m.* ~*man,* ~*woman,* irlandese, *m.f.* ~ *Sea,* Mare d'Irlanda, *m.* ¶ *(language) n.* l'irlandese, *m.*
irksome, *a.* noioso, fastidioso, penoso, tedioso.
iron, *n. (metal, wrought, for linen, golf, &c.)* ferro, *m.*; *(cast, pig)* ghisa, *f.*; *(sheet)* lamiera di ferro, latta, *f.* ¶ *a.* ferreo, di ferro, in ferro. ~ *(& steel) constructional work,* costruzione in ferro, *f.* ~ *(or steel) bridge),* ponte di ferro, *m.* ~ *& steel shares,* valori siderurgici, v. metallurgici, *m.pl.* ~ *clad (ship),* corazzata, *f.* ~ *constitution,* salute di ferro, *f.*, costituzione ferrea, *f.* ~ *master,* proprietario di ferriere, *m.* ~*monger (small),* chincagliere, *m.*; *(big.)* negoziante in ferramenta, negoziante di ferravecchi, *m.* ~*mongery,* chincaglieria, ferravecchi, *m.pl.*, articoli in ferro, *m.pl.* ~ *ore,* minerale di ferro, *m.* ~*shod,* ferrato. ~*work,* lavoro in ferro, *m.*, *(girders, &c.)* costruzione in ferro, *f.* ~ *worker,* lavoratore in ferro, ferraio, fabbro, *m.* ~ *works;* ferriera, *f.* ¶ *v.t.* ferrare; *(linen)* stirare. ~ *out,* spianare, lisciare. ~**er,** *n.* stiratore, *m.*, -trice, *f.*; macchina per stirare, *f.* ~**ing,** *n.* stiratura, *f.*
ironic(al), *a.* ironico. **irony,** *n.* ironia, *f.*
irradiation, *n.* irradiazione, *f.*
irrational, *a.* irrazionale, poco ragionevole, assurdo.
irreclaimable, *a. (pers.)* incorreggibile; *(land)* incoltivabile.
irreconcilable, *a.* irreconciliabile.
irrecoverable, *a.* irrecuperabile. ~ *arrears (taxes),* credito inesigibile, *m.*, arretrati inesigibili, *m.pl.*

irredeemable, *a.* irredimibile.
irredentism, *n.* irredentismo, *m.*
irreducible, *a.* irriducibile.
irrefutable, *a.* irrefutabile.
irregular, *a.* irregolare, sregolato, disordinato; asimmetrico. **~ity,** *n.* irregolarità, sregolatezza, *f.*; disordine, *m.*; anormalità, *f.*
irrelevant, *a.* irrilevante, fuor di proposito, senza rapporto con; *(Law)* non pertinente.
irreligious, *a.* irreligioso, indevoto, profano, empio, miscredente.
irremediable, *a.* irrimediabile.
irremovable, *a.* irremovibile, fisso.
irreparable, *a.* irreparabile.
irrepressible, *a.* irreprimibile, che non si può reprimere; *(laughter)* smoderato, inestinguibile.
irreproachable, *a.* irreprensibile.
irresistible, *a.* irresistibile.
irresolute, *a.* irresoluto, indeciso.
irrespective of, indipendente da, senza riguardo per, *a.*
irresponsible, *a.* irresponsabile.
irretrievable, *a.* irreparabile, irrimediabile.
irreverent, *a.* irriverente.
irrevocable, *a.* irrevocabile.
irrigate, *v.t.* irrigare. **irrigation,** *n.* irrigazione, *f.* **irrigator,** *n.* irrigatore, *m.*
irritable, *a.* irritabile. **irritate,** *v.t.* irritare. **irritation,** *n.* irritazione, *f.*
irruption, *n.* irruzione, *f.*
isinglass, *n.* colla di pesce, *f.*
Islam, *n.* Islam, islamismo, *m.*; la religione di Maometto, *f.*
island, *n.* isola, *f.*; *(houses)* isolato, *m.* *street* **~,** salvagente, *m.* **~er,** *n.* isolano, *m.*, **-a,** *f.* **isle,** *n.* isola, *f.*
islet, *n.* isoletta, *f.*
isolate, *v.t.* isolare. **isolation,** *n.* isolamento, *m.* **~** *hospital,* ospedale d'isolamento, *m.*
Israel, *n.* Israele, *m.*
Israelite, *n.* israelita, *m.f.*
issue, *n.* uscita, *f.*, sbocco, sfogo, esito, risultato, *m.*; *(notes, &c.)* emissione, *f.*, rilascio, *m.*, distribuzione, *f.*; conclusione, questione, *f.*; punto in dibattito, *m.*; *(publications)* pubblicazione, stampa, tiratura, edizione, *f.*; numero, *(offspring)* discendenza, prole, figliazione, *f.*; discendenti, *m.pl.*; *(Med.)* scolo, *m.* at **~,** in lite; di cui si tratta. **¶** *v.i.* uscire; zampillare, scaturire; emanare; terminare, sboccare; *(v.t.)* pubblicare, emettere, rilasciare.
isthmus, *n.* istmo, *m.*

it, *pn.* esso, egli, *m.*, essa, *f.*; lo, *m.*, la, *f.*; ciò. **~** *is I,* sono io. **~** *is you,* siete voi. **~** *is said that* . . ., si dice che . . . **~** *is six o'clock,* sono le sei. *about* **~,** ne, ci. *at* **~,** ci, vi, a tal passo; a tal punto. *by* **~,** ne, ci. *for* **~,** ne, per ciò. *from* **~,** ne, da esso. *in* **~,** ci, vi, in esso. *of* **~,** ne, di esso. *to* **~,** ci, vi, a ciò, ad esso.
Italian, *a.* italiano. **¶** *n. (pers.)* italiano, *m.*, **-a,** *f.*; *(language)* l'italiano, *m.*, lingua italiana, *f.*
italic, *a.* italico. **~s,** *n.pl.* corsivo, carattere corsivo, *m.* **italicize,** *v.t.* stampare in corsivo; *(fig.)* accentuare.
Italy, *n.* l'Italia, *f.*
itch, *v.i.* prudere; *(fig.)* aver gran voglia (di). *my arm itches,* il braccio mi prude, sento (un) prurito al braccio. **~[ing],** *n.* prurito, *m.*; rogna, scabbia, *f.* **~y,** *a.* che prude, rognoso.
item, *n.* articolo, elemento, *m.*; partita, particola, voce, cosa, qualchecosa, *f.*; capo, *m.* **¶** *ad.* parimenti, similmente.
itinerant, *a.* girovago, ambulante. **itinerary,** *n.* itinerario, *m.*
its, *a.* il suo, suo, la sua, i suoi, le sue, ne.
itself, *pn.* esso stesso, essa stessa, si, sé, sé medesimo, sé stesso.
ivory, *n.* avorio, *m.* *the I* **~** *Coast,* la Costa d'Avorio, *f.*
ivy, *n.* edera, ellera, *f.*

J

jabber, *v.i. & t.* ciarlare, cicalare, chiacchierare; borbottare; parlare rapidamente od incoerentemente.
jacinth, *n.* giacinto, *m.*
jack, *n. (Mach.)* cricco, martinetto, *m.*, binda, *f.*; *(spit)* girarrosto, spiedo, *m.*; *(fish)* luccio, *m.*; *(Cards)* fante, *m.*; *(Bowls)* boccino, *m.* *J* **~,** Gianni. *Yellow J* **~,** febbre gialla, *f.* **~ass,** somaro, *m.*; *(fig.)* scioccone, goffone, *m.* **~boot,** stivalone, *m.* **~daw,** gracchia, *f.* *J* **~** *in office,* piccolo funzionario pieno della sua importanza, *m.* **~-in-the-box,** gi[u]ocattolo a sorpresa; saltamartino, *m.* **~knife,** coltello a serramanico tascabile, *m.* *J* **~** *of all trades* (or *work*) *and master of none,* guastamestieri, *m.inv.* **~-o-lantern,**

fuoco fatuo, *m.* ~ *plane*, pialletto, *m.*
before you could say J ~ *Robinson*,
in men che non si dice, in un
attimo, in un batter d'occhio.
~ *tar*, marinaio, *m.* ~ *towel*, asciugamano, *m.*

jackal, *n.* sciacallo, *m.*

jackanapes, *n.* sciocchino, vispetto,
birboncello; zerbino.

jacket, *n.* (*lounge*) giacca, giubba, *f.*;
(*short*) giacchetta, giubbettina, *f.*;
(*cardigan*) panciotto di lana tessuto
a maglia, *m.*; (*book*) copertina, *f.*;
(*steam, water*) camicia, *f.* ~ *potatoes*,
patate in camicia, *f.pl.*

jacobin, *n.* giacobino, *m.*

jade, *n.* (*horse*) rozza, brenna, *f.*,
brocco, *m.*; (*woman*) donnaccia,
sgualdrina, megera, *f.*; (*Min.*) giada,
f. ~**d,** *a.* affaticato, stracco, stanco.

jag, *v.t.* intaccare, frastagliare,
dentellare.

jaguar, *n.* giaguaro, *m.*

jail, &*c.,* Same as *gaol,* &*c.*

jam, *n.* (*fruit*) marmellata, conserva, *f.*;
(*squeeze*) serra, pigia, calca, *f.*;
(*Mach.*) incaglio, *m.*; (*traffic*) ostruzione, *f.* ~ *pot*, vaso per la
conserva, *m.* ¶ *v.t.* serrare, pigiare;
incagliare, bloccare; (*Radio*) disturbare.

Jamaica, *n.* la Giammaica, *f.*

jamb, *n.* stipite, *m.* ~ *lining*, guarnizione degli stipiti, *f.*

jangle, *n.* stonatura; discordia, *f.*
¶ *v.i.* stonare; leticare, altercare;
(*v.t.*) stonare; fare discordare, rendere
discordante.

janitor, *n.* custode; portinaio, *m.*

January, *n.* gennaio, *m.*

japan, *n.* vernice giapponese, lacca del
Giappone, *f.* ¶ *v.t.* laccare, inverniciare. **Japan,** *n.* il Giappone, *m.*
Japanese, *a.* giapponese. ~ *curios*,
&*c.,* oggetti (vasi, bronzi; ricami,
&c.) giapponesi, *m.pl.* ~ *paper* &
~ *porcelain*, carta del Giappone, *f.*,
porcellana del G~, *f.* ¶ *n.* (*pers.*)
giapponese, *m.f.*; (*language*) il giapponese, *m.*, lingua giapponese, *f.*

jar, *n.* giara, *f.*, vaso, *m.*, brocca, *f.*,
boccale, *m.*, bottiglia, *f.*; (*jolt*) urto,
m., scossa, vibrazione, *f.* ¶ *v.i.*
stonare, mandare un suono aspro
e discorde; riuscire sgradevole; non
accordarsi. ~ *upon*, offendere,
irritare, urtare; (*nerves*) dare in.

jardiniere, *n.* (*stand*) portafiori, *m.inv.*

jargon, *n.* gergo; linguaggio professionale, *m.*; parlare poco
intelligibile, *m.*

jarring, *a.* discordante, stonato; in
conflitto.

jasmin[e], *n.* gelsomino, *m.*

jasper, *n.* diaspro, *m.*

jaundice, *n.* itterizia, *f.* ~**d,** *a.*
itterico; (*fig.*) geloso, astioso,
presentato sotto falsa luce.

jaunt, *n.* gita, scampagnata, *f.* ~**y,** *a.*
gaio, vivace, attillato.

Java, *n.* Giava, *f.* **Javanese,** *a.*
giavanese. ¶ *n.* giavanese, *m.f.*;
(*language*) il giavanese, *m.*, lingua
giavanese, *f.*

javelin, *n.* giavellotto, *m.*

jaw, *n.* mascella; ganascia, *f.*; (*pl.
animal*) fauci, *f.pl.*; (*Anat.*) mandibola, *f.*; (*pl. of death*) braccia della
morte, fauci della morte, *f.pl.*
~*-bone*, osso mascellare, osso della
mascella, *m.*

jay (*bird*), *n.* ghiandaia, *f.* ~*walker*,
pedone disattento, *m.*

jealous, *a.* geloso. ~**y,** *n.* gelosia,
f.

jeep, *n.* camionetta, *f.*, gip, *m.*

jeer, *n.* rinfaccio, sarcasmo, *m.*,
beffa, *f.* ¶ *v.i.* beffarsi, farsi giuoco,
~ *at*, beffarsi di, farsi giuoco di;
(*pers.*) burlarsi di; schernire, rinfacciare; ridere alle spalle di.

jejune, *a.* insipido, privo d'interesse.

jelly, *n.* gelatina; conserva, *f.* ~*fish*,
medusa, *f.*

jemmy, *n.* grimaldello, *m.*

jennet, *n.* ginnetto, *m.*

jeopardize, *v.t.* mettere in pericolo,
mettere a repentaglio, arrischiare.
jeopardy, *n.* repentaglio, pericolo.

jerboa, *n.* gerboa, *f.*

jeremiad, *n.* geremiade, *f.*

jerk, *n.* stratta, spinta, *f.*, strappo,
scatto; urto, *m.*; scossa, *f.* ¶ *v.t.*
fare saltare, spingere, scuotere,
strappare. ~**y,** *a.* a scatti, a scosse,
a strappi.

jerry-build, *v.t.* costruire in fretta
e con cattivi materiali. ~**er,** *n.*
costruttore di case per speculazione,
m. ~**ing,** *n.* costruzione frettolosa, *f.*
jerry-built, *a.* non solido, costrutto
in fretta, c. con lo sputo. **jerry-
work** *n.* lavoro mal fatto, abbor-
racciamento, *m.*

jersey, *n.* camiciotto di lana, *m.*,
maglia, *f.* *J* ~ (*Geog.*), *n.* Jersey, *f.*
J ~ *cow*, vacca di Jersey, *f.*

Jerusalem, *n.* Gerusalemme, *f.*

jessamin[e], *n.* gelsomino, *m.*

jest, *n.* scherzo, motteggio, frizzo,
tiro, *m.*, celia, arguzia, burla, *f.*
¶ *v.i.* scherzare, motteggiare, celiare,

burlare. ~er, *n.* burlone, celiatore; (*court*) buffone, *m.*

Jesuit, *n.* gesuita, *m.* ~ical, *a.* gesuitico.

Jesus, *n.* Gesú, *m.* *Jesus Christ*, Gesú Cristo, *m.*

jet, *n.* getto, zampillo; becco (di gas); tubo di scarico; *m.*, zaffata, *f.*; (*lignite*) giaietto, *m.*, ambra nera, *f.* ~(*-black*), nero come l'ambra nera, color nero cupo. ~*plane*, aeroplano a reazione,, *m.* ~ *propulsion*, propulsione a reazione, *f.*

jetsam, *n.* relitti di mare, *m.pl.* **jettison,** *n.* gettito (in mare), *m.* ¶ *v.t.* fare gettito, gettare fuori bordo.

jetty, *n.* gettata, *f.*, molo, *m.*

Jew, *n.* ebreo, israelita, *m.* ~'*s harp*, scacciapensieri, *m.inv.*

jewel, *n.* gioiello, *m.*, gioia, *f.*; (*Horol.*) rubino, *m.* ~ *case*, scrigno, cofanetto, *m.*; (*travelling*) portagioielli, *m.inv.* **jeweller,** *n.* gioielliere, *m.* **jewel[le]ry,** *n.* gioielli, *m.pl.*, gioie, *f.pl.*; (*trade, art*) gioielleria, *f.*

Jewess, *n.* ebrea, israelita, *f.* **Jewish,** *a.* ebreo, giudeo; giudaico, israelita. **Jewry,** *n.* gli Ebrei, *m.pl.*

jib, *n.* (*sail*) fiocco, *m.*; (*crane*) braccio (di gru), *m.* ¶ *v.i.* mostrarsi ricalcitrante; (*horse*) accularsi.

jibe, *n. & v.i.* Same as *gibe*.

jiffy, *n.* (*slang*) attimo, istante, batter d'occhio, *m.*

jig, *n.* (*Mus., dance*) giga, *f.* ~*-saw*, sega verticale, mossa da una leva. ~*-saw puzzle*, giuoco di pazienza, *m.*

jilt, *v.t.* mancare alla promessa di matrimonio, essere infedele a.

jingle, *n.* tintinnio, *m.*, consonanza, *f.*; rima (o poesia) senza significato, *f.* ¶ *v.i. & t.* tintinnare, fare tintinnare; far rima.

jingoism, *n.* sciovinismo, *m.*, megalomania patriottica, *f.*

jinricksha, *n.* risciò, *m.inv.*

jiu-jitsu, *n.* lotta giapponese, *f.*

job, *n.* compito, lavoro, affare, *m.*; bisogna, impresa, opera, *f.*; maneggio, intrigo, raggiro, *m.* *a good* ~ *that*, meno male che. ~ *line* or ~ *lot*, mercanzie d'occasione, *f.pl.*, soldo, *m.* ~ *master*, noleggiatore di carrozze (*or* di cavalli). ~ *work*, lavoro a cottimo, *m.*; (*Typ.*) lavoro vario, *m.* **jobber** (*shady*), *n.* intrigante, sfruttatore, speculatore di Borsa, *m.*

jobbery, *n.* raggiro, *m.*; impresa equivoca, *f.* **jobbing** (*tailor, &c.*), *p.a.* a cottimo, cottimista.

jockey (*Turf*), *n.* fantino, *m.* *J~ Club*, circolo di amatori di cavalli e che ne organizzano le corse.

jocose, *a.* giocoso, allegro, burlesco.

jocular, *a.* faceto, scherzoso, motteggiatore. ~ly, *ad.* a modo faceto, giocosamente, scherzosamente.

jocund, *a.* giocondo, gaio; allegro.

jog, *v.t.* spingere, scuotere (leggermente); (*attention, memory*) eccitare, stimolare. ~ *along*, far cammino, trotterellare. ~ *on*, procedere lentamente, avviarsi. ~*-trot*, piccolo trotto, trotterello, *m.*; (*fig.*)

joggle, *n.* leggera scossa, *f.*; (*Carp., Build.*) immorsatura, caletta, *f.* ¶ *v.t.* scuotere leggermente.

John, *n.* Giovanni, *m.* *J~ Dory*, pesce di San Pietro, *m.*

join, *v.t.* giungere, congiungere, legare insieme, collegare, unire; accoppiare; associare. ~ *battle*, attaccare battaglia. ~ *in*, partecipare a, entrare in; unirsi in, unirsi per. ~er, *n.* falegname, legnai[u]olo, *m.* ~ery, *n.* falegnameria, *f.*; lavoro da falegname, *m.* **joint,** *n.* giuntura, *f.*, giunto, *m.*, articolazione, *f.*; nodo (*Bot.*), *m.*; accoppiamento, *m.*, cerniera (*hinge*), *f.*; (*fishing-rod, &c.*) commettitura, incastratura, *f.*; (*meat*) pezzo, *m. to put out of* ~, slogare. ¶ *v.t.* unire a mezzo di giunture od articolazioni. ¶ *a.* congiunto, indiviso, comune, collettivo, unito; co-, con-, com-. ~ (*commission, committee*), misto. *on* ~ *account*, in conto comune, in compartecipazione. ~ *& several*, solidale. ~ *& several liability*, responsabilità solidale, *f.* ~ *manager*, condirettore, *m.* ~ *estate*, ~ *ownership*, proprietà indivisa, *f.* ~ *tenant*, coinquilino, casigliano, *m.* ~*-stock bank*, banca a tipo anonimo, società anonima che esercita il commercio bancario, *f.* ~*-stock company*, società anonima, *f.* **jointure,** *n.* beni dotali, *m.pl.*, sopraddote, *f.*

joist, *n.* trave, *f.*, travicello, corrente, *m.*

joke, *n.* scherzo, *m.*; celia, facezia, *f.*, motto spiritoso, *m.*; (*feeble*) freddura, *f.* ¶ *v.i.* scherzare, celiare, dire facezie, d. freddure. **joker,** *n.* burlone, celione, motteggiatore, *m.*; persona faceta, *f.*

jollification & jollity, *nn.* festa,

baldoria, *f.*, giubilo, *m.*, giubilazione, gaiezza, *f.* **jolly**, *a.* allegro, gaio, gioioso; gioviale. ~ *well*, ben ben. *to be* ~ (*in drink*), essere brillo, alticcio, mezzo cotto.
jolt, *n.* scossa, *f.*, sobbalzo, trabalzo, *m.* ¶ *v.i.* sobbalzare; *v.t.* far sobbalzare, scuotere.
Jonah (*fig.*), *n.* iettatore, *m.*
jonquil, *n.* giunchiglia odorosa, *f.*
Jordan (**the**), *n.* Giordano, il fiume G., *m.*
Joseph, *n.* Giuseppe, *m.*
jostle, *v.t.* spingere, urtarsi contro, dar di gomito a.
jot, *n.* particella, iota, ette, *f.*, nulla, *m.* ~ *down*, gettare giú, prendere nota di.
journal, *n.* giornale, diario, *m.*; (*shaft*) perno, *m.*; (*axle*) collo dell'asse, *m.* ~**ism**, *n.* giornalismo, *m.* ~**ist**, *n.* giornalista, *m.f.*
journey, *n.* viaggio; (*distance*) giornata, marcia, tappa, *f.* ~*man*, giornaliero, operaio avventizio, *m.*
joust, *n.* torneo, *m.*, giostra, *f.* ¶ *v.i.* giostrare, torneare.
jovial, *a.* gioviale. ~**ity**, *n.* giovialità, *f.*
jowl, *n.* mascella, gota, guancia, *f.* *cheek by* ~, guancia a guancia.
joy, *n.* gioia, letizia, allegrezza, *f.* ~**ful** & ~**ous**, *a.* gioioso, lieto. ~**fulness**, *n.* allegrezza, gioia, *f.*
jubilation, *n.* esultanza, *f.*, giubilo, *m.*
jubilee, *n.* giubileo, *m.* ~ *year*, anno del giubileo, *m.*
Judaic, *a.* giudaico, ebreo.
Judas, *n.* Giuda, *m.*
judge, *n.* giudice; magistrato; conoscitore, intenditore, esperto, *m.* ¶ *v.t.* & *i.* giudicare. **judg**[**e**]**ment**, *n.* giudizio, *m.*, sentenza, *f.*; decreto; avviso; senno, discernimento, *m.* **Judges** (*Bible*), *n.pl.* Libro dei Giudici, *m.*
judicature, *n.* giudicatura, *f.*, potere giudiziario, *m.* **judicial**, *a.* giudiziario; legale.
judicious, *a.* giudizioso, accorto, assennato, sagace, prudente.
judo (*or* **jiu-jitsu**), *n.* lotta giapponese, *f.*
jug, *n.* brocca, *f.*; boccale, *m.*; caraffa, *f.* ~**ful**, *n.* brocca piena, *f.* *jugged hare*, un intingolo di lepre, *m.*
juggle, *v.i.* giocolare, fare il prestigiatore. ¶ ~ & ~**ry**, *n.* giuoco di destrezza, *m.*, prestidigitazione, *f.*
juggler, *n.* prestigiatore, giocoliere, *m.*

Jugo-Slav, *a.* iugoslavo. ¶ *n.* iugoslavo, *m.*, -a, *f.* **Jugo-Slavia**, *n.* la Iugoslavia, *f.*
jugular [**vein**], *n.* [vena] giugulare, *f.*
juice, *n.* succo, sugo, *m.* **juicy**, *a.* succoso.
jujube, *n.* giuggiola, pastiglia dolce, *f.* ~ [*shrub*], giuggiolo, *m.*
ju-jutsu, *n.* lotta giapponese, *f.*
julep, *n.* giulebbe, *m.*
July, *n.* luglio, *m.*
jumble, *n.* miscuglio, guazzabuglio, *m.*; confusione, *f.* ~ *sale*, vendita di oggetti spaiati, *f.* ~ *shop*, negozio di cianfrusaglie, *m.* ¶ *v.t.* confondere, mescolare; mischiare.
jump, *n.* salto, sbalzo, *m.* ¶ *v.i.* & *t.* saltare, fare un salto, balzare; precipitarsi. ~ *over*, saltare, scavalcare, attraversare saltando. ~**er**, *n.* (*pers.*) saltatore, *m.*, -trice, *f.*; (*sailor's*) camiciotto di lana, *m.*; (*woman's*) giubbettino (di lana), golf, *m.*; (*bus*) controllore, *m.* ~**ing** : ~ *jack*, saltamartino, *m.* ~-*off ground* (*fig.*), trampolino, *m.* ~ *skis*, sci di salto, *m.pl.*
junction, *n.* congiunzione, unione, *f.*; (*Rly. line*, &c.) diramazione, *f.*, nodo ferroviario, *m.*; (*Rly. station*) stazione di diramazione, *f.*
juncture, *n.* congiuntura, circostanza, *f.*; punto, momento, *m.*; crisi, *f.*
June, *n.* giugno, *m.*
jungle, *n.* giungla, *f.*; (*att.*) della giungla.
junior, *a.* iuniore, piú giovane; minore; assistente, subalterno; (*partner*) (socio) subordinato; (*clerk*) secondo commesso. ~ *officer*, ufficiale subalterno. ¶ *n.* iuniore, (il) giovane, cadetto; (*son*) figlio, iuniore; (*Sport*) iuniore, *m.*
juniper, *n.* (*genus*) ginepro, *m.*
junk, *n.* (*Chinese*) giunca, *f.*; (*tow*) gomena vecchia, *f.*; (*refuse*) oggetti di rifiuto, *m.pl.*
junket, *n.* giuncata, *f.* ¶ *v.i.* far festa, banchettare, dare trattenimento.
juridicial, *a.* giuridico. **jurisdiction**, *n.* giurisdizione, *f.* **jurist**, *n.* giurista, *m.*
juror, juryman, *n.* giurato, *m.* **jury**, *n.* giurati, *m.pl.*; giuria, *f.*, giurí, *m.* ~ *mast*, albero di fortuna, *m.*
just, *a.* giusto, equo, imparziale; meritato; appropriato; esatto, preciso. ¶ *ad.* giusto, appena, appunto, proprio, precisamente; recentissimamente, *or* ora; non . . . che; tutto.

~ *as*, tutto come; proprio quando; così, altrettanto. ~ *now*, or ora, proprio adesso, un momento fa. ~ *so*, proprio così, già. *I have* ~, ho appena . . . **justice**, *n.* giustizia, *f.*; (*as to a meal*) onore, *m.*; (*pers.*) giudice, *m.*

justifiable, *a.* giustificabile; (*homicide*) colposo. **justification**, *n.* giustificazione, *f.* **justify**, *v.t.* giustificare; motivare.

justly, *ad.* giustamente, a buon diritto, con ragione. **justness**, *n.* giustizia; giustezza, precisione, esattezza, *f.*

jut [out], *v.i.* sporgere, aggettare, avanzarsi, proiettarsi.

jute, *n.* iuta, *f.* ~ *works*, iutificio, *m.*

juvenile, *a.* giovanile; giovane; (*books*) per la gioventú. ~ *offender*, imputato minorenne, *m.* ¶ *n.* giovane; minorenne, *m.f.*; fanciullo, *m.*, -a, *f.*; bambino, *m.*, -a, *f.*

juxtapose, *v.t.* giustapporre.

K

kale, *n.* cavolo, *m.*

kaleidoscope, *n.* caleidoscopio, *m.*

kangaroo, *n.* canguro, *m.*

kaolin, *n.* caolino, *m.*

kedge [anchor], *n.* ancorotto, *m.*

keel, *n.* chiglia, *f.* **ke[e]lson**, *n.* paramezzale, *m.*

keen, *a.* (*edge*, *point*, &c.) affilato, aguzzo; acuminato, acuto; tagliente; (*fig.*) sottile, penetrante, accorto; ardente; scaltro; grande, intenso; pungente, mordente; avido; vivo; aspro, piccante, caustico; (*sportsman*, &c.) appassionato. *a* ~ *disappointment*, un vivo disappunto. ~*ly*, *ad.* vivamente, acutamente. ~**ness**, *n.* acutezza, finezza, sottigliezza, *f.*; ardore, *m.*; avidità, *f.*

keep, *n.* mantenimento, *m.*; (*castle*) maschio, torrione, *m.* ¶ *v.t. ir.* tenere, mantenere; serbare, conservare, preservare; avere, fare; condurre, gestire; seguire; celebrare, osservare; (*v.i. ir.*) tenersi, mantenersi; stare, restare, rimanere; continuare (a), non cessare (da); conservarsi. ~ *a saint's day*, celebrare, osservare una festa. ~ *away*, assentarsi; tenersi lontano, t. a distanza; (*v.t.*) tenere lontano,

allontanare. ~ *back*, *v.t.* tenere indietro, ritenere, trattenere; celare, nascondere; reprimere; (*v.i.*) tenersi indietro, t. in disparte. ~ *in* (*Sch.*), impedire (proibire) d'uscire. ~ *in with*, mantenersi in buona relazione con, nelle buone grazie di. ~ *off*, *v.i.* allontanarsi, tenersi lontano. (*please*) ~ *off the grass*, è vietato camminare sull'erba. ~ (*on*), continuare, proseguire. ~ *one's hand in*, tenersi in pratica, t. in esercizio. ~ *to oneself*, starsene da solo, tenersi in disparte. ~ *the type standing*, conservare la composizione. ~ *watch & ward*, fare la ronda. ~**er**, *n.* custode, guardiano, *m.*; (*game*) guardacaccia, *m.* ~**ing**, *n.* custodia, protezione, conservazione; tenuta; armonia, *f.*, accordo, *m.* ~ *apples*, mele da confetturare, *f.pl. in* ~*with*, in armonia con; d'accordo con.

keepsake, *n.* ricordo, pegno d'affetto, p. d'amicizia, *m.*

keg, *n.* barilotto, *m.*

ken, *n.* conoscenza, vista, *f.*

kennel, *n.* canile, covo, *m.*; (*hounds*) muta, *f.*; (*street gutter*) grondaia, cunetta, *f.*

Kenya, *n.* la Chenia, *f.* ~ *Colony & Protectorate*, la colonia e protettorato di C.

kerb, *n.* bordo del lastricato, cordone del marciapiede, *m.* ~ *stone*, paracarro, *m.*

kerchief, *n.* fazzoletto, fisciù, *m.*

kernel, *n.* (*of nut*, *stone fruit*, *seed*) mandorla, *f.*, nocciolo, *m.*; (*nucleus*) nucleo, *m.*; (*gist*) essenza, sostanza, *f.*, nocciolo, *m.*

kerosene, *n.* petrolio raffinato, p. illuminante, *m.*

kestrel, *n.* gheppio, *m.*

ketch, *n.* piccolo veliero a due alberi, *m.*

kettle, *n.* caldaia, *f.*; calderotto, *m.*; bricco, *m.* ~ *drum*, timballo, timpano, *m.* ~ *drummer*, timpanista, suonatore di timballi, *m.*

key, *n.* chiave, *f.*; (*watch*, &c.) chiavetta, *f.* (*piano*, &c.) tasto, *m.*; (*to school book*) chiave; (*Mus.*) chiave, *f.*; tono, *m.*; (*Mech.*) chiavetta, bietta, *f.* ~*board*, tastiera, *f.* ~ *chain*, catenella per le chiavi, *f.* ~*hole*, buco della serratura, *m.* ~*hole saw*, gattuccio, *m.* ~ *industria*, industria chiave, *f.* ~ *money*, caparra, *f.* ~*note*, tonica, *f.*; (*fig.*) nota dominante, *f.*, motivo principale, *m.* ~*-ring*, (anello) portachiavi, *m.*

signature (*Mus.*), armatura, *f.* ~
stone, chiave di volta, *f.* ~ *way*,
alloggiamento per chiavetta, *m.* ¶
v.t. chiudere a chiave; (*Mus.*) intonare, accordare. *to* ~ *up*, stimolare,
incitare. ~*ed*, *p.a.* a chiave. ~*less*,
a. senza chiave; (*watch*) a remontcir.
khaki, *n.* kaki, *m.*
Khedive, *n.* kedivè, *m.*
kibble (*Min.*), *n.* secchia di ferro, *f.*
kick, *n.* calcio, *m.*, pedata, *f.*, colpo di
piede, *m.*; (*horse*) calcio, *m.*; (*gun*)
rinculo, *m.* ~-*off* (*Foot.*), calcio
d'inizio, *m.* *corner* ~ (*Foot.*), c.
d'angolo, *m.* *free* ~ (*Foot.*), c. di
punizione, *m.* *penalty* ~ (*Foot.*),
c. di rigore, *m.* ¶ *v.t.* colpire col
piede, prendere a calci, spingere col
piede; (*a goal*) segnare; (*v.i.*) (*horse*,
&c.) calciare; menar calci, tirar
calci; (*gun*) rinculare. ~ *about*, *v.i.*
sgambettare; *v.t.* sballottare (con
colpi di piede). ~ *at* (*fig.*),
dibattersi contro. ~*er*, *n.* (*pers.*)
calciante; (*animal*) calcitrante.
kid, *n.* capretto, *m.* ~ *gloves*, guanti
glacés, g. di pelle di capretto, *m.pl.*
kiddy, *n.* bambino, bimbo, *m.*
kidnap, *v.t.* rapire, involare, portar
via a forza.
kidney, *n.* (*Anat.*) rene, *m.*; (*meat*)
rognone, *m.*; (*fig.*) tempra, indole, *f.*,
umore, *m.* ~ *bean*, fagiolino, *m.*
kill, *n.* caccia, cacciagione ,*f.* ¶ *v.t*
uccidere, ammazzare, abbattere;
assassinare; far morire; spegnere.
killed in action, ucciso in combattimento. *the killed*, i morti, i caduti,
m.pl. ~-*joy*, guastafeste, *m.f.inv.*
~*er*, *n.* uccisore, *m.*, -sora, *f.*; assas
sino, omicida, *m.* ~*ing*, *n.* uccisione, *f.*; assassinio, omicidio, *m.*;
(*animals*) macellazione, *f.* ¶ *a.*
mortale, che uccide, assassino;
(*bewitching*) affascinante, assassino.
kiln, *n.* forno, *m.*; fornace, *f.* ~-*dry*,
seccare al forno.
kilo *&* **kilogramme**, *n.* chilo, chilogramma, *m.* **kilocycle**, *n.* chilo-
ciclo, *m.* **kilometer** *&* **kilometre**,
n. chilometro, *m.* **kilometric**(**al**), *a.*
chilometrico. **kilowatt**, *n.* chilowatt, *m.inv.*
kilt, *n.* gonnellino, *m.*, gonnella alla
scozzese, *f.* ¶ *v.t.* raccogliere in
pieghe.
kimono, *n.* chimono, *m.*
kin, *n.* parenti, congiunti, *m.pl.*;
parentela, *f.*
kind, *a.* gentile, cortese; amabile;
benevolo; buono; tenero; compia-

cente, indulgente. ~ *regards*,
saluti, complimenti, ossequi, *m.pl.*
¶ *n.* genere, *m.*; specie; sorta; razza,
f. in ~, in natura.
kindergarten, *n.* giardino d'infanzia,
asilo infantile, *m.*
kindle, *v.t.* accendere; (*fig.*) destare,
eccitare, infiammare.
kindliness, *n.* amabilità, benevolenza,
bontà di cuore, *f.* **kindly**, *a.*
benevolo; benefico, favorevole. ¶ *ad.*
gentilmente, benevolmente; con
gentilezza; in buona parte. **kindness**, *n.* bontà; gentilezza; benevolenza; compiacenza, *f.*
kindred, *n.* parentela, *f.*; parenti,
congiunti, *m.pl.* ¶ *a.* della stessa
famiglia; (*fig.*) analogo, dello stesso
ordine.
king, *n.* re, *m.inv.*; (*Draughts*) dama, *f.*
~-*bolt*, perno, *m.* ~-*cup*, bottone
d'oro, *m.* ~-*fisher*, martin pescatore,
m. ~-*post*, monaco, *m.* *oil*, *steel*, ~,
~*dom*, *n.* (*lit. & fig.*) regno, *m.*
~*let*, *n.* reuccio, *m.* ~*ly*, *a.*
regale, reale; da re.
kink, *n.* attorcigliamento, *m.*; (*fig.*)
ghiribizzo, grillo, *m.* ¶ *v.t.* attorcigliare; (*v.i.*) attorcigliarsi, *v.refl.*
kinship, *n.* parentela, *f.* **kinsman**,
~**woman**, *n.* parente, *m.f.*,
congiunto, *m.*, -a, *f.*
kiosk, *n.* chiosco, *m.*; (*news-stall*)
edicola, *f.*
kipper, *n.* aringa affumicata, *f.* ¶ *v.t.*
affumicare e conservare.
kiss, *n.* bacio, *m.* ¶ *v.t.* baciare;
(*repeatedly*) baciucchiare; (*embrace*)
abbracciare, accarezzare. ~*ing*
crust, orliccio, *m.*
kit, *n.* corredo; arredo, *m.* ~*bag*,
valigia inglese, *f.*; (*Mil.*) sacco, *m.*
kitchen, *n.* cucina, *f.* ~ *boy*, sguattero, *m.*, lavapiatti, *m.inv.* ~ *garden*,
orto, *m.* ~ *maid*, sguattera, serva, *f.*
~*er*, *n.* fornello da cucina, *m.*
kite, *n.* (*bird*) nibbio, *m.*; (*toy*)
aquilone, cervo volante, *m.*; (*Com.*)
cambiale di comodo, *f.*
kith *&* **kin**, amici e parenti, *m.pl.*
kitten, *n.* gattino, micio, micino, *m.*
kleptomania, *n.* cleptomania, *f.*
kleptomaniac, *n.* cleptomane, *m.f.*
knack, *n.* dono, colpo, *m.*; abilità,
destrezza, *f.*; (*slightingly*) abitudine,
f.; trucco, *m.*
knacker, *n.* negoziante o macellatore
di cavalli fuori uso, *m.*
knapsack, *n.* zaino, *m.*
knave, *n.* briccone, ` furfante,
impostore, *m.*; (*Cards*) fante, *m.*

~**ry**, *n.* bricconeria, furfanteria, *f.*
knavish, *a.* furbo, malizioso, da mariuolo.
knead, *v.t.* impastare. ~*ing trough*, madia, *f.*
knee, *n.* ginocchio, *m.* ~ *breeches*, calzoni fino al ginocchio, calzoncini, *m.pl.* ~*cap* (*Anat.*), rotella, rotula, *f.*; (*pad*) ginocchiello, *m.*
kneel [**down**], *v.i. ir.* inginocchiarsi, mettersi in ginocchio. *kneeling desk*, inginocchiatoio, *m.*
knell, *n.* rintocco (funebre), suono a morte, *m.*
knickerbockers & **knickers**, *n.pl.* calzoni larghi e raccolti sotto il ginocchio, calzettoni, *m.pl.*
knick-knack, *n.* ninnolo, gingillo, *m.*
knife, *n.* coltello, *m* ~*board*, lustra-coltelli, *m.* ~ *cleaner*, macchina per pulire i coltelli, *f.* ~ *edge*, filo (d'un coltello), *m.* ~, *fork*, & *spoon*, posata, *f.* ~ *grinder*, arrotino, *m.* ~ *rest*, reggiposata; portacoltelli, *m.inv. before you can say* ~, in un attimo, in un batter d'occhio. *to the* ~ (*war*), (guerra) accanita, (lotta) mortale. ¶ *v.t.* dare una coltellata a, pugnalare.
knight, *n.* cavaliere, *m.*; (*Chess*) cavallo, *m.* ~ *errant*, cavaliere errante; (*fig.*) paladino, *m.* ~ *errantry*, cavalleria errante *f.* ~*hood*, cavalleria, *f.*; titolo di cavaliere, *m.* ~ *Templar*, Templare, *m.* **knightly**, *a.* cavalleresco.
knit, *v.t. & i.ir.* lavorare a maglia, fare a maglia; fare la calza; (*brow*) aggrottare (le ciglia); (*fig.*) legare, unire. **knitted** (*vest*, &*c.*), fatto (lavorato, tessuto) a maglia. ~ *garment*, indumento fatto a maglia, *m.* **knitter**, *n.* tessitore, *m.*, -trice, *f.*, a maglia. **knitting**, *n.* lavoro a maglia, tessuto a m., *m.* ~ *needle*, ~ *pin*, ferro da calza, ago per lavori a maglia, *m.* **knitwear**, *n.* lavori a maglia, *m.pl.*
knob, *n.* bottone, pomo; bernoccolo; nodo, *m.*; (*Radio*) manopola, *f.*
knock, *n.* colpo, *m.*; (*at the door*) bussata, *f.*; picchio, *m.* ¶ *v.t. & i.* colpire; urtare; bussare, picchiare; dare una bussata un picchio. ~*-about comedian*, buffone, *m.* ~ *down*, abbattere; atterrare; abbassare; (*auction*) aggiudicare. ~*kneed*, colle gambe a iccasse. ~*out* (*Box.*), knock-out, fuori combattimento, *m.* ~**ed up**, spossato, rifinito. ~**er** (*door*), *n.* martello, picchiottolo, *m.*

knoll, *n.* monticello, poggio, *m.*, collinetta, *f.*
knot, *n.* nodo; (*cluster*) gruppo; (*tangle*) garbuglio, *m.* *running* ~, n. scorsoio, n. scorrevole. ¶ *v.t.* annodare. **knotty**, *a.* nodoso; nocchiuto; (*fig.*) spinoso.
know, *v.t. & i.ir.* conoscere; sapere; essere informato (di). ~ (*again*), riconoscere. ~ *how to*, sapere. *not to* ~, ignorare. ~*ing*, *a.* scaltro, fino, furbo; accorto, perspicace. ~**ingly**, *ad.* consciamente, scientemente, a bello studio. **knowledge**, *n.* conoscenza; cognizione, *f.*; sapere, *m.*, erudizione; notorietà, *f. to my* ~, a mia saputa. *without my* ~, a mia insaputa. **known**, *a.* noto; *p.a.* conosciuto, saputo.
knuckle, *n.* nocca, *f.*; (*veal*) garetto, *m.* ~ [*bone*] [*mutton*], garetto, *m.* ~ *bones* (*game*), aliossi, *m.pl.* ~*-duster*, pugno di ferro, *m.* ~ (*joint*) (*Mech.*), giunto a cerniera, *m. knuckle under* or *down*, cedere, sottomettersi.
knurl, *n.* godronatura, zigrinatura, *f.* ¶ *v.t.* zigrinare.
kohlrabi, *n.* cavolrapa, *f.*
Koran, *n.* corano, alcorano, *m.*
Korea, *n.* la Corea, *f.*
kosher, *a.* (cibo) preparato secondo la legge ebraica.
kudos, *n.* fama, gloria, *f.*
kursaal, *n.* casino, *m.*

L

label, *n.* etichetta, *f.*; cartellino, *m.* ¶ *v.t.* attaccare l'etichetta a, contrassegnare con etichetta; (*pastᵉ on*) incollare l'e. su; (*fig.*) denominare, descrivere.
labial, *a.* labiale. ¶ *n.* labiale, *f.*
laboratory, *n.* laboratorio, *m.*; officina, *f.*
laborious, *a.* laborioso, faticoso, penoso. **labour**, *n.* lavoro, *m.*, fatica, pena, *f.*; impresa, *f.*; mano d'opera, *f.*; le classi operaie, *f.pl.* ~ *exchange*, ufficio impieghi, ufficio statale di collocamento dei lavoratori, *m.* ~ *market*, ~ *supply*, mercato del lavoro., *m.* ~ (*pains*), doglie, *f.pl.* ~ *party*, partito dei lavoratori, partito laburista, *m.*

~ *question*, questione operaia, *f.*
~-*saving*, *a.* che risparmia la mano
d'opera.   ~ *troubles*, conflitti tra
operai e datori di lavoro. ¶ *v.i. & t.*
lavorare, sforzarsi, affaticarsi; (*land*)
arare; (*ship*) travagliare; rullare.
~*ed*, (*fig.*) *p.a.* elaborato, stentato.
~*er*, *n.* lavoratore, operaio, manovale, bracciante; cantoniere; uomo di
fatica; giornaliero, *m.*; (*farm*)
lavoratore agricolo, *m.*
laburnum, *n.* avornio, laburno, *m.*
labyrinth, *n.* labirinto, dedalo, *m.*
lac, *n.* lacca, *f.*   ~, *lak of rupees*,
centomila rupie.
lace, *n.* merletto, pizzo, *m.*, trina, *f.*;
(*boot*, *&c.*) laccio (da scarpe), *m.*;
stringa, *f.*; (*leather*) coreggiolo, *m.*
~ *boots*, stivali, scarpe coi lacci.
~ *insertion*, applicazione in pizzo,
f.   ~-*up shoes*, scarpe con stringhe,
f.pl.   ¶ *v.t.* allacciare, allacciarsi;
gallonare.   guarnire di pizzo.   ~
oneself tight(*ly*), serrarsi.   ~*d paper*,
carta traforata, *f.*
lacerate, *v.t.* lacerare.
lack, *n.* mancanza, deficienza, scarsità,
f. ¶ *v.t.* mancare di.   ~*ing in*, che
manca di, senza, digiuno di.   ~
lustre, a, atono, smorto, appannato.
lackadaisical, *a.* lezioso, smorfioso,
sentimentale.
lackey, *n.* lacchè, valletto, *m.*; (*fig.*)
adulatore, *m.*
laconic, *a.* laconico.
lacquer, *n. & ~ work*, lacca, *f.*
¶ *v.t.* verniciare, laccare.
lacrosse, *n.* lacrosse, *f.*
lacteal, *a.* latteo.
lacuna, *n.* lacuna, *f.*, vuoto, *m.*
lacustrine, *a.* lacustre.
lad, *n.* giovanetto, giovane, ragazzo,
fanciullo, *m.*
ladder, *n.* scala (a piuoli), *f.*; (*stocking*,
&c.) sfilatura, maglia caduta, *f.*
~*proof*, indemagliabile.   ¶ *v.i.*
smagliarsi.
lade, *v.t. ir.* caricare.
ladle, *n.* mestolo, ramaiuolo, cucchiaione, *m.*   ~*ful*, *n.* mestolata, *f.*
lady, *n.* signora, dama, padrona di
casa; nobildonna, *f.*   *ladies' &
children's wear*, novità, *f.pl. Ladies
& Gentlemen!* Signore! Signori!
ladies first! prima le signore!
~*bird*, coccinella, *f.*   ~ *bookkeeper*,
contabile, *f.*   ~ *cashier*, cassiera, *f.*
L~ chapel, cappella della Madonna,
f.   ~ *clerk*, impiegata, *f.*   ~ *companion*, dama (damigella) di compagnia, *f.*   *L~ Day*, festa del-

l'Annunziata, *f.*; il 25 marzo.   ~
doctor, medichessa, dottoressa, *f.*
~*killer*, dongiovanni, damerino,
m.   *his* (*my*) ~ *love*, donna dei
suoi (dei miei) pensieri, *f.*   ~ *of
the manor*, castellana, *f.*   ~ *secretary*, segretaria, *f.*   ~*'s hand
bag*, borsetta da signora, *f.*   ~*'s
maid*, cameriera, *f.*   ~*'s* (or
ladies') *man*, damerino, cavaliere,
beniamino delle signore, cicisbeo, *m.*
~*like*, da signora, distinto; effeminato.
lag, *v.i.* indugiare, trascinarsi; (*v.t.*)
fasciare, rivestire.   ~ *behind*,
restare indietro.
lager [**beer**], *n.* birra leggera (tipo
tedesco), *f.*
lagoon, *n.* laguna, *f.*
laic, *n. & laic*(**al**), *a.* laico, *a. & m.*
laid paper, carta vergata, *f.* **laid up**
(*in bed*), ammalato, obbligato a
tenere il letto; (*ship*) disarmato.
lair, *n.* tana, *f.*; covo, nascondiglio, *m.*
laity, *n.* laici, *m.pl.*
lake, *n.* lago, *m.*; (*paint*) (pigmento)
rosso scuro.   ~ *dwelling*, abitazione
lacustre (costruita su palafitte), *f.*
lama, *n.* lama, *m. Grand Lama*, Gran
Lama, *m.*
lamb, *n.* agnello, *m.*; (*pers.*) chi è
innocente come l'agnello.   ¶ *v.t.*
figliare (agnelli).   ~*kin*, agnellino,
agnelletto, *m.*
lambent, *a.* (*light*) blando, dolce,
diffuso.
lame, *a.* zoppo; storpio; claudicane;
(*fig.*) imperfetto, incompleto.   ¶ *v.t.*
storpiare; rendere zoppo.
lamé, *a. & n.* laminato, *a. & m.*
lameness, *n.* zoppaggine, *f.*; l'essere
zoppo, *m.*
lament, *n.* lamento, pianto, *m.*;
querela, elegia, *f.*; canto funebre,
m.; aria lamentosa, *f.*   ¶ *v.i.*
lamentarsi, dolersi; (*v.t.*) rimpiangere; deplorare.   ~*able*, *a.*
lamentevole, deplorevole.   ~*ation*,
n. lamento, *m.*, grida di dolore, *f.pl.*
the (*late*) ~*ed*, il (la) compianto, -a.
lamina, *n.* lamina, piastra di metallo,
f. **laminate**, *v.t.* laminare.
lammergeyer, *n.* avvoltoio barbuto,
m.
lamp, *n.* lampada, lucerna, *f.*, fanale,
m.; (*street*) lampione, *m.*   ~ *black*,
nero (di) fumo, *m.*   ~ *ighter*,
lampionaio, *m.*   ~ *man*, lampista,
m.   ~ *oil*, olio da ardere, olio per
lampade, *m.*   ~ *post*, ~ *standard*,
lampione, palo per lampione, *m.*

~ *room*, lampisteria, *f.* ~ *shade*, paralume, *m.*

lampoon, *n.* pasquinata, satira personale, *f.*; libello, *m.* *v.t.* fare oggetto d'una pasquinata, deridere. ~**er,** *n.* scrittore di pasquinate, *m.*

lamprey, *n.* lampreda, *f.*

lance, *n.* lancia, *f.* ¶ (*Surg.*) *v.t.* aprire con una lancetta. **lancers** (*Dance*), *n.pl.*, lancieri (specie di quadriglia). **lancet,** *n.* lancetta, *f.* ~ *window*, finestra ogivale, *f.*

land, *n.* terra, *f.*; terreno; paese, *m.*; contrada, proprietà, *f.* ~ *bank*, banca di credito agrario, *f.* *Crown* ~*s*, terreni demaniali, *m.pl.* ~*fall*, approdo, *m.*; (*fig.*) eredità improvvisa, *f.* ~ *carriage*, trasporto per terra, *m.* ~ *locked* (*sea*, *&c.*), circondato da terra; (*Law*) rinchiuso da terre, intercluso. ~ *locked property*, fondo intercluso, *m.* ~*lord*, ~*lady*, possidente, *m.f.* padrone, *m.*, -a, *f.*; oste, *m.*, ostessa, *f.*; proprietario d'immobili, *m.*; locatore, *m.* ~*lubber*, marinaio d'acqua dolce, *m.* ~*mark*, punto di riferimento, segno di confine, limite, *m.* ~ *of milk & honey*, ~ *of plenty*, (paese di) cuccagna, *m*, ~*owner*, possidente, *m.f.*; proprietario fondiario, *m.* ~ *reclamation*, bonifica, *f.* ~*scape* & ~ *scape painting*, paesaggio, *m.* ~*scape garden*, giardino all'inglese, *m.* ~*scape gardener*, disegnatore di giardini, *m.* ~*scape painter*, paesista, *m.* ~*slide*, ~*slip*, frana, *f.* ~*slide* (*Pol.*), sfacelo, *m.*; rovina, *f.* ~ *tax*, imposta fondiaria, *f.* ¶ *v.t.* sbarcare, mettere a terra; (*ball*) piazzare; (*blow*) dirigere, vibrare; (*fish*) tirare a terra; (*v.i.*) approdare, sbarcare, scendere a terra.

landau, *n.* landò, *m.* ~**let,** *n.* landaulet (*Fr.*), *m.*

landed property, proprietà fondiaria, *f.* **landing,** *n.* approdo, sbarco, scalo; (*quay*) sbarcatoio, *m.*; banchina *f.*; (*aircraft*) atterraggio, *m.*; (*stairs*) pianerottolo, *m.* ~ *gear* (*Aero.*), treno d'atterraggio, *m.* ~ *net*, vangaiola, *f.* ~ *place*, ~ *stage*, approdo, sbarcatoio, scalo, *m.*; banchina, *f.*; pontile, sbarcatoio galleggiante, *m.* ~ *ticket*, carta di sbarco, *f.* **landsman,** *n.* chi vive in terraferma, uomo di terra, *m.*

lane, *n.* sentiero, vicolo, passaggio, *m.*; viuzza, stradicciola, *f.*; (*running*) corridoio, *m.*

language, *n.* lingua, *f.*; linguaggio, *m.*, favella, *f.*

languid, *a.* languido. **languish,** *v.i.* languire. ~**ing,** *a.* languente, tenero, dolce, pieno di languore. **languor,** *n.* lang\`ore, abbattimento, struggimento di desiderio, *m.*; apatia, *f.* ~**ous,** pieno di languore, sonnacchioso; seducente, carezzevole.

lank, *a.* magro, sparuto, sottile; (*hair*) liscio, piatto. ~**y,** *a.* alto e magro.

lantern, *n.* lanterna, *f.*, fanale, faro, *m.* ~ *jawed*, con le guancie infossate. ~ *slide*, proiezione luminosa, *f.*

lanyard, *n.* (*Naut.*) drizza, sagola, *f.*

lap, *n.* (*of pers.*) grembo, *m.*, ginocchia, *f.pl.*; (*of luxury*) mezzo, seno, *m.*; (*of dress*) falda, piega, *f.*; (*layer*) letto, *m.*; (*overlap*) ricoprimento, *m.*; (*sport*) giro (della pista), *m.*; (*polisher*) smerigliatrice, *f.* ~ *dog* cagnolino (di lusso), *m.* ¶ *v.t.* lambire, leccare; (*grind*) smerigliare. ~ *over*, *v.i.* ricoprire, ripiegarsi (su). ~ [*up*], *v.t.* leccare.

lapel, *n.* falda, risvolta, *f.*; rovescio, *m.*

lapidary, *a. & n.* lapidario, *a. & m.*

lapis lazuli, *n.* lapislazzuli, *m.*

Lapland, *n.* la Lapponia, *f.* **Lapp,** *a.* lappone. **Lapp, Lapplander,** *n.* lappone, *m.f.*

lappet, *n.* falda, *f.*, lembo, *m.*

lapse, *n.* decorrenza, *f.*; decorso, passaggio, *m.*; (*moral*) errore, fallo, sbaglio, *m.*; (*expiration*) decadenza, scadenza, *f.*; (*time*) volgere, trascorso, intervallo, *m.* ¶ *v.i.* passare, trascorrere; decadere.

lapwing, *n.* pavoncella, *f.*

larceny, *n.* ladrocinio, furto, *m.*

larch, *n.* larice, *m.*

lard, *n.* lardo, strutto, *m.*; sugna, *f.* ¶ *v.t.* (*Cook.*) lardellare; (*fig.*) arricchire, condire. ~**er,** *n.* dispensa, *f.*

Lares, *n.pl.* lari, *m.pl.*

large, *a.* grande, ampio, grosso, largo; abbondante, copioso; spazioso; raguardevole, rilevante; considerevole. ~ *hand* (*writing*), scrittura grossa, *f.*, larghi caratteri, *m.pl.* *at* ~, libero, in libertà, alla larga. *as* ~ *as life*, di grandezza naturale. ~**ly,** *ad.* in gran parte. ~**ness,** *n.* grandezza; importanza, *f.* **largess[e],** *n.* dono, regalo, *m.*; liberalità, *f.*

lark, *n.* (*bird*) allodola, *f.*; (*frolic*) scappata, *f.*, scherzo, *m.* ~**spur,**

fior cappuccio, *m.*, consolida reale, *f.*
larva, *n.* larva, *f.*
laryingitis, *n.* laringite, *f.* **larynx,** *n.*
laringe, *f.*
lascivious, *a.* lascivo.
lash, *n.* (*of whip*) corda, cordicella,
striscia (di cuoio), *f.*; (*cut with a
whip*) colpo di frusta, *m.*, sferzata, *f.*;
(*eye*) ciglio, *m.* (-a, *pl.f.*); (*fig.*)
bastone, sarcasmo, *m.*   ¶ *v.t.*
frustare, sferzare; flagellare; satireggiare; attaccare, legare, rizzare;
(*Naut.*) amarrare, rizzare. ~ *its tail*,
agitare, dimenare (la coda), battersi
i fianchi. ~ *out*, scattar fuori, fare
delle stranezze; (*horse*) sferrare calci.
lass[ie], *n.* ragazza, fanciulla, giovanetta, *f.*
lassitude, *n.* lassitudine, stanchezza, *f.*
lasso, *n.* laccio, *m.*   ¶ *v.t.* prendere,
(acchiappare) col laccio.
last, *a.* ultimo; passato, scorso;
(*honours*) estremo.   ~ *but one*,
a. & *n.* penultimo, *a.* & *m.* ~ *night*,
la notte scorsa, la notte passata, ieri
notte.   ~ *piece* (*left on dish*),
bocconcino della creanza, *m.*   ~
resource, ultimo appello, *m.* ~ *straw*,
il colmo, *m.*   ~ *week*, la settimana
passata, la settimana scorsa. ~ *will
& testament*, atto di ultima volontà,
m., ultime volontà, *f.pl. the* ~ *word*,
l'ultima parola, *f. the* ~ *word in*
(as *elegance*), la perfezione di. ¶ *ad.*
finalmente, alla fine, per ultimo.
¶ *n.* ultimo, *m.*, ultimo respiro, *m.*,
ultima lettera, *f.*, fine, *f.*; (*shoe*)
forma, *f. at* ~, finalmente, alla fine.
¶ *v.i.* durare.   ~**ing,** *a.* durevole,
duraturo.   ~**ly,** *ad.* per ultimo,
alla fine, in conclusione.
latch, *n.* (*gate*) stanghetta, *f.*; (*door*)
saliscendi, *m.*, nottola, *f.* ~ *catch*,
boncinello, *m.*   ~**key,** chiave
comune, chiave di casa, *f.*
late, *a.* tardo, tardivo, in ritardo;
recente, ultimo, avanzato, ex-, già;
(*deceased*) fu, defunto, deceduto.
~*comer*, nuovo venuto, ritardatario,
m. ~ *fee*, sopratassa per la levata
eccezionale, *f.*   ~ *season*, stagione
avanzata, *f.* ¶ *ad.* tardi, in ritardo.
~ *in the day* & ~ *in life*, ad un'ora
avanzata del giorno; sul tardi.
B, late, A, A, B succéssore. ~**ly,**
ad. recentemente, di recente, poco
fa. ~**ness,** *n.* ritardo, tempo
avanzato, *m.*, epoca recente, *f. the*
~ *of the hour*, l'ora inoltrata, l'ora
avanzata, *f.*
latent, *a.* latente; nascosto, **segreto.**

later, *a.* piú tardo, piú recente,
posteriore, susseguente. ~ [on], *ad.*
piú tardi, dopo, piú innanzi.
lateral, *a.* laterale.
latest, *a.* ultimo, il piú recente.
~ *style* (*in dress*), ultima moda, *f.*
at the ~, al piú tardi. ~ (*thing out*),
ultime notizie, *f.pl.*   ~ *time for
posting*, ultima levata della posta, *f.*
latex, *n.* latice, *m.*
lath, *n.* assicella, *f.*, panconcello, listello, *m.*; (*blind*) stecca, *f.* ¶ *v.t.*
coprire con assicelle.
lathe, *n.* tornio, *m.*
lather, *n.* schiuma, saponata, *f.* ¶ *v.i.*
formare schiuma; (*v.t.*) insaponare.
lathing, *n.* listellatura, *f.*
Latin, *a.* & *n.* latino, *a.* & *m.*
latitude, *n.* latitudine, *f.*; libertà di
azione, *f.*
latrine, *n.* latrina, *f.*
latter (**the**), questo, quest'ultimo,
l'ultimo menzionato; il secondo.
~**ly,** *ad.* di recente, recentemente,
ultimamente.
lattice, *n.* traliccio, *m.*, graticciata, *f.*
¶ *v.t.* graticciare, intrecciare.
Latvia, *n.* la Lettonia, *f.* **Latvian,** *a.*
& *n.* lettone, *a.* & *m.*
laud, *v.t.* lodare, elogiare. ~ (*to the
skies*), portare alle stelle. ~**able,** *a.*
lodevole. **laudatory,** *a.* laudativo.
laugh, *n.* riso, *m.*, risata, *f.* ¶ *v.i.*
ridere, ridersi.   ~ *derisively*,
sghignazzare.   ~**able,** *a.* risibile,
ridicolo. *it is no* ~*ing matter*, non
c'è da ridere, non è il caso di
ridere. ~*ing stock*, zimbello, oggetto
di riso, *m.* **laughter,** *n.* riso, *m.*
launch, *n.* lancia, scialuppa, *f.* ¶ *v.t.*
lanciare, fondare; (*attack*) sferrare;
(*ship*) varare.   ~[ing], *n.* varo, *m.*
~ *out*, lanciarsi, avventurarsi.
launder, *v.t.* lavare (i panni).
laundress, *n.* stiratrice, lavandaia, *f.*
laundry, *n.* lavanderia, *f.*; (*wash*)
bucato, *m.*
laureate, *a.* laureato.
laurel, *n.* alloro, lauro, *m.*; (*pl. fig.*)
allori, *m.pl.*
lava, *n.* lava, *f.*
lavatory, *n.* lavatoio, lavabo, gabinetto da toletta, *m.*
lavender, *n.* lavanda, *f.*
lavish, *a.* prodigo, profuso. ¶ *v.t.*
prodigare, profondere.   ~**ly,** *ad.*
prodigamente.   ~**ness,** *n.* prodigalità, *f.*
law, *n.* diritto, *m.*, legge, *f.*, statuto,
decreto, *m.*; giustizia, giurispru-
denza, *f.* ~ *abiding*, ubbidiente alla

legge. ~ & order, ordine pubblico, m. ~ case, processo civile, m. ~ costs, spese di giudizio, f.pl. ~ courts, palazzo di giustizia, tribunale, m.; corte di giustizia, f. ~ giver, legislatore, m. ~ of nations, diritto delle genti, m. ~ officers, magistrati, m.pl. ~suit, processo, m., azione in giudizio, f. ~ term, termine legale, t. giuridico, m.; sessione, f. ~ful, a. legittimo, lecito, legale. ~fulness, n. legalità, f. ~less, a. senza legge, arbitrario, sfrenato.

lawn, n. tappeto verde, praticello, m., radura, f.; zolla erbosa, f.; (linen) rensa, batista, f., linone, m. ~ grass, erba folta e corta, f. ~ mower, falciatrice da prato, f. ~ tennis, tennis, m.; pallacorda, f.

lawyer, n. avvocato; giureconsulto, giurista, legista; forense, legale, m.

lax, a. rilassato, sciolto, molle, fiacco, vago. ~ative, a. & n. lassativo, a. & m. ~ity, n. rilassatezza, f.

lay, a: ~ brother, frate laico, frate servente, converso. ~man, laico, secolare, m. ~ habit, abito secolare, m. ~ sister, suora laica, conversa, f, ¶ n. canzone, ballata, f.; canto, lamento, m.; elegia, f.; (of ground) configurazione, direzione, f. ¶ v.t. ir. porre, posare, mettere, collocare; gettare; tendere; ordire; apparecchiare; (fire) preparare; (gun) puntare, mirare; (eggs) deporre, fare; (a wager) scommettere, fare una scommessa; (to stake) giuocare. ~ bare, mettere a nudo, svelare, scoprire. ~ before (court), sottomettere; ~ down, deporre, posare, mettere a terra; lasciare, abbandonare, rinunziare; (law, rule) formulare, dettare, imporre, stabilire; (plan, project) proporre, esporre, concepire, tracciare; (in bed, on the ground) coricare; (life) dare, fare sacrifizio di. ~ hold of, afferrare, prendere, impadronirsi di. ~ in [a stock of], approvvigionarsi di. ~ on, applicare, sovrapporre; attribuire a, addossare a; colpire, battere fortemente; (Typ.) marginare. ~ out, sborsare, spendere; costruire; disporre, stendere; preparare; tracciare; spiegare; (cards) scartare. ~ up, ammassare; mettre da parte; (ship) disarmare; costringere a letto.

lay day (Ship), n. stallia, f.

layer, n. (pipes, rails, &c.), montatore, m. (carpets, &c.) tappezziere, m.;

(stratum, bed) strato, letto, m.; (Hort.) margotta, f.

lay figure, n. manichino, fantoccio, m.

laying, n. posa, messa, f.; il porre, il mettere, m.; montaggio, m.; imposizione, f.; (eggs) covata, f.

layout, n. disegno, piano; (Typ.) progetto, m.

lazaretto, lazaret, n. lazzaretto, m.

laze, v.i. oziare, essere ozioso, vivere nell'inerzia, nell'indolenza. lazily, ad. pigramente, indolentemente, neghittosamente. laziness, n. indolenza, pigrizia, f. lazy, a. indolente, pigro, neghittoso. ~-bones, gran pigro, infingardo, fannullone, m.

lea (Poet.), n. campo, prato, m., pianura, f.

leach, v.t. & i. lisciviare.

lead, n. piombo, m.; (for pencils) matita, f.; (Typ.) interlinea, f.; (Naut.) scandaglio, m. ~ pencil, matita, f. ~ poisoning, colica saturnina, f., colica degli imbianchini, f. ~ work & ~ works, fonderia di piombo, f. ¶ v.t. impiombare, piombare; (Typ.) interlineare.

lead, n. direzione, f., comando, m., condotta, iniziativa, f., esempio, vantaggio, primato, m.; (Cards) mano, f., primo posto, primo colpo; (leash) guinzaglio, laccio, m. ~ in (Radio) discesa, f. ¶ v.t. & i.ir. condurre, menare, guidare; indurre; portare a, mirare a, tendere a, comandare, dirigere, dominare; esordire; (Cards, &c.) cominciare. ~ astray, sviare, indurre in errore. ~ back, ricondurre. ~ up to (fig.), (v.t.) avviare verso, indurre verso; (v.i.) preludere (a).

leaden, a. di piombo, plumbeo, pesante; (sky) di piombo.

leader, n. capo, m., guida, f., conduttore, m., duce, m., capofila, m.; (political) capopartito, m.; (orchestra) direttore, primo violino, m.; (news) articolo di fondo, m.; (Anat.) tendine, m.; (pl. Typ.) puntini di guida, m.pl. ~ship, n. condotta, direzione, f., comando, m. leading, a. importante, che guida, che dirige, dominante, principale. ~ article, articolo di fondo, m. ~ lady (Theat.) prima attrice; (Revue) prima attrice. ~ man, primo attore. ~ part (Theat.), parte principale, f. ~ people, notabilità, f.pl. ~ rein, corda per guidare, f. ~ question, domanda suggestiva, *f.* ~ *seaman*, marinaio scelto, *m.* ~ *strings*, dande, *f.pl.*

leadsman, *n.* scandagliatore, *m.*

leaf, *n.* (*Bot.*) foglia, *f.*; (*paper*, *metal*) foglio, *m.*; (*door*) battente, *m.*; (*table*) aggiunta, *f.*; (*rifle*) alzo, *m.* ~ *mould*, terriccio di foglie, *m.* ~ *stalk*, picciolo, peziolo, *m.* *turn over a new* ~, svoltare la pagina, (*fig.*) mutar vita, cambiare metodo di vita, migliorare. *turn over the leaves of* (*a book*), sfogliare, sfogliettare. ~**age**, *n.* fogliame, *m.* ~**let**, *n.* foglietto, *m.*; (*Bot.*) piccola foglia, *f.* ~**y**, *a.* fronzuto, frondoso, coperto di foglie.

league, *n.* lega, associazione, unione, alleanza, confederazione, *f.*; (*of Nations*) società, *f.*; (*Meas.*) lega, *f.*; (*land l.* = metri 4828, *naut. l.* = metri 5561.838). ¶ *v.t.* confederare, unire in lega.

leak & ~**age**, *n.* falla, via d'acqua, perdita, *f.*; colaggio, ammanco, filtramento, *m.* *to spring a* ~, aprire una falla, far acqua. *to stop a* ~, accecare una falla, tappare una falla. ¶ *v.i.* colare, sfuggire; (*ship*) far acqua. *to leak out*, trapelare, traspirare, divulgarsi. ~**y**, *a.* sdruscito, fesso, che fa acqua, che cola.

lean, *a.* magro; sottile; smunto, scarno, sparuto; povero, sterile, stentato. ¶ *n.* carne magra, *f.*, magro, *m.* ¶ *v.t. ir.* appoggiare, far pendere, inclinare, piegare; (*v.i. ir.*) (*rest*) appoggiarsi; (*slope*) pendere, inclinarsi; essere disposto a, essere propenso a, restar ligio a. ~ *back in*, inclinarsi indietro in, sdraiarsi in. ~ *on one's elbow(s)*, appoggiarsi sul gomito. ~ *out of*, sporgersi da, fuori di. ~**ing** (*fig.*), *n.* inclinazione, propensione, disposizione, *f.* ~ *tower* (Pisa), torre pendente, *f.* ~**ness**, *n.* magrezza, *f.* ~ **-to**, *n.* tettoia, *f.*

leap, *n.* salto, balzo, sbalzo, slancio, *m.* *by* ~*s* & *bounds*, a passi di gigante, a salti e a sbalzi. ¶ *v.t.* & *i.* balzare, saltare, spiccare un salto, precipitarsi, slanciarsi. ~*frog*, saltamontone, *m.* ~ *year*, anno bisestile, *m.* **leaper**, *n.* saltatore, *m.*

learn, *v.t.* & *i.ir.* apprendere; imparare; venire a sapere, sentire, istruirsi. ~**ed**, *a.* dotto, erudito, istruito; (*profession*) liberale. ~**edly**, *ad.* dottamente, eruditamente. ~**er**,

n. principiante, allievo, chi impara, chi apprende. ~**ing** *n.* cultura, dottrina, erudizione, scienza, *f.*, sapere, *m.*

lease, *n.* affitto, contratto d' affitto (d'immobile, &c.), *m.* ¶ *v.t.* affittare; (*grant*) dare in affitto; (*take*) prendere in affitto. ~*holder*, *n.* affittuario, *m.* *lend* ~, affitti e prestiti, *m.pl.*

leash, *n.* guinzaglio, laccio, *m.*; (*set of dogs*) muta, *f.* ¶ *v.t.* legare (tenere, condurre, menare) col guinzaglio.

least (**the**), *a.* il minimo, *m.*, la minima, *f.*, il piú piccolo, *m.* ¶ *ad.* il meno. *at* ~, almeno, per lo meno, ad ogni modo. *not in the* ~, niente affatto, affatto, per nulla, in niun (nessun) modo.

leat, *n.* canale di diversione, *m.*

leather, *n.* cuoio, *m.* ~ *bottle*, otre, *m.* ~ *dressing*, concia del cuoio, *f.* ~*ette*, *n.* imitazione cuoio, *f.* ~**y**, *a.* come di cuoio, coriaceo.

leave, *n.* permesso, *m.*, licenza, autorizzazione, *f.*; congedo, commiato, *m.* *by your* ~! con vostro permesso, con vostra licenza! permesso! *on* ~, in licenza, in permesso, in congedo. ¶ *v.t. ir.* lasciare, abbandonare; legare, lasciare per testamento, in eredità; (*v.i. ir.*) partire, andarsene. ~ *off*, smettere, cessare, rinunciare a, desistere. ~ *out*, lasciar fuori, omettere, escludere, tralasciare. *on leaving*, quando me ne andai, se ne andò, &c.; all' uscita di.

leaven, *n.* lievito, *m.* ¶ *v.t.* lievitare; (*fig.*) temperare, modificare.

leavings, *n.pl.* rimasugli, avanzi, *m.pl.*

lecherous, *a.* lascivo,l ibidinoso.

lectern, *n.* leggio, *m.*

lecture, *n.* lezione, *f.*, discorso, *m.*, conferenza, *f.*; (*scolding*) sgridata, ramanzina, *f.* ¶ *v.t.* tenere (una conferenza, una lezione, un corso di conferenze); ammonire, rimproverare. ~ *on*, tenere (fare) una conferenza, un corso di . . . su . . . **lecturer**, *n.* conferenziere, lettore, *m.*

ledge, *n.* ripiano, orlo, sporto, *m.*; tavola, *f.*, strato, *m.*; scogli, *m.pl.*, catena di rocce, *f.*; (*window*) davanzale, *m.*

ledger, *n.* libro mastro, *m.*; (*Building*) sostegno orizzontale, *m.*

lee [**side**], *n.* sottovento, lato di sottovento, *m.*

leech, *n.* sanguisuga, mignatta, *f.*

leek, *n.* porro, *m.*

leer, *n.* sguardo bieco, *m.*, occhiata maliziosa, smorfia, *f.* *to ~ at,* sbirciare, guardare sott'occhio, schernire.

lees, *n.pl.* feccia, *f.*, sedimento, fondaccio, *m.*

leeward, *a.* a sottovento, verso sottovento. *L~ Islands,* (le) Isole Sottovento, *f.pl.* leeway, *n.* deriva, *f.*; (*fig.*) perdita di tempo, *f.*, lavoro arretrato, *m.*

left, *a. & n.* sinistro, manco; sinistra, mano sinistra, *f.* *the ~ (Box.),* pugno sinistro, *m.* ¶ *ad.* a sinistra, sulla sinistra, verso sinistra. *~ -hand page,* verso, *m.* *~-handed,* *a.,* & *~-hander* (*pers. or player*), *n.* mancino, *m.*

left (to be), restare. *left luggage office,* consegna dei bagagli *f.* *left-off wearing apparel,* vestiti usati, *m.pl.* *left-overs, n.pl.* rimasugli, resti, *m.pl*

leg, *n.* gamba, *f.*; (*birds, insects, &c.*) zampa, *f.*; (*fowl*) coscia, *f.*; (*mutton*) coscio, *m.*; (*table, &c.*) piede, *m.*; (*compass*) gamba, *f.*; (*boot, stocking*) forma, *f.* *~ of beef,* coscio, *m.* *on one ~,* su una gamba sola.

legacy, *n.* legato, lascito, *m.*, eredità di beni mobili, *f.*

legal, *a.* legale, giuridico. *~ aid,* assistenza legale, *f.* *~ charges,* spese giudiziali, *f.pl.* *~ entity,* persona giuridica, *f.* *~ maxim,* massima giuridica, *f.* *~ tender* [*currency*], (*value*) valuta, moneta, a corsa legale; (*money*) moneta a corso legale, *f.* *~ize, v.t.* legalizzare, regolarizzare.

legate, *n.* legato pontificio, *m.* legatee, *n.* legatario, *m.*, erede di beni mobili, *m.f.* legation, *n.* legazione, *f.*

legend, *n.* leggenda, *f.* *~ary, a.* leggendario.

legerdemain, *n.* prestidigitazione, *f.*, giuoco di prestigio, *m.*, giuoco di mano, *m.* *feat of ~,* gherminella, *f.*

legging, *n.* gambale, *m.*; (*pl.*) ghettoni, *m.pl.*; uose, *f.pl.*

Leghorn, *n.* Livorno, *f.*

legible, *a.* leggibile.

legion, *n.* legione, *f.* *their name is ~,* sono legione.

legislate, *v.i.* fare (creare, formare, emanare) delle leggi. *~ for,* dare leggi a. legislation, *n.* legislazione, *f.* legislator, *n.* legislatore, *m.* legislature, *n.* legislatura, *f.*, corpo

legislativo; parlamento, *m.* legist, *n.* giureconsulto, *m.*

legitimacy, *n.* legittimità, *f.* legitimate, *a.* legittimo, autentico, lecito. legitim[at]ize, *v.t.* legittimare, dichiarare legittimo.

legume[n], *n.* legume, *m.* leguminous, *a.* leguminoso.

leisure, *n.* ozio, agio, comodo, riposo. *at ~,* libero, in libertà, a bell'agio. *at your ~,* con vostro comodo. *a ~ly man,* un uomo tranquillo e posato, un (uomo) indolente, *m.* [*in a*] *~ly* [*way*], *ad.* a bell'agio, senza fretta, con comodo, con calma.

leitmotiv, -if, *n.* tema, *m.*, melodia principale, *f.*

lemon, *m.* limone, *m.* *~ squash,* spremuta di limone, *f.* *~ squeezer,* spremilimoni, strizzalimoni, *m.* *~ tree,* limone, *m.* *~ade,* limonata, *f.*

lemon sole, sogliola fritta (con limone), *f.*

lend, *v.t. ir.* prestare, imprestare, mutuare, dare a mutuo; fornire, dare. *~er, n.* prestatore, mutuante, *m.* *~ing,* *n.* l'imprestare, *m.*, prestito, *m.* *lend-lease,* affitti e prestiti. *~ library,* biblioteca circolante, biblioteca di prestito, *f.*

length, *n.* lunghezza, *f.*, spazio, periodo, *m.*; (*time*) durata, durazione, *f.*; (*piece of stuff*) taglio, *m.*; (*of service*) anzianità, *f.* *at ~,* alla lunga; alla fine, finalmente. *at great ~,* per disteso. *~en, v.t.* allungare, distendere, prolungare. *~ening piece,* aggiunta, *f.* *~ways,* *~wise, ad.* in lungo, per il lungo. *~y, a.* lungo, prolisso.

lenient, *a.* indulgente, mite, clemente. leniency, *n.* indulgenza, mitezza, *f.*

Leningrad, *n.* Leningrado, *f.*

lens, *n.* lente, *f.*; (*camera, microscope*) obiettivo *m.*; (*eye*) cristallino, *m.*

lent, *n.* quaresima, *f.* *to keep ~,* fare quaresima. *~en, a.* di quaresima, quaresimale; magro.

lenticular, *a.* lenticolare.

lentil, *n.* lenticchia, *f.*

leonine, *a.* leonino.

leopard, *n.* leopardo, *m.* *~ess, n.* leopardo femmina, *f.*

leper, *n.* lebbroso, *m.*, -a, *f.* *~ hospital,* lebbrosario *m.*

Lepidoptera, *n.pl.* lepidotteri, *m.pl.*

leprosy, *n* lebbra, *f.* leprous, *a.* lebbroso.

lesion, *n.* lesione, *f.*

less, *a.* minore, inferiore, piú piccolo. -~ (*suffix*), senza. ¶ *ad.* meno, in grado inferiore, in misura inferiore, non tanto.

lessee, *n.* affittuario, locatario, *m.*

lesser, *a.* minore, inferiore, piú piccolo, meno importante.

lesson, *n.* lezione, *f.*, compito; esempio, *m.*

lessor, *n.* locatore, *m.*, -trice, *f.*

lest, *c.* per paura che, per timore che, per tema che, affinché non.

let (*Ten.*), *n.* colpo nullo, *m.* ¶ *v.t. & aux. ir.* lasciare, permettere; fare; locare, affittare. *to* (*be*) ~, da affittare, da affittarsi, appigionasi, si loca, da locare. ~ *down*, abbassare, lasciar discendere, calare, scendere; (*fail pers. at need*) lasciare, abbandonare. ~ *fall*, lasciar cadere. ~ *go* (*hold*), allentare, rilasciare, lasciar sfuggire; (*anchor*) affondare; (*rope*) mollare. ~ *have*, dare, cedere. ~ *have back*, restituire, rendere. ~ *loose*, sciogliere, lasciar libero. ~ *in*, far entrare, lasciar entrare, introdurre; incastonare. ~ *off*, perdonare, scusare, fare grazia; (*gun*) tirare, sparare; (*epigram*) scoccare. ~ *out*, fare (lasciare) uscire; rallentare; divulgare; (*clothes*) allargare; (*fire*) lasciar spegnersi.

lethal, *a.* letale. ~ *weapon*, arma micidiale, *f.*

lethargic, *a.* letargico. **lethargy,** *n.* letargo, *m.*, letargia, *f.* **Lethe** *n.* Lete, *m.*

let's pretend set (*child's*), panoplia, *f.*

letter, *n.* lettera, *f.*; carattere, *m.* ~ *book*, copialettere, registro, *m.* ~ *box*, buca delle lettere, *f.* ~ *card*, carta lettera, *f.* ~ *case*, portafogli, *m.* ~ *missive*, lettera missiva, *f.* *registered* ~, lettera raccomandata, *f.* ~ *paper*, carta da lettere, *f.* ~ *post*, corrispondenza postale, *f.* ~*press*, stampato, *m.*, impressione tipografica, *f.*; calcalettere, *m.* ~*press printing*, tipografia, *f.* ~ *scales*, bilancia per le lettere, *f.* ~ *writer* (*pers.*) scrittore di lettere; scrivano (pubblico), *m.* ¶ *v.t.* imprimere (lettere), improntare, bollare; (*book, cover*) imprimere. ~ *ed* (*man, woman*), letterato, *m.*, -a, *f.* ~*ing*, *n.* iscrizione, soprascritta, *f.*; (*on binding*) titolo, *m.*; impressioni, *f.pl.*

letting, *n.* affitto, nolo, *m.*, locazione, *f.* ~ *value*, valore locativo, *m.*

lettuce, *n.* lattuga, *f.*

Levant, *n.* Levante, *m.* **Levantine,** *a.* levantino; (*ports*) del Levante. ¶ *n.* levantino, *m.*, -a, *f.*

levee, *n.* ricevimento (reale), *m.*

level, *a.* piano, a livello; orizzontale; levigato. ~ *crossing*, passaggio a livello, *m.* *a* ~*-headed person*, una mente bene equilibrata, un uomo assennato. ~ *with*, a livello con, a fior di, all' altezza di. ¶ *n.* livello, *m.*, altezza, *f.*; (*instr. mason's*) livella, *f.*; (*Min.*) galleria, *f.* ¶ *v.t.* livellare, spianare, appianare, levigare, mettere a livello; abbattere, rovesciare; eguagliare; (*gun, &c.*) puntare. **levelling,** *n.* livellamento, *m.*, livellazione, *f.* ~ *staff*, stadia, *f.*

lever, *n.* leva; manetta, *f.* ~ *watch*, orologio ad ancora, o con leva vibrante, *m.* ~ [*up*], *v.t.* sollevare per mezzo di una leva. ~*age*, *n.* potenza d'una leva, *f.*, giuoco d'una leva, *m.*; (*fig.*) pressione, influenza, *f.*, vantaggio, *m.*

leveret, *n.* leprotto, *m.*

leviathan, *n.* leviatano, *m.*

Levite, *n.* levita, *m.* **Leviticus,** *n.* il Levitico, *m.* (*O.T.*).

levity, *n.* leggerezza, *f.*

levy, *n.* (*troops*) leva, *f.*; (*taxes*) imposizione, *f.*; riscotimento, *m.* ¶ *v.t.* levare; (*war*) fare; (*taxes*) imporre; esigere, riscuotere.

lewd, *a.* impudico, lascivo. ~*ness*, *n.* impudicizia, lascivia, *f.*

lexicographer, *n.* lessicografo, *m.*

lexicon, *n.* lessico, dizionario, *m.*

Leyden, *n.* Leida, *f.*

liability, *n.* responsabilità, *f.*, obbligo, *m.*, impegno, *m.*; (*pl. Fin.*) passivo, *m.*, passività, *f.pl.*, debiti, *m.pl.* *to incur a* ~, incorrere in una responsabilità. **liable,** *a.* responsabile (di); esposto (a); soggetto (a), tenuto (a).

liaison officer, ufficiale di collegamento, *m.*

liana, liane, *n.* liana, *f.*

liar, *n.* bugiardo, *m.*, -a, *f.*, mentitore, *m.*, -trice, *f.*

lias, *n.* (*Geol.*) lias, *m.* **liassic,** *a.* liassico.

libation, *n.* libazione, *f.*

libel, *n.* diffamazione, *f.*, libello, *m.* ~ *action*, causa per diffamazione, *f.* ¶ *v.t.* diffamare. **libellous,** *a.* diffamatorio.

liberal, *a.* liberale, abbondante; copioso, largo; generoso, libero, franco, aperto. ¶ *n.* liberale, *m.f.*

~ism, *n.* liberalismo, *m.* ~ity, *n.* liberalità, *f.*

liberate, *v.t.* liberare.

libertine, *a. & n.* libertino, *a. & m.*

liberty, *n.* libertà, *f.* at ~, libero, in libertà.

librarian, *n.* bibliotecario, *m.*, -a, *f.*

library, *n.* biblioteca, *f.*

librettist, *n.* librettista, *m.f.* **libretto,** *n.* libretto, *m.*

licence, *n.* licenza, *f.*, permesso, *m.*, autorizzazione, *f.*, concessione, *f.*; patente, *f.*; eccesso, *m.* driving ~, patente di abilitazione, *f.*; (*motor*) patente per condurre automobili, *f.* ~ to sell, patente di vendita, *f.*; (*tobacco,* *spirits,* *&c.*) licenza (patente) per lo spaccio di tabacchi, di bevande alcooliche, &c., *f.*

license, *v.t.* autorizzare, licenziare, brevettare, patentare; dispensare (da). ~d victualler, oste, trattore, *m.*

licentiate, *n.* licenziato, *m.* ~'s degree, licenza (*Sch.*), *f.* **licentious,** *a.* licenzioso, scostumato, dissoluto. ~ness, *n.* dissolutezza, scostumatezza, *f.*

lichen, *n.* lichene, *m.*

licit *a.* lecito.

lick, *v.t.* leccare. ~ up, leccare, lambire; divorare.

lictor, *n.* (*Hist.*) littore, *m.*

lid, *n.* coperchio, *m.*; (*eye*) pa¹pebra, *f.*

lie, *n.* bugia, menzogna, *f.* give the ~ to, smentire, dare una smentita a. ¶ *v.i.* mentire, dire bugie.

lie, *n.* (*of ground*) configurazione, *f.*; (*Golf, &c.*) posizione, *f.*; ¶ *v.i.* ir. giacere; stare, essere situato; trovarsi; consistere. ~ back in, sdraiarsi in. ~ dormant, essere in giacenza, inattivo. ~ down, mettersi a giacere, riposare, coricarsi, sdraiarsi. ~ idle, essere disoccupato; (*land*) e. incolto. ~ in wait, essere in agguato. ~ to (*Naut.*) cappeggiare.

liege, *a.* ligio, fedele. ¶ *n.* vassallo, *m.*

lien, *n.* diritto privilegiato, diritto di ritenzione, *m.*, pegno, privilegio, *m.*

lieu of (**in**), in luogo di.

lieutenant, *n.* tenente; luogotenente, (*second*) sottotenente, *m.*; (*Naval*) tenente di vascello, *m.* ~-colonel, tenente colonnello, *m.* ~-commander, capitano di corvetta, *m.* ~-general, generale di corpo d'armata; tenente generale, *m.*

life, *n.* vita, esistenza; attività, vivacità, *f.* for ~, a vita, vitalizio, per la vita, per tutta la vita from ~ (*Art*), dal vero. to the ~, al vivo, al naturale. 2 lives lost, 2 morti, vittime, periti. ~ [& soul] (*of the party*), animatore della festa, ~ annuity, [assegno] vitalizio, *m.*, pensione vitalizia, *f.* ~belt, cintura di salvataggio, *f.* ~boat, battello di salvataggio, *m.* ~buoy, salvagente, gavitello di salvataggio, *m.* ~ giving, vivificante, fecondo. ~ insurance, assicurazione sulla vita, *f.* ~ jacket, cintura di salvataggio, *f.* ~ preserver, rompitesta, mazza piombata, *f.* ~ saving, salvataggio, *m.* ~ size, in grandezza naturale. ~ table, tavola di mortalità, *f.* ~ time, vita, durata della vita, *f.* ~less, *a.* esanime; senza spirito. ~like, *a.* vivo, naturale, pieno di vita. ~long, *a.* durante la vita, per tutta la vita.

lift, *n.* ascensore, *m.*; (*goods*) montacarichi, *m.inv.*; (*of the hand*) gesto, cenno, *m.* ~man, ~ girl, ascensorista, *m.f.* ¶ *v.t.* alzare; elevare; sollevare; levare, portar via.

ligament, *n.* legamento, *m.* **ligature,** (*Mus.,* *Surg.*) *n.* legatura, *f.*

light, *a.* leggero; agile, lesto; gaio, divertente; facile; piccolo; frugale; frivolo; lieve; (*ship unladen*) senza carico, in zavorra; vuoto; (*colour*) chiaro, biondo; (*earth*) mobile. ~ car, automobile leggera, vetturetta, *f.* ~-fingered gentleman, borsaiuolo, baro, *m.* ~ fishing, pesca del piccolo pesce, *f.* ~ headed, stordito, sventato, delirante, ~ headedness, *n.* balordaggine, *f.*, delirio, *m.*, giramento di testa, *m.* ~ heavyweight (*Box.*), peso mediomassimo, *m.* ~ lager, birra chiara, *f.* ~ lorry, camion leggero, *m.* ~ meal, pasto leggero, pasto frugale, *m.* ~ opera, operetta, *f.* ~ railway, ferrovia a scartamento ridotto, *f.* ~ reading, lettura amena, *f.* ~ refreshments, rinfreschi, *m.pl.*, merenda, *f.* ~ weight (*Box.*), peso leggero, *m.* ¶ *n.* luce, illuminazione, *f.*, chiarore, giorno, *m.*; fanale, *m.*, lampada, *f.*, lume, *m.*; aspetto, *m.*, finestra, *f.* against the ~, controluce. ~s out (*Mil.*) riposo; coprifuoco, *m.* ~ & shade (*Art.*), chiaroscuro, *m.*; (*pl.* *Mus.,* *&c.*) sfumature, *f.pl.* ~house, faro, *m.* ~ship, nave faro, *f.*, faro galleggiante, *m.* ¶ *v.t.* ir. accendere; illuminare; rischiarare. ~ up, illuminare. ~ [up]on, imbattersi in, incontrare; posarsi su.

lighten, *v.t* alleggerire; scaricare;

alleviare, lenire; sollevare; illuminare; (v.imp.) rischiararsi; lampeggiare, balenare.

lighter, a. piú leggero, &c. ~ than air aviation or branch (army), aerostazione, f. ~ than air machine [apparecchio] piú leggero dell'aria, aerostato, m.

lighter, n. (pers.) accenditore, m.; (petrol) accenditore (a benzina); (boat) alleggio, m., chiatta, f. ~man, chiattaiuolo, m. ~age, n. scaricamento, m., prezzo di carico, prezzo di scarico, m. **lighting,** n. illuminazione; (fire) accensione, f. ~ up time, l'ora d'accendere le luci, f.

lightly, ad. leggermente; lievemente.

lightness, n. leggerezza, f.

lightning, n. fulmine, lampo, baleno, m. ~ conductor, parafulmine, m. ~ strike, sciopero di sorpresa, m.

lights, (animal lungs) n.pl. corata, f.

ligneous, a. ligneo. **lignite,** n. lignite, f. lignum vitae, [legno di] guaiaco, legno santo, m.

likable, a. simpatico. **like,** a. simile, somigliante, rassomigliante; pari, uguale, analogo; tale, quale; stesso, medesimo. to be ~, rassomigliare a, essere somigliante a, essere simile a. to look ~, somigliare; parere, sembrare, aver l'aria di. ¶ n. altrettanto, simile, m., la stessa cosa, cosa eguale, pariglia, f. the ~ (treatment, &c), pari, simile, di tal sorta; & the ~, ed altrettanto, ed una cosa simile, eccetera. ~s & dislikes, simpatie ed antipatie, f.pl. ¶ pr. ad. come, da, alla maniera di. ¶ v.t. & i. gustare, voler bene a, avere simpatia per, essere contento di, approvare, trovare; (of the obj.) piacere a, andare a genio, gradire.

likelihood, n. probabilità; verosimiglianza, f. **likely,** a. probabile, verosimile; very ~, molto probabilmente, verosimilmente.

liken, v.t. paragonare, comparare, confrontare.

likeness, n. rassomiglianza, somiglianza, f.; ritratto, m.

likewise, ad. parimenti, similmente.

liking, n. (things) gusto, m., inclinazione, f.; (pers.) affezione, simpatia, f. that is to my ~, ciò mi va a genio.

lilac, n. & a. lilla, a. & m.

liliaceous, a. gigliaceo, liliaceo.

Lilliputian, a. lillipuziano.

lily, n. giglio, m.; (Her.) fiordaliso, m. ~ of the valley, mughetto, m.

limb, n. membro, m., pl.f. -a; (tree) tronco, m.; (Math., &c.) limbo, m. **limbed,** a. avente membri. strong ~, membruto.

limber, a. flessibile. ¶ n. avantreno, m. ~ up, rimettere l'avantreno.

limbo, n. limbo, m.

lime, n. calce, calcina, f. ~ burner, fornaciaio, m. ~ juice, succo di limone, m., acqua cedrata, f. ~ kiln, forno da calce, m. ~light, lume ossidrico, m. to be in the ~light, essere sotto i lumi della ribalta. (fig.) essere in vista. ~stone, pietra calcarea, f. ~ [tree] (citrus), cedro, limone, m.; (linden) tiglio, m. ~ twig, fuscello impaniato, m. ¶ v.t. (Agric.) concimare, ingrassare con calce; (twig) invischiare, impaniare.

limit, n. limite, termine, confine, m.; fine, f., perimetro, m. ¶ v.t. restringere, limitare, contenere. ~s, pl. limiti, m.pl., circoscrizione, f. ~ation, n. limitazione, f. **limited,** p.p. & p.a. limitato, ristretto; (monarchy) (monarchia) costituzionale; (edition) a tiratura ridotta. ~ company (public) società anonima, f.; (private) società per azioni a responsabilità limitata, f. ~ partnership, [società in] accomandita, f.

limousine, n. limousine, (Fr.) f.

limp, a. flaccido, floscio; (binding) flessibile, pieghevole. ¶ n. zoppicamento, m. ¶ v.i. zoppicare.

limpet, n. patella, f.

limpid, a. limpido. ~ity, n. limpidezza, f.

linchpin, n. acciarino, m., chiavetta passante, f., chiodo di ruota, m.

linden, n. tiglio, m.

line, n. linea, riga; serie, f.; ordine, m., successione, regola, norma, f.; corda, cordicella, funicella, f.; dinastia, famiglia, f., lignaggio, m.; genere, m.; specialità, f.; (fishing) lenza, f.; (Poet.) verso, m.; (Teleph. subscriber's) linea dell'abbonato, f. (Rly.) binario, m., linea, strada ferrata, f. ~ block, cliché al tratto, m. ~ engraving, incisione a tratto, f. ¶ v.t. foderare, guarnire; rivestire, rinfiancare, incrostare; allineare; rigare, segnare. ~ up, schierare. ~ one's stomach, riempire lo stomaco, mangiare a sazietà.

lineage, n. casato, lignaggio, m.

lineal, *a.* lineare; (*pers.*) in linea diretta. **lineament,** *n.* lineamento, *m.* **linear,** *a.* lineare.

linen, *n.* tela di lino, *f.*, tessuto di lino, *m.*; (*made up*) biancheria, *f.* *baby* ∼, corredino per neonato, *m.* ∼ *draper*, mercante di tele, *m.* ∼ *embroidery*, tela operata, biancheria operata, *f.* ∼ *press*, ∼ *room*, armadio della biancheria, *m.* ∼ (*thread*), filo di lino, *m.* ∼ *trade*, commercio di tele, *m.*

liner, *n.* piroscafo di linea regolare; transatlantico, *m.*

linesman, *n.* (*Mil.*) soldato di fanteria di linea, *m.*; (*Teleg., Teleph.*) guardafili, *m.inv.*; (*Foot.*) guardalinee, *m.inv.*

ling, *n.* (*Fish*) molva, *f.* (*Bot.*) erica comune, *f.*

linger, *v.i.* indugiare, attardarsi, restare indietro, esitare. ∼*ing death*, morte lenta, *f.* ∼ *over*, tirare in lungo.

lingerie, *n.* biancheria, *f.*; pannolino, *m.* ∼ *maker*, ∼ *dealer*, cucitrice in bianco, *f.*, mercante di biancheria, *m.*

lingo, *a.* gergo, *m.*, lingua barbara, *f.* **lingual,** *a.* linguale. ¶ *n.* linguale, *f.* **linguist,** *n.* linguista, *m.f.* ∼*ics,* *n.* linguistica, *f.*

liniment, *n.* linimento, *m.*

lining, *n.* fodera, foderatura, *f.*, rivestimento, *m.*; (*hat*) guarnizione, *f.*

link, *n.* anello, *m.*, maglia, *f.*; (*Mach.*) bielletta, *f.*, giunto, uncino, *m.*; (*fig.*) vincolo, legame, tratto d'unione, *m.* ∼ *motion*, settore articolato, *m.*, articolazione, *f.* ¶ *v.t.* legare, collegare, unire, allacciare, attaccare, congiungere, connettere, vincolare. ∼ *up*, unire, collegare, congiungere.

links, *n.pl.* landa, *f.*, terreno aperto, *m.*; (*Golf*) campo, terreno, *m.*

linnet, *n.* fanello, *m.*

linoleum, *n.* also **lino** *abb.* linoleum, *m.*, tela cerata, *f.*

linotype, *n. & att.* linotipo, *m.*, linotipia, *f.*

linseed, *n.* seme di lino, *m.* ∼ *oil*, olio di (seme di) lino, *m.* ∼ *poultice*, cataplasma di seme di lino, *m.*

lint, *n.* filaccia di cotone, garza, *f.*

lintel, *n.* architrave, *m.*

lion, ∼*ess,* *n.* leone, *m.*, leonessa, *f.* ∼ *cub*, ∼ *whelp*, leoncello, *m.* ∼*'s share*, parte del leone, *f.*

lip, *n.* labbro, *m.*, *pl.* labbri, *m.*,

labbra, *f.*; (*fig.*) bordo, orlo, *m.*; (*Mech.*) coprimozzo, *m.* ∼*stick*, rossetto (per le labbra), *m.*

liquefaction, *n.* liquefazione, *f.* **liquefy,** *v.t.* liquefare.

liqueur, *n.* liquore, *m.* ∼ *brandy*, cognac fino, *m.* ∼ *case*, ∼ *set*, portaliquori, *m.inv.*

liquid, *a.* liquido, fluido, scorrevole; (*Com. Fin.*) liquido, attivo; (*fig.*) chiaro, limpido, trasparente. ∼ *ammonia*, spirito d'ammoniaca, *m.* ∼ *assets*, attività liquide, *f.pl.* ∼ *paraffin* (*Phar.*), olio di paraffina, *m.* ¶ *n.* liquido, *m.*; (*Gram.*) liquida, *f.*

liquidate, *v.t.* liquidare. **liquidation,** *n.* liquidazione, *f.* **liquidator,** *n.* liquidatore, *m.*

liquor, *n.* liquore, *m.*

liquorice, *n.* liquirizia, *f.*

Lisbon, *n.* Lisbona, *f.*

lisp, *v.i.* bisbigliare, balbettare, balbuziare, essere bleso, parlare con una pronuncia b'esa.

lissom[e], *a.* svelto, pieghevole.

list, *n.* lista, *f.*, catalogo, *m.*, elenco, *m.*, tavola, *f.*, inventario, *m.*, ruolo, bollettino, controllo, *m.*; (*army, Navy, &c.*) annuario militare, *a.* della marina, *m.*; (*Naut.*) falsa banda, *f.*, guardamano, sbandamento, *m.*; (*selvage*) lisiera, *f.*, vivagno, *m.*; (*pl.*) lizza, arena, palizzata, *f.* ∼ *of dishes* (*menu*), carta (lista) delle vivande, *f.* ∼ *slipper*, ciabatta (pantofola) fatta di vivagni di stoffa, *f.* ¶ *v.t.* mettere (iscrivere) in lista, registrare, catalogare; (*door*) calafatare; (*v.i.*) (*Naut.*) sbandare.

listen, *v.i. & ∼ in* (*Radio*), ascoltare. ∼*er,* *n.* (*hearer, & Radio*), ascoltatore, *m.*; (*spy*)

listless, *a.* languido, disattento, indifferente.

litany, *n.* litania, *j.*; -*ic,* *f. pl.*

literal, *a.* letterale, alla lettera. ∼ [*error*], errore di stampa, *m.* ∼ *sense*, (*passage*) significato letterale, *m.*; (*word*) senso proprio, *m.*

literary. *a,* letterario. ∼ *man*, letterato, *m.* ∼ *woman*, letterata, *f.* **literate,** *a.* letterato, erudito. **literature,** *n.* letteratura, *f.*

litharge, *n.* litargirio, *m.*

lithe, *a.* snello, svelto, lesto, agile.

lithia, *n.* litina, *f.* **lithium,** *n.* litio, *m.* **lithograph** *&* ∼*y,* *n.* litografia, *f.* ¶ *v.t.* litografare. ∼*er,* *n.* litografo, *m.* ∼*ic,* *a.* litografico.

Lithuania, *n.* la Lituania, *f.*

litigant, *n.* litigante, *m.f.*, parte in causa, *f.* **litigation,** *n.*, lite, *f.*, causa, controversia, *f.*, processo, *m.* **litigious,** *a.* litigioso.

litmus, *n.* tornasole, *m.*

litter, *n.* (*palanquin*) lettiga, barella, *f.*; (*straw & dung*) lettiera, *f.*, strame, pattume, *m.*, roba disordinata, *f.*, **s**compiglio, *m.*; (*young animals*) figliata, ventrata, *f.*; (*pigs*) figliata di maialini. ¶ *v.t.* figliare; metter in disordine, sparpagliare; sporcare.

little, *a.* piccolo, poco, scarso, esiguo, tenue, breve. [*dear*] ~ *brother,* fratellino, fratelluccio, *m.* ~ *chap,* bimbo, bambino, *m.* ~ *devil,* diavoletto, diavolino, *m.* ~ *dinner,* pranzino, pranzetto, *m.* ~ *finger,* mignolo, dito mignolo, *m.* ~ *ones,* bambini, piccini, piccoli, *m.pl.*; piccolo mondo, *m.*; (*cubs*) piccoli, piccoli nati, *m.pl.* ~ *place,* (w.c.) luogo comodo, gabinetto, *m.* L~ *Red Riding Hood,* Cappuccetto Rosso, *m.* [*dear*] ~ *sister,* sorellina, *f.* *a very* ~, un pochino. ~ *by* ~, a poco a poco. *as* ~ *as possible,* il meno possibile. *be it ever so* ~, per poco che sia. *a* ~ [*while*] *longer,* un poco piú, ancora un poco. ¶ *ad.* poco. ¶ *n.* poco, *m.*, poca cosa, piccola quantità, *f.*, piccolo spazio, *m.*, breve distanza, *f.*, breve tempo, *m.* ~**ness,** piccolezza; mediocrità, *f.*

live, *a.* vivo, vivente, attivo; (*coal*) carboni ardenti, *m.pl.*, bragia, *f.* (*axle*) girante; (*Elec.*) sottotensione; (*shell*) carico. ~*-bait fishing,* pesca con esca viva, *f.* ~*stock,* bestiame, *m.*

live, *v.i. & t.* vivere, campare, dimorare, abitare, essere domiciliato, risiedere, stare di casa, alloggiare; condurre, menare una vita; nutrirsi (*on milk, &c.* = di). ~ *again in,* sopravvivere in, rivivere in.

livelihood, *n.* vita, sussistenza, *f.* *to afford a* ~, dare da vivere. *to earn a* ~, guadagnarsi la vita.

liveliness, *n.* vivacità, gaiezza, *f.*, movimento, *m.* **lively,** *a.* animato, vivace, allegro, brioso.

liver, (*Anat.*) fegato, *m.*

livery, *n.* livrea, *f.* ~ *stables,* stallaggio, *m.*, scuderia, *f.*, pensione per cavalli, *f.*

livid, *a.* livido. ~**ity,** *n.* lividezza, *f.*

living, *a.* vivo, vivente, in vita; (*force*) vivo. ~ *being,* vivente, vivo, *m.*, persona viva, persona vivente, *f.* *within* ~ *memory,*

a memoria d'uomo. ¶ *n.* mezzi di sussistenza, *m.pl.*, rendita, *f.*, vivere, *m*,. vita, *f.*; (*fare*) trattamento, *m.*; (*Eccl.*) benefizio, *m.*, cura, *f.* ~ *expenses,* spesa pel vitto, *f.*, spese domestiche, *f.pl.* ~*-in,* internato, *m.* ~ *room,* stanza di soggiorno, *f.* *the* ~, i viventi, i vivi, *m.pl.*

lizard, *n.* lucertola, *f.*

llama, *n.* lama, *m.*

Lloyd's, *n.* il Lloyd, *m.* ~ *agent,* agente (rappresentante) del Lloyd, *m.*

loach, *n.*, ghiozzo, *m.*

load, *n.* carico, *m.*, soma, *f.*, peso, fardello, *m.* ~ *draught* (*ship*), pescaggio con carico, *m.* ~ *star,* stella polare, *f.*; (*fig.*) buona stella, *f.* ~ *stone,* calamita, siderite, *f.*; (*fig.*) magnete, *m.*, attrazione, *f.* ~ [*water*] *line,* linea di carico, linea d'immersione d'una nave carica, *f.* ¶ *v.t.* caricare; ingombrare; (*fig.*) colmare (di), opprimere (con); (*dice*) falsare; (*v.i.*) caricare, ricever il carico. ~**ed,** *p.p.* caricato, carico; piombato; falsato; ingombrato. ~ *stick,* bastone piombato, *m.* ~**er,** *n.* caricatore. *m.* ~**ing,** *n.* caricamento, *m.* [*now*] ~ (*ship*), in carica.

loaf, *n. & ~ of bread,* pane, *m.*, (*round loaf*), pagnotta, *f.* ~ *sugar,* zucchero in pani, *m.*

loaf, *v.i.* oziare, vagabondare, andare a zonzo. ~**er,** *n.* perdigiorno, fannullone, *m.*

loam, *n.* terra grassa, argilla, *f.*, terriccio, *m.*

loan, *n.* prestito, imprestito, mutuo, *m.*

loath (**to be**), essere avverso, essere poco disposto; (*imp.*) ripugnare a. **loathe,** *v.t.* aborrire, avere in odio, avere a schifo. **loathing,** *n.* ripugnanza, *f.*, schifo, aborrimento, *m.* **loathsome,** *a.* ripugnante, odioso, stomachevole.

lob (*Ten.*), *n.* pallonetto, *m.*

lobby, *n.* corridoio, vestibolo, *m.*, sala d'aspetto, *f.*; (*Theat.*), ridotto, *m.* ~**ing,** *n.* manovre di corridoio, *f.pl.*

lobe, *n.* lobo, *m.*

lobelia, *n.* lobelia, *f.*, fiore di cardinale, *m.*

lobster, *n.* aragosta, *f.*, gambero di mare, *m.* ~ *pot,* ~ *basket,* nassa, paniere, *m.*

local, *a.* locale; del paese; di campanile; (*custom*) del luogo, del paese; (*on letter*) città. ~ *line,* **linea**

secondaria, *f.* ～ *time*, ora locale, *f.*
～ [e], *n.* scena, *f.* luogo, *m.* ～**ity**,
n. località, *f.* ～**ize**, *v.t.* localizzare.
～**ly**, *ad.* localmente.
locate, *v.t.* collocare, locare, localizzare; fissare; individuare.
lock, *n.* serratura, toppa, *f.*; (*canal*)
chiusa, *f.*; (*hair*) ciocca, *f.*, ricciolo,
ciuffo, *m.* (*pl.*) capelli, *m.pl.*,
capigliatura, *f.* *under* ～ *& key*, sotto
chiave. ～ *hospital*, sifilicomio, *m.*
～ *jaw*, tetano, *m.* ～ *nut*, contro-
dado, *m.* ～ *out*, serrata, *f.* ～*smith*,
chiavaio, *m.* ～*-up* (*police*), cella,
prigione provvisoria, *f.*; (*garage*)
rimessa, *f.* ¶ *v.t.* chiudere a chiave;
serrare; bloccare, (*fig.*) stringere,
abbracciare. ～ *out*, chiudere fuori,
impedire d'entrare; (*men*) chiudere
le officine, serrare. ～ *up*, mettere
sotto chiave, rinchiudere, chiudere
sotto chiave; imprigionare; (*Fin.*)
bloccare, inmobilizzare.
locker, *n.* armadietto; cassone, cassetto; ripostiglio, *m.* *he has not a shot
in his* ～, non gli resta piú niente.
locket, *n.* medaglione, *m.*
locomotion, *n.* locomozione, *f.*
locomotive, *a.* locomotivo, loco-
motore. ¶ *n.* locomotiva, *f.*
locomotor ataxy, atassia locomotrice,
f.
loculus, *n.* alveolo; loculo, *m.*
locum tenens, *n.* supplente, *m.f.*,
sostituto, *m.*
locust, *n.* locusta, *f.* ～ [*bean*],
carruba, *f.*
locution, *n.* locuzione, *f.*
lode, *n.* filone, *m.*, vena, *f.* ～ *star*,
～ *stone*, same as *loadstar*, *loadstone*.
lodge, *n.* casetta; (*freemasons*) loggia;
(*shooting*) casina da caccia, *f.* ¶ *v.t.*
alloggiare, dare alloggio a; depositare; collocare; (*appeal*) fare, presentare; (*v.i.*) alloggiare, abitare. **lodger**, *n.* inquilino, *m.*, -a, *f.* **lodging**,
n. alloggio, *m.*; camera d'affitto,
f.; (*pl.*) alloggio, *m.*; camere d'affitto,
f.pl. *board & ～(s)*, alloggio e vitto.
m. ～ *house*, pensione; casa a quartieri (da affitto), *f.* *house keeper*,
padrone, *m.*, -a, *f.* (d'una pensione).
loft, *n.* soffitta, *f.*, solaio; granaio,
fienile, *m.*; (*organ*) tribuna, *f.* ¶
(*Golf*) *v.t.* mandare in aria. **loftiness**, *n.* altezza, grandezza, maestà,
f.; (*of manners*) alterigia, arroganza,
f. **lofty**, *a.* alto, elevato, nobile;
altero, arrogante; (*style*) maestoso.
log, *n.* ciocco, ceppo, tronco, *m.*;
(*Naut. inst.*) solcometro, *m.* ～

[*book*], giornale di bordo, *m.* ～
cabin, ～ *hut*, capanna di tronchi
d'alberi, *f.* ～ *wood* (legno di)
campeggio, *m.*
logan (**stone**], *n.* pietra o roccia
barcollante, *f.*
logarithm, *n.* logaritmo, *m.*
loggerheads [*at*], alle prese, in
disaccordo, in lite.
logic, *n.* logica, *f.* ～*al*, *a.* logico.
～**ian**, *n.* logico, *m.* **logistics**, *n.pl.*
logistica, *f.*
loin, *n.* (*veal*, *mutton*) lombata, *f.*;
lombo, *m.* (*pl.*) lombi, *m.pl.*, reni,
f.pl. ～ *chop*, braciola di filetto, *f.*
～ *cloth*, perizoma, *m.*
loiter, *v.i.* indugiare, attardarsi;
andare a zonzo, bighellonare. ～**er**,
n. bighellone, perdigiorno, *m.*
loll, *v.i.* reclinarsi indolentemente,
sdraiarsi, appoggiarsi con abbandono; (*tongue*) penzolare, lasciar
penzolare.
Lombardy, *n.* la Lombardia, *f.*
London, *n.* Londra, *f.*; (*att.*) di
Londra. ～**er**, *n.* londinese, *m.f.*
loneliness, *n.* solitudine, *f.*, isolamento, *m.* **lonely** *& lone*[**some**],
a. solitario, desolato; solo, solingo.
lone cottage, capanna solitaria, *f.*
～*ly dwelling*, abitazione solitaria, *f.*
long, *a.* lungo, esteso, allungato;
lento, tardo, tedioso, prolungato;
(*Measure*) lungo, di lunghezza, in
lunghezza, della lunghezza di.
～ *boat*, scialuppa, *f.* ～ *clothes*,
fasce, *f.pl.* ～*-distance race*, corsa
di fondo, *f.* ～*-drawn*, prolungato,
(*argument*) avviluppato. ～*-haired*,
capelluto. ～ *jump*, salto in lunghezza, *m.* ～*-legged* (*man*), alto di
gambe, che ha le gambe lunghe.
～*-lived*, longevo; (*things*) duraturo.
～ *service*, servizio lungo, *m.*; anzianità, *f.* ～*shoreman*, giornaliere del
porto, *m.* ～ *sighted* (*person*), pres-
bite, *m.f.*, che ha la vista lunga.
～ [*syllable*], sillaba lunga, *f.* ～
vacation, vacanze lunghe, *f.pl.* *a ～
while*, un lungo tempo, un pezzo. *in
the ～ run*, a lungo andare, alla lunga.
～*-winded*, prolisso, verboso,
interminabile. ¶ *ad.* lungamente,
a lungo, per lungo tempo, da lungo
tempo. ～ *ago*, molto tempo fa.
before ～, fra breve, fra non molto.
not ～ since, non guari ～ *the long
and the short of it is . . .*, per farla
breve. ～*-suffering*, *a.* paziente,
tollerante. ¶ *in the ～ & the short
of it*, i minimi particolari, *m.pl.*

¶ *v.i. I* ~ *to*, ho gran voglia di, mi par mill'anni che (*subj.*), non vedo l'ora di. ~ *for*, desiderare vivamente, sospirare per, aspettare con impazienza. *to be* ~ (*delay*), essere lento a, tardare (a). *longest way round*, la strada piú lunga.

longevity, *n.* longevità, *f.*

longing, *n.* vivo desiderio, *m.*, brama, voglia, impazienza, *f.*

longish, *a.* lunghetto, piuttosto lungo.

longitude, *n.* longitudine, *f.* **longitudinal**, *a.* longitudinale.

look, *n.* sguardo, colpo d'occhio, *m.*, occhiata, *f.*; aria, apparenza, sembianza, faccia, *f.*, aspetto, *m.* ~-*out*, sorveglianza, vigilanza, *f.*; vedetta, *f.*; (*box*, *post*) posto d'osservazione, *m.*; garitta, *f.*; casotto, *m.*; (*man*) guardia, vedetta, *f.* ¶ *v.i.* guardare; apparire, parere, sembrare; avere l'aspetto di, avere l'aria di, mostrarsi. ~ *after*, badare a, aver cura di, governare, maneggiare, fare attenzione a, sorvegliare. ~ *at*, guardare, mirare, fissare. ~ *alive* (*fam.*), sbrigarsi. ~ *down*, (*from on high*) guardare in basso, guardare dall'alto. ~ *down* [*up*]*on*, disprezzare, sprezzare. ~ *for*, cercare, aspettare. ~ *into*, guardar dentro; esaminare, investigare, scrutare. ~ *like*, rassomigliare a, avere l'aria di. ~ *on*, considerare; assistere a; (*front*) dare su. ~ *out* (*post*, *man*, *Rly. car*), vedetta, *f. to* ~ *out, to be on the* ~ *out*, stare in guardia, stare in agguato, stare alle vedette, stare accorto. ~ *out!* badate! badi! stia atento! attenzione! state attenti! ~ *out for*, cercare di scorgere, stare in attesa per, ricercare. ~ *out of the window*, guardare dalla finestra. ~ *over*, ripassare, scorrere. ~ *up a word in the dictionary*, cercare una parola nel dizionario. *to translate by looking up every other word in the dictionary*, tradurre consultando ogni momento il dizionario. ~**er-on**, *n.* spettatore, astante, *m.* ~**er-in**, *n.* televisore, *m.* ~**ing glass**, specchio, *m.*; (*cheval glass*, *full-length mirror*) psiche, *f.*

loom, *n.* telaio, *m.*

loom, *v.i.* apparire indistintamente, disegnarsi in lontananza.

loop, *n.* cappio, cappiello; nodo scorsoio; anello; alamaro; laccio, *m.*; maglia, *f.*, (*letter*) occhiello, *m.*; (*road*,

movement) raddoppiamento, rigiro, *m.*, ripiegatura, *f.*; (*hair*) treccia, *f.* ~*hole*, feritoia, apertura, *f.*; (*fig.*) scappatoia, *f.*, sotterfugio, *m.* ~ [*line*], scambi, binari di raccordo, *m.pl.* ¶ *v.t.* fare cappio in; legare con nodi; aggiustare in trecce. ~ *up*, allacciare, rannodare. ~ *the* ~, compiere il salto della morte in aeroplano.

loose, *a.* sciolto, libero, rilasciato; slacciato, slegato; mal riunito; poco solido; dissoluto; licenzioso; vago, poco esatto; (*fig.*) scucito, illogico; (*pulley*) folle; (*in bulk*) in blocco. ~ *cash*, moneta spicciola, *f. to be at a* ~ *end*, essere a spasso. ~-*leaf ledger*, mastro a fogli staccati, *m.* **loose**[**n**], *v.t.* sciogliere, slegare; rilassare, rallentare, allentare; snodare, staccare, liberare, disserrare; (*sail*) mollare.

loot, *n.* saccheggio, bottino, *m.* ¶ *v.t. & i.* saccheggiare.

lop, *v.t.* tagliare, potare, mozzare, troncare. ~-*ear*[*ed rabbit*], coniglio dalle orecchie pendenti, *m.* ~*sided*, asimmetrico, non equilibrato, di fianco falso. *lopped tree*, albero troncato, con rami potati, *m.*

loquacious, *a.* loquace. **loquacity**, *n.* loquacità, *f.*

lord, *n.* signore; (*Eng.*) pari, lord, *m.* L~ *Mayor* (*Eng.*) (*London, York, Dublin*), It. sindaco, *m.* ~ *of creation*, Re del creato, *m.* ~ *of the manor*, castellano, *m.* *the Lord* (*God*), il Signore, *m.* *Lord's prayer*, preghiera domenicale, *f.*, paternostro, *m.* *Lord's supper*, (sacramento dell') Eucaristia, Santissimo Sacramento, *m.* ~ *it over*, dominare, signoreggiare, tiranneggiare. ~**ly**, *a.* signorile, grande, nobile; altero, fiero, superbo; sfarzoso, sontuoso. ~**ship**, *n.* signoria, *f. Your L*~, la Signoria vostra, Vossignoria.

lore, *n.* scienza, erudizione, *f.*

lorgnette, *n.* occhialetto, occhialino col manico, *m.*

Lorraine, *n.* la Lorena, *f.*

lorry, *n.* carro (senza lati), autocarro, carromatto, camion, *m.* ~ *driver*, camionista, *m.*

lose, *v.t. & i.ir.* perdere, smarrire, subire perdite, una perdita, essere battuto; (*train*) perdere; (*clock*) ritardare (di). ~ *heart*, perdersi di coraggio, d'animo. **loser**, *n.* perdente, *m.f.*, perditore, *m.*, -trice, f.; (good, bad) giuocatore, m., -trice, f. be a ~, perdere, essere in perdita. **loss**, n. perdita, f.; danno, deperimento, scapito, m.; rovina, disfatta, f. ~ of appetite, inappetenza, f. ~ of voice, l'esser senza voce. at a ~, con perdita; (fig.) imbarazzato, soncertato, messo nel sacco. be at a ~, non sapere che fare, non sapere, non comprendere. **lost**, p.p. & p.a. perduto, smarrito; mancato; scomparso; decesso, defunto; naufragato; perplesso, confuso; (in thought) immerso. ~ property office, ufficio degli oggetti smarriti, m.

lot, n. sorte, fortuna, porzione, f.; fato, destino, m.; (land) lotto, appezzamento, m.; (goods) partita, f. a ~, ~s, (gran) quantità; gran copia, f.; gran numero, m.; (of people) molta gente, moltissima gente, f. the ~, il tutto. to draw ~s, tirare a sorte. ~ [out], v.t. dividere in lotti.

loth (to be), essere avverso, essere poco disposto; (impers.) ripugnare a.

lotion, n. lozione, f.

lottery, n. lotto, m.; lotteria, estrazione a sorte, f. public ~, lotto pubblico, m.

lotto, n. lotto, m.

lotus, n. loto, m.

loud, a. alto, forte, grande (ref. to sound, suono, rumore); rumoroso, sonoro; (colour, dress) vistoso, sgargiante, chiassoso. ~ cheers, grande applauso, m.; vive acclamazioni, f.pl. ~ pedal, pedale forte, m. ~ speaker, altoparlante, m. ~[ly], ad. forte, fortemente, ad alta voce.

Louisiana, n. la Luigiana, f.

lounge, n. (hotel, &c.) vestibolo (d'albergo); (Music hall) passeggio (coperto), m. ~ bed, canapè, letto a divano, m. ~ chair, poltrona a sdraio, seggiola a sdraio, f. ~ suit, abito (completo), m., giacchetta, f. ¶ v.i. gironzare, andare a zonzo, bighellonare, oziare.

lounger, n. bighellone, infingardo, perdigiorno, m.

lour, v.i. See lower.

louse, n. pidocchio, m. **lousy**, a. pidocchioso; sporco, sozzo, vile.

lout, n. & ~ish, a. zotico, a. & m., zoticone, m., goffo, grossolano, maleducato, a.

lovable, a. amabile. **love**, n. amore, m.; affezione, carità, tenerezza, f.; amante, m.f. for ~ or money, per

tutto l'oro del mondo. in ~, innamorato (di). fall in ~, innamorarsi (di), invaghirsi (di). make ~ to, fare la corte a, amoreggiare, corteggiare, fare all'amore con, vezzeggiare. play for ~, giuocare per amore, per chiasso. [with] [best] ~ (letter), con affettuosi saluti. ~ all (Ten.), zero pari. ~bird, psittaco, m. ~-in-a-mist (Bot.), fior del finocchio, m. ~ knot, nodo d'amore, m. ~ letter, biglietto amoroso, m., lettera d'amore, f. ~-lock (as worn by a man), ciuffetto, m.; (by a woman) ricciolo, m., ciocca di capelli, f. ~ match, matrimonio d'inclinazione, matrimonio d'amore, m. ~ potion, filtro d'amore, m. ~-sick, languente d'amore, ammalato d'amore. ~ story, storia d'amore, romanzo, racconto galante. ~ tragedy, tragedia d'amore, f. ¶ v.t. & i. amare, essere appassionato di, essere affezionato a, voler bene a. ~ one another, amarsi [reciprocamente].

loveliness, n. bellezza, grazia, vaghezza, f., incanto, m. **lovely**, a. grazioso, bello, vago, vezzoso, incantevole, seducente.

lover, n. amante, m.f., innamorato, m., -a, f., galante, m., amico, m., -a, f., amatore, m. ~ of old books, amatore di vecchi libri. **loving**, a. affezionato, affettuoso, amoroso, buono, tenero.

low, a. basso, di bassa condizione; triviale, volgare, abbietto, vile, ignobile; (fever, speed) lento; (bow) profondo. L~ Countries, Paesi Bassi, m.pl. ~ gear, prima velocità, f. ~ mass, messa bassa, piana, f. very ~ neck, (vestito) molto scollato. in ~ spirits, abbattuto. ~ relief, bassorilievo, m. ~ Sunday, Domenica in Albis, Domenica dopo Pasqua. ~-water mark (sea), livello di bassa marea, m.; (river) magra, f. ¶ ad. basso, in basso; a voce bassa; profondamente. ~-bred, mal educato. ~-necked (dress), scollato. ~-spirited, abbattuto, scoraggiato. to be ~ waisted (dress), aver la vita bassa.

low, v.i. muggire, mugghiare.

lower, a. inferiore, più basso, di sotto, di basso, minore. ~ case (Typ.) (letters), le minuscole, f.pl. ~ register (Mus.), grave. ~ tooth, dente inferiore, m. ¶ v.t. abbassare, calare, fare discendere, diminuire, ridurre; (flags, sails) ammainare.

~ *oneself* (*fig.*), abbassarsi, avvilirsi. *award*, *&c.*, *to the lowest tenderer*, aggiudicare al ribasso. **lower** *or* **lour**, *v.i.* minacciare, aggrottare le ciglia; rannuvolarsi, oscurarsi.

lowlands, *n.pl.* terreni bassi, *m.pl.*; bassopiano, *m.*

lowliness, *n.* umiltà, *f.* **lowly**, *a.* umile, dimesso; basso, piccolo.

lowness, *n.* sito basso, stato basso; (*voice*) tono basso, *m.*; (*sound*) gravità, *f.*; (*spirits*) abbattimento, *m.*; (*price*, *&c.*) modicità, *f.*; (*vileness*) bassezza, *f.*

loyal, *a.* leale, ligio, fedele, costante, ~**ism**, *n.* lealismo, *m.*, fedeltà al sovrano, *f.* ~**ist**, *n.* suddito leale o fedele, aderente del re, *m.* ~**ty**, *n.* lealtà, *f.*; (*to sovereign*) lealismo, *m.*

lozenge, *n.* pastiglia, tavoletta, *f.*; (*Geom.*) rombo, *m.*, losanga, *f.*

lubber, *n.* goffone, tanghero, zoticone, *m.*

lubricate, *v.t.* lubrificare. *lubricating oil*, olio lubrificante, *m.* **lubricator**, *n.* lubrificatore, *m.*

Lucca, *n.* Lucca, *f. of* ~, lucchese.

lucern[e], *n.* erba medica, *f.*

Lucerne (Lake of), lago di Lucerna, lago dei Quattro Cantoni, *m.*

lucid, *a.* lucido. ~**ity**, *n.* lucidità, *f.*

luck, *n.* fortuna, ventura, *f.*, successo; azzardo, caso, *m.* ~**less**, *a.* sfortunato, sventurato. ~**y**, *a.* fortunato, propizio, favorevole. ~ *star*, buona stella, *f.*

lucrative, *a.* lucroso, lucrativo, profittevole. **lucre**, *n.* lucro *m.*

lucubration, *n.* elucubrazione, *f.*

ludicrous, *a.* ridicolo, comico.

luff, *n.* orzata, *f.*; sopravvento, *m.* ¶ *v.t.* orzare.

lug, *n.* verme da pesca, *m.*; lobo dell'orecchio, *m.* ¶ *v.t.* tirare, trascinare. ~ *sail*, vela aurica, *f.*

luge, *n.* piccola slitta, *f.* ¶ *v.i.* slittare.

luggage, *n.* bagaglio, *m.* ~ *carrier*, facchino, portabagagli, *m.* ~ *van*, carro bagagli, bagagliaio, *m.*

lugger, *n.* trabaccolo, *m.*

lugubrious, *a.* lugubre.

lukewarm, *a.* tiepido, tepido (*fig.*) indifferente. ~**ness**, *n.* tepidezza, *f.*, poco fervore, *m.*

lull, *n.* bonaccia, calma, *f.*; intervallo di calma, *m.* ¶ *v.t.* calmare, cullare, acquetare. ~ *to sleep*, addormentare cullando. **lullaby**, *n.* ninna nanna, *f.*

lumbago, *n.* lombaggine, *f.* **lumbar**, *a.* lombare.

lumber, *n.* rifiuti, arnesi od oggetti inutili, *m.pl.*; cose non usate, *f.pl.*; (*Amer.*) legname da costruzione, *m.* ~*man*, boscaiuolo, *m.* ~ *room*, ripostiglio, *m.*, soffitta, *f.*

luminary, *n.* luminare, astro, lume, corpo luminoso, *m.* (*pers.*) luminare, *m.* **luminous**, *a.* luminoso. ~ *dial* (*watch*), quadrante luminoso, *m.*

lump, *n.* blocco, pezzo, *m.*, zolla, massa, *f.*, nodo, *m.*, escrescenza, enfiagione, natta, *f.* ~ *sugar*, zucchero in pezzi, *m.* ~ *sum*, somma globale, *f.* *in a* ~ *sum* (*opp.* by instalments), tutto in una volta. ¶ *v.t.* prendere in blocco, mettere in massa; trattare senza distinzione. ~**ish**, *a.* pesante, massiccio, inerte, stupido.

lunacy, *n.* alienazione mentale, pazzia, follia, mania, demenza, *f.*

lunar, *a.* lunare.

lunatic, *n.* pazzo, -a, alienato, -a, *m.f.* *asylum*, manicomio, *m.*

lunch *&* **luncheon**, *n.* colazione, seconda colazione, *f.* *lunch*[*eon*] *basket*, cestino delle provvigioni; (*Rly.*) cestino da viaggio, *m.* *luncheon set*, servizio da colazione, *m.* **lunch**, *v.i.* fare colazione.

lung, *n.* polmone, *m.*

lunge, *n.* botta, *f.*

lupin[e], *n.* (*Bot.*) lupino, *m.*

lupus, (*Med.*) n. lupus, *m.*

lurch, *n.* scarto; traballamento, *m.* *leave in the* ~, lasciare nelle difficoltà, nell'imbarazzo, lasciare in asso, piantare. ¶ *v.i.* scartare, traballare.

lure, *n.* esca, *f.*, allettamento, *m.* ¶ *v.t.* adescare allettare; (*birds*) richiamare.

lurid, *a.* livido, fosco; torvo; spettrale; terribile, sinistro.

lurk, *v.i.* nascondersi, stare in agguato, covare.

luscious, *a.* delizioso, molto dolce, sdolcinato, melato; mellifluo.

lush, *a.* lussureggiante, grasso.

lust, *n.* concupiscenza, lussuria, brama, incontinenza, *f.* ~ *after*, agognare, bramare, desiderare ardentemente. ~**ful**, *a.* libidinoso, lascivo, voluttuoso.

lustre, *n.* lustro, splendore; candelabro, *m.*; (*fig.*) decoro, vanto, *m.*, gloria, *f.* ¶ *v.t.* lustrare, verniciare. ~**less**, *a.* senza lustro, appannato, offuscato.

lusty, *a.* gagliardo, sano, vigoroso, robusto.

lute, n. (*Mus.*) liuto, m.; (*cement*) luto, m. ¶ v.t. lutare.
Lutheran, a. & n. luterano, a. & m.
Luxemburg, n. il Lussemburgo, m.; (*city*) L~, f.
luxuriance, n. esuberanza, f., rigoglio, lussureggiamento, m. **luxuriant,** a. esuberante, rigoglioso, fertilissimo. **luxurious,** a. sontuoso, fastoso, di lusso. **luxury,** n. lusso, m., profusione, sontuosità, f.
lye, n. lisciva, f.
lying, a. mendace, bugiardo, menzognero. ¶ n. menzogna, bugia, f.
lying-in, n. parto, puerperio, m. ¶ a. partoriente. ~ hospital, ospedale, m. (casa, f.) di maternità.
lymph, n. linfa, f.; vaccino, m.
lynch, v.t. linciare. ~ing, ~ law, linciaggio, m., giustizia sommaria, f.
lynx, n. lince, f.; (*common*) lupo cerviero, m.
Lyons, n. Lione, f.
lyre, n. lira, f. ~ bird, uccello lira, m. *Eolian lyre*, arpa di Eolo, f.
lyric & lyrical, a. lirico. **lyric,** n. [poesia] lirica, f. **lyricism,** n. lirismo, m.

M

macabre, a. macabro.
macaco or **macaque,** n. macaco, m.
macadam, n. macadam, m. ~ize, v.t. macadamizzare.
macaroni, n. maccheroni, m.pl.
macaroon, n. amaretto, m.
macaw, n. macao, m., ara, f.
mace, n. mazza, f.; (*spice*) mace, m. ~ bearer, mazziere, m.
macerate, v.t. macerare.
Machiavellian, a. machiavellico.
machination, n. macchinazione, f., complotto, intrigo, m.
machine, n. macchina, f. ~ cut, tagliato a macchina. ~ gun, mitragliatrice, f. ~ gunner, mitragliere, m. ~ made, fatto a macchina. ~ oil, olio da macchinario. ~ tool, macchina utensile, f. ¶ v.t. lavorare a macchina; (*Typ.*) stampare (a macchina), tirare. (v.i.) far rotolare il torchio. **machinery,** n. macchinario, meccanismo, m., macchine, f.pl., apparecchi, m.pl.; (*fig.*)

mezzo, strumento, m. **machining** (*Typ.*), n. tiratura, impressione, f. **machinist,** n. macchinista; meccanico, m.; (*Sewing*) punteggiatrice, f.
mackerel, n. sgombro, m. ~ sky, cielo a pecorelle, m.
mackintosh, n. impermeabile, m.
mad, a. matto, pazzo, alienato, folle; insensato, scervellato; furioso, frenetico; infuriato (*pers. & bull*); arrabbiato (*pers. & dog*). ~ cap, testa matta, f., ragazza scaltra, f. ~man, ~woman, pazzo, m., -a, f., forsennato, m., -a, f.
madam, n. signora, f.
madapollam, n. madapolam, m.
madden, v.t. rendere furioso; fare impazzire; fare arrabbiare. ~ing, p.a. che fa rabbia, irritante.
madder, n. robbia, f.
Madeira, n. Madera, f.; (*wine*) (vino di) Madera, m.
madly, ad. pazzamente; disperatamente. **madness,** n. pazzia, demenza, alienazione, follia, f., furore, m.; (*dog's*) idrofobia, rabbia, f.
madonna, n. Madonna, f.
madrepore, n. madrepora, f.
madrigal, n. madrigale, m.
magazine, n. magazzino, deposito; fondaco, arsenale, m.; rivista, f. ~ camera, (macchina fotografica) a magazzino, f. ~ rifle, ~ gun, fucile a ripetizione, m. powder ~, polveriera; santabarbara, f.
Maggiore (Lago), lago Maggiore, m.
maggot, n. verme, baco, bruco, m.; (*fig.*) capriccio, ghiribizzo, m.; ubbia, f. ~y, a. verminoso, bacato.
Magi, n.pl. Magi, m.pl.
magic, a. magico; meraviglioso. ~ lantern, lanterna magica, f. ~ wand, bacchetta magica, f. ¶ n. magia, arte magica, f.; incanto, incantesimo, m. ~al, a. magico. ~ally, ad. magicamente. ~ian, n. mago, stregone, m.
magisterial, a. di magistrato, di maestro; (*fig.*) magistrale. ~ly, ad. da magistrato, magistralmente, da maestro. **magistracy,** n. magistratura, f. **magistrate,** n. giudice, magistrato.
magnanimity, n. magnanimità, f.
magnanimous, a. magnanimo.
magnate, n. magnate; (*fam.*) pezzo grosso, m.
magnesia, n. magnesia, f. **magnesium,** n. magnesio, m. ~ light, luce al magnesio, f.

magnet, *n.* calamita, *f.*, magnete, *m.*
~ic, *a.* magnetico; *(bar, needle)* ago magnetico, *m.*; *(fig.)* attraente, attrattivo. **~ics,** *n.* & **~ism,** *n.* magnetismo, *m.* **~ize,** *v.t.* calamitare; magnetizzare. **magneto,** *n.*, magnete, *m.*; *(in comps.)* magneto. **~ electric,** *a.* magnetoelettrico.

magnificat, *n.* magnificat, *m.*

magnificence, *n.* magnificenza, *f.* **magnificent,** *a.* magnifico.

magnify, *v.t.* amplificare, ingrandire, ingrossare; *(the Lord)* magnificare. *magnifying glass,* lente d'ingrandimento, *f.*

magniloquence, *n.* magniloquenza, ampollosità, *f.* **magniloquent,** *a.* magniloquente.

magnitude, *n.* grandezza; importanza, *f.*

magnolia, *n.* magnolia, *f.*

magot *(Chinese figure & ape),* *n.* macaco, *m.*

magpie, *n.* gazza, *f.*

mahogany, *n.* mogano, *m.*

mahout, *n.* conduttore d'elefanti, *m.*

maid, *n.* fanciulla, ragazza, giovanetta; nubile, vergine; cameriera, donna di servizio, *f.* ~*(servant),* fantesca, serva, persona di servizio, domestica. *maid of all work,* domestica, donna a tutto servizio, *f.* *maid's room,* camera della domestica, *f.* **maiden,** *n.* fanciulla, ragazza, vergine, pulzella, *f.* ~ *(lady),* signorina, *f.* ¶ *a.* di fanciulla, di ragazza, verginale; *(speech)* primo; *(trip)* primo, inaugurale. ~ *hair,* *(fern)* capelvenere, *m.* ~ *name,* nome di fanciulla, nome da signorina, *m.* **~hood,** *n.* verginità, *f.* **~ly,** *a.* verginale.

mail, *n.* *(armour)* maglia di ferro, cotta di maglia, *f.*; *(Post)* corriere (postale), *m.*, posta, corrispondenza, *f.* ~*bag,* valigia postale, *f.*, sacco di corrispondenza, *m.* ~ *boat,* ~ *steamer,* vapore postale, piroscafo postale, *m.* ~ *carriage* *(Rly.),* vagone postale, *m.* ~ *cart* *(child's),* carrozzella leggera, *f.* ~ *cart,* ~ *coach,* furgone, vagone postale, *m.* ~ *coach,* *(stage)* vettura della posta, *f.* ~ *order business,* ordinazioni per posta, *f.pl.* ~ *(train),* treno postale.

maim, *v.t.* storpiare, mutilare.

main, *a.* principale, primo, capitale, essenziale, più importante. ~ *[portion of]* building, edificio principale, *m.* *the* ~ *chance,* il solido, *m.* ~ *deck,* ponte principale, primo

ponte, *m.* ~ *drain,* collettore di fognatura, *m.* *by* ~ *force,* a viva forza. ~ *hall,* *(body of building)* sala principale, *f.*, salone, *m.*, *(Sch.)* aula magna, *f.* *the* ~ *idea* *(of a book),* concetto generale, *m.* ~ *issue* *(Law),* fondo, *m.* ~*land,* terraferma, *f.*, continente, *m.* ~ *line* *(Rly.),* linea principale, *f.* ~ *mast,* albero maestro, *m.* *the* ~ *point,* punto essenziale, punto capitale, *m.* ~ *road,* strada maestra, strada principale, *f.* ~ *sail,* vela (di) maestra, *f.* ~ *spring,* molla principale, molla; *(fig.)* agente principale, *m.*, causa prima, *f.*, movente, *m.* ~*stay,* *(fig.)* sostegno principale, appoggio principale, *m.* ~ *structure* *(of a building),* edificio principale, *m.* *the* ~ *thing,* la cosa essenziale, *f.* l'essenziale, *m.* ~ *walls,* muri esterni, *m.pl.*, mura, *f.pl.* muraglione, *m.* ¶ *n.* *(pipe)* conduttura principale, *f.*; *(pl.)* canalizzazione, *f.*; *(Elec.)* conduttore principale, *m.*; *(sea, Poet.)* oceano, *m.*, onda, *f.*, alto mare, *m.* *in the* ~, in generale, in fondo, in sostanza. **the M~** *(river),* il Meno, *m.* **~ly,** *ad.* principalmente; sopratutto.

maintain, *v.t.* mantenere, sostenere; asserire; nutrire; conservare, rimanere fedele a. **maintenance,** *n.* mantenimento, *m.*; vitto, *m.*, alimenti, *m.pl.*; *(Mach.)* manutenzione, *f.*

Mainz, *n.* Magonza, *f.*

maisonette, *n.* casetta, casettina, *f.*

maize, *n.* mais, granturco, *m.*

majestic, *a.* maestoso. **majesty,** *n.* maestà, *f.* *His, Her M~,* Sua Maestà.

majolica, *n.* maiolica, *f.*

major, *a.* maggiore, più anziano; *(prophet)* grande; *(pers.)* anziano, maggiore. ~ *planet,* principale. ~ *road,* strada maestra, *f.* ¶ *(Mil.)* *n.* maggiore, capo di battaglione, di uno squadrone, *m.* ~ *general,* maggiore-generale, *m.*

Majorca, *n.* Maiorca, *f.*

majority, *n.* maggioranza, *f.*, i più *m.pl.*, la parte più grande, *f.*, età maggiore, *f.*; grado di maggiore, *m.*

make, *n.* fabbricazione, fattura, costruzione; forma, struttura, corporatura; *f.* ~*believe,* finta, *f.*, sembiante, *m.* ~*shift,* espediente, *m.* ~*up,* travestimento, *m.*, truccatura, *f.* ~*weight,* complemento di peso, *m.*, aggiunta, *f.*;

(*butcher's*) contentino, *m.*; (*fig.*) riempitivo, ripieno, *m.* ¶ *v.t. ir.* fare, creare, causare, produrre, fabbricare, confezionare, costruire, operare, eseguire, effettuare; rendere, costringere; (*inquiries*) prendere, assumere (informazioni); fare indagini; (*v.i. ir.*) dirigersi. ~ *away with*, far sparire, disfarsi di, uccidere. ~ *faces*, fare le smorfie. ~ *good* (*damage*), risarcire; (*loss*) riparare a, rifarsi di. ~ *hay*, tagliare, raccogliere il fieno; (*fig.*) battere il ferro (mentre è caldo). ~ *it up*, riconciliarsi, comporre una lite, rappattumarsi. ~ *light of*, prendere alla leggera, non far caso di, attribuire poca importanza a, svalutare. ~ *money*, arricchirsi, guadagnare denaro. ~ *much of*, tener gran conto di; far mille carezze a, vezzeggiare. ~ *one's will*, fare testamento, eseguire un testamento. ~ *off*, andarsene, svignarsela. ~ *out*, comprendere, capire; scoprire, scorgere; decifrare; distinguere; giustificare, provare; accertare; redigere; regolare. ~ *the most of*, attribuire la massima importanza a, trarre il miglior partito da. ~ *up*, fare, completare; riparare, colmare, compensare; preparare, metter insieme, confezionare; fingere, inventare; (*a/c*) regolare; (*face*) tingersi, imbellettarsi; (*Theat.*) travestirsi, mascherarsi; (*Typ.*) impaginare. ~ *up for*, supplire a, rimpiazzare. ~ *up one's mind*, decidersi, risolversi.

maker, *n.* creatore, fattore, autore, *m.*; costruttore, fabbricante, *m.* ~-*up* (*Typ.*), impaginatore, *m.*

making, *n.* fabbricazione, fattura, confezione, costruzione, *f.* ~ *ready* (*Typ.*), mettere in pronto. ~-*up price* (*Stk. Ex.*), prezzo corrente al giorno di riporto (*Contango day*).

malachite, *n.* malachite, *f.*

maladministration, *n.* mal governo, *m.*; cattiva amministrazione, *f.*

maladroit, *a.* malaccorto.

malady, *n.* malattia, *f.*

Malagasy, *a.* malgascio. ¶ *n.* (*pers.*) malgascio, *m.* (*language*), il malgascio, *m.*

malaprop[ism], *n.* incongruità di parole, cacologia, *f.*

malar, *a.* della guancia. ¶ *n.* osso della guancia, *m.*

malaria, *n.* malaria, *f.* **malarial**, *a.* malarico.

Malay[an], *a.* malese. ¶ *n.* (*pers.*) malese, *m.f.*; (*language*) il malese, *m.*

Malaysia, *n.* Malesia, *f.*

malcontent, *a. & n.* malcontento, *a. & m.*

male, *n.* maschio, *m.* ¶ *a.* maschio, maschile. ~ *descent*, discendenza maschile, *f.* ~ *nurse*, infermiere, *m.*

malediction, *n.* maledizione, *f.*

malefactor, *n.* malfattore, *m.*

malevolent, *a.* malevolo.

malformation, *n.* deformità, struttura anormale, *f.*

malice, *n.* malignità, cattiveria, *f.*, rancore, *m.* ~ *aforethought*, ~ *prepense*, premeditazione, *f.*

malicious, *a.* malizioso.

malign, *v.t.* diffamare, parlar male di.

malign, **malignant**, *a.* maligno, virulento.

malinger, *v.i.* fingersi malato.

mallard, *n.* anitra selvatica, *f.*, maschio dell' a. s., *m.*

malleable, *a.* malleabile.

mallet, *n.* maglio, martello di legno, *m.*

mallow, *n.* malva, *f.*

malt, *n.* malto, *m.* ~ *house*, germinatoio, *m.* ¶ *v.t.* convertire in malto. ~*ing*, *n.* fabbricazione di malto, *f.* ~*ster*, *n.* fabbricante di malto, *m.*

Malta, *n.* Malta, *f.* **Maltese**, *a.* maltese. ~ *cross*, croce di Malta, *f.* ~ (*dog*, *bitch*), cane maltese, *m.*, cagna maltese, *f.* ¶ *n.* (*pers.*) maltese, *m.f.*; (*language*) il maltese, *m.*

maltreat, *v.t.* maltrattare, malmenare. ~*ment*, *n.* maltrattamento, *m.*

mamillary, *a.* mammillare.

mam[m]a, *n.* mamma, *f.*

mammal, *n.* mammifero, *m.* **mammalia**, *n.pl.* mammiferi, *m.pl.*, mammali, *m.pl.*

mammoth, *n.* mammut, *m. inv.*

man, *n.* uomo; signore; servitore, domestico; operaio, impiegato; il genere umano, *m.*; (*Draughts*) pedina, *f.*; (*Chess*) pezzo, *m.* ~ *& wife*, marito e moglie. ~ *at the wheel*, timoniere, *m.* ~ *child*, figlio maschio, *m.* ~-*eater*, antropofago, cannibale, *m.* ~ *Friday*, seguace devoto, uomo buono a tutto, factotum, *m.* ~*hole* (*Mach.*), passo d'uomo, portello, *m.*; (*sewer*, *&c.*) botola, bocca d'accesso, *f.* *the* ~ *in the street*, uomo qualunque, uomo ordinario, il passante, *m.* ~ *of all work*, factotum, uomo buono a tutto, *m.* ~ *of colour*, negro, *m.* ~ *of deeds*, uomo d'azione, *m.* ~ *of fashion*, elegante, *m.* ~ *of straw*, uomo di paglia, *m.*, persona fittizia, *f.* ~ *of substance*, uomo agiato, *m.* ~*-of-war*, nave da guerra, *f.* ~*'s estate*, età maggiore, *f.* ~*'s part acted by a woman*, parte travestita, *f.* ~ (*servant*), servitore, domestico, *m.* ~*slaughter*, omicidio colposo, preterintenzionale, &c. (tutte le figure di omicidio che sono *felonies* e che non assurgono a *murder*). *men's single, double* (*Ten.*), singolare uomini, doppio uomini. ¶ *v.t.* (*boat, &c.*) armare, equipaggiare; (*prize ship*) ammarinare (una presa). ~hood, ~kind, ~ly, &c. See below.

manacle, *v.t.* ammanettare; (*fig.*) incatenare. ~s, *n.pl.* manette, *f.pl.*

manage, *v.t.* gestire, amministrare; condurre, dirigere; (*machines, &c.*) manovrare, governare; (*horses, &c.*) maneggiare; (*v.i.*) sapere, aggiustarsi. ~ *to*, riuscire a, fare in modo da, pervenire a. ~ment, *n.* amministrazione, direzione, gestione, condotta, *f.*; maneggio, *m.* **manager**, ~ess, *n.* amministratore, *m.*, -trice, *f.*; direttore, *m.*, -trice, *f.*; gerente, gestore; (*farm*) massaio, *m.*, -a, *f.*; (*ship's*) armatore, *m. managing director*, amministratore delegato, *m.*

manatee, *n.* lamantino, *m.*

Manchukuo, *n.* Man-chu-kwo, *f.* **Manchuria**, *n.* la Manciuria, *f.* **Manchu[rian]**, *a.* manciuriano. ¶ *n.* manciuriano, *m.*, -a, *f.*

mandarin, *n.* mandarino, *m.*; (*toy*) pagoda, *f.*

mandarin[e] [orange], *n.* mandarino, *m.*, arancia mandarina, *f.*

mandatary, -ory, *n.* mandatario, *m.* **mandate**, *n.* mandato, incarico, *m.* ~*d territory*, paese sotto mandato, *m.* **mandator**, *n.* mandante, *m.f.*

mandible, *n.* mandibola, *f.*

mandolin[e], *n.* mandolino, *m.*

mandrake, *n.* mandragora, *f.*

mandrel, -il (*lathe*), *n.* mandrino, *m.*

mandrill (*baboon*), *n.* mandrillo, *m.*

mane, *n.* criniera, *f.*

manège, -ege, *n.* maneggio, *m.*

manes, *n.pl.* mani, *m.pl.*

manfully, *ad.* da uomo, coraggiosamente, intrepidamente, virilmente.

manganese, *n.* manganese, *m.*

mange, *n.* rogna, scabbia, *f.*

mangel[-wurzel] *or* **mangold [-wurzel]**, *n.* barbabietola campestre, *f.*

manger, *n.* mangiatoia, greppia, *f.*; presepio, *m.*

mangle, *n.* mangano; cilindro, *m.* ¶ *v.t.* mutilare; (*in carving*) sciupare tagliando; (*linen*) manganare; cilindrare; (*language*) straziare.

mango, *n.* mango, *m.*

mangrove, *n.* rizoforea, *f.*

mangy, *a.* rognoso, scabbioso.

manhood, *n.* virilità, età virile, *f.* ~ *suffrage*, voto a tutti i cittadini maggiorenni, *m.*

mania, *n.* mania, *f.* **maniac**, *n.* & ~al, *a.* maniaco, *a.* & *m.*

manicure, *n.* manicura, *f.* ~ *set*, astuccio, servizio da manicura, *m.* ~ *the hands*, fare una manicura. **manicurist**, *n.* manicure, *m.f.*

manifest, *a.* manifesto, noto, evidente. ¶ (*ship*) *n.* manifesto, *m.*, nota di carico, *f.* ¶ *v.t.* manifestare.

manifesto, *n.* manifesto, *m.*

manifold, *a.* molteplice, vario. ~ *book*, copialettere, *m.inv.*

manikin, *n.* nano, omiciattolo, *m.*; (*lay figure*) manichino, fantoccio, *m.*

Manil[l]a, *n.* (*Geog.*) Manilla, *f.*; (*cheroot*) manilla, *m.*, sigaro di Manilla, *m.*

manioc, *n.* manioc, *m.*

manipulate, *v.t.* manipolare, manovrare; (*pers.*) abbindolare, raggirare.

mankind, *n.* genere umano, *m.*, umanità, *f.*, gli uomini, *m.pl.* **manliness**, *n.* coraggio virile, *m.*, virilità, dignità di uomo, *f.* **manly**, *a.* virile, da uomo, coraggioso, maschile; (*woman*) maschile.

manna, *n.* manna, *f.*

mannequin, *n.* (*pers.*) manichino, *m.*; indossatrice, *f.*

manner, *n.* maniera, guisa, *f.*, modo, portamento, *m.*; aria, via, foggia, *f.*; genere, metodo, stile, *m.*; specie, abitudine, *f.*; (*pl.*) maniere, *f.pl.*; modi, costumi, *m.pl.* ~ed (*style, &c.*), *a.* ricercato, manierato. ~ism, *n.* manierismo, *m.*, affettazione, *f.* ~ly, *a.* garbato, cortese.

mannish, *a.* da uomo, maschile.

manoeuvre, *n.* manovra, *f.* ¶ *v.i.* & *t.* manovrare.

manometer, *n.* manometro, *m.*

manor, *n.* maniero, *m.*; (*or* ~ *house*) casa signorile, *f.*; (*Law*) feudo. *m.*; zona territoriale di cui una persona ha la libera proprietà.

mansard roof, tetto a mansarda, *m.*

mansion, *n.* palazzo, castello, *m.*, casa signorile, *f.*; (*pl.*) appartamenti, *m.pl.*

mant[e]let, *n.* mantellina, *f.*

mantelpiece, *n.* caminetto, *m.*

mantelshelf, *n.* cappa del camino, *f.*, piano del caminetto, *m.*

mantilla, *n.* mantiglia, *f.*

mantle, *n.* mantello, *m.*; (*gas*) reticella (per gas), *f.* ~*maker,* sarto da donna, *m.*; sarta, *f.* ¶ *v.t.* coprire, velare.

Mantua, *n.* Mantova, *f.* ~**n,** *a.* mantovano.

manual, *a.* manuale. ~ (*exercise*) (*Mil.*) maneggio delle armi, *m.* ¶ *n.* manuale, libretto, compendio, *m.*; (*organ*) tastiera, *f.*

manufactory, *n.* fabbrica, *f.* **manufacture,** *n.* fabbricazione, manifattura, confezione; industria, *f.* **manufacturer,** *n.* fabbricante, manifattore, industriale, *m.* ~'*s price,* prezzo di fabbrica, *m.* **manufacturing,** *p.a.* manifatturiero, industriale.

manure, *n.* concime, ingrasso, *m.* ¶ *v.t.* concimare, ingrassare.

manuscript, *n.* & *a.* manoscritto, *a.* & *m.*

Manx, *a.* dell'isola di Man.

many, *a.* molti, molte, piú (*inv.*); parecchi, parecchie; un gran numero di, numerosi, numerose. ~ *coloured,* multicolore. ~ *a,* piú d'un(o) . . . , parecchi. ~-*sided,* moltilatero, (*fig.*) complesso, complicato, di gran capacità, molto istruito. *a great* ~, moltissimi, *a. as* ~, tanti, altrettanti. *as* ~ *as,* tanto . . . quanto. ~ *people,* molta gente, *f.*, molte persone, *f.pl. so* ~, tanti. *the* ~, la moltitudine, la folla, *f. too* ~, troppo.

map, *n.* carta, *f.* ~ *case,* portacarte, *m.inv.* ~ *of the heavens,* carta celeste, *f.* ~ *of the heavens in hemispheres,* mappamondo celeste, *m.* ~ *of the world in hemispheres,* mappamondo, *m. outline* ~, *skeleton* ~, carta muta, *f.* ~ *producer,* cartografo, *m.* ¶ *v.t.* fare una carta di, disegnare la carta di. ~ *out,* tracciare.

maple, *n.* acero, *m.*

mar, *v.t.* guastare; deformare; danneggiare; turbare.

marabou & **marabout,** *n.* marabú, *m.* inv.

maraschino, *n.* maraschino, *m.*

marasmus, *n.* marasma, *m.*

Marathon [*race*], *n.* [corsa di] maratona, *f.*

maraud, *v.t.* razziare, predare. ~**er,**

n. razziatore, predone, ladro, *m.* ~**ing,** *n.* saccheggio, predamento, ladroneggio, *m.*

marble, *n.* marmo, *m.*; (*games*) pallina di marmo, *f.* ~ *mason* & ~ *merchant,* marmista, *m.* ~ *quarry,* cava di marmo, *f.* ~*work* & ~ *works,* lavoro di marmo, laboratorio da marmista, *m.*; segheria di marmi, *f.* ¶ *v.t.* marmorizzare. **marbler,** *n.* marmorizzatore, *m.* **marbling,** *n.* marezzamento, marezzo, *m.*

marc, (*fruit, refuse*) *n.* fondaccio, *m.*, feccia, *f.*

marcasite, *n.* marcassite, *f.*

March, *n.* marzo, *m.*

march, *n.* marcia, *f.*; (*frontier*) marca, frontiera, *f.* ~ *past,* sfilata, *f.* ¶*v.i.* marciare. ~ *in,* entrare. ~ *off,* mettersi in marcia. ~ *out,* sortire. ~ *past,* sfilare. ~**ing,** *n.* marcia, *f.* ~ *song,* canzone di marcia, *f.*

marchioness, *n.* marchesa, *f.*

mare, *n.* cavalla; giumenta, *f. he has found a* ~'*s nest,* ha fatto una scoperta assurda, ha trovato il nido di un topo nell'orecchio di un gatto.

margarine, *n.* margarina, *f.*

margin, *n.* margine, *m.*, bordo, *m.*; (*book page*) margine, *m.* ~**al,** *a.* marginale, a margine.

marguerite, *n.* margherita, *f.*

marigold, *n.* calendula, *f.*, fiorrancio, *m.*

marine, *a.* marino, marittimo. ~ *glue,* colla da marina, *f.* ~ *stores,* forniture marittime, *f.pl.* ~ *superintendent,* capitano del porto, *m.* ¶ *n.* (*shipping*) marina, *f.*; (*pers.*) soldato di marina, *m.* **mariner,** *n.* marinaio, *m.* ~'*s compass,* bussola di navigazione, *f.*

marionette, *n.* marionetta, *f.*

marital, *a.* maritale.

maritime, *a.* marittimo.

marjoram, *n.* maggiorana, *f.*

mark, *n.* segno, *m.*, marca, *f.*; distintivo, bollo, marchio, *m.*; impronta, traccia, *f.*; indizio, segnale, contrassegno, pegno, *m.*; prova, testimonianza, *f.*; confine, limite; bersaglio, *m.*; mira, *f.*; scopo, punto, *m.*; (*Sch.*) punto, voto, *m.* ~ *flag,* bandierina, *f.* ~ *of origin,* bollo, certificato d'origine, *m. book* ~, segnalibro, *m. post* ~, timbro postale, *m. trade* ~, marca di fabbrica, *f. low water* ~, linea di fondo, *f.* ¶ *v.t.* marcare, segnare; contrassegnare; notare, rimarcare, fare attenzione a, osservare; (*card*) segnare. ~ *out*, tracciare, delimitare. ~ *time*, battere il tempo, segnare il passo. ~**ed**, *p.a.* marcato, accentuato, notato, notevole; (*cheque*) notato, contrassegnato; (*man*) notabile; uomo sotto vigilanza; (*cards*) segnato. ~**er**, *n.* marcatore, segnatore; osservatore, *m.*; (*Mil.*) canneggiatore, *m.*; (*book*) segnalibro, segnapagina, *m.*

market, *n.* mercato, *m.*, piazza, *f.*, sbocco, *m.*, Borsa, *f.*, fiera, *f.*; (*covered*) mercato coperto, *m.* ~ *garden*, orto, *m.* ~ *gardener*, ortolano, *m.*, -a, *f.* ~ *gardening*, orticoltura, *f.* ~ *place* (piazza del) mercato. ~ *porter*, facchino, *m.* ~ *price*, prezzo corrente, prezzo di mercato, *m.* ~ *trader*, mercante, *m.* ~ *town*, borgo, *m.*, borgata, città dove ha luogo il mercato, *f.* ~ *value*, valore di mercato, valore mercantile, *m.* ~**able**, *a.* vendibile. ¶ *v.t.* vendere sul mercato, spacciare; (*v.i.*) fare le spese, mercanteggiare. ~**ing**, *n.* mercatura, *f.*

marking, *n.* marcatura, *f.* ~ *ink*, inchiostro indelebile, *m.*

marksman, *n.* tiratore, scelto, *m.*

marl, *n.* marna, *f.* ~ *pit*, marniera, *f.* ¶ *v.t.* marnare.

marline, *n.* merlino, *m.* ~ *spike*, *marlinspike*, caviglia da impiombare, *f.*

marly, *a.* marnoso.

marmalade, *n.* marmellata d'arance, *f.*

Marmora (Sea of), Mar di Marmara, *m.*

marmot (*Zool.*), *n.* marmotta, *f.*

Marne, *n.* Marna, *f.*

maroon, *a.* marrone. ¶ *n.* colore marrone, *m.*; (*firework*) castagnola, *f.*; (*pers.*) negro marrone, *m.*

marquee, *n.* padiglione, *m.*

marquet[e]ry, *n.* intarsio, *m.*, intarsiatura, *f.*

marquis, -quess, *n.* marchese, *m.*

marriage, *n.* matrimonio, sposalizio, *m.*; nozze, *f.pl.* ~ *articles*, convenzioni matrimoniali, contratto nuziale, *m.* ~ *licence*, dispensa di matrimonio, *f.* ~ *of convenience*, matrimonio di convenienza, *m.* ~ *portion*, dote, *f.* ~ *settlement*, contratto di matrimonio, *m.*, costituzione di dote, *f.* ~ *tie*, vincolo coniugale, *m.* *cousin*, &c., *by* ~, cugino acquistato, -a, *m.f.* ~**able**,

a. nubile, da marito. ~ *daughter*, figlia da marito, *f.* **married**, *p.a.* maritata, ammogliato, sposato, -a, coniugale; (*newly*) ~ *couple*, sposi, *m.pl.* ~ *life*, vita coniugale, *f.* *get* ~, sposarsi, maritarsi, prender marito, ammogliarsi, prender moglie.

marrow, *n.* midolla, *f.*, midollo, *m.*; (*vegetable*) zucca ovifera, *f.* ~ *bone*, ossobuco, *m.* ~ *fats*, genere di pisello primaticcio. ~**y**, *a.* midolloso.

marry, *v.t.* sposare, sposarsi con; maritare, ammogliare, dare moglie a, dare in isposa; (*v.i.*) sposarsi, maritarsi, prender moglie, prender marito. ~ *a second, a third time*, passare a seconde, a terze nozze. ~ *again*, risposarsi, passare a seconde nozze, rimaritarsi, riprender moglie, riprender marito. ~ *into*, imparentarsi con.

Marseillais, *e, a.* di Marsiglia, marsigliese. ¶ *n.* marsigliese, *m.f.* *the Marseillaise* (hymn), la Marsigliese, *f.* **Marseilles**, *n.* Marsiglia, *f.*

marsh, *n.* palude, *f.*, pantano, stagno, acquitrino, *m.* ~ *gas*, metano, *m.* ~ *mallow*, altea, bismalva, *f.* ~ *marigold*, fiorrancio delle paludi, *m.*

marshal, *n.* (*Mil.*) maresciallo, *m.*; (*Sport*) cerimoniere, *m.* ¶ *v.t.* ordinare, schierare. ~**ship**, *n.* grado (rango) di maresciallo, *m.*

marshy, *a.* paludoso, di palude, pantanoso.

marsupial, *n.* marsupiale, *m.*

mart, *n.* fiera, *f.*, emporio, *m.*, sala di vendita all'incanto, *f.*; (*Poet.*) mercato, *m.*

marten, *n.* martora; faina, *f.*

martial, *a.* marziale, militare, guerresco; (*pers.*) guerriero. ~ *law* (*in a town*), stato d'assedio, *m.*

martin, *n.* rondine, rondinella, *f.*

martinet, *n.* rigorista, ufficiale severo, *m.*

martingale (*Harness, Betting*), *n.* martingala, *f.*

Martinmas, *n.* il San Martino, *m.*, festa di San Martino, *f.*

martyr, *n.* martire, *m.f.* ~**dom**, *n.* martirio, *m.* ~**[ize]**, *v.t.* martirizzare. ~**ology** (*list*), *n.* martirologio, *m.*

marvel, *n.* meraviglia, *f.*, prodigio, *m.* ¶ *v.i.* meravigliarsi (di). **marvellous**, *a.* meraviglioso.

marzipan, *n.* marzapane, *m.*

mascot, *n.* portafortuna, *m.f.*

masculine, *a.* maschile; mascolino,

(*woman*) che ha del maschio, dell'uomo. ~ (*gender*), (genere) maschile, *m.* **masculinity,** *n.* mascolinità, *f.*

mash, *n.* mescolanza, *f.*, miscuglio, *m.*, miscela, *f.*; (*cattle*) pastone, beverone, *m.*; (*poultry*) pastone, *m.*; (*Cook.*) passata, *f.* ~ *tub,* tinozza in cui si preparano i grani pel malto. ¶ *v.t.* mescolare, pestare, ridurre in massa polposa. ~*ed potatoes,* turnips, purè di patate, di rape, *m.*

mask, *n.* maschera, *f.*; (*Arch.*) mascherone, *m.*; (*Phot.*) velo di carta, *m.* ¶ *v.t.* mascherare. ~*ed ball,* ballo mascherato, ballo in maschera, *m.* **masker,** ~**quer,** (*pers.*) *n.* maschera, *f.*

mason, *n.* muratore, *m.* *free* ~, frammassone, massone, *m.* *master* ~, capomastro, *m.* ~**ic,** *a.* massonico. ~**ry,** *n.* muratura, *f.* *free* ~, massoneria, frammassoneria, *f.*

masquerade, *n.* mascherata, *f.*; (*fig.*) mascherata, pantalonata, *f.*, travestimento, *m.* ¶ *v.i.* mascherarsi, travestirsi.

mass, *n.* massa, *f.*, ammasso, *m.*, quantità grande, *f.*, mole, *f.*, il tutto, *m.*; (*Relig.*) messa, *f.* *high* ~, messa grande, *m.* solenne, *f.* *low* ~, messa bassa, piana, *f.* ~ *production,* produzione in serie, *f.* *the* ~ *of the people,* la maggioranza del popolo, *f.* ¶ *v.t.* ammassare, disporre in massa; aggruppare, adunare.

massacre, *n.* massacro, *m.*, strage, *f.*, macello, *m.* ¶ *v.t.* massacrare.

massage, *n.* massaggio, *m.* ¶ *v.t.* massaggiare, fare i massaggi a. **masseur, -euse,** *n.* massaggiatore, *m.*, -trice, *f.*

massive, *a.* massiccio; solido.

mast, *n.* albero, *m.*; (*pl.*) alberatura, *f.* alberi, *m.pl.*; (*beech*) faggiuola, *f.*; (*oak*) ghianda, *f.* ~ *head,* testa dell'albero, cima dell'albero, *f.* ¶ *v.t.* alberare.

master, *n.* maestro; capo; padrone; direttore; professore; conoscitore, intenditore; capitano; signore, *m.* *be* ~ *of,* essere padrone di, disporre di; possedere, conoscere a fondo. *be one's own* ~, essere indipendente, essere libero. *M* ~ *A* (*boy*), il signorino A, *m.* ~ *card,* carta maestra, *f.* ~ *key,* passapertutto, *m.*, chiave maestra, *f.* ~ *mariner,* capitano di nave mercantile, *m.*

~ *mind,* mente superiore, mente direttiva, *f.* *M* ~ *of Ceremonies,* Maestro del cerimoniale, *m.* ~ *of foreign-going vessel,* capitano di lungo corso, *m.* ~ *of hounds,* capocaccia, *m.* ~ *passion,* passione dominante, *f.* ~*piece,* capolavoro, *m.* ~ *stroke,* colpo da maestro, *m.* ¶ *v.t.* dominare, sopraffare; rendersi padrone di, possedere, impadronirsi di. ~**ful,** *a.* (*tone, &c.*) imperioso, magistrale. ~ *man,* ~ *woman,* prepotente, *m.f.* ~**ly,** *a.* da maestro, abilissimo. *in a* ~ *way,* da maestro, con mano maestra. ~**ship,** *n.* posto di maestro, *m.* ~**y,** *n.* maestria, padronanza; supremazia, *f.*

mastic, *n.* mastice, *m.* ~ (*tree*), lentischio, *m.*

masticate, *v.t.* masticare. **mastication,** *n.* masticazione, *f.*

mastiff, *n.* mastino, *m.*

masting, *n.* & ~ *house,* alberatura, *f.*

mastodon, *n.* mastodonte, *m.*

mastoid, *n.* mastoide, *f.*

mat, *a.* smorto, bruno, matto. ¶ *n.* stuoia, *f.*, stoino, pagliericcio, *m.*; (*plate*) sottopiatto, *m.* ~ *maker,* fabbricante di stuoie, stuoiaio, *m.* ¶ *v.t.* stoiare. *matted hair,* capelli arruffati, *m.pl.*

matador, (*pers. & games*) *n.* mattadore, *m.*

match, *n.* (*light*) fiammifero, zolfanello, cerino, *m.*; (*fuse*) miccia, *f.*; (*marriage*) matrimonio, *m.*; (*pers.*) uguale; (*for marriage*) partito, *m.* (*Ten., &c.*) partita, *f.*; (*Box., Wrestling*) lotta, gara, *f.* ~ *board,* perlina, *f.* ~ *box,* scatola di fiammiferi, *f.* ~ *maker,* agente matrimoniale; chi combina matrimoni, *m.f.* ~ *play* (*Golf*), partita a buche, *f.* ¶ *v.t.* uguagliare, pareggiare, proporzionare; (*colours*) appaiare, assortire, combinare; (*in pairs*) appaiare, accoppiare, maritare. *to* ~, (*adv.*), bene assortito. *to be a* ~ *for,* far fronte a. ~**less,** *a.* senza pari, impareggiabile.

mate, *n.* compagno, camerata; assistente, *m.*; (*Naut.*) secondo di bordo; (*Chess*) scaccomatto, *m.* ¶ *v.t.* accoppiare, appaiare, unire; (*Chess*) dare scaccomatto a.

material, *a.* materiale. ¶ *n.* materia, sostanza, *f.*, materiale, *m.*; roba, stoffa, *f.*; (*pl.*) materiali, *m.pl,* oggetti, *m.pl.*, (*made up*) confezioni, *f.pl.* ~**ism,** *n.* materialismo, *m.*

~ist, *n.* materialista, *m.f.* ~istic, *a.* materialistico. ~ize, *v.t.* materializzare; (*v.i.*) materializzarsi, riuscire, far capo.

maternal, *a.* materno. **maternity**, *n.* maternità, *f.* ~ *hospital*, casa di maternità, *f.* ~ *doctor*, ostetrico, *m.*

mathematical, *a.* matematico; (*precise*) geometrico; (*instruments*) di matematica. **mathematician**, *n.* matematico, *m.*, -a, *f.* **mathematics**, *n.pl.* matematica, *f.*

matinée, *n.* mattinata, *f.* **matins**, *n.pl.* mattutino, *m.*

matriarchy, *n.* matriarcato, *m.*

matriculate, *v.i.* iscriversi, prendere l'iscrizione, immatricolarsi. **matriculation**, *n.* immatricolazione, iscrizione, *f.*

matrimonial, *a.* coniugale; (*Law*, *agent*, &c.) matrimoniale. ~ *triangle*, ménage à trois, (*Fr.*), *m.* **matrimony**, *n.* matrimonio, *m.*

matrix, *n.* matrice, *f.*

matron, *n.* matrona, *f.*; (*hospital*) infermiera (in capo), direttrice, *f.* ~ly, *a.* da matrona, d'età matura.

matter, *n.* materia, cosa; faccenda; questione, *f.*; caso; soggetto, argomento, contenuto, *m.*; (*Med.*) pus, *m.* *as a* ~ *of course*, come una cosa che va da sé, come cosa evidente. *as a* ~ *of fact*, per dir vero, difatti, infatti. ~-*of-fact*, positivo, prosaico. ~ *of history*, fatto storico, *m.* *be the* ~, trattarsi (di). *be the* ~ *with*, avere, esserci. ¶ *v.i.* importare, premere, avere importanza. *No* ~! non importa! non fa niente!

Matterhorn (the), il Monte Cervino, *m.*

mattery, *a.* purulento.

matting, *n.* stuoie, *f.pl.*, stuoiame, pagliericcio, *m.*; tessuto fatto di giunco, paglia, spartea, *m.*, fibra di cocco (coco[a]nut); (*pl.*) capannuccia, *f.*

mattins, *n.pl.* mattutino, *m.*, *or* azioni del mattino, *f.pl.*

mattock, *n.* zappone, piccone, *m.*, gravina, *f.*

mattress, *n.* materasso, *m.* ~ *maker*, materassaio, *m.*

mature, *a.* maturo. ¶ *v.i.* & *t.* maturare; (*Com.*) scadere. **maturity**, *n.* maturità, scadenza, *f.*

maudlin, *a.* piagnucoloso, lagrimoso, ipersensibile; (*in drink*) brillo, semiubbriaco.

maul, *v.t.* battere, percuotere,

malmenare. ~ *stick*, bacchetta (dei pittori), *f.*, appoggiamano, *m.*

Mauritius, *n.* Maurizio, *m.*

mausoleum, *n.* mausoleo, *m.*

mauve, *n.* & *a.* malva, *a.* & *f.*, color malva, *a.*

mawkish, *a.* insipido, sdolcinato, scipito.

maxim, *n.* massima, sentenza, *f.*

maximum, *n.* massimo, *m.* ¶ *a.* massimo.

May (*month*), *n.* maggio, *m.* *May Day*, il primo di maggio, *m.* *May fly*, effimera, *f.* *maypole*, albero (del primo) di maggio, *m.*

may (*Bot.*), *n.* fiore del biancospino, *m.* ~ (*bush*), biancospino, *m.*

may, *v.aux.ir.* potere; ~ *be*, ad. forse. *it* ~ *be*, può darsi, può essere, sarà.

Mayence, see **Mainz**, *n.* Magonza, *f.*

mayonnaise, *n.* & *att.* maionese, *f.*; salsa maionese, *f.*

mayor, *n.* sindaco, *m.* ~alty, *n.* sindacato, *m.*; ufficio, *m.*, carica di sindaco, *f.* ~ess, *f.* moglie del sindaco, *f.*

maze, *n.* dedalo, labirinto, *m.*; (*fig.*) imbroglio, impiccio, *m.*

mazurka, *n.* mazurca, *f.*

me, *pn.* mi, me.

meadow & (*Poet.*) **mead**, *n.* prato, *m.*, prateria, *f.* *meadow-sweet*, spirea, regina dei prati, *f.*

meagre, *a.* magro, povero, scarso, insufficiente; scialbo, scarno, sparuto; breve, succinto. ~ness, *n.* magrezza; povertà, scarsità, *f.*

meal, *n.* pasto, *m.*; (*flour*) farina, *f.* ~ *time*, ora dei pasti, ora del pasto, *f.* *at* ~ *times*, alle ore dei pasti. ~y, *a.* farinoso, cosparso di farina. ~-*mouthed*, che ha parola melata, mellifluo.

mean, *a.* meschino; gretto; avaro, tirato; basso; ignobile; umile, mediocre; (*average*) medio. *in the* ~*time* (or *while*) or ~*time*, ~*while*, *ad.* nell'intervallo, frattanto, nel frattempo, nell'attesa; in quel mentre. ¶ *n.* mezzo, punto intermedio, *m.*; (*Math.*) media, *f.* *golden* ~, giusto mezzo, *m.*; (*pl.*) mezzi, *m.pl.*; risorse, rendite, entrate, *f.pl.* *by no* ~s, niente affatto, in nessun modo, altro che. *by all* ~, con ogni mezzo, con tutti i mezzi; pure, ad ogni modo. *by any* ~, con qualsiasi mezzo. ¶ *v.t.* & *i.ir.* voler dire, intendere, significare; proporsi di, avere l'intenzione di;

fare a bella posta, fare a proposito; valere. ~ *for*, destinare a.

meander, *n.* meandro, *m.* ¶ *v.i.* serpeggiare; vagare.

meaning, *n.* significato, senso, *m.*, intenzione, *f.* **meaning,** *a.* intenzionato. ~ *look*, sguardo significativo, *m.* ~*less, a.* senza significato.

meanness, *n.* bassezza; avarizia; grettezza, *f.*

measles, *n.pl.* morbillo, *m.*; (*German*) rosolia, *f.*

measurable, *a.* misurabile. **measure,** *n.* misura, *f.*; provvedimento, *m.*; proporzione; capacità; moderazione, *f.*; metro, ritmo, *m.*; (*tape*) nastro, metrico, *m.* (*bill* progetto di legge, *m.*; (*pl. Geol.*) strati, *m.pl.*, letto, *m. to* ~ (clothes, &c.), su misura. ¶ *v.t. & i.* misurare; (*for fitting*) prendere la misura (o le misure) a qualcuno per . . ~ *out*, misurare, distribuire; dosare. ~*less, a.* smisurato. ~*ment, n.* misura; misurazione, *f.*

meat, *n.* carne, *f.* ~ *breakfast*, colazione alla forchetta, *f.* ~ *day* (*Eccl.*), giorno (di) grasso, *m.* ~ *diet*, carne, *f.*, alimento di carne, *m.* ~ *safe*, guardavivande, *m.inv.*; dispensa, *f.* ~*y, a.* carnoso; (*food*) di carne; grasso.

Mecca, *n.* Mecca, *f.*

mechanic, *n.* meccanico, macchinista; artigiano, *m.* ~*al, a.* meccanico; (*fig.*) macchinale. ~ *dentistry*, dentisteria meccanica, *f.* ~ *drawing*, disegno d'officina, disegno lineare, *m.* ~ *engineer*, ingegnere meccanico, *m.* ~ *engineering*, ingegneria meccanica, *f.* **mechanician & mechanist,** *n.* meccanico, *m.* **mechanics,** *n.pl.* meccanica, *f.* **mechanism,** *n.* meccanismo, congegno, *m.*; **mechanization,** *n.* meccanizzazione, *f.* ~ *farming*, agricoltura motorizzata, *f.* **mechanize,** *v.t.* meccanizzare.

Mechlin [**lace**], *n.* merletto di Malines, *m.*

medal, *n.* medaglia, *f.* ~ *cabinet* & *collection of* ~*s*, medagliere, *m.* ~ *maker* or *medallist*, medagliaio, incisore di medaglie, *m.* ~ *play* (*Golf*), partita alla medaglia, *f.* *award a* ~ *to*, conferire una medaglia a, premiare con (una) medaglia. **medalled,** *a.* decorato (premiato) con medaglia. **medallion,** *n.* medaglione, *m.* **medallist**

(*recipient*), *n.* premiato con medaglia, *m.*

meddle, *v.i.* immischiarsi (in), intromettersi (in), ingerirsi. ~ *with*, toccare. **meddler,** *n.* or **meddlesome person,** faccendiere, ficcanaso, intrigante, *m.* **meddling,** *n.* ingerenza, intromissione, *f.*, intervento officioso, *m.*

mediaeval, *a.* medioevale, del medioevo. ~*ist, n.* studioso (o scrittore) della storia medioevale, *m.*

mediate, *v.i.* intervenire, fare da mediatore, intercedere. **mediation,** *n.* mediazione, *f.* **mediator, -trix,** *n.* mediatore, *m.*, -trice, *f.*

medical, *a.* medico; (*school, &c.*) scuola (facoltà) di medicina, *f.*; (*student*) studente in medicina, *m.* ~ *examination* (*recruits*), visita medica, *f.* ~ *jurisprudence*, medicina legale, *f.* ~ *man*, ~ *officer*, medico, dottore in medicina, *m.* **medicament,** *n.* medicamento, *m.* **medicated,** *p.a.* medicato. **medicinal,** *a.* medicinale. **medicine,** *n.* medicina, *f.*, droga, *f.*, farmaco, *m.* ~ *cabinet*, armadietto farmaceutico, *m.* ~ *chest*, cassetta di medicazione, scatola di droghe, farmacia portatile, *f.* ~ *man*, stregone, *m.* **medicojudicial,** *a.* medico-legale.

medieval, *&c.* Same as *mediaeval, &c.*

mediocre, *a.* mediocre, di second'ordine. **mediocrity,** *n.* (*quality*) mediocrità, *f.*; (*pers.*) mediocre, *m.*

meditate ([**up**]**on**), *v.t. & i.* meditare (su), contemplare. **meditation,** *n.* meditazione, *f.* **meditative,** *a.* meditativo.

mediterranean, *a.* mediterraneo. M~, *a.* mediterraneo. **the M**~ [**Sea**], il [Mare] Mediterraneo, *m.*

medium, *a.* medio. ¶ *n.* mezzo, espediente, modo, veicolo; (*ether*) atmosfera, *f.*; (*agency*) intermediario; tramite; mezzano, *m.*; (*Spiritualism*) medium, *m.inv.*

medlar, *n.* nespola, *f.* ~ [*tree*], nespolo, *m.*

medley, *n.* miscela, *f.*, miscuglio, guazzabuglio, *m.*; (*colours*) varietà, *f.*; (*Mus., Lit.*), *f.*, centone, *m.* ¶ *a.* mischiato, confuso. ¶ *v.t.* mescolare, frammischiare.

medullary, *a.* midollare.

medusa (*jelly fish*) *n.* medusa, *f.*

meek, *a.* mite, dolce, sottomesso,

umile. ~ly, *ad.* in modo sottomesso, umilmente. ~ness, *n.* sottomissione, umiltà, *f.*

meerschaum, *n.* schiuma di mare, *f.*

meet, (*Hunt.*) *n.* riunione di cacciatori, assemblea, *f.* ¶ *v.t. ir.* incontrare; trovare; affrontare, affacciarsi a, fare fronte a, battersi con; sostenere, soddisfare; fare onore a; corrispondere a; adempiere; pagare; (*v.i. ir.*) incontrarsi, imbattersi, convenire, accozzarsi, scontrarsi, adunarsi, riunirsi, vedersi; convergersi (verso); (*extremes*) toccarsi. ~ *with,* incontrare; ricevere; provare; trovare; subire. ~ing, *n.* incontro, *m.*; assemblea, adunanza, *f.*; comizio, *m.*; riunione, seduta, *f.*; convegno, *m.*, convocazione, *f.*; (*rivers*) confluenza, *f.*; (*roads*) congiunzione, *f.*; (*of engagements, bills of exchange*) adempimento, pagamento, soddisfacimento, *m.* ~ *house,* cappella, casa di riunione dei Quacqueri, *f.*

megaphone, *n.* megafono, portavoce, *m.*

melancholia & **melancholy,** *n.* malinconia, *f.* **melancholic** & **melancholy,** *a.* malinconico; tetro; abbattuto.

Melanesia, *n.* la Melanesia, *f.*

mellow, *a.* maturo; stagionato; tenero; melodioso; (*earth*) soffice. ¶ *v.t.* far maturare; stagionare; ammollire, addolcire, render soffice.

melodious, *a.* melodioso. **melody,** *n.* melodia, *f.*, canto, *m.*

melon, *n.* melone, popone; (*water*) cocomero, *m.*

melt, (*Foundry*) *n.* fusione, *f.* ¶ *v.t.* fondere; sciogliere, struggere; liquefare; intenerire; (*v.i.*) fondersi, sciogliersi, &c. *that* ~*s in the mouth* (*as a pear*), succoso, fondente. ~er, *n.* fonditore, *m.* ~ing, *n.* fusione; liquefazione, *f.* ~ *point,* punto di fusione, *m.* ~ *pot,* crogiuolo, *m.*

member, *n.* membro, socio, associato; rappresentante, *m.* ~ *of a* (or *the*) *congress,* congressista, *m.f.* ~ *of a mutual society* or *association,* mutualista, *m.f.* ~ *of parliament,* membro, deputato, *m.* ~ship, *n.* qualità (funzione) di membro; iscrizione, *f.*; (*parliament*) deputazione, *f.*; l'insieme dei membri, dei deputati, *m.*

membrane, *n.* membrana, *f.*

memento, *n.* ricordo, memento, memoriale, *m.*

memoir, *n.* memoria, *f.*, ricordo, *m.*, notizia, *f.*; (*pl. book*) ricordi, *m.pl.*; memorie, ricordanze, *f.pl.*

memorable, *a.* memorabile. **memorandum,** *n.* nota, *f.*, promemoria, *m.*, appunto, *m.*, memorandum, *m. as a* ~, per memoria. ~ *book,* taccuino, libretto per gli appunti, memorandum, *m.* ~ (*of association*), atto costitutivo d'una società anonima, *m.* **memorial,** *n.* memoriale, ricordo; monumento commemorativo, *m.*; petizione, *f.*

memorize, *v.t.* apprendere a memoria, mandare a mente, imparare a memoria, a mente.

memory, *n.* memoria, ricordanza, *f.*; (*pl.*) memorie, ricordanze, *f.pl. from* ~, a memoria.

menace, *n.* minaccia, *f. public* ~ (*pers.*), malfattore libero, *m.* pubblico. ¶ *v.t.* minacciare.

menagerie, *n.* serraglio (parco per bestiami), *m.*

mend, *v.t.* raccomodare, racconciare, rammendare, riparare; correggere, migliorare, riformare.

mendacious, *a.* mendace. **mendacity** *n.* mendacia, falsità, *f.*

mender, *n.* racconciatore, *m.*, -trice, *f.*; raccomodatore, *m.*, -trice, *f.*; riparatore, *m.*, -trice, *f.*

mendicancy & **mendicity,** *n.* accattonaggio, *m.*, mendicità, *f.* **mendicant,** *a.* & *n.* mendicante, *m.f.* pitocco, *m.*, accattone, *m.*, pezzente, *m.f.*

mending, *n.* racconciatura, riparazione, *f.*

menhir, *n.* menir, *m.*

menial, *a.* servile. ¶ *n.* domestico, servo; valletto, lacchè, *m.*

meningitis, *n.* meningite, *f.*

mensuration, *n.* misurazione, *f.*, misuramento, *m.*; (*science*) misure, *f.pl.*; (*of the body*) misura, *f.*

mental, *a.* mentale; intellettuale. ~ *arithmetic,* calcolo mentale, *m.* ~ *institution,* manicomio, asilo di alienati, *m.*, casa di alienati, *f.* ~ *patient,* alienato, *m.*, -a, *f.* ~ *reservation,* riserva mentale, *f.*, restrizione mentale, *f.*; secondo fine, *m.* ~ *specialist,* alienista, psichiatra, *m.* ~ity, *n.* mentalità, *f.* ~ly, *ad.* mentalmente, intellettualmente. ~ *deficient,* di scarsa mentalità.

menthol, *n.* mentolo, *m.*

mention, *n.* menzione, allusione, *f.*; cenno, riferimento, *m.* ¶ *v.t.* fare menzione di ,accennare a, alludere a, riferirsi a; mentovare, nominare. *don't* ~ *it!* non parlatene! prego! grazie! niente affatto!

Mentone, *n.* Mentone, *f.*

menu, *n.* carta delle vivande, lista delle vivande, lista dei piatti, *f.*

mercantile, *a.* mercantile, commerciale; (*mercenary*), mercantile, interessato. ~ *marine,* marina mercantile, *f.* ~ *office,* ~ *agency,* agenzia commerciale, *f.*, ufficio d'informazioni commerciali, *m.*

Mercator's projection, carta Mercatore, *f.*

mercenary, *a.* mercenario, venale. ¶ *n.* mercenario, *m.*

mercer, *n.* merciaio, mercante di seterie, nastri, &c., *m.* ~*ized,* *a.* mercerizzato.

merchandise, *n.* mercanzia, merce, *f.*

merchant, *n.* commerciante, mercante, negoziante, *m.* *the* ~ *class,* il ceto commerciale, *m.*, la classe commerciale, *f.* ~*man,* nave mercantile, *f.* ~ *service,* ~ *shipping,* marina mercantile, *f.*

merciful, *a.* pietoso, clemente.

merciless, *a.* spietato, senza pietà.

mercurial, *a.* (*Chem.*) mercuriale; (*barometer,* &c.) a mercurio; (*fig.*) vivace, vivo. **mercury,** *n.* (*metal*) mercurio, *m.*; (*Bot.*) mercuriale, *f.*

mercy, *n.* misericordia, pietà, clemenza; mercè, grazia, compassione, *f.* *at the* ~ *of,* alla mercè di. ~ *on us!* per pietà! ~ *seat,* propiziatorio, *m.*, trono di Dio, *m.* *sister of* ~, suora di carità, *f.*

mere, *a.* semplice; puro, mero; pretto; solo. *a* ~ *nothing,* niente, nulla, un nonnulla. ¶ *n.* laghetto, *m.*

meretricious, *a.* fittizio, falso; attraente.

merge, *v.t.* immergere, fondere, fare assorbire. **merger** (*Law*), *n.* confusione, *f.*; (*Com.*) fusione, *f.*, incorporamento, *m.*

meridian, *n.* & *a.* meridiano, *m.* & *a.* **meridional,** *a.* & *n.* meridionale, *a.* & *m.f.*

meringue, *n.* meringa, *f.*

merino, *n.* merino, *m.*

merit, *n.* merito, valore, pregio, *m.*, benemerenza, *f.* ¶ *v.t.* meritare. **meritorious,** *a.* meritorio; (*of pers.*) meritevole, benemerente.

merlin (*bird*), *n.* smeriglio, *m.*

mermaid, *n.* sirena, *f.* **merman,** *n.* tritone, *m.*

merrily, *ad.* allegramente, gaiamente.

merriment, *n.* allegrezza, allegria,

f. **merry,** *a.* allegro, gaio, giocondo. *a* ~ *Christmas!* buon Natale! felice Natale! *make* ~, fare festa, fare baldoria, stare allegri, divertirsi. *make* ~ *over,* ridersi di, ridere a spese di, farsi giuoco di. ~ *andrew,* buffone, pagliaccio, *m.* ~*-go-round,* carosello, *m.*, giostra (con cavalli di legno), *f.* ~ *making,* festa, *f.*, festeggiamento, *m.* ~ *thought,* forcella, *f.*, sterno di pollo, *m.*

merry (*wild cherry*), *n.* visciola, ciliegia selvatica, *f.*

mesh, *n.* maglia, *f.*; in ~ (*Mech.*), in ingranaggio. ¶ *v.t.* ingranare; (*fig.*) arretire.

mesmeric, *a.* mesmerico, magnetico. **mesmerism,** *n.* mesmerismo, *m.* **mesmerist,** *n.* mesmerista, *m.f.* **mesmerize,** *v.t.* ipnotizzare.

mess, *n.* porzione, *f.*, piatto, *m.*; (*Mil.*, *Nav.*) tavola, mensa, *f.*; piatto, rancio, *m.*; (*fig.*) disordine, *m.*, confusione, *f.*, guazzabuglio, imbroglio, pasticcio, impaccio, *m.*; imbrattatura, sporcizia, *f.* ~ *mate,* commensale, *m.* ~*room,* sala da pranzo, *f.* ~ *tin,* gavetta, gamella, *f.* ¶ *v.t.* guastare, sporcare; (*v.i.*) mangiare insieme, far camerata, prendere i pasti in comune. ~ *about,* rimescolare, manipolare, mestare. ~ *up,* guastare, rovinare, fare la zuppa in . . . , fare un pasticcio di.

message, *n.* messaggio, *m.*, comunicazione, commissione, *f.*, notizie, *f.pl.*, avviso, *m.* **messenger,** *n.* messaggero, *m.*, -a, *f.*; messo, fattorino, *m.*

Messiah, *n.* Messia, *m.*

Messina, *n.* Messina, *f.*

messuage, *n.* casa con annessi e connessi, *f.*

messy, *a.* imbrogliato, sudicio, imbrattato.

metal, *n.* metallo, *m.*; (*for roads*) brecciame, pietrisco, *m.*, (*pl. Rly.*) rotaie, *f.pl.* ~ *saw,* ~ *screw,* sega, vite per metalli, *f.* ~ *worker,* operaio metallurgico, *m.*, ¶ (*road*) *v.t.* ricoprire con brecciame. **metallic,** *a.* metallico, (*voice*) metallico. **metalliferous,** *a.* metallifero. **metallurgist,** *n.* metallurgo, *m.* **metallurgy,** *n.* metallurgia, *f.*

metamorphose, *v.t.* cambiare forma, trasmutare. **metamorphosis,** *n.* metamorfosi, *f.*

metaphor, *n.* metafora, *f.* ~*ical,* *a.* metaforico.

metaphysical, *a.* metafisico. **metaphysician,** *n.* metafisico, *m.* **metaphysics,** *n.pl.* metafisica, *f.*
mete [out], *v.t.* misurare, dosare.
meteor, *n.* meteora, *f.* ~ic, *a.* meteorico. ~ite, *n.* meteorite, *f.* ~ologic(al), *a.* meteorologico. ~ology, *n.* meteorologia, *f.*
meter, *n.* contatore, misuratore, *m.*
method, *n.* metodo, modo; ordine, *m.*, maniera, *f.* ~ical, *a.* metodico. ~ism, *n.* metodismo. ~ist, *n.* metodista, *m.f.*
methyl (*Chem.*), metile, *m.* ~ated spirit, alcool (spirito) da bruciare (spirito di vino misto al 10% con metile), *m.*, alcool denaturato, *m.*
meticulous, *a.* meticoloso.
metonymy, *n.* metonimia, *f.*
metre (*Poet.*), *n.* metro, verso, *m.* ~-gauge railway, ferrovia a scartamento di 1 metro, *f.* **metric** & **metrical,** *a.* metrico. **metrics** (*Poet.*), *n.* metrica, *f.*
metronome, *n.* metronomo, *m.*
metropolis, *n.* metropoli, *f.* **metropolitan,** *a.* metropolitano.
mettle, *n.* ardore, *m.*, foga, *f.*, spirito, coraggio, fuoco, *m.* ~some, *a.* focoso, ardente, pieno di coraggio.
mew, *n.* (*sea gull*) gabbiano, *m.*; (*cage for hawks*) gabbia, *f.* ¶ *v.i.* miagolare. ~[ing], *n.* miagolio, *m.* **mews,** *n.* stallaggio, *m.*, scuderie, *f.pl.*
Mexican, *a.* messicano. ¶ *n.* messicano, *m.* **Mexico** (*country*), *n.* il Messico, *m.* ~ [City], Messico, *f.*
mezzanine [floor], *n.* mezzanino, *m.* **mezzo-relievo,** *n.* mezzo-rilievo, *m.* **mezzo-soprano,** *n.* mezzosoprano, *m.* **mezzotint,** *n.* mezzatinta, *f.*
miaow, *n.* miao, *m.*
miasma, *n.* miasma, *m.*
mica, *n.* mica, *f.*
Michaelmas, *n.* il San Michele, giorno, *m.* (festa, *f.*) di San Michele. ~ daisy, astero selvatico, *m.*, verga d'argento, *f.*
microbe, *n.* microb[i]o, *m.*
micrometer, *n.* micrometro, *m.*
microphone, *n.* microfono, *m.*
microscope, *n.* microscopio, *m.* **microscopic**[al], *a.* microscopico.
mid, *a.*: in ~ air, nel mezzo dell'aria; in pieno cielo. in mid Channel (Straits of Dover), nel mezzo della Manica. in ~ channel, a mezzo canale. ~day, mezzogiorno, *m.* ~ Lent, mezza quaresima, metà quaresima, *f.* ~night, mezzanotte, *f.* ~shipman, aspirante (di marina), *m.* ~summer, mezza estate, *f.*, mezzo dell'estate, *m.* Midsummer day, festa di San Giovanni, *f.* ~ way, *ad.* a mezza strada, nel mezzo della via. ~wife, levatrice, *f.* ~wifery, ostetricia, *f.* in ~ winter, nel cuore dell'inverno, in pieno inverno, nel forte dell'inverno, nel mezzo inverno.
middle, *a.* mezzo, di mezzo; centrale; mediano, mezzano; medio. ~-aged, di mezza età. ~ ages, Medio Evo, *m.* ~ class[es], classe media, borghesia, gente mezzana, *f.*; medio ceto, *m.* ~-class house, casa borghese, *f.* ~ class man, woman, borghese, *m.f.* ~ course (conduct), via di mezzo, *f.* ~ distance, secondo piano, *m.* ~-distance race, corsa di mezzo fondo, *f.* the M~ East, il Medio Oriente, *m.* ~ finger, dito medio, *m.* ~ man, intermediario, *m.* ~ register (Mus.), registro di mezzo, *m.* ~ [term] (Log.), mezzo termine, *m.* ~weight (Box.), peso medio, *m.* ¶ *n.* mezzo, centro, *m.*, parte mediana, *f.*; (waist) vita, cintura, *f.* in the very ~, nel bel mezzo.
middling, *a.* medio, mediocre, passabile. ¶ *ad.* così così, discretamente, mediocremente. ~s (flour), *n.pl.* cascami, *m.pl.*
midge, *n.* moscerino, moschino, *m.*
midget, *n.* nanerottolo, pigmeo, *m.*
midnight, midshipman, &c. See under mid.
midst, *n.* mezzo, centro, *m.*; (fig.) cuore, forte, *m.* in our ~, in mezzo a noi, fra noi.
mien, *n.* aria, cera, figura, *f.*, aspetto, viso, portamento, *m.*
might, *n.* forza, potenza, possanza, *f.*, potere, vigore, *m.* with ~ & main, a corpo morto, a corpo perduto, con tutte le (sue) forze. one ~ as well, tanto sarebbe, tanto vale. a ~-have-been, un grand'uomo mancato. **mightiness,** *n.* potenza, grandezza; (title) altezza, *f.* **mighty,** *a.* forte, grande, possente, potente; numeroso; vasto. the ~ ones, i potenti, i grandi, *m.pl.*
mignonette, *n.* (Bot.) reseda odorosa, *f.*, amorino, *m.*
migrant, *a.* migratore. **migrate,** *v.i.* migrare, emigrare, passare. **migration,** *n.* migrazione, *f.* **migratory,** *a.* migratore, di passo.

Milan, *n.* Milano, *f.* ~**ese,** *a.* milanese. ¶ *n.* milanese, *m.f.*

milch cow, mucca, vacca da latte, *f.*

mild, *a.* mite; dolce; leggero; benigno.

mildew, *n.* muffa, macchia di umidità, *f.*; (*blight on plants*) ruggine, *f.*; (*on wines*) peronospora, *f.* ¶ *v.t.* colpire di ruggine, ammuffire; (*v.i.*) ammuffire.

mildness, *n.* mitezza, dolcezza, *f.*

mile, *n.* miglio, *m.* (Eng. mile = 1.6093 kilometres). (*Note.—To convert miles to kilometres, approximately, multiply miles by 8 and divide by 5.*) (*long way*) lega, *f.* a ~ off, lontano un miglio, a una lega, a un miglio (di distanza). ~ *stone,* pietra miliare, *f.*

milfoil, *n.* millefoglie, *f.inv.*

militant, *a. & n.* militante, *a. & m.f.* **militarize,** *v.t.* militarizzare. **military,** *a. & ~ man,* militare, *a. & m.* the ~, i militari, *m.pl.* ~ *pageant,* parata militare, *f.* **militate** (*against*), *v.i.* opporsi, militare contro. **militia,** *n.* milizia, *f.* ~ *man,* milite, *m.* ~ *men,* guardia nazionale, *f.*

milk, *n.* latte, *m.* ~ *& water,* latte misto (tagliato) con acqua; (*fig.*) insipido, indeciso. ~ *chocolate,* cioccolata al latte. ~ *diet,* regime a latte, dieta lattea. ~ *fever,* febbre di latte, *f.* ~ *food,* latticini, *m.pl.* ~ *jug,* lattiera, *f.*, vaso da latte, *m.* ~*maid,* lattaia, *f.* ~*man,* ~*woman,* lattivendolo, *m.*, lattivendola, *f.* ~*sop* (*pers.*), pulcino bagnato, *m.* ~ *tooth,* dente di latte, *m.* ~ *van* (*Rly.*), vagone per il trasporto del latte. *to give* ~, allattare. ¶ *v.t.* mungere. ~**er,** *n.* mungitore, *m.*, -trice, -tora, *f.*; (*cow*) vacca lattifera, *f.* ~**ing,** *n.* mungitura, *f.* **milky,** *a.* latteo. M~ Way, Via Lattea, *f.*

mill, *a.* mulino, *m.*; fabbrica, officina; filanda, *f.*; opificio, stabilimento, *m.* ~ *board,* cartone forte, *m.* ~ *hand.* operaio (di stabilimento, &c.), -a, *m.f.* ~ *owner,* proprietario, *m.* (di fabbrica &c.). ~*stone,* macina di mulino, mola, *f.* ~*stone grit &* ~*stone grit quarry,* selce molare, *f.,* alberese, *m.,* cava d'alberese, *f.* ¶ *v.t.* macinare; (*ore, &c.*) martellare; (*cloth*) feltrare, follare, gualcare; (*to knurl*) zigrinare; (*to slot*) fresare; (*a coin*) granire. ~*ed edge,* granitura, *f. milling machine,* fresatrice, *f.*

millenary, *a.* millenario. **millenium,**

n. millennio; (*fig.*) paradiso terrestre, *m.*

millepede, *n.* millepiedi, *m.inv.*

miller, *n.* mugnaio, *m.*

millet, *n.* miglio, *m.* ~ *grass,* miglio, *m.*

milliard, (1.000,000,000) *n.* miliardo, *m.*

milliner, *n.* modista, crestaia, *f.* ~*'s head.* modello, *m.* ~**y,** *n.* mercerie, mode, *f.pl.* articoli di moda *m.pl.*

milling *n.* (*flour*) macinatura, *f.*; (*ore*) martellatura, *f.*; (*cloth*) feltratura, *f.*; (*metal*) fresatura, *f.*; (*coins*) granitura, *f.* ~ *cutter,* fresa, fresatrice, *f.* ~ *machine,* fresatrice. *f.*

million, *n.* milione, *m.* the ~, la moltitudine, *f.,* le masse, *f.pl.* **millionaire,** *n.* milionario, *m.* **millionth,** *a. & n.* milionesimo, *a. & m.*

milt, *n.* (*in mammals*) milza, *f.*; (*in fish*) latte di pesce, *m.* ¶ *v.t.* fecondare.

mime, *n.* mimo, *m.*; (*pers.*) mimo, *m.*, -a, *f.* ¶ *v.i.* imitare, esprimersi coi gesti. **mimic,** *a.* mimico, imitativo; (*pers.*) imitatore, *m.*, -trice, *f.* ~ *war,* guerra finta, *f.* ¶ *n.* mimo, imitatore, *m.*, -trice, *f.* ¶ *v.t.* imitare, contraffare. **mimicry,** *n.* mimica, *f.* **mimicry or mimesis** (*Zool.*), *n.* mimetismo, *m.* mimesi, *f.*

mimosa, *n.* mimosa, *f.*

mince, *n.* carne tritata, *f.*; battuto, ammorsellato, *m.* ~*meat,* carne tritata, *f.* ¶ *v.t.* (*meat*) tritare, sminuzzare; (*v.i.*) civettare, fare il vezzo, vezzeggiare. *not to ~ one's words,* non misurare le parole. *not to ~ matters,* parlare chiaro e senza riguardi. **mincer,** *n.* tagliere, *m.* **mincing,** (*fig.*) *n.* affettazione, smanceria, *f.* ¶ *a.* affettato, lezioso, smancioso.

mind, *n.* mente, intelligenza, ragione, *f.*; spirito, cervello, animo, *m.*; decisione, intenzione, voglia, opinione, *f.*; avviso, *m.*; memoria, *f.* *go out of one's* ~, perdere la ragione, impazzire. ¶ *v.t.* fare attenzione a, occuparsi di, curare, non dimenticare, badare a, tenere conto di, sorvegliare. ~ *your own business!* badate ai fatti vostri! ~! attenzione! bada! bada! ~**ed,** *a.* disposto, incline, intenzionato. ~**er,** *n.* sorvegliante, *m.f.*, guardiano, *m.* ~**ful,** *a.* attento, pieno di riguardi, premuroso. ~ *of,* memore di. *to be* ~ *of,* ricordarsi di, pensare sempre a.

mine, *pn.* mio, il mio, mia, la mia, miei, i miei, mie, le mie. *a friend of* ~, un mio amico.

mine, *n.* miniera, *f.*; (*fig.*) sorgente, *f.* (*War*) mina, *f.* ~ *crater,* cavità, *f.* ~*layer,* [nave] posamine, *m.* ~*sweeper,* spazzamine. ¶ *v.t. & i.* scavare, minare. **miner,** *n.* minatore, *m.* **mineral,** *a. & n.* minerale, *a. & m.* ~ *vater,* acqua minerale, *f.* **mineralogical,** *a.* mineralogico. **mineralogist,** *n.* mineralogista, *m.* **mineralogy,** *n.* mineralogia, *f.*

minever, -iver, *n.* vaio, *m.*, pelliccia di vaio, *f.*

mingle, *v.t.* mescolare, mischiare; (*v.i.*) mescolarsi. ~ *with,* mescolarsi a.

miniature, *n.* miniatura, *f.* **miniaturist,** *n.* miniaturista, *m.f.*

minim, *n.* (*Mus.*) minima, *f.*; (*apothecaries' measure*) = 0.059 millilitro; (*fig.*) goccia, *f.* **minimum,** *n. & a.* minimo, *a. & m.*

minimize, *v.t.* ridurre al minimo; menomare, mettere a non cale.

mining, *n.* scavi di miniere, *m.pl.*; sfruttamento di miniera, *m.*; (*att.*) minerario, di miniera. ~ *engineer,* ingegnere minerario; *m.*

minion, *n.* mignone, favorito, *m.* ~*s of the law,* assistenti giudiziari, *m.pl.*

minister, *n.* ministro, *m.*; ambasciatore, *m.*; pastore, *m.* *tb* ~, ~ *to,* provvedere (a), venire in soccorso (di), servire; (*Eccl.*) ufficiare, compiere i doveri di, celebrare. ~**ial,** *a.* ministeriale; sacerdotale, ecclesiastico. ~*ing angel,* angelo di bontà, spirito consolatore, *m.* **ministration,** *n.* servizio, *m.* **ministry,** *n.* ministero, *m.*; dipartimento, sacerdozio, *m.* M~ *of Defence, of Labour, &c.,* Ministero della Difesa, del Lavoro, &c.

mink, *n.* (*Zool. & fur*) visone, *m.*, pelliccia di visone, *f.*

minnow, *n.* pesciolino d'acqua dolce, argentino, *m.*, varione, *m.*

minor, *a.* minore; piú piccolo; secondario; subalterno; poco importante, lieve; accessorio; (*repairs*) minuto, piccolo; (*planet*) telescopico; (*pers.*) minore, giovane, cadetto; (*Poet*) di second'ordine. ¶ *n.* (*pers.*) minore, minorenne, *m.f.*; (*Mus.*) minore, *m.*

Minorca, *n.* Minorca, *f.*

minority, *n.* minoranza; età minore, *f.*

minster, *n.* cattedrale, chiesa abbaziale, *f.*

minstrel, *n.* (*Hist.*) menestrello; cantore, musico.

mint, *n.* zecca, *f.*; (*fig.*) tesoro, *m.*, miniera, *f.*; (*Bot.*) menta, *f. a* ~ *of money,* tesoro, *m.* ¶ *v.t.* coniare, battere, monetare. ~**er,** *n.* coniatore, *m.*

minuet, *n.* minuetto, *m.*

minus, *pr.* meno, senza. ~ *quantity,* quantità negativa, *f.*; (*fig.*) meno di nulla, *m.* ~ [*sign*] segno di sottrazione, *m.*

minute, *a.* minuto, piccolissimo, minuscolo, minimo. ¶ *n.* minuto, momento, istante, *m.*, nota, *f.*, minuta, *f.*, processo verbale, *m.*; (*pl.*) verbale, *m.*, verbali, *m.pl.* ~ *book,* registro dei [processi] verbali, *m.* ~ *gun,* cannone che spara ad intervalli di un minuto, *m.* ~ *hand,* lancetta dei minuti, *f.* ¶ *v.t.* stendere verbale di; prendere nota di. ~**ly,** *ad.* minutamente, minuziosamente. ~**ness** & **minutia,** *n.* piccolezza, minuzia, *f.*

minx, *n.* birichina, bricconcella, birbona, *f.*

miracle, *n.* miracolo, prodigio, *m.*, meraviglia, *f.* ~ (*play*), mistero, *m.* **miraculous,** *a.* miracoloso.

mirage, *n.* miraggio, *m.*

mire, *n.* melma, mota, *f.*, fango, *m.* ¶ *v.t.* infangare, sporcare di mota.

mirror, *n.* specchio, *m.*; psiche, *f.* ¶ *v.t.* rispecchiare, riflettere.

mirth, *n.* allegria, gaiezza, ilarità, *f.* ~**ful,** *a.* allegro, gaio, ilare.

miry, *a.* fangoso, melmoso, motoso.

misadventure, *n.* contrattempo, *m.*, disgrazia, *f.*

misalliance, *n.* matrimonio sconveniente, *m.*, unione fra persone di classi diverse, *f.* *make a* ~, contrarre un matrimonio sconveniente. **misally,** *v.t.* far fare un matrimonio sconveniente.

misanthrope, -pist, *n.* misantropo, *m.* **misanthropic(al),** *a.* misantropico.

misapply, *v.t.* applicar male; intendere male, sbagliare; appropriarsi fraudolentemente. **misapprehension,** *n.* malinteso, equivoco, *m.*

misappropriate, *v.t.* appropriarsi fraudolentemente; dilapidare.

misbehave [oneself], comportarsi

male, condursi male. **mis-behaviour**, *n.* cattiva condotta, *f.*

miscalculate, *v.i.* sbagliarsi, ingannarsi. **miscalculation**, *n.* calcolo erroneo, errore di calcolo, *m.*

miscarriage, *n.* (*letter*, *&c.*) disguido, *f.*, smarrimento, *m.*; (*Med.*) aborto, *m.*; (*failure*) fiasco, insuccesso, colpo mancato, *m.* ~ *of justice*, errore giudiziario, *m.* **miscarry**, *v.i.* smarrirsi, perdersi; (*Med.*) abortire; (*fail*) fallire, non riuscire.

miscellaneous, *a.* miscellaneo, misto, vario. ~ *works* or **miscellany**, raccolta di scritti vari, miscellanea, *f.* **miscellanea**, *n.* miscellanea, *f.*

mischance, *n.* infortunio, *m.*, disgrazia, sventura, *f.*

mischief, *n.* male, danno, torto, *m.*, discordia, malizia, *f.*; (*playful*) birichinata, *f.* ~ *maker*, attaccabrighe, mettimale, *m.f.inv.* **mischievous**, *a.* cattivo, nocivo, funesto; furbo.

misconceive, *v.t. & i.* concepire male, intendere male, giudicare male. **misconception**, *n.* idea sbagliata, concezione erronea, *f.*, malinteso, *m.*

misconduct, *n.* cattiva condotta, *f.* ~ *oneself*, condursi male.

misconstruction, *n.* falsa interpretazione, *f.* **misconstrue**, *v.t.* interpretare male; tradurre a torto.

miscreant, *n.* scellerato, miserabile, malfattore, *m.*

miscue, *n.* colpo sbagliato (al biliardo), *m.*

misdeal (*Cards*), *n.* distribuzione erronea, *f.*

misdeed, *n.* misfatto, *m.*

misdeliver, *v.t.* distribuire in errore, d. a un indirizzo sbagliato.

misdemeanant, *n.* delinquente, *m.f.* **misdemeanour**, *n.* fallo, *m.*, (*Law*) reato, *m.*

misdirect, *v.t.* dirigere male, informare male; (*a letter*) sbagliare l'indirizzo di.

miser, *n.* avaro, *m.*, -a, *f.*

miserable, *a.* miserabile, disgraziato, infelice; meschino.

misère (*Cards*), *n.* miseria, *f.*

miserere, *n.* miserere, *m.*

misericord, *n.* misericordia, *f.*

miserly, *a.* avaro, sordido, gretto.

misery, *n.* miseria, infelicità, *f.*, sofferenze, *f.pl.*, supplizio, *m.*

misfire, *n.* scatto a vuoto, *m.*; (*fig.*) cilecca, *f.* ¶ *v.i.* scattare a vuoto; (*fig.*) fare cilecca.

misfit, *n.* abito che non va bene, scarpa che non calza bene, &c.; (*fig.*) pesce fuor d'acqua.

misfortune, *n.* disgrazia, sfortuna, calamità, *f.*

misgiving, *n.* dubbio, sospetto, timore, *m.*

misgovern, *v.t.* governare male, amministrare male. ~**ment**, *n.* malgoverno, *m.*

misguide, *v.t.* sviare, traviare, dirigere male. **misguided**, *a.* traviato, ingannato; cieco.

mishap, *n.* disgrazia, *f.*, contrattempo, *m.*

misinform, *v.t.* informare male, dare delle informazioni errate.

misinterpret, *v.t.* interpretare male, ingannarsi sul vero senso di. **misinterpretation**, *n.* falsa interpretazione, *f.*

misjudge, *v.t.* giudicare male, sbagliarsi sul conto di.

mislay, *v.t.* smarrire.

mislead, *v.t.* sviare, traviare; (*fig.*) ingannare, indurre in errore. ~**ing**, *p.a.* ingannevole, fallace.

mismanage, *v.t.* dirigere male, condurre male, amministrare male, fare male. ~**ment**, *n.* cattiva amministrazione, *f.*

misnamed, *p.p.* chiamato a torto, denominato erroneamente.

misnomer, *n.* termine improprio, titolo sbagliato, errore di nome, *m.*

misogynist, *n.* misogino, *m.*

misplace, *v.t.* collocare male, spostare.

misprint, *n.* errore di stampa, errore tipografico, *m.*

mispronounce, *v.t.* pronunziar male. **mispronunciation**, *n.* pronuncia scorretta, cattiva pronuncia, *f.*

misquotation, *n.* citazione inesatta, citazione erronea, *f.* **misquote**, *v.t.* citare inesattamente, scorrettamente.

misrepresent, *v.t.* travisare, esporre sotto una falsa luce, storcere, snaturare. ~**ation**, *n.* esposizione inesatta, *f.*, falso rapporto, *m.*

misrule, *n.* malgoverno, *m.*

miss, *n.* colpo mancato, *m.*; signorina, *f.* M~, Signorina, *f.* ¶ *v.t. & i.* non colpire, non dare nel segno; fallire, mancare; non ottenere, non raggiungere; smarrire, lasciar sfuggire, perdere; aver bisogno di, sentire la mancanza di; rimpiangere. ~ *fire*, fallire il colpo, scattare a vuoto; (*fig.*) fare cilecca. ~ *the point*, tralasciare l'essenziale.

missal, *n.* messale, *m.*
missel thrush, tordella, *f.*
misshapen, *a.* deforme, mal fatto.
missile, *n.* proiettile, *m.*
missing, *a.* mancante, smarrito, scomparso, assente; (*ship*) [perduto] senza notizie.   ~ *link*, anello mancante, *m.*   *the* ~ (*Mil.*), gli scomparsi, *m.pl.*   *be* ~, mancare, scomparire, essere assente.
mission, *n.* missione, ambasciata, *f.* ~**ary,** missionario, *m.*, -a, *f.*
missive, *n.* missiva, *f.*
misspell, *v.t. & abs.* compitare male, fare errori di ortografia. ~**ing,** *n.* ortografia scorretta o sbagliata, *f.*, errore di ortografia, *m.*
misstatement,   *n.*   dichiarazione inesatta, falsa rappresentazione, *f.*
mist, *n.* nebbia, bruma, pioggerella, *f.*, vapore, *m.*
mistake, *n.* sbaglio, errore, equivoco, malinteso, *m.* ¶ *v.t. ir.* intendere male, capire male, sbagliare, smarrire, prendere in un senso erroneo, ingannarsi su, confondere.
mistaken, *a.* erroneo, sbagliato, mal inteso, mal compreso.   ~ *identity*, identità sbagliata, *f.*   ~ *kindness*, eccesso di bontà, *m.*   *be* ~, sbagliare, sbagliarsi, essere in errore.
mister, *n.* signore, *m.*
mistletoe, *n.* vischio, *m.*
mistranslation, *n.* versione errata, *f.*, controsenso, *m.*
mistress,   *n.*   signora;   padrona; istitutrice, maestra; direttrice; amante, *f.*   *be one's own* ~, essere libera, essere indipendente.
mistrust, *n.* sospetto, *m.*, sfiducia, diffidenza, *f.* ¶ *v.t.* sospettare, diffidare di, dubitare. ~**ful,** *a.* diffidente, sospettoso.
misty, *a.* nebbioso, brumoso, oscuro.
misunderstand, *v.t. ir.* fraintendere, comprendere male, ingannarsi su, prendere in senso erroneo. ~**ing,** *n.* malinteso, equivoco; disaccordo, *m.*   **misunderstood,** (*pers.*) *p.a.* incompreso.
misuse, *n.* abuso, *m.*, falsa applicazione, *f.*, maltrattamento, *m.* ¶ *v.t.* maltrattare; guastare; usare male, abusare di.
mite, *n.* (*farthing*) centesimo, *m.*, somma piccolissima, *f.*; (*child*) piccino, *m.*; (*insect*) acaro; baco, bacolino, *m.*
mitigate, *v.t.* mitigare, moderare, attenuare.

mitre, *n.* (*bishop's*) mitra, *f.*; (*Carp.*) ugnatura, *f.*   ~**d,** *a.* mitrato; (*Carp.*) ugnato, tagliato con un angolo di 45 gradi.
mitt[en], *n.* mezzo guanto, *m.*
mix, *v.t.* mescolare, mischiare, confondere; (*salad*) rimescolare. **mixed,** *a.* mescolato, mischiato, misto.   ~ *bathing*, bagni misti, *m.pl.*   ~ *double* (*Ten.*), doppio misto.   ~ *ice*, gelato misto, *m.*   ~ *metaphor*, metafora incoerente, *f.*   ~ *school*, scuola mista, *f.*   **mixture,** *n.* mescolanza, *f.*, miscuglio, *m.*; (*blend*) miscela, *f.*; (*Med.*) mistura, *f.*; (*fodder*) farragine, *f.*; (*cloth*) tessuto misto di lana e cotone.
miz[z]en [sail], *n. &* **miz[z]en mast,** mezzana, *f.*, vela di mezzana, *f.*, albero di mezzana, *m.*
mizzle, *n.* pioggerella, pioggia fine, *f.* ¶ *v.imp.* piovigginare.
mnemonic, *a.* mnemonico. ~**s,** *n.pl.* mnemonica, *f.*
moan, *n.* gemito, lamento, pianto, *m.* ¶ *v.i.* gemere, lamentarsi.
moat, *n.* fosso, fossato, *m.*
mob, *n.* folla, plebe, canaglia, *f.*   ~ *law*, legge della folla, *f.*; linciaggio, *m.* ¶ *v.t.* assalire, attaccare, inseguire urlando.
mobile, *a.* mobile.   **mobility,** *n.* mobilità, *f.*
Mocha, *n.* Moca, *f.*   *Mocha coffee* or **mocha,** moca, caffè moca, *m.*
mock, *v.t.* deridere, beffare, canzonare, burlarsi di, schernire.   ~ *fight*, battaglia finta, *f.*   ~-*heroic*, eroicomico.   ~**er,** *n.* beffeggiatore, burlone, beffardo, *m.*   ~**ery,** *n.* derisione, beffa, *f.*; oggetto di scherno, *m.*   ~*ing bird*, mimo; merlo poliglotta, tordo beffeggiatore, *m.*
mode, *n.* (*fashion*) moda, *f.*; (*way, form, method*) modo, *m.*, maniera, forma, *f.*, genere, mezzo, sistema, *m.*
model, *n.* modello, tipo, *m.*; riproduzione, *f.*; (*att.*) modello, *m.* ¶ *v.t.* modellare.   **modeller,** *n.* modellatore, *m.*, -trice, *f.*
moderate, *a.* moderato, mediocre, modesto; (*price*) modico. ¶ *v.t.* moderare. ~**ly,** *ad.* moderatamente, mediocremente; modicamente.   ~**ness,** *n.* modicità, *f.*   **moderation,** *n.* moderazione, *f.*
modern, *a. & n.* moderno, *a. & m.*   ~ *language*, lingua vivente, l. moderna, *f.*   ~**ism,** *n.* modernismo, *m.*   ~**ize,** *v.t.* modernizzare.

modest, *a.* modesto. ~**y,** *n.* modestia, *f.*

modicum, *n.* piccola quantità, *f.*, pocolino, *m.*

modification, *n.* modificazione, *f.* **modify,** *v.t.* modificare.

modish, *a.* di moda, alla moda. ~**ly,** *ad.* alla moda.

modulate, *v.t.* modulare. **modulation,** *n.* modulazione, *f.* **module** *&* **modulus,** *n.* modulo, *m.*

modus operandi, modo d'operazione, *m.*

modus vivendi, modus vivendi, *m.*

mohair, *n.* pelo di capra d'Angora, *m.*

Mohammedan, *n. & a.* maomettano, *a. & m.* ~**ism,** *n.* maomettismo, *m.*

moiety, *n.* metà, *f.*

moil, *v.i.* affaticarsi, lavorare duramente.

moire, *n.* moerre, -o, *m.* **moiré,** *v.t.* marezzare. ~ *silk,* seta marezzata, *f.*

moist, *a.* umido; madido. ~**en,** *v.t.* umettare, inumidire. ~**ness,** *&* ~**ure,** *n.* umidità, umidezza, *f.*; madore, *m.*

molar, *a. & n.* molare, *a. & m.*

molasses, *n.* melassa, *f.*

mole, *n.* neo, *m.*, verruca, *f.*; (*jetty*) molo, *m.*; (*Zool.*) talpa, *f.* ~*hill,* mucchio di terra scavato dalla talpa, *m.* ~*skin,* pelle di talpa, *f.*, tessuto di fustagno, *m.* ~ *trap,* trappola per le talpe, *f.*

molecular, *a.* molecolare. **molecule,** *n.* molecola, *f.*

molest, *v.t.* molestare, turbare, vessare. ~**ation,** *n.* molestia, *f.*

mollify, *v.t.* ammollire, mollificare; addolcire.

mollusc, *n.* mollusco, *m.*

molly, *n.* baggeo, effeminato, *m.* ~*coddle,* donnetta, persona effeminata, *f.*, pulcino bagnato, *m.* (*iron*). ¶ *v.t.* vezzeggiare, trattare delicatamente.

molten, *p.p.* fuso.

Moluccas (the), le Molucche, *f.pl.*

moment, *n.* momento, istante, *m.*; importanza, *f.* *a* ~ *ago,* un momento fa. ~**ary,** *a.* momentaneo. ~**ous,** *a.* di grande importanza, grave, critico. **momentum,** *n.* (*Mech.*) momento, impulso, *m.*; (*impetus*) impeto, slancio, *m.*

monarch, *n.* monarca, *m.* ~**ic(al),** *a.* monarchico. ~**ist,** *n.* monarchico, *m.* ~**y,** *n.* monarchia, *f.*

monastery, *n.* monastero, convento, *m.* **monastic,** *a.* monastico.

monastically, *ad.* monasticamente.

Monday, *n.* lunedì, *m.*

monetary, *a.* monetario. **monetize,** *v.t.* dare il valore di moneta, adoperare ad uso monetario. **money,** *n.* danaro, *m.*, contanti, quattrini, *m.pl.*; moneta, valuta, *f.*; fondi, valori, *m.pl.*; capitale, *m.* ~ *changer,* cambiamonete, cambiavalute, *m.inv.* ~ *box,* salvadanaio, *m.* ~ *grubber,* accumulatore di danaro, *m.* ~ *lender,* usuraio, prestatore di danaro, *m.* ~ *market,* borsa, *f.*, mercato monetario, *m.* ~ *order,* vaglia, *m.* ~**ed,** *a.* danaroso, ricco. -**monger,** *n.* mercante, negoziante, *m.*

Mongolia, *n.* la Mongolia, *f.* **Mongol[ian],** *a.* mongolo. ¶ *n.* mongolo, *m.*, -a, *f.*

mongoose, *n.* mangusta, *f.*

mongrel, *a.* bastardo; meticcio, di razza mista. ¶ *n.* meticcio, *m.*, -a, *f.*; bastardo, *m.*, -a, *f.*; (*cur*) cane di razza mista, *m.*

monk, *n.* monaco, *m.* ~**'s hood** (*Bot.*), aconito, *m.* ~**ery** *&* ~**hood,** *n.* monachismo, *m.*, i monaci, *m.pl.*; vita monastica *f.* ~**ish,** *a.* monacale.

monkey, *n.* scimmia, *f.*; (*she*) bertuccia, scimmia femmina, *f.*; (*pile driving*) (scatto del) battipalo, *m.* *young* ~, scimmiotto, *m.*; (*child*) birichino, *m.* ~ *house,* gabbia delle scimmie, *f.* ~ *nut,* arachide, *f.* ~ *puzzle,* araucaria, *f.* ~ *trick,* scimmiottata, buffoneria, *f.* ~ *wrench,* chiave inglese, *f.*

monochord, *n.* monocordo, *m.* **monochrome,** *a.* monocromo. **monocle,** *n.* monocolo, *m.*; caramella, *f.* **monogamy,** *n.* monogamia, *f.* **monogram,** *n.* monogramma, *m.* **monograph,** *n.* monografia, *f.* **monolith,** *n. &* ~**ic,** *a.* monolito, *m.*, monolitico, *a.* **monologize,** *v.i.* monologare. **monologue,** *n.* monologo, *m.* **monomania,** *n.* monomania, *f.* **monoplane,** *n.* monoplano, *m.* **monopolist,** *n.* monopolista, accaparratore, *m.* **monopolize,** *v.t.* monopolizzare, accaparrare. **monopoly,** *n.* monopolio, *m.* **monosyllabic,** *a.* monosillabico. **monosyllable,** *n.* monosillabo, *m.* **monotonist** (*pers.*), *n.* monocordo, *m.* **monotonous,** *a.* monotono. **monotony,** *n.* monotonia, *f.* **monotype,** *n.* monotipia, *f.*

monsoon, *n.* monsone, *m.*

monster, *n. & a.* mostro, *m. & a.*
monstrance, *n.* ostensorio, *m.*
monstrosity, *n.* mostruosità, *f.*
monstrous, *a.* mostruoso, enorme; orribile.
Mont Blanc, il Monte Bianco, *m.*
Montenegrin, *a.* montenegrino. ¶ *n.* montenegrino, *m.*, -a, *f.*
Montenegro, *n.* il Montenegro, *m.*
Monte Rosa, il Monte Rosa, *m.*
month, *n.* mese, *m.* ~'s *pay, rent*, or *like*, mensile, *m.* **monthly**, *a.* mensile, a mese, al mese. ~ *nurse*, levatrice, *f.* ~ *payment, drawing, salary*, or *like*, mensile, *m.* ~ *statement* (*Com.*), bilancio mensile, *m.* ¶ *n.* rivista mensile, *f.* ¶ *ad.* mensilmente, per mese, una volta al mese, tutti i mesi.
monument, *n.* monumento, *m.* **monumental**, *a.* monumentale. ~ *mason*, marmista, lavoratore in marmo, *m.*
moo, *v.i.* mugghiare, muggire. ¶ *n.* mugghio, muggito.
mood, *n.* umore, *m.*, disposizione, *f.*; (*Gram.*) modo, *m.* ~y, *a.* di cattivo umore, impensierito, cupo.
moon, *n.* luna, *f.* ~*beam*, raggio di luna, raggio lunare, *m.* ~*light*, chiaro di luna, *m.* ~*lit*, illuminato dalla luna. ~*shine* (*fig.*), baie, bagattelle, *f.pl.*, illusione, *f.* ~*stone*, adularia, pietra di luna, *f.* ~*struck*, lunatico. ~ [*about*], *v.i.* bighellonare, gironzare.
moor, & ~*land*, *n.* brughiera, landa, *f.* ~ *cock*, gallo di brughiera, *m.*, lagopiede rosso di Scozia, *m.* ~*hen*, gallina d'acqua, *f.*
Moor (*pers.*) *n.* Moro, *m.*
moor, *v.t.* ammarrare, ormeggiare. ~*ing*, *n.* ormeggio, *m.*; (*pl.*) ormeggi, *m.pl.*, ancoraggio, *m.*; (*dolphin*) corpo-morto, *m.*, boa di ormeggio, *f.*
Moorish, *a.* moresco.
moose, *n.* alce americano, *m.*
moot, *a.* discutibile, dubbio, incerto. ¶ *v.t.* proporre per discussione, mettere in campo.
mop, *n.* radazza di cenci, *f.*; (*of hair*) massa compatta, *f.* ~ *broom*, scopa, *f.* ¶ *v.t.* nettare, pulire, lavare. ~ *up*, rasciugare.
mope, *v.i.* stare triste e tacito, annoiarsi, stupidirsi. *in the* ~*s*, annoiato, malinconico.
moraine, *n.* morena, *f.*
moral, *a.* morale, virtuoso. ¶ *n.* (*of story, of fable*) lezione, morale, *f.*;

(*pl. manners*) costumi, *m.pl.*; (*pl. ethics*) morale, etica, *f.* ~[e], *n.* morale, *m.* ~*ist*, *n.* moralista, *m.* ~*ity*, *n.* moralità, *f.* ~*ize*, *v.i. & t.* moralizzare.
morass, *n.* palude, *f.*, pantano, *m.*
moratorium, *n.* moratoria, *f.*
Moravia, *n.* la Moravia, *f.*
morbid, *a.* morboso. **morbidezza**, *n.* morbidezza, *f.* **morbidity**, *n.* moraleggiare, moralizzare.
mordant, *a. & n.* mordente, *a. & m.*
more, *a.* piú, maggiore, piú numeroso, piú grande, in maggiore quantità. ¶ *ad.* piú, di piú, in piú, maggiormente, ancora, in aggiunta. *much* ~, vieppiú. *one* ~, ancora uno. *all the more*, tanto piú. ~*over*, *ad.* inoltre, oltre a ciò, di piú, d'altronde, d'altra parte.
Moresque, *a.* moresco.
morganatic, *a.* morganatico.
moribund, *a.* moribondo.
morning, & (*Poet.*) **morn**, *n.* mattino, *m.*, mattina, *f.*; (*course*) mattinata, *f.* ~ *coat*, giacca, *f.* ~ *dress*, abito da passeggio, *m.* ~ *performance*, mattinata, *f.* ~ *star*, stella del mattino, stella mattutina, *f.* ~ *suit*, vestito completo da mattina, *m.*
Moroccan, *a.* marocchino. ¶ *n.* marocchino, *m.*, -a, *f.* **Morocco**, *n.* il Marocco, *m.* *morocco* [*leather*], marocchino, *m.*
morose, *a.* tetro, sgarbato, stizzoso. ~*ness*, *n.* tetraggine, *f.*
Morpheus, *n.* Morfeo, *m.* **morphia**, **-phine**, morfina, *f.* **morphinomaniac**, *n.* morfinomane, *m.f.*
morris [*dance*], (*Moorish*) *n.* danza moresca, *f.*
morrow (**the**), & **on the** ~, l'indomani, all'indomani.
morsel, *n.* boccone; pezzetto; briciolo; tozzo, *m.*
mortal, *a.* mortale; (*strife*) a morte, ad oltranza. ¶ *n.* mortale, *m.* ~*ity*, *n.* mortalità, *f.*
mortar, *n.* (*plaster*) malta, calcina, *f.*; (*vessel & Mil.*) mortaio, *m.*
mortgage, *n.* ipoteca, *f.* ~ *deed*, contratto, titolo ipotecario, *m.* ¶ *v.t.* ipotecare. **mortgagee**, *n.* creditore ipotecario, *m.* **mortgagor**, *n.* debitore ipotecario, *m.*
mortification, *n.* mortificazione, vessazione, *f.*; (*Med.*) cancrena, *f.* **mortify**, *v.t.* mortificare, umiliare; incancrenire.
mortise, **-ice**, *n.* mortisa, *f.*, incavo,

incastro, *m.* ~ *lock,* serratura incastrata, *f.* ¶ *v.t.* incastrare; congiungere a mortisa.

mortmain, *n.* manomorta, *f. property in* ~, beni inalienabili, *m.pl.*

mortuary, *a.* mortuario. ~ *chapel,* cappella mortuaria, *f.* ¶ *n.* camera mortuaria, *f.*

Mosaic (*of Moses*), *a.* mosaico, di Mosè.

mosaic, *n.* mosaico, *m.*

Moscow, *n.* Mosca, *f.*

Moslem, *n. & a.* maomettano, *a. & m.,* mussulmano, *a. & m.*

mosque, *n.* moschea, *f.*

mosquito, *n.* zanzara, *f.* ~ *net,* ~ *curtain,* zanzariera, *f.*

moss, *n.* musco, *m.,* borracina, *f.* ~ *grown,* coperto di musco. ~ *rose,* rosa muscosa, rosa borracina, *f.* ~*y,* *a.* muscoso, coperto di musco.

most, *a.* il piú (di), il massimo, la maggior parte (di), la massima parte (di). ~ *eminent,* eminentissimo. ~ *illustrious,* illustrissimo. ~ *reverend, right reverend,* reverendissimo. ¶ *ad.* il piú. ~ *of all,* sopra tutto. ~ *ly, ad.* principalmente, il piú sovente, il piú delle volte, per la piú parte, per lo piú.

mote, *n.* (*dust*) atomo, *m.;* (*in eye, fig.*) festuca, pagliuzza, *f.*

moth, *n.* falena, farfalla notturna, tarma, tignola, *f.* ~-*eaten,* tarmato.

mother, *n.* madre, *f.* ~ *church,* Madre Chiesa; chiesa metropolitana, *f.* ~ *country,* [madre] patria, *f.,* paese natio, *m.* ~ *earth,* nostra madre comune, *f.* ~-*in-law,* suocera, *f.* ~ *of pearl,* madreperla, *f.* ~'*s side* (*family*), parte di madre, *f.* ~ *superior,* madre superiore, *f.* ~ *tongue* (*native*), lingua materna, *f.;* (*original*) lingua madre, *f.* ~ *wit,* buon senso, spirito naturale, *m.* ¶ *v.t.* fare da madre a, adottare; (*fig.*) covare. ~*less,* *a.* senza madre, orfano di madre. ~*ly,* *a.* materno, di madre.

motif, *n.* (*Art, Need.*) motivo, *m.;* (*literary*) tema, *m.,* argomento, *m.*

motion, *n.* moto, movimento, *m.;* iniziativa, *f.;* (*proposal*) mozione, proposta, *f.;* (*Med.*) scarica, andata di corpo, *f.* ¶ *v.i.* fare cenno, fare segno. ~*less,* *a.* immoto, immobile. **motive,** *a.* motore. ~ *power,* forza motrice, *f.* ¶ *n.* motivo, *m.,* ragione, *f.*

motley, *a.* screziato, variopinto,

misto. ¶ *n.* screziatura, *f.;* abito d'arlecchino, *m.*

motor, *n.* motore, *m.;* automobile, *f.* ~ (*bi*)*cycle,* motocicletta, *f.,* motociclo, *m.* ~ *boat,* motoscafo, *m.,* motobarca, *f.;* mas, *m.inv.* ~ *body builder,* carrozziere, *m.* ~ *bus,* autobus, *m.* ~ (*car*), automobile, *f.,* macchina, *f.,* auto, *m.* ~ (*car*) *insurance,* assicurazione delle automobili, *f.* ~ *coach,* vettura automobile, *f.,* autobus, *m.* ~ *combination,* motocarrozzetta, *f.* ~ *cyclist,* motociclista, *m.f.* ~ *lorry,* autocarro, *m.* ~ *man,* (train, tram) macchinista, *m.;* conducente d'automobile, autista, *m.* ~ *road,* autostrada, *f.* ~-*scooter,* motopattino, *m.* ~ *ship,* motonave, *f.* ~ *show,* mostra automobilistica, *f.* ¶ *v.i.* andare in automobile. ~*ing,* *n.* automobilismo, *m.* ~*ist,* *n.* motorista, automobilista, *m.* ~*ize,* *v.t.* motorizzare.

mottled soap, sapone marmorizzato, s. venato, *m.*

motto, *n.* motto, *m.,* divisa, *f.;* (*of a device*) (*prefixed to book or chapter*) epigrafe, *f.;* (*Mus.*) motivo, *m.*

mould, *n.* modello, stampo, *m.,* forma, *f.;* (*fig.*) carattere, *m.;* (*Typ.*) forma, *f.;* (*vegetable*) terra vegetale, *f.,* terriccio; (*ship*) garbo, *m.;* (*decay*) muffa, *f.* ¶ *v.t.* modellare, formare; (*Typ.*) gettare in forma. ~*er,* *n.* modellatore; gettatore, *m.* ~ (*away*), ridursi in polvere, consumarsi. **mouldiness,** *n.* muffa, *f.* **moulding,** *n.* (*act*) modellamento, *m.,* modellatura, *f.;* (*ornamental strip*) modanatura, *f.* **mouldy,** *a.* muffito, ammuffito. *turn* ~, muffare, muffire.

moult, *v.i.* mudare. ~[*ing*], *n.* muda, *f.*

mound, *n.* monticello, poggio, tumulo, *m.*

mount, *n.* (*as Etna*) monte, *m.;* (*photo*) cartone, *m.,* montatura, *f.;* (*horse, &c.*) cavalcatura, *f.;* (*Horse Racing*) monta, *f.* ¶ *v.i.* montare, salire, ascendere; (*on calico or linen*) incollare; (*jewels*) incastonare, montare; (*play*) mettere in scena.

mountain, *n.* montagna, *f.* ~ *ash,* sorbo, *m.* ~ *sickness,* mal di montagna, *m.* ~*eer,* *n.* (*dweller*) montanaro, *m.,* -a, *f.;* (*climber*) alpinista, *m.f.* ~*eering,* *n.* alpinismo, *m.* ~*ous,* *a.* montagnoso; enorme.

mountebank, *n.* saltimbanco, *m.*; (*fig.*) ciarlatano, *m.*

mounted, *p.a.* a cavallo, montato.

mounter, *n.* montatore, *m.*, -trice, *f.*

mounting, *n.* montaggio, *m.*; montatura, incastonatura, *f.*; messa in scena, *f.*

mourn, *v.t. & i.* piangere, rimpiangere, lamentare, lamentarsi. **the ~ers**, il convoglio, il corteo funebre, *m.* [**hired**] **~er**, prefica, *f.* **~ful**, *a.* triste, lugubre. **~ing**, *n.* lutto, *m.* **~ band**, fascia da lutto, *f.* **~ coach**, carro funebre, *m.* **~ paper**, carta da lutto, *f.* **to be in ~**, essere in lutto, vestire a lutto.

mouse, *n.* topo, sorcio, *m.*; (*young*) topolino, *m.* **~ trap**, trappola per topi, *f.*

moustache, *n.* baffi, mustacchi, *m.pl.* **~d**, *a.* con baffi, baffuto.

mouth, *n.* bocca; gola, *f.*; fauci, *f.pl.*; imboccatura, foce, apertura, entrata, *f.*; orifizio, *m.*; (*grimace*) smorfia, *f.* **~ organ**, armonica, *f.* **~piece**, imboccatura, *f.*; bocchino, *m.*; (*pers.*) portavoce, interprete, *m.* **~wash**, acqua dentifricia, *f.* **~ful**, *n.* boccone, *m.*, boccata, *f.*

movable, *a.* mobile; (*Law*) mobiliare.

move, *n.* mossa, *f.*, movimento, *m.*; (*Chess, &c.*) turno, *m.* **whose ~ is it?** a chi tocca giuocare? ¶ *v.t.* muovere, rimuovere, far muovere; commuovere, intenerire; traslocare, trasportare; spingere; indurre; proporre; (*v.i.*) muoversi, mettersi in moto, portarsi, dirigersi. **~ along**, avanzare, allontanarsi. **~ back**, indietreggiare, ritirare. **~ in** (*house*), entrare (in), occupare, trasportare i mobili (in). **~ off**, allontanarsi. **~ on!** circolate! **~ [out]** (*house*), cambiare domicilio, sgombrare. **~ment**, *n.* movimento, giro, moto, *m.*; marcia *f.*; gesto, cenno, *m.* **moving**, *a.* commovente. **~ body** (*Mech.*), corpo mobile, *m.* **~ picture**, cinema, cinematografo, *m.* **~ spirit**, animatore, *m.*, -trice, *f.* **~ staircase**, scala mobile, *f.* **moving van**, furgone, *m.*

mow, *n.* pagliaio, mucchio, *m.*; smorfia, boccaccia, *f.* ¶ *v.t.* ir. falciare, mietere; (*turf*) tagliare. **~ down**, falciare, mietere. **~er**, *n.* (*pers.*) falciatore, mietitore, *m.*, -trice, *f.*; (*Mach.*) falciatrice, *f.*; (*lawn*) falciatrice da prato, *f.*

Mr., Signor(e), *m.*, il Signor . . .

(*courtesy title of lawyers*). **Mrs.**, Signora, *f.* (*Note.—As a form of address on envelope or in letter* Signore *or* Signora *should not be abbreviated.*)

much, *a. & ad.* molto, assai, grande; caro; di molto, a lungo, bene. **as ~**, lo stesso, in uguale quantità, altrettanto, la stessa cosa. **as ~ as**, tanto . . . quanto, tanto da, abbastanza per, altrettanto. **so ~**, tanto. **very ~**, estremamente, bene, assai. **to make ~ of**, fare gran caso di, fare mille carezze a, tener gran conto di.

mucilage, *n.* mucilaggine, *f.*

muck, *n.* fango, letame, concime, *m.*; porcheria, *f.*

mucous, *a.* mucoso. **~ membrane**, [membrana] mucosa, *f.* **mucus**, *n.* muco, *m.*

mud, *n.* fango, *m.*, mota, melma, *f.*; (*river*) limo, *m.* **~ bath**, bagno di fango, *m.* **~ brush** (*boots*), spazzola da scarpe, *f.* **~guard**, parafango, *m.* **~ lark**, fognaiuolo, *m.* **~ pie**, pasta, *f.* (di fango). **~ spring**, polla fangosa, *f.*

muddle, *n.* confusione, *f.*, disordine, guazzabuglio, imbroglio, pasticcio, scombussolio, *m.* ¶ *v.t.* confondere, far pasticci, scombinare, scombussolare, impasticciare; (*with drinks*) inebriare, stupidire. **~ up**, impasticciare, impappinare. **muddler**, *n.* guastamestieri, pasticcione, *m.*

muddy, *a.* fangoso, melmoso, torbido. ¶ *v.t.* imbrattare di fango, intorbidare.

muezzin, *n.* muezzino, *m.*

muff, *n.* manicotto, *m.*; (*pers.*) grullo, minchione, individuo maldestro, *m.* **muffle** (*Chem.*), *n.* muffola, *f.* ¶ *v.t.* assordare; (*drum*) velare. **~ up**, avviluppare, imbaccucare. **~d**, *p.a.* assordato, velato; avviluppato, bendato. **muffler**, *n.* sciarpa da collo, *f.*

mufti (**in**), in borghese, in abito civile.

mug, *n.* bicchiere, *m.*, tazza, *f.*, boccale, *m.*; (*slang*) bocca, faccia, *f.*; semplicione, *m.*

muggy, *a.* umido, afoso.

mulatto, *n.* mulatto, *m.*, -a, *f.* ¶ *a.* mulatto.

mulberry, *n.* mora, gelsa, *f.* **~ [tree]**, moro, gelso, *m.*

mulch, *n.* strato di paglia o letame, *m.*, lettiera, *f.* ¶ *v.t.* impagliare.

mulct, *v.t.* colpire di multa, multare.

mule, *n.* (*he & pers.*) mulo, *m.*; (*she*) mula, *f.*; (*pl. slippers*) ciabatte, *f.pl.* ~ *track*, strada mulattiera, *f.*

muleteer, *n.* mulattiere, *m.*

mulish, *a.* da mulo, ostinato come un mulo.

mulled wine, vino caldo, *m.*

muller (*grinding*), *n.* macinello, *m.*

mullet, *n.* (*grey*) muggine, *f.*; (*red*) triglia, *f.*

mullion, *n.* regolo, *m.*, traversa, *f.*, tramezzo verticale, *m.* ~*ed window*, finestra divisa per compartimenti, finestra a regoli, *f.*

multicolour[ed], *a.* multicolore, variopinto.

multifarious, *a.* molti e vari, numeroso, molteplice.

multi-light standard, candelabro, lampadario, *m.*

multi-millionaire, *n. & a.* multimilionario, *m.*, -a, *f.*

multiple, *n. & a.* multiplo, *a. & m.* ~ *firm*, casa con succursali, *f.* ~ *fork* (*of roads*), incrocio di parecchie strade, *m.*; (*fig.*) zampa d'oca, *f.* ~ *shop*, negozio con succursali, *m.* **multiplicand**, *n.* moltiplicando, *m.* **multiplication**, *n.* moltiplicazione, *f.* ~ *table*, tavola pitagorica, tavola di Pitagora, *f.* **multiplicity**, *n.* moltiplicità, *f.* **multiplier**, *n.* moltiplicatore, *m.* **multiply**, *v.t.* moltiplicare; (*v.i.*) moltiplicarsi.

multitude, *n.* moltitudine, *f.*

mum ['s the word], zitto! non profferite sillaba!

mumble, *v.i.* borbottare.

mummer, *n.* persona mascherata, *f.*, attore, *m.* ~**y**, *n.* pagliacciata, stupidaggine, *f.*

mummify, *v.t.* mummificare.

mummy, *n.* mummia, *f.*; (*mother*) mamma, *f.*

mumps, *n.* (*Med.*) orecchioni, *m.pl.*; (*sulks*) broncio, cattivo umore, *m.*

munch, *v.t. & i.* masticare.

mundane, *a.* mondano.

Munich, *n.* Monaco, *f.*

municipal, *a.* municipale. ~**ity**, *n.* municipalità, *f.*, comune municipale, *m.*

munificence, *n.* munificenza, *f.* **munificent**, *a.* munificente.

muniment, *n.* titolo, atto, *m.* ~ *room*, archivio, *m.*

munitions, *n.pl.* munizioni; provvigioni, *f.pl.*

mural, *a.* murale.

murder, *n.* omicidio, assassinio, *m.*

~! all'assassino! ¶ *v.t.* ammazzare, assassinare, uccidere; (*fig.*) massacrare; (*language*) storpiare. ~**er**, ~**ess**, *n.* assassino, *m.*, -a, *f.*, omicida, *m.f.* ~**ous**, *a.* micidiale, omicida, assassino.

muriatic, *a.* muriatico, cloridrico.

murky, *a.* buio, fosco, tenebroso.

murmur, *n.* mormorio, *m.*; lagnanza, *f.* ¶ *v.i. & t.* mormorare, brontolare.

murrain, *n.* peste, malattia contagiosa del bestiame; moria, *f.*

muscat (*grape*, *wine*) moscato, *m.* **muscatels**, *n.pl.* moscatelli, *m.pl.*

muscle, *n.* muscolo, *m.* **muscled**, *a.* muscoloso. **muscular**, *a.* (*force*) muscolare; (*pers.*) muscoloso.

Muse, *n.* Musa, *f.*

muse, *v.i.* meditare; riflettere; sognare.

museum, *n.* museo, *m.*; (*natural history*) museo di storia naturale, *m.*

mush, *n.* poltiglia, *f.*; intriso, *m.*; pappa, *f.*

mushroom, *n.* fungo (prataiuolo), f. mangereccio, *m.*; (*pers.*) villano rifatto, uomo nuovo, *m.*; (*att.*) effimero, di un giorno. ~ *bed*, fungaia, *f.* ~ *growth*, (*fig.*) sviluppo rapido, *m.* ~ *spawn*, micelio, *m.*

music, *n.* musica, *f.* ~ *cabinet*, casellario per la musica, *m.* ~ *case*, portamusica, *m.inv.* ~ *hall*, caffè concerto, *m.* ~ *master*, maestro di musica, *m.* ~ *stand*, leggio da musica, scaffale per musica, *m.* ~ *stool*, sgabello per piano, *m.* **musical**, *a.* musicale; (*pers.*) musico, *m.* ~ *box*, scatola armonica, *f.* ~ *clock*, orologio a cariglione, *m.* ~ *comedy*, operetta, *f.* ~ *director*, capomusica, *m.inv.*, direttore d'orchestra, *m.* ~ *ear*, orecchio musicale, orecchio sensibile alla musica, *m.* ~ *evening*, serata musicale, *f.* ~ *glasses*, armonica, *f.* ~ *instrument*, strumento musicale, *m.* ~ *instrument maker*, fabbricante di strumenti musicali, *m.* ~ *instrument making*, fabbricazione di strumenti musicali. ~ *interlude*, intermezzo musicale, *m.* ~ *play*, operetta, *f.*

musician, *n.* musico, *m.*, musicista, *m.f.*, musicante, *m.f.*

musing, *n.* meditazione, riflessione, *f.*, sogno, *m.*

musk, *n.* muschio, *m.* ~ *deer*, muschio, *m.*, cervo muschio, *m.* ~ *rat*, ondatra, *f.* ~ *rose*, rosa muschiata, *f.* to [*perfume with*] ~, muschiare.

musket, *n.* moschetto, *m.* ~**eer** (*Hist.*), *n.* moschettiere, *m.* ~**ry** (*Mil.*), *n.* tiro, *m.*, fucileria, *f.* ~ *instructor*, istruttore di tiro, *m.*

Muslim, *n. & a.* maomettano, *m. & a.*

muslin, *n.* mussolina, *f.*

musquash, *n.* ondatra, *f.*; (*fur*) pelliccia di ondatra, *f.*

mussel, *n.* dattero di mare, *m.*, arsella, cozza, *f.*

Mussulman, *n. & a.* mussulmano, *a. & m.*

must, *v.aux.ir.* dovere; bisognare (*impers.*).

must, *n.* mosto, *m.*

mustard, *n.* mostarda; senapa, -e, *f.*; (*Bot.*) senapa, *f.* ~ *gas*, iprite, *f.* ~ *maker*, fabbricante di mostarda, *m.* ~ *plaster*, ~ *poultice*, senapismo, *m.* ~ *pot*, mostardiera, *f.* ~ *sauce*, salsa di mostarda, *f.* ~ *seed*, seme di senape, *m.* ~ *spoon*, cucchiaino da mostarda, *m.*

muster, *n.* appello, *m.*, rivista, adunata, *f.* ~ *roll*, appello, controllo, ruolo, *m.* ¶ *v.t.* fare l'appello di; passare in rivista, radunare, contare. ~ *courage*, riprendere coraggio.

musty, *a.* ammuffito, muffato, intanfito; (*smell*) con odore di muffa, di rinchiuso.

mutability, *n.* mutabilità, incostanza, *f.* **mutation,** *n.* mutamento, *m.*; mutazione, *f.*

mute, *a.* muto, silenzioso. ¶ *n.* muto, *m.*, -a, *f.*; (*Gram.*) muta, lettera muta, *f.*; (*Mus.*) sordina, *f.* ~**d,** *p.a.* in sordina. ~**ly,** *ad.* mutamente, in silenzio.

mutilate, *v.t.* mutilare. **mutilation,** *n.* mutilazione, *f.*

mutineer, *n.* ammutinato, *m.* **mutinous,** *a.* ribelle. **mutiny,** *n.* ammutinamento, *m.*, rivolta, ribellione, *f.* ¶ *v.i.* ammutinarsi, ribellarsi.

mutter, *v.i.* borbottare, brontolare; (*of thunder*) rumoreggiare.

mutton, *n.* montone, castrato, *m.* ~ *cutlet*, cotoletta di castrato, di montone, *f.*

mutual, *a.* reciproco, corrisposto; comune; mutuo. ~ *association*, mutualità, società di mutuo soccorso, *f.* ~ *loan association*, mutualità di credito, *f.* on ~ *terms* (*engagement*), alla pari. ~**ity,** *n.* mutualità; reciprocità, *f.*

muzzle, *n.* (*animal*) muso, ceffo, grugno, *m.*; (*gun*) bocca, *f.*; (*for dog*) museruola, *f.* ~*-loading,* ad

avancarica. ¶ *v.t.* mettere la museruola a; (*fig.*) fare tacere, imbavagliare.

my, *a.* (il) mio, (la) mia, (i) miei, (le) mie.

myopia, *n.* miopia, *f.* **myopic,** *a.* miope.

myriad, *n.* miriade, *f.*

myriapod, *n.* miriapodo, *m.*

myrmidon, *n.* mirmidone; (*fig.*) sbirro, *m.*

myrrh, *n.* mirra, *f.*

myrtle, *n.* mirto, *m* ~*berry,* bacca del mirto, *f.*

myself, *pn.* io stesso, me stesso; mi, me.

mysterious, *a.* misterioso. ~ *appeal* (*as of the olden times*), mistica, *f.*

mystery, *n.* mistero, *m.* ~ (*play*), mistero, *m.* **mystic** (*pers.*), *n.* mistico. ~(**al**), *a.* mistico. **mysticalness,** *n.* misticità, *f.* **mysticism,** *n.* misticismo, *m.* **mistify,** *v.t.* mistificare.

myth, *n.* mito, *m.* ~**ic(al),** *a.* mitico. ~**ologic(al),** *a.* mitologico. ~**ologist,** *n.* mitologista, *m.f.* ~**ology** *n.* mitologia, *f.*

N

nabob, *n.* nababbo, *m.*

nadir, *n.* nadir, *m.*; (*fig.*) punto piú basso.

naevus, *n.* neo, *m.*, voglia, *f.*

nag, *n.* ronzino, cavalluccio, *m.* ~ (**at**), *v.t. & i.* rimbrottare, stuzzicare, infastidire. **nagging,** *p.a.* rimbrottante, irritante, brontolone.

naiad, *n.* naiade, *f.*

nail, *n.* (*finger, toe*) unghia, *f.*; (*metal*) chiodo, *m.* ~ *brush*, spazzolino per le unghie, *m.* ~ *extractor*, cacciachiodo, *m.* ~ *file*, lima per le unghie, *f.* ~ *maker*, chiodaio, *m.* ~ *making & works*, chioderia, fabbrica di chiodi, *f.* ~ *scissors*, forbici per le unghie, *f.pl.* (pay) on the ~, per contanti. ~ [up], *v.t.* inchiodare.

naive, *a.* ingenuo, semplice. **naivety,** *n.* ingenuità, *f.*

naked, *a.* nudo, ignudo. with the ~ *eye*, ad occhio nudo. ~**ly** (*fig.*), *ad.* nudamente, a nudo, allo scoperto. ~**ness,** *n.* nudità, *f.*

namby-pamby, *a.* sentimentale, affettato, scipito.

name, *n.* nome, *m.*; denominazione, *f.*, titolo, *m.*; rinomanza, reputazione, *f.*

by ∼, (*to mention*) di nome; (*be
called on*) per nome. *my* ∼ *is Adam,*
mi chiamo Adamo. ∼*plate,* targa
col nome, *f.* ∼*sake,* omonimo, *m.*
¶ *v.t.* nominare, chiamare; dare
nome a, battezzare; intitolare;
menzionare, accennare, indicare;
parlare di. ∼**less,** *a.* senza nome,
innominato; anonimo. ∼**ly,** *ad.*
cioè, vale a dire; (*of pers.*) nominatamente.

nankeen, *n.* nanchino, *m.*

nanny, *n.* bambinaia, balia, *f.* ∼
[*goat*], capra, *f.*

nap, *n.* (*sleep*) sonnellino, *m.*, siesta, *f.*;
(*pile*) peluria, *f.* *to catch napping,*
prendere alla sprovvista.

nape [**of the neck**], *n.* nuca, *f.*

naphtha, *n.* nafta, *f.* **naphthalene,
-ine,** *n.* naftalina, *f.*

napkin, *n.* tovagli[u]olo, *m.*, salvietta,
f.; (*baby's*) pannicello, *m.* ∼ *ring,*
anello per tovagli[u]olo, *m.*

Naples, *n.* Napoli, *f.*

narcissus, *n.* narcisò, *m.*

narcotic, *a. & n.* narcotico, *a. & m.*

narrate, *v.t.* narrare, raccontare.
narration *&* **narrative,** *n.*
racconto, *m.*, narrativa, narrazione,
esposizione, *f.* **narrative,** *a.*
narrativo. **narrator, -tress,** *n.*
raccontatore, *m.*, -trice, *f.*, narratore,
m., -trice, *f.*

narrow, *a.* stretto, serrato, ristretto,
angusto; esiguo, limitato; gretto,
meschino; esatto, minuzioso. *to have
a* ∼ *escape,* scapparla belle,
scamparla per miracolo. ∼*-gauge
railway,* ferrovia a scartamento
ridotto, *f.* ∼*-minded,* di mentalità
ristretta, illiberale, di corte vedute.
¶ *n.* (*Naut.*) *often pl.,* stretto, *m.*,
gola, *f.* ¶ *v.t.* restringere; accorciare;
limitare. ∼**ness,** *n.* strettezza,
ristrettezza, *f.*

narwhal, *n.* narvalo, *m.*

nasal, *a.* nasale. ¶(*Gram.*) *n.* nasale,
lettera nasale, *f.*

nascent, *a.* nascente.

nastiness, *n.* sporcizia; schifezza;
oscenità, *f.*

nasturtium, *n.* nasturzio, *m.*

nasty, *a.* schifoso, brutto; cattivo;
sgradevole; stomachevole. *Often
rendered by the suffix* -accio, -accia.

natal, *a.* natale.

natation, *n.* nuoto, *m.*

nation, *n.* nazione, *f.*, popolo, *m.*
∼**al,** *a.* nazionale; pubblico. ∼
capital (*Economics*), ricchezza pubblica, *f.* ∼ *debt,* debito pubblico, *m.*

∼ *monument,* monumento nazionale,
monumento storico, *m.* **nationalism,** *n.* nazionalismo, *m.* **nationalist,** *n. & att.* nazionalista, *m.f. & a.*
nationality, *n.* nazionalità, *f.*
nationals, *n.pl.* connazionali, *m.pl.*

native, *a.* nativo, natio; materno;
natale; indigeno; originario, oriundo.
∼ *land,* ∼ *country,* patria, *f.*, paese
natio, *m.* ¶ *n.* nativo, *m.*, -a, *f.*;
indigeno, *m.*, -a, *f.*; (*pl. oysters*)
ostriche del paese, *f.pl.* **nativity,** *n.*
natività, nascita, *f.*; oroscopo, *m.*

natty, *a.* attillato, ben tenuto.

natural, *a.* naturale. ¶ *n.* idiota, *m.f.*;
(*Mus.*) bequadro, *m.* ∼ *history museum,* museo di storia naturale, *m.*
∼**ist,** *n.* naturalista, *m.f.* ∼**ization,**
n. naturalizzazione, *f.* ∼ *papers,*
lettere di n., *f.pl.* ∼**ize,** *v.t.*
naturalizzare. ∼**ness,** *n.* naturalezza, *f.* **nature,** *n.* natura, *f.*;
naturale, *m.*, indole, *f.*, carattere,
temperamento, *m.* **-natured,** *a.* di
un (buon, cattivo) naturale, temperamento.

naughtiness, *n.* cattiveria, *f.*
naughty, *a.* cattivo; (*indecent*)
sconveniente, grossolano.

nausea, *n.* nausea, *f.* **nauseate,** *v.t.*
nauseare, stomacare. **nauseating,**
a. nauseabondo, stomachevole.
nauseous, *a.* nauseabondo, disgustoso.

nautical, *a.* nautico. ∼ *almanac,*
effemeridi astronomiche, *f.pl.* ∼
mile, miglio marino, m. nautico, *m.*
∼ *science, n.* nautica, *f.*

nautilus, *n.* nautilo, *m.*

naval, *a.* navale; marittimo; di
marina, della marina. ∼ *cadet,*
allievo della scuola navale, *m.*
∼ *dockyard,* arsenale marittimo,
cantiere navale, *m.* ∼ *officer,*
ufficiale di marina, *m.* ∼ *port,*
∼ *base,* ∼ *station,* porto militare.

nave, *n.* (*wheel*) mozzo, *m.*; (*church*)
navata, *f.*

navel, *n.* ombelico, *m.*

navigable, *a.* navigabile. **navigate,**
v.i. navigare; fare rotta (*v.t.*)
navigare in; percorrere; (*steer*)
dirigere. **navigation,** *n.* navigazione, *f.* **navigator,** *n.* navigatore,
m.

navvy, *n.* terrazziere, sterratore, *m.*

navy, *n.* marina [militare], *f.* ∼ *blue,*
blu marino, *m.*

nay, *neg. particle,* no; anzi. ¶ *n.*
diniego, rifiuto, *m.*

Nazareth, *n.* Nazaret, *f.*

Neapolitan, *a.* napoletano. ¶ *n.* napoletano, *m.,* -a, *f.*

neap tide, bassa marea, *f.*

near, *a.* vicino; prossimo; stretto; intimo; breve, corte; gretto, avaro. *the* N~ *East,* il Levante, il vicino Oriente, *m.* ~ *relations,* parenti prossimi, *m.pl.* ~ *relationship,* parentela stretta, *f.* ~ *side,* lato sinistro (della vettura); (*Riding*) lato della briglia, *m.* ~ *sight,* miopia, vista corta, *f.* ~-*sighted* (*person*), miope, *a. & m.f.* ¶ *ad.* presso; accanto, allato, a fianco. ¶ *pr.* presso di, vicino a, accanto (a). ~ *the wind* (*Naut.*), stretto al vento. ¶ *v.i.* avvicinarsi. ~**ly,** *ad.* quasi; circa, a un dipresso, press'a poco. *he* ~ *fell,* poco mancò che non cadesse. *I* ~ *missed the train,* ho fallito mancare il treno. ~**ness,** *n.* prossimità, *f.*

neat, *a.* netto, pulito, lindo; ben tenuto; pretto; puro; destro. ~ [*cattle*], grosso bestiame, *m.* ~ *herd,* bovaro, vaccaro, *m.* ~'*s foot,* piede di bue, *m.* ~'*s foot oil,* olio di piede di bue, *m.* ~'*s leather,* pelle di vacca, *f.* ~**ness,** *n.* nettezza, pulizia, eleganza, *f.*

nebula (*Astr.*), *n.* nebulosa, *f.* **nebulous,** *a.* nebuloso.

necessarily, *ad.* necessariamente, di (tutta) necessità. **necessary,** *a.* necessario. *if* ~, se è n., se bisogna. ¶ *n. &* **necessaries,** *n.pl.* necessario, *m.,* cose necessarie, *f.pl.*; necessità, *f. & f.pl.* **necessitate,** *v.t.* rendere necessario; costringere. **necessitous,** *a.* bisognoso, indigente. *in* ~ *circumstances,* nel bisogno. **necessity,** *n.* necessità, *f.*

neck, *n.* collo, *m.*; (*land*) braccio, istmo, *m.*; lingua, *f.*; (*violin*) manico, *m.*; (*Racing*) incollatura, *f.* ~ *band,* colletto (di camicia), *m.* ~*lace,* collana, *f.* ~ *measurement,* ~ *size,* giro del collo, *m.* ~*tie,* cravatta, *f. to win by a* ~, vincere (guadagnare) per un'incollatura. **neckerchief,** *n.* fazzoletto (da collo), *m.* ~**let,** *n.* collanetta, *f.*

necrology, *n.* (*notice*) necrologia, *f.*; (*roll, book*) necrologio, registro dei morti, *m.* **necromancer,** *n.* negromante, *m.f.* **necromancy,** *n.* negromanzia, *f.* **necropolis,** *n.* necropoli, *f.* **necrosis,** *n.* necrosi, *f.*

nectar, *n.* nettare, *m.* ~**ine,** *n.* pesca noce, *f.* ~**y,** *n.* (*Bot.*) nettario, *m.*

need, *n.* bisogno, *m.*; necessità; indigenza, miseria, povertà, *f.* ¶ *v.t. & t.* avere bisogno (di), mancare (di); volere; dovere, essere obbligato (a); (*impers.*) bisognare, abbisognare, occorrere. *at* ~, *if* ~ *be,* al bisogno. *I* ~, mi occorre, mi abbisogna, ho bisogno di. *How much do you* ~? Quanto Le occorre? ~ *you ask?* bisogna domandarlo? *You* ~ *not laugh,* non c'è di che ridere. **needful,** *a. & n.* necessario, *a. & m.*

needle, *n.* ago, *m.* ~ *case,* astuccio per aghi; agoraio, *m.* ~-*made lace,* merletti all'ago, *m.pl.* ~ *maker,* fabbricante di aghi, *m.* ~*woman,* cucitrice, *f.*, lingerista, *f.* ~*work,* lavoro d'ago, cucito, *m. art* ~*work,* lavori d'ago fino, *m.pl. knitting* ~, ago da calza, *m. gramophone* ~, puntina per gramofono, *f.* ~**ful,** *n.* gugliata, *f.*

needless, *a.* inutile, superfluo. **needs,** *ad.* necessariamente. **needy,** *a.* indigente, bisognoso.

ne'er (*Poet.*), *ad.* mai, giammai, non . . . mai. ~-*do-well,* -*weel,* a. buono a nulla. *a* ~-*do-well, -weel,* un buono a nulla, un fannullone, un perdigiorno, *m.*

nefarious, *a.* nefario, ribaldo, scellerato.

negation, *n.* negazione, *f.* **negative,** *a.* negativo. ¶ *n.* negativa, *f.* ¶ *v.t.* rigettare, dare il veto a; annullare.

neglect, *v.t.* negligere, dimenticare, trascurare; abbandonare. **neglect** *&* **negligence,** *n.* negligenza, trascuranza, *f.*; oblio, abbandono, *m.* **neglectful** *&* **negligent,** *a.* negligente, trascurato, disattento. **negligible,** *a.* negligibile, trascurabile.

negotiable, *a.* negoziabile. ~ *instrument,* titolo negoziabile, *m.* **negotiate,** *v.t. & i.* negoziare; trattare; contrattare; trafficare. **negotiation,** *n.* negoziato, *m.,* trattativa; *f.* (*gen. pl.*); (*Com.*) negoziazione, *f. by* ~, amichevolmente. **negotiator, -tress,** *or* -**trix,** *n.* negoziatore, *m.,* -trice, *f*

negress, *n.* negra, *f.* **negro,** *n.* negro, *m.* ¶ *a.* negro, nero.

neigh, *v.i.* nitrire. ~[**ing**], *n.* nitrito, *m.*

neighbour, *n.* vicino, *m.,* -a, *f.,* prossimo, *m.,* -a *f.* ~**hood,** *n.* vicinanza, *f.,* vicinato, *m.*; dintorni,

m.pl., pressi, *m.pl.*; quartiere, *m.*
~ing, *a.* vicino, prossimo; adiacente; (*country*) limitrofo. *in a* ~*ly*
way, da buon vicino.
neither, *pn. & a.*, né l'uno (l'una) né
l'altro (l'altra). ¶ *c.* né; non;
neanche, nemmeno; non piú. ¶ *ad.*
non piú, neanche, nemmeno.
Nemesis, *n.* Nemesi, *f.*
nemine contradicente (abb. *nem.*
con.), all'unanimità.
neologism, *n.* neologismo, *m.*
neon, *n.* neon, *m.* ~ *light*, luce di ~;
(*lamp*) lampada al n., *f.*
neophyte, *n.* neofito, *m.*, -a, *f.*
nephew, *n.* nipote, *m.*
ne plus ultra, nec plus ultra.
nepotism, *n.* nepotismo, *m.*
Nereid, *n.* nereide, *f.*
nerve, *n.* nervo, *m.*; (*Bot.*) nervatura,
f.; (*fig.*) coraggio, sangue freddo, *m.*
~ *specialist*, neurologo, *m.* ~less,
a. snervato, sfibrato; debole.
nervous, *a.* timido, eccitabile;
nervoso; energico. ~ *breakdown*,
prostrazione nervosa, *f.* ~ness, *n.*
apprensione, timidità, *f.*
nest, *n.* nido, *m.*; (*tubes, &c.*) fascio,
m.; (*fig.*) riparo, covo, covile,
ricettacolo, *m.* ~ *egg*, nidiandolo,
endice, guardanido, *m.*; (*savings*)
denaro messo da parte come riserva,
m. ~ *of drawers*, cassette, *f.pl.*
~ *of pigeon-holes*, casellario, *m.*
¶ *v.i.* nidificare; annidarsi. ~[ful],
n. nidiata, *f.* nestle, *v.i.* annidarsi.
~ *close to*, stringersi a. nestling,
n. nidiace, *m.*
net, *n.* rete; reticella, *f.*; (*material*)
tulle, *m.*, (*fig.*) rete, trappola, *f.*,
laccio, *m.* *drag*~, tramaglio, *m.*
sweep-~, giacchio, *m.* ~ *bag*, rete
per la spesa, *f.* ~*maker*, fabbricante
di reti, *m.* ~ *sinker*, ~ *weight* (*Fish.*),
piombo, *m.* ~work, reticolato, *m.*;
rete; reticella, *f.* ¶ (*Com.*) *a.* netto.
¶ (*catch*) *v.t.* prendere con la rete.
nether, *a.* inferiore, basso. ~
millstone (*fig.*), fondo; cuor di sasso,
m. ~ *regions*, inferno, *m.* Nether-
lander, *n.* neerlandese, *m.f.*
Netherlandish, *a.* neerlandese.
the Netherlands, i Paesi Bassi,
m.pl. nethermost, *a.* il piú basso.
netting, *n.* rete, *f.*; lavoro in maglia,
m.; (*wire*) reticolato *m.*, rete
metallica, *f.*
nettle, *n.* ortica, *f.* ~ *rash*, orticaria,
f. ¶ *v.t.* pungere, irritare,
esasperare.
neuralgia, *n.* nevralgia, *f.* neuralgic,

a. nevralgico. neurasthenia, *n.*
neurastenia, *f.* neuritis, *n.* neurite,
f. neurologist, *n.* neurologo, *m.*
neurosis, *n.* neurosi, *f.* neurotic,
a. neurotico.
neuter, *a. & n.* neutro, *a. & m.*,
genere neutro, *m.* neutral, *a. & n.*,
neutrale, *a. & m.*; (*Chem., Elec.*) *a.*
neutro. ~ity, *n.* neutralità, *f.* ~ize,
v.t. neutralizzare.
never, *ad.* mai, giammai, non . . . mai.
~ *again*, mai piú. ~*-ending*,
infinito, senza fine. nevertheless,
ad. & c. nondimeno; ciò nonostante,
tuttavia, ad ogni modo, pure,
pertanto.
new, *a.* nuovo; fresco; recente;
novello, tenero. *brand* ~, nuovo di
zecca. ~*-born* (*child*), neonato, *m.*,
-nata, *f.* ~*comer*, nuovo venuto, *m.*,
nuova venuta, *f.* Newfoundland
[*dog*], cane di Terranuova, *m.*
~ *growth* (*Forestry*), rimessa, *f.*
~ *guard* (*Mil.*), guardia montante, *f.*
~*-laid* (*eggs*), fresco. ~ *lease of*
life, vita nuova, *f.*, ritorno di forze,
m. ~ *member* (*of a society*), nuovo
ammesso, *m.*, ~a, *f.* ~
par[*agraph*], alinea, *m.* N~
Testament, Nuovo Testamento, *m.*
the ~ *woman*, la donna moderna.
~ *year card*, cartolina d'auguri di
capo d'anno, *f.* ~ *year's day*, capo
d'anno, *m.* ~ *year's eve*, vigilia del
capo d'anno, *f.*, San Silvestro, *m.*
~ *year's gift*, strenna, *f.* ~ *year's*
wishes, auguri di buon anno, a. di
capo d'anno, *m.pl.*
New (*Geog.*), *a.* ~ *Brunswick*, il
Nuovo Brunswick. ~*foundland*,
Terranuova, *f.* ~ *Guinea*, la
Nuova Guinea. ~ *Orleans*, Nuova
Orleans, *f.* ~ *South Wales*, la
Nuova Galles del Sud. ~ *York*,
Nuova York, *f.* ~ *Zealand*, la
Nuova Zelanda; (*att.*) della N~ Z~.
~ *Zealander*, Nuova-zelandese, *m.f.*
newel, *n.* nocciolo; pilastrino, *m.*
newly, *ad.* novellamente, frescamente,
di fresco; recentemente, ultimamente. newness, *n.* novità, *f.*
news, *n.* notizia, *f.*, *oft. pl.* notizie;
nuova, novella, *f.*; informazioni,
f.pl.; (*Cinema*) attualità, *f.pl. what's*
the ~? che c'è di nuovo? ~ *agency*,
agenzia d'informazioni, *f.* ~ *agent*,
venditore di giornali, *m.* ~*boy*,
giornalaio, strillone, *m.* ~ [*bulletin*]
(*Radio*), giornale radio, *m.*, informazioni, *f.pl.* ~ *film*, film di attualità,
m. ~ *items* (*in paper*), fatti diversi,

echi di cronaca, *m.pl.*   ~*monger,* cronista, gazzettista, *m.*   ~*paper,* giornale, foglio, *m.*, gazzetta, *f.* ~*paper rate,* tariffa postale per le stampe, *f.* ~*print,* carta da giornali, *f.*   ~ *room,* sala di lettura, *f.*, gabinetto di l., *m.*   *stop-press* ~, ultime notizie, **n.** dell'ultimo momento, *f.pl.*

newt, *n.* tritone, *m.*, salamandra acquaiola, *f.*

next, *a.* prossimo, venturo; vicino, contiguo, adiacente; seguente, successivo; primo; *(world)* altro. *the* ~ *day,* l'indomani, il giorno seguente. *the* ~ *day but one,* due giorni dopo. ~ *door to,* accanto a, vicino a, nella casa accanto, (a) porta a porta. ¶ *ad.* dopo, in secondo luogo, in seguito, poi, appresso.   ~ *the skin,* sulla pelle.   ~ *to,* vicino a, accanto a; quasi, press'a poco. ¶ ~ *of kin,* piú prossimo parente, *m.*, i parenti piú prossimi, *m.pl.*

nib, *n.* pennino, *m.*; punta, *f.*

nibble (*Fish.*), *n.* piccolo morso, *m.* ¶ *v.t.* & *i.* rosicare, rosicchiare, morsicare; *(grass)* brucare; *(fish)* abboccare; mordere.

nice, *a.* buono, amabile, attraente; gentile, simpatico; gradevole; delicato, grazioso; bello, carino, piacevole; esigente, difficile; esatto, puntiglioso, preciso.   ~*ly,* *ad.* molto bene, gradevolmente; esattamente, acconciatamente,

Nicene Creed (the), il credo di Nicea, il simbolo di N., *m.*

nicety, *n.* precisione, esattezza, *f.*; *(pl.)* delicatezze; sfumature, *f.pl.* *to a* ~, di punto, alla perfezione. *to fit to a* ~, andare a capello.

niche, *n.* nicchia, *f.*

nick, *n.* tacca, intaccatura, *f.* *in the* ~ *of time,* nel momento giusto, all'istante preciso. *Old N*~, il diavolo. ¶ *v.t.* intaccare, fare una tacca a.

nickel, *n.* nichel, *m.* ¶ *v.t.* nichelare. ~ *plated,* nichelato.

nick-nack, *n.* ninnolo, gingillo, *m.*, bazzecola, *f.*

nickname, *n.* soprannome, nomignolo, *m.* ¶ *v.t.* soprannominare, chiamare col nomignolo.

nicotine, *n.* nicotina, *f.*

niece, *n.* nipote, *f.*

niello, *n.* niello, *m.*

niggard, *n.* spilorcio, avaro, *m.* ~*ly,* *a.* gretto, avaro, spilorcio, taccagno.

nigger, *n.* negro, *m.*, -a, *f.*   ~ *boy, girl,* negretto; -etta, *m.f.*

nigh, *a.* vicino, prossimo; pronto. ¶ *ad.* presso, dappresso, in prossimità; quasi.

night, *n.* notte; sera, *f.* *at* ~, la notte, durante la notte; *(hour)* della notte. *by* ~, di notte. *the* ~ *before last,* l'altra notte, avant'ieri notte. ~*cap,* berretto da notte, *m.*; *(fig.)* bevanda calda presa al momento di coricarsi. ~*club,* ritrovo notturno, *m.* ~ *commode,* seggetta, *f.* ~*dress,* ~*gown,* camicia da notte, *f.* ~ *fall* crepuscolo, tramonto, *m.*, sera, *f.*, fare di notte, *m.* *at* ~*fall,* sul cader(e) della notte, sull'imbrunire. ~ *lamp* & ~*light,* lampadina da notte, *f.*, lumino da notte, *m.* ~ *man,* v[u]otacessi, *m.inv.* ~*mare,* incubo, *m.* ~ *nurse,* infermiera di notte, *f.* ~ *nursing,* veglia notturna, *f.* ~*shade,* morella, *f.* ~*shirt,* camicia da notte, *f.* ~*'s lodging,* alloggio per la notte, *m.* ~ *soil,* immondizie, *f.pl.*

nightingale, *n.* usign[u]olo, *m.*

nightly, *a.* di notte, notturno; di sera, serale. ¶ *ad.* ogni notte, tutte le notti.

nihilist, *n.* nichilista, *m.f.*

nil, *n.* nulla, niente, *m.*

Nile (the), il Nilo, *m.*

nimble, *a.* agile, svelto, lesto, leggero, sciolto.   ~*ness,* *n.* sveltezza, agilità, *f.*

nimbus, *n.* nimbo, *m.*, aureola, *f.*; *(Meteor.)* nemb·, *m.*

nincompoop, *n.* baggeo, semplicione, *m.*

nine, *a.* & *n.* nove, *a.* & *m.* *9-hole course* (golf), percorso (golf) di 9 buche, *m.* ~*pins,* birilli, *m.pl.* ~ *times out of ten,* nove volte su dieci.

nineteen, *a.* & *n.* diciannove, *a.* & *m.* **nineteenth,** *a.* & *n.* diciannovesimo, decimo nono, *a.* & *m.*, diciannove, *m.* **ninetieth,** *a.* & *n.* novantesimo, *a.* & *m.* **ninety,** *a.* & *n.* novanta, *a.* & *m.* 91, 92, &c., novantuno, novantadue, &c.

Nineveh, *n.* Ninive, *f.*

ninny, *n.* scioccherello, semplicione, *m.*

ninth, *a.* & *n.* nono, *a.* & *m.*; nove, *m.* ~*ly,* *ad.* in (al) nono luogo.

nip, *n.* *(pinch)* pizzicotto; *(liquor)* bicchierino, *m.* ¶ *v.t.* pizzicare; morsicare; bruciare; piccare.

nipper, *n.* *(boy)* ragazzino, *m.*; *(of crustacean, &c.)* pinza, *f.*; *(pl.)* tanaglie; pinzette, *f.pl.*

nipple, *n.* capezzolo, *m.*, poppa, *f.*; (*feeding bottle*) poppatoio, *m.*

nit, *n.* lendine, *m.*

nitrate, *n.* nitrato, azotato, *m.* **nitre,** *n.* nitro, *m.* **nitric,** *a.* nitrico, azotico. **nitrogen,** *n.* azoto, *m.* **nitroglycerin[e],** *n.* nitro-glicerina, *f.* **nitrous,** *a.* nitroso.

no, *ad.* no; non; punto, mica, niente. ¶ *n.* no; voto contrario, *m.*; (*fig.*) palla nera, *f.* ¶ *a.* nessuno, niuno; non . . . alcuno veruno; non; niente. ~ *admittance* [*except on business*], è proibito l'ingresso, è vietato l'i., divieto d'entrata (senza autorizzazione). ~ *case to answer* (*Law*), non luogo (a procedere). ~ *entry* [*one way street*], divieto di transito (senso unico). ~ *flowers, by request,* si dispensa dal mandare fiori, né fiori, né corone. ~ *hands wanted,* non si accettano richiesti di lavoro. ~ *occupation,* senza occupazione fissa, s. professione. ~ *parking,* divieto di sosta. ~ *performance,* (oggi) riposo. ~ *reply* (*Teleph.*), non risponde. ~ *smoking,* vietato fumare. ~ *thoroughfare,* divieto di transito. ~ *value* (*in account*), assegno vuoto.

Noah's ark, arca di Noè, *f.*

nobiliary, *a.* nobiliare. **nobility,** *n.* nobiltà, *f.*, i nobili, *m.pl.*; grandezza, *f.* **noble,** *a.* nobile; grande. ~[*man*], nobile, signore; nobiluomo, gentiluomo, *m.* ~*woman,* nobile, signora nobile; nobildonna, *f.* ~*ness,* *n.* nobiltà; grandezza, magnificenza, *f.*

nobody, *n.* nessuno, *pn.m* a ~, un nulla, uno zero, *m.*

nocturnal, *a. &* **nocturne,** *n.* notturno, *a. & m.*

nocuous, *a.* nocivo.

nod, *n.* cenno, segno (con la testa), *m.*; inclinazione della testa, *f.* ¶ *v.i.* fare cenno; inclinare la testa; dondolare, tentennare; assopirsi.

node, *n.* nodo, *m.* **nodule,** *n.* nodulo, *m.*

noggin, *n.* bicchierino, *m.*; (*Meas.*) ½ pint.

noise, *n.* rumore; baccano; chiasso; fracasso, frastuono, strepito, *m.*; (*in ears*) ronzio; (*fig.*) rumore, *m.*, fama, voce, *f.* ~ *abroad,* *v.t.* divulgare; strombazzare. ~*less,* *a.* senza rumore, silenzioso.

noisome, *a.* nocivo, malsano.

noisy, *a.* rumoroso, strepitoso, chiassoso; (*colour*) forte, vivo.

nolens volens, volente o nolente.

nomad, *n. &* ~(*ic*), *a.* nomade, *m. & a.*

nomenclature, *n.* nomenclatura, *f.*

nominal, *a.* nominale; (*of* [*the*] *names, as a list*) nominativo.

nominate, *v.t.* nominare, designare; proporre come candidato. **nomination,** *n.* nominazione, designazione, (*appointment*) nomina, *f.* **nominative** [*case*], (caso) nominativo, *m.* **nominee,** *n.* persona nominata, *f.* *in a* ~*'s name,* a nome di.

non, *prefix:* ~-*alcoholic drinks,* bevande non-alcooliche, *f.pl.* ~*combatant,* *n. & att.,* non-combattente; civile, *m. & a.* ~-*commissioned officer,* sottufficiale, *m.* ~*committal,* che rifiuta d'impegnarsi. *to be* ~, non dir né sì né no, restare neutro. ~-*copying ribbon* (*typewriter*), nastro fisso, *m.* ~-*effective* (*Mil.*), inabile al servizio. ~-*existence,* inesistenza, *f.*; (*Philos.*) non essere, *m.* ~-*existent,* inesistente. ~-*interference,* ~-*intervention,* non-intervento, *m.* ~-*payment,* mancato pagamento, *m.* ~-*performance,* mancata esecuzione, *f.*; inadempimento, *m.* ~-*skid,* *a.* antisdrucciolevole. ~-*stop,* *a.* continuo, senza tregua; (*Aviat.*) senza scalo. (*train*) diretto, senza fermata. ~-*vintage wine,* vino senza data, *m.*

nonage, *n.* minorità, età minore, *f.*

nonagenarian, *a. & n.* nonagenario, *a. & m.*

nonce, *n.* circostanza, *f.*; (*att.*) di circostanza. *for the* ~, per questa volta.

nonchalance, *n.* noncuranza, svogliatezza, *f.* **nonchalant,** *a.* non-curante, svogliato, indifferente. ~*ly,* *ad.* svogliatamente.

nonconformist, *n. & att.* non-conformista, *m.f. & att.*

nondescript, *a.* indefinibile.

none, *a. & pn.* nessuno, niuno, veruno; niente.

nonentity, *n.* (*Phil.*) non essere, *m.*; inesistenza, *f.*; (*pers.*) nullità, persona da nulla, *f.*, (uno) zero, *m.*

nonplus, *n.* imbarazzo, *m.* ¶ *v.t.* imbarazzare, sconcertare.

nonsense, *n.* controsenso, nonsenso, *m.*; sciocchezza, assurdità, *f.*; bagattelle, frottole, *f.pl.* *all* ~, un nonsenso. ¶ *i.* macchè! non dica sciocchezza! che bestialità!

nonsuit, *v.t.* condannare per desistenza da un'azione, mettere fuori ruolo.

noodle, *n.* baggeo, semplicione, scimunito, *m.*

nook, *n.* angolo, canto, cantuccio; ritiro, ripostiglio, *m.*

noon *&* **noonday** *&* **noontide,** *n.* mezzogiorno, mezzodì, *m.*

noose, *n.* laccio, nodo scorsoio, cappio, *m.*

nor, *c.* né, neanche, neppure, nemmeno, e non.

Nordic, *a.* nordico.

norm, *n.* norma, *f.*; modello, tipo, *m.* **normal,** *a.* normale.

Norman, *a.* normanno. ¶ *n.* normanno, *m.*, -a, *f.* **Normandy,** *n.* la Normandia, *f.*

Norse, *a.* *&* *n.* *&* **~man,** *n.* norvegese, *a.* *&* *m.* *Old Norse* (*language*), scandinavo antico, *m.*, lingua scandinava antica, *f.*

north, *n.* nord, settentrione, *m.* ¶ *ad.* a nord, verso il n., a settentrione, verso s. ¶ *a.* del nord, settentrionale. *N~ Africa,* Africa del Nord, A~ s~. *N~ America,* A~ del Nord, A~ s~. *N~ Britain,* Scozia, *f.* *~-east,* *n.* nordest, *m.* *~ easter* (*wind*), grecale, *m.* *N~ Pole,* Polo Nord, *m.* *N~ Sea,* Mare del Nord, *m.* *N~ Wales,* Galles del Nord, *m.* *~-west,* *n.* nord-ovest, *m.* *~-wester* (*wind*), *n.* maestrale; vento di nord-ovest, *m.* **northerly,** *a.* del nord, settentrionale. **northern,** *a.* nord, settentrionale, situato a nord; boreale. *~ lights,* aurora boreale, *f.* **northerner,** *n.* nordico, abitante del nord, *m.* **northward[s],** *ad.* a nord, verso il nord, verso nord.

Norway, *n.* la Norvegia, *f.* **Norwegian,** *a.* norvegese. ¶ *n.* (*pers.*) norvegese, *m.f.*; (*language*) norvegese, *m.*, la lingua norvegese, *f.*

nose, *n.* naso (*beast*) muso; (*tool*) becco; (*scent*) fiuto, odorato, *m.* *to blow one's ~,* soffiarsi il naso. *to turn up one's ~,* arricciare il naso, fare boccuccia. *~-bag,* sacchetto mangiatoia, *m.* *~-band,* museruola, *f.* *~-dive* (*Aero.*), *n.* picchiata, *f;* *v.i.* scendere in picchiata. *~gay,* *n.* mazzetto (*or* mazzolino) di fiori, *m.* *~* [*out*], *v.t.* fiutare. *~ about.* mettere il naso negli affari altrui.

nostalgia, *n.* nostalgia, *f.* **nostalgic,** *a.* nostalgico. **nostril,** *n.* nàrice (*horse*) frogia, *f.*

nostrum, *n.* rimedio segreto, r. ciarlatanesco, *m.*; panacea, *f.*

not, **n't,** *ad.* non, mica, niente, punto, per nulla, di no. *~ at all,* niente affatto. (*to be*) *~ at home,* non essere a (in) casa. *~ competing* [*for prize*], fuori (di) concorso. *~ exceeding,* che non eccede, che non sorpassa. *~ guilty,* non colpevole, innocente. *to find ~ guilty,* dichiarare innocente. *~ negotiable* (*cheque*), non negoziabile. *~ to be confused with,* da non confondersi con. *~ to be taken* (*Med.*), per uso esterno. *~ transferable,* non trasferibile, non cedibile.

nota bene (*abb.* N.B.), nota bene.

notability, *n.* notabilità, *f.* **notable,** *a.* notevole, notabile, segnalato; distinto; considerevole.

notarial charges (*on bill*), spese notarili, *f.pl.* **notary,** *n.* notaio, *m.*

notation, *n.* notazione; numerazione, *f.*

notch, *n.* tacca, intaccatura, incisione, *f.* ¶ *v.t.* intaccare.

note, *n.* nota, annotazione, *f.*; appunto; scontrino, *m.*; polizza; marca, *f.*, segno, contrassegno; biglietto, *m.*, letterina, *f.*; conto, *m.*, fattura, *f.*; lista, *f.*, listino, *m.*; riguardo, *m.*, reputazione, importanza, *f.*; punto, *m.*; (*Mus.*) nota, *f.*; (*please observe*) nota (bene). (*pers.*) *of ~,* di riguardo, distinto, notevole. *~book,* taccuino, quaderno (di note), *m.* *~case,* portafoglio, *m.* *~ of hand,* pagherò (cambiario), *m.* *~paper,* carta da lettera, *f.* *~worthy,* *a.* degno di nota, notevole. ¶ *v.t.* notare; osservare; rilevare; prendere una nota di; rimarcare; registrare. **noted,** *p.p.* noto, [ben] conosciuto, insigne.

nothing, *n.* nulla, niente; zero, *m.*; nessuna cosa, *f.* *~ at all,* niente affatto; nulla a. *make ~ of,* non capire affatto. *a mere ~,* una cosa da nulla, una bagattella, un'inezia. **~ness,** *n.* nullità, *f.*; oblio; *m.*

notice, *n.* avviso, preavviso, avvertimento, *m.*; notifica, *f.*; annunzio, manifesto, *m.*; notizia, informazione; attenzione, osservazione, *f.*; riguardi, *m.pl.* *at short ~,* all'improvviso, con breve dilazione; (*loan*) a breve scadenza. [*term of*] *~,* termine della disdetta, *m.* *~ board,* cartello, *m.* *~ of meeting,* avviso di riunione, *m.*, convocazione di assemblea, *f.* *previous ~,* preavviso, *m.* *~* [*to quit*], congedo, *m.*; disdetta, *f.* ¶ *v.t.* osservare, accorgersi di; constatare; badare a; fare menzione di; occuparsi di, trattare con riguardi

~able, *a.* notevole, percettibile.
notify, *v.t.* notificare, avvertire, intimare.
notion, *n.* nozione, idea, *f.*, concetto, *m.*
notoriety, *n.* notorietà. *f.* **notorious,** *a.* notorio; malfamato.
notwithstanding, *pr.* nonostante, malgrado; ad onta di, a dispetto di. ¶ *ad.* tuttavia, ciò non ostante.
nought, *n.* nulla; (*Arith.*) zero, *m.*
noun, *n.* nome, sostantivo, *m.*
nourish, *v.t.* nutrire, alimentare; (*fig.*) sostenere; fomentare. **~ing,** *a.* nutriente, nutritivo. **~ment,** *n.* nutrimento, *m.*
nous, *n.* intelletto, spirito, *m.*, mente, *f.*
Nova Scotia, la Nuova Scozia, *f.*
Nova Zembla, la Nuova Zembla, *f.*
novel, *a.* novello, nuovo, strano. ¶ *n.* romanzo, *m.* *~ with a sex interest,* r. sentimentale, r. d'amore. **~ette,** *n.* novella, *f.* **~ist,** *n.* romanziere, *m.* **~ty,** *n.* novità, *f.*
November, *n.* novembre, *m.*
novice, *n.* novizio, *m.*, -a, *f.*; principiante, *m.f.* **noviciate,** *n.* noviziato; tirocinio, *m.*
now, *ad.* ora, adesso; attualmente, al presente; ancora; (*after past tenses*) allora; dunque. ¶ *c.* ora che. ¶ *n.* presente, tempo p.; tempo attuale; questo momento, *m.* ¶ *i.* oibò! via! macchè! *~ then!* ebbene! *before* ~, *ere* ~, prima d'ora, già, pel passato. *just* ~, *or* ora, all'istante, proprio ora, poco fa. *~ & again,* di tempo in tempo, di quando in quando; qualche volta, alle volte, talvolta. *~ & henceforth,* oramai, ormai, d'ora innanzi. *between* ~ *& then,* di qui a lí. [*every*] ~ *& then,* ogni tanto, di quando in quando. *from* ~ *until to-morrow,* di qui a domani. *from* ~ *onward,* per l'avvenire, d'ora innanzi. **nowadays,** *ad.* oggidí, oggigiorno, al presente, ai nostri giorni.
nowhere, *ad.* in nessun luogo, da nessuna parte. *~ near,* tutt'altro che vicino. **nowise,** *ad.* in nessun modo.
noxious, *a.* nocivo, dannoso, pernicioso.
noyau, *n.* acqua di nocciolo, *f.*, cordiale aromatizzato, *m.*
nozzle, *n.* becco, beccuccio; tubo; ugello, *m.*
Nubia, *n.* la Nubia. **Nubian,** *a.* nubiano. ¶ *n.* nubiano *m.*, -a, *f.*

nubile, *a.* nubile.
nucleus, *n.* nucleo, *m.*
nude, *a. & n.* nudo, *a. & m.*
nudge, *n.* colpo leggero col gomito, *m.*, piccola gomitata, *f.* ¶ *v.t.* spingere leggermente, toccare col gomito (per richiamare l'attenzione).
nudity, *n.* nudità, *f.*
nugatory, *a.* futile, vano, senza effetto.
nugget, *n.* pepita, *f.*
nuisance, *n.* noia, seccatura, *f.*; incomodo, disturbo, fastidio; abuso; supplizio, *m.*; cosa spiacevole; *f.*; (*Law, &c.*) danno, *m.*, molestia, *f.*; (*pers.*) persona noiosa, *f.*, importuna, *f.*, seccatore, *m.*, -trice, *f.*, scocciatore, *m.*, -trice, *f.*
null, *a.* nullo, non valido. *~ & void,* nullo e di nessun effetto. ¶ *n.* nullo, *m.* **nullify,** *v.t.* annullare, rendere nullo. **nullity,** *n.* nullità, *f.*
numb, *a.* intorpidito, torpido, intirizzito. ¶ *v.t.* intorpidire, intirizzire; paralizzare.
number, *n.* numero, *m.*; quantità; cifra, *f.*; (*publication*) fascicolo, *m.*, dispensa, puntata, *f.*; foglio, *m.* *even* ~, numero pari. *odd* ~, numero dispari. **N~s** (*Bible*), i Numeri, *m.pl.* *~ one,* se stesso. *~ plate* (*motor car*), targa di riconoscimento, *f.* ¶ *v.t.* numerare, assegnare un numero a; ammontare a. **~ing,** *n.* numerazione, *f.* **~less,** *a.* innumerevole.
numbness, *n.* intorpidimento, torpore, *m.* (*of fingers*) intirizzimento, *m.*
numeral, *a.* numerale. ¶ *n.* cifra, *f.* **numerary,** *a.* numerario. **numerator,** *n.* (*Arith.*) numeratore, *m.* **numerical,** *a.* numerico. **numerous,** *a.* numeroso.
numismatics, *n.* numismatica, *f.* **numismatist,** *n.* numismatico, *m.*
numskull, *n.* babbeo, minchione, *m.*
nun, *n.* religiosa, monaca, suora, *f.*
nunciature, *n.* nunziatura, *f.* **nuncio,** *n.* nunzio, *m.*
nunnery, *n.* convento, monastero, *m.*
nuptial, *a.* nuziale. **~s,** *n.pl.* nozze, *f.pl.*
Nuremberg, *n.* Norimberga, *f.*
nurse, *n.* nutrice, balia; infermiera, *f.*; (*male*) infermiere, *m.* **~(maid),** bambinaia, *f.* ¶ *v.t.* allattare; allevare; curare; tenere in collo, t. in braccio; (*fig.*) coltivare; accarezzare. **nursery,** *n.* camera dei bambini, *f.*; asilo infantile, *m.*;

(*Hort. & fig.*) semenzaio, vivaio, *m.*
~ *language*, linguaggio infantile, *m.*
~*man*, *n.* giardiniere, *m.* ~ *rhymes*,
rime per l'infanzia, filastrocche, *f.pl.*
~ *tale*, racconto per bambini, *m.*;
nursing, *n.* allattamento, *m.*; cura, *f.*
~ *home*, casa di salute; clinica, *f.*
~ *mother* (*wet nurse*), balia, *f.*
nurs[e]ling, *n.* lattante, *m.f.* (*fig.*)
favorito, beniamino, *m.* **nursy**, *n.*
tata, *f.*
nurture, *n.* allevamento; nutrimento,
m.; cura, educazione, *f.* ¶ *v.t.*
nutrire; allevare; educare.
nut, *n.* noce, nocci[u]ola, *f.*; (*violin*,
&c.) capotasto, *m.*; (*for bolt*)
madrevite, rotella d'arresto, *f.*,
dado, *m.*; (*pl. coal*) carbone in
piccoli pezzi, *m.* ~ *brown*, color
nocci[u]ola; (*hair*) castagno. ~
cracker (*bird*), nucifraga, *f.* ~-
cracker face, faccia tosta, f. di
bronzo, *f.* ~ *crackers*, schiaccianoci,
m.inv. ~ *gall*, noce di galla, *f.*
~-*hatch & ~-pecker*, picchio, *m.*
~ *shell*, guscio di noce, *m.* ~ *tree*,
noce, *m.*
nutmeg, *n.* noce moscata,*f.* ~ [*tree*],
albero di noce moscata, *m.*
nutriment, *n.* nutrimento, *m.* **nutrition**, *n.* nutrizione, *f.* **nutritious
& nutritive**, *a.* nutritivo, nutriente.
nutting, *n.* raccolta delle noci, *f.*;
abbacchiamento delle noci, *m.*
nutty, *a.* che ha un gusto (un odore)
di noci.
nux vomica, noce vomica, *f.*
nuzzle, *v.i. & t.* (*animals*) grufolarsi,
scavare col muso (*swine*, col grugno),
fregare il muso (il grugno) contro;
(*child*) rannicchiarsi, nascondersi nel
seno.
nymph, *n.* ninfa; pastorella, *f.*

O

O, o, *i.* o! oh! ~ *dear!* (*of pain*), ahi!
oaf, *n.* tanghero, zoticone, *m.*
oak [tree], *n.* quercia, *f.* ~ (*wood or
timber*), legno di quercia, *m.* ~
apple, galla, *f. Turkey* ~, cerro, *m.*
¶ *att. &* ~**en**, *a.* di quercia.
oakum, *n.* stoppa, *f.* (da calafato).
oar, *n.* remo, *m.* **oarsman**, *n.*
rematore, vogatore, canottiere, *m.*
oarswoman, *n.* rematrice, *f.*
oasis (*lit. & fig.*), *n.* oasi, *f.*
oast, *n.* torno da luppolo, *m.* ~*house*,
essiccatoio da luppolo, da malto, *m.*

oat, *n.* (*pl.*) avena, (*pop.*, *Poet.*) vena,
f. ~ *cake*, focaccia di avena, *f.*,
pasticcio di avena, *m.* ~*meal*, farina
di avena, *f.*, tritello di avena, *m. to
sow one's wild* ~*s*, darsi ai piaceri
della giovinezza, condurre vita dissi-
pata, correre la cavallina.
oath, *n.* giuramento, *m.*; (*profane*)
bestemmia, imprecazione, *f.*
obbligato, *a.* obbligato. ¶ *n.*
obbligato, *m.*
obdurate, *a.* ostinato, testardo,
caparbio; impenitente (*Eccl.*).
obedience, *n.* ubbidienza, *f.*, sottomissione, *f.* **obedient**, *a.* ubbidiente; rispettoso. ~**ly**, *ad.*
ubbidientemente. **obeisance**, *n.*
riverenza, *f.*, saluto rispettoso, *m.*
obelisk, *n.* obelisco, *m.*; (*Typ.*) croce,
f., asterisco, *m.*
obese, *a.* obeso. **obesity**, *n.* obesità, *f.*
obey, *v.t.* ubbidire a; (*v.i.*) ubbidire.
obfuscate, *v.t.* offuscare.
obituary, *n.* necrologia, *f.*
object, *n.* oggetto; scopo, *m.*, fine, *m.*,
mira, *f.*; (*fright*) orrore, *m.*; (*Gram.*)
complemento (diretto), *m.* ~ *glass*,
lente obbiettiva, *f.* ~ *lesson*,
lezione visuale, *f.*; (*fig.*) illustrazione
pratica, *f.* ¶ *v.i. & t.* fare una
obiezione; sollevare obiezioni;
obiettare, opporsi (a), contestare;
avere da ridire. **objection**, *n.*
obiezione, *f.*; inconveniente, *m.*
~**able**, *a.* ripugnante, spiacevole,
riprensibile. **objective**, *a.* oggettivo, obiettivo. ¶ (*aim*, *Opt.*) *n.*
obiettivo, *m.* ~ [*case*], caso
oggettivo, *m.* *the* ~ (*Phil.*),
l'oggettivo, *m.*
objurgation, *n.* rimprovero, *m.*,
riprensione, sgridata, *f.*
oblation, *n.* oblazione, *f.*
obligate, *v.t.* obbligare. **obligation**,
n. obbligazione, *f.*; obbligo, impegno,
m. **obligatory**, *a.* obbligatorio,
oblige, *v.t.* costringere; obbligare;
favorire, rendere servizio a. **obliging**, *a.* compiacente, gentile. ~**ly**,
ad. in modo compiacente.
oblique, *a.* obliquo. ~**ly**, *ad.*
obliquamente. **obliquity**, *n.* obliquità, *f.*
obliterate, *v.t.* cancellare, far sparire,
obliterare.
oblivion, *n.* oblio, *m.*; (*Pol.*) amnistia, *f.* **oblivious**, *a.* dimentico,
immemore.
oblong, *a.* oblungo, bislungo. ¶ *n.*,
figura oblunga, *f.*; rettangolo, *m.*
obloquy, *n.* ingiuria, censura, maldi-

cenza, *f.* ; disonore, *m.* vergogna, *f.*

obnoxious, *a.* odioso, spiacente, sgradevole ; riprensibile, colpevole; nocivo, pernicioso.

oboe. *n.* oboe, *m.* **oboist**, *n.* oboista, *m.*

obscene, *a.* osceno. **obscenity**, *n.* oscenità, *f.*

obscure, *a.* oscuro; inintelligibile; poco noto, sconosciuto; umile. *v.t.* oscurare; ecclissare; offuscare. **~ly**, *ad.* oscuramente. **obscurity**, *n.* oscurità, *f.*, tenebre, *f. pl.*

obsequies, *n.*, *pl.* esequie, *f. pl.* **obsequious**, *a.* ossequioso, ossequente, sottomesso, servile. **~ness**, *n.* servilità, osservanza servile, *f.*, sottomissione, *f.*

observance, *n.* osservanza, *f.*, compimento riguardo, *m.*; osservazione; (*Theol.*) osservanza, *f.*; (*religious*) pratica, *f.* **observant**, *a.* osservatore, attento. **observation**, *n.* osservazione, *f.* **~post** (*Mil.*) & **observatory**, *n.* osservatorio, posto di osservazione, *m.* **observe**, *v.t.* osservare, scorgere, fare attenzione a; celebrare, praticare; rimarcare. **observer**, *n.* osservatore, *m.*, -trice, *f.*

obsess, *v.t.* ossessionare. *to be ~ed by*, *with*, essere ossessionato da. **~ion**, *n.* ossessione, *f.*

obsolescent, *a.* che cade in disuso. **obsolete**, *a.* caduto in disuso; antiquato.

obstacle, *n.* ostacolo, impedimento, *m.* **~race**, corsa con ostacoli, *f.*

obstetric(al), *a.* ostetrico. **obstetrics**, *n.pl.* ostetricia, ginecologia, *f.*

obstinacy, *n.* ostinatezza, ostinazione, caparbietà, *f.* **obstinate**, *a.* ostinato, testardo, accanito, caparbio; (*Med.*) ribelle. **~ly**, *ad.* ostinatamente.

obstreperous, *a.* strepitoso, chiassoso, turbolento; insofferente di disciplina.

obstruct, *v.t.* ostruire, impedire, impacciare; creare ostacoli a; (*v.i.*) fare ostruzionismo. **~ion**, *n.* ostruzione, *f.*, ostacolo, *m.*; (*fig.*) difficoltà, *f.*

obtain, *v.t.* ottenere, acquistare, conseguire; (*v.i.*) prevalere, essere di moda.

obtrude, *v.t.* imporre, intrudere; (*v.i.*) imporsi, insinuarsi, ficcarsi.

obturator, *n.* otturatore, *m.*

obtuse, *a.* ottuso, (*fig.*) stupido, poco penetrante. **~** *angle*, angolo ottuso, *m.*

obverse (*coin*), *n.* faccia, *f.*, diritto, *m.* **obviate**, *v.t.* ovviare a.

obvious, *a.* ovvio, evidente, chiaro **ocarina**, *n.* ocarina, *f.*

occasion, *n.* occasione; circostanza, *f.*; cagione, *f.*; motivo *m.*; ragione, *f.*; volta, *f.*; ¶ *v.t.* causare, cagionare, recare, far nascere; **~al**, *a.* occasionale, incidentale, saltuario; (*occupation*) d'occasione; di tempo in tempo; (*cause*, *Phil.*) (causa) occasionale, *f.* **~** *expenses*, spese incidentali, spese accessorie, *f.pl.* **~** *table*, (piccolo) tavolino, *m.*, tavolino fantasia, *m.* **~** *verses*, versi di circostanza, *m.pl.* **~** *ally*, *ad.* alle volte, di quando in quando.

occiput, *n.* occipite, *m.*

occult, *a.* occulto. **~ing light**, luce intermittente, *f.*, faro ad ecclissi, *m.* **~ism**, *n.* occultismo, *m.*

occupant, *n.* abitante, *m.f.*; possessore, occupante, *m.f.*; titolare, *m.* **occupation**, *n.* occupazione, *f.*, possesso, *m.*; impiego, *m.*, professione, *f.*, mestiere, *m.* **occupier**, *n.* occupante, possessore, locatario, *m.* **occupy**, *v.t.* occupare, prendere possesso di; avere in possesso; essere l'occupante di; (*Chair*, *Univ.*, *&c.*) tenere.

occur, *v.i.* accadere, succedere; occorrere. **occurrence**, *n.* avvenimento, evento, caso, incidente, *m.*; occorrenza, *f.* *it ~s to me*, mi viene l'idea, mi pare, mi viene in mente. *it did not ~ to me*, non mi venne in mente, non mi è venuta l'idea, non ci ho pensato.

ocean, *n.* oceano, *m.* **~[going]**, *a.* di lungo corso. **~** *greyhound* (*fig.*), transatlantico veloce, *m.* **Oceania**, *n.* l'Oceania, *f.*

ochre, *n.* ocra, *f.*

o'clock, ora, *f.*, ore, *f.pl.*

octagon, *n.* ottagono, *m.* **~al**, *a.* ottagonale. **~al nut**, dado ottagonale, *m.* **octave**, *n.* ottava, *f.* **octavo**, *a.* & *n.* (*abb.* 8vo), ottavo, *m.*, in ottavo, *a.* **October**, *n.* ottobre, *m.* **octodecimo**, *a.* & *n.* in ottodecimo, *a.*, diciottesimo, *m.* **octogenarian**, *a.* & *n.* ottuagenario, *a.* & *m.* **octopus**, *n.* ottopode, polpo, *m.*, piovra, *f.* **octoroon**, *n.* figlio di un meticcio e di una bianca.

ocular, *a.* & *n.* oculare. **oculist**, *n.* oculista, *m.*

odd, *a.* (*number*) impari, dispari; (*queer*) barocco, bizzarro, strambo, strano; casuale; (*pair or set*) spaiato, scompagnato; ~jobs, lavorucci, lavoretti, *m.pl.* ~money, resto, residuo, *m.*, gli spiccioli, *m.pl. at* ~ *times*, a tempo perso, nei momenti di ozio. -ity, *n.* singolarità, *f.*; (*pers.*) originale, eccentrico, *m.*, macchietta, *f.* -ly, *ad.* stranamente, fantasticamente. -ments, *n.pl.* pezzi spaiati, scampoli, articoli spaiati, ritagli di panno, *m.pl.* -ness, *n.* bizzarria, stranezza, *f.* odds, *n.pl.* probabilità, *f.pl.* ; forza superiore, f.; (*turf*) vantaggio, *m.*, quota, *f.*, punti di vantaggio, *m.pl. at* ~, in contesa, in discordia, in lite. *to lay* ~ *of 3 to 1*, fare una scommessa di tre contro uno, scommettere tre contro uno. *the* ~ *are that*, è probabile che. ~ *& ends*, pezzi e bocconi, *m.pl.*; ritagli, *m.pl.*; miscellanea, cianfrusaglia, *f.*

ode, *n.* ode; canzone, *f.*

odious, *a.* odioso. **odium,** *n.* odio, *m.*; colpa, *f.*

odoriferous, *a.* odorifero. **odour,** *n.* odore, *m.*; (*fig.*) considerazione, stima, riputazione, *f.* ~less, *a.* senza odore, inodoro.

Odyssey, (*fig.*) *n.* odissea, *f.*

oesophagus, *n.* esofago, *m.*

oestrus *or* **oestrum,** *n.* estro, *m.*

of, *pr.* di; tra; fra; in; a; da; per.

off, *pr.* da, d'addosso, di su; all'altezza di. 1 ~ 3, 1 ~ 2 (*Golf*) meno 3, m. 2. ~ *colour*, indisposto, malaticcio. ~hand, *a. & ad.* disinvolto, con disinvoltura, senza esitazione, di primo acchito, sull'istante. ~handedness, *n.* maniere disinvolte, *f.pl.* ~print, estratto, *m.* ~season, stagione morta, *f.* ~shore fishing, pesca al largo, *f.* ~side, lato destro, m. ¶ *ad.* lontano, discosto; via, a distanza, di qui; *to be* ~, andarsene, partire; staccarsi; (*dish at restaurant*) essere esaurito; (*Elec. switch*) essere disinserito. ~duty, fuori servizio. ~side (*Foot.*) fuori giuoco. *the match is* ~, il matrimonio è rotto, il matrimonio è andato a monte, è andato all'aria; (*sport*) la partita è sospesa. *to set* ~, *v.t.* mettere in rilievo, (*v.i.*) partire.

offal, *n.* frattaglie, *f.pl.*, avanzo, rifiuto, *m.*

offcut, *n.* (*Bookb.*) piccolo cartone, *m.*; (*Typ.*) ritagli di carta, *m.pl.*

offence, *n.* offesa, colpa, *f.*, delitto, *m.*, reato, *m.*, contravvenzione, infrazione, *f. to take* ~, offendersi (per), sentirsi offeso (per). **offend,** *v.t.*

offendere; ferire, nuocere; (*v.i.*) trasgredire. ~er, *n.* offensore, *m.*, delinquente, colpevole, *m.f.*; reo, *m.* *juvenile* ~, delinquente minorile. *m.f.* **offensive,** *a.* offensivo; sgradevole, spiacevole; aggressivo. ¶ *n.* (*Mil.*) offensiva, *f.*

offer, *n.* offerta; proposta, *f.* ¶ *v.t.*, offrire, presentare, proporre; rivolgere. ~ *up*, offrire, rendere. ~ing, *n.* offerta; oblazione, *f.*; sacrificio, *m.* ~tory, *n.* (*Lit.*) offertorio, *m.*; (*collection*) colletta, questua, *f.*

office, *n.* ufficio, impiego, incarico, posto, *m.*; carica, funzione, commissione, *f.*; studio, gabinetto, *m.*; cassa, *f.*; ministero; servizio divino; potere, *m.* ~-*boy*, piccolo commesso, ragazzo, *m.* ~ *hours*, orario d'ufficio, *m.* *O* ~ *of Works*, Ministero dei Lavori pubblici, *m.* **officer,** *n.* ufficiale; funzionario; agente, *m.* ¶ *v.t.* fornire di ufficiali, di funzionari; comandare. **official,** *a.* ufficiale, d'ufficio. ~ *statement* (to press), comunicato ufficiale, bollettino, *m.* ¶ *n.* funzionario; impiegato, *m.*; (*Sport*, *&c.*) ufficiale, commissario, *m.* -dom *&* -ism, *n.* burocrazia, *f.*, funzionarismo, *m.* **officiate,** *v.i.* (*Eccl.*) ufficiare, officiare; esercitare le funzioni (*as* = di). **officious,** *a.* ufficioso, inframmettente; (*Diplomacy*) ufficioso. ~ *adviser*, consigliere, *m.* ~ *person*, ficcanaso, faccendone, *m.*

offing, *n.* largo, *m.*; mare aperto, *m.*, distanza [dalla terra], *f. in the* ~, al largo.

offscourings, (*fig.*) *n.pl.* feccia, *f.*, rifiuto, *m.*

offset, *n.* compenso, equivalente, *m.*; (*Hort.*) germoglio; rampollo, *m.*; (*Arch.*) risega, *f.*; (*Typ.*) ~ *process*, rotocalcografia, *f.*

offshoot, *n.* germoglio, rampollo, *m.*

offspring, *n.* progenie, prole, *f.*, discendenti, posteri, *m.pl.*, frutto, *m.*

often *&* (*Poet.*) **oft,** *ad.* spesso, sovente, spesse volte, molte volte. *how often*? quante volte?

ogee, *n.* modanatura a S., *f.* **ogive,** *n.* ogiva, *f.*

ogle, *n.* occhiata, *f.*, sguardo amoroso, s. di traverso, *m.* ¶ *v.t.* adocchiare, occhieggiare.

ogre, ogress, *n.* orco, *m.*, orchessa, *f.*

oh, *i.* oh! ah! ahimè! ahi!

oil, *n.* olio; petrolio, *m.*; essenza, *f.* ~*cak*?, panello (di sansa), *m.* ~*can* (*Storag.*), bidone, *m.*, latta da petrolio, *f.*; (*nozzled*) oliatore (a mano), *m.* ~*cloth*, (*table*, &*c.*) tela cerata, *f.*; (*floor*) linoleo, *m.*; ~*colour*, ~*paint*, colore ad olio, *m.* ~ *engine*, motore a petrolio, *m.* ~*field*, giacimento di petrolio, *m.*; giacimento petrolifero, *m.* ~ *fuel*, petrolio combustibile, olio pesante, *m.* ~*heater*, stufa a petrolio, *f.* ~*hole*, buco ingrassatore, *m.* ~*man*, oliandolo, negoziante d'olio, *m.* ~*mill*, ~*press*, frantoio, torchio per olio, *m.* ~*painting*, pittura ad olio, *f.* ~*seed*, seme oleoso, *m.* ~ *shares*, valori di petrolio, *m.pl.* ~ *ship*, nave cisterna, *f.* ~ *shop*, spaccio di olio, magazzino da olio, *m.* ~*skin*, tela cerata, *f.*; (*garment*) impermeabile, *m.* ~*stone*, pietra ad olio, *f.* ~ *stove*, stufa a petrolio, *f.* ~*varnish*, vernice ad olio, *f.* ~*well*, pozzo di petrolio, pozzo petrolifero, *m.*, sorgente di petrolio, *f. castor* ~, olio di ricino, *m. cod-liver* ~, olio di fegato di merluzzo, *m. cooking* ~, olio commestibile, *m.* ¶ *v.t.* ungere; lubrificare; spalmare. -y, *a.* oleoso, untuoso, oleaginoso.

ointment, *n.* unguento, *m.*

old, *a.* vecchio, attempato; antico; antiquato. *how* ~ *is he? he is* 10 *years* ~, che età ha? quanti anni ha? ha dieci anni. *the* ~, (*opp. new*) il vecchio, *m.*; (*people*) i vecchi, *m.pl.* ~ & *young*, grandi e piccoli, vecchi e giovani, *m.pl. of* ~, una volta, già, tempo già fu, anticamente. ~ *age*, vecchiaia, *f.*; (*decay*) vetustà, *f.* ~ *age pension fund*, Cassa Nazionale delle Assicurazioni Sociali, Cassa di assicurazione contro la vecchiaia; *f.* ~ *clothes*, abiti usati, *m.pl.* ~ *established*, vecchio, fondato da lungo tempo; di lunga mano; fisso. ~ *fashioned*, alla vecchia moda, all'antica, di foggia antica; (*man*) passata, antiquato, passato di moda. ~ *fellow*, ~ *boy*, ~ *chap* (*as form of address*), caro mio. ~ *gold*, oro vecchio, *m.* ~ *guard* (*Mil.*), vecchia guardia, *f.* ~ *iron*, rottami di ferro, *m.pl.* ~ *maid*; vecchia zitella, *f.* ~ *man*, vecchio; (*in comedy*) pantalone, *m.* ~ *master* (*Art.*), antico maestro, *m.* ~ *offender*, recidivo, *m.* ~ *paper*(s), *waste paper*, cartaccia, *f.* ~ *salt* (*sailor*), lupo di mare, *m. the same* ~ *story*, la stessa storia, la solita canzone, *f.* O ~ *Testament*, Antico Testamento, *m.* ~ *things*, anticaglia,

f., vecchiume, *m. the good* ~ *times*, il buon tempo antico, il tempo che Berta filava, *m.*, l'età d'oro, *f.* ~ *woman*, vecchia, *f. in the* ~*en time*, ai tempi antichi, anticamente. -ish, *a.* vecchiotto, piuttosto vecchio.

oleaginous, *a.* oleaginoso.

oleander, *n.* oleandro, *m.*

olfactory, *a.* olfattivo.

oligarchy, *n.* oligarchia, *f.*

olive, *n.* oliva & uliva, *f.* ~[*tree*, *wood*], olivo, *m.* legno d'olivo, *m.* ~ (*complexion*, &*c.*), olivastro. ~[-*green*], verde oliva. ~ *grove*, oliveto, *m.* ~ *oil*, olio d'oliva, *m.*

Olympic games, giuochi olimpici, *m.pl.* Le Olimpiadi, *f.pl.* **Olympus**, (*fig.*) *n.* olimpo, *m.*

omega, *n.* omega, *f.*

omelet[te], *n.* frittata, *f.*

omen, *n.* presagio, augurio, *m.* **ominous**, *a.* sinistro, di cattivo augurio, infausto.

omission, *n.* omissione; lacuna, *f.* **omit**, *v.t.* omettere; trascurare, tralasciare.

omnibus, *n.* omnibus, *m. inv.*

omnipotence, *n.* onnipotenza, *f.* **omnipotent**, *a.* onnipotente. *the Omnipotent*, l'Onnipotente, l'Essere Supremo, *m.* **omniscience**, *n.* onniscienza, *f.* **omniscient**, *a.* onnisciente.

omnivorous, *a.* onnivoro.

on, *pr.* su, sopra; a, in; di, da; per; dopo. ~ & *after*, a datare di ...., a partire da ...., ~*deck*, in coperta, ~*hand* (*work*), in preparazione, in corso; (*Typ.*) in corso di stampa, in pressione; (*orders*) in portafoglio; (*cash*) in cassa; disponibile; (*goods uncollected*) in magazzino; [*goods left*] ~ *hand*, *refused*, lasciate per conto. ~ *sale or return*, da vendere o rimandare. ~ *on that*, poi, dopo questo; ci. *to live* ~ *income*, vivere di rendita, di reddito. ¶ *ad.* sopra; indosso; innanzi; via; avanti. *and so* ~, e cosí via, e via discorrendo, e cosí di seguito.

once, *ad.* una volta, già, un tempo. ~ *again*, ~ *more*, ancora una volta. ~ *a year*, una volta all'anno. ~ & *for all*, una volta per sempre, una buona volta. ~ *upon a time*, già, una volta, c'era una volta.

one, *a.* uno; (& *only*) unico; solo. ~ *act play*, atto unico, *m.* ~*armed* & ~*handed* (*person*), monco, *m.*, *a.*, *f.* ~*class liner*, transatlantico a classe unica, *m.* ~*eyed*, che ha un solo occhio, monocolo. ∼-horse (carriage), ad un solo cavallo. ∼-price shop, magazzino a prezzo unico. ∼-sided, unilaterale; (fig.) parziale. ∼-way street, via a senso unico, f. ∼-way traffic, circolazione a senso unico, f. ¶ n. il numero uno at ∼ [o'clock], all'una, al tocco. ¶ pn. uno, una, un tale; qualcuno, -a, un certo, una certa. ∼ & all, tutti quanti, tutti senza eccezione, dal primo all'ultimo. ∼ by ∼, or ∼ after another, uno per uno, uno dopo l'altro. he is ∼ of us, egli è uno di noi, uno dei nostri. -ness, n. unità, f.

onerous, a. oneroso, gravoso.

one's, pn. suo, sua, suoi, sue, il suo, &c.; proprio, propria, propri, proprie. oneself, pn. se stesso, se stessa; si.

onion, n. cipolla, f. ∼ bed, cipollaio, m. ∼ sauce, salsa cipollenta, f. ∼ skin, ∼ peel, buccia di cipolla, f.

onlooker, n. spettatore, m., -trice, f., assistente, m.f.

only, a. solo, unico. ¶ ad. solo, soltanto, solamente, non . . . che.

onomatopoeia, n. onomatopea, -peia, f.

onset, onrush, onslaught, n. assalto, attacco, m., carica, irruzione, f.

onus, n. onere, gravame, peso, m. ∼ of proof, onere della prova, m.

onward, a. progressivo, in progresso, avanzato. -[s], ad. avanti, in avanti, in su. to move ∼, avanzarsi; circolare.

onyx, n. onice, m.

ooze, n. fango, m., fanghiglia, f., limo, m., melma, f. ¶ v.i. percolare, trapelare. ∼ out, essudare.

opacity, n. opacità, f.

opal, n. opale, m. -ine, a. opalino.

opaque, a. opaco. -ness, n. opacità, f.

open, v.t. aprire, schiudere, svelare; iniziare; inaugurare; incominciare; intavolare; (bottle) sturare; (oysters) sgusciare; (Med) sezionare, salassare; (v.i.) aprirsi, schiudersi, avere inizio, esordire; (flowers) sbocciarsi, aprirsi. ∼ out (pers., fig.) sbottonarsi, sfogarsi, aprirsi. ∼ sesame! Sesamo, apriti! ¶ a. aperto, scoperto; accessibile; possibile; manifesto; esposto; chiaro; franco; (climate) mite; (account) corrente; (enemy) dichiarato; (field) libero; (boat) senza ponte, scoperto. in the ∼ [air], all'aria aperta, all'aperto, a cielo scoperto. in the ∼ [country],

in aperta campagna, in piena campagna. in the ∼ (publicly), in pieno giorno, apertamente. ∼-end tie, cravatta da regata, f. ∼-handed, generoso, largo, liberale. ∼-hearted, franco, sincero, dal cuore aperto. ∼ house, casa aperta, tavola aperta, f. ∼ mind, mente aperta, ∼-mouthed, a bocca aperta, con la bocca aperta. in the ∼ sea, in alto mare. ∼ space, spazio libero. ∼ warfare, guerra aperta, guerra dichiarata; guerra manovrata. ∼ [work], att. a giorno, a traforo. ∼work (Need.), (lavoro) a traforo, sfilato, m. -er, n. (pers.) chi apre, apritore, m. -trice, f.; primo (oratore, &c.); (instrument) arnese per aprire, apritrice, f. -ing, n. apertura, f., passaggio, m.; breccia, feritoia, f.; buco, orifizio; esordio, inizio, principio; sbocco, m.; (neck) scollatura, f., scollo, m. ¶ a. nascente, primo, iniziale, inaugurale, d'apertura. (Med.) lassativo. -ness, n. (fig.), franchezza, f.; (climate) mitezza. -ly, ad. apertamente, francamente, pubblicamente.

opera, n. & -house, opera, f. ∼ cloak, mantello da sera (portato dalle signore per il teatro) m. ∼ glass[es], binocolo (da teatro), m. ∼ hat, gibus, m.

operate, v.t. operare, effettuare; (v.i.) agire, funzionare. ∼on (Surg.), operare, eseguire un'operazione (su).

operatic, a. d'opera, lirico.

operating room or theatre, sala operatoria, f., teatro operatorio, m.

operation, n. operazione, azione, f.

operative, n. operaio, m., -aia, f.; lavorante, m.f. ¶ a. operativo, efficace; (surgery) operatorio. operator, n. operatore, m. -trice, f.; sfruttatore; proiettatore; giocatore; borsista, m.

operetta, n. operetta, f.

ophthalmia, n. oftalmia, f. ophthalmic, a. oftalmico.

opiate, n. oppiato, m. narcotico, m. (fig.) soporifero. -d, a. oppiato.

opine, v.i. opinare, ritenere. opinion, n. opinione, f. parere, concetto, avviso, m.; sentenza, f. (legal) consulto, m.; consiglio, m. -ated, a. ostinato alla propria opinione, dommatico.

opium, n. oppio, m. ∼ addict, oppiomane, m. ∼ den, casa per fumatori d'oppio, f. ∼ poppy, papavero sonnifero, m.

Oporto, *n.* Oporto, *f.*

opossum, *n.* opossum, *m.*; sariga, *f.*

opponent, *n.* avversario, opponente, *m.* ¶ *a.* contrario, opposto.

opportune, *a.* opportuno. **-ly,** *ad.* opportunamente, a proposito. **-ness,** *n.* opportunità, *f.* **opportunism,** *n.* opportunismo, *m.* **opportunist,** *n.* opportunista, *m.f.* **opportunity,** *n.* opportunità, occasione, *f.*

oppose, *v.t.* opporre, opporsi a, fare opposizione a; resistere a; contestare, contrariare. **-ed,** *p.p.* opposto, contrapposto; avverso, contrario. **opposing,** *p.a.* opposto, avverso. **opposite,** *n.* opposto, *m.* (il) contrario, *m.*, cosa contraria, *f.* ~ (to), *a.*, *pr.*, *ad.* di fronte (a), in faccia (a), dirimpetto (a); (*sex*) l'altro (sesso), *m.* **opposition,** *n.* opposizione, *f.*; contrasto, *m.*; (*Com.*) concorrenza, *f.*

oppress, *v.t.* opprimere. **-ion,** *n.* oppressione, *f.*; abbattimento, *m.* **-ive,** *a.* oppressivo, opprimente; tirannico. **-or,** *n.* oppressore, tiranno, *m.*

opprobrious, *a.* obbrobrioso. **opprobrium** *n.* obbrobrio, *m.*

optic, *a.* ottico. **-al,** *a.* ottico; (*glass, instruments, illusion*) ottico. ~ *lantern,* lanterna di proiezione, lanterna magica, *f.* **optician,** *n.* ottico, *m.* **optics,** *n.* ottica, *f.*

optimism, *n.* ottimismo, *m.* **optimist,** *n,* & **-(ic),** *a.* ottimista, *m.f.* & *a.* ottimistico, *a.*

option, *n.* opzione, *f.*; diritto di scelta, *m.*, scelta, alternativa, facoltà, *f.* (*Stk. Ex.*) opzione, *f.*, contratto a premio, *m.* **-al,** *a.* facoltativo.

opulence, *n.* opulenza, *f.* **opulent,** *a.* opulente.

or, *c.* o, od, oppure; sia; (*neg.*) né. ~ *else,* altrimenti, o bene, oppure; *either* ~, o . . . o, sia . . . sia. 2 *or* 3 *times a day,* 3 o 4 volte al giorno.

oracle, *n.* oracolo, *m.*

oral, *a.* orale. ~ *examination,* esame orale, *m.*

orange, *n.* arancia, *f.*; (*colour*) arancio, color d'arancio, *m.* ¶ *a.* arancio, d'arancio, arancino. ~ (*tree*) arancio, *m.* ~ *blossom,* fiore d'arancio, *m.* ~ *marmalade,* marmellata di arance, *f.* ~ *peel,* scorza d'arancia, *f.* **-ade,** *n.* aranciata, *f.* **-ry,** *n.* aranciera, *f.*; (*grove*) aranceto, *m.*

orang-outang, *n.* orangutan, *m.inv.*

oration, *n.* orazione; arringa, *f.*; discorso, *m.*; (*funeral*) orazione

funebre, *f.* **orator,** *n.* oratore, *m.* **-ical,** *a.* oratorio. **oratorio,** *n.* oratorio, *m.* **oratory,** *n.* eloquenza, (arte) oratoria, *f.*; (*chapel*) oratorio, *m.*

orb, *n.* orbe, globo, *m.*, sfera, *f.* **orbit,** *n.* orbita, *f.*

orc, *n.* orca, *f.*; (*Poet.*) orco, *m.*

orchard, *n.* frutteto, *m.*

orchestra, *n.* orchestra, *f.* ~ *stall,* poltrona, *f.* **orchestral,** *a.* orchestrale, d'orchestra. **orchestrate,** *v.t.* orchestrare.

orchid, *n.* orchidea, *f.* **orchis,** *n.* orchidea, *f.*

ordain, *v.t.* decretare, comandare; ordinare.

ordeal, *n.* prova, *f.*, cimento, *m.*; (*Hist.*) giudizio di Dio, *m.*

order, *n.* ordine, assetto, *m.*; scala, serie, fila, successione, *f.*; metodo, *m.*, regola; classe, specie, *f.*, genere, *m.*; decreto, regolamento, comando, *m.*; ordinazione, commissione; ordinanza, sentenza, *f.*; mandato, vaglia; permesso, biglietto, *m.*; (*Mil.*) ordine, comando, *m.*; (*pl.*, *Mil.*) ordine del giorno, *m.* ~! all'ordine! zitto! in ~ *that,* acciocché, affinché, perché, allo scopo che, al fin che. in ~ *to,* per, a fine di, allo scopo di. ~ *book,* libro delle (di) ordinazioni, *m.* ~ *form,* bollettino d'ordinazione, *m.* ¶ *v.t.* ordinare, mettere in ordine; comandare, dirigere, regolare; (*goods*) ordinare, comandare; farsi fare; (*arms, Mil.*) riposarsi su. *made to order,* fatto su ordinazione. **-ing,** *n.* disposizione, ordinanza, *f.* **-ly,** *a.* ordinato, metodico, regolare; pacifico, tranquillo. ¶ *n.* (*Mil.*) ordinanza, staffetta, *f.*; (*hospital*) inserviente, *m.* *on* ~ *duty,* di servizio, di piantone. ~ *officer,* ufficiale di giornata, *m.* ~ *room,* ufficio di compagnia, *m.*

ordinal [number], *n.* [numero] ordinale, *m.*

ordinance, *n.* ordinanza, *f.*, decreto, regolamento, *m.*; rito, *m.*, cerimonia, *f.*

ordinary, *a.* ordinario, solito, normale; mediocre. ~ (*bicycle*), bicicletta, *f.* ~ *seaman,* marinaio semplice, *m.* ¶ *n.* tavola rotonda, *f.*

ordination, *n.* ordinazione, *f.*

ordnance, *n.* artiglieria, *f.* ~ (*survey*) *map,* carta dello Stato Maggiore, *f.* ~ *surveyor,* *n.* topografo militare, *m.*

ordure, *n.* escremento, *m.*; lordura; oscenità, *f.*

ore, *n.* minerale; metallo grezzo, *m.*

organ, *n.* organo, *m.*; (*Mus.*) organo, *m.* ~ *grinder,* sonatore d'organetto (di Barberia), *m.* ~ *loft,* tribuna dell'organo, *f.* ~ *pipe,* canna d'organo, *f.*

organdie, *n.* battista, *f.*

organic, *a.* organico. **organization,** *n.* organizzazione, *f.*; (*fête,* &c.) ordinamento, *m.* **organize,** *v.t.* organizzare; ordinare. **organizer,** *n.* organizzatore, *m.,* -trice, *f.*

oriel [window], *n.* finestra (gotica) sporgente, *f.*

orient, *n.* oriente, *m.* *the O* ~ (*Geog.*), l'Oriente, *m.* ~**al,** *a.* orientale; ¶ *n.* orientale, *m.f.* ~**[ate],** *v.t.* orientare.

orifice, *n.* orifizio, *m.,* apertura, *f.*

oriflamme, *n.* orifiamma, *f.*

origin, *n.* origine, *f.*; provenienza, *f.* ~**al,** *a.* (*not copied*) originale; (*primitive*) originario. ¶ *n.* originale, *m.* ~**ality,** *n.* originalità, *f.* ~**ate,** *v.t.* originare, far nascere; (*v.i.*) nascere, trarre origine (da), provenire (da). **originator,** *n.* autore, *m.*

Orinoco (the), l'Orinoco, *m.*

oriole (*bird*), *n.* rigogolo, *m.*

Orion, *n.* (*Astr., Myth.*) Orione, *m.*

Orkneys (the), le Orcadi, *f.pl.*

Orleans, *n.* Orleans, *f.*

orlop [deck], *n.* ponte di corridoio, *m.,* falso ponte, *m.*

ormolu, *n.* bronzo dorato, *m.*

ornament, *n.* ornamento, *m.* ¶ *v.t.* ornare, abbellire, decorare. ~**al,** *a.* ornamentale. ~ *border,* vignetta, *f.,* fregio, *m.*; (*Hort.*) bordura di fiori, *f.* ~ *lake,* laghetto, specchio d'acqua, *m.* ~ *trees,* alberi di alto fusto, *m.pl.* **ornamentalist,** *n.* decoratore, *m.* **ornamentation,** *n.* ornamentazione, *f.* **ornate,** *a.* ornato, adorno, decorativo.

ornithologist, *n.* ornitologo, *m.* **ornithology,** *n.* ornitologia, *f.*

orphan, *n.* & *a.* orfano, *a.* & *m.* orfana, *f.* ~**age** (*asylum*) orfanotrofio, *m.*

Orpheus, *n.* Orfeo, *m.*

orrery, *n.* planetario, *m.*

orris root, *n.* radice di giaggiolo, *f.*

orthodox, *a.* ortodosso. ~**y,** *n.* ortodossia, *f.* **orthography,** *n.* ortografia, *f.* (*Arch.*) ortografia, *f.* **orthopaedic,** *a.* ortopedico. **orthopaedy,** *n.* ortopedia, *f.*

ortolan, *n.* ortolano, *m.*

orts, *n.pl.* resti, rifiuti, rilievi, *m.pl.*

oscillate, *v.i.* oscillare; (*v.t.*) fare

oscillare. **oscillation,** *n.* oscillazione, *f.* *oscillating current,* corrente oscillatoria, *f.*

osier, *n.* vimine, vinco, *m.* ~ *bed,* vincheto, *m.*

osmium, *n.* osmio, *m.*

osprey, *n.* ossifraga, *f.,* falco pescatore, *m.*

osseous, *a.* osseo. **ossicle,** *n.* ossicino, *m.* **ossify,** *v.t.* ossificare. **ossuary,** *n.* ossario, *m.*

Ostend, *n.* Ostenda, *f.*

ostensible, *a.* ostensibile, preteso. **ostensibly,** *ad.* ostensibilmente, siccome si pretende. **ostensory,** *n.,* ostensorio, *m.* **ostentation,** *n.* ostentazione, *f.,* fasto, *m.,* vana pompa, *f.* **ostentatious,** *a.* pieno d'ostentazione, fastoso, pomposo.

ostler, *n.* stalliere; mozzo di stalla, *m.*

ostracism, *n.* ostracismo, *m.* **ostracize,** *v.t.* ostracizzare.

ostrich, *n.* struzzo, *m.* ~ *feather,* piuma di struzzo, *f.*

otary, *n.* otaria, *f.*

other, *a.* & *pn.* altro. *every* ~ *day,* ogni due giorni (secondo giorno), un giorno su due, un giorno sì e l'altro no, tutti i due giorni. *the* ~ *side* (opinion, pers.) la parte opposta. *on the* ~ *side* or *hand,* d'altra parte, dall'altra parte, dall'altro canto. ~**s,** ~ *people,* altri, altre persone, altrui, gli altri. *in* ~ *respects,* sotto altri riguardi. ~**wise,** *ad.* altrimenti, in altra maniera, d'altronde.

otter, *n.* lontra, *f.*

Ottoman, *a.* ottomano. ¶ *n.* ottomano, *m.* o ~, *n.* (*sofa*) ottomana, *f.*

otto of roses, essenza di rose, *f.*

oubliette, *n.* trabocchetto, carcere perpetuo, *m.*

ought, *n.* zero, *m.* ¶ *v.aux.i.* dovere, bisognare (*impers.*).

ounce, *n.* (*Zool.*) lonza, pantera dei monti, *f.*; (*Meas.*) oncia, *f.* (*avoirdupois*) = 28.350 grammes; (*troy* & *apothecaries'* weight) = 31.1035 grammes; (*apothecaries' measure*) = 2.84123 centilitres.

our, *a.* nostro, il nostro, &c. *Our Lady,* Nostra Signora, la Madonna, *f.* *Our Lord,* Nostro Signore, *m.* ~**s,** *pn.* il nostro, la nostra, i nostri, le nostre, a noi, di noi. **ourselves,** *pn.* noi stessi, noi stesse; ci.

ousel, *n.* merlo, *m.*

oust, *v.t.* sloggiare, snidare; mettere fuori, scacciare; spossessare, soppiantare.

out, *ad.* & *pr.* fuori, al di fuori; uscito;

assente; spento; estinto; sbocciato; pubblicato; nell'errore; in isciopero; ad oltranza. ~ & *out*, a fondo, completamente; assolutamente; matricolato, arci-. ~ *loud*, ad alta voce. ~ [*see copy*] (*Typ.*) lasciatura, *f*. ~ *there*, laggiú. **out of**, *comps:* ~ *action*, fuori servizio; fuori di combattimento. ~ *bounds*, fuori dei limiti, oltre i limiti; ~ *commission*, (*ship*) in disarmo; (*Mech.*) fuori servizio. ~ *date*, disusato, caduto in disuso, non piú di moda; arretrato; (*ticket*, &*c.*) troppo vecchio, prescritto. ~ *doors*, all'aperto, all'aria aperta. ~ *fashion*, fuori (di) moda, passato di moda, antiquato. ~ *hand*, indisciplinato; subito, incontanente. ~ *one's element*, spostato, pesce fuor d'acqua, fuori del proprio elemento. ~ *one's reckoning*, non torna il conto, sbagliato nel computo. ~ *order*, in cattivo stato, sregolato, che non funziona, guasto, rotto. ~ *place* (*fig.*), mal posto, mal detto, male a proposito; inopportuno. ~ *pocket*, in perdita. ~ *pocket expenses*, sborsamenti, *m.pl.*, spese incidentali, *s.* casuali, *f.pl.* ~ *practice*, fuori esercizio, arrugginito, (*aver*) perduto la pratica. ~ *print*, esaurito; ~ *shape*, sformato. ~ *sight*, lontano dagli occhi, fuori di vista, perduto di vista. ~ *sorts*, indisposto, malaticcio. *to be* ~ *stock of*, essere a corto di, mancare. ~ *the common*. raro, fuori del comune. ~ *of the way*, a. raro, insolito; lontano, remoto. ~ *true*, incurvato, sviato, storto. ~ *tune*, stonato, falso, fuori d'accordo. *to be* ~ *work*, essere disoccupato, licenziato, senza lavoro. *out*, *i.* fuori! via di qui!; (*Box.*) fuori! ~ *with him!* alla porta! mettetelo fuori! ~ *with it!* dite! parlate!

outbid, *v.t.ir.* offrire piú di, fare un'offerta superiore.

outboard, *ad.* fuori bordo. ~ *motor*, motore fuoribordo.

outbreak, *n.* scoppio, *m.*, eruzione, *f.*; (*riot*) sommossa, *f.*, tumulto, *m.*; (*disease*) epidemia, *f.* ~ *of fire*, incendio, *m. at the* ~ *of war*, quando scoppiò la guerra, allo scoppiar della guerra.

outbuilding, *n.* dipendenza, *f.*, [fabbricato] annesso, *m.*

outburst, *n.* esplosione, *f.*, scoppio; accesso, scatenamento, *m.*; tirata, *f.*

outcast, *n.* reietto, espulso, proscritto, vagabondo, *m.*

outcaste, *n.* paria, *m.inv.*

outcome, *n.* risultato, esito, portato, prodotto, *m.*, conseguenza, *f.*

outcrop, (*Geol.*) *n.* affioramento, *m.*

outcry, *n.* grido, *m.*, grida, *f.pl.*, clamore, *m.*

outdistance, *v.t.* sorpassare, lasciar indietro.

outdo, *v.t.ir.* superare, sorpassare.

outdoor, *a.* all'aperto, all'aria aperta, all'aria libera. ~ *relief*, assistenza domiciliare, *f.*

outer, *a.* esterno, esteriore. ~ *cover* (tyre), copertura, *f.* ~ *harbour*, avamporto, *m.*

outfall, *n.* scarico, *m.*; (*mouth*) foce, imboccatura, *f.*

outfit, *n.* corredo; armamento, equipaggiamento, *m.* **outfitter,** *n.* negoziante di corredi, fornitore, *m.*

outflank, *v.t.* aggirare, girare.

outflow, *n.* effiusso; sgorgamento; scaricamento; deflusso, *m.*; corrente, *f.* ~ (*tide*) (marea) calante, *f.*

outgoing, *a.* uscente; antico (*tenant*, &*c.*). ~s, *n.pl.* uscite, spese, *f.pl.*

outgrow, *v.t.ir.* sorpassare in crescita, diventare troppo grande per; (*fig.*) ricredersi.

outhouse, *n.* tettoia; capanna; rimessa, *f.*

outing, *n.* scampagnata, gita, passeggiata, escursione, *f.*, giro, *m.*

outlandish, *a.* strano, bizzarro.

outlast, *v.t.* durare piú di; sopravvivere a.

outlaw, *n.* proscritto, bandito, *m.* ¶ *v.t.* proscrivere, bandire, mettere fuori della legge. ~**ry,** *n.* proscrizione, perdita dei diritti civili, *f.*

outlay, *n.* spesa, *f.*, sborso, *m.* or *pl.* sborsi.

outlet, *n.* sbocco, scarico; sfogo, *m.*; uscita, *f.*; via di scolo, *f.*

outline, *n.* contorno, profilo; sbozzo, schizzo, (*fig.*) grandi linee, *f.pl.*, tracciato, abbozzo, *m.* ~ *drawing*, sagoma, *f.*; disegno lineare, tracciato, *m.* ~ ¶ *v.t.* sbozzare, tracciare le grandi linee di. ~ *map*, carta muta, *f.*

outlive, *v.t.* sopravvivere a.

outlook, *n.* prospettiva, *f.*, prospetto, *m.*, vista, visione, *f.*; avvenire, *m.*

outlying, *a.* distante, lontano; isolato; (*Mil.*) avanzato.

outnumber, *v.t.* superare in numero, sorpassare in numero, essere piú numeroso di.

outmanoeuvre, *v.t.* sventare; manovrare piú abilmente di.

out-patient, *n.* malato esterno, *m.*

outpost, *n.* avamposto, posto avanzato, *m.*

outport, *n.* avamporto, *m.*

outpouring, *n.* effusione, *f.*, spargimento, *m.*

output, *n.* produzione, *f.*

outrage, *n.* oltraggio; attentato, *m.* ¶ *v.t.* oltraggiare, fare oltraggio a; violare. **~ous,** *a.* oltraggioso, violento, atroce, eccessivo, esagerato.

outrider, *n.* battistrada, *m.inv.*

outrigger, *n.* (*boat*), imbarcazione (barchetta) da corsa con scalmiere sporgenti, *f.*; (*for rowlocks*) buttafuori, *m.inv.*

outright, *a.* completo, matricolato. ¶ *ad.* senza ritegno, schietto e retto; sgangheratamente; (*opp. by instalments*), in blocco.

outrival, *v.t.* superare, sorpassare.

outset, *n.* inizio, principio; avviamento, *m.*

outshine, *v.t.ir.* sorpassare in splendore, brillare piú di, ecclissare.

outside, *a.* esterno, esteriore. ~ *broker,* chi opera in titoli senza appartenere all'Associazione (della Borsa). ~ [*cut*], primo pezzo tagliato, *m.* ~ *edge* (*Skating*), curva esterna, *f.* ~ *margins* (book), margini esteriori, *m.pl.* ~ *shutter,* controvento, *m.* ¶ *ad.* fuori, all'esterno, al di fuori. ~ *text* (*plate, map, &c.*), fuori testo. ¶ *n.* esterno, *m.*, parte esterna, *f.* il di fuori, *m.*; superficie; (*bus*) imperiale, *f.*; (*café*) terrazza, *f.* *at the ~,* al piú, tutt'al piú; al massimo. **outsider,** *n.* (*pers.*) estraneo, *m.*; (*horse*) cavallo non classificato, *m.*

outsize, *n.* taglio fuori misura, *m.*

outskirts, *n.pl.* dintorni, sobborghi, *m.pl.*, periferia, *f.*

outspoken, *a.* chiaro e lindo, franco, retto; ardito. **~ness,** *n.* franchezza, libertà di parola, *f.*

outspread, *a.* spiegato, esteso.

outstanding, *a.* prominente, cospicuo, spiccante; in pendenza; arretrato, non pagato; in sospeso. ~ *bills* (*Com.*), effetti in circolazione, *m.pl.* ~ *debts* (*Com.*) crediti attivi, *m.pl.*

outstretched, *a.* steso, allungato.

outstrip, *v.t.* oltrepassare, distanziare; vincere.

out-turn, *n.* rendimento, *m.*

outward, *a.* esteriore, esterno; d'us-cita, di sortita. *for ~ application* (*Med.*), per uso esterno. ~ *bound,* in partenza (per l'estero), diretto all'estero. ~[s], *ad.* verso l'esterno, all'infuori.

outwit, *v.t.* acchiappare; sorpassare in finezza; gabbare, truffare, mettere in sacco, essere il piú furbo.

outwork, *n.* opera avanzata, *f.*, antimuro, *m.*; lavoro esterno, *m.*; (*pl. Mil.*) fortificazione esterna, *f.* ~**er,** *n.* lavorante esterno, *m.*, l. esterna, *f.*

ouzel, *n.* merlo, *m.*

oval, *a. & n.* ovale, *a. & m.*

ovary, *n.* ovaia, *f.*, ovario, *m.*

ovation, *n.* ovazione, *f.*

oven, *n.* forno, *m.*; (*fig.*) stufa, *f.*

over, *ad.* sopra, al di sopra, per di sopra, al di là; in piú, per sopram-mercato; troppo, eccessivamente, piú che; (*prefix*) stra-, ultra-; finito, passato. ~ *again,* di nuovo, nuovamente; ancora una volta. ~*board,* in mare; fuori bordo. ~ *& above,* inoltre, di piú, in su; ~ *there,* laggiú. ¶ *pr.* su, sopra; al di sopra di; piú di, in aggiunta a; oltre, al di là di; dall'altra parte di; attraverso; per; durante. ~*all* (*Meas.*) per tutto, fuori tutto. ¶ *n.* (*Cricket*) numero di mandate (palle) successive di cui dispone il lanciatore (*bowler*).

overact, *v.t.* esagerare (la parte).

overall, *n.* copritutto, *m.*, tenuta da lavoro, *f.*; (*pl.*) tuta, *f.*, calzoni da lavoro, *m.pl.*

overarm stroke, taglio, *m.*

overassess, *v.t.* tassare eccessivamente. **overassessment,** *n.* imposizione eccessiva (di tasse); sopratassa, *f.*

overawe, *v.t.* intimidire; mettere in soggezione, tenere in soggezione, far stare a segno.

overbalance, *v.i.* sbilanciarsi; perdere l'equilibrio.

overbearing, *a.* prepotente, arrogante.

overboard (*Naut.*) *ad.* fuori bordo; in mare; in acqua. [*a*] *man ~!* uomo in mare!

overburden (*Min.*) *n.* terreni di copertura, *m.pl.* ¶ *v.t.* sovraccaricare.

overcast, *a.* coperto, nuvoloso, offuscato. ¶ *v.t.ir.* offuscare; cucire a sopraggitto. ¶ (*Emb.*) *n.* sopraggitto, *m.*

overcautious, *a.* troppo cauto, timido.

overcharge, *n.* sovraccarico; prezzo eccessivo, *m.* ¶ *v.t. & i.,* sovraccaricare; far pagare troppo caro; (*Stk. Ex.*) estorcere.

overcoat, *n.* soprabito, *m.*; (*Mil.*) cappotto, *m.*

overcome, *v.t.ir.* superare; vincere; sormontare; sopraffare.

overcrowd, *v.t.* ingombrare (con troppa roba o gente).

overdo, *v.t.ir.* esagerare; spingere troppo oltre; sopraccaricare; (*Cook.*) far cuocere troppo. **overdone,** *a.* esagerato, spinto troppo oltre; troppo cotto.

overdose, *n.* dose eccessiva, *f.*

overdraft, *n.* scoperto, credito allo scoperto, *m.* **overdraw,** *v.t.ir.* (*an a/c*) superare il credito, trarre allo scoperto; (*fig.*) esagerare.

overdrive, *v.t.ir.* strapazzare, esaurire; affaticare; spingere troppo forte.

overdue, *a.* in ritardo; in sofferenza; scaduto, arretrato.

overelaborate, *v.t.* sforzare; leccare, rifinire, levigare.

overestimate, *v.t.* stimare in eccesso, stimare oltre il valore, valutare eccessivamente.

overexcite, *v.t.* sovreccitare.

overexposure (*Phot.*) *n.* eccesso di posa, *m.*

overfeed, *v.t.ir.* dare troppo da mangiare, satollare, rimpinzare.

overflow, *n.* scarico, traboccamento; troppo pieno; (*fig.*) sfogo, *m.,* espansione, *f.* ¶ *v.i.* traboccare, straripare.

overgrow, *v.t.ir.* coprire, ricoprire; crescere sopra; invadere. **overgrown,** *p.a.* coperto, ricoperto (di), ingombrato; troppo grande, cresciuto a dismisura. **overgrowth,** *n.* crescita eccessiva, *f.,* aumento smisurato, *m.*

overhang, *n.* strapiombo, aggetto, *m.* ¶ *v.i. & t., ir.* strapiombare, sovrastare, impendere sopra, essere sospeso sopra.

overhaul, *v.t.* esaminare, visitare, ispezionare; (*Mech.*) revisionare, smontare; ripassare; raggiungere.

overhead, *a.* aereo; di soffitto. ~ *charges,* [tutte le] spese aggiunte [al prezzo base], *f.pl.* ~ *expenses,* spese generali, spese vive, *f.pl.* ~ *price,* prezzo tutto compreso. ¶ *ad.* in su, in alto; sopra la testa; al piano di sopra.

overhear, *v.t.ir.* sentire per caso, carpire; sorprendere.

overheat, *v.t.* riscaldare troppo, surriscaldare.

overindulgence, *n.* indulgenza eccessiva; intemperanza; mollezza, *f.*

overjoyed, *p.p.* lietissimo, colmo di gioia.

overladen, *p.p.* sovraccarico, sovraccaricato.

overland, *ad. & a.* per terra, di terra; terrestre. ~ *route,* via di terra, *f.*

overlap, *v.t. & i.* accavalcare, sovrapporre a, sovrapporsi, sporgere, ricoprire.

overlay, *n.* coperta da letto; piccola tovaglia, *f.* ¶ *v.t.* coprire, ricoprire; soffocare; incrostare.

overleaf, *ad.* dall'altra parte della pagina, al rovescio, al verso.

overload, *v.t.* sovraccaricare.

overlook, *v.t.* dare su; dominare; sorvegliare; passare sopra, chiudere gli occhi sopra, trascurare, non accorgersi di; perdonare.

overmantel, *n.* intelaiatura sopra il camino, *f.*

overmuch, *ad.* troppo, all'eccesso, oltre misura.

overnight, *ad.* durante la notte, durante la sera precedente.

overpay, *v.t.ir.* pagare troppo, ricompensare troppo largamente.

overplus, *n.* soprappiù, eccesso, *m.*

over-polite, *a.* ceremonioso.

overpower, *v.t.* sopraffare, vincere. ~**ing,** *a.* irresistibile, schiacciante.

overproduction, *n.* sopraproduzione, *f.,* eccesso di produzione, *m.*

overrate, *v.t.* stimare più del valore. ~ *oneself* (*fig.*) presumere troppo; stendersi troppo avanti.

overreach, *v.t.* oltrepassare; truffare, ingannare.

override, *v.t.ir.* strapazzare; scartare, non far niente di; mettere da parte.

overripe, *a.* marcio, strafatto, troppo maturo.

overrule, *v.t.* rigettare, annullare; riformare, decidere contro.

overrun, *v.t.ir.* scorrere; percorrere; spandersi sopra, infestare; (*Typ.*) rimaneggiare.

oversea[s], *a.* d'oltre mare. ¶ *ad.* oltremare.

overseer, *n.* sorvegliante, *m.f.,* ispettore, *m.,* -trice, *f.,* soprintendente, *m.f.* (*Typ.*) proto, *m.*

overset, *v.t.* rovesciare, capovolgere, mettere sossopra, far ribaltare.

oversewing stitch, sopraggitto, *m.*

overshadow, *v.t.* ombreggiare; (*fig.*) oscurare, ecclissare.

overshoe, *n.* soprascarpa, scarpa di gomma, galoscia, *f.*

overshoot, *v.t.ir.* oltrepassare, sorpassare, portare al di là (del segno).

oversight, *n.* svista, *f.*, sbaglio, *m.*, inavvertenza, *f.*; sorveglianza, *f.*

oversleep oneself (to), *v. reflexive ir.* dormire troppo a lungo, svegliarsi troppo tardi.

overspread, *v.t.ir.* spandersi sopra.

overstate, *v.t.* esagerare; caricare.

overstep, *v.t.* oltrepassare; eccedere; trasgredire.

overstock, *v.t.* ingombrare; approvvigionare all'eccesso.

overstrain, *v.t.* forzare, sforzare; stringere all'eccesso.

overstrung, *a.* sovreccitato.

overt, *a.* manifesto, aperto.

overtake, *v.t.ir.* raggiungere; ripigliare; sorprendere; (*Motor*) oltrepassare.

overtax, *v.t.* sovraccaricare; abusare di.

overthrow, *v.t.ir.* rovesciare, sconvolgere; distruggere, rovinare.

overtime, *n.* ore di lavoro straordinario, *f.pl.*

overtop, *v.t.* soprastare, sorpassare, dominare.

overtraining, *n.* allenamento eccessivo, allenamento troppo prolungato, *m.*

overture, *n.* offerta, proposizione, *f.*; (*Mus.*) preludio, *m.*

overturn, *v.t.* capovolgere, rovesciare, ribaltare; sovvertire.

overvalue, *v.t.* stimare piú del valore, valutare troppo.

overweening, *a.* presuntuoso.

overweight, *n.* eccedenza di peso, *f.*

overwhelm, *v.t.* sopraffare, caricare; opprimere; atterrare; rovinare su; colmare.

overwork, *v.t.* sovraccaricare di lavoro; strapazzare; far lavorare troppo.

ovine, *a.* ovino.

oviparous, *a.* oviparo.

owe, *v.t.* dovere, essere indebito di.

owing, *a.* dovuto; scaduto, arretrato. ~ *to,* a causa di, grazie a, da attribuirsi a.

owl, *n.* gufo, *m.*, civetta, *f.*, barbagianni, *m.inv.* ~**ish,** *a.* da gufo.

own, *a.* proprio; (*brother,* *sister*) (fratello) germano, *m.*, (sorella) germana, *f. not my* ~, non . . . a me, non il mio. *one's* ~, suo (proprio); a sé; ¶ *v.t.* possedere, essere proprietario di; (*v.i.*) confessare. **owner,**

n. proprietario, *m.*, -a, *f.*; (*ship's manager*) armatore; gerente, *m.*; (*ship's proprietor*) proprietario, *m.* ~**-driver,** proprietario conducente, *m. at* ~*'s risk,* al rischio e pericolo del destinatario. ~**ship,** *n.* proprietà, *f.*, diritto di proprietà, *m.*

ox, *n.* (*pl.* **oxen**) bue (*pl.* buoi), bove, *m.*; ~*-eye daisy,* margherita dei campi, *f.*

oxide, *n.* ossido, *m.* **oxidize,** *v.t.* ossidare. **oxygen,** *n.* ossigeno, *m.* **oxyhydrogen** (*blowpipe,* &*c.*) *att.* ossidrico.

oyster, *n.* ostrica, *f.* ~ *bed,* ostricaio, banco di ostriche, *m.* ~ *culture,* ostricultura, *f.* ~ *man,* ~ *woman,* ostricaio, -caro, *m.*, -a, *f.*

ozone, *n.* ozono, *m.*

P

pace, *n.* passo, *m.*; andatura; velocità, *f. to keep* ~ *with,* camminare di pari passo. (*fig.*) mantenersi di passo con. ~*maker,* cavallo che dà l'andatura di partenza (alle corse); allenatore, *m.* ¶ *v.t.* misurare a passi; percorrere; allenare.

pachyderm, *n.* pachiderma, *m.*

pacific, *a.* pacifico. **P**~ [**ocean**], [Oceano] Pacifico, *m.* **pacificist, pacifist,** *n.* & *att.* pacifista, *m.f.* & *att.* **pacify,** *v.t.* pacificare. **pacifying,** *p.a.* pacificatore, -trice.

pack, *n.* pacco, fardello, fagotto, peso, *m.*; balla, *f.*; (*soldier's*) zaino, *m.*; (*hounds*) muta, *f.*; (*Cards*) mazzo, giuoco, *m.*; (*ice*) ammasso, lastrone, *m.*; (*thieves*) mano, banda, *f.* ~ *horse,* cavallo da soma, *m.* ~ *man,* merciaiolo ambulante, *m.* ~ *saddle,* basto, *m.* ~ *thread,* spago, filo, *m.*, cordicella, *f.* ¶ *v.t.* imballare, impaccare, impacchettare; incassare; fare fagotto; fare le valigie; serrare; premere insieme; (*hounds*) fare una muta. ~ [*up*] impaccare, imballare, incassare; fare il baule, fare le valigie. ~**age,** *n.* pacchetto, collo, *m.* ~**ed,** *p.a.* impaccato, disposto in pacchi; accalcato, pigiato. ~ *like sardines* (*people*), pieno zeppo, pieno straboccante. ~**er,** *n.* imballatore, *m.*, -trice, *f.* ~**et,** *n.* pacchetto, involto, *m.* ~ (*boat*), piroscafo postale, vapore postale, *m.* ~**ing,** *n.*

imballaggio, *m.*; guarnizione, (di pistone, &c.), *f.* ~ *case*, cassa, *f.* ~ *case maker*, cassettaio, bossolaio, *m.*

pact, *n.* patto, *m.*

pad, *n.* guancialetto, cuscinetto; batuffolo, tampone; (*Med.*) stuello, *m.*; (*for carrier's* ʀeaɪ) cercine, *m.*; (*stamp*) cuscinetto, tampone, *m.* (*blotting*) cartella di carta sugante.; (*writing*) sottomano, *m.inv.* cartella da scrittoio, *f.* ¶ *v.t.* imbottire, ovattare, riempire di borra.; (*verses*) infarcire. **padding**, *n.* borra, ovatta, imbottitura, *f.* *padded cell*, cella imbottita, *f.*

paddle (*canoe*) *n.* pagaia, *f.* ~ (*board*) pala, paletta, *f.* (*water wheel*) pala, *f.* ~*boat*, vapore a ruote, *m.* ~ *box*, tamburo, *m.* ~ *wheel*, ruota a pale, *f.* ¶ *v.i.* remare con la pagaia; (*splash about*) guazzare. **paddler**, *n.* pagaiatore, rematore con la pagaia, *m.* **paddling**, *n.* (*child*) guazzamento, *m.* (*canoe*) navigazione con la pagaia, *f.*

paddock, *n.* chiuso, recinto di chiusura, *m.*; (*Turf*) passeggiatoio, *m.*

padlock, *n.* catenaccio, lucchetto, *m.* ¶ *v.t.* allucchettare, chiudere a catenaccio.

Padua, *n.* Padova, *f.*

paean, *n.* peana, *m.*

pagan, *a. & n.* pagano, *a. & m.* ~**ism** *& ~***dom**, *n.* paganesimo, *m.*

page, *n.* (*book*) pagina, *f.*; (*Hist., noble youth*) paggio, *m.*; (*boy*) fattorino, *m.* *left-hand* (*even*) ~, verso. *right-hand* (*odd*) ~, recto, *m.* ~ *proof*, messa in pagina, *f.* **page** or **paginate**, *v.t.* numerare le pagine di.

pageant, *n.* corteo, *m.*, parata, processione, *f.*; spettacolo, *m.* ~**ry**, *n.*, fasto, *m.*, pompa, *f.*

paid, *p.p.* pagato, saldato; per quietanza. ~ *up* (*capital*), versato; (*shares*) versato.

pail, *n.* secchia, *f.*; bigonciolo, *m.* ~(**ful**), *n.* una secchia piena.

paillasse, *n.* pagliericcio, saccone, *m.*

pain, *n.* male, *m.*, sofferenza, *f.*; dolore, *m.*; pena, *f.*; dispiacere, *m.* *in* ~, sofferente; (*fig.*) in pena. ¶ *v.t.* far male a, far soffrire, causare dolore a; affiggere, amareggiare, contristare. ~**ful**, *a.* doloroso; penoso; faticoso. ~**less**, *a.* senza dolore. **pains**, *n.pl.* pena, cura, applicazione, *f.*; sforzi, *m.pl.*, fatica; premura, *f.* *to take* ~, darsi cura, affaticarsi, sforzarsi. ~**taking**, *a.*

laborioso, diligente, sollecito, premuroso.

paint, *n.* colore, *m.*; (*industry*) vernice, *f.*; (*face*) belletto, rossetto, *m.* ~*brush*, pennello, *m.* ¶ *v.t.* dipingere; imbellettare (*face*); verniciare. ~**er**, *n.* pittore, *m.*; verniciatore; (*house*) imbianchino, *m.*; (*boat*) barbetta, *f.* ~**ing**, *n.* pittura, *f.*; verniciatura, *f.*; (*picture*) quadro, *m.* **paintress**, *n.* pittrice, *f.*

pair, *n.* paio, *m.* (*pl.* paia, *f.*), coppia, *f.*; (*horses*) pariglia, *f.* ~ *of compasses*, compasso, *m.* ~ *of scales*, bilancia, *f.* ~ *of scissors*, forbici, *f.pl.*, paio di forbici, *m.* ~ *of steps*, scala doppia, *f.* ~ *of trousers*, calzoni, *m.pl.*; paio di calzoni, *m.* the ~ (*pictures*, &c.) i (due) pendenti, i due che si fanno riscontro, *m.pl.* ¶ *v.t.* appaiare, accoppiare; (*v.i.*) appaiarsi, accoppiarsi; farsi riscontro.

palace, *n.* palazzo, *m.*

paladin, *n.* paladino, cavaliere errante, *m.*

palaeo-. Same as *paleo-*.

palatable, *a.* gradevole [al palato], saporito. **palatal**, *a.* palatale; *palat(al)ized consonant*, consonante palatale, *f.* **palate**, *n.* palato, *m.*; gusto, *m.*

palatial, *a.* grandioso.

palaver, *n.* diceria, *f.*; storie, *f.pl.* discorsi frivoli, *m.pl.*; colloquio, *m.* ¶ *v.i.* cicalare; confabulare.

pale, *a.* pallido, smorto, scialbo; biondo. ¶ *n.* palo, *m.*; limiti, confini, *m.pl.* ¶ *v.i.* impallidire, diventare pallido. ~**ness**, *n.* pallidezza, *f.*; pallore, *m.*

paleography, *n.* paleografia, *f.*

paleontology, *n.* paleontologia, *f.*

Palermo, *n.* Palermo, *f.*

Palestine, *n.* la Palestina, *f.*

palette, *n.* tavolozza, *f.* ~*knife*, mestichino, *m.*

palfrey, (*Poet.*) *n.* palafreno, *m.*

palimpsest, *n. & a.* palinsesto, *n. & a.*

paling, *n.* stecconato, impalancato, *m.*

palisade, *n.* stecconaia, palizzata, *f.* ¶ *v.t.* stecconare, circondare con una palizzata.

palish, *a.* pallidetto.

pall, *n.* coltre mortuaria, *f.*, drappo funebre, *m.* ~ *bearers*, chi reggono i cordoni (gli angoli) di un drappo funebre. ~*on*, saziare, satollare; diventare insipido a.

pallet, *n.* pagliericcio; *(bed)* lettuccio, *m.*, *(Poet.)* coltrice, *f.*

palliasse, *n.* pagliericcio, saccone, *m.*

palliate, *v.t.* palliare. **palliative,** *a. & n.* palliativo, *a. & m.*

pallid, *a.* pallidetto. **pallor,** *n.* pallore, *m.*

palm, *(hand)* *n.* palmo, *m.* ~ *(branch)* palma, *f.* ~[*tree*] palmizio, *m.*, palma, *f.* ~ *grove,* palmeto, *m.* ~ *house,* serra per palme, *f.* ~ *oil,* olio di palma, *m.*; *(fig.)* mancia, *f.* *P* ~ *Sunday,* Domenica delle Palme, *f.* ~ **off,** fare credere a, far passare, imporre colla frode. ~ate[d], *a.* palmato. ~**ist,** *n.* chiromante, *m.f.* ~**istry,** *n.* chiromanzia, *f.* ~*y days,* giorni felici, giorni gloriosi, *m.pl.*

palp[us], *n.* palpo, *m.* **palpable,** *a.* palpabile. **palpitate,** *v.i.* palpitare. **palpitation,** *n.* palpitazione, *f.*

palter, *v.i.* equivocare, tergiversare. ~ *with,* non essere franco con.

paltry, *a.* piccolo, meschino; povero.

pampas, *n.pl.* pampa, *f.*

pamper, *v.t.* impinzare, satollare; trattare delicatamente, vezzeggiare.

pamphlet, *n.* opuscolo; libello, *m.* ~**eer,** *n.* libellista *(satirical).*

pan, *n.* padella, casseruola, *f.*; scodellino, tegame, *m.*; teglia, terrina, *f.*; *(brain)* cranio, *m.*; *(scale)* piatto, *m.*, coppa, *f.* *(w.c.)* catino, *m.*

panacea, *n.* panacea, *f.*

panama, *n.* or *Panama hat,* panama, *m.*

pancake, *n.* frittella, *f.*

pancreas, *n.* pancreas, *m.*

pandemonium, *n.* pandemonio, diavolìo, *m.*

pander to, prestarsi a, fare il compiacente, mostrare una compiacenza indegna.

Pandora's box, vaso di Pandora, *m.*

pane, *n.* *(glass)* vetro, quadrato di vetro, *m.*; *(side or face)* faccetta; *(hammer)* penna, *f.*

panegyric, *n.* panegirico, *m.*

panel, *n.* pannello, *m.*, tavola, *f.*; quadretto, scompartimento, *m.*; *(Radio)* cassa; lista, *f.* ~ *envelope,* busta a cellofane, *f.* ¶ *v.t.* rivestire di legno, rivestire con pannelli.

pang, *n.* spasimo, dolore acuto, *m.*, angoscia, *f.*; *(pl.)* doglie, *f.pl.*; terrori, *m.pl.*

pan-Germanism, *n.* pangermanesimo, *m.*

panic, *n.* panico, *m.* ¶ *a.* panico. ¶ *v.i.* essere colto (preso) dal panico; ~*struck,* esterrefatto.

panjandrum, *n.* funzionario arrogante, *m.*

pannier, *n.* paniere, cesto, *m.*; *(on back)* gerla, *f.*

pannikin, *n.* piccolo tegame, piccolo vaso, *m.*

panoply, *n.* panoplia, *f.*

panorama, *n.* panorama, *m.*

pansy, *n.* viola del pensiero, *f.*

pant, *v.i.* ansare, ansimare. ~ *for,* *(fig.)* anelare.

pantechnicon (van), furgone, *m.*

pantheism, *n.* panteismo, *m.*

pantheon, *n.* Panteon, *m.*

panther, *n.* pantera, *f.*

panting, *p.a.* ansante, ansimante; anelante.

pantograph, *n.* pantografo, *m.*

pantomime *(dumb show),* *n.* mimica, pantomima, *f.* **pantomimist,** *n.* pantomimo, *m.*

pantry, *n.* dispensa, *f.*

pants, *n.pl.* calzoni, *m.pl.*

pap, *n.* panbollito; *(nipple)* capezzolo, *m.*

papa, *n.* babbo, papà, *m.*

papacy, *n.* papato, *m.* **papal,** *a.* papale. ~ *nuncio,* nunzio pontificio, *m.* ~ *states,* Stati Pontifici, *m.pl.*

paper, *n.* carta, *f.*; *(news)* giornale, foglio, *m.* *(wall)* tappezzeria, *f.*; *(learned)* articolo, saggio, *m.*, dissertazione, *f.*; *(Sch.)* tema, *m.*; composizione, *f.*; esercizio, *m.*; foglio di esame, *m.*; *(voting)* scheda di votazione, *f.* ~ *case,* cartella, *f.* ~*chase,* caccia nella quale la traccia è fornita da striscie di carta. *in* ~ *covers,* cartolinato, legato alla rustica. ~*clip,* ~ *fastener,* serracarte, fermacarte, *m.inv.* ~ *hanger,* tappezziere in carta, incollatore, *m.*; ~ *hat* *(Danc.)* cappello di carta, *m.* ~ *knife,* tagliacarte, *m.inv.* ~ *lantern* (Chinese, Japanese), lanternino di carta, *m.* ~ *maker,* cartaio,-fabbricante di carta, *m.* ~ *making & ~ trade,* fabbricazione della carta, *f.*, commercio della carta, *m.* ~ *money,* *(convertible)* valuta cartacea, *f.* *(inconvertible)* carta moneta, *f.* ~ *streamer,* stella filante, *f.* ~ *warfare,* polemica per iscritto, guerra della penna, *f.* ~*weight,* calcafogli, *m.inv.*; pressacarte, *m.inv.* ~ *wrappered,* cartolinato. ~ *wrappered, turned over,* involto di carta, avvolto in carta. ¶ *v.t.* *(wall)* tappezzare.

papier mâché, cartapesta, *f.*
papist, *n.* papista, *m.f.*
papyrus, *n.* papiro, *m.*
par, *n.* pari, *f.* (See also *paragraph.*)
parable & **parabola,** *n.* parabola, *f.*
  parabolic(al), *a.* in forma di parabola; allegorico; (*Geom.*) parabolico.
parachute, *n.* paracadute, *m.inv.*
parade, *n.* parata, *f.*; sfoggio, *m.*;
  ostentazione, *f.*; (*of mannequins*)
  mostra, sfilata, *f.*; ~ *ground,* piazza
  d'armi, *f.*; campo di Marte, *m.*
paradise, *n.* paradiso, *m.*; (*Eden*) il
  paradiso (terrestre), *m.*
paradox, *n.* paradosso, *m.* ~**ical,** *a.*
  paradossale.
paraffin [oil], *n.* olio di paraffina, *m.*;
  petrolio combustibile, *m.* ~**[wax],**
  n. paraffina, *f.*
paragon, *n.* paragone, modello perfetto, *m.*, fenice, *f.*
paragraph (*abb.* par.) *n.* paragrafo,
  m.; alinea, *m.*; capoverso, trafiletto,
  m. par writer, cronista, *m.*
parakeet, *n.* pappagallo, *m.*
parallax, *n.* parallasse, *f.*
parallel, *a.* parallelo; (*drill shank,* &*c.*)
  cilindrico; (*fig.*) simile, somigliante.
  ~ *bars,* parallele, *f.pl.* ~ *ruler,*
  regolo per tracciare parallele, *m.*
  ¶ *n.* (*Geom., Mil.*) parallela, *f.*; (*of
  latitude*) parallelo, *m.*; (*comparison*)
  parallelo, confronto, paragone, *m.*
parallelepiped, *n.* parallelepipedo,
  m. **parallelogram,** *n.* parallelo-
  gramma, *m.*
paralyse, *v.t.* paralizzare. **paralysis,**
  n. paralisi, *f.* **paralytic,** *a.* & *n.*
  paralitico, *a.* & *m.* ~ *stroke,* attacco
  di paralisi, *m.*
paramount, *a.* sovrano, sommo,
  supremo.
paramour, *n.* amante, *m.f.*, drudo, *m.*,
  -a, *f.*
parapet, *n.* parapetto, *m.*
paraphernalia, *n.pl.* roba, *f.*, apparato, *m.*
paraphrase, *n.* parafrasi, *f.* ¶ *v.t.* & *i.*
  parafrasare.
parasite, *n.* parassita, *m.*; (*pers.*)
  parassita, *m.f.* **parasitic(al),** *a.*
  parassitico; (*animal, plant*) parassita.
parasol, *n.* parasole, *m.inv.*, ombrellino, *m.*
parboil, *v.t.* far bollire (o cuocere) a
  mezzo; (*fig.*) riscaldare, sobbollire.
parbuckle, *n.* lentia, braca da botte,
  f.; treviro, *m.* ¶ *v.t.* lentiare,
  sollevare per mezzo della lentia.
parcel, *n.* pacco, involto, collo, *m.*;
  (*land*) lotto, pezzo (di terreno) *m.*

~ *post,* servizio dei pacchi postali,
  m. by ~ *post,* per pacco postale. ~*s
delivery,* consegna di pacchi (di colli)
  (per espresso o a mezzo corriere), *f.*
  ~(*s*) *office,* ufficio di messaggeria, *m.*
  ~ **[out],** *v.t.* spartire, distribuire.
parch, *v.t.* essiccare; abbruciacchiare.
parchment, *n.* cartapecora, pergamena, *f.*
pardon, *n.* perdono, *m.*, grazia,
  amnistia, *f.*; (*Eccl.*) indulgenza, *f.*
  I beg your ~, scusate, scusi. ¶ *v.t.*
  perdonare; scusare; (*Leg.*) graziare.
  ~**able,** *a.* scusabile, perdonabile.
pare, *v.t.* (*nails*) tagliarsi (le unghie);
  (*fruit*) sbucciare; (*vegetable*) pelare,
  mondare, sbaccellare, nettare; (*turf*)
  tosare.
paregoric, *a.* paregorico.
parent, *n.* genitore, *m.*, genitrice, *f.*;
  padre, *m.*; madre, *f.*; (*fig.*) cagione,
  sorgente, *f.*; progenitore, *m.*; (*att.*)
  madre, principale. ~**s,** *pl.* genitori,
  m.pl. ~ *state,* madrepatria, *f.* ~
  stock, lignaggio, tronco, *m.* ~**age,**
  n. nascita; famiglia, stirpe, *f.*;
  genitori, *m.pl.* ~**al,** *a.* dei genitori;
  di padre, di madre.
parenthesis, *n.* parentesi, *f.* **paren-
thetic(al),** *a.* fra parentesi. **paren-
thetically,** *ad.* per parentesi; quasi
  per parentesi.
pariah, *n.* paria, *m.f.*
paring, *n.* ritagliamento, *m.*; mondatura, buccia, *f.*
pari passu, *ad.* pari passo. *to rank* ~,
  essere considerato pari (a).
Paris, *n.* Parigi, *f.* **Parisian,** *a.*
  parigino, di Parigi. ¶ *n.* parigino, *m*,
  -a, *f.*
parish, *n.* (*civil*) comune, municipio,
  m.; (*Eccl.*) parrocchia, *f.*; (*att.*)
  comunale, municipale; parrocchiale.
  ~ *church,* chiesa parrocchiale,
  parrocchia, *f.* **parishioner,** *n.*
  parrocchiano, *m.*, -a, *f.*
parity, *n.* parità, *f.*
park, *n.* parco; bosco, *m.* ~**keeper,**
  custode (guardiano) del parco, *m.*
  ¶ *v.t.* parcare, posteggiare; radunare; (*v.i.*) stazionare. ¶ *v.i.*
  parcheggio, *m.* ~*place,* posteggio
  [per automobili], *m.* *no* ~, proibizione di sosta, *f.*, divieto di sosta, *m.*
parlance, *n.* linguaggio, *m.*
parley, *n.* trattativa, conferenza, *f.*;
  abboccamento, *m.* ¶ *v.i.* parlamentare, conferire, venire a trattative
  (con).
parliament, *n.* parlamento, *m.* ~**ary,**
  a. (*government*) parlamentare; (*elec-*

tion) parlamentare, legislativo; (*candidate*) (candidato) alla Camera. ~ **division,** circoscrizione elettorale, *f.*

parlour, *n.* salotto, *m.*; (*convent, school*) parlatorio, *m.* ~ *games,* giuochi di sala, *m.pl.* ~*maid,* fantesca che serve in tavola, cameriera, *f.*

Parma, *n.* Parma, *f.* ~ *violet,* viola (o violetta) di Parma, *f.* **Parmesan,** *a. & n.* parmigiano, *a. & m.* ~ *cheese,* formaggio parmigiano, *m.*

Parnassus, *n.* Parnaso, *m.*

parochial, *a.* (*civil*) comunale; (*Eccl.*) parrocchiale; (*fig.*) di campanile.

parodist, *n.* parodista, scrittore di parodie, *m.* **parody,** *n.* parodia, *f.* ¶ *v.t.* parodiare.

parole, *n.* parola, parola d'onore, *f.*

paroxysm, *n.* parossismo, *m.*

parquet, *n.* pavimento di legno, *m.* ¶ *v.t.* pavimentare in legno.

parricidal, *a.* parricida. **parricide,** *n.* (*pers.*) parricida, *m.f.*; (*act*) parricidio, *m.*

parrot, *n.* pappagallo, *m.*; (*hen*) pappagallo femmina, *f.*

parry, *v.t.* parare; schermire; evitare. ~*ing,* *n.* parata, *f.*

parse, *v.t.* analizzare (grammaticalmente).

Parsee, *n.* parso, *m.*, -a, *f.* ¶ *a.* parso.

parsimonious, *a.* economo, gretto, parsimonioso, parco. **parsimony,** *n.* parsimonia, ristrettezza, *f.*

parsing, *n.* analisi (grammaticale), *f.*

parsley, *n.* prezzemolo, *m.*

parsnip, *n.* pastinaca, *f.*

parson, *n.* prete; curato, parroco, ecclesiastico, *m.*; (*Protestant*) ministro, *m.* ~'s *nose,* groppone di pollo, *m.* ~*age,* *n.* casa parrocchiale, *f.*; presbiterio, *m.*

part, *n.* parte, porzione, *f.*; pezzo, *m.*; quartiere, luogo, *m.*; località, *f.*; dovere, *m.*; (*side*) partito, *m.*; (*Theat.*), parte, *f.*; (*book*) fascicolo, *m.*; dispensa, *f.* *to take the* ~ *of,* (*Theat.*) rappresentare, fare la parte di, impersonare; (*side with*) prendere le parti di, tenere, prendere da parte. *to take in good* ~, prendere in buona parte. ~s, *n.pl.* capacità, intelligenza, *f.* ¶ *v.t.* separare, dividere; (*Metals*) rompere, ripartire. ~ *one's hair,* farsi la scriminatura. (*v.i.*) separarsi (da); partire, andarsene. ~ *with,* rinunciare, disfarsi di.

partake, *v.i.ir.* partecipare. ~ *of,* fare, mangiare; accettare.

partial, *a.* (*biased*) parziale; (*not entire*)

parziale. *to be* ~ *to,* avere un debole per. ~**ity,** *n.* parzialità, predilezione, *f.*, debole, *m.*

participate, *v.i.* partecipare.

participial adjective, (*present*) aggettivo verbale; (*past*) participio passato (usato come aggettivo), *m.* **participle,** *n.* participio, *m.*

particle, *n.* particella, *f.*, atomo minimo, *m.*; (*Gram.*) particella, *f.*

particoloured, *a.* variopinto, screziato.

particular, *a.* particolare, speciale; esatto, preciso, distinto; fastidioso, esigente, difficile; intimo. ¶ *n.* dettaglio, particolare, *m.*; circostanza, *f.*; (*pl.*) dettagli, particolari, ragguagli, *m.pl.*; informazioni, *f.pl.* ~**ity,** *n.* particolarità, singolarità, *f.* ~**ize,** *v.t.* particolareggiare, dettagliare.

parting, *n.* separazione; rottura; (*hair*) scriminatura, *f.*; addio, *m.* *at the* ~ *of the ways,* al bivio.

partisan, *n.* partigiano, *m.*

partition, *n.* divisione, spartizione, *f.*; tramezzo, *m.*; paratia, *f.*; (*Mus.*) spartito, *m.* ~ *off,* separare (dividere) con paratia o tramezzo.

partitive (*Gram.*) *a.* partitivo.

partly, *ad.* in parte, parte, parzialmente. ~ *paid share,* azione non liberata, non interamente versata, *f.*

partner, *n.* (*Com.*) socio, *m.*; (*Sports, Games, Danc. & husband*), compagno, *m.*; (*wife*) compagna, moglie, *f.*; (*Danc.*) cavaliere, *m.*, dama, *f.* ¶ (*a lady, Danc.*) *v.t.* menare, condurre; ballare con. ~*ship,* *n.* associazione, società, *f.* *to enter into* ~ *with,* associarsi, entrare in società con.

partridge, *n.* pernice, *f.* (*young*) perniciotto, *m.*

party, *n.* (*body united in cause*) partito, *m.*; (*united in pleasure*) partita (di piacere); festa; briga, riunione, comitiva; serata, *f.*; gruppo, crocchio, *m.*; (*Mil.*) reparto, plotone, distaccamento, *m.* ~ *at fault* (*accident*) autore, *m.*, parte implicata, *f.* ~*-coloured,* screziato, variopinto. *to the* ~ (*entitled*) (*Law*), a chi di diritto. ~ (*entitled*) avente diritto, *m.f.* ~ *to a* (*or the*) *marriage* (*Law*), coniuge, *m.f.* ~ *rights* (*Law*), comproprietà, *f.* *to be a* ~ *to a crime,* essere complice in un delitto. ~ *spirit,* spirito di parte, *m.* ~ *wall,* muro divisorio, *m.*

paschal, *a.* pasquale, di Pasqua.

pass, *n.* passo; varco, *m.*, gola, *f.*,

passaggio, *m.*; circostanza, condizione, *f.*; punto; permesso, *m.*, lasciapassare, *m.inv.*; salvacondotto, *m.*; (*fencing*) passata, stoccata, botta, *f.*; (*Mil.*) permesso, *m.* ~ *book*, libretto di banca, l. di deposito, l. di conto corrente, *m.*; (*motors*) libretto per i transiti doganali, *m.* ~ *list* (exams), lista dei promossi (*or* ammessi),*f.* ~ *sheet* (*motors at Cust.*) carta di confine, *f.*, trittico, *m.* ~*word*, parola d'ordine (*Mil.*) *f.* ¶ *v.i.* & *t.* passare, trascorrere; finire, scomparire, svanire; ammettere, lasciar passare; pronunciare, fare rivolgere; adottare, prendere; approvare; collaudare, verificare, appurare; votare; oltrepassare; varcare. ~ *along!* circolate! ~ *away*, passare, trascorrere, scomparire, svanire; morire, trapassare. ~ *by*, passare davanti a; passar sotto silenzio, negligere. ~ *for payment*, dar l'ordine di pagare. ~ *on*, (*v.i.*) passare oltre, proseguire il cammino, andare avanti; (*v.t.*) fare passare, trasmettere, rimettere in circolazione; ~*-out check* (*Theat.*), contromarca, *f.* ~**able**, *a.* passabile, tollerabile; (*road*, &*c.*) praticabile. ~**age**, *n.* passaggio; corridoio; andito; viaggio, tragitto, *m.*; traversata, *f.*; (*book, letter*, &*c.*) brano, passo, *m.* ~ *money*, prezzo del viaggio, *m.*, prezzo del tragitto, *m.* *bird of* ~, uccello migratorio, *m.*

passenger, *n.* (*land, sea, or air*) viaggiatore, *m.*, -trice, *f.*; (*sea or air*) passeggero, *m.*, -a, *f.* ~*lift*, ascensore, *m.* ~*ship*, battello (per passeggeri, *m.* ~ *steamer*, piroscafo passeggeri, *m.* ~ *train*, treno viaggiatori, *m.* ~ *traffic*, movimento di viaggiatori, *m.* *by* ~ *train*, a gran velocità.

passer-by, *n.* passante, *m.f.*; (*pl.*) viandanti, *m.f.pl.* **passing,** *n.* passaggio, *m.*; (*Parl. bill*) approvazione, *f.*; (*time*) decorso; (*death*) decesso, *m.*, morte, *f.* *in* ~, di passata. ~ *bell*, rintocco, *m.* ¶ *a.* passeggero, fugace; presente, attuale. ~ *events*, attualità, *f.pl.* ~ *fancy*, capriccio, *m.*; (*liaison*) amoretto, amoruccio, *m.* ~ *note* (*Mus.*), passaggio, *m.*

passion, *n.* passione; collera, *f.* ~*play*, rappresentazione della Passione, *f.* ~ *flower*, passiflora, *f.* ~ *week*, Settimana Santa, *f.* ~**ate**, *a.* appassionato; collerico; ardente, vivo.

~**ately,** *ad.* appassionatamente, ardentemente, alla follia. ~ *fond of*, che ama perdutamente, che ama alla follia.

passive, *a.* passivo. ~ (*voice*) *n.* passivo, *m.* **passivity,** *n.* passività,*f.*

passover, *n.* pasqua (degli Ebrei) (dei Giudei), *f.*

passport, *n.* passaporto, *m.*

past, *n.* passato, *m.* ¶ *a.* & *p.p.* passato, trascorso, scorso; finito. ~ *master*, maestro perfetto, padrone (di), *m.*; matricolato (*with appropriate noun*). *e.g.* un briccone matricolato, *a past master in roguery, an arrant rogue.* ~ (*tense*) passato, tempo passato, *m.* *it is* ~ *ten*, sono le dieci passate. *for some time* ~, da qualche tempo.

paste, *n.* pasta; colla; gemma falsa, *f.*; diamante artificiale, *m.* ~*board*, cartone, *m.* ¶ *v.t.* incollare. ~*-on album*, album per incollare, *m.* ~*up* affissare, affiggere. ~*-on mount*, cartone per incollare le fotografie, le incisioni, *m.* ~*pot*, vaso da colla, *m.*

pastel, *n.* pastello, *m.* ~**ist,** *n.* pastellista, *m.f.*

pastern, *n.* pastoia, *f.*, pasturale, *f.*

Pasteurize, *v.t.* pastorizzare.

pastil[le], *n.* pastiglia, *f.*

pastime, *n.* passatempo, *m.*; distrazione, *f.*; divertimento, *m.*

pastor, *n.* pastore, *m.* ~**al,** *a.* pastorale. ~*al* & ~**ale,** *n.* pastorale, *f.*

pastry, *n.* pasticceria, *f.*; paste, *f.pl.*; articoli di pasta, *m.pl.* ~ *board*, tavola per fare la pasticceria, *f.* ~*cook* (& *confectioner*) pasticciere, *m.* ~ *shop*, pasticceria, *f.* ~ *server*, paletta, *f.*

pasturage, *n.* pastura, *f.* **pasture,** *n.* pastura, *f.*; pascolo, *m.*; (*uncut*) erbaggio, *m.* ¶ *v.t.* far pascere, pascolare; condurre al pascolo; (*fig.*) nutrire.

pasty, *a.* pastoso. ¶ *n.* pasticcio, *m.*

pat, *a.* & *ad.* esatto, opportuno; a proposito, a punto. ¶ *n.* colpetto, colpettino, *m.*; (*butter*) panetto, *m.* ¶ *v.t.* dare un piccolo colpo su, dare un buffetto a; (*an animal*) accarezzare. ~ *oneself on the back*, lodarsi, fare il proprio elogio.

patch, *n.* (*ground*) pezzo (di terra, di terreno); (*cabbages*, &*c.*) quadrato, *m.*; (*face*) neo, *m.*; (*tyre*) rappezzatura (*outer cover*); impiastro di gomma (*inner tube*). ~ *pocket*, tasca sovrapposta, *f.* ~*work*, rappezzatura, rattoppatura, *f.* (*fig.*) miscuglio, mosaico, *m.* ¶ *v.t.* rattoppare, rappezzare, raccommodare, ~**up**, rammendare; accomodare, aggiustare.

pate, *n.* zucca, testa, *f.*

paten, *n.* patena, *f.*

patent, *a.* brevettato; (*obvious*) patente, ovvio. ~ *leather*, pelle verniciata, *f.*, cuoio verniciato, *m.*; (*att.*) verniciato. ~ *medicine*, specialità farmaceutica, *f.* ¶ *n.* brevetto; titolo, diploma, *m.* ¶ *v.t.* brevettare.

paternal, *a.* paterno. **paternity**, *n.* paternità, *f.* **paternoster**, *n.* paternostro, *m.*

path, *n.* sentiero, viale; cammino, *m.*; (*storm, &c.*) corso, *m.*; traiettoria, *f.*

pathetic, *a.* patetico.

pathological, *a.* patologico. **pathologist**, *n.* patologo, *m.* **pathology**, *n.* patologia, *f.*

pathos, *n.* patetico, *m.*

patience, *n.* pazienza; (*Cards*) pazienza, *f. to put out of* ~, far perdere la pazienza a. **patient**, *a.* paziente. ¶ *n.* paziente, *m.f.*; malato sotto cura, *m.*

patina, *n.* patina, *f.* **patinated**, *a.* patinato.

patriarch, *n.* patriarca, *m.* ~**al**, *a.* patriarcale.

patrician, *a. & n.* patrizio, *a. & m.*

patrimony, *n.* patrimonio, *m.*

patriot, *n.* patriota, *m.f.* ~**ic**, *a.* patriottico. ~**ism**, *n.* patriottismo, *m.*

patrol, *n.* pattuglia, *f.* ¶ *v.i.* fare la ronda; (*v.t.*) perlustrare

patron, *n.* patrono, protettore, *m.*; (*fig.*) mecenate, *m.*; (*shop*) avventore, compratore, *m.* ~ (*saint*), patrono, *m.*, -a, *f.*, santo (protettore) *m.*, santa protettrice, *f.* ~ *saint's day*, festa patronale, *f.* ~**age**, *n.* patronato, *m.*; protezione, *f.*; (*shop*) avviamento, concorso di avventori, *m.* ~**ess**, *n.* patronessa, *f.*, protettrice, *f.*; (*fête, &c.*) patrona, *f.* **patronize**, *v.t.* patrocinare, proteggere; servirsi di. ~**d**, (*shop*) *p.p.* avviato. *well* ~, ben avviato, che ha molti avventori. **patronizing**, *a.* (*air, &c.*) di condiscendenza.

patronymic, *n.* [nome] patronimico, *m.*

patten, *n.* zoccolo, *m.*, pattino, *m.*

patter, *n.* rumore, scroscio, scalpitio, *m.*; (*in song*) parlata, *f.*; (*showman's*) cicalio, cicaleccio, *m.* ¶ *v.i.* trottare a piccoli passi; (*rain*) picchiare. *a*

~*ing of feet*, un rumore di passi lievi e rapidi, *m.*

pattern, *n.* modello; campione; saggio, disegno, *m.* ~ *maker* (*Foundry*), modellatore, *m.* ~ *making*, modellamento, *m.* ¶ *v.t.* modellare.

patty, *n.* pasticcetto, *m.*, piccola torta, *f.*

Paul Pry, *n.* frugatore, ficcanaso, *m.*

paunch, *n.* pancia, *f.*

pauper, *n.* povero, *m.*, -a, *f.*, indigente, *m.f.*, mendicante, *m.f.* ~**ism**, *n.* pauperismo, *m.*, indigenza, *f.*

pause, *n.* pausa, *f.*, intervallo, *m.*; silenzio, *m.*; fermata, *f.* ¶ *v.i.* fare una pausa, arrestarsi.

pave, *v.t.* lastricare, pavimentare; (*fig.*) preparare, spianare (la via, &c.). ~**ment**, *n.* lastrico, selciato, pavimento, *m.*; marciapiede, *m.*; (*outside café*) terrazza, *f.* ~ *glass*, lucernario, *m.* ~ *display* (shop), bancarella, *f.* **paver**, **paviour**, *n.* selciatore; lastricatore, *m.*

Pavia, *n.* Pavia, *f.*

pavilion, *n.* padiglione, *m.*, tendone, *m.*

paving, *n.* lastrico, pavimento, *m.*; lastricamento, *m.*, pavimentazione, *f.* ~ *stone*, lastra, *f.*, calce, *m.*

paw, *n.* zampa, *f. to* ~ *the ground*, calpestare, scalpitare.

pawl, *n.* (*Mech.*) dente d'arresto, rottolino d'arresto, *m.*

pawn, *n.* pegno, *m.*; (*Fin.*) pegno, *m.*; (*Chess*) pedina, *f.* ~*broker*, chi presta su pegno; commissionario del Monte di Pietà, *m.* ¶ *v.t.* dare in pegno, impegnare. ~*shop*, Monte di Pietà, *m.*

pax, *n.* pace, *f.*

pay, *n.* paga, *f.*, salario, stipendio, emolumento, *m.*; soldo, *m.*, mercede, *f.* ~ *office*, cassa, *f.* ~*master*, pagatore, tesoriere, commissario, *m.* ~ *packet*, busta paga, *f.* ¶ *v.t. & i.* pagare, saldare; rimunerare, ricompensare; fruttare, tornar conto; (*attention*) fare, prestare; usare; (*visit*) fare; (*respects*) fare; salutare; (*homage*) rendere, presentare. ~ *back*, restituire; ricambiare. ~ *cash* (cheque crossing) pagare in contanti. ~ *for*, pagare; (*fig.*) scontare. ~ *in*, versare. ~ *off*, licenziare; (*debt*) pagare, ammortizzare; sdebitarsi; (*mortgage*), estinguere; (*ship*) disarmare. ~*out*, sborsare; (cable) filare, lasciar scorrere; (*someone*) rendere la pariglia a, rendere pane per focaccia. ~ *up*, (*v.t.*) pagare, versare, soddisfare; (*v.i.*) pagare a saldo. ~**able**, *a.* pagabile, esigibile. ~**ee**, *n.* beneficiario, *m.*, -a, *f.*; (*cheque*) portatore, latore, *m.* ~**er**, *n.* pagatore, *m.* -trice, *f.*; chi paga; (*good, bad*) buon pagatore, cattivo pagatore, *m.* ~**ing**, *a.* fruttifero, produttivo, lucrativo, rimunerativo. ~ *guest*, pensionario, *m.*, pensionante, *m.f.* ~*in slip*, cedola di versamento, *f.* ~**ment**, *n.* pagamento, versamento, *m.*

pea, *n.* pisello, *m.* ~ *chick*, cece, *m.* ~*cock*, pavone, *m.* ~*hen*, pavona, pavonessa, *f.* ~*cock butterfly*, pavoncella, pavona, *f.* ~*nut*, pistacchio, *m.*, arachide, *f.* ~*shooter*, cerbottana, *f.* ~ *soup*, passata di piselli, *f.* ~ *stick*, palo, *m.*

peace, *n.* pace, tranquillità, *f.*; ordine pubblico, *m.* ~*maker*, conciliatore, *m.*, -trice, *f.*; pacificatore, *m.*, -trice, *f.*; paciere, *m.*, -a, *f.* ~**able** & ~**ful**, *a.* pacifico, tranquillo.

peach, *n.* pesca, *f.* ~ (*tree*) pesco, *m.*

peak, *n.* cima, vetta, sommità, *f.*, vertice, picco, *m.*; punta, *f.*; pizzo, *m.*; massimo, *m.*; (*cap.*) visiera, *f.*, tesa, *f.* ~ *hours*, ore di punta, *f.pl.*

peal, *n.* (*bells*) scampanata, *f.*; concerto, cariglione, *m.*; (*laughter*) scoppio, *m.*; (*hunter's horn*) voce, *f.*, suono, *m.*; (*thunder*) scoppio, rimbombo, *m.* ¶ *v.i.* suonare, risuonare; rimbombare, tuonare.

pear, *n.* pera, *f.* ~*tree* & ~*wood*, pero, *m.*

pearl, *n.* perla, *f.* ~ *button*, bottone di madreperla, *m.* ~ *barley*, orzo perlato, *m.* ~ *knitting*, punto rovescio, *m.* ~ *oyster*, ostrica perlifera, *f.* ~**y**, *a.* perlato, di perla.

peasant, *n.* contadino, *m.*, -a, *f.*, campagnuolo, *m.*, -a, *f.* ¶ *a.* contadinesco, campagnuolo. ~**ry**, *n.* contadini, *m.pl.*, gente di campagna, *f.*

peat, *n.* torba, *f.*; (*fuel*) formella, *f.* ~ *bog*, ~*ery*, *n.* torbiera, *f.* ~**y**, *a.* torboso.

pebble, *n.* ciottolo, sasso, sassolino. **pebbly,** *a.* sassoso, pieno di ciottoli.

peccadillo, *n.* peccatuccio, *m.*

peccary, *n.* pecari, *m.inv.*

peccavi, *n.* mea culpa, *m.*

peck, *n.* colpo di becco, *m.*, beccata, *f.*; Meas. = 9.092 litri. ¶ *v.t.* beccare; (*v.i.*) dare colpi di becco. *to be* ~*ish*, essere affamato.

pecten, (*Mol.*) *n.* pettine, *m.*

peculate, *v.t.* appropriarsi. **peculation,** *n.* peculato, *m.*

peculiar, *a.* peculiare, particolare; singolare, bizzarro. ~**ity**, *n.* particolarità, *f.*

pecuniary, *a.* pecuniario.

pedagogue, *n.* pedagogo, *m.*

pedal, *n.* pedale, *m.* ~ [*key*]*board*, pedaliera, *f.* ¶ *v.i.* (*cycle*) pedalare; (*Mus.*) pedaleggiare.

pedant, *n.* pedante, *m.f.* ~**ic,** *a.* (*pers.*) pedante; (*thing*) pedantesco. ~**ry,** *n.* pedanteria, *f.*

peddle, *v.i.* & *t.* fare il merciaiolo ambulante; vendere al dettaglio.

pedestal, *n.* piedestallo, *m.*; piede; zoccolo, *m.*; portavasi, *m.inv.* ~ *cupboard*, comodino, tavolino da notte, *m.* ~ *table*, tavola a piede centrale, *f.*

pedestrian, *n.* pedone, *m.* ~ *crossing*, passaggio per pedoni, *f.* ¶ *a.* a piedi, dei pedoni; (*Statue*) pedestre; (*fig.*) comune, prosaico.

pedigree, *n.* genealogia, *f.*; albero genealogico, *m.*; stirpe, *f.*

pediment, *n.* frontone, *m.*

pedlar, *n.* venditore ambulante, merciai[u]olo, *m.*

pedometer, *n.* pedometro, *m.*

peel, *n.* buccia, scorza, *f.* ¶ *v.t.* sbucciare, scortecciare, mondare. ~ (*off*) *v.i.* squamarsi, scorticarsi. ~**ings,** *n.pl.* mondatura, *f.*, bucce, *f.pl.*

peep, *n.* occhiata, *f.*, sguardo furtivo, *m. at* ~ *of day*, allo spuntare del giorno, alla punta del giorno. ~*hole*, spia, *f.*; spioncino, spiraglio, *m.* ¶ *v.i.* far capolino, gettare un'occhiata furtiva; (*chirp*) pigolare. ~ *at*, guardare sott'occhio, guardare di nascosto, adocchiare, guardare colla coda dell'occhio.

peer, *n.* pari, *m.* ~ *into*, scrutare, guardare curiosamente; frugare, rovistare. ~**age,** *n.* dignità di pari, *f.*; (*book*) almanacco nobiliare, *m.* ~**ess,** *n.* moglie d'un pari, *f.* ~**less,** *a.* senza pari, imparagonabile.

peevish, *a.* petulante, bisbetico, stizzoso, permaloso.

peewit, *n.* pavoncella, *f.*

peg, *n.* caviglia, *f.*, cavicchio; piuolo, *m.*; (*degree*) grado, gradino, punto, *m.*; (*violin, &c.*) bischero, *m.* ~ *top*, trottola, *f.* ¶ *v.t.* incavigliare, attaccare con caviglie; (*Com. Fin.*) stabilizzare. ~ (*away*). tirar via, tirar sempre avanti, persistere.

pegamoid, *n.* pegamoide, *f.*

Pegasus, (*fig.*) *n.* Pegaso, *m.*
peggy (*tooth*, *Nursery talk*), *n.* dentino, *m.*
pekin (*fabric*), *n.* pechino, *m.* **Pechinese** *or* **peke** (*dog*), *n.* cane pechinese, *m.* **Pekin[g]** (*Geog.*), *n.* Pechino, *f.*
pelargonium, *n.* pelargonio, *m.*
pelf, *n.* ricchezze, *f.pl.*, lucro, *m.*
pelican, *n.* pellicano, *m.*
pelisse, *n.* pelliccia, *f.*
pellet, *n.* pallottola, pallina, *f.*
pellicle, *n.* pellicola, *f.*
pell-mell, *ad.* alla rinfusa; promiscuamente; sfrenatamente.
pellucid, *a.* limpidissimo, chiaro e trasparente.
pelt, *n.* pelle greggia, pelle col pelo, *f* ¶ *v.t.* assalire a colpi (*with* = di), lanciare contro. ~*ing rain,* pioggia dirotta, *f.* ~**ry,** *n.* pelletteria, *f.*
pelvis, *n.* pelvi, *f.*; bacino, *m.*
pemmican, *n.* carne seccata, *f.*
pen, *n.* penna, *f.*; pecorile, chiuso, *m.* ~ *& ink drawing,* disegno a penna, *m.* fountain ~, penna stilografica, *f.* ~ *holder,* portapenne, *m.inv.*, cannuccia, *f.* quill ~, penna d'oca, *f.* ~ *knife,* temperino, *m.* ~*manship,* calligrafia, *f.* ~ *name,* nome letterario, pseudonimo, *m.* ~ *rack,* portapenne (a piani), *m.inv.* ~ *dealer,* ~ *driver,* pennaiuolo, *m.* ~ *wiper,* asciugapenne, *m.inv.* ¶ *v.t.* scrivere (a penna); mettere in carta; comporre, redigere; rinchiudere, confinare, parcare.
penal, *a.* penale. ~**ty,** *n.* pena; penalità; sanzione, *f.* ~ *area* (*Foot.*), area di rigore, *f.* ~ *clause,* clausola penale, *f.* ~ *kick,* calcio di rigore, *m.* **penance,** *n.* penitenza, *f.*
Penates, *n.pl.* penati, *m.pl.*
pencil, *n.* lapis, *m.inv.*, matita, *f.*; (*Opt.*) fascio di raggi, pennello, *m.* ~ *case* portalapis, portamatite, *m.inv.* ~ *sharpener,* taglialapis, tagliamatite, *m.inv.* ¶ *v.t.* disegnare (scrivere) a matita.
pendant, ~**ent,** *n.* pendente; ciondolo; orecchino; pendaglio, *m.*; (*Nav.*) fiamma, *f.*; gagliardetto; penzolo, *m.* **pendent,** ~**ant,** *a.* pendente. **pendentive** (*Arch.*), *n.* pennacchio, *m.* **pending,** *a.* pendente, indeciso, non risolto, in corso, in pendenza. ¶ *pr.* in attesa di, fino a, durante. **pendulum,** *n.* pendolo, *m.*; bilanciere, *m.*; (*Horol.*) pendolo, *m.* ~ *clock,* pendola, *f.*
penetrate, *v.t. & i.* penetrare.

penguin, *n.* pinguino, *m.*
penicillin, *n.* penicillina, *f.*
peninsula, *n.* penisola, *f.* **peninsular,** *a.* peninsulare.
penitence, *n.* penitenza, *f.* **penitent,** *a. & n.* penitente, *a. & m.f.* ~**ial,** *a.* penitenziale. **penitentiary,** *a.* penitenziale; penitenziario. ¶ *n.* penitenziario, *m.*
pennant, *n.* fiamma, *f.*
penniless, *a.* senza un soldo, senza danaro; (*pop.*) squattrinato, al verde.
pennon, *n.* fiamma, *f.*, pennone, *m.*
Pennsylvania, *n.* la Pensilvania, *f.*
penny, *n.* penny = $\frac{1}{12}$th of a shilling, *m.*; due soldi, *m.pl.*; denaro, *m.* (*very little money*) soldo. ~*-a-liner,* scrittorello, *m.*; gazzettiere, *m.* ~ *dreadful,* romanzo da due soldi, *m.* ~*-royal,* puleggio, *m.* ~ *weight,* Meas. = 1·5552 grammes.
pension, *n.* pensione, *f.* ¶ *v.t.* pensionare. ~ *off,* giubilare, collocare a riposo, mettere in ritiro. ~**er,** *n.* pensionato, *m.*; (*Mil.*) invalido, *m.*
pensive, *a.* pensieroso, preoccupato.
Pentateuch (the), il Pentateuco, *m.*
Pentecost, *n.* Pentecoste, *f.*
penthouse, *n.* tettoia (addossata ad un muro), *f.*
penultimate, *a.* penultimo.
penumbra, *a.* penombra, *f.*
penurious, *a.* gretto, parsimonioso; povero. **penury,** *n.* penuria, indigenza, miseria, *f.*
peony, *n.* peonia, *f.*
people, *n.* (*individuals*) gente, *f.*; (*nation*) popolo, *m.* ~ *say,* si dice, corre voce. ¶ *v.t.* popolare.
pepper, *n.* pepe, *m.* ~ *box,* pepaiuola, *f.* ~*corn,* granello di pepe, *m.* ~*mint,* menta peperina, *f.* ~*mint* [*lozenge*], pasticca di menta, *f.* ~ *plant,* albero del pepe, *m.* ¶ *v.t.* impepare, condire con pepe; (*shot*) crivellare; (*questions*) tempestare. ~*y,* *a.* ben pepato; (*fig.*) irascibile.
per, *pr.* per, per mezzo di, pel tramite di, secondo. ~ *annum,* per anno, all'anno; ogni anno. ~ *cent,* per cento. ~ *contra,* in contropartita.
perambulate, *v.t.* percorrere (a piedi). **perambulator** (*abb.* **pram**), *n.* carrozzino, *m.*, carrozzella, *f.*
perceive, *v.t.* scorgere, accorgersi di, vedere; notare, rilevare; (*Phil.*) percepire.
percentage, *n.* percentuale, *f.*, percento, *m.*; (*part*) saggio percentuale, *m.*
perceptible, *a.* percettibile, visibile,

sensibile. **perception,** *n.* percezione, *f.*

perch, *n.* (*bird's*) posatoio, *m.*, bastone, *m.*, cannuccia, *f.*; (*Meas.* = 25·293 sq. metres); pertica, *f.*; (*fig.*) posatoio, *m.*, (*fish*) pesce persico, *m.* ¶ *v.i.* posarsi, mettersi; appollaiarsi.

perchance, *ad.* forse, per caso.

percolate, *v.i. & t.* filtrare, colare.

percussion, *n.* percussione, *f.*; percossa, *f.* ~ *cap,* capsula di percussione, *f.*, fulminante, *m.* ~ *instruments,* strumenti a percussione, *m.pl.* **percussive,** *a.* percussivo.

perdition, *n.* perdizione, rovina, *f.*

peregrination, *n.* peregrinazione, *f.* **peregrine [falcon],** *n.* falcone pellegrino, *m.*, falco migratorio, *m.*

peremptory, *a.* perentorio, deciso, risoluto.

perennial, *a.* perenne; perpetuo; continuo. ¶ *n.* pianta vivace, pianta perenne, *f.*

perfect, *a.* perfetto, puro, pretto, vero, completo, finito, esatto. ¶ *n.* (*Gram.*) tempo perfetto. ¶ *v.t.* perfezionare, rendere perfetto, dare l'ultima mano a. ~*ly sweet* (*pers.*), (gente) da baci. ~*ion,* *n.* perfezione, *f.*

perfidious, *a.* perfido, sleale. **perfidy,** *n.* perfidia, *f.*

perforate, *v.t.* perforare, bucare.

perforce, *ad.* per forza, forzatamente.

perform, *v.t. & i.* fare, eseguire, compiere; adempiere; (*Theat.*) rappresentare, recitare; (*Mus.*) eseguire. ~*ance,* *n.* esecuzione, *f.*, adempimento, *m.*; (*Sport*) forma, *f.*, risultato, *m.*; (*Theat.*) rappresentazione, recita, *f.* (*Cinema, &c.*), spettacolo, *m.* no ~, riposo, *m.* ~*er,* *n.* esecutore, *m.*, -trice, *f.*; attore, *m.*, -trice, *f.*; artista, musicante, *m.f.* ~*ing dog,* cane sapiente, *m.*

perfume, *n.* profumo, *m.*; (*fig.*) odore, *m.*, fragranza, *f.* ~ *distiller,* profumiere, *m.* ¶ *v.t.* profumare. **perfumer,** *n.* profumiere, *m.*, -a, *f.*, profumatore, *m.*, -trice, *f.* ~*y,* *n.* profumeria, *f.*

perfunctory, *a.* negligente; senza zelo; fatto per la forma, sbrigativo.

pergola, *n.* pergola, *f.*

perhaps, *ad.* forse, per avventura, per caso.

peril, *n.* rischio, pericolo, *m.* ~*ous,* *a.* pericoloso, rischioso.

perimeter, *n.* perimetro, *m.*

period, *n.* periodo, *m.*, spazio di tempo, *m.*; epoca, *f.*; fase, *f.*; durata, *f.*; tempo, limite, termine, *m.* ~*ic,* *& ~ical,* *a.* periodico. ~*ical,* *n.* periodico, giornale, *m.*, rivista, *f.*

periphery, *n.* periferia, *f.*

periphrasis, *n.* perifrasi, *f.*

periscope, *n.* periscopio, *m.*

perish, *v.i.* perire, deperire, morire, guastarsi, cadere in rovina. ~*able,* *a.* deperibile, che si guasta presto, soggetto a decadere; mortale.

peristyle, *n.* peristilio, *m.*

peritonitis, *n.* peritonite, *f.*

periwinkle, *n.* (*Mol.*) littorina, *f.*; (*Bot.*) pervinca, *f.*

perjure oneself, spergiurare. ~*d,* *p.a.* spergiurato. **perjurer,** *n.* spergiuro, *m.*, -a, *f.*; (*Law*) chi giura il falso. **perjury,** *n.* spergiuro; giuramento falso, *m.*

perky, *a.* impertinente, vispetto, vivace; civettuolo.

permanence, *n.* permanenza, *f.* **permanent,** *a.* permanente; duraturo; immutabile. ~ *wave,* ondulazione permanente, *f.* ~ *way* (*Rly.*) rotaie, *f.pl.* ~ *works, structures,* costruzioni permanenti, *f.pl.* ~*ly,* *a.* permanentemente, in permanenza.

permanganate, *n.* permanganato, *m.*

permeable, *a.* permeabile. **permeate,** *v.t.* penetrare; permeare.

permissible, *a.* permissibile. **permission,** *n.* permesso, *m.*, permissione, *f.* **permit,** *n.* permesso, *m.*, lasciapassare, *m.* ¶ *v.t.* permettere; lasciare; soffrire; tollerare; concedere; accordare.

pernicious, *a.* pernicioso, nocivo.

peroration, *n.* perorazione, *f.*

peroxide, *n.* perossido, *m.*

perpendicular, *a. & n.* perpendicolare, *a. & f.*

perpetrate, *v.t.* perpetrare, commettere. **perpetrator,** (*crime*) *n.* autore, *m.*

perpetual, *a.* perpetuo. **perpetuate,** *v.t.* perpetuare. **perpetuity,** *n.* perpetuità, *f.* *in* ~, in perpetuo.

perplex, *v.t.* confondere, rendere perplesso, mettere nell'imbarazzo, imbrogliare. ~*ed,* *a.* perplesso. ~*ing,* *a.* imbarazzante. ~*ity,* *n.* perplessità, *f.*

perquisite, *n.* gratificazione, *f.*, emolumento casuale, *m.* (*pl.*) proventi, incerti, *m.pl.*, guadagni casuali, *m.pl.*; mance, *f.pl.*

perry, *n.* sidro di pere, *m.*

persecute, *v.t.* perseguitare; (*fig.*) importunare. **persecution,** *n.*

persecuzione, *f.*; **persecutor,** *n.*
persecutore, *m.*, -trice, *f.*
perseverance, *n.* perseveranza, *f.*
persevere, *v.i.* perseverare.
Persia, *n.* la Persia, *f.* **Persian**
(*modern*) *a.* persiano. ~ *blind,*
persiana, *f.*; gelosia, *f.*, scuri, *m.pl.*;
~ *carpet,* tappeto persiano, *m.* ~
cat, gatto persiano, g. d'Angora, *m.*
~ *Gulf,* Golfo persico, *m.* ¶ *n.*
(*pers.*) persiano, *m.*, -a, f.; (*language*)
persiano, *m.*
persiflage, *n.* canzonatura, ironia
leggera e sottile, *f.*
persist, *v.i.* persistere; perseverare;
ostinarsi. ~ence, ~ency, *n.*
persistenza, ostinazione, *f.* ~ent,
a. persistente.
person, *n.* persona, *f.* ~ *of indepen-*
dent means, reddituario, *m.*, -a, *f.*
~ *opposite,* persona che sta (o siede)
di rimpetto, *f.* ~age, *n.* personaggio, *m.* ~al, *a.* personale; (*property*)
mobile, mobiliare. ~ality, *n.*
personalità, *f.* ~alty, *n.* beni
mobili, *m.pl.* ~ate, *v.t.* rappresentare; farsi passare per. ~nel, *n.*
personale, *m.* **personify,** *v.t.* per-
sonificare.
perspective, *n.* prospettiva, f.; (*Theat.*)
prospettiva, ottica, *f.*
perspicacious, *a.* perspicace. **pers-**
picacity, *n.* perspicacia, *f.* **perspi-**
cuous, *a.* perspicuo.
perspiration, *n.* traspirazione, *f.*;
sudore, *m.* *bathed in* ~, madido di
sudore. **perspire,** *v.i.* sudare;
traspirare.
persuade, *v.t.* persuadere. **persua-**
sion, *n.* persuasione; fede, *f.*
persuasive, *a.* persuasivo.
pert, *a.* vispetto, impertinente.
pertain, *v.i.* appartenere, spettare,
riferirsi (a).
pertinacious, *a.* pertinace. **pertina-**
city, *n.* pertinacia, *f.*
pertinent, *a.* a proposito, opportuno,
proprio. **-ly,** *ad.* a proposito.
pertness, *n.* impertinenza, *f.*, vivacità,
insolenza, *f.*
perturb, *v.t.* perturbare. **-ation,** *n.*
perturbazione, *f.*, perturbamento,
m.
Perú, *n.* il Perú, *m.*
Perugia, *n.* Perugia, *f.*
perusal, *n.* lettura (attenta) *f.* **peruse,**
v.t. leggere attentamente.
Peruvian, *a.* peruviano. ~ *bark,*
china, *f.* ¶ *n.* peruviano, *m.*, -a,
f.
pervade, *v.t.* pervadere, compene-

trare, diffondersi per. **pervasive,** *a.*
diffuso.
perverse, *a.* perverso, cattivo. **per-**
version, *n.* pervertimento, *m.* **per-**
versity, *n.* perversità, *f.* **pervert**
(*apostate*), *n.* apostata, pervertito, *m.*
¶ *v.t.* pervertire; svisare, snaturare;
corrompere.
pervious, *a.* permeabile.
pessimism, *n.* pessimismo, *m.* **pes-**
simist, *n.* & **-ic,** *a.* pessimista,
a. & *m.f.*
pest, *n.* peste, pestilenza, *f.*
pester, *v.t.* importunare, seccare,
tormentare.
pestilence, *n.* pestilenza, *f.* **pestilent,**
~ial, *a.* pestilenziale, pernicioso.
pestle, *n.* pestello, *m.* ¶ *v.t.* pestare.
pet, *n.* favorito, *m.*, -a, *f.*, beniamino,
m., -a, *f.*, carino, *m.*, -a, *f.*; animale
favorito, *m.*; accesso di cattivo
umore, *m.*, stizza, *f.* ~ *argument,*
argomento prediletto, *m.*; cavallo di
battaglia, *m.* ~ *aversion,* incubo, *m.*
~ *dog,* cane favorito, *m.* ~ *name,*
vezzeggiativo, *m.* ~ *scheme,* piano
favorito, *m.* ~ *subject,* idea predi-
letta, *f.*, soggetto prediletto, *m.*
~ *theory,* fissazione, *f.* ~ *vice,*
peccatuccio prediletto, *m.* ¶ *v.t.*
accarezzare, vezzeggiare.
petal, *n.* petalo, *m.*
Peter's pence, l'obolo di San Pietro,
m.
petiole, *n.* picciuolo (di foglia), *m.*
petite, *a.* piccolina, carina.
petition, *n.* petizione, supplica; istanza; richiesta, *f.* ¶ *v.t.* supplicare,
sollecitare, presentare istanza; (*v.i.*)
presentare una petizione, stendere
una petizione. ~er, *n.* supplicante,
postulante, istante, *m.f.*
petitio principii, petizione di principio, *f.*
petrel, *n.* procellaria, *f.*
petrifaction, *n.* pietrificazione, *f.*
petrify, *v.t.* pietrificare; (*fig.*) stupire, stordire, sbalordire.
petrol, *n.* benzina, *f.* ~ *tank,* serbatoio di benzina, *m.*, cisterna di b.,
f. ~ *tin,* bidone (da benzina) *n.*
petroleum, *n.* petrolio, *m.*
petticoat, *n.* gonnella, sottana, *f.*;
sottoveste, *f.*
pettifoggery, *n.* professione di legu-
leio, *f.*; cavilli, *m.pl.*; litigiosità, *f.*
pettifogging, *a.* cavilloso.
pettiness, *n.* piccolezza, meschinità,
f.
pettish, *a.* irritabile, bisbetico, stizzito.
petty, *a.* piccolo, piccino, meschino,

insignificante. ~ *officer*, sotto'ufficiale di marina, *m.*
petulance, *n.* scontrosità, irascibilità, *f.* **petulant**, *a.* scontroso, bizzoso.
petunia, *n.* petunia, *f.*
pew, *n.* banco (di chiesa), *m.*
pewit, *n.* pavoncella, *f.*
pewter, *n.* peltro, *m.*, lega di stagno, *f.* ~**er**, *n.* stagnaio, *m.*
phaeton, *n.* calessino, *m.*
phalanx, *n.* falange, *f.*
phantasm, *n.* fantasma, *m.* **phantasy**, *n.* fantasia, *f.* **phantasmagoria**, *n.* fantasmagoria, *f.* **phantom**, *n.* fantasma, spettro, *m.*; larva, *f.* ¶ *a.* spettrale, irreale; fantastico. ~ *ship*, nave fantasma, *f.*
Pharaoh, *n.* Faraone, *m.*
Pharisaic(al), *a.* farisaico. **Pharisee**, *n.* fariseo, *m.*, -a, *f.*
pharmaceutical, *a.* farmaceutico. **pharmacist**, *n.* farmacista, *m.f.* **pharmacy**, *n.* farmacia, *f.*
pharingitis, *n.* faringite, *f.* **pharynx**, *n.* faringe, *f.*
phase, *n.* fase, *f.*
pheasant, *n.* fagiano, *m.*, -a, *f.*; (*young*) fagianotto, *m.* ~**ry**, *n.* fagianaia, *f.*
phenacetin, *n.* fenacetina, *f.*
phenol, *n.* (*Chem.*) fenolo, *m.*
phenomenal, *a.* fenomenale. **phenomenon**, *n.* fenomeno, *m.*
phial, *n.* fiala, boccetta, *f.*
Phidias, *n.* Fidia, *m.*
Philadelphia, *n.* Filadelfia, *f.*
philander, *v.i.* civettare, fare il cascamorto, fare il galante. ~**er**, *n.* cascamorto, galante, *m.*
philanthropic, *a.* filantropico. **philanthropist**, *n.* filantropo, *m.*, -a, *f.* **philanthropy**, *n.* filantropia, *f.*
philatelist, *n.* filatelico, *m.*, -a, *f.* **philately**, *n.* filatelia, *f.*; filatelica, *f.*
philharmonic, *a.* filarmonico.
philippic, *n.* filippica, *f.*
Philistine, *n.* filisteo, *m.*
philologist, *n.* filologo, *m.* **philology**, *n.* filologia, *f.*
philosopher, *n.* filosofo, *m.* ~'*s stone*, pietra filosofale, *f.* **philosophic(al)**, *a.* filosofico. ~ (*calm*), serenità, tranquillità dell'animo, *f.* **philosophize**, *v.i.* filosofare. **philosophy**, *n.* filosofia, *f.*
philtre, ~**ter**, *n.* filtro, *m.*
phlebitis, *n.* flebite, *f.*
phlegm, *n.* muco, *m.*; pituita, *f.*; (*fig.*) flemma, *f.*, sangue freddo, *m.* ~**atic**, *a.* flemmatico.
phlox, *n.* flosside, *f.*, flocs, *m.*

ph[o]enix, *n.* fenice, *f.*
phonetic, *a.* fonetico. ~**s**, *n.pl.* fonetica, *f.*
phonograph, *n.* fonografo, *m.*
phosphate, *n.* fosfato, *m.* **phosphorescence**, *n.* fosforescenza, *f.* **phosphorescent**, *a.* fosforescente. **phosphorus**, *n.* fosforo, *m.*
photograph, *n.* fotografia, *f.* ~ *frame*, cornice, *f.* ¶ *v.t.* fotografare. ~**er**, *n.* fotografo, *m.* ~**ic**, *a.* fotografico. ~**y**, *n.* fotografia, *f.* **photogravure**, *n.* fotoincisione, *f.*
phrase, *n.* frase, locuzione, *f.*; (*Mus.*) frase (musicale) *f.*; periodo, *m.*; ¶ *v.t.* esprimere; chiamare, (*v.i.*) fraseggiare. **phraseology**, *n.* fraseologia, *f.*
phrenologist, *n.* frenologo, *m.* **phrenology**, *n.* frenologia, *f.*
phthisis, *n.* tisi, *f.*
physic, *n.* medicina, *f.* ¶ *v.t.* somministrare medicine a, medicare. ~**al**, *a.* fisico, *m.* ~**ian**, *n.* medico, *m.* ~**ist**, *n.* fisico, *m.* ~**s**, *n.pl.* fisica, *f.*
physiognomy, *n.* fisionomia, *f.*
physiology, *n.* fisiologia, *f.*
physique, *n.* fisico, *m.*
Piacenza, *n.* Piacenza, *f.*
pianist, *n.* pianista, *m.f.* **piano[forte]**, *n.* pianoforte, *m.* *piano organ*, & ~ *player*, pianoforte meccanico, *m.* ~ *wire*, corda del pianoforte, *f.*
piccaninny, *n.* bambino negro, *m.*
piccolo, *n.* ottavino, *m.*
pick, *n.* piccone, *m.*; (*choice*) scelta, *f.*, fiore, *m.*; (*of the basket*) parte migliore, *f.* ~ *axe*, piccone, *m.*; gravina, *f.* ~ *lock* (*inst.*) grimaldello, *m.*; (*pers.*) scassinatore, *m.* ~-*me-up*, bicchierino, ristorativo, *m.* *the* ~ *of the bunch*, il fior fiore, *m.* ~*pocket*, borsaio[u]olo, *m.*, tagliaborse, *m.inv.* ¶ *v.t.* cogliere, raccogliere; piluccare; scegliere; (*bone*) rodere, rosicchiare; (*lock*) aprire, scassinare (col grimaldello); (*teeth*) nettarsi, pulirsi, stuzzicarsi; (*quarrel*) attaccar (briga), cercare (contesa). ~ *at one's food*, sbocconcellare, mangiucchiare, spilluzzicare. ~ *up*, raccattare, raccogliere; rialzare; rimettersi in salute, rifarsi; imparare; (*passengers*) prendere; (*news*) raccogliere; (*Radio*) captare.
pickaback, *ad.* addosso, sul dorso.
picked, *p.a.* colto, raccolto; scelto; distinto; mondato, pulito. **picker**, *n.* raccoglitore, *m.*, -trice, *f.*; spigolatore, *m.*, -trice, *f.*

picket, *n.* picchetto, *m.* ¶ *v.t.* mettere picchetti, picchettare.

picking, *n.* colta, raccolta, *f.*, cernita, scelta, *f.*; (*pl. pilferings*) risorse del mestiere, *f.pl.*; guadagni casuali, *m.pl.*

pickle, *n.* (*brine*) salamoia, *f.*; (*plight*) imbroglio, *m.*, situazione imbarazzante, *f.*; (*child*) diavoletto, *m.*; (*pl.*) legumi in aceto, *m.pl.*, sott'aceti; acetini, *m.pl.* ¶ *v.t.* salare, mettere sott'aceto. ~**d,** *a.* (*vegetables*) in accto, sott'aceto; (*meat*) salato.

picnic, *n.* merenda all'aperto, colazione sull'erba, *f.* ~ *basket*, cestino, *m.* ¶ *v.i.* fare merenda in campagna; accozzare i pentolini.

pictorial, *a.* pittorico, della pittura; (*journal*) illustrato; (*plan, map*) figurativo, figurato. ¶ *n.* giornale illustrato, *m.* **picture,** *n.* quadro, dipinto, ritratto, *m.*; pittura, *f.*; tela, *f.* ~ *book*, libro illustrato, l. figurato, *m.* ~ *gallery*, galleria di quadri, pinacoteca, *f.* ~ *palace* or ~*s*, cinema, *m.* ~ *postcard*, cartolina illustrata, *f.* ~ *puzzle*, rebus, *m.inv.* ~ *writing*, scrittura figurativa, *f.*; dipinto simbolico, *m.* ¶ *v.t.* dipingere; descrivere; figurare; rappresentare. ~ *to oneself*, figurarsi, immaginarsi. **picturesque,** *a.* pittoresco. ~**ness,** *n.* pittoresco, *m.*

pie, *n.* (*meat*) pasticcio, *m.*; (*fruit*) torta, *f.* ,crostata, *f.* (*printers'*) refusi, *m.pl.* massa confusa di caratteri, *f.* [*state of*] ~, (*fig.*) confusione, *f.*, disordine, *m.* ~*dish*, tortiera; terrina, *f.*

piebald, *a.* pezzato, pomellato.

piece, *n.* pezzo, frammento, brano, tozzo, boccone, *m.*; squarcio, *m.*; pezza, *f.*; scampolo, *m.*; (*drama*) dramma, *m.*, commedia, *f.* ~ *of business*, affare, *m.* ~ *of furniture*, mobile, *m.* ~ *of ice*, ghiaccio, *m.* ~ *of impertinence*, impertinenza, *f.* ~ *of news*, notizia, *f.* ~ *of ordnance*, pezzo (d'artiglieria) *m.*; bocca da fuoco, *f.* ~ *of poetry*, poesia, *f.* ~ *work*, lavoro a cottimo, *m.* ¶ *v.t.* rappezzare; ~ *together* (*fig.*) formarsi un'idea d'insieme. **piecemeal,** *ad.* pezzo a pezzo, poco a poco, a pezzi e a bocconi.

pied, *a.* screziato, variegato; pezzato.

Piedmont, *n.* il Piemonte, *m.* **Piedmontese,** *a. & n.* piemontese, *a. & m.*

pier, *n.* molo, *m.*, banchina, *f.*; calata, gettata, *f.*; sbarcatoio, *m.*; pila, *f.*,

pilone, *m.*; contrafforte, pilastro, *m.*; ~*head*, testa di molo, *f.*, capo del molo, *m.*

pierce, *v.t. & i.* trafiggere, attraversare; forare, traforare; penetrare. **piercing,** *p.a.* penetrante, pungente, acuto; commovente; (*cold*) pungente; (*sound*) squillante.

piety, *n.* pietà, devozione, riverenza, *f.*

pig, *n.* porco, maiale, *m.*; (*child*) porcellino, porchetto, *m.* (*Founding*) pane di ghisa, massello, *m.*; verga, *f.* ~ *breeding*, allevamento suino, *m.* ~*-headed*, ostinato, testardo, stupido. ~(*iron*) ferro crudo, *m.*, ghisa, *f.* ~ *meat*, carne di porco, di maiale, *f.* ~*skin*, pelle di porco, *f.* ~*sty* or **piggery,** *n.* porcile, *m.* ~*tail* (hair) codino, *m.*

pigeon, *n.* piccione, colombo, *m.*, -a, *f.*; (*young*) piccioncino, *m.* ~*hole*, casella, *f.*; (*in desk*) casella. [*set of*] ~ *holes*, casellario, *m.* ~**ry,** *n.* colombaia, *f.*

piglet, *n.* porcellino, *m.*

pigment, *n.* pigmento, *m.*

pigmy, *n.* pigmeo, *m.*

pike, *n.* picca, *f.*; (*fish*) luccio, *m.*

pilaster, *n.* pilastro, *m.*

pilchard, *n.* sardella, *f.*

pile, *n.* mucchio, *m.*, pila, catasta, *f.*, monte, monticello, *m.*; (*mass of building*) casamento, gruppo di costruzioni, ammasso, *m.*; (*wood*) catasta, *f.*; mucchio, *m.*, legnaia, *f.*; (*arms*) fascio, *m.*; (*Stake*) palo, *m.*, palafitta, *f.*; (*nap*) pelo, *m.* ~ *driver*, maglio, scatto, battipalo, *m.*; berta, *f.* *man who has made his* ~, uomo che ha fatto fortuna, che ha ammassato ricchezze. ~ [*up*] *v.t.* ammonticchiare, ammucchiare, accumulare. *pile arms*, mettere in fascio, disporre in fasci.

piles (*Med.*) *n.pl.* emorroidi, *f.pl.*

pilfer, *v.t.* rubacchiare, sottrarre.

pilgrim, *n.* pellegrino, *m.*, -a, *f.* ~**age,** *n. & place of pilgrimage*, pellegrinaggio, *m.*

piling, *n.* (*pile work*) palafittata, *f.* ~ *up of taxation*, fiscalità, *f.*

pill, *n.* pillola, *f.* ~ *box*, scatoletta per pillole, *f.*; (*Mil.*) fortino in cemento, *m.*

pillage, *n.* saccheggio, *m.* ¶ *v.t.* saccheggiare.

pillar, *n.* colonna, *f.*, pilastro, sostegno, *m.* ~ *box*, buca delle lettere, *f.*

pillion, *n.* (*Motor*) *n.* sedile di tandem; cuscinetto, *m.*; sella da donna, *f.*

~ *rider*, passeggero (-a) al sedile di tandem, *m.f.*

pillory, *n.* berlina, gogna, *f.* ¶ *v.t.* mettere alla berlina.

pillow, *n.* guanciale, origliere, cuscino, capezzale, *m.*; (*lace making*) tombolo, *m.*; (*Mech.*) cuscinetto, *m.* ~*case*, ~*slip*, federa (di guanciale), *f.* ~ *lace*, merletto al tombolo, *m.*

pilot, *n.* pilota, *m.* ~ *balloon*, (*fig.*) tentativo, *m.*, prova, *f.*, pallone di prova, *m.* ~ *boat*, battello pilota, *m.* ~ *lamp*, lampada spia, *f.* ¶ *v.t.* pilotare; (*fig.*) condurre. ~**age**, *n.* pilotaggio, *m.*

pimpernel, *n.* anagallide, erba grisellina, *f.*

pimple, *n.* pustola, vescichetta, *f.*, foruncolo, *m.* *to break out in* ~*s*, coprirsi di pustole.

pin, *n.* spillo, *m.*; (*peg*) caviglia, *f.*, cavicchio, *m.*; (*fig.*) bagatella, *f.*, spilla, *f.*; (*Mech.*) pernio, asse, *m.*, spina; chiavetta, *f.*; (*watch*) copiglia, *f.* *drawing* ~, puntina, *f.* ~*s & needles* (*fig.*) formicolio, *m.* ~ *cushion*, portaspilli, *m.*, guancialetto per gli spilli, *m.* ~ *money*, spillatico, *m.* ~ *prick*, puntura di spillo, *f.*; (*fig.*) colpo di spillo, *m.* ~ *table*, biliardo americano, *m.* ¶ *v.t.* attaccare con spilli; incavigliare, appuntare, imperniare.

pinafore, *n.* grembiulino, *m.*

pincers, *n.pl.* tanaglie (*or* tenaglie); (*smith's*) tanaglie da falegname, *f.pl.*

pinch, *n.* (*of salt*) pizzico, *m.*; (*sr.uff*) presa, *f.* *at a* ~, al bisogno, in caso di necessità. ¶ *v.t.* pizzicare, dare un pizzicotto a; serrare, stringere; far soffrire; risparmiare, privare del necessario, ridurre alle strettezze. ~**ed**, *p.a.* (*face*) sparuto; (*for money*) stretto a danaro.

pine[**apple**], *n.* ananasso, *m.* **pine** [**tree**], *n.* pino, *m.* *pinewood* (forest), pineta, *f.*

pine, *v.i.* languire; deperire. ~ *for*, *v.t.* sospirare dietro, struggersi per, bramare.

ping-pong, *n.* ping-pong, tennis da tavola, *m.* ~ *set*, giuoco di p.-p., giuoco di t. da t., *m.*

pining, *n.* languore, deperimento; struggimento; desiderio ardente, *m.*; nostalgia, *f.*

pinion, *n.* punta dell'ala, *f.*; (*fig. & poet.*) ala, *f.*; (*Mech.*) pignone, rocchetto, *m.* ¶ *v.t.* tarpare le ali a; tagliare la punta dell'ala a; (*pers.*) legare le braccia a.

pink, *a.* rosa, color rosa. ¶ *n.* color rosa, *m.*; (*fig.*) fiore; modello, *m.*, perfezione, *f.*; (*Bot.*) garofano, *m.*

pinnace, *n.* scialuppa, *f.*, grande canotto, *m.*

pinnacle, *n.* pinnacolo, *m.*, cima, *f.*; (*fig.*) sommità a punta, *f.*; sommo, apogeo, *m.*

pint, *n.* pinta, *f.*, mezzo litro, *m.*; *Imperial Meas.* = 0.568 litre.

pintle, *n.* cardine; spillo del perno, *m.*; (*Naut.*) agugliotto, *m.*

pioneer, *n.* pioniere; precursore, *m.*

pious, *a.* pio, devoto.

pip, *n.* (*seed*) seme, chicco, granello, acino, vinacciuolo, *m.*; (*cards, dominoes*) macchia, *f.*, punto, *m.*; (*disease*) pipita, *f.*

pipe, *n.* tubo, condotto, *m.*; (*organ*) canna, *f.*; (*key*) canna, *f.*; (*tobacco*) pipa, *f.*; (*Mus. instr.*) zampogna; fistola, *f.*; zufolo; piffero; flauto, *m.*; (*boatswain's*) fischietto (del nostromo), *m.* ~ *clay*, terra da pipa, *f.*, argilla per pipe, *f.* ~ *light*, fiammifero per accendere la pipa, legnetto, *m.* ~ *lighter*, accendisigaro, *m.inv.* ~ *line*, tubazione, *f.*; condotto, *m.* ¶ *v.i. & t.* suonare la zampogna, pifferare, suonare sul flauto, sul piffero; zufolare; fischiare. **piping**, (*braid*) *n.* filetto, *m.*

pipit, *n.* calandra; pispola, *f.*

pipkin, *n.* pentolino, tegame, *m.*

pippin, *n.* mela renetta, *f.*

piquancy, *n.* gusto piccante, *m.*; (*fig.*) sale, piccante; il bello, il più bello. **piquant**, *a.* piccante, acre, pungente; arguto, spiritoso. **pique**, *n.* malumore, *m.*, irritazione, picca, *f.*, puntiglio, *m.* ¶ *v.t.* irritare, offendere. ~ *oneself on*, vantarsi di, piccarsi di. **piquet**, *n.* picchetto, *m.*

piracy, *n.* pirateria; contraffazione, *f.* **pirate**, *n.* pirata, *m.f.*; (*fig.*) pirata, succhione, *m.* ~ *publisher*, editore pirata, *m.* ¶ *v.t.* contraffare, stampare alla macchia; (*v.i.*) pirateggiare. ~**d**, (*publication*) stampato alla macchia.

Piraeus, *n.* il Pireo, *m.*

pirouette, *n.* piroetta, *f.* ¶ *v.i.* far piroetta, piroettare.

Pisa, *n.* Pisa, *f.*

pisciculture, *f.* piscicoltura, *f.*

pistachio, *n.* (*nut*) pistacchio, *m.*, (*tree*) pistacchio, *m.*

pistil, *n.* pistillo, *m.*

pistol, *n.* pistola, *f.* *to hold a* ~ *at one's head*, (*fig.*) star con la pistola alla mano, rivolgere una minaccia a.

piston, n. pistone, stantuffo, m. ~ rod, asta (gambo, stelo, m.) dello stantuffo, f.

pit, n. fossa, buca, f., scavo, m.; pozzo; abisso, m.; miniera, cava, cavità, f.; (stomach) cavo, m.; (in metal, &c.) forellino, bucolino, m.; (pock) buttero, segno, m., traccia, pustola, f.; (Theat.) platea, f. ~fall, trabocchetto, m., buca cieca, f.; (fig.) tranello, m., trappola, f. ~ saw, segone, m., sega lunga, f. ¶ v.t. marcare, segnare; butterare; bucare; punteggiare; mettere alle prese (con), mettere contro, mettere in gara. ~ted, a. butterato.

pit-[a]-pat (to go), palpitare; fare tic-tac.

pitch, n. (material) pece, f., bitume, m.; (degree, &c.) grado, m.; elevazione, pendenza (d'un tetto), f., m.; (Mus.) tono, m.; voce, estensione, f.; altezza, f.; diapason, m.; (Mech.) passo, m.; (Naut.) movimento della prua, m.; (angler's) colpo, m.; ~ dark, buio come la pece, nero come la pece, buio pesto. ~ fork (Mus.) diapason, m.; (Agr.) forca, f., forcone, m. ~fork someone into an office, lanciare qualcuno in un uffizio. ~ pine, abete rosso, m. ~ pipe, diapason a fiato, m. ¶ v.t. gettare, lanciare, precipitare; (tent, camp, &c.) piantare, porre, rizzare; (net) tendere. v.i. cadere, abbattersi, tuffarsi; (ship) beccheggiare. ~ upon, abbattersi in, decidersi per, fermare la scelta su. ~ed battle, battaglia campale, f.

pitcher, n. brocca, secchia, f.

piteous, a. pietoso; lamentevole.

pith, n. midollo, m.; (palm tree) cefaglione, m.; (fig.) succo, m., essenza, quintessenza; forza, f.; vigore, m.; (of a story) parte essenziale, f., nodo, m. ~ helmet, casco coloniale, m. ~y, a. midolloso; (fig.) molto sugoso, pieno di vigore.

pitiable & **pitiful,** a. pietoso, degno di pietà. **pitiless,** a. spietato, senza pietà.

pittance, n. pietanza, piccola porzione, f.

pity, n. pietà, compassione, f. what a ~! che peccato! to move to ~, muovere a pietà; destare pietà. ¶ v.t. compatire, compiangere, commiserare, aver pietà di.

pivot, n. perno, pernio, m.; asse, f.; cardine, m. ¶ v.i. imperniare, girare su.

pixy, ~xie, n. fata, f.

placard, n. affisso, cartello, m., cartellone, manifesto, m. ¶ v.t. affiggere (dei cartelli), annunziare a mezzo di cartello.

place, n. luogo, posto, sito, m.; piazza, terrazza, viuzza, f.; impiego, m., carica, f.; rango, m.; condizione, posizione, f.; vece; villa, f. to take ~, aver luogo, accadere. to take the ~ of, fare le veci di, tener luogo di, sostituire, rimpiazzare. ¶ v.t. collocare, mettere, porre, posare, situare. ~d horse, cavallo piazzato, m.

placer, (Min.) n. terreno aurifero, m.

placid, a. placido, sereno. ~ity, n. placidità, f.

plagiarism, n. plagio, m. **plagiarist,** n. plagiario, m., -a, f. **plagiarize,** v.t. plagiare.

plague, n. peste, pestilenza, f.; flagello, tormento, m. ~ stricken (person) colpito dalla peste. ¶ (fig.) v.t. tormentare, importunare, molestare; (tease) stuzzicare, provocare.

plaice, n. pesce passera, m.

plain, a. semplice; nudo; liscio, eguale, piatto, piano; (cigarettes, &c.) ordinario; chiaro, evidente, manifesto; franco, schietto, puro; (of one colour) unito; al naturale; alla buona; brutto. ~[-boiled], al naturale, senza salsa. in ~ clothes, in abito civile, in borghese. ~ cooking, cucina casalinga, f. ~ dealing, franchezza, lealtà, f. in ~ figures, in cifre chiare. ~ girl, ragazza bruttina, f. ~ knitting, lavoro (a maglia) semplice, m. ~ language (Teleg.), chiaro. ~ sewing, cucitura (alla mano), f. ~-song, canto fermo, canto gregoriano, m. ¶ n. piano, m., pianura, f. ~ly, ad. chiaramente, evidentemente, manifestamente, visibilmente; francamente, schiettamente, apertamente; semplicemente; al naturale, alla buona. ~ness, n. franchezza, schiettezza; semplicità; naturalezza; bruttezza, f.

plaintiff, n. attore, m., -trice, f.; parte civile, f.; querelante, m.f. **plaintive,** a. lamentevole, querulo.

plait, n. piega, treccia, f. ¶ v.t. pieghettare. to ~ one's hair, intrecciare.

plan, n. piano, progetto, disegno; sistema, m.; mezzo, partito, m.; (building &c.) pianta, f. ¶ v.t. progettare; disegnare; pianificare.

plane, a. piano. ¶ n. piano, m., superficie piana, f.; (tool) pialla, f.

aeroplano, *m.* ~ *table*, tavoletta, assicella, *f.*; banco, *m.* ~ [*tree*] platano, *m.* ¶ *v.t.* piallare. ~ *down*, appianare, livellare.

planet, *n.* pianeta, *m.* **planetarium,** *n.* planetario, *m.* **planetary,** *a.* planetario.

planing machine, *n.* piallatrice (meccanica), *f.*

planish, *v.t.* appiattire; (*wood*) piallare; (*metal*) martellare, incartare.

plank, *n.* tavola, asse, *f.*; tavolone, pancone.*m*

plankton, *n.* plankton, *m.*

planner, *n.* progettista, *m.f.* **planning,** *n.* pianificazione, *f.* *post-war* ~, pianificazioni postbelliche, *f.pl.*

plant, *n.* pianta, *f.*; erba, *f.*; (*Mech.*) impianto, materiale, *m.*; attrezzi, arnesi, *m.pl.* ~ *life*, vita vegetale, *f.* ¶ *v.t.* piantare, (*fig.*) piantare, impiantare, fissare, fondare. ~ *out*, trapiantare.

plantain, *n.* piantaggine, *f.*; (*banana*) banano, fico d'Adamo, *m.*

plantation, *n.* piantagione, *f.*, albereto, boschetto, *m.* **planter** *n.* colono; piantatore, *m.*, -trice, *f.*

plaque, *n.* placca, *f.*

plash, *n.* pozza, pozzanghera, *f.* ¶ *v.i.* spruzzare, far maretta.

plaster, *n.* gesso, intonaco, *m.*; calcina, *f.*; ((*Med.*) impiastro, *m.*, cataplasma, *f.* ~ *cast*, gesso, *m.*; maschera, *f.* ~ *of Paris*, gesso da scultore, stucco, *m.* ¶ *v.t.* intonacare, ingessare, spalmare; applicare un impiastro a. ~er, *n.* gessaio, *m.*

plastic, *a.* plastico. ~s, *n.pl.* [*materiali*] plastici, *m.pl.* **plasticity,** *n.*, plasticità, *f.*

plat, *n.* treccia; aiuola, *f.*; pezzo di terra, *m.* ¶ *v.t.* intrecciare, intessere.

plate, *n.* lamina, lamiera, lastra, placca, piastra, targa, *f.*; (*dish*) piatto, *m.* (*coll.*) vasellame, *m.*; argenteria, *f.*; (*Phot.*) lastra; negativa, *f.*; (*book*) incisione, illustrazione, tavola, *f.*; (*Turf*) coppa, *f.*; [*book of*] ~s, albo, atlante, *m.* *fish*-~, (*Rly.*) ganascia, *f.* ~s & *dishes*, vasellame, *m.* ~ *basket*, cesto per piatti, cestino per le posate, *m.* ~ *glass*, cristallo, cristallo in lastre, *m.* ~ *glass insurance*, assicurazione contro le rotture di cristalli, *f.* ~layer, (*Rly.*) montatore (dei binari), *m.* ~ *rack*, portapiatti, scolapiatti, *m.inv.* ¶ *v.t.* placcare, inargentare; (*Ship*) corazzare, ~[-ful], *n.* piatto pieno, *m.*; scodellata, *f.*

plateau, *n.* altopiano, *m.*

platen, *n.* (*Typ.*) platina, *f.*, (*type-writer*) rullo, *m.*

platform, *n.* piattaforma, terrazza, tribuna, *f.*; palco, *m.*; (*Rly.*) marciapiede, *m.*, banchina, *f.*; scalo (*goods*), *m.*; (*Pol.*) programma, *m.*; piattaforma, *f.* ~ *car* (*Rly.*), pianale, *m.* ~ *scales*, bascula, *f.*

platinotype, *n.* platinotipia, *f.* **platinum,** *n.* platino, *m.* ~ *blonde* (colour), biondo platino, *m.*

platitude, *n.* banalità, insulsaggine, insipidezza, *f.*

Plato, *n.* Platone, *m.* **Platonic,** *a.* platonico.

platoon, *n.* plotone, *m.*

plaudit, *n.* applauso, *m.*

plausible, *a.* plausibile.

play, *n.* giuoco; divertimento, spasso, *m.*, ricreazione, *f.*; spettacolo, *m.*; commedia, *f.*; dramma; *m.*; rappresentazione, *f.*; (*pl.*) teatro, *m.*; (*Mech.*) giuoco, movimento, *m.*, oscillazioni, *f.pl.*; (*room*) slancio, scopo, *m.*, libertà d'azione, *f.* ~ *bill*, programma (dello spettacolo), affisso teatrale, *m.* ~fellow, ~mate, compagno di giuoco, *m.*, compagna di giuoco, *f.*; camerata, *m.f.* ~goer, pratico di teatri, frequentatore di spettacoli, *m.* ~ground, (*Sch.*) corte di ricreazione, *f.*; (*covered*) chiostro, *m.* ~ *house*, teatro, *m.*; sala di spettacolo, *f.* ~ *of colours*, giuoco di colori, *m.* ~ *of features*, giuochi di fisionomia, *m.pl.* ~ *of light*, giuochi di luce, *m.pl.* ~ *on words*, bisticcio di parole, giuoco di parole, *m.* ~pen, girello, *m.* ~thing, giocattolo, trastullo, balocco, *m.* ~time, ore di ricreazione, *f.pl.* ~wright, autore drammatico, drammaturgo, *m.* ¶ *v.i.* giocare, trastullarsi; divertirsi; agire; comportarsi; (*v.t.*) giocare, fare; recitare, rappresentare; (*harp*, &*c.*) pizzicare; (*Mus. instr.*) suonare, tasteggiare; ~ *about*, ruzzare, scherzare, divertirsi. ~ [*for*] *low* [*stakes*] giocare piccole poste, fare piccolo giuoco. ~ *a little* (music), strimpellare. ~er, *n.* giocatore, *m.*, -trice, *f.*; attore, *m.*, -trice, *f.*; sonatore, *m.*, -trice, *f.* ~ *piano*, pianoforte meccanico, *m.* ~ful, *a.* scherzoso, allegro, faceto. ~fulness, *n.* umore scherzoso, umore faceto, *m.* allegria, gaiezza, *f.* *playing cards*, carte da giuoco, *f.pl.* *playing off* (tie), partita decisiva, *f.*

plea, *n.* scusa, *f.*, pretesto, *m.*; preg-

hiera, *f.*; (*Law*) causa; eccezione, *f.*
plead, *v.t. & i.* appellarsi, fare
appello a, invocare; intercedere;
allegare; scusarsi; far valere, patrocinare; sostenere, perorare, svolgere
una difesa; (*draw pleadings*) istruire.
~ *guilty,* dichiararsi colpevole.
~ *not guilty,* dichiararsi, protestarsi
innocente. ~**ing,** (*Law*) *n.* (*oral
advocacy*) arringa, difesa, *f.*; (*preparatory formalities*) istruzione, *f.*,
-i, *f.pl.* (*pl. statement*) difese scritte,
f.pl.
pleasant, *a.* piacevole, grato, gradevole; ameno, attraente, leggiadro.
~**ness,** *n.* piacevolezza, amenità, *f.*
~**ry,** *n.* facezia, *f.*, detto arguto,
scherzo, *m.* **please,** *v.t.* piacere a,
far piacere a; compiacere, gradire,
aggradare, garbare a; accontentare,
soddisfare; divertire, svagare; (*abs.*)
piacere. ¶ *imperative,* se vi piace,
per piacere, per favore, di grazia,
favorisca, abbia (abbiate) la bontà di.
~**d,** *p.a.* contento, soddisfatto,
felice. **pleasing,** *a.* piacevole,
gradevole; attraente; ameno; grazioso. **pleasurable,** *a.* gradevole,
piacevole. **pleasure,** *n.* piacere;
divertimento; diletto, *m.* attrattiva,
f.; godimento, *m.*, voluttà; *f.*; bene-
placito; gradimento, grado, *m.*;
voglia, volontà, *f.* ~ *boat,* battello
da diporto, canotto di piacere,
m. ~ *grounds,* parco, giardino
inglese, *m.* ~ *resort,* luogo di
ricreazione, *m.* ~ *trip,* ~ *party,*
gita di piacere, *f.*, viaggio di piacere,
m., partita di piacere, *f.*
pleat, *n.* piega, ripiegatura, *f.* ¶ *v.t.*
ripiegare, piegare.
plebeian, *a.* plebeo. **plebiscite,** *n.*
plebiscito, *m.*
pledge, *n.* pegno, *m.*, arra, garanzia,
cauzione; promessa; professione di
fede, *f.*; voto di temperanza, *m.*;
brindisi, *m.* ¶ *v.t.* impegnare, dare
in pegno, garantire; fare un brindisi
a, brindare a.
plenary, *a.* plenario, pieno. **plenipotentiary,** *a. & n.* plenipotenziario, *a. & m.* **plenitude,** *n.*
pienezza, *f.* **plenteous & plentiful,**
a. abbondante, copioso. *to be
plentiful,* abbondare; brulicare, pullulare. **plenty,** *n.* abbondanza,
copia, *f.* ~ *of,* molto, tanto, abbondanza di, in abbondanza. *with* ~ *of,*
a furia di. **plenum,** *n.* pieno, *m.*
pleonasm, *n.* pleonasmo, *m.*
plethora, *n.* pletora, *f.*

pleura, *n.* pleura, *f.* **pleurisy,** *n.*
pleurite, *f.*
plexus, *n.* plesso, *m.*
pliable, pliant, *a.* pieghevole, flessibile; (*fig.*) arrendevole, compiacente.
pliancy, *n.* pieghevolezza, *f.*
pliers, *n.* pinza, *f.*; pinzette, *f.pl.*
plight, *n.* stato, *m.*, condizione, *f.*,
situazione, *f.* ¶ *v.t.* impegnare,
giurare (fede), dare (la parola
d'onore).
plinth, *n.* plinto, zoccolo, *m.*
plod on, along, *v.i.* camminare penosamente, a fatica, a stento; sgobbare.
plodder, *n.* sgobbone, *m.*, -a, *f.*;
lavoratore assiduo, *m.*; lavoratrice
assidua, *f.*
plomb, (*Cust.*) *n.* piombo, *m.* ¶ *v.t.*
piombare.
plot, *n.* appezzamento (di terreno), *m.*,
aiuola, *f.*; congiura, trama, cospirazione, *f.*, complotto, *m.*; (*novel,
play*) intreccio, *m.* ¶ *v.t. & i.* fare il
piano di, fare l'ordito di; rilevare;
complottare, cospirare, macchinare,
tramare. **plotter,** *n.* cospiratore,
macchinatore, congiurato, *m.* *plotting paper,* foglio quadrettato, *m.*
plough, *n.* aratro, *m.*; (*Elec.*) aratrice
elettrica, *f.* ~ *land,* terra arativa, *f.*
~**man,** bifolco, aratore, *m.* ~ *share,*
vomere, *m.* snow-~, spazzaneve,
m.inv. ¶ *v.t. & i.* arare; (*fig.*) solcare,
fendere; (*Exam.*) bocciare; respingere. ~ *back* (profits) *into the
business,* rimettere nell'azienda.
~**ing,** *n.* aratura, *f.*
plover, *n.* piviere, *m.*, pavoncella, *f.*
~*s' eggs,* (*Cook.*), uova di pavoncella, *f.pl.*
pluck, *n.* coraggio, *m.*; (*Butchery*)
frattaglia, *f.*, or *pl.* frattaglie. ¶ *v.t.*
cogliere, svellere, strappare, tirare,
(*fowl*) spennare, spiumare; (*Mus.
strings*) pizzicare, (*Exam.*) bocciare,
respingere. ~ *up,* (*spirit*) farsi
animo. ~**y,** *a.* coraggioso; (*Phot.*)
vigoroso.
plug, *n.* tampone, turacciolo, tappo,
zaffo, *m.*; (*bath*) valvola, *f.*; (*Elec.*)
spina, *f.*; (*sparking, Motor*) candela,
f.; (*bottle left in pipe*) deposito, *m.*;
(*twist of tobacco*) tabacco compresso,
m. ~ *hole,* graticola, *f.* ¶ *v.t.*
tamponare, turare; stoppare, zaffare;
otturare.
plum, *n.* prugna, susina, *f.*; (*dried*)
prugna secca, *f.* ~ *orchard,* pru-
gneto, *m.* ~ *pudding,* budino all'inglese, *m.* ~ [*tree*], prugno,
susino, *m.*

plumage, *n.* piume, penne, *f.pl.*, piumaggio, *m.* **plumassier,** *n.* piumaio, *m.*, pennaiuolo, *m.*

plumb, *a.* verticale, perpendicolare. ¶ *ad.* a piombo, a dirittura; tutto ad un tratto. ¶ *n.* piombo, piombino, *m.* ∼ *line*, filo a piombo, *m.*; linea verticale, *f.* ¶ *v.t.* scandagliare, piombinare; piombare. **plumbago,** *n.* piombaggine, *f.* **plumber,** *n.* stagnaio, trombaio, idraulico, *m.* **plumbing,** *n.* piombatura, impiombatura, *f.*

plume, *n.* penna, piuma, *f.*; pennacchio, *m.*; piumino, *m.*; (*fig.*) palma, *f.*; trofeo, *m.* ¶ *v.t.* piumare, impennacchiare, ornare. ∼ *its feathers*, pulirsi le penne. ∼ *oneself on*, vantarsi di, piccarsi di.

plummer block, cuscinetto di perno, *m.*

plummet, *n.* piombino, *m.*

plump, *a.* grassoccio, grassotto; pienotto; paffuto; diretto; netto; (*chicken*) grasso. *to* ∼ *for*, votare in massa per, votare esclusivamente per. ∼*ness,* *n.* grassezza, *f.*

plunder, *n.* saccheggio, *m.*; depredazione, *f.*; (*booty*) bottino, *m.* ¶ *v.t.* saccheggiare, spogliare, depredare. ∼**er,** *n.* saccheggiatore, predone, *m.*

plunge, *n.* sbalzo; (*Swim.*) tuffo, *m.* *to take the* ∼, (*fig.*) saltare il fosso. *the first* ∼, (*fig.*) il primo passo. ¶ *v.t.* tuffare, immergere; gettare; (*v.i.*) tuffarsi, fare il tuffo; immergersi; slanciarsi, precipitarsi; (*gambling*) giuocare grosso. **plunger,** *n.* tuffatore; speculatore rischioso, *m.*; (*Mech.*) stantuffo, pistone, *m.*

pluperfect, *n.* trapassato prossimo, piú che perfetto, *m.*

plural, *a.* (*Gram.*) plurale. ¶ *n.* plurale, *m.* ∼**ity,** *n.* pluralità, *f.*; (*of votes*) maggioranza, *f.*; (*of offices*) cumulo (di funzioni, &c.), *m.*

plus, *pr.* piú; con l'aggiunta di. *he is* 10, 12, ∼, ha 10, 12 anni passati. ∼*-fours,* calzoni alla zuava, *m.pl.* ∼ [*sign*], [simbolo] piú, segno piú, s. di addizione, *m.*

plush, *n.* felpa, *f.*, peluzza, *m.*

plutocracy, *n.* plutocrazia, *f.* **plutocrat,** *n.* plutocrate, *m.*

ply, *n.* piega, *f.*, indirizzo, *m.* ∼*wood,* legno compensato, *m.* ¶ *v.t.* (*tool*) maneggiare, manipolare; (*questions*) incalzare, importunare; (*trade*) esercitare, occuparsi di, attendere a; (*v.i.*) andare, fare il percorso, fare tragitti regolari; bordeggiare; fare il servizio.

pneumatic, *a.* pneumatico. ∼ (*tyre*) pneumatico, *m.*; gomma, *f.*

pneumonia, *n.* pneumonia, polmonite, *f.*

Po (the), il Po, *m.*

poach, *v.t.* prendere (*game*, *fish*), rubare; (*eggs*) affogare; (*v.i.*) cacciare di frodo. ∼**er,** *n.* cacciatore di frodo, *m.*

pocket, *n.* tasca; saccoccia, scarsella, *f.*; (*vest*) taschino, *m.*; (*Min.*) cavità, *f.*; (*Bil.*) buca, bilia, *f.*; (*air*) vuoto, *m.*, sacca, *f.* ∼ *book*, taccuino, portafoglio, *m.* ∼*-handkerchief*, fazzoletto, *m.* ∼ *money*, danaro per i minuti piaceri, *m.*, spiccioli, *m.pl.*; spillatico, *m. in* ∼, in guadagno. *out of* ∼, in perdita. *in one's* ∼, (*fig.*) in tasca. ∼ *dictionary*, ∼ *edition*, dizionario, edizione tascabile. ¶ *v.t.* intascare; mettere in tasca; (*fig.*) subire, tollerare, ingoiare. ∼**ful,** *n.* tascata, tasca piena, *f.*

pock-marked, *a.* butterato.

pod, *n.* baccello, guscio, *m.*

poem, *n.* (*long*, *narrative*) poema, *m*;. poemetto, *m.*; (*Short*, *gen. lyrical*) poesia, *f.* **poet,** *n.* poeta, *m.* ∼**aster,** *n.* poetastro, *m.* ∼**ess,** *n.* poetessa, *f.* ∼**ic,** ∼**ical,** *a.* poetico. ∼**ry,** *n.* poesia, *f.*

poignant, *a.* cocente, violento, straziante; mordace.

point, *n.* punto, momento, istante, *m.*; punta, *f.*; scopo, *m.*, mira, *f.*; fatto; essenziale, *m*; angolo; (*compass*) quarta, *f.*, rombo, punto, *m.*; (*Rly.*) ago (dello scambio); (*pl.*) scambio, deviatoio, *m.*; promontorio, *m.*; estremità, *f.* ∼*-blank*, *ad.* di punto in bianco, a bruciapelo; chiaro e tondo. ∼ *lace*, pizzo, merletto, *m.*, trina a punta d'ago, *f.* ∼ *of law*, incidente; cavillo giudiziario, *m.* ∼ *of the compass*, (*Naut.*) quarta, *f.*; rombo, *m. boiling* ∼, punto d'ebollizione. *flash* ∼, p. d'infiammabilità; *freezing* ∼, p. di congelamento, *m. starting* ∼, (*race*) punto di partenza; (*fig.*) p. di riferimento, *m. one* ∼ *letter-spaced* (*Typ.*), spaziato a un punto. 6, 8, ∼ [*size*] (*Typ.*), corpo 6, 8; corpi di 6, di 8, punti. *decimal* ∼, virgola decimale, *f. to the* ∼, a proposito, al fatto, alla questione. ¶ *v.t.* (*sharpen*) appuntare, fare la punta a; (*punctuate*) punteggiare; (*masonry*) affilettare; stuccare i giunti; (*direct*) dirigere, indirizzare;

(*emphasize*) dar rilievo a. (*v.t. & abs. of dog, &c.*) puntare. ~ *at*, additare, mostrare a dito. ~ *out*, indicare, mostrare; additare; osservare, far osservare. ~ed, *a.* appuntito, acuto, aguzzo; (*fig.*) arguto; netto; personale; piccante. ~ *arch*, ogiva, *f.* ~er, *n.*, indice, *m.*; lancetta; bacchetta, *f.*; cane da punta, *m.* ~less, *a.* (*fig.*) scipito, insulso, insipido, inutile. pointsman (*Rly.*), *n.* deviatore, *m.*

poise, *n.* equilibrio; peso, *m.* ¶ *v.t.* equilibrare, mettere in equilibrio.

poison, *n.* veleno, tossico, *m.* ~ *gas*, gas asfissiante, g. velenoso, *m.* ¶ *v.t.* avvelenare, attossicare; (*fig.*) corrompere. ~er, *n.* avvelenatore, *m.*, -trice, *f.* ~ing, *n.* avvelenamento, *m.* ~ous, *a.* velenoso, tossico.

poke, *n.* spinta, *f.*, spintone, *m.*; sacco, *m.*; scarsella, *f.* *a pig in a* ~, acquisto alla cieca, la gatta nel sacco. ¶ *v.t.* frugare; dare uno spintone a; ficcare; (*fire*) attizzare. ~ *about*, frugare, rovistare, frugacchiare. poker, *n.* attizzatoio, *m.*; (*cards*) poker, *m.* ~ *work*, pirografia, *f.*; lavoro in pirografia, *m.* poky, *a.* stretto, meschino.

Poland, *n.* la Polonia, *f.*

polar, *a.* polare. ~ *bear*, orso polare, orso bianco, *m.* pole, *m.* palo; (*hop, &c.*) pertica, *f.*; (*carriage*) timone, *m.* (*Astr. Phys., &c.*) polo, *m.*; *Meas.* = (perch) 25·293 sq. metres. P~, *n.* polacco, *m.*, -a, *f.* ~axe, ascia del beccaio, mazza piombata, *f.*; (*Hist.*) ascia d'armi, *f.* ~cat, puzzola, *f.* ~ *jump*, salto della pertica, *m.* ~ *star*, stella polare, *f.* ¶ *v.t.* sostenere con pali.

polemic(al), *a.* polemico. polemic, *n. &* ~s, *n.pl.* polemica, *f.*

police, ~, *n.* polizia; gendarmeria, *f.* ~ *court*, tribunale correzionale, *m.* ~man, agente di polizia, poliziotto; carabiniere, *m.*; guardia, *f.* ~ *records*, casellario giudiziario, *m.* ~ *station*, posto di polizia, *m.*, polizia, *f.*; (*divisional*) commissariato, ufficio di questura, *m.* ~ *van*, carro della polizia, *m.*, vettura cellulare, *f.*

policy, *n.* linea di condotta, *f.*, piano d'azione, sistema, *m.*; (*public*) politica, *f.*; (*Insce*) polizza (d'assicurazione), *f.*

Polish, *a.* polacco. ¶ *n.* polacco, *m.*, lingua polacca, *f.*

polish, *n.* lustro, lucido, *m.*; vernice, brunitura; eleganza, raffinatezza; finitura, *f.* ¶ *v.t.* pulire, lisciare; lucidare; forbire, brunire, levigare, lustrare, verniciare; ingentilire. ~ *off*, sbrigare, sbarazzarsi di, spedire. ~ing brush, (boots), spazzola per lucidare, *f.*

polite, *a.* cortese, gentile, garbato, civile. politely, *ad.* cortesemente, gentilmente. ~ness, *n.* cortesia, gentilezza, *f.*, garbo, *m.*; (*to women*) galanteria, *f.*

politic & political, *a.* politico. ~ian, *n.* politico, uomo politico, *m.*; (*as a trade*) politicante, *m.* ~s, *n.pl. &* polity, *n.* politica, *f.*, regime politico, *m.* *to talk politics*, palare di politica.

polka, *n.* polca, *f.*

poll, *n.* ballottaggio, *m.*, votazione, *f.*, voto, *m.*, voti, *m.pl.*; scrutinio, *m.*; lista, testa, *f.* ~ *tax*, imposta di capitazione, *f.*; testatico, *m.* ~ing *station*, sezione elettorale, *f.*, luogo per votare, *m.*, sala di votazione, *f.*

pollard, *n.* capitozza, *f.* ¶ *v.t.* scapezzare, scapitozzare; cimare.

pollen, *n.* polline, *m.*

pollute, *v.t.* contaminare, sporcare; corrompere, violare, profanare.

polo, *n. &* ~ *cap*, polo, *m.*

polonaise, *n.* polonese, *f.*

poltroon, *n.* vigliacco, codardo, poltrone, *m.*

polyanthus, *n.* polianto, *m.* polygamist, *n. &* polygamous, *a.*, poligamo, *m. & a.* polygamy, *n.* poligamia, *f.* polyglot, *a. & n.* poliglotta, *a. & m.f.* polygon, *n.* poligono, *m.* Polynesia, *n.* la Polinesia, *f.* polyp & polypus, *n.* polipo, *m.* polysyllabic, *a., &* polysyllable, *n.* polisillabo, *a. & m.* polytechnic, *a.* politecnico. polytheism, *n.* politeismo, *m.*

pomade, ~atum, *n.* pomata, *f.* ¶ *v.t.* impomatare, applicare la pomata a.

pomegranate, *n.* melagrana, *f.* ~ [*tree*] melograno, melo granato, *m.*

Pomeranian [dog], *n.* or pom. *abb.* cane di Pomerania, *m.*

pommel, *n.* pomo, pomolo, *m.* ¶ *v.t.* battere, malmenare, dare pugni a.

pomp, *n.* pompa, *f.*, fasto, sfarzo, sfoggio, *m.*

Pompeii, *n.* Pompei, *m.*

pomposity, *n.* pomposità, burbanza, enfasi, *f.* pompous, *a.* pomposo, gonfio, ampolloso.

pond, *n.* stagno, laghetto, vivaio, *m.*, peschiera, *f.*; serbatoio d'acqua, *m.*; (*of canal*) gora, *f.*
ponder, *v.i.* meditare, riflettere; (*v.t.*) pesare, meditare su, considerare. ~**able,** *a.* ponderabile. ~**ous,** *a.* ponderoso, pesante, massiccio.
pons asinorum, ponte dell'asino, *m.*
pontiff, *n.* pontefice, *m.* **pontifical,** *a. & n.* pontificale, *a. & m.* **pontificate,** *n.* pontificato, *m.*
pontoon, *n.* pontone, *m.*, chiatta, *f.* ~ *bridge,* ponte su barconi, su pontoni, ponte di chiatte, *m.*
pony, *n.* cavallino, *m.*
poodle, *n.* cane barbone, cane maltese, *m.*
pooh, *i.* poh! oibò! **pooh-pooh,** *v.t.* trattare con leggerezza o derisione.
pool, *n.* laghetto, stagno, *m.*, pozzanghera, gora, *f.*; (*bathing*) piscina, *f.*; (*Cards, &c.*) pool, l'ammontare delle poste, *m.*; (*Com.*) fondo comune, *m.*; (*Fin.*) sindacato, *m.* ~ *betting,* (il) totalizzatore; totocalcio, *m.* ¶ *v.t.* mettere in comune.
poop, *n. & ~ deck,* poppa, *f.*, cassero, *m.*
poor, *a.* povero, indigente; magro, scarno; meschino; modesto; mediocre. ~ *box,* cassetta dei poveri, *f.* ~ *health,* salute malferma, cattiva salute, *f.* ~ *little thing* (*pers.*) poveretto, *m.* ~ *rate,* imposta (tributo, *m.*) locale per l'assistenza dei poveri, *f.* ~ *spirited,* pusillanime. *the* ~, i poveri, *m.pl.* ~**ly,** *ad.* scarsamente, poveramente, malamente. ¶ *a.* indisposto, sofferente. ~**ness,** *n.* povertà, magrezza, sterilità, mediocrità, *f.*
pope, *n.* papa, *m.* ~**ry,** *n.* papismo, *m.*
pop gun, pistola ad aria compressa (per bambini), *f.*
popinjay, *n.* (*Hist.*) pappagallo, *m.*; (*fig.*) damerino, vagheggino, *m.*
popish, *a.* papistico, di papista.
poplar, *n.* pioppo, *m.*
poplin, *n.* poplina, *f.*
poppy, *n.* papavero, *m.*
populace, *n.* popolo, volgo, *m.*, plebaglia, *f.*, popolaccio, basso popolo, *m.* **popular,** *a.* popolare, volgare; popolano; alla moda; (*treatise*) popolare, ad uso del popolo. ~ *edition,* edizione popolare, *f.* ~**ity,** *n.* popolarità, *f.* ~**ize,** *v.t.* popolarizzare. **populate,** *v.t.* popolare. **population,** *n.* popolazione, *f.* **populous,** *a.* popoloso.
porcelain, *n.* porcellana, *f.*

porch, *n.* portico, *m.*
porcupine, *n.* istrice, *f.*, porcospino, *m.*
pore, *n.* poro, *m.* ~ *over,* divorare, leggere (studiare) attentamente.
pork, *n.* carne di maiale, di porco, *f.* ~ *butcher,* *n.* pizzicagnolo, salumaio, *m.* ~**er,** *n.* porco, porchetto, *m.*
porosity, *n.* porosità, *f.* **porous,** *a.* poroso.
porphyry, *n.* porfirio, porfido, *m.*
porpoise, *n.* marsovino, porco di mare, porco marino, *m.*, focena, *f.*
porridge, *n.* farinata, *f.*; (*oatmeal*) farinata d'avena, *f.* **porringer,** *n.* scodella, ciotola, gavetta, *f.*
port, *n.* porto, *m.*; (*side*) babordo, *m.*, sinistra, *f.* ~(*hole*), oblò, portello, *m.*; cannoniera, *f.* ~ *lid,* portello, *m.* ~ *of call,* approdo, porto di scalo, porto d'ordini, *m.* ~ *of registry,* porto d'iscrizione, *m.* ~ [*wine*] vino di Oporto, *m.* ~-*wine mark,* macchia di vino, *f.*
portable, *a.* portabile, portatile.
portal, *n.* porta, *f.*, portone, *m.*
portcullis, *n.* saracinesca, *f.*
portend, *v.t.* presagire, augurare.
portent, *n.* presagio, augurio; portento, prodigio, *m.* **portentous,** *a.* portentoso; funesto, di cattivo augurio.
porter, *n.* facchino, portabagagli, portinaio, *m.*; birra nera, *f.* ~**age,** *n.* porto, facchinaggio, *m.*
portfolio, *n.* cartella, *f.*; (*Pol.*) portafoglio, *m.*
portico, *n.* portico, *m.*
portion, *n.* porzione, parte, *f.*; (*city*) quartiere, rione, *m.*; (*marriage*) dote, *f.* ¶ *v.t.* ripartire, dividere, distribuire; dotare.
Portland cement, cemento Portland, *m.*
portliness, *n.* grassezza, corpulenza, *f.*; nobile portamento, *m.* **portly,** *a.* corpulento, grassoccio; maestoso.
portmanteau, *n.* valigia, *f.*, baule per viaggio, *m.*
portrait & ~ure, *n.* ritratto, *m.*, pittura, *f.*; ritratti, *m.pl.*; (*fig.*) descrizione, *f.* **portray,** *v.t.* dipingere, fare il ritratto di. **portrayal,** *n.* pittura, descrizione, *f.*
portress, *n.* portinaia, *f.*
Portugal, *n.* il Portogallo, *m.* **Portuguese,** *a.* portoghese. ¶ *n.* (*pers.*) portoghese, *m.f.*; (*language*) il portoghese, *m.*, lingua portoghese, *f.*
pose, *n.* posa, *f.*, atteggiamento, *m.*;

affettazione, *f.* ¶ *v.i.* posare, assumere una posa; (*v.t.*) far posare, mettere in posa; atteggiare; (*question*) fare. **poser,** *n.* enigma, problema, *m.*, questione alla quale non c'è da rispondere, domanda imbarazzante, *f.* **position,** *n.* posizione, condizione; situazione, positura, *f.*; grado, rango; impiego, *m.*; classificazione, classifica (*sport*), *f.* ¶ *v.t.* classificare.

positive, *a.* positivo, assoluto, certo.

posse, *n.* squadra, compagnia, forza, *f.*, manipolo, *m.*

possess, *v.t.* possedere; godere; occupare. **~ed,** *p.p.* posseduto, impadronitosi di, in preda (di); dotato (di)! invasato. (*as if* ~), (come) indiavolato. *one* ~, ossesso, *m.* **~ion,** *n.* possesso, godimento, *m.*, possessione; ossessione, *f.*; (*pl.*) possedimenti, *m.pl.*, beni, *m.pl. with immediate* ~, con possesso immediato. **~ive,** *a.* possessivo. **~or,** *n.* possessore, *m.*; posseditore, *m.*, -trice, *f.*

possibility, *n.* possibilità, *f.* **possible,** *a.* & *n.* possibile, *a.* & *m. as soon as* ~, appena possibile, al più presto possibile. *as far as* ~, nei limiti del possibile. *to be* ~, essere possibile, poter essere, poter darsi. **possibly,** *ad.* forse, possibilmente, può darsi, può essere. *he cannot* ~, non è possibile che (egli).

post, *n.* (*upright*) palo, *m.*, colonna, *f.*; stipite, montante, *m.*; (*place*) posto, *m.*, situazione, tappa, *f.*, impiego, *m.*; (*P.O.*) posta, *f.*, ufficio postale, *m.*; (*letters*) corriere, *m.*, corrispondenza, posta, *f. by return of* ~, a volta di corriere. **~card,** cartolina postale, *f.* **~ free,** franco di posta, franco di porto. *to go* **~-haste,** andare in gran fretta, andare a tutta briglia. **~man,** portalettere, *m.inv.*, postino, *m.* **~mark,** bollo della posta, timbro postale, *m.*; (*v.t.*) timbrare. **~ master,** **~ mistress,** direttore (-trice) d'ufficio postale. **~master general,** Ministro delle Poste e Telecomunicazioni, *m.* **~ office,** ufficio postale, *m.*, posta, *f.* **~ office guide,** indicatore. **~ office order,** vaglia postale, *m.* **~ office savings bank,** cassa [di risparmio] postale, *f.* **~ woman,** portalettere, *f.* ¶ *v.t.* impostare; affiggere; affissare; postare, porre, collocare; (*Bkkpg.*) riportare (registrare) a mastro; (*men*) postare. **~age,** *n.* porto, *m.*, spese postali, *f.pl.*; affrancazione; tariffa, *f.*

~ *stamp,* francobollo, *m.* **~al,** *a.* postale. ~ *order,* vaglia postale, *m.*

postdate, *n.* data posteriore, *f.* ¶ *v.t.* posdatare.

poster, *n.* affisso, cartellone, manifesto, *m.*

posterior, *a.* & *n.* posteriore, *a.* & *m.*

posterity, *n.* i posteri, *m.pl.*, posterità, *f.*

postern, *n.* (*Hist.*) postierla, *f.*

posthumous, *a.* postumo.

postillion, *n.* postiglione, *m.*

posting, *n.* (*letters*) impostazione, *f.*; (*bills*) affissione, *f.*; (*Bkkpg.*) registrazione a mastro, *f.*; (*sentry*) posa, *f.* **~box,** buca (cassetta) postale, *f.*

post meridiem (*abb.* p.m.) pomeridiano, *a.*, pomeriggio, *m.*

post mortem, *n.* autopsia, *f.*

postpone, *v.t.* posporre, rimandare, rimettere, rinviare. **~ment,** *n.* rinvio, *m.*, posposizione, *f.*, differimento, *m.*

postscript, *n.* (*abb.* P.S.) *n.* poscritto, *m.*

postulant, *n.* postulante, *m.f.*

posture, *n.* postura, posa, attitudine, *f.*, atteggiamento, *m.*, stato, *m.* **~er,** *n.* acrobata, *m.f.*; tipo affettato, lezioso, *m.*

post-war, *a.* di dopoguerra, posbellico, postbellico.

posy, *n.* mazzo, mazzetto (di fiori), *m.*

pot, *n.* vaso, *m.*, brocca, *f.*, boccale, barattolo, *m.*, pentola, pignatta, terrina, marmitta, *f.*; (*sport*) coppa, *f.* ~ *bellied,* panciuto. ~ *boy,* ~ *man,* garzone d'osteria, di bettola, *m.* ~ *herb,* erba d'orto, *f.* (*pl.*) ortaggi, *m.pl.* ~ *hole,* buca, marmitta, *f.* ~ *hook,* gancio del camino, *m.*; (*writing*) asta (della lettera), *f.* ~ *house,* bettola, osteria, *f.* ~ *hunter,* cacciatore di premi, *m. to take* ~ *luck,* mangiare alla buona. ¶ *v.t.* mettere (conservare) in vaso, piantare in vasi. **~ful,** *n.* vaso pieno, *m.*

potable, *a.* potabile.

potash, *n.* potassa, *f.* **potassium,** *n.* potassio, *n.*

potato, *n.* patata, *f.*

potency, *n.* potenza, efficacia, *f.* **potent,** *a.* possente, efficace. **potentate,** *n.* potentato, *m.* **potential,** *a.* & *n.* potenziale, *a.* & *m.*

pother, *n.* confusione, *f.*, frastuono, schiamazzo, *m.*

potion, *n.* pozione, bevanda, *f.*

potted, *p.a.* in vaso, in scatola, conservato in vaso. ~ *meats*, carne in scatola, carne conservata, *f.*

potter, *n.* vasaio; pentolaio; stovigliaio, *m.* ~'*s wheel*, ruota del vasaio, *f.*, tornio da vasai, *m.* ¶ *v.i.* gingillare, gironzolare, perdersi in bagattelle, baloccarsi. ~**y**, *n.* ceramica, *f.*, vasellame, *m.*, terraglie, *f.pl.*

pottle, *n.* cestellino, paniere, *m.*

pouch, *n.* scarsella, borsa, tasca; carniera, *f.*; tascapane, *m.*; giberna, cartuccera, *f.*; (*tobacco*) borsa, borsetta, *f.*

pouf, *n.* puf, *m.*

poulterer, *n.* pollaiuolo, pollivendolo, *m.*

poultice, *n.* cataplasma, impiastro, *m.*

poultry, *n.* pollame, *m.*, volatili, *m.pl.* ~ *yard*, pollaio, *m.*, cortile pel pollame, *m.*

pounce, *n.* spolvero, polverino, *m.* ¶ *v.t.* spolverare, fregare con pomice. ~*on*, piombare su.

pound, *n.* (*for cattle*) chiuso, *m.*; (£) lira sterlina, *f.*; (*avoirdupois weight*) libbra (inglese), *f.* = 0.45359243 kilogramme. ¶ *v.t.* pestare, battere; tritare; frantumare; stritolare. ~*age*, *n.* commissione, *f.* percentuale, *f.*; tassa per l'emissione di vaglia, *f.*

pour, *n.* acquazzone, diluvio, *m.* ~ [*out*], *v.t.* versare, mescere; spandere, far cadere, far piovere, far traboccare; dar fuori, emettere; (*Metall.*) colare; (*oil on waves*) filare. *it is* ~*ing*, piove dirottamente, piove a rovesci. ~*ing rain*, pioggia torrenziale, pioggia dirotta, *f.*

pout, *v.i.* fare il broncio, fare il grugno, fare il muso, fare il labbro. ~*er* [*pigeon*], *n.* piccione gozzuto, *m.*

poverty, *n.* povertà, *f.* ~*-stricken* (person), indigente, ridotto in povertà.

powder, *n.* polvere, polverina, *f.*; (*face*) cipria, *f.* ~ *bowl & ~ box*, scatola da cipria, *f.* ~ *magazine*, polveriera; (*ship*) santabarbara, *f.* ~ *mill*, polverificio, *m.* ~ *puff*, piumino per la cipria, *m.* ¶ *v.t.* impolverare; polverizzare; aspergere (di), cospargere (di); salare; incipriare. ~**y**, *a.* polveroso, friabile, ridotto in polvere.

power, *n.* potere, *m.* potenza, forza, energia; facoltà; corrente industriale, *f.*; talento, *m.*; autorità, *f.*, dominio, *m.*; (*att.*) meccanico. ~ *hammer*, martello-pilone; maglio a vapore, *m.* ~ *house*, ~ *station*, stazione genera-

trice di corrente, di forza motrice, *f.* (*Elec.*) centrale elettrica, *f.* ~ *of attorney*, procura, *f.* ~**ful**, *a.* potente; poderoso; possente, forte. ~**less**, *a.* impotente; senza potere; senza forza.

practicable, *a.* praticabile, fattibile, attuabile. **practical**, *a.* pratico; (*pers.*) pratico, positivo, realista. ~ *joke*, brutto tiro, *m.*, farsa, sbeffa, *f.* ~ *joker*, burlone, capo ameno, mistificatore, corbellatore, *m.* **practice**, *n.* pratica, abitudine, *f.*, uso, esercizio, *m.*; regola, norma; clientela, *f.*; metodo, tiro, *m.*; (*sport*) allenamento, *m.* **practician**, *n.* praticante, *m.* **practise**, *v.t.* praticare; professare, fare, esercitare; osservare; usare. **practitioner**, *n.* professionista, praticante; (*esp.*) medico, *m.*

Prague, *n.* Praga, *f.*

prairie, *n.* prateria, *f.*

praise, *n.* lode, *f.*, encomio, elogio, *m.* ¶ *v.t.* lodare, fare l'elogio di, elogiare. ~*worthy*, lodevole.

prance, *v.i.* (*horse*) impennarsi; (*child*) saltellare; balzellare; pavoneggiarsi.

prank, *n.* scappata; burla, birichinata, *f.*, tiro, *m.*

prate, *v.i.* ciarlare, cianciare, chiacchierare; ridire.

pratique, *n.* libera pratica, *f.*

prattle, *n.* ciarla, ciancia, *f.*, cicaleccio, *m.* ¶ *v.i.* cianciare, cinguettare.

prawn, *n.* palemone, *m.*

pray, *v.t. & i.* pregare; implorare; domandare. ¶ (*form of address*) prego! per favore! **prayer**, *n.* preghiera; orazione; domanda, *f.* ~ *book*, libro di preghiere, *m.* ~ *wheel*, cilindro girevole, *m.*

preach, *v.t. & i.* predicare. ~*er*, *n.* predicatore, *m.*; (*protestant*) pastore, *m.* ~*ing*, *n.* predica, predicazione, *f.*

preamble, *n.* preambolo, *m.*

prebend, *n.* prebenda, *f.* ~*ary*, *n.* prebendario, *m.*

precarious, *a.* precario.

precaution, *n.* precauzione, cautela, *f.* ~*ary*, *a.* precauzionale, di cautela.

precede, *v.t.* precedere. **precedence**, *n.* precedenza, *f.* **precedent**, *n. &* **preceding**, *a.* precedente, *a. & m.*

precentor, *n.* precentore, capocoro, *m.*

precept, *n.* precetto, *m.* ~**or**, *n.* precettore, *m.*

precinct, *n.* precinto, *m.*; (*pl.*) confini, limiti, *m.pl.*

precious, *a.* prezioso.

precipice, *n.* precipizio, *m.* **precipitancy** & **precipitation,** *n.* precipitazione, *f.* **precipitate,** *v.t.* & *i.* precipitare. ¶ *a.* & *n.* precipitato, *a.* & *m.* ~**ly,** *ad.* precipitatamente. **precipitous,** *a.* erto, ripido, a picco.

precise, *a.* preciso, esatto. ~**ly,** *ad.* precisamente. *to state* ~, precisare, specificare. **precision,** *n.* precisione, esattezza, *f.*

preclude, *v.t.* precludere, prevenire.

precocious, *a.* precoce; (*too knowing*) scaltro, furbo, fino; (*in vice*) discolo. ~**ness,** *n.* precocità, *f.*

preconceived, preconcerted, *a.* preconcetto.

precursor, *n.* & ~**y,** *a.* precursore, *a.* & *m.*

predatory, *a.* predatorio, rapace.

predecease, *n.* (*Law*) premorienza, *f.* ¶ *v.i.* premorire.

predecessor, *n.* predecessore, antecessore, *m.*

predestination, *n.* predestinazione, *f.*

predicament, *n.* mal passo, *m.*, situazione difficile, *f.*; (*Log.*) categoria, *f.*

predicate, (*Log.* & *Gram.*) *n.* predicato, attributo, *m.* ¶ *v.t.* affermare, predicare. *predicative adjective,* aggettivo attributo, *m.*

predict, *v.t.* predire. ~**ion,** *n.* predizione, *f.*

predilection, *n.* predilezione, preferenza, *f.*

predispose, *v.t.* predisporre.

predominance, *n.* predominio, ascendente, *m.* **predominant,** *a.* predominante. **predominate,** *v.i.* predominare.

pre-eminent, *a.* preminente. ~**ly,** *ad.* preminentemente, per eccellenza.

pre-emption, *n.* pre-acquisto, *m.*

preen, *v.t.* pulire, adornare. ~ *its feathers,* lisciarsi (aggiustare) le penne.

preface, *n.* prefazione, *f.,* proemio, *m.,* preambolo, *m.* ¶ *v.t.* fare la prefazione a, fare precedere. **prefatory,** *a.* preliminare, di prefazione.

prefect, *n.* prefetto, *m.* ~**ure,** *n.* prefettura, *f.*

prefer, *v.t.* preferire; anteporre; (*complaint, charge*) presentare, portare. ~**able,** *a.* preferibile. ~**ence,** *n.* preferenza, *f.*; (*Cust.*) preferenza, *f.* ~ *shares or preferred stock,* azioni privilegiate, *f.pl.* **preferential,** *a.* di preferenza, privile-

giato. **preferment,** *n.* avanzamento, *m.,* promozione, *f.*

prefix, *n.* prefisso, *m.* ¶ *v.t.* premettere; mettere come prefisso. ~**ed,** (*Gram.*) *p.a.* prefisso.

pregnable, *a.* espugnabile, prendibile.

pregnancy, *n.* gravidanza, *f.* **pregnant,** *a.f.* incinta, grossa; (*animal*) gravida; (*fig.*) fecondo, fertile, pregno.

prehensile, *a.* prensile. ~ *tail,* coda prensile, *f.*

prehistoric, *a.* preistorico.

prejudge, *v.t.* pregiudicare. **prejudice,** *n.* pregiudizio, *m.,* prevenzione, *f.*; torto, danno, *m. without* ~ *to,* senza pregiudizio di, senza danno di. ¶ *v.t.* nuocere a, far torto a; pregiudicare, mettere in prevenzione. **prejudicial,** *a.* dannoso, nocivo, pregiudiziale, pregiudizievole.

prelacy, *n.* prelatura, *f.* **prelate,** *n.* prelato, *m.*

preliminary, *a.* preliminare. ~ *expenses* (*company*), spese preliminari, *f.pl.* ~ *trial* (*Racing*), prova preliminare, *f.,* criterio, *m.* **preliminaries,** *n.pl.* preliminari, *m.pl,* introduzione, *f.*

prelude, *n.* preludio, *m.* ¶ *v.i.* preludere; (*v.t.*) preludere a.

premature, *a.* prematuro. ~ [*child*]-*birth,* parto prematuro.

premeditate, *v.t.* premeditare. **premeditation,** *n.* premeditazione, *f.*

premier, *a.* primo, primario, primiero. ¶ *n.* primo ministro, Presidente del Consiglio (dei Ministri) *m.* ~**ship,** *n.* presidenza del Consiglio, *f.*

premise, *v.t.* premettere. ¶ ~ *or* **premiss,** *n.* premessa, *f.* ~**s,** *n.pl.,* locali, *m.pl.*; casa e sue attinenze, *f.pl.*; stabili con annessi e connessi, *m.pl.*; (*deed*) articoli innanzi detti, *m.pl.* premis[s]es, (*Log.*) *n.pl.* premesse, *f.pl.*

premium, *n.* premio, *m.*; (*Letting*) ricompensa, *f. at a* ~, sopra la pari.

premonition, *n.* premonizione, *f.* **premonitory,** *a.* premonitorio, foriero. ~ *symptom,* prodromo, sintomo foriero, *m.*

preoccupation, *n.* preoccupazione, *f.* **preoccupy,** *v.t.* preoccupare.

preparation, *n.* preparazione, *f.*; (*Sch.*) studio, *m.*; (*pl.*) preparativi, *m.pl.* **preparatory,** *a.* preparatorio. ~ *work* (*Min.*) dispositivi di mine. *m.pl.* **prepare,** *v.t.* preparare; allestire. ~**d,** (*ready*) *p.a.* pronto.

prepay, *v.t.* pagare anticipatamente, in anticipo; (*letter*) affrancare.

preponderance, *n.* preponderanza, *f.* **to preponderate over**, preponderare su; superare; pesare più di.

preposition, *n.* preposizione, *f.*

prepossess, *v.t.* impressionare; ispirare. **~ing**, *a.* attraente, insinuante, simpatico. **~ion**, *n.* prevenzione, preoccupazione, *f.*; pregiudizio, *m.*

preposterous, *a.* irragionevole, assurdo, strambo, mostruoso.

prerogative, *n.* prerogativa, *f.*

presage, *n.* presagio, *m.* ¶ *v.t.* presagire.

Presbyterian, *n. & a.* presbiteriano, *a. & m.*

prescience, *n.* prescienza, *f.* **prescient**, *a.* presciente.

prescribe, *v.t.* prescrivere; (*Med.*) fare (dare) una ricetta, ordinare. **prescription**, *n.* prescrizione, *f.*; (*Med.*) ricetta, *f.*

presence, *n.* presenza; aria, *f.*, aspetto, *m.*; apparizione, *f.* **present**, *a.* presente, attuale, corrente. **~day fashions**, mode d'oggigiorno, *f.pl.* ¶ *n.* presente, *m*; (*gift*) dono, regalo, *m.* **at ~**, al presente, presentemente; attualmente, oggi. ¶ *v.t.* presentare, offrire; donare, regalare. **~able**, *a.* presentabile. **presentation**, *n.* presentazione; rappresentazione, *f.* **~ copy**, copia (esemplare, *m.*), in omaggio, *f.*

presentiment, *n.* presentimento, *m.* **to have a ~ of**, presentire.

presently, *ad.* fra poco, subito, quanto prima; adesso.

preservation, *n.* conservazione, preservazione, *f.* **preservative**, *n. & a.* preservativo, *a. & m.*; (*for food*) preservante; antisettico, *a. & m.* **preserve**, *n.* (*game &c.*) bandita, riserva, *f.*; (*jam, &c.*) confettura, conserva, marmellata, *f.*; (*pl.*) riserva, caccia riservata, *f.*; (*pl. Opt.*) occhiali di conserva, *m.pl.* ¶ *v.t.* preservare; salvare; conservare, confetturare; (*plant*) naturalizzare.

preside, *v.i.* presiedere. **~at, over**, presiedere [a]. **presidency**, *n.* presidenza, *f.* **president**, *n.* presidente, *m.* P ~ *of the Board of Education* (*Eng.*) ministro della Pubblica Istruzione, *m.* P ~ *of the Board of Trade*, ministro dell'Industria e del Commercio, *m.* **presiding judge**, presidente, *m.*

press, *n.* (*Mech.*) pressa, *f.*; torchio; strettoio; armadio, guardaroba, *m.*; credenza; calca, folla; urgenza, *f.*; giornalismo, *m.*; (*of sail*) forza, *f.*, sforzo, *m.* **the ~** (*newspapers*), (la) stampa, *f.* (*for*) **~**, pronto per la stampa. **in the ~**, in corso di stampa, sotto stampa. **~ agency**, agenzia d'informazioni, *f.* **~ copy**, (letter), copia alla stampa, *f.* (*book*) esemplare per la stampa, *m.* **~ cutting**, ritaglio di giornale, *m.* **~man**, giornalista, *m.*; (*Typ.*) macchinista, *m.* ¶ *v.t. & i.* premere, stringere; pigiare, serrare, incalzare; spingere; costringere, forzare; pressare, sollecitare, urgere, far accettare; pregare, insistere; cilindrare; pesare. **~ on**, **~ forward**, farsi avanti, farsi strada, affrettarsi, aprirsi un passaggio. **~ out**, spremere, estrarre. **~ing**, *a.* urgente, pressante; (*debt*) vergognoso. **pressure**, *n.* pressione; urgenza, *f.*; peso, impulso, *m.* **~ gauge**, manometro, *m.*

prestige, *n.* prestigio, *m.*

presume, *v.t. & i.* presumere. **~ [up]on**, prevalersi di. **presumption**, *n.* presunzione, supposizione; arroganza, *f.* **presumptuous**, *a.* presuntuoso. **~ness**, *n.* presuntuosità, presunzione, *f.*

presuppose, *v.t.* presupporre.

pretence, *n.* pretesa, *f.*; pretesto, *m.*; finta, apparenza, *f.* **pretend**, *v.t. & i.* pretendere, fingere, far vista di, far sembiante, simulare, far mostra di. **~er**, *n.* pretendente, *m.f.* **pretension**, *n.* pretensione, pretesa, *f.* **pretentious**, *a.* pretensioso.

preterite, *n.* preterito, passato remoto, *m.*

preternatural, *a.* soprannaturale.

pretext, *n.* pretesto, *m.*

prettiness, *n.* leggiadria, eleganza, grazia, gentilezza, *f.* **pretty**, *a.* leggiadro, bello, grazioso, bellino, vezzoso, delizioso. ¶ *ad.* abbastanza, passabilmente. **~ good**, abbastanza buono, discreto, passabile. **~ much**, abbastanza, press'a poco. **~ nearly**, press'a poco, quasi.

prevail over, prevalere su, trionfare su, vincerla su, soverchiare. **prevail [up]on**, persuadere, indurre. **prevailing**, *p.a.* prevalente, predominante; in voga, alla moda. **prevalence**, *n.* prevalenza, *f.* **prevalent**, *a.* prevalente, generale, diffuso. **to be ~**, regnare, esser prevalente.

prevaricate, *v.i.* tergiverequivocare.

prevarication, *n.* equivoco, tergiversazione, *f.*, equivoco, *m.*
prevent, *v.t.* impedire, ostacolare; ovviare a. ~**ion,** *n.* prevenzione, *f.*, l'impedire, *m. society for the ~ of cruelty to animals,* società protettrice degli animali, *f.* ~**ive,** *n.* preventivo; preservativo, *m.*
previous, *a.* precedente, previo, antecedente. ~ *speaker,* oratore precedente. ~ *question,* questione pregiudiziale, *f.*
prevision, *n.* previsione, *f.*
pre-war, *a.* d'anteguerra.
prey, *n.* preda, *f.* ~ [*up*]*on,* divorare, far preda; di vivere a spese di; minare, infestare; (*the mind*) rodere, tormentare, ossessionare.
price, *n.* prezzo, *m. all at the same ~,* (*shop*) a scelta. ~ *list,* listino, *m.,* distinta, tariffa, *f. market ~ list,* mercuriale, *m.* ¶ *v.t.* valutare, fissare il prezzo di; informarsi del prezzo di. ~**less,** *a.* inestimabile, senza prezzo, impagabile.
prick, *n.* puntura, *f.*; (*conscience*) rimorso, *m.* ¶ *v.t.* pungere; (*card*) puntare, punteggiare; (*conscience*) rimordere. ~ *up* (*ears*) drizzare, rizzare. **prickle,** *n.* aculeo, pungiglione, *m.* **prickly,** *a.* spinoso, pungente. ~ *pear,* fico d'India, *m.*
pride, *n.* orgoglio, *m.*, fierezza, superbia, alterigia, *f.*; (*fig.*) splendore, *m.* gloria, *f.*; (*collection of animals*) gruppo, *m.* ~ *oneself* [*up*] *on,* vantarsi di, farsi gloria di, piccarsi di.
priest, *n.* prete, sacerdote, *m.* ~**ess,** *n.* sacerdotessa, *f.* ~**hood,** *n.* clero, sacerdozio, *m.* ~**ly,** *a.* sacerdotale, pretesco.
prig, *n.* saputello, saccentone, pedante, *m.* **priggish,** *a.* saccente, vanitoso, affettato.
prim, *a.* preciso, formale; attillato; modestino; riservato.
primacy, *n.* primazia, *f.*, primato, *m.*, supremazia, *f.*
prima donna, prima donna, diva, *f.*
prima facie, prima facie, a prima vista.
primary, *a.* primario, elementare, fondamentale. **primate,** *n.* primate, *m.* **prime,** *a.* primo, di prima qualità, di primo ordine. ~ *cost,* costo di produzione, *m.* ~ *minister,* primo ministro, Presidente del Consiglio, *m.* ~ *mover,* promotore, *m.*; (*fig.*) causa prima, *f.* ~ *of life,*

fiore dell'età, *m.* ¶ *v.t.* (*pump, Blasting*) adescare; (*paint*) ammannire; mesticare, dare la mestica a; (*pers.*) preparare, istruire. **primer,** *n.* abecedario, sillabario; manuale; *m.*; (*Expl.*) innesco, *m. long ~* (*Typ.*) garamone, *m.*, 10 punti.
primeval, *a.* primitivo, pristino, primevo. **priming,** *n.* innesco, adescamento, *m.*; (*paint*) mestica. imprimitura, *f.* **primitive,** *a.* primitivo. **primogeniture,** *n.* primogenitura, *f.* **primordial,** *a.* primordiale. **primrose,** *n.* primula, *f.*
prince, *n.* principe, *m.* ~**ly,** *a.* principesco. **princess,** *n.* principessa, *f.*
principal, *a.* principale, capitale ¶ *n.* capo, direttore, *m.,* -trice, *f.,* rettore, padrone, principale; committente, mandante, *m.*; (*of debt*) capitale, *m.* ~**ity,** *n.* principato, *m.*
principle, *n.* principio, *m.*
prink, *v.t.* ornare, infronzolare, acconciare.
print, *n.* incisione, stampa, impressione, impronta, *f.*; giornale, foglio, *m.*; (*Phot.*) prova, *f.*; (*type*) carattere, *m. & pl.* -i. *in ~,* a stampa, in vendita; *out of ~,* esaurito. ¶ *v.t.* stampare, imprimere; (*with pen*) improntare. ~(*-ed cotton fabric*), tela indiana, *f.* ~(*-ed fabric*), stoffa stampata, *f.* ~*ed paper & ~ed book & ~ed form,* stampato, *m.* ~**er,** *n.* tipografo, *m.* ~*'s error,* errore tipografico, *m.*, errore di stampa, *m.* ~*'s imprint,* nome del tipografo, *m.* ~**ing,** *n.* impressione, stampa, tiratura, *f.*; (*art*) tipografia, arte tipografica, *f.* ~ *frame* (*Phot.*) torchietto, *m.* ~ *ink,* inchiostro da stampa, *m.* ~ *office,* ~ *works,* tipografia, *f.*, stabilimento tipografico, *m.* ~ *out paper* (*Phot.*) carta ad annerimento diretto, *f.*
prior, *a.* anteriore, precedente. ¶ *n.* priore, *m.* ~**ess,** *n.* priora, badessa, *f.* ~ *to,* prima di. ~**ity,** *b.* priorità, precedenza, *f.* **priory,** *n.* prioria, *f.*
prise, *n.* leva, *f.* ¶ *v.t.* aprire, forzare.
prism, *n.* prisma, *m.* ~**atic,** *a.* prismatico.
prison, *n.* prigione, *f.*, carcere, *m.* ~ *breaking,* evasione, *f.* ~**er,** *n.* prigioniero, *m.*, -a, *f.*, detenuto, *m.*, -a, *f.* ~ *at the bar,* accusato, imputato, *m.*, -a, *f.* ~*s' bar,* ~*s' base,* barriera, bomba, *f.*
pristine, *a.* pristino.

privacy, *n.* segreto, ritiro, *m.*, solitudine, intimità, *f.* **private,** *a.* privato, intimo, particolare, personale, segreto; semplice; (*on door*) è proibito l'ingresso. ~ (*soldier*) soldato semplice, fante, fantaccino, *m. by* ~ *treaty,* amichevolmente. ~ *view* (*Art*), anteprima, *f.* **privateer,** *n.* corsaro patentato, *m.*; nave corsara, *f.* **privateering,** *n.* mestiere di corsaro, *m.* **privately,** *ad.* privatamente, in forma privata, intimamente, personalmente.

privation, *n.* privazione, *f.* **privative** (*Gram.*) *a. & n.* privativo, *a. & m.*

privet, *n.* ligustro, *m.*

privilege, *n.* privilegio, *m.*; prerogativa, *f.* ¶ *v.t.* privilegiare.

privily, *ad.* segretamente, in segreto.

privy, (*Law*) *a.* privato, segreto. ~ *purse,* lista civile del re, *f.* ~ *to,* consapevole di. ¶ *n.* cesso, luogo comodo, *m.*, ritirata, *f.*

prize, *n.* premio; guiderdone, *m.*; (*Nav.*) presa, nave catturata, *f.*; (*lottery*) premio, lotto, *m.*; (*leverage*) sforzo, giuoco d'una leva, *m.* ~ *bull,* toro premiato, *m.* ~ *court,* tribunale delle prese, *m.* ~ *fight(ing),* pugilato, *m.*, partita di pugilato, *f.* ~ *fighter,* pugilatore (professionista), *m.* ~ *giving,* distribuzione dei premi, *f.* ~ *list,* elenco dei premiati, *m.* ~ *man,* premiato, laureato, *m.* ~ *medal,* medaglia d'onore, *f.* ~ *money,* taglia, *f.* ~ *winner,* premiato, laureato, *m.* ¶ *v.t.* (*value*) apprezzare, stimare, far caso di; (*lever,* ~ *open*) aprire con una leva.

pro, *pr.* pro, per. *the* ~*s & cons,* i pro e i contro.

probability, *n.* probabilità, *f.* **probable,** *a.* probabile.

probate, *n.* verificazione d'un testamento, *f.*

probation, *n.* prova, *f.*; (*Eccl.*) noviziato, *m. on* ~, di prova. ~*er, n.* candidato, novizio, *m.*

probe, *n.* sonda, tenta, *f.* ¶ *v.t.* tentare, sondare, scandagliare, scrutare.

probity, *n.* probità, integrità, *f.*

problem, *n.* problema, *m.* ~ *play,* dramma a tesi, *m.* ~**atic(al),** *a.* problematico.

proboscis, *n.* proboscide, *f.*

pro-British, *a.* anglofilo.

procedure, *n.* procedimento, *m.*; (*Law*) procedura, *f.* **proceed,** *v.i.* procedere; avanzare; continuare; derivare, provenire, emanare; recarsi, ricorrere, passare; agire. ~ *against* (*Law*) procedere contro, perseguire. ~ *on & ~ with,* proseguire. ~**ing,** *n.* procedimento, *m.*; (*pl.*) atti, *m.pl.*, processo verbale, *r.* **proceeds,** *n.pl.* provento, ricavo, *m.*

process, *n.* processo, corso, andamento, *m.*; via, *f.*; (*Law*) processo, *m.*, citazione, *f. in ~ of time,* in processo di tempo, col tempo, in seguito. ~ *engraving,* fotoincisione, *f.*

procession, *n.* processione, *f.*, corteo, *m.*

proclaim, *v.t.* proclamare; bandire.

proclamation, *n.* proclama, bando, decreto, *m.*

proclivity, *n.* proclività, *f.*

procrastinate, *v.i.* procrastinare. **procrastination,** *n.* procrastinazione, *f.*

procreate, *v.t.* procreare.

proctor (*Univ.*) *n.* censore, *m.*

procuration, *n.* procura, *f.* **procure,** *v.t.* procurarsi, acquistare, ottenere; cagionare.

prod, *v.t.* pungolare; spingere; frugare; (*fig.*) stimolare, irritare.

prodigal, *a. & n.* prodigo, *a.m.* ~ *son,* figliuol prodigo, *m.* ~**ity,** *n.* prodigalità, *f.*

prodigious, *a.* prodigioso, mostruoso. **prodigy,** *n.* prodigio, *m.*

produce, *n.* prodotti, *m.pl.*; frutto, profitto, *m.*; generi, *m.pl.*; derrate, *f.pl.* ~ *broker,* agente di produzione, *m.* ~ *exchange,* borsa di commercio, *f.* ~ *market,* mercato commerciale, *m.* ¶ *v.t.* produrre, arrecare; fornire; esibire, mostrare; fabbricare; rappresentare, mettere in scena; causare; (*Geom.*) prolungare. **producer,** *n.* produttore; (*Theat.*) impresario, *m.* ~ *gas,* gas di generatore, g. povero, *m.* **product,** *n.* prodotto, *m.* ~**ion,** *n.* produzione, *f.*; prodotto, *m.*; esibizione; messa in scena, *f.* ~**ive,** *a.* produttivo, fertile.

profanation, *n.* profanazione, *f.* **profane,** *a.* profano, empio. ¶ *v.t.* profanare, bestemmiare. **profanity,** *n.* profanità, bestemmia, irriverenza, *f.*

profess, *v.t.* professare, fare professione di; dichiarare; esercitare; pretendere. ~**ed,** *a.* dichiarato, professo, preteso. ~**ion,** *n.* professione, dichiarazione, *f.*, stato, mestiere, *m.* ~**ional,** *a. & n.* professionale, professionista. ~

accountant, esperto-contabile, *m.*
~ *jealousy,* gelosia di mestiere, *f.*
~**or,** *n.* professore, *m.,* -essa, *f.*
~**orship,** professorato, *m.;* cattedra, *f.*
proficiency, *n.* perizia, abilità, destrezza, *f.* **proficient,** *a.* abile, esperto, forte.
profile, *n.* profilo, *m.* ¶ *v.t.* profilare.
profit, *n.* profitto, guadagno, frutto; vantaggio, utile, *m.* ~ *sharing,* compartecipazione agli utili, interessenza, *f.* ¶ *v.i. & t.* profittare, giovare a, giovarsi (di). ~**able,** *a.* profittevole, utile. ~**ably,** *ad.* profittevolmente. ~**eer,** *n.* (*fig.*) péscecane, *m.*
profligacy, *n.* dissolutezza, sregolatezza, *f.,* libertinaggio, *m.* **profligate,** *a.* sregolato, dissoluto, libertino. ¶ *n.* libertino; prodigo, *m.*
pro forma, (*invoice*) pro-forma; figurato, simulato.
profound, *a.* profondo; cupo; alto. ~**ly,** *ad.* profondamente. **profundity,** *n.* profondità, *f.*
profuse, *a.* profuso, abbondante, prodigo, copioso. ~**ly,** *ad.* profusamente, a profusione. **profusion,** *n.* profusione, abbondanza, copia, *f.;* lusso, *m.*
progenitor, *n.* progenitore, *m. our* ~*s,* i nostri avi, i nostri antenati, *m.pl.*
progeny, *n.* progenie, prole, *f.,* i figli, *m.pl.*
prognathous, *a.* prognato.
prognosticate, *v.t.* pronosticare. **prognostic[ation],** *n.* pronostico, *m.,* pronosticazione, *f.*
programme, *n.* programma, *m.*
progress, *n.* progresso, progredimento, *m.,* avanzata, *f.;* andamento, corso, *m. in* ~, in corso. ¶ *v.i.* progredire, avanzarsi, far progressi. ~**ion,** *n.* progressione, *f.* ~**ive,** *a.* progressivo, crescente; (*party*) progressista.
prohibit, *v.t.* proibire, vietare. ~**ion,** *n.* proibizione, *f.,* divieto, *m.* ~**ionist,** *n.* proibizionista, *m.f.* ~**ive** *& ~***ory,** *a.* proibitivo.
project, *n.* progetto, disegno; divisamento, piano, *m.* ¶ *v.t.* progettare; (*Geom.*) proiettare (*v.i.*) aggettare. sporgere. ~ *beyond,* sporgere in fuori. ~**ile,** *n. & a.* proiettile, *a. & m.* ~**ing,** *p.a.* sporgente. ~**ion,** *n.* proiezione, *f.;* (*protruding*) sporgenza, *f.,* sporto, risalto, rilievo, aggetto, *m.* ' ~ *lantern,* lanterna magica, *f.* ~**or,** (*Opt.*) proiettore, *m.*

proletarian, *a. & n.* proletario, *a. & m.* **proletariat[e],** *n.* proletariato, *m.*
prolific, *a.* prolifico; fecondo, fertile.
prolix, *a.* prolisso. ~**ity,** *n.* prolissità, *f.*
prologue, *n.* prologo, *m.*
prolong, *v.t.* prolungare. ~**ation,** *n.* prolungazione, *f.,* prolungamento, *m. prolonged applause,* applauso prolungato, *a.* nutrito, *m.*
promenade, *n.* passeggio, *m.,* passeggiata, *f.* ~ *deck,* prima coperta, *f.*
prominence, *n.* prominenza, *f.,* risalto, *m.* **prominent,** *a.* prominente. cospicuo; sporgente, spiccato
promiscuity, *n.* promiscuità, *f.* **promiscuous,** *a.* promiscuo. ~**ly,** *ad.* promiscuamente.
promise, *n.* promessa, *f.* ¶ *v.t. & i.* promettere, fare una promessa; predire; dare a sperare. ~*d land,* land *of* ~, terra promessa, *f.* **promising,** *a.* promettente, che promette bene. *promissory note,* pagherò, *m.*
promontory, *n.* promontorio, *m.*
promote, *v.t.* promuovere; facilitare. **promoter,** *n.* promotore, *m.* **promotion,** *n.* promozione, *f.;* (*of a public company, &c.*) lancio, *m.*
prompt, *a.* pronto, sollecito; lesto, subito, puntuale. ~ *cash,* contante, *m.* or *pl.* contanti. ¶ *v.t.* suggerire, ispirare; incitare, spingere; (*Theat.*), *&c.*) suggerire. ~ *book,* testo del suggeritore, *m.* ~**er,** *n.* suggeritore, *m.* ~**itude,** *n.* prontezza, sollecitudine, *f.*
promulgate, *v.t.* promulgare.
prone, *a.* prono; disposto (a), incline (a). ¶ *ad.* bocconi. ~**ness,** *n.* inclinazione, propensità, *f.*
prong, *n.* rebbio, *m.;* punta, *f.*
pronominal, *a.* pronominale. **pronoun,** *n.* pronome, *m.*
pronounce, *v.t. & i.* pronunziare. **pronunciation,** *n.* pronunzia, *f.*
proof, *n.* prova, dimostrazione, *f.;* titolo, *m.;* (*spirit*) grado, *m.;* (*print*) bozza, *f.* in ~ *of which,* a prova di ciò. ~ *against,* a prova di, superiore a. ~ *reader,* correttore di bozze, *m.* ~ *reading,* correzione (revisione) di bozze, *f.* ~ *spirit,* alcool a 56 gradi, *m.* ¶ *v.t.* rendere impermeabile.
prop, *n.* puntello, appoggio; sostegno, *m.* ¶ *v.t.* puntellare, sostenere.
propaganda, *n.* propaganda, *f.*
propagate, *v.t.* propagare; spargere, diffondere.
propel, *v.t.* spingere innanzi, impel-

lere, propulsare. **propeller,** *n.* propulsore, *m.*; (*screw*) elica, *f.*
propensity, *n.* propensione, *f.*
proper, *a.* proprio; convenevole, confacente; giusto, esatto. ~**ty,** *n.* proprietà, *f.*, avere, *m.*; beni, fondi, beni mobili ed immobili, *m.pl.*; (*pl. Theat.*) vestiario, *m.* ~ *market,* mercato immobiliario, *m.* ~ *tax,* imposta fondiaria, *f.*
prophecy, *n.* profezia, *f.* **prophesy,** *v.t. & i.* profetizzare, predire, profetare. **prophet,** *n.* profeta, *m.* ~**ess,** *n.* profetessa, *f.* ~**ic(al),** *a.* profetico.
propinquity, *n.* propinquità, *f*; (*relationship*) parentela, *f.*
propitiate, *v.t.* propiziare. **propitious,** *a.* propizio.
proportion, *n.* proporzione, *f.* ¶ *v.t.* proporzionare. ~**al,** *a.* proporzionale.
proposal, *n.* proposta, offerta, *f.* **propose,** *v.t. & i.* proporre, offrire, intendere, proporsi; (*toast*) fare; (*marriage to woman*) domandare la mano di; (*to man*) offrire la mano a. **proposer,** *n.* proponente, *m.f.* **proposition,** *n.* proposizione, *f.*; affare, *m.*
propound, *v.t.* esporre, mettere in campo, proporre.
proprietary, *a.* (*rights*) di proprietà. ~ *medicine,* specialità farmaceutica, *f.* **proprietor, -tress,** *n.* proprietario, *m.* -*a,* *f.* **propriety,** *n.* convenienza, decenza, *f.* **proprieties,** *n.pl.* buone creanze, *f.pl.*
propulsion, *n.* propulsione, *f.* jet ~, propulsione a reazione.
pro rata, *ad.* in proporzione. ~ *to,* in proporzione a.
prorogue, *v.t.* prorogare.
prosaic, *a.* prosaico.
proscenium, *n.* proscenio, *m.*
proscribe, *v.t.* proscrivere.
prose, *n.* prosa, *f.* ~ *writer,* prosatore, *m.* ~ *writings,* *n.pl.* prose; opere in prosa, *f.pl.*
prosecute, *v.t.* far processare, procedere contro; proseguire, continuare. **prosecution,** *n.* accusa, querela, *f.*, parte civile, *f.*; prosecuzione, *f.*, proseguimento, *m.*, continuazione, *f.* **prosecutor,** *n.* (*Law*) attore, *m.* parte civile, *f.* *public* ~, pubblico ministero, *m.*
proselyte, *n.* proselito, *m.*
prosiness, *n.* prosaicità; verbosità, *f.*
prosody, *n.* prosodia, *f.*
prospect, *n.* prospetto, *m.*, prospet-

tiva, esposizione, vista; aspettativa, speranza, *f.* ¶ *v.t.* esplorare. ~ *for,* andare alla ricerca di. ~**ing,** *n.* esplorazione, ricerca, *f.* ~**ive,** *a.* previsto, anticipato, probabile. ~**or,** *n.* ricercatore (di metalli preziosi), *m.*
prospectus, *n.* prospetto, progetto, programma, *m.*
prosper, *v.i.* prosperare, riuscire. ~**ity,** *n.* prosperità, *f.* ~**ous,** *a.* prospero, fortunato, fiorente.
prostate [**gland**], *n.* prostata, *f.*
prostitute, *v.t.* prostituire.
prostrate, *a.* prostrato, prosternato. ¶ *v.t.* prostrare. ~ *oneself,* prostrarsi. **prostration,** *n.* prostrazione, *f.*; (*Med.*) abbattimento, *m.*
prosy, *a.* prosaico; stucchevole, tedioso.
protagonist, *n.* protagonista, *m.f.*
protect, *v.t.* proteggere, difendere; tutelare. ~**ion,** *n.* protezione, difesa; tutela, *f.* ~**ionist,** *n. & att.* protezionista, *m. & a.* ~**ive,** difensivo, protettore, di protezione. ~ *colouring,* mimetizzamento, mimetismo, *m.* **protector, -tress,** protettore, *m.,* -trice, *f.* ~**ate,** *n.* protettorato, *m.*
protein, *n.* proteina, *f.*
pro tempore, (*abb.* pro tem.) *ad.* in via provvisoria, a titolo provvisorio.
protest, *n.* protesta, *f.*; (*bill*) protesto, *m.* ¶ *v.t. & i.* protestare. ~**ant,** *n. & a.* protestante. *a. & m.* **Protestantism,** *n.* protestantesimo, *m.* religione protestante, *f.*
protocol, *n.* protocollo, *m.*
prototype, *n.* prototipo, *m.*
protract, *v.t.* protrarre; prolungare. ~**or,** *n.* rapportatore, goniometro, *m.*
protrude, *v.i.* sporgere, aggettare, spingersi fuori.
protuberance, *n.* protuberanza, *f.*
proud, *a.* fiero, orgoglioso, altero, superbo; (*fig.*) grande, magnifico. ~ *flesh,* cicciolo, *m.*
prove, *v.t.* dimostrare, provare, mettere alla prova; ratificare, confermare; (*will*) omologare, verificare. (*v.i.*) tornare, riuscire, mostrarsi.
Provençal, *a.* provenzale.
provender, *n.* foraggio, *m.,* provvigioni, *f.pl.*
proverb, *n.* proverbio, *m.* ~**ial,** *a.* proverbiale.
provide, *v.t.* provvedere, fornire, munire; stipulare, pattuire. ~ *against,* premunirsi contro, prendere delle misure contro. ~*d* [*that*],

purché, a condizione che. **provi-dence,** *n.* provvidenza, *f.*; (*God*) Provvidenza, *f.* **provident,** *a.* provvido, previdente. ∼ *fund,* fondo di previdenza, *m.* ∼**ial,** *a.* provvidenziale. **provider,** *n.* provveditore, *m.*

province, *n.* provincia, *f.*; (*pl.*) province, *f.pl.*; (*sphere*) sfera, competenza, *f.*; limiti, *m.pl.*; giurisdizione, *f.* **provincial,** *a.* provinciale, di provincia.

provision, *n.* provvedimento, preparativo, *m.*; disposizione, *f.*; (*pl.*) provviste; provvigioni, *f.pl.*; viveri, generi alimentari, *m.pl.* ¶ *v.t.* approvvigionare. ∼**al,** *a.* provvisorio, provvisionale.

proviso, *n.* stipulazione, clausola condizionale, *f.*, patto, *m.*

provocation, *n.* provocazione, *f.* **provoke,** *v.t.* provocare, eccitare, stimolare, stizzire.

provost, *n.* prevosto, proposto (*Eccl.*); rettore; sindaco, *m.*

prow, *n.* prora, prua, *f.*

prowess, *n.* prodezza, *f.*, valore, *m.*

prowl, *v.i.* andare in busca, cercare la preda, girare intorno. ∼**er,** *n.* girellone, nottolone, *m.*

proximate, *a.* prossimo, immediato. **proximity,** *n.* prossimità, *f.* **proximo,** *ad.* del mese venturo.

proxy, *n.* procura, *f.*; procuratore, *m.*, **prude,** *n.* ritrosetta, finta modesta, schizzinosa, *f.*

prudence, *n.* prudenza, *f.* **prudent,** *a.* prudente, savio. ∼**ial,** *a.* prudenziale.

prudery, *n.* ritrosia, schifiltà, *f.* **prudish,** *a.* ritrosetto, schifiltoso.

prune, *n.* prugna secca, pruna, *f.* ¶ *v.t.* potare, mondare. **pruning,** *n.* potatura, *f.* ∼ *hook,* potatoio, *m.* ∼ *knife,* coltello per potare, *m.* ∼ *shears,* forbici da giardino, *f.pl.*

pruriency, *n.* libidine, sensualità, *f.* **prurient,** *a.* lascivo, libidinoso. **pruritus,** *n.* prurito, *m.*

Prussia, *n.* la Prussia, *f.* **Prussian,** *a.* prussiano. ∼ *blue,* azzurro di Prussia. ¶ *n.* prussiano, *m.* **prussic,** *a.* prussico.

pry into, *v.t.* spiare, scrutare, ficcare il naso (in). ∼**ing,** *a.* inquisitivo, curioso, indiscreto.

psalm, *n.* salmo, cantico, *m.* ∼**ist,** *n.* salmista, *m.* **psalter,** *n.* salterio, *m.*

pseudonym, *n.* -**ous,** *a.* pseudonimo, *a. & m.*

pshaw, *i.* puh! uff!

psychiater, psychiatrist, *n.* psichia-

tra, *m.* **psychic(al),** *a.* psichico. **psycho-analysis,** *n.*, psicoanalisi, *f.* **psychological,** *a.* psicologico. **psychologist,** *n.* psicologo, *m.* **psychology,** *n.* psicologia, *f.* **ptarmigan,** *n.* pernice di montagna, *f.*

ptomaine, *n.* ptomaina, *f.* ∼ *poisoning,* avvelenamento per le ptomaine, *m.*

puberty, *n.* pubertà, *f.*

public, *a.* pubblico. ∼ *assistance,* ∼ *relief,* assistenza pubblica, *f.* ∼ *assistance institution,* istituzione di beneficenza pubblica, *f.* ∼ *convenience,* luogo comodo, *m.* ∼ *holiday,* giorno festivo, giorno di festa, *m.* ∼ *house,* bettola, osteria, mescita, *f.*, spaccio di bevande alcooliche, *m.* ∼ *prosecutor,* pubblico ministero, *m.* ¶ *n.* pubblico, *m.*, clientela, *f.* ∼**an,** *n.* bettoliere, oste, liquorista, *m.*; (*Bible*) pubblicano, *m.* ∼**ation,** *n.* pubblicazione, *f.* ∼**ist,** *n.* pubblicista, *m.* ∼**ity,** *n.* pubblicità, *f.* **publish,** *v.t.* pubblicare; promulgare; render pubblico; *to be* ∼*ed,* (book) sotto stampa. *just* ∼*ed,* novità editoriale, *f.* ∼**er,** *n.* editore, *m.* ∼*'s imprint,* nome dell'editore, *m.* ∼**ing,** *n.* pubblicazione, *f.* ∼ *house,* casa editrice, libreria, *f.*

puce, *a.* color pulce.

puck, *n.* folletto, demonietto, *m.*; (*Ice hockey*), disco, *m.*, piastrella, *f.* ∼**ish,** *a.* furbetto, maliziosetto.

pucker, *n.* grinza, crespa, ruga; *f.* ¶ *v.t.* raggrinzare, increspare, corrugare; (*v.i.*) raggrinzarsi.

pudding, *n.* budino, *m.*

puddle, *n.* pozza, pozzanghera, *f.* ¶ *v.t.* (*clay*) rimescolare, impastare; (*Metall.*) pudellare.

puerile, *a.* puerile.

puff, *n.* soffio, sbuffo, *m.*, buffata, *f.*; (*dress*) sboffo, *m.*; (*powder*) piumino, *m.*; (*pastry*) sfoglia, pasta sfogliata, *f.* ∼ *paragraph,* reclame, *f.*, soffietto, *m.* ¶ *v.t. & i.* soffiare, gonfiare, sbuffare, lanciare (tirare) buffate (di). ∼ *one's goods,* fare della pubblicità a . . ., fare la reclame a. . . .

puffin, *n.* puffino, *m.*

puffy, *a.* gonfiato, paffuto.

pug (*clay*), *n.* argilla, impastata, *f.* ∼ [*dog*], cagnolino, can bolognese, *m.* ∼ *nose,* naso camuso, *m.* ¶ *v.t.* impastare; murare alla grossa.

pugilism, *n.* pugilato, *m.*; pugilistica, *f.* **pugilist,** *n.* pugilatore, *m.* **pugnacious,** *a.* pugnace, combattivo.

pule, *v.i.* piagnucolare.
pull, *n.* tiro, *m.*, tirata, *f.*, strappo, *m.*,
strappata, *f.*, colpo, sforzo, *m.*;
(*drink*) sorsata, *f.*, sorso, *m.*; (*Typ.*)
bozza; impressione, tiratura, *f.*; (*bell*)
colpo; (*rope, bell*) cordone, *m.*; (*fig.*)
vantaggio, *m.* ~-*over*, pullover, *m.*
¶ *v.t. & i.* tirare; trascinare; strappare; cavare, estrarre; vogare, remare; (*proof, Typ.*) fare. ~ *the
wires for,* (*fig.*) intrigare nell'interesse
di. ~ *to one side* (traffic) tirare da
parte. ~ *to pieces,* fare a pezzi,
squartare; (*fig.*) sparlare di.
pullet, *n.* pollastro, *m.*; pollastrella, *f.*
pulley, *n.* puleggia; carrucola, girella,
f. ~ *block,* paranco, *m.*
Pullman [car], *n.* vettura Pullman,
carrozza-salone, *f.*
pullulate, *v.i.* pullulare.
pulmonary, *a.* polmonare.
pulp, *n.* polpa, *f.*; (*Paper making*)
pasta, *f.* ¶ *v.t.* ridurre in polpa, in
pasta.
pulpit, *n.* pulpito; pergamo, *m.* ~
eloquence, oratoria sacra, *f.* ~
orator, oratore sacro, *m.*
pulsate, *v.i.* pulsare; battere. **pulsation,** *n.* pulsazione, *f.* **pulse,** *n.*
(*Anat.*) polso, *m.*; (*food*) semi legumi-
nosi (cece, pisello, ecc.), *m.pl.* ~
rate, ritmo del polso, *m.*
pulverize, *v.t.* polverizzare.
puma, *n.* puma, coguaro, *m.*
pumice [stone], *n.* pomice, pietra
pomice, *f.* ¶ *v.t.* fregare con la pomice.
pump, *n.* pompa, *f.*; (*dress shoe*)
scarpettina da ballo, *f.* ~ *handle,*
manovella, leva di pompa, *f.* ~
maker, fabbricatore di pompe, *m.*
~ *room* (at spa) sala delle sorgenti, *f.*
¶ *v.t. & i.* pompare; (*fig.*) strappare
un segreto a. ~ *up* (tyre), gonfiare.
pumpkin, *n.* zucca, *f.*, popone, *m.*
pun, *n.* bisticcio, giuoco di parole, *m.*
¶ *v.i.* far giuochi di parole.
punch, *n.* pugno, colpo di pugno, *m.*;
(*tool*) punzone, *m.*, stampino, stampo, *m.*, cacciatoia, *f.*; (*drink*) ponce,
m. ~ *bowl,* bicchiere da ponce, *m.*
P~, *m.* Pulcinella, *m.* ~ *& Judy*
[show], i burattini, *m.pl.*, teatro di
Pulcinella, *m.* ¶ *v.t.* dare un pugno
a; (*Mech.*) punzonare; perforare.
punching ball, palla usata negli
esercizi dei pugilatori, *f.*
punctilio, *n.* puntiglio, *m.*, formalità,
f. **punctilious,** *a.* puntiglioso,
minuzioso, formalista.
punctual, *a.* puntuale. ~**ity,** *n.*
puntualità, *f.* **punctuate,** *v.t. &*

abs. punteggiare. **punctuation,** *n.*
punteggiatura, interpunzione, *f.* ~
marks, segni di interpunzione, *m.pl.*
puncture, *n.* puntura, *f.*; (*Surg.*)
puntura, *f.*; (*tyre*) buco, *m.*, foratura,
f. ¶ *v.t. & i.* pungere; (*tyre*) forare.
pundit, *n.* dotto indiano; (*fig.*) dotto,
m.
pungency, *n.* agrezza, acrimonia, *f.*,
gusto piccante, *m.* **pungent,** *a.*
pungente, piccante, acre; (*fig.*)
sarcastico.
punish, *v.t.* punire. ~**able,** *a.* puni-
bile. ~**ment,** *n.* punizione, pena, *f.*
punster, *n.* bisticcione, chi fa giuochi
di parole, *m.*
punt, (*boat*) *n.* chiatta, *f.*, barchino, *m.*
¶ *v.i.* (*Cards*) puntare; (*Betting*)
scommettere; (*v.t.*) (*Boating*) spingere (una barca piatta) con le per-
tiche. ~**er,** *n.* (*Cards*) puntatore, *m.*;
(*Betting*) scommettitore, *m.*
puny, *a.* piccino, debole, malaticcio,
meschino.
pup, *n.* cucciolo, cane lattante, *m.*
sell a ~, (*fig.*) raggirare. ¶ *v.i.*
figliare.
pupa, *n.* crisalide, *f.*
pupil, *n.* (*eye*) pupilla, *f.*; (*scholar*)
allievo, alunno, scolaro, *m.*
puppet, *n.* burattino, *m.*, marionetta,
f.
puppy, *n.* cagnolino, *m.*; (*pers.*)
vanerello, damerino, *m.*
purblind, *a.* miope, mezzo cieco;
ottuso.
purchase, *n.* acquisto, *m.*, acquisi-
zione, *f.*; (*shopping*) compra, *f.*; (*hold*)
presa, stretta, *f.*; (*tackle*) paranco, *m.*
¶ *v.t.* comprare, acquistare. **purchaser,** *n.* acquirente, *m.f.*, compratore, *m.*, -trice, *f.*, avventore, *m.*
pure, *a.* puro, mero, pretto; illibato,
innocente. ~ *mechanics,* meccanica
teorica, *f.* ~**ness,** *n.* purezza, *f.*
purgative, *a.* purgativo. ¶ *n.* purgante, *m.* **purgatory,** *n.* purgatorio,
m. **purge,** *v.t.* purgare. **purge,**
purging, *n.* purgante, *m.*, purga,
purgazione, *f.*
purify, *v.t.* purificare. **purist,** *n.*
purista, *m.* **Puritan,** *n. & a., &*
puritanic(al), *a.* puritano, *a. & m.*,
puritanico, *a.* **purity,** *n.* purità,
purezza; illibatezza; castità, *f.*
purl, *v.i.* mormorare, gorgogliare,
sussurrare. ~ *knitting,* lavoro a
punto rovescio, *m.*
purlieus, *n.pl.* dintorni, *m.pl.*, vici-
nanze, *f.pl.*, confini, *m.pl.*
purlin, *n.* (*Arch.*) arcareccio, *m.*

purloin, *v.t.* sottrarre, involare, rubare; (*fig.*) plagiare.

purple, *n.* porpora, *f.*; (*robe*) porpora, *f. born in the* ~, di sangue reale. ¶ *a.* purpureo. ~ *red*, rosso purpureo. ¶ (*fig.*) *v.t.* imporporare, fare arrossire. **purplish,** *a.* porporino.

purport, *n.* tenore, *m.* portata; sostanza, *f.*; significato, scopo, *m.* ¶ *v.t.* significare; aver per scopo; indicare; pretendere.

purpose, *n.* mira, *f.*, scopo, intento, fine, proposito, *m.*, intenzione, *f.*, proponimento; risultato, vantaggio, *m. on* ~, apposta, di proposito, espressamente, a bella posta. *to no* ~, invano, inutilmente, senza risultato. ¶ *v.t.* proporsi di, mirare a, avere l'intenzione di. ~*ly, ad.* di proposito, intenzionalmente, a bello studio.

purr, purring, *n.* fusa, *f.pl.* ¶ *v.i.* far le fusa.

purse, *n.* borsa, *f.* ¶ (*lips*) *v.t.* contrarre, fare il bocchino bello; (*brow*) corrugare, raggrinzare. **purser,** *n.* commissario, *m.*

purslane, (*Bot.*) *n.* porcellana, *f.*

pursuant to, in pursuance of, conforme a, in seguito di, (a).

pursue, *v.t.* inseguire, proseguire, continuare, seguire, perseguire, seguitare. **pursuit,** *n.* inseguimento, *m.*; ricerca; occupazione, *f.*

purulent, a. purulento.

purvey, *v.t.* provvedere, fornire. ~*or,* *n.* provveditore, *m.*, fornitore, *m.*, -trice, *f.*

purview, *n.* limiti, *m.pl.*, circoscrizione, *f.*; (*Law*), dispositivo, *m.*

pus, *n.* pus, *m.*, marcia, *f.*

push, *n.* spinta, *f.*, colpo, attacco, impulso, urto, *m.*; iniziativa, energia, *f.*; caso urgente, momento critico, *m.* ~ (-*button*) bottone, *m.*; (*Elec.*) pulsante, *m.* ¶ *v.t.* spingere; urtare; (*fig.*) promuovere, dare impulso a. ~-*cart*, carretto a mano, *m.* ~ *about*, urtacchiare; spingere qua e là. ~ *back*, respingere, far indietreggiare. ~ *off* (*Naut.*) partire, pigliare il largo. ~ *on*, avanzare, proseguire la strada, farsi avanti. ~*ing, a.* operoso, intraprendente, energico.

pusillanimous, *a.* pusillanime.

puss[y], *n.* micio, micino, *m. Puss in Boots*, il Gatto con gli stivali, *m.*

pustule, *n.* pustola, *f.*

put, *v.t.ir,* mettere, porre, collocare, posare; proporre, offrire, presentare

esprimere.   ~   (*things*) *away*, mettere via, mettere al sicuro. ~ *down*, deporre; sopprimere; prender nota di, mettere in iscritto; proporre, fare anticipare. ~ *forward*, mettere innanzi. ~ *in*, mettere dentro, introdurre; (*Naut.*) prender porto. ~ *off*, differire, rinviare, rimandare. ~ *on*, mettere sopra, avanzare; (*clothes*) indossare, mettersi, vestirsi di; (*brake*) chiudere, serrare, stringere. ~ *out*, mettere fuori, mettere alla porta; emettere; spegnere; incomodare, imbarazzare; (*tongue*) tirar fuori. ~ *out of joint*, slogare. ~ *out of order*, guastare, disordinare, disturbare. ~ *out of tune*, scordare. ~ *the shot*, lanciare il peso. ~ *up* (*money*), contribuire; (*money at cards*), giocare a soldi, puntare; (*vehicle*) rimettere, riporre in rimessa; (*at hotel*) scendere, alloggiarsi. ~-*up job*, affare concertato prima, colpo preparato, *m.* ~ *up with*, sopportare, tollerare.

put[t] (*Golf*) *n.* colpo leggero (per far entrar la palla in buca), *m.* ¶ *v.t.* colpire leggermente (per far entrar la palla in buca).

putlog, *n.* traversa orizzontale, *f.*

putrefaction, *n.* putrefazione, *f.* **putrefy,** *v.t.* putrefare; (*v.i.*) putrefarsi. **putrid,** *a.* putrido, stagnante.

puttee, *n.* mollettiera, *f.*

putter, (*club*) *n.* mazza per far arrivare la palla nelle buche (*Golf*). *putting green*, tratto vicino alla buca (*Golf*). *putting the shot*, lanciamento del peso, *m.*

putty, *n.* mastice; stucco, *m.* ~ *powder*, ossido di stagno, *m.* ¶ *v.t.* immasticare, turare con mastice; stuccare.

puzzle, *n.* rompicapo, indovinello, enigma, *m.* ¶ *v.t.* sconcertare, render perplesso, ingarbugliare. ~*d, p.a.* perplesso, sconcertato, imbarazzato.

pygmy, *a. & n.* pigmeo, *a.m..*

pyjamas, *n.pl.* pigiama, *m.*

pylon, *n.* pilone, *m.*

pyorrhoea, *n.* (*Med.*) piorrea (alveolare), *f.*

pyramid, *n.* piramide, *f.*

pyre, *n.* pira, *f.*, rogo, *m.*

Pyrenees (**the**), i Pirenei, *m.pl.*

pyrethrum, *n.* piretro, *m.*

pyrites, *n.* pirite, *f.*

pyrotechnics, *n.pl.* pirotecnica, *f.* **pyrotechnist,** *n.* pirotecnico, *m.*

python, *n.* pitone, *m.*

pyx, *n.* pisside, coppella, *f.*, ciborio, *m.*

Q

qua, *c.* in qualità di, in forza di.

quack [doctor], *n.* ciarlatano; empirico, *m.* ~ery, *n.* ciarlataneria, *f.*

quadrangle, *n.* quadrangolo, *m.*; corte, *f.*

quadrant, *n.* quadrante; quarto di cerchio, *m.*

quadroon, *n.* meticcio, quarterone, *m.*

quadruped, *n. & a.* quadrupede, *m. & a.*

quadruple, *a. & n.* quadruplo, *a. & m.* **quadruplets**, *n.pl.* quattro nati in un solo parto, *m.pl.*

quaff, *v.t.* tracannare, bere a lunghi tratti.

quag[mire], *n.* acquitrino, pantano, *m.*; palude, *f.*, terreno paludoso, *m.*

quail, *n.* quaglia, *f.* ¶ *v.i.* tremare; aver paura, sgomentarsi.

quaint, *a.* singolare, pittoresco, vecchiotto; barocco, strano, curioso. ~ness, *n.* singolarità, stranezza, natura bizzarra, *f.*

quake, *v.i.* tremare, fremere. **Quaker**, *n.* quacchero, *m.*, -a, *f.*

qualification, *n.* titolo, *m.*; qualità, *f.*; qualifica; capacità, *f.*; modificazione, riserva, *f.*; (*in shares*) cauzione, *f.* **qualified**, *p.a.* qualificato; capace, atto, competente; in grado di; modificato, condizionale, con riserva. **qualify**, *v.t.* qualificare; abilitare, preparare; modificare; restringere. **quality**, *n.* qualità, *f.*; stato, rango, ceto distinto, *m.*; capacità, *f.*; carattere, *m.*

qualms, *n.pl.* mal di cuore; (*of conscience*) scrupolo, *m.*, rimorsi, *m.pl.*

quandary, *n.* imbarazzo, *m.*; perplessità; situazione difficile, *f.*

quantity, *n.* quantità, *f.* ~ surveying, misurazione, *f.* ~ surveyor, misuratore, *m.*

quantum, *n.* quanto, *m.*, suffic[i]enza, *f.* ~ theory (*Phys.*), teoria dei quanta, *f.*

quarantine, *n.* quarantena, *f.*; (*station*) lazzaretto, *m.* ¶ *v.t.* mettere in quarantena.

quarrel, *n.* questione, contesa, disputa, *f.*; alterco, bisticcio, *m.*; rissa; lite, *f.* ¶ *v.i.* altercare, bisticciarsi; disputare, litigare, questionare. *to pick a quarrel with*, attaccar briga con. ~some, *a.* rissoso, litigioso. ~person, accattabrighe, *m.f.*

quarry, *n.* cava, *f.*; preda, *f.* ~ man,

cavatore, *m.* ¶ *v.t.* scavare, estrarre.

quart, *n.* Imperial Meas. = 1·136 litres.

quarter, *n.* quartiere; parte, *f.*; lato, *m.*; (¼th) quarto; (*3 months*) trimestre, *m.*; (*28 lb.*) = 12·70 kilos; (*8 bushels*) = 2·909 hectolitres; (*pl.*) alloggio; appartamento, *m.*; (*Mil.*) quartieri, *m.pl.*, accantonamento, *m.*; (*horse*) stalla, *f.*, scuderie, *f.pl. a* ~ *of an hour*, un quarto d'ora. ~ *binding*, mezza legatura. ~ *day*, giorno della pigione, *m.* ~ *deck*, cassero, *m.* ~master, (*Mil.*) furiere; (*Naut.*) secondo capo timoniere, *m.* ¶ *v.t.* dividere in quarti; (*tear in pieces*) squartare; (*lodge*) alloggiare; (*Mil.*) acquartierare, accantonare. ~ly, *a.* trimestrale; (*ad.*) al trimestre.

quartet[te], *n.* quartetto, *m.*

quarto *or* **4to** *or* **4°**, *n. & att.* in-quarto, in 4to, *m. & a.m.*

quartz, *n.* quarzo, *m.*

quash, *v.t.* cassare, annullare, invalidare.

quasi, *c. & quasi-*, *prefix*, quasi (*ad.*), come se, poco meno che, per pochissimo; mezzo, tinto, quasi-.

quassia, *n.* (*tree & bark*) quassia, *f.*

quatrain, *n.* quartina, *f.*

quaver, (*Mus.*) *n.* croma, *f.* ¶ *v.i.* cantare o parlare con voce tremola, tremolare.

quay, *n.* banchina, *f.*, molo, scalo, *m.*

queen, *n.* regina; (*Cards*, *Chess*) regina, *f.* ~ *bee*, ape regina, *f.* ¶ (*Chess*) *v.t.* convertire in regina. ~ly, *a.* di regina, da r., degno d'una r.

queer, *a.* strambo, bizzarro, originale, strano; singolare, sorprendente; indisposto. *a* ~ *fellow*, un tipo strano, bel tipo!

quell, *v.t.* sopprimere, reprimere; sottomettere; estinguere; acquietare.

quench, *v.t.* spegnere; (*thirst*) dissetare.

querulous, *a.* querulo, lamentevole.

query, *n.* domanda, *f.*; quesito, *m.*

quest, *n.* ricerca, busca, *f.* **question**, *n.* domanda; questione, *f.*; dubbio; affare, soggetto, *m.*; vertenza, *f.*; problema, *m.*; disputa, discussione; interpellanza, *f.* ¶ *v.t.* interrogare, esaminare; contestare; mettere in dubbio, dubitare di. **questionable**, *a.* contestabile, dubbio, incerto; sospetto.

queue, *n.* coda, *f. to* ~ [*up*], far coda.

quibble, *n.* cavillo, sofisma, *m.*;

equivoco, *m.* ¶ *v.i.* cavillare, sofisticare, equivocare.
quick, *a.* rapido; svelto, agile, lesto; pronto; attivo; sollecito; vivo; fino; spiritoso, acuto. ~*-change artist,* trasformista, *m.f.* ~*-firing,* a tiro rapido. ~ *lime,* calce viva, *f.* ~ *march,* passo accelerato, *m.* ~ *sand,* sabbia mobile, *f.* ~*set hedge,* siepe di piante vive, *f.* ~*silver,* argento vivo, mercurio, *m.* ~*-tempered,* collerico, impetuoso, capriccioso. ¶ *ad.* presto; subito. *be* ~! sbrigatevi! presto! ¶ *n.* vivo *m.,* carne viva, *f.* ~**en,** *v.t.* vivificare, animare; accelerare, sbrigare, affrettare. ~**ly,** *ad.* presto, subito, tosto; rapidamente, prontamente. ~**ness,** *n.* prestezza, rapidità; vivacità; svegliatezza; prontezza, *f.*
quid (*tobacco*), *n.* cicca, *f.*
quidnunc, *n.* saccente, curioso, *m.*
quid pro quo, *n.* compenso, equivalente, ricambio, *m.*
quiescent, *a.* quiescente, a riposo.
quiet, *a.* quieto, calmo, tranquillo; silenzioso; modesto, semplice, composto, dimesso. *be* ~! (sta) zitto! tacete! ¶ *n.* quiete, calma, tranquillità, *f.*; riposo, *m.* ¶ *v.t.* acquietare, calmare; far tacere. ~(**-ness**) *&* ~**ude,** *n.* quiete, calma, tranquillità, *f.*; silenzio; riposo, *m.*
quietus, *n.* colpo mortale, colpo di grazia, *m.*
quill, *n.* cannello, *m.*; (*porcupine*) punta, *f.* ~ *driver,* scribacchino, imbrattacarte, *m.* ~ [*feather*], penna, *f.* ~ [*pen*], penna d'oca, *f.*
quilt, *n.* trapunta, coltre, *f.*; (*eiderdown*) piumino, *m.* ¶ *v.t.* trapuntare; imbottire. ~**ing,** *n.* imbottitura trapunta, *f.*
quince, *n.* (mela) cotogna, *f.* ~ [*tree*], cotogno, *m.*
quincunx, *n.* quinconce, *f.*
quinine, *n.* chinino, *m.,* chinina, *f.*
quinquennial, *a.* quinquennale.
quinsy, *n.* squinanzia, angina, *f.*
quint, *n.* quinta, *f.*
quintessence, *n.* quintessenza, *f.*
quintet[te], *n.* quintetto, *m.*
quip, *n.* frizzo, motteggio, *m.,* bottata, *f.*
quire, *n.* quaderno (*24 sheets*); coro, *m.*
quirk, *n.* (*quip*) capriccio, detto arguto, *m.*; (*Carp.*) svolta, *f.*
quit, *a.* libero, sbarazzato, sdebitato. ¶ *v.t.* lasciare, abbandonare.
quite, *ad.* affatto, del tutto, tutto,

bene, completamente, perfettamente; proprio; piú di. ~ *so,* proprio cosí.
quits, *a.* pari, pari e patta.
quiver, (*for arrows*) *n.* faretra, *f.* ¶ *v.i.* tremolare, fremere, palpitare; avere i brividi. ~[**ing**], *n.* tremito, fremito, *m.*
Quixote, *n.* Don Chisciotte, *m.*
quixotic, *a.* stravagante, donchisciottesco. ~**ally,** *ad.* donchisciottescamente.
quiz, *v.t.* burlare, canzonare, corbellare. **quizzical,** *a.* canzonatorio, faceto.
quoin, *n.* spigolo, cantone, *m.*; (*Typ.*) cuneo, *m.*
quoit, *n.* *&* ~**s,** *n.pl.,* disco, *m.,* piastrella, *f.*
quondam, *a.* antico, d'altre volte.
quorum, *n.* numero legale (d'un comitato), *m.*
quota, *n.* quota, quota parte; rata; proporzione, *f.*; contingente, *m.*
quotation, *n.* citazione; (*Com., Fin.*) quotazione, *f.,* corso, *m.*; (*in Stk. Ex. list*) prezzo, *m.* ~ *marks,* virgolette, *f.pl.* **quote,** *v.t.* citare; quotare.
quoth he, disse lui, fece lui.
quotient, *n.,* quoziente, *m.*

R

rabbet, *n.* scanalatura, *f.* ~ *plane.* pialletto per scanalare, *m.*
rabbi, *n.* rabbino, *m.*
rabbit, *n.* coniglio, *m.*; (*young*) coniglietto, *m.*; (*pers. at game*) schiappa, *f.* ~ *burrow,* ~ *hole,* tana di coniglio selvatico, *f.* ~ *hutch,* conigliera, *f.* ~**ry,** *n.* conigliera, *f.*
rabble, *n.* canaglia, plebaglia, *f.*
rabid, *a.* furioso, violento, arrabbiato; rabbioso; fanatico. **rabies,** *n.* rabbia, idrofobia, *f.*
rac[c]oon, *n.* tasso americano, procione, *m.*
race, *n.* (*tribe*) razza; schiatta, stirpe, *f.*; lignaggio, *m.*; (*contest, &c.*) corsa, *f.*; palio, *m.*; (*sea*) corrente (di marea) *f.* ~ *card,* programma delle corse, *m.* ~ *course,* campo (terreno) di corse, *m.*; pista, *f.* ~ *horse,* cavallo da corsa, *m.* ~ *meeting,* riunione di corse, *f.*; periodo di corse, *m.* ~ *suicide,* suicidio del genere umano, *m.* ~ [*way*], canale, *m.,* gora, *f.* ¶ *v.i.* correre, fare una corsa; (*v.t.*)

far correre. **racer,** *n.* corridore, *m.*; cavallo da corsa, *m.* **racial,** *a.* di razza. **racing,** *n.* corse, *f.pl.*; (*horse*) corse di cavalli, *f.pl.* ∼ *boat*, canotto da corsa; motoscafo da corsa, *m.* ∼ *calendar*, calendario delle corse, *m.* ∼ *cyclist*, corridore ciclista, *m.* ∼*-world*, mondo ippico, *m.*

rack, *n.* (*fodder*) rastrelliera, *f.*; (*plates*, *bottles*) scolapiatti, scolabottiglie, *m.inv.*; sostegno, *m.*; (*letters*, *cards*) casellario, *m.*, portacarte, portabiglietti, *m.inv.*; (*cogged*) cremagliera, dentiera, ruota dentata, *f.*; (*luggage*, *Rly.*) rete, reticella, *f.*; (*punishment*, *Hist.*) ruota, *f.*, cavalletto, *m.*, tortura della ruota, *f.* ∼ & *pinion*, ingranaggio a dentiera, *m.* ∼ *railway*, ferrovia a cremagliera, a dentiera, *f.* to ∼ *and ruin*, in rovina, in malora, a monte, a rotoli. ∼ [**off**], *v.t.* travasare. to ∼ *one's brains*, lambiccarsi il cervello, stillarsi il c.

racket, *n.* schiamazzo, chiasso, fracasso, *m.* **racket or racquet,** *n.* racchetta, *f.* ∼ *press*, pressa per racchetta, *f.*

racy, (*fig.*) *a.* piccante, brioso, vigoroso, vivace.

radar, *n.* radar, *m.* ∼ *station*, posto r., *m.*

radial, *a.* radiale. **radiance** & **radiation,** *n.* splendore, *m.*, irradiamento, *m.*, irradiazione, *f.* **radiancy,** *n.* splendore, *m.*, fulgidezza, *f.* **radiant,** *a.* radiante, raggiante, radioso. **radiate,** *v.i.* irradiarsi, emettere raggi. **radiator,** *n.* radiatore, *m.*, calorifero, *m.*

radical, *a.* & *n.* radicale, *a.* & *m.*

radio, *n.* radio, *f.*; apparecchio radio, *m.* ∼ *beacon*, radiofaro, *m.* **radioactive,** *a.* radioattivo. **radiogram,** *n.* radiogramma, *m.* **radiogramophone,** *n.* radiogrammofono, *m.* **radiography,** *n.* radiografia, *f.* **radiolocation,** *n.* radiolocalizzazione, *f.* **radiotelegraphy,** *n.* radiotelegrafia, *f.*

radish, *n.* rafano, radicchio, ravanello, *m.*

radium, *n.* radio, *m.*

radius, *n.* raggio, *m.*, portata, *f.*; (*Anat.*) radio, *m.*

raffle, *n.* lotteria (privata), estrazione a sorte, riffa, *f.*

raffle, *v.t.* estrarre a sorte, mettere in lotteria, riffare.

raft, *n.* zattera, chiatta, *f.* **rafter,** *n.* trave, *f.*, travetto; puntone, *m.*

rafting, *n.* trasporto con zattere, *m.*

raftsman, *n.* chiattaiuolo, *m.*

rag, *n.* cencio, straccio; brandello; cascame, *m.*; (*pl. for paper making*) stracci, *m.pl.*; (*newspaper*) giornalaccio, giornalucolo, *m.*; (*Sch.*) baccano, *m.* ∼ *picker*, ∼ *merchant*, ∼ (& *bone*) *man*, raccoglitore di stracci, straccivendolo, cenciaiolo, *m.*, negoziante di stracci, *m.* ∼*tag* (& *bobtail*), canaglia, plebaglia, *f.* ∼*time*, musica sincopata, *f.* ∼*wort*, erba (di) S. Giacomo, *f.*

ragamuffin, *n.* pezzente, straccione; biricchino, ragazzaccio, *m.*

rage, *n.* rabbia, collera, *f.*, furore, *m.*, violenza, forza, *f.*

rage, *v.i.* arrabbiarsi, infuriarsi; (*war*, *fever*, &c.) infierire.

ragged, *a.* in cenci, a brandelli, lacero, cencioso, stracciato.

raging, *a.* furioso, furibondo, violento, imbestialito. ∼ *fever*, febbre ardente, *f.* ∼ *toothache*, forte dolor di denti, *m.*

raglan, *n.* soprabito (raglan), *m.*

ragout, *n.* intingolo, guazzetto, *m.*

raid, *n.* razzia, scorreria, incursione, *f.* *air* ∼, incursione aerea, *f.* *air*∼ *precautions*, protezione antiaerea, *f.*

raid, *v.t.* razziare, fare una incursione in, attaccare.

rail, *n.* sbarra, inferriata, *f.*, cancello, *m.*, traversone, *m.*; balustrata, *f.*, ringhiera, *f.*, bracciuolo, *m.*; (*hand*) corrimano, *m.*; (*ship's*) battagliola, *f.*; (*Rly.*) rotaia; guida, *f.*; (*bird*) gallinella, *f.*; ∼*car*, vettura automotrice, *f.*

rail, *v.t.* circondare con cancelli, con una cancellata. ∼ *at*, ingiuriare, deridere, svillaneggiare. ∼ *in*, circondare con una cancellata. ∼**ing,** *n.* cancellata, *f.*, ringhiera, grata, inferriata, *f.*; corrimano, *m.*, steccato, *m.*; ingiurie, *f.pl.*, maldicenza, *f.*

raillery, *n.* canzonatura, beffa, *f.*, motteggio, *m.*

railway & **railroad,** *n.* ferrovia, strada ferrata, *f.* ∼*man*, ferroviere, *m.*, impiegato ferroviario, *m.* ∼ *strike*, sciopero ferroviario, dei ferrovieri, *m.*

raiment, *n.* abbigliamento, *m.*, vestiti, *m.pl.*

rain, *n.* pioggia, *f.*, acqua, *f.* ∼*bow*, arcobaleno, *m.*; (*halo*) iride, *f.* ∼*coat*, impermeabile, *m.* ∼*fall*, pioggia, caduta di pioggia, *f.* ∼ *gauge*, pluviometro, *m.* ~ *water*, acqua piovana, *f.*

rain, *v.i.* piovere; (*v.t.*) far piovere, spandere, versare. ~y, *a.* piovoso, di pioggia. ~ (*day*) giorno di pioggia, *m.* ~ (*weather*) tempo piovoso, *m.*

raise, *v.t.* alzare, levare, sollevare; elevare; erigere; (far) costruire; formulare; creare; eccitare, evocare, far nascere; suscitare, provocare; aumentare, rialzare, far salire; allevare, coltivare, produrre; issare; (*cry*) gettare, dare, emettere, far sentire; (*hat*) levarsi; (*flag*) alzare, issare; (*objections*) muovere; (*money for some purpose*) procurare, raccogliere; (*money for oneself*) procurarsi; (*the dead*) risuscitare.

raised, *p.a.* in rilievo, rilevato, saliente, che risalta. ~ *satin stitch*, plumetis in rilievo, *m.*, ~ *stitch*, punto in rilievo, *m.*

raisin, *n.* uva secca, uva passa, *f.*

rajah, *n.* raià, *m.*

rake, *n.* rastrello, *m.*; (*fire*) riavolo, attizzatoio, *m.*; (*pers.*) libertino.

rake, *v.t.* rastrellare; raschiare, frugare; infilare; raccogliere, rimuovere. ~ *up*, ravvivare, risvegliare, richiamare alla luce. *raking fire*, (*Mil.*) fuoco d'infilata, *m. raking shore*, arco di sostegno, puntello, *m.*

rakish, *a.* libertino, dissoluto.

rally, *n.* raccolta, riunione, *f.*; ripresa, *f.* ricupero di forze, *m.*; (*Ten.*) turno, *m.*; (*race meeting*) adunata, *f.* ¶ *v.t.* radunare, riunire; beffare, canzonare; (*v.i.*) riunirsi, adunarsi; ricuperarsi, rimettersi.

ram, *n.* montone, *m.*, ariete, *m.*; (*pile driving*) berta, *f.* battipalo a scatto, ariete, *m.*; (*battleship*) sperone, *m.* **ram**, *v.t.* battere; pigiare; impinzare; mazzerangare; speronare.

ramble, *n.* passeggiata, gita, *f.*; giro, *m.*, escursione, *f.* ¶ *v.i.* vagare, girare, gironzolare; (*rave*) delirare. **rambler**, *n.* (*rose*) rosaio rampicante, *m.* **rambling**, *a.* errante, girovago; (*discourse*) sconnesso, incoerente, a vanvera.

ramification, *n.* ramificazione, *f.* **ramify**, *v.i.* ramificare.

rammer, *n.* berta, mazzaranga, *f.*, battipalo, pillo, pestello, pestone, *m.*; (*cannon*) calcatoio, *m.*

ramp, *n.* salita, rampa, *f.*

rampant, *a.* (*Her.*) rampante. *to be* ~, infierire, far strage.

rampart, *n.* baluardo, riparo, *m.*

ramrod, *n.* bacchetta, *f.*; calcatoio, *m.*

ramshackle, *a.* malfermo, cadente, sgangherato.

ranch, *n.* fattoria, *f.*; (*Amer.*) grande fattoria per allevamento del bestiame.

rancid, *a.* rancido. ~ness, *n.* rancidità, rancidezza, *f.*

rancorous, *a.* pieno di rancore, invelenito. **rancour**, *n.* rancore, *m.*

random, *a.* & *at* ~, a caso, a casaccio, alla cieca, alla ventura.

range, *n.* portata, *f.*; ordine, *m.*, serie, *f.*; campo, *m.*; campo di tiro, *m.*, tiro, *m.*; spazio, *m.*, distesa, *f.*; fornello, *m.*, cucina economica, graticola, *f.*, sfera, *f.*; (*musical*) tastiera, *f.*, scala, *f.*; (*hills*) catena, *f.* ~ *finder*, telemetro, *m.* ~ *pole*, biffa, *f.* ¶ *v.t.* ordinare, schierare; classificare; percorrere. *v.i.* errare, vagare; schierarsi, correre nel numero (di), estendersi; portare, avere la portata (di). **ranger**, *n.* guardia forestale, *f.*

Rangoon, *n.* Rangun, *f.*

rank, *n.* rango, grado, ceto, *m.*, classe, fila, *f.*; (*cab*) stazione, *f.* ~ & *file*, soldati semplici, *m.pl.*

rank, *v.t.* assegnare un grado a; classificare, collocare. ¶ *v.i.* essere nel grado (di), nel rango (di)

rank, *a.* ricco, fertile, rigoglioso, esuberante; rancido, puzzolente; puro, vero, or with the prefix *arci-.*

rankle, *v.i.* inasprirsi, esacerbarsi.

ransack, *v.t.* frugare, perquisire, rovistare.

ransom, *n.* riscatto, *m.*, taglia, *f.*

ransom, *v.t.* riscattare, redimere, pagare una taglia per.

rant, *n.* vana declamazione, *f.*, discorso ampolloso, *m.* ¶ *v.i.* urlare, smaniare, declamare a voce altissima.

ranunculus, *n.* ranuncolo, *m.*

rap, *n.* picchiata, *f.*, pacca, *f.*, colpo secco, *m.*; (*fig.*) centesimo, fico, cosa senza valore.

rap, *v.t.* & *v.i.* picchiare, bussare.

rapacious, *a.* rapace.

rape, *n.* ratto, rapimento, stupro, *m.*; (*Law*) violenza carnale, violazione, *f.*, ratto, *m.*; (*oil seed plant*) rapa, *f.*; (*colerape*) ravizzone, *m.*

rapid, *a.* rapido, celere, veloce; (*pulse, &c.*) frequente, rapido.

rapid, *n.* corrente rapide, *f.*, cascata, *f.* (*oft. pl.*). ~ity, *n.* rapidità, *f.*

rapier, *n.* fioretto, spadino, *m.*

rapine, *n.* rapina, *f.*
rapt, *a.* rapito, estasiato, in estasi.
rapture, *n.* estasi, *f.*, rapimento, *m.*
rapturous, *a.* estatico.
rara avis, rara avis, *f.*, uccello raro, *m.*
rare, *a.* raro, rado, scarso; (*word*) poco usato.
rarefy, *v.t.* rarefare.
rareness, rarity, *n.* rarità, radezza, *f.*
rascal, *n.* briccone, birbante, birbone, furfante, mariuolo, *m.* ~ **ity,** *n.* bricconeria, birbanteria, furfanteria, *f.* ~**ly,** *a.* furfantesco, birbonesco, birbantesco.
rash, *a.* temerario, imprudente, avventato.
rash, *n.* eruzione (cutanea), *f.* ~**ness,** *n.* temerità, arditezza, imprudenza, *f.*
rasher, *n.* fetta di lardo, di prosciutto, *f.*
rasp, *n.* raspa, grattugia, *f.*
rasp, *v.t.* raspare, raschiare, grattugiare.
raspberry, & ~ **bush,** *n.* lampone, *m.*
rat, *n.* topo, *m.*, ratto, *m.*; (*young*) topino, *m.*; (*pers.*) rinnegato; crumiro (*blackleg*), *m.*; (*Pol.*) girella, *m.*, banderuola, *f.* ~ *catcher,* cacciatore di topi, *m.* ~ *poison,* veleno per i topi. ~ *trap,* trappola per topi, *f.* ~*trap pedal,* pedale a sega, *m.*
rat, *v.i.* uccidere i topi; (*Pol.*) voltar casacca.
ratable, *a.* tassabile, gravabile, imponibile; (*land*) catastale; soggetto a tributo locale.
ratchet, *n.* dente d'arresto, nottolino d'arresto, *m.* ~ *brace,* trapano a cricco, *m.* ~ *drill,* trapano a nottolino, *m.* ~ *spanner,* ruota d'arresto, *f.* ~ *wheel,* ruota d'arresto, *f.* *v.t.* munire di denti d'arresto.
rate, *n.* prezzo, *m.*, tariffa; proporzione, ragione, aliquota, contribuzione media, *f.*; tributo, *m.*; passo, andamento, *m.*, velocità; classe, *f.* ordine, rango, *m.*; corso, tasso, saggio; modo, caso, *m.*; qualifica, *f.* ~ *payer,* contribuente, *m.f.* *at any* ~, ad ogni modo, in ogni caso, comunque. *at this rate,* in questa maniera, se così è. ~ *of exchange,* corso dei cambi, *m.* ~ *of interest,* tasso d'interesse, *m.* ~ *of depreciation,* percentuale dell'ammortamento, *f. death* ~*s,* mortalità, *f. local* ~*s,* tributi locali, *m.pl.* ~*s & taxes,* tributi e tasse.
rate, *v.t.* valutare; classificare; (*tax*)

tassare; (*esteem*) apprezzare; (*scold*) sgridare, dare lavate di capo.
rather, *ad.* piuttosto, alquanto, un po'. ~ *nice,* graziosetto, gentilino. ~ *slowly,* (*Mus.*) adagio. ~! sicuro; senza dubbio!
ratification, *n.* ratifica, *f.* **ratify,** *v.t.* ratificare.
rating, *n.* valutazione, tassazione, *f.*; tassamento, *m.*; (*Naut.*) grado, *m.*; sgridata, *f.*, rimprovero, *m.*
ratio, *n.* rapporto, *m.*, proporzione, ragione, *f.*
ration, *n.* razione, *f.*, rancio, *m.*; (*pl.*) viveri, *m.pl.*, razione, *f.* ~ *book,* libretto d'alimentazione, *m.* ~ *card,* tessera annonaria, *f.*
ration, *v.t.* razionare. ~**al,** *a.* razionale, ragionevole.
rationalism, *n.* razionalismo, *m.*
rationalization, *n.* razionalizzazione, *f.*
rat[t]an, *n.* & ~ *cane,* canna d'India, *f.*
rat-tat(-tat), *n.* pum! pum!
ratter, *n.* cane da topi, *m.*
rattle, *n.* sonaglio; tintinnio; strepito, rumore, *m.*; (*baby's*) raganella, *f.*, sonaglietto, *m.*; (*fig.*) chiacchierona, *f.*; (*throat*) rantolo, *m.* ~*snake,* serpente a sonagli, *m.* ~ *trap,* macchina guasta, *f.*; (*vehicle*) vetturaccia, *f.* ¶ *v.i.* & *v.t.* tintinnare, far tintinnare; scuotere con strepito; ciarlare.
raucous, *a.* rauco.
ravage, *v.t.* devastare, depredare, guastare, saccheggiare. ~**s,** *n.pl.* strage, *f.*, guasto, *m.*, devastazione, *f.*; (*of time*) ingiurie, *f.pl.*
rave, *v.i.* delirare, farneticare, esser furioso.
ravel, *v.t.* imbrogliare, ingarbugliare, avviluppare.
ravellings, *n.pl.* filaccie, *f.pl.*
raven, *n.* corvo (maggiore), *m.*
Ravenna, *n.* Ravenna, *f. native of* ~, *n.* & *a.* ravennate, *a.m.* & *f.*
ravenous, *a.* vorace, divorante, affamato.
ravine, *n.* burrone, *m.*, borro, *m.*, fossa, *f.*
raving, *n.* delirio, *m.*, frenesia, *f.*, furore, *m.* ~ *mad,* pazzo furioso, matto da legare.
ravish, *v.t.* rapire, estasiare; violare, stuprare. **ravishing,** *a.* incantevole.
ravishingly, *ad.* incantevolmente, d'incanto.
raw, *a.* crudo, rozzo, brutto, immaturo, grezzo, (*silk*) greggia; verde,

nudo, nuovo, puro; (*meat, wound*) sanguinante; (*material*) primo, greggio; (*fig.*) inesperto, zotico; novizio, imberbe; (*weather*) freddo ed umido. **~ness,** *n.* crudezza; inesperienza, rozzezza, *f.* (*weather*) rigore, *m.*

ray, *n.* raggio, *m.*; (*fish*) razza, *f.*

rayon, *n.* raion, *m.*, seta artificiale, *f.*

raze, *v.t.* radere (a terra), spianare.

razor, *n.* rasoio, *m.*

re (in) *pr.* nella causa di, nell'affare di.

reach, *n.* portata, distanza, bordata, estensione, *f.*, tratto d'un fiume, *m.* gora (di mulino); capacità, *f.* potere, *m.* penetrazione, *f.*

reach, *v.t.* giungere a, pervenire a, raggiungere, toccare. **~ [out],** *v.t.* tendere, stendere, porgere; (*v.i.*) estendersi, spandere.

react, *v.i.* reagire. **~ion,** *n.* reazione, *f.* **~ionary,** *a. & n.* reazionario, *a. & m.*

reactive, *a.* reattivo.

read, *v.t. & i.* leggere; (*fig.*) indovinare; (*report*) dare lettura di (una relazione); (*Law, &c.*) studiare.; (*meter*) rilevare. **~ for (***exam***),** preparare. **~ over,** percorrere (leggendo). **~able,** *a.* leggibile.

readdress, *v.t.* indirizzare di nuovo, rispedire.

reader, *n.* lettore, *m.*, -trice, *f.*; (*Sch.*) libro di lettura, (*Typ.*) correttore di bozze, *m.* **~ship,** letterato, *m.*

readiness, *n.* prontezza, buona volontà, premura, *f.* **reading,** *n.* lettura; lezione; (*fig.*) interpretazione, *f.* **~ desk,** leggio, *m.*; (*church*) leggio. **~ glass,** lente biconvessa, *f.* **~ lamp,** lampada da studio, *f.*, **~room;** sala di lettura, *f.*, gabinetto di l., *m.*

ready, *a.* pronto; disposto; disinvolto; facile. **~-made,** fatto, confezionato. **~ money,** contanti, *m.pl.* **~ reckoner,** libretto calcolatore, *m.*

reagent, *n.* reagente, *m.*

real, *a.* reale, vero, effettivo; (*Law*) immobile. **~ estate,** proprietà fondiaria, *f.*; beni immobili, *m.pl.* **~ist,** *n.* realista, *m.f.*; **~istic,** *a.* realistico. **~ity,** *n.* realtà, *f.*; il reale, *m.* **~ize,** *v.t.* realizzare.

realm, *n.* regno, reame, *m.*

realty, *n.* beni immobili, *m.pl.*

ream, *n.* risma (*c.* 500 *sheets*), *f.* ¶ *v.t.* alesare. **~er,** *n.* alesatore, *m.*

reap, *v.t.* mietere, falciare; (*fig.*) raccogliere, fare il raccolto. **reaper,** *n.* mietitore, *m.*, -trice, *f.* **reaping,** *n.* falciatura, mietitura, *f.* **~ hook,**

falce, *f.*, falcetto, *m.* **~ machine** or **reaper,** *n.* mietitrice, *f.* **~ & threshing machine (***combined harvester***),** mietitrice-trebbiatrice, *f.*

reappear, *v.i.* ricomparire, riapparire. **~ance,** *n.* ricomparsa, *f.*; (*Law*) ricomparizione, *f.*

reappoint, *v.t.* rinominare.

rear, *n.* il di dietro, tergo, *m.*; spalle, *f.pl.*; coda, *f.* **~ admiral,** contrammiraglio, ammiraglio di divisione, *m.* **at the ~, in the ~,** a tergo, alle spalle, indietro, per di dietro. **~ guard,** retroguardia, *f.* **~ lamp,** fanalino posteriore, *m.* **~ rank,** ultima fila, *f.* ¶ *v.t.* innalzare, levare, elevare, erigere; allevare; coltivare; (*v.i.*) (*horse*) impennarsi. **~ing of children,** allevamento di bambini, *m.*

rearrangement, *n.* riordinamento, *m.*

reason, *n.* ragione, causa, *f.*, motivo, *m.* **to state the ~ for,** motivare. ¶ *v.i.* ragionare, discorrere, argomentare. **~ with,** discutere con, argomentare. **~able,** *a.* ragionevole. **~er,** *n.* ragionatore, *m.*, -trice, *f.* **~ing,** *n.* ragionamento, *m.*; argomentazione, *f.*

reassert, *v.t.* riaffermare.

reassure, *v.t.* rassicurare, riassicurare.

rebate, *n.* sconto, ribasso, *m.*, bonifica, *f.*; (*Carp.*) scanalatura, *f.*; incastro (in un pezzo di legno), *m.*

rebel, *n.* ribelle, *m.f.* ¶ *v.i.* ribellarsi, rivoltarsi, sollevarsi. **rebellion,** *n.* ribellione, rivolta, *f.* **rebellious,** *a.* ribelle.

rebind, *v.t.ir.* legare di nuovo.

rebirth, *n.* rinascimento, *m.*, rinascita, rinascenza, *f.*

rebound, *n.* rimbalzo, *m.* ¶ *v.i.* rimbalzare.

rebuff, *n.* rifiuto, scacco, *m.*; rabbuffo, *m.* ¶ *v.t.* respingere.

rebuild, *v.t.ir.* ricostruire.

rebuke, *n.* rimprovero, *m.*, rabbuffo, *m.*, sgridata, *f.* ¶ *v.t.* riprendere, sgridare.

rebut, *v.t.* ributtare, confutare.

recalcitrant, *a. & n.*, ricalcitrante, *a. & m.f.*

recall, *n.* richiamo, *m.* ¶ *v.t.* richiamare; (*recollect*) ricordarsi.

recant, *v.t.* ritrattare, rinnegare, disdire. **~ation,** *n.* ritrattazione, rinnegazione; palinodia, *f.*

recapitulate, *v.t.* ricapitolare; riassumere.

recapture, *n.* ripresa, *f.* ¶ *v.t.* riprendere, ricatturare.

recast, *v.t.ir.* rifondere; rifare.
recede, *v.i.* indietreggiare, ritrarsi; recedere. **receding** (*forehead*), depresso; (*chin*) fuggente.
receipt, *n.* (*act of reception*) ricevimento, *m.*; (*acknowledgement*) ricevuta, quietanza, *f.*; (*recipe*, *prescription*) ricetta, *f.*; (*pl.*) incasso, *m.*; entrate, *f.pl.* ~ *stamp*, marca da bollo, *f.* ¶ *v.t.* quietanzare. **receive**, *v.t.* ricevere, accogliere; (*money*) ricevere, riscuotere, toccare; (*stolen goods*) ricettare. **receiver**, *n.* ricevitore, destinatario, recipiente; (*stolen goods*) ricettatore; (*Ten.*) ribattitore, *m.*; (*Teleph.*) ricevitore, *m.*; (*vessel*) recipiente, *m.*; *official* ~ (*bankruptcy*), curatore fallimentare, *m.* *receiving office* (*Rly.*), ufficio di ricevimento, *m.*
recent, *a.* recente.
receptacle, *n.* ricettacolo, recipiente, *m.* **reception**, *n.* ricevimento, *m.*; (*Radio*) ricezione, *f.*; accoglienza, *f.* ~ *room*, sala di ricevimento, *f.* **receptive** (*mind*, *Radio*, &c.), *a.* ricettivo, *a.*
recess, *n.* recesso, *m.*; nicchia, *f.*; alcova, *f.*; svano, *m.*; (*holidays*) vacanze, *f.pl.*; (*pl. heart*, &c.) latebra, *f.*; recessi, *m.pl.* ¶ *v.t.* sfondare.
recipe, *n.* ricetta, *f.*; (*Phar.*) formula, *f.*
recipient, *n.* destinatario, *m.*; recipiente, *m.f.*
reciprocal, *a.* reciproco. **reciprocate**, *v.t.* contraccambiare. **reciprocating**, *p.a.* (*Mech.*) alternativo. **reciprocity**, *n.* reciprocità, *f.*
recital, *a.* racconto, *m.*, narrazione, relazione; enumerazione; (*Mus.*) recita, *f.* **recitation**, *n.* recitazione, recita, *f.* **recitative**, *n.*, recitativo, *m.* **recite**, *v.t.* recitare; declamare; enumerare.
reckless, *a.* temerario, sfrenato; indifferente. ~ *driving*, condotta incurante, *f.* ~**ly**, *ad.* temerariamente, insensatamente, noncurantemente.
reckon, *v.t. & i.* contare, computare, calcolare, stimare. ~**ing**, *n.* conto, calcolo, computo, *m.*; regolamento dei conti; scotto, *m.* *day of* ~, giorno di retribuzione, *m.*
reclaim, *v.t.* riformare, correggere; (*Law*) rivendicare; (*uncultivated land*) dissodare, bonificare; (*submerged land*) prosciugare, metter a secco.
recline, *v.i.* reclinarsi; appoggiarsi; riposarsi.

recluse, *n.* eremita, solitario, - *m.*
reclusion, *n.* reclusione, *f.*
recognition, *n.* riconoscimento, *m.*; ammissione, *f.* **recognizable**, *a.* riconoscibile. **recognisance**, *n.* scrittura d'obbligo, *f.* **recognize**, *v.t.* riconoscere; ammettere.
recoil, *n.* rinculo, rinculamento, *m.* ¶ *v.i.* rinculare.
recoin, *v.t.* riconiare, coniare di nuovo.
recollect, *v.t.* ricordarsi, rammentarsi. ~**ion**, *n.* ricordo, *m.*; memoria, ricordanza, *f.*; riflessione, *f.*
recommence, *v.t. & i.* ricominciare.
recommend, *v.t.* raccomandare; proporre. ~**ation**, *n.* raccomandazione, *f.*; (*for election*) proposta, *f.* ~**er**, *n.* proponente, presentatore; raccomandatore, *m.*
recompense, *n.* ricompensa, *f.* ¶ *v.t.* ricompensare, risarcire; indennizzare.
reconcile, *v.t.* riconciliare.
recondite, *a.* recondito, astruso, oscuro.
reconnoitre, *v.t.* riconoscere; fare una recognizione, *m.*; perlustrare.
reconsider, *v.t.* riconsiderare, considerare di nuovo, rivedere; riesaminare.
reconstruct, *v.t.* ricostruire; (*fig.*) ricostituire. ~**ion**, *n.* ricostruzione, *f.*; ricostituzione (*fig.*), *f.*
record, *n.* registro; rapporto; atto pubblico registrato; protocollo; atto autentico, *m.*; nota, *f.*, ricordo, *m.*; memoriale, *m.*; (*pl.*) archivi; annali; atti; verbali, *m.pl.* (*Sport*, &c.) record; massimo, primato *m.*; (*gramophone*) disco, *m.* ~ *office*, archivio, *m.*; cancelleria, *f.* ~ *ribbon* (typewriter), nastro fisso, *m.* ¶ *v.t.* registrare; iscrivere; notare; celebrare; (*vote*) votare. ~**er**, *n.* registratore; giudice, *m.*
recount, *v.t.* raccontare, narrare; contare di nuovo. ¶ *n.* nuovo computo, *m.*
recoup, *v.t.* ricuperare, risarcire. ~ *oneself for* (a loss), rifarsi di.
recourse, *n.* ricorso, *m.*; *have* ~ *to*, ricorrere a.
recover, *v.t.* ricuperare, riacquistare; riprendere; riparare; ricoprire, rilegare; risordetare; salvare; (*v.i.*) ristabilirsi, guarire; rimettersi. ~**y**, *n.* ricupero, *m.*; ripresa, *f.*; guarigione, *f.*; ristabilimento, *f.*
recreant, *a. & n.* vigliacco, poltrone; apostata, *m.*
re-create, *v.t.* ricreare, creare di nuovo.

recreate, *v.t.* ricreare, divertire.
recreation, *n.* passatempo, divertimento, *m.*; ricreazione, *f.*
recrimination, *n.* recriminazione, *f.*
recrudescence, *n.* recrudescenza, *f.*
recruit, *n.* recluta, *f.* ¶ *v.t.* reclutare, (*v.i.*) rimettersi in salute; rifarsi; ~*ing sergeant,* sottufficiale di reclutamento, *m.*
rectangle, *n.* rettangolo, *m.* **rectangular,** *a.* rettangolare.
rectify, *v.t.* rettificare, correggere; raddrizzare.
rectilinear, *a.* rettilineo.
rectitude, *n.* rettitudine, dirittura, *f.*
recto, *n.* recto, retto, *m.*
rector, *n.* rettore; (*Eccl.*) pievano, parroco, *m.* ~**ship,** *n.* rettorato, *m.* ~**y,** *n.* presbiterio, *m.*; pievania, *f.*
rectum, *n.* retto, *m.*
recumbent, *a.* sdraiato, coricato, disteso. ~ *figure* (statue), giacente.
recuperate, *v.i.* ricuperarsi, rifarsi, ristabilirsi.
recur, *v.i.* ricorrere, tornare, ritornare; **recurrence,** *n.* ricorrenza; ripetizione, *f. recurring decimal,* frazione periodica, *f.*
red, *a. & n.* rosso, *a. & m.*; (*hair, &c.*) rosso, rossiccio. *the* ~s (*Pol.*) i rossi, *m.pl.* ~ *breast,* pettirosso, *m. the* R~ *Cross,* la Croce Rossa, *f.* ~*-faced* (*person*), rubicondo. ~*-haired* (*person*) dai capelli rossi, che ha i capelli rossi. ~*-handed,* (*fig.*) sul fatto, in flagrante (delitto). ~ *herring,* (*fig.*) traccia falsa, idea capricciosa, *f.* ~*-hot,* rovente. ~ *Indian* ot ~*skin,* pellerossa, *m.f.* ~ *lead,* minio, *m. to be a* ~*-letter day,* fare epoca. ~ *mullet,* triglia, *f.* ~ *pepper,* pepe rosso, p. di Caienna, *m.* R~ *sea,* Mar Rosso, *m.* ~ *spot* (skin) rossore, *m.* ~*start,* codirosso, *m.* ~ *tape,* (*fig.*) burocrazia (pedantica), *f*; quisquiglie, *f.pl.* ~*wing,* tordo sassello, *m.* **redden,** *v.t. & i.* arrossire. **reddish,** *a.* rossiccio, rossastro.
redeem, *v.t.* redimere; riscattare; riparare; rimborsare; ammortizzare; disimpegnare; (*promise*) adempiere. **Redeemer,** *n.* Redentore, *m.* **redemption,** *n.* redenzione, *f.*; riscatto; ricupero, *m.*; (*mortgage*) estinzione, *f.*, ammortamento, *m.*; (*Relig.*) redenzione, *f.*
redness, *n.* rossezza, *f.*; rossore, *m.*
redolent of, che sente . . .
redoubt, *n.* ridotta, *f.*, fortino, *m.*

redoubtable, *a.* formidabile.
redound, *v.i.* ridondare (a), contribuire (a), tendere (a).
redress, *n.* riparazione, *f.*; risarcimento, compenso, *m.* ¶ *v.t.* riparare, rettificare, correggere.
reduce, *v.t.* ridurre, diminuire, abbassare, impoverire. ~ *the staff,* ridurre il personale. ~ *to lower rank,* (*Mil.*) far retrocedere. ~ *to the ranks,* degradare. **reduction,** *n.* riduzione, diminuzione; (*tax*) riduzione, *f.*, abbattimento; (*of staff*) sfollamento, *m.* ~ *to the absurd* or *reductio ad absurdum,* riduzione all'assurdo. ~ *to the ranks,* retrocessione; degradazione, *f.*
redundant, *a.* ridondante.
re-echo, *v.i.* riecheggiare, echeggiare; rimbombare, risonare.
reed, *n.* canna, *f.*, giunco, *m.*; (*pipe*) fistola, *f.*, zampogna, *f.*; (*Mus.*) linguetta; ancia, *f.*; (*Arch.*) tondino, bastoncello, *m.*; (*Weaving*) pettine, *m.* ~ *mace,* giunco, *m.*
reef, *n.* scoglio, *m.*, scogliera, *f.*; (*coral*) banco, *m.*; (*Min.*) vena, *f.*; (*in sail*) terzaruolo, *m.* ~ *knot,* nodo piano, *m.*; nodo di terzaruolo, *m.*
reek, *n.* fumo, *m.*, esalazione, *f.*; odore fetido, *m.* ~ *with,* ~ *of,* esalare un odore di. ~*ing with,* puzzante di.
reel, *n.* aspo, arcolaio, guindolo; gomitolo, *m.*, bobina, *f.*, rocchetto, *m.*; (*dance*) trescone scozzese, *m.*; (*film*) rotolo, *m.*; (*Fish*) gomitolo, *m.* ¶ *v.t.* annaspare, aggomitolare; (*v.i.*) barcollare, vacillare. ~ *off* (*fig.*) ripetere tutto d'un fiato, spacciare.
re-elect, *v.t.* rieleggere. ~**ion,** *n.* rielezione, *f.* **re-eligible,** *a.* rieleggibile.
re-embark, *v.t.* rimbarcare; (*v.i.*) rimbarcarsi.
re-enact, *v.t.* promulgare di nuovo.
re-enforce, *v.t.* rimettere in vigore.
re-engage, *v.t.* ringaggiare, ingaggiare di nuovo.
re-enlist, *v.i.* riarruolarsi.
re-enter, *v.i.* rientrare; (*v.t.*) rientrare in; registrare di nuovo. **re-entrant,** *a.* rientrante. **re-entry,** *n.* rientrata; nuova registrazione, *f.*
re-establish, *v.t.* ristabilire.
reeve, *n.* (*Naut.*) *v.t.ir.* infilare, passare; assicurare.
re-examine, *v.t.* riesaminare.
re-export, *v.t.* riesportare.
refectory, *n.* refettorio, *m.*
refer, *v.t.* riferire, rimettere, riman-

dar?. ~ *to*, riferirsi a; consultare, rimettere al giudizio di; alludere a. ~**ee**, *n.* arbitro, *m.*; (*Box*) arbitro, *m.* ¶ *v.t.* arbitrare. **reference**, *n.* referenza, *f.*; riferimento, *m.*, rapporto, *m.*; relazione, *f.*; allusione, *f.*, menzione, *f.*; considerazione, *f.* ~ *library*, sala di consultazione (d'una biblioteca), *f.* ~ [*mark*], segno di richiamo, *m.* ~ *note* (on map), leggenda, *f.* with ~ *to*, a proposito di, in merito a. **referendum**, *n.* referendum, plebiscito, *m.*

refine, *v.t.* raffinare; affinare; (*v.i.*) raffinarsi, affinarsi; ~**d**, *p.a.* colto, distinto, gentile; raffinato. ~**ment**, (*fig.*) *n.* eleganza, grazia, gentilezza, *f.* **refiner**, *n.* raffinatore, *m.* **refinery**, *n.* raffineria, *f.*

refit, *v.t.* riattare, (*ship*) raddobbare.

reflect, *v.t. & i.* riflettere; ripensare, meditare. ~ *on*, meditare su. ~ *upon*, gettare discredito su. ~**ion**, *n.* riflessione, *f.*, riflesso, *m.*; immagine, censura, *f.* ~**ive**, *a.* riflessivo. ~**or**, *n.* riflettore, *m.* **reflex**, *a.* riflesso. ~ *camera*, camera riflessa, *f.* ¶ *n.* riflesso, *m.* **reflexion**, *n.* riflessione, *f.* **reflexive** (*Gram.*) *a.* riflessivo.

refloat (*ship*), *v.t.* rimettere a galla.

reflux, *n.* riflusso, *m.*

re-form, *v.t.* formare di nuovo, riformare.

reform, *n.* riforma, *f.* ¶ *v.t.* riformare. ~**ation**, *n.* riformazione; riforma, *f.* ~**atory**, *n.* casa di correzione, *f.* ~**er**, *n.* riformatore, *m.*, -trice, *f.*

refract, *v.t.* rifrangere. ~*ing telescope*, telescopio a rifrazione, *m.* **refractoriness**, *n.* natura refrattaria; caparbietà, *f.*; renitenza, ostinatezza, *f.* **refractory**, *a.* refrattario, renitente, *m.*

refrain, *n.* ritornello, *m.*; aria, cantilena, *f.* ¶ *v.i.* astenersi, trattenersi, raffrenarsi.

refresh, *v.t.* rinfrescare; ricreare; rifocillare, ristorare. **refreshment**, *n.* rinfresco, rinfrescamento, ristoro, *m.* ~ *bar*, ~ *room*, mescita, *f.*; caffè, ristorante, *m.*

refrigerate, *v.t.* refrigerare. **refrigeration**, *n.* refrigerazione, *f.* **refrigerator**, *n.* frigorifero, *m.*; ghiacciaia, *f.*

refuel, *v.t. & i.* rifornirsi di combus-

tibile; (*Aviat.*) rifornire di carburante.

refuge, *n.* rifugio, asilo, *m.* *to take* ~, rifugiarsi. **refugee**, *n.* rifugiato, *m.*, -a, *f.*; esule, profugo, *m.*

refulgent, *a.* fulgido, splendente, rifulgente.

refund, *v.t.* rimborsare.

refurnish, *v.t.* ammobigliare di nuovo, a nuovo.

refusal, *n.* rifiuto; diritto di prelazione, di scelta, *m.* **refuse**, *n.* rifiuto, scarto, *m.*; feccia, *f.*, immondizie, *f.pl.*, spazzatura, *f.* ~ *dump*, mondezzaio, *m.* ¶ *v.t. & i.* rifiutare, rifiutarsi; ricusare. ~ *admittance*, vietare l'entrata, non lasciare entrare, negare l'accesso (a).

refute, *v.t.* confutare; ribattere; dimostrare falso.

regain, *v.t.* riguadagnare, riacquistare; ricuperare.

regal, *a.* regale.

regale, *v.t.* festeggiare.

regalia, *n.* insegne reali, *f.pl.*

regard, *n.* riguardo, rispetto, *m.*; deferenza, considerazione, stima, simpatia, *f.* *out of* ~ *for*, per riguardo a. ~**s**, *m.pl.* complimenti, ossequi, *m.pl.* with ~ *to*, ~*ing*, con riguardo a, in merito a, a proposito di, per quanto riguarda. ¶ *v.t.* riguardare, considerare; riferirsi a; spettare a; toccare a. ~**less**, *a.* senza riguardo, noncurante, indifferente.

regatta, *n.* regata, *f.*

regency, *n.* reggenza, *f.*

regenerate, *v.t.* rigenerare. **regeneration**, *n.* rigenerazione, *f.*

regent, *n. & a.* reggente, *m. & a.*

regicidal, *a. &* **regicide**, *a. & n.* regicida, *a. & m.f.* **regicide** (*act*), *n.* regicidio, *m.*

regild, *v.t.ir.* dorare di nuovo, ridorare.

regimen, *n.* regime, *m.*; dieta, *f.*

regiment, *n.* reggimento, *m.* **regimental**, *a.* reggimentale.

region, *n.* regione; contrada, *f.* ~**al**, *a.* regionale.

register, *n.* registro; libro; repertorio, *m.*, matricola, *f.*; estensione, portata, *f.*; (*book mark*) segnacarte, segno, *m.* ~ *of voters*, lista elettorale, *f.* ¶ *v.t.* registrare, iscrivere, matricolare; (*design, &c.*) depositare, brevettare; (*Post*) raccomandare. ~**ed**, *p.a.* (*capital, office*) sociale; (*shares*) (azioni) nominative, *f.pl.* ~ *letter* envelope, busta di lettera raccomandata, f. ~ packet, pacco raccomandato, m. ~ manager (of a ship), armatore, m. register[ed] tonnage], tonnellaggio netto, tonnellaggio di registro, m. ~ trade mark, marca depositata, f. registrar, n. segretario; cancelliere, m.; attuario, m.; (births, &c.) ufficiale dello Stato Civile, m. registry [office], n. (marriage) ufficio dello Stato civile; (servants) ufficio di collocamento, m.

regret, n. rincrescimento, rammarico, m. ¶ v.t. rimpiangere, rammaricarsi per, pentirsi di. I ~ that, mi rincresce che.

regular, a. regolare, normale, abituale; assiduo; regolato; vero; matricolato. ~ channel(s) (fig.) trafila, f.; vie regolari, f.pl. ~ity, n. regolarità, f. ~ize, v.t. regolarizzare.

regulate, v.t. regolare. regulation, n. regolamento, m., regola, f.; ordinanza, f.; (att.) d'ordine, regolamentare. regulator, n. regolatore, m.

rehabilitate, v.t. riabilitare.

rehandle, v.t. rimaneggiare.

rehearsal, n. prova, ripetizione, f.

rehearse, v.t. ripetere, far le prove di; enumerare.

rehousing, n. rialloggiamento, rialloggiare, m.

reign, n. regno, m. ¶ v.i. regnare. ~ing, a. regnante.

reimburse, v.t. rimborsare.

reimport, v.t. reimportare.

reimpose, v.t. reimporre, imporre di nuovo.

rein, n. redine; guida, f.

reindeer, n. renna, f.

reinforce, v.t. rinforzare; (Mech.) rafforzare; (concrete) armare. ~d concrete, cemento armato, m. ~ment, n. rinforzamento, rinforzo; consolidamento, m.; armatura, f.; (men) rinforzo, m., oft. pl.

reinstate, v.t. ristabilire, reintegrare.

reinsure, v.t. riassicurare.

reinvest (Fin.), v.t. reinvestire.

reinvigorate, v.t. rinvigorire.

reissue, n. (book) ristampa, f.; (Fin.) nuova emissione, f.

reiterate, v.t. reiterare.

reject, v.t. rigettare, respingere. ~ion, n. rigetto, rifiuto, m.

rejoice, v.t. rallegrare, allietare; (v.i.) rallegrarsi, esultare, gioire, giubilare.

rejoicing, n. allegrezza, festa, f.

~s, n.pl. feste, f.pl., festeggiamenti, m.pl.

re-join, v.t. unire di nuovo, riunire; (one's regiment, &c.) raggiungere; (v.i.) rispondere, replicare. rejoinder, n. replica, risposta, f.

rejuvenate, v.t. & i. ringiovanire.

rekindle, v.t. riaccendere.

relapse, n. (Med., &c.) ricaduta, f. (Fin.) caduta, f.; (crime) recidiva, f. ¶ v.i. ricadere, ricascare. ~ into crime, ricadere nel delitto, recidivare.

relate, v.t. raccontare; riferire; rapportare; (v.i.) riferirsi, aver rapporto. ~d to, parente di, imparentato con, legato di parentela (con).

relation, n. rapporto, m., relazione, f.; parente, m.f., congiunto, m., -a, f. ~ship, n. parentela, f. relative, a. relativo. ¶. n. parente, m.f.; congiunto, m., -a, f. relativity, n. relatività, f.

relax, v.t. allentare, rilassare, mollare; mitigare; (Med.) rallentare; (v.i.) allentarsi; riposarsi, ricrearsi. ~ed throat, faringite, f. ~ation, n. ricreazione, f., divertimento, m.; allentamento, m. ~ing, (climate) a. snervante.

re-lay, v.t.ir. ricollocare, rimettere.

relay, n. ricambio; (Elec.) relè, m.; muta, posta, f. ~ race, corsa staffetta, c. di staffete, f. ¶ v.t. sostituire, alternare; (Radio) ritrasmettere.

release, n. liberazione, f.; scarico, m.; rilasciamento, m.; (Law) cessione, esecuzione, f.; scarcerazione, f.; (pigeons) lanciare, lanciamento, m.; (Mech.) scarico, m.; scatto, m. ¶ v.t. rilasciare, liberare, sciogliere; scarcerare, scatenare; svincolare; esentare, esonerare; scaricare; lanciare.

relegate, v.t. relegare.

relent, v.i. piegarsi, cedere; intenerirsi, pentirsi. ~less, a. spietato; inflessibile.

relet, v.t.ir. affittare di nuovo, riaffittare. reletting, n. riaffitto, m.

relevant, a. pertinente, apposito, acconcio, a proposito, che ha rapporto a.

reliability, n. sicurezza; fidatezza; solvibilità, f. ~ trial, prova di resistenza, f. reliable, a. sicuro; solido; degno di fiducia; attendibile. reliance, n. fiducia, fede, f.

relic, n. reliquia, f.; resto, avanzo, m.

relict, n. vedova, f.

relief, n. sollievo, conforto, m.;

alleviamento, alleggerimento, *m.*; soccorso, *m. oft. pl.*; assistenza, *f.*; *(tax)* esenzione, *f.* *(for dependants, Inc. Tax)* abbattimento, *m.*; *(Art., Geog.)* rilievo, *m.*; *(Mil.)* cambio, *m.*; muta, *f.* ~ *fund,* fondo di soccorso, *m.* ~ *train,* treno supplementare, *m.*

relieve, *v.t.* alleviare, alleggerire, mitigare; soccorrere; sollevare; dispensare; esentare (da) (Mil.) rilevare, dare il cambio a.

relight, *v.t.* riaccendere.

religion, *n.* religione, *f.* **religious**, *a.* religioso, pio, devoto; *(book. &c.)* devoto, di devozione. ~**ness**, *n.* religiosità, *f.*

relinquish, *v.t.* abbandonare, cedere, rinunziare a.

reliquary, *n.* reliquario, *m.*

relish, *n.* gusto, sapore; condimento; buon appetito, *m.* ¶ *v.t.* gustare, trovar buono, prediligere. *I do not* ~, non mi garba.

re-load, *v.t.* ricaricare.

reluctance, *n.* riluttanza, ripugnanza, *f. I am reluctant to,* mi ripugna di . . . **reluctantly**, *ad.* con riluttanza.

rely, *v.i.* fidarsi (di); far assegnamento (su); contare (su).

remain, *v.i.* rimanere, restare; stare. ~ *over*, avanzare. **remainder**, *n.* resto, residuo, avanzo, *m.*; rimanenza, *f.*; scampolo, *m.* ¶ *v.t. (books)* vendere con ribasso. **remains**, *n.pl.* resti, avanzi, *m.pl.*; ceneri, spoglie, *f.pl.*; *(Lit.)* opere postume, *f.pl.*

remake, *v.t.ir.* rifare.

remand, *v.t.* rimandare; *(Law)* rinviare. ¶ *n.* rinvio, *m.*

remark, *n.* osservazione, nota, *f.*; commento, *m.* **remark**, *v.t.* osservare, notare, rilevare. **re-mark**, *v.t.* rimarcare, marcare di nuovo. ~**able**, *a.* rimarchevole.

remedy, *n.* rimedio, riparo, *m.*; *(Law)* azione, *f.*, ricorso, mezzo giuridico, *m.* ¶ *v.t.* rimediare a, porre rimedio a.

remember, *v.t.* ricordarsi di, rammentarsi di; sovvenirsi di. **remembrance**, *n.* rimembranza, memoria, *f.*, ricordo, *m.*

remind of, rammentare a, richiamare alla memoria di, ricordare a. *You* ~*me of someone*, mi fa pensare a qualcuno. ~**er**, *n.* ricordo; memento; consiglio, *m.*

reminiscence, *n.* reminiscenza, *f.*

remiss, *a.* negligente, trascurato. ~**ion**, *n.* remissione; riduzione (di pena). **remit**, *v.t.* rimettere,

inviare, consegnare. **remittance**, *n.* rimessa (di danaro),*f.*

remnant, *n.* resto; avanzo; scampolo, *m.*

remodel, *v.t.* rimodellare.

remonstrance, *n.* rimostranza, *f.* **remonstrate**, *v.i.* rimostrare, fare delle rimostranze *(with* = con).

remorse, *n.* rimorso, *m.* ~**less**, *a.* spietato. ~**lessly**, *ad.* spietatamente, senza rimorso.

remote, *a.* remoto, lontano; *(antiquity)* remoto. ~**ness**, *n.* lontananza, distanza, *f.*

remount, *n.* rimonta, *f.* ¶ *v.t.* rimontare, risalire.

removable, *a.* amovibile, trasportabile. **removal**, *n.* trasferimento, trasloco; spostamento; trasporto; sgombro, *m*; rimozione, *f.*; presa, *f.*; ritiro, *m.*; estrazione, *f.*; *(of office)* destituzione, *f.* ~ *contractor*, *[furniture]* *remover*, sgomberatore, *m.*

remove, *v.t.* rimuovere, muovere, levare, sgombrare; spostare; traslocare; allontanare, togliere, far sparire; eliminare, sopprimere; destituire.

remunerate, *v.t.* rimunerare. **remuneration**, *n.* rimunerazione,*f.*

renaissance, *n.* rinascimento, *m.*; rinascenza, rinascita, *f.*

rename, *v.t.* ribattezzare; rinominare.

rend, *v.t.ir.* stracciare; squarciare; lacerare, spezzare; *(the air)* fendere.

render, *v.t.* rendere, dare, prestare, consegnare, fornire; interpretare, tradurre; far divenire; *(plaster)* spalmare. ~ *void*, rendere nullo, annullare, ridurre a nulla. ~**ing**, *n.* *(accounts)* rendimento, *m.*; *(Art.)* esecuzione, *f.*; interpretazione, traduzione, *f.* *(plaster)* spalmo, *m.*

rendezvous, *n.* ritrovo, appuntamento, convegno, *m.*

renegade, *n.* rinnegato, *m.*

renew, *v.t.* rinnovare; rinnovellare; rimettere a nuovo; ricominciare; rifare; ravvivare; ripetere; sostituire. ~**al**, *n.* rinnovamento, *m.*; rinnovazione, ripresa, *f.*

rennet, *n.* presame, *m.*; *(apple)* mela renetta, *f.*

renounce, *v.t.* rinunziare a; abiurare; rinnegare; ripudiare.

renovate, *v.t.* rinnovare.

renown, *n.* rinomanza, fama, *f.* ~**ed**, *a.* rinomato, famoso, celebre.

rent, *n.* *(tear)* strappo, squarcio, straccio, *m.*; lacerazione; fessura, *f.*; *(periodical payment)* pigione, *f.*, fitto, affitto, prezzo di affitto, *m.*; rendita. ~ *collector*, esattore delle pigioni, *m.* ¶ *v.t.* dare in affitto; prendere in affitto; tenere in affitto; pigionare, prendere a pigione. ~al, *n.* affitto, *m.*; rendita fondiaria, *f.*; (*Law*) ammontare del canone d'affitto, valore locativo, *m.* ~er, *n.* affittuario, locatario, pigionale, *m.*

renunciation, *n.* rinunzia, *f.*

reopen, *v.t.* riaprire; (*v.i.*) riaprirsi, ~ing, *n.* riapertura, *f.*

reorganize, *v.t.* riorganizzare.

rep or **repp** or **reps**, *n.* reps, *m.inv.*, bastoncino, cannellato, *m.*

repack, *v.t.* imballare di nuovo, impaccare di nuovo.

repair, *n.* riparazione, *f.*, restauro; (*ship*) raddobbo; (*good*, *bad*) stato, *m.* ¶ *v.t.* riparare, raccomodare, restaurare. (*v.i.*) riparare; recarsi, trasferirsi, andare. ~able, *a.* riparabile. **reparable**, *a.* riparabile. **reparation**, *n.* riparazione, *f.*, risarcimento, compenso, *m.*

repartee, *n.* replica arguta, risposta pronta, *f.*

repast, *n.* pasto; banchetto, *m.*

repatriate, *v.t.* rimpatriare, far rimpatriare.

repay, *v.t.ir.* rimborsare, ripagare, ricompensare; rendere; (*fig.*) valere la pena di. ~ment, *n.* rimborso, *m.*

repeal, *n.* abrogazione, revoca, *f.* ¶ *v.t.* abrogare, revocare.

repeat, (*Mus.*) *ad.* bis. ¶ (*Mus.*) *n.* ripresa, *f.* ¶ *v.t.* ripetere, ridire; recitare. ~edly, *ad.* ripetutamente, frequentemente, spesse volte. ~ing, (*rifle*, *watch*) *p.a.* a ripetizione.

repel, *v.t.* respingere, repellere. **repellent**, *a.* repulsivo, repellente; (*Phys.*) repulsivo.

repent, *v.i.* pentirsi; (*v.t.*) pentirsi di; ~ance, *n.* pentimento, *m.*

repeople, *v.t.* ripopolare.

repercussion, *n.* ripercussione, *f.*

repertory, *n.* repertorio, *m.*

repetend, *n.* decimale ricorrente, *m.*; parola (frase) ripetuta, *f.* **repetition**, *n.* ripetizione, *f.*; recitazione, *f.*; replica, *f.*

repine, *v.i.* dolersi, lagnarsi, querelarsi; mormorare.

replace, *v.t.* rimettere, ricollocare; sostituire.

replant, *v.t.* ripiantare.

replay, *v.t.* giocare di nuovo; ripetere (una partita); (*Mus.*) sonare di nuovo.

replenish, *v.t.* riempire. **replete**, *a.*

pieno, ripieno, zeppo. **repletion**, *n.* pienezza, sazietà, *f.*

replica, *n.* replica, *f.*

reply, *n.* risposta, *f.* ~ *paid*, con risposta pagata. *in* ~ (*Law*), in replica. ¶ *v.t.* & *i.* rispondere, replicare.

report, *n.* rapporto, *m.*; relazione, cronaca, *f.*; rendiconto, resoconto; rumore, strepito; scoppio, *m.*; detonazione, *f.*; notizia, *f.*; voce, fama, diceria, *f.*, riputazione, *f.* ¶ *v.t.* rapportare, riferire, rendere conto di, fare un rapporto di; denunziare; (*press*) fare la cronaca di. (*v.i.*) (*newspaper*) fare il cronista. ~er (*news*), *n.* cronista, corrispondente; (*Law*, *&c.*) relatore, *m.* ~ing, *n.* servizio d'informazione, *m.*

repose, *n.* riposo, *m.*; tranquillità, pace, *f.* ¶ *v.i.* riposarsi, riposare.

repository, *n.* deposito, magazzino; ripostiglio, *m.*; (*fig.*) repertorio, *m.*

repot, *v.t.* rinvasare.

repoussé **work**, lavoro a sbalzo, lavoro di rilièvo, *m.*

reprehend, *v.t.* riprendere, rimproverare. **reprehensible**, *a.* riprensibile.

represent, *v.t.* rappresentare. ~ation, *n.* rappresentazione, *f.* ~ative, *a.* rappresentativo. ¶ *n.* rappresentante; deputato, *m.*

repress, *v.t.* reprimere. ~ion, *n.* repressione, *f.*

reprieve, *n.* dilazione, *f.* ¶ *v.t.* accordare una dilazione a.

reprint, *n.* ristampa, *f.* ¶ *v.t.* ristampare.

reprisal, *n.* oft.pl. rappresaglia, *f.* *to take* ~s, usare rappresaglie.

reproach, *n.* rimprovero, *m.*; onta, vergogna, *f.*, vituperio, *m.* ¶ *v.t.* rimproverare, rinfacciare. ~ful, *a.* ingiurioso, pieno di rimproveri, vituperativo. ~fully, *ad.* in tono di rimprovero.

reprobate, *n.* reprobo, malvagio, *m.* ¶ *v.t.* riprovare. **reprobation**, *n.* riprovazione, *f.*

reproduce, *v.t.* riprodurre. **reproduction**, *n.* riproduzione, *f.*

reproof, *n.* rimprovero, *m.*, censura, riprensione, *f.* **reprove**, *v.t.* riprendere, censurare, biasimare.

reptile, *n.* rettile, *m.* ¶ *a.* rettile.

republic, *n.* repubblica, *f.* ~an, *a.* & *n.* repubblicano, *a.* & *m.*

republish, *v.t.* ripubblicare; ristampare.

repudiate, *v.t.* ripudiare.

repugnance, *n.* ripugnanza, *f.* **repugnant,** *a.* ripugnante. *to be* ~ *to,* ripugnare a.

repulse, *n.* ripulsa, sconfitta, *f.* ¶ *v.t.* respingere. **repulsion,** *n.* ripulsione; (*Phys.*) repulsione, *f.* **repulsive,** *a.* repellente; schifoso; (*Phys.*) repulsivo.

repurchase, *n.* ricompra, *f.* ¶ *v.t.* ricomprare.

reputable, *a.* rispettabile, onorevole, stimabile. **reputation** & **repute,** *n.* riputazione, *f.*, rinomanza, *f.*; onore, *m.* *of repute,* riputato, in fama. **reputed,** *a.* supposto; putativo.

request, *n.* domanda, richiesta, preghiera, *f.*; invito, *m.*; voga, *f.* *by* ~, *on* ~, a richiesta. *at the* ~ *of,* su domanda di. *in* ~, in voga, alla moda; domandato, ricercato. ¶ *v.t.* chiedere, richiedere, domandare; pregare; invitare.

requiem, *n.* requie, *f.*, requiem, *m.*; messa di requiem, *f.*

require, *v.t.* richiedere, esigere, volere; aver bisogno di; requisire; (*v.i.*) dovere, essere necessario, bisognare. *be* ~*d,* occorrere, far bisogno, far d'uopo; mancare. ~**ment,** *n.* bisogno, *m.*, esigenza, *f.*; necessità, *f.*; requisito, *m.*, condizione, *f.* **requisite,** *a.* requisito, necessario. ¶ *n.* fabbisogno, occorrente, *m.* **requisition,** *n.* requisizione; domanda, richiesta, *f.* ¶ *v.t.* requisire.

requital, *n.* ricompensa, *f.*, contraccambio, *m.* **requite,** *v.t.* ricompensare; contraccambiare.

reredos, *n.* dossale, *m.*

resale, *n.* rivendita, *f.*

rescind, *v.t.* rescindere. **rescission,** *n.* rescissione, *f.*

rescript, *n.* rescritto, *m.*

rescue, *n.* liberazione, *f.*; soccorso; ricupero, *m.*; (*Mil.*) riscossa, *f.*; (*sea*) salvataggio, *m.* *to the* ~, al soccorso! ¶ *v.t.* salvare; liberare; scampare; strappare, ricuperare.

research, *n.* ricerca, indagine, inchiesta, *f.*; studio, *m.* ~ *worker,* ricercatore, investigatore, *m.*, -trice, *f.*

reseat, *v.t.* rimettere a sedere; rimettere il fondo a.

resemblance, *n.* rassomiglianza, *f.*; immagine, *f.* **resemble,** *v.t.* rassomigliare a.

resent, *v.t.* risentirsi di, risentire; prendere in mala parte. ~**ful,** *a.*

sdegnoso, vendicativo, pieno di risentimento; risentito. ~**ment,** *n.* risentimento, *m.*

reservation, *n.* riserva, eccezione, *f.*; (*mental*) restrizione, *f.*; (*seats*) locazione, *f.* **reserve,** *n.* riserva, *f.*; riserbo, *m.*, ritenutezza; reticenza, *f.* ~ (*price*) prezzo di riserva, *m.* ¶ *v.t.* riservare, riserbare; ritenere; locare. ~**d,** *a.* (*pers.*) chiuso. ~*d seat,* posto riservato, posto prenotato, *m.* ~*d seat ticket,* biglietto per un posto riservato, b. di prenotazione, *m.* **reservist,** *n.* riservista, soldato della riserva, *m.* **reservoir,** *n.* serbatoio, *m.*, cisterna; recipiente, *f.*

reset, *v.t.ir.* (*jewels*) incastonare di nuovo; (*Typ.*) ricomporre. **resetting,** (*Typ.*) *n.* ricomposizione, *f.*

reship, *v.t.* rimbarcare; rispedire, ricaricare.

reshuffle, *v.t.* rimescolare.

reside, *v.i.* abitare, risiedere, dimorare, stare di casa. **residence,** *n.* residenza, dimora, *f.*; soggiorno, *m.*; domicilio, *m.* **resident,** *n.* abitante, *m.f.*; interno, *m.*; (*diplomatic*) residente, *m.*

residuary legatee, erede universale, *m.f.* **residue,** *n.* residuo, resto, *m.*

resign, *v.t.* rassegnare, rimettere, rinunziare a; abbandonare; (*v.i.*) dimettersi, dare le dimissioni; rassegnarsi. **resignation,** *n.* dimissione, *f.*; (*submission*) rassegnazione, *f.*

resilient, *a.* elastico; rimbalzante.

resin, *n.* resina; ragia, *f.*; (*for violin*) colofonia, *f.* ~**ous,** *a.* resinoso.

resist, *v.t.* resistere a, opporsi a, contrastare; (*v.i.*) resistere, opporre resistenza. ~**ance,** *n.* resistenza, *f.*

resole, *v.t.* rimettere le suole a, risolare.

resolute, *a.* risoluto. **resolution,** *n.* risoluzione, decisione; deliberazione; conclusione; risolutezza; energia; proposta, *f.*; scioglimento, *m.* **resolve,** *n.* determinazione, *f.* ¶ *v.t.* decidere, concludere, risolvere, determinare; sciogliere; chiarire. ~ *on,* decidere (di), decidersi (a).

resonance, *n.* risonanza, *f.* **resonant,** *a.* risonante.

resort, *n.* (luogo di) convegno, ritrovo, luogo frequentato, *m.*; centro, *m.*; stazione, *f.*; soggiorno, *m.*; ricorso, *m.*, appello, *m.*; risorsa, *f.*; (*Law*) giurisdizione, *f.* *in the last* ~, in ultimo. ~ *to*, ricorrere a, aver ricorso a; frequentare, recarsi a.

resound, *v.i.* risonare, (ri)echeggiare; rimbombare.

resource, *n.* risorsa, *f.*; mezzo; espediente, *m.* ~**ful,** *a.* pieno di risorse, pieno di espedienti.

respect, *n.* rispetto; riguardo; rapporto, *m.*; (*pl.*) ossequi, *m.pl.* ¶ *v.t.* rispettare; riguardare. ~**able,** *a.* rispettabile, ragguardevole. ~**ably,** *ad.* decentemente; bene, passabilmente. ~**ful,** *a.* rispettoso. ~**ing,** *pr.* in rapporto a, riguardo a, in merito a. ~**ive,** *a.* rispettivo.

respiration, *n.* respirazione, *f.* **respirator,** *n.* respiratore, *m.*

respite, *n.* respiro, indugio, *m.*, pausa, tregua; (*Law*) dilazione, *f.* ¶ *v.t.* concedere una dilazione a.

resplendent, *a.* risplendente.

respond, *v.i.* rispondere; ubbidire; (*Phys.*) reagire. ~**ent,** *n.* chi risponde; (*Law*) convenuto, *m.*, -a, *f.* co-~, correo, coimputato, *m.*, -a, *f.* **response,** *n.* risposta, *f.*; (*Eccl.*) responso, *m.* **responsibility,** *n.* responsabilità, *f.* **responsible,** *a.* responsabile. **responsive,** *a.* responsivo.

rest, *n.* riposo, *m.*; (*Mus.*) silenzio, *m.*, pausa, *f.*; appoggio, sostegno, *m.*; (*Bil. &c.*) ponticino; (remainder) resto, rimanente, *m.*, (gli) altri, *m.pl.* & all the ~ of it, eccetera (*abb.* ecc.). ¶ *v.i.* riposare, riposarsi; appoggiarsi; stare; incombere (*upon* = a); (*v.t.*) riposare, far riposare, dare del riposo a; appoggiare, porre; posare; basare; fondare; riporre. to ~ with, dipendere da, spettare a.

re-stage, *v.t.* rimettere in scena.

restaurant, *n.* ristorante, *m.*; trattoria, *f.* ~ keeper, trattore, oste, padrone (d'un ristorante), *m.*

restful, *a.* tranquillo, quieto, che dà riposo. **resting place,** luogo di riposo; sepolcro, *m.*

restitch, *v.t.* ricucire.

restitution, *n.* restituzione, *f.*

restive, *a.* restio.

restless, *a.* irrequieto, inquieto; incessante.

restock, *v.t.* rifornire; ripopolare.

restoration, *n.* restauro, *m.*, restaurazione, *f.*, ristabilimento, *m.*; restituzione, *f.* **restorative,** *a. & n.* ristorativo, *a. & m.* **restore,** *v.t.* restaurare; ristabilire; rinnovare; ricostituire, reintegrare; rendere, restituire, rimettere, ridare; riporre.

restorer, *n.* restauratore, *m.*, -trice' *f.* picture ~, restauratore di quadri *m.*

restrain, *v.t.* trattenere, contenere, frenare, raffrenare, reprimere, ritenere. **restraint,** *n.* costringimento, freno; ritegno, riserbo, *m.*; detenzione, *f.* to place (lunatic) under ~, rinchiudere, mettere sotto controllo.

restrict, *v.t.* restringere, limitare. ~**ion,** *n.* restrizione, *f.*

restring, *v.t.i.ir.* (violin, &c.) rimettere le corde a.

result, *n.* risultato, esito, *m.*; conseguenza, *f.* ¶ *v.i.* risultare; riuscire; seguire.

resume, *v.t.* riprendere, riassumere, ripigliare; rioccupare; (*v.i.*) ricominciare. **resumption,** *n.* ripresa, *f.*

resurrection, *n.* risurrezione, *f.* ~ pie, avanzi di mensa, rimasugli, *m.pl.*

resurvey, *n.* controperizia, revisione, *f.*; rimisuramento, *m.*

resuscitate, *v.t.* risuscitare.

retail, *n.* [commercio] al minuto, al dettaglio, *m.*; vendita al minuto, *f.* ¶ *v.t.* vendere al minuto. ~**er,** *n.*; venditore al minuto, dettagliante, *m.*

retain, *v.t.* ritenere; serbare, conservare. **retaining wall,** muro di sostegno, *m.* ~**er,** *n.* (fee) anticipo, *m.*; (*pl.*) i suoi, dipendenti, servitori, *m.pl.*

retake, *v.t.ir.* riprendere.

retaliate, *v.i.* (upon, against) rendere la pariglia (a); usare rappresaglie (verso). **retaliation,** *n.* rappresaglie, *f.pl.*; taglione, contraccambio, *m.* **retaliatory,** *a.* di rappresaglia.

retard, *v.t.* ritardare.

retch, *v.i.* recere.

retention, *n.* conservazione; (*Med.*) ritenzione, *f.* **retentive,** *a.* ritentivo, tenace.

reticence, *n.* reticenza, *f.*; to be reticent, essere reticente, tacere.

reticle & **reticule,** *n.* reticella, borsetta, *f.*

retina, *n,* retina, *f.*

retinue, *n.* seguito; corteggio, *m.*

retire, *v.t.* ritirare, collocare a riposo; (officer) riformare; congedare; giubilare; (*v.i.*) ritirarsi; dimettersi; indietreggiare. ~**d,** *p.p.* ritirato, solitario, appartato; collocato a riposo. officer on the ~ list, (ufficiale) collocato a riposo; giubilato, in ritiro. ~-pay, assegno di quiescenza, *m.*; pensione, *f.* ~-ment, *n.* ritiro, *m.*, dimissione, *f.*; collocamento a riposo, *m.*; solitudine, *f.* **retiring,** *p.a.* (*pers.*) riservato, schivo; (*manners*) pieno di riserbo, circospetto, modesto; (*director, &c.*) uscente; (*pension*) di riposo, di quiescenza.

retort, *n.* replica, risposta pronta, rimbecco, *m.*; (*Chem.*) storta, *f.* ¶ *v.t. & i.* ritorcere; rispondere vivamente, ribattere.

retouch, *v.t.* ritoccare. ~[ing], *n.* ritocco, *m.*, ritoccatura, *f.*

retrace, *v.t.* rintracciare; (*one's steps*) rifare (la strada), tornare indietro.

retract, *v.t.* ritrattare, sconfessare; (*v.i.*) disdirsi.

retreat, *n.* (*Mil.*) ritirata, *f.*; ritiro, *m.*; eremo, *m.*; (*glacier*) discesa, *f.* ¶ *v.i.* ritirarsi; rifugiarsi.

retrench, *v.t.* diminuire, ridurre, restringere; (*v.i.*) economizzare.

retribution, *n.* retribuzione, *f.*

retrieve, *v.t.* ritrovare, ricuperare, riparare, ristabilire, riabilitare; (*game*) riportare. **retriever** (*dog*) *n.* retriever, cane da caccia, *m.* a good ~, un cane che riporta bene.

retroactive, *a.* retroattivo.

retrograde, *a.* retrogrado.

retrospect, *n.* sguardo retrospettivo, esame del passato; *m.* **-ive,** *a.* retrospettivo; (*effect of a law*) retroattivo.

return, *n.* ritorno, *m.* rientrata, ripresa, *f.*; rinvio, *m.*, restituzione; rimessa, *f.*, rimborso, *m.*; contraccambio, *m.*; compenso, *m.*; ricompensa, *f.*; frutto, guadagno; prodotto, incasso, *m.*; resoconto, rapporto, *m.*, relazione; statistica, *f.*; elezione, *f.*; (*pl.*) (*books, newspapers*), rimesse, *f.pl.*; (*Com.*) provento, *m.* ~ *match*, (partita di) rivincita, *f.* by ~ of post, a volta di corriere. ~ of spring, nuova stagione, primavera, *f.* ~ *ticket*, biglietto di (andata e) ritorno, *m.* ¶ *v.t.* restituire, ritornare, rinviare, rimandare; rimettere; rispondere, replicare; rimborsare, contraccambiare; fare (una relazione, un rapporto, &c.); riportare; eleggere (al parlamento); (*Ten.*) ribattere, rimandare; (*v.i.*) ritornare, rientrare, riapparire; rinnovarsi, ripetersi, ricorrere. ~**able,** *a.* restituibile, di rimando; (*packings*) da rimandarsi; (*Law*) di rinvio. ~*ed letter*, lettera respinta, lettera giacente, *f.* ~*ed letter office*, ufficio delle lettere con destinatario introvabile *m.*

reunion, *n.* riunione, *f.* **reunite,** *v.t.* riunire.

reveal (*Arch.*), *n.* strombatura; mazzetta, *f.* ¶ *v.t.* rivelare, palesare.

reveille, *n.* diana, sveglia, *f.*

revel, *n.* *oft.pl.* festa, baldoria, *f.*, festino, *m.*, festa rumorosa, *f.* ¶ *v.i.* far baldoria, gozzovigliare, darsi bel tempo, godersi. ~ *in*, dilettarsi (di, in), compiacersi (di), godersi (di).

revelation, *n.* rivelazione, *f.* R~ (*Bible*), l'Apocalisse, *f.*

reveller, *n.* festaiolo, *m.*; gozzovigliatore, *m.*, -trice, *f.* **revelry,** *n.* allegrezza, baldoria, orgia, *f.*

revenge, *n.* vendetta, *f.*; (*for defeat*) rivincita, *f.* ~ *oneself,* vendicarsi (*for* = di, *on* = su). ~**ful,** *a.* vendicativo.

revenue, *n.* entrata, *f.* (*oft.pl.* -e); reddito, *m.*; rendita, *f.* ~ *cutter,* barca della Dogana, barca doganiera, *f.* ~*-earning house,* casa di vendita, *f.* ~ *stamp,* marca da bollo, *f.*

reverberate, *v.t. & i.* riverberare, -arsi, rimbombare, risonare; *reverberatory furnace,* forno a riverbero, *m.*

revere, *v.t.* riverire, onorare. **reverence,** *n.* riverenza, *f.*; venerazione, *f.*; (*pers.*) reverendo, *m.* ¶ *v.t.* riverire, venerare. **reverend,** *a.* reverendo. **reverent,** *a.* riverente. **reverential,** *a.* riverenziale, riverente. **reverentially,** *ad.* riverenzialmente, riverentemente.

reverie, *n.* meditazione, *f.*, astrazione di mente, *f.*; fantasticheria, *f.*

reversal, *n.* inversione, *f.*, rovesciamento, *m.*; annullamento, *m.* **reverse,** *n.* rovescio, *m.*; parte opposta, *f.*, (il) contrario, *m.*; sconfitta, *f.*; (*of coin or medal*) rovescio, *m.*; (*page*) verso, *m.* ¶ *v.t.* rovesciare, rivoltare, invertire; (*Law*) annullare, cassare; riformare.

reversible, *a.* riversibile, invertibile; (*cloth, &c.*) a due facce, a due diritti. **reversing,** *n. & ~ gear,* meccanismo d'inversione, *m.* **reversion,** *n.* riversione, successione, *f.*

revert, *v.i.* ritornare, rivenire.

revet, *v.t.* rivestire. ~**ment,** *n.* rivestimento, *m.*

revictual, *v.t.* rifornire di viveri, vettovagliare.

review, *n.* rivista, *f.*, revisione, *f.*; (*book*) recensione, critica; notizia; *f*; resoconto, *m.* ¶ *v.t.* rivedere, esaminare; (*Mil.*) passare in rivista; (*book*) fare la recensione di, criticare, fare il resoconto di. ~er, *n.* recensore, critico.

revile, *v.t.* ingiuriare, insultare; oltraggiare, sparlare di.

revise (*Typ.*) *n.* seconda bozza, *f.*; riscontro, *m.* ¶ *v.t.* correggere; rivedere. **revision,** *n.* revisione, *f.*

revival, *n.* ravvivamento, ricupero, risorgimento, *m.*; ripresa, *f.*; rinascenza, *f.*, rinnovamento, *m.*; (*Relig.*) risveglie (religioso), *m.* **revive,** *v.t.* ravvivare, rianimare, far rivivere; risvegliare, rimettere in vigore.

revoke, *v.t.* revocare. (*v.i.*) (*Cards*) rifiutare.

revolt, *n.* rivolta, insurrezione, *f.* ¶ *v.i.* rivoltarsi, ribellarsi. ~**ing,** *a.* ributtante, che fa ribrezzo, stomachevole.

revolution, *n.* rivoluzione, *f.*; giro, *m.* ~*s per minute,* giri al minuto; ~**ary,** *a. & n.,* rivoluzionario, *a. & m.,* -a *f.* ~**ize,** *v.t.* rivoluzionare. **revolve,** *v.t. & i.* rivolgere, far girare, girare, rotare.

revolver, *n.* rivoltella, *f.,* revolver, *m.inv.* **revolving,** *a.* rotante, roteante; girevole; a rotazione, rotatorio; ricorrente. ~ *light,* faro a luce mobile, *m.*

revue, *n.* rivista, *f.*

revulsion, *n.* (*Med.*) revulsione; improvvisa reazione; ripugnanza, *f.*

reward, *n.* ricompensa, *f.,* premio, *m.* ¶ *v.t.* ricompensare, premiare.

rewrite, *v.t. ir.* riscrivere.

rhapsody, *n.* rapsodia, *f.*

Rheims, *n.* Reims, *f.*

rhetoric, *n.* retorica, *f.* ~**al,** *a.* retorico.

rheumatic, *a.* reumatico. **rheumatism,** *n.* reumatismo, *m.*

Rhine (**the**), il Reno, *m.* ¶ *att.* del Reno; (*wine*) vino del Reno, *m.*; *the* ~ *land,* la Renania, *f.*

rhinoceros, *n.* rinoceronte, *m.*

rhododendron, *n.* rododendro, *m.*

rhomb[us], *n.* rombo, *m.*

Rhone (**the**), il Rodano, *m.*

rhubarb, *n.* rabarbaro, *m.*

rhyme, *n.* rima, *f.*; (*fig.*) verso, *m.*; versi, *m.pl.*; poesia, *f.* ¶ *v.i.* rimare, far versi, far rime. **rhym[est]er,** *n.* rimatore, poetastro, *m.* **rhythm,** *n.* ritmo, *m.* ~**ic[al],** *a.* ritmico.

rib, *n.* costola, *f.*; puntello, *m.*; nervatura; ordinata, *f.*; (*ship*) costa, *f.*; (*umbrella*) stecca, *f.* ~ *steak,* costoletta, intracosta, *f.*

ribald, *a.* scurrile, sboccato, osceno.

ribbed, *a.* vergato, fatto a costole; costoluto, a nervature.

ribbon or **riband,** *n.* nastro, *m.*; benda, *f.,* cordone, *m.*;(*fig.*) fettuccia, striscia, *f.* ~ *book mark*[*er*], segnacarte, *m.* ~**s,** (*fig.*) brandelli, *m.pl.*; redini, *f.pl.* ~*maker,* fabbricante di nastri, *m.* ~ *trade,* commercio dei nastri, *m.*

rice, *n.* riso, *m.* ~ *field,* risaia, *f.* ~ *paper,* carta cinese, *f.*

rich, *a.* ricco, opulento; (*food*) grasso, succulento; sontuoso, dovizioso; abbondante; fertile; fecondo; ubertoso; (*colour*) brillante, smagliante, vivace, vivo. *the* ~, i ricchi, *m.pl.*; **riches,** *n.pl.* ricchezze, *f.pl.* **richness,** *n.* ricchezza; grassezza; sontuosità, *f.*; abbondanza; fertilità; fecondità; vivacità (*colour*), *f.*

rick, *n.* (*hay*) catasta, *f.,* mucchio, pagliaio, *m.*; (*strain*) sforzo, *m.* ~ *cloth,* copertone, *m.*

rickets, *n.* rachitide, *f.,* rachitismo, *m.* **rickety,** *a.* malfermo, poco stabile, zoppicante; rachitico.

ricksha[w], *n.* risciò, *m.inv.*

ricochet, *n.* rimbalzo, *m.* ¶ *v.i.* rimbalzare.

rid, *v.t. ir.* disfare, liberare, sbarazzare. **riddance,** *n.* liberazione, *f.*; sbarazzamento, *m.*

riddle, *n.* indovinello, *m.*, enigma, *m.*; (*sieve*) vaglio, crivello, *m.* ¶ *v.t.* vagliare, crivellare.

ride, *n.* passeggiata a cavallo, cavalcata, *f.* ¶ *v.t. & i.* cavalcare, andare a cavallo, montare (*horse*); fare un viaggio a cavallo; passeggiare (in carrozza, a cavallo, &c.). ~ *at anchor,* essere all'ancora. ~ *side-saddle,* montare da amazzone, cavalcare all'amazzone. ~ *to death* (*fig.*) abusare. **rider,** *n.* cavaliere, cavalcatore, *m.*; (*jockey*) fantino, *m.*; (*P.S.*) aggiunta, *f.*, poscritto, *m.*; (*Com.*) clausola addizionale, *f.*; (*to bill of exchange*), coda, allunga, *f.*

ridge, *n.* cresta, *f.*, rialzo, rialto, *m.*; elevazione, *f.*; giogo; banco, scoglio, *m.*; piega, *f.*; (*roof*) colmo, comignolo, *m.*; (*hill*) cima, *f.*, crinale; giogo, *m.*; (*Agric.*) solco, *m.*; colmo, *m.*; (*left by plough*) porca, *f.* ~ *capping,* copertura del colmo, *f.* ~ *pole,* spina del tetto, trave di colmo, *f.*; (*tent*) comignolo, *m.* ~ *tile,* tegola di colmo, *f.*; ¶ (*Agric.*) *v.t.* reinterrare, rincalzare.

ridicule, *n.* ridicolo; scherno, *m.* ¶ *v.t.* mettere in ridicolo, rendere ridicolo, canzonare; sbeffare, sbeffeggiare. **ridiculous**, *a.* ridicolo. ~**ness**, *n.* ridicolo, *m.*

riding, *n.* equitazione, *f.*; maneggio, *m.*; cavalcata, *f.*; (*Turf*) corsa, *f.* ~ *boots*, stivaloni; stivali per equitazione, *m.pl.* ~ *breeches*, calzoni da equitazione, *m.pl.* ~ *habit*, amazzone, *f.* ~ *school*, scuola d'equitazione, *f.*; maneggio, *m.*; cavallerizza, *f.* ~ *whip*, frustino, *m.*

rife (to be), infierire, imperversare; correre.

riff-raff, *n.* canaglia, plebaglia, marmaglia, *f.*

rifle, *n.* fucile, *m.* carabina, *f.* ~ *drill*, esercitazione col fucile, *f.*, maneggio d'armi, *m.* ~*man*, bersagliere, fuciliere, *m.* ~ *range*, campo del tiro (a segno); (*gallery*) tiro, tiro alla carabina, *m.* ¶ *v.t.* (*rob*) svaligiare, spogliare; (*groove*) rigare.

rift, *n.* fessura, spaccatura, crepatura, *f.*; (*fig.*) apertura, *f.*; dissenso, *m.*, divisione, *f.*

rig, *v.t.* allestire, equipaggiare; (*ship*) attrezzare; guarnire. ~ *out*, vestire alla meglio. ~ *the market*, rarefare il mercato. **rigging**, *n.* sartiame, *m.*; attrezzi, *m.pl.*, attrezzatura, *f.* ~ *the market*, rarefazione del mercato; truffa di borsa, *f.*

right, *a.* retto, diritto, in linea, retta; destro; corretto; esatto; regolare; giusto; vero; equo; proprio; propizio; conveniente; adatto; opportuno; addicevole; dovuto; voluto. ~-*angled*, rettangolo. ~ *handed person or player*, chi usa la mano destra. ~-*minded*, retto; ben pensante. *at the* ~ *moment*, al momento opportuno, a tempo. ~ *side* (*fabric*), diritto, *m.* *the* ~ *time*, l'ora giusta, *f.*; il tempo propizio, *m.* *to be* ~, avere ragione. ¶ *ad.* diritto; bene; tutto; come si deve, in linea retta, a destra, proprio, correttamente. ~ *about*, nella direzione opposta; (*Mil.*) per fianco destro! dietro front! ~ *honourable*, onorevolissimo. ~ *reverend*, reverendissimo. ~ *& left*, *ad.* a destra ed a sinistra. ~ *through*, da parte a parte, interamente. ¶ *n.* diritto, privilegio, *m.*; rettitudine; giustizia; ragione, *f.*; bene, *m.*; (*side*) destra, man destra, parte destra, *f.*; (*pl.*) diritti, *m.pl.*; proprietà letteraria, *f.* ~ *of way*, diritto di passaggio, *m.* *by* ~*s*, a rigore. ¶ *v.t.* correggere, riparare, raddrizzare.

righteous, *a.* giusto, retto; santo, virtuoso. ~**ly**, *ad.* giustamente; rettamente; santamente. ~**ness**, *n.* rettitudine; santità; giustizia, *f.*

rightful, *a.* legittimo, equo, giusto. **rightly**, *ad.* giustamente, a giusto titolo, bene.

rigid, *a.* rigido; severo. ~**ity**, *n.* rigidezza, rigidità, *f.*

rigmarole, *n.* guazzabuglio di parole, *m.*, filastrocca, tiritera, *f.*

rigor mortis, rigidità cadaverica, *f.*

rigorous, *a.* rigoroso. **rigour**, *n.* rigore, *m.*

rill, *n.* ruscelletto, rigagnolo, *m.*

rim, *n.* bordo, orlo, margine, *m.*; (*wheel*) quarto, cerchione, *m.*, corona, *f.*; (*watch*) cerchio, *m.* ~ *brake*, freno sul (al) cerchione, sui cerchioni, *m.* ~ *lock*, serratura a cassetta, *f.* ¶ *v.t.* bordare, orlare. ~**less** (*glasses*) *a*, (occhialini) senza montatura, *m.pl.*

rime, *n.* brina, *f.*

rind, *n.* scorza, buccia, corteccia, *f.*; (*cheese*) crosta, *f.*; (*bacon*) cotenna, *f.*

rinderpest, *n.* peste bovina, *f.*

ring, *n.* anello, cerchio, cerchietto, orecchino; suono, scampanio; colpo di campanello, *m.*, scampanellata; cinta, *f.*, circolo, *m.*; (*gathering*) crocchio, *m.*, cricca, combriccola; arena, *f.*; (*Box.*) recinto del combattimento, *m.* ~ *bolt*, golfare ad anello, *m.* ~ *dove*, colombo, *m.* ~ *finger*, (dito) anulare, *m.* ~ *leader*, caporione, agitatore, *m.* ~ *quoits*, giuoco d'anelli, ~ *degli anelli*, *m.* ~*s under the eyes*, occhiaie, *f.pl.*, occhi pesti, *m.pl.* ~ *worm*, empetigine, *f.*, tigna tonsurante, *f.* ¶ *v.t. & i.ir.* far suonare, tintinnire, far tintinnire, risonare; circondare, formar un cerchio, cerchiare, accerchiare; (*bull, &c.*) mettere un anello a. ~ *a peal*, scampanare. ~ *for*, suonare a, suonare per. ~ *up*, chiamare al telefono.

ringlet, *n.* riccio, *m.*

rink, *n.* impianto di pattinaggio, *m.*, pista, *f.*

rinse, *& ~ out*, *v.t.* risciacquare. **rinsings**, *n.pl.* risciacquate, *f.pl.*

riot, *n.* sommossa, *f.*, tumulto, *m.*, rissa, *f.*, (*fig.*) baccano, chiasso, eccesso, *m.*, schiamazzo, *m*, orgia, *f.*; (*Leg.*) assembramento, *m.* ¶ *v.i.* tumultuare, far baccano, far chiasso, sollevarsi. ~**er**, *n.* sovvertitore, sedizioso, rivoltoso, *m.* ~**ous**, *a.*

ŕottoso, chiassoso, sregolato, discolo.
rip, *n.* scucitura, *f.*, squarcio; mascalzone, *m.* ¶ *v.t.* stracciare, squarciare, strappare; fendere, scucire,
sdrucire. ~ *saw*, sega da rifendere, *f.*
riparian, *a.* rivierasco.
ripe, *a.* maturo; perfetto, compito.
ripen, *v.t. & i.* maturare, far
maturare. **ripeness,** *n.* maturità,
perfezione, *f.* **ripening,** *n.* matura-
zione, *f.*
ripple, *n.* crespa, maretta, increspa-
tura, *f.*, increspamento, *m.* ¶ *v.t.*
far increspare, increspare. (*v.i.*)
incresparsi. **rippling,** *n.* increspa-
tura, *f.*
riposte, *n.* risposta, *f.* ¶ *v.t.* rispondere, rendere colpo per colpo,
rimbeccare.
rise, *n.* ascensione, elevazione, *f.*;
avanzamento, *m.*; erta, salita, levata,
altura, *f.*; l'alzarsi, il sorgere;
aumento, rincaro, rialzo, gonfiamento, *m.*; piena, *f.* (*water*); (*temperature*) aumento, *m.*; (*of a step*)
altezza di gradino, *f. give ~ to*, far
nascere, cagionare. ¶ *v.i. ir.* alzarsi,
levarsi, sorgere; spuntare, nascere;
provenire; sollevarsi; rivoltarsi, insorgere; gonfiarsi; lievitare, crescere,
ingrossare, aumentare, aumentarsi,
rincarare; (*dead*) risorgere, risuscitare; (*fish*) venire a fior d'acqua;
(*meeting*) chiudersi, sciogliersi. **rising,** *n.* levata, ascensione, risurrezione, *f.*; risorgimento, *m.*; solleva-
zione, *f.*, sollevamento, *m.*; insurrezione, rivolta, *f.*; tumore,
gonfiamento, *m.*; (*meeting*) scioglimento, *m.*, chiusura, *f.* ¶ *p.a.*
montante, crescente, nascente. ~
generation, sorgente generazione, *f.*,
i giovani, *m.pl.* ~ *sun*, sole nascente,
levante. ~ *tide*, marea montante, *f.*
risk, *n.* rischio, azzardo, *m.* ¶ *v.t.*
arrischiare, azzardare. *I'll ~ it*, a
casaccio. ~**y,** *a.* rischioso, pericoloso.
rissole, *n.* crocchetta, frittella, pol-
petta, *f.*
rite, *n.* rito, *m.*, cerimonia, *f.* **ritual,**
a. & n. rituale, *a. & m.*
rival, *a.* rivale. ¶ *n.* rivale, *m.f.* ¶ *v.t.*
rivaleggiare con; eguagliare. ~**ry,**
n. rivalità, emulazione, *f.*
rive, *v.t. ir.* fendere, spaccare; (*v.i. ir.*)
fendersi, spaccarsi.
river, *n.* fiume, *m.*, riviera, *f.*; (*att.*)
di fiume, fluviale. ~ *god*, divinità
del fiume, *f.* ~ *side*, riva, sponda, *f.*;
(*att.*) rivierasco.

rivet, *n.* chiodo (ribadito) *m.* ¶ *v.t.*
ribadire, inchiodare, chiodare; (*fig.*)
tener fisso; scolpire.
Riviera (the), la Riviera, *f.*
rivulet, *n.* ruscel'etto, *m.*
roach (*fish*), lasc *f.*
road, *n.* strada, via, ; ~ *code*, codice
stradale, *m.* ~ *hog*, conducente
sconsiderato, *m.* ~ *man* or ~ *mender*,
cantoniere, *m.* ~ *map*, carta stradale,
pianta stradale, *f.* ~ *race*, corsa
stradale, *f.* ~ *side*, margine della
strada, *m.*; (*att.*) sulla strada. ~*side
inn & road house*, locanda sulla
strada, *f.* ~*side station*, stazione di
passaggio, *f.* ~[*stead*], rada, *f.*,
ancoraggio, *m.* ~ *stones*, acciotto-
lato, selciato, *m.* ~(*way*) carreggiata, *f.* **roadster,** *n.* bicicletta da
turismo, *f.*
roam, *v.i.* errare, vagare, andar
attorno, gironzare, girovagare.
roan, *a.* (*animal*) roano; (*shoes*) uso
marocchino. ¶ *n.* (*animal*) roano, *m.*;
(*sheepskin*) bazzana, *f.*
roar, *v.i. & t.* ruggire; mugghiare;
urlare; muggire; gridare, vociferare;
rimbombare. ¶ *n.* ruggito, muggito,
grido, urlo, *m.*
roast, *v.t. & i.* arrostire; arrostirsi;
(*coffee, &c.*) torrefare. ~ *beef*,
arrosto di manzo, manzo arrosto,
rosbif[fe], *m.* ~ (*meat*) & ~ *meat
course*, arrosto, *m.* ~ *mutton*, arrosto
di castrato, *m.* ~*ing jack*, girarrosto,
m.
rob, *v.t.* rubare, derubare, svaligiare.
robber, *n.* ladro, brigante, *m.* ~**y,**
n. ladreria, ruberia, *f.* brigantaggio,
m., rapina, *f.* ~ *with violence*, furto
a mano armata, *m.*
robe, *n.* veste, *f.*; vestito, *m.*; toga, *f.*
robin [**redbreat**] *n.* pettirosso, *m.*
robing room, vestiario, *m.*
robot, *n.* automa, *m.*
Rob Roy canoe, piroga, *f.*
robust, *a.* robusto, forte, vigoroso.
rock, *n.* roccia, *f.*, scoglio, *m.*; rupe,
balza, *f.*; sasso, *m.*; macigno, *m.*;
(*fig.*) rocca, *f.* ~ *crystal*, cristallo, *m.*
~ *drill*, perforatrice, *f.* ~ *garden*,
giardino alpino, *m.* ~ *salt*, sal-
gemma, *f.* ~ *work*, roccia artificiale,
f. ¶ *v.t.* cullare, dondolare; (*v.i.*)
barcollare. ~**er,** *n.* altalena, *f.*;
(*pers.*) cullatrice, *f.* ~**ery,** *n.* roccia
artificiale, *f.* ~**et,** *n.* razzo, *m.* (*Bot.*)
ruchetta, *f.* ~ *apparatus*, razzo di
salvataggio, *m.* ~**ing,** *n.* cullamen-
to, dondolamento, *m.* ~ *chair*, sedia
a dondolo, *f.* ~ *horse*, cavallo a

dondolo, *m.* ~ *stone*, roccia instabile, *f.* ~**y**, *a.* roccioso, di sasso, di macigno. *R*~ *Mountains*, le Montagne Rocciose, *f.pl.*

rococo, *n. & a.*, rococò, *a. & m.*

rod, *n.* bacchetta, asta, barra, stecca, *f.*; bordone, bastoncello, *m.*, verga, *f.*; staffile, *m.*; canna (da pesca) *f.*; scettro, *m.*; *Meas.* = 25.293 sq. metres.

rodent, *n. & a.*, rosicante, *a. & m.f.*

roe, *n.* (*fish*). See *hard*, *soft*. ~*buck*, capriolo, *m.* ~-*doe*, capriola, *f.*

rogations, *n.pl.* rogazioni, *f.pl.*

rogue, *n.* furfante, briccone, birbante, mariuolo, imbroglione, *m.*; (*Law*) vagabondo, *m.*; (*child*) birichino, *m*, -a, *f.* **roguish**, *a.* birbantesco, malizioso, scaltro, buffonesco; furbesco. **roguishness & roguery**, *n.* bricconeria, furfanteria, mariuoleria, buffoneria, *f.*

roisterer, *n.* chiassone, *m.*

roll, *n.* rotolo, rocchetto; registro, ruolo; elenco, *m.*; lista, matricola, *f.*; panino, *m.*; (*package*) involto, *m.*; (*butter*) panetto, *m.* ~ *call*, appello, *m.* ~ *of honour*, ruolo d'onore, *m.* ~ *of the drum*, rullo, rullio, (di tamburo). ¶ *v.t. & i.* rotolare, rotolarsi, girare, ruzzolare, far ruzzolare, rullare; involgere; stendere (*dough*); stralunare (*eyes*); laminare (*metal*). ~-*top desk*, scrittoio americano, *n.* ~-*film camera*, macchina fotografica per pellicole su rocchetti, *f.* ~-*film developing tank*, vaschetta per sviluppare le pellicole su rocchetti, *f.* ~ *up*, arrotolare, fare un rotolo di; avvolgere; (*sleeve*, *&c.*) rimboccare. ~-*up manicure set*, completo (or trousse) per manicure, *m.* ~**ed gold**, oro laminato, *m.* **roller**, *n.* rullo, *m.*; appianatoio, *m.*; (*garden*) cilindro, *m.*; (*Mech.*, *Metal.*) laminatoio, *m.*; (*map*) rullo, *m.*; (*bird*) ghiandaia marina, *f.*; (*wave*) cavallone, *m.* ~ *skates*, pattini a rotelle, *m.pl.* ~ *skating*, pattinaggio a rotelle, *m.* ~ *towel*, bandinella, *f.*, asciugamano a rotolo, *m.*

rollick, *v.i.* fare baldoria, far festa, gozzovigliare. ~**ing**, *a.* brioso, giocondo, fanfarone.

rolling, *n.* rotolamento, *m.*; (*ship*) rullio, *m.* ~ *in wealth*, ricchissimo. ~ *mill*, laminatoio, *m.* ~ *pin*, matterello, *m.* ~ *stock*, (*Rly.*) materiale rotabile, *m.*

Roman, *a.* romano; romanesco (*Mod.*

Roman dialect); (*nose*) aquilino. ~ *candle*, candela romana, *f.* ~ *Catholic*, *a. & n.* cattolico [romano], *a. & m.* ~ *Catholicism*, *n.* cattolicismo [romano], *m.* ¶ *n.* (*pers.*) romano, *m.* -a *f.*; (*Typ.*) caratteri romani, *m.pl.*

romance, *n.* romanzo, idillio, *m.*; favola, *f.*; (*Mus.*) romanza, *f.*; *R*~, *a. & n.*, romanzo, *a. & m.* ~ *languages*, lingue romanze, *f.pl.* ¶ *v.i.* fantasticare, fare dei romanzi, favoleggiare.

Romanesque (*Arch.*), *a.* romanico. **Romansch**, *a. & n.*, romanico, retico romano, *a. & m.*

romantic, *a.* romantico, romanzesco. **Rome**, *n.* Roma, *f.*

romp, *n.* trambusto, gioco chiassoso, *m.*; monella chiassosa, *f.* ¶ *v.i.* ruzzare, folleggiare, fare il monello. ~**ers**, (*child's*) *n.pl.* grembiule da bambino, *m.*

rood, *n.* croce, *f.*, crocefisso, *m.*; *Meas.* = 10.117 ares. ~ *screen*, tramezzo fra la navata e il coro di una chiesa (su cui è esposto il crocefisso).

roof, *n.* tetto, *m.*; volta, *f.*; cielo, *m.*; (*coach*) imperiale, *m.* ~ *garden*, giardino pensile, *m.* ~ *of the month*, palato, *m.* ¶ *v.t.* coprire (con tetto). ~**ing**, *n.* copertura, *f.*, tetto, *m.*; spina del tetto, *f.*; il fare il tetto, *m.*

rook, *n.* cornacchia, *f.*, cornacchione, *m.*; (*chess*) rocco, *m.*, torre, *f.* ~**ery**, *n.* cornacchiaia, *f.*; gruppo di casupole poverissime, *m.*

room, *n.* stanza, camera, sala, *f.*; salotto; posto, spazio; luogo; margine; motivo; locale, *m.*; occasione, *f.*; (*School*) aula, *f.*; (*pl.*) appartamento, alloggio, *m.* *boiler* ~, locale caldaie, *m.* *engine* ~, sala macchine, *f.* ~ *mate*, compagno di camera, camerata, *m.* ~**ful**, *n.* stanza piena, *f.*, quanta gente può stare in una stanza. ~**y**, *a.* spazioso, ampio.

roost, *n.* posatoio, *m.* ¶ *v.i.* appollaiarsi. ~**er**, *n.* gallo, *m.*

root, *n.* radice, *f.*; barba, *f.* ¶ *v.i.* radicarsi, pigliar (mettere) radice, abbarbicarsi. ~ *out*, ~ *up*, sradicare, svellere, estirpare.

rope, *n.* fune, corda, *f.*; cavo, *m.*; (*bell*) cordone, *m.* (*pearls*) filza, *f.* ~ *dancer*, funambolo, *m.*, -a, *f.* ~ *end*, capo della fune, *m.*; corda, sferza, *f.* ~ *maker*, funaio, cordaio, *m.* ~ *making & ~ works*, corderia, *f.* ~ *walker*, funambolo, *m.*,

-a, *f.* ¶ *v.t.* legare con fune; assicurare con funi; (unire) con corda, attaccare. **ropiness** (*wine*), *n.* grasso, *m.*; viscosità, filosità, *f.* **ropy**, *a.* (*liquid*) filante, viscoso; (*wine*) inspessito, grasso.

roquet (*croquet*) *v.t.* colpire la palla di un altro giocatore con la propria.

rosary, *n.* rosario, *m.*, corona, *f.*; (*rose garden*) roseto, *m.* **rose**, *n.* rosa, *f.*; (*colour*) rosa, *m.*, color (di) rosa, *m.*; (*ceiling*) rosone, *m.*; (*watering can*) rosetta, *f.*, pomo, *m.*; (*pipe*) doccia, *f.* ~*bud*, bottone di rosa, *m.* ~ *diamond*, rosetta, *f.* ~ *grower*, coltivatore di rosai, di rose, *m.* ~ *tree*, rosaio, *m.* ~ *window*, rosone, finestrone a rosa, *m.* ~ *wood*, palissandro, *m.* under the ~, in segreto, di nascosto. **roseate**, *a.* roseo. **rosemary**, *n.* rosmarino, *m.* **rosette**, *n.* rosetta, coccarda, *f.*; (*Arch.*) rosetta, *f.*; rosone, *m.*

rosin, *n.* resina, *f.*, ragia, *f.*; (*for violin*) colofonia, *f.*

roster, *n.* turno di servizio, orario, *m.*

rostrum, *n.* rostro, *m.*; tribuna, *f.*

rosy, *a.* roseo, color di rosa.

rot, *n.* putrefazione, *m.*, fradiciume, *m.*, carie, *f.*; sciocchezze, *f.pl.* ¶ (*v.i.*) putrefare, imputridire, infradicire; cariare; (*v.t.*) fare imputridire, far marcire; cariare.

rota, *n.* lista, *f.*; ruolo, *m.* **rotary**, *a.* rotante, rotativo, rotatorio, girevole. **rotate**, *v.t. & i.* girare, roteare. **rotation**, *n.* rotazione, *f.*; giro, *m.*; successione, *f.*; (*in office*) turno, *m.*; (*crops*) giro (delle sementi), *m.* in ~, a turno.

rote (by), a memoria.

rotten, *a.* marcio, fradicio, putrefatto, cariato; (*egg, &c.*) guasto. ~**ness**, *n.* fracidezza, *f.* putridume, fradiciume *m.*; carie, *f.*

rotund, *a.* rotondo. **rotunda**, *n.* rotonda, *f.* **rotundity**, *n.* rotondità, *f.*

rouge, *n.* belletto, rossetto, *m.* ~ *et noir*, trenta e quaranta, *m.* ¶ *v.i.* imbellettare.

rough, *a.* aspro, ruvido, ispido, scabro[so], rozzo, rude; brusco, brutale, grossolano, villano; greggio, grezzo, crudo; violento; (*sea*) grosso, agitato, burrascoso, tempestoso. ~ *account*, ~ *guess*, calcolo approssimativo, *m.* in a ~ & ready fashion, fatto coll'accetta, coll'ascia. ~ & *tumble*, mischia, zuffa, *f.* ~-*cast* (*walls*), *n.* arricciato, *m.* *v.t.* arric-

ciare. ~ *draft*, brutta copia, *f.*; schizzo, *m.* ~ *estimate*, valutazione approssimativa, *f.* at (or on) a ~ *estimate*, ad un dipresso. ~-*haired*, dal pelo duro. ~-*rider*, scozzone, *m.* ~ *shod* (horse) ferrato a ghiaccio. *to ride* ~*shod over*, calpestare. ¶ *n.* becero, chiassone, giovinastro sregolato, *m.* the ~ (*Golf*), erba lunga, *f.* ¶ ~, ~**down**, ~**out**, ~**hew**, *v.t.* sgrossare, sbozzare, abbozzare. ~ **ness**, *n.* asprezza, asperità, rozzezza; violenza, *f.*, modi bruschi, *m.pl.*

R[o]umania, *n.* la Rumenia, *f.* **R[o]umanian**, *a.* rumeno. ¶ *n.* (*pers.*) rumeno, *m.*, -a, *f.*; (*language*) il rumeno, *m.*

round, *a.* rotondo, circolare, tondo; franco, schietto; buono. ~ *hand* (writing), rondo, *m.*; (*Typ.*) formatello, *m.* ~-*shouldered*, curvo (di spalle), dalle spalle curve. ~ *voyage*, andata e ritorno. ¶ *n.* ronda, *f.*; (*slice*) fetta (rotonda), *f.*; (*rung*) piuolo, *m.*; (*tour*) giro, *m.*; (*applause*) scoppio, *m.*; salva, *f.*; (*lap*) giro (della pista), *m.*; (*Sport*) partita, volta, *f.*; (*Box.*) ripresa, *f.*; ~ *of ammunition*, cartuccia, *f.* ~ *of toast*, crostino, *m.* ¶ *ad.* intorno, in giro, di circonferenza, all'intorno, d'intorno. ~ *about*, tutt'intorno. ¶ *pr.* intorno a; nei dintorni di. ¶ *v.t.* arrotondare; fare il giro di, doppiare. ~ *up*, raccogliere; (*thieves*) fare una retata di. **round-about**, *a.* tortuoso, indiretto; (*traffic*) rotatorio, giratorio. ¶ *n.* giostra, *f.*; carosello, *m.*; (*traffic*) senso giratorio, circolazione, *f.* **roundelay**, *n.* rondò, *m.* **rounders**, *n.pl.* specie di giuoco alla palla. **roundish**, *a.* tondetto, rotondetto. **roundly**, *ad.* schiettamente, francamente, chiaro e tondo. **roundness**, *n.* rotondità, *f.* **roundsman**, *n.* distributore, *m.*

rouse, *v.t.* svegliare, risvegliare, destare; incitare, provocare; (*game*) scovare.

rout, *n.* rotta, sconfitta, *f.*, sbaraglio, *m.* ¶ *v.t.* mettere in rotta, sconfiggere, sbaragliare.

route, *n.* via, rotta, direzione, strada, *f.* ~ *march*, marcia di addestramento, *f.*; ordine di marcia, *m.* ¶ *v.t.* avviare, incamminare, instradare.

routine, *n.* uso, *m.*, pratica, *f.*; usanza, abitudine, *f.*

rove, *v.i.* errare, divagare, gironzolare; (*v.t.*) infilare, torcere (il filo). **rover**, *n.* vagabondo, giramondo, *m.*; (*sea*) pirata, *m.*; corsaro, *m.*; (*Croquet*) corsaro, *m.* **roving**, *a.* vagabondo, girovago; incostante.

row, *n.* fila, linea, *f.*; ordine, filare, *m.*; (*fig.*) colonna, *f.*; gita in barca, vogata, *f.*; baruffa, *f.*, baccano, *m.*; rissa, *f.*; tumulto, *m.*; tafferuglio, *m.*; scenata, *f.*; (*of stitches*, Knit., &c.) girò, *m.* a ~ *of trees, houses,* &c., filare, *m.* ¶ *v.i.* remare, vogare. ~[*ing*] *boat*, barca a remi, *f.*

rowdy, *a.* & *n.* chiassone, *m.*, chiassoso, *a.*

rowel, *n.* stella di sperone, spronella, *f.*

rower, *n.* rematore, vogatore, canottiere, *m.* **rowing**, *n.* (*il*) remare, vogare, *m.*; voga, *f.*; canottaggio, *m.*; (*att.*) a remi. ~ *club*, circolo di canottieri, *m.* **rowlock**, *n.* scalmo, *m.*; scalmiera, *f.*

royal, *a.* reale; regio. *His, Your, R* ~ *Highness*, Sua Altezza Reale, Vostra Altezza Reale, *f.* ~**ist**, *n.* & *att.* realista, *m.f.* & *a.* ~**ty**, *n.* dignità reale; famiglia reale, *f.*; (*rent*) diritto, censo, *m.*; canone, livello, *m.*; (*author's*) diritti d'autore, *m.pl.*

rub, *n.* (*with a cloth*) strofinamento, colpo di strofinaccio, *m.*; fregata, fregatina, *f.*; (*fig.*) difficoltà, *f.*, (*il*) difficile, *m.*, nodo, busillis, *m.* ¶ *v.t.* & *i.* fregare, strofinare; stropicciare; applicare; fregarsi, strofinarsi; (*Med.*) far frizioni (a), frizionare; (*inscription*) improntare. ~ *down* (*horse*), strigliare. ~ *one's hands*, fregarsi le mani. ~ *out*, cancellare, raschiare. ~ *shoulders with*, fregarsi a, bazzicare, frequentare. ~ *up* (*fig.*), rinfrescare. ~ [*up*] *the wrong way* (*fig.*), offendere, contrariare. **rubber**, *n.* fregatore, strofinaccio, *m.*; caucciù, *m.*; gomma (elastica), *f.*; (*Cards*) partita tripla, *f.*; (*3rd game*) bella, *f.* ~ *floating toys*, animali marini galleggianti, animali di caucciù, *m.pl.* ~ *heels*, salvatacchi, *m.pl.* ~ *shares*, valori di caucciù. ~ *stamp*, stampino di gomma, *m.* ~ *tyre*, pneumatico, *m.*, gomma, *f.* ~*-tyre* & ~[*ize*;, *v.t.* spalmare di caucciù, rinnovare la gomma. **rubbing**, *n.* fregamento, attrito, *m.*, frizione, *f.* (*oft. pl.*); (*with oil*) unzione, lubrificazione, *f.*; (*copy*) impronta, *f.*

rubbish, *n.* robaccia, *f.*, rottame, *m.*; detriti, *m.pl.*; macerie, *f.pl.*; vecchiume, *m.*; (*dirt*) immondizie, spazzature, *f.pl.*; (*trash*) rifiuti, scarti, *m.pl.*;

(*nonsense*) sciocchezze, *f.pl.*, assurdità, insulsaggine, *f.*

rubble [*stone*] *n.* frammenti di pietra, ciottoli, rottami, *m.pl.*; pietra greggia, *f.* ~ [*work*] *n.* muratura in pietre di cava, *f.*

rubicund, *a.* rubicondo.

rubric, *n.* rubrica, *f.*

ruby, *n.* rubino, *m.* ¶ (*lips*) *a.* vermiglio.

ruck, *n.* mucchio, *m.*; folla, *f.*

rucksack, *n.* sacco da montagna, *m.*

rudder, *n.* timone, *m.*

ruddy, *a.* rubicondo, rosso, vermiglio.

rude, *a.* rozzo, rude, informe; grossolano; scortese; sgarbato; (*health*) robusto. ~**ness**, *n.* scortesia, sgarbatezza, grossolanità, *f.*

rudiment, *n.* rudimento, *m.* (*pl. of a science, an art*), elementi, *m.pl.* ~**ary**, *a.* rudimentale.

rue (*Bot.*), *n.* ruta, *f.* ¶ *v.t.* pentirsi di. ~**ful**, *a.* triste, lamentevole, lugubre.

ruff (*Hist. dress*), *n.* gorgiera, *f.*

ruffian, *n.* bandito, furfante, malandrino, scellerato, sgherro, assassino, *m.* ~**ly**, *a.* scellerato, brutale, brigantesco.

ruffle, *n.* manichino, *m.* ¶ *v.t.* increspare; agitare, urtare, disturbare; mettere in disordine; (*hair*) scompigliare, arruffare.

rug, *n.* tappetino, *m.*; scendiletto, *m.*; (*travelling*) coperta (da viaggio), *f.* ~ *work*, tappeti, *m.pl.*; tappezzeria, *f.*

Rugby [**football**], *n.* (*ball*) palla ovale, *f.*; (*game*) giuoco del pallone ovale, *m.*

rugged, *a.* ruvido, aspro, irregolare, scabro[so], irsuto, peloso; rude; ineguale; aggrottato. ~**ness**, *n.* ruvidezza, rozzezza, scabrosità; asprezza; irregolarità, *f.*

ruin, *n.* rovina, *f.* ¶ *v.t.* rovinare. ~**ous**, *a.* in rovina; dannoso, rovinoso.

rule, *n.* regola, *f.*; norma, *f.*; regime, *m.*; governo, dominio, *m.*; (*inst.*) regolo, *m.*; (*Typ.*) filetto, *m.* ~ *of the road*, regolamento stradale; modo di circolare, *m.* ~ *of thumb*, processo empirico, *m.*; (*att.*) empirico. *by* ~ *of thumb*, empiricamente. *as a* ~, *as a general* ~, di regola, in massima, come regola generale. ¶ *v.t.* governare, reggere; regolare, dirigere; (*with lines*) rigare; (*v.i.*) governare, regnare; essere di regola; (*prices*) mantenersi, aggirarsi (*intorno a* = about). **ruler**, *n.*

governante; sovrano; dominatore, *m.*;
(*for lines*) regolo, *m.* **ruling,** *p.a.*
dominante; regnante; (*price*) corrente, del giorno. ～ *passion,*
passione dominante, *f.* ¶ *n.* rigatura;
decisione, *f.*
rum, *n.* rum, *m.*
Rumania, *&c.* Same as *Roumania,*
&c.
rumble, *v.i.* rumoreggiare, mormorare; (*bowels*) gorgogliare.
ruminant, *n. & a.* ruminante, *a. &*
m.f. **ruminate,** *v.t. & i.* ruminare.
rummage, *v.t. & i.* rovistare, frugare.
rumour, *n.* rumore, *m.* diceria; voce,
f., dire, *m. it is ～ed that,* si dice che,
corre voce che.
rump, *n.* groppa, *f.*; (*bird*) codione, *m.*;
(*beef*) coscia, culatta, *f.* ～ *steak,*
fetta di culatta, *f.*, culaccio, *m.*
rumple, *v.t.* spiegazzare, sgualcire.
run, *n.* corsa, *f.*, corso, *m.*, corrente, *f.*;
percorso, *m.*; tragitto, *m.*; passeggiata, *f.*; trottata, *f.*; caccia, *f.*; distanza
percorsa; affluenza, *f.*; concorso; periodo; seguito, *m.*; serie, *f.*; ripetizione,
f.; generalità, *f.*; comune, *m.*;
durata, voga, vena, *f.*; accesso libero,
m.; entrata libera, *f. a ～ on the*
banks, un assedio alle banche, *m.*
in the long ～, a lungo andare, in
ultima analisi. ～*-off* (from dead
heat), decisione, *f.* ～ (*-up*) (*Jump.*),
rincorsa, *f.* ¶ *v.i. ir.* correre, fuggire;
filare, percorrere, passare, fare,
navigare; (*Mach.*) funzionare, girare,
marciare; estendersi; decorrere; ammontare; colare, liquefarsi, fondersi;
scorrere, fluire; fare il servizio;
circolare; diffondersi, spargersi; (*v.t.*
ir.) correre; far correre, far funzionare, far girare, far rotolare;
spingere, conficcare, infilzare; fondere, gettare; colare, versare, spargere; condurre, tenere, esercire.
～ *about,* correre qua e là. ～
against, imbattersi in; urtare contro. ～ *aground,* arrenarsi, investire in secca; incagliarsi. ～ *along,*
stendersi lungo. ～ *away,* fuggire,
fuggirsene; (*horse*) prendere la mano.
～ *into,* incontrare, imbattersi in;
(*debt*) incorrere, ingolfarsi. ～ *on*
(*Typ.*) seguire. ～ *out of* (*stock*)
mancare di. *to be ～ out of,* esaurirsi;
～ *out of petrol,* mancare di benzina.
～ *over,* scorrere; traboccare. *to be*
～ *over,* essere abbattuto, investito.
～ *stock against one's clients,* fare
la controparte. ～ *the streets,* far
birichinate. ～ *through,* percorrere;

trafiggere; pervadere; (*money, &c.*)
dissipare, scialacquare. ～ *to earth,*
scovare, ritrovare le traccie di. ～ *to*
seed, fare il seme, andare in seme,
tallire. ～ *up against* (pers.), incontrare inaspettatamente. **run-**
about, *n.* discolo, *m.*, -a, *f.*; (*car*)
vetturetta, *f.* **runaway,** *n. & a.*
fuggitivo, *m.*, -a, *f.*; fuggiasco, *m.*,
-a, *f.* ～ *match,* matrimonio clandestino, furtivo, *m.*
rune, *n.* runa, *f.*, carattere runico, *m.*
rung, *n.* piuolo, *m.*
runner, *n.* corridore, *m.*; (*tout*)
piazzista, *m.*; messaggero, *m.*; (*slide*)
cursore, *m.*; (*millstone*) macina
superiore, *f.*; (*for shelf*) anello
mobile, *a.* scorrevole, *m.*; (*Hort.*
Bot.) tralcio, viticcio, *m.*; (*slider*
of sledge) pattino, *m.* ～ *bean,*
fagiuolo, fagiuolo rampicante, *f.* di
Spagna. *m.* **running,** *n.* corsa, *f.*;
movimento, *m.*; scorrimento, rotamento, *m.*; scolo, *m.*; funzionamento,
m.; marcia, *f.* ¶ *p.a.* corrente;
scorrevole; (*knot*) scorsoio; (*sore*)
suppurante; consecutivo, di seguito.
～ *buffet,* buffet, *m.* ～*-commentary*
(*Radio*), cronaca radiofonica, *f.* ～
dive, tuffo con slancio, *m.* ～ *fire,*
fuoco a volontà, *f.*, f. continuo, *m.*
～ *from to-day,* a decorrere da oggi.
～ *board* (*motor, car, &c.*), montatoio, *m.* ～ *gear,* parti mobili (di
una macchina), *f.pl.* ～ *hand,* corsivo
(carattere), *m.* ～ *number,* numero
d'ordine, *m.* **runway,** *n.* (*Aviat.*)
pista di decollo, p. di lancio, *f.*
rupee, *n.* rupia, *f.*
rupture, *n.* rottura, *f.*; (*Med.*) ernia, *f.*
¶ *v.t.* rompere. *to be ～d,* avere
un'ernia.
rural, *a.* rurale, campestre.
ruse, *n.* astuzia, *f.* artificio, *m.*;
stratagemma, *m.*
rush, *n.* (*Bot.*) giunco, *m.*; (*pl. Golf*)
ginestre, *f.pl.*; assalto, attacco;
slancio, *m.*, corsa impetuosa, *f.*;
impeto; afflusso, *m.*; ressa, *f.* ～ *of*
blood to the head, congestione
cerebrale, *f.* ～ *chair,* sedia impagliata, *f.* ～ *hours,* ore di punta, ore
di maggior traffico, *f.pl.* ¶ *v.t.*
precipitare; spicciare, affrettare; (*v.i.*)
precipitarsi, slanciarsi, scagliarsi,
avventarsi, gettarsi; accorrere,
affrettarsi; affollarsi, affluire, salire.
～ *down,* fare a precipizio, precipitarsi giù.
rusk, *n.* biscotto, *m.*
russet, *a.* rossetto, rossiccio. ¶ *n.*

(*colour*) rossetto, *m.*; (*apple*) renetta, *f.*

Russia, *n.* la Russia, *f.* **Russian,** *a.* russo. ¶ *n.* (*pers.*) russo, *m.*, -a, *f.*; (*language*) il russo, *m.*; lingua russa, *f.*

rust, *n.* ruggine, *f. to rub off the ~ from,* srugginire. ¶ *v.t.* arrugginire; (*v.i.*) arrugginirsi. **rustiness,** *n.* ruggine, *f.* **rustless,** *a.* inossidabile.

rustic, *a.* rustico, agreste, rurale, rozzo. ¶ *n.* villano, contadino, zoticone, *m.* **rusticate,** *v.i.* villeggiare.

rustle, *v.i.* stormire, fremere; (*dress*) far fruscio.

rusty, *a.* rugginoso, arrugginito, irrugginito.

rut, *n.* solco, *m.*; traccia, *f.*; (*groove*) scanalatura, *f.*; (*of animals*) frega, *f.*, calore, *m.*

ruthless, *a.* spietato.

rye, *n.* segala, *f. ~ grass,* loglio, *m.*

S

S, *n. & S hook,* esse, *f.*

sabbath, *n.* (*Jewish*) sabato, *m.*; (*Christian*) domenica, *f.*

sable, *n.* (*Zool.*) zibellino; (*fur*) zibellino, *m.*; (*Her.*) nero, *m.*

sabotage, *n.* sabotaggio, *m.* ¶ *v.t.* sabotare.

sabre, *n.* sciabola, *f.* ¶ *v.t.* sciabolare.

sac, *n.* sacco, *m.*, borsa, *f.*

saccharin[e], *n.* saccarina, *f.*

sacerdotal, *a.* sacerdotale.

sachet, *n.* sacchetto, *m.*; cuscinetto di profumi, *m.*

sack, *n.* sacco, *m.*; saccheggio, *m.* ~*cloth, sacking,* tela da sacco, *f.* (*fig.*) cilicio, *m.*; (*Theol.*) sacco, *m. in ~cloth & ashes,* con aria penitente. ~ *race,* corsa degli insaccati, *f.* ¶ *v.t.* saccheggiare; congedare. ~*ful, m.* sacco pieno *m.*, saccata, *f.*

sacrament, *n.* sacramento, *m.* ~*al, a. & m.* sacramentale. **sacred,** *a.* sacro, **santo**; inviolabile; (*song, &c.*) sacro; (*concert*) sacro; (*to the memory of*) consacrato a, dedicato a. **sacrifice,** *n.* sacrifizio, *m.* ¶ *v.t. & i.* sacrificare; immolare; abbandonare. **sacrificial,** *a.* di sacrifizio, espiatorio. **sacrilege,** *n.* sacrilegio, *m.* **sacrilegious,** *a.* sacrilego. **sacristy,** *n.* sagrestia, *f.* **sacristan,** *n.*

sagrestano, *m.* **sacrosanct,** *a.* sacrosanto.

sad, *a.* triste, mesto, doloroso; lugubre; deplorevole, tristo, funesto. **sadden,** *v.t.* rattristare, attristare, contristare.

saddle, *n.* sella, *f.*; (*mountain*) gola, *f.*, cresta, giogaia, *f.* ~*-backed,* sellato. ~*bag,* bisaccia, *f.*; (*stuff*) mocchetto, *m.* ~*bow,* arcione, *m.* ~ *horse,* cavallo da sella, *m.* ¶ *v.t.* sellare; (*pack animal*) mettere il basto a.; (*fig.*) gravare, caricare. **saddler,** *n.* sellaio, *m.* **saddlery,** *n.* selleria, *f.*; oggetti di selleria, *m.pl.*

sadly, *ad.* tristemente, dolorosamente. **sadness,** *n.* tristezza, *f.*

safe, *a.* salvo, sicuro; al coperto, al sicuro; (*investment*) sicuro; (*arrival*) in salvo, felice. ~ *& sound,* sano e salvo, incolume. ~ *conduct,* salvacondotto, *m. in ~ custody,* (sotto) buona guardia, (in) buona custodia. ~ *keeping,* buona guardia, *f.* ¶ *n.* cassaforte, *f.*; (*meat*) guardavivande, *m.inv.* ~ *deposit,* camera di sicurezza, *f.* ~*guard,* salvaguardia, *f.*; (*v.t.*) salvaguardare. ~*ly, ad.* in salvo, senza incidenti; sicuramente, al sicuro, in luogo sicuro. ~*ty, n.* sicurezza; salvezza, salute, *f.* ~ *belt,* cintura di salvataggio, *f.* ~ *bicycle,* bicicletta, *f.* ~ *catch,* dente d'arresto; dispositivo di sicurezza, *m.*; (*fire-arm*) sicura, *f.* ~ *curtain,* sipario di sicurezza, *m.* ~ *first,* la sicurezza anzitutto. ~ *lamp,* lampada di sicurezza, *f.* ~ *pin,* spillo di sicurezza, *m.* ~ *razor,* rasoio di sicurezza, *m.* ~ *valve* (*lit. & fig.*) valvola di sicurezza, *f.*

saffron, *n.* zafferano, *m.*

sag, *n.* depressione, insellatura, *f.* ¶ *v.i.* piegarsi (in giú), vacillare, penzolare; abbassarsi.

sagacious, *a.* sagace. **sagacity,** *n.* sagacia, sagacità, *f.*

sage, *n.* (*pers.*) saggio, savio, erudito, *m.*; (*herb*) salvia, *f.* ¶ *a.* savio, saggio, erudito.

sago, *n.* sago, sagú, *m.* ~ *palm,* palma del sagú, *f.*

said (**the**) (*Law*), *p.a.* il detto, il suddetto.

sail, *n.* vela, *f.*; gita sull'acqua, *f.*; (*fig.*) bastimento, *m.*; (*windmill*) ala (di mulino), *f.* ~ *cloth,* tela da vele, tela olona, *f.* ~ *loft & ~ making,* veleria, *f.* ~ *maker,* velaio, *m.* ¶ *v.i.* veleggiare, andare a vela; navigare, far vela; salpare; (*v.t.*) veleggiare, navigare; navigare su.

~**er**, *n.* veliero, *m.*   ~**ing**, *n.* navigazione, arte del navigare; partenza, *f.*   ~ *ship*, nave a vela; imbarcazione a vela, *f.*; veliero, *m.* ~**or**, *n.* marinaio, *m.*   ~ *suit*, costume da marinaio, *m.*

sainfoin, *n.* lupinella, *f.*

saint, *a.* santo. ¶ *n.* santo, *m.*, santa, *f.* *St. Anthony's fire*, fuoco di Sant'Antonio, *m.*   ~*'s day*, festa, *f.* *St. Bernard dog*, cane di San Bernardo, *m.* *Saint Helena*, Sant'Elena, *f.* *St. John's-wort*, erba di San Giovanni, *f.*   *Saint Lawrence*, San Lorenzo. *St. Vitus's dance*, ballo di San Vito, *m.* ¶ *v.t.* canonizzare. ~**ed**, *p.p.* santo, canonizzato. **saintliness**, *n.* santità, *f.*   **saintly**, *a.* santo, di santo, pio, devoto.

sake, *n.* causa, *f.*, riguardo, amore, *m.*; ragioni, *f.pl.*; interesse, *m.*

sal, *n.* sale, *m.*   ~*-ammoniac*, sal ammoniaco. ~ *volatile*, sal volatile.

salaam, *n.* salamelecco, *m.*

salable, *a.* vendibile.

salacious, *a.* salace, lascivo, lubrico.

salad, *n.* insalata, *f.*   ~ *bowl*, insalatiera, *f.*   ~ *oil*, olio da tavola, olio commestibile, *m.*

Salamanca, *n.* Salamanca, *f.*

salamander, *n.* salamandra, *f.*

salaried, *p.a.* salariato, stipendiato.

salary, *n.* stipendio; salario; onorario, *m.*; (*M.P.'s*) indennità, *f.* *to put on a* ~ *basis*, stipendiare.

sale, *n.* vendita, *f.*; spaccio, smercio; esito, *m.*; messa in vendita, *f.* (*clearance*) liquidazione, *f.*   ~ *by private treaty*, vendita all'amichevole. *on* ~, in vendita. *on* ~ *or return*, da vendere o rimandare.

Salerno, *n.* Salerno, *f.*   *of* ~, salernitano.

salesman, ~**woman**, *n.* commesso, commesso alla vendita, *m.*; commessa, venditrice, commessa alla vendita, *f.*; (*market*) piazzista, *m.* ~**ship**, l'arte di vendere.

Salic law, legge salica, *f.*

salient, *a. & n.* saliente, *a. & m.*

saline, *a.* salino, salso.

saliva, *n.* saliva, *f.*   **salivate**, *v.i.* salivare.

sallow, *a.* giallognolo, giallastro, smorto. ¶ *n.* salcio, *m.*

sally, *n.* (*Mil.*) sortita, *f.*; (*wit*) arguzia, *f.*, frizzo, motto, tratto di spirito, *m.*

salmon, *n.* salmone, *m.*; (*young*) salmoncino, *m.*   ~ *pink*, rosa

salmone, *m.*   ~ *trout*, trota salmonata, *f.*

Salonica, *n.* Salonicco, *f.*

saloon, *n.* salone, *m.*   ~ *car*, vagonesalotto, *m.*, vettura salone, *f.*

salt, *n.* sale, *m.*   ~ *cellar*, saliera, *f.* *old* ~, lupo di mare, vecchio marinaio, *m.*   ~ *industry*, fabbricazione di sale, *f.*   ~ *lake*, lago salato, *m.*   ~*-meadow sheep & ~-meadow mutton*, castrato di maremma, *m.*   ~ *pan*, salina, *f.*   ~ *pork*, maiale salato, *m.*   ~ *provisions*, salumi, *m.pl.*, carni salate, *f.pl.*   ~ *spoon*, cucchiaino pel (per) sale, *m.*   ~ *water*, acqua salata, acqua di mare, *f.* ~*-water fish*, pesce di mare, *m.*; (*caught & fresh*) pesci di mare freschi, *m.pl.*   ~*-water fishing*, pesca di mare, *f.*   ~ *works*, saline, *f.pl.* ¶ *v.t.* salare, condire con sale. ~**ing**, *n.* salatura, salata, *f.*, (il) salare, *m.* ~**ness**, *n.* salsedine, *f.*, gusto salato, *m.* **saltern**, *n.* salina, *f.* **saltpetre**, *n.* salnitro, *m.*

salubrious, *a.* salubre.

saluki, *n.* levriere d'Africa, *m.*

salutary, *a.* salutare. **salutation**, *n.* saluto, *m.*; salutazione, *f.*; inchino, *m.*, riverenza, *f.* **salute**, *n.* saluto, *m.*; (*guns*) salva, *f.* ¶ *v.t.* salutare; fare gli onori a, inchinarsi a; dare il benvenuto a.

salvage, *n.* salvataggio; ricupero, *m.* (da naufragio). ¶ *v.t.* salvare, ricuperare. ~ *money*, diritti di ricupero, *m.pl.*   **salvation**, *n.* salvazione, salute, *f.* *S* ~ *Army*, Esercito della Salute, *m.*   **salve**, *n.* unguento, balsamo, *m.* ¶ (*fig.*) *v.t.* salvare; calmare, rimediare a.

salver, *n.* vassoio, *m.*, sottocoppa, *m.inv.*

salvo, *n.* salva, *f.*

salvor, *n.* salvatore, *m.*

Salzburg, *m.* Salisburgo, *f.*

same, *a.* stesso, medesimo. *much the* ~, press'a poco.   ~**ness**, *n.* uniformità, monotonia, *f.*

sample, *n.* campione, *m.*; mostra, *f.*, saggio, esempio, esemplare; tipo, *m.* *book of* ~, campionario, *m.* ¶ *v.t.* assaggiare, prendere saggio di, provare; campionare; subire; (*taste wines, &c.*) assaggiare. **sampler**, *n.* modello di ricamo, *m.*; assaggiatore, *m.*

Samson, *n.* Sansone, *m.*

sanatorium, *n.* sanatorio, *m.*, casa di salute, *f.*

sanctify, *v.t.* santificare. **sanctimo-**

nious, *a. &* ~ *person,* n., santocchio, santerello, bigotto, bacchettone, graffiasanti, pinzochero, *m.* **sanction,** *n.* sanzione, *f.*; permesso, *m.* ¶ *v.t.* sanzionare; permettere; sancire. **sanctity,** *n.*, santità, *f.* **sanctuary,** *n.* santuario, asilo, rifugio, *m.* **sanctum,** *n.* gabinetto, santo dei santi, *m.*

sand, *n.* sabbia, rena, *f.*; (*pl.*) spiaggia, *f.* *quick*~(*s*), sabbia mobile, *f.* ~*bag,* sacco di terra, *m.* ~*bank,* banco di sabbia, *m.* ~ *blast,* getto di sabbia, *m.* ~*flats,* piano sabbioso, *m.* ~*fly,* specie di moscerino. ~ *glass,* oriolo a polvere, *m.* ~ *hill,* duna, *f.* ~ *martin,* rondinella di mare, delle rive, *f.* ~*paper,* *n.* carta vetro, carta vetrata, *f.* (*v.t.*) soffregare con carta vetro. ~ *piper,* beccaccino, *m.* ~ *pit,* renaio, *m.*, cava di rena, di sabbia, *f.* ~*stone,* arenaria, *f.* ¶ *v.t.* sabbiare, cospargere di rena, di sabbia; ~ (*up*), insabbiare.

sandal, *n.* sandalo, *m.* ~(*wood*), [legno di] sandalo, *m.*

sandwich, *n.* panino gravido, *m.* ~*man,* uomo reclame, *m.*

sandy, *a.* sabbioso, arenoso; granuloso. ~ *hair,* capelli rossi, *m.pl.*

sane, *a.* sano (di mente), ragionevole, equilibrato.

sanguinary, *a.* sanguinario. **sanguine,** *a.* ottimistico, confidente, pieno di speranza; (*full-blooded*) sanguigno.

sanitary, *a.* sanitario; igienico. ~ *dust bin,* secchia igienica, *f.* ~ *inspector,* ispettore sanitario, *m.* ~ *pipe,* tubo igienico, *m.* ~ *towel,* pannilino, *m.* **sanitate,** *v.t.* rendere igienico. **sanitation,** *n.* regime sanitario, *m.*, igiene, *f.*

sanity, *n.* sanità di mente, *f.*, buon senso, equilibrio, *m.*

Santa Claus, Befana, *f.*

sap, *n.* succo, *m.*; linfa, *f.*; (*Mil.*) trincea, *f.*; scavo d'approccio, *m.* ~ *wood,* alburno, *m.* ¶ *v.t.* zappare, minare; sottominare. **sapling,** *n.* arboscello, *m.* **sapper,** *n.* zappatore, *m.*; ~s, (*Mil.*) *n.pl.* genio, *m.*

sapphire, *n.* zaffiro, *m.*

sappy, *a.* sugoso, succoso.

Saragossa, *n.* Saragozza, *f.*

Saratoga [**trunk**], *n.* grosso baule, *m.*

sarcasm, *n.* sarcasmo, *m.* **sarcastic,** *a.* sarcastico.

sarcophagus, *n.* sarcofago, *m.* (*pl.* -agi).

sardine, *n.* sardina, *f.*

Sardinia, *n.* la Sardegna, *f.* **Sardinian,** *a.* sardo. ¶ *n.* sardo, *m.*, -a, *f.*

sardonic, *a.* sardonico.

sardonyx, *n.* sardonice, *f.*

sarsaparilla, *n.* salsapariglia, *f.*

sarsenet, *n.* taffetà, *m.*

sash, *n.* fascia (di seta), sciarpa, *f.*; (*window*) intelaio, *m.* ~ *window,* finestra all'inglese, finestra a cateratta, *f.*

Satan, *n.* Satana, *m.* ~*ic,* *a.* satanico.

satchel, *n.* borsa, *f.*, sacchetto, *m.*, cartella, *f.*

sate, *v.t.* saziare.

sateen *or* **satinet**[**te**], *n.* rasato, satinato, *m.*

satellite, *n. & att.* satellite, *m.*, *att.*

satiate, *v.t.* saziare, satollare. **satiety,** *n.* sazietà, *f.*

satin, *n.* raso, *m.* ~ *stitch* (*Emb.*) plumetis, *m.* punto raso, *m.* ~*wood,* legno satinato, *m.* ~*y,* *a.* rasato, lustro.

satire, *n.* satira, *f.* **satiric** *& ~al,* *a.* satirico. **satirist,** *n.* satirico, *m.* **satirize,** *v.t.* satireggiare.

satisfaction, *n.* soddisfazione; contentezza, *f.*; appagamento, *m.* **satisfactorily,** *ad.* in modo soddisfacente. **satisfactory,** *a.* soddisfacente. **satisfy,** *v.t.* soddisfare, soddisfare a, appagare, contentare; convincere.

saturate, *v.t.* saturare.

Saturday, *n.* sabato, *m.*

saturnalia, *n.pl.* saturnali, *m.pl.*

saturnine, *a.* fosco, cupo, taciturno, tetro; (*Med.*) saturnino.

satyr, *n.* satiro, *m.*

sauce, *n.* salsa, *f.*; condimento, *m.*; (*fig.*) impertinenza, *f.* ~ *boat,* salsiera, *f.* ~ *ladle,* cucchiaio per la salsa, *m.* ~*pan,* casseruola, *f.* **saucer,** *n.* sottocoppa, *m.inv.*, piattello, *m.*; (*artist's*) ciotola, *f.* **saucy,** *a.* impertinente, furbetto.

sauerkraut, *n.* salcrautte, *m.*

saunter, *v.i.* girandolare, andare a zonzo, bighellonare. ~*ing,* *n.* girandolamento, il girovagare, il girandolare, *m.*, passeggiata oziosa, *f.*

sausage, *n.* (*fresh*) salsiccia, *f.*; mortadella (di Bologna); (*smoked*) salame, *m.* ~ *balloon,* pallone frenato, *m.*

sauté potatoes, patate sautées, *f.pl.*

savage, *a.* selvaggio; barbaro, crudele, fiero, feroce. ¶ *n.* selvaggio, *m.*, -a, *f.*, barbaro, *m.*, -a, *f.*, cannibale, *m.f.*

~**ry,** *n.* stato selvaggio, *m.*; brutalità, ferocia, *f.*

savant, *n.* sapiente, dotto, erudito, *m.*

save, *v.t.* salvare, campare; economizzare, mettere da parte, conservare, guadagnare, non perdere; evitare. (*v.i.*) risparmiare, economizzare. ¶ *pr.* salvo, eccetto, fuorché, ad eccezione di. **saving,** *n.* risparmio, *m.*, economia, *f.* ~ *clause,* clausola restrittiva, *f.* ~*s bank,* cassa di risparmio, *f.* **the Saviour,** il Salvatore, il Redentore, *m.*

savory (*Bot.*), *n.* santoreggia, *f.* **savour,** *n.* sapore, gusto, *m.* *to* ~ *of,* sapere di, sentire (di). **savoury,** *a.* saporito, gustoso, squisito; soave; ¶ *n.* piatto salato, *m.* ~ *herbs,* verdura, *f.* ~ *omelet(te),* frittata di verdura, *f.*

Savoy, *n.* la Savoia, *f.* **s** ~, (*cavolo*) cappuccio, *m.*

saw, *n.* sega, *f.*; proverbio, motto, adagio, *m.* ~ *bones,* studente in medicina, *m.* ~*dust,* segatura, *f.* ~*mill,* segheria, *f.* ¶ *v.t. ir.* segare. ~ *off,* segare. ~*ing,* *n.* segatura, *f.* ~*yer,* *n.* segantino, segatore, *m.*

saxhorn, *n.* bas[so] tuba, *f.*

saxifrage, *n.* sassifraga, *f.*

Saxon, *a.* sassone. ¶ *n.* sassone, *m.f.* **Saxony,** *n.* la Sassonia, *f.*

saxophone, *n.* sassofono, *m.*

say, *n.* dire, *m.*, parola, *f.*, discorso, *m.* ¶ *v.t. & i. ir.* dire; recitare; parlare. ¶ (*so much*) diciamo; come dire; ossia, cioè; *I* ~*!* Senta! senti! dica! dimmi un po'! dite dunque! *you don't* ~ *so!* non è possibile! non mi fa celia! ~ *again,* ridire, ripetere. **saying,** *n.* motto, detto; adagio, proverbio, *m.* ~*s & doings,* parole e fatti.

scab, *n.* crosta, *f.* (*Med.*) tigna, *f.*; (*Vet.*) rogna, scabbia, *f.*; (*Hort.*) rogna, *f.*

scabbard, *n.* fodero, *m.*

scabby *&* **scabious,** *a.* rognoso, scabbioso; coperto di croste; tignoso; **scabious** (*Bot.*), *n.* scabbiosa, *f.*

scaffold, *n.* palco, ponteggio; patibolo, *m.* ~**ing,** *n.,* impalcatura, *f.* ~ *pole,* antenna, *f.*

scald, *n.* scottatura, *f.* ¶ *v.t.* scottare; ustionare.

scale, *n.* scaglia, squama; piastra (*metal*), *f.*; scala, proporzione, *f.*; (*Mus.*) gamma, *f.* ~(*pan*), piatto, *m.*; (*pl.*) bilancia, *f.*, basculla, *f.* ~ *maker,* bilanciaio, *m.* ¶ *v.t.* scalare; salire; (*Mech.*) graduare, pesare;

(*wall*) scavalcare, arrampicarsi su; (*boiler*) forare, scrostare; (*v.i.*) squamarsi.

scallop, *n.* (*Mol.*) petonchio, *m.*, pettine, *m.*; (*edging*) dentellatura, *f.*, festone, *m.*, smerlo, *m.* ¶ *v.t.* festonare, tagliare a festoni; smerlare.

scalp, *n.* cuoio capelluto, cranio, *m.*; (*trophy*) cotenna, *f.*; pelle del cranio, *f.* ~ *massage,* frizione, *f.* ¶ *v.t.* scotennare.

scalpel, *n.* scalpello, *m.*

scaly, *a.* squamoso, scaglioso.

scamp, *n.* furfante, mascalzone, cialtrone, farabutto, gaglioffo, tristo, cattivo soggetto, *m.* ¶ *v.t.* acciabattare, abborracciare.

scamper away, svignarsela (correndo); darsela a gambe, battersela.

scan, *v.t.* scrutare, guardare da vicino; (*fig. of conduct*) sindacare; (*verse*) scandire.

scandal, *n.* scandalo, *m.*; rumore, *m.*; maldicenza, *f.*; vergogna, *f.* ~*monger,* maldicente, *m.f.*, malalingua, *f.* ~*ize,* *v.t.* scandalizzare. ~*ous,* *a.* ontoso; scandaloso, calunnioso.

Scandinavia, *n.* la Scandinavia, *f.* **Scandinavian,** *a.* scandinavo. ¶ *n.* scandinavo, *m.*, -a, *f.*

scansion, *n.* scansione, *f.*

scant[y], *a.* scarso, esiguo, ristretto; povero, meschino; (*attire*) sommario.

scape (*Bot.*), *n.* peduncolo, *m.* ~*goat,* capro espiatorio, *m.* ~*grace,* scapestrato, cattivo soggetto, *m.*; (*child*) birichino, monello, *m.*

scar, *n.* cicatrice, *f.*, sfregio, frinzello, *m.*; rupe scoscesa, *f.* ¶ *v.t.* sfregiare, cicatrizzare, sfigurare.

scarab, *n.* scarabeo, *m.*

scarce, *a.* scarso, raro; (*time*) breve. ~*ly,* *a.* appena; scarsamente. ~ *anyone,* ~ *anything,* quasi nessuno, quasi nulla. ~ *ever,* quasi mai. **scarcity,** *n.* scarsezza, *f.*, rarità, *f.*; carestia, penuria, *f.*

scare, *n.* spavento, allarme, *m.* ¶ *v.t.* spaventare, impaurire, sgomentare. ~*crow,* *n.* spauracchio, *m.*

scarf, *n.* sciarpa; cravatta; ciarpa, *f.*; fazzoletto da collo, *m.*

scarify, *v.t.* scarificare.

scarlatina, *n.* or **scarlet fever,** scarlattina, *f.* **scarlet,** *n. & a.,* scarlatto, *m. & a.* ~ *runner,* fagiuolo di Spagna, *m.*

scarp, *n.* scarpa, scarpata, *f.*

scatheless, *a.* illeso, incolume, **senza**

danno. **scathing,** *a.* scottante, mordace, feroce, fiero. ~ *attack* (*fig.*) stroncatura, *f.*

scatter, *v.t.* spargere, sparpagliare, disseminare, disperdere; sconfiggere, sbaragliare. (*v.i.*) spargersi; spergersi; disperdersi, sbandarsi.

scavenge, *v.t.* spazzare, scopare. **scavenger,** *n.* spazzino, spazzaturaio, *m.*

scenario, *n.* scenario; canovaccio (d'una commedia), *m.* **scene,** *n.* scena, quinta, *f.*; teatro, *m.*; spettacolo, quadro, *m.*; veduta, *f.*, colpo d'occhio, *m. behind the* ~s, dietro le scene, dietro le quinte. ~ *painter,* scenografo, *m.*, pittore di scenari, *m.* ~ *shifter,* macchinista, *m.* ~ *shifting,* cambiamento di scena, *m.* ~**ry,** *n.* paesaggi, *m.pl.*; (*Theat.*) scenario, *m.* **scenic,** *a.* scenico. ~ *railway,* montagne russe, *f.pl.*

scent, *n.* odore, profumo; odorato, fiuto, sentore, *m.*; pista, *f.* ~*bag,* sacchetto profumato, *m.* ~ *bottle,* boccetta di profumo, boccetta da odori, *f. to throw off the* ~, far perdere la traccia a. ¶ *v.t.* profumare; fiutare, sentire, seguire la pista (la traccia) di. ~**ed,** *a.* profumato, odoroso. ~**less,** *a.* inodoro.

sceptic, *n.* & ~**al,** *a.* scettico. **scepticism,** *n.* scetticismo.

sceptre, *n.* scettro, *m.*

Schaffhausen, *n.* Sciaffusa, *f.*

schedule, *n.* lista, *f.*, inventario annesso, *m.*, bilancio, listino, *m.*; (*Inc. Tax*) cedola, *f.*

Scheldt (the), la Schelda, *f.*

scheme, *n.* piano, progetto, disegno, prospetto, *m.*; schema, *m.*; combinazione, disposizione, *f.* ¶ *v.t.* divisare, progettare; macchinare. (*v.i.*) fare (dei) progetti; intrigare. **schemer,** *n.* progettista; intrigante, *m.f.* **scheming,** *n.* progetti, *m.pl.*; macchinazioni, *f.pl.* ¶ *a.* astuto, intrigante, scaltro.

schism, *n.* scisma, *m.*

schist, *n.* schisto, *m.* ~**ose,** *a.* schistoso.

schizophrenia, *n.* schizofrenia, *f.* ~**phrenic,** *a.* & *m.* schizofrenico, *a.m.*

scholar, *n.* (*pupil*) allievo, *m.*, -a, *f.*, alunno, *m.*, -a, *f.*, scolaro, *m.*, -a, *f.*, studente, *m.*, -essa, *f.*; (*learned person*) erudito, *m.*, -a, *f.*, letterato, *m*, -a, *f.*, studioso, *m.*, -a, *f.* ~**ly,** *a.* erudito ,dotto, scienziato. ~**ship,** *n.*

erudizione, scienza, *f.*, sapere, *m.*; borsa (di studio), *f.* **scholastic,** *a.* scolastico. **school,** *n.* scuola; liceo, collegio, ginnasio, *m.*; classe, *f.*; corso, *m.*; seminario, *m.*; convitto, *m.*; accademia, *f.*; (*music*) conservatorio, *m.*; (*of fish*) banco, *m.*; sciame, *m.* ~ *book,* libro scolastico, *m.* ~*boy,* ~*girl,* scolaro, *m.*, -a, *f.*, alunno, *m.*, -a, *f.* ~ *fees,* tasse scolastiche, *f.pl.* ~ *fellow,* condiscepolo, *m.*, compagno di scuola, *m.*, compagna di scuola, *f.* ~ *for defective children,* scuola di anormali, *f.* ~*master,* ~*mistress,* maestro (di scuola), *m.*, maestra (di scuola), *f.*, insegnante, *m.f.*, istitutore, *m.*, -trice, *f.*; direttore (di convitto, pensionato, &c.), *m.*, direttrice, *f.* ~ *of dancing,* scuola di ballo, *f.* ~*room,* classe, aula scolastica, *f.* **schooling,** *n.* insegnamento, *m.*, istruzione, *f.*; lezioni, *f.pl.*

schooner, *n.* goletta (a tre alberi), *f.*

sciatic, *a.* sciatico. **sciatica,** *n.* sciatica, *f.*

science, *n.* scienza, *f.* **scientific,** *a.* scientifico, (*instruments*) scientifico, di precisione. **scientist,** *n.* scienziato, *m.*, -a, *f.*

Scilly Islands, or **Isles,** le isole Sorlinghe, *f.pl.*

scimitar, *n.* scimitarra, *f.*

scintillate, *v.i.* scintillare.

sciolist, *n.* semidotto, saputello, *m.*

scion, *n.* (*Hort.*) pollone, *m.*, rimessiticcio; (*pers.*) rampollo, *m.*, discendente, *m.*

scissors, *n.pl.* forbici, *f.pl.* (*large*) cesoie, *f.pl.*, cesoia, *f.*; with ~ & *paste,* (*fig.*) lavoro di compilazione.

sclerosis, *n.* sclerosi, *f.*

scoff at, sbeffeggiare, deridere, farsi giuoco di, schernire. **scoffer,** *n.* canzonatore, burlone, beffardo, schernitore, cinico, *m.* **scoffing,** *n.* derisione, canzonatura, *f.*

scold, *n.* brontolona, megera, *f.* ¶ *v.t.* sgridare, rampognare, dare una lavata di capo a; (*v.i.*) bisticciare, strillare, schiamazzare, vociare.

scollop, *n.* & *v.* Same as *scallop.*

sconce, *n.* sostegno a bracci, mensola, *f.*; candelabro a muro, *m.*

scoop, *n.* votazza, paletta, *f.*, cucchiaione, *m.*, sonda, *f.*, sassola, *f.*; (*fig.*, *Press*) colpo, *m.* ~ **out,** scavare.

scooter, *n.* (*child's*) monopattino, *m.*; (*motor*) motopattino, *m.*

scope, *n.* scopo, disegno, *m.*; portata

estensione, *f.*, spazio, *m.*, limiti, *m.pl.* *free* ~, libertà d'azione, *f.*, campo libero, *m.*

scorch, *v.t.* abbruciacchiare, scottare, ustionare, *(skin, face)* abbronzire.

score, *n.* tacca, linea, tratta, *f.*; scotto, conto; debito, *m.*; *(20)* ventina, *f.*; ragione, *f.*; punto, numero dei punti, punteggio, *m.*; *(Mus.)* spartito, *m.*, partitura, *f.*; orchestrazione, *f.* ¶ *v.t.* intaccare; marcare, segnare, fare; *(Mus.)* orchestrare. **scorer,** *n.* marcatore, segnatore (dei punti), *m.*

scoria, *n.* scoria, *f.*

scoring, *n.* segnatura, *f.*; orchestrazione, *f.* ~ *board* (*Bil.*), pallottoliere, *m.* ~ *card* (*Golf*), carta di risultati, *f.*

scorn, *n.* disdegno, sdegno, disprezzo, scherno, ludibrio; scorno, *m.* *laugh to* ~, deridere, farsi beffa di. ¶ *v.t.* schernire, sdegnare, disprezzare; sprezzare; scornare, dispregiare, tenere a vile. ~**er,** *n.* schernitore, *m.*, -trice, *f.*; sprezzatore, *m.*, -trice, *f.*; ~**ful,** *a.* sdegnoso, sprezzante.

scorpion, *n.* scorpione, *m.*

scotch, *v.t.* sfregiare; sopprimere.

Scotch or **Scots,** *a.* scozzese. ~*man,* ~*woman,* & *Scot,* scozzese, *m.f.* *the* ~, gli scozzesi, il popolo scozzese. ~ *mist,* nebbia spessa, pioggerella, *f.*

scot-free, *a.* immune, indenne, impunito.

Scotland, *n.* la Scozia, *f.* ~ *Yard,* [sede della] polizia metropolitana londinese, *f.* **Scottish,** *a.* scozzese.

scoundrel, *n.* ribaldo, scellerato, malandrino, gaglioffo, miserabile, *m.*

scour, *n.* flusso; *(wool)* detersivo, *m.* ¶ *v.t.* ripulire, forbire; sgrassare; scorrere, percorrere, perlustrare, girare per; *(seas)* solcare, percorrere; *(country)* battere.

scourge, *n.* *(whip)* sferza, frusta, *f.*; *(plague)* flagello, *m.* ¶ *v.t.* sferzare, frustare; flagellare.

scout, *n.* esploratore, *m.*; scolta, *f.*; *(warship)* vedetta, nave in vedetta, nave esploratrice, *f.* *boy* ~, giovane esploratore, *m.* ~ *master,* capo esploratore, *m.* ¶ *v.i.* andare alla scoperta, esplorare. *(v.t.)* deridere, respingere con disdegno.

scowl, *v.i.* aggrottar le ciglia, guardar torvo. ¶ *n.* sguardo torvo, *m.* ~**ing,** *a.* torvo, arcigno, accigliato.

scrag, *n.* *(mutton)* collottola, *f.*; *(pers.)* scheletro, *m.* ~ *end,* collo, *m.* **scraggy,** *a.* scarno, mag.¿, pelle e ossa.

scramble, *n.* parapiglia, confusione, zuffa, *f.*; *(for place)*, lotta, *f.*; scalata affrettata. ¶ *v.i.* dibattersi, urtarsi, avventarsi. ~ *up,* arrampicarsi, inerpicarsi. ~*d eggs,* uova strapazzate, *f.pl.*

scrap, *n.* pezzettino, tozzo, frammento, briciolo; resto, squarcio, *m.*; *(metal)* rottame; *(pl.)* rifiuti, rimasugli, *m.pl.* ~ *book,* libro di squarci, album, *m.* ~ *iron,* rottami di ferro, *m.pl.*, ferraccio, *m.* ¶ *v.t.* rigettare, gettare al rottame; fare a meno di.

scrape, *v.t.* raschiare, grattare; razzolare, raspare, sfangare; *(Golf)* scalfire. ¶ *n.* impiccio, imbroglio, *m.* **scraper,** *n.* raschietto, raschiatoio, *m.*; *(mat)* pulisciscarpe, *m.inv.* **scrapings,** *n.pl.* raschiature, spazzature, *f.pl.*; *(savings)* risparmi, *pl.m.*, economie, *f.pl.*

scratch, *n.* graffiatura, *f.*, graffio, *m.*, sgraffiata, scalfittura, *f.*; colpo di zampa, *m.*; *(Sport)* ~ & ~ *line,* linea di partenza, *f.* *to come up to* ~, *(fig.)* far fronte ai propri impegni. ~ *race,* corsa a pari condizioni per tutti i concorrenti, *f.* ¶ *v.t.* grattare, graffiare, raspare; scarabocchiare, scalfire; *(Sport)* ritirare. ~ *out,* scancellare, grattare.

scrawl, *n.* scarabocchio, *m.* ¶ *v.t.* & *i.* scarabocchiare.

scream & **screech,** *n.* grido (acuto), strido, strillo, urlo, *m.* ¶ *v.i.* & *t.* strillare, gridare, vociare. *screech owl,* barbagianni, *m.*, civetta, *f.*

screed, *n.* letterone, *m.*, tirata, filastrocca, *f.*

screen, *n.* paravento, parafuoco, *m.*, cortina, *f.*; riparo, *m.*, difesa, *f.*; schermo, *m.*; *(choir)* tramezzo, *m.*; *(sieve)* crivello, *m.*; *(cinema)* schermo, *m.* ~ *door,* controporta, *f.* ¶ *v.t.* riparare, mettere al coperto; difendere, proteggere; sottrarre; vagliare; *(cinema)* proiettare. - ~*ings,* *n.pl.* mondiglia, *f.*

screw, *n.* vite; elica, *f.*; *(on ball)* effetto, *m.*; *(pers.)* spilorcio, avaraccio, *m.* ~ *cutting,* impanatura, *f.* ~*driver,* cacciavite, *m.* ~ *eye,* occhiello della vite, *m.*; ~ *jack,* martinetto a vite, *m.*, binda a vite, *f.* ~ *plate,* filiera, *f.* ~ *steamer,* vapore ad elica, *m.* ¶ *v.t.* avvitare.

scribble, *n.* scarabocchio, *m.* ¶ *v.t.* scarabocchiare, scribacchiare; *(v.i. of author)* scribacchiare. **scribbler,** *n.* scribacchino, imbrattacarte, scrittoruccio, *m. scribbling block,* carta (da lettere) in blocco, *f.* **scribe,** *n.* scrivano, scriba, *m.*

scrimmage, *n.* mischia, zuffa, *f.,* tafferuglio, *m.*

scrip, *n.* certificato provvisorio, *m.;* titoli, valori, *m.pl.* ~ *of paper,* pezzo di carta, *m.*

Scripture, *n. oft pl.* Sacra Scrittura, la Bibbia, *f.*

scrofula, *n.* scrofola, *f.* **scrofulous,** *a.* scrofoloso.

scroll, *n.* pergamena, *f.;* rotolo, *m.; (Arch.)* voluta, *f.*

scrub *(bush), n.* macchia, *f.* ¶ *v.t.* spazzolare; lavare, fregare. ~**bing,** *n.* spazzolata, strofinata, *f. scrubbing brush,* spazzola dura, *f.,* setolino, *m.*

scruff of the neck, nuca, *f.,* pelle del collo, *f.*

scrum[mage], *n.* mischia, *f.;* scompiglio, *m.*

scrunch, *v.t.* schiacciare, sgretolare.

scruple, *n.* scrupolo, *m.; (apothecaries' measure)* = 1·184 millilitres; *(apothecaries' weight)* = 1·296 grammes. ~ *to,* farsi scrupolo di, esitare. **scrupulous,** *a.* scrupoloso.

scrutineer, *n.* scrutatore, *m.* **scrutinize,** *v.t.* scrutare, scrutinare, esaminare minuziosamente. **scrutiny,** *n.* esame minuzioso; *(votes)* scrutinio, *m.*

scuffle, *n.* zuffa, rissa, baruffa, *f.;* tafferuglio, *m.*

scull, *n.* piccolo remo (a due pale), *m.,* pagaia, *f.; (stern oar)* remo a pertica, *m.* ¶ *v.t.* remare; *(v.i.)* vogare all'inglese. ~**er,** *n.* rematore, *m.*

scullery, *n.* lavatoio (di cucina), *m.* ~ *maid,* sguattera, *f.*

scullion, *n.* sguattero, *m.*

sculptor, *n.* scultore, *m.* **sculptress,** *n.* scultrice, *f.* **sculpture,** *n.* scultura, *f.* ¶ *v.t.* scolpire.

scum, *n.* schiuma, *f.; (fig.)* schiuma; feccia, *f.,* rifiuto, sudiciume, *m.*

scumble, *n.* smorzatura di tinte, di colori. ¶ *v.t.* smorzare, attenuare le tinte di.

scupper, *n.* ombrinale, *m.* ¶ *v.t.* affondare.

scurf, *n.* forfora; scabbia, crosta di piaga, *f.* ~ *comb,* piccolo pettine, pettine per togliere la forfora, *m.*

scurrilous, *a.* scurrile, oltraggioso, contumelioso, sboccato.

scurvy, *n.* scorbuto, *m.* ¶ *a.* meschino, basso, sprezzabile.

scutcheon, *n.* stemma, *m.,* scudo, *m.*

scuttle, *n.* secchio, *m. (coal); (Naut.)* portello, piccolo boccaporto, *m.* ¶ *v.t.* perforare una nave per affondarla; *v.i.* andarsene in gran fretta, fuggire alla chetichella.

scythe, *n.* falce, *f.*

sea, *n.* mare, *m.;* colpo di mare, *m.;* ondata, *f.,* maroso, *m., choppy* ~, mare corto. *cross* ~, mare confuso. *head* ~, mare di prua. ~*board,* litorale, *m.* ~ *boots,* stivaloni impermeabili, *m.pl.* ~ *bream,* reina di mare, *f.,* pagello, *m.* ~ *breeze,* brezza marina, *f.* ~ *coast,* costa del mare, *f.* ~ *cow,* vacca marina, *f.,* lamantino, *m.;* ~*-damaged,* avariato. ~*farer* or ~*faring man,* marinaio, uomo di mare, *m.* ~*faring people,* gente di mare, *f.;* popolo marinaro, *m.* ~ *fishing,* pesca di mare, *f.* ~*going* (ship), di mare. ~*gull,* gabbiano, *m.* ~*horse,* cavallo marino; ippocampo, *m.* ~ *kale,* cavolo marino, *m. to have got one's* ~ *legs,* (avere) il piede marino. ~ *level,* livello del mare, *m.* ~ *lion,* otaria, *f.* ~ *man,* marinaio, uomo di mare, *m.; (skilful)* buon marinaio, manovratore, *m. in a* ~*manlike manner,* da buon marinaio. ~*manship,* arte marinaresca; manovra, *f.* ~ *mark,* meda, *m.;* faro, *m.* ~*men,* gente di mare, *f.* ~*nymph,* ninfa marina, nereide, sirena, *f.* ~*plane,* idroplano, idrovolante, *m.* ~*power,* potere sul mare, *m.;* potenza marittima, *f.* ~*scape,* ~ *piece,* marina, *f.* ~ *shore,* riva del mare, *f.* ~ *sickness,* mal di mare, *m. to be* ~*sick,* soffrire di m. di. m. ~*side,* spiaggia, *f.,* lido, *m.* ~*side resort,* spiaggia, *(bathing),* stazione balneare, *f.* ~ *urchin,* riccio di mare, *m.* ~ *wall,* diga, *f.* ~*ware,* relitti, *m.pl.* ~*weed,* pianta marina, alga, *f.,* fuco, *m.* ~*worthy,* atto al mare, atto alla navigazione.

seal, *n.* suggello; sigillo; timbro, bollo, *m.; (bottle)* capsula, *f.; (fig.)* impronta, *f.; (Zool.)* foca, *f.,* vitello marino, *m.* ~*skin,* pelle di foca, *f.* ¶ *v.t.* sigillare, suggellare; confermare *(fig.).* ~*ed book (fig.),* mistero, *m.* ~*ing wax,* ceralacca, *f.*

seam, *n.* cucitura, costura, *f.; (Geol.)* vena, *f.,* giacimento, strato, *m.,* filone, *m.* ~ *stitch,* (Need.) sopraggitto, *m.* ¶ *v.t.* far la costura a, cucire. ~**less,** *a.* senza cucitura. **seamstress,** *n.* cucitrice, *f. the seamy side (lit. & fig.),* il rovescio, *m.*

seance, *n.* seduta, *f.*

sear, *a.* disseccato, appassito, avvizzito. ¶ *v.t.* bruciare, cauterizzare, disseccare.

search, *n.* ricerca, inchiesta, *f.* (*customs*) visita, *f.*; (*Law*) perquisizione, *f.* ~*light*, proiettore, *m.* ~ *warrant*, mandato di perquisizione, *m.* ¶ *v.t.* scrutare, esaminare, frugare, ricercare; (*customs*) visitare, (*Law*) perquisire. ~**er,** *n.* ricercatore, *m.*, -trice, *f.*, indagatore, investigatore, frugatore, *m.* ~**ing,** *a.* penetrante, scrutatore, incalzante.

season, *n.* stagione, *f.*; tempo, tempo opportuno, *m.* ~ *ticket*, biglietto d'abbonamento, *m.* ¶ *v.t.* condire; acconciare, ammanire; stagionare, abituare, acclimare; (*wood*) stagionare; (*fig.*) agguerrire. ~**able,** *a.* di stagione, opportuno. ~**ably,** *ad.* a proposito, a modo, convenevolmente. ~**ing,** (*Cook*) *n.* condimento, *m.*

seat, *n.* sede, *f.*, posto, *m.*; sedia, seggiola, *f.*, sedile, *m.*; banco, seggio, scanno, *m.*; casa, residenza, villa, *f.*, castello; centro; teatro (*war*), *m.*; (*trousers, chair*) fondo, *m.*; (*on horse*) portamento, *m.* ¶ *v.t.* far sedere, porre a sedere; mettere il fondo a . . ., riparare il fondo a. 2-, 3-*seater*, vettura a due, a tre posti, *f.*

secede, *v.i.* ritirarsi, separarsi, fare secessione.

secluded, *p.a.* ritirato, appartato. **seclusion,** *n.* ritiro, *m.*, solitudine, reclusione, *f.*

second, *a.* secondo; (*cousin*) in secondo grado. ~ *childhood*, seconda infanzia, senilità, *f.* ~ *finger*, dito medio, *m.* ~-*hand*, d'occasione, di seconda mano, vecchio, usato. ~ *hand dealer*, rivenditore, *m.*, -trice, *f.*, rigattiere, *m.*, -a, *f.* ~ *lieutenant*, sottotenente, *m.* ~ *one's* ~ *self*, un altro sé stesso. *on* ~ *thoughts*, tutto ben considerato, dopo averci ripensato, dopo matura riflessione. *Charles the S*~, Carlo Secondo. [*on*] *the* ~ *of September*, il due [di] settembre. ¶ *n.* secondo, *m.*; appoggio, protettore, spalleggiatore, *m.*; (*Box.*) secondo, *m.*; (*duel*) padrino, *m.*; (*time*) secondo, minuto secondo. ~ *hand*, lancetta dei secondi, *f.* ~ *of exchange*, seconda di cambio, *f.* ¶ *v.t.* assecondare, favorire, appoggiare, spalleggiare; fare da padrino, da secondo. ~**ary,** *a.* secondario;

accessorio. ~ *school*, scuola media, *f.*; liceo, *m.*; ginnasio, *m.*

secrecy, *n.* segretezza, *f.*, riserbo, segreto, *m.*; discrezione, *f.* **secret,** *a.* segreto; nascosto. ~ *spring*, segreto, *m.* ¶ *n.* segreto, *m.* **secretary,** *n.*, segretario, *m.*, segretaria, *f.* ~ *bird*, serpentario, segretario, *m.* *S*~ *of State for Foreign Affairs* (*Eng.*), Ministro degli Affari Esteri. *Home Secretary* (*Eng.*), Ministro dell'Interno (*It.*). *S*~ *of State for War*, Ministro della Guerra. ~**ship** & **secretariat[e],** *n.* segretariato, *m.* **secrete,** *v.t.* nascondere, separare, segregare; (*Physiol.*) secernere. **secretion,** *n.* secrezione, *f.* **secretive,** *a.* riservato, poco comunicativo, dissimulato. **secretly,** *ad.* segretamente, in segreto, di nascosto, al coperto.

sect, *n.* setta, *f.* ~**arian,** *n.* & *a.* settario, *m.* & *a.*

section, *n.* sezione; divisione, *f.*; spaccato, taglio, *m.*; profilo, *m.* articolo, *m.*; rubrica, *f.* ~ *mark* (§), paragrafo, *m.* ~**al,** *a.* sezionale; parziale; smontabile; (*iron*) profilato; di campanile; (*paper*) a quadretti, a scacchi. **sector,** *n.* settore, *m.*

secular, *a.* secolare, laico; profano; (*100*) secolare.

secure, *a.* sicuro; salvo; certo; al sicuro. ¶ *v.t.* assicurare, far sicuro; render sicuro; fermare; arrestare; garantire; prenotare; impadronirsi di; ottenere. **security,** *n.* sicurezza; sicurtà, cauzione; garanzia, *f.*; (*pl.*) titoli, valori, *m.pl.*; *securities clerk*, cassiere dei titoli, *m.* *collective* ~, sicurezza collettiva, *f.*

sedan [**chair**], *n.* portantina, *f.*

sedate, *a.* posato, calmo, placido, pacato. **sedative,** *n.* & *a.* sedativo, *m.* & *a.*, calmante, *a.* & *m.f.* **sedentary,** *a.* sedentario.

sedge, *n.* carice, *f.*; giunco, *m.* ~ *warbler*, capinera dei giunchi, *f.*

sediment, *n.* sedimento; fondaccio, *m.*

sedition, *n.* sedizione, *f.* **seditious,** *a.* sedizioso.

seduce, *v.t.* sedurre. ~ *from duty*, sviare, distogliere. **seducer,** *n.* seduttore, *m.*, -trice, *f.* **seduction,** *n.* seduzione, *f.* **seductive,** *a.* seducente, seduttore.

sedulous, *a.* assiduo, diligente. ~**ly,** *ad.* assiduamente.

see, *v.t.* & *i.*, *ir.* vedere. ~ *home,* ricondurre, riaccompagnare. ~

through, penetrare; assistere, dare aiuto a. ~ *to*, pensare a, badare a, occuparsi di. ¶ (*vide*) *v. imperative*, vedi, vedere.

seed, *n.* seme, *m.*; semenza, *f.*; chicco, granello, *m.*; (*fig.*) germe, *m.*; razza, progenie, *f.* ~ *corn*, grano per la semina, *m.* ~ *pearls*, perlettine, *f.pl.*, semenza di perle, *f.* ~ *time* (stagione della) semina, *f.* ¶ *v.i.* granire; (*v.t.*) sgranare; ~ *the players* (*Ten.*) selezionare i capiserie. ~*ed player*, caposerie, *m.inv. to run to* ~, tallire. ~**ling**, *n.* pianticella, *f.* (*pl. &* ~-**plot**) semenzaio, *m.* **seedsman**, *n.* granaiolo, semaio, *m.*

seeing, *n.* vista, *f.*, visione, *f.*; (il) vedere, *m.* ~-*in*, televisione, *f.* ~ *that*, visto che, stante che, poiché.

seek, *v.t. & i., ir.* cercare, ricercare; sforzarsi. ~**er**, *n.* cercatore, *m.*, -trice, *f.*

seem, *v.i.* sembrare, parere. **seeming**, *n.* apparenza, *f.*, parere, *m. the* ~ *& the real*, l'essere e il non essere, l'essere e il parere. ¶ *p.a.* apparente, finto, specioso. **seemingly**, *ad.* apparentemente, in apparenza, a ciò che pare. **seemly**, *a.* decente, convenevole, conveniente.

seer, *n.* profeta, *m.*; veggente, *m.f.*; indovino, *m.*

seesaw, *n.* altalena, *f.* ¶ *v.i.* dondolarsi, giocare all'altalena.

seethe, *v.i.* bollire, essere in agitazione.

segment, *n.* segmento, *m.*

segregate, *v.t.* segregare. **segregation**, *n.* segregazione, *f.*

Seidlitz powder, polvere di Sidlitz, *f.*

Seine, (**the**), *n.* (la) Senna, *f.*

seine, (*net*) *n.* sagena, *f.*, sciabica, *f.*

seismic, *a.* sismico. **seismograph**, *n.* sismografo, *m.*

seize, *v.t.* afferrare, acchiappare, agguantare, prendere; cogliere; dare di piglio a; abbrancare; impadronirsi di; impossessarsi di; staggire; sequestrare; confiscare; (*of dog*) pigliare; (*Naut.*) amarrare; (*v.i. Mech.*) grippare; ingranarsi. **seizure**, *n.* presa; cattura; confisca, *f.*; afferramento, *f.*; sequestro; accesso, attacco (di paralisi), *m.*

seldom, *ad.* raramente, di rado.

select, *a.* scelto, eletto. ~ *committee*, commissione d'inchiesta, *f.*; giuria, *f.* ~ *party*, crocchio (d'amici), *m.* ¶ *v.t.* scegliere, eleggere; (*Sport*) selezionare. ~**ion**, *n.* scelta; selezione, raccolta, *f.*; (*pl. from*

writings) brani scelti, *m.pl.*, scelta, *f.* (*Betting*) pronostico, *m.*

self, *n.* persona, *f.*, individuo, *m.*; l'io, io stesso, sé stesso, stesso. ~-*acting*, automatico, semovente. ~-*communion*, raccoglimento, *m.* meditazione, *f.* ~-*conceit*, fatuità, presunzione, *f.* ~-*contained*, indipendente. ~-*control*, padronanza di sé, autocontrollo, *m.* ~-*defence*, legittima difesa, difesa personale. ~-*denial*, abnegazione, astinenza, *f.* ~-*esteem*, amor proprio, *m.* ~-*government*, autonomia, *f.* ~-*importance*, boria, presunzione, elevata opinione di sé stesso. ~-*made man*, figlio del proprio lavoro, delle proprie opere. ~-*opinionated*, ostinato, caparbio. ~-*possession*, sangue freddo, *m.*, disinvoltura, *f.* ~-*reliance*, fiducia in sé stesso, *f.* ~-*respect*, amor proprio, *m.*, giusta fierezza, *f.* ~-*sacrifice*, sacrifizio di sé stesso. ~-*satisfied*, soddisfatto di sé, vanesio; beato. ~-*styled*, sedicente. ~-*taught*, (person) autodidatta, *m.f.* ~-*toning* (*Phot.*) autovirante. ~-*willed*, ostinato, testardo, pertinace.

selfish, *a.* egoista, egoistico; interessato. ~**ness**, *n.* egoismo, *m.*

sell, *v.t. ir.* vendere; esitare; alienare; smerciare; cedere; realizzare; (*v.i.ir*) vendere, vendersi, spacciarsi. ~ *off*, liquidare; spacciare. ~ *up*, vendere, vendere giudiziariamente.

seller, *n.* venditore, *m.*, -trice, *f.*

seltzer [**water**], *n.* acqua di Seltz, *f.*

selvage, -**edge**, *n.* vivagno, *m.*, cimosa, *f.*

semaphore, *n.* semaforo, *m.*

semblance, *n.* sembianza, apparenza, *f.*

semi, *prefix:* ~*breve*, semibreve, *f.* ~*circle*, semicerchio, *m.* ~*colon*, punto e virgola (;), *m.* ~-*detached*, gemello. ~-*final*, semifinale, *f.* ~-*official*, semiufficiale, ufficioso. ~*quaver*, biscroma, *f.* ~*tone*, semitono, *m.*

seminary, *n.* seminario, *m.*

Semitic, *a.* semitico.

semolina, *n.* semolino, *m.*

sempstress, *n.* cucitrice, sarta, *f.*

senate, *n.* senato, *m.* **senator**, *n.* senatore, *m.*

send, *v.t. & i., ir.* mandare, inviare, spedire; lanciare. ~ *away*, mandar via, congedare, licenziare. ~ *back*, rimandare, rimettere, rinviare. ~ *for*, mandare a cercare, fare chiamare, fare venire, mandare a pren-

dere. ~ *to sleep*, addormentare.
~ *to sleep again*, riaddormentare.
~er, *n.* (*of letter*, *parcel*, *&c.*),
mittente, *m.f.*; speditore, *m.*, -trice, *f.*
Senegal, *n.* (il) Senegal, *m.*
senile, *n.* senile. ~ *decay*, decrepitezza, caducità, *f.* **senility,** *n.*,
senilità, *f.*
senior, *a.* seniore, anziano, maggiore;
piú vecchio; principale; primo; capo.
he is ten years my ~, egli ha dieci
anni piú di me. ¶ *n.* maggiore, *m.f.*;
decano, *m.*, -a, *f.*; (*Sports*) seniore,
m. **~ity,** *n.* anzianità, *f.*
senna, *n.* senna, *f.*
sensation, *n.* sensazione, impressione, *f.* **~al,** *a.* sensazionale,
a sensazione. ~ *affair*, dramma, *m.*
sense, *n.* senso; senno, sentimento,
giudizio, *m.*; ragione, *f.*; significato,
m.; buon senso, *m.* ¶ *v.t.* presentire,
indovinare. **~less,** *a.* insensibile;
insulso; insensato; sciocco; assurdo;
senza significato. **sensibility,** *n.*
sensibilità, *f.* **sensible,** *a.* assennato,
giudizioso, ragionevole; saggio; percettibile, sensibile, impressionabile.
sensibly, *ad.* sensibilmente; assennatamente. **sensitive,** *a.* sensitivo,
sensibile; tenero; suscettibile, permaloso. **~ness,** *n.* sensibilità,
delicatezza, suscettibilità, *f.* **sensitized** (*Phot.*), *a.* sensibilizzato.
sensual, *a.* sensuale, carnale. **~ist,** *n.*
uomo sensuale, *m.*; (*Phil.*) sensualista, *m.f.* **~ity,** *n.* sensualità, *f.*
sentence, *n.* sentenza, *f.*, giudizio, *m.*,
condanna, *f.*; (*Gram.*) proposizione,
f., periodo, *m.*, frase, *f.* ¶ *v.t.*
condannare. **sententious,** *a.* sentenzioso.
sentient, *a.* sensibile, cosciente.
sentiment, *n.* sentimento, *m.*;
opinione, idea, *f.* **~al,** *a.* sentimentale. **~ality,** *n.* sentimentalità,
f.
sentinel, *n.* sentinella, *f.* **sentry,** *n.*
sentinella, *f.*; (*mounted*) vedetta, *f.*
~ *box*, garitta, *f.* ~ *duty*, guardia,
fazione, *f.*
separate, *a.* separato, distinto, a
parte. ~ *cell system*, carcerazione
cellulare, *f.* ¶ *v.t.* separare. **separation,** *n.* separazione, *f.*
sepia, *n.* seppia, *f.*
sepoy, *n.* cipai, *m.*
September, *n.* settembre, *m.*
septet[te], *n.* settetto, gruppo di sette,
m.
septic, *a.* settico.
septum, *n.* (*Anat.*) setto, *m.*

sepulchral, *a.* sepolcrale. **sepulchre,**
n. sepolcro, *m.*
sequel, *n.* seguito, *m.*, conseguenza, *f.*
sequence, *n.* serie, successione;
sequela, *f.*; treno, *m.*; (*Cards*)
sequenza, *f.*
sequestered, *p.p.* appartato, ritirato,
isolato, romito. **sequestration**
(*Law*) *n.* sequestro, *m.*
seraglio, *n.* serraglio, *m.*
seraph, *n.* serafino, *m.* **~ic,** *a.*
serafico.
Serbia, *n.* la Serbia, *f.* **Serb[ian],** *a.*
serbo. ¶ *n.* (*pers.*) serbo, *m.*, -a, *f.*;
(*language*) il serbo, *m.*, lingua serba,
f.
sere, *a.* secco, disseccato, adusto,
appassito.
serenade, *n.* serenata, *f.* ¶ *v.t.* fare una
serenata a, fare delle serenate a.
serene, *a.* sereno, calmo. **serenity,** *n.*
serenità, *f.*
serf, *n.* (*Hist.*) servo della gleba;
schiavo, *m.* **~dom,** *n.* servaggio, *m.*;
schiavitú, *f.*
serge, *n.* rascia; saia, *f.*
sergeant, *n.* sergente, *m.*; (*Cavalry*)
sergente (di cavalleria), *m.*; (*Police*)
brigadiere, *m.* ~ *major*, sergente
maggiore, *m.* *lance* ~, caporale
maggiore, *m.*
serial, *a.* di serie, in serie; appartenente
ad una serie, pubblicato a fascicoli.
~ *rights*, diritti di riproduzione nei
giornali e periodici, *m.pl.* ~ [*story*],
romanzo d'appendice, *m.* **seriatim,**
ad. successivamente. **series,** *n.*
serie, *f.*
serif, *n.* (*Typ.*) terminazione obliqua, *f.*
serious, *a.* serio, grave. **~ness,** *n.*
serietà, gravità, *f.* **~ly,** *ad.* sul
serio.
sermon, *n.* predica, *f.*; sermone, *m.*,
orazione, *f.* **~ize,** *v.t.* fare la
predica a, sermoneggiare. **~izer,** *n.*
predicatore tedioso, *m.*
serosity, *n.* sierosità, *f.* **serous,** *a.*
sieroso.
serpent, *n.* serpe, *f.*, serpente, *m.*
serpentine, *a.* serpentino. ¶ *n.*
serpentina, *f.*
serration, *n.* dentellatura, *f.* **serrate[d],** *a.* dentellato, a denti di sega.
serried, *a.* serrato.
serum, *n.* siero, *m.*
servant, *n.* domestico, servitore;
servo, fante; fam'glio; impiegato,
m.; (*pl.*) personale, *m.*, persone di
servizio, *f.pl.*; impiegati, *m.pl.*,
gente; servitú, *f.* *civil* ~, statale, *m.*
~ *girl*, domestica, fantesca, *f.*

~*s' hall*, sala dei domestici, *f.*
serve, *v.t. & i.* servire, prestare servizio; assistere; assecondare; soddisfare; fungere, fare; agire; tener luogo (di) (da); trattare; (*a sentence*) subire, scontare; (*ball*) mandare; (*at table*) portare, apparecchiare, (*worship*) rendere culto a; (*a notice*) notificare, comunicare, intimare a, eseguire. ~ *up*, servire, portare. ¶ (*Ten.*) *n.* servizio, *m.* **server**, (*Ten.*) *n.* battitore, mandatore, *m.*
service, *n.* servizio, impiego, *m.*; ufficio (divino), *m.*; messa, *f.* pratica, *f.*; opera, *f.*, ufficio, ministero, *m.*; vantaggio, *m.*, beneficio, favore, *m.* *civil* ~, pubblica amministrazione, *f.*; (*domestic*) servitú, *f.*, servizio, *m.*; (*china, &c.*) servizio, vasellame, *m.*; (*of writ*) intimazione, notifica, citazione, *f.* *to grow grey in the* ~, invecchiare nel mestiere. ~ *hatch*, sportello della credenza, *m.* ~ *lift*, montavivande, *m.inv.* ~ *line* (*Ten.*) linea di servizio, *f.* ~ *station*, stazione di servizio, *f.* ~ *table*, credenzina, *f.* ~ *tree*, sorbo, *m.* ~ *wagon*, credenzina mobile, *f.* ~**able**, *a.* utile, giovevole, atto al servizio.
serviette, *n.* tovagliolo, *m.* ~ *ring*, anello per tovagliolo, *m.*
servile, *a.* servile. **servility**, *n.* servilità, *f.* **servitude**, *n.* servitú, *f.*, schiavitú, *f.* *penal* ~, lavori forzati, *m.pl.*
sesame, *n.* sesamo, *m.*
session, *n.* sessione; seduta, *f.*
set, *n.* serie, *f.*; assortimento, arredo, treno, seguito, *m.*; collezione, raccolta, *f.*; batteria (da cucina); guarnizione (*buttons, curtains, &c.*); astuccio (*surgical instr., &c.*); vezzo, finimento, guarnimento (*pearls, diamonds, &c.*); insieme, *m.*; servizio (*tea, china*); vasellame; giuoco, *m.*, partita, *f.*; (*group*) circolo, *m.*, brigata; combriccola, cricca, *f.*; (*Elec., Radio*) apparecchio, *m.*; (*paving stone*), ciottolo, selciato, lastrico, *m.*; (*of saw*) allicciatura, *f.*; (*of current*) moto, *m.*; direzione, *f.*; (*sapling*) pollone, *m.*, barbatella, *f.*; (*Theat., television*) scenario, *m.*; (*Ten.*) partita, *f.* ~ *of* (*artificial*) *teeth*, dentiera, *f.*; (*natural*) dentatura, *f.* ~-*back*, arresto, regresso, *m.* (*Arch.*) risega, *f.*; (*illness*) ricaduta, *f.* ~-*off*, compenso, contrappeso, *m.*; (*foil*) incastonatura, *f.*, ciò che **serve** a porre in risalto; (*Arch.*)

risalto, *m.*; (*Law*) controquerela, *f.* ~-*out*, esordio, *m.*; mostra, *f.* ~-*to*, baruffa, zuffa, *f.*, tafferuglio, *m.* ~-*up*, sistemazione, messa a punto, *f.*; portamento, *m.* ¶ *v.t.* *ir.* mettere, porre, collocare; posare; fissare; piantare; mettere a sedere; (*bone*) rimettere; (*dog on, fashion, &c.*) lanciare; (*of dog*), puntare; (*gem*) incastonare, incassare, montare; (*hen*) far covare, mettere a covare; (*sail*) spiegare (le vele), partire; (*saw*) allicciare; (*seal*) apporre; (*shutter* ~ *Phot.*) armare; (*task, example, &c.*), dare; (*tools, razor*) affilare; (*trap*) mettere; tendere; (*type*) comporre; (*watch*) regolare; (*v.i. ir.*) (*thicken, coagulate*) rassegarsi, rappigliarsi; (*harden*) rassodarsi; (*sun*) tramontare; — *about* (*it*), accingersi a (farlo), incominciare. ~ *about*, mettersi a, porsi a; ~ (*pers.*) *against* (*pers.*), ispirare con mala voglia per. ~ *down in writing*, mettere in iscritto, ~ *off* (*figure*) dare risalto a, far risaltare. ~ *on* (*pers.*) lapidare. ~ *out*, partire. ~ *out again*, ripartire. ~ *up*, montare, erigere, stabilire. ¶ *p.a.* ~ *face*, viso immobile, *m.* ~ (*pers.*) *against* (*pers.*), ispirare con mala voglia per. fermo risoluzione, *f.* ~ *screw*, vite di arresto, *v.* di pressione, *f.* ~ *smile*, sorriso fisso, *m.* ~ *speech*, discorso preparato, *m.*
settee, *n.* canapè, divano, *m.*
setter, *n.* cane da fermo, *m.* **setting**, *n.* posa, *f.*, collocamento, *m.* (*bones*) rimessa a posto; (*cement*) presa, *f.*; (*gem*) montatura, incastonatura, *f.*; castone, *m.*; (*Mus.*) messa, *f.* (*Theat.*) messa in scena; (*sun*) tramonto, *m.*, calare, *m.*; (*Typ.*) composizione, *f.* ~ *up* (*Mech.*), montaggio, *m.*, sistemazione, messa a punto, *f.* ~ *aside*, lasciando stare, prescindendo (da), astrazione fatta da. ~ *stick* (*Typ.*) compositoio, *m.* ~ *sun*, sole che tramonta, tramonto, *m.*
settle, *n.* panca, *f.*, sedile, *m.* ¶ *v.t.* fissare, stabilire; decidere, determinare, concludere; accomodare; provvedere; regolare; sistemare; comporre; conciliare, calmare; assegnare; maritare; allogare, colonizzare, popolare; (*account*) saldare; liquidare; accusare, convenire, pattuire; (*property*) intestare, costituire; (*v.i.*) riposare, posare; posarsi,

fissarsi; stabilirsi; **accasarsi**, maritarsi, ammogliarsi; cadere, cessare; accingersi, mettersi; decidersi; calmarsi; (*ground*), cedere, avvallarsi. ~**d**, *p.a.* fisso, stabile; deciso, determinato, concluso; (*weather*) sereno, bello, costante. ~**ment**, *n.* contratto, accomodamento, accordo, *m.*; soluzione, decisione, *f.*; sistemazione, *f.*; regolamento, *m.*; liquidazione, *f.*; accasamento, insediamento; saldo di conti, *m.*; colonia, colonizzazione, *f.* (*Stk. Ex.*) liquidazione, *f.* **settler**, *n.* colono, *m.*

seven, *a. & n.* sette, *a. & m.* **seventeen**, *a. & n.* diciassette, *a. & m.* **seventeenth**, *a. & n.* diciassettesimo, *a. & m.*; diciassette, *m.* ~**ly**, *ad.* in diciassettesimo luogo. **seventh**, *a. & n.* settimo, *a. & m.*; sette, *m.* ~**ly**, *ad.* in settimo luogo, settimo. **seventieth**, *a. & n.* settantesimo, *a. & m.* **seventy**, *a. & n.* settanta, *a. & m.* 71, 72, settantuno, settantadue.

sever, *v.t.* separare; staccare; tagliare. ~**al**, *a.* parecchi, -ie; diversi; distinti. ~**ance**, *n.* separazione, disgiunzione, *f.*, distacco, *m.*

severe, *a.* severo, rigoroso, austero, rigido; forte, grave. **severity**, *n.* severità, *f.*, rigore, *m.*

Seville, *f.* Siviglia, *f.* ~ *orange*, arancia amara, *f.*

sew, *v.t. ir.* cucire. ~**er**, *n.* cucitore, *m.*, -trice, *f.*

sewer, *n.* fogna, *f.*, smaltitoio, *m.* ~ *man*, fognaiuolo, *m.* **sew[er]age**, *n.* fognatura, scolatura, *f.*; immondizie, *f.pl.*; acqua da smaltitoio, *f.*

sewing, *n.* cucitura, *f.* ~ *machine*, macchina da cucire, *f.*

sex, *n.* sesso, *m.* ~ *appeal*, attrazione del sesso, *f.*

sextant, *n.* sestante, *m.*

sextet[te], *n.* sestetto, *m.*

sexton, *n.* sagrestano, *m.*

sexual, *a.* sessuale.

shabby, *a.* meschino, gretto, spregevole; logoro, frusto; malvestito, cencioso.

shackle, *n.* (*Mech.*) anello di trazione, *m.*; (*Naut.*) maniglia, *f.*; pastoia, *f.*; (*fig.*) catene, *f.pl.*; ferri, ceppi, *m.pl.*, manette, *f.pl.* ¶ *v.t.* incatenare; ammanettare; (*fig.*) impacciare, inceppare.

shade, *n.* ombra, *f.*; tenebre, *f.pl.*; scuro, *m.*; tinta, sfumatura, gradazione, *f.*; (*fig.*) tantino, *m.*; schermo,

riparo; spettro, *m.*; (*pl. spirits*) mani, spiriti, *m.pl.* *lamp* ~, paralume, *m.*, ventola, *f.* ¶ *v.t.* ombreggiare, adombrare; riparare, proteggere; (*Art.*) ombreggiare. ~ *off*, digradare, sfumare. **shadow**, *n.* ombra, *f.*; oscurità, *f.*; sembianza, traccia, *f.* ~ *boxing*, pugilato finto, *m.* ¶ *v.t.* ombreggiare; oscurare, velare; (*fig.*) pedinare. **shady**, *a.* ombreggiato; oscuro, ombrato; (*Poet.*) ombroso; (*disreputable*) equivoco, sospetto, losco, bieco. *to be on the* ~ *side of* 40, avere oltreppassato la quarantina.

shaft, *n.* (*arrow*) freccia, saetta, *f.*; (*spear, &c*) asta, *f.*; (*smoke*) camino, fumaiolo, *m.*; (*of chimney*) torretta, *f.*; (*cart*) stanga, *f.*, timone, *m.*; (*Arch.*) fusto, *m.* (*Mech.*) albero, *m.*; asse, semiasse, *f.*; (*Min. & lift*) pozzo, *m.* ~ *horse*, cavallo a stanga, *m. ventilating* ~, (*Min.*) pozzo di aerazione, *m.*

shaggy, *a.* irsuto, peloso.

shagreen, *n.* zigrino, *m.*

shah, *n.* scià, *m.*

shake, *n.* scossa, *f.*; tremito; crollo, *m.*; (*head*) scrollata, *f.*; (*hand*) stretta, *f.*; (*Mus.*) trillo, *m.* ¶ *v.t. ir.* scuotere, agitare, dimenare; scrollare, far crollare; dondolare; intimidire; (*hand*) stringere; (*Mus.*) trillare. (*v.i. ir.*) agitarsi, scuotersi, dimenarsi, tremare; tentennare; barcollare. **shaky**, *a.* malfermo; poco solido; vacillante.

Shakespeare, *n.* Shakespeare, *m.* **Shakespearian**, *a.* scespiriano.

shale, *n.* argilla schistosa, *f.* ~ *oil*, olio minerale, o. di schisto, *m.*

shall, *v. aux. ir.*, is expressed in It. by future tense. Also by *dovere*.

shallot, *n.* scalogno, *m.*

shallow, *a.* poco profondo; basso; piatto; (*fig.*) superficiale, frivolo. ~**s**, *n.pl.* bassifondi, *m.pl.*

sham, *n.* finta, imitazione, impostura, *f.*, pretesa, *f.*; pretesto, *m.* ¶ *a.* finto, falso, fittizio, simulato. ~ *fight*, battaglia finta, *f.* ¶ *v.t. & i.* fingere, simulare, far vista (di).

shambles, *n.* macello, *m.*; carneficina, *f.*

shambling, *p.a.* goffo, strascicante, che cammina con passo pesante e goffo.

shame, *n.* vergogna, onta, *f.*; disonore, scandalo, *m.* *for* ~! vergogna! eh via, vergogna! ¶ *v.t.* svergognare, fare onta a, far arrossire; disonorare. ~ **faced**, *a.* vergognoso, confuso. ~**ful**, 1. vergognoso, infame, disonesto. ~less, a. svergognato, sfacciato, sfrontato. ~lessly, ad. sfacciatamente, sfrontatamente.

shammy [leather], n. pelle di camoscio, f.

shampoo, n. (wet) shampoo, m.; (dry) frizione, f. ¶ v.t. fare uno shampoo, una frizione (a).

shamrock, n. trifoglio, m. (emblema dell'Irlanda).

Shanghai, n. Sciangài, f.

shank, n. gamba, f.; tibia, f., stinco, m.; fusto, gambo, m.; ~ bone, osso della gamba, m.

shanty, n. baracca, f.; canzone marinaresca, f.

shape, n. forma, figura, foggia; taglio, m., vita, f.; modello, m.; (Arch., &c.) sagoma, f. ¶ v.t. formare; foggiare; dare forma a; modellare; dirigere; regolare; determinare. ~less, a. informe; sformato. shaping machine, limatrice, f.

share, n. porzione, parte, quota, f.; (Fin.) azione, f., valore, titolo, m.; (plough) vomero, m. ~ capital, capitale azionario, m. ~holder, azionista, m.f. ~ pusher, piazzista, m. ¶ v.t. & i. spartire, dividere; condividere; partecipare (a), aver parte (in), prendere parte (a). ~ out, distribuire.

shark (fish & rapacious person), n. pescecane, m. (also war profiteer).

sharp, a. tagliente, affilato; acuto, appuntito, aguzzo; brusco, violento; piccante, mordace, acerbo, pungente; astuto, accorto; chiaro, netto; svegliato, fino, scaltro; (acid) agro; (frost) forte; (rebuke) aspro, solenne, (blow) secco; (features) dimagrato; marcato; (watch, look-out) vigilante. ~ practices, indelicatezze, trufferie, f.pl. ~-shooter, tiratore scelto, m. ¶ ad. (hour) preciso. look ~! sbrigatevi! presto! ¶ (Mus.) n. diesis, m. ~en, v.t. affilare, arrotare, aguzzare; appuntare; stimolare; (wits) aguzzare, scaltrire. ~er, n. scroccone, cavaliere d'industria, truffatore, m. ~ener (tool) n. affilatoio, m.; (Mach.) affilatrice, f. ~ly, ad. vivacemente; vivamente; nettamente, recisamente. ~ness, n. acutezza, f., acume, m.; finezza; acredine, acrimonia, asprezza, f.; nettezza, chiarezza, f.; oculatezza, scaltrezza, f.

shatter, v.t. fracassare, frantumare, sfracellare; (fig.) infrangere; rovinare.

shave, v.t. radere; fare la barba a;

rasare; (crown of the head), tonsurare. (v.i.) radersi; farsi la barba, rasarsi.

shaving, n. (il) radere, radersi, m.; la barba, f. (chip) ritaglio, truciolo, m. ~ brush, pennello per (or da) barba, m. ~ cream, crema per rasarsi, f. ~ stick, bastoncello di sapone per (la) barba, m.

shawl, n. scialle, m.

she, pn. ella, essa, lei; colei; quella. ¶ n. femmina, f. att. e.g. il leopardo f., or la f. del leopardo. ~-ass, asina, f. ~-bear, orsa, f. ~-camel, cammella, f. ~-devil, diavola, diavolessa, f. ~-goat, capra, f. ~-monkey, bertuccia, f. ~-wolf, lupa, f.

sheaf, n. covone, m.; manna, manata, f.; fascio, m. ¶ v.t. accovonare.

shear, v.t. ir. (sheep, &c.) tondere, tosare; (Mech.) tagliare, tranciare. ~er, n. tosatore, m., -trice, f. ~ing, n. tosatura, f.; taglio, m. ~ machine, tosatrice; (Mech.) cesoia meccanica, f.; **shears**, n.pl. cesoie, f.pl.

sheath, n. guaina, f., fodero; astuccio, m. **sheathe**, v.t. (ri)mettere nel fodero; inguainare; rivestire.

sheave, n. carrucola, puleggia, f.

shed, n. tettoia, f.; baraccone, m.; capanna; rimessa, f. ¶ v.t. ir. versare, spandere, spargere; spogliarsi di; gettare. **shedding** (blood), n. effusione, f., spargimento, m.

sheen, n. lustro, splendore, m.

sheep, n. pecora, f., pecore, f.pl.; ovino, m. ~ dog, cane da pastore, m. ~ fold, ovile, m. ~ like (pers.) pecoresco. ~ pox, chiavello, m. ~ [skin] pelle di pecora, f. ~ish, a. pecoresco; timido, mogio, sciocco.

sheer, a. puro, pretto, mero; netto; affatto; (force) vivo, estremo; perpendicolare. ~ off, prendere il largo; allontanarsi.

sheet, n. foglio, m.; (metal, &c.) lamiera, lastra, f.; (water) distesa, f., specchio, m.; (tarpaulin) copertone, m.; (flame) fiammata, f.; (Naut.) scotta, f.; (bed) lenzuolo, m. (f.pl. le lenzuola). ~ anchor, ancora di speranza, f.; (fig.) ancora di salvezza, f. ~ glass, lastra di vetro, f. ~ iron, lamiera [di ferro], f. ~ lead, piombo in fogli, m. ~ lightning, baleno a secco, m. ~ piling, palancola, f. ~ing, n. tela da lenzuola, f.; (Civil Engin.), blindaggio, m.

sheik[h], n. sceicco, m.

shekel, (*Bible*), *n.* siclo, *m.*

sheldrake, *n.* tadorna, *m.*

shelf, *n.* ripiano, *m.;* tavola, mensola, *f.;* palchetto; (piano di) scaffale, *m.;* (*Naut.*) banco, scoglio, *m.* [*set of*] *shelves,* scaffale, *m.,* scansia, *f.*

shell, *n.* conchiglia, *f.;* nicchio, *m.,* conca, *f.;* guscio, *m.;* baccello, *m.;* corteccia, *f.,* scorza, *f.;* involucro, *m.* (*building*) ossatura, *f.;* (*coffin*) cassa, *f.;* (*Artil.*) proiettile, obice, *m.* (*ship*) scafo, fasciame, *m.* ~*fish,* mollusco, crostaceo, *m.* ~ *hole,* cratere, *m.* ~ *shock,* commozione, psicosi traumatica, *f.* ¶ *v.t.* sgusciare, sbaccllare, sgranare, sgranellare; (*Artil.*) bombardare, cannoneggiare.

shellac, *n.* gomma lacca, *f.;* scaglie di lacca, *f.pl.*

shelter, *n.* coperto; asilo, rifugio, ricovero, *m.;* protezione, *f.,* schermo, *m. under* ~, al coperto. ¶ *v.t.* mettere al coperto, ricoverare, riparare, proteggere, dare asilo a.

shelve, *v.i.* essere in pendio, pendere; (*v.t.*) fornire di scansie; (*fig.*) mettere da parte, sbarazzarsi di, rimandare.

shepherd, *n.* pastore, pecoraio, *m.;* ~*'s crook,* vincastro, *m.* ~*'s purse,* borsa da pastore, *f.* ~**ess,** *n.* pastorella, *f.*

sherry, *n.* vino di Xeres, *m.*

shew, *n. & v.ir.* Same as *show.*

shield, *n.* scudo; schermo; protettore, *m.;* (*armour*) scudo; (*Her.*) scudo, stemma, *m.* ¶ *v.t.* riparare; proteggere, fare scudo a; mettere al coperto.

shift, *n.* spostamento; cambiamento; sotterfugio, *m.;* (*Naut.,* *of wind*) salto, *m.;* mezzo, espediente, *m.;* risorsa, *f.;* tiro, *m.,* gherminella, *f.;* (*work, workmen*) turno, *m.;* muta, *f.* ¶ *v.t. & i.* spostare, spostarsi; cambiare, cambiare di posto, traslocare; girare; saltare; (*cargo*) spostarsi. ~ *for oneself,* fare da sé; guadagnare la propria vita; ~**ing,** *p.a.* cambiante, fuggente, mutevole; (*sand*) mobile; (*wind*) variabile. ~**y,** *a.,* furbo, furtivo, pieno di espedienti.

shilling (⅟₂₀ *of a £*), *n.* scellino, *m.*

shilly-shally, *v.i.* titubare, gingillare, vacillare.

shimmer, *v.i.* luccicare. ¶ *n.* luce tremolante, *f.,* barlume, luccichio, *m.*

shin, *n.* stinco, *m.;* (*beef*) garretto, *m.,* coscia, *f.* ~ *bone,* tibia, *f.* ~*guard,* ghettone, gambale, *m.*

shindy, *n.* baccano, chiasso, *m.,* chiassata, baruffa, rissa chiassosa, *f.,* schiamazzo, *m.*

shine, *n.* lustro, splendore; lucido; bel tempo, *m.* ¶ *v.i.* *ir.* brillare, (ri)splendere, rifulgere, rilucere; raggiare.

shingle, *n.* ghiaia, *f.,* ciottoli, selci, *m.pl.;* (*Build.*) assicella, tegola di legno, *f.* ~**s** (*Med.*), *n.pl.* erpete zonario, *m.,* zona ignea, *f.* ¶ (*Metall.*) *v.t.* eliminare la scoria. ~[*d hair*], taglio di capelli alla garçonne, *m.*

shining *&* **shiny,** *a.* lucente, rilucente, risplendente, brillante.

ship, *n.* nave, *f.,* bastimento, vascello, battello, *m.* ~ *biscuit,* galletta, *f.,* biscotto di mare, *m.* ~ *broker,* sensale marittimo, *m.* ~ *builder,* costruttore di navi, c. navale, *m.* ~ *building,* costruzione navale, *f.* ~ *canal,* canale navigabile, *m.* ~ *chandler,* fornitore navale, *m.,* fornitore di bordo, *m.* ~ *flying the British flag,* nave battente bandiera inglese. ~*mate,* compagno di bordo, *m.* ~ *owner,* armatore, proprietario di nave, *m.* ~ *quoits,* giuoco di anelli, *m.* ~*shape,* in buon assetto, in ordine. ~*wreck,* naufragio, *m. to be* ~*wrecked,* naufragare, far naufragio. ~*wright,* capo carpentiere; carpentiere d'arsenale, *m.* ~*yard,* cantiere navale, cantiere di costruzione, arsenale, *m.* ¶ *v.t.* imbarcare, caricare, mettere a bordo; prendere a bordo; spedire; (*oars*) armare, disarmare; ~ *water,* ~ *a sea,* imbarcare, **shipment,** *n.* imbarco, carico, *m.;* spedizione, *f.*

shipper, *n.* caricatore, speditore, esportatore, *m.* **shipping,** *n.* navi, *f.pl.;* naviglio, *m.,* marina, *f.;* navigazione, *f.;* imbarco, *m.,* spedizione, *f.,* trasporto marittimo; tonnellaggio, *m.* ~ *agent,* agente di trasporti marittimi, spedizioniere marittimo, *m.* ~ *charges,* spese di spedizione, *f.pl.* ~ *clerk,* spedizioniere, *m.*

shire, *n.* contea, *f.*

shirk, *v.t.* eludere, scansare, sottrarsi a, schivare; (*v.i.*) imboscarsi, rimpiattarsi. ~[*er*], scansafatiche, *m.inv.* imboscato, *m.*

shirt, *n.* camicia, *f.* ~ *collar,* collo di camicia, colletto, *m.* ~ *maker,* camiciaio, *m.,* -a, *f.* ~**ing,** *n.* tela da camicia, tela per camicie, *f.*

shiver, *v.t.* frantumare, spezzare; (*v.i.*) tremare (di freddo), rabbrividire.

shoal, *n.* (*sand*, *fish*) banco, *m.*; (*shallow*) bassofondo, *m.* ~s *of people*, un nuvolo di gente, *m.*

shock, *n.* cozzo, urto, *m.*, scossa, *f.*; colpo, attacco, *m.*; sensazione violenta, prostrazione nervosa, *f.*, sorpresa spiacevole, *f.* (*hair*) zazzera, *f.*, massa, *f.*; (*corn*) covone, *m.* ~ *absorber*, smorzatore di scosse, *m.*, para-urti, *m.inv.* ~ *headed*, dai capelli arruffati, scapigliato. ¶ *v.t.* scuotere, urtare, dare di cozzo a; (*fig.*) urtare, offendere, scandalizzare, disgustare, fare schifo a, fare stordire. ~*ing*, *a.* ributtante, orribile, orrido, spaventevole.

shoddy, *n.* robaccia, *f.*, stoffa di stracci di lana, *f.*

shoe, *n.* scarpa, *f.*; (*wooden*, *clog*) zoccolo, *m.* (*horse*) ferro, *m.* ~ *black*, lustrascarpe, *m.inv.* ~ *brush*, spazzola da scarpe, *f.* ~ *horn*, calzatoia, *f.* ~*maker*, calzolaio, *m.* ¶ *v.t. ir.* calzare; (*horse*) ferrare.

shoeing, *n.* (*horse*) ferratura, *f.* ~*smith*, maniscalco, *m.*

shoot, *n.* rampollo, pollone, germoglio, *m.*; caccia, *f.*, partita di caccia, *f.*; gara di tiro, *f.*; scivolo; doccione, *m.*; cascata, *f.* ¶ *v.t. ir.* tirare, sparare; scoccare; lanciare, gettare; saettare; colpire; caccia; (*film*) girare; scaricare; uccidere (con un colpo di fucile, &c.), (*spy*, *deserter*) fucilare. (*tip*) rovesciare; (*rapids*) superare. (*v.i. ir.*) tirare, sparare; cacciare; slanciarsi, precipitarsi; proiettarsi; filare, passare di slancio; balenare; (*grow*) spuntare, crescere, germogliare; (*Foot.*) tirare un colpo secco, un calcio secco. (*pain*) dare, causare un dolore lancinante. **shooting,** *n.* tiro, sparo, *m.*, caccia; fucilazione, *f.* ~ *box*, padiglione da caccia, *m.*, casina da caccia, *f.* ~ *gallery*, tiro, locale del tiro, *m.* ~ (*game*, *match*) gara di tiro, *f.* concorso di tiro, *m.* ~ *pains*, dolore lancinante, *m.* ~ *star*, meteora, stella filante, *f.*

shop, *n.* bottega, *f.*, negozio, magazzino, fondaco, *m.*; (*works*) officina, *f.* ~ *assistant*, commesso, *m.*, commessa, *f.* (*di negozio*). ~ *foreman*, capo reparto, *m.* ~ *front*, vetrina [di mostra], *f.* ~ *keeper*, bottegaio, *m.*, negoziante, *m.f.* ~ *lifter*, taccheggiatore, *m.*, -trice, *f.* ~*lifting*, taccheggiamento, *m.* ~ *parlour*, retrobottega, *m.* ~*-soiled*, sciupato, sbiadito. ~ *walker*, ispettore di reparto, *m.* ~ *window*, vetrina, *f.*

¶ *v.i.* (andar a) fare delle compre, fare acquisti, far provviste, far la spesa, girar le botteghe. *shopping basket*, paniere per la provvigione, *m.*

shore, *n.* spiaggia, *f.*, costa, *f.*, lido, *m.*; riva, sponda, *f.* ~ *fishing*, pesca dalla (alla, verso) spiaggia. *on* ~, a terra. *off* ~, al largo. ¶ ~ *or* ~ *up*, *v.t.* puntellare.

short, *a.* corto; piccolo; breve; ridotto; succinto; basso; insufficiente; reciso, brusco; (*pastry*) croccante. ~ *circuit*, corto circuito, *m.* ~*coming*, deficienza, *f.*; mancanza, *f.*, fallo, *m.*; (*pl.*) manchevolezze, *f.pl.*, difetti, *m.pl.* ~ *curtain* (for window), tendina, *f.* ~ *cut*, scorciatoia, *f.* ~ *dated*, a breve data, a breve scadenza. ~*-haired* (dog, &c.) dal pelo raso, dal pelo corto. ~ *hand*, stenografia, *f.* ~ *handed*, a corto di personale. ~*hand typist*, stenodattilografo, *m.*, -a, *f.* ~*hand writer*, stenografo, *m.*, -a, *f.* ~ *length* (stuff), taglio corto, *m.* ~*-lived*, a breve durata, passeggero, effimero. *are* ~*-lived*, . . . hanno vita breve, vivono poco. ~*-sighted*, di vista corta, miope; (*fig.*) imprevidente. ~ *story*, racconto, *m.*, novella, *f.* ~ [*syllable*], breve, *f.* ¶ *ad.* corto, di botto, improvvisamente. *in* ~, in breve, insomma, infine. ~*age*, *n.* deficienza, mancanza, scarsità, *f.* ~*en*, *v.t.* raccorciare, abbreviare, diminuire; (*sail*) serrare. ~*ly*, *ad.* in poche parole, brevemente; presto, fra poco, fra breve, prossimamente, di qui a poco. ~ *after*, poco dopo; ~ *before*, poco prima. ~*ness*, *n.* brevità, *f.*; breve durata, *f.*; piccolezza (di statura, &c). ~ *of breath*, respiro corto, *m.*

shot, *n.* colpo, sparo (di fucile, di cannone), *m.*; scarica (di fucile da caccia); palla (da cannone), *f.*; pallino (da fucile), *m.*; pallottola, *f.*; proiettile, *m.*; piombo, *m.*; tiratore *m.*; tiro, *m.*, portata, *f.* (*putting the shot*) peso. ~*gun*, fucile da caccia, *m.*

shot (*fabrics*), *p.p.* cangiante.

should, *v.aux.* is expressed in It. by conditional mood. Also by *dovere*.

shoulder, *n.* spalla, *f.*; (*Mech.*) spallamento, *m.* ~ *blade*, scapola, *f.*; (*horse*, *ox*), paletta, *f.* ~ *of mutton*, spalla di castrato, *f.* ~*-strap*, bretella, *f.*; spallina, *f.* ¶ *v.t.* prendere sulle spalle; spingere con la

spalla; (*arms*) portare; (*fig.*) indossare.
~ *arms!* (*Mil.*), spall'arm!

shout, *n.* grido, urlo, *m.*; (*v.t. & i.*)
gridare, vociare, urlare.

shove, *n.* spinta, *f.* ¶ *v.t. & i.*, spingere. ~ *back*, respingere. ~ *off*,
spingere dalla riva; spingersi al largo.

shovel, *n.* pala; paletta, *f.* ¶ *v.t.*
spalare; paleggiare. ~**ful,** *n.* palata,
f.

show, *n.* mostra, *f.*, spettacolo, *m.*;
esposizione; fiera, *f.*; concorso,
salone, *m.*; sembianza, *f.*; apparenza,
f.; pompa, parata, *f.*; fasto, *m.* ~ *of
hands*, voto a mano levata, voto per
alzata e seduta, *m.* ~*card*, cartello,
cartellone, manifesto, *m.* ~*case*,
vetrina, *f.* ~*man*, fierai[u]olo; saltimbanco. ~*room*, sala di mostra, *f.*
¶ *v.t.* mostrare, far vedere, mettere
in mostra; esporre; manifestare;
spiegare; dimostrare, provare;
rappresentare; (*v.i.ir.*) mostrarsi,
apparire. ~ *in*, fare entrare; introdurre. ~ *off*, far mostra (di); (*abs.*)
pavoneggiarsi. ~ *out*, condurre alla
porta, accompagnare alla porta.
~ *round*, fare da guida a. ~ *the
white feather*, mancare di coraggio.
~ *up*, smascherare; mettere a nudo,
sventare; far salire; far risaltare;
mettere alla berlina.

shower, *n.* acquazzone, *m.*, acquata,
pioggia, *f.*; (*hail*) grandinata, *f.*;
(*missiles*) grandine, *f.* ~ *bath*, doccia,
f.; bagno a doccia, *m.* ~ *proof*,
impermeabile. ¶ *v.t.* far piovere;
versare; spargere; (*v.i.*) diluviare.
showery weather, tempo piovoso, *m.*

showy, *a.* pomposo, fastoso; appariscente, vistoso.

shrapnel, *n.* shrapnel, *m.*; granata a
pallette, *f.*

shred, *n.* ritaglio; brandello; squarcio,
m.; (*pl.*) brandelli, *m.pl.*; filacce, *f.pl.*
¶ *v.t.* tagliuzzare, sminuzzare;
stracciare.

shrew, *n.* bisbetica, brontolona, santippe, *f.* ~ (*mouse*) toporagno, *m.*

shrewd, *a.* sagace, astuto, perspicace,
scaltro. ~**ness,** *n.* acume, *m.*,
sagacita, astuzia, *f.*

shriek, *n.* strillo, strido, grido acuto,
m. ¶ *v.i.* strillare, gettare grida
acute.

shrike, *n.* velia, *f.*

shrill, *a.* acuto, squillante, stridente,
stridulo. ~**ness,** *n.* acutezza (di
suono), *f.*

shrimp, *n.* gamberettino (di mare),
m.; (*pers.*) mingherlino, nanerottolo,

m. ~**ing,** *n.* pesca di gamberettini,
f.

shrine, *n.* reliquario; tabernacolo;
santuario, *m.*

shrink, *v.i. ir.* contrarsi; stringersi il
cuore; restringersi, ritirarsi, raccorciarsi; (*v.t. ir.*) restringere, raccorciare, diminuire. ~**age,** *n.* contrazione, *f.*, restringimento, scemamento, (*Com.*) calò; (*Mech.*) ritiro, *m.*

shrivel, *v.t.* raggrinzare; (*v.i.*) raggrinzarsi, accartocciarsi.

shroud, *n.* sudario, lenzuolo mortuario, *m.*; (*Naut.*) sartia, *f.* (*f.pl.*
sartie). ¶ *v.t.* avvolgere, inviluppare;
annebbiare, celare.

Shrovetide, *n.* ultimi giorni di carnevale, *m.pl. Shrove Tuesday*, martedí
grasso, *m.*

shrub, *n.* arboscello, arbusto, *m.*
shrubbery, *n.* piantagione d'arbusti, *f.*, boschetto, *m.*

shrug, *n.* stretta di spalle, *f.* ¶ *v.t.*
stringersi nelle spalle, alzare le
spalle.

shudder, *v.i.* rabbrividire, fremere.
¶ *n.* brivido, fremito, *m.*

shuffle, *v.t.* scompigliare, confondere;
mescolare; battere; (*cards*) scozzare,
mescolare. (*v.i.*) andar a sghembo;
tergiversare, vacillare; cavarsela.
~ *along*, strascicare i piedi; camminare strascicando i piedi. ¶
(*excuse*) *n.* sotterfugio, pretesto, *m.*
shuffling gait, andatura trascinante,
f., passo strascinante, *m.*

shun, *v.t.* evitare, scansare, sfuggire.

shunt (*Elec.*) *n.* derivazione, *f.* ¶ *v.t.*
(*Rly.*) smistare; scambiare; (*Elec.*)
derivare. ~**er,** *n.* deviatore, *m.*

shut, *v.t. ir.* chiudere; serrare; (*v.i.*)
chiudersi. ~ *in*, rinchiudere. ~
out, escludere. ~ *up*, chiudere,
rinchiudere; tacere, far tacere.

shutter, *n.* scurino, *m.*; imposta;
persiana, *f.*; (*roller*) saracinesca;
serranda avvolgibile, *f.*; (*Phot.*)
otturatore, *m.*

shuttle, *n.* spola, *f.*; navetta, *f.* ~
cock, volano, volante, *m.*

shy, *a.* timido, schivo; selvatico;
diffidente, riservato, sospettoso;
(*horse*) ombroso. ¶ *v.i.* pigliar
ombra; fare uno scarto; (*v.t.*)
lanciare. ~**ness,** *n.* timidezza,
diffidenza, ritrosia; selvatichezza, *f.*

Shylock, *n.* (*fig.*) usuraio, *m.*

Siam, *n.* il Siam, *m.* **Siamese,** *a.*
siamese. ~ *cat*, gatto del Siam, *m.*
¶ *n.* (*pers.*) siamese, *m.f.*; (*language*)
siamese, *m.*

Siberia, *n.* la Siberia, *f.* **Siberian,** *a.* siberiano. ¶ *n.* siberiano, *m.*, -a, *f.*

sibyl, *n.* sibilla, *f.*

Sicilian, *a.* siciliano. ¶ *n.* siciliano, *m.*, -a, *f.* **Sicily,** *n.* la Sicilia, *f.*

sick, *a.* malato, indisposto, infermo; stomacato, nauseato. *to be* ~, essere malato; (*stomach*) provare nausea, vomitare. *the* ~, gli ammalati, *m.pl.* ~ *bay*, infermeria (di bordo), *f.* ~ *& tired*, stanco morto, sopraffatto. ~ *bed*, letto d'infermo, letto di dolore, *m.* ~ *headache*, emicrania, *f.*, mal di capo accompagnato con nausea, *m.* ~ *leave*, congedo per malattia, *m.*, licenza per *m.*, *f.* ~ *list*, lista degli ammalati, *f.* ~ *room*, camera d'infermo, *f.* (*Sch.*, *&c.*) infermeria, *f.* ~en, *v.i.* ammalarsi; (*v.t.*) nauseare; disgustare; fare schifo a.

sickle, *n.* falce, *f.*, falcetto, *m.*, roncola, *f.*

sickly, *a.* malaticcio; (di salute) cagionevole; (*sweet*) sdolcinato. **sickness,** *n.* malattia, *f.*, morbo, *m.*, infermità, *f.*; (*stomach*) nausea, *f.*

side, *n.* lato, canto, *m.*, banda, *f.*, fianco, *m.*; parte, *f.* partito, *m.*; versante, *m.*; facciata, *f.*; bordo, *m.*, parete, *f.* ~ *by* ~, l'uno accanto all'altro, l'uno allato all'altro, a lato, a fianco. ~ *arm*, arma bianca, *f.* (~*s*, armi bianche). ~*board*, credenza, *f.* ~*car*, carrozzetta laterale. ~ *dish*, entremets, *m.* ~ *door*, porta laterale, *f.* ~ *face*, profilo, *m.* ~ *glance*, occhiata obliqua, *f.*, occhiolino, *m.* ~ *issue*, questione di interesse secondario, *f.* ~*line*, esercizio secondario, *m.* ~*long*, obliquo, a traverso, di fianco; (*glance*) occhiolino, *m.* ~ *note*, nota marginale, *f.* ~ *saddle*, sella da donna, *f.* ~ *scene*, retroscena, *f.* ~*show*, spettacolo a pagamento; (*fair*) teatro da fiera, *m.* ~-*slip*, *v.i.* sdrucciolare; (*Aero.*) scivolare d'ala. ¶ *n.* sdrucciolata, scivolata, *f.* ~-*step*, tirarsi in disparte, fare un passo obliquo, a sghembo; (*fig.*) scansare, eludere. ~ *stroke*, nuotata sul fianco, *f.* ~ *walk*, controviale; marciapiede, *m.* ~ *ways*, a traverso, a sghembo, da canto; lateralmente. ~ *whiskers*, fedine, *f.pl.* ~ *with*, tener da, prendere le parti di, schierarsi dalla parte di, abbracciare il parere di.

sidereal, *a.* sidereo.

siding, *n.* binario morto; raccordo, *m.* (*private*) raccordo privato, *m.*

sidle in, entrare a sghembo. **sidle up,** accostarsi con esitazione, accostarsi camminando di fianco.

siege, *n.* assedio, *m.* ~ *gun*, cannone da assedio, *m.* *to lay* ~ *to*, assediare.

Sien[n]a, *n.* Siena, *f.* s~, *n.* terra di Siena, *f.*, giallo di Siena, *m.*

siesta, *n.* siesta, *f.*, sonno meridiano, *m.*

sieve, *n.* staccio, crivello, vaglio; (*flour*) buratto; (*hair*) setaccio, *m.* **sift,** *v.t.* stacciare, vagliare, crivellare, abburattare; (*question*) vagliare. **siftings,** *n.pl.* mondiglia, vagliatura, stacciatura, *f.*

sigh, *n.* sospiro, *m.* ¶ *v.i.* sospirare.

sight, *n.* vista, veduta, *f.*; prospetto, aspetto, spettacolo, *m.*; curiosità, *f.*; (*Surv.*) mira, *f.*; (*gun*) mirino, *m.* *at* ~, a prima vista; (*reading*) a libro aperto; (*Com.*) a vista. ~*seer*, curioso, *m.*, -a, *f.*; turista, *m.f.* ~ [*vane*], traguardo, *m.* ¶ *v.t.* aggiustare la mira di; mirare, scorgere; (*land*) avvistare.

sign, *n.* segno, indizio, sintomo, *m.* ~(*board*), insegna, *f.* ~ *of expression* (*Mus.*) sfumatura, *f.* ~*post*, palo indicatore, *m.* ~*writer*, pittore di insegne, *m.* ¶ *v.t. & i.* firmare, sottoscrivere; segnare, far segno (a), accennare (a); (*in the margin*) firmare in margine. ~ [*on*], impegnare, scritturare.

signal, *n.* segnale, *m.*; segnalazione; (*traffic*) semaforo, *m.* ~ *box*, cabina dei segnali, *f.* ~*man* (*Rly.*) segnalatore, *m.*; casellante, *m.* ¶ *a.* segnalato, eminente, insigne; rimarchevole. ¶ *v.i.* fare segnalazioni; *v.t. & ~ize*, segnalare. **signaller** (*Mil.*), *n.* segnalatore, *m.* **signatory** or **signer,** *n.* firmatario, *m.*, -a, *f.* **signature,** *n.* firma, *f.*, sottoscrizione, *f.*; (*Mus.*) armatura, *f.*; (*Typ.*) segnatura, *f.* **signet,** *n.* suggello, sigillo, *m.* ~ *ring*, anello con sigillo, *m.* ~ *wafer*, ostia gommata, ostia da sigillare, *f.*

significance, *n.* significato, senso, *m.*; importanza, portata, *f.* *look of deep* ~, sguardo molto significativo. **significant,** *a.* significativo. **signify,** *v.t. & i.* significare, voler dire; importare.

silence, *n.* silenzio, *m.* ¶ *v.t.* far tacere; (*enemy's fire*) spegnere. **silencer,** *n.* silenziatore, *m.* **silent,** *a.* silenzioso, tacito, taciturno;

(*Gram.*, *&c.*) muto. ~ *partner*, (socio) accomandante, s. occulto, *m.* *to be* ~, tacere. ~**ly**, *ad.* in silenzio, tacitamente, senza rumore, pian piano.

Silesia, *n.* la Slesia, *f.* **Silesian**, *a.* slesiano.

silhouette, *n.* siluetta, *f.*; profilo, *m.*

silica, *n.* silice, *f.* **silicate**, *n.* silicato, *m.* **silicon**, *n.* silicio, *m.*

silk, *n.* seta, *f.* ~ *coloured handkerchief*, fazzoletto di seta in colore, *m.* ~ *goods* or *silks*, seterie, *f.pl.* ~ *hat*, cappello di seta, *m.*; cappello alto, cilindro, *m.* ~ *square*, fazzoletto da collo, *m.* **silkworm**, *n.* baco da seta, bigatto, filugello, *m.* ~ *breeding*, allevamento di bachi da seta, *m.*; sericultura, *f.* ~ *breeding ground*, bigattiera, *f.* ~ *gut*, crine di Firenze, *m.* ~*s' eggs*, seme [di] bachi [da seta], *m.* **silky**, *a.* morbido, (fino) come la seta; serico.

sill, *n.* soglia, *f.*; davanzale, *m.*

silliness, *n.* sciocchezza, scempiaggine, stupidaggine; melensaggine, semplicioneria, *f.* **silly**, *a.* sciocco, semplice, goffo, scempio, scemo, stupido, scimunito. ¶ *n.* sciocco, scioccone, *m.*, stupido, *m.*, -a, *f.*, stupidella, *f.*, scimunito, *m.*, -a, *f.*

silo, *n.* silo, *m.* ¶ *v.t.* mettere nel silo.

silt, *n.* limo, fango, *m.*; mota, *f.*; deposito di sabbia, di rena, *m.* ~ *up*, infangarsi, colmare di sabbia.

silver, *n.* argento, *m.*; moneta d'argento, *f.* ~ *birch*, betulla bianca, *f.* ~ *fox*, volpe argentata, *f.* ~*-gilt*, d'argento dorato. ~ *mine*, miniera d'argento, *f.* ~*-plate*, argenteria, *f.*; vasellame d'argento, *m.*; (*v.t.*) inargentare. ~ *sand*, sabbia bianca, *f.* ~ *side*, girello di bue, *m.* ~ *smith*, argentiere, *m.* ~ [*smith's*; *work*, argenteria, *f.* ~ *thaw*, nevischio, *m.* ~ *wedding*, nozze d'argento, *f.pl.* ¶ *v.t.* [in]argentare; (*mirror*) spalmare di stagno. ~**ing** (*for mirror*), *n.* stagnatura, *f.* ~**y**, *a.* argenteo, argentino.

simian, *a.* scimmiesco.

similar, *a.* simile, somigliante, pari, uguale. ~**ity** *&* **similitude**, *n.* somiglianza, rassomiglianza, similitudine, *f.* ~**ly**, *ad.* similmente, parimenti. **simile**, *n.* similitudine, *f.*

simmer, *v.i. & t.* sobbollire.

simony, *n.* simonia, *f.*

simoom, **simoon**, *n.* simun, *m.inv.*

simper, *n.* sorriso affettato, *m.* ¶ *v.i.*

civettare, far vezzi, sorridere con smorfie.

simple, *a. & n.* semplice, *a. & m.*; erba medicinale, *f.* ~ *contract*, contratto non formale, contratto per scrittura privata, *m.* ~ *good natured man*, *woman*, bonomo, [uomo] bonaccione, uomo di buona pasta, *m.*; buona donna, *f.* ~ *hearted*, a cuore schietto, candido, franco, col cuore in mano. ~ *minded*, semplice, ingenuo. **simpleton**, *n.* semplicione; scioccone, scimunito, *m.* **simplicity**, *n.* semplicità, *f.* **simplify**, *v.t.* semplificare.

Simplon, *n.* Sempione, *m.*

simulacrum, *n.* simulacro, *m.* **simulate**, *v.t.* simulare, fingere.

simultaneous, *a.* simultaneo.

sin, *n.* peccato, male, vizio, *m.*; iniquità, malvagità, *f.*; (*shame*) vergogna, *f.* ¶ *v.i.* peccare.

Sinai (**Mount**), *n.* il monte Sinai, *m.*

since, *ad. & pr.* dopo; (*ad.*) dipoi, d'allora in poi, da tempo; fa; (*pr.*) da. ¶ *c.* poiché, dacché, giacché, da quando. *long* ~, da molto tempo.

sincere, *a.* sincero, schietto, franco, vero. **sincerity**, sincerità, *f.*

sine, *n.* seno, *m.*

sine die, sine die, indefinitamente, a data da stabilirsi.

sine qua non, sine qua non, *m.*

sinew, *n.* nervo, tendine, *m.*; (*in meat*) muscolo, *m.*; (*pl. of war*) nerbo, *m.* **sinful**, *a.* peccaminoso, colpevole, iniquo, corrotto.

sing, *v.t. & i. ir.* cantare. ~ *small*, sgonfiarsi, abbassar la cresta, calar di pretensione. ~ *to sleep*, addormentar cantando.

Singapore, *n.* Singapore, *f.*

singe, *v.t.* abbrustolire, rosolare, scottare, bruciacchiare.

singer, *n.* cantante, *m.f.*; (*church*) cantore, *m.* **singing**, *n.* canto, *m.*; (*ears*) ronzio, tintinnio, zufolamento, *m.*; (*att.*) di canto, cantante; (*kettle*) che borbotta.

single, *a.* solo, semplice; unico; isolato; nubile, celibe. ~ *bed*, letto a un posto, letto a uno, *m.* ~ *blessedness*, (la felicità del) celibato. ~*-breasted*, ad un petto. ~ *combat*, singolare tenzone, *f.*, combattimento singolare, *m.* ~*-handed*, solo, senza aiuto. *a* ~ *life*, il celibato, lo stato nubile, *m.* ~ *man*, celibe; scapolo, *m.* ~ *oar*, (scull) remo corto, *m.*

~ *room*, camera per una persona, camera ad un letto, *f.* ~ *stick*, bastone, *m.* giuoco del bastone, *m.* ~-*string instrument*, monocordo, *m.* ~ *ticket*, biglietto semplice, *m.* ~ *width* (cloth), altezza, *f.* ~ *woman*, donna nubile; zitella, *f.* ¶ (*sport*) *n.* (partita) semplice, *f.* ~ *out*, prescegliere, distinguere. **singly,** *ad.* ad uno ad uno, separatamente.

singsong, *a.* monotono. ¶ *n.* canto monotono, *m.*; salmodia, *f.*; piccola riunione per il canto, *f.*

singular, *a. & n.* singolare, *a. & m.*

sinister, *a.* sinistro, funesto, truce, di cattivo augurio; cupo, fosco, tetro; (*Her.*) sinistro.

sink, *n.* acquaio, lavatoio, scolatoio; piombo, *m.*; fogna, *f.* (*fig.*) cloaca, sentina, *f.* ¶ *v.i. ir.* affondare, affondarsi, sprofondarsi, immergersi, sommergersi, attuffarsi; declinare, indebolirsi; estinguersi; calare, diminuire; abbassarsi; cedere; cadere; (*ship*) affondare, colare a picco, andar a fondo; (*v.t. ir.*) affondare; sprofondare; infossare, scavare; approfondire; sommergere, mandare a picco; (*die*) incidere; (*money, a fortune*), collocare, investire, mettere; impiegare a fondo perduto; (*loan, national debt*) ammortizzare, estinguere. ~ *in*[to], penetrare, cadere in; imbeversi, inzupparsi. *in a sinking condition* (ship), in perdizione. *sinking fund*, fondo di ammortamento, *m.*

sinless, *a.* senza peccato, innocente. **sinner,** *n.* peccatore, *m.*, -trice, *f.*

sinuous, *a.* sinuoso.

sinus, *n.* seno, *m.*; cavità, *f.*

sip, *n.* sorso, centellino, gocciolo, *m.* ¶ *v.t. & i.* sorseggiare, bere a centellini, bere a sorsi.

siphon, *n.* sifone, *m.*

sippet, *m.* fettolina (di pane), *f.*, crostino, *m.* (da immergere nel vino, &c.).

sir, *n.* signore, cavaliere, baronetto (*title*), *m.* *no*, ~, (*Army*), no, signor Capitano, Generale, ecc.; (*Navy*), no, signor Tenente, ecc. **sire,** *n.* padre, *m.*; (*to kings*) Sire, Signore, *m.*, Maestà, *f.* ¶ *v.t.* generare.

siren, *n.* (*Myth. & hooter*) sirena, *f.*

sirloin, *n.* lombo, *m.* *a roast* ~, arrosto di lombo (di bue), *m.*

siskin, *n.* lucherino, *m.*

sister, *n.* sorella; suora, *f.* ~-*in-law*,

cognata, *f.* ~ *ship*, nave gemella, *f.* ~*hood*, comunità di religiose, di monache, *f.* ~**ly**, *a.* da sorella.

sit, *v.i. ir.* sedere, sedersi, star seduto; (*portrait*) posare; (*court, &c.*) sedere, tener seduta, aver sede; (*hen*) covare. ~ *down*, sedersi, mettersi a sedere, porsi a sedere. ~ *down again*, rimettersi a sedere. ~-*down supper* (ball), cena servita a tavola, *f.* ~ *for* (*portrait*) posare per; (*Pol.*) rappresentare. ~ *enthroned & * ~ *in state*, troneggiare. ~ *on* (eggs), covare. ~ *out*, restare fino alla conclusione. ~ *out a dance*, fare da comparsa (a un ballo). ~ *up*, tenersi dritto; vegliare.

site, *n.* sito, *m.*; area, *f.*, terreno, *m.*, posizione, *f.*

sitter, *n.* modello, *m.*, -a, *f.*; chi posa, *m.f.*

sitting, *n.* seduta, sessione; adunanza, udienza; posa, *f.* ~ *hen*, chioccia, gallina covatrice, *f.* ~ *posture*, sedere, *m.*, posa, *f.* ~ *room*, salottino, *m.* ~ *time*, cova, covatura, *f.*

situated, *a.* situato, posto, collocato; (*pers.*) in una posizione. **situation,** *n.* situazione, *f.*; sito, posto, *m.*; impiego, *m.*; posizione, *f.* ~ *vacant*, offerta d'impiego, *f.* ~ *wanted*, domanda d'impiego, *f.*

sitz bath, *n.* semicupio, *m.*

six, *a. & n.* sei, *a. & m.* **sixteen,** *a. & n.* sedici, *a. & m.* ~ *mo or* 16-*mo*, *a. & m.* sedicesimo, *m. & in* 16-*mo* (*abb.*). **sixteenth,** *a. & n.* sedicesimo, *a. & m.*; (il) sedici, *m.* **sixth,** *a. & n.* sesto, *a.m.* (il) sei, *m.* (*Mus.*) sesta, *f.* **sixtieth,** *a. & n.* sessantesimo, *a. & m.* **sixty,** *a. & n.* sessanta, *a. & m.*

size, *n.* dimensione, *f.* *oft. pl.*); grandezza, mole; statura, altezza, misura, *f.*; numero; calibro, *m.*; (*book*) formato, *m.*; (*glue, &c.*) colla, *f.*; appretto, *m.* ¶ *v.t.* incollare; imbozzimare; dare l'appretto a; fare la cernita di, pezzare. ~ *up* (*pers.*) misurare la capacità di.

skate, *n.* pattino, *m.*; (*fish*) razza, *f.* ¶ *v.i.* pattinare. **skater,** *n.* pattinatore, *m.*, -trice, *f.* *skating rink*, pista di pattinaggio, *f.*, pattinaggio, *m.*

skedaddle, *v.i.* spulezzare, darsela a gambe.

skein, *n.* matassa, *f.*

skeleton, *n.* scheletro, *m.*; (*fig.*) ossatura, *f.*; carcassa, *f.* ~ *in the cupboard*, segreta onta di famiglia, *f.*

~ *key*, grimaldello, *m.*, chiave maestra, *f.* ~ *map*, carta muta, *f.*

sketch, *n.* abbozzo, schizzo, bozzetto, disegno, *m.*; macchia, *f.*; (*playlet*) macchietta, commedietta, *f.* ~ *book*, album (libretto) per abbozzi, *m.* ¶ *v.t.* abbozzare, schizzare; disegnare.

skew, *a.* obliquo, sbieco.

skewer, *n.* spiedino, schidione, spiedo, *m.*

ski, *n.* sci, *m.inv.* ~ *stick*, bastone da sci, *m.* ¶ *v.i.* sciare. **skiing**, *n.* corse con gli sci, *f.pl.*

skid, *n.* scarpa; catena (da ruota), *f.*; (*Aero.*) pattino, *m.*; (*slip*) slittamento, *m.*, slittata, *f.* ¶ *v.t.* frenare con la scarpa; (*v.i.*) scivolare, slittare.

skiff, *n.* schifo, *m.*; barchettina, *f.*

skilful, *a.* abile, esperto, destro, lesto.

skill, *n.* abilità, destrezza, perizia, *f.* ~ed, *a.* pratico, esperimentato, esperto, perito; (*work*) provetto, specializzato.

skim, *v.t.* schiumare, scremare, spannare, digrassare; sfiorare; rasentare. ~ *milk*, latte scremato, l. spannato, *m.* **skimmer**, *n.*, schiumatoio, *m.* **skimmings**, *n.pl.* schiuma, *f.*

skimp, *v.t.* restringere; tenere a stecchetto.

skin, *n.* pelle, *f.*; (*pl.*) pelli, *f.pl.*, pellame, *m.*; pelliccie, *f.pl.*; cuoio, *m.*; (*Anat.*) cute, *f.*; buccia, scorza, *f.*; pelliccia, *f.*; spoglia, *f.*; crosta, *f.*; involucro, *m.* ~ *deep*, superficiale. ~ *disease*, malattia cutanea, *f.* ~ *dresser*, pellicciaio, *m.*, -a, *f.*; cuoiaio, *m.*, -a, *f.* ~ *dressing*, cuoieria, *f.* ~ *mat*, tappeto di pelle, *m.* ~ *specialist*, specialista delle malattie cutanee, *m.* ¶ *v.t.* scorticare, spelare, scuoiare. ~*flint*, spilorcio; usuraio, *m.* ~ *over*, cicatrizzarsi. ~*less pea*, or *bean*, pisello, baccellone, *m.* **skinny**, *a.* macilento, scarno.

skip, *n.* salterello, balzello, sgambetto, *m.* ¶ *v.t. & i.* saltare; omettere; saltellare; svolazzare. ~ *about*, sgambettare. **skipper**, *n.* padrone, capitano, *m.* (di nave mercantile). *'s daughters* (waves), pecorelle, *f.pl.*, cavalloni, *m.pl. skipping rope*, corda per saltellare, *f.*

skirmish, *a.* scaramuccia, *f.* ¶ *v.i.* scaramucciare. ~er, *n.* tiratore, cacciatore, *m.*

skirt, *n.* gonnella, gonna; sottana, *f.*; falda, *f.*; lembo, *m.*; (*of a wood*) margine, orlo, *m.* ¶ *v.t.* rasentare;

confinare con; costeggiare. ~ing [**board**], *n.* plinto, zoccolino, *m.*

skit, *n.* burla, *f.*, scherzo, frizzo, *m.*

skittish, *a.* (*horse*) ombroso.

skittles, *n.pl.* birilli, *m.pl.* ~ *alley*, andito per giocare ai birilli, *m.*

skulk, *v.i.* nascondersi, tenersi nascosto furtivamente. ~er, *n.* scansapericolo, scansafatiche, *m.inv.*; poltrone, *m.*

skull, *n.* cranio, teschio, *m.* ~ *cap*, papalina, calotta, *f.*

skunk, *n.* moffetta; (*fur*) pelliccia di moffetta, *f.*; (*pers.*) vigliacco, *m.*

sky, *n.* cielo, firmamento, *m.*; (*pl.* Poet.) nubi, nuvole, *f.pl.* ~ *blue*, celeste. ~*lark*, allodola, *f.* ~*light*, abbaino, lucernario, *m.* ~*line*, [filo dell']orizzonte, *m.* ~ *rocket*, razzo volante, *m.* ~*scraper*, grattacielo, *m.* ~ *writing*, pubblicità sulle nuvole, *f.*

slab, *n.* lastra, piastra; tavola, tavoletta, *f.*; pezzo, *m.*; (*Typ.*) marmo, *m.*

slack, *a.* allentato, lento; negligente; infingardo; fiacco, rilassato. ~ *tide*, ~ *water* (*Naut.*), marea stanca, acqua ferma, *f.* ¶ *n.* (*Naut.*) imbando, *m.* ¶ ~ *& ~en*, *v.t. & i.* allentare, allentarsi, rallentare, rallentarsi; mollare; rilasciare; diminuire, moderarsi; (*lime*) spegnere. ~er, *n.* infingardo, *m.* ~s, *n.pl.* calzoni, *m.pl.*

slag, *n.* scoria, *f.* (*oft. pl.*), rosticci, *m.pl.*, loppa, *f.*

slake, *v.t.* (*lime*) spegnere, estinguere; (*thirst*) dissetarsi; cavarsi la sete.

slam (*Cards*) *n.* stramazzo, (*grand*) cappotto, *m.* ¶ (*bang*) *v.i. & t.* sbatacchiare, chiudere con violenza.

slander, *v.t.* calunniare, diffamare. ¶ *n.* calunnia, maldicenza, *f.*; diffamazione, *f.* ~ous, *a.* calunnioso, diffamatorio.

slang, *n.* gergo, *m.*; lingua furbesca, *f.*

slant, *n.* pendio, declivio, *m.*, inclinazione, direzione obliqua, *f.* ¶ *v.i. & t.* inclinare.

slap, *n.* schiaffo, *m.*; pacca, *f.*, ceffone, *m.* ¶ *v.t.* schiaffeggiare.

slash, *v.t.* sfregiare, tagliare con violenza, squarciare; ~ *about*, colpire a casaccio. ~ed, (*dress*) *p.a.* sfregiato.

slat, *n.* assicella, *f.*; (*blind*) stecca, *f.*

slate, *n.* ardesia; lavagna; tegola d'ardesia, *f.* ~*-coloured*, del colore dell'ardesia. ~ *pencil*, **matita**

d'ardesia, *f.* ~ *quarry*, cava d'ardesia, *f.*, cava di lavagne, *f.* ¶ *v.t.* coprire con tegole d'ardesia, *(fig.)* sgridare, stroncare. ~er, *n.* conciatetti, *m.inv.*

slattern, *n.* sciattona, *f.*, sudiciona, *f.*

slaughter, *n.* strage, *f.*, massacro, eccidio, *m.*; carneficina, *f.*; uccisione, *f.*; macellazione, *f.* ~ *house*, macello, ammazzatoio, *m.* ~ *man*, macellatore, abbattitore, *m.* ¶ *v.t.* ammazzare, uccidere, massacrare, trucidare; scannare; sgozzare; *(cattle)* macellare, abbattere.

Slav, *a.* slavo. ¶ *n.* slavo, *m.*, -a, *f.*

slave, *n.* schiavo, *m.*, -a, *f.* ~*driver* & ~ *trader* & **slaver,** *n.* negriere, mercante di negri, *m.* ~ *trade*, tratta dei negri, *f.* **slave,** *v.i.* sfacchinare; sgobbare, affaticarsi.

slaver, *n.* bava, *f.* ¶ *v.i.* sbavare.

slavery, *n.* schiavitù, *f.* **slavish,** *a.* servile. ~**ness,** *n.* servilità, *f.*

slay, *v.t. ir.* uccidere, ammazzare, trucidare; immolare; sacrificare. ~**er,** *n.* uccisore, *m.*; omicida, *m.*; trucidatore, *m.*

sledge, *n.* slitta, *f.*; treggia, *f.*; traino, *m.* ~*(hammer)*, mazza, *f.*; martellone da fabbro, *m.* **sledging,** *n.* lo slittare, *m.*

sleek, *a.* liscio; levigato; morbido; lucente.

sleep, *n.* sonno, *m.*; riposo. ~ *walker*, sonnambulo, *m.*, -a, *f.* ¶ *v.i.* & *t.ir.* dormire. ~ *out*, dormire fuori di casa. ~**er,** *n.* dormiente, *m.f.*; *(Rly.)* traversina, *f.*; vagone letto, *m.* **sleepiness,** *n.* sonnolenza, *f.* **sleeping,** *p.a.* addormentato. ~ *bag*, sacco a pelo, *m. the S*~ *Beauty*, la Bella Addormentata, *f.* ~ *berth*, cuccetta, *f.* ~ *car*, vagone-letto, *m.* ~ *doll*, bambola dormiente, *f.* ~ *compartment*, scompartimento a letti, *m.* ~ *draught*, pozione calmante, *f.*, sonnifero, *m.* ~ *partner*, socio accomandante, socio occulto, *m.* ~ *sickness*, malattia del sonno, *f.* ~ *suit*, pigiama, *m.* **sleepless,** *a.* insonne; senza riposo. ~**ness,** *n.* insonnia, *f.* **sleepy,** *a.* sonnacchioso, sonnolento; assonnato. ~ *head*, bimbo sonnacchioso, *m.*

sleet, *n.* nevischio, *m.* ¶ *v.i.* cader nevischio.

sleeve, *n.* manica, *f.*; *(Mech.)* manicotto, *m.* ~ *links*, bottoni, gemelli da polsino, *m.pl. to laugh up one's* ~, ridere sotto i baffi. ~**less,** *a.* senza maniche.

sleigh, *n.* slitta (leggera), *f.* ~**ing,** *n.* lo slittare, andare in slitta.

sleight-of-hand, *n.* giuoco di prestigio, g. di mano, *m.*

slender, *a.* sottile, esile, tenue; smilzo, mingherlino; gracile; fino; svelto; debole; fievole; esiguo, scarso.

sleuth hound, segugio, *m.*

slew, *v.t.* girare, rotare.

slice, *n.* fetta, *f.*; *(fruit)* spicchio, *m.* ~ *of bread* & *butter*, fetta di pane col burro, tartina, *f.* ¶ *v.t.* tagliare (a fette), affettare; *(ball)* tagliare.

slide, *n.* sdrucciolo, *m.*; scivolo, *m.*, scivolata, *f.*; *(instr.)* cursore, *m.*; *(Mech.)* scorrimento, *m.*; *(land)* frana, *f.*; *(microscope)* porta-oggettivo, *m.inv.*; preparazione, *f.*; *(lantern)* vetro, *m.*; proiezione, *f.* ~ *fastener* (zip), chiusura scorrevole, c. lampo, *f.* ~ *lantern*, lanterna magica, *f.* ~ *rest*, sostegno scorrevole, *m.* ~ *rule*, regolo calcolatore, *m.* ~ *valve*, valvola a cassetto, *f.* ¶ *v.i. ir.* scivolare; sdrucciolare, scorrere. **sliding,** *p.a.* scorrevole; mobile. ~ *door*, porta scorrevole, *f.* ~ *roof*, tetto mobile, *m.* ~ *scale*, scala mobile, *f.* ~ *seat* (boat), sedile scorrevole, *m.*

slight, *a.* leggero, esiguo, insignificante; tenue, sottile, minuto; piccolo, magretto. ¶ *n.* offesa, mancanza di riguardo, *f.* ¶ *v.t.* offendere, mancare di riguardo a. *the* ~*est*, il minimo, il più piccolo, la minima, la più piccola.

slim, *a.* smilzo, gracile, slanciato, *m.*

slime, *a.* melma, *f.*, limaccio, *m.*, mota, bava, *f.* **slimy,** *a.* melmoso, limaccioso, viscoso, bavoso.

sling, *n.* fionda, *f.*; frombola; *(hoist)* braca, imbracatura, *f.* ¶ *v.t. ir.* lanciare, scagliare, gettare; imbracare; sospendere. *slung* [*over the shoulders*], a bandoliera, ad armacollo.

slink away, *v.i. ir.* sottrarsi, svignarsela, uscire furtivamente.

slip, *n.* sdrucciolo, scivolone; passo falso; sbaglio, *m.*, svista, *f.*, errore, peccatuccio, *m.*; foglietto *(paper, &c.)* *m.*, pezzo, *m.*; striscia, *f.*, lista, *f.*; *(library, &c.)* scheda, distinta, *f.*; *(Typ.)* colonna (di bozze), *f.*; *(leash)* guinzaglio, *m.* *(drawers)* sottogonna, gonnella, *f.*; *(pillow)* federa, *f.*; *(twig)* ramoscello, *m.*; *(Hort.)* piantone, pollone, rampollo, *m.*; *(Naut.)* scalo di costruzione, *m.* *(Box.)* scanso, *m.*; *(pl. Theat.)*

quinte, *f.pl.* ~ *carriage*, vagone staccato, *m.* ~-*in album*, album a passe-partout, *m.* ~-*in mount*, montatura passe-partout, *f.* ~*knot*, nodo scorsoio, *m. a slip of a woman*, un pezzetto di donna, *m.* ~*shod*, in ciabatte, trascurato; sconnesso; negligente; sguaiato. ~*stream* (*Aero.*), *n.* corrente d'aria prodotta dall'elica, *f.* ¶ *v.i. & t.* scivolare, sdrucciolare, far scivolare; (*Mech.*) slittare; fare un passo falso; sbagliare; sfuggire, scorrere; guizzare; scappare; (*dog*) sguinzagliare; (*rope*) allentare. ~ *in*, *v.t.* far scivolare in, far scorrere in; (*v.i.*) entrare, introdursi, insinuarsi. ~ *on* (garment), infilare, *v.t.* **slipper**, *n.* pantofola, ciabatta, pianella, *f.*; zoccolo (di ruota), *m.* ~ *chin*, bazza, *f.* **slippery**, *a.* sdrucciolevole; incerto, instabile.

slit, *n.* fessura, *f.*, fesso, spacco, *m.*; finestrino, *m.* ¶ (*dress*) *p.a.* sfregiato. ¶ *v.t. ir.* fendere, spaccare.

slobber, *n.* bava, *f.* ¶ *v.i.* sbavare.

sloe, *n.* prugnola, *f.*; prugna salvatica, *f.* ~ *gin*, (liquore di) prugnola, *m.* ~ (*tree*), prugnolo, *m.*

slogan, *n.* grido di guerra (scozzese), *m.*; divisa di pubblicità, *f.*

sloop, *n.* scialuppa; corvetta, *f.*

slop [over], *v.i.* traboccare. *slop-pail*, secchio per l'acqua sporca, *m.*

slope, *n.* pendenza, *f.* pendio, versante, declivio, *m.* ¶ *v.i.* inchinarsi, essere in pendenza.

sloppiness, (*fig.*) *n.* sciattaggine, *f.* **sloppy**, *a.* bagnato, umido; sporco; (*fig.*) sciatto. **slops**, *n.pl.* lavatura, risciacquatura, acque sporche; (*thin soup*) brodo, *m.*; (*liquid diet*) pappa, *f.*; cibo liquido, *m.*

slot, *n.* fessura, scanalatura, buca, *f.*; traccia di cervo, *f.*; (*of a slot machine, &c.*) buca, *f.* ~ *machine*, distributore automatico, *m.* ~ *meter*, contatore a pagamento anticipato, *m.*

sloth, *n.* pigrizia, infingardaggine, accidia, indolenza, *f.*; (*Zool.*) tardigrado, *m.* ~*ful*, *a.* pigro, infingardo, indolente.

slouch, *v.i.* camminare dinoccolato, muoversi goffamente, pendere da una parte ~ *hat*, feltro floscio a tesa larga, *m.*

slough, *n.* pantano, *m.*, pozzanghera, *f.*; (*snake*) spoglia, *f.* (*Med.*) escara, *f.* ¶ *v.i.* spogliarsi.

sloven, *n.* sciattone, sudicione, *m.* ~*ly*, *a.* sciatto, trascurato, goffo, negligente.

slow, *a.* lento, tardo; pesante; noioso; ottuso; (*train*) omnibus; (*goods*) piccola velocità; (*clock*) in ritardo, che ritarda; indietro. *to be* ~ (tedious), essere noioso, tedioso, mancare di brio, di vivacità. ~ *coach*, badalone, cincischione, ninnolone, pigrone, perdigiorno, *m.* ~-*combustion stove*, stufa a combustione continua, *f.* ~-*motion picture*, film al rallentatore. ¶ *ad.* lentamente, adagio. *go* ~! (*traffic sign*) rallentare! ~ **down**, rallentare. **slowness**, *n.* lentezza, *f.*; lungaggine, *f.*; ritardo, indugio, *m.*

slow-worm, *n.* cecilia, *f.*

sludge, *n.* fango, *m.*; fanghiglia, *f.*

slug, *n.* lumaca, *f.*; (*bullet & Typ.*), pallottola, *f.*

sluggard, *n.* dormiglione, infingardo, fannullone, *m.* **sluggish**, *a.* pigro, inerte, apatico.

sluice, *n.* canale, *m.*; chiusa, *f.*, cateratta, *f.* ~ *gate*, paratoia, saracinesca, *f.* ~ *gates of heaven*, cateratte del cielo, *f.pl.*

slum, *n.* quartiere basso, *m.*, via stretta e sporca, *f.*; vicolo lurido, *m.*; casupola inabitabile, *f.* ~ *area*, bassifondi, *m.pl.*

slumber, *n.* sonno, riposo, *m.* ¶ *v.i.* dormire.

slump, *n.* (*in prices*) abbassamento generale, ribasso improvviso, *m.*; caduta rapida, *f.*; (*in trade*) crisi, *f.*, vendita affrettata, *f.* ¶ *v.i.* precipitare (dei titoli); affondare, abbassarsi.

slur, *n.* macchia, *f.*; (*Mus.*) legatura, *f.* *to cast a* ~ *upon*, denigrare, macchiare. ¶ *v.t.* articolar male; (*Mus.*) legare; (*v.i., Typ.*) increspare, strisciare. ~ *over*, passar sopra.

slush, *n.* neve dimoiata; melma, fanghiglia, *f.*

slut, *n.* baldracca; sudiciona, sciattona, *f.*

sly, *a.* sornione, astuto, fino, furbo, scaltro. ~ *boots*, furbetto, *m. on the* ~, di nascosto, alla chetichella, in sordina, furtivamente.

smack, *n.* sapore, gusto, *m.*; schiocco, schiaffo, *m.*; sculacciata, *f.*; baciozzo, *m.*; tinta, infarinatura, *f.*; pochino, *m.*; barca da pesca, *f.* ¶ *v.t.* schiaffeggiare, sculacciare, fare schioccare; (*tongue*) schioccare; (*lips*) leccarsi. *to* ~ *of*, sentire di, avere il sapore di.

small, *a.* piccolo, minuto, piccino; tenue; fine; lieve; corto; basso;

stretto; scarso; (*intestine*) tenue; (*Arms*, *Mil.*) portatili. ~ *craft*, bastimento di piccola portata. ~ *fry* (*fig.*) sceltume, *m.*, rifiuti, *m.pl.* ~*hand* (*writing*), scrittura fine, *f.*, caratteri minuti, *m.pl.* ~ *part* (*Theat.*) piccola parte, parte insignificante, *f.* ~*pox*, vaiolo, *m.* ~*pox case* (*pers.*) vaioloso, *m.*, -a, *f.* ~ *stones*, pietrame, *m.* ~ *talk*, conversazione banale, *f.*. piccole chiacchiere, *f.pl.* ¶ ~ *of the back*, parte piú bassa del dosso, *f.* ~*ness*, *n.* piccolezza, tenuità, *f.*, piccolo volume, piccolo numero, *m.*

smart, *n.* bruciore, dolore, *m.* ¶ *v.i.* bruciarsi, cuocere, dolersi. ¶ *a.* vivo, acuto, vivace, vispo; bello, attillato, galante, spiritoso, ben vestito, azzimato, elegante, alla moda, piccante; svegliato. *the* ~ *set*, il bel mondo, *m.* ~*en oneself up*, azzimarsi, attillarsi, farsi bello. ~**ing**, *n.* bruciore, *m.* ¶ *p.a.* cocente, bruciante, acuto. ~**ness**, *n.* finezza, acutezza, eleganza, *f.*; brio *m.*, prontezza, vivacità, *f.*

smash, *n.* fracasso, crollo, fiasco, *m.*; catastrofe, disgrazia, *f.*; (*Fin.*) fallimento, *m.*; (*Ten.*) colpo schiacciato, *m. to go* ~ (*bank*, *&c.*), fallire, far fallimento. ¶ *v.t.* frantumare, fracassare, schiacciare; (*Ten.*) schiacciare.

smattering, *n.* infarinatura, conoscenza superficiale, *f.*

smear, *v.t.* spalmare; imbrattare.

smell, *n.* odore, odorato, *m.* ¶ *v.t. & i. ir.* sentire, odorare, fiutare; mandare un odore; olezzare; puzzare. *smelling bottle*, fiaschetto d'odori, *m.*, boccetta di profumo, *f.* *smelling salts*, sale ammoniaco odoroso, *m.*, i sali (da aspirare), *m.pl.*

smelt, *n.* eperlano, *m.*

smelt, *v.t.* fondere. ~*ing works*, fonderia, *f.*

smilax, *n.* smilace, *m.*; salsapariglia, *f.*

smile, *n.* sorriso, *m.* ¶ *v.i.* sorridere. **smiling**, *a.* sorridente.

smirch, *v.t.* sporcare, insudiciare, (*fig.*) macchiare.

smirk, *n.* sorriso affettato, *m.* ¶ *v.i.* civettare, far vezzi, far smorfie.

smite, *v.t. ir.* percuotere, ferire, battere, colpire. (Cf. *smitten*).

smith, *n.* fabbro, *m.*, fabbro ferraio, *m.* ~**y**, *n.* fucina, ferriera, *f.*

smitten, *p.p.* (*remorse*) preso; (*love*) invaghito, innamorato.

smock [**frock**], *n.* camiciotto, *m.*, sopravveste, *f.* **smocking**, *n.* ricamo pieghettato, *m.*

smoke, *n.* fumo, *m.*; fumata, *f.*; (*fig.*) fumo, vapore, *m.*; esalazione, *f.* ~*-consuming*, fumivoro. ~ *helmet*, maschera contro il fumo, *f.* ~ *house*, fumatoio, *m.* ~ *screen*, cortina di fumo, *f.* ~ *stack*, fumaiolo, *m.* ciminiera, *f.* ¶ *v.i. & t.* fumare; far fumo; emettere, *f.*; (*chimney*) buttar fumo; affumicare; (*lamp*) filare. ~*d herring*, aringa affumicata, *f.* ~*d sausage*, salame, *m.* ~**less**, *a.* senza fumo. **smoker**, *n.* fumatore, *m.*, -trice, *f.* **smoking**, *n.* (il) fumare, *m.* ~ *compartment*, scompartimento per fumatori, *m.* ~ *room*, fumatoio, *m.* ~ *strictly prohibited*, è rigorosamente vietato fumare. **smoky**, *a.* fumoso, pieno di fumo.

smooth, *a.* liscio, piano, levigato; soave, dolce; (*sea*) calmo, piatto. ~*-bore*, a canna liscia. ~*-haired* (dog), dal pelo raso. ~*-tongued*, dal parlare dolce, con voce melata, con parole melate. ¶ *v.t.* spianare, levigare, lisciare, appianare; calmare; disfare le pieghe di. ~ *faced*, sbarbato, imberbe. ~*ing plane*, pialla, *f.* ~**ly**, *ad.* soavemente, facilmente, semplicemente. ~**ness**, *n.* eguaglianza (di superficie), levigatezza; dolcezza, soavità, *f.*

smother, *v.t.* soffocare; sopprimere, estinguere.

smoulder, *v.i.* covare, bruciare lentamente.

smudge, *n.* macchia leggera, imbrattatura, *f.* ¶ *v.t.* imbrattare, sporcare, sgorbiare.

smug, *a.* soddisfatto di sé (stesso), impudente, beato, vanitoso.

smuggle, *v.t.* far passare di contrabbando, contrabbandare, introdurre clandestinamente; (*v.i.*) far contrabbando, esercitare il contrabbando. ~ *in*, (*v.t.*) introdurre di contrabbando. **smuggler**, *n.* contrabbandiere, *m.*

smut, *n.* particella di fuliggine, macchia di nero, *f.*; (*Agric.*) golpe, *f.*, carbonchio, *m.* **smutty**, *a.* annerito, imbrattato, sporco; golpato; (*obscene*) sconcio, osceno.

Smyrna, *n.* Smirne, *f.*

snack, *n.* bocconcino, *m.*, merenda, *f.*, spuntino, *m. to have a* ~, mangiare un bocconcino, fare uno spuntino. ~ *bar*, spuntino, *m.*

snaffle, *n.* morso snodato, *m.*

snag, *n.* toppo (d'albero); (*fig.*) ostacolo, intoppo, inciampo, *m.*

snail, *n.* lumaca, chiocciola, *f.*; (*edible*) chiocciola, lumaca commestibile, *f.* *at a ~'s pace,* a passo di lumaca, a passi di formicola.

snake, *n.* biscia, serpe, *f.*, colubro, *m.*; (*young*) serpentello, *m.* *there is a ~ in the grass,* gatta ci cova.

snap, *n.* crac, cric-crac, *m.*, rottura subitanea, *f.*, scocco, colpo secco, colpo di dente, *m.*; fibbia a scatto, *f.*, fermaglio, *m.* *~dragon,* bocca di leone, *f.*, antirrino, *m.* *~ fastener,* bottone automatico, *m.* *~ hook,* moschettone, gancio a molla, *m.* *~[shot]* istantanea, *f.* *to ~ one's fingers at* (*fig.*), schernire, farsi beffe di. ¶ *v.t.* spezzare, fracassare, rompere, scoccare, far scoppiettare. *~ at,* tentare di mordere; gettarsi su; dir parolacce a. *~ up,* chiappare, rubare, prendere. **snapper** (*whip*), *n.* sferzino, *m.*, codetta, *f.* **snappy** or **snappish,** *a.* arcigno, ringhioso, stizzoso, bisbetico.

snare, *n.* laccio, *m.*; trappola, insidia, *f.*; (*drum*) timbro, *m.* *~ drum,* tamburo, *m.* ¶ *v.t.* tendere insidie a, prendere al laccio.

snarl, *v.i.* grugnire, ringhiare, brontolare. *~ing,* *p.a.* ringhioso, bronto lone.

snatch, (*scrap*) *n.* pezzetto, frammento, brano, squarcio, *m.* ¶ *v.t.* afferrare, strappare, ghermire, agguantare; (*kiss*) strappare.

sneak, *n.* sornione, trappolone, *m.*; (*Sch.*) spia, *f.* *~ away,* svignarsela, andarsene furtivamente. *to have a ~ing fondness for,* avere un debole per.

sneer, *n.* ghigno, sogghigno, riso di dileggio, di scherno, *m.* ¶ *v.i.* ghignare, sogghignare. *~ at,* canzonare, sbeffare, schernire, farsi beffe di.

sneeze, *v.i.* starnutire; (*animal*) sbuffare.

sniff, *v.i. & t.* fiutare, annusare. *~ up,* aspirare.

snigger, *v.i.* ridacchiare, ridere sotto i baffi.

snip, *n.* forbiciata, *f.*; pezzettino, *m.* ¶ *v.t.* tagliare con le forbici.

snipe, *n.* beccaccino, *m.* ¶ *v.t.* sparare (contro qualcuno) (da luogo sicuro). **sniper,** *n.* tiratore isolato, franco tiratore, *m.* **snippet,** *n.* pezzettino, *m.*

snivel, *v.i.* piagnucolare, frignare.

snob, *n.* millantatore, snob, parassita, *m.*

snobbery & **snobbishness,** *n.* snobbismo, *m.*

snooze, *n.* sonnellino, *m.* ¶ *v.i.* sonnecchiare.

snore, *v.i.* russare.

snort, *v.i.* sbuffare.

snout, *n.* muso, ceffo; (*pig*) grugno; (*boar*) grifo, *m.*

snow, *n.* neve, *f.* *~ball,* palla di neve, *f.* *~ blindness,* cecità dovuta al riflesso della neve, *f.*, ambliopia, *f.* *~boots,* calzature per la neve, *f.pl.* *~-capped,* coronato di neve. *~-bound.* circondato, impedito dalla neve. *~drift,* ammasso di neve, cumulo di neve, *m.* *~flake,* fiocco di neve, *m.* *~ fall,* nevicata, *f.* *~drop,* bucaneve, *m.inv.* *~ leopard,* lonza, *f.* *~ line,* limite delle nevi (perpetue), *m.* *~plough,* spartineve, spazzaneve, *m.inv.* *~ shoes,* racchette per la neve, *f.pl.* *~ squall,* raffica di neve, *f.* *~ storm,* tempesta di neve, forte nevicata, *f.* ¶ *v.i.* nevicare. *~y,* *a.* nevoso, di neve. *~ weather,* tempo di neve, *m.*

snub, *n.* rabbuffo, rimprovero, affronto, smacco, *m.* *~-nosed,* [dal naso] camuso. ¶ *v.t.* rintuzzare, rimbeccare, respingere sgarbatamente.

snuff, *n.* tabacco da naso, da fiuto, *m.* *to take ~,* prendere tabacco, pizzicar tabacco. *pinch of ~,* presa di tabacco, *f.* *~ box,* tabacchiera, *f.* *~ taker,* tabaccone, *m.*, -a, *f.* ¶ *v.t.* (*candle, &c.*) smoccolare; (*smell*) fiutare. *~ up,* prendere, aspirare.

snuffle, *v.i.* parlare nel naso, aspirare forte per il naso. *~s,* *n.pl.* intasatura (del naso), *f.*, catarro nasale, *m.*

snug, *a.* piccolo e comodo, caldo e comodo.

snuggle, *v.i.* accostarsi, stringersi, rannicchiarsi.

so, *ad. c. & pn.* così, in questo modo, tanto; perciò, pertanto, quindi, dunque, adunque; tale, lo, ciò. *~ & ~,* un tale, una tale. *Mr. ~ & ~,* il signor tal dei tali, *m.* *~ called,* sedicente, preteso. *~ as to,* in modo da, così da, allo scopo di, al fine di. *~ ~,* passabilmente, così così. *~ soon as,* tosto che, appena che, a condizione che. *~ that,* di modo che, per modo che, tanto che, affinché, cosicché. *~ to speak,* per così dire.

soak, *v.t.* inzuppare, bagnare, macerare; (*dirty linen*) immergere, ammollare.

soap, *n.* sapone, *m.* *cake of ~,*

saponetta, *f.* ~ *dish*, portasapone, *m.inv.* ~ *maker*, fabbricante di sapone, saponaio, *m.* ~ *making & ~ works*, saponeria, *f.* ~ *stone*, steatite, *f.* ~ *suds*, saponata, *f.*, bolle di sapone, *f.pl.*; acqua di sapone, *f.* ¶ *v.t.* insaponare. ~y, *a.* saponaceo, insaponato.

ᵗoar, *v.i.* alzarsi, innalzarsi, librarsi, salire; volare, spiccare il volo, spaziare; prendere l'aria.

sob, *n.* singhiozzo, *m.* ~-*stuff*, dramma piagnucoloso, racconto piagnucoloso, *m.* ¶ *v.i.* singhiozzare.

sober, *a.* sobrio; non ubriaco; ragionevole, calmo, grave, serio. he is *never* ~, è sempre ubriaco. ¶ *v.t.* render sobrio, moderare, calmare, render ragionevole; disilludere. ~ness, *n.* sobrietà, serietà, *f.*

sociable, *a.* socievole, affabile. social, *a.* sociale, della società. ~ *events*, (news) mondanità, *f.pl.* ~ism, *n.* socialismo, *m.* ~ist, *n. & a.* socialista, *m.f. & a.* society, *n.* società, *f.*, (l') ordine sociale, *m.*; compagnia, brigata, lega, *f.*; (*fashionable world*), società (elegante), *f.*, bel mondo, *m.*; (*att.*) mondano. ~*man, woman*, mondano, *m.*, -a, *f.* sociology, *n.* sociologia, *f.*

sock, *n.* calzino, *m. ankle* ~, soletta, *f.* ~ *suspenders*, giarrettiere, *f.pl.*

socket, *n.* bocciolo, *m.*; manico, manicotto, *m.*; (*eye*) occhiaia, orbita, *f.*; base, *f.*, zoccolo, incastramento; (*pipe*) bicchiere; (*tooth, &c.*) alveolo, *m.* ¶ *v.t.* incastrare.

Socrates, *m.* Socrate, *m.*

sod, *n.* piota, zolla, *f.*

soda, *n.* soda, *f.*; (*washing*) cristalli di soda, *m.pl.* ~[*water*], acqua gassosa, acqua di Seltz, *f.*

sodden, *a.* bagnato, inzuppato, floscio; bollito.

sodium, *n.* sodio, *m.*

sofa, *n.* sofà, *m.*, canapè, *m.*, divano, *m.*

soffit, *n.* soffitta, *f.*; (*Arch.*) intradosso, *m.*

soft, *a.* morbido, soffice; tenero, mite, dolce; molle; effeminato, semplicione; (*fruit*) mézzo. ~-*boiled* (*eggs*), uova bazzotte, *f.pl.* ~ *collar*, colletto morbido, *m.* ~ *corn*, occhio di pernice, *m.* ~ *felt* (hat), feltro floscio, *m.* ~ *furnishings*, tessuti di ammobigliamento, *m.pl. a* ~ *job*, impiego facile, *m.* ~ *nothings*, galanterie, paroline, *f.pl.* ~ *palate*, palatino, *m.* ~ *pedal*, sordina, *f.* ~ *roe*, latte (di pesce) *m.* ~-*roed*, di

latte. ~*sawder & ~ soap* (*fig.*), piaggeria, lisciatura, *f.*; (*v.t.*) allettare, lusingare. ~ *solder*, saldatura dolce, *f.*; (*v.t.*) saldare a stagno. ~ *soap*, sapone tenero, *m.* ~-*witted*, incretinito, rimbecillito. ~en, *v.t.* rammollire, addolcire, raddolcire; calmare; moderare; intenerire. ~*ening of the brain*, rammollimento cerebrale, *m.* ~ish, *a.* molliccio, morbidetto. ~ly, *ad.* pian piano, adagio, a voce bassa. ~ness, *n.* morbidezza, delicatezza; mollezza; tenerezza; stupidaggine, *f.*

soil, *n.* suolo, terreno, *m.*;terra, gleba, *f.*; letame, *m.* ¶ *v.t.* sporcare, insudiciare, macchiare, imbrattare, insozzare. ~ed, *p.a.* (*linen*) sudicio; (*shop goods*) appassito, sbiadito.

sojourn, *n.* soggiorno, *m.* ¶ *v.i.* soggiornare.

solace, *n.* consolazione, *f.*, conforto, *m.* ¶ *v.t.* consolare, confortare.

solar, *a.* solare. ~ *plexus*, plesso solare, *m.*

sola topi, ~ee (*India*), *n.* elmo di sughero, *m.*

solder & ~ing, *n.* saldatura, *f.* ¶ *v.t.* saldare. ~*ing iron*, saldatoio, *m.*

soldier, *n.* soldato, milite, militare, *m.* ~y, *n.* militari, *m.pl.*; (*unruly*) soldatesca, *f.*

sole, *a.* solo, unico; tutto; esclusivo. ~ *agent*, rappresentante esclusivo, *m.* ¶ *n.* (*foot*) pianta, *f.*; (*shoe*) suola, *f.*; (*fish*) sogliola, *f.* ¶ (*shoes*) *v.t.* risolare.

solecism, *n.* solecismo, *m.*

solemn, *a.* solenne, grave. ~ity, *n.* solennità, *f.* ~ize, *v.t.* solennizzare; (*wedding, &c.*) celebrare.

sol-fa, *n.* solfa, *f.*, solfeggio, *m.* ¶ *v.t. & i.* solfeggiare.

solicit, *v.t.* sollecitare, pregare, chiedere. ~or, *n.* legale, avvocato, notaio, procuratore, *m.* ~ous, *a.* desideroso, premuroso, sollecito. ~ude, *n.* sollecitudine, premura, *f.*

solid, *a.* solido, compatto; fermo, saldo; sodo, massiccio; pieno. ~ *rock*, roccia viva, *f.* ¶ *n.* solido, *m.* ~ify, *v.t.* solidificare. ~ity, *n.* solidità, *f.*

soliloquize, *v.i.* fare un soliloquio, parlare con sé stesso. soliloquy, *n.* soliloquio; monologo, *m.*

soling, *n.* (*shoes*) solatura, *f.*

solitaire, (*gem, game*) *n.* solitario, *m.* solitary, *a.* solitario, ritirato. ~ *confinement*, segregazione cellulare, *f.*, segreta, *f.* ~ *imprisonment*, segreta, reclusione, *f.* **solitude,** *n.* solitudine, *f.*

solo, *n.* solo; assolo, *m.* ~ *dance,* passo a solo, *m.* ~ *violin,* solo di violino, *m.* ~**ist,** *n.* solista, *m.f.*

solstice, *n.* solstizio, *m.*

soluble, *a.* solubile. **solution,** *n.* soluzione; risoluzione, *f.* **solve,** *v.t.* risolvere. **solvency,** *n.* solvibilità, *f.* **solvent,** *a.* solvente; (*Com.*) solvibile. ¶ *n.* solvente; dissolvente, *m.*

sombre, *a.* fosco, tetro, cupo; triste.

some, *a.* qualche, alcuno; certi, parecchi; del, della . . ., dei . . ., delle . . ., un po' di. ¶ *pn.* alcuni, alcune; certi, -e; parecchi, -ie; gli uni, altri; ne. **somebody** & **someone,** *n.* qualcuno, qualcheduno, taluno. ~ *else,* qualche altro, -a. to be *somebody,* essere un personaggio, qualchecosa, una persona importante. **somehow** [or other], *ad.* in qualche modo, in un modo o nell'altro, tanto bene che male, in una maniera o nell'altra, comunque, alla meglio, non saprei dire come.

somersault, *n.* capitombolo, salto mortale, *m.*

something, *n.* qualchecosa, qualche cosa di, qualcosa, (un) non so che, alcunché. ~ *in the wind,* qualche cosa per aria. **sometimes,** *ad.* qualche volta, talvolta, alcune volte, alle volte, di quando in quando. **somewhat,** *ad.* alquanto, un po'. **somewhere,** *ad.* in qualche luogo, da qualche parte; ~ *else,* altrove, in qualche altro luogo. ~ *in the world,* in qualche parte del mondo. ~ *to stay,* alloggio, *m.,* osteria, *f.*

somnambulism, *n.* sonnambulismo, *m.* **somnambulist,** *n.,* sonnambulo, *m.,* -a, *f.* **somnolent,** *a.,* sonnolento.

son, *n.* figlio, figli[u]olo, *m.* ~*-in-law,* *m.,* genero, *m.*

sonata, *n.* sonata, *f.*

song, *n.* canto, *m.,* canzone, *f.;* romanza, aria, *f.* (*sacred*) cantico; (*of birds*), canto, gorgheggio, *m.;* (*mere trifle*) nulla, *m.,* bagatella, *f.,* poco o nulla. ~ *bird,* uccello canoro, *m.* ~ *book,* canzoniere, *m.* ~ *thrush,* tordo canoro, *m.* ~ *without words,* romanza senza parole, *f.* ~ *writer,* compositore di canzoni, *m.* ~**ster,** ~**stress,** *n.,* uccello canoro, *m.;* cantatore, *m.;* cantatrice, *f.,* cantante, *m.f.*

sonnet, *n.* sonetto, *m.*

sonorous, *a.* sonoro.

soon, *ad.* tosto, presto; fra poco, prossimamente; volentieri. as ~ as, appena [che], tosto che, subito che. as ~ as possible, al piú presto possibile, quanto prima; ~ after, poco dopo. ~**er,** *ad.* piú presto, piú tosto, prima; (*rather*) piuttosto. ~ *or later,* prima o poi, tosto o tardi. no ~ *said than done,* detto fatto.

soot, *n.* fuliggine, *f.* ~**y,** *a.* fuligginoso; nero.

soothe, *v.t.* addolcire, calmare, rasserenare; blandire; consolare; lusingare.

soothsayer, *n.* indovino, *m.,* -a, *f.*

sop, *n.* pezzo (di pane) bagnato, crostino inzuppato, *m.;* (*fig.*) osso da rodere, *m.,* offa (a Cerbero), *f.*

sophism, *n.* sofismo, *m.* **sophisticate,** *v.t.* sofisticare. ~**d,** *p.a.* sofisticato, affettato. **sophistry,** *n.* sofisticheria, *f.;* (*Phil.*) sofistica, *f.*

soporific, *a.* & *n.* soporifico, *a.* & *m.*

soprano (*voice* & *pers.*), *n.* soprano, *m.*

sorcerer, *n.* mago, stregone, *m.* ~**ess,** maga, stregona, strega, *f.* **sorcery,** *n.* stregoneria, magia, *f.*

sordid, *a.* sordido. ~**ness,** *n.* sordidezza, *f.*

sore, *a.* doloroso, penoso; severo, grave, crudele; indispettito, stizzito, irritato; sensitivo, permaloso. *I have a ~ finger,* ho male a un dito, il dito mi fa male. ~ *eyes,* male agli occhi, mal d'occhi, *m.* ~ *point,* punto doloroso, punto sensibile, *m.* ~ *throat,* mal di gola, male alla gola, *m.* ¶ *n.* piaga, *f.;* (*gathering*) piaga maligna, *f.*

sorrel, *n.* acetosa, romice, *f.* ¶ *a.* sauro.

sorrily, *ad.* miseramente, meschinamente. **sorrow,** *n.* dolore; dispiacere, *m.;* tristezza, afflizione, *f.,* affanno; cordoglio, *m.;* pena, *f.* ¶ *v.i.* addolorarsi, affliggersi, dolersi. ~**ful,** *a.* afflitto, addolorato, triste; doloroso. ~**fully,** *ad.* dolorosamente, tristemente. **sorry,** *a.* dispiacente, spiacente, dolente; cattivo, povero, meschino, misero, triste; pietoso. to be ~, feel ~, rincrescersi, [di]spiacersi, dolersi (*all used impersonally*); pentirsi; essere [di]spiacente. *I am ~ for it,* me ne rincresce, me ne spiace. *they will be ~ for it,* se ne pentiranno. *I am ~ to say,* mi [di]spiace di dire, mi rincresce dire, mi duole dire. *in a ~ plight,* malconcio, malandato, ridotto a mal partito.

sort, *n.* sorta, *f.*, genere, *m.*; specie; classe, natura, condizione, *f.*; (*pl. Typ.*) assortimento, *m.*; ¶ *v.t.* assortire, classificare, scegliere, cernere. ~**er,** *n.* cernitore, *m.*, -trice, *f.*; classificatore, *m.*, -trice, *f.*

sortie, *n.* sortita, *f.*

sot, *n.* ubriacone, *m.*, -a, *f.*, beone, *m.*, -a, *f.* **sottish,** *a.* abbrutito, imbrutito.

sough, *v.i.* sussurrare, mormorare.

sought after, ricercato.

soul, *n.* anima, *f.*; (*fig.*) creatura; vita, incarnazione, *f.* ~**less,** *a.* senza anima.

sound, *a.* sano; saldo; integro, intero; buono, perfetto; robusto; saggio; solenne; vero, legittimo; (*sleep*) profondo. ¶ *n.* suono, rumore, *m.*; (*Geog.*) stretto, braccio di mare, *m.*; (*probe*) sonda, *f.* ~[ing] *board*; cielo (di pulpito), *m.*; (*Mus.*) cassa armonica. ~ *film,* film sonoro, *m.* ~ *hole,* apertura (di violino, *&c.*), *f.* ~ *post,* anima, *f.* ~*proof,* impenetrabile al suono. ~*proofing,* isolamento acustico, *m.* ~ *track* (cinema), colonna sonora, *f.* ¶ *v.t.* suonare, far risonare, far sentire; scandagliare, tastare; (*Med.*) ascoltare, esplorare, sondare; (*Mil., retreat*), battere; (*v.i.*) suonare, risonare. ~**ly,** *ad.* bene. ~**ness,** *n.* saldezza, integrità, *f.*

soup, *n.* zuppa, minestra, *f.*; brodo, *m.* ~ *kitchen,* cucina economica, *f.* ~ *ladle,* cucchiaione; mestolo, *m.* ~ *plate,* scodella, *f.* ~ *tureen,* zuppiera, *f.*

sour, *a.* agro, acerbo, acido, brusco; acre; (*milk, &c.*) acido, rappreso; (*wine*) inacetito. ¶ *v.t.* far inacidire; (*fig.*) inasprire, esacerbare. ~**ish,** *a.* acidulo, agretto, acidetto. ~**ly,** *ad.* acerbamente; stizzosamente. ~**ness,** *n.* acidità, agrezza, acetosità; acrimonia, *f.*

source, *n.* sorgente, fonte; origine, *f.*

souse, *n.* salamoia; carne marinata, *f.* ¶ *v.t.* marinare; immergere, tuffare, inzuppare.

south, *n.* sud, mezzodí, mezzogiorno, *m.* ¶ *ad.* a sud, verso (il) sud. ¶ *a.* sud, del sud; meridionale; australe. *S~ Africa,* l'Africa del Sud, A. meridionale, Sud-Africa, *f. S~ African,* sudafricano. *S~ America,* l'America del Sud. *S~ American,* sud-americano. *S~ Australia,* l'Australia meridionale, *f.* ~*-east,*

sud-est, *m. S~ polo,* polo sud, *m. S~ Sea Islands,* Isole del Pacifico, *f.pl. S~ Wales,* la Galles del Sud, *f. New S~ Wales,* la Nuova Galles del Sud, *f.* ~*-west,* sud-ovest, *m.*

southern, *a.* [del] sud; meridionale; australe. ~**er,** *n.* meridionale, *m.f. the* ~ *Cross,* la Croce del Sud, *f. the* ~ *hemisphere,* l'emisfero australe, *m.* **southward[s],** *ad.* verso (il) sud, a sud.

souvenir, *n.* ricordo, *m.*

sou'wester, *n.* (*wind*) vento di sud-ovest, libeccio, *m.*; libecciata, *f.*

sovereign, *a. & (pers.)* *n.* sovrano, -a, *a. & m.f.*; (*£*) lira sterlina, *f.* ~**ty,** *n.*, sovranità, *f.*

soviet, *n.* soviet, *m.inv.*; (*att.*) sovietico, *a.*

sow, *n.* scrofa, troia, *f.*; (*wild*) cinghiala, *f.*

sow, *v.t. & i. ir.* seminare, far la sementa. ~**er,** *n.* seminatore, *m.*, -trice, *f.* **sowing,** *n.* seminagione; semina; sementa, *f.* ~ *machine,* seminatrice, *f.* ~ *time,* stagione della semina.

soy[a] bean, soia, *f.*

spa, *n.* stazione termale, *f.*; terme, *f.pl.*; bagni, *m.pl.*; sorgente minerale, *f.*

space, *n.* spazio; intervallo; vuoto, *m.*; posto; distesa, *f.*; (*Mus.*) spazio, *m.*, interlinea, *f.*; (*Typ.*) spazio, *m.* ~ *between lines,* interlinea, *f.* ¶ ~ *& ~ out,* *v.t.* disporre ad intervalli; spaziare; (*fig.*) diradare; (*Typ.*) spazieggiare. **spacious,** *a.* spazioso, ampio, largo, vasto.

spade, *n.* vanga, *f.*; (*pl. Cards*) picche, spade, *f.pl.* ¶ *v.t.* vangare. ~**ful,** *n.* vangata, palata, *f.*

Spain, *n.* la Spagna, *f.*

span, *n.* larghezza, lunghezza; estensione; apertura, portata, durata; (*arch., bridge*), luce, *f.*; *wing* ~ (*Aero.*) *n.* larghezza d'ala; apertura d'ali, *f.* ¶ *v.t.* stendersi (su, attraverso); traversare; abbracciare.

spandrel, *n.* timpano, *m.*

spangle, *n.* lustrino, *m.*; paglietta, *f.* ~**d,** *p.p.* ornato (di stelle, con lustrini, pagliette, etc.); stellato.

Spaniard, *n.* spagnuolo, *m.*, -a, *f.*

spaniel, *n.* bracco spagnuolo, *m.*

Spanish, *a.* spagnuolo, di Spagna. ~ *fly,* cantaride, *f.* ~ *mahogany,* acagiú delle Antille, *m.* ~ *onion,* cipolla dolce (di Spagna), *f.* ¶ *n.* il spagnuolo, *m.*, la lingua spagnuola, *f.*

spank, *v.t.* sculacciare. ~**ing,** *n.* sculacciata, *f.*

spanner, *n.* chiave inglese, chiave per dadi (*box-spanner*), chiave a viti, *f.*

spar, *n.* (*Naut.*) antenna, *f.*; alberetto, *m.*, asta, *f.*, pennoncino, *m.*; (*Miner.*) spato, *m.* ~ *deck,* controcoperta, *f.*, falso ponte, *m.* ~**s,** (*Naut.*) alberatura, *f.* ¶ *v.i.* esercitarsi al pugilato.

spare, *a.* magro, smilzo, sparuto; parco, frugale; di reserva; di rispetto; di ricambio; d'avanzo; (*time*) libero, disponibile. ~ [*bed*] *room,* camera libera, camera degli ospiti, *f.* ~ [*part*], pezzo di ricambio. ~ *time,* tempo libero, tempo avanzato, *m.*; ore d'ozio, *f.pl.* ~ *wheel,* ruota di ricambio, *f.* ¶ *v.t.* risparmiare; (*feeling*) aver cura di, aver riguardo a; concedere; (*life*) dare, accordare; (*time*) trovare. *to have enough & to* ~, aver piú che abbastanza. **sparing,** *a.* economo, parco, frugale, avaro.

spark, *n.* scintilla, favilla, *f.*; (*pers.*) damerino, galante, *m.* ~*ing plug,* candela d'accensione, *f.* **sparkle,** *v.i.* scintillare, sfavillare, brillare, luccicare. **sparkling,** *a.* scintillante, luccicante; (*wine*) spumante.

sparring, *n.* allenamento di pugilatori, *m.*

sparrow, *n.* passero, *m.* ~ *hawk,* sparviero, astore, *m.*

sparse, *a.* rado, sparso, poco spesso. **Spartan,** *a. & n.* spartano, *a. & m.*

spasm, *n.* spasimo, *m.* **spasmodic,** *a.* irregolare, saltuario, fatto a scatto; (*Med.*) spasmodico. ~*ally,* *ad.* spasmodicamente, a scatti.

spate, *n.* piena, corrente impetuoso, *f.*

spats, *n.pl.* ghette di città, *f.pl.*

spatter, *v.t.* spruzzare, spargere; inzaccherare.

spatula, *n.* spatola, *f.*

spawn, *n.* (*fish*) uova, *f.pl.*; (*mushroom*) micelio bianco, *m.* ¶ *v.i.* deporre le uova.

speak, *v.i. & t.ir.* parlare; dire; rivolgere parole (a); prendere la parola; conversare; pronunziare, esprimere; (*ship*) parlamentare, chiamare (a parlamento). ~ *one's mind,* sbottonarsi, sfogarsi; esprimere la propria opinione. ~*er,* *n.* parlatore; oratore; presidente (*Parl.*), *m.*; (*in dialogue*) interlocutore, *m.*; *loud* ~, altoparlante, *m.* **speaking,** *n.* parola, *f.*, (il) parlare, *m.* X ~ (*Teleph.*) parla X. **without** ~, senza parlare. ~ *likeness,* ritratto parlante, *m. we are not on* ~ *terms,* non ci parliamo. ~ *trumpet,*

portavoce, *m.inv.* ~ *tube,* tubo acustico, *m.*

spear, *n.* lancia, *f.*; (*fig.*) asta, *f.*; (*fish*) arpione, *m.* ~*head,* punta della lancia, *f.* ~*mint,* menta verde, *f.* ¶ *v.t.* trafiggere; (*fish*) arpionare.

special, *a.* speciale; particolare; straordinario. ~ *correspondent,* inviato speciale, *m.* ~ *dish for the day,* piatto del giorno, *m.* ~*ist,* *n.* specialista, *m.f.* ~*ity,* *n.* specialità, *f.*; prodotto speciale, *m.* ~*ize in,* specializzarsi in.

specie, *n.* numerario, *m.*, contanti, *m.pl.*, moneta metallica, *f.*

species, *n.* specie; classe, *f.*

specific, *a.* specifico; particolare. ~ *gravity,* peso specifico, *m.* ~ *legatee,* legatario di un oggetto determinato, *m.* ¶ *n.* specifico, *m.* ~*ation,* *n.* specificazione, *f.* **specify,** *v.t.* specificare. **specimen,** *n.* campione; esemplare, saggio; modello, *m.* ~ *page* (*Typ.*), foglio di prova, *m.* **specious,** *a.* specioso, plausibile.

speck, *n.* macchietta, *f.*; punto; grano, *m.*; particella, *f.* ~*le,* *v.t.* chiazzare, screziare; macchiettare.

spectacle, *n.* spettacolo, *m.*; (*pl.*) occhiali, *m.pl.* ~ *case,* astuccio per occhiali, *m.* ~ *maker,* fabbricante di occhiali, occhialaio, ottico, *m.* **spectacular,** *a.* spettacoloso; teatrale. **spectator,** *n.* spettatore, *m.*, -trice, *f.*; assistente, *m.f.*

spectral, *a.* spettrale, di spettro. **spectre,** *n.* spettro, fantasma, *m.* **spectroscope,** *n.* spettroscopio, *m.* **spectrum,** *n.* spettro, *m.* ~ *analysis,* analisi spettrale, *f.*

speculate, *v.i.* speculare; meditare; giuocare. **speculation,** *n.* speculazione, congettura, *f.* **speculative,** *a.* speculativo. **speculator,** *n.* speculatore, *m.*

speech, *n.* parola, *f.*; parlare, *m.*; favella, *f.*; linguaggio, *m.*; discorso, *m.*, allocuzione, *f.* ~ *day,* (*Sch.*) distribuzione dei premi, *f. figure of* ~, figura retorica, *f.* ~ *for the defence,* arringa, *f.* ~*ify,* *v.i.* perorare, far discorsi lunghi. ~*less,* *a.* senza parola, muto.

speed, *n.* velocità; fretta; rapidità; celerità; prestezza, *f.* ~*boat,* idroscivolante. ~ *counter,* contagiri, *m.inv. 3-speed gear,* ingranaggio a tre velocità, *m.* ~ *swim,* corsa di velocità, *f.* ~*way,* autostrada, *f.* ¶ *v.i. ir.* affrettarsi, affrettare il passo, volare. ~ *up*, accelerare, affrettare. **speedometer**, *n.* indicatore di velocità, tachimetro, *m.* **speedwell**, (*Bot.*) *n.* veronica, *f.* **speedy**, *a.* pronto, tosto; rapido, spedito, celere, veloce.

spell, *n.* incanto, fascino, incantesimo, sortilegio, *m.*; parole magiche, *f.pl.*; malia, *f.*; breve periodo; turno [di servizio], *m.* ~ *bound*, affascinato, incantato. ¶ *v.t. & i.ir.* compitare, scrivere. **spelling**, *n.* ortografia, grafia, *f.*; compitazione, *f.* ~ *bee*, concorso ortografico, *m.* ~ *book*, sillabario, abbecedario, *m.*

spelter, *n.* zinco commerciale, *m.*

spencer, *n.* giacchetta, *f.*; panciotto, *m.*; spenser, *m.*

spend, *v.t. & i.ir.* spendere; sborsare; consumare; esaurire; (*time*) passare, trascorrere. ~*thrift*, *n. & att.* prodigo, sprecone, *m.* **spent bullet**, pallottola morta, *f.*

sperm, *n.* sperma, *m.* ~ *oil*, olio di spermaceto, *m.* ~ *whale*, capidoglio, *m.* **spermaceti**, *n.* spermaceti, *m.pl.*; bianco di balena, *m.* **spermatozoon**, *n.* spermatozoo, *m.*

spew, *v.t. & i.* vomitare.

sphere, *n.* sfera, *f.* **spherical**, *a.* sferico.

sphincter, *n.* sfintere, *m.*

sphinx, *n.* sfinge, *f.*

spice, *n.* spezie, spezierie, *f.pl.*; (*fig.*) grano, *m.*, tintura, *f.*, pochino, *m.*

spick & span, *a.* nuovo di zecca, inappuntabile, attillato.

spicy, *a.* aromatico, piccante.

spider, *n.* ragno, *m.* ~('*s*) *web*, ragnatelo, *m.*, -a, *f.*

spigot, *n.* zaffo, tappo; zipolo, *m.*

spike, *n.* aculeo, *m.*; punta, *f.*; chiodo grosso, *m.*, caviglia; (*pl. on wall*) punte di ferro, *m.pl.*; lancia, *f.*; (*of flower*) spigo, *m.* ¶ (*gun*) *v.t.* inchiodare.

spill (*pipe light*), *n.* fidibus, legnetto, *m. to have a* ~, cadere. ¶ *v.t. ir.* spargere, versare, rovesciare.

spin, *n.* (*on ball*) effetto, *m.*; (*Aero.*) avvitamento, *m.* ¶ *v.t. ir.* filare; (*top*) far girare, far roteare; (*v.i.*) rotare, girare; trottolare. ~ *out*, protrarre, prolungare, estendere. ~ *yarns*, recitare storielle, spifferar fandonie.

spinach, ~**age**, *n.* spinacio, *m.*; (*Cook.*) gli spinaci, *m.pl.*

spinal, *a.* spinale. ~ *column*, colonna vertebrale, *f.* ~ *cord*, midollo spinale, *m.* ~ *complaint*, malattia del midollo spinale, *f.*

spindle, *n.* fuso; perno; asse, *m.* ~ *tree*, fusaggine, *f.*

spindrift, *n.* spruzzo del mare, *m.*

spine, *n.* spina, *f.* (*Bot.*); (*Anat.*) spina dorsale, colonna vertebrale, *f.*; (*of book*) dorso, *m.* ~**less**, (*fig.*) *a.* fiacco, infingardo.

spinel, *n.* spinello, *m.*

spinner, *n.* filatore, *m.*, -trice, *f.*

spinney, *n.* boschetto, *m.*

spinning, *n.* filatura, *f.* ~ *jenny*, filatoio, *m.*, filatrice meccanica, *f.*; ~ *mill*, filanda, *f.* ~ *wheel*, filatoio, *m.*

spinster, *n.* zitella: (donna) nubile, *f.*

spiny, *a.* spinoso. ~ *lobster*, aragosta, *f.*

spiral, *a.* spirale; (*spring*) a spirale; (*stairs*) a chiocciola. ¶ *n.* spirale, *f.*

spire, *n.* guglia; cuspide, *f.*; vertice, *m.*; (*whorl*) spira, *f.*

spirit, *n.* spirito, *m.*; anima, *f.*; genio; brio, *m.*; essenza; disposizione, natura, *f.*; fantasma, spettro, *m.*; alcool, liquore alcoolico, *m.*; (*pl.*) umore, *m.*; spiriti; liquori alcoolici, *m.pl.* ~ *lamp*, lampada a spirito, ad alcool, *f.* ~ *level*, livella a bolla d'aria, *f.* ~(*s*) *of salt*, of *wine*, spirito di sale, di vino, *m.* ~ *stove*, stufa ad alcool, *f.* ~ *varnish*, vernice a spirito, (ad) all'alcool, *f.* ~ *away*, far scomparire (come per incanto), rapire, sedurre. ~**ed**, *a.* ardente, brioso, vivace; focoso, impetuoso; coraggioso. ~**less**, *a.* senza spirito, abbattuto, pigro. **spiritual**, *a.* spirituale. **spiritualism**, *n.* (*Psychics*), spiritismo, *m.*; (*Philos*) spiritualismo, *m.* **spiritualist**, *n.* (*Psychics*) spiritista, *m.f.*; (*Philos*) spiritualista, *m.f.* **spirituous**, *a.* alcoolico, spiritoso.

spirt, *n.* getto, *m.* ¶ *v.i.* schizzare, spruzzare; zampillare; (*pen*) sprizzare.

spit, *n.* (*roasting*) spiedo, schidione *m.*; (*Geog.*) lingua di terra (littorale), *f.*; (*Cust.*) scandaglio, *m.* ¶ *v.t.* infilzare (sullo spiedo); trafiggere.

spit, *v.i. & t.ir.* sputare, sputacchiare.

spite, *n.* dispetto, astio, rancore, *m.*; cattiveria; malizia, *f.*; risentimento, *m. in* ~ *of*, malgrado, in dispetto di, ad onta di. ¶ *v.t.* far dispiacere, contrariare, far dispetto a, voler male a, tormentare. ~**ful**, *a.* astioso, vendicativo, malizioso.

spitfire, *n.* persona irascibile, stizzosa, collerica. (*Aera.*) spitfire, *m.inv.*

spittle, *n.* saliva, *f.*, sputo, *m.* **spittoon**, *n.* sputacchiera, *f.*

splash, *n.* (*of water*) schizzo; (*into water*) tonfo, tuffo, *m.*; (*mud, &c.*)

schizzo, spruzzo, *m.*; zacchera, *f.*; (*colour*, *&c.*) chiazza, macchia, *f.* ~*board*, parafango, *m.*, paraspruzzi, *m.inv. to make a* ~ (*pop.*), ostentare, fare effetto. ¶ *v.t.* inzaccherare, schizzare; (*v.i.*) sguazzare, schizzare, batter l'acqua; (*tap*) sputare. ~ *about*, agitarsi, sguazzare.

splay, *v.t.* (*Arch.*) strombare, sguanciare; (*dislocate*) spallare.

spleen, *n.* (*Anat.*) milza, *f.*; (*dumps*) malinconia, noia, *f.*, umor nero, *m.*; (*spite*) bile, animosità, stizza, *f.*

splendid, *a.* splendido, lauto, magnifico. **splendour**, *n.* splendore, *m.*

splice, *n.* unione, intrecciatura, *f.*; (*Naut.*) impiombatura, *f.* ¶ *v.t.* impiombare, unire, riunire.

splint, *n.* stecca, *f.* ~ [*bone*] fibula, *f.*

splinter, *n.* scheggia; (*bone*) scheggia (d'osso), *f.* ~ *bar*, bilancino (di carrozza), *m.* ¶ *v.t.* scheggiare, spezzare.

split, *n.* fessura, spaccatura, *f.*; (*fig.*) divergenza, divisione, separazione, *f.* ¶ *v.t. ir.* fendere, spaccare, dividere; (*ears with noise*) lacerare, rompere (il cranio); (*v.i.*) fendersi, spaccarsi, dividersi, separarsi; crepare, scoppiare. ~ *hairs*, cavillare, sofisticare, cercare il pelo nell'uovo. ~ *peas*(*e*), piselli spaccati, sbucciati, *m.pl.* ~*-wood*, stecca, assicella, *f. splitting headache*, mal di testa da impazzire, *m.*

splutter, *n.* barbugliamento, discorso interrotto e confuso, *m.* ¶ *v.i.* barbugliare, sputacchiare parlando.

spoil, *n.* spoglie, *f.pl.*, preda, *f.*; bottino, *m.* ¶ *v.t.* guastare, danneggiare, rovinare; corrompere, viziare. ~ *sport*, guastafeste, *m.inv.*

spoke, *n.* raggio, *m.* ~ *shave*, piccola pialla, *f.* ¶ *v.t.* incastrare i raggi in una ruota.

spokesman, *n.* rappresentante, portavoce.

spoliation, *n.* spogliazione, *f.*

sponge, *n.* spugna, *f.*; (*gun*) scovolo, *m.* ~ *bag*, sacchetto per la spugna, *m.* ~ *cake*, biscotto spugnoso, *m.* ~ *cloth*, tessuto a spugna, *m.* ~*down*, spugnatura, *f.* ¶ *v.t.* passare la spugna sopra, pulire, nettare con la spugna; scroccare. **sponger**, *n.* scroccone, parassita, *m.* **spongy**, *a.* spugnoso.

sponsor, *m.* garante, *m.f.*, mallevadore, *m.*, -drice, *f.*; (*Eccl.*) padrino, *m.*, madrina, *f.*

spontaneous, *a.* spontaneɔ

spook, *n.* spettro, fantasma, *m.*, larva, *f.*

spool, *n.* rocchetto, *m.*, bobina, *f.* ¶ *v.t.* bobinare.

spoon, *n.* cucchiaio, *m.* ~ *bill*, spatola, *f.* ~ *brake*, freno sul pneumatico, *m.* ~*ful*, cucchiaiata, *f.*

spoor, *n.* traccia, *f.*

sporadic, *a.* sporadico.

spore, *n.* spora, *f.*

sport, *n.* giuoco; scherzo, *m.*; caccia, *f.* (*s. & pl.*) lo sport, *m.* ~*s editor*, redattore sportivo, *m.* ~*s ground*, stadio; campo (di calcio, di golf, di tennis, ecc.), *m.* ~*s suit*, vestito da sport, completo per lo sport, *m.* ~*s outfitter*, fornitore di indumenti sportivi, *m.* ¶ *v.i.* giuocare; divertirsi, svagarsi. ~*ing*, *a.* (*dog*, *gun*, *&c.*) da caccia; (*editor*, *spirit*, *&c.*) sportivo. **sportsman**, *n.* cultore dello sport, [uomo] sportivo; cacciatore, *m.*

spot, *n.* luogo, posto, sito; punto, segno, *m.*; macchia, *f.*; (*Bil.*) segno, *m.*; (*Com.*) contante, disponibile. *on the* ~, sul luogo, immediatamente, immantinente, senz'altro, d'un colpo. ~*light*, proiettore [orientabile], *m.* ¶ *v.t.* macchiare; scorgere, scoprire, riconoscere. **spotted**, *a.* macchiato; chiazzato; punteggiato. **spotless**, *a.* senza macchia, immacolato.

spouse, *n.* speso, *m.*, sposa, *f.*

spout, *n.* getto, zampillo, *m.*; colonna, *f.*; tubo, becco, beccuccio, *m.*; gronda, grondaia, doccia, *f.* *water* ~, (*Naut.*) tromba marina, *f.* ¶ *v.i. & t.* sgorgare, scaturire, schizzare; gettare, lanciare; (*fig.*) declamare.

sprain, *n.* storta, *f. to* ~ *one's* . . ., storcersi il, la . . .

sprat, *n.* piccolo pesce simile all'aringa, *m.*; specie di cheppia.

sprawl, *v.i.* sdraiarsi in modo scomposto.

spray, *n.* spruzzo, *m.*, gocciolette, *f.pl.*; ramicello, *m.*, frasca, *f.*; (*sea*) spruzzo del mare, *m.*; (*jewels*) spiga, *f.*; (*flowers*) mazzo, fascio, *f.*; (*squirt*) vaporizzatore, spruzzatore, *m.* ¶ *v.t.* spruzzare; vaporizzare.

spread, *n.* estensione, diffusione, distesa, propagazione, *f.*; sviluppo, *m.*; (*pop.*) pasto, banchetto, *m.* ¶ *v.t.* stendere, spandere, spargere, allargare, disseminare, propagare; (*table*) apparecchiare, mettere; (*wings*, *&c.*) spiegare. (*v.i.*) stendersi, allargarsi, diffondersi, spiegarsi, spandersi.

spree, *n.* baldoria, scappata, ribotta, *f.*
sprig, *n.* ramoscello, rampollo, *m.*
sprightly, *a.* gaio, vivace, allegro, brioso.
spring, *n.* balzo, slancio, salto, *m.*; elasticità; molla; sorgente, polla, fonte, *f.*; (*season*) primavera, *f.*; (*att.*) primaverile, della primavera. ~ *balance,* bilancia a molla, *f.* ~*board,* trampolino, *m.* ~ *chicken,* pulcino, *m.* ~ *cleaning,* grande ripulitura, *f.* ~ *knife, clasp k.,* coltello a molla, *m.* ~ *mattress,* materasso elastico, *m.,* cassa elastica, *f.* ~ *onion,* cipollina, *f.* ~ *tide,* marea grande, marea massima, marea di plenilunio, di novilunio, *f.* ¶ *v.i.* ir. saltare, balzare; slanciarsi. ~ (*from*), derivare; discendere; provenire. ~ *up,* nascere; spuntare; sorgere. *to* ~ *a mast,* consentire un albero. ~**er,** (*Arch.*) *n.* imposta, *f.* ~**y,** *a.* elastico.
sprinkle, *v.t.* spruzzare, spargere, cospargere, aspergere; (*book-edges*) screziare. **sprinkler,** *n.* spruzzatore, *m.,* (*Eccl.*) aspersorio, *m.*
sprint, *n.* corsa di velocità, *f.*; scatto, *m.* ~**er,** *n.* velocista, *m.*
sprite, *n.* folletto, *m.*
sprocket wheel, rocchetto a denti, *m.*
sprout, *n.* germoglio; tallo, *m.* ¶ *v.i.* germogliare. *Brussels* ~*s,* broccoletti di Brusselle, *m.pl.*
spruce, *a.* attillato, lindo, vivace. ¶ *n.* abete rosso, *m.*
sprung (*provided with springs*) *p.a.* a molle.
spud (*Agric.*) *n.* zappetta, *f.*; sarchio, sarchiello, *m.*; (*pop.*) patata, *f.*
spur, *n.* sperone, sprone, *m.*; (*bird*) sperone (di gallo); (*mountain*) contrafforte; (*fig.*) stimolo, pungolo, incitamento; (*Build.*) arco di sostegno, *m.* *on the* ~ *of the moment,* sotto l'impulso del momento. ¶ *v.t.* spronare, dare di sprone a; incitare, aizzare.
spurious, *a.* spurio, falso, contraffatto.
spurn, *v.t.* respingere (con disprezzo), sdegnare.
spurt, *v.i.* sgorgare, zampillare, schizzare; (*price*) balzare, salire, subire un rialzo improvviso. ¶ *n.* schizzo, scatto, salto, *m.*; (*Running*) sforzo, scatto, *m.,* volata, *f.*
sputter, *n.* spruzzo; scoppiettìo; balbettamento, *m.* ¶ *v.i.* sputacchiare, schizzare, scoppiettare.
spy, *n.* spia, *f.*; (*police*) spione, delatore, *m.* ~*-glass,* piccolo cannocchiale, *m.*

~*-hole,* spioncino, *m.* ¶ *v.t. & i.* (or ~ *upon*) spiare. ~ *into,* scrutare; ~ *out,* scoprire, scorgere.
squab, *n.* cuscinetto; piccioncino, *m.*
squabble, *n.* contesa, zuffa, *f.*; alterco, *m.* ¶ *v.i.* altercare, questionarsi.
squab[by], *a.* grassotto, paffuto, tozzo.
squad, *n.* squadra, *f.*; drappello, plotone, *m.* **squadron,** (*Cavalry*) squadrone, *m.*; (*Navy*) squadriglia; (*Air*) squadriglia, *f.*
squalid, *a.* lurido, sudicio, sporco.
squall, *n.* raffica, burrasca, *f.*; colpo di vento, *m.* ¶ *v.i.* sbraitare, vociare, strillare. ~**y,** *a.* a raffiche, burrascoso.
squalor, *n.* miseria, *f.,* sudiciume, fango, *m.*
squander, *v.t.* sprecare, sciupare, dissipare, scialacquare, sperperare.
square, *a.* quadro, quadrato; (*fig.*) regolato; pareggiato; giusto, onesto; pari. *all* ~, al pari. ~ *foot,* piede quadrato, *m.* = 9.2903 sq. decimetres. ~ *inch,* pollice quadrato, *m.* = 6.4516 sq. centimetres. ~ *meal,* pasto sostanzioso, *m.* ~ *measure,* misura di superficie, *f.* ~ *mile,* miglio quadrato, *m.* = 259.00 hectares. ~ *root,* radice quadrata, *f.* ~ *ruler &* ~ *file,* quadrello, *m.* ~*-shouldered,* dalle spalle quadre. ~ *yard,* iarda quadrata, *f.* = 0.836126 sq. metre. (*of the circle*) quadratura, *f.* ¶ *n.* quadro, quadrato, *m.*; (*instrument & at right angles,* squadra, *f.*; (*town*) piazza, *f.*; (*parvis*) sacrato, *m.*; (*chessboard*) scacco, *m.* ¶ *v.t.* quadrare, squadrare; (*Math.*) elevare al quadrato; conformare; regolare, sistemare. ~*d paper,* carta a quadretti. ~**[ly],** *ad.* chiaro e tondo, schietto e netto.
squash, *v.t.* schiacciare; appiattire.
squat, *v.i.* acquattarsi; accoccolarsi; accosciarsi; rannicchiarsi. ¶ *a.* tozzo, tarchiato, atticciato.
squeak, *n.* piccolo strido, pigolìo, *m.* ¶ *v.i.* fare piccoli stridi; pigolare; (*of things*) cigolare, stridere, scricchiolare. ~**er,** (*Punch's*) *n.* fischietto, *m.*
squeal, *n.* strido acuto, grido di dolore. ¶ *v.i.* strillare; lamentarsi.
squeamish, *a.* soggetto a nausee; fastidioso, schizzinoso.
squeegee, *n.* asciugatoio di gomma, *m.*; (*Naut.*) radazza, *f.*
squeeze, *n.* strizzata; stretta, *f.*; (*fam.*) calca, pressa, serra, *f.* ¶ *v.t.* strizzare; stringere; serrare, pigiare.

~ *out*, spremere; (*fig.*) strappare (a), cavare (a).

squelch, *v.t.* (*fam.*) schiacciare; sconcertare; ridurre al silenzio.

squib, *n.* razzetto, salterello, *m.*; pasquinata, *f.*

squid, *n.* seppia, *f.*, calamaro, *m.*

squint, *v.i.* guardar di traverso; (*Med.*) essere affetto da strabismo. ¶ *n.* sguardo bieco, sguardo losco, *m.*

squire, *n.* gentiluomo di campagna; (*Hist.*) scudiero, *m.*

squirrel, *n.* scoiattolo, *m.*

squirt, *n.* siringa, *f.*, schizzetto, *m.* ¶ *v.t.* schizzare; (*v.i.*) scaturire, zampillare.

stab, *n.* stoccata, pugnalata, coltellata, *f.* ¶ *v.t.* pugnalare, stilettare, trafiggere, dare una coltellata a.

Stabat Mater, *n.* Stabat Mater, *m.*

stability, *n.* stabilità; consistenza, *f.*

stabilize, *v.t.* stabilizzare, rendere stabile; (*Fin.*) stabilizzare. **stable**, *a.* stabile, saldo; costante, fermo. ¶ *n.* (*horses*) scuderia, *f.*; (*cattle*), stalla, *f.* ~ *boy*, mozzo di stalla; (*Turf*) lad, *m.* ¶ *v.t.* mettere in istalla, mettere nella scuderia.

staccato, *a.* (*note*) punto; (*voice*) staccato.

stack, *n.* (*Agric.*) pagliaio, *m.*; (*heap*) mucchio, *m.*, bica, catasta, *f.*; (*arms*) fascio, *m.*; (*chimney*) camino, *m.*, gola di camino, *f.* ¶ *v.t.* accatastare, abbicare, ammucchiare, mettere in fascio.

stadium, *n.* stadio, *m.*

staff, *n.* bastone, *m.*, asta, *f.*; (*pilgrim's*) bordone, *m.*; (*Mus.*) rigo, *m.*; personale, *m.*, impiegati, *m.pl.*; (*Mil.*) Stato Maggiore, *m.* ~ *officer*, ufficiale d'ordinanza, ufficiale di Stato Maggiore, *m.*

stag, *n.* cervo, *m.*; (*young*) cerbiatto, *m.* ~ *beetle*, cervo volante, *m.*

stage, *n.* tappa, fase, *f.*, grado; periodo; stadio, *m.*; scena, *f.*, teatro, palcoscenico, *m.* ~ *box*, palco di proscenio, *m.* ~*coach*, posta, diligenza, *f.* ~ *directions*, didascalia, *f.* ~ *effect*, effetto scenico, colpo di scena, *m.* ~ *manager*, direttore (di scena), *m.* ~ *name*, nome d'arte, nome di teatro, *m.* ~ *trick*, gioco di scena, colpo di teatro, *m.* ~ *whisper*, a parte. ¶ *v.t.* mettere in scena, rappresentare. *old stager*, volpe vecchia, *f.*, volpone, *m.*

stagger, *v.i.* barcollare, vacillare, tentennare; (*v.t.*) stupefare, far strabiliare.

staging, *n.* (*scaffolding*) impalcatura *f.*, ponteggio, *m.*; (*Theat.*) messa in scena, *f.*

stagnant, *a.* stagnante; inattivo; cheto.

stagnation, *n.* ristagno, *m.*, inattività, *f.*

staid, *a.* grave, posato; sobrio.

stain, *n.* macchia, chiazza; magagna, *f.*; colore, *m.*, tinta, *f.* ¶ *v.t.* macchiare; tingere, colorare; dipingere. *stained glass*, vetro colorato; (*Church, &c.*) vetrate dipinte, *f.pl.*, vetro cattedrale, *m.* *stained glass artist*, pittore vetraio, *m.* *stained glass window*, vetrata dipinta, *f.* **stainless**, *a.* senza macchia, immacolato; (*steel*) inossidabile.

stair, *n.* (*step*) gradino, scalino, *m.* ~ *carpet*, tappeto di scala, *m.* ~*case* & ~[*s*], scala, *f.*, scalinata, *f.*, scalone, *m.* ~ *rail*, corrimano, *m.* *down*~*s*, giú, da basso; al pianterreno. ~*way*, gabbia, tromba (delle scale). *moving* ~, scala mobile, *f.* *up*~*s*, di sopra; ai piani superiori.

stake, *n.* palo, steccone, *m.*; palanca, *f.*; biffa, *f.*; pi[u]olo, *m.*; (*fig.*) rogo, martirio, *m.*; (*Turf*) posta, scommessa, *f.* ¶ *v.t.* giocare, porre, puntare, scommettere; rischiare. ~ *out*, segnare con pali, con pioli; (*fig. claim, &c.*) reclamare, pretendere a.

stalactite, *n.* stalattite, *f.*

stalagmite, *n.* stalagmite, *f.*

stale, *a.* stantio, vecchio, guasto, insipido, scipito, trito. (*bread*) raffermo; (*cheque*) vecchio, prescritto.

stalemate, *n.* (*Chess*) stallo, *m.* ¶ *v.t.* far stallo.

stalk, *n.* stelo, gambo; (*cabbage*) torsolo; piede, *m.* ¶ *v.t.* cacciare (all'agguato, all'aspetto). ~*ing horse* (*fig.*), maschera, *f.*, pretesto, *m.*

stall, *n.* stalla, *f.*; stallo, *m.*; baracca, *f.*; mostra, *f.*; banco, *m.*, bancarella, *f.*; edicola, *f.*, chiosco, *m.*; (*Theat.*) poltrona, *f.*; scanno, sedile; canonicato, *m.* ~ *holder*, rivendugliolo, *m.* ¶ *v.t.* mettere nella stalla, *v.i.* (*engine*) fermarsi; (*Aero.*) andare al disotto della velocità che consente il controllo dell'apparecchio.

stallion, *n.* stallone, *m.*

stalwart, *a.* robusto, gagliardo; prode, fiero.

stamen, *n.* stame, *m.*

stamina, *n.* forza di resistenza, gagliardia, robustezza, *f.*

stammer, *v.i.* & *t.* balbettare, (*stutter*) tartagliare. ~*er*, *n.*

balbuziente, *m.f.*; tartaglione, *m.*, -ona, *f.*

stamp, *n.* stampo, *m.*; impronta, *f.*; marchio; segno, bollo; timbro; punzone, maglio, *m.*; tempra, *f.*; carattere, *m.* *postage* ~, francobollo, *m.* ~ *duty,* tassa di bollo, *f.* ~ *office,* ufficio del bollo, *m.* ¶ *v.t. & i.* improntare; bollare, affrancare, timbrare; imprimere, scolpire; coniare; suggellare; (*feet*) battere, pestare; (*horse*) scalpitare. ~*ed addressed envelope,* busta affrancata per la risposta, *f.*

stampede, *n.* fuga precipitosa, *f.*

stance, *n.* posizione, posa, *f.*

stanch, *a. & v.t.* Same as **staunch.**

stanchion, *n.* puntello, sostegno, *m.*

stand, *n.* posizione, stazione, sosta, *f.*; posto, posteggio, sostegno; banco, *m.*; tribuna, *f.*; pausa; resistenza, *f.*; tavolato, palco, *m.*; (*music*) leggio, *m.*; (*exhibition*) mostra, *f.*, banco di mostra, *m.*; affusto; piede, zoccolo, piedestallo, *m.*; (*stall*) baracca, *f.* ~ *point,* punto di vista, *m.* ~*still,* arresto, ristagno, *m.* ¶ *v.i.* stare in piedi, essere in piedi, rimanere in piedi, stare; tenere, tenersi; essersi; trovarsi; fermarsi; farsi; porsi; mettersi; presentarsi; difendersi; reggersi; durare; essere valido; (*v.t. ir.*) sopportare, sostenere, mantenere; subire; resistere a; tollerare; soffrire; adattarsi a; (*drink, &c.*) pagare. ~ *aside,* far luogo, far posto, appartarsi, scansarsi, farsi in là; ~ *back!* dietro! scansatevi! ~ *down* (*from witness box*) ritirarsi; (*from candidature*) rinunziare. ~ *idle,* essere disoccupato. ~ *in the way of,* fare ostacolo a, opporsi a. ~ *on end* (hair), rizzare. ~ *out,* risaltare; resistere; tener duro; stare sulle sue; ~ *up,* tenersi dritto, alzarsi, stare in piedi. ~*-up collar,* colletto dritto, colletto duro, c. inamidato (*starched*).

standard, *n.* bandiera, *f.*, stendardo, *m.*; insegna, *f.*; modello, *m.*; criterio, tipo, *m.*, norma, *f.*; grado, *m.*; classe, *f.*; tenore, livello, *m.*; misura, *f.*; piede, *m.*; (*weight, measure*) matrice, *f.*; (*gold*) titolo, *m.*; (*of coin*) legge, *f.*; corso legale, *m.* ~ *bearer,* portabandiera, portastendardo, *m.inv.,* gonfaloniere, *m.* ¶ *att.* modello, tipo; classico, autorevole; legale; (*gauge*) normale; (*edition*) definitivo; (*charge*) fissato; (*gold*) al titolo; (*solution*) titolato; (*lamp*) a

piede; (*time*) medio legale. ~*ize,* *v.t.* unificare, standardizzare; (*Chem.*) titolare.

standing, *n.* posizione, *f.*, rango, *m.*; durata; riputazione, *f.* *of long* ~, di lunga mano, vecchio; che data da molto tempo. ¶ *a.* in piedi, ritto; stabile; fisso; permanente; (*crops*) in erba, non falciato; (*Law*) frutti pendenti, *m.pl.*; (*Naut.*) dormiente; (*water*) stagnante; (*orders, army, &c.*) permanente; (*expenses*) generale, ordinario; (*jump, dive*) a piedi giunti, da fermo; (*start*) fermato. ~ *room only!* soltanto posti in piedi! ~ *start mile,* miglio, partenza fermata. ~ *type,* conservazione, *f.*

stand-offish, *a.* riservato, poco comunicativo, distante. ~*ness,* *n.* riserva, *f.*

stanza, *n.* stanza, strofa, *f.*

staple, *n.* (*wall*) grappa, *f.*; (*wire*) gancio, filo metallico ad U, *m.*; (*lock*) staffa, *f.*; (*to fasten papers*) fermaglio, *m.*, serracarte, *m.inv.*; ~ (*product*) prodotto principale, *m.* ~ (*of conversation*), soggetto principale, *m.*

star, *n.* stella, *f.*, astro, *m.*; (*lucky*) buona stella, *f.*; (*Theat.*) stella, *f.*; (*Cinema*) diva, *f.*; (*Typ.*) asterisco, *m.* ~*fish,* asteria, stella marina, *f.* ~*gaze,* stare a bada, baloccarsi, ~ *map,* carta celeste, *f.* ~ *of Bethlehem,* ornitogalo, *m.* ~ *shell,* razzo, *m.* ~ *turn,* la maggiore attrattiva, *f.*, numero principale, *m.*

starboard, *n.* tribordo, *m.*; dritta, *f.*; fianco dritto, *m.*

starch, *n.* amido, *m.*; (*paste*) colla d'amido, *f.* ¶ *v.t.* inamidare. ~*y* (*food*) *a.* feculento.

stare, *n.* sguardo fisso, *m.* ¶ *v.i.* fissare gli occhi, spalancare gli occhi. ~ *at,* guardare fissamente.

stark, *a.* rigido, inflessibile; assoluto. ~ *mad,* pazzo da legare, pazzo a catene. ~ *naked,* tutto nudo, nudo come un verme.

starling, *n.* (*bird*) stornello, *m.*

starry, *a.* stellato, seminato di stelle; fulgido.

start, *n.* sobbalzo; soprassalto, *m.*; scossa, *f.*; slancio, scatto, *m.*; primo passo, avviamento; inizio, principio, *m.*; partenza, *f.*; vantaggio, *m.* ¶ *v.i.* sussultare, trasalire; balzare, dare un salto; partire; prendere le mosse; cominciare; (*v.t.*) iniziare, far nascere, avviare; aprire; lanciare; fondare; partire, dare il segnale della partenza; mettere in moto; (*quarry*) levare, scovare. **~er**, *n.* (*signal giver*), mossiere, *m.*; (*horse, runner*), partente, *m.f.*, (*Elec.*) avviatore, *m.* **~***ing line*, linea di partenza, *f.* **~***ing post*, palo di partenza, *m.*

startle, *v.t.* far trasalire, mettere in allarme, sorprendere. **startling**, *a.* sorprendente, allarmante, spaventoso.

starvation, *n.* morte di fame, inedia, fame, *f.* **~** *diet*, dieta assoluta, *f.* **~** *wage*, salario da fame, *m.* **starve**, *v.t.* affamare, far morire di fame; (*v.i.*) morir di fame. **~ling**, *n.* affamato, *m.*, -a, *f.* **starving**, *p.a.* affamato, famelico.

state, *n.* stato, *m.*, condizione, *f.*; apparato, *m.*, gala, *f.*, pompa, *f.*; (*stage of engraved or etched plate*) stato, *m.* *to lie in* **~** (of body), essere esposto sul letto mortuario. **~** *controlled*, **~** *managed*, statizzato, sotto l'amministrazione dello stato. **~** *insurance*, previdenza sociale, *f.* **~** *railway*, ferrovia dello Stato, *f.* **~** *reception*, ricevimento solenne, *m.* **~** *rooms*, **~** *apartments* (palace), grandi appartamenti, *m.pl.* (*ship*) appartamenti di lusso, *m.pl.* *S*~ *socialism*, socialismo di Stato, *m.* ¶ *v.t.* affermare, esporre, dire, dichiarare, enunciare, formulare, constatare, porre; fissare. **~d**, *p.a.* fisso, determinato. **~li-ness**, *n.* maestà. **~ly**, *a.* magnifico, imponente, maestoso. **statement**, *n.* affermazione, asserzione; dichiarazione; deposizione, relazione, *f.*; rendiconto, *m.*; rivista, *f.*; (*Com.*) prospetto, quadro, *m.*, distinta, *f.* **~** *of affairs*, bilancio, *m.* **~** *of claim* (*Law*) libello, *m.*, comparsa, memoria, *f.* **statesman**, *n.* uomo di Stato, statista, *m.*

static(**al**), *a.* statico. **statics**, *n.pl.* statica, *f.*

station, *n.* stazione, *f.*; grado, stato, posto, *m.*, condizione, *f.*, rango, *m.*; (*police*) questura; **~s** *of the Cross*, stazioni della Via Crucis, *f.pl.*, cammino della Croce, *m.* **~***master*, capo-stazione, *m.inv.* ¶ *v.t.* stanziare, appostare, assegnare un posto a, collocare. **~ary**, *a.* stazionario, fisso, immobile.

stationer, *n.* cartolaio, *m.* **~y**, *n.* cartoleria, *f.*, articoli di cartoleria, *m.pl.* **~** *case*, portafogli, *m.inv.*, cartella, *f.* **~** *rack*, portacarte, *m.inv.*

statistic(**al**), *a.* statistico. **statistician**, *n.* studioso di statistica, *m.* **statistics**, *n.pl.* statistica, *f.*

statuary, *a.* statuario. ¶ *n.* statue, *f.pl.*; (*Art*) scultura, statuaria, *f.*; (*pers.*) statuario, *m.* **statue**, *n.* statua, *f.* **statuette**, *n.* figurina, *f.* stucchino, *m.*

stature, *n.* statura, taglia, *f.*

status, *n.* stato, titolo, grado, *m.*; condizione civile, *f.*; *legal* **~**, posizione o condizione giuridica, *f.*

statute, *n.* statuto, *m.*, legge (scritta), *f.* **~***-barred*, caduco, decaduto. *to be* **~***-barred*, prescriversi, andar in prescrizione; **~** *book*, codice, *m.* **~** *law*, legge scritta, *f.* **statutory**, *a.* statutario, regolato dalla legge (scritta).

staunch, *a.* fermo, devoto, fido. ¶ *v.t.* ristagnare; (*thirst*) levarsi, estinguere.

stave, *n.* doga, *f.*; stanza, strofa, *f.*; versetto, *m.*; (*Mus.*) rigo, *m.* **~** *in*, *v.t.* *ir.* sfondare. **~** *off*, respingere, parare, scansare.

stay, *n.* soggiorno, *m.*, dimora, *f.*; indugio; puntello, tirante, *m*; straglio, *m.*; (*Law*) sospensione, *f.*; (*pl.*) busto, corsetto, *m.* **~** *in the country*, villeggiatura, *f.* ¶ *v.i.* stare, rimanere, fermarsi; aspettare; soggiornare, dimorare; (*v.t.*) ritardare, arrestare, trattenere; calmare; puntellare. **~***at-home*, *a.* & *n.* casalingo, *a.* & *m.*, persona casalinga, *f.* **~** *away*, assentarsi, allontanarsi. **~***-in strike*, sciopero bianco, *m.* **~** *the course*, fare la corsa. **~** *up*, vegliare. **~***ing power*, forza di resistenza, *f.*

stead, *n.* luogo, posto, *m.*; vece, *f.* *stand in good* **~**, giovare, essere di grande utilità a.

steadfast, *a.* fermo, costante, risoluto. **~ly**, *ad* fermamente, costantemente. **~ness**, *n.* costanza, risolutezza, *f.*

steady, *a.* costante, fermo; saldo; fisso; assiduo, regolare, regolato. ¶ *i.* così! piano! rimanete tranquillo! (*Mil.*) fissi!

steak, *n.* fetta (di carne), costoletta, *f.*; (*beef*) bistecca, *f.*

steal, *v.t.* & *i.* *ir.* rubare, involare, derubare, svaligiare. **~** *away*, sottrarsi, svignarsela, andarsene furtivamente, involarsi. **~** *in*, introdursi furtivamente, insinuarsi. **~ing**, *n.* furto, *m.* **by stealth**, furtivamente, di soppiatto. **stealthy**, *a.* furtivo, segreto, clandestino.

steam, *n.* vapore, *m.*; (*att.*) a vapore, di vapore. **~** *room* (bath), bagno a vapore, *m.* ¶ *v.t.* (*Cook*) (far) cuocere a vapore; (*v.i.*) emettere vapore; fumare; navigare (a vapore). ~er or ~boat or ~ship, *n.* nave a vapore, *f.*, vapore, piroscafo, battello a vapore, vaporetto, *m.* ~er or ~ cooker, *n.* marmitta a vapore, autoclave, *f.* ~ing, *n.* (*Cook*), cottura a vapore, *f.*

stearin, *n.* stearina, *f.* **steatite**, *n.* steatite, *f.*

steed (*Poet.*) *n.* corsiero, destriero, *m.*

steel, *n.* acciaio, *m.*; (*of tinder box*) acciarino, *m.*; (*sharpener*) acciaiolo, *m.*; (*corset*) stecca, *f.*; (*att.*) di acciaio, d'acciaio. ~ works, acciaieria, *f.*, -ie, *f.pl.* ~yard, stadera, bilancia romana, *f.* ¶ *v.t.* acciaiare, rivestire d'acciaio; (*fig.*) indurire, fortificare, corrazzare.

steep, *a.* erto, scosceso, ripido, a picco. ¶ *v.t.* immergere, tuffare; immollare; macerare; bagnare; imbevere, inzuppare. ~ed in (*fig.*), pieno di, gonfio di. **steeple**, *n.* guglia, *f.*, campanile aguzzo, *m.* ~chase, corsa ad ostacoli, *f.* **steepness**, *n.* ripidezza, ripida pendenza, *f.*

steer, *n.* giovenco, *m.* ¶ *v.t. & i.* dirigere, condurre, guidare, governare, dirigersi. ~ clear of, evitare. **steerage**, *n.* posti dei passeggeri di terza (classe), *m.pl.* ~ passenger, passeggero di terza (classe), *m.* **steering**, *n.* direzione, *f.* (*Naut.*) governo, *m.* ~ compass, bussola di rotta, *f.* ~ wheel (*Motor*), volante di direzione, v. di guida, *m.* **steersman**, *n.* timoniere, *m.*

stellar, *a.* stellare.

stem, *n.* stelo, gambo; picciuolo; piede, *m.*; stirpe, *f.*; ramo, rampollo, *m.*; (*ship*) prua, prora, *f.*; (*Gram.*) tema, *m.* ~ stitch, punto di gambo, *m.* ¶ *v.t.* arrestare, resistere a, andar contro a.

stench, *n.* puzzo, fetore, *m.*

stencil, *n.* stampino, *m.*; marchio, *m.*; (*Typing*) stencil, *m.* ¶ *v.t.* imprimere collo stampino.

stenographer, ~phist, *n.* stenografo, *m.*, -a, *f.* **stenography**, *n.* stenografia, *f.*

stentorian, *a.* stentoreo.

step, *n.* passo; gradino, scalino, *m.*; (*of ladder*) piuolo, *m.*; (*carriage*) predellino, montatoio, *m.*; (*footstep*) pianta, orma, pedata, *f.*; (*door*) soglia, *f.*; andatura, *f.*; (*pl.*) scala, *f.*; (*pair of*) scala doppia. ~brother, fratellastro, *m.* ~ dance, punta e

tacco, *m.* ~daughter, figliastra, *f.* ~father, patrigno, *m.* ~mother, matrigna, *f.* (*cruel*) (*fig.*) matrigna, *f.* ~sister, sorellastra, *f.* ~son, figliastro, *m.* ¶ *v.i.* fare un passo; camminare, andare, venire, montare. keep ~ with, andare (marciare) al passo con. ~ forward, avanzarsi. ~ in, entrare; intervenire; ~ down, scendere. ~ out, uscire. stepping stone, pietra a guado, pietra da passaggio, *f.*; (*fig.*) marciapiede, *m.*; piuolo, scalino, *m.*

stereoscope, *n.* stereoscopio, *m.*

stereotype, *n.* stereotipia, *f.* ¶ *v.t.* stereotipare.

sterile, *n.* sterile, *m.* **sterility**, *n.* sterilità, *f.* **sterilize**, *v.t.* sterilizzare.

sterling, *a.* (*Eng. money*) sterlina; (*fig.*) di buona lega, genuino. ¶ *n.* lira sterlina, *f.*

stern, *a.* austero, duro, severo, rigoroso, torvo. ¶ *n.* poppa, *f.* ~ fast, ormeggio poppiero. ~ post, dritto di poppa, *m.* ~ sheets, camera, *f.* ~ tube, tubo dell'elica, *m.* **sternness**, *n.* austerità, fierezza, severità; cera torva, *f.*

sternum, *n.* sterno, *m.*

stet (*Typ.*), stet; correzione cancellata.

stethoscope, *n.* stetoscopio, *m.*

stevedore, *n.* stivatore, *m.* **stevedoring**, *n.* lo stivare.

stew, *n.* umido, intingolo, *m.*; carne stufata, *f.*; stufato, *m.* ~pan, casseruola, *f.*; tegame, *m.*; stufaiola, *f.*; ¶ *v.t.* stufare, (far) cuocere a fuoco lento; (*abs.*) cuocere in stufato. ~ed, *p.p.* stufato, umido di; (*fruit*) composto di.

steward, *n.* fattore, agente, intendente; maggiordomo; dispensiere; economo; (*ship*) cameriere di bordo; (*deck*) inserviente di ponte, *m.* ~'s mate, (*ship*), cambusiere, *m.* ~'s room, (*ship*), cambusa, *f.* ~ess (*ship*) *n.* cameriera (di bordo), *f.*

stick, *n.* bastone, *m.*; mazza; bacchetta; canna, *f.*; (*umbrella*) asta (d'ombrello), *f.*; (*sealing wax, chocolate, &c.*) bastoncino, *m.*; (*pl.*) stecchi, ramoscelli, *m.pl.*; legna, legne, *f.pl.* bundle of ~, fastello di legna, *m.* ¶ *v.t. ir.* appiccicare, attaccare; incollare; ingommare; fare aderire; (*in*) inserire, piantare; (*bills*) affiggere; (*Hort.*) palare; (*pig*) scannare; (*v.i. ir.*) aderire, ficcarsi, impigliarsi, attaccarsi; arrestarsi; applicarsi, attenersi. ~ in the mud, (*fig.*) impelagarsi, impaniarsi, impasticciarsi. ~ no *bills*, è proibita l'affissione. **sticki-ness**, *n.* viscosità, glutinosità, gommosità, *f.* *sticking plaster*, cerotto adesivo, taffetà, *m.*

stickleback, *n.* spinarello, *m.*

sticky, *a.* colloso, viscoso, glutinoso; attaccaticcio.

stiff, *a.* duro, rigido, inflessibile; ostinato; indurito; irrigidito, stecchito; (*from fatigue*) indolenzito, pesto, rotto; (*from cold*) intirizzito, assiderato; (*strained*) impettito, impalato; contegnoso; (*price*) salato, eccessivo; (*paste*, &c.) consistente, spesso. ~ *collar*, colletto (rigido), *m.* ~ *neck*, torcicollo, *m.* ~**en**, *v.t.* indurire, irrigidire, intirizzire, (*paste*, *liquid*, &c.) ispessire. ~**ness**, *n.* rigidezza, inflessibilità; durezza, *f.*; (*in the joints of the body*) indolenzimento, *m.*; tensione; (*horse*) bolsaggine, *f.*; ostinatezza, *f.*

stifle, *v.t.* reprimere, soffocare.

stigma, *n.* stigma, marchio d'infamia, *m.* **stigmatize**, *v.t.* stigmatizzare, stimmatizzare.

stile, *n.* barriera, *f.*; (*door*) stipite, *m.*

stiletto, *n.* stiletto, *m.*

still, *a.* calmo, tranquillo, cheto, quieto, silenzioso; immobile; (*water*) stagnante, cheto; (*wine*) non spumante; (*lemonade*) non gassosa; ~*-born*, nato morto. ~ *life* (*Art.*), natura morta, *f.* ¶ *ad.* tuttora, sempre; pure, anche, ancora; tuttavia, per altro, ma poi. ¶ *n.* alambicco, *m.* ~*room*, cantina, *f.*; laboratorio d'una distilleria, *m.* ¶ *v.t.* calmare, acquietare, tranquillare; sopprimere. ~**ness**, *n.* calma, tranquillità, *f.*; silenzio, riposo, *m.*

stilt, *n.* trampolo, *m.* ~**ed**, *a.* pomposo, affettato, ampolloso.

stimulant, *n.* stimolante, *m.* **stimulate**, *v.t.* stimolare. **stimulus**, *n.* stimolo, *m.*

sting, *n.* pungiglione, *m.*, puntura, morsicatura, *f.*; pungolo, *m.*; (*fig.*) (*of conscience*) rimorso; stimolo, *m.* ¶ *v.t.* & *i.ir* pungere; (*of conscience*) rimordere. **stinging**, *p.a.* pungente. ~ *nettle*, ortica bruciante, ortica pungente, *f.*

stingy, *a.* taccagno, gretto, tirchio, meschino.

stink, *n.* puzzo, fetore, *m.* ¶ *v.i.* ir. puzzare.

stint, *n.* limite, *m.*; restrizione, *f.* ¶ *v.t.* restringere, limitare; privare. ~ *oneself*, privarsi, stare a stecchetto, mettersi a razione.

stipend, *n.* stipendio, *m.*

stipple, *n.* punteggiatura, *f.* ¶ *v.t.* punteggiare.

stipulate, *v.t.* stipulare.

stir, *n.* moto, movimento; baccano, *m.*; agitazione, *f.*; scompiglio, *m.* *make a* ~, far furore. ¶ *v.t.* muovere, agitare; (ri)svegliare; perturbare; rimescolare; (*fire*) attizzare; (*the blood*) far bollire; (*v.i.*) muoversi; risvegliarsi; essere in piedi; ~ *up*, eccitare, concitare, incitare, aizzare. **stirring**, *p.a.* commovente, vibrato, vivo; pieno di incidenti.

stirrup, *n.* staffa, *f.* ~ *cup*, bicchiere della staffa, *m.* ~ *leather*, cinghia della staffa, *f.*, staffile, *m.*

stitch, *n.* punto, *m.*; (*Knit.*, *Crochet*, &c.) maglia, *f.* ~ *in the side* (*Med.*), punta al fianco, *f.* ¶ *v.t.* cucire; (*leather*) impuntire. (*books*) legare alla rustica. ~ *together*, cucire insieme. ~*ed hem*, orlo impuntito, *m.* ~**er**, *n.* cucitrice, punteggiatrice, *f.* ~**ing**, *n.* cucitura, *f.*, punti, *m.pl.*; il cucire, *m.*

stiver (*fig.*) *n.* centesimo, obolo, *m.*

stoat, *n.* ermellino, *m.*

stock, *n.* (*descent*) razza, schiatta, prosapia, *f.*; lignaggio, casato, *m.*; (*tree*, &c.) ceppo, tronco, *m.*; (*rifle*) cassa, *f.*, calcio, *m.*; (*anchor*) ceppo, *m.*; (*bit*) menarola, *f.*; trapano, *m.*; (*die*) filiera, *f.*; (*Hort.*) innesto, *m.*, mazza, *f.*; (*wild*) piantone, *m.*; pollone selvatico, *m.*; (*vine*) ceppo; (*flower*) violacciocca, *f.*; (*Com.*) fondo, assortimento, *m.*; esistenza, giacenza; provvista, *f.*, provvigione, *f.*; merci, *f.pl.*; materiali, *m.pl.*; riserva, *f.*; (*Fin.*) valore, *oft.pl.*, titolo, *m.* *oft pl.*, fondi, *m.pl.*, azioni, *f.pl.*; (*Cook*) consumato, *m.*; carne da brodo, *f.*; (*pl. Naut.*) scalo (di costruzione) *m.*, cantiere, *m.*; (*pl. Hist*) ceppi, *m.pl.* *in* ~, in magazzino, di *m.* ~ & *diss*, filiera guarnita, *f.* ~*s* & *shares*, titoli ed azioni, valori mobili, *m.pl.* ~*broker*, agente di cambio, mediatore in borsa, *m.* ~ *exchange*, Borsa [Valori], *f.* ~ *exchange committee*, deputazione di Borsa, *f.* ~ *exchange daily*, *official list*, bollettino della Borsa, *m.*, listino ufficiale della Borsa, *m.* ~ *breeder*, allevatore di bestiame, *m.* ~ *breeding*, ~ *farming*, allevamento di bestiame, *m.* ~ *fish*, stoccafisso, *m.* ~ *holder*, possessore di titoli (nominativi), *m.* ~ *in trade*, merci in magazzino, *f.pl.*;

mercanzie, *f.pl.*; consistenza di magazzino, *f.* ~ *jobbing*, aggiotaggio, *m.*; speculazione di borsa, *f.pl.* ~ *phrase*, espressione bell'e fatta, *f.*, luogo comune, *m.* ~ *piece*, commedia del repertorio, *f.* ~ *pot*, marmitta, *f.* ~ *solution* (*Phot.*) soluzione madre, di riserva, *f.* ~*-still*, immobile. ~*taking*, compilazione dell'inventario, *f.* ~*yard* (*cattle*) recinto per il bestiame, *m.* (*materials*) deposito di materiali, *m.* ¶ *v.t.* approvvigionare; far provvigione di, far provvista di; rifornire; tenere in magazzino; provvedere; riempire; immettere, popolare; ammobiliare. ~*ed by*, presso.

stockade, *n.* stecconato *m.*, palizzata, *f.*
stockinet, *n.* tessuto a maglia, *m.*
stocking, *n.* calza, calzetta, *f.*
stocky, *a.* tozzo, tarchiato.
Stoic, *n. & att.* stoico, *m. & a.* **stoical,** *a.* stoico. **stoicism,** *n.* stoicismo, *m.*
stoke, *v.t.* attizzare, scaldare. ~*hole*, ~*hold*, camera delle caldaie, *f.*
stoker, *n.* fochista, *m.*; (*Mechanical*) caricatore, alimentatore automatico (di combustibile), *m.*
stole, *n.* stola, *f.*
stolid, *a.* stolido. ~**ity,** *n.* stolidezza, stolidità, *f.*
stomach, *n.* stomaco, *m.*; (*fig.*) appetito, *m.*; cuore, *m.*, voglia, *f.* ~*ache*, mal di stomaco, *m.* ~*pump*, pompa stomacale, *f.* ¶ *v.t.* digerire, ingoiare, inghiottire; tollerare. ~**ic,** *a. & n.* stomachico, *a. & m.*
stone, *n.* pietra, *f.*; sasso, macigno, *m.*; roccia, *f.*; ciottolo, *m.*; (*Med.*) calcolo, *m.*; (*fruit*) nocciolo, *m.*; (*grape*) acino, chicco, vinacciolo, *m.*; (*Meas.*) (14 lbs =) 6·350 kilos. ~*breaker*, spaccapietre, *m.inv.* ~*crop*, erba da calli, *f.*, favagello, *m.* ~ *dead*, morto stecchito. ~ *fruit*, frutto a nocciolo, *m.* ~ *jar*, giara di pietra arenaria, *f.* ~ (*gem*) (*setter*) legatore, *m.* ~*'s throw*, tiro di pietra, tiro di mano. ~ *ware*, vasselame di pietra arenaria, -di creta, *m.* ~*work*, muratura, *f.* ¶ *v.t.* (*to death*) lapidare; (*fruit*) togliere il nocciolo da. **stony,** *a.* pietroso, sassoso, roccioso, di macigno; (*fig.*) duro, insensibile; (*heart, &c.*) di pietra, di sasso; (*look*) freddo.
stool, *n.* sgabello; panchetto, *m.*; (*Med.*) seggetta; evacuazione, *f.*
stoop, *v.i.* abbassarsi, chinarsi, curvarsi; umiliarsi, sottomettersi.

stop, *n.* fermata, sosta, pausa, *f.*; stazione, *f.*; arresto, *m.* interruzione, opposizione, *f.*; (*buffer*) respingente; (*Mech.*) arresto; (*organ*) registro; (*Phot.*) diaframma, *m.*; apertura, *f.*; (*Typ.*) punto (fermo). *to put a* ~ *to*, mettere fine a, tagliar corto. ~ *& go lights*, semaforo, *m.* ~ *blocks* (*Rly.*) paracolpi, *m.inv.* ~*cock*, rubinetto d'arresto, *m.* ~*gap*, turabuchi, *m.inv.* ~*press* [*news*] (informazioni dell') ultima ora, *f.pl.* ~*watch*, cronometro, *m.* ¶ *v.t.* fermare, arrestare; (*Naut., &c.*) fermare; interrompere, far cessare; sospendere, impedire; otturare; (*wages*) fare una trattenuta (sul salario); (*leak*) turare, accecare (una falla); (*teeth*) impiombare; (*v.i.*) fermarsi, arrestarsi, sostare, cessare; smettere (di); *all cars* ~ *here*, tram ~, fermata obbligatoria, *f. cars* ~ (*here*) *if required*, ~ *on request*, fermata facoltativa, *f.* ~ *up*, turare; otturare; intasare; ostruire. ¶ *i.* alto! alto-là!; (*Naut., in telegrams, &c.*) stop.
stope, (*Min.*) *n.* scavo d'estrazione, *m.*
stoppage, *n.* arresto, *m.*, sospensione, *f.*; cessazione, *f.*; ostruzione; interruzione; intasatura, *f.* **stopper,** *n.* turacciolo, tappo, tampone, *m.* ¶ *v.t.* otturare, turare; tamponare, tappare.
storage, *n.* magazzinaggio, *m.* **store,** *n.* magazzino; deposito, emporio, *m.*; abbondanza, provvista, *f.*; materiale, *m.*; (*pl.*) provvigioni, provviste, munizioni, *f.pl.*; magazzino di mode, bazar, emporio, *m.* ~ *curtain*, stoia, *f.* ~ *keeper*, magazziniere; negoziante, *m.* ~ *room*, locale di deposito, *m.* ¶ *v.t.* approvvigionare, immagazzinare; (*fig.*) conservare, accumulare.
storer, *n.* depositario, *m.*
storey, *n.* piano, *m.* *3-storied*, di tre piani.
stork, *n.* cicogna, *f.*
storm, *n.* temporale, *m.*, burrasca, *f.*, fortunale, uragano, *m.*, tempesta, *f.* ~ *cloud*, nembo, *m.*, nuvola di tempesta, *f.* ~ *of abuse*, sfuriata, *f.* ¶ *v.t.* prendere d'assalto; (*v.i.*) tempestare, infuriarsi, andar sulle furie.
stormy, *a.* tempestoso, burrascoso; violento. ~ *petrel*, procellaria, *f. at* ~ (*barometer*), alla tempesta.
story, *n.* storia, *f.*, racconto, *m.*; novella, *f.*; aneddoto, *m.*; favola, *f.*; fandonia, frottola, *f.*; (*floor*) piano, *m.* ~ *book*, libro di racconti, *m.* ~ *teller*, novelliere, *m.*, -a, *f.*;

narratore di storielle, raccontatore, *m.*

stoup, *n.* acquasantiera, *f.*; boccale, *m.*

stout, *a.* forte, vigoroso, robusto; rinforzato; coraggioso; corpulento; grosso, grasso. ¶ (*beer*) *n.* birra nera, *f.*, birrone, *m.* ~**ness** (*of body*), *n.* grassezza, pinguedine, *f.*

stove, *n.* stufa, *f.*, fornello, *m.*; (*central heating*) calorifero, *m.* ~ *& range maker,* stufaiolo, *m.* ~ *brush,* spazzola per la stufa, *f.*

stow, (*Naut.*) *v.t.* stivare. ~ *away,* *v.t.* rinchiudere, riporre; (*v.i.*) imbarcarsi clandestinamente. ~ *away,* *n.* passeggero clandestino, *m.*, -a, *f.*

straddle, *v.t. & i.* mettersi a cavalcioni (sopra), essere a cavalcioni, inforcare.

straggle, *v.i.* sbandarsi, sbrancarsi, andare alla spicciolata. **straggler,** *n.* ritardatario, soldato sbrancato, *m.* **straggling,** *a.* (*houses*) (case) sparpagliate. (*village*) irregolare, colle case sparse; (*beard*) negletto.

straight, *a.* dritto, diritto, retto, difilato; (*hair*) piatti; (*respectable*) onesto; franco; schietto; sincero. *a* ~ *left, right* (*Box.*), un sinistro diretto, un destro diretto. ¶ *ad.* diritto, direttamente. ¶ *or* ~ *line,* *n.* linea retta; dirittura, *f.* ~**en,** *v.t.* raddrizzare; mettere in ordine; rassettare. **straightforward,** *a.* schietto, diritto; probo; retto. **straightforwardly,** *ad.* schiettamente; rettamente. **straightforwardness,** *n.* schiettezza; franchezza; rettitudine, *f.* **straightness,** *n.* dirittura, *f.*

strain, *n.* (*molecular*) tensione; (*Mech.*) deformazione, *f.*; storcimento, *m.*; (*overstrain*) fatica, *f.*; (*Med.*) sforzo, *m.*; (*Vet.*) storta, *f.*; (*descent*) razza, *f.*; (*dash*) tinta, *f.*; (*pl.*) accenti, accordi, *m.pl.*, concento, *m.* ~ *in the back,* reumatismo lombare, *m.* ¶ *v.t.* tendere, stringere, storcere; affaticare, fare male a; (*Med.*, *&c.*) sforzare, slogare; (*filter*) filtrare, passare, spremere, colare, far colare. ~**ed,** (*fig.*) *p.a.* affettato, forzato, stentato. ~ *relations,* rapporti tesi, *m.pl.* ~**er,** *n.* filtro; colatoio; colino, *m.*

strait, *n.* (*s. & pl.*) stretto, passo, braccio di mare, *m.*; (*pl.*) strettezze, *f.pl.*, difficoltà, *f.pl.*; strette, *f.pl.*; stretto, passo, *m.* S~*s of Dover,* il passo di Calais. S~*s of Gibraltar,*

stretto di Gibilterra, *m.* **strait-laced,** *a.* (*fig.*) (*to be* ~), star sul grave. **strait waistcoat,** camicia di forza, *f.* **in straitened circumstances,** nelle strettezze.

strand, *n.* riva, spiaggia; sponda, *f.*; lido, *m.*; (*rope*) filo di corda; cordone, *m.* ¶ *v.t. & i.* far[e] arenare, incagliarsi, tirare in secco; arenarsi, dare in secco.

strange, *a.* strano; estraneo; bizzarro; sconosciuto. *he is a* ~ *mixture,* è un tipo straordinario, un tipo bizzarro. **stranger,** *n.* straniero, *m.*, -a, *f.*; forestiero, sconosciuto, *m.*, -a, *f.* **strangeness,** *n.* singolarità, novità, stranezza, *f.*

strangle, *v.t.* strozzare, strangolare. ~**s,** (*Vet.*) *n.pl.* stranguglioni, *m.pl.*, cimurro, *m.* **strangulation,** *n.*, strangolazione, *f.*; strangolamento, strozzamento, *m.*

strap, *n.* cinghia, cigna; correggia; striscia di cuoio, *f.*; guinzaglio, *m.* ~ *watch,* orologio braccialetto, *m.* ¶ *v.t.* legare, cignare, attaccare (con cinghie); frustare, staffilare, battere colla correggia.

Strasburg, *n.* Strasburgo, *f.*

stratagem, *n.* stratagemma, *m.* **strategic(al),** *a.* strategico. **strategist,** *n.* stratega, *m.* **strategy,** *n.* strategia, *f.*

stratified, *p.p.* stratificato. **stratum,** *n.* strato, *m.*

straw, *n.* paglia; pagliuzza; festuca, *f.*; (*drinking*) pagliuzza, cannuccia, *f.*; (*fig.*) fico; fuscello, *m. the last* ~, (*fig.*) la maggior disgrazia. ~*board,* cartone di paglia, *m.* ~*-colour*(*ed*), del colore della paglia, color paglia. ~ *envelope* (bottle), rivestimento di paglia, *m.*; veste di paglia, *f.* ~ *hat,* cappello di paglia, *m.*, paglietta, *f.* ~ *mattress,* pagliericcio, *m.*

strawberry, *n.* (*plant & fruit*) fragola, *f.* ~ *bed,* fragoleto, *m.* ~ *ice,* gelato alle fragole, *m.*

stray, *v.i.* smarrirsi, sviare, traviare; errare, vagare. ¶ *a.* smarrito.

streak, *n.* striscia; stria; riga; screziatura; piccola traccia; *f.*; raggio [di luna, &c.], *m.*; ena, *f.* ¶ *v.t.* rigare, striare, screziare; solcare. ~**y,** (*meat*) *a.* lardellato.

stream, *n.* fiume, ruscello, corso d'acqua, *m.*, corrente, *f.*; (*fig.*) torrente, *m.*; marea, *f.*, fiotto, *m.*; successione, *f.* ~*-lined,* affusolato, aerodinamico. ~*lining,* aerodinamismo, *m.* ¶ *v.i.* scorrere, fluire;

colare, spiovere; emanare. ~er, n.
pennoncello, m.; banderuola, f.;
albore, m.; (paper) stella filante, f.
street, n. strada, via, f.; (s. & pl. fig.)
lastrico, m. ~ child, ~ arab,
monello, birichino; ragazzo abbandonato, m. ~ lamp, lampione,
fanale, m. ~ musician, musicante
girovago, cantatore della strada, m.
strength, n. forza, f., vigore, m.;
potenza; resistenza, robustezza, intensità, f.; (of a solution) titolo, m.
(men) effettivi, m.pl.; quadri, m.pl.;
forze, f.pl. ~en, v.t. rinforzare,
rafforzare, consolidare; rinvigorire;
fortificare.
strenuous, a. strenuo, energico,
vigoroso; (life) attivo, intenso.
streptomycine, n. streptomicina, f.
stress, n. sforzo, m., tensione, f.;
travaglio; carico, m.; fatica; enfasi, f.;
accento, m.; sollecitazione, f.;
(weather) violenza, f. to be in ~
(Mech.), essere sollecitato. ¶ v.t.
insistere su; mettere l'accento su;
assoggettare a tensione; (Mech.)
sollecitare; (Mus.) scandire.
stretch, n. estensione, f.; tratto,
percorso, m.; lunghezza, f.; (of
person's arms), larghezza, f.; (Mech.)
allungamento, m.; tensione, f. ¶ v.t
tendere, stendere, estendere; allargare, allungare; stirare; forzare;
esagerare. ~ oneself, stirarsi,
sdraiarsi. stretcher, n. barella,
lettiga, (boat) pedagna, f., punta-
piedi, m.inv.; (glove) allargaguanti,
m.inv.; (shoe) forma, f.; (Mech.)
tenditore, allargatore; (for painter's
canvas) telaio, m. ~ bearer, porta-
barella, m.inv.
strew, v.t. ir. spargere, cospargere;
sparpagliare; seminare.
stria, n. stria, f. striate[d], a. striato.
striation, n. striazione, striatura, f.
strickle, n. rasiera, f.
strict, a. stretto, rigido; rigoroso;
severo; formale; esatto. ~ness, n.
rigore, m.; rigidezza; severità;
esattezza, precisione, f. ~ure, n.
censura, f., rimprovero, m.; (Med.)
restringimento, m.
stride, n. passo (lungo), m.; andatura,
f.; (fig.) slancio, progresso, m.
~ along, v.i. ir. camminare a passi
lunghi, a gran passi.
strident, a. stridente, stridulo.
strife, n. guerra; discordia, f.
strike, n. (of pers.) sciopero, m.; (att.)
scioperante. ~s & lock-outs, scio-
peri e serrate. ¶ v.t. ir. colpire,

battere, percuotere; urtare; impressionare; suonare; raggiungere; rendere; scoprire, trovare; (coin, medal)
coniare, battere; (match) accendere;
(root, v.t. & abs.) mettere, prendere;
(tent) levare; (sail) abbassare, ammainare, calare; (colours) calare,
ammainare; (a balance) stabilire,
fare; (v.i. ir.) colpire; suonare; scioperare, far sciopero. it ~s me, mi
pare, mi è venuta l'idea. how does it
~ you? che ne pensate? ~ down,
abbattere. ~ off, tagliare; dedurre;
cancellare; (copies) tirare. ~ out,
cancellare. ~ up (tune) intonare.
~er, scioperante, m.f. ~ing, p.a.
impressionante, sorprendente, cospicuo, rimarchevole. ~ clock,
orologio a suoneria, m.
string, n. spago, m., corda, cordicella,
(beads) corona, f., rosario, m.; (fig.)
apparato, treno, m.; fuga, infilata,
fila, filza, f.; (Bil.) pallottoliere, m.
the ~s (Mus.) le corde, f.pl. ~ bag,
borsa a rete, f. ~ band, orchestra
d'archi, f. ¶ v.t. ir. infilare, infilzare;
(violin) mettere le corde a. ~ed, p.a.
a corda, a corde.
stringent, a. rigoroso, severo, preciso.
stringy, a. fibroso, filamentoso.
strip, n. striscia, lista, f.; nastro, m.
¶ v.t. spogliare, denudare; sguarnire;
scorzare, disattrezzare, smontare.
(v.i.) spogliarsi, svestirsi.
stripe, n. riga, lista, linea, striscia, f.;
sferzata, staffilata, f.; (N.C.O.'s Navy)
gallone, m. ~ed, a. rigato, vergato;
a liste, a righe; zebrato.
strive, v.i. ir. sforzarsi; ingegnarsi;
contendere, lottare.
stroke, n. colpo, m.; botta, percossa, f.;
tratto, m.; pennata, f., pennellata, f.;
riga, linea, asta, f.; tocco, rintocco;
attacco, m.; (piston) corsa, f.; (swim)
nuoto, m., bracciata, f.; (apoplexy)
colpo di sangue, m.; breast ~ (Swim.)
nuoto a ranocchio, m.; side ~, nuoto
alla marinara, m.; (Rowing) palata,
remata, f.; colpo (di remo), m.; (pers.)
capo-voga, m. ~ play (Golf);
partita a colpi, f. on the ~ of time,
all'ora sonante. ¶ v.t. passare la
mano su; lisciare, accarezzare.
stroll, n. passeggiatina, passeggiata, f.;
giro, giretto, m. ¶ v.i. fare una
passeggiatina, girandolare, girovagare. strolling, p.a. girovago,
ambulante, vagabondo.
strong, a. forte, vigoroso, robusto;
gagliardo; energico; valido; resistente; saldo, solido; potente; (flavour)

piccante; (*wind, &c.*) forte, violento; (*language*) forte; (*well up in*) ferrato, forte. ~ *box,* cassaforte, *f.* ~ *drink,* liquori forti, *m.pl.,* bevande alcooliche, *f.pl.* ~ *hold,* fortezza, roccaforte, *f.* ~ *man,* (professional) ercole, *m.* ~*-minded person,* spirito forte, *m.* ~*-minded woman,* donna di mente virile, *f.* ~ *point,* forte, *m.* ~*room,* camera blindata; (*ship*) camera dei valori, *f.*

strop, *n.* cuoio (da rasoio), *m.;* coramella, *f.*; (*safety blade*) stecca per affilare il rasoio, *f.* ¶ *v.t.* ripassare, affilare.

structural, *a.* strutturale; da costruzioni; (*repairs*) grosso. **structure,** *n.* struttura; costruzione, formazione, *f.*; edifizio, monumento, *m.*; (*fig.*) impalcatura, *f.*

struggle, *n.* lotta, *f.*; sforzo, *m.*; agonia, *f.* ¶ *v.i.* lottare, dibattersi; sforzarsi.

strum, *v.t. & i.* strimpellare.

strut, *n.* pezzo di rinforzo, *m.*; biella, *f.*; puntone, puntello, *m.* ¶ *v.i.* pavoneggiarsi, camminare impettito, andar pettoruto.

strychnin[e], *n.* stricnina, *f.*

stub, *n.* ceppo, tronco; (*Mech.*) mozzicone, *m.*; (*cheque book, &c.*) madre, *f.*

stubble, *n.* stoppia, seccia, *f.*

stubborn, *a.* ostinato, caparbio, testardo; inflessibile, tenace; duro; difficile. ~**ness,** *n.* ostinazione, ostinatezza, caparbietà; inflessibilità, tenacia, *f.*

stucco & stucco work, *n.* stucco, *m. worker in* ~, *decorator,* stuccatore; (*figure maker*) stucchinaio, *m.*

stuck-up, *a.* arrogante, borioso, altero.

stud, *n.* chiodo, chiodino, chiodetto, *m.*; borchia, bulletta, *f.*; bottone, bottoncino, *m.*; (*horses*) scuderia, *f.*; (*breeding*) stabilimento di allevamento, *m.* ~ *bolt,* vite prigioniera, *f.* ~ *book,* registro di animali puro sangue, *m.* ~ *earring,* orecchino, *m.* ~ *farm,* stazione d'allevamento (di cavalli). *f.* ~ *groom,* capoallevatore, *m.* ~ *horse,* stallone, cavallo di razza, *m.* ¶ *v.t.* guarnire di borchie, &c.; (*fig.*) seminare, spargere. *studded crossing* (pedestrian), passaggio tracciato da chiodi, *m.*

student, *n.* (*pupil*) studente, *m.*, studentessa, *f.*; allievo, *m.*, -a, *f.*; (*disinterested scholar*) studioso, *m.*

studied, *pp.* studiato 'cercato; affet-

tato; (*deliberate*) premeditato, voluto, calcolato. ~ *elegance,* ricercatezza, *f.*

studio, *n.* studio, *m.* **studious,** *a.* studioso, attento, applicato. **study,** *n.* studio; gabinetto, *m.* ¶ *v.t. & i.* studiare.

stuff, *n.* stoffa, *f.*, tessuto, *m.*, materia, *f.*; materiali, *m.pl.*, roba, *f.*, robaccia, *f.*; (*fig.*) sciocchezza, stupidaggine, *f.* ~ & *nonsense,* futilità, insulsaggini, *f.pl.* ¶ *v.t.* imbottire; stivare; [r]impinzare; caricare; (*dead animal*) impagliare; (*Cook.*) infarcire. ~**ing,** *n.* borra, *f.*; (*Cook.*) ripieno, *m.* ~**y,** *a.* soffocante, mal aerato, senz'aria.

stultify, *v.t.* rendere inefficace, neutralizzare l'effetto di.

stumble, *v.i.* inciampare, fare un passo falso, incespicare. *stumbling block,* inciampo, *m. stumbling stone,* pietra d'inciampo, *f.*

stump, *n.* ceppo, toppo, tronco, troncone, *m.*; moncone, moncherino, torso, *m.*; (*cigar*) mozzicone, pezzettino, *m.*; (*cricket*) sbarra, *f.* (*tooth*) dente rotto, *m.*; (*Art.*) sfumino, *m.* ~ *orator,* declamatore, oratore popolare, *m.* ~**y,** *a.* tozzo.

stun, *v.t.* stordire, intronare, assordare; sbalordire. *stunning blow,* colpo che stordisce, colpo assordante, *m.*; mazzata, *f.*

stunt, *n.* (*Aero.*) acrobazia, *f.*

stunted, *p.p.* intristito, imbozzacchito, abortito; malfatto, mal cresciuto; smilzo.

stupefy, *v.t.* inebetire, istupidire, ottundere; (*narcotize*) stupefare.

stupendous, *a.* stupendo, prodigioso.

stupid, *a.* stolto, stupido, balordo, ottuso, sciocco, melenso; (*things*) scipito, insipido. · ~**ity,** *n.* sciocchezza, stoltezza, melensaggine, *f.* **stupore,** *n.* stupore, *m.*

sturdy, *a.* vigoroso, robusto; tarchiato; gagliardo, forte.

sturgeon, *n.* storione, *m.*

stutter, *v.i. & t.* tartagliare, balbettare. ~**er,** *n.* tartaglione, *m.*, -ona, *f.*, balbuziente, *m.f.*

sty, *n.* porcile, *m.* ¶ *v.t.* mettere nel porcile.

sty[e] (*on the eye*), *n.* orzaiuolo, *m*

style, *n.* stile, modo, genere, *m.*; maniera, *f.*; gusto, *m.*; moda, *f.*; cerimoniale; titolo, *m.*; (*Bot.*; *gnomon of sundial, &c., stylus*) stilo, *m.*; (*firm name*) ragione (sociale), ditta, *f.* ~ *of hair-dressing,* acconciatura, *f.* ¶ *v.t.* [de]nominare, qualificare, chiamare.

stylet, *n,* stiletto, *m.*
stylish, *a.* alla moda, distinto, elegante.
stylograph, *n.* penna stilografica, *f.*
suave, *a.* blando, dolce, cortese.
suavity, *n.* dolcezza, gentilezza, cortesia, *f.*
sub-acid, *a.* acidetto, acidulo, agrodolce.
subaltern, *a. & n.* subalterno, *a. & m.*
sub-committee, *n.* sottocomitato, *m.,* sottocommissione, *f.*
subconscious, *a. & n.* subcosciente, *a. & m.* ~ness, *n.* subcoscienza, *f.*
subcontract, *n.* subappalto, *m.* ~or, *n.* subappaltatore, *m.*
subcutaneous, *a.* sottocutaneo.
subdivide, *v.t.* suddividere.
subdue, *v.t.* assoggettare, sottomettere; conquistare, soggiogare; moderare, temperare; *(light)* smorzare, abbassare, attenuare.
sub-editor, *n.* vice-direttore; redattore assistente, segretario di redazione, *m.*
subject, *n.* soggetto, argomento, proposito; *(pers.)* suddito, *m.,* -a, *f.* ~ catalogue, catalogo per materie, *m.* ¶ *v.t.* sottomettere, sottoporre; assoggettare. ¶ ~ to, soggetto a, esposto a, sottoposto a; sotto benefizio di, con riserva di. ~ion, *n.* assoggettamento, *m.,* soggezione, dipendenza, *f.* ~ive, *a. & n.,* soggettivo, *a. & m.*
subjoined, *p.p.* aggiunto, soggiunto.
subjugate, *v.t.* soggiogare.
subjunctive [mood], *n.* modo congiuntivo, *m.*
sublet, *v.t. ir.* subaffittare; riaffittare.
sub-lietenant, *n.* sottotenente, *m.*
sublime, *a. & n.* sublime, *a. & m.*
sublimity, *n.* sublimità, *f*
sublunar[y], *a.* sublunare.
submarine, *a.* sottomarino. ¶ *n.* sommergibile, *m.*
submerge, *v.t.* sommergere; *(v.i.)* sommergersi.
submission, *n.* sommissione, sottomissione, deferenza, *f.;* rispetto, *m.* **submissive,** *a.* sommesso, deferente, rassegnato. ~ness, *n.* rassegnazione, deferenza, *f.* **submit,** *v.t.* sottomettere, sottoporre. ~ to, sottomettersi a, sottoporsi a, rassegnarsi a, acconsentire, ubbidire a, subire.
sub-order, *n.* sottordine, *m.,* suddivisione, *f.*
subordinate, *a.* subordinato, subalterno, dipendente. ¶ *n.* subordinato, subalterno, *m.* ¶ *v.t.* subordinare.
suborn, *v.t.* subornare, sedurre. ~er, *n.* subornatore, *m.,* -trice, *f.*
subpoena, *n.* citazione (di testimone), *f.* ¶ *v.t.* citare.
subrogate, *v.t.* surrogare.
subscribe, *v.t. & i.* sottoscrivere; abbonarsi; contribuire; *(fig.)* aderire, consentire. **subscriber,** *n.* sottoscrittore, *m.,* -trice, *f.;* contribuente, *m.f.;* abbonato, *m.,* -a, *f.* **subscription,** *n.* sottoscrizione, *f.,* abbonamento, *m.* ~ dance, ballo per sottoscrizione, *m.*
subsection, *n.* sottosezione; alinea, *f.,* comma, *m.*
subsequent, *a.* susseguente, successivo; ulteriore.
subservience, *n.* subordinazione; dipendenza; servilità, *f.* **subservient,** *a.* subordinato; dipendente; servile.
subside, *v.i.* abbassarsi, sgonfiarsi; decrescere *(waters);* avvallarsi, cedere, sprofondare *(ground);* diminuire, calmarsi, cessare *(disorder, wind, &c.).* **subsidence,** *n.* abbassamento, avvallamento, *m.;* cedimento, sprofondamento, *m.*
subsidiary, *a.* sussidiario, ausiliario. ~ *[company],* succursale, *f.*
subsidize, *v.t.* sovvenzionare, sussidiare. **subsidy,** *n.* sovvenzione, *f.,* sussidio, *m.;* assistenza, *f.*
subsist, *v.i.* sussistere, esistere; mantenersi, vivere (on = di). ~ence, *n.* sussistenza, *f.;* alimento, cibo, *m.;* mezzi di sussistenza, *m.pl.* ~ allowance, *(Com.)* indennità di trasferta, *f.*
sub-soil, *n.* sottosuolo, *m.*
substance, *n.* sostanza, *f.;* fondo, corpo; avere, *m.,* beni, *m.pl.; (fig.)* contenuto, *m.;* essenza, realtà, *f.* **substantial,** *a.* sostanziale, solido, fondato, sicuro; benestante, agiato, ricco; *(meal, lunch)* sostanzioso. ~ly, *ad.* sostanzialmente, essenzialmente. **substantiate,** *v.t.* confermare, corroborare, provare; convalidare; stabilire. **substantive,** *a. & n.* sostantivo, *a. & m.*
substitute, *n.* sostituto; surrogato; succedaneo, *m.; (pers.)* sostituto, supplente, surrogante, *m.* ¶ *v.t.* sostituire *(replace, take the place of);* rimpiazzare. ~ for, sostituire a.
substratum, *n.* substrato; fondo, *m.*
substructure, *n.* fondamenta, *f.pl.;* base *f.; (road, Rly.)* piano di posa, *m.*

subtenant, *n.* subaffittuario, *m.*, subinquilino, *m.*, -a, *f.*

subterfuge, *n.* sotterfugio; equivoco; raggiro, *m.*

subterranean, *a.* sotterraneo.

subtilize, *v.t. & i.* sottilizzare, (*fig.*) assottigliare.

subtitle, *n.* sottotitolo, secondo titolo, *m.*

subtle, *a.* fino, delicato, sottile; astuto, scaltro. **~ty,** *n.* sottigliezza, finezza, astuzia, *f.*

subtract, *v.t.* sottrarre; dedurre. **~ion,** *n.* sottrazione, *f.*

suburb, *n.* sobborgo, suburbio, *m.*; (*pl.*) sobborghi; dintorni, *m.pl.*; periferia, *f.* **~an,** *a.* suburbano.

subvention, *n.* sovvenzione, *f.*, sussidio, *m.*

subversive, *a.* sovversivo. **subvert,** *v.t.* sovvertire.

subway, *n.* sottopassaggio, *m.*; galleria, *f.*

succeed, *v.t.* succedere a, seguire; (*v.i.*) succedere; (*prosper*) riuscire. **~ing,** *p.a.* seguente, susseguente.

success, *n.* riuscita, *f.*, successo, *m.*, **~ful,** *a.* fortunato, felice, ben riuscito. **succession,** *n.* successione, *f.*, seguito, *m.* **successive,** *a.* successivo, consecutivo. **successor,** *n.* successore, *m.*; erede, *m.f.*

succinct, *a.* succinto; conciso. **~ness,** *n.* concisione, *f.*

succour, *n.* soccorso, aiuto, *m.* ¶ *v.t.* soccorrere, aiutare.

succulent, *a.* succulento, succoso.

succumb, *v.i.* soccombere.

such, *a.* tale, simile, siffatto; (*so great*) tanto. **~ as,** tale che, come; quale; quelli che.

suck, *v.t. & i.* succhiare; (*infant*) poppare. **~ in,** (*Mech.*) aspirare. **~ up,** assorbire, sorbire. **~er,** *n.* (*of insect*) succhiatoio, *m.*; (*of leech*) ventosa, *f.*; (*Hort.*) pollone, rimessiticcio, *m.* **~ing pig,** porcellino di latte, *m.* **~le,** *v.t.* allattare. **~ling,** *n.* [bambino] lattante, *m.* **suction,** *n.* aspirazione, *f.*, succhiamento, *m.* **~ pump,** pompa aspirante, *f.*

sudden, *a.* subitaneo, repentino; improvviso, brusco. **~ turn** (road), svolta repentina, *f.* **all of a ~,** di botto, tutto d'un tratto, improvvisamente. **~ly,** *ad.* subito, subitamente. **~ness,** *n.* subitaneità; impetuosità, *f.*

suds, *n.pl.* saponata, acqua saponata, *f.*

sue, *v.t.* citare in giudizio, querelare, intentar lite a. **~ for,** chiedere, supplicare.

suède gloves, guanti di Svezia, *m.pl.*

suet, *n.* grasso (di bove), *m.*

suffer, *v.t.* sopportare; subire; tollerare; (*v.i.*) soffrire, patire. **~able,** *a.* sopportabile. **~ance,** *n.* tolleranza, *f.* **~er,** *n.* sofferente, paziente, *m.f.*; vittima, *f.* **~ing,** *n.* sofferenza, *f.*, pena, *f.*, dolore, *m.* **~ing,** *p.a.* sofferente.

suffice, *v.i.* bastare, esser sufficiente.

sufficiency, *n.* sufficienza, *f.*; mezzi sufficienti, *m.pl.* **sufficient,** *a.* sufficiente, bastevole.

suffix, *n.* suffisso, *m.* **~ed,** *p.a.*, aggiunto (come suffisso).

suffocate, *v.t.* soffocare; asfissiare. **suffocation,** *n.* soffocazione; asfissia, *f.*

suffragan, *a. & n.* suffraganeo, *a. & m.*

suffrage, *n.* suffragio, [diritto di] voto, *m.* **suffragette,** *n.* sufi getta, *f.*

suffuse, *v.t.* spandersi su, coprire, bagnare. **suffusion,** *n.* suffusione, *f.*

sugar, *n.* zucchero, *m.* **~ almond,** mandorla inzuccherata, *f.* **~ basin,** zuccheriera, *f.* vaso per lo zucchero, *m.* **~ beet,** barbabietola da z., *f.* **~ candy,** candito, *m.* **~ cane,** canna da z., *f.* **~ refiner,** raffinatore di z., *m.* **~ industry,** industria dello zucchero, *f.* **~ sifter,** zuccheriera a spruzzo, *f.* **~ tongs,** mollette per z., *f.pl.* ¶ *v.t.* inzuccherare; addolcire. **~y,** *a.* zuccherino; inzuccherato.

suggest, *v.t.* suggerire; proporre; ispirare; dettare. **~ion,** *n.* suggerimento, *m.*; proposta; (*hypnotic, &c.*) suggestione, *f.* **~ive,** *a.* suggestivo.

suicide, *n.* suicidio, *m.*; (*pers.*) suicida, *m.f.* **to commit ~,** suicidarsi.

suit, *n.* preghiera, domanda, richiesta, *f.*; corte; (*Law*) causa, *f.*; processo, *m.*; (*Card*) colore, *m.*; serie, *f.* **~ case,** valigia, *f.* **~ of armour,** armatura, *f.* **~ of clothes,** [abito] completo, *m.* **~ to measure,** vestito su misura, *m.* ¶ *v.t.* adattare, appropriare; conformare; convenire a; andare a; andare a genio di; accomodare; (*v.i.*) convenire; accordarsi, confarsi, quadrare, accomodare; attagliarsi; piacere. **~ability,** *n.* convenienza, *f.* **~able,** *a. &* **~ed,** *p.p.* conveniente, conforme, appropriato, adatto, acconcio, adeguato, opportuno.

suite, *n.* seguito, corteo, *m.*; (*of*

furniture) ammobigliamento completo, *m.*; ∼ (*of rooms*), appartamento, *m.*

suitings, *n.pl.* tessuti per vestiti, *m.pl.*

suitor, *n.* (*Law*) litigante, *m.f.*, attore, *m.*, parte in causa, *f.*; (*wooer*) aspirante, corteggiatore, *m.*

sulk, *v.i.* tenersi il broncio, metter su muso, essere di malumore, stare in malumore. ∼y, *a.* musone, imbronciato, di cattivo umore, malgrazioso.

sullen, *a.* arcigno, cupo, tetro, fosco, ritroso. ∼ness, *n.* umor cupo, umor nero, *m.*; musoneria, *f.*

sully, *v.t.* macchiare; sporcare; appannare; offuscare.

sulphate, *n.* solfato, *m.* **sulphide,** *n.* solfuro, *m.* **sulphite,** *n.* solfito, *m.* **sulphur,** *n.* zolfo, *m.* ∼ *bath,* bagno solforoso, *m.* ∼ *mine,* miniera di zolfo, solfatara, *f.* **sulphuretted,** *a.* solforato. **sulphuric,** *a.* solforico. **sulphurous,** *a.* solforoso.

sultan, *n.* sultano; (*Hist.*) soldano, Gran Turco, *m.* **sultana,** *n.* sultana, *f.*; (*pl.*) uve sultane, *f.pl.*

sultry, *a.* (*weather*) afoso; (*heat*) soffocante; pesante.

sum, *n.* somma, *f.*, montante; calcolo, *m.* ∼ *total,* somma globale, *f.* ∼ *up,* sommare; riassumere. **summarize,** *v.t.* riassumere, fare un sunto di. **summary,** *a.* sommario. ¶ *n.* riassunto, sunto; compendio; sommario, *m.*

summer, *n.* estate, state, *f.* ∼ *holidays,* vacanze estive, *f.pl.* ∼ *house,* padiglione, pergolato, frascato, *m.*; casa d'estate, *f.* ∼ *lightning,* balenare a secco, *m.* ∼ *resort,* stazione estiva, *f.* ∼ *time,* ora estiva, *f.* ¶ *v.i.* passare l'estate, villeggiare; (*v.t.*) pascolare durante l'estate.

summing up, riassunto, *m.*; esposizione riassuntiva, *f.*

summit, *n.* vetta, cima, *f.*; colmo, vertice, *m.*; sommità, *f.*, sommo, *m.*

summon, *v.t.* chiamare, far venire, convocare, (*Law*) citare; ∼ *up courage,* riprendere coraggio, farsi animo. ∼ *back & ∼ up,* richiamare.

summons, *n.* (*Law*) citazione, *f.*; mandato di comparizione, *m.* ¶ *v.t.* citare; convenire in giudizio, *m.*

sump, *n.* (*Min.*) pozzo di scarico, *m.*

sumptuous, *a.* sontuoso; (*fare*) lauto. ∼ness, *n.* sontuosità, *f.*; lusso, *m.*

sun, *n.* sole, *m.* ∼ *bath,* bagno di sole, *m.* ∼ *bathing,* [la cura dei] bagni di

sole, *m.pl.* ∼ *beam,* raggio di sole, *m.* ∼ *blind,* stoia, *f.*, tendina, *f.* ∼ *bonnet,* cuffia, *f.* ∼ *burn,* abbronzatura del sole, *f.* ∼ *burnt,* abbronzato (dal sole). *to get* ∼ *burnt,* abbronzarsi. ∼ *dial,* meridiana, *f.*, quadrante solare, *m.* ∼ *flower,* girasole, *m.* ∼ *helmet,* casco coloniale, *m.* ∼ *light,* luce solare, *f.* ∼ *light treatment,* cura medica mediante il sole, *f.* ∼ *lit,* illuminato dal sole, soleggiato. ∼ *rise,* levar del sole, *m.* ∼ *set,* tramonto, *m.* ∼ *-shade,* ombrellino, parasole, *m.* ∼ *shine,* sole, *m.* ∼ *shine roof,* tetto mobile, *m.* ∼ *shiny day,* giorno di sole, *m.* ∼ *shutter,* persiana, gelosia, *f.* ∼ *spot,* macchia solare, *f.* ∼ *stroke,* colpo di sole, *m.*; insolazione, *f.* ¶ *v.t.* soleggiare. ∼ *oneself,* soleggiarsi.

Sunday, *n.* domenica, *f. to put on one's* ∼ *best,* vestirsi da festa. ∼ *closing,* chiusura domenicale, *f.* ∼ *rest,* riposo domenicale, *m.*

sunder, *v.t.* separare.

sundries, *n.pl.* [articoli] diversi, *m.pl.*; spese casuali, *f.pl.* **sundry,** *a.* parecchi, diversi.

sunken, *p.a.* infossato, incavato; affondato.

sunless, *a.* senza sole. **sunny,** *a.* aprico, esposto al sole, soleggiato, solatio; (*fig.*) allegro, felice.

sup, *v.i.* cenare.

superabundant, *a.* sovrabbondante.

superannuated, *p.p.* (*thing*) disusato, desueto; (*pers.*) giubilato, collocato a riposo. *superannuation fund,* cassa delle pensioni, *f.*

superb, *a.* superbo.

supercargo, *n.* sopraccarico, *m.*

supercilious, *a.* sdegnoso, arrogante, sprezzante.

superficial, *a.* superficiale. **superficies,** *n.* superficie, *f.*

superfine, *a.* sopraffino.

superfluity, *n.* superfluità, *f.* **superfluous,** *a.* superfluo.

superheat, *v.t.* surriscaldare.

superhuman, *a.* sovrumano.

super[im]pose, *v.t.* sovrapporre.

superintend, *v.t.* soprintendere, a, sorvegliare. ∼ence, *n.* soprintendenza, sorveglianza, *f.* ∼ent, *n.* soprintendente, capo, sorvegliante, *m.*; (*police*) commissario, *m.*; (*restaurant*) sorvegliante, *m.*

superior, *a. & n.* superiore, *a. & m.f.* ∼ity, *n.* superiorità, *f.*

superlative, *a.* superlativo, supremo;

(*Gram.*) superlativo. ¶ *n.* super-lativo, *m.*

superman, *n.* superuomo, *m.*

supernatural, *a. & n.* soprannaturale, *a. & m.*

supernumerary, *a. & n.* soprannumerario, *a. & m.* ~ *officer,* ufficiale del seguito, *m.* ¶ (*Theat.*) *n.* comparsa, *f.*, figurante, *m.f.*

superscription, *n.* soprascritta, leggenda, *f.*

supersede, *v.t.* sostituire, rimpiazzare.

superstition, *n.* superstizione, *f.* **superstitious,** *a.* superstizioso.

supertax, *n.* soprattassa, *f.*

supervene, *v.i.* sopravvenire.

supervise, *v.t.* sorvegliare, soprintendere a. **supervision,** *n.* sorveglianza, *f.* **supervisor,** *n.* sorvegliante, *m.f.*, controllore, ispettore, *m.*

supine, *a.* supino; (*fig.*) indolente, negligente.

supper, *n.* cena, *f.* *to have* ~, cenare. ~ *time,* ora di cena, *f.* ~**less,** *a.* senza cena.

supplant, *v.t.* soppiantare.

supple, *a.* pieghevole, flessibile; arrendevole; agile. *to make* ~, piegare, rendere flessibile.

supplement, *n.* supplemento, *m.* ¶ *v.t.* fare aggiunte a, supplementare; aumentare. ~**ary,** *a.* supplementare.

suppleness, *n.* flessibilità, pieghevolezza, *f.*

suppliant, *a. & n.* supplicante, *a. & m.f.* **supplicate,** *v.t.* supplicare. **supplication,** *n.* supplicazione, supplica, preghiera, *f.*

supplier, *n.* provveditore, fornitore, *m.* **supply,** *n.* provvista, *f.*, approvigionamento, rifornimento, *m.*, fornitura, *f.*, arrivo (di merci), *m.*; (*pl.*) provviste, *f.pl.*, viveri; fondi, crediti, arrivi, *m.pl.* ~ *& demand,* l'offerta e la domanda. ~ (*work*), supplenza, *f.* ¶ *v.t.* provvedere, approvigionare, fornire.

support, *n.* sostegno, appoggio; aiuto, soccorso, *m.*; mantenimento, *m.* ¶ *v.t.* sostenere, reggere; appoggiare, sostentare; aiutare; mantenere. ~**er,** *n.* sostegno, sostenitore; aderente; seguace; partigiano; difensore, *m.*

suppose, *v.t.* supporre, credere, presumere. *supposing* (*that*), supposto che. **supposition,** *n.* supposizione,

congettura, *f.* **supposititious,** *a.* spurio, supposto, putativo.

suppress, *v.t.* sopprimere, reprimere; trattenere; nascondere. ~*ed rage,* ira non sfogata, *f.* ~**ion,** *n.* soppressione, *f.*

suppurate, *v.i.* suppurare.

supremacy, *n.* supremazia, *f.*; primato, *m.* **supreme,** *a.* supremo, sommo, sovrano.

surcharge, *n.* sopratassa, *f.*

sure, *a.* sicuro, certo; fermo. *to make* ~ *of,* assicurarsi di. ~**ness,** *n.* sicurezza, certezza, *f.* ~**ty,** *n.* cauzione, *f.*; (*pers.*) garante, mallevadore, *m.*

surf, *n.* risacca; spuma, *f.*; frangenti, *m.pl.* ~**board,** acquaplano, *m.* ~ *boat* (*native*), piroga, *f.* ~ *fishing,* pesca di spiaggia, *f.* ~ *riding,* lo sport dell'acquaplano, *m.*

surface, *n.* superficie, *f.*; esterno, *m.* ~ *mine,* cava a cielo aperto, *f.* ~ *plate,* (*Mech.*) piano di riscontro, *m.*

surfeit, *n.* sazietà, *f.* ¶ *v.t.* saziare; satollare, rimpinzare; stuccare.

surge, *n.* maroso, mareggio, *m.*, ondata, *f.* ¶ *v.i.* gonfiarsi, ingrossarsi; rifluire; ondeggiare.

surgeon, *n.* chirurgo, *m.* **surgery,** *n.* chirurgia, *f.*; gabinetto (di un chirurgo), *m.*, clinica, *f.* **surgical,** *a.* chirurgico. ~ *case* (*pers.*), operato, *m.*, -a, *f.*

surging, *p.a.* ondoso, mosso, agitato, di leva.

surly, *a.* arcigno, burbero, scontroso; cupo, tetro, accigliato; (*dog,* &*c.*) ringhioso.

surmise, *n.* supposizione, congettura, *f.* ¶ *v.t.* supporre, congetturare.

surmount, *v.t.* sormontare.

surname, *n.* cognome, soprannome, nome di famiglia, *m.*

surpass, *v.t.* sorpassare. ~**ing,** *a.* raro, supremo, sovrano, insuperabile.

surplice, *n.* cotta, *f.*; roccetto, *m.*

surplus, *n.* soprappiú, avanzo, *m.*; eccedenza, *f.* ~ *stock,* saldo, *m.*, scampoli, *m.pl.*

surprise, *n.* sorpresa, *f.*; stupore, *m.*, meraviglia, *f.* ~ *attack,* assalto improvviso, attacco fatto all'improvviso, colpo di mano, *m.* ¶ *v.t.* sorprendere; stupire; meravigliare. **surprising,** *a.* sorprendente, stupendo, meraviglioso ~**ly,** *ad.* sorprendentemente; stupendamente.

surrender, *n.* resa, *f.*; abbandono, *m.*, rinunzia, *f.*; cessione, consegna, *f.*; (*Insce.*) riscatto, *m.* ¶ *v.t.* cedere; consegnare, abbandonare, rinunziare a; (*insurance policy*) riscattare; (*v.i.*) arrendersi.

surreptitious, *a.* furtivo, clandestino, surrettizio.

surrogate, *n.* sostituto, delegato, surrogato, *m.*

surround, *v.t.* circondare, cingere, accerchiare, attorniare. ¶ *n.* contorno, *m.* ~ing, *p.a.* circostante. ~ings, *n.pl.* dintorni, *m.pl.*

surtax, *n.* sopratassa, *f.* ¶ *v.t.* imporre una sopratassa a, (su).

survey, *n.* vista, visita, *f.*, esame, *m.*, ispezione, *f.*, sorveglianza, *f.*; misurazione, perizia, *f.*, rilevamento, *m.*; (*land*) agrimensura, *f.* ¶ *v.t.* contemplare, guardare; sorvegliare; esaminare, ispezionare, misurare, rilevare. ~or, *n.* ispettore, *m.*; controllore; (*land*) perito, agrimensore, geometra, *m.*; (*quantity*) misuratore, *m.*; (*roads*) ispettore stradale, *m.*

survival, *n.* sopravvivenza, *f.* ~ of the fittest, selezione naturale, *f.*

survive, *v.t.* sopravvivere a; (*v.i.*) sopravvivere. **survivor,** *n.* (*shipwreck, &c.*) superstite, *m.f.* sopravvivente, *m.f.*

susceptible, *a.* suscettibile; sensibile; impressionabile.

suspect, *a.* sospetto, *m.*, -a, *f.* ¶ *n.* sospetto, *m.*, -a, *f.* ¶ *v.t.* sospettare, diffidare di.

suspend, *v.t.* sospendere. ~er[s], *n.* bretelle, giarrettiere, cigne, *f.pl.* sock ~, cigne da calzini, *f.pl.* ~ belt, cinta porta-bretelle, *f.* **suspense,** *n.* incertezza, *f.*, dubbio, *m.* in ~, nell'incertezza; in sospeso. ~ account, conto crediti contestati, *m.* **suspension,** *n.* sospensione, *f.* ~ bridge, ponte sospeso, *m.* **suspensory bandage,** sospensorio, *m.*

suspicion, *n.* sospetto, dubbio, *m.*; (*Law*) sospetto, *m.* **suspicious,** *a.* sospettoso, diffidente; sospetto.

sustain, *v.t.* sostenere, reggere; subire; mantenere. ~ing, *p.a.* (*power*) sostenitore; (*food*) che sostiene, nutriente. **sustenance,** *n.* nutrimento, vitto, *m.*

sutler, *n.* vivandiere, *m.*

suture, *n.* sutura, *f.*

suzerain, *n. & a.* sovrano, *m. & a.*

swab, *n.* strofinaccio, *m.*; (*Naut.*) radazza, *f.*; (*Surg.*) tampone, *m.*

swaddling clothes, (*lit. & fig.*) fasce, *f.pl.*

swage, *n.* stampo (da latta, &c.), *m.* ¶ *v.t.* stampare.

swagger, *v.i.* fare il fanfarone, far lo spaccone, pavoneggiarsi; millantare, bravazzare. ~er, *n.* fanfarone, smargiasso, millantatore, bravazzo, *m.*

swain, *n.* pastorello; amante, *m.*

swallow, *n.* rondine; gola, *f.*; (*river*) perdita, *f.* ~-tail (coat), (abito) a coda di rondine. ¶ *v.t.* inghiottire, ingoiare.

swamp, *n.* acquitrino, *m.*; palude, *f.* ¶ *v.t.* riempire d'acqua, inondare; sommergere. be ~ed (boat), riempirsi. ~y, *a.* paludoso, pantanoso, aquitrinoso.

swan, *n.* cigno, *m.* ~'s down, piuma di cigno, *f.* (*cloth*) vigogna *f.*; molletone, *m.* ~ song, canto del cigno, *m.*

sward, *n.* tappeto d'erba, *m.*; erbetta, erbuccia, *f.*

swarm, *n.* (*bees*) sciame, *m.*; (*multitude*) folla, frotta, *f.* nuvolo, *m.*, calca, *f.*, sciame, *m.* ¶ *v.i.* (*bees*) far sciame, sciamare; brulicare; pullulare, formicolare, abbondare.

swarthy, *a.* bruno, nericcio, moretto, abbronzato.

swash, *v.i.* far maretta; sciabordare. ~buckler, *n.* fanfarone, spaccone, spadaccino, *m.*

swastika, *n.* croce uncinata, *f.*

swat, *v.t.* (*fly*) uccidere. fly swat[ter], scacciamosche, *m.inv.*

swath, *n.* falciata, *f.*, mannello, *m.*; (*path cut*) passaggio aperto con la falce, *m.*

swathe, *v.t.* fasciare.

sway, *n.* dominio, potere, *m.*; preponderanza, influenza, *f.* ¶ *v.t.* fare oscillare, dondolare, scuotere; signoreggiare, dominare, governare; piegare, influenzare.

swear, *v.i. & t. ir.* giurare; bestemmiare; (*witness, &c.*) attestare, testificare, prestare giuramento. ~ in, far prestare giuramento.

sweat, *n.* sudore, *m.* ¶ *v.i. & t.* sudare; (*fig.*) sfruttare. ~ profusely, sudare come un cavallo. ~er, *n.* sfruttatore, *m.*; (*vest*) maglia a maniche lunghe, *f.* ~ing room (bath), stanza da sudare, *f.* ~y, *a.* sudato, madido di sudore, sudicio dal sudore.

Swede, *n.* svedese, *m.f.* s~, *n.* rapa svedese, *f.* **Sweden,** *n.* la Svezia, *f.*

Swedish, *a.* svedese. ~ *drill,* ginnastica svedese, *f.* ¶ *n.* lo svedese, *m.*

sweep, *n.* scopata, *f.*, tratto, colpo, slancio, *m.*; curva, *f.*, circuito, *m.*, passaggio rapido, *m.*; razzia; portata, *f.*; (*pers.*) spazzacamino, *m.* ¶ *v.t. & i. ir.* scopare, spazzare, passare rapidamente; (*chimney*) spazzare; (*Naut.*) dragare. *a clean* ~, tavola rasa, *f.* ~ *away,* portar via, spazzar via. ~ *the board,* raccogliere le poste. ~**er,** *n.* spazzatore, spazzino; scopatore, *m.*; (*Mach.*) spazzatrice meccanica, *f.*; *chimney sweep*[*er*], spazzacamino, *m.* ~**ing** *gesture,* gesto largo, *m.* ~**ings,** *n.pl.* spazzature, immondizie, *f.pl.* ~**stake**[*s*], *n.* puglia, *f.*, gara in cui il premio è costituito dalle poste dei singoli concorrenti; lotteria, *f.*

sweet, *a.* dolce, zuccherino; soave; aromatico, odoroso; carino, delizioso; (*wine*) dolce. ~ *bread,* animella, *f.* ~ *briar,* rosa canina, rosa di macchia, *f.*; (*bush*) rosaio di macchia, *m.* ~**heart,** innamorato, *m.*, -a, *f.*, amante, *m.f.* ~ *herbs,* erbe aromatiche, erbucce, *f.pl.* ~ *omelet*(*te*), frittata inzuccherata, *f.* ~**meat,** zuccherino, dolce, confetto, *m.* ~ *oil,* olio dolce, olio d'oliva, *m.* ~ *pea,* pisello odoroso, *m.* ~ *potato,* patata dolce, *f.* ~ *scented,* odoroso, profumato. *to have a* ~ *tooth,* essere amante dei dolci. ~*-william,* garofano screziato, *m.* *the* ~ (*opp.* the bitter), il dolce. ¶ *n.* dolce, *m.*; (*pl.*) zuccherini, dolci, dolciumi, *m.pl.* ~**en,** *v.t.* addolcire, inzuccherare; profumare, purificare. ~**ies,** *n.pl.* galanteria, *f.*; confetti, dolciumi, *m.pl.* ~**ish,** *a.* dolciastro, piuttosto dolce. ~**ness,** *n.* dolcezza, soavità, *f.*; gusto zuccherino; aroma, profumo, *m.*

swell, *n.* convessità, *f.*, gonfiamento, *m.*; (*sea*) ondeggiamento, *m.*, levata, *f.*, mar nuovo, mar di leva, *m.*; (*pers.*) elegante, *m.f.*, gran signore, pezzo grosso, *m.* ¶ *a.* alla moda, elegante. ~ *mob*[*s men*], borsaiuoli eleganti, ben vestiti, *m.pl.* ¶ *v.t. & i.ir.* gonfiare, enfiare, ingrossare, ingrandire; crescere, gonfiarsi, (*Mus.*) risonare. **swelling,** *n.* gonfiamento; tumore, *m.*, enfiagione, *f.*

swelter, *v.i.* fare un caldo soffocante; soffocare per l'eccessivo calore.

swerve, *n.* giro; scarto; *m.*, sterzata,

deviazione, *f.* ¶ *v.i.* sterzare, fare una sterzata, piegarsi, scostarsi.

swift, *a.* rapido, lesto, svelto, veloce, celere, presto. ~*-footed,* a piede leggero. ¶ *n.* rondone, *m.* ~**ness,** *n.* celerità, rapidità, leggerezza, *f.*

swig, *v.t.* tracannare, bere d'un fiato, bere a lunghi tratti.

swill, *v.t.* lavare a più acque, risciacquare; (*drink*) tracannare.

swim, *n.* nuotata, *f.* *in the* ~, al corrente (di affari, &c.), della partita. ¶ *v.i. & t.ir.* nuotare. ~ *across,* passare a nuoto, attraversare a nuoto. ~ *under water,* nuotare sott'acqua. **swimmer,** *n.* nuotatore, *m.*, -trice, *f.* **swimming,** *n.* nuoto, *m.* *my head is* ~, mi gira la testa. ~ *bath,* ~ *pool,* piscina, *f.* ~ *costume,* *swim suit,* costume da bagno, *m.*

swindle, *n.* truffa, frode, *f.*; raggiro, *m.* ¶ *v.t.* truffare, raggirare. **swindler,** *n.* truffatore, *m.*

swine, *n.* porco, maiale, *m.* ~*herd,* porcaio, *m.*

swing, *n.* altalena, *f.*; oscillazione, *f.*; dondolamento, *m.*; slancio, libero corso, sfogo, *m.* *in full* ~, in piena attività. ~ *bridge,* ponte girante, ponte girevole, *m.* ~ *door,* porta battente, porta volante; (*Naut.*) botola, *f.* ¶ *v.t. & i. ir.* oscillare, far oscillare; dondolare; fare l'altalena; girare, dondolarsi, agitarsi; penzolare; girare sull'ancora.

swingletree, *n.* bilancino, *m.*

swirl, *n.* turbine, vortice, risucchio, *m.* ¶ *v.i.* turbinare, roteare.

swish, *n.* fruscio, fischio, scroscio, *m.* ¶ *v.t.* far fischiare; sferzare; (*tail*) agitare.

Swiss, *a. & n.* svizzero, *a. & m.* ~ *guard,* guardia svizzera, *f.*

switch, *n.* verghetta, bacchetta, mazzettina, *f.*; (*Rly.*) scambio, deviatoio; (*Elec.*) interruttore, commutatore, *m.* ~*back,* montagne russe, *f.pl.* ~*board,* tavola di commutazione, *f.*, quadro di comando, *m.* ¶ *v.t.* sferzare, bacchettare; dimenare; far deviare; (*Rly.*) smistare. ~ *off,* tagliare, rompere il circuito, chiudere la corrente, disinserire; (*lights*) spegnere. ~ *on,* aprire (la corrente), girare l'interruttore, inserire; (*light*) accendere.

Switzerland, *n.* la Svizzera, *f.*

swivel, *n.* parte girevole, *f.*, anello g., *m.*; molinello, *m.* ¶ *v.i.* imperniarsi, girare.

swollen glands, glandole gonfiate (al collo), *f.pl.*

swoon, *n.* svenimento, deliquio, *m.* ¶ *v.i.* svenire.

swoop down on, piombare su, p. addosso a.

sword, *n.* spada, *f.*; (*Poet.*) ferro, brando, *m.*; (*in fun*), spadone, *m.*, durlindana, *f.* ~ *belt,* cinturone, *m.* ~*fish,* pescespada, *m.* ~ *rattler,* spadaccino, *m.* ~ *stick,* bastone animato, *m.* **swordsman,** *n.* spadaccino, schermitore, *m.* **swordsmanship,** *n.* scherma, *f.*

Sybarite, *n.* sibarita, *m.*

sycamore, *n.* sicomoro, *m.*

sycophant, *n.* sicofante, *m.*

syllabize, *v.t.* sillabare. **syllable,** *n.* sillaba, *f.*

syllabus, *n.* programma, *m.*; (*Eccl.*) sillabo, *m.*

syllogism, *n.* sillogismo, *m.*

sylph, *n.*, silfo, *m.*, silfide, *f.*

sylvan, *a.* silvano, boschereccio.

symbol, *n.* simbolo, *m.* ~**ic(al),** *a.* simbolico. ~**ism,** *n.* simbolismo, *m.* ~**ize,** *v.t.* simboleggiare.

symmetric(al), *a.* simmetrico. **symmetry,** *n.* simmetria, *f.*

sympathetic, *a.* tenero; pieno di simpatia; indulgente; gentile. ~ *strike,* sciopero di solidarietà, *m.* **sympathize,** *v.i.* simpatizzare, compatire. **sympathy,** *n.* simpatia, *f.*

symphony, *n.* sinfonia, *f.*

symptom, *n.* sintomo, *m.*

synagogue, *n.* sinagoga, *f.*

synchronous, *a.* sincrono.

syncopate, *v.t.* sincopare. **syncopation,** *n.* sincopatura, *f.* **syncope,** *n.* sincope, *f.*

syndicate, *n.* sindacato, *m.* ¶ *v.t.* costituire in sindacato.

synod, *n.* sinodo, *m.* ~**ic(al),** *a.* sinodico.

synonym, *n.* & **synonymous,** *a.* sinonimo, *a.* & *m.*

synopsis, *n.* sinossi, *f.*, sommario, sunto, *m.*

synovitis, *n.* sinovite, *f.*

syntax, *n.* sintassi, *f.*

synthesis, *n.* sintesi, *f.* **synthetic(al),** *a.* sintetico.

Syracuse, *n.* Siracusa, *f.*

Syria, *n.* la Siria, *f.* **Syrian,** *a.* siriano, della Siria. ¶ *n.* siriano, *m.*, -a, *f.*

syringa, *n.* siringa, *f.*

syringe, *n.* siringa, *f.*; schizzetto, *m.* ¶ *v.t.* siringare.

syrup, *n.* sciroppo, *m.* ~**y,** *a.* sciropposo, come lo sciroppo.

system, *n.* sistema, *m.*, regime, *m.* rete, *f.*; impianto, *m.* *railway* ~, rete ferroviaria, *f.* *telephone* ~, rete telefonica, *f.* *heating* ~, impianto di riscaldamento, *m.* ~**atic,** *a.* sistematico, ragionato, regolare.

T

T, *n.* T, ti, *f.* ~ *square,* riga a T, *f.* *to a* ~, a pennello.

tab, *n.* linguetta, striscettina, aletta, *f.*

tabby cat, gatta tigrata, g. grigiastra, g. soriana, *f.*

tabernacle, *n.* tabernacolo, *m.*

tabes, *n.* (*Med.*) tabe, *f.*

table, *n.* tavola, *f.*, tavolo, *m.*; quadro, elenco, indice, prospetto, *m.*; tabella, *f.* ~ *centre,* centro da tavola, *m.* ~ *cloth,* tovaglia, *f.* ~ *companion,* commensale, *m.f.*; convitato, *m.*, -a, *f.* ~ *cover,* tappeto da tavola, *m.* ~*cut* (gem), a piatto. ~ *fowl,* pollo, pollastro, *m.* ~ *fruit,* frutta da tavola, *f.* ~ *gramophone,* fonografo a cassetta, *m.* ~ *knife,* coltello da tavola, *m.* ~ *land,* altipiano, *m.* ~ *mat,* sopratovaglia, *f.* ~ *napkin,* tovagliolo, *m.* ~ *salt,* sale fino, *m.* ~*spoon,* cucchiaio da tavola, *m.* ~*spoonful,* cucchiaiata, *f.* ~ *talk,* discorsi fatti a tavola, *m.pl.*; chiacchiere, *f.pl.* ~ *water,* acqua minerale, *f.* ¶ *v.t.* mettere innanzi, intavolare. **tableau,** *n.* quadro, *m.*

tablet, *n.* tavoletta, *f.*, placca, *f.*; pezzo, *m.*; (*Pharm.*) pastiglia, *f.* ~ *for inscription,* lapide, *f.*

taboo, *n.* tabù, *m.* *he, it, is* ~, è tabù. ¶ *v.t.* proibire, interdire, dichiarare tabù.

tabular, *a.* in forma di tavole, di tabelle, in tavole. ~ *matter* (*Typ.*), composizione delle tabelle. **tabulate,** *v.t.* far elenco di, classificare; ridurre in tavole, disporre in tabelle.

tacit, *a.* tacito; implicito. **taciturn,** *a.* taciturno. ~**ity,** *n.* taciturnità, *f.*

tack, *n.* bulletta, *f.* (*Naut.*) bordata, *f.*, bordo, *m.*; (*of sail*) mura, *f.* ¶ *v.t.* attaccare con bullette; fissare con puntine; aggiungere; (*Need.*) imbastire; cucire; (*v.i.*) bordeggiare, virar di bordo. ~*ing cotton,* cotone da imbastire, *m.*

tackle, *n.* arnesi, finimenti, *m.pl.*; roba, *f.*; attrezzi, *m.pl.*; (*Naut.*) paranco; sartiame, *m.* ~ *block,* taglia, puleggia, *f.*; bozzello, *m.* ~ *fall,* tirante di paranco, *m.* ¶ *v.t.*

metter mano a, intraprendere; (*pers. fig.*) indirizzarsi a, rivolgersi a, cercare di convincere.

tacky, *a.* colloso, vischioso.

tact, *n.* tatto, *m.*, accortezza, *f.*, riguardo, *m.* (*cft. pl.*). **~ful,** *a.* pieno di tatto, accorto, premuroso. **~less,** *a.* senza tatto, malaccorto, goffo.

tactical, *a.* tattico. **tactician,** *n.* tattico, *m.* **tactics,** *n.pl.* tattica, *f.*; evoluzioni, *f.pl.*

tactile, tactual, *a.* tattile.

tadpole, *n.* girino, *m.*

taffeta, *n.* taffetà, *m.*

taffrail, *n.* coronamento (della poppa), *m.*

tag, *n.* (*lace, &c.*) puntale, aghetto; (*boot*) tirante, *m.*; (*stock phrase*) luogo comune, *m.*, espressione bell'e fatta, *f.*; (*old story*) ritornello, *m.*, vecchia antifona, *f.* **~ label,** cartellino (di spedizione), *m.* **~-rag** (*& bobtail*), canaglia, *f.* ¶ *v.t.* mettere l'aghetto a; attaccare, unire.

Tagus, (the), il Tago, *m.*

Taihiti, *n.* Taiti, *m.*, l'isola di T., *f.*

tail, *n.* coda, *f.*; estremità, *f.*; (*coat, &c.*) coda, falda, *f.*; (*coin*) rovescio, *m.*; (*book page*) coda, *f.*, taglio inferiore, *m.* **~ coat** or **tails** (evening), abito a coda di rondine, *m.*; (*morning*) abito a falda, *m.* **~piece,** vignetta, *f.* **~ stock** (lathe), contropunta, *f.* **to turn ~,** darsela a gambe, menar le calcagna. **to return with one's ~ between one's legs,** tornare a piè zoppo, tornare con le pive nel sacco. **~ings,** *n.pl.* rifiuti di miniera; residui di scarto, *m.pl.*; (*grain*) mondiglia, lolla, *f.*

tailor, *n.* sarto, *m.* **~-made** or **~ed,** fatto da un sarto. **~ess,** *n.* sarta, *f.* **~ing,** *n.* sartoria, *f.*

taint, *n.* infezione; macchia, magagna, *f.*; difetto, *m.*; tintura, tinta, *f.* ¶ *v.t.* infettare, guastare, corrompere, intaccare, macchiare, appestare. **~ed** (*meat, &c.*) *p.a.* guastato, corrotto.

take, *v.t. ir.* prendere; pigliare; portare; condurre, menare; acchiappare; afferrare; accettare; scegliere; fare; seguire; provare; mettere; impiegare; comprendere; intendere; ritenere; (*v.i.*) prendere; supporre; credere; immaginarsi. **~** (*a degree*), conseguire; laurearsi. **~ away,** togliere; levare, portar via; condur via; rimuovere; sottrarre. **~ back,** riprendere; riportare; ricondurre; ritrattare. **~ cover,** rifugiarsi. **~**

~ down, abbassare; ammainare; sganciare; staccare; smontare; scrivere; far nota di; (*pop.*) umiliare; abbattere, demolire. **~ down** [*in shorthand*] stenografare. **~ in,** ricevere, introdurre, far entrare; tirar dentro; abbracciare, comprendere, includere; raccorciare; fare; ingannare. **~ off,** levare; togliere; levarsi; (*a pers.*) imitare, contraffare, beffarsi di; (*Jump.*) spiccare; (*Aero.*) decollare, ¶ *n.* decollo, *m.* **~ on** (hands), ingaggiare. **~ out,** cavare, estrarre; cancellare; far sparire; ritirare; levare, toglier via; (*Insce. policy*) fare, effettuare. **~ over,** prendere, assumere; incaricarsi di; acquistare, trasportare. **~ shape,** rivelarsi, manifestarsi. **~ to,** applicarsi a, darsi a, mettersi a; occuparsi di; aver gusto per, provar simpatia per, affezionarsi a. **~ to pieces,** smontare, sconnettere. **~ to task,** rimproverare, biasimare, ammonire, fare una paternale a. **~ up,** raccogliere; rilevare; accettare; attendere a, occuparsi di; assorbire; occupare; raccattare; prendere; tenere; (*shares*) acquistare; rilevare; (*option*) consolidare. **~ your seats!** (in carriage), in vettura! **taker,** *n.* prenditore, *m.*, -trice, *f.* **taking,** *a.* seducente, attraente. ¶ *n.* presa, *f.*; (*pl.*) incasso, *m.*, ricavo, *m.* **~ off** (*Aero.*), decollaggio, *m.*

talc, *n.* talco, *m.*

tale, *n.* novella; storiella, *f.*; racconto, *m.*; narrazione; favola, fiaba, *f.*; numero, *m.* **~ bearer,** spifferone, chiacchierone, *m.*, -ona, *f.*

talent, *n.* ingegno, talento, *m.* **~ed,** *a.* d'ingegno, che ha del talento.

talisman, *n.* talismano, *m.*

talk, *n.* conversazione, *f.*; colloquio; abboccamento; discorso, *m.*, ragionamento, *m.*; propositi, *m.pl.*; ciarla, diceria, *f.* ¶ *v.i. & t.* parlare; discorrere (su, di); conversare; ciarlare, chiacchierare **~ative,** *a.* loquace, chiacchierone. **~er,** *n.* chi parla, parlatore, *m.*, -trice, *f.*; chiacchierone, *m.*, -a, *f.* **~ing,** *a.* parlante; (*film*) parlante, sonoro.

tall, *a.* grande, alto. **~ness,** *n.* (*pers.*) statura alta; statura, *f.*; (*steeple, &c.*) altezza, *f.*

tallow, *n.* sego, *m.* ¶ *v.t.* spalmare con sego; ingrassare.

tally, *n.* (*stick*) taglia, *f.*; (*check*) riscontro, *m.*; tessera; segnatura; (*label*) etichetta, *f.* **~ trade,** vendita

a pagamenti rateali. ¶ *v.i.* comba-
ciare (con), corrispondere (a); accordarsi, quadrare. ~-ho, *i.* grido
d'incitamento ai cani, *m.*

talon, *n.* artiglio, *m.*; (*counterfoil*)
madre, matrice, *f.* (d'un foglio di
tagliandi).

talus, *n.* pendio, *m.*, scarpata, *f.*;
materiale accumulatosi alla base
d'un luogo scosceso.

tamarind, *n.* tamarindo, *m.* **tamarisk,** *n.* tamerice, *f.*, tamarisco, *m.*

tambour, *m.* tamburo, *m.* ~ine, *n.*
tamburello, *m.*

tame, *a.* addomesticato, ammansito;
(*fig.*) docile, mansueto; innocuo;
domestico; sottomesso; sbiadito.
~ *rabbit,* coniglio domestico. ¶ *v.t.*
ammansare, domare, addomesticare.
tamer, *n.* domatore, *m.*, -trice, *f.*

tam-o'-shanter, *n.* berretto scozzese,
m.

tamp, *v.t.* turare, tamponare; pigiare,
pestare.

tamper with, immischiarsi di; falsificare; (*witness*) subornare.

tampon, *n.* tampone, stuello, *m.*

tan, *n.* concia, *f.* ~yard, conceria, *f.*
¶ *v.t.* conciare, abbronzare. ¶ *a.*
color tanè, castagno; abbronzato.

tandem, *n.* tandem, *m.* ¶ *a. & ad.* a
tandem.

tang, *n.* gusto, sapore piccante, *m.*;
salsedine, *f.*; suono, *m.*; (*shank*)
codolo, *m. There is a ~ in the air,*
l'aria è frizzante.

tangent, *n.* tangente, *f.* ~[ial], *a.*
tangenziale.

tangerine, *n.* mandarino, *m.*

tangible, *a.* tangibile.

Tangier, *n.* Tangeri, *f.*

tangle, *n.* garbuglio, viluppo, affare
intricato, *m.*; alga marina, *f.*;
complicazione, *f.*, arruffio, *m.* ¶ *v.t.*
ingarbugliare, impigliare; avvilup-
parsi, confondere.

tango, *n.* tango, *m.*

tank, *n.* cisterna, *f.*, serbatoio, *m.*;
(*Mil.*) carro armato; (*pop.*) auto-
bruco, *m.* ~ steamer, or **tanker,**
nave cisterna, [nave] petroliera, *f.*

tankard, *n.* boccale, bricco, *m.*

tanner, *n.* conciatore, *m.* ~y, *n.*
conceria, *f.* **tannin,** *n.* tannino,
m.

tantalize, *v.t.* frustrare, far soffrire il
supplizio di Tantalo. **tantalum,** *n.*
tantalio, *m.* **tantalus,** *n.* tantalo, *m.*,
cassettina da liquori, *f.*

tantamount to (to be), equivalere a,
essere equivalente a (*or* di).

tantrums, *n.pl.* furie, *f.pl.*; nervi,
m.pl.; burrasche, *f.pl.*

tap, *n.* colpo leggero, colpetto, *m.*
(*water, &c.*) rubinetto, *m.*; cannella,
f.; (*plug*) tappo, *m.*, spina, *f.*;
(*screw*) maschio, *m.* ~ *dance,* punta
e tacco. ~ *root,* radice principale, *f.*,
fittone, *m.*, barba maestra, *f.* ¶ *v.t.
& i.* picchiare, toccare, battere;
(*screw*) maschiare; (*cask*) spillare;
(*tree, &c.*) far incisione a; (*Surg.*)
far la paracentesi a.

tape, *n.* nastro, *m.*; fettuccia, *f.*
~ *machine,* telegrafo stampatore, *m.*
~ *measure,* metro a nastro, *m.*,
rotella metrica, *f.* ~worm, tenia, *f.*

taper, *n.* piccola candela, *f.*, moccolo,
cerino; (*coiled*) stoppino, lucignolo,
m.; (*church*) cero, *m.* ¶ *v.t.* affusolare,
acuminare; (*v.i.*) terminare in punta,
assottigliarsi verso l'estremità.
~[ing], *a.* a punta, conico, affusolato, acuminato.

tapestry, *n. & ~ work,* tappezzeria,
f., arazzo, *m.*

tapioca, *n.* tapioca, *f.*

tapir, *n.* tapiro, *m.*

tapis (to be on the), essere in discussione.

tar, *n.* catrame, *m.*, pece liquida, *f.*;
(*pers.*) marinaio, lupo di mare, *m.*
~ *macadam,* macadam al catrame, *m.*
~ *spraying,* incatramazione, inca-
tramatura, *f.* ¶ *v.t.* incatramare,
spalmare di catrame, impeciare.

tarantella, *n.* tarantella, *f.* **tarantula,**
n. tarantola, *f.*

tardy, *a.* tardo, lento, tardivo.

tare, *n.* veccia, *f.*; (*pl. fig.*) loglio, *m.*,
zizzania, *f.*; (*Com.*) tara, *f.*

target, *n.* bersaglio, segno, *m.*; (*fig.*)
scopo, fine, obiettivo, *m.*, meta,
mira, *f.* ~ *practice,* tiro al bersaglio,
m.

tariff, *n.* tariffa, *f.* ¶ *v.t.* tariffare.

tarn, *n.* laghetto (in montagna), *m.*

tarnish, *v.t.* appannare, offuscare,
scolorire, insozzare; (*v.i.*) appan-
narsi, offuscarsi, insozzarsi.

tarpaulin, *n.* tela incatramata, *f.*;
copertone, *m.*

tarragon, *n.* (*Bot.*) artemisia, *f.*

Tarragona, *n.* Tarragona, *f.*

tarry, *a.* catramato; bituminoso.

tarry, *v.i.* indugiare, tardare.

tarsus, *n.* tarso, *m.*

tart, *a.* agro, acerbo, acido; brusco,
aspro, mordace. ¶ *n.* (*open*) torta,
pasta; (*covered*) crostata, *f.*

tartan, *n.* (*Naut.*) tartana, *f.*; (*cloth*)
tessuto di lana a righe, *m.*

tartar, *n.* tartaro, *m.* ~**ic,** *a.* tartarico.

tartness, *n.* acidezza, acerbezza, acredine, *f.*; (*fig.*) mordacità, asprezza, *f.*

task, *n.* compito, lavoro, *m.*; lezione, *f.*; carico, *m.*, incarico, *m.* *to take to* ~, rimproverare, biasimare, lavare il capo a. ¶ *v.t.* mettere alla prova, assegnare un compito a; essere a carico di, opprimere, esaurire.

Tasmania, *n.* la Tasmania, *f.*

tassel, *n.* fiocco, *m.*, nappina, *f.*; (*book*) segnalibro, *m.*

taste, *n.* gusto, sapore; saggio, genio; pochino, tantino; bocconcino, *m.* ¶ *v.t. & i.* gustare, assaporare, sentire, provare; avere un sapore, un gusto; (*tea, wine, &c.*) assaggiare, degustare. ~ *of,* sapere di, avere il gusto di. ~**ful,** *a.* di buon gusto. ~**less,** *a.* senza gusto, insipido; di cattivo gusto. **taster,** *n.* assaggiatore, *m.*, degustatore, *m.*, -trice, *f.*; (*cheese*) sonda, *f.* **tasting,** *n.* degustazione, *f.*, assaggio, *m.* **tasty,** *a.* saporito.

tata, *i.* addio; (*pop.*) ciào.

tatter, *n.* (*gen. pl.*) cencio, brandello, straccio, *m.* ~**ed,** *a.* stracciato, a brandelli, lacero. **tatterdemalion,** *n.* pezzente, straccione, *m.*

tatting, *n.* frivolezza, *f.*

tattle, *n.* ciancia, ciarla, chiacchiera, *f.* ¶ *v.i.* cianciare, ciarlare, chiacchierare. **tattler,** *n. & tattling,** *a.* ciarlone, *a. & m.*, ciarlona, *a. & f.*; chiacchierone, *a.m.*, -a, *a.f.*

tattoo, *n.* tatuaggio, *m.*; (*Mil.*) ritirata, *f.* ¶ *v.t.* tatuare; (*v.i.*) tamburinare.

taunt, *n.* rinfaccio, sarcasmo, *m.*; rampogna, *f.*; scherno, *m.* ¶ *v.t.* rinfacciare, gettare alla faccia, rampognare, farsi beffa di. ~ *with,* rimproverare.

taut, *a.* teso; rigido. ~**en,** *v.t.* tendere; irrigidire.

tautologic(al), *a.* tautologico. **tautology,** *n.* tautologia, *f.*

tavern, *n.* bettola, taverna, osteria, mescita, *f.* ~ *with gardens & dance hall,* bettola, *f.*

taw, *v.t.* conciare (con allume).

tawdriness, *n.* falso splendore, sfarzo senza eleganza, *m.*, orpellatura, *f.*, sfoggio volgare, *m.* **tawdry,** *a.* d'orpello, vistoso, pretenzioso. ~ *finery,* orpello, *m.*, cenci guarniti d'orpello, *m.pl.*

tawny, *a.* fulvo, rossiccio, abbronzato. ~ *owl,* barbagianni, gufo, *m.*

tax, *n.* tassa, imposta, *f.* ~ *collector,* esattore delle imposte, agente del fisco, *m.* ~ *dodger,* chi evade una tassa, *m.f.*, frodatore dei diritti del fisco, *m.* ~ *free,* esente da tassa, da imposta. ~*payer,* contribuente, *m.f.* ¶ *v.t.* tassare, (*fig.*) accusare, tacciare (*with* = di). *Why do you* ~ *me with it?* Perché se la rifà con me? ~**able,** *a.* tassabile, imponibile. ~ *income,* reddito, imponibile, *m.* ~**ation,** *n.* tassazione, *f.*; tasse, imposte, *f.pl.*

taxi, *v.i.* (*Aero.*) rullare; (*sea-plane*) flottare. ~[*cab*], *taxi,* tassí, *m.*, autopubblica, *f.* ~ *driver,* ~*man,* autista di tassi, *m.* ~ *meter,* tassametro, *m.*

taxidermist, *n.* impagliatore, *m.* **taxidermy,** *n.* tassidermia, *f.*

tea, *n.* tè, *m.* ~ *caddy,* scatola da tè, *f.* ~ *cloth,* tovaglia da tè, *f.* ~ *cosy,* copriteiera, *f.inv.* ~*cup,* tazza da tè, *f.* ~*gown,* toletta pel tè, vestito da casa. ~ *party,* tè, *m.* ~ *plant,* pianta del tè, *f.* ~*pot,* teiera, *f.* ~ *roll, & butter,* tè completo, *m.* ~ *room(s),* ~ *shop,* sala da tè, *f.*, pasticceria, *f.* ~ *rose,* rosa tè, *f.* ~*spoon,* cucchiaino (da tè), *m.* ~*time,* ora del tè, *f.*

teach, *v.t. & i. ir.* insegnate, istruire; ammaestrare; professare; mostrare (a); fare, tenere (una lezione); (*bird*) imbeccare, insegnare a ripetere. ~ *someone a lesson,* fare una lezione a qualcuno. ~ *someone manners,* fare a qualcuno una lezione di cortesia. ~**er,** *n.* insegnante, *m.f.*; istitutore, *m.*, -trice, *f.*; maestro, *m.*, -a, *f.*; professore, *m.*, -essa, *f.*; precettore, *m.* ~**ing,** *n.*, insegnamento, *m.*, istruzione, *f.*; dottrina, *f.*

teak, *n.* (legno) tec, *m.*

teal, *n.* arzavola, *f.*

team, *n.* (*draught animals*) tiro, *m.*; (*workmen, sport, &c.*) squadra, *f.*, (*pair*) pariglia, *f.* ~ *race,* corsastaffetta, *f.* ~ *spirit,* spirito di corpo, *m.* ~ *work,* sforzo combinato, *m.*

tear, *n.* squarcio, sdrucio, strappo, *m.*; stracciatura, lacerazione, laceratura, *f.* ¶ *v.t.* lacerare, stracciare. ~ *off* or ~ *out* strappare. ~ *up,* squarciare; sradicare; fare a pezzi. ~ *one another to pieces,* dilaniarsi l'un l'altro.

tear, *n.* lagrima, *f.* ~**s,** *pl.* pianto, *m.*

~ *gas*, gas lacrimogeno, *m.* ~**ful**, *a.* lagrimoso.

tease, *v.t.* tormentare, contrariare; stuzzicare, punzecchiare; (*textiles*) pettinare, cardare. ¶ (*pers.*) *n.* stuzzichino, *m.*, seccatore, *m.*, -trice, *f.*

teasel, *n.* cardo, scardasso, labbro di Venere, *m.* ¶ *v.t.* cardare.

teaser, *n.* (*pers.*) stuzzichino, tormentatore, *m.*; (*fig.*) problema, rompicapo, *m.*; cardatore, *m.*, -trice, *f.* **teasing**, *n.* malizia, *f.*, importunità, *f.*

teat, *n.* capezzolo, *m.*, mammella, poppa, tetta, *f.*

technical, *a.* tecnico. ~ *offence*, quasi-delitto, *m.* ~ *school*, scuola tecnica, scuola pratica, *f.* **technicolour**, *n.* tecnicolore, *m.* **technique**, *n.* tecnica, *f.*; arte, *f.*; meccanismo, *m.* **technology**, *n.* tecnologia, *f.*

ted, *v.t.* rivoltare (il fieno). **tedder**, *n.* (*Mech.*) spandifieno, *m.*

Teddy bear, orso di felpa, *m.*

Te Deum, *n.* Te Deum, *m.*

tedious, *a.* tedioso, noioso. ~**ness** & **tedium**, *n.* tedio, *m.*, noia, *f.*, uggia, *f.*

tee, *n.* ti, T, *f.*; (*Golf*) monticello, mucchietto di rena per la palla. *to a* ~, a pennello. ¶ (*Golf*) *v.t.* mettere la palla sul mucchietto di rena. ~*ing ground* (*Golf*), piazzuola di partenza, *f.*

teem with, formicolare di, brulicare di, abbondare di.

teens (in one's), adolescente, giovinetto (dai tredici ai diciannove anni).

teethe, *v.i.* mettere i denti. **teething**, *n.* dentizione, *f.*

teetotal, *a.* antialcoolico, non alcoolico, astemio. ~**ism**, *n.* antialcoolismo, *m.*, astensione dall'alcool, *f.* **teetotaller**, *n.* bevilacqua, *m.f.*, astemio, *m.*, -a, *f.*

teetotum, *n.* trottola (a quattro facce), *f.*

tegument, *n.* tegumento, *m.*

telegram, *n.* telegramma, dispaccio, *m.* **telegraph**, *n.* telegrafo, *m.* ~ *board* (sport) indicatore, *m.* ~ *boy*, ~ *messenger*, fattorino del telegrafo, *m.* ~ *office*, ufficio telegrafico, *m.* ¶ *v.t.* & *i.* telegrafare. ~**ese**, *n.* linguaggio telegrafico, stile telegrafico, *m.* ~**ic**, *a.* telegrafico. ~**y**, *n.* telegrafia, *f* *wireless* ~, telegrafia senza fili, *f.*

telepathy, *n.* telepatia, *f.*

telephone, *n.* telefono, *m.* ¶ *v.t.* & *i.*

telefonare. ¶ *att.* & **telephonic**, *a.* telefonico. **telephony**, *n.* telefonia, *f.* **telephotograph** & **telephotography**, *n.* telefotografia, *f.*

teleprinter, *n.* telescrivente, *m.*

telescope, *n.* (*reflecting*) telescopio a riflessione; (*refracting*) t. a. rifrazione; (*spy-glass*) cannocchiale, *m.* ¶ *v.i.* inserirsi, infilarsi. **telescopic**, *a.* telescopico; (*sliding*) a corsoio.

televise, *v.t.* trasmettere per televisione. **television**, *n.* televisione, *f.*

tell, *v.t.* & *i.* *ir.* dire, raccontare, ripetere, narrare; riferire, indicare, svelare; riconoscere, distinguere, scoprire; farsi sentire; contare; sapere; (*of remark*, &c.) portar effetto, far colpo; (*in one's favour*) militare. ~**er**, *n.* (*voting*) scrutatore, scrutinatore, *m.*; (*bank*) cassiere, *m.* ~**ing**, *a.* efficace, che colpisce, che porta effetto. *there is no* ~, non si può sapere, non si sa. ~*tale*, *n.* (*pers.*) informatore, *m.*, -trice, *f.*; rifischione, *m.*; (*Mach.*) contatore, *m.*

temerity, *n.* temerità, *f.*

temper, *n.* carattere, *m.*, disposizione, *f.*, umore, *m.*, indole, *f.*, tempra, *f.*; (*bad*) cattivo umore, *m.*, collera, *f.* ¶ *v.t.* (*metal*) temperare, dare la tempera; (*mortar*) stemperare; (*fig.*) temperare, moderare. **temperament**, *n.* temperamento, *m.*, complessione, costituzione, *f.* ~**al**, *a.* costituzionale; capriccioso, impressionabile. **temperance**, *n.* temperanza, *f.* **temperate**, *a.* temperante, sobrio; (*climate*, *speech*) temperato. **temperature**, *n.* temperatura, *f.*

tempest, *n.* tempesta, burrasca, *f.* **tempestuous**, *a.* tempestoso.

template, ~**plet**, *n.* sagoma, forma, maschera, *f.*; cuscino d'appoggio, *m.*

temple, *n.* tempio, *m.*; (*Anat.*) tempia, *f.*

temporal, *a.* temporale. **temporary**, *a.* temporaneo, transitorio, provvisorio. **temporize**, *v.i.* temporeggiare.

tempt, *v.t.* tentare; invitare; allettare, sedurre. **-ation**, *n.*, tentazione, *f.* **tempter**, **-tress**, tentatore, *m.* -trice *f.* seduttore, *m.*, -trice *f.* **tempting**, *a.*, attraente, seducente, allettante, (*food*), appetitoso, gustoso.

ten, *a.* dieci. ¶*n.* dieci, (una) decina, *f.* **-fold**, *a.* & *ad.* decuplo, dieci volte. *to increase*-, rendere dieci volte maggiore, decuplicare.

tenable, *a.* sostenibile. **tenacious,** *a.* tenace. ~**ly,** *ad.* tenacemente.

tenancy, *n.* affitto, *m.*, locazione, *f.*; usufrutto, *m.* **tenant,** *n.* fittaiolo, *m.*, -a, *f.*; pigionale, *m.f.*; locatario, *m.*, -a, *f.*; inquilino, *m.*, -a, *f.*; (*Law*) affittuario, locatario, usufruttuario, *m.*, -a, *f.*; (*farm*) affittuario d'un fondo. ~ *farmer*, affittuario (di fondi rustici). ~'*s repairs*, riparazioni locative, *f.pl.* ~**able,** *a.* abitabile.

tench, *n.* tinca, *f.*

tend, *v.t.* curare, sorvegliare, attendere a, aver cura di, vegliare su; (*v.i.*) tendere, aver tendenza, esser diretto, mirare. ~**ency,** *n.* tendenza, disposizione, *f.* **tendentious,** *a.* tendenzioso. **tender,** *n.* offerta, *f.* (per prendere in appalto); (*boat*) bastimento ausiliare; (*Rly.*) carro di scorta, *m.*, tender, *m.* *legal* ~, corso legale, *m.*, valuta legale, *f.* ¶ *v.t.* offrire, deferire. ~ *for*, fare offerta per prendere in appalto; concorrere ad un appalto.

tender, *a.* tenero, dolce, delicato; affettuoso; sensibile; sensitivo; (*meat*) frollo, tenero. ~**ness,** *n.* tenerezza, *f.*, affetto, *m.*; delicatezza; fragilità; sensibilità, *f.*

tendon, *n.* tendine, *m.*

tendril, *n.* viticcio, *m.*

tenement, *n.* abitazione, *f.*, alloggio, *m.*; tenuta, *f.*; casa, *f.*, appartamento (di basso valore), *m.* ~ *house*, casa popolare d'affitto, casa di reddito, *f.*

Teneriffe, *n.* Teneriffa, *f.*

tenet, *n.* dogma, *m.*; dottrina, *f.*

tennis, *n.* tennis, *m.* ~ *court*, campo di tennis, *m.*

tenon, *n.* tenone, *m.* ~ *saw*, sega per incastri, *f.*; saracco a dorso, *m.*

tenor, *n.* tenore, senso, *m.*, portata, *f.*; (*bill*) scadenza, *f.*; (*voice, singer*) tenore, *m.* ~ *clef*, chiave di tenore (di dò).

tense, *a.* teso, rigido. ¶ *n.* tempo, *m.* **tension,** *n.* tensione, *f.*

tent, *n.* tenda, *f.*, padiglione, *m.*; (*Surg.*) tasta, *f.* ~ *pole*, albero di tenda. ~ *umbrella*, parasole, *m.*

tentacle, *n.* tentacolo, *m.*

tentative [effort], tentativo, *m.*

tenterhook, *n.* uncino, *m.* *on* ~*s*, sulle spine, sui carboni ardenti, sulla brace.

tenth, *a.* decimo. ¶ *n.* decimo, *m.*, decima (parte), *f.*; (il) dieci, *m.*

tenuity, *n.* tenuità, *f.* **tenuous,** *a.* tenue; esile; sottile.

tenure, *n.* possesso, *m.*, godimento, *m.*, occupazione, *f.*; diritto di occupazione, *m.*, escrcizio, *m.* *during his* ~ *cf office*, durante l'esercizio delle sue funzioni.

tepid, *a.* tiepido. ~**ness,** *n.* tiepidezza, *f.*

term, *n.* termine, limite, *m.*; durata; sessione, *f.*; (*Sch.*) trimestre, *m.*; (*pl.*) condizioni, *f.pl.*; patti, *m.pl.*; prezzo, *m.*; (*pl.*) rapporti, *m.pl.*; tenore, accordo, *m.* ¶ *v.t.* chiamare, denominare, qualificare. **on equal** ~**s,** del pari, sopra un piede di uguaglianza.

termagant, *n.* megera, virago, *f.*

terminable, *a.* a termine, terminabile. **terminal,** *a.* estremo, ultimo; terminale, a testa di linea. ¶ *n.* (*Elec.*) terminale, *m.* **terminate,** *v.t.* terminare. **termination,** *n.* fine, conclusione; terminazione, desinenza, *f.* **terminus,** *n.* limite, termine, *m.*; stazione capolinea, *f.*

termite, *n.* termite, *f.*

tern, *n.* sterna, rondine di mare, *f.*

terrace, *n.* terrazza, terrazzina, *f.*; terrapieno, *m.*, ripiano, *n.* ¶ *v.t.* terrazzare. ~*d vineyard*, vigna a balze.

terracotta, *n.* terracotta, *f.* *a* ~, una terracotta.

terra firma, *n.* terraferma, *f.*

terrapin, *n.* tartaruga acquatica, *f.*

terrestrial, *a.* terrestre.

terrible, *a.* terrible, spaventoso.

terrier, *n.* [cane] terrier, *m.*

terrific, *a.* spaventevole, spaventoso; terribile. **terrify,** *v.t.* spaventare, atterrire.

territorial, *a. & n.*, territoriale, *a. & m.* **territory,** *n.* territorio, *m.*

terror, *n.* terrore, spavento, *m.* ~**ize,** *v.t.* terrorizzare, atterrire, intimidire.

terse, *a.* terso, nitido, conciso. ~**ness,** *n.* concisione, *f.*

tessellated pavement, pavimento a mosaico, mosaico, *m.*

test, *n.* prova, *f.*, assaggio, saggio; [e]sperimento, *n.*; pietra di paragone, *f.*, criterio, *m.* ~ *glass & test tube & ~ piece*, provino, *m.*, provetta, *f.* ~ *paper*, carta reattiva, *f.* ~ *piece* (*Music, &c.*) pezzo di concorso, *m.* ¶ *v.t.* provare, assaggiare; (*eggs*) prendere di mira; (*Mech.*) collaudare.

testament, *n.* testamento, *m.* ~**ary,** *a.* testamentario. **testator,** ~**trix,** *n.* testatore, *m.*, -trice, *f.* **testicle,** *n.* testicolo, *m.* **testify,** *v.t. & i.*

testificare, testimoniare, attestare, deporre. **testimonial,** *n.* attestato, certificato, *m.* **testimony,** *n.* testimonianza, *f.*

testy, *a.* irascibile, irritabile.

tetanus, *n.* tetano, *m.*

tether, *n.* pastoia, *f.* *at the end of one's* ~, non sapere piú che dire o che fare, aver vuotato il sacco. ¶ *v.t.* impastoiare, legare.

Teutonic, *a.* teutonico.

text, *n.* testo, *m.* ~*book*, manuale, *m.* ~ *hand*, scrittura grossa, *f.*

textile, *n.* tessuto, *m.*; materia tessile, *f.* ¶ *a.* tessile.

textual, *a.* testuale; (error) del testo.

texture, *n.* tessitura, *f.*; tessuto, *m.*

Thames (the), il Tamigi, *m.*

than, *c. & pr.* che, di.

thank, *v.t.* ringraziare. ~ *God!* grazie a Dio, sia ringraziato Iddio! ~ *Heaven!* grazie al cielo! ~ *oneself*, pigliarsela con sé stesso. ~ *you!* (& *no thank you!*), grazie! *he has only himself to* ~ *for it*, è colpa sua. ~*ful*, *a.* riconoscente, grato. ~*fully*, *ad.* con riconoscenza. ~*fulness*, *n.* riconoscenza, gratitudine, *f.* ~*less*, *a.* ingrato, poco stimato. **thanks,** *n.pl.* ringraziamenti, *m.pl.* ¶ *i.* grazie. ~ *to*, grazie a, a cagione di. **thanksgiving,** *n.* rendimento di grazie, *m.*

that, *a. & pn.* quello, *m.*, quella, *f.*, ciò; (*rel. pn.*) che, il quale, la quale. *i quali, le quali* ~ *is all*, questo è tutto, non c'è altro. ~ *is to say*, cioè, vale a dire. ¶ *c.* che, affinché, perché.

thatch, *n.* paglia, stoppia, *f.* ¶ *v.t.* coprire di paglia, di stoppia. ~*ed cottage*, capanna (coperta di paglia), *f.* ~*er*, *n.* chi fa coperture di paglia.

thaw, *n.* sgelo, *m.* ¶ *v.t. & i.* sgelare, sgelarsi; (*fig.*) sciogliere, sciogliersi, commuovere, commuoversi, intenerire, intenerirsi.

the, *def. art.* il, lo, l', *m.*; la, l', *f.*; i, gli, *m.pl.*; le, *f.pl.*; *of* ~, del, dello, dell', della, dell', dei, de', degli, delle. *to* ~, *at* ~, al, allo, all', alla, all', ai, agli, alle.

theatre, *n.* teatro, *m.*, scena, *f.* **theatrical,** *a.* di teatro, del teatro, teatrale, scenico. ~ *& fancy costumier*, vestiarista, *m.* **theatricals,** *n.pl.* rappresentazioni teatrali, *f.pl.*

thee, *pn.*, ti, te.

theft, *n.* furto, *m.*

their, *a.* il loro, la loro, i loro, le loro.

theirs, il loro, la loro, i loro, le loro; di loro.

theism, *n.* teismo, *m.* **theistic(al),** *a.* teistico.

them, *pn.* li, le, loro; essi, esse. ~*selves*, se stessi, se stesse; essi stessi, esse stesse; sé, si.

theme, *n.* tema, argomento, soggetto, *m.*; (*Mus.*) motivo, *m.*

then, *ad.* allora, a quel tempo, poscia, poi, in seguito, su questo, di quell'epoca, d'allora; dunque, quindi; da questo, ne. **thence,** *ad.* indi, di là. **thenceforth, thenceforward,** *a.* d'allora in poi.

theodolite, *n.* teodolito, *m.*

theologian, *n.* teologo, *m.* **theological,** *a.* teologico. **theology,** *n.* teologia, *f.*

theorem, *n.* teorema, *m.* **theoretic(al),** *a.* teoretico, teorico. **theorist,** *n.* teorico, *m.* **theorize,** *v.i.* teorizzare. **theory,** *n.* teoria, *f.*

theosophy, *n.* teosofia, *f.*

therapeutic, *a.* terapeutico. ~*s*, *n.pl.* terapeutica, *f.*

there, *ad.* lí, là, colà; vi, ci; ivi, in ciò, ecco! ~ *& back*, andata e ritorno. ~ *& then*, subito, sul posto, seduta stante, a tempo e luogo, lí per lí. ~ *is* ~ *are*, vi è, vi sono, c'è, ci sono. ~ *about*, ~ *abouts*, là intorno; all'incirca, a un dipresso. ~*by*, con tal mezzo, cosí, da ciò. ~*fore*, perciò, per conseguenza, per tale ragione, quindi, laonde, onde, dunque, ne segue che. ~*on*, su di ciò, sopra di ciò, a tal proposito. ~*upon*, su di ciò, su questo, in conseguenza, immediatamente dopo. ~*withal*, inoltre, in piú, con ciò, con tutto questo, nello stesso tempo.

thermal, *a.* termale. **thermometer,** *n.* termometro, *m.*

these, *a. & pn.* questi, *m.pl.*; queste, *f.pl.*; cotesti, *m.pl.*; coteste, *f.pl.*

thesis, *n.* tesi, *f.*; dissertazione, *f.*

thews, *n.pl.* muscoli, tendini, *m.pl.*; (*fig.*) forza (muscolare), *f.*

they, *pn.* essi, *m.pl.*; esse, *f.pl.*; loro, coloro, costoro, *m.f.pl.*; si (*indef.*).

thick, *a.* spesso; denso; torbido; grosso; fitto, folto, serrato; (*with someone*) stretto, intimo. ~ *or clear* (soup)? [zuppa] crema o brodo? ~*lipped*, a labbra grosse, dalle labbra grosse. ~*set*, tozzo, tarchiato, atticciato; (*trees, &c.*) fitto. ~ *stroke*, grosso. ~**[ly]**, *ad.* fittamente; densamente. *in the* ~ *of*, nel piú forte di, nel cuore di. *through*

~ & *thin*, malgrado tutti (or tutto), attraverso tutti gli ostacoli, nella buona e nella cattiva sorte. ~**en**, *v.t.* [i]spessire, addensare; (*v.i.*) addensarsi; oscurarsi; (*sauce*) legare. ~**ening**, *n.* ispessimento, condensamento, *m.*; (*for sauce*) legamento, *m.*

thicket, *n.* boschetto, *m.*, macchia folta, *f.*

thickness, *n.* spessore, *m.*, grossezza, densità; torbidezza, oscurità, *f.*

thief, *n.* ladro, *m.*, ladra, *f.*, ladrone, *m.*, rubatore, *m.* **thieve**, *v.t.* rubare. *thieves' kitchen*, officina, *f.* **thievish**, *a.* di ladro; (*pers.*) ladro, ladresco.

thigh, *n.* coscia, *f.* ~*bone*, femore, *m.* ~ *boots*, cosciali, *m.pl.*

thill, *n.* stanga, *f.*

thimble, *n.* ditale, *m.*; (*Naut.*) radancia, *f.* ~ *rigger*, giuocatore di bussolotti, *m.*, ~**ful**, *n.* dito, *m.*

thin, *a.* sottile; magro, smunto; fine, delicato, tenue; chiaro; leggero; fievole, rarefatto; lungo (*soup*); (*hair, grass, &c.*) sparso, rado; (*legs, voice*) esile, debole, sottile. ~ *air* (*fig.*) fumo, *m.* *to be* ~ *skinned* (*fig.*) essere impressionabile, essere permaloso. ~ *slice*, fettuccina, *f.* ~ *stroke*, filetto, *m.* ¶ *v.t.* assottigliare; diradare; far dimagrire; rarefare.

thine, *pn.* il tuo, la tua, i tuoi, le tue; a te.

thing, *n.* cosa, *f.*, affare, *m.*, oggetto, *m.*, fatto, *m.*; (*pers.*) essere, *m.*, creatura, *f.*; (*pl.*) effetti, vestimenti, *m.pl.*; roba, *f.*, affari, *m.pl.*; *the* ~ (in fashion), ciò che occorre, l'ultima moda.

think, *v.t. & i. ir.* pensare; credere; giudicare; riflettere; ritenere, stimare, trovare; immaginarsi. ~**er**, *n.* pensatore, *m.*, -trice, *f.* **thinking**, *a.* pensante, che riflette, di giudizio. ¶ *n.* pensiero, *m.*, riflessione, opinione, *f.*; parere, *m.*

thinly, *qd.* scarsamente, leggermente, sparsamente, appena. ~ *sown*, rado, seminato qua e là. **thinness**, *n.*, sottigliezza; magrezza; radezza; tenuità, esilità, *f.* **thinnish**, *a.* magretto, mingherlino.

third, *a.* terzo. ~ *finger*, (dito) anulare, *m.* ~ *person*, terzo, *m.*, terza persona, *f.*; (*Gram.*) terza persona, *f.* ¶ *n.* terzo, (il) tre, *m.*, terza parte, *f.* ~ *of exchange*, terza di cambio.

thirst, *n.* sete, *f.* ~*-creating*, che dà sete. ~ *for*, aver sete di, essere assetato di, agognare a. **thirsty**, *a.* assetato; (*fig.*) sitibondo, avido, arido; (*country*) della sete, arido. *to be* ~, aver sete.

thirteen, *a. & n.* tredici, *a. & m.* ~**th**, *a. & n.* tredicesimo, *a. & m.*, tredici, *m.*

thirtieth, *a. & n.* trentesimo, *a. & m.* **thirty**, *a. & n.* trenta, *a. & m.*, trentina, *f.* ~*-two-mo* or *32mo*, *a. & n.* in trentaduesimo, 32mo.

this, *a. & pn.* questo, *m.*, questa, *f.*; codesto, *m.*, codesta, *f.*; presente, *m.f.*, ciò. ~ *day week*, oggi a otto. ~ *way!* di qui, di qua! ~ *way & that*, qua e là.

thistle, *n.* cardo, cardone, *m.* ~*down*, lanugine del cardo, del cardone, *f.*

thong, *n.* striscia di cuoio, cinghia, coreggia.

thorax, *n.* torace, *m.*

thorn, *n.* spina, *f.* ~ *bush*, spineto, *m.* ~**y**, *a.* spinoso.

thorough, *a.* compiuto, perfetto, consumato, profondo; matricolato; *often referred by prefix* **arci-** *or abs.* **super, -issimo**. ~*bred* (horse), di puro sangue, di razza. ~*fare*, via pubblica, via di transito, via battuta *f.*; diritto di passaggio, *m.* ~**ly**, *ad.* completamente, perfettamente, a fondo.

those, *a. & pn.* quelli, quelle; cotesti, coteste; coloro.

thou, *pn.* tu. ¶ *v.t.* dare del tu a.

though, *c.* benché, quantunque, sebbene, ancorché, tuttoché, pertanto, però, pure. *as* ~, come se.

thought, *n.* pensiero, *m.*, riflessione, idea, *f.* ~ *reader*, ipnotizzatore, *m.*, lettore (-trice) del pensiero, *m.f.* ~**ful**, *a.* pensieroso, pensoso; previdente, premuroso. ~**less**, *a.* spensierato, sconsiderato, trascurato. ~**lessness**, *n.* spensieratezza, leggerezza, trascuratezza, *f.*

thousand, *a.* mille. ¶ *n.* mille, migliaio, *m.*; (*pls.*) mila, migliaia. ~**th**, *a. & n.* millesimo, *a. & m.*, millesima parte, *f.*

thraldom, *n.* schiavitú, *f.* **thrall**, *n.* schiavo, *m.*, -a, *f.*

thrash, *v.t.* bastonare, sferzare, battere. ~**ing**, *n.* bastonatura, bastonata, sferzata, *f.*

thread, *n.* filo, refe, *m.*; corda, *f.*; filamento, filato, *m.*; (*screw*) filetto, *m.*; (*screw pitch*) pane, *m.*; (*of life*) filo, *m.* ~ *bare*, logoro; consumato; (*fig.*) trito, fritto e rifritto. ¶ *v.t.* infilare; (*screw*) filettare.

threat, *n.* minaccia, *f.* ~en, *v.t.* minacciare.

three, *a. & n.* tre, *a. & m.* ~-colour process, tricromía, *f.* ~-master, trealberi, *m.* ~-ply [wood], legno compensato (a tre strati), *m.* ~-quarter binding, rilegatura in mezza pelle, in mezza tela e carta, *f.* ~score [years] & ten, settant'anni, *m.pl.* ~some, partita di tre, *f.* ~-speed gear, ingranaggio a tre velocità, *m.* ~fold, *a.* triplice, triplo.

thresh, *v.t.* trebbiare, battere (il grano). ~ out (fig.) or thrash out, esaurire, risolvere, sciogliere. ~er, (pers.) *n.* battitore, *m.*, -trice, *f.*; trebbiatore, *m.*, -trice, *f.* ~ing machine, trebbiatrice, *f.*

threshold, *n.* soglia, *f.*

thrice, *ad.* tre volte.

thrift, *n.* economia, *f.*, risparmio, *m.* ~less, *a.* prodigo, spendereccio, scialacquatore. ~y, *a.* frugale, economico.

thrill, *n.* brivido, fremito, trasalimento, sussulto, *m.* ❡ *v.t.* elettrizzare, far trasalire, commuovere; (v.i.) trasalire, fremere, palpitare. ~ing, *a.* palpitante, commoventissimo.

thrive, *v.i.* ir. prosperare; (plant) allignare, attecchire. not to ~, intisichire. tàriving, *a.* prospero, fiorente.

throat, *n.* gola, strozza, *f.*; (neck) collo, *m.*; ~ register, voce di gola, *f.*

throb, *v.i.* battere, palpitare, pulsare; (Med.) spasimare. ❡ *n.* battito, palpito, *m.*, pulsazione, *f.*; spasimo, *m.*

throe, *n.* dolore, *m.*; (pl.) angoscia, *f.*, doglie, *f pl.*; affanni, *m.pl.*; (death) agonía, *f*

thrombosis, *n.* (Med.) trombosi, *f.*

throne, *n.* trono, *m.*; (bishop's) cattedra, *f.*

throng, *n.* folla calca, turba, ressa, *f.* ❡ *v.t.* affollare, accalcare; ingombrare; (sail) far forza di vele; (v.i.) affollarsi, accalcarsi, affluire.

throstle, *n.* tordo, *m.*

throttle, *n.* strozza, *f.*; (valve) valvola di immissione, v. a farfalla, *f.* ❡ *v.t.* strozzare, strangolare.

through, *pr.* attraverso, per; a mezzo di; per colpa di; a seguito di, dietro. ~ thick & thin, nella buona e nella cattiva sorte. ❡ *ad.* da banda a banda, da parte a parte, da una parte all'altra; sino alla fine; a buon fine,

completamente, interamente, tutto. ❡ *a.* diretto. ~ portion (Rly.), vetture dirette, *f.pl.* ~ rate, tariffa per trasporti in servizio cumulativo, *f.* ~ ticket (to final destination), biglietto diretto, *m.*; (sea-land-sea) biglietto cumulativo. ~ bookings, servizi cumulativi. ~out, *pr.* per tutto, durante tutto; (ad.) dappertutto, da un capo all'altro, interamente.

throw, *n.* getto, lancio, tiro, *m.*; (Mech.) corsa, *f.*; eccentricità, *f.* ❡ *v.t.* ir. gettare, lanciare, scagliare; buttare, atterrare, mettere. ~ away, gettar via, dissipare, scialacquare. ~ back, riversare, rigettare, respingere. ~ down, ~ over, rovesciare, abbattere, buttar giú, gettar per terra. ~ open, aprire. ~ out, scacciare; rigettare; respingere, espellere. ~ up, gettare, lanciare in aria; rinunziare a; (a post) dimettersi da. ~ing, *n.* lanciamento, *m.*

thrum, *v.t.* strimpellare; (v.i.) tamburinare.

thrush, *n.* tordo, *m.*

thrust, *n.* spinta, botta, *f.*; (Fenc.) colpo, *m.*; botta, stoccata, *f.*; (Mech.) spinta, *f.*, colpo, *m.* ❡ *v.t.* spingere; tuffare; ficcare; (sword) cacciare; (Fenc.) colpire, dare una botta. ~ aside, respingere. ~ at, (Fenc.) assestare una stoccata, un colpo, (una botta) a, aggiustare.

thud, *n.* colpo sordo, *m.*; suono cupo, *m.*

thug, *n.* strangolatore, *m.*

thumb, *n.* pollice, *m.* ~ mark, impronta del pollice, *f.* ~ nut, dado ad alette, *m.* ~ stall, ditale, *m.* ❡ *v.t.* sfogliare; lasciare l'impronta del pollice su.

thump, *n.* colpo sordo; pugno, *m.*; botta, percossa, *f.* ❡ *v.t.* battere, percuotere con pugni.

thunder, *n.* tuono, *m.* ~bolt, fulmine, colpo di fulmine, *m.* (pl. Jove's) fulmini, *m.pl.*, strali, *m.pl.* ~clap, colpo di tuono, scoppio di tuono, *m.* ~cloud, nuvolone, *m.* ~storm, temporale, *m.* ~struck, fulminato. ❡ *v.i. & t.* tuonare; fulminare. ~y, *a.* tempestoso, che minaccia il tuono.

Thursday, *n.* giovedí, *m.*

thus, *ad.* cosí, in questo modo, in tal modo. ~ far, fin qui, fin qua, fino a tal punto.

thwack, *n.* colpo secco, *m.*, percossa, *f.* ❡ *v.t.* colpire, bussare, percuotere.

thwart, *n.* banco di rematore, *m.* ¶ *v.t.* contrariare, opporsi a, frustrare.

thy, *a.* (il) tuo, (la) tua; (*pl.*) i tuoi, le tue.

thyme, *n.* timo, *m.*; (*wild*) serpillo, *m.*

thyroid, *n.* tiroide, *f.* ~ *gland*, glandola tiroidea, *f.*

thyself, *pn.* tu stesso, tu stessa, te stesso, te stessa; ti.

tiara, *n.* tiara, *f.*

Tiber (the), (il) Tevere, *m.*

tibia, *n.* tibia, *f.*

tic, *n.* tic; ticchio, *m.*

Ticino (the), (il) Ticino, *m.*

tick, *n.* battito, tic-tac, tic; segno, segnetto, punto, *m.*; (*insect*) zecca, *f.* ~ *or* ~*ing*, *n.* bordatino, traliccio, *m.*; tela da materassi, *f.*; ticchettio, *m.* ~-*tack*, tic-tac, *m.* ¶ *v.i.* battere, far tic-tac; (*v.t.*) segnare, notare con un punto.

ticket, *n.* biglietto, *m.*; etichetta, cedola, bolletta, carta, tessera, scheda, *f.*; cartellino, scontrino, buono, *m.*; ~ *collector*, controllore, *m.* ~ *window*, ~ *office*, sportello (dei biglietti); ufficio biglietti, *m.*; biglietteria, *f.* ¶ *v.t.* metter l'etichetta a, segnare con etichetta.

tickle, *v.t. & i.* solleticare, titillare.

ticklish, *a.* sensitivo al solletico; critico, delicato, scabroso.

tidal, *a.* ~ *basin*, bacino di marea, *m.* ~ *water*, acque a marea, *f.pl.*; ~ *wave*, maremoto, *m.*, onda di marea, *f.*, maroso straordinario, *m.* **tide,** *n.* marea; corrente di marea, *f.* ~*way*, filo di corrente, *m. to tide over a difficulty*, cavarsi dall'impiccio.

tidiness, *n.* pulitezza, proprietà, *f.*; buon ordine, *m.*

tidings, *n.pl.* notizie, *f.pl.*

tidy, *a.* netto, pulito, lindo, in buon ordine; (*pers.*) ordinato, vestito con proprietà. ¶ *n.* copertura (di seggiola o poltrona), *f.* ¶ *v.t.* ordinare, mettere in ordine, assettare. ~ *oneself up*, attillarsi, acconciarsi, fare toletta.

tie, *n.* legame; vincolo; tirante, *m.*; cravatta, *f.*, nodo, *m.*; (*Mus.*) legatura, *f.*; (*Voting*) parità di voti, *f.*; (*sport*) parità di punti, partita nulla, *f.* ~ *pin*, spilla da cravatta, *f.* ¶ *v.t.* ir. legare; vincolare; attaccare; unire; (*knot*) fare; (*v.i.*) (*Sport*) fare partita nulla, partita pari; (*Exams.*) essere classificato ex aequo. ~ *down*, legare; attaccare; costringere, obbligare; ~ *up*, legare, fasciare, serrare, avviluppare; (*Law*) rendere inalienabile.

tier, *n.* fila, *f.*; piano, ordine, gradino, scalino, *m.*; (*pl.*) gradinata, scalinata, *f.*, -e, *f.pl.*

tierce, *n.* terza, *f.*

Tierra del Fuego, la Terra del Fuoco, *f.*

tiff, *n.* bisticcio, battibecco, malumore, *m.*

tiger, *n.* tigre, *f.* ~ *cat*, gatto tigre, *m.*, gatto selvaggio, *m.* ~ *lily*, giglio tigrino (or tigrato), *m.*

tight, *a.* serrato; teso; stretto; giusto; attillato. *water*~, impermeabile; stagno. *to drive into a* ~ *corner*, mettere con le spalle al muro, mettere alle strette. ~*en*, *v.t.* stringere, serrare, rinserrare; tendere. ~[*ly*], *ad.* stretto, strettamente, fortemente, fermo, attillatamente. ~*ness*, *n.* strettezza; tensione; oppressione (al petto), *f.* **tights,** *n.pl.* maglia, *f.*

tigress, *n.* tigre, *f.*

Tigris (the), il Tigri, *m.*

tile, *n.* tegola, embrice, mattonella, *f.*; quadrello, *m.*; (*pl.*, *roof*) gronde, *f.pl.*; grondaia, *f.* ~ *floor*[*ing*], ammattonato, *m.* ~ *maker*, tegolaio, *m.* ~ *works*, fabbrica di tegole, mattonaia, *f.* ¶ *v.t.* coprire di tegole, di mattonelle.

till, *n.* cassa, *f.* cassetto, *m.* ¶ *v.t.* coltivare, lavorare. ¶ *pr.* fino, fino a, infino, sino, sino a, insino a. ¶ *c.* finché. **tillage,** *n.* coltivazione, aratura, *f.* **tiller,** *n.* coltivatore, *m.*; barra del timone, *f.*

tilt, *n.* copertone, *m.*, tenda, *f.*, tendone, *m.*; giostra, *f.*; inclinazione, *f.*, pendenza, *f.* ¶ *v.t.* inclinare, chinare, rovesciare; (*v.i.*) inclinarsi, ribaltare, giostrare. **tilting,** (*Hist.*) *n.* giostra, *f.* ~ *at the ring*, giostra all'anello, *f.*

timber, *n.* legname, *m.* alberi (d'alto fusto), *m.pl.*; trave, *f.*; (*ship*) ordinata, costola, *f.* ~ *tree*, albero d'alto fusto, *m.* ~-*tree forest*, bosco, *m.*, foresta, *f.* ~ *work*, costruzione in legno, *f.* ~ *yard*, cantiere (da carpentiere), *m.* ¶ *v.t.* costruire in legname (in legno); provvedere di legname; piantar alberi in. ~*ing*, *n.* rivestimento in legno, *m.*

timbre, *n.* timbro, suono, metallo (della voce), *m.*

Timbuctoo, *n.* Timbuktú, *f.*

time, *n.* tempo, momento, *m.*; occasione, epoca, stagione, *f.*; secolo, *m.*;

ora, *f.*; volta, ripresa, durata, *f.*; termine, *m.*; scadenza, *f.*; misura, *f.*, cadenza, *f.*, passo, *m.* at ~*s*, qualche volta, talvolta, a volte. [*just*] *in* ~, (proprio) a tempo, in buon punto. (*work*, &c.) *of* ~, di lunga lena. ~ *bargain*, vendita a termine, *f.*; (*Stk. Ex.*) contratto a termine, *m.* ~ *bomb*, bomba a scoppio ritardato, *f.* ~ *fuse*, spoletta a tempo, *f.* ~-*honoured*, secolare, venerando. ~ *keeper* (*pers.*), controllore, *m.*; (*Sport*) cronometrista, *m.* ~ *piece*, pendola, *f.* ~-*server*, opportunista, *m.f.* ~*sheet*, foglio di presenza, *m.* ~ *signal*, segnale orario, *m.* ~*table* (*book*), indicatore, *m.*; (*placard & scheme of work*) orario, *m.* ¶ *v.t.* (*watch*) regolare; (*Sport*) misurare sul cronometro, cronometrare. **timing**, *n.* determinazione dei tempi; verifica (dell'ora, &c.); (*engine*) messa in fase, *f.* **timeliness**, *n.* opportunità, *f.*; il tornar opportuno. **timely**, *a.* opportuno.

timid, *a.* timido, pauroso. ~**ity**, *n.* timidità, timidezza, *f.* **timorous**, *a.* timoroso.

tin, *n.* stagno, *m.*, latta, *f.*; (*can*) scatola di latta, *f.* ~*foil*, foglio di stagno, *m.*, stagnola, *f.* ~ *loaf*, pane oblungo, *m.* ~ *opener*, apriscatole, *m.inv.* ~ (*plate*), ferro bianco, *m.* ~ *soldier*, soldato di piombo, *m.* ~*smith*, lattaio, stagnaio, *m.* ~*tack* (*s. & pl.*) bulletta, *f.*, bullette, *f.pl.* ~*ware*, oggetti di stagno, di ferro bianco, *m.pl.*; chincaglieria, *f.* ¶ *v.t.* stagnare; mettere in scatola, mettere in conserva. *tinned foods*, conserve in scatola, *f.pl. tinned salmon*, salmone in scatola, *m.*

tincture, *n.* tintura; tinta, *f.* ¶ *v.t.* tingere.

tinder, *n.* esca, *f.* ~ *box*, acciarino, *m.*

tine, *n.* dente (di ferro); (*deer*) palco, *m.*

tinge, *n.* tinta, sfumatura, *f.*; sapore leggero, *m.* ¶ *v.t.* tingere, colorire.

tingle, *v.i.* sentire un formicolio, pizzicare; (*ears*) zufolare.

tinkle, *v.i.* tintinnire.

tinker, *n.* calderaio ambulante, *m.*

tinsel, *n.* orpello, *m.*, cenci guarniti d'orpello, *m.pl.*; broccatello, *m.*; (*fig.*) falso splendore.

tint, *n.* tinta, *f.*, colorito, *m.* ¶ *v.t.* tingere, colorire.

tiny, *a.* minuscolo, piccolino, minuto.

~ *bit*, tantino, *m.* ~ *drop*, gocciolina, *f.*

tip, *n.* punta, estremità, *f.*; buffetto, piccolo colpo, *m.*; (*wing*) estremità; (*Bil. cue*) cuoio, *m.*; (*gratuity*) mancia, *f.*; (*information*) informazione privata, informazione speciale, *f.*; (*dump*) scarico, *m.* ¶ *v.t.* mettere (fare) una punta a; coprire la punta di; dare una mancia a; dare informazioni speciali a; sbilanciare, ribaltare, versare. ~ *cart*, carro a bilico, *m.* ~-*up seat*, strapuntino, *m.*

tipcat, *n.* lippa, *f.*

tippet, *n.* pellegrina, mantellina, *f.*

tipple, *v.i.* bevucchiare, centellinare, sbevazzare. **tippler**, *n.* beone, *m.*

tipsy, *a.* brillo, mezzo cotto, alticcio. ~ *cake*, dolce con mandorle bagnato nel vino.

tiptoe (**on**), in punta di piedi.

tiptop, *n.* colmo, *m.*, cima, *f.* ¶ *a.* eccellente, perfetto; di prima salute.

tirade, *n.* tirata, *f.*; arringa declamatoria, *f.*

tire, *n.* see *tyre* (pneumatico, *m.*).

tire, *v.t.* stancare, affaticare; annoiare; (*v.i.*) stancarsi, affaticarsi; annoiarsi. ~*d out*, esaurito, stanco morto. ~**less**, *a.* instancabile, infaticabile. ~*some*, *a.* noioso, importuno, seccante.

tiro, *n.* principiante, *m.f.*; novizio, *m.*

tissue, *n.* tessuto; broccato; ordito, *m.* ~ *paper*, carta seta, carta velina, *f.*

tit, (*bird*) *n.* cinciallegra *or* cingallegra, *f.* ~ *for tat*, pan per focaccia, niente per niente, dai e ricevi.

titbit, *n.* bocconcino, boccone ghiotto, *m.*; leccornia, *f.*

tithe, *n.* decima parte, decima, *f.*

titillate, *v.t.* titillare, solleticare.

titivate, *v.t.* fare toletta, mettersi in ordine, attillarsi, azzimarsi, rinfronzolarsi.

titlark, *n.* pispola, *f.*

title, *n.* titolo; diritto, *m.* ~ (*deed*) titolo, titolo di proprietà, *m.* ~ *page*, frontispizio; (*Typ.*) titolo principale, *m.* *half* ~, titolo abbreviato, *m.* ~*d*, *a.* titolato.

titmouse, *n.* cinciallegra, cincia, *f.*

titter, *v.i.* ridere scioccamente, ridere sotto i baffi, sogghignare.

tittle, *n.* iota, ettè, nulla, *m.* ~-*tattle*, chiacchiere, *f.pl.*; ciancia, *f.*, pettegolezzi, *m. pl.*

titular, *a.* titolare.

to, *pr.* a, in; verso, fino a; per; di; da; su; contro; presso, accanto a; (*of the hours*) meno. *to go* ~ *& fro*, andare avanti e indietro, andare su e giú. ~ *be called for*, ferma in posta, fermo stazione, da ritirarsi. ~ *be kept cool, dry*, or *in a cool, dry place*, tenere al fresco, all'asciutto o in luogo fresco, asciutto. ~ *be taken after meals*, da prendersi dopo i pasti.' ~ *boot*, per di piú, per giunta. ~ *match*, pari, simile, bene assortito. ~ *measure*, su misura. ~ *wit*, cioè; (*of pers.*) nominatamente.

toad, *n.* rospo, *m.*; botta, *f.* ~*hole*, luogo pieno di rospi, *m.* ~*stone*, bufonite, *f.* ~*stool*, fungo velenoso, *m.* **toady,** *n.* parassita, sicofante, piaggiatore, *m.*, -trice, *f.*; ~ *to*, piaggiare, lisciare, leccare gli stivali a. ~*ism*, *n.* piaggeria, *f.*

toast, *n.* crostino, *m.* (fetta di) pane abbrustolito, *f.*; (*buttered*) crostino imburrato, pane abbrustolito con burro, *m.*; (*health*) brindisi, *m.* ~ *rack*, portacrostini, *m.inv.* ¶ *v.t.* abbrustolire, tostare; (*health*) fare un brindisi a, brindare. ~**er,** *n.* graticola, gratella, *f.* ~**ing fork,** forchetta per crostini.

tobacco, *n.* tabacco, *m.* ~ *pouch*, borsa per tabacco, *f.* **tobacconist,** *n.* tabaccaio, *m.* ~'*s shop*, tabaccheria, *f.* spaccio di tabacchi, *m.*

toboggan, *n.* toboga, *f.*; traino, *m.*, slitta, *f.* ~ *run*, pista di toboga, *f.*

to-day, *ad. & n.* oggi, *ad. & m.* ~'*s gossip*, chiacchiere odierne, *f.pl.* ~ *week*, ~ *fortnight*, oggi a otto, a quindici.

toddle, *v.i.* trotterellare, sgambettare.

to-do, *n.* gran daffare, *m.*, commozione, *f.*, cerimonie, *f.pl.*

toe, *n.* dito (del piede), *m.*; (*shoe*, *sock*) punta, *f.* ~*nail*, unghia del piede, *f.*

toga, *n.* toga, *f.*

together, *ad.* insieme, unitamente, in una volta, di concerto. ~ *with*, con, in compagnia di, come pure.

toil, *n.* lavoro, *m.*, fatica, *f.*, travaglio, *m.*; (*pl.*) trappole, *f.pl.*; laccio, *m.*, rete, *f.* ¶ *v.i.* lavorare, affaticarsi. ~ *& moil*, affaticarsi, sgobbare. ~**er,** *n.* lavoratore indefesso; sgobbone (*oft. iron.*), *m.*

toilet, *n.* toletta, *f.* ~ *paper*, carta igienica, *f.* ~ *powder*, cipria, *f.* ~ *roll*, rotolo di carta igienica, rotolo igienico, *m.*

toilsome, *a.* faticoso, penoso.

token, *n.* segno, contrassegno, *m.*; marca, testimonianza, prova, *f.*;

attestato, pegno, omaggio, *m.*; medaglia, *f.*

Toledo, *n.* Toledo, *f.*

tolerable, *a.* tollerabile, passabile. **tolerably,** *ad.* passabilmente, tollerabilmente. **tolerance & toleration,** *n.* tolleranza, *f.* **tolerate,** *v.t.* tollerare.

toll, *n.* tassa, *f.*; tributo, diritto, *m.*; imposta, *f.*; pedaggio, *m.* ~ *call* (*Teleph.*) chiamata (comunicazione) regionale, *f.* ¶ *v.t. & i.* suonare a rintocchi. ~**ing,** *n.* rintocco (funebre), *m.*

tom: ~*boy* maschietta, sfacciatella, *f.*; ~*cat*, gatto, gattone, *m.* ~*foolery*, stupidaggine, *f.*, inezie, *f.pl.*, buffonate, *f.pl.* *T*~ *Thumb umbrella*, ombrellino, *m.* ~*tit*, cinciallegra, *f.*

tomato, *n.* pomodoro, *m.* ~ *sauce*, salsa di pomidoro, *f.*

tomb, *n.* tomba, *f.*, sepolcro, *m.*, avello, *m.* ~*stone*, lapide, *f.*

tome, *n.* tomo, volume, *m.*

tommy [bar], *n.* spillo, fermaglio, *m.* *tommy gun*, *n.* fucile mitragliatore, *m.*

to-morrow, *ad. & n.* domani, *ad. & m.* ~ *morning*, domattina, domani mattina. ~ *night*, ~ *evening*, domani sera, *f.*

tompion, *n.* turacciolo, *m.*

tomtom, *n.* tam-tam, *m.*

ton, *n.* tonnellata, *f.* *Eng. ton* (2240 lbs) = 1016 kilos.

tone, *n.* tono, suono, accento, *m.*; gamma, *f.*, registro, *m.*; disposizione, *f.*; (*Phot.*) intonazione, *f.* ¶ (*v.t. Phot.*) virare, intonare; (*v.i.*) armonizzarsi. ~ *down*, ammorzare; attenuare; sfumare. ~**d** (*paper*) *p.p.* tinto.

tongs, *n.pl.* molle; pinze; tenaglie, *f.pl.*

tongue, *n.* lingua, *f.*; (*strip*, *slip*) linguetta, *f.*; (*of bell*) battaglio, *m.*; (*of buckle*) ardiglione, *m.*

tonic, *a.* tonico. ~ *sol-fa*, solfa tonica, *f.* ¶ *n.* (*Med. & drink*) tonico, ricostituente, *m.*; (*Mus.*) tonica, *f.*

to-night, *ad. & n.* stanotte, stasera, questa notte, questa sera, *ad. & f.*

toning (*Phot.*) *n.* viraggio, *m.*

tonnage, *n.* tonnellaggio, *m.*

Tonquin, *n.* Tonchino, *m.*

tonsil, *n.* tonsilla, *f.* **tonsilitis,** *n.* tonsillite, *f.*

tonsure, *n.* tonsura, *f.* ¶ *v.t.* tonsurare.

too, *ad.* troppo. ¶ *c.* anche, egualmente, pure, ancora, altresi. ~ *long* (*length*), troppo lungo; (*time*) troppo,

troppo a lungo. ¶ *a.* ~ *much,* ~ *many,* troppo, *m.; -a, f.* troppi, *m.pl.,* troppe, *f.pl.*

tool, *n.* arnese, ordigno o utensile, strumento, ferro, *m.; (Bookb.)* ferro, *m.; (pers.)* fautore, *m.,* agente, *m.* ~ *box,* scatola degli utensili, cassetta dei ferri, *f.* ~ *maker,* fabbricante di utensili, di ferri, fabbroferraio, *m.* ¶ *v.t. (Mach.)* lavorare; *(Bookb.)* bulinare. **~ing,** *n. (Bookb.)* fregiatura, *f.*

tooth, *n.* dente, *m.* ~*ache,* mal di denti, *m.; (violent)* fierissimo dolor di denti, *m.* ~*brush,* spazzolino da denti, *m.* ~*brush moustache,* mustacchio a spazzola, *m.* ~*paste,* pasta dentifricia, *f.* ~*pick,* stuzzicadenti, *m.inv.* ~ *powder,* dentifricio in polvere, *m.* ¶ *v.t.* munire di denti, addentellare, ingranare. **~some,** *a.* ghiottone.

tootsy [-wootsy], *(Nursery talk) n.* piedino, *m.*

top, *n.* cima, vetta, sommità, *f.;* colmo, vertice, apice, *m.;* cocuzzolo, capo; lato superiore, il di sopra, *m.;* sommo, alto, coperchio, *m.; (bus)* imperiale, *f.; (Naut.)* gabbia, coffa, *f.; (turnip, &c.)* cima, *f.; (book page)* testa, *f.,* taglio superiore, *m.; (toys)* trottola, palla, *f. at the ~ of one's voice,* a squarciagola. ~ *boots,* stivali a risvolta, *m.pl.* ~ *coat,* soprabito, *m.* ~ *figure,* cifra massima, *f.* ~ *gallant (Mast)* pappafico, rocchetto, *m.* ~ *hamper,* attrezzatura ingombrante, *f.* ~ *hat,* [capello a] cilindro, *m.* ~*-heavy,* troppo pesante in cima, squilibrato. ~ *man (Naut.),* gabbiere, *m.* ~ *margin* (book), margine superiore, bianco di testa, *m.* ~ *mast,* albero di gabbia, *m.* ~ *sail,* gabbia, vela di gabbia, *f.* ¶ *v.t.* coronare; coprire; sovrastare, dominare; sormontare, sorpassare; essere alla testa di, essere in cima a; *(tree)* cimare, svettare, scapezzare.

topaz, *n.* topazio, *m.*

toper, *n.* ubriacone, beone, *m.*

topic, *n.* soggetto, argomento, tema, *m.* ~*al film,* film di attualità, *m.* ~*al song,* canzone che tratta soggetti del giorno, *f.*

topographic(al), *a.* topografico. **topography,** *n.* topografia, *f.*

topple over, *v.i.* capitombolare, *(v.t.)* fare capitombolare.

topsy turvy, *ad.* sossopra.

torch, *n.* fiaccola, torcia, *f. electric* ~, lampadina tascabile, *f.* ~ *bearer,* portafiaccola, *m.inv. by* ~ *light,* alla luce delle fiaccole. ~*light procession,* ~ *tattoo,* fiaccolata, *f.*

toreador, *n.* toreadore, *m.*

torment, *n.* tormento, supplizio, strazio, *m.;* tortura, *f.* ¶ *v.t.* tormentare; affliggere. **tormentor,** *n.* tormentatore, *m.,* -trice, *f.*

tornado, *n.* turbine, ciclone, uragano, *m.*

torpedo, *n.* torpedine, *f.;* siluro, *m.* ~ *boat,* torpediniera, *f.;* silurante. ~ *tube,* [tubo] lanciasiluri, *m.* ¶ *v.t.* torpedinare, silurare.

torpid, *a.* torpido, intorpidito. **torpor,** *n.* torpore, *m.*

torrent, *n.* torrente, *m. in* ~*s,* a torrenti. **~ial,** *a.* torrenziale.

torrid, *a.* torrido.

torsion, *n.* torsione, *f.*

torso, *n.* torso, *m.*

tort *(Law), n.* torto, delitto o quasi-delitto civile, *m.*

tortoise, *n.* tartaruga; testuggine, *f.* ~*shell,* [guscio di] tartaruga, *m.* ~*shell butterfly,* tartaruga, *f.* ~*shell cat,* gatto di Spagna, *m.*

tortuous, *a.* tortuoso. **torture,** *n.* tortura, pena, *f.;* tormento, *m. instrument of* ~, strumento di tortura, *m.* ¶ *v.t.* torturare. **torturer,** *n.* boia; tormentatore, aguzzino, *m.* **torturous,** *a.* che serve a torturare.

torus & **tore,** *n.* toro, *m.*

toss, *v.t.* & *i.* lanciare, gettare (in aria); sbalzare, sballottare; trabalzare; scuotere, far saltare, agitarsi; *(head)* scrollare, tentennare; *(oars)* alberare. ~ *in blanket,* trabalzare in una coperta; ~ *off* (drink) bere d'un sorso, d'un fiato, tracannare. ~ *[up]* (coin), gi[u]ocare a pila e croce, a palle e santi.

tot, *n. (child)* piccino, *m.; (rum, &c.)* bicchierino, *m.; (Arith.)* somma, *f.*

total, *a.* totale, globale; completo, pieno, assoluto. ¶ *n.* totale, *m.;* somma totale, *f.* **totalizer, totalizator,** *n.* totalizzatore, *m.*

totter, *v.i.* barcollare; vacillare; traballare; crollare.

toucan, *n.* tucano, *m.*

touch, *n.* tatto, contatto, tocco, *m.;* comunicazione, *f.,* tratto, *m.,* colpo leggero, attacco leggero; saggio, accenno, *m.;* tintura, tinta, *f.;* tantino, (un) po' di, *m.; (Art.)* tratto di pennello, *m.,* pennellata, *f.;* tocco,

m. ~ *needle*, ago d'assaggio, *m.*
~*stone*, pietra di paragone, *f.*
~*wood*, esca, *f.* ¶ *v.t.* & *i.* toccare;
combaciarsi; tastare; palpare; maneggiare; essere in contatto; raggiungere; commuovere; sfiorare; interessare; riguardare; spettare; eguagliare.
~ *at*, fare scalo a, toccare, approdare
a. ~ *up*, ritoccare, rinfrescare. ~*ed*
(*crazy*), *p.p.* tocco (nel cervello), un
po' matto. ~*iness*, *n.* sucettibilità, *f.*
~*ing*, *a.* commovente. ¶ *pr.* ri-
guardante, in riguardo a, in fatto di,
circa, in merito a, quanto a. ~*y*,
a. suscettibile, irritabile, sensitivo.
tough, *a.* duro, resistente, tenace,
coriaceo; (*meat*) tiglioso. ~*en*, *v.t.*
indurire, render duro. ~*ness*, *n.*
durezza; tenacita; resistenza; qualità
coriacea; q. tigliosa, *f.*; solidità, *f.*
tour, *n.* giro, circuito, viaggio (circolare), *m.* ~*ing*, *n.* turismo, *m.*
~ *car*, vettura da turismo, *f.*;
torpedone, *m.* ~*ist*, *n.* turista, *m.f.*
~ *agency*, ufficio viaggi, *m.*; agenzia
di turismo, *f.* ~ *ticket*, biglietto
circolare, b. turistico, *m.*
tournament, *n.* torneo, concorso, *m.*;
giostra, *f.* **tourney**, *n.* torneo, *m.*
tourniquet, *n.* tornichetto, *m.*
tousle, *v.t.* scompigliare, arruffare,
mettere in disordine.
tout, *n.* sollecitatore; commissionario
d'albergo; piazzista, *m.* ~ *for*,
cercare clienti fare; la piazza.
tow, *n.* stoppa, *f.*; (*boat*) rimorchio, *m.*
in ~, a rimorchio. ¶ *v.t.* rimorchi-
are. ~ *boat*, rimorchio, rimorchiatore, *m.* ~[*ing*] *path*, banchina di
rimorchio, *f.*
toward[*s*], *pr.* verso, verso di, alla
volta di; a, su, per.
towel, *n.* asciugamano, *m.*, ~ *horse*,
~ *rail*, porta-asciugamano, *m.* **towel-
ling**, *n.* tela per asciugamani, *f.*
tower, *n.* torre, *f.*; pilone, *m.* ~ *above*,
dominare. ~*ing rage*, collera pazza,
f.
town, *n.* città, *f.*; (*country*) borgo, *m.*,
città di provincia, *f.* ~ *clerk*,
segretario comunale, *m.* ~ *clerk's
office*, municipio, *m.* ~ *council*,
consiglio comunale, *m.* ~ *crier*,
banditore pubblico, *m.* ~ *hall*,
municipio, palazzo municipale, *m.*
~ *house*, casa in città, *f.* ~ *planning*,
pianificazione cittadina, *f.* **townsman**, *n.* cittadino, *m.*
toxic, *a.* tossico. **toxin**, *n.* tossina, *f.*
toy, *n.* giocattolo, balocco, ninnolo, *m.*;
(*fig.*) bagatella, *f.*, zimbello, tras-

tullo, *m.* ¶ *v.i.* giocolare, baloccarsi,
scherzare.
trace, *n.* traccia, orma, *f.*; vestigio, *m.*;
(*Harness*) tirella, *f.* ¶ *v.t.* tracciare,
delineare, calcare; seguire la traccia
di; scoprire. ~ *back*, rintracciare,
rimontare, risalire (all'origine, alla
sorgente, &c.); far risalire. ~*d*
pattern, tracciato, *m.* ~*ry*, *n.*
ornamento a rete, merletto, *m.*
trachea, *n.* trachea, *f.*
tracing, *n.* calco; tracciato, *m.* ~
cloth, tela da calco, *f.* ~ *paper*, carta
da calco, *f.*
track, *n.* traccia, pista; pedata; via,
rotta, orbita, *f.*; cammino, sentiero,
m.; rotaia, carreggiata, *f.*; binario;
solco, *m.*; scia, *f.* ~ *race*, corsa su
pista, *f.* ¶ *v.t.* seguire la pista di,
scoprire la traccia di, tracciare.
~ *down* (*game*), scovare, ritrovare le
tracce di; (*criminal*) snidare, essere
sulle piste di.
tract, *n.* tratto, *m.*, regione, *f.*; (*leaflet*)
opuscoletto, *m.*, trattatello, *m.*
~*able*, *a.* trattabile, docile; maneggevole. **traction**, *n.* trazione, *f.*
~ *engine*, locomobile, *f.* **tractor**, *n.*
trattore, *m.* *caterpillar* ~, t. a
cingoli. *farm* ~, t. agricolo. ~
driver, trattorista, *m.* ~ *farming*,
motocultura, *f.*
trade, *n.* commercio, negozio, traffico,
m.; tratta, *f.*; mestiere, *m.*; industria,
f.; i commercianti, i negozianti,
gli esercenti, *m.pl.* ~ *discount*,
sconto commerciale, *m.* ~ *mark*,
marca di fabbrica, *f.*, marchio di f.,
m. ~ *price*, prezzo all'ingrosso, *f.*
~ *route*, rotta commerciale, *f.*
~ *union*, camera del lavoro, *f.*,
sindacato operaio, *m.* ~ *unionist*,
sindacalista, *m.f.* ~ *winds*, (venti)
alisei, *m.pl.* ¶ *v.i.* trafficare (*tre =
in*), fare il commercio (*in = di*),
fare affari (in). **trader**, *n.* commerciante, negoziante, fornitore, *m.*;
(*col. pl.*) commercianti, *m.pl.*; ceto
commerciale, *m.* **trading**, *n.* commercio, *m.*, tratta, *f.*, esercizio, *m.*
~ *account*, conto esercizio commerciale, *m.* ~ *capital*, capitale impegnato, l'insieme dei capitale fisso e
circolante, *m.* ~ *concern*, azienda
commerciale, *f.* ~ *station*, stazior e
di commercio, *f.* **tradesman**, *n.*
negoziante, bottegaio, fornitore, *m.*
tradesmen's entrance, porta di servizio, *f.*
tradition, *n.* tradizione, *f.* ~*al*, *a.*
tradizionale.

traduce, *v.t.* diffamare, calunniare.
~er, *n.* diffamatore, *m.*, -trice, *f.*

traffic, *n.* traffico; commercio; movimento, *m.*; circolazione, *f.* ~ **block,** traffico ostruito, *m.* ~ **lights,** semaforo, *m.* ~ **police,** polizia di circolazione, *f.* ~ **roundabout,** ~ **circus,** piazza a traffico circolare, *f.* ~ **sign,** segnale di traffico, *m.*
trafficker, *n.* mercante, trafficante, *m.f.*

tragedian, *n.* (autore) tragico, *m.*; attore tragico, *m.* **tragedienne,** attrice tragica, *f.* **tragedy,** *n.* tragedia, *f.* **tragic(al),** *a.* tragico. **tragicomedy,** *n.* tragicommedia, *f.* **tragicomic,** *a.* tragicomico.

trail, *n.* traccia, pista; striscia, coda, *f.*; solco, *m.*; (*gun carriage*) coda d'affusto, *f.* ~ **rope,** (*Aero.*) fune (di pallone), *f.* ¶ *v.t.* trascinare, strascicare; seguire sulle piste di. **~er,** *n.* rimorchio, carro rimorchiato, *m.*; giardiniera, *f.*

train, *n.* treno, convoglio; seguito, corteggio, corteo, *m.*; striscia, *f.*; tenore, *m.*; fila, serie, *f.*; (*dress*) strascico, *m.*, coda, *f.*; (*comet*) coda, *f.*; (*powder*) traccia, striscia, *f.*; (*events*) serie, *m.*, concatenamento, *m.* ~ **bearer,** caudatario, paggio, *m.* ~ **ferry,** pontone trasbordatore, *m.* ~ **oil,** olio di balena, *m.* ¶ *v.t.* ammaestrare, allenare, addestrare, esercitare, istruire, educare, abituare; (*plant*) disporre; (*gun*) dirigere, puntare; **~er,** *n.* allenatore; istruttore; (*animals*) domatore, *m.* **training,** *n.* addestramento, *m.*, esercitazione, *f.*, istruzione, *f.*, allenamento, *m.*, ammaestramento, *f.* ~ **centre,** scuola professionale, *f.* ~ **college,** scuola normale, *f.* ~ **ship,** nave scuola, *f.*

trait, *n.* tratto, *m.*, caratteristica, *f.*

traitor, **~tress,** *n.* traditore, *m.*, traditrice, *f.* **~ous,** *a.* traditore, -trice. **~ously,** *ad.* a tradimento.

trajectory, *n.* traiettoria, *f.*

tram (*Tapestry work*), *v.t.* ricavare campioni (da una pezza di stoffa).

tram[car], *n.* tramvai, *m.* **tramway** [line], tranvia, *f.*

trammel, *n.* (*net*) tramaglio, *m.*; (*pl.*) pastoie, *f.pl.* ¶ *v.t.* inceppare; impastoiare; imbarazzare.

tramp, *n.* rumore di passi; viaggio pedestre, *m.*; (*horses*) calpestio, *m.*; (*pers.*) vagabondo, *m.*, -a, *f.*; mendicante, *m.f.* ~ (*steamer*), vapore che non ha linea regolare. ¶ *v.i.* vaga-

bondare; battere il selciato; camminare pesantemente; (*v.t.*) misurare (a grandi passi). ~ **up & down,** percorrere.

trample [on] [down], *v.t.* calpestare; conculcare, pestare.

trance, *n.* estasi, *f.*; (*hypnotic*) stato ipnotico, *m.*, catalessi, *f.*

tranquil, *a.* tranquillo. **tranquillity,** *n.* tranquillità, *f.*

transact, *v.t.* fare, negoziare, trattare. **~ion,** *n.* affare, *m.*, operazione, transazione, *f.*; (*pl.*) atti, *m pl.*; memorie, *f.pl.*; verbali, *m.pl.*

transatlantic, *a.* transatlantico.

transcend, *v.t.* trascendere. **~ent,** *a.* trascendente.

transcribe, *v.t.* trascrivere. **transcript & transcription,** *n.* copia, trascrizione, *f.*, apografo, *m.*

transept, *n.* transetto, *m.*

transfer, *n.* trasferimento, *m.*, cessione, *f.*; storno; trapasso, *m.*; trasferta (*of pers.*); trasmissione, *f.*; (*Emb., &c.*) decalco, *m.*; (*for china & as toy*) decalcomania, *f.*; (*tram, bus*) corrispondenza, *f.* ~ [deed], atto di cessione, *m.* ¶ *v.t.* trasferire, trasmettere; cedere, stornare; trasportare; (*tracing*) decalcare; riportare. **~able,** *a.* trasferibile. **~ee,** *n.* cessionario, *m.* **~or,** *n.* cedente, *m.f.*

transfiguration, *n.* trasfigurazione, *f.*

transfix, *v.t.* trafiggere, trapassare.

transform, *v.t.* trasformare. **~ation,** *n.* trasformazione, *f.* ~ **scene,** trasformazione a vista, *f.* **~er,** *n.* trasformatore, *m.*

transfuse, *v.t.* trasfondere.

transgress, *v.t.* trasgredire; contravvenire a. **~or,** *n.* trasgressore, violatore, *m.*; peccatore, *m.*, -trice, *f.*

tran[s]ship, *v.t.* trasbordare; (*v.i.*) trasbordarsi, trasferirsi. **~ment,** *n.* trasbordo, *m.* ~ **bond,** bolletta di transito, *f.*

transient, *a.* transitorio, fugace, passeggero.

transire (*Cust.*) *n.* lasciapassare doganale, *m.*

transit, *n.* (*Astr., Cust.*) transito, *m. in* ~, in transito. **~ion,** *n.* transizione, *f.* **~ive,** *a.* transitivo. **~ory,** *a.* transitorio, passeggero.

translate, *v.t.* tradurre, volgere; (*bishop*) trasferire, traslocare. **translation,** *n.* traduzione, versione, *f.*; (*bishop*) traslazione, *f.* **translator,** *n.* traduttore, *m.*, -trice, *f.*

translucent, *a.* trasparente, diafano.

transmigration, *n.* trasmigrazione, *f.*

transmission, *n.* trasmissione, *f.* **transmit,** *v.t.* trasmettere. **transmitter,** *n.* trasmettitore, *m.*

transmute, *v.t.* trasmutare.

transom, *n.* traversa, *f.*

transparency, *n.* trasparenza, *f.*; *(picture)* trasparente, *m.* **transparente,** *a.* trasparente.

transpire, *v.i.* traspirare.

transplant, *v.t.* trapiantare.

transport, *n.* trasporto, *m.*; navetrasporto, *f.*; *(rage)* furia, *f.*, accesso di collera, *m.* ¶ *v.t.* trasportare. **~ation,** *n.* deportazione, *f.*

transpose, *v.t.* trasporre; *(Mus.)* trasportare.

transubstantiation, *n.* transustanziazione, *f.*

transverse, *a.* trasversale, trasverso.

trap, *n.* trappola; tagliola, *f.*; trabocchetto, tranello, *m.*; insidia, *f.*, agguato, *m.*; *(drain)* valvola, *f.*; sifone, *m.*; carrozzetta, *f.*; *(pl.)* bagaglio, *m.*; effetti, *m.pl.* ~ *ball,* valvola a sfera, *f.*; regolatore a galleggiante, *m.* ~*door,* botola, *f.*, trabocchetto, *m.* ¶ *v.t.* prendere in trappola; *(fig.)* ingannare.

trapeze, *n.* trapezio, *m.*

trapper, *n.* cacciatore (di pelli), *m.*

trappings, *n.pl.* finimenti, ornamenti, *m.pl.*; bardatura, *f.*

trash, *n.* robaccia, *f.*; oggetti di rifiuto, *m.pl.*; ciarpame, *m.*; *(worthless contents of books)* robaccia, *f.*; futilità, *f.pl.*

travail, *n.* doglie (del parto), *f.pl.*

travel, *n.* viaggio, *m.*, il viaggiare. ¶ *v.i.* viaggiare, camminare, girare; *(Mech.)* scorrere *(rings),* rullare; *(fig.)* propagarsi. ~ *over,* percorrere. **traveller,** *n.* viaggiatore, *m.*, -trice, *f.*; *(Com.)* piazzista, commesso viaggiatore, *m.* ~*'s cheque,* assegno per viaggiatore, *m.* **travelling,** *p.a.* ambulante; di (da) viaggio. ~ *crane,* gru a ponte, g. mobile, *f.* ~ *dress,* abito da viaggio, *m.* ~ *journeyman,* giornaliero ambulante, *m.* ~ *expenses,* spese di viaggio, *f.pl.* ~ *rug,* coperta da viaggio, *f.*

traverse, *v.t.* traversare, attraversare; contestare; *(Law)* negare, respingere.

travesty, *n.* parodia, *f.*; travestimento, *m.* ¶ *v.t.* parodiare.

trawl [net], *n.* rete a sacco, draga, *f.* ¶ *v.i.* pescare con la rete a sacco, con la draga. ~**er,** *n.* nave da pesca con la draga. ~**ing,** *n.* pesca con la draga, *f.*

tray, *n.* vassoio, *m.*; *(Phot.)* bacinella, *f.* ~ *cloth,* tovagliolino, *m.*

treacherous, *a.* perfido, sleale, traditore. **treachery,** *n.* tradimento, *m.*, perfidia, slealtà, *f.*

treacle, *n.* melassa, *f.*

tread, *n.* passo; incesso, *m.*; andatura, *f.*; *(of stair step)* pedata, *f.*; *(tyre)* battistrada, *m.inv.* *(egg)* germe, *m.* ¶ *v.i. ir.* mettere il piede, camminare; *(v.t. ir.)* pigiare, pestare, calcare, calpestare; ~ *water,* nuotare in piedi. ~**le,** *n.* pedale, *m.*

treason, *n.* tradimento, *m.*

treasure, *n. & ~ trove,* tesoro, *m.* ¶ *v.t.* tesoreggiare; custodire, conservare come tesoro. **treasurer,** *n.* tesoriere, cassiere, *m.* **treasury,** *n.* tesoro, *m.*, tesoreria, *f.*, erario, *m.*; dicastero delle finanze, *m.*, cassa, *f.*, fisco, *m.* T~ *Board,* *(Eng.)* Consiglio del Tesoro, *m.*

treat, *n.* regalo, *m.*, festa, *f.*, convito, *m.*, piacere fuori del comune, *m.* ¶ *v.t. & i.* trattare; dar trattenimento a; far festa; pagare da bere; discorrere; curare, medicare. **treatise,** *n.* trattato, *m.* **treatment,** *n.* trattamento, *m.*; accoglienza, *f.*; cura, *f.*; *(Music, Art)* esecuzione, *f.*; fattura, *f.* **treaty,** *n.* trattato, *m.* *by private* ~, a trattativa privata, amichevolmente.

treble, *a.* triplice, triplicato, di soprano acuto. ¶ *n.* triplo; *(Mus.)* soprano, *m.* *(Crochet)* nastri, *m.* ~ *clef,* chiave ai sol, *f.* ¶ *v.t.* triplicare.

tree, *n.* albero, *m.* ~ *fern,* felce arborea, *f.* ~ *nail,* caviglia, *f.* ~ *sparrow,* passera mattugia, *f.* ~**less,** *a.* senza alberi.

trefoil, *n.* trifoglio, *m.*

trellis, *n.* graticolato, *m.*; [in]gratticciata, rete, *f.*; traliccio, *m.*; pergolato, *m.* ¶ *v.t.* ingraticciare.

tremble, *v.i.* tremare, fremere. **trembling,** *n.* tremito, *m.*, tremolio, *m.*

tremendous, *a.* tremendo, enorme, formidabile, terribile.

tremolo, *n.* tremolo, *m.* **tremor,** *n.* tremore, fremito, *m.* **tremulous,** *a.* tremulo, tremante.

trench, *n.* trincea, *f.*, fosso, *m.*, fossato, *m.* ~ *mortar,* lanciabombe, *m.inv.* ~ *warfare,* guerra di trincea, guerra di posizione, *f.* ¶ *v.t.* scavare (una trincea), solcare; *(Mil.)* trincerare. ~ *upon,* invadere; rasentare. ~**ant,** *a.* tagliente, incisivo.

trencher, *n.* tagliere, piatto; berretto (tocco) universitario, *m.* **trencherman,** *n.* mangiatore, *m.*, buona forchetta, *f.*

trend, *n.* direzione, tendenza, *f.*; ¶ *v.i.* inclinarsi, dirigersi, tendere (a, verso).

Trent, *n.* Trento, *f.* **the Trentino,** il Trentino, *m.*

trepan, *n.* trapano, *m.* ¶ *v.t.* trapanare.

trepidation, *n.* trepidazione, *f.*

trespass, *n.* intrusione, offesa, trasgressione, *f.*; peccato, *m.*; infrazione, contravvenzione, violazione; (*Law*) turbativa di possesso, *f.* ¶ ~ *against*, offendere, recare offesa a, far torto a. ~ *on*, trasgredire, violare; (*fig.*) usurpare, abusare di. ~**er,** *n.* intruso, *m.* ~*s will be prosecuted,* (è) vietato l'ingresso, divieto di entrare sotto pena d'ammenda.

tress, *n.* treccia, *f.*

trestle, *n.* cavalletto, trespolo, *m.*; capra, *f.*; traliccio, *m.*

Treves, *n.* Treviri, *f.*

trial, *n.* prova, *f.*; saggio, esperimento, *m.*; giudizio, processo, *m.*; (*pl.*) pena, sofferenza, tribolazione, *f.* ~ *& error*, tastoni, tentoni, *m.pl.* ~ *balance*, bilancio di verificazione, *m.* ~ *trip*, viaggio di prova, *m.*

triangle, *n.* (*Geom. & Mus.*) triangolo, *m.* **triangular,** *a.* triangolare.

tribe, *n.* tribù; famiglia, classe, specie, *f.*

tribulation, *n.* tribolazione, *f.*

tribunal, *n.* tribunale, *m.* **tribune,** *n.* tribuna, galleria, *f.*; (*Hist. pers.*) tribuno, *m.*

tributary, *a.* tributario. ¶ *n.* tributario, affluente, *m.* **tribute,** *n.* tributo; omaggio, *m.*

trice, *n.* istante, attimo, batter d'occhio, *m.*

triceps, *a. & n.* tricipite, *a. & m.*

trick, *n.* tiro, trucco, scherzo, *m.*; gherminella, astuzia, *f.*; stratagemma, artifizio, inganno, *m.*; illusione, *f.*; (*Cards*) alzata, *f.*; (*habit*) ticchio, vizio, *m.* ~ *riding*, volteggio, *m.* ¶ *v.t.* ingannare, gabbare. ~**ery,** *n.* furberia, *f.*

trickle, *n.* filo d'acqua, *m.*; gocciolio; ruscelletto, *m.* ¶ *v.i.* gocciolare, colare, grondare.

trickster, *n.* baro, briccone, mariolo, truffatore, raggiratore; giocoliere, *m.* **tricky,** *a.* furbo, astuto; scabro; difficile.

tricycle, *n.* triciclo, *m.*

trident, *n.* tridente, *m.*

triennial, *a.* triennale.

trifle, *n.* bagattella, inezia, bazzecola, minuzia, *f.*; nonnulla, *m.*; (*Cook.*) zuppa inglese, *f.* ¶ *v.i.* frivoleggiare, baloccarsi, perdersi in inezie. ~ *with,* prendersi giuoco di, farsi beffe di. **trifler,** *n.* baloccone, tentennone, *m.*, persona frivola, *f.* **trifling,** *a.* di poca importanza, insignificante, minimo.

triforium, *m.* triforio, *m.*

trigger, *n.* grilletto, *m.*; (*Mech.*) scatto, *m.*, molla, levetta di comando, *f.*

triglyph, *n.* (*Arch.*) triglifo, *m.*

trigonometry, *n.* trigonometria, *f.*

Trilby [hat], *n.* feltro (cappello) floscio, *m.*

trill, *n.* trillo, *m.* ¶ *v.t.* trillare, ornare di trilli.

trilogy, *n.* trilogia, *f.*

trim, *a.* lindo, netto, ben messo, attillato, ben tenuto, ben assettato. ¶ *n.* assetto, ordine, stato, *m.*; abbigliamento; equilibrio; portamento, *m.*; andatura, posizione, *f.*; stivamento, *m.* ¶ *v.t.* assettare, aggiustare, allestire, abbigliare; guarnire; (*edges*) raffilare, tosare; (*book edges, &c.*) ritagliare, tosare; (*hair, &c.*) tagliare, spuntare; (*candle*) smoccolare; (*wood*) grossare, piallare; (*ship*) equilibrare, stivare; (*sails*) orientare. **trimmer,** *n.* opportunista, chi esita tra due opinioni, *m.f.*; (*Naut.*) stivatore, *m.* **trimming,** *n.* raffilatura, *f.* (*Typ.*) margine di taglio, *m.* **trimmings,** *n.pl.* guarnizioni, *f.pl.*; passamanteria, *f.*; nastri, *m.pl.*; ritagli, *m.pl.*; (*Cook.*) contorno, *m.*

Trinidad, *n. & the Trinity,* la Trinità, *f.*

trinket, *n.* ciondolo, gioiellino, ninnolo, gingillo, *m.*

trio, *n.* trio, *m.*

trip, *n.* gita, *f.*, giro, breve viaggio, *m.*, escursione, *f.*; passo falso; sgambetto, *m.* ~ [up], *v.t.* dare lo sgambetto a, far inciampare; (*Mech.*) lasciar cadere, liberare; (*v.i.*) inciampare, mettere il piede in fallo, incespicare. ~ *along,* saltellare.

tripartite, *a.* tripartito.

tripe, *n.* trippa, *f.* ~ *dresser*, trippaiolo, *m.*, -a, *f.* ~ *shop*, tripperia, *f.*

triple, *a.* triplo, triplice. ~*-expansion engine,* macchina a triplice espansione, *f.* ¶ *v.t. & i.* triplicare, triplicarsi. **triplet,** *n.* terzetto, *m.*,

terzina, *f.*; (*pl.*) trigemini, *m.pl.*
triplicate, *n.* triplicato, *m.*
tripod, *n.* treppiede, *m.*, treppiedi, *m.inv.*
tripoli, *n.* tripoli, *m.* **Tripoli**, *n.* Tripoli, *f.*
tripper, *n.* escursionista, *m.f.*
triptych, *n.* trittico, *m.*
trite, *a.* banale, comune, trito. ~**ness**, *n.* banalità, *f.*
triton, *n.* tritone, *m.*
triumph, *n.* trionfo, *m.* ¶ *v.i.* trionfare. ~**al**, *a.* trionfale, di trionfo. ~**ant**, *a.* trionfante. ~**antly**, *ad.* trionfalmente.
trivet, *n.* treppiede, *m.*
trivial, *a.* insignificante, senza importanza, da nulla, minimo, frivolo, leggero.
troat, *v.i.* bramire.
troglodyte, *n.* troglodita, *m.*
Trojan, *a.* troiano, *a.* & *m.*; (*war*) di Troia.
troll (*Fish.*), *v.i.* pescare con esca girante.
troll[e]y, *n.* carrello; carretto da scalo, *m.*; (*Elec.*) asta di presa, *f.* ~**bus**, filobus, *m.*
trolling, *n.* pesca con esca girante, *f.*
trombone, *n.* trombone, *m.*
troop, *n.* truppa; banda, frotta, *f.*; squadrone, *m.*; compagnia teatrale, *f.* ~**ship**, trasporto, *m.* ~ *train*, treno militare, *m.* ~**er**, *n.* soldato di cavalleria, *m.*
trope, *n.* tropo, *m.*
trophy, *n.* trofeo, *m.*
tropic, *n.* tropico, *m.* ~ *of Cancer, of Capricorn*, tropico del Cancro, del Capricorno, *m.* ~**al**, *a.* tropicale, dei tropici.
trot, *n.* trotto, *m.* ¶ *v.i.* & *t.* trottare, andare al trotto, fare andare al trotto.
troth, *n.* fede, *f.*
trotter, *n.* trottatore, *m.*, -trice, *f.*; (*pl.*) piedi; zampini, *m.pl.*
troubadour, *n.* trovatore, *m.*
trouble, *n.* pena; afflizione, *f.*; disturbo; fastidio; imbarazzo; incomodo, *m.*; molestia, *f.*; male, *m.* ¶ *v.t.* disturbare, incomodare; infastidire; inquietare, perturbare; affliggere. ~**d**, *p.a.* agitato, mosso; commosso; inquieto, travagliato, tribolato. ~ *waters* (*fig.*) acque torbide, *f.pl.*; torbido, *m.* ~**some**, *a.* importuno, noioso, seccante.
trough, *n.* trogolo, *m.*; madia, *f.*; (*of wave*) avvallamento, *m.*; (*sea*) spazio fra due onde, *m.*

trounce, *v.t.* malmenare, castigare.
troupe, *n.* compagnia, *f.*
trousers, *n.pl.* calzoni, *m.pl.* ~ *stretcher*, stiracalzoni, *m.inv.* ~**ed**, *p.p.* che porta i calzoni, coi calzoni.
trousseau, *n.* corredo, *m.*
trout, *n.* trota, *f.* ~ *fishing*, pesca delle trote, *f.*
trowel, *n.* cazzuola; mestola, *f.*; (*Hort.*) spiantatore, trapiantatoio, *m.*
truancy, *n.* vagabondaggio, *m.*; assenza, *f.* **truant**, *a.* vagabondo. *to play* ~, marinare la scuola, fare forca.
truce, *n.* tregua, *f.*
truck, *n.* (*barter*) baratto, scambio, *m.*; (*Rly.*) carro merci, vagone merci, *m.*; (*lorry*) carro, carro matto; (*motor*) autocarro, *m*; (*hand*) carretto da scalo, *m.* ~ *load*, vagone completo, *m.* ¶ *v.t.* barattare, scambiare; trasportare.
truckle, *v.i.* strisciarsi, umiliarsi, abbassarsi.
truculent, *a.* truculento, feroce.
trudge, *v.i.* andare a piedi, camminare penosamente.
trudgen (*Swim.*), *n.* doppio braccetto, nuoto all' indiana, *m.*
true, *a.* vero, verace, veritiero; leale, fedele; schietto, genuino, sincero; buono, giusto; esatto; rettilineo, corretto. [*certified*] *a* ~ *copy*, copia conforme, copia legalizzata, *f.* *in one's* ~ *colours*, nella propria vera luce, in veste da camera. ~*-love*[*r's*] *knot*, nodo d'amore, *m.* ~ *to life*, al naturale. *come* ~, avverarsi. ¶ *v.t.* spianare, rettificare, raddrizzare.
truffle, *n.* tartufo, *m.*
truism, *n.* verità evidente (da sé stessa), verità banale, *f.* **truly**, *ad.* veramente, in verità, veracemente, sinceramente; (*letters*) devotissimo.
trump, *n.* tromba, *f.*; (*fam.*) brav'uomo, *m.* ~[*card*], *n.* & ~**s**, *n.pl.* trionfo, *m.*; (*fig.*) caval di battaglia, *m.* ~ *up*, fabbricare, inventare.
trumpery, *n.* frottole, *f.pl.*; orpello, *m.*; anticaglie; bubbole, *f.pl.* ¶ *a.* di poco valore, meschino, insignificante.
trumpet, *n.* tromba, *f.*; (*ear*) corno acustico, *m.* ~ *call*, suono di tromba, squillo di tromba, *m.* ¶ *v.t.* & *i.* (*fig.*) pubblicare a suon di tromba, strombazzare, strombettare; (*elephant*) barrire; (*Mus.*) suonare la tromba. ~**er**, *n.* trombettiere, *m.*

truncate, *v.t.* troncare, mozzare.

truncheon, *n.* bastone, randello, *m.*; mazza, *f.*

trundle, *n.* ruzzola, *f.* ¶ *v.t.* far ruzzolare.

trunk, *n.* baule; tronco; fusto; pedale; torso, *m.*; (*elephant*) proboscide, *f.*; (*pl.*) calzoni, *m.pl.*; brache, *f.pl.* ~ *& bag manufacturer,* fabbricante di bauli e di valigie, baulaio, valigiaio, *m.* ~ *call,* (*Teleph.*) comunicazione intercomunale, *f.* ~ *line,* linea principale, *f.*

trunnion, *n.* orecchione, *m.*

truss, *n.* fascio, fastello, fagotto, *m.*; cinto erniario, *m.* (*Build.*) travatura, capriata; (*Arch.*) mensola, *f.* ¶ *v.t.* accosciare; legare; (*hay*) affastellare; (*Build.*) armare.

trust, *n.* fiducia, confidenza, fede, *f.*; credito, *m.*, credenza, *f.*; deposito, carico, custodia, *f.*; (*oil, steel*) sindacato, consorzio, *m.* ~ *deed,* atto di fidecommesso, contratto fiduciario, *m.* ¶ *v.t. & i.* fidarsi di, aver fiducia in, far credito a, credere (a), aver fede (in); confidare; sperare. ~**ed,** *p.a.* di confidenza, di fiducia. ~**ee,** *n.* amministratore fiduciario; curatore, *m.*, -trice, *f.*; depositario; tutore, *m.* ~**ful,** *a.* confidente, fiducioso. ~**worthy,** *a.* degno di fede, di fiducia, fedele; leale. ~**y,** *a.* fedele, fidato, a tutta prova.

truth, *n.* verità, *f.*; (il) vero, *m.* ~**ful,** *a.* verace, veridico, vero; ~**fulness,** *n.* veracità; sincerità, *f.*

try, *n.* tentativo, *m.*; prova, *f.*; colpo, *m.*; saggio, *m.* ¶ *v.t. & i.* provare, mettere alla prova, saggiare; sperimentare, fare, assaggiare; tentare, tastare, esaminare; cercare, sforzarsi di; raffinare, epurare; stancare; (*law case*) processare, mettere sotto processo, giudicare; (*patience*) provare, stancare, esaurire. ~ *on,* provare. ~**ing,** *a.* difficile; penoso; critico; fastidioso, noioso. ~ *time,* brutto quarto d'ora, tempo critico, *m.*

tub, *n.* vasca, tinozza, *f.*; tino, *m.*; conca, *f.*; bagno, *m.*; (*plants*) cassa, *f.*; (*bad ship*) barcaccia, *f.* tub[by man], pancione, *m.*

tuba, *n.* tuba, *f.*

tube, *n.* tubo, *m.*; (*Rly., London, &c.*) ferrovia sotterranea, *f.*

tuber, *n.* tubero, *m.* **tubercle,** *n.* tubercolo, *m.* **tuberculosis,** *n.*

tubercolosi, tisi, *f.* **tuberculous'** *a.* tubercoloso. **tuberose,** n· tuberosa, *f.*

tubular, *a.* tubolare. ~ *boiler,* caldaia tubolare, *f.* ~ *tyre,* gomma, *f.*, pneumatico, *m.*

tuck, *n.* basta; piega, *f.* ¶ *v.t.* fare una basta in. ~ *in,* avviluppare, rincalzare. ~ *up* (*sleeves, &c.*), rimboccare, tirar su.

Tuesday, *n.* martedí, *m.*

tuft, *n.* ciuffetto, fiocco, ciuffo, pennacchio, *m.*; ciocca, *f.*; nappina, *f.*, mazzo (di fiori, di piume), *m.*; macchia (d'alberi), *f.*; (*on chin*) mosca, *f.* ~**ed,** *a.* crestato, fronduto, folto, capelluto, col ciuffo.

tug, *n.* tirata, strappata, *f.*; strappo, *m.*; (*boat*) rimorchiatore, *m.* ~ *of war,* lotta alla corda, *f.*; tiro alla fune, *m.*; (*fig.*) sforzo supremo, *m.* ¶ *v.t.* tirar con forza, strappare.

tuition, *n.* insegnamento, *m.*; istruzione, *f.*

tulip, *n.* tulipano, *m.* ~ *tree,* tulipifero, *m.*

tulle, *n.* tulle, *m.*; rezza, *f.*

tumble, *n.* cascata, caduta, *f.*; capitombolo, *m.* ~**down,** (*v.i.*) cadere, cascare, capitombolare, ruzzolare, crollare. ~**-down,** *a.* crollante, caduco, diroccato, rovinato. **tumbler,** *n.* (*pers.*) saltimbanco, acrobata, *m.*; (*glass*) bicchiere (di vetro), *m.*; (*toy*) pancione, *m.* **tumbrel** ~**il,** *n.* carretta, *f.*, furgone, *m.*

tumour, *n.* tumore, *m.*

tumult, *n.* tumulto, *m.* **tumultous,** *a.* tumultuoso.

tumulus, *n.* tumulo, *m.*

tun, *n.* botte, *f.*

tune, *n.* aria, *f.*; accordo, *m.*; cadenza, *f.*; (*fig.*) armonia, nota, *f.*; tono; registro, *m.*; vena; disposizione, *f.* *v.t.* accordare, mettere d'accordo. **tuner,** *n.* accordatore, *m.* **tuneful,** *a.* armonioso, melodioso.

tungsten, *n.* tungsteno, *m.*

tunic, *n.* tunica, *f.*

tuning, *n.* accordatura, *f.* ~ *fork,* diapason, corista, *m.*

Tunis, *n.* (*State*) la Tunisia, *f.*; (*capital*) Tunisi, *f.* **Tunisian,** *a.* tunisino. ¶ *n.* tunisino, *m.*, -a, *f.*

tunnel, *n.* galleria, *f.*; traforo, *m.* ¶ *v.t.* traforare, fare una galleria sotto.

tunny, *n.* tonno, *m.*

tup, *n.* montone, *m.*; (*pile driving*) berta, *f.*; battipalo, *m.*

turban, *n.* turbante, *m.*

turbid, *a.* torbido.

turbine, *n.* turbina, *f.* **turbo-jet,** *att.*:
~ *engine,* motore a reazione, *m.*;
~ *plane,* aeroplano a reazione, *m.*

turbot, *n.* rombo, *m.*; (*young*) rombetto, *m.*

turbulence, *n.* turbolenza, *f.* **turbulent,** *a.* turbolento.

tureen, *n.* zuppiera, *f.*

turf, *n.* tappeto verde, *m.*; piota, zolla erbosa, *f.*; *the* ~ (*Racing*), le corse, *f.pl.*, il mondo ippico, *m.* ¶ *v.t.* rivestire d'erba, piotare.

turgid, *a.* turgido, gonfio, ampolloso.

Turin, *n.* Torino, *f. of* ~, torinese.

Turk, *n.* turco, *m.*, -a, *f.* **Turkey,** *n.* la Turchia, *f.* ~ *carpet,* tappeto turco, *m.* *t* ~ [*cock*], tacchino, *m.* *t* ~ [*hen*], tacchina, *f.* *t* ~ *poult,* tacchinotto, *m.* **Turkish,** *a.* turco. ~ *bath,* bagno turco, *m.* ¶ (*language*) *n.* il turco, *m.*, la lingua turca, *f.*

Turkoman (*pers.*), *n.* turcomanno, *m.*

turmeric, *n.* curcuma, *f.*; zafferano delle Indie, *m.*

turmoil, *n.* tumulto, disordine, scompiglio, *m.*

turn, *n.* giro, *m.*; curva, voltata, piega, svolta, *f.*; passeggiata, *f.*; inclinazione, tendenza, *f.*; turno, *m.*; volta; rivoluzione; vicenda, *f.*; (*tide*) cambiamento, *m.* ~ *of the scale,* tratto della bilancia, *m.* *sharp* ~ (*road traffic*), curva stretta, *f. at every* ~, ad ogni istante, in ogni occasione. *in* ~, a turno, per turno, a vicenda, in successione. *to a* ~, a perfezione. ¶ *v.t. & i.* volgere, voltare, svoltare, girare, far girare; rivolgere, rivoltare, rivolgersi, rivoltarsi; trasformare, convertire; cambiare; tradurre; rendere; (*Mech.*) tornire, lavorare al tornio; (*discussion*) aggirarsi (sopra), riferirsi (a), rigirarsi (a). ~ *aside,* sviare, scartare, stornare; rivolgere altrove; sconsigliare; voltarsi da un'altra parte. ~ *back,* tornare indietro, rifare il cammino. ~ *off* (*tap*), chiudere; (*water*) tagliare; (*light*) spegnere. ~ *on* (*tap*), aprire; (*water*) far colare; aprire il rubinetto di; (*light*) accendere. ~ *out badly,* andar male, riuscir male. ~ *right over,* rovesciare, capovolgere, capovolgersi. ~ *round,* girare, voltare, rivoltare, voltarsi in là; virare. ~ *the scale,* fare trabocc-

care la bilancia. ~ *up,* sollevare; rimboccare (*trousers, sleeves*); (*v.i.*) capitare, presentarsi, sopravvenire. ~-*up* (*card*) carta voltata, *f.*; ~ed-*up moustache,* baffi arricciati, *m.pl.*

turncoat, *n.* voltacasacca, rinnegato, *m.*, banderuola, *f.*

turncock, *n.* fontaniere, *m.*

turn-down (*collar*), *a.* colletto doppio, *c.* rivoltato, *m.*

turned (*a certain age*), *p.p.* oltrepassato, passato; (*tanti anni*) suonati.

turner, *n.* tornitore, *m.* **turning,** *n.* (*bend*) curva, svolta, svoltata, *f.*; gomito, *m.*; (*street*) cantonata, *f.* ~ *about,* giravolta, *f.*; voltafaccia, *m.* ~ *point & ~ space,* volta, *f.*; punto di cambiamento; momento critico, *m.*

turnip, *n.* rapa, *f.*; ravone, *m.* ~ *tops,* foglie di rapa, cime di rapa, *f.pl.*

turnkey, *n.* sottocarceriere, secondino, *m.*

turnout, (*Rly.*) *n.* diramazione, *f.*; binario laterale, *m.*

turnover, *n.* mutamento, *m.* (*Com.*) ciclo di affari, *m.*; (*Fin.*) cifra d'affari, circolazione, *f.*; (*Cook.*) pasticcino (con marmellata di mele), *m.*; (*stocking, &c.*) rivolta, *f.*; (*upset*) ribaltamento, *m.*

turnpike, *n.* barriera (di strada), *f.*

turnstile, *n.* (*X on post*) arganello, mulinello, *m.*; (*admission*) tornichetto, *m.*; contatore, *m.*

turntable, *n.* piattaforma girevole, *f.*; voltacarro, *m.*

turpentine, *n.* trementina, *f.*

turpitude, *n.* turpitudine, *f.*

turquoise, *n. & att.* turchese, *f. & att.*

turret, *n.* torretta, piccola torre, *f.* ~ *lathe,* tornio a revolver, *m.* ~ *ship,* nave a torrette, *f.*

turtle, *n.* tartaruga; testuggine di mare, *f.* ~ *dove,* tortora, *f.*; (*young*) tortorella, *f.* ~ *soup,* zuppa di tartaruga, *f. to turn* ~, capovolgersi.

Tuscan, *a.* toscano. ~**y,** *n.* la Toscana, *f.*

tusk, *n.* zanna, *f.*

tussle, *n.* zuffa, lotta, *f.*

tut, *i.* oibò! pst! ta!

tutelage, *n.* tutela, *f.* **tutelar[y],** *a.* tutelare. **tutor,** *n.* precettore, insegnante, ripetitore; tutore, *m.* ¶ *v.t.* istruire, fare da precettore a, insegnare a. **tutorship,** *n.* precettorato, *m.*; tutela, *f.*

twaddle, *n.* frottole, fole, *f.pl.*;

pettegolezzi, *m.pl.*; stupidaggine, *f.*; chiacchieramento, *m.*

twang, *n.* accento nasale; suono acuto, *m.* ¶ *v.i.* far stridere; parlare con voce nasale. ~ [*on*] (stringed instrument), pizzicare le corde di.

tweak, *v.t.* pizzicare, tirare.

tweed, *n.* tela scozzese, *f.*

'tween-decks, *n.* sottocoperta, *f.*, interponte, *m.*

tweezers, *n.pl.* pinzette, *f.pl.*

twelfth, *a. & n.* dodicesimo, *a. & m.*, il dodici, *m.* **twelve**, *a. & n.* dodici, *a. & m.* ~*mo* or *12mo*, *a. & n.* in dodicesimo. ~ *month*, anno, *m.* ~ *o'clock* (*in the day*), mezzogiorno, *m.*; (*at night*) mezzanotte, *f.*

twentieth, *a. & n.* ventesimo, *a. & m.*, il venti, *m.* **twenty**, *a. & n.* venti, *a. & m.*

twice, *ad.* due volte. ~ *as much*, il doppio, due volte tanto.

twiddle, *v.t.* far girare.

twig, *n.* ramoscello, *m.*; (*pl.*) ramoscelli, *m.pl.*; fraschette, *f.pl.*

twilight, *n.* crepuscolo, *m.*; penombra, *f.* ~ *sleep*, anestesia alla regina, *f.*

twill, *n.* saia, *f.*; tessuto, spinato, *m.*, levantina, *f.*

twill, *n.* saia, *f.*; spigato, *m.* ¶ *v.t.* spigare.

twin, *a.* gemello; doppio. ¶ *n.* gemello, *m.*, -a, *f.*; (*pl.*) gemelli, *m.pl.* ~ *screw*, *att.* a due eliche.

twine, *n.* spago, *m.* ¶ *v.t.* allacciare, tessere, intrecciare, attorcigliare, avviticchiare.

twinge, *n.* spasimo, *m.*, fitta, *f.*

twining (*Bot.*), *p.a.* rampicante; volubile.

twinkle, *v.i.* scintillare; tremolare; batter gli occhi. *in the twinkling of an eye*, in un batter d'occhio.

twirl, *v.t.* far rotare, prillare; (*stick*) fare il mulinello con; (*moustache*) attorcigliare; (*v.i.*) piroettare.

twist, *n.* torsione, *f.*; torcimento, *m.*; svolta, *f.*; tessuto a spire, cordoncino, *m.*, spago torto, filo ritorto, *m.*; (*of straw*) cencio, *m.*; (*tobacco*, *&c.*), rotolo, *m.*; (*Bil.*) effetto, *m.* ~*s & turns*, (*fig.*) vicende, *f.pl.* ~ *drill*, punta a elica (di trapano), *f.* ¶ *v.t.* torcere, contorcere, attorcigliare, intrecciare, avvolgere. ~**ed**, *pp. & p.a.* torto, ritorto, contorto; attorcigliato; avvolto; (*column*) a spirale.

twit, *v.t.* rimbrottare, rimproverare, rinfacciare.

twitch, *v.i.* avere un tic, palpitare; (*v.t.*) far saltare (dalla mano).

~ [**grass**], *n.* gramigna, *f.* ~**ing**, *p.a.* palpitante. ~**ing**, *n.* tic, contrazione spasmodica, *f.*; (*of conscience*), rimorso, *m.*

twitter, *v.i.* cinguettare. ~**ing**, *n.* cinguettio, *m.*

two, *a. & n.* due, *a. & m.* ~ *days before*, antivigilia, *f.* ~**-footed**, ~ *legged*, bipede. ~**-headed**, a due teste. ~**-master** (ship), due alberi, *m.inv.* ~**-seater** (car, &c.), biposto, *m.* ~**-way** *collar*, colletto doppio, *m.* ~**-way** *switch*, interruttore bipolare, *m.* ~**fold**, doppio, duplice, duplicato.

tympan *&* **tympanum**, *n.* timpano, *m.*

type, *n.* tipo, genere, *m.*; (*Typ.*) carattere, *m.* ~ *face*, occhio dei caratteri, *m.* ~ *founder*, fonditore di caratteri, *m.* ~ *metal*, metallo per caratteri, *m.*, lega tipografica per c., *f.* ~ *setting*, composizione, *f.* ~ *specimen*, campione del carattere, *m.* ~[*write*], *v.t.* scrivere a macchina, dattilografare. ~*writer*, macchina da scrivere, *f.* ~*writing*, dattilografia, *f.* ~*written*, dattilografato, scritto a macchina.

typhoid [**fever**], *n.* febbre tifoidea, *f.*; tifoide, *f.*

typhoon, *n.* tifone, *m.*

typhus, *n.* tifo, *m.*

typical, *a.* tipico. **typify**, *v.t.* figurare, simbolizzare, rappresentare.

typist, *n.* dattilografo, *m.*, -a, *f.*

typografic(al), *a.* tipografico. **typography**, *n.* tipografia, *f.*

tyrannic(al), *a.* tirannico. **tyrannize** [**over**], tiranneggiare. **tyranny**, *n.* tirannia, *f.* **tyrant**, *n.* tiranno, *m.*

tyre, (*pneumatic*), *n.* pneumatico, *m.*, gomma, *f.* *to put on a* ~, applicare un ~ a (*una ruota*). *the* ~ *has burst*, è scoppiato il (lo) pneumatico; *is punctured*, è lesionato, c'è un buco nel p.

tyro, *n.* Same as *tiro*.

Tyrol (the), il Tirolo, *m.* **Tyrolese**, *a.* tirolese. ¶ *n.* tirolese, *m.f.*

Tyrrhenian, *a.* tirreno.

U

ubiquity, *n.* ubiquità, *f.*

udder, *n.* mammella, poppa, *f.*

ugh, *i.* puh! oibò!

ugliness, *n.* bruttezza, laidezza, deformità, *f.* **ugly**, *a.* brutto; laido;

deforme; ripulsivo. (*as*) ~ *as sin*, brutto come il peccato.

ukulele, *n.* ukulele, *m.*, chitarra di Hawaii, *f.*

ulcer, *n.* ulcera, *f.* ~**ate,** *v.i.* ulcerarsi.

ullage, *n.* votatura, *f.*, calo (del vino nelle botti), *m.*

ulterior, *a.* ulteriore. ~ *motive*, secondo fine, pensiero segreto.

ultimate, *a.* ultimo, finale, definitivo. **uitimatum,** *n.* ultimatum, *m.* **ultimo,** *ad.* del mese passato, del mese scorso.

ultramarine, *n.* azzurro oltremarino, *m.* ¶ *a.* oltremarino.

ultra-violet, *a.* ultravioletto. ~ *rays*, raggi ultravioletti, *m.pl.*

ultravires, eccesso di potere; extra-statutario.

umber, *n.* terra d'ombra, *f.*

umbrage, *n.* ombra, *f.* sospetto, *m.* *take* ~ (*at*), adombrarsi (per), essere offeso (da).

umbrella, *n.* ombrello, *m.*; (*garden, beach, hold over potentate*) parasole, *m.* ~ *ring*, ghiera d'ombrello, *f.* ~ *stand*, porta-ombrelli, *m.inv.* ~ *sunshade*, parasole, *m.*

umpire, *n.* arbitro, *m.* ¶ *v.i.* arbitrare, far l'arbitro.

unabated, *a.* sostenuto, non diminuito, senza diminuzione, non scemato; infaticabile.

unable, *a.* incapace, inabile. **to be** ~ *to*, non potere.

unabridged, *a.* completo.

unacceptable, *a.* inaccettabile. **unaccepted,** *a.* (*bill*) respinto.

unaccompanied, *a.* solo, senza compagno.

unaccountable, *a.* inesplicabile.

unaccustomed, *a.* poco abituato; insolito.

unacquainted with (**to be**), non conoscere; ignorare; essere poco versato in, essere ignaro di.

unadorned, *a.* senza ornamenti; disadorno; semplice; naturale.

unadulterated, *a.* non adulterato; puro.

unaffected, *a.* naturale, semplice, senza affettazione; non affettato; inalterabile.

unafraid, *a.* senza paura.

unalloyed, *a.* puro, senza lega.

unalterable, *a.* inalterabile, invariabile.

unambiguous, *a.* non ambiguo, non equivoco; preciso.

unambitious, *a.* senza ambizione, senza pretese.

unanimous, *a.* unanime. ~**ly,** *ad.* all'unanimità, unanimemente.

unanswerable, *a.* inconfutabile, irrefutabile, incontestabile. **unanswered,** *a.* senza risposta.

unappreciated, *a.* poco apprezzato; incompreso.

unapproachable, *a.* inaccessibile.

unarmed, *a.* inerme, senza armi.

unasked, *a.* senza invito; non richiesto.

unassailable, *a.* inattaccabile; inespugnabile; incontestabile.

unassuming, *a.* modesto, semplice, senza pretese.

unattached (*Mil.*), *a.* in disponibilità.

unattainable, *a.* irraggiungibile, che non si può raggiungere, inaccessibile.

unattended, *a.* senza seguito, solo, negletto.

unattractive, *a.* poco attraente, senza attrattive.

unavailable, *a.* non disponibile.

unavailing, *a.* inutile, vano, inefficace.

unavoidable, *a.* inevitabile.

unaware of (**to be**), ignorare, essere inconscio di. **unawares,** *ad.* all'improvviso, per inavvertenza, inconsciamente.

unbalanced, *a.* non equilibrato; (*account*) non pareggiato.

unballast, *v.t.* scaricare della zavorra, sbarcare la zavorra.

unbandage, *v.t.* sbendare, togliere la benda a.

unbar, *v.t.* levare le sbarre a.

unbearable, *a.* insopportabile.

unbecoming, *a.* sconveniente, indecoroso; disdicevole, che non va, che non s'addice. **to be** ~, disdire, non confarsi, sconvenire.

unbelief, *n.* incredulità, *f.*, scetticismo, *m.* **unbeliever,** *n.* miscredente, incredulo, scettico, *m.*

unbend, *v.t. ir.* raddrizzare; allentare; (*v.i. ir.*) raddrizzarsi, allentarsi, rilassarsi; (*fig.*) essere affabile, usare condiscendenza. ~**ing,** *a.* inflessibile, rigido, austero.

unbias(s)ed, *a.* imparziale, senza prevenzioni.

unbind, *v.t. ir.* sciogliere, slegare.

unbleached, *a.* non imbiancato, non candeggiato; greggio.

unblemished, *a.* senza taccia, intatto.

unblushing, *a.* sfacciato, sfrontato.

unbolt, *v.t.* aprire, levare il catenaccio, levare il paletto a.

unborn, *a.* non ancora nato, futuro, da venire.

unbosom oneself, sfogarsi confidarsi (con), aprirsi (con).

unbound (*book*), *a.* non rilegato.

unbounded, *a.* illimitato, smisurato; sconfinato; sfrenato.

unbreakable, *a.* infrangibile, che non si può rompere.

unbridled, *a.* sbrigliato, sfrenato.

unbroken, *a.* non rotto, intero, intatto; non interrotto, continuo, consecutivo; (*horse*) non domato.

unbuckle, *v.t.* sfibbiare.

unbuilt on, non costruito, aperto, libero.

unburden oneself, aprirsi (con).

unburied, *a.* insepolto.

unbusinesslike, *a.* poco pratico, senza metodo.

unbutton, *v.t.* sbottonare.

uncalled for remark, osservazione fuori di posto, fuori di proposito, *f.*

uncanny, *a.* strano, fantastico, misterioso.

uncapsizable, *a.* che non si può capovolgere.

uncared for, negletto, abbandonato, trascurato.

unceasing, *a.* incessante. ~ly, *ad.* incessantemente.

unceremoniously, *ad.* alla buona, senza cerimonie.

uncertain, *a.* incerto. ~ty, *n.* incertezza, *f.*

unchain, *v.t.* scatenare, sciogliere dalle catene; liberare.

unchangeable, *a.* immutabile. **un- changing**, *a.* costante, invariabile, invariato.

uncharitable, *a.* senza carità, poco caritatevole.

unchaste, *a.* impudico; licenzioso.

unchecked, *a.* sfrenato, senza freno, incontrollato.

uncircumcised, *a.* incirconciso.

uncivil, *a.* scortese, sgarbato, incivile. ~ized, *a.* barbaro.

unclad, *a.* nudo, spogliato, senza vesti.

unclaimed, *a.* non reclamato; (*divi- dend*) arretrato.

unclassified, *a.* non classificato.

uncle, *n.* zio, *m.*

unclean, *a.* sporco, sudicio, sozzo; impuro, immondo.

unclothed, *a.* spogliato, svestito, nudo.

unclouded, *a.* senza nuvole, sereno, chiaro.

uncock (*gun*), *v.t.* disarmare.

uncoil, *v.t.* svolgere.

uncomely, *a.* sgraziato; poco attra- ente.

uncomfortable, *a.* incomodo, sco- modo, sgradevole; (*of pers.*) a disagio, inquieto.

uncommon, *a.* poco comune, fuori del comune, raro. ~ly, *ad.* assai, molto.

uncommunicative, *a.* poco comuni- cativo, riservato, taciturno.

uncomplaining, *a.* rassegnato. *the* ~ *poor*, i poveri vergognosi, *m.pl.*

uncompleted, *a.* incompiuto; incom- pleto.

uncompromising, *a.* intransigente, intrattabile.

unconcern, *n.* indifferenza, noncu- anza, *f.*

unconditional, *a. &* ~ly, *ad.* senza condizione.

unconfirmed, *a.* non confermato.

unconnected (*desultory*), *a.* scucito, sconnesso.

unconquerable, *a.* invincibile, in- domabile.

unconscious, *a.* inconscio; (*dead faint*) senza conoscenza. ~ness, *n.* incoscienza; perdita della conos- cenza, *f.*; svenimento, *m.*

unconsecrated ground, terra non consacrata, *f.*

unconstitutional, *a.* incostitu- zionale, contrario alla costituzione.

unconstrained, *a.* spontaneo, disin- volto; spigliato. **unconstraint**, *n.* disinvoltura, scioltezza, *f.*, abandono, *m.*

uncontested, *a.* incontestato, incon- trastato.

uncontrollable, *a.* irrefrenabile, in- governabile; inestinguibile.

unconventional, *a.* non convenzio- nale; senza soggezione; disinvolto.

unconvincing, *a.* poco verosimile, poco soddisfacente.

uncork, *v.t.* stappare, sturare.

uncorrected, *a.* non riveduto, non corretto.

uncouple, *v.t.* disgiungere, staccare; spaiare.

uncouth, *a.* strambo, goffo, rozzo.

uncover, *v.t.* scoprire, svelare, (*v.i.*) scoprirsi.

uncreated, *a.* increato, non creato.

uncrossed (*cheque*), *a.* non sbarrato.

unction, *n.* unzione, *f.* **unctuous**, *a.* untuoso.

uncultivated & uncultured, *a.* incolto.

uncurbed, *a.* indomito.

uncurl, *v.t.* disfare, svolgere.

uncustomary, *a.* insolito, inusitato.

uncustomed, *a.* (*not liable to duty*) esente da dazio; non soggetto a dazio; (*having paid no duty*) non sdoganato, non dichiarato in dogana.

uncut, *a.* (*gem*) non tagliato; (*cake*) intero; ~ *edges* (*book*) intonso.

undamaged, *a.* non danneggiato, non avariato; intatto.

undated, *a.* senza data.

undaunted, *a.* intrepido.

undeceive, *v.t.* disingannare.

undecided, *a.* indeciso, incerto.

undecipherable, *a.* indecifrabile.

undefended, *a.* indifeso, senza difesa, senza difensore; (*law case*) non contestato; (*heard ex parte*) giudicato in contumacia.

undefiled, *a.* senza taccia, senza macchia, puro, immacolato.

undefined, *a.* indefinito, indeterminato.

undeliverable, *a.* con destinatario introvabile, giacente. **undelivered,** *a.* non consegnato; non liberato.

undeniable, *a.* innegabile, incontestabile.

undenominational, *a.* laico, neutro.

under, *pr.* sotto; di sotto; al di sotto di; in; a; mediante; dopo; meno di; per virtú di. ~ *there,* vi sotto, laggiú. ~ *water,* sott'acqua, tra due acque. ¶ *ad.* sotto; al di sotto; a meno di; troppo poco, insufficientemente. ~ *way,* in cammino, in marcia.

underassessment, *n.* insufficienza d'imposizione, *f.*

underbred, *a.* malcreato, maleducato, volgare.

under-carriage (*Aero.*), *n.* carrello d'atterraggio, *m.*

underclothing, *n.* (*women's*) panni di sotto, *m.pl.*; (*men's*) sottovesti, *f.pl.*; sottovestiario, *m.*; biancheria personale, *f.*

undercurrent, *n.* corrente sottomarina, *f.*; (*in air*) corrente inferiore, *f.*; (*fig.*) fondo, *m.*, corrente segreta, *f.*

undercut (*meat*), *n.* filetto, *m.*; (*Box.*) colpo di taglio, *m.*

underdeveloped, *a.* non abbastanza sviluppato.

underdone, *a.* poco cotto, al sangue.

under-estimate, *v.t.* stimare sotto il valore, stimare poco, svalutare.

under-exposure (*Phot.*), *n.* posa insufficiente, *f.*

undergarment, *n.* (*men's*) sottoveste, *f.*; (*women's*) copribusto, *m.*

undergo, *v.t. ir.* subire, soffrire, patire.

undergraduate, *n.* studente, aspirante ai gradi universitari, *m.*

underground, *a.* sotterraneo. ¶ *ad.* sottoterra.

undergrowth, *n.* macchie, *f.pl.*, fratta, *f.*, arboscelli, cespugli, *m.pl.*

underhand, *a.* clandestino, segreto, nascosto, sordo; (*Ten. service*). inverso. ¶ *ad.* sottomano, clandestinamente.

underlease, *n.* subaffitto, *m.*

underlet, *v.t. ir.* subaffittare.

underline, *v.t.* sottolineare.

underling, *n.* (impiegato) subalterno, inferiore, strumento, *m.*

underlying, *a.* giacente sotto, sottostante.

undermentioned, *a.* sottomenzionato, sottonominato.

undermine, *v.t.* minare.

undermost, *a.* (il) piú basso.

underneath, *ad.* sotto, al di sotto. ¶ *pr.* sotto, al di sotto di.

underpay, *v.t. ir.* pagare insufficientemente, pagare troppo poco, pagare male.

underpin, *v.t.* puntellare, sottomurare.

underprop, *v.t.* puntellare.

underrate, *v.t.* stimare troppo poco, deprezzare.

underscore, *v.t.* sottolineare.

under-sea, *a.* sottomarino.

under-secretary, *n.* sottosegretario, *m.*

undersell, *v.t. ir.* vendere meno caro di.

underside, *n.* disotto, *m.*; parte inferiore, *f.*; rovescio, *m.*

undersigned, *a. & n.* sottoscritto, *a. & m.*

understand, *v.t. & i. ir.* capire, comprendere, intendere; intendersi (di); apprendere, essere informato, sentire, sapere, sottintendere. ~**ing,** *n.* intelligenza, comprensione, *f.*, intelletto, *m.*, sapere, *m.*; intesa, *f.*, accordo, *m.*

understatement, *n.* litote, affermazione incompleta, *f.*

understrapper, *n.* impiegato subalterno, *m.*

understudy, *n.* sostituto, *m.*; (attore), supplente, *m.*, (attrice) s., *f.* ¶ *v.t.* fare da supplente, sostituire.

undertake, *v.t. ir.* intraprendere, imprendere, assumere, impegnarsi (a), farsi responsabile (di), incaricarsi (di); osare. **undertaker,** *n.*

imprenditore di pompe funebri, *m.*
undertaking, *n.* promessa, obbligazione; impresa, *f.* *written* ∼, impegno scritto, *m.*
undertone (in an), a bassa voce, a mezza voce.
undertow, *n.* risacca, *f.*
undervalue, *v.t.* stimare sotto il valore, far poco conto di, svalutare.
underwear, *n.* Same as *underclothing.*
underwood, *n.* boscaglia, *f.*, bosco ceduo, *m.*
underworld, *n.* inferno, *m.*; i bassi fondi (della società), *m.pl.*
underwrite, *v.t.* *ir.* (*Insce.*) sottoscrivere, sottoscrivere per; (*Fin.*) garantire. **underwriter,** *n.* assicuratore (marittimo), assuntore (delle azioni di una società); (*Fin.*) mallevadore, garante, *m.* **underwriting,** *n.* sottoscrizione; assicurazione, *f.*
undeserved, *a.* immeritato. **undeserving,** *a.* immeritevole; indegno (of = di).
undesirable, *a. & n.* non desiderabile, poco desiderabile, *a.*, poco conveniente, *a.*; persona sgradita, *f.*
undetermined, *a.* indeterminato.
undeveloped, *a.* poco (non) sviluppato; incolto.
undigested, *a.* non digerito, (*fig.*) indigesto, crudo.
undignified, *a.* senza dignità; poco dignitoso.
undisciplined, *a.* indisciplinato.
undiscoverable, *a.* introvabile. **undiscovered,** *a.* non scoperto.
undismayed, *a.* intrepido, non sgomentato, senza paura, senza essere scoraggiato.
undisputed, *a.* incontrastato, fuori discussione.
undisturbed, *a.* tranquillo, placido; non interrotto.
undo, *v.t.* *ir.* disfare; sciogliere; staccare; annullare, rovinare; (*knitting*) smagliare, disfare. ∼**ing,** *n.* rovina, *f.*; disfacimento; scioglimento, *m.* *to come undone*, disfarsi. *to leave undone*, trascurare di fare, tralasciare.
undoubted, *a.* indubitato, indubitabile, certo.
undress, *n.* abito da camera, *m.*; (*Mil. Nav.*) piccola divisa; divisa di servizio, bassa tenuta, *f.* ¶ *v.t.* svestire, spogliare; (*v.i.*) svestirsi.
undrinkable, *a.* non potabile, imbevibile.

undue, *a.* indebito; eccessivo, esagerato.
undulate, *v.i.* ondeggiare, ondulare. **undulating,** *a.* ondulato, ondeggiante. **undulation,** *n.* ondulazione, *f.*
unduly, *ad.* indebitamente; troppo, eccessivamente.
undutiful, *a.* che manca al proprio dovere; poco rispettoso, cattivo.
undying, *a.* imperituro, immortale.
unearned, *a.* non guadagnato; immeritato. ∼ *increment*, plus-valore, maggior valore, *m.*
unearth, *v.t.* dissotterrare; (*fig.*) scoprire, trovare. ∼**ly,** *a.* spettrale, che ha del fantasma; non terreno.
uneasiness, *n.* inquietudine, ansia, *f.* **uneasy,** *a.* inquieto; incomodo; preoccupato.
uneatable, *a.* immangiabile.
uneducated, *a.* senza istruzione.
unemployable (the), coloro che sono disadatti per l'impiego; le mani inutili. **unemployed,** *a.* non impiegato, non usato; (*pers.*) disoccupato, senza lavoro. *on the* ∼ *list* (*Mil.*) in disponibilità. *the* ∼, i disoccupati, *m.pl.* **unemployment,** *n.* disoccupazione, *f.* ∼ *benefit*, indennità di disoccupazione, *f.*, sussidio (ai) disoccupati, *m.* ∼ *insurance*, assicurazione contro la disoccupazione, *f.*
unending, *a.* interminabile, senza fine; sterminato.
unenterprising, *a.* poco intraprendente, senza iniziativa.
unenviable, *a.* poco invidiabile, da non invidiarsi.
unequal, *a.* ineguale. ∼ *to* (task), impari a, incapace di. **unequalled,** *a.* incomparabile, senza eguale.
unequivocal, *a.* non equivoco, chiaro, franco.
unerring, *a.* infallibile, certo, sicuro.
uneven, *a.* ineguale, non piano; scabro; (*number*) dispari. ∼**ness,** *n.* ineguaglianza, *f.*; (*number*) imparità, *f.*
unexceptionable, *a.* ineccepibile, irrecusabile, irreprensibile.
unexpected, *a.* inatteso, imprevisto, inaspettato.
unexpired, *a.* non ancora scaduto.
unexplained, *a.* non spiegato.
unexplored, *a.* inesplorato.
unexpurgated, *a.* integrale.
unfailing, *a.* immancabile; inesauribile; (*spring*) perenne.
unfair, *a.* ingiusto, iniquo, parziale.

~**ness,** *n.* ingiustizia, parzialità, mala fede, *f.*

unfaithful, *a.* infedele. ~**ness,** *n.* infedeltà, *f.*

unfamiliar, *a.* poco familiare, poco noto, strano.

unfasten, *v.t.* sciogliere, disfare; allentare, slegare; staccare; disserrare; sfibbiare.

unfathomable, *a.* insondabile, senza fondo; (*fig.*) inscrutabile, impenetrabile.

unfavourable, *a.* sfavorevole. ~ *light,* cattiva luce (*lit. & fig.*), *f.*

unfederated Malay States (the), gli Stati malesi non federati, *m.pl.*

unfeeling, *a.* insensibile; duro, crudele; senza pietà.

unfeigned, *a* sincero.

unfenced, *a.* senza chiusa, senza muri, senza siepi.

unfettered, *a.* senza ceppi, senza pastoie, senza impacci; (*fig.*) illimitato, pieno.

unfinished, *a.* incompiuto, incompleto.

unfit, *a.* disadatto; improprio; incapace, inabile; *the* ~, gli inabili, gli incapaci, *m.pl.* ~ *for use,* fuori uso. ~**ness,** *n.* incapacità, inattitudine, *f.* **unfitting,** *a.* sconveniente.

unflagging, *a.* instancabile; sostenuto.

unfledged, *a.* senza piume.

unflinching, *a.* fermo, risoluto; a tutta prova.

unfold, *v.t.* aprire, spiegare; distendere; esporre; svolgere; svelare.

unforeseen, *a.* impreveduto, imprevisto.

unforgettable, *a.* indimenticabile.

unforgivable, *a.* imperdonabile.

unfortified, *a.* non fortificato; (*town*) aperto.

unfortunate, *a.* sfortunato, disgraziato, sventurato, infelice. *the* ~, gli sfortunati, i disgraziati, *m.pl.*

unfounded, *a.* senza fondamento, infondato, ingiustificato.

unfrequented, *a.* infrequentato, poco praticato.

unfriendly, *a.* non amichevole, poco benevolo, poco gentile, mal disposto. ~ *to,* contrario a.

unfrock, *v.t.* sfratare, spretare.

unfruitful, *a.* infruttuoso, sterile, infecondo. ~**ness,** *n.* sterilità, *f.*

unfulfilled, *a.* inadempiuto, incompiuto; non esaudito.

unfurl, *v.t.* spiegare.

unfurnished, *a.* non ammobigliato; sprovvisto (di).

ungainly, *a.* goffo, maldestro, sguaiato, dinoccolato.

ungathered, *a.* non colto; non raccolto.

ungenerous, *a.* poco generoso; meschino.

ungodliness, *n.* empietà, *f.* **ungodly,** *a.* empio, irreligioso.

ungovernable, *a.* infrenabile, ingovernabile; violento.

ungraceful, *a.* sgraziato, senza grazia, goffo.

ungracious, *a.* scortese, sgarbato.

ungrafted, *a.* non innestato, senza innesti.

ungrammatical, *a.* sgrammaticato, scorretto. ~**ly,** *ad.* incorrettamente; con spropositi di grammatica. *to speak or write* ~, sgrammaticare.

ungrateful, *a.* ingrato. ~**ness,** *n.* ingratitudine, *f.*

ungrudgingly, *ad.* di buon cuore, molto volentieri.

unguarded, *a.* senza difesa; indiscreto.

unhair (*skins*), *v.t.* togliere il pelo a; depilare.

unhallowed, *a.* empio, profano.

unhappiness, *n.* infelicità, *f.* **unhappy,** *a.* infelice.

unharmed, *a.* illeso; indenne, senza danno.

unharness, *v.t.* staccare, levare la bardatura, i finimenti (al cavallo).

unhatched, *a.* non uscito dall'uovo; non schiuso.

unhealthiness, *n.* insalubrità, *f.* **unhealthy,** *a.* insalubre; malsano.

unheard of, inaudito.

unheated, *a.* non riscaldato.

unheeded, *a.* negletto, poco riguardato; non ascoltato.

unhesitatingly, *ad.* senza esitazione, prontamente, risolutamente.

unhewn, *a.* non tagliato.

unhindered, *a.* senza impaccio, non impedito.

unhinge, *v.t.* scardinare, sgangherare; (*fig.*) sconvolgere.

unholiness, *n.* empietà, *f.* **unholy,** *a.* profano, empio.

unhonoured, *a.* inonorato, non apprezzato; senza onore.

unhook, *v.t.* sganciare; staccare; sfibbiare.

unhoped for, insperato.

unhorse, *v.t.* scavalcare.

unhurt, *a.* illeso, indenne, incolume, salvo.

unicorn, *n.* liocorno.

uniform, *a.* uniforme. ¶ *n.* divisa

tenuta, uniforme, *f.* ~**ity,** *n.* uniformità, *f.* ~**ly,** *ad.* uniformemente; invariabilmente; regolarmente. **unify,** *v.t.* unificare.

unilateral, *a.* unilaterale.

unimaginable, *a.* inimmaginabile.

unimpaired, *a.* in pieno vigore.

unimpeachable, *a.* incontestabile, indiscutibile.

unimpeded, *a.* senza ostacoli, senza impedimento.

unimportant, *a.* insignificante, non importante.

uninflammable, *a.* non infiammabile.

uninhabitable, *a.* inabitabile. **uninhabited,** *a.* (*house*) disabitato; (*island, country*) inabitato.

unitiated person, persona non iniziata, *f.*; profano, *m.*

uninjured, *a.* illeso, indenne, incolume.

uninstructed, *a.* senza istruzione, ignorante; senza ordini.

uninsured, *a.* non assicurato; (*Post.*) senza valore dichiarato.

unintelligent, *a.* poco intelligente. **unintelligible,** *a.* inintelligibile, incomprensibile.

unintentional, *a.* non intenzionale; involontario.

uninterested, *a.* non interessato, indifferente, disinteressato. **uninteresting,** *a.* poco interessante, senza interesse.

uninterrupted, *a.* ininterrotto, continuo, senza interruzione. ~**ly,** *ad.* senza interruzione, senza fermata, continuamente.

uninvited, *a.* non invitato, senza invito. **uninviting,** *a.* poco attraente; poco appetitoso.

union, *n.* unione, società, alleanza, lega, federazione, *f.*; (*Mech.*) raccordo, collegamento, *m. union of linen and cotton,* tela mista. *U*~ *of South Africa,* Unione sud-africana, *f.* U~ of Soviet Socialist Republics (contr. U.S.S.R.), Unione Repubbliche Socialiste Sovietiche (U.R.S.S.). *trade* ~, camera del lavoro, sindacato operaio, *m.*

unique, *a.* unico, solo.

unison, *n.* unisono, *n. in* ~, all'unisono.

unissued (*stocks, shares*), *a.* non emesso.

unit, *n.* unità, *f.* ~ *price,* prezzo unitario, *m.* **unite,** *v.t.* unire; riunire, congiungere; legare, collegare; accoppiare; maritare; radunare. **united,** *a.* unito; congiunto;

U~ *Kingdom* [of Great Britain and Northern Ireland], Regno Unito [di Gran Bretagna e Irlanda del Nord], *m. U*~ *Nations Organisation* (abb. *U.N.O.*), Organizzazione delle Nazioni Unite (O.N.U.), *f. U*~ *States* [of America], Gli Stati Uniti, *m.pl.* **unity,** *n.* unità; unione; armonia, concordia, *f.*; insieme, *m.*

universal, *a.* universale. ~**ity,** *n.* universalità, *f.* **universe,** *n.* universo, *m.* **university,** *n.* università, *f.*; (*att.*) universitario.

unjust, *a.* ingiusto; iniquo. **unjustifiable,** *a.* ingiustificabile.

unkempt, *a.* mal pettinato, incolto, ruvido.

unkind, *a.* non amabile, poco gentile; duro, crudele, cattivo. ~**ness,** *n.* mancanza di gentilezza, scortesia, cattiveria, crudeltà, *f.*

unknown, *a.* sconosciuto. ~ *person,* sconosciuto, *m.,* -a, *f.* ignoto, *m.,* -a, *f.* ~ (*quantity*), quantità sconosciuta, *f.* ~ *to,* all'insaputa di. *the* ~, l'ignoto; *the U*~ *Warrior,* or *Soldier,* il Milite Ignoto, *m.*

unlace, *v.t.* slacciare.

unlawful, *a.* illegale, vietato dalla legge, illecito; ~ *assembly to the disturbance of the peace,* attruppamento, *m.,* riunione vietata dalla legge, *f.* ~**ness,** *n.* illegalità, *f.*

unlearn, *v.t.* disimparare. ~**ed,** *a.* ignorante, illetterato.

unleavened, *a.* senza lievito; (*Jewish*) azzimo. ~ *bread,* pane azzimo, *m.*

unless, *c.* a meno che non, se non; salvo che.

unlettered, *a.* illetterato, ignorante.

unlicensed, *a.* non autorizzato, senza licenza, senza permesso.

unlicked cub, ragazzo sgarbato, *m.*

unlike, *a.* dissimile, differente, diverso. *to be* ~, non assomigliare a. ¶ *pr.* all'inverso di, tutto al contrario di. **unlikelihood,** *n.* inverosimiglianza; improbabilità, *f.* **unlikely,** *a.* poco probabile, inverosimile.

unlimber, *v.i.* staccare l'avantreno.

unlimited, *a.* illimitato.

unlined, *a.* non foderato; (*paper*) senza righe;(*face*) senza rughe.

unload, *v.t.* scaricare; (*Fin.*) disfarsi di.

unlock, *v.t.* aprire, disserrare.

unlooked for, inatteso, inaspettato.

unloose, *v.t.* scatenare, slegare, snodare, sciogliere; sguinzagliare, lasciare andare.

unlovely, *a.* poco amabile, non attraente.

unlucky, *a.* disgraziato, sfortunato, sventurato, malaugurato, sinistro.

unmake, *v.t. ir.* disfare.

unman, *v.t.* privare di coraggio, snervare, abbattere.

unmanageable, *a.* non maneggiabile; intrattabile; indomabile, ingovernabile.

unmanly, *a.* indegno di un uomo; effeminato; pusillanime, vile.

unmannerly, *a.* malcreato, screanzato, sgarbato, scortese.

unmanufactured, *a.* crudo, greggio.

unmarketable, *a.* invendibile.

unmarried, *a.* non maritato; *(man)* celibe, scapolo; *(woman)* nubile; **unmarry,** *v.t.* sciogliere il matrimonio di.

unmask, *v.t.* smascherare.

unmentionable, *a.* di cui non si parla.

unmerciful, *a.* spietato, inumano, senza misericordia.

unmerited, *a.* immeritato.

unmethodical, *a.* senza metodo, non metodico.

unmindful, *a.* immemore; negligente, disattento; dimentico.

unmingled, *a.* non mescolato; puro.

unmistakable, *a.* chiaro, evidente, manifesto; da non sbagliarsi.

unmitigated, *a.* assoluto, completo, intero; non mitigato.

unmixed, *a.* non mescolato, non misto; completo.

unmolested, *a.* non molestato, in pace.

unmoor, *v.t.* disormeggiare.

unmounted, *a.* non montato; senza incorniciatura; *(gem)* non incastonato; *(pers.)* a piedi.

unmoved, *a.* immobile; impassibile.

unmusical, *a.* poco armonioso, discordante; senza un orecchio musicale.

unmuzzle, *v.t.* togliere la museruola a.

unnamable, *a.* innominabile. **unnamed,** *a.* innominato.

unnatural, *a.* snaturato, innaturale, contro natura.

unnavigable, *a.* innavigabile.

unnecessary, *a.* non necessario, inutile.

unneighbourly way (in an), non da buon vicino, da cattivo vicino.

unnerve, *v.t.* snervare, far perdere il coraggio a, togliere la forza a.

unnoticed, unobserved, *a.* inosser-

vato. **unobservant,** *a.* disattento, distratto.

unobstructed, *a.* non impedito, senza ostacoli; *(view)* aperto.

unobtainable, *a.* che non si può ottenere *or* procurare.

unobtrusive, *a.* modesto, discreto, riservato. ~**ly,** *ad.* discretamente, modestamente.

unoccupied, *a.* inoccupato; libero, disponibile.

unoffending, *a.* inoffensivo.

unofficial, *a.* non ufficiale; *(information)*, privato; ufficioso.

unopened, *a.* non aperto; non dissigillato.

unopposed, *a.* senza opposizione, incontrastato.

unorganized, *a.* non organizzato.

unorthodox, *a.* poco ortodosso, eterodosso.

unostentatious, *a. & ~ly, ad.* senza ostentazione.

unpack, *v.t.* sballare, disimballare, spacchettare, disfare. ~**ed,** *a.* sballato, aperto.

unpaid, *a. (bill, &c.)* non pagato, insoluto; *(capital, &c.)* non versato; *(carriage, &c.)* non affrancato; *(no salary)* gratuito.

unpalatable, *a.* sgradevole al gusto, poco saporito.

unparalleled, *a.* senza pari, incomparabile, impareggiabile.

unpardonable, *a.* imperdonabile.

unparliamentary, *a.* poco civile, rude, non parlamentare.

unpatriotic, *a.* poco patriottico, antipatriottico, senza patriottismo.

unpave, *v.t.* disselciare, smattonare. ~**d,** *a.* senza selciato.

unperceived, *a.* inosservato.

unphilosophical, *a.* poco filosofico.

unpin, *v.t.* togliere gli spilli a, staccare.

unplaced horse, cavallo non piazzato, non fra i tre primi alle corse.

unpleasant, *a.* sgradevole, spiacevole; doloroso; ingrato. ~**ness,** *n.* dispiacere, fastidio, *m.,* noia, molestia, *f.*

unpleasing, *a.* spiacente, spiacevole, ingrato.

unpoetic(al), *a.* non poetico, poco poetico.

unpolished, *a.* non ripulito; matto, non levigato; ruvido; rozzo, incolto.

unpolluted, *a.* incontaminato, puro.

unpopular, *a.* impopolare, ~**ity,** *n.* impopolarità, *f.*

unpractical, *a.* poco pratico.

unpractised, *a.* inesercitato; inesperto, novizio.

unprecedented, *a.* senza precedenti, inaudito.

unprejudiced, *a.* senza pregiudizi, senza prevenzione, imparziale.

unpremeditated, *a.* non premeditato, senza premeditazione.

unprepared, *a.* senza essere preparato; spontaneo, all'improvviso, alla sprovvista.

unprepossessing, *a.* poco avvenente.

unpretentious, *a.* senza pretensione; modesto, discreto.

unprincipled, *a.* senza principi morali.

unprintable, *a.* non stampabile; non adatto per la stampa.

unprocurable, *a.* che non si può procurare; introvabile.

unproductive, *a.* improduttivo; sterile.

unprofessional, *a.* contrario agli usi di una professione; indegno d'un professionista.

unprofitable, *a.* poco lucrativo; inutile; ingrato; senza profitto; **unprofitably,** *ad.* senza profitto; inutilmente.

unpromising, *a.* poco promettente, che promette poco.

unpronounceable, *a.* che non si sa pronunziare; impronunziabile.

unpropitious, *a.* poco propizio, sfavorevole.

unprotected, *a.* senza protezione, senza difesa.

unprovided, *a.* sprovvisto, sfornito (with = *di*).

unprovoked, *a.* senza provocazione, non provocato.

unpublished (*book, MS.*), *a.* inedito.

unpunctual, *a.* poco puntuale. ~**ity,** *n.* mancanza di puntualità, inesattezza, *f.*

unpunished, *a.* impunito.

unqualified, *a.* senza le qualità volute, senza i requisiti necessari; senza riserva, pieno, senza condizione.

unquenchable, *a.* inestinguibile; insaziabile.

unquestionable, *a.* incontestabile, indiscutibile, indubitabile.

unravel, *v.t.* districare, sfilacciare; snodare, sciogliere; sbrogliare, dipanare; disfare.

unread, *a.* non letto, senza essere letto; illetterato. ~**able,** *a.* (*writing, unsupportable book*), *a.* illeggibile.

unreal, *a.* irreale. ~**ity,** *n.* irrealtà, *f.*

unrealizable, *a.* irrealizzabile.

unreasonable, *a.* irragionevole; intrattabile. ~**ness,** *n.* irragionevolezza, *f.* **unreasoning,** *a.* irragionevole.

unrecognizable, *a.* irriconoscibile.

unredeemable, *a.* irredimibile, non riscattabile. **unredeemed,** *a.* (*stock*) non ammortizzato; (*pledge*) non disimpegnato.

unrefined, *a.* non raffinato; impuro, greggio; maleducato.

unrefuted, *a.* irrefutato.

unregistered, *a.* non registrato; (*Post*) non raccomandato; (*trade mark*) (marca) non depositata.

unrelenting, *a.* inesorabile.

unreliable, *a.* poco sicuro, incerto; sul quale non si può contare.

unremitting, *a.* incessante, continuo, senza sosta, senza tregua.

unremunerative, *a.* poco rimunerativo.

unrepealed, *a.* non abrogato, non revocato; in vigore.

unrepentant, *a.* impenitente.

unreservedly, *ad.* senza riserva; francamente.

unrest, *n.* agitazione; inquietudine, *f.*

unrestrained, *a.* senza freno, sfrenato, immoderato.

unrestricted, *a.* senza restrizioni, senza limitazione, assoluto.

unretentive (*memory*), *a.* fiacco, corto, che ritiene poco.

unrewarded, *a.* senza ricompensa.

unrighteous, *a.* ingiusto, iniquo; malvagio. ~**ness,** *n.* ingiustizia.

unripe, *a.* verde, acerbo, immaturo. ~**ness,** *n.* immaturità, *f.*

unrivalled, *a.* senza pari, senza rivale, impareggiabile.

unrivet, *v.t.* schiodare.

unroll, *v.t.* svolgere; spiegare.

unruffled, *a.* imperturbabile, imperturbato; composto, calmo, tranquillo.

unruled, *a.* senza righe.

unruly, *a.* sregolato, indisciplinato; turbolento.

unsaddle, *v.t.* dissellare; buttar dalla sella; (*pack animal*) levar il basto a.

unsafe, *a.* poco sicuro, malsicuro; rischioso.

unsalable, *a.* invendibile.

unsalaried, *a.* non stipendiato, senza stipendio.

unsalted, *a.* non salato.

unsanitary, *a.* malsano, insalubre.

unsatisfactorily, *ad.* in un modo poco soddisfacente. **unsatisfactory,**

a. poco soddisfacente, punto soddisfacente, non soddisfacente.

unsavoury, *a.* (*fig.*) stomachevole, schifoso.

unsay, *v.t. ir.* disdire.   *to leave unsaid,* tacere.

unscathed, *a.* incolume, indenne.

unscientific, *a.* non scientifico, poco scientifico.

unscrew, *v.t.* svitare.   *to come ∼ed,* svitarsi.

unscrupulous, *a.* poco scrupoloso, indelicato. ∼**ly,** *ad.* senza scrupoli.

unseal, *v.t.* dissigillare, levare i sigilli a.

unseasonable, *a.* fuori (di) stagione; intempestivo; mal a proposito, inopportuno.   **unseasonably,** *ad.* intempestivamente, inopportunamente.   **unseasoned** (*wood*), *a.* verde.

unseat, *v.t.* (*fig.*) invalidare; (*rider*) scavalcare, buttar giú dalla sella.

unseaworthy, *a.* innavigabile, non atto alla navigazione.

unsecured, *a.* senza garanzia, non assicurato, allo scoperto.

unseemly, *a.* disdicevole, indecoroso, sconvenevole.

unseen, *a.* inosservato; invisibile. ∼ (*translation*), versione a libro aperto, *f.*

unselfish, *a.* disinteressato, altruista, che pensa agli altri.

unserviceable, *a.* inservibile, fuori servizio.

unsettle, *v.t.* disordinare, sconvolgere, scompigliare, dissestare; (*pers.*) sgomentare, scomodare, disturbare, tenere in sospeso. ∼**d,** *a.* (*weather*) incostante, mutevole, variabile; (*question*) indeciso; (*bill*) non pagato, non regolato.

unshakable, *a.* incrollabile.

unshapely, *a.* deforme.

unshaven, *a.* non raso, non sbarbato.

unsheathe, *v.t.* sguainare.

unsheltered, *a.* senza riparo, esposto, non protetto.

unship, *v.t.* sbarcare; togliere dalla barca; (*oars*) disarmare.

unshoe (*horse*), *v.t. ir.* sferrare.

unshrinkable, *a.* (*cloth*) (panno) che non si ritira, non si restringe, irrestringibile.

unsightliness, *n.* bruttezza, *f.* **unsightly,** *a.* brutto, poco vistoso, sgradevole alla vista.

unsigned, *a.* non firmato, senza firma

unsinkable, *a.* insommergibile, non affondabile.

unskilful, *a.* poco abile, inesperto, malaccorto. ∼**ness,** *n.* malaccortezza, inettezza, goffaggine, *f.* **unskilled,** *a.* inesperto, poco pratico; non specializzato. ∼ *labour,* lavoro manuale, *m.*

unsla[c]ked lime, calce viva, *f.*

unsociable, *a.* insociabile, insocievole.

unsocial, *a.* antisociale.

unsold, *a.* invenduto; non venduto.

unsolicited, *a.* non richiesto, non sollecitato; spontaneo.

unsolved, *a.* insoluto.

unsophisticated, *a.* non sofisticato, semplice, ingenuo; non adulterato.

unsought, *a.* senza essere ricercato.

unsound, *a.* guasto, vizioso, difettoso; poco solido, non fermo; malsano; cattivo; cagionevole; agitato; erroneo. *of* ∼ *mind,* non sano di mente, malato di mente.

unsparing, *a.* prodigo, largo, liberale; spietato, inesorabile.

unspeakable, *a.* ineffabile, indicibile.

unspent, *a.* non speso, non sborsato; non esaurito.

unspillable (*ink bottle*), *a.* che non si può rovesciare.

unspotted, *a.* senza macchia, immacolato.

unstable, *a.* poco stabile, instabile; incostante, variabile.

unstained, *a.* non tinto; senza macchia.

unstamped, *a.* non stampato, non timbrato, senza francobollo; (*paper with no revenue stamps on*) carta non bollata, *c.* libera, *f.*; (*letter*) lettera non affrancata, *f.*

unsteadiness, *n.* instabilità; vacillazione, incostanza, irresoluzione; irregolarità, *f.* **unsteady,** *a.* instabile; incostante; malfermo; irregolare.

unstinted, *a.* abbondante, illimitato; a volontà; di pien cuore.

unstitch, *v.t.* scucire.

unstop, *v.t.* stasare.

unstressed (*Gram.*) *a.* atono, non accentato.

unstudied, *a.* naturale; spontaneo.

unsubdued, *a.* indomato, non sottomesso.

unsubstantial, *a.* poco sostanziale, immateriale; chimerico; leggero, poco solido, poco sostanzioso.

unsuccessful, *a.* non riuscito, vano;

(*pers.*) mancato. ~**ly**, *ad.* senza successo, vanamente.

unsuitable, *a.* disadatto, sconveniente, inopportuno; improprio. **unsuited**, *a.* mal adatto, inetto, male assortito, non fatto (per).

unsullied, *a.* immacolato, senza macchia.

unsupported, *a.* non appoggiato, senza sostegno; (*Mil.*) senza mezzi di rinforzo.

unsurpassed, *a.* (non) mai sorpassato.

unsuspected, *a.* non sospettato, insospettato. **unsuspecting** & **unsuspicious**, *a.* poco sospettoso, senza sospetto. **unsuspectingly**, *ad.* senza sospetto, senza diffidenza.

unsweetened, *a.* non addolcito; (*wine*) brusco.

unswerving, *a.* che non devia, che non si lascia deviare; fermo, incrollabile.

unsymmetrical, *a.* asimmetrico, non simmetrico.

untack (*Need.*) *v.t.* scucire, disfare l'imbastitura di.

untainted, *a.* non corrotto, non infettato; fresco, non guasto.

untamable, *a.* indomabile, che non si può addomesticare. **untamed**, *a.* indomato, non addomesticato.

untarnished, *a.* non appannato, non oscurato; senza macchia.

untaught, *a.* senza istruzione, incolto.

untenable, *a.* (*position*, &*c.*) non difensibile; (*assertion*, &*c.*) insostenibile.

untenanted, *a.* disabitato; non affittato, libero, vuoto.

unthinkable, *a.* inimmaginabile, impensabile. **unthinking**, *a.* irriflessivo, spensierato.

unthread, *v.t.* sfilare.

untidiness, *n.* disordine, *m.*, sciatteria, *f.* **untidy**, *a.* sciatto, disordinato, mal tenuto.

untie, *v.t.* sciogliere, slegare, disfare.

until, *pr.* fino a, sino a, prima di. ¶ *c.* finché (non), prima che, fino a quando. *not* ~, non prima che, senza prima, non prima di.

untimely, *a.* intempestivo; inopportuno; prematuro; (*hour*) inopportuno.

untiring, *a.* instancabile, infaticabile, indefesso.

untold, *a.* indicibile, innumerevole, senza numero. ~ *gold*, mucchi d'oro, monti d'oro, *m. pl.*

untouchable, *n.* paria, *m.* **untouched**,

a. intatto; senza toccarlo; insensibile, non commosso.

untoward, *a.* malcapitato, malaugurato, inconveniente, fastidioso; di cattivo augurio.

untrained, *a.* non esercitato, non istruito, inesperto; (*animal*) non ammaestrato.

untranslatable, *a.* intraducibile.

untravelled, *a.* (*country*) inesplorato; non attraversato; (*pers.*) che non ha mai viaggiato.

untried, *a.* non provato, non tentato, intentato; non processato.

untrimmed, *a.* senza guarnimento; non tosato; (*ship*) non stivato; (*Typ.*) intonso.

untrodden, *a.* non calpestato, non (mai) battuto, non frequentato.

untroubled, *a.* non turbato; calmo, tranquillo, placido.

untrue, *a.* falso; sleale; erroneo. **untruly**, *ad.* falsamente.

untrustworthy, *a.* indegno di fede, di fiducia.

untruth, *n.* menzogna, bugia, falsità, *f.* ~**ful**, *a.* menzognero, bugiardo.

untuck, *v.t.* scucire, disfare una piega.

untutored, *a.* senza istruzione, incolto; naturale, spontaneo.

untwist, *v.t.* storcere, strigare, sciogliere.

unused, *a.* non usato, non impiegato. ~ *to*, malpratico di, nuovo, poco abituato a. **unusual**, *a.* poco comune, insolito, inusitato, strano, raro. ~**ly**, *ad.* straordinariamente.

unutterable, *a.* indicibile, ineffabile.

unvarnished, *a.* non verniciato, senza vernice, (*fig.*) naturale, semplice.

unvarying, *a.* uniforme, invariabile.

unveil, *v.t.* svelare, scoprire; inaugurare.

unventilated, *a.* non ventilato, non aerato, senza ventilazione.

unversed in, poco versato in.

unwarily, *ad.* incautamente, senza precauzione, imprudentemente.

unwarlike, *a.* poco bellicoso, imbelle.

unwarrantable, *a.* ingiustificabile, inescusabile.

unwary, *a.* incauto, malaccorto, poco circospetto.

unwashed, *a.* non lavato, sporco, sudicio. *the great* ~, la plebaglia, *f.*

unwavering, *a.* fermo, deciso, incrollabile.

unweaned, *a.* non divezzato, non spoppato, non slattato.

unwearied, *a.* indefesso, instancabile, infaticabile.
unwelcome, *a.* malaccolto, sgradito.
unwell, *a.* indisposto, sofferente.
unwholesome, *a.* malsano; insalubre; nocivo.
unwieldy, *a.* poco maneggevole; pesante; poco comodo.
unwilling, *a.* poco disposto, mal disposto. ~**ly,** *ad.* malvolentieri, di malavoglia, con ripugnanza. ~**ness,** *n.* malavoglia, avversione, ripugnanza, *f.*
unwind, *v.t. ir.* dipanare, disfare, sgomitolare, sciogliere.
unwisdom, *n.* mancanza di saggezza, imprudenza, *f.* **unwise,** *a.* poco saggio, imprudente, mal accorto. ~**ly,** *ad.* imprudentemente, malaccortamente; a torto; senza giudizio.
unwittingly, *ad.* inconsciamente, inconsapevolmente, per inavvertenza.
unwonted, *a.* insolito.
unworkable, *a.* ineseguibile, impraticabile; non lavorabile; incoltivabile. **unworked,** *a.* non sfruttato, incoltivato. *in an unworkmanlike manner,* in un modo inesperto, alla ventura.
unworn, *a.* non usato; mai indossato; non logoro.
unworthiness, *n.* indegnità, mancanza di merito, *f.* **unworthy,** *a.* immeritevole, indegno.
unwounded, *a.* illeso, non ferito.
unwrap, *v.t.* sfasciare, disfare.
unwrinkled, *a.* senza rughe.
unwritten, *a.* non scritto. ~ *law,* legge tradizionale, *f.*; diritto consuetudinario, *m.*
unwrought, *a.* non lavorato; greggio, bruto.
unyielding, *a.* inflessibile, ostinato; duro, rigido.
unyoke, *v.t.* staccare, sciogliere dal giogo, togliere il giogo a.
up, *a.* ascendente, in salita. ~ *grade,* salita, *f.* ~ *stroke* (writing), filetto, *m.* ~ *train,* treno ascendente; treno in arrivo, *m.* ¶ *ad.* su, in su, in alto; in piedi, alzato; sorto; spirato; scaduto; scorso; trascorso; finito; in rivolta; *(prices)* salito, in rialzo, al rialzo; *(risen)* levato. ~ *& down,* in alto e in basso, su e giú. ~ *stairs,* in alto, in su. ~ *stream,* a monte; ~ *there,* lassú. ~ *to,* fino a, sino a; *(a)* uguale a, capace di. ~ *to date,* a giorno, aggiornato; *(att.)* modernissimo, alla moda, di moda. *so many holes* ~. *(Golf),* tante buche di

vantaggio. *higher* ~, fin su; *well up in* (subject), forte in, bene informato su, all'altezza di. ¶ *ups & downs,* vicende, *f.pl.,* oscillazioni, *f.pl.,* alti e bassi, *m.pl.*; ¶ *up!,* su! su in piedi! all'erta! levatevi!
upbraid, *v.t.* rimproverare, rimbrottare.
upheaval, *n. (Geol.)* sollevamento, *m.* *(fig.)* sconvolgimento, *m.,* confusione, convulsione, *f.*
uphill, *a.* montante, in salita; arduo, faticoso. ¶ *ad.* in salita, in su, all'insú. *to go* ~, salire.
uphold, *v.t. ir.* sostenere, mantenere, difendere. ~**er,** *n.* sostegno, appoggio, partigiano, *m.*
upholster, *v.t.* tappezzare, imbottire. ~**er,** *n.* tappezziere, *m.,* -a, *f.*
upkeep, *n.* mantenimento, *m.*; *(building, &c.)* manutenzione, *f.*
upland, *n.* altipiano, *m.*
uplift, *v.t.* alzare, sollevare; nobilitare, esaltare.
upon, *pr.* su, sopra; a; di; da; all'atto di; verso.
upper, *a.* superiore; alto; di sopra. ~ *case letters* (caps. *&* small caps), maiuscole e maiuscolette, *f.pl.* ~*circle* (Theat.), seconda galleria, *f.* the ~ *classes,* le classi piú elevate; le classi superiori, *f.pl.* ~*cut* (Box.) colpo montante, *m.* ~ *deck,* ponte di coperta, *m.*; *(bus)* imperiale, *m.* *U*~ *Egypt,* l'Alto Egitto, *m., the* ~ *hand (fig.),* il disopra, il vantaggio, *m.* ~ *register (Mus.)* gli acuti, *m.pl. the* ~ *ten,* il gran mondo, *m.* ~ *tooth,* dente superiore, *m.* ¶ *(shoe) n.* tomaio, *m. (pl.* -a). ~*most,* *a.* il piú alto, il piú elevato; *(fig.)* il piú forte, predominante.
upright, *a. & ad.* ritto, diritto; in piedi; eretto, verticale; *(fig.)* integro, onesto, retto. ~ *piano,* pianoforte verticale, *m.* ~**ness,** *n.* perpendicolarità; dirittura; integrità, *f.*
uprising, *n.* sollevamento, *m.*; rivolta, insurrezione, *f.*
uproar, *n.* baccano, tumulto, chiasso, strepito, schiamazzo, *m.*; cagnara, gazzarra, *f.* ~**ious,** *a.* chiassoso, tumultuoso, rumoroso.
uproot, *v.t.* sradicare, svellere, estirpare.
upset, *n.* sconvolgimento, rovesciamento, *m.*; scompiglio; trambusto, tramestio, *m.* ¶ *v.t.* rovesciare, sconvolgere, capovolgere; ribaltare; far ribaltare; agitare, sbalordire, dis-

turbare; ~ price, prezzo d'apertura, prezzo iniziale (sale).
upshot, n. risultato, esito, m., fine, f.
upside down, ad. sottosopra, sossopra, ritto rovescio, a catafascio.
upstart, n. villano rifatto, pretendente, nuovo pervenuto, nuovo ricco.
upstroke, n. (piston) corsa ascendente, salita (dello stantuffo), f.; (writing) filetto, m.
upward, a. ascendente, che sale, rivolto in su. ~[s], ad. in alto, verso l'alto, in su, all'insú. ~s of, piú di.
Ural (the), l'Urale, m. the ~ Mountains, gli Urali, m.pl.
uranium, n. uranio, m.
urban, a. urbano. **urbane**, a. cortese, gentile. ~ly, ad. con urbanità, cortesemente, gentilmente.
urchin, n. biricchino, monello, ragazzino, marmocchio, m. sea ~, echino, riccio di mare, m.
urethra, n. uretra, f.
urge, n. impulso, desiderio, istinto; m. ¶ v.t. spingere, incalzare; premere; sollecitare; esortare; addurre, allegare.
urgency, n. urgenza, f. **urgent**, a. urgente, incalzante, pressante. ~ly, ad. urgentemente, d'urgenza, con istanza.
uric, a. urico. **urinal**, n. orinatoio; vespasiano, m. (vessel) orinale, vaso da notte, m. **urinate**, v.i. orinare. **urine**, n. orina, f.
urn, n. urna, f. (tea, &c.) bricco; samovar, m.
us, pr. noi; ci; ce.
usage, n. uso, m., usanza, consuetudine, abitudine, f.; trattamento, m.
usance, n. usanza, f. **use**, n. uso; impiego; godimento, possesso, consumo, m.; utilità, f. valore, vantaggio, m. ~ & wont, usi e costumi, m.pl. to be of ~, servire. ¶ v.t. usare, impiegare, fare uso di; adoperare, consumare; utilizzare; trattare. ~ no hooks, non servirsi di uncinetti. ~d, p.a. usato, consunto; abituato, avvezzo; adoperato; rotto, consumato, logorato, smesso. ~ful, a. utile. ~fulness, n. utilità, f. ~less, a. inuti e; vano. ~ person, zero, m. ~ things, inutilità, f.pl. ~lessness, n. inutilità, f. **user**, n. chi usa (adopera, impiega, si serve di).
Ushant, n. Ushanti, m.
usher, n. usciere, m.; ripetitore, m.

~ in, far entrare, introdurre, annunziare; (fig.) inaugurare.
usual, a. solito, usuale, abituale, ordinario. as ~, come al solito, come d'uso. more than ~, piú dell'usato, piú del consueto.
usufruct, n. usufrutto, m.
usurer, n. usuraio; strozzino, m. **usurious**, a. da usuraio.
usurp, v.t. usurpare. ~ation, n. usurpazione, f. ~er, n. usurpatore, m., -trice, f.
usury, n. usura, f.
utensil, n. utensile, arnese, ordigno; vaso, m.
uterine, a. uterino. **uterus**, n. utero, m.
utilitarian, a. & n. utilitario, a. & m.
utility, n. utilità, f. **utilize**, v.t. utilizzare, servirsi di.
utmost, a. massimo, estremo, ultimo, sommo. one's (very) ~, tutto il (suo) possibile, l'impossibile, m. to the ~, ad oltranza, a tutt'oltranza.
utopia, n. utopia, f. **utopian**, a. utopistico. ¶ n. utopista, m.f.
utter, a. completo, intero, totale, assoluto; estremo, ultimo. ¶ v.t. pronunziare, proferire, dire; (cry) gettare, mandare fuori, cacciare, emettere; (money) passare, mettere in circolazione. **utterance**, n. articolazione, pronunzia; f.; modo di parlare; detto, m., parole, f.pl., discorso, m. ~most, a. estremo, ultimo, il piú lontano.
uvula, n. ugola, f.

V

vacancy, n. vacanza, f.; vuoto, m.
vacant, a. vacante, vuoto; libero, non occupato; distratto. **vacate**, v.t. (office) lasciare, dimettersi da, ritirarsi da; (premises) lasciar vuoto, sgomb[e]rare. **vacation**, n. vacanze, f.pl.; (Law) periodo feriale, m., vacanze dei tribunali, f.pl.
vaccinate, v.t. vaccinare. **vaccination**, n. vaccinazione, f. **vaccine**, n. vaccino, m.
vacillate, v.i. vacillare. **vacillation**, n. vacillazione; incostanza, f.
vacuity, n. vacuità, inanità, f. **vacuous**, a. vacuo, inane. **vacuum**, n. vuoto, m. ~ brake, freno a

depressione, *m.* ～ *cleaner*, aspira·polvere, *m.* ～ *flask*, termos, *m.*

vade-mecum, *n.* vade-mecum, libretto tascabile, *m.*

vagabond, *n. & a.* vagabondo, *a. & m.*

vagary, *n.* capriccio, ghiribizzo, *m.*, fantasia, *f.*

vagrancy, *n.* accattonaggio, vagabondaggio, *m.* **vagrant,** *n.* accattone, *m. & f.* ¶ *a.* vagabondo; ambulante.

vague, *a.* vago, impreciso. ～**ness,** *n.* vago, *m.* imprecisione, incertezza, *f.*

vain, *a.* vano, inutile; vanitoso. ～**glorious,** vanaglorioso. ～**glory,** *n.* vanagloria, *f.*

valance, *n.* pendaglio di letto, *m.*, balza, *f.*

vale, *n.* valle, vallata, *f.*

valedictory, *a.* d'addio, di commiato.

valence, ～**cy** (*Chem.*) *n.* valenza, *f.*

valence, *n.* tornaletto, *m.*

Valencia, *n.* Valenza, *f.*

valet, *n.* valletto, servitore, *m.* *v.t.* fare il valletto di; fare il servitore di.

Valetta, *n.* La Valletta, *f.*

valetudinarian, *a. & n.* valetudinario, *a. & m.*

valiant, *a.* valoroso, prode.

valid, *a.* valido; (*ticket*) valevole. ～**ate,** *v.t.* rendere valido, convalidare. ～**ity,** *n.* validità, *f.*

valise, *n.* valigia, *f.*

valley, *n.* valle, *f.*, vallata, *f.*, vallone, *m.*; (*of roof*) conversa, *f.*

valorous, *a.* valoroso, prode.

valour, *n.* coraggio, valore, *m.*, prodezza, bravura, *f.*

valuable, *a.* di [gran] valore, di prezzo; prezioso; costoso. ～**s,** *n.pl.* valori, oggetti di valore, *m.pl.*

valuation, *n.* valutazione, stima, *f.*, apprezzamento, *m.*; perizia, *f.*; estimo, *m.* ～ *list*, catasto, *m.*

value, *n.* valore, prezzo, *m.*, (*Com*) valuta, *f.*; importanza, utilità, *f.* ～ *parcel*, pacco-valori, *m.* ¶ *v.t.* valutare; apprezzare; stimare; far caso di.

valueless, *a.* senza valore.

valuer, *n.* [e]stimatore, apprezzatore (perito), *m.*

valve, *n.* valvola. ～ *set*, apparecchio a valvole, *m.*

vamp (*shoe*), *n.* tomaia, *f.* ¶ *v.t. & i.* improvvisare.

vampire, *n.* vampiro.

van, *n.* furgone, furgoncino; carro,

vagone; (*Rly.*) bagagliaio, *m.* ～ [*guard*], avanguardia, *f.*

vanadium, *n.* vanadio, *m.*

vandal, *a. & n.* vandalo, *a. & m.* ～**ism,** *n.* vandalismo, *m.*

vane, *n.* banderuola, *f.*, mostravento, *m.*; pala, *f.*

vanilla, *n.* vaniglia, *f.* ～ *ice*, gelato alla vaniglia, *m.*

vanish, *v.i.* svanire, sparire, scomparire; fuggire, dileguarsi, eclissarsi, volatilizzarsi. ～*ing point*, punto di sparizione, *m.*

vanity, *n.* vanità, *f.* ～ *case*, *n.* portacipria, *m.inv.*

vanner (*horse*), *n.* conduttore di carro, *m.*

vanquish, *v.t.* vincere. *the* ～*ed*, i vinti, *m.pl.*

vantage (*Ten.*), *n.* vantaggio, *m.*; ～ *ground*, posizione elevata, *f.*

vapid, *a.* insipido, insulso, scipito.

vaporize, *v.t.* vaporizzare. **vaporizer,** *n.* vaporizzatore, spruzzatore, *m.*

vaporous, ～**ry,** *a.* vaporoso.

vapour, *n.* vapore, *m.* ～ *bath*, bagno a vapore, *m.*

variable, *a.* variabile, mutevole, incostante. *at variance*, in disaccordo (con). **variant,** *n.* variante, *f.* **variation,** *n.* variazione, *f.*; cambiamento, *m.*; modifica, *f.*

varicose vein, vena varicosa, *f.*

variegate, *v.t.* variare; screziare, pichiettare. **varieties** (*Theat.*), *n.pl.* spettacoli di varietà, *m.pl.*

variety, *n.* varietà, *f.* ～ *actress*, cantante (in un caffè concerto), *f.* ～ *theatre*, teatro di varietà; caffè concerto, *m.*

various, *a.* vario; diverso; cangiante, variegato; certo, parecchio.

varlet (*Hist.*), *n.* donzello, paggio, *m.*

varnish, *n.* vernice, *f.* ¶ *v.t.* [in]verniciare. ～**ing,** *n.* verniciatura, *f.* ～ *day*, *n.* la vernice, *f.*

vary, *v.t. & i.* variare; diversificare; modificare; essere diverso.

vascular, *a.* vascolare.

vase, *n.* vaso, *m.*; (*Chinese, etc.*) vaso di porcellana, &*c.*

vaseline (*proprietary term*), *n.* vasellina, *f.*

vassal (*Hist*), *n.* vassallo, *m.*

vast, *a.* immenso, enorme. ～**ly,** *ad.* grandemente, enormemente, ～**ness,** *n.* immensità, *f.*

vat, *n.* tino, *m.* ¶ *v.t.* mettere nel tino.

Vaucluse, *n.* Valchiusa, *f.*

vaudeville, *n.* operetta, farsa, *f.*

vault, *n.* volta, *f.*; sotterraneo, *m.*, cantina; tomba, *f.*, (*leap*) salto, *m.* *turrel* ~ (*Arch.*) volta a botte. *cross* ~ (or *vaulting*), v. a crociera. *fan[tail]* ~ (or *vaulting*), v. a ventaglio. ¶ *v.t.* coprire con una volta, costruire a volta; (*v.i.*) saltare, balzare; volteggiare. *vaulting horse,* *n.* cavallo di legno per ginnastica, *m.*

vaunt, *n.* vanto. ¶ *v.t.* vantarsi di, (*v.i.*) vantarsi.

veal, *n.* vitello, *m.* carne di vitello, *f.* ~ *cutlet,* costoletta di vitello, *f.*

vector, *n.* vettore, *m.*

veer, *v.i.* (*wind*) cambiare direzione; (*opinion*) mutare di opinione; (*ship*) virare di bordo. ~ *out,* filare, allentare. ~*ing* (*opinion*) *n.* cambiamento di opinione, *m.*

vegetable, *n.* legume, *m.* ~*s,* *n.pl.* legumi, ortaggi, *m.pl.*, verdura, *f.* ¶ *a.* vegetale. ~ *dish,* *n.* piatto per servire i legumi, *m.* ~ *marrow,* zucchino, *m.* ~ *soup,* minestra di verdura, *f.* **vegetarian,** *a. & n.* vegetariano, *a. & m.* **vegetarianism,** vegetarianismo, regime vegetariano, *m.* **vegetate,** *v.i.* vegetare; **vegetation,** *n.* vegetazione, *f.*

vehemence, *n.* veemenza, *f.* **vehement,** *a.* veemente.

vehicle, *n.* (*carriage*) veicolo, *m.*, vettura, *f.* (*medium*) mezzo, tramite, *m.* *vehicular traffic,* circolazione dei veicoli, *f.*

veil, *n.* velo, *m.*, veletta, *f.*; (*fig.*) velo, *m.*, cortina, *f.*; pretesto, *m.* ¶ *v.t.* velare; (*fig.*) celare, nascondere.

vein, *n.* vena, *f.*; (*leaf*) nervatura, *f.* ¶ *v.t.* venare.

vellum, *n.* cartapecora, pergamena fine, *f.*

velocipede, *n.* velocipede, *m.*

velocity, *n.* velocità, *f.*

velours, *n.* feltro floscio, feltro velluto, *m.*

velum (*Anat.*), *n.* velo, *m.*

velvet, *n.* velluto, *m.* ~ *pile* (*carpet*), *n.* tappeto con pelo lungo e soffice, *m.* **velveteen,** *n.* velluto di cotone, *m.* **velvet[y],** *a.* di velluto, vellutato.

venal, *a.* venale. **venality,** *n.* venalità, *f.*

vender, *n.* mercante, negoziante, *m.*

vendor, *n.* venditore, *m.*, venditrice, *f.*; (*Law*) apportatore. ~ *company,* *n.* società apportatrice, *f.* ~'s *assets,* *n.* valori d'apporto, *m.pl.*

veneer & ~*ing,* *n.* impiallacciatura;

(*fig.*) vernice, *f.* ¶ *v.t.* impiallacciare; (*fig.*) verniciare.

venerable, *a.* venerabile. **venerate,** *v.t.* venerare. **veneration,** *n.* venerazione.

venereal, *a.* venereo.

Venetia, *n.* la Venezia, *f.*, il Veneto, *m.*

Venetian, *a.* veneziano, di Venezia. ~ *blind,* *n.* gelosia, persiana, *f.*; ¶ *n.* veneziano, *m.*, veneziana, *f.*

vengeance, *n.* vendetta, *f.* **vengeful,** *a.* vendicativo.

venial, *a.* veniale.

Venice, *n.* Venezia, *f.*

venison, *n.* carne di cervo o capriolo, cacciagione, *f.*

venom, *n.* veleno, *m.* ~*ous,* *a.* velenoso; (*fig.*) malevolo, maldicente.

vent, *n.* (*Mech., Phys.*) feritoia, *f.*, forellino, foro, *m.*; spiraglio; (*fig.*), passaggio; libero corso, sfogo, sbocco, *m.* ~ *hole* (*cask*), buco (di botte), *m.* ~ *peg,* zipolo (di botte), *m.* ¶ *v.t.* dare sfogo a, sfogare; palesare; emettere; esalare.

ventilate, *v.t.* ventilare; (*fig.*) far conoscere, pubblicare. *well-*~*d,* arioso. **ventilation,** *n.* ventilazione, *f.* **ventilator,** *n.* ventilatore, *m.*; (*ship*) manica a vento, *f.*

ventral, *a.* ventrale.

ventricle, *n.* ventricolo, *m.*

ventriloquism, ~*quy,* *n.* ventriloquio, *m.* **ventriloquist,** *n.* ventriloquo, *m.*, -a, *f.*

venture, *n.* ventura; impresa; speculazione, *f.*; azzardo, rischio; caso, *m.* ¶ *v.t.* avventurare, arrischiare, azzardare. ~ *to,* osare; permettersi (di). ~*some,* *a.* ardito; avventuroso; azzardoso; intraprendente.

Venus, *n.* Venere, *f.*

veracious, *a.* verace, veridico.

veracity, *n.* veracità, *f.*

veranda[h], *n.* veranda, *f.*

verb, *n.* verbo, *m.* **verbal,** *a.* verbale; orale. ~*ly,* *ad.* verbalmente. **verbatim,** *ad. & a.* parola per parola. **verbiage,** *n.* parole inutili, *f.pl.*, sproloquio, *m.*, verbosità, *f.* **verbose,** *a.* verboso. **verbosity,** *n.* verbosità, *f.*

verdant, *a.* verdeggiante.

verdict, *n.* verdetto, *m.*

verdigris, *n.* verderame, *m.*

verdure, *n.* verzura, *f.*

verge, *n.* orlo, bordo, *m.*; (*road*) orlo, limite, *m.*; estremità, bordura, *f.*; (*fig.*) orlo, procinto, *m.*; (*rod*) verga, *f.* ¶ ~ *on,* essere vicino a; confinare con; (*ruin*) tendere verso.

verger, *n.* bidello; sagrestano; mazziere, *m.*

verification, *m.* verifica, *f.*, controllo, *m.* **verify,** *v.t.* verificare, confermare, avverare, controllare.

verisimilitude, *n.* verosimiglianza, *f.*

veritable, *a.* vero; reale, genuino; vero e proprio.

verity, *n.* verità, *f.*

vermicelli, *n.* vermicelli, *m.pl.*, spaghettini, *m.pl.*

vermilion, *n.* cinabro; vermiglione, *m.* ¶ *a.* vermiglio.

vermin, *n.* animali nocivi, *m.pl.* **verminous,** *a.* verminoso.

verm[o]uth, *n.* vermut, *m.*

vernacular, *a.* volgare, vernacolo. ¶ *n.* lingua volgare, *f.*, vernacolo, *m.*

vernal, *a.* primaverile; (*equinox*) (equinozio) di primavera.

vernier, *n.* verniero, *m.*

Verona, *n.* Verona, *f.*

veronica, *n.* veronica, *f.*

Versailles, *n.* Versaglia, *f.*

versatile, *a.* versatile. **versatility,** *n.* versatilità, *f.*

verse, *n.* verso, *m.* (also a line of poetry), strofa *or* strofetta, stanza, *f.*; versi, *m.pl.*; versetto, *m.* **versed in,** versato in, pratico di, valente in.

versicle (*Lit.*) *n.* versetto, *m.* **versifier,** *n.* versificatore, *m.*, -trice, *f.*

versify, *v.t.* versificare, ridurre in versi. **version,** *n.* versione, traduzione, *f.* **verso,** *n.* verso, *m.*

versus, *pr.* contro.

vertebra, *n.* vertebra, *f.* **vertebral,** *a.* vertebrale. **vertebrata,** *n.pl.* vertebrati, *m.pl.* **vertebrate,** *a.* & *n.* vertebrato *a.* & *m.*

vertex, *n.* vertice, *m.*, cima, *f.*, apice, *m.*, sommità, *f.*, zenit, *m.* **vertical,** *a.* verticale, perpendicolare. ¶ *n.* verticale, *f.* ~**ity,** verticalità, *f.* ~**ly,** *ad.* verticalmente.

vertiginous, *a.* vertiginoso. **vertigo,** *n.* vertigine, *f.*, capogiro, *m.*

vervain, *n.* verbena, *f.*

verve, *n.* brio, entusiasmo; vigore, *m.*

very, *a.* stesso; solo; vero; esatto; puro. ¶ *ad.* assai, molto; bene; proprio; tutto; persino; *abs. sup. in* -issimo. ~ *much,* assai, molto.

vesicle, *n.* vescichetta, *f.*

vespers, *n.pl.* vespri, *m.pl.*

vessel, *n.* vaso, recipiente, *m.*; (*blood, &c.*) vaso, *m.*; (*ship*) vascello, bastimento, *m.*, nave, *f.*

vest, *n.* (*man's*) panciotto, *m.*, sottoveste, *f.*; (*woman's*) camiciola, *f.*; (*baby's*) camicina, *f.* ~ *pocket*

camera, macchina fotografica tascabile, *f.* ¶ *v.t.* investire; affidare; conferire, porre in possesso (di); ~*ed rights,* diritti acquisiti, *m.pl.*

vesta, *n.* cerino, *m.*

vestal [**virgin**], *n.* vestale, *f.*

vestibule, *n.* vestibolo, *m.*

vestige, *n.* vestigio, *m.*, traccia, *f.*

vestment, *n.* paramento sacerdotale; abito di prete, *m.*

vestry, *n.* sagrestia, *f.*; (*council*) fabbriceria, *f.*

Vesuvian, *a.* vesuviano. **Vesuvius,** *n.* Vesuvio, *m.*

vetch, *n.* cicerchia, *f.*; (*tare*) veccia, *f.*

veteran, *n.* veterano, reduce, *m.* ¶ *a.* veterano; anziano; vecchio.

veterinary, *a.* veterinario. ~ (*surgeon*) veterinario, *m.*

veto, *n.* veto, *m.* ¶ *v.t.* mettere il veto a.

vex, *v.t.* irritare, contrariare; annoiare. ~**ation,** *n.* irritazione, *f.*, dispiacere, fastidio, *m.*, noia, molestia, *f.* **vexatious,** *a.* molesto, fastidioso, noioso, irritante. **vexed** (*question*), *p.a.* (argomento) controverso, dibattuto a lungo.

via, *pr.* per la via di, via.

viability, *n.* vitalità; viabilità, *f.* **viable,** *a.* vitale; viabile.

viaduct, *n.* viadotto, *m.*

vial, *n.* fiala, boccetta, *f.*

viand, *n.* cibo, piatto, *m.* ~**s,** *n.pl.*, vivande, *f.pl.*, commestibili, *m.pl.*

vibrate, *v.i.* (*Phys. & fig.*) vibrare; risonare.; (*machinery, car, &c.*) oscillare. **vibration,** *n.* (*Phys.*) vibrazione, *f.*; (*Mach., &c.*) oscillazione, *f.*

vicar, *n.* vicario; pievano, parroco, *m.* ~**age,** *n.* presbiterio, *m.*, casa parrocchiale, *f.* ~**ship,** *n.* vicariato, *m.*

vice, *n.* (*depravity*), vizio, *m.*; (*tool*) morsa, *f.*

vice-, (*prefix*), vice-, ~ *chairman,* ~ *presidente,* vice-presidente, *m.* ~ *consul,* vice-console, *m.*, ~ *principal* (college), vice-rettore, *m.* ~*reine,* vice-regina, *f.* ~*roy,* viceré, *m.*

Vicenza, *n.* Vicenza, *f.*

vice versa, *ad.* viceversa, reciprocamente.

vicinity, *n.* vicinanza, prossimità, *f.*; pressi, dintorni, *m.pl.*

vicious, *a.* vizioso; cattivo; corrotto; (*style, &c.*) scorretto. ~ *circle,* circolo vizioso, *m.* ~**ness,** *n.* viziosità, corruttéla, depravazione, *f.*

vicissitude, *n.* (*often pl.*) vicenda, vicissitudine; traversia, *f.*
victim, *n.* vittima, *f.* ~ize, *v.t.* fare (una) vittima di.
victor, *n.* vincitore *m.* victoria (*carriage*), *n.* vittoria, *f.* victorious, *a.* vittorioso. victory, *n.* vittoria, *f.*
victual, *v.t.* vettovagliare, rifornire di viveri, approvvigionare. ~s, *n.pl.* viveri, *m.pl.*, vettovaglie, *f.pl.*
vicugna, ~uña, *n.* vigogna, *f.*
vide, *v. imperative,* vedi, vedere.
vie, *v.i.* gareggiare; rivaleggiare.
Vienna, *n.* Vienna, *f.* Viennese, *a.* viennese. ¶ *n.* viennese, *m.f.*
Vietnam, *n.* il Vietnam, *m.* Vietnamese, *a. & n.* vietnamese, *a. & m.*
view, *n.* veduta, vista, *f.*, prospetto, *m.*, prospettiva, *f.*, colpo d'occhio, quadro, paesaggio; aspetto, scopo, *m.*; mira, intenzione; idea, opinione, *f.*, parere, *m. to have in* ~, avere in vista, mirare a, aspirare a. ~ *finder,* mirino, *m.* ¶ *v.t.* guardare, riguardare; contemplare; considerare.
vigil, *n.* veglia, *f.*; (*Eccl.*) vigilia, *f.* ~ance, *n.* vigilanza, *f.* ~ant, *a.* vigilante. ~antly, *ad.* con vigilanza.
vignette, *n.* vignetta, *f.* ¶ *v.t.* fare una vignetta di, digradare. vignetter, *n.* vignettista, *m.f.*
vigorous, *a.* vigoroso. vigour, *n.* vigore, *m.*
vile, *a.* vile, abbietto, basso. ~ness, *n.* viltà, bassezza, *f.* vilify, *v.t.* diffamare, denigrare, calunniare.
villa, *n.* casino, villino, *m.*, casetta, villa suburbana, *f.* village, *n.* villaggio, paese *m.*, borgata, *f.*; (*att.*) di villaggio. villager, *n.* abitante di villaggio; (*Lit.*) villico, *m.*
villain, *n.* mascalzone, furfante, ribaldo, briccone, mariuolo, birbante, scellerato; (*Hist.*) villano, *m.* ~ous, *a.* scellerato, infame, vile, *m.* ~y, *n.* scelleratezza, infamia, viltà, *f.* villein, *n.*, villano, *m.*
vindicate, *v.t.* giustificare; rivendicare. vindication, *n.*, giustificazione; rivendicazione, *f.*
vindictive, *a.* vendicativo.
vine, *n.* vite, *f.* ~ *shoot,* pampano, tralcio, sarmento, *m.* vinegar, *n.* aceto, *m.* ~ *works,* fabbrica d'aceto, *f.* ¶ *v.t.* condire con aceto. vinery, *n.* serra da viti, *f.*
vineyard, *n.* vigna, *f.*, vigneto, *m.*
vinosity, *n.* vinosità, *f.* vinous, *a.* vinoso. vintage, *n.* (*growth*) raccolto, *m.*, vini, *m.pl.*, vendemmia,

f.; (*season*) vendemmia, *f.*; (*crop*) anno, *m.*, annata, *f.* ~ *wine,* vino con data, *m.* ~ *year,* annata di buon raccolto, *f.* vintager, *n.* vendemmiatore, *m.*, -trice, *f.*
viola, *n.* (*Mus.*) viola; (*Bot.*) viola, *f.*
violaceae, *n.pl.* violacee, *f.pl.* violaceous, *a.* violaceo.
violate, *v.t.* violare; contravvenire a; venire meno a; trasgredire; infrangere. violation, *n.* violazione, *f.*; (*rape*) violenza carnale, *f.* violator, *n.* violatore, *m.*, -trice, *f.* violence, *n.* violenza, *f. do* ~ *to,* violentare; fare violenza a. violent, *a.* violento.
violet, *n.* (*Bot.*) violetta, (viola) mammola, *f.*; (*colour*) colore [di] viola mammola, *m.* ¶ *a.* violetto.
violin, *n.* violino, *m.* ~ist, *n.* violinista, *m.f.* violoncellist, *n.* violoncellista, *m.f.* violoncello, *n.* violoncello, *m.*
viper, *n.* vipera, *f.*
virago, *n.* virago, donnaccia, megera, *f.*
Virgil, *n.* Virgilio, *m.*
virgin, *n.* vergine, *f.* ¶ *a.* vergine, di vergine. ~al, *a.* verginale. Virginia, (*Geog.*), *n.* la Virginia, *f.* ~ *creeper,* vite del Canadà, *f.* ~ (*tobacco*) tabacco Virginia, *m.* virginity, *n.* verginità, *f.*
virile, *a.* virile, maschio, forte. virility, *n.* virilità, *f.*
virtual, *a.* virtuale. virtue, *n.* virtù, *f.* virtuosity, *n.* virtuosità, *f.* virtuoso, *n.* amatore, virtuoso, *m.* virtuous, *a.* virtuoso, buono, casto, onesto.
virulence, *n.* virulenza, *f.* virulent, *a.* virulento. virus, *n.* virus, *m.inv.*
visa, *n.* visto, *m.*; vidimazione, *f.* ¶ *v.t.* vistare, vidimare.
visage, *n.* viso, volto, *m.*, cera, faccia, figura, *f.*; aspetto, *m.*
viscera, *n.pl.* viscere, *f.pl.*; (*Zool., Med.*) visceri, *m.pl.*
viscid, *a.* viscido. viscous, *a.* viscoso. viscose, *n.* viscosa, *f.* viscosity, *n.* viscosità, *f.*
viscount, *n.* visconte, *m.* ~ess, *n.* viscontessa, *f.*
visibility, *n.* visibilità, *f.* visible, *a.* visibile. visibly, *ad.* visibilmente.
vision, *n.* visione; apparizione; (*faculty of sight*) vista, *f.* ~ary, *a.* visionario. ¶ *n.* visionario, *m.*, -a, *f.*
visit, *n.* visita, *f.* ¶ *v.t.* passare da; visitare, far visita a; andare a vedere; (*Cust.*) fare la visita dei bagagli. ~ation, *n.* visita, ispezione, *f*

(*Eccl.*) visitazione, *f.*   ~*ing card,* ɔiglietto da visita, *m.*   ~**or,** *n.* ʋisitatore, *m.,* -trice, *f.*; ospite, *m.f.*; turista, *m.f. district* ~, visitatrice, *f.* ~*s' tax,* tassa di soggiorno, *f.*
visor, *n.* visiera, *f.*
vista, *n.* vista, prospettiva, *f.*
Vistula (the), la Vistola, *f.*
visual, *a.* visuale, visivo.
vital, *a.* vitale; vivo; (*fig.*) essenziale, importante.   ~**ity,** *n.* vitalità, *f.* ~**ize,** *v.t.* dar vita a; vivificare. ~**s,** *n.pl.* organi vitali, *m.pl.*
vitamin, *n.* vitamina, *f.*
vitiate, *v.t.* viziare, alterare, corrompere, guastare; **vitiation,** *n.* corruzione, alterazione, *f.*, guasto, *m.*
viticultural, *a.* viticolo. **viticultur-**[al]**ist,** *n.* viticultore, *m.*   **viticulture,** *n.* viticultura, *f.*
vitreous, *a.* vitreo; (*humour*) (umore) vitreo, *m.* **vitrify,** *v.t.* vetrificare.
vitriol, *n.* vetriolo, *m.*   ~**ic,** *a.* vetriolico.
vituperate, *v.t.* vituperare; ingiuriare. **vituperation,** *n.* vituperazione, *f.*; ingiurie, *f.pl.*
vivacious, *a.* vivace, vispo. *to be* ~, essere vivace.   ~**ly,** *ad.* con vivacità, vivacemente. **viva voce,** *ad.* a (*or* di) viva voce; ¶ *a.* orale. ¶ *n.* esame orale, *m.* **vivid,** *a.* vivo, vivente, vivace. **vividness,** *n.* animazione, vivacità, *f.* **vivify,** *v.t.* vivificare. **viviparous,** *a.* viviparo. **vivisection,** *n.* vivisezione, *f.*
vixen, *n.* volpe (femmina), *f.*; (*woman*) megera, donnaccia, Santippe, *f.*
viz., *ad. abb.* cioè, vale a dire.
vizi[e]**r,** *n.* visir, visire, *m.*
vocable, *n.* parola, voce, *f.* **vocabulary,** *n.* vocabolario, *m.* **vocal,** *a.* vocale.   ~**ist,** *n.* cantante, *m.f.,* cantatore, *m.,* -trice, *f.* ~**ize,** *v.t.* vocalizzare. **vocation,** *n.* vocazione, *f.* **vocative [case],** *n.* (caso) vocativo, *m.*
vociferate, *v.i.* vociferare, vociare. **vociferous,** *a.* clamoroso, rumoroso, strepitoso.   ~**ly,** *ad.* rumorosamente, chiassosamente, strepitosamente.
vogue, *n.* voga, moda, *f.*
voice, *n.* voce, *f.* ¶ *v.t.* esprimere, dar voce a.
void, *a.* vuoto, vano, vacuo; nullo, invalido. ¶ *n.* vuoto, *m.*; lacuna, *f.* ¶ *v.t.* vuotare, espellere, scaricare; annullare, liberare.
voile (*textile*), *n.* velo, *m.*
volatile, *a.* volatile. **volatilize,** *t.t.* volatilizzare.

volcanic, *a.* vulcanico. **volcano,** *n.* vulcano, *m.*
vole (*Zool.*), *n.* campagnolo, topo d'acqua, *m.*
volition, *n.* volizione, *f.*
volley, *n.* (*Mil.*) scarica, raffica; (*Ten.*) volata, *f.*; (*fig.*) carico, diluvio, torrente, *m.*, salva, grandinata, *f.* ~ *firing,* fuoco collettivo, *m.* ¶ (*Ten.*) *v.t.* colpire la palla in piena volata (prima dello sbalzo) (*abs.*) prendere la battuta a volo.
volplane, *n.* (*Aero.*) volo planato, *m.* ¶ *v.i.* fare un volo planato, planare.
volt, *n.* volta, *m.inv.* ~**age,** *n.* voltaggio, *m.* **voltaic,** *a.* voltaico. **voltmeter,** *n.* voltametro, *m.*
volubility, *n.* fluidità; loquacità, *f.* **voluble,** *a.* fluente, loquace.
volume, *n.* volume, *m.*, massa, mole, quantità, *f.*; (*book*) tomo, volume, *m.*; (*of smoke, &c.*) turbine, nuvolo, *m.*
voluminous, *a.* voluminoso; copioso, diffuso.
voluntary, *a.* volontario. ¶ (*organ*), *n.* (*before service*) preludio, *m.*; (*during*) interludio, *m.*; (*after*) uscita, *f.*; (*between credo & sanctus*) offertorio, *m.* **volunteer,** *n.* (*Mil.*) volontario, *m.*; (*for task*) uomo di buona volontà, *m.* ~ *corps,* corpo di volontari, *m.*
voluptuary, *n.* epicureo; libertino, *m.*
voluptuous, *a.* voluttuoso. ~**ness,** *n.* voluttà, sensualità, lussuria, *f.*
volute, *n.* voluta, *f.*
vomit, *n.* vomito, *m.* ¶ *v.t. & i.* vomitare.
voracious, *a.* vorace. ~**ly,** *ad.* voracemente. ~**ness, voracity,** *n.* voracità, *f.*
vortex, *n.* vortice; turbine, gorgo, *m.*
Vosges (the), *n.pl.* i Vosgi, *m.pl.*
votary, *n.* devoto, *m.,* -a, *f.,* adoratore, *m.,* -trice, *f.*; settario, *m.,* -a, *f.,* seguace, *m.f.* **vote,** *n.* voto; scrutinio, suffragio, *m.* ~*s for women,* suffragio femminile, *m.* ¶ *v.t. & i.* votare; andare ai voti. ~ *by a show of hands,* votare per alzata e seduta. **voter,** *n.* votante, *m.f.*, elettore, *m.,* -trice, *f.* **voting,** *n.* votazione, *f.* ~ *paper,* scheda di votazione, *f.*, bollettino di votazione, *m.* **votive,** *a.* votivo.
vouch, *v.t.* attestare; verificare. ~ *for,* rispondere di, garantire (di, per), esser mallevadore di. ~**er,** *n.* documento giustificativo, *m.*, pezza di appoggio; ricevuta, quietanza, *f.*; bono, scontrino, polizzino, *m.* ~ *copy,* (*Typ.*) giustificativo, *m.* ~-

safe, *v.t.* accordare; degnarsi di; accondiscendere, concedere.
voussoir, *n.* mattone a cuneo, *m.*
vow, *n.* voto, *m.* ¶ *v.t.* giurare; (*v.i.*) fare un voto.
vowel, *n.* vocale, *f.*
voyage, *n.* viaggio (per mare), *m.* ¶ *v.i.* viaggiare.
vulcanite, *n.* gomma vulcanizzata, *f.*
vulcanize, *v.t.* vulcanizzare.
vulgar, *a.* volgare, plebeo, popolaresco; comune, triviale; basso; meschino; (*fraction*) ordinario, proprio. *the* ~ [*herd*], il volgo. ~**ism,** *n.* espressione del volgo, trivialità, *f.* ~**ity,** *n.* volgarità, trivialità, *f.* ~**ize,** *v.t.* render popolare; rendere banale. *the Vulgate,* la Volgata, *f.*
vulnerable, *a.* vulnerabile.
vulture, *n.* avvoltoio, *m.*

W

wad, *n.* borra, *f.*, turacciolo, cuscinetto, *m.*; (*gun*) stoppaccio, *m.*; (*surgery*) piumacciolo, *m.* **wadding,** *n.* ovatta, *f.*, batuffolo, *m.*, bambagia, *f.*; (*action*) imbottitura, *f.*
waddle, *n.* dondolamento, *m.* ¶ *v.i.* camminare dondolandosi (come l'anitra), barcollare.
wade, *v.i.* guadare; (*in the sea*) sguazzare. ~ *through* (ford), passare a guado. ~ *through a book,* leggere tutto un libro lungo e noioso; farsi strada con difficoltà.
wader, *n.* (*bird*) trampoliere, *m.*; (*pl.*) stivaloni impermeabili per la pesca, *m.pl.*
wafer, *n.* (*flat biscuit*) brigidino, *m.*; (*cornet biscuit*) cialdone, *m.*; (*signet*) ostia per sigillar, *f.*; (*Eccl.*) ostia, *f.*
waffle, *n.* cialda, *f.* ~ *irons,* ferro da cialde, *m.*
waft, *n.* soffio, *m.* ¶ *v.t.* portare (in aria), spandere, diffondere.
wag, *n.* uomo faceto, capo ameno, celione, burlone, *m.* ¶ *v.t.* (*tail*) muovere, agitare (la coda), scodinzolare; (*head*) scuotere, tentennare, scrollare.
wage, *n. oft. pl.* salario, stipendio, *m.*, paga, *f.* ~ *earner,* salariato, *m.*, -a, *f.* *to pay a* ~ *to,* salariare, stipendiare. *to* ~ *war,* muovere guerra, guerreggiare.
wager, *n.* scommessa, *f.* ¶ *v.t.* scommettere.

waggish, *a.* faceto, giocoso, scherzevole.
waggle, *v.t.* & *i.* tentennare, dimenare, dimenarsi.
wag[g]on, *n.* carro, barroccio, furgone, *m.*; (*Rly.*) vagone, *m.* ~ *load,* carrettata, *f.* ~**er,** *n.* carraio, carrettiere, *m.* ~**ette,** *m.* carrozzetta, *f.*
wagtail, *n.* cutrettola, batticoda, *f.*
waif, *n.* fanciullo abbandonato, *m.* *waifs* & *strays,* relitti, rifiuti, oggetti smarriti, *m.pl.*
wail, *n.* gemito, lamento, *m.* ¶ *v.i.* gemere, lamentarsi; (*of baby*) vagire, mandar vagiti.
wain, *n.* carro, *m.*
wainscot, *n.* intavolato, rivestimento, zoccolo (di legno), *m.* ¶ *v.t.* rivestire, intavolare.
waist, *n.* vita, *f.*, busto, *m.*, cintola, *f.* ~**band,** cintura; fascia dei calzoni, *f.* ~**coat,** panciotto, corpetto, *m.* ~ *lock* (*Wrestling*), cintura, *f.* ~ *measurement,* misura della cintola, *f.*
wait, *n.* attesa, *f.*, indugio; agguato, *m.* *to lie in* ~, stare in agguato, imboscarsi, appostarsi. ¶ *v.t.* & *i.* aspettare, attendere; rimanere, indugiare. ~-&-*see,* *a.* di attesa. ~ [*up*]*on,* servire; andare a vedere' presentarsi da. **waiter,** *n.* cameriere, *m.* ~! cameriere! **waiting,** *n.* attesa, *f.* ~ *maid* (*Theat.*), domestica, *f.* ~ *room,* anticamera, *f.*; (*Rly.*, &*c.*) sala d'aspetto, *f.* **waitress,** *n.* cameriera, *f.* ~! cameriera!
waive, *v.t.* rinunziare a, non insistere su, abbandonare.
wake, *n.* scia, *f.*; (*fig.*) orma, traccia, *f.*; (*Irish*) veglia, *f.* *follow in the* ~ *of,* (*Naut.* & *fig.*) seguire nella scia di, sulle orme di, sulle tracce di. ¶ *v.t. ir.* & **waken,** *v.t.* destare, svegliare, risvegliare; (*v.i.*) destarsi, svegliarsi. ~**ful,** *a.* sveglio, insonne; vigilante. ~**fulness,** *n.* vigile, insonnia, *f.*
Wales, *n.* (il) Galles, il paese di G., *m.*
walk, *n.* camminata, passeggiata, *f.*; passeggio, passo, *m.*; andatura, *f.*, cammino, sentiero, viale, *m.* *to go for a* ~, andare a spasso. ~ *of life,* carriera, professione, *f.* ~ *over* (*Sport*), vincita per mancanza di un concorrente; (*fig.*) facile vittoria, *f.* ~ [*s*] *clerk* (bank), riscotitore, *m.* ¶ *v.i.* camminare, andare a piedi, passeggiare, andare al passo. ~ *about,* passeggiare. ~ *in,* entrare. ~ *off,* andarsene, allontanarsi,

svignarsela. ~ *out*, uscire. **walker,**
n. camminatore, *m.*, -trice, *f.*;
pedone, *m.*, passeggiatore, *m.*, -trice,
f. ~ *on*, figurante, *m.*, comparsa, *f.*
walkie-talkie, *n.* (*pop.*) radiotele-
fono da passeggio, *m.* **walking,** *n.*
marcia, *f.*; passeggio, *m.* ¶ *p.a. or att.*
ambulante; (*dress*) da passeggio;
(*boots*) di fatica, di marcia. ~-*on*
part, parte di figurante, parte di
comparsa, *f.* ~ *stick*, bastone, *m.*
~ *tour*, escursione a piedi; passeggiata, *f.*

wall, *n.* muro, *m.*; muraglia; parete, *f.*
~ *cupboard*, armadio a muro, *m.*
~*flower*, viola gialla, violacciocca, *f.*
to be a ~*flower*, fare da comparsa.
~ *map*, carta murale, *f.* ~*paper*,
tappezzeria (in carta); carta da
parati, *f.* ~ *plate*, trave di bordo,
f., piano di posa, *m.*; mensola a
muro, *f.*, dormiente, *m.* ~ *plug*,
innesto, *m.* ~ *tree*, albero di
spalliera, *m.* ¶ *v.t.* murare; circondare di muri.

wallet, *n.* bisaccia, borsa, *f.*; portafoglio, *m.*

wallow, *n.* andatura dondolante, *f.*;
(*ship*) rullio, *m.* ¶ *v.i.* avvoltolarsi;
guazzare.

walnut, *n.* noce, *f.*; (*tree*, *wood*) noce,
m.

walrus, *n.* tricheco, *m.*

waltz, *n.* valzer, *m.* ¶ *v.t.* ballare il
valzer. ~**er,** *n.* chi balla il valzer,
m.f.; ballerino, (-a) di valzer, *m.* (*f.*)

wan, *a.* pallido, smorto, scialbo; (*face*)
pallido.

wand, *n.* bacchetta, verga, *f.*

wander, *v.i.* vagare, errare, girovagare; deviare, scostarsi, divagare;
delirare. ~ *around*, girare e rigirare,
rigirarsi; ronzare. ~**er,** *n.* vagabondo, *m.*, -a, *f.*; vagante, *m.f.*;
nomade, *m.f.* *the* W*andering Jew*,
l'Ebreo errante, *m.*

wane, *n.* declino; decadimento, *m.*
¶ *v.i.* decrescere, declinare, sce-
marsi. **waning,** *a.* decadente,
declinante; (*moon*) calante.

want, *n.* bisogno, *m.*, mancanza,
deficienza; indigenza, *f.*, strettezze,
f.pl. ¶ *v.t.* avere bisogno di, mancare
di; desiderare, volere; (*v.i.*) mancare,
occorrere. ~**ed** (*advt.*), cercasi, si
chiede.

wanton, *a.* lascivo, licenzioso; marcia,
f.; passeggio, *m.*; scherzevole, spensierato, capriccioso; gratuito, senza
motivo. ~ *destruction*, vandalismo,
m. out of sheer ~*ness*, a cuor leggero.

war, warfare, *n.* guerra, *f.* ~ *correspondent*, corrispondente di guerra,
m. ~ *dance*, danza di guerra, danza
guerresca, *f.* ~ *horse*, cavallo di
battaglia, *m.* W~ *Loan*, prestito di
guerra, *m.* ~ *memorial*, monumento
ai caduti in guerra, *m.* ~ *of attrition*, guerra di logoramento, *f.* W~
Office, Ministero della Guerra, *m.*
~*ship*, nave da guerra, *f.* ~*monger*,
guerrafondaio, guerraiuolo, *m.* ¶ *v.i.*
guerreggiare, fare la guerra.

warble, *v.i.* gorgheggiare, trillare,
canterellare; (*v.t.*) cantare. **warbler,**
n. (*bird*) capinera, *f.*, beccafico, *m.*

ward, *n.* pupillo, *m.*, -a, *f.*, minore,
m.f.; custodia, tutela, *f.*; rione,
quartiere, *m.*; (*fencing*) guardia, *f.*;
(*hospital*) sala, corsia, *f.*; padiglione,
m.; (*lock*) nottolino, *m.* ~*room*,
quadrato degli ufficiali, *m.* ~ [**off**],
v.t. parare, respingere, tener lontano.
~**en,** *n.* custode, guardiano; conservatore; direttore, *m.* **warder.**
~**dress,** *n.* guardiano, *m.*, -a, *f.*;
carceriere, *m.*, -a, *f.* **wardrobe,** *n.*
guardaroba, *m.inv.*, armadio, *m.*;
vestiario, *m.* ~ *dealer*, mercante
d'abiti usati, *m.* ~ *keeper*, guardaroba, *m.f. inv.*; (*Theat.*) trovarobe,
m.f. inv., vestiarista, *m.f.* ~ *trunk*,
baule armadio, *m.*

warehouse, *n.* magazzino, deposito,
magazzino di deposito, *m.* ~
keeper, (bonded), magazziniere, *m.*
~*man*, magazziniere, *m.*; commerciante all'ingrosso, *m.* ¶ *v.t.*
[im]magazzinare, mettere (depositare) in magazzino.

wares, *n.pl.* merci, *f.pl.*; mercanzia, *f.*;
derrate, *f.pl.*; articoli, *m.pl. small* ~,
mercerie, *f.pl.*

warily, *ad.* con circospezione, accor-
tamente, a tastoni, tentoni. **wariness,** *n.* precauzione, accortezza,
circospezione, *f.*

warlike, *a.* guerriero, guerresco,
bellicoso; marziale. ~ *stores*,
munizioni di guerra, *f.pl.*

warm, *a.* caldo; (*fig.*) caloroso, ardente,
violento. *to be* ~, (of pers.) avere
caldo. ¶ *v.t.* scaldare, riscaldare.
~**ing pan,** scaldino, scaldaletto, *m.*
~**th,** *n.* calore; ardore; zelo, *m.*

warn, *v.t.* avvertire, ammonire, premunire; (*Com. Law*) diffidare. ~**ing,**
n. avvertimento, ammonimento; preavviso; allarme, *m.*; diffida, *f.*

warp, *n.* ordito, *m.*; contrazione, *f.*
difetto, *m.*, perversione, *f.*; (*Naut.*)
or ~ *line*, cavo da tonneggio, *m.*

¶ *v.t.* curvare, storcere; sviare, pervertire; (*yarn*) ordire; (*Naut.*) tonneggiare; (*v.i.*) curvarsi, deformarsi; tonneggiarsi.

warrant, *n.* autorizzazione, giustificazione, *f.*; ordine, mandato, *m.*; fede, *f.*; certificato, *m.*; cedola, *f.*; buono, *m.*; nota di pegno, *f.*; titolo, *m.* ~ *of arrest*, mandato di arresto, *m.* *search* ~, ordine di perquisizione domiciliare, *m.* ¶ *v.t.* garantire; giustificare; attestare; assicurare. ~**able,** *a.* giustificabile. ~**y,** *n.* garanzia, *f.*

warren, *n.* garenna, *f.*

warrior, *n.* guerriero, *m.*

Warsaw, *n.* Varsavia, *f.*

wart, *n.* verruca, *f.*; porro, *m.* ~**y,** *a.* verrucoso.

wary, *a.* circospetto, diffidente; scaltro, accorto.

wash, *n.* lavata, *f.*; (*linen*) bucato, *m.*, biancheria da lavarsi, *f.*; (*Art.*) acquerello, *m.*; (*mouth*) acqua, *f.*; (*ship*) onda, *f.*; (*slops*) lavatura (di piatti), acqua di lavatura, *f.* *to have a* ~, lavarsi. ~ *& brush up*, lavarsi e pulirsi, toletta e spazzolata. ~ *basin*, catinella, *f.*, catino, lavabo, *m.* ~ *drawing*, acquerello, *m.* ~*house*, lavatoio, *m.*, lavanderia, *f.* ~*leather*, pelle scamosciata, pelle lavabile, *f.* ~*stand*, lavabo, porta-catino, *m.* ~*tub*, conca (del bucato), *f.* ¶ *v.t. & i.* lavare, lavarsi; fare il bucato; imbiancare; bagnare. ~ *away*, portar via, lavar via. ~ *out*, lavare, risciacquare. ~ *up*, rigettare sulla sponda; lavare. ~**able,** *a.* lavabile. *washed overboard*, travolto in mare, spazzato in mare. **washer,** *n.* (*pers.*) lavatore, *m.*, -trice, *f.*; (*Mach.*) lavatrice, *f.*; (*ring*) rondella, rosetta, *f.* ~ *woman*, lavandaia, *f.* **washing,** *n.* lavatura, *f.*; bucato, *m.*; imbiancatura; toletta, abluzione, *f.* ~*board*, asse per lavare, *m.*, tavola per lavare, *f.* ~*day*, giorno del bucato, *m.*

wasp, *n.* vespa, *f.* ~'*s nest*, vespaio, *m.* **waspish,** *a.* (*fig.*) stizzoso, irascibile.

waste, *a.* incolto, deserto; (*gas, heat*) perduto; (*matter*) di scarto. *to lay* ~, devastare, guastare, rovinare. ¶ *n.* scarto, *m.*, rifiuti, *m.pl.*, sperpero, spreco, sciupio, *m.*; perdita, *f.*, calo, consumo inutile, *m.* ¶ *comps.*: ~ *book*, scartafaccio, brogliazzo, *m.* ~ *heap*, mucchio di spazzature, di rifiuti, *m.* ~ *paper*, carta straccia, *f.* ~ *paper basket*, cestino per la carta

straccia, *m.* ~ *pipe*, tubo di scarico, *m.* ~ *water*, acqua di rifiuto, *f.* ¶ *v.t.* sciupare, sc alacquare, sprecare, dissipare. ~ *away*, consumarsi, sciuparsi, deperire, dimagrare, atrofizzarsi. ~*d life*, vita mancata, *f.* **waster,** *n.* guastatore, *m.*, -trice, *f.*; sprecone, *m.*, -a, *f.*; dissipatore, *m.*, -trice, *f.*; prodigo, *m.* **wasteful,** *a.* prodigo, spendereccio, dissipatore. **wastefulness,** *n.* prodigalità, *f.*, sciupio, *m.*

watch, *n.* sorveglianza; veglia; attenzione; guardia, sentinella, *f.*; (*Naut.*) guardia, *f.*; (*Horol.*) orologio, oriolo, *m. on the* ~, all'erta, in guardia, in agguato, alla posta, attento. ~ *chain*, catena da orologio, *f.* ~*dog*, cane da guardia, *m.* ~ *fire*, bivacco, *m.* ~ *guard*, cordoncino da orologio, *m.* ~*maker*, orologiaio, oriolaio *m.*, ~*man*, guardia (notturna), *f.*, guardiano, *m.* ~ *on bracelet*, orologio [sul] braccialetto, *m.* ~ *stand*, porta-orologio, *m.inv.* ~*word*, parola d'ordine, *f.* ¶ *v.t. & i.* vegliare, sorvegliare, far (la) guardia a; osservare, tener d'occhio, spiare, guardare, star desto, vigilare. ~**er,** *n.* vegliatore, *m.*, -trice, *f.*; osservatore, *m.* -trice, *f.*; infermiere, *m.*, -a, *f.* ~**ful,** *a.* vigilante, attento. ~**fulness,** *n.* vigilanza, attenzione, *f.*

water, *n.* acqua, *f.*; (*tide*) marea, *f.*; (*pl.*) acque, *f.pl. drinking* ~, acqua potabile, *f.* ~ *bath*, (*Chem., &c.*) bagno-maria, *m.* ~ *bed*, materassa da acqua, *f.* ~ *bottle*, caraffa, *f.*; (*Mil.*) borraccia, *f.* ~ *butt*, botte da acqua, *f.* ~ *cart*, carretto da inaffiare, *m.* ~ *closet*, gabinetto, cesso, luogo comodo, *m.* ~ *colour*, acquerello, *m.* ~ *course*, corso d'acqua, scolatoio, canale, *m.* ~ *cress*, crescione, *m.* ~ *diviner*, rabdomante, *m.* ~ *divining*, rabdomanzia, *f.* ~*fall*, caduta d'acqua, cascata, *f.* ~ *fowl*, uccello acquatico, *m.* ~ *gauge*, tubo di livello, idro-metro, *m.* ~ *glass* (*Hist.*) clessidra, *f.*; (*Chem.*) soluzione silicea, *f.*, silicato di potassio, *m.* ~ *hammer* [*ing*], martello d'acqua, colpo d'ariete, *m.* ~ *hazard* (*Golf*) fossatello, *m.* ~ *ice*, sorbetto, *m.* ~ *jacket*, camicia d'acqua, *f.* ~ *jug*, brocca, *f.* ~ *jump* (*Turf*), fossatello, *m.* ~ *level*, livello dell'acqua, *m.*; (*instrument*) livella a bolla d'aria, *f.* ~ *lily*, nenufar, *m.*, ninfea, *f.* ~ *line*, linea d'acqua; (*Naut.*) linea di galleggiamento, *f.* ~*logged*, pieno d'acqua, imbevuto d'acqua; inzuppato. ~*man*, battelliere, barcaiolo, *m.* ~*mark* (*tidal*), livello dell'acqua, *m.*; (*paper*) filigrana, *f.* ~ *meadow*, prateria irrigabile, p. inondabile, *f.* ~ *melon*, cocomero, *m.* ~ *meter*, contatore dell'acqua, *m.* ~ *mill*, mulino ad acqua, *m.* ~ *nymph*, naiade, *f.* ~ [*omni*]*bus*, battello omnibus, vaporetto, *m.* ~ *on the brain*, idrocefalia, *f.* ~ *on the knee*, travaso di sinovia, *m.* ~ *pipe*, condotto d'acqua, *m.* ~ *power*, forza idrica, energia idraulica, *f.*; carbone bianco, *m.* ~*proof*, *a.* impermeabile (all'acqua); (*n.*) impermeabile, *m.*; (*v.t.*) rendere impermeabile. ~ *polo*, polo ad acqua, sull'acqua, *m.* ~ *rat*, topo acquaiolo, *m.* ~ *rate*, tariffa per la fornitura dell'acqua, *f.* ~ *shed*, spartiacque, *m.inv.*, versante, *m.* ~*side*, sponda, riva, *f.*, bordo dell'acqua, *m.* (*att.*) rivierasco, littoraneo. ~ *spout*, (*rain*) doccia, gronda, *f.*; (*Meteor.*) tromba (d'acqua), t. marina, *f.* ~*tight*, stagno, *m.* ~ *tournament*, giostra sull'acqua, *f.* ~ *tower*, castello d'acqua, *m.* ~ *way*, canale navigabile, *m.*; (*bridge*) sbocco, *m.* ~ *wheel*, ruota idraulica; turbina idraulica, *f.* ~ *works*, impianto idrico, *m.* ¶ *v.t.* (*garden*, *&c.*) innaffiare; (*horse*) abbeverare; (*drink*) annacquare, diluire, mettere acqua in, tagliare; battezzare; (*stock*, *Fin.*); diluire; (*silk*) marezzare; (*v.i.*) (*eyes*) piangere; (*take in water*) fare acqua. *it makes one's mouth* ~, fa venire l'acquolina in bocca. ~*ed silk*, seta marezzata, *f.* ~*ing*, *n.* innaffiamento, abbeveramento, *m.*; irrigazione; marezzatura, *f.* ~ *place*, stazione balneare, stazione termale, *f.*; acque, *f.pl.*; (*animal*) abbeveratoio, *m.* ~ *pot*, innaffiatoio, *m.* ~*less*, *a.* senz'acqua, privo d'acqua. ~*y*, *a.* acqueo, acquoso, umido; (*fluid*) tenue.

watt, *n.* (*Elec.*) watt, *m. inv.*

wattle, *n.* (*rods & twigs*) canniccio, graticcio, *m.*; vimini, *m.pl.*; (*birds*) bargiglio, *m.*, caruncola, *f.*; (*fish*) barbetta, *f.* ¶ *v.t.* legare con vimini, intrecciare, ingraticciare.

wave, *n.* onda, *f.*, flutto, maroso, cavallone, *m.*; ondulazione, *f.*; (*hand*) segno, gesto, cenno, *m.*; (*wand*) colpo, *m.* ¶ *v.i.* ondeggiare, fluttuare; far segno; (*v.t.*) agitare; brandire;

far segno di; ondula e. *to have one's hair* ~*d*, farsi ondulare i capelli.

waver, *v.i.* vacillare, esitare, titubare, tentennare. ~*ing*, *a.* esitante, fluttuante. wavy, *a.* ondeggiante, ondulato; serpeggiante; (*line*) tremolante.

wax, *n.* cera, *f.*; (*cobbler's*) pece, *f.* ~ *chandler*, ceraiuolo, *m.* ~ *vesta*, cerino, *m.* ~*works*, figure di cera, *f.pl.*; museo di figure di cera, *m.* ¶ *v.t.* incerare. (*v.i.*) crescere, divenire, farsi. ~*en*, *a.* di cera, ceroso, come cera. ~*ed thread*, filo impeciato, *m.* ~*y*, *a.* come cera, cereo.

way, *n.* modo, mezzo, *m.*; maniera, guisa, aria, *f.*; tono, *m.*; abitudine, usanza, pratica, *f.*; cammino, passo, passaggio, *m.*; via, strada, rotta, *f.*; progresso; luogo; stato, *m.*; direzione, distanza, parte, *f.*; senso, *m.*; (*Naut.*) abbrivo, *m.*; velocità, *f.* *by the* ~, di passaggio, cammin facendo; (*fig.*) a proposito. *in the* ~, ingombrante, incomodo, molesto, di disturbo, a noia. *over the* ~, dall'altra parte della strada, dirimpetto, in faccia. ~ *bill*, foglio di rotta, *m.* ~*farer*, viandante, *m.f.*; viaggiatore, *m.*, -trice, *f.* ~ *in*, entrata, *f.* ~*lay*, porre agguato per, tendere insidie a; fare la posta a, attendere. ~ *out*, uscita, *f.* ~*side*, margine della strada, bordo della strada, *m.* (*att.*) sul bordo della strada, di campagna. (*Rly. station*) stazione di passaggio, s. di campagna, fermata, *f.*

wayward, *a.* capriccioso, caparbietto, ritroso, scapestrato. ~*ness*, *n.* ritrosia, *f.*

we, *pn.* noi, noi altri, si.

weak, *a.* debole, fiacco, infermo, fievole, fioco; (*tea*) debole, leggero. ~ *spot* (*fig. of pers.*), debole, lato debole, punto debole, *m.* ~*en*, *v.t.* indebolire, affievolire, infiacchire; attenuare; (*blow*) ammortire; (*v.i.*) indebolirsi; scemare. ~*ling*, *n.* creatura debole. ~*ly*, *a.* debole, infermo, poco robusto. ~*ness*, *n.* debolezza, *f.*; debole, lato debole, *m.*

weal, *n.* bene, benessere, *m.* (Cf. *the common* ~, il benessere pubblico); *for* ~ *& woe*, nella fortuna come nella disgrazia.

wealth, *n.* ricchezze, *f.pl.* (or ricchezza, *f.*); opulenza, *f.* beni, *m.pl.*; dovizie, *f.pl.* ~*y*, *a.* ricco, opulento.

wean, *v.t.* svezzare, spoppare. ~*ing*, *n.* spoppamento, divezzamento, *m.*

weapon, *n.* arma, *f.* (*pl.* armi). ∼less, *n.* disarmato, senz'armi.

wear, *n.* uso, *m.*; durata (*durability*), *f.*; logorio, consumo, *m.*; moda, *f.*, vestito, abbigliamento, *m.* *the worse for* ∼, guasto, molto logoro. ∼ & *tear,* logorio, *m.* ¶ *v.t.* & *i.* portare, indossare, avere; durare; scavare. ∼ *out,* (*v.i.*) usarsi, logorarsi, consumarsi; (*v.t.*) logorare, esaurire; spossare, stancare. ∼ *well,* fare buon uso, avere lunga durata, essere in (buon) assetto. ∼**able,** *a.* portabile, da portarsi, che si può indossare.

weariness, *n.* stanchezza, spossatezza, fatica, *f.*; tedio, *m.*, noia, *f.*, disgusto, *m.*

wearing, *n.* uso, *m.*, usura, *f.*

wearisome, *a.* soporifero, noioso, tedioso, penoso, seccante, faticoso. ∼**ness,** *n.* tedio, *m.*, noia, uggia, *f.*

weary, *a.* affaticato, stanco; noioso. ¶ *v.t.* stancare, affaticare; annoiare, stufare. ∼ *for,* agognare, languire (per), parer mille anni (che), non veder l'ora (di), struggersi dal desiderio di.

weasel, *n.* donnola, *f.*

weather, *n.* tempo, *m.*; (*pl.* varieties of weather) intemperie, *f.pl.* *exposed to all* ∼s, esposto a tutte le intemperie. ∼ & *news* (*Radio*), giornale radio, *m.* ∼**beaten,** sbattuto dalla tempesta (or *pl.* -e), logoro. ∼**cock,** banderuola, ventarola, *f.*; (*fig.*) banderuola, ventarola, *f.*, uomo volubile, arlecchino, *m.* ∼ *forecast,* bollettino meteorologico, *m.* ∼ *permitting,* tempo permettendo. ∼ *side,* lato del vento, *m.* ∼ *strip,* tendina, *f.* ¶ *v.t.* resistere a, reggere a, uscire da; (*cape*) doppiare, oltrepassare; (*Geol.*) alterare, disgregare.

weave, *n.* tessuto, *m.* ¶ *v.t.* *ir.* tessere; (*basket*) intrecciare; (*fig.*) ordire, tramare, inventare. **weaver,** *n.* tessitore, *m.*, -trice, *f.* **weaving,** *n.* tessitura, *f.*

web, *n.* tela, *f.*, tessuto, *m.*, struttura, *f.*; (*bird's foot*) membrana, *f.*; (*spider's*) ragnatela, *f.*; (*girder,* &*c.*) parete verticale, *f.*; (*key*) ingegno, *m.*; (*of life*) trama, *f.* ∼**footed,** palmipede. **webbed,** *a.* palmato. **webbing,** *n.* tela da cigna, *f.*

wed, *v.t.* sposare, impalmare; (*v.i.*) maritarsi; ammogliarsi; sposarsi. **wedded,** *a.* coniugale; (*to opinion*) attaccato, legato. **wedding,** *n.* nozze, *f.pl.*; matrimonio, sposalizio, *m.* ∼ *breakfast,* banchetto nuziale, *m.* ∼ *cake,* "gateau" nuziale, *m.* ∼ *day,* giorno dello sposalizio, dí delle nozze, *m.* ∼ *dress,* veste nuziale, *f.* ∼ *festivities* & ∼ *party,* nozze, *f.pl.*; corteo nuziale, *m.*, invitati alle nozze, *m.pl.* ∼ *march,* marcia nuziale, *f.* ∼ *present,* regalo di nozze, *m.*; (*bridegroom's*) regali (per la futura sposa), *m.pl.* ∼ *ring,* anello nuziale, anello matrimoniale, *m.*, fede, *f.*

wedge, *n.* cuneo, *m.*; bietta, *f.* ¶ *v.t.* incuneare, imbiettare.

wedlock, *n.* matrimonio, stato coniugale, *m.*

Wednesday, *n.* mercoledí, *m.*

wee, *a.* piccolino, minuscolo.

weed, *n.* malerba, erbaccia, *f.* ¶ *v.t.* sarchiare. *widow's* ∼s, bruno di vedova, *m.* ∼ *out,* sradicare, estirpare. ∼**er,** *n.* (*pers.*) sarchiatore, *m.*, -trice, *f.*; (*hoe*) sarchio, *m.*

week, *n.* settimana, *f.*; (*e.g. Friday to Friday*) settimana, *f.*, otto gorni, *m.pl.* *next* ∼, la settimana ventura, *f.* ∼ *day,* giorno feriale, giorno di lavoro, *m.* *this day* ∼, oggi a otto; *to-morrow* ∼, domani a otto. ∼**end** *cottage,* villino, *m.* ∼**end** *ticket,* biglietto (ferroviario) a prezzo ridotto, *m.* ∼**ly,** *a.* & *n.* settimanale, *a.* & *m.*

weep, *v.i.* & *t.* *ir.* & ∼ *for,* piangere. ∼**er,** *n.* chi piange; piagnone, *m.*, -a, *f.* **weeping,** *n.* pianto, *m.*; lagrime, *f.pl.* ¶ *a.* che piange, piangente, lacrimoso; (*tree*) piangente.

weevil, *n.* punteruolo, *m.* ∼**y,** *a.* bacato.

weft, *n.* trama, *f.*

weigh, *v.t.* pesare; (*fig.*) ponderare; valutare; (*anchor*) salpare; levare. (*v.i.*) pesare, aver peso. ∼ *bridge,* ponte a bascula, *m.* ∼ *down,* far piegare; aggravare, accasciare, opprimere. *to get under* ∼, salpare, levar l'ancora. ∼**er,** *n.* pesatore, *m.* **weighing,** *n.* pesatura, *f.* ∼ *in* & ∼*in room,* pesaggio, recinto del peso, *m.* ∼ *machine,* pesatrice, *f.* **weight,** *n.* peso, *m.*; gravità, pesantezza, *f.*; importanza, *f.* ∼ *allowed free,* franchigia del bagaglio, *f.*, peso (del bagaglio) che ha il beneficio della franchigia, *m.* *he (it) is worth his, (its)* ∼ *in gold,* vale (tanto) oro quanto pesa. *in* ∼, pesante, di peso. ∼ *handicap,* eccesso di peso, *m.* ∼**y,** *a.* pesante; grave, importante.

weir, *n.* chiusa, traversa, diga, *f.*; sbarramento, *m.*

weird, *a.* fantastico, strano.

welcome, *a.* grato, gradito, ben accetto, (*pers.*) benvenuto. ¶ *n.* benvenuto, *m.*; (buona) accoglienza, *f.* ¶ *v.t.* dare il benvenuto a, far le feste a, accogliere cordialmente.

weld, *n.* & ~**ing,** saldatura, *f.* ¶ *v.t.* saldare (a fuoco).

welfare, *n.* benessere, bene, *m.*; (*public*) salute (pubblica), *f.*

well, *n.* pozzo, *m.*; sorgente; fontana, *f.*, serbatoio, *m.*, vivaio, *m.*; (*of ship*) sentina, *f.*; (*of court*) banco degli avvocati, *m.* ~ *sinker,* [s]cavapozzi, *m.inv.* ~ *spring,* fontana, sorgente, *f.* ¶ *v.i.* or ~ *up,* scaturire, sorgere, sgorgare, zampillare.

well, *a.* bene, buono, sano, in buona salute. ¶ *ad.* bene. *to do oneself* ~, godersela, amare i propri comodi. *to live* ~, vivere agiatamente; far baldoria. ~-*advised,* ben consigliato, prudente. ~ & *good,* alla buon'ora. ~-*attended,* ben frequentato, ben seguito, che fa gente. ~-*balanced,* bene equilibrato, assennato; (*style, prose*) armonioso. ~-*behaved,* ben costumato, saggio, che si comporta bene. ~-*being,* benessere, *m.* ~ *beloved,* *a.* & *n.* benamato, *a.* & *m.*, -a, *f.* ~-*bred,* beneducato. ~-*built,* ~ *knit,* ben costruito, solido. ~-*disposed* & ~ *meaning,* ben disposto, bene intenzionato. ~ *done,* ben fatto; (*Cookery*) ben cotto. ~ *done!* ben fatto! bravo! ~-*finished,* ben messo, bene finito. ~-*informed,* bene informato. ~ *known,* ben noto, ben conosciuto. ~-*marked,* spiccato, che risalta. ~ *off* & ~ *to do,* agiato, danaroso, benestante. ~ *read,* istruito, letterato, erudito. ~-*spoken,* facondo. ~-*timed,* opportuno, a proposito.

wellingtons, *n.pl.* stivaloni, *m.pl.*

Welsh, *a.* gallese, del Paese di Galles. ¶ *n.* gallese, *m.*, lingua gallese, *f.* ~*man,* ~*woman,* gallese, *m.f.* ~ *rabbit,* ~ *rarebit,* crostino di formaggio arrostito, *m.* ~*er,* *n.* truffatore di somme scommesse, *m.*

welt, *n.* (*shoe*) trapunta, tramezza, *f.*

welter, *v.i.* nuotare, avvoltolarsi, essere sballottato. ~ *weight* (*Box.*), peso medio-leggero.

wen, *n.* natta, *f.*; gozzo, *m.*

wench, *n.* zitella, ragazza, *f.*

wend, *v.i.* proseguire, continuare; (*one's way*) prender la strada.

wer[e]wolf, *n.* lupo mannaro, *m.*

west, *n.* ovest, occidente, ponente, *m.* ¶ *a.* dell'ovest, d'occidente, di ponente, dell'occidente, occidentale. *W* ~ *Africa,* l'Africa Occidentale, *f.* *the W* ~ *Indies,* le Indie Occidentali, *f.pl.* **westerly,** *a.* d'ovest, dell'ovest. **western,** *a.* dell'ovest, occidentale, d'occidente. *W* ~ *Australia,* l'Australia Occidenta'e, *f.* ~**er,** *n.* occidentale, *m.f.* **westward,** *ad.* verso occidente, verso ponente, v. l'ovest.

Westphalia, *n.* la Vestfalia, *f.*

wet, *a.* bagnato, umido; acquitrinoso; fradicio, molle; piovoso, piovigginoso; (*goods*) liquido; (*paint, ink*) fresco. ~ *blanket* (*fig.*), spegnitoio, *m.*; guastafeste, *m.inv.* ~ *dock,* bacino a chiusa, *m.*, darsena, *f.* ~ *fish,* pesci freschi, *m.pl.* ~ *nurse,* balia, nutrice (che allatta), *f.* ~ *through,* tutto bagnato, inzuppato. **wet** & ~**ness,** *n.* umidità, *f.*; tempo piovoso, *m.* *out in the wet,* alla pioggia. ¶ *v.t.* bagnare, inumidire, imbevere, inzuppare; umettare; annaffiare.

wether, *n.* (montone) castrato, *m.*

whack, *n.* bussa, *f.*, colpo sonoro, *m.* ¶ *v.t.* bastonare.

whale, *n.* balena, *f.* ~*boat,* baleniera, *f.* ~*bone,* osso di balena, *n.* ~ *calf,* balenotto, *m.* **whaler,** *n.* baleniere, *m.*

wharf, *n.* scalo, *m.*, banchina, calata, *f.*, molo, *m.* **wharfinger,** *n.* intendente di (un) molo, guardiano di molo, *m.*

what, *a.* *pn.* & *ad.* quale, che; che cosa, ciò che, quel[lo] che; (tanto) quanto; che cosa? come? ~ *a,* che...! ~ *a relief!* ah! ~ *for?* perché? ~ *do you call* it? come lo chiamate? **whatever** & **whatsoever,** *pn.* & *a.* qualunque (cosa), qualsisia (cosa), checché, tutto ciò che, per quanto.

whatnot, *n.* scaffaletto, *m.*

wheat, *n.* frumento, grano, *m.* ~**en,** *a.* di frumento, di grano.

wheedle, *v.t.* vezzeggiare, accarezzare; blandire.

wheel, *n.* ruota, *f.*; volante, disco, *m.*, rotella, *f.*; (*emery,* &c.) mola, *f.*; (*helm*) barra, ruota (del timone), *f.*; (*Mil.*) conversione, *f.* *driving* ~, (*Mech.*) ruota motrice, *f.* ~ *barrow,* carriola (a mano), *f.* ~ *base,* interasse, *m.* ~ *work,* wheels, meccanismo, ingranaggio, *m.*; (*watch*) castello, *m.* ~*wright,* *n.* carraio, carradore, *m.* ¶ *v.t.* far rotare, far girare; trasportare (in un veicolo); (*v.i.*) (*birds*, *&c.*) muoversi in giro, svolazzare; (*Mil.*) fare una conversione. ~ **wheeled**, *a.*, a ruote. **wheeler**, *n.* cavallo del timone. *m.*

wheeze, *v.i.* ansimare, soffiare, soffrire d'asma. **wheezy**, *a.* ansimante, sibilante; bolso; (*pers.*) asmatico.

whelk, *n.* buccina, trombetta, *f.*

when, *ad.* quando, allorché, mentre; dopo che; in cui, a che ora. **whence**, *ad.* donde, onde. **whenever**, *ad.*, ogni volta che, tutte le volte che, sempre che, ogniqualvolta, qualora, quando che sia.

where, *ad.* dove, ove, laddove. ~ *to fish*, dove si può pescare. **whereabouts**, *ad.* dove, in che posto. *one's* ~, luogo dove si trova [qualcuno], dove si pratica. **whereas**, *ad.* mentre, quando invece, laddove, mentre che; atteso che, visto che. **whereat**, *ad.* al che, su di che. **whereby**, *ad.* da cui, per cui, per il quale. **wherefore**, *ad.* perciò, quindi, onde; per quale ragione? **wherein**, *ad.* in che, nel quale; dove?, in che cosa? **whereof**, *ad.* di cui, del quale. **where[up]on**, *ad.* al che, su cui, sul quale, sopra di che, sopra del quale, su ciò. **wherever**, *a.* in qualunque luogo, dove che sia, dovunque. *the wherewithal*, i mezzi, *m.pl.*; danaro, *m.*

wherry, *n.* barchetta, *f.*, barchino, *m.* ~*man*, barcaiuolo, *m.*

whet, *n.* aperitivo, *m.* ¶ *v.t.* (*tools*) affilare, arrotare; (*appetite*) aguzzare, stimolare. ~ *stone*, cote, pietra per affilare, *f.*

whether, *c.* se, sia che, sia.

whey, *n.* siero (di latte), *m.*

which, *pn.* & *a.* che, il quale, la quale, i quali, le quali, cui, quale?, quali? ~ *way?* per dove? **whichever**, *a.* & *pn.* qualunque, qualsisia, sia l'uno sia l'altro, non importa che.

whiff, *n.* buffata, *f.*; soffio, alito, sbuffo, *m.*

while, *n.* tempo, pezzo, *m.* *it is worth* ~, vale la pena. **while** & **whilst**, *c.* mentre (che), nel[lo stesso] tempo che, intanto che. *to while away*, far passare.

whim, *n.* capriccio, ghiribizzo, *m.*, fantasia, *f.*; (*Mach.*) mulinello, *m.*

whimper, *v.i.* piagnucolare, pigolare, gemere. ~*er*, *n.* piagnone, *m.*, -a, *f.*, piagnucolone, *m.*

whimsical, *a.* capriccioso, bizzarro, fantastico, fantasioso.

whin, *n.* ginestra spinosa, *f.*

whine, *v.i.* gemere, piagnucolare, lagnarsi; (*dog*) uggiolare.

whinny, *n.* nitrito, *m.* ¶ *v.i.* nitrire.

whip, *n.* frusta, sferza, *f.*, scudiscio, *m.* ~*cord*, corda da frusta, *f.* ~ *hand* (*fig.*), sopravvento, vantaggio, *m.* ¶ *v.t.* & *i.* frustare, sferzare; fustigare, flagellare; (*cream*, *&c.*) sbattere. **whipper-in**, *n.* capocaccia, *m.* **whipper-snapper**, *n.* vanerello, uomo presuntuoso; monello, *m.* **whipping**, *n.* bastonatura, sferzata, *f.* ~ *top*, paleo, *m.*

whir[r], *v.i.* frusciare, ronzare.

whirl, *n.* giro rapido, turbine, *m.*; agitazione, *f.*; bolli-bolli, *m.* ~*pool*, vortice (d'acqua), gorgo, *m.* ~*wind*, turbine, vortice (di vento), *m.*; tromba, *f.*, tifone, *m.* ¶ *v.i.* roteare, girare, turbinare, essere trasportato da un vortice. **whirligig**, *n.* girello, *m.*, girandola, *f.*, carosello, *m.*, giostra, *f.*

whisk, *n.* (*brush*, *broom*) spolveracciolo, granatino, *m.*; (*egg*) frullino, *m.* ¶ *v.t.* (*dust*) spolverare; (*eggs*) sbattere, frullare.

whiskers, *n.pl.* bassette, fedine, *f.pl.*; (*cat*) baffi, *m.pl.*

whisky, *n.* whisky, *m.*

whisper, *n.* bisbiglio; sussurro, mormorio, *m.* ¶ *v.i.* & *t.* bisbigliare; sussurrare, mormorare. ~*er*, bisbiglione, *m.*, bisbigliatore, *m.*, -trice, *f.* ~*ing*, *n.* bisbiglio, sussurrio, *m.* ~ *gallery*, galleria acustica, *f.*

whist (*Cards*), *n.* whist, *m.*

whistle, *n.* fischio; fischietto; colpo di fischietto; zufolo, *m.* ¶ *v.t.* & *i.* fischiare, fischiettare, zufolare, sibilare; (*wind*) muggire, mugghiare. **whistler**, *n.* fischiatore, *m.*, -trice, *f.*

whit, *n.* ette, iota, *m.* *not a* ~, niente affatto. *W*~ *Monday*, lunedì di Pentecoste.

white, *a.* bianco, candido. ~ *ant*, termite, *f.* ~ *bait*, pesciolini, *m.pl. show the* ~ *feather*, dar prova di vigliaccheria. ~ *horses* (*sea*), pecorelle, *f.pl.* ~ *heat*, incandescenza, *f.* ~-*hot*, incandescente. ~ *lead*, cerussa, *f.*, bianco di cerussa, *m.* ~ *lie*, bugia innocente, *f.* *W*~ *Sea*, (il) Mar Bianco, *m.* ~-*throat*, capinera grigia, *f.* ~*wash*, n. calce (da imbiancare); (*v.t.*) imbiancare; (*fig.*) riabilitare, nascondere i difetti di. ¶ *n.* (*colour, man*) bianco, *m.*; (*ball, woman*), bianca, *f.* ~ *of egg*, chiaro d'uovo; (*boiled*) bianco, *m.* ~ *sale*, vendita del bianco, *f.* **white[n]**, *v.t.* imbiancare. **whiteness**, *n.* bianchezza, *f.*, candore, *m.*; (*hair*) canizie, *f.*

whither, *ad.* dove, per dove.

whiting, *n.* bianco di creta, bianco di Spagna, *m.*; (*fish*) merlano, *m.*

whitish, *a.* biancastro, bianchiccio.

whitlow, *n.* patereccio, *m.*

Whitsuntide, *n.* (la) Pentecoste, Pasqua delle Rose, *f.* *Whit Sunday,* domenica di Pentecoste, *f.*

whittle, *v.t.* tagliuzzare. ~ *down*, attenuare; ridurre, assottigliare.

whiz[z], *n.* fischio, sibilo, *m.* ¶ *v.i.* fischiare, sibilare.

who, *pn.* che, il quale, la quale, i quali, le quali; chi? ~ *goes there?* chi è? chi è là? ~ *knows!* chi sa! chi lo sa!

whoa, *i.* fermo!

whoever, *pn.* chiunque, qualunque (persona).

whole, *a.* tutto; intero; integrale; intatto; compiuto, completo; totale, globale; pieno. ~ *binding*, legatura, rilegatura completa, *f.* ~*-length* (portrait), in piedi. ~*meal bread*, pane integrale, *m.* ¶ *n.* il tutto, l'insieme, il totale, *m.* *as a* ~, in complesso, nell'insieme. [*up*] *on the* ~, tutto sommato, in fin dei conti, dopo tutto, tutto ben considerato.

wholesale, *a.* all'ingrosso. ~ [*trade*], commercio all'ingrosso, *m.*

wholesome, *a.* sano, salubre; salutare. **wholly**, *ad.* interamente, integralmente, completamente, del tutto, in tutto, tutto.

whom, *pn.* che, chi, il quale, la quale, i quali, le quali. **whomsoever**, *pn.* qualunque, chiunque, chicchessia.

whoop, *n.* urlo, *m.*, urlata, *f.*, grido, *m.* ¶ *v.i.* urlare, gridare. ~*ing cough*, tosse canina, *f.*

whorl, *n.* verticello, *m.*, spira, *f.*

whortleberry, *n.* mirtillo, *m.*

whose, *pn.* di cui, il cui, la cui, del quale, della quale, dei quali, delle quali; di chi?, a chi? **whosoever**, *pn.* chiunque.

why, *ad. c. & n.* perché, *ad. c. & m.* ¶ *i.* ma! come! ebbene!

wick, *n.* stoppino, lucignolo, *m.*

wicked, *a.* malvagio, tristo, scellerato, maligno, cattivo. ~*ness*, *n.* malvagità, malignità, scelleratezza, nequizia, cattiveria, *f.*

wicker, *n.* vimine, vinco, *m.* ~ *cradle*, zana, *f.* ~ *work*, viminata, *f.*, lavoro in vimini, *m.*; arte del panieraio, *f.* ¶ *v.t.* incannucciare; rivestire di vimini.

wicket, *n.* sportello, *m.*; (*Cricket*) (le) sbarre, *f.pl.*; (*Croquet*) archetto, *m.*

wide, *a.* largo, vasto, grande, ampio, spazioso, esteso; (*Meas.*) largo, di larghezza. *to be* ~ *awake*, essere interamente sveglio. ~*-awake*, (ben) svegliato, sveglio, desto; furbo, scaltro; in guardia, all'erta, sull'avviso. ~ *of the mark*, lontano dal vero, dal segno. ~*-spread*, largamente diffuso, molto diffuso. ~ *ly*, *ad.* largamente, grandemente, molto. ~ *known*, assai conosciuto.

widen, *v.t.* allargare; dilatare; estendere. **in a wider sense**, per estensione.

widgeon, *n.* fischione, *m.*, anitra selvatica, *f.*

widow, *n.* vedova, *f.* *the* ~*'s mite*, l'obolo della vedova, *f.* ~*'s weeds*, abiti da lutto, (d'una vedova), *m.pl.* ~*ed*, *p.p.* vedovato, vedovo; (*fig.*) privato. ~*er*, *n.* vedovo, *m.* ~*hood*, *n.* vedovanza, *f.*, stato vedovile, *m.*

width, *n.* larghezza, ampiezza, estensione, *f.*; (*cloth*) altezza, *f.*

wield, *v.t.* maneggiare; (*power*) esercitare.

wife, *n.* moglie, sposa, *f.*

wig, *n.* parrucca, *f.* ~ *maker*, parrucchiere, *m.*

wight, *n.* individuo, uomo, *m.*

wild, *a.* selvaggio; selvatico; incolto, deserto; barbaro; furioso, impetuoso; tempestoso; sregolato, dissoluto; stravagante, incoerente, pazzo; (*look*) smarrito. ~ *beast*, fiera, bestia feroce, *f.*; (*pl.*) belve, *f.pl.* ~ *boar*, cinghiale, cignale, *m.*; (*young*) cignaletto, *m.* ~ *cherry*, marasca, visciola, *f.*; (*tree*) marasco, visciolo, *m.* ~ *flowers*, fiori dei campi, fiori dei prati, fiori selvatici, *m.pl.* ~ *goose chase*, folle impresa, impresa temeraria, *f.* *to sow one's* ~ *oats*, correr la cavallina, menare una vita scapestrata. ~ *rabbit*, coniglio selvatico, *m.* ~ *raspberry* (bush), lampone selvatico, *m.*; mora, *f.* ~ *rose*, rosa di macchia, *f.*; (*bush*) rosaio di macchia, *m.* ~ *sow*, cignala, scrofa, *f.* **wild & wilderness**, *n.* deserto, luogo selvaggio, *m.*, solitudine, *f.* ~*ing*, *n.* pollone selvatico, frutto selvatico, *m.* ~*ly*, *ad.* furiosamente, impetuosamente; stravagantemente; sfrenatamente.

~ness, n. selvatichezza, f.; stato selvaggio, m.; scapataggine, f.

wile & **wiliness**, n. artificio, m., astuzia, malizia, furberia, f.; (pl.) sottigliezze, f.pl.

wilful, a. ostinato, testardo, caparbio, cocciuto; intenzionale, premeditato, volontario. ~ misrepresentation, dolo, m. ~ murder, omicidio premeditato, o. volontario, assassinio, m. ~ly, ad. apposta, volontariamente, con premeditazione; da caparbio, cocciutamente. ~ness, n. ostinazione, testardaggine, f.

will, n. volontà, f., volere, m.; discrezione, f.; piacere, arbitrio; cuore, animo, carattere, m.; (Law) testamento, m. ¶ v.t. ir. volere; disporre per testamento, lasciare (per testamento). v.aux. is expressed in It. by future tense, also by volere. **willing**, a. pronto (a), disposto (a), desideroso (di); volontario, spontaneo, compiacente, volenteroso; (hands) di volontari. to be ~, volere (bene). ~ly, ad. volentieri. ~ness, n. compiacenza, f., consentimento, m., buona volontà, f.

will-o'-the-wisp, n. fuoco fatuo, m.

willow, n. salice, salce, m. ~ plantation, salceto, m.

willynilly, ad. buon grado, mal grado. ¶ a. volente o nolente.

wilt, v.t. far appassire, far avvizzire; (v.i.) appassire, avvizzire, imbozzacchire; (pers.) languire.

wily, a. astuto, furbo, scaltro.

wimple, n. soggolo, m.

win, n. vincita, vittoria, f. ~ on points, vittoria ai punti, f. ¶ v.t. ir. guadagnare, vincere; cattivarsi, conciliare; acquistare, riportare.

wince, v.i. trasalire (dal dolore, dalla paura); indietreggiare; fremere; fare una smorfia.

winch, n. argano; verricello, m.; manovella, f.

wind, n. vento, fiato, m.; (Med.) flatulenza, flatuosità, f. ~bag, parlatore vano, fanfarone, mulino a vento, m. ~ egg, uovo chiaro, uovo non fertilizzato, m. ~ erosion, erosione eolica, f. ~fall, frutto abbattuto dal vento; (fig) buona fortuna, f., guadagno inaspettato, m., bazza, f. ~mill, mulino a vento, m. ~pipe, trachea, f. ~ row, falciata, f. ~screen, paravento, parabrezza, m. gust of ~, raffica, f., colpo di vento, m. ~screen wiper, tergicristallo, m.

to get ~ of, fiutare, scoprire, sventare. ¶ v.t. fare sfiatare, far trafelare.

wind, v.t. ir. avvolgere, aggomitolare, attorcigliare, annaspare; (off) dipanare; (Min.) rimontare; (v.i. ir.) serpeggiare; girare, muovere in giro; fare delle svolte. ~ up (clock, watch), caricare; finire, concludere, terminare, liquidare. ~ing, a. sinuoso, serpeggiante, tortuoso. ¶ n. (turn) svolta, svoltata, giravolta; sinuosità, f.; (maze, lit. & fig.) meandro, m. ~ sheet, sudario, lenzuolo mortuario, m. ~ stair, ~ staircase, scala a spirale, scala a chiocciola, f.

windlass, n. argano, verricello, m.

window, n. finestra, f.; (pl. col.) vetri, m.pl.; vetrate, invetriate, f.pl.; (casement) finestra a gangheri, f.; (leaded) vetrata; (carriage) sportello, finestrino, m., portiera, f.; (shop) vetrina, mostra, f. ~ box, giardino di finestra, m. ~ dresser, vetrinista, m.f. ~ dressing (fig.) inganno, m., illusione, f. ~ glass, vetro da finestra, m., invetriata, f. ~ ledge, ~ sill, davanzale, m. ~ mirror, spia, f. ~ pane, vetro, m.

windward, n. lato del vento, m.; (a.) al vento; (ad.) a sopravvento, contro vento. **windy**, a. ventoso; (day) di vento, di gran vento. to be ~, tirar vento.

wine, n. vino; liquore, m. ~ & spirit merchant, liquorista, m. ~ merchant, mercante di vino, m. ~glass, bicchiere da vino; m. ~ grapes, uva da vino, f. ~ grower, viticultore, vignaiuolo, m. ~ growing, n. viticultura, f. ~-growing, a. vinicolo, viticolo. ~ list, lista dei vini, f. ~ of the country, vino del paese, m. ~ trade, commercio dei vini, m.

wing, n. ala, f.; volo, m., volata, f.; (pl. Theat.) quinte, f.pl., retroscena, f. ~ dam, stecconaia, f. ~ nut, dado ad alette, m. ~ spread, ~span, apertura d'ali, f. ~ed, a. alato, veloce; ferito nell'ala. ~ creature, volatile, m.

wink, n. batter d'occhio, cenno, ammicco, m.; occhiata, f. ¶ v.i. ammiccare, batter le palpebre, strizzar l'occhio. ~ at, (fig.) chiuder un occhio a.

winkle (Crust.) n. chiocciola di mare, f.

winner, n. vincitore, m., -trice, f. **winning**, a. vincente, vincitore, -trice; (number) estratto; attraente,

seducente. ~ *post*, traguardo, *m.*
winning, *n. & ~s, n.pl.*, vincita,
f., vincite, *f.pl.*, guadagno, *m.*
winnow, *v.t.* vagliare, sventolare,
spulare. **~ing**, *n.* vagliatura,
spulatura, *f.*
winsome, *a.* amabile, attraente,
piacente.
winter, *n.* inverno, verno, *m.* ¶ *v.i.*
& t. svernare, passare l'inverno.
¶ ~, *att. &* **wintry**, *a.* d'inverno,
invernale.
wipe, *n.* strofinata, *f.*, colpo di cencio,
di fazzoletto, *&c.*, *m.* ~ **[up]**, *v.t.*
strofinare, asciugare, pulire, forbire.
~ *off* (debt, &c.), saldare, liquidare.
~ *out*, cancellare; oscurare.
wire, *n.* filo, *m.* (di ferro) (metallico);
(*Mus.*) corda, *f.*; telegramma,
dispaccio, *m.* barbed ~, filo spinato,
m. ~ *cutter*, tagliafili, *m.inv.*, pinza
tagliafili, *f.* ~*draw*, trafilare; (*fig.*)
lambiccare. ~ *edge*, filo morto, *m.*
~ *entanglement*, reticolato, *m.* ~
fence, barriera di reticolato, siepe
metallica, *f.* ~ *gauge*, calibro del
filo, *m.* ~ *gauze*, tela metallica, *f.*
~ *haired* (dog), dal pelo ruvido.
~ *nail*, puntina, *f.* ~ *netting*, rete
metallica, *f.*, reticolato, *m.* ~ *puller*,
intrigante, mestatore, *m.* ~ *rope*,
fune metallica, fune di fil di ferro, *f.*
~*-spring mattress*, cassa elastica, *f.*
¶ *v.t.* (*house, Elec.*) porre (montare)
dei fili in; ingraticolare; telegrafare.
wiring, *n.* montaggio (or posa) di
condutture elettriche, *m.* (*f.*). **wireless**, *a.* senza fili. ~ (*telegram*),
radio(tele)gramma, *m.* ~ (*telegraphy*), telegrafia senza fili, radiotelegrafia, *f.* ~ *cabinet*, ~ *set*,
apparecchio radio, *m.*; radio, *f.*
~ *operator*, radiotelegrafista, *m.*
¶ *n.* radio, *f.* **wiry**, *a.* magro, secco,
nerboruto.
wisdom, *n.* saggezza, sapienza, prudenza, *f.*, giudizio, *m.* ~ *tooth*, dente
del giudizio, *m.* **wise**, *a.* saggio,
savio, sensato, prudente, giudizioso,
avveduto. ~ *acre*, saccentone,
saccente, *m.* ¶ *n.* modo, *m.*, guisa,
maniera, *f.*   .
wish, *n.* voglia, *f.*, desiderio; augurio,
voto, *m.* ¶ *v.t. & i.* desiderare;
bramare; volere; augurare. ~
*someone many happy returns [of the
day]*, augurare una buona festa a
qualcuno. **~ful**, *a.* desideroso.
~ing bone, forcella, *f.*, sterno di
pollo, *m.* **~ing cap**, berretto
magico, *m.*

wish-wash, *n.* sciacquatura, *f.* **wishy-
washy**, *a.* insipido, debole, povero.
wisp, *n.* ciuffo, ciuffetto, *f.*, ciocca,
striscia, *f.*; (*straw*) pugnello (di
paglia), *m.*
wistaria, *n.* glicine, *f.*
wistful, *a.* pensoso, preoccupato,
pieno di nostalgia o d'un vago
desiderio. **~ly**, *ad.* da pensoso.
wit, *n.* spirito, *m.*, arguzia, *f.*, sale, *m.*;
(*pers.*) bello spirito, uomo arguto, *m.*;
(*pl.*) ingegno, cervello, *m.*, testa, *f.*
at one's ~s' end, essere agli estremi,
non sapere più che cosa fare. *to ~*,
cioè.
witch, *n.* strega, *f.* ~*craft*, stregoneria, *f.*, sortilegio, *m.* ~*doctor*,
stregone, *m.* ~*ery*, *n.* fascino,
incanto, *m.*
with, *pr.* con, da, fra, a, in, presso, di,
per, contro.
withdraw, *v.t. ir.* ritirare; ritrarre;
richiamare; rinunziare (a); (*v.i. ir.*)
ritirarsi; ritrarsi; rinchiudersi, trin-
cerarsi; andarsene; (*candidature*)
rinunziare (a). **~al**, *n.* ritiro, *m.*,
rinunzia, *f.*
withe, *n.* vimine, vinco, *m.*, ritorta, *f.*
wither, *v.t.* far avvizzire, far deperire,
disseccare; (*v.i.*) avvizzire, appas-
sirsi, disseccarsi; languire. **~ing**
(*look*), *a.* fulminante, sprezzante.
withers, *n.pl.* garrese, *m.*
withhold, *v.t. ir.* ritenere, rattenere,
trattenere; rifiutare.
within, *pr.* entro, in; sotto; a portata di; fra; in meno di. ¶ *ad.* per
entro, dentro, qui accluso. ~ *call*,
a portata di voce. *from ~*, di
dentro.
without, *pr.* senza, senza che, a meno
che, fuori di. *from ~*, dall'esterno,
di fuori. *to do ~*, fare a meno di, far
senza, astenersi da.
withstand, *v.t. ir.* resistere a, opporsi
a, subire.
withy, *n.* vimine, vinco, *m.*, ritorta, *f.*
witless, *a.* senza spirito, stupido,
sciocco. **witling**, *n.* saccentello,
saccentuzzo, *m.*
witness, *n.* testimonianza, prova, *f.*,
attestato, segno, *m.*; (*pers.*) testimone,
m.f., testimonio, *m.*, teste, *m.f.*
~ *box*, banco dei testi, b. riservato
ai testimoni, *m.* ~ *for the defence*,
teste a discarico, *m.f.* ~ *for the
prosecution*, teste a carico, *m.f.*
¶ *v.t.* testimoniare, deporre come
testimone; esser testimone di; attestare; certificare, sottoscrivere; assistere a, essere presente a; vedere.

witticism, *n.* facezia, *f.*; frizzo, bisticcio, tratto di spirito, *m.*

wittingly, *ad.* scientemente, consapevolmente; apposta, a bello studio.

witty, *a.* spiritoso, arguto.

wizard, *n.* mago, stregone, *m.* ~**ry,** *n.* magia, *f.*

wizened, *a.* raggrinzito, disseccato, avvizzito, magro.

wo (or **whoa**), *i.* fermo!

woad, *n.* guado, *m.*

wobble, *v.i.* vacillare, tentennare.

woe, *n.* guaio, dolore, *m.*, affanno, *m.*; tristezza, *f.* ~**begone** & ~**ful,** *a.* addolorato, pieno di guai, dolente, doloroso, triste, infelice.

wolf, *n.* lupo, *m.*, -a, *f.* ~ **cub** (*Zool.* & *Scouting*), lupacchiotto, *m.* ~'**s bane,** aconito, *m.*

wolfram, *n.* volframio, tungsteno, *m.*

woman, *n.* donna, femmina, *f.* ~ **barrister,** avvocatessa, *f.* ~ **doctor,** medichessa, *f.* ~ **driver,** conduttrice (d'automobile, &c.), *f.* ~ **hater,** misogino, nemico delle donne, *m.* ~ **of fashion,** donna elegante, *f.* ~ **suffrage,** suffragio femminile, suffragio delle donne, diritto di voto alle donne, *m.* **women's single, double** (*Ten.*), singolare, doppio, signore, *m.* ~**ish,** *a.* effeminato; (*voice*) femminile, *f.* ~**ly,** *a.* di donna, degno di donna, da vera donna, femminile, *f.*

womb, *n.* seno, utero, *m.*; matrice, *f.*, grembo, *m.*

wonder, *n.* meraviglia; sorpresa, *f.*, prodigio, miracolo, *m.*, cosa meravigliosa, *f.* ¶ *v.i.* meravigliarsi; stupirsi (*at* = di); domandarsi (*why* = perché). ~**ful,** *a.* meraviglioso, prodigioso, sorprendente.

wont, *n.* uso, costume, *m.* ~**ed,** *a.* solito, abituale.

woo, *v.t.* corteggiare, fare la corte a.

wood, *n.* bosco, *m.*, foresta, *f.*; legno, legname, *m.*, legna, *f.*; (*Bowls*) boccino, *m.* **in the** ~ (wine), nel barile. **from the** ~, dal barile. ~**bine,** caprifoglio, *m.* ~**carver,** scultore in legno, *m.* ~**cock,** beccaccia, *f.* ~**cut,** incisione su legno, *f.* ~**land,** terreno boscoso, *m.*, boschi, *m.pl.*; (*att.*) di bosco, dei boschi, silvestre. ~**louse,** porcellino terrestre, p. di terra, *m.* ~**man,** boscaiuolo, guardaboschi, *m.* ~ **nymph,** ninfa dei boschi, driade, *f.* ~ **owl,** allocco, *m.* ~**pecker,** picchio, *m.* ~ **pigeon,** colombo selvatico, colombaccio, *m.* ~ **screw,** vite a

legno, *f.* ~**shed,** tettoia da legna, *f.* ~ **spirit,** alcool metilico, *m.* **the** ~ [~**wind**], i legni, *m.pl.* ~**wool,** paglia di legno, *f.* ~**work,** lavoro in legno, *m.* ~**worker,** lavoratore del legno, *m.* ~**ed,** *a.* boscoso, coperto di boschi, selvoso. ~**en,** *a.* di legno, in legno; (*fig.*) rigido. ~**y,** *a.* legnoso; boscoso.

wooer, *n.* corteggiatore, pretendente, innamorato.

woof, *n.* trama, tessitura, *f.*

wool, *n.* lana, *f.*; (*animal's coat*) pellame, *m.*, mantello, *m.* ~**shop,** laneria, *f.* **woollen,** *a.* di lana; (*trade*) laniero. ~ **goods or** ~**s,** *n.pl.* laneria, *f.*, lanerie, *f.pl.*, tessuti di lana, *m.pl.* ~ **manufacturer,** lanaiuolo, *m.* ~ **mill,** lanificio, *m.*, fabbrica di tessuti di lana, *f.* ~ **trade,** industria laniera, *f.* **woolly,** *a.* lanoso; (*fruit, style*) cotonoso; (*hair*) crespo; (*outline, sound*) morbido.

word, *n.* parola, voce, *f.*, termine, vocabolo; avviso, *m.*, notizia, promessa, *f.*, segnale, *m.* ~ **square,** quadrato magico, *m.* **by** ~ **of mouth,** di bocca, oralmente, a viva voce. **the Word** (*Theol.*) il Verbo, *m.* ¶ *v.t.* formulare, redigere, esprimere.

wordiness, *n.* verbosità, *f.*

wording, *n.* modo di dire, *m.*, termini, *m.pl.* **wordy,** *a.* verboso, parolaio.

work, *n.* lavoro, *m.* (*oft. pl.*); azione, *f.*, funzionamento, *m.*, opera, *f.*, effetto, impiego, compito, pezzo, daffare, *m.*, faccenda, *f.*; (*social*) opere, *f.pl.*; (*of art*) opera, *f.*, oggetto, *m.* (*col. pl.* of *an artist*) opere, *f.pl.*; (*pl.*) lavori, *m.pl.*, opere, *f.pl.*; congegno, meccanismo, movimento, *m.*; (*pl.* & *s.*) fabbrica, officina, *f.*, stabilimento, *m.*, cantiere, *m.* ~ **bag,** borsetta, *f.* ~ **basket,** cestino da lavoro, *m.* ~ **box,** cassetta da lavoro, *f.*, scatola da lavoro, *f.* ~**man,** ~**woman,** operaio, *m.*, -a, *f.*; artigiano, artefice, *m.* ~**manlike,** ben fatto, ben lavorato, da bravo lavorante, da buon operaio, da perito artefice. ~**manship,** fattura, mano d'opera, esecuzione, *f.* ~**men's compensation insurance,** assicurazione contro gli infortuni sul lavoro, *f.* ~ **room,** stanza da lavoro, officina, *f.*; (*convent*) laboratorio, *m.* ~**s manager,** direttore della fabbrica, capo dell'officina, *m.* ~**shop,** officina, *f.* ~ **stand,** tavola da lavoro, *f.*, reggilavoro, *m.inv.* ¶ *v.t.* lavorare, operare; fare, esercire;

sfuttare; far funzionare; far fermentare; far correre, mettere in moto, mettere in esecuzione; manovrare, manipolare; ricamare; (v.i.) lavorare, funzionare, agire; operarsi, prodursi; fermentare; bollire; andare; fare effetto. ~ *hard*, faticare, lavorare di sgobbo, lavorare a tutt'uomo, sgobbare. ~ *loose*, prender giuoco. ~ *out*, v.t. elaborare; effettuare; esaurire; calcolare; (v.i.) dare certi risultati, riuscire. ~ *up*, eccitare, stimolare; far uso di; mescolare, preparare, affinare. ~**able**, *a.* eseguibile; che si può lavorare; sfruttabile; praticabile, pratico. ~**er**, *n.* lavoratore, *m.*, -trice, *f.*; lavorante, *m.f.*; operaio, *m.*, -a, *f.*; (*unskilled*) manovale, *m.* ~ *bee*, ape operaia, *f.* ~**ing**, *n.* operazione, *f.*; funzionamento, *m.*; attività; lavorazione, *f.*; esercizio; giuoco, *m.*; manovra, *f.* ~ *capital*, capitale d'esercizio, capitale circolante, *m.* ~ *class(es)*, classe operaia, *f.*, classi operaie, *f.pl.*, classe lavoratrice, *f.*, classi lavoratrici, *f.pl.* ~ *clothes*, vestiti da lavoro, abiti da lavoro, *m.pl.* ~ *day*, giorno di lavoro, giorno lavorativo, giorno feriale, *m.*; giornata lavorativa, *f.* ~ *drawing*, disegno d'officina, *m.*; (*Build.*) piano (costruttivo), *m.* ~ *expenses*, spese di gestione, spese d'esercizio, *f.pl.* the ~*less*, i disoccupati, *m.pl.*

world, *n.* mondo; secolo, *m.* ~(*-wide*) *a.* mondiale, universale. **worldliness.** *n.* mondanità, *f.*, spirito mondano, *m.* **worldling**, *n. & worldly*, *a.* mondano, *m. & a. all one's worldly goods*, tutta la sua roba.

worm, *n.* verme, *m.*; (*screw*) filetto, *m.*; (*corkscrew*) chiocciola, *f.*; (*Mach.*) vite senza fine, *f.*; (*still*) storta, *f.*, serpentino, *m.* ~*-eaten*, bacato, tarlato, roso dai vermi. ~ *fishing*, pesca al verme, *f.* ~**wood**, assenzio, *m.* ~ **oneself into**, insinuarsi in. ~**y**, *a.* verminoso, pieno di vermi.

worry, *n.* dispiacere, fastidio, *m.*, noia, perplessità, *f.*; tormento, *m.* ¶ *v.t.* disturbare, tormentare, infastidire, seccare, annoiare; (*of dogs*) dilaniare, sbranare.

worse, *a.* peggio, peggiore; (*Machine, &c.*) guasto, *m.* the ~ *for wear*. sgangherato. ¶ *ad.* peggio. *grow* ~, peggiorare. *make* ~, rendere peggiore, **far diventare peggiore.**

worship, *n.* culto, *m.*, adorazione, *f.*; uffizio (divino), *m. your*, *his W* ~, Signor Giudice, Signor Sindaco. ¶ *v.t. & i.* (*God, gods*) adorare; (*saints, relics*) venerare. **worshipper**, *m.*, adoratore, *m.*, -trice, *f.*, *pl.* fedeli, *m.pl.*

worst, *a.* il peggiore, il peggio, il più cattivo, il più grave. ¶ *ad. & n.* il peggio. *at the* ~, alla peggio.

worsted, *n.* lana filata, lana pettinata, roba di lana, *f.*

wort, *n.* (*of beer*), mosto, *m.*; (*plant*) erba, pianta, *f.*

worth, *n.* valore; pregio; prezzo; merito, *m.*; (*money's*) per (la somma di). ¶ *a.* del valore di; degno di; ricco di; che merita. *to be* ~, valere; meritare, possedere. ~**less**, *a.* senza valore, di nessun valore, senza merito; vile, spregevole; (*cheque*) senza provvisione. ~**lessness**, *n.* mancanza di valore; indegnità; inutilità, *f.* ~**y**, *a.* degno.

would, *v.aux. is expressed in It. by the conditional mood. Also by* volere; ~ *heaven that*, volesse il cielo! volesse Iddio! piaccia a Dio! ~**-be**, *a.* sedicente, preteso.

wound, *n.* ferita; piaga, *f.* ¶ *v.t.* ferire; offendere. *the* ~*ed*, i feriti, *m.pl.*

wove paper, carta velina, *f.*

wrack, *n.* rifiuti di mare, *m.pl.*; fuco, *m.*, alga, *f.*

wrangle, *n.* alterco, *m.*, disputa, rissa, *f.* ¶ *v.i.* leticare, bisticciarsi, disputare, contrastarsi. **wrangling**, *n.* disputazione, *f.*, litigio, *m.*

wrap, *n.* scialle, mantello (da sera), *m.*; (*bath*, &c.) accappatoio; boa, *m.* ~ [*up*], *v.t.* avvolgere; arrotolare; avviluppare, inviluppare; incartare, impaccare. ~ [*oneself*] *up*, avvolgersi, coprirsi. ~*-round corset*, fascetta, *f.* **wrapper**, *n.* involto, *m.*, tela o carta da involto, *f.*, involucro, *m.*; accappatoio, *m.*; (*newspaper*) fascia, fascetta, *f.*; (*cigar*) copertina, *f.*

wrath, *n.* ira, collera, rabbia, *f.*, sdegno, *m.* ~**ful**, *a.* adirato, sdegnato, incollerito, stizzoso.

wreak, *v.t.* eseguire; sfogare; infliggere. ~ *vengeance*, vendicarsi.

wreath, *n.* ghirlanda, corona; corona funeraria, c. mortuaria, *f.*; (*smoke*) turbine, *m.* **wreathe**, *v.t.* inghirlandare, intrecciare.

wreck, *n.* naufragio; bastimento naufragato, *m.*; (*fig.*) rovina, distruzione, *f.* ~[**age**], *n.* avanzi di un naufragio, relitti di mare, *m.pl.* **wreck,** *v.t.* fare naufragare, rovinare, distruggere; (*a train*) sabotare. *to be ~ed,* naufragare.

wren, *n.* scricciolo, re di macchia, *m.*

wrench, *n.* (*Med.*) storta, slogatura, *f.*; (*twist*) strappo, *m.*, torsione, *f.*, storcimento, sforzo violento, *m.*; (*tool*) chiave, madre vite, *f.* ¶ *v.t.* storcere; strappare; slogare; svisare. *~ open,* sforzare.

wrest, *v.t.* torcere; strappare; svisare.

wrestle, *v.i.* lottare. **wrestler,** *n.* lottatore, *m.* **wrestling,** *n.* lotta, *f.* *~ match,* incontro di lotta, *m.*

wretch, *n.* disgraziato, *m.*, -a, *f.*; sciagurato, *m.*, -a, *f.*; miserabile, *m.f.*; povero diavolo; scellerato, *m.* *~ed,* *a.* misero, sfortunato, sciagurato; meschino, povero, pietoso; cattivo. *~edness,* *n.* miseria, *f.*

wrick, *n.* storta, *f.* *to ~ one's back,* storcersi il dorso.

wriggle, *v.i.* contorcersi, dimenarsi, dibattersi, divincolarsi.

wring, *v.t.* *ir.* torcere, torcersi; attorcere; estorcere; stringere; spremere; (*linen*) torcere. *~er,* *n.* cilindro da bucato; torcitoio, *m.* *~ing wet,* da torcersi, inzuppato (bagnato).

wrinkle, *n.* ruga, grinza; piega, crespa, *f.*; (*tip*) buona idea, informazione speciale, *f.*; (*how to do something*) avviso utile, *m.* ¶ *v.t.* aggrinzare, corrugare, increspare, spiegazzare.

wrist, *n.* polso, *m.* *~ band,* polsino, manichino, *m.* *~[let]* watch, orologio da polso, orologio braccialetto, *m.* *~let,* *n.* braccialetto, *m.*

writ, *n.* citazione, *f.*, mandato, *m.*; breve, ordinanza, *f.*, decreto, rescritto, ordine, *m.* *Holy W~,* la Sacra Scrittura, *f.*

write, *v.t. & i. ir.* scrivere; inscrivere; redigere. *~ back,* rispondere, riscrivere; (*Bkkpg.*) rigirare. *~ for* (*journal*) scrivere in, collaborare a. *~ off,* ammortizzare, estinguere, mettere al passivo. *~ out,* copiare, trascrivere; tracciare; redigere, formulare, stendere. **writer,** *n.* scrivente, *m.f.*; scrittore, *m.*, -trice, *f.* autore, *m.*, -trice, *f.*

writhe, *v.i.* torcersi, contorcersi.

writing, *n.* scrittura, calligrafia, *f.*, scritto, documento, *m.*, iscrizione, *f.* *~ case,* portafogli, *m.inv.*, cartella con l'occorrente per scrivere, *f.* *~ desk,* *~ table,* scrittoio, *m.*, scrivania, tavola da scrivere, *f.* *~ ink,* inchiostro per scrivere, *m.*

~ materials, [articoli] da scrivere, *m.pl.* *~ pad,* carta da lettere in blocco, cartella per scrivere, cartella da scrittoio, *f.* **written,** *p.p.* scritto, in iscritto, per iscritto.

wrong, *a.* erroneo; ingiusto; indiretto; falso; sbagliato; cattivo, inequo; storto; scorretto, inesatto; improprio. *~ fount,* (*abb.* w.f.), (*Typ.*) refuso. *~ side* (fabric), rovescio, *m.* *~ side out,* alla rovescia. *~ side up,* sottosopra. *the ~ way,* *ad.* a rovescio, a controsenso, a contropelo. ¶ *ad.* male, malamente, a torto, a traverso. ¶ *n.* torto, male, danno, *m.*, ingiuria, colpa, *f.* ¶ *v.t.* far torto a, essere ingiusto con; ledere, nuocere, maltrattare. *~ful,* *a.* ingiusto, *~ly,* *ad.* a torto; falsamente.

wrought iron, ferro battuto, *m.*

wry, *a.* (*neck*) torto; (*mouth, smile*) storto; affettato; sbieco; ironico. *~ face,* smorfia, *f.* *~ neck* (bird), torcicollo, *m.* *~ness,* *n.* distorsione, contorsione, *f.*

wych-elm, *n.* olmo di montagna, olmo della Scozia, *m.*

X

Xanthippe, *n.* Santippe, *f.*

Xenophon, *n.* Senofonte, *m.*

Xmas, *abb.* See *Christmas.*

X-rays, *n.pl.* raggi X, *m.pl.*

xylography, *n.* silografia, *f.*

xylonite, *n.* celluloide, *f.*

xylophone, *n.* silofono, *m.*

Y

yacht, *n.* yacht, *m.*; nave da diporto, *f.* panfilo, *m.* *~ing,* *n.* crociera su (una) nave da diporto, *f.*

yam, *n.* igname, *m.*

yap, *v.i.* guaire, squittire, abbaiare.

yard, *n.* cortile; parco, recinto; (*Build., Shipbldg.*) cantiere, *m.* (*Rly. goods*) scalo merci; (*Naut.*) pennone, *m.*, antenna, *f.*; (*Meas.*) iarda *f.* = 0.914 399 metres.

yarn, *n.* (*thread*) filato, *m.*; (*tale*) racconto, *m.*, storia; filastrocca, *f.*

yarrow, *n.* millefoglie, *m.inv.*

yaw, *n.* (*Naut.*) straorzata, deviazione dalla rotta. ¶ *v.i.* deviare, straorzarsi.

yawl, *n.* iole, *f.*

yawn, *v.i.* sbadigliare; (*fig.*) spalancarsi. *~ing,* *a.* (*fig.*) spalancato.

ye, *pn.* (*Poet.*) voi.
yean, *v.i.* partorire.
year, *n.* anno, *m.*; annata, *f.*; (*Fin.*) esercizio, *m.* ~-*book*, annuario, *m.* ~*s of discretion,* età della ragione, e. della discrezione, *f.* ~**ly,** *a.* annuale; (*ad.*) annualmente, ogni anno, tutti gli anni.
yearn for, sospirare, agognare, struggersi di, non veder l'ora di.
yeast, *n.* lievito, *m.*
yell, *n.* urlo, strillo, *m.* ¶ *v.i.* urlare, strillare.
yellow, *a. & n.* giallo, *a. & m.* *the* ~ *races,* le razze gialle, *f.pl.,* i gialli, *m.pl.* Y~ *sea,* Mar Giallo, *m.* ¶ *v.t. & i.* ingiallire, ~**ish,** *a.* giallastro.
yelp, *v.i.* guaire, squittire.
yes, *particle,* sì, già. ¶ *n.* sì, *m.*
yesterday, *n.* ieri, *m.* *yester year,* una volta; l'anno passato. *the day before* ~, avant'ieri, ieri l'altro.
yet, *c.* pure, eppure, tuttavia, nondimeno, però, nonostante. ¶ *ad.* ancora. *as* ~, finora, fino al presente.
yew [*tree*], *n.* tasso, *m.*
yield, *n.* raccolto, prodotto, *m.*; rendita, *f.*; frutto, *m.* ¶ *v.t.* rendere, produrre; dare; offrire; (*v.i.*) cedere, arrendersi; acconsentire.
yoke, *n.* giogo; paio *m.*, coppia, *f.*; tiro, *m.*, muta, *f.*; ~ *elm,* carpino, *m.* ¶ *v.t.* aggiogare.
yokel, *n.* villano, zoticone, *m.*
yolk, *n.* torlo (d'uovo), giallo (d'uovo), *m.*
yonder, *a.* quello . . . là. ¶ *ad.* di là; laggiú, lassú.
yore (*of*), altre volte, anticamente, tempo già fu.
you, *pn.* voi, tu; vi, ve, ti, te; Loro; Ella, Lei.
young, *a.* giovane; piccolo. ~ *lady,* signorina; giovane signora, *f.* ~ *one,* piccolo, *-a, f.* *the* ~, (*pers.*) i giovani, *m.pl.,* la gioventú, *f.*; (*animals*) i nati, i piccoli, *m.pl.* ~**er,** *a.* (piú) giovane, minore. ~ *brother,* ~ *sister,* fratello minore, sorella m. *to make look* ~, ringiovanire. ~**ster,** *n.* ragazzo, *m.*
your, *a.* (il) vostro, (la) vostra, (i)

vostri, (le) vostre; (il) tuo, (la) tua, (i) tuoi, (le) tue; (il) suo, (la) sua, (i) suoi, (le) sue. **yours,** *pn. & your own,* il vostro, la vostra, &c.; a voi, di voi. ~ *affectionately,* tuo affezionatissimo. ~ *faithfully,* ~ *truly* [il] vostro (Suo) devotissimo (*abb.* devmo). ~ *very truly,* colla massima stima, Suo devmo. **yourself, yourselves,** *pn.* voi stesso, voi stessa, voi stessi, voi stesse; tu stesso, tu stessa, te stesso, te stessa; (*refl.*) vi.
youth, *n.* giovinezza; gioventú; adolescenza, *f.*; giovane, giovanotto, adolescente, *m.* ~**ful,** *a.* giovane, giovanile, di (della) giovinezza.
yule[**tide**], *n.* Natale, *m.*, festa di Natale, *f.* *yule log,* ceppo di Natale, *m.*

Z

zeal, *n.* zelo, *m.* **zealot,** *n.* zelatore, *m.*, -trice, *f.*, fanatico, *m.*, -a, *f.* **zealous,** *a.* zelante, premuroso, sollecito. ~**ly,** *ad.* con zelo.
zebra, *n.* zebra, *f.*
zenith, *n.* zenit; (*fig.*) zenit, culmine, apogeo, *m.*
zephyr, *n.* zeffiro, *m.*; (*vest*) maglia, *f.*
Zeppelin, *n.* dirigibile, *m.*
zero, *n.* zero, *m.*
zest, *n.* sapore piccante; gusto, ardore, *m.*
zigzag, *n.* zigzag, *m.* ¶ *v.i.* andare a zigzag.
zinc, *n.* zinco, *m.* ~ *worker,* zincatore, *m.* **zincography,** *n.* zincografia, *f.*
zip[**p**] **fastener,** chiusura scorrevole, chiusura lampo, *f.*
zircon, *n.* zircone, *m.*
zither, *n.* cetra, *f.*
zodiac, *n.* zodiaco, *m.* ~**al,** *a.* zodiacale, dello zodiaco.
zone, *n.* zona, *f.*
zoological, *a.* zoologico. **zoologist,** *n.* zoologo, *m.* **zoology,** *n.* zoologia, *f.*
Zulu, *a.* zulú ¶ *n.* zulú, *m.f.*
Zuyder Zee (**the**), lo Zuiderzee, *m.*